To Douglas and Betty
in loving appreciation
of much kindness
Peter and Isobel.
Christmas 1990.

The BIBLE in ONE YEAR

The BIBLE in ONE YEAR

NEW INTERNATIONAL VERSION

HODDER & STOUGHTON
LONDON SYDNEY AUCKLAND TORONTO

First published in Great Britain 1979
This edition 1988

ISBN 0 340 41917 2

British Library Cataloguing in Publication Data

The Bible in one year: New International Version.
1. Bible—Daily readings
242'.2

 Photoset by Rowland Phototypesetting Ltd, Bury St Edmunds, Suffolk. Printed in Great Britain for Hodder and Stoughton Ltd, Mill Road, Dunton Green, Sevenoaks, Kent by Richard Clay Ltd, Bungay, Suffolk.

FOREWORD

THE BIBLE IN ONE YEAR is a new arrangement of the Bible designed to let the reader get the most out of reading the complete Bible methodically in the space of one year. For every day in the year, readings are given from the Old Testament, the New Testament, and from Psalms or Proverbs. Reading may begin at any time during the year; but the Old Testament books are placed in broadly chronological order, starting on January 1st. However, in the interests of smooth reading, and to keep the individual character of different books, the books themselves are not broken up but are generally read in sequence. For the same reason, the New Testament is presented in traditional Bible order. A time chart is included in the notes and maps at the end of the book, and reference to this will help the reader to see the flow of biblical history.

Psalms and Proverbs have been divided evenly over the whole year. Because of the poetic nature of the Psalms, and the pithy wisdom of Proverbs, they are presented in regular, short sections to encourage reflection at the end of the day's reading.

This Bible may also be used for reference, and the contents pages show where each book begins.

The notes and maps at the end of the book will be especially useful to those who are less familiar with the Bible. The section called *What is the Bible* is a helpful introduction to Bible reading, and other sections give background information, a summary of the individual books, an index to well known passages, and five useful Bible maps.

PREFACE

TO THE NEW INTERNATIONAL VERSION

THE NEW INTERNATIONAL VERSION is a completely new translation of the Holy Bible made by over a hundred scholars working directly from the best available Hebrew, Aramaic and Greek texts. It had its beginning in 1965 when, after several years of exploratory study by committees from the Christian Reformed Church and the National Association of Evangelicals, a group of scholars met at Palos Heights, Illinois, and concurred in the need for a new translation of the Bible in contemporary English. This group, though not made up of official church representatives, was transdenominational. Its conclusion was endorsed by a large number of leaders from many denominations who met in Chicago in 1966.

Responsibility for the new version was delegated by the Palos Heights group to a self-governing body of fifteen, the Committee on Bible Translation, composed for the most part of biblical scholars from colleges, universities and seminaries. In 1967 the New York Bible Society (now the International Bible Society) generously undertook the financial sponsorship of the project—a sponsorship that made it possible to enlist the help of many distinguished scholars. The fact that participants from the United States, Great Britain, Canada, Australia and New Zealand worked together gave the project its international scope. That they were from many denominations—including Anglican, Assemblies of God, Baptist, Brethren, Christian Reformed, Church of Christ, Evangelical Free, Lutheran, Mennonite, Methodist, Nazarene, Presbyterian, Wesleyan and other churches—helped to safeguard the translation from sectarian bias.

How it was made helps to give the New International Version its distinctiveness. The translation of each book was assigned to a team of scholars. Next, one of the Intermediate Editorial Committees revised the initial translation, with constant reference to the Hebrew, Aramaic or Greek. Their work then went to one of the General Editorial Committees, which checked it in detail and made another thorough revision. This revision in turn was carefully reviewed by the Committee on Bible Translation, which made further changes and then released the final version for publication. In this way the entire Bible underwent three revisions, during each of which the translation was examined for its faithfulness to the original languages and for its English style.

All this involved many thousands of hours of research and discussion regarding the meaning of the texts and the precise way of putting them into English. It may well be that no other translation has been made by a more thorough process of review and revision from committee to committee than this one.

From the beginning of the project, the Committee on Bible Translation held to certain goals for the New International Version: that it would be an accurate translation and one that would have clarity and literary quality and so prove suitable for public and private reading, teaching, preaching, memorising and liturgical use. The Committee also sought to preserve some measure of continuity with the long tradition of translating the Scriptures into English.

In working towards these goals, the translators were united in their commitment to the authority and infallibility of the Bible as God's Word in written form. They believe that it contains the divine answer to the deepest needs of humanity, that it sheds unique light on our path in a dark world, and that it sets forth the way to our eternal well-being.

The first concern of the translators has been the accuracy of the translation and its fidelity to the thought of the biblical writers. They have weighed the significance of the lexical and grammatical details of the Hebrew, Aramaic and Greek texts. At the same time, they have striven for more than a word-for-word translation. Because thought patterns and syntax differ from language to language, faithful communication of the meaning of the writers of the Bible demands frequent modifications in sentence structure and constant regard for the contextual meanings of words.

A sensitive feeling for style does not always accompany scholarship. Accordingly the Committee on Bible Translation submitted the developing version to a number of stylistic consultants. Two of them read every book of both Old and New Testaments twice—once before and once after the last major revision—and made invaluable suggestions. Samples of the translation were tested for clarity and ease of reading by various kinds of people—young and old, highly educated and less well educated, ministers and laymen.

Concern for clear and natural English—that the New International Version should be idiomatic but not idiosyncratic, contemporary but not dated—motivated the translators and consultants. At the same time, they tried to reflect the differing styles of the biblical writers. In view of the international use of English, the translators sought to avoid obvious Americanisms on the one hand and obvious Anglicisms on the other. A British edition reflects the comparatively few differences of significant idiom and of spelling.

As for the traditional pronouns "thou", "thee" and "thine" in reference to the Deity, the translators judged that to use these archaisms (along with old verb forms such as "doest", "wouldest" and "hadst") would violate accuracy in translation. Neither Hebrew, Aramaic nor Greek uses special pronouns for the persons of the Godhead. A present-day translation is not enhanced by forms that in the time of the King James Version were used in everyday speech, whether referring to God or man.

For the Old Testament the standard Hebrew text, the Masoretic Text as published in the latest editions of *Biblia Hebraica*, was used throughout. The Dead Sea Scrolls contain material bearing on an earlier stage of the Hebrew text. They were consulted, as were the Samaritan Pentateuch and the ancient scribal traditions relating to textual changes. Sometimes a variant Hebrew reading in the margin of the Masoretic Text was followed instead of the text itself. Such instances, being variants within the Masoretic tradition, are not specified by footnotes. In rare cases, words in the consonantal text were divided differently from the way they appear in the Masoretic Text. Footnotes indicate this. The translators also consulted the more important early versions—the Septuagint; Aquila, Symmachus and Theodotion; the Vulgate; the Syriac Peshitta; the Targums; and for the Psalms the *Juxta Hebraica* of Jerome. Readings from these versions were occasionally followed where the Masoretic Text seemed doubtful and where accepted principles of textual criticism showed that one or more of these textual witnesses appeared to provide the correct reading. Such instances are footnoted. Sometimes vowel letters and vowel signs did not, in the judgment of the translators, represent the correct vowels for the original consonantal text. Accordingly some words were read with a different set of vowels. These instances are usually not indicated by footnotes.

The Greek text used in translating the New Testament was an eclectic one. No other piece of ancient literature has such an abundance of manuscript witnesses as does the New Testament. Where existing manuscripts differ, the translators made their choice of readings according to accepted principles of New Testament textual criticism. Footnotes call attention to places where there was uncertainty about what the original text was. The best current printed texts of the Greek New Testament were used.

There is a sense in which the work of translation is never wholly finished. This applies to all great literature and uniquely so to the Bible. In 1973 the New Testament in the New International Version was published. Since then, suggestions for corrections and revisions have been received from various sources. The Committee on Bible Translation carefully considered the suggestions and adopted a number of them. These were incorporated in the first printing of the entire Bible in 1978. Additional revisions were made by the Committee on Bible Translation in 1983 and appear in printings after that date.

As in other ancient documents, the precise meaning of the biblical texts is sometimes uncertain. This is more often the case with the Hebrew and Aramaic texts than with the Greek text. Although archaeological and linguistic discoveries in this century aid in understanding difficult passages, some uncertainties remain. The more significant of these have been called to the reader's attention in the footnotes.

In regard to the divine name *YHWH*, commonly referred to as the *Tetragrammaton*, the translators adopted the device used in most English versions of rendering that name as "LORD" in capital letters to distinguish it from *Adonai*, another Hebrew word rendered "Lord", for which small letters are used. Wherever the two names stand together in the Old Testament as a compound name of God, they are rendered "Sovereign LORD".

Because for most readers today the phrases "the LORD of hosts" and "God of hosts" have little meaning, this version renders them "the LORD Almighty" and "God Almighty". These renderings convey the sense of the Hebrew, namely, "he who is sovereign over all the 'hosts' (powers) in heaven and on earth, especially over the 'hosts' (armies) of Israel." For readers unacquainted with Hebrew this does not make clear the distinction between *Sabaoth* ("hosts" or "Almighty") and *Shaddai* (which can also be translated "Almighty"), but the latter occurs infrequently and is always footnoted. When *Adonai* and *YHWH Sabaoth* occur together, they are rendered "the Lord, the LORD Almighty".

As for other proper nouns, the familiar spellings of the Authorised Version are generally retained. Names traditionally spelled with "ch", except where it is final, are usually spelled in this translation with "k" or "c", since the biblical languages do not have the sound that "ch" frequently indicates in English—for example, in *chant*. For well-known names such as Zechariah, however, the traditional spelling has been retained. Variation in the spelling of names in the original languages has usually not been indicated. Where a person or place has two or more different names in the Hebrew, Aramaic or Greek texts, the more familiar one has generally been used, with footnotes where needed.

To achieve clarity the translators sometimes supplied words not in the original texts but required by the context. If there was uncertainty about such material, it is enclosed in brackets. Also for the sake of clarity or style, nouns, including some proper nouns, are sometimes substituted for pronouns, and vice versa. And though the Hebrew writers often shifted back and forth between first, second and third personal pronouns without change of antecedent, this translation often makes them uniform, in accordance with English style and without the use of footnotes.

Poetical passages are printed as poetry, that is, with indentation of lines and with separate stanzas. These are generally designed to reflect the structure of Hebrew poetry. This poetry is normally characterised by parallelism in balanced lines. Most of the poetry in the Bible is in the Old Testament, and scholars differ regarding the scansion of Hebrew lines. The translators determined the stanza divisions for the most part by analysis of the subject matter. The stanzas therefore serve as poetic paragraphs.

As an aid to the reader, italicised sectional headings are inserted in most of the books. They are not to be regarded as part of the NIV text, are not for oral reading, and are not intended to dictate the interpretation of the sections they head.

The footnotes in this version are of several kinds, most of which need no explanation. Those giving alternative translations begin with "Or" and generally introduce the alternative with the last word preceding it in the text, except when it is a single-word alternative; in poetry quoted in a footnote a slant mark indicates a line division. Footnotes introduced by "Or" do not have uniform significance. In some cases two possible translations were considered to have about equal validity. In other cases, though the translators were convinced that the translation in the text was correct, they judged that another interpretation was possible and of sufficient importance to be represented in a footnote.

In the New Testament, footnotes that refer to uncertainty regarding the original text are introduced by "Some manuscripts" or similar expressions. In the Old Testament, evidence for the reading chosen is given first and evidence for the alternative is added after a semicolon (for example: Septuagint; Hebrew *father*). In such notes the term "Hebrew" refers to the Masoretic Text.

It should be noted that minerals, flora and fauna, architectural details, articles of clothing and jewellery, musical instruments and other articles cannot always be identified with precision. Also measures of capacity in the biblical period are particularly uncertain (see the table of weights and measures following the text).

Like all translations of the Bible, made as they are by imperfect man, this one undoubtedly falls short of its goals. Yet we are grateful to God for the extent to which he has enabled us to realise these goals and for the strength he has given us and our colleagues to complete our task. We offer this version of the Bible to him in whose name and for whose glory it has been made. We pray that it will lead many into a better understanding of the Holy Scriptures and a fuller knowledge of Jesus Christ the incarnate Word, of whom the Scriptures so faithfully testify.

The Committee on Bible Translation

June 1978
(Revised August 1983)

Names of the translators and editors may be secured
from the International Bible Society
144 Tices Lane, East Brunswick, New Jersey 08816, U.S.A.

Note The footnotes to the New International Version are not included in this edition, which is intended for general Bible reading. They are to be found in other editions of this Bible, also available from Hodder and Stoughton.

CONTENTS

The page numbers given indicate where the first reading from a particular book begins. Psalms and Proverbs are spread throughout the year – see separate index overleaf.

THE BOOKS OF THE OLD TESTAMENT

THE BOOKS OF THE NEW TESTAMENT

INDEX TO PSALMS AND PROVERBS

JANUARY 1

DAY 1

OLD TESTAMENT READING
Genesis 1:1–2:17

The Beginning

1 In the beginning God created
the heavens and the earth. 2Now
the earth was formless and empty,
darkness was over the surface of
the deep, and the Spirit of God was
hovering over the waters.
3And God said, "Let there be light,"
and there was light. 4God saw that
the light was good, and he separated the light from the darkness.
5God called the light "day", and
the darkness he called "night".
And there was evening, and there
was morning—the first day.
6And God said, "Let there be an expanse between the waters to separate water from water." 7So God
made the expanse and separated
the water under the expanse from
the water above it. And it was so.
8God called the expanse "sky".
And there was evening, and there
was morning—the second day.
9And God said, "Let the water under
the sky be gathered to one place,
and let dry ground appear." And it
was so. 10God called the dry
ground "land", and the gathered
waters he called "seas". And God
saw that it was good.
11Then God said, "Let the land
produce vegetation: seed-bearing
plants and trees on the land that
bear fruit with seed in it, according
to their various kinds." And it was
so. 12The land produced vegetation: plants bearing seed according
to their kinds and trees bearing
fruit with seed in it according
to their kinds. And God saw
that it was good. 13And there
was evening, and there was
morning—the third day.
14And God said, "Let there be lights in
the expanse of the sky to separate
the day from the night, and let
them serve as signs to mark seasons
and days and years, 15and let them
be lights in the expanse of the sky
to give light on the earth." And it
was so. 16God made two great
lights—the greater light to govern
the day and the lesser light to govern the night. He also made the
stars. 17God set them in the expanse of the sky to give light on the
earth, 18to govern the day and the
night, and to separate light from
darkness. And God saw that it was
good. 19And there was evening,
and there was morning—the
fourth day.
20And God said, "Let the water teem
with living creatures, and let birds
fly above the earth across the expanse of the sky." 21So God created the great creatures of the sea
and every living and moving thing
with which the water teems,
according to their kinds, and every
winged bird according to its kind.
And God saw that it was good.
22God blessed them and said, "Be
fruitful and increase in number and
fill the water in the seas, and let the
birds increase on the earth." 23And
there was evening, and there was
morning—the fifth day.
24And God said, "Let the land produce
living creatures according to their
kinds: livestock, creatures that
move along the ground, and wild
animals, each according to its
kind." And it was so. 25God made
the wild animals according to their
kinds, the livestock according to
their kinds, and all the creatures
that move along the ground

according to their kinds. And God
saw that it was good.
26Then God said, "Let us make
man in our image, in our likeness,
and let them rule over the fish of
the sea and the birds of the air, over
the livestock, over all the earth,
and over all the creatures that
move along the ground."

27So God created man
in his own image,
in the image of God
he created him;
male and female
he created them.

28God blessed them and said to
them, "Be fruitful and increase in
number; fill the earth and subdue
it. Rule over the fish of the sea and
the birds of the air and over every
living creature that moves on the
ground."
29Then God said, "I give you
every seed-bearing plant on the
face of the whole earth and every
tree that has fruit with seed in it.
They will be yours for food. 30And
to all the beasts of the earth and all
the birds of the air and all the creatures that move on the ground—
everything that has the breath of
life in it—I give every green plant
for food." And it was so.
31God saw all that he had made,
and it was very good. And there
was evening, and there was morning—the sixth day.

2 Thus the heavens and the earth
were completed in all their vast
array.

2By the seventh day God had finished
the work he had been doing; so on
the seventh day he rested from all
his work. 3And God blessed the
seventh day and made it holy,
because on it he rested from all
the work of creating that he had
done.

Adam and Eve

4This is the account of the heavens
and the earth when they were created.

When the LORD God made the earth
and the heavens—5and no shrub of the
field had yet appeared on the earth and
no plant of the field had yet sprung up,
for the LORD God had not sent rain
on the earth and there was no man to
work the ground, 6but streams came up
from the earth and watered the whole
surface of the ground—7the LORD God
formed the man from the dust of the
ground and breathed into his nostrils
the breath of life, and the man became
a living being.
8Now the LORD God had planted a
garden in the east, in Eden; and there
he put the man he had formed. 9And the
LORD God made all kinds of trees grow
out of the ground—trees that were
pleasing to the eye and good for food. In
the middle of the garden were the tree
of life and the tree of the knowledge of
good and evil.
10A river watering the garden flowed
from Eden; from there it was separated
into four headwaters. 11The name of the
first is the Pishon; it winds through the
entire land of Havilah, where there is
gold. 12(The gold of that land is good;
aromatic resin and onyx are also there.)
13The name of the second river is the
Gihon; it winds through the entire land
of Cush. 14The name of the third river is
the Tigris; it runs along the east side of
Asshur. And the fourth river is the
Euphrates.
15The LORD God took the man and
put him in the Garden of Eden to work
it and take care of it. 16And the LORD
God commanded the man, "You are
free to eat from any tree in the garden;
17but you must not eat from the tree of
the knowledge of good and evil, for
when you eat of it you will surely die."

NEW TESTAMENT READING
Matthew 1:1–25

The Genealogy of Jesus

1 A record of the genealogy of Jesus Christ the son of David, the son of Abraham:

2Abraham was the father of Isaac,
Isaac the father of Jacob,
Jacob the father of Judah and his brothers,
3Judah the father of Perez and Zerah, whose mother was Tamar,
Perez the father of Hezron,
Hezron the father of Ram,
4Ram the father of Amminadab,
Amminadab the father of Nahshon,
Nahshon the father of Salmon,
5Salmon the father of Boaz, whose mother was Rahab,
Boaz the father of Obed, whose mother was Ruth,
Obed the father of Jesse,
6and Jesse the father of King David.

David was the father of Solomon, whose mother had been Uriah's wife,
7Solomon the father of Rehoboam,
Rehoboam the father of Abijah,
Abijah the father of Asa,
8Asa the father of Jehoshaphat,
Jehoshaphat the father of Jehoram,
Jehoram the father of Uzziah,
9Uzziah the father of Jotham,
Jotham the father of Ahaz,
Ahaz the father of Hezekiah,
10Hezekiah the father of Manasseh,
Manasseh the father of Amon,
Amon the father of Josiah,
11and Josiah the father of Jeconiah and his brothers at the time of the exile to Babylon.

12After the exile to Babylon:
Jeconiah was the father of Shealtiel,
Shealtiel the father of Zerubbabel,
13Zerubbabel the father of Abiud,
Abiud the father of Eliakim,
Eliakim the father of Azor,
14Azor the father of Zadok,
Zadok the father of Akim,
Akim the father of Eliud,
15Eliud the father of Eleazar,
Eleazar the father of Matthan,
Matthan the father of Jacob,
16and Jacob the father of Joseph, the husband of Mary, of whom was born Jesus, who is called Christ.

17Thus there were fourteen generations in all from Abraham to David, fourteen from David to the exile to Babylon, and fourteen from the exile to the Christ.

The Birth of Jesus Christ

18This is how the birth of Jesus Christ
came about: His mother Mary was
pledged to be married to Joseph, but
before they came together, she was
found to be with child through the Holy
Spirit. 19Because Joseph her husband
was a righteous man and did not want to
expose her to public disgrace, he had in
mind to divorce her quietly.
20But after he had considered this, an
angel of the Lord appeared to him in a
dream and said, "Joseph son of David,
do not be afraid to take Mary home as
your wife, because what is conceived in
her is from the Holy Spirit. 21She will
give birth to a son, and you are to give
him the name Jesus, because he will
save his people from their sins."
22All this took place to fulfil what the
Lord had said through the prophet:
23"The virgin will be with child and will
give birth to a son, and they will call him
Immanuel"—which means, "God with
us."
24When Joseph woke up, he did what

the angel of the Lord had commanded him and took Mary home as his wife. 25But he had no union with her until she gave birth to a son. And he gave him the name Jesus.

READING FROM PSALMS
Psalm 1:1–6

1Blessed is the man
who does not walk in the counsel
of the wicked
or stand in the way of sinners
or sit in the seat of mockers.
2But his delight is in the law of the
LORD,
and on his law he meditates day
and night.

3He is like a tree planted by streams of
water,
which yields its fruit in season
and whose leaf does not wither.
Whatever he does prospers.

4Not so the wicked!
They are like chaff
that the wind blows away.
5Therefore the wicked will not stand
in the judgment,
nor sinners in the assembly of the
righteous.

6For the LORD watches over the way
of the righteous,
but the way of the wicked will
perish.

DAY 2

JANUARY 2

OLD TESTAMENT READING
Genesis 2:18–4:16

18The LORD God said, "It is not good for the man to be alone. I will make a helper suitable for him."

19Now the LORD God had formed out of the ground all the beasts of the field and all the birds of the air. He brought them to the man to see what he would name them; and whatever the man called each living creature, that was
its name. 20So the man gave names to
all the livestock, the birds of the air and all the beasts of the field.

But for Adam no suitable helper was
found. 21So the LORD God caused the man to fall into a deep sleep; and while he was sleeping, he took one of the man's ribs and closed up the place with
flesh. 22Then the LORD God made a woman from the rib he had taken out of the man, and he brought her to the man.
23The man said,

"This is now bone of my bones
and flesh of my flesh;
she shall be called 'woman',
for she was taken out of man."

24For this reason a man will leave his father and mother and be united to his wife, and they will become one flesh.
25The man and his wife were both naked, and they felt no shame.

The Fall of Man

3 Now the serpent was more crafty than any of the wild animals the LORD God had made. He said to the woman, "Did God really say, 'You must not eat from any tree in the garden'?"

2The woman said to the serpent, "We may eat fruit from the trees in the gar-
den, 3but God did say, 'You must not eat fruit from the tree that is in the middle of the garden, and you must not touch it, or you will die.'"

4"You will not surely die," the ser-
pent said to the woman. 5"For God knows that when you eat of it your eyes will be opened, and you will be like God, knowing good and evil."

6When the woman saw that the fruit
of the tree was good for food and pleasing to the eye, and also desirable for
gaining wisdom, she took some and ate
it. She also gave some to her husband,
who was with her, and he ate it. 7Then
the eyes of both of them were opened,
and they realised that they were naked;
so they sewed fig leaves together and
made coverings for themselves.
8Then the man and his wife heard the
sound of the LORD God as he was walking in the garden in the cool of the day,
and they hid from the LORD God among
the trees of the garden. 9But the LORD
God called to the man, "Where are
you?"
10He answered, "I heard you in the
garden, and I was afraid because I was
naked; so I hid."
11And he said, "Who told you that
you were naked? Have you eaten from
the tree from which I commanded you
not to eat?"
12The man said, "The woman you put
here with me—she gave me some fruit
from the tree, and I ate it."
13Then the LORD God said to the
woman, "What is this you have done?"
The woman said, "The serpent deceived me, and I ate."
14So the LORD God said to the serpent, "Because you have done this,

"Cursed are you above all the
livestock
and all the wild animals!
You will crawl on your belly
and you will eat dust
all the days of your life.
15And I will put enmity
between you and the woman,
and between your offspring and
hers;
he will crush your head,
and you will strike his heel."

16To the woman he said,

"I will greatly increase your pains in
childbearing;
with pain you will give birth to
children.
Your desire will be for your husband,
and he will rule over you."

17To Adam he said, "Because you
listened to your wife and ate from the
tree about which I commanded you,
'You must not eat of it,'

"Cursed is the ground because of
you;
through painful toil you will eat of
it
all the days of your life.
18It will produce thorns and thistles for
you,
and you will eat the plants of the
field.
19By the sweat of your brow
you will eat your food
until you return to the ground,
since from it you were taken;
for dust you are
and to dust you will return."

20Adam named his wife Eve, because
she would become the mother of all the
living.
21The LORD God made garments of
skin for Adam and his wife and clothed
them. 22And the LORD God said, "The
man has now become like one of us,
knowing good and evil. He must not be
allowed to reach out his hand and take
also from the tree of life and eat, and
live for ever." 23So the LORD God
banished him from the Garden of Eden
to work the ground from which he had
been taken. 24After he drove the man
out, he placed on the east side of the
Garden of Eden cherubim and a flaming
sword flashing back and forth to guard
the way to the tree of life.

Cain and Abel

4 Adam lay with his wife Eve, and
she became pregnant and gave
birth to Cain. She said, "With the help
of the LORD I have brought forth a

man." 2Later she gave birth to his
brother Abel.
Now Abel kept flocks, and Cain
worked the soil. 3In the course of time
Cain brought some of the fruits of the
soil as an offering to the LORD. 4But
Abel brought fat portions from some of
the firstborn of his flock. The LORD
looked with favour on Abel and his
offering, 5but on Cain and his offering
he did not look with favour. So Cain
was very angry, and his face was downcast.
6Then the LORD said to Cain, "Why
are you angry? Why is your face downcast? 7If you do what is right, will you
not be accepted? But if you do not do
what is right, sin is crouching at your
door; it desires to have you, but you
must master it."
8Now Cain said to his brother Abel,
"Let's go out to the field." And while
they were in the field, Cain attacked his
brother Abel and killed him.
9Then the LORD said to Cain, "Where
is your brother Abel?"
"I don't know," he replied. "Am I
my brother's keeper?"
10The LORD said, "What have you
done? Listen! Your brother's blood
cries out to me from the ground. 11Now
you are under a curse and driven from
the ground, which opened its mouth to
receive your brother's blood from your
hand. 12When you work the ground, it
will no longer yield its crops for you.
You will be a restless wanderer on the
earth."
13Cain said to the LORD, "My punishment is more than I can bear. 14Today
you are driving me from the land, and I
will be hidden from your presence; I will
be a restless wanderer on the earth, and
whoever finds me will kill me."
15But the LORD said to him, "Not so;
if anyone kills Cain, he will suffer
vengeance seven times over." Then the
LORD put a mark on Cain so that no-one
who found him would kill him. 16So
Cain went out from the LORD's presence and lived in the land of Nod, east of
Eden.

NEW TESTAMENT READING
Matthew 2:1–18

The Visit of the Magi

2 After Jesus was born in Bethlehem
in Judea, during the time of King
Herod, Magi from the east came to
Jerusalem 2and asked, "Where is the
one who has been born king of the
Jews? We saw his star in the east and
have come to worship him."
3When King Herod heard this he was
disturbed, and all Jerusalem with him.
4When he had called together all the
people's chief priests and teachers of
the law, he asked them where the Christ
was to be born. 5"In Bethlehem in
Judea," they replied, "for this is what
the prophet has written:

6" 'But you, Bethlehem, in the land of
Judah,
are by no means least among the
rulers of Judah;
for out of you will come a ruler
who will be the shepherd of my
people Israel.' "

7Then Herod called the Magi secretly
and found out from them the exact time
the star had appeared. 8He sent them to
Bethlehem and said, "Go and make a
careful search for the child. As soon as
you find him, report to me, so that I too
may go and worship him."
9After they had heard the king, they
went on their way, and the star they had
seen in the east went ahead of them
until it stopped over the place where the
child was. 10When they saw the star,
they were overjoyed. 11On coming to
the house, they saw the child with his
mother Mary, and they bowed down
and worshipped him. Then they opened
their treasures and presented him with
gifts of gold and of incense and of
myrrh. 12And having been warned in a
dream not to go back to Herod, they
returned to their country by another
route.

The Escape to Egypt

13When they had gone, an angel of the Lord appeared to Joseph in a dream. "Get up," he said, "take the child and his mother and escape to Egypt. Stay there until I tell you, for Herod is going to search for the child to kill him."

14So he got up, took the child and his mother during the night and left for
Egypt, 15where he stayed until the death of Herod. And so was fulfilled what the Lord had said through the prophet: "Out of Egypt I called my son."

16When Herod realised that he had been outwitted by the Magi, he was furious, and he gave orders to kill all the boys in Bethlehem and its vicinity who were two years old and under, in accordance with the time he had
learned from the Magi. 17Then what was said through the prophet Jeremiah was fulfilled:

18"A voice is heard in Ramah,
weeping and great mourning,
Rachel weeping for her children
and refusing to be comforted,
because they are no more."

READING FROM PSALMS

Psalm 2:1–12

1Why do the nations conspire
and the peoples plot in vain?
2The kings of the earth take their stand
and the rulers gather together against the LORD
and against his Anointed One.
3"Let us break their chains," they say,
"and throw off their fetters."

4The One enthroned in heaven laughs;
the Lord scoffs at them.
5Then he rebukes them in his anger
and terrifies them in his wrath, saying,
6"I have installed my King
on Zion, my holy hill."

7I will proclaim the decree of the LORD:

He said to me, "You are my Son;
today I have become your Father.
8Ask of me,
and I will make the nations your inheritance,
the ends of the earth your possession.
9You will rule them with an iron sceptre;
you will dash them to pieces like pottery."

10Therefore, you kings, be wise;
be warned, you rulers of the earth.
11Serve the LORD with fear
and rejoice with trembling.
12Kiss the Son, lest he be angry
and you be destroyed in your way,
for his wrath can flare up in a moment.
Blessed are all who take refuge in him.

DAY 3

JANUARY 3

OLD TESTAMENT READING
Genesis 4:17–6:22

[17]Cain lay with his wife, and she became pregnant and gave birth to Enoch.
Cain was then building a city, and he
named it after his son Enoch. [18]To
Enoch was born Irad, and Irad was the
father of Mehujael, and Mehujael was
the father of Methushael, and
Methushael was the father of Lamech.
[19]Lamech married two women, one
named Adah and the other Zillah.
[20]Adah gave birth to Jabal; he was the
father of those who live in tents and
raise livestock. [21]His brother's name
was Jubal; he was the father of all who
play the harp and flute. [22]Zillah also had
a son, Tubal-Cain, who forged all kinds
of tools out of bronze and iron. Tubal-
Cain's sister was Naamah.
[23]Lamech said to his wives,

"Adah and Zillah, listen to me;
  wives of Lamech, hear my words.
I have killed a man for wounding me,
  a young man for injuring me.
[24]If Cain is avenged seven times,
  then Lamech seventy-seven
    times."

[25]Adam lay with his wife again, and
she gave birth to a son and named him
Seth, saying, "God has granted me
another child in place of Abel, since
Cain killed him." [26]Seth also had a son,
and he named him Enosh.

At that time men began to call on the
name of the LORD.

From Adam to Noah

5 This is the written account of
Adam's line.

When God created man, he made
him in the likeness of God. [2]He created
them male and female and blessed
them. And when they were created, he
called them "man".
[3]When Adam had lived 130 years, he
had a son in his own likeness, in his own
image; and he named him Seth. [4]After
Seth was born, Adam lived 800 years
and had other sons and daughters. [5]Al-
together, Adam lived 930 years, and
then he died.
[6]When Seth had lived 105 years, he
became the father of Enosh. [7]And after
he became the father of Enosh, Seth
lived 807 years and had other sons and
daughters. [8]Altogether, Seth lived 912
years, and then he died.
[9]When Enosh had lived 90 years, he
became the father of Kenan. [10]And
after he became the father of Kenan,
Enosh lived 815 years and had other
sons and daughters. [11]Altogether,
Enosh lived 905 years, and then he died.
[12]When Kenan had lived 70 years, he
became the father of Mahalalel. [13]And
after he became the father of Mahalalel,
Kenan lived 840 years and had other
sons and daughters. [14]Altogether,
Kenan lived 910 years, and then he
died.
[15]When Mahalalel had lived 65 years,
he became the father of Jared. [16]And
after he became the father of Jared,
Mahalalel lived 830 years and had other
sons and daughters. [17]Altogether,
Mahalalel lived 895 years, and then he
died.
[18]When Jared had lived 162 years, he
became the father of Enoch. [19]And
after he became the father of Enoch,
Jared lived 800 years and had other sons
and daughters. [20]Altogether, Jared
lived 962 years, and then he died.
[21]When Enoch had lived 65 years, he
became the father of Methuselah.
[22]And after he became the father of
Methuselah, Enoch walked with God
300 years and had other sons and daughters. [23]Altogether, Enoch lived 365
years. [24]Enoch walked with God; then

he was no more, because God took him
away.
25 When Methuselah had lived 187
years, he became the father of Lamech.
26 And after he became the father of
Lamech, Methuselah lived 782 years
and had other sons and daughters.
27 Altogether, Methuselah lived 969
years, and then he died.
28 When Lamech had lived 182 years,
he had a son. 29 He named him Noah and
said, "He will comfort us in the labour
and painful toil of our hands caused by
the ground the LORD has cursed."
30 After Noah was born, Lamech lived
595 years and had other sons and daughters. 31 Altogether, Lamech lived 777
years, and then he died.
32 After Noah was 500 years old, he
became the father of Shem, Ham and
Japheth.

The Flood

6 When men began to increase in
number on the earth and daughters
were born to them, 2 the sons of God
saw that the daughters of men were
beautiful, and they married any of them
they chose. 3 Then the LORD said, "My
Spirit will not contend with man for
ever, for he is mortal; his days will be a
hundred and twenty years."
4 The Nephilim were on the earth in
those days—and also afterwards—
when the sons of God went to the
daughters of men and had children by
them. They were the heroes of old, men
of renown.
5 The LORD saw how great man's
wickedness on the earth had become,
and that every inclination of the
thoughts of his heart was only evil all
the time. 6 The LORD was grieved that
he had made man on the earth, and his
heart was filled with pain. 7 So the LORD
said, "I will wipe mankind, whom I
have created, from the face of the earth
—men and animals, and creatures that
move along the ground, and birds of the
air—for I am grieved that I have made
them." 8 But Noah found favour in the
eyes of the LORD.

9 This is the account of Noah.

Noah was a righteous man, blameless
among the people of his time, and he
walked with God. 10 Noah had three
sons: Shem, Ham and Japheth.
11 Now the earth was corrupt in God's
sight and was full of violence. 12 God saw
how corrupt the earth had become, for
all the people on earth had corrupted
their ways. 13 So God said to Noah, "I
am going to put an end to all people, for
the earth is filled with violence because
of them. I am surely going to destroy
both them and the earth. 14 So make
yourself an ark of cypress wood; make
rooms in it and coat it with pitch inside
and out. 15 This is how you are to build
it: The ark is to be 450 feet long, 75 feet
wide and 45 feet high. 16 Make a roof for
it and finish the ark to within 18 inches
of the top. Put a door in the side of the
ark and make lower, middle and upper
decks. 17 I am going to bring floodwaters
on the earth to destroy all life under the
heavens, every creature that has the
breath of life in it. Everything on earth
will perish. 18 But I will establish my
covenant with you, and you will enter
the ark—you and your sons and your
wife and your sons' wives with you.
19 You are to bring into the ark two of all
living creatures, male and female, to
keep them alive with you. 20 Two of
every kind of bird, of every kind of
animal and of every kind of creature
that moves along the ground will come
to you to be kept alive. 21 You are to
take every kind of food that is to be
eaten and store it away as food for you
and for them."
22 Noah did everything just as God
commanded him.

NEW TESTAMENT READING

Matthew 2:19–3:17

The Return to Nazareth

19 After Herod died, an angel of the
Lord appeared in a dream to Joseph in
Egypt 20 and said, "Get up, take the

child and his mother and go to the land
of Israel, for those who were trying to
take the child's life are dead."
21So he got up, took the child and his
mother and went to the land of Israel.
22But when he heard that Archelaus was
reigning in Judea in place of his father
Herod, he was afraid to go there.
Having been warned in a dream, he
withdrew to the district of Galilee,
23and he went and lived in a town called
Nazareth. So was fulfilled what was
said through the prophets: "He will be
called a Nazarene."

John the Baptist Prepares the Way

3 In those days John the Baptist
came, preaching in the Desert of
Judea 2and saying, "Repent, for the
kingdom of heaven is near." 3This is he
who was spoken of through the prophet
Isaiah:

"A voice of one calling in the desert,
'Prepare the way for the Lord,
make straight paths for him.'"

4John's clothes were made of camel's
hair, and he had a leather belt round his
waist. His food was locusts and wild
honey. 5People went out to him from
Jerusalem and all Judea and the whole
region of the Jordan. 6Confessing their
sins, they were baptised by him in the
Jordan River.
7But when he saw many of the Pharisees and Sadducees coming to where he
was baptising, he said to them: "You
brood of vipers! Who warned you to flee
from the coming wrath? 8Produce fruit
in keeping with repentance. 9And do
not think you can say to yourselves, 'We
have Abraham as our father.' I tell you
that out of these stones God can raise up
children for Abraham. 10The axe is
already at the root of the trees, and
every tree that does not produce good
fruit will be cut down and thrown into
the fire.
11"I baptise you with water for repentance. But after me will come one
who is more powerful than I, whose
sandals I am not fit to carry. He will
baptise you with the Holy Spirit and
with fire. 12His winnowing fork is in his
hand, and he will clear his threshing-
floor, gathering his wheat into the barn
and burning up the chaff with unquenchable fire."

The Baptism of Jesus

13Then Jesus came from Galilee to
the Jordan to be baptised by John. 14But
John tried to deter him, saying, "I need
to be baptised by you, and do you come
to me?"
15Jesus replied, "Let it be so now; it is
proper for us to do this to fulfil all
righteousness." Then John consented.
16As soon as Jesus was baptised, he
went up out of the water. At that
moment heaven was opened, and he
saw the Spirit of God descending like a
dove and lighting on him. 17And a voice
from heaven said, "This is my Son,
whom I love; with him I am well
pleased."

READING FROM PSALMS
Psalm 3:1–8

A psalm of David. When he fled from his son Absalom.

1O LORD, how many are my foes!
How many rise up against me!
2Many are saying of me,
"God will not deliver him."
Selah

3But you are a shield around me, O LORD;
you bestow glory on me and lift up my head.
4To the LORD I cry aloud,
and he answers me from his holy hill. *Selah*

5I lie down and sleep;
I wake again, because the LORD sustains me.

[6]I will not fear the tens of thousands
drawn up against me on every
side.

[7]Arise, O LORD!
Deliver me, O my God!
Strike all my enemies on the jaw;
break the teeth of the wicked.

[8]From the LORD comes deliverance.
May your blessing be on your
people. *Selah*

JANUARY 4

DAY 4

OLD TESTAMENT READING

Genesis 7:1–9:17

7 The LORD then said to Noah, "Go
into the ark, you and your whole
family, because I have found you righteous in this generation. [2]Take with you
seven of every kind of clean animal, a
male and its mate, and two of every kind
of unclean animal, a male and its mate,
[3]and also seven of every kind of bird,
male and female, to keep their various
kinds alive throughout the earth.
[4]Seven days from now I will send rain on
the earth for forty days and forty nights,
and I will wipe from the face of the earth
every living creature I have made."

[5]And Noah did all that the LORD commanded him.

[6]Noah was six hundred years old
when the floodwaters came on the
earth. [7]And Noah and his sons and his
wife and his sons' wives entered the ark
to escape the waters of the flood. [8]Pairs
of clean and unclean animals, of birds
and of all creatures that move along the
ground, [9]male and female, came to
Noah and entered the ark, as God had
commanded Noah. [10]And after the
seven days the floodwaters came on the
earth.

[11]In the six hundredth year of Noah's
life, on the seventeenth day of the
second month—on that day all the
springs of the great deep burst forth,
and the floodgates of the heavens were
opened. [12]And rain fell on the earth for
forty days and forty nights.

[13]On that very day Noah and his sons,
Shem, Ham and Japheth, together with
his wife and the wives of his three sons,
entered the ark. [14]They had with them
every wild animal according to its kind,
all livestock according to their kinds,
every creature that moves along the
ground according to its kind and every
bird according to its kind, everything
with wings. [15]Pairs of all creatures that
have the breath of life in them came to
Noah and entered the ark. [16]The animals going in were male and female of
every living thing, as God had commanded Noah. Then the LORD shut him in.

[17]For forty days the flood kept coming on the earth, and as the waters
increased they lifted the ark high above
the earth. [18]The waters rose and increased greatly on the earth, and the ark
floated on the surface of the water.
[19]They rose greatly on the earth, and all
the high mountains under the entire
heavens were covered. [20]The waters
rose and covered the mountains to a
depth of more than twenty feet. [21]Every
living thing that moved on the earth
perished—birds, livestock, wild animals, all the creatures that swarm over
the earth, and all mankind. [22]Every-
thing on dry land that had the breath of
life in its nostrils died. [23]Every living
thing on the face of the earth was wiped
out; men and animals and the creatures
that move along the ground and the
birds of the air were wiped from the
earth. Only Noah was left, and those
with him in the ark.

24The waters flooded the earth for a
hundred and fifty days.

8 But God remembered Noah and all
the wild animals and the livestock
that were with him in the ark, and he
sent a wind over the earth, and the
waters receded. 2Now the springs of
the deep and the floodgates of the
heavens had been closed, and the rain
had stopped falling from the sky. 3The
water receded steadily from the earth.
At the end of the hundred and fifty days
the water had gone down, 4and on the
seventeenth day of the seventh month
the ark came to rest on the mountains of
Ararat. 5The waters continued to re-
cede until the tenth month, and on the
first day of the tenth month the tops of
the mountains became visible.

6After forty days Noah opened the
window he had made in the ark 7and
sent out a raven, and it kept flying back
and forth until the water had dried up
from the earth. 8Then he sent out a dove
to see if the water had receded from the
surface of the ground. 9But the dove
could find no place to set its feet because
there was water over all the surface of
the earth; so it returned to Noah in the
ark. He reached out his hand and took
the dove and brought it back to himself
in the ark. 10He waited seven more days
and again sent out the dove from the
ark. 11When the dove returned to him in
the evening, there in its beak was a
freshly plucked olive leaf! Then Noah
knew that the water had receded from
the earth. 12He waited seven more days
and sent the dove out again, but this
time it did not return to him.

13By the first day of the first month of
Noah's six hundred and first year, the
water had dried up from the earth.
Noah then removed the covering from
the ark and saw that the surface of the
ground was dry. 14By the twenty-
seventh day of the second month the
earth was completely dry.

15Then God said to Noah, 16"Come
out of the ark, you and your wife and
your sons and their wives. 17Bring out
every kind of living creature that is with
you—the birds, the animals, and all the
creatures that move along the ground
—so they can multiply on the earth and
be fruitful and increase in number upon
it."

18So Noah came out, together with
his sons and his wife and his sons' wives.
19All the animals and all the creatures
that move along the ground and all the
birds—everything that moves on the
earth—came out of the ark, one kind
after another.

20Then Noah built an altar to the
LORD and, taking some of all the clean
animals and clean birds, he sacrificed
burnt offerings on it. 21The LORD smelled the pleasing aroma and said in his
heart: "Never again will I curse the
ground because of man, even though
every inclination of his heart is evil from
childhood. And never again will I
destroy all living creatures, as I have
done.

22"As long as the earth endures,
seedtime and harvest,
cold and heat,
summer and winter,
day and night
will never cease."

God's Covenant With Noah

9 Then God blessed Noah and his
sons, saying to them, "Be fruitful
and increase in number and fill the
earth. 2The fear and dread of you will
fall upon all the beasts of the earth and
all the birds of the air, upon every creature that moves along the ground, and
upon all the fish of the sea; they are
given into your hands. 3Everything that
lives and moves will be food for you.
Just as I gave you the green plants, I
now give you everything.

4"But you must not eat meat that has
its lifeblood still in it. 5And for your
lifeblood I will surely demand an
accounting. I will demand an accounting from every animal. And from each
man, too, I will demand an accounting
for the life of his fellow man.

6"Whoever sheds the blood of man,
by man shall his blood be shed;
for in the image of God
has God made man.

7As for you, be fruitful and increase in
number; multiply on the earth and increase upon it."
8Then God said to Noah and to his
sons with him: 9"I now establish my
covenant with you and with your descendants after you 10and with every
living creature that was with you—the
birds, the livestock and all the wild
animals, all those that came out of the
ark with you—every living creature on
earth. 11I establish my covenant with
you: Never again will all life be cut off
by the waters of a flood; never again will
there be a flood to destroy the earth."
12And God said, "This is the sign of
the covenant I am making between me
and you and every living creature with
you, a covenant for all generations to
come: 13I have set my rainbow in the
clouds, and it will be the sign of the
covenant between me and the earth.
14Whenever I bring clouds over the
earth and the rainbow appears in the
clouds, 15I will remember my covenant
between me and you and all living creatures of every kind. Never again will the
waters become a flood to destroy all life.
16Whenever the rainbow appears in the
clouds, I will see it and remember the
everlasting covenant between God and
all living creatures of every kind on the
earth."
17So God said to Noah, "This is the
sign of the covenant I have established
between me and all life on the earth."

NEW TESTAMENT READING
Matthew 4:1–22

The Temptation of Jesus

4 Then Jesus was led by the Spirit
into the desert to be tempted by the
devil. 2After fasting for forty days and
forty nights, he was hungry. 3The tempter came to him and said, "If you are the
Son of God, tell these stones to become
bread."
4Jesus answered, "It is written: 'Man
does not live on bread alone, but on
every word that comes from the mouth
of God.'"
5Then the devil took him to the holy
city and had him stand on the highest
point of the temple. 6"If you are the Son
of God," he said, "throw yourself
down. For it is written:

"'He will command his angels
concerning you,
and they will lift you up in their
hands,
so that you will not strike your foot
against a stone.'"

7Jesus answered him, "It is also written: 'Do not put the Lord your God to
the test.'"
8Again, the devil took him to a very
high mountain and showed him all the
kingdoms of the world and their splendour. 9"All this I will give you," he said,
"if you will bow down and worship me."
10Jesus said to him, "Away from me,
Satan! For it is written: 'Worship the
Lord your God, and serve him only.'"
11Then the devil left him, and angels
came and attended him.

Jesus Begins to Preach

12When Jesus heard that John had
been put in prison, he returned to
Galilee. 13Leaving Nazareth, he went
and lived in Capernaum, which was by
the lake in the area of Zebulun and
Naphtali—14to fulfil what was said
through the prophet Isaiah:

15"Land of Zebulun and land of
Naphtali,
the way to the sea, along the
Jordan,
Galilee of the Gentiles—

[16]the people living in darkness
have seen a great light;
on those living in the land of the
shadow of death
a light has dawned."

[17]From that time on Jesus began to
preach, "Repent, for the kingdom of
heaven is near."

The Calling of the First Disciples

[18]As Jesus was walking beside the Sea
of Galilee, he saw two brothers, Simon
called Peter and his brother Andrew.
They were casting a net into the lake,
for they were fishermen. [19]"Come, follow me," Jesus said, "and I will make
you fishers of men." [20]At once they left
their nets and followed him.

[21]Going on from there, he saw two
other brothers, James son of Zebedee
and his brother John. They were in a
boat with their father Zebedee, preparing their nets. Jesus called them,
[22]and immediately they left the boat and
their father and followed him.

READING FROM PROVERBS
Proverbs 1:1–7

Prologue: Purpose and Theme

1 The proverbs of Solomon son of David, king of Israel:

[2]for attaining wisdom and discipline;
for understanding words of insight;
[3]for acquiring a disciplined and
prudent life,
doing what is right and just and
fair;
[4]for giving prudence to the simple,
knowledge and discretion to the
young—
[5]let the wise listen and add to their
learning,
and let the discerning get
guidance—
[6]for understanding proverbs and
parables,
the sayings and riddles of the wise.

[7]The fear of the LORD is the beginning
of knowledge,
but fools despise wisdom and
discipline.

DAY 5

JANUARY 5

OLD TESTAMENT READING
Genesis 9:18–11:9

The Sons of Noah

[18]The sons of Noah who came out of
the ark were Shem, Ham and Japheth.
(Ham was the father of Canaan.)
[19]These were the three sons of Noah,
and from them came the people who
were scattered over the earth.

[20]Noah, a man of the soil, proceeded
to plant a vineyard. [21]When he drank
some of its wine, he became drunk and
lay uncovered inside his tent. [22]Ham,
the father of Canaan, saw his father's
nakedness and told his two brothers
outside. [23]But Shem and Japheth took a
garment and laid it across their shoulders; then they walked in backwards
and covered their father's nakedness.
Their faces were turned the other way
so that they would not see their father's
nakedness.

[24]When Noah awoke from his wine
and found out what his youngest son
had done to him, [25]he said,

"Cursed be Canaan!
The lowest of slaves
will he be to his brothers."

[26]He also said,

"Blessed be the LORD, the God of
Shem!
May Canaan be the slave of Shem.
[27]May God extend the territory of
Japheth;
may Japheth live in the tents of
Shem,
and may Canaan be his slave."

[28]After the flood Noah lived 350
years. [29]Altogether, Noah lived 950
years, and then he died.

The Table of Nations

10 This is the account of Shem,
Ham and Japheth, Noah's sons,
who themselves had sons after the
flood.

The Japhethites

[2]The sons of Japheth:
Gomer, Magog, Madai, Javan,
Tubal, Meshech and Tiras.
[3]The sons of Gomer:
Ashkenaz, Riphath and Togarmah.
[4]The sons of Javan:
Elishah, Tarshish, the Kittim
and the Rodanim. [5](From these
the maritime peoples spread out
into their territories by their
clans within their nations, each
with its own language.)

The Hamites

[6]The sons of Ham:
Cush, Mizraim, Put and Canaan.
[7]The sons of Cush:
Seba, Havilah, Sabtah, Raamah
and Sabteca.
The sons of Raamah:
Sheba and Dedan.

[8]Cush was the father of Nimrod, who
grew to be a mighty warrior on the
earth. [9]He was a mighty hunter before
the LORD; that is why it is said, "Like
Nimrod, a mighty hunter before the
LORD." [10]The first centres of his kingdom were Babylon, Erech, Akkad and
Calneh, in Shinar. [11]From that land he
went to Assyria, where he built
Nineveh, Rehoboth Ir, Calah [12]and Re-
sen, which is between Nineveh and
Calah; that is the great city.

[13]Mizraim was the father of
the Ludites, Anamites, Lehabites, Naphtuhites, [14]Pathrusites,
Casluhites (from whom the Philistines came) and Caphtorites.
[15]Canaan was the father of
Sidon his firstborn, and of the
Hittites, [16]Jebusites, Amorites,
Girgashites, [17]Hivites, Arkites,
Sinites, [18]Arvadites, Zemarites
and Hamathites.

Later the Canaanite clans scattered
[19]and the borders of Canaan reached
from Sidon towards Gerar as far as
Gaza, and then towards Sodom,
Gomorrah, Admah and Zeboiim, as far
as Lasha.
[20]These are the sons of Ham by their
clans and languages, in their territories
and nations.

The Semites

[21]Sons were also born to Shem,
whose older brother was Japheth; Shem
was the ancestor of all the sons of Eber.

[22]The sons of Shem:
Elam, Asshur, Arphaxad, Lud
and Aram.
[23]The sons of Aram:
Uz, Hul, Gether and Meshech.
[24]Arphaxad was the father of Shelah,
and Shelah the father of Eber.
[25]Two sons were born to Eber:
One was named Peleg, because
in his time the earth was divided;
his brother was named Joktan.
[26]Joktan was the father of
Almodad, Sheleph, Hazar-
maveth, Jerah, [27]Hadoram,

Uzal, Diklah, 28Obal, Abimael,
Sheba, 29Ophir, Havilah and
Jobab. All these were sons of
Joktan.

30The region where they lived stretched
from Mesha towards Sephar, in the
eastern hill country.
31These are the sons of Shem by their
clans and languages, in their territories
and nations.

32These are the clans of Noah's sons,
according to their lines of descent,
within their nations. From these the
nations spread out over the earth after
the flood.

The Tower of Babel

11 Now the whole world had one
language and a common speech.
2As men moved eastward, they found a
plain in Shinar and settled there.
3They said to each other, "Come,
let's make bricks and bake them
thoroughly." They used brick instead of
stone, and bitumen for mortar. 4Then
they said, "Come, let us build ourselves
a city, with a tower that reaches to the
heavens, so that we may make a name
for ourselves and not be scattered over
the face of the whole earth."
5But the LORD came down to see the
city and the tower that the men were
building. 6The LORD said, "If as one
people speaking the same language they
have begun to do this, then nothing they
plan to do will be impossible for them.
7Come, let us go down and confuse their
language so they will not understand
each other."
8So the LORD scattered them from
there over all the earth, and they
stopped building the city. 9That is why
it was called Babel—because there the
LORD confused the language of the
whole world. From there the LORD
scattered them over the face of the
whole earth.

NEW TESTAMENT READING
Matthew 4:23–5:20

Jesus Heals the Sick

23Jesus went throughout Galilee,
teaching in their synagogues, preaching
the good news of the kingdom, and
healing every disease and sickness
among the people. 24News about him
spread all over Syria, and people
brought to him all who were ill with
various diseases, those suffering severe
pain, the demon-possessed, those
having seizures, and the paralysed, and
he healed them. 25Large crowds from
Galilee, the Decapolis, Jerusalem,
Judea and the region across the Jordan
followed him.

The Beatitudes

5 Now when he saw the crowds, he
went up on a mountainside and sat
down. His disciples came to him, 2and
he began to teach them, saying:

3"Blessed are the poor in spirit,
for theirs is the kingdom of
heaven.
4Blessed are those who mourn,
for they will be comforted.
5Blessed are the meek,
for they will inherit the earth.
6Blessed are those who hunger and
thirst for righteousness,
for they will be filled.
7Blessed are the merciful,
for they will be shown mercy.
8Blessed are the pure in heart,
for they will see God.
9Blessed are the peacemakers,
for they will be called sons of God.
10Blessed are those who are persecuted
because of righteousness,
for theirs is the kingdom of heaven.

11"Blessed are you when people insult you, persecute you and falsely say
all kinds of evil against you because of
me. 12Rejoice and be glad, because
great is your reward in heaven, for in

the same way they persecuted the prophets who were before you.

Salt and Light

13"You are the salt of the earth. But if the salt loses its saltiness, how can it be made salty again? It is no longer good for anything, except to be thrown out and trampled by men.
14"You are the light of the world. A city on a hill cannot be hidden.
15Neither do people light a lamp and put it under a bowl. Instead they put it on its stand, and it gives light to everyone in the house. 16In the same way, let your light shine before men, that they may see your good deeds and praise your Father in heaven.

The Fulfilment of the Law

17"Do not think that I have come to abolish the Law or the Prophets; I have not come to abolish them but to fulfil
them. 18I tell you the truth, until heaven and earth disappear, not the smallest letter, not the least stroke of a pen, will by any means disappear from the Law until everything is accomplished.
19Anyone who breaks one of the least of these commandments and teaches others to do the same will be called least in the kingdom of heaven, but whoever practises and teaches these commands will be called great in the kingdom of
heaven. 20For I tell you that unless your righteousness surpasses that of the Pharisees and the teachers of the law, you will certainly not enter the kingdom of heaven.

READING FROM PSALMS
Psalm 4:1–8

For the director of music. With stringed instruments. A psalm of David.

1Answer me when I call to you,
O my righteous God.
Give me relief from my distress;
be merciful to me and hear my prayer.

2How long, O men, will you turn my glory into shame?
How long will you love delusions
and seek false gods? *Selah*
3Know that the LORD has set apart the godly for himself;
the LORD will hear when I call to him.

4In your anger do not sin;
when you are on your beds,
search your hearts and be silent. *Selah*
5Offer right sacrifices
and trust in the LORD.

6Many are asking, "Who can show us any good?"
Let the light of your face shine
upon us, O LORD.
7You have filled my heart with greater joy
than when their grain and new wine abound.
8I will lie down and sleep in peace,
for you alone, O LORD,
make me dwell in safety.

DAY 6

JANUARY 6

OLD TESTAMENT READING
Genesis 11:10–13:18

From Shem to Abram

10This is the account of Shem.

Two years after the flood, when Shem was 100 years old, he became the father of Arphaxad. 11And after he became the father of Arphaxad, Shem lived 500 years and had other sons and daughters.

12When Arphaxad had lived 35 years, he became the father of Shelah. 13And after he became the father of Shelah, Arphaxad lived 403 years and had other sons and daughters.

14When Shelah had lived 30 years, he became the father of Eber. 15And after he became the father of Eber, Shelah lived 403 years and had other sons and daughters.

16When Eber had lived 34 years, he became the father of Peleg. 17And after he became the father of Peleg, Eber lived 430 years and had other sons and daughters.

18When Peleg had lived 30 years, he became the father of Reu. 19And after he became the father of Reu, Peleg lived 209 years and had other sons and daughters.

20When Reu had lived 32 years, he became the father of Serug. 21And after he became the father of Serug, Reu lived 207 years and had other sons and daughters.

22When Serug had lived 30 years, he became the father of Nahor. 23And after he became the father of Nahor, Serug lived 200 years and had other sons and daughters.

24When Nahor had lived 29 years, he became the father of Terah. 25And after he became the father of Terah, Nahor lived 119 years and had other sons and daughters.

26After Terah had lived 70 years, he became the father of Abram, Nahor and Haran.

27This is the account of Terah.

Terah became the father of Abram, Nahor and Haran. And Haran became the father of Lot. 28While his father Terah was still alive, Haran died in Ur of the Chaldeans, in the land of his birth. 29Abram and Nahor both married. The name of Abram's wife was Sarai, and the name of Nahor's wife was Milcah; she was the daughter of Haran, the father of both Milcah and Iscah. 30Now Sarai was barren; she had no children.

31Terah took his son Abram, his grandson Lot son of Haran, and his daughter-in-law Sarai, the wife of his son Abram, and together they set out from Ur of the Chaldeans to go to Canaan. But when they came to Haran, they settled there.

32Terah lived 205 years, and he died in Haran.

The Call of Abram

12 The LORD had said to Abram, "Leave your country, your people and your father's household and go to the land I will show you.

2"I will make you into a great nation
  and I will bless you;
I will make your name great,
  and you will be a blessing.
3I will bless those who bless you,
  and whoever curses you I will
    curse;
and all peoples on earth
  will be blessed through you."

4So Abram left, as the LORD had told him; and Lot went with him. Abram was seventy-five years old when he set out from Haran. 5He took his wife

Sarai, his nephew Lot, all the possessions they had accumulated and the people they had acquired in Haran, and they set out for the land of Canaan, and they arrived there.

6Abram travelled through the land as far as the site of the great tree of Moreh at Shechem. At that time the Canaanites were in the land. 7The LORD appeared to Abram and said, "To your offspring I will give this land." So he built an altar there to the LORD, who had appeared to him.

8From there he went on towards the hills east of Bethel and pitched his tent, with Bethel on the west and Ai on the east. There he built an altar to the LORD and called on the name of the LORD. 9Then Abram set out and continued towards the Negev.

Abram in Egypt

10Now there was a famine in the land, and Abram went down to Egypt to live there for a while because the famine was severe. 11As he was about to enter Egypt, he said to his wife Sarai, "I know what a beautiful woman you are. 12When the Egyptians see you, they will say, 'This is his wife.' Then they will kill me but will let you live. 13Say you are my sister, so that I will be treated well for your sake and my life will be spared because of you."

14When Abram came to Egypt, the Egyptians saw that she was a very beautiful woman. 15And when Pharaoh's officials saw her, they praised her to Pharaoh, and she was taken into his palace. 16He treated Abram well for her sake, and Abram acquired sheep and cattle, male and female donkeys, menservants and maidservants, and camels.

17But the LORD inflicted serious diseases on Pharaoh and his household because of Abram's wife Sarai. 18So Pharaoh summoned Abram. "What have you done to me?" he said. "Why didn't you tell me she was your wife? 19Why did you say, 'She is my sister,' so that I took her to be my wife? Now then, here is your wife. Take her and go!" 20Then Pharaoh gave orders about Abram to his men, and they sent him on his way, with his wife and everything he had.

Abram and Lot Separate

13 So Abram went up from Egypt to the Negev, with his wife and everything he had, and Lot went with him. 2Abram had become very wealthy in livestock and in silver and gold.

3From the Negev he went from place to place until he came to Bethel, to the place between Bethel and Ai where his tent had been earlier 4and where he had first built an altar. There Abram called on the name of the LORD.

5Now Lot, who was moving about with Abram, also had flocks and herds and tents. 6But the land could not support them while they stayed together, for their possessions were so great that they were not able to stay together. 7And quarrelling arose between Abram's herdsmen and the herdsmen of Lot. The Canaanites and Perizzites were also living in the land at that time.

8So Abram said to Lot, "Let's not have any quarrelling between you and me, or between your herdsmen and mine, for we are brothers. 9Is not the whole land before you? Let's part company. If you go to the left, I'll go to the right; if you go to the right, I'll go to the left."

10Lot looked up and saw that the whole plain of the Jordan was well watered, like the garden of the LORD, like the land of Egypt, towards Zoar. (This was before the LORD destroyed Sodom and Gomorrah.) 11So Lot chose for himself the whole plain of the Jordan and set out towards the east. The two men parted company: 12Abram lived in the land of Canaan, while Lot lived among the cities of the plain and pitched his tents near Sodom. 13Now the men of Sodom were wicked and were sinning greatly against the LORD.

14The LORD said to Abram after Lot

had parted from him, "Lift up your eyes from where you are and look north and south, east and west. [15]All the land that you see I will give to you and your offspring for ever. [16]I will make your offspring like the dust of the earth, so that if anyone could count the dust, then your offspring could be counted. [17]Go, walk through the length and breadth of the land, for I am giving it to you."

[18]So Abram moved his tents and went to live near the great trees of Mamre at Hebron, where he built an altar to the LORD.

NEW TESTAMENT READING
Matthew 5:21–42

Murder

[21]"You have heard that it was said to the people long ago, 'Do not murder, and anyone who murders will be subject to judgment.' [22]But I tell you that anyone who is angry with his brother will be subject to judgment. Again, anyone who says to his brother, 'Raca,' is answerable to the Sanhedrin. But anyone who says, 'You fool!' will be in danger of the fire of hell.

[23]"Therefore, if you are offering your gift at the altar and there remember that your brother has something against you, [24]leave your gift there in front of the altar. First go and be reconciled to your brother; then come and offer your gift.

[25]"Settle matters quickly with your adversary who is taking you to court. Do it while you are still with him on the way, or he may hand you over to the judge, and the judge may hand you over to the officer, and you may be thrown into prison. [26]I tell you the truth, you will not get out until you have paid the last penny.

Adultery

[27]"You have heard that it was said, 'Do not commit adultery.' [28]But I tell you that anyone who looks at a woman lustfully has already committed adultery with her in his heart. [29]If your right eye causes you to sin, gouge it out and throw it away. It is better for you to lose one part of your body than for your whole body to be thrown into hell. [30]And if your right hand causes you to sin, cut it off and throw it away. It is better for you to lose one part of your body than for your whole body to go into hell.

Divorce

[31]"It has been said, 'Anyone who divorces his wife must give her a certificate of divorce.' [32]But I tell you that anyone who divorces his wife, except for marital unfaithfulness, causes her to become an adulteress, and anyone who marries the divorced woman commits adultery.

Oaths

[33]"Again, you have heard that it was said to the people long ago, 'Do not break your oath, but keep the oaths you have made to the Lord.' [34]But I tell you, Do not swear at all: either by heaven, for it is God's throne; [35]or by the earth, for it is his footstool; or by Jerusalem, for it is the city of the Great King. [36]And do not swear by your head, for you cannot make even one hair white or black. [37]Simply let your 'Yes' be 'Yes', and your 'No', 'No'; anything beyond this comes from the evil one.

An Eye for an Eye

[38]"You have heard that it was said, 'Eye for eye, and tooth for tooth.' [39]But I tell you, Do not resist an evil person. If someone strikes you on the right cheek, turn to him the other also. [40]And if someone wants to sue you and take your tunic, let him have your cloak as well. [41]If someone forces you to go one mile, go with him two miles. [42]Give to the one who asks you, and do not turn away from the one who wants to borrow from you.

READING FROM PSALMS
Psalm 5:1–12

For the director of music. For flutes.
A psalm of David.

1Give ear to my words, O LORD,
consider my sighing.
2Listen to my cry for help,
my King and my God,
for to you I pray.
3In the morning, O LORD, you hear
my voice;
in the morning I lay my requests
before you
and wait in expectation.

4You are not a God who takes
pleasure in evil;
with you the wicked cannot dwell.
5The arrogant cannot stand in your
presence;
you hate all who do wrong.
6You destroy those who tell lies;
bloodthirsty and deceitful men
the LORD abhors.

7But I, by your great mercy,
will come into your house;
in reverence will I bow down
towards your holy temple.
8Lead me, O LORD, in your
righteousness
because of my enemies—
make straight your way before me.

9Not a word from their mouth can be
trusted;
their heart is filled with
destruction.
Their throat is an open grave;
with their tongue they speak
deceit.
10Declare them guilty, O God!
Let their intrigues be their
downfall.
Banish them for their many sins,
for they have rebelled against you.

11But let all who take refuge in you be
glad;
let them ever sing for joy.
Spread your protection over them,
that those who love your name may
rejoice in you.
12For surely, O LORD, you bless the
righteous;
you surround them with your
favour as with a shield.

JANUARY 7

DAY 7

OLD TESTAMENT READING
Genesis 14:1–16:16

Abram Rescues Lot

14 At this time Amraphel king of
Shinar, Arioch king of Ellasar,
Kedorlaomer king of Elam and Tidal
king of Goiim 2went to war against Bera
king of Sodom, Birsha king of Gomorrah, Shinab king of Admah, Shemeber
king of Zeboiim, and the king of Bela
(that is, Zoar). 3All these latter kings
joined forces in the Valley of Siddim
(the Salt Sea). 4For twelve years they
had been subject to Kedorlaomer, but
in the thirteenth year they rebelled.
5In the fourteenth year, Kedorlaomer and the kings allied with him
went out and defeated the Rephaites in
Ashteroth Karnaim, the Zuzites in
Ham, the Emites in Shaveh Kiriathaim
6and the Horites in the hill country of
Seir, as far as El Paran near the desert.
7Then they turned back and went to En
Mishpat (that is, Kadesh), and they
conquered the whole territory of the
Amalekites, as well as the Amorites
who were living in Hazezon Tamar.
8Then the king of Sodom, the king of

Gomorrah, the king of Admah, the king of Zeboiim and the king of Bela (that is, Zoar) marched out and drew up their battle lines in the Valley of Siddim 9against Kedorlaomer king of Elam, Tidal king of Goiim, Amraphel king of Shinar and Arioch king of Ellasar—four kings against five. 10Now the Valley of Siddim was full of tar pits, and when the kings of Sodom and Gomorrah fled, some of the men fell into them and the rest fled to the hills. 11The four kings seized all the goods of Sodom and Gomorrah and all their food; then they went away. 12They also carried off Abram's nephew Lot and his possessions, since he was living in Sodom.

13One who had escaped came and reported this to Abram the Hebrew. Now Abram was living near the great trees of Mamre the Amorite, a brother of Eshcol and Aner, all of whom were allied with Abram. 14When Abram heard that his relative had been taken captive, he called out the 318 trained men born in his household and went in pursuit as far as Dan. 15During the night Abram divided his men to attack them and he routed them, pursuing them as far as Hobah, north of Damascus. 16He recovered all the goods and brought back his relative Lot and his possessions, together with the women and the other people.

17After Abram returned from defeating Kedorlaomer and the kings allied with him, the king of Sodom came out to meet him in the Valley of Shaveh (that is, the King's Valley).

18Then Melchizedek king of Salem brought out bread and wine. He was priest of God Most High, 19and he blessed Abram, saying,

"Blessed be Abram by God Most
    High,
  Creator of heaven and earth.
20And blessed be God Most High,
  who delivered your enemies into
    your hand."

Then Abram gave him a tenth of everything.

21The king of Sodom said to Abram, "Give me the people and keep the goods for yourself."

22But Abram said to the king of Sodom, "I have raised my hand to the LORD, God Most High, Creator of heaven and earth, and have taken an oath 23that I will accept nothing belonging to you, not even a thread or the thong of a sandal, so that you will never be able to say, 'I made Abram rich.' 24I will accept nothing but what my men have eaten and the share that belongs to the men who went with me—to Aner, Eshcol and Mamre. Let them have their share."

God's Covenant With Abram

15 After this, the word of the LORD came to Abram in a vision:

"Do not be afraid, Abram.
  I am your shield,
  your very great reward."

2But Abram said, "O Sovereign LORD, what can you give me since I remain childless and the one who will inherit my estate is Eliezer of Damascus?" 3And Abram said, "You have given me no children; so a servant in my household will be my heir."

4Then the word of the LORD came to him: "This man will not be your heir, but a son coming from your own body will be your heir." 5He took him outside and said, "Look up at the heavens and count the stars—if indeed you can count them." Then he said to him, "So shall your offspring be."

6Abram believed the LORD, and he credited it to him as righteousness.

7He also said to him, "I am the LORD, who brought you out of Ur of the Chaldeans to give you this land to take possession of it."

8But Abram said, "O Sovereign LORD, how can I know that I shall gain possession of it?"

9So the LORD said to him, "Bring me a heifer, a goat and a ram, each three

years old, along with a dove and a young
pigeon."
[10]Abram brought all these to him, cut
them in two and arranged the halves
opposite each other; the birds, however, he did not cut in half. [11]Then birds
of prey came down on the carcasses, but
Abram drove them away.
[12]As the sun was setting, Abram fell
into a deep sleep, and a thick and dreadful darkness came over him. [13]Then the
LORD said to him, "Know for certain
that your descendants will be strangers
in a country not their own, and they will
be enslaved and ill-treated four hundred years. [14]But I will punish the nation they serve as slaves, and afterwards
they will come out with great possessions. [15]You, however, will go to your
fathers in peace and be buried at a good
old age. [16]In the fourth generation your
descendants will come back here, for
the sin of the Amorites has not yet
reached its full measure."
[17]When the sun had set and darkness
had fallen, a smoking brazier with a
blazing torch appeared and passed between the pieces. [18]On that day the
LORD made a covenant with Abram and
said, "To your descendants I give this
land, from the river of Egypt to the great
river, the Euphrates—[19]the land of the
Kenites, Kenizzites, Kadmonites,
[20]Hittites, Perizzites, Rephaites,
[21]Amorites, Canaanites, Girgashites
and Jebusites."

Hagar and Ishmael

16 Now Sarai, Abram's wife, had
borne him no children. But she
had an Egyptian maidservant named
Hagar; [2]so she said to Abram, "The
LORD has kept me from having children. Go, sleep with my maidservant;
perhaps I can build a family through
her."
Abram agreed to what Sarai said. [3]So
after Abram had been living in Canaan
ten years, Sarai his wife took her Egyptian maidservant Hagar and gave her to
her husband to be his wife. [4]He slept
with Hagar, and she conceived.
When she knew she was pregnant,
she began to despise her mistress.
[5]Then Sarai said to Abram, "You are
responsible for the wrong I am suffering. I put my servant in your arms, and
now that she knows she is pregnant, she
despises me. May the LORD judge between you and me."
[6]"Your servant is in your hands,"
Abram said. "Do with her whatever
you think best." Then Sarai ill-treated
Hagar; so she fled from her.
[7]The angel of the LORD found Hagar
near a spring in the desert; it was the
spring that is beside the road to Shur.
[8]And he said, "Hagar, servant of Sarai,
where have you come from, and where
are you going?"
"I'm running away from my mistress
Sarai," she answered.
[9]Then the angel of the LORD told her,
"Go back to your mistress and submit to
her." [10]The angel added, "I will so increase your descendants that they will
be too numerous to count."
[11]The angel of the LORD also said to
her:

"You are now with child
and you will have a son.
You shall name him Ishmael,
for the LORD has heard of your
misery.
[12]He will be a wild donkey of a man;
his hand will be against everyone
and everyone's hand against him,
and he will live in hostility
towards all his brothers."

[13]She gave this name to the LORD who
spoke to her: "You are the God who
sees me," for she said, "I have now seen
the One who sees me." [14]That is why
the well was called Beer Lahai Roi; it is
still there, between Kadesh and Bered.
[15]So Hagar bore Abram a son, and
Abram gave the name Ishmael to the
son she had borne. [16]Abram was eighty-
six years old when Hagar bore him
Ishmael.

NEW TESTAMENT READING
Matthew 5:43–6:24

Love for Enemies

43“You have heard that it was said,
‘Love your neighbour and hate your
enemy.’ 44But I tell you: Love your
enemies and pray for those who persecute you, 45that you may be sons of your
Father in heaven. He causes his sun to
rise on the evil and the good, and sends
rain on the righteous and the unrighteous. 46If you love those who love you,
what reward will you get? Are not even
the tax collectors doing that? 47And if
you greet only your brothers, what are
you doing more than others? Do not
even pagans do that? 48Be perfect,
therefore, as your heavenly Father is
perfect.

Giving to the Needy

6 “Be careful not to do your ‘acts of
righteousness’ before men, to be
seen by them. If you do, you will have
no reward from your Father in heaven.
2“So when you give to the needy, do
not announce it with trumpets, as the
hypocrites do in the synagogues and on
the streets, to be honoured by men. I
tell you the truth, they have received
their reward in full. 3But when you give
to the needy, do not let your left hand
know what your right hand is doing, 4so
that your giving may be in secret. Then
your Father, who sees what is done in
secret, will reward you.

Prayer

5“And when you pray, do not be like
the hypocrites, for they love to pray
standing in the synagogues and on the
street corners to be seen by men. I tell
you the truth, they have received their
reward in full. 6But when you pray, go
into your room, close the door and pray
to your Father, who is unseen. Then
your Father, who sees what is done in
secret, will reward you. 7And when you
pray, do not keep on babbling like
pagans, for they think they will be heard
because of their many words. 8Do not
be like them, for your Father knows
what you need before you ask him.
9“This, then, is how you should pray:

“ ‘Our Father in heaven,
hallowed be your name,
10your kingdom come,
your will be done
on earth as it is in heaven.
11Give us today our daily bread.
12Forgive us our debts,
as we also have forgiven our
debtors.
13And lead us not into temptation,
but deliver us from the evil one.’

14For if you forgive men when they sin
against you, your heavenly Father will
also forgive you. 15But if you do not
forgive men their sins, your Father will
not forgive your sins.

Fasting

16“When you fast, do not look som-
bre as the hypocrites do, for they dis-
figure their faces to show men they are
fasting. I tell you the truth, they have
received their reward in full. 17But
when you fast, put oil on your head and
wash your face, 18so that it will not be
obvious to men that you are fasting, but
only to your Father, who is unseen; and
your Father, who sees what is done in
secret, will reward you.

Treasures in Heaven

19“Do not store up for yourselves
treasures on earth, where moth and rust
destroy, and where thieves break in and
steal. 20But store up for yourselves treasures in heaven, where moth and rust do
not destroy, and where thieves do not
break in and steal. 21For where your
treasure is, there your heart will be also.
22“The eye is the lamp of the body. If
your eyes are good, your whole body
will be full of light. 23But if your eyes are

bad, your whole body will be full of
darkness. If then the light within you is
darkness, how great is that darkness!
24“No-one can serve two masters.
Either he will hate the one and love the
other, or he will be devoted to the one
and despise the other. You cannot serve
both God and Money.

READING FROM PSALMS
Psalm 6:1–10

For the director of music. With stringed instruments. According to *sheminith*. A psalm of David.

1O LORD, do not rebuke me in your
anger
or discipline me in your wrath.
2Be merciful to me, LORD, for I am
faint;
O LORD, heal me, for my bones are
in agony.
3My soul is in anguish.
How long, O LORD, how long?

4Turn, O LORD, and deliver me;
save me because of your unfailing
love.
5No-one remembers you when he is
dead.
Who praises you from his grave?

6I am worn out from groaning;
all night long I flood my bed with
weeping
and drench my couch with tears.
7My eyes grow weak with sorrow;
they fail because of all my foes.

8Away from me, all you who do evil,
for the LORD has heard my
weeping.
9The LORD has heard my cry for
mercy;
the LORD accepts my prayer.
10All my enemies will be ashamed and
dismayed;
they will turn back in sudden
disgrace.

JANUARY 8

DAY 8

OLD TESTAMENT READING
Genesis 17:1–18:33

The Covenant of Circumcision

17 When Abram was ninety-nine
years old, the LORD appeared to
him and said, “I am God Almighty;
walk before me and be blameless. 2I
will confirm my covenant between me
and you and will greatly increase your
numbers.”
3Abram fell face down, and God said
to him, 4“As for me, this is my covenant
with you: You will be the father of many
nations. 5No longer will you be called
Abram; your name will be Abraham,
for I have made you a father of many
nations. 6I will make you very fruitful; I
will make nations of you, and kings will
come from you. 7I will establish my
covenant as an everlasting covenant between me and you and your descendants after you for the generations to
come, to be your God and the God of
your descendants after you. 8The whole
land of Canaan, where you are now an
alien, I will give as an everlasting possession to you and your descendants
after you; and I will be their God.”
9Then God said to Abraham, “As for
you, you must keep my covenant, you
and your descendants after you for the
generations to come. 10This is my covenant with you and your descendants
after you, the covenant you are to keep:
Every male among you shall be circumcised. 11You are to undergo circumcision, and it will be the sign of the
covenant between me and you. 12For

the generations to come every male
among you who is eight days old must
be circumcised, including those born in
your household or bought with money
from a foreigner—those who are not
your offspring. 13Whether born in your
household or bought with your money,
they must be circumcised. My covenant
in your flesh is to be an everlasting
covenant. 14Any uncircumcised male,
who has not been circumcised in the
flesh, will be cut off from his people; he
has broken my covenant."

15God also said to Abraham, "As for
Sarai your wife, you are no longer to call
her Sarai; her name will be Sarah. 16I
will bless her and will surely give you a
son by her. I will bless her so that she
will be the mother of nations; kings of
peoples will come from her."

17Abraham fell face down; he
laughed and said to himself, "Will a son
be born to a man a hundred years old?
Will Sarah bear a child at the age of
ninety?" 18And Abraham said to God,
"If only Ishmael might live under your
blessing!"

19Then God said, "Yes, but your wife
Sarah will bear you a son, and you will
call him Isaac. I will establish my covenant with him as an everlasting covenant for his descendants after him.
20And as for Ishmael, I have heard you:
I will surely bless him; I will make him
fruitful and will greatly increase his
numbers. He will be the father of twelve
rulers, and I will make him into a great
nation. 21But my covenant I will establish with Isaac, whom Sarah will bear to
you by this time next year." 22When he
had finished speaking with Abraham,
God went up from him.

23On that very day Abraham took his
son Ishmael and all those born in his
household or bought with his money,
every male in his household, and circumcised them, as God told him.
24Abraham was ninety-nine years old
when he was circumcised, 25and his son
Ishmael was thirteen; 26Abraham and
his son Ishmael were both circumcised
on that same day. 27And every male in
Abraham's household, including those
born in his household or bought from a
foreigner, was circumcised with him.

The Three Visitors

18 The LORD appeared to Abraham near the great trees of
Mamre while he was sitting at the entrance to his tent in the heat of the day.
2Abraham looked up and saw three
men standing nearby. When he saw
them, he hurried from the entrance of
his tent to meet them and bowed low to
the ground.

3He said, "If I have found favour in
your eyes, my lord, do not pass your
servant by. 4Let a little water be
brought, and then you may all wash
your feet and rest under this tree. 5Let
me get you something to eat, so you can
be refreshed and then go on your way
—now that you have come to your
servant."

"Very well," they answered, "do as
you say."

6So Abraham hurried into the tent to
Sarah. "Quick," he said, "get three
seahs of fine flour and knead it and bake
some bread."

7Then he ran to the herd and selected
a choice, tender calf and gave it to a
servant, who hurried to prepare it. 8He
then brought some curds and milk and
the calf that had been prepared, and set
these before them. While they ate, he
stood near them under a tree.

9"Where is your wife Sarah?" they
asked him.

"There, in the tent," he said.

10Then the LORD said, "I will surely
return to you about this time next year,
and Sarah your wife will have a son."

Now Sarah was listening at the entrance to the tent, which was behind
him. 11Abraham and Sarah were
already old and well advanced in years,
and Sarah was past the age of childbearing. 12So Sarah laughed to herself as she
thought, "After I am worn out and my
master is old, will I now have this
pleasure?"

13Then the LORD said to Abraham,
"Why did Sarah laugh and say, 'Will I
really have a child, now that I am old?'
14Is anything too hard for the LORD? I
will return to you at the appointed time
next year and Sarah will have a son."
15Sarah was afraid, so she lied and
said, "I did not laugh."

But he said, "Yes, you did laugh."

Abraham Pleads for Sodom

16When the men got up to leave, they
looked down towards Sodom, and
Abraham walked along with them to
see them on their way. 17Then the LORD
said, "Shall I hide from Abraham what I
am about to do? 18Abraham will surely
become a great and powerful nation,
and all nations on earth will be blessed
through him. 19For I have chosen him,
so that he will direct his children and his
household after him to keep the way of
the LORD by doing what is right and
just, so that the LORD will bring about
for Abraham what he has promised
him."
20Then the LORD said, "The outcry
against Sodom and Gomorrah is so
great and their sin so grievous 21that I
will go down and see if what they have
done is as bad as the outcry that has
reached me. If not, I will know."
22The men turned away and went towards Sodom, but Abraham remained
standing before the LORD. 23Then
Abraham approached him and said:
"Will you sweep away the righteous
with the wicked? 24What if there are
fifty righteous people in the city? Will
you really sweep it away and not spare
the place for the sake of the fifty righteous people in it? 25Far be it from you to
do such a thing—to kill the righteous
with the wicked, treating the righteous
and the wicked alike. Far be it from
you! Will not the Judge of all the earth
do right?"
26The LORD said, "If I find fifty righteous people in the city of Sodom, I will
spare the whole place for their sake."
27Then Abraham spoke up again:
"Now that I have been so bold as to
speak to the Lord, though I am nothing
but dust and ashes, 28what if the number
of the righteous is five less than fifty?
Will you destroy the whole city because
of five people?"

"If I find forty-five there," he said, "I will not destroy it."

29Once again he spoke to him, "What
if only forty are found there?"

He said, "For the sake of forty, I will not do it."

30Then he said, "May the Lord not be
angry, but let me speak. What if only
thirty can be found there?"

He answered, "I will not do it if I find thirty there."

31Abraham said, "Now that I have
been so bold as to speak to the Lord,
what if only twenty can be found
there?"

He said, "For the sake of twenty, I will not destroy it."

32Then he said, "May the Lord not be
angry, but let me speak just once more.
What if only ten can be found there?"

He answered, "For the sake of ten, I will not destroy it."

33When the LORD had finished speaking with Abraham, he left, and Abraham returned home.

NEW TESTAMENT READING
Matthew 6:25–7:23

Do Not Worry

25"Therefore I tell you, do not worry
about your life, what you will eat or
drink; or about your body, what you
will wear. Is not life more important
than food, and the body more important than clothes? 26Look at the birds of
the air; they do not sow or reap or store
away in barns, and yet your heavenly
Father feeds them. Are you not much
more valuable than they? 27Who of you
by worrying can add a single hour to his
life?
28"And why do you worry about
clothes? See how the lilies of the field
grow. They do not labour or spin. 29Yet

I tell you that not even Solomon in all
his splendour was dressed like one of
these. 30If that is how God clothes the
grass of the field, which is here today
and tomorrow is thrown into the fire,
will he not much more clothe you, O
you of little faith? 31So do not worry,
saying, 'What shall we eat?' or 'What
shall we drink?' or 'What shall we
wear?' 32For the pagans run after all
these things, and your heavenly Father
knows that you need them. 33But seek
first his kingdom and his righteousness,
and all these things will be given to you
as well. 34Therefore do not worry about
tomorrow, for tomorrow will worry
about itself. Each day has enough
trouble of its own.

Judging Others

7 "Do not judge, or you too will be
judged. 2For in the same way as
you judge others, you will be judged,
and with the measure you use, it will be
measured to you.

3"Why do you look at the speck of
sawdust in your brother's eye and pay
no attention to the plank in your own
eye? 4How can you say to your brother,
'Let me take the speck out of your eye,'
when all the time there is a plank in your
own eye? 5You hypocrite, first take the
plank out of your own eye, and then you
will see clearly to remove the speck
from your brother's eye.

6"Do not give dogs what is sacred; do
not throw your pearls to pigs. If you do,
they may trample them under their feet,
and then turn and tear you to pieces.

Ask, Seek, Knock

7"Ask and it will be given to you; seek
and you will find; knock and the door
will be opened to you. 8For everyone
who asks receives; he who seeks finds;
and to him who knocks, the door will be
opened.

9"Which of you, if his son asks for
bread, will give him a stone? 10Or if he
asks for a fish, will give him a snake? 11If
you, then, though you are evil, know
how to give good gifts to your children,
how much more will your Father in
heaven give good gifts to those who ask
him! 12So in everything, do to others
what you would have them do to you,
for this sums up the Law and the
Prophets.

The Narrow and Wide Gates

13"Enter through the narrow gate.
For wide is the gate and broad is the
road that leads to destruction, and
many enter through it. 14But small is the
gate and narrow the road that leads to
life, and only a few find it.

A Tree and Its Fruit

15"Watch out for false prophets.
They come to you in sheep's clothing,
but inwardly they are ferocious wolves.
16By their fruit you will recognise them.
Do people pick grapes from thornbushes, or figs from thistles? 17Like-
wise every good tree bears good fruit,
but a bad tree bears bad fruit. 18A
good tree cannot bear bad fruit, and
a bad tree cannot bear good fruit.
19Every tree that does not bear good
fruit is cut down and thrown into the
fire. 20Thus, by their fruit you will
recognise them.

21"Not everyone who says to me,
'Lord, Lord,' will enter the kingdom of
heaven, but only he who does the will of
my Father who is in heaven. 22Many will
say to me on that day, 'Lord, Lord, did
we not prophesy in your name, and in
your name drive out demons and perform many miracles?' 23Then I will tell
them plainly, 'I never knew you. Away
from me, you evildoers!'

READING FROM PROVERBS

Proverbs 1:8–19

Exhortations to Embrace Wisdom

Warning Against Enticement

8Listen, my son, to your father's
instruction

and do not forsake your mother's
teaching.
9They will be a garland to grace your
head
and a chain to adorn your neck.

10My son, if sinners entice you,
do not give in to them.
11If they say, "Come along with us;
let's lie in wait for someone's
blood,
let's waylay some harmless soul;
12let's swallow them alive, like the
grave,
and whole, like those who go down
to the pit;
13we will get all sorts of valuable things
and fill our houses with plunder;
14throw in your lot with us,
and we will share a common
purse"—
15my son, do not go along with them,
do not set foot on their paths;
16for their feet rush into sin,
they are swift to shed blood.
17How useless to spread a net
in full view of all the birds!
18These men lie in wait for their own
blood;
they waylay only themselves!
19Such is the end of all who go after
ill-gotten gain;
it takes away the lives of those who
get it.

JANUARY 9

DAY 9

OLD TESTAMENT READING

Genesis 19:1–20:18

Sodom and Gomorrah Destroyed

19 The two angels arrived at
Sodom in the evening, and Lot
was sitting in the gateway of the city.
When he saw them, he got up to meet
them and bowed down with his face to
the ground. 2"My lords," he said,
"please turn aside to your servant's
house. You can wash your feet and
spend the night and then go on your way
early in the morning."

"No," they answered, "we will spend
the night in the square."

3But he insisted so strongly that they
did go with him and entered his house.
He prepared a meal for them, baking
bread without yeast, and they ate.
4Before they had gone to bed, all the
men from every part of the city of
Sodom—both young and old—
surrounded the house. 5They called to
Lot, "Where are the men who came
to you tonight? Bring them out to us so
that we can have sex with them."

6Lot went outside to meet them and
shut the door behind him 7and said,
"No, my friends. Don't do this wicked
thing. 8Look, I have two daughters who
have never slept with a man. Let me
bring them out to you, and you can do
what you like with them. But don't do
anything to these men, for they have
come under the protection of my roof."

9"Get out of our way," they replied.
And they said, "This fellow came here
as an alien, and now he wants to play the
judge! We'll treat you worse than
them." They kept bringing pressure on
Lot and moved forward to break down
the door.

10But the men inside reached out and
pulled Lot back into the house and shut
the door. 11Then they struck the men
who were at the door of the house,
young and old, with blindness so that
they could not find the door.

12The two men said to Lot, "Do you
have anyone else here—sons-in-law,
sons or daughters, or anyone else in the

city who belongs to you? Get them out
of here, [13]because we are going to destroy this place. The outcry to the
LORD against its people is so great that
he has sent us to destroy it."
[14]So Lot went out and spoke to his
sons-in-law, who were pledged to marry
his daughters. He said, "Hurry and get
out of this place, because the LORD is
about to destroy the city!" But his sons-
in-law thought he was joking.
[15]With the coming of dawn, the
angels urged Lot, saying, "Hurry! Take
your wife and your two daughters who
are here, or you will be swept away
when the city is punished."
[16]When he hesitated, the men
grasped his hand and the hands of his
wife and of his two daughters and led
them safely out of the city, for the LORD
was merciful to them. [17]As soon as they
had brought them out, one of them said,
"Flee for your lives! Don't look back,
and don't stop anywhere in the plain!
Flee to the mountains or you will be
swept away!"
[18]But Lot said to them, "No, my
lords, please! [19]Your servant has found
favour in your eyes, and you have shown
great kindness to me in sparing my life.
But I can't flee to the mountains; this
disaster will overtake me, and I'll die.
[20]Look, here is a town near enough to
run to, and it is small. Let me flee to
it—it is very small, isn't it? Then my life
will be spared."
[21]He said to him, "Very well, I will
grant this request too; I will not overthrow the town you speak of. [22]But flee
there quickly, because I cannot do anything until you reach it." (That is why
the town was called Zoar.)
[23]By the time Lot reached Zoar, the
sun had risen over the land. [24]Then the
LORD rained down burning sulphur on
Sodom and Gomorrah—from the LORD
out of the heavens. [25]Thus he overthrew
those cities and the entire plain, including all those living in the cities—and
also the vegetation in the land. [26]But
Lot's wife looked back, and she became
a pillar of salt.
[27]Early the next morning Abraham
got up and returned to the place where
he had stood before the LORD. [28]He
looked down towards Sodom and
Gomorrah, towards all the land of
the plain, and he saw dense smoke
rising from the land, like smoke from
a furnace.
[29]So when God destroyed the cities of
the plain, he remembered Abraham,
and he brought Lot out of the catastrophe that overthrew the cities where
Lot had lived.

Lot and His Daughters

[30]Lot and his two daughters left Zoar
and settled in the mountains, for he was
afraid to stay in Zoar. He and his two
daughters lived in a cave. [31]One day the
older daughter said to the younger,
"Our father is old, and there is no man
around here to lie with us, as is the
custom all over the earth. [32]Let's get our
father to drink wine and then lie with
him and preserve our family line
through our father."
[33]That night they got their father to
drink wine, and the older daughter went
in and lay with him. He was not aware of
it when she lay down or when she got
up.
[34]The next day the older daughter
said to the younger, "Last night I lay
with my father. Let's get him to drink
wine again tonight, and you go in and lie
with him so we can preserve our family
line through our father." [35]So they got
their father to drink wine that night
also, and the younger daughter went
and lay with him. Again he was not
aware of it when she lay down or when
she got up.
[36]So both of Lot's daughters became
pregnant by their father. [37]The older
daughter had a son, and she named him
Moab; he is the father of the Moabites
of today. [38]The younger daughter also
had a son, and she named him Ben-
Ammi; he is the father of the Ammonites of today.

Abraham and Abimelech

20 Now Abraham moved on from
there into the region of the
Negev and lived between Kadesh and
Shur. For a while he stayed in Gerar,
2and there Abraham said of his wife
Sarah, "She is my sister." Then
Abimelech king of Gerar sent for Sarah
and took her.
3But God came to Abimelech in a
dream one night and said to him, "You
are as good as dead because of the
woman you have taken; she is a married
woman."
4Now Abimelech had not gone near
her, so he said, "Lord, will you destroy
an innocent nation? 5Did he not say to
me, 'She is my sister,' and didn't she
also say, 'He is my brother'? I have
done this with a clear conscience and
clean hands."
6Then God said to him in the dream,
"Yes, I know you did this with a clear
conscience, and so I have kept you from
sinning against me. That is why I did not
let you touch her. 7Now return the
man's wife, for he is a prophet, and he
will pray for you and you will live. But if
you do not return her, you may be sure
that you and all yours will die."
8Early the next morning Abimelech
summoned all his officials, and when he
told them all that had happened, they
were very much afraid. 9Then
Abimelech called Abraham in and said,
"What have you done to us? How have I
wronged you that you have brought
such great guilt upon me and my kingdom? You have done things to me that
should not be done." 10And Abimelech
asked Abraham, "What was your
reason for doing this?"
11Abraham replied, "I said to myself,
'There is surely no fear of God in this
place, and they will kill me because of
my wife.' 12Besides, she really is my
sister, the daughter of my father though
not of my mother; and she became my
wife. 13And when God caused me to
wander from my father's household, I
said to her, 'This is how you can show
your love to me: Everywhere we go, say
of me, "He is my brother."'"
14Then Abimelech brought sheep and
cattle and male and female slaves and
gave them to Abraham, and he returned Sarah his wife to him. 15And
Abimelech said, "My land is before
you; live wherever you like."
16To Sarah he said, "I am giving your
brother a thousand shekels of silver.
This is to cover the offence against you
before all who are with you; you are
completely vindicated."
17Then Abraham prayed to God, and
God healed Abimelech, his wife and his
slave girls so they could have children
again, 18for the LORD had closed up
every womb in Abimelech's household
because of Abraham's wife Sarah.

NEW TESTAMENT READING

Matthew 7:24–8:22

The Wise and Foolish Builders

24"Therefore everyone who hears
these words of mine and puts them into
practice is like a wise man who built his
house on the rock. 25The rain came
down, the streams rose, and the winds
blew and beat against that house; yet it
did not fall, because it had its foundation on the rock. 26But everyone who
hears these words of mine and does not
put them into practice is like a foolish
man who built his house on sand. 27The
rain came down, the streams rose, and
the winds blew and beat against that
house, and it fell with a great crash."

28When Jesus had finished saying
these things, the crowds were amazed at
his teaching, 29because he taught as one
who had authority, and not as their
teachers of the law.

The Man With Leprosy

8 When he came down from the
mountainside, large crowds followed him. 2A man with leprosy came

and knelt before him and said, "Lord, if
you are willing, you can make me
clean."
3Jesus reached out his hand and
touched the man. "I am willing," he
said. "Be clean!" Immediately he was
cured of his leprosy. 4Then Jesus said to
him, "See that you don't tell anyone.
But go, show yourself to the priest and
offer the gift Moses commanded, as a
testimony to them."

The Faith of the Centurion

5When Jesus had entered Capernaum, a centurion came to him, asking
for help. 6"Lord," he said, "my servant
lies at home paralysed and in terrible
suffering."
7Jesus said to him, "I will go and heal
him."
8The centurion replied, "Lord, I do
not deserve to have you come under my
roof. But just say the word, and my
servant will be healed. 9For I myself am
a man under authority, with soldiers
under me. I tell this one, 'Go,' and he
goes; and that one, 'Come,' and he
comes. I say to my servant, 'Do this,'
and he does it."
10When Jesus heard this, he was
astonished and said to those following
him, "I tell you the truth, I have not
found anyone in Israel with such great
faith. 11I say to you that many will come
from the east and the west, and will take
their places at the feast with Abraham,
Isaac and Jacob in the kingdom of
heaven. 12But the subjects of the kingdom will be thrown outside, into the
darkness, where there will be weeping
and gnashing of teeth."
13Then Jesus said to the centurion,
"Go! It will be done just as you believed
it would." And his servant was healed at
that very hour.

Jesus Heals Many

14When Jesus came into Peter's
house, he saw Peter's mother-in-law
lying in bed with a fever. 15He touched
her hand and the fever left her, and she
got up and began to wait on him.
16When evening came, many who
were demon-possessed were brought to
him, and he drove out the spirits with a
word and healed all the sick. 17This was
to fulfil what was spoken through the
prophet Isaiah:

"He took up our infirmities
and carried our diseases."

The Cost of Following Jesus

18When Jesus saw the crowd around
him, he gave orders to cross to the other
side of the lake. 19Then a teacher of the
law came to him and said, "Teacher, I
will follow you wherever you go."
20Jesus replied, "Foxes have holes
and birds of the air have nests, but the
Son of Man has nowhere to lay his
head."
21Another disciple said to him,
"Lord, first let me go and bury my
father."
22But Jesus told him, "Follow me,
and let the dead bury their own dead."

READING FROM PSALMS
Psalm 7:1–9

A *shiggaion* of David, which he sang to the
LORD concerning Cush, a Benjamite.

1O LORD my God, I take refuge in
you;
save and deliver me from all who
pursue me,
2or they will tear me like a lion
and rip me to pieces with no-one to
rescue me.

3O LORD my God, if I have done this
and there is guilt on my hands—
4if I have done evil to him who is at
peace with me
or without cause have robbed my
foe—
5then let my enemy pursue and
overtake me;

let him trample my life to the
ground
and make me sleep in the dust.
Selah

6Arise, O LORD, in your anger;
rise up against the rage of my
enemies.
Awake, my God; decree justice.
7Let the assembled peoples gather
round you.
Rule over them from on high;
8 let the LORD judge the peoples.
Judge me, O LORD, according to my
righteousness,
according to my integrity, O Most
High.
9O righteous God,
who searches minds and hearts,
bring to an end the violence of the
wicked
and make the righteous secure.

JANUARY 10

DAY 10

OLD TESTAMENT READING

Genesis 21:1–23:20

The Birth of Isaac

21 Now the LORD was gracious to
Sarah as he had said, and the
LORD did for Sarah what he had promised. 2Sarah became pregnant and bore
a son to Abraham in his old age, at the
very time God had promised him.
3Abraham gave the name Isaac to the
son Sarah bore him. 4When his son
Isaac was eight days old, Abraham circumcised him, as God commanded him.
5Abraham was a hundred years old
when his son Isaac was born to him.
6Sarah said, "God has brought me
laughter, and everyone who hears
about this will laugh with me." 7And
she added, "Who would have said to
Abraham that Sarah would nurse children? Yet I have borne him a son in his
old age."

Hagar and Ishmael Sent Away

8The child grew and was weaned, and
on the day Isaac was weaned Abraham
held a great feast. 9But Sarah saw that
the son whom Hagar the Egyptian had
borne to Abraham was mocking, 10and
she said to Abraham, "Get rid of that
slave woman and her son, for that slave
woman's son will never share in the
inheritance with my son Isaac."
11The matter distressed Abraham
greatly because it concerned his son.
12But God said to him, "Do not be so
distressed about the boy and your maidservant. Listen to whatever Sarah tells
you, because it is through Isaac that
your offspring will be reckoned. 13I will
make the son of the maidservant into a
nation also, because he is your
offspring."
14Early the next morning Abraham
took some food and a skin of water and
gave them to Hagar. He set them on her
shoulders and then sent her off with the
boy. She went on her way and wandered
in the desert of Beersheba.
15When the water in the skin was
gone, she put the boy under one of the
bushes. 16Then she went off and sat
down nearby, about a bow-shot away,
for she thought, "I cannot watch the
boy die." And as she sat there nearby,
she began to sob.
17God heard the boy crying, and the
angel of God called to Hagar from
heaven and said to her, "What is the
matter, Hagar? Do not be afraid; God
has heard the boy crying as he lies there.
18Lift the boy up and take him by the
hand, for I will make him into a great
nation."

19Then God opened her eyes and she
saw a well of water. So she went and
filled the skin with water and gave the
boy a drink.
20God was with the boy as he grew up.
He lived in the desert and became an
archer. 21While he was living in the
Desert of Paran, his mother got a wife
for him from Egypt.

The Treaty at Beersheba

22At that time Abimelech and Phicol
the commander of his forces said to
Abraham, "God is with you in everything you do. 23Now swear to me here
before God that you will not deal falsely
with me or my children or my descendants. Show to me and the country where
you are living as an alien the same kindness that I have shown to you."
24Abraham said, "I swear it."
25Then Abraham complained to
Abimelech about a well of water
that Abimelech's servants had seized.
26But Abimelech said, "I don't know
who has done this. You did not tell
me, and I heard about it only today."
27So Abraham brought sheep and
cattle and gave them to Abimelech, and
the two men made a treaty. 28Abraham
set apart seven ewe lambs from the
flock, 29and Abimelech asked Abraham, "What is the meaning of these
seven ewe lambs you have set apart by
themselves?"
30He replied, "Accept these seven
lambs from my hand as a witness that I
dug this well."
31So that place was called Beersheba,
because the two men swore an oath
there.
32After the treaty had been made at
Beersheba, Abimelech and Phicol the
commander of his forces returned to the
land of the Philistines. 33Abraham
planted a tamarisk tree in Beersheba,
and there he called upon the name of
the LORD, the Eternal God. 34And
Abraham stayed in the land of the
Philistines for a long time.

Abraham Tested

22 Some time later God tested
Abraham. He said to him,
"Abraham!"
"Here I am," he replied.
2Then God said, "Take your son,
your only son, Isaac, whom you love,
and go to the region of Moriah. Sacrifice
him there as a burnt offering on one of
the mountains I will tell you about."
3Early the next morning Abraham
got up and saddled his donkey. He took
with him two of his servants and his son
Isaac. When he had cut enough wood
for the burnt offering, he set out for the
place God had told him about. 4On the
third day Abraham looked up and saw
the place in the distance. 5He said to his
servants, "Stay here with the donkey
while I and the boy go over there. We
will worship and then we will come back
to you."
6Abraham took the wood for the
burnt offering and placed it on his son
Isaac, and he himself carried the fire
and the knife. As the two of them went
on together, 7Isaac spoke up and said to
his father Abraham, "Father?"
"Yes, my son?" Abraham replied.
"The fire and wood are here," Isaac
said, "but where is the lamb for the
burnt offering?"
8Abraham answered, "God himself
will provide the lamb for the burnt
offering, my son." And the two of them
went on together.
9When they reached the place God
had told him about, Abraham built an
altar there and arranged the wood on it.
He bound his son Isaac and laid him on
the altar, on top of the wood. 10Then he
reached out his hand and took the knife
to slay his son. 11But the angel of the
LORD called out to him from heaven,
"Abraham! Abraham!"
"Here I am," he replied.
12"Do not lay a hand on the boy," he
said. "Do not do anything to him. Now I
know that you fear God, because you
have not withheld from me your son,
your only son."

13Abraham looked up and there in a
thicket he saw a ram caught by its horns.
He went over and took the ram and
sacrificed it as a burnt offering instead
of his son. 14So Abraham called that
place The LORD Will Provide. And to
this day it is said, "On the mountain of
the LORD it will be provided."

15The angel of the LORD called to
Abraham from heaven a second time
16and said, "I swear by myself, declares
the LORD, that because you have done
this and have not withheld your son,
your only son, 17I will surely bless you
and make your descendants as numerous as the stars in the sky and as the sand
on the seashore. Your descendants will
take possession of the cities of their
enemies, 18and through your offspring
all nations on earth will be blessed,
because you have obeyed me."

19Then Abraham returned to his ser-
vants, and they set off together for
Beersheba. And Abraham stayed in
Beersheba.

Nahor's Sons

20Some time later Abraham was told,
"Milcah is also a mother; she has borne
sons to your brother Nahor: 21Uz the
firstborn, Buz his brother, Kemuel (the
father of Aram), 22Kesed, Hazo, Pil-
dash, Jidlaph and Bethuel." 23Bethuel
became the father of Rebekah. Milcah
bore these eight sons to Abraham's
brother Nahor. 24His concubine, whose
name was Reumah, also had sons:
Tebah, Gaham, Tahash and Maacah.

The Death of Sarah

23 Sarah lived to be a hundred and
twenty-seven years old. 2She
died at Kiriath Arba (that is, Hebron) in
the land of Canaan, and Abraham went
to mourn for Sarah and to weep over
her.

3Then Abraham rose from beside his
dead wife and spoke to the Hittites. He
said, 4"I am an alien and a stranger
among you. Sell me some property for a
burial site here so that I can bury my
dead."

5The Hittites replied to Abraham,
6"Sir, listen to us. You are a mighty
prince among us. Bury your dead in the
choicest of our tombs. None of us will
refuse you his tomb for burying your
dead."

7Then Abraham rose and bowed
down before the people of the land, the
Hittites. 8He said to them, "If you are
willing to let me bury my dead, then
listen to me and intercede with Ephron
son of Zohar on my behalf 9so that he
will sell me the cave of Machpelah,
which belongs to him and is at the end
of his field. Ask him to sell it to me for
the full price as a burial site among
you."

10Ephron the Hittite was sitting
among his people and he replied to
Abraham in the hearing of all the Hittites who had come to the gate of his
city. 11"No, my lord," he said. "Listen
to me; I give you the field, and I give you
the cave that is in it. I give it to you in the
presence of my people. Bury your
dead."

12Again Abraham bowed down before the people of the land 13and he said
to Ephron in their hearing, "Listen to
me, if you will. I will pay the price of the
field. Accept it from me so that I can
bury my dead there."

14Ephron answered Abraham,
15"Listen to me, my lord; the land is
worth four hundred shekels of silver,
but what is that between me and you?
Bury your dead."

16Abraham agreed to Ephron's terms
and weighed out for him the price he
had named in the hearing of the Hittites: four hundred shekels of silver,
according to the weight current among
the merchants.

17So Ephron's field in Machpelah
near Mamre—both the field and the
cave in it, and all the trees within the
borders of the field—was legally made
over 18to Abraham as his property in the
presence of all the Hittites who had

come to the gate of the city. 19After-
wards Abraham buried his wife Sarah
in the cave in the field of Machpelah
near Mamre (which is at Hebron) in the
land of Canaan. 20So the field and
the cave in it were legally made over to
Abraham by the Hittites as a burial site.

NEW TESTAMENT READING

Matthew 8:23–9:13

Jesus Calms the Storm

23Then he got into the boat and his
disciples followed him. 24Without warning, a furious storm came up on the
lake, so that the waves swept over the
boat. But Jesus was sleeping. 25The disciples went and woke him, saying,
"Lord, save us! We're going to drown!"

26He replied, "You of little faith, why
are you so afraid?" Then he got up and
rebuked the winds and the waves, and it
was completely calm.

27The men were amazed and asked,
"What kind of man is this? Even the
winds and the waves obey him!"

The Healing of Two Demon-possessed Men

28When he arrived at the other side
in the region of the Gadarenes, two
demon-possessed men coming from the
tombs met him. They were so violent
that no-one could pass that way.
29"What do you want with us, Son of
God?" they shouted. "Have you come
here to torture us before the appointed
time?"

30Some distance from them a large
herd of pigs was feeding. 31The demons
begged Jesus, "If you drive us out, send
us into the herd of pigs."

32He said to them, "Go!" So they
came out and went into the pigs, and the
whole herd rushed down the steep bank
into the lake and died in the water.
33Those tending the pigs ran off, went
into the town and reported all this,
including what had happened to the
demon-possessed men. 34Then the
whole town went out to meet Jesus.
And when they saw him, they pleaded
with him to leave their region.

Jesus Heals a Paralytic

9 Jesus stepped into a boat, crossed
over and came to his own town.
2Some men brought to him a paralytic,
lying on a mat. When Jesus saw their
faith, he said to the paralytic, "Take
heart, son; your sins are forgiven."

3At this, some of the teachers of the
law said to themselves, "This fellow is
blaspheming!"

4Knowing their thoughts, Jesus said,
"Why do you entertain evil thoughts in
your hearts? 5Which is easier: to say,
'Your sins are forgiven,' or to say, 'Get
up and walk'? 6But so that you may
know that the Son of Man has authority
on earth to forgive sins. . . ." Then he
said to the paralytic, "Get up, take your
mat and go home." 7And the man got
up and went home. 8When the crowd
saw this, they were filled with awe; and
they praised God, who had given such
authority to men.

The Calling of Matthew

9As Jesus went on from there, he saw
a man named Matthew sitting at the tax
collector's booth. "Follow me," he told
him, and Matthew got up and followed
him.

10While Jesus was having dinner at
Matthew's house, many tax collectors
and "sinners" came and ate with him
and his disciples. 11When the Pharisees
saw this, they asked his disciples, "Why
does your teacher eat with tax collectors
and 'sinners'?"

12On hearing this, Jesus said, "It is
not the healthy who need a doctor, but
the sick. 13But go and learn what this
means: 'I desire mercy, not sacrifice.'
For I have not come to call the righteous, but sinners."

READING FROM PSALMS

Psalm 7:10–17

10My shield is God Most High,
who saves the upright in heart.
11God is a righteous judge,
a God who expresses his wrath
every day.
12If he does not relent,
he will sharpen his sword;
he will bend and string his bow.
13He has prepared his deadly
weapons;
he makes ready his flaming arrows.
14He who is pregnant with evil
and conceives trouble gives birth to
disillusionment.
15He who digs a hole and scoops it out
falls into the pit he has made.
16The trouble he causes recoils on
himself;
his violence comes down on his
own head.

17I will give thanks to the LORD
because of his righteousness
and will sing praise to the name of
the LORD Most High.

JANUARY 11

DAY 11

OLD TESTAMENT READING

Genesis 24:1–67

Isaac and Rebekah

24 Abraham was now old and well
advanced in years, and the LORD
had blessed him in every way. 2He said
to the chief servant in his household, the
one in charge of all that he had, "Put
your hand under my thigh. 3I want you
to swear by the LORD, the God of
heaven and the God of earth, that you
will not get a wife for my son from the
daughters of the Canaanites, among
whom I am living, 4but will go to my
country and my own relatives and get a
wife for my son Isaac."
5The servant asked him, "What if the
woman is unwilling to come back with
me to this land? Shall I then take your
son back to the country you came
from?"
6"Make sure that you do not take my
son back there," Abraham said. 7"The
LORD, the God of heaven, who brought
me out of my father's household and my
native land and who spoke to me and
promised me on oath, saying, 'To your
offspring I will give this land'—he will
send his angel before you so that you
can get a wife for my son from there. 8If
the woman is unwilling to come back
with you, then you will be released from
this oath of mine. Only do not take my
son back there." 9So the servant put his
hand under the thigh of his master
Abraham and swore an oath to him
concerning this matter.
10Then the servant took ten of his
master's camels and left, taking with
him all kinds of good things from his
master. He set out for Aram Naharaim
and made his way to the town of Nahor.
11He made the camels kneel down near
the well outside the town; it was towards evening, the time the women go
out to draw water.
12Then he prayed, "O LORD, God of
my master Abraham, give me success
today, and show kindness to my master
Abraham. 13See, I am standing beside
this spring, and the daughters of the
townspeople are coming out to draw
water. 14May it be that when I say to a
girl, 'Please let down your jar that I may
have a drink,' and she says, 'Drink, and
I'll water your camels too'—let her be
the one you have chosen for your servant Isaac. By this I will know that you
have shown kindness to my master."

15Before he had finished praying, Rebekah came out with her jar on her
shoulder. She was the daughter of
Bethuel son of Milcah, who was the wife
of Abraham's brother Nahor. 16The girl
was very beautiful, a virgin; no man had
ever lain with her. She went down to the
spring, filled her jar and came up again.
17The servant hurried to meet her and
said, "Please give me a little water from
your jar."
18"Drink, my lord," she said, and
quickly lowered the jar to her hands and
gave him a drink.
19After she had given him a drink, she
said, "I'll draw water for your camels
too, until they have finished drinking."
20So she quickly emptied her jar into the
trough, ran back to the well to draw
more water, and drew enough for all his
camels. 21Without saying a word, the
man watched her closely to learn
whether or not the LORD had made his
journey successful.
22When the camels had finished
drinking, the man took out a gold nose
ring weighing a beka and two gold
bracelets weighing ten shekels. 23Then
he asked, "Whose daughter are you?
Please tell me, is there room in your
father's house for us to spend the
night?"
24She answered him, "I am the
daughter of Bethuel, the son that Milcah bore to Nahor." 25And she added,
"We have plenty of straw and fodder, as
well as room for you to spend the
night."
26Then the man bowed down and
worshipped the LORD, 27saying, "Praise
be to the LORD, the God of my master
Abraham, who has not abandoned his
kindness and faithfulness to my master.
As for me, the LORD has led me on the
journey to the house of my master's
relatives."
28The girl ran and told her mother's
household about these things. 29Now
Rebekah had a brother named Laban,
and he hurried out to the man at the
spring. 30As soon as he had seen the
nose ring, and the bracelets on his
sister's arms, and had heard Rebekah
tell what the man said to her, he went
out to the man and found him standing
by the camels near the spring. 31"Come,
you who are blessed by the LORD," he
said. "Why are you standing out here?
I have prepared the house and a place
for the camels."
32So the man went to the house, and
the camels were unloaded. Straw and
fodder were brought for the camels,
and water for him and his men to wash
their feet. 33Then food was set before
him, but he said, "I will not eat until I
have told you what I have to say."
"Then tell us," ⌊Laban⌋ said.
34So he said, "I am Abraham's servant. 35The LORD has blessed my master
abundantly, and he has become
wealthy. He has given him sheep and
cattle, silver and gold, menservants and
maidservants, and camels and donkeys.
36My master's wife Sarah has borne him
a son in her old age, and he has given
him everything he owns. 37And my master made me swear an oath, and said,
'You must not get a wife for my son
from the daughters of the Canaanites,
in whose land I live, 38but go to my
father's family and to my own clan, and
get a wife for my son.'
39"Then I asked my master, 'What if
the woman will not come back with
me?'
40"He replied, 'The LORD, before
whom I have walked, will send his angel
with you and make your journey a success, so that you can get a wife for my
son from my own clan and from my
father's family. 41Then, when you go to
my clan, you will be released from my
oath even if they refuse to give her to
you—you will be released from my
oath.'
42"When I came to the spring today, I
said, 'O LORD, God of my master Abraham, if you will, please grant success to
the journey on which I have come.
43See, I am standing beside this spring;
if a maiden comes out to draw water and
I say to her, "Please let me drink a little
water from your jar," 44and if she says

to me, "Drink, and I'll draw water for your camels too," let her be the one the LORD has chosen for my master's son.'

45"Before I finished praying in my heart, Rebekah came out, with her jar on her shoulder. She went down to the spring and drew water, and I said to her, 'Please give me a drink.'

46"She quickly lowered her jar from her shoulder and said, 'Drink, and I'll water your camels too.' So I drank, and she watered the camels also.

47"I asked her, 'Whose daughter are you?'

"She said, 'The daughter of Bethuel son of Nahor, whom Milcah bore to him.'

"Then I put the ring in her nose and the bracelets on her arms, 48and I bowed down and worshipped the LORD. I praised the LORD, the God of my master Abraham, who had led me on the right road to get the granddaughter of my master's brother for his son. 49Now if you will show kindness and faithfulness to my master, tell me; and if not, tell me, so I may know which way to turn."

50Laban and Bethuel answered, "This is from the LORD; we can say nothing to you one way or the other. 51Here is Rebekah; take her and go, and let her become the wife of your master's son, as the LORD has directed."

52When Abraham's servant heard what they said, he bowed down to the ground before the LORD. 53Then the servant brought out gold and silver jewellery and articles of clothing and gave them to Rebekah; he also gave costly gifts to her brother and to her mother. 54Then he and the men who were with him ate and drank and spent the night there.

When they got up the next morning, he said, "Send me on my way to my master."

55But her brother and her mother replied, "Let the girl remain with us ten days or so; then you may go."

56But he said to them, "Do not detain me, now that the LORD has granted success to my journey. Send me on my way so I may go to my master."

57Then they said, "Let's call the girl and ask her about it." 58So they called Rebekah and asked her, "Will you go with this man?"

"I will go," she said.

59So they sent their sister Rebekah on her way, along with her nurse and Abraham's servant and his men. 60And they blessed Rebekah and said to her,

"Our sister, may you increase
to thousands upon thousands;
may your offspring possess
the gates of their enemies."

61Then Rebekah and her maids got ready and mounted their camels and went back with the man. So the servant took Rebekah and left.

62Now Isaac had come from Beer Lahai Roi, for he was living in the Negev. 63He went out to the field one evening to meditate, and as he looked up, he saw camels approaching. 64Rebekah also looked up and saw Isaac. She got down from her camel 65and asked the servant, "Who is that man in the field coming to meet us?"

"He is my master," the servant answered. So she took her veil and covered herself.

66Then the servant told Isaac all he had done. 67Isaac brought her into the tent of his mother Sarah, and he married Rebekah. So she became his wife, and he loved her; and Isaac was comforted after his mother's death.

NEW TESTAMENT READING

Matthew 9:14–38

Jesus Questioned About Fasting

14Then John's disciples came and asked him, "How is it that we and the Pharisees fast, but your disciples do not fast?"

15Jesus answered, "How can the guests of the bridegroom mourn while

he is with them? The time will come
when the bridegroom will be taken from
them; then they will fast.
16"No-one sews a patch of unshrunk
cloth on an old garment, for the patch
will pull away from the garment, making the tear worse. 17Neither do men
pour new wine into old wineskins. If
they do, the skins will burst, the wine
will run out and the wineskins will
be ruined. No, they pour new wine
into new wineskins, and both are
preserved."

A Dead Girl and a Sick Woman

18While he was saying this, a ruler
came and knelt before him and said,
"My daughter has just died. But come
and put your hand on her, and she will
live." 19Jesus got up and went with him,
and so did his disciples.
20Just then a woman who had been
subject to bleeding for twelve years
came up behind him and touched the
edge of his cloak. 21She said to herself,
"If I only touch his cloak, I will be
healed."
22Jesus turned and saw her. "Take
heart, daughter," he said, "your faith
has healed you." And the woman was
healed from that moment.
23When Jesus entered the ruler's
house and saw the flute players and the
noisy crowd, 24he said, "Go away. The
girl is not dead but asleep." But they
laughed at him. 25After the crowd had
been put outside, he went in and took
the girl by the hand, and she got up.
26News of this spread through all that
region.

Jesus Heals the Blind and Mute

27As Jesus went on from there, two
blind men followed him, calling out,
"Have mercy on us, Son of David!"
28When he had gone indoors, the
blind men came to him, and he asked
them, "Do you believe that I am able to
do this?"
"Yes, Lord," they replied.
29Then he touched their eyes and
said, "According to your faith will it be
done to you"; 30and their sight was restored. Jesus warned them sternly, "See
that no-one knows about this." 31But
they went out and spread the news
about him all over that region.
32While they were going out, a man
who was demon-possessed and could
not talk was brought to Jesus. 33And
when the demon was driven out, the
man who had been mute spoke. The
crowd was amazed and said, "Nothing
like this has ever been seen in Israel."
34But the Pharisees said, "It is by the
prince of demons that he drives out
demons."

The Workers Are Few

35Jesus went through all the towns
and villages, teaching in their synagogues, preaching the good news of the
kingdom and healing every disease and
sickness. 36When he saw the crowds, he
had compassion on them, because they
were harassed and helpless, like sheep
without a shepherd. 37Then he said to
his disciples, "The harvest is plentiful
but the workers are few. 38Ask the Lord
of the harvest, therefore, to send out
workers into his harvest field."

READING FROM PSALMS
Psalm 8:1–9

For the director of music. According to
gittith. A psalm of David.

1O LORD, our Lord,
how majestic is your name in all
the earth!

You have set your glory
above the heavens.
2From the lips of children and infants
you have ordained praise
because of your enemies,
to silence the foe and the avenger.

[3]When I consider your heavens,
the work of your fingers,
the moon and the stars,
which you have set in place,
[4]what is man that you are mindful of him,
the son of man that you care for him?
[5]You made him a little lower than the heavenly beings
and crowned him with glory and honour.
[6]You made him ruler over the works of your hands;
you put everything under his feet:
[7]all flocks and herds,
and the beasts of the field,
[8]the birds of the air,
and the fish of the sea,
all that swim the paths of the seas.

[9]O LORD, our Lord,
how majestic is your name in all the earth!

JANUARY 12

DAY 12

OLD TESTAMENT READING

Genesis 25:1–26:35

The Death of Abraham

25 Abraham took another wife, whose name was Keturah. [2]She bore him Zimran, Jokshan, Medan, Midian, Ishbak and Shuah. [3]Jokshan was the father of Sheba and Dedan; the descendants of Dedan were the Asshurites, the Letushites and the Leummites. [4]The sons of Midian were Ephah, Epher, Hanoch, Abida and Eldaah. All these were descendants of Keturah.

[5]Abraham left everything he owned to Isaac. [6]But while he was still living, he gave gifts to the sons of his concubines and sent them away from his son Isaac to the land of the east.

[7]Altogether, Abraham lived a hundred and seventy-five years. [8]Then Abraham breathed his last and died at a good old age, an old man and full of years; and he was gathered to his people. [9]His sons Isaac and Ishmael buried him in the cave of Machpelah near Mamre, in the field of Ephron son of Zohar the Hittite, [10]the field Abraham had bought from the Hittites. There Abraham was buried with his wife Sarah. [11]After Abraham's death, God blessed his son Isaac, who then lived near Beer Lahai Roi.

Ishmael's Sons

[12]This is the account of Abraham's son Ishmael, whom Sarah's maidservant, Hagar the Egyptian, bore to Abraham.

[13]These are the names of the sons of Ishmael, listed in the order of their birth: Nebaioth the firstborn of Ishmael, Kedar, Adbeel, Mibsam, [14]Mishma, Dumah, Massa, [15]Hadad, Tema, Jetur, Naphish and Kedemah. [16]These were the sons of Ishmael, and these are the names of the twelve tribal rulers according to their settlements and camps. [17]Altogether, Ishmael lived a hundred and thirty-seven years. He breathed his last and died, and he was gathered to his people. [18]His descendants settled in the area from Havilah to Shur, near the border of Egypt, as you go towards Asshur. And they lived in hostility towards all their brothers.

Jacob and Esau

[19]This is the account of Abraham's son Isaac.

Abraham became the father of Isaac,
[20]and Isaac was forty years old when he
married Rebekah daughter of Bethuel
the Aramean from Paddan Aram and
sister of Laban the Aramean.
[21]Isaac prayed to the LORD on behalf
of his wife, because she was barren. The
LORD answered his prayer, and his wife
Rebekah became pregnant. [22]The
babies jostled each other within her,
and she said, "Why is this happening to
me?" So she went to enquire of the
LORD.
[23]The LORD said to her,

"Two nations are in your womb,
  and two peoples from within you
    will be separated;
one people will be stronger than the
    other,
  and the older will serve the
    younger."

[24]When the time came for her to give
birth, there were twin boys in her
womb. [25]The first to come out was red,
and his whole body was like a hairy
garment; so they named him Esau.
[26]After this, his brother came out, with
his hand grasping Esau's heel; so he was
named Jacob. Isaac was sixty years old
when Rebekah gave birth to them.
[27]The boys grew up, and Esau became a skilful hunter, a man of the open
country, while Jacob was a quiet man,
staying among the tents. [28]Isaac, who
had a taste for wild game, loved Esau,
but Rebekah loved Jacob.
[29]Once when Jacob was cooking
some stew, Esau came in from the open
country, famished. [30]He said to Jacob,
"Quick, let me have some of that red
stew! I'm famished!" (That is why he
was also called Edom.)
[31]Jacob replied, "First sell me your
birthright."
[32]"Look, I am about to die," Esau
said. "What good is the birthright to
me?"
[33]But Jacob said, "Swear to me first."
So he swore an oath to him, selling his
birthright to Jacob.
[34]Then Jacob gave Esau some bread
and some lentil stew. He ate and drank,
and then got up and left.
So Esau despised his birthright.

Isaac and Abimelech

26 Now there was a famine in
the land—besides the earlier
famine of Abraham's time—and Isaac
went to Abimelech king of the Philistines in Gerar. [2]The LORD appeared to
Isaac and said, "Do not go down to
Egypt; live in the land where I tell you
to live. [3]Stay in this land for a while, and
I will be with you and will bless you. For
to you and your descendants I will give
all these lands and will confirm the oath
I swore to your father Abraham. [4]I will
make your descendants as numerous as
the stars in the sky and will give them all
these lands, and through your offspring
all nations on earth will be blessed,
[5]because Abraham obeyed me and kept
my requirements, my commands, my
decrees and my laws." [6]So Isaac stayed
in Gerar.
[7]When the men of that place asked
him about his wife, he said, "She is my
sister," because he was afraid to say,
"She is my wife." He thought, "The
men of this place might kill me on
account of Rebekah, because she is
beautiful."
[8]When Isaac had been there a long
time, Abimelech king of the Philistines
looked down from a window and saw
Isaac caressing his wife Rebekah. [9]So
Abimelech summoned Isaac and said,
"She is really your wife! Why did you
say, 'She is my sister'?"
Isaac answered him, "Because I
thought I might lose my life on account
of her."
[10]Then Abimelech said, "What is this
you have done to us? One of the men
might well have slept with your wife,
and you would have brought guilt upon
us."
[11]So Abimelech gave orders to all the
people: "Anyone who molests this man
or his wife shall surely be put to death."

12Isaac planted crops in that land and
the same year reaped a hundredfold,
because the LORD blessed him. 13The
man became rich, and his wealth continued to grow until he became very
wealthy. 14He had so many flocks and
herds and servants that the Philistines
envied him. 15So all the wells that his
father's servants had dug in the time of
his father Abraham, the Philistines
stopped up, filling them with earth.
16Then Abimelech said to Isaac,
"Move away from us; you have become
too powerful for us."
17So Isaac moved away from there
and encamped in the Valley of Gerar
and settled there. 18Isaac reopened the
wells that had been dug in the time of his
father Abraham, which the Philistines
had stopped up after Abraham died,
and he gave them the same names his
father had given them.
19Isaac's servants dug in the valley
and discovered a well of fresh water
there. 20But the herdsmen of Gerar
quarrelled with Isaac's herdsmen and
said, "The water is ours!" So he named
the well Esek, because they disputed
with him. 21Then they dug another well,
but they quarrelled over that one also;
so he named it Sitnah. 22He moved on
from there and dug another well, and
no-one quarrelled over it. He named it
Rehoboth, saying, "Now the LORD has
given us room and we will flourish in the
land."
23From there he went up to Beersheba. 24That night the LORD appeared
to him and said, "I am the God of your
father Abraham. Do not be afraid, for I
am with you; I will bless you and will
increase the number of your descendants for the sake of my servant
Abraham."
25Isaac built an altar there and called
on the name of the LORD. There he
pitched his tent, and there his servants
dug a well.
26Meanwhile, Abimelech had come
to him from Gerar, with Ahuzzath his
personal adviser and Phicol the commander of his forces. 27Isaac asked
them, "Why have you come to me,
since you were hostile to me and sent
me away?"
28They answered, "We saw clearly
that the LORD was with you; so we said,
'There ought to be a sworn agreement
between us'—between us and you. Let
us make a treaty with you 29that you will
do us no harm, just as we did not molest
you but always treated you well and sent
you away in peace. And now you are
blessed by the LORD."
30Isaac then made a feast for them,
and they ate and drank. 31Early the next
morning the men swore an oath to each
other. Then Isaac sent them on their
way, and they left him in peace.
32That day Isaac's servants came and
told him about the well they had dug.
They said, "We've found water!" 33He
called it Shibah, and to this day the
name of the town has been Beersheba.
34When Esau was forty years old, he
married Judith daughter of Beeri the
Hittite, and also Basemath daughter of
Elon the Hittite. 35They were a source
of grief to Isaac and Rebekah.

NEW TESTAMENT READING
Matthew 10:1–31

Jesus Sends Out the Twelve

10 He called his twelve disciples to
him and gave them authority to
drive out evil spirits and to heal every
disease and sickness.
2These are the names of the twelve
apostles: first, Simon (who is called
Peter) and his brother Andrew; James
son of Zebedee, and his brother John;
3Philip and Bartholomew; Thomas
and Matthew the tax collector; James
son of Alphaeus, and Thaddaeus;
4Simon the Zealot and Judas Iscariot,
who betrayed him.
5These twelve Jesus sent out with the
following instructions: "Do not go
among the Gentiles or enter any town of
the Samaritans. 6Go rather to the lost
sheep of Israel. 7As you go, preach this

message: 'The kingdom of heaven is near.' 8Heal the sick, raise the dead, cleanse those who have leprosy, drive out demons. Freely you have received, freely give. 9Do not take along any gold or silver or copper in your belts; 10take no bag for the journey, or extra tunic, or sandals or a staff; for the worker is worth his keep.

11"Whatever town or village you enter, search for some worthy person there and stay at his house until you leave. 12As you enter the home, give it your greeting. 13If the home is deserving, let your peace rest on it; if it is not, let your peace return to you. 14If anyone will not welcome you or listen to your words, shake the dust off your feet when you leave that home or town. 15I tell you the truth, it will be more bearable for Sodom and Gomorrah on the day of judgment than for that town. 16I am sending you out like sheep among wolves. Therefore be as shrewd as snakes and as innocent as doves.

17"Be on your guard against men; they will hand you over to the local councils and flog you in their synagogues. 18On my account you will be brought before governors and kings as witnesses to them and to the Gentiles. 19But when they arrest you, do not worry about what to say or how to say it. At that time you will be given what to say, 20for it will not be you speaking, but the Spirit of your Father speaking through you.

21"Brother will betray brother to death, and a father his child; children will rebel against their parents and have them put to death. 22All men will hate you because of me, but he who stands firm to the end will be saved. 23When you are persecuted in one place, flee to another. I tell you the truth, you will not finish going through the cities of Israel before the Son of Man comes.

24"A student is not above his teacher, nor a servant above his master. 25It is enough for the student to be like his teacher, and the servant like his master. If the head of the house has been called Beelzebub, how much more the members of his household!

26"So do not be afraid of them. There is nothing concealed that will not be disclosed, or hidden that will not be made known. 27What I tell you in the dark, speak in the daylight; what is whispered in your ear, proclaim from the roofs. 28Do not be afraid of those who kill the body but cannot kill the soul. Rather, be afraid of the One who can destroy both soul and body in hell. 29Are not two sparrows sold for a penny? Yet not one of them will fall to the ground apart from the will of your Father. 30And even the very hairs of your head are all numbered. 31So don't be afraid; you are worth more than many sparrows.

READING FROM PROVERBS

Proverbs 1:20–33

Warning Against Rejecting Wisdom

20Wisdom calls aloud in the street,
she raises her voice in the public squares;
21at the head of the noisy streets she cries out,
in the gateways of the city she makes her speech:

22"How long will you simple ones love your simple ways?
How long will mockers delight in mockery
and fools hate knowledge?
23If you had responded to my rebuke,
I would have poured out my heart to you
and made my thoughts known to you.
24But since you rejected me when I called
and no-one gave heed when I stretched out my hand,
25since you ignored all my advice
and would not accept my rebuke,
26I in turn will laugh at your disaster;
I will mock when calamity overtakes you—

[27]when calamity overtakes you like a storm,
when disaster sweeps over you like a whirlwind,
when distress and trouble overwhelm you.

[28]"Then they will call to me but I will not answer;
they will look for me but will not find me.
[29]Since they hated knowledge
and did not choose to fear the LORD,
[30]since they would not accept my advice
and spurned my rebuke,
[31]they will eat the fruit of their ways
and be filled with the fruit of their schemes.
[32]For the waywardness of the simple will kill them,
and the complacency of fools will destroy them;
[33]but whoever listens to me will live in safety
and be at ease, without fear of harm."

JANUARY 13

DAY 13

OLD TESTAMENT READING

Genesis 27:1–28:22

Jacob Gets Isaac's Blessing

27 When Isaac was old and his eyes
were so weak that he could no
longer see, he called for Esau his older
son and said to him, "My son."

"Here I am," he answered.

[2]Isaac said, "I am now an old man
and don't know the day of my death.
[3]Now then, get your weapons—your
quiver and bow—and go out to the
open country to hunt some wild game
for me. [4]Prepare me the kind of tasty
food I like and bring it to me to eat, so
that I may give you my blessing before I
die."

[5]Now Rebekah was listening as Isaac
spoke to his son Esau. When Esau left
for the open country to hunt game and
bring it back, [6]Rebekah said to her son
Jacob, "Look, I overheard your father
say to your brother Esau, [7]'Bring me
some game and prepare me some tasty
food to eat, so that I may give you my
blessing in the presence of the LORD
before I die.' [8]Now, my son, listen carefully and do what I tell you: [9]Go out to
the flock and bring me two choice young
goats, so that I can prepare some tasty
food for your father, just the way he
likes it. [10]Then take it to your father to
eat, so that he may give you his blessing
before he dies."

[11]Jacob said to Rebekah his mother,
"But my brother Esau is a hairy man,
and I'm a man with smooth skin. [12]What
if my father touches me? I would appear
to be tricking him and would bring
down a curse on myself rather than a
blessing."

[13]His mother said to him, "My son,
let the curse fall on me. Just do what I
say; go and get them for me."

[14]So he went and got them and
brought them to his mother, and she
prepared some tasty food, just the way
his father liked it. [15]Then Rebekah took
the best clothes of Esau her older son,
which she had in the house, and put
them on her younger son Jacob. [16]She
also covered his hands and the smooth
part of his neck with the goatskins.
[17]Then she handed to her son Jacob the
tasty food and the bread she had made.

[18]He went to his father and said, "My
father."

"Yes, my son," he answered. "Who
is it?"

19Jacob said to his father, "I am Esau
your firstborn. I have done as you told
me. Please sit up and eat some of my
game so that you may give me your
blessing."
20Isaac asked his son, "How did you
find it so quickly, my son?"
"The LORD your God gave me success," he replied.
21Then Isaac said to Jacob, "Come
near so I can touch you, my son, to
know whether you really are my son
Esau or not."
22Jacob went close to his father Isaac,
who touched him and said, "The voice
is the voice of Jacob, but the hands are
the hands of Esau." 23He did not recognise him, for his hands were hairy like
those of his brother Esau; so he blessed
him. 24"Are you really my son Esau?"
he asked.
"I am," he replied.
25Then he said, "My son, bring me
some of your game to eat, so that I may
give you my blessing."
Jacob brought it to him and he ate;
and he brought some wine and he
drank. 26Then his father Isaac said to
him, "Come here, my son, and kiss
me."
27So he went to him and kissed him.
When Isaac caught the smell of his
clothes, he blessed him and said,

"Ah, the smell of my son
is like the smell of a field
that the LORD has blessed.
28May God give you of heaven's dew
and of earth's richness—
an abundance of grain and new
wine.
29May nations serve you
and peoples bow down to you.
Be lord over your brothers,
and may the sons of your mother
bow down to you.
May those who curse you be cursed
and those who bless you be
blessed."

30After Isaac finished blessing him
and Jacob had scarcely left his father's
presence, his brother Esau came in
from hunting. 31He too prepared some
tasty food and brought it to his father.
Then he said to him, "My father, sit up
and eat some of my game, so that you
may give me your blessing."
32His father Isaac asked him, "Who
are you?"
"I am your son," he answered, "your
firstborn, Esau."
33Isaac trembled violently and said,
"Who was it, then, that hunted game
and brought it to me? I ate it just before
you came and I blessed him—and indeed he will be blessed!"
34When Esau heard his father's
words, he burst out with a loud and
bitter cry and said to his father, "Bless
me—me too, my father!"
35But he said, "Your brother came
deceitfully and took your blessing."
36Esau said, "Isn't he rightly named
Jacob? He has deceived me these two
times: He took my birthright, and now
he's taken my blessing!" Then he asked,
"Haven't you reserved any blessing for
me?"
37Isaac answered Esau, "I have made
him lord over you and have made all his
relatives his servants, and I have sustained him with grain and new wine. So
what can I possibly do for you, my
son?"
38Esau said to his father, "Do you
have only one blessing, my father?
Bless me too, my father!" Then Esau
wept aloud.
39His father Isaac answered him,

"Your dwelling will be
away from the earth's richness,
away from the dew of heaven
above.
40You will live by the sword
and you will serve your brother.
But when you grow restless,
you will throw his yoke
from off your neck."

Jacob Flees to Laban

41Esau held a grudge against Jacob
because of the blessing his father had

given him. He said to himself, "The
days of mourning for my father are
near; then I will kill my brother Jacob."
42When Rebekah was told what her
older son Esau had said, she sent for her
younger son Jacob and said to him,
"Your brother Esau is consoling himself with the thought of killing you.
43Now then, my son, do what I say: Flee
at once to my brother Laban in Haran.
44Stay with him for a while until your
brother's fury subsides. 45When your
brother is no longer angry with you and
forgets what you did to him, I'll send
word for you to come back from there.
Why should I lose both of you in one
day?"

46Then Rebekah said to Isaac, "I'm
disgusted with living because of these
Hittite women. If Jacob takes a wife
from among the women of this land,
from Hittite women like these, my life
will not be worth living."

28 So Isaac called for Jacob and
blessed him and commanded
him: "Do not marry a Canaanite
woman. 2Go at once to Paddan Aram,
to the house of your mother's father
Bethuel. Take a wife for yourself there,
from among the daughters of Laban,
your mother's brother. 3May God
Almighty bless you and make you fruitful and increase your numbers until you
become a community of peoples. 4May
he give you and your descendants the
blessing given to Abraham, so that you
may take possession of the land where
you now live as an alien, the land God
gave to Abraham." 5Then Isaac sent
Jacob on his way, and he went to Paddan Aram, to Laban son of Bethuel the
Aramean, the brother of Rebekah, who
was the mother of Jacob and Esau.

6Now Esau learned that Isaac had
blessed Jacob and had sent him to Paddan Aram to take a wife from there, and
that when he blessed him he commanded him, "Do not marry a Canaanite
woman," 7and that Jacob had obeyed
his father and mother and had gone to
Paddan Aram. 8Esau then realised how
displeasing the Canaanite women were
to his father Isaac; 9so he went to
Ishmael and married Mahalath, the sister of Nebaioth and daughter of Ishmael
son of Abraham, in addition to the
wives he already had.

Jacob's Dream at Bethel

10Jacob left Beersheba and set out for
Haran. 11When he reached a certain
place, he stopped for the night because
the sun had set. Taking one of the
stones there, he put it under his head
and lay down to sleep. 12He had a dream
in which he saw a stairway resting on the
earth, with its top reaching to heaven,
and the angels of God were ascending
and descending on it. 13There above it
stood the LORD, and he said: "I am the
LORD, the God of your father Abraham
and the God of Isaac. I will give you and
your descendants the land on which you
are lying. 14Your descendants will be
like the dust of the earth, and you will
spread out to the west and to the east, to
the north and to the south. All peoples
on earth will be blessed through you and
your offspring. 15I am with you and will
watch over you wherever you go, and I
will bring you back to this land. I will
not leave you until I have done what I
have promised you."

16When Jacob awoke from his sleep,
he thought, "Surely the LORD is in this
place, and I was not aware of it." 17He
was afraid and said, "How awesome is
this place! This is none other than the
house of God; this is the gate of
heaven."

18Early the next morning Jacob took
the stone he had placed under his head
and set it up as a pillar and poured oil on
top of it. 19He called that place Bethel,
though the city used to be called Luz.

20Then Jacob made a vow, saying, "If
God will be with me and will watch over
me on this journey I am taking and will
give me food to eat and clothes to wear
21so that I return safely to my father's
house, then the LORD will be my God
22and this stone that I have set up as a
pillar will be God's house, and of all that
you give me I will give you a tenth."

NEW TESTAMENT READING

Matthew 10:32–11:15

32“Whoever acknowledges me before men, I will also acknowledge him before my Father in heaven. 33But whoever disowns me before men, I will disown him before my Father in heaven.

34“Do not suppose that I have come to bring peace to the earth. I did not come to bring peace, but a sword. 35For I have come to turn

“ ‘a man against his father,
  a daughter against her mother,
 a daughter-in-law against her
   mother-in-law—
36 a man’s enemies will be the
   members of his own
   household.’

37“Anyone who loves his father or mother more than me is not worthy of me; anyone who loves his son or daughter more than me is not worthy of me; 38and anyone who does not take his cross and follow me is not worthy of me. 39Whoever finds his life will lose it, and whoever loses his life for my sake will find it.

40“He who receives you receives me, and he who receives me receives the one who sent me. 41Anyone who receives a prophet because he is a prophet will receive a prophet’s reward, and anyone who receives a righteous man because he is a righteous man will receive a righteous man’s reward. 42And if anyone gives even a cup of cold water to one of these little ones because he is my disciple, I tell you the truth, he will certainly not lose his reward.”

Jesus and John the Baptist

11 After Jesus had finished instructing his twelve disciples, he went on from there to teach and preach in the towns of Galilee.

2When John heard in prison what Christ was doing, he sent his disciples 3to ask him, “Are you the one who was to come, or should we expect someone else?”

4Jesus replied, “Go back and report to John what you hear and see: 5The blind receive sight, the lame walk, those who have leprosy are cured, the deaf hear, the dead are raised, and the good news is preached to the poor. 6Blessed is the man who does not fall away on account of me.”

7As John’s disciples were leaving, Jesus began to speak to the crowd about John: “What did you go out into the desert to see? A reed swayed by the wind? 8If not, what did you go out to see? A man dressed in fine clothes? No, those who wear fine clothes are in kings’ palaces. 9Then what did you go out to see? A prophet? Yes, I tell you, and more than a prophet. 10This is the one about whom it is written:

“ ‘I will send my messenger ahead of
   you,
  who will prepare your way before
   you.’

11I tell you the truth: Among those born of women there has not risen anyone greater than John the Baptist; yet he who is least in the kingdom of heaven is greater than he. 12From the days of John the Baptist until now, the kingdom of heaven has been forcefully advancing, and forceful men lay hold of it. 13For all the Prophets and the Law prophesied until John. 14And if you are willing to accept it, he is the Elijah who was to come. 15He who has ears, let him hear.

READING FROM PSALMS

Psalm 9:1–6

For the director of music. To ⌞the tune of⌟ “The Death of the Son”. A psalm of David.

1I will praise you, O Lord, with all my
   heart;
  I will tell of all your wonders.
2I will be glad and rejoice in you;

I will sing praise to your name, O
Most High.
3My enemies turn back;
they stumble and perish before
you.
4For you have upheld my right and my
cause;
you have sat on your throne,
judging righteously.
5You have rebuked the nations and
destroyed the wicked;
you have blotted out their name
for ever and ever.
6Endless ruin has overtaken the
enemy,
you have uprooted their
cities;
even the memory of them has
perished.

JANUARY 14

DAY 14

OLD TESTAMENT READING

Genesis 29:1–30:43

Jacob Arrives in Paddan Aram

29 Then Jacob continued on his
journey and came to the land of
the eastern peoples. 2There he saw a
well in the field, with three flocks of sheep lying near it because the flocks were watered from that well. The stone over the mouth of the well was large.
3When all the flocks were gathered
there, the shepherds would roll the stone away from the well's mouth and water the sheep. Then they would return the stone to its place over the mouth of the well.

4Jacob asked the shepherds, "My brothers, where are you from?"

"We're from Haran," they replied.

5He said to them, "Do you know Laban, Nahor's grandson?"

"Yes, we know him," they answered.

6Then Jacob asked them, "Is he well?"

"Yes, he is," they said, "and here comes his daughter Rachel with the sheep."

7"Look," he said, "the sun is still high; it is not time for the flocks to be gathered. Water the sheep and take them back to pasture."

8"We can't," they replied, "until all the flocks are gathered and the stone has been rolled away from the mouth of the well. Then we will water the sheep."

9While he was still talking with them,
Rachel came with her father's sheep,
for she was a shepherdess. 10When
Jacob saw Rachel daughter of Laban, his mother's brother, and Laban's sheep, he went over and rolled the stone away from the mouth of the well
and watered his uncle's sheep. 11Then
Jacob kissed Rachel and began to weep
aloud. 12He had told Rachel that he
was a relative of her father and a son of Rebekah. So she ran and told her father.

13As soon as Laban heard the news about Jacob, his sister's son, he hurried to meet him. He embraced him and kissed him and brought him to his home, and there Jacob told him all
these things. 14Then Laban said to him,
"You are my own flesh and blood."

Jacob Marries Leah and Rachel

After Jacob had stayed with him for
a whole month, 15Laban said to him,
"Just because you are a relative of mine, should you work for me for nothing? Tell me what your wages should be."

16Now Laban had two daughters; the name of the older was Leah, and the
name of the younger was Rachel.
17Leah had weak eyes, but Rachel was

lovely in form, and beautiful. 18Jacob
was in love with Rachel and said, "I'll
work for you seven years in return for
your younger daughter Rachel."
19Laban said, "It's better that I give
her to you than to some other man. Stay
here with me." 20So Jacob served seven
years to get Rachel, but they seemed
like only a few days to him because of
his love for her.
21Then Jacob said to Laban, "Give
me my wife. My time is completed, and
I want to lie with her."
22So Laban brought together all the
people of the place and gave a feast.
23But when evening came, he took his
daughter Leah and gave her to Jacob,
and Jacob lay with her. 24And Laban
gave his servant girl Zilpah to his daughter as her maidservant.
25When morning came, there was
Leah! So Jacob said to Laban, "What is
this you have done to me? I served you
for Rachel, didn't I? Why have you
deceived me?"
26Laban replied, "It is not our custom
here to give the younger daughter in
marriage before the older one. 27Finish
this daughter's bridal week; then we will
give you the younger one also, in return
for another seven years of work."
28And Jacob did so. He finished the
week with Leah, and then Laban gave
him his daughter Rachel to be his wife.
29Laban gave his servant girl Bilhah to
his daughter Rachel as her maidservant.
30Jacob lay with Rachel also, and he
loved Rachel more than Leah. And he
worked for Laban another seven years.

Jacob's Children

31When the LORD saw that Leah was
not loved, he opened her womb, but
Rachel was barren. 32Leah became
pregnant and gave birth to a son. She
named him Reuben, for she said, "It is
because the LORD has seen my misery.
Surely my husband will love me now."
33She conceived again, and when she
gave birth to a son she said, "Because
the LORD heard that I am not loved, he
gave me this one too." So she named
him Simeon.
34Again she conceived, and when she
gave birth to a son she said, "Now at last
my husband will become attached to
me, because I have borne him three
sons." So he was named Levi.
35She conceived again, and when she
gave birth to a son she said, "This time I
will praise the LORD." So she named
him Judah. Then she stopped having
children.

30 When Rachel saw that she was
not bearing Jacob any children,
she became jealous of her sister. So she
said to Jacob, "Give me children, or I'll
die!"
2Jacob became angry with her and
said, "Am I in the place of God, who
has kept you from having children?"
3Then she said, "Here is Bilhah, my
maidservant. Sleep with her so that she
can bear children for me and that
through her I too can build a family."
4So she gave him her servant Bilhah
as a wife. Jacob slept with her, 5and she
became pregnant and bore him a son.
6Then Rachel said, "God has vindicated me; he has listened to my plea and
given me a son." Because of this she
named him Dan.
7Rachel's servant Bilhah conceived
again and bore Jacob a second son.
8Then Rachel said, "I have had a great
struggle with my sister, and I have
won." So she named him Naphtali.
9When Leah saw that she had stopped having children, she took her maidservant Zilpah and gave her to Jacob as
a wife. 10Leah's servant Zilpah bore
Jacob a son. 11Then Leah said, "What
good fortune!" So she named him Gad.
12Leah's servant Zilpah bore Jacob a
second son. 13Then Leah said, "How
happy I am! The women will call me
happy." So she named him Asher.
14During wheat harvest, Reuben
went out into the fields and found some
mandrake plants, which he brought to
his mother Leah. Rachel said to Leah,
"Please give me some of your son's
mandrakes."

15But she said to her, "Wasn't it
enough that you took away my husband? Will you take my son's mandrakes too?"
"Very well," Rachel said, "he can
sleep with you tonight in return for your
son's mandrakes."
16So when Jacob came in from the
fields that evening, Leah went out to
meet him. "You must sleep with me,"
she said. "I have hired you with my
son's mandrakes." So he slept with her
that night.
17God listened to Leah, and she became pregnant and bore Jacob a fifth
son. 18Then Leah said, "God has rewarded me for giving my maidservant to
my husband." So she named him
Issachar.
19Leah conceived again and bore
Jacob a sixth son. 20Then Leah said,
"God has presented me with a precious
gift. This time my husband will treat me
with honour, because I have borne him
six sons." So she named him Zebulun.
21Some time later she gave birth to a
daughter and named her Dinah.
22Then God remembered Rachel; he
listened to her and opened her womb.
23She became pregnant and gave birth
to a son and said, "God has taken away
my disgrace." 24She named him Joseph,
and said, "May the LORD add to me
another son."

Jacob's Flocks Increase

25After Rachel gave birth to Joseph,
Jacob said to Laban, "Send me on my
way so that I can go back to my own
homeland. 26Give me my wives and
children, for whom I have served you,
and I will be on my way. You know how
much work I've done for you."
27But Laban said to him, "If I have
found favour in your eyes, please stay. I
have learned by divination that the
LORD has blessed me because of you."
28He added, "Name your wages, and I
will pay them."
29Jacob said to him, "You know how
I have worked for you and how your
livestock has fared under my care.
30The little you had before I came has
increased greatly, and the LORD has
blessed you wherever I have been. But
now, when may I do something for my
own household?"
31"What shall I give you?" he asked.
"Don't give me anything," Jacob replied. "But if you will do this one thing
for me, I will go on tending your flocks
and watching over them: 32Let me go
through all your flocks today and remove from them every speckled or spotted sheep, every dark-coloured lamb
and every spotted or speckled goat.
They will be my wages. 33And my honesty will testify for me in the future,
whenever you check on the wages you
have paid me. Any goat in my possession that is not speckled or spotted, or
any lamb that is not dark-coloured, will
be considered stolen."
34"Agreed," said Laban. "Let it be as
you have said." 35That same day he
removed all the male goats that were
streaked or spotted, and all the speckled or spotted female goats (all that had
white on them) and all the dark-
coloured lambs, and he placed them in
the care of his sons. 36Then he put a
three-day journey between himself and
Jacob, while Jacob continued to tend
the rest of Laban's flocks.
37Jacob, however, took fresh-cut
branches from poplar, almond and
plane trees and made white stripes on
them by peeling the bark and exposing
the white inner wood of the branches.
38Then he placed the peeled branches in
all the watering troughs, so that they
would be directly in front of the flocks
when they came to drink. When the
flocks were in heat and came to drink,
39they mated in front of the branches.
And they bore young that were
streaked or speckled or spotted. 40Jacob
set apart the young of the flock by themselves, but made the rest face the
streaked and dark-coloured animals
that belonged to Laban. Thus he made
separate flocks for himself and did not
put them with Laban's animals.

41Whenever the stronger females were
in heat, Jacob would place the branches
in the troughs in front of the animals so
that they would mate near the branches,
42but if the animals were weak, he
would not place them there. So the
weak animals went to Laban and the
strong ones to Jacob. 43In this way
the man grew exceedingly prosperous
and came to own large flocks, and maidservants and menservants, and camels
and donkeys.

NEW TESTAMENT READING
Matthew 11:16–30

16"To what can I compare this generation? They are like children sitting in
the market-places and calling out to
others:

17" 'We played the flute for you,
    and you did not dance;
  we sang a dirge,
    and you did not mourn.'

18For John came neither eating nor
drinking, and they say, 'He has a demon.' 19The Son of Man came eating
and drinking, and they say, 'Here is a
glutton and a drunkard, a friend of tax
collectors and "sinners".' But wisdom is
proved right by her actions."

Woe on Unrepentant Cities

20Then Jesus began to denounce the
cities in which most of his miracles had
been performed, because they did not
repent. 21"Woe to you, Korazin! Woe
to you, Bethsaida! If the miracles that
were performed in you had been performed in Tyre and Sidon, they would
have repented long ago in sackcloth and
ashes. 22But I tell you, it will be more
bearable for Tyre and Sidon on the day
of judgment than for you. 23And you,
Capernaum, will you be lifted up to the
skies? No, you will go down to the
depths. If the miracles that were performed in you had been performed in
Sodom, it would have remained to this
day. 24But I tell you that it will be more
bearable for Sodom on the day of judgment than for you."

Rest for the Weary

25At that time Jesus said, "I praise
you, Father, Lord of heaven and earth,
because you have hidden these things
from the wise and learned, and revealed
them to little children. 26Yes, Father,
for this was your good pleasure.

27"All things have been committed to
me by my Father. No-one knows the
Son except the Father, and no-one
knows the Father except the Son and
those to whom the Son chooses to reveal him.

28"Come to me, all you who are
weary and burdened, and I will give you
rest. 29Take my yoke upon you and
learn from me, for I am gentle and
humble in heart, and you will find rest
for your souls. 30For my yoke is easy and
my burden is light."

READING FROM PSALMS
Psalm 9:7–12

7The LORD reigns for ever;
  he has established his throne for
    judgment.
8He will judge the world in
    righteousness;
  he will govern the peoples with
    justice.
9The LORD is a refuge for the
    oppressed,
  a stronghold in times of trouble.
10Those who know your name will trust
    in you,
  for you, LORD, have never
    forsaken those who seek you.

11Sing praises to the LORD, enthroned
    in Zion;
  proclaim among the nations what
    he has done.
12For he who avenges blood
    remembers;
  he does not ignore the cry of the
    afflicted.

JANUARY 15

OLD TESTAMENT READING

Genesis 31:1–55

Jacob Flees From Laban

31 Jacob heard that Laban's sons were saying, "Jacob has taken everything our father owned and has gained all this wealth from what belonged to our father." 2And Jacob noticed that Laban's attitude towards him was not what it had been.

3Then the LORD said to Jacob, "Go back to the land of your fathers and to your relatives, and I will be with you."

4So Jacob sent word to Rachel and Leah to come out to the fields where his flocks were. 5He said to them, "I see that your father's attitude towards me is not what it was before, but the God of my father has been with me. 6You know that I've worked for your father with all my strength, 7yet your father has cheated me by changing my wages ten times. However, God has not allowed him to harm me. 8If he said, 'The speckled ones will be your wages,' then all the flocks gave birth to speckled young; and if he said, 'The streaked ones will be your wages,' then all the flocks bore streaked young. 9So God has taken away your father's livestock and has given them to me.

10"In the breeding season I once had a dream in which I looked up and saw that the male goats mating with the flock were streaked, speckled or spotted. 11The angel of God said to me in the dream, 'Jacob.' I answered, 'Here I am.' 12And he said, 'Look up and see that all the male goats mating with the flock are streaked, speckled or spotted, for I have seen all that Laban has been doing to you. 13I am the God of Bethel, where you anointed a pillar and where you made a vow to me. Now leave this land at once and go back to your native land.'"

14Then Rachel and Leah replied, "Do we still have any share in the inheritance of our father's estate? 15Does he not regard us as foreigners? Not only has he sold us, but he has used up what was paid for us. 16Surely all the wealth that God took away from our father belongs to us and our children. So do whatever God has told you."

17Then Jacob put his children and his wives on camels, 18and he drove all his livestock ahead of him, along with all the goods he had accumulated in Paddan Aram, to go to his father Isaac in the land of Canaan.

19When Laban had gone to shear his sheep, Rachel stole her father's household gods. 20Moreover, Jacob deceived Laban the Aramean by not telling him he was running away. 21So he fled with all he had, and crossing the River, he headed for the hill country of Gilead.

Laban Pursues Jacob

22On the third day Laban was told that Jacob had fled. 23Taking his relatives with him, he pursued Jacob for seven days and caught up with him in the hill country of Gilead. 24Then God came to Laban the Aramean in a dream at night and said to him, "Be careful not to say anything to Jacob, either good or bad."

25Jacob had pitched his tent in the hill country of Gilead when Laban overtook him, and Laban and his relatives camped there too. 26Then Laban said to Jacob, "What have you done? You've deceived me, and you've carried off my daughters like captives in war. 27Why did you run off secretly and deceive me? Why didn't you tell me, so that I could send you away with joy and singing to the music of tambourines and harps? 28You didn't even let me kiss my grandchildren and my daughters good-bye. You have done a foolish thing. 29I have

the power to harm you; but last night
the God of your father said to me, 'Be
careful not to say anything to Jacob,
either good or bad.' 30Now you have
gone off because you longed to return to
your father's house. But why did you
steal my gods?"
31Jacob answered Laban, "I was
afraid, because I thought you would
take your daughters away from me by
force. 32But if you find anyone who has
your gods, he shall not live. In the presence of our relatives, see for yourself
whether there is anything of yours here
with me; and if so, take it." Now Jacob
did not know that Rachel had stolen the
gods.
33So Laban went into Jacob's tent and
into Leah's tent and into the tent of the
two maidservants, but he found nothing. After he came out of Leah's tent,
he entered Rachel's tent. 34Now Rachel
had taken the household gods and put
them inside her camel's saddle and was
sitting on them. Laban searched
through everything in the tent but found
nothing.
35Rachel said to her father, "Don't be
angry, my lord, that I cannot stand up in
your presence; I'm having my period."
So he searched but could not find the
household gods.
36Jacob was angry and took Laban to
task. "What is my crime?" he asked
Laban. "What sin have I committed
that you hunt me down? 37Now that you
have searched through all my goods,
what have you found that belongs to
your household? Put it here in front of
your relatives and mine, and let them
judge between the two of us.
38"I have been with you for twenty
years now. Your sheep and goats have
not miscarried, nor have I eaten rams
from your flocks. 39I did not bring you
animals torn by wild beasts; I bore the
loss myself. And you demanded payment from me for whatever was stolen
by day or night. 40This was my situation:
The heat consumed me in the daytime
and the cold at night, and sleep fled
from my eyes. 41It was like this for the
twenty years I was in your household. I
worked for you fourteen years for your
two daughters and six years for your
flocks, and you changed my wages ten
times. 42If the God of my father, the
God of Abraham and the Fear of Isaac,
had not been with me, you would surely
have sent me away empty-handed. But
God has seen my hardship and the toil
of my hands, and last night he rebuked
you."
43Laban answered Jacob, "The
women are my daughters, the children
are my children, and the flocks are my
flocks. All you see is mine. Yet what can
I do today about these daughters of
mine, or about the children they have
borne? 44Come now, let's make a covenant, you and I, and let it serve as a
witness between us."
45So Jacob took a stone and set it up
as a pillar. 46He said to his relatives,
"Gather some stones." So they took
stones and piled them in a heap, and
they ate there by the heap. 47Laban
called it Jegar Sahadutha, and Jacob
called it Galeed.
48Laban said, "This heap is a witness
between you and me today." That is
why it was called Galeed. 49It was also
called Mizpah, because he said, "May
the LORD keep watch between you and
me when we are away from each other.
50If you ill-treat my daughters or if you
take any wives besides my daughters,
even though no-one is with us, remember that God is a witness between you
and me."
51Laban also said to Jacob, "Here is
this heap, and here is this pillar I have
set up between you and me. 52This heap
is a witness, and this pillar is a witness,
that I will not go past this heap to your
side to harm you and that you will not go
past this heap and pillar to my side to
harm me. 53May the God of Abraham
and the God of Nahor, the God of their
father, judge between us."
So Jacob took an oath in the name of
the Fear of his father Isaac. 54He
offered a sacrifice there in the hill country and invited his relatives to a meal.

After they had eaten, they spent the
night there.
55Early the next morning Laban kissed his grandchildren and his daughters
and blessed them. Then he left and
returned home.

NEW TESTAMENT READING
Matthew 12:1–21

Lord of the Sabbath

12 At that time Jesus went through
the cornfields on the Sabbath.
His disciples were hungry and began to
pick some ears of corn and eat them.
2When the Pharisees saw this, they said
to him, "Look! Your disciples are doing
what is unlawful on the Sabbath."
3He answered, "Haven't you read
what David did when he and his companions were hungry? 4He entered the
house of God, and he and his companions ate the consecrated bread—which
was not lawful for them to do, but only
for the priests. 5Or haven't you read in
the Law that on the Sabbath the priests
in the temple desecrate the day and yet
are innocent? 6I tell you that one greater
than the temple is here. 7If you had
known what these words mean, 'I desire
mercy, not sacrifice,' you would not
have condemned the innocent. 8For the
Son of Man is Lord of the Sabbath."
9Going on from that place, he went
into their synagogue, and 10a man with a
shrivelled hand was there. Looking
for a reason to accuse Jesus, they
asked him, "Is it lawful to heal on the
Sabbath?"
11He said to them, "If any of you has a
sheep and it falls into a pit on the Sabbath, will you not take hold of it and lift
it out? 12How much more valuable is a
man than a sheep! Therefore it is lawful
to do good on the Sabbath."
13Then he said to the man, "Stretch
out your hand." So he stretched it out
and it was completely restored, just as
sound as the other. 14But the Pharisees
went out and plotted how they might
kill Jesus.

God's Chosen Servant

15Aware of this, Jesus withdrew from
that place. Many followed him, and he
healed all their sick, 16warning them not
to tell who he was. 17This was to fulfil
what was spoken through the prophet
Isaiah:

18"Here is my servant whom I have
chosen,
the one I love, in whom I delight;
I will put my Spirit on him,
and he will proclaim justice to the
nations.
19He will not quarrel or cry out;
no-one will hear his voice in the
streets.
20A bruised reed he will not break,
and a smouldering wick he will not
snuff out,
till he leads justice to victory.
21 In his name the nations will put
their hope."

READING FROM PSALMS
Psalm 9:13–20

13O LORD, see how my enemies
persecute me!
Have mercy and lift me up from
the gates of death,
14that I may declare your praises
in the gates of the Daughter of
Zion
and there rejoice in your salvation.
15The nations have fallen into the pit
they have dug;
their feet are caught in the net they
have hidden.
16The LORD is known by his justice;
the wicked are ensnared by the
work of their hands.
Higgaion. Selah

17The wicked return to the grave,
all the nations that forget God.
18But the needy will not always be
forgotten,
nor the hope of the afflicted ever
perish.

19Arise, O LORD, let not man triumph;
let the nations be judged in your
presence.

20Strike them with terror, O LORD;
let the nations know they are but
men. *Selah*

DAY 16

JANUARY 16

OLD TESTAMENT READING
Genesis 32:1–33:20

Jacob Prepares to Meet Esau

32 Jacob also went on his way, and
the angels of God met him.
2When Jacob saw them, he said, "This
is the camp of God!" So he named that
place Mahanaim.
3Jacob sent messengers ahead of him
to his brother Esau in the land of Seir,
the country of Edom. 4He instructed
them: "This is what you are to say to my
master Esau: 'Your servant Jacob says,
I have been staying with Laban and
have remained there till now. 5I have
cattle and donkeys, sheep and goats,
menservants and maidservants. Now I
am sending this message to my lord,
that I may find favour in your eyes.'"
6When the messengers returned to
Jacob, they said, "We went to your
brother Esau, and now he is coming to
meet you, and four hundred men are
with him."
7In great fear and distress Jacob divided the people who were with him into
two groups, and the flocks and herds
and camels as well. 8He thought, "If
Esau comes and attacks one group, the
group that is left may escape."
9Then Jacob prayed, "O God of my
father Abraham, God of my father
Isaac, O LORD, who said to me, 'Go
back to your country and your relatives,
and I will make you prosper,' 10I am
unworthy of all the kindness and faithfulness you have shown your servant. I
had only my staff when I crossed this
Jordan, but now I have become two
groups. 11Save me, I pray, from the
hand of my brother Esau, for I am
afraid he will come and attack me, and
also the mothers with their children.
12But you have said, 'I will surely make
you prosper and will make your descendants like the sand of the sea, which
cannot be counted.'"
13He spent the night there, and from
what he had with him he selected a gift
for his brother Esau: 14two hundred
female goats and twenty male goats,
two hundred ewes and twenty rams,
15thirty female camels with their young,
forty cows and ten bulls, and twenty
female donkeys and ten male donkeys.
16He put them in the care of his servants, each herd by itself, and said to his
servants, "Go ahead of me, and keep
some space between the herds."
17He instructed the one in the lead:
"When my brother Esau meets you and
asks, 'To whom do you belong, and
where are you going, and who owns all
these animals in front of you?' 18then
you are to say, 'They belong to your
servant Jacob. They are a gift sent to my
lord Esau, and he is coming behind
us.'"
19He also instructed the second, the
third and all the others who followed
the herds: "You are to say the same
thing to Esau when you meet him.
20And be sure to say, 'Your servant
Jacob is coming behind us.'" For he
thought, "I will pacify him with these
gifts I am sending on ahead; later, when
I see him, perhaps he will receive me."
21So Jacob's gifts went on ahead of him,
but he himself spent the night in the
camp.

Jacob Wrestles with God

22 That night Jacob got up and took his
two wives, his two maidservants and his
eleven sons and crossed the ford of the
Jabbok. 23 After he had sent them across
the stream, he sent over all his possessions. 24 So Jacob was left alone, and a
man wrestled with him till daybreak.
25 When the man saw that he could not
overpower him, he touched the socket
of Jacob's hip so that his hip was
wrenched as he wrestled with the man.
26 Then the man said, "Let me go, for it
is daybreak."

But Jacob replied, "I will not let you
go unless you bless me."

27 The man asked him, "What is your
name?"

"Jacob," he answered.

28 Then the man said, "Your name
will no longer be Jacob, but Israel, because you have struggled with God and
with men and have overcome."

29 Jacob said, "Please tell me your
name."

But he replied, "Why do you ask my
name?" Then he blessed him there.

30 So Jacob called the place Peniel,
saying, "It is because I saw God face to
face, and yet my life was spared."

31 The sun rose above him as he passed Peniel, and he was limping because
of his hip. 32 Therefore to this day the
Israelites do not eat the tendon attached
to the socket of the hip, because the
socket of Jacob's hip was touched near
the tendon.

Jacob Meets Esau

33 Jacob looked up and there was
Esau, coming with his four hundred men; so he divided the children
among Leah, Rachel and the two maidservants. 2 He put the maidservants and
their children in front, Leah and her
children next, and Rachel and Joseph in
the rear. 3 He himself went on ahead and
bowed down to the ground seven times
as he approached his brother.

4 But Esau ran to meet Jacob and
embraced him; he threw his arms
around his neck and kissed him. And
they wept. 5 Then Esau looked up and
saw the women and children. "Who are
these with you?" he asked.

Jacob answered, "They are the children God has graciously given your
servant."

6 Then the maidservants and their
children approached and bowed down.
7 Next, Leah and her children came and
bowed down. Last of all came Joseph
and Rachel, and they too bowed down.

8 Esau asked, "What do you mean by
all these droves I met?"

"To find favour in your eyes, my
lord," he said.

9 But Esau said, "I already have
plenty, my brother. Keep what you
have for yourself."

10 "No, please!" said Jacob. "If I have
found favour in your eyes, accept this
gift from me. For to see your face is like
seeing the face of God, now that you
have received me favourably. 11 Please
accept the present that was brought to
you, for God has been gracious to me
and I have all I need." And because
Jacob insisted, Esau accepted it.

12 Then Esau said, "Let us be on our
way; I'll accompany you."

13 But Jacob said to him, "My lord
knows that the children are tender and
that I must care for the ewes and cows
that are nursing their young. If they are
driven hard just one day, all the animals
will die. 14 So let my lord go on ahead of
his servant, while I move along slowly at
the pace of the droves before me and
that of the children, until I come to my
lord in Seir."

15 Esau said, "Then let me leave some
of my men with you."

"But why do that?" Jacob asked.
"Just let me find favour in the eyes of
my lord."

16 So that day Esau started on his way
back to Seir. 17 Jacob, however, went to
Succoth, where he built a place for himself and made shelters for his livestock.
That is why the place is called Succoth.

18 After Jacob came from Paddan

Aram, he arrived safely at the city of Shechem in Canaan and camped within sight of the city. 19For a hundred pieces of silver, he bought from the sons of Hamor, the father of Shechem, the plot of ground where he pitched his tent. 20There he set up an altar and called it El Elohe Israel.

NEW TESTAMENT READING

Matthew 12:22–45

Jesus and Beelzebub

22Then they brought him a demon-possessed man who was blind and mute, and Jesus healed him, so that he could both talk and see. 23All the people were astonished and said, "Could this be the Son of David?"

24But when the Pharisees heard this, they said, "It is only by Beelzebub, the prince of demons, that this fellow drives out demons."

25Jesus knew their thoughts and said to them, "Every kingdom divided against itself will be ruined, and every city or household divided against itself will not stand. 26If Satan drives out Satan, he is divided against himself. How then can his kingdom stand? 27And if I drive out demons by Beelzebub, by whom do your people drive them out? So then, they will be your judges. 28But if I drive out demons by the Spirit of God, then the kingdom of God has come upon you.

29"Or again, how can anyone enter a strong man's house and carry off his possessions unless he first ties up the strong man? Then he can rob his house.

30"He who is not with me is against me, and he who does not gather with me scatters. 31And so I tell you, every sin and blasphemy will be forgiven men, but the blasphemy against the Spirit will not be forgiven. 32Anyone who speaks a word against the Son of Man will be forgiven, but anyone who speaks against the Holy Spirit will not be forgiven, either in this age or in the age to come.

33"Make a tree good and its fruit will be good, or make a tree bad and its fruit will be bad, for a tree is recognised by its fruit. 34You brood of vipers, how can you who are evil say anything good? For out of the overflow of the heart the mouth speaks. 35The good man brings good things out of the good stored up in him, and the evil man brings evil things out of the evil stored up in him. 36But I tell you that men will have to give account on the day of judgment for every careless word they have spoken. 37For by your words you will be acquitted, and by your words you will be condemned."

The Sign of Jonah

38Then some of the Pharisees and teachers of the law said to him, "Teacher, we want to see a miraculous sign from you."

39He answered, "A wicked and adulterous generation asks for a miraculous sign! But none will be given it except the sign of the prophet Jonah. 40For as Jonah was three days and three nights in the belly of a huge fish, so the Son of Man will be three days and three nights in the heart of the earth. 41The men of Nineveh will stand up at the judgment with this generation and condemn it; for they repented at the preaching of Jonah, and now one greater than Jonah is here. 42The Queen of the South will rise at the judgment with this generation and condemn it; for she came from the ends of the earth to listen to Solomon's wisdom, and now one greater than Solomon is here.

43"When an evil spirit comes out of a man, it goes through arid places seeking rest and does not find it. 44Then it says, 'I will return to the house I left.' When it arrives, it finds the house unoccupied, swept clean and put in order. 45Then it goes and takes with it seven other spirits more wicked than itself, and they go in and live there. And the final condition of that man is worse than the first. That is how it will be with this wicked generation."

READING FROM PROVERBS
Proverbs 2:1–11

Moral Benefits of Wisdom

2 My son, if you accept my words
and store up my commands within
you,
2 turning your ear to wisdom
and applying your heart to
understanding,
3 and if you call out for insight
and cry aloud for understanding,
4 and if you look for it as for silver
and search for it as for hidden
treasure,
5 then you will understand the fear of
the LORD
and find the knowledge of God.
6 For the LORD gives wisdom,
and from his mouth come
knowledge and understanding.
7 He holds victory in store for the
upright,
he is a shield to those whose walk is
blameless,
8 for he guards the course of the just
and protects the way of his faithful
ones.

9 Then you will understand what is
right and just
and fair—every good path.
10 For wisdom will enter your heart,
and knowledge will be pleasant to
your soul.
11 Discretion will protect you,
and understanding will guard you.

JANUARY 17

DAY 17

OLD TESTAMENT READING
Genesis 34:1–35:29

Dinah and the Shechemites

34 Now Dinah, the daughter Leah
had borne to Jacob, went out to
visit the women of the land. 2 When
Shechem son of Hamor the Hivite, the
ruler of that area, saw her, he took her
and raped her. 3 His heart was drawn to
Dinah daughter of Jacob, and he loved
the girl and spoke tenderly to her. 4 And
Shechem said to his father Hamor,
"Get me this girl as my wife."
5 When Jacob heard that his daughter
Dinah had been defiled, his sons were in
the fields with his livestock; so he kept
quiet about it until they came home.
6 Then Shechem's father Hamor went
out to talk with Jacob. 7 Now Jacob's
sons had come in from the fields as soon
as they heard what had happened. They
were filled with grief and fury, because
Shechem had done a disgraceful thing in
Israel by lying with Jacob's daughter
—a thing that should not be done.
8 But Hamor said to them, "My son
Shechem has his heart set on your
daughter. Please give her to him as his
wife. 9 Intermarry with us; give us your
daughters and take our daughters for
yourselves. 10 You can settle among us;
the land is open to you. Live in it, trade
in it, and acquire property in it."
11 Then Shechem said to Dinah's
father and brothers, "Let me find
favour in your eyes, and I will give you
whatever you ask. 12 Make the price for
the bride and the gift I am to bring as
great as you like, and I'll pay whatever
you ask me. Only give me the girl as my
wife."
13 Because their sister Dinah had been
defiled, Jacob's sons replied deceitfully
as they spoke to Shechem and his father
Hamor. 14 They said to them, "We can't
do such a thing; we can't give our sister
to a man who is not circumcised. That
would be a disgrace to us. 15 We will give

our consent to you on one condition only: that you become like us by circumcising all your males. 16Then we will give you our daughters and take your daughters for ourselves. We'll settle among you and become one people with you. 17But if you will not agree to be circumcised, we'll take our sister and go."

18Their proposal seemed good to Hamor and his son Shechem. 19The young man, who was the most honoured of all his father's household, lost no time in doing what they said, because he was delighted with Jacob's daughter. 20So Hamor and his son Shechem went to the gate of their city to speak to their fellow townsmen. 21"These men are friendly towards us," they said. "Let them live in our land and trade in it; the land has plenty of room for them. We can marry their daughters and they can marry ours. 22But the men will consent to live with us as one people only on the condition that our males be circumcised, as they themselves are. 23Won't their livestock, their property and all their other animals become ours? So let us give our consent to them, and they will settle among us."

24All the men who went out of the city gate agreed with Hamor and his son Shechem, and every male in the city was circumcised.

25Three days later, while all of them were still in pain, two of Jacob's sons, Simeon and Levi, Dinah's brothers, took their swords and attacked the unsuspecting city, killing every male. 26They put Hamor and his son Shechem to the sword and took Dinah from Shechem's house and left. 27The sons of Jacob came upon the dead bodies and looted the city where their sister had been defiled. 28They seized their flocks and herds and donkeys and everything else of theirs in the city and out in the fields. 29They carried off all their wealth and all their women and children, taking as plunder everything in the houses.

30Then Jacob said to Simeon and Levi, "You have brought trouble on me by making me a stench to the Canaanites and Perizzites, the people living in this land. We are few in number, and if they join forces against me and attack me, I and my household will be destroyed."

31But they replied, "Should he have treated our sister like a prostitute?"

Jacob Returns to Bethel

35 Then God said to Jacob, "Go up to Bethel and settle there, and build an altar there to God, who appeared to you when you were fleeing from your brother Esau."

2So Jacob said to his household and to all who were with him, "Get rid of the foreign gods you have with you, and purify yourselves and change your clothes. 3Then come, let us go up to Bethel, where I will build an altar to God, who answered me in the day of my distress and who has been with me wherever I have gone." 4So they gave Jacob all the foreign gods they had and the rings in their ears, and Jacob buried them under the oak at Shechem. 5Then they set out, and the terror of God fell upon the towns all around them so that no-one pursued them.

6Jacob and all the people with him came to Luz (that is, Bethel) in the land of Canaan. 7There he built an altar, and he called the place El Bethel, because it was there that God revealed himself to him when he was fleeing from his brother.

8Now Deborah, Rebekah's nurse, died and was buried under the oak below Bethel. So it was named Allon Bacuth.

9After Jacob returned from Paddan Aram, God appeared to him again and blessed him. 10God said to him, "Your name is Jacob, but you will no longer be called Jacob; your name will be Israel." So he named him Israel.

11And God said to him, "I am God Almighty; be fruitful and increase in number. A nation and a community of

nations will come from you, and kings
will come from your body. 12The land I
gave to Abraham and Isaac I also give to
you, and I will give this land to your
descendants after you." 13Then God
went up from him at the place where he
had talked with him.

14Jacob set up a stone pillar at the
place where God had talked with him,
and he poured out a drink offering on it;
he also poured oil on it. 15Jacob called
the place where God had talked with
him Bethel.

The Deaths of Rachel and Isaac

16Then they moved on from Bethel.
While they were still some distance
from Ephrath, Rachel began to give
birth and had great difficulty. 17And as
she was having great difficulty in childbirth, the midwife said to her, "Don't
be afraid, for you have another son."
18As she breathed her last—for she was
dying—she named her son Ben-Oni.
But his father named him Benjamin.

19So Rachel died and was buried on
the way to Ephrath (that is, Bethlehem). 20Over her tomb Jacob set up a
pillar, and to this day that pillar marks
Rachel's tomb.

21Israel moved on again and pitched
his tent beyond Migdal Eder. 22While
Israel was living in that region, Reuben
went in and slept with his father's concubine Bilhah, and Israel heard of it.

Jacob had twelve sons:

23The sons of Leah:
Reuben the firstborn of Jacob,
Simeon, Levi, Judah, Issachar
and Zebulun.

24The sons of Rachel:
Joseph and Benjamin.

25The sons of Rachel's maidservant
Bilhah:
Dan and Naphtali.

26The sons of Leah's maidservant
Zilpah:
Gad and Asher.

These were the sons of Jacob, who
were born to him in Paddan Aram.

27Jacob came home to his father Isaac
in Mamre, near Kiriath Arba (that is,
Hebron), where Abraham and Isaac
had stayed. 28Isaac lived a hundred and
eighty years. 29Then he breathed his last
and died and was gathered to his people, old and full of years. And his sons
Esau and Jacob buried him.

NEW TESTAMENT READING

Matthew 12:46–13:17

Jesus' Mother and Brothers

46While Jesus was still talking to the
crowd, his mother and brothers stood
outside, wanting to speak to him.
47Someone told him, "Your mother and
brothers are standing outside, wanting
to speak to you."

48He replied to him, "Who is my
mother, and who are my brothers?"
49Pointing to his disciples, he said,
"Here are my mother and my brothers.
50For whoever does the will of my
Father in heaven is my brother and
sister and mother."

The Parable of the Sower

13 That same day Jesus went out of
the house and sat by the lake.
2Such large crowds gathered round him
that he got into a boat and sat in it, while
all the people stood on the shore. 3Then
he told them many things in parables,
saying: "A farmer went out to sow his
seed. 4As he was scattering the seed,
some fell along the path, and the birds
came and ate it up. 5Some fell on rocky
places, where it did not have much soil.
It sprang up quickly, because the soil
was shallow. 6But when the sun came
up, the plants were scorched, and they
withered because they had no root.
7Other seed fell among thorns, which
grew up and choked the plants. 8Still
other seed fell on good soil, where it
produced a crop—a hundred, sixty or

thirty times what was sown. 9He who
has ears, let him hear."
10The disciples came to him and
asked, "Why do you speak to the
people in parables?"
11He replied, "The knowledge of the
secrets of the kingdom of heaven has
been given to you, but not to them.
12Whoever has will be given more, and
he will have an abundance. Whoever
does not have, even what he has will be
taken from him. 13This is why I speak to
them in parables:

"Though seeing, they do not see;
though hearing, they do not hear
or understand.

14In them is fulfilled the prophecy of
Isaiah:

" 'You will be ever hearing but never
understanding;
you will be ever seeing but never
perceiving.
15For this people's heart has become
calloused;
they hardly hear with their ears,
and they have closed their eyes.
Otherwise they might see with their
eyes,
hear with their ears,
understand with their hearts
and turn, and I would heal them.'

16"But blessed are your eyes because
they see, and your ears because they
hear. 17For I tell you the truth, many
prophets and righteous men longed to
see what you see but did not see it, and
to hear what you hear but did not hear
it.

READING FROM PSALMS

Psalm 10:1–11

1Why, O LORD, do you stand far off?
Why do you hide yourself in times
of trouble?

2In his arrogance the wicked man
hunts down the weak,
who are caught in the schemes he
devises.
3He boasts of the cravings of his heart;
he blesses the greedy and reviles
the LORD.
4In his pride the wicked does not seek
him;
in all his thoughts there is no room
for God.
5His ways are always prosperous;
he is haughty and your laws are far
from him;
he sneers at all his enemies.
6He says to himself, "Nothing will
shake me;
I'll always be happy and never
have trouble."
7His mouth is full of curses and lies
and threats;
trouble and evil are under his
tongue.
8He lies in wait near the villages;
from ambush he murders the
innocent,
watching in secret for his victims.
9He lies in wait like a lion in cover;
he lies in wait to catch the helpless;
he catches the helpless and drags
them off in his net.
10His victims are crushed, they
collapse;
they fall under his strength.
11He says to himself, "God has
forgotten;
he covers his face and never sees."

OLD TESTAMENT READING
Genesis 36:1–37:36

Esau's Descendants

36 This is the account of Esau (that is, Edom).

2Esau took his wives from the
women of Canaan: Adah daughter
of Elon the Hittite, and Oholibamah daughter of Anah and granddaughter of Zibeon the Hivite—
3also Basemath daughter of
Ishmael and sister of Nebaioth.
4Adah bore Eliphaz to Esau,
Basemath bore Reuel, 5and Oholibamah bore Jeush, Jalam and
Korah. These were the sons of
Esau, who were born to him in
Canaan.
6Esau took his wives and sons
and daughters and all the members
of his household, as well as his
livestock and all his other animals
and all the goods he had acquired
in Canaan, and moved to a land
some distance from his brother
Jacob. 7Their possessions were too
great for them to remain together;
the land where they were staying
could not support them both because of their livestock. 8So Esau
(that is, Edom) settled in the hill
country of Seir.

9This is the account of Esau the father
of the Edomites in the hill country of
Seir.

10These are the names of Esau's
sons:
Eliphaz, the son of Esau's wife
Adah, and Reuel, the son of
Esau's wife Basemath.
11The sons of Eliphaz:
Teman, Omar, Zepho, Gatam
and Kenaz.
12Esau's son Eliphaz also had a
concubine named Timna, who
bore him Amalek. These were
grandsons of Esau's wife Adah.
13The sons of Reuel:
Nahath, Zerah, Shammah and
Mizzah. These were grandsons
of Esau's wife Basemath.
14The sons of Esau's wife Oholibamah daughter of Anah and granddaughter of Zibeon, whom she
bore to Esau:
Jeush, Jalam and Korah.

15These were the chiefs among Esau's
descendants:
The sons of Eliphaz the firstborn
of Esau:
Chiefs Teman, Omar, Zepho,
Kenaz, 16Korah, Gatam and
Amalek. These were the chiefs
descended from Eliphaz in
Edom; they were grandsons of
Adah.
17The sons of Esau's son Reuel:
Chiefs Nahath, Zerah, Shammah and Mizzah. These were the
chiefs descended from Reuel in
Edom; they were grandsons of
Esau's wife Basemath.
18The sons of Esau's wife Oholibamah:
Chiefs Jeush, Jalam and Korah.
These were the chiefs descended
from Esau's wife Oholibamah
daughter of Anah.
19These were the sons of Esau (that
is, Edom), and these were their chiefs.

20These were the sons of Seir the
Horite, who were living in the region:
Lotan, Shobal, Zibeon, Anah,
21Dishon, Ezer and Dishan.
These sons of Seir in Edom were
Horite chiefs.
22The sons of Lotan:
Hori and Homam. Timna was
Lotan's sister.

[23]The sons of Shobal:
Alvan, Manahath, Ebal, Shepho and Onam.
[24]The sons of Zibeon:
Aiah and Anah. This is the Anah who discovered the hot springs in the desert while he was grazing the donkeys of his father Zibeon.
[25]The children of Anah:
Dishon and Oholibamah daughter of Anah.
[26]The sons of Dishon:
Hemdan, Eshban, Ithran and Keran.
[27]The sons of Ezer:
Bilhan, Zaavan and Akan.
[28]The sons of Dishan:
Uz and Aran.
[29]These were the Horite chiefs:
Lotan, Shobal, Zibeon, Anah,
[30]Dishon, Ezer and Dishan.
These were the Horite chiefs, according to their divisions, in the land of Seir.

The Rulers of Edom

[31]These were the kings who reigned in Edom before any Israelite king reigned:
[32]Bela son of Beor became king of Edom. His city was named Dinhabah.
[33]When Bela died, Jobab son of Zerah from Bozrah succeeded him as king.
[34]When Jobab died, Husham from the land of the Temanites succeeded him as king.
[35]When Husham died, Hadad son of Bedad, who defeated Midian in the country of Moab, succeeded him as king. His city was named Avith.
[36]When Hadad died, Samlah from Masrekah succeeded him as king.
[37]When Samlah died, Shaul from Rehoboth on the river succeeded him as king.
[38]When Shaul died, Baal-Hanan son of Acbor succeeded him as king.
[39]When Baal-Hanan son of Acbor died, Hadad succeeded him as king. His city was named Pau, and his wife's name was Mehetabel daughter of Matred, the daughter of Me-Zahab.

[40]These were the chiefs descended from Esau, by name, according to their clans and regions:
Timna, Alvah, Jetheth, [41]Oholi-
bamah, Elah, Pinon, [42]Kenaz,
Teman, Mibzar, [43]Magdiel and
Iram. These were the chiefs of Edom, according to their settlements in the land they occupied.

This was Esau the father of the Edomites.

Joseph's Dreams

37 Jacob lived in the land where his father had stayed, the land of Canaan.

[2]This is the account of Jacob.

Joseph, a young man of seventeen, was tending the flocks with his brothers, the sons of Bilhah and the sons of Zilpah, his father's wives, and he brought their father a bad report about them.
[3]Now Israel loved Joseph more than any of his other sons, because he had been born to him in his old age; and he made a richly ornamented robe for him.
[4]When his brothers saw that their father loved him more than any of them, they hated him and could not speak a kind word to him.

[5]Joseph had a dream, and when he told it to his brothers, they hated him all
the more. [6]He said to them, "Listen to
this dream I had: [7]We were binding sheaves of corn out in the field when suddenly my sheaf rose and stood upright, while your sheaves gathered round mine and bowed down to it."
[8]His brothers said to him, "Do you

intend to reign over us? Will you actually rule us?" And they hated him all
the more because of his dream and what
he had said.
9Then he had another dream, and he
told it to his brothers. "Listen," he said,
"I had another dream, and this time the
sun and moon and eleven stars were
bowing down to me."
10When he told his father as well as
his brothers, his father rebuked him and
said, "What is this dream you had? Will
your mother and I and your brothers
actually come and bow down to the
ground before you?" 11His brothers
were jealous of him, but his father kept
the matter in mind.

Joseph Sold by His Brothers

12Now his brothers had gone to graze
their father's flocks near Shechem,
13and Israel said to Joseph, "As you
know, your brothers are grazing the
flocks near Shechem. Come, I am going
to send you to them."
"Very well," he replied.
14So he said to him, "Go and see if all
is well with your brothers and with the
flocks, and bring word back to me."
Then he sent him off from the Valley of
Hebron.
When Joseph arrived at Shechem, 15a
man found him wandering around in the
fields and asked him, "What are you
looking for?"
16He replied, "I'm looking for my
brothers. Can you tell me where they
are grazing their flocks?"
17"They have moved on from here,"
the man answered. "I heard them say,
'Let's go to Dothan.'"
So Joseph went after his brothers and
found them near Dothan. 18But they
saw him in the distance, and before he
reached them, they plotted to kill him.
19"Here comes that dreamer!" they
said to each other. 20"Come now, let's
kill him and throw him into one of these
cisterns and say that a ferocious animal
devoured him. Then we'll see what
comes of his dreams."
21When Reuben heard this, he tried
to rescue him from their hands. "Let's
not take his life," he said. 22"Don't shed
any blood. Throw him into this cistern
here in the desert, but don't lay a hand
on him." Reuben said this to rescue him
from them and take him back to his
father.
23So when Joseph came to his
brothers, they stripped him of his robe
—the richly ornamented robe he was
wearing—24and they took him and
threw him into the cistern. Now the
cistern was empty; there was no water in
it.
25As they sat down to eat their meal,
they looked up and saw a caravan of
Ishmaelites coming from Gilead. Their
camels were loaded with spices, balm
and myrrh, and they were on their way
to take them down to Egypt.
26Judah said to his brothers, "What
will we gain if we kill our brother and
cover up his blood? 27Come, let's sell
him to the Ishmaelites and not lay our
hands on him; after all, he is our
brother, our own flesh and blood." His
brothers agreed.
28So when the Midianite merchants
came by, his brothers pulled Joseph up
out of the cistern and sold him for
twenty shekels of silver to the Ishmaelites, who took him to Egypt.
29When Reuben returned to the cistern and saw that Joseph was not there,
he tore his clothes. 30He went back to
his brothers and said, "The boy isn't
there! Where can I turn now?"
31Then they got Joseph's robe,
slaughtered a goat and dipped the robe
in the blood. 32They took the
ornamented robe back to their father
and said, "We found this. Examine it to
see whether it is your son's robe."
33He recognised it and said, "It is my
son's robe! Some ferocious animal has
devoured him. Joseph has surely been
torn to pieces."
34Then Jacob tore his clothes, put on
sackcloth and mourned for his son many
days. 35All his sons and daughters came
to comfort him, but he refused to be

comforted. “No,” he said, “in mourning will I go down to the grave to my
son.” So his father wept for him.
36Meanwhile, the Midianites sold
Joseph in Egypt to Potiphar, one of
Pharaoh’s officials, the captain of the
guard.

NEW TESTAMENT READING
Matthew 13:18–35

18“Listen then to what the parable of
the sower means: 19When anyone hears
the message about the kingdom and
does not understand it, the evil one
comes and snatches away what was
sown in his heart. This is the seed sown
along the path. 20The one who received
the seed that fell on rocky places is the
man who hears the word and at once
receives it with joy. 21But since he has
no root, he lasts only a short time.
When trouble or persecution comes because of the word, he quickly falls away.
22The one who received the seed that
fell among the thorns is the man who
hears the word, but the worries of this
life and the deceitfulness of wealth
choke it, making it unfruitful. 23But the
one who received the seed that fell on
good soil is the man who hears the word
and understands it. He produces a crop,
yielding a hundred, sixty or thirty times
what was sown.”

The Parable of the Weeds

24Jesus told them another parable:
“The kingdom of heaven is like a man
who sowed good seed in his field. 25But
while everyone was sleeping, his enemy
came and sowed weeds among the
wheat, and went away. 26When the
wheat sprouted and formed ears, then
the weeds also appeared.
27“The owner’s servants came to him
and said, ‘Sir, didn’t you sow good seed
in your field? Where then did the weeds
come from?’
28“ ‘An enemy did this,’ he replied.
“The servants asked him, ‘Do you
want us to go and pull them up?’
29“ ‘No,’ he answered, ‘because while
you are pulling the weeds, you may root
up the wheat with them. 30Let both
grow together until the harvest. At that
time I will tell the harvesters: First collect the weeds and tie them in bundles to
be burned; then gather the wheat and
bring it into my barn.’ ”

The Parables of the Mustard Seed and the Yeast

31He told them another parable:
“The kingdom of heaven is like a mustard seed, which a man took and
planted in his field. 32Though it is the
smallest of all your seeds, yet when it
grows, it is the largest of garden plants
and becomes a tree, so that the birds of
the air come and perch in its branches.”
33He told them still another parable:
“The kingdom of heaven is like yeast
that a woman took and mixed into a
large amount of flour until it worked all
through the dough.”
34Jesus spoke all these things to the
crowd in parables; he did not say anything to them without using a parable.
35So was fulfilled what was spoken
through the prophet:

“I will open my mouth in parables,
I will utter things hidden since the
creation of the world.”

READING FROM PSALMS
Psalm 10:12–18

12Arise, LORD! Lift up your hand, O
God.
Do not forget the helpless.
13Why does the wicked man revile
God?
Why does he say to himself,
“He won’t call me to account”?
14But you, O God, do see trouble and
grief;

you consider it to take it in hand.
The victim commits himself to you;
you are the helper of the fatherless.
15Break the arm of the wicked and evil
man;
call him to account for his
wickedness
that would not be found out.

16The LORD is King for ever and ever;
the nations will perish from his
land.
17You hear, O LORD, the desire of the
afflicted;
you encourage them, and you
listen to their cry,
18defending the fatherless and the
oppressed,
in order that man, who is of the
earth, may terrify no more.

JANUARY 19

DAY 19

OLD TESTAMENT READING

Genesis 38:1–39:23

Judah and Tamar

38 At that time, Judah left his
brothers and went down to stay
with a man of Adullam named Hirah.
2There Judah met the daughter of a
Canaanite man named Shua. He married her and lay with her; 3she became
pregnant and gave birth to a son, who
was named Er. 4She conceived again
and gave birth to a son and named him
Onan. 5She gave birth to still another
son and named him Shelah. It was at
Kezib that she gave birth to him.

6Judah got a wife for Er, his firstborn,
and her name was Tamar. 7But Er,
Judah's firstborn, was wicked in the
LORD's sight; so the LORD put him to
death.

8Then Judah said to Onan, "Lie with
your brother's wife and fulfil your duty
to her as a brother-in-law to produce
offspring for your brother." 9But Onan
knew that the offspring would not be
his; so whenever he lay with his
brother's wife, he spilled his semen on
the ground to keep from producing
offspring for his brother. 10What he did
was wicked in the LORD's sight; so he
put him to death also.

11Judah then said to his daughter-in-
law Tamar, "Live as a widow in your
father's house until my son Shelah
grows up." For he thought, "He may
die too, just like his brothers." So
Tamar went to live in her father's
house.

12After a long time Judah's wife, the
daughter of Shua, died. When Judah
had recovered from his grief, he went
up to Timnah, to the men who were
shearing his sheep, and his friend Hirah
the Adullamite went with him.

13When Tamar was told, "Your
father-in-law is on his way to Timnah to
shear his sheep," 14she took off her
widow's clothes, covered herself with a
veil to disguise herself, and then sat
down at the entrance to Enaim, which is
on the road to Timnah. For she saw
that, though Shelah had now grown up,
she had not been given to him as his
wife.

15When Judah saw her, he thought
she was a prostitute, for she had
covered her face. 16Not realising that
she was his daughter-in-law, he went
over to her by the roadside and said,
"Come now, let me sleep with you."

"And what will you give me to sleep
with you?" she asked.

17"I'll send you a young goat from my
flock," he said.

"Will you give me something as a
pledge until you send it?" she asked.

18He said, "What pledge should I give
you?"

"Your seal and its cord, and the staff in your hand," she answered. So he gave them to her and slept with her, and she became pregnant by him. 19After she left, she took off her veil and put on her widow's clothes again.

20Meanwhile Judah sent the young goat by his friend the Adullamite in order to get his pledge back from the woman, but he did not find her. 21He asked the men who lived there, "Where is the shrine-prostitute who was beside the road at Enaim?"

"There hasn't been any shrine-prostitute here," they said.

22So he went back to Judah and said, "I didn't find her. Besides, the men who lived there said, 'There hasn't been any shrine-prostitute here.'"

23Then Judah said, "Let her keep what she has, or we will become a laughing-stock. After all, I did send her this young goat, but you didn't find her."

24About three months later Judah was told, "Your daughter-in-law Tamar is guilty of prostitution, and as a result she is now pregnant."

Judah said, "Bring her out and have her burned to death!"

25As she was being brought out, she sent a message to her father-in-law. "I am pregnant by the man who owns these," she said. And she added, "See if you recognise whose seal and cord and staff these are."

26Judah recognised them and said, "She is more righteous than I, since I wouldn't give her to my son Shelah." And he did not sleep with her again.

27When the time came for her to give birth, there were twin boys in her womb. 28As she was giving birth, one of them put out his hand; so the midwife took a scarlet thread and tied it on his wrist and said, "This one came out first." 29But when he drew back his hand, his brother came out, and she said, "So this is how you have broken out!" And he was named Perez. 30Then his brother, who had the scarlet thread on his wrist, came out and he was given the name Zerah.

Joseph and Potiphar's Wife

39 Now Joseph had been taken down to Egypt. Potiphar, an Egyptian who was one of Pharaoh's officials, the captain of the guard, bought him from the Ishmaelites who had taken him there.

2The LORD was with Joseph and he prospered, and he lived in the house of his Egyptian master. 3When his master saw that the LORD was with him and that the LORD gave him success in everything he did, 4Joseph found favour in his eyes and became his attendant. Potiphar put him in charge of his household, and he entrusted to his care everything he owned. 5From the time he put him in charge of his household and of all that he owned, the LORD blessed the household of the Egyptian because of Joseph. The blessing of the LORD was on everything Potiphar had, both in the house and in the field. 6So he left in Joseph's care everything he had; with Joseph in charge, he did not concern himself with anything except the food he ate.

Now Joseph was well-built and handsome, 7and after a while his master's wife took notice of Joseph and said, "Come to bed with me!"

8But he refused. "With me in charge," he told her, "my master does not concern himself with anything in the house; everything he owns he has entrusted to my care. 9No-one is greater in this house than I am. My master has withheld nothing from me except you, because you are his wife. How then could I do such a wicked thing and sin against God?" 10And though she spoke to Joseph day after day, he refused to go to bed with her or even to be with her.

11One day he went into the house to attend to his duties, and none of the household servants was inside. 12She caught him by his cloak and said, "Come to bed with me!" But he left his

cloak in her hand and ran out of the
house.
13When she saw that he had left his
cloak in her hand and had run out of the
house, 14she called her household servants. "Look," she said to them, "this
Hebrew has been brought to us to make
sport of us! He came in here to sleep
with me, but I screamed. 15When he
heard me scream for help, he left his
cloak beside me and ran out of the
house."
16She kept his cloak beside her until
his master came home. 17Then she told
him this story: "That Hebrew slave you
brought us came to me to make sport of
me. 18But as soon as I screamed for
help, he left his cloak beside me and ran
out of the house."
19When his master heard the story his
wife told him, saying, "This is how your
slave treated me," he burned with anger. 20Joseph's master took him and put
him in prison, the place where the king's
prisoners were confined.
But while Joseph was there in the
prison, 21the LORD was with him; he
showed him kindness and granted him
favour in the eyes of the prison warder.
22So the warder put Joseph in charge of
all those held in the prison, and he was
made responsible for all that was done
there. 23The warder paid no attention to
anything under Joseph's care, because
the LORD was with Joseph and gave him
success in whatever he did.

NEW TESTAMENT READING
Matthew 13:36–58

The Parable of the Weeds Explained

36Then he left the crowd and went
into the house. His disciples came to
him and said, "Explain to us the parable
of the weeds in the field."
37He answered, "The one who sowed
the good seed is the Son of Man. 38The
field is the world, and the good seed
stands for the sons of the kingdom. The
weeds are the sons of the evil one, 39and
the enemy who sows them is the devil.
The harvest is the end of the age, and
the harvesters are angels.
40"As the weeds are pulled up and
burned in the fire, so it will be at the end
of the age. 41The Son of Man will send
out his angels, and they will weed out of
his kingdom everything that causes sin
and all who do evil. 42They will throw
them into the fiery furnace, where there
will be weeping and gnashing of teeth.
43Then the righteous will shine like the
sun in the kingdom of their Father. He
who has ears, let him hear.

The Parables of the Hidden Treasure and the Pearl

44"The kingdom of heaven is like
treasure hidden in a field. When a man
found it, he hid it again, and then in his
joy went and sold all he had and bought
that field.
45"Again, the kingdom of heaven is
like a merchant looking for fine pearls.
46When he found one of great value, he
went away and sold everything he had
and bought it.

The Parable of the Net

47"Once again, the kingdom of
heaven is like a net that was let down
into the lake and caught all kinds of fish.
48When it was full, the fishermen pulled
it up on the shore. Then they sat down
and collected the good fish in baskets,
but threw the bad away. 49This is how it
will be at the end of the age. The angels
will come and separate the wicked from
the righteous 50and throw them into the
fiery furnace, where there will be weeping and gnashing of teeth.
51"Have you understood all these
things?" Jesus asked.
"Yes," they replied.
52He said to them, "Therefore every
teacher of the law who has been instructed about the kingdom of heaven is
like the owner of a house who brings out
of his storeroom new treasures as well
as old."

A Prophet Without Honour

53When Jesus had finished these parables, he moved on from there.
54Coming to his home town, he began
teaching the people in their synagogue,
and they were amazed. "Where did this
man get this wisdom and these miraculous powers?" they asked. 55"Isn't this
the carpenter's son? Isn't his mother's
name Mary, and aren't his brothers
James, Joseph, Simon and Judas?
56Aren't all his sisters with us? Where
then did this man get all these things?"
57And they took offence at him.
But Jesus said to them, "Only in his
home town and in his own house is a
prophet without honour."
58And he did not do many miracles
there because of their lack of faith.

READING FROM PSALMS
Psalm 11:1–7

For the director of music. Of David.

1In the LORD I take refuge.
How then can you say to me:
"Flee like a bird to your mountain.
2For look, the wicked bend their
bows;
they set their arrows against the
strings
to shoot from the shadows
at the upright in heart.
3When the foundations are being
destroyed,
what can the righteous do?"

4The LORD is in his holy temple;
the LORD is on his heavenly
throne.
He observes the sons of men;
his eyes examine them.
5The LORD examines the righteous,
but the wicked and those who love
violence
his soul hates.
6On the wicked he will rain
fiery coals and burning sulphur;
a scorching wind will be their
lot.

7For the LORD is righteous,
he loves justice;
upright men will see his face.

DAY 20

JANUARY 20

OLD TESTAMENT READING
Genesis 40:1–41:40

The Cupbearer and the Baker

40 Some time later, the cupbearer
and the baker of the king of
Egypt offended their master, the king of
Egypt. 2Pharaoh was angry with his two
officials, the chief cupbearer and the
chief baker, 3and put them in custody in
the house of the captain of the guard, in
the same prison where Joseph was confined. 4The captain of the guard
assigned them to Joseph, and he
attended them.
After they had been in custody for
some time, 5each of the two men—the
cupbearer and the baker of the king of
Egypt, who were being held in prison
—had a dream the same night, and each
dream had a meaning of its own.
6When Joseph came to them the next
morning, he saw that they were dejected. 7So he asked Pharaoh's officials
who were in custody with him in his
master's house, "Why are your faces so
sad today?"
8"We both had dreams," they

answered, "but there is no-one to interpret them."

Then Joseph said to them, "Do not interpretations belong to God? Tell me your dreams."

9So the chief cupbearer told Joseph his dream. He said to him, "In my dream I saw a vine in front of me, 10and on the vine were three branches. As soon as it budded, it blossomed, and its clusters ripened into grapes. 11Pharaoh's cup was in my hand, and I took the grapes, squeezed them into Pharaoh's cup and put the cup in his hand."

12"This is what it means," Joseph said to him. "The three branches are three days. 13Within three days Pharaoh will lift up your head and restore you to your position, and you will put Pharaoh's cup in his hand, just as you used to do when you were his cupbearer. 14But when all goes well with you, remember me and show me kindness; mention me to Pharaoh and get me out of this prison. 15For I was forcibly carried off from the land of the Hebrews, and even here I have done nothing to deserve being put in a dungeon."

16When the chief baker saw that Joseph had given a favourable interpretation, he said to Joseph, "I too had a dream: On my head were three baskets of bread. 17In the top basket were all kinds of baked goods for Pharaoh, but the birds were eating them out of the basket on my head."

18"This is what it means," Joseph said. "The three baskets are three days. 19Within three days Pharaoh will lift off your head and hang you on a tree. And the birds will eat away your flesh."

20Now the third day was Pharaoh's birthday, and he gave a feast for all his officials. He lifted up the heads of the chief cupbearer and the chief baker in the presence of his officials: 21He restored the chief cupbearer to his position, so that he once again put the cup into Pharaoh's hand, 22but he hanged the chief baker, just as Joseph had said to them in his interpretation.

23The chief cupbearer, however, did not remember Joseph; he forgot him.

Pharaoh's Dreams

41 When two full years had passed, Pharaoh had a dream: He was standing by the Nile, 2when out of the river there came up seven cows, sleek and fat, and they grazed among the reeds. 3After them, seven other cows, ugly and gaunt, came up out of the Nile and stood beside those on the riverbank. 4And the cows that were ugly and gaunt ate up the seven sleek, fat cows. Then Pharaoh woke up.

5He fell asleep again and had a second dream: Seven ears of corn, healthy and good, were growing on a single stalk. 6After them, seven other ears of corn sprouted—thin and scorched by the east wind. 7The thin ears of corn swallowed up the seven healthy, full ears. Then Pharaoh woke up; it had been a dream.

8In the morning his mind was troubled, so he sent for all the magicians and wise men of Egypt. Pharaoh told them his dreams, but no-one could interpret them for him.

9Then the chief cupbearer said to Pharaoh, "Today I am reminded of my shortcomings. 10Pharaoh was once angry with his servants, and he imprisoned me and the chief baker in the house of the captain of the guard. 11Each of us had a dream the same night, and each dream had a meaning of its own. 12Now a young Hebrew was there with us, a servant of the captain of the guard. We told him our dreams, and he interpreted them for us, giving each man the interpretation of his dream. 13And things turned out exactly as he interpreted them to us: I was restored to my position, and the other man was hanged."

14So Pharaoh sent for Joseph, and he was quickly brought from the dungeon. When he had shaved and changed his clothes, he came before Pharaoh.

15Pharaoh said to Joseph, "I had a

dream, and no-one can interpret it. But I have heard it said of you that when you hear a dream you can interpret it."

16"I cannot do it," Joseph replied to Pharaoh, "but God will give Pharaoh the answer he desires."

17Then Pharaoh said to Joseph, "In my dream I was standing on the bank of the Nile, 18when out of the river there came up seven cows, fat and sleek, and they grazed among the reeds. 19After them, seven other cows came up—scrawny and very ugly and lean. I had never seen such ugly cows in all the land of Egypt. 20The lean, ugly cows ate up the seven fat cows that came up first. 21But even after they ate them, no-one could tell that they had done so; they looked just as ugly as before. Then I woke up.

22"In my dreams I also saw seven ears of corn, full and good, growing on a single stalk. 23After them, seven other ears sprouted—withered and thin and scorched by the east wind. 24The thin ears of corn swallowed up the seven good ears. I told this to the magicians, but none could explain it to me."

25Then Joseph said to Pharaoh, "The dreams of Pharaoh are one and the same. God has revealed to Pharaoh what he is about to do. 26The seven good cows are seven years, and the seven good ears of corn are seven years; it is one and the same dream. 27The seven lean, ugly cows that came up afterwards are seven years, and so are the seven worthless ears of corn scorched by the east wind: They are seven years of famine.

28"It is just as I said to Pharaoh: God has shown Pharaoh what he is about to do. 29Seven years of great abundance are coming throughout the land of Egypt, 30but seven years of famine will follow them. Then all the abundance in Egypt will be forgotten, and the famine will ravage the land. 31The abundance in the land will not be remembered, because the famine that follows it will be so severe. 32The reason the dream was given to Pharaoh in two forms is that the matter has been firmly decided by God, and God will do it soon.

33"And now let Pharaoh look for a discerning and wise man and put him in charge of the land of Egypt. 34Let Pharaoh appoint commissioners over the land to take a fifth of the harvest of Egypt during the seven years of abundance. 35They should collect all the food of these good years that are coming and store up the grain under the authority of Pharaoh, to be kept in the cities for food. 36This food should be held in reserve for the country, to be used during the seven years of famine that will come upon Egypt, so that the country may not be ruined by the famine."

37The plan seemed good to Pharaoh and to all his officials. 38So Pharaoh asked them, "Can we find anyone like this man, one in whom is the spirit of God?"

39Then Pharaoh said to Joseph, "Since God has made all this known to you, there is no-one so discerning and wise as you. 40You shall be in charge of my palace, and all my people are to submit to your orders. Only with respect to the throne will I be greater than you."

NEW TESTAMENT READING
Matthew 14:1–21

John the Baptist Beheaded

14 At that time Herod the tetrarch heard the reports about Jesus, 2and he said to his attendants, "This is John the Baptist; he has risen from the dead! That is why miraculous powers are at work in him."

3Now Herod had arrested John and bound him and put him in prison because of Herodias, his brother Philip's wife, 4for John had been saying to him: "It is not lawful for you to have her." 5Herod wanted to kill John, but he was afraid of the people, because they considered him a prophet.

6On Herod's birthday the daughter of

Herodias danced for them and pleased
Herod so much 7that he promised with
an oath to give her whatever she asked.
8Prompted by her mother, she said,
"Give me here on a platter the head of
John the Baptist." 9The king was distressed, but because of his oaths and his
dinner guests, he ordered that her request be granted 10and had John beheaded in the prison. 11His head was
brought in on a platter and given to the
girl, who carried it to her mother.
12John's disciples came and took his
body and buried it. Then they went and
told Jesus.

Jesus Feeds the Five Thousand

13When Jesus heard what had happened, he withdrew by boat privately to
a solitary place. Hearing of this, the
crowds followed him on foot from the
towns. 14When Jesus landed and saw a
large crowd, he had compassion on
them and healed their sick.

15As evening approached, the disciples came to him and said, "This is a
remote place, and it's already getting
late. Send the crowds away, so that they
can go to the villages and buy themselves some food."

16Jesus replied, "They do not need to
go away. You give them something to
eat."

17"We have here only five loaves of
bread and two fish," they answered.

18"Bring them here to me," he said.
19And he directed the people to sit
down on the grass. Taking the five
loaves and the two fish and looking up
to heaven, he gave thanks and broke the
loaves. Then he gave them to the disciples, and the disciples gave them to the
people. 20They all ate and were satisfied, and the disciples picked up twelve
basketfuls of broken pieces that were
left over. 21The number of those who
ate was about five thousand men, besides women and children.

READING FROM PROVERBS

Proverbs 2:12–22

12Wisdom will save you from the ways
of wicked men,
from men whose words are
perverse,
13who leave the straight paths
to walk in dark ways,
14who delight in doing wrong
and rejoice in the perverseness of
evil,
15whose paths are crooked
and who are devious in their ways.

16It will save you also from the
adulteress,
from the wayward wife with her
seductive words,
17who has left the partner of her youth
and ignored the covenant she made
before God.
18For her house leads down to death
and her paths to the spirits of the
dead.
19None who go to her return
or attain the paths of life.

20Thus you will walk in the ways of
good men
and keep to the paths of the
righteous.
21For the upright will live in the land,
and the blameless will remain in it;
22but the wicked will be cut off from
the land,
and the unfaithful will be torn from
it.

DAY 21

JANUARY 21

OLD TESTAMENT READING

Genesis 41:41–42:38

Joseph in Charge of Egypt

41So Pharaoh said to Joseph, "I
hereby put you in charge of the whole
land of Egypt." 42Then Pharaoh took
his signet ring from his finger and put it
on Joseph's finger. He dressed him in
robes of fine linen and put a gold chain
around his neck. 43He had him ride in a
chariot as his second-in-command, and
men shouted before him, "Make way!"
Thus he put him in charge of the whole
land of Egypt.

44Then Pharaoh said to Joseph, "I am
Pharaoh, but without your word no-one
will lift hand or foot in all Egypt."
45Pharaoh gave Joseph the name
Zaphenath-Paneah and gave him Asenath daughter of Potiphera, priest of
On, to be his wife. And Joseph went
throughout the land of Egypt.

46Joseph was thirty years old when he
entered the service of Pharaoh king of
Egypt. And Joseph went out from Pharaoh's presence and travelled throughout Egypt. 47During the seven years of
abundance the land produced plenti-
fully. 48Joseph collected all the food
produced in those seven years of abundance in Egypt and stored it in the
cities. In each city he put the food grown
in the fields surrounding it. 49Joseph
stored up huge quantities of grain, like
the sand of the sea; it was so much that
he stopped keeping records because it
was beyond measure.

50Before the years of famine came,
two sons were born to Joseph by Asenath daughter of Potiphera, priest of
On. 51Joseph named his firstborn Manasseh and said, "It is because God has
made me forget all my trouble and all
my father's household." 52The second
son he named Ephraim and said, "It is
because God has made me fruitful in the
land of my suffering."

53The seven years of abundance in
Egypt came to an end, 54and the seven
years of famine began, just as Joseph
had said. There was famine in all the
other lands, but in the whole land of
Egypt there was food. 55When all Egypt
began to feel the famine, the people
cried to Pharaoh for food. Then Pharaoh told all the Egyptians, "Go to
Joseph and do what he tells you."

56When the famine had spread over
the whole country, Joseph opened the
storehouses and sold grain to the Egyptians, for the famine was severe
throughout Egypt. 57And all the countries came to Egypt to buy grain from
Joseph, because the famine was severe
in all the world.

Joseph's Brothers Go to Egypt

42 When Jacob learned that there
was grain in Egypt, he said to his
sons, "Why do you just keep looking at
each other?" 2He continued, "I have
heard that there is grain in Egypt. Go
down there and buy some for us, so that
we may live and not die."

3Then ten of Joseph's brothers went
down to buy grain from Egypt. 4But
Jacob did not send Benjamin, Joseph's
brother, with the others, because he
was afraid that harm might come to
him. 5So Israel's sons were among those
who went to buy grain, for the famine
was in the land of Canaan also.

6Now Joseph was the governor of the
land, the one who sold grain to all its
people. So when Joseph's brothers arrived, they bowed down to him with
their faces to the ground. 7As soon as
Joseph saw his brothers, he recognised
them, but he pretended to be a stranger
and spoke harshly to them. "Where do
you come from?" he asked.

"From the land of Canaan," they replied, "to buy food."
8Although Joseph recognised his
brothers, they did not recognise him.
9Then he remembered his dreams about
them and said to them, "You are spies!
You have come to see where our land is
unprotected."
10"No, my lord," they answered.
"Your servants have come to buy food.
11We are all the sons of one man. Your
servants are honest men, not spies."
12"No!" he said to them. "You have
come to see where our land is unprotected."
13But they replied, "Your servants
were twelve brothers, the sons of one
man, who lives in the land of Canaan.
The youngest is now with our father,
and one is no more."
14Joseph said to them, "It is just as I
told you: You are spies! 15And this is
how you will be tested: As surely as
Pharaoh lives, you will not leave this
place unless your youngest brother
comes here. 16Send one of your number
to get your brother; the rest of you will
be kept in prison, so that your words
may be tested to see if you are telling the
truth. If you are not, then as surely as
Pharaoh lives, you are spies!" 17And he
put them all in custody for three days.
18On the third day, Joseph said to
them, "Do this and you will live, for I
fear God: 19If you are honest men, let
one of your brothers stay here in prison,
while the rest of you go and take grain
back for your starving households.
20But you must bring your youngest
brother to me, so that your words may
be verified and that you may not die."
This they proceeded to do.
21They said to one another, "Surely
we are being punished because of our
brother. We saw how distressed he was
when he pleaded with us for his life, but
we would not listen; that's why this
distress has come upon us."
22Reuben replied, "Didn't I tell you
not to sin against the boy? But you
wouldn't listen! Now we must give an
accounting for his blood." 23They did
not realise that Joseph could understand them, since he was using an
interpreter.
24He turned away from them and began to weep, but then turned back and
spoke to them again. He had Simeon
taken from them and bound before
their eyes.
25Joseph gave orders to fill their bags
with grain, to put each man's silver back
in his sack, and to give them provisions
for their journey. After this was done
for them, 26they loaded their grain on
their donkeys and left.
27At the place where they stopped for
the night one of them opened his sack to
get feed for his donkey, and he saw his
silver in the mouth of his sack. 28"My
silver has been returned," he said to his
brothers. "Here it is in my sack."
Their hearts sank and they turned to
each other trembling and said, "What is
this that God has done to us?"
29When they came to their father
Jacob in the land of Canaan, they told
him all that had happened to them.
They said, 30"The man who is lord over
the land spoke harshly to us and treated
us as though we were spying on the
land. 31But we said to him, 'We are
honest men; we are not spies. 32We
were twelve brothers, sons of one
father. One is no more, and the
youngest is now with our father in
Canaan.'
33"Then the man who is lord over the
land said to us, 'This is how I will know
whether you are honest men: Leave one
of your brothers here with me, and take
food for your starving households and
go. 34But bring your youngest brother
to me so I will know that you are not
spies but honest men. Then I will give
your brother back to you, and you can
trade in the land.'"
35As they were emptying their sacks,
there in each man's sack was his pouch
of silver! When they and their father
saw the money pouches, they were
frightened. 36Their father Jacob said to
them, "You have deprived me of my
children. Joseph is no more and Simeon

is no more, and now you want to take
Benjamin. Everything is against me!"
37Then Reuben said to his father,
"You may put both of my sons to death
if I do not bring him back to you. Entrust him to my care, and I will bring
him back."
38But Jacob said, "My son will not go
down there with you; his brother is dead
and he is the only one left. If harm
comes to him on the journey you are
taking, you will bring my grey head
down to the grave in sorrow."

NEW TESTAMENT READING
Matthew 14:22–15:9

Jesus Walks on the Water

22Immediately Jesus made the disciples get into the boat and go on ahead of
him to the other side, while he dismissed the crowd. 23After he had dismissed
them, he went up on a mountainside by
himself to pray. When evening came, he
was there alone, 24but the boat was
already a considerable distance from
land, buffeted by the waves because the
wind was against it.
25During the fourth watch of the night
Jesus went out to them, walking on the
lake. 26When the disciples saw him
walking on the lake, they were terrified.
"It's a ghost," they said, and cried out in
fear.
27But Jesus immediately said to them:
"Take courage! It is I. Don't be afraid."
28"Lord, if it's you," Peter replied,
"tell me to come to you on the water."
29"Come," he said.
Then Peter got down out of the boat,
walked on the water and came towards
Jesus. 30But when he saw the wind, he
was afraid and, beginning to sink, cried
out, "Lord, save me!"
31Immediately Jesus reached out his
hand and caught him. "You of little
faith," he said, "why did you doubt?"
32And when they climbed into the
boat, the wind died down. 33Then those
who were in the boat worshipped him,
saying, "Truly you are the Son of God."
34When they had crossed over, they
landed at Gennesaret. 35And when the
men of that place recognised Jesus, they
sent word to all the surrounding country. People brought all their sick to him
36and begged him to let the sick just
touch the edge of his cloak, and all who
touched him were healed.

Clean and Unclean

15 Then some Pharisees and
teachers of the law came to Jesus
from Jerusalem and asked, 2"Why do
your disciples break the tradition of the
elders? They don't wash their hands
before they eat!"
3Jesus replied, "And why do you
break the command of God for the sake
of your tradition? 4For God said, 'Honour your father and mother' and 'Anyone who curses his father or mother
must be put to death.' 5But you say that
if a man says to his father or mother,
'Whatever help you might otherwise
have received from me is a gift devoted
to God,' 6he is not to 'honour his father'
with it. Thus you nullify the word of
God for the sake of your tradition. 7You
hypocrites! Isaiah was right when he
prophesied about you:

8" 'These people honour me with their
lips,
but their hearts are far from me.
9They worship me in vain;
their teachings are but rules taught
by men.' "

READING FROM PSALMS
Psalm 12:1–8

For the director of music. According to
sheminith. A psalm of David.

1Help, LORD, for the godly are no
more;
the faithful have vanished from
among men.

2Everyone lies to his neighbour;
their flattering lips speak with deception.

3May the LORD cut off all flattering lips
and every boastful tongue
4that says, "We will triumph with our tongues;
we own our lips—who is our master?"

5"Because of the oppression of the weak
and the groaning of the needy,
I will now arise," says the LORD.
"I will protect them from those who malign them."
6And the words of the LORD are flawless,
like silver refined in a furnace of clay,
purified seven times.

7O LORD, you will keep us safe
and protect us from such people for ever.
8The wicked freely strut about
when what is vile is honoured among men.

JANUARY 22

DAY 22

OLD TESTAMENT READING
Genesis 43:1–44:34

The Second Journey to Egypt

43 Now the famine was still severe
in the land. 2So when they had
eaten all the grain they had brought
from Egypt, their father said to them,
"Go back and buy us a little more
food."
3But Judah said to him, "The man
warned us solemnly, 'You will not see
my face again unless your brother is
with you.' 4If you will send our brother
along with us, we will go down and buy
food for you. 5But if you will not send
him, we will not go down, because the
man said to us, 'You will not see my face
again unless your brother is with you.' "
6Israel asked, "Why did you bring
this trouble on me by telling the man
you had another brother?"
7They replied, "The man questioned
us closely about ourselves and our family. 'Is your father still living?' he asked
us. 'Do you have another brother?' We
simply answered his questions. How
were we to know he would say, 'Bring
your brother down here'?"
8Then Judah said to Israel his father,
"Send the boy along with me and we
will go at once, so that we and you and
our children may live and not die. 9I
myself will guarantee his safety; you can
hold me personally responsible for him.
If I do not bring him back to you and set
him here before you, I will bear the
blame before you all my life. 10As it is, if
we had not delayed, we could have gone
and returned twice."
11Then their father Israel said to
them, "If it must be, then do this: Put
some of the best products of the land in
your bags and take them down to the
man as a gift—a little balm and a little
honey, some spices and myrrh, some
pistachio nuts and almonds. 12Take
double the amount of silver with you,
for you must return the silver that was
put back into the mouths of your sacks.
Perhaps it was a mistake. 13Take your
brother also and go back to the man at
once. 14And may God Almighty grant
you mercy before the man so that he will
let your other brother and Benjamin
come back with you. As for me, if I am
bereaved, I am bereaved."
15So the men took the gifts and
double the amount of silver, and

Benjamin also. They hurried down to
Egypt and presented themselves to
Joseph. 16When Joseph saw Benjamin
with them, he said to the steward of his
house, "Take these men to my house,
slaughter an animal and prepare dinner;
they are to eat with me at noon."
17The man did as Joseph told him and
took the men to Joseph's house. 18Now
the men were frightened when they
were taken to his house. They thought,
"We were brought here because of the
silver that was put back into our sacks
the first time. He wants to attack us and
overpower us and seize us as slaves and
take our donkeys."
19So they went up to Joseph's steward
and spoke to him at the entrance to the
house. 20"Please, sir," they said, "we
came down here the first time to buy
food. 21But at the place where we stopped for the night we opened our sacks
and each of us found his silver—the
exact weight—in the mouth of his sack.
So we have brought it back with us.
22We have also brought additional silver
with us to buy food. We don't know who
put our silver in our sacks."
23"It's all right," he said. "Don't be
afraid. Your God, the God of your
father, has given you treasure in your
sacks; I received your silver." Then he
brought Simeon out to them.
24The steward took the men into
Joseph's house, gave them water to
wash their feet and provided fodder for
their donkeys. 25They prepared their
gifts for Joseph's arrival at noon, because they had heard that they were to
eat there.
26When Joseph came home, they presented to him the gifts they had brought
into the house, and they bowed down
before him to the ground. 27He asked
them how they were, and then he said,
"How is your aged father you told me
about? Is he still living?"
28They replied, "Your servant our
father is still alive and well." And they
bowed low to pay him honour.
29As he looked about and saw his
brother Benjamin, his own mother's
son, he asked, "Is this your youngest
brother, the one you told me about?"
And he said, "God be gracious to you,
my son." 30Deeply moved at the sight of
his brother, Joseph hurried out and
looked for a place to weep. He went
into his private room and wept there.
31After he had washed his face, he
came out and, controlling himself, said,
"Serve the food."
32They served him by himself, the
brothers by themselves, and the Egyptians who ate with him by themselves,
because Egyptians could not eat with
Hebrews, for that is detestable to Egyptians. 33The men had been seated before him in the order of their ages, from
the firstborn to the youngest; and they
looked at each other in astonishment.
34When portions were served to them
from Joseph's table, Benjamin's portion was five times as much as anyone
else's. So they feasted and drank freely
with him.

A Silver Cup in a Sack

44 Now Joseph gave these instructions to the steward of his house:
"Fill the men's sacks with as much food
as they can carry, and put each man's
silver in the mouth of his sack. 2Then
put my cup, the silver one, in the mouth
of the youngest one's sack, along with
the silver for his grain." And he did as
Joseph said.
3As morning dawned, the men were
sent on their way with their donkeys.
4They had not gone far from the city
when Joseph said to his steward, "Go
after those men at once, and when you
catch up with them, say to them, 'Why
have you repaid good with evil? 5Isn't
this the cup my master drinks from and
also uses for divination? This is a wicked
thing you have done.'"
6When he caught up with them, he
repeated these words to them. 7But
they said to him, "Why does my lord say
such things? Far be it from your servants to do anything like that! 8We even
brought back to you from the land of

Canaan the silver we found inside the
mouths of our sacks. So why would we
steal silver or gold from your master's
house? 9If any of your servants is found
to have it, he will die; and the rest of us
will become my lord's slaves."

10"Very well, then," he said, "let it be
as you say. Whoever is found to have it
will become my slave; the rest of you
will be free from blame."

11Each of them quickly lowered his
sack to the ground and opened it.
12Then the steward proceeded to
search, beginning with the oldest and
ending with the youngest. And the cup
was found in Benjamin's sack. 13At this,
they tore their clothes. Then they all
loaded their donkeys and returned to
the city.

14Joseph was still in the house when
Judah and his brothers came in, and
they threw themselves to the ground
before him. 15Joseph said to them,
"What is this you have done? Don't you
know that a man like me can find things
out by divination?"

16"What can we say to my lord?"
Judah replied. "What can we say? How
can we prove our innocence? God has
uncovered your servants' guilt. We are
now my lord's slaves—we ourselves
and the one who was found to have the
cup."

17But Joseph said, "Far be it from me
to do such a thing! Only the man who
was found to have the cup will become
my slave. The rest of you, go back to
your father in peace."

18Then Judah went up to him and
said: "Please, my lord, let your servant
speak a word to my lord. Do not be
angry with your servant, though you are
equal to Pharaoh himself. 19My lord
asked his servants, 'Do you have a
father or a brother?' 20And we
answered, 'We have an aged father, and
there is a young son born to him in his
old age. His brother is dead, and he is
the only one of his mother's sons left,
and his father loves him.'

21"Then you said to your servants,
'Bring him down to me so I can see him
for myself.' 22And we said to my lord,
'The boy cannot leave his father; if he
leaves him, his father will die.' 23But
you told your servants, 'Unless your
youngest brother comes down with you,
you will not see my face again.' 24When
we went back to your servant my father,
we told him what my lord had said.

25"Then our father said, 'Go back
and buy a little more food.' 26But we
said, 'We cannot go down. Only if our
youngest brother is with us will we go.
We cannot see the man's face unless our
youngest brother is with us.'

27"Your servant my father said to us,
'You know that my wife bore me two
sons. 28One of them went away from
me, and I said, "He has surely been torn
to pieces." And I have not seen him
since. 29If you take this one from me too
and harm comes to him, you will bring
my grey head down to the grave in
misery.'

30"So now, if the boy is not with us
when I go back to your servant my
father and if my father, whose life is
closely bound up with the boy's life,
31sees that the boy isn't there, he will
die. Your servants will bring the grey
head of our father down to the grave in
sorrow. 32Your servant guaranteed the
boy's safety to my father. I said, 'If I do
not bring him back to you, I will bear
the blame before you, my father, all my
life!'

33"Now then, please let your servant
remain here as my lord's slave in place
of the boy, and let the boy return with
his brothers. 34How can I go back to my
father if the boy is not with me? No! Do
not let me see the misery that would
come upon my father."

NEW TESTAMENT READING
Matthew 15:10–39

10Jesus called the crowd to him and
said, "Listen and understand. 11What
goes into a man's mouth does not make
him 'unclean', but what comes out of

his mouth, that is what makes him
'unclean'."
12Then the disciples came to him and
asked, "Do you know that the Pharisees
were offended when they heard this?"
13He replied, "Every plant that my
heavenly Father has not planted will be
pulled up by the roots. 14Leave them;
they are blind guides. If a blind man
leads a blind man, both will fall into a
pit."
15Peter said, "Explain the parable to
us."
16"Are you still so dull?" Jesus asked
them. 17"Don't you see that whatever
enters the mouth goes into the stomach
and then out of the body? 18But the
things that come out of the mouth come
from the heart, and these make a man
'unclean'. 19For out of the heart come
evil thoughts, murder, adultery, sexual
immorality, theft, false testimony, slander. 20These are what make a man 'unclean'; but eating with unwashed hands
does not make him 'unclean'."

The Faith of the Canaanite Woman

21Leaving that place, Jesus withdrew
to the region of Tyre and Sidon. 22A
Canaanite woman from that vicinity
came to him, crying out, "Lord, Son of
David, have mercy on me! My daughter
is suffering terribly from demon-
possession."
23Jesus did not answer a word. So his
disciples came to him and urged him,
"Send her away, for she keeps crying
out after us."
24He answered, "I was sent only to
the lost sheep of Israel."
25The woman came and knelt before
him. "Lord, help me!" she said.
26He replied, "It is not right to take
the children's bread and toss it to their
dogs."
27"Yes, Lord," she said, "but even
the dogs eat the crumbs that fall from
their masters' table."
28Then Jesus answered, "Woman,
you have great faith! Your request is
granted." And her daughter was healed
from that very hour.

Jesus Feeds the Four Thousand

29Jesus left there and went along the
Sea of Galilee. Then he went up on a
mountainside and sat down. 30Great
crowds came to him, bringing the lame,
the blind, the crippled, the mute and
many others, and laid them at his feet;
and he healed them. 31The people were
amazed when they saw the mute speaking, the crippled made well, the lame
walking and the blind seeing. And they
praised the God of Israel.
32Jesus called his disciples to him and
said, "I have compassion for these people; they have already been with me
three days and have nothing to eat. I do
not want to send them away hungry, or
they may collapse on the way."
33His disciples answered, "Where
could we get enough bread in this remote place to feed such a crowd?"
34"How many loaves do you have?"
Jesus asked.
"Seven," they replied, "and a few
small fish."
35He told the crowd to sit down on the
ground. 36Then he took the seven
loaves and the fish, and when he had
given thanks, he broke them and gave
them to the disciples, and they in turn to
the people. 37They all ate and were
satisfied. Afterwards the disciples
picked up seven basketfuls of broken
pieces that were left over. 38The number of those who ate was four thousand,
besides women and children. 39After
Jesus had sent the crowd away, he got
into the boat and went to the vicinity of
Magadan.

READING FROM PSALMS

Psalm 13:1–6

For the director of music. A psalm of David.

1How long, O LORD? Will you forget
me for ever?
How long will you hide your face
from me?

2How long must I wrestle with my
thoughts
and every day have sorrow in my
heart?
How long will my enemy triumph
over me?

3Look on me and answer, O LORD my
God.
Give light to my eyes, or I will
sleep in death;
4my enemy will say, "I have overcome
him,"
and my foes will rejoice when I
fall.

5But I trust in your unfailing love;
my heart rejoices in your
salvation.
6I will sing to the LORD,
for he has been good to me.

JANUARY 23

DAY 23

OLD TESTAMENT READING
Genesis 45:1–47:12

Joseph Makes Himself Known

45 Then Joseph could no longer
control himself before all his
attendants, and he cried out, "Make
everyone leave my presence!" So there
was no-one with Joseph when he made
himself known to his brothers. 2And he
wept so loudly that the Egyptians heard
him, and Pharaoh's household heard
about it.
3Joseph said to his brothers, "I am
Joseph! Is my father still living?" But
his brothers were not able to answer
him, because they were terrified at his
presence.
4Then Joseph said to his brothers,
"Come close to me." When they had
done so, he said, "I am your brother
Joseph, the one you sold into Egypt!
5And now, do not be distressed and do
not be angry with yourselves for selling
me here, because it was to save lives
that God sent me ahead of you. 6For
two years now there has been famine in
the land, and for the next five years
there will not be ploughing and reaping.
7But God sent me ahead of you to preserve for you a remnant on earth and to
save your lives by a great deliverance.
8"So then, it was not you who sent me
here, but God. He made me father to
Pharaoh, lord of his entire household
and ruler of all Egypt. 9Now hurry back
to my father and say to him, 'This is
what your son Joseph says: God has
made me lord of all Egypt. Come down
to me; don't delay. 10You shall live in
the region of Goshen and be near me
—you, your children and grandchildren, your flocks and herds, and all you
have. 11I will provide for you there,
because five years of famine are still to
come. Otherwise you and your household and all who belong to you will
become destitute.'
12"You can see for yourselves, and so
can my brother Benjamin, that it is
really I who am speaking to you. 13Tell
my father about all the honour accorded
me in Egypt and about everything you
have seen. And bring my father down
here quickly."
14Then he threw his arms around his
brother Benjamin and wept, and Benjamin embraced him, weeping. 15And
he kissed all his brothers and wept over
them. Afterwards his brothers talked
with him.
16When the news reached Pharaoh's
palace that Joseph's brothers had come,
Pharaoh and all his officials were
pleased. 17Pharaoh said to Joseph,

"Tell your brothers, 'Do this: Load
your animals and return to the land of
Canaan, 18and bring your father and
your families back to me. I will give you
the best of the land of Egypt and you
can enjoy the fat of the land.'

19"You are also directed to tell them,
'Do this: Take some carts from Egypt
for your children and your wives, and
get your father and come. 20Never mind
about your belongings, because the best
of all Egypt will be yours.' "

21So the sons of Israel did this. Joseph
gave them carts, as Pharaoh had commanded, and he also gave them provisions for their journey. 22To each of
them he gave new clothing, but to Benjamin he gave three hundred shekels of
silver and five sets of clothes. 23And this
is what he sent to his father: ten donkeys
loaded with the best things of Egypt,
and ten female donkeys loaded with
grain and bread and other provisions for
his journey. 24Then he sent his brothers
away, and as they were leaving he said
to them, "Don't quarrel on the way!"

25So they went up out of Egypt and
came to their father Jacob in the land of
Canaan. 26They told him, "Joseph is
still alive! In fact, he is ruler of all
Egypt." Jacob was stunned; he did not
believe them. 27But when they told him
everything Joseph had said to them, and
when he saw the carts Joseph had sent
to carry him back, the spirit of their
father Jacob revived. 28And Israel said,
"I'm convinced! My son Joseph is still
alive. I will go and see him before I die."

Jacob Goes to Egypt

46 So Israel set out with all that was
his, and when he reached Beersheba, he offered sacrifices to the God
of his father Isaac.

2And God spoke to Israel in a vision
at night and said, "Jacob! Jacob!"

"Here I am," he replied.

3"I am God, the God of your father,"
he said. "Do not be afraid to go down to
Egypt, for I will make you into a great
nation there. 4I will go down to Egypt
with you, and I will surely bring you
back again. And Joseph's own hand will
close your eyes."

5Then Jacob left Beersheba, and
Israel's sons took their father Jacob and
their children and their wives in the
carts that Pharaoh had sent to transport
him. 6They also took with them their
livestock and the possessions they had
acquired in Canaan, and Jacob and all
his offspring went to Egypt. 7He took
with him to Egypt his sons and grandsons and his daughters and granddaugh-
ters—all his offspring.

8These are the names of the sons of
Israel (Jacob and his descendants) who
went to Egypt:

Reuben the firstborn of Jacob.
9The sons of Reuben:
Hanoch, Pallu, Hezron and
Carmi.
10The sons of Simeon:
Jemuel, Jamin, Ohad, Jakin,
Zohar and Shaul the son of a
Canaanite woman.
11The sons of Levi:
Gershon, Kohath and Merari.
12The sons of Judah:
Er, Onan, Shelah, Perez and
Zerah (but Er and Onan had
died in the land of Canaan).
The sons of Perez:
Hezron and Hamul.
13The sons of Issachar:
Tola, Puah, Jashub and Shim-
ron.
14The sons of Zebulun:
Sered, Elon and Jahleel.

15These were the sons Leah bore to
Jacob in Paddan Aram, besides his
daughter Dinah. These sons and daughters of his were thirty-three in all.

16The sons of Gad:
Zephon, Haggi, Shuni, Ezbon,
Eri, Arodi and Areli.
17The sons of Asher:
Imnah, Ishvah, Ishvi and Be-
riah.
Their sister was Serah.

The sons of Beriah:
Heber and Malkiel.
18These were the children born to Jacob by Zilpah, whom Laban had given to his daughter Leah—sixteen in all.

19The sons of Jacob's wife Rachel:
Joseph and Benjamin. 20In Egypt, Manasseh and Ephraim were born to Joseph by Asenath daughter of Potiphera, priest of On.
21The sons of Benjamin:
Bela, Beker, Ashbel, Gera, Naaman, Ehi, Rosh, Muppim, Huppim and Ard.
22These were the sons of Rachel who were born to Jacob—fourteen in all.

23The son of Dan:
Hushim.
24The sons of Naphtali:
Jahziel, Guni, Jezer and Shillem.
25These were the sons born to Jacob by Bilhah, whom Laban had given to his daughter Rachel—seven in all.

26All those who went to Egypt with
Jacob—those who were his direct descendants, not counting his sons' wives
—numbered sixty-six persons. 27With
the two sons who had been born to Joseph in Egypt, the members of Jacob's family, which went to Egypt, were seventy in all.

28Now Jacob sent Judah ahead of him to Joseph to get directions to Goshen. When they arrived in the region of
Goshen, 29Joseph had his chariot made
ready and went to Goshen to meet his father Israel. As soon as Joseph appeared before him, he threw his arms around his father and wept for a long time.
30Israel said to Joseph, "Now I am ready to die, since I have seen for myself that you are still alive."
31Then Joseph said to his brothers and to his father's household, "I will go up and speak to Pharaoh and will say to him, 'My brothers and my father's household, who were living in the land
of Canaan, have come to me. 32The men
are shepherds; they tend livestock, and they have brought along their flocks and herds and everything they own.'
33When Pharaoh calls you in and asks,
'What is your occupation?' 34you should
answer, 'Your servants have tended livestock from our boyhood on, just as our fathers did.' Then you will be allowed to settle in the region of Goshen, for all shepherds are detestable to the Egyptians."

47 Joseph went and told Pharaoh, "My father and brothers, with their flocks and herds and everything they own, have come from the land of
Canaan and are now in Goshen." 2He
chose five of his brothers and presented them before Pharaoh.
3Pharaoh asked the brothers, "What is your occupation?"
"Your servants are shepherds," they replied to Pharaoh, "just as our fathers
were." 4They also said to him, "We
have come to live here awhile, because the famine is severe in Canaan and your servants' flocks have no pasture. So now, please let your servants settle in Goshen."
5Pharaoh said to Joseph, "Your father and your brothers have come to
you, 6and the land of Egypt is before
you; settle your father and your brothers in the best part of the land. Let them live in Goshen. And if you know of any among them with special ability, put them in charge of my own livestock."
7Then Joseph brought his father Jacob in and presented him before Pharaoh. After Jacob blessed Pharaoh,
8Pharaoh asked him, "How old are you?"
9And Jacob said to Pharaoh, "The years of my pilgrimage are a hundred and thirty. My years have been few and difficult, and they do not equal the years
of the pilgrimage of my fathers." 10Then
Jacob blessed Pharaoh and went out from his presence.

11So Joseph settled his father and his
brothers in Egypt and gave them property in the best part of the land, the
district of Rameses, as Pharaoh
directed. 12Joseph also provided his
father and his brothers and all his
father's household with food, according
to the number of their children.

NEW TESTAMENT READING
Matthew 16:1–20

The Demand for a Sign

16 The Pharisees and Sadducees
came to Jesus and tested him by
asking him to show them a sign from
heaven.
2He replied, "When evening comes,
you say, 'It will be fair weather, for the
sky is red,' 3and in the morning, 'Today
it will be stormy, for the sky is red and
overcast.' You know how to interpret
the appearance of the sky, but you cannot interpret the signs of the times. 4A
wicked and adulterous generation looks
for a miraculous sign, but none will be
given it except the sign of Jonah." Jesus
then left them and went away.

The Yeast of the Pharisees and Sadducees

5When they went across the lake, the
disciples forgot to take bread. 6"Be
careful," Jesus said to them. "Be on
your guard against the yeast of the Pharisees and Sadducees."
7They discussed this among themselves and said, "It is because we didn't
bring any bread."
8Aware of their discussion, Jesus
asked, "You of little faith, why are you
talking among yourselves about having
no bread? 9Do you still not understand?
Don't you remember the five loaves for
the five thousand, and how many
basketfuls you gathered? 10Or the seven
loaves for the four thousand, and how
many basketfuls you gathered? 11How
is it you don't understand that I was not
talking to you about bread? But be on
your guard against the yeast of the Pharisees and Sadducees." 12Then they
understood that he was not telling them
to guard against the yeast used in bread,
but against the teaching of the Pharisees
and Sadducees.

Peter's Confession of Christ

13When Jesus came to the region of
Caesarea Philippi, he asked his disciples, "Who do people say the Son of
Man is?"
14They replied, "Some say John the
Baptist; others say Elijah; and still
others, Jeremiah or one of the
prophets."
15"But what about you?" he asked.
"Who do you say I am?"
16Simon Peter answered, "You are
the Christ, the Son of the living God."
17Jesus replied, "Blessed are you,
Simon son of Jonah, for this was not
revealed to you by man, but by my
Father in heaven. 18And I tell you that
you are Peter, and on this rock I will
build my church, and the gates of Hades
will not overcome it. 19I will give you the
keys of the kingdom of heaven; whatever you bind on earth will be bound in
heaven, and whatever you loose on
earth will be loosed in heaven." 20Then
he warned his disciples not to tell anyone that he was the Christ.

READING FROM PSALMS
Psalm 14:1–7

For the director of music. Of David.

1The fool says in his heart,
"There is no God."
They are corrupt, their deeds are
vile;
there is no-one who does good.
2The LORD looks down from heaven
on the sons of men
to see if there are any who
understand,
any who seek God.

3All have turned aside,
they have together become
corrupt;
there is no-one who does good,
not even one.

4Will evildoers never learn—
those who devour my people as
men eat bread
and who do not call on the LORD?
5There they are, overwhelmed with
dread,
for God is present in the company
of the righteous.
6You evildoers frustrate the plans of
the poor,
but the LORD is their refuge.

7Oh, that salvation for Israel would
come out of Zion!
When the LORD restores the
fortunes of his people,
let Jacob rejoice and Israel be
glad!

JANUARY 24

DAY 24

OLD TESTAMENT READING
Genesis 47:13–48:22

Joseph and the Famine

13There was no food, however, in the
whole region because the famine was
severe; both Egypt and Canaan wasted
away because of the famine. 14Joseph
collected all the money that was to be
found in Egypt and Canaan in payment
for the grain they were buying, and he
brought it to Pharaoh's palace. 15When
the money of the people of Egypt and
Canaan was gone, all Egypt came to
Joseph and said, "Give us food. Why
should we die before your eyes? Our
money is used up."
16"Then bring your livestock," said
Joseph. "I will sell you food in exchange
for your livestock, since your money is
gone." 17So they brought their livestock
to Joseph, and he gave them food in
exchange for their horses, their sheep
and goats, their cattle and donkeys.
And he brought them through that
year with food in exchange for all their
livestock.
18When that year was over, they
came to him the following year and
said, "We cannot hide from our lord the
fact that since our money is gone and
our livestock belongs to you, there is
nothing left for our lord except our
bodies and our land. 19Why should we
perish before your eyes—we and our
land as well? Buy us and our land in
exchange for food, and we with our
land will be in bondage to Pharaoh.
Give us seed so that we may live and
not die, and that the land may not
become desolate."
20So Joseph bought all the land in
Egypt for Pharaoh. The Egyptians, one
and all, sold their fields, because the
famine was too severe for them. The
land became Pharaoh's, 21and Joseph
reduced the people to servitude, from
one end of Egypt to the other.
22However, he did not buy the land of
the priests, because they received a regular allotment from Pharaoh and had
food enough from the allotment Pharaoh gave them. That is why they did not
sell their land.
23Joseph said to the people, "Now
that I have bought you and your land
today for Pharaoh, here is seed for you
so you can plant the ground. 24But when
the crop comes in, give a fifth of it to
Pharaoh. The other four-fifths you may
keep as seed for the fields and as food
for yourselves and your households and
your children."

25“You have saved our lives,” they
said. “May we find favour in the eyes
of our lord; we will be in bondage to
Pharaoh.”
26So Joseph established it as a law
concerning land in Egypt—still in force
today—that a fifth of the produce belongs to Pharaoh. It was only the land
of the priests that did not become
Pharaoh’s.
27Now the Israelites settled in Egypt
in the region of Goshen. They acquired
property there and were fruitful and
increased greatly in number.
28Jacob lived in Egypt seventeen
years, and the years of his life were a
hundred and forty-seven. 29When the
time drew near for Israel to die, he
called for his son Joseph and said to
him, “If I have found favour in your
eyes, put your hand under my thigh and
promise that you will show me kindness
and faithfulness. Do not bury me in
Egypt, 30but when I rest with my
fathers, carry me out of Egypt and bury
me where they are buried.”
“I will do as you say,” he said.
31“Swear to me,” he said. Then
Joseph swore to him, and Israel worshipped as he leaned on the top of his
staff.

Manasseh and Ephraim

48 Some time later Joseph was
told, “Your father is ill.” So he
took his two sons Manasseh and
Ephraim along with him. 2When Jacob
was told, “Your son Joseph has come to
you,” Israel rallied his strength and sat
up on the bed.
3Jacob said to Joseph, “God Almighty appeared to me at Luz in the
land of Canaan, and there he blessed
me 4and said to me, ‘I am going to make
you fruitful and will increase your numbers. I will make you a community of
peoples, and I will give this land as an
everlasting possession to your descendants after you.’
5“Now then, your two sons born to
you in Egypt before I came to you here
will be reckoned as mine; Ephraim and
Manasseh will be mine, just as Reuben
and Simeon are mine. 6Any children
born to you after them will be yours; in
the territory they inherit they will be
reckoned under the names of their
brothers. 7As I was returning from Paddan, to my sorrow Rachel died in the
land of Canaan while we were still on
the way, a little distance from Ephrath.
So I buried her there beside the road to
Ephrath” (that is, Bethlehem).
8When Israel saw the sons of Joseph,
he asked, “Who are these?”
9“They are the sons God has given
me here,” Joseph said to his father.
Then Israel said, “Bring them to me
so that I may bless them.”
10Now Israel’s eyes were failing because of old age, and he could hardly
see. So Joseph brought his sons close to
him, and his father kissed them and
embraced them.
11Israel said to Joseph, “I never expected to see your face again, and now
God has allowed me to see your children too.”
12Then Joseph removed them from
Israel’s knees and bowed down with his
face to the ground. 13And Joseph took
both of them, Ephraim on his right towards Israel’s left hand and Manasseh
on his left towards Israel’s right hand,
and brought them close to him. 14But
Israel reached out his right hand and put
it on Ephraim’s head, though he was
the younger, and crossing his arms, he
put his left hand on Manasseh’s head,
even though Manasseh was the firstborn.
15Then he blessed Joseph and said,

“May the God before whom my
fathers
Abraham and Isaac walked,
the God who has been my
shepherd
all my life to this day,
16the Angel who has delivered me
from all harm
—may he bless these boys.

May they be called by my name
  and the names of my fathers
    Abraham and Isaac,
and may they increase greatly
  upon the earth."

17When Joseph saw his father placing
his right hand on Ephraim's head he was
displeased; so he took hold of his
father's hand to move it from Ephraim's
head to Manasseh's head. 18Joseph said
to him, "No, my father, this one is the
firstborn; put your right hand on his
head."
19But his father refused and said, "I
know, my son, I know. He too will
become a people, and he too will become great. Nevertheless, his younger
brother will be greater than he, and his
descendants will become a group of nations." 20He blessed them that day and
said,

"In your name will Israel pronounce
    this blessing:
  'May God make you like Ephraim
    and Manasseh.'"

So he put Ephraim ahead of Manasseh.
21Then Israel said to Joseph, "I am
about to die, but God will be with you
and take you back to the land of your
fathers. 22And to you, as one who is
over your brothers, I give the ridge of
land I took from the Amorites with my
sword and my bow."

NEW TESTAMENT READING
Matthew 16:21–17:13

Jesus Predicts His Death

21From that time on Jesus began to
explain to his disciples that he must go
to Jerusalem and suffer many things at
the hands of the elders, chief priests and
teachers of the law, and that he must be
killed and on the third day be raised to
life.
22Peter took him aside and began to
rebuke him. "Never, Lord!" he said.
"This shall never happen to you!"
23Jesus turned and said to Peter, "Get
behind me, Satan! You are a stumbling-
block to me; you do not have in mind
the things of God, but the things of
men."
24Then Jesus said to his disciples, "If
anyone would come after me, he must
deny himself and take up his cross and
follow me. 25For whoever wants to save
his life will lose it, but whoever loses his
life for me will find it. 26What good will
it be for a man if he gains the whole
world, yet forfeits his soul? Or what can
a man give in exchange for his soul?
27For the Son of Man is going to come in
his Father's glory with his angels, and
then he will reward each person according to what he has done. 28I tell you the
truth, some who are standing here will
not taste death before they see the Son
of Man coming in his kingdom."

The Transfiguration

17 After six days Jesus took with
him Peter, James and John the
brother of James, and led them up a
high mountain by themselves. 2There
he was transfigured before them. His
face shone like the sun, and his clothes
became as white as the light. 3Just then
there appeared before them Moses and
Elijah, talking with Jesus.
4Peter said to Jesus, "Lord, it is good
for us to be here. If you wish, I will put
up three shelters—one for you, one for
Moses and one for Elijah."
5While he was still speaking, a bright
cloud enveloped them, and a voice from
the cloud said, "This is my Son, whom I
love; with him I am well pleased. Listen
to him!"
6When the disciples heard this, they
fell face down to the ground, terrified.
7But Jesus came and touched them.
"Get up," he said. "Don't be afraid."
8When they looked up, they saw no-one
except Jesus.
9As they were coming down the
mountain, Jesus instructed them,

"Don't tell anyone what you have seen, until the Son of Man has been raised from the dead."
10The disciples asked him, "Why then do the teachers of the law say that Elijah must come first?"
11Jesus replied, "To be sure, Elijah comes and will restore all things. 12But I
tell you, Elijah has already come, and they did not recognise him, but have done to him everything they wished. In the same way the Son of Man is going to suffer at their hands." 13Then the disciples understood that he was talking to them about John the Baptist.

READING FROM PROVERBS
Proverbs 3:1–10

Further Benefits of Wisdom

3 My son, do not forget my
teaching,
but keep my commands in your
heart,
2for they will prolong your life many
years
and bring you prosperity.
3Let love and faithfulness never leave
you;
bind them around your neck,
write them on the tablet of your
heart.
4Then you will win favour and a good
name
in the sight of God and man.

5Trust in the LORD with all your heart
and lean not on your own
understanding;
6in all your ways acknowledge him,
and he will make your paths
straight.

7Do not be wise in your own eyes;
fear the LORD and shun evil.
8This will bring health to your body
and nourishment to your bones.

9Honour the LORD with your wealth,
with the firstfruits of all your
crops;
10then your barns will be filled to
overflowing,
and your vats will brim over with
new wine.

DAY 25

JANUARY 25

OLD TESTAMENT READING
Genesis 49:1–50:26

Jacob Blesses His Sons

49 Then Jacob called for his sons and said: "Gather round so that I can tell you what will happen to you in days to come.

2"Assemble and listen, sons of Jacob;
listen to your father Israel.

3"Reuben, you are my firstborn,
my might, the first sign of my
strength,
excelling in honour, excelling in
power.
4Turbulent as the waters, you will no
longer excel,
for you went up onto your father's
bed,
onto my couch and defiled it.

5"Simeon and Levi are brothers—
their swords are weapons of
violence.
6Let me not enter their council,
let me not join their assembly,
for they have killed men in their
anger
and hamstrung oxen as they
pleased.

7Cursed be their anger, so fierce,
and their fury, so cruel!
I will scatter them in Jacob
and disperse them in Israel.

8"Judah, your brothers will praise you;
your hand will be on the neck of your enemies;
your father's sons will bow down to you.
9You are a lion's cub, O Judah;
you return from the prey, my son.
Like a lion he crouches and lies down,
like a lioness—who dares to rouse him?
10The sceptre will not depart from Judah,
nor the ruler's staff from between his feet,
until he comes to whom it belongs
and the obedience of the nations is his.
11He will tether his donkey to a vine,
his colt to the choicest branch;
he will wash his garments in wine,
his robes in the blood of grapes.
12His eyes will be darker than wine,
his teeth whiter than milk.

13"Zebulun will live by the seashore
and become a haven for ships;
his border will extend towards Sidon.

14"Issachar is a scrawny donkey
lying down between two saddlebags.
15When he sees how good is his resting place
and how pleasant is his land,
he will bend his shoulder to the burden
and submit to forced labour.

16"Dan will provide justice for his people
as one of the tribes of Israel.
17Dan will be a serpent by the roadside,
a viper along the path,
that bites the horse's heels
so that its rider tumbles backwards.

18"I look for your deliverance, O LORD.

19"Gad will be attacked by a band of raiders,
but he will attack them at their heels.

20"Asher's food will be rich;
he will provide delicacies fit for a king.

21"Naphtali is a doe set free
that bears beautiful fawns.

22"Joseph is a fruitful vine,
a fruitful vine near a spring,
whose branches climb over a wall.
23With bitterness archers attacked him;
they shot at him with hostility.
24But his bow remained steady,
his strong arms stayed supple,
because of the hand of the Mighty One of Jacob,
because of the Shepherd, the Rock of Israel,
25because of your father's God, who helps you,
because of the Almighty, who blesses you
with blessings of the heavens above,
blessings of the deep that lies below,
blessings of the breast and womb.
26Your father's blessings are greater
than the blessings of the ancient mountains,
than the bounty of the age-old hills.
Let all these rest on the head of Joseph,
on the brow of the prince among his brothers.

27"Benjamin is a ravenous wolf;
in the morning he devours the prey,
in the evening he divides the plunder."

28All these are the twelve tribes of
Israel, and this is what their father said
to them when he blessed them, giving
each the blessing appropriate to him.

The Death of Jacob

29Then he gave them these instructions: "I am about to be gathered to my
people. Bury me with my fathers in the
cave in the field of Ephron the Hittite,
30the cave in the field of Machpelah,
near Mamre in Canaan, which Abraham bought as a burial place from
Ephron the Hittite, along with the field.
31There Abraham and his wife Sarah
were buried, there Isaac and his wife
Rebekah were buried, and there I
buried Leah. 32The field and the cave in
it were bought from the Hittites."
33When Jacob had finished giving instructions to his sons, he drew his feet
up into the bed, breathed his last and
was gathered to his people.
50 Joseph threw himself upon his
father and wept over him and
kissed him. 2Then Joseph directed the
physicians in his service to embalm his
father Israel. So the physicians embalmed him, 3taking a full forty days,
for that was the time required for
embalming. And the Egyptians
mourned for him seventy days.
4When the days of mourning had
passed, Joseph said to Pharaoh's court,
"If I have found favour in your eyes,
speak to Pharaoh for me. Tell him, 5'My
father made me swear an oath and said,
"I am about to die; bury me in the tomb
I dug for myself in the land of Canaan."
Now let me go up and bury my father;
then I will return.'"
6Pharaoh said, "Go up and bury your
father, as he made you swear to do."
7So Joseph went up to bury his father.
All Pharaoh's officials accompanied
him—the dignitaries of his court and all
the dignitaries of Egypt—8besides all
the members of Joseph's household and
his brothers and those belonging to his
father's household. Only their children
and their flocks and herds were left in
Goshen. 9Chariots and horsemen also
went up with him. It was a very large
company.
10When they reached the threshing-
floor of Atad, near the Jordan, they
lamented loudly and bitterly; and there
Joseph observed a seven-day period of
mourning for his father. 11When the
Canaanites who lived there saw the
mourning at the threshing-floor of
Atad, they said, "The Egyptians are
holding a solemn ceremony of mourning." That is why that place near the
Jordan is called Abel Mizraim.
12So Jacob's sons did as he had commanded them: 13They carried him to the
land of Canaan and buried him in the
cave in the field of Machpelah, near
Mamre, which Abraham had bought as
a burial place from Ephron the Hittite,
along with the field. 14After burying his
father, Joseph returned to Egypt,
together with his brothers and all the
others who had gone with him to bury
his father.

Joseph Reassures His Brothers

15When Joseph's brothers saw that
their father was dead, they said, "What
if Joseph holds a grudge against us and
pays us back for all the wrongs we did to
him?" 16So they sent word to Joseph,
saying, "Your father left these instructions before he died: 17'This is what you
are to say to Joseph: I ask you to forgive
your brothers the sins and the wrongs
they committed in treating you so
badly.' Now please forgive the sins of
the servants of the God of your father."
When their message came to him,
Joseph wept.
18His brothers then came and threw
themselves down before him. "We are
your slaves," they said.
19But Joseph said to them, "Don't be
afraid. Am I in the place of God? 20You
intended to harm me, but God intended
it for good to accomplish what is now
being done, the saving of many lives.
21So then, don't be afraid. I will provide
for you and your children." And he

reassured them and spoke kindly to
them.

The Death of Joseph

[22]Joseph stayed in Egypt, along with
all his father's family. He lived a hundred and ten years [23]and saw the third
generation of Ephraim's children. Also
the children of Makir son of Manasseh
were placed at birth on Joseph's knees.
[24]Then Joseph said to his brothers, "I
am about to die. But God will surely
come to your aid and take you up out of
this land to the land he promised on
oath to Abraham, Isaac and Jacob."
[25]And Joseph made the sons of Israel
swear an oath and said, "God will surely
come to your aid, and then you must
carry my bones up from this place."
[26]So Joseph died at the age of a hundred and ten. And after they embalmed
him, he was placed in a coffin in Egypt.

NEW TESTAMENT READING
Matthew 17:14–18:9

The Healing of a Boy With a Demon

[14]When they came to the crowd, a
man approached Jesus and knelt before
him. [15]"Lord, have mercy on my son,"
he said. "He has seizures and is suffering greatly. He often falls into the fire or
into the water. [16]I brought him to your
disciples, but they could not heal him."
[17]"O unbelieving and perverse generation," Jesus replied, "how long shall I
stay with you? How long shall I put up
with you? Bring the boy here to me."
[18]Jesus rebuked the demon, and it came
out of the boy, and he was healed from
that moment.
[19]Then the disciples came to Jesus in
private and asked, "Why couldn't we
drive it out?"
[20]He replied, "Because you have so
little faith. I tell you the truth, if you
have faith as small as a mustard seed,
you can say to this mountain, 'Move
from here to there' and it will move.
Nothing will be impossible for you."
[22]When they came together in
Galilee, he said to them, "The Son of
Man is going to be betrayed into the
hands of men. [23]They will kill him, and
on the third day he will be raised to
life." And the disciples were filled with
grief.

The Temple Tax

[24]After Jesus and his disciples arrived
in Capernaum, the collectors of the
two-drachma tax came to Peter and
asked, "Doesn't your teacher pay the
temple tax?"
[25]"Yes, he does," he replied.
When Peter came into the house,
Jesus was the first to speak. "What do
you think, Simon?" he asked. "From
whom do the kings of the earth collect
duty and taxes—from their own sons or
from others?"
[26]"From others," Peter answered.
"Then the sons are exempt," Jesus
said to him. [27]"But so that we may not
offend them, go to the lake and throw
out your line. Take the first fish you
catch; open its mouth and you will find a
four-drachma coin. Take it and give it to
them for my tax and yours."

The Greatest in the Kingdom of Heaven

18 At that time the disciples came
to Jesus and asked, "Who is the
greatest in the kingdom of heaven?"
[2]He called a little child and had him
stand among them. [3]And he said: "I tell
you the truth, unless you change and
become like little children, you will
never enter the kingdom of heaven.
[4]Therefore, whoever humbles himself
like this child is the greatest in the kingdom of heaven.
[5]"And whoever welcomes a little
child like this in my name welcomes me.
[6]But if anyone causes one of these little
ones who believe in me to sin, it would
be better for him to have a large millstone hung around his neck and to be
drowned in the depths of the sea.
[7]"Woe to the world because of the
things that cause people to sin! Such

things must come, but woe to the man through whom they come! 8If your hand or your foot causes you to sin, cut it off and throw it away. It is better for you to enter life maimed or crippled than to have two hands or two feet and be thrown into eternal fire. 9And if your eye causes you to sin, gouge it out and throw it away. It is better for you to enter life with one eye than to have two eyes and be thrown into the fire of hell.

READING FROM PSALMS
Psalm 15:1–5

A psalm of David.

1LORD, who may dwell in your
sanctuary?
Who may live on your holy hill?

2He whose walk is blameless
and who does what is righteous,
who speaks the truth from his
heart
3 and has no slander on his
tongue,
who does his neighbour no wrong
and casts no slur on his
fellow-man,
4who despises a vile man
but honours those who fear the
LORD,
who keeps his oath
even when it hurts,
5who lends his money without usury
and does not accept a bribe against
the innocent.

He who does these things
will never be shaken.

DAY 26

JANUARY 26

OLD TESTAMENT READING
Job 1:1–3:26

Prologue

1 In the land of Uz there lived a man whose name was Job. This man was blameless and upright; he feared God and shunned evil. 2He had seven sons and three daughters, 3and he owned seven thousand sheep, three thousand camels, five hundred yoke of oxen and five hundred donkeys, and had a large number of servants. He was the greatest man among all the people of the East.

4His sons used to take turns holding feasts in their homes, and they would invite their three sisters to eat and drink with them. 5When a period of feasting had run its course, Job would send and have them purified. Early in the morning he would sacrifice a burnt offering for each of them, thinking, "Perhaps my children have sinned and cursed God in their hearts." This was Job's regular custom.

Job's First Test

6One day the angels came to present themselves before the LORD, and Satan also came with them. 7The LORD said to Satan, "Where have you come from?"

Satan answered the LORD, "From roaming through the earth and going to and fro in it."

8Then the LORD said to Satan, "Have you considered my servant Job? There is no-one on earth like him; he is blameless and upright, a man who fears God and shuns evil."

9"Does Job fear God for nothing?" Satan replied. 10"Have you not put a hedge around him and his household and everything he has? You have blessed the work of his hands, so that his flocks and herds are spread throughout the land. 11But stretch out your hand

and strike everything he has, and he will
surely curse you to your face."
12The LORD said to Satan, "Very
well, then, everything he has is in your
hands, but on the man himself do not
lay a finger."
Then Satan went out from the presence of the LORD.
13One day when Job's sons and
daughters were feasting and drinking
wine at the oldest brother's house, 14a
messenger came to Job and said, "The
oxen were ploughing and the donkeys
were grazing nearby, 15and the Sabeans
attacked and carried them off. They put
the servants to the sword, and I am the
only one who has escaped to tell you!"
16While he was still speaking, another
messenger came and said, "The fire of
God fell from the sky and burned up the
sheep and the servants, and I am the
only one who has escaped to tell you!"
17While he was still speaking, another
messenger came and said, "The Chaldeans formed three raiding parties and
swept down on your camels and carried
them off. They put the servants to the
sword, and I am the only one who has
escaped to tell you!"
18While he was still speaking, yet
another messenger came and said,
"Your sons and daughters were feasting
and drinking wine at the oldest
brother's house, 19when suddenly a
mighty wind swept in from the desert
and struck the four corners of the
house. It collapsed on them and they
are dead, and I am the only one who has
escaped to tell you!"
20At this, Job got up and tore his robe
and shaved his head. Then he fell to the
ground in worship 21and said:

"Naked I came from my mother's
womb,
and naked I shall depart.
The LORD gave and the LORD has
taken away;
may the name of the LORD be
praised."

22In all this, Job did not sin by charging God with wrongdoing.

Job's Second Test

2 On another day the angels came to
present themselves before the
LORD, and Satan also came with them to
present himself before him. 2And the
LORD said to Satan, "Where have you
come from?"
Satan answered the LORD, "From
roaming through the earth and going to
and fro in it."
3Then the LORD said to Satan, "Have
you considered my servant Job? There
is no-one on earth like him; he is blameless and upright, a man who fears God
and shuns evil. And he still maintains
his integrity, though you incited me
against him to ruin him without any
reason."
4"Skin for skin!" Satan replied. "A
man will give all he has for his own life.
5But stretch out your hand and strike his
flesh and bones, and he will surely curse
you to your face."
6The LORD said to Satan, "Very well,
then, he is in your hands; but you must
spare his life."
7So Satan went out from the presence
of the LORD and afflicted Job with painful sores from the soles of his feet to the
top of his head. 8Then Job took a piece
of broken pottery and scraped himself
with it as he sat among the ashes.
9His wife said to him, "Are you still
holding on to your integrity? Curse God
and die!"
10He replied, "You are talking like a
foolish woman. Shall we accept good
from God, and not trouble?"
In all this, Job did not sin in what he
said.

Job's Three Friends

11When Job's three friends, Eliphaz
the Temanite, Bildad the Shuhite and
Zophar the Naamathite, heard about all
the troubles that had come upon him,
they set out from their homes and met
together by agreement to go and sympathise with him and comfort him.
12When they saw him from a distance,

they could hardly recognise him; they began to weep aloud, and they tore their robes and sprinkled dust on their heads. 13Then they sat on the ground with him for seven days and seven nights. No-one said a word to him, because they saw how great his suffering was.

Job Speaks

3 After this, Job opened his mouth and cursed the day of his birth. 2He said:

3"May the day of my birth perish,
and the night it was said, 'A boy is born!'
4That day—may it turn to darkness;
may God above not care about it;
may no light shine upon it.
5May darkness and deep shadow claim it once more;
may a cloud settle over it;
may blackness overwhelm its light.
6That night—may thick darkness seize it;
may it not be included among the days of the year
nor be entered in any of the months.
7May that night be barren;
may no shout of joy be heard in it.
8May those who curse days curse that day,
those who are ready to rouse Leviathan.
9May its morning stars become dark;
may it wait for daylight in vain
and not see the first rays of dawn,
10for it did not shut the doors of the womb on me
to hide trouble from my eyes.

11"Why did I not perish at birth,
and die as I came from the womb?
12Why were there knees to receive me
and breasts that I might be nursed?
13For now I would be lying down in peace;
I would be asleep and at rest
14with kings and counsellors of the earth,
who built for themselves places now lying in ruins,
15with rulers who had gold,
who filled their houses with silver.
16Or why was I not hidden in the ground like a stillborn child,
like an infant who never saw the light of day?
17There the wicked cease from turmoil,
and there the weary are at rest.
18Captives also enjoy their ease;
they no longer hear the slave driver's shout.
19The small and the great are there,
and the slave is freed from his master.

20"Why is light given to those in misery,
and life to the bitter of soul,
21to those who long for death that does not come,
who search for it more than for hidden treasure,
22who are filled with gladness
and rejoice when they reach the grave?
23Why is life given to a man
whose way is hidden,
whom God has hedged in?
24For sighing comes to me instead of food;
my groans pour out like water.
25What I feared has come upon me;
what I dreaded has happened to me.
26I have no peace, no quietness;
I have no rest, but only turmoil."

NEW TESTAMENT READING
Matthew 18:10–35

The Parable of the Lost Sheep

10"See that you do not look down on one of these little ones. For I tell you that their angels in heaven always see the face of my Father in heaven.
12"What do you think? If a man owns

a hundred sheep, and one of them wanders away, will he not leave the ninety-
nine on the hills and go to look for the
one that wandered off? [13]And if he
finds it, I tell you the truth, he is happier
about that one sheep than about the
ninety-nine that did not wander off. [14]In
the same way your Father in heaven is
not willing that any of these little ones
should be lost.

A Brother Who Sins Against You

[15]"If your brother sins against you, go
and show him his fault, just between the
two of you. If he listens to you, you have
won your brother over. [16]But if he will
not listen, take one or two others along,
so that 'every matter may be established
by the testimony of two or three witnesses.' [17]If he refuses to listen to them,
tell it to the church; and if he refuses to
listen even to the church, treat him as
you would a pagan or a tax collector.
[18]"I tell you the truth, whatever you
bind on earth will be bound in heaven,
and whatever you loose on earth will be
loosed in heaven.
[19]"Again, I tell you that if two of you
on earth agree about anything you ask
for, it will be done for you by my Father
in heaven. [20]For where two or three
come together in my name, there am I
with them."

The Parable of the Unmerciful Servant

[21]Then Peter came to Jesus and
asked, "Lord, how many times shall I
forgive my brother when he sins against
me? Up to seven times?"
[22]Jesus answered, "I tell you, not
seven times, but seventy-seven times.
[23]"Therefore, the kingdom of heaven
is like a king who wanted to settle
accounts with his servants. [24]As he began the settlement, a man who owed
him ten thousand talents was brought to
him. [25]Since he was not able to pay, the
master ordered that he and his wife and
his children and all that he had be sold
to repay the debt.
[26]"The servant fell on his knees before him. 'Be patient with me,' he begged, 'and I will pay back everything.'
[27]The servant's master took pity on him,
cancelled the debt and let him go.
[28]"But when that servant went out,
he found one of his fellow-servants
who owed him a hundred denarii. He
grabbed him and began to choke him.
'Pay back what you owe me!' he demanded.
[29]"His fellow-servant fell to his knees
and begged him, 'Be patient with me,
and I will pay you back.'
[30]"But he refused. Instead, he went
off and had the man thrown into prison
until he could pay the debt. [31]When the
other servants saw what had happened,
they were greatly distressed and went
and told their master everything that
had happened.
[32]"Then the master called the servant
in. 'You wicked servant,' he said, 'I
cancelled all that debt of yours because
you begged me to. [33]Shouldn't you have
had mercy on your fellow-servant just
as I had on you?' [34]In anger his master
turned him over to the jailers to be
tortured, until he should pay back all he
owed.
[35]"This is how my heavenly Father
will treat each of you unless you forgive
your brother from your heart."

READING FROM PSALMS
Psalm 16:1–11

A *miktam* of David.

[1]Keep me safe, O God,
for in you I take refuge.

[2]I said to the LORD, "You are my
Lord;
apart from you I have no good
thing."
[3]As for the saints who are in the land,
they are the glorious ones in whom
is all my delight.

4The sorrows of those will increase
who run after other gods.
I will not pour out their libations of
blood
or take up their names on my lips.

5LORD, you have assigned me my
portion and my cup;
you have made my lot secure.
6The boundary lines have fallen for
me in pleasant places;
surely I have a delightful
inheritance.

7I will praise the LORD, who counsels
me;
even at night my heart instructs
me.

8I have set the LORD always before
me.
Because he is at my right hand,
I shall not be shaken.

9Therefore my heart is glad and my
tongue rejoices;
my body also will rest secure,
10because you will not abandon me to
the grave,
nor will you let your Holy One see
decay.
11You have made known to me the
path of life;
you will fill me with joy in your
presence,
with eternal pleasures at your right
hand.

DAY 27

JANUARY 27

OLD TESTAMENT READING
Job 4:1–7:21

Eliphaz

4 Then Eliphaz the Temanite replied:

2"If someone ventures a word with
you, will you be impatient?
But who can keep from speaking?
3Think how you have instructed
many,
how you have strengthened feeble
hands.
4Your words have supported those
who stumbled;
you have strengthened faltering
knees.
5But now trouble comes to you, and
you are discouraged;
it strikes you, and you are
dismayed.
6Should not your piety be your
confidence
and your blameless ways your
hope?

7"Consider now: Who, being
innocent, has ever perished?
Where were the upright ever
destroyed?
8As I have observed, those who
plough evil
and those who sow trouble reap it.
9At the breath of God they are
destroyed;
at the blast of his anger they
perish.
10The lions may roar and growl,
yet the teeth of the great lions are
broken.
11The lion perishes for lack of prey,
and the cubs of the lioness are
scattered.

12"A word was secretly brought to me,
my ears caught a whisper of it.
13Amid disquieting dreams in the
night,
when deep sleep falls on men,

14fear and trembling seized me
and made all my bones shake.
15A spirit glided past my face,
and the hair on my body stood on end.
16It stopped,
but I could not tell what it was.
A form stood before my eyes,
and I heard a hushed voice:
17'Can a mortal be more righteous than God?
Can a man be more pure than his Maker?
18If God places no trust in his servants,
if he charges his angels with error,
19how much more those who live in houses of clay,
whose foundations are in the dust,
who are crushed more readily than a moth!
20Between dawn and dusk they are broken to pieces;
unnoticed, they perish for ever.
21Are not the cords of their tent pulled up,
so that they die without wisdom?'

5 "Call if you will, but who will answer you?
To which of the holy ones will you turn?
2Resentment kills a fool,
and envy slays the simple.
3I myself have seen a fool taking root,
but suddenly his house was cursed.
4His children are far from safety,
crushed in court without a defender.
5The hungry consume his harvest,
taking it even from among thorns,
and the thirsty pant after his wealth.
6For hardship does not spring from the soil,
nor does trouble sprout from the ground.
7Yet man is born to trouble
as surely as sparks fly upward.

8"But if it were I, I would appeal to God;
I would lay my cause before him.
9He performs wonders that cannot be fathomed,
miracles that cannot be counted.
10He bestows rain on the earth;
he sends water upon the countryside.
11The lowly he sets on high,
and those who mourn are lifted to safety.
12He thwarts the plans of the crafty,
so that their hands achieve no success.
13He catches the wise in their craftiness,
and the schemes of the wily are swept away.
14Darkness comes upon them in the daytime;
at noon they grope as in the night.
15He saves the needy from the sword in their mouth;
he saves them from the clutches of the powerful.
16So the poor have hope,
and injustice shuts its mouth.

17"Blessed is the man whom God corrects;
so do not despise the discipline of the Almighty.
18For he wounds, but he also binds up;
he injures, but his hands also heal.
19From six calamities he will rescue you;
in seven no harm will befall you.
20In famine he will ransom you from death,
and in battle from the stroke of the sword.
21You will be protected from the lash of the tongue,
and need not fear when destruction comes.
22You will laugh at destruction and famine,
and need not fear the beasts of the earth.
23For you will have a covenant with the stones of the field,
and the wild animals will be at peace with you.

24You will know that your tent is
secure;
you will take stock of your
property and find nothing
missing.
25You will know that your children will
be many,
and your descendants like the grass
of the earth.
26You will come to the grave in full
vigour,
like sheaves gathered in season.

27"We have examined this, and it is
true.
So hear it and apply it to yourself."

Job

6 Then Job replied:

2"If only my anguish could be weighed
and all my misery be placed on the
scales!
3It would surely outweigh the sand of
the seas—
no wonder my words have been
impetuous.
4The arrows of the Almighty are in
me,
my spirit drinks in their poison;
God's terrors are marshalled
against me.
5Does a wild donkey bray when it has
grass,
or an ox bellow when it has
fodder?
6Is tasteless food eaten without salt,
or is there flavour in the white of
an egg?
7I refuse to touch it;
such food makes me ill.

8"Oh, that I might have my request,
that God would grant what I hope
for,
9that God would be willing to crush
me,
to let loose his hand and cut me
off!
10Then I would still have this
consolation—
my joy in unrelenting pain—
that I had not denied the words of
the Holy One.

11"What strength do I have, that I
should still hope?
What prospects, that I should be
patient?
12Do I have the strength of stone?
Is my flesh bronze?
13Do I have any power to help myself,
now that success has been driven
from me?

14"A despairing man should have the
devotion of his friends,
even though he forsakes the fear of
the Almighty.
15But my brothers are as undependable
as intermittent streams,
as the streams that overflow
16when darkened by thawing ice
and swollen with melting snow,
17but that cease to flow in the dry
season,
and in the heat vanish from their
channels.
18Caravans turn aside from their
routes;
they go up into the wasteland and
perish.
19The caravans of Tema look for water,
the travelling merchants of Sheba
look in hope.
20They are distressed, because they had
been confident;
they arrive there, only to be
disappointed.
21Now you too have proved to be of no
help;
you see something dreadful and are
afraid.
22Have I ever said, 'Give something on
my behalf,
pay a ransom for me from your
wealth,
23deliver me from the hand of the
enemy,
ransom me from the clutches of the
ruthless'?

24"Teach me, and I will be quiet;
show me where I have been wrong.

25How painful are honest words!
But what do your arguments prove?
26Do you mean to correct what I say,
and treat the words of a despairing man as wind?
27You would even cast lots for the fatherless
and barter away your friend.

28"But now be so kind as to look at me.
Would I lie to your face?
29Relent, do not be unjust;
reconsider, for my integrity is at stake.
30Is there any wickedness on my lips?
Can my mouth not discern malice?

7 "Does not man have hard service on earth?
Are not his days like those of a hired man?
2Like a slave longing for the evening shadows,
or a hired man waiting eagerly for his wages,
3so I have been allotted months of futility,
and nights of misery have been assigned to me.
4When I lie down I think, 'How long before I get up?'
The night drags on, and I toss till dawn.
5My body is clothed with worms and scabs,
my skin is broken and festering.

6"My days are swifter than a weaver's shuttle,
and they come to an end without hope.
7Remember, O God, that my life is but a breath;
my eyes will never see happiness again.
8The eye that now sees me will see me no longer;
you will look for me, but I will be no more.
9As a cloud vanishes and is gone,
so he who goes down to the grave does not return.
10He will never come to his house again;
his place will know him no more.

11"Therefore I will not keep silent;
I will speak out in the anguish of my spirit,
I will complain in the bitterness of my soul.
12Am I the sea, or the monster of the deep,
that you put me under guard?
13When I think my bed will comfort me
and my couch will ease my complaint,
14even then you frighten me with dreams
and terrify me with visions,
15so that I prefer strangling and death,
rather than this body of mine.
16I despise my life; I would not live for ever.
Let me alone; my days have no meaning.

17"What is man that you make so much of him,
that you give him so much attention,
18that you examine him every morning
and test him every moment?
19Will you never look away from me,
or let me alone even for an instant?
20If I have sinned, what have I done to you,
O watcher of men?
Why have you made me your target?
Have I become a burden to you?
21Why do you not pardon my offences
and forgive my sins?
For I shall soon lie down in the dust;
you will search for me, but I shall be no more."

NEW TESTAMENT READING
Matthew 19:1–15

Divorce

19 When Jesus had finished saying these things, he left Galilee and went into the region of Judea to the

other side of the Jordan. 2Large crowds
followed him, and he healed them
there.
3Some Pharisees came to him to test
him. They asked, "Is it lawful for a man
to divorce his wife for any and every
reason?"
4"Haven't you read," he replied,
"that at the beginning the Creator
'made them male and female', 5and
said, 'For this reason a man will leave
his father and mother and be united to
his wife, and the two will become one
flesh'? 6So they are no longer two, but
one. Therefore what God has joined
together, let man not separate."
7"Why then," they asked, "did
Moses command that a man give his
wife a certificate of divorce and send her
away?"
8Jesus replied, "Moses permitted you
to divorce your wives because your
hearts were hard. But it was not this way
from the beginning. 9I tell you that anyone who divorces his wife, except for
marital unfaithfulness, and marries
another woman commits adultery."
10The disciples said to him, "If this is
the situation between a husband and
wife, it is better not to marry."
11Jesus replied, "Not everyone can
accept this word, but only those to
whom it has been given. 12For some are
eunuchs because they were born that
way; others were made that way by
men; and others have renounced marriage because of the kingdom of heaven.
The one who can accept this should
accept it."

The Little Children and Jesus

13Then little children were brought to
Jesus for him to place his hands on them
and pray for them. But the disciples
rebuked those who brought them.
14Jesus said, "Let the little children
come to me, and do not hinder them,
for the kingdom of heaven belongs to
such as these." 15When he had placed
his hands on them, he went on from
there.

READING FROM PSALMS
Psalm 17:1–5

A prayer of David.

1Hear, O LORD, my righteous plea;
listen to my cry.
Give ear to my prayer—
it does not rise from deceitful lips.
2May my vindication come from you;
may your eyes see what is right.

3Though you probe my heart and
examine me at night,
though you test me, you will find
nothing;
I have resolved that my mouth will
not sin.
4As for the deeds of men—
by the word of your lips
I have kept myself
from the ways of the violent.
5My steps have held to your paths;
my feet have not slipped.

OLD TESTAMENT READING
Job 8:1–10:22

Bildad

8 Then Bildad the Shuhite replied:

2"How long will you say such things?
Your words are a blustering wind.
3Does God pervert justice?
Does the Almighty pervert what is right?
4When your children sinned against him,
he gave them over to the penalty of their sin.
5But if you will look to God
and plead with the Almighty,
6if you are pure and upright,
even now he will rouse himself on your behalf
and restore you to your rightful place.
7Your beginnings will seem humble,
so prosperous will your future be.

8"Ask the former generations
and find out what their fathers learned,
9for we were born only yesterday and know nothing,
and our days on earth are but a shadow.
10Will they not instruct you and tell you?
Will they not bring forth words from their understanding?
11Can papyrus grow tall where there is no marsh?
Can reeds thrive without water?
12While still growing and uncut,
they wither more quickly than grass.
13Such is the destiny of all who forget God;
so perishes the hope of the godless.
14What he trusts in is fragile;
what he relies on is a spider's web.
15He leans on his web, but it gives way;
he clings to it, but it does not hold.
16He is like a well-watered plant in the sunshine,
spreading its shoots over the garden;
17it entwines its roots around a pile of rocks
and looks for a place among the stones.
18But when it is torn from its spot,
that place disowns it and says, 'I never saw you.'
19Surely its life withers away,
and from the soil other plants grow.

20"Surely God does not reject a blameless man
or strengthen the hands of evildoers.
21He will yet fill your mouth with laughter
and your lips with shouts of joy.
22Your enemies will be clothed in shame,
and the tents of the wicked will be no more."

Job

9 Then Job replied:

2"Indeed, I know that this is true.
But how can a mortal be righteous before God?
3Though one wished to dispute with him,
he could not answer him one time out of a thousand.
4His wisdom is profound, his power is vast.
Who has resisted him and come out unscathed?
5He moves mountains without their knowing it
and overturns them in his anger.
6He shakes the earth from its place
and makes its pillars tremble.

7He speaks to the sun and it does not
shine;
he seals off the light of the stars.
8He alone stretches out the heavens
and treads on the waves of the sea.
9He is the Maker of the Bear and
Orion,
the Pleiades and the constellations
of the south.
10He performs wonders that cannot be
fathomed,
miracles that cannot be counted.
11When he passes me, I cannot see him;
when he goes by, I cannot perceive
him.
12If he snatches away, who can stop
him?
Who can say to him, 'What are you
doing?'
13God does not restrain his anger;
even the cohorts of Rahab cowered
at his feet.

14"How then can I dispute with him?
How can I find words to argue with
him?
15Though I were innocent, I could not
answer him;
I could only plead with my Judge
for mercy.
16Even if I summoned him and he
responded,
I do not believe he would give me a
hearing.
17He would crush me with a storm
and multiply my wounds for no
reason.
18He would not let me regain my breath
but would overwhelm me with
misery.
19If it is a matter of strength, he is
mighty!
And if it is a matter of justice, who
will summon him?
20Even if I were innocent, my mouth
would condemn me;
if I were blameless, it would
pronounce me guilty.

21"Although I am blameless,
I have no concern for myself;
I despise my own life.
22It is all the same; that is why I say,
'He destroys both the blameless
and the wicked.'
23When a scourge brings sudden death,
he mocks the despair of the
innocent.
24When a land falls into the hands of
the wicked,
he blindfolds its judges.
If it is not he, then who is it?

25"My days are swifter than a runner;
they fly away without a glimpse of
joy.
26They skim past like boats of papyrus,
like eagles swooping down on their
prey.
27If I say, 'I will forget my complaint,
I will change my expression, and
smile,'
28I still dread all my sufferings,
for I know you will not hold me
innocent.
29Since I am already found guilty,
why should I struggle in vain?
30Even if I washed myself with soap
and my hands with washing soda,
31you would plunge me into a slime pit
so that even my clothes would
detest me.

32"He is not a man like me that I might
answer him,
that we might confront each other
in court.
33If only there were someone to
arbitrate between us,
to lay his hand upon us both,
34someone to remove God's rod from
me,
so that his terror would frighten me
no more.
35Then I would speak up without fear
of him,
but as it now stands with me, I
cannot.

10 "I loathe my very life;
therefore I will give free rein to
my complaint
and speak out in the bitterness of
my soul.

2I will say to God: Do not condemn
me,
but tell me what charges you have
against me.
3Does it please you to oppress me,
to spurn the work of your hands,
while you smile on the schemes of
the wicked?
4Do you have eyes of flesh?
Do you see as a mortal sees?
5Are your days like those of a mortal
or your years like those of a man,
6that you must search out my faults
and probe after my sin—
7though you know that I am not guilty
and that no-one can rescue me
from your hand?

8"Your hands shaped me and made
me.
Will you now turn and destroy me?
9Remember that you moulded me like
clay.
Will you now turn me to dust
again?
10Did you not pour me out like milk
and curdle me like cheese,
11clothe me with skin and flesh
and knit me together with bones
and sinews?
12You gave me life and showed me
kindness,
and in your providence watched
over my spirit.

13"But this is what you concealed in
your heart,
and I know that this was in your
mind:
14If I sinned, you would be watching
me
and would not let my offence go
unpunished.
15If I am guilty—woe to me!
Even if I am innocent, I cannot lift
my head,
for I am full of shame
and drowned in my affliction.
16If I hold my head high, you stalk me
like a lion
and again display your awesome
power against me.
17You bring new witnesses against me
and increase your anger towards
me;
your forces come against me wave
upon wave.

18"Why then did you bring me out of
the womb?
I wish I had died before any eye
saw me.
19If only I had never come into being,
or had been carried straight from
the womb to the grave!
20Are not my few days almost over?
Turn away from me so that I can
have a moment's joy
21before I go to the place of no return,
to the land of gloom and deep
shadow,
22to the land of deepest night,
of deep shadow and disorder,
where even the light is like
darkness."

NEW TESTAMENT READING
Matthew 19:16–30

The Rich Young Man

16Now a man came up to Jesus and
asked, "Teacher, what good thing must
I do to get eternal life?"
17"Why do you ask me about what is
good?" Jesus replied. "There is only
One who is good. If you want to enter
life, obey the commandments."
18"Which ones?" the man enquired.
Jesus replied, "'Do not murder, do
not commit adultery, do not steal, do
not give false testimony, 19honour your
father and mother,' and 'love your
neighbour as yourself.'"
20"All these I have kept," the young
man said. "What do I still lack?"
21Jesus answered, "If you want to be
perfect, go, sell your possessions and
give to the poor, and you will have

treasure in heaven. Then come, follow
me."
22When the young man heard this, he
went away sad, because he had great
wealth.
23Then Jesus said to his disciples, "I
tell you the truth, it is hard for a rich
man to enter the kingdom of heaven.
24Again I tell you, it is easier for a camel
to go through the eye of a needle than
for a rich man to enter the kingdom of
God."
25When the disciples heard this, they
were greatly astonished and asked,
"Who then can be saved?"
26Jesus looked at them and said,
"With man this is impossible, but with
God all things are possible."
27Peter answered him, "We have left
everything to follow you! What then
will there be for us?"
28Jesus said to them, "I tell you the
truth, at the renewal of all things, when
the Son of Man sits on his glorious
throne, you who have followed me will
also sit on twelve thrones, judging the
twelve tribes of Israel. 29And everyone
who has left houses or brothers or sisters or father or mother or children or
fields for my sake will receive a hundred
times as much and will inherit eternal
life. 30But many who are first will be
last, and many who are last will be first.

READING FROM PROVERBS

Proverbs 3:11–20

11My son, do not despise the LORD's
discipline
and do not resent his rebuke,
12because the LORD disciplines those he
loves,
as a father the son he delights in.

13Blessed is the man who finds wisdom,
the man who gains understanding,
14for she is more profitable than silver
and yields better returns than gold.
15She is more precious than rubies;
nothing you desire can compare
with her.
16Long life is in her right hand;
in her left hand are riches and
honour.
17Her ways are pleasant ways,
and all her paths are peace.
18She is a tree of life to those who
embrace her;
those who lay hold of her will be
blessed.

19By wisdom the LORD laid the earth's
foundations,
by understanding he set the
heavens in place;
20by his knowledge the deeps were
divided,
and the clouds let drop the dew.

DAY 29

JANUARY 29

OLD TESTAMENT READING

Job 11:1–14:22

Zophar

11 Then Zophar the Naamathite
replied:

2"Are all these words to go
unanswered?
Is this talker to be vindicated?
3Will your idle talk reduce men to
silence?
Will no-one rebuke you when you
mock?
4You say to God, 'My beliefs are
flawless
and I am pure in your sight.'
5Oh, how I wish that God would
speak,
that he would open his lips against
you

[6]and disclose to you the secrets of
wisdom,
for true wisdom has two sides.
Know this: God has even forgotten
some of your sin.

[7]"Can you fathom the mysteries of
God?
Can you probe the limits of the
Almighty?
[8]They are higher than the
heavens—what can you do?
They are deeper than the depths of
the grave—what can you
know?
[9]Their measure is longer than the
earth
and wider than the sea.

[10]"If he comes along and confines you
in prison
and convenes a court, who can
oppose him?
[11]Surely he recognises deceitful men;
and when he sees evil, does he not
take note?
[12]But a witless man can no more
become wise
than a wild donkey's colt can be
born a man.

[13]"Yet if you devote your heart to him
and stretch out your hands to him,
[14]if you put away the sin that is in your
hand
and allow no evil to dwell in your
tent,
[15]then you will lift up your face without
shame;
you will stand firm and without
fear.
[16]You will surely forget your trouble,
recalling it only as waters gone by.
[17]Life will be brighter than noonday,
and darkness will become like
morning.
[18]You will be secure, because there is
hope;
you will look about you and take
your rest in safety.
[19]You will lie down, with no-one to
make you afraid,
and many will court your favour.
[20]But the eyes of the wicked will fail,
and escape will elude them;
their hope will become a dying
gasp."

Job

12 Then Job replied:

[2]"Doubtless you are the people,
and wisdom will die with you!
[3]But I have a mind as well as you;
I am not inferior to you.
Who does not know all these
things?

[4]"I have become a laughing-stock to
my friends,
though I called upon God and he
answered—
a mere laughing-stock, though
righteous and blameless!
[5]Men at ease have contempt for
misfortune
as the fate of those whose feet are
slipping.
[6]The tents of marauders are
undisturbed,
and those who provoke God are
secure—
those who carry their god in their
hands.

[7]"But ask the animals, and they will
teach you,
or the birds of the air, and they will
tell you;
[8]or speak to the earth, and it will teach
you,
or let the fish of the sea inform
you.
[9]Which of all these does not know
that the hand of the LORD has done
this?
[10]In his hand is the life of every
creature
and the breath of all mankind.
[11]Does not the ear test words
as the tongue tastes food?
[12]Is not wisdom found among the
aged?
Does not long life bring
understanding?

[13]"To God belong wisdom and power;
counsel and understanding are his.
[14]What he tears down cannot be rebuilt;
the man he imprisons cannot be released.
[15]If he holds back the waters, there is drought;
if he lets them loose, they devastate the land.
[16]To him belong strength and victory;
both deceived and deceiver are his.
[17]He leads counsellors away stripped
and makes fools of judges.
[18]He takes off the shackles put on by kings
and ties a loincloth round their waist.
[19]He leads priests away stripped
and overthrows men long established.
[20]He silences the lips of trusted advisers
and takes away the discernment of elders.
[21]He pours contempt on nobles
and disarms the mighty.
[22]He reveals the deep things of darkness
and brings deep shadows into the light.
[23]He makes nations great, and destroys them;
he enlarges nations, and disperses them.
[24]He deprives the leaders of the earth of their reason;
he sends them wandering through a trackless waste.
[25]They grope in darkness with no light;
he makes them stagger like drunkards.

13 "My eyes have seen all this,
my ears have heard and understood it.
[2]What you know, I also know;
I am not inferior to you.
[3]But I desire to speak to the Almighty
and to argue my case with God.
[4]You, however, smear me with lies;
you are worthless physicians, all of you!
[5]If only you would be altogether silent!
For you, that would be wisdom.
[6]Hear now my argument;
listen to the plea of my lips.
[7]Will you speak wickedly on God's behalf?
Will you speak deceitfully for him?
[8]Will you show him partiality?
Will you argue the case for God?
[9]Would it turn out well if he examined you?
Could you deceive him as you might deceive men?
[10]He would surely rebuke you
if you secretly showed partiality.
[11]Would not his splendour terrify you?
Would not the dread of him fall on you?
[12]Your maxims are proverbs of ashes;
your defences are defences of clay.

[13]"Keep silent and let me speak;
then let come to me what may.
[14]Why do I put myself in jeopardy
and take my life in my hands?
[15]Though he slay me, yet will I hope in him;
I will surely defend my ways to his face.
[16]Indeed, this will turn out for my deliverance,
for no godless man would dare come before him!
[17]Listen carefully to my words;
let your ears take in what I say.
[18]Now that I have prepared my case,
I know I will be vindicated.
[19]Can anyone bring charges against me?
If so, I will be silent and die.

[20]"Only grant me these two things, O God,
and then I will not hide from you:
[21]Withdraw your hand far from me,
and stop frightening me with your terrors.
[22]Then summon me and I will answer,
or let me speak, and you reply.
[23]How many wrongs and sins have I committed?
Show me my offence and my sin.

24Why do you hide your face
and consider me your enemy?
25Will you torment a wind-blown leaf?
Will you chase after dry chaff?
26For you write down bitter things
against me
and make me inherit the sins of my
youth.
27You fasten my feet in shackles;
you keep close watch on all my
paths
by putting marks on the soles of my
feet.

28"So man wastes away like something
rotten,
like a garment eaten by moths.

14 "Man born of woman
is of few days and full of
trouble.
2He springs up like a flower and
withers away;
like a fleeting shadow, he does not
endure.
3Do you fix your eye on such a one?
Will you bring him before you for
judgment?
4Who can bring what is pure from the
impure?
No-one!
5Man's days are determined;
you have decreed the number of
his months
and have set limits he cannot
exceed.
6So look away from him and let him
alone,
till he has put in his time like a
hired man.

7"At least there is hope for a tree:
If it is cut down, it will sprout
again,
and its new shoots will not fail.
8Its roots may grow old in the ground
and its stump die in the soil,
9yet at the scent of water it will bud
and put forth shoots like a plant.
10But man dies and is laid low;
he breathes his last and is no more.
11As water disappears from the sea
or a river bed becomes parched
and dry,
12so man lies down and does not rise;
till the heavens are no more, men
will not awake
or be roused from their sleep.

13"If only you would hide me in the
grave
and conceal me till your anger has
passed!
If only you would set me a time
and then remember me!
14If a man dies, will he live again?
All the days of my hard service
I will wait for my renewal to come.
15You will call and I will answer you;
you will long for the creature your
hands have made.
16Surely then you will count my steps
but not keep track of my sin.
17My offences will be sealed up in a
bag;
you will cover over my sin.

18"But as a mountain erodes and
crumbles
and as a rock is moved from its
place,
19as water wears away stones
and torrents wash away the soil,
so you destroy man's hope.
20You overpower him once for all, and
he is gone;
you change his countenance and
send him away.
21If his sons are honoured, he does not
know it;
if they are brought low, he does not
see it.
22He feels but the pain of his own body
and mourns only for himself."

NEW TESTAMENT READING
Matthew 20:1–19

The Parable of the Workers in the Vineyard

20 "For the kingdom of heaven is
like a landowner who went out
early in the morning to hire men to work

in his vineyard. 2He agreed to pay them
a denarius for the day and sent them
into his vineyard.
3"About the third hour he went out
and saw others standing in the market-
place doing nothing. 4He told them,
'You also go and work in my vineyard,
and I will pay you whatever is right.' 5So
they went.
"He went out again about the sixth
hour and the ninth hour and did the
same thing. 6About the eleventh hour
he went out and found still others standing around. He asked them, 'Why have
you been standing here all day long
doing nothing?'
7" 'Because no-one has hired us,' they
answered.
"He said to them, 'You also go and
work in my vineyard.'
8"When evening came, the owner of
the vineyard said to his foreman, 'Call
the workers and pay them their wages,
beginning with the last ones hired and
going on to the first.'
9"The workers who were hired about
the eleventh hour came and each received a denarius. 10So when those
came who were hired first, they expected to receive more. But each one of
them also received a denarius. 11When
they received it, they began to grumble
against the landowner. 12'These men
who were hired last worked only one
hour,' they said, 'and you have made
them equal to us who have borne the
burden of the work and the heat of the
day.'
13"But he answered one of them,
'Friend, I am not being unfair to you.
Didn't you agree to work for a denarius? 14Take your pay and go. I want
to give the man who was hired last the
same as I gave you. 15Don't I have the
right to do what I want with my own
money? Or are you envious because I
am generous?'
16"So the last will be first, and the first
will be last."

Jesus Again Predicts His Death

17Now as Jesus was going up to Jerusalem, he took the twelve disciples aside
and said to them, 18"We are going up to
Jerusalem, and the Son of Man will be
betrayed to the chief priests and the
teachers of the law. They will condemn
him to death 19and will turn him over to
the Gentiles to be mocked and flogged
and crucified. On the third day he will
be raised to life!"

READING FROM PSALMS
Psalm 17:6–12

6I call on you, O God, for you will
answer me;
give ear to me and hear my prayer.
7Show the wonder of your great love,
you who save by your right hand
those who take refuge in you from
their foes.
8Keep me as the apple of your eye;
hide me in the shadow of your
wings
9from the wicked who assail me,
from my mortal enemies who
surround me.

10They close up their callous hearts,
and their mouths speak with
arrogance.
11They have tracked me down, they
now surround me,
with eyes alert, to throw me to the
ground.
12They are like a lion hungry for prey,
like a great lion crouching in cover.

JANUARY 30

OLD TESTAMENT READING
Job 15:1–18:21

Eliphaz

15 Then Eliphaz the Temanite replied:

2"Would a wise man answer with
empty notions
or fill his belly with the hot east
wind?
3Would he argue with useless words,
with speeches that have no value?
4But you even undermine piety
and hinder devotion to God.
5Your sin prompts your mouth;
you adopt the tongue of the crafty.
6Your own mouth condemns you, not
mine;
your own lips testify against you.

7"Are you the first man ever born?
Were you brought forth before the
hills?
8Do you listen in on God's council?
Do you limit wisdom to yourself?
9What do you know that we do not
know?
What insights do you have that we
do not have?
10The grey-haired and the aged are on
our side,
men even older than your father.
11Are God's consolations not enough
for you,
words spoken gently to you?
12Why has your heart carried you
away,
and why do your eyes flash,
13so that you vent your rage against
God
and pour out such words from your
mouth?

14"What is man, that he could be pure,
or one born of woman, that he
could be righteous?
15If God places no trust in his holy
ones,
if even the heavens are not pure in
his eyes,
16how much less man, who is vile and
corrupt,
who drinks up evil like water!

17"Listen to me and I will explain to
you;
let me tell you what I have seen,
18what wise men have declared,
hiding nothing received from their
fathers
19(to whom alone the land was given
when no alien passed among
them):
20All his days the wicked man suffers
torment,
the ruthless through all the years
stored up for him.
21Terrifying sounds fill his ears;
when all seems well, marauders
attack him.
22He despairs of escaping the darkness;
he is marked for the sword.
23He wanders about—food for
vultures;
he knows the day of darkness is at
hand.
24Distress and anguish fill him with
terror;
they overwhelm him, like a king
poised to attack,
25because he shakes his fist at God
and vaunts himself against the
Almighty,
26defiantly charging against him
with a thick, strong shield.

27"Though his face is covered with fat
and his waist bulges with flesh,
28he will inhabit ruined towns
and houses where no-one lives,
houses crumbling to rubble.
29He will no longer be rich and his
wealth will not endure,

nor will his possessions spread over
the land.
30He will not escape the darkness;
a flame will wither his shoots,
and the breath of God's mouth will
carry him away.
31Let him not deceive himself by
trusting what is worthless,
for he will get nothing in return.
32Before his time he will be paid in full,
and his branches will not flourish.
33He will be like a vine stripped of its
unripe grapes,
like an olive tree shedding its
blossoms.
34For the company of the godless will
be barren,
and fire will consume the tents of
those who love bribes.
35They conceive trouble and give birth
to evil;
their womb fashions deceit."

Job

16 Then Job replied:

2"I have heard many things like these;
miserable comforters are you all!
3Will your long-winded speeches
never end?
What ails you that you keep on
arguing?
4I also could speak like you,
if you were in my place;
I could make fine speeches against
you
and shake my head at you.
5But my mouth would encourage you;
comfort from my lips would bring
you relief.

6"Yet if I speak, my pain is not
relieved;
and if I refrain, it does not go
away.
7Surely, O God, you have worn me
out;
you have devastated my entire
household.
8You have bound me—and it has
become a witness;
my gauntness rises up and testifies
against me.
9God assails me and tears me in his
anger
and gnashes his teeth at me;
my opponent fastens on me his
piercing eyes.
10Men open their mouths to jeer at me;
they strike my cheek in scorn
and unite together against me.
11God has turned me over to evil men
and thrown me into the clutches of
the wicked.
12All was well with me, but he
shattered me;
he seized me by the neck and
crushed me.
He has made me his target;
13 his archers surround me.
Without pity, he pierces my kidneys
and spills my gall on the ground.
14Again and again he bursts upon me;
he rushes at me like a warrior.

15"I have sewed sackcloth over my skin
and buried my brow in the dust.
16My face is red with weeping,
deep shadows ring my eyes;
17yet my hands have been free of
violence
and my prayer is pure.

18"O earth, do not cover my blood;
may my cry never be laid to rest!
19Even now my witness is in heaven;
my advocate is on high.
20My intercessor is my friend
as my eyes pour out tears to God;
21on behalf of a man he pleads with
God
as a man pleads for his friend.

22"Only a few years will pass
before I go on the journey of no
return.

17 1My spirit is broken,
my days are cut short,
the grave awaits me.
2Surely mockers surround me;
my eyes must dwell on their
hostility.

3"Give me, O God, the pledge you
demand.
Who else will put up security for
me?
4You have closed their minds to
understanding;
therefore you will not let them
triumph.
5If a man denounces his friends for
reward,
the eyes of his children will fail.

6"God has made me a byword to
everyone,
a man in whose face people spit.
7My eyes have grown dim with grief;
my whole frame is but a shadow.
8Upright men are appalled at this;
the innocent are aroused against
the ungodly.
9Nevertheless, the righteous will hold
to their ways,
and those with clean hands will
grow stronger.

10"But come on, all of you, try again!
I will not find a wise man among
you.
11My days have passed, my plans are
shattered,
and so are the desires of my heart.
12These men turn night into day;
in the face of darkness they say,
'Light is near.'
13If the only home I hope for is the
grave,
if I spread out my bed in darkness,
14if I say to corruption, 'You are my
father,'
and to the worm, 'My mother' or
'My sister',
15where then is my hope?
Who can see any hope for me?
16Will it go down to the gates of death?
Will we descend together into the
dust?"

Bildad

18 Then Bildad the Shuhite replied:

2"When will you end these speeches?
Be sensible, and then we can talk.
3Why are we regarded as cattle
and considered stupid in your
sight?
4You who tear yourself to pieces in
your anger,
is the earth to be abandoned for
your sake?
Or must the rocks be moved from
their place?

5"The lamp of the wicked is snuffed
out;
the flame of his fire stops burning.
6The light in his tent becomes dark;
the lamp beside him goes out.
7The vigour of his step is weakened;
his own schemes throw him down.
8His feet thrust him into a net
and he wanders into its mesh.
9A trap seizes him by the heel;
a snare holds him fast.
10A noose is hidden for him on the
ground;
a trap lies in his path.
11Terrors startle him on every side
and dog his every step.
12Calamity is hungry for him;
disaster is ready for him when he
falls.
13It eats away parts of his skin;
death's firstborn devours his limbs.
14He is torn from the security of his
tent
and marched off to the king of
terrors.
15Fire resides in his tent;
burning sulphur is scattered over
his dwelling.
16His roots dry up below
and his branches wither above.
17The memory of him perishes from the
earth;
he has no name in the land.
18He is driven from light into darkness
and is banished from the world.
19He has no offspring or descendants
among his people,
no survivor where once he lived.
20Men of the west are appalled at his
fate;
men of the east are seized with
horror.

[21]Surely such is the dwelling of an evil man;
such is the place of one who knows not God."

NEW TESTAMENT READING
Matthew 20:20–34

A Mother's Request

[20]Then the mother of Zebedee's sons came to Jesus with her sons and, kneeling down, asked a favour of him.

[21]"What is it you want?" he asked.

She said, "Grant that one of these two sons of mine may sit at your right and the other at your left in your kingdom."

[22]"You don't know what you are asking," Jesus said to them. "Can you drink the cup I am going to drink?"

"We can," they answered.

[23]Jesus said to them, "You will indeed drink from my cup, but to sit at my right or left is not for me to grant. These places belong to those for whom they have been prepared by my Father."

[24]When the ten heard about this, they
were indignant with the two brothers.
[25]Jesus called them together and said, "You know that the rulers of the Gentiles lord it over them, and their high officials exercise authority
over them. [26]Not so with you. Instead, whoever wants to become great
among you must be your servant, [27]and
whoever wants to be first must be your
slave—[28]just as the Son of Man did not come to be served, but to serve, and to give his life as a ransom for many."

Two Blind Men Receive Sight

[29]As Jesus and his disciples were leaving Jericho, a large crowd followed him.
[30]Two blind men were sitting by the roadside, and when they heard that Jesus was going by, they shouted, "Lord, Son of David, have mercy on us!"

[31]The crowd rebuked them and told them to be quiet, but they shouted all the louder, "Lord, Son of David, have mercy on us!"

[32]Jesus stopped and called them. "What do you want me to do for you?" he asked.

[33]"Lord," they answered, "we want our sight."

[34]Jesus had compassion on them and touched their eyes. Immediately they received their sight and followed him.

READING FROM PSALMS
Psalm 17:13–15

[13]Rise up, O LORD, confront them, bring them down;
rescue me from the wicked by your sword.
[14]O LORD, by your hand save me from such men,
from men of this world whose reward is in this life.

You still the hunger of those you cherish;
their sons have plenty,
and they store up wealth for their children.
[15]And I—in righteousness I shall see your face;
when I awake, I shall be satisfied with seeing your likeness.

JANUARY 31

OLD TESTAMENT READING
Job 19:1–21:34

Job

19 Then Job replied:

2"How long will you torment me
and crush me with words?
3Ten times now you have reproached me;
shamelessly you attack me.
4If it is true that I have gone astray,
my error remains my concern alone.
5If indeed you would exalt yourselves above me
and use my humiliation against me,
6then know that God has wronged me
and drawn his net around me.

7"Though I cry, 'I've been wronged!' I get no response;
though I call for help, there is no justice.
8He has blocked my way so that I cannot pass;
he has shrouded my paths in darkness.
9He has stripped me of my honour
and removed the crown from my head.
10He tears me down on every side till I am gone;
he uproots my hope like a tree.
11His anger burns against me;
he counts me among his enemies.
12His troops advance in force;
they build a siege ramp against me
and encamp around my tent.

13"He has alienated my brothers from me;
my acquaintances are completely estranged from me.
14My kinsmen have gone away;
my friends have forgotten me.
15My guests and my maidservants count me a stranger;
they look upon me as an alien.
16I summon my servant, but he does not answer,
though I beg him with my own mouth.
17My breath is offensive to my wife;
I am loathsome to my own brothers.
18Even the little boys scorn me;
when I appear, they ridicule me.
19All my intimate friends detest me;
those I love have turned against me.
20I am nothing but skin and bones;
I have escaped by only the skin of my teeth.

21"Have pity on me, my friends, have pity,
for the hand of God has struck me.
22Why do you pursue me as God does?
Will you never get enough of my flesh?

23"Oh, that my words were recorded,
that they were written on a scroll,
24that they were inscribed with an iron tool on lead,
or engraved in rock for ever!
25I know that my Redeemer lives,
and that in the end he will stand upon the earth.
26And after my skin has been destroyed,
yet in my flesh I will see God;
27I myself will see him
with my own eyes—I, and not another.
How my heart yearns within me!

28"If you say, 'How we will hound him,
since the root of the trouble lies in him,'
29you should fear the sword yourselves;
for wrath will bring punishment by the sword,

and then you will know that there
is judgment."

Zophar

20 Then Zophar the Naamathite
replied:

2"My troubled thoughts prompt me to
answer
because I am greatly disturbed.
3I hear a rebuke that dishonours me,
and my understanding inspires me
to reply.

4"Surely you know how it has been
from of old,
ever since man was placed on the
earth,
5that the mirth of the wicked is brief,
the joy of the godless lasts but a
moment.
6Though his pride reaches to the
heavens
and his head touches the clouds,
7he will perish for ever, like his own
dung;
those who have seen him will say,
'Where is he?'
8Like a dream he flies away, no more
to be found,
banished like a vision of the night.
9The eye that saw him will not see him
again;
his place will look on him no more.
10His children must make amends to
the poor;
his own hands must give back his
wealth.
11The youthful vigour that fills his
bones
will lie with him in the dust.

12"Though evil is sweet in his mouth
and he hides it under his tongue,
13though he cannot bear to let it go
and keeps it in his mouth,
14yet his food will turn sour in his
stomach;
it will become the venom of
serpents within him.
15He will spit out the riches he
swallowed;
God will make his stomach vomit
them up.
16He will suck the poison of serpents;
the fangs of an adder will kill him.
17He will not enjoy the streams,
the rivers flowing with honey and
cream.
18What he toiled for he must give back
uneaten;
he will not enjoy the profit from his
trading.
19For he has oppressed the poor and
left them destitute;
he has seized houses he did not
build.

20"Surely he will have no respite from
his craving;
he cannot save himself by his
treasure.
21Nothing is left for him to devour;
his prosperity will not endure.
22In the midst of his plenty, distress will
overtake him;
the full force of misery will come
upon him.
23When he has filled his belly,
God will vent his burning anger
against him
and rain down his blows upon him.
24Though he flees from an iron
weapon,
a bronze-tipped arrow pierces
him.
25He pulls it out of his back,
the gleaming point out of his liver.
Terrors will come over him;
26 total darkness lies in wait for his
treasures.
A fire unfanned will consume him
and devour what is left in his tent.
27The heavens will expose his guilt;
the earth will rise up against him.
28A flood will carry off his house,
rushing waters on the day of God's
wrath.
29Such is the fate God allots the
wicked,
the heritage appointed for them by
God."

Job

21 Then Job replied:

2"Listen carefully to my words;
let this be the consolation you give me.
3Bear with me while I speak,
and after I have spoken, mock on.

4"Is my complaint directed to man?
Why should I not be impatient?
5Look at me and be astonished;
clap your hand over your mouth.
6When I think about this, I am terrified;
trembling seizes my body.
7Why do the wicked live on,
growing old and increasing in power?
8They see their children established around them,
their offspring before their eyes.
9Their homes are safe and free from fear;
the rod of God is not upon them.
10Their bulls never fail to breed;
their cows calve and do not miscarry.
11They send forth their children as a flock;
their little ones dance about.
12They sing to the music of tambourine and harp;
they make merry to the sound of the flute.
13They spend their years in prosperity
and go down to the grave in peace.
14Yet they say to God, 'Leave us alone!
We have no desire to know your ways.
15Who is the Almighty, that we should serve him?
What would we gain by praying to him?'
16But their prosperity is not in their own hands,
so I stand aloof from the counsel of the wicked.

17"Yet how often is the lamp of the wicked snuffed out?
How often does calamity come upon them,
the fate God allots in his anger?
18How often are they like straw before the wind,
like chaff swept away by a gale?
19⌞It is said,⌟ 'God stores up a man's punishment for his sons.'
Let him repay the man himself, so that he will know it!
20Let his own eyes see his destruction;
let him drink of the wrath of the Almighty.
21For what does he care about the family he leaves behind
when his allotted months come to an end?

22"Can anyone teach knowledge to God,
since he judges even the highest?
23One man dies in full vigour,
completely secure and at ease,
24his body well nourished,
his bones rich with marrow.
25Another man dies in bitterness of soul,
never having enjoyed anything good.
26Side by side they lie in the dust,
and worms cover them both.

27"I know full well what you are thinking,
the schemes by which you would wrong me.
28You say, 'Where now is the great man's house,
the tents where wicked men lived?'
29Have you never questioned those who travel?
Have you paid no regard to their accounts—
30that the evil man is spared from the day of calamity,
that he is delivered from the day of wrath?
31Who denounces his conduct to his face?
Who repays him for what he has done?

32He is carried to the grave,
and watch is kept over his tomb.
33The soil in the valley is sweet to him;
all men follow after him,
and a countless throng goes before
him.

34"So how can you console me with
your nonsense?
Nothing is left of your answers but
falsehood!"

NEW TESTAMENT READING
Matthew 21:1–17

The Triumphal Entry

21 As they approached Jerusalem
and came to Bethphage on the
Mount of Olives, Jesus sent two disciples, 2saying to them, "Go to the village
ahead of you, and at once you will find a
donkey tied there, with her colt by her.
Untie them and bring them to me. 3If
anyone says anything to you, tell him
that the Lord needs them, and he will
send them right away."
4This took place to fulfil what was
spoken through the prophet:

5"Say to the Daughter of Zion,
'See, your king comes to you,
gentle and riding on a donkey,
on a colt, the foal of a donkey.'"

6The disciples went and did as Jesus
had instructed them. 7They brought the
donkey and the colt, placed their cloaks
on them, and Jesus sat on them. 8A very
large crowd spread their cloaks on the
road, while others cut branches from
the trees and spread them on the road.
9The crowds that went ahead of him and
those that followed shouted,

"Hosanna to the Son of David!"

"Blessed is he who comes in the
name of the Lord!"

"Hosanna in the highest!"

10When Jesus entered Jerusalem, the
whole city was stirred and asked, "Who
is this?"
11The crowds answered, "This is
Jesus, the prophet from Nazareth in
Galilee."

Jesus at the Temple

12Jesus entered the temple area and
drove out all who were buying and selling there. He overturned the tables of
the money changers and the benches of
those selling doves. 13"It is written," he
said to them, "'My house will be called
a house of prayer,' but you are making it
a 'den of robbers'."
14The blind and the lame came to him
at the temple, and he healed them.
15But when the chief priests and the
teachers of the law saw the wonderful
things he did and the children shouting
in the temple area, "Hosanna to the Son
of David," they were indignant.
16"Do you hear what these children
are saying?" they asked him.
"Yes," replied Jesus, "have you
never read,

"'From the lips of children and
infants
you have ordained praise'?"

17And he left them and went out of
the city to Bethany, where he spent the
night.

READING FROM PSALMS
Psalm 18:1–6

For the director of music. Of David the servant of the LORD. He sang to the LORD the words of this song when the LORD delivered him from the hand of all his enemies and from the hand of Saul. He said:

1I love you, O LORD, my strength.

2The LORD is my rock, my fortress and
my deliverer;

my God is my rock, in whom I take
refuge.
He is my shield and the horn of my
salvation, my stronghold.
3I call to the LORD, who is worthy of
praise,
and I am saved from my enemies.

4The cords of death entangled
me;
the torrents of destruction
overwhelmed me.
5The cords of the grave coiled around
me;
the snares of death confronted me.
6In my distress I called to the LORD;
I cried to my God for help.
From his temple he heard my voice;
my cry came before him, into his
ears.

FEBRUARY 1

DAY 32

OLD TESTAMENT READING

Job 22:1–24:25

Eliphaz

22 Then Eliphaz the Temanite replied:

2"Can a man be of benefit to God?
Can even a wise man benefit him?
3What pleasure would it give the
Almighty if you were
righteous?
What would he gain if your ways
were blameless?

4"Is it for your piety that he rebukes
you
and brings charges against you?
5Is not your wickedness great?
Are not your sins endless?
6You demanded security from your
brothers for no reason;
you stripped men of their clothing,
leaving them naked.
7You gave no water to the weary
and you withheld food from the
hungry,
8though you were a powerful man,
owning land—
an honoured man, living on it.
9And you sent widows away
empty-handed
and broke the strength of the
fatherless.
10That is why snares are all around you,
why sudden peril terrifies you,
11why it is so dark that you cannot see,
and why a flood of water covers
you.

12"Is not God in the heights of heaven?
And see how lofty are the highest
stars!
13Yet you say, 'What does God know?
Does he judge through such
darkness?
14Thick clouds veil him, so he does not
see us
as he goes about in the vaulted
heavens.'
15Will you keep to the old path
that evil men have trod?
16They were carried off before their
time,
their foundations washed away by
a flood.
17They said to God, 'Leave us alone!
What can the Almighty do to us?'
18Yet it was he who filled their houses
with good things,
so I stand aloof from the counsel of
the wicked.

19"The righteous see their ruin and
rejoice;
the innocent mock them, saying,
20'Surely our foes are destroyed,
and fire devours their wealth.'

21"Submit to God and be at peace with
him;
in this way prosperity will come to
you.
22Accept instruction from his mouth
and lay up his words in your heart.
23If you return to the Almighty, you
will be restored:
If you remove wickedness far from
your tent
24and assign your nuggets to the dust,
your gold of Ophir to the rocks in
the ravines,
25then the Almighty will be your gold,
the choicest silver for you.
26Surely then you will find delight in
the Almighty
and will lift up your face to God.
27You will pray to him, and he will hear
you,
and you will fulfil your vows.
28What you decide on will be done,
and light will shine on your ways.
29When men are brought low and you
say, 'Lift them up!'
then he will save the downcast.
30He will deliver even one who is not
innocent,
who will be delivered through the
cleanness of your hands."

Job

23 Then Job replied:

2"Even today my complaint is bitter;
his hand is heavy in spite of my
groaning.
3If only I knew where to find him;
if only I could go to his dwelling!
4I would state my case before him
and fill my mouth with arguments.
5I would find out what he would
answer me,
and consider what he would say.
6Would he oppose me with great
power?
No, he would not press charges
against me.
7There an upright man could present
his case before him,
and I would be delivered for ever
from my judge.
8"But if I go to the east, he is not
there;
if I go to the west, I do not find him.
9When he is at work in the north, I do
not see him;
when he turns to the south, I catch
no glimpse of him.
10But he knows the way that I take;
when he has tested me, I shall
come forth as gold.
11My feet have closely followed his
steps;
I have kept to his way without
turning aside.
12I have not departed from the
commands of his lips;
I have treasured the words of his
mouth more than my daily
bread.

13"But he stands alone, and who can
oppose him?
He does whatever he pleases.
14He carries out his decree against me,
and many such plans he still has in
store.
15That is why I am terrified before him;
when I think of all this, I fear him.
16God has made my heart faint;
the Almighty has terrified me.
17Yet I am not silenced by the
darkness,
by the thick darkness that covers
my face.

24 "Why does the Almighty not
set times for judgment?
Why must those who know him
look in vain for such days?
2Men move boundary stones;
they pasture flocks they have
stolen.
3They drive away the orphan's donkey
and take the widow's ox in pledge.
4They thrust the needy from the path
and force all the poor of the land
into hiding.
5Like wild donkeys in the desert,
the poor go about their labour of
foraging food;
the wasteland provides food for
their children.

6They gather fodder in the fields
and glean in the vineyards of the wicked.
7Lacking clothes, they spend the night naked;
they have nothing to cover themselves in the cold.
8They are drenched by mountain rains
and hug the rocks for lack of shelter.
9The fatherless child is snatched from the breast;
the infant of the poor is seized for a debt.
10Lacking clothes, they go about naked;
they carry the sheaves, but still go hungry.
11They crush olives among the terraces;
they tread the winepresses, yet suffer thirst.
12The groans of the dying rise from the city,
and the souls of the wounded cry out for help.
But God charges no-one with wrongdoing.

13"There are those who rebel against the light,
who do not know its ways
or stay in its paths.
14When daylight is gone, the murderer rises up
and kills the poor and needy;
in the night he steals forth like a thief.
15The eye of the adulterer watches for dusk;
he thinks, 'No eye will see me,'
and he keeps his face concealed.
16In the dark, men break into houses,
but by day they shut themselves in;
they want nothing to do with the light.
17For all of them, deep darkness is their morning;
they make friends with the terrors of darkness.

18"Yet they are foam on the surface of the water;
their portion of the land is cursed,
so that no-one goes to the vineyards.
19As heat and drought snatch away the melted snow,
so the grave snatches away those who have sinned.
20The womb forgets them,
the worm feasts on them;
evil men are no longer remembered
but are broken like a tree.
21They prey on the barren and childless woman,
and to the widow show no kindness.
22But God drags away the mighty by his power;
though they become established,
they have no assurance of life.
23He may let them rest in a feeling of security,
but his eyes are on their ways.
24For a little while they are exalted,
and then they are gone;
they are brought low and gathered up like all others;
they are cut off like ears of corn.

25"If this is not so, who can prove me false
and reduce my words to nothing?"

NEW TESTAMENT READING
Matthew 21:18–32

The Fig-Tree Withers

18Early in the morning, as he was on
his way back to the city, he was hungry.
19Seeing a fig-tree by the road, he went
up to it but found nothing on it except
leaves. Then he said to it, "May you
never bear fruit again!" Immediately
the tree withered.
20When the disciples saw this, they
were amazed. "How did the fig-tree
wither so quickly?" they asked.
21Jesus replied, "I tell you the truth, if
you have faith and do not doubt, not
only can you do what was done to the
fig-tree, but also you can say to this
mountain, 'Go, throw yourself into the

sea,' and it will be done. 22If you believe, you will receive whatever you ask
for in prayer."

The Authority of Jesus Questioned

23Jesus entered the temple courts,
and, while he was teaching, the chief
priests and the elders of the people
came to him. "By what authority are
you doing these things?" they asked.
"And who gave you this authority?"
24Jesus replied, "I will also ask you
one question. If you answer me, I will
tell you by what authority I am doing
these things. 25John's baptism—where
did it come from? Was it from heaven,
or from men?"
They discussed it among themselves
and said, "If we say, 'From heaven', he
will ask, 'Then why didn't you believe
him?' 26But if we say, 'From men'—we
are afraid of the people, for they all hold
that John was a prophet."
27So they answered Jesus, "We don't
know."
Then he said, "Neither will I tell you
by what authority I am doing these
things.

The Parable of the Two Sons

28"What do you think? There was a
man who had two sons. He went to the
first and said, 'Son, go and work today
in the vineyard.'
29" 'I will not,' he answered, but later
he changed his mind and went.
30"Then the father went to the other
son and said the same thing. He
answered, 'I will, sir,' but he did not go.
31"Which of the two did what his
father wanted?"
"The first," they answered.
Jesus said to them, "I tell you the
truth, the tax collectors and the prostitutes are entering the kingdom of God
ahead of you. 32For John came to you to
show you the way of righteousness, and
you did not believe him, but the tax
collectors and the prostitutes did. And
even after you saw this, you did not
repent and believe him.

READING FROM PROVERBS
Proverbs 3:21–35

21My son, preserve sound judgment
and discernment,
do not let them out of your sight;
22they will be life for you,
an ornament to grace your neck.
23Then you will go on your way in
safety,
and your foot will not stumble;
24when you lie down, you will not be
afraid;
when you lie down, your sleep will
be sweet.
25Have no fear of sudden disaster
or of the ruin that overtakes the
wicked,
26for the LORD will be your confidence
and will keep your foot from being
snared.

27Do not withhold good from those
who deserve it,
when it is in your power to act.
28Do not say to your neighbour,
"Come back later; I'll give it
tomorrow"—
when you now have it with you.

29Do not plot harm against your
neighbour,
who lives trustfully near you.
30Do not accuse a man for no reason—
when he has done you no harm.

31Do not envy a violent man
or choose any of his ways,
32for the LORD detests a perverse man
but takes the upright into his
confidence.

33The LORD's curse is on the house of
the wicked,
but he blesses the home of the
righteous.
34He mocks proud mockers
but gives grace to the humble.
35The wise inherit honour,
but fools he holds up to shame.

FEBRUARY 2

OLD TESTAMENT READING
Job 25:1–29:25

Bildad

25 Then Bildad the Shuhite replied:

2"Dominion and awe belong to God;
he establishes order in the heights of heaven.
3Can his forces be numbered?
Upon whom does his light not rise?
4How then can a man be righteous before God?
How can one born of woman be pure?
5If even the moon is not bright
and the stars are not pure in his eyes,
6how much less man, who is but a maggot—
a son of man, who is only a worm!"

Job

26 Then Job replied:

2"How you have helped the powerless!
How you have saved the arm that is feeble!
3What advice you have offered to one without wisdom!
And what great insight you have displayed!
4Who has helped you utter these words?
And whose spirit spoke from your mouth?

5"The dead are in deep anguish,
those beneath the waters and all that live in them.
6Death is naked before God;
Destruction lies uncovered.
7He spreads out the northern ⌊skies⌋ over empty space;
he suspends the earth over nothing.
8He wraps up the waters in his clouds,
yet the clouds do not burst under their weight.
9He covers the face of the full moon,
spreading his clouds over it.
10He marks out the horizon on the face of the waters
for a boundary between light and darkness.
11The pillars of the heavens quake,
aghast at his rebuke.
12By his power he churned up the sea;
by his wisdom he cut Rahab to pieces.
13By his breath the skies became fair;
his hand pierced the gliding serpent.
14And these are but the outer fringe of his works;
how faint the whisper we hear of him!
Who then can understand the thunder of his power?"

27 And Job continued his discourse:

2"As surely as God lives, who has denied me justice,
the Almighty, who has made me taste bitterness of soul,
3as long as I have life within me,
the breath of God in my nostrils,
4my lips will not speak wickedness,
and my tongue will utter no deceit.
5I will never admit you are in the right;
till I die, I will not deny my integrity.
6I will maintain my righteousness and never let go of it;
my conscience will not reproach me as long as I live.

7"May my enemies be like the wicked,
my adversaries like the unjust!

8For what hope has the godless when
he is cut off,
when God takes away his life?
9Does God listen to his cry
when distress comes upon him?
10Will he find delight in the Almighty?
Will he call upon God at all times?

11"I will teach you about the power of
God;
the ways of the Almighty I will not
conceal.
12You have all seen this yourselves.
Why then this meaningless talk?

13"Here is the fate God allots to the
wicked,
the heritage a ruthless man
receives from the Almighty:
14However many his children, their
fate is the sword;
his offspring will never have
enough to eat.
15The plague will bury those who
survive him,
and their widows will not weep for
them.
16Though he heaps up silver like dust
and clothes like piles of clay,
17what he lays up the righteous will
wear,
and the innocent will divide his
silver.
18The house he builds is like a moth's
cocoon,
like a hut made by a watchman.
19He lies down wealthy, but will do so
no more;
when he opens his eyes, all is gone.
20Terrors overtake him like a flood;
a tempest snatches him away in the
night.
21The east wind carries him off, and he
is gone;
it sweeps him out of his place.
22It hurls itself against him without
mercy
as he flees headlong from its
power.
23It claps its hands in derision
and hisses him out of his place.

28 "There is a mine for silver
and a place where gold is
refined.
2Iron is taken from the earth,
and copper is smelted from ore.
3Man puts an end to the darkness;
he searches the farthest recesses
for ore in the blackest darkness.
4Far from where people dwell he cuts
a shaft,
in places forgotten by the foot of
man;
far from men he dangles and
sways.
5The earth, from which food comes,
is transformed below as by fire;
6sapphires come from its rocks,
and its dust contains nuggets of
gold.
7No bird of prey knows that hidden
path,
no falcon's eye has seen it.
8Proud beasts do not set foot on it,
and no lion prowls there.
9Man's hand assaults the flinty rock
and lays bare the roots of the
mountains.
10He tunnels through the rock;
his eyes see all its treasures.
11He searches the sources of the rivers
and brings hidden things to light.

12"But where can wisdom be found?
Where does understanding dwell?
13Man does not comprehend its worth;
it cannot be found in the land of
the living.
14The deep says, 'It is not in me';
the sea says, 'It is not with me.'
15It cannot be bought with the finest
gold,
nor can its price be weighed in
silver.
16It cannot be bought with the gold of
Ophir,
with precious onyx or sapphires.
17Neither gold nor crystal can compare
with it,
nor can it be had for jewels of
gold.
18Coral and jasper are not worthy of
mention;

the price of wisdom is beyond
rubies.
19The topaz of Cush cannot compare
with it;
it cannot be bought with pure gold.

20"Where then does wisdom come
from?
Where does understanding dwell?
21It is hidden from the eyes of every
living thing,
concealed even from the birds of
the air.
22Destruction and Death say,
'Only a rumour of it has reached
our ears.'
23God understands the way to it
and he alone knows where it
dwells,
24for he views the ends of the earth
and sees everything under the
heavens.
25When he established the force of the
wind
and measured out the waters,
26when he made a decree for the rain
and a path for the thunderstorm,
27then he looked at wisdom and
appraised it;
he confirmed it and tested it.
28And he said to man,
'The fear of the Lord—that is
wisdom,
and to shun evil is
understanding.'"

29 Job continued his discourse:
2"How I long for the months gone by,
for the days when God watched
over me,
3when his lamp shone upon my head
and by his light I walked through
darkness!
4Oh, for the days when I was in my
prime,
when God's intimate friendship
blessed my house,
5when the Almighty was still with me
and my children were around me,
6when my path was drenched with
cream
and the rock poured out for me
streams of olive oil.

7"When I went to the gate of the city
and took my seat in the public
square,
8the young men saw me and stepped
aside
and the old men rose to their feet;
9the chief men refrained from
speaking
and covered their mouths with
their hands;
10the voices of the nobles were hushed,
and their tongues stuck to the roof
of their mouths.
11Whoever heard me spoke well of me,
and those who saw me commended
me,
12because I rescued the poor who cried
for help,
and the fatherless who had none to
assist him.
13The man who was dying blessed me;
I made the widow's heart sing.
14I put on righteousness as my clothing;
justice was my robe and my turban.
15I was eyes to the blind
and feet to the lame.
16I was a father to the needy;
I took up the case of the stranger.
17I broke the fangs of the wicked
and snatched the victims from
their teeth.

18"I thought, 'I shall die in my own
house,
my days as numerous as the grains
of sand.
19My roots will reach to the water,
and the dew will lie all night on my
branches.
20My glory will remain fresh in me,
the bow ever new in my hand.'

21"Men listened to me expectantly,
waiting in silence for my counsel.
22After I had spoken, they spoke no
more;
my words fell gently on their ears.
23They waited for me as for showers
and drank in my words as the
spring rain.

24When I smiled at them, they scarcely
believed it;
the light of my face was precious to
them.
25I chose the way for them and sat as
their chief;
I dwelt as a king among his troops;
I was like one who comforts
mourners.

NEW TESTAMENT READING
Matthew 21:33–22:14

The Parable of the Tenants

33"Listen to another parable: There
was a landowner who planted a
vineyard. He put a wall around it, dug a
winepress in it and built a watchtower.
Then he rented the vineyard to some
farmers and went away on a journey.
34When the harvest time approached,
he sent his servants to the tenants to
collect his fruit.

35"The tenants seized his servants;
they beat one, killed another, and
stoned a third. 36Then he sent other
servants to them, more than the first
time, and the tenants treated them in
the same way. 37Last of all, he sent his
son to them. 'They will respect my son,'
he said.

38"But when the tenants saw the son,
they said to each other, 'This is the heir.
Come, let's kill him and take his inheritance.' 39So they took him and threw him
out of the vineyard and killed him.

40"Therefore, when the owner of the
vineyard comes, what will he do to
those tenants?"

41"He will bring those wretches to a
wretched end," they replied, "and he
will rent the vineyard to other tenants,
who will give him his share of the crop at
harvest time."

42Jesus said to them, "Have you
never read in the Scriptures:

" 'The stone the builders rejected
has become the capstone;
the Lord has done this,
and it is marvellous in our eyes'?

43"Therefore I tell you that the kingdom of God will be taken away from
you and given to a people who will
produce its fruit. 44He who falls on this
stone will be broken to pieces, but he on
whom it falls will be crushed."

45When the chief priests and the
Pharisees heard Jesus' parables, they
knew he was talking about them. 46They
looked for a way to arrest him, but
they were afraid of the crowd because
the people held that he was a prophet.

The Parable of the Wedding Banquet

22 Jesus spoke to them again in
parables, saying: 2"The kingdom of heaven is like a king who prepared a wedding banquet for his son.
3He sent his servants to those who had
been invited to the banquet to tell them
to come, but they refused to come.

4"Then he sent some more servants
and said, 'Tell those who have been
invited that I have prepared my dinner:
My oxen and fattened cattle have been
slaughtered, and everything is ready.
Come to the wedding banquet.'

5"But they paid no attention and
went off—one to his field, another to
his business. 6The rest seized his servants, ill-treated them and killed them.
7The king was enraged. He sent his
army and destroyed those murderers
and burned their city.

8"Then he said to his servants, 'The
wedding banquet is ready, but those I
invited did not deserve to come. 9Go to
the street corners and invite to the banquet anyone you find.' 10So the servants
went out into the streets and gathered
all the people they could find, both good
and bad, and the wedding hall was filled
with guests.

11"But when the king came in to see
the guests, he noticed a man there who
was not wearing wedding clothes.
12'Friend,' he asked, 'how did you get in
here without wedding clothes?' The
man was speechless.

13"Then the king told the attendants,
'Tie him hand and foot, and throw him

outside, into the darkness, where there will be weeping and gnashing of teeth.'

14"For many are invited, but few are chosen."

READING FROM PSALMS
Psalm 18:7–15

7The earth trembled and quaked,
and the foundations of the mountains shook;
they trembled because he was angry.
8Smoke rose from his nostrils;
consuming fire came from his mouth,
burning coals blazed out of it.
9He parted the heavens and came down;
dark clouds were under his feet.
10He mounted the cherubim and flew;
he soared on the wings of the wind.
11He made darkness his covering, his canopy around him—
the dark rain clouds of the sky.
12Out of the brightness of his presence clouds advanced,
with hailstones and bolts of lightning.
13The LORD thundered from heaven;
the voice of the Most High resounded.
14He shot his arrows and scattered ⌞the enemies⌟,
great bolts of lightning and routed them.
15The valleys of the sea were exposed
and the foundations of the earth laid bare
at your rebuke, O LORD,
at the blast of breath from your nostrils.

FEBRUARY 3

DAY 34

OLD TESTAMENT READING
Job 30:1–32:22

30 "But now they mock me,
men younger than I,
whose fathers I would have disdained
to put with my sheep dogs.
2Of what use was the strength of their hands to me,
since their vigour had gone from them?
3Haggard from want and hunger,
they roamed the parched land
in desolate wastelands at night.
4In the brush they gathered salt herbs,
and their food was the root of the broom tree.
5They were banished from their fellow-men,
shouted at as if they were thieves.
6They were forced to live in the dry stream beds,
among the rocks and in holes in the ground.
7They brayed among the bushes
and huddled in the undergrowth.
8A base and nameless brood,
they were driven out of the land.

9"And now their sons mock me in song;
I have become a byword among them.
10They detest me and keep their distance;
they do not hesitate to spit in my face.
11Now that God has unstrung my bow and afflicted me,
they throw off restraint in my presence.
12On my right the tribe attacks;
they lay snares for my feet,

they build their siege ramps against
me.
13They break up my road;
they succeed in destroying me—
without anyone's helping them.
14They advance as through a gaping
breach;
amid the ruins they come rolling in.
15Terrors overwhelm me;
my dignity is driven away as by the
wind,
my safety vanishes like a cloud.

16"And now my life ebbs away;
days of suffering grip me.
17Night pierces my bones;
my gnawing pains never rest.
18In his great power ⌞God⌟ becomes
like clothing to me;
he binds me like the neck of my
garment.
19He throws me into the mud,
and I am reduced to dust and
ashes.

20"I cry out to you, O God, but you do
not answer;
I stand up, but you merely look at
me.
21You turn on me ruthlessly;
with the might of your hand you
attack me.
22You snatch me up and drive me
before the wind;
you toss me about in the storm.
23I know you will bring me down to
death,
to the place appointed for all the
living.

24"Surely no-one lays a hand on a
broken man
when he cries for help in his
distress.
25Have I not wept for those in trouble?
Has not my soul grieved for the
poor?
26Yet when I hoped for good, evil
came;
when I looked for light, then came
darkness.
27The churning inside me never stops;
days of suffering confront me.
28I go about blackened, but not by the
sun;
I stand up in the assembly and cry
for help.
29I have become a brother of jackals,
a companion of owls.
30My skin grows black and peels;
my body burns with fever.
31My harp is tuned to mourning,
and my flute to the sound of
wailing.

31 "I made a covenant with my
eyes
not to look lustfully at a girl.
2For what is man's lot from God
above,
his heritage from the Almighty on
high?
3Is it not ruin for the wicked,
disaster for those who do wrong?
4Does he not see my ways
and count my every step?

5"If I have walked in falsehood
or my foot has hurried after
deceit—
6let God weigh me in honest scales
and he will know that I am
blameless—
7if my steps have turned from the
path,
if my heart has been led by my
eyes,
or if my hands have been defiled,
8then may others eat what I have
sown,
and may my crops be uprooted.

9"If my heart has been enticed by a
woman,
or if I have lurked at my
neighbour's door,
10then may my wife grind another
man's grain,
and may other men sleep with her.
11For that would have been shameful,
a sin to be judged.
12It is a fire that burns to Destruction;
it would have uprooted my harvest.

13"If I have denied justice to my
menservants and maidservants

when they had a grievance against
me,
14what will I do when God confronts
me?
What will I answer when called to
account?
15Did not he who made me in the
womb make them?
Did not the same one form us both
within our mothers?

16"If I have denied the desires of the
poor
or let the eyes of the widow grow
weary,
17if I have kept my bread to myself,
not sharing it with the fatherless—
18but from my youth I reared him as
would a father,
and from my birth I guided the
widow—
19if I have seen anyone perishing for
lack of clothing,
or a needy man without a garment,
20and his heart did not bless me
for warming him with the fleece
from my sheep,
21if I have raised my hand against the
fatherless,
knowing that I had influence in
court,
22then let my arm fall from the
shoulder,
let it be broken off at the joint.
23For I dreaded destruction from God,
and for fear of his splendour I
could not do such things.

24"If I have put my trust in gold
or said to pure gold, 'You are my
security,'
25if I have rejoiced over my great
wealth,
the fortune my hands had gained,
26if I have regarded the sun in its
radiance
or the moon moving in splendour,
27so that my heart was secretly enticed
and my hand offered them a kiss of
homage,
28then these also would be sins to be
judged,
for I would have been unfaithful to
God on high.

29"If I have rejoiced at my enemy's
misfortune
or gloated over the trouble that
came to him—
30I have not allowed my mouth to sin
by invoking a curse against his
life—
31if the men of my household have
never said,
'Who has not had his fill of Job's
meat?'—
32but no stranger had to spend the
night in the street,
for my door was always open to the
traveller—
33if I have concealed my sin as men do,
by hiding my guilt in my heart
34because I so feared the crowd
and so dreaded the contempt of the
clans
that I kept silent and would not go
outside—

35("Oh, that I had someone to hear
me!
I sign now my defence—let the
Almighty answer me;
let my accuser put his indictment in
writing.
36Surely I would wear it on my
shoulder,
I would put it on like a crown.
37I would give him an account of my
every step;
like a prince I would approach
him.)—

38"if my land cries out against me
and all its furrows are wet with
tears,
39if I have devoured its yield without
payment
or broken the spirit of its tenants,
40then let briers come up instead of
wheat
and weeds instead of barley."

The words of Job are ended.

Elihu

32 So these three men stopped
answering Job, because he was
righteous in his own eyes. 2But Elihu
son of Barakel the Buzite, of the family
of Ram, became very angry with Job for
justifying himself rather than God. 3He
was also angry with the three friends,
because they had found no way to refute
Job, and yet had condemned him. 4Now
Elihu had waited before speaking to Job
because they were older than he. 5But
when he saw that the three men had
nothing more to say, his anger was
aroused.
6So Elihu son of Barakel the Buzite
said:

"I am young in years,
and you are old;
that is why I was fearful,
not daring to tell you what I know.
7I thought, 'Age should speak;
advanced years should teach
wisdom.'
8But it is the spirit in a man,
the breath of the Almighty, that
gives him understanding.
9It is not only the old who are wise,
not only the aged who understand
what is right.

10"Therefore I say: Listen to me;
I too will tell you what I know.
11I waited while you spoke,
I listened to your reasoning;
while you were searching for words,
12 I gave you my full attention.
But not one of you has proved Job
wrong;
none of you has answered his
arguments.
13Do not say, 'We have found wisdom;
let God refute him, not man.'
14But Job has not marshalled his words
against me,
and I will not answer him with your
arguments.

15"They are dismayed and have no
more to say;
words have failed them.
16Must I wait, now that they are silent,
now that they stand there with no
reply?
17I too will have my say;
I too will tell what I know.
18For I am full of words,
and the spirit within me compels
me;
19inside I am like bottled-up wine,
like new wineskins ready to burst.
20I must speak and find relief;
I must open my lips and reply.
21I will show partiality to no-one,
nor will I flatter any man;
22for if I were skilled in flattery,
my Maker would soon take me
away.

NEW TESTAMENT READING
Matthew 22:15–46

Paying Taxes to Caesar

15Then the Pharisees went out and
laid plans to trap him in his words.
16They sent their disciples to him along
with the Herodians. "Teacher," they
said, "we know you are a man of integrity and that you teach the way of God
in accordance with the truth. You aren't
swayed by men, because you pay no
attention to who they are. 17Tell us
then, what is your opinion? Is it right to
pay taxes to Caesar or not?"
18But Jesus, knowing their evil intent,
said, "You hypocrites, why are you
trying to trap me? 19Show me the coin
used for paying the tax." They brought
him a denarius, 20and he asked them,
"Whose portrait is this? And whose
inscription?"
21"Caesar's," they replied.
Then he said to them, "Give to
Caesar what is Caesar's, and to God
what is God's."
22When they heard this, they were
amazed. So they left him and went
away.

Marriage at the Resurrection

23That same day the Sadducees, who
say there is no resurrection, came to

him with a question. 24"Teacher," they
said, "Moses told us that if a man dies
without having children, his brother
must marry the widow and have children for him. 25Now there were seven
brothers among us. The first one married and died, and since he had no children, he left his wife to his brother.
26The same thing happened to the
second and third brother, right on down
to the seventh. 27Finally, the woman
died. 28Now then, at the resurrection,
whose wife will she be of the seven,
since all of them were married to her?"

29Jesus replied, "You are in error
because you do not know the Scriptures
or the power of God. 30At the resurrection people will neither marry nor be
given in marriage; they will be like the
angels in heaven. 31But about the resurrection of the dead—have you not read
what God said to you, 32'I am the God
of Abraham, the God of Isaac, and the
God of Jacob'? He is not the God of the
dead but of the living."

33When the crowds heard this, they
were astonished at his teaching.

The Greatest Commandment

34Hearing that Jesus had silenced the
Sadducees, the Pharisees got together.
35One of them, an expert in the law,
tested him with this question:
36"Teacher, which is the greatest commandment in the Law?"

37Jesus replied: " 'Love the Lord your
God with all your heart and with all
your soul and with all your mind.' 38This
is the first and greatest commandment.
39And the second is like it: 'Love your
neighbour as yourself.' 40All the Law
and the Prophets hang on these two
commandments."

Whose Son Is the Christ?

41While the Pharisees were gathered
together, Jesus asked them, 42"What do
you think about the Christ? Whose son
is he?"

"The son of David," they replied.

43He said to them, "How is it then
that David, speaking by the Spirit, calls
him 'Lord'? For he says,

44" 'The Lord said to my Lord:
"Sit at my right hand
until I put your enemies
under your feet." '

45If then David calls him 'Lord', how
can he be his son?" 46No-one could say a
word in reply, and from that day on
no-one dared to ask him any more
questions.

READING FROM PSALMS
Psalm 18:16–24

16He reached down from on high and
took hold of me;
he drew me out of deep waters.
17He rescued me from my powerful
enemy,
from my foes, who were too strong
for me.
18They confronted me in the day of my
disaster,
but the LORD was my support.
19He brought me out into a spacious
place;
he rescued me because he
delighted in me.

20The LORD has dealt with me
according to my righteousness;
according to the cleanness of my
hands he has rewarded me.
21For I have kept the ways of the LORD;
I have not done evil by turning
from my God.
22All his laws are before me;
I have not turned away from his
decrees.
23I have been blameless before him
and have kept myself from sin.
24The LORD has rewarded me
according to my righteousness,
according to the cleanness of my
hands in his sight.

FEBRUARY 4

OLD TESTAMENT READING
Job 33:1–34:37

33 "But now, Job, listen to my words;
pay attention to everything I say.
2I am about to open my mouth;
my words are on the tip of my tongue.
3My words come from an upright heart;
my lips sincerely speak what I know.
4The Spirit of God has made me;
the breath of the Almighty gives me life.
5Answer me then, if you can;
prepare yourself and confront me.
6I am just like you before God;
I too have been taken from clay.
7No fear of me should alarm you,
nor should my hand be heavy upon you.

8"But you have said in my hearing—
I heard the very words—
9'I am pure and without sin;
I am clean and free from guilt.
10Yet God has found fault with me;
he considers me his enemy.
11He fastens my feet in shackles;
he keeps close watch on all my paths.'

12"But I tell you, in this you are not right,
for God is greater than man.
13Why do you complain to him
that he answers none of man's words?
14For God does speak—now one way, now another—
though man may not perceive it.
15In a dream, in a vision of the night,
when deep sleep falls on men
as they slumber in their beds,
16he may speak in their ears
and terrify them with warnings,
17to turn man from wrongdoing
and keep him from pride,
18to preserve his soul from the pit,
his life from perishing by the sword.
19Or a man may be chastened on a bed of pain
with constant distress in his bones,
20so that his very being finds food repulsive
and his soul loathes the choicest meal.
21His flesh wastes away to nothing,
and his bones, once hidden, now stick out.
22His soul draws near to the pit,
and his life to the messengers of death.

23"Yet if there is an angel on his side
as a mediator, one out of a thousand,
to tell a man what is right for him,
24to be gracious to him and say,
'Spare him from going down to the pit;
I have found a ransom for him'—
25then his flesh is renewed like a child's;
it is restored as in the days of his youth.
26He prays to God and finds favour with him,
he sees God's face and shouts for joy;
he is restored by God to his righteous state.
27Then he comes to men and says,
'I have sinned, and perverted what was right,
but I did not get what I deserved.
28He redeemed my soul from going down to the pit,
and I shall live to enjoy the light.'

29"God does all these things to a man—
twice, even three times—

30to turn back his soul from the pit,
that the light of life may shine on him.

31"Pay attention, Job, and listen to me;
be silent, and I will speak.
32If you have anything to say, answer me;
speak up, for I want you to be cleared.
33But if not, then listen to me;
be silent, and I will teach you wisdom."

34 Then Elihu said:

2"Hear my words, you wise men;
listen to me, you men of learning.
3For the ear tests words
as the tongue tastes food.
4Let us discern for ourselves what is right;
let us learn together what is good.

5"Job says, 'I am innocent,
but God denies me justice.
6Although I am right,
I am considered a liar;
although I am guiltless,
his arrow inflicts an incurable wound.'
7What man is like Job,
who drinks scorn like water?
8He keeps company with evildoers;
he associates with wicked men.
9For he says, 'It profits a man nothing
when he tries to please God.'

10"So listen to me, you men of understanding.
Far be it from God to do evil,
from the Almighty to do wrong.
11He repays a man for what he has done;
he brings upon him what his conduct deserves.
12It is unthinkable that God would do wrong,
that the Almighty would pervert justice.
13Who appointed him over the earth?
Who put him in charge of the whole world?
14If it were his intention
and he withdrew his spirit and breath,
15all mankind would perish together
and man would return to the dust.

16"If you have understanding, hear this;
listen to what I say.
17Can he who hates justice govern?
Will you condemn the just and mighty One?
18Is he not the One who says to kings,
'You are worthless,'
and to nobles, 'You are wicked,'
19who shows no partiality to princes
and does not favour the rich over the poor,
for they are all the work of his hands?
20They die in an instant, in the middle of the night;
the people are shaken and they pass away;
the mighty are removed without human hand.

21"His eyes are on the ways of men;
he sees their every step.
22There is no dark place, no deep shadow,
where evildoers can hide.
23God has no need to examine men further,
that they should come before him for judgment.
24Without enquiry he shatters the mighty
and sets up others in their place.
25Because he takes note of their deeds,
he overthrows them in the night
and they are crushed.
26He punishes them for their wickedness
where everyone can see them,
27because they turned from following him
and had no regard for any of his ways.

28They caused the cry of the poor to
come before him,
so that he heard the cry of the
needy.
29But if he remains silent, who can
condemn him?
If he hides his face, who can see
him?
Yet he is over man and nation alike,
30 to keep a godless man from ruling,
from laying snares for the people.

31"Suppose a man says to God,
'I am guilty but will offend no
more.
32Teach me what I cannot see;
if I have done wrong, I will not do
so again.'
33Should God then reward you on your
terms,
when you refuse to repent?
You must decide, not I;
so tell me what you know.

34"Men of understanding declare,
wise men who hear me say to me,
35'Job speaks without knowledge;
his words lack insight.'
36Oh, that Job might be tested to the
utmost
for answering like a wicked man!
37To his sin he adds rebellion;
scornfully he claps his hands
among us
and multiplies his words against
God."

NEW TESTAMENT READING

Matthew 23:1–39

Seven Woes

23 Then Jesus said to the crowds
and to his disciples: 2"The
teachers of the law and the Pharisees sit
in Moses' seat. 3So you must obey them
and do everything they tell you. But do
not do what they do, for they do not
practise what they preach. 4They tie up
heavy loads and put them on men's
shoulders, but they themselves are not
willing to lift a finger to move them.

5"Everything they do is done for men
to see: They make their phylacteries
wide and the tassels on their garments
long; 6they love the place of honour at
banquets and the most important seats
in the synagogues; 7they love to be
greeted in the market-places and to
have men call them 'Rabbi'.

8"But you are not to be called
'Rabbi', for you have only one Master
and you are all brothers. 9And do not
call anyone on earth 'father', for you
have one Father, and he is in heaven.
10Nor are you to be called 'teacher', for
you have one Teacher, the Christ. 11The
greatest among you will be your servant. 12For whoever exalts himself will
be humbled, and whoever humbles
himself will be exalted.

13"Woe to you, teachers of the law
and Pharisees, you hypocrites! You
shut the kingdom of heaven in men's
faces. You yourselves do not enter, nor
will you let those enter who are trying
to.

15"Woe to you, teachers of the law
and Pharisees, you hypocrites! You
travel over land and sea to win a single
convert, and when he becomes one, you
make him twice as much a son of hell as
you are.

16"Woe to you, blind guides! You
say, 'If anyone swears by the temple, it
means nothing; but if anyone swears by
the gold of the temple, he is bound by
his oath.' 17You blind fools! Which is
greater: the gold, or the temple that
makes the gold sacred? 18You also say,
'If anyone swears by the altar, it means
nothing; but if anyone swears by the gift
on it, he is bound by his oath.' 19You
blind men! Which is greater: the gift, or
the altar that makes the gift sacred?
20Therefore, he who swears by the altar
swears by it and by everything on it.
21And he who swears by the temple
swears by it and by the one who dwells
in it. 22And he who swears by heaven
swears by God's throne and by the one
who sits on it.

23"Woe to you, teachers of the law
and Pharisees, you hypocrites! You give

a tenth of your spices—mint, dill and
cummin. But you have neglected the
more important matters of the law—
justice, mercy and faithfulness. You
should have practised the latter, without neglecting the former. 24You blind
guides! You strain out a gnat but
swallow a camel.
25"Woe to you, teachers of the law
and Pharisees, you hypocrites! You
clean the outside of the cup and dish,
but inside they are full of greed and
self-indulgence. 26Blind Pharisee! First
clean the inside of the cup and dish, and
then the outside also will be clean.
27"Woe to you, teachers of the law
and Pharisees, you hypocrites! You are
like whitewashed tombs, which look
beautiful on the outside but on the inside are full of dead men's bones and
everything unclean. 28In the same way,
on the outside you appear to people as
righteous but on the inside you are full
of hypocrisy and wickedness.
29"Woe to you, teachers of the law
and Pharisees, you hypocrites! You
build tombs for the prophets and decorate the graves of the righteous. 30And
you say, 'If we had lived in the days of
our forefathers, we would not have
taken part with them in shedding the
blood of the prophets.' 31So you testify
against yourselves that you are the descendants of those who murdered the
prophets. 32Fill up, then, the measure of
the sin of your forefathers!
33"You snakes! You brood of vipers!
How will you escape being condemned
to hell? 34Therefore I am sending you
prophets and wise men and teachers.
Some of them you will kill and crucify;
others you will flog in your synagogues
and pursue from town to town. 35And so
upon you will come all the righteous
blood that has been shed on earth, from
the blood of righteous Abel to the blood
of Zechariah son of Berakiah, whom
you murdered between the temple and
the altar. 36I tell you the truth, all this
will come upon this generation.
37"O Jerusalem, Jerusalem, you who
kill the prophets and stone those sent to
you, how often I have longed to gather
your children together, as a hen gathers
her chicks under her wings, but you
were not willing. 38Look, your house is
left to you desolate. 39For I tell you, you
will not see me again until you say,
'Blessed is he who comes in the name of
the Lord.'"

READING FROM PSALMS

Psalm 18:25–36

25To the faithful you show yourself
faithful,
to the blameless you show yourself
blameless,
26to the pure you show yourself pure,
but to the crooked you show
yourself shrewd.
27You save the humble
but bring low those whose eyes are
haughty.
28You, O LORD, keep my lamp
burning;
my God turns my darkness into
light.
29With your help I can advance against
a troop;
with my God I can scale a wall.

30As for God, his way is perfect;
the word of the LORD is flawless.
He is a shield
for all who take refuge in him.
31For who is God besides the LORD?
And who is the Rock except our
God?
32It is God who arms me with strength
and makes my way perfect.
33He makes my feet like the feet of a
deer;
he enables me to stand on the
heights.
34He trains my hands for battle;
my arms can bend a bow of bronze.
35You give me your shield of victory,
and your right hand sustains me;
you stoop down to make me great.
36You broaden the path beneath me,
so that my ankles do not turn over.

FEBRUARY 5

OLD TESTAMENT READING

Job 35:1–37:24

35 Then Elihu said:

2"Do you think this is just?
You say, 'I shall be cleared by God.'
3Yet you ask him, 'What profit is it to me,
and what do I gain by not sinning?'

4"I would like to reply to you
and to your friends with you.
5Look up at the heavens and see;
gaze at the clouds so high above you.
6If you sin, how does that affect him?
If your sins are many, what does that do to him?
7If you are righteous, what do you give to him,
or what does he receive from your hand?
8Your wickedness affects only a man like yourself,
and your righteousness only the sons of men.

9"Men cry out under a load of oppression;
they plead for relief from the arm of the powerful.
10But no-one says, 'Where is God my Maker,
who gives songs in the night,
11who teaches more to us than to the beasts of the earth
and makes us wiser than the birds of the air?'
12He does not answer when men cry out
because of the arrogance of the wicked.
13Indeed, God does not listen to their empty plea;
the Almighty pays no attention to it.
14How much less, then, will he listen
when you say that you do not see him,
that your case is before him
and you must wait for him,
15and further, that his anger never punishes
and he does not take the least notice of wickedness.
16So Job opens his mouth with empty talk;
without knowledge he multiplies words."

36 Elihu continued:

2"Bear with me a little longer and I will show you
that there is more to be said on God's behalf.
3I get my knowledge from afar;
I will ascribe justice to my Maker.
4Be assured that my words are not false;
one perfect in knowledge is with you.

5"God is mighty, but does not despise men;
he is mighty, and firm in his purpose.
6He does not keep the wicked alive
but gives the afflicted their rights.
7He does not take his eyes off the righteous;
he enthrones them with kings
and exalts them for ever.
8But if men are bound in chains,
held fast by cords of affliction,
9he tells them what they have done—
that they have sinned arrogantly.
10He makes them listen to correction
and commands them to repent of their evil.
11If they obey and serve him,
they will spend the rest of their days in prosperity
and their years in contentment.

[12]But if they do not listen,
they will perish by the sword
and die without knowledge.

[13]"The godless in heart harbour resentment;
even when he fetters them, they do not cry for help.
[14]They die in their youth,
among male prostitutes of the shrines.
[15]But those who suffer he delivers in their suffering;
he speaks to them in their affliction.

[16]"He is wooing you from the jaws of distress
to a spacious place free from restriction,
to the comfort of your table laden with choice food.
[17]But now you are laden with the judgment due to the wicked;
judgment and justice have taken hold of you.
[18]Be careful that no-one entices you by riches;
do not let a large bribe turn you aside.
[19]Would your wealth
or even all your mighty efforts
sustain you so you would not be in distress?
[20]Do not long for the night,
to drag people away from their homes.
[21]Beware of turning to evil,
which you seem to prefer to affliction.

[22]"God is exalted in his power.
Who is a teacher like him?
[23]Who has prescribed his ways for him,
or said to him, 'You have done wrong'?
[24]Remember to extol his work,
which men have praised in song.
[25]All mankind has seen it;
men gaze on it from afar.
[26]How great is God—beyond our understanding!
The number of his years is past finding out.

[27]"He draws up the drops of water,
which distil as rain to the streams;
[28]the clouds pour down their moisture
and abundant showers fall on mankind.
[29]Who can understand how he spreads out the clouds,
how he thunders from his pavilion?
[30]See how he scatters his lightning about him,
bathing the depths of the sea.
[31]This is the way he governs the nations
and provides food in abundance.
[32]He fills his hands with lightning
and commands it to strike its mark.
[33]His thunder announces the coming storm;
even the cattle make known its approach.

37 "At this my heart pounds
and leaps from its place.
[2]Listen! Listen to the roar of his voice,
to the rumbling that comes from his mouth.
[3]He unleashes his lightning beneath the whole heaven
and sends it to the ends of the earth.
[4]After that comes the sound of his roar;
he thunders with his majestic voice.
When his voice resounds,
he holds nothing back.
[5]God's voice thunders in marvellous ways;
he does great things beyond our understanding.
[6]He says to the snow, 'Fall on the earth,'
and to the rain shower, 'Be a mighty downpour.'
[7]So that all men he has made may know his work,
he stops every man from his labour.
[8]The animals take cover;
they remain in their dens.

[9]The tempest comes out from its
chamber,
the cold from the driving winds.
[10]The breath of God produces ice,
and the broad waters become
frozen.
[11]He loads the clouds with moisture;
he scatters his lightning through
them.
[12]At his direction they swirl around
over the face of the whole earth
to do whatever he commands
them.
[13]He brings the clouds to punish men,
or to water his earth and show his
love.

[14]"Listen to this, Job;
stop and consider God's wonders.
[15]Do you know how God controls the
clouds
and makes his lightning flash?
[16]Do you know how the clouds hang
poised,
those wonders of him who is
perfect in knowledge?
[17]You who swelter in your clothes
when the land lies hushed under
the south wind,
[18]can you join him in spreading out the
skies,
hard as a mirror of cast bronze?

[19]"Tell us what we should say to him;
we cannot draw up our case
because of our darkness.
[20]Should he be told that I want to
speak?
Would any man ask to be
swallowed up?
[21]Now no-one can look at the sun,
bright as it is in the skies
after the wind has swept them
clean.
[22]Out of the north he comes in golden
splendour;
God comes in awesome majesty.
[23]The Almighty is beyond our reach
and exalted in power;
in his justice and great
righteousness, he does not
oppress.
[24]Therefore, men revere him,
for does he not have regard for all
the wise in heart?"

NEW TESTAMENT READING
Matthew 24:1–31

Signs of the End of the Age

24 Jesus left the temple and was
walking away when his disciples
came up to him to call his attention to its
buildings. [2]"Do you see all these
things?" he asked. "I tell you the truth,
not one stone here will be left on
another; every one will be thrown
down."
[3]As Jesus was sitting on the Mount of
Olives, the disciples came to him privately. "Tell us," they said, "when will
this happen, and what will be the sign of
your coming and of the end of the age?"
[4]Jesus answered: "Watch out that no-
one deceives you. [5]For many will come
in my name, claiming, 'I am the Christ,'
and will deceive many. [6]You will hear of
wars and rumours of wars, but see to it
that you are not alarmed. Such things
must happen, but the end is still to
come. [7]Nation will rise against nation,
and kingdom against kingdom. There
will be famines and earthquakes in
various places. [8]All these are the
beginning of birth-pains.
[9]"Then you will be handed over to be
persecuted and put to death, and you
will be hated by all nations because of
me. [10]At that time many will turn away
from the faith and will betray and hate
each other, [11]and many false prophets
will appear and deceive many people.
[12]Because of the increase of wickedness, the love of most will grow cold,
[13]but he who stands firm to the end will
be saved. [14]And this gospel of the kingdom will be preached in the whole
world as a testimony to all nations, and
then the end will come.
[15]"So when you see standing in the
holy place 'the abomination that causes
desolation', spoken of through the

prophet Daniel—let the reader understand—16then let those who are in
Judea flee to the mountains. 17Let no-
one on the roof of his house go down to
take anything out of the house. 18Let
no-one in the field go back to get his
cloak. 19How dreadful it will be in those
days for pregnant women and nursing
mothers! 20Pray that your flight will not
take place in winter or on the Sabbath.
21For then there will be great distress,
unequalled from the beginning of the
world until now—and never to be
equalled again. 22If those days had not
been cut short, no-one would survive,
but for the sake of the elect those days
will be shortened. 23At that time if anyone says to you, 'Look, here is the
Christ!' or, 'There he is!' do not believe
it. 24For false Christs and false prophets
will appear and perform great signs and
miracles to deceive even the elect—if
that were possible. 25See, I have told
you ahead of time.

26"So if anyone tells you, 'There he is,
out in the desert,' do not go out; or,
'Here he is, in the inner rooms,' do not
believe it. 27For as lightning that comes
from the east is visible even in the west,
so will be the coming of the Son of Man.
28Wherever there is a carcass, there the
vultures will gather.

29"Immediately after the distress of
those days

" 'the sun will be darkened,
  and the moon will not give its light;
the stars will fall from the sky,
  and the heavenly bodies will be
    shaken.'

30"At that time the sign of the Son of
Man will appear in the sky, and all the
nations of the earth will mourn. They
will see the Son of Man coming on the
clouds of the sky, with power and great
glory. 31And he will send his angels with
a loud trumpet call, and they will gather
his elect from the four winds, from one
end of the heavens to the other.

READING FROM PROVERBS
Proverbs 4:1–9

Wisdom Is Supreme

4 Listen, my sons, to a father's
    instruction;
  pay attention and gain
    understanding.
2I give you sound learning,
  so do not forsake my teaching.
3When I was a boy in my father's
    house,
  still tender, and an only child of my
    mother,
4he taught me and said,
  "Lay hold of my words with all
    your heart;
  keep my commands and you will
    live.
5Get wisdom, get understanding;
  do not forget my words or swerve
    from them.
6Do not forsake wisdom, and she will
    protect you;
  love her, and she will watch over
    you.
7Wisdom is supreme; therefore get
    wisdom.
  Though it cost all you have, get
    understanding.
8Esteem her, and she will exalt you;
  embrace her, and she will honour
    you.
9She will set a garland of grace on
    your head
  and present you with a crown of
    splendour."

OLD TESTAMENT READING

Job 38:1–40:2

The Lord Speaks

38 Then the LORD answered Job out of the storm. He said:

2"Who is this that darkens my counsel
with words without knowledge?
3Brace yourself like a man;
I will question you,
and you shall answer me.

4"Where were you when I laid the earth's foundation?
Tell me, if you understand.
5Who marked off its dimensions?
Surely you know!
Who stretched a measuring line across it?
6On what were its footings set,
or who laid its cornerstone—
7while the morning stars sang together
and all the angels shouted for joy?

8"Who shut up the sea behind doors
when it burst forth from the womb,
9when I made the clouds its garment
and wrapped it in thick darkness,
10when I fixed limits for it
and set its doors and bars in place,
11when I said, 'This far you may come and no farther;
here is where your proud waves halt'?

12"Have you ever given orders to the morning,
or shown the dawn its place,
13that it might take the earth by the edges
and shake the wicked out of it?
14The earth takes shape like clay under a seal;
its features stand out like those of a garment.
15The wicked are denied their light,
and their upraised arm is broken.

16"Have you journeyed to the springs of the sea
or walked in the recesses of the deep?
17Have the gates of death been shown to you?
Have you seen the gates of the shadow of death?
18Have you comprehended the vast expanses of the earth?
Tell me, if you know all this.

19"What is the way to the abode of light?
And where does darkness reside?
20Can you take them to their places?
Do you know the paths to their dwellings?
21Surely you know, for you were already born!
You have lived so many years!

22"Have you entered the storehouses of the snow
or seen the storehouses of the hail,
23which I reserve for times of trouble,
for days of war and battle?
24What is the way to the place where the lightning is dispersed,
or the place where the east winds are scattered over the earth?
25Who cuts a channel for the torrents of rain,
and a path for the thunderstorm,
26to water a land where no man lives,
a desert with no-one in it,
27to satisfy a desolate wasteland
and make it sprout with grass?
28Does the rain have a father?
Who fathers the drops of dew?
29From whose womb comes the ice?
Who gives birth to the frost from the heavens
30when the waters become hard as stone,
when the surface of the deep is frozen?

31"Can you bind the beautiful
Pleiades?
Can you loose the cords of Orion?
32Can you bring forth the constellations
in their seasons
or lead out the Bear with its cubs?
33Do you know the laws of the
heavens?
Can you set up ⌊God's⌋ dominion
over the earth?

34"Can you raise your voice to the
clouds
and cover yourself with a flood of
water?
35Do you send the lightning bolts on
their way?
Do they report to you, 'Here we
are'?
36Who endowed the heart with wisdom
or gave understanding to the mind?
37Who has the wisdom to count the
clouds?
Who can tip over the water jars of
the heavens
38when the dust becomes hard
and the clods of earth stick
together?

39"Do you hunt the prey for the lioness
and satisfy the hunger of the lions
40when they crouch in their dens
or lie in wait in a thicket?
41Who provides food for the raven
when its young cry out to God
and wander about for lack of food?

39 "Do you know when the
mountain goats give birth?
Do you watch when the doe bears
her fawn?
2Do you count the months till they
bear?
Do you know the time they give
birth?
3They crouch down and bring forth
their young;
their labour pains are ended.
4Their young thrive and grow strong
in the wilds;
they leave and do not return.

5"Who let the wild donkey go free?
Who untied his ropes?
6I gave him the wasteland as his home,
the salt flats as his habitat.
7He laughs at the commotion in the
town;
he does not hear a driver's shout.
8He ranges the hills for his pasture
and searches for any green thing.

9"Will the wild ox consent to serve
you?
Will he stay by your manger at
night?
10Can you hold him to the furrow with
a harness?
Will he till the valleys behind you?
11Will you rely on him for his great
strength?
Will you leave your heavy work to
him?
12Can you trust him to bring in your
grain
and gather it to your
threshing-floor?

13"The wings of the ostrich flap
joyfully,
but they cannot compare with the
pinions and feathers of the
stork.
14She lays her eggs on the ground
and lets them warm in the sand,
15unmindful that a foot may crush
them,
that some wild animal may trample
them.
16She treats her young harshly, as if
they were not hers;
she cares not that her labour was in
vain,
17for God did not endow her with
wisdom
or give her a share of good sense.
18Yet when she spreads her feathers to
run,
she laughs at horse and rider.

19"Do you give the horse his strength
or clothe his neck with a flowing
mane?
20Do you make him leap like a locust,

striking terror with his proud
snorting?
21He paws fiercely, rejoicing in his
strength,
and charges into the fray.
22He laughs at fear, afraid of nothing;
he does not shy away from the
sword.
23The quiver rattles against his side,
along with the flashing spear and
lance.
24In frenzied excitement he eats up the
ground;
he cannot stand still when the
trumpet sounds.
25At the blast of the trumpet he snorts,
'Aha!'
He catches the scent of battle from
afar,
the shout of commanders and the
battle cry.

26"Does the hawk take flight by your
wisdom
and spread his wings towards the
south?
27Does the eagle soar at your command
and build his nest on high?
28He dwells on a cliff and stays there at
night;
a rocky crag is his stronghold.
29From there he seeks out his food;
his eyes detect it from afar.
30His young ones feast on blood,
and where the slain are, there is
he."

40 The LORD said to Job:

2"Will the one who contends with the
Almighty correct him?
Let him who accuses God answer
him!"

NEW TESTAMENT READING
Matthew 24:32–25:13

32"Now learn this lesson from the
fig-tree: As soon as its twigs get tender
and its leaves come out, you know that
summer is near. 33Even so, when you
see all these things, you know that it is
near, right at the door. 34I tell you the
truth, this generation will certainly not
pass away until all these things have
happened. 35Heaven and earth will pass
away, but my words will never pass
away.

The Day and Hour Unknown

36"No-one knows about that day or
hour, not even the angels in heaven, nor
the Son, but only the Father. 37As it was
in the days of Noah, so it will be at the
coming of the Son of Man. 38For in the
days before the flood, people were eating and drinking, marrying and giving in
marriage, up to the day Noah entered
the ark; 39and they knew nothing about
what would happen until the flood came
and took them all away. That is how it
will be at the coming of the Son of Man.
40Two men will be in the field; one will
be taken and the other left. 41Two
women will be grinding with a hand
mill; one will be taken and the other
left.

42"Therefore keep watch, because
you do not know on what day your Lord
will come. 43But understand this: If the
owner of the house had known at what
time of night the thief was coming, he
would have kept watch and would not
have let his house be broken into. 44So
you also must be ready, because the Son
of Man will come at an hour when you
do not expect him.

45"Who then is the faithful and wise
servant, whom the master has put in
charge of the servants in his household
to give them their food at the proper
time? 46It will be good for that servant
whose master finds him doing so when
he returns. 47I tell you the truth, he will
put him in charge of all his possessions.
48But suppose that servant is wicked
and says to himself, 'My master is
staying away a long time,' 49and he then
begins to beat his fellow-servants and to
eat and drink with drunkards. 50The
master of that servant will come on a
day when he does not expect him and at

an hour he is not aware of. [51]He will cut him to pieces and assign him a place with the hypocrites, where there will be weeping and gnashing of teeth.

The Parable of the Ten Virgins

25 "At that time the kingdom of heaven will be like ten virgins who took their lamps and went out to
meet the bridegroom. [2]Five of them
were foolish and five were wise. [3]The
foolish ones took their lamps but did not
take any oil with them. [4]The wise,
however, took oil in jars along with
their lamps. [5]The bridegroom was a
long time in coming, and they all became drowsy and fell asleep.

[6]"At midnight the cry rang out: 'Here's the bridegroom! Come out to meet him!'

[7]"Then all the virgins woke up and
trimmed their lamps. [8]The foolish ones
said to the wise, 'Give us some of your oil; our lamps are going out.'

[9]" 'No,' they replied, 'there may not be enough for both us and you. Instead, go to those who sell oil and buy some for yourselves.'

[10]"But while they were on their way to buy the oil, the bridegroom arrived. The virgins who were ready went in with him to the wedding banquet. And the door was shut.

[11]"Later the others also came. 'Sir! Sir!' they said. 'Open the door for us!'

[12]"But he replied, 'I tell you the truth, I don't know you.'

[13]"Therefore keep watch, because you do not know the day or the hour.

READING FROM PSALMS
Psalm 18:37–42

[37]I pursued my enemies and overtook them;
I did not turn back till they were destroyed.
[38]I crushed them so that they could not rise;
they fell beneath my feet.
[39]You armed me with strength for battle;
you made my adversaries bow at my feet.
[40]You made my enemies turn their backs in flight,
and I destroyed my foes.
[41]They cried for help, but there was no-one to save them—
to the LORD, but he did not answer.
[42]I beat them as fine as dust borne on the wind;
I poured them out like mud in the streets.

FEBRUARY 7

DAY 38

OLD TESTAMENT READING
Job 40:3–42:17

[3]Then Job answered the LORD:

[4]"I am unworthy—how can I reply to you?
I put my hand over my mouth.
[5]I spoke once, but I have no answer—
twice, but I will say no more."

[6]Then the LORD spoke to Job out of the storm:

[7]"Brace yourself like a man;
I will question you,
and you shall answer me.

[8]"Would you discredit my justice?
Would you condemn me to justify yourself?

9Do you have an arm like God's,
and can your voice thunder like his?
10Then adorn yourself with glory and splendour,
and clothe yourself in honour and majesty.
11Unleash the fury of your wrath,
look at every proud man and bring him low,
12look at every proud man and humble him,
crush the wicked where they stand.
13Bury them all in the dust together;
shroud their faces in the grave.
14Then I myself will admit to you
that your own right hand can save you.

15"Look at the behemoth,
which I made along with you
and which feeds on grass like an ox.
16What strength he has in his loins,
what power in the muscles of his belly!
17His tail sways like a cedar;
the sinews of his thighs are close-knit.
18His bones are tubes of bronze,
his limbs like rods of iron.
19He ranks first among the works of God,
yet his Maker can approach him with his sword.
20The hills bring him their produce,
and all the wild animals play nearby.
21Under the lotus plant he lies,
hidden among the reeds in the marsh.
22The lotuses conceal him in their shadow;
the poplars by the stream surround him.
23When the river rages, he is not alarmed;
he is secure, though the Jordan should surge against his mouth.
24Can anyone capture him by the eyes,
or trap him and pierce his nose?

41 "Can you pull in the leviathan with a fishhook
or tie down his tongue with a rope?
2Can you put a cord through his nose
or pierce his jaw with a hook?
3Will he keep begging you for mercy?
Will he speak to you with gentle words?
4Will he make an agreement with you
for you to take him as your slave for life?
5Can you make a pet of him like a bird
or put him on a leash for your girls?
6Will traders barter for him?
Will they divide him up among the merchants?
7Can you fill his hide with harpoons
or his head with fishing spears?
8If you lay a hand on him,
you will remember the struggle and never do it again!
9Any hope of subduing him is false;
the mere sight of him is overpowering.
10No-one is fierce enough to rouse him.
Who then is able to stand against me?
11Who has a claim against me that I must pay?
Everything under heaven belongs to me.

12"I will not fail to speak of his limbs,
his strength and his graceful form.
13Who can strip off his outer coat?
Who would approach him with a bridle?
14Who dares open the doors of his mouth,
ringed about with his fearsome teeth?
15His back has rows of shields
tightly sealed together;
16each is so close to the next
that no air can pass between.
17They are joined fast to one another;
they cling together and cannot be parted.
18His snorting throws out flashes of light;
his eyes are like the rays of dawn.

[19]Firebrands stream from his mouth;
sparks of fire shoot out.
[20]Smoke pours from his nostrils
as from a boiling pot over a fire of reeds.
[21]His breath sets coals ablaze,
and flames dart from his mouth.
[22]Strength resides in his neck;
dismay goes before him.
[23]The folds of his flesh are tightly joined;
they are firm and immovable.
[24]His chest is hard as rock,
hard as a lower millstone.
[25]When he rises up, the mighty are terrified;
they retreat before his thrashing.
[26]The sword that reaches him has no effect,
nor does the spear or the dart or the javelin.
[27]Iron he treats like straw
and bronze like rotten wood.
[28]Arrows do not make him flee;
slingstones are like chaff to him.
[29]A club seems to him but a piece of straw;
he laughs at the rattling of the lance.
[30]His undersides are jagged potsherds,
leaving a trail in the mud like a threshing-sledge.
[31]He makes the depths churn like a boiling cauldron
and stirs up the sea like a pot of ointment.
[32]Behind him he leaves a glistening wake;
one would think the deep had white hair.
[33]Nothing on earth is his equal—
a creature without fear.
[34]He looks down on all that are haughty;
he is king over all that are proud."

Job

42 Then Job replied to the LORD:

[2]"I know that you can do all things;
no plan of yours can be thwarted.
[3]⌞You asked,⌟ 'Who is this that obscures my counsel without knowledge?'
Surely I spoke of things I did not understand,
things too wonderful for me to know.

[4]⌞"You said,⌟ 'Listen now, and I will speak;
I will question you,
and you shall answer me.'
[5]My ears had heard of you
but now my eyes have seen you.
[6]Therefore I despise myself
and repent in dust and ashes."

Epilogue

[7]After the LORD had said these things
to Job, he said to Eliphaz the Temanite,
"I am angry with you and your two
friends, because you have not spoken of
me what is right, as my servant Job has.
[8]So now take seven bulls and seven
rams and go to my servant Job and
sacrifice a burnt offering for yourselves.
My servant Job will pray for you, and I
will accept his prayer and not deal with
you according to your folly. You have
not spoken of me what is right, as my
servant Job has." [9]So Eliphaz the
Temanite, Bildad the Shuhite and
Zophar the Naamathite did what the
LORD told them; and the LORD accepted
Job's prayer.
[10]After Job had prayed for his
friends, the LORD made him prosperous
again and gave him twice as much as he
had before. [11]All his brothers and sisters and everyone who had known him
before came and ate with him in his
house. They comforted and consoled
him over all the trouble the LORD had
brought upon him, and each one gave
him a piece of silver and a gold ring.
[12]The LORD blessed the latter part of
Job's life more than the first. He had
fourteen thousand sheep, six thousand
camels, a thousand yoke of oxen and a
thousand donkeys. [13]And he also had

seven sons and three daughters. 14The
first daughter he named Jemimah, the
second Keziah and the third Keren-
Happuch. 15Nowhere in all the land
were there found women as beautiful as
Job's daughters, and their father
granted them an inheritance along with
their brothers.
16After this, Job lived a hundred and
forty years; he saw his children and their
children to the fourth generation.
17And so he died, old and full of years.

NEW TESTAMENT READING
Matthew 25:14–46

The Parable of the Talents

14"Again, it will be like a man going
on a journey, who called his servants
and entrusted his property to them.
15To one he gave five talents of money,
to another two talents, and to another
one talent, each according to his ability.
Then he went on his journey. 16The man
who had received the five talents went
at once and put his money to work and
gained five more. 17So also, the one with
the two talents gained two more. 18But
the man who had received the one
talent went off, dug a hole in the ground
and hid his master's money.
19"After a long time the master of
those servants returned and settled
accounts with them. 20The man who had
received the five talents brought the
other five. 'Master,' he said, 'you entrusted me with five talents. See, I have
gained five more.'
21"His master replied, 'Well done,
good and faithful servant! You have
been faithful with a few things; I will put
you in charge of many things. Come and
share your master's happiness!'
22"The man with the two talents also
came. 'Master,' he said, 'you entrusted
me with two talents; see, I have gained
two more.'
23"His master replied, 'Well done,
good and faithful servant! You have
been faithful with a few things; I will put
you in charge of many things. Come and
share your master's happiness!'
24"Then the man who had received
the one talent came. 'Master,' he said, 'I
knew that you are a hard man, harvesting where you have not sown and
gathering where you have not scattered
seed. 25So I was afraid and went out and
hid your talent in the ground. See, here
is what belongs to you.'
26"His master replied, 'You wicked,
lazy servant! So you knew that I harvest
where I have not sown and gather where
I have not scattered seed? 27Well then,
you should have put my money on deposit with the bankers, so that when I
returned I would have received it back
with interest.
28" 'Take the talent from him and give
it to the one who has the ten talents.
29For everyone who has will be given
more, and he will have an abundance.
Whoever does not have, even what he
has will be taken from him. 30And throw
that worthless servant outside, into the
darkness, where there will be weeping
and gnashing of teeth.'

The Sheep and the Goats

31"When the Son of Man comes in his
glory, and all the angels with him, he
will sit on his throne in heavenly glory.
32All the nations will be gathered before
him, and he will separate the people one
from another as a shepherd separates
the sheep from the goats. 33He will put
the sheep on his right and the goats on
his left.
34"Then the King will say to those on
his right, 'Come, you who are blessed
by my Father; take your inheritance,
the kingdom prepared for you since the
creation of the world. 35For I was hungry and you gave me something to eat, I
was thirsty and you gave me something
to drink, I was a stranger and you invited me in, 36I needed clothes and you
clothed me, I was sick and you looked
after me, I was in prison and you came
to visit me.'

37“Then the righteous will answer
him, ‘Lord, when did we see you hungry
and feed you, or thirsty and give you
something to drink? 38When did we see
you a stranger and invite you in, or
needing clothes and clothe you?
39When did we see you sick or in prison
and go to visit you?’
40“The King will reply, ‘I tell you the
truth, whatever you did for one of the
least of these brothers of mine, you did
for me.’
41“Then he will say to those on his
left, ‘Depart from me, you who are
cursed, into the eternal fire prepared for
the devil and his angels. 42For I was
hungry and you gave me nothing to eat,
I was thirsty and you gave me nothing to
drink, 43I was a stranger and you did not
invite me in, I needed clothes and you
did not clothe me, I was sick and in
prison and you did not look after me.’
44“They also will answer, ‘Lord,
when did we see you hungry or thirsty or
a stranger or needing clothes or sick or
in prison, and did not help you?’
45“He will reply, ‘I tell you the truth,
whatever you did not do for one of the
least of these, you did not do for me.’
46“Then they will go away to eternal
punishment, but the righteous to eternal life.”

READING FROM PSALMS
Psalm 18:43–50

43You have delivered me from the
attacks of the people;
you have made me the head of
nations;
people I did not know are subject
to me.
44As soon as they hear me, they obey
me;
foreigners cringe before me.
45They all lose heart;
they come trembling from their
strongholds.

46The LORD lives! Praise be to my
Rock!
Exalted be God my Saviour!
47He is the God who avenges me,
who subdues nations under me,
48 who saves me from my enemies.
You exalted me above my foes;
from violent men you rescued me.
49Therefore I will praise you among the
nations, O LORD;
I will sing praises to your name.
50He gives his king great victories;
he shows unfailing kindness to his
anointed,
to David and his descendants for
ever.

FEBRUARY 8

DAY 39

OLD TESTAMENT READING
Exodus 1:1–3:22

The Israelites Oppressed

1 These are the names of the sons of
Israel who went to Egypt with
Jacob, each with his family: 2Reuben,
Simeon, Levi and Judah; 3Issachar,
Zebulun and Benjamin; 4Dan and
Naphtali; Gad and Asher. 5The descendants of Jacob numbered seventy in
all; Joseph was already in Egypt.
6Now Joseph and all his brothers and
all that generation died, 7but the
Israelites were fruitful and multiplied
greatly and became exceedingly numerous, so that the land was filled with
them.
8Then a new king, who did not know
about Joseph, came to power in Egypt.
9“Look,” he said to his people, “the
Israelites have become much too
numerous for us. 10Come, we must deal
shrewdly with them or they will become
even more numerous and, if war breaks

out, will join our enemies, fight against us and leave the country."

11So they put slave masters over them to oppress them with forced labour, and they built Pithom and Rameses as store cities for Pharaoh. 12But the more they were oppressed, the more they multiplied and spread; so the Egyptians came to dread the Israelites 13and worked them ruthlessly. 14They made their lives bitter with hard labour in brick and mortar and with all kinds of work in the fields; in all their hard labour the Egyptians used them ruthlessly.

15The king of Egypt said to the Hebrew midwives, whose names were Shiphrah and Puah, 16"When you help the Hebrew women in childbirth and observe them on the delivery stool, if it is a boy, kill him; but if it is a girl, let her live." 17The midwives, however, feared God and did not do what the king of Egypt had told them to do; they let the boys live. 18Then the king of Egypt summoned the midwives and asked them, "Why have you done this? Why have you let the boys live?"

19The midwives answered Pharaoh, "Hebrew women are not like Egyptian women; they are vigorous and give birth before the midwives arrive."

20So God was kind to the midwives and the people increased and became even more numerous. 21And because the midwives feared God, he gave them families of their own.

22Then Pharaoh gave this order to all his people: "Every boy that is born you must throw into the Nile, but let every girl live."

The Birth of Moses

2 Now a man of the house of Levi married a Levite woman, 2and she became pregnant and gave birth to a son. When she saw that he was a fine child, she hid him for three months. 3But when she could hide him no longer, she got a papyrus basket for him and coated it with tar and pitch. Then she placed the child in it and put it among the reeds along the bank of the Nile. 4His sister stood at a distance to see what would happen to him.

5Then Pharaoh's daughter went down to the Nile to bathe, and her attendants were walking along the river bank. She saw the basket among the reeds and sent her slave girl to get it. 6She opened it and saw the baby. He was crying, and she felt sorry for him. "This is one of the Hebrew babies," she said.

7Then his sister asked Pharaoh's daughter, "Shall I go and get one of the Hebrew women to nurse the baby for you?"

8"Yes, go," she answered. And the girl went and got the baby's mother. 9Pharaoh's daughter said to her, "Take this baby and nurse him for me, and I will pay you." So the woman took the baby and nursed him. 10When the child grew older, she took him to Pharaoh's daughter and he became her son. She named him Moses, saying, "I drew him out of the water."

Moses Flees to Midian

11One day, after Moses had grown up, he went out to where his own people were and watched them at their hard labour. He saw an Egyptian beating a Hebrew, one of his own people. 12Glancing this way and that and seeing no-one, he killed the Egyptian and hid him in the sand. 13The next day he went out and saw two Hebrews fighting. He asked the one in the wrong, "Why are you hitting your fellow Hebrew?"

14The man said, "Who made you ruler and judge over us? Are you thinking of killing me as you killed the Egyptian?" Then Moses was afraid and thought, "What I did must have become known."

15When Pharaoh heard of this, he tried to kill Moses, but Moses fled from Pharaoh and went to live in Midian, where he sat down by a well. 16Now a priest of Midian had seven daughters, and they came to draw water and fill the

troughs to water their father's flock.
17Some shepherds came along and
drove them away, but Moses got up and
came to their rescue and watered their
flock.
18When the girls returned to Reuel
their father, he asked them, "Why have
you returned so early today?"
19They answered, "An Egyptian rescued us from the shepherds. He even
drew water for us and watered the
flock."
20"And where is he?" he asked his
daughters. "Why did you leave him?
Invite him to have something to eat."
21Moses agreed to stay with the man,
who gave his daughter Zipporah to
Moses in marriage. 22Zipporah gave
birth to a son, and Moses named him
Gershom, saying, "I have become an
alien in a foreign land."
23During that long period, the king of
Egypt died. The Israelites groaned in
their slavery and cried out, and their cry
for help because of their slavery went up
to God. 24God heard their groaning and
he remembered his covenant with
Abraham, with Isaac and with Jacob.
25So God looked on the Israelites and
was concerned about them.

Moses and the Burning Bush

3 Now Moses was tending the flock
of Jethro his father-in-law, the
priest of Midian, and he led the flock to
the far side of the desert and came to
Horeb, the mountain of God. 2There
the angel of the LORD appeared to him
in flames of fire from within a bush.
Moses saw that though the bush was on
fire it did not burn up. 3So Moses
thought, "I will go over and see this
strange sight—why the bush does not
burn up."
4When the LORD saw that he had
gone over to look, God called to him
from within the bush, "Moses! Moses!"
And Moses said, "Here I am."
5"Do not come any closer," God
said. "Take off your sandals, for the
place where you are standing is holy
ground." 6Then he said, "I am the God
of your father, the God of Abraham,
the God of Isaac and the God of Jacob."
At this, Moses hid his face, because he
was afraid to look at God.
7The LORD said, "I have indeed seen
the misery of my people in Egypt. I have
heard them crying out because of their
slave drivers, and I am concerned about
their suffering. 8So I have come down to
rescue them from the hand of the Egyptians and to bring them up out of that
land into a good and spacious land, a
land flowing with milk and honey—the
home of the Canaanites, Hittites, Am-
onites, Perizzites, Hivites and Jebusites.
9And now the cry of the Israelites has
reached me, and I have seen the way the
Egyptians are oppressing them. 10So
now, go. I am sending you to Pharaoh to
bring my people the Israelites out of
Egypt."
11But Moses said to God, "Who am I,
that I should go to Pharaoh and bring
the Israelites out of Egypt?"
12And God said, "I will be with you.
And this will be the sign to you that it is I
who have sent you: When you have
brought the people out of Egypt, you
will worship God on this mountain."
13Moses said to God, "Suppose I go
to the Israelites and say to them, 'The
God of your fathers has sent me to you,'
and they ask me, 'What is his name?'
Then what shall I tell them?"
14God said to Moses, "I AM WHO I AM.
This is what you are to say to the
Israelites: 'I AM has sent me to you.'"
15God also said to Moses, "Say to the
Israelites, 'The LORD, the God of your
fathers—the God of Abraham, the
God of Isaac and the God of Jacob
—has sent me to you.' This is my name
for ever, the name by which I am to
be remembered from generation to
generation.
16"Go, assemble the elders of Israel
and say to them, 'The LORD, the God of
your fathers—the God of Abraham,
Isaac and Jacob—appeared to me and
said: I have watched over you and have
seen what has been done to you in

Egypt. 17And I have promised to bring you up out of your misery in Egypt into the land of the Canaanites, Hittites, Amorites, Perizzites, Hivites and Jebusites—a land flowing with milk and honey.'

18"The elders of Israel will listen to you. Then you and the elders are to go to the king of Egypt and say to him, 'The LORD, the God of the Hebrews, has met with us. Let us take a three-day journey into the desert to offer sacrifices to the LORD our God.' 19But I know that the king of Egypt will not let you go unless a mighty hand compels him. 20So I will stretch out my hand and strike the Egyptians with all the wonders that I will perform among them. After that, he will let you go.

21"And I will make the Egyptians favourably disposed towards this people, so that when you leave you will not go empty-handed. 22Every woman is to ask her neighbour and any woman living in her house for articles of silver and gold and for clothing, which you will put on your sons and daughters. And so you will plunder the Egyptians."

NEW TESTAMENT READING

Matthew 26:1–30

The Plot Against Jesus

26 When Jesus had finished saying all these things, he said to his disciples, 2"As you know, the Passover is two days away—and the Son of Man will be handed over to be crucified."

3Then the chief priests and the elders of the people assembled in the palace of the high priest, whose name was Caiaphas, 4and they plotted to arrest Jesus in some sly way and kill him. 5"But not during the Feast," they said, "or there may be a riot among the people."

Jesus Anointed at Bethany

6While Jesus was in Bethany in the home of a man known as Simon the Leper, 7a woman came to him with an alabaster jar of very expensive perfume, which she poured on his head as he was reclining at the table.

8When the disciples saw this, they were indignant. "Why this waste?" they asked. 9"This perfume could have been sold at a high price and the money given to the poor."

10Aware of this, Jesus said to them, "Why are you bothering this woman? She has done a beautiful thing to me. 11The poor you will always have with you, but you will not always have me. 12When she poured this perfume on my body, she did it to prepare me for burial. 13I tell you the truth, wherever this gospel is preached throughout the world, what she has done will also be told, in memory of her."

Judas Agrees to Betray Jesus

14Then one of the Twelve—the one called Judas Iscariot—went to the chief priests 15and asked, "What are you willing to give me if I hand him over to you?" So they counted out for him thirty silver coins. 16From then on Judas watched for an opportunity to hand him over.

The Lord's Supper

17On the first day of the Feast of Unleavened Bread, the disciples came to Jesus and asked, "Where do you want us to make preparations for you to eat the Passover?"

18He replied, "Go into the city to a certain man and tell him, 'The Teacher says: My appointed time is near. I am going to celebrate the Passover with my disciples at your house.'" 19So the disciples did as Jesus had directed them and prepared the Passover.

20When evening came, Jesus was reclining at the table with the Twelve. 21And while they were eating, he said, "I tell you the truth, one of you will betray me."

22 They were very sad and began to
say to him one after the other, "Surely
not I, Lord?"
23 Jesus replied, "The one who has
dipped his hand into the bowl with me
will betray me. 24 The Son of Man will go
just as it is written about him. But woe
to that man who betrays the Son of
Man! It would be better for him if he
had not been born."
25 Then Judas, the one who would
betray him, said, "Surely not I,
Rabbi?"
Jesus answered, "Yes, it is you."
26 While they were eating, Jesus took
bread, gave thanks and broke it, and
gave it to his disciples, saying, "Take
and eat; this is my body."
27 Then he took the cup, gave thanks
and offered it to them, saying, "Drink
from it, all of you. 28 This is my blood of
the covenant, which is poured out for
many for the forgiveness of sins. 29 I tell
you, I will not drink of this fruit of the
vine from now on until that day when I
drink it anew with you in my Father's
kingdom."
30 When they had sung a hymn, they
went out to the Mount of Olives.

READING FROM PSALMS
Psalm 19:1–6

For the director of music. A psalm of David.

1 The heavens declare the glory of God;
the skies proclaim the work of his hands.
2 Day after day they pour forth speech;
night after night they display knowledge.
3 There is no speech or language
where their voice is not heard.
4 Their voice goes out into all the earth,
their words to the ends of the world.

In the heavens he has pitched a tent for the sun,
5 which is like a bridegroom coming forth from his pavilion,
like a champion rejoicing to run his course.
6 It rises at one end of the heavens
and makes its circuit to the other;
nothing is hidden from its heat.

FEBRUARY 9

DAY 40

OLD TESTAMENT READING
Exodus 4:1–6:12

Signs for Moses

4 Moses answered, "What if they do
not believe me or listen to me and
say, 'The LORD did not appear to you'?"
2 Then the LORD said to him, "What is
that in your hand?"
"A staff," he replied.
3 The LORD said, "Throw it on the
ground."
Moses threw it on the ground and it
became a snake, and he ran from it.
4 Then the LORD said to him, "Reach out
your hand and take it by the tail." So
Moses reached out and took hold of the
snake and it turned back into a staff in
his hand. 5 "This," said the LORD, "is so
that they may believe that the LORD, the
God of their fathers—the God of Abraham, the God of Isaac and the God of
Jacob—has appeared to you."
6 Then the LORD said, "Put your hand
inside your cloak." So Moses put his
hand into his cloak, and when he took it
out, it was leprous, like snow.
7 "Now put it back into your cloak,"

he said. So Moses put his hand back into
his cloak, and when he took it out, it was
restored, like the rest of his flesh.
8Then the LORD said, "If they do not
believe you or pay attention to the first
miraculous sign, they may believe the
second. 9But if they do not believe these
two signs or listen to you, take some
water from the Nile and pour it on the
dry ground. The water you take from
the river will become blood on the
ground."
10Moses said to the LORD, "O Lord, I
have never been eloquent, neither in
the past nor since you have spoken to
your servant. I am slow of speech and
tongue."
11The LORD said to him, "Who gave
man his mouth? Who makes him deaf or
mute? Who gives him sight or makes
him blind? Is it not I, the LORD? 12Now
go; I will help you speak and will teach
you what to say."
13But Moses said, "O Lord, please
send someone else to do it."
14Then the LORD's anger burned
against Moses and he said, "What about
your brother, Aaron the Levite? I know
he can speak well. He is already on his
way to meet you, and his heart will be
glad when he sees you. 15You shall
speak to him and put words in his
mouth; I will help both of you speak and
will teach you what to do. 16He will
speak to the people for you, and it will
be as if he were your mouth and as if you
were God to him. 17But take this staff
in your hand so that you can perform
miraculous signs with it."

Moses Returns to Egypt

18Then Moses went back to Jethro his
father-in-law and said to him, "Let me
go back to my own people in Egypt to
see if any of them are still alive."
Jethro said, "Go, and I wish you
well."
19Now the LORD had said to Moses in
Midian, "Go back to Egypt, for all the
men who wanted to kill you are dead."
20So Moses took his wife and sons, put
them on a donkey and started back to
Egypt. And he took the staff of God in
his hand.
21The LORD said to Moses, "When
you return to Egypt, see that you perform before Pharaoh all the wonders I
have given you the power to do. But I
will harden his heart so that he will not
let the people go. 22Then say to Pharaoh, 'This is what the LORD says: Israel
is my firstborn son, 23and I told you,
"Let my son go, so that he may worship
me." But you refused to let him go; so I
will kill your firstborn son.'"
24At a lodging place on the way, the
LORD met ⌞Moses⌟ and was about to kill
him. 25But Zipporah took a flint knife,
cut off her son's foreskin and touched
⌞Moses'⌟ feet with it. "Surely you are a
bridegroom of blood to me," she said.
26So the LORD let him alone. (At that
time she said "bridegroom of blood",
referring to circumcision.)
27The LORD said to Aaron, "Go into
the desert to meet Moses." So he met
Moses at the mountain of God and
kissed him. 28Then Moses told Aaron
everything the LORD had sent him to
say, and also about all the miraculous signs he had commanded him to
perform.
29Moses and Aaron brought together
all the elders of the Israelites, 30and
Aaron told them everything the LORD
had said to Moses. He also performed
the signs before the people, 31and they
believed. And when they heard that the
LORD was concerned about them and
had seen their misery, they bowed down
and worshipped.

Bricks Without Straw

5 Afterwards Moses and Aaron went
to Pharaoh and said, "This is what
the LORD, the God of Israel, says: 'Let
my people go, so that they may hold a
festival to me in the desert.'"
2Pharaoh said, "Who is the LORD,
that I should obey him and let Israel go?

I do not know the LORD and I will not let
Israel go."
3 Then they said, "The God of the
Hebrews has met with us. Now let us
take a three-day journey into the desert
to offer sacrifices to the LORD our God,
or he may strike us with plagues or with
the sword."
4 But the king of Egypt said, "Moses
and Aaron, why are you taking the
people away from their labour? Get
back to your work!" 5 Then Pharaoh
said, "Look, the people of the land are
now numerous, and you are stopping
them from working."
6 That same day Pharaoh gave this
order to the slave drivers and foremen
in charge of the people: 7 "You are no
longer to supply the people with straw
for making bricks; let them go and
gather their own straw. 8 But require
them to make the same number of
bricks as before; don't reduce the
quota. They are lazy; that is why they
are crying out, 'Let us go and sacrifice to
our God.' 9 Make the work harder for
the men so that they keep working and
pay no attention to lies."
10 Then the slave drivers and the foremen went out and said to the people,
"This is what Pharaoh says: 'I will not
give you any more straw. 11 Go and get
your own straw wherever you can find
it, but your work will not be reduced at
all.'" 12 So the people scattered all over
Egypt to gather stubble to use for straw.
13 The slave drivers kept pressing them,
saying, "Complete the work required
of you for each day, just as when you
had straw." 14 The Israelite foremen
appointed by Pharaoh's slave drivers
were beaten and were asked, "Why
didn't you meet your quota of bricks
yesterday or today, as before?"
15 Then the Israelite foremen went
and appealed to Pharaoh: "Why have
you treated your servants this way?
16 Your servants are given no straw, yet
we are told, 'Make bricks!' Your servants are being beaten, but the fault is
with your own people."
17 Pharaoh said, "Lazy, that's what
you are—lazy! That is why you keep
saying, 'Let us go and sacrifice to the
LORD.' 18 Now get to work. You will not
be given any straw, yet you must produce your full quota of bricks."
19 The Israelite foremen realised they
were in trouble when they were told,
"You are not to reduce the number of
bricks required of you for each day."
20 When they left Pharaoh, they found
Moses and Aaron waiting to meet them,
21 and they said, "May the LORD look
upon you and judge you! You have
made us a stench to Pharaoh and his
officials and have put a sword in their
hand to kill us."

God Promises Deliverance

22 Moses returned to the LORD and
said, "O Lord, why have you brought
trouble upon this people? Is this why
you sent me? 23 Ever since I went to
Pharaoh to speak in your name, he has
brought trouble upon this people, and
you have not rescued your people at
all."
6 Then the LORD said to Moses,
"Now you will see what I will do to
Pharaoh: Because of my mighty hand
he will let them go; because of my
mighty hand he will drive them out of
his country."
2 God also said to Moses, "I am the
LORD. 3 I appeared to Abraham, to
Isaac and to Jacob as God Almighty,
but by my name the LORD I did not
make myself known to them. 4 I also
established my covenant with them to
give them the land of Canaan, where
they lived as aliens. 5 Moreover, I have
heard the groaning of the Israelites,
whom the Egyptians are enslaving, and
I have remembered my covenant.
6 "Therefore, say to the Israelites: 'I
am the LORD, and I will bring you out
from under the yoke of the Egyptians. I
will free you from being slaves to them,
and I will redeem you with an outstretched arm and with mighty acts of
judgment. 7 I will take you as my own
people, and I will be your God. Then

you will know that I am the LORD your
God, who brought you out from under
the yoke of the Egyptians. 8And I will
bring you to the land I swore with uplifted hand to give to Abraham, to Isaac
and to Jacob. I will give it to you as a
possession. I am the LORD.' "
9Moses reported this to the Israelites,
but they did not listen to him because
of their discouragement and cruel
bondage.
10Then the LORD said to Moses,
11"Go, tell Pharaoh king of Egypt to let
the Israelites go out of his country."
12But Moses said to the LORD, "If the
Israelites will not listen to me, why
would Pharaoh listen to me, since I
speak with faltering lips?"

NEW TESTAMENT READING
Matthew 26:31–46

Jesus Predicts Peter's Denial

31Then Jesus told them, "This very
night you will all fall away on account of
me, for it is written:

" 'I will strike the shepherd,
and the sheep of the flock will be
scattered.'

32But after I have risen, I will go ahead
of you into Galilee."
33Peter replied, "Even if all fall away
on account of you, I never will."
34"I tell you the truth," Jesus
answered, "this very night, before the
cock crows, you will disown me three
times."
35But Peter declared, "Even if I have
to die with you, I will never disown
you." And all the other disciples said
the same.

Gethsemane

36Then Jesus went with his disciples
to a place called Gethsemane, and he
said to them, "Sit here while I go over
there and pray." 37He took Peter and
the two sons of Zebedee along with
him, and he began to be sorrowful and
troubled. 38Then he said to them, "My
soul is overwhelmed with sorrow to the
point of death. Stay here and keep
watch with me."
39Going a little farther, he fell with his
face to the ground and prayed, "My
Father, if it is possible, may this cup be
taken from me. Yet not as I will, but as
you will."
40Then he returned to his disciples
and found them sleeping. "Could you
men not keep watch with me for one
hour?" he asked Peter. 41"Watch and
pray so that you will not fall into temptation. The spirit is willing, but the body
is weak."
42He went away a second time and
prayed, "My Father, if it is not possible
for this cup to be taken away unless I
drink it, may your will be done."
43When he came back, he again found
them sleeping, because their eyes were
heavy. 44So he left them and went away
once more and prayed the third time,
saying the same thing.
45Then he returned to the disciples
and said to them, "Are you still sleeping
and resting? Look, the hour is near, and
the Son of Man is betrayed into the
hands of sinners. 46Rise, let us go! Here
comes my betrayer!"

READING FROM PROVERBS
Proverbs 4:10–19

10Listen, my son, accept what I say,
and the years of your life will be
many.
11I guide you in the way of wisdom
and lead you along straight paths.
12When you walk, your steps will not
be hampered;
when you run, you will not
stumble.
13Hold on to instruction, do not let it
go;
guard it well, for it is your life.
14Do not set foot on the path of the
wicked

or walk in the way of evil men.
15Avoid it, do not travel on it;
turn from it and go on your way.
16For they cannot sleep till they do evil;
they are robbed of slumber till they
make someone fall.
17They eat the bread of wickedness
and drink the wine of violence.
18The path of the righteous is like the
first gleam of dawn,
shining ever brighter till the full
light of day.
19But the way of the wicked is like deep
darkness;
they do not know what makes them
stumble.

FEBRUARY 10

DAY 41

OLD TESTAMENT READING
Exodus 6:13–8:32

Family Record of Moses and Aaron

13Now the LORD spoke to Moses and Aaron about the Israelites and Pharaoh king of Egypt, and he commanded them to bring the Israelites out of Egypt.

14These were the heads of their families:

The sons of Reuben the firstborn son of Israel were Hanoch and Pallu, Hezron and Carmi. These were the clans of Reuben.

15The sons of Simeon were Jemuel, Jamin, Ohad, Jakin, Zohar and Shaul the son of a Canaanite woman. These were the clans of Simeon.

16These were the names of the sons of Levi according to their records: Gershon, Kohath and Merari. Levi lived 137 years.

17The sons of Gershon, by clans, were Libni and Shimei.

18The sons of Kohath were Amram, Izhar, Hebron and Uzziel. Kohath lived 133 years.

19The sons of Merari were Mahli and Mushi.

These were the clans of Levi according to their records.

20Amram married his father's sister Jochebed, who bore him Aaron and Moses. Amram lived 137 years.

21The sons of Izhar were Korah, Nepheg and Zicri.

22The sons of Uzziel were Mishael, Elzaphan and Sithri.

23Aaron married Elisheba, daughter of Amminadab and sister of Nahshon, and she bore him Nadab and Abihu, Eleazar and Ithamar.

24The sons of Korah were Assir, Elkanah and Abiasaph. These were the Korahite clans.

25Eleazar son of Aaron married one of the daughters of Putiel, and she bore him Phinehas.

These were the heads of the Levite families, clan by clan.

26It was this same Aaron and Moses
to whom the LORD said, "Bring the
Israelites out of Egypt by their divisions." 27They were the ones who spoke
to Pharaoh king of Egypt about bringing the Israelites out of Egypt. It was the
same Moses and Aaron.

Aaron to Speak for Moses

28Now when the LORD spoke to
Moses in Egypt, 29he said to him, "I am
the LORD. Tell Pharaoh king of Egypt
everything I tell you."
30But Moses said to the LORD, "Since

I speak with faltering lips, why would Pharaoh listen to me?"

7 Then the LORD said to Moses, "See, I have made you like God to Pharaoh, and your brother Aaron will be your prophet. 2You are to say everything I command you, and your brother Aaron is to tell Pharaoh to let the Israelites go out of his country. 3But I will harden Pharaoh's heart, and though I multiply my miraculous signs and wonders in Egypt, 4he will not listen to you. Then I will lay my hand on Egypt and with mighty acts of judgment I will bring out my divisions, my people the Israelites. 5And the Egyptians will know that I am the LORD when I stretch out my hand against Egypt and bring the Israelites out of it."

6Moses and Aaron did just as the LORD commanded them. 7Moses was eighty years old and Aaron eighty-three when they spoke to Pharaoh.

Aaron's Staff Becomes a Snake

8The LORD said to Moses and Aaron, 9"When Pharaoh says to you, 'Perform a miracle,' then say to Aaron, 'Take your staff and throw it down before Pharaoh,' and it will become a snake."

10So Moses and Aaron went to Pharaoh and did just as the LORD commanded. Aaron threw his staff down in front of Pharaoh and his officials, and it became a snake. 11Pharaoh then summoned the wise men and sorcerers, and the Egyptian magicians also did the same things by their secret arts: 12Each one threw down his staff and it became a snake. But Aaron's staff swallowed up their staffs. 13Yet Pharaoh's heart became hard and he would not listen to them, just as the LORD had said.

The Plague of Blood

14Then the LORD said to Moses, "Pharaoh's heart is unyielding; he refuses to let the people go. 15Go to Pharaoh in the morning as he goes out to the water. Wait on the bank of the Nile to meet him, and take in your hand the staff that was changed into a snake. 16Then say to him, 'The LORD, the God of the Hebrews, has sent me to say to you: Let my people go, so that they may worship me in the desert. But until now you have not listened. 17This is what the LORD says: By this you will know that I am the LORD: With the staff that is in my hand I will strike the water of the Nile, and it will be changed into blood. 18The fish in the Nile will die, and the river will stink; the Egyptians will not be able to drink its water.'"

19The LORD said to Moses, "Tell Aaron, 'Take your staff and stretch out your hand over the waters of Egypt—over the streams and canals, over the ponds and all the reservoirs'—and they will turn to blood. Blood will be everywhere in Egypt, even in the wooden buckets and stone jars."

20Moses and Aaron did just as the LORD had commanded. He raised his staff in the presence of Pharaoh and his officials and struck the water of the Nile, and all the water was changed into blood. 21The fish in the Nile died, and the river smelled so bad that the Egyptians could not drink its water. Blood was everywhere in Egypt.

22But the Egyptian magicians did the same things by their secret arts, and Pharaoh's heart became hard; he would not listen to Moses and Aaron, just as the LORD had said. 23Instead, he turned and went into his palace, and did not take even this to heart. 24And all the Egyptians dug along the Nile to get drinking water, because they could not drink the water of the river.

The Plague of Frogs

25Seven days passed after the LORD

8 struck the Nile. 1Then the LORD said to Moses, "Go to Pharaoh and say to him, 'This is what the LORD says: Let my people go, so that they may worship me. 2If you refuse to let them go, I will plague your whole country with frogs. 3The Nile will teem with

frogs. They will come up into your
palace and your bedroom and onto your
bed, into the houses of your officials and
on your people, and into your ovens and
kneading troughs. 4The frogs will go up
on you and your people and all your
officials.'"

5Then the LORD said to Moses, "Tell
Aaron, 'Stretch out your hand with
your staff over the streams and canals
and ponds, and make frogs come up on
the land of Egypt.'"

6So Aaron stretched out his hand
over the waters of Egypt, and the frogs
came up and covered the land. 7But the
magicians did the same things by their
secret arts; they also made frogs come
up on the land of Egypt.

8Pharaoh summoned Moses and
Aaron and said, "Pray to the LORD to
take the frogs away from me and my
people, and I will let your people go to
offer sacrifices to the LORD."

9Moses said to Pharaoh, "I leave to
you the honour of setting the time for
me to pray for you and your officials and
your people that you and your houses
may be rid of the frogs, except for those
that remain in the Nile."

10"Tomorrow," Pharaoh said.

Moses replied, "It will be as you say,
so that you may know there is no-one
like the LORD our God. 11The frogs will
leave you and your houses, your officials and your people; they will remain
only in the Nile."

12After Moses and Aaron left Pharaoh, Moses cried out to the LORD about
the frogs he had brought on Pharaoh.
13And the LORD did what Moses asked.
The frogs died in the houses, in the
courtyards and in the fields. 14They
were piled into heaps, and the land
reeked of them. 15But when Pharaoh
saw that there was relief, he hardened
his heart and would not listen to Moses
and Aaron, just as the LORD had said.

The Plague of Gnats

16Then the LORD said to Moses, "Tell
Aaron, 'Stretch out your staff and strike
the dust of the ground,' and throughout
the land of Egypt the dust will become
gnats." 17They did this, and when
Aaron stretched out his hand with the
staff and struck the dust of the ground,
gnats came upon men and animals. All
the dust throughout the land of Egypt
became gnats. 18But when the magicians tried to produce gnats by their
secret arts, they could not. And the
gnats were on men and animals.

19The magicians said to Pharaoh,
"This is the finger of God." But Pharaoh's heart was hard and he would not
listen, just as the LORD had said.

The Plague of Flies

20Then the LORD said to Moses, "Get
up early in the morning and confront
Pharaoh as he goes to the water and say
to him, 'This is what the LORD says: Let
my people go, so that they may worship
me. 21If you do not let my people go, I
will send swarms of flies on you and
your officials, on your people and into
your houses. The houses of the Egyptians will be full of flies, and even the
ground where they are.

22"'But on that day I will deal differently with the land of Goshen, where
my people live; no swarms of flies will
be there, so that you will know that I,
the LORD, am in this land. 23I will make
a distinction between my people and
your people. This miraculous sign will
occur tomorrow.'"

24And the LORD did this. Dense
swarms of flies poured into Pharaoh's
palace and into the houses of his officials, and throughout Egypt the land
was ruined by the flies.

25Then Pharaoh summoned Moses
and Aaron and said, "Go, sacrifice to
your God here in the land."

26But Moses said, "That would not be
right. The sacrifices we offer the LORD
our God would be detestable to the
Egyptians. And if we offer sacrifices
that are detestable in their eyes, will
they not stone us? 27We must take a
three-day journey into the desert to

offer sacrifices to the LORD our God, as
he commands us."
28Pharaoh said, "I will let you go to
offer sacrifices to the LORD your God in
the desert, but you must not go very far.
Now pray for me."
29Moses answered, "As soon as I
leave you, I will pray to the LORD, and
tomorrow the flies will leave Pharaoh
and his officials and his people. Only be
sure that Pharaoh does not act deceitfully again by not letting the people go
to offer sacrifices to the LORD."
30Then Moses left Pharaoh and
prayed to the LORD, 31and the LORD did
what Moses asked: The flies left Pharaoh and his officials and his people; not
a fly remained. 32But this time also
Pharaoh hardened his heart and would
not let the people go.

NEW TESTAMENT READING
Matthew 26:47–68

Jesus Arrested

47While he was still speaking, Judas,
one of the Twelve, arrived. With him
was a large crowd armed with swords
and clubs, sent from the chief priests
and the elders of the people. 48Now the
betrayer had arranged a signal with
them: "The one I kiss is the man; arrest
him." 49Going at once to Jesus, Judas
said, "Greetings, Rabbi!" and kissed
him.
50Jesus replied, "Friend, do what you
came for."
Then the men stepped forward,
seized Jesus and arrested him. 51With
that, one of Jesus' companions reached
for his sword, drew it out and struck the
servant of the high priest, cutting off his
ear.
52"Put your sword back in its place,"
Jesus said to him, "for all who draw the
sword will die by the sword. 53Do you
think I cannot call on my Father, and he
will at once put at my disposal more
than twelve legions of angels? 54But
how then would the Scriptures be
fulfilled that say it must happen in this
way?"
55At that time Jesus said to the crowd,
"Am I leading a rebellion, that you
have come out with swords and clubs to
capture me? Every day I sat in the temple courts teaching, and you did not
arrest me. 56But this has all taken place
that the writings of the prophets might
be fulfilled." Then all the disciples deserted him and fled.

Before the Sanhedrin

57Those who had arrested Jesus took
him to Caiaphas, the high priest, where
the teachers of the law and the elders
had assembled. 58But Peter followed
him at a distance, right up to the courtyard of the high priest. He entered and
sat down with the guards to see the
outcome.
59The chief priests and the whole
Sanhedrin were looking for false evidence against Jesus so that they could
put him to death. 60But they did not find
any, though many false witnesses came
forward.
Finally two came forward 61and declared, "This fellow said, 'I am able to
destroy the temple of God and rebuild it
in three days.'"
62Then the high priest stood up and
said to Jesus, "Are you not going to
answer? What is this testimony that
these men are bringing against you?"
63But Jesus remained silent.
The high priest said to him, "I charge
you under oath by the living God: Tell
us if you are the Christ, the Son of
God."
64"Yes, it is as you say," Jesus replied. "But I say to all of you: In the
future you will see the Son of Man
sitting at the right hand of the Mighty
One and coming on the clouds of
heaven."
65Then the high priest tore his clothes
and said, "He has spoken blasphemy!
Why do we need any more witnesses?
Look, now you have heard the blasphemy. 66What do you think?"

"He is worthy of death," they answered.

67Then they spat in his face and struck him with their fists. Others slapped him 68and said, "Prophesy to us, Christ. Who hit you?"

READING FROM PSALMS
Psalm 19:7–14

7The law of the LORD is perfect,
reviving the soul.
The statutes of the LORD are trustworthy,
making wise the simple.
8The precepts of the LORD are right,
giving joy to the heart.
The commands of the LORD are radiant,
giving light to the eyes.
9The fear of the LORD is pure,
enduring for ever.
The ordinances of the LORD are sure
and altogether righteous.
10They are more precious than gold,
than much pure gold;
they are sweeter than honey,
than honey from the comb.
11By them is your servant warned;
in keeping them there is great reward.

12Who can discern his errors?
Forgive my hidden faults.
13Keep your servant also from wilful sins;
may they not rule over me.
Then will I be blameless,
innocent of great transgression.

14May the words of my mouth and the meditation of my heart
be pleasing in your sight,
O LORD, my Rock and my Redeemer.

FEBRUARY 11

DAY 42

OLD TESTAMENT READING
Exodus 9:1–10:29

The Plague on Livestock

9 Then the LORD said to Moses, "Go to Pharaoh and say to him, 'This is what the LORD, the God of the Hebrews, says: "Let my people go, so that they may worship me." 2If you refuse to let them go and continue to hold them back, 3the hand of the LORD will bring a terrible plague on your livestock in the field—on your horses and donkeys and camels and on your cattle and sheep and goats. 4But the LORD will make a distinction between the livestock of Israel and that of Egypt, so that no animal belonging to the Israelites will die.'"

5The LORD set a time and said, "Tomorrow the LORD will do this in the land." 6And the next day the LORD did it: All the livestock of the Egyptians died, but not one animal belonging to the Israelites died. 7Pharaoh sent men to investigate and found that not even one of the animals of the Israelites had died. Yet his heart was unyielding and he would not let the people go.

The Plague of Boils

8Then the LORD said to Moses and Aaron, "Take handfuls of soot from a furnace and have Moses toss it into the air in the presence of Pharaoh. 9It will become fine dust over the whole land of Egypt, and festering boils will break out on men and animals throughout the land."

10So they took soot from a furnace and stood before Pharaoh. Moses

tossed it into the air, and festering
boils broke out on men and animals.
11The magicians could not stand before
Moses because of the boils that were
on them and on all the Egyptians.
12But the LORD hardened Pharaoh's
heart and he would not listen to Moses
and Aaron, just as the LORD had said
to Moses.

The Plague of Hail

13Then the LORD said to Moses, "Get
up early in the morning, confront Pharaoh and say to him, 'This is what the
LORD, the God of the Hebrews, says:
Let my people go, so that they may
worship me, 14or this time I will send the
full force of my plagues against you and
against your officials and your people,
so you may know that there is no-one
like me in all the earth. 15For by now I
could have stretched out my hand and
struck you and your people with a plague that would have wiped you off the
earth. 16But I have raised you up for this
very purpose, that I might show you my
power and that my name might be proclaimed in all the earth. 17You still set
yourself against my people and will not
let them go. 18Therefore, at this time
tomorrow I will send the worst hailstorm that has ever fallen on Egypt,
from the day it was founded till now.
19Give an order now to bring your livestock and everything you have in the
field to a place of shelter, because the
hail will fall on every man and animal
that has not been brought in and is still
out in the field, and they will die.' "

20Those officials of Pharaoh who
feared the word of the LORD hurried to
bring their slaves and their livestock
inside. 21But those who ignored the
word of the LORD left their slaves and
livestock in the field.

22Then the LORD said to Moses,
"Stretch out your hand towards the sky
so that hail will fall all over Egypt—on
men and animals and on everything
growing in the fields of Egypt." 23When
Moses stretched out his staff towards
the sky, the LORD sent thunder and hail,
and lightning flashed down to the
ground. So the LORD rained hail on the
land of Egypt; 24hail fell and lightning
flashed back and forth. It was the worst
storm in all the land of Egypt since it
had become a nation. 25Throughout
Egypt hail struck everything in the
fields—both men and animals; it beat
down everything growing in the fields
and stripped every tree. 26The only
place it did not hail was the land of
Goshen, where the Israelites were.

27Then Pharaoh summoned Moses
and Aaron. "This time I have sinned,"
he said to them. "The LORD is in the
right, and I and my people are in the
wrong. 28Pray to the LORD, for we have
had enough thunder and hail. I will
let you go; you don't have to stay any
longer."

29Moses replied, "When I have gone
out of the city, I will spread out my
hands in prayer to the LORD. The thunder will stop and there will be no more
hail, so you may know that the earth is
the LORD's. 30But I know that you and
your officials still do not fear the LORD
God."

31(The flax and barley were destroyed, since the barley was in the ear
and the flax was in bloom. 32The wheat
and spelt, however, were not destroyed, because they ripen later.)

33Then Moses left Pharaoh and went
out of the city. He spread out his hands
towards the LORD; the thunder and hail
stopped, and the rain no longer poured
down on the land. 34When Pharaoh saw
that the rain and hail and thunder had
stopped, he sinned again: He and his
officials hardened their hearts. 35So
Pharaoh's heart was hard and he would
not let the Israelites go, just as the LORD
had said through Moses.

The Plague of Locusts

10 Then the LORD said to Moses,
"Go to Pharaoh, for I have hardened his heart and the hearts of his
officials so that I may perform these

miraculous signs of mine among them
2that you may tell your children and
grandchildren how I dealt harshly with
the Egyptians and how I performed my
signs among them, and that you may
know that I am the LORD."
3So Moses and Aaron went to Pharaoh and said to him, "This is what the
LORD, the God of the Hebrews, says:
'How long will you refuse to humble
yourself before me? Let my people go,
so that they may worship me. 4If you
refuse to let them go, I will bring locusts
into your country tomorrow. 5They will
cover the face of the ground so that it
cannot be seen. They will devour what
little you have left after the hail, including every tree that is growing in your
fields. 6They will fill your houses and
those of all your officials and all the
Egyptians—something neither your
fathers nor your forefathers have ever
seen from the day they settled in this
land till now.'" Then Moses turned and
left Pharaoh.
7Pharaoh's officials said to him,
"How long will this man be a snare to
us? Let the people go, so that they may
worship the LORD their God. Do you
not yet realise that Egypt is ruined?"
8Then Moses and Aaron were
brought back to Pharaoh. "Go, worship
the LORD your God," he said. "But just
who will be going?"
9Moses answered, "We will go with
our young and old, with our sons and
daughters, and with our flocks and
herds, because we are to celebrate a
festival to the LORD."
10Pharaoh said, "The LORD be with
you—if I let you go, along with your
women and children! Clearly you are
bent on evil. 11No! Let only the men go;
and worship the LORD, since that's what
you have been asking for." Then Moses
and Aaron were driven out of Pharaoh's
presence.
12And the LORD said to Moses,
"Stretch out your hand over Egypt so
that locusts will swarm over the land
and devour everything growing in the
fields, everything left by the hail."
13So Moses stretched out his staff
over Egypt, and the LORD made an east
wind blow across the land all that day
and all that night. By morning the wind
had brought the locusts; 14they invaded
all Egypt and settled down in every area
of the country in great numbers. Never
before had there been such a plague of
locusts, nor will there ever be again.
15They covered all the ground until it
was black. They devoured all that was
left after the hail—everything growing
in the fields and the fruit on the trees.
Nothing green remained on tree or
plant in all the land of Egypt.
16Pharaoh quickly summoned Moses
and Aaron and said, "I have sinned
against the LORD your God and against
you. 17Now forgive my sin once more
and pray to the LORD your God to take
this deadly plague away from me."
18Moses then left Pharaoh and prayed
to the LORD. 19And the LORD changed
the wind to a very strong west wind,
which caught up the locusts and carried
them into the Red Sea. Not a locust was
left anywhere in Egypt. 20But the LORD
hardened Pharaoh's heart, and he
would not let the Israelites go.

The Plague of Darkness

21Then the LORD said to Moses,
"Stretch out your hand towards the sky
so that darkness will spread over Egypt
—darkness that can be felt." 22So
Moses stretched out his hand towards
the sky, and total darkness covered all
Egypt for three days. 23No-one could
see anyone else or leave his place for
three days. Yet all the Israelites had
light in the places where they lived.
24Then Pharaoh summoned Moses
and said, "Go, worship the LORD. Even
your women and children may go with
you; only leave your flocks and herds
behind."
25But Moses said, "You must allow us
to have sacrifices and burnt offerings to
present to the LORD our God. 26Our
livestock too must go with us; not a hoof
is to be left behind. We have to use

some of them in worshipping the LORD
our God, and until we get there we will
not know what we are to use to worship
the LORD."
27But the LORD hardened Pharaoh's
heart, and he was not willing to let them
go. 28Pharaoh said to Moses, "Get out
of my sight! Make sure you do not
appear before me again! The day you
see my face you will die."
29"Just as you say," Moses replied, "I
will never appear before you again."

NEW TESTAMENT READING
Matthew 26:69–27:10

Peter Disowns Jesus

69Now Peter was sitting out in the
courtyard, and a servant girl came to
him. "You also were with Jesus of
Galilee," she said.
70But he denied it before them all. "I
don't know what you're talking about,"
he said.
71Then he went out to the gateway,
where another girl saw him and said to
the people there, "This fellow was with
Jesus of Nazareth."
72He denied it again, with an oath: "I
don't know the man!"
73After a little while, those standing
there went up to Peter and said, "Surely
you are one of them, for your accent
gives you away."
74Then he began to call down curses
on himself and he swore to them, "I
don't know the man!"
Immediately a cock crowed. 75Then
Peter remembered the word Jesus had
spoken: "Before the cock crows, you
will disown me three times." And he
went outside and wept bitterly.

Judas Hangs Himself

27 Early in the morning, all the
chief priests and the elders of the
people came to the decision to put Jesus
to death. 2They bound him, led him
away and handed him over to Pilate, the
governor.
3When Judas, who had betrayed him,
saw that Jesus was condemned, he was
seized with remorse and returned the
thirty silver coins to the chief priests and
the elders. 4"I have sinned," he said,
"for I have betrayed innocent blood."
"What is that to us?" they replied.
"That's your responsibility."
5So Judas threw the money into the
temple and left. Then he went away and
hanged himself.
6The chief priests picked up the coins
and said, "It is against the law to put this
into the treasury, since it is blood
money." 7So they decided to use the
money to buy the potter's field as a
burial place for foreigners. 8That is why
it has been called the Field of Blood to
this day. 9Then what was spoken by
Jeremiah the prophet was fulfilled:
"They took the thirty silver coins, the
price set on him by the people of Israel,
10and they used them to buy the potter's
field, as the Lord commanded me."

READING FROM PSALMS
Psalm 20:1–9

For the director of music. A psalm of
David.

1May the LORD answer you when you
are in distress;
may the name of the God of Jacob
protect you.
2May he send you help from the
sanctuary
and grant you support from Zion.
3May he remember all your sacrifices
and accept your burnt offerings.
Selah
4May he give you the desire of your
heart
and make all your plans succeed.
5We will shout for joy when you are
victorious
and will lift up our banners in the
name of our God.
May the LORD grant all your
requests.

6Now I know that the LORD saves his
anointed;
he answers him from his holy
heaven
with the saving power of his right
hand.
7Some trust in chariots and some in
horses,
but we trust in the name of the
LORD our God.
8They are brought to their knees and
fall,
but we rise up and stand firm.
9O LORD, save the king!
Answer us when we call!

FEBRUARY 12

DAY 43

OLD TESTAMENT READING
Exodus 11:1–12:51

The Plague on the Firstborn

11 Now the LORD said to Moses, "I
will bring one more plague on
Pharaoh and on Egypt. After that, he
will let you go from here, and when he
does, he will drive you out completely.
2Tell the people that men and women
alike are to ask their neighbours for
articles of silver and gold." 3(The LORD
made the Egyptians favourably disposed towards the people, and Moses
himself was highly regarded in Egypt by
Pharaoh's officials and by the people.)
4So Moses said, "This is what the
LORD says: 'About midnight I will go
throughout Egypt. 5Every firstborn son
in Egypt will die, from the firstborn son
of Pharaoh, who sits on the throne, to
the firstborn son of the slave girl, who is
at her hand mill, and all the firstborn of
the cattle as well. 6There will be loud
wailing throughout Egypt—worse than
there has ever been or ever will be
again. 7But among the Israelites not a
dog will bark at any man or animal.'
Then you will know that the LORD
makes a distinction between Egypt and
Israel. 8All these officials of yours will
come to me, bowing down before me
and saying, 'Go, you and all the people
who follow you!' After that I will
leave." Then Moses, hot with anger,
left Pharaoh.
9The LORD had said to Moses, "Pharaoh will refuse to listen to you—so that
my wonders may be multiplied in
Egypt." 10Moses and Aaron performed
all these wonders before Pharaoh, but
the LORD hardened Pharaoh's heart,
and he would not let the Israelites go
out of his country.

The Passover

12 The LORD said to Moses and
Aaron in Egypt, 2"This month is
to be for you the first month, the first
month of your year. 3Tell the whole
community of Israel that on the tenth
day of this month each man is to take a
lamb for his family, one for each household. 4If any household is too small for a
whole lamb, they must share one with
their nearest neighbour, having taken
into account the number of people there
are. You are to determine the amount
of lamb needed in accordance with what
each person will eat. 5The animals you
choose must be year-old males without
defect, and you may take them from the
sheep or the goats. 6Take care of them
until the fourteenth day of the month,
when all the people of the community of
Israel must slaughter them at twilight.
7Then they are to take some of the
blood and put it on the sides and tops of
the door-frames of the houses where
they eat the lambs. 8That same night
they are to eat the meat roasted over the

fire, along with bitter herbs, and bread
made without yeast. 9Do not eat the
meat raw or cooked in water, but roast
it over the fire—head, legs and inner
parts. 10Do not leave any of it till morning; if some is left till morning, you must
burn it. 11This is how you are to eat it:
with your cloak tucked into your belt,
your sandals on your feet and your staff
in your hand. Eat it in haste; it is the
LORD's Passover.

12"On that same night I will pass
through Egypt and strike down every
firstborn—both men and animals—and
I will bring judgment on all the gods of
Egypt. I am the LORD. 13The blood will
be a sign for you on the houses where
you are; and when I see the blood, I will
pass over you. No destructive plague
will touch you when I strike Egypt.

14"This is a day you are to commemorate; for the generations to come you
shall celebrate it as a festival to the
LORD—a lasting ordinance. 15For seven
days you are to eat bread made without
yeast. On the first day remove the yeast
from your houses, for whoever eats anything with yeast in it from the first day
until the seventh must be cut off from
Israel. 16On the first day hold a sacred
assembly, and another one on the
seventh day. Do no work at all on these
days, except to prepare food for everyone to eat—that is all you may do.

17"Celebrate the Feast of Unleavened Bread, because it was on this
very day that I brought your divisions
out of Egypt. Celebrate this day as a
lasting ordinance for the generations to
come. 18In the first month you are to eat
bread made without yeast, from the
evening of the fourteenth day until the
evening of the twenty-first day. 19For
seven days no yeast is to be found in
your houses. And whoever eats anything with yeast in it must be cut off
from the community of Israel, whether
he is an alien or native-born. 20Eat nothing made with yeast. Wherever you
live, you must eat unleavened bread."

21Then Moses summoned all the
elders of Israel and said to them, "Go at
once and select the animals for your
families and slaughter the Passover
lamb. 22Take a bunch of hyssop, dip it
into the blood in the basin and put some
of the blood on the top and on both
sides of the door-frame. Not one of you
shall go out of the door of his house until
morning. 23When the LORD goes
through the land to strike down the
Egyptians, he will see the blood on the
top and sides of the door-frame and will
pass over that doorway, and he will not
permit the destroyer to enter your
houses and strike you down.

24"Obey these instructions as a lasting ordinance for you and your descendants. 25When you enter the land that
the LORD will give you as he promised,
observe this ceremony. 26And when
your children ask you, 'What does this
ceremony mean to you?' 27then tell
them, 'It is the Passover sacrifice to the
LORD, who passed over the houses of
the Israelites in Egypt and spared our
homes when he struck down the Egyptians.'" Then the people bowed down
and worshipped. 28The Israelites did
just what the LORD commanded Moses
and Aaron.

29At midnight the LORD struck down
all the firstborn in Egypt, from the
firstborn of Pharaoh, who sat on the
throne, to the firstborn of the prisoner,
who was in the dungeon, and the
firstborn of all the livestock as well.
30Pharaoh and all his officials and all the
Egyptians got up during the night, and
there was loud wailing in Egypt, for
there was not a house without someone
dead.

The Exodus

31During the night Pharaoh summoned Moses and Aaron and said,
"Up! Leave my people, you and the
Israelites! Go, worship the LORD as you
have requested. 32Take your flocks and
herds, as you have said, and go. And
also bless me."

33The Egyptians urged the people to
hurry and leave the country. "For
otherwise," they said, "we will all die!"

34So the people took their dough before
the yeast was added, and carried it on
their shoulders in kneading troughs
wrapped in clothing. 35The Israelites
did as Moses instructed and asked the
Egyptians for articles of silver and gold
and for clothing. 36The LORD had made
the Egyptians favourably disposed towards the people, and they gave them
what they asked for; so they plundered
the Egyptians.
37The Israelites journeyed from
Rameses to Succoth. There were about
six hundred thousand men on foot, besides women and children. 38Many
other people went up with them, as well
as large droves of livestock, both flocks
and herds. 39With the dough they had
brought from Egypt, they baked cakes
of unleavened bread. The dough was
without yeast because they had been
driven out of Egypt and did not have
time to prepare food for themselves.
40Now the length of time the Israelite
people lived in Egypt was 430 years.
41At the end of the 430 years, to the very
day, all the LORD's divisions left Egypt.
42Because the LORD kept vigil that night
to bring them out of Egypt, on this night
all the Israelites are to keep vigil to
honour the LORD for the generations to
come.

Passover Restrictions

43The LORD said to Moses and
Aaron, "These are the regulations for
the Passover:
"No foreigner is to eat of it. 44Any
slave you have bought may eat of it after
you have circumcised him, 45but a temporary resident and a hired worker may
not eat of it.
46"It must be eaten inside one house;
take none of the meat outside the
house. Do not break any of the bones.
47The whole community of Israel must
celebrate it.
48"An alien living among you who
wants to celebrate the LORD's Passover
must have all the males in his household
circumcised; then he may take part like
one born in the land. No uncircumcised
male may eat of it. 49The same law
applies to the native-born and to the
alien living among you."

50All the Israelites did just what the
LORD had commanded Moses and
Aaron. 51And on that very day the
LORD brought the Israelites out of
Egypt by their divisions.

NEW TESTAMENT READING
Matthew 27:11–44

Jesus Before Pilate

11Meanwhile Jesus stood before the
governor, and the governor asked him,
"Are you the king of the Jews?"
"Yes, it is as you say," Jesus replied.
12When he was accused by the chief
priests and the elders, he gave no
answer. 13Then Pilate asked him,
"Don't you hear the testimony they are
bringing against you?" 14But Jesus
made no reply, not even to a single
charge—to the great amazement of the
governor.
15Now it was the governor's custom at
the Feast to release a prisoner chosen by
the crowd. 16At that time they had a
notorious prisoner, called Barabbas.
17So when the crowd had gathered,
Pilate asked them, "Which one do you
want me to release to you: Barabbas, or
Jesus who is called Christ?" 18For he
knew it was out of envy that they had
handed Jesus over to him.
19While Pilate was sitting on the
judge's seat, his wife sent him this message: "Don't have anything to do with
that innocent man, for I have suffered a
great deal today in a dream because of
him."
20But the chief priests and the elders
persuaded the crowd to ask for Barabbas and to have Jesus executed.
21"Which of the two do you want me
to release to you?" asked the governor.
"Barabbas," they answered.
22"What shall I do, then, with Jesus
who is called Christ?" Pilate asked.
They all answered, "Crucify him!"

23“Why? What crime has he committed?” asked Pilate.
But they shouted all the louder,
“Crucify him!”
24When Pilate saw that he was getting
nowhere, but that instead an uproar was
starting, he took water and washed his
hands in front of the crowd. “I am innocent of this man’s blood,” he said. “It is
your responsibility!”
25All the people answered, “Let his
blood be on us and on our children!”
26Then he released Barabbas to
them. But he had Jesus flogged, and
handed him over to be crucified.

The Soldiers Mock Jesus

27Then the governor’s soldiers took
Jesus into the Praetorium and gathered
the whole company of soldiers round
him. 28They stripped him and put a
scarlet robe on him, 29and then twisted
together a crown of thorns and set it on
his head. They put a staff in his right
hand and knelt in front of him and
mocked him. “Hail, king of the Jews!”
they said. 30They spat on him, and took
the staff and struck him on the head
again and again. 31After they had
mocked him, they took off the robe
and put his own clothes on him. Then
they led him away to crucify him.

The Crucifixion

32As they were going out, they met a
man from Cyrene, named Simon, and
they forced him to carry the cross.
33They came to a place called Golgotha
(which means The Place of the Skull).
34There they offered Jesus wine to
drink, mixed with gall; but after tasting
it, he refused to drink it. 35When they
had crucified him, they divided up his
clothes by casting lots. 36And sitting
down, they kept watch over him there.
37Above his head they placed the written charge against him: THIS IS JESUS,
THE KING OF THE JEWS. 38Two robbers
were crucified with him, one on his right
and one on his left. 39Those who passed
by hurled insults at him, shaking their
heads 40and saying, “You who are going
to destroy the temple and build it in
three days, save yourself! Come down
from the cross, if you are the Son of
God!”
41In the same way the chief priests,
the teachers of the law and the elders
mocked him. 42“He saved others,” they
said, “but he can’t save himself! He’s
the King of Israel! Let him come down
now from the cross, and we will believe
in him. 43He trusts in God. Let God
rescue him now if he wants him, for he
said, ‘I am the Son of God.’” 44In the
same way the robbers who were crucified with him also heaped insults on
him.

READING FROM PSALMS

Psalm 21:1–7

For the director of music. A psalm of David.

1O LORD, the king rejoices in your
strength.
How great is his joy in the victories
you give!
2You have granted him the desire of
his heart
and have not withheld the request
of his lips. *Selah*
3You welcomed him with rich
blessings
and placed a crown of pure gold on
his head.
4He asked you for life, and you gave it
to him—
length of days, for ever and ever.
5Through the victories you gave, his
glory is great;
you have bestowed on him
splendour and majesty.
6Surely you have granted him eternal
blessings
and made him glad with the joy of
your presence.
7For the king trusts in the LORD;
through the unfailing love of the
Most High
he will not be shaken.

FEBRUARY 13

DAY 44

OLD TESTAMENT READING
Exodus 13:1–14:31

Consecration of the Firstborn

13 The LORD said to Moses, 2"Consecrate to me every firstborn male. The first offspring of every womb among the Israelites belongs to me, whether man or animal."

3Then Moses said to the people, "Commemorate this day, the day you came out of Egypt, out of the land of slavery, because the LORD brought you out of it with a mighty hand. Eat nothing containing yeast. 4Today, in the month of Abib, you are leaving. 5When the LORD brings you into the land of the Canaanites, Hittites, Amorites, Hivites and Jebusites—the land he swore to your forefathers to give you, a land flowing with milk and honey—you are to observe this ceremony in this month: 6For seven days eat bread made without yeast and on the seventh day hold a festival to the LORD. 7Eat unleavened bread during those seven days; nothing with yeast in it is to be seen among you, nor shall any yeast be seen anywhere within your borders. 8On that day tell your son, 'I do this because of what the LORD did for me when I came out of Egypt.' 9This observance will be for you like a sign on your hand and a reminder on your forehead that the law of the LORD is to be on your lips. For the LORD brought you out of Egypt with his mighty hand. 10You must keep this ordinance at the appointed time year after year.

11"After the LORD brings you into the land of the Canaanites and gives it to you, as he promised on oath to you and your forefathers, 12you are to give over to the LORD the first offspring of every womb. All the firstborn males of your livestock belong to the LORD. 13Redeem with a lamb every firstborn donkey, but if you do not redeem it, break its neck. Redeem every firstborn among your sons.

14"In days to come when your son asks you, 'What does this mean?' say to him, 'With a mighty hand the LORD brought us out of Egypt, out of the land of slavery. 15When Pharaoh stubbornly refused to let us go, the LORD killed every firstborn in Egypt, both man and animal. This is why I sacrifice to the LORD the first male offspring of every womb and redeem each of my firstborn sons.' 16And it will be like a sign on your hand and a symbol on your forehead that the LORD brought us out of Egypt with his mighty hand."

Crossing the Sea

17When Pharaoh let the people go, God did not lead them on the road through the Philistine country, though that was shorter. For God said, "If they face war, they might change their minds and return to Egypt." 18So God led the people around by the desert road towards the Red Sea. The Israelites went up out of Egypt armed for battle.

19Moses took the bones of Joseph with him because Joseph had made the sons of Israel swear an oath. He had said, "God will surely come to your aid, and then you must carry my bones up with you from this place."

20After leaving Succoth they camped at Etham on the edge of the desert. 21By day the LORD went ahead of them in a pillar of cloud to guide them on their way and by night in a pillar of fire to give them light, so that they could travel by day or night. 22Neither the pillar of cloud by day nor the pillar of fire by night left its place in front of the people.

14 Then the LORD said to Moses, 2"Tell the Israelites to turn back and camp near Pi Hahiroth, between Migdol and the sea. They are to camp by the sea, directly opposite Baal

Zephon. 3Pharaoh will think, 'The Israelites are wandering around the land in confusion, hemmed in by the desert.' 4And I will harden Pharaoh's heart, and he will pursue them. But I will gain glory for myself through Pharaoh and all his army, and the Egyptians will know that I am the LORD." So the Israelites did this.

5When the king of Egypt was told that the people had fled, Pharaoh and his officials changed their minds about them and said, "What have we done? We have let the Israelites go and have lost their services!" 6So he had his chariot made ready and took his army with him. 7He took six hundred of the best chariots, along with all the other chariots of Egypt, with officers over all of them. 8The LORD hardened the heart of Pharaoh king of Egypt, so that he pursued the Israelites, who were marching out boldly. 9The Egyptians—all Pharaoh's horses and chariots, horsemen and troops—pursued the Israelites and overtook them as they camped by the sea near Pi Hahiroth, opposite Baal Zephon.

10As Pharaoh approached, the Israelites looked up, and there were the Egyptians, marching after them. They were terrified and cried out to the LORD. 11They said to Moses, "Was it because there were no graves in Egypt that you brought us to the desert to die? What have you done to us by bringing us out of Egypt? 12Didn't we say to you in Egypt, 'Leave us alone; let us serve the Egyptians'? It would have been better for us to serve the Egyptians than to die in the desert!"

13Moses answered the people, "Do not be afraid. Stand firm and you will see the deliverance the LORD will bring you today. The Egyptians you see today you will never see again. 14The LORD will fight for you; you need only to be still."

15Then the LORD said to Moses, "Why are you crying out to me? Tell the Israelites to move on. 16Raise your staff and stretch out your hand over the sea to divide the water so that the Israelites can go through the sea on dry ground. 17I will harden the hearts of the Egyptians so that they will go in after them. And I will gain glory through Pharaoh and all his army, through his chariots and his horsemen. 18The Egyptians will know that I am the LORD when I gain glory through Pharaoh, his chariots and his horsemen."

19Then the angel of God, who had been travelling in front of Israel's army, withdrew and went behind them. The pillar of cloud also moved from in front and stood behind them, 20coming between the armies of Egypt and Israel. Throughout the night the cloud brought darkness to the one side and light to the other; so neither went near the other all night long.

21Then Moses stretched out his hand over the sea, and all that night the LORD drove the sea back with a strong east wind and turned it into dry land. The waters were divided, 22and the Israelites went through the sea on dry ground, with a wall of water on their right and on their left.

23The Egyptians pursued them, and all Pharaoh's horses and chariots and horsemen followed them into the sea. 24During the last watch of the night the LORD looked down from the pillar of fire and cloud at the Egyptian army and threw it into confusion. 25He made the wheels of their chariots come off so that they had difficulty driving. And the Egyptians said, "Let's get away from the Israelites! The LORD is fighting for them against Egypt."

26Then the LORD said to Moses, "Stretch out your hand over the sea so that the waters may flow back over the Egyptians and their chariots and horsemen." 27Moses stretched out his hand over the sea, and at daybreak the sea went back to its place. The Egyptians were fleeing towards it, and the LORD swept them into the sea. 28The water flowed back and covered the chariots and horsemen—the entire army of Pharaoh that had followed the Israelites

into the sea. Not one of them survived.
29But the Israelites went through the
sea on dry ground, with a wall of water
on their right and on their left. 30That
day the LORD saved Israel from the
hands of the Egyptians, and Israel saw
the Egyptians lying dead on the shore.
31And when the Israelites saw the great
power the LORD displayed against the
Egyptians, the people feared the LORD
and put their trust in him and in Moses
his servant.

NEW TESTAMENT READING

Matthew 27:45–66

The Death of Jesus

45From the sixth hour until the ninth
hour darkness came over all the land.
46About the ninth hour Jesus cried out
in a loud voice, "*Eloi, Eloi, lama sabachthani?*"—which means, "My
God, my God, why have you forsaken
me?"
47When some of those standing there
heard this, they said, "He's calling
Elijah."
48Immediately one of them ran and
got a sponge. He filled it with wine
vinegar, put it on a stick, and offered it
to Jesus to drink. 49The rest said, "Now
leave him alone. Let's see if Elijah
comes to save him."
50And when Jesus had cried out again
in a loud voice, he gave up his spirit.
51At that moment the curtain of the
temple was torn in two from top to
bottom. The earth shook and the rocks
split. 52The tombs broke open and the
bodies of many holy people who had
died were raised to life. 53They came
out of the tombs, and after Jesus' resurrection they went into the holy city and
appeared to many people.
54When the centurion and those with
him who were guarding Jesus saw the
earthquake and all that had happened,
they were terrified, and exclaimed,
"Surely he was the Son of God!"
55Many women were there, watching
from a distance. They had followed
Jesus from Galilee to care for his needs.
56Among them were Mary Magdalene,
Mary the mother of James and Joses,
and the mother of Zebedee's sons.

The Burial of Jesus

57As evening approached, there came
a rich man from Arimathea, named
Joseph, who had himself become a disciple of Jesus. 58Going to Pilate, he
asked for Jesus' body, and Pilate
ordered that it be given to him. 59Joseph
took the body, wrapped it in a clean
linen cloth, 60and placed it in his own
new tomb that he had cut out of the
rock. He rolled a big stone in front of
the entrance to the tomb and went
away. 61Mary Magdalene and the other
Mary were sitting there opposite the
tomb.

The Guard at the Tomb

62The next day, the one after Preparation Day, the chief priests and the
Pharisees went to Pilate. 63"Sir," they
said, "we remember that while he was
still alive that deceiver said, 'After three
days I will rise again.' 64So give the
order for the tomb to be made secure
until the third day. Otherwise, his disciples may come and steal the body and
tell the people that he has been raised
from the dead. This last deception will
be worse than the first."
65"Take a guard," Pilate answered.
"Go, make the tomb as secure as you
know how." 66So they went and made
the tomb secure by putting a seal on the
stone and posting the guard.

READING FROM PROVERBS

Proverbs 4:20–27

20My son, pay attention to what I say;
listen closely to my words.
21Do not let them out of your sight,
keep them within your heart;

[22]for they are life to those who find
them
and health to a man's whole
body.
[23]Above all else, guard your heart,
for it is the wellspring of life.
[24]Put away perversity from your
mouth;
keep corrupt talk far from your
lips.
[25]Let your eyes look straight ahead,
fix your gaze directly before you.
[26]Make level paths for your feet
and take only ways that are firm.
[27]Do not swerve to the right or the left;
keep your foot from evil.

DAY 45

FEBRUARY 14

OLD TESTAMENT READING
Exodus 15:1–16:36

The Song of Moses and Miriam

15 Then Moses and the Israelites
sang this song to the LORD:

"I will sing to the LORD,
for he is highly exalted.
The horse and its rider
he has hurled into the sea.
[2]The LORD is my strength and my
song;
he has become my salvation.
He is my God, and I will praise him,
my father's God, and I will exalt
him.
[3]The LORD is a warrior;
the LORD is his name.
[4]Pharaoh's chariots and his army
he has hurled into the sea.
The best of Pharaoh's officers
are drowned in the Red Sea.
[5]The deep waters have covered them;
they sank to the depths like a
stone.

[6]"Your right hand, O LORD,
was majestic in power.
Your right hand, O LORD,
shattered the enemy.
[7]In the greatness of your majesty
you threw down those who
opposed you.
You unleashed your burning anger;
it consumed them like stubble.
[8]By the blast of your nostrils
the waters piled up.
The surging waters stood firm like a
wall;
the deep waters congealed in the
heart of the sea.

[9]"The enemy boasted,
'I will pursue, I will overtake them.
I will divide the spoils;
I will gorge myself on them.
I will draw my sword
and my hand will destroy them.'
[10]But you blew with your breath,
and the sea covered them.
They sank like lead
in the mighty waters.

[11]"Who among the gods is like you, O
LORD?
Who is like you—
majestic in holiness,
awesome in glory,
working wonders?
[12]You stretched out your right hand
and the earth swallowed them.

[13]"In your unfailing love you will lead
the people you have redeemed.
In your strength you will guide them
to your holy dwelling.
[14]The nations will hear and tremble;
anguish will grip the people of
Philistia.

15The chiefs of Edom will be terrified,
the leaders of Moab will be seized
with trembling,
the people of Canaan will melt away;
16 terror and dread will fall upon
them.
By the power of your arm
they will be as still as a stone—
until your people pass by, O LORD,
until the people you bought pass
by.
17You will bring them in and plant
them
on the mountain of your
inheritance—
the place, O LORD, you made for
your dwelling,
the sanctuary, O Lord, your hands
established.
18The LORD will reign
for ever and ever."

19When Pharaoh's horses, chariots
and horsemen went into the sea, the
LORD brought the waters of the sea back
over them, but the Israelites walked
through the sea on dry ground. 20Then
Miriam the prophetess, Aaron's sister,
took a tambourine in her hand, and all
the women followed her, with tambourines and dancing. 21Miriam sang to
them:

"Sing to the LORD,
for he is highly exalted.
The horse and its rider
he has hurled into the sea."

The Waters of Marah and Elim

22Then Moses led Israel from the Red
Sea and they went into the Desert of
Shur. For three days they travelled in
the desert without finding water.
23When they came to Marah, they could
not drink its water because it was bitter.
(That is why the place is called Marah.)
24So the people grumbled against
Moses, saying, "What are we to drink?"
25Then Moses cried out to the LORD,
and the LORD showed him a piece of
wood. He threw it into the water, and
the water became sweet.
There the LORD made a decree and a
law for them, and there he tested them.
26He said, "If you listen carefully to the
voice of the LORD your God and do
what is right in his eyes, if you pay
attention to his commands and keep all
his decrees, I will not bring on you any
of the diseases I brought on the Egyptians, for I am the LORD, who heals
you."
27Then they came to Elim, where
there were twelve springs and seventy
palm trees, and they camped there near
the water.

Manna and Quail

16 The whole Israelite community
set out from Elim and came to
the Desert of Sin, which is between
Elim and Sinai, on the fifteenth day of
the second month after they had come
out of Egypt. 2In the desert the whole
community grumbled against Moses
and Aaron. 3The Israelites said to them,
"If only we had died by the LORD's hand
in Egypt! There we sat round pots of
meat and ate all the food we wanted,
but you have brought us out into this
desert to starve this entire assembly to
death."
4Then the LORD said to Moses, "I will
rain down bread from heaven for you.
The people are to go out each day and
gather enough for that day. In this way I
will test them and see whether they will
follow my instructions. 5On the sixth
day they are to prepare what they bring
in, and that is to be twice as much as
they gather on the other days."
6So Moses and Aaron said to all the
Israelites, "In the evening you will
know that it was the LORD who brought
you out of Egypt, 7and in the morning
you will see the glory of the LORD,
because he has heard your grumbling
against him. Who are we, that you
should grumble against us?" 8Moses
also said, "You will know that it was the

LORD when he gives you meat to eat in the evening and all the bread you want in the morning, because he has heard your grumbling against him. Who are we? You are not grumbling against us, but against the LORD."

9Then Moses told Aaron, "Say to the entire Israelite community, 'Come before the LORD, for he has heard your grumbling.'"

10While Aaron was speaking to the whole Israelite community, they looked towards the desert, and there was the glory of the LORD appearing in the cloud.

11The LORD said to Moses, 12"I have heard the grumbling of the Israelites. Tell them, 'At twilight you will eat meat, and in the morning you will be filled with bread. Then you will know that I am the LORD your God.'"

13That evening quail came and covered the camp, and in the morning there was a layer of dew around the camp. 14When the dew was gone, thin flakes like frost on the ground appeared on the desert floor. 15When the Israelites saw it, they said to each other, "What is it?" For they did not know what it was.

Moses said to them, "It is the bread the LORD has given you to eat. 16This is what the LORD has commanded: 'Each one is to gather as much as he needs. Take an omer for each person you have in your tent.'"

17The Israelites did as they were told; some gathered much, some little. 18And when they measured it by the omer, he who gathered much did not have too much, and he who gathered little did not have too little. Each one gathered as much as he needed.

19Then Moses said to them, "No-one is to keep any of it until morning."

20However, some of them paid no attention to Moses; they kept part of it until morning, but it was full of maggots and began to smell. So Moses was angry with them.

21Each morning everyone gathered as much as he needed, and when the sun grew hot, it melted away. 22On the sixth day, they gathered twice as much—two omers for each person—and the leaders of the community came and reported this to Moses. 23He said to them, "This is what the LORD commanded: 'Tomorrow is to be a day of rest, a holy Sabbath to the LORD. So bake what you want to bake and boil what you want to boil. Save whatever is left and keep it until morning.'"

24So they saved it until morning, as Moses commanded, and it did not stink or get maggots in it. 25"Eat it today," Moses said, "because today is a Sabbath to the LORD. You will not find any of it on the ground today. 26Six days you are to gather it, but on the seventh day, the Sabbath, there will not be any."

27Nevertheless, some of the people went out on the seventh day to gather it, but they found none. 28Then the LORD said to Moses, "How long will you refuse to keep my commands and my instructions? 29Bear in mind that the LORD has given you the Sabbath; that is why on the sixth day he gives you bread for two days. Everyone is to stay where he is on the seventh day; no-one is to go out." 30So the people rested on the seventh day.

31The people of Israel called the bread manna. It was white like coriander seed and tasted like wafers made with honey. 32Moses said, "This is what the LORD has commanded: 'Take an omer of manna and keep it for the generations to come, so they can see the bread I gave you to eat in the desert when I brought you out of Egypt.'"

33So Moses said to Aaron, "Take a jar and put an omer of manna in it. Then place it before the LORD to be kept for the generations to come."

34As the LORD commanded Moses, Aaron put the manna in front of the Testimony, that it might be kept. 35The Israelites ate manna for forty years, until they came to a land that was settled; they ate manna until they reached the border of Canaan.

36(An omer is one tenth of an ephah.)

NEW TESTAMENT READING
Matthew 28:1–20

The Resurrection

28 After the Sabbath, at dawn on
the first day of the week, Mary
Magdalene and the other Mary went to
look at the tomb.
2There was a violent earthquake, for
an angel of the Lord came down from
heaven and, going to the tomb, rolled
back the stone and sat on it. 3His
appearance was like lightning, and his
clothes were white as snow. 4The guards
were so afraid of him that they shook
and became like dead men.
5The angel said to the women, "Do
not be afraid, for I know that you are
looking for Jesus, who was crucified.
6He is not here; he has risen, just as he
said. Come and see the place where he
lay. 7Then go quickly and tell his disciples: 'He has risen from the dead and is
going ahead of you into Galilee. There
you will see him.' Now I have told you."
8So the women hurried away from the
tomb, afraid yet filled with joy, and ran
to tell his disciples. 9Suddenly Jesus met
them. "Greetings," he said. They came
to him, clasped his feet and worshipped
him. 10Then Jesus said to them, "Do not
be afraid. Go and tell my brothers to go
to Galilee; there they will see me."

The Guards' Report

11While the women were on their
way, some of the guards went into the
city and reported to the chief priests
everything that had happened. 12When
the chief priests had met with the elders
and devised a plan, they gave the soldiers a large sum of money, 13telling
them, "You are to say, 'His disciples
came during the night and stole him
away while we were asleep.' 14If this
report gets to the governor, we will
satisfy him and keep you out of
trouble." 15So the soldiers took the
money and did as they were instructed.
And this story has been widely circu-
lated among the Jews to this very day.

The Great Commission

16Then the eleven disciples went to
Galilee, to the mountain where Jesus
had told them to go. 17When they saw
him, they worshipped him; but some
doubted. 18Then Jesus came to them
and said, "All authority in heaven and
on earth has been given to me.
19Therefore go and make disciples of all
nations, baptising them in the name of
the Father and of the Son and of the
Holy Spirit, 20and teaching them to
obey everything I have commanded
you. And surely I am with you always,
to the very end of the age."

READING FROM PSALMS
Psalm 21:8–13

8Your hand will lay hold on all your
enemies;
your right hand will seize your
foes.
9At the time of your appearing
you will make them like a fiery
furnace.
In his wrath the LORD will swallow
them up,
and his fire will consume them.
10You will destroy their descendants
from the earth,
their posterity from mankind.
11Though they plot evil against you
and devise wicked schemes, they
cannot succeed;
12for you will make them turn their
backs
when you aim at them with drawn
bow.

13Be exalted, O LORD, in your
strength;
we will sing and praise your might.

DAY 46

FEBRUARY 15

OLD TESTAMENT READING
Exodus 17:1–18:27

Water From the Rock

17 The whole Israelite community set out from the Desert of Sin, travelling from place to place as the LORD commanded. They camped at Rephidim, but there was no water for the people to drink. 2So they quarrelled with Moses and said, "Give us water to drink."

Moses replied, "Why do you quarrel with me? Why do you put the LORD to the test?"

3But the people were thirsty for water there, and they grumbled against Moses. They said, "Why did you bring us up out of Egypt to make us and our children and livestock die of thirst?"

4Then Moses cried out to the LORD, "What am I to do with these people? They are almost ready to stone me."

5The LORD answered Moses, "Walk on ahead of the people. Take with you some of the elders of Israel and take in your hand the staff with which you struck the Nile, and go. 6I will stand there before you by the rock at Horeb. Strike the rock, and water will come out of it for the people to drink." So Moses did this in the sight of the elders of Israel. 7And he called the place Massah and Meribah because the Israelites quarrelled and because they tested the LORD saying, "Is the LORD among us or not?"

The Amalekites Defeated

8The Amalekites came and attacked the Israelites at Rephidim. 9Moses said to Joshua, "Choose some of our men and go out to fight the Amalekites. Tomorrow I will stand on top of the hill with the staff of God in my hands."

10So Joshua fought the Amalekites as Moses had ordered, and Moses, Aaron and Hur went to the top of the hill. 11As long as Moses held up his hands, the Israelites were winning, but whenever he lowered his hands, the Amalekites were winning. 12When Moses' hands grew tired, they took a stone and put it under him and he sat on it. Aaron and Hur held his hands up—one on one side, one on the other—so that his hands remained steady till sunset. 13So Joshua overcame the Amalekite army with the sword.

14Then the LORD said to Moses, "Write this on a scroll as something to be remembered and make sure that Joshua hears it, because I will completely blot out the memory of Amalek from under heaven."

15Moses built an altar and called it The LORD is my Banner. 16He said, "For hands were lifted up to the throne of the LORD. The LORD will be at war against the Amalekites from generation to generation."

Jethro Visits Moses

18 Now Jethro, the priest of Midian and father-in-law of Moses, heard of everything God had done for Moses and for his people Israel, and how the LORD had brought Israel out of Egypt.

2After Moses had sent away his wife Zipporah, his father-in-law Jethro received her 3and her two sons. One son was named Gershom, for Moses said, "I have become an alien in a foreign land"; 4and the other was named Eliezer, for he said, "My father's God was my helper; he saved me from the sword of Pharaoh."

5Jethro, Moses' father-in-law, together with Moses' sons and wife, came to him in the desert, where he was camped near the mountain of God.

6Jethro had sent word to him, "I, your
father-in-law Jethro, am coming to you
with your wife and her two sons."
7So Moses went out to meet his
father-in-law and bowed down and kissed him. They greeted each other and
then went into the tent. 8Moses told his
father-in-law about everything the
LORD had done to Pharaoh and the
Egyptians for Israel's sake and about all
the hardships they had met along the
way and how the LORD had saved them.
9Jethro was delighted to hear about
all the good things the LORD had done
for Israel in rescuing them from the
hand of the Egyptians. 10He said,
"Praise be to the LORD, who rescued
you from the hand of the Egyptians and
of Pharaoh, and who rescued the people
from the hand of the Egyptians. 11Now I
know that the LORD is greater than all
other gods, for he did this to those who
had treated Israel arrogantly." 12Then
Jethro, Moses' father-in-law, brought a
burnt offering and other sacrifices to
God, and Aaron came with all the
elders of Israel to eat bread with Moses'
father-in-law in the presence of God.
13The next day Moses took his seat to
serve as judge for the people, and they
stood round him from morning till evening. 14When his father-in-law saw all
that Moses was doing for the people, he
said, "What is this you are doing for the
people? Why do you alone sit as judge,
while all these people stand round you
from morning till evening?"
15Moses answered him, "Because the
people come to me to seek God's will.
16Whenever they have a dispute, it is
brought to me, and I decide between
the parties and inform them of God's
decrees and laws."
17Moses' father-in-law replied,
"What you are doing is not good. 18You
and these people who come to you will
only wear yourselves out. The work is
too heavy for you; you cannot handle it
alone. 19Listen now to me and I will give
you some advice, and may God be with
you. You must be the people's representative before God and bring their
disputes to him. 20Teach them the decrees and laws, and show them the way
to live and the duties they are to perform. 21But select capable men from all
the people—men who fear God, trustworthy men who hate dishonest gain
—and appoint them as officials over
thousands, hundreds, fifties and tens.
22Have them serve as judges for the
people at all times, but have them bring
every difficult case to you; the simple
cases they can decide themselves. That
will make your load lighter, because
they will share it with you. 23If you do
this and God so commands, you will be
able to stand the strain, and all these
people will go home satisfied."
24Moses listened to his father-in-law
and did everything he said. 25He chose
capable men from all Israel and made
them leaders of the people, officials
over thousands, hundreds, fifties and
tens. 26They served as judges for the
people at all times. The difficult cases
they brought to Moses, but the simple
ones they decided themselves.
27Then Moses sent his father-in-law
on his way, and Jethro returned to his
own country.

NEW TESTAMENT READING

Mark 1:1–28

John the Baptist Prepares the Way

1 The beginning of the gospel about
Jesus Christ, the Son of God.

2It is written in Isaiah the prophet:

"I will send my messenger ahead of
you,
who will prepare your way"—
3"a voice of one calling in the desert,
'Prepare the way for the Lord,
make straight paths for him.'"

4And so John came, baptising in the
desert region and preaching a baptism
of repentance for the forgiveness of
sins. 5The whole Judean countryside

and all the people of Jerusalem went out
to him. Confessing their sins, they were
baptised by him in the Jordan River.
6John wore clothing made of camel's
hair, with a leather belt round his waist,
and he ate locusts and wild honey. 7And
this was his message: "After me will
come one more powerful than I, the
thongs of whose sandals I am not
worthy to stoop down and untie. 8I baptise you with water, but he will baptise
you with the Holy Spirit."

The Baptism and Temptation of Jesus

9At that time Jesus came from
Nazareth in Galilee and was baptised by
John in the Jordan. 10As Jesus was coming up out of the water, he saw heaven
being torn open and the Spirit descending on him like a dove. 11And a voice
came from heaven: "You are my Son,
whom I love; with you I am well
pleased."

12At once the Spirit sent him out into
the desert, 13and he was in the desert for
forty days, being tempted by Satan. He
was with the wild animals, and angels
attended him.

The Calling of the First Disciples

14After John was put in prison, Jesus
went into Galilee, proclaiming the good
news of God. 15"The time has come,"
he said. "The kingdom of God is near.
Repent and believe the good news!"

16As Jesus walked beside the Sea of
Galilee, he saw Simon and his brother
Andrew casting a net into the lake, for
they were fishermen. 17"Come, follow
me," Jesus said, "and I will make you
fishers of men." 18At once they left their
nets and followed him.

19When he had gone a little farther,
he saw James son of Zebedee and his
brother John in a boat, preparing their
nets. 20Without delay he called them,
and they left their father Zebedee in the
boat with the hired men and followed
him.

Jesus Drives Out an Evil Spirit

21They went to Capernaum, and
when the Sabbath came, Jesus went into
the synagogue and began to teach.
22The people were amazed at his
teaching, because he taught them as one
who had authority, not as the teachers
of the law. 23Just then a man in their
synagogue who was possessed by an evil
spirit cried out, 24"What do you want
with us, Jesus of Nazareth? Have you
come to destroy us? I know who you
are—the Holy One of God!"

25"Be quiet!" said Jesus sternly.
"Come out of him!" 26The evil spirit
shook the man violently and came out
of him with a shriek.

27The people were all so amazed that
they asked each other, "What is this? A
new teaching—and with authority! He
even gives orders to evil spirits and they
obey him." 28News about him spread
quickly over the whole region of
Galilee.

READING FROM PSALMS
Psalm 22:1–11

For the director of music. To ⌞the tune of⌟ "The Doe of the Morning". A psalm of David.

1My God, my God, why have you
forsaken me?
Why are you so far from saving
me,
so far from the words of my
groaning?
2O my God, I cry out by day, but you
do not answer,
by night, and am not silent.

3Yet you are enthroned as the Holy
One;
you are the praise of Israel.
4In you our fathers put their trust;
they trusted and you delivered
them.
5They cried to you and were saved;
in you they trusted and were not
disappointed.

6But I am a worm and not a man,
scorned by men and despised by the people.
7All who see me mock me;
they hurl insults, shaking their heads:
8"He trusts in the LORD;
let the LORD rescue him.
Let him deliver him,
since he delights in him."
9Yet you brought me out of the womb;
you made me trust in you
even at my mother's breast.
10From birth I was cast upon you;
from my mother's womb you have been my God.
11Do not be far from me,
for trouble is near
and there is no-one to help.

FEBRUARY 16

DAY 47

OLD TESTAMENT READING

Exodus 19:1–20:26

At Mount Sinai

19 In the third month after the
Israelites left Egypt—on the
very day—they came to the Desert of
Sinai. 2After they set out from Rephidim, they entered the Desert of Sinai,
and Israel camped there in the desert in
front of the mountain.
3Then Moses went up to God, and the
LORD called to him from the mountain
and said, "This is what you are to say to
the house of Jacob and what you are to
tell the people of Israel: 4'You
yourselves have seen what I did to
Egypt, and how I carried you on eagles'
wings and brought you to myself. 5Now
if you obey me fully and keep my covenant, then out of all nations you will be
my treasured possession. Although the
whole earth is mine, 6you will be for me
a kingdom of priests and a holy nation.'
These are the words you are to speak to
the Israelites."
7So Moses went back and summoned
the elders of the people and set before
them all the words the LORD had commanded him to speak. 8The people all
responded together, "We will do everything the LORD has said." So Moses
brought their answer back to the LORD.
9The LORD said to Moses, "I am
going to come to you in a dense cloud,
so that the people will hear me speaking
with you and will always put their trust
in you." Then Moses told the LORD
what the people had said.
10And the LORD said to Moses, "Go
to the people and consecrate them today and tomorrow. Make them wash
their clothes 11and be ready by the third
day, because on that day the LORD will
come down on Mount Sinai in the sight
of all the people. 12Put limits for the
people around the mountain and tell
them, 'Be careful that you do not go up
the mountain or touch the foot of it.
Whoever touches the mountain shall
surely be put to death. 13He shall surely
be stoned or shot with arrows; not a
hand is to be laid on him. Whether man
or animal, he shall not be permitted to
live.' Only when the ram's horn sounds
a long blast may they go up to the
mountain."
14After Moses had gone down the
mountain to the people, he consecrated
them, and they washed their clothes.
15Then he said to the people, "Prepare
yourselves for the third day. Abstain
from sexual relations."
16On the morning of the third day
there was thunder and lightning, with a
thick cloud over the mountain, and a
very loud trumpet blast. Everyone in

the camp trembled. 17Then Moses led
the people out of the camp to meet with
God, and they stood at the foot of the
mountain. 18Mount Sinai was covered
with smoke, because the LORD descended on it in fire. The smoke bil-
lowed up from it like smoke from a
furnace, the whole mountain trembled
violently, 19and the sound of the trumpet grew louder and louder. Then
Moses spoke and the voice of God
answered him.

20The LORD descended to the top of
Mount Sinai and called Moses to the top
of the mountain. So Moses went up
21and the LORD said to him, "Go down
and warn the people so they do not
force their way through to see the LORD
and many of them perish. 22Even the
priests, who approach the LORD, must
consecrate themselves, or the LORD will
break out against them."

23Moses said to the LORD, "The people cannot come up Mount Sinai, because you yourself warned us, 'Put
limits around the mountain and set it
apart as holy.'"

24The LORD replied, "Go down and
bring Aaron up with you. But the
priests and the people must not force
their way through to come up to the
LORD, or he will break out against
them."

25So Moses went down to the people
and told them.

The Ten Commandments

20 And God spoke all these words:

2"I am the LORD your God, who brought you out of Egypt, out of the land of slavery.

3"You shall have no other gods before me.

4"You shall make for yourself an idol in the form of anything in heaven above or on the earth beneath or in the
waters below. 5You shall not
bow down to them or worship
them; for I, the LORD your
God, am a jealous God,
punishing the children for the
sin of the fathers to the third
and fourth generation of
those who hate me, 6but
showing love to a thousand
⌞generations⌟ of those who
love me and keep my commandments.

7"You shall not misuse the name of the LORD your God, for the LORD will not hold anyone guiltless who misuses his name.

8"Remember the Sabbath day by
keeping it holy. 9Six days you
shall labour and do all your
work, 10but the seventh day is
a Sabbath to the LORD your
God. On it you shall not do
any work, neither you, nor
your son or daughter, nor
your manservant or maidservant, nor your animals, nor
the alien within your gates.
11For in six days the LORD
made the heavens and the
earth, the sea, and all that is
in them, but he rested on the
seventh day. Therefore the
LORD blessed the Sabbath
day and made it holy.

12"Honour your father and your mother, so that you may live long in the land the LORD your God is giving you.

13"You shall not murder.

14"You shall not commit adultery.

15"You shall not steal.

16"You shall not give false testimony against your neighbour.

17"You shall not covet your neighbour's house. You shall not covet your neighbour's wife, or his manservant or maidservant, his ox or donkey, or anything that belongs to your neighbour."

18When the people saw the thunder
and lightning and heard the trumpet

and saw the mountain in smoke, they trembled with fear. They stayed at a distance 19and said to Moses, "Speak to us yourself and we will listen. But do not have God speak to us or we will die."

20Moses said to the people, "Do not be afraid. God has come to test you, so that the fear of God will be with you to keep you from sinning."

21The people remained at a distance, while Moses approached the thick darkness where God was.

Idols and Altars

22Then the LORD said to Moses, "Tell the Israelites this: 'You have seen for yourselves that I have spoken to you from heaven: 23Do not make any gods to be alongside me; do not make for yourselves gods of silver or gods of gold.

24"'Make an altar of earth for me and sacrifice on it your burnt offerings and fellowship offerings, your sheep and goats and your cattle. Wherever I cause my name to be honoured, I will come to you and bless you. 25If you make an altar of stones for me, do not build it with dressed stones, for you will defile it if you use a tool on it. 26And do not go up to my altar on steps, lest your nakedness be exposed on it.'

NEW TESTAMENT READING

Mark 1:29–2:17

Jesus Heals Many

29As soon as they left the synagogue, they went with James and John to the home of Simon and Andrew. 30Simon's mother-in-law was in bed with a fever, and they told Jesus about her. 31So he went to her, took her hand and helped her up. The fever left her and she began to wait on them.

32That evening after sunset the people brought to Jesus all the sick and demon-possessed. 33The whole town gathered at the door, 34and Jesus healed many who had various diseases. He also drove out many demons, but he would not let the demons speak because they knew who he was.

Jesus Prays in a Solitary Place

35Very early in the morning, while it was still dark, Jesus got up, left the house and went off to a solitary place, where he prayed. 36Simon and his companions went to look for him, 37and when they found him, they exclaimed: "Everyone is looking for you!"

38Jesus replied, "Let us go somewhere else—to the nearby villages—so that I can preach there also. That is why I have come." 39So he travelled throughout Galilee, preaching in their synagogues and driving out demons.

A Man With Leprosy

40A man with leprosy came to him and begged him on his knees, "If you are willing, you can make me clean."

41Filled with compassion, Jesus reached out his hand and touched the man. "I am willing," he said. "Be clean!" 42Immediately the leprosy left him and he was cured.

43Jesus sent him away at once with a strong warning: 44"See that you don't tell this to anyone. But go, show yourself to the priest and offer the sacrifices that Moses commanded for your cleansing, as a testimony to them." 45Instead he went out and began to talk freely, spreading the news. As a result, Jesus could no longer enter a town openly but stayed outside in lonely places. Yet the people still came to him from everywhere.

Jesus Heals a Paralytic

2 A few days later, when Jesus again entered Capernaum, the people heard that he had come home. 2So many gathered that there was no room left, not even outside the door, and he preached the word to them. 3Some men

came, bringing to him a paralytic, carried by four of them. 4Since they could not get him to Jesus because of the crowd, they made an opening in the roof above Jesus and, after digging through it, lowered the mat the paralysed man was lying on. 5When Jesus saw their faith, he said to the paralytic, "Son, your sins are forgiven."

6Now some teachers of the law were sitting there, thinking to themselves, 7"Why does this fellow talk like that? He's blaspheming! Who can forgive sins but God alone?"

8Immediately Jesus knew in his spirit that this was what they were thinking in their hearts, and he said to them, "Why are you thinking these things? 9Which is easier: to say to the paralytic, 'Your sins are forgiven,' or to say, 'Get up, take your mat and walk'? 10But that you may know that the Son of Man has authority on earth to forgive sins. . . ." He said to the paralytic, 11"I tell you, get up, take your mat and go home." 12He got up, took his mat and walked out in full view of them all. This amazed everyone and they praised God, saying, "We have never seen anything like this!"

The Calling of Levi

13Once again Jesus went out beside the lake. A large crowd came to him, and he began to teach them. 14As he walked along, he saw Levi son of Alphaeus sitting at the tax collector's booth. "Follow me," Jesus told him, and Levi got up and followed him.

15While Jesus was having dinner at Levi's house, many tax collectors and "sinners" were eating with him and his disciples, for there were many who followed him. 16When the teachers of the law who were Pharisees saw him eating with the "sinners" and tax collectors, they asked his disciples: "Why does he eat with tax collectors and 'sinners'?"

17On hearing this, Jesus said to them, "It is not the healthy who need a doctor, but the sick. I have not come to call the righteous, but sinners."

READING FROM PSALMS

Psalm 22:12–21

12Many bulls surround me;
strong bulls of Bashan encircle me.
13Roaring lions tearing their prey
open their mouths wide against me.
14I am poured out like water,
and all my bones are out of joint.
My heart has turned to wax;
it has melted away within me.
15My strength is dried up like a potsherd,
and my tongue sticks to the roof of my mouth;
you lay me in the dust of death.
16Dogs have surrounded me;
a band of evil men has encircled me,
they have pierced my hands and my feet.
17I can count all my bones;
people stare and gloat over me.
18They divide my garments among them
and cast lots for my clothing.

19But you, O LORD, be not far off;
O my Strength, come quickly to help me.
20Deliver my life from the sword,
my precious life from the power of the dogs.
21Rescue me from the mouth of the lions;
save me from the horns of the wild oxen.

FEBRUARY 17

DAY 48

OLD TESTAMENT READING
Exodus 21:1–22:31

21 “These are the laws you are to set before them:

Hebrew Servants

2“If you buy a Hebrew servant, he is to serve you for six years. But in the seventh year, he shall go free, without paying anything. 3If he comes alone, he is to go free alone; but if he has a wife when he comes, she is to go with him. 4If his master gives him a wife and she bears him sons or daughters, the woman and her children shall belong to her master, and only the man shall go free.

5“But if the servant declares, ‘I love my master and my wife and children and do not want to go free,’ 6then his master must take him before the judges. He shall take him to the door or the doorpost and pierce his ear with an awl. Then he will be his servant for life.

7“If a man sells his daughter as a servant, she is not to go free as menservants do. 8If she does not please the master who has selected her for himself, he must let her be redeemed. He has no right to sell her to foreigners, because he has broken faith with her. 9If he selects her for his son, he must grant her the rights of a daughter. 10If he marries another woman, he must not deprive the first one of her food, clothing and marital rights. 11If he does not provide her with these three things, she is to go free, without any payment of money.

Personal Injuries

12“Anyone who strikes a man and kills him shall surely be put to death. 13However, if he does not do it intentionally, but God lets it happen, he is to flee to a place I will designate. 14But if a man schemes and kills another man deliberately, take him away from my altar and put him to death.

15“Anyone who attacks his father or his mother must be put to death.

16“Anyone who kidnaps another and either sells him or still has him when he is caught must be put to death.

17“Anyone who curses his father or mother must be put to death.

18“If men quarrel and one hits the other with a stone or with his fist and he does not die but is confined to bed, 19the one who struck the blow will not be held responsible if the other gets up and walks around outside with his staff; however, he must pay the injured man for the loss of his time and see that he is completely healed.

20“If a man beats his male or female slave with a rod and the slave dies as a direct result, he must be punished, 21but he is not to be punished if the slave gets up after a day or two, since the slave is his property.

22“If men who are fighting hit a pregnant woman and she gives birth prematurely but there is no serious injury, the offender must be fined whatever the woman’s husband demands and the court allows. 23But if there is serious injury, you are to take life for life, 24eye for eye, tooth for tooth, hand for hand, foot for foot, 25burn for burn, wound for wound, bruise for bruise.

26“If a man hits a manservant or maidservant in the eye and destroys it, he must let the servant go free to compensate for the eye. 27And if he knocks out the tooth of a manservant or maidservant, he must let the servant go free to compensate for the tooth.

28“If a bull gores a man or a woman to death, the bull must be stoned to death, and its meat must not be eaten. But the owner of the bull will not be held responsible. 29If, however, the bull has had the habit of goring and the owner has been warned but has not kept it penned up and it kills a man or woman, the bull must be stoned and the owner also must be put to death. 30However, if payment is demanded of him, he may redeem his life by paying whatever is demanded. 31This law also applies if the bull gores a son or a daughter. 32If the bull gores a male or female slave, the owner must pay thirty shekels of silver to the master of the slave, and the bull must be stoned.

33"If a man uncovers a pit or digs one and fails to cover it and an ox or a donkey falls into it, 34the owner of the pit must pay for the loss; he must pay its owner, and the dead animal will be his.

35"If a man's bull injures the bull of another and it dies, they are to sell the live one and divide both the money and the dead animal equally. 36However, if it was known that the bull had the habit of goring, yet the owner did not keep it penned up, the owner must pay, animal for animal, and the dead animal will be his.

Protection of Property

22 "If a man steals an ox or a sheep and slaughters it or sells it, he must pay back five head of cattle for the ox and four sheep for the sheep.

2"If a thief is caught breaking in and is struck so that he dies, the defender is not guilty of bloodshed; 3but if it happens after sunrise, he is guilty of bloodshed.

"A thief must certainly make restitution, but if he has nothing, he must be sold to pay for his theft.

4"If the stolen animal is found alive in his possession—whether ox or donkey or sheep—he must pay back double.

5"If a man grazes his livestock in a field or vineyard and lets them stray and they graze in another man's field, he must make restitution from the best of his own field or vineyard.

6"If a fire breaks out and spreads into thornbushes so that it burns shocks of grain or standing corn or the whole field, the one who started the fire must make restitution.

7"If a man gives his neighbour silver or goods for safekeeping and they are stolen from the neighbour's house, the thief, if he is caught, must pay back double. 8But if the thief is not found, the owner of the house must appear before the judges to determine whether he has laid his hands on the other man's property. 9In all cases of illegal possession of an ox, a donkey, a sheep, a garment, or any other lost property about which somebody says, 'This is mine,' both parties are to bring their cases before the judges. The one whom the judges declare guilty must pay back double to his neighbour.

10"If a man gives a donkey, an ox, a sheep or any other animal to his neighbour for safekeeping and it dies or is injured or is taken away while no-one is looking, 11the issue between them will be settled by the taking of an oath before the LORD that the neighbour did not lay hands on the other person's property. The owner is to accept this, and no restitution is required. 12But if the animal was stolen from the neighbour, he must make restitution to the owner. 13If it was torn to pieces by a wild animal, he shall bring in the remains as evidence and he will not be required to pay for the torn animal.

14"If a man borrows an animal from his neighbour and it is injured or dies while the owner is not present, he must make restitution. 15But if the owner is with the animal, the borrower will not have to pay. If the animal was hired, the money paid for the hire covers the loss.

Social Responsibility

16"If a man seduces a virgin who is not pledged to be married and sleeps with her, he must pay the bride-price, and she shall be his wife. 17If her father absolutely refuses to give her to him, he must still pay the bride-price for virgins.

18"Do not allow a sorceress to live.

19“Anyone who has sexual relations
with an animal must be put to death.
20“Whoever sacrifices to any god
other than the LORD must be destroyed.
21“Do not ill-treat an alien or oppress
him, for you were aliens in Egypt.
22“Do not take advantage of a widow
or an orphan. 23If you do and they cry
out to me, I will certainly hear their cry.
24My anger will be aroused, and I will
kill you with the sword; your wives will
become widows and your children
fatherless.
25“If you lend money to one of my
people among you who is needy, do not
be like a money-lender; charge him no
interest. 26If you take your neighbour’s
cloak as a pledge, return it to him by
sunset, 27because his cloak is the only
covering he has for his body. What else
will he sleep in? When he cries out to
me, I will hear, for I am compassionate.
28“Do not blaspheme God or curse
the ruler of your people.
29“Do not hold back offerings from
your granaries or your vats.
“You must give me the firstborn of
your sons. 30Do the same with your
cattle and your sheep. Let them stay
with their mothers for seven days, but
give them to me on the eighth day.
31“You are to be my holy people. So
do not eat the meat of an animal torn by
wild beasts; throw it to the dogs.

NEW TESTAMENT READING
Mark 2:18–3:30

Jesus Questioned About Fasting

18Now John’s disciples and the Pharisees were fasting. Some people came
and asked Jesus, “How is it that John’s
disciples and the disciples of the Pharisees are fasting, but yours are not?”
19Jesus answered, “How can the
guests of the bridegroom fast while he is
with them? They cannot, so long as they
have him with them. 20But the time will
come when the bridegroom will be
taken from them, and on that day they
will fast.
21“No-one sews a patch of unshrunk
cloth on an old garment. If he does, the
new piece will pull away from the old,
making the tear worse. 22And no-one
pours new wine into old wineskins. If he
does, the wine will burst the skins, and
both the wine and the wineskins will be
ruined. No, he pours new wine into new
wineskins.”

Lord of the Sabbath

23One Sabbath Jesus was going
through the cornfields, and as his disciples walked along, they began to pick
some ears of corn. 24The Pharisees said
to him, “Look, why are they doing what
is unlawful on the Sabbath?”
25He answered, “Have you never
read what David did when he and his
companions were hungry and in need?
26In the days of Abiathar the high
priest, he entered the house of God and
ate the consecrated bread, which is lawful only for priests to eat. And he also
gave some to his companions.”
27Then he said to them, “The Sabbath was made for man, not man for the
Sabbath. 28So the Son of Man is Lord
even of the Sabbath.”
3 Another time he went into the
synagogue, and a man with a
shrivelled hand was there. 2Some of
them were looking for a reason to accuse Jesus, so they watched him closely
to see if he would heal him on the
Sabbath. 3Jesus said to the man with the
shrivelled hand, “Stand up in front of
everyone.”
4Then Jesus asked them, “Which is
lawful on the Sabbath: to do good or to
do evil, to save life or to kill?” But they
remained silent.
5He looked round at them in anger
and, deeply distressed at their stubborn
hearts, said to the man, “Stretch out
your hand.” He stretched it out, and his
hand was completely restored. 6Then
the Pharisees went out and began to

plot with the Herodians how they might
kill Jesus.

Crowds Follow Jesus

7Jesus withdrew with his disciples to
the lake, and a large crowd from Galilee
followed. 8When they heard all he was
doing, many people came to him from
Judea, Jerusalem, Idumea, and the regions across the Jordan and around
Tyre and Sidon. 9Because of the crowd
he told his disciples to have a small boat
ready for him, to keep the people from
crowding him. 10For he had healed
many, so that those with diseases were
pushing forward to touch him.
11Whenever the evil spirits saw him,
they fell down before him and cried out,
"You are the Son of God." 12But he
gave them strict orders not to tell who
he was.

The Appointing of the Twelve Apostles

13Jesus went up on a mountainside
and called to him those he wanted, and
they came to him. 14He appointed
twelve—designating them apostles—
that they might be with him and that he
might send them out to preach 15and to
have authority to drive out demons.
16These are the twelve he appointed:
Simon (to whom he gave the name
Peter); 17James son of Zebedee and
his brother John (to them he gave the
name Boanerges, which means Sons of
Thunder); 18Andrew, Philip, Bartholomew, Matthew, Thomas, James
son of Alphaeus, Thaddaeus, Simon
the Zealot 19and Judas Iscariot, who
betrayed him.

Jesus and Beelzebub

20Then Jesus entered a house, and
again a crowd gathered, so that he and
his disciples were not even able to eat.
21When his family heard about this,
they went to take charge of him, for
they said, "He is out of his mind."

22And the teachers of the law who
came down from Jerusalem said, "He is
possessed by Beelzebub! By the prince
of demons he is driving out demons."
23So Jesus called them and spoke to
them in parables: "How can Satan drive
out Satan? 24If a kingdom is divided
against itself, that kingdom cannot
stand. 25If a house is divided against
itself, that house cannot stand. 26And if
Satan opposes himself and is divided, he
cannot stand; his end has come. 27In
fact, no-one can enter a strong man's
house and carry off his possessions unless he first ties up the strong man. Then
he can rob his house. 28I tell you the
truth, all the sins and blasphemies of
men will be forgiven them. 29But whoever blasphemes against the Holy Spirit
will never be forgiven; he is guilty of an
eternal sin."
30He said this because they were
saying, "He has an evil spirit."

READING FROM PROVERBS
Proverbs 5:1–14

Warning Against Adultery

5 My son, pay attention to my
wisdom,
listen well to my words of insight,
2that you may maintain discretion
and your lips may preserve
knowledge.
3For the lips of an adulteress drip
honey,
and her speech is smoother than
oil;
4but in the end she is bitter as gall,
sharp as a double-edged sword.
5Her feet go down to death;
her steps lead straight to the grave.
6She gives no thought to the way of
life;
her paths are crooked, but she
knows it not.

7Now then, my sons, listen to me;
do not turn aside from what I say.

8Keep to a path far from her,
do not go near the door of her
house,
9lest you give your best strength to
others
and your years to one who is cruel,
10lest strangers feast on your wealth
and your toil enrich another man's
house.
11At the end of your life you will groan,
when your flesh and body are
spent.
12You will say, "How I hated
discipline!
How my heart spurned correction!
13I would not obey my teachers
or listen to my instructors.
14I have come to the brink of utter ruin
in the midst of the whole
assembly."

FEBRUARY 18

DAY 49

OLD TESTAMENT READING
Exodus 23:1–24:18

Laws of Justice and Mercy

23 "Do not spread false reports.
Do not help a wicked man by
being a malicious witness.
2"Do not follow the crowd in doing
wrong. When you give testimony in a
lawsuit, do not pervert justice by siding
with the crowd, 3and do not show
favouritism to a poor man in his lawsuit.
4"If you come across your enemy's ox
or donkey wandering off, be sure to
take it back to him. 5If you see the
donkey of someone who hates you
fallen down under its load, do not leave
it there; be sure you help him with it.
6"Do not deny justice to your poor
people in their lawsuits. 7Have nothing
to do with a false charge and do not put
an innocent or honest person to death,
for I will not acquit the guilty.
8"Do not accept a bribe, for a bribe
blinds those who see and twists the
words of the righteous.
9"Do not oppress an alien; you
yourselves know how it feels to be
aliens, because you were aliens in
Egypt.

Sabbath Laws

10"For six years you are to sow your
fields and harvest the crops, 11but
during the seventh year let the land lie
unploughed and unused. Then the poor
among your people may get food from
it, and the wild animals may eat what
they leave. Do the same with your
vineyard and your olive grove.
12"Six days do your work, but on the
seventh day do not work, so that your
ox and your donkey may rest and the
slave born in your household, and the
alien as well, may be refreshed.
13"Be careful to do everything I have
said to you. Do not invoke the names of
other gods; do not let them be heard on
your lips.

The Three Annual Festivals

14"Three times a year you are to celebrate a festival to me.

15"Celebrate the Feast of Unleavened Bread; for seven days eat bread made without yeast, as I commanded you. Do this at the appointed time in the month of Abib, for in that month you came out of Egypt.

"No-one is to appear before me empty-handed.

16"Celebrate the Feast of Harvest with the firstfruits of the crops you sow in your field.

"Celebrate the Feast of Ingathering at the end of the year, when you gather in your crops from the field.

17“Three times a year all the men are
to appear before the Sovereign LORD.
18“Do not offer the blood of a sacrifice to me along with anything containing yeast.
“The fat of my festival offerings must
not be kept until morning.
19“Bring the best of the firstfruits of
your soil to the house of the LORD your
God.
“Do not cook a young goat in its
mother’s milk.

God’s Angel to Prepare the Way

20“See, I am sending an angel ahead
of you to guard you along the way and to
bring you to the place I have prepared.
21Pay attention to him and listen to what
he says. Do not rebel against him; he
will not forgive your rebellion, since my
Name is in him. 22If you listen carefully
to what he says and do all that I say, I
will be an enemy to your enemies and
will oppose those who oppose you.
23My angel will go ahead of you and
bring you into the land of the Amorites,
Hittites, Perizzites, Canaanites, Hivites
and Jebusites, and I will wipe them out.
24Do not bow down before their gods or
worship them or follow their practices.
You must demolish them and break
their sacred stones to pieces. 25Worship
the LORD your God, and his blessing
will be on your food and water. I will
take away sickness from among you,
26and none will miscarry or be barren in
your land. I will give you a full life span.
27“I will send my terror ahead of you
and throw into confusion every nation
you encounter. I will make all your
enemies turn their backs and run. 28I
will send the hornet ahead of you to
drive the Hivites, Canaanites and Hittites out of your way. 29But I will not
drive them out in a single year, because
the land would become desolate and the
wild animals too numerous for you.
30Little by little I will drive them out
before you, until you have increased
enough to take possession of the land.
31“I will establish your borders from
the Red Sea to the Sea of the Philistines,
and from the desert to the River. I will
hand over to you the people who live in
the land and you will drive them out
before you. 32Do not make a covenant
with them or with their gods. 33Do not
let them live in your land, or they will
cause you to sin against me, because the
worship of their gods will certainly be a
snare to you.”

The Covenant Confirmed

24 Then he said to Moses, “Come
up to the LORD, you and Aaron,
Nadab and Abihu, and seventy of the
elders of Israel. You are to worship at a
distance, 2but Moses alone is to
approach the LORD; the others must not
come near. And the people may not
come up with him.”
3When Moses went and told the people all the LORD’s words and laws, they
responded with one voice, “Everything
the LORD has said we will do.” 4Moses
then wrote down everything the LORD
had said.
He got up early the next morning and
built an altar at the foot of the mountain
and set up twelve stone pillars representing the twelve tribes of Israel.
5Then he sent young Israelite men, and
they offered burnt offerings and sacrificed young bulls as fellowship offerings to the LORD. 6Moses took half of
the blood and put it in bowls, and the
other half he sprinkled on the altar.
7Then he took the Book of the Covenant and read it to the people. They
responded, “We will do everything the
LORD has said; we will obey.”
8Moses then took the blood, sprinkled it on the people and said, “This is
the blood of the covenant that the LORD
has made with you in accordance with
all these words.”
9Moses and Aaron, Nadab and
Abihu, and the seventy elders of Israel
went up 10and saw the God of Israel.
Under his feet was something like a
pavement made of sapphire, clear as the
sky itself. 11But God did not raise his

hand against these leaders of the Israelites; they saw God, and they ate and drank.

12The LORD said to Moses, "Come up to me on the mountain and stay here, and I will give you the tablets of stone, with the law and commands I have written for their instruction."

13Then Moses set out with Joshua his assistant, and Moses went up on the mountain of God. 14He said to the elders, "Wait here for us until we come back to you. Aaron and Hur are with you, and anyone involved in a dispute can go to them."

15When Moses went up on the mountain, the cloud covered it, 16and the glory of the LORD settled on Mount Sinai. For six days the cloud covered the mountain, and on the seventh day the LORD called to Moses from within the cloud. 17To the Israelites the glory of the LORD looked like a consuming fire on top of the mountain. 18Then Moses entered the cloud as he went on up the mountain. And he stayed on the mountain forty days and forty nights.

NEW TESTAMENT READING
Mark 3:31–4:29

Jesus' Mother and Brothers

31Then Jesus' mother and brothers arrived. Standing outside, they sent someone in to call him. 32A crowd was sitting around him, and they told him, "Your mother and brothers are outside looking for you."

33"Who are my mother and my brothers?" he asked.

34Then he looked at those seated in a circle around him and said, "Here are my mother and my brothers! 35Whoever does God's will is my brother and sister and mother."

The Parable of the Sower

4 Again Jesus began to teach by the lake. The crowd that gathered round him was so large that he got into a boat and sat in it out on the lake, while all the people were along the shore at the water's edge. 2He taught them many things by parables, and in his teaching said: 3"Listen! A farmer went out to sow his seed. 4As he was scattering the seed, some fell along the path, and the birds came and ate it up. 5Some fell on rocky places, where it did not have much soil. It sprang up quickly, because the soil was shallow. 6But when the sun came up, the plants were scorched, and they withered because they had no root. 7Other seed fell among thorns, which grew up and choked the plants, so that they did not bear grain. 8Still other seed fell on good soil. It came up, grew and produced a crop, multiplying thirty, sixty, or even a hundred times."

9Then Jesus said, "He who has ears to hear, let him hear."

10When he was alone, the Twelve and the others around him asked him about the parables. 11He told them, "The secret of the kingdom of God has been given to you. But to those on the outside everything is said in parables 12so that,

" 'they may be ever seeing but never
perceiving,
and ever hearing but never
understanding;
otherwise they might turn and be
forgiven!' "

13Then Jesus said to them, "Don't you understand this parable? How then will you understand any parable? 14The farmer sows the word. 15Some people are like seed along the path, where the word is sown. As soon as they hear it, Satan comes and takes away the word that was sown in them. 16Others, like seed sown on rocky places, hear the word and at once receive it with joy. 17But since they have no root, they last only a short time. When trouble or persecution comes because of the word, they quickly fall away. 18Still others,

like seed sown among thorns, hear the
word; 19but the worries of this life, the
deceitfulness of wealth and the desires
for other things come in and choke the
word, making it unfruitful. 20Others,
like seed sown on good soil, hear the
word, accept it, and produce a crop
—thirty, sixty or even a hundred times
what was sown."

A Lamp on a Stand

21He said to them, "Do you bring in a
lamp to put it under a bowl or a bed?
Instead, don't you put it on its stand?
22For whatever is hidden is meant to be
disclosed, and whatever is concealed is
meant to be brought out into the open.
23If anyone has ears to hear, let him
hear."
24"Consider carefully what you
hear," he continued. "With the
measure you use, it will be measured to
you—and even more. 25Whoever has
will be given more; whoever does not
have, even what he has will be taken
from him."

The Parable of the Growing Seed

26He also said, "This is what the kingdom of God is like. A man scatters seed
on the ground. 27Night and day,
whether he sleeps or gets up, the seed
sprouts and grows, though he does not
know how. 28All by itself the soil produces corn—first the stalk, then the
ear, then the full grain in the ear. 29As
soon as the grain is ripe, he puts the
sickle to it, because the harvest has
come."

READING FROM PSALMS
Psalm 22:22–31

22I will declare your name to my brothers;
in the congregation I will praise you.
23You who fear the LORD, praise him!
All you descendants of Jacob, honour him!
Revere him, all you descendants of Israel!
24For he has not despised or disdained
the suffering of the afflicted one;
he has not hidden his face from him
but has listened to his cry for help.

25From you comes the theme of my praise in the great assembly;
before those who fear you will I fulfil my vows.
26The poor will eat and be satisfied;
they who seek the LORD will praise him—
may your hearts live for ever!
27All the ends of the earth
will remember and turn to the LORD,
and all the families of the nations
will bow down before him,
28for dominion belongs to the LORD
and he rules over the nations.

29All the rich of the earth will feast and worship;
all who go down to the dust will kneel before him—
those who cannot keep themselves alive.
30Posterity will serve him;
future generations will be told about the Lord.
31They will proclaim his righteousness
to a people yet unborn—
for he has done it.

OLD TESTAMENT READING
Exodus 25:1–26:37

Offerings for the Tabernacle

25 The LORD said to Moses, 2"Tell the Israelites to bring me an offering. You are to receive the offering for me from each man whose heart prompts him to give. 3These are the offerings you are to receive from them: gold, silver and bronze; 4blue, purple and scarlet yarn and fine linen; goat hair; 5ram skins dyed red and hides of sea cows; acacia wood; 6olive oil for the light; spices for the anointing oil and for the fragrant incense; 7and onyx stones and other gems to be mounted on the ephod and breastpiece.

8"Then have them make a sanctuary for me, and I will dwell among them. 9Make this tabernacle and all its furnishings exactly like the pattern I will show you.

The Ark

10"Have them make a chest of acacia wood—two and a half cubits long, a cubit and a half wide, and a cubit and a half high. 11Overlay it with pure gold, both inside and out, and make a gold moulding around it. 12Cast four gold rings for it and fasten them to its four feet, with two rings on one side and two rings on the other. 13Then make poles of acacia wood and overlay them with gold. 14Insert the poles into the rings on the sides of the chest to carry it. 15The poles are to remain in the rings of this ark; they are not to be removed. 16Then put in the ark the Testimony, which I will give you.

17"Make an atonement cover of pure gold—two and a half cubits long and a cubit and a half wide. 18And make two cherubim out of hammered gold at the ends of the cover. 19Make one cherub on one end and the second cherub on the other; make the cherubim of one piece with the cover, at the two ends. 20The cherubim are to have their wings spread upwards, overshadowing the cover with them. The cherubim are to face each other, looking towards the cover. 21Place the cover on top of the ark and put in the ark the Testimony, which I will give you. 22There, above the cover between the two cherubim that are over the ark of the Testimony, I will meet with you and give you all my commands for the Israelites.

The Table

23"Make a table of acacia wood—two cubits long, a cubit wide and a cubit and a half high. 24Overlay it with pure gold and make a gold moulding around it. 25Also make around it a rim a handbreadth wide and put a gold moulding on the rim. 26Make four gold rings for the table and fasten them to the four corners, where the four legs are. 27The rings are to be close to the rim to hold the poles used in carrying the table. 28Make the poles of acacia wood, overlay them with gold and carry the table with them. 29And make its plates and dishes of pure gold, as well as its pitchers and bowls for the pouring out of offerings 30Put the bread of the Presence on this table to be before me at all times.

The Lampstand

31"Make a lampstand of pure gold and hammer it out, base and shaft; its flowerlike cups, buds and blossoms shall be of one piece with it. 32Six branches are to extend from the sides of the lampstand—three on one side and three on the other. 33Three cups shaped like almond flowers with buds and blossoms are to be on one branch, three on the next branch, and the same for all six branches extending from the lampstand. 34And on the lampstand there are to be four cups shaped like almond flowers with buds and blossoms. 35One bud shall be under the first pair of branches extending from the lampstand, a second bud under the second pair, and a third bud under the third pair—six branches in all. 36The buds and branches shall all be of one piece with the lampstand, hammered out of pure gold.

37"Then make its seven lamps and set them up on it so that they light the space in front of it. 38Its wick trimmers and trays are to be of pure gold. 39A talent of pure gold is to be used for the lampstand and all these accessories. 40See that you make them according to the pattern shown you on the mountain.

The Tabernacle

26 "Make the tabernacle with ten curtains of finely twisted linen and blue, purple and scarlet yarn, with cherubim worked into them by a skilled craftsman. 2All the curtains are to be the same size—twenty-eight cubits long and four cubits wide. 3Join five of the curtains together, and do the same with the other five. 4Make loops of blue material along the edge of the end curtain in one set, and do the same with the end curtain in the other set. 5Make fifty loops on one curtain and fifty loops on the end curtain of the other set, with the loops opposite each other. 6Then make fifty gold clasps and use them to fasten the curtains together so that the tabernacle is a unit.

7"Make curtains of goat hair for the tent over the tabernacle—eleven altogether. 8All eleven curtains are to be the same size—thirty cubits long and four cubits wide. 9Join five of the curtains together into one set and the other six into another set. Fold the sixth curtain double at the front of the tent. 10Make fifty loops along the edge of the end curtain in one set and also along the edge of the end curtain in the other set. 11Then make fifty bronze clasps and put them in the loops to fasten the tent together as a unit. 12As for the additional length of the tent curtains, the half curtain that is left over is to hang down at the rear of the tabernacle. 13The tent curtains will be a cubit longer on both sides; what is left will hang over the sides of the tabernacle so as to cover it. 14Make for the tent a covering of ram skins dyed red, and over that a covering of hides of sea cows.

15"Make upright frames of acacia wood for the tabernacle. 16Each frame is to be ten cubits long and a cubit and a half wide, 17with two projections set parallel to each other. Make all the frames of the tabernacle in this way. 18Make twenty frames for the south side of the tabernacle 19and make forty silver bases to go under them—two bases for each frame, one under each projection. 20For the other side, the north side of the tabernacle, make twenty frames 21and forty silver bases—two under each frame. 22Make six frames for the far end, that is, the west end of the tabernacle, 23and make two frames for the corners at the far end. 24At these two corners they must be double from the bottom all the way to the top, and fitted into a single ring; both shall be like that. 25So there will be eight frames and sixteen silver bases—two under each frame.

26"Also make crossbars of acacia wood: five for the frames on one side of the tabernacle, 27five for those on the other side, and five for the frames on the west, at the far end of the tabernacle. 28The centre crossbar is to extend from end to end at the middle of the frames. 29Overlay the frames with gold and make gold rings to hold the crossbars. Also overlay the crossbars with gold.

30"Set up the tabernacle according to the plan shown you on the mountain.

31"Make a curtain of blue, purple and scarlet yarn and finely twisted linen, with cherubim worked into it by a skilled craftsman. 32Hang it with gold hooks on four posts of acacia wood overlaid with gold and standing on four silver bases. 33Hang the curtain from the clasps and place the ark of the Testimony behind the curtain. The curtain will separate the Holy Place from the Most Holy Place. 34Put the atonement cover on the ark of the Testimony in the Most Holy Place. 35Place the table outside the curtain on the north side of the tabernacle and put the lampstand opposite it on the south side.

36"For the entrance to the tent make a curtain of blue, purple and scarlet yarn and finely twisted linen—the work of an embroiderer. 37Make gold hooks for this curtain and five posts of acacia wood overlaid with gold. And cast five bronze bases for them.

NEW TESTAMENT READING
Mark 4:30–5:20

The Parable of the Mustard Seed

30Again he said, "What shall we say the kingdom of God is like, or what parable shall we use to describe it? 31It is like a mustard seed, which is the smallest seed you plant in the ground. 32Yet when planted, it grows and becomes the largest of all garden plants, with such big branches that the birds of the air can perch in its shade."

33With many similar parables Jesus spoke the word to them, as much as they could understand. 34He did not say anything to them without using a parable. But when he was alone with his own disciples, he explained everything.

Jesus Calms the Storm

35That day when evening came, he said to his disciples, "Let us go over to the other side." 36Leaving the crowd behind, they took him along, just as he was, in the boat. There were also other boats with him. 37A furious squall came up, and the waves broke over the boat, so that it was nearly swamped. 38Jesus was in the stern, sleeping on a cushion. The disciples woke him and said to him, "Teacher, don't you care if we drown?"

39He got up, rebuked the wind and said to the waves, "Quiet! Be still!" Then the wind died down and it was completely calm.

40He said to his disciples, "Why are you so afraid? Do you still have no faith?"

41They were terrified and asked each other, "Who is this? Even the wind and the waves obey him!"

The Healing of a Demon-possessed Man

5 They went across the lake to the region of the Gerasenes. 2When Jesus got out of the boat, a man with an evil spirit came from the tombs to meet him. 3This man lived in the tombs, and no-one could bind him any more, not even with a chain. 4For he had often been chained hand and foot, but he tore the chains apart and broke the irons on his feet. No-one was strong enough to subdue him. 5Night and day among the tombs and in the hills he would cry out and cut himself with stones.

6When he saw Jesus from a distance, he ran and fell on his knees in front of him. 7He shouted at the top of his voice, "What do you want with me, Jesus, Son of the Most High God? Swear to God that you won't torture me!" 8For Jesus had said to him, "Come out of this man, you evil spirit!"

9Then Jesus asked him, "What is your name?"

"My name is Legion," he replied, "for we are many." 10And he begged Jesus again and again not to send them out of the area.

11A large herd of pigs was feeding on the nearby hillside. 12The demons begged Jesus, "Send us among the pigs;

allow us to go into them." [13]He gave them permission, and the evil spirits came out and went into the pigs. The herd, about two thousand in number, rushed down the steep bank into the lake and were drowned.

[14]Those tending the pigs ran off and reported this in the town and countryside, and the people went out to see what had happened. [15]When they came to Jesus, they saw the man who had been possessed by the legion of demons, sitting there, dressed and in his right mind; and they were afraid. [16]Those who had seen it told the people what had happened to the demon-possessed man—and told about the pigs as well. [17]Then the people began to plead with Jesus to leave their region.

[18]As Jesus was getting into the boat, the man who had been demon-possessed begged to go with him. [19]Jesus did not let him, but said, "Go home to your family and tell them how much the Lord has done for you, and how he has had mercy on you." [20]So the man went away and began to tell in the Decapolis how much Jesus had done for him. And all the people were amazed.

READING FROM PSALMS
Psalm 23:1–6

A psalm of David.

[1]The LORD is my shepherd, I shall not
be in want.
[2] He makes me lie down in green
pastures,
he leads me beside quiet waters,
[3] he restores my soul.
He guides me in paths of
righteousness
for his name's sake.
[4]Even though I walk
through the valley of the shadow of
death,
I will fear no evil,
for you are with me;
your rod and your staff,
they comfort me.

[5]You prepare a table before me
in the presence of my enemies.
You anoint my head with oil;
my cup overflows.
[6]Surely goodness and love will follow
me
all the days of my life,
and I will dwell in the house of the
LORD
for ever.

DAY 51

FEBRUARY 20

OLD TESTAMENT READING
Exodus 27:1–28:43

The Altar of Burnt Offering

27 "Build an altar of acacia wood, three cubits high; it is to be square, five cubits long and five cubits wide. [2]Make a horn at each of the four corners, so that the horns and the altar are of one piece, and overlay the altar with bronze. [3]Make all its utensils of bronze—its pots to remove the ashes, and its shovels, sprinkling bowls, meat forks and firepans. [4]Make a grating for it, a bronze network, and make a bronze ring at each of the four corners of the network. [5]Put it under the ledge of the altar so that it is halfway up the altar. [6]Make poles of acacia wood for the altar and overlay them with bronze. [7]The poles are to be inserted into the rings so they will be on two sides of the altar when it is carried. [8]Make the altar hollow, out of boards. It is to be

made just as you were shown on the
mountain.

The Courtyard

[9]"Make a courtyard for the tabernacle. The south side shall be a hundred
cubits long and is to have curtains of
finely twisted linen, [10]with twenty posts
and twenty bronze bases and with silver
hooks and bands on the posts. [11]The
north side shall also be a hundred cubits
long and is to have curtains, with twenty
posts and twenty bronze bases and with
silver hooks and bands on the posts.

[12]"The west end of the courtyard
shall be fifty cubits wide and have curtains, with ten posts and ten bases. [13]On
the east end, towards the sunrise, the
courtyard shall also be fifty cubits wide.
[14]Curtains fifteen cubits long are to be
on one side of the entrance, with three
posts and three bases, [15]and curtains
fifteen cubits long are to be on the other
side, with three posts and three bases.

[16]"For the entrance to the courtyard,
provide a curtain twenty cubits long, of
blue, purple and scarlet yarn and finely
twisted linen—the work of an embroiderer—with four posts and four
bases. [17]All the posts around the courtyard are to have silver bands and hooks,
and bronze bases. [18]The courtyard shall
be a hundred cubits long and fifty cubits
wide, with curtains of finely twisted
linen five cubits high, and with bronze
bases. [19]All the other articles used in the
service of the tabernacle, whatever
their function, including all the tent
pegs for it and those for the courtyard,
are to be of bronze.

Oil for the Lampstand

[20]"Command the Israelites to bring
you clear oil of pressed olives for the
light so that the lamps may be kept
burning. [21]In the Tent of Meeting, outside the curtain that is in front of the
Testimony, Aaron and his sons are to
keep the lamps burning before the
LORD from evening till morning. This is
to be a lasting ordinance among the
Israelites for the generations to come.

The Priestly Garments

28 "Have Aaron your brother
brought to you from among the
Israelites, with his sons Nadab and
Abihu, Eleazar and Ithamar, so that
they may serve me as priests. [2]Make
sacred garments for your brother
Aaron, to give him dignity and honour.
[3]Tell all the skilled men to whom I have
given wisdom in such matters that they
are to make garments for Aaron, for his
consecration, so that he may serve me
as priest. [4]These are the garments they
are to make: a breastpiece, an ephod, a
robe, a woven tunic, a turban and a
sash. They are to make these sacred
garments for your brother Aaron and
his sons, so that they may serve me as
priests. [5]Make them use gold, and blue,
purple and scarlet yarn, and fine linen.

The Ephod

[6]"Make the ephod of gold, and of
blue, purple and scarlet yarn, and of
finely twisted linen—the work of a skilled craftsman. [7]It is to have two shoulder pieces attached to two of its corners,
so that it can be fastened. [8]Its skilfully
woven waistband is to be like it—of one
piece with the ephod and made with
gold, and with blue, purple and scarlet
yarn, and with finely twisted linen.

[9]"Take two onyx stones and engrave
on them the names of the sons of Israel
[10]in the order of their birth—six names
on one stone and the remaining six on
the other. [11]Engrave the names of the
sons of Israel on the two stones the way
a gem cutter engraves a seal. Then
mount the stones in gold filigree settings
[12]and fasten them on the shoulder
pieces of the ephod as memorial stones
for the sons of Israel. Aaron is to bear

the names on his shoulders as a memorial before the LORD. 13Make gold filigree settings 14and two braided chains of pure gold, like a rope, and attach the chains to the settings.

The Breastpiece

15"Fashion a breastpiece for making decisions—the work of a skilled craftsman. Make it like the ephod: of gold, and of blue, purple and scarlet yarn, and of finely twisted linen. 16It is to be square—a span long and a span wide—and folded double. 17Then mount four rows of precious stones on it. In the first row there shall be a ruby, a topaz and a beryl; 18in the second row a turquoise, a sapphire and an emerald; 19in the third row a jacinth, an agate and an amethyst; 20in the fourth row a chrysolite, an onyx and a jasper. Mount them in gold filigree settings. 21There are to be twelve stones, one for each of the names of the sons of Israel, each engraved like a seal with the name of one of the twelve tribes.

22"For the breastpiece make braided chains of pure gold, like a rope. 23Make two gold rings for it and fasten them to two corners of the breastpiece. 24Fasten the two gold chains to the rings at the corners of the breastpiece, 25and the other ends of the chains to the two settings, attaching them to the shoulder pieces of the ephod at the front. 26Make two gold rings and attach them to the other two corners of the breastpiece on the inside edge next to the ephod. 27Make two more gold rings and attach them to the bottom of the shoulder pieces on the front of the ephod, close to the seam just above the waistband of the ephod. 28The rings of the breastpiece are to be tied to the rings of the ephod with blue cord, connecting it to the waistband, so that the breastpiece will not swing out from the ephod.

29"Whenever Aaron enters the Holy Place, he will bear the names of the sons of Israel over his heart on the breastpiece of decision as a continuing memorial before the LORD. 30Also put the Urim and the Thummim in the breastpiece, so they may be over Aaron's heart whenever he enters the presence of the LORD. Thus Aaron will always bear the means of making decisions for the Israelites over his heart before the LORD.

Other Priestly Garments

31"Make the robe of the ephod entirely of blue cloth, 32with an opening for the head in its centre. There shall be a woven edge like a collar around this opening, so that it will not tear. 33Make pomegranates of blue, purple and scarlet yarn around the hem of the robe, with gold bells between them. 34The gold bells and the pomegranates are to alternate around the hem of the robe. 35Aaron must wear it when he ministers. The sound of the bells will be heard when he enters the Holy Place before the LORD and when he comes out, so that he will not die.

36"Make a plate of pure gold and engrave on it as on a seal: HOLY TO THE LORD. 37Fasten a blue cord to it to attach it to the turban; it is to be on the front of the turban. 38It will be on Aaron's forehead, and he will bear the guilt involved in the sacred gifts the Israelites consecrate, whatever their gifts may be. It will be on Aaron's forehead continually so that they will be acceptable to the LORD.

39"Weave the tunic of fine linen and make the turban of fine linen. The sash is to be the work of an embroiderer. 40Make tunics, sashes and headbands for Aaron's sons, to give them dignity and honour. 41After you put these clothes on your brother Aaron and his sons, anoint and ordain them. Consecrate them so they may serve me as priests.

42"Make linen undergarments as a covering for the body, reaching from the waist to the thigh. 43Aaron and his sons must wear them whenever they enter the Tent of Meeting or approach the altar to minister in the Holy Place, so that they will not incur guilt and die.

"This is to be a lasting ordinance for Aaron and his descendants.

NEW TESTAMENT READING

Mark 5:21–6:6a

A Dead Girl and a Sick Woman

[21]When Jesus had again crossed over by boat to the other side of the lake, a large crowd gathered round him while he was by the lake. [22]Then one of the synagogue rulers, named Jairus, came there. Seeing Jesus, he fell at his feet [23]and pleaded earnestly with him, "My little daughter is dying. Please come and put your hands on her so that she will be healed and live." [24]So Jesus went with him.

A large crowd followed and pressed around him. [25]And a woman was there who had been subject to bleeding for twelve years. [26]She had suffered a great deal under the care of many doctors and had spent all she had, yet instead of getting better she grew worse. [27]When she heard about Jesus, she came up behind him in the crowd and touched his cloak, [28]because she thought, "If I just touch his clothes, I will be healed." [29]Immediately her bleeding stopped and she felt in her body that she was freed from her suffering.

[30]At once Jesus realised that power had gone out from him. He turned around in the crowd and asked, "Who touched my clothes?"

[31]"You see the people crowding against you," his disciples answered, "and yet you can ask, 'Who touched me?' "

[32]But Jesus kept looking around to see who had done it. [33]Then the woman, knowing what had happened to her, came and fell at his feet and, trembling with fear, told him the whole truth. [34]He said to her, "Daughter, your faith has healed you. Go in peace and be freed from your suffering."

[35]While Jesus was still speaking, some men came from the house of Jairus, the synagogue ruler. "Your daughter is dead," they said. "Why bother the teacher any more?"

[36]Ignoring what they said, Jesus told the synagogue ruler, "Don't be afraid; just believe."

[37]He did not let anyone follow him except Peter, James and John the brother of James. [38]When they came to the home of the synagogue ruler, Jesus saw a commotion, with people crying and wailing loudly. [39]He went in and said to them, "Why all this commotion and wailing? The child is not dead but asleep." [40]But they laughed at him.

After he put them all out, he took the child's father and mother and the disciples who were with him, and went in where the child was. [41]He took her by the hand and said to her, *"Talitha koum!"* (which means, "Little girl, I say to you, get up!"). [42]Immediately the girl stood up and walked around (she was twelve years old). At this they were completely astonished. [43]He gave strict orders not to let anyone know about this, and told them to give her something to eat.

A Prophet Without Honour

6 Jesus left there and went to his home town, accompanied by his disciples. [2]When the Sabbath came, he began to teach in the synagogue, and many who heard him were amazed.

"Where did this man get these things?" they asked. "What's this wisdom that has been given him, that he even does miracles! [3]Isn't this the carpenter? Isn't this Mary's son and the brother of James, Joseph, Judas and Simon? Aren't his sisters here with us?" And they took offence at him.

[4]Jesus said to them, "Only in his home town, among his relatives and in his own house is a prophet without honour." [5]He could not do any miracles

there, except lay his hands on a few sick people and heal them. 6And he was amazed at their lack of faith.

READING FROM PSALMS
Psalm 24:1–10

Of David. A psalm.

1The earth is the LORD's, and
everything in it,
the world, and all who live in it;
2for he founded it upon the seas
and established it upon the waters.

3Who may ascend the hill of the
LORD?
Who may stand in his holy place?
4He who has clean hands and a pure
heart,
who does not lift up his soul to an
idol
or swear by what is false.
5He will receive blessing from the
LORD
and vindication from God his
Saviour.
6Such is the generation of those who
seek him,
who seek your face, O God of
Jacob. *Selah*

7Lift up your heads, O you gates;
be lifted up, you ancient doors,
that the King of glory may come in.
8Who is this King of glory?
The LORD strong and mighty,
the LORD mighty in battle.
9Lift up your heads, O you gates;
lift them up, you ancient doors,
that the King of glory may come in.
10Who is he, this King of glory?
The LORD Almighty—
he is the King of glory. *Selah*

DAY 52

FEBRUARY 21

OLD TESTAMENT READING
Exodus 29:1–30:38

Consecration of the Priests

29 "This is what you are to do to
consecrate them, so that they
may serve me as priests: Take a young
bull and two rams without defect. 2And
from fine wheat flour, without yeast,
make bread, and cakes mixed with oil,
and wafers spread with oil. 3Put them in
a basket and present them in it—along
with the bull and the two rams. 4Then
bring Aaron and his sons to the entrance to the Tent of Meeting and wash
them with water. 5Take the garments
and dress Aaron with the tunic, the robe
of the ephod, the ephod itself and the
breastpiece. Fasten the ephod on him
by its skilfully woven waistband. 6Put
the turban on his head and attach the
sacred diadem to the turban. 7Take the
anointing oil and anoint him by pouring
it on his head. 8Bring his sons and dress
them in tunics 9and put headbands on
them. Then tie sashes on Aaron and his
sons. The priesthood is theirs by a lasting ordinance. In this way you shall
ordain Aaron and his sons.
10"Bring the bull to the front of the
Tent of Meeting, and Aaron and his
sons shall lay their hands on its head.
11Slaughter it in the LORD's presence at
the entrance to the Tent of Meeting.
12Take some of the bull's blood and put
it on the horns of the altar with your
finger, and pour out the rest of it at the
base of the altar. 13Then take all the fat
around the inner parts, the covering of
the liver, and both kidneys with the fat
on them, and burn them on the altar.
14But burn the bull's flesh and its hide

and its offal outside the camp. It is a sin offering.

15"Take one of the rams, and Aaron and his sons shall lay their hands on its head. 16Slaughter it and take the blood and sprinkle it against the altar on all sides. 17Cut the ram into pieces and wash the inner parts and the legs, putting them with the head and the other pieces. 18Then burn the entire ram on the altar. It is a burnt offering to the LORD, a pleasing aroma, an offering made to the LORD by fire.

19"Take the other ram, and Aaron and his sons shall lay their hands on its head. 20Slaughter it, take some of its blood and put it on the lobes of the right ears of Aaron and his sons, on the thumbs of their right hands, and on the big toes of their right feet. Then sprinkle blood against the altar on all sides. 21And take some of the blood on the altar and some of the anointing oil and sprinkle it on Aaron and his garments and on his sons and their garments. Then he and his sons and their garments will be consecrated.

22"Take from this ram the fat, the fat tail, the fat around the inner parts, the covering of the liver, both kidneys with the fat on them, and the right thigh. (This is the ram for the ordination.) 23From the basket of bread made without yeast, which is before the LORD, take a loaf, and a cake made with oil, and a wafer. 24Put all these in the hands of Aaron and his sons and wave them before the LORD as a wave offering. 25Then take them from their hands and burn them on the altar along with the burnt offering for a pleasing aroma to the LORD, an offering made to the LORD by fire. 26After you take the breast of the ram for Aaron's ordination, wave it before the LORD as a wave offering, and it will be your share.

27"Consecrate those parts of the ordination ram that belong to Aaron and his sons: the breast that was waved and the thigh that was presented. 28This is always to be the regular share from the Israelites for Aaron and his sons. It is the contribution the Israelites are to make to the LORD from their fellowship offerings.

29"Aaron's sacred garments will belong to his descendants so that they can be anointed and ordained in them. 30The son who succeeds him as priest and comes to the Tent of Meeting to minister in the Holy Place is to wear them seven days.

31"Take the ram for the ordination and cook the meat in a sacred place. 32At the entrance to the Tent of Meeting, Aaron and his sons are to eat the meat of the ram and the bread that is in the basket. 33They are to eat these offerings by which atonement was made for their ordination and consecration. But no-one else may eat them, because they are sacred. 34And if any of the meat of the ordination ram or any bread is left over till morning, burn it up. It must not be eaten, because it is sacred.

35"Do for Aaron and his sons everything I have commanded you, taking seven days to ordain them. 36Sacrifice a bull each day as a sin offering to make atonement. Purify the altar by making atonement for it, and anoint it to consecrate it. 37For seven days make atonement for the altar and consecrate it. Then the altar will be most holy, and whatever touches it will be holy.

38"This is what you are to offer on the altar regularly each day: two lambs a year old. 39Offer one in the morning and the other at twilight. 40With the first lamb offer a tenth of an ephah of fine flour mixed with a quarter of a hin of oil from pressed olives, and a quarter of a hin of wine as a drink offering. 41Sacrifice the other lamb at twilight with the same grain offering and its drink offering as in the morning—a pleasing aroma, an offering made to the LORD by fire.

42"For the generations to come this burnt offering is to be made regularly at the entrance to the Tent of Meeting before the LORD. There I will meet you and speak to you; 43there also I will

meet with the Israelites, and the place
will be consecrated by my glory.
44"So I will consecrate the Tent of
Meeting and the altar and will consecrate Aaron and his sons to serve me as
priests. 45Then I will dwell among the
Israelites and be their God. 46They will
know that I am the LORD their God,
who brought them out of Egypt so that I
might dwell among them. I am the
LORD their God.

The Altar of Incense

30 "Make an altar of acacia wood
for burning incense. 2It is to be
square, a cubit long and a cubit wide,
and two cubits high—its horns of one
piece with it. 3Overlay the top and all
the sides and the horns with pure gold,
and make a gold moulding around it.
4Make two gold rings for the altar below
the moulding—two on opposite sides
—to hold the poles used to carry it.
5Make the poles of acacia wood and
overlay them with gold. 6Put the altar in
front of the curtain that is before the ark
of the Testimony—before the atonement cover that is over the Testimony
—where I will meet with you.
7"Aaron must burn fragrant incense
on the altar every morning when he
tends the lamps. 8He must burn incense
again when he lights the lamps at twilight so that incense will burn regularly
before the LORD for the generations to
come. 9Do not offer on this altar any
other incense or any burnt offering or
grain offering, and do not pour a drink
offering on it. 10Once a year Aaron shall
make atonement on its horns. This
annual atonement must be made with
the blood of the atoning sin offering for
the generations to come. It is most holy
to the LORD."

Atonement Money

11Then the LORD said to Moses,
12"When you take a census of the
Israelites to count them, each one must
pay the LORD a ransom for his life at the
time he is counted. Then no plague will
come on them when you number them.
13Each one who crosses over to those
already counted is to give a half shekel,
according to the sanctuary shekel,
which weighs twenty gerahs. This half
shekel is an offering to the LORD. 14All
who cross over, those twenty years old
or more, are to give an offering to the
LORD. 15The rich are not to give more
than a half shekel and the poor are not
to give less when you make the offering
to the LORD to atone for your lives.
16Receive the atonement money from
the Israelites and use it for the service of
the Tent of Meeting. It will be a memorial for the Israelites before the LORD,
making atonement for your lives."

Basin for Washing

17Then the LORD said to Moses,
18"Make a bronze basin, with its bronze
stand, for washing. Place it between the
Tent of Meeting and the altar, and put
water in it. 19Aaron and his sons are to
wash their hands and feet with water
from it. 20Whenever they enter the Tent
of Meeting, they shall wash with water
so that they will not die. Also, when
they approach the altar to minister by
presenting an offering made to the
LORD by fire, 21they shall wash their
hands and feet so that they will not die.
This is to be a lasting ordinance for
Aaron and his descendants for the generations to come."

Anointing Oil

22Then the LORD said to Moses,
23"Take the following fine spices: 500
shekels of liquid myrrh, half as much
(that is, 250 shekels) of fragrant cinnamon, 250 shekels of fragrant cane, 24500
shekels of cassia—all according to the
sanctuary shekel—and a hin of olive oil.
25Make these into a sacred anointing
oil, a fragrant blend, the work of a
perfumer. It will be the sacred anointing
oil. 26Then use it to anoint the Tent of

Meeting, the ark of the Testimony, 27the table and all its articles, the lampstand and its accessories, the altar of incense, 28the altar of burnt offering and all its utensils, and the basin with its stand. 29You shall consecrate them so they will be most holy, and whatever touches them will be holy.

30"Anoint Aaron and his sons and consecrate them so they may serve me as priests. 31Say to the Israelites, 'This is to be my sacred anointing oil for the generations to come. 32Do not pour it on men's bodies and do not make any oil with the same formula. It is sacred, and you are to consider it sacred. 33Whoever makes perfume like it and whoever puts it on anyone other than a priest must be cut off from his people.' "

Incense

34Then the LORD said to Moses, "Take fragrant spices—gum resin, onycha and galbanum—and pure frankincense, all in equal amounts, 35and make a fragrant blend of incense, the work of a perfumer. It is to be salted and pure and sacred. 36Grind some of it to powder and place it in front of the Testimony in the Tent of Meeting, where I will meet with you. It shall be most holy to you. 37Do not make any incense with this formula for yourselves; consider it holy to the LORD. 38Whoever makes any like it to enjoy its fragrance must be cut off from his people."

NEW TESTAMENT READING
Mark 6:6b–29

Jesus Sends Out the Twelve

Then Jesus went round teaching from village to village. 7Calling the Twelve to him, he sent them out two by two and gave them authority over evil spirits.

8These were his instructions: "Take nothing for the journey except a staff—no bread, no bag, no money in your belts. 9Wear sandals but not an extra tunic. 10Whenever you enter a house, stay there until you leave that town. 11And if any place will not welcome you or listen to you, shake the dust off your feet when you leave, as a testimony against them."

12They went out and preached that people should repent. 13They drove out many demons and anointed many sick people with oil and healed them.

John the Baptist Beheaded

14King Herod heard about this, for Jesus' name had become well known. Some were saying, "John the Baptist has been raised from the dead, and that is why miraculous powers are at work in him."

15Others said, "He is Elijah."

And still others claimed, "He is a prophet, like one of the prophets of long ago."

16But when Herod heard this, he said, "John, the man I beheaded, has been raised from the dead!"

17For Herod himself had given orders to have John arrested, and he had him bound and put in prison. He did this because of Herodias, his brother Philip's wife, whom he had married. 18For John had been saying to Herod, "It is not lawful for you to have your brother's wife." 19So Herodias nursed a grudge against John and wanted to kill him. But she was not able to, 20because Herod feared John and protected him, knowing him to be a righteous and holy man. When Herod heard John, he was greatly puzzled; yet he liked to listen to him.

21Finally the opportune time came. On his birthday Herod gave a banquet for his high officials and military commanders and the leading men of Galilee. 22When the daughter of Herodias came in and danced, she pleased Herod and his dinner guests.

The king said to the girl, "Ask me for anything you want, and I'll give it to you." 23And he promised her with an oath, "Whatever you ask I will give you, up to half my kingdom."

24She went out and said to her mother, "What shall I ask for?"

"The head of John the Baptist," she answered.

25At once the girl hurried in to the king with the request: "I want you to give me right now the head of John the Baptist on a platter."

26The king was greatly distressed, but because of his oaths and his dinner guests, he did not want to refuse her.
27So he immediately sent an executioner with orders to bring John's head. The man went, beheaded John in
the prison, 28and brought back his head on a platter. He presented it to the girl,
and she gave it to her mother. 29On
hearing of this, John's disciples came and took his body and laid it in a tomb.

READING FROM PROVERBS
Proverbs 5:15–23

15Drink water from your own cistern,
running water from your own well.
16Should your springs overflow in the streets,
your streams of water in the public squares?
17Let them be yours alone,
never to be shared with strangers.
18May your fountain be blessed,
and may you rejoice in the wife of your youth.
19A loving doe, a graceful deer—
may her breasts satisfy you always,
may you ever be captivated by her love.
20Why be captivated, my son, by an adulteress?
Why embrace the bosom of another man's wife?

21For a man's ways are in full view of the LORD,
and he examines all his paths.
22The evil deeds of a wicked man ensnare him;
the cords of his sin hold him fast.
23He will die for lack of discipline,
led astray by his own great folly.

DAY 53

FEBRUARY 22

OLD TESTAMENT READING
Exodus 31:1–33:6

Bezalel and Oholiab

31 Then the LORD said to Moses,
2"See I have chosen Bezalel son of Uri, the son of Hur, of the tribe of
Judah, 3and I have filled him with the Spirit of God, with skill, ability and
knowledge in all kinds of crafts—4to make artistic designs for work in gold,
silver and bronze, 5to cut and set stones, to work in wood, and to engage in all
kinds of craftsmanship. 6Moreover, I have appointed Oholiab son of Ahisamach, of the tribe of Dan, to help him. Also I have given skill to all the craftsmen to make everything I have commanded you:
7the Tent of Meeting, the ark of the Testimony with the atonement cover on it, and all the other furnishings of the tent—
8the table and its articles, the pure gold lampstand and all its accessories, the altar of incense,
9the altar of burnt offering and all its utensils, the basin with its stand—
10and also the woven garments, both the sacred garments for Aaron the priest and the garments for his sons when they serve as priests,
11and the anointing oil and fragrant incense for the Holy Place. They are to make them just as I commanded you."

The Sabbath

12Then the LORD said to Moses, 13"Say to the Israelites, 'You must observe my Sabbaths. This will be a sign between me and you for the generations to come, so that you may know that I am the LORD, who makes you holy.

14" 'Observe the Sabbath, because it is holy to you. Anyone who desecrates it must be put to death; whoever does any work on that day must be cut off from his people. 15For six days, work is to be done, but the seventh day is a Sabbath of rest, holy to the LORD. Whoever does any work on the Sabbath day must be put to death. 16The Israelites are to observe the Sabbath, celebrating it for the generations to come as a lasting covenant. 17It will be a sign between me and the Israelites for ever, for in six days the LORD made the heavens and the earth, and on the seventh day he abstained from work and rested.' "

18When the LORD finished speaking to Moses on Mount Sinai, he gave him the two tablets of the Testimony, the tablets of stone inscribed by the finger of God.

The Golden Calf

32 When the people saw that Moses was so long in coming down from the mountain, they gathered round Aaron and said, "Come, make us gods who will go before us. As for this fellow Moses who brought us up out of Egypt, we don't know what has happened to him."

2Aaron answered them, "Take off the gold ear-rings that your wives, your sons and your daughters are wearing, and bring them to me." 3So all the people took off their ear-rings and brought them to Aaron. 4He took what they handed him and made it into an idol cast in the shape of a calf, fashioning it with a tool. Then they said, "These are your gods, O Israel, who brought you up out of Egypt."

5When Aaron saw this, he built an altar in front of the calf and announced, "Tomorrow there will be a festival to the LORD." 6So the next day the people rose early and sacrificed burnt offerings and presented fellowship offerings. Afterwards they sat down to eat and drink and got up to indulge in revelry.

7Then the LORD said to Moses, "Go down, because your people, whom you brought up out of Egypt, have become corrupt. 8They have been quick to turn away from what I commanded them and have made themselves an idol cast in the shape of a calf. They have bowed down to it and sacrificed to it and have said, 'These are your gods, O Israel, who brought you up out of Egypt.'

9"I have seen these people," the LORD said to Moses, "and they are a stiff-necked people. 10Now leave me alone so that my anger may burn against them and that I may destroy them. Then I will make you into a great nation."

11But Moses sought the favour of the LORD his God. "O LORD," he said, "why should your anger burn against your people, whom you brought out of Egypt with great power and a mighty hand? 12Why should the Egyptians say, 'It was with evil intent that he brought them out, to kill them in the mountains and to wipe them off the face of the earth'? Turn from your fierce anger; relent and do not bring disaster on your people. 13Remember your servants Abraham, Isaac and Israel, to whom you swore by your own self: 'I will make your descendants as numerous as the stars in the sky and I will give your descendants all this land I promised them, and it will be their inheritance for ever.' " 14Then the LORD relented and did not bring on his people the disaster he had threatened.

15Moses turned and went down the mountain with the two tablets of the Testimony in his hands. They were inscribed on both sides, front and back. 16The tablets were the work of God; the writing was the writing of God, engraved on the tablets.

17When Joshua heard the noise of the
people shouting, he said to Moses,
"There is the sound of war in the
camp."
18Moses replied:

"It is not the sound of victory,
it is not the sound of defeat;
it is the sound of singing that I
hear."

19When Moses approached the camp
and saw the calf and the dancing, his
anger burned and he threw the tablets
out of his hands, breaking them to
pieces at the foot of the mountain.
20And he took the calf they had made
and burned it in the fire; then he ground
it to powder, scattered it on the water
and made the Israelites drink it.
21He said to Aaron, "What did these
people do to you, that you led them into
such great sin?"
22"Do not be angry, my lord," Aaron
answered. "You know how prone these
people are to evil. 23They said to me,
'Make us gods who will go before us. As
for this fellow Moses who brought us up
out of Egypt, we don't know what has
happened to him.' 24So I told them,
'Whoever has any gold jewellery, take it
off.' Then they gave me the gold, and I
threw it into the fire, and out came this
calf!"
25Moses saw that the people were
running wild and that Aaron had let
them get out of control and so become a
laughing-stock to their enemies. 26So he
stood at the entrance to the camp and
said, "Whoever is for the LORD, come
to me." And all the Levites rallied to
him.
27Then he said to them, "This is what
the LORD, the God of Israel, says: 'Each
man strap a sword to his side. Go back
and forth through the camp from one
end to the other, each killing his brother
and friend and neighbour.'" 28The Levites did as Moses commanded, and
that day about three thousand of the
people died. 29Then Moses said, "You
have been set apart to the LORD today,
for you were against your own sons and
brothers, and he has blessed you this
day."
30The next day Moses said to the
people, "You have committed a great
sin. But now I will go up to the LORD;
perhaps I can make atonement for your
sin."
31So Moses went back to the LORD
and said, "Oh, what a great sin these
people have committed! They have
made themselves gods of gold. 32But
now, please forgive their sin—but if
not, then blot me out of the book you
have written."
33The LORD replied to Moses, "Whoever has sinned against me I will blot
out of my book. 34Now go, lead the
people to the place I spoke of, and
my angel will go before you. However, when the time comes for me to
punish, I will punish them for their
sin."
35And the LORD struck the people
with a plague because of what they did
with the calf Aaron had made.

33 Then the LORD said to Moses,
"Leave this place, you and the
people you brought up out of Egypt,
and go up to the land I promised on oath
to Abraham, Isaac and Jacob, saying,
'I will give it to your descendants.' 2I
will send an angel before you and drive
out the Canaanites, Amorites, Hittites,
Perizzites, Hivites and Jebusites. 3Go
up to the land flowing with milk and
honey. But I will not go with you, because you are a stiff-necked people and
I might destroy you on the way."
4When the people heard these dis-
tressing words, they began to mourn
and no-one put on any ornaments. 5For
the LORD had said to Moses, "Tell the
Israelites, 'You are a stiff-necked people. If I were to go with you even for a
moment, I might destroy you. Now take
off your ornaments and I will decide
what to do with you.'" 6So the Israelites
stripped off their ornaments at Mount
Horeb.

NEW TESTAMENT READING
Mark 6:30–56

Jesus Feeds the Five Thousand

[30]The apostles gathered round Jesus
and reported to him all they had done
and taught. [31]Then, because so many
people were coming and going that they
did not even have a chance to eat, he
said to them, "Come with me by
yourselves to a quiet place and get some
rest."

[32]So they went away by themselves in
a boat to a solitary place. [33]But many
who saw them leaving recognised them
and ran on foot from all the towns and
got there ahead of them. [34]When Jesus
landed and saw a large crowd, he had
compassion on them, because they were
like sheep without a shepherd. So he
began teaching them many things.

[35]By this time it was late in the day, so
his disciples came to him. "This is a
remote place," they said, "and it's
already very late. [36]Send the people
away so that they can go to the surrounding
countryside and villages and
buy themselves something to eat."

[37]But he answered, "You give them
something to eat."

They said to him, "That would take eight months of a man's wages! Are we to go and spend that much on bread and give it to them to eat?"

[38]"How many loaves do you have?"
he asked. "Go and see."

When they found out, they said, "Five—and two fish."

[39]Then Jesus directed them to have
all the people sit down in groups on the
green grass. [40]So they sat down in
groups of hundreds and fifties. [41]Taking
the five loaves and the two fish and
looking up to heaven, he gave thanks
and broke the loaves. Then he gave
them to his disciples to set before the
people. He also divided the two fish
among them all. [42]They all ate and were
satisfied, [43]and the disciples picked up
twelve basketfuls of broken pieces of
bread and fish. [44]The number of the
men who had eaten was five thousand.

Jesus Walks on the Water

[45]Immediately Jesus made his disciples
get into the boat and go on ahead of
him to Bethsaida, while he dismissed
the crowd. [46]After leaving them, he
went up on a mountainside to pray.

[47]When evening came, the boat was
in the middle of the lake, and he was
alone on land. [48]He saw the disciples
straining at the oars, because the wind
was against them. About the fourth
watch of the night he went out to them,
walking on the lake. He was about to
pass by them, [49]but when they saw him
walking on the lake, they thought he
was a ghost. They cried out, [50]because
they all saw him and were terrified.

Immediately he spoke to them and
said, "Take courage! It is I. Don't be
afraid." [51]Then he climbed into the boat
with them, and the wind died down.
They were completely amazed, [52]for
they had not understood about the
loaves; their hearts were hardened.

[53]When they had crossed over, they
landed at Gennesaret and anchored
there. [54]As soon as they got out of the
boat, people recognised Jesus. [55]They
ran throughout that whole region and
carried the sick on mats to wherever
they heard he was. [56]And wherever he
went—into villages, towns or countryside—they
placed the sick in the
market-places. They begged him to let
them touch even the edge of his cloak,
and all who touched him were healed.

READING FROM PSALMS
Psalm 25:1–7

Of David.

[1]To you, O LORD, I lift up my soul;
[2] in you I trust, O my God.
Do not let me be put to shame,
nor let my enemies triumph over me.
[3]No-one whose hope is in you
will ever be put to shame,

but they will be put to shame
who are treacherous without
excuse.

4Show me your ways, O LORD,
teach me your paths;
5guide me in your truth and teach me,
for you are God my Saviour,
and my hope is in you all day long.
6Remember, O LORD, your great
mercy and love,
for they are from of old.
7Remember not the sins of my youth
and my rebellious ways;
according to your love remember me,
for you are good, O LORD.

DAY 54

FEBRUARY 23

OLD TESTAMENT READING

Exodus 33:7–34:35

The Tent of Meeting

7Now Moses used to take a tent and
pitch it outside the camp some distance
away, calling it the "tent of meeting".
Anyone enquiring of the LORD would
go to the tent of meeting outside the
camp. 8And whenever Moses went out
to the tent, all the people rose and stood
at the entrances to their tents, watching
Moses until he entered the tent. 9As
Moses went into the tent, the pillar of
cloud would come down and stay at the
entrance, while the LORD spoke with
Moses. 10Whenever the people saw the
pillar of cloud standing at the entrance
to the tent, they all stood and worshipped, each at the entrance to his tent.
11The LORD would speak to Moses face
to face, as a man speaks with his friend.
Then Moses would return to the camp,
but his young assistant Joshua son of
Nun did not leave the tent.

Moses and the Glory of the LORD

12Moses said to the LORD, "You have
been telling me, 'Lead these people,'
but you have not let me know whom you
will send with me. You have said, 'I
know you by name and you have found
favour with me.' 13If you are pleased
with me, teach me your ways so I may
know you and continue to find favour
with you. Remember that this nation is
your people."

14The LORD replied, "My Presence
will go with you, and I will give you
rest."

15Then Moses said to him, "If your
Presence does not go with us, do not
send us up from here. 16How will anyone know that you are pleased with me
and with your people unless you go with
us? What else will distinguish me and
your people from all the other people
on the face of the earth?"

17And the LORD said to Moses, "I will
do the very thing you have asked, because I am pleased with you and I know
you by name."

18Then Moses said, "Now show me
your glory."

19And the LORD said, "I will cause all
my goodness to pass in front of you, and
I will proclaim my name, the LORD, in
your presence. I will have mercy on
whom I will have mercy, and I will have
compassion on whom I will have compassion. 20But," he said, "you cannot
see my face, for no-one may see me and
live."

21Then the LORD said, "There is a
place near me where you may stand on a
rock. 22When my glory passes by, I will
put you in a cleft in the rock and cover
you with my hand until I have passed
by. 23Then I will remove my hand and
you will see my back; but my face must
not be seen."

The New Stone Tablets

34 The LORD said to Moses,
"Chisel out two stone tablets
like the first ones, and I will write on
them the words that were on the first
tablets, which you broke. 2Be ready in
the morning, and then come up on
Mount Sinai. Present yourself to me
there on top of the mountain. 3No-one
is to come with you or be seen anywhere
on the mountain; not even the flocks
and herds may graze in front of the
mountain."
4So Moses chiselled out two stone
tablets like the first ones and went up
Mount Sinai early in the morning, as the
LORD had commanded him; and he carried the two stone tablets in his hands.
5Then the LORD came down in the cloud
and stood there with him and proclaimed his name, the LORD. 6And he
passed in front of Moses, proclaiming,
"The LORD, the LORD, the compassionate and gracious God, slow to anger,
abounding in love and faithfulness,
7maintaining love to thousands, and
forgiving wickedness, rebellion and sin.
Yet he does not leave the guilty unpunished; he punishes the children and
their children for the sin of the fathers to
the third and fourth generation."
8Moses bowed to the ground at once
and worshipped. 9"O Lord, if I have
found favour in your eyes," he said,
"then let the Lord go with us. Although
this is a stiff-necked people, forgive our
wickedness and our sin, and take us as
your inheritance."
10Then the LORD said: "I am making
a covenant with you. Before all your
people I will do wonders never before
done in any nation in all the world. The
people you live among will see how
awesome is the work that I, the LORD,
will do for you. 11Obey what I command
you today. I will drive out before you
the Amorites, Canaanites, Hittites,
Perizzites, Hivites and Jebusites. 12Be
careful not to make a treaty with those
who live in the land where you are
going, or they will be a snare among
you. 13Break down their altars, smash
their sacred stones and cut down their
Asherah poles. 14Do not worship any
other god, for the LORD, whose name is
Jealous, is a jealous God.
15"Be careful not to make a treaty
with those who live in the land; for when
they prostitute themselves to their gods
and sacrifice to them, they will invite
you and you will eat their sacrifices.
16And when you choose some of their
daughters as wives for your sons and
those daughters prostitute themselves
to their gods, they will lead your sons to
do the same.
17"Do not make cast idols.
18"Celebrate the Feast of Unleavened Bread. For seven days eat
bread made without yeast, as I commanded you. Do this at the appointed
time in the month of Abib, for in that
month you came out of Egypt.
19"The first offspring of every womb
belongs to me, including all the
firstborn males of your livestock,
whether from herd or flock. 20Redeem
the firstborn donkey with a lamb, but if
you do not redeem it, break its neck.
Redeem all your firstborn sons.
"No-one is to appear before me
empty-handed.
21"Six days you shall labour, but on
the seventh day you shall rest; even
during the ploughing season and harvest you must rest.
22"Celebrate the Feast of Weeks with
the firstfruits of the wheat harvest, and
the Feast of Ingathering at the turn
of the year. 23Three times a year all your
men are to appear before the Sovereign
LORD, the God of Israel. 24I will drive
out nations before you and enlarge your
territory, and no-one will covet your
land when you go up three times each
year to appear before the LORD your
God.
25"Do not offer the blood of a sacrifice to me along with anything containing yeast, and do not let any of the
sacrifice from the Passover Feast remain until morning.
26"Bring the best of the firstfruits of

your soil to the house of the LORD your
God.
"Do not cook a young goat in its
mother's milk."
27Then the LORD said to Moses,
"Write down these words, for in accordance with these words I have made a
covenant with you and with Israel."
28Moses was there with the LORD forty
days and forty nights without eating
bread or drinking water. And he wrote
on the tablets the words of the covenant
—the Ten Commandments.

The Radiant Face of Moses

29When Moses came down from
Mount Sinai with the two tablets of the
Testimony in his hands, he was not
aware that his face was radiant because
he had spoken with the LORD. 30When
Aaron and all the Israelites saw Moses,
his face was radiant, and they were
afraid to come near him. 31But Moses
called to them; so Aaron and all the
leaders of the community came back to
him, and he spoke to them. 32After-
wards all the Israelites came near him,
and he gave them all the commands the
LORD had given him on Mount Sinai.
33When Moses finished speaking to
them, he put a veil over his face. 34But
whenever he entered the LORD's presence to speak with him, he removed
the veil until he came out. And when he
came out and told the Israelites what he
had been commanded, 35they saw that
his face was radiant. Then Moses would
put the veil back over his face until he
went in to speak with the LORD.

NEW TESTAMENT READING
Mark 7:1–30

Clean and Unclean

7 The Pharisees and some of the
teachers of the law who had come
from Jerusalem gathered round Jesus
and 2saw some of his disciples eating
food with hands that were "unclean",
that is, unwashed. 3(The Pharisees and
all the Jews do not eat unless they give
their hands a ceremonial washing, holding to the tradition of the elders. 4When
they come from the market-place they
do not eat unless they wash. And they
observe many other traditions, such as
the washing of cups, pitchers and
kettles.)
5So the Pharisees and teachers of the
law asked Jesus, "Why don't your disciples live according to the tradition of
the elders instead of eating their food
with 'unclean' hands?"
6He replied, "Isaiah was right when
he prophesied about you hypocrites; as
it is written:

" 'These people honour me with their
lips,
but their hearts are far from me.
7They worship me in vain;
their teachings are but rules taught
by men.'

8You have let go of the commands of
God and are holding on to the traditions
of men."
9And he said to them: "You have a
fine way of setting aside the commands
of God in order to observe your own
traditions! 10For Moses said, 'Honour
your father and your mother,' and,
'Anyone who curses his father or
mother must be put to death.' 11But you
say that if a man says to his father or
mother: 'Whatever help you might
otherwise have received from me is
Corban' (that is, a gift devoted to God),
12then you no longer let him do anything
for his father or mother. 13Thus you
nullify the word of God by your tradition that you have handed down. And
you do many things like that."
14Again Jesus called the crowd to him
and said, "Listen to me, everyone, and
understand this. 15Nothing outside a
man can make him 'unclean' by going
into him. Rather, it is what comes out of
a man that makes him 'unclean'."
17After he had left the crowd and
entered the house, his disciples asked

him about this parable. [18]"Are you so
dull?" he asked. "Don't you see that
nothing that enters a man from the outside can make him 'unclean'? [19]For it
doesn't go into his heart but into his
stomach, and then out of his body." (In
saying this, Jesus declared all foods
"clean".)

[20]He went on: "What comes out of a
man is what makes him 'unclean'. [21]For
from within, out of men's hearts, come
evil thoughts, sexual immorality, theft,
murder, adultery, [22]greed, malice, deceit, lewdness, envy, slander, arrogance
and folly. [23]All these evils come from
inside and make a man 'unclean'."

The Faith of a Syro-Phoenician Woman

[24]Jesus left that place and went to the
vicinity of Tyre. He entered a house and
did not want anyone to know it; yet he
could not keep his presence secret. [25]In
fact, as soon as she heard about him, a
woman whose little daughter was possessed by an evil spirit came and fell at
his feet. [26]The woman was a Greek,
born in Syrian Phoenicia. She begged
Jesus to drive the demon out of her
daughter.

[27]"First let the children eat all they
want," he told her, "for it is not right to
take the children's bread and toss it to
their dogs."

[28]"Yes, Lord," she replied, "but
even the dogs under the table eat the
children's crumbs."

[29]Then he told her, "For such a reply,
you may go; the demon has left your
daughter."

[30]She went home and found her child
lying on the bed, and the demon gone.

READING FROM PSALMS
Psalm 25:8–15

[8]Good and upright is the LORD;
therefore he instructs sinners in his ways.
[9]He guides the humble in what is right
and teaches them his way.
[10]All the ways of the LORD are loving and faithful
for those who keep the demands of his covenant.
[11]For the sake of your name, O LORD,
forgive my iniquity, though it is great.
[12]Who, then, is the man that fears the LORD?
He will instruct him in the way chosen for him.
[13]He will spend his days in prosperity,
and his descendants will inherit the land.
[14]The LORD confides in those who fear him;
he makes his covenant known to them.
[15]My eyes are ever on the LORD,
for only he will release my feet from the snare.

DAY 55

FEBRUARY 24

OLD TESTAMENT READING
Exodus 35:1–36:38

Sabbath Regulations

35 Moses assembled the whole
Israelite community and said to
them, "These are the things the LORD
has commanded you to do: 2For six
days, work is to be done, but the
seventh day shall be your holy day, a
Sabbath of rest to the LORD. Whoever
does any work on it must be put to
death. 3Do not light a fire in any of your
dwellings on the Sabbath day."

Materials for the Tabernacle

4Moses said to the whole Israelite
community, "This is what the LORD has
commanded: 5From what you have,
take an offering for the LORD. Everyone who is willing is to bring to the
LORD an offering of gold, silver and
bronze; 6blue, purple and scarlet yarn
and fine linen; goat hair; 7ram skins
dyed red and hides of sea cows; acacia
wood; 8olive oil for the light; spices for
the anointing oil and for the fragrant
incense; 9and onyx stones and other
gems to be mounted on the ephod and
breastpiece.

10"All who are skilled among you are
to come and make everything the LORD
has commanded: 11the tabernacle with
its tent and its covering, clasps, frames,
crossbars, posts and bases; 12the ark
with its poles and the atonement cover
and the curtain that shields it; 13the
table with its poles and all its articles
and the bread of the Presence; 14the
lampstand that is for light with its accessories, lamps and oil for the light; 15the
altar of incense with its poles, the
anointing oil and the fragrant incense;
the curtain for the doorway at the entrance to the tabernacle; 16the altar of
burnt offering with its bronze grating,
its poles and all its utensils; the bronze
basin with its stand; 17the curtains of the
courtyard with its posts and bases, and
the curtain for the entrance to the
courtyard; 18the tent pegs for the tabernacle and for the courtyard, and their
ropes; 19the woven garments worn for
ministering in the sanctuary—both the
sacred garments for Aaron the priest
and the garments for his sons when they
serve as priests."

20Then the whole Israelite community withdrew from Moses' presence,
21and everyone who was willing and
whose heart moved him came and
brought an offering to the LORD for the
work on the Tent of Meeting, for all its
service, and for the sacred garments.
22All who were willing, men and women
alike, came and brought gold jewellery
of all kinds: brooches, ear-rings, rings
and ornaments. They all presented their
gold as a wave offering to the LORD.
23Everyone who had blue, purple or
scarlet yarn or fine linen, or goat hair,
ram skins dyed red or hides of sea cows
brought them. 24Those presenting an
offering of silver or bronze brought it as
an offering to the LORD, and everyone
who had acacia wood for any part of the
work brought it. 25Every skilled woman
spun with her hands and brought what
she had spun—blue, purple or scarlet
yarn or fine linen. 26And all the women
who were willing and had the skill spun
the goat hair. 27The leaders brought
onyx stones and other gems to be
mounted on the ephod and breastpiece.
28They also brought spices and olive oil
for the light and for the anointing oil
and for the fragrant incense. 29All the
Israelite men and women who were
willing brought to the LORD freewill
offerings for all the work the LORD
through Moses had commanded them
to do.

Bezalel and Oholiab

30Then Moses said to the Israelites, "See, the LORD has chosen Bezalel son of Uri, the son of Hur, of the tribe of Judah, 31and he has filled him with the Spirit of God, with skill, ability and knowledge in all kinds of crafts—32to make artistic designs for work in gold, silver and bronze, 33to cut and set stones, to work in wood and to engage in all kinds of artistic craftsmanship. 34And he has given both him and Oholiab son of Ahisamach, of the tribe of Dan, the ability to teach others. 35He has filled them with skill to do all kinds of work as craftsmen, designers, embroiderers in blue, purple and scarlet yarn and fine linen, and weavers—all of them master craftsmen and designers.

36 1So Bezalel, Oholiab and every skilled person to whom the LORD has given skill and ability to know how to carry out all the work of constructing the sanctuary are to do the work just as the LORD has commanded."

2Then Moses summoned Bezalel and Oholiab and every skilled person to whom the LORD had given ability and who was willing to come and do the work. 3They received from Moses all the offerings the Israelites had brought to carry out the work of constructing the sanctuary. And the people continued to bring freewill offerings morning after morning. 4So all the skilled craftsmen who were doing all the work on the sanctuary left their work 5and said to Moses, "The people are bringing more than enough for doing the work the LORD commanded to be done."

6Then Moses gave an order and they sent this word throughout the camp: "No man or woman is to make anything else as an offering for the sanctuary." And so the people were restrained from bringing more, 7because what they already had was more than enough to do all the work.

The Tabernacle

8All the skilled men among the workmen made the tabernacle with ten curtains of finely twisted linen and blue, purple and scarlet yarn, with cherubim worked into them by a skilled craftsman. 9All the curtains were the same size—twenty-eight cubits long and four cubits wide. 10They joined five of the curtains together and did the same with the other five. 11Then they made loops of blue material along the edge of the end curtain in one set, and the same was done with the end curtain in the other set. 12They also made fifty loops on one curtain and fifty loops on the end curtain of the other set, with the loops opposite each other. 13Then they made fifty gold clasps and used them to fasten the two sets of curtains together so that the tabernacle was a unit.

14They made curtains of goat hair for the tent over the tabernacle—eleven altogether. 15All eleven curtains were the same size—thirty cubits long and four cubits wide. 16They joined five of the curtains into one set and the other six into another set. 17Then they made fifty loops along the edge of the end curtain in one set and also along the edge of the end curtain in the other set. 18They made fifty bronze clasps to fasten the tent together as a unit. 19Then they made for the tent a covering of ram skins dyed red, and over that a covering of hides of sea cows.

20They made upright frames of acacia wood for the tabernacle. 21Each frame was ten cubits long and a cubit and a half wide, 22with two projections set parallel to each other. They made all the frames of the tabernacle in this way. 23They made twenty frames for the south side of the tabernacle 24and made forty silver bases to go under them—two bases for each frame, one under each projection. 25For the other side, the north side of the tabernacle, they made twenty frames 26and forty silver bases—two under each frame. 27They made six frames for the far end, that is, the west

end of the tabernacle, 28and two frames
were made for the corners of the
tabernacle at the far end. 29At these two
corners the frames were double from
the bottom all the way to the top and
fitted into a single ring; both were made
alike. 30So there were eight frames and
sixteen silver bases—two under each
frame.
31They also made crossbars of acacia
wood: five for the frames on one side of
the tabernacle, 32five for those on the
other side, and five for the frames on the
west, at the far end of the tabernacle.
33They made the centre crossbar so that
it extended from end to end at the middle of the frames. 34They overlaid the
frames with gold and made gold rings to
hold the crossbars. They also overlaid
the crossbars with gold.
35They made the curtain of blue, purple and scarlet yarn and finely twisted
linen, with cherubim worked into it by a
skilled craftsman. 36They made four
posts of acacia wood for it and overlaid
them with gold. They made gold hooks
for them and cast their four silver bases.
37For the entrance to the tent they made
a curtain of blue, purple and scarlet
yarn and finely twisted linen—the work
of an embroiderer; 38and they made five
posts with hooks for them. They overlaid the tops of the posts and their bands
with gold and made their five bases of
bronze.

NEW TESTAMENT READING
Mark 7:31–8:13

The Healing of a Deaf and Mute Man

31Then Jesus left the vicinity of Tyre
and went through Sidon, down to the
Sea of Galilee and into the region of
the Decapolis. 32There some people
brought to him a man who was deaf and
could hardly talk, and they begged him
to place his hand on the man.
33After he took him aside, away from
the crowd, Jesus put his fingers into the
man's ears. Then he spat and touched
the man's tongue. 34He looked up to
heaven and with a deep sigh said to him,
"*Ephphatha!*" (which means, "Be
opened!"). 35At this, the man's ears
were opened, his tongue was loosened
and he began to speak plainly.
36Jesus commanded them not to tell
anyone. But the more he did so, the
more they kept talking about it.
37People were overwhelmed with
amazement. "He has done everything
well," they said. "He even makes the
deaf hear and the mute speak."

Jesus Feeds the Four Thousand

8 During those days another large
crowd gathered. Since they had
nothing to eat, Jesus called his disciples
to him and said, 2"I have compassion
for these people; they have already
been with me three days and have nothing to eat. 3If I send them home
hungry, they will collapse on the way,
because some of them have come a long
distance."
4His disciples answered, "But where
in this remote place can anyone get
enough bread to feed them?"
5"How many loaves do you have?"
Jesus asked.
"Seven," they replied.
6He told the crowd to sit down on the
ground. When he had taken the seven
loaves and given thanks, he broke them
and gave them to his disciples to set
before the people, and they did so.
7They had a few small fish as well; he
gave thanks for them also and told the
disciples to distribute them. 8The people ate and were satisfied. Afterwards
the disciples picked up seven basketfuls
of broken pieces that were left over.
9About four thousand men were present. And having sent them away, 10he
got into the boat with his disciples and
went to the region of Dalmanutha.
11The Pharisees came and began to
question Jesus. To test him, they asked
him for a sign from heaven. 12He sighed
deeply and said, "Why does this generation ask for a miraculous sign? I tell you

the truth, no sign will be given to it."
13Then he left them, got back into the
boat and crossed to the other side.

READING FROM PSALMS
Psalm 25:16–22

16Turn to me and be gracious to me,
for I am lonely and afflicted.
17The troubles of my heart have multiplied;
free me from my anguish.
18Look upon my affliction and my distress
and take away all my sins.
19See how my enemies have increased
and how fiercely they hate me!
20Guard my life and rescue me;
let me not be put to shame,
for I take refuge in you.
21May integrity and uprightness protect me,
because my hope is in you.

22Redeem Israel, O God,
from all their troubles!

FEBRUARY 25

DAY 56

OLD TESTAMENT READING
Exodus 37:1–38:31

The Ark

37 Bezalel made the ark of acacia
wood—two and a half cubits
long, a cubit and a half wide, and a cubit
and a half high. 2He overlaid it with pure
gold, both inside and out, and made
a gold moulding around it. 3He cast
four gold rings for it and fastened them
to its four feet, with two rings on one
side and two rings on the other. 4Then
he made poles of acacia wood and overlaid them with gold. 5And he inserted
the poles into the rings on the sides of
the ark to carry it.

6He made the atonement cover of
pure gold—two and a half cubits long
and a cubit and a half wide. 7Then he
made two cherubim out of hammered
gold at the ends of the cover. 8He made
one cherub on one end and the second
cherub on the other; at the two ends he
made them of one piece with the cover.
9The cherubim had their wings spread
upwards, overshadowing the cover with
them. The cherubim faced each other,
looking towards the cover.

The Table

10They made the table of acacia wood
—two cubits long, a cubit wide, and a
cubit and a half high. 11Then they overlaid it with pure gold and made a gold
moulding around it. 12They also made
around it a rim a handbreadth wide and
put a gold moulding on the rim. 13They
cast four gold rings for the table and
fastened them to the four corners,
where the four legs were. 14The rings
were put close to the rim to hold the
poles used in carrying the table. 15The
poles for carrying the table were made
of acacia wood and were overlaid with
gold. 16And they made from pure gold
the articles for the table—its plates and
dishes and bowls and its pitchers for the
pouring out of drink offerings.

The Lampstand

17They made the lampstand of pure
gold and hammered it out, base and
shaft; its flowerlike cups, buds and blossoms were of one piece with it. 18Six
branches extended from the sides of the
lampstand—three on one side and
three on the other. 19Three cups shaped

like almond flowers with buds and blossoms were on one branch, three on the
next branch and the same for all six
branches extending from the lampstand. 20And on the lampstand were
four cups shaped like almond flowers
with buds and blossoms. 21One bud was
under the first pair of branches extending from the lampstand, a second bud
under the second pair, and a third bud
under the third pair—six branches in
all. 22The buds and the branches were
all of one piece with the lampstand,
hammered out of pure gold.
23They made its seven lamps, as well
as its wick trimmers and trays, of pure
gold. 24They made the lampstand and
all its accessories from one talent of
pure gold.

The Altar of Incense

25They made the altar of incense out
of acacia wood. It was square, a cubit
long and a cubit wide, and two cubits
high—its horns of one piece with it.
26They overlaid the top and all the sides
and the horns with pure gold, and made
a gold moulding around it. 27They made
two gold rings below the moulding—
two on opposite sides—to hold the
poles used to carry it. 28They made the
poles of acacia wood and overlaid them
with gold.
29They also made the sacred anointing oil and the pure, fragrant incense
—the work of a perfumer.

The Altar of Burnt Offering

38 They built the altar of burnt
offering of acacia wood, three
cubits high; it was square, five cubits
long and five cubits wide. 2They made a
horn at each of the four corners, so that
the horns and the altar were of one
piece, and they overlaid the altar with
bronze. 3They made all its utensils of
bronze—its pots, shovels, sprinkling
bowls, meat forks and firepans. 4They
made a grating for the altar, a bronze
network, to be under its ledge, halfway
up the altar. 5They cast bronze rings to
hold the poles for the four corners of the
bronze grating. 6They made the poles of
acacia wood and overlaid them with
bronze. 7They inserted the poles into
the rings so they would be on the sides
of the altar for carrying it. They made it
hollow, out of boards.

Basin for Washing

8They made the bronze basin and its
bronze stand from the mirrors of the
women who served at the entrance to
the Tent of Meeting.

The Courtyard

9Next they made the courtyard. The
south side was a hundred cubits long and
had curtains of finely twisted linen,
10with twenty posts and twenty bronze
bases, and with silver hooks and bands
on the posts. 11The north side was also a
hundred cubits long and had twenty
posts and twenty bronze bases, with
silver hooks and bands on the posts.
12The west end was fifty cubits wide
and had curtains, with ten posts and ten
bases, with silver hooks and bands on
the posts. 13The east end, towards the
sunrise, was also fifty cubits wide.
14Curtains fifteen cubits long were on
one side of the entrance, with three
posts and three bases, 15and curtains
fifteen cubits long were on the other
side of the entrance to the courtyard,
with three posts and three bases. 16All
the curtains around the courtyard were
of finely twisted linen. 17The bases for
the posts were bronze. The hooks and
bands on the posts were silver, and their
tops were overlaid with silver; so all the
posts of the courtyard had silver bands.
18The curtain for the entrance to the
courtyard was of blue, purple and scarlet yarn and finely twisted linen—the
work of an embroiderer. It was twenty
cubits long and, like the curtains of the
courtyard, five cubits high, 19with four

posts and four bronze bases. Their
hooks and bands were silver, and their
tops were overlaid with silver. [20]All the
tent pegs of the tabernacle and of the
surrounding courtyard were bronze.

The Materials Used

[21]These are the amounts of the materials used for the tabernacle, the
tabernacle of the Testimony, which
were recorded at Moses' command by
the Levites under the direction of Ithamar son of Aaron, the priest. [22](Bezalel
son of Uri, the son of Hur, of the tribe of
Judah, made everything the LORD commanded Moses; [23]with him was Oholiab
son of Ahisamach, of the tribe of Dan
—a craftsman and designer, and an
embroiderer in blue, purple and scarlet
yarn and fine linen.) [24]The total amount
of the gold from the wave offering used
for all the work on the sanctuary was 29
talents and 730 shekels, according to the
sanctuary shekel.
[25]The silver obtained from those of
the community who were counted in the
census was 100 talents and 1,775
shekels, according to the sanctuary
shekel—[26]one beka per person, that is,
half a shekel, according to the sanctuary
shekel, from everyone who had crossed
over to those counted, twenty years old
or more, a total of 603,550 men. [27]The
100 talents of silver were used to cast the
bases for the sanctuary and for the curtain—100 bases from the 100 talents,
one talent for each base. [28]They used
the 1,775 shekels to make the hooks for
the posts, to overlay the tops of the
posts, and to make their bands.
[29]The bronze from the wave offering
was 70 talents and 2,400 shekels. [30]They
used it to make the bases for the entrance to the Tent of Meeting, the
bronze altar with its bronze grating and
all its utensils, [31]the bases for the surrounding courtyard and those for its
entrance and all the tent pegs for the
tabernacle and those for the surrounding courtyard.

NEW TESTAMENT READING
Mark 8:14–9:1

The Yeast of the Pharisees and Herod

[14]The disciples had forgotten to bring
bread, except for one loaf they had with
them in the boat. [15]"Be careful," Jesus
warned them. "Watch out for the yeast
of the Pharisees and that of Herod."
[16]They discussed this with one
another and said, "It is because we have
no bread."
[17]Aware of their discussion, Jesus
asked them: "Why are you talking
about having no bread? Do you still not
see or understand? Are your hearts hardened? [18]Do you have eyes but fail to
see, and ears but fail to hear? And don't
you remember? [19]When I broke the five
loaves for the five thousand, how many
basketfuls of pieces did you pick up?"

"Twelve," they replied.

[20]"And when I broke the seven
loaves for the four thousand, how many
basketfuls of pieces did you pick up?"

They answered, "Seven."

[21]He said to them, "Do you still not
understand?"

The Healing of a Blind Man at Bethsaida

[22]They came to Bethsaida, and some
people brought a blind man and begged
Jesus to touch him. [23]He took the blind
man by the hand and led him outside the
village. When he had spat on the man's
eyes and put his hands on him, Jesus
asked, "Do you see anything?"
[24]He looked up and said, "I see
people; they look like trees walking
around."
[25]Once more Jesus put his hands on
the man's eyes. Then his eyes were
opened, his sight was restored, and he
saw everything clearly. [26]Jesus sent
him home, saying, "Don't go into the
village."

Peter's Confession of Christ

[27]Jesus and his disciples went on to
the villages around Caesarea Philippi.

On the way he asked them, "Who do
people say I am?"
28They replied, "Some say John the
Baptist; others say Elijah; and still
others, one of the prophets."
29"But what about you?" he asked.
"Who do you say I am?"
Peter answered, "You are the
Christ."
30Jesus warned them not to tell anyone about him.

Jesus Predicts His Death

31He then began to teach them that
the Son of Man must suffer many things
and be rejected by the elders, chief
priests and teachers of the law, and that
he must be killed and after three days
rise again. 32He spoke plainly about
this, and Peter took him aside and began to rebuke him.
33But when Jesus turned and looked
at his disciples, he rebuked Peter. "Get
behind me, Satan!" he said. "You do
not have in mind the things of God, but
the things of men."
34Then he called the crowd to him
along with his disciples and said: "If
anyone would come after me, he must
deny himself and take up his cross and
follow me. 35For whoever wants to save
his life will lose it, but whoever loses his
life for me and for the gospel will save it.
36What good is it for a man to gain the
whole world, yet forfeit his soul? 37Or
what can a man give in exchange for his
soul? 38If anyone is ashamed of me and
my words in this adulterous and sinful
generation, the Son of Man will be
ashamed of him when he comes in his
Father's glory with the holy angels."
9 And he said to them, "I tell you the
truth, some who are standing here
will not taste death before they see the
kingdom of God come with power."

READING FROM PROVERBS
Proverbs 6:1–11

Warnings Against Folly

6 My son, if you have put up
security for your neighbour,
if you have struck hands in pledge
for another,
2if you have been trapped by what you
said,
ensnared by the words of your
mouth,
3then do this, my son, to free
yourself,
since you have fallen into your
neighbour's hands:
Go and humble yourself;
press your plea with your
neighbour!
4Allow no sleep to your eyes,
no slumber to your eyelids.
5Free yourself, like a gazelle from the
hand of the hunter,
like a bird from the snare of the
fowler.

6Go to the ant, you sluggard;
consider its ways and be wise!
7It has no commander,
no overseer or ruler,
8yet it stores its provisions in summer
and gathers its food at harvest.

9How long will you lie there, you
sluggard?
When will you get up from your
sleep?
10A little sleep, a little slumber,
a little folding of the hands to
rest—
11and poverty will come on you like a
bandit
and scarcity like an armed man.

FEBRUARY 26 DAY 57

OLD TESTAMENT READING
Exodus 39:1–40:38

The Priestly Garments

39 From the blue, purple and scar-
let yarn they made woven gar-
ments for ministering in the sanctuary.
They also made sacred garments for
Aaron, as the LORD commanded
Moses.

The Ephod

2They made the ephod of gold, and of
blue, purple and scarlet yarn, and of
finely twisted linen. 3They hammered
out thin sheets of gold and cut strands to
be worked into the blue, purple and
scarlet yarn and fine linen—the work of
a skilled craftsman. 4They made shoulder pieces for the ephod, which were
attached to two of its corners, so that it
could be fastened. 5Its skilfully woven
waistband was like it—of one piece
with the ephod and made with gold,
and with blue, purple and scarlet yarn,
and with finely twisted linen, as the
LORD commanded Moses.
6They mounted the onyx stones in
gold filigree settings and engraved them
like a seal with the names of the sons of
Israel. 7Then they fastened them on the
shoulder pieces of the ephod as memorial stones for the sons of Israel, as the
LORD commanded Moses.

The Breastpiece

8They fashioned the breastpiece—
the work of a skilled craftsman. They
made it like the ephod: of gold, and of
blue, purple and scarlet yarn, and of
finely twisted linen. 9It was square—a
span long and a span wide—and folded
double. 10Then they mounted four rows
of precious stones on it. In the first row
there was a ruby, a topaz and a beryl;
11in the second row a turquoise, a
sapphire and an emerald; 12in the third
row a jacinth, an agate and an amethyst;
13in the fourth row a chrysolite, an onyx
and a jasper. They were mounted in
gold filigree settings. 14There were
twelve stones, one for each of the names
of the sons of Israel, each engraved like
a seal with the name of one of the twelve
tribes.
15For the breastpiece they made
braided chains of pure gold, like a rope.
16They made two gold filigree settings
and two gold rings, and fastened the
rings to two of the corners of the breastpiece. 17They fastened the two gold
chains to the rings at the corners of the
breastpiece, 18and the other ends of the
chains to the two settings, attaching
them to the shoulder pieces of the
ephod at the front. 19They made two
gold rings and attached them to the
other two corners of the breastpiece on
the inside edge next to the ephod.
20Then they made two more gold rings
and attached them to the bottom of the
shoulder pieces on the front of the
ephod, close to the seam just above
the waistband of the ephod. 21They tied
the rings of the breastpiece to the rings
of the ephod with blue cord, connecting
it to the waistband so that the breastpiece would not swing out from the
ephod—as the LORD commanded
Moses.

Other Priestly Garments

22They made the robe of the ephod
entirely of blue cloth—the work of a
weaver—23with an opening in the centre of the robe like the opening of a
collar, and a band around this opening,
so that it would not tear. 24They made
pomegranates of blue, purple and scarlet yarn and finely twisted linen around
the hem of the robe. 25And they made
bells of pure gold and attached them

around the hem between the pomegranates. 26The bells and pomegranates
alternated around the hem of the robe
to be worn for ministering, as the LORD
commanded Moses.

27For Aaron and his sons, they made
tunics of fine linen—the work of a
weaver—28and the turban of fine linen,
the linen headbands and the undergarments of finely twisted linen. 29The sash
was of finely twisted linen and blue,
purple and scarlet yarn—the work of an
embroiderer—as the LORD commanded Moses.

30They made the plate, the sacred
diadem, out of pure gold and engraved
on it, like an inscription on a seal: HOLY
TO THE LORD. 31Then they fastened a
blue cord to it to attach it to the turban,
as the LORD commanded Moses.

Moses Inspects the Tabernacle

32So all the work on the tabernacle,
the Tent of Meeting, was completed.
The Israelites did everything just as the
LORD commanded Moses. 33Then they
brought the tabernacle to Moses: the
tent and all its furnishings, its clasps,
frames, crossbars, posts and bases;
34the covering of ram skins dyed red,
the covering of hides of sea cows and the
shielding curtain; 35the ark of the Testimony with its poles and the atonement
cover; 36the table with all its articles and
the bread of the Presence; 37the pure
gold lampstand with its row of lamps
and all its accessories, and the oil for the
light; 38the gold altar, the anointing oil,
the fragrant incense, and the curtain for
the entrance to the tent; 39the bronze
altar with its bronze grating, its poles
and all its utensils; the basin with its
stand; 40the curtains of the courtyard
with its posts and bases, and the curtain
for the entrance to the courtyard; the
ropes and tent pegs for the courtyard;
all the furnishings for the tabernacle,
the Tent of Meeting; 41and the woven
garments worn for ministering in the
sanctuary, both the sacred garments for
Aaron the priest and the garments for
his sons when serving as priests.

42The Israelites had done all the work
just as the LORD had commanded
Moses. 43Moses inspected the work and
saw that they had done it just as the
LORD had commanded. So Moses blessed them.

Setting Up the Tabernacle

40 Then the LORD said to Moses:
2"Set up the tabernacle, the
Tent of Meeting, on the first day of the
first month. 3Place the ark of the Testimony in it and shield the ark with the
curtain. 4Bring in the table and set out
what belongs on it. Then bring in the
lampstand and set up its lamps. 5Place
the gold altar of incense in front of the
ark of the Testimony and put the curtain
at the entrance to the tabernacle.

6"Place the altar of burnt offering in
front of the entrance to the tabernacle,
the Tent of Meeting; 7place the basin
between the Tent of Meeting and the
altar and put water in it. 8Set up the
courtyard around it and put the curtain
at the entrance to the courtyard.

9"Take the anointing oil and anoint
the tabernacle and everything in it; consecrate it and all its furnishings, and it
will be holy. 10Then anoint the altar of
burnt offering and all its utensils; consecrate the altar, and it will be most holy.
11Anoint the basin and its stand and
consecrate them.

12"Bring Aaron and his sons to the
entrance to the Tent of Meeting and
wash them with water. 13Then dress
Aaron in the sacred garments, anoint
him and consecrate him so that he may
serve me as priest. 14Bring his sons and
dress them in tunics. 15Anoint them just
as you anointed their father, so that
they may serve me as priests. Their
anointing will be to a priesthood that
will continue for all generations to
come." 16Moses did everything just as
the LORD commanded him.

17So the tabernacle was set up on the
first day of the first month in the second
year. 18When Moses set up the tabernacle, he put the bases in place, erected

the frames, inserted the crossbars and set up the posts. 19Then he spread the tent over the tabernacle and put the covering over the tent, as the LORD commanded him.

20He took the Testimony and placed it in the ark, attached the poles to the ark and put the atonement cover over it. 21Then he brought the ark into the tabernacle and hung the shielding curtain and shielded the ark of the Testimony, as the LORD commanded him.

22Moses placed the table in the Tent of Meeting on the north side of the tabernacle outside the curtain 23and set out the bread on it before the LORD, as the LORD commanded him.

24He placed the lampstand in the Tent of Meeting opposite the table on the south side of the tabernacle 25and set up the lamps before the LORD, as the LORD commanded him.

26Moses placed the gold altar in the Tent of Meeting in front of the curtain 27and burned fragrant incense on it, as the LORD commanded him. 28Then he put up the curtain at the entrance to the tabernacle.

29He set the altar of burnt offering near the entrance to the tabernacle, the Tent of Meeting, and offered on it burnt offerings and grain offerings, as the LORD commanded him.

30He placed the basin between the Tent of Meeting and the altar and put water in it for washing, 31and Moses and Aaron and his sons used it to wash their hands and feet. 32They washed whenever they entered the Tent of Meeting or approached the altar, as the LORD commanded Moses.

33Then Moses set up the courtyard around the tabernacle and altar and put up the curtain at the entrance to the courtyard. And so Moses finished the work.

The Glory of the LORD

34Then the cloud covered the Tent of Meeting, and the glory of the LORD filled the tabernacle. 35Moses could not enter the Tent of Meeting because the cloud had settled upon it, and the glory of the LORD filled the tabernacle.

36In all the travels of the Israelites, whenever the cloud lifted from above the tabernacle, they would set out; 37but if the cloud did not lift, they did not set out—until the day it lifted. 38So the cloud of the LORD was over the tabernacle by day, and fire was in the cloud by night, in the sight of all the house of Israel during all their travels.

NEW TESTAMENT READING

Mark 9:2–32

The Transfiguration

2After six days Jesus took Peter, James and John with him and led them up a high mountain, where they were all alone. There he was transfigured before them. 3His clothes became dazzling white, whiter than anyone in the world could bleach them. 4And there appeared before them Elijah and Moses, who were talking with Jesus.

5Peter said to Jesus, "Rabbi, it is good for us to be here. Let us put up three shelters—one for you, one for Moses and one for Elijah." 6(He did not know what to say, they were so frightened.)

7Then a cloud appeared and enveloped them, and a voice came from the cloud: "This is my Son, whom I love. Listen to him!"

8Suddenly, when they looked round, they no longer saw anyone with them except Jesus.

9As they were coming down the mountain, Jesus gave them orders not to tell anyone what they had seen until the Son of Man had risen from the dead. 10They kept the matter to themselves, discussing what "rising from the dead" meant.

11And they asked him, "Why do the teachers of the law say that Elijah must come first?"

12Jesus replied, "To be sure, Elijah

does come first, and restores all things.
Why then is it written that the Son of
Man must suffer much and be rejected?
13But I tell you, Elijah has come, and
they have done to him everything they
wished, just as it is written about him."

The Healing of a Boy With an Evil Spirit

14When they came to the other disciples, they saw a large crowd around
them and the teachers of the law
arguing with them. 15As soon as all the
people saw Jesus, they were overwhelmed with wonder and ran to greet
him.

16"What are you arguing with them
about?" he asked.

17A man in the crowd answered,
"Teacher, I brought you my son, who is
possessed by a spirit that has robbed
him of speech. 18Whenever it seizes
him, it throws him to the ground. He
foams at the mouth, gnashes his teeth
and becomes rigid. I asked your disciples to drive out the spirit, but they
could not."

19"O unbelieving generation," Jesus
replied, "how long shall I stay with you?
How long shall I put up with you? Bring
the boy to me."

20So they brought him. When the
spirit saw Jesus, it immediately threw
the boy into a convulsion. He fell to the
ground and rolled around, foaming at
the mouth.

21Jesus asked the boy's father, "How
long has he been like this?"

"From childhood," he answered.
22"It has often thrown him into fire or
water to kill him. But if you can do
anything, take pity on us and help us."

23" 'If you can'?" said Jesus. "Everything is possible for him who believes."

24Immediately the boy's father exclaimed, "I do believe; help me overcome my unbelief!"

25When Jesus saw that a crowd was
running to the scene, he rebuked the
evil spirit. "You deaf and mute spirit,"
he said, "I command you, come out of
him and never enter him again."

26The spirit shrieked, convulsed him
violently and came out. The boy looked
so much like a corpse that many said,
"He's dead." 27But Jesus took him by
the hand and lifted him to his feet, and
he stood up.

28After Jesus had gone indoors, his
disciples asked him privately, "Why
couldn't we drive it out?"

29He replied, "This kind can come
out only by prayer."

30They left that place and passed
through Galilee. Jesus did not want
anyone to know where they were,
31because he was teaching his disciples.
He said to them, "The Son of Man is
going to be betrayed into the hands of
men. They will kill him, and after three
days he will rise." 32But they did not
understand what he meant and were
afraid to ask him about it.

READING FROM PSALMS
Psalm 26:1–12

Of David.

1Vindicate me, O LORD,
for I have led a blameless life;
I have trusted in the LORD
without wavering.
2Test me, O LORD, and try me,
examine my heart and my mind;
3for your love is ever before me,
and I walk continually in your
truth.
4I do not sit with deceitful men,
nor do I consort with hypocrites;
5I abhor the assembly of evildoers
and refuse to sit with the wicked.
6I wash my hands in innocence,
and go about your altar, O LORD,
7proclaiming aloud your praise
and telling of all your wonderful
deeds.
8I love the house where you live, O
LORD,
the place where your glory dwells.

9 Do not take away my soul along with
sinners,
my life with bloodthirsty men,
10 in whose hands are wicked schemes,
whose right hands are full of
bribes.

11 But I lead a blameless life;
redeem me and be merciful to me.

12 My feet stand on level ground;
in the great assembly I will praise
the LORD.

FEBRUARY 27

DAY 58

OLD TESTAMENT READING

Leviticus 1:1–3:17

The Burnt Offering

1 The LORD called to Moses and
spoke to him from the Tent of
Meeting. He said, 2 "Speak to the
Israelites and say to them: 'When any of
you brings an offering to the LORD,
bring as your offering an animal from
either the herd or the flock.
3 " 'If the offering is a burnt offering
from the herd, he is to offer a male
without defect. He must present it at the
entrance to the Tent of Meeting so that
it will be acceptable to the LORD. 4 He is
to lay his hand on the head of the burnt
offering, and it will be accepted on his
behalf to make atonement for him. 5 He
is to slaughter the young bull before the
LORD, and then Aaron's sons the priests
shall bring the blood and sprinkle it
against the altar on all sides at the entrance to the Tent of Meeting. 6 He is to
skin the burnt offering and cut it into
pieces. 7 The sons of Aaron the priest
are to put fire on the altar and arrange
wood on the fire. 8 Then Aaron's sons
the priests shall arrange the pieces, including the head and the fat, on the
burning wood that is on the altar. 9 He is
to wash the inner parts and the legs with
water, and the priest is to burn all of it
on the altar. It is a burnt offering, an
offering made by fire, an aroma pleasing to the LORD.
10 " 'If the offering is a burnt offering
from the flock, from either the sheep or
the goats, he is to offer a male without
defect. 11 He is to slaughter it at the
north side of the altar before the LORD,
and Aaron's sons the priests shall
sprinkle its blood against the altar on all
sides. 12 He is to cut it into pieces, and
the priest shall arrange them, including
the head and the fat, on the burning
wood that is on the altar. 13 He is to wash
the inner parts and the legs with water,
and the priest is to bring all of it and
burn it on the altar. It is a burnt offering, an offering made by fire, an aroma
pleasing to the LORD.
14 " 'If the offering to the LORD is a
burnt offering of birds, he is to offer a
dove or a young pigeon. 15 The priest
shall bring it to the altar, wring off the
head and burn it on the altar; its blood
shall be drained out on the side of the
altar. 16 He is to remove the crop with its
contents and throw it to the east side of
the altar, where the ashes are. 17 He
shall tear it open by the wings, not
severing it completely, and then the
priest shall burn it on the wood that is on
the fire on the altar. It is a burnt offering, an offering made by fire, an aroma
pleasing to the LORD.

The Grain Offering

2 " 'When someone brings a grain
offering to the LORD, his offering is
to be of fine flour. He is to pour oil on it,

put incense on it 2and take it to Aaron's
sons the priests. The priest shall take a
handful of the fine flour and oil,
together with all the incense, and burn
this as a memorial portion on the altar,
an offering made by fire, an aroma
pleasing to the LORD. 3The rest of the
grain offering belongs to Aaron and his
sons; it is a most holy part of the offerings made to the LORD by fire.
4" 'If you bring a grain offering baked
in an oven, it is to consist of fine flour:
cakes made without yeast and mixed
with oil, or wafers made without yeast
and spread with oil. 5If your grain offering is prepared on a griddle, it is to be
made of fine flour mixed with oil, and
without yeast. 6Crumble it and pour oil
on it; it is a grain offering. 7If your grain
offering is cooked in a pan, it is to be
made of fine flour and oil. 8Bring the
grain offering made of these things to
the LORD; present it to the priest, who
shall take it to the altar. 9He shall take
out the memorial portion from the grain
offering and burn it on the altar as an
offering made by fire, an aroma pleasing to the LORD. 10The rest of the grain
offering belongs to Aaron and his sons;
it is a most holy part of the offerings
made to the LORD by fire.
11" 'Every grain offering you bring to
the LORD must be made without yeast,
for you are not to burn any yeast or
honey in an offering made to the LORD
by fire. 12You may bring them to the
LORD as an offering of the firstfruits, but
they are not to be offered on the altar as
a pleasing aroma. 13Season all your
grain offerings with salt. Do not leave
the salt of the covenant of your God out
of your grain offerings; add salt to all
your offerings.
14" 'If you bring a grain offering of
firstfruits to the LORD, offer crushed
heads of new grain roasted in the fire.
15Put oil and incense on it; it is a grain
offering. 16The priest shall burn the
memorial portion of the crushed grain
and the oil, together with all the incense, as an offering made to the LORD
by fire.

The Fellowship Offering

3 " 'If someone's offering is a fellowship offering, and he offers an animal from the herd, whether male or
female, he is to present before the LORD
an animal without defect. 2He is to lay
his hand on the head of his offering and
slaughter it at the entrance to the Tent
of Meeting. Then Aaron's sons the
priests shall sprinkle the blood against
the altar on all sides. 3From the fellowship offering he is to bring a sacrifice
made to the LORD by fire: all the fat that
covers the inner parts or is connected to
them, 4both kidneys with the fat on
them near the loins, and the covering of
the liver, which he will remove with the
kidneys. 5Then Aaron's sons are to
burn it on the altar on top of the burnt
offering that is on the burning wood, as
an offering made by fire, an aroma
pleasing to the LORD.
6" 'If he offers an animal from the
flock as a fellowship offering to the
LORD, he is to offer a male or female
without defect. 7If he offers a lamb, he
is to present it before the LORD. 8He is
to lay his hand on the head of his offering and slaughter it in front of the Tent
of Meeting. Then Aaron's sons shall
sprinkle its blood against the altar on all
sides. 9From the fellowship offering he
is to bring a sacrifice made to the LORD
by fire: its fat, the entire fat tail cut off
close to the backbone, all the fat that
covers the inner parts or is connected to
them, 10both kidneys with the fat on
them near the loins, and the covering of
the liver, which he will remove with the
kidneys. 11The priest shall burn them on
the altar as food, an offering made to
the LORD by fire.
12" 'If his offering is a goat, he is to
present it before the LORD. 13He is to
lay his hand on its head and slaughter it
in front of the Tent of Meeting. Then
Aaron's sons shall sprinkle its blood
against the altar on all sides. 14From
what he offers he is to make this offering
to the LORD by fire: all the fat that
covers the inner parts or is connected to

them, 15both kidneys with the fat on them near the loins, and the covering of the liver, which he will remove with the kidneys. 16The priest shall burn them on the altar as food, an offering made by fire, a pleasing aroma. All the fat is the LORD's.

17" 'This is a lasting ordinance for the generations to come, wherever you live: You must not eat any fat or any blood.' "

NEW TESTAMENT READING
Mark 9:33–10:12

Who Is the Greatest?

33They came to Capernaum. When he was in the house, he asked them, "What were you arguing about on the road?" 34But they kept quiet because on the way they had argued about who was the greatest.

35Sitting down, Jesus called the Twelve and said, "If anyone wants to be first, he must be the very last, and the servant of all."

36He took a little child and had him stand among them. Taking him in his arms, he said to them, 37"Whoever welcomes one of these little children in my name welcomes me; and whoever welcomes me does not welcome me but the one who sent me."

Whoever Is Not Against Us Is for Us

38"Teacher," said John, "we saw a man driving out demons in your name and we told him to stop, because he was not one of us."

39"Do not stop him," Jesus said. "No-one who does a miracle in my name can in the next moment say anything bad about me, 40for whoever is not against us is for us. 41I tell you the truth, anyone who gives you a cup of water in my name because you belong to Christ will certainly not lose his reward.

Causing to Sin

42"And if anyone causes one of these little ones who believe in me to sin, it would be better for him to be thrown into the sea with a large millstone tied around his neck. 43If your hand causes you to sin, cut it off. It is better for you to enter life maimed than with two hands to go into hell, where the fire never goes out. 45And if your foot causes you to sin, cut it off. It is better for you to enter life crippled than to have two feet and be thrown into hell. 47And if your eye causes you to sin, pluck it out. It is better for you to enter the kingdom of God with one eye than to have two eyes and be thrown into hell, 48where

" 'their worm does not die,
and the fire is not quenched.'

49Everyone will be salted with fire.

50"Salt is good, but if it loses its saltiness, how can you make it salty again? Have salt in yourselves, and be at peace with each other."

Divorce

10 Jesus then left that place and went into the region of Judea and across the Jordan. Again crowds of people came to him, and as was his custom, he taught them.

2Some Pharisees came and tested him by asking, "Is it lawful for a man to divorce his wife?"

3"What did Moses command you?" he replied.

4They said, "Moses permitted a man to write a certificate of divorce and send her away."

5"It was because your hearts were hard that Moses wrote you this law," Jesus replied. 6"But at the beginning of creation God 'made them male and female'. 7'For this reason a man will leave his father and mother and be united to his wife, 8and the two will become one flesh.' So they are no longer

two, but one. 9Therefore what God has
joined together, let man not separate."
10When they were in the house again,
the disciples asked Jesus about this.
11He answered, "Anyone who divorces
his wife and marries another woman
commits adultery against her. 12And if
she divorces her husband and marries
another man, she commits adultery."

READING FROM PSALMS
Psalm 27:1–6

Of David.

1The LORD is my light and my
salvation—
whom shall I fear?
The LORD is the stronghold of my
life—
of whom shall I be afraid?
2When evil men advance against me
to devour my flesh,
when my enemies and my foes attack
me,
they will stumble and fall.
3Though an army besiege me,
my heart will not fear;
though war break out against me,
even then will I be confident.

4One thing I ask of the LORD,
this is what I seek:
that I may dwell in the house of the
LORD
all the days of my life,
to gaze upon the beauty of the LORD
and to seek him in his temple.
5For in the day of trouble
he will keep me safe in his
dwelling;
he will hide me in the shelter of his
tabernacle
and set me high upon a rock.
6Then my head will be exalted
above the enemies who surround
me;
at his tabernacle will I sacrifice with
shouts of joy;
I will sing and make music to the
LORD.

DAY 59

FEBRUARY 28

OLD TESTAMENT READING
Leviticus 4:1–5:13

The Sin Offering

4 The LORD said to Moses, 2"Say to
the Israelites: 'When anyone sins
unintentionally and does what is forbidden in any of the LORD's commands—

3" 'If the anointed priest sins, bringing guilt on the people, he must bring to
the LORD a young bull without defect as
a sin offering for the sin he has committed. 4He is to present the bull at the
entrance to the Tent of Meeting before
the LORD. He is to lay his hand on its
head and slaughter it before the LORD.
5Then the anointed priest shall take
some of the bull's blood and carry it into
the Tent of Meeting. 6He is to dip his
finger into the blood and sprinkle some
of it seven times before the LORD, in
front of the curtain of the sanctuary.
7The priest shall then put some of
the blood on the horns of the altar of
fragrant incense that is before the LORD
in the Tent of Meeting. The rest of the
bull's blood he shall pour out at the base
of the altar of burnt offering at the
entrance to the Tent of Meeting. 8He
shall remove all the fat from the bull of
the sin offering—the fat that covers the
inner parts or is connected to them,
9both kidneys with the fat on them near
the loins, and the covering of the liver,

which he will remove with the kidneys
—10just as the fat is removed from the
ox sacrificed as a fellowship offering.
Then the priest shall burn them on the
altar of burnt offering. 11But the hide of
the bull and all its flesh, as well as the
head and legs, the inner parts and offal
—12that is, all the rest of the bull—he
must take outside the camp to a place
ceremonially clean, where the ashes are
thrown, and burn it in a wood fire on the
ash heap.

13" 'If the whole Israelite community
sins unintentionally and does what is
forbidden in any of the LORD's commands,
even though the community is
unaware of the matter, they are guilty.
14When they become aware of the sin
they committed, the assembly must
bring a young bull as a sin offering and
present it before the Tent of Meeting.
15The elders of the community are to lay
their hands on the bull's head before the
LORD, and the bull shall be slaughtered
before the LORD. 16Then the anointed
priest is to take some of the bull's blood
into the Tent of Meeting. 17He shall dip
his finger into the blood and sprinkle it
before the LORD seven times in front of
the curtain. 18He is to put some of the
blood on the horns of the altar that is
before the LORD in the Tent of Meeting.
The rest of the blood he shall pour out at
the base of the altar of burnt offering at
the entrance to the Tent of Meeting.
19He shall remove all the fat from it and
burn it on the altar, 20and do with this
bull just as he did with the bull for the
sin offering. In this way the priest will
make atonement for them, and they will
be forgiven. 21Then he shall take the
bull outside the camp and burn it as he
burned the first bull. This is the sin
offering for the community.

22" 'When a leader sins unintentionally
and does what is forbidden in
any of the commands of the LORD his
God, he is guilty. 23When he is made
aware of the sin he committed, he
must bring as his offering a male goat
without defect. 24He is to lay his hand
on the goat's head and slaughter it at
the place where the burnt offering is
slaughtered before the LORD. It is a sin
offering. 25Then the priest shall take
some of the blood of the sin offering
with his finger and put it on the horns of
the altar of burnt offering and pour out
the rest of the blood at the base of the
altar. 26He shall burn all the fat on the
altar as he burned the fat of the fellowship
offering. In this way the priest
will make atonement for the man's sin,
and he will be forgiven.

27" 'If a member of the community
sins unintentionally and does what is
forbidden in any of the LORD's commands,
he is guilty. 28When he is made
aware of the sin he committed, he must
bring as his offering for the sin he committed
a female goat without defect.
29He is to lay his hand on the head of the
sin offering and slaughter it at the place
of the burnt offering. 30Then the priest
is to take some of the blood with his
finger and put it on the horns of the altar
of burnt offering and pour out the rest
of the blood at the base of the altar.
31He shall remove all the fat, just as the
fat is removed from the fellowship
offering, and the priest shall burn it on
the altar as an aroma pleasing to the
LORD. In this way the priest will make
atonement for him, and he will be
forgiven.

32" 'If he brings a lamb as his sin offering,
he is to bring a female without
defect. 33He is to lay his hand on its head
and slaughter it for a sin offering at the
place where the burnt offering is
slaughtered. 34Then the priest shall take
some of the blood of the sin offering
with his finger and put it on the horns of
the altar of burnt offering and pour out
the rest of the blood at the base of the
altar. 35He shall remove all the fat, just
as the fat is removed from the lamb of
the fellowship offering, and the priest
shall burn it on the altar on top of the
offerings made to the LORD by fire. In
this way the priest will make atonement

for him for the sin he has committed,
and he will be forgiven.

5 " 'If a person sins because he does
not speak up when he hears a public charge to testify regarding something
he has seen or learned about, he will be
held responsible.
2" 'Or if a person touches anything
ceremonially unclean—whether the
carcasses of unclean wild animals or of
unclean livestock or of unclean creatures that move along the ground—
even though he is unaware of it, he has
become unclean and is guilty.
3" 'Or if he touches human uncleanness—anything that would make him
unclean—even though he is unaware of
it, when he learns of it he will be guilty.
4" 'Or if a person thoughtlessly takes
an oath to do anything, whether good or
evil—in any matter one might care-
lessly swear about—even though he is
unaware of it, in any case when he
learns of it he will be guilty.
5" 'When anyone is guilty in any of
these ways, he must confess in what way
he has sinned 6and, as a penalty for the
sin he has committed, he must bring to
the LORD a female lamb or goat from
the flock as a sin offering; and the priest
shall make atonement for him for his
sin.
7" 'If he cannot afford a lamb, he is to
bring two doves or two young pigeons to
the LORD as a penalty for his sin—one
for a sin offering and the other for a
burnt offering. 8He is to bring them to
the priest, who shall first offer the one
for the sin offering. He is to wring its
head from its neck, not severing it completely, 9and is to sprinkle some of the
blood of the sin offering against the side
of the altar; the rest of the blood must
be drained out at the base of the altar. It
is a sin offering. 10The priest shall then
offer the other as a burnt offering in the
prescribed way and make atonement
for him for the sin he has committed,
and he will be forgiven.
11" 'If, however, he cannot afford two
doves or two young pigeons, he is to
bring as an offering for his sin a tenth of
an ephah of fine flour for a sin offering.
He must not put oil or incense on it,
because it is a sin offering. 12He is to
bring it to the priest, who shall take a
handful of it as a memorial portion and
burn it on the altar on top of the offerings made to the LORD by fire. It is a sin
offering. 13In this way the priest will
make atonement for him for any of
these sins he has committed, and he will
be forgiven. The rest of the offering will
belong to the priest, as in the case of the
grain offering.' "

NEW TESTAMENT READING
Mark 10:13–31

The Little Children and Jesus

13People were bringing little children
to Jesus to have him touch them, but the
disciples rebuked them. 14When Jesus
saw this, he was indignant. He said to
them, "Let the little children come to
me, and do not hinder them, for the
kingdom of God belongs to such as
these. 15I tell you the truth, anyone who
will not receive the kingdom of God like
a little child will never enter it." 16And
he took the children in his arms, put his
hands on them and blessed them.

The Rich Young Man

17As Jesus started on his way, a man
ran up to him and fell on his knees
before him. "Good teacher," he asked,
"what must I do to inherit eternal life?"
18"Why do you call me good?" Jesus
answered. "No-one is good—except
God alone. 19You know the commandments: 'Do not murder, do not commit
adultery, do not steal, do not give false
testimony, do not defraud, honour your
father and mother.' "
20"Teacher," he declared, "all these I
have kept since I was a boy."
21Jesus looked at him and loved him.
"One thing you lack," he said. "Go, sell
everything you have and give to the

poor, and you will have treasure in
heaven. Then come, follow me."
22At this the man's face fell. He went
away sad, because he had great wealth.
23Jesus looked around and said to his
disciples, "How hard it is for the rich to
enter the kingdom of God!"
24The disciples were amazed at his
words. But Jesus said again, "Children,
how hard it is to enter the kingdom of
God! 25It is easier for a camel to go
through the eye of a needle than for a
rich man to enter the kingdom of God."
26The disciples were even more
amazed, and said to each other, "Who
then can be saved?"
27Jesus looked at them and said,
"With man this is impossible, but not
with God; all things are possible with
God."
28Peter said to him, "We have left
everything to follow you!"
29"I tell you the truth," Jesus replied,
"no-one who has left home or brothers
or sisters or mother or father or children
or fields for me and the gospel 30will fail
to receive a hundred times as much in
this present age (homes, brothers, sisters, mothers, children and fields—and
with them, persecutions) and in the age
to come, eternal life. 31But many who
are first will be last, and the last first."

READING FROM PSALMS
Psalm 27:7–14

7Hear my voice when I call, O LORD;
be merciful to me and answer me.
8My heart says of you, "Seek his
face!"
Your face, LORD, I will seek.
9Do not hide your face from me,
do not turn your servant away in
anger;
you have been my helper.
Do not reject me or forsake me,
O God my Saviour.
10Though my father and mother
forsake me,
the LORD will receive me.
11Teach me your way, O LORD;
lead me in a straight path
because of my oppressors.
12Do not hand me over to the desire of
my foes,
for false witnesses rise up against
me,
breathing out violence.

13I am still confident of this:
I will see the goodness of the LORD
in the land of the living.
14Wait for the LORD;
be strong and take heart
and wait for the LORD.

MARCH 1

DAY 60

OLD TESTAMENT READING
Leviticus 5:14–7:10

The Guilt Offering

14The LORD said to Moses: 15"When a
person commits a violation and sins unintentionally in regard to any of the
LORD's holy things, he is to bring to the
LORD as a penalty a ram from the flock,
one without defect and of the proper
value in silver, according to the sanctuary shekel. It is a guilt offering. 16He
must make restitution for what he has
failed to do in regard to the holy things,
add a fifth of the value to that and give it
all to the priest, who will make atonement for him with the ram as a guilt
offering, and he will be forgiven.
17"If a person sins and does what is
forbidden in any of the LORD's commands, even though he does not know
it, he is guilty and will be held responsible. 18He is to bring to the priest as a
guilt offering a ram from the flock, one
without defect and of the proper value.

In this way the priest will make atonement for him for the wrong he has committed unintentionally, and he will be forgiven. [19]It is a guilt offering; he has been guilty of wrongdoing against the LORD."

6 The LORD said to Moses: [2]"If anyone sins and is unfaithful to the LORD by deceiving his neighbour about something entrusted to him or left in his care or stolen, or if he cheats him, [3]or if he finds lost property and lies about it, or if he swears falsely, or if he commits any such sin that people may do—[4]when he thus sins and becomes guilty, he must return what he has stolen or taken by extortion, or what was entrusted to him, or the lost property he found, [5]or whatever it was he swore falsely about. He must make restitution in full, add a fifth of the value to it and give it all to the owner on the day he presents his guilt offering. [6]And as a penalty he must bring to the priest, that is, to the LORD, his guilt offering, a ram from the flock, one without defect and of the proper value. [7]In this way the priest will make atonement for him before the LORD, and he will be forgiven for any of these things he did that made him guilty."

The Burnt Offering

[8]The LORD said to Moses: [9]"Give Aaron and his sons this command: 'These are the regulations for the burnt offering: The burnt offering is to remain on the altar hearth throughout the night, till morning, and the fire must be kept burning on the altar. [10]The priest shall then put on his linen clothes, with linen undergarments next to his body, and shall remove the ashes of the burnt offering that the fire has consumed on the altar and place them beside the altar. [11]Then he is to take off these clothes and put on others, and carry the ashes outside the camp to a place that is ceremonially clean. [12]The fire on the altar must be kept burning; it must not go out. Every morning the priest is to add firewood and arrange the burnt offering on the fire and burn the fat of the fellowship offerings on it. [13]The fire must be kept burning on the altar continuously; it must not go out.

The Grain Offering

[14]" 'These are the regulations for the grain offering: Aaron's sons are to bring it before the LORD, in front of the altar. [15]The priest is to take a handful of fine flour and oil, together with all the incense on the grain offering, and burn the memorial portion on the altar as an aroma pleasing to the LORD. [16]Aaron and his sons shall eat the rest of it, but it is to be eaten without yeast in a holy place; they are to eat it in the courtyard of the Tent of Meeting. [17]It must not be baked with yeast; I have given it as their share of the offerings made to me by fire. Like the sin offering and the guilt offering, it is most holy. [18]Any male descendant of Aaron may eat it. It is his regular share of the offerings made to the LORD by fire for the generations to come. Whatever touches it will become holy.' "

[19]The LORD also said to Moses, [20]"This is the offering Aaron and his sons are to bring to the LORD on the day he is anointed: a tenth of an ephah of fine flour as a regular grain offering, half of it in the morning and half in the evening. [21]Prepare it with oil on a griddle; bring it well-mixed and present the grain offering broken in pieces as an aroma pleasing to the LORD. [22]The son who is to succeed him as anointed priest shall prepare it. It is the LORD's regular share and is to be burned completely. [23]Every grain offering of a priest shall be burned completely; it must not be eaten."

The Sin Offering

[24]The LORD said to Moses, [25]"Say to Aaron and his sons: 'These are the

regulations for the sin offering: The sin
offering is to be slaughtered before the
LORD in the place where the burnt offering is slaughtered; it is most holy. 26The
priest who offers it shall eat it; it is to be
eaten in a holy place, in the courtyard
of the Tent of Meeting. 27Whatever
touches any of the flesh will become
holy, and if any of the blood is spattered
on a garment, you must wash it in a holy
place. 28The clay pot that the meat is
cooked in must be broken; but if it is
cooked in a bronze pot, the pot is to be
scoured and rinsed with water. 29Any
male in a priest's family may eat it; it is
most holy. 30But any sin offering whose
blood is brought into the Tent of Meeting to make atonement in the Holy
Place must not be eaten; it must be
burned.

The Guilt Offering

7 " 'These are the regulations for the
guilt offering, which is most holy:
2The guilt offering is to be slaughtered
in the place where the burnt offering is
slaughtered, and its blood is to be
sprinkled against the altar on all sides.
3All its fat shall be offered: the fat tail
and the fat that covers the inner parts,
4both kidneys with the fat on them near
the loins, and the covering of the liver,
which is to be removed with the kidneys. 5The priest shall burn them on the
altar as an offering made to the LORD
by fire. It is a guilt offering. 6Any male
in a priest's family may eat it, but it
must be eaten in a holy place; it is most
holy.
7" 'The same law applies to both the
sin offering and the guilt offering: They
belong to the priest who makes atonement with them. 8The priest who offers
a burnt offering for anyone may keep its
hide for himself. 9Every grain offering
baked in an oven or cooked in a pan or
on a griddle belongs to the priest who
offers it, 10and every grain offering,
whether mixed with oil or dry, belongs
equally to all the sons of Aaron.

NEW TESTAMENT READING
Mark 10:32–52

Jesus Again Predicts His Death

32They were on their way up to Jerusalem, with Jesus leading the way, and
the disciples were astonished, while
those who followed were afraid. Again
he took the Twelve aside and told them
what was going to happen to him.
33"We are going up to Jerusalem," he
said, "and the Son of Man will be betrayed to the chief priests and teachers
of the law. They will condemn him to
death and will hand him over to the
Gentiles, 34who will mock him and spit
on him, flog him and kill him. Three
days later he will rise."

The Request of James and John

35Then James and John, the sons of
Zebedee, came to him. "Teacher,"
they said, "we want you to do for us
whatever we ask."
36"What do you want me to do for
you?" he asked.
37They replied, "Let one of us sit at
your right and the other at your left in
your glory."
38"You don't know what you are
asking," Jesus said. "Can you drink the
cup I drink or be baptised with the
baptism I am baptised with?"
39"We can," they answered.
Jesus said to them, "You will drink
the cup I drink and be baptised with the
baptism I am baptised with, 40but to sit
at my right or left is not for me to grant.
These places belong to those for whom
they have been prepared."
41When the ten heard about this, they
became indignant with James and John.
42Jesus called them together and said,
"You know that those who are regarded
as rulers of the Gentiles lord it over
them, and their high officials exercise
authority over them. 43Not so with you.
Instead, whoever wants to become
great among you must be your servant,
44and whoever wants to be first must be

slave of all. 45 For even the Son of Man
did not come to be served, but to serve,
and to give his life as a ransom for
many."

Blind Bartimaeus Receives His Sight

46 Then they came to Jericho. As
Jesus and his disciples, together with a
large crowd, were leaving the city, a
blind man, Bartimaeus (that is, the Son
of Timaeus), was sitting by the roadside
begging. 47 When he heard that it was
Jesus of Nazareth, he began to shout,
"Jesus, Son of David, have mercy on
me!"
48 Many rebuked him and told him to
be quiet, but he shouted all the more,
"Son of David, have mercy on me!"
49 Jesus stopped and said, "Call him."
So they called to the blind man,
"Cheer up! On your feet! He's calling
you." 50 Throwing his cloak aside, he
jumped to his feet and came to Jesus.
51 "What do you want me to do for
you?" Jesus asked him.
The blind man said, "Rabbi, I want to
see."
52 "Go," said Jesus, "your faith has
healed you." Immediately he received
his sight and followed Jesus along the
road.

READING FROM PROVERBS
Proverbs 6:12–19

12 A scoundrel and villain,
who goes about with a corrupt
mouth,
13 who winks with his eye,
signals with his feet
and motions with his fingers,
14 who plots evil with deceit in his
heart—
he always stirs up dissension.
15 Therefore disaster will overtake him
in an instant;
he will suddenly be destroyed—
without remedy.

16 There are six things the LORD
hates,
seven that are detestable to him:
17 haughty eyes,
a lying tongue,
hands that shed innocent
blood,
18 a heart that devises wicked
schemes,
feet that are quick to rush into
evil,
19 a false witness who pours out lies
and a man who stirs up
dissension among brothers.

DAY 61

MARCH 2

OLD TESTAMENT READING
Leviticus 7:11–8:36

The Fellowship Offering

11 " 'These are the regulations for the
fellowship offering a person may present to the LORD:
12 " 'If he offers it as an expression of
thankfulness, then along with this
thank-offering he is to offer cakes of
bread made without yeast and mixed
with oil, wafers made without yeast and
spread with oil, and cakes of fine flour
well-kneaded and mixed with oil.
13 Along with his fellowship offering of
thanksgiving he is to present an offering
with cakes of bread made with yeast.
14 He is to bring one of each kind as an
offering, a contribution to the LORD; it
belongs to the priest who sprinkles the
blood of the fellowship offerings. 15 The
meat of his fellowship offering of
thanksgiving must be eaten on the day it
is offered; he must leave none of it till
morning.

16"'If, however, his offering is the result of a vow or is a freewill offering, the sacrifice shall be eaten on the day he offers it, but anything left over may be eaten on the next day. 17Any meat of the sacrifice left over till the third day must be burned up. 18If any meat of the fellowship offering is eaten on the third day, it will not be accepted. It will not be credited to the one who offered it, for it is impure; the person who eats any of it will be held responsible.

19"'Meat that touches anything ceremonially unclean must not be eaten; it must be burned up. As for other meat, anyone ceremonially clean may eat it. 20But if anyone who is unclean eats any meat of the fellowship offering belonging to the LORD, that person must be cut off from his people. 21If anyone touches something unclean—whether human uncleanness or an unclean animal or any unclean, detestable thing—and then eats any of the meat of the fellowship offering belonging to the LORD, that person must be cut off from his people.'"

Eating Fat and Blood Forbidden

22The LORD said to Moses, 23"Say to the Israelites: 'Do not eat any of the fat of cattle, sheep or goats. 24The fat of an animal found dead or torn by wild animals may be used for any other purpose, but you must not eat it. 25Anyone who eats the fat of an animal from which an offering by fire may be made to the LORD must be cut off from his people. 26And wherever you live, you must not eat the blood of any bird or animal. 27If anyone eats blood, that person must be cut off from his people.'"

The Priests' Share

28The LORD said to Moses, 29"Say to the Israelites: 'Anyone who brings a fellowship offering to the LORD is to bring part of it as his sacrifice to the LORD. 30With his own hands he is to bring the offering made to the LORD by fire; he is to bring the fat, together with the breast, and wave the breast before the LORD as a wave offering. 31The priest shall burn the fat on the altar, but the breast belongs to Aaron and his sons. 32You are to give the right thigh of your fellowship offerings to the priest as a contribution. 33The son of Aaron who offers the blood and the fat of the fellowship offering shall have the right thigh as his share. 34From the fellowship offerings of the Israelites, I have taken the breast that is waved and the thigh that is presented and have given them to Aaron the priest and his sons as their regular share from the Israelites.'"

35This is the portion of the offerings made to the LORD by fire that were allotted to Aaron and his sons on the day they were presented to serve the LORD as priests. 36On the day they were anointed, the LORD commanded that the Israelites give this to them as their regular share for the generations to come.

37These, then, are the regulations for the burnt offering, the grain offering, the sin offering, the guilt offering, the ordination offering and the fellowship offering, 38which the LORD gave Moses on Mount Sinai on the day he commanded the Israelites to bring their offerings to the LORD, in the Desert of Sinai.

The Ordination of Aaron and His Sons

8 The LORD said to Moses, 2"Bring Aaron and his sons, their garments, the anointing oil, the bull for the sin offering, the two rams and the basket containing bread made without yeast, 3and gather the entire assembly at the entrance to the Tent of Meeting." 4Moses did as the LORD commanded him, and the assembly gathered at the entrance to the Tent of Meeting.

5Moses said to the assembly, "This is what the LORD has commanded to be done." 6Then Moses brought Aaron and his sons forward and washed them with water. 7He put the tunic on Aaron, tied the sash around him, clothed him with the robe and put the ephod on him. He also tied the ephod to him by its skilfully woven waistband; so it was fastened on him. 8He placed the breastpiece on him and put the Urim and Thummim in the breastpiece. 9Then he placed the turban on Aaron's head and set the gold plate, the sacred diadem, on the front of it, as the LORD commanded Moses.

10Then Moses took the anointing oil and anointed the tabernacle and everything in it, and so consecrated them. 11He sprinkled some of the oil on the altar seven times, anointing the altar and all its utensils and the basin with its stand, to consecrate them. 12He poured some of the anointing oil on Aaron's head and anointed him to consecrate him. 13Then he brought Aaron's sons forward, put tunics on them, tied sashes around them and put headbands on them, as the LORD commanded Moses.

14He then presented the bull for the sin offering, and Aaron and his sons laid their hands on its head. 15Moses slaughtered the bull and took some of the blood, and with his finger he put it on all the horns of the altar to purify the altar. He poured out the rest of the blood at the base of the altar. So he consecrated it to make atonement for it. 16Moses also took all the fat around the inner parts, the covering of the liver, and both kidneys and their fat, and burned it on the altar. 17But the bull with its hide and its flesh and its offal he burned up outside the camp, as the LORD commanded Moses.

18He then presented the ram for the burnt offering, and Aaron and his sons laid their hands on its head. 19Then Moses slaughtered the ram and sprinkled the blood against the altar on all sides. 20He cut the ram into pieces and burned the head, the pieces and the fat. 21He washed the inner parts and the legs with water and burned the whole ram on the altar as a burnt offering, a pleasing aroma, an offering made to the LORD by fire, as the LORD commanded Moses.

22He then presented the other ram, the ram for the ordination, and Aaron and his sons laid their hands on its head. 23Moses slaughtered the ram and took some of its blood and put it on the lobe of Aaron's right ear, on the thumb of his right hand and on the big toe of his right foot. 24Moses also brought Aaron's sons forward and put some of the blood on the lobes of their right ears, on the thumbs of their right hands and on the big toes of their right feet. Then he sprinkled blood against the altar on all sides. 25He took the fat, the fat tail, all the fat around the inner parts, the covering of the liver, both kidneys and their fat and the right thigh. 26Then from the basket of bread made without yeast, which was before the LORD, he took a cake of bread, and one made with oil, and a wafer; he put these on the fat portions and on the right thigh. 27He put all these in the hands of Aaron and his sons and waved them before the LORD as a wave offering. 28Then Moses took them from their hands and burned them on the altar on top of the burnt offering as an ordination offering, a pleasing aroma, an offering made to the LORD by fire. 29He also took the breast —Moses' share of the ordination ram —and waved it before the LORD as a wave offering, as the LORD commanded Moses.

30Then Moses took some of the anointing oil and some of the blood from the altar and sprinkled them on Aaron and his garments and on his sons and their garments. So he consecrated Aaron and his garments and his sons and their garments.

31Moses then said to Aaron and his sons, "Cook the meat at the entrance to the Tent of Meeting and eat it there with the bread from the basket of ordination offerings, as I commanded, saying, 'Aaron and his sons are to eat it.' 32Then burn up the rest of the meat and the bread. 33Do not leave the entrance to the Tent of Meeting for seven days,

until the days of your ordination are
completed, for your ordination will last
seven days. 34What has been done today
was commanded by the LORD to make
atonement for you. 35You must stay at
the entrance to the Tent of Meeting day
and night for seven days and do what
the LORD requires, so that you will not
die; for that is what I have been commanded." 36So Aaron and his sons did
everything the LORD commanded
through Moses.

NEW TESTAMENT READING
Mark 11:1–25

The Triumphal Entry

11 As they approached Jerusalem
and came to Bethphage and
Bethany at the Mount of Olives, Jesus
sent two of his disciples, 2saying to
them, "Go to the village ahead of you,
and just as you enter it, you will find a
colt tied there, which no-one has ever
ridden. Untie it and bring it here. 3If
anyone asks you, 'Why are you doing
this?' tell him, 'The Lord needs it and
will send it back here shortly.'"

4They went and found a colt outside
in the street, tied at a doorway. As they
untied it, 5some people standing there
asked, "What are you doing, untying
that colt?" 6They answered as Jesus had
told them to, and the people let them
go. 7When they brought the colt to
Jesus and threw their cloaks over it, he
sat on it. 8Many people spread their
cloaks on the road, while others spread
branches they had cut in the fields.
9Those who went ahead and those who
followed shouted,

"Hosanna!"

"Blessed is he who comes in the
name of the Lord!"

10"Blessed is the coming kingdom of
our father David!"

"Hosanna in the highest!"

11Jesus entered Jerusalem and went
to the temple. He looked around at
everything, but since it was already late,
he went out to Bethany with the
Twelve.

Jesus Clears the Temple

12The next day as they were leaving
Bethany, Jesus was hungry. 13Seeing in
the distance a fig-tree in leaf, he went to
find out if it had any fruit. When he
reached it, he found nothing but leaves,
because it was not the season for figs.
14Then he said to the tree, "May no-one
ever eat fruit from you again." And his
disciples heard him say it.

15On reaching Jerusalem, Jesus entered the temple area and began driving
out those who were buying and selling
there. He overturned the tables of the
money changers and the benches of
those selling doves, 16and would not
allow anyone to carry merchandise
through the temple courts. 17And as he
taught them, he said, "Is it not written:

"'My house will be called
a house of prayer for all nations'?

But you have made it 'a den of
robbers'."

18The chief priests and the teachers of
the law heard this and began looking for
a way to kill him, for they feared him,
because the whole crowd was amazed at
his teaching.

19When evening came, they went out
of the city.

The Withered Fig-Tree

20In the morning, as they went along,
they saw the fig-tree withered from the
roots. 21Peter remembered and said to
Jesus, "Rabbi, look! The fig-tree you
cursed has withered!"

22"Have faith in God," Jesus
answered. 23"I tell you the truth, if anyone says to this mountain, 'Go, throw
yourself into the sea,' and does not
doubt in his heart but believes that what

he says will happen, it will be done for him. 24Therefore I tell you, whatever you ask for in prayer, believe that you have received it, and it will be yours. 25And when you stand praying, if you hold anything against anyone, forgive him, so that your Father in heaven may forgive you your sins."

READING FROM PSALMS

Psalm 28:1–9

Of David.

1To you I call, O LORD my Rock;
do not turn a deaf ear to me.
For if you remain silent,
I shall be like those who have gone down to the pit.
2Hear my cry for mercy
as I call to you for help,
as I lift up my hands
towards your Most Holy Place.

3Do not drag me away with the wicked,
with those who do evil,
who speak cordially with their neighbours
but harbour malice in their hearts.
4Repay them for their deeds
and for their evil work;
repay them for what their hands have done
and bring back upon them what they deserve.
5Since they show no regard for the works of the LORD
and what his hands have done,
he will tear them down
and never build them up again.

6Praise be to the LORD,
for he has heard my cry for mercy.
7The LORD is my strength and my shield;
my heart trusts in him, and I am helped.
My heart leaps for joy
and I will give thanks to him in song.

8The LORD is the strength of his people,
a fortress of salvation for his anointed one.
9Save your people and bless your inheritance;
be their shepherd and carry them for ever.

DAY 62

MARCH 3

OLD TESTAMENT READING

Leviticus 9:1–10:20

The Priests Begin Their Ministry

9 On the eighth day Moses summoned Aaron and his sons and the elders of Israel. 2He said to Aaron, "Take a bull calf for your sin offering and a ram for your burnt offering, both without defect, and present them before the LORD. 3Then say to the Israelites: 'Take a male goat for a sin offering, a calf and a lamb—both a year old and without defect—for a burnt offering, 4and an ox and a ram for a fellowship offering to sacrifice before the LORD, together with a grain offering mixed with oil. For today the LORD will appear to you.' "

5They took the things Moses commanded to the front of the Tent of Meeting, and the entire assembly came near and stood before the LORD. 6Then Moses said, "This is what the LORD has commanded you to do, so that the glory of the LORD may appear to you."

7Moses said to Aaron, "Come to the

altar and sacrifice your sin offering and
your burnt offering and make atonement for yourself and the people; sacrifice the offering that is for the people
and make atonement for them, as the
LORD has commanded."
8So Aaron came to the altar and
slaughtered the calf as a sin offering for
himself. 9His sons brought the blood to
him, and he dipped his finger into the
blood and put it on the horns of the
altar; the rest of the blood he poured
out at the base of the altar. 10On the
altar he burned the fat, the kidneys and
the covering of the liver from the sin
offering, as the LORD commanded
Moses; 11the flesh and the hide he
burned up outside the camp.
12Then he slaughtered the burnt
offering. His sons handed him the
blood, and he sprinkled it against the
altar on all sides. 13They handed him
the burnt offering piece by piece, including the head, and he burned them
on the altar. 14He washed the inner
parts and the legs and burned them on
top of the burnt offering on the altar.
15Aaron then brought the offering
that was for the people. He took the
goat for the people's sin offering and
slaughtered it and offered it for a sin
offering as he did with the first one.
16He brought the burnt offering and
offered it in the prescribed way. 17He
also brought the grain offering, took a
handful of it and burned it on the altar
in addition to the morning's burnt
offering.
18He slaughtered the ox and the ram
as the fellowship offering for the people. His sons handed him the blood, and
he sprinkled it against the altar on all
sides. 19But the fat portions of the ox
and the ram—the fat tail, the layer of
fat, the kidneys and the covering of the
liver—20these they laid on the breasts,
and then Aaron burned the fat on the
altar. 21Aaron waved the breasts and
the right thigh before the LORD as a
wave offering, as Moses commanded.
22Then Aaron lifted his hands towards the people and blessed them.
And having sacrificed the sin offering,
the burnt offering and the fellowship
offering, he stepped down.
23Moses and Aaron then went into
the Tent of Meeting. When they came
out, they blessed the people; and the
glory of the LORD appeared to all the
people. 24Fire came out from the presence of the LORD and consumed the
burnt offering and the fat portions on
the altar. And when all the people saw
it, they shouted for joy and fell face
down.

The Death of Nadab and Abihu

10 Aaron's sons Nadab and Abihu
took their censers, put fire in
them and added incense; and they
offered unauthorised fire before the
LORD, contrary to his command. 2So
fire came out from the presence of the
LORD and consumed them, and they
died before the LORD. 3Moses then said
to Aaron, "This is what the LORD spoke
of when he said:

"'Among those who approach me
I will show myself holy;
in the sight of all the people
I will be honoured.'"

Aaron remained silent.
4Moses summoned Mishael and
Elzaphan, sons of Aaron's uncle Uzziel,
and said to them, "Come here; carry
your cousins outside the camp, away
from the front of the sanctuary." 5So
they came and carried them, still in their
tunics, outside the camp, as Moses
ordered.
6Then Moses said to Aaron and his
sons Eleazar and Ithamar, "Do not let
your hair become unkempt, and do not
tear your clothes, or you will die and the
LORD will be angry with the whole community. But your relatives, all the house
of Israel, may mourn for those the LORD
has destroyed by fire. 7Do not leave the
entrance to the Tent of Meeting or you
will die, because the LORD's anointing
oil is on you." So they did as Moses said.

8Then the LORD said to Aaron,
9"You and your sons are not to drink
wine or other fermented drink whenever you go into the Tent of Meeting, or
you will die. This is a lasting ordinance
for the generations to come. 10You must
distinguish between the holy and the
common, between the unclean and
the clean, 11and you must teach the
Israelites all the decrees the LORD has
given them through Moses."
12Moses said to Aaron and his remaining sons, Eleazar and Ithamar,
"Take the grain offering left over from
the offerings made to the LORD by fire
and eat it prepared without yeast beside
the altar, for it is most holy. 13Eat it in a
holy place, because it is your share and
your sons' share of the offerings made
to the LORD by fire; for so I have been
commanded. 14But you and your sons
and your daughters may eat the breast
that was waved and the thigh that was
presented. Eat them in a ceremonially
clean place; they have been given to you
and your children as your share of the
Israelites' fellowship offerings. 15The
thigh that was presented and the breast
that was waved must be brought with
the fat portions of the offerings made by
fire, to be waved before the LORD as a
wave offering. This will be the regular
share for you and your children, as the
LORD has commanded."
16When Moses enquired about the
goat of the sin offering and found that it
had been burned up, he was angry with
Eleazar and Ithamar, Aaron's remaining sons, and asked, 17"Why didn't you
eat the sin offering in the sanctuary
area? It is most holy; it was given to you
to take away the guilt of the community
by making atonement for them before
the LORD. 18Since its blood was not
taken into the Holy Place, you should
have eaten the goat in the sanctuary
area, as I commanded."
19Aaron replied to Moses, "Today
they sacrificed their sin offering and
their burnt offering before the LORD,
but such things as this have happened to
me. Would the LORD have been pleased
if I had eaten the sin offering today?"
20When Moses heard this, he was
satisfied.

NEW TESTAMENT READING
Mark 11:27–12:12

The Authority of Jesus Questioned

27They arrived again in Jerusalem,
and while Jesus was walking in the temple courts, the chief priests, the teachers
of the law and the elders came to him.
28"By what authority are you doing
these things?" they asked. "And who
gave you authority to do this?"
29Jesus replied, "I will ask you one
question. Answer me, and I will tell you
by what authority I am doing these
things. 30John's baptism—was it from
heaven, or from men? Tell me!"
31They discussed it among themselves
and said, "If we say, 'From heaven', he
will ask, 'Then why didn't you believe
him?' 32But if we say, 'From
men'. . . ." (They feared the people,
for everyone held that John really was a
prophet.)
33So they answered Jesus, "We don't
know."
Jesus said, "Neither will I tell you by
what authority I am doing these
things."

The Parable of the Tenants

12 He then began to speak to them
in parables: "A man planted a
vineyard. He put a wall around it, dug a
pit for the winepress and built a watchtower. Then he rented the vineyard to
some farmers and went away on a journey. 2At harvest time he sent a servant
to the tenants to collect from them some
of the fruit of the vineyard. 3But they
seized him, beat him and sent him away
empty-handed. 4Then he sent another
servant to them; they struck this man on
the head and treated him shamefully.
5He sent still another, and that one they

killed. He sent many others; some of
them they beat, others they killed.
6"He had one left to send, a son,
whom he loved. He sent him last of all,
saying, 'They will respect my son.'
7"But the tenants said to one
another, 'This is the heir. Come, let's
kill him, and the inheritance will be
ours.' 8So they took him and killed him,
and threw him out of the vineyard.
9"What then will the owner of the
vineyard do? He will come and kill
those tenants and give the vineyard
to others. 10Haven't you read this
scripture:

"'The stone the builders rejected
has become the capstone;
11the Lord has done this,
and it is marvellous in our eyes'?"

12Then they looked for a way to arrest
him because they knew he had spoken
the parable against them. But they were
afraid of the crowd; so they left him and
went away.

READING FROM PSALMS

Psalm 29:1–11

A psalm of David.

1Ascribe to the LORD, O mighty ones,
ascribe to the LORD glory and
strength.
2Ascribe to the LORD the glory due to
his name;
worship the LORD in the splendour
of his holiness.

3The voice of the LORD is over the
waters;
the God of glory thunders,
the LORD thunders over the mighty
waters.
4The voice of the LORD is powerful;
the voice of the LORD is majestic.
5The voice of the LORD breaks the
cedars;
the LORD breaks in pieces the
cedars of Lebanon.
6He makes Lebanon skip like a calf,
Sirion like a young wild ox.
7The voice of the LORD strikes
with flashes of lightning.
8The voice of the LORD shakes the
desert;
the LORD shakes the Desert of
Kadesh.
9The voice of the LORD twists the oaks
and strips the forests bare.
And in his temple all cry, "Glory!"

10The LORD sits enthroned over the
flood;
the LORD is enthroned as King for
ever.
11The LORD gives strength to his
people;
the LORD blesses his people with
peace.

DAY 63

MARCH 4

OLD TESTAMENT READING

Leviticus 11:1–12:8

Clean and Unclean Food

11 The LORD said to Moses and
Aaron, 2"Say to the Israelites:
'Of all the animals that live on land,
these are the ones you may eat: 3You
may eat any animal that has a split hoof
completely divided and that chews the
cud.
4" 'There are some that only chew the
cud or only have a split hoof, but you
must not eat them. The camel, though it
chews the cud, does not have a split
hoof; it is ceremonially unclean for you.
5The coney, though it chews the cud,
does not have a split hoof; it is unclean
for you. 6The rabbit, though it chews
the cud, does not have a split hoof; it is
unclean for you. 7And the pig, though it
has a split hoof completely divided,
does not chew the cud; it is unclean for
you. 8You must not eat their meat or
touch their carcasses; they are unclean
for you.
9" 'Of all the creatures living in the
water of the seas and the streams, you
may eat any that have fins and scales.
10But all creatures in the seas or streams
that do not have fins and scales—
whether among all the swarming things
or among all the other living creatures
in the water—you are to detest. 11And
since you are to detest them, you must
not eat their meat and you must detest
their carcasses. 12Anything living in the
water that does not have fins and scales
is to be detestable to you.
13" 'These are the birds you are to
detest and not eat because they are
detestable: the eagle, the vulture, the
black vulture, 14the red kite, any kind of
black kite, 15any kind of raven, 16the
horned owl, the screech owl, the gull,
any kind of hawk, 17the little owl, the
cormorant, the great owl, 18the white
owl, the desert owl, the osprey, 19the
stork, any kind of heron, the hoopoe
and the bat.
20" 'All flying insects that walk on all
fours are to be detestable to you.
21There are, however, some winged
creatures that walk on all fours that you
may eat: those that have jointed legs for
hopping on the ground. 22Of these you
may eat any kind of locust, katydid,
cricket or grasshopper. 23But all other
winged creatures that have four legs you
are to detest.
24" 'You will make yourselves unclean by these; whoever touches their
carcasses will be unclean till evening.
25Whoever picks up one of their carcasses must wash his clothes, and he
will be unclean till evening.
26" 'Every animal that has a split hoof
not completely divided or that does not
chew the cud is unclean for you; whoever touches ⌞the carcass of⌟ any of
them will be unclean. 27Of all the animals that walk on all fours, those that
walk on their paws are unclean for you;
whoever touches their carcasses will be
unclean till evening. 28Anyone who
picks up their carcasses must wash his
clothes, and he will be unclean till evening. They are unclean for you.
29" 'Of the animals that move about
on the ground, these are unclean for
you: the weasel, the rat, any kind of
great lizard, 30the gecko, the monitor
lizard, the wall lizard, the skink and the
chameleon. 31Of all those that move
along the ground, these are unclean for
you. Whoever touches them when they
are dead will be unclean till evening.
32When one of them dies and falls on
something, that article, whatever its
use, will be unclean, whether it is made
of wood, cloth, hide or sackcloth. Put it
in water; it will be unclean till evening,
and then it will be clean. 33If one of

them falls into a clay pot, everything in it will be unclean, and you must break the pot. 34Any food that could be eaten but has water on it from such a pot is unclean, and any liquid that could be drunk from it is unclean. 35Anything that one of their carcasses falls on becomes unclean; an oven or cooking pot must be broken up. They are unclean, and you are to regard them as unclean. 36A spring, however, or a cistern for collecting water remains clean, but anyone who touches one of these carcasses is unclean. 37If a carcass falls on any seeds that are to be planted, they remain clean. 38But if water has been put on the seed and a carcass falls on it, it is unclean for you.

39" 'If an animal that you are allowed to eat dies, anyone who touches the carcass will be unclean till evening. 40Anyone who eats some of the carcass must wash his clothes, and he will be unclean till evening. Anyone who picks up the carcass must wash his clothes, and he will be unclean till evening.

41" 'Every creature that moves about on the ground is detestable; it is not to be eaten. 42You are not to eat any creature that moves about on the ground, whether it moves on its belly or walks on all fours or on many feet; it is detestable. 43Do not defile yourselves by any of these creatures. Do not make yourselves unclean by means of them or be made unclean by them. 44I am the LORD your God; consecrate yourselves and be holy, because I am holy. Do not make yourselves unclean by any creature that moves about on the ground. 45I am the LORD who brought you up out of Egypt to be your God; therefore be holy, because I am holy.

46" 'These are the regulations concerning animals, birds, every living thing that moves in the water and every creature that moves about on the ground. 47You must distinguish between the unclean and the clean, between living creatures that may be eaten and those that may not be eaten.' "

Purification After Childbirth

12 The LORD said to Moses, 2"Say to the Israelites: 'A woman who becomes pregnant and gives birth to a son will be ceremonially unclean for seven days, just as she is unclean during her monthly period. 3On the eighth day the boy is to be circumcised. 4Then the woman must wait thirty-three days to be purified from her bleeding. She must not touch anything sacred or go to the sanctuary until the days of her purification are over. 5If she gives birth to a daughter, for two weeks the woman will be unclean, as during her period. Then she must wait sixty-six days to be purified from her bleeding.

6" 'When the days of her purification for a son or daughter are over, she is to bring to the priest at the entrance to the Tent of Meeting a year-old lamb for a burnt offering and a young pigeon or a dove for a sin offering. 7He shall offer them before the LORD to make atonement for her, and then she will be ceremonially clean from her flow of blood.

" 'These are the regulations for the woman who gives birth to a boy or a girl. 8If she cannot afford a lamb, she is to bring two doves or two young pigeons, one for a burnt offering and the other for a sin offering. In this way the priest will make atonement for her, and she will be clean.' "

NEW TESTAMENT READING

Mark 12:13–27

Paying Taxes to Caesar

13Later they sent some of the Pharisees and Herodians to Jesus to catch him in his words. 14They came to him and said, "Teacher, we know you are a man of integrity. You aren't swayed by men, because you pay no attention to who they are; but you teach the way of God in accordance with the truth. Is it right to pay taxes to Caesar or not? 15Should we pay or shouldn't we?"

But Jesus knew their hypocrisy.
"Why are you trying to trap me?" he
asked. "Bring me a denarius and let me
look at it." 16They brought the coin, and
he asked them, "Whose portrait is this?
And whose inscription?"
"Caesar's," they replied.
17Then Jesus said to them, "Give to
Caesar what is Caesar's and to God
what is God's."
And they were amazed at him.

Marriage at the Resurrection

18Then the Sadducees, who say there
is no resurrection, came to him with
a question. 19"Teacher," they said,
"Moses wrote for us that if a man's
brother dies and leaves a wife but no
children, the man must marry the
widow and have children for his
brother. 20Now there were seven
brothers. The first one married and died
without leaving any children. 21The
second one married the widow, but he
also died, leaving no child. It was the
same with the third. 22In fact, none of
the seven left any children. Last of all,
the woman died too. 23At the resurrection whose wife will she be, since the
seven were married to her?"
24Jesus replied, "Are you not in error
because you do not know the Scriptures
or the power of God? 25When the dead
rise, they will neither marry nor be
given in marriage; they will be like the
angels in heaven. 26Now about the dead
rising—have you not read in the book
of Moses, in the account of the bush,
how God said to him, 'I am the God of
Abraham, the God of Isaac, and the
God of Jacob'? 27He is not the God of
the dead, but of the living. You are
badly mistaken!"

READING FROM PSALMS
Psalm 30:1–7

A psalm. A song. For the dedication of the temple. Of David.

1I will exalt you, O LORD,
for you lifted me out of the depths
and did not let my enemies gloat
over me.
2O LORD my God, I called to you for
help
and you healed me.
3O LORD, you brought me up from the
grave;
you spared me from going down
into the pit.

4Sing to the LORD, you saints of his;
praise his holy name.
5For his anger lasts only a moment,
but his favour lasts a lifetime;
weeping may remain for a night,
but rejoicing comes in the
morning.

6When I felt secure, I said,
"I shall never be shaken."
7O LORD, when you favoured me,
you made my mountain stand firm;
but when you hid your face,
I was dismayed.

MARCH 5

DAY 64

OLD TESTAMENT READING

Leviticus 13:1–59

Regulations About Infectious Skin Diseases

13 The LORD said to Moses and Aaron, 2"When anyone has a swelling or a rash or a bright spot on his skin that may become an infectious skin disease, he must be brought to Aaron the priest or to one of his sons who is a priest. 3The priest is to examine the sore on his skin, and if the hair in the sore has turned white and the sore appears to be more than skin deep, it is an infectious skin disease. When the priest examines him, he shall pronounce him ceremonially unclean. 4If the spot on his skin is white but does not appear to be more than skin deep and the hair in it has not turned white, the priest is to put the infected person in isolation for seven days. 5On the seventh day the priest is to examine him, and if he sees that the sore is unchanged and has not spread in the skin, he is to keep him in isolation another seven days. 6On the seventh day the priest is to examine him again, and if the sore has faded and has not spread in the skin, the priest shall pronounce him clean; it is only a rash. The man must wash his clothes, and he will be clean. 7But if the rash does spread in his skin after he has shown himself to the priest to be pronounced clean, he must appear before the priest again. 8The priest is to examine him, and if the rash has spread in the skin, he shall pronounce him unclean; it is an infectious disease.

9"When anyone has an infectious skin disease, he must be brought to the priest. 10The priest is to examine him, and if there is a white swelling in the skin that has turned the hair white and if there is raw flesh in the swelling, 11it is a chronic skin disease and the priest shall pronounce him unclean. He is not to put him in isolation, because he is already unclean.

12"If the disease breaks out all over his skin and, so far as the priest can see, it covers all the skin of the infected person from head to foot, 13the priest is to examine him, and if the disease has covered his whole body, he shall pronounce that person clean. Since it has all turned white, he is clean. 14But whenever raw flesh appears on him, he will be unclean. 15When the priest sees the raw flesh, he shall pronounce him unclean. The raw flesh is unclean; he has an infectious disease. 16Should the raw flesh change and turn white, he must go to the priest. 17The priest is to examine him, and if the sores have turned white, the priest shall pronounce the infected person clean; then he will be clean.

18"When someone has a boil on his skin and it heals, 19and in the place where the boil was, a white swelling or reddish-white spot appears, he must present himself to the priest. 20The priest is to examine it, and if it appears to be more than skin deep and the hair in it has turned white, the priest shall pronounce him unclean. It is an infectious skin disease that has broken out where the boil was. 21But if, when the priest examines it, there is no white hair in it and it is not more than skin deep and has faded, then the priest is to put him in isolation for seven days. 22If it is spreading in the skin, the priest shall pronounce him unclean; it is infectious. 23But if the spot is unchanged and has not spread, it is only a scar from the boil, and the priest shall pronounce him clean.

24"When someone has a burn on his skin and a reddish-white or white spot appears in the raw flesh of the burn,

25the priest is to examine the spot, and if
the hair in it has turned white, and it
appears to be more than skin deep, it is
an infectious disease that has broken
out in the burn. The priest shall pronounce him unclean; it is an infectious
skin disease. 26But if the priest examines it and there is no white hair in
the spot and if it is not more than skin
deep and has faded, then the priest is to
put him in isolation for seven days. 27On
the seventh day the priest is to examine
him, and if it is spreading in the skin, the
priest shall pronounce him unclean; it is
an infectious skin disease. 28If, however, the spot is unchanged and has not
spread in the skin but has faded, it is a
swelling from the burn, and the priest
shall pronounce him clean; it is only a
scar from the burn.

29"If a man or woman has a sore on
the head or on the chin, 30the priest is to
examine the sore, and if it appears to be
more than skin deep and the hair in it is
yellow and thin, the priest shall pronounce that person unclean; it is an itch,
an infectious disease of the head or
chin. 31But if, when the priest examines
this kind of sore, it does not seem to be
more than skin deep and there is no
black hair in it, then the priest is to put
the infected person in isolation for
seven days. 32On the seventh day the
priest is to examine the sore, and if the
itch has not spread and there is no yellow hair in it and it does not appear to be
more than skin deep, 33he must be
shaved except for the diseased area, and
the priest is to keep him in isolation
another seven days. 34On the seventh
day the priest is to examine the itch, and
if it has not spread in the skin and
appears to be no more than skin deep,
the priest shall pronounce him clean.
He must wash his clothes, and he will be
clean. 35But if the itch does spread in the
skin after he is pronounced clean, 36the
priest is to examine him, and if the itch
has spread in the skin, the priest does
not need to look for yellow hair; the
person is unclean. 37If, however, in his
judgment it is unchanged and black hair
has grown in it, the itch is healed. He is
clean, and the priest shall pronounce
him clean.

38"When a man or woman has white
spots on the skin, 39the priest is to examine them, and if the spots are dull
white, it is a harmless rash that has
broken out on the skin; that person is
clean.

40"When a man has lost his hair and is
bald, he is clean. 41If he has lost his hair
from the front of his scalp and has a bald
forehead, he is clean. 42But if he has a
reddish-white sore on his bald head or
forehead, it is an infectious disease
breaking out on his head or forehead.
43The priest is to examine him, and if
the swollen sore on his head or forehead
is reddish-white like an infectious skin
disease, 44the man is diseased and is
unclean. The priest shall pronounce
him unclean because of the sore on his
head.

45"The person with such an infectious
disease must wear torn clothes, let his
hair be unkempt, cover the lower part of
his face and cry out, 'Unclean! Unclean!' 46As long as he has the infection
he remains unclean. He must live alone;
he must live outside the camp.

Regulations About Mildew

47"If any clothing is contaminated
with mildew—any woollen or linen
clothing, 48any woven or knitted material of linen or wool, any leather or
anything made of leather—49and if the
contamination in the clothing, or leather,
or woven or knitted material, or any
leather article, is greenish or reddish, it
is a spreading mildew and must be
shown to the priest. 50The priest is to
examine the mildew and isolate the
affected article for seven days. 51On the
seventh day he is to examine it, and if
the mildew has spread in the clothing,
or the woven or knitted material, or the
leather, whatever its use, it is a destructive mildew; the article is unclean. 52He
must burn up the clothing, or the woven
or knitted material of wool or linen, or

any leather article that has the contamination in it, because the mildew is
destructive; the article must be burned
up.
53"But if, when the priest examines it,
the mildew has not spread in the clothing, or the woven or knitted material,
or the leather article, 54he shall order
that the contaminated article be
washed. Then he is to isolate it for
another seven days. 55After the affected
article has been washed, the priest is to
examine it, and if the mildew has not
changed its appearance, even though it
has not spread, it is unclean. Burn it
with fire, whether the mildew has
affected one side or the other. 56If,
when the priest examines it, the mildew
has faded after the article has been
washed, he is to tear the contaminated
part out of the clothing, or the leather,
or the woven or knitted material. 57But
if it reappears in the clothing, or in the
woven or knitted material, or in the
leather article, it is spreading, and whatever has the mildew must be burned
with fire. 58The clothing, or the woven
or knitted material, or any leather
article that has been washed and is rid
of the mildew, must be washed again,
and it will be clean."
59These are the regulations concerning contamination by mildew in woollen
or linen clothing, woven or knitted
material, or any leather article, for pro-
nouncing them clean or unclean.

NEW TESTAMENT READING
Mark 12:28–44

The Greatest Commandment

28One of the teachers of the law came
and heard them debating. Noticing that
Jesus had given them a good answer, he
asked him, "Of all the commandments,
which is the most important?"
29"The most important one,"
answered Jesus, "is this: 'Hear, O
Israel, the Lord our God, the Lord is
one. 30Love the Lord your God with all
your heart and with all your soul and
with all your mind and with all your
strength.' 31The second is this: 'Love
your neighbour as yourself.' There is no
commandment greater than these."
32"Well said, teacher," the man replied. "You are right in saying that God
is one and there is no other but him.
33To love him with all your heart, with
all your understanding and with all your
strength, and to love your neighbour as
yourself is more important than all
burnt offerings and sacrifices."
34When Jesus saw that he had
answered wisely, he said to him, "You
are not far from the kingdom of God."
And from then on no-one dared ask him
any more questions.

Whose Son Is the Christ?

35While Jesus was teaching in the
temple courts, he asked, "How is it that
the teachers of the law say that the
Christ is the son of David? 36David
himself, speaking by the Holy Spirit,
declared:

"'The Lord said to my Lord:
"Sit at my right hand
until I put your enemies
under your feet."'

37David himself calls him 'Lord'. How
then can he be his son?"
The large crowd listened to him with
delight.
38As he taught, Jesus said, "Watch
out for the teachers of the law. They like
to walk around in flowing robes and be
greeted in the market-places, 39and
have the most important seats in the
synagogues and the places of honour at
banquets. 40They devour widows'
houses and for a show make lengthy
prayers. Such men will be punished
most severely."

The Widow's Offering

41Jesus sat down opposite the place
where the offerings were put and

watched the crowd putting their money into the temple treasury. Many rich people threw in large amounts. 42But a poor widow came and put in two very small copper coins, worth only a fraction of a penny.

43Calling his disciples to him, Jesus said, "I tell you the truth, this poor widow has put more into the treasury than all the others. 44They all gave out of their wealth; but she, out of her poverty, put in everything—all she had to live on."

READING FROM PROVERBS
Proverbs 6:20–29

Warning Against Adultery

20My son, keep your father's
commands
and do not forsake your mother's
teaching.
21Bind them upon your heart for ever;
fasten them around your neck.
22When you walk, they will guide you;
when you sleep, they will watch
over you;
when you awake, they will speak to
you.
23For these commands are a lamp,
this teaching is a light,
and the corrections of discipline
are the way to life,
24keeping you from the immoral
woman,
from the smooth tongue of the
wayward wife.
25Do not lust in your heart after her
beauty
or let her captivate you with her
eyes,
26for the prostitute reduces you to a
loaf of bread,
and the adulteress preys upon your
very life.
27Can a man scoop fire into his lap
without his clothes being burned?
28Can a man walk on hot coals
without his feet being scorched?
29So is he who sleeps with another
man's wife;
no-one who touches her will go
unpunished.

DAY 65

MARCH 6

OLD TESTAMENT READING
Leviticus 14:1–57

Cleansing From Infectious Skin Diseases

14 The LORD said to Moses,
2"These are the regulations for
the diseased person at the time of his
ceremonial cleansing, when he is
brought to the priest: 3The priest is to go
outside the camp and examine him. If
the person has been healed of his infectious skin disease, 4the priest shall order
that two live clean birds and some cedar wood, scarlet yarn and hyssop be brought for the one to be cleansed.
5Then the priest shall order that one of
the birds be killed over fresh water in a
clay pot. 6He is then to take the live bird
and dip it, together with the cedar wood, the scarlet yarn and the hyssop, into the blood of the bird that was killed
over the fresh water. 7Seven times he
shall sprinkle the one to be cleansed of the infectious disease and pronounce him clean. Then he is to release the live bird in the open fields.

8"The person to be cleansed must
wash his clothes, shave off all his hair and bathe with water; then he will be ceremonially clean. After this he may come into the camp, but he must stay
outside his tent for seven days. 9On the

seventh day he must shave off all his hair; he must shave his head, his beard, his eyebrows and the rest of his hair. He must wash his clothes and bathe himself with water, and he will be clean.

10"On the eighth day he must bring two male lambs and one ewe lamb a year old, each without defect, along with three-tenths of an ephah of fine flour mixed with oil for a grain offering, and one log of oil. 11The priest who pronounces him clean shall present both the one to be cleansed and his offerings before the LORD at the entrance to the Tent of Meeting.

12"Then the priest is to take one of the male lambs and offer it as a guilt offering, along with the log of oil; he shall wave them before the LORD as a wave offering. 13He is to slaughter the lamb in the holy place where the sin offering and the burnt offering are slaughtered. Like the sin offering, the guilt offering belongs to the priest; it is most holy. 14The priest is to take some of the blood of the guilt offering and put it on the lobe of the right ear of the one to be cleansed, on the thumb of his right hand and on the big toe of his right foot. 15The priest shall then take some of the log of oil, pour it in the palm of his own left hand, 16dip his right forefinger into the oil in his palm, and with his finger sprinkle some of it before the LORD seven times. 17The priest is to put some of the oil remaining in his palm on the lobe of the right ear of the one to be cleansed, on the thumb of his right hand and on the big toe of his right foot, on top of the blood of the guilt offering. 18The rest of the oil in his palm the priest shall put on the head of the one to be cleansed and make atonement for him before the LORD.

19"Then the priest is to sacrifice the sin offering and make atonement for the one to be cleansed from his uncleanness. After that, the priest shall slaughter the burnt offering 20and offer it on the altar, together with the grain offering, and make atonement for him, and he will be clean.

21"If, however, he is poor and cannot afford these, he must take one male lamb as a guilt offering to be waved to make atonement for him, together with a tenth of an ephah of fine flour mixed with oil for a grain offering, a log of oil, 22and two doves or two young pigeons, which he can afford, one for a sin offering and the other for a burnt offering.

23"On the eighth day he must bring them for his cleansing to the priest at the entrance to the Tent of Meeting, before the LORD. 24The priest is to take the lamb for the guilt offering, together with the log of oil, and wave them before the LORD as a wave offering. 25He shall slaughter the lamb for the guilt offering and take some of its blood and put it on the lobe of the right ear of the one to be cleansed, on the thumb of his right hand and on the big toe of his right foot. 26The priest is to pour some of the oil into the palm of his own left hand, 27and with his right forefinger sprinkle some of the oil from his palm seven times before the LORD. 28Some of the oil in his palm he is to put on the same places he put the blood of the guilt offering—on the lobe of the right ear of the one to be cleansed, on the thumb of his right hand and on the big toe of his right foot. 29The rest of the oil in his palm the priest shall put on the head of the one to be cleansed, to make atonement for him before the LORD. 30Then he shall sacrifice the doves or the young pigeons, which the person can afford, 31one as a sin offering and the other as a burnt offering, together with the grain offering. In this way the priest will make atonement before the LORD on behalf of the one to be cleansed."

32These are the regulations for anyone who has an infectious skin disease and who cannot afford the regular offerings for his cleansing.

Cleansing From Mildew

33The LORD said to Moses and Aaron, 34"When you enter the land of Canaan, which I am giving you as your

possession, and I put a spreading mildew in a house in that land, 35the owner
of the house must go and tell the priest,
'I have seen something that looks like
mildew in my house.' 36The priest is to
order the house to be emptied before he
goes in to examine the mildew, so that
nothing in the house will be pronounced
unclean. After this the priest is to go in
and inspect the house. 37He is to examine the mildew on the walls, and if it
has greenish or reddish depressions that
appear to be deeper than the surface of
the wall, 38the priest shall go out of the
doorway of the house and close it up for
seven days. 39On the seventh day the
priest shall return to inspect the house.
If the mildew has spread on the walls,
40he is to order that the contaminated
stones be torn out and thrown into an
unclean place outside the town. 41He
must have all the inside walls of the
house scraped and the material that is
scraped off dumped into an unclean
place outside the town. 42Then they are
to take other stones to replace these and
take new clay and plaster the house.

43"If the mildew reappears in the
house after the stones have been torn
out and the house scraped and plastered, 44the priest is to go and examine it
and, if the mildew has spread in the
house, it is a destructive mildew; the
house is unclean. 45It must be torn down
—its stones, timbers and all the plaster
—and taken out of the town to an unclean place.

46"Anyone who goes into the house
while it is closed up will be unclean till
evening. 47Anyone who sleeps or eats in
the house must wash his clothes.

48"But if the priest comes to examine
it and the mildew has not spread after
the house has been plastered, he shall
pronounce the house clean, because the
mildew is gone. 49To purify the house he
is to take two birds and some cedar
wood, scarlet yarn and hyssop. 50He
shall kill one of the birds over fresh
water in a clay pot. 51Then he is to take
the cedar wood, the hyssop, the scarlet
yarn and the live bird, dip them into the
blood of the dead bird and the fresh
water, and sprinkle the house seven
times. 52He shall purify the house with
the bird's blood, the fresh water, the
live bird, the cedar wood, the hyssop
and the scarlet yarn. 53Then he is to
release the live bird in the open fields
outside the town. In this way he will
make atonement for the house, and it
will be clean."

54These are the regulations for any
infectious skin disease, for an itch, 55for
mildew in clothing or in a house, 56and
for a swelling, a rash or a bright spot,
57to determine when something is clean
or unclean.

These are the regulations for infectious skin diseases and mildew.

NEW TESTAMENT READING

Mark 13:1–31

Signs of the End of the Age

13 As he was leaving the temple,
one of his disciples said to him,
"Look, Teacher! What massive stones!
What magnificent buildings!"

2"Do you see all these great buildings?" replied Jesus. "Not one stone
here will be left on another; every one
will be thrown down."

3As Jesus was sitting on the Mount of
Olives opposite the temple, Peter,
James, John and Andrew asked him
privately, 4"Tell us, when will these
things happen? And what will be
the sign that they are all about to be
fulfilled?"

5Jesus said to them: "Watch out that
no-one deceives you. 6Many will come
in my name, claiming, 'I am he,' and
will deceive many. 7When you hear of
wars and rumours of wars, do not be
alarmed. Such things must happen, but
the end is still to come. 8Nation will rise
against nation, and kingdom against
kingdom. There will be earthquakes in
various places, and famines. These are
the beginning of birth-pains.

9"You must be on your guard. You

will be handed over to the local councils
and flogged in the synagogues. On
account of me you will stand before
governors and kings as witnesses to
them. [10]And the gospel must first be
preached to all nations. [11]Whenever
you are arrested and brought to trial, do
not worry beforehand about what to
say. Just say whatever is given you at the
time, for it is not you speaking, but the
Holy Spirit.

[12]"Brother will betray brother to
death, and a father his child. Children
will rebel against their parents and have
them put to death. [13]All men will hate
you because of me, but he who stands
firm to the end will be saved.

[14]"When you see 'the abomination
that causes desolation' standing where it
does not belong—let the reader understand—then let those who are in Judea
flee to the mountains. [15]Let no-one on
the roof of his house go down or enter
the house to take anything out. [16]Let
no-one in the field go back to get his
cloak. [17]How dreadful it will be in those
days for pregnant women and nursing
mothers! [18]Pray that this will not take
place in winter, [19]because those will be
days of distress unequalled from the
beginning, when God created the
world, until now—and never to be
equalled again. [20]If the Lord had not cut
short those days, no-one would survive.
But for the sake of the elect, whom he
has chosen, he has shortened them.
[21]At that time if anyone says to you,
'Look, here is the Christ!' or, 'Look,
there he is!' do not believe it. [22]For false
Christs and false prophets will appear
and perform signs and miracles to deceive the elect—if that were possible.
[23]So be on your guard; I have told you
everything ahead of time.

[24]"But in those days, following that
distress,

" 'the sun will be darkened,
and the moon will not give its light;
[25]the stars will fall from the sky,
and the heavenly bodies will be
shaken.'

[26]"At that time men will see the Son
of Man coming in clouds with great
power and glory. [27]And he will send his
angels and gather his elect from the four
winds, from the ends of the earth to the
ends of the heavens.

[28]"Now learn this lesson from the
fig-tree: As soon as its twigs get tender
and its leaves come out, you know that
summer is near. [29]Even so, when you
see these things happening, you know
that it is near, right at the door. [30]I tell
you the truth, this generation will certainly not pass away until all these
things have happened. [31]Heaven and
earth will pass away, but my words will
never pass away.

READING FROM PSALMS
Psalm 30:8–12

[8]To you, O LORD, I called;
to the Lord I cried for mercy:
[9]"What gain is there in my
destruction,
in my going down into the pit?
Will the dust praise you?
Will it proclaim your faithfulness?
[10]Hear, O LORD, and be merciful to
me;
O LORD, be my help."

[11]You turned my wailing into dancing;
you removed my sackcloth and
clothed me with joy,
[12]that my heart may sing to you and not
be silent.
O LORD my God, I will give you
thanks for ever.

OLD TESTAMENT READING
Leviticus 15:1–16:34

Discharges Causing Uncleanness

15 The LORD said to Moses and
Aaron, 2"Speak to the Israelites
and say to them: 'When any man has a
bodily discharge, the discharge is unclean. 3Whether it continues flowing
from his body or is blocked, it will make
him unclean. This is how his discharge
will bring about uncleanness:
4" 'Any bed the man with a discharge
lies on will be unclean, and anything he
sits on will be unclean. 5Anyone who
touches his bed must wash his clothes
and bathe with water, and he will be
unclean till evening. 6Whoever sits on
anything that the man with a discharge
sat on must wash his clothes and bathe
with water, and he will be unclean till
evening.
7" 'Whoever touches the man who
has a discharge must wash his clothes
and bathe with water, and he will be
unclean till evening.
8" 'If the man with the discharge spits
on someone who is clean, that person
must wash his clothes and bathe with
water, and he will be unclean till
evening.
9" 'Everything the man sits on when
riding will be unclean, 10and whoever
touches any of the things that were
under him will be unclean till evening;
whoever picks up those things must
wash his clothes and bathe with water,
and he will be unclean till evening.
11" 'Anyone the man with a discharge
touches without rinsing his hands with
water must wash his clothes and bathe
with water, and he will be unclean till
evening.
12" 'A clay pot that the man touches
must be broken, and any wooden article
is to be rinsed with water.
13" 'When a man is cleansed from his
discharge, he is to count off seven days
for his ceremonial cleansing; he must
wash his clothes and bathe himself with
fresh water, and he will be clean. 14On
the eighth day he must take two doves
or two young pigeons and come before
the LORD to the entrance to the Tent of
Meeting and give them to the priest.
15The priest is to sacrifice them, the one
for a sin offering and the other for a
burnt offering. In this way he will make
atonement before the LORD for the man
because of his discharge.
16" 'When a man has an emission of
semen, he must bathe his whole body
with water, and he will be unclean till
evening. 17Any clothing or leather that
has semen on it must be washed with
water, and it will be unclean till evening. 18When a man lies with a woman
and there is an emission of semen, both
must bathe with water, and they will be
unclean till evening.
19" 'When a woman has her regular
flow of blood, the impurity of her
monthly period will last seven days, and
anyone who touches her will be unclean
till evening.
20" 'Anything she lies on during her
period will be unclean, and anything she
sits on will be unclean. 21Whoever
touches her bed must wash his clothes
and bathe with water, and he will be
unclean till evening. 22Whoever touches
anything she sits on must wash his
clothes and bathe with water, and he
will be unclean till evening. 23Whether
it is the bed or anything she was sitting
on, when anyone touches it, he will be
unclean till evening.
24" 'If a man lies with her and her
monthly flow touches him, he will be
unclean for seven days; any bed he lies
on will be unclean.
25" 'When a woman has a discharge of
blood for many days at a time other than
her monthly period or has a discharge
that continues beyond her period, she

will be unclean as long as she has the discharge, just as in the days of her period. 26Any bed she lies on while her discharge continues will be unclean, as is her bed during her monthly period, and anything she sits on will be unclean, as during her period. 27Whoever touches them will be unclean; he must wash his clothes and bathe with water, and he will be unclean till evening.

28" 'When she is cleansed from her discharge, she must count off seven days, and after that she will be ceremonially clean. 29On the eighth day she must take two doves or two young pigeons and bring them to the priest at the entrance to the Tent of Meeting. 30The priest is to sacrifice one for a sin offering and the other for a burnt offering. In this way he will make atonement for her before the LORD for the uncleanness of her discharge.

31" 'You must keep the Israelites separate from things that make them unclean, so they will not die in their uncleanness for defiling my dwelling-place, which is among them.' "

32These are the regulations for a man with a discharge, for anyone made unclean by an emission of semen, 33for a woman in her monthly period, for a man or a woman with a discharge, and for a man who lies with a woman who is ceremonially unclean.

The Day of Atonement

16 The LORD spoke to Moses after the death of the two sons of Aaron who died when they approached the LORD. 2The LORD said to Moses: "Tell your brother Aaron not to come whenever he chooses into the Most Holy Place behind the curtain in front of the atonement cover on the ark, or else he will die, because I appear in the cloud over the atonement cover.

3"This is how Aaron is to enter the sanctuary area: with a young bull for a sin offering and a ram for a burnt offering. 4He is to put on the sacred linen tunic, with linen undergarments next to his body; he is to tie the linen sash around him and put on the linen turban. These are sacred garments; so he must bathe himself with water before he puts them on. 5From the Israelite community he is to take two male goats for a sin offering and a ram for a burnt offering.

6"Aaron is to offer the bull for his own sin offering to make atonement for himself and his household. 7Then he is to take the two goats and present them before the LORD at the entrance to the Tent of Meeting. 8He is to cast lots for the two goats—one lot for the LORD and the other for the scapegoat. 9Aaron shall bring the goat whose lot falls to the LORD and sacrifice it for a sin offering. 10But the goat chosen by lot as the scapegoat shall be presented alive before the LORD to be used for making atonement by sending it into the desert as a scapegoat.

11"Aaron shall bring the bull for his own sin offering to make atonement for himself and his household, and he is to slaughter the bull for his own sin offering. 12He is to take a censer full of burning coals from the altar before the LORD and two handfuls of finely ground fragrant incense and take them behind the curtain. 13He is to put the incense on the fire before the LORD, and the smoke of the incense will conceal the atonement cover above the Testimony, so that he will not die. 14He is to take some of the bull's blood and with his finger sprinkle it on the front of the atonement cover; then he shall sprinkle some of it with his finger seven times before the atonement cover.

15"He shall then slaughter the goat for the sin offering for the people and take its blood behind the curtain and do with it as he did with the bull's blood: He shall sprinkle it on the atonement cover and in front of it. 16In this way he will make atonement for the Most Holy Place because of the uncleanness and rebellion of the Israelites, whatever their sins have been. He is to do the same for the Tent of Meeting, which is

among them in the midst of their uncleanness. 17No-one is to be in the Tent
of Meeting from the time Aaron goes in
to make atonement in the Most Holy
Place until he comes out, having made
atonement for himself, his household
and the whole community of Israel.

18"Then he shall come out to the altar
that is before the LORD and make atonement for it. He shall take some of the
bull's blood and some of the goat's
blood and put it on all the horns of the
altar. 19He shall sprinkle some of the
blood on it with his finger seven times to
cleanse it and consecrate it from the
uncleanness of the Israelites.

20"When Aaron has finished making
atonement for the Most Holy Place, the
Tent of Meeting and the altar, he shall
bring forward the live goat. 21He is to
lay both hands on the head of the live
goat and confess over it all the wickedness and rebellion of the Israelites—all
their sins—and put them on the goat's
head. He shall send the goat away into
the desert in the care of a man
appointed for the task. 22The goat will
carry on itself all their sins to a solitary
place; and the man shall release it in the
desert.

23"Then Aaron is to go into the Tent
of Meeting and take off the linen garments he put on before he entered the
Most Holy Place, and he is to leave
them there. 24He shall bathe himself
with water in a holy place and put on his
regular garments. Then he shall come
out and sacrifice the burnt offering for
himself and the burnt offering for the
people, to make atonement for himself and for the people. 25He shall also
burn the fat of the sin offering on the
altar.

26"The man who releases the goat as a
scapegoat must wash his clothes and
bathe himself with water; afterwards he
may come into the camp. 27The bull and
the goat for the sin offerings, whose
blood was brought into the Most Holy
Place to make atonement, must be
taken outside the camp; their hides,
flesh and offal are to be burned up.
28The man who burns them must wash
his clothes and bathe himself with
water; afterwards he may come into
the camp.

29"This is to be a lasting ordinance for
you: On the tenth day of the seventh
month you must deny yourselves and
not do any work—whether native-born
or an alien living among you—
30because on this day atonement will be
made for you, to cleanse you. Then,
before the LORD, you will be clean from
all your sins. 31It is a sabbath of rest, and
you must deny yourselves; it is a lasting
ordinance. 32The priest who is anointed
and ordained to succeed his father as
high priest is to make atonement. He is
to put on the sacred linen garments
33and make atonement for the Most
Holy Place, for the Tent of Meeting and
the altar, and for the priests and all the
people of the community.

34"This is to be a lasting ordinance for
you: Atonement is to be made once a
year for all the sins of the Israelites."

And it was done, as the LORD commanded Moses.

NEW TESTAMENT READING
Mark 13:32–14:16

The Day and Hour Unknown

32"No-one knows about that day or
hour, not even the angels in heaven, nor
the Son, but only the Father. 33Be on
guard! Be alert! You do not know when
that time will come. 34It's like a man
going away: He leaves his house and
puts his servants in charge, each with his
assigned task, and tells the one at the
door to keep watch.

35"Therefore keep watch because
you do not know when the owner
of the house will come back—whether
in the evening, or at midnight, or when
the cock crows, or at dawn. 36If he
comes suddenly, do not let him find you
sleeping. 37What I say to you, I say to
everyone: 'Watch!'"

Jesus Anointed at Bethany

14 Now the Passover and the Feast
of Unleavened Bread were only
two days away, and the chief priests and
the teachers of the law were looking for
some sly way to arrest Jesus and kill
him. 2"But not during the Feast," they
said, "or the people may riot."
3While he was in Bethany, reclining
at the table in the home of a man known
as Simon the Leper, a woman came with
an alabaster jar of very expensive perfume, made of pure nard. She broke the
jar and poured the perfume on his head.
4Some of those present were saying
indignantly to one another, "Why this
waste of perfume? 5It could have been
sold for more than a year's wages and
the money given to the poor." And they
rebuked her harshly.
6"Leave her alone," said Jesus.
"Why are you bothering her? She has
done a beautiful thing to me. 7The poor
you will always have with you, and you
can help them any time you want. But
you will not always have me. 8She did
what she could. She poured perfume on
my body beforehand to prepare for my
burial. 9I tell you the truth, wherever
the gospel is preached throughout the
world, what she has done will also be
told, in memory of her."
10Then Judas Iscariot, one of the
Twelve, went to the chief priests to
betray Jesus to them. 11They were delighted to hear this and promised to give
him money. So he watched for an
opportunity to hand him over.

The Lord's Supper

12On the first day of the Feast of
Unleavened Bread, when it was customary to sacrifice the Passover lamb,
Jesus' disciples asked him, "Where do
you want us to go and make preparations for you to eat the Passover?"
13So he sent two of his disciples, telling them, "Go into the city, and a man
carrying a jar of water will meet you.
Follow him. 14Say to the owner of the
house he enters, 'The Teacher asks:
Where is my guest room, where I may
eat the Passover with my disciples?'
15He will show you a large upper room,
furnished and ready. Make preparations for us there."
16The disciples left, went into the city
and found things just as Jesus had told
them. So they prepared the Passover.

READING FROM PSALMS

Psalm 31:1–8

For the director of music. A psalm of David.

1In you, O LORD, I have taken refuge;
  let me never be put to shame;
  deliver me in your righteousness.
2Turn your ear to me,
  come quickly to my rescue;
be my rock of refuge,
  a strong fortress to save me.
3Since you are my rock and my fortress,
  for the sake of your name lead and guide me.
4Free me from the trap that is set for me,
  for you are my refuge.
5Into your hands I commit my spirit;
  redeem me, O LORD, the God of truth.

6I hate those who cling to worthless idols;
  I trust in the LORD.
7I will be glad and rejoice in your love,
  for you saw my affliction
  and knew the anguish of my soul.
8You have not handed me over to the enemy
  but have set my feet in a spacious place.

DAY 67

MARCH 8

OLD TESTAMENT READING
Leviticus 17:1–18:30

Eating Blood Forbidden

17 The LORD said to Moses,
2“Speak to Aaron and his sons
and to all the Israelites and say to them:
‘This is what the LORD has commanded:
3Any Israelite who sacrifices an ox, a
lamb or a goat in the camp or outside of
it 4instead of bringing it to the entrance
to the Tent of Meeting to present it as an
offering to the LORD in front of the
tabernacle of the LORD—that man shall
be considered guilty of bloodshed; he
has shed blood and must be cut off from
his people. 5This is so that the Israelites
will bring to the LORD the sacrifices they
are now making in the open fields. They
must bring them to the priest, that is, to
the LORD, at the entrance to the Tent of
Meeting and sacrifice them as fellowship offerings. 6The priest is to
sprinkle the blood against the altar of
the LORD at the entrance to the Tent of
Meeting and burn the fat as an aroma
pleasing to the LORD. 7They must no
longer offer any of their sacrifices to the
goat idols to whom they prostitute
themselves. This is to be a lasting ordinance for them and for the generations
to come.’

8“Say to them: ‘Any Israelite or any
alien living among them who offers a
burnt offering or sacrifice 9and does not
bring it to the entrance to the Tent of
Meeting to sacrifice it to the LORD—
that man must be cut off from his
people.

10“ ‘Any Israelite or any alien living
among them who eats any blood—I will
set my face against that person who eats
blood and will cut him off from his
people. 11For the life of a creature is in
the blood, and I have given it to you to
make atonement for yourselves on the
altar; it is the blood that makes atonement for one’s life. 12Therefore I say to
the Israelites, “None of you may eat
blood, nor may an alien living among
you eat blood.”

13“ ‘Any Israelite or any alien living
among you who hunts any animal or
bird that may be eaten must drain out
the blood and cover it with earth,
14because the life of every creature is its
blood. That is why I have said to the
Israelites, “You must not eat the blood
of any creature, because the life of
every creature is its blood; anyone
who eats it must be cut off.”

15“ ‘Anyone, whether native-born or
alien, who eats anything found dead or
torn by wild animals must wash his
clothes and bathe with water, and he
will be ceremonially unclean till evening; then he will be clean. 16But if he
does not wash his clothes and bathe
himself, he will be held responsible.’ ”

Unlawful Sexual Relations

18 The LORD said to Moses,
2“Speak to the Israelites and say
to them: ‘I am the LORD your God.
3You must not do as they do in Egypt,
where you used to live, and you must
not do as they do in the land of Canaan,
where I am bringing you. Do not follow
their practices. 4You must obey my laws
and be careful to follow my decrees. I
am the LORD your God. 5Keep my decrees and laws, for the man who obeys
them will live by them. I am the LORD.

6“ ‘No-one is to approach any close
relative to have sexual relations. I am
the LORD.

7“ ‘Do not dishonour your father by
having sexual relations with your
mother. She is your mother; do not
have relations with her.

8“ ‘Do not have sexual relations with
your father’s wife; that would dishonour your father.

9" 'Do not have sexual relations with your sister, either your father's daughter or your mother's daughter, whether she was born in the same home or elsewhere.

10" 'Do not have sexual relations with your son's daughter or your daughter's daughter; that would dishonour you.

11" 'Do not have sexual relations with the daughter of your father's wife, born to your father; she is your sister.

12" 'Do not have sexual relations with your father's sister; she is your father's close relative.

13" 'Do not have sexual relations with your mother's sister, because she is your mother's close relative.

14" 'Do not dishonour your father's brother by approaching his wife to have sexual relations; she is your aunt.

15" 'Do not have sexual relations with your daughter-in-law. She is your son's wife; do not have relations with her.

16" 'Do not have sexual relations with your brother's wife; that would dishonour your brother.

17" 'Do not have sexual relations with both a woman and her daughter. Do not have sexual relations with either her son's daughter or her daughter's daughter; they are her close relatives. That is wickedness.

18" 'Do not take your wife's sister as a rival wife and have sexual relations with her while your wife is living.

19" 'Do not approach a woman to have sexual relations during the uncleanness of her monthly period.

20" 'Do not have sexual relations with your neighbour's wife and defile yourself with her.

21" 'Do not give any of your children to be sacrificed to Molech, for you must not profane the name of your God. I am the LORD.

22" 'Do not lie with a man as one lies with a woman; that is detestable.

23" 'Do not have sexual relations with an animal and defile yourself with it. A woman must not present herself to an animal to have sexual relations with it; that is a perversion.

24" 'Do not defile yourselves in any of these ways, because this is how the nations that I am going to drive out before you became defiled. 25Even the land was defiled; so I punished it for its sin, and the land vomited out its inhabitants. 26But you must keep my decrees and my laws. The native-born and the aliens living among you must not do any of these detestable things, 27for all these things were done by the people who lived in the land before you, and the land became defiled. 28And if you defile the land, it will vomit you out as it vomited out the nations that were before you.

29" 'Everyone who does any of these detestable things—such persons must be cut off from their people. 30Keep my requirements and do not follow any of the detestable customs that were practised before you came and do not defile yourselves with them. I am the LORD your God.' "

NEW TESTAMENT READING

Mark 14:17–42

17When evening came, Jesus arrived with the Twelve. 18While they were reclining at the table eating, he said, "I tell you the truth, one of you will betray me—one who is eating with me."

19They were saddened, and one by one they said to him, "Surely not I?"

20"It is one of the Twelve," he replied, "one who dips bread into the bowl with me. 21The Son of Man will go just as it is written about him. But woe to that man who betrays the Son of Man! It would be better for him if he had not been born."

22While they were eating, Jesus took bread, gave thanks and broke it, and gave it to his disciples, saying, "Take it; this is my body."

23Then he took the cup, gave thanks and offered it to them, and they all drank from it.

24"This is my blood of the covenant, which is poured out for many," he said

to them. 25“I tell you the truth, I will not
drink again of the fruit of the vine until
that day when I drink it anew in the
kingdom of God.”
26When they had sung a hymn, they
went out to the Mount of Olives.

Jesus Predicts Peter's Denial

27“You will all fall away,” Jesus told
them, “for it is written:

“ ‘I will strike the shepherd,
and the sheep will be scattered.’

28But after I have risen, I will go ahead
of you into Galilee.”
29Peter declared, “Even if all fall
away, I will not.”
30“I tell you the truth,” Jesus
answered, “today—yes, tonight—
before the cock crows twice you yourself will disown me three times.”
31But Peter insisted emphatically,
“Even if I have to die with you, I will
never disown you.” And all the others
said the same.

Gethsemane

32They went to a place called Gethsemane, and Jesus said to his disciples,
“Sit here while I pray.” 33He took
Peter, James and John along with him,
and he began to be deeply distressed
and troubled. 34“My soul is overwhelmed with sorrow to the point of
death,” he said to them. “Stay here
and keep watch.”
35Going a little farther, he fell to the
ground and prayed that if possible the
hour might pass from him. 36“*Abba*,
Father,” he said, “everything is possible for you. Take this cup from me. Yet
not what I will, but what you will.”
37Then he returned to his disciples
and found them sleeping. “Simon,” he
said to Peter, “are you asleep? Could
you not keep watch for one hour?
38Watch and pray so that you will not
fall into temptation. The spirit is willing, but the body is weak.”
39Once more he went away and
prayed the same thing. 40When he came
back, he again found them sleeping,
because their eyes were heavy. They did
not know what to say to him.
41Returning the third time, he said to
them, “Are you still sleeping and resting? Enough! The hour has come.
Look, the Son of Man is betrayed into
the hands of sinners. 42Rise! Let us go!
Here comes my betrayer!”

READING FROM PSALMS

Psalm 31:9–18

9Be merciful to me, O LORD, for I am
in distress;
my eyes grow weak with sorrow,
my soul and my body with grief.
10My life is consumed by anguish
and my years by groaning;
my strength fails because of my
affliction,
and my bones grow weak.
11Because of all my enemies,
I am the utter contempt of my
neighbours;
I am a dread to my friends—
those who see me on the street flee
from me.
12I am forgotten by them as though I
were dead;
I have become like broken pottery.
13For I hear the slander of many;
there is terror on every side;
they conspire against me
and plot to take my life.

14But I trust in you, O LORD;
I say, “You are my God.”
15My times are in your hands;
deliver me from my enemies
and from those who pursue me.
16Let your face shine on your servant;
save me in your unfailing love.
17Let me not be put to shame, O LORD,
for I have cried out to you;
but let the wicked be put to shame
and lie silent in the grave.
18Let their lying lips be silenced,
for with pride and contempt
they speak arrogantly against the
righteous.

MARCH 9 DAY 68

OLD TESTAMENT READING
Leviticus 19:1–20:27

Various Laws

19 The LORD said to Moses,
2"Speak to the entire assembly
of Israel and say to them: 'Be holy
because I, the LORD your God, am holy.
3" 'Each of you must respect his
mother and father, and you must
observe my Sabbaths. I am the LORD
your God.
4" 'Do not turn to idols or make gods
of cast metal for yourselves. I am the
LORD your God.
5" 'When you sacrifice a fellowship
offering to the LORD, sacrifice it in such
a way that it will be accepted on your
behalf. 6It shall be eaten on the day you
sacrifice it or on the next day; anything
left over until the third day must be
burned up. 7If any of it is eaten on the
third day, it is impure and will not be
accepted. 8Whoever eats it will be held
responsible because he has desecrated
what is holy to the LORD; that person
must be cut off from his people.
9" 'When you reap the harvest of your
land, do not reap to the very edges of
your field or gather the gleanings of
your harvest. 10Do not go over your
vineyard a second time or pick up the
grapes that have fallen. Leave them for
the poor and the alien. I am the LORD
your God.
11" 'Do not steal.
" 'Do not lie.
" 'Do not deceive one another.
12" 'Do not swear falsely by my name
and so profane the name of your God. I
am the LORD.
13" 'Do not defraud your neighbour
or rob him.
" 'Do not hold back the wages of a
hired man overnight.
14" 'Do not curse the deaf or put a
stumbling-block in front of the blind,
but fear your God. I am the LORD.
15" 'Do not pervert justice; do not
show partiality to the poor or favouritism to the great, but judge your neighbour fairly.
16" 'Do not go about spreading slander among your people.
" 'Do not do anything that endangers
your neighbour's life. I am the LORD.
17" 'Do not hate your brother in your
heart. Rebuke your neighbour frankly
so that you will not share in his guilt.
18" 'Do not seek revenge or bear a
grudge against one of your people, but
love your neighbour as yourself. I am
the LORD.
19" 'Keep my decrees.
" 'Do not mate different kinds of
animals.
" 'Do not plant your field with two
kinds of seed.
" 'Do not wear clothing woven of two
kinds of material.
20" 'If a man sleeps with a woman who
is a slave girl promised to another man
but who has not been ransomed or given
her freedom, there must be due punishment. Yet they are not to be put to
death, because she had not been freed.
21The man, however, must bring a ram
to the entrance to the Tent of Meeting
for a guilt offering to the LORD. 22With
the ram of the guilt offering the priest is
to make atonement for him before the
LORD for the sin he has committed, and
his sin will be forgiven.
23" 'When you enter the land and
plant any kind of fruit tree, regard its
fruit as forbidden. For three years you
are to consider it forbidden; it must not
be eaten. 24In the fourth year all its fruit
will be holy, an offering of praise to the
LORD. 25But in the fifth year you may
eat its fruit. In this way your harvest will
be increased. I am the LORD your God.
26" 'Do not eat any meat with the
blood still in it.
" 'Do not practise divination or
sorcery.

27“ ‘Do not cut the hair at the sides of
your head or clip off the edges of your
beard.
28“ ‘Do not cut your bodies for the
dead or put tattoo marks on yourselves.
I am the LORD.
29“ ‘Do not degrade your daughter by
making her a prostitute, or the land will
turn to prostitution and be filled with
wickedness.
30“ ‘Observe my Sabbaths and have
reverence for my sanctuary. I am the
LORD.
31“ ‘Do not turn to mediums or seek
out spiritists, for you will be defiled by
them. I am the LORD your God.
32“ ‘Rise in the presence of the aged,
show respect for the elderly and revere
your God. I am the LORD.
33“ ‘When an alien lives with you in
your land, do not ill-treat him. 34The
alien living with you must be treated as
one of your native-born. Love him as
yourself, for you were aliens in Egypt. I
am the LORD your God.
35“ ‘Do not use dishonest standards
when measuring length, weight or
quantity. 36Use honest scales and honest weights, an honest ephah and an
honest hin. I am the LORD your God,
who brought you out of Egypt.
37“ ‘Keep all my decrees and all my
laws and follow them. I am the LORD.’ ”

Punishments for Sin

20 The LORD said to Moses, 2“Say
to the Israelites: ‘Any Israelite
or any alien living in Israel who gives
any of his children to Molech must be
put to death. The people of the community are to stone him. 3I will set my
face against that man and I will cut him
off from his people; for by giving his
children to Molech, he has defiled my
sanctuary and profaned my holy name.
4If the people of the community close
their eyes when that man gives one of
his children to Molech and they fail to
put him to death, 5I will set my face
against that man and his family and will
cut off from their people both him and
all who follow him in prostituting themselves to Molech.
6“ ‘I will set my face against the person who turns to mediums and spiritists
to prostitute himself by following them,
and I will cut him off from his people.
7“ ‘Consecrate yourselves and be
holy, because I am the LORD your God.
8Keep my decrees and follow them. I
am the LORD, who makes you holy.
9“ ‘If anyone curses his father or
mother, he must be put to death. He has
cursed his father or his mother, and his
blood will be on his own head.
10“ ‘If a man commits adultery with
another man’s wife—with the wife of
his neighbour—both the adulterer and
the adulteress must be put to death.
11“ ‘If a man sleeps with his father’s
wife, he has dishonoured his father.
Both the man and the woman must be
put to death; their blood will be on their
own heads.
12“ ‘If a man sleeps with his daughter-
in-law, both of them must be put to
death. What they have done is a perversion; their blood will be on their own
heads.
13“ ‘If a man lies with a man as one lies
with a woman, both of them have done
what is detestable. They must be put to
death; their blood will be on their own
heads.
14“ ‘If a man marries both a woman
and her mother, it is wicked. Both he
and they must be burned in the fire, so
that no wickedness will be among you.
15“ ‘If a man has sexual relations with
an animal, he must be put to death, and
you must kill the animal.
16“ ‘If a woman approaches an animal
to have sexual relations with it, kill both
the woman and the animal. They must
be put to death; their blood will be on
their own heads.
17“ ‘If a man marries his sister, the
daughter of either his father or his
mother, and they have sexual relations,
it is a disgrace. They must be cut off
before the eyes of their people. He has
dishonoured his sister and will be held
responsible.

18"'If a man lies with a woman during
her monthly period and has sexual relations with her, he has exposed the
source of her flow, and she has also
uncovered it. Both of them must be cut
off from their people.
19"'Do not have sexual relations with
the sister of either your mother or your
father, for that would dishonour a close
relative; both of you would be held
responsible.
20"'If a man sleeps with his aunt, he
has dishonoured his uncle. They will be
held responsible; they will die childless.
21"'If a man marries his brother's
wife, it is an act of impurity; he has
dishonoured his brother. They will be
childless.
22"'Keep all my decrees and laws and
follow them, so that the land where I am
bringing you to live may not vomit you
out. 23You must not live according to
the customs of the nations I am going to
drive out before you. Because they did
all these things, I abhorred them. 24But
I said to you, "You will possess their
land; I will give it to you as an inheritance, a land flowing with milk and
honey." I am the LORD your God, who
has set you apart from the nations.
25"'You must therefore make a distinction between clean and unclean
animals and between unclean and clean
birds. Do not defile yourselves by any
animal or bird or anything that moves
along the ground—those which I have
set apart as unclean for you. 26You are
to be holy to me because I, the LORD,
am holy, and I have set you apart from
the nations to be my own.
27"'A man or woman who is a
medium or spiritist among you must be
put to death. You are to stone them;
their blood will be on their own
heads.'"

NEW TESTAMENT READING

Mark 14:43–72

Jesus Arrested

43Just as he was speaking, Judas, one
of the Twelve, appeared. With him was
a crowd armed with swords and clubs,
sent from the chief priests, the teachers
of the law, and the elders.
44Now the betrayer had arranged a
signal with them: "The one I kiss is the
man; arrest him and lead him away
under guard." 45Going at once to Jesus,
Judas said, "Rabbi!" and kissed him.
46The men seized Jesus and arrested
him. 47Then one of those standing near
drew his sword and struck the servant of
the high priest, cutting off his ear.
48"Am I leading a rebellion," said
Jesus, "that you have come out with
swords and clubs to capture me?
49Every day I was with you, teaching in
the temple courts, and you did not
arrest me. But the Scriptures must be
fulfilled." 50Then everyone deserted
him and fled.
51A young man, wearing nothing but
a linen garment, was following Jesus.
When they seized him, 52he fled naked,
leaving his garment behind.

Before the Sanhedrin

53They took Jesus to the high priest,
and all the chief priests, elders and
teachers of the law came together.
54Peter followed him at a distance, right
into the courtyard of the high priest.
There he sat with the guards and
warmed himself at the fire.
55The chief priests and the whole
Sanhedrin were looking for evidence
against Jesus so that they could put him
to death, but they did not find any.
56Many testified falsely against him, but
their statements did not agree.
57Then some stood up and gave this
false testimony against him: 58"We
heard him say, 'I will destroy this man-
made temple and in three days will build
another, not made by man.'" 59Yet
even then their testimony did not agree.
60Then the high priest stood up before them and asked Jesus, "Are you
not going to answer? What is this testimony that these men are bringing
against you?" 61But Jesus remained
silent and gave no answer.

Again the high priest asked him, "Are you the Christ, the Son of the Blessed One?"

62"I am," said Jesus. "And you will see the Son of Man sitting at the right hand of the Mighty One and coming on the clouds of heaven."

63The high priest tore his clothes. "Why do we need any more witnesses?" he asked. 64"You have heard the blasphemy. What do you think?"

They all condemned him as worthy of death. 65Then some began to spit at him; they blindfolded him, struck him with their fists, and said, "Prophesy!" And the guards took him and beat him.

Peter Disowns Jesus

66While Peter was below in the courtyard, one of the servant girls of the high priest came by. 67When she saw Peter warming himself, she looked closely at him.

"You also were with that Nazarene, Jesus," she said.

68But he denied it. "I don't know or understand what you're talking about," he said, and went out into the entrance.
69When the servant girl saw him there, she said again to those standing around, "This fellow is one of them."
70Again he denied it.

After a little while, those standing near said to Peter, "Surely you are one of them, for you are a Galilean."

71He began to call down curses on himself, and he swore to them, "I don't know this man you're talking about."

72Immediately the cock crowed the second time. Then Peter remembered the word Jesus had spoken to him: "Before the cock crows twice you will disown me three times." And he broke down and wept.

READING FROM PROVERBS
Proverbs 6:30–35

30Men do not despise a thief if he steals
to satisfy his hunger when he is starving.
31Yet if he is caught, he must pay sevenfold,
though it costs him all the wealth of his house.
32But a man who commits adultery lacks judgment;
whoever does so destroys himself.
33Blows and disgrace are his lot,
and his shame will never be wiped away;
34for jealousy arouses a husband's fury,
and he will show no mercy when he takes revenge.
35He will not accept any compensation;
he will refuse the bribe, however great it is.

DAY 69

MARCH 10

OLD TESTAMENT READING
Leviticus 21:1–22:33

Rules for Priests

21 The LORD said to Moses, "Speak to the priests, the sons of Aaron, and say to them: 'A priest must not make himself ceremonially unclean for any of his people who die, 2except
for a close relative, such as his mother or father, his son or daughter, his brother, 3or an unmarried sister who is dependent on him since she has no husband—for her he may make himself unclean. 4He must not make himself unclean for people related to him by marriage, and so defile himself.

5" 'Priests must not shave their heads or shave off the edges of their beards or

cut their bodies. 6They must be holy to
their God and must not profane the
name of their God. Because they present the offerings made to the LORD by
fire, the food of their God, they are to
be holy.
7" 'They must not marry women defiled by prostitution or divorced from
their husbands, because priests are holy
to their God. 8Regard them as holy,
because they offer up the food of your
God. Consider them holy, because I the
LORD am holy—I who make you holy.
9" 'If a priest's daughter defiles herself by becoming a prostitute, she disgraces her father; she must be burned in
the fire.
10" 'The high priest, the one among
his brothers who has had the anointing
oil poured on his head and who has been
ordained to wear the priestly garments,
must not let his hair become unkempt or
tear his clothes. 11He must not enter a
place where there is a dead body. He
must not make himself unclean, even
for his father or mother, 12nor leave the
sanctuary of his God or desecrate it,
because he has been dedicated by the
anointing oil of his God. I am the LORD.
13" 'The woman he marries must be a
virgin. 14He must not marry a widow, a
divorced woman, or a woman defiled by
prostitution, but only a virgin from his
own people, 15so that he will not defile
his offspring among his people. I am the
LORD, who makes him holy.' "
16The LORD said to Moses, 17"Say to
Aaron: 'For the generations to come
none of your descendants who has a
defect may come near to offer the food
of his God. 18No man who has any
defect may come near: no man who is
blind or lame, disfigured or deformed;
19no man with a crippled foot or hand,
20or who is hunchbacked or dwarfed, or
who has any eye defect, or who has
festering or running sores or damaged
testicles. 21No descendant of Aaron the
priest who has any defect is to come
near to present the offerings made to
the LORD by fire. He has a defect; he
must not come near to offer the food of
his God. 22He may eat the most holy
food of his God, as well as the holy
food; 23yet because of his defect, he
must not go near the curtain or
approach the altar, and so desecrate my
sanctuary. I am the LORD, who makes
them holy.' "
24So Moses told this to Aaron and his
sons and to all the Israelites.

22 The LORD said to Moses, 2"Tell
Aaron and his sons to treat with
respect the sacred offerings the
Israelites consecrate to me, so that they
will not profane my holy name. I am the
LORD.
3"Say to them: 'For the generations
to come, if any of your descendants is
ceremonially unclean and yet comes
near the sacred offerings that the
Israelites consecrate to the LORD, that
person must be cut off from my presence. I am the LORD.
4" 'If a descendant of Aaron has an
infectious skin disease or a bodily discharge, he may not eat the sacred offerings until he is cleansed. He will also be
unclean if he touches something defiled
by a corpse or by anyone who has an
emission of semen, 5or if he touches any
crawling thing that makes him unclean,
or any person who makes him unclean,
whatever the uncleanness may be. 6The
one who touches any such thing will be
unclean till evening. He must not eat
any of the sacred offerings unless he has
bathed himself with water. 7When the
sun goes down, he will be clean, and
after that he may eat the sacred offerings, for they are his food. 8He must not
eat anything found dead or torn by wild
animals, and so become unclean
through it. I am the LORD.
9" 'The priests are to keep my requirements so that they do not become
guilty and die for treating them with
contempt. I am the LORD, who makes
them holy.
10" 'No-one outside a priest's family
may eat the sacred offering, nor may the
guest of a priest or his hired worker eat
it. 11But if a priest buys a slave with

money, or if a slave is born in his household, that slave may eat his food. 12If a priest's daughter marries anyone other than a priest, she may not eat any of the sacred contributions. 13But if a priest's daughter becomes a widow or is divorced, yet has no children, and she returns to live in her father's house as in her youth, she may eat of her father's food. No unauthorised person, however, may eat any of it.

14" 'If anyone eats a sacred offering by mistake, he must make restitution to the priest for the offering and add a fifth of the value to it. 15The priests must not desecrate the sacred offerings the Israelites present to the LORD 16by allowing them to eat the sacred offerings and so bring upon them guilt requiring payment. I am the LORD, who makes them holy.' "

Unacceptable Sacrifices

17The LORD said to Moses, 18"Speak to Aaron and his sons and to all the Israelites and say to them: 'If any of you—either an Israelite or an alien living in Israel—presents a gift for a burnt offering to the LORD, either to fulfil a vow or as a freewill offering, 19you must present a male without defect from the cattle, sheep or goats in order that it may be accepted on your behalf. 20Do not bring anything with a defect, because it will not be accepted on your behalf. 21When anyone brings from the herd or flock a fellowship offering to the LORD to fulfil a special vow or as a freewill offering, it must be without defect or blemish to be acceptable. 22Do not offer to the LORD the blind, the injured or the maimed, or anything with warts or festering or running sores. Do not place any of these on the altar as an offering made to the LORD by fire. 23You may, however, present as a freewill offering an ox or a sheep that is deformed or stunted, but it will not be accepted in fulfilment of a vow. 24You must not offer to the LORD an animal whose testicles are bruised, crushed, torn or cut. You must not do this in your own land, 25and you must not accept such animals from the hand of a foreigner and offer them as the food of your God. They will not be accepted on your behalf, because they are deformed and have defects.' "

26The LORD said to Moses, 27"When a calf, a lamb or a goat is born, it is to remain with its mother for seven days. From the eighth day on, it will be acceptable as an offering made to the LORD by fire. 28Do not slaughter a cow or a sheep and its young on the same day.

29"When you sacrifice a thank-offering to the LORD, sacrifice it in such a way that it will be accepted on your behalf. 30It must be eaten that same day; leave none of it till morning. I am the LORD.

31"Keep my commands and follow them. I am the LORD. 32Do not profane my holy name. I must be acknowledged as holy by the Israelites. I am the LORD, who makes you holy 33and who brought you out of Egypt to be your God. I am the LORD."

NEW TESTAMENT READING
Mark 15:1–32

Jesus Before Pilate

15 Very early in the morning, the chief priests, with the elders, the teachers of the law and the whole Sanhedrin, reached a decision. They bound Jesus, led him away and turned him over to Pilate.

2"Are you the king of the Jews?" asked Pilate.

"Yes, it is as you say," Jesus replied.

3The chief priests accused him of many things. 4So again Pilate asked him, "Aren't you going to answer? See how many things they are accusing you of."

5But Jesus still made no reply, and Pilate was amazed.

6Now it was the custom at the Feast to

release a prisoner whom the people requested. 7A man called Barabbas was in
prison with the insurrectionists who had
committed murder in the uprising. 8The
crowd came up and asked Pilate to do
for them what he usually did.
9"Do you want me to release to you
the king of the Jews?" asked Pilate,
10knowing it was out of envy that the
chief priests had handed Jesus over to
him. 11But the chief priests stirred up
the crowd to have Pilate release Barabbas instead.
12"What shall I do, then, with the one
you call the king of the Jews?" Pilate
asked them.
13"Crucify him!" they shouted.
14"Why? What crime has he committed?" asked Pilate.
But they shouted all the louder,
"Crucify him!"
15Wanting to satisfy the crowd, Pilate
released Barabbas to them. He had
Jesus flogged, and handed him over to
be crucified.

The Soldiers Mock Jesus

16The soldiers led Jesus away into the
palace (that is, the Praetorium) and
called together the whole company of
soldiers. 17They put a purple robe on
him, then twisted together a crown of
thorns and set it on him. 18And they
began to call out to him, "Hail, king of
the Jews!" 19Again and again they
struck him on the head with a staff and
spat on him. Falling on their knees, they
paid homage to him. 20And when they
had mocked him, they took off the purple robe and put his own clothes on him.
Then they led him out to crucify him.

The Crucifixion

21A certain man from Cyrene, Simon,
the father of Alexander and Rufus, was
passing by on his way in from the country, and they forced him to carry the
cross. 22They brought Jesus to the place
called Golgotha (which means The
Place of the Skull). 23Then they offered
him wine mixed with myrrh, but he did
not take it. 24And they crucified him.
Dividing up his clothes, they cast lots to
see what each would get.
25It was the third hour when they
crucified him. 26The written notice of
the charge against him read: THE KING OF
THE JEWS. 27They crucified two robbers
with him, one on his right and one on his
left. 29Those who passed by hurled insults at him, shaking their heads and
saying, "So! You who are going to destroy the temple and build it in three
days, 30come down from the cross and
save yourself!"
31In the same way the chief priests
and the teachers of the law mocked him
among themselves. "He saved others,"
they said, "but he can't save himself!
32Let this Christ, this King of Israel,
come down now from the cross, that we
may see and believe." Those crucified
with him also heaped insults on him.

READING FROM PSALMS

Psalm 31:19–24

19How great is your goodness,
which you have stored up for those
who fear you,
which you bestow in the sight of men
on those who take refuge in you.
20In the shelter of your presence you
hide them
from the intrigues of men;
in your dwelling you keep them safe
from accusing tongues.

21Praise be to the LORD,
for he showed his wonderful love
to me
when I was in a besieged city.
22In my alarm I said,
"I am cut off from your sight!"
Yet you heard my cry for mercy
when I called to you for help.

23Love the LORD, all his saints!
The LORD preserves the faithful,
but the proud he pays back in full.
24Be strong and take heart,
all you who hope in the LORD.

DAY 70

MARCH 11

OLD TESTAMENT READING

Leviticus 23:1–24:23

23 The LORD said to Moses,
2"Speak to the Israelites and say
to them: 'These are my appointed
feasts, the appointed feasts of the
LORD, which you are to proclaim as
sacred assemblies.

The Sabbath

3" 'There are six days when you may
work, but the seventh day is a Sabbath
of rest, a day of sacred assembly. You
are not to do any work; wherever you
live, it is a Sabbath to the LORD.

The Passover and Unleavened Bread

4" 'These are the LORD's appointed
feasts, the sacred assemblies you are to
proclaim at their appointed times: 5The
LORD's Passover begins at twilight on
the fourteenth day of the first month.
6On the fifteenth day of that month the
LORD's Feast of Unleavened Bread begins; for seven days you must eat bread
made without yeast. 7On the first day
hold a sacred assembly and do no regular work. 8For seven days present an
offering made to the LORD by fire. And
on the seventh day hold a sacred assembly and do no regular work.' "

Firstfruits

9The LORD said to Moses, 10"Speak
to the Israelites and say to them: 'When
you enter the land I am going to give
you and you reap its harvest, bring to
the priest a sheaf of the first grain you
harvest. 11He is to wave the sheaf before
the LORD so that it will be accepted on
your behalf; the priest is to wave it on
the day after the Sabbath. 12On the day
you wave the sheaf, you must sacrifice
as a burnt offering to the LORD a lamb a
year old without defect, 13together with
its grain offering of two-tenths of an
ephah of fine flour mixed with oil—an
offering made to the LORD by fire, a
pleasing aroma—and its drink offering
of a quarter of a hin of wine. 14You must
not eat any bread, or roasted or new
grain, until the very day you bring this
offering to your God. This is to be a
lasting ordinance for the generations to
come, wherever you live.

Feast of Weeks

15" 'From the day after the Sabbath,
the day you brought the sheaf of the
wave offering, count off seven full
weeks. 16Count off fifty days up to the
day after the seventh Sabbath, and then
present an offering of new grain to the
LORD. 17From wherever you live, bring
two loaves made of two-tenths of an
ephah of fine flour, baked with yeast, as
a wave offering of firstfruits to the
LORD. 18Present with this bread seven
male lambs, each a year old and without
defect, one young bull and two rams.
They will be a burnt offering to the
LORD, together with their grain offerings and drink offerings—an offering
made by fire, an aroma pleasing to the
LORD. 19Then sacrifice one male goat
for a sin offering and two lambs, each a
year old, for a fellowship offering. 20The
priest is to wave the two lambs before
the LORD as a wave offering, together
with the bread of the firstfruits. They
are a sacred offering to the LORD for the
priest. 21On that same day you are to
proclaim a sacred assembly and do no
regular work. This is to be a lasting
ordinance for the generations to come,
wherever you live.

22" 'When you reap the harvest of
your land, do not reap to the very edges
of your field or gather the gleanings of
your harvest. Leave them for the poor

and the alien. I am the LORD your
God.' "

Feast of Trumpets

23The LORD said to Moses, 24"Say to
the Israelites: 'On the first day of the
seventh month you are to have a day of
rest, a sacred assembly commemorated
with trumpet blasts. 25Do no regular
work, but present an offering made to
the LORD by fire.' "

Day of Atonement

26The LORD said to Moses, 27"The
tenth day of this seventh month is the
Day of Atonement. Hold a sacred
assembly and deny yourselves, and present an offering made to the LORD by
fire. 28Do no work on that day, because
it is the Day of Atonement, when atonement is made for you before the LORD
your God. 29Anyone who does not deny
himself on that day must be cut off from
his people. 30I will destroy from among
his people anyone who does any work
on that day. 31You shall do no work at
all. This is to be a lasting ordinance for
the generations to come, wherever you
live. 32It is a sabbath of rest for you, and
you must deny yourselves. From the
evening of the ninth day of the month
until the following evening you are to
observe your sabbath."

Feast of Tabernacles

33The LORD said to Moses, 34"Say to
the Israelites: 'On the fifteenth day of
the seventh month the LORD's Feast of
Tabernacles begins, and it lasts for
seven days. 35The first day is a sacred
assembly; do no regular work. 36For
seven days present offerings made to
the LORD by fire, and on the eighth day
hold a sacred assembly and present an
offering made to the LORD by fire. It is
the closing assembly; do no regular
work.
37(" 'These are the LORD's appointed
feasts, which you are to proclaim as
sacred assemblies for bringing offerings
made to the LORD by fire—the burnt
offerings and grain offerings, sacrifices
and drink offerings required for each
day. 38These offerings are in addition to
those for the LORD's Sabbaths and in
addition to your gifts and whatever you
have vowed and all the freewill offerings you give to the LORD.)
39" 'So beginning with the fifteenth
day of the seventh month, after you
have gathered the crops of the land,
celebrate the festival to the LORD for
seven days; the first day is a day of rest,
and the eighth day also is a day of rest.
40On the first day you are to take choice
fruit from the trees, and palm fronds,
leafy branches and poplars, and rejoice
before the LORD your God for seven
days. 41Celebrate this as a festival to the
LORD for seven days each year. This is
to be a lasting ordinance for the generations to come; celebrate it in the seventh month. 42Live in booths for seven
days: All native-born Israelites are to
live in booths 43so that your descendants
will know that I made the Israelites live
in booths when I brought them out of
Egypt. I am the LORD your God.' "
44So Moses announced to the
Israelites the appointed feasts of the
LORD.

Oil and Bread Set Before the LORD

24 The LORD said to Moses,
2"Command the Israelites to
bring you clear oil of pressed olives for
the light so that the lamps may be kept
burning continually. 3Outside the curtain of the Testimony in the Tent of
Meeting, Aaron is to tend the lamps
before the LORD from evening till morning, continually. This is to be a lasting
ordinance for the generations to come.
4The lamps on the pure gold lampstand before the LORD must be tended
continually.
5"Take fine flour and bake twelve
loaves of bread, using two-tenths of an
ephah for each loaf. 6Set them in two
rows, six in each row, on the table of
pure gold before the LORD. 7Along each

row put some pure incense as a memorial portion to represent the bread and
to be an offering made to the LORD by
fire. 8This bread is to be set out before
the LORD regularly, Sabbath after Sabbath, on behalf of the Israelites, as a
lasting covenant. 9It belongs to Aaron
and his sons, who are to eat it in a holy
place, because it is a most holy part of
their regular share of the offerings made
to the LORD by fire."

A Blasphemer Stoned

10Now the son of an Israelite mother
and an Egyptian father went out among
the Israelites, and a fight broke out in
the camp between him and an Israelite.
11The son of the Israelite woman blasphemed the Name with a curse; so they
brought him to Moses. (His mother's
name was Shelomith, the daughter of
Dibri the Danite.) 12They put him in
custody until the will of the LORD
should be made clear to them.

13Then the LORD said to Moses:
14"Take the blasphemer outside the
camp. All those who heard him are to
lay their hands on his head, and the
entire assembly is to stone him. 15Say to
the Israelites: 'If anyone curses his God,
he will be held responsible; 16anyone
who blasphemes the name of the LORD
must be put to death. The entire assembly must stone him. Whether an alien or
native-born, when he blasphemes the
Name, he must be put to death.

17" 'If anyone takes the life of a human being, he must be put to death.
18Anyone who takes the life of someone's animal must make restitution—
life for life. 19If anyone injures his
neighbour, whatever he has done must
be done to him: 20fracture for fracture,
eye for eye, tooth for tooth. As he has
injured the other, so he is to be injured.
21Whoever kills an animal must make
restitution, but whoever kills a man
must be put to death. 22You are to have
the same law for the alien and the
native-born. I am the LORD your
God.' "

23Then Moses spoke to the Israelites,
and they took the blasphemer outside
the camp and stoned him. The Israelites
did as the LORD commanded Moses.

NEW TESTAMENT READING
Mark 15:33–47

The Death of Jesus

33At the sixth hour darkness came
over the whole land until the ninth
hour. 34And at the ninth hour Jesus
cried out in a loud voice, "*Eloi, Eloi,
lama sabachthani?*"—which means,
"My God, my God, why have you forsaken me?"

35When some of those standing near
heard this, they said, "Listen, he's calling Elijah."

36One man ran, filled a sponge with
wine vinegar, put it on a stick, and
offered it to Jesus to drink. "Now leave
him alone. Let's see if Elijah comes to
take him down," he said.

37With a loud cry, Jesus breathed his
last.

38The curtain of the temple was torn
in two from top to bottom. 39And when
the centurion, who stood there in front
of Jesus, heard his cry and saw how he
died, he said, "Surely this man was the
Son of God!"

40Some women were watching from a
distance. Among them were Mary Magdalene, Mary the mother of James the
younger and of Joses, and Salome. 41In
Galilee these women had followed him
and cared for his needs. Many other
women who had come up with him to
Jerusalem were also there.

The Burial of Jesus

42It was Preparation Day (that is, the
day before the Sabbath). So as evening
approached, 43Joseph of Arimathea, a
prominent member of the Council, who
was himself waiting for the kingdom of
God, went boldly to Pilate and asked
for Jesus' body. 44Pilate was surprised

to hear that he was already dead. Summoning the centurion, he asked him if Jesus had already died. [45]When he learned from the centurion that it was so, he gave the body to Joseph. [46]So Joseph bought some linen cloth, took down the body, wrapped it in the linen, and placed it in a tomb cut out of rock. Then he rolled a stone against the entrance of the tomb. [47]Mary Magdalene and Mary the mother of Joses saw where he was laid.

READING FROM PSALMS
Psalm 32:1–11

Of David. A *maskil.*

[1]Blessed is he
whose transgressions are forgiven,
whose sins are covered.
[2]Blessed is the man
whose sin the LORD does not count against him
and in whose spirit is no deceit.

[3]When I kept silent,
my bones wasted away
through my groaning all day long.
[4]For day and night
your hand was heavy upon me;
my strength was sapped
as in the heat of summer. *Selah*
[5]Then I acknowledged my sin to you
and did not cover up my iniquity.
I said, "I will confess
my transgressions to the LORD"—
and you forgave
the guilt of my sin. *Selah*

[6]Therefore let everyone who is godly pray to you
while you may be found;
surely when the mighty waters rise,
they will not reach him.
[7]You are my hiding-place;
you will protect me from trouble
and surround me with songs of deliverance. *Selah*

[8]I will instruct you and teach you in the way you should go;
I will counsel you and watch over you.
[9]Do not be like the horse or the mule,
which have no understanding
but must be controlled by bit and bridle
or they will not come to you.
[10]Many are the woes of the wicked,
but the LORD's unfailing love
surrounds the man who trusts in him.

[11]Rejoice in the LORD and be glad, you righteous;
sing, all you who are upright in heart!

MARCH 12

DAY 71

OLD TESTAMENT READING
Leviticus 25:1–26:13

The Sabbath Year

25 The LORD said to Moses on Mount Sinai, [2]"Speak to the Israelites and say to them: 'When you enter the land I am going to give you, the land itself must observe a sabbath to the LORD. [3]For six years sow your fields, and for six years prune your vineyards and gather their crops. [4]But in the seventh year the land is to have a sabbath of rest, a sabbath to the LORD. Do not sow your fields or prune your vineyards. [5]Do not reap what grows of itself or harvest the grapes of your untended vines. The land is to have a year of rest. [6]Whatever the land yields

during the sabbath year will be food for
you—for yourself, your manservant
and maidservant, and the hired worker
and temporary resident who live among
you, 7as well as for your livestock and
the wild animals in your land. Whatever
the land produces may be eaten.

The Year of Jubilee

8" 'Count off seven sabbaths of years
—seven times seven years—so that the
seven sabbaths of years amount to a
period of forty-nine years. 9Then have
the trumpet sounded everywhere on the
tenth day of the seventh month; on the
Day of Atonement sound the trumpet
throughout your land. 10Consecrate the
fiftieth year and proclaim liberty
throughout the land to all its inhabitants. It shall be a jubilee for you; each
one of you is to return to his family
property and each to his own clan.
11The fiftieth year shall be a jubilee for
you; do not sow and do not reap what
grows of itself or harvest the untended
vines. 12For it is a jubilee and is to be
holy for you; eat only what is taken
directly from the fields.

13" 'In this Year of Jubilee everyone
is to return to his own property.

14" 'If you sell land to one of your
countrymen or buy any from him, do
not take advantage of each other. 15You
are to buy from your countryman on the
basis of the number of years since the
Jubilee. And he is to sell to you on
the basis of the number of years left for
harvesting crops. 16When the years are
many, you are to increase the price, and
when the years are few, you are to
decrease the price, because what he is
really selling you is the number of crops.
17Do not take advantage of each other,
but fear your God. I am the LORD your
God.

18" 'Follow my decrees and be careful
to obey my laws, and you will live safely
in the land. 19Then the land will yield its
fruit, and you will eat your fill and live
there in safety. 20You may ask, "What
will we eat in the seventh year if we do
not plant or harvest our crops?" 21I will
send you such a blessing in the sixth year
that the land will yield enough for three
years. 22While you plant during the
eighth year, you will eat from the old
crop and will continue to eat from it
until the harvest of the ninth year comes
in.

23" 'The land must not be sold per-
manently, because the land is mine and
you are but aliens and my tenants.
24Throughout the country that you hold
as a possession, you must provide for
the redemption of the land.

25" 'If one of your countrymen becomes poor and sells some of his property, his nearest relative is to come and
redeem what his countryman has sold.
26If, however, a man has no-one to redeem it for him but he himself prospers
and acquires sufficient means to redeem
it, 27he is to determine the value for the
years since he sold it and refund the
balance to the man to whom he sold it;
he can then go back to his own property.
28But if he does not acquire the means
to repay him, what he sold will remain
in the possession of the buyer until the
Year of Jubilee. It will be returned in
the Jubilee, and he can then go back to
his property.

29" 'If a man sells a house in a walled
city, he retains the right of redemption a
full year after its sale. During that time
he may redeem it. 30If it is not redeemed
before a full year has passed, the house
in the walled city shall belong per-
manently to the buyer and his descendants. It is not to be returned in the
Jubilee. 31But houses in villages without
walls round them are to be considered
as open country. They can be redeemed, and they are to be returned in
the Jubilee.

32" 'The Levites always have the right
to redeem their houses in the Levitical
towns, which they possess. 33So the
property of the Levites is redeemable
—that is, a house sold in any town they
hold—and is to be returned in the
Jubilee, because the houses in the towns
of the Levites are their property among

the Israelites. 34But the pasture-land
belonging to their towns must not be
sold; it is their permanent possession.
35“ ‘If one of your countrymen becomes poor and is unable to support
himself among you, help him as you
would an alien or a temporary resident,
so that he can continue to live among
you. 36Do not take interest of any kind
from him, but fear your God, so that
your countryman may continue to live
among you. 37You must not lend him
money at interest or sell him food at a
profit. 38I am the LORD your God, who
brought you out of Egypt to give you the
land of Canaan and to be your God.
39“ ‘If one of your countrymen becomes poor among you and sells himself
to you, do not make him work as a
slave. 40He is to be treated as a hired
worker or a temporary resident among
you; he is to work for you until the Year
of Jubilee. 41Then he and his children
are to be released, and he will go back to
his own clan and to the property of his
forefathers. 42Because the Israelites are
my servants, whom I brought out of
Egypt, they must not be sold as slaves.
43Do not rule over them ruthlessly, but
fear your God.
44“ ‘Your male and female slaves are
to come from the nations around you;
from them you may buy slaves. 45You
may also buy some of the temporary
residents living among you and members of their clans born in your country,
and they will become your property.
46You can will them to your children as
inherited property and can make them
slaves for life, but you must not rule
over your fellow Israelites ruthlessly.
47“ ‘If an alien or a temporary resident among you becomes rich and one
of your countrymen becomes poor and
sells himself to the alien living among
you or to a member of the alien’s clan,
48he retains the right of redemption
after he has sold himself. One of his
relatives may redeem him: 49An uncle
or a cousin or any blood-relative in his
clan may redeem him. Or if he prospers,
he may redeem himself. 50He and his
buyer are to count the time from the
year he sold himself up to the Year of
Jubilee. The price for his release is to be
based on the rate paid to a hired man for
that number of years. 51If many years
remain, he must pay for his redemption
a larger share of the price paid for him.
52If only a few years remain until the
Year of Jubilee, he is to compute that
and pay for his redemption accordingly.
53He is to be treated as a man hired from
year to year; you must see to it that his
owner does not rule over him ruthlessly.
54“ ‘Even if he is not redeemed in any
of these ways, he and his children are to
be released in the Year of Jubilee, 55for
the Israelites belong to me as servants.
They are my servants, whom I brought
out of Egypt. I am the LORD your God.

Reward for Obedience

26 “ ‘Do not make idols or set up an
image or a sacred stone for
yourselves, and do not place a carved
stone in your land to bow down before
it. I am the LORD your God.
2“ ‘Observe my Sabbaths and have
reverence for my sanctuary. I am the
LORD.
3“ ‘If you follow my decrees and are
careful to obey my commands, 4I will
send you rain in its season, and the
ground will yield its crops and the trees
of the field their fruit. 5Your threshing
will continue until grape harvest and the
grape harvest will continue until planting, and you will eat all the food you
want and live in safety in your land.
6“ ‘I will grant peace in the land, and
you will lie down and no-one will make
you afraid. I will remove savage beasts
from the land, and the sword will not
pass through your country. 7You will
pursue your enemies, and they will fall
by the sword before you. 8Five of you
will chase a hundred, and a hundred of
you will chase ten thousand, and your
enemies will fall by the sword before
you.
9“ ‘I will look on you with favour and

make you fruitful and increase your
numbers, and I will keep my covenant
with you. 10You will still be eating last
year's harvest when you will have to
move it out to make room for the new.
11I will put my dwelling-place among
you, and I will not abhor you. 12I will
walk among you and be your God, and
you will be my people. 13I am the LORD
your God, who brought you out of
Egypt so that you would no longer be
slaves to the Egyptians; I broke the bars
of your yoke and enabled you to walk
with heads held high.

NEW TESTAMENT READING
Mark 16:1–20

The Resurrection

16 When the Sabbath was over,
Mary Magdalene, Mary the
mother of James, and Salome bought
spices so that they might go to anoint
Jesus' body. 2Very early on the first day
of the week, just after sunrise, they
were on their way to the tomb 3and they
asked each other, "Who will roll the
stone away from the entrance of the
tomb?"

4But when they looked up, they saw
that the stone, which was very large,
had been rolled away. 5As they entered
the tomb, they saw a young man dressed
in a white robe sitting on the right side,
and they were alarmed.

6"Don't be alarmed," he said. "You
are looking for Jesus the Nazarene, who
was crucified. He has risen! He is not
here. See the place where they laid him.
7But go, tell his disciples and Peter, 'He
is going ahead of you into Galilee.
There you will see him, just as he told
you.'"

8Trembling and bewildered, the
women went out and fled from the
tomb. They said nothing to anyone,
because they were afraid.

[The most reliable early manuscripts and other ancient witnesses do not have Mark 16:9–20.]

9When Jesus rose early on the first
day of the week, he appeared first to
Mary Magdalene, out of whom he had
driven seven demons. 10She went and
told those who had been with him and
who were mourning and weeping.
11When they heard that Jesus was alive
and that she had seen him, they did not
believe it.

12Afterwards Jesus appeared in a
different form to two of them while they
were walking in the country. 13These
returned and reported it to the rest; but
they did not believe them either.

14Later Jesus appeared to the Eleven
as they were eating; he rebuked them
for their lack of faith and their stubborn
refusal to believe those who had seen
him after he had risen.

15He said to them, "Go into all the
world and preach the good news to all
creation. 16Whoever believes and is
baptised will be saved, but whoever
does not believe will be condemned.
17And these signs will accompany those
who believe: In my name they will drive
out demons; they will speak in new
tongues; 18they will pick up snakes with
their hands; and when they drink deadly
poison, it will not hurt them at all; they
will place their hands on sick people,
and they will get well."

19After the Lord Jesus had spoken to
them, he was taken up into heaven and
he sat at the right hand of God. 20Then
the disciples went out and preached
everywhere, and the Lord worked with
them and confirmed his word by the
signs that accompanied it.

READING FROM PSALMS
Psalm 33:1–11

1Sing joyfully to the LORD, you
    righteous;
  it is fitting for the upright to praise
    him.
2Praise the LORD with the harp;

make music to him on the
ten-stringed lyre.
3Sing to him a new song;
play skilfully, and shout for joy.
4For the word of the LORD is right and
true;
he is faithful in all he does.
5The LORD loves righteousness and
justice;
the earth is full of his unfailing
love.
6By the word of the LORD were the
heavens made,
their starry host by the breath of
his mouth.
7He gathers the waters of the sea into
jars;
he puts the deep into storehouses.
8Let all the earth fear the LORD;
let all the people of the world
revere him.
9For he spoke, and it came to be;
he commanded, and it stood firm.
10The LORD foils the plans of the
nations;
he thwarts the purposes of the
peoples.
11But the plans of the LORD stand firm
for ever,
the purposes of his heart through
all generations.

MARCH 13

DAY 72

OLD TESTAMENT READING
Leviticus 26:14–27:34

Punishment for Disobedience

14" 'But if you will not listen to me and
carry out all these commands, 15and if
you reject my decrees and abhor my
laws and fail to carry out all my commands and so violate my covenant,
16then I will do this to you: I will bring
upon you sudden terror, wasting diseases and fever that will destroy your
sight and drain away your life. You will
plant seed in vain, because your enemies will eat it. 17I will set my face
against you so that you will be defeated
by your enemies; those who hate you
will rule over you, and you will flee even
when no-one is pursuing you.

18" 'If after all this you will not listen
to me, I will punish you for your sins
seven times over. 19I will break down
your stubborn pride and make the sky
above you like iron and the ground
beneath you like bronze. 20Your
strength will be spent in vain, because
your soil will not yield its crops, nor will
the trees of the land yield their fruit.

21" 'If you remain hostile towards me
and refuse to listen to me, I will multiply
your afflictions seven times over, as
your sins deserve. 22I will send wild
animals against you, and they will rob
you of your children, destroy your cattle
and make you so few in number that
your roads will be deserted.

23" 'If in spite of these things you do
not accept my correction but continue
to be hostile towards me, 24I myself will
be hostile towards you and will afflict
you for your sins seven times over.
25And I will bring the sword upon you to
avenge the breaking of the covenant.
When you withdraw into your cities, I
will send a plague among you, and you
will be given into enemy hands. 26When
I cut off your supply of bread, ten
women will be able to bake your bread
in one oven, and they will dole out the
bread by weight. You will eat, but you
will not be satisfied.

27" 'If in spite of this you still do not
listen to me but continue to be hostile
towards me, 28then in my anger I will be
hostile towards you, and I myself will
punish you for your sins seven times

over. 29You will eat the flesh of your
sons and the flesh of your daughters. 30I
will destroy your high places, cut down
your incense altars and pile your dead
bodies on the lifeless forms of your
idols, and I will abhor you. 31I will turn
your cities into ruins and lay waste your
sanctuaries, and I will take no delight in
the pleasing aroma of your offerings. 32I
will lay waste the land, so that your
enemies who live there will be appalled.
33I will scatter you among the nations
and will draw out my sword and pursue
you. Your land will be laid waste, and
your cities will lie in ruins. 34Then the
land will enjoy its sabbath years all the
time that it lies desolate and you are in
the country of your enemies; then the
land will rest and enjoy its sabbaths.
35All the time that it lies desolate, the
land will have the rest it did not have
during the sabbaths you lived in it.

36" 'As for those of you who are left, I
will make their hearts so fearful in the
lands of their enemies that the sound of
a wind-blown leaf will put them to
flight. They will run as though fleeing
from the sword, and they will fall, even
though no-one is pursuing them. 37They
will stumble over one another as though
fleeing from the sword, even though
no-one is pursuing them. So you will not
be able to stand before your enemies.
38You will perish among the nations;
the land of your enemies will devour
you. 39Those of you who are left will
waste away in the lands of their enemies
because of their sins; also because of
their fathers' sins they will waste away.

40" 'But if they will confess their sins
and the sins of their fathers—their
treachery against me and their hostility
towards me, 41which made me hostile
towards them so that I sent them into
the land of their enemies—then when
their uncircumcised hearts are humbled
and they pay for their sin, 42I will remember my covenant with Jacob and
my covenant with Isaac and my covenant with Abraham, and I will remember the land. 43For the land will be
deserted by them and will enjoy its
sabbaths while it lies desolate without
them. They will pay for their sins because they rejected my laws and abhorred my decrees. 44Yet in spite of this,
when they are in the land of their enemies, I will not reject them or abhor
them so as to destroy them completely,
breaking my covenant with them. I am
the LORD their God. 45But for their sake
I will remember the covenant with their
ancestors whom I brought out of Egypt
in the sight of the nations to be their
God. I am the LORD.' "

46These are the decrees, the laws and
the regulations that the LORD established on Mount Sinai between himself
and the Israelites through Moses.

Redeeming What Is the LORD's

27 The LORD said to Moses,
2"Speak to the Israelites and say
to them: 'If anyone makes a special vow
to dedicate persons to the LORD by giving equivalent values, 3set the value of a
male between the ages of twenty and
sixty at fifty shekels of silver, according
to the sanctuary shekel; 4and if it is a
female, set her value at thirty shekels.
5If it is a person between the ages of five
and twenty, set the value of a male at
twenty shekels and of a female at ten
shekels. 6If it is a person between one
month and five years, set the value of a
male at five shekels of silver and that of
a female at three shekels of silver. 7If it
is a person sixty years old or more, set
the value of a male at fifteen shekels and
of a female at ten shekels. 8If anyone
making the vow is too poor to pay the
specified amount, he is to present the
person to the priest, who will set
the value for him according to what the
man making the vow can afford.

9" 'If what he vowed is an animal that
is acceptable as an offering to the LORD,
such an animal given to the LORD becomes holy. 10He must not exchange it
or substitute a good one for a bad one,
or a bad one for a good one; if he should
substitute one animal for another, both
it and the substitute become holy. 11If

what he vowed is a ceremonially unclean animal—one that is not acceptable as an offering to the LORD—the animal must be presented to the priest, 12who will judge its quality as good or bad. Whatever value the priest then sets, that is what it will be. 13If the owner wishes to redeem the animal, he must add a fifth to its value.

14“ ‘If a man dedicates his house as something holy to the LORD, the priest will judge its quality as good or bad. Whatever value the priest then sets, so it will remain. 15If the man who dedicates his house redeems it, he must add a fifth to its value, and the house will again become his.

16“ ‘If a man dedicates to the LORD part of his family land, its value is to be set according to the amount of seed required for it—fifty shekels of silver to a homer of barley seed. 17If he dedicates his field during the Year of Jubilee, the value that has been set remains. 18But if he dedicates his field after the Jubilee, the priest will determine the value according to the number of years that remain until the next Year of Jubilee, and its set value will be reduced. 19If the man who dedicates the field wishes to redeem it, he must add a fifth to its value, and the field will again become his. 20If, however, he does not redeem the field, or if he has sold it to someone else, it can never be redeemed. 21When the field is released in the Jubilee, it will become holy, like a field devoted to the LORD; it will become the property of the priests.

22“ ‘If a man dedicates to the LORD a field he has bought, which is not part of his family land, 23the priest will determine its value up to the Year of Jubilee, and the man must pay its value on that day as something holy to the LORD. 24In the Year of Jubilee the field will revert to the person from whom he bought it, the one whose land it was. 25Every value is to be set according to the sanctuary shekel, twenty gerahs to the shekel.

26“ ‘No-one, however, may dedicate the firstborn of an animal, since the firstborn already belongs to the LORD; whether an ox or a sheep, it is the LORD’s. 27If it is one of the unclean animals, he may buy it back at its set value, adding a fifth of the value to it. If he does not redeem it, it is to be sold at its set value.

28“ ‘But nothing that a man owns and devotes to the LORD—whether man or animal or family land—may be sold or redeemed; everything so devoted is most holy to the LORD.

29“ ‘No person devoted to destruction may be ransomed; he must be put to death.

30“ ‘A tithe of everything from the land, whether grain from the soil or fruit from the trees, belongs to the LORD; it is holy to the LORD. 31If a man redeems any of his tithe, he must add a fifth of the value to it. 32The entire tithe of the herd and flock—every tenth animal that passes under the shepherd’s rod—will be holy to the LORD. 33He must not pick out the good from the bad or make any substitution. If he does make a substitution, both the animal and its substitute become holy and cannot be redeemed.’ ”

34These are the commands the LORD gave Moses on Mount Sinai for the Israelites.

NEW TESTAMENT READING
Luke 1:1–25

Introduction

1 Many have undertaken to draw up an account of the things that have been fulfilled among us, 2just as they were handed down to us by those who from the first were eye-witnesses and servants of the word. 3Therefore, since I myself have carefully investigated everything from the beginning, it seemed good also to me to write an orderly account for you, most excellent Theophilus, 4so that you may know the certainty of the things you have been taught.

The Birth of John the Baptist Foretold

5 In the time of Herod king of Judea
there was a priest named Zechariah,
who belonged to the priestly division of
Abijah; his wife Elizabeth was also a
descendant of Aaron. 6 Both of them
were upright in the sight of God,
observing all the Lord's commandments and regulations blamelessly.
7 But they had no children, because
Elizabeth was barren; and they were
both well on in years.

8 Once when Zechariah's division was
on duty and he was serving as priest
before God, 9 he was chosen by lot,
according to the custom of the priesthood, to go into the temple of the Lord
and burn incense. 10 And when the time
for the burning of incense came, all the
assembled worshippers were praying
outside.

11 Then an angel of the Lord appeared
to him, standing at the right side of the
altar of incense. 12 When Zechariah saw
him, he was startled and was gripped
with fear. 13 But the angel said to him:
"Do not be afraid, Zechariah; your
prayer has been heard. Your wife
Elizabeth will bear you a son, and you
are to give him the name John. 14 He will
be a joy and delight to you, and many
will rejoice because of his birth, 15 for he
will be great in the sight of the Lord. He
is never to take wine or other fermented
drink, and he will be filled with the Holy
Spirit even from birth. 16 Many of the
people of Israel will he bring back to the
Lord their God. 17 And he will go on
before the Lord, in the spirit and
power of Elijah, to turn the hearts of
the fathers to their children and the
disobedient to the wisdom of the
righteous—to make ready a people
prepared for the Lord."

18 Zechariah asked the angel, "How
can I be sure of this? I am an old man
and my wife is well on in years."

19 The angel answered, "I am Gabriel.
I stand in the presence of God, and I
have been sent to speak to you and to
tell you this good news. 20 And now you
will be silent and not able to speak until
the day this happens, because you did
not believe my words, which will come
true at their proper time."

21 Meanwhile, the people were waiting for Zechariah and wondering why
he stayed so long in the temple. 22 When
he came out, he could not speak to
them. They realised he had seen a vision
in the temple, for he kept making signs
to them but remained unable to speak.

23 When his time of service was completed, he returned home. 24 After this
his wife Elizabeth became pregnant and
for five months remained in seclusion.
25 "The Lord has done this for me," she
said. "In these days he has shown his
favour and taken away my disgrace
among the people."

READING FROM PROVERBS

Proverbs 7:1–5

Warning Against the Adulteress

7 My son, keep my words
  and store up my commands
    within you.
2 Keep my commands and you will
    live;
  guard my teachings as the apple of
    your eye.
3 Bind them on your fingers;
  write them on the tablet of your
    heart.
4 Say to wisdom, "You are my sister,"
  and call understanding your
    kinsman;
5 they will keep you from the
    adulteress,
  from the wayward wife with her
    seductive words.

OLD TESTAMENT READING
Numbers 1:1–2:9

The Census

1 The LORD spoke to Moses in the Tent of Meeting in the Desert of Sinai on the first day of the second month of the second year after the Israelites came out of Egypt. He said:
2"Take a census of the whole Israelite community by their clans and families, listing every man by name, one by one.
3You and Aaron are to number by their divisions all the men in Israel twenty years old or more who are able to serve in the army.
4One man from each tribe, each the head of his family, is to help you.
5These are the names of the men who are to assist you:

from Reuben, Elizur son of Shedeur;
6from Simeon, Shelumiel son of Zurishaddai;
7from Judah, Nahshon son of Amminadab;
8from Issachar, Nethanel son of Zuar;
9from Zebulun, Eliab son of Helon;
10from the sons of Joseph:
from Ephraim, Elishama son of Ammihud;
from Manasseh, Gamaliel son of Pedahzur;
11from Benjamin, Abidan son of Gideoni;
12from Dan, Ahiezer son of Ammishaddai;
13from Asher, Pagiel son of Ocran;
14from Gad, Eliasaph son of Deuel;
15from Naphtali, Ahira son of Enan."

16These were the men appointed from the community, the leaders of their ancestral tribes. They were the heads of the clans of Israel.

17Moses and Aaron took these men
whose names had been given, 18and
they called the whole community together on the first day of the second month. The people indicated their ancestry by their clans and families, and the men twenty years old or more were
listed by name, one by one, 19as the
LORD commanded Moses. And so he counted them in the Desert of Sinai:

20From the descendants of Reuben the firstborn son of Israel:
All the men twenty years old or more who were able to serve in the army were listed by name, one by one, according to the records of their clans and families.
21The number from the tribe of Reuben was 46,500.

22From the descendants of Simeon:
All the men twenty years old or more who were able to serve in the army were counted and listed by name, one by one, according to the records of their clans and
families. 23The number from the tribe of Simeon was 59,300.

24From the descendants of Gad:
All the men twenty years old or more who were able to serve in the army were listed by name, according to the records of their
clans and families. 25The number from the tribe of Gad was 45,650.

26From the descendants of Judah:
All the men twenty years old or more who were able to serve in the army were listed by name, according to the records of their
clans and families. 27The number from the tribe of Judah was 74,600.

28From the descendants of Issachar:
All the men twenty years old or
more who were able to serve in
the army were listed by name,
according to the records of their
clans and families. 29The number
from the tribe of Issachar was
54,400.

30From the descendants of Zebulun:
All the men twenty years old or
more who were able to serve in
the army were listed by name,
according to the records of their
clans and families. 31The number
from the tribe of Zebulun was
57,400.

32From the sons of Joseph:
From the descendants of Ephraim:
All the men twenty years old or
more who were able to serve in
the army were listed by name,
according to the records of their
clans and families. 33The number
from the tribe of Ephraim was
40,500.

34From the descendants of Manasseh:
All the men twenty years old or
more who were able to serve in
the army were listed by name,
according to the records of their
clans and families. 35The number
from the tribe of Manasseh was
32,200.

36From the descendants of Benjamin:
All the men twenty years old or
more who were able to serve in
the army were listed by name,
according to the records of their
clans and families. 37The number
from the tribe of Benjamin was
35,400.

38From the descendants of Dan:
All the men twenty years old or
more who were able to serve in
the army were listed by name,
according to the records of their
clans and families. 39The number
from the tribe of Dan was
62,700.

40From the descendants of Asher:
All the men twenty years old or
more who were able to serve in
the army were listed by name,
according to the records of their
clans and families. 41The number
from the tribe of Asher was
41,500.

42From the descendants of Naphtali:
All the men twenty years old or
more who were able to serve in
the army were listed by name,
according to the records of their
clans and families. 43The number
from the tribe of Naphtali was
53,400.

44These were the men counted by
Moses and Aaron and the twelve leaders of Israel, each one representing his
family. 45All the Israelites twenty years
old or more who were able to serve in
Israel's army were counted according to
their families. 46The total number was
603,550.

47The families of the tribe of Levi,
however, were not counted along with
the others. 48The LORD had said to
Moses: 49"You must not count the tribe
of Levi or include them in the census of
the other Israelites. 50Instead, appoint
the Levites to be in charge of the
tabernacle of the Testimony—over all
its furnishings and everything belonging
to it. They are to carry the tabernacle
and all its furnishings; they are to take
care of it and encamp round it.
51Whenever the tabernacle is to move,
the Levites are to take it down, and
whenever the tabernacle is to be set up,
the Levites shall do it. Anyone else who
goes near it shall be put to death. 52The
Israelites are to set up their tents by
divisions, each man in his own camp
under his own standard. 53The Levites,
however, are to set up their tents round
the tabernacle of the Testimony so that

wrath will not fall on the Israelite community. The Levites are to be responsible for the care of the tabernacle of the
Testimony."
54The Israelites did all this just as the
LORD commanded Moses.

The Arrangement of the Tribal Camps

2 The LORD said to Moses and
Aaron: 2"The Israelites are to
camp round the Tent of Meeting some
distance from it, each man under his
standard with the banners of his
family."

3On the east, towards the sunrise, the divisions of the camp of
Judah are to encamp under their
standard. The leader of the people
of Judah is Nahshon son of Amminadab. 4His division numbers
74,600.
5The tribe of Issachar will camp
next to them. The leader of the
people of Issachar is Nethanel son
of Zuar. 6His division numbers
54,400.
7The tribe of Zebulun will be
next. The leader of the people of
Zebulun is Eliab son of Helon.
8His division numbers 57,400.
9All the men assigned to the
camp of Judah, according to their
divisions, number 186,400. They
will set out first.

NEW TESTAMENT READING
Luke 1:26–38

The Birth of Jesus Foretold

26In the sixth month, God sent the
angel Gabriel to Nazareth, a town in
Galilee, 27to a virgin pledged to be married to a man named Joseph, a descendant of David. The virgin's name was
Mary. 28The angel went to her and said,
"Greetings, you who are highly
favoured! The Lord is with you."
29Mary was greatly troubled at his
words and wondered what kind of
greeting this might be. 30But the angel
said to her, "Do not be afraid, Mary,
you have found favour with God. 31You
will be with child and give birth to a son,
and you are to give him the name Jesus.
32He will be great and will be called the
Son of the Most High. The Lord God
will give him the throne of his father
David, 33and he will reign over the
house of Jacob for ever; his kingdom
will never end."
34"How will this be," Mary asked the
angel, "since I am a virgin?"
35The angel answered, "The Holy
Spirit will come upon you, and the
power of the Most High will over-
shadow you. So the holy one to be born
will be called the Son of God. 36Even
Elizabeth your relative is going to have
a child in her old age, and she who was
said to be barren is in her sixth month.
37For nothing is impossible with God."
38"I am the Lord's servant," Mary
answered. "May it be to me as you have
said." Then the angel left her.

READING FROM PSALMS
Psalm 33:12–22

12Blessed is the nation whose God is
the LORD,
the people he chose for his
inheritance.
13From heaven the LORD looks down
and sees all mankind;
14from his dwelling-place he watches
all who live on earth—
15he who forms the hearts of all,
who considers everything they do.
16No king is saved by the size of his
army;
no warrior escapes by his great
strength.
17A horse is a vain hope for
deliverance;
despite all its great strength it
cannot save.
18But the eyes of the LORD are on those
who fear him,

on those whose hope is in his
unfailing love,
19to deliver them from death
and keep them alive in famine.

20We wait in hope for the LORD;
he is our help and our shield.
21In him our hearts rejoice,
for we trust in his holy name.
22May your unfailing love rest upon us,
O LORD,
even as we put our hope in you.

DAY 74

MARCH 15

OLD TESTAMENT READING

Numbers 2:10–3:51

10On the south will be the divisions of the camp of Reuben under their standard. The leader of the people of Reuben is Elizur son of Shedeur. 11His division numbers 46,500.
12The tribe of Simeon will camp next to them. The leader of the people of Simeon is Shelumiel son of Zurishaddai. 13His division numbers 59,300.
14The tribe of Gad will be next. The leader of the people of Gad is Eliasaph son of Deuel. 15His division numbers 45,650.
16All the men assigned to the camp of Reuben, according to their divisions, number 151,450. They will set out second.

17Then the Tent of Meeting and the camp of the Levites will set out in the middle of the camps. They will set out in the same order as they encamp, each in his own place under his standard.

18On the west will be the divisions of the camp of Ephraim under their standard. The leader of the people of Ephraim is Elishama son of Ammihud. 19His division numbers 40,500.
20The tribe of Manasseh will be next to them. The leader of the people of Manasseh is Gamaliel son of Pedahzur. 21His division numbers 32,200.
22The tribe of Benjamin will be next. The leader of the people of Benjamin is Abidan son of Gideoni. 23His division numbers 35,400.
24All the men assigned to the camp of Ephraim, according to their divisions, number 108,100. They will set out third.

25On the north will be the divisions of the camp of Dan, under their standard. The leader of the people of Dan is Ahiezer son of Ammishaddai. 26His division numbers 62,700.
27The tribe of Asher will camp next to them. The leader of the people of Asher is Pagiel son of Ocran. 28His division numbers 41,500.
29The tribe of Naphtali will be next. The leader of the people of Naphtali is Ahira son of Enan. 30His division numbers 53,400.
31All the men assigned to the camp of Dan number 157,600. They will set out last, under their standards.

32These are the Israelites, counted according to their families. All those in the camps, by their divisions, number 603,550. 33The Levites, however, were not counted along with the other Israelites, as the LORD commanded Moses.

34So the Israelites did everything the LORD commanded Moses; that is the way they encamped under their standards, and that is the way they set out, each with his clan and family.

The Levites

3 This is the account of the family of Aaron and Moses at the time the LORD talked with Moses on Mount Sinai.

2The names of the sons of Aaron were Nadab the firstborn and Abihu, Eleazar and Ithamar. 3Those were the names of Aaron's sons, the anointed priests, who were ordained to serve as priests. 4Nadab and Abihu, however, fell dead before the LORD when they made an offering with unauthorised fire before him in the Desert of Sinai. They had no sons; so only Eleazar and Ithamar served as priests during the lifetime of their father Aaron.

5The LORD said to Moses, 6"Bring the tribe of Levi and present them to Aaron the priest to assist him. 7They are to perform duties for him and for the whole community at the Tent of Meeting by doing the work of the tabernacle. 8They are to take care of all the furnishings of the Tent of Meeting, fulfilling the obligations of the Israelites by doing the work of the tabernacle. 9Give the Levites to Aaron and his sons; they are the Israelites who are to be given wholly to him. 10Appoint Aaron and his sons to serve as priests; anyone else who approaches the sanctuary must be put to death."

11The LORD also said to Moses, 12"I have taken the Levites from among the Israelites in place of the first male offspring of every Israelite woman. The Levites are mine, 13for all the firstborn are mine. When I struck down all the firstborn in Egypt, I set apart for myself every firstborn in Israel, whether man or animal. They are to be mine. I am the LORD."

14The LORD said to Moses in the Desert of Sinai, 15"Count the Levites by their families and clans. Count every male a month old or more." 16So Moses counted them, as he was commanded by the word of the LORD.

17These were the names of the sons of Levi:
Gershon, Kohath and Merari.

18These were the names of the Gershonite clans:
Libni and Shimei.

19The Kohathite clans:
Amram, Izhar, Hebron and Uzziel.

20The Merarite clans:
Mahli and Mushi.

These were the Levite clans, according to their families.

21To Gershon belonged the clans of the Libnites and Shimeites; these were the Gershonite clans. 22The number of all the males a month old or more who were counted was 7,500. 23The Gershonite clans were to camp on the west, behind the tabernacle. 24The leader of the families of the Gershonites was Eliasaph son of Lael. 25At the Tent of Meeting the Gershonites were responsible for the care of the tabernacle and tent, its coverings, the curtain at the entrance to the Tent of Meeting, 26the curtains of the courtyard, the curtain at the entrance to the courtyard surrounding the tabernacle and altar, and the ropes—and everything related to their use.

27To Kohath belonged the clans of the Amramites, Izharites, Hebronites and Uzzielites; these were the Kohathite clans. 28The number of all the males a month old or more was 8,600. The Kohathites were responsible for the care of the sanctuary. 29The

Kohathite clans were to camp on the south side of the tabernacle. 30The leader of the families of the Kohathite clans was Elizaphan son of Uzziel. 31They were responsible for the care of the ark, the table, the lampstand, the altars, the articles of the sanctuary used in ministering, the curtain, and everything related to their use. 32The chief leader of the Levites was Eleazar son of Aaron, the priest. He was appointed over those who were responsible for the care of the sanctuary.

33To Merari belonged the clans of the Mahlites and the Mushites; these were the Merarite clans. 34The number of all the males a month old or more who were counted was 6,200. 35The leader of the families of the Merarite clans was Zuriel son of Abihail; they were to camp on the north side of the tabernacle. 36The Merarites were appointed to take care of the frames of the tabernacle, its crossbars, posts, bases, all its equipment, and everything related to their use, 37as well as the posts of the surrounding courtyard with their bases, tent pegs and ropes.

38Moses and Aaron and his sons were to camp to the east of the tabernacle, towards the sunrise, in front of the Tent of Meeting. They were responsible for the care of the sanctuary on behalf of the Israelites. Anyone else who approached the sanctuary was to be put to death.

39The total number of Levites counted at the LORD's command by Moses and Aaron according to their clans, including every male a month old or more, was 22,000.

40The LORD said to Moses, "Count all the firstborn Israelite males who are a month old or more and make a list of their names. 41Take the Levites for me in place of all the firstborn of the Israelites, and the livestock of the Levites in place of all the firstborn of the livestock of the Israelites. I am the LORD."

42So Moses counted all the firstborn of the Israelites, as the LORD commanded him. 43The total number of firstborn males a month old or more, listed by name, was 22,273.

44The LORD also said to Moses, 45"Take the Levites in place of all the firstborn of Israel, and the livestock of the Levites in place of their livestock. The Levites are to be mine. I am the LORD. 46To redeem the 273 firstborn Israelites who exceed the number of the Levites, 47collect five shekels for each one, according to the sanctuary shekel, which weighs twenty gerahs. 48Give the money for the redemption of the additional Israelites to Aaron and his sons."

49So Moses collected the redemption money from those who exceeded the number redeemed by the Levites. 50From the firstborn of the Israelites he collected silver weighing 1,365 shekels, according to the sanctuary shekel. 51Moses gave the redemption money to Aaron and his sons, as he was commanded by the word of the LORD.

NEW TESTAMENT READING
Luke 1:39–56

Mary Visits Elizabeth

39At that time Mary got ready and hurried to a town in the hill country of Judea, 40where she entered Zechariah's home and greeted Elizabeth. 41When Elizabeth heard Mary's greeting, the baby leaped in her womb, and Elizabeth was filled with the Holy Spirit. 42In a loud voice she exclaimed: "Blessed are you among women, and blessed is the child you will bear! 43But why am I so favoured, that the mother of my Lord should come to me? 44As soon as the sound of your greeting reached my ears, the baby in my womb leaped for joy. 45Blessed is she who has believed that what the Lord has said to her will be accomplished!"

Mary's Song

46 And Mary said:

"My soul glorifies the Lord
47 and my spirit rejoices in God my Saviour,
48 for he has been mindful
of the humble state of his servant.
From now on all generations will call me blessed,
49 for the Mighty One has done great things for me—
holy is his name.
50 His mercy extends to those who fear him,
from generation to generation.
51 He has performed mighty deeds with his arm;
he has scattered those who are proud in their inmost thoughts.
52 He has brought down rulers from their thrones
but has lifted up the humble.
53 He has filled the hungry with good things
but has sent the rich away empty.
54 He has helped his servant Israel,
remembering to be merciful
55 to Abraham and his descendants for ever,
even as he said to our fathers."

56 Mary stayed with Elizabeth for about three months and then returned home.

READING FROM PSALMS

Psalm 34:1–10

Of David. When he pretended to be insane before Abimelech, who drove him away, and he left.

1 I will extol the LORD at all times;
his praise will always be on my lips.
2 My soul will boast in the LORD;
let the afflicted hear and rejoice.
3 Glorify the LORD with me:
let us exalt his name together.

4 I sought the LORD, and he answered me;
he delivered me from all my fears.
5 Those who look to him are radiant;
their faces are never covered with shame.
6 This poor man called, and the LORD heard him;
he saved him out of all his troubles.
7 The angel of the LORD encamps around those who fear him,
and he delivers them.

8 Taste and see that the LORD is good;
blessed is the man who takes refuge in him.
9 Fear the LORD, you his saints,
for those who fear him lack nothing.
10 The lions may grow weak and hungry,
but those who seek the LORD lack no good thing.

DAY 75 **MARCH 16**

OLD TESTAMENT READING
Numbers 4:1–5:10

The Kohathites

4 The LORD said to Moses and
Aaron: 2“Take a census of the
Kohathite branch of the Levites by their
clans and families. 3Count all the men
from thirty to fifty years of age who
come to serve in the work in the Tent of
Meeting.
4“This is the work of the Kohathites
in the Tent of Meeting: the care of the
most holy things. 5When the camp is to
move, Aaron and his sons are to go in
and take down the shielding curtain and
cover the ark of the Testimony with it.
6Then they are to cover this with hides
of sea cows, spread a cloth of solid blue
over that and put the poles in place.
7“Over the table of the Presence they
are to spread a blue cloth and put on it
the plates, dishes and bowls, and the
jars for drink offerings; the bread that is
continually there is to remain on it.
8Over these they are to spread a scarlet
cloth, cover that with hides of sea cows
and put its poles in place.
9“They are to take a blue cloth and
cover the lampstand that is for light,
together with its lamps, its wick trimmers and trays, and all its jars for the oil
used to supply it. 10Then they are to
wrap it and all its accessories in a covering of hides of sea cows and put it on a
carrying frame.
11“Over the gold altar they are to
spread a blue cloth and cover that with
hides of sea cows and put its poles in
place.
12“They are to take all the articles
used for ministering in the sanctuary,
wrap them in a blue cloth, cover that
with hides of sea cows and put them on a
carrying frame.
13“They are to remove the ashes from
the bronze altar and spread a purple
cloth over it. 14Then they are to place on
it all the utensils used for ministering at
the altar, including the firepans, meat
forks, shovels and sprinkling bowls.
Over it they are to spread a covering of
hides of sea cows and put its poles in
place.
15“After Aaron and his sons have
finished covering the holy furnishings
and all the holy articles, and when the
camp is ready to move, the Kohathites
are to come to do the carrying. But they
must not touch the holy things or they
will die. The Kohathites are to carry
those things that are in the Tent of
Meeting.
16“Eleazar son of Aaron, the priest, is
to have charge of the oil for the light,
the fragrant incense, the regular grain
offering and the anointing oil. He is to
be in charge of the entire tabernacle and
everything in it, including its holy furnishings and articles.”
17The LORD said to Moses and
Aaron, 18“See that the Kohathite tribal
clans are not cut off from the Levites.
19So that they may live and not die when
they come near the most holy things, do
this for them: Aaron and his sons are to
go into the sanctuary and assign to each
man his work and what he is to carry.
20But the Kohathites must not go in to
look at the holy things, even for a moment, or they will die.”

The Gershonites

21The LORD said to Moses, 22“Take a
census also of the Gershonites by their
families and clans. 23Count all the men
from thirty to fifty years of age who
come to serve in the work at the Tent of
Meeting.
24“This is the service of the Gershonite clans as they work and carry burdens: 25They are to carry the curtains of
the tabernacle, the Tent of Meeting, its
covering and the outer covering of hides
of sea cows, the curtains for the entrance to the Tent of Meeting, 26the

curtains of the courtyard surrounding the tabernacle and altar, the curtain for the entrance, the ropes and all the equipment used in its service. The Gershonites are to do all that needs to be done with these things. [27]All their service, whether carrying or doing other work, is to be done under the direction of Aaron and his sons. You shall assign to them as their responsibility all they are to carry. [28]This is the service of the Gershonite clans at the Tent of Meeting. Their duties are to be under the direction of Ithamar son of Aaron, the priest.

The Merarites

[29]"Count the Merarites by their clans and families. [30]Count all the men from thirty to fifty years of age who come to serve in the work at the Tent of Meeting. [31]This is their duty as they perform service at the Tent of Meeting: to carry the frames of the tabernacle, its crossbars, posts and bases, [32]as well as the posts of the surrounding courtyard with their bases, tent pegs, ropes, all their equipment and everything related to their use. Assign to each man the specific things he is to carry. [33]This is the service of the Merarite clans as they work at the Tent of Meeting under the direction of Ithamar son of Aaron, the priest."

The Numbering of the Levite Clans

[34]Moses, Aaron and the leaders of the community counted the Kohathites by their clans and families. [35]All the men from thirty to fifty years of age who came to serve in the work in the Tent of Meeting, [36]counted by clans, were 2,750. [37]This was the total of all those in the Kohathite clans who served in the Tent of Meeting. Moses and Aaron counted them according to the LORD's command through Moses.

[38]The Gershonites were counted by their clans and families. [39]All the men from thirty to fifty years of age who came to serve in the work at the Tent of Meeting, [40]counted by their clans and families, were 2,630. [41]This was the total of those in the Gershonite clans who served at the Tent of Meeting. Moses and Aaron counted them according to the LORD's command.

[42]The Merarites were counted by their clans and families. [43]All the men from thirty to fifty years of age who came to serve in the work at the Tent of Meeting, [44]counted by their clans, were 3,200. [45]This was the total of those in the Merarite clans. Moses and Aaron counted them according to the LORD's command through Moses.

[46]So Moses, Aaron and the leaders of Israel counted all the Levites by their clans and families. [47]All the men from thirty to fifty years of age who came to do the work of serving and carrying the Tent of Meeting [48]numbered 8,580. [49]At the LORD's command through Moses, each was assigned his work and told what to carry.

Thus they were counted, as the LORD commanded Moses.

The Purity of the Camp

5 The LORD said to Moses, [2]"Command the Israelites to send away from the camp anyone who has an infectious skin disease or a discharge of any kind, or who is ceremonially unclean because of a dead body. [3]Send away male and female alike; send them outside the camp so that they will not defile their camp, where I dwell among them." [4]The Israelites did this; they sent them outside the camp. They did just as the LORD had instructed Moses.

Restitution for Wrongs

[5]The LORD said to Moses, [6]"Say to the Israelites: 'When a man or woman wrongs another in any way and so is unfaithful to the LORD, that person is guilty [7]and must confess the sin he has committed. He must make full restitution for his wrong, add one fifth to it and give it all to the person he has wronged. [8]But if that person has no close relative

to whom restitution can be made for the
wrong, the restitution belongs to the
LORD and must be given to the priest,
along with the ram with which atonement is made for him. 9All the sacred
contributions the Israelites bring to a
priest will belong to him. 10Each man's
sacred gifts are his own, but what he
gives to the priest will belong to the
priest.'"

NEW TESTAMENT READING
Luke 1:57–80

The Birth of John the Baptist

57When it was time for Elizabeth to
have her baby, she gave birth to a son.
58Her neighbours and relatives heard
that the Lord had shown her great
mercy, and they shared her joy.

59On the eighth day they came to
circumcise the child, and they were
going to name him after his father
Zechariah, 60but his mother spoke up
and said, "No! He is to be called John."

61They said to her, "There is no-one
among your relatives who has that
name."

62Then they made signs to his father,
to find out what he would like to name
the child. 63He asked for a writing
tablet, and to everyone's astonishment
he wrote, "His name is John."
64Immediately his mouth was opened
and his tongue was loosed, and he
began to speak, praising God. 65The
neighbours were all filled with awe, and
throughout the hill country of Judea
people were talking about all these
things. 66Everyone who heard this wondered about it, asking, "What then is
this child going to be?" For the Lord's
hand was with him.

Zechariah's Song

67His father Zechariah was filled with
the Holy Spirit and prophesied:

68"Praise be to the Lord, the God of
Israel,
because he has come and has
redeemed his people.
69He has raised up a horn of salvation
for us
in the house of his servant David
70(as he said through his holy prophets
of long ago),
71salvation from our enemies
and from the hand of all who hate
us—
72to show mercy to our fathers
and to remember his holy
covenant,
73 the oath he swore to our father
Abraham:
74to rescue us from the hand of our
enemies,
and to enable us to serve him
without fear
75 in holiness and righteousness
before him all our days.

76And you, my child, will be called a
prophet of the Most High;
for you will go on before the Lord
to prepare the way for him,
77to give his people the knowledge of
salvation
through the forgiveness of their
sins,
78because of the tender mercy of our
God,
by which the rising sun will come to
us from heaven
79to shine on those living in darkness
and in the shadow of death,
to guide our feet into the path of
peace."

80And the child grew and became
strong in spirit; and he lived in the
desert until he appeared publicly to
Israel.

READING FROM PSALMS
Psalm 34:11–22

11Come, my children, listen to me;
I will teach you the fear of the
LORD.
12Whoever of you loves life
and desires to see many good days,

13keep your tongue from evil
and your lips from speaking lies.
14Turn from evil and do good;
seek peace and pursue it.

15The eyes of the LORD are on the righteous
and his ears are attentive to their cry;
16the face of the LORD is against those who do evil,
to cut off the memory of them from the earth.

17The righteous cry out, and the LORD hears them;
he delivers them from all their troubles.

18The LORD is close to the broken-hearted
and saves those who are crushed in spirit.

19A righteous man may have many troubles,
but the LORD delivers him from them all;
20he protects all his bones,
not one of them will be broken.

21Evil will slay the wicked;
the foes of the righteous will be condemned.
22The LORD redeems his servants;
no-one will be condemned who takes refuge in him.

MARCH 17

DAY 76

OLD TESTAMENT READING
Numbers 5:11–6:27

The Test for an Unfaithful Wife

11Then the LORD said to Moses,
12"Speak to the Israelites and say to
them: 'If a man's wife goes astray and is
unfaithful to him 13by sleeping with
another man, and this is hidden from
her husband and her impurity is undetected (since there is no witness
against her and she has not been caught
in the act), 14and if feelings of jealousy
come over her husband and he suspects
his wife and she is impure—or if he is
jealous and suspects her even though
she is not impure—15then he is to take
his wife to the priest. He must also take
an offering of a tenth of an ephah of
barley flour on her behalf. He must not
pour oil on it or put incense on it, because it is a grain offering for jealousy, a
reminder offering to draw attention to
guilt.
16" 'The priest shall bring her and
make her stand before the LORD.
17Then he shall take some holy water in
a clay jar and put some dust from the
tabernacle floor into the water. 18After
the priest has made the woman stand
before the LORD, he shall loosen her
hair and place in her hands the reminder
offering, the grain offering for jealousy,
while he himself holds the bitter water
that brings a curse. 19Then the priest
shall put the woman under oath and say
to her, "If no other man has slept with
you and you have not gone astray and
become impure while married to your
husband, may this bitter water that
brings a curse not harm you. 20But if you
have gone astray while married to your
husband and you have defiled yourself
by sleeping with a man other than your
husband"—21here the priest is to put
the woman under this curse of the oath
—"may the LORD cause your people to
curse and denounce you when he causes
your thigh to waste away and your
abdomen to swell. 22May this water that
brings a curse enter your body so that

your abdomen swells and your thigh
wastes away."

"'Then the woman is to say, "Amen.
So be it."

23"'The priest is to write these curses
on a scroll and then wash them off into
the bitter water. 24He shall make the
woman drink the bitter water that
brings a curse, and this water will enter
her and cause bitter suffering. 25The
priest is to take from her hands the grain
offering for jealousy, wave it before the
LORD and bring it to the altar. 26The
priest is then to take a handful of the
grain offering as a memorial offering
and burn it on the altar; after that, he is
to make the woman drink the water. 27If
she has defiled herself and been unfaithful to her husband, then when she is
made to drink the water that brings a
curse, it will go into her and cause bitter
suffering; her abdomen will swell and
her thigh waste away, and she will become accursed among her people. 28If,
however, the woman has not defiled
herself and is free from impurity, she
will be cleared of guilt and will be able
to have children.

29"'This, then, is the law of jealousy
when a woman goes astray and defiles
herself while married to her husband,
30or when feelings of jealousy come
over a man because he suspects his wife.
The priest is to make her stand before
the LORD and is to apply this entire law
to her. 31The husband will be innocent
of any wrongdoing, but the woman will
bear the consequences of her sin.'"

The Nazirite

6 The LORD said to Moses, 2"Speak
to the Israelites and say to them: 'If
a man or woman wants to make a
special vow, a vow of separation to the
LORD as a Nazirite, 3he must abstain
from wine and other fermented drink
and must not drink vinegar made from
wine or from other fermented drink. He
must not drink grape juice or eat grapes
or raisins. 4As long as he is a Nazirite,
he must not eat anything that comes
from the grapevine, not even the seeds
or skins.

5"'During the entire period of his
vow of separation no razor may be used
on his head. He must be holy until the
period of his separation to the LORD is
over; he must let the hair of his head
grow long. 6Throughout the period of
his separation to the LORD he must not
go near a dead body. 7Even if his own
father or mother or brother or sister
dies, he must not make himself ceremonially unclean on account of them,
because the symbol of his separation to
God is on his head. 8Throughout the
period of his separation he is consecrated to the LORD.

9"'If someone dies suddenly in his
presence, thus defiling the hair he has
dedicated, he must shave his head on
the day of his cleansing—the seventh
day. 10Then on the eighth day he must
bring two doves or two young pigeons to
the priest at the entrance to the Tent of
Meeting. 11The priest is to offer one as a
sin offering and the other as a burnt
offering to make atonement for him
because he sinned by being in the presence of the dead body. That same day
he is to consecrate his head. 12He must
dedicate himself to the LORD for the
period of his separation and must bring
a year-old male lamb as a guilt offering.
The previous days do not count, because he became defiled during his
separation.

13"'Now this is the law for the Nazirite when the period of his separation is
over. He is to be brought to the entrance to the Tent of Meeting. 14There
he is to present his offerings to the
LORD: a year-old male lamb without
defect for a burnt offering, a year-old
ewe lamb without defect for a sin offering, a ram without defect for a fellowship offering, 15together with their grain
offerings and drink offerings, and a
basket of bread made without yeast—
cakes made of fine flour mixed with oil,
and wafers spread with oil.

16"'The priest is to present them before the LORD and make the sin offering

and the burnt offering. 17He is to present the basket of unleavened bread and
is to sacrifice the ram as a fellowship
offering to the LORD, together with its
grain offering and drink offering.
18" 'Then at the entrance to the Tent
of Meeting, the Nazirite must shave off
the hair that he dedicated. He is to take
the hair and put it in the fire that is
under the sacrifice of the fellowship
offering.
19" 'After the Nazirite has shaved off
the hair of his dedication, the priest is to
place in his hands a boiled shoulder of
the ram, and a cake and a wafer from
the basket, both made without yeast.
20The priest shall then wave them before the LORD as a wave offering; they
are holy and belong to the priest,
together with the breast that was waved
and the thigh that was presented. After
that, the Nazirite may drink wine.
21" 'This is the law of the Nazirite who
vows his offering to the LORD in accordance with his separation, in addition to
whatever else he can afford. He must
fulfil the vow he has made, according to
the law of the Nazirite.' "

The Priestly Blessing

22The LORD said to Moses, 23"Tell
Aaron and his sons, 'This is how you are
to bless the Israelites. Say to them:

24" ' "The LORD bless you
and keep you;
25the LORD make his face shine upon
you
and be gracious to you;
26the LORD turn his face towards you
and give you peace." '

27"So they will put my name on the
Israelites, and I will bless them."

NEW TESTAMENT READING

Luke 2:1–20

The Birth of Jesus

2 In those days Caesar Augustus
issued a decree that a census should
be taken of the entire Roman world.
(2This was the first census that took
place while Quirinius was governor of
Syria.) 3And everyone went to his own
town to register.
4So Joseph also went up from the
town of Nazareth in Galilee to Judea, to
Bethlehem the town of David, because
he belonged to the house and line of
David. 5He went there to register with
Mary, who was pledged to be married to
him and was expecting a child. 6While
they were there, the time came for the
baby to be born, 7and she gave birth to
her firstborn, a son. She wrapped him in
cloths and placed him in a manger, because there was no room for them in the
inn.

The Shepherds and the Angels

8And there were shepherds living out
in the fields near by, keeping watch over
their flocks at night. 9An angel of the
Lord appeared to them, and the glory of
the Lord shone around them, and they
were terrified. 10But the angel said to
them, "Do not be afraid. I bring you
good news of great joy that will be for all
the people. 11Today in the town of
David a Saviour has been born to you;
he is Christ the Lord. 12This will be
a sign to you: You will find a baby
wrapped in cloths and lying in a
manger."
13Suddenly a great company of the
heavenly host appeared with the angel,
praising God and saying,

14"Glory to God in the highest,
and on earth peace to men on
whom his favour rests."

15When the angels had left them and
gone into heaven, the shepherds said to
one another, "Let's go to Bethlehem
and see this thing that has happened,
which the Lord has told us about."
16So they hurried off and found Mary
and Joseph, and the baby, who was
lying in the manger. 17When they had
seen him, they spread the word concerning what had been told them about

this child, [18]and all who heard it were
amazed at what the shepherds said to
them. [19]But Mary treasured up all these
things and pondered them in her heart.
[20]The shepherds returned, glorifying
and praising God for all the things they
had heard and seen, which were just as
they had been told.

READING FROM PROVERBS

Proverbs 7:6–20

[6]At the window of my house
I looked out through the lattice.
[7]I saw among the simple,
I noticed among the young men,
a youth who lacked judgment.
[8]He was going down the street near
her corner,
walking along in the direction of
her house
[9]at twilight, as the day was fading,
as the dark of night set in.
[10]Then out came a woman to meet him,
dressed like a prostitute and with
crafty intent.
[11](She is loud and defiant,
her feet never stay at home;
[12]now in the street, now in the squares,
at every corner she lurks.)
[13]She took hold of him and kissed him
and with a brazen face she said:

[14]"I have fellowship offerings at home;
today I fulfilled my vows.
[15]So I came out to meet you;
I looked for you and have found
you!
[16]I have covered my bed
with coloured linens from Egypt.
[17]I have perfumed my bed
with myrrh, aloes and cinnamon.
[18]Come, let's drink deep of love till
morning;
let's enjoy ourselves with love!
[19]My husband is not at home;
he has gone on a long journey.
[20]He took his purse filled with money
and will not be home till full
moon."

DAY 77

MARCH 18

OLD TESTAMENT READING

Numbers 7:1–65

Offerings at the Dedication of the Tabernacle

7 When Moses finished setting up the
tabernacle, he anointed it and consecrated it and all its furnishings. He
also anointed and consecrated the altar
and all its utensils. [2]Then the leaders of
Israel, the heads of families who were
the tribal leaders in charge of those who
were counted, made offerings. [3]They
brought as their gifts before the LORD
six covered carts and twelve oxen—an
ox from each leader and a cart from
every two. These they presented before
the tabernacle.

[4]The LORD said to Moses, [5]"Accept
these from them, that they may be used
in the work at the Tent of Meeting. Give
them to the Levites as each man's work
requires."

[6]So Moses took the carts and oxen
and gave them to the Levites. [7]He gave
two carts and four oxen to the Gershonites, as their work required, [8]and he
gave four carts and eight oxen to the
Merarites, as their work required. They
were all under the direction of Ithamar
son of Aaron, the priest. [9]But Moses
did not give any to the Kohathites, because they were to carry on their shoulders the holy things, for which they
were responsible.

[10]When the altar was anointed, the

leaders brought their offerings for its
dedication and presented them before
the altar. 11For the LORD had said to
Moses, "Each day one leader is to bring
his offering for the dedication of the
altar."

12The one who brought his offering on
the first day was Nahshon son of Amminadab of the tribe of Judah.

13His offering was one silver plate
weighing a hundred and thirty
shekels, and one silver sprinkling
bowl weighing seventy shekels,
both according to the sanctuary
shekel, each filled with fine flour
mixed with oil as a grain offering;
14one gold dish weighing ten
shekels, filled with incense; 15one
young bull, one ram and one male
lamb a year old, for a burnt offering; 16one male goat for a sin offering; 17and two oxen, five rams, five
male goats and five male lambs a
year old, to be sacrificed as a
fellowship offering. This was the
offering of Nahshon son of Amminadab.

18On the second day Nethanel son of
Zuar, the leader of Issachar, brought
his offering.

19The offering he brought was one
silver plate weighing a hundred and
thirty shekels, and one silver
sprinkling bowl weighing seventy
shekels, both according to the
sanctuary shekel, each filled with
fine flour mixed with oil as a grain
offering; 20one gold dish weighing
ten shekels, filled with incense;
21one young bull, one ram and one
male lamb a year old, for a burnt
offering; 22one male goat for a sin
offering; 23and two oxen, five rams,
five male goats and five male lambs
a year old, to be sacrificed as a
fellowship offering. This was the
offering of Nethanel son of Zuar.

24On the third day, Eliab son of Helon,
the leader of the people of Zebulun,
brought his offering.

25His offering was one silver plate
weighing a hundred and thirty
shekels, and one silver sprinkling
bowl weighing seventy shekels,
both according to the sanctuary
shekel, each filled with fine flour
mixed with oil as a grain offering;
26one gold dish weighing ten
shekels, filled with incense; 27one
young bull, one ram and one male
lamb a year old, for a burnt offering; 28one male goat for a sin offering; 29and two oxen, five rams, five
male goats and five male lambs a
year old, to be sacrificed as a
fellowship offering. This was the
offering of Eliab son of Helon.

30On the fourth day Elizur son of
Shedeur, the leader of the people of
Reuben, brought his offering.

31His offering was one silver plate
weighing a hundred and thirty
shekels, and one silver sprinkling
bowl weighing seventy shekels,
both according to the sanctuary
shekel, each filled with fine flour
mixed with oil as a grain offering;
32one gold dish weighing ten
shekels, filled with incense; 33one
young bull, one ram and one male
lamb a year old, for a burnt offering; 34one male goat for a sin offering; 35and two oxen, five rams, five
male goats and five male lambs a
year old, to be sacrificed as a
fellowship offering. This was the
offering of Elizur son of Shedeur.

36On the fifth day Shelumiel son of
Zurishaddai, the leader of the people of
Simeon, brought his offering.

37His offering was one silver plate
weighing a hundred and thirty
shekels, and one silver sprinkling
bowl weighing seventy shekels,
both according to the sanctuary
shekel, each filled with fine flour
mixed with oil as a grain offering;
38one gold dish weighing ten
shekels, filled with incense; 39one
young bull, one ram and one male

lamb a year old, for a burnt offering; 40one male goat for a sin offering; 41and two oxen, five rams, five
male goats and five male lambs a
year old, to be sacrificed as a
fellowship offering. This was the
offering of Shelumiel son of
Zurishaddai.

42On the sixth day Eliasaph son of
Deuel, the leader of the people of Gad,
brought his offering.
43His offering was one silver plate
weighing a hundred and thirty
shekels, and one silver sprinkling
bowl weighing seventy shekels,
both according to the sanctuary
shekel, each filled with fine flour
mixed with oil as a grain offering;
44one gold dish weighing ten
shekels, filled with incense; 45one
young bull, one ram and one male
lamb a year old, for a burnt offering; 46one male goat for a sin offering; 47and two oxen, five rams, five
male goats and five male lambs a
year old, to be sacrificed as a
fellowship offering. This was the
offering of Eliasaph son of Deuel.

48On the seventh day Elishama son of
Ammihud, the leader of the people of
Ephraim, brought his offering.
49His offering was one silver plate
weighing a hundred and thirty
shekels, and one silver sprinkling
bowl weighing seventy shekels,
both according to the sanctuary
shekel, each filled with fine flour
mixed with oil as a grain offering;
50one gold dish weighing ten
shekels, filled with incense; 51one
young bull, one ram and one male
lamb a year old, for a burnt offering; 52one male goat for a sin offering; 53and two oxen, five rams, five
male goats and five male lambs a
year old, to be sacrificed as a
fellowship offering. This was the
offering of Elishama son of Ammihud.

54On the eighth day Gamaliel son of
Pedahzur, the leader of the people of
Manasseh, brought his offering.
55His offering was one silver plate
weighing a hundred and thirty
shekels, and one silver sprinkling
bowl weighing seventy shekels,
both according to the sanctuary
shekel, each filled with fine flour
mixed with oil as a grain offering;
56one gold dish weighing ten
shekels, filled with incense; 57one
young bull, one ram and one male
lamb a year old, for a burnt offering; 58one male goat for a sin offering; 59and two oxen, five rams, five
male goats and five male lambs a
year old, to be sacrificed as a
fellowship offering. This was the
offering of Gamaliel son of
Pedahzur.

60On the ninth day Abidan son of
Gideoni, the leader of the people of
Benjamin, brought his offering.
61His offering was one silver plate
weighing a hundred and thirty
shekels, and one silver sprinkling
bowl weighing seventy shekels,
both according to the sanctuary
shekel, each filled with fine flour
mixed with oil as a grain offering;
62one gold dish weighing ten
shekels, filled with incense; 63one
young bull, one ram and one male
lamb a year old, for a burnt offering; 64one male goat for a sin offering; 65and two oxen, five rams, five
male goats and five male lambs a
year old, to be sacrificed as a
fellowship offering. This was the
offering of Abidan son of Gideoni.

NEW TESTAMENT READING
Luke 2:21–40

Jesus Presented in the Temple

21On the eighth day, when it was time
to circumcise him, he was named Jesus,
the name the angel had given him before he had been conceived.

22When the time of their purification
according to the Law of Moses had been
completed, Joseph and Mary took him
to Jerusalem to present him to the Lord
23(as it is written in the Law of the Lord,
"Every firstborn male is to be consecrated to the Lord"), 24and to offer a
sacrifice in keeping with what is said in
the Law of the Lord: "a pair of doves or
two young pigeons".

25Now there was a man in Jerusalem
called Simeon, who was righteous and
devout. He was waiting for the consolation of Israel, and the Holy Spirit was
upon him. 26It had been revealed to him
by the Holy Spirit that he would not die
before he had seen the Lord's Christ.
27Moved by the Spirit, he went into the
temple courts. When the parents
brought in the child Jesus to do for him
what the custom of the Law required,
28Simeon took him in his arms and
praised God, saying:

29"Sovereign Lord, as you have
promised,
you now dismiss your servant in
peace.
30For my eyes have seen your
salvation,
31 which you have prepared in the
sight of all people,
32a light for revelation to the Gentiles
and for glory to your people
Israel."

33The child's father and mother marvelled at what was said about him.
34Then Simeon blessed them and said to
Mary, his mother: "This child is destined to cause the falling and rising of
many in Israel, and to be a sign that
will be spoken against, 35so that the
thoughts of many hearts will be revealed. And a sword will pierce your
own soul too."

36There was also a prophetess, Anna,
the daughter of Phanuel, of the tribe of
Asher. She was very old; she had lived
with her husband seven years after her
marriage, 37and then was a widow until
she was eighty-four. She never left the
temple but worshipped night and day,
fasting and praying. 38Coming up to
them at that very moment, she gave
thanks to God and spoke about the
child to all who were looking forward to
the redemption of Jerusalem.

39When Joseph and Mary had done
everything required by the Law of the
Lord, they returned to Galilee to their
own town of Nazareth. 40And the child
grew and became strong; he was filled
with wisdom, and the grace of God was
upon him.

READING FROM PSALMS

Psalm 35:1–10

Of David.

1Contend, O LORD, with those who
contend with me;
fight against those who fight
against me.
2Take up shield and buckler;
arise and come to my aid.
3Brandish spear and javelin
against those who pursue me.
Say to my soul,
"I am your salvation."

4May those who seek my life
be disgraced and put to shame;
may those who plot my ruin
be turned back in dismay.
5May they be like chaff before the
wind,
with the angel of the LORD driving
them away;
6may their path be dark and slippery,
with the angel of the LORD
pursuing them.
7Since they hid their net for me
without cause
and without cause dug a pit for me,
8may ruin overtake them by
surprise—
may the net they hid entangle
them,
may they fall into the pit, to their
ruin.

9Then my soul will rejoice in the LORD
and delight in his salvation.
10My whole being will exclaim,
"Who is like you, O LORD?
You rescue the poor from those too strong for them,
the poor and needy from those who rob them."

DAY 78

MARCH 19

OLD TESTAMENT READING
Numbers 7:66–9:14

66On the tenth day Ahiezer son of Ammishaddai, the leader of the people of Dan, brought his offering.

67His offering was one silver plate weighing a hundred and thirty shekels, and one silver sprinkling bowl weighing seventy shekels, both according to the sanctuary shekel, each filled with fine flour mixed with oil as a grain offering;
68one gold dish weighing ten shekels, filled with incense; 69one young bull, one ram and one male lamb a year old, for a burnt offering; 70one male goat for a sin offering; 71and two oxen, five rams, five male goats and five male lambs a year old, to be sacrificed as a fellowship offering. This was the offering of Ahiezer son of Ammishaddai.

72On the eleventh day Pagiel son of Ocran, the leader of the people of Asher, brought his offering.

73His offering was one silver plate weighing a hundred and thirty shekels, and one silver sprinkling bowl weighing seventy shekels, both according to the sanctuary shekel, each filled with fine flour mixed with oil as a grain offering;
74one gold dish weighing ten shekels, filled with incense; 75one young bull, one ram and one male lamb a year old, for a burnt offering; 76one male goat for a sin offering; 77and two oxen, five rams, five male goats and five male lambs a year old, to be sacrificed as a fellowship offering. This was the offering of Pagiel son of Ocran.

78On the twelfth day Ahira son of Enan, the leader of the people of Naphtali, brought his offering.

79His offering was one silver plate weighing a hundred and thirty shekels, and one silver sprinkling bowl weighing seventy shekels, both according to the sanctuary shekel, each filled with fine flour mixed with oil as a grain offering;
80one gold dish weighing ten shekels, filled with incense; 81one young bull, one ram and one male lamb a year old, for a burnt offering; 82one male goat for a sin offering; 83and two oxen, five rams, five male goats and five male lambs a year old, to be sacrificed as a fellowship offering. This was the offering of Ahira son of Enan.

84These were the offerings of the Israelite leaders for the dedication of the altar when it was anointed: twelve silver plates, twelve silver sprinkling bowls and twelve gold dishes. 85Each silver plate weighed a hundred and thirty shekels, and each sprinkling bowl seventy shekels. Altogether, the silver dishes weighed two thousand four hundred shekels, according to the sanctuary shekel. 86The twelve gold dishes filled with incense weighed ten shekels each, according to the sanctuary shekel. Altogether, the gold dishes weighed a hundred and twenty shekels. 87The total number of animals for the burnt offering came to twelve young bulls, twelve rams and twelve male lambs a year old, together with their grain offering. Twelve male goats were used for the sin offering. 88The total number of animals for the sacrifice of the fellowship offering came to twenty-four oxen, sixty rams, sixty male goats and sixty male lambs a year old. These were the offerings for the dedication of the altar after it was anointed.

89When Moses entered the Tent of Meeting to speak with the LORD, he heard the voice speaking to him from between the two cherubim above the atonement cover on the ark of the Testimony. And he spoke with him.

Setting Up the Lamps

8 The LORD said to Moses, 2"Speak to Aaron and say to him, 'When you set up the seven lamps, they are to light the area in front of the lampstand.' "

3Aaron did so; he set up the lamps so that they faced forward on the lampstand, just as the LORD commanded Moses. 4This is how the lampstand was made: It was made of hammered gold—from its base to its blossoms. The lampstand was made exactly like the pattern the LORD had shown Moses.

The Setting Apart of the Levites

5The LORD said to Moses: 6"Take the Levites from among the other Israelites and make them ceremonially clean. 7To purify them, do this: Sprinkle the water of cleansing on them; then make them shave their whole bodies and wash their clothes, and so purify themselves. 8Make them take a young bull with its grain offering of fine flour mixed with oil; then you are to take a second young bull for a sin offering. 9Bring the Levites to the front of the Tent of Meeting and assemble the whole Israelite community. 10You are to bring the Levites before the LORD, and the Israelites are to lay their hands on them. 11Aaron is to present the Levites before the LORD as a wave offering from the Israelites, so that they may be ready to do the work of the LORD.

12"After the Levites lay their hands on the heads of the bulls, use the one for a sin offering to the LORD and the other for a burnt offering, to make atonement for the Levites. 13Make the Levites stand in front of Aaron and his sons and then present them as a wave offering to the LORD. 14In this way you are to set the Levites apart from the other Israelites, and the Levites will be mine.

15"After you have purified the Levites and presented them as a wave offering, they are to come to do their work at the Tent of Meeting. 16They are the Israelites who are to be given wholly to me. I have taken them as my own in place of the firstborn, the first male offspring from every Israelite woman. 17Every firstborn male in Israel, whether man or animal, is mine. When I struck down all the firstborn in Egypt, I set them apart for myself. 18And I have taken the Levites in place of all the firstborn sons in Israel. 19Of all the Israelites, I have given the Levites as gifts to Aaron and his sons to do the work at the Tent of Meeting on behalf of the Israelites and to make atonement for them so that no plague will strike the Israelites when they go near the sanctuary."

20Moses, Aaron and the whole Israelite community did with the Levites just as the LORD commanded Moses. 21The Levites purified themselves and washed their clothes. Then Aaron presented them as a wave offering before the LORD and made atonement for them to purify them. 22After that, the Levites came to do their work at the Tent of Meeting under the supervision of Aaron and his sons. They did with the Levites just as the LORD commanded Moses.

23The LORD said to Moses, 24"This applies to the Levites: Men twenty-five years old or more shall come to take part in the work at the Tent of Meeting, 25but at the age of fifty, they must retire from their regular service and work no longer. 26They may assist their brothers in performing their duties at the Tent of Meeting, but they themselves must not do the work. This, then, is how you are to assign the responsibilities of the Levites."

The Passover

9 The LORD spoke to Moses in the Desert of Sinai in the first month of the second year after they came out of Egypt. He said, 2"Make the Israelites celebrate the Passover at the appointed time. 3Celebrate it at the appointed time, at twilight on the fourteenth day of this month, in accordance with all its rules and regulations."

4So Moses told the Israelites to celebrate the Passover, 5and they did so in the Desert of Sinai at twilight on the fourteenth day of the first month. The Israelites did everything just as the LORD commanded Moses.

6But some of them could not celebrate the Passover on that day because they were ceremonially unclean on account of a dead body. So they came to Moses and Aaron that same day 7and said to Moses, "We have become unclean because of a dead body, but why should we be kept from presenting the LORD's offering with the other Israelites at the appointed time?"

8Moses answered them, "Wait until I find out what the LORD commands concerning you."

9Then the LORD said to Moses, 10"Tell the Israelites: 'When any of you or your descendants are unclean because of a dead body or are away on a journey, they may still celebrate the LORD's Passover. 11They are to celebrate it on the fourteenth day of the second month at twilight. They are to eat the lamb, together with unleavened bread and bitter herbs. 12They must not leave any of it till morning or break any of its bones. When they celebrate the Passover, they must follow all the regulations. 13But if a man who is ceremonially clean and not on a journey fails to celebrate the Passover, that person must be cut off from his people because he did not present the LORD's offering at the appointed time. That man will bear the consequences of his sin.

14" 'An alien living among you who wants to celebrate the LORD's Passover must do so in accordance with its rules and regulations. You must have the same regulations for the alien and the native-born.' "

NEW TESTAMENT READING
Luke 2:41–52

The Boy Jesus at the Temple

41Every year his parents went to Jerusalem for the Feast of the Passover. 42When he was twelve years old, they went up to the Feast, according to the custom. 43After the Feast was over, while his parents were returning home, the boy Jesus stayed behind in Jerusalem, but they were unaware of it. 44Thinking he was in their company, they travelled on for a day. Then they began looking for him among their relatives and friends. 45When they did not find him, they went back to Jerusalem to look for him. 46After three days they found him in the temple courts, sitting among the teachers, listening to them and asking them questions. 47Everyone who heard him was amazed at his understanding and his answers. 48When his parents saw him, they were astonished. His mother said to him, "Son, why have you treated us like this? Your father and I have been anxiously searching for you."

49"Why were you searching for me?" he asked. "Didn't you know I had to be in my Father's house?" 50But they did not understand what he was saying to them.

51Then he went down to Nazareth

with them and was obedient to them. But his mother treasured all these things in her heart. 52And Jesus grew in wisdom and stature, and in favour with God and men.

READING FROM PSALMS
Psalm 35:11–18

11Ruthless witnesses come forward;
they question me on things I know nothing about.
12They repay me evil for good
and leave my soul forlorn.
13Yet when they were ill, I put on sackcloth
and humbled myself with fasting.
When my prayers returned to me unanswered,
14 I went about mourning
as though for my friend or brother.
I bowed my head in grief
as though weeping for my mother.
15But when I stumbled, they gathered in glee;
attackers gathered against me when I was unaware.
They slandered me without ceasing.
16Like the ungodly they maliciously mocked;
they gnashed their teeth at me.
17O Lord, how long will you look on?
Rescue my life from their ravages,
my precious life from these lions.
18I will give you thanks in the great assembly;
among throngs of people I will praise you.

MARCH 20

DAY 79

OLD TESTAMENT READING
Numbers 9:15–11:3

The Cloud Above the Tabernacle

15On the day the tabernacle, the Tent of the Testimony, was set up, the cloud covered it. From evening till morning the cloud above the tabernacle looked like fire. 16That is how it continued to be; the cloud covered it, and at night it looked like fire. 17Whenever the cloud lifted from above the Tent, the Israelites set out; wherever the cloud settled, the Israelites encamped. 18At the LORD's command the Israelites set out, and at his command they encamped. As long as the cloud stayed over the tabernacle, they remained in camp. 19When the cloud remained over the tabernacle a long time, the Israelites obeyed the LORD's order and did not set out. 20Sometimes the cloud was over the tabernacle only a few days; at the LORD's command they would encamp, and then at his command they would set out. 21Sometimes the cloud stayed only from evening till morning, and when it lifted in the morning, they set out. Whether by day or by night, whenever the cloud lifted, they set out. 22Whether the cloud stayed over the tabernacle for two days or a month or a year, the Israelites would remain in camp and not set out; but when it lifted, they would set out. 23At the LORD's command they encamped, and at the LORD's command they set out. They obeyed the LORD's order, in accordance with his command through Moses.

The Silver Trumpets

10 The LORD said to Moses: 2"Make two trumpets of hammered silver, and use them for calling the community together and for having the camps set out. 3When both are

sounded, the whole community is to
assemble before you at the entrance to
the Tent of Meeting. 4If only one is
sounded, the leaders—the heads of the
clans of Israel—are to assemble before
you. 5When a trumpet blast is sounded,
the tribes camping on the east are to set
out. 6At the sounding of a second blast,
the camps on the south are to set out.
The blast will be the signal for setting
out. 7To gather the assembly, blow the
trumpets, but not with the same signal.
8"The sons of Aaron, the priests, are
to blow the trumpets. This is to be a
lasting ordinance for you and the generations to come. 9When you go into
battle in your own land against an
enemy who is oppressing you, sound a
blast on the trumpets. Then you will be
remembered by the LORD your God and
rescued from your enemies. 10Also at
your times of rejoicing—your appointed feasts and New Moon festivals
—you are to sound the trumpets over
your burnt offerings and fellowship
offerings, and they will be a memorial
for you before your God. I am the LORD
your God."

The Israelites Leave Sinai

11On the twentieth day of the second
month of the second year, the cloud
lifted from above the tabernacle of the
Testimony. 12Then the Israelites set out
from the Desert of Sinai and travelled
from place to place until the cloud came
to rest in the Desert of Paran. 13They set
out, this first time, at the LORD's command through Moses.
14The divisions of the camp of Judah
went first, under their standard. Nahshon son of Amminadab was in command. 15Nethanel son of Zuar was over
the division of the tribe of Issachar,
16and Eliab son of Helon was over the
division of the tribe of Zebulun. 17Then
the tabernacle was taken down, and the
Gershonites and Merarites, who carried
it, set out.
18The divisions of the camp of
Reuben went next, under their standard. Elizur son of Shedeur was in command. 19Shelumiel son of Zurishaddai
was over the division of the tribe of
Simeon, 20and Eliasaph son of Deuel
was over the division of the tribe of
Gad. 21Then the Kohathites set out,
carrying the holy things. The tabernacle
was to be set up before they arrived.
22The divisions of the camp of
Ephraim went next, under their standard. Elishama son of Ammihud was in
command. 23Gamaliel son of Pedahzur
was over the division of the tribe of
Manasseh, 24and Abidan son of
Gideoni was over the division of the
tribe of Benjamin.
25Finally, as the rear guard for all the
units, the divisions of the camp of Dan
set out, under their standard. Ahiezer
son of Ammishaddai was in command.
26Pagiel son of Ocran was over the division of the tribe of Asher, 27and Ahira
son of Enan was over the division of the
tribe of Naphtali. 28This was the order
of march for the Israelite divisions as
they set out.
29Now Moses said to Hobab son of
Reuel the Midianite, Moses' father-in-
law, "We are setting out for the place
about which the LORD said, 'I will give it
to you.' Come with us and we will treat
you well, for the LORD has promised
good things to Israel."
30He answered, "No, I will not go; I
am going back to my own land and my
own people."
31But Moses said, "Please do not
leave us. You know where we should
camp in the desert, and you can be our
eyes. 32If you come with us, we will
share with you whatever good things the
LORD gives us."
33So they set out from the mountain
of the LORD and travelled for three
days. The ark of the covenant of the
LORD went before them during those
three days to find them a place to rest.
34The cloud of the LORD was over them
by day when they set out from the camp.
35Whenever the ark set out, Moses
said,

"Rise up, O LORD!
May your enemies be scattered;
may your foes flee before you."
36Whenever it came to rest, he said,

"Return, O LORD,
to the countless thousands of
Israel."

Fire From the LORD

11 Now the people complained about their hardships in the hearing of the LORD, and when he heard them his anger was aroused. Then fire from the LORD burned among them and consumed some of the outskirts of the camp. 2When the people cried out to Moses, he prayed to the LORD and the fire died down. 3So that place was called Taberah, because fire from the LORD had burned among them.

NEW TESTAMENT READING
Luke 3:1–22

John the Baptist Prepares the Way

3 In the fifteenth year of the reign of Tiberius Caesar—when Pontius Pilate was governor of Judea, Herod tetrarch of Galilee, his brother Philip tetrarch of Iturea and Traconitis, and Lysanias tetrarch of Abilene—2during the high priesthood of Annas and Caiaphas, the word of God came to John son of Zechariah in the desert.
3He went into all the country around the Jordan, preaching a baptism of repentance for the forgiveness of sins. 4As is written in the book of the words of Isaiah the prophet:

"A voice of one calling in the desert,
'Prepare the way for the Lord,
make straight paths for him.
5Every valley shall be filled in,
every mountain and hill made low.
The crooked roads shall become
straight,
the rough ways smooth.
6And all mankind will see God's
salvation.'"

7John said to the crowds coming out to be baptised by him, "You brood of vipers! Who warned you to flee from the coming wrath? 8Produce fruit in keeping with repentance. And do not begin to say to yourselves, 'We have Abraham as our father.' For I tell you that out of these stones God can raise up children for Abraham. 9The axe is already at the root of the trees, and every tree that does not produce good fruit will be cut down and thrown into the fire."

10"What should we do then?" the crowd asked.

11John answered, "The man with two tunics should share with him who has none, and the one who has food should do the same."

12Tax collectors also came to be baptised. "Teacher," they asked, "what should we do?"

13"Don't collect any more than you are required to," he told them.

14Then some soldiers asked him, "And what should we do?"

He replied, "Don't extort money and don't accuse people falsely—be content with your pay."

15The people were waiting expectantly and were all wondering in their hearts if John might possibly be the Christ. 16John answered them all, "I baptise you with water. But one more powerful than I will come, the thongs of whose sandals I am not worthy to untie. He will baptise you with the Holy Spirit and with fire. 17His winnowing fork is in his hand to clear his threshing-floor and to gather the wheat into his barn, but he will burn up the chaff with unquenchable fire." 18And with many other words John exhorted the people and preached the good news to them.

19But when John rebuked Herod the tetrarch because of Herodias, his brother's wife, and all the other evil things he had done, 20Herod added this to them all: He locked John up in prison.

The Baptism and Genealogy of Jesus

21When all the people were being baptised, Jesus was baptised too. And as he was praying, heaven was opened
22and the Holy Spirit descended on him in bodily form like a dove. And a voice came from heaven: "You are my Son, whom I love; with you I am well pleased."

READING FROM PSALMS
Psalm 35:19–28

19Let not those gloat over me
who are my enemies without cause;
let not those who hate me without
reason
maliciously wink the eye.
20They do not speak peaceably,
but devise false accusations
against those who live quietly in
the land.
21They gape at me and say, "Aha!
Aha!
With our own eyes we have seen
it."

22O LORD, you have seen this; be not
silent.
Do not be far from me, O Lord.
23Awake, and rise to my defence!
Contend for me, my God and
Lord.
24Vindicate me in your righteousness,
O LORD my God;
do not let them gloat over me.
25Do not let them think, "Aha, just
what we wanted!"
or say, "We have swallowed him
up."

26May all who gloat over my distress
be put to shame and confusion;
may all who exalt themselves over me
be clothed with shame and
disgrace.
27May those who delight in my
vindication
shout for joy and gladness;
may they always say, "The LORD be
exalted,
who delights in the well-being of
his servant."
28My tongue will speak of your
righteousness
and of your praises all day long.

DAY 80

MARCH 21

OLD TESTAMENT READING
Numbers 11:4–13:25

Quail From the LORD

4The rabble with them began to crave other food, and again the Israelites started wailing and said, "If only we had meat to eat!
5We remember the fish we ate in Egypt at no cost—also the cucumbers, melons, leeks, onions and garlic.
6But now we have lost our appetite; we never see anything but this manna!"

7The manna was like coriander seed and looked like resin.
8The people went around gathering it, and then ground it in a hand mill or crushed it in a mortar. They cooked it in a pot or made it into cakes. And it tasted like something made with olive oil.
9When the dew settled on the camp at night, the manna also came down.

10Moses heard the people of every family wailing, each at the entrance to

his tent. The LORD became exceedingly
angry, and Moses was troubled. 11He
asked the LORD, "Why have you
brought this trouble on your servant?
What have I done to displease you that
you put the burden of all these people
on me? 12Did I conceive all these people? Did I give them birth? Why do you
tell me to carry them in my arms, as a
nurse carries an infant, to the land you
promised on oath to their forefathers?
13Where can I get meat for all these
people? They keep wailing to me, 'Give
us meat to eat!' 14I cannot carry all these
people by myself; the burden is too
heavy for me. 15If this is how you are
going to treat me, put me to death right
now—if I have found favour in your
eyes—and do not let me face my own
ruin."

16The LORD said to Moses: "Bring me
seventy of Israel's elders who are
known to you as leaders and officials
among the people. Make them come to
the Tent of Meeting, that they may
stand there with you. 17I will come down
and speak with you there, and I will take
of the Spirit that is on you and put the
Spirit on them. They will help you carry
the burden of the people so that you will
not have to carry it alone.

18"Tell the people: 'Consecrate
yourselves in preparation for tomorrow, when you will eat meat. The LORD
heard you when you wailed, "If only we
had meat to eat! We were better off in
Egypt!" Now the LORD will give you
meat, and you will eat it. 19You will not
eat it for just one day, or two days, or
five, ten or twenty days, 20but for a
whole month—until it comes out of
your nostrils and you loathe it—
because you have rejected the LORD,
who is among you, and have wailed
before him, saying, "Why did we ever
leave Egypt?"'"

21But Moses said, "Here I am among
six hundred thousand men on foot, and
you say, 'I will give them meat to eat for
a whole month!' 22Would they have
enough if flocks and herds were slaughtered for them? Would they have
enough if all the fish in the sea were
caught for them?"

23The LORD answered Moses, "Is the
LORD's arm too short? You will now see
whether or not what I say will come true
for you."

24So Moses went out and told the
people what the LORD had said. He
brought together seventy of their elders
and made them stand round the Tent.
25Then the LORD came down in the
cloud and spoke with him, and he took
of the Spirit that was on him and put the
Spirit on the seventy elders. When the
Spirit rested on them, they prophesied,
but they did not do so again.

26However, two men, whose names
were Eldad and Medad, had remained
in the camp. They were listed among
the elders, but did not go out to the
Tent. Yet the Spirit also rested on them,
and they prophesied in the camp. 27A
young man ran and told Moses, "Eldad
and Medad are prophesying in the
camp."

28Joshua son of Nun, who had been
Moses' assistant since youth, spoke up
and said, "Moses, my lord, stop them!"

29But Moses replied, "Are you
jealous for my sake? I wish that all the
LORD's people were prophets and that
the LORD would put his Spirit on them!"
30Then Moses and the elders of Israel
returned to the camp.

31Now a wind went out from the
LORD and drove quail in from the sea. It
brought them down all around the camp
to about three feet above the ground, as
far as a day's walk in any direction. 32All
that day and night and all the next day
the people went out and gathered quail.
No-one gathered less than ten homers.
Then they spread them out all around
the camp. 33But while the meat was still
between their teeth and before it could
be consumed, the anger of the LORD
burned against the people, and he
struck them with a severe plague.
34Therefore the place was named Kibroth Hattaavah, because there they
buried the people who had craved other
food.

[35]From Kibroth Hattaavah the people travelled to Hazeroth and stayed there.

Miriam and Aaron Oppose Moses

12 Miriam and Aaron began to talk against Moses because of his Cushite wife, for he had married a Cushite. [2]"Has the LORD spoken only through Moses?" they asked. "Hasn't he also spoken through us?" And the LORD heard this.

[3](Now Moses was a very humble man, more humble than anyone else on the face of the earth.)

[4]At once the LORD said to Moses, Aaron and Miriam, "Come out to the Tent of Meeting, all three of you." So the three of them came out. [5]Then the LORD came down in a pillar of cloud; he stood at the entrance to the Tent and summoned Aaron and Miriam. When both of them stepped forward, [6]he said, "Listen to my words:

"When a prophet of the LORD is
among you,
I reveal myself to him in visions,
I speak to him in dreams.
[7]But this is not true of my servant
Moses;
he is faithful in all my house.
[8]With him I speak face to face,
clearly and not in riddles;
he sees the form of the LORD.
Why then were you not afraid
to speak against my servant
Moses?"

[9]The anger of the LORD burned against them, and he left them.

[10]When the cloud lifted from above the Tent, there stood Miriam—leprous, like snow. Aaron turned towards her and saw that she had leprosy; [11]and he said to Moses, "Please, my lord, do not hold against us the sin we have so foolishly committed. [12]Do not let her be like a stillborn infant coming from its mother's womb with its flesh half eaten away."

[13]So Moses cried out to the LORD, "O God, please heal her!"

[14]The LORD replied to Moses, "If her father had spat in her face, would she not have been in disgrace for seven days? Confine her outside the camp for seven days; after that she can be brought back." [15]So Miriam was confined outside the camp for seven days, and the people did not move on till she was brought back.

[16]After that, the people left Hazeroth and encamped in the Desert of Paran.

Exploring Canaan

13 The LORD said to Moses, [2]"Send some men to explore the land of Canaan, which I am giving to the Israelites. From each ancestral tribe send one of its leaders."

[3]So at the LORD's command Moses sent them out from the Desert of Paran. All of them were leaders of the Israelites. [4]These are their names:

from the tribe of Reuben, Shammau son of Zaccur;
[5]from the tribe of Simeon, Shaphat son of Hori;
[6]from the tribe of Judah, Caleb son of Jephunneh;
[7]from the tribe of Issachar, Igal son of Joseph;
[8]from the tribe of Ephraim, Hoshea son of Nun;
[9]from the tribe of Benjamin, Palti son of Raphu;
[10]from the tribe of Zebulun, Gaddiel son of Sodi;
[11]from the tribe of Manasseh (a tribe of Joseph), Gaddi son of Susi;
[12]from the tribe of Dan, Ammiel son of Gemalli;
[13]from the tribe of Asher, Sethur son of Michael;
[14]from the tribe of Naphtali, Nahbi son of Vophsi;
[15]from the tribe of Gad, Geuel son of Maki.

[16]These are the names of the men Moses sent to explore the land. (Moses gave Hoshea son of Nun the name Joshua.)

[17]When Moses sent them to explore
Canaan, he said, "Go up through the
Negev and on into the hill country.
[18]See what the land is like and whether
the people who live there are strong or
weak, few or many. [19]What kind of land
do they live in? Is it good or bad? What
kind of towns do they live in? Are they
unwalled or fortified? [20]How is the soil?
Is it fertile or poor? Are there trees on it
or not? Do your best to bring back some
of the fruit of the land." (It was the
season for the first ripe grapes.)
[21]So they went up and explored the
land from the Desert of Zin as far as
Rehob, towards Lebo Hamath. [22]They
went up through the Negev and came to
Hebron, where Ahiman, Sheshai and
Talmai, the descendants of Anak, lived.
(Hebron had been built seven years before Zoan in Egypt.) [23]When they
reached the Valley of Eshcol, they cut
off a branch bearing a single cluster of
grapes. Two of them carried it on a pole
between them, along with some pomegranates and figs. [24]That place was
called the Valley of Eshcol because of
the cluster of grapes the Israelites cut
off there. [25]At the end of forty days they
returned from exploring the land.

NEW TESTAMENT READING
Luke 3:23–4:13

[23]Now Jesus himself was about thirty
years old when he began his ministry.
He was the son, so it was thought, of
Joseph,

the son of Heli, [24]the son of Matthat,
the son of Levi, the son of Melki,
the son of Jannai, the son of Joseph,
[25]the son of Mattathias, the son of
Amos,
the son of Nahum, the son of Esli,
the son of Naggai, [26]the son of
Maath,
the son of Mattathias, the son of
Semein,
the son of Josech, the son of Joda,
[27]the son of Joanan, the son of Rhesa,
the son of Zerubbabel, the son of
Shealtiel,
the son of Neri, [28]the son of Melki,
the son of Addi, the son of Cosam,
the son of Elmadam, the son of Er,
[29]the son of Joshua, the son of Eliezer,
the son of Jorim, the son of Matthat,
the son of Levi, [30]the son of Simeon,
the son of Judah, the son of Joseph,
the son of Jonam, the son of Eliakim,
[31]the son of Melea, the son of Menna,
the son of Mattatha, the son of
Nathan,
the son of David, [32]the son of Jesse,
the son of Obed, the son of Boaz,
the son of Salmon, the son of
Nahshon,
[33]the son of Amminadab, the son of
Ram,
the son of Hezron, the son of Perez,
the son of Judah, [34]the son of Jacob,
the son of Isaac, the son of Abraham,
the son of Terah, the son of Nahor,
[35]the son of Serug, the son of Reu,
the son of Peleg, the son of Eber,
the son of Shelah, [36]the son of
Cainan,
the son of Arphaxad, the son of
Shem,
the son of Noah, the son of Lamech,
[37]the son of Methuselah, the son of
Enoch,
the son of Jared, the son of
Mahalalel,
the son of Kenan, [38]the son of Enosh,
the son of Seth, the son of Adam,
the son of God.

The Temptation of Jesus

4 Jesus, full of the Holy Spirit, returned from the Jordan and was led
by the Spirit in the desert, [2]where for
forty days he was tempted by the devil.
He ate nothing during those days, and
at the end of them he was hungry.
[3]The devil said to him, "If you are the
Son of God, tell this stone to become
bread."
[4]Jesus answered, "It is written: 'Man
does not live on bread alone.'"
[5]The devil led him up to a high place

and showed him in an instant all the
kingdoms of the world. 6And he said to
him, "I will give you all their authority
and splendour, for it has been given to
me, and I can give it to anyone I want to.
7So if you worship me, it will all be
yours."

8Jesus answered, "It is written:
'Worship the Lord your God and serve
him only.'"

9The devil led him to Jerusalem and
had him stand on the highest point of
the temple. "If you are the Son of
God," he said, "throw yourself down
from here. 10For it is written:

"'He will command his angels
concerning you
to guard you carefully;
11they will lift you up in their hands,
so that you will not strike your foot
against a stone.'"

12Jesus answered, "It says: 'Do not
put the Lord your God to the test.'"
13When the devil had finished all this
tempting, he left him until an opportune
time.

READING FROM PROVERBS
Proverbs 7:21–27

21With persuasive words she led him
astray;
she seduced him with her smooth
talk.
22All at once he followed her
like an ox going to the slaughter,
like a deer stepping into a noose
23 till an arrow pierces his liver,
like a bird darting into a snare,
little knowing it will cost him his
life.

24Now then, my sons, listen to me;
pay attention to what I say.
25Do not let your heart turn to her ways
or stray into her paths.
26Many are the victims she has brought
down;
her slain are a mighty throng.
27Her house is a highway to the grave,
leading down to the chambers of
death.

DAY 81

MARCH 22

OLD TESTAMENT READING
Numbers 13:26–14:45

Report on the Exploration

26They came back to Moses and
Aaron and the whole Israelite community at Kadesh in the Desert of Paran.
There they reported to them and to the
whole assembly and showed them the
fruit of the land. 27They gave Moses this
account: "We went into the land to
which you sent us, and it does flow with
milk and honey! Here is its fruit. 28But
the people who live there are powerful,
and the cities are fortified and very
large. We even saw descendants of
Anak there. 29The Amalekites live in
the Negev; the Hittites, Jebusites and
Amorites live in the hill country; and the
Canaanites live near the sea and along
the Jordan."

30Then Caleb silenced the people before Moses and said, "We should go up
and take possession of the land, for we
can certainly do it."

31But the men who had gone up with
him said, "We can't attack those people; they are stronger than we are."
32And they spread among the Israelites
a bad report about the land they had
explored. They said, "The land we explored devours those living in it. All the
people we saw there are of great size.

33We saw the Nephilim there (the descendants of Anak come from the
Nephilim). We seemed like grasshoppers in our own eyes, and we looked
the same to them."

The People Rebel

14 That night all the people of the
community raised their voices
and wept aloud. 2All the Israelites
grumbled against Moses and Aaron,
and the whole assembly said to them,
"If only we had died in Egypt! Or in this
desert! 3Why is the LORD bringing us to
this land only to let us fall by the sword?
Our wives and children will be taken as
plunder. Wouldn't it be better for us to
go back to Egypt?" 4And they said to
each other, "We should choose a leader
and go back to Egypt."
5Then Moses and Aaron fell face
down in front of the whole Israelite
assembly gathered there. 6Joshua son of
Nun and Caleb son of Jephunneh, who
were among those who had explored
the land, tore their clothes 7and said to
the entire Israelite assembly, "The land
we passed through and explored is exceedingly good. 8If the LORD is pleased
with us, he will lead us into that land, a
land flowing with milk and honey, and
will give it to us. 9Only do not rebel
against the LORD. And do not be afraid
of the people of the land, because we
will swallow them up. Their protection
is gone, but the LORD is with us. Do not
be afraid of them."
10But the whole assembly talked
about stoning them. Then the glory of
the LORD appeared at the Tent of Meeting to all the Israelites. 11The LORD said
to Moses, "How long will these people
treat me with contempt? How long will
they refuse to believe in me, in spite of
all the miraculous signs I have performed among them? 12I will strike
them down with a plague and destroy
them, but I will make you into a nation
greater and stronger than they."
13Moses said to the LORD, "Then the
Egyptians will hear about it! By your
power you brought these people up
from among them. 14And they will tell
the inhabitants of this land about it.
They have already heard that you, O
LORD, are with these people and that
you, O LORD, have been seen face to
face, that your cloud stays over them,
and that you go before them in a pillar
of cloud by day and a pillar of fire by
night. 15If you put these people to death
all at one time, the nations who have
heard this report about you will say,
16'The LORD was not able to bring these
people into the land he promised them
on oath; so he slaughtered them in the
desert.'
17"Now may the Lord's strength be
displayed, just as you have declared:
18'The LORD is slow to anger, abounding in love and forgiving sin and rebellion. Yet he does not leave the guilty
unpunished; he punishes the children
for the sin of the fathers to the third and
fourth generation.' 19In accordance
with your great love, forgive the sin of
these people, just as you have pardoned
them from the time they left Egypt until
now."
20The LORD replied, "I have forgiven
them, as you asked. 21Nevertheless, as
surely as I live and as surely as the glory
of the LORD fills the whole earth, 22not
one of the men who saw my glory and
the miraculous signs I performed in
Egypt and in the desert but who disobeyed me and tested me ten times
—23not one of them will ever see the
land I promised on oath to their forefathers. No-one who has treated me
with contempt will ever see it. 24But
because my servant Caleb has a different spirit and follows me wholeheartedly, I will bring him into the land
he went to, and his descendants will
inherit it. 25Since the Amalekites and
Canaanites are living in the valleys, turn
back tomorrow and set out towards the
desert along the route to the Red Sea."
26The LORD said to Moses and
Aaron: 27"How long will this wicked
community grumble against me? I have

heard the complaints of these grumbling Israelites. 28 So tell them, 'As surely as I live, declares the LORD, I will do to you the very things I heard you say: 29 In this desert your bodies will fall—every one of you twenty years old or more who was counted in the census and who has grumbled against me. 30 Not one of you will enter the land I swore with uplifted hand to make your home, except Caleb son of Jephunneh and Joshua son of Nun. 31 As for your children that you said would be taken as plunder, I will bring them in to enjoy the land you have rejected. 32 But you—your bodies will fall in this desert. 33 Your children will be shepherds here for forty years, suffering for your unfaithfulness, until the last of your bodies lies in the desert. 34 For forty years—one year for each of the forty days you explored the land—you will suffer for your sins and know what it is like to have me against you.' 35 I, the LORD, have spoken, and I will surely do these things to this whole wicked community, which has banded together against me. They will meet their end in this desert; here they will die."

36 So the men Moses had sent to explore the land, who returned and made the whole community grumble against him by spreading a bad report about it—37 these men responsible for spreading the bad report about the land were struck down and died of a plague before the LORD. 38 Of the men who went to explore the land, only Joshua son of Nun and Caleb son of Jephunneh survived.

39 When Moses reported this to all the Israelites, they mourned bitterly. 40 Early the next morning they went up towards the high hill country. "We have sinned," they said. "We will go up to the place the LORD promised."

41 But Moses said, "Why are you disobeying the LORD's command? This will not succeed! 42 Do not go up, because the LORD is not with you. You will be defeated by your enemies, 43 for the Amalekites and Canaanites will face you there. Because you have turned away from the LORD, he will not be with you and you will fall by the sword."

44 Nevertheless, in their presumption they went up towards the high hill country, though neither Moses nor the ark of the LORD's covenant moved from the camp. 45 Then the Amalekites and Canaanites who lived in that hill country came down and attacked them and beat them down all the way to Hormah.

NEW TESTAMENT READING
Luke 4:14–37

Jesus Rejected at Nazareth

14 Jesus returned to Galilee in the power of the Spirit, and news about him spread through the whole countryside. 15 He taught in their synagogues, and everyone praised him.

16 He went to Nazareth, where he had been brought up, and on the Sabbath day he went into the synagogue, as was his custom. And he stood up to read. 17 The scroll of the prophet Isaiah was handed to him. Unrolling it, he found the place where it is written:

18 "The Spirit of the Lord is on me,
because he has anointed me
to preach good news to the poor.
He has sent me to proclaim freedom
for the prisoners
and recovery of sight for the blind,
to release the oppressed,
19 to proclaim the year of the Lord's
favour."

20 Then he rolled up the scroll, gave it back to the attendant and sat down. The eyes of everyone in the synagogue were fastened on him, 21 and he began by saying to them, "Today this scripture is fulfilled in your hearing."

22 All spoke well of him and were amazed at the gracious words that came from his lips. "Isn't this Joseph's son?" they asked.

23 Jesus said to them, "Surely you will
quote this proverb to me: 'Physician,
heal yourself! Do here in your home
town what we have heard that you did in
Capernaum.'"
24 "I tell you the truth," he continued,
"no prophet is accepted in his home
town. 25 I assure you that there were
many widows in Israel in Elijah's time,
when the sky was shut for three and a
half years and there was a severe famine
throughout the land. 26 Yet Elijah was
not sent to any of them, but to a widow
in Zarephath in the region of Sidon.
27 And there were many in Israel with
leprosy in the time of Elisha the
prophet, yet not one of them was
cleansed—only Naaman the Syrian."
28 All the people in the synagogue
were furious when they heard this.
29 They got up, drove him out of the
town, and took him to the brow of the
hill on which the town was built, in
order to throw him down the cliff. 30 But
he walked right through the crowd and
went on his way.

Jesus Drives Out an Evil Spirit

31 Then he went down to Capernaum,
a town in Galilee, and on the Sabbath
began to teach the people. 32 They were
amazed at his teaching, because his
message had authority.
33 In the synagogue there was a man
possessed by a demon, an evil spirit. He
cried out at the top of his voice, 34 "Ha!
What do you want with us, Jesus of
Nazareth? Have you come to destroy
us? I know who you are—the Holy One
of God!"
35 "Be quiet!" Jesus said sternly.
"Come out of him!" Then the demon
threw the man down before them all
and came out without injuring him.
36 All the people were amazed and
said to each other, "What is this
teaching? With authority and power he
gives orders to evil spirits and they come
out!" 37 And the news about him spread
throughout the surrounding area.

READING FROM PSALMS

Psalm 36:1–12

For the director of music. Of David the servant of the LORD.

1 An oracle is within my heart
concerning the sinfulness of the wicked:
There is no fear of God
before his eyes.
2 For in his own eyes he flatters himself
too much to detect or hate his sin.
3 The words of his mouth are wicked and deceitful;
he has ceased to be wise and to do good.
4 Even on his bed he plots evil;
he commits himself to a sinful course
and does not reject what is wrong.

5 Your love, O LORD, reaches to the heavens,
your faithfulness to the skies.
6 Your righteousness is like the mighty mountains,
your justice like the great deep.
O LORD, you preserve both man and beast.
7 How priceless is your unfailing love!
Both high and low among men
find refuge in the shadow of your wings.
8 They feast in the abundance of your house;
you give them drink from your river of delights.
9 For with you is the fountain of life;
in your light we see light.

10 Continue your love to those who know you,
your righteousness to the upright in heart.
11 May the foot of the proud not come against me,
nor the hand of the wicked drive me away.
12 See how the evildoers lie fallen—
thrown down, not able to rise!

DAY 82

MARCH 23

OLD TESTAMENT READING
Numbers 15:1–16:35

Supplementary Offerings

15 The LORD said to Moses,
2"Speak to the Israelites and say
to them: 'After you enter the land I am
giving you as a home 3and you present
to the LORD offerings made by fire,
from the herd or the flock, as an aroma
pleasing to the LORD—whether burnt
offerings or sacrifices, for special vows
or freewill offerings or festival offerings
—4then the one who brings his offering
shall present to the LORD a grain offering of a tenth of an ephah of fine flour
mixed with a quarter of a hin of oil.
5With each lamb for the burnt offering
or the sacrifice, prepare a quarter of a
hin of wine as a drink offering.

6" 'With a ram prepare a grain offering of two-tenths of an ephah of fine
flour mixed with a third of a hin of oil,
7and a third of a hin of wine as a drink
offering. Offer it as an aroma pleasing
to the LORD.

8" 'When you prepare a young bull as
a burnt offering or sacrifice, for a special
vow or a fellowship offering to the
LORD, 9bring with the bull a grain offering of three-tenths of an ephah of fine
flour mixed with half a hin of oil. 10Also
bring half a hin of wine as a drink offering. It will be an offering made by fire,
an aroma pleasing to the LORD. 11Each
bull or ram, each lamb or young goat,
is to be prepared in this manner. 12Do
this for each one, for as many as you
prepare.

13" 'Everyone who is native-born
must do these things in this way when he
brings an offering made by fire as an
aroma pleasing to the LORD. 14For the
generations to come, whenever an alien
or anyone else living among you presents an offering made by fire as an
aroma pleasing to the LORD, he must do
exactly as you do. 15The community is
to have the same rules for you and for
the alien living among you; this is a
lasting ordinance for the generations to
come. You and the alien shall be the
same before the LORD: 16The same laws
and regulations will apply both to you
and to the alien living among you.' "

17The LORD said to Moses, 18"Speak
to the Israelites and say to them: 'When
you enter the land to which I am taking
you 19and you eat the food of the land,
present a portion as an offering to the
LORD. 20Present a cake from the first of
your ground meal and present it as an
offering from the threshing-floor.
21Throughout the generations to come
you are to give this offering to the LORD
from the first of your ground meal.

Offerings for Unintentional Sins

22" 'Now if you unintentionally fail to
keep any of these commands the LORD
gave Moses—23any of the LORD's commands to you through him, from the day
the LORD gave them and continuing
through the generations to come—
24and if this is done unintentionally
without the community being aware of
it, then the whole community is to offer
a young bull for a burnt offering as an
aroma pleasing to the LORD, along with
its prescribed grain offering and drink
offering, and a male goat for a sin offering. 25The priest is to make atonement
for the whole Israelite community, and
they will be forgiven, for it was not
intentional and they have brought to the
LORD for their wrong an offering made
by fire and a sin offering. 26The whole
Israelite community and the aliens living among them will be forgiven, because all the people were involved in the
unintentional wrong.

27" 'But if just one person sins unintentionally, he must bring a year-old

female goat for a sin offering. [28]The priest is to make atonement before the LORD for the one who erred by sinning unintentionally, and when atonement has been made for him, he will be forgiven. [29]One and the same law applies to everyone who sins unintentionally, whether he is a native-born Israelite or an alien.

[30]" 'But anyone who sins defiantly, whether native-born or alien, blasphemes the LORD, and that person must be cut off from his people. [31]Because he has despised the LORD's word and broken his commands, that person must surely be cut off; his guilt remains on him.' "

The Sabbath-Breaker Put to Death

[32]While the Israelites were in the desert, a man was found gathering wood on the Sabbath day. [33]Those who found him gathering wood brought him to Moses and Aaron and the whole assembly, [34]and they kept him in custody, because it was not clear what should be done to him. [35]Then the LORD said to Moses, "The man must die. The whole assembly must stone him outside the camp." [36]So the assembly took him outside the camp and stoned him to death, as the LORD commanded Moses.

Tassels on Garments

[37]The LORD said to Moses, [38]"Speak to the Israelites and say to them: 'Throughout the generations to come you are to make tassels on the corners of your garments, with a blue cord on each tassel. [39]You will have these tassels to look at and so you will remember all the commands of the LORD, that you may obey them and not prostitute yourselves by going after the lusts of your own hearts and eyes. [40]Then you will remember to obey all my commands and will be consecrated to your God. [41]I am the LORD your God, who brought you out of Egypt to be your God. I am the LORD your God.' "

Korah, Dathan and Abiram

16 Korah son of Izhar, the son of Kohath, the son of Levi, and certain Reubenites—Dathan and Abiram, sons of Eliab, and On son of Peleth—became insolent [2]and rose up against Moses. With them were 250 Israelite men, well-known community leaders who had been appointed members of the council. [3]They came as a group to oppose Moses and Aaron and said to them, "You have gone too far! The whole community is holy, every one of them, and the LORD is with them. Why then do you set yourselves above the LORD's assembly?"

[4]When Moses heard this, he fell face down. [5]Then he said to Korah and all his followers: "In the morning the LORD will show who belongs to him and who is holy, and he will make that person come near him. The man he chooses he will cause to come near him. [6]You, Korah, and all your followers are to do this: Take censers [7]and tomorrow put fire and incense in them before the LORD. The man the LORD chooses will be the one who is holy. You Levites have gone too far!"

[8]Moses also said to Korah, "Now listen, you Levites! [9]Isn't it enough for you that the God of Israel has separated you from the rest of the Israelite community and brought you near himself to do the work at the LORD's tabernacle and to stand before the community and minister to them? [10]He has brought you and all your fellow Levites near himself, but now you are trying to get the priesthood too. [11]It is against the LORD that you and all your followers have banded together. Who is Aaron that you should grumble against him?"

[12]Then Moses summoned Dathan and Abiram, the sons of Eliab. But they said, "We will not come! [13]Isn't it enough that you have brought us up out of a land flowing with milk and honey to kill us in the desert? And now you also want to lord it over us? [14]Moreover, you haven't brought us into a land flowing

with milk and honey or given us an
inheritance of fields and vineyards. Will
you gouge out the eyes of these men?
No, we will not come!"
15Then Moses became very angry and
said to the LORD, "Do not accept their
offering. I have not taken so much as a
donkey from them, nor have I wronged
any of them."
16Moses said to Korah, "You and all
your followers are to appear before the
LORD tomorrow—you and they and
Aaron. 17Each man is to take his censer
and put incense in it—250 censers in
all—and present it before the LORD.
You and Aaron are to present your
censers also." 18So each man took his
censer, put fire and incense in it, and
stood with Moses and Aaron at the
entrance to the Tent of Meeting.
19When Korah had gathered all his followers in opposition to them at the entrance to the Tent of Meeting, the glory
of the LORD appeared to the entire assembly. 20The LORD said to Moses and
Aaron, 21"Separate yourselves from
this assembly so that I can put an end to
them at once."
22But Moses and Aaron fell face
down and cried out, "O God, God of
the spirits of all mankind, will you be
angry with the entire assembly when
only one man sins?"
23Then the LORD said to Moses,
24"Say to the assembly, 'Move away
from the tents of Korah, Dathan and
Abiram.'"
25Moses got up and went to Dathan
and Abiram, and the elders of Israel
followed him. 26He warned the assembly, "Move back from the tents of these
wicked men! Do not touch anything
belonging to them, or you will be swept
away because of all their sins." 27So
they moved away from the tents of
Korah, Dathan and Abiram. Dathan
and Abiram had come out and were
standing with their wives, children and
little ones at the entrances to their tents.
28Then Moses said, "This is how you
will know that the LORD has sent me to
do all these things and that it was not my
idea: 29If these men die a natural death
and experience only what usually happens to men, then the LORD has not sent
me. 30But if the LORD brings about
something totally new, and the earth
opens its mouth and swallows them,
with everything that belongs to them,
and they go down alive into the grave,
then you will know that these men have
treated the LORD with contempt."
31As soon as he finished saying all
this, the ground under them split apart
32and the earth opened its mouth and
swallowed them, with their households
and all Korah's men and all their possessions. 33They went down alive into the
grave, with everything they owned; the
earth closed over them, and they
perished and were gone from the community. 34At their cries, all the
Israelites around them fled, shouting,
"The earth is going to swallow us too!"
35And fire came out from the LORD
and consumed the 250 men who were
offering the incense.

NEW TESTAMENT READING

Luke 4:38–5:16

Jesus Heals Many

38Jesus left the synagogue and went to
the home of Simon. Now Simon's
mother-in-law was suffering from a high
fever, and they asked Jesus to help her.
39So he bent over her and rebuked the
fever, and it left her. She got up at once
and began to wait on them.
40When the sun was setting, the
people brought to Jesus all who had
various kinds of sickness, and laying his
hands on each one, he healed them.
41Moreover, demons came out of many
people, shouting, "You are the Son of
God!" But he rebuked them and would
not allow them to speak, because they
knew he was the Christ.
42At daybreak Jesus went out to a
solitary place. The people were looking
for him and when they came to where he
was, they tried to keep him from leaving
them. 43But he said, "I must preach the

good news of the kingdom of God to the
other towns also, because that is why I
was sent." 44And he kept on preaching
in the synagogues of Judea.

The Calling of the First Disciples

5 One day as Jesus was standing by
the Lake of Gennesaret, with the
people crowding round him and listening to the word of God, 2he saw at the
water's edge two boats, left there by the
fishermen, who were washing their
nets. 3He got into one of the boats, the
one belonging to Simon, and asked him
to put out a little from shore. Then he
sat down and taught the people from the
boat.

4When he had finished speaking, he
said to Simon, "Put out into deep water,
and let down the nets for a catch."

5Simon answered, "Master, we've
worked hard all night and haven't
caught anything. But because you say
so, I will let down the nets."

6When they had done so, they caught
such a large number of fish that their
nets began to break. 7So they signalled
to their partners in the other boat to
come and help them, and they came and
filled both boats so full that they began
to sink.

8When Simon Peter saw this, he fell
at Jesus' knees and said, "Go away from
me, Lord; I am a sinful man!" 9For he
and all his companions were astonished
at the catch of fish they had taken, 10and
so were James and John, the sons of
Zebedee, Simon's partners.

Then Jesus said to Simon, "Don't be
afraid; from now on you will catch
men." 11So they pulled their boats up on
shore, left everything and followed him.

The Man With Leprosy

12While Jesus was in one of the towns,
a man came along who was covered with
leprosy. When he saw Jesus, he fell with
his face to the ground and begged him,
"Lord, if you are willing, you can make
me clean."

13Jesus reached out his hand and
touched the man. "I am willing," he
said. "Be clean!" And immediately the
leprosy left him.

14Then Jesus ordered him, "Don't
tell anyone, but go, show yourself to the
priest and offer the sacrifices that Moses
commanded for your cleansing, as a
testimony to them."

15Yet the news about him spread all
the more, so that crowds of people came
to hear him and to be healed of their
sicknesses. 16But Jesus often withdrew
to lonely places and prayed.

READING FROM PSALMS

Psalm 37:1–9

Of David.

1Do not fret because of evil men
or be envious of those who do
wrong;
2for like the grass they will soon
wither,
like green plants they will soon die
away.

3Trust in the LORD and do good;
dwell in the land and enjoy safe
pasture.
4Delight yourself in the LORD
and he will give you the desires of
your heart.

5Commit your way to the LORD;
trust in him and he will do this:
6He will make your righteousness
shine like the dawn,
the justice of your cause like the
noonday sun.

7Be still before the LORD and wait
patiently for him;
do not fret when men succeed in
their ways,
when they carry out their wicked
schemes.

8Refrain from anger and turn from
wrath;
do not fret—it leads only to evil.
9For evil men will be cut off,
but those who hope in the LORD
will inherit the land.

DAY 83

MARCH 24

OLD TESTAMENT READING
Numbers 16:36–18:32

36The LORD said to Moses, 37"Tell
Eleazar son of Aaron, the priest, to take
the censers out of the smouldering remains and scatter the coals some distance away, for the censers are holy
—38the censers of the men who sinned
at the cost of their lives. Hammer the
censers into sheets to overlay the altar,
for they were presented before the
LORD and have become holy. Let them
be a sign to the Israelites."
39So Eleazar the priest collected the
bronze censers brought by those who
had been burned up, and he had them
hammered out to overlay the altar, 40as
the LORD directed him through Moses.
This was to remind the Israelites that
no-one except a descendant of Aaron
should come to burn incense before the
LORD, or he would become like Korah
and his followers.
41The next day the whole Israelite
community grumbled against Moses
and Aaron. "You have killed the
LORD's people," they said.
42But when the assembly gathered in
opposition to Moses and Aaron and
turned towards the Tent of Meeting,
suddenly the cloud covered it and the
glory of the LORD appeared. 43Then
Moses and Aaron went to the front of
the Tent of Meeting, 44and the LORD
said to Moses, 45"Get away from this
assembly so that I can put an end to
them at once." And they fell face down.
46Then Moses said to Aaron, "Take
your censer and put incense in it, along
with fire from the altar, and hurry to the
assembly to make atonement for them.
Wrath has come out from the LORD; the
plague has started." 47So Aaron did as
Moses said, and ran into the midst of the
assembly. The plague had already
started among the people, but Aaron
offered the incense and made atonement for them. 48He stood between the
living and the dead, and the plague
stopped. 49But 14,700 people died from
the plague, in addition to those who had
died because of Korah. 50Then Aaron
returned to Moses at the entrance to the
Tent of Meeting, for the plague had
stopped.

The Budding of Aaron's Staff

17 The LORD said to Moses,
2"Speak to the Israelites and get
twelve staffs from them, one from the
leader of each of their ancestral tribes.
Write the name of each man on his staff.
3On the staff of Levi write Aaron's
name, for there must be one staff for the
head of each ancestral tribe. 4Place
them in the Tent of Meeting in front of
the Testimony, where I meet with you.
5The staff belonging to the man I choose
will sprout, and I will rid myself of this
constant grumbling against you by the
Israelites."
6So Moses spoke to the Israelites, and
their leaders gave him twelve staffs, one
for the leader of each of their ancestral
tribes, and Aaron's staff was among
them. 7Moses placed the staffs before
the LORD in the Tent of the Testimony.
8The next day Moses entered the
Tent of the Testimony and saw that
Aaron's staff, which represented the
house of Levi, had not only sprouted
but had budded, blossomed and produced almonds. 9Then Moses brought
out all the staffs from the LORD's presence to all the Israelites. They looked at
them, and each man took his own staff.
10The LORD said to Moses, "Put back
Aaron's staff in front of the Testimony,
to be kept as a sign to the rebellious.
This will put an end to their grumbling
against me, so that they will not die."
11Moses did just as the LORD commanded him.

[12]The Israelites said to Moses, "We shall die! We are lost, we are all lost! [13]Anyone who even comes near the tabernacle of the LORD will die. Are we all going to die?"

Duties of Priests and Levites

18 The LORD said to Aaron, "You, your sons and your father's family are to bear the responsibility for offences against the sanctuary, and you and your sons alone are to bear the responsibility for offences against the priesthood. [2]Bring your fellow Levites from your ancestral tribe to join you and assist you when you and your sons minister before the Tent of the Testimony. [3]They are to be responsible to you and are to perform all the duties of the Tent, but they must not go near the furnishings of the sanctuary or the altar, or both they and you will die. [4]They are to join you and be responsible for the care of the Tent of Meeting—all the work at the Tent—and no-one else may come near where you are.

[5]"You are to be responsible for the care of the sanctuary and the altar, so that wrath will not fall on the Israelites again. [6]I myself have selected your fellow Levites from among the Israelites as a gift to you, dedicated to the LORD to do the work at the Tent of Meeting. [7]But only you and your sons may serve as priests in connection with everything at the altar and inside the curtain. I am giving you the service of the priesthood as a gift. Anyone else who comes near the sanctuary must be put to death."

Offerings for Priests and Levites

[8]Then the LORD said to Aaron, "I myself have put you in charge of the offerings presented to me; all the holy offerings the Israelites give me I give to you and your sons as your portion and regular share. [9]You are to have the part of the most holy offerings that is kept from the fire. From all the gifts they bring me as most holy offerings, whether grain or sin or guilt offerings, that part belongs to you and your sons. [10]Eat it as something most holy; every male shall eat it. You must regard it as holy.

[11]"This also is yours: whatever is set aside from the gifts of all the wave offerings of the Israelites. I give this to you and your sons and daughters as your regular share. Everyone in your household who is ceremonially clean may eat it.

[12]"I give you all the finest olive oil and all the finest new wine and grain they give to the LORD as the firstfruits of their harvest. [13]All the land's firstfruits that they bring to the LORD will be yours. Everyone in your household who is ceremonially clean may eat it.

[14]"Everything in Israel that is devoted to the LORD is yours. [15]The first offspring of every womb, both man and animal, that is offered to the LORD is yours. But you must redeem every firstborn son and every firstborn male of unclean animals. [16]When they are a month old, you must redeem them at the redemption price set at five shekels of silver, according to the sanctuary shekel, which weighs twenty gerahs.

[17]"But you must not redeem the firstborn of an ox, a sheep or a goat; they are holy. Sprinkle their blood on the altar and burn their fat as an offering made by fire, an aroma pleasing to the LORD. [18]Their meat is to be yours, just as the breast of the wave offering and the right thigh are yours. [19]Whatever is set aside from the holy offerings the Israelites present to the LORD I give to you and your sons and daughters as your regular share. It is an everlasting covenant of salt before the LORD for both you and your offspring."

[20]The LORD said to Aaron, "You will have no inheritance in their land, nor will you have any share among them; I am your share and your inheritance among the Israelites.

[21]"I give to the Levites all the tithes in Israel as their inheritance in return for the work they do while serving at the

Tent of Meeting. 22From now on the
Israelites must not go near the Tent of
Meeting, or they will bear the consequences of their sin and will die. 23It is
the Levites who are to do the work at
the Tent of Meeting and bear the responsibility for offences against it. This
is a lasting ordinance for the generations to come. They will receive no
inheritance among the Israelites.
24Instead, I give to the Levites as their
inheritance the tithes that the Israelites
present as an offering to the LORD. That
is why I said concerning them: 'They
will have no inheritance among the
Israelites.'"

25The LORD said to Moses, 26"Speak
to the Levites and say to them: 'When
you receive from the Israelites the tithe
I give you as your inheritance, you must
present a tenth of that tithe as the
LORD's offering. 27Your offering will be
reckoned to you as grain from the
threshing-floor or juice from the winepress. 28In this way you also will present
an offering to the LORD from all the
tithes you receive from the Israelites.
From these tithes you must give the
LORD's portion to Aaron the priest.
29You must present as the LORD's portion the best and holiest part of everything given to you.'

30"Say to the Levites: 'When you present the best part, it will be reckoned to
you as the product of the threshing-floor
or the winepress. 31You and your
households may eat the rest of it anywhere, for it is your wages for your work
at the Tent of Meeting. 32By presenting
the best part of it you will not be guilty
in this matter; then you will not defile
the holy offerings of the Israelites, and
you will not die.'"

NEW TESTAMENT READING
Luke 5:17–32

Jesus Heals a Paralytic

17One day as he was teaching, Pharisees and teachers of the law, who had
come from every village of Galilee and
from Judea and Jerusalem, were sitting
there. And the power of the Lord was
present for him to heal the sick. 18Some
men came carrying a paralytic on a mat
and tried to take him into the house to
lay him before Jesus. 19When they could
not find a way to do this because of the
crowd, they went up on the roof and
lowered him on his mat through the tiles
into the middle of the crowd, right in
front of Jesus.

20When Jesus saw their faith, he said,
"Friend, your sins are forgiven."

21The Pharisees and the teachers of
the law began thinking to themselves,
"Who is this fellow who speaks blasphemy? Who can forgive sins but God
alone?"

22Jesus knew what they were thinking
and asked, "Why are you thinking these
things in your hearts? 23Which is easier:
to say, 'Your sins are forgiven,' or to
say, 'Get up and walk'? 24But that you
may know that the Son of Man has
authority on earth to forgive sins. . . ."
He said to the paralysed man, "I tell
you, get up, take your mat and go
home." 25Immediately he stood up in
front of them, took what he had been
lying on and went home praising God.
26Everyone was amazed and gave praise
to God. They were filled with awe and
said, "We have seen remarkable things
today."

The Calling of Levi

27After this, Jesus went out and saw a
tax collector by the name of Levi sitting
at his tax booth. "Follow me," Jesus
said to him, 28and Levi got up, left
everything and followed him.

29Then Levi held a great banquet for
Jesus at his house, and a large crowd of
tax collectors and others were eating
with them. 30But the Pharisees and the
teachers of the law who belonged to
their sect complained to his disciples,
"Why do you eat and drink with tax
collectors and 'sinners'?"

31Jesus answered them, "It is not the

healthy who need a doctor, but the sick. 32I have not come to call the righteous, but sinners to repentance."

READING FROM PSALMS
Psalm 37:10–20

10A little while, and the wicked will be
no more;
though you look for them, they will
not be found.
11But the meek will inherit the land
and enjoy great peace.

12The wicked plot against the righteous
and gnash their teeth at them;
13but the Lord laughs at the wicked,
for he knows their day is coming.

14The wicked draw the sword
and bend the bow
to bring down the poor and needy,
to slay those whose ways are
upright.
15But their swords will pierce their own
hearts,
and their bows will be broken.

16Better the little that the righteous
have
than the wealth of many wicked;
17for the power of the wicked will be
broken,
but the LORD upholds the
righteous.

18The days of the blameless are known
to the LORD,
and their inheritance will endure
for ever.
19In times of disaster they will not
wither;
in days of famine they will enjoy
plenty.

20But the wicked will perish:
The LORD's enemies will be like
the beauty of the fields,
they will vanish—vanish like
smoke.

MARCH 25

DAY 84

OLD TESTAMENT READING
Numbers 19:1–21:3

The Water of Cleansing

19 The LORD said to Moses and
Aaron: 2"This is a requirement
of the law that the LORD has commanded: Tell the Israelites to bring you a red heifer without defect or blemish and that has never been under a yoke.
3Give
it to Eleazar the priest; it is to be taken outside the camp and slaughtered in his presence.
4Then Eleazar the priest is to
take some of its blood on his finger and sprinkle it seven times towards the front of the Tent of Meeting.
5While he
watches, the heifer is to be burned—its hide, flesh, blood and offal.
6The priest
is to take some cedar wood, hyssop and scarlet wool and throw them onto the burning heifer.
7After that, the priest
must wash his clothes and bathe himself with water. He may then come into the camp, but he will be ceremonially unclean till evening.
8The man who burns
it must also wash his clothes and bathe with water, and he too will be unclean till evening.

9"A man who is clean shall gather up the ashes of the heifer and put them in a ceremonially clean place outside the camp. They shall be kept by the Israelite community for use in the water of cleansing; it is for purification from sin.
10The man who gathers up the ashes
of the heifer must also wash his clothes, and he too will be unclean till evening.

This will be a lasting ordinance both for the Israelites and for the aliens living among them.

11“Whoever touches the dead body of anyone will be unclean for seven days. 12He must purify himself with the water on the third day and on the seventh day; then he will be clean. But if he does not purify himself on the third and seventh days, he will not be clean. 13Whoever touches the dead body of anyone and fails to purify himself defiles the LORD’s tabernacle. That person must be cut off from Israel. Because the water of cleansing has not been sprinkled on him, he is unclean; his uncleanness remains on him.

14“This is the law that applies when a person dies in a tent: Anyone who enters the tent and anyone who is in it will be unclean for seven days, 15and every open container without a lid fastened on it will be unclean.

16“Anyone out in the open who touches someone who has been killed with a sword or someone who has died a natural death, or anyone who touches a human bone or a grave, will be unclean for seven days.

17“For the unclean person, put some ashes from the burned purification offering into a jar and pour fresh water over them. 18Then a man who is ceremonially clean is to take some hyssop, dip it in the water and sprinkle the tent and all the furnishings and the people who were there. He must also sprinkle anyone who has touched a human bone or a grave or someone who has been killed or someone who has died a natural death. 19The man who is clean is to sprinkle the unclean person on the third and seventh days, and on the seventh day he is to purify him. The person being cleansed must wash his clothes and bathe with water, and that evening he will be clean. 20But if a person who is unclean does not purify himself, he must be cut off from the community, because he has defiled the sanctuary of the LORD. The water of cleansing has not been sprinkled on him, and he is unclean. 21This is a lasting ordinance for them.

“The man who sprinkles the water of cleansing must also wash his clothes, and anyone who touches the water of cleansing will be unclean till evening. 22Anything that an unclean person touches becomes unclean, and anyone who touches it becomes unclean till evening.”

Water From the Rock

20 In the first month the whole Israelite community arrived at the Desert of Zin, and they stayed at Kadesh. There Miriam died and was buried.

2Now there was no water for the community, and the people gathered in opposition to Moses and Aaron. 3They quarrelled with Moses and said, “If only we had died when our brothers fell dead before the LORD! 4Why did you bring the LORD’s community into this desert, that we and our livestock should die here? 5Why did you bring us up out of Egypt to this terrible place? It has no grain or figs, grapevines or pomegranates. And there is no water to drink!”

6Moses and Aaron went from the assembly to the entrance to the Tent of Meeting and fell face down, and the glory of the LORD appeared to them. 7The LORD said to Moses, 8“Take the staff, and you and your brother Aaron gather the assembly together. Speak to that rock before their eyes and it will pour out its water. You will bring water out of the rock for the community so that they and their livestock can drink.”

9So Moses took the staff from the LORD’s presence, just as he commanded him. 10He and Aaron gathered the assembly together in front of the rock and Moses said to them, “Listen, you rebels, must we bring you water out of this rock?” 11Then Moses raised his arm and struck the rock twice with his staff. Water gushed out, and the community and their livestock drank.

12But the LORD said to Moses and
Aaron, "Because you did not trust in
me enough to honour me as holy in the
sight of the Israelites, you will not bring
this community into the land I give
them."
13These were the waters of Meribah,
where the Israelites quarrelled with the
LORD and where he showed himself
holy among them.

Edom Denies Israel Passage

14Moses sent messengers from
Kadesh to the king of Edom, saying:

> "This is what your brother Israel
> says: You know about all the
> hardships that have come upon us.
> 15Our forefathers went down into
> Egypt, and we lived there many
> years. The Egyptians ill-treated us
> and our fathers, 16but when we
> cried out to the LORD, he heard our
> cry and sent an angel and brought
> us out of Egypt.
> "Now we are here at Kadesh, a
> town on the edge of your territory.
> 17Please let us pass through your
> country. We will not go through
> any field or vineyard, or drink
> water from any well. We will travel
> along the king's highway and not
> turn to the right or to the left until
> we have passed through your
> territory."

18But Edom answered:

> "You may not pass through
> here; if you try, we will march out
> and attack you with the sword."

19The Israelites replied:

> "We will go along the main road,
> and if we or our livestock drink any
> of your water, we will pay for it.
> We only want to pass through on
> foot—nothing else."

20Again they answered:

> "You may not pass through."

Then Edom came out against them
with a large and powerful army. 21Since
Edom refused to let them go through
their territory, Israel turned away from
them.

The Death of Aaron

22The whole Israelite community set
out from Kadesh and came to Mount
Hor. 23At Mount Hor, near the border
of Edom, the LORD said to Moses and
Aaron, 24"Aaron will be gathered to his
people. He will not enter the land I give
the Israelites, because both of you rebelled against my command at the
waters of Meribah. 25Call Aaron and his
son Eleazar and take them up Mount
Hor. 26Remove Aaron's garments and
put them on his son Eleazar, for Aaron
will be gathered to his people; he will
die there."
27Moses did as the LORD commanded: They went up Mount Hor in the
sight of the whole community. 28Moses
removed Aaron's garments and put
them on his son Eleazar. And Aaron
died there on top of the mountain. Then
Moses and Eleazar came down from the
mountain, 29and when the whole community learned that Aaron had died,
the entire house of Israel mourned for
him thirty days.

Arad Destroyed

21 When the Canaanite king of
Arad, who lived in the Negev,
heard that Israel was coming along the
road to Atharim, he attacked the
Israelites and captured some of them.
2Then Israel made this vow to the LORD:
"If you will deliver these people into
our hands, we will totally destroy their
cities." 3The LORD listened to Israel's
plea and gave the Canaanites over to
them. They completely destroyed them
and their towns; so the place was named
Hormah.

NEW TESTAMENT READING
Luke 5:33–6:11

Jesus Questioned About Fasting

33They said to him, "John's disciples
often fast and pray, and so do the disciples of the Pharisees, but yours go on
eating and drinking."
34Jesus answered, "Can you make the
guests of the bridegroom fast while he is
with them? 35But the time will come
when the bridegroom will be taken from
them; in those days they will fast."
36He told them this parable: "No-one
tears a patch from a new garment and
sews it on an old one. If he does, he will
have torn the new garment, and the
patch from the new will not match the
old. 37And no-one pours new wine into
old wineskins. If he does, the new wine
will burst the skins, the wine will run out
and the wineskins will be ruined. 38No,
new wine must be poured into new
wineskins. 39And no-one after drinking
old wine wants the new, for he says,
'The old is better.'"

Lord of the Sabbath

6 One Sabbath Jesus was going
through the cornfields, and his disciples began to pick some ears of corn,
rub them in their hands and eat the
grain. 2Some of the Pharisees asked,
"Why are you doing what is unlawful on
the Sabbath?"
3Jesus answered them, "Have you
never read what David did when he and
his companions were hungry? 4He entered the house of God, and taking the
consecrated bread, he ate what is lawful
only for priests to eat. And he also gave
some to his companions." 5Then Jesus
said to them, "The Son of Man is Lord
of the Sabbath."
6On another Sabbath he went into
the synagogue and was teaching, and
a man was there whose right hand
was shrivelled. 7The Pharisees and the
teachers of the law were looking for a
reason to accuse Jesus, so they watched
him closely to see if he would heal on
the Sabbath. 8But Jesus knew what they
were thinking and said to the man with
the shrivelled hand, "Get up and stand
in front of everyone." So he got up and
stood there.
9Then Jesus said to them, "I ask you,
which is lawful on the Sabbath: to do
good or to do evil, to save life or to
destroy it?"
10He looked round at them all, and
then said to the man, "Stretch out your
hand." He did so, and his hand was
completely restored. 11But they were
furious and began to discuss with one
another what they might do to Jesus.

READING FROM PROVERBS
Proverbs 8:1–11

Wisdom's Call

8 Does not wisdom call out?
Does not understanding raise her
voice?
2On the heights along the way,
where the paths meet, she takes
her stand;
3beside the gates leading into the city,
at the entrances, she cries aloud:
4"To you, O men, I call out;
I raise my voice to all mankind.
5You who are simple, gain prudence;
you who are foolish, gain
understanding.
6Listen, for I have worthy things to
say;
I open my lips to speak what is
right.
7My mouth speaks what is true,
for my lips detest wickedness.
8All the words of my mouth are just;
none of them is crooked or
perverse.
9To the discerning all of them are
right;
they are faultless to those who
have knowledge.
10Choose my instruction instead of
silver,
knowledge rather than choice gold,
11for wisdom is more precious than
rubies,
and nothing you desire can
compare with her.

OLD TESTAMENT READING
Numbers 21:4–22:20

The Bronze Snake

4They travelled from Mount Hor
along the route to the Red Sea, to go
round Edom. But the people grew impatient on the way; 5they spoke against
God and against Moses, and said, "Why have you brought us up out of Egypt to die in the desert? There is no bread! There is no water! And we detest this miserable food!"
6Then the LORD sent venomous
snakes among them; they bit the people
and many Israelites died. 7The people
came to Moses and said, "We sinned when we spoke against the LORD and against you. Pray that the LORD will take the snakes away from us." So Moses prayed for the people.
8The LORD said to Moses, "Make a
snake and put it up on a pole; anyone
who is bitten can look at it and live." 9So
Moses made a bronze snake and put it up on a pole. Then when anyone was bitten by a snake and looked at the bronze snake, he lived.

The Journey to Moab

10The Israelites moved on and
camped at Oboth. 11Then they set out
from Oboth and camped in Iye Abarim, in the desert that faces Moab towards
the sunrise. 12From there they moved
on and camped in the Zered Valley.
13They set out from there and camped
alongside the Arnon, which is in the desert extending into Amorite territory. The Arnon is the border of Moab, between Moab and the Amorites.
14That is why the Book of the Wars of
the LORD says:

"... Waheb in Suphah and the
ravines,
the Arnon 15and the slopes of the
ravines
that lead to the site of Ar
and lie along the border of Moab."

16From there they continued on to Beer, the well where the LORD said to Moses, "Gather the people together and I will give them water."
17Then Israel sang this song:

"Spring up, O well!
Sing about it,
18about the well that the princes dug,
that the nobles of the people sank—
the nobles with sceptres and staffs."

Then they went from the desert to Mattanah, 19from Mattanah to Nahaliel,
from Nahaliel to Bamoth, 20and from
Bamoth to the valley in Moab where the top of Pisgah overlooks the wasteland.

Defeat of Sihon and Og

21Israel sent messengers to say to
Sihon king of the Amorites:

22"Let us pass through your country. We will not turn aside into any field or vineyard, or drink water from any well. We will travel along the king's highway until we have passed through your territory."

23But Sihon would not let Israel pass
through his territory. He mustered his entire army and marched out into the desert against Israel. When he reached
Jahaz, he fought with Israel. 24Israel,
however, put him to the sword and took over his land from the Arnon to the Jabbok, but only as far as the Ammonites, because their border was fortified. 25Israel captured all the cities of
the Amorites and occupied them, including Heshbon and all its surrounding
settlements. 26Heshbon was the city of

Sihon king of the Amorites, who had fought against the former king of Moab and had taken from him all his land as far as the Arnon.

27That is why the poets say:

"Come to Heshbon and let it be rebuilt;
let Sihon's city be restored.

28"Fire went out from Heshbon,
a blaze from the city of Sihon.
It consumed Ar of Moab,
the citizens of Arnon's heights.
29Woe to you, O Moab!
You are destroyed, O people of Chemosh!
He has given up his sons as fugitives
and his daughters as captives
to Sihon king of the Amorites.

30"But we have overthrown them;
Heshbon is destroyed all the way to Dibon.
We have demolished them as far as Nophah,
which extends to Medeba."

31So Israel settled in the land of the Amorites.

32After Moses had sent spies to Jazer,
the Israelites captured its surrounding settlements and drove out the Amorites
who were there. 33Then they turned and
went up along the road towards Bashan, and Og king of Bashan and his whole army marched out to meet them in battle at Edrei.

34The LORD said to Moses, "Do not be afraid of him, for I have handed him over to you, with his whole army and his land. Do to him what you did to Sihon king of the Amorites, who reigned in Heshbon."

35So they struck him down, together with his sons and his whole army, leaving them no survivors. And they took possession of his land.

Balak Summons Balaam

22 Then the Israelites travelled to the plains of Moab and camped along the Jordan across from Jericho.

2Now Balak son of Zippor saw all that
Israel had done to the Amorites, 3and
Moab was terrified because there were so many people. Indeed, Moab was filled with dread because of the Israelites.

4The Moabites said to the elders of Midian, "This horde is going to lick up everything around us, as an ox licks up the grass of the field."

So Balak son of Zippor, who was king
of Moab at that time, 5sent messengers
to summon Balaam son of Beor, who was at Pethor, near the River, in his native land. Balak said:

"A people has come out of Egypt; they cover the face of the land and have settled next to me.
6Now come and put a curse on
these people, because they are too powerful for me. Perhaps then I will be able to defeat them and drive them out of the country. For I know that those you bless are blessed, and those you curse are cursed."

7The elders of Moab and Midian left, taking with them the fee for divination. When they came to Balaam, they told him what Balak had said.

8"Spend the night here," Balaam said to them, "and I will bring you back the answer the LORD gives me." So the Moabite princes stayed with him.

9God came to Balaam and asked, "Who are these men with you?"

10Balaam said to God, "Balak son of Zippor, king of Moab, sent me this
message: 11'A people that has come out
of Egypt covers the face of the land. Now come and put a curse on them for me. Perhaps then I will be able to fight them and drive them away.'"

12But God said to Balaam, "Do not go with them. You must not put a curse on those people, because they are blessed."

13The next morning Balaam got up and said to Balak's princes, "Go back to your own country, for the LORD has refused to let me go with you."

[14]So the Moabite princes returned to
Balak and said, "Balaam refused to
come with us."
[15]Then Balak sent other princes,
more numerous and more distinguished
than the first. [16]They came to Balaam
and said:

"This is what Balak son of Zippor says: Do not let anything keep
you from coming to me, [17]because I
will reward you handsomely and do
whatever you say. Come and put a
curse on these people for me."

[18]But Balaam answered them, "Even
if Balak gave me his palace filled with
silver and gold, I could not do anything
great or small to go beyond the command of the LORD my God. [19]Now stay
here tonight as the others did, and I will
find out what else the LORD will tell
me."
[20]That night God came to Balaam
and said, "Since these men have come
to summon you, go with them, but do
only what I tell you."

NEW TESTAMENT READING
Luke 6:12–36

The Twelve Apostles

[12]One of those days Jesus went out to
a mountainside to pray, and spent the
night praying to God. [13]When morning
came, he called his disciples to him and
chose twelve of them, whom he also
designated apostles: [14]Simon (whom he
named Peter), his brother Andrew,
James, John, Philip, Bartholomew,
[15]Matthew, Thomas, James son of
Alphaeus, Simon who was called the
Zealot, [16]Judas son of James, and Judas
Iscariot, who became a traitor.

Blessings and Woes

[17]He went down with them and stood
on a level place. A large crowd of his
disciples was there and a great number
of people from all over Judea, from
Jerusalem, and from the coast of Tyre
and Sidon, [18]who had come to hear him
and to be healed of their diseases.
Those troubled by evil spirits were
cured, [19]and the people all tried to
touch him, because power was coming
from him and healing them all.
[20]Looking at his disciples, he said:

"Blessed are you who are poor,
for yours is the kingdom of God.
[21]Blessed are you who hunger now,
for you will be satisfied.
Blessed are you who weep now,
for you will laugh.
[22]Blessed are you when men hate you,
when they exclude you and insult you
and reject your name as evil,
because of the Son of Man.

[23]"Rejoice in that day and leap for
joy, because great is your reward in
heaven. For that is how their fathers
treated the prophets.

[24]"But woe to you who are rich,
for you have already received your comfort.
[25]Woe to you who are well fed now,
for you will go hungry.
Woe to you who laugh now,
for you will mourn and weep.
[26]Woe to you when all men speak well of you,
for that is how their fathers treated the false prophets.

Love for Enemies

[27]"But I tell you who hear me: Love
your enemies, do good to those who
hate you, [28]bless those who curse you,
pray for those who ill-treat you. [29]If
someone strikes you on one cheek, turn
to him the other also. If someone takes
your cloak, do not stop him from taking
your tunic. [30]Give to everyone who asks
you, and if anyone takes what belongs
to you, do not demand it back. [31]Do to
others as you would have them do to
you.

32"If you love those who love you,
what credit is that to you? Even 'sinners' love those who love them. 33And if
you do good to those who are good to
you, what credit is that to you? Even
'sinners' do that. 34And if you lend to
those from whom you expect repay-
ment, what credit is that to you? Even
'sinners' lend to 'sinners', expecting to
be repaid in full. 35But love your enemies, do good to them, and lend to
them without expecting to get anything
back. Then your reward will be great,
and you will be sons of the Most High,
because he is kind to the ungrateful and
wicked. 36Be merciful, just as your
Father is merciful.

READING FROM PSALMS

Psalm 37:21–31

21The wicked borrow and do not repay,
but the righteous give generously;
22those the LORD blesses will inherit
the land,
but those he curses will be cut off.

23If the LORD delights in a man's way,
he makes his steps firm;
24though he stumble, he will not fall,
for the LORD upholds him with his
hand.

25I was young and now I am old,
yet I have never seen the righteous
forsaken
or their children begging bread.
26They are always generous and lend
freely;
their children will be blessed.

27Turn from evil and do good;
then you will dwell in the land for
ever.
28For the LORD loves the just
and will not forsake his faithful
ones.

They will be protected for ever,
but the offspring of the wicked will
be cut off;
29the righteous will inherit the land
and dwell in it for ever.

30The mouth of the righteous man
utters wisdom,
and his tongue speaks what is just.
31The law of his God is in his heart;
his feet do not slip.

DAY 86

MARCH 27

OLD TESTAMENT READING

Numbers 22:21–23:26

Balaam's Donkey

21Balaam got up in the morning,
saddled his donkey and went with the
princes of Moab. 22But God was very
angry when he went, and the angel of
the LORD stood in the road to oppose
him. Balaam was riding on his donkey,
and his two servants were with him.
23When the donkey saw the angel of the
LORD standing in the road with a drawn
sword in his hand, she turned off the
road into a field. Balaam beat her to get
her back on the road.
24Then the angel of the LORD stood in
a narrow path between two vineyards,
with walls on both sides. 25When the
donkey saw the angel of the LORD, she
pressed close to the wall, crushing
Balaam's foot against it. So he beat her
again.
26Then the angel of the LORD moved
on ahead and stood in a narrow place
where there was no room to turn, either
to the right or to the left. 27When the
donkey saw the angel of the LORD, she
lay down under Balaam, and he was

angry and beat her with his staff. 28Then
the LORD opened the donkey's mouth,
and she said to Balaam, "What have I
done to you to make you beat me these
three times?"
29Balaam answered the donkey,
"You have made a fool of me! If I had a
sword in my hand, I would kill you right
now."
30The donkey said to Balaam, "Am I
not your own donkey, which you have
always ridden, to this day? Have I been
in the habit of doing this to you?"
"No," he said.
31Then the LORD opened Balaam's
eyes, and he saw the angel of the LORD
standing in the road with his sword
drawn. So he bowed low and fell face
down.
32The angel of the LORD asked him,
"Why have you beaten your donkey
these three times? I have come here to
oppose you because your path is a reckless one before me. 33The donkey saw
me and turned away from me these
three times. If she had not turned away,
I would certainly have killed you by
now, but I would have spared her."
34Balaam said to the angel of the
LORD, "I have sinned. I did not realise
you were standing in the road to oppose
me. Now if you are displeased, I will go
back."
35The angel of the LORD said to
Balaam, "Go with the men, but speak
only what I tell you." So Balaam went
with the princes of Balak.
36When Balak heard that Balaam was
coming, he went out to meet him at the
Moabite town on the Arnon border, at
the edge of his territory. 37Balak said to
Balaam, "Did I not send you an urgent
summons? Why didn't you come to me?
Am I really not able to reward you?"
38"Well, I have come to you now,"
Balaam replied. "But can I say just
anything? I must speak only what God
puts in my mouth."
39Then Balaam went with Balak to
Kiriath Huzoth. 40Balak sacrificed cattle and sheep, and gave some to Balaam
and the princes who were with him.
41The next morning Balak took Balaam
up to Bamoth Baal, and from there he
saw part of the people.

Balaam's First Oracle

23 Balaam said, "Build me seven
altars here, and prepare seven
bulls and seven rams for me." 2Balak
did as Balaam said, and the two of them
offered a bull and a ram on each altar.
3Then Balaam said to Balak, "Stay
here beside your offering while I go
aside. Perhaps the LORD will come to
meet with me. Whatever he reveals to
me I will tell you." Then he went off to a
barren height.
4God met with him, and Balaam said,
"I have prepared seven altars, and on
each altar I have offered a bull and a
ram."
5The LORD put a message in Balaam's
mouth and said, "Go back to Balak and
give him this message."
6So he went back to him and found
him standing beside his offering, with
all the princes of Moab. 7Then Balaam
uttered his oracle:

"Balak brought me from Aram,
the king of Moab from the eastern
mountains.
'Come,' he said, 'curse Jacob for me;
come, denounce Israel.'
8How can I curse
those whom God has not cursed?
How can I denounce
those whom the LORD has not
denounced?
9From the rocky peaks I see them,
from the heights I view them.
I see people who live apart
and do not consider themselves
one of the nations.
10Who can count the dust of Jacob
or number the fourth part of
Israel?
Let me die the death of the righteous,
and may my end be like theirs!"

11Balak said to Balaam, "What have
you done to me? I brought you to curse

my enemies, but you have done nothing
but bless them!"
12He answered, "Must I not speak
what the LORD puts in my mouth?"

Balaam's Second Oracle

13Then Balak said to him, "Come
with me to another place where you can
see them; you will see only a part but
not all of them. And from there, curse
them for me." 14So he took him to the
field of Zophim on the top of Pisgah,
and there he built seven altars and
offered a bull and a ram on each altar.
15Balaam said to Balak, "Stay here
beside your offering while I meet with
him over there."
16The LORD met with Balaam and
put a message in his mouth and said,
"Go back to Balak and give him this
message."
17So he went to him and found him
standing beside his offering, with the
princes of Moab. Balak asked him,
"What did the LORD say?"
18Then he uttered his oracle:

"Arise, Balak, and listen;
hear me, son of Zippor.
19God is not a man, that he should lie,
nor a son of man, that he should
change his mind.
Does he speak and then not act?
Does he promise and not fulfil?
20I have received a command to bless;
he has blessed, and I cannot
change it.

21"No misfortune is seen in Jacob,
no misery observed in Israel.
The LORD their God is with them;
the shout of the King is among
them.
22God brought them out of Egypt;
they have the strength of a wild ox.
23There is no sorcery against Jacob,
no divination against Israel.
It will now be said of Jacob
and of Israel, 'See what God has
done!'
24The people rise like a lioness;
they rouse themselves like a lion
that does not rest till he devours his
prey
and drinks the blood of his
victims."

25Then Balak said to Balaam,
"Neither curse them at all nor bless
them at all!"
26Balaam answered, "Did I not tell
you I must do whatever the LORD
says?"

NEW TESTAMENT READING
Luke 6:37–7:10

Judging Others

37"Do not judge, and you will not be
judged. Do not condemn, and you will
not be condemned. Forgive, and you
will be forgiven. 38Give, and it will be
given to you. A good measure, pressed
down, shaken together and running
over, will be poured into your lap. For
with the measure you use, it will be
measured to you."
39He also told them this parable:
"Can a blind man lead a blind man?
Will they not both fall into a pit? 40A
student is not above his teacher, but
everyone who is fully trained will be like
his teacher.
41"Why do you look at the speck of
sawdust in your brother's eye and pay
no attention to the plank in your own
eye? 42How can you say to your brother,
'Brother, let me take the speck out of
your eye,' when you yourself fail to see
the plank in your own eye? You hypocrite, first take the plank out of your
eye, and then you will see clearly to
remove the speck from your brother's
eye.

A Tree and Its Fruit

43"No good tree bears bad fruit, nor
does a bad tree bear good fruit. 44Each
tree is recognised by its own fruit. People do not pick figs from thornbushes,
or grapes from briers. 45The good man

brings good things out of the good
stored up in his heart, and the evil man
brings evil things out of the evil stored
up in his heart. For out of the overflow
of his heart his mouth speaks.

The Wise and Foolish Builders

46"Why do you call me, 'Lord, Lord,'
and do not do what I say? 47I will show
you what he is like who comes to me and
hears my words and puts them into
practice. 48He is like a man building a
house, who dug down deep and laid the
foundation on rock. When the flood
came, the torrent struck that house but
could not shake it, because it was well
built. 49But the one who hears my words
and does not put them into practice is
like a man who built a house on the
ground without a foundation. The
moment the torrent struck that house,
it collapsed and its destruction was
complete."

The Faith of the Centurion

7 When Jesus had finished saying all
this in the hearing of the people, he
entered Capernaum. 2There a centurion's servant, whom his master valued
highly, was sick and about to die. 3The
centurion heard of Jesus and sent some
elders of the Jews to him, asking him to
come and heal his servant. 4When they
came to Jesus, they pleaded earnestly
with him, "This man deserves to have
you do this, 5because he loves our
nation and has built our synagogue."
6So Jesus went with them.

He was not far from the house when
the centurion sent friends to say to him:
"Lord, don't trouble yourself, for I do
not deserve to have you come under my
roof. 7That is why I did not even consider myself worthy to come to you. But
say the word, and my servant will be
healed. 8For I myself am a man under
authority, with soldiers under me. I tell
this one, 'Go', and he goes; and that
one, 'Come', and he comes. I say to my
servant, 'Do this', and he does it."

9When Jesus heard this, he was
amazed at him, and turning to the
crowd following him, he said, "I tell
you, I have not found such great faith
even in Israel." 10Then the men who
had been sent returned to the house and
found the servant well.

READING FROM PSALMS
Psalm 37:32–40

32The wicked lie in wait for the
righteous,
seeking their very lives;
33but the LORD will not leave them in
their power
or let them be condemned when
brought to trial.

34Wait for the LORD
and keep his way.
He will exalt you to inherit the land;
when the wicked are cut off, you
will see it.

35I have seen a wicked and ruthless
man
flourishing like a green tree in its
native soil,
36but he soon passed away and was no
more;
though I looked for him, he could
not be found.

37Consider the blameless, observe the
upright;
there is a future for the man of
peace.
38But all sinners will be destroyed;
the future of the wicked will be cut
off.

39The salvation of the righteous comes
from the LORD;
he is their stronghold in time of
trouble.
40The LORD helps them and delivers
them;
he delivers them from the wicked
and saves them,
because they take refuge in him.

OLD TESTAMENT READING

Numbers 23:27–26:11

Balaam's Third Oracle

27Then Balak said to Balaam, "Come, let me take you to another place. Perhaps it will please God to let you curse them for me from there."
28And Balak took Balaam to the top of Peor, overlooking the wasteland.
29Balaam said, "Build me seven altars here, and prepare seven bulls and seven rams for me."
30Balak did as Balaam had said, and offered a bull and a ram on each altar.

24 Now when Balaam saw that it pleased the LORD to bless Israel, he did not resort to sorcery as at other times, but turned his face towards the desert.
2When Balaam looked out and saw Israel encamped tribe by tribe, the Spirit of God came upon him
3and he uttered his oracle:

"The oracle of Balaam son of Beor,
the oracle of one whose eye sees clearly,
4the oracle of one who hears the words of God,
who sees a vision from the Almighty,
who falls prostrate, and whose eyes are opened:

5"How beautiful are your tents, O Jacob,
your dwelling-places, O Israel!

6"Like valleys they spread out,
like gardens beside a river,
like aloes planted by the LORD,
like cedars beside the waters.
7Water will flow from their buckets;
their seed will have abundant water.

"Their king will be greater than Agag;
their kingdom will be exalted.

8"God brought them out of Egypt;
they have the strength of a wild ox.
They devour hostile nations
and break their bones in pieces;
with their arrows they pierce them.
9Like a lion they crouch and lie down,
like a lioness—who dares to rouse them?

"May those who bless you be blessed
and those who curse you be cursed!"

10Then Balak's anger burned against Balaam. He struck his hands together and said to him, "I summoned you to curse my enemies, but you have blessed them these three times.
11Now leave at once and go home! I said I would reward you handsomely, but the LORD has kept you from being rewarded."
12Balaam answered Balak, "Did I not tell the messengers you sent me,
13'Even if Balak gave me his palace filled with silver and gold, I could not do anything of my own accord, good or bad, to go beyond the command of the LORD—and I must say only what the LORD says'?
14Now I am going back to my people, but come, let me warn you of what this people will do to your people in days to come."

Balaam's Fourth Oracle

15Then he uttered his oracle:

"The oracle of Balaam son of Beor,
the oracle of one whose eye sees clearly,
16the oracle of one who hears the words of God,
who has knowledge from the Most High,
who sees a vision from the Almighty,
who falls prostrate, and whose eyes are opened:

17“I see him, but not now;
I behold him, but not near.
A star will come out of Jacob;
a sceptre will rise out of Israel.
He will crush the foreheads of Moab,
the skulls of all the sons of Sheth.
18Edom will be conquered;
Seir, his enemy, will be conquered,
but Israel will grow strong.
19A ruler will come out of Jacob
and destroy the survivors of the
city.”

Balaam's Final Oracles

20Then Balaam saw Amalek and
uttered his oracle:

“Amalek was first among the
nations,
but he will come to ruin at last.”

21Then he saw the Kenites and
uttered his oracle:

“Your dwelling-place is secure,
your nest is set in a rock;
22yet you Kenites will be destroyed
when Asshur takes you captive.”

23Then he uttered his oracle:

“Ah, who can live when God does
this?
24 Ships will come from the shores of
Kittim;
they will subdue Asshur and Eber,
but they too will come to ruin.”

25Then Balaam got up and returned
home and Balak went his own way.

Moab Seduces Israel

25 While Israel was staying in
Shittim, the men began to indulge in sexual immorality with
Moabite women, 2who invited them to
the sacrifices to their gods. The people
ate and bowed down before these gods.
3So Israel joined in worshipping the
Baal of Peor. And the LORD's anger
burned against them.
4The LORD said to Moses, “Take all
the leaders of these people, kill them
and expose them in broad daylight before the LORD, so that the LORD's fierce
anger may turn away from Israel.”
5So Moses said to Israel's judges,
“Each of you must put to death those of
your men who have joined in worshipping the Baal of Peor.”
6Then an Israelite man brought to his
family a Midianite woman right before
the eyes of Moses and the whole assembly of Israel while they were weeping at
the entrance to the Tent of Meeting.
7When Phinehas son of Eleazar, the son
of Aaron, the priest, saw this, he left the
assembly, took a spear in his hand 8and
followed the Israelite into the tent. He
drove the spear through both of them
—through the Israelite and into the
woman's body. Then the plague against
the Israelites was stopped; 9but those
who died in the plague numbered
24,000.
10The LORD said to Moses,
11“Phinehas son of Eleazar, the son of
Aaron, the priest, has turned my anger
away from the Israelites; for he was as
zealous as I am for my honour among
them, so that in my zeal I did not put an
end to them. 12Therefore tell him I am
making my covenant of peace with him.
13He and his descendants will have a
covenant of a lasting priesthood, because he was zealous for the honour of
his God and made atonement for the
Israelites.”
14The name of the Israelite who was
killed with the Midianite woman was
Zimri son of Salu, the leader of a
Simeonite family. 15And the name of
the Midianite woman who was put to
death was Cozbi daughter of Zur, a
tribal chief of a Midianite family.
16The LORD said to Moses, 17“Treat
the Midianites as enemies and kill them,
18because they treated you as enemies
when they deceived you in the affair of
Peor and their sister Cozbi, the daughter of a Midianite leader, the woman

who was killed when the plague came as
a result of Peor."

The Second Census

26 After the plague the LORD said
to Moses and Eleazar son of
Aaron, the priest, 2"Take a census of
the whole Israelite community by families—all those twenty years old or
more who are able to serve in the army
of Israel." 3So on the plains of Moab by
the Jordan across from Jericho, Moses
and Eleazar the priest spoke with them
and said, 4"Take a census of men
twenty years old or more, as the LORD
commanded Moses."

These were the Israelites who came
out of Egypt:

5The descendants of Reuben, the
firstborn son of Israel, were:
through Hanoch, the Hanochite clan;
through Pallu, the Palluite clan;
6through Hezron, the Hezronite clan;
through Carmi, the Carmite clan.
7These were the clans of Reuben; those
numbered were 43,730.
8The son of Pallu was Eliab, 9and the
sons of Eliab were Nemuel, Dathan and
Abiram. The same Dathan and Abiram
were the community officials who rebelled against Moses and Aaron and
were among Korah's followers when
they rebelled against the LORD. 10The
earth opened its mouth and swallowed
them along with Korah, whose followers died when the fire devoured the 250
men. And they served as a warning sign.
11The line of Korah, however, did not
die out.

NEW TESTAMENT READING
Luke 7:11–35

Jesus Raises a Widow's Son

11Soon afterwards, Jesus went to a
town called Nain, and his disciples and a
large crowd went along with him. 12As
he approached the town gate, a dead
person was being carried out—the only
son of his mother, and she was a widow.
And a large crowd from the town was
with her. 13When the Lord saw her, his
heart went out to her and he said,
"Don't cry."

14Then he went up and touched the
coffin, and those carrying it stood still.
He said, "Young man, I say to you, get
up!" 15The dead man sat up and began
to talk, and Jesus gave him back to his
mother.

16They were all filled with awe and
praised God. "A great prophet has
appeared among us," they said. "God
has come to help his people." 17This
news about Jesus spread throughout
Judea and the surrounding country.

Jesus and John the Baptist

18John's disciples told him about all
these things. Calling two of them, 19he
sent them to the Lord to ask, "Are you
the one who was to come, or should we
expect someone else?"

20When the men came to Jesus, they
said, "John the Baptist sent us to you to
ask, 'Are you the one who was to come,
or should we expect someone else?'"

21At that very time Jesus cured many
who had diseases, sicknesses and evil
spirits, and gave sight to many who were
blind. 22So he replied to the messengers, "Go back and report to John what
you have seen and heard: The blind
receive sight, the lame walk, those who
have leprosy are cured, the deaf hear,
the dead are raised, and the good news
is preached to the poor. 23Blessed is the
man who does not fall away on account
of me."

24After John's messengers left, Jesus
began to speak to the crowd about
John: "What did you go out into the
desert to see? A reed swayed by the
wind? 25If not, what did you go out to
see? A man dressed in fine clothes? No,
those who wear expensive clothes and
indulge in luxury are in palaces. 26But

what did you go out to see? A prophet?
Yes, I tell you, and more than a
prophet. 27This is the one about whom it
is written:

"'I will send my messenger ahead of
you,
who will prepare your way before
you.'

28I tell you, among those born of women
there is no-one greater than John; yet
the one who is least in the kingdom of
God is greater than he."

(29All the people, even the tax collectors, when they heard Jesus' words, acknowledged that God's way was right,
because they had been baptised by
John. 30But the Pharisees and experts in
the law rejected God's purpose for
themselves, because they had not been
baptised by John.)

31"To what, then, can I compare the
people of this generation? What are
they like? 32They are like children sitting in the market-place and calling out
to each other:

"'We played the flute for you,
and you did not dance;
we sang a dirge,
and you did not cry.'

33For John the Baptist came neither
eating bread nor drinking wine, and you
say, 'He has a demon.' 34The Son of
Man came eating and drinking, and you
say, 'Here is a glutton and a drunkard, a
friend of tax collectors and "sinners".'
35But wisdom is proved right by all her
children."

READING FROM PSALMS

Psalm 38:1–12

A psalm of David. A petition.

1O LORD, do not rebuke me in your anger
or discipline me in your wrath.
2For your arrows have pierced me,
and your hand has come down upon me.
3Because of your wrath there is no health in my body;
my bones have no soundness because of my sin.
4My guilt has overwhelmed me
like a burden too heavy to bear.

5My wounds fester and are loathsome
because of my sinful folly.
6I am bowed down and brought very low;
all day long I go about mourning.
7My back is filled with searing pain;
there is no health in my body.
8I am feeble and utterly crushed;
I groan in anguish of heart.

9All my longings lie open before you, O Lord;
my sighing is not hidden from you.
10My heart pounds, my strength fails me;
even the light has gone from my eyes.
11My friends and companions avoid me
because of my wounds;
my neighbours stay far away.
12Those who seek my life set their traps,
those who would harm me talk of my ruin;
all day long they plot deception.

MARCH 29

OLD TESTAMENT READING
Numbers 26:12–27:11

12The descendants of Simeon by their clans were:
through Nemuel, the Nemuelite clan;
through Jamin, the Jaminite clan;
through Jakin, the Jakinite clan;
13through Zerah, the Zerahite clan;
through Shaul, the Shaulite clan.
14These were the clans of Simeon; there were 22,200 men.

15The descendants of Gad by their clans were:
through Zephon, the Zephonite clan;
through Haggi, the Haggite clan;
through Shuni, the Shunite clan;
16through Ozni, the Oznite clan;
through Eri, the Erite clan;
17through Arodi, the Arodite clan;
through Areli, the Arelite clan.
18These were the clans of Gad; those numbered were 40,500.

19Er and Onan were sons of Judah, but they died in Canaan.
20The descendants of Judah by their clans were:
through Shelah, the Shelanite clan;
through Perez, the Perezite clan;
through Zerah, the Zerahite clan.
21The descendants of Perez were:
through Hezron, the Hezronite clan;
through Hamul, the Hamulite clan.
22These were the clans of Judah; those numbered were 76,500.

23The descendants of Issachar by their clans were:
through Tola, the Tolaite clan;
through Puah, the Puite clan;
24through Jashub, the Jashubite clan;
through Shimron, the Shimronite clan.
25These were the clans of Issachar; those numbered were 64,300.

26The descendants of Zebulun by their clans were:
through Sered, the Seredite clan;
through Elon, the Elonite clan;
through Jahleel, the Jahleelite clan.
27These were the clans of Zebulun; those numbered were 60,500.

28The descendants of Joseph by their clans through Manasseh and Ephraim were:

29The descendants of Manasseh:
through Makir, the Makirite clan (Makir was the father of Gilead);
through Gilead, the Gileadite clan.
30These were the descendants of Gilead:
through Iezer, the Iezerite clan;
through Helek, the Helekite clan;
31through Asriel, the Asrielite clan;
through Shechem, the Shechemite clan;
32through Shemida, the Shemidaite clan;
through Hepher, the Hepherite clan.
33(Zelophehad son of Hepher had no sons; he had only daughters, whose names were Mahlah, Noah, Hoglah, Milcah and Tirzah.)
34These were the clans of Manasseh; those numbered were 52,700.

35These were the descendants of Ephraim by their clans:
through Shuthelah, the Shuthelahite clan;
through Beker, the Bekerite clan;
through Tahan, the Tahanite clan.
36These were the descendants of Shuthelah:
through Eran, the Eranite clan.

37These were the clans of Ephraim; those numbered were 32,500.

These were the descendants of Joseph by their clans.

38The descendants of Benjamin by their clans were:
through Bela, the Belaite clan;
through Ashbel, the Ashbelite clan;
through Ahiram, the Ahiramite clan;
39through Shupham, the Shuphamite clan;
through Hupham, the Huphamite clan.
40The descendants of Bela through Ard and Naaman were:
through Ard, the Ardite clan;
through Naaman, the Naamite clan.
41These were the clans of Benjamin; those numbered were 45,600.

42These were the descendants of Dan by their clans:
through Shuham, the Shuhamite clan.
These were the clans of Dan: 43All of them were Shuhamite clans; and those numbered were 64,400.

44The descendants of Asher by their clans were:
through Imnah, the Imnite clan;
through Ishvi, the Ishvite clan;
through Beriah, the Beriite clan;
45and through the descendants of Beriah:
through Heber, the Heberite clan;
through Malkiel, the Malkielite clan.
46(Asher had a daughter named Serah.)
47These were the clans of Asher; those numbered were 53,400.

48The descendants of Naphtali by their clans were:
through Jahzeel, the Jahzeelite clan;
through Guni, the Gunite clan;
49through Jezer, the Jezerite clan;
through Shillem, the Shillemite clan.
50These were the clans of Naphtali; those numbered were 45,400.

51The total number of the men of Israel was 601,730.

52The LORD said to Moses, 53"The land is to be allotted to them as an
inheritance based on the number of
names. 54To a larger group give a larger
inheritance, and to a smaller group a
smaller one; each is to receive its inheritance according to the number of those
listed. 55Be sure that the land is distributed by lot. What each group inherits
will be according to the names for its
ancestral tribe. 56Each inheritance is to
be distributed by lot among the larger
and smaller groups."

57These were the Levites who were counted by their clans:
through Gershon, the Gershonite clan;
through Kohath, the Kohathite clan;
through Merari, the Merarite clan.
58These also were Levite clans:
the Libnite clan,
the Hebronite clan,
the Mahlite clan,
the Mushite clan,
the Korahite clan.
(Kohath was the forefather of
Amram; 59the name of Amram's
wife was Jochebed, a descendant of
Levi, who was born to the Levites
in Egypt. To Amram she bore
Aaron, Moses and their sister
Miriam. 60Aaron was the father of
Nadab and Abihu, Eleazar and
Ithamar. 61But Nadab and Abihu
died when they made an offering before the LORD with unauthorised fire.)

62All the male Levites a month old or more numbered 23,000. They were not counted along with the other Israelites because they received no inheritance among them.

63These are the ones counted by
Moses and Eleazar the priest when they
counted the Israelites on the plains of
Moab by the Jordan across from
Jericho. 64Not one of them was among
those counted by Moses and Aaron the
priest when they counted the Israelites
in the Desert of Sinai. 65For the LORD
had told those Israelites they would
surely die in the desert, and not one of
them was left except Caleb son of
Jephunneh and Joshua son of Nun.

Zelophehad's Daughters

27 The daughters of Zelophehad
son of Hepher, the son of
Gilead, the son of Makir, the son of
Manasseh, belonged to the clans
of Manasseh son of Joseph. The names
of the daughters were Mahlah, Noah,
Hoglah, Milcah and Tirzah. They
approached 2the entrance to the Tent of
Meeting and stood before Moses,
Eleazar the priest, the leaders and the
whole assembly, and said, 3"Our father
died in the desert. He was not among
Korah's followers, who banded
together against the LORD, but he died
for his own sin and left no sons. 4Why
should our father's name disappear
from his clan because he had no son?
Give us property among our father's
relatives."

5So Moses brought their case before
the LORD 6and the LORD said to him,
7"What Zelophehad's daughters are
saying is right. You must certainly give
them property as an inheritance among
their father's relatives and give their
father's inheritance over to them.

8"Say to the Israelites, 'If a man dies
and leaves no son, give his inheritance
over to his daughter. 9If he has no
daughter, give his inheritance to his
brothers. 10If he has no brothers, give
his inheritance to his father's brothers.
11If his father had no brothers, give his
inheritance to the nearest relative in his
clan, that he may possess it. This is to be
a legal requirement for the Israelites, as
the LORD commanded Moses.'"

NEW TESTAMENT READING
Luke 7:36–50

Jesus Anointed by a Sinful Woman

36Now one of the Pharisees invited
Jesus to have dinner with him, so he
went to the Pharisee's house and reclined at the table. 37When a woman
who had lived a sinful life in that town
learned that Jesus was eating at the
Pharisee's house, she brought an alabaster jar of perfume, 38and as she stood
behind him at his feet weeping, she
began to wet his feet with her tears.
Then she wiped them with her hair,
kissed them and poured perfume on
them.

39When the Pharisee who had invited
him saw this, he said to himself, "If this
man were a prophet, he would know
who is touching him and what kind of
woman she is—that she is a sinner."

40Jesus answered him, "Simon, I
have something to tell you."

"Tell me, teacher," he said.

41"Two men owed money to a certain
money-lender. One owed him five
hundred denarii, and the other fifty.
42Neither of them had the money to pay
him back, so he cancelled the debts of
both. Now which of them will love him
more?"

43Simon replied, "I suppose the one
who had the bigger debt cancelled."

"You have judged correctly," Jesus
said.

44Then he turned towards the woman
and said to Simon, "Do you see this
woman? I came into your house. You
did not give me any water for my feet,
but she wet my feet with her tears and
wiped them with her hair. 45You did not
give me a kiss, but this woman, from the
time I entered has not stopped kissing
my feet. 46You did not put oil on my
head, but she has poured perfume on
my feet. 47Therefore, I tell you, her
many sins have been forgiven—for she
loved much. But he who has been forgiven little loves little."

48Then Jesus said to her, "Your sins
are forgiven."

[49]The other guests began to say among themselves, "Who is this who even forgives sins?"

[50]Jesus said to the woman, "Your faith has saved you; go in peace."

READING FROM PROVERBS

Proverbs 8:12–21

[12]"I, wisdom, dwell together with
  prudence;
 I possess knowledge and
  discretion.
[13]To fear the LORD is to hate evil;
 I hate pride and arrogance,
 evil behaviour and perverse
  speech.
[14]Counsel and sound judgment are
  mine;
 I have understanding and power.
[15]By me kings reign
 and rulers make laws that are just;
[16]by me princes govern,
 and all nobles who rule on earth.
[17]I love those who love me,
 and those who seek me find me.
[18]With me are riches and honour,
 enduring wealth and prosperity.
[19]My fruit is better than fine gold;
 what I yield surpasses choice silver.
[20]I walk in the way of righteousness,
 along the paths of justice,
[21]bestowing wealth on those who love
  me
 and making their treasuries full.

MARCH 30

DAY 89

OLD TESTAMENT READING

Numbers 27:12–29:11

Joshua to Succeed Moses

[12]Then the LORD said to Moses, "Go up this mountain in the Abarim Range and see the land I have given the Israelites. [13]After you have seen it, you too will be gathered to your people, as your brother Aaron was, [14]for when the community rebelled at the waters in the Desert of Zin, both of you disobeyed my command to honour me as holy before their eyes." (These were the waters of Meribah Kadesh, in the Desert of Zin.)

[15]Moses said to the LORD, [16]"May the LORD, the God of the spirits of all mankind, appoint a man over this community [17]to go out and come in before them, one who will lead them out and bring them in, so that the LORD's people will not be like sheep without a shepherd."

[18]So the LORD said to Moses, "Take Joshua son of Nun, a man in whom is the spirit, and lay your hand on him. [19]Make him stand before Eleazar the priest and the entire assembly and commission him in their presence. [20]Give him some of your authority so that the whole Israelite community will obey him. [21]He is to stand before Eleazar the priest, who will obtain decisions for him by enquiring of the Urim before the LORD. At his command he and the entire community of the Israelites will go out, and at his command they will come in."

[22]Moses did as the LORD commanded him. He took Joshua and made him stand before Eleazar the priest and the whole assembly. [23]Then he laid his hands on him and commissioned him, as the LORD instructed through Moses.

Daily Offerings

28 The LORD said to Moses, [2]"Give this command to the Israelites and say to them: 'See that you present to me at the appointed time the food for my offerings made by fire, as an aroma

pleasing to me.' 3Say to them: 'This is the offering made by fire that you are to present to the LORD: two lambs a year old without defect, as a regular burnt offering each day. 4Prepare one lamb in the morning and the other at twilight, 5together with a grain offering of a tenth of an ephah of fine flour mixed with a quarter of a hin of oil from pressed olives. 6This is the regular burnt offering instituted at Mount Sinai as a pleasing aroma, an offering made to the LORD by fire. 7The accompanying drink offering is to be a quarter of a hin of fermented drink with each lamb. Pour out the drink offering to the LORD at the sanctuary. 8Prepare the second lamb at twilight, along with the same kind of grain offering and drink offering that you prepare in the morning. This is an offering made by fire, an aroma pleasing to the LORD.

Sabbath Offerings

9" 'On the Sabbath day, make an offering of two lambs a year old without defect, together with its drink offering and a grain offering of two-tenths of an ephah of fine flour mixed with oil. 10This is the burnt offering for every Sabbath, in addition to the regular burnt offering and its drink offering.

Monthly Offerings

11" 'On the first of every month, present to the LORD a burnt offering of two young bulls, one ram and seven male lambs a year old, all without defect. 12With each bull there is to be a grain offering of three-tenths of an ephah of fine flour mixed with oil; with the ram, a grain offering of two-tenths of an ephah of fine flour mixed with oil; 13and with each lamb, a grain offering of a tenth of an ephah of fine flour mixed with oil. This is for a burnt offering, a pleasing aroma, an offering made to the LORD by fire. 14With each bull there is to be a drink offering of half a hin of wine; with the ram, a third of a hin; and with each lamb, a quarter of a hin. This is the monthly burnt offering to be made at each new moon during the year. 15Besides the regular burnt offering with its drink offering, one male goat is to be presented to the LORD as a sin offering.

The Passover

16" 'On the fourteenth day of the first month the LORD's Passover is to be held. 17On the fifteenth day of this month there is to be a festival; for seven days eat bread made without yeast. 18On the first day hold a sacred assembly and do no regular work. 19Present to the LORD an offering made by fire, a burnt offering of two young bulls, one ram and seven male lambs a year old, all without defect. 20With each bull prepare a grain offering of three-tenths of an ephah of fine flour mixed with oil; with the ram, two-tenths; 21and with each of the seven lambs, one-tenth. 22Include one male goat as a sin offering to make atonement for you. 23Prepare these in addition to the regular morning burnt offering. 24In this way prepare the food for the offering made by fire every day for seven days as an aroma pleasing to the LORD; it is to be prepared in addition to the regular burnt offering and its drink offering. 25On the seventh day hold a sacred assembly and do no regular work.

Feast of Weeks

26" 'On the day of firstfruits, when you present to the LORD an offering of new grain during the Feast of Weeks, hold a sacred assembly and do no regular work. 27Present a burnt offering of two young bulls, one ram and seven male lambs a year old as an aroma pleasing to the LORD. 28With each bull there is to be a grain offering of three-tenths of an ephah of fine flour mixed with oil; with the ram, two-tenths; 29and with each of the seven lambs, one-tenth. 30Include one male goat to make atonement for you. 31Prepare these together with their drink offerings, in addition to the regular burnt offering and its grain offering. Be sure the animals are without defect.

Feast of Trumpets

29 " 'On the first day of the seventh month hold a sacred assembly and do no regular work. It is a day for you to sound the trumpets. 2As an aroma pleasing to the LORD, prepare a burnt offering of one young bull, one ram and seven male lambs a year old, all without defect. 3With the bull prepare a grain offering of three-tenths of an ephah of fine flour mixed with oil; with the ram, two-tenths; 4and with each of the seven lambs, one-tenth. 5Include one male goat as a sin offering to make atonement for you. 6These are in addition to the monthly and daily burnt offerings with their grain offerings and drink offerings as specified. They are offerings made to the LORD by fire—a pleasing aroma.

Day of Atonement

7" 'On the tenth day of this seventh month hold a sacred assembly. You must deny yourselves and do no work. 8Present as an aroma pleasing to the LORD a burnt offering of one young bull, one ram and seven male lambs a year old, all without defect. 9With the bull prepare a grain offering of three-tenths of an ephah of fine flour mixed with oil; with the ram, two-tenths; 10and with each of the seven lambs, one-tenth. 11Include one male goat as a sin offering, in addition to the sin offering for atonement and the regular burnt offering with its grain offering, and their drink offerings.

NEW TESTAMENT READING
Luke 8:1–18

The Parable of the Sower

8 After this, Jesus travelled about from one town and village to another, proclaiming the good news of the kingdom of God. The Twelve were with him, 2and also some women who had been cured of evil spirits and diseases: Mary (called Magdalene) from whom seven demons had come out; 3Joanna the wife of Chuza, the manager of Herod's household; Susanna; and many others. These women were helping to support them out of their own means.

4While a large crowd was gathering and people were coming to Jesus from town after town, he told this parable: 5"A farmer went out to sow his seed. As he was scattering the seed, some fell along the path; it was trampled on, and the birds of the air ate it up. 6Some fell on rock, and when it came up, the plants withered because they had no moisture. 7Other seed fell among thorns, which grew up with it and choked the plants. 8Still other seed fell on good soil. It came up and yielded a crop, a hundred times more than was sown."

When he said this, he called out, "He who has ears to hear, let him hear."

9His disciples asked him what this parable meant. 10He said, "The knowledge of the secrets of the kingdom of God has been given to you, but to others I speak in parables, so that,

" 'though seeing, they may not see;
though hearing, they may not
understand.'

11"This is the meaning of the parable: The seed is the word of God. 12Those along the path are the ones who hear, and then the devil comes and takes away the word from their hearts, so that they may not believe and be saved. 13Those on the rock are the ones who receive the word with joy when they hear it, but they have no root. They believe for a while, but in the time of testing they fall away. 14The seed that fell among thorns stands for those who hear, but as they go on their way they are choked by life's worries, riches and pleasures, and they do not mature. 15But the seed on good soil stands for those with a noble and good heart, who hear the word, retain it, and by persevering produce a crop.

A Lamp on a Stand

[16]"No-one lights a lamp and hides it in a jar or puts it under a bed. Instead, he puts it on a stand, so that those who come in can see the light. [17]For there is nothing hidden that will not be disclosed, and nothing concealed that will not be known or brought out into the open. [18]Therefore consider carefully how you listen. Whoever has will be given more; whoever does not have, even what he thinks he has will be taken from him."

READING FROM PSALMS

Psalm 38:13–22

[13]I am like a deaf man, who cannot
hear,
like a mute, who cannot open his
mouth;
[14]I have become like a man who does
not hear,
whose mouth can offer no reply.
[15]I wait for you, O LORD;
you will answer, O Lord my God.
[16]For I said, "Do not let them gloat
or exalt themselves over me when
my foot slips."

[17]For I am about to fall,
and my pain is ever with me.
[18]I confess my iniquity;
I am troubled by my sin.
[19]Many are those who are my vigorous
enemies;
those who hate me without reason
are numerous.
[20]Those who repay my good with evil
slander me when I pursue what is
good.

[21]O LORD, do not forsake me;
be not far from me, O my God.
[22]Come quickly to help me,
O Lord my Saviour.

DAY 90

MARCH 31

OLD TESTAMENT READING

Numbers 29:12–31:24

Feast of Tabernacles

[12]" 'On the fifteenth day of the seventh month, hold a sacred assembly and do no regular work. Celebrate a festival to the LORD for seven days. [13]Present an offering made by fire as an aroma pleasing to the LORD, a burnt offering of thirteen young bulls, two rams and fourteen male lambs a year old, all without defect. [14]With each of the thirteen bulls prepare a grain offering of three-tenths of an ephah of fine flour mixed with oil; with each of the two rams, two-tenths; [15]and with each of the fourteen lambs, one-tenth. [16]Include one male goat as a sin offering, in addition to the regular burnt offering with its grain offering and drink offering.

[17]" 'On the second day prepare twelve young bulls, two rams and fourteen male lambs a year old, all without defect. [18]With the bulls, rams and lambs, prepare their grain offerings and drink offerings according to the number specified. [19]Include one male goat as a sin offering, in addition to the regular burnt offering with its grain offering, and their drink offerings.

[20]" 'On the third day prepare eleven bulls, two rams and fourteen male lambs a year old, all without defect. [21]With the bulls, rams and lambs, prepare their grain offerings and drink

offerings according to the number specified. 22Include one male goat as a sin
offering, in addition to the regular burnt
offering with its grain offering and
drink offering.
23" 'On the fourth day prepare ten
bulls, two rams and fourteen male
lambs a year old, all without defect.
24With the bulls, rams and lambs, prepare their grain offerings and drink
offerings according to the number specified. 25Include one male goat as a sin
offering, in addition to the regular burnt
offering with its grain offering and
drink offering.
26" 'On the fifth day prepare nine
bulls, two rams and fourteen male
lambs a year old, all without defect.
27With the bulls, rams and lambs, prepare their grain offerings and drink
offerings according to the number specified. 28Include one male goat as a sin
offering, in addition to the regular burnt
offering with its grain offering and
drink offering.
29" 'On the sixth day prepare eight
bulls, two rams and fourteen male
lambs a year old, all without defect.
30With the bulls, rams and lambs, prepare their grain offerings and drink
offerings according to the number specified. 31Include one male goat as a sin
offering, in addition to the regular burnt
offering with its grain offering and
drink offering.
32" 'On the seventh day prepare
seven bulls, two rams and fourteen male
lambs a year old, all without defect.
33With the bulls, rams and lambs, prepare their grain offerings and drink
offerings according to the number specified. 34Include one male goat as a sin
offering, in addition to the regular burnt
offering with its grain offering and
drink offering.
35" 'On the eighth day hold an assembly and do no regular work. 36Present
an offering made by fire as an aroma
pleasing to the LORD, a burnt offering of
one bull, one ram and seven male lambs
a year old, all without defect. 37With the
bull, the ram and the lambs, prepare
their grain offerings and drink offerings
according to the number specified.
38Include one male goat as a sin offering, in addition to the regular burnt
offering with its grain offering and
drink offering.
39" 'In addition to what you vow and
your freewill offerings, prepare these
for the LORD at your appointed feasts:
your burnt offerings, grain offerings, drink offerings and fellowship
offerings.' "
40Moses told the Israelites all that the
LORD commanded him.

Vows

30 Moses said to the heads of the
tribes of Israel: "This is what the
LORD commands: 2When a man makes
a vow to the LORD or takes an oath to
bind himself by a pledge, he must not
break his word but must do everything
he said.
3"When a young woman still living in
her father's house makes a vow to the
LORD or binds herself by a pledge 4and
her father hears about her vow or
pledge but says nothing to her, then all
her vows and every pledge by which she
bound herself will stand. 5But if her
father forbids her when he hears about
it, none of her vows or the pledges by
which she bound herself will stand; the
LORD will release her because her father
has forbidden her.
6"If she marries after she makes a
vow or after her lips utter a rash promise
by which she binds herself 7and her
husband hears about it but says nothing
to her, then her vows or the pledges by
which she bound herself will stand. 8But
if her husband forbids her when he
hears about it, he nullifies the vow that
binds her or the rash promise by which
she binds herself, and the LORD will
release her.
9"Any vow or obligation taken by a
widow or divorced woman will be binding on her.
10"If a woman living with her husband makes a vow or binds herself by a

pledge under oath 11and her husband hears about it but says nothing to her and does not forbid her, then all her vows or the pledges by which she bound herself will stand. 12But if her husband nullifies them when he hears about them, then none of the vows or pledges that came from her lips will stand. Her husband has nullified them, and the LORD will release her. 13Her husband may confirm or nullify any vow she makes or any sworn pledge to deny herself. 14But if her husband says nothing to her about it from day to day, then he confirms all her vows or the pledges binding on her. He confirms them by saying nothing to her when he hears about them. 15If, however, he nullifies them some time after he hears about them, then he is responsible for her guilt."

16These are the regulations the LORD gave Moses concerning relationships between a man and his wife, and between a father and his young daughter still living in his house.

Vengeance on the Midianites

31 The LORD said to Moses, 2"Take vengeance on the Midianites for the Israelites. After that, you will be gathered to your people."

3So Moses said to the people, "Arm some of your men to go to war against the Midianites and to carry out the LORD's vengeance on them. 4Send into battle a thousand men from each of the tribes of Israel." 5So twelve thousand men armed for battle, a thousand from each tribe, were supplied from the clans of Israel. 6Moses sent them into battle, a thousand from each tribe, along with Phinehas son of Eleazar, the priest, who took with him articles from the sanctuary and the trumpets for signalling.

7They fought against Midian, as the LORD commanded Moses, and killed every man. 8Among their victims were Evi, Rekem, Zur, Hur and Reba—the five kings of Midian. They also killed Balaam son of Beor with the sword. 9The Israelites captured the Midianite women and children and took all the Midianite herds, flocks and goods as plunder. 10They burned all the towns where the Midianites had settled, as well as all their camps. 11They took all the plunder and spoils, including the people and animals, 12and brought the captives, spoils and plunder to Moses and Eleazar the priest and the Israelite assembly at their camp on the plains of Moab, by the Jordan across from Jericho.

13Moses, Eleazar the priest and all the leaders of the community went to meet them outside the camp. 14Moses was angry with the officers of the army—the commanders of thousands and commanders of hundreds—who returned from the battle.

15"Have you allowed all the women to live?" he asked them. 16"They were the ones who followed Balaam's advice and were the means of turning the Israelites away from the LORD in what happened at Peor, so that a plague struck the LORD's people. 17Now kill all the boys. And kill every woman who has slept with a man, 18but save for yourselves every girl who has never slept with a man.

19"All of you who have killed anyone or touched anyone who was killed must stay outside the camp seven days. On the third and seventh days you must purify yourselves and your captives. 20Purify every garment as well as everything made of leather, goat hair or wood."

21Then Eleazar the priest said to the soldiers who had gone into battle, "This is the requirement of the law that the LORD gave Moses: 22Gold, silver, bronze, iron, tin, lead 23and anything else that can withstand fire must be put through the fire, and then it will be clean. But it must also be purified with the water of cleansing. And whatever cannot withstand fire must be put through that water. 24On the seventh day wash your clothes and you will be clean. Then you may come into the camp."

NEW TESTAMENT READING
Luke 8:19–39

Jesus' Mother and Brothers

19Now Jesus' mother and brothers
came to see him, but they were not able
to get near him because of the crowd.
20Someone told him, "Your mother and
brothers are standing outside, wanting
to see you."

21He replied, "My mother and
brothers are those who hear God's word
and put it into practice."

Jesus Calms the Storm

22One day Jesus said to his disciples,
"Let's go over to the other side of the
lake." So they got into a boat and set
out. 23As they sailed, he fell asleep. A
squall came down on the lake, so that
the boat was being swamped, and they
were in great danger.

24The disciples went and woke him,
saying, "Master, Master, we're going to
drown!"

He got up and rebuked the wind and
the raging waters; the storm subsided,
and all was calm. 25"Where is your
faith?" he asked his disciples.

In fear and amazement they asked one another, "Who is this? He commands even the winds and the water, and they obey him."

The Healing of a Demon-possessed Man

26They sailed to the region of the
Gerasenes, which is across the lake from
Galilee. 27When Jesus stepped ashore,
he was met by a demon-possessed man
from the town. For a long time this man
had not worn clothes or lived in a house,
but had lived in the tombs. 28When he
saw Jesus, he cried out and fell at his
feet, shouting at the top of his voice,
"What do you want with me, Jesus, Son
of the Most High God? I beg you, don't
torture me!" 29For Jesus had commanded the evil spirit to come out of the
man. Many times it had seized him, and
though he was chained hand and foot
and kept under guard, he had broken
his chains and had been driven by the
demon into solitary places.

30Jesus asked him, "What is your
name?"

"Legion," he replied, because many
demons had gone into him. 31And they
begged him repeatedly not to order
them to go into the Abyss.

32A large herd of pigs was feeding
there on the hillside. The demons begged Jesus to let them go into them, and
he gave them permission. 33When the
demons came out of the man, they went
into the pigs, and the herd rushed down
the steep bank into the lake and was
drowned.

34When those tending the pigs saw
what had happened, they ran off and
reported this in the town and countryside, 35and the people went out to see
what had happened. When they came to
Jesus, they found the man from whom
the demons had gone out, sitting at
Jesus' feet, dressed and in his right
mind; and they were afraid. 36Those
who had seen it told the people how the
demon-possessed man had been cured.
37Then all the people of the region of
the Gerasenes asked Jesus to leave
them, because they were overcome with
fear. So he got into the boat and left.

38The man from whom the demons
had gone out begged to go with him, but
Jesus sent him away, saying, 39"Return
home and tell how much God has done
for you." So the man went away and
told all over the town how much Jesus
had done for him.

READING FROM PSALMS
Psalm 39:1–13

For the director of music. For Jeduthun. A psalm of David.

1I said, "I will watch my ways
and keep my tongue from sin;
I will put a muzzle on my mouth
as long as the wicked are in my
presence."

[2]But when I was silent and still,
not even saying anything good,
my anguish increased.
[3]My heart grew hot within me,
and as I meditated, the fire burned;
then I spoke with my tongue:

[4]"Show me, O LORD, my life's end
and the number of my days;
let me know how fleeting is my life.
[5]You have made my days a mere
handbreadth;
the span of my years is as nothing
before you.
Each man's life is but a breath.
Selah
[6]Man is a mere phantom as he goes to
and fro:
He bustles about, but only in vain;
he heaps up wealth, not knowing
who will get it.

[7]"But now, Lord, what do I look for?
My hope is in you.
[8]Save me from all my transgressions;
do not make me the scorn of fools.
[9]I was silent; I would not open my
mouth,
for you are the one who has done
this.
[10]Remove your scourge from me;
I am overcome by the blow of your
hand.
[11]You rebuke and discipline men for
their sin;
you consume their wealth like a
moth—
each man is but a breath. *Selah*

[12]"Hear my prayer, O LORD,
listen to my cry for help;
be not deaf to my weeping.
For I dwell with you as an alien,
a stranger, as all my fathers were.
[13]Look away from me, that I may
rejoice again
before I depart and am no more."

DAY 91

APRIL 1

OLD TESTAMENT READING
Numbers 31:25–32:42

Dividing the Spoils

[25]The LORD said to Moses, [26]"You and Eleazar the priest and the family heads of the community are to count all the people and animals that were captured. [27]Divide the spoils between the soldiers who took part in the battle and the rest of the community. [28]From the soldiers who fought in the battle, set apart as tribute for the LORD one out of every five hundred, whether persons, cattle, donkeys, sheep or goats. [29]Take this tribute from their half share and give it to Eleazar the priest as the LORD's part. [30]From the Israelites' half, select one out of every fifty, whether persons, cattle, donkeys, sheep, goats or other animals. Give them to the Levites, who are responsible for the care of the LORD's tabernacle." [31]So Moses and Eleazar the priest did as the LORD commanded Moses.

[32]The plunder remaining from the spoils that the soldiers took was 675,000 sheep, [33]72,000 cattle, [34]61,000 donkeys [35]and 32,000 women who had never slept with a man.

[36]The half share of those who fought in the battle was:

337,500 sheep, [37]of which the tribute
for the LORD was 675;
[38]36,000 cattle, of which the tribute for
the LORD was 72;
[39]30,500 donkeys, of which the tribute
for the LORD was 61;
[40]16,000 people, of which the tribute
for the LORD was 32.

41Moses gave the tribute to Eleazar
the priest as the LORD's part, as the
LORD commanded Moses.
42The half belonging to the Israelites,
which Moses set apart from that of the
fighting men— 43the community's half
—was 337,500 sheep, 4436,000 cattle,
4530,500 donkeys 46and 16,000 people.
47From the Israelites' half, Moses
selected one out of every fifty persons
and animals, as the LORD commanded
him, and gave them to the Levites, who
were responsible for the care of the
LORD's tabernacle.
48Then the officers who were over the
units of the army—the commanders of
thousands and commanders of hundreds—went to Moses 49and said to
him, "Your servants have counted the
soldiers under our command, and not
one is missing. 50So we have brought
as an offering to the LORD the gold
articles each of us acquired—armlets,
bracelets, signet rings, ear-rings and
necklaces—to make atonement for
ourselves before the LORD."
51Moses and Eleazar the priest
accepted from them the gold—all the
handcrafted articles. 52All the gold from
the commanders of thousands and commanders of hundreds that Moses and
Eleazar presented as a gift to the LORD
weighed 16,750 shekels. 53Each soldier
had taken plunder for himself. 54Moses
and Eleazar the priest accepted the gold
from the commanders of thousands and
commanders of hundreds and brought it
into the Tent of Meeting as a memorial
for the Israelites before the LORD.

The Transjordan Tribes

32 The Reubenites and Gadites,
who had very large herds and
flocks, saw that the lands of Jazer and
Gilead were suitable for livestock. 2So
they came to Moses and Eleazar the
priest and to the leaders of the community, and said, 3"Ataroth, Dibon, Jazer,
Nimrah, Heshbon, Elealeh, Sebam,
Nebo and Beon—4the land the LORD
subdued before the people of Israel—
are suitable for livestock, and your servants have livestock. 5If we have found
favour in your eyes," they said, "let this
land be given to your servants as our
possession. Do not make us cross the
Jordan."
6Moses said to the Gadites and Reubenites, "Shall your countrymen go to
war while you sit here? 7Why do you
discourage the Israelites from going
over into the land the LORD has given
them? 8This is what your fathers did
when I sent them from Kadesh Barnea
to look over the land. 9After they went
up to the Valley of Eshcol and viewed
the land, they discouraged the Israelites
from entering the land the LORD had
given them. 10The LORD's anger was
aroused that day and he swore this oath:
11'Because they have not followed me
wholeheartedly, not one of the men
twenty years old or more who came up
out of Egypt will see the land I promised
on oath to Abraham, Isaac and Jacob
—12not one except Caleb son of
Jephunneh the Kenizzite and Joshua
son of Nun, for they followed the LORD
wholeheartedly.' 13The LORD's anger
burned against Israel and he made them
wander in the desert for forty years,
until the whole generation of those who
had done evil in his sight was gone.
14"And here you are, a brood of sinners, standing in the place of your
fathers and making the LORD even more
angry with Israel. 15If you turn away
from following him, he will again leave
all this people in the desert, and you will
be the cause of their destruction."
16Then they came up to him and said,
"We would like to build pens here for
our livestock and cities for our women
and children. 17But we are ready to arm
ourselves and go ahead of the Israelites
until we have brought them to their
place. Meanwhile our women and children will live in fortified cities, for protection from the inhabitants of the land.
18We will not return to our homes until
every Israelite has received his inheritance. 19We will not receive any inheritance with them on the other side of

the Jordan, because our inheritance
has come to us on the east side of the
Jordan."
20Then Moses said to them, "If you
will do this—if you will arm yourselves
before the LORD for battle, 21and if all of
you will go armed over the Jordan before the LORD until he has driven his
enemies out before him—22then when
the land is subdued before the LORD,
you may return and be free from your
obligation to the LORD and to Israel.
And this land will be your possession
before the LORD.
23"But if you fail to do this, you will
be sinning against the LORD; and you
may be sure that your sin will find you
out. 24Build cities for your women and
children, and pens for your flocks, but
do what you have promised."
25The Gadites and Reubenites said to
Moses, "We your servants will do as our
lord commands. 26Our children and
wives, our flocks and herds will remain
here in the cities of Gilead. 27But your
servants, every man armed for battle,
will cross over to fight before the LORD,
just as our lord says."
28Then Moses gave orders about
them to Eleazar the priest and Joshua
son of Nun and to the family heads of
the Israelite tribes. 29He said to them,
"If the Gadites and Reubenites, every
man armed for battle, cross over the
Jordan with you before the LORD, then
when the land is subdued before
you, give them the land of Gilead as
their possession. 30But if they do not
cross over with you armed, they must
accept their possession with you in
Canaan."
31The Gadites and Reubenites
answered, "Your servants will do what
the LORD has said. 32We will cross over
before the LORD into Canaan armed,
but the property we inherit will be on
this side of the Jordan."
33Then Moses gave to the Gadites,
the Reubenites and the half-tribe of
Manasseh son of Joseph the kingdom of
Sihon king of the Amorites and the
kingdom of Og king of Bashan—the
whole land with its cities and the territory around them.
34The Gadites built up Dibon, Ataroth, Aroer, 35Atroth Shophan, Jazer,
Jogbehah, 36Beth Nimrah and Beth
Haran as fortified cities, and built pens
for their flocks. 37And the Reubenites
rebuilt Heshbon, Elealeh and
Kiriathaim, 38as well as Nebo and Baal
Meon (these names were changed) and
Sibmah. They gave names to the cities
they rebuilt.
39The descendants of Makir son of
Manasseh went to Gilead, captured it
and drove out the Amorites who were
there. 40So Moses gave Gilead to the
Makirites, the descendants of Manasseh, and they settled there. 41Jair, a
descendant of Manasseh, captured their
settlements and called them Havvoth
Jair. 42And Nobah captured Kenath and
its surrounding settlements and called it
Nobah after himself.

NEW TESTAMENT READING
Luke 8:40–9:9

A Dead Girl and a Sick Woman

40Now when Jesus returned, a crowd
welcomed him, for they were all expecting him. 41Then a man named Jairus, a
ruler of the synagogue, came and fell at
Jesus' feet, pleading with him to come
to his house 42because his only daughter, a girl of about twelve, was dying.
As Jesus was on his way, the crowds
almost crushed him. 43And a woman
was there who had been subject to
bleeding for twelve years, but no-one
could heal her. 44She came up behind
him and touched the edge of his cloak,
and immediately her bleeding stopped.
45"Who touched me?" Jesus asked.
When they all denied it, Peter said,
"Master, the people are crowding and
pressing against you."
46But Jesus said, "Someone touched
me; I know that power has gone out
from me."
47Then the woman, seeing that she

could not go unnoticed, came trembling
and fell at his feet. In the presence of all
the people, she told why she had
touched him and how she had been
instantly healed. 48Then he said to her,
"Daughter, your faith has healed you.
Go in peace."
49While Jesus was still speaking,
someone came from the house of Jairus,
the synagogue ruler. "Your daughter is
dead," he said. "Don't bother the
teacher any more."
50Hearing this, Jesus said to Jairus,
"Don't be afraid; just believe, and she
will be healed."
51When he arrived at the house of
Jairus, he did not let anyone go in with
him except Peter, John and James,
and the child's father and mother.
52Meanwhile, all the people were wailing and mourning for her. "Stop wailing," Jesus said. "She is not dead but
asleep."
53They laughed at him, knowing that
she was dead. 54But he took her by the
hand and said, "My child, get up!"
55Her spirit returned, and at once she
stood up. Then Jesus told them to give
her something to eat. 56Her parents
were astonished, but he ordered them
not to tell anyone what had happened.

Jesus Sends Out the Twelve

9 When Jesus had called the Twelve
together, he gave them power and
authority to drive out all demons and to
cure diseases, 2and he sent them out to
preach the kingdom of God and to heal
the sick. 3He told them: "Take nothing
for the journey—no staff, no bag, no
bread, no money, no extra tunic.
4Whatever house you enter, stay there
until you leave that town. 5If people do
not welcome you, shake the dust off
your feet when you leave their town, as
a testimony against them." 6So they set
out and went from village to village,
preaching the gospel and healing people
everywhere.
7Now Herod the tetrarch heard about
all that was going on. And he was perplexed, because some were saying that
John had been raised from the dead,
8others that Elijah had appeared, and
still others that one of the prophets of
long ago had come back to life. 9But
Herod said, "I beheaded John. Who,
then, is this I hear such things about?"
And he tried to see him.

READING FROM PSALMS

Psalm 40:1–8

For the director of music. Of David.
A psalm.

1I waited patiently for the LORD;
he turned to me and heard my cry.
2He lifted me out of the slimy pit,
out of the mud and mire;
he set my feet on a rock
and gave me a firm place to stand.
3He put a new song in my mouth,
a hymn of praise to our God.
Many will see and fear
and put their trust in the LORD.

4Blessed is the man
who makes the LORD his trust,
who does not look to the proud,
to those who turn aside to false
gods.
5Many, O LORD my God,
are the wonders you have done.
The things you planned for us
no-one can recount to you;
were I to speak and tell of them,
they would be too many to declare.

6Sacrifice and offering you did not
desire,
but my ears you have pierced;
burnt offerings and sin offerings
you did not require.
7Then I said, "Here I am, I have
come—
it is written about me in the scroll.
8I desire to do your will, O my God;
your law is within my heart."

DAY 92

APRIL 2

OLD TESTAMENT READING

Numbers 33:1–34:29

Stages in Israel's Journey

33 Here are the stages in the journey of the Israelites when they
came out of Egypt by divisions under
the leadership of Moses and Aaron.
2 At the LORD's command Moses recorded the stages in their journey. This
is their journey by stages:

3 The Israelites set out from
Rameses on the fifteenth day of the
first month, the day after the Passover. They marched out boldly in
full view of all the Egyptians, 4 who
were burying all their firstborn,
whom the LORD had struck down
among them; for the LORD had
brought judgment on their gods.
5 The Israelites left Rameses and
camped at Succoth.
6 They left Succoth and camped
at Etham, on the edge of the
desert.
7 They left Etham, turned back to
Pi Hahiroth, to the east of Baal
Zephon, and camped near Migdol.
8 They left Pi Hahiroth and
passed through the sea into the
desert, and when they had travelled for three days in the Desert
of Etham, they camped at Marah.
9 They left Marah and went to
Elim, where there were twelve
springs and seventy palm trees, and
they camped there.
10 They left Elim and camped by
the Red Sea.
11 They left the Red Sea and
camped in the Desert of Sin.
12 They left the Desert of Sin and
camped at Dophkah.
13 They left Dophkah and
camped at Alush.
14 They left Alush and camped at
Rephidim, where there was no
water for the people to drink.
15 They left Rephidim and
camped in the Desert of Sinai.
16 They left the Desert of Sinai
and camped at Kibroth Hattaavah.
17 They left Kibroth Hattaavah
and camped at Hazeroth.
18 They left Hazeroth and
camped at Rithmah.
19 They left Rithmah and camped
at Rimmon Perez.
20 They left Rimmon Perez and
camped at Libnah.
21 They left Libnah and camped
at Rissah.
22 They left Rissah and camped at
Kehelathah.
23 They left Kehelathah and
camped at Mount Shepher.
24 They left Mount Shepher and
camped at Haradah.
25 They left Haradah and camped
at Makheloth.
26 They left Makheloth and
camped at Tahath.
27 They left Tahath and camped
at Terah.
28 They left Terah and camped at
Mithcah.
29 They left Mithcah and camped
at Hashmonah.
30 They left Hashmonah and
camped at Moseroth.
31 They left Moseroth and
camped at Bene Jaakan.
32 They left Bene Jaakan and
camped at Hor Haggidgad.
33 They left Hor Haggidgad and
camped at Jotbathah.
34 They left Jotbathah and
camped at Abronah.
35 They left Abronah and camped
at Ezion Geber.
36 They left Ezion Geber and
camped at Kadesh, in the Desert of
Zin.

37They left Kadesh and camped
at Mount Hor, on the border of
Edom. 38At the LORD's command
Aaron the priest went up Mount
Hor, where he died on the first day
of the fifth month of the fortieth
year after the Israelites came out of
Egypt. 39Aaron was a hundred and
twenty-three years old when he
died on Mount Hor.
40The Canaanite king of Arad,
who lived in the Negev of Canaan,
heard that the Israelites were
coming.
41They left Mount Hor and
camped at Zalmonah.
42They left Zalmonah and
camped at Punon.
43They left Punon and camped at
Oboth.
44They left Oboth and camped at
Iye Abarim, on the border of
Moab.
45They left Iyim and camped at
Dibon Gad.
46They left Dibon Gad and
camped at Almon Diblathaim.
47They left Almon Diblathaim
and camped in the mountains of
Abarim, near Nebo.
48They left the mountains of
Abarim and camped on the plains
of Moab by the Jordan across from
Jericho. 49There on the plains of
Moab they camped along the Jordan from Beth Jeshimoth to Abel
Shittim.

50On the plains of Moab by the Jordan across from Jericho the LORD said
to Moses, 51"Speak to the Israelites and
say to them: 'When you cross the Jordan into Canaan, 52drive out all the
inhabitants of the land before you. Destroy all their carved images and their
cast idols, and demolish all their high
places. 53Take possession of the land
and settle in it, for I have given you the
land to possess. 54Distribute the land by
lot, according to your clans. To a larger
group give a larger inheritance, and to a
smaller group a smaller one. Whatever
falls to them by lot will be theirs. Distribute it according to your ancestral
tribes.
55" 'But if you do not drive out the
inhabitants of the land, those you allow
to remain will become barbs in your
eyes and thorns in your sides. They will
give you trouble in the land where you
will live. 56And then I will do to you
what I plan to do to them.' "

Boundaries of Canaan

34 The LORD said to Moses,
2"Command the Israelites and
say to them: 'When you enter Canaan,
the land that will be allotted to you as an
inheritance will have these boundaries:

3" 'Your southern side will include
some of the Desert of Zin along the
border of Edom. On the east, your
southern boundary will start from the
end of the Salt Sea, 4cross south of
Scorpion Pass, continue on to Zin and
go south of Kadesh Barnea. Then it will
go to Hazar Addar and over to Azmon,
5where it will turn, join the Wadi of
Egypt and end at the Sea.
6" 'Your western boundary will be the
coast of the Great Sea. This will be your
boundary on the west.
7" 'For your northern boundary, run
a line from the Great Sea to Mount Hor
8and from Mount Hor to Lebo Hamath.
Then the boundary will go to Zedad,
9continue to Ziphron and end at Hazar
Enan. This will be your boundary on the
north.
10" 'For your eastern boundary, run a
line from Hazar Enan to Shepham.
11The boundary will go down from
Shepham to Riblah on the east side of
Ain and continue along the slopes east
of the Sea of Kinnereth. 12Then the
boundary will go down along the Jordan
and end at the Salt Sea.
" 'This will be your land, with its
boundaries on every side.' "
13Moses commanded the Israelites:
"Assign this land by lot as an inheritance. The LORD has ordered that it be
given to the nine and a half tribes,

14because the families of the tribe of
Reuben, the tribe of Gad and the half-
tribe of Manasseh have received their
inheritance. 15These two and a half
tribes have received their inheritance
on the east side of the Jordan of Jericho,
towards the sunrise."

16The LORD said to Moses, 17"These
are the names of the men who are to
assign the land for you as an inheritance: Eleazar the priest and Joshua son
of Nun. 18And appoint one leader from
each tribe to help assign the land.
19These are their names:

Caleb son of Jephunneh,
from the tribe of Judah;
20Shemuel son of Ammihud,
from the tribe of Simeon;
21Elidad son of Kislon,
from the tribe of Benjamin;
22Bukki son of Jogli,
the leader from the tribe of Dan;
23Hanniel son of Ephod,
the leader from the tribe of Manasseh son of Joseph;
24Kemuel son of Shiphtan,
the leader from the tribe of Ephraim son of Joseph;
25Elizaphan son of Parnach,
the leader from the tribe of Zebulun;
26Paltiel son of Azzan,
the leader from the tribe of Issachar;
27Ahihud son of Shelomi,
the leader from the tribe of Asher;
28Pedahel son of Ammihud,
the leader from the tribe of Naphtali."

29These are the men the LORD commanded to assign the inheritance to the Israelites in the land of Canaan.

NEW TESTAMENT READING
Luke 9:10–27

Jesus Feeds the Five Thousand

10When the apostles returned, they
reported to Jesus what they had done.
Then he took them with him and they
withdrew by themselves to a town called
Bethsaida, 11but the crowds learned
about it and followed him. He welcomed them and spoke to them about
the kingdom of God, and healed those
who needed healing.

12Late in the afternoon the Twelve
came to him and said, "Send the crowd
away so they can go to the surrounding
villages and countryside and find food
and lodging, because we are in a remote
place here."

13He replied, "You give them something to eat."

They answered, "We have only five
loaves of bread and two fish—unless we
go and buy food for all this crowd."
14(About five thousand men were
there.)

But he said to his disciples, "Make
them sit down in groups of about fifty
each." 15The disciples did so, and everybody sat down. 16Taking the five loaves
and the two fish and looking up to
heaven, he gave thanks and broke
them. Then he gave them to the disciples to set before the people. 17They all
ate and were satisfied, and the disciples
picked up twelve basketfuls of broken
pieces that were left over.

Peter's Confession of Christ

18Once when Jesus was praying in
private and his disciples were with him,
he asked them, "Who do the crowds say
I am?"

19They replied, "Some say John the
Baptist; others say Elijah; and still
others, that one of the prophets of long
ago has come back to life."

20"But what about you?" he asked.
"Who do you say I am?"

Peter answered, "The Christ of
God."

21Jesus strictly warned them not to
tell this to anyone. 22And he said, "The
Son of Man must suffer many things and
be rejected by the elders, chief priests
and teachers of the law, and he must be
killed and on the third day be raised to
life."

[23]Then he said to them all: "If anyone
would come after me, he must deny
himself and take up his cross daily and
follow me. [24]For whoever wants to save
his life will lose it, but whoever loses his
life for me will save it. [25]What good is it
for a man to gain the whole world, and
yet lose or forfeit his very self? [26]If
anyone is ashamed of me and my words,
the Son of Man will be ashamed of him
when he comes in his glory and in the
glory of the Father and of the holy
angels. [27]I tell you the truth, some who
are standing here will not taste death
before they see the kingdom of God."

READING FROM PROVERBS
Proverbs 8:22–31

[22]"The LORD brought me forth as the
first of his works,
before his deeds of old;
[23]I was appointed from eternity,
from the beginning, before the
world began.
[24]When there were no oceans, I was
given birth,
when there were no springs
abounding with water;
[25]before the mountains were settled in
place,
before the hills, I was given birth,
[26]before he made the earth or its fields
or any of the dust of the world.
[27]I was there when he set the heavens
in place,
when he marked out the horizon
on the face of the deep,
[28]when he established the clouds above
and fixed securely the fountains of
the deep,
[29]when he gave the sea its boundary
so that the waters would not
overstep his command,
and when he marked out the
foundations of the earth.
[30] Then I was the craftsman at his
side.
I was filled with delight day after day,
rejoicing always in his presence,
[31]rejoicing in his whole world
and delighting in mankind.

APRIL 3

DAY 93

OLD TESTAMENT READING
Numbers 35:1–36:13

Towns for the Levites

35 On the plains of Moab by the
Jordan across from Jericho,
the LORD said to Moses, [2]"Command
the Israelites to give the Levites towns
to live in from the inheritance the
Israelites will possess. And give them
pasture-lands around the towns. [3]Then
they will have towns to live in and pasture-lands for their cattle, flocks and all
their other livestock.
[4]"The pasture-lands around the
towns that you give the Levites will
extend out fifteen hundred feet from the
town wall. [5]Outside the town, measure
three thousand feet on the east side,
three thousand on the south side, three
thousand on the west and three
thousand on the north, with the town in
the centre. They will have this area as
pasture-land for the towns.

Cities of Refuge

[6]"Six of the towns you give the Levites will be cities of refuge, to which a
person who has killed someone may
flee. In addition, give them forty-two
other towns. [7]In all you must give the
Levites forty-eight towns, together with

their pasture-lands. 8The towns you
give the Levites from the land the
Israelites possess are to be given in
proportion to the inheritance of each
tribe: Take many towns from a tribe
that has many, but few from one that
has few."
9Then the LORD said to Moses:
10"Speak to the Israelites and say to
them: 'When you cross the Jordan into
Canaan, 11select some towns to be your
cities of refuge, to which a person who
has killed someone accidentally may
flee. 12They will be places of refuge
from the avenger, so that a person accused of murder may not die before he
stands trial before the assembly.
13These six towns you give will be your
cities of refuge. 14Give three on this side
of the Jordan and three in Canaan as
cities of refuge. 15These six towns will
be a place of refuge for Israelites, aliens
and any other people living among
them, so that anyone who has killed
another accidentally can flee there.
16" 'If a man strikes someone with an
iron object so that he dies, he is a
murderer; the murderer shall be put to
death. 17Or if anyone has a stone in his
hand that could kill, and he strikes
someone so that he dies, he is a murderer; the murderer shall be put to
death. 18Or if anyone has a wooden
object in his hand that could kill, and he
hits someone so that he dies, he is a
murderer; the murderer shall be put to
death. 19The avenger of blood shall put
the murderer to death; when he meets
him, he shall put him to death. 20If
anyone with malice aforethought
pushes another or throws something at
him intentionally so that he dies 21or if
in hostility he hits him with his fist so
that he dies, that person shall be put to
death; he is a murderer. The avenger of
blood shall put the murderer to death
when he meets him.
22" 'But if without hostility someone
suddenly pushes another or throws
something at him unintentionally 23or,
without seeing him, drops a stone on
him that could kill him, and he dies,
then since he was not his enemy and he
did not intend to harm him, 24the assembly must judge between him and the
avenger of blood according to these
regulations. 25The assembly must protect the one accused of murder from the
avenger of blood and send him back to
the city of refuge to which he fled. He
must stay there until the death of the
high priest, who was anointed with holy
oil.
26" 'But if the accused ever goes outside the limits of the city of refuge to
which he has fled 27and the avenger of
blood finds him outside the city, the
avenger of blood may kill the accused
without being guilty of murder. 28The
accused must stay in his city of refuge
until the death of the high priest; only
after the death of the high priest may he
return to his own property.
29" 'These are to be legal requirements for you throughout the generations to come, wherever you live.
30" 'Anyone who kills a person is to be
put to death as a murderer only on the
testimony of witnesses. But no-one is to
be put to death on the testimony of only
one witness.
31" 'Do not accept a ransom for the
life of a murderer, who deserves to die.
He must surely be put to death.
32" 'Do not accept a ransom for anyone who has fled to a city of refuge and
so allow him to go back and live on his
own land before the death of the high
priest.
33" 'Do not pollute the land where
you are. Bloodshed pollutes the land,
and atonement cannot be made for the
land on which blood has been shed,
except by the blood of the one who shed
it. 34Do not defile the land where you
live and where I dwell, for I, the LORD,
dwell among the Israelites.' "

Inheritance of Zelophehad's Daughters

36 The family heads of the clan of
Gilead son of Makir, the son of
Manasseh, who were from the clans

of the descendants of Joseph, came and
spoke before Moses and the leaders, the
heads of the Israelite families. 2They
said, "When the LORD commanded my
lord to give the land as an inheritance to
the Israelites by lot, he ordered you to
give the inheritance of our brother
Zelophehad to his daughters. 3Now
suppose they marry men from other
Israelite tribes; then their inheritance
will be taken from our ancestral inheritance and added to that of the tribe they
marry into. And so part of the inheritance allotted to us will be taken away.
4When the Year of Jubilee for the
Israelites comes, their inheritance will
be added to that of the tribe into which
they marry, and their property will be
taken from the tribal inheritance of our
forefathers."

5Then at the LORD's command Moses
gave this order to the Israelites: "What
the tribe of the descendants of Joseph is
saying is right. 6This is what the LORD
commands for Zelophehad's daughters:
They may marry anyone they please as
long as they marry within the tribal clan
of their father. 7No inheritance in Israel
is to pass from tribe to tribe, for every
Israelite shall keep the tribal land inherited from his forefathers. 8Every daughter who inherits land in any Israelite
tribe must marry someone in her
father's tribal clan, so that every
Israelite will possess the inheritance
of his fathers. 9No inheritance may
pass from tribe to tribe, for each
Israelite tribe is to keep the land it
inherits."

10So Zelophehad's daughters did
as the LORD commanded Moses.
11Zelophehad's daughters—Mahlah,
Tirzah, Hoglah, Milcah and Noah—
married their cousins on their father's
side. 12They married within the clans of
the descendants of Manasseh son of
Joseph, and their inheritance remained
in their father's clan and tribe.

13These are the commands and regulations the LORD gave through Moses to
the Israelites on the plains of Moab by
the Jordan across from Jericho.

NEW TESTAMENT READING
Luke 9:28–56

The Transfiguration

28About eight days after Jesus said
this, he took Peter, John and James
with him and went up onto a mountain
to pray. 29As he was praying, the
appearance of his face changed, and his
clothes became as bright as a flash of
lightning. 30Two men, Moses and Elijah, 31appeared in glorious splendour,
talking with Jesus. They spoke about his
departure, which he was about to bring
to fulfilment at Jerusalem. 32Peter and
his companions were very sleepy, but
when they became fully awake, they
saw his glory and the two men standing
with him. 33As the men were leaving
Jesus, Peter said to him, "Master, it is
good for us to be here. Let us put up
three shelters—one for you, one for
Moses and one for Elijah." (He did not
know what he was saying.)

34While he was speaking, a cloud
appeared and enveloped them, and
they were afraid as they entered the
cloud. 35A voice came from the cloud,
saying, "This is my Son, whom I have
chosen; listen to him." 36When the
voice had spoken, they found that Jesus
was alone. The disciples kept this to
themselves, and told no-one at that time
what they had seen.

The Healing of a Boy With an Evil Spirit

37The next day, when they came
down from the mountain, a large crowd
met him. 38A man in the crowd called
out, "Teacher, I beg you to look at my
son, for he is my only child. 39A spirit
seizes him and he suddenly screams; it
throws him into convulsions so that he
foams at the mouth. It scarcely ever
leaves him and is destroying him. 40I
begged your disciples to drive it out, but
they could not."

41"O unbelieving and perverse generation," Jesus replied, "how long shall

I stay with you and put up with you? Bring your son here."

42Even while the boy was coming, the demon threw him to the ground in a convulsion. But Jesus rebuked the evil spirit, healed the boy and gave him back to his father. 43And they were all amazed at the greatness of God.

While everyone was marvelling at all that Jesus did, he said to his disciples, 44"Listen carefully to what I am about to tell you: The Son of Man is going to be betrayed into the hands of men." 45But they did not understand what this meant. It was hidden from them, so that they did not grasp it, and they were afraid to ask him about it.

Who Will Be the Greatest?

46An argument started among the disciples as to which of them would be the greatest. 47Jesus, knowing their thoughts, took a little child and made him stand beside him. 48Then he said to them, "Whoever welcomes this little child in my name welcomes me; and whoever welcomes me welcomes the one who sent me. For he who is least among you all—he is the greatest."

49"Master," said John, "we saw a man driving out demons in your name and we tried to stop him, because he is not one of us."

50"Do not stop him," Jesus said, "for whoever is not against you is for you."

Samaritan Opposition

51As the time approached for him to be taken up to heaven, Jesus resolutely set out for Jerusalem. 52And he sent messengers on ahead, who went into a Samaritan village to get things ready for him; 53but the people there did not welcome him, because he was heading for Jerusalem. 54When the disciples James and John saw this, they asked, "Lord, do you want us to call fire down from heaven to destroy them?" 55But Jesus turned and rebuked them, 56and they went to another village.

READING FROM PSALMS

Psalm 40:9–17

9I proclaim righteousness in the great assembly;
I do not seal my lips,
as you know, O LORD.
10I do not hide your righteousness in my heart;
I speak of your faithfulness and salvation.
I do not conceal your love and your truth
from the great assembly.

11Do not withhold your mercy from me, O LORD;
may your love and your truth always protect me.
12For troubles without number surround me;
my sins have overtaken me, and I cannot see.
They are more than the hairs of my head,
and my heart fails within me.

13Be pleased, O LORD, to save me;
O LORD, come quickly to help me.
14May all who seek to take my life
be put to shame and confusion;
may all who desire my ruin
be turned back in disgrace.
15May those who say to me, "Aha! Aha!"
be appalled at their own shame.
16But may all who seek you
rejoice and be glad in you;
may those who love your salvation always say,
"The LORD be exalted!"

17Yet I am poor and needy;
may the Lord think of me.
You are my help and my deliverer;
O my God, do not delay.

APRIL 4

OLD TESTAMENT READING

Deuteronomy 1:1–2:23

The Command to Leave Horeb

1 These are the words Moses spoke to all Israel in the desert east of the Jordan—that is, in the Arabah—opposite Suph, between Paran and Tophel, Laban, Hazeroth and Dizahab. 2(It takes eleven days to go from Horeb to Kadesh Barnea by the Mount Seir road.)

3In the fortieth year, on the first day of the eleventh month, Moses proclaimed to the Israelites all that the LORD had commanded him concerning them. 4This was after he had defeated Sihon king of the Amorites, who reigned in Heshbon, and at Edrei had defeated Og king of Bashan, who reigned in Ashtaroth.

5East of the Jordan in the territory of Moab, Moses began to expound this law, saying:

6The LORD our God said to us at Horeb, "You have stayed long enough at this mountain. 7Break camp and advance into the hill country of the Amorites; go to all the neighbouring peoples in the Arabah, in the mountains, in the western foothills, in the Negev and along the coast, to the land of the Canaanites and to Lebanon, as far as the great river, the Euphrates. 8See, I have given you this land. Go in and take possession of the land that the LORD swore he would give to your fathers—to Abraham, Isaac and Jacob—and to their descendants after them."

The Appointment of Leaders

9At that time I said to you, "You are too heavy a burden for me to carry alone. 10The LORD your God has increased your numbers so that today you are as many as the stars in the sky. 11May the LORD, the God of your fathers, increase you a thousand times and bless you as he has promised! 12But how can I bear your problems and your burdens and your disputes all by myself? 13Choose some wise, understanding and respected men from each of your tribes, and I will set them over you."

14You answered me, "What you propose to do is good."

15So I took the leading men of your tribes, wise and respected men, and appointed them to have authority over you—as commanders of thousands, of hundreds, of fifties and of tens and as tribal officials. 16And I charged your judges at that time: Hear the disputes between your brothers and judge fairly, whether the case is between brother Israelites or between one of them and an alien. 17Do not show partiality in judging; hear both small and great alike. Do not be afraid of any man, for judgment belongs to God. Bring me any case too hard for you, and I will hear it. 18And at that time I told you everything you were to do.

Spies Sent Out

19Then, as the LORD our God commanded us, we set out from Horeb and went towards the hill country of the Amorites through all that vast and dreadful desert that you have seen, and so we reached Kadesh Barnea. 20Then I said to you, "You have reached the hill country of the Amorites, which the LORD our God is giving us. 21See, the LORD your God has given you the land. Go up and take possession of it as the LORD, the God of your fathers, told you. Do not be afraid; do not be discouraged."

22Then all of you came to me and said, "Let us send men ahead to spy out the land for us and bring back a report

about the route we are to take and the
towns we will come to."
[23]The idea seemed good to me; so I
selected twelve of you, one man from
each tribe. [24]They left and went up into
the hill country, and came to the Valley
of Eshcol and explored it. [25]Taking with
them some of the fruit of the land, they
brought it down to us and reported, "It
is a good land that the LORD our God is
giving us."

Rebellion Against the LORD

[26]But you were unwilling to go up;
you rebelled against the command of
the LORD your God. [27]You grumbled in
your tents and said, "The LORD hates
us; so he brought us out of Egypt to
deliver us into the hands of the Amorites to destroy us. [28]Where can we go?
Our brothers have made us lose heart.
They say, 'The people are stronger and
taller than we are; the cities are large,
with walls up to the sky. We even saw
the Anakites there.'"
[29]Then I said to you, "Do not be
terrified; do not be afraid of them.
[30]The LORD your God, who is going
before you, will fight for you, as he did
for you in Egypt, before your very eyes,
[31]and in the desert. There you saw how
the LORD your God carried you, as a
father carries his son, all the way you
went until you reached this place."
[32]In spite of this, you did not trust in
the LORD your God, [33]who went ahead
of you on your journey, in fire by night
and in a cloud by day, to search out
places for you to camp and to show you
the way you should go.
[34]When the LORD heard what you
said, he was angry and solemnly swore:
[35]"Not a man of this evil generation
shall see the good land I swore to give
your forefathers, [36]except Caleb son of
Jephunneh. He will see it, and I will give
him and his descendants the land he set
his feet on, because he followed the
LORD wholeheartedly."
[37]Because of you the LORD became
angry with me also and said, "You shall
not enter it, either. [38]But your assistant,
Joshua son of Nun, will enter it. Encourage him, because he will lead Israel
to inherit it. [39]And the little ones that
you said would be taken captive, your
children who do not yet know good
from bad—they will enter the land. I
will give it to them and they will take
possession of it. [40]But as for you, turn
round and set out towards the desert
along the route to the Red Sea."
[41]Then you replied, "We have sinned
against the LORD. We will go up and
fight, as the LORD our God commanded
us." So every one of you put on his
weapons, thinking it easy to go up into
the hill country.
[42]But the LORD said to me, "Tell
them, 'Do not go up and fight, because I
will not be with you. You will be defeated by your enemies.'"
[43]So I told you, but you would not
listen. You rebelled against the LORD's
command and in your arrogance you
marched up into the hill country. [44]The
Amorites who lived in those hills came
out against you; they chased you like a
swarm of bees and beat you down from
Seir all the way to Hormah. [45]You came
back and wept before the LORD, but he
paid no attention to your weeping and
turned a deaf ear to you. [46]And so you
stayed in Kadesh many days—all the
time you spent there.

Wanderings in the Desert

2 Then we turned back and set out
towards the desert along the route
to the Red Sea, as the LORD had
directed me. For a long time we made
our way around the hill country of Seir.
[2]Then the LORD said to me, [3]"You
have made your way around this hill
country long enough; now turn north.
[4]Give the people these orders: 'You are
about to pass through the territory of
your brothers the descendants of Esau,
who live in Seir. They will be afraid of
you, but be very careful. [5]Do not provoke them to war, for I will not give you
any of their land, not even enough to
put your foot on. I have given Esau the
hill country of Seir as his own. [6]You are

to pay them in silver for the food you eat
and the water you drink.'"
7The LORD your God has blessed you
in all the work of your hands. He has
watched over your journey through this
vast desert. These forty years the LORD
your God has been with you, and you
have not lacked anything.
8So we went on past our brothers the
descendants of Esau, who live in Seir.
We turned from the Arabah road,
which comes up from Elath and Ezion
Geber, and travelled along the desert
road of Moab.
9Then the LORD said to me, "Do not
harass the Moabites or provoke them to
war, for I will not give you any part of
their land. I have given Ar to the descendants of Lot as a possession."
10(The Emites used to live there—a
people strong and numerous, and as tall
as the Anakites. 11Like the Anakites,
they too were considered Rephaites,
but the Moabites called them Emites.
12Horites used to live in Seir, but the
descendants of Esau drove them out.
They destroyed the Horites from before
them and settled in their place, just as
Israel did in the land the LORD gave
them as their possession.)
13And the LORD said, "Now get up
and cross the Zered Valley." So we
crossed the valley.
14Thirty-eight years passed from the
time we left Kadesh Barnea until we
crossed the Zered Valley. By then, that
entire generation of fighting men had
perished from the camp, as the LORD
had sworn to them. 15The LORD's hand
was against them until he had completely eliminated them from the camp.
16Now when the last of these fighting
men among the people had died, 17the
LORD said to me, 18"Today you are to
pass by the region of Moab at Ar.
19When you come to the Ammonites,
do not harass them or provoke them to
war, for I will not give you possession of
any land belonging to the Ammonites. I
have given it as a possession to the
descendants of Lot."
20(That too was considered a land of
the Rephaites, who used to live there;
but the Ammonites called them Zam-
zummites. 21They were a people strong
and numerous, and as tall as the Anakites. The LORD destroyed them from
before the Ammonites, who drove
them out and settled in their place.
22The LORD had done the same for the
descendants of Esau, who lived in Seir,
when he destroyed the Horites from
before them. They drove them out and
have lived in their place to this day.
23And as for the Avvites who lived in
villages as far as Gaza, the Caphtorites
coming out from Caphtor destroyed
them and settled in their place.)

NEW TESTAMENT READING
Luke 9:57–10:24

The Cost of Following Jesus

57As they were walking along the
road, a man said to him, "I will follow
you wherever you go."
58Jesus replied, "Foxes have holes
and birds of the air have nests, but the
Son of Man has nowhere to lay his
head."
59He said to another man, "Follow
me."
But the man replied, "Lord, first let
me go and bury my father."
60Jesus said to him, "Let the dead
bury their own dead, but you go and
proclaim the kingdom of God."
61Still another said, "I will follow
you, Lord; but first let me go back and
say good-bye to my family."
62Jesus replied, "No-one who puts his
hand to the plough and looks back is fit
for service in the kingdom of God."

Jesus Sends Out the Seventy-two

10 After this the Lord appointed
seventy-two others and sent
them two by two ahead of him to every
town and place where he was about to
go. 2He told them, "The harvest is
plentiful, but the workers are few. Ask
the Lord of the harvest, therefore, to

send out workers into his harvest field.
3Go! I am sending you out like lambs
among wolves. 4Do not take a purse or
bag or sandals; and do not greet anyone
on the road.
5"When you enter a house, first say,
'Peace to this house.' 6If a man of peace
is there, your peace will rest on him; if
not, it will return to you. 7Stay in that
house, eating and drinking whatever
they give you, for the worker deserves
his wages. Do not move around from
house to house.
8"When you enter a town and are
welcomed, eat what is set before you.
9Heal the sick who are there and tell
them, 'The kingdom of God is near
you.' 10But when you enter a town and
are not welcomed, go into its streets and
say, 11'Even the dust of your town that
sticks to our feet we wipe off against
you. Yet be sure of this: The kingdom of
God is near.' 12I tell you, it will be more
bearable on that day for Sodom than for
that town.
13"Woe to you, Korazin! Woe to you,
Bethsaida! For if the miracles that were
performed in you had been performed
in Tyre and Sidon, they would have
repented long ago, sitting in sackcloth
and ashes. 14But it will be more bearable for Tyre and Sidon at the judgment
than for you. 15And you, Capernaum,
will you be lifted up to the skies? No,
you will go down to the depths.
16"He who listens to you listens to
me; he who rejects you rejects me; but
he who rejects me rejects him who sent
me."
17The seventy-two returned with joy
and said, "Lord, even the demons submit to us in your name."
18He replied, "I saw Satan fall like
lightning from heaven. 19I have given
you authority to trample on snakes
and scorpions and to overcome all the
power of the enemy; nothing will harm
you. 20However, do not rejoice that the
spirits submit to you, but rejoice that
your names are written in heaven."
21At that time Jesus, full of joy
through the Holy Spirit, said, "I praise
you, Father, Lord of heaven and earth,
because you have hidden these things
from the wise and learned, and revealed
them to little children. Yes, Father, for
this was your good pleasure.
22"All things have been committed to
me by my Father. No-one knows who
the Son is except the Father, and no-one
knows who the Father is except the Son
and those to whom the Son chooses to
reveal him."
23Then he turned to his disciples and
said privately, "Blessed are the eyes
that see what you see. 24For I tell you
that many prophets and kings wanted to
see what you see but did not see it, and
to hear what you hear but did not hear
it."

READING FROM PSALMS
Psalm 41:1–6

For the director of music. A psalm of David.

1Blessed is he who has regard for the weak;
the LORD delivers him in times of trouble.
2The LORD will protect him and preserve his life;
he will bless him in the land
and not surrender him to the desire of his foes.
3The LORD will sustain him on his sick-bed
and restore him from his bed of illness.

4I said, "O LORD, have mercy on me;
heal me, for I have sinned against you."
5My enemies say of me in malice,
"When will he die and his name perish?"
6Whenever one comes to see me,
he speaks falsely, while his heart gathers slander;
then he goes out and spreads it abroad.

APRIL 5

DAY 95

OLD TESTAMENT READING
Deuteronomy 2:24–4:14

Defeat of Sihon King of Heshbon

24“Set out now and cross the Arnon
Gorge. See, I have given into your hand
Sihon the Amorite, king of Heshbon,
and his country. Begin to take possession of it and engage him in battle.
25This very day I will begin to put the
terror and fear of you on all the nations
under heaven. They will hear reports of
you and will tremble and be in anguish
because of you.”
26From the desert of Kedemoth I sent
messengers to Sihon king of Heshbon
offering peace and saying, 27“Let us
pass through your country. We will stay
on the main road; we will not turn aside
to the right or to the left. 28Sell us food
to eat and water to drink for their price
in silver. Only let us pass through on
foot—29as the descendants of Esau,
who live in Seir, and the Moabites, who
live in Ar, did for us—until we cross the
Jordan into the land the LORD our God
is giving us.” 30But Sihon king of Heshbon refused to let us pass through. For
the LORD your God had made his spirit
stubborn and his heart obstinate in
order to give him into your hands, as he
has now done.
31The LORD said to me, “See, I have
begun to deliver Sihon and his country
over to you. Now begin to conquer and
possess his land.”
32When Sihon and all his army came
out to meet us in battle at Jahaz, 33the
LORD our God delivered him over to us
and we struck him down, together with
his sons and his whole army. 34At that
time we took all his towns and completely destroyed them—men, women
and children. We left no survivors.
35But the livestock and the plunder
from the towns we had captured we
carried off for ourselves. 36From Aroer
on the rim of the Arnon Gorge, and
from the town in the gorge, even as far
as Gilead, not one town was too strong
for us. The LORD our God gave us all of
them. 37But in accordance with the
command of the LORD our God, you did
not encroach on any of the land of the
Ammonites, neither the land along the
course of the Jabbok nor that around
the towns in the hills.

Defeat of Og King of Bashan

3 Next we turned and went up along
the road towards Bashan, and Og
king of Bashan with his whole army
marched out to meet us in battle at
Edrei. 2The LORD said to me, “Do not
be afraid of him, for I have handed him
over to you with his whole army and his
land. Do to him what you did to Sihon
king of the Amorites, who reigned in
Heshbon.”
3So the LORD our God also gave into
our hands Og king of Bashan and all his
army. We struck them down, leaving no
survivors. 4At that time we took all his
cities. There was not one of the sixty
cities that we did not take from them
—the whole region of Argob, Og’s
kingdom in Bashan. 5All these cities
were fortified with high walls and with
gates and bars, and there were also a
great many unwalled villages. 6We completely destroyed them, as we had done
with Sihon king of Heshbon, destroying
every city—men, women and children.
7But all the livestock and the plunder
from their cities we carried off for
ourselves.
8So at that time we took from these
two kings of the Amorites the territory
east of the Jordan, from the Arnon
Gorge as far as Mount Hermon.
9(Hermon is called Sirion by the Sidonians; the Amorites call it Senir.) 10We
took all the towns on the plateau, and
all Gilead, and all Bashan as far as

Salecah and Edrei, towns of Og's kingdom in Bashan. 11(Only Og king of
Bashan was left of the remnant of the
Rephaites. His bed was made of iron
and was more than thirteen feet long
and six feet wide. It is still in Rabbah of
the Ammonites.)

Division of the Land

12Of the land that we took over at that
time, I gave the Reubenites and the
Gadites the territory north of Aroer by
the Arnon Gorge, including half the hill
country of Gilead, together with its
towns. 13The rest of Gilead and also all
of Bashan, the kingdom of Og, I gave to
the half-tribe of Manasseh. (The whole
region of Argob in Bashan used to be
known as a land of the Rephaites.
14Jair, a descendant of Manasseh, took
the whole region of Argob as far as the
border of the Geshurites and the
Maacathites; it was named after him, so
that to this day Bashan is called Havvoth Jair.) 15And I gave Gilead to
Makir. 16But to the Reubenites and the
Gadites I gave the territory extending
from Gilead down to the Arnon Gorge
(the middle of the gorge being the border) and out to the Jabbok River, which
is the border of the Ammonites. 17Its
western border was the Jordan in the
Arabah, from Kinnereth to the Sea of
the Arabah (the Salt Sea), below the
slopes of Pisgah.

18I commanded you at that time:
"The LORD your God has given you
this land to take possession of it. But
all your able-bodied men, armed for
battle, must cross over ahead of your
brother Israelites. 19However, your
wives, your children and your livestock
(I know you have much livestock) may
stay in the towns I have given you,
20until the LORD gives rest to your
brothers as he has to you, and they too
have taken over the land that the LORD
your God is giving them, across the
Jordan. After that, each of you may go
back to the possession I have given
you."

Moses Forbidden to Cross the Jordan

21At that time I commanded Joshua:
"You have seen with your own eyes all
that the LORD your God has done to
these two kings. The LORD will do the
same to all the kingdoms over there
where you are going. 22Do not be afraid
of them; the LORD your God himself
will fight for you."

23At that time I pleaded with the
LORD: 24"O Sovereign LORD, you have
begun to show to your servant your
greatness and your strong hand. For
what god is there in heaven or on earth
who can do the deeds and mighty works
you do? 25Let me go over and see the
good land beyond the Jordan—that fine
hill country and Lebanon."

26But because of you the LORD was
angry with me and would not listen to
me. "That is enough," the LORD said.
"Do not speak to me any more about
this matter. 27Go up to the top of Pisgah
and look west and north and south and
east. Look at the land with your own
eyes, since you are not going to cross
this Jordan. 28But commission Joshua,
and encourage and strengthen him, for
he will lead this people across and will
cause them to inherit the land that you
will see." 29So we stayed in the valley
near Beth Peor.

Obedience Commanded

4 Hear now, O Israel, the decrees
and laws I am about to teach you.
Follow them so that you may live and
may go in and take possession of the
land that the LORD, the God of your
fathers, is giving you. 2Do not add to
what I command you and do not sub-
tract from it, but keep the commands of
the LORD your God that I give you.

3You saw with your own eyes what
the LORD did at Baal Peor. The LORD
your God destroyed from among you
everyone who followed the Baal of
Peor, 4but all of you who held fast to the
LORD your God are still alive today.

5See, I have taught you decrees and

laws as the LORD my God commanded
me, so that you may follow them in the
land you are entering to take possession
of it. 6Observe them carefully, for this
will show your wisdom and understanding to the nations, who will hear about
all these decrees and say, "Surely this
great nation is a wise and understanding
people." 7What other nation is so great
as to have their gods near them the way
the LORD our God is near us whenever
we pray to him? 8And what other nation
is so great as to have such righteous
decrees and laws as this body of laws I
am setting before you today?

9Only be careful, and watch
yourselves closely so that you do not
forget the things your eyes have seen or
let them slip from your heart as long as
you live. Teach them to your children
and to their children after them.
10Remember the day you stood before
the LORD your God at Horeb, when he
said to me, "Assemble the people before me to hear my words so that they
may learn to revere me as long as they
live in the land and may teach them to
their children." 11You came near and
stood at the foot of the mountain while
it blazed with fire to the very heavens,
with black clouds and deep darkness.
12Then the LORD spoke to you out of the
fire. You heard the sound of words but
saw no form; there was only a voice.
13He declared to you his covenant, the
Ten Commandments, which he commanded you to follow and then wrote
them on two stone tablets. 14And the
LORD directed me at that time to teach
you the decrees and laws you are to
follow in the land that you are crossing
the Jordan to possess.

NEW TESTAMENT READING
Luke 10:25–11:4

The Parable of the Good Samaritan

25On one occasion an expert in the
law stood up to test Jesus. "Teacher,"
he asked, "what must I do to inherit
eternal life?"

26"What is written in the Law?" he
replied. "How do you read it?"

27He answered: "'Love the Lord
your God with all your heart and with
all your soul and with all your strength
and with all your mind'; and, 'Love your
neighbour as yourself.'"

28"You have answered correctly,"
Jesus replied. "Do this and you will
live."

29But he wanted to justify himself,
so he asked Jesus, "And who is my
neighbour?"

30In reply Jesus said: "A man was
going down from Jerusalem to Jericho,
when he fell into the hands of robbers.
They stripped him of his clothes, beat
him and went away, leaving him half-
dead. 31A priest happened to be going
down the same road, and when he saw
the man, he passed by on the other side.
32So too, a Levite, when he came to the
place and saw him, passed by on the
other side. 33But a Samaritan, as he
travelled, came where the man was; and
when he saw him, he took pity on him.
34He went to him and bandaged his
wounds, pouring on oil and wine. Then
he put the man on his own donkey,
brought him to an inn and took care of
him. 35The next day he took out two
silver coins and gave them to the inn-
keeper. 'Look after him,' he said, 'and
when I return, I will reimburse you for
any extra expense you may have.'

36"Which of these three do you think
was a neighbour to the man who fell into
the hands of robbers?"

37The expert in the law replied, "The
one who had mercy on him."

Jesus told him, "Go and do likewise."

At the Home of Martha and Mary

38As Jesus and his disciples were on
their way, he came to a village where a
woman named Martha opened her
home to him. 39She had a sister called
Mary, who sat at the Lord's feet listening to what he said. 40But Martha was
distracted by all the preparations that

had to be made. She came to him and
asked, "Lord, don't you care that my
sister has left me to do the work by
myself? Tell her to help me!"
41"Martha, Martha," the Lord
answered, "you are worried and upset
about many things, 42but only one thing
is needed. Mary has chosen what is
better, and it will not be taken away
from her."

Jesus' Teaching on Prayer

11 One day Jesus was praying in a
certain place. When he finished,
one of his disciples said to him, "Lord,
teach us to pray, just as John taught his
disciples."
2He said to them, "When you pray,
say:

"'Father,
hallowed be your name,
your kingdom come.
3Give us each day our daily bread.
4Forgive us our sins,
for we also forgive everyone who
sins against us.
And lead us not into temptation.'"

READING FROM PSALMS
Psalm 41:7–13

7All my enemies whisper together
against me;
they imagine the worst for me,
saying,
8"A vile disease has beset him;
he will never get up from the place
where he lies."
9Even my close friend, whom I
trusted,
he who shared my bread,
has lifted up his heel against me.

10But you, O LORD, have mercy on me;
raise me up, that I may repay
them.
11I know that you are pleased with me,
for my enemy does not triumph
over me.
12In my integrity you uphold me
and set me in your presence for
ever.

13Praise be to the LORD, the God of
Israel,
from everlasting to everlasting.
Amen and Amen.

DAY 96

APRIL 6

OLD TESTAMENT READING
Deuteronomy 4:15–5:33

Idolatry Forbidden

15You saw no form of any kind the
day the LORD spoke to you at Horeb out
of the fire. Therefore watch yourselves
very carefully, 16so that you do not become corrupt and make for yourselves
an idol, an image of any shape, whether
formed like a man or a woman, 17or like
any animal on earth or any bird that flies
in the air, 18or like any creature that
moves along the ground or any fish in
the waters below. 19And when you look
up to the sky and see the sun, the moon
and the stars—all the heavenly array
—do not be enticed into bowing down
to them and worshipping things the
LORD your God has apportioned to all
the nations under heaven. 20But as for
you, the LORD took you and brought
you out of the iron-smelting furnace,
out of Egypt, to be the people of his
inheritance, as you now are.
21The LORD was angry with me because of you, and he solemnly swore
that I would not cross the Jordan and
enter the good land the LORD your God

is giving you as your inheritance. 22I will
die in this land; I will not cross the
Jordan; but you are about to cross over
and take possession of that good land.
23Be careful not to forget the covenant
of the LORD your God that he made
with you; do not make for yourselves an
idol in the form of anything the LORD
your God has forbidden. 24For the
LORD your God is a consuming fire, a
jealous God.

25After you have had children and
grandchildren and have lived in the land
a long time—if you then become corrupt and make any kind of idol, doing
evil in the eyes of the LORD your God
and provoking him to anger, 26I call
heaven and earth as witnesses against
you this day that you will quickly perish
from the land that you are crossing the
Jordan to possess. You will not live
there long but will certainly be destroyed. 27The LORD will scatter you
among the peoples, and only a few of
you will survive among the nations to
which the LORD will drive you. 28There
you will worship man-made gods of
wood and stone, which cannot see or
hear or eat or smell. 29But if from there
you seek the LORD your God, you will
find him if you look for him with all your
heart and with all your soul. 30When
you are in distress and all these things
have happened to you, then in later
days you will return to the LORD your
God and obey him. 31For the LORD your
God is a merciful God; he will not abandon or destroy you or forget the covenant with your forefathers, which he
confirmed to them by oath.

The LORD Is God

32Ask now about the former days,
long before your time, from the day
God created man on the earth; ask from
one end of the heavens to the other. Has
anything so great as this ever happened,
or has anything like it ever been heard
of? 33Has any other people heard the
voice of God speaking out of fire, as you
have, and lived? 34Has any god ever
tried to take for himself one nation out
of another nation, by testings, by miraculous signs and wonders, by war, by a
mighty hand and an outstretched arm,
or by great and awesome deeds, like all
the things the LORD your God did for
you in Egypt before your very eyes?

35You were shown these things so
that you might know that the LORD is
God; besides him there is no other.
36From heaven he made you hear his
voice to discipline you. On earth he
showed you his great fire, and you heard
his words from out of the fire. 37Because
he loved your forefathers and chose
their descendants after them, he
brought you out of Egypt by his Presence and his great strength, 38to drive
out before you nations greater and
stronger than you and to bring you into
their land to give it to you for your
inheritance, as it is today.

39Acknowledge and take to heart this
day that the LORD is God in heaven
above and on the earth below. There is
no other. 40Keep his decrees and commands, which I am giving you today, so
that it may go well with you and your
children after you and that you may live
long in the land the LORD your God
gives you for all time.

Cities of Refuge

41Then Moses set aside three cities
east of the Jordan, 42to which anyone
who had killed a person could flee if he
had unintentionally killed his neighbour
without malice aforethought. He could
flee into one of these cities and save his
life. 43The cities were these: Bezer in
the desert plateau, for the Reubenites;
Ramoth in Gilead, for the Gadites; and
Golan in Bashan, for the Manassites.

Introduction to the Law

44This is the law Moses set before the
Israelites. 45These are the stipulations,
decrees and laws Moses gave them
when they came out of Egypt 46and

were in the valley near Beth Peor east of
the Jordan, in the land of Sihon king of
the Amorites, who reigned in Heshbon
and was defeated by Moses and the
Israelites as they came out of Egypt.
47They took possession of his land and
the land of Og king of Bashan, the two
Amorite kings east of the Jordan. 48This
land extended from Aroer on the rim of
the Arnon Gorge to Mount Siyon (that
is, Hermon), 49and included all the Arabah east of the Jordan, as far as the Sea
of the Arabah, below the slopes of
Pisgah.

The Ten Commandments

5 Moses summoned all Israel and
said:
Hear, O Israel, the decrees and the laws
I declare in your hearing today. Learn
them and be sure to follow them. 2The
LORD our God made a covenant with us
at Horeb. 3It was not with our fathers
that the LORD made this covenant, but
with us, with all of us who are alive here
today. 4The LORD spoke to you face to
face out of the fire on the mountain.
5(At that time I stood between the LORD
and you to declare to you the word of
the LORD, because you were afraid of
the fire and did not go up the mountain.) And he said:

6"I am the LORD your God, who
brought you out of Egypt, out
of the land of slavery.
7"You shall have no other gods
before me.
8"You shall not make for yourself
an idol in the form of anything in heaven above or on
the earth beneath or in the
waters below. 9You shall not
bow down to them or worship
them; for I, the LORD your
God, am a jealous God,
punishing the children for the
sin of the fathers to the third
and fourth generation of
those who hate me, 10but
showing love to a thousand
⌊generations⌋ of those who
love me and keep my com-
mandments.
11"You shall not misuse the name of
the LORD your God, for the
LORD will not hold anyone
guiltless who misuses his
name.
12"Observe the Sabbath day by
keeping it holy, as the LORD
your God has commanded
you. 13Six days you shall
labour and do all your work,
14but the seventh day is a Sabbath to the LORD your God.
On it you shall not do any
work, neither you, nor your
son or daughter, nor your
manservant or maidservant,
nor your ox, your donkey or
any of your animals, nor the
alien within your gates, so
that your manservant and
maidservant may rest, as you
do. 15Remember that you
were slaves in Egypt and that
the LORD your God brought
you out of there with a mighty
hand and an outstretched
arm. Therefore the LORD
your God has commanded
you to observe the Sabbath
day.
16"Honour your father and your
mother, as the LORD your
God has commanded you, so
that you may live long and
that it may go well with you in
the land the LORD your God
is giving you.
17"You shall not murder.
18"You shall not commit adultery.
19"You shall not steal.
20"You shall not give false testimony against your neigh-
bour.
21"You shall not covet your neighbour's wife. You shall not set
your desire on your neighbour's house or land, his
manservant or maidservant,

his ox or donkey, or anything
that belongs to your neighbour."

22These are the commandments the
LORD proclaimed in a loud voice to your
whole assembly there on the mountain
from out of the fire, the cloud and the
deep darkness; and he added nothing
more. Then he wrote them on two stone
tablets and gave them to me.
23When you heard the voice out of the
darkness, while the mountain was
ablaze with fire, all the leading men of
your tribes and your elders came to me.
24And you said, "The LORD our God
has shown us his glory and his majesty,
and we have heard his voice from the
fire. Today we have seen that a man can
live even if God speaks with him. 25But
now, why should we die? This great fire
will consume us, and we will die if we
hear the voice of the LORD our God any
longer. 26For what mortal man has ever
heard the voice of the living God speaking out of fire, as we have, and survived? 27Go near and listen to all that
the LORD our God says. Then tell us
whatever the LORD our God tells you.
We will listen and obey."
28The LORD heard you when you
spoke to me and the LORD said to me, "I
have heard what this people said to you.
Everything they said was good. 29Oh,
that their hearts would be inclined to
fear me and keep all my commands
always, so that it might go well with
them and their children for ever!
30"Go, tell them to return to their
tents. 31But you stay here with me so
that I may give you all the commands,
decrees and laws that you are to teach
them to follow in the land I am giving
them to possess."
32So be careful to do what the LORD
your God has commanded you; do not
turn aside to the right or to the left.
33Walk in all the way that the LORD
your God has commanded you, so that
you may live and prosper and prolong
your days in the land that you will
possess.

NEW TESTAMENT READING

Luke 11:5–32

5Then he said to them, "Suppose one
of you has a friend, and he goes to him
at midnight and says, 'Friend, lend me
three loaves of bread, 6because a friend
of mine on a journey has come to me,
and I have nothing to set before him.'
7"Then the one inside answers,
'Don't bother me. The door is already
locked, and my children are with me in
bed. I can't get up and give you anything.' 8I tell you, though he will not get
up and give him the bread because he is
his friend, yet because of the man's
boldness he will get up and give him as
much as he needs.
9"So I say to you: Ask and it will be
given to you; seek and you will find;
knock and the door will be opened to
you. 10For everyone who asks receives;
he who seeks finds; and to him who
knocks, the door will be opened.
11"Which of you fathers, if your son
asks for a fish, will give him a snake
instead? 12Or if he asks for an egg, will
give him a scorpion? 13If you then,
though you are evil, know how to give
good gifts to your children, how much
more will your Father in heaven give the
Holy Spirit to those who ask him!"

Jesus and Beelzebub

14Jesus was driving out a demon that
was mute. When the demon left, the
man who had been mute spoke, and the
crowd was amazed. 15But some of them
said, "By Beelzebub, the prince of
demons, he is driving out demons."
16Others tested him by asking for a sign
from heaven.
17Jesus knew their thoughts and said
to them: "Any kingdom divided against
itself will be ruined, and a house divided
against itself will fall. 18If Satan is divided against himself, how can his kingdom stand? I say this because you claim
that I drive out demons by Beelzebub.
19Now if I drive out demons by Beelzebub, by whom do your followers drive

them out? So then, they will be your
judges. 20But if I drive out demons by
the finger of God, then the kingdom of
God has come to you.
21"When a strong man, fully armed,
guards his own house, his possessions
are safe. 22But when someone stronger
attacks and overpowers him, he takes
away the armour in which the man
trusted and divides up the spoils.
23"He who is not with me is against
me, and he who does not gather with
me, scatters.
24"When an evil spirit comes out of a
man, it goes through arid places seeking
rest and does not find it. Then it says, 'I
will return to the house I left.' 25When it
arrives, it finds the house swept clean
and put in order. 26Then it goes and
takes seven other spirits more wicked
than itself, and they go in and live there.
And the final condition of that man is
worse than the first."
27As Jesus was saying these things, a
woman in the crowd called out, "Blessed is the mother who gave you birth
and nursed you."
28He replied, "Blessed rather are
those who hear the word of God and
obey it."

The Sign of Jonah

29As the crowds increased, Jesus said,
"This is a wicked generation. It asks for
a miraculous sign, but none will be
given it except the sign of Jonah. 30For
as Jonah was a sign to the Ninevites, so
also will the Son of Man be to this
generation. 31The Queen of the South
will rise at the judgment with the men of
this generation and condemn them; for
she came from the ends of the earth to
listen to Solomon's wisdom, and now
one greater than Solomon is here. 32The
men of Nineveh will stand up at the
judgment with this generation and
condemn it; for they repented at
the preaching of Jonah, and now one
greater than Jonah is here.

READING FROM PROVERBS
Proverbs 8:32–36

32"Now then, my sons, listen to me;
blessed are those who keep my
ways.
33Listen to my instruction and be wise;
do not ignore it.
34Blessed is the man who listens to me,
watching daily at my doors,
waiting at my doorway.
35For whoever finds me finds life
and receives favour from the
LORD.
36But whoever fails to find me harms
himself;
all who hate me love death."

DAY 97

APRIL 7

OLD TESTAMENT READING
Deuteronomy 6:1–8:20

Love the LORD Your God

6 These are the commands, decrees
and laws the LORD your God
directed me to teach you to observe
in the land that you are crossing the
Jordan to possess, 2so that you, your
children and their children after them
may fear the LORD your God as long as
you live by keeping all his decrees and
commands that I give you, and so that
you may enjoy long life. 3Hear, O
Israel, and be careful to obey so that it
may go well with you and that you may
increase greatly in a land flowing with

milk and honey, just as the LORD, the
God of your fathers, promised you.
4Hear, O Israel: The LORD our God,
the LORD is one. 5Love the LORD your
God with all your heart and with all
your soul and with all your strength.
6These commandments that I give you
today are to be upon your hearts.
7Impress them on your children. Talk
about them when you sit at home and
when you walk along the road, when
you lie down and when you get up. 8Tie
them as symbols on your hands and bind
them on your foreheads. 9Write them
on the door-frames of your houses and
on your gates.
10When the LORD your God brings
you into the land he swore to your
fathers, to Abraham, Isaac and Jacob,
to give you—a land with large,
flourishing cities you did not build,
11houses filled with all kinds of good
things you did not provide, wells you
did not dig, and vineyards and olive
groves you did not plant—then when
you eat and are satisfied, 12be careful
that you do not forget the LORD, who
brought you out of Egypt, out of the
land of slavery.
13Fear the LORD your God, serve him
only and take your oaths in his name.
14Do not follow other gods, the gods of
the peoples around you; 15for the LORD
your God, who is among you, is a
jealous God and his anger will burn
against you, and he will destroy you
from the face of the land. 16Do not test
the LORD your God as you did at Massah. 17Be sure to keep the commands of
the LORD your God and the stipulations
and decrees he has given you. 18Do
what is right and good in the LORD's
sight, so that it may go well with you and
you may go in and take over the good
land that the LORD promised on oath to
your forefathers, 19thrusting out all
your enemies before you, as the LORD
said.
20In the future, when your son asks
you, "What is the meaning of the stipulations, decrees and laws the LORD our
God has commanded you?" 21tell him:
"We were slaves of Pharaoh in Egypt,
but the LORD brought us out of Egypt
with a mighty hand. 22Before our eyes
the LORD sent miraculous signs and
wonders—great and terrible—upon
Egypt and Pharaoh and his whole
household. 23But he brought us out
from there to bring us in and give us the
land that he promised on oath to our
forefathers. 24The LORD commanded us
to obey all these decrees and to fear the
LORD our God, so that we might always
prosper and be kept alive, as is the case
today. 25And if we are careful to obey
all this law before the LORD our God, as
he has commanded us, that will be our
righteousness."

Driving Out the Nations

7 When the LORD your God brings
you into the land you are entering
to possess and drives out before you
many nations—the Hittites, Girgashites, Amorites, Canaanites, Perizzites, Hivites and Jebusites, seven
nations larger and stronger than you
—2and when the LORD your God has
delivered them over to you and you
have defeated them, then you must destroy them totally. Make no treaty with
them, and show them no mercy. 3Do
not intermarry with them. Do not give
your daughters to their sons or take
their daughters for your sons, 4for they
will turn your sons away from following
me to serve other gods, and the LORD's
anger will burn against you and will
quickly destroy you. 5This is what you
are to do to them: Break down their
altars, smash their sacred stones, cut
down their Asherah poles and burn
their idols in the fire. 6For you are a
people holy to the LORD your God. The
LORD your God has chosen you out of
all the peoples on the face of the earth to
be his people, his treasured possession.
7The LORD did not set his affection on
you and choose you because you were
more numerous than other peoples, for
you were the fewest of all peoples. 8But
it was because the LORD loved you and

kept the oath he swore to your forefathers that he brought you out with a
mighty hand and redeemed you from
the land of slavery, from the power of
Pharaoh king of Egypt. 9Know therefore that the LORD your God is God; he
is the faithful God, keeping his covenant of love to a thousand generations
of those who love him and keep his
commands. 10But

those who hate him he will repay to
their face by destruction;
he will not be slow to repay to their
face those who hate him.

11Therefore, take care to follow the
commands, decrees and laws I give you
today.

12If you pay attention to these laws
and are careful to follow them, then the
LORD your God will keep his covenant
of love with you, as he swore to your
forefathers. 13He will love you and bless
you and increase your numbers. He will
bless the fruit of your womb, the crops
of your land—your grain, new wine and
oil—the calves of your herds and the
lambs of your flocks in the land that he
swore to your forefathers to give you.
14You will be blessed more than any
other people; none of your men or
women will be childless, nor any of your
livestock without young. 15The LORD
will keep you free from every disease.
He will not inflict on you the horrible
diseases you knew in Egypt, but he will
inflict them on all who hate you. 16You
must destroy all the peoples the LORD
your God gives over to you. Do not look
on them with pity and do not serve their
gods, for that will be a snare to you.

17You may say to yourselves, "These
nations are stronger than we are. How
can we drive them out?" 18But do not be
afraid of them; remember well what the
LORD your God did to Pharaoh and to
all Egypt. 19You saw with your own eyes
the great trials, the miraculous signs and
wonders, the mighty hand and outstretched arm, with which the LORD
your God brought you out. The LORD
your God will do the same to all the
peoples you now fear. 20Moreover, the
LORD your God will send the hornet
among them until even the survivors
who hide from you have perished. 21Do
not be terrified by them, for the LORD
your God, who is among you, is a great
and awesome God. 22The LORD your
God will drive out those nations before
you, little by little. You will not be
allowed to eliminate them all at once, or
the wild animals will multiply around
you. 23But the LORD your God will deliver them over to you, throwing them
into great confusion until they are destroyed. 24He will give their kings into
your hand, and you will wipe out their
names from under heaven. No-one will
be able to stand up against you; you will
destroy them. 25The images of their
gods you are to burn in the fire. Do not
covet the silver and gold on them, and
do not take it for yourselves, or you will
be ensnared by it, for it is detestable to
the LORD your God. 26Do not bring a
detestable thing into your house or you,
like it, will be set apart for destruction.
Utterly abhor and detest it, for it is set
apart for destruction.

Do Not Forget the LORD

8 Be careful to follow every command I am giving you today, so that
you may live and increase and may enter and possess the land that the LORD
promised on oath to your forefathers.
2Remember how the LORD your God
led you all the way in the desert these
forty years, to humble you and to test
you in order to know what was in your
heart, whether or not you would keep
his commands. 3He humbled you, causing you to hunger and then feeding you
with manna, which neither you nor your
fathers had known, to teach you that
man does not live on bread alone but on
every word that comes from the mouth
of the LORD. 4Your clothes did not wear
out and your feet did not swell during
these forty years. 5Know then in your
heart that as a man disciplines his son,
so the LORD your God disciplines you.

6Observe the commands of the LORD
your God, walking in his ways and revering him. 7For the LORD your God is
bringing you into a good land—a land
with streams and pools of water, with
springs flowing in the valleys and hills;
8a land with wheat and barley, vines and
fig-trees, pomegranates, olive oil and
honey; 9a land where bread will not be
scarce and you will lack nothing; a land
where the rocks are iron and you can dig
copper out of the hills.
10When you have eaten and are satisfied, praise the LORD your God for the
good land he has given you. 11Be careful
that you do not forget the LORD your
God, failing to observe his commands,
his laws and his decrees that I am giving
you this day. 12Otherwise, when you eat
and are satisfied, when you build fine
houses and settle down, 13and when
your herds and flocks grow large and
your silver and gold increase and all you
have is multiplied, 14then your heart will
become proud and you will forget the
LORD your God, who brought you out
of Egypt, out of the land of slavery.
15He led you through the vast and
dreadful desert, that thirsty and waterless land, with its venomous snakes
and scorpions. He brought you water
out of hard rock. 16He gave you manna
to eat in the desert, something your
fathers had never known, to humble
and to test you so that in the end it
might go well with you. 17You may
say to yourself, "My power and the
strength of my hands have produced
this wealth for me." 18But remember
the LORD your God, for it is he who
gives you the ability to produce wealth,
and so confirms his covenant, which
he swore to your forefathers, as it is
today.
19If you ever forget the LORD your
God and follow other gods and worship
and bow down to them, I testify against
you today that you will surely be destroyed. 20Like the nations the LORD
destroyed before you, so you will be
destroyed for not obeying the LORD
your God.

NEW TESTAMENT READING
Luke 11:33–54

The Lamp of the Body

33"No-one lights a lamp and puts it in
a place where it will be hidden, or under
a bowl. Instead he puts it on its stand, so
that those who come in may see the
light. 34Your eye is the lamp of your
body. When your eyes are good, your
whole body also is full of light. But
when they are bad, your body also is full
of darkness. 35See to it, then, that the
light within you is not darkness.
36Therefore, if your whole body is full of
light, and no part of it dark, it will be
completely lighted, as when the light of
a lamp shines on you."

Six Woes

37When Jesus had finished speaking,
a Pharisee invited him to eat with him;
so he went in and reclined at the table.
38But the Pharisee, noticing that Jesus
did not first wash before the meal, was
surprised.
39Then the Lord said to him, "Now
then, you Pharisees clean the outside of
the cup and dish, but inside you are full
of greed and wickedness. 40You foolish
people! Did not the one who made the
outside make the inside also? 41But give
what is inside ⌊the dish⌋ to the poor, and
everything will be clean for you.
42"Woe to you Pharisees, because
you give God a tenth of your mint, rue
and all other kinds of garden herbs, but
you neglect justice and the love of God.
You should have practised the latter
without leaving the former undone.
43"Woe to you Pharisees, because
you love the most important seats in the
synagogues and greetings in the market-
places.
44"Woe to you, because you are like
unmarked graves, which men walk over
without knowing it."
45One of the experts in the law
answered him, "Teacher, when you say
these things, you insult us also."
46Jesus replied, "And you experts in

the law, woe to you, because you load
people down with burdens they can
hardly carry, and you yourselves will
not lift one finger to help them.
47"Woe to you, because you build
tombs for the prophets, and it was your
forefathers who killed them. 48So you
testify that you approve of what your
forefathers did; they killed the
prophets, and you build their tombs.
49Because of this, God in his wisdom
said, 'I will send them prophets and
apostles, some of whom they will kill
and others they will persecute.'
50Therefore this generation will be held
responsible for the blood of all the
prophets that has been shed since
the beginning of the world, 51from the
blood of Abel to the blood of Zechariah, who was killed between the altar
and the sanctuary. Yes, I tell you, this
generation will be held responsible for it
all.
52"Woe to you experts in the law,
because you have taken away the key to
knowledge. You yourselves have not
entered, and you have hindered those
who were entering."
53When Jesus left there, the Pharisees
and the teachers of the law began to
oppose him fiercely and to besiege him
with questions, 54waiting to catch him in
something he might say.

READING FROM PSALMS
Psalm 42:1–6a

For the director of music. A *maskil* of the Sons of Korah.

1As the deer pants for streams of
water,
so my soul pants for you, O God.
2My soul thirsts for God, for the living
God.
When can I go and meet with God?
3My tears have been my food
day and night,
while men say to me all day long,
"Where is your God?"
4These things I remember
as I pour out my soul:
how I used to go with the multitude,
leading the procession to the house
of God,
with shouts of joy and thanksgiving
among the festive throng.

5Why are you downcast, O my soul?
Why so disturbed within me?
Put your hope in God,
for I will yet praise him,
my Saviour and 6my God.

DAY 98

APRIL 8

OLD TESTAMENT READING
Deuteronomy 9:1–10:22

Not Because of Israel's Righteousness

9 Hear, O Israel. You are now about
to cross the Jordan to go in and
dispossess nations greater and stronger
than you, with large cities that have
walls up to the sky. 2The people are
strong and tall—Anakites! You know
about them and have heard it said:
"Who can stand up against the Anakites?" 3But be assured today that the
LORD your God is the one who goes
across ahead of you like a devouring
fire. He will destroy them; he will subdue them before you. And you will
drive them out and annihilate them
quickly, as the LORD has promised you.
4After the LORD your God has driven
them out before you, do not say to
yourself, "The LORD has brought me
here to take possession of this land because of my righteousness." No, it is on
account of the wickedness of these nations that the LORD is going to drive
them out before you. 5It is not because

of your righteousness or your integrity
that you are going in to take possession
of their land; but on account of the
wickedness of these nations, the LORD
your God will drive them out before
you, to accomplish what he swore to
your fathers, to Abraham, Isaac and
Jacob. 6 Understand, then, that it is not
because of your righteousness that the
LORD your God is giving you this good
land to possess, for you are a stiff-
necked people.

The Golden Calf

7 Remember this and never forget
how you provoked the LORD your God
to anger in the desert. From the day you
left Egypt until you arrived here, you
have been rebellious against the LORD.
8 At Horeb you aroused the LORD's
wrath so that he was angry enough to
destroy you. 9 When I went up on the
mountain to receive the tablets of stone,
the tablets of the covenant that the
LORD had made with you, I stayed on
the mountain forty days and forty
nights; I ate no bread and drank no
water. 10 The LORD gave me two stone
tablets inscribed by the finger of God.
On them were all the commandments
the LORD proclaimed to you on the
mountain out of the fire, on the day of
the assembly.

11 At the end of the forty days and
forty nights, the LORD gave me the two
stone tablets, the tablets of the covenant. 12 Then the LORD told me, "Go
down from here at once, because your
people whom you brought out of Egypt
have become corrupt. They have turned
away quickly from what I commanded
them and have made a cast idol for
themselves."

13 And the LORD said to me, "I have
seen this people, and they are a stiff-
necked people indeed! 14 Let me alone,
so that I may destroy them and blot out
their name from under heaven. And I
will make you into a nation stronger and
more numerous than they."

15 So I turned and went down from the
mountain while it was ablaze with fire.
And the two tablets of the covenant
were in my hands. 16 When I looked, I
saw that you had sinned against the
LORD your God; you had made for
yourselves an idol cast in the shape of a
calf. You had turned aside quickly from
the way that the LORD had commanded
you. 17 So I took the two tablets and
threw them out of my hands, breaking
them to pieces before your eyes.

18 Then once again I fell prostrate before the LORD for forty days and forty
nights; I ate no bread and drank no
water, because of all the sin you had
committed, doing what was evil in the
LORD's sight and so provoking him to
anger. 19 I feared the anger and wrath of
the LORD, for he was angry enough with
you to destroy you. But again the LORD
listened to me. 20 And the LORD was
angry enough with Aaron to destroy
him, but at that time I prayed for Aaron
too. 21 Also I took that sinful thing of
yours, the calf you had made, and
burned it in the fire. Then I crushed it
and ground it to powder as fine as dust
and threw the dust into a stream that
flowed down the mountain.

22 You also made the LORD angry at
Taberah, at Massah and at Kibroth
Hattaavah.

23 And when the LORD sent you out
from Kadesh Barnea, he said, "Go up
and take possession of the land I have
given you." But you rebelled against
the command of the LORD your God.
You did not trust him or obey him.
24 You have been rebellious against the
LORD ever since I have known you.

25 I lay prostrate before the LORD
those forty days and forty nights because the LORD had said he would destroy you. 26 I prayed to the LORD and
said, "O Sovereign LORD, do not destroy your people, your own inheritance
that you redeemed by your great power
and brought out of Egypt with a mighty
hand. 27 Remember your servants Abraham, Isaac and Jacob. Overlook the
stubbornness of this people, their wickedness and their sin. 28 Otherwise, the
country from which you brought us will

say, 'Because the LORD was not able to take them into the land he had promised them, and because he hated them, he brought them out to put them to death in the desert.' 29But they are your people, your inheritance that you brought out by your great power and your outstretched arm."

Tablets Like the First Ones

10 At that time the LORD said to me, "Chisel out two stone tablets like the first ones and come up to me on the mountain. Also make a wooden chest. 2I will write on the tablets the words that were on the first tablets, which you broke. Then you are to put them in the chest."

3So I made the ark out of acacia wood and chiselled out two stone tablets like the first ones, and I went up on the mountain with the two tablets in my hands. 4The LORD wrote on these tablets what he had written before, the Ten Commandments he had proclaimed to you on the mountain, out of the fire, on the day of the assembly. And the LORD gave them to me. 5Then I came back down the mountain and put the tablets in the ark I had made, as the LORD commanded me, and they are there now.

6(The Israelites travelled from the wells of the Jaakanites to Moserah. There Aaron died and was buried, and Eleazar his son succeeded him as priest. 7From there they travelled to Gudgodah and on to Jotbathah, a land with streams of water. 8At that time the LORD set apart the tribe of Levi to carry the ark of the covenant of the LORD, to stand before the LORD to minister and to pronounce blessings in his name, as they still do today. 9That is why the Levites have no share or inheritance among their brothers; the LORD is their inheritance, as the LORD your God told them.)

10Now I had stayed on the mountain forty days and nights, as I did the first time, and the LORD listened to me at this time also. It was not his will to destroy you. 11"Go," the LORD said to me, "and lead the people on their way, so that they may enter and possess the land that I swore to their fathers to give them."

Fear the LORD

12And now, O Israel, what does the LORD your God ask of you but to fear the LORD your God, to walk in all his ways, to love him, to serve the LORD your God with all your heart and with all your soul, 13and to observe the LORD's commands and decrees that I am giving you today for your own good?

14To the LORD your God belong the heavens, even the highest heavens, the earth and everything in it. 15Yet the LORD set his affection on your forefathers and loved them, and he chose you, their descendants, above all the nations, as it is today. 16Circumcise your hearts, therefore, and do not be stiff-necked any longer. 17For the LORD your God is God of gods and Lord of lords, the great God, mighty and awesome, who shows no partiality and accepts no bribes. 18He defends the cause of the fatherless and the widow, and loves the alien, giving him food and clothing. 19And you are to love those who are aliens, for you yourselves were aliens in Egypt. 20Fear the LORD your God and serve him. Hold fast to him and take your oaths in his name. 21He is your praise; he is your God, who performed for you those great and awesome wonders you saw with your own eyes. 22Your forefathers who went down into Egypt were seventy in all, and now the LORD your God has made you as numerous as the stars in the sky.

NEW TESTAMENT READING

Luke 12:1–34

Warnings and Encouragements

12 Meanwhile, when a crowd of many thousands had gathered, so that they were trampling on one

another, Jesus began to speak first to his
disciples, saying: "Be on your guard
against the yeast of the Pharisees, which
is hypocrisy. 2There is nothing concealed that will not be disclosed, or
hidden that will not be made known.
3What you have said in the dark will be
heard in the daylight, and what you
have whispered in the ear in the inner
rooms will be proclaimed from the
roofs.

4"I tell you, my friends, do not be
afraid of those who kill the body and
after that can do no more. 5But I will
show you whom you should fear: Fear
him who, after the killing of the body,
has power to throw you into hell. Yes, I
tell you, fear him. 6Are not five sparrows sold for two pennies? Yet not one
of them is forgotten by God. 7Indeed,
the very hairs of your head are all numbered. Don't be afraid; you are worth
more than many sparrows.

8"I tell you, whoever acknowledges
me before men, the Son of Man will also
acknowledge him before the angels of
God. 9But he who disowns me before
men will be disowned before the angels
of God. 10And everyone who speaks
a word against the Son of Man will
be forgiven, but anyone who blasphemes against the Holy Spirit will not
be forgiven.

11"When you are brought before
synagogues, rulers and authorities, do
not worry about how you will defend
yourselves or what you will say, 12for
the Holy Spirit will teach you at that
time what you should say."

The Parable of the Rich Fool

13Someone in the crowd said to him,
"Teacher, tell my brother to divide the
inheritance with me."

14Jesus replied, "Man, who appointed me a judge or an arbiter between you?" 15Then he said to them,
"Watch out! Be on your guard against
all kinds of greed; a man's life does
not consist in the abundance of his
possessions."

16And he told them this parable:
"The ground of a certain rich man produced a good crop. 17He thought to
himself, 'What shall I do? I have no
place to store my crops.'

18"Then he said, 'This is what I'll do. I
will tear down my barns and build bigger ones, and there I will store all my
grain and my goods. 19And I'll say to
myself, "You have plenty of good
things laid up for many years. Take life
easy; eat, drink and be merry." '

20"But God said to him, 'You fool!
This very night your life will be demanded from you. Then who will get
what you have prepared for yourself?'

21"This is how it will be with anyone
who stores up things for himself but is
not rich towards God."

Do Not Worry

22Then Jesus said to his disciples:
"Therefore I tell you, do not worry
about your life, what you will eat; or
about your body, what you will wear.
23Life is more than food, and the body
more than clothes. 24Consider the
ravens: They do not sow or reap, they
have no storeroom or barn; yet God
feeds them. And how much more valuable you are than birds! 25Who of you by
worrying can add a single hour to his
life? 26Since you cannot do this very
little thing, why do you worry about the
rest?

27"Consider how the lilies grow. They
do not labour or spin. Yet I tell you, not
even Solomon in all his splendour was
dressed like one of these. 28If that is how
God clothes the grass of the field, which
is here today, and tomorrow is thrown
into the fire, how much more will he
clothe you, O you of little faith! 29And
do not set your heart on what you will
eat or drink; do not worry about it.
30For the pagan world runs after all such
things, and your Father knows that you
need them. 31But seek his kingdom, and
these things will be given to you as well.

32"Do not be afraid, little flock, for
your Father has been pleased to give

you the kingdom. 33Sell your possessions and give to the poor. Provide purses for yourselves that will not wear out, a treasure in heaven that will not be exhausted, where no thief comes near and no moth destroys. 34For where your treasure is, there your heart will be also.

READING FROM PSALMS
Psalm 42:6b–11

My soul is downcast within me;
therefore I will remember you
from the land of the Jordan,
the heights of Hermon—from
Mount Mizar.
7Deep calls to deep
in the roar of your waterfalls;
all your waves and breakers
have swept over me.

8By day the LORD directs his love,
at night his song is with me—
a prayer to the God of my life.

9I say to God my Rock,
"Why have you forgotten me?
Why must I go about mourning,
oppressed by the enemy?"
10My bones suffer mortal agony
as my foes taunt me,
saying to me all day long,
"Where is your God?"

11Why are you downcast, O my soul?
Why so disturbed within me?
Put your hope in God,
for I will yet praise him,
my Saviour and my God.

DAY 99

APRIL 9

OLD TESTAMENT READING
Deuteronomy 11:1–12:32

Love and Obey the LORD

11 Love the LORD your God and keep his requirements, his decrees, his laws and his commands always. 2Remember today that your children were not the ones who saw and experienced the discipline of the LORD your God: his majesty, his mighty hand, his outstretched arm; 3the signs he performed and the things he did in the heart of Egypt, both to Pharaoh king of Egypt and to his whole country; 4what he did to the Egyptian army, to its horses and chariots, how he overwhelmed them with the waters of the Red Sea as they were pursuing you, and how the LORD brought lasting ruin on them. 5It was not your children who saw what he did for you in the desert until you arrived at this place, 6and what he did to Dathan and Abiram, sons of Eliab the Reubenite, when the earth opened its mouth right in the middle of all Israel and swallowed them up with their households, their tents and every living thing that belonged to them. 7But it was your own eyes that saw all these great things the LORD has done.

8Observe therefore all the commands I am giving you today, so that you may have the strength to go in and take over the land that you are crossing the Jordan to possess, 9and so that you may live long in the land that the LORD swore to your forefathers to give to them and their descendants, a land flowing with milk and honey. 10The land you are entering to take over is not like the land of Egypt, from which you have come, where you planted your seed and irrigated it by foot as in a vegetable garden.
11But the land you are crossing the Jordan to take possession of is a land of

mountains and valleys that drinks rain
from heaven. 12It is a land the LORD
your God cares for; the eyes of the
LORD your God are continually on it
from the beginning of the year to its
end.
13So if you faithfully obey the commands I am giving you today—to love
the LORD your God and to serve him
with all your heart and with all your
soul—14then I will send rain on your
land in its season, both autumn and
spring rains, so that you may gather in
your grain, new wine and oil. 15I will
provide grass in the fields for your cattle, and you will eat and be satisfied.
16Be careful, or you will be enticed to
turn away and worship other gods and
bow down to them. 17Then the LORD's
anger will burn against you, and he will
shut the heavens so that it will not rain
and the ground will yield no produce,
and you will soon perish from the good
land the LORD is giving you. 18Fix these
words of mine in your hearts and minds;
tie them as symbols on your hands and
bind them on your foreheads. 19Teach
them to your children, talking about
them when you sit at home and when
you walk along the road, when you lie
down and when you get up. 20Write
them on the door-frames of your houses
and on your gates, 21so that your days
and the days of your children may be
many in the land that the LORD swore to
give your forefathers, as many as the
days that the heavens are above the
earth.
22If you carefully observe all these
commands I am giving you to follow
—to love the LORD your God, to walk in
all his ways and to hold fast to him
—23then the LORD will drive out all
these nations before you, and you will
dispossess nations larger and stronger
than you. 24Every place where you set
your foot will be yours: Your territory
will extend from the desert to Lebanon,
and from the Euphrates River to the
western sea. 25No man will be able to
stand against you. The LORD your God,
as he promised you, will put the terror
and fear of you on the whole land,
wherever you go.
26See, I am setting before you today a
blessing and a curse—27the blessing if
you obey the commands of the LORD
your God that I am giving you today;
28the curse if you disobey the commands
of the LORD your God and turn from the
way that I command you today by following other gods, which you have not
known. 29When the LORD your God has
brought you into the land you are entering to possess, you are to proclaim on
Mount Gerizim the blessings, and on
Mount Ebal the curses. 30As you know,
these mountains are across the Jordan,
west of the road, towards the setting
sun, near the great trees of Moreh, in
the territory of those Canaanites living
in the Arabah in the vicinity of Gilgal.
31You are about to cross the Jordan to
enter and take possession of the land
the LORD your God is giving you. When
you have taken it over and are living
there, 32be sure that you obey all the
decrees and laws I am setting before you
today.

The One Place of Worship

12 These are the decrees and laws
you must be careful to follow in
the land that the LORD, the God of your
fathers, has given you to possess—as
long as you live in the land. 2Destroy
completely all the places on the high
mountains and on the hills and under
every spreading tree where the nations
you are dispossessing worship their
gods. 3Break down their altars, smash
their sacred stones and burn their
Asherah poles in the fire; cut down the
idols of their gods and wipe out their
names from those places.
4You must not worship the LORD
your God in their way. 5But you are to
seek the place the LORD your God will
choose from among all your tribes to
put his Name there for his dwelling. To
that place you must go; 6there bring
your burnt offerings and sacrifices, your
tithes and special gifts, what you have

vowed to give and your freewill offerings, and the firstborn of your herds and
flocks. 7There, in the presence of the
LORD your God, you and your families
shall eat and shall rejoice in everything
you have put your hand to, because the
LORD your God has blessed you.

8You are not to do as we do here
today, everyone as he sees fit, 9since
you have not yet reached the resting
place and the inheritance the LORD your
God is giving you. 10But you will cross
the Jordan and settle in the land the
LORD your God is giving you as an
inheritance, and he will give you rest
from all your enemies around you so
that you will live in safety. 11Then to the
place the LORD your God will choose as
a dwelling for his Name—there you are
to bring everything I command you:
your burnt offerings and sacrifices, your
tithes and special gifts, and all the
choice possessions you have vowed to
the LORD. 12And there rejoice before
the LORD your God, you, your sons and
daughters, your menservants and maidservants, and the Levites from your
towns, who have no allotment or inheritance of their own. 13Be careful not to
sacrifice your burnt offerings anywhere
you please. 14Offer them only at the
place the LORD will choose in one of
your tribes, and there observe everything I command you.

15Nevertheless, you may slaughter
your animals in any of your towns and
eat as much of the meat as you want, as
if it were gazelle or deer, according to
the blessing the LORD your God gives
you. Both the ceremonially unclean and
the clean may eat it. 16But you must not
eat the blood; pour it out on the ground
like water. 17You must not eat in your
own towns the tithe of your grain and
new wine and oil, or the firstborn of
your herds and flocks, or whatever you
have vowed to give, or your freewill
offerings or special gifts. 18Instead, you
are to eat them in the presence of the
LORD your God at the place the LORD
your God will choose—you, your sons
and daughters, your menservants and
maidservants, and the Levites from
your towns—and you are to rejoice before the LORD your God in everything
you put your hand to. 19Be careful not
to neglect the Levites as long as you live
in your land.

20When the LORD your God has enlarged your territory as he promised
you, and you crave meat and say, "I
would like some meat," then you may
eat as much of it as you want. 21If the
place where the LORD your God
chooses to put his Name is too far away
from you, you may slaughter animals
from the herds and flocks the LORD has
given you, as I have commanded you,
and in your own towns you may eat as
much of them as you want. 22Eat them
as you would gazelle or deer. Both the
ceremonially unclean and the clean may
eat. 23But be sure you do not eat the
blood, because the blood is the life, and
you must not eat the life with the meat.
24You must not eat the blood; pour it
out on the ground like water. 25Do not
eat it, so that it may go well with you and
your children after you, because you
will be doing what is right in the eyes of
the LORD.

26But take your consecrated things
and whatever you have vowed to give,
and go to the place the LORD will
choose. 27Present your burnt offerings
on the altar of the LORD your God, both
the meat and the blood. The blood of
your sacrifices must be poured beside
the altar of the LORD your God, but you
may eat the meat. 28Be careful to obey
all these regulations I am giving you, so
that it may always go well with you and
your children after you, because you
will be doing what is good and right in
the eyes of the LORD your God.

29The LORD your God will cut off
before you the nations you are about to
invade and dispossess. But when you
have driven them out and settled in
their land, 30and after they have been
destroyed before you, be careful not to
be ensnared by enquiring about their
gods, saying, "How do these nations
serve their gods? We will do the same."

31You must not worship the LORD your
God in their way, because in worshipping their gods, they do all kinds of
detestable things the LORD hates. They
even burn their sons and daughters in
the fire as sacrifices to their gods.
32See that you do all I command you;
do not add to it or take away from it.

NEW TESTAMENT READING

Luke 12:35–59

Watchfulness

35"Be dressed ready for service and
keep your lamps burning, 36like men
waiting for their master to return from a
wedding banquet, so that when he
comes and knocks they can immediately
open the door for him. 37It will be good
for those servants whose master finds
them watching when he comes. I tell
you the truth, he will dress himself to
serve, will have them recline at the table
and will come and wait on them. 38It will
be good for those servants whose master finds them ready, even if he comes in
the second or third watch of the night.
39But understand this: If the owner of
the house had known at what hour the
thief was coming, he would not have let
his house be broken into. 40You also
must be ready, because the Son of Man
will come at an hour when you do not
expect him."
41Peter asked, "Lord, are you telling
this parable to us, or to everyone?"
42The Lord answered, "Who then is
the faithful and wise manager, whom
the master puts in charge of his servants
to give them their food allowance at the
proper time? 43It will be good for that
servant whom the master finds doing so
when he returns. 44I tell you the truth,
he will put him in charge of all his
possessions. 45But suppose the servant
says to himself, 'My master is taking a
long time in coming,' and he then begins
to beat the menservants and maidservants and to eat and drink and get
drunk. 46The master of that servant will
come on a day when he does not expect
him and at an hour he is not aware of.
He will cut him to pieces and assign him
a place with the unbelievers.
47"That servant who knows his master's will and does not get ready or does
not do what his master wants will be
beaten with many blows. 48But the one
who does not know and does things
deserving punishment will be beaten
with few blows. From everyone who has
been given much, much will be demanded; and from the one who has
been entrusted with much, much more
will be asked.

Not Peace but Division

49"I have come to bring fire on the
earth, and how I wish it were already
kindled! 50But I have a baptism to
undergo, and how distressed I am until
it is completed! 51Do you think I came
to bring peace on earth? No, I tell you,
but division. 52From now on there will
be five in one family divided against
each other, three against two and two
against three. 53They will be divided,
father against son and son against
father, mother against daughter and
daughter against mother, mother-
in-law against daughter-in-law and
daughter-in-law against mother-in-
law."

Interpreting the Times

54He said to the crowd: "When you
see a cloud rising in the west, immediately you say, 'It's going to rain,'
and it does. 55And when the south wind
blows, you say, 'It's going to be hot,'
and it is. 56Hypocrites! You know how
to interpret the appearance of the earth
and the sky. How is it that you don't
know how to interpret this present
time?
57"Why don't you judge for
yourselves what is right? 58As you are
going with your adversary to the magis-
trate, try hard to be reconciled to him
on the way, or he may drag you off to

the judge, and the judge turn you over to the officer, and the officer throw you into prison. [59]I tell you, you will not get out until you have paid the last penny."

READING FROM PSALMS
Psalm 43:1–5

[1]Vindicate me, O God,
and plead my cause against an ungodly nation;
rescue me from deceitful and wicked men.
[2]You are God my stronghold.
Why have you rejected me?
Why must I go about mourning,
oppressed by the enemy?
[3]Send forth your light and your truth,
let them guide me;
let them bring me to your holy mountain,
to the place where you dwell.
[4]Then will I go to the altar of God,
to God, my joy and my delight.
I will praise you with the harp,
O God, my God.

[5]Why are you downcast, O my soul?
Why so disturbed within me?
Put your hope in God,
for I will yet praise him,
my Saviour and my God.

DAY 100

APRIL 10

OLD TESTAMENT READING
Deuteronomy 13:1–14:29

Worshipping Other Gods

13 If a prophet, or one who foretells by dreams, appears among you and announces to you a miraculous sign or wonder, [2]and if the sign or wonder of which he has spoken takes place, and he says, "Let us follow other gods" (gods you have not known) "and let us worship them," [3]you must not listen to the words of that prophet or dreamer. The LORD your God is testing you to find out whether you love him with all your heart and with all your soul. [4]It is the LORD your God you must follow, and him you must revere. Keep his commands and obey him; serve him and hold fast to him. [5]That prophet or dreamer must be put to death, because he preached rebellion against the LORD your God, who brought you out of Egypt and redeemed you from the land of slavery; he has tried to turn you from the way the LORD your God commanded you to follow. You must purge the evil from among you.

[6]If your very own brother, or your son or daughter, or the wife you love, or your closest friend secretly entices you, saying, "Let us go and worship other gods" (gods that neither you nor your fathers have known, [7]gods of the peoples around you, whether near or far, from one end of the land to the other), [8]do not yield to him or listen to him. Show him no pity. Do not spare him or shield him. [9]You must certainly put him to death. Your hand must be the first in putting him to death, and then the hands of all the people. [10]Stone him to death, because he tried to turn you away from the LORD your God, who brought you out of Egypt, out of the land of slavery. [11]Then all Israel will hear and be afraid, and no-one among you will do such an evil thing again.

[12]If you hear it said about one of the towns the LORD your God is giving you to live in [13]that wicked men have arisen among you and have led the people of their town astray, saying, "Let us go and worship other gods" (gods you have not known), [14]then you must enquire, probe and investigate it thoroughly.

And if it is true and it has been proved
that this detestable thing has been done
among you, 15you must certainly put to
the sword all who live in that town.
Destroy it completely, both its people
and its livestock. 16Gather all the plunder of the town into the middle of the
public square and completely burn the
town and all its plunder as a whole burnt
offering to the LORD your God. It is to
remain a ruin for ever, never to be
rebuilt. 17None of those condemned
things shall be found in your hands, so
that the LORD will turn from his fierce
anger; he will show you mercy, have
compassion on you, and increase your
numbers, as he promised on oath to
your forefathers, 18because you obey
the LORD your God, keeping all his
commands that I am giving you today
and doing what is right in his eyes.

Clean and Unclean Food

14 You are the children of the
LORD your God. Do not cut
yourselves or shave the front of your
heads for the dead, 2for you are a people holy to the LORD your God. Out of
all the peoples on the face of the earth,
the LORD has chosen you to be his
treasured possession.

3Do not eat any detestable thing.
4These are the animals you may eat: the
ox, the sheep, the goat, 5the deer, the
gazelle, the roe deer, the wild goat,
the ibex, the antelope and the mountain
sheep. 6You may eat any animal that has
a split hoof divided in two and that
chews the cud. 7However, of those that
chew the cud or that have a split hoof
completely divided you may not eat the
camel, the rabbit or the coney.
Although they chew the cud, they do
not have a split hoof; they are ceremonially unclean for you. 8The pig is
also unclean; although it has a split
hoof, it does not chew the cud. You are
not to eat their meat or touch their
carcasses.

9Of all the creatures living in the
water, you may eat any that has fins
and scales. 10But anything that does not
have fins and scales you may not eat; for
you it is unclean.

11You may eat any clean bird. 12But
these you may not eat: the eagle, the
vulture, the black vulture, 13the red
kite, the black kite, any kind of falcon,
14any kind of raven, 15the horned owl,
the screech owl, the gull, any kind of
hawk, 16the little owl, the great owl, the
white owl, 17the desert owl, the osprey,
the cormorant, 18the stork, any kind of
heron, the hoopoe and the bat.

19All flying insects that swarm are
unclean to you; do not eat them. 20But
any winged creature that is clean you
may eat.

21Do not eat anything you find
already dead. You may give it to an
alien living in any of your towns, and
he may eat it, or you may sell it to a
foreigner. But you are a people holy
to the LORD your God.

Do not cook a young goat in its
mother's milk.

Tithes

22Be sure to set aside a tenth of all
that your fields produce each year.
23Eat the tithe of your grain, new wine
and oil, and the firstborn of your herds
and flocks in the presence of the LORD
your God at the place he will choose as a
dwelling for his Name, so that you may
learn to revere the LORD your God always. 24But if that place is too distant
and you have been blessed by the LORD
your God and cannot carry your tithe
(because the place where the LORD will
choose to put his Name is so far away),
25then exchange your tithe for silver,
and take the silver with you and go to
the place the LORD your God will
choose. 26Use the silver to buy whatever
you like: cattle, sheep, wine or other
fermented drink, or anything you wish.
Then you and your household shall eat
there in the presence of the LORD your
God and rejoice. 27And do not neglect
the Levites living in your towns, for they
have no allotment or inheritance of
their own.

28At the end of every three years,
bring all the tithes of that year's produce
and store it in your towns, 29so that the
Levites (who have no allotment or inheritance of their own) and the aliens,
the fatherless and the widows who live
in your towns may come and eat and be
satisfied, and so that the LORD your
God may bless you in all the work of
your hands.

NEW TESTAMENT READING
Luke 13:1–30

Repent or Perish

13 Now there were some present at
that time who told Jesus about
the Galileans whose blood Pilate had
mixed with their sacrifices. 2Jesus
answered, "Do you think that these
Galileans were worse sinners than all
the other Galileans because they suffered this way? 3I tell you, no! But
unless you repent, you too will all
perish. 4Or those eighteen who died
when the tower in Siloam fell on them
—do you think they were more guilty
than all the others living in Jerusalem?
5I tell you, no! But unless you repent,
you too will all perish."
6Then he told this parable: "A man
had a fig-tree, planted in his vineyard,
and he went to look for fruit on it, but
did not find any. 7So he said to the man
who took care of the vineyard, 'For
three years now I've been coming to
look for fruit on this fig-tree and haven't
found any. Cut it down! Why should it
use up the soil?'
8" 'Sir,' the man replied, 'leave it
alone for one more year, and I'll dig
round it and fertilise it. 9If it bears
fruit next year, fine! If not, then cut it
down.' "

A Crippled Woman Healed on the Sabbath

10On a Sabbath Jesus was teaching in
one of the synagogues, 11and a woman
was there who had been crippled by a
spirit for eighteen years. She was bent
over and could not straighten up at all.
12When Jesus saw her, he called her
forward and said to her, "Woman, you
are set free from your infirmity."
13Then he put his hands on her, and
immediately she straightened up and
praised God.
14Indignant because Jesus had healed
on the Sabbath, the synagogue ruler
said to the people, "There are six days
for work. So come and be healed on
those days, not on the Sabbath."
15The Lord answered him, "You
hypocrites! Doesn't each of you on the
Sabbath untie his ox or donkey from the
stall and lead it out to give it water?
16Then should not this woman, a daughter of Abraham, whom Satan has kept
bound for eighteen long years, be set
free on the Sabbath day from what
bound her?"
17When he said this, all his opponents
were humiliated, but the people were
delighted with all the wonderful things
he was doing.

The Parables of the Mustard Seed and the Yeast

18Then Jesus asked, "What is the
kingdom of God like? What shall I compare it to? 19It is like a mustard seed,
which a man took and planted in his
garden. It grew and became a tree,
and the birds of the air perched in its
branches."
20Again he asked, "What shall I compare the kingdom of God to? 21It is like
yeast that a woman took and mixed into
a large amount of flour until it worked
all through the dough."

The Narrow Door

22Then Jesus went through the towns
and villages, teaching as he made his
way to Jerusalem. 23Someone asked
him, "Lord, are only a few people going
to be saved?"
He said to them, 24"Make every

effort to enter through the narrow door, because many, I tell you, will try to enter and will not be able to.
25Once the owner of the house gets up and closes the door, you will stand outside knocking and pleading, 'Sir, open the door for us.'

"But he will answer, 'I don't know you or where you come from.'

26"Then you will say, 'We ate and drank with you, and you taught in our streets.'

27"But he will reply, 'I don't know you or where you come from. Away from me, all you evildoers!'

28"There will be weeping there, and gnashing of teeth, when you see Abraham, Isaac and Jacob and all the prophets in the kingdom of God, but you yourselves thrown out.
29People will come from east and west and north and south, and will take their places at the feast in the kingdom of God.
30Indeed there are those who are last who will be first, and first who will be last."

READING FROM PROVERBS

Proverbs 9:1–12

Invitations of Wisdom and of Folly

9 Wisdom has built her house;
she has hewn out its seven pillars.
2She has prepared her meat and mixed her wine;
she has also set her table.
3She has sent out her maids, and she calls
from the highest point of the city.
4"Let all who are simple come in here!"
she says to those who lack judgment.
5"Come, eat my food
and drink the wine I have mixed.
6Leave your simple ways and you will live;
walk in the way of understanding.

7"Whoever corrects a mocker invites insult;
whoever rebukes a wicked man incurs abuse.
8Do not rebuke a mocker or he will hate you;
rebuke a wise man and he will love you.
9Instruct a wise man and he will be wiser still;
teach a righteous man and he will add to his learning.

10"The fear of the LORD is the beginning of wisdom,
and knowledge of the Holy One is understanding.
11For through me your days will be many,
and years will be added to your life.
12If you are wise, your wisdom will reward you;
if you are a mocker, you alone will suffer."

DAY 101

APRIL 11

OLD TESTAMENT READING
Deuteronomy 15:1–16:20

The Year for Cancelling Debts

15 At the end of every seven years
you must cancel debts. 2This is
how it is to be done: Every creditor shall
cancel the loan he has made to his fellow
Israelite. He shall not require payment
from his fellow Israelite or brother, because the LORD's time for cancelling
debts has been proclaimed. 3You may
require payment from a foreigner, but
you must cancel any debt your brother
owes you. 4However, there should be
no poor among you, for in the land the
LORD your God is giving you to possess
as your inheritance, he will richly bless
you, 5if only you fully obey the LORD
your God and are careful to follow all
these commands I am giving you today.
6For the LORD your God will bless you
as he has promised, and you will lend to
many nations but will borrow from
none. You will rule over many nations
but none will rule over you.
7If there is a poor man among your
brothers in any of the towns of the land
that the LORD your God is giving you,
do not be hard-hearted or tight-fisted
towards your poor brother. 8Rather be
open-handed and freely lend him whatever he needs. 9Be careful not to harbour this wicked thought: "The seventh
year, the year for cancelling debts, is
near," so that you do not show ill will
towards your needy brother and give
him nothing. He may then appeal to the
LORD against you, and you will be found
guilty of sin. 10Give generously to him
and do so without a grudging heart;
then because of this the LORD your God
will bless you in all your work and in
everything you put your hand to.
11There will always be poor people in
the land. Therefore I command you to
be open-handed towards your brothers
and towards the poor and needy in your
land.

Freeing Servants

12If a fellow Hebrew, a man or
woman, sells himself to you and serves
you six years, in the seventh year you
must let him go free. 13And when you
release him, do not send him away
empty-handed. 14Supply him liberally
from your flock, your threshing-floor
and your winepress. Give to him as the
LORD your God has blessed you.
15Remember that you were slaves in
Egypt and the LORD your God redeemed you. That is why I give you this
command today.
16But if your servant says to you, "I
do not want to leave you," because he
loves you and your family and is well off
with you, 17then take an awl and push it
through his ear lobe into the door, and
he will become your servant for life. Do
the same for your maidservant.
18Do not consider it a hardship to set
your servant free, because his service to
you these six years has been worth twice
as much as that of a hired hand. And the
LORD your God will bless you in everything you do.

The Firstborn Animals

19Set apart for the LORD your God
every firstborn male of your herds and
flocks. Do not put the firstborn of your
oxen to work, and do not shear the
firstborn of your sheep. 20Each year you
and your family are to eat them in the
presence of the LORD your God at the
place he will choose. 21If an animal has a
defect, is lame or blind, or has any
serious flaw, you must not sacrifice it to
the LORD your God. 22You are to eat it
in your own towns. Both the ceremonially unclean and the clean may eat
it, as if it were gazelle or deer. 23But you

must not eat the blood; pour it out on
the ground like water.

Passover

16 Observe the month of Abib and
celebrate the Passover of the
LORD your God, because in the month
of Abib he brought you out of Egypt by
night. 2Sacrifice as the Passover to the
LORD your God an animal from your
flock or herd at the place the LORD will
choose as a dwelling for his Name. 3Do
not eat it with bread made with yeast,
but for seven days eat unleavened
bread, the bread of affliction, because
you left Egypt in haste—so that all the
days of your life you may remember the
time of your departure from Egypt.
4Let no yeast be found in your possession in all your land for seven days. Do
not let any of the meat you sacrifice on
the evening of the first day remain until
morning.
5You must not sacrifice the Passover
in any town the LORD your God gives
you 6except in the place he will choose
as a dwelling for his Name. There you
must sacrifice the Passover in the evening, when the sun goes down, on the
anniversary of your departure from
Egypt. 7Roast it and eat it at the place
the LORD your God will choose. Then in
the morning return to your tents. 8For
six days eat unleavened bread and on
the seventh day hold an assembly to the
LORD your God and do no work.

Feast of Weeks

9Count off seven weeks from the time
you begin to put the sickle to the standing corn. 10Then celebrate the Feast of
Weeks to the LORD your God by giving
a freewill offering in proportion to the
blessings the LORD your God has given
you. 11And rejoice before the LORD
your God at the place he will choose as a
dwelling for his Name—you, your sons
and daughters, your menservants and
maidservants, the Levites in your
towns, and the aliens, the fatherless
and the widows living among you.
12Remember that you were slaves in
Egypt, and follow carefully these
decrees.

Feast of Tabernacles

13Celebrate the Feast of Tabernacles
for seven days after you have gathered
the produce of your threshing-floor and
your winepress. 14Be joyful at your
Feast—you, your sons and daughters,
your menservants and maidservants,
and the Levites, the aliens, the fatherless and the widows who live in your
towns. 15For seven days celebrate the
Feast to the LORD your God at the place
the LORD will choose. For the LORD
your God will bless you in all your harvest and in all the work of your hands,
and your joy will be complete.
16Three times a year all your men
must appear before the LORD your God
at the place he will choose: at the Feast
of Unleavened Bread, the Feast of
Weeks and the Feast of Tabernacles.
No man should appear before the LORD
empty-handed: 17Each of you must
bring a gift in proportion to the way the
LORD your God has blessed you.

Judges

18Appoint judges and officials for
each of your tribes in every town the
LORD your God is giving you, and they
shall judge the people fairly. 19Do not
pervert justice or show partiality. Do
not accept a bribe, for a bribe blinds the
eyes of the wise and twists the words of
the righteous. 20Follow justice and justice alone, so that you may live and
possess the land the LORD your God is
giving you.

NEW TESTAMENT READING
Luke 13:31–14:14

Jesus' Sorrow for Jerusalem

31At that time some Pharisees came
to Jesus and said to him, "Leave this

place and go somewhere else. Herod wants to kill you."

32He replied, "Go tell that fox, 'I will drive out demons and heal people today and tomorrow, and on the third day I
will reach my goal.' 33In any case, I must keep going today and tomorrow and the next day—for surely no prophet can die outside Jerusalem!

34"O Jerusalem, Jerusalem, you who kill the prophets and stone those sent to you, how often I have longed to gather your children together, as a hen gathers her chicks under her wings, but you
were not willing! 35Look, your house is left to you desolate. I tell you, you will not see me again until you say, 'Blessed is he who comes in the name of the Lord.'"

Jesus at a Pharisee's House

14 One Sabbath, when Jesus went to eat in the house of a prominent Pharisee, he was being carefully
watched. 2There in front of him was a
man suffering from dropsy. 3Jesus asked the Pharisees and experts in the law, "Is it lawful to heal on the Sabbath
or not?" 4But they remained silent. So taking hold of the man, he healed him and sent him away.

5Then he asked them, "If one of you has a son or an ox that falls into a well on the Sabbath day, will you not immediately pull him out?" 6And they had nothing to say.

7When he noticed how the guests picked the places of honour at the table,
he told them this parable: 8"When someone invites you to a wedding feast, do not take the place of honour, for a person more distinguished than you
may have been invited. 9If so, the host who invited both of you will come and say to you, 'Give this man your seat.' Then, humiliated, you will have to take
the least important place. 10But when you are invited, take the lowest place, so that when your host comes, he will say to you, 'Friend, move up to a better place.' Then you will be honoured in the
presence of all your fellow guests. 11For everyone who exalts himself will be humbled, and he who humbles himself will be exalted."

12Then Jesus said to his host, "When you give a luncheon or dinner, do not invite your friends, your brothers or relatives, or your rich neighbours; if you do, they may invite you back and so you
will be repaid. 13But when you give a banquet, invite the poor, the crippled,
the lame, the blind, 14and you will be blessed. Although they cannot repay you, you will be repaid at the resurrection of the righteous."

READING FROM PSALMS

Psalm 44:1–12

For the director of music. Of the Sons of Korah. A *maskil.*

1We have heard with our ears, O God;
our fathers have told us
what you did in their days,
in days long ago.
2With your hand you drove out the
nations
and planted our fathers;
you crushed the peoples
and made our fathers flourish.
3It was not by their sword that they
won the land,
nor did their arm bring them
victory;
it was your right hand, your arm,
and the light of your face, for you
loved them.

4You are my King and my God,
who decrees victories for Jacob.
5Through you we push back our
enemies;
through your name we trample our
foes.
6I do not trust in my bow,
my sword does not bring me
victory;
7but you give us victory over our
enemies,
you put our adversaries to shame.

8In God we make our boast all day
long,
and we will praise your name for
ever. *Selah*

9But now you have rejected and
humbled us;
you no longer go out with our
armies.

10You made us retreat before the
enemy,
and our adversaries have
plundered us.
11You gave us up to be devoured like
sheep
and have scattered us among the
nations.
12You sold your people for a pittance,
gaining nothing from their sale.

APRIL 12

DAY 102

OLD TESTAMENT READING
Deuteronomy 16:21–18:22

Worshipping Other Gods

21Do not set up any wooden Asherah
pole beside the altar you build to the
LORD your God, 22and do not erect a
sacred stone, for these the LORD your
God hates.

17 Do not sacrifice to the LORD
your God an ox or a sheep that
has any defect or flaw in it, for that
would be detestable to him.
2If a man or woman living among you
in one of the towns the LORD gives you
is found doing evil in the eyes of the
LORD your God in violation of his covenant, 3and contrary to my command
has worshipped other gods, bowing
down to them or to the sun or the moon
or the stars of the sky, 4and this has been
brought to your attention, then you
must investigate it thoroughly. If it is
true and it has been proved that this
detestable thing has been done in Israel,
5take the man or woman who has done
this evil deed to your city gate and stone
that person to death. 6On the testimony
of two or three witnesses a man shall be
put to death, but no-one shall be put to
death on the testimony of only one witness. 7The hands of the witnesses must
be the first in putting him to death, and
then the hands of all the people. You
must purge the evil from among you.

Law Courts

8If cases come before your courts that
are too difficult for you to judge—
whether bloodshed, lawsuits or assaults
—take them to the place the LORD your
God will choose. 9Go to the priests,
who are Levites, and to the judge who is
in office at that time. Enquire of them
and they will give you the verdict. 10You
must act according to the decisions they
give you at the place the LORD will
choose. Be careful to do everything
they direct you to do. 11Act according to
the law they teach you and the decisions
they give you. Do not turn aside from
what they tell you, to the right or to the
left. 12The man who shows contempt for
the judge or for the priest who stands
ministering there to the LORD your God
must be put to death. You must purge
the evil from Israel. 13All the people will
hear and be afraid, and will not be
contemptuous again.

The King

14When you enter the land the LORD
your God is giving you and have taken
possession of it and settled in it, and you
say, "Let us set a king over us like all the

nations around us," 15be sure to appoint
over you the king the LORD your God
chooses. He must be from among your
own brothers. Do not place a foreigner
over you, one who is not a brother
Israelite. 16The king, moreover, must
not acquire great numbers of horses for
himself or make the people return to
Egypt to get more of them, for the LORD
has told you, "You are not to go back
that way again." 17He must not take
many wives, or his heart will be led
astray. He must not accumulate large
amounts of silver and gold.
18When he takes the throne of his
kingdom, he is to write for himself on a
scroll a copy of this law, taken from that
of the priests, who are Levites. 19It is to
be with him, and he is to read it all the
days of his life so that he may learn to
revere the LORD his God and follow
carefully all the words of this law and
these decrees 20and not consider himself
better than his brothers and turn from
the law to the right or to the left. Then
he and his descendants will reign a long
time over his kingdom in Israel.

Offerings for Priests and Levites

18 The priests, who are Levites—
indeed the whole tribe of Levi
—are to have no allotment or inheritance with Israel. They shall live on the
offerings made to the LORD by fire, for
that is their inheritance. 2They shall
have no inheritance among their
brothers; the LORD is their inheritance,
as he promised them.
3This is the share due to the priests
from the people who sacrifice a bull or a
sheep: the shoulder, the jowls and the
inner parts. 4You are to give them the
firstfruits of your grain, new wine and
oil, and the first wool from the shearing
of your sheep, 5for the LORD your God
has chosen them and their descendants
out of all your tribes to stand and
minister in the LORD's name always.
6If a Levite moves from one of your
towns anywhere in Israel where he is
living, and comes in all earnestness to
the place the LORD will choose, 7he may
minister in the name of the LORD his
God like all his fellow Levites who serve
there in the presence of the LORD. 8He
is to share equally in their benefits even
though he has received money from the
sale of family possessions.

Detestable Practices

9When you enter the land the LORD
your God is giving you, do not learn to
imitate the detestable ways of the nations there. 10Let no-one be found
among you who sacrifices his son or
daughter in the fire, who practises divination or sorcery, interprets omens, en-
gages in witchcraft, 11or casts spells, or
who is a medium or spiritist or who
consults the dead. 12Anyone who does
these things is detestable to the LORD,
and because of these detestable practices the LORD your God will drive out
those nations before you. 13You must
be blameless before the LORD your
God.

The Prophet

14The nations you will dispossess listen to those who practise sorcery or
divination. But as for you, the LORD
your God has not permitted you to do
so. 15The LORD your God will raise up
for you a prophet like me from among
your own brothers. You must listen to
him. 16For this is what you asked of the
LORD your God at Horeb on the day of
the assembly when you said, "Let us not
hear the voice of the LORD our God nor
see this great fire any more, or we will
die."
17The LORD said to me: "What they
say is good. 18I will raise up for them a
prophet like you from among their
brothers; I will put my words in his
mouth, and he will tell them everything
I command him. 19If anyone does not
listen to my words that the prophet
speaks in my name, I myself will call
him to account. 20But a prophet who
presumes to speak in my name anything

I have not commanded him to say, or a prophet who speaks in the name of other gods, must be put to death."

21You may say to yourselves, "How can we know when a message has not been spoken by the LORD?" 22If what a prophet proclaims in the name of the LORD does not take place or come true, that is a message the LORD has not spoken. That prophet has spoken presumptuously. Do not be afraid of him.

NEW TESTAMENT READING
Luke 14:15–35

The Parable of the Great Banquet

15When one of those at the table with him heard this, he said to Jesus, "Blessed is the man who will eat at the feast in the kingdom of God."

16Jesus replied: "A certain man was preparing a great banquet and invited many guests. 17At the time of the banquet he sent his servant to tell those who had been invited, 'Come, for everything is now ready.'

18"But they all alike began to make excuses. The first said, 'I have just bought a field, and I must go and see it. Please excuse me.'

19"Another said, 'I have just bought five yoke of oxen, and I'm on my way to try them out. Please excuse me.'

20"Still another said, 'I have just got married, so I can't come.'

21"The servant came back and reported this to his master. Then the owner of the house became angry and ordered his servant, 'Go out quickly into the streets and alleys of the town and bring in the poor, the crippled, the blind and the lame.'

22" 'Sir,' the servant said, 'what you ordered has been done, but there is still room.'

23"Then the master told his servant, 'Go out to the roads and country lanes and make them come in, so that my house will be full. 24I tell you, not one of those men who were invited will get a taste of my banquet.' "

The Cost of Being a Disciple

25Large crowds were travelling with Jesus, and turning to them he said: 26"If anyone comes to me and does not hate his father and mother, his wife and children, his brothers and sisters—yes, even his own life—he cannot be my disciple. 27And anyone who does not carry his cross and follow me cannot be my disciple.

28"Suppose one of you wants to build a tower. Will he not first sit down and estimate the cost to see if he has enough money to complete it? 29For if he lays the foundation and is not able to finish it, everyone who sees it will ridicule him, 30saying, 'This fellow began to build and was not able to finish.'

31"Or suppose a king is about to go to war against another king. Will he not first sit down and consider whether he is able with ten thousand men to oppose the one coming against him with twenty thousand? 32If he is not able, he will send a delegation while the other is still a long way off and will ask for terms of peace. 33In the same way, any of you who does not give up everything he has cannot be my disciple.

34"Salt is good, but if it loses its saltiness, how can it be made salty again? 35It is fit neither for the soil nor for the manure heap; it is thrown out.

"He who has ears to hear, let him hear."

READING FROM PSALMS
Psalm 44:13–26

13You have made us a reproach to our
 neighbours,
 the scorn and derision of those
 around us.
14You have made us a byword among
 the nations;
 the peoples shake their heads at us.
15My disgrace is before me all day long,
 and my face is covered with shame
16at the taunts of those who reproach
 and revile me,

because of the enemy, who is bent
on revenge.

17All this happened to us,
though we had not forgotten you
or been false to your covenant.
18Our hearts had not turned back;
our feet had not strayed from your
path.
19But you crushed us and made us a
haunt for jackals
and covered us over with deep
darkness.

20If we had forgotten the name of our
God
or spread out our hands to a
foreign god,
21would not God have discovered it,
since he knows the secrets of the
heart?
22Yet for your sake we face death all
day long;
we are considered as sheep to be
slaughtered.

23Awake, O Lord! Why do you sleep?
Rouse yourself! Do not reject us
for ever.
24Why do you hide your face
and forget our misery and
oppression?

25We are brought down to the dust;
our bodies cling to the ground.
26Rise up and help us;
redeem us because of your
unfailing love.

DAY 103

APRIL 13

OLD TESTAMENT READING
Deuteronomy 19:1–20:20

Cities of Refuge

19 When the LORD your God has
destroyed the nations whose
land he is giving you, and when you
have driven them out and settled in
their towns and houses, 2then set aside
for yourselves three cities centrally lo-
cated in the land the LORD your God is
giving you to possess. 3Build roads to
them and divide into three parts the
land the LORD your God is giving you as
an inheritance, so that anyone who kills
a man may flee there.
4This is the rule concerning the man
who kills another and flees there to save
his life—one who kills his neighbour
unintentionally, without malice aforethought. 5For instance, a man may go
into the forest with his neighbour to cut
wood, and as he swings his axe to fell a
tree, the head may fly off and hit his
neighbour and kill him. That man may
flee to one of these cities and save his
life. 6Otherwise, the avenger of blood
might pursue him in a rage, overtake
him if the distance is too great, and kill
him even though he is not deserving of
death, since he did it to his neighbour
without malice aforethought. 7This is
why I command you to set aside for
yourselves three cities.
8If the LORD your God enlarges your
territory, as he promised on oath to
your forefathers, and gives you the
whole land he promised them, 9because
you carefully follow all these laws I
command you today—to love the LORD
your God and to walk always in his
ways—then you are to set aside three
more cities. 10Do this so that innocent
blood will not be shed in your land,
which the LORD your God is giving you
as your inheritance, and so that you will
not be guilty of bloodshed.
11But if a man hates his neighbour
and lies in wait for him, assaults and
kills him, and then flees to one of these

cities, 12the elders of his town shall send
for him, bring him back from the city,
and hand him over to the avenger of
blood to die. 13Show him no pity. You
must purge from Israel the guilt of shedding innocent blood, so that it may go
well with you.
14Do not move your neighbour's
boundary stone set up by your prede-
cessors in the inheritance you receive in
the land the LORD your God is giving
you to possess.

Witnesses

15One witness is not enough to convict a man accused of any crime or
offence he may have committed. A matter must be established by the testimony
of two or three witnesses.
16If a malicious witness takes the
stand to accuse a man of a crime, 17the
two men involved in the dispute must
stand in the presence of the LORD before the priests and the judges who are
in office at the time. 18The judges must
make a thorough investigation, and if
the witness proves to be a liar, giving
false testimony against his brother,
19then do to him as he intended to do to
his brother. You must purge the evil
from among you. 20The rest of the people will hear of this and be afraid, and
never again will such an evil thing be
done among you. 21Show no pity: life
for life, eye for eye, tooth for tooth,
hand for hand, foot for foot.

Going to War

20 When you go to war against your
enemies and see horses and
chariots and an army greater than
yours, do not be afraid of them, because
the LORD your God, who brought you
up out of Egypt, will be with you.
2When you are about to go into battle,
the priest shall come forward and
address the army. 3He shall say: "Hear,
O Israel, today you are going into battle
against your enemies. Do not be faint-
hearted or afraid; do not be terrified or
give way to panic before them. 4For the
LORD your God is the one who goes
with you to fight for you against your
enemies to give you victory."
5The officers shall say to the army:
"Has anyone built a new house and not
dedicated it? Let him go home, or he
may die in battle and someone else may
dedicate it. 6Has anyone planted a
vineyard and not begun to enjoy it? Let
him go home, or he may die in battle
and someone else enjoy it. 7Has anyone
become pledged to a woman and not
married her? Let him go home, or he
may die in battle and someone else
marry her." 8Then the officers shall
add, "Is any man afraid or faint-
hearted? Let him go home so that his
brothers will not become disheartened
too." 9When the officers have finished
speaking to the army, they shall appoint
commanders over it.
10When you march up to attack a city,
make its people an offer of peace. 11If
they accept and open their gates, all the
people in it shall be subject to forced
labour and shall work for you. 12If they
refuse to make peace and they engage
you in battle, lay siege to that city.
13When the LORD your God delivers it
into your hand, put to the sword all the
men in it. 14As for the women, the
children, the livestock and everything
else in the city, you may take these as
plunder for yourselves. And you may
use the plunder the LORD your God
gives you from your enemies. 15This is
how you are to treat all the cities that
are at a distance from you and do not
belong to the nations nearby.
16However, in the cities of the nations
the LORD your God is giving you as
an inheritance, do not leave alive
anything that breathes. 17Completely
destroy them—the Hittites, Amorites,
Canaanites, Perizzites, Hivites and
Jebusites—as the LORD your God has
commanded you. 18Otherwise, they will
teach you to follow all the detestable
things they do in worshipping their
gods, and you will sin against the LORD
your God.

19When you lay siege to a city for a
long time, fighting against it to capture
it, do not destroy its trees by putting an
axe to them, because you can eat their
fruit. Do not cut them down. Are the
trees of the field people, that you should
besiege them? 20However, you may cut
down trees that you know are not fruit
trees and use them to build siege works
until the city at war with you falls.

NEW TESTAMENT READING
Luke 15:1–32

The Parable of the Lost Sheep

15 Now the tax collectors and "sinners" were all gathering round
to hear him. 2But the Pharisees and the
teachers of the law muttered, "This
man welcomes sinners, and eats with
them."
3Then Jesus told them this parable:
4"Suppose one of you has a hundred
sheep and loses one of them. Does he
not leave the ninety-nine in the open
country and go after the lost sheep until
he finds it? 5And when he finds it, he
joyfully puts it on his shoulders 6and
goes home. Then he calls his friends and
neighbours together and says, 'Rejoice
with me; I have found my lost sheep.' 7I
tell you that in the same way there will
be more rejoicing in heaven over one
sinner who repents than over ninety-
nine righteous persons who do not need
to repent.

The Parable of the Lost Coin

8"Or suppose a woman has ten silver
coins and loses one. Does she not light a
lamp, sweep the house and search carefully until she finds it? 9And when she
finds it, she calls her friends and neighbours together and says, 'Rejoice with
me; I have found my lost coin.' 10In the
same way, I tell you, there is rejoicing in
the presence of the angels of God over
one sinner who repents."

The Parable of the Lost Son

11Jesus continued: "There was a man
who had two sons. 12The younger one
said to his father, 'Father, give me my
share of the estate.' So he divided his
property between them.
13"Not long after that, the younger
son got together all he had, set off for a
distant country and there squandered
his wealth in wild living. 14After he had
spent everything, there was a severe
famine in that whole country, and he
began to be in need. 15So he went and
hired himself out to a citizen of that
country, who sent him to his fields to
feed pigs. 16He longed to fill his stomach
with the pods that the pigs were eating,
but no-one gave him anything.
17"When he came to his senses, he
said, 'How many of my father's hired
men have food to spare, and here I am
starving to death! 18I will set out and go
back to my father and say to him:
Father, I have sinned against heaven
and against you. 19I am no longer
worthy to be called your son; make me
like one of your hired men.' 20So he got
up and went to his father.
"But while he was still a long way off,
his father saw him and was filled with
compassion for him; he ran to his son,
threw his arms around him and kissed
him.
21"The son said to him, 'Father, I
have sinned against heaven and against
you. I am no longer worthy to be called
your son.'
22"But the father said to his servants,
'Quick! Bring the best robe and put it on
him. Put a ring on his finger and sandals
on his feet. 23Bring the fattened calf and
kill it. Let's have a feast and celebrate.
24For this son of mine was dead and is
alive again; he was lost and is found.' So
they began to celebrate.
25"Meanwhile, the older son was in
the field. When he came near the house,
he heard music and dancing. 26So he
called one of the servants and asked him
what was going on. 27'Your brother has
come,' he replied, 'and your father has

killed the fattened calf because he has him back safe and sound.'

28"The older brother became angry and refused to go in. So his father went out and pleaded with him. 29But he answered his father, 'Look! All these years I've been slaving for you and never disobeyed your orders. Yet you never gave me even a young goat so I could celebrate with my friends. 30But when this son of yours who has squandered your property with prostitutes comes home, you kill the fattened calf for him!'

31"'My son,' the father said, 'you are always with me, and everything I have is yours. 32But we had to celebrate and be glad, because this brother of yours was dead and is alive again; he was lost and is found.'"

READING FROM PSALMS
Psalm 45:1–9

For the director of music. To ⌊the tune of⌋ "Lilies". Of the Sons of Korah. A *maskil*. A wedding song.

1My heart is stirred by a noble theme
as I recite my verses for the king;
my tongue is the pen of a skilful writer.
2You are the most excellent of men
and your lips have been anointed with grace,
since God has blessed you for ever.
3Gird your sword upon your side, O mighty one;
clothe yourself with splendour and majesty.
4In your majesty ride forth victoriously
on behalf of truth, humility and righteousness;
let your right hand display awesome deeds.
5Let your sharp arrows pierce the hearts of the king's enemies;
let the nations fall beneath your feet.
6Your throne, O God, will last for ever and ever;
a sceptre of justice will be the sceptre of your kingdom.
7You love righteousness and hate wickedness;
therefore God, your God, has set you above your companions
by anointing you with the oil of joy.
8All your robes are fragrant with myrrh and aloes and cassia;
from palaces adorned with ivory
the music of the strings makes you glad.
9Daughters of kings are among your honoured women;
at your right hand is the royal bride in gold of Ophir.

APRIL 14

DAY 104

OLD TESTAMENT READING
Deuteronomy 21:1–22:30

Atonement for an Unsolved Murder

21 If a man is found slain, lying in a field in the land the LORD your God is giving you to possess, and it is not known who killed him, 2your elders and judges shall go out and measure the distance from the body to the neighbouring towns. 3Then the elders of the town nearest the body shall take a heifer that has never been worked and has never worn a yoke 4and lead her down to a valley that has not been ploughed or planted and where there is a flowing stream. There in the valley they are to break the heifer's neck. 5The priests,

the sons of Levi, shall step forward, for the LORD your God has chosen them to minister and to pronounce blessings in the name of the LORD and to decide all cases of dispute and assault. 6Then all the elders of the town nearest the body shall wash their hands over the heifer whose neck was broken in the valley, 7and they shall declare: "Our hands did not shed this blood, nor did our eyes see it done. 8Accept this atonement for your people Israel, whom you have redeemed, O LORD, and do not hold your people guilty of the blood of an innocent man." And the bloodshed will be atoned for. 9So you will purge from yourselves the guilt of shedding innocent blood, since you have done what is right in the eyes of the LORD.

Marrying a Captive Woman

10When you go to war against your enemies and the LORD your God delivers them into your hands and you take captives, 11if you notice among the captives a beautiful woman and are attracted to her, you may take her as your wife. 12Bring her into your home and make her shave her head, trim her nails 13and put aside the clothes she was wearing when captured. After she has lived in your house and mourned her father and mother for a full month, then you may go to her and be her husband and she shall be your wife. 14If you are not pleased with her, let her go wherever she wishes. You must not sell her or treat her as a slave, since you have dishonoured her.

The Right of the Firstborn

15If a man has two wives, and he loves one but not the other, and both bear him sons but the firstborn is the son of the wife he does not love, 16when he wills his property to his sons, he must not give the rights of the firstborn to the son of the wife he loves in preference to his actual firstborn, the son of the wife he does not love. 17He must acknowledge the son of his unloved wife as the firstborn by giving him a double share of all he has. That son is the first sign of his father's strength. The right of the firstborn belongs to him.

A Rebellious Son

18If a man has a stubborn and rebellious son who does not obey his father and mother and will not listen to them when they discipline him, 19his father and mother shall take hold of him and bring him to the elders at the gate of his town. 20They shall say to the elders, "This son of ours is stubborn and rebellious. He will not obey us. He is a profligate and a drunkard." 21Then all the men of his town shall stone him to death. You must purge the evil from among you. All Israel will hear of it and be afraid.

Various Laws

22If a man guilty of a capital offence is put to death and his body is hung on a tree, 23you must not leave his body on the tree overnight. Be sure to bury him that same day, because anyone who is hung on a tree is under God's curse. You must not desecrate the land the LORD your God is giving you as an inheritance.

22 If you see your brother's ox or sheep straying, do not ignore it but be sure to take it back to him. 2If the brother does not live near you or if you do not know who he is, take it home with you and keep it until he comes looking for it. Then give it back to him. 3Do the same if you find your brother's donkey or his cloak or anything he loses. Do not ignore it.

4If you see your brother's donkey or his ox fallen on the road, do not ignore it. Help him to get it to its feet.

5A woman must not wear men's clothing, nor a man wear women's clothing, for the LORD your God detests anyone who does this.

6If you come across a bird's nest beside the road, either in a tree or on the ground, and the mother is sitting on the young or on the eggs, do not take the mother with the young. 7You may take the young, but be sure to let the mother go, so that it may go well with you and you may have a long life.

8When you build a new house, make a parapet around your roof so that you may not bring the guilt of bloodshed on your house if someone falls from the roof.

9Do not plant two kinds of seed in your vineyard; if you do, not only the crops you plant but also the fruit of the vineyard will be defiled.

10Do not plough with an ox and a donkey yoked together.

11Do not wear clothes of wool and linen woven together.

12Make tassels on the four corners of the cloak you wear.

Marriage Violations

13If a man takes a wife and, after lying with her, dislikes her 14and slanders her and gives her a bad name, saying, "I married this woman, but when I approached her, I did not find proof of her virginity," 15then the girl's father and mother shall bring proof that she was a virgin to the town elders at the gate. 16The girl's father will say to the elders, "I gave my daughter in marriage to this man, but he dislikes her. 17Now he has slandered her and said, 'I did not find your daughter to be a virgin.' But here is the proof of my daughter's virginity." Then her parents shall display the cloth before the elders of the town, 18and the elders shall take the man and punish him. 19They shall fine him a hundred shekels of silver and give them to the girl's father, because this man has given an Israelite virgin a bad name. She shall continue to be his wife; he must not divorce her as long as he lives.

20If, however, the charge is true and no proof of the girl's virginity can be found, 21she shall be brought to the door of her father's house and there the men of her town shall stone her to death. She has done a disgraceful thing in Israel by being promiscuous while still in her father's house. You must purge the evil from among you.

22If a man is found sleeping with another man's wife, both the man who slept with her and the woman must die. You must purge the evil from Israel.

23If a man happens to meet in a town a virgin pledged to be married and he sleeps with her, 24you shall take both of them to the gate of that town and stone them to death—the girl because she was in a town and did not scream for help, and the man because he violated another man's wife. You must purge the evil from among you.

25But if out in the country a man happens to meet a girl pledged to be married and rapes her, only the man who has done this shall die. 26Do nothing to the girl; she has committed no sin deserving death. This case is like that of someone who attacks and murders his neighbour, 27for the man found the girl out in the country, and though the betrothed girl screamed, there was no-one to rescue her.

28If a man happens to meet a virgin who is not pledged to be married and rapes her and they are discovered, 29he shall pay the girl's father fifty shekels of silver. He must marry the girl, for he has violated her. He can never divorce her as long as he lives.

30A man is not to marry his father's wife; he must not dishonour his father's bed.

NEW TESTAMENT READING

Luke 16:1–18

The Parable of the Shrewd Manager

16 Jesus told his disciples: "There was a rich man whose manager was accused of wasting his possessions. 2So he called him in and asked him, 'What is this I hear about you? Give an

account of your management, because
you cannot be manager any longer.'
3"The manager said to himself,
'What shall I do now? My master is
taking away my job. I'm not strong
enough to dig, and I'm ashamed to beg
—4I know what I'll do so that, when I
lose my job here, people will welcome
me into their houses.'
5"So he called in each one of his
master's debtors. He asked the first,
'How much do you owe my master?'
6"'Eight hundred gallons of olive oil,'
he replied.
"The manager told him, 'Take your
bill, sit down quickly, and make it four
hundred.'
7"Then he asked the second, 'And
how much do you owe?'
"'A thousand bushels of wheat,' he
replied.
"He told him, 'Take your bill and
make it eight hundred.'
8"The master commended the dishonest manager because he had acted
shrewdly. For the people of this world
are more shrewd in dealing with their
own kind than are the people of the
light. 9I tell you, use worldly wealth to
gain friends for yourselves, so that when
it is gone, you will be welcomed into
eternal dwellings.
10"Whoever can be trusted with very
little can also be trusted with much, and
whoever is dishonest with very little will
also be dishonest with much. 11So if you
have not been trustworthy in handling
worldly wealth, who will trust you with
true riches? 12And if you have not been
trustworthy with someone else's property, who will give you property of your
own?
13"No servant can serve two masters.
Either he will hate the one and love the
other, or he will be devoted to the one
and despise the other. You cannot serve
both God and Money."
14The Pharisees, who loved money,
heard all this and were sneering at
Jesus. 15He said to them, "You are the
ones who justify yourselves in the eyes
of men, but God knows your hearts.
What is highly valued among men is
detestable in God's sight.

Additional Teachings

16"The Law and the Prophets were
proclaimed until John. Since that time,
the good news of the kingdom of God is
being preached, and everyone is forcing
his way into it. 17It is easier for heaven
and earth to disappear than for the least
stroke of a pen to drop out of the Law.
18"Anyone who divorces his wife and
marries another woman commits adultery, and the man who marries a divorced woman commits adultery.

READING FROM PROVERBS
Proverbs 9:13–18

13The woman Folly is loud;
she is undisciplined and without
knowledge.
14She sits at the door of her house,
on a seat at the highest point of the
city,
15calling out to those who pass by,
who go straight on their way.
16"Let all who are simple come in
here!"
she says to those who lack
judgment.
17"Stolen water is sweet;
food eaten in secret is delicious!"
18But little do they know that the dead
are there,
that her guests are in the depths of
the grave.

APRIL 15

DAY 105

OLD TESTAMENT READING

Deuteronomy 23:1–25:19

Exclusion From the Assembly

23 No-one who has been emascu-
lated by crushing or cutting may
enter the assembly of the LORD.
2No-one born of a forbidden marriage
nor any of his descendants may enter
the assembly of the LORD, even down to
the tenth generation.
3No Ammonite or Moabite or any of
his descendants may enter the assembly
of the LORD, even down to the tenth
generation. 4For they did not come to
meet you with bread and water on your
way when you came out of Egypt, and
they hired Balaam son of Beor from
Pethor in Aram Naharaim to pronounce
a curse on you. 5However, the LORD
your God would not listen to Balaam
but turned the curse into a blessing for
you, because the LORD your God loves
you. 6Do not seek a treaty of friendship
with them as long as you live.
7Do not abhor an Edomite, for he is
your brother. Do not abhor an Egyptian, because you lived as an alien in his
country. 8The third generation of children born to them may enter the assembly of the LORD.

Uncleanness in the Camp

9When you are encamped against
your enemies, keep away from everything impure. 10If one of your men is
unclean because of a nocturnal emission, he is to go outside the camp and
stay there. 11But as evening approaches
he is to wash himself, and at sunset he
may return to the camp.
12Designate a place outside the camp
where you can go to relieve yourself.
13As part of your equipment have something to dig with, and when you relieve
yourself, dig a hole and cover up your
excrement. 14For the LORD your God
moves about in your camp to protect
you and to deliver your enemies to you.
Your camp must be holy, so that he will
not see among you anything indecent
and turn away from you.

Miscellaneous Laws

15If a slave has taken refuge with you,
do not hand him over to his master.
16Let him live among you wherever he
likes and in whatever town he chooses.
Do not oppress him.
17No Israelite man or woman is to
become a shrine-prostitute. 18You must
not bring the earnings of a female
prostitute or of a male prostitute into
the house of the LORD your God to pay
any vow, because the LORD your God
detests them both.
19Do not charge your brother interest, whether on money or food or
anything else that may earn interest.
20You may charge a foreigner interest,
but not a brother Israelite, so that the
LORD your God may bless you in everything you put your hand to in the land
you are entering to possess.
21If you make a vow to the LORD your
God, do not be slow to pay it, for the
LORD your God will certainly demand it
of you and you will be guilty of sin.
22But if you refrain from making a vow,
you will not be guilty. 23Whatever your
lips utter you must be sure to do, because you made your vow freely to the
LORD your God with your own mouth.
24If you enter your neighbour's
vineyard, you may eat all the grapes you
want, but do not put any in your basket.
25If you enter your neighbour's corn-
field, you may pick the ears with your
hands, but you must not put a sickle to
his standing corn.

24 If a man marries a woman who
becomes displeasing to him because he finds something indecent
about her, and he writes her a certificate of divorce, gives it to her and

sends her from his house, [2]and if after she leaves his house she becomes the wife of another man, [3]and her second husband dislikes her and writes her a certificate of divorce, gives it to her and sends her from his house, or if he dies, [4]then her first husband, who divorced her, is not allowed to marry her again after she has been defiled. That would be detestable in the eyes of the LORD. Do not bring sin upon the land the LORD your God is giving you as an inheritance.

[5]If a man has recently married, he must not be sent to war or have any other duty laid on him. For one year he is to be free to stay at home and bring happiness to the wife he has married.

[6]Do not take a pair of millstones—not even the upper one—as security for a debt, because that would be taking a man's livelihood as security.

[7]If a man is caught kidnapping one of his brother Israelites and treats him as a slave or sells him, the kidnapper must die. You must purge the evil from among you.

[8]In cases of leprous diseases be very careful to do exactly as the priests, who are Levites, instruct you. You must follow carefully what I have commanded them. [9]Remember what the LORD your God did to Miriam along the way after you came out of Egypt.

[10]When you make a loan of any kind to your neighbour, do not go into his house to get what he is offering as a pledge. [11]Stay outside and let the man to whom you are making the loan bring the pledge out to you. [12]If the man is poor, do not go to sleep with his pledge in your possession. [13]Return his cloak to him by sunset so that he may sleep in it. Then he will thank you, and it will be regarded as a righteous act in the sight of the LORD your God.

[14]Do not take advantage of a hired man who is poor and needy, whether he is a brother Israelite or an alien living in one of your towns. [15]Pay him his wages each day before sunset, because he is poor and is counting on it. Otherwise he may cry to the LORD against you, and you will be guilty of sin.

[16]Fathers shall not be put to death for their children, nor children put to death for their fathers; each is to die for his own sin.

[17]Do not deprive the alien or the fatherless of justice, or take the cloak of the widow as a pledge. [18]Remember that you were slaves in Egypt and the LORD your God redeemed you from there. That is why I command you to do this.

[19]When you are harvesting in your field and you overlook a sheaf, do not go back to get it. Leave it for the alien, the fatherless and the widow, so that the LORD your God may bless you in all the work of your hands. [20]When you beat the olives from your trees, do not go over the branches a second time. Leave what remains for the alien, the fatherless and the widow. [21]When you harvest the grapes in your vineyard, do not go over the vines again. Leave what remains for the alien, the fatherless and the widow. [22]Remember that you were slaves in Egypt. That is why I command you to do this.

25 When men have a dispute, they are to take it to court and the judges will decide the case, acquitting the innocent and condemning the guilty. [2]If the guilty man deserves to be beaten, the judge shall make him lie down and have him flogged in his presence with the number of lashes his crime deserves, [3]but he must not give him more than forty lashes. If he is flogged more than that, your brother will be degraded in your eyes.

[4]Do not muzzle an ox while it is treading out the grain.

[5]If brothers are living together and one of them dies without a son, his widow must not marry outside the family. Her husband's brother shall take her and marry her and fulfil the duty of a brother-in-law to her. [6]The first son she bears shall carry on the name of the dead brother so that his name will not be blotted out from Israel.

7However, if a man does not want to
marry his brother's wife, she shall go to
the elders at the town gate and say, "My
husband's brother refuses to carry on
his brother's name in Israel. He will not
fulfil the duty of a brother-in-law to
me." 8Then the elders of his town shall
summon him and talk to him. If he
persists in saying, "I do not want to
marry her," 9his brother's widow shall
go up to him in the presence of the
elders, take off one of his sandals, spit in
his face and say, "This is what is done to
the man who will not build up his
brother's family line." 10That man's line
shall be known in Israel as The Family
of the Unsandalled.

11If two men are fighting and the wife
of one of them comes to rescue her
husband from his assailant, and she
reaches out and seizes him by his private
parts, 12you shall cut off her hand. Show
her no pity.

13Do not have two differing weights
in your bag—one heavy, one light.
14Do not have two differing measures in
your house—one large, one small.
15You must have accurate and honest
weights and measures, so that you may
live long in the land the LORD your God
is giving you. 16For the LORD your God
detests anyone who does these things,
anyone who deals dishonestly.

17Remember what the Amalekites
did to you along the way when you came
out of Egypt. 18When you were weary
and worn out, they met you on your
journey and cut off all who were lagging
behind; they had no fear of God.
19When the LORD your God gives you
rest from all the enemies around you in
the land he is giving you to possess as an
inheritance, you shall blot out the memory of Amalek from under heaven. Do
not forget!

NEW TESTAMENT READING

Luke 16:19–17:10

The Rich Man and Lazarus

19"There was a rich man who was
dressed in purple and fine linen and
lived in luxury every day. 20At his gate
was laid a beggar named Lazarus,
covered with sores 21and longing to eat
what fell from the rich man's table.
Even the dogs came and licked his
sores.

22"The time came when the beggar
died and the angels carried him to Abraham's side. The rich man also died and
was buried. 23In hell, where he was in
torment, he looked up and saw Abraham far away, with Lazarus by his side.
24So he called to him, 'Father Abraham,
have pity on me and send Lazarus to dip
the tip of his finger in water and cool my
tongue, because I am in agony in this
fire.'

25"But Abraham replied, 'Son, remember that in your lifetime you received your good things, while Lazarus
received bad things, but now he is comforted here and you are in agony. 26And
besides all this, between us and you a
great chasm has been fixed, so that
those who want to go from here to you
cannot, nor can anyone cross over from
there to us.'

27"He answered, 'Then I beg you,
father, send Lazarus to my father's
house, 28for I have five brothers. Let
him warn them, so that they will not also
come to this place of torment.'

29"Abraham replied, 'They have
Moses and the Prophets; let them listen
to them.'

30" 'No, father Abraham,' he said,
'but if someone from the dead goes to
them, they will repent.'

31"He said to him, 'If they do not
listen to Moses and the Prophets, they
will not be convinced even if someone
rises from the dead.' "

Sin, Faith, Duty

17 Jesus said to his disciples:
"Things that cause people to sin
are bound to come, but woe to that
person through whom they come. 2It
would be better for him to be thrown
into the sea with a millstone tied round
his neck than for him to cause one of

these little ones to sin. 3So watch yourselves.

"If your brother sins, rebuke him, and if he repents, forgive him. 4If he sins against you seven times in a day, and seven times comes back to you and says, 'I repent,' forgive him."

5The apostles said to the Lord, "Increase our faith!"

6He replied, "If you have faith as small as a mustard seed, you can say to this mulberry tree, 'Be uprooted and planted in the sea,' and it will obey you.

7"Suppose one of you had a servant ploughing or looking after the sheep. Would he say to the servant when he comes in from the field, 'Come along now and sit down to eat'? 8Would he not rather say, 'Prepare my supper, get yourself ready and wait on me while I eat and drink; after that you may eat and drink'? 9Would he thank the servant because he did what he was told to do? 10So you also, when you have done everything you were told to do, should say, 'We are unworthy servants; we have only done our duty.'"

READING FROM PSALMS
Psalm 45:10–17

10Listen, O daughter, consider and give
ear:
Forget your people and your
father's house.
11The king is enthralled by your
beauty;
honour him, for he is your lord.
12The Daughter of Tyre will come with
a gift,
men of wealth will seek your
favour.

13All glorious is the princess within
⌞her chamber⌟;
her gown is interwoven with gold.
14In embroidered garments she is led to
the king;
her virgin companions follow her
and are brought to you.
15They are led in with joy and
gladness;
they enter the palace of the
king.

16Your sons will take the place of your
fathers;
you will make them princes
throughout the land.
17I will perpetuate your memory
through all generations;
therefore the nations will praise
you for ever and ever.

DAY 106

APRIL 16

OLD TESTAMENT READING
Deuteronomy 26:1–28:14

Firstfruits and Tithes

26 When you have entered the land that the LORD your God is giving you as an inheritance and have taken possession of it and settled in it, 2take some of the firstfruits of all that you produce from the soil of the land that the LORD your God is giving you and put them in a basket. Then go to the place that the LORD your God will choose as a dwelling for his Name 3and say to the priest in office at the time, "I declare today to the LORD your God that I have come to the land that the LORD swore to our forefathers to give us." 4The priest shall take the basket from your hands and set it down in front of the altar of the LORD your God. 5Then you shall declare before the LORD your God: "My father was a

wandering Aramean, and he went down into Egypt with a few people and lived there and became a great nation, powerful and numerous. 6But the Egyptians ill-treated us and made us suffer, putting us to hard labour. 7Then we cried out to the LORD, the God of our fathers, and the LORD heard our voice and saw our misery, toil and oppression. 8So the LORD brought us out of Egypt with a mighty hand and an outstretched arm, with great terror and with miraculous signs and wonders. 9He brought us to this place and gave us this land, a land flowing with milk and honey; 10and now I bring the firstfruits of the soil that you, O LORD, have given me." Place the basket before the LORD your God and bow down before him. 11And you and the Levites and the aliens among you shall rejoice in all the good things the LORD your God has given to you and your household.

12When you have finished setting aside a tenth of all your produce in the third year, the year of the tithe, you shall give it to the Levite, the alien, the fatherless and the widow, so that they may eat in your towns and be satisfied. 13Then say to the LORD your God: "I have removed from my house the sacred portion and have given it to the Levite, the alien, the fatherless and the widow, according to all you commanded. I have not turned aside from your commands nor have I forgotten any of them. 14I have not eaten any of the sacred portion while I was in mourning, nor have I removed any of it while I was unclean, nor have I offered any of it to the dead. I have obeyed the LORD my God; I have done everything you commanded me. 15Look down from heaven, your holy dwelling-place, and bless your people Israel and the land you have given us as you promised on oath to our forefathers, a land flowing with milk and honey."

Follow the LORD's Commands

16The LORD your God commands you this day to follow these decrees and laws; carefully observe them with all your heart and with all your soul. 17You have declared this day that the LORD is your God and that you will walk in his ways, that you will keep his decrees, commands and laws, and that you will obey him. 18And the LORD has declared this day that you are his people, his treasured possession as he promised, and that you are to keep all his commands. 19He has declared that he will set you in praise, fame and honour high above all the nations he has made and that you will be a people holy to the LORD your God, as he promised.

The Altar on Mount Ebal

27 Moses and the elders of Israel commanded the people: "Keep all these commands that I give you today. 2When you have crossed the Jordan into the land the LORD your God is giving you, set up some large stones and coat them with plaster. 3Write on them all the words of this law when you have crossed over to enter the land the LORD your God is giving you, a land flowing with milk and honey, just as the LORD, the God of your fathers, promised you. 4And when you have crossed the Jordan, set up these stones on Mount Ebal, as I command you today, and coat them with plaster. 5Build there an altar to the LORD your God, an altar of stones. Do not use any iron tool upon them. 6Build the altar of the LORD your God with stones from the field and offer burnt offerings on it to the LORD your God. 7Sacrifice fellowship offerings there, eating them and rejoicing in the presence of the LORD your God. 8And you shall write very clearly all the words of this law on these stones you have set up."

Curses From Mount Ebal

9Then Moses and the priests, who are Levites, said to all Israel, "Be silent, O Israel, and listen! You have now become the people of the LORD your God. 10Obey the LORD your God and follow his commands and decrees that I give you today."

11On the same day Moses commanded the people:

12When you have crossed the Jordan, these tribes shall stand on Mount Gerizim to bless the people: Simeon, Levi, Judah, Issachar, Joseph and Benjamin.
13And these tribes shall stand on Mount Ebal to pronounce curses: Reuben, Gad, Asher, Zebulun, Dan and Naphtali.

14The Levites shall recite to all the people of Israel in a loud voice:

15"Cursed is the man who carves an image or casts an idol—a thing detestable to the LORD, the work of the craftsman's hands—and sets it up in secret."
Then all the people shall say,
"Amen!"
16"Cursed is the man who dishonours his father or his mother."
Then all the people shall say,
"Amen!"
17"Cursed is the man who moves his neighbour's boundary stone."
Then all the people shall say,
"Amen!"
18"Cursed is the man who leads the blind astray on the road."
Then all the people shall say,
"Amen!"
19"Cursed is the man who withholds justice from the alien, the fatherless or the widow."
Then all the people shall say,
"Amen!"
20"Cursed is the man who sleeps with his father's wife, for he dishonours his father's bed."
Then all the people shall say,
"Amen!"
21"Cursed is the man who has sexual relations with any animal."
Then all the people shall say,
"Amen!"
22"Cursed is the man who sleeps with his sister, the daughter of his father or the daughter of his mother."
Then all the people shall say,
"Amen!"
23"Cursed is the man who sleeps with his mother-in-law."
Then all the people shall say,
"Amen!"
24"Cursed is the man who kills his neighbour secretly."
Then all the people shall say,
"Amen!"
25"Cursed is the man who accepts a bribe to kill an innocent person."
Then all the people shall say,
"Amen!"
26"Cursed is the man who does not uphold the words of this law by carrying them out."
Then all the people shall say,
"Amen!"

Blessings for Obedience

28 If you fully obey the LORD your God and carefully follow all his commands that I give you today, the LORD your God will set you high above all the nations on earth.
2All these blessings will come upon you and accompany you if you obey the LORD your God:

3You will be blessed in the city and blessed in the country.
4The fruit of your womb will be blessed, and the crops of your land and the young of your livestock —the calves of your herds and the lambs of your flocks.
5Your basket and your kneading trough will be blessed.
6You will be blessed when you come in and blessed when you go out.

7The LORD will grant that the enemies who rise up against you will be defeated before you. They will come at you from one direction but flee from you in seven.
8The LORD will send a blessing on your barns and on everything you put your hand to. The LORD your God will bless you in the land he is giving you.

9The LORD will establish you as his holy people, as he promised you on oath, if you keep the commands of the LORD your God and walk in his ways. 10Then all the peoples on earth will see that you are called by the name of the LORD, and they will fear you. 11The LORD will grant you abundant prosperity—in the fruit of your womb, the young of your livestock and the crops of your ground—in the land he swore to your forefathers to give you.

12The LORD will open the heavens, the storehouse of his bounty, to send rain on your land in season and to bless all the work of your hands. You will lend to many nations but will borrow from none. 13The LORD will make you the head, not the tail. If you pay attention to the commands of the LORD your God that I give you this day and carefully follow them, you will always be at the top, never at the bottom. 14Do not turn aside from any of the commands I give you today, to the right or to the left, following other gods and serving them.

NEW TESTAMENT READING
Luke 17:11–37

Ten Healed of Leprosy

11Now on his way to Jerusalem, Jesus travelled along the border between Samaria and Galilee. 12As he was going into a village, ten men who had leprosy met him. They stood at a distance 13and called out in a loud voice, "Jesus, Master, have pity on us!"

14When he saw them, he said, "Go, show yourselves to the priests." And as they went, they were cleansed.

15One of them, when he saw he was healed, came back, praising God in a loud voice. 16He threw himself at Jesus' feet and thanked him—and he was a Samaritan.

17Jesus asked, "Were not all ten cleansed? Where are the other nine? 18Was no-one found to return and give praise to God except this foreigner?" 19Then he said to him, "Rise and go; your faith has made you well."

The Coming of the Kingdom of God

20Once, having been asked by the Pharisees when the kingdom of God would come, Jesus replied, "The kingdom of God does not come with your careful observation, 21nor will people say, 'Here it is,' or 'There it is,' because the kingdom of God is within you."

22Then he said to his disciples, "The time is coming when you will long to see one of the days of the Son of Man, but you will not see it. 23Men will tell you, 'There he is!' or 'Here he is!' Do not go running off after them. 24For the Son of Man in his day will be like the lightning, which flashes and lights up the sky from one end to the other. 25But first he must suffer many things and be rejected by this generation.

26"Just as it was in the days of Noah, so also will it be in the days of the Son of Man. 27People were eating, drinking, marrying and being given in marriage up to the day Noah entered the ark. Then the flood came and destroyed them all.

28"It was the same in the days of Lot. People were eating and drinking, buying and selling, planting and building. 29But the day Lot left Sodom, fire and sulphur rained down from heaven and destroyed them all.

30"It will be just like this on the day the Son of Man is revealed. 31On that day no-one who is on the roof of his house, with his goods inside, should go down to get them. Likewise, no-one in the field should go back for anything. 32Remember Lot's wife! 33Whoever tries to keep his life will lose it, and whoever loses his life will preserve it. 34I tell you, on that night two people will be in one bed; one will be taken and the other left. 35Two women will be grinding grain together; one will be taken and the other left."

37"Where, Lord?" they asked.

He replied, "Where there is a dead body, there the vultures will gather."

READING FROM PSALMS
Psalm 46:1–11

For the director of music. Of the Sons of Korah. According to *alamoth*. A song.

1God is our refuge and strength,
an ever-present help in trouble.
2Therefore we will not fear, though the earth give way
and the mountains fall into the heart of the sea,
3though its waters roar and foam
and the mountains quake with their surging. *Selah*

4There is a river whose streams make glad the city of God,
the holy place where the Most High dwells.
5God is within her, she will not fall;
God will help her at break of day.
6Nations are in uproar, kingdoms fall;
he lifts his voice, the earth melts.

7The LORD Almighty is with us;
the God of Jacob is our fortress. *Selah*

8Come and see the works of the LORD,
the desolations he has brought on the earth.
9He makes wars cease to the ends of the earth;
he breaks the bow and shatters the spear,
he burns the shields with fire.
10"Be still, and know that I am God;
I will be exalted among the nations,
I will be exalted in the earth."

11The LORD Almighty is with us;
the God of Jacob is our fortress. *Selah*

DAY 107

APRIL 17

OLD TESTAMENT READING
Deuteronomy 28:15–68

Curses for Disobedience

15However, if you do not obey the LORD your God and do not carefully follow all his commands and decrees I am giving you today, all these curses will come upon you and overtake you:

16You will be cursed in the city
and cursed in the country.
17Your basket and your kneading trough will be cursed.
18The fruit of your womb will be cursed, and the crops of your land, and the calves of your herds and the lambs of your flocks.
19You will be cursed when you come in and cursed when you go out.

20The LORD will send on you curses, confusion and rebuke in everything you put your hand to, until you are destroyed and come to sudden ruin because of the evil you have done in forsaking him.
21The LORD will plague you with diseases until he has destroyed you from the land you are entering to possess.
22The LORD will strike you with wasting disease, with fever and inflammation, with scorching heat and drought, with blight and mildew, which will plague you until you perish.
23The sky over your head will be bronze, the ground beneath you iron.
24The LORD will turn the rain of your country into dust and powder; it will come down from the skies until you are destroyed.

25The LORD will cause you to be defeated before your enemies. You will come at them from one direction but flee from them in seven, and you will

become a thing of horror to all the
kingdoms on earth. 26Your carcasses
will be food for all the birds of the air
and the beasts of the earth, and there
will be no-one to frighten them away.
27The LORD will afflict you with the boils
of Egypt and with tumours, festering
sores and the itch, from which you cannot be cured. 28The LORD will afflict you
with madness, blindness and confusion
of mind. 29At midday you will grope
about like a blind man in the dark. You
will be unsuccessful in everything you
do; day after day you will be oppressed
and robbed, with no-one to rescue you.

30You will be pledged to be married
to a woman, but another will take her
and ravish her. You will build a house,
but you will not live in it. You will plant
a vineyard, but you will not even begin
to enjoy its fruit. 31Your ox will be
slaughtered before your eyes, but you
will eat none of it. Your donkey will be
forcibly taken from you and will not be
returned. Your sheep will be given to
your enemies, and no-one will rescue
them. 32Your sons and daughters will be
given to another nation, and you will
wear out your eyes watching for them
day after day, powerless to lift a hand.
33A people that you do not know will eat
what your land and labour produce, and
you will have nothing but cruel oppression all your days. 34The sights you see
will drive you mad. 35The LORD will
afflict your knees and legs with painful
boils that cannot be cured, spreading
from the soles of your feet to the top of
your head.

36The LORD will drive you and the
king you set over you to a nation unknown to you or your fathers. There
you will worship other gods, gods of
wood and stone. 37You will become a
thing of horror and an object of scorn
and ridicule to all the nations where the
LORD will drive you.

38You will sow much seed in the field
but you will harvest little, because locusts will devour it. 39You will plant
vineyards and cultivate them but you
will not drink the wine or gather the
grapes, because worms will eat them.
40You will have olive trees throughout
your country but you will not use the oil,
because the olives will drop off. 41You
will have sons and daughters but you
will not keep them, because they will go
into captivity. 42Swarms of locusts will
take over all your trees and the crops of
your land.

43The alien who lives among you will
rise above you higher and higher, but
you will sink lower and lower. 44He will
lend to you, but you will not lend to
him. He will be the head, but you will be
the tail.

45All these curses will come upon
you. They will pursue you and overtake you until you are destroyed, because you did not obey the LORD your
God and observe the commands and
decrees he gave you. 46They will be a
sign and a wonder to you and your
descendants for ever. 47Because you did
not serve the LORD your God joyfully
and gladly in the time of prosperity,
48therefore in hunger and thirst, in
nakedness and dire poverty, you will
serve the enemies the LORD sends
against you. He will put an iron yoke on
your neck until he has destroyed you.

49The LORD will bring a nation
against you from far away, from the
ends of the earth, like an eagle swooping down, a nation whose language you
will not understand, 50a fierce-looking
nation without respect for the old or
pity for the young. 51They will devour
the young of your livestock and the
crops of your land until you are destroyed. They will leave you no grain,
new wine or oil, nor any calves of your
herds or lambs of your flocks until you
are ruined. 52They will lay siege to all
the cities throughout your land until the
high fortified walls in which you trust
fall down. They will besiege all the cities
throughout the land the LORD your God
is giving you.

53Because of the suffering that your
enemy will inflict on you during the
siege, you will eat the fruit of the womb,
the flesh of the sons and daughters the

LORD your God has given you. 54Even
the most gentle and sensitive man
among you will have no compassion on
his own brother or the wife he loves or
his surviving children, 55and he will not
give to one of them any of the flesh of his
children that he is eating. It will be all he
has left because of the suffering that
your enemy will inflict on you during
the siege of all your cities. 56The most
gentle and sensitive woman among
you—so sensitive and gentle that she
would not venture to touch the ground
with the sole of her foot—will begrudge
the husband she loves and her own
son or daughter 57the afterbirth from
her womb and the children she bears.
For she intends to eat them secretly
during the siege and in the distress
that your enemy will inflict on you in
your cities.

58If you do not carefully follow all the
words of this law, which are written in
this book, and do not revere this glorious and awesome name—the LORD
your God—59the LORD will send fearful
plagues on you and your descendants,
harsh and prolonged disasters, and
severe and lingering illnesses. 60He will
bring upon you all the diseases of Egypt
that you dreaded, and they will cling to
you. 61The LORD will also bring on you
every kind of sickness and disaster not
recorded in this Book of the Law, until
you are destroyed. 62You who were as
numerous as the stars in the sky will be
left but few in number, because you did
not obey the LORD your God. 63Just as it
pleased the LORD to make you prosper
and increase in number, so it will please
him to ruin and destroy you. You will be
uprooted from the land you are entering
to possess.

64Then the LORD will scatter you
among all nations, from one end of the
earth to the other. There you will
worship other gods—gods of wood and
stone, which neither you nor your
fathers have known. 65Among those nations you will find no repose, no resting
place for the sole of your foot. There the
LORD will give you an anxious mind,
eyes weary with longing, and a despairing heart. 66You will live in constant
suspense, filled with dread both night
and day, never sure of your life. 67In the
morning you will say, "If only it were
evening!" and in the evening, "If only it
were morning!"—because of the terror
that will fill your hearts and the sights
that your eyes will see. 68The LORD will
send you back in ships to Egypt on a
journey I said you should never make
again. There you will offer yourselves
for sale to your enemies as male and
female slaves, but no-one will buy you.

NEW TESTAMENT READING
Luke 18:1–30

The Parable of the Persistent Widow

18 Then Jesus told his disciples a
parable to show them that they
should always pray and not give up. 2He
said: "In a certain town there was a
judge who neither feared God nor cared
about men. 3And there was a widow in
that town who kept coming to him with
the plea, 'Grant me justice against my
adversary.'

4"For some time he refused. But
finally he said to himself, 'Even though I
don't fear God or care about men, 5yet
because this widow keeps bothering
me, I will see that she gets justice, so
that she won't eventually wear me out
with her coming!'"

6And the Lord said, "Listen to what
the unjust judge says. 7And will not
God bring about justice for his chosen
ones, who cry out to him day and night?
Will he keep putting them off? 8I tell
you, he will see that they get justice, and
quickly. However, when the Son of
Man comes, will he find faith on the
earth?"

The Parable of the Pharisee and the Tax Collector

9To some who were confident of their
own righteousness and looked down on

everybody else, Jesus told this parable:
10"Two men went up to the temple to
pray, one a Pharisee and the other a tax
collector. 11The Pharisee stood up and
prayed about himself: 'God, I thank
you that I am not like other men—
robbers, evildoers, adulterers—or even
like this tax collector. 12I fast twice a
week and give a tenth of all I get.'
13"But the tax collector stood at a
distance. He would not even look up to
heaven, but beat his breast and said,
'God, have mercy on me, a sinner.'
14"I tell you that this man, rather than
the other, went home justified before
God. For everyone who exalts himself
will be humbled, and he who humbles
himself will be exalted."

The Little Children and Jesus

15People were also bringing babies to
Jesus to have him touch them. When
the disciples saw this, they rebuked
them. 16But Jesus called the children to
him and said, "Let the little children
come to me, and do not hinder them,
for the kingdom of God belongs to such
as these. 17I tell you the truth, anyone
who will not receive the kingdom of
God like a little child will never enter
it."

The Rich Ruler

18A certain ruler asked him, "Good
teacher, what must I do to inherit
eternal life?"
19"Why do you call me good?" Jesus
answered. "No-one is good—except
God alone. 20You know the commandments: 'Do not commit adultery, do not
murder, do not steal, do not give false
testimony, honour your father and
mother.'"
21"All these I have kept since I was a
boy," he said.
22When Jesus heard this, he said to
him, "You still lack one thing. Sell
everything you have and give to the
poor, and you will have treasure in
heaven. Then come, follow me."
23When he heard this, he became
very sad, because he was a man of great
wealth. 24Jesus looked at him and said,
"How hard it is for the rich to enter the
kingdom of God! 25Indeed, it is easier
for a camel to go through the eye of a
needle than for a rich man to enter the
kingdom of God."
26Those who heard this asked, "Who
then can be saved?"
27Jesus replied, "What is impossible
with men is possible with God."
28Peter said to him, "We have left all
we had to follow you!"
29"I tell you the truth," Jesus said to
them, "no-one who has left home or
wife or brothers or parents or children
for the sake of the kingdom of God
30will fail to receive many times as much
in this age and, in the age to come,
eternal life."

READING FROM PSALMS
Psalm 47:1–9

For the director of music. Of the Sons of Korah. A psalm.

1Clap your hands, all you nations;
shout to God with cries of joy.
2How awesome is the LORD Most High,
the great King over all the earth!
3He subdued nations under us,
peoples under our feet.
4He chose our inheritance for us,
the pride of Jacob, whom he loved.
Selah

5God has ascended amid shouts of joy,
the LORD amid the sounding of trumpets.
6Sing praises to God, sing praises;
sing praises to our King, sing praises.

7For God is the King of all the earth;
sing to him a psalm of praise.
8God reigns over the nations;
God is seated on his holy throne.

[9]The nobles of the nations assemble
as the people of the God of
Abraham,
for the kings of the earth belong to
God;
he is greatly exalted.

DAY 108

APRIL 18

OLD TESTAMENT READING
Deuteronomy 29:1–30:10

Renewal of the Covenant

29 These are the terms of the covenant the LORD commanded Moses to make with the Israelites in Moab, in addition to the covenant he had made with them at Horeb.

[2]Moses summoned all the Israelites and said to them:

Your eyes have seen all that the LORD did in Egypt to Pharaoh, to all his officials and to all his land. [3]With your
own eyes you saw those great trials, those miraculous signs and great wonders. [4]But to this day the LORD has not
given you a mind that understands or
eyes that see or ears that hear. [5]During
the forty years that I led you through the desert, your clothes did not wear out, nor did the sandals on your feet. [6]You
ate no bread and drank no wine or other fermented drink. I did this so that you might know that I am the LORD your God.

[7]When you reached this place, Sihon king of Heshbon and Og king of Bashan came out to fight against us, but we
defeated them. [8]We took their land and
gave it as an inheritance to the Reubenites, the Gadites and the half-tribe of Manasseh.

[9]Carefully follow the terms of this covenant, so that you may prosper in
everything you do. [10]All of you are
standing today in the presence of the LORD your God—your leaders and chief men, your elders and officials, and all the other men of Israel, [11]together
with your children and your wives, and the aliens living in your camps who chop
your wood and carry your water. [12]You
are standing here in order to enter into a covenant with the LORD your God, a covenant the LORD is making with you
this day and sealing with an oath, [13]to
confirm you this day as his people, that he may be your God as he promised you and as he swore to your fathers, Abraham, Isaac and Jacob. [14]I am making
this covenant, with its oath, not only
with you [15]who are standing here with
us today in the presence of the LORD our God but also with those who are not here today.

[16]You yourselves know how we lived in Egypt and how we passed through the
countries on the way here. [17]You saw
among them their detestable images and idols of wood and stone, of silver
and gold. [18]Make sure there is no man
or woman, clan or tribe among you today whose heart turns away from the LORD our God to go and worship the gods of those nations; make sure there is no root among you that produces such bitter poison.

[19]When such a person hears the words of this oath, he invokes a blessing on himself and therefore thinks, "I will be safe, even though I persist in going my own way." This will bring disaster
on the watered land as well as the dry.
[20]The LORD will never be willing to forgive him; his wrath and zeal will burn against that man. All the curses written in this book will fall upon him, and the LORD will blot out his name from under
heaven. [21]The LORD will single him out

from all the tribes of Israel for disaster, according to all the curses of the covenant written in this Book of the Law.

22Your children who follow you in later generations and foreigners who come from distant lands will see the calamities that have fallen on the land and the diseases with which the LORD has afflicted it. 23The whole land will be a burning waste of salt and sulphur—nothing planted, nothing sprouting, no vegetation growing on it. It will be like the destruction of Sodom and Gomorrah, Admah and Zeboiim, which the LORD overthrew in fierce anger. 24All the nations will ask: "Why has the LORD done this to this land? Why this fierce, burning anger?"

25And the answer will be: "It is because this people abandoned the covenant of the LORD, the God of their fathers, the covenant he made with them when he brought them out of Egypt. 26They went off and worshipped other gods and bowed down to them, gods they did not know, gods he had not given them. 27Therefore the LORD's anger burned against this land, so that he brought on it all the curses written in this book. 28In furious anger and in great wrath the LORD uprooted them from their land and thrust them into another land, as it is now."

29The secret things belong to the LORD our God, but the things revealed belong to us and to our children for ever, that we may follow all the words of this law.

Prosperity After Turning to the LORD

30 When all these blessings and curses I have set before you come upon you and you take them to heart wherever the LORD your God disperses you among the nations, 2and when you and your children return to the LORD your God and obey him with all your heart and with all your soul according to everything I command you today, 3then the LORD your God will restore your fortunes and have compassion on you and gather you again from all the nations where he scattered you. 4Even if you have been banished to the most distant land under the heavens, from there the LORD your God will gather you and bring you back. 5He will bring you to the land that belonged to your fathers, and you will take possession of it. He will make you more prosperous and numerous than your fathers. 6The LORD your God will circumcise your hearts and the hearts of your descendants, so that you may love him with all your heart and with all your soul, and live. 7The LORD your God will put all these curses on your enemies who hate and persecute you. 8You will again obey the LORD and follow all his commands I am giving you today. 9Then the LORD your God will make you most prosperous in all the work of your hands and in the fruit of your womb, the young of your livestock and the crops of your land. The LORD will again delight in you and make you prosperous, just as he delighted in your fathers, 10if you obey the LORD your God and keep his commands and decrees that are written in this Book of the Law and turn to the LORD your God with all your heart and with all your soul.

NEW TESTAMENT READING
Luke 18:31–19:10

Jesus Again Predicts His Death

31Jesus took the Twelve aside and told them, "We are going up to Jerusalem, and everything that is written by the prophets about the Son of Man will be fulfilled. 32He will be turned over to the Gentiles. They will mock him, insult him, spit on him, flog him and kill him. 33On the third day he will rise again."

34The disciples did not understand any of this. Its meaning was hidden from them, and they did not know what he was talking about.

A Blind Beggar Receives His Sight

35As Jesus approached Jericho, a
blind man was sitting by the roadside
begging. 36When he heard the crowd
going by, he asked what was happening.
37They told him, "Jesus of Nazareth is
passing by."
38He called out, "Jesus, Son of
David, have mercy on me!"
39Those who led the way rebuked him
and told him to be quiet, but he shouted
all the more, "Son of David, have
mercy on me!"
40Jesus stopped and ordered the man
to be brought to him. When he came
near, Jesus asked him, 41"What do you
want me to do for you?"
"Lord, I want to see," he replied.
42Jesus said to him, "Receive your
sight; your faith has healed you."
43Immediately he received his sight and
followed Jesus, praising God. When all
the people saw it, they also praised
God.

Zacchaeus the Tax Collector

19 Jesus entered Jericho and was
passing through. 2A man was
there by the name of Zacchaeus; he
was a chief tax collector and was
wealthy. 3He wanted to see who Jesus
was, but being a short man he could not,
because of the crowd. 4So he ran ahead
and climbed a sycamore-fig tree to see
him, since Jesus was coming that way.
5When Jesus reached the spot, he
looked up and said to him, "Zacchaeus,
come down immediately. I must stay at
your house today." 6So he came down
at once and welcomed him gladly.
7All the people saw this and began to
mutter, "He has gone to be the guest of
a 'sinner'."
8But Zacchaeus stood up and said to
the Lord, "Look, Lord! Here and now I
give half of my possessions to the poor,
and if I have cheated anybody out of
anything, I will pay back four times the
amount."
9Jesus said to him, "Today salvation
has come to this house, because this
man, too, is a son of Abraham. 10For
the Son of Man came to seek and to save
what was lost."

READING FROM PROVERBS

Proverbs 10:1–10

Proverbs of Solomon

10 The proverbs of Solomon:

A wise son brings joy to his father,
but a foolish son grief to his
mother.

2Ill-gotten treasures are of no value,
but righteousness delivers from
death.

3The LORD does not let the righteous
go hungry
but he thwarts the craving of the
wicked.

4Lazy hands make a man poor,
but diligent hands bring wealth.

5He who gathers crops in summer is a
wise son,
but he who sleeps during harvest is
a disgraceful son.

6Blessings crown the head of the
righteous,
but violence overwhelms the
mouth of the wicked.

7The memory of the righteous will be
a blessing,
but the name of the wicked will
rot.

8The wise in heart accept commands,
but a chattering fool comes to ruin.

9The man of integrity walks securely,
but he who takes crooked paths
will be found out.

10He who winks maliciously causes
grief,
and a chattering fool comes to ruin.

APRIL 19

DAY 109

OLD TESTAMENT READING
Deuteronomy 30:11–31:29

The Offer of Life or Death

[11]Now what I am commanding you
today is not too difficult for you or
beyond your reach. [12]It is not up in
heaven, so that you have to ask, "Who
will ascend into heaven to get it and
proclaim it to us so that we may obey
it?" [13]Nor is it beyond the sea, so that
you have to ask, "Who will cross the sea
to get it and proclaim it to us so that we
may obey it?" [14]No, the word is very
near you; it is in your mouth and in your
heart so that you may obey it.

[15]See, I set before you today life and
prosperity, death and destruction. [16]For
I command you today to love the LORD
your God, to walk in his ways, and to
keep his commands, decrees and laws;
then you will live and increase, and the
LORD your God will bless you in the
land you are entering to possess.

[17]But if your heart turns away and
you are not obedient, and if you are
drawn away to bow down to other gods
and worship them, [18]I declare to you
this day that you will certainly be destroyed. You will not live long in the
land you are crossing the Jordan to
enter and possess.

[19]This day I call heaven and earth as
witnesses against you that I have set
before you life and death, blessings and
curses. Now choose life, so that you and
your children may live [20]and that you
may love the LORD your God, listen to
his voice, and hold fast to him. For the
LORD is your life, and he will give you
many years in the land he swore to give
to your fathers, Abraham, Isaac and
Jacob.

Joshua to Succeed Moses

31 Then Moses went out and spoke
these words to all Israel: [2]"I am
now a hundred and twenty years old and
I am no longer able to lead you. The
LORD has said to me, 'You shall not
cross the Jordan.' [3]The LORD your God
himself will cross over ahead of you. He
will destroy these nations before you,
and you will take possession of their
land. Joshua also will cross over ahead
of you, as the LORD said. [4]And the
LORD will do to them what he did to
Sihon and Og, the kings of the Amorites, whom he destroyed along with
their land. [5]The LORD will deliver them
to you, and you must do to them all that
I have commanded you. [6]Be strong and
courageous. Do not be afraid or terrified because of them, for the LORD
your God goes with you; he will never
leave you nor forsake you."

[7]Then Moses summoned Joshua and
said to him in the presence of all Israel,
"Be strong and courageous, for you
must go with this people into the land
that the LORD swore to their forefathers
to give them, and you must divide it
among them as their inheritance. [8]The
LORD himself goes before you and will
be with you; he will never leave you nor
forsake you. Do not be afraid; do not be
discouraged."

The Reading of the Law

[9]So Moses wrote down this law and
gave it to the priests, the sons of Levi,
who carried the ark of the covenant of
the LORD, and to all the elders of Israel.
[10]Then Moses commanded them: "At
the end of every seven years, in the year
for cancelling debts, during the Feast of
Tabernacles, [11]when all Israel comes to
appear before the LORD your God at the
place he will choose, you shall read this
law before them in their hearing.
[12]Assemble the people—men, women
and children, and the aliens living in
your towns—so that they can listen and
learn to fear the LORD your God and
follow carefully all the words of this law.
[13]Their children, who do not know this

law, must hear it and learn to fear the
LORD your God as long as you live in
the land you are crossing the Jordan to
possess."

Israel's Rebellion Predicted

14The LORD said to Moses, "Now the
day of your death is near. Call Joshua
and present yourselves at the Tent of
Meeting, where I will commission
him." So Moses and Joshua came and
presented themselves at the Tent of
Meeting.
15Then the LORD appeared at the
Tent in a pillar of cloud, and the cloud
stood over the entrance to the Tent.
16And the LORD said to Moses: "You
are going to rest with your fathers, and
these people will soon prostitute themselves to the foreign gods of the land
they are entering. They will forsake me
and break the covenant I made with
them. 17On that day I will become angry
with them and forsake them; I will hide
my face from them, and they will be
destroyed. Many disasters and difficulties will come upon them, and on that
day they will ask, 'Have not these disasters come upon us because our God is
not with us?' 18And I will certainly hide
my face on that day because of all their
wickedness in turning to other gods.
19"Now write down for yourselves
this song and teach it to the Israelites
and make them sing it, so that it may be
a witness for me against them. 20When I
have brought them into the land flowing
with milk and honey, the land I promised on oath to their forefathers, and
when they eat their fill and thrive, they
will turn to other gods and worship
them, rejecting me and breaking my
covenant. 21And when many disasters
and difficulties come upon them, this
song will testify against them, because it
will not be forgotten by their descendants. I know what they are disposed to
do, even before I bring them into the
land I promised them on oath." 22So
Moses wrote down this song that day
and taught it to the Israelites.
23The LORD gave this command to
Joshua son of Nun: "Be strong and
courageous, for you will bring the
Israelites into the land I promised them
on oath, and I myself will be with you."
24After Moses finished writing in a
book the words of this law from beginning to end, 25he gave this command to
the Levites who carried the ark of the
covenant of the LORD: 26"Take this
Book of the Law and place it beside the
ark of the covenant of the LORD your
God. There it will remain as a witness
against you. 27For I know how rebellious and stiff-necked you are. If you
have been rebellious against the LORD
while I am still alive and with you, how
much more will you rebel after I die!
28Assemble before me all the elders of
your tribes and all your officials, so that
I can speak these words in their hearing
and call heaven and earth to testify
against them. 29For I know that after my
death you are sure to become utterly
corrupt and to turn from the way I have
commanded you. In days to come, disaster will fall upon you because you will
do evil in the sight of the LORD and
provoke him to anger by what your
hands have made."

NEW TESTAMENT READING

Luke 19:11–44

The Parable of the Ten Minas

11While they were listening to this, he
went on to tell them a parable, because
he was near Jerusalem and the people
thought that the kingdom of God was
going to appear at once. 12He said: "A
man of noble birth went to a distant
country to have himself appointed king
and then to return. 13So he called ten of
his servants and gave them ten minas.
'Put this money to work,' he said, 'until
I come back.'
14"But his subjects hated him and
sent a delegation after him to say, 'We
don't want this man to be our king.'
15"He was made king, however, and
returned home. Then he sent for the
servants to whom he had given the

money, in order to find out what they
had gained with it.
16"The first one came and said, 'Sir,
your mina has earned ten more.'
17" 'Well done, my good servant!' his
master replied. 'Because you have been
trustworthy in a very small matter, take
charge of ten cities.'
18"The second came and said, 'Sir,
your mina has earned five more.'
19"His master answered, 'You take
charge of five cities.'
20"Then another servant came and
said, 'Sir, here is your mina; I have kept
it laid away in a piece of cloth. 21I was
afraid of you, because you are a hard
man. You take out what you did not put
in and reap what you did not sow.'
22"His master replied, 'I will judge
you by your own words, you wicked
servant! You knew, did you, that I am a
hard man, taking out what I did not put
in, and reaping what I did not sow?
23Why then didn't you put my money on
deposit, so that when I came back, I
could have collected it with interest?'
24"Then he said to those standing by,
'Take his mina away from him and give
it to the one who has ten minas.'
25" 'Sir,' they said, 'he already has
ten!'
26"He replied, 'I tell you that to
everyone who has, more will be given,
but as for the one who has nothing, even
what he has will be taken away. 27But
those enemies of mine who did not want
me to be a king over them—bring them
here and kill them in front of me.' "

The Triumphal Entry

28After Jesus had said this, he went
on ahead, going up to Jerusalem. 29As
he approached Bethphage and Bethany
at the hill called the Mount of Olives, he
sent two of his disciples, saying to them,
30"Go to the village ahead of you, and
as you enter it, you will find a colt tied
there, which no-one has ever ridden.
Untie it and bring it here. 31If anyone
asks you, 'Why are you untying it?' tell
him, 'The Lord needs it.' "

32Those who were sent ahead went
and found it just as he had told them.
33As they were untying the colt, its
owners asked them, "Why are you untying the colt?"
34They replied, "The Lord needs it."
35They brought it to Jesus, threw
their cloaks on the colt and put Jesus on
it. 36As he went along, people spread
their cloaks on the road.
37When he came near the place where
the road goes down the Mount of
Olives, the whole crowd of disciples
began joyfully to praise God in loud
voices for all the miracles they had seen:

38"Blessed is the king who comes in the
name of the Lord!"

"Peace in heaven and glory in the
highest!"

39Some of the Pharisees in the crowd
said to Jesus, "Teacher, rebuke your
disciples!"
40"I tell you," he replied, "if they
keep quiet, the stones will cry out."
41As he approached Jerusalem and
saw the city, he wept over it 42and said,
"If you, even you, had only known on
this day what would bring you peace
—but now it is hidden from your eyes.
43The days will come upon you when
your enemies will build an embankment
against you and encircle you and hem
you in on every side. 44They will dash
you to the ground, you and the children
within your walls. They will not leave
one stone on another, because you did
not recognise the time of God's coming
to you."

READING FROM PSALMS

Psalm 48:1–8

A song. A psalm of the Sons of Korah.

1Great is the LORD, and most worthy
of praise,
in the city of our God, his holy
mountain.

[2]It is beautiful in its loftiness,
the joy of the whole earth.
Like the utmost heights of Zaphon is
Mount Zion,
the city of the Great King.
[3]God is in her citadels;
he has shown himself to be her
fortress.

[4]When the kings joined forces,
when they advanced together,
[5]they saw ⌞her⌟ and were astounded;
they fled in terror.
[6]Trembling seized them there,
pain like that of a woman in
labour.
[7]You destroyed them like ships of
Tarshish
shattered by an east wind.

[8]As we have heard,
so have we seen
in the city of the LORD Almighty,
in the city of our God:
God makes her secure for ever.
Selah

DAY 110

APRIL 20

OLD TESTAMENT READING
Deuteronomy 31:30–32:52

The Song of Moses

[30]And Moses recited the words of this song from beginning to end in the hearing of the whole assembly of Israel:

32 Listen, O heavens, and I will
speak;
hear, O earth, the words of my
mouth.
[2]Let my teaching fall like rain
and my words descend like dew,
like showers on new grass,
like abundant rain on tender
plants.

[3]I will proclaim the name of the LORD.
Oh, praise the greatness of our
God!
[4]He is the Rock, his works are perfect,
and all his ways are just.
A faithful God who does no wrong,
upright and just is he.

[5]They have acted corruptly towards
him;
to their shame they are no longer
his children,
but a warped and crooked
generation.
[6]Is this the way you repay the LORD,
O foolish and unwise people?
Is he not your Father, your Creator,
who made you and formed you?

[7]Remember the days of old;
consider the generations long past.
Ask your father and he will tell you,
your elders, and they will explain
to you.
[8]When the Most High gave the
nations their inheritance,
when he divided all mankind,
he set up boundaries for the peoples
according to the number of the
sons of Israel.
[9]For the LORD's portion is his people,
Jacob his allotted inheritance.

[10]In a desert land he found him,
in a barren and howling waste.
He shielded him and cared for him;
he guarded him as the apple of his
eye,
[11]like an eagle that stirs up its nest
and hovers over its young,
that spreads its wings to catch them
and carries them on its pinions.
[12]The LORD alone led him;
no foreign god was with him.

13He made him ride on the heights of the land
and fed him with the fruit of the fields.
He nourished him with honey from the rock,
and with oil from the flinty crag,
14with curds and milk from herd and flock
and with fattened lambs and goats,
with choice rams of Bashan
and the finest grains of wheat.
You drank the foaming blood of the grape.

15Jeshurun grew fat and kicked;
filled with food, he became heavy and sleek.
He abandoned the God who made him
and rejected the Rock his Saviour.
16They made him jealous with their foreign gods
and angered him with their detestable idols.
17They sacrificed to demons, which are not God—
gods they had not known,
gods that recently appeared,
gods your fathers did not fear.
18You deserted the Rock, who fathered you;
you forgot the God who gave you birth.

19The LORD saw this and rejected them
because he was angered by his sons and daughters.
20"I will hide my face from them," he said,
"and see what their end will be;
for they are a perverse generation,
children who are unfaithful.
21They made me jealous by what is no god
and angered me with their worthless idols.
I will make them envious by those who are not a people;
I will make them angry by a nation that has no understanding.
22For a fire has been kindled by my wrath,
one that burns to the realm of death below.
It will devour the earth and its harvests
and set on fire the foundations of the mountains.

23"I will heap calamities upon them
and expend my arrows against them.
24I will send wasting famine against them,
consuming pestilence and deadly plague;
I will send against them the fangs of wild beasts,
the venom of vipers that glide in the dust.
25In the street the sword will make them childless;
in their homes terror will reign.
Young men and young women will perish,
infants and grey-haired men.
26I said I would scatter them
and blot out their memory from mankind,
27but I dreaded the taunt of the enemy,
lest the adversary misunderstand
and say, 'Our hand has triumphed;
the LORD has not done all this.'"

28They are a nation without sense,
there is no discernment in them.
29If only they were wise and would understand this
and discern what their end will be!
30How could one man chase a thousand,
or two put ten thousand to flight,
unless their Rock had sold them,
unless the LORD had given them up?
31For their rock is not like our Rock,
as even our enemies concede.
32Their vine comes from the vine of Sodom
and from the fields of Gomorrah.
Their grapes are filled with poison,
and their clusters with bitterness.

33Their wine is the venom of serpents,
the deadly poison of cobras.

34"Have I not kept this in reserve
and sealed it in my vaults?
35It is mine to avenge; I will repay.
In due time their foot will slip;
their day of disaster is near
and their doom rushes upon
them."

36The LORD will judge his people
and have compassion on his
servants
when he sees their strength is gone
and no-one is left, slave or free.
37He will say: "Now where are their
gods,
the rock they took refuge in,
38the gods who ate the fat of their
sacrifices
and drank the wine of their drink
offerings?
Let them rise up to help you!
Let them give you shelter!

39"See now that I myself am He!
There is no god besides me.
I put to death and I bring to life,
I have wounded and I will heal,
and no-one can deliver out of my
hand.
40I lift my hand to heaven and declare:
As surely as I live for ever,
41when I sharpen my flashing sword
and my hand grasps it in judgment,
I will take vengeance on my
adversaries
and repay those who hate me.
42I will make my arrows drunk with
blood,
while my sword devours flesh:
the blood of the slain and the
captives,
the heads of the enemy leaders."

43Rejoice, O nations, with his people,
for he will avenge the blood of his
servants;
he will take vengeance on his enemies
and make atonement for his land
and people.

44Moses came with Joshua son of Nun
and spoke all the words of this song in
the hearing of the people. 45When
Moses finished reciting all these words
to all Israel, 46he said to them, "Take to
heart all the words I have solemnly declared to you this day, so that you may
command your children to obey carefully all the words of this law. 47They are
not just idle words for you—they are
your life. By them you will live long in
the land you are crossing the Jordan to
possess."

Moses to Die on Mount Nebo

48On that same day the LORD told
Moses, 49"Go up into the Abarim
Range to Mount Nebo in Moab, across
from Jericho, and view Canaan, the
land I am giving the Israelites as their
own possession. 50There on the mountain that you have climbed you will die
and be gathered to your people, just as
your brother Aaron died on Mount Hor
and was gathered to his people. 51This is
because both of you broke faith with me
in the presence of the Israelites at the
waters of Meribah Kadesh in the Desert
of Zin and because you did not uphold
my holiness among the Israelites.
52Therefore, you will see the land only
from a distance; you will not enter the
land I am giving to the people of Israel."

NEW TESTAMENT READING
Luke 19:45–20:26

Jesus at the Temple

45Then he entered the temple area
and began driving out those who were
selling. 46"It is written," he said to
them, "'My house will be a house of
prayer'; but you have made it 'a den of
robbers'."

47Every day he was teaching at the
temple. But the chief priests, the
teachers of the law and the leaders
among the people were trying to kill

him. 48Yet they could not find any way
to do it, because all the people hung on
his words.

The Authority of Jesus Questioned

20 One day as he was teaching the
people in the temple courts and
preaching the gospel, the chief priests
and the teachers of the law, together
with the elders, came up to him. 2"Tell
us by what authority you are doing these
things," they said. "Who gave you this
authority?"
3He replied, "I will also ask you a
question. Tell me, 4John's baptism—
was it from heaven, or from men?"
5They discussed it among themselves
and said, "If we say, 'From heaven', he
will ask, 'Why didn't you believe him?'
6But if we say, 'From men', all the
people will stone us, because they are
persuaded that John was a prophet."
7So they answered, "We don't know
where it was from."
8Jesus said, "Neither will I tell you by
what authority I am doing these
things."

The Parable of the Tenants

9He went on to tell the people this
parable: "A man planted a vineyard,
rented it to some farmers and went
away for a long time. 10At harvest time
he sent a servant to the tenants so they
would give him some of the fruit of the
vineyard. But the tenants beat him and
sent him away empty-handed. 11He sent
another servant, but that one also they
beat and treated shamefully and sent
away empty-handed. 12He sent still a
third, and they wounded him and threw
him out.
13"Then the owner of the vineyard
said, 'What shall I do? I will send my
son, whom I love; perhaps they will
respect him.'
14"But when the tenants saw him,
they talked the matter over. 'This is the
heir,' they said. 'Let's kill him, and the
inheritance will be ours.' 15So they
threw him out of the vineyard and killed
him.
"What then will the owner of the
vineyard do to them? 16He will come
and kill those tenants and give the
vineyard to others."
When the people heard this, they
said, "May this never be!"
17Jesus looked directly at them and
asked, "Then what is the meaning of
that which is written:

" 'The stone the builders rejected
has become the capstone' ?

18Everyone who falls on that stone will
be broken to pieces, but he on whom it
falls will be crushed."
19The teachers of the law and the
chief priests looked for a way to arrest
him immediately, because they knew he
had spoken this parable against them.
But they were afraid of the people.

Paying Taxes to Caesar

20Keeping a close watch on him, they
sent spies, who pretended to be honest.
They hoped to catch Jesus in something
he said so that they might hand him over
to the power and authority of the governor. 21So the spies questioned him:
"Teacher, we know that you speak and
teach what is right, and that you do not
show partiality but teach the way of
God in accordance with the truth. 22Is it
right for us to pay taxes to Caesar or
not?"
23He saw through their duplicity and
said to them, 24"Show me a denarius.
Whose portrait and inscription are on
it?"
25"Caesar's," they replied.
He said to them, "Then give to
Caesar what is Caesar's, and to God
what is God's."
26They were unable to trap him in
what he had said there in public. And
astonished by his answer, they became
silent.

READING FROM PSALMS
Psalm 48:9–14

9Within your temple, O God,
we meditate on your unfailing
love.
10Like your name, O God,
your praise reaches to the ends of
the earth;
your right hand is filled with
righteousness.
11Mount Zion rejoices,
the villages of Judah are glad
because of your judgments.

12Walk about Zion, go round her,
count her towers,
13consider well her ramparts,
view her citadels,
that you may tell of them to the
next generation.
14For this God is our God for ever and
ever;
he will be our guide even to the
end.

DAY 111

APRIL 21

OLD TESTAMENT READING
Deuteronomy 33:1–34:12

Moses Blesses the Tribes

33 This is the blessing that Moses
the man of God pronounced on
the Israelites before his death. 2He said:

"The LORD came from Sinai
and dawned over them from Seir;
he shone forth from Mount Paran.
He came with myriads of holy ones
from the south, from his mountain
slopes.
3Surely it is you who love the people;
all the holy ones are in your hand.
At your feet they all bow down,
and from you receive instruction,
4the law that Moses gave us,
the possession of the assembly of
Jacob.
5He was king over Jeshurun
when the leaders of the people
assembled,
along with the tribes of Israel.

6"Let Reuben live and not die,
nor his men be few."

7And this he said about Judah:

"Hear, O LORD, the cry of Judah;
bring him to his people.
With his own hands he defends his
cause.
Oh, be his help against his foes!"

8About Levi he said:

"Your Thummim and Urim belong
to the man you favoured.
You tested him at Massah;
you contended with him at the
waters of Meribah.
9He said of his father and mother,
'I have no regard for them.'
He did not recognise his brothers
or acknowledge his own children,
but he watched over your word
and guarded your covenant.
10He teaches your precepts to Jacob
and your law to Israel.
He offers incense before you
and whole burnt offerings on your
altar.
11Bless all his skills, O LORD,
and be pleased with the work of his
hands.
Smite the loins of those who rise up
against him;
strike his foes till they rise no
more."

12About Benjamin he said:

"Let the beloved of the LORD rest
secure in him,
for he shields him all day long,
and the one the LORD loves rests
between his shoulders."

13About Joseph he said:

"May the LORD bless his land
with the precious dew from heaven
above
and with the deep waters that lie
below;
14with the best the sun brings forth
and the finest the moon can yield;
15with the choicest gifts of the ancient
mountains
and the fruitfulness of the
everlasting hills;
16with the best gifts of the earth and its
fulness
and the favour of him who dwelt in
the burning bush.
Let all these rest on the head of
Joseph,
on the brow of the prince among
his brothers.
17In majesty he is like a firstborn bull;
his horns are the horns of a wild ox.
With them he will gore the nations,
even those at the ends of the earth.
Such are the ten thousands of
Ephraim;
such are the thousands of
Manasseh."

18About Zebulun he said:

"Rejoice, Zebulun, in your going
out,
and you, Issachar, in your tents.
19They will summon peoples to the
mountain
and there offer sacrifices of
righteousness;
they will feast on the abundance of
the seas,
on the treasures hidden in the
sand."

20About Gad he said:

"Blessed is he who enlarges Gad's
domain!
Gad lives there like a lion,
tearing at arm or head.
21He chose the best land for himself;
the leader's portion was kept for
him.
When the heads of the people
assembled,
he carried out the LORD's righteous
will,
and his judgments concerning
Israel."

22About Dan he said:

"Dan is a lion's cub,
springing out of Bashan."

23About Naphtali he said:

"Naphtali is abounding with the
favour of the LORD
and is full of his blessing;
he will inherit southward to the
lake."

24About Asher he said:

"Most blessed of sons is Asher;
let him be favoured by his
brothers,
and let him bathe his feet in oil.
25The bolts of your gates will be iron
and bronze,
and your strength will equal your
days.

26"There is no-one like the God of
Jeshurun,
who rides on the heavens to help
you
and on the clouds in his majesty.
27The eternal God is your refuge,
and underneath are the everlasting
arms.
He will drive out your enemy before
you,
saying, 'Destroy him!'

[28]So Israel will live in safety alone;
Jacob's spring is secure
in a land of grain and new wine,
where the heavens drop dew.
[29]Blessed are you, O Israel!
Who is like you,
a people saved by the LORD?
He is your shield and helper
and your glorious sword.
Your enemies will cower before you,
and you will trample down their
high places."

The Death of Moses

34 Then Moses climbed Mount Nebo from the plains of Moab to the top of Pisgah, across from Jericho. There the LORD showed him the whole land—from Gilead to Dan, [2]all of Naphtali, the territory of Ephraim and Manasseh, all the land of Judah as far as the western sea, [3]the Negev and the whole region from the Valley of Jericho, the City of Palms, as far as Zoar. [4]Then the LORD said to him, "This is the land I promised on oath to Abraham, Isaac and Jacob when I said, 'I will give it to your descendants.' I have let you see it with your eyes, but you will not cross over into it."

[5]And Moses the servant of the LORD died there in Moab, as the LORD had said. [6]He buried him in Moab, in the valley opposite Beth Peor, but to this day no-one knows where his grave is. [7]Moses was a hundred and twenty years old when he died, yet his eyes were not weak nor his strength gone. [8]The Israelites grieved for Moses in the plains of Moab thirty days, until the time of weeping and mourning was over.

[9]Now Joshua son of Nun was filled with the spirit of wisdom because Moses had laid his hands on him. So the Israelites listened to him and did what the LORD had commanded Moses.

[10]Since then, no prophet has risen in Israel like Moses, whom the LORD knew face to face, [11]who did all those miraculous signs and wonders the LORD sent him to do in Egypt—to Pharaoh and to all his officials and to his whole land. [12]For no-one has ever shown the mighty power or performed the awesome deeds that Moses did in the sight of all Israel.

NEW TESTAMENT READING
Luke 20:27–21:4

The Resurrection and Marriage

[27]Some of the Sadducees, who say there is no resurrection, came to Jesus with a question. [28]"Teacher," they said, "Moses wrote for us that if a man's brother dies and leaves a wife but no children, the man must marry the widow and have children for his brother. [29]Now there were seven brothers. The first one married a woman and died childless. [30]The second [31]and then the third married her, and in the same way the seven died, leaving no children. [32]Finally, the woman died too. [33]Now then, at the resurrection whose wife will she be, since the seven were married to her?"

[34]Jesus replied, "The people of this age marry and are given in marriage. [35]But those who are considered worthy of taking part in that age and in the resurrection from the dead will neither marry nor be given in marriage, [36]and they can no longer die; for they are like the angels. They are God's children, since they are children of the resurrection. [37]But in the account of the bush, even Moses showed that the dead rise, for he calls the Lord 'the God of Abraham, and the God of Isaac, and the God of Jacob'. [38]He is not the God of the dead, but of the living, for to him all are alive."

[39]Some of the teachers of the law responded, "Well said, teacher!" [40]And no-one dared to ask him any more questions.

Whose Son Is the Christ?

[41]Then Jesus said to them, "How is it that they say the Christ is the Son of

David? 42David himself declares in the
Book of Psalms:

" 'The Lord said to my Lord:
"Sit at my right hand
43until I make your enemies
a footstool for your feet." '

44David calls him 'Lord'. How then can
he be his son?"
45While all the people were listening,
Jesus said to his disciples, 46"Beware of
the teachers of the law. They like to
walk around in flowing robes and love
to be greeted in the market-places and
have the most important seats in the
synagogues and the places of honour at
banquets. 47They devour widows'
houses and for a show make lengthy
prayers. Such men will be punished
most severely."

The Widow's Offering

21 As he looked up, Jesus saw the
rich putting their gifts into the
temple treasury. 2He also saw a poor
widow put in two very small copper
coins. 3"I tell you the truth," he said,
"this poor widow has put in more than
all the others. 4All these people gave
their gifts out of their wealth; but she
out of her poverty put in all she had to
live on."

READING FROM PSALMS
Psalm 49:1–20

For the director of music. Of the Sons of Korah. A psalm.

1Hear this, all you peoples;
listen, all who live in this world,
2both low and high,
rich and poor alike:
3My mouth will speak words of
wisdom;
the utterance from my heart will
give understanding.

4I will turn my ear to a proverb;
with the harp I will expound my
riddle:

5Why should I fear when evil days
come,
when wicked deceivers surround
me—
6those who trust in their wealth
and boast of their great riches?
7No man can redeem the life of
another
or give to God a ransom for him—
8the ransom for a life is costly,
no payment is ever enough—
9that he should live on for ever
and not see decay.

10For all can see that wise men die;
the foolish and the senseless alike
perish
and leave their wealth to others.
11Their tombs will remain their houses
for ever,
their dwellings for endless
generations,
though they had named lands after
themselves.

12But man, despite his riches, does not
endure;
he is like the beasts that perish.

13This is the fate of those who trust in
themselves,
and of their followers, who
approve their sayings. *Selah*
14Like sheep they are destined for the
grave,
and death will feed on them.
The upright will rule over them in the
morning;
their forms will decay in the grave,
far from their princely mansions.
15But God will redeem my life from the
grave;
he will surely take me to himself.
Selah

16Do not be overawed when a man
grows rich,
when the splendour of his house
increases;

[17]for he will take nothing with him
when he dies,
his splendour will not descend with
him.
[18]Though while he lived he counted
himself blessed—
and men praise you when you
prosper—
[19]he will join the generation of his
fathers,
who will never see the light ⌞of
life⌟.

[20]A man who has riches without
understanding
is like the beasts that perish.

DAY 112

APRIL 22

OLD TESTAMENT READING
Joshua 1:1–2:24

The LORD Commands Joshua

1 After the death of Moses the servant of the LORD, the LORD said to
Joshua son of Nun, Moses' assistant:
[2]"Moses my servant is dead. Now then,
you and all these people, get ready to
cross the Jordan River into the land I
am about to give to them—to the
Israelites. [3]I will give you every place
where you set your foot, as I promised
Moses. [4]Your territory will extend from
the desert to Lebanon, and from the
great river, the Euphrates—all the Hittite country—to the Great Sea on the
west. [5]No-one will be able to stand up
against you all the days of your life. As I
was with Moses, so I will be with you; I
will never leave you nor forsake you.

[6]"Be strong and courageous, because
you will lead these people to inherit the
land I swore to their forefathers to give
them. [7]Be strong and very courageous.
Be careful to obey all the law my servant
Moses gave you; do not turn from it to
the right or to the left, that you may be
successful wherever you go. [8]Do not let
this Book of the Law depart from your
mouth; meditate on it day and night, so
that you may be careful to do everything
written in it. Then you will be prosperous and successful. [9]Have I not
commanded you? Be strong and
courageous. Do not be terrified; do not
be discouraged, for the LORD your God
will be with you wherever you go."

[10]So Joshua ordered the officers of
the people: [11]"Go through the camp
and tell the people, 'Get your supplies
ready. Three days from now you will
cross the Jordan here to go in and take
possession of the land the LORD your
God is giving you for your own.' "

[12]But to the Reubenites, the Gadites
and the half-tribe of Manasseh, Joshua
said, [13]"Remember the command that
Moses the servant of the LORD gave
you: 'The LORD your God is giving you
rest and has granted you this land.'
[14]Your wives, your children and your
livestock may stay in the land that
Moses gave you east of the Jordan, but
all your fighting men, fully armed, must
cross over ahead of your brothers. You
are to help your brothers [15]until the
LORD gives them rest, as he has done for
you, and until they too have taken possession of the land that the LORD your
God is giving them. After that, you may
go back and occupy your own land,
which Moses the servant of the LORD
gave you east of the Jordan towards the
sunrise."

[16]Then they answered Joshua,
"Whatever you have commanded us we
will do, and wherever you send us we
will go. [17]Just as we fully obeyed Moses,
so we will obey you. Only may the LORD
your God be with you as he was with
Moses. [18]Whoever rebels against your

word and does not obey your words,
whatever you may command them, will
be put to death. Only be strong and
courageous!"

Rahab and the Spies

2 Then Joshua son of Nun secretly
sent two spies from Shittim. "Go,
look over the land," he said, "especially
Jericho." So they went and entered the
house of a prostitute named Rahab and
stayed there.
2The king of Jericho was told, "Look!
Some of the Israelites have come here
tonight to spy out the land." 3So the
king of Jericho sent this message to
Rahab: "Bring out the men who came
to you and entered your house, because
they have come to spy out the whole
land."
4But the woman had taken the two
men and hidden them. She said, "Yes,
the men came to me, but I did not know
where they had come from. 5At dusk,
when it was time to close the city gate,
the men left. I don't know which way
they went. Go after them quickly. You
may catch up with them." 6(But she had
taken them up to the roof and hidden
them under the stalks of flax she had
laid out on the roof.) 7So the men set
out in pursuit of the spies on the road
that leads to the fords of the Jordan, and
as soon as the pursuers had gone out,
the gate was shut.
8Before the spies lay down for the
night, she went up on the roof 9and said
to them, "I know that the LORD has
given this land to you and that a great
fear of you has fallen on us, so that all
who live in this country are melting in
fear because of you. 10We have heard
how the LORD dried up the water of the
Red Sea for you when you came out of
Egypt, and what you did to Sihon and
Og, the two kings of the Amorites east
of the Jordan, whom you completely
destroyed. 11When we heard of it, our
hearts sank and everyone's courage
failed because of you, for the LORD your
God is God in heaven above and on the
earth below. 12Now then, please swear
to me by the LORD that you will show
kindness to my family, because I have
shown kindness to you. Give me a sure
sign 13that you will spare the lives of my
father and mother, my brothers and
sisters, and all who belong to them, and
that you will save us from death."
14"Our lives for your lives!" the men
assured her. "If you don't tell what we
are doing, we will treat you kindly and
faithfully when the LORD gives us the
land."
15So she let them down by a rope
through the window, for the house she
lived in was part of the city wall. 16Now
she had said to them, "Go to the hills so
that the pursuers will not find you. Hide
yourselves there three days until they
return, and then go on your way."
17The men said to her, "This oath you
made us swear will not be binding on us
18unless, when we enter the land, you
have tied this scarlet cord in the window
through which you let us down, and
unless you have brought your father and
mother, your brothers and all your
family into your house. 19If anyone goes
outside your house into the street, his
blood will be on his own head; we will
not be responsible. As for anyone who
is in the house with you, his blood will
be on our head if a hand is laid on him.
20But if you tell what we are doing, we
will be released from the oath you made
us swear."
21"Agreed," she replied. "Let it be as
you say." So she sent them away and
they departed. And she tied the scarlet
cord in the window.
22When they left, they went into the
hills and stayed there three days, until
the pursuers had searched all along the
road and returned without finding
them. 23Then the two men started back.
They went down out of the hills, forded
the river and came to Joshua son of Nun
and told him everything that had happened to them. 24They said to Joshua,
"The LORD has surely given the whole
land into our hands; all the people are
melting in fear because of us."

NEW TESTAMENT READING
Luke 21:5–38

Signs of the End of the Age

[5]Some of his disciples were remark-
ing about how the temple was adorned
with beautiful stones and with gifts
dedicated to God. But Jesus said, [6]"As
for what you see here, the time will
come when not one stone will be left
on another; every one of them will
be thrown down."
[7]"Teacher," they asked, "when will
these things happen? And what will be
the sign that they are about to take
place?"
[8]He replied: "Watch out that you are
not deceived. For many will come in my
name, claiming, 'I am he,' and 'The
time is near.' Do not follow them.
[9]When you hear of wars and revolu-
tions, do not be frightened. These
things must happen first, but the end
will not come right away."
[10]Then he said to them: "Nation will
rise against nation, and kingdom
against kingdom. [11]There will be great
earthquakes, famines and pestilences in
various places, and fearful events and
great signs from heaven.
[12]"But before all this, they will lay
hands on you and persecute you. They
will deliver you to synagogues and prisons, and you will be brought before
kings and governors, and all on account
of my name. [13]This will result in your
being witnesses to them. [14]But make up
your mind not to worry beforehand how
you will defend yourselves. [15]For I will
give you words and wisdom that none of
your adversaries will be able to resist or
contradict. [16]You will be betrayed even
by parents, brothers, relatives and
friends, and they will put some of you to
death. [17]All men will hate you because
of me. [18]But not a hair of your head will
perish. [19]By standing firm you will gain
life.
[20]"When you see Jerusalem being
surrounded by armies, you will know
that its desolation is near. [21]Then let
those who are in Judea flee to the mountains, let those in the city get out, and let
those in the country not enter the city.
[22]For this is the time of punishment in
fulfilment of all that has been written.
[23]How dreadful it will be in those days
for pregnant women and nursing
mothers! There will be great distress in
the land and wrath against this people.
[24]They will fall by the sword and will be
taken as prisoners to all the nations.
Jerusalem will be trampled on by the
Gentiles until the times of the Gentiles
are fulfilled.
[25]"There will be signs in the sun,
moon and stars. On the earth, nations
will be in anguish and perplexity at the
roaring and tossing of the sea. [26]Men
will faint from terror, apprehensive of
what is coming on the world, for the
heavenly bodies will be shaken. [27]At
that time they will see the Son of Man
coming in a cloud with power and great
glory. [28]When these things begin to take
place, stand up and lift up your heads,
because your redemption is drawing
near."
[29]He told them this parable: "Look at
the fig-tree and all the trees. [30]When
they sprout leaves, you can see for
yourselves and know that summer is
near. [31]Even so, when you see these
things happening, you know that the
kingdom of God is near.
[32]"I tell you the truth, this generation
will certainly not pass away until all
these things have happened. [33]Heaven
and earth will pass away, but my words
will never pass away.
[34]"Be careful, or your hearts will be
weighed down with dissipation, drunkenness and the anxieties of life, and that
day will close on you unexpectedly like
a trap. [35]For it will come upon all those
who live on the face of the whole earth.
[36]Be always on the watch, and pray that
you may be able to escape all that is
about to happen, and that you may be
able to stand before the Son of Man."
[37]Each day Jesus was teaching at the
temple, and each evening he went out to
spend the night on the hill called the

Mount of Olives, 38and all the people came early in the morning to hear him at the temple.

READING FROM PROVERBS
Proverbs 10:11–20

11The mouth of the righteous is a
fountain of life,
but violence overwhelms the
mouth of the wicked.

12Hatred stirs up dissension,
but love covers over all wrongs.

13Wisdom is found on the lips of the
discerning,
but a rod is for the back of him who
lacks judgment.

14Wise men store up knowledge,
but the mouth of a fool invites ruin.

15The wealth of the rich is their
fortified city,
but poverty is the ruin of the
poor.

16The wages of the righteous bring
them life,
but the income of the wicked
brings them punishment.

17He who heeds discipline shows the
way to life,
but whoever ignores correction
leads others astray.

18He who conceals his hatred has lying
lips,
and whoever spreads slander is a
fool.

19When words are many, sin is not
absent,
but he who holds his tongue is
wise.

20The tongue of the righteous is choice
silver,
but the heart of the wicked is of
little value.

APRIL 23

DAY 113

OLD TESTAMENT READING
Joshua 3:1–5:12

Crossing the Jordan

3 Early in the morning Joshua and all
the Israelites set out from Shittim
and went to the Jordan, where they
camped before crossing over. 2After
three days the officers went throughout
the camp, 3giving orders to the people:
"When you see the ark of the covenant
of the LORD your God, and the priests,
who are Levites, carrying it, you are to
move out from your positions and follow it. 4Then you will know which way
to go, since you have never been this
way before. But keep a distance of
about a thousand yards between you
and the ark; do not go near it."
5Joshua told the people, "Consecrate
yourselves, for tomorrow the LORD will
do amazing things among you."
6Joshua said to the priests, "Take up
the ark of the covenant and pass on
ahead of the people." So they took it up
and went ahead of them.
7And the LORD said to Joshua, "Today I will begin to exalt you in the eyes
of all Israel, so that they may know that
I am with you as I was with Moses. 8Tell
the priests who carry the ark of the
covenant: 'When you reach the edge of
the Jordan's waters, go and stand in the
river.' "
9Joshua said to the Israelites, "Come

here and listen to the words of the LORD your God. [10]This is how you will know that the living God is among you and that he will certainly drive out before you the Canaanites, Hittites, Hivites, Perizzites, Girgashites, Amorites and Jebusites. [11]See, the ark of the covenant of the Lord of all the earth will go into the Jordan ahead of you. [12]Now then, choose twelve men from the tribes of Israel, one from each tribe. [13]And as soon as the priests who carry the ark of the LORD—the Lord of all the earth —set foot in the Jordan, its waters flowing downstream will be cut off and stand up in a heap."

[14]So when the people broke camp to cross the Jordan, the priests carrying the ark of the covenant went ahead of them. [15]Now the Jordan is in flood all during harvest. Yet as soon as the priests who carried the ark reached the Jordan and their feet touched the water's edge, [16]the water from upstream stopped flowing. It piled up in a heap a great distance away, at a town called Adam in the vicinity of Zarethan, while the water flowing down to the Sea of the Arabah (the Salt Sea) was completely cut off. So the people crossed over opposite Jericho. [17]The priests who carried the ark of the covenant of the LORD stood firm on dry ground in the middle of the Jordan, while all Israel passed by until the whole nation had completed the crossing on dry ground.

4 When the whole nation had finished crossing the Jordan, the LORD said to Joshua, [2]"Choose twelve men from among the people, one from each tribe, [3]and tell them to take up twelve stones from the middle of the Jordan from right where the priests stood and to carry them over with you and put them down at the place where you stay tonight."

[4]So Joshua called together the twelve men he had appointed from the Israelites, one from each tribe, [5]and said to them, "Go over before the ark of the LORD your God into the middle of the Jordan. Each of you is to take up a stone on his shoulder, according to the number of the tribes of the Israelites, [6]to serve as a sign among you. In the future, when your children ask you, 'What do these stones mean?' [7]tell them that the flow of the Jordan was cut off before the ark of the covenant of the LORD. When it crossed the Jordan, the waters of the Jordan were cut off. These stones are to be a memorial to the people of Israel for ever."

[8]So the Israelites did as Joshua commanded them. They took twelve stones from the middle of the Jordan, according to the number of the tribes of the Israelites, as the LORD had told Joshua; and they carried them over with them to their camp, where they put them down. [9]Joshua set up the twelve stones that had been in the middle of the Jordan at the spot where the priests who carried the ark of the covenant had stood. And they are there to this day.

[10]Now the priests who carried the ark remained standing in the middle of the Jordan until everything the LORD had commanded Joshua was done by the people, just as Moses had directed Joshua. The people hurried over, [11]and as soon as all of them had crossed, the ark of the LORD and the priests came to the other side while the people watched. [12]The men of Reuben, Gad and the half-tribe of Manasseh crossed over, armed, in front of the Israelites, as Moses had directed them. [13]About forty thousand armed for battle crossed over before the LORD to the plains of Jericho for war.

[14]That day the LORD exalted Joshua in the sight of all Israel; and they revered him all the days of his life, just as they had revered Moses.

[15]Then the LORD said to Joshua, [16]"Command the priests carrying the ark of the Testimony to come up out of the Jordan."

[17]So Joshua commanded the priests, "Come up out of the Jordan."

[18]And the priests came up out of the river carrying the ark of the covenant of the LORD. No sooner had they set their

feet on the dry ground than the waters of the Jordan returned to their place and ran in flood as before.

19On the tenth day of the first month the people went up from the Jordan and camped at Gilgal on the eastern border of Jericho. 20And Joshua set up at Gilgal the twelve stones they had taken out of the Jordan. 21He said to the Israelites, "In the future when your descendants ask their fathers, 'What do these stones mean?' 22tell them, 'Israel crossed the Jordan on dry ground.' 23For the LORD your God dried up the Jordan before you until you had crossed over. The LORD your God did to the Jordan just what he had done to the Red Sea when he dried it up before us until we had crossed over. 24He did this so that all the peoples of the earth might know that the hand of the LORD is powerful and so that you might always fear the LORD your God."

Circumcision at Gilgal

5 Now when all the Amorite kings west of the Jordan and all the Canaanite kings along the coast heard how the LORD had dried up the Jordan before the Israelites until we had crossed over, their hearts sank and they no longer had the courage to face the Israelites.

2At that time the LORD said to Joshua, "Make flint knives and circumcise the Israelites again." 3So Joshua made flint knives and circumcised the Israelites at Gibeath Haaraloth.

4Now this is why he did so: All those who came out of Egypt—all the men of military age—died in the desert on the way after leaving Egypt. 5All the people that came out had been circumcised, but all the people born in the desert during the journey from Egypt had not. 6The Israelites had moved about in the desert forty years until all the men who were of military age when they left Egypt had died, since they had not obeyed the LORD. For the LORD had sworn to them that they would not see the land that he had solemnly promised their fathers to give us, a land flowing with milk and honey. 7So he raised up their sons in their place, and these were the ones Joshua circumcised. They were still uncircumcised because they had not been circumcised on the way. 8And after the whole nation had been circumcised, they remained where they were in camp until they were healed.

9Then the LORD said to Joshua, "Today I have rolled away the reproach of Egypt from you." So the place has been called Gilgal to this day.

10On the evening of the fourteenth day of the month, while camped at Gilgal on the plains of Jericho, the Israelites celebrated the Passover. 11The day after the Passover, that very day, they ate some of the produce of the land: unleavened bread and roasted grain. 12The manna stopped the day after they ate this food from the land; there was no longer any manna for the Israelites, but that year they ate of the produce of Canaan.

NEW TESTAMENT READING

Luke 22:1–38

Judas Agrees to Betray Jesus

22 Now the Feast of Unleavened Bread, called the Passover, was approaching, 2and the chief priests and the teachers of the law were looking for some way to get rid of Jesus, for they were afraid of the people. 3Then Satan entered Judas, called Iscariot, one of the Twelve. 4And Judas went to the chief priests and the officers of the temple guard and discussed with them how he might betray Jesus. 5They were delighted and agreed to give him money. 6He consented, and watched for an opportunity to hand Jesus over to them when no crowd was present.

The Last Supper

7Then came the day of Unleavened Bread on which the Passover lamb had

to be sacrificed. 8Jesus sent Peter and
John, saying, "Go and make preparations for us to eat the Passover."
9"Where do you want us to prepare
for it?" they asked.
10He replied, "As you enter the city,
a man carrying a jar of water will meet
you. Follow him to the house that he
enters, 11and say to the owner of the
house, 'The Teacher asks: Where is the
guest room, where I may eat the Passover with my disciples?' 12He will show
you a large upper room, all furnished.
Make preparations there."
13They left and found things just as
Jesus had told them. So they prepared
the Passover.
14When the hour came, Jesus and his
apostles reclined at the table. 15And he
said to them, "I have eagerly desired to
eat this Passover with you before I
suffer. 16For I tell you, I will not eat it
again until it finds fulfilment in the kingdom of God."
17After taking the cup, he gave
thanks and said, "Take this and divide it
among you. 18For I tell you I will not
drink again of the fruit of the vine until
the kingdom of God comes."
19And he took bread, gave thanks
and broke it, and gave it to them,
saying, "This is my body given for you;
do this in remembrance of me."
20In the same way, after the supper he
took the cup, saying, "This cup is the
new covenant in my blood, which is
poured out for you. 21But the hand of
him who is going to betray me is with
mine on the table. 22The Son of Man
will go as it has been decreed, but woe
to that man who betrays him." 23They
began to question among themselves
which of them it might be who would do
this.
24Also a dispute arose among them as
to which of them was considered to be
greatest. 25Jesus said to them, "The
kings of the Gentiles lord it over them;
and those who exercise authority over
them call themselves Benefactors.
26But you are not to be like that. Instead, the greatest among you should be
like the youngest, and the one who rules
like the one who serves. 27For who is
greater, the one who is at the table or
the one who serves? Is it not the one
who is at the table? But I am among you
as one who serves. 28You are those who
have stood by me in my trials. 29And I
confer on you a kingdom, just as my
Father conferred one on me, 30so that
you may eat and drink at my table in my
kingdom and sit on thrones, judging the
twelve tribes of Israel.
31"Simon, Simon, Satan has asked to
sift you as wheat. 32But I have prayed
for you, Simon, that your faith may not
fail. And when you have turned back,
strengthen your brothers."
33But he replied, "Lord, I am ready
to go with you to prison and to death."
34Jesus answered, "I tell you, Peter,
before the cock crows today, you will
deny three times that you know me."
35Then Jesus asked them, "When I
sent you without purse, bag or sandals,
did you lack anything?"
"Nothing," they answered.
36He said to them, "But now if you
have a purse, take it, and also a bag; and
if you don't have a sword, sell your
cloak and buy one. 37It is written: 'And
he was numbered with the transgressors'; and I tell you that this must be
fulfilled in me. Yes, what is written
about me is reaching its fulfilment."
38The disciples said, "See, Lord, here
are two swords."
"That is enough," he replied.

READING FROM PSALMS
Psalm 50:1–15

A psalm of Asaph.

1The Mighty One, God, the LORD,
speaks and summons the earth
from the rising of the sun to the
place where it sets.
2From Zion, perfect in beauty,
God shines forth.
3Our God comes and will not be
silent;

a fire devours before him,
and around him a tempest rages.
4He summons the heavens above,
and the earth, that he may judge
his people:
5"Gather to me my consecrated
ones,
who made a covenant with me by
sacrifice."
6And the heavens proclaim his
righteousness,
for God himself is judge. *Selah*

7"Hear, O my people, and I will
speak,
O Israel, and I will testify against
you:
I am God, your God.
8I do not rebuke you for your
sacrifices
or your burnt offerings, which are
ever before me.
9I have no need of a bull from your
stall
or of goats from your pens,
10for every animal of the forest is mine,
and the cattle on a thousand hills.
11I know every bird in the mountains,
and the creatures of the field are
mine.
12If I were hungry I would not tell you,
for the world is mine, and all that is
in it.
13Do I eat the flesh of bulls
or drink the blood of goats?
14Sacrifice thank-offerings to God,
fulfil your vows to the Most High,
15and call upon me in the day of
trouble;
I will deliver you, and you will
honour me."

APRIL 24

DAY 114

OLD TESTAMENT READING
Joshua 5:13–7:26

The Fall of Jericho

13Now when Joshua was near Jericho,
he looked up and saw a man standing in
front of him with a drawn sword in his
hand. Joshua went up to him and asked,
"Are you for us or for our enemies?"
14"Neither," he replied, "but as commander of the army of the LORD I have
now come." Then Joshua fell face down
to the ground in reverence, and asked
him, "What message does my Lord
have for his servant?"
15The commander of the LORD's
army replied, "Take off your sandals,
for the place where you are standing is
holy." And Joshua did so.
6 Now Jericho was tightly shut up
because of the Israelites. No-one
went out and no-one came in.
2Then the LORD said to Joshua, "See,
I have delivered Jericho into your
hands, along with its king and its
fighting men. 3March around the city
once with all the armed men. Do this for
six days. 4Make seven priests carry
trumpets of rams' horns in front of the
ark. On the seventh day, march around
the city seven times, with the priests
blowing the trumpets. 5When you hear
them sound a long blast on the trumpets, make all the people give a loud
shout; then the wall of the city will
collapse and the people will go up,
every man straight in."
6So Joshua son of Nun called the
priests and said to them, "Take up the
ark of the covenant of the LORD and
make seven priests carry trumpets in
front of it." 7And he ordered the people, "Advance! March around the city,
with the armed guard going ahead of the
ark of the LORD."
8When Joshua had spoken to the people, the seven priests carrying the seven

trumpets before the LORD went forward, blowing their trumpets, and the
ark of the LORD's covenant followed
them. 9The armed guard marched
ahead of the priests who blew the trumpets, and the rear guard followed the
ark. All this time the trumpets were
sounding. 10But Joshua had commanded the people, "Do not give a war cry,
do not raise your voices, do not say a
word until the day I tell you to shout.
Then shout!" 11So he had the ark of the
LORD carried around the city, circling it
once. Then the people returned to camp
and spent the night there.

12Joshua got up early the next morning and the priests took up the ark of the
LORD. 13The seven priests carrying the
seven trumpets went forward, marching
before the ark of the LORD and blowing
the trumpets. The armed men went
ahead of them and the rear guard followed the ark of the LORD, while the
trumpets kept sounding. 14So on the
second day they marched around
the city once and returned to the
camp. They did this for six days.

15On the seventh day, they got up at
daybreak and marched around the city
seven times in the same manner, except
that on that day they circled the city
seven times. 16The seventh time
around, when the priests sounded the
trumpet blast, Joshua commanded the
people, "Shout! For the LORD has given
you the city! 17The city and all that is in
it are to be devoted to the LORD. Only
Rahab the prostitute and all who are
with her in her house shall be spared,
because she hid the spies we sent. 18But
keep away from the devoted things, so
that you will not bring about your own
destruction by taking any of them.
Otherwise you will make the camp of
Israel liable to destruction and bring
trouble on it. 19All the silver and gold
and the articles of bronze and iron are
sacred to the LORD and must go into his
treasury."

20When the trumpets sounded, the
people shouted, and at the sound of the
trumpet, when the people gave a loud
shout, the wall collapsed; so every man
charged straight in, and they took the
city. 21They devoted the city to the
LORD and destroyed with the sword
every living thing in it—men and
women, young and old, cattle, sheep
and donkeys.

22Joshua said to the two men who had
spied out the land, "Go into the prostitute's house and bring her out and all
who belong to her, in accordance with
your oath to her." 23So the young men
who had done the spying went in and
brought out Rahab, her father and
mother and brothers and all who belonged to her. They brought out her
entire family and put them in a place
outside the camp of Israel.

24Then they burned the whole city
and everything in it, but they put the
silver and gold and the articles of bronze
and iron into the treasury of the LORD's
house. 25But Joshua spared Rahab the
prostitute, with her family and all who
belonged to her, because she hid the
men Joshua had sent as spies to Jericho
—and she lives among the Israelites to
this day.

26At that time Joshua pronounced
this solemn oath: "Cursed before the
LORD is the man who undertakes to
rebuild this city, Jericho:

"At the cost of his firstborn son
   will he lay its foundations;
at the cost of his youngest
   will he set up its gates."

27So the LORD was with Joshua, and
his fame spread throughout the land.

Achan's Sin

7 But the Israelites acted unfaithfully
in regard to the devoted things;
Achan son of Carmi, the son of Zimri,
the son of Zerah, of the tribe of Judah,
took some of them. So the LORD's anger
burned against Israel.

2Now Joshua sent men from Jericho
to Ai, which is near Beth Aven to the
east of Bethel, and told them, "Go up

and spy out the region." So the men
went up and spied out Ai.
3When they returned to Joshua, they
said, "Not all the people will have to go
up against Ai. Send two or three
thousand men to take it and do not
weary all the people, for only a few men
are there." 4So about three thousand
men went up; but they were routed by
the men of Ai, 5who killed about thirty-
six of them. They chased the Israelites
from the city gate as far as the stone
quarries and struck them down on the
slopes. At this the hearts of the people
melted and became like water.
6Then Joshua tore his clothes and fell
face down to the ground before the ark
of the LORD, remaining there till evening. The elders of Israel did the same,
and sprinkled dust on their heads. 7And
Joshua said, "Ah, Sovereign LORD,
why did you ever bring this people
across the Jordan to deliver us into the
hands of the Amorites to destroy us? If
only we had been content to stay on the
other side of the Jordan! 8O Lord, what
can I say, now that Israel has been
routed by its enemies? 9The Canaanites
and the other people of the country will
hear about this and they will surround
us and wipe out our name from the
earth. What then will you do for your
own great name?"
10The LORD said to Joshua, "Stand
up! What are you doing down on your
face? 11Israel has sinned; they have
violated my covenant, which I commanded them to keep. They have taken
some of the devoted things; they have
stolen, they have lied, they have put
them with their own possessions. 12That
is why the Israelites cannot stand
against their enemies; they turn their
backs and run because they have been
made liable to destruction. I will not be
with you any more unless you destroy
whatever among you is devoted to
destruction.
13"Go, consecrate the people. Tell
them, 'Consecrate yourselves in preparation for tomorrow; for this is what the
LORD, the God of Israel, says: That
which is devoted is among you, O
Israel. You cannot stand against your
enemies until you remove it.
14" 'In the morning, present yourselves tribe by tribe. The tribe that the
LORD takes shall come forward clan by
clan; the clan that the LORD takes shall
come forward family by family; and the
family that the LORD takes shall come
forward man by man. 15He who is
caught with the devoted things shall be
destroyed by fire, along with all that
belongs to him. He has violated the
covenant of the LORD and has done a
disgraceful thing in Israel!' "
16Early the next morning Joshua had
Israel come forward by tribes, and
Judah was taken. 17The clans of Judah
came forward, and he took the Zerahites. He had the clan of the Zerahites
come forward by families, and Zimri
was taken. 18Joshua had his family come
forward man by man, and Achan son of
Carmi, the son of Zimri, the son of
Zerah, of the tribe of Judah, was taken.
19Then Joshua said to Achan, "My
son, give glory to the LORD, the God of
Israel, and give him the praise. Tell me
what you have done; do not hide it from
me."
20Achan replied, "It is true! I have
sinned against the LORD, the God of
Israel. This is what I have done: 21When
I saw in the plunder a beautiful robe
from Babylonia, two hundred shekels of
silver and a wedge of gold weighing fifty
shekels, I coveted them and took them.
They are hidden in the ground inside my
tent, with the silver underneath."
22So Joshua sent messengers, and
they ran to the tent, and there it was,
hidden in his tent, with the silver underneath. 23They took the things from the
tent, brought them to Joshua and all the
Israelites and spread them out before
the LORD.
24Then Joshua, together with all
Israel, took Achan son of Zerah, the
silver, the robe, the gold wedge, his
sons and daughters, his cattle, donkeys
and sheep, his tent and all that he had,
to the Valley of Achor. 25Joshua said,

"Why have you brought this trouble on
us? The LORD will bring trouble on you
today."

Then all Israel stoned him, and after
they had stoned the rest, they burned
them. 26Over Achan they heaped up a
large pile of rocks, which remains to this
day. Then the LORD turned from his
fierce anger. Therefore that place has
been called the Valley of Achor ever
since.

NEW TESTAMENT READING
Luke 22:39–62

Jesus Prays on the Mount of Olives

39Jesus went out as usual to the
Mount of Olives, and his disciples followed him. 40On reaching the place, he
said to them, "Pray that you will not fall
into temptation." 41He withdrew about
a stone's throw beyond them, knelt
down and prayed, 42"Father, if you are
willing, take this cup from me; yet not
my will, but yours be done." 43An angel
from heaven appeared to him and
strengthened him. 44And being in
anguish, he prayed more earnestly, and
his sweat was like drops of blood falling
to the ground.

45When he rose from prayer and went
back to the disciples, he found them
asleep, exhausted from sorrow. 46"Why
are you sleeping?" he asked them. "Get
up and pray so that you will not fall into
temptation."

Jesus Arrested

47While he was still speaking a crowd
came up, and the man who was called
Judas, one of the Twelve, was leading
them. He approached Jesus to kiss him,
48but Jesus asked him, "Judas, are you
betraying the Son of Man with a kiss?"

49When Jesus' followers saw what
was going to happen, they said, "Lord,
should we strike with our swords?"
50And one of them struck the servant of
the high priest, cutting off his right ear.

51But Jesus answered, "No more of
this!" And he touched the man's ear
and healed him.

52Then Jesus said to the chief priests,
the officers of the temple guard, and the
elders, who had come for him, "Am I
leading a rebellion, that you have come
with swords and clubs? 53Every day I
was with you in the temple courts, and
you did not lay a hand on me. But this is
your hour—when darkness reigns."

Peter Disowns Jesus

54Then seizing him, they led him
away and took him into the house of the
high priest. Peter followed at a distance.
55But when they had kindled a fire in the
middle of the courtyard and had sat
down together, Peter sat down with
them. 56A servant girl saw him seated
there in the firelight. She looked closely
at him and said, "This man was with
him."

57But he denied it. "Woman, I don't
know him," he said.

58A little later someone else saw him
and said, "You also are one of them."

"Man, I am not!" Peter replied.

59About an hour later another
asserted, "Certainly this fellow was
with him, for he is a Galilean."

60Peter replied, "Man, I don't know
what you're talking about!" Just as he
was speaking, the cock crowed. 61The
Lord turned and looked straight at
Peter. Then Peter remembered the
word the Lord had spoken to him:
"Before the cock crows today, you will
disown me three times." 62And he went
outside and wept bitterly.

READING FROM PSALMS
Psalm 50:16–23

16But to the wicked, God says:

"What right have you to recite my
laws
or take my covenant on your lips?

17You hate my instruction
and cast my words behind you.
18When you see a thief, you join with him;
you throw in your lot with adulterers.
19You use your mouth for evil
and harness your tongue to deceit.
20You speak continually against your brother
and slander your own mother's son.
21These things you have done and I kept silent;
you thought I was altogether like you.
But I will rebuke you
and accuse you to your face.

22"Consider this, you who forget God,
or I will tear you to pieces, with none to rescue:
23He who sacrifices thank-offerings honours me,
and he prepares the way
so that I may show him the salvation of God."

APRIL 25

DAY 115

OLD TESTAMENT READING
Joshua 8:1–9:15

Ai Destroyed

8 Then the LORD said to Joshua, "Do not be afraid; do not be discouraged. Take the whole army with you, and go up and attack Ai. For I have delivered into your hands the king of Ai, his people, his city and his land.
2You shall do to Ai and its king as you did to Jericho and its king, except that you may carry off their plunder and livestock for yourselves. Set an ambush behind the city."
3So Joshua and the whole army moved out to attack Ai. He chose thirty thousand of his best fighting men and sent them out at night
4with these orders: "Listen carefully. You are to set an ambush behind the city. Don't go very far from it. All of you be on the alert.
5I and all those with me will advance on the city, and when the men come out against us, as they did before, we will flee from them.
6They will pursue us until we have lured them away from the city, for they will say, 'They are running away from us as they did before.' So when we flee from them,
7you are to rise up from ambush and take the city. The LORD your God will give it into your hand.
8When you have taken the city, set it on fire. Do what the LORD has commanded. See to it; you have my orders."
9Then Joshua sent them off, and they went to the place of ambush and lay in wait between Bethel and Ai, to the west of Ai—but Joshua spent that night with the people.
10Early the next morning Joshua mustered his men, and he and the leaders of Israel marched before them to Ai.
11The entire force that was with him marched up and approached the city and arrived in front of it. They set up camp north of Ai, with the valley between them and the city.
12Joshua had taken about five thousand men and set them in ambush between Bethel and Ai, to the west of the city.
13They had the soldiers take up their positions—all those in the camp to the north of the city and the ambush to the west of it. That night Joshua went into the valley.
14When the king of Ai saw this, he and all the men of the city hurried out early in the morning to meet Israel in battle at a certain place overlooking the

Arabah. But he did not know that an
ambush had been set against him behind the city. 15Joshua and all Israel let
themselves be driven back before them,
and they fled towards the desert. 16All
the men of Ai were called to pursue
them, and they pursued Joshua and
were lured away from the city. 17Not a
man remained in Ai or Bethel who did
not go after Israel. They left the city
open and went in pursuit of Israel.

18Then the LORD said to Joshua,
"Hold out towards Ai the javelin that is
in your hand, for into your hand I will
deliver the city." So Joshua held out his
javelin towards Ai. 19As soon as he did
this, the men in the ambush rose quickly
from their position and rushed forward.
They entered the city and captured it
and quickly set it on fire.

20The men of Ai looked back and saw
the smoke of the city rising against the
sky, but they had no chance to escape in
any direction, for the Israelites who had
been fleeing towards the desert had
turned back against their pursuers.
21For when Joshua and all Israel saw
that the ambush had taken the city and
that smoke was going up from the city,
they turned round and attacked the men
of Ai. 22The men of the ambush also
came out of the city against them, so
that they were caught in the middle,
with Israelites on both sides. Israel cut
them down, leaving them neither survivors nor fugitives. 23But they took the
king of Ai alive and brought him to
Joshua.

24When Israel had finished killing all
the men of Ai in the fields and in the
desert where they had chased them, and
when every one of them had been put to
the sword, all the Israelites returned to
Ai and killed those who were in it.
25Twelve thousand men and women fell
that day—all the people of Ai. 26For
Joshua did not draw back the hand that
held out his javelin until he had destroyed all who lived in Ai. 27But Israel
did carry off for themselves the livestock and plunder of this city, as the
LORD had instructed Joshua.

28So Joshua burned Ai and made it a
permanent heap of ruins, a desolate
place to this day. 29He hung the king of
Ai on a tree and left him there until
evening. At sunset, Joshua ordered
them to take his body from the tree and
throw it down at the entrance of the city
gate. And they raised a large pile of
rocks over it, which remains to this day.

The Covenant Renewed at Mount Ebal

30Then Joshua built on Mount Ebal
an altar to the LORD, the God of Israel,
31as Moses the servant of the LORD had
commanded the Israelites. He built it
according to what is written in the Book
of the Law of Moses—an altar of uncut
stones, on which no iron tool had been
used. On it they offered to the LORD
burnt offerings and sacrificed fellowship
offerings. 32There, in the presence of
the Israelites, Joshua copied on stones
the law of Moses, which he had written.
33All Israel, aliens and citizens alike,
with their elders, officials and judges,
were standing on both sides of the ark of
the covenant of the LORD, facing those
who carried it—the priests, who were
Levites. Half of the people stood in
front of Mount Gerizim and half of
them in front of Mount Ebal, as Moses
the servant of the LORD had formerly
commanded when he gave instructions
to bless the people of Israel.

34Afterwards, Joshua read all the
words of the law—the blessings and the
curses—just as it is written in the Book
of the Law. 35There was not a word of
all that Moses had commanded that
Joshua did not read to the whole assembly of Israel, including the women and
children, and the aliens who lived
among them.

The Gibeonite Deception

9 Now when all the kings west of the
Jordan heard about these things
—those in the hill country, in the western foothills, and along the entire coast
of the Great Sea as far as Lebanon

(the kings of the Hittites, Amorites,
Canaanites, Perizzites, Hivites and
Jebusites)—2they came together to
make war against Joshua and Israel.
3However, when the people of Gibeon heard what Joshua had done to
Jericho and Ai, 4they resorted to a
ruse: They went as a delegation whose
donkeys were loaded with worn-out
sacks and old wineskins, cracked and
mended. 5The men put worn and
patched sandals on their feet and wore
old clothes. All the bread of their food
supply was dry and mouldy. 6Then they
went to Joshua in the camp at Gilgal and
said to him and the men of Israel, "We
have come from a distant country; make
a treaty with us."
7The men of Israel said to the Hivites,
"But perhaps you live near us. How
then can we make a treaty with you?"
8"We are your servants," they said to
Joshua.
But Joshua asked, "Who are you and
where do you come from?"
9They answered: "Your servants
have come from a very distant country
because of the fame of the LORD your
God. For we have heard reports of him:
all that he did in Egypt, 10and all that he
did to the two kings of the Amorites east
of the Jordan—Sihon king of Heshbon,
and Og king of Bashan, who reigned in
Ashtaroth. 11And our elders and all
those living in our country said to us,
'Take provisions for your journey; go
and meet them and say to them, "We
are your servants; make a treaty with
us."' 12This bread of ours was warm
when we packed it at home on the day
we left to come to you. But now see how
dry and mouldy it is. 13And these wineskins that we filled were new, but see
how cracked they are. And our clothes
and sandals are worn out by the very
long journey."
14The men of Israel sampled their
provisions but did not enquire of the
LORD. 15Then Joshua made a treaty of
peace with them to let them live, and
the leaders of the assembly ratified it by
oath.

NEW TESTAMENT READING
Luke 22:63–23:25

The Guards Mock Jesus

63The men who were guarding Jesus
began mocking and beating him. 64They
blindfolded him and demanded,
"Prophesy! Who hit you?" 65And they
said many other insulting things to him.

Jesus Before Pilate and Herod

66At daybreak the council of the
elders of the people, both the chief
priests and teachers of the law, met
together, and Jesus was led before
them. 67"If you are the Christ," they
said, "tell us."
Jesus answered, "If I tell you, you
will not believe me, 68and if I asked you,
you would not answer. 69But from now
on, the Son of Man will be seated at the
right hand of the mighty God."
70They all asked, "Are you then the
Son of God?"
He replied, "You are right in saying I
am."
71Then they said, "Why do we need
any more testimony? We have heard it
from his own lips."
23 Then the whole assembly rose
and led him off to Pilate. 2And
they began to accuse him, saying, "We
have found this man subverting our
nation. He opposes payment of taxes to
Caesar and claims to be Christ, a king."
3So Pilate asked Jesus, "Are you the
king of the Jews?"
"Yes, it is as you say," Jesus replied.
4Then Pilate announced to the chief
priests and the crowd, "I find no basis
for a charge against this man."
5But they insisted, "He stirs up the
people all over Judea by his teaching.
He started in Galilee and has come all
the way here."
6On hearing this, Pilate asked if the
man was a Galilean. 7When he learned
that Jesus was under Herod's jurisdic-
tion, he sent him to Herod, who was
also in Jerusalem at that time.

[8]When Herod saw Jesus, he was
greatly pleased, because for a long time
he had been wanting to see him. From
what he had heard about him, he hoped
to see him perform some miracle. [9]He
plied him with many questions, but
Jesus gave him no answer. [10]The chief
priests and the teachers of the law were
standing there, vehemently accusing
him. [11]Then Herod and his soldiers ridiculed and mocked him. Dressing him in
an elegant robe, they sent him back to
Pilate. [12]That day Herod and Pilate became friends—before this they had
been enemies.

[13]Pilate called together the chief
priests, the rulers and the people, [14]and
said to them, "You brought me this man
as one who was inciting the people to
rebellion. I have examined him in your
presence and have found no basis for
your charges against him. [15]Neither has
Herod, for he sent him back to us; as
you can see, he has done nothing to
deserve death. [16]Therefore, I will punish him and then release him."

[18]With one voice they cried out,
"Away with this man! Release Barabbas to us!" ([19]Barabbas had been
thrown into prison for an insurrection in
the city, and for murder.)

[20]Wanting to release Jesus, Pilate
appealed to them again. [21]But they kept
shouting, "Crucify him! Crucify him!"

[22]For the third time he spoke to them:
"Why? What crime has this man committed? I have found in him no grounds
for the death penalty. Therefore I will
have him punished and then release
him."

[23]But with loud shouts they insist-
ently demanded that he be crucified,
and their shouts prevailed. [24]So Pilate
decided to grant their demand. [25]He
released the man who had been thrown
into prison for insurrection and murder,
the one they asked for, and surrendered
Jesus to their will.

READING FROM PSALMS
Psalm 51:1–9

For the director of music. A psalm of David. When the prophet Nathan came to him after David had committed adultery with Bathsheba.

[1]Have mercy on me, O God,
according to your unfailing love;
according to your great compassion
blot out my transgressions.
[2]Wash away all my iniquity
and cleanse me from my sin.

[3]For I know my transgressions,
and my sin is always before me.
[4]Against you, you only, have I sinned
and done what is evil in your sight,
so that you are proved right when you speak
and justified when you judge.
[5]Surely I was sinful at birth,
sinful from the time my mother conceived me.
[6]Surely you desire truth in the inner parts;
you teach me wisdom in the inmost place.

[7]Cleanse me with hyssop, and I shall be clean;
wash me, and I shall be whiter than snow.
[8]Let me hear joy and gladness;
let the bones you have crushed rejoice.
[9]Hide your face from my sins
and blot out all my iniquity.

APRIL 26

OLD TESTAMENT READING

Joshua 9:16–10:43

16Three days after they made the treaty with the Gibeonites, the Israelites heard that they were neighbours, living near them. 17So the Israelites set out and on the third day came to their cities: Gibeon, Kephirah, Beeroth and Kiriath Jearim. 18But the Israelites did not attack them, because the leaders of the assembly had sworn an oath to them by the LORD, the God of Israel.

The whole assembly grumbled against the leaders, 19but all the leaders answered, "We have given them our oath by the LORD, the God of Israel, and we cannot touch them now. 20This is what we will do to them: We will let them live, so that wrath will not fall on us for breaking the oath we swore to them." 21They continued, "Let them live, but let them be woodcutters and water-carriers for the entire community." So the leaders' promise to them was kept.

22Then Joshua summoned the Gibeonites and said, "Why did you deceive us by saying, 'We live a long way from you,' while actually you live near us? 23You are now under a curse: You will never cease to serve as woodcutters and water-carriers for the house of my God."

24They answered Joshua, "Your servants were clearly told how the LORD your God had commanded his servant Moses to give you the whole land and to wipe out all its inhabitants from before you. So we feared for our lives because of you, and that is why we did this. 25We are now in your hands. Do to us whatever seems good and right to you."

26So Joshua saved them from the Israelites, and they did not kill them. 27That day he made the Gibeonites woodcutters and water-carriers for the community and for the altar of the LORD at the place the LORD would choose. And that is what they are to this day.

The Sun Stands Still

10 Now Adoni-Zedek king of Jerusalem heard that Joshua had taken Ai and totally destroyed it, doing to Ai and its king as he had done to Jericho and its king, and that the people of Gibeon had made a treaty of peace with Israel and were living near them. 2He and his people were very much alarmed at this, because Gibeon was an important city, like one of the royal cities; it was larger than Ai, and all its men were good fighters. 3So Adoni-Zedek king of Jerusalem appealed to Hoham king of Hebron, Piram king of Jarmuth, Japhia king of Lachish and Debir king of Eglon. 4"Come up and help me attack Gibeon," he said, "because it has made peace with Joshua and the Israelites."

5Then the five kings of the Amorites—the kings of Jerusalem, Hebron, Jarmuth, Lachish and Eglon—joined forces. They moved up with all their troops and took up positions against Gibeon and attacked it.

6The Gibeonites then sent word to Joshua in the camp at Gilgal: "Do not abandon your servants. Come up to us quickly and save us! Help us, because all the Amorite kings from the hill country have joined forces against us."

7So Joshua marched up from Gilgal with his entire army, including all the best fighting men. 8The LORD said to Joshua, "Do not be afraid of them; I have given them into your hand. Not one of them will be able to withstand you."

9After an all-night march from Gilgal, Joshua took them by surprise.

10The LORD threw them into confusion
before Israel, who defeated them in a
great victory at Gibeon. Israel pursued
them along the road going up to Beth
Horon and cut them down all the way to
Azekah and Makkedah. 11As they fled
before Israel on the road down from
Beth Horon to Azekah, the LORD
hurled large hailstones down on them
from the sky, and more of them died
from the hailstones than were killed by
the swords of the Israelites.

12On the day the LORD gave the
Amorites over to Israel, Joshua said to
the LORD in the presence of Israel:

"O sun, stand still over Gibeon,
  O moon, over the Valley of
    Aijalon."
13So the sun stood still,
  and the moon stopped,
  till the nation avenged itself on its
    enemies,

as it is written in the Book of Jashar.

The sun stopped in the middle of the
sky and delayed going down about a full
day. 14There has never been a day like it
before or since, a day when the LORD
listened to a man. Surely the LORD was
fighting for Israel!

15Then Joshua returned with all Israel
to the camp at Gilgal.

Five Amorite Kings Killed

16Now the five kings had fled and
hidden in the cave at Makkedah.
17When Joshua was told that the five
kings had been found hiding in the cave
at Makkedah, 18he said, "Roll large
rocks up to the mouth of the cave, and
post some men there to guard it. 19But
don't stop! Pursue your enemies, attack
them from the rear and don't let them
reach their cities, for the LORD your
God has given them into your hand."

20So Joshua and the Israelites destroyed them completely—almost to a
man—but the few who were left
reached their fortified cities. 21The
whole army then returned safely to
Joshua in the camp at Makkedah, and
no-one uttered a word against the
Israelites.

22Joshua said, "Open the mouth of
the cave and bring those five kings out
to me." 23So they brought the five kings
out of the cave—the kings of Jerusalem, Hebron, Jarmuth, Lachish and
Eglon. 24When they had brought these
kings to Joshua, he summoned all the
men of Israel and said to the army commanders who had come with him,
"Come here and put your feet on the
necks of these kings." So they came
forward and placed their feet on their
necks.

25Joshua said to them, "Do not be
afraid; do not be discouraged. Be strong
and courageous. This is what the LORD
will do to all the enemies you are going
to fight." 26Then Joshua struck and
killed the kings and hung them on
five trees, and they were left hanging on
the trees until evening.

27At sunset Joshua gave the order and
they took them down from the trees and
threw them into the cave where they
had been hiding. At the mouth of the
cave they placed large rocks, which are
there to this day.

28That day Joshua took Makkedah.
He put the city and its king to the sword
and totally destroyed everyone in it. He
left no survivors. And he did to the king
of Makkedah as he had done to the king
of Jericho.

Southern Cities Conquered

29Then Joshua and all Israel with him
moved on from Makkedah to Libnah
and attacked it. 30The LORD also gave
that city and its king into Israel's hand.
The city and everyone in it Joshua put to
the sword. He left no survivors there.
And he did to its king as he had done to
the king of Jericho.

31Then Joshua and all Israel with him
moved on from Libnah to Lachish; he
took up positions against it and attacked
it. 32The LORD handed Lachish over to
Israel, and Joshua took it on the second

day. The city and everyone in it he put
to the sword, just as he had done to
Libnah. 33Meanwhile, Horam king of
Gezer had come up to help Lachish, but
Joshua defeated him and his army—
until no survivors were left.

34Then Joshua and all Israel with him
moved on from Lachish to Eglon; they
took up positions against it and attacked
it. 35They captured it that same day and
put it to the sword and totally destroyed
everyone in it, just as they had done to
Lachish.

36Then Joshua and all Israel with him
went up from Eglon to Hebron and
attacked it. 37They took the city and put
it to the sword, together with its king, its
villages and everyone in it. They left no
survivors. Just as at Eglon, they totally
destroyed it and everyone in it.

38Then Joshua and all Israel with him
turned round and attacked Debir.
39They took the city, its king and its
villages, and put them to the sword.
Everyone in it they totally destroyed.
They left no survivors. They did to Debir and its king as they had done to
Libnah and its king and to Hebron.

40So Joshua subdued the whole region, including the hill country, the
Negev, the western foothills and the
mountain slopes, together with all their
kings. He left no survivors. He totally
destroyed all who breathed, just as the
LORD, the God of Israel, had commanded. 41Joshua subdued them from
Kadesh Barnea to Gaza and from the
whole region of Goshen to Gibeon.
42All these kings and their lands Joshua
conquered in one campaign, because
the LORD, the God of Israel, fought for
Israel.

43Then Joshua returned with all Israel
to the camp at Gilgal.

NEW TESTAMENT READING
Luke 23:26–56

The Crucifixion

26As they led him away, they seized
Simon from Cyrene, who was on his
way in from the country, and put the
cross on him and made him carry it
behind Jesus. 27A large number of people followed him, including women who
mourned and wailed for him. 28Jesus
turned and said to them, "Daughters of
Jerusalem, do not weep for me; weep
for yourselves and for your children.
29For the time will come when you will
say, 'Blessed are the barren women, the
wombs that never bore and the breasts
that never nursed!' 30Then

" 'they will say to the mountains,
"Fall on us!"
and to the hills "Cover us!" '

31For if men do these things when the
tree is green, what will happen when it is
dry?"

32Two other men, both criminals,
were also led out with him to be executed. 33When they came to the place
called the Skull, there they crucified
him, along with the criminals—one on
his right, the other on his left. 34Jesus
said, "Father, forgive them, for they do
not know what they are doing." And
they divided up his clothes by casting
lots.

35The people stood watching, and the
rulers even sneered at him. They said,
"He saved others; let him save himself if
he is the Christ of God, the Chosen
One."

36The soldiers also came up and
mocked him. They offered him wine
vinegar 37and said, "If you are the king
of the Jews, save yourself."

38There was a written notice above
him, which read: THIS IS THE KING OF THE
JEWS.

39One of the criminals who hung
there hurled insults at him: "Aren't you
the Christ? Save yourself and us!"

40But the other criminal rebuked
him. "Don't you fear God," he said,
"since you are under the same sentence? 41We are punished justly, for
we are getting what our deeds deserve.
But this man has done nothing wrong."

42Then he said, "Jesus, remember me
when you come into your kingdom."

[43]Jesus answered him, "I tell you the truth, today you will be with me in paradise."

Jesus' Death

[44]It was now about the sixth hour, and
darkness came over the whole land until
the ninth hour, [45]for the sun stopped
shining. And the curtain of the temple
was torn in two. [46]Jesus called out with a
loud voice, "Father, into your hands I
commit my spirit." When he had said
this, he breathed his last.
[47]The centurion, seeing what had
happened, praised God and said,
"Surely this was a righteous man."
[48]When all the people who had gathered
to witness this sight saw what took
place, they beat their breasts and went
away. [49]But all those who knew him,
including the women who had followed
him from Galilee, stood at a distance,
watching these things.

Jesus' Burial

[50]Now there was a man named
Joseph, a member of the Council, a
good and upright man, [51]who had not
consented to their decision and action.
He came from the Judean town of Arimathea and he was waiting for the kingdom of God. [52]Going to Pilate, he asked
for Jesus' body. [53]Then he took it down,
wrapped it in linen cloth and placed it in
a tomb cut in the rock, one in which
no-one had yet been laid. [54]It was
Preparation Day, and the Sabbath
was about to begin.
[55]The women who had come with
Jesus from Galilee followed Joseph and
saw the tomb and how his body was laid
in it. [56]Then they went home and prepared spices and perfumes. But they
rested on the Sabbath in obedience to
the commandment.

READING FROM PROVERBS

Proverbs 10:21–30

[21]The lips of the righteous nourish
many,
but fools die for lack of judgment.

[22]The blessing of the LORD brings
wealth,
and he adds no trouble to it.

[23]A fool finds pleasure in evil conduct,
but a man of understanding
delights in wisdom.

[24]What the wicked dreads will overtake
him;
what the righteous desire will be
granted.

[25]When the storm has swept by, the
wicked are gone,
but the righteous stand firm for
ever.

[26]As vinegar to the teeth and smoke to
the eyes,
so is a sluggard to those who send
him.

[27]The fear of the LORD adds length to
life,
but the years of the wicked are cut
short.

[28]The prospect of the righteous is joy,
but the hopes of the wicked come
to nothing.

[29]The way of the LORD is a refuge for
the righteous,
but it is the ruin of those who do
evil.

[30]The righteous will never be uprooted,
but the wicked will not remain in
the land.

APRIL 27

DAY 117

OLD TESTAMENT READING

Joshua 11:1–12:24

Northern Kings Defeated

11 When Jabin king of Hazor heard of this, he sent word to Jobab king of Madon, to the kings of Shimron and Acshaph, [2]and to the northern kings who were in the mountains, in the Arabah south of Kinnereth, in the western foothills and in Naphoth Dor on the west; [3]to the Canaanites in the east and west; to the Amorites, Hittites, Perizzites and Jebusites in the hill country; and to the Hivites below Hermon in the region of Mizpah. [4]They came out with all their troops and a large number of horses and chariots—a huge army, as numerous as the sand on the seashore. [5]All these kings joined forces and made camp together at the Waters of Merom, to fight against Israel.

[6]The LORD said to Joshua, "Do not be afraid of them, because by this time tomorrow I will hand all of them over to Israel, slain. You are to hamstring their horses and burn their chariots."

[7]So Joshua and his whole army came against them suddenly at the Waters of Merom and attacked them, [8]and the LORD gave them into the hand of Israel. They defeated them and pursued them all the way to Greater Sidon, to Misrephoth Maim, and to the Valley of Mizpah on the east, until no survivors were left. [9]Joshua did to them as the LORD had directed: He hamstrung their horses and burned their chariots.

[10]At that time Joshua turned back and captured Hazor and put its king to the sword. (Hazor had been the head of all these kingdoms.) [11]Everyone in it they put to the sword. They totally destroyed them, not sparing anything that breathed, and he burned up Hazor itself.

[12]Joshua took all these royal cities and their kings and put them to the sword. He totally destroyed them, as Moses the servant of the LORD had commanded. [13]Yet Israel did not burn any of the cities built on their mounds—except Hazor, which Joshua burned. [14]The Israelites carried off for themselves all the plunder and livestock of these cities, but all the people they put to the sword until they completely destroyed them, not sparing anyone that breathed. [15]As the LORD commanded his servant Moses, so Moses commanded Joshua, and Joshua did it; he left nothing undone of all that the LORD commanded Moses.

[16]So Joshua took this entire land: the hill country, all the Negev, the whole region of Goshen, the western foothills, the Arabah and the mountains of Israel with their foothills, [17]from Mount Halak, which rises towards Seir, to Baal Gad in the Valley of Lebanon below Mount Hermon. He captured all their kings and struck them down, putting them to death. [18]Joshua waged war against all these kings for a long time. [19]Except for the Hivites living in Gibeon, not one city made a treaty of peace with the Israelites, who took them all in battle. [20]For it was the LORD himself who hardened their hearts to wage war against Israel, so that he might destroy them totally, exterminating them without mercy, as the LORD had commanded Moses.

[21]At that time Joshua went and destroyed the Anakites from the hill country: from Hebron, Debir and Anab, from all the hill country of Judah, and from all the hill country of Israel. Joshua totally destroyed them and their towns. [22]No Anakites were left in Israelite territory; only in Gaza, Gath and Ashdod did any survive. [23]So Joshua took the entire land, just as the LORD had directed Moses, and he gave

it as an inheritance to Israel according to their tribal divisions.

Then the land had rest from war.

List of Defeated Kings

12 These are the kings of the land whom the Israelites had defeated and whose territory they took over east of the Jordan, from the Arnon Gorge to Mount Hermon, including all the eastern side of the Arabah:

2Sihon king of the Amorites,
who reigned in Heshbon. He ruled from Aroer on the rim of the Arnon Gorge—from the middle of the gorge—to the Jabbok River, which is the border of the Ammonites. This included half of Gilead.
3He also ruled over the eastern Arabah from the Sea of Kinnereth to the Sea of the Arabah (the Salt Sea), to Beth Jeshimoth, and then southward below the slopes of Pisgah.

4And the territory of Og king of Bashan,
one of the last of the Rephaites, who reigned in Ashtaroth and Edrei. 5He ruled over Mount Hermon, Salecah, all of Bashan to the border of the people of Geshur and Maacah, and half of Gilead to the border of Sihon king of Heshbon.

6Moses, the servant of the LORD, and the Israelites conquered them. And Moses the servant of the LORD gave their land to the Reubenites, the Gadites and the half-tribe of Manasseh to be their possession.

7These are the kings of the land that Joshua and the Israelites conquered on the west side of the Jordan, from Baal Gad in the Valley of Lebanon to Mount Halak, which rises towards Seir (their lands Joshua gave as an inheritance to the tribes of Israel according to their tribal divisions—8the hill country, the western foothills, the Arabah, the mountain slopes, the desert and the Negev—the lands of the Hittites, Amorites, Canaanites, Perizzites, Hivites and Jebusites):

9the king of Jericho	one
the king of Ai (near Bethel)	one
10the king of Jerusalem	one
the king of Hebron	one
11the king of Jarmuth	one
the king of Lachish	one
12the king of Eglon	one
the king of Gezer	one
13the king of Debir	one
the king of Geder	one
14the king of Hormah	one
the king of Arad	one
15the king of Libnah	one
the king of Adullam	one
16the king of Makkedah	one
the king of Bethel	one
17the king of Tappuah	one
the king of Hepher	one
18the king of Aphek	one
the king of Lasharon	one
19the king of Madon	one
the king of Hazor	one
20the king of Shimron Meron	one
the king of Acshaph	one
21the king of Taanach	one
the king of Megiddo	one
22the king of Kedesh	one
the king of Jokneam in Carmel	one
23the king of Dor (in Naphoth Dor)	one
the king of Goyim in Gilgal	one
24the king of Tirzah	one

thirty-one kings in all.

NEW TESTAMENT READING

Luke 24:1–35

The Resurrection

24 On the first day of the week, very early in the morning, the women took the spices they had prepared and went to the tomb. 2They

found the stone rolled away from the
tomb, 3but when they entered, they did
not find the body of the Lord Jesus.
4While they were wondering about this,
suddenly two men in clothes that
gleamed like lightning stood beside
them. 5In their fright the women bowed
down with their faces to the ground, but
the men said to them, "Why do you
look for the living among the dead? 6He
is not here; he has risen! Remember
how he told you, while he was still with
you in Galilee: 7'The Son of Man must
be delivered into the hands of sinful
men, be crucified and on the third day
be raised again.'" 8Then they remembered his words.

9When they came back from the
tomb, they told all these things to the
Eleven and to all the others. 10It was
Mary Magdalene, Joanna, Mary the
mother of James, and the others with
them who told this to the apostles. 11But
they did not believe the women, because their words seemed to them like
nonsense. 12Peter, however, got up and
ran to the tomb. Bending over, he saw
the strips of linen lying by themselves,
and he went away, wondering to himself
what had happened.

On the Road to Emmaus

13Now that same day two of them
were going to a village called Emmaus,
about seven miles from Jerusalem.
14They were talking with each other
about everything that had happened.
15As they talked and discussed these
things with each other, Jesus himself
came up and walked along with them;
16but they were kept from recognising
him.

17He asked them, "What are you discussing together as you walk along?"

They stood still, their faces downcast.
18One of them, named Cleopas, asked
him, "Are you only a visitor to Jerusalem and do not know the things that
have happened there in these days?"

19"What things?" he asked.

"About Jesus of Nazareth," they replied. "He was a prophet, powerful in
word and deed before God and all the
people. 20The chief priests and our rulers handed him over to be sentenced to
death, and they crucified him; 21but we
had hoped that he was the one who was
going to redeem Israel. And what is
more, it is the third day since all this
took place. 22In addition, some of our
women amazed us. They went to the
tomb early this morning 23but didn't
find his body. They came and told us
that they had seen a vision of angels,
who said he was alive. 24Then some of
our companions went to the tomb and
found it just as the women had said, but
him they did not see."

25He said to them, "How foolish you
are, and how slow of heart to believe all
that the prophets have spoken! 26Did
not the Christ have to suffer these things
and then enter his glory?" 27And beginning with Moses and all the Prophets,
he explained to them what was said
in all the Scriptures concerning himself.

28As they approached the village
to which they were going, Jesus acted
as if he were going further. 29But they
urged him strongly, "Stay with us,
for it is nearly evening; the day is
almost over." So he went in to stay
with them.

30When he was at the table with them,
he took bread, gave thanks, broke it
and began to give it to them. 31Then
their eyes were opened and they recognised him, and he disappeared from
their sight. 32They asked each other,
"Were not our hearts burning within us
while he talked with us on the road and
opened the Scriptures to us?"

33They got up and returned at once to
Jerusalem. There they found the
Eleven and those with them, assembled
together 34and saying, "It is true! The
Lord has risen and has appeared to
Simon." 35Then the two told what had
happened on the way, and how Jesus
was recognised by them when he broke
the bread.

READING FROM PSALMS
Psalm 51:10–19

10Create in me a pure heart, O God,
and renew a steadfast spirit within me.
11Do not cast me from your presence
or take your Holy Spirit from me.
12Restore to me the joy of your salvation
and grant me a willing spirit, to sustain me.

13Then I will teach transgressors your ways,
and sinners will turn back to you.
14Save me from bloodguilt, O God,
the God who saves me,
and my tongue will sing of your righteousness.
15O Lord, open my lips,
and my mouth will declare your praise.
16You do not delight in sacrifice, or I would bring it;
you do not take pleasure in burnt offerings.
17The sacrifices of God are a broken spirit;
a broken and contrite heart,
O God, you will not despise.

18In your good pleasure make Zion prosper;
build up the walls of Jerusalem.
19Then there will be righteous sacrifices,
whole burnt offerings to delight you;
then bulls will be offered on your altar.

DAY 118

APRIL 28

OLD TESTAMENT READING
Joshua 13:1–14:15

Land Still to Be Taken

13 When Joshua was old and well advanced in years, the LORD said to him, "You are very old, and there are still very large areas of land to be taken over.

2"This is the land that remains: all the regions of the Philistines and Geshurites: 3from the Shihor River on the east of Egypt to the territory of Ekron on the north, all of it counted as Canaanite (the territory of the five Philistine rulers in Gaza, Ashdod, Ashkelon, Gath and Ekron—that of the Avvites); 4from the south, all the land of the Canaanites, from Arah of the Sidonians as far as Aphek, the region of the Amorites, 5the area of the Gebalites; and all Lebanon to the east, from Baal Gad below Mount Hermon to Lebo Hamath.

6"As for all the inhabitants of the mountain regions from Lebanon to Misrephoth Maim, that is, all the Sidonians, I myself will drive them out before the Israelites. Be sure to allocate this land to Israel for an inheritance, as I have instructed you, 7and divide it as an inheritance among the nine tribes and half of the tribe of Manasseh."

Division of the Land East of the Jordan

8The other half of Manasseh, the Reubenites and the Gadites had received the inheritance that Moses had given them east of the Jordan, as he, the servant of the LORD, had assigned it to them.

9It extended from Aroer on the rim of the Arnon Gorge, and from the

town in the middle of the gorge,
and included the whole plateau of
Medeba as far as Dibon, 10and all
the towns of Sihon king of the
Amorites, who ruled in Heshbon,
out to the border of the Ammonites. 11It also included Gilead, the
territory of the people of Geshur
and Maacah, all of Mount Hermon
and all Bashan as far as Salecah
—12that is, the whole kingdom of
Og in Bashan, who had reigned in
Ashtaroth and Edrei and had survived as one of the last of the
Rephaites. Moses had defeated
them and taken over their land.
13But the Israelites did not drive
out the people of Geshur and
Maacah, so they continue to live
among the Israelites to this day.

14But to the tribe of Levi he gave no
inheritance, since the offerings made by
fire to the LORD, the God of Israel, are
their inheritance, as he promised them.

15This is what Moses had given to the
tribe of Reuben, clan by clan:

16The territory from Aroer on the
rim of the Arnon Gorge, and from
the town in the middle of the gorge,
and the whole plateau past Medeba
17to Heshbon and all its towns on
the plateau, including Dibon,
Bamoth Baal, Beth Baal Meon,
18Jahaz, Kedemoth, Mephaath,
19Kiriathaim, Sibmah, Zereth Sha-
har on the hill in the valley, 20Beth
Peor, the slopes of Pisgah, and
Beth Jeshimoth 21—all the towns
on the plateau and the entire realm
of Sihon king of the Amorites, who
ruled at Heshbon. Moses had defeated him and the Midianite
chiefs, Evi, Rekem, Zur, Hur and
Reba—princes allied with Sihon
—who lived in that country. 22In
addition to those slain in battle, the
Israelites had put to the sword
Balaam son of Beor, who practised
divination. 23The boundary of the
Reubenites was the bank of the
Jordan. These towns and their villages were the inheritance of the
Reubenites, clan by clan.

24This is what Moses had given to the
tribe of Gad, clan by clan:

25The territory of Jazer, all the
towns of Gilead and half the
Ammonite country as far as Aroer,
near Rabbah; 26and from Heshbon
to Ramath Mizpah and Betonim,
and from Mahanaim to the territory of Debir; 27and in the valley,
Beth Haram, Beth Nimrah, Succoth and Zaphon with the rest of
the realm of Sihon king of Heshbon
(the east side of the Jordan, the
territory up to the end of the Sea of
Kinnereth). 28These towns and
their villages were the inheritance
of the Gadites, clan by clan.

29This is what Moses had given to the
half-tribe of Manasseh, that is, to half
the family of the descendants of Manasseh, clan by clan:

30The territory extending from
Mahanaim and including all of
Bashan, the entire realm of Og
king of Bashan—all the settlements of Jair in Bashan, sixty
towns, 31half of Gilead, and
Ashtaroth and Edrei (the royal
cities of Og in Bashan). This was
for the descendants of Makir son of
Manasseh—for half of the sons of
Makir, clan by clan.

32This is the inheritance Moses had
given when he was in the plains of Moab
across the Jordan east of Jericho. 33But
to the tribe of Levi, Moses had given no
inheritance; the LORD, the God of
Israel, is their inheritance, as he promised them.

Division of the Land West of the Jordan

14 Now these are the areas the
Israelites received as an inheritance in the land of Canaan, which

Eleazar the priest, Joshua son of Nun
and the heads of the tribal clans of Israel
allotted to them. 2Their inheritances
were assigned by lot to the nine-and-a-
half tribes, as the LORD had commanded through Moses. 3Moses had
granted the two-and-a-half tribes their
inheritance east of the Jordan but had
not granted the Levites an inheritance
among the rest, 4for the sons of Joseph
had become two tribes—Manasseh and
Ephraim. The Levites received no share
of the land but only towns to live in,
with pasture-lands for their flocks and
herds. 5So the Israelites divided the
land, just as the LORD had commanded
Moses.

Hebron Given to Caleb

6Now the men of Judah approached
Joshua at Gilgal, and Caleb son of
Jephunneh the Kenizzite said to him,
"You know what the LORD said to
Moses the man of God at Kadesh Barnea about you and me. 7I was forty
years old when Moses the servant of the
LORD sent me from Kadesh Barnea to
explore the land. And I brought him
back a report according to my convic-
tions, 8but my brothers who went up
with me made the hearts of the people
sink. I, however, followed the LORD my
God wholeheartedly. 9So on that day
Moses swore to me, 'The land on which
your feet have walked will be your inheritance and that of your children for
ever, because you have followed the
LORD my God wholeheartedly.'

10"Now then, just as the LORD promised, he has kept me alive for forty-five
years since the time he said this to
Moses, while Israel moved about in the
desert. So here I am today, eighty-five
years old! 11I am still as strong today as
the day Moses sent me out; I'm just as
vigorous to go out to battle now as I was
then. 12Now give me this hill country
that the LORD promised me that day.
You yourself heard then that the Anakites were there and their cities were
large and fortified, but, the LORD helping me, I will drive them out just as he
said."

13Then Joshua blessed Caleb son of
Jephunneh and gave him Hebron as his
inheritance. 14So Hebron has belonged
to Caleb son of Jephunneh the Kenizzite ever since, because he followed
the LORD, the God of Israel, wholeheartedly. 15(Hebron used to be called
Kiriath Arba after Arba, who was the
greatest man among the Anakites.)

Then the land had rest from war.

NEW TESTAMENT READING
Luke 24:36–53

Jesus Appears to the Disciples

36While they were still talking about
this, Jesus himself stood among them
and said to them, "Peace be with you."

37They were startled and frightened,
thinking they saw a ghost. 38He said to
them, "Why are you troubled, and why
do doubts rise in your minds? 39Look at
my hands and my feet. It is I myself!
Touch me and see; a ghost does not
have flesh and bones, as you see I
have."

40When he had said this, he showed
them his hands and feet. 41And while
they still did not believe it because of
joy and amazement, he asked them,
"Do you have anything here to eat?"
42They gave him a piece of broiled fish,
43and he took it and ate it in their
presence.

44He said to them, "This is what I told
you while I was still with you: Everything must be fulfilled that is written
about me in the Law of Moses, the
Prophets and the Psalms."

45Then he opened their minds so they
could understand the Scriptures. 46He
told them, "This is what is written: The
Christ will suffer and rise from the dead
on the third day, 47and repentance and
forgiveness of sins will be preached in
his name to all nations, beginning at
Jerusalem. 48You are witnesses of these

things. 49I am going to send you what
my Father has promised; but stay in the
city until you have been clothed with
power from on high."

The Ascension

50When he had led them out to the
vicinity of Bethany, he lifted up his
hands and blessed them. 51While he was
blessing them, he left them and was
taken up into heaven. 52Then they worshipped him and returned to Jerusalem
with great joy. 53And they stayed continually at the temple, praising God.

READING FROM PSALMS
Psalm 52:1–9

For the director of music. A *maskil* of David. When Doeg the Edomite had gone to Saul and told him: "David has gone to the house of Ahimelech."

1Why do you boast of evil, you mighty man?
Why do you boast all day long,
you who are a disgrace in the eyes of God?
2Your tongue plots destruction;
it is like a sharpened razor,
you who practise deceit.
3You love evil rather than good,
falsehood rather than speaking the truth. *Selah*
4You love every harmful word,
O you deceitful tongue!

5Surely God will bring you down to everlasting ruin:
He will snatch you up and tear you from your tent;
he will uproot you from the land of the living. *Selah*
6The righteous will see and fear;
they will laugh at him, saying,
7"Here now is the man
who did not make God his stronghold
but trusted in his great wealth
and grew strong by destroying others!"

8But I am like an olive tree
flourishing in the house of God;
I trust in God's unfailing love
for ever and ever.
9I will praise you for ever for what you have done;
in your name I will hope, for your name is good.
I will praise you in the presence of your saints.

APRIL 29

DAY 119

OLD TESTAMENT READING
Joshua 15:1–16:10

Allotment for Judah

15 The allotment for the tribe of
Judah, clan by clan, extended
down to the territory of Edom, to the
Desert of Zin in the extreme south.
2Their southern boundary
started from the bay at the southern end of the Salt Sea, 3crossed
south of Scorpion Pass, continued
on to Zin and went over to the
south of Kadesh Barnea. Then it
ran past Hezron up to Addar and
curved around to Karka. 4It then
passed along to Azmon and joined
the Wadi of Egypt, ending at
the sea. This is their southern
boundary.
5The eastern boundary is the
Salt Sea as far as the mouth of the
Jordan.
The northern boundary started
from the bay of the sea at the

mouth of the Jordan, 6went up to
Beth Hoglah and continued north
of Beth Arabah to the Stone of
Bohan son of Reuben. 7The
boundary then went up to Debir
from the Valley of Achor and
turned north to Gilgal, which faces
the Pass of Adummim south of the
gorge. It continued along to the
waters of En Shemesh and came
out at En Rogel. 8Then it ran up the
Valley of Ben Hinnom along the
southern slope of the Jebusite city
(that is, Jerusalem). From there it
climbed to the top of the hill west of
the Hinnom Valley at the northern
end of the Valley of Rephaim.
9From the hilltop the boundary
headed towards the spring of the
waters of Nephtoah, came out at
the towns of Mount Ephron and
went down towards Baalah (that is,
Kiriath Jearim). 10Then it curved
westward from Baalah to Mount
Seir, ran along the northern slope
of Mount Jearim (that is, Kesalon),
continued down to Beth Shemesh
and crossed to Timnah. 11It went
to the northern slope of Ekron,
turned towards Shikkeron, passed
along to Mount Baalah and
reached Jabneel. The boundary
ended at the sea.
12The western boundary is the
coastline of the Great Sea.

These are the boundaries around the
people of Judah by their clans.

13In accordance with the LORD's command to him, Joshua gave to Caleb son
of Jephunneh a portion in Judah—
Kiriath Arba, that is, Hebron. (Arba
was the forefather of Anak.) 14From
Hebron Caleb drove out the three Anakites—Sheshai, Ahiman and Talmai—
descendants of Anak. 15From there he
marched against the people living in
Debir (formerly called Kiriath Sepher).
16And Caleb said, "I will give my
daughter Acsah in marriage to the man
who attacks and captures Kiriath
Sepher." 17Othniel son of Kenaz,
Caleb's brother, took it; so Caleb gave
his daughter Acsah to him in marriage.
18One day when she came to Othniel,
she urged him to ask her father for a
field. When she got off her donkey,
Caleb asked her, "What can I do for
you?"
19She replied, "Do me a special
favour. Since you have given me land in
the Negev, give me also springs of
water." So Caleb gave her the upper
and lower springs.

20This is the inheritance of the tribe of
Judah, clan by clan:

21The southernmost towns of the tribe
of Judah in the Negev towards the
boundary of Edom were:
Kabzeel, Eder, Jagur, 22Kinah,
Dimonah, Adadah, 23Kedesh,
Hazor, Ithnan, 24Ziph, Telem,
Bealoth, 25Hazor Hadattah,
Kerioth Hezron (that is, Hazor),
26Amam, Shema, Moladah,
27Hazar Gaddah, Heshmon, Beth
Pelet, 28Hazar Shual, Beersheba,
Biziothiah, 29Baalah, Iim, Ezem,
30Eltolad, Kesil, Hormah,
31Ziklag, Madmannah, Sansan-
nah, 32Lebaoth, Shilhim, Ain and
Rimmon—a total of twenty-nine
towns and their villages.

33In the western foothills:
Eshtaol, Zorah, Ashnah,
34Zanoah, En Gannim, Tappuah,
Enam, 35Jarmuth, Adullam,
Socoh, Azekah, 36Shaaraim,
Adithaim and Gederah (or Geder-
othaim)—fourteen towns and their
villages.
37Zenan, Hadashah, Migdal
Gad, 38Dilean, Mizpah, Joktheel,
39Lachish, Bozkath, Eglon,
40Cabbon, Lahmas, Kitlish,
41Gederoth, Beth Dagon, Naamah
and Makkedah—sixteen towns
and their villages.
42Libnah, Ether, Ashan,
43Iphtah, Ashnah, Nezib, 44Keilah,
Aczib and Mareshah—nine towns
and their villages.

[45]Ekron, with its surrounding settlements and villages; [46]west of Ekron, all that were in the vicinity of Ashdod, together with their villages; [47]Ashdod, its surrounding settlements and villages; and Gaza, its settlements and villages, as far as the Wadi of Egypt and the coastline of the Great Sea.

[48]In the hill country:
Shamir, Jattir, Socoh,
[49]Dannah, Kiriath Sannah (that is,
Debir), [50]Anab, Eshtemoh, Anim,
[51]Goshen, Holon and Giloh—
eleven towns and their villages.
[52]Arab, Dumah, Eshan,
[53]Janim, Beth Tappuah, Aphekah,
[54]Humtah, Kiriath Arba (that is,
Hebron) and Zior—nine towns
and their villages.
[55]Maon, Carmel, Ziph, Juttah,
[56]Jezreel, Jokdeam, Zanoah,
[57]Kain, Gibeah and Timnah—ten
towns and their villages.
[58]Halhul, Beth Zur, Gedor,
[59]Maarath, Beth Anoth and Eltekon—six towns and their villages.
[60]Kiriath Baal (that is, Kiriath Jearim) and Rabbah—two towns and their villages.

[61]In the desert:
Beth Arabah, Middin, Secacah,
[62]Nibshan, the City of Salt and En Gedi—six towns and their villages.
[63]Judah could not dislodge the Jebusites, who were living in Jerusalem; to this day the Jebusites live there with the people of Judah.

Allotment for Ephraim and Manasseh

16 The allotment for Joseph began at the Jordan of Jericho, east of the waters of Jericho, and went up from there through the desert into the hill country of Bethel. [2]It went on from
Bethel (that is, Luz), crossed over to the territory of the Arkites in Ataroth, [3]descended westward to
the territory of the Japhletites as far as the region of Lower Beth Horon and on to Gezer, ending at the sea.
[4]So Manasseh and Ephraim, the descendants of Joseph, received their inheritance.

[5]This was the territory of Ephraim, clan by clan:
The boundary of their inheritance went from Ataroth Addar in the east to Upper Beth Horon [6]and
continued to the sea. From Micmethath on the north it curved eastward to Taanath Shiloh, passing by it to Janoah on the east.
[7]Then it went down from Janoah to
Ataroth and Naarah, touched Jericho and came out at the Jordan. [8]From Tappuah the border
went west to the Kanah Ravine and ended at the sea. This was the inheritance of the tribe of the Ephraimites, clan by clan. [9]It also
included all the towns and their villages that were set aside for the Ephraimites within the inheritance of the Manassites.
[10]They did not dislodge the Canaanites living in Gezer; to this day the Canaanites live among the people of Ephraim but are required to do forced labour.

NEW TESTAMENT READING
John 1:1–28

The Word Became Flesh

1 In the beginning was the Word, and the Word was with God, and the Word was God. [2]He was with God
in the beginning.
[3]Through him all things were made; without him nothing was made that has been made. [4]In him was life, and that
life was the light of men. [5]The light
shines in the darkness, but the darkness has not understood it.
[6]There came a man who was sent from God; his name was John. [7]He
came as a witness to testify concerning that light, so that through him all men

might believe. 8He himself was not the
light; he came only as a witness to the
light. 9The true light that gives light to
every man was coming into the world.
10He was in the world, and though the
world was made through him, the world
did not recognise him. 11He came to
that which was his own, but his own did
not receive him. 12Yet to all who received him, to those who believed in his
name, he gave the right to become children of God—13children born not of
natural descent, nor of human decision
or a husband's will, but born of God.
14The Word became flesh and made
his dwelling among us. We have seen his
glory, the glory of the One and Only,
who came from the Father, full of grace
and truth.
15John testifies concerning him. He
cries out, saying, "This was he of whom
I said, 'He who comes after me has
surpassed me because he was before
me.' " 16From the fulness of his grace we
have all received one blessing after
another. 17For the law was given
through Moses; grace and truth came
through Jesus Christ. 18No-one has ever
seen God, but God the One and Only,
who is at the Father's side, has made
him known.

John the Baptist Denies Being the Christ

19Now this was John's testimony
when the Jews of Jerusalem sent priests
and Levites to ask him who he was. 20He
did not fail to confess, but confessed
freely, "I am not the Christ."
21They asked him, "Then who are
you? Are you Elijah?"

He said, "I am not."

"Are you the Prophet?"

He answered, "No."

22Finally they said, "Who are you?
Give us an answer to take back to those
who sent us. What do you say about
yourself?"
23John replied in the words of Isaiah
the prophet, "I am the voice of one
calling in the desert, 'Make straight the
way for the Lord.' "
24Now some Pharisees who had been
sent 25questioned him, "Why then do
you baptise if you are not the Christ, nor
Elijah, nor the Prophet?"
26"I baptise with water," John replied, "but among you stands one you
do not know. 27He is the one who comes
after me, the thongs of whose sandals I
am not worthy to untie."
28This all happened at Bethany on the
other side of the Jordan, where John
was baptising.

READING FROM PSALMS

Psalm 53:1–6

For the director of music. According to *mahalath*. A *maskil* of David.

1The fool says in his heart,
"There is no God."
They are corrupt, and their ways are vile;
there is no-one who does good.

2God looks down from heaven
on the sons of men
to see if there are any who understand,
any who seek God.
3Everyone has turned away,
they have together become corrupt;
there is no-one who does good,
not even one.

4Will the evildoers never learn—
those who devour my people as men eat bread
and who do not call on God?
5There they were, overwhelmed with dread,
where there was nothing to dread.
God scattered the bones of those who attacked you;
you put them to shame, for God despised them.

6Oh, that salvation for Israel would come out of Zion!
When God restores the fortunes of his people,
let Jacob rejoice and Israel be glad!

APRIL 30 DAY 120

OLD TESTAMENT READING
Joshua 17:1–18:28

17 This was the allotment for the
tribe of Manasseh as Joseph's
firstborn, that is, for Makir, Manasseh's
firstborn. Makir was the ancestor of the
Gileadites, who had received Gilead
and Bashan because the Makirites were
great soldiers. 2So this allotment was for
the rest of the people of Manasseh—the
clans of Abiezer, Helek, Asriel,
Shechem, Hepher and Shemida. These
are the other male descendants of Manasseh son of Joseph by their clans.
3Now Zelophehad son of Hepher, the
son of Gilead, the son of Makir, the son
of Manasseh, had no sons but only
daughters, whose names were Mahlah,
Noah, Hoglah, Milcah and Tirzah.
4They went to Eleazar the priest,
Joshua son of Nun, and the leaders and
said, "The LORD commanded Moses to
give us an inheritance among our
brothers." So Joshua gave them an inheritance along with the brothers of
their father, according to the LORD's
command. 5Manasseh's share consisted
of ten tracts of land besides Gilead and
Bashan east of the Jordan, 6because the
daughters of the tribe of Manasseh received an inheritance among the sons.
The land of Gilead belonged to the rest
of the descendants of Manasseh.

7The territory of Manasseh extended from Asher to Micmethath
east of Shechem. The boundary
ran southward from there to include the people living at En Tappuah. 8(Manasseh had the land of
Tappuah, but Tappuah itself, on
the boundary of Manasseh, belonged to the Ephraimites.) 9Then
the boundary continued south to
the Kanah Ravine. There were
towns belonging to Ephraim lying
among the towns of Manasseh, but
the boundary of Manasseh was the
northern side of the ravine and ended at the sea. 10On the south the
land belonged to Ephraim, on the
north to Manasseh. The territory
of Manasseh reached the sea and
bordered Asher on the north and
Issachar on the east.
11Within Issachar and Asher,
Manasseh also had Beth Shan,
Ibleam and the people of Dor,
Endor, Taanach and Megiddo,
together with their surrounding
settlements (the third in the list is
Naphoth).

12Yet the Manassites were not able to
occupy these towns, for the Canaanites
were determined to live in that region.
13However, when the Israelites grew
stronger, they subjected the Canaanites
to forced labour but did not drive them
out completely.
14The people of Joseph said to
Joshua, "Why have you given us only
one allotment and one portion for an
inheritance? We are a numerous
people and the LORD has blessed us
abundantly."
15"If you are so numerous," Joshua
answered, "and if the hill country of
Ephraim is too small for you, go up into
the forest and clear land for yourselves
there in the land of the Perizzites and
Rephaites."
16The people of Joseph replied, "The
hill country is not enough for us, and all
the Canaanites who live in the plain
have iron chariots, both those in Beth
Shan and its settlements and those in
the Valley of Jezreel."
17But Joshua said to the house of
Joseph—to Ephraim and Manasseh—
"You are numerous and very powerful.
You will have not only one allotment
18but the forested hill country as well.
Clear it, and its farthest limits will be
yours; though the Canaanites have iron

chariots and though they are strong,
you can drive them out."

Division of the Rest of the Land

18 The whole assembly of the
Israelites gathered at Shiloh and
set up the Tent of Meeting there. The
country was brought under their control, 2but there were still seven Israelite
tribes who had not yet received their
inheritance.
3So Joshua said to the Israelites:
"How long will you wait before you
begin to take possession of the land that
the LORD, the God of your fathers, has
given you? 4Appoint three men from
each tribe. I will send them out to make
a survey of the land and to write a
description of it, according to the inheritance of each. Then they will return
to me. 5You are to divide the land into
seven parts. Judah is to remain in its
territory on the south and the house of
Joseph in its territory on the north.
6After you have written descriptions of
the seven parts of the land, bring them
here to me and I will cast lots for you in
the presence of the LORD our God. 7The
Levites, however, do not get a portion
among you, because the priestly service
of the LORD is their inheritance. And
Gad, Reuben and the half-tribe of Manasseh have already received their inheritance on the east side of the Jordan.
Moses the servant of the LORD gave it to
them."
8As the men started on their way to
map out the land, Joshua instructed
them, "Go and make a survey of the
land and write a description of it. Then
return to me, and I will cast lots for you
here at Shiloh in the presence of the
LORD." 9So the men left and went
through the land. They wrote its description on a scroll, town by town, in
seven parts, and returned to Joshua in
the camp at Shiloh. 10Joshua then cast
lots for them in Shiloh in the presence of
the LORD, and there he distributed the
land to the Israelites according to their
tribal divisions.

Allotment for Benjamin

11The lot came up for the tribe of Benjamin, clan by clan. Their allotted territory lay between the tribes of Judah and
Joseph:
12On the north side their boundary began at the Jordan, passed the
northern slope of Jericho and
headed west into the hill country,
coming out at the desert of Beth
Aven. 13From there it crossed to
the south slope of Luz (that is,
Bethel) and went down to Ataroth
Addar on the hill south of Lower
Beth Horon.
14From the hill facing Beth
Horon on the south the boundary
turned south along the western side
and came out at Kiriath Baal (that
is, Kiriath Jearim), a town of the
people of Judah. This was the western side.
15The southern side began at the
outskirts of Kiriath Jearim on the
west, and the boundary came out at
the spring of the waters of Nephtoah. 16The boundary went down
to the foot of the hill facing the
Valley of Ben Hinnom, north of
the Valley of Rephaim. It continued down the Hinnom Valley
along the southern slope of the
Jebusite city and so to En Rogel.
17It then curved north, went to En
Shemesh, continued to Geliloth,
which faces the Pass of Adummim,
and ran down to the Stone of
Bohan son of Reuben. 18It continued to the northern slope of
Beth Arabah and on down into the
Arabah. 19It then went to the
northern slope of Beth Hoglah and
came out at the northern bay of the
Salt Sea, at the mouth of the Jordan
in the south. This was the southern
boundary.
20The Jordan formed the boundary on the eastern side.
These were the boundaries that marked
out the inheritance of the clans of Benjamin on all sides.

[21]The tribe of Benjamin, clan by clan, had the following cities:

Jericho, Beth Hoglah, Emek Keziz, [22]Beth Arabah, Zemaraim, Bethel, [23]Avvim, Parah, Ophrah, [24]Kephar Ammoni, Ophni and Geba—twelve towns and their villages.

[25]Gibeon, Ramah, Beeroth, [26]Mizpah, Kephirah, Mozah, [27]Rekem, Irpeel, Taralah, [28]Zelah, Haeleph, the Jebusite city (that is, Jerusalem), Gibeah and Kiriath—fourteen towns and their villages.

This was the inheritance of Benjamin for its clans.

NEW TESTAMENT READING
John 1:29–51

Jesus the Lamb of God

[29]The next day John saw Jesus coming towards him and said, "Look, the Lamb of God, who takes away the sin of the world! [30]This is the one I meant when I said, 'A man who comes after me has surpassed me because he was before me.' [31]I myself did not know him, but the reason I came baptising with water was that he might be revealed to Israel."

[32]Then John gave this testimony: "I saw the Spirit come down from heaven as a dove and remain on him. [33]I would not have known him, except that the one who sent me to baptise with water told me, 'The man on whom you see the Spirit come down and remain is he who will baptise with the Holy Spirit.' [34]I have seen and I testify that this is the Son of God."

Jesus' First Disciples

[35]The next day John was there again with two of his disciples. [36]When he saw Jesus passing by, he said, "Look, the Lamb of God!"

[37]When the two disciples heard him say this, they followed Jesus. [38]Turning round, Jesus saw them following and asked, "What do you want?"

They said, "Rabbi" (which means Teacher), "where are you staying?"

[39]"Come," he replied, "and you will see."

So they went and saw where he was staying, and spent that day with him. It was about the tenth hour.

[40]Andrew, Simon Peter's brother, was one of the two who heard what John had said and who had followed Jesus. [41]The first thing Andrew did was to find his brother Simon and tell him, "We have found the Messiah" (that is, the Christ). [42]And he brought him to Jesus.

Jesus looked at him and said, "You are Simon son of John. You will be called Cephas" (which, when translated, is Peter).

Jesus Calls Philip and Nathanael

[43]The next day Jesus decided to leave for Galilee. Finding Philip, he said to him, "Follow me."

[44]Philip, like Andrew and Peter, was from the town of Bethsaida. [45]Philip found Nathanael and told him, "We have found the one Moses wrote about in the Law, and about whom the prophets also wrote—Jesus of Nazareth, the son of Joseph."

[46]"Nazareth! Can anything good come from there?" Nathanael asked.

"Come and see," said Philip.

[47]When Jesus saw Nathanael approaching, he said of him, "Here is a true Israelite, in whom there is nothing false."

[48]"How do you know me?" Nathanael asked.

Jesus answered, "I saw you while you were still under the fig-tree before Philip called you."

[49]Then Nathanael declared, "Rabbi, you are the Son of God; you are the King of Israel."

[50]Jesus said, "You believe because I told you I saw you under the fig-tree. You shall see greater things than that."

51He then added, "I tell you the truth, you shall see heaven open, and the angels of God ascending and descending on the Son of Man."

READING FROM PROVERBS
Proverbs 10:31–11:8

31The mouth of the righteous brings
forth wisdom,
but a perverse tongue will be cut
out.

32The lips of the righteous know what is
fitting,
but the mouth of the wicked only
what is perverse.

11 The LORD abhors dishonest
scales,
but accurate weights are his
delight.

2When pride comes, then comes
disgrace,
but with humility comes wisdom.

3The integrity of the upright guides
them,
but the unfaithful are destroyed by
their duplicity.

4Wealth is worthless in the day of
wrath,
but righteousness delivers from
death.

5The righteousness of the blameless
makes a straight way for them,
but the wicked are brought down
by their own wickedness.

6The righteousness of the upright
delivers them,
but the unfaithful are trapped by
evil desires.

7When a wicked man dies, his hope
perishes;
all he expected from his power
comes to nothing.

8The righteous man is rescued from
trouble,
and it comes on the wicked
instead.

DAY 121

MAY 1

OLD TESTAMENT READING
Joshua 19:1–21:19

Allotment for Simeon

19 The second lot came out for the
tribe of Simeon, clan by clan.
Their inheritance lay within the territory of Judah. 2It included:
Beersheba (or Sheba), Moladah,
3Hazar Shual, Balah, Ezem,
4Eltolad, Bethul, Hormah,
5Ziklag, Beth Marcaboth, Hazar
Susah, 6Beth Lebaoth and Shar-
uhen—thirteen towns and their
villages;
7Ain, Rimmon, Ether and
Ashan—four towns and their
villages—8and all the villages
around these towns as far as Baalath
Beer (Ramah in the Negev).
This was the inheritance of the tribe of
the Simeonites, clan by clan. 9The inheritance of the Simeonites was taken
from the share of Judah, because
Judah's portion was more than they
needed. So the Simeonites received
their inheritance within the territory of
Judah.

Allotment for Zebulun

10The third lot came up for Zebulun,
clan by clan:
The boundary of their inheritance went as far as Sarid. 11Going

west it ran to Maralah, touched
Dabbesheth, and extended to the
ravine near Jokneam. 12It turned
east from Sarid towards the sunrise
to the territory of Kisloth Tabor
and went on to Daberath and up to
Japhia. 13Then it continued eastward to Gath Hepher and Eth
Kazin; it came out at Rimmon and
turned towards Neah. 14There the
boundary went round on the north
to Hannathon and ended at the
Valley of Iphtah El. 15Included
were Kattath, Nahalal, Shimron,
Idalah and Bethlehem. There were
twelve towns and their villages.
16These towns and their villages were
the inheritance of Zebulun, clan by
clan.

Allotment for Issachar

17The fourth lot came out for Issachar,
clan by clan. 18Their territory included:
Jezreel, Kesulloth, Shunem,
19Hapharaim, Shion, Anaharath,
20Rabbith, Kishion, Ebez,
21Remeth, En Gannim, En Had-
dah and Beth Pazzez. 22The boundary touched Tabor, Shahazumah
and Beth Shemesh, and ended at
the Jordan. There were sixteen
towns and their villages.
23These towns and their villages were
the inheritance of the tribe of Issachar,
clan by clan.

Allotment for Asher

24The fifth lot came out for the tribe of
Asher, clan by clan. 25Their territory
included:
Helkath, Hali, Beten, Acshaph,
26Allammelech, Amad and Mishal.
On the west the boundary touched
Carmel and Shihor Libnath. 27It
then turned east towards Beth
Dagon, touched Zebulun and the
Valley of Iphtah El, and went
north to Beth Emek and Neiel,
passing Cabul on the left. 28It went
to Abdon, Rehob, Hammon and
Kanah, as far as Greater Sidon.
29The boundary then turned back
towards Ramah and went to the
fortified city of Tyre, turned towards Hosah and came out at the
sea in the region of Aczib, 30Um-
mah, Aphek and Rehob. There
were twenty-two towns and their
villages.
31These towns and their villages were
the inheritance of the tribe of Asher,
clan by clan.

Allotment for Naphtali

32The sixth lot came out for Naphtali,
clan by clan:
33Their boundary went from
Heleph and the large tree in
Zaanannim, passing Adami Nekeb
and Jabneel to Lakkum and ending
at the Jordan. 34The boundary ran
west through Aznoth Tabor and
came out at Hukkok. It touched
Zebulun on the south, Asher on
the west and the Jordan on the east.
35The fortified cities were Ziddim,
Zer, Hammath, Rakkath, Kinnereth, 36Adamah, Ramah,
Hazor, 37Kedesh, Edrei, En
Hazor, 38Iron, Migdal El, Horem,
Beth Anath and Beth Shemesh.
There were nineteen towns and
their villages.
39These towns and their villages were
the inheritance of the tribe of Naphtali,
clan by clan.

Allotment for Dan

40The seventh lot came out for the tribe
of Dan, clan by clan. 41The territory of
their inheritance included:
Zorah, Eshtaol, Ir Shemesh,
42Shaalabbin, Aijalon, Ithlah,
43Elon, Timnah, Ekron, 44Eltekeh,
Gibbethon, Baalath, 45Jehud,
Bene Berak, Gath Rimmon, 46Me
Jarkon and Rakkon, with the area
facing Joppa.
47(But the Danites had difficulty
taking possession of their territory, so

they went up and attacked Leshem, took it, put it to the sword and occupied it. They settled in Leshem and named it Dan after their forefather.)
48These towns and their villages were the inheritance of the tribe of Dan, clan by clan.

Allotment for Joshua

49When they had finished dividing the land into its allotted portions, the Israelites gave Joshua son of Nun an inheritance among them, 50as the LORD had commanded. They gave him the town he asked for—Timnath Serah in the hill country of Ephraim. And he built up the town and settled there.

51These are the territories that Eleazar the priest, Joshua son of Nun and the heads of the tribal clans of Israel assigned by lot at Shiloh in the presence of the LORD at the entrance to the Tent of Meeting. And so they finished dividing the land.

Cities of Refuge

20 Then the LORD said to Joshua: 2"Tell the Israelites to designate the cities of refuge, as I instructed you through Moses, 3so that anyone who kills a person accidentally and unintentionally may flee there and find protection from the avenger of blood.

4"When he flees to one of these cities, he is to stand in the entrance of the city gate and state his case before the elders of that city. Then they are to admit him into their city and give him a place to live with them. 5If the avenger of blood pursues him, they must not surrender the one accused, because he killed his neighbour unintentionally and without malice aforethought. 6He is to stay in that city until he has stood trial before the assembly and until the death of the high priest who is serving at that time. Then he may go back to his own home in the town from which he fled."

7So they set apart Kedesh in Galilee in the hill country of Naphtali, Shechem in the hill country of Ephraim, and Kiriath Arba (that is, Hebron) in the hill country of Judah. 8On the east side of the Jordan of Jericho they designated Bezer in the desert on the plateau in the tribe of Reuben, Ramoth in Gilead in the tribe of Gad, and Golan in Bashan in the tribe of Manasseh. 9Any of the Israelites or any alien living among them who killed someone accidentally could flee to these designated cities and not be killed by the avenger of blood prior to standing trial before the assembly.

Towns for the Levites

21 Now the family heads of the Levites approached Eleazar the priest, Joshua son of Nun, and the heads of the other tribal families of Israel 2at Shiloh in Canaan and said to them, "The LORD commanded through Moses that you give us towns to live in, with pasture-lands for our livestock." 3So, as the LORD had commanded, the Israelites gave the Levites the following towns and pasture-lands out of their own inheritance:

4The first lot came out for the Kohathites, clan by clan. The Levites who were descendants of Aaron the priest were allotted thirteen towns from the tribes of Judah, Simeon and Benjamin. 5The rest of Kohath's descendants were allotted ten towns from the clans of the tribes of Ephraim, Dan and half of Manasseh.

6The descendants of Gershon were allotted thirteen towns from the clans of the tribes of Issachar, Asher, Naphtali and the half-tribe of Manasseh in Bashan.

7The descendants of Merari, clan by clan, received twelve towns from the tribes of Reuben, Gad and Zebulun.

8So the Israelites allotted to the Levites these towns and their pasture-lands, as the LORD had commanded through Moses.

9From the tribes of Judah and Simeon they allotted the following towns by name 10(these towns were assigned to the descendants of Aaron who were from the Kohathite clans of the Levites, because the first lot fell to them):

11They gave them Kiriath Arba (that is, Hebron), with its surrounding pasture-land, in the hill country of Judah. (Arba was the forefather of Anak.) 12But the fields and villages around the city they had given to Caleb son of Jephunneh as his possession.

13So to the descendants of Aaron the priest they gave Hebron (a city of refuge for one accused of murder), Libnah, 14Jattir, Eshtemoa, 15Holon, Debir, 16Ain, Juttah and Beth Shemesh, together with their pasture-lands—nine towns from these two tribes.

17And from the tribe of Benjamin they gave them Gibeon, Geba, 18Anathoth and Almon, together with their pasture-lands—four towns.

19All the towns for the priests, the descendants of Aaron, were thirteen, together with their pasture-lands.

NEW TESTAMENT READING
John 2:1–25

Jesus Changes Water to Wine

2 On the third day a wedding took place at Cana in Galilee. Jesus' mother was there, 2and Jesus and his disciples had also been invited to the wedding. 3When the wine was gone, Jesus' mother said to him, "They have no more wine."

4"Dear woman, why do you involve me?" Jesus replied, "My time has not yet come."

5His mother said to the servants, "Do whatever he tells you."

6Nearby stood six stone water jars, the kind used by the Jews for ceremonial washing, each holding from twenty to thirty gallons.

7Jesus said to the servants, "Fill the jars with water"; so they filled them to the brim.

8Then he told them, "Now draw some out and take it to the master of the banquet."

They did so, 9and the master of the banquet tasted the water that had been turned into wine. He did not realise where it had come from, though the servants who had drawn the water knew. Then he called the bridegroom aside 10and said, "Everyone brings out the choice wine first and then the cheaper wine after the guests have had too much to drink; but you have saved the best till now."

11This, the first of his miraculous signs, Jesus performed at Cana in Galilee. He thus revealed his glory, and his disciples put their faith in him.

Jesus Clears the Temple

12After this he went down to Capernaum with his mother and brothers and his disciples. There they stayed for a few days.

13When it was almost time for the Jewish Passover, Jesus went up to Jerusalem. 14In the temple courts he found men selling cattle, sheep and doves, and others sitting at tables exchanging money. 15So he made a whip out of cords, and drove all from the temple area, both sheep and cattle; he scattered the coins of the money changers and overturned their tables. 16To those who sold doves he said, "Get these out of here! How dare you turn my Father's house into a market!"

17His disciples remembered that it is written, "Zeal for your house will consume me."

18Then the Jews demanded of him, "What miraculous sign can you show us to prove your authority to do all this?"

19Jesus answered them, "Destroy this temple, and I will raise it again in three days."

20The Jews replied, "It has taken forty-six years to build this temple, and you are going to raise it in three days?"

[21]But the temple he had spoken of was
his body. [22]After he was raised from the
dead, his disciples recalled what he had
said. Then they believed the Scripture
and the words that Jesus had spoken.
[23]Now while he was in Jerusalem at
the Passover Feast, many people saw
the miraculous signs he was doing and
believed in his name. [24]But Jesus would
not entrust himself to them, for he knew
all men. [25]He did not need man's testimony about man, for he knew what was
in a man.

READING FROM PSALMS
Psalm 54:1–7

For the director of music. With stringed instruments. A *maskil* of David. When the Ziphites had gone to Saul and said, "Is not David hiding among us?"

[1]Save me, O God, by your name;
vindicate me by your might.

[2]Hear my prayer, O God;
listen to the words of my mouth.

[3]Strangers are attacking me;
ruthless men seek my life—
men without regard for God. *Selah*

[4]Surely God is my help;
the Lord is the one who sustains me.

[5]Let evil recoil on those who slander me;
in your faithfulness destroy them.

[6]I will sacrifice a freewill offering to you;
I will praise your name, O LORD,
for it is good.
[7]For he has delivered me from all my troubles,
and my eyes have looked in triumph on my foes.

DAY 122

MAY 2

OLD TESTAMENT READING
Joshua 21:20–22:34

[20]The rest of the Kohathite clans of the
Levites were allotted towns from the
tribe of Ephraim:
[21]In the hill country of Ephraim
they were given Shechem (a city of
refuge for one accused of murder)
and Gezer, [22]Kibzaim and Beth
Horon, together with their pasture-lands—four towns.
[23]Also from the tribe of Dan they
received Eltekeh, Gibbethon,
[24]Aijalon and Gath Rimmon,
together with their pasture-lands
—four towns.
[25]From half the tribe of Manasseh they received Taanach and
Gath Rimmon, together with their
pasture-lands—two towns.

[26]All these ten towns and their pasture-
lands were given to the rest of the
Kohathite clans.

[27]The Levite clans of the Gershonites
were given:
from the half-tribe of Manasseh,
Golan in Bashan (a city of refuge
for one accused of murder) and Be
Eshtarah, together with their pasture-lands—two towns;
[28]from the tribe of Issachar,
Kishion, Daberath, [29]Jarmuth and
En Gannim, together with their
pasture-lands—four towns;
[30]from the tribe of Asher,
Mishal, Abdon, [31]Helkath and Rehob, together with their pasture-
lands—four towns;
[32]from the tribe of Naphtali,
Kedesh in Galilee (a city of refuge

for one accused of murder), Hammoth Dor and Kartan, together with their pasture-lands—three towns.
33All the towns of the Gershonite clans were thirteen, together with their pasture-lands.

34The Merarite clans (the rest of the Levites) were given:
from the tribe of Zebulun,
Jokneam, Kartah, 35Dimnah and Nahalal, together with their pasture-lands—four towns;
36from the tribe of Reuben,
Bezer, Jahaz, 37Kedemoth and Mephaath, together with their pasture-lands—four towns;
38from the tribe of Gad,
Ramoth in Gilead (a city of refuge for one accused of murder), Mahanaim, 39Heshbon and Jazer, together with their pasture-lands —four towns in all.
40All the towns allotted to the Merarite clans, who were the rest of the Levites, were twelve.

41The towns of the Levites in the territory held by the Israelites were forty-eight in all, together with their pasture-lands. 42Each of these towns had pasture-lands surrounding it; this was true for all these towns.

43So the LORD gave Israel all the land he had sworn to give their forefathers, and they took possession of it and settled there. 44The LORD gave them rest on every side, just as he had sworn to their forefathers. Not one of their enemies withstood them; the LORD handed all their enemies over to them. 45Not one of all the LORD's good promises to the house of Israel failed; every one was fulfilled.

Eastern Tribes Return Home

22 Then Joshua summoned the Reubenites, the Gadites and the half-tribe of Manasseh 2and said to them, "You have done all that Moses the servant of the LORD commanded, and you have obeyed me in everything I commanded. 3For a long time now—to this very day—you have not deserted your brothers but have carried out the mission the LORD your God gave you. 4Now that the LORD your God has given your brothers rest as he promised, return to your homes in the land that Moses the servant of the LORD gave you on the other side of the Jordan. 5But be very careful to keep the commandment and the law that Moses the servant of the LORD gave you: to love the LORD your God, to walk in all his ways, to obey his commands, to hold fast to him and to serve him with all your heart and all your soul."

6Then Joshua blessed them and sent them away, and they went to their homes. 7(To the half-tribe of Manasseh Moses had given land in Bashan, and to the other half of the tribe Joshua gave land on the west side of the Jordan with their brothers.) When Joshua sent them home, he blessed them, 8saying, "Return to your homes with your great wealth—with large herds of livestock, with silver, gold, bronze and iron, and a great quantity of clothing—and divide with your brothers the plunder from your enemies."

9So the Reubenites, the Gadites and the half-tribe of Manasseh left the Israelites at Shiloh in Canaan to return to Gilead, their own land, which they had acquired in accordance with the command of the LORD through Moses.

10When they came to Geliloth near the Jordan in the land of Canaan, the Reubenites, the Gadites and the half-tribe of Manasseh built an imposing altar there by the Jordan. 11And when the Israelites heard that they had built the altar on the border of Canaan at Geliloth near the Jordan on the Israelite side, 12the whole assembly of Israel gathered at Shiloh to go to war against them.

13So the Israelites sent Phinehas son of Eleazar, the priest, to the land of

Gilead—to Reuben, Gad and the half-
tribe of Manasseh. 14With him they sent
ten of the chief men, one for each of the
tribes of Israel, each the head of a family division among the Israelite clans.
15When they went to Gilead—to
Reuben, Gad and the half-tribe of Manasseh—they said to them: 16"The
whole assembly of the LORD says: 'How
could you break faith with the God of
Israel like this? How could you turn
away from the LORD and build yourselves an altar in rebellion against him
now? 17Was not the sin of Peor enough
for us? Up to this very day we have not
cleansed ourselves from that sin, even
though a plague fell on the community
of the LORD! 18And are you now turning
away from the LORD?
"'If you rebel against the LORD today, tomorrow he will be angry with the
whole community of Israel. 19If the land
you possess is defiled, come over to the
LORD's land, where the LORD's tabernacle stands, and share the land with us.
But do not rebel against the LORD or
against us by building an altar for
yourselves, other than the altar of the
LORD our God. 20When Achan son of
Zerah acted unfaithfully regarding the
devoted things, did not wrath come
upon the whole community of Israel?
He was not the only one who died for his
sin.'"
21Then Reuben, Gad and the half-
tribe of Manasseh replied to the heads
of the clans of Israel: 22"The Mighty
One, God, the LORD! The Mighty One,
God, the LORD! He knows! And let
Israel know! If this has been in rebellion
or disobedience to the LORD, do not
spare us this day. 23If we have built our
own altar to turn away from the LORD
and to offer burnt offerings and grain
offerings, or to sacrifice fellowship
offerings on it, may the LORD himself
call us to account.
24"No! We did it for fear that some
day your descendants might say to ours,
'What do you have to do with the LORD,
the God of Israel? 25The LORD has
made the Jordan a boundary between
us and you—you Reubenites and Gadites! You have no share in the LORD.' So
your descendants might cause ours to
stop fearing the LORD.
26"That is why we said, 'Let us get
ready and build an altar—but not for
burnt offerings or sacrifices.' 27On the
contrary, it is to be a witness between us
and you and the generations that follow, that we will worship the LORD at
his sanctuary with our burnt offerings,
sacrifices and fellowship offerings.
Then in the future your descendants will
not be able to say to ours, 'You have no
share in the LORD.'
28"And we said, 'If they ever say this
to us, or to our descendants, we will
answer: Look at the replica of the
LORD's altar, which our fathers built,
not for burnt offerings and sacrifices,
but as a witness between us and you.'
29"Far be it from us to rebel against
the LORD and turn away from him today
by building an altar for burnt offerings,
grain offerings and sacrifices, other than
the altar of the LORD our God that
stands before his tabernacle."
30When Phinehas the priest and the
leaders of the community—the heads
of the clans of the Israelites—heard
what Reuben, Gad and Manasseh had
to say, they were pleased. 31And
Phinehas son of Eleazar, the priest, said
to Reuben, Gad and Manasseh, "Today
we know that the LORD is with us, because you have not acted unfaithfully
towards the LORD in this matter. Now
you have rescued the Israelites from the
LORD's hand."
32Then Phinehas son of Eleazar, the
priest, and the leaders returned to Canaan from their meeting with the
Reubenites and Gadites in Gilead and
reported to the Israelites. 33They were
glad to hear the report and praised God.
And they talked no more about going
to war against them to devastate the
country where the Reubenites and the
Gadites lived.
34And the Reubenites and the Gadites gave the altar this name: A Witness
Between Us that the LORD is God.

NEW TESTAMENT READING

John 3:1–21

Jesus Teaches Nicodemus

3 Now there was a man of the Pharisees named Nicodemus, a member
of the Jewish ruling council. 2He came
to Jesus at night and said, "Rabbi, we
know you are a teacher who has come
from God. For no-one could perform
the miraculous signs you are doing if
God were not with him."
3In reply Jesus declared, "I tell you
the truth, no-one can see the kingdom
of God unless he is born again."
4"How can a man be born when he is
old?" Nicodemus asked. "Surely he
cannot enter a second time into his
mother's womb to be born!"
5Jesus answered, "I tell you the truth,
no-one can enter the kingdom of God
unless he is born of water and the Spirit.
6Flesh gives birth to flesh, but the Spirit
gives birth to spirit. 7You should not be
surprised at my saying, 'You must be
born again.' 8The wind blows wherever
it pleases. You hear its sound, but you
cannot tell where it comes from or
where it is going. So it is with everyone
born of the Spirit."
9"How can this be?" Nicodemus
asked.
10"You are Israel's teacher," said
Jesus, "and do you not understand
these things? 11I tell you the truth, we
speak of what we know, and we testify
to what we have seen, but still you
people do not accept our testimony. 12I
have spoken to you of earthly things and
you do not believe; how then will you
believe if I speak of heavenly things?
13No-one has ever gone into heaven
except the one who came from heaven
—the Son of Man. 14Just as Moses lifted
up the snake in the desert, so the Son of
Man must be lifted up, 15that everyone
who believes in him may have eternal
life.
16"For God so loved the world that he
gave his one and only Son, that whoever
believes in him shall not perish but have
eternal life. 17For God did not send his
Son into the world to condemn the
world, but to save the world through
him. 18Whoever believes in him is not
condemned, but whoever does not believe stands condemned already because he has not believed in the name of
God's one and only Son. 19This is the
verdict: Light has come into the world,
but men loved darkness instead of
light because their deeds were evil.
20Everyone who does evil hates the
light, and will not come into the light for
fear that his deeds will be exposed.
21But whoever lives by the truth comes
into the light, so that it may be seen
plainly that what he has done has been
done through God."

READING FROM PSALMS

Psalm 55:1–11

For the director of music. With stringed instruments. A *maskil* of David.

1Listen to my prayer, O God,
do not ignore my plea;
2 hear me and answer me.
My thoughts trouble me and I am
distraught
3 at the voice of the enemy,
at the stares of the wicked;
for they bring down suffering upon
me
and revile me in their anger.

4My heart is in anguish within me;
the terrors of death assail me.
5Fear and trembling have beset me;
horror has overwhelmed me.
6I said, "Oh, that I had the wings of a
dove!
I would fly away and be at rest—
7I would flee far away
and stay in the desert; *Selah*
8I would hurry to my place of shelter,
far from the tempest and storm."

9Confuse the wicked, O Lord,
confound their speech,
for I see violence and strife in the
city.

10Day and night they prowl about on its
walls;
malice and abuse are within
it.

11Destructive forces are at work in the
city;
threats and lies never leave its
streets.

DAY 123

MAY 3

OLD TESTAMENT READING
Joshua 23:1–24:33

Joshua's Farewell to the Leaders

23 After a long time had passed and
the LORD had given Israel rest
from all their enemies around them,
Joshua, by then old and well advanced
in years, 2summoned all Israel—their
elders, leaders, judges and officials—
and said to them: "I am old and well
advanced in years. 3You yourselves
have seen everything the LORD your
God has done to all these nations for
your sake; it was the LORD your God
who fought for you. 4Remember how I
have allotted as an inheritance for your
tribes all the land of the nations that
remain—the nations I conquered—
between the Jordan and the Great Sea
in the west. 5The LORD your God himself will drive them out of your way. He
will push them out before you, and you
will take possession of their land, as the
LORD your God promised you.

6"Be very strong; be careful to obey
all that is written in the Book of the Law
of Moses, without turning aside to the
right or to the left. 7Do not associate
with these nations that remain among
you; do not invoke the names of their
gods or swear by them. You must not
serve them or bow down to them. 8But
you are to hold fast to the LORD your
God, as you have until now.

9"The LORD has driven out before
you great and powerful nations; to this
day no-one has been able to withstand
you. 10One of you routs a thousand,
because the LORD your God fights for
you, just as he promised. 11So be very
careful to love the LORD your God.

12"But if you turn away and ally
yourselves with the survivors of these
nations that remain among you and if
you intermarry with them and associate
with them, 13then you may be sure that
the LORD your God will no longer drive
out these nations before you. Instead,
they will become snares and traps for
you, whips on your backs and thorns in
your eyes, until you perish from this
good land, which the LORD your God
has given you.

14"Now I am about to go the way of
all the earth. You know with all your
heart and soul that not one of all the
good promises the LORD your God gave
you has failed. Every promise has been
fulfilled; not one has failed. 15But just as
every good promise of the LORD your
God has come true, so the LORD will
bring on you all the evil he has
threatened, until he has destroyed you
from this good land he has given you.
16If you violate the covenant of the
LORD your God, which he commanded
you, and go and serve other gods and
bow down to them, the LORD's anger
will burn against you, and you will
quickly perish from the good land he
has given you."

The Covenant Renewed at Shechem

24 Then Joshua assembled all the
tribes of Israel at Shechem. He
summoned the elders, leaders, judges
and officials of Israel, and they presented themselves before God.

2Joshua said to all the people, "This is
what the LORD, the God of Israel, says:
'Long ago your forefathers, including
Terah the father of Abraham and
Nahor, lived beyond the River and worshipped other gods. 3But I took your
father Abraham from the land beyond
the River and led him throughout Canaan and gave him many descendants. I
gave him Isaac, 4and to Isaac I gave
Jacob and Esau. I assigned the hill
country of Seir to Esau, but Jacob and
his sons went down to Egypt.

5" 'Then I sent Moses and Aaron, and
I afflicted the Egyptians by what I did
there, and I brought you out. 6When I
brought your fathers out of Egypt, you
came to the sea, and the Egyptians pursued them with chariots and horsemen
as far as the Red Sea. 7But they cried to
the LORD for help, and he put darkness
between you and the Egyptians; he
brought the sea over them and covered
them. You saw with your own eyes what
I did to the Egyptians. Then you lived in
the desert for a long time.

8" 'I brought you to the land of the
Amorites who lived east of the Jordan.
They fought against you, but I gave
them into your hands. I destroyed them
from before you, and you took possession of their land. 9When Balak son of
Zippor, the king of Moab, prepared to
fight against Israel, he sent for Balaam
son of Beor to put a curse on you. 10But
I would not listen to Balaam, so
he blessed you again and again, and I
delivered you out of his hand.

11" 'Then you crossed the Jordan and
came to Jericho. The citizens of Jericho
fought against you, as did also the
Amorites, Perizzites, Canaanites, Hittites, Girgashites, Hivites and Jebusites, but I gave them into your hands.
12I sent the hornet ahead of you, which
drove them out before you—also the
two Amorite kings. You did not do it
with your own sword and bow. 13So I
gave you a land on which you did not
toil and cities you did not build; and you
live in them and eat from vineyards and
olive groves that you did not plant.'

14"Now fear the LORD and serve him
with all faithfulness. Throw away the
gods your forefathers worshipped
beyond the River and in Egypt, and
serve the LORD. 15But if serving the
LORD seems undesirable to you, then
choose for yourselves this day whom
you will serve, whether the gods your
forefathers served beyond the River, or
the gods of the Amorites, in whose land
you are living. But as for me and my
household, we will serve the LORD."

16Then the people answered, "Far be
it from us to forsake the LORD to serve
other gods! 17It was the LORD our God
himself who brought us and our fathers
up out of Egypt, from that land of slavery, and performed those great signs
before our eyes. He protected us on our
entire journey and among all the nations through which we travelled. 18And
the LORD drove out before us all the
nations, including the Amorites, who
lived in the land. We too will serve the
LORD, because he is our God."

19Joshua said to the people, "You are
not able to serve the LORD. He is a holy
God; he is a jealous God. He will not
forgive your rebellion and your sins. 20If
you forsake the LORD and serve foreign
gods, he will turn and bring disaster on
you and make an end of you, after he
has been good to you."

21But the people said to Joshua, "No!
We will serve the LORD."

22Then Joshua said, "You are witnesses against yourselves that you have
chosen to serve the LORD."

"Yes, we are witnesses," they replied.

23"Now then," said Joshua, "throw
away the foreign gods that are among
you and yield your hearts to the LORD,
the God of Israel."

24And the people said to Joshua, "We
will serve the LORD our God and obey
him."

25On that day Joshua made a covenant for the people, and there at
Shechem he drew up for them decrees
and laws. 26And Joshua recorded these
things in the Book of the Law of God.

Then he took a large stone and set it up
there under the oak near the holy place
of the LORD.
27“See!” he said to all the people.
“This stone will be a witness against us.
It has heard all the words the LORD has
said to us. It will be a witness against
you if you are untrue to your God.”

Buried in the Promised Land

28Then Joshua sent the people away,
each to his own inheritance.
29After these things, Joshua son of
Nun, the servant of the LORD, died at
the age of a hundred and ten. 30And
they buried him in the land of his inheritance, at Timnath Serah in the hill country of Ephraim, north of Mount Gaash.
31Israel served the LORD throughout
the lifetime of Joshua and of the elders
who outlived him and who had experienced everything the LORD had done
for Israel.
32And Joseph's bones, which the
Israelites had brought up from Egypt,
were buried at Shechem in the tract of
land that Jacob bought for a hundred
pieces of silver from the sons of Hamor,
the father of Shechem. This became the
inheritance of Joseph's descendants.
33And Eleazar son of Aaron died and
was buried at Gibeah, which had been
allotted to his son Phinehas in the hill
country of Ephraim.

NEW TESTAMENT READING

John 3:22–36

John the Baptist's Testimony About Jesus

22After this, Jesus and his disciples
went out into the Judean countryside,
where he spent some time with them,
and baptised. 23Now John also was baptising at Aenon near Salim, because
there was plenty of water, and people
were constantly coming to be baptised.
24(This was before John was put in
prison.) 25An argument developed between some of John's disciples and a
certain Jew over the matter of ceremonial washing. 26They came to John
and said to him, “Rabbi, that man who
was with you on the other side of the
Jordan—the one you testified about—
well, he is baptising, and everyone is
going to him.”
27To this John replied, “A man can
receive only what is given him from
heaven. 28You yourselves can testify
that I said, ‘I am not the Christ but am
sent ahead of him.’ 29The bride belongs
to the bridegroom. The friend who
attends the bridegroom waits and
listens for him, and is full of joy when
he hears the bridegroom's voice. That
joy is mine, and it is now complete.
30He must become greater; I must
become less.
31“The one who comes from above is
above all; the one who is from the earth
belongs to the earth, and speaks as one
from the earth. The one who comes
from heaven is above all. 32He testifies
to what he has seen and heard, but
no-one accepts his testimony. 33The
man who has accepted it has certified
that God is truthful. 34For the one
whom God has sent speaks the words of
God, for God gives the Spirit without
limit. 35The Father loves the Son and
has placed everything in his hands.
36Whoever believes in the Son has eternal life, but whoever rejects the Son will
not see life, for God's wrath remains on
him.”

READING FROM PSALMS

Psalm 55:12–23

12If an enemy were insulting me,
  I could endure it;
 if a foe were raising himself against
   me,
  I could hide from him.
13But it is you, a man like myself,
  my companion, my close friend,
14with whom I once enjoyed sweet
   fellowship
  as we walked with the throng at the
   house of God.

[15]Let death take my enemies by
surprise;
let them go down alive to the grave,
for evil finds lodging among them.

[16]But I call to God,
and the LORD saves me.
[17]Evening, morning and noon
I cry out in distress,
and he hears my voice.
[18]He ransoms me unharmed
from the battle waged against me,
even though many oppose me.
[19]God, who is enthroned for ever,
will hear them and afflict
them— *Selah*
men who never change their ways
and have no fear of God.

[20]My companion attacks his friends;
he violates his covenant.
[21]His speech is smooth as butter,
yet war is in his heart;
his words are more soothing than oil,
yet they are drawn swords.

[22]Cast your cares on the LORD
and he will sustain you;
he will never let the righteous fall.
[23]But you, O God, will bring down the
wicked
into the pit of corruption;
bloodthirsty and deceitful men
will not live out half their days.

But as for me, I trust in you.

MAY 4

DAY 124

OLD TESTAMENT READING
Judges 1:1–2:5

Israel Fights the Remaining Canaanites

1 After the death of Joshua, the
Israelites asked the LORD, "Who
will be the first to go up and fight for us
against the Canaanites?"
[2]The LORD answered, "Judah is to
go; I have given the land into their
hands."
[3]Then the men of Judah said to the
Simeonites their brothers, "Come up
with us into the territory allotted to us,
to fight against the Canaanites. We in
turn will go with you into yours." So the
Simeonites went with them.
[4]When Judah attacked, the LORD
gave the Canaanites and Perizzites into
their hands and they struck down ten
thousand men at Bezek. [5]It was there
that they found Adoni-Bezek and
fought against him, putting to rout the
Canaanites and Perizzites. [6]Adoni-
Bezek fled, but they chased him and
caught him, and cut off his thumbs and
big toes.
[7]Then Adoni-Bezek said, "Seventy
kings with their thumbs and big toes cut
off have picked up scraps under my
table. Now God has paid me back for
what I did to them." They brought him
to Jerusalem, and he died there.
[8]The men of Judah attacked Jerusalem also and took it. They put the city
to the sword and set it on fire.
[9]After that, the men of Judah went
down to fight against the Canaanites
living in the hill country, the Negev and
the western foothills. [10]They advanced
against the Canaanites living in Hebron
(formerly called Kiriath Arba) and defeated Sheshai, Ahiman and Talmai.
[11]From there they advanced against
the people living in Debir (formerly
called Kiriath Sepher). [12]And Caleb
said, "I will give my daughter Acsah in
marriage to the man who attacks and
captures Kiriath Sepher." [13]Othniel son
of Kenaz, Caleb's younger brother,
took it; so Caleb gave his daughter
Acsah to him in marriage.
[14]One day when she came to Othniel,
she urged him to ask her father for a

field. When she got off her donkey, Caleb asked her, "What can I do for you?"

15She replied, "Do me a special favour. Since you have given me land in the Negev, give me also springs of water." Then Caleb gave her the upper and lower springs.

16The descendants of Moses' father-in-law, the Kenite, went up from the City of Palms with the men of Judah to live among the people of the Desert of Judah in the Negev near Arad.

17Then the men of Judah went with the Simeonites their brothers and attacked the Canaanites living in Zephath, and they totally destroyed the city. Therefore it was called Hormah. 18The men of Judah also took Gaza, Ashkelon and Ekron—each city with its territory.

19The LORD was with the men of Judah. They took possession of the hill country, but they were unable to drive the people from the plains, because they had iron chariots. 20As Moses had promised, Hebron was given to Caleb, who drove from it the three sons of Anak. 21The Benjamites, however, failed to dislodge the Jebusites, who were living in Jerusalem; to this day the Jebusites live there with the Benjamites.

22Now the house of Joseph attacked Bethel, and the LORD was with them. 23When they sent men to spy out Bethel (formerly called Luz), 24the spies saw a man coming out of the city and they said to him, "Show us how to get into the city and we will see that you are treated well." 25So he showed them, and they put the city to the sword but spared the man and his whole family. 26He then went to the land of the Hittites, where he built a city and called it Luz, which is its name to this day.

27But Manasseh did not drive out the people of Beth Shan or Taanach or Dor or Ibleam or Megiddo and their surrounding settlements, for the Canaanites were determined to live in that land. 28When Israel became strong, they pressed the Canaanites into forced labour but never drove them out completely. 29Nor did Ephraim drive out the Canaanites living in Gezer, but the Canaanites continued to live there among them. 30Neither did Zebulun drive out the Canaanites living in Kitron or Nahalol, who remained among them; but they did subject them to forced labour. 31Nor did Asher drive out those living in Acco or Sidon or Ahlab or Aczib or Helbah or Aphek or Rehob, 32and because of this the people of Asher lived among the Canaanite inhabitants of the land. 33Neither did Naphtali drive out those living in Beth Shemesh or Beth Anath; but the Naphtalites too lived among the Canaanite inhabitants of the land, and those living in Beth Shemesh and Beth Anath became forced labourers for them. 34The Amorites confined the Danites to the hill country, not allowing them to come down into the plain. 35And the Amorites were determined also to hold out in Mount Heres, Aijalon and Shaalbim, but when the power of the house of Joseph increased, they too were pressed into forced labour. 36The boundary of the Amorites was from Scorpion Pass to Sela and beyond.

The Angel of the LORD at Bokim

2 The angel of the LORD went up from Gilgal to Bokim and said, "I brought you up out of Egypt and led you into the land that I swore to give to your forefathers. I said, 'I will never break my covenant with you, 2and you shall not make a covenant with the people of this land, but you shall break down their altars.' Yet you have disobeyed me. Why have you done this? 3Now therefore I tell you that I will not drive them out before you; they will be ⌊thorns⌋ in your sides and their gods will be a snare to you."

4When the angel of the LORD had spoken these things to all the Israelites, the people wept aloud, 5and they called that place Bokim. There they offered sacrifices to the LORD.

NEW TESTAMENT READING
John 4:1–26

Jesus Talks With a Samaritan Woman

4 The Pharisees heard that Jesus was
gaining and baptising more disciples than John, 2although in fact it was
not Jesus who baptised, but his disciples. 3When the Lord learned of this,
he left Judea and went back once more
to Galilee.
4Now he had to go through Samaria.
5So he came to a town in Samaria called
Sychar, near the plot of ground Jacob
had given to his son Joseph. 6Jacob's
well was there, and Jesus, tired as he
was from the journey, sat down by the
well. It was about the sixth hour.
7When a Samaritan woman came to
draw water, Jesus said to her, "Will you
give me a drink?" 8(His disciples had
gone into the town to buy food.)
9The Samaritan woman said to him,
"You are a Jew and I am a Samaritan
woman. How can you ask me for a
drink?" (For Jews do not associate with
Samaritans.)
10Jesus answered her, "If you knew
the gift of God and who it is that asks
you for a drink, you would have asked
him and he would have given you living
water."
11"Sir," the woman said, "you have
nothing to draw with and the well is
deep. Where can you get this living
water? 12Are you greater than our
father Jacob, who gave us the well and
drank from it himself, as did also his
sons and his flocks and herds?"
13Jesus answered, "Everyone who
drinks this water will be thirsty again,
14but whoever drinks the water I give
him will never thirst. Indeed, the water
I give him will become in him a spring of
water welling up to eternal life."
15The woman said to him, "Sir, give
me this water so that I won't get thirsty
and have to keep coming here to draw
water."
16He told her, "Go, call your husband
and come back."
17"I have no husband," she replied.
Jesus said to her, "You are right
when you say you have no husband.
18The fact is, you have had five husbands, and the man you now have is not
your husband. What you have just said
is quite true."
19"Sir," the woman said, "I can see
that you are a prophet. 20Our fathers
worshipped on this mountain, but you
Jews claim that the place where we must
worship is in Jerusalem."
21Jesus declared, "Believe me,
woman, a time is coming when you will
worship the Father neither on this
mountain nor in Jerusalem. 22You
Samaritans worship what you do not
know; we worship what we do know, for
salvation is from the Jews. 23Yet a time
is coming and has now come when the
true worshippers will worship the
Father in spirit and truth, for they are
the kind of worshippers the Father
seeks. 24God is spirit, and his worshippers must worship in spirit and in
truth."
25The woman said, "I know that Messiah" (called Christ) "is coming. When
he comes, he will explain everything to
us."
26Then Jesus declared, "I who speak
to you am he."

READING FROM PROVERBS
Proverbs 11:9–18

9With his mouth the godless destroys
his neighbour,
but through knowledge the
righteous escape.

10When the righteous prosper, the city
rejoices;
when the wicked perish, there are
shouts of joy.

11Through the blessing of the upright a
city is exalted,
but by the mouth of the wicked it is
destroyed.

[12]A man who lacks judgment derides
his neighbour,
but a man of understanding holds
his tongue.

[13]A gossip betrays a confidence,
but a trustworthy man keeps a
secret.

[14]For lack of guidance a nation falls,
but many advisers make victory
sure.

[15]He who puts up security for another
will surely suffer,
but whoever refuses to strike hands
in pledge is safe.

[16]A kind-hearted woman gains respect,
but ruthless men gain only wealth.

[17]A kind man benefits himself,
but a cruel man brings trouble on
himself.

[18]The wicked man earns deceptive
wages,
but he who sows righteousness
reaps a sure reward.

DAY 125

MAY 5

OLD TESTAMENT READING
Judges 2:6–3:31

Disobedience and Defeat

[6]After Joshua had dismissed the
Israelites, they went to take possession
of the land, each to his own inheritance.
[7]The people served the LORD throughout the lifetime of Joshua and of the
elders who outlived him and who had
seen all the great things the LORD had
done for Israel.

[8]Joshua son of Nun, the servant of the
LORD, died at the age of a hundred and
ten. [9]And they buried him in the land of
his inheritance, at Timnath Heres in the
hill country of Ephraim, north of Mount
Gaash.

[10]After that whole generation had
been gathered to their fathers, another
generation grew up, who knew neither
the LORD nor what he had done for
Israel. [11]Then the Israelites did evil in
the eyes of the LORD and served the
Baals. [12]They forsook the LORD, the
God of their fathers, who had brought
them out of Egypt. They followed and
worshipped various gods of the peoples
around them. They provoked the LORD
to anger [13]because they forsook him and
served Baal and the Ashtoreths. [14]In his
anger against Israel the LORD handed
them over to raiders who plundered
them. He sold them to their enemies all
around, whom they were no longer able
to resist. [15]Whenever Israel went out to
fight, the hand of the LORD was against
them to defeat them, just as he had
sworn to them. They were in great
distress.

[16]Then the LORD raised up judges,
who saved them out of the hands of
these raiders. [17]Yet they would not listen to their judges but prostituted themselves to other gods and worshipped
them. Unlike their fathers, they quickly
turned from the way in which their
fathers had walked, the way of obedience to the LORD's commands. [18]When-
ever the LORD raised up a judge for
them, he was with the judge and saved
them out of the hands of their enemies
as long as the judge lived; for the LORD
had compassion on them as they
groaned under those who oppressed
and afflicted them. [19]But when the
judge died, the people returned to ways
even more corrupt than those of their

fathers, following other gods and serving and worshipping them. They refused to give up their evil practices and
stubborn ways.
20Therefore the LORD was very angry
with Israel and said, "Because this nation has violated the covenant that I laid
down for their forefathers and has not
listened to me, 21I will no longer drive
out before them any of the nations
Joshua left when he died. 22I will use
them to test Israel and see whether they
will keep the way of the LORD and walk
in it as their forefathers did." 23The
LORD had allowed those nations to remain; he did not drive them out at once
by giving them into the hands of Joshua.
3 These are the nations the LORD left
to test all those Israelites who had
not experienced any of the wars in Canaan 2(he did this only to teach warfare
to the descendants of the Israelites who
had not had previous battle experience): 3the five rulers of the Philistines,
all the Canaanites, the Sidonians, and
the Hivites living in the Lebanon mountains from Mount Baal Hermon to Lebo
Hamath. 4They were left to test the
Israelites to see whether they would
obey the LORD's commands, which he
had given their forefathers through
Moses.
5The Israelites lived among the
Canaanites, Hittites, Amorites, Perizzites, Hivites and Jebusites. 6They took
their daughters in marriage and gave
their own daughters to their sons, and
served their gods.

Othniel

7The Israelites did evil in the eyes of
the LORD; they forgot the LORD their
God and served the Baals and the
Asherahs. 8The anger of the LORD
burned against Israel so that he sold
them into the hands of Cushan-
Rishathaim king of Aram Naharaim, to
whom the Israelites were subject for
eight years. 9But when they cried out to
the LORD, he raised up for them a deliverer, Othniel son of Kenaz, Caleb's
younger brother, who saved them.
10The Spirit of the LORD came upon
him, so that he became Israel's judge
and went to war. The LORD gave
Cushan-Rishathaim king of Aram into
the hands of Othniel, who overpowered
him. 11So the land had peace for forty
years, until Othniel son of Kenaz died.

Ehud

12Once again the Israelites did evil in
the eyes of the LORD, and because they
did this evil the LORD gave Eglon king
of Moab power over Israel. 13Getting
the Ammonites and Amalekites to join
him, Eglon came and attacked Israel,
and they took possession of the City of
Palms. 14The Israelites were subject to
Eglon king of Moab for eighteen years.
15Again the Israelites cried out to the
LORD, and he gave them a deliverer
—Ehud, a left-handed man, the son of
Gera the Benjamite. The Israelites sent
him with tribute to Eglon king of Moab.
16Now Ehud had made a double-edged
sword about a foot and a half long,
which he strapped to his right thigh
under his clothing. 17He presented the
tribute to Eglon king of Moab, who was
a very fat man. 18After Ehud had presented the tribute, he sent on their way
the men who had carried it. 19At the
idols near Gilgal he himself turned back
and said, "I have a secret message for
you, O king."
The king said, "Quiet!" And all his
attendants left him.
20Ehud then approached him while
he was sitting alone in the upper room
of his summer palace and said, "I have a
message from God for you." As the
king rose from his seat, 21Ehud reached
with his left hand, drew the sword from
his right thigh and plunged it into the
king's belly. 22Even the handle sank in
after the blade, which came out of his
back. Ehud did not pull the sword out,
and the fat closed in over it. 23Then
Ehud went out to the porch; he shut the
doors of the upper room behind him
and locked them.

[24]After he had gone, the servants
came and found the doors of the upper
room locked. They said, "He must be
relieving himself in the inner room of
the house." [25]They waited to the point
of embarrassment, but when he did not
open the doors of the room, they took a
key and unlocked them. There they saw
their lord fallen to the floor, dead.
[26]While they waited, Ehud got away.
He passed by the idols and escaped to
Seirah. [27]When he arrived there, he
blew a trumpet in the hill country of
Ephraim, and the Israelites went down
with him from the hills, with him leading them.
[28]"Follow me," he ordered, "for the
LORD has given Moab, your enemy,
into your hands." So they followed him
down and, taking possession of the
fords of the Jordan that led to Moab,
they allowed no-one to cross over. [29]At
that time they struck down about ten
thousand Moabites, all vigorous and
strong; not a man escaped. [30]That day
Moab was made subject to Israel, and
the land had peace for eighty years.

Shamgar

[31]After Ehud came Shamgar son of
Anath, who struck down six hundred
Philistines with an ox-goad. He too
saved Israel.

NEW TESTAMENT READING
John 4:27–42

The Disciples Rejoin Jesus

[27]Just then his disciples returned and
were surprised to find him talking with a
woman. But no-one asked, "What do
you want?" or "Why are you talking
with her?"
[28]Then, leaving her water jar, the
woman went back to the town and said
to the people, [29]"Come, see a man who
told me everything I ever did. Could
this be the Christ?" [30]They came out of
the town and made their way towards
him.
[31]Meanwhile his disciples urged him,
"Rabbi, eat something."
[32]But he said to them, "I have food to
eat that you know nothing about."
[33]Then his disciples said to each
other, "Could someone have brought
him food?"
[34]"My food," said Jesus, "is to do the
will of him who sent me and to finish his
work. [35]Do you not say, 'Four months
more and then the harvest'? I tell you,
open your eyes and look at the fields!
They are ripe for harvest. [36]Even now
the reaper draws his wages, even now
he harvests the crop for eternal life, so
that the sower and the reaper may be
glad together. [37]Thus the saying 'One
sows and another reaps' is true. [38]I sent
you to reap what you have not worked
for. Others have done the hard work,
and you have reaped the benefits of
their labour."

Many Samaritans Believe

[39]Many of the Samaritans from that
town believed in him because of the
woman's testimony, "He told me everything I ever did." [40]So when the Samaritans came to him, they urged him to
stay with them, and he stayed two days.
[41]And because of his words many more
became believers.
[42]They said to the woman, "We no
longer believe just because of what you
said; now we have heard for ourselves,
and we know that this man really is the
Saviour of the world."

READING FROM PSALMS
Psalm 56:1–13

For the director of music. To ⌊the tune of⌋ "A Dove on Distant Oaks". Of David. A *miktam.* When the Philistines had seized him in Gath.

[1]Be merciful to me, O God, for men
hotly pursue me;
all day long they press their attack.

[2]My slanderers pursue me all day
long;
many are attacking me in their
pride.

[3]When I am afraid,
I will trust in you.
[4]In God, whose word I praise,
in God I trust; I will not be
afraid.
What can mortal man do to me?

[5]All day long they twist my words;
they are always plotting to harm
me.
[6]They conspire, they lurk,
they watch my steps,
eager to take my life.

[7]On no account let them escape;
in your anger, O God, bring down
the nations.

[8]Record my lament;
list my tears on your scroll—
are they not in your record?

[9]Then my enemies will turn back
when I call for help.
By this I will know that God is for
me.
[10]In God, whose word I praise,
in the LORD, whose word I
praise—
[11]in God I trust; I will not be afraid.
What can man do to me?

[12]I am under vows to you, O God;
I will present my thank-offerings to
you.
[13]For you have delivered me from
death
and my feet from stumbling,
that I may walk before God
in the light of life.

MAY 6

DAY 126

OLD TESTAMENT READING
Judges 4:1–5:31

Deborah

4 After Ehud died, the Israelites
once again did evil in the eyes of
the LORD. [2]So the LORD sold them into
the hands of Jabin, a king of Canaan,
who reigned in Hazor. The commander
of his army was Sisera, who lived in
Harosheth Haggoyim. [3]Because he had
nine hundred iron chariots and had
cruelly oppressed the Israelites for
twenty years, they cried to the LORD for
help.
[4]Deborah, a prophetess, the wife of
Lappidoth, was leading Israel at that
time. [5]She held court under the Palm of
Deborah between Ramah and Bethel in
the hill country of Ephraim, and the
Israelites came to her to have their disputes decided. [6]She sent for Barak son
of Abinoam from Kedesh in Naphtali
and said to him, "The LORD, the God of
Israel, commands you: 'Go, take with
you ten thousand men of Naphtali and
Zebulun and lead the way to Mount
Tabor. [7]I will lure Sisera, the commander of Jabin's army, with his chariots
and his troops to the Kishon River and
give him into your hands.'"
[8]Barak said to her, "If you go with
me, I will go; but if you don't go with
me, I won't go."
[9]"Very well," Deborah said, "I will
go with you. But because of the way you
are going about this, the honour will not
be yours, for the LORD will hand Sisera
over to a woman." So Deborah went
with Barak to Kedesh, [10]where he
summoned Zebulun and Naphtali. Ten
thousand men followed him, and
Deborah also went with him.
[11]Now Heber the Kenite had left the

other Kenites, the descendants of
Hobab, Moses' brother-in-law, and
pitched his tent by the great tree in
Zaanannim near Kedesh.
12When they told Sisera that Barak
son of Abinoam had gone up to Mount
Tabor, 13Sisera gathered together his
nine hundred iron chariots and all the
men with him, from Harosheth Haggoyim to the Kishon River.
14Then Deborah said to Barak, "Go!
This is the day the LORD has given
Sisera into your hands. Has not the
LORD gone ahead of you?" So Barak
went down Mount Tabor, followed by
ten thousand men. 15At Barak's advance, the LORD routed Sisera and all
his chariots and army by the sword,
and Sisera abandoned his chariot and
fled on foot. 16But Barak pursued the
chariots and army as far as Harosheth
Haggoyim. All the troops of Sisera fell
by the sword; not a man was left.
17Sisera, however, fled on foot to the
tent of Jael, the wife of Heber the
Kenite, because there were friendly
relations between Jabin king of Hazor
and the clan of Heber the Kenite.
18Jael went out to meet Sisera and
said to him, "Come, my lord, come
right in. Don't be afraid." So he entered
her tent, and she put a covering over
him.
19"I'm thirsty," he said. "Please give
me some water." She opened a skin of
milk, gave him a drink, and covered him
up.
20"Stand in the doorway of the tent,"
he told her. "If someone comes by and
asks you, 'Is anyone here?' say 'No.'"
21But Jael, Heber's wife, picked up a
tent peg and a hammer and went quietly
to him while he lay fast asleep, exhausted. She drove the peg through his
temple into the ground, and he died.
22Barak came by in pursuit of Sisera,
and Jael went out to meet him.
"Come," she said, "I will show you the
man you're looking for." So he went in
with her, and there lay Sisera with the
tent peg through his temple—dead.
23On that day God subdued Jabin,
the Canaanite king, before the
Israelites. 24And the hand of the
Israelites grew stronger and stronger
against Jabin, the Canaanite king, until
they destroyed him.

The Song of Deborah

5 On that day Deborah and Barak
son of Abinoam sang this song:

2"When the princes in Israel take the
lead,
when the people willingly offer
themselves—
praise the LORD!

3"Hear this, you kings! Listen, you
rulers!
I will sing to the LORD, I will sing;
I will make music to the LORD, the
God of Israel.

4"O LORD, when you went out from
Seir,
when you marched from the land
of Edom,
the earth shook, the heavens
poured,
the clouds poured down water.
5The mountains quaked before the
LORD, the One of Sinai,
before the LORD, the God of
Israel.

6"In the days of Shamgar son of
Anath,
in the days of Jael, the roads were
abandoned;
travellers took to winding paths.
7Village life in Israel ceased,
ceased until I, Deborah, arose,
arose a mother in Israel.
8When they chose new gods,
war came to the city gates,
and not a shield or spear was seen
among forty thousand in Israel.
9My heart is with Israel's princes,
with the willing volunteers among
the people.
Praise the LORD!

10"You who ride on white donkeys,
sitting on your saddle blankets,
and you who walk along the road,
consider 11the voice of the singers at
the watering places.
They recite the righteous acts of
the LORD,
the righteous acts of his warriors in
Israel.

"Then the people of the LORD
went down to the city gates.
12'Wake up, wake up, Deborah!
Wake up, wake up, break out in
song!
Arise, O Barak!
Take captive your captives, O son
of Abinoam.'

13"Then the men who were left
came down to the nobles;
the people of the LORD
came to me with the mighty.
14Some came from Ephraim, whose
roots were in Amalek;
Benjamin was with the people who
followed you.
From Makir captains came down,
from Zebulun those who bear a
commander's staff.
15The princes of Issachar were with
Deborah;
yes, Issachar was with Barak,
rushing after him into the valley.
In the districts of Reuben
there was much searching of heart.
16Why did you stay among the
campfires
to hear the whistling for the flocks?
In the districts of Reuben
there was much searching of heart.
17Gilead stayed beyond the Jordan.
And Dan, why did he linger by the
ships?
Asher remained on the coast
and stayed in his coves.
18The people of Zebulun risked their
very lives;
so did Naphtali on the heights of
the field.

19"Kings came, they fought;
the kings of Canaan fought
at Taanach by the waters of Megiddo,
but they carried off no silver, no
plunder.
20From the heavens the stars fought,
from their courses they fought
against Sisera.
21The river Kishon swept them away,
the age-old river, the river Kishon.
March on, my soul; be strong!
22Then thundered the horses' hoofs—
galloping, galloping go his mighty
steeds.
23'Curse Meroz,' said the angel of the
LORD.
'Curse its people bitterly,
because they did not come to help the
LORD,
to help the LORD against the
mighty.'

24"Most blessed of women be Jael,
the wife of Heber the Kenite,
most blessed of tent-dwelling
women.
25He asked for water, and she gave him
milk;
in a bowl fit for nobles she brought
him curdled milk.
26Her hand reached for the tent peg,
her right hand for the workman's
hammer.
She struck Sisera, she crushed his
head,
she shattered and pierced his
temple.
27At her feet he sank,
he fell; there he lay.
At her feet he sank, he fell;
where he sank, there he
fell—dead.

28"Through the window peered Sisera's
mother;
behind the lattice she cried out,
'Why is his chariot so long in coming?
Why is the clatter of his chariots
delayed?'
29The wisest of her ladies answer her;
indeed, she keeps saying to herself,
30'Are they not finding and dividing the
spoils:
a girl or two for each man,

colourful garments as plunder for
Sisera,
colourful garments embroidered,
highly embroidered garments for
my neck—
all this as plunder?'

31"So may all your enemies perish, O
LORD!
But may they who love you be like
the sun
when it rises in its strength."

Then the land had peace for forty years.

NEW TESTAMENT READING
John 4:43–5:15

Jesus Heals the Official's Son

43After the two days he left for
Galilee. 44(Now Jesus himself had
pointed out that a prophet has no
honour in his own country.) 45When he
arrived in Galilee, the Galileans welcomed him. They had seen all that he
had done in Jerusalem at the Passover
Feast, for they also had been there.
46Once more he visited Cana in
Galilee, where he had turned the water
into wine. And there was a certain royal
official whose son lay sick at Capernaum. 47When this man heard that
Jesus had arrived in Galilee from Judea,
he went to him and begged him to come
and heal his son, who was close to
death.
48"Unless you people see miraculous
signs and wonders," Jesus told him,
"you will never believe."
49The royal official said, "Sir, come
down before my child dies."
50Jesus replied, "You may go. Your
son will live."
The man took Jesus at his word and
departed. 51While he was still on the
way, his servants met him with the news
that his boy was living. 52When he enquired as to the time when his son got
better, they said to him, "The fever left
him yesterday at the seventh hour."
53Then the father realised that this
was the exact time at which Jesus had
said to him, "Your son will live." So he
and all his household believed.
54This was the second miraculous sign
that Jesus performed, having come
from Judea to Galilee.

The Healing at the Pool

5 Some time later, Jesus went up to
Jerusalem for a feast of the Jews.
2Now there is in Jerusalem near the
Sheep Gate a pool, which in Aramaic is
called Bethesda and which is surrounded by five covered colonnades.
3Here a great number of disabled people used to lie—the blind, the lame, the
paralysed. 5One who was there had
been an invalid for thirty-eight years.
6When Jesus saw him lying there and
learned that he had been in this condition for a long time, he asked him,
"Do you want to get well?"
7"Sir," the invalid replied, "I have
no-one to help me into the pool when
the water is stirred. While I am trying to
get in, someone else goes down ahead
of me."
8Then Jesus said to him, "Get up!
Pick up your mat and walk." 9At once
the man was cured; he picked up his mat
and walked.
The day on which this took place was
a Sabbath, 10and so the Jews said to the
man who had been healed, "It is the
Sabbath; the law forbids you to carry
your mat."
11But he replied, "The man who
made me well said to me, 'Pick up your
mat and walk.'"
12So they asked him, "Who is this
fellow who told you to pick it up and
walk?"
13The man who was healed had no
idea who it was, for Jesus had slipped
away into the crowd that was there.
14Later Jesus found him at the temple
and said to him, "See, you are well
again. Stop sinning or something worse

may happen to you." 15The man went
away and told the Jews that it was Jesus
who had made him well.

READING FROM PSALMS
Psalm 57:1–6

For the director of music. ⌞To the tune of⌟ "Do Not Destroy". Of David. A *miktam*. When he had fled from Saul into the cave.

1Have mercy on me, O God, have
mercy on me,
for in you my soul takes refuge.
I will take refuge in the shadow of
your wings
until the disaster has passed.

2I cry out to God Most High,
to God, who fulfils ⌞his purpose⌟
for me.

3He sends from heaven and saves me,
rebuking those who hotly pursue
me; *Selah*
God sends his love and his
faithfulness.

4I am in the midst of lions;
I lie among ravenous beasts—
men whose teeth are spears and
arrows,
whose tongues are sharp swords.

5Be exalted, O God, above the
heavens;
let your glory be over all the earth.

6They spread a net for my feet—
I was bowed down in distress.
They dug a pit in my path—
but they have fallen into it
themselves. *Selah*

MAY 7

DAY 127

OLD TESTAMENT READING
Judges 6:1–7:8a

Gideon

6 Again the Israelites did evil in the
eyes of the LORD, and for seven
years he gave them into the hands of the
Midianites. 2Because the power of Midian was so oppressive, the Israelites
prepared shelters for themselves in
mountain clefts, caves and strongholds.
3Whenever the Israelites planted their
crops, the Midianites, Amalekites and
other eastern peoples invaded the country. 4They camped on the land and
ruined the crops all the way to Gaza and
did not spare a living thing for Israel,
neither sheep nor cattle nor donkeys.
5They came up with their livestock and
their tents like swarms of locusts. It
was impossible to count the men and
their camels; they invaded the land to
ravage it. 6Midian so impoverished the
Israelites that they cried out to the
LORD for help.
7When the Israelites cried to the
LORD because of Midian, 8he sent them
a prophet, who said, "This is what the
LORD, the God of Israel, says: I brought
you up out of Egypt, out of the land of
slavery. 9I snatched you from the power
of Egypt and from the hand of all your
oppressors. I drove them from before
you and gave you their land. 10I said to
you, 'I am the LORD your God; do not
worship the gods of the Amorites, in
whose land you live.' But you have not
listened to me."
11The angel of the LORD came and sat
down under the oak in Ophrah that
belonged to Joash the Abiezrite, where
his son Gideon was threshing wheat
in a winepress to keep it from the

Midianites. 12When the angel of the
LORD appeared to Gideon, he said,
"The LORD is with you, mighty
warrior."
13"But sir," Gideon replied, "if the
LORD is with us, why has all this happened to us? Where are all his wonders
that our fathers told us about when they
said, 'Did not the LORD bring us up out
of Egypt?' But now the LORD has abandoned us and put us into the hand of
Midian."
14The LORD turned to him and said,
"Go in the strength you have and save
Israel out of Midian's hand. Am I not
sending you?"
15"But Lord," Gideon asked, "how
can I save Israel? My clan is the weakest
in Manasseh, and I am the least in my
family."
16The LORD answered, "I will be with
you, and you will strike down all the
Midianites together."
17Gideon replied, "If now I have
found favour in your eyes, give me a
sign that it is really you talking to me.
18Please do not go away until I come
back and bring my offering and set it
before you."
And the LORD said, "I will wait until
you return."
19Gideon went in, prepared a young
goat, and from an ephah of flour he
made bread without yeast. Putting the
meat in a basket and its broth in a pot,
he brought them out and offered them
to him under the oak.
20The angel of God said to him,
"Take the meat and the unleavened
bread, place them on this rock, and
pour out the broth." And Gideon did
so. 21With the tip of the staff that was in
his hand, the angel of the LORD touched
the meat and the unleavened bread.
Fire flared from the rock, consuming
the meat and the bread. And the angel
of the LORD disappeared. 22When Gideon realised that it was the angel of the
LORD, he exclaimed, "Ah, Sovereign
LORD! I have seen the angel of the LORD
face to face!"
23But the LORD said to him, "Peace!
Do not be afraid. You are not going to
die."
24So Gideon built an altar to the
LORD there and called it The LORD is
Peace. To this day it stands in Ophrah of
the Abiezrites.
25That same night the LORD said to
him, "Take the second bull from your
father's herd, the one seven years old.
Tear down your father's altar to Baal
and cut down the Asherah pole beside
it. 26Then build a proper kind of altar to
the LORD your God on the top of this
height. Using the wood of the Asherah
pole that you cut down, offer the second
bull as a burnt offering."
27So Gideon took ten of his servants
and did as the LORD told him. But because he was afraid of his family and the
men of the town, he did it at night rather
than in the daytime.
28In the morning when the men of the
town got up, there was Baal's altar,
demolished, with the Asherah pole beside it cut down and the second bull
sacrificed on the newly-built altar!
29They asked each other, "Who did
this?"
When they carefully investigated,
they were told, "Gideon son of Joash
did it."
30The men of the town demanded of
Joash, "Bring out your son. He must
die, because he has broken down Baal's
altar and cut down the Asherah pole
beside it."
31But Joash replied to the hostile
crowd around him, "Are you going to
plead Baal's cause? Are you trying to
save him? Whoever fights for him shall
be put to death by morning! If Baal
really is a god, he can defend himself
when someone breaks down his altar."
32So that day they called Gideon
"Jerub-Baal", saying, "Let Baal contend with him," because he broke down
Baal's altar.

33Now all the Midianites, Amalekites
and other eastern peoples joined forces
and crossed over the Jordan and
camped in the Valley of Jezreel. 34Then
the Spirit of the LORD came upon

Gideon, and he blew a trumpet, summoning the Abiezrites to follow him. 35He sent messengers throughout Manasseh, calling them to arms, and also into Asher, Zebulun and Naphtali, so that they too went up to meet them.

36Gideon said to God, "If you will save Israel by my hand as you have promised—37look, I will place a wool fleece on the threshing-floor. If there is dew only on the fleece and all the ground is dry, then I will know that you will save Israel by my hand, as you said." 38And that is what happened. Gideon rose early the next day; he squeezed the fleece and wrung out the dew—a bowlful of water.

39Then Gideon said to God, "Do not be angry with me. Let me make just one more request. Allow me one more test with the fleece. This time make the fleece dry and the ground covered with dew." 40That night God did so. Only the fleece was dry; all the ground was covered with dew.

Gideon Defeats the Midianites

7 Early in the morning, Jerub-Baal (that is, Gideon) and all his men camped at the spring of Harod. The camp of Midian was north of them in the valley near the hill of Moreh. 2The LORD said to Gideon, "You have too many men for me to deliver Midian into their hands. In order that Israel may not boast against me that her own strength has saved her, 3announce now to the people, 'Anyone who trembles with fear may turn back and leave Mount Gilead.'" So twenty-two thousand men left, while ten thousand remained.

4But the LORD said to Gideon, "There are still too many men. Take them down to the water, and I will sift them out for you there. If I say, 'This one shall go with you,' he shall go; but if I say, 'This one shall not go with you,' he shall not go."

5So Gideon took the men down to the water. There the LORD told him, "Separate those who lap the water with their tongues like a dog from those who kneel down to drink." 6Three hundred men lapped with their hands to their mouths. All the rest got down on their knees to drink.

7The LORD said to Gideon, "With the three hundred men that lapped I will save you and give the Midianites into your hands. Let all the other men go, each to his own place." 8So Gideon sent the rest of the Israelites to their tents but kept the three hundred, who took over the provisions and trumpets of the others.

NEW TESTAMENT READING
John 5:16–30

Life Through the Son

16So, because Jesus was doing these things on the Sabbath, the Jews persecuted him. 17Jesus said to them, "My Father is always at his work to this very day, and I, too, am working." 18For this reason the Jews tried all the harder to kill him; not only was he breaking the Sabbath, but he was even calling God his own Father, making himself equal with God.

19Jesus gave them this answer: "I tell you the truth, the Son can do nothing by himself; he can do only what he sees his Father doing, because whatever the Father does the Son also does. 20For the Father loves the Son and shows him all he does. Yes, to your amazement he will show him even greater things than these. 21For just as the Father raises the dead and gives them life, even so the Son gives life to whom he is pleased to give it. 22Moreover, the Father judges no-one, but has entrusted all judgment to the Son, 23that all may honour the Son just as they honour the Father. He who does not honour the Son does not honour the Father, who sent him.

24"I tell you the truth, whoever hears my word and believes him who sent me has eternal life and will not be condemned; he has crossed over from death to life. 25I tell you the truth, a time is coming and has now come when the dead will hear the voice of the Son of God and those who hear will live. 26For as the Father has life in himself, so he has granted the Son to have life in himself. 27And he has given him authority to judge because he is the Son of Man.

28"Do not be amazed at this, for a time is coming when all who are in their graves will hear his voice 29and come out—those who have done good will rise to live, and those who have done evil will rise to be condemned. 30By myself I can do nothing; I judge only as I hear, and my judgment is just, for I seek not to please myself but him who sent me.

READING FROM PSALMS
Psalm 57:7–11

7My heart is steadfast, O God,
my heart is steadfast;
I will sing and make music.
8Awake, my soul!
Awake, harp and lyre!
I will awaken the dawn.

9I will praise you, O Lord, among the nations;
I will sing of you among the peoples.
10For great is your love, reaching to the heavens;
your faithfulness reaches to the skies.

11Be exalted, O God, above the heavens;
let your glory be over all the earth.

DAY 128

MAY 8

OLD TESTAMENT READING
Judges 7:8b–8:35

Now the camp of Midian lay below him in the valley. 9During that night the LORD said to Gideon, "Get up, go down against the camp, because I am going to give it into your hands. 10If you are afraid to attack, go down to the camp with your servant Purah 11and listen to what they are saying. Afterwards, you will be encouraged to attack the camp." So he and Purah his servant went down to the outposts of the camp. 12The Midianites, the Amalekites and all the other eastern peoples had settled in the valley, thick as locusts. Their camels could no more be counted than the sand on the seashore.

13Gideon arrived just as a man was telling a friend his dream. "I had a dream," he was saying. "A round loaf of barley bread came tumbling into the Midianite camp. It struck the tent with such force that the tent overturned and collapsed."

14His friend responded, "This can be nothing other than the sword of Gideon son of Joash, the Israelite. God has given the Midianites and the whole camp into his hands."

15When Gideon heard the dream and its interpretation, he worshipped God. He returned to the camp of Israel and called out, "Get up! The LORD has given the Midianite camp into your hands." 16Dividing the three hundred men into three companies, he placed trumpets and empty jars in the hands of all of them, with torches inside.

17"Watch me," he told them. "Follow my lead. When I get to the edge of the camp, do exactly as I do. 18When I and all who are with me blow our trumpets, then from all around the camp

blow yours and shout, 'For the LORD
and for Gideon.'"
19Gideon and the hundred men with
him reached the edge of the camp at the
beginning of the middle watch, just
after they had changed the guard. They
blew their trumpets and broke the jars
that were in their hands. 20The three
companies blew the trumpets and
smashed the jars. Grasping the torches
in their left hands and holding in their
right hands the trumpets they were to
blow, they shouted, "A sword for the
LORD and for Gideon!" 21While each
man held his position around the camp,
all the Midianites ran, crying out as they
fled.
22When the three hundred trumpets
sounded, the LORD caused the men
throughout the camp to turn on each
other with their swords. The army fled
to Beth Shittah towards Zererah as far
as the border of Abel Meholah near
Tabbath. 23Israelites from Naphtali,
Asher and all Manasseh were called
out, and they pursued the Midianites.
24Gideon sent messengers throughout
the hill country of Ephraim, saying,
"Come down against the Midianites
and seize the waters of the Jordan ahead
of them as far as Beth Barah."
So all the men of Ephraim were called
out and they took the waters of the
Jordan as far as Beth Barah. 25They also
captured two of the Midianite leaders,
Oreb and Zeeb. They killed Oreb at the
rock of Oreb, and Zeeb at the winepress
of Zeeb. They pursued the Midianites and brought the heads of Oreb
and Zeeb to Gideon, who was by the
Jordan.

Zebah and Zalmunna

8 Now the Ephraimites asked Gideon, "Why have you treated us
like this? Why didn't you call us when
you went to fight Midian?" And they
criticised him sharply.
2But he answered them, "What have
I accomplished compared to you?
Aren't the gleanings of Ephraim's
grapes better than the full grape harvest
of Abiezer? 3God gave Oreb and Zeeb,
the Midianite leaders, into your hands.
What was I able to do compared to
you?" At this, their resentment against
him subsided.
4Gideon and his three hundred men,
exhausted yet keeping up the pursuit,
came to the Jordan and crossed it. 5He
said to the men of Succoth, "Give my
troops some bread; they are worn out,
and I am still pursuing Zebah and Zalmunna, the kings of Midian."
6But the officials of Succoth said,
"Do you already have the hands of
Zebah and Zalmunna in your possession? Why should we give bread to your
troops?"
7Then Gideon replied, "Just for that,
when the LORD has given Zebah and
Zalmunna into my hand, I will tear your
flesh with desert thorns and briers."
8From there he went up to Peniel and
made the same request of them, but
they answered as the men of Succoth
had. 9So he said to the men of Peniel,
"When I return in triumph, I will tear
down this tower."
10Now Zebah and Zalmunna were in
Karkor with a force of about fifteen
thousand men, all that were left of the
armies of the eastern peoples; a hundred and twenty thousand swordsmen
had fallen. 11Gideon went up by the
route of the nomads east of Nobah and
Jogbehah and fell upon the unsuspecting army. 12Zebah and Zalmunna, the
two kings of Midian, fled, but he pursued them and captured them, routing
their entire army.
13Gideon son of Joash then returned
from the battle by the Pass of Heres.
14He caught a young man of Succoth
and questioned him, and the young man
wrote down for him the names of the
seventy-seven officials of Succoth, the
elders of the town. 15Then Gideon came
and said to the men of Succoth, "Here
are Zebah and Zalmunna, about whom
you taunted me by saying, 'Do you
already have the hands of Zebah and
Zalmunna in your possession? Why

should we give bread to your exhausted
men?'" 16He took the elders of the
town and taught the men of Succoth a
lesson by punishing them with desert
thorns and briers. 17He also pulled
down the tower of Peniel and killed the
men of the town.
18Then he asked Zebah and Zalmunna, "What kind of men did you
kill at Tabor?"
"Men like you," they answered,
"each one with the bearing of a prince."
19Gideon replied, "Those were my
brothers, the sons of my own mother.
As surely as the LORD lives, if you had
spared their lives, I would not kill you."
20Turning to Jether, his oldest son, he
said, "Kill them!" But Jether did not
draw his sword, because he was only a
boy and was afraid.
21Zebah and Zalmunna said, "Come,
do it yourself. 'As is the man, so is his
strength.'" So Gideon stepped forward
and killed them, and took the ornaments off their camels' necks.

Gideon's Ephod

22The Israelites said to Gideon,
"Rule over us—you, your son and your
grandson—because you have saved us
out of the hand of Midian."
23But Gideon told them, "I will not
rule over you, nor will my son rule over
you. The LORD will rule over you."
24And he said, "I do have one request,
that each of you give me an ear-ring
from your share of the plunder." (It was
the custom of the Ishmaelites to wear
gold ear-rings.)
25They answered, "We'll be glad to
give them." So they spread out a garment, and each man threw a ring from
his plunder onto it. 26The weight of the
gold rings he asked for came to seventeen hundred shekels, not counting the
ornaments, the pendants and the purple
garments worn by the kings of Midian
or the chains that were on their camels'
necks. 27Gideon made the gold into an
ephod, which he placed in Ophrah, his
town. All Israel prostituted themselves
by worshipping it there, and it became a
snare to Gideon and his family.

Gideon's Death

28Thus Midian was subdued before
the Israelites and did not raise its head
again. During Gideon's lifetime, the
land enjoyed peace for forty years.
29Jerub-Baal son of Joash went back
home to live. 30He had seventy sons of
his own, for he had many wives. 31His
concubine, who lived in Shechem, also
bore him a son, whom he named
Abimelech. 32Gideon son of Joash died
at a good old age and was buried in the
tomb of his father Joash in Ophrah of
the Abiezrites.
33No sooner had Gideon died than
the Israelites again prostituted themselves to the Baals. They set up Baal-
Berith as their god and 34did not
remember the LORD their God, who
had rescued them from the hands of all
their enemies on every side. 35They also
failed to show kindness to the family of
Jerub-Baal (that is, Gideon) for all the
good things he had done for them.

NEW TESTAMENT READING
John 5:31–47

Testimonies About Jesus

31"If I testify about myself, my testimony is not valid. 32There is another
who testifies in my favour, and I know
that his testimony about me is valid.
33"You have sent to John and he has
testified to the truth. 34Not that I accept
human testimony; but I mention it that
you may be saved. 35John was a lamp
that burned and gave light, and you
chose for a time to enjoy his light.
36"I have testimony weightier than
that of John. For the very work that the
Father has given me to finish, and which
I am doing, testifies that the Father has
sent me. 37And the Father who sent me
has himself testified concerning me.
You have never heard his voice nor seen

his form, 38nor does his word dwell in
you, for you do not believe the one he
sent. 39You diligently study the Scriptures because you think that by them
you possess eternal life. These are the
Scriptures that testify about me, 40yet
you refuse to come to me to have life.

41"I do not accept praise from men,
42but I know you. I know that you do
not have the love of God in your hearts.
43I have come in my Father's name, and
you do not accept me; but if someone
else comes in his own name, you will
accept him. 44How can you believe if
you accept praise from one another, yet
make no effort to obtain the praise that
comes from the only God?

45"But do not think I will accuse you
before the Father. Your accuser is
Moses, on whom your hopes are set. 46If
you believed Moses, you would believe
me, for he wrote about me. 47But since
you do not believe what he wrote, how
are you going to believe what I say?"

READING FROM PROVERBS
Proverbs 11:19–28

19The truly righteous man attains life,
but he who pursues evil goes to his death.

20The LORD detests men of perverse heart
but he delights in those whose ways are blameless.

21Be sure of this: The wicked will not go unpunished,
but those who are righteous will go free.

22Like a gold ring in a pig's snout
is a beautiful woman who shows no discretion.

23The desire of the righteous ends only in good,
but the hope of the wicked only in wrath.

24One man gives freely, yet gains even more;
another withholds unduly, but comes to poverty.

25A generous man will prosper;
he who refreshes others will himself be refreshed.

26People curse the man who hoards grain,
but blessing crowns him who is willing to sell.

27He who seeks good finds goodwill,
but evil comes to him who searches for it.

28Whoever trusts in his riches will fall,
but the righteous will thrive like a green leaf.

DAY 129

MAY 9

OLD TESTAMENT READING
Judges 9:1–57

Abimelech

9 Abimelech son of Jerub-Baal went
to his mother's brothers in
Shechem and said to them and to all his
mother's clan, 2"Ask all the citizens of
Shechem, 'Which is better for you: to
have all seventy of Jerub-Baal's sons
rule over you, or just one man?' Remember, I am your flesh and blood."
3When the brothers repeated all this
to the citizens of Shechem, they were
inclined to follow Abimelech, for they
said, "He is our brother." 4They gave
him seventy shekels of silver from the
temple of Baal-Berith, and Abimelech
used it to hire reckless adventurers, who
became his followers. 5He went to his
father's home in Ophrah and on one
stone murdered his seventy brothers,
the sons of Jerub-Baal. But Jotham, the
youngest son of Jerub-Baal, escaped by
hiding. 6Then all the citizens of
Shechem and Beth Millo gathered beside the great tree at the pillar in
Shechem to crown Abimelech king.
7When Jotham was told about this, he
climbed up on the top of Mount Gerizim and shouted to them, "Listen to
me, citizens of Shechem, so that God
may listen to you. 8One day the trees
went out to anoint a king for themselves. They said to the olive tree, 'Be
our king.'
9"But the olive tree answered,
'Should I give up my oil, by which both
gods and men are honoured, to hold
sway over the trees?'
10"Next, the trees said to the fig-tree,
'Come and be our king.'
11"But the fig-tree replied, 'Should I
give up my fruit, so good and sweet, to
hold sway over the trees?'
12"Then the trees said to the vine,
'Come and be our king.'
13"But the vine answered, 'Should I
give up my wine, which cheers both
gods and men, to hold sway over the
trees?'
14"Finally all the trees said to the
thornbush, 'Come and be our king.'
15"The thornbush said to the trees, 'If
you really want to anoint me king over
you, come and take refuge in my shade;
but if not, then let fire come out of the
thornbush and consume the cedars of
Lebanon!'
16"Now if you have acted honourably
and in good faith when you made
Abimelech king, and if you have been
fair to Jerub-Baal and his family, and if
you have treated him as he deserves
—17and to think that my father fought
for you, risked his life to rescue you
from the hand of Midian 18(but today
you have revolted against my father's
family, murdered his seventy sons on a
single stone, and made Abimelech, the
son of his slave girl, king over the
citizens of Shechem because he is your
brother)—19if then you have acted honourably and in good faith towards
Jerub-Baal and his family today, may
Abimelech be your joy, and may you be
his, too! 20But if you have not, let fire
come out from Abimelech and consume
you, citizens of Shechem and Beth
Millo, and let fire come out from
you, citizens of Shechem and Beth
Millo, and consume Abimelech!"
21Then Jotham fled, escaping to
Beer, and he lived there because he was
afraid of his brother Abimelech.
22After Abimelech had governed
Israel for three years, 23God sent an evil
spirit between Abimelech and the
citizens of Shechem, who acted
treacherously against Abimelech.
24God did this in order that the crime
against Jerub-Baal's seventy sons, the
shedding of their blood, might be
avenged on their brother Abimelech
and on the citizens of Shechem, who

had helped him murder his brothers.
25 In opposition to him these citizens of
Shechem set men on the hilltops to
ambush and rob everyone who passed
by, and this was reported to Abimelech.
26 Now Gaal son of Ebed moved with
his brothers into Shechem, and its
citizens put their confidence in him.
27 After they had gone out into the fields
and gathered the grapes and trodden
them, they held a festival in the temple
of their god. While they were eating and
drinking, they cursed Abimelech.
28 Then Gaal son of Ebed said, "Who is
Abimelech, and who is Shechem, that
we should be subject to him? Isn't he
Jerub-Baal's son, and isn't Zebul his
deputy? Serve the men of Hamor,
Shechem's father! Why should we serve
Abimelech? 29 If only this people were
under my command! Then I would get
rid of him. I would say to Abimelech,
'Call out your whole army!' "
30 When Zebul the governor of the
city heard what Gaal son of Ebed said,
he was very angry. 31 Under cover he
sent messengers to Abimelech, saying,
"Gaal son of Ebed and his brothers
have come to Shechem and are stirring
up the city against you. 32 Now then,
during the night you and your men
should come and lie in wait in the fields.
33 In the morning at sunrise, advance
against the city. When Gaal and his men
come out against you, do whatever your
hand finds to do."
34 So Abimelech and all his troops set
out by night and took up concealed
positions near Shechem in four companies. 35 Now Gaal son of Ebed had
gone out and was standing at the entrance to the city gate just as Abimelech
and his soldiers came out from their
hiding-place.
36 When Gaal saw them, he said to
Zebul, "Look, people are coming down
from the tops of the mountains!"
Zebul replied, "You mistake the
shadows of the mountains for men."
37 But Gaal spoke up again: "Look,
people are coming down from the
centre of the land, and a company is
coming from the direction of the sooth-
sayers' tree."
38 Then Zebul said to him, "Where is
your big talk now, you who said, 'Who
is Abimelech that we should be subject
to him?' Aren't these the men you ridiculed? Go out and fight them!"
39 So Gaal led out the citizens of
Shechem and fought Abimelech.
40 Abimelech chased him, and many fell
wounded in the flight—all the way to
the entrance to the gate. 41 Abimelech
stayed in Arumah, and Zebul drove
Gaal and his brothers out of Shechem.
42 The next day the people of
Shechem went out to the fields, and this
was reported to Abimelech. 43 So he
took his men, divided them into three
companies and set an ambush in the
fields. When he saw the people coming
out of the city, he rose to attack them.
44 Abimelech and the companies with
him rushed forward to a position at the
entrance to the city gate. Then two companies rushed upon those in the fields
and struck them down. 45 All that day
Abimelech pressed his attack against
the city until he had captured it and
killed its people. Then he destroyed the
city and scattered salt over it.
46 On hearing this, the citizens in the
tower of Shechem went into the stronghold of the temple of El-Berith. 47 When
Abimelech heard that they had assembled there, 48 he and all his men went up
Mount Zalmon. He took an axe and cut
off some branches, which he lifted to his
shoulders. He ordered the men with
him, "Quick! Do what you have seen
me do!" 49 So all the men cut branches
and followed Abimelech. They piled
them against the stronghold and set it
on fire over the people inside. So all the
people in the tower of Shechem, about a
thousand men and women, also died.
50 Next Abimelech went to Thebez
and besieged it and captured it. 51 Inside
the city, however, was a strong tower,
to which all the men and women—all
the people of the city—fled. They
locked themselves in and climbed up
on the tower roof. 52 Abimelech went

to the tower and stormed it. But
as he approached the entrance to the
tower to set it on fire, 53a woman
dropped an upper millstone on his head
and cracked his skull.

54Hurriedly he called to his armour-
bearer, "Draw your sword and kill me,
so that they can't say, 'A woman killed
him.'" So his servant ran him through,
and he died. 55When the Israelites saw
that Abimelech was dead, they went
home.

56Thus God repaid the wickedness
that Abimelech had done to his father
by murdering his seventy brothers.
57God also made the men of Shechem
pay for all their wickedness. The curse
of Jotham son of Jerub-Baal came on
them.

NEW TESTAMENT READING
John 6:1–24

Jesus Feeds the Five Thousand

6 Some time after this, Jesus crossed
to the far shore of the Sea of
Galilee (that is, the Sea of Tiberias),
2and a great crowd of people followed
him because they saw the miraculous
signs he had performed on the sick.
3Then Jesus went up on a mountainside
and sat down with his disciples. 4The
Jewish Passover Feast was near.

5When Jesus looked up and saw a
great crowd coming towards him, he
said to Philip, "Where shall we buy
bread for these people to eat?" 6He
asked this only to test him, for he
already had in mind what he was going
to do.

7Philip answered him, "Eight
months' wages would not buy enough
bread for each one to have a bite!"

8Another of his disciples, Andrew,
Simon Peter's brother, spoke up,
9"Here is a boy with five small barley
loaves and two small fish, but how far
will they go among so many?"

10Jesus said, "Make the people sit
down." There was plenty of grass in that
place, and the men sat down, about five
thousand of them. 11Jesus then took the
loaves, gave thanks, and distributed to
those who were seated as much as they
wanted. He did the same with the fish.

12When they had all had enough to
eat, he said to his disciples, "Gather the
pieces that are left over. Let nothing be
wasted." 13So they gathered them and
filled twelve baskets with the pieces of
the five barley loaves left over by those
who had eaten.

14After the people saw the miraculous sign that Jesus did, they began to
say, "Surely this is the Prophet who is to
come into the world." 15Jesus, knowing
that they intended to come and make
him king by force, withdrew again to a
mountain by himself.

Jesus Walks on the Water

16When evening came, his disciples
went down to the lake, 17where they got
into a boat and set off across the lake for
Capernaum. By now it was dark, and
Jesus had not yet joined them. 18A
strong wind was blowing and the waters
grew rough. 19When they had rowed
three or three and a half miles, they saw
Jesus approaching the boat, walking on
the water; and they were terrified. 20But
he said to them, "It is I; don't be
afraid." 21Then they were willing to
take him into the boat, and immediately
the boat reached the shore where they
were heading.

22The next day the crowd that had
stayed on the opposite shore of the lake
realised that only one boat had been
there, and that Jesus had not entered it
with his disciples, but that they had
gone away alone. 23Then some boats
from Tiberias landed near the place
where the people had eaten the bread
after the Lord had given thanks. 24Once
the crowd realised that neither Jesus
nor his disciples were there, they got
into the boats and went to Capernaum
in search of Jesus.

READING FROM PSALMS
Psalm 58:1–11

For the director of music. ⌞To the tune of⌟ "Do Not Destroy". Of David. A *miktam*.

1Do you rulers indeed speak justly?
Do you judge uprightly among men?
2No, in your heart you devise injustice,
and your hands mete out violence on the earth.
3Even from birth the wicked go astray;
from the womb they are wayward and speak lies.
4Their venom is like the venom of a snake,
like that of a cobra that has stopped its ears,
5that will not heed the tune of the charmer,
however skilful the enchanter may be.

6Break the teeth in their mouths, O God;
tear out, O LORD, the fangs of the lions!
7Let them vanish like water that flows away;
when they draw the bow, let their arrows be blunted.
8Like a slug melting away as it moves along,
like a stillborn child, may they not see the sun.

9Before your pots can feel ⌞the heat of⌟ the thorns—
whether they be green or dry—the wicked will be swept away.
10The righteous will be glad when they are avenged,
when they bathe their feet in the blood of the wicked.
11Then men will say,
"Surely the righteous still are rewarded;
surely there is a God who judges the earth."

MAY 10

DAY 130

OLD TESTAMENT READING
Judges 10:1–11:40

Tola

10 After the time of Abimelech a
man of Issachar, Tola son of
Puah, the son of Dodo, rose to save
Israel. He lived in Shamir, in the hill
country of Ephraim. 2He led Israel for
twenty-three years; then he died, and
was buried in Shamir.

Jair

3He was followed by Jair of Gilead,
who led Israel for twenty-two years.
4He had thirty sons, who rode thirty
donkeys. They controlled thirty towns
in Gilead, which to this day are called
Havvoth Jair. 5When Jair died, he was
buried in Kamon.

Jephthah

6Again the Israelites did evil in the
eyes of the LORD. They served the Baals
and the Ashtoreths, and the gods of
Aram, the gods of Sidon, the gods of
Moab, the gods of the Ammonites and
the gods of the Philistines. And because
the Israelites forsook the LORD and no
longer served him, 7he became angry

with them. He sold them into the hands
of the Philistines and the Ammonites,
8who that year shattered and crushed
them. For eighteen years they oppressed all the Israelites on the east side of
the Jordan in Gilead, the land of the
Amorites. 9The Ammonites also crossed the Jordan to fight against Judah,
Benjamin and the house of Ephraim;
and Israel was in great distress. 10Then
the Israelites cried out to the LORD,
"We have sinned against you, forsaking
our God and serving the Baals."

11The LORD replied, "When the
Egyptians, the Amorites, the Ammonites, the Philistines, 12the Sidonians,
the Amalekites and the Maonites
oppressed you and you cried to me for
help, did I not save you from their
hands? 13But you have forsaken me and
served other gods, so I will no longer
save you. 14Go and cry out to the gods
you have chosen. Let them save you
when you are in trouble!"

15But the Israelites said to the LORD,
"We have sinned. Do with us whatever
you think best, but please rescue us
now." 16Then they got rid of the foreign
gods among them and served the LORD.
And he could bear Israel's misery no
longer.

17When the Ammonites were called
to arms and camped in Gilead, the
Israelites assembled and camped at
Mizpah. 18The leaders of the people of
Gilead said to each other, "Whoever
will launch the attack against the
Ammonites will be the head of all those
living in Gilead."

11 Jephthah the Gileadite was a
mighty warrior. His father was
Gilead; his mother was a prostitute.
2Gilead's wife also bore him sons, and
when they were grown up, they drove
Jephthah away. "You are not going to
get any inheritance in our family," they
said, "because you are the son of
another woman." 3So Jephthah fled
from his brothers and settled in the land
of Tob, where a group of adventurers
gathered around him and followed
him.

4Some time later, when the Ammonites made war on Israel, 5the elders of
Gilead went to get Jephthah from the
land of Tob. 6"Come," they said, "be
our commander, so we can fight the
Ammonites."

7Jephthah said to them, "Didn't you
hate me and drive me from my father's
house? Why do you come to me now,
when you're in trouble?"

8The elders of Gilead said to him,
"Nevertheless, we are turning to you
now; come with us to fight the Ammonites, and you will be our head over all
who live in Gilead."

9Jephthah answered, "Suppose you
take me back to fight the Ammonites
and the LORD gives them to me—will I
really be your head?"

10The elders of Gilead replied, "The
LORD is our witness; we will certainly do
as you say." 11So Jephthah went with
the elders of Gilead, and the people
made him head and commander over
them. And he repeated all his words
before the LORD in Mizpah.

12Then Jephthah sent messengers to
the Ammonite king with the question:
"What do you have against us that you
have attacked our country?"

13The king of the Ammonites
answered Jephthah's messengers,
"When Israel came up out of Egypt,
they took away my land from the Arnon
to the Jabbok, all the way to the Jordan.
Now give it back peaceably."

14Jephthah sent back messengers to
the Ammonite king, 15saying:

"This is what Jephthah says: Israel
did not take the land of Moab or
the land of the Ammonites. 16But
when they came up out of Egypt,
Israel went through the desert to
the Red Sea and on to Kadesh.
17Then Israel sent messengers to
the king of Edom, saying, 'Give us
permission to go through your
country,' but the king of Edom
would not listen. They sent also to
the king of Moab, and he refused.
So Israel stayed at Kadesh.

18"Next they travelled through
the desert, skirted the lands of
Edom and Moab, passed along the
eastern side of the country of
Moab, and camped on the other
side of the Arnon. They did not
enter the territory of Moab, for the
Arnon was its border.
19"Then Israel sent messengers
to Sihon king of the Amorites, who
ruled in Heshbon, and said to him,
'Let us pass through your country
to our own place.' 20Sihon, however, did not trust Israel to pass
through his territory. He mustered
all his men and encamped at Jahaz
and fought with Israel.
21"Then the LORD, the God of
Israel, gave Sihon and all his men
into Israel's hands, and they defeated them. Israel took over
all the land of the Amorites who
lived in that country, 22capturing
all of it from the Arnon to the
Jabbok and from the desert to the
Jordan.
23"Now since the LORD, the God
of Israel, has driven the Amorites
out before his people Israel, what
right have you to take it over?
24Will you not take what your god
Chemosh gives you? Likewise,
whatever the LORD our God has
given us, we will possess. 25Are you
better than Balak son of Zippor,
king of Moab? Did he ever quarrel
with Israel or fight with them?
26For three hundred years Israel
occupied Heshbon, Aroer, the surrounding settlements and all the
towns along the Arnon. Why didn't
you retake them during that time?
27I have not wronged you, but you
are doing me wrong by waging war
against me. Let the LORD, the
Judge, decide the dispute this day
between the Israelites and the
Ammonites."

28The king of Ammon, however, paid
no attention to the message Jephthah
sent him.

29Then the Spirit of the LORD came
upon Jephthah. He crossed Gilead and
Manasseh, passed through Mizpah of
Gilead, and from there he advanced
against the Ammonites. 30And Jephthah made a vow to the LORD: "If you
give the Ammonites into my hands,
31whatever comes out of the door of my
house to meet me when I return in
triumph from the Ammonites will be
the LORD's, and I will sacrifice it as a
burnt offering."
32Then Jephthah went over to
fight the Ammonites, and the LORD
gave them into his hands. 33He
devastated twenty towns from Aroer
to the vicinity of Minnith, as far as
Abel Karamim. Thus Israel subdued
Ammon.
34When Jephthah returned to his
home in Mizpah, who should come
out to meet him but his daughter,
dancing to the sound of tambourines!
She was an only child. Except for
her he had neither son nor daughter.
35When he saw her, he tore his
clothes and cried, "Oh! My daughter!
You have made me miserable and
wretched, because I have made a
vow to the LORD that I cannot
break."
36"My father," she replied, "you
have given your word to the LORD. Do
to me just as you promised, now that the
LORD has avenged you of your enemies,
the Ammonites. 37But grant me this
one request," she said. "Give me two
months to roam the hills and weep
with my friends, because I will never
marry."
38"You may go," he said. And he let
her go for two months. She and the girls
went into the hills and wept because she
would never marry. 39After the two
months, she returned to her father and
he did to her as he had vowed. And she
was a virgin.
From this comes the Israelite custom
40that each year the young women of
Israel go out for four days to commemorate the daughter of Jephthah the
Gileadite.

NEW TESTAMENT READING
John 6:25–59

Jesus the Bread of Life

25When they found him on the other
side of the lake, they asked him,
"Rabbi, when did you get here?"
26Jesus answered, "I tell you the
truth, you are looking for me, not because you saw miraculous signs but because you ate the loaves and had your
fill. 27Do not work for food that spoils,
but for food that endures to eternal life,
which the Son of Man will give you. On
him God the Father has placed his seal
of approval."
28Then they asked him, "What must
we do to do the works God requires?"
29Jesus answered, "The work of God
is this: to believe in the one he has
sent."
30So they asked him, "What miraculous sign then will you give that we may
see it and believe you? What will you
do? 31Our forefathers ate the manna in
the desert; as it is written: 'He gave
them bread from heaven to eat.'"
32Jesus said to them, "I tell you the
truth, it is not Moses who has given you
the bread from heaven, but it is my
Father who gives you the true bread
from heaven. 33For the bread of God is
he who comes down from heaven and
gives life to the world."
34"Sir," they said, "from now on give
us this bread."
35Then Jesus declared, "I am the
bread of life. He who comes to me will
never go hungry, and he who believes in
me will never be thirsty. 36But as I told
you, you have seen me and still you do
not believe. 37All that the Father gives
me will come to me, and whoever comes
to me I will never drive away. 38For I
have come down from heaven not to do
my will but to do the will of him who
sent me. 39And this is the will of him
who sent me, that I shall lose none of all
that he has given me, but raise them up
at the last day. 40For my Father's will is
that everyone who looks to the Son and
believes in him shall have eternal life,
and I will raise him up at the last day."
41At this the Jews began to grumble
about him because he said, "I am the
bread that came down from heaven."
42They said, "Is this not Jesus, the son
of Joseph, whose father and mother we
know? How can he now say, 'I came
down from heaven'?"
43"Stop grumbling among yourselves," Jesus answered. 44"No-one can
come to me unless the Father who sent
me draws him, and I will raise him up at
the last day. 45It is written in the
Prophets: 'They will all be taught by
God.' Everyone who listens to the
Father and learns from him comes to
me. 46No-one has seen the Father except the one who is from God; only he
has seen the Father. 47I tell you the
truth, he who believes has everlasting
life. 48I am the bread of life. 49Your
forefathers ate the manna in the desert,
yet they died. 50But here is the bread
that comes down from heaven, which a
man may eat and not die. 51I am the
living bread that came down from
heaven. If anyone eats of this bread, he
will live for ever. This bread is my flesh,
which I will give for the life of the
world."
52Then the Jews began to argue
sharply among themselves, "How can
this man give us his flesh to eat?"
53Jesus said to them, "I tell you the
truth, unless you can eat the flesh of the
Son of Man and drink his blood, you
have no life in you. 54Whoever eats my
flesh and drinks my blood has eternal
life, and I will raise him up at the last
day. 55For my flesh is real food and my
blood is real drink. 56Whoever eats my
flesh and drinks my blood remains in
me, and I in him. 57Just as the living
Father sent me and I live because of the
Father, so the one who feeds on me will
live because of me. 58This is the bread
that came down from heaven. Your
forefathers ate manna and died, but he
who feeds on this bread will live for
ever." 59He said this while teaching in
the synagogue in Capernaum.

READING FROM PSALMS
Psalm 59:1–8

For the director of music. ⌊To the tune of⌋ "Do Not Destroy". Of David. A *miktam*. When Saul had sent men to watch David's house in order to kill him.

1Deliver me from my enemies, O God;
protect me from those who rise up against me.
2Deliver me from evildoers
and save me from bloodthirsty men.

3See how they lie in wait for me!
Fierce men conspire against me
for no offence or sin of mine, O LORD.
4I have done no wrong, yet they are ready to attack me.
Arise to help me; look on my plight!
5O LORD God Almighty, the God of Israel,
rouse yourself to punish all the nations;
show no mercy to wicked traitors.
Selah

6They return at evening,
snarling like dogs,
and prowl about the city.
7See what they spew from their mouths—
they spew out swords from their lips,
and they say, "Who can hear us?"
8But you, O LORD, laugh at them;
you scoff at all those nations.

MAY 11

DAY 131

OLD TESTAMENT READING
Judges 12:1–13:25

Jephthah and Ephraim

12 The men of Ephraim called out their forces, crossed over to Zaphon and said to Jephthah, "Why did you go to fight the Ammonites without calling us to go with you? We're going to burn down your house over your head."

2Jephthah answered, "I and my people were engaged in a great struggle with the Ammonites, and although I called, you didn't save me out of their hands.
3When I saw that you wouldn't help, I took my life in my hands and crossed over to fight the Ammonites, and the LORD gave me the victory over them. Now why have you come up today to fight me?"

4Jephthah then called together the men of Gilead and fought against Ephraim. The Gileadites struck them down because the Ephraimites had said, "You Gileadites are renegades from Ephraim and Manasseh."
5The Gileadites captured the fords of the Jordan leading to Ephraim, and whenever a survivor of Ephraim said, "Let me cross over," the men of Gilead asked him, "Are you an Ephraimite?" If he replied, "No,"
6they said, "All right, say 'Shibboleth'." If he said, "Sibboleth", because he could not pronounce the word correctly, they seized him and killed him at the fords of the Jordan. Forty-two thousand Ephraimites were killed at that time.

7Jephthah led Israel for six years. Then Jephthah the Gileadite died, and was buried in a town in Gilead.

Ibzan, Elon and Abdon

8After him, Ibzan of Bethlehem led Israel.
9He had thirty sons and thirty daughters. He gave his daughters away

in marriage to those outside his clan, and for his sons he brought in thirty young women as wives from outside his clan. Ibzan led Israel for seven years. 10Then Ibzan died, and was buried in Bethlehem.

11After him, Elon the Zebulunite led Israel for ten years. 12Then Elon died, and was buried in Aijalon in the land of Zebulun.

13After him, Abdon son of Hillel, from Pirathon, led Israel. 14He had forty sons and thirty grandsons, who rode on seventy donkeys. He led Israel for eight years. 15Then Abdon son of Hillel died, and was buried at Pirathon in Ephraim, in the hill country of the Amalekites.

The Birth of Samson

13 Again the Israelites did evil in the eyes of the LORD, so the LORD delivered them into the hands of the Philistines for forty years.

2A certain man of Zorah, named Manoah, from the clan of the Danites, had a wife who was sterile and remained childless. 3The angel of the LORD appeared to her and said, "You are sterile and childless, but you are going to conceive and have a son. 4Now see to it that you drink no wine or other fermented drink and that you do not eat anything unclean, 5because you will conceive and give birth to a son. No razor may be used on his head, because the boy is to be a Nazirite, set apart to God from birth, and he will begin the deliverance of Israel from the hands of the Philistines."

6Then the woman went to her husband and told him, "A man of God came to me. He looked like an angel of God, very awesome. I didn't ask him where he came from, and he didn't tell me his name. 7But he said to me, 'You will conceive and give birth to a son. Now then, drink no wine or other fermented drink and do not eat anything unclean, because the boy will be a Nazirite of God from birth until the day of his death.'"

8Then Manoah prayed to the LORD: "O Lord, I beg you, let the man of God you sent to us come again to teach us how to bring up the boy who is to be born."

9God heard Manoah, and the angel of God came again to the woman while she was out in the field; but her husband Manoah was not with her. 10The woman hurried to tell her husband, "He's here! The man who appeared to me the other day!"

11Manoah got up and followed his wife. When he came to the man, he said, "Are you the one who talked to my wife?"

"I am," he said.

12So Manoah asked him, "When your words are fulfilled, what is to be the rule for the boy's life and work?"

13The angel of the LORD answered, "Your wife must do all that I have told her. 14She must not eat anything that comes from the grapevine, nor drink any wine or other fermented drink nor eat anything unclean. She must do everything I have commanded her."

15Manoah said to the angel of the LORD, "We would like you to stay until we prepare a young goat for you."

16The angel of the LORD replied, "Even though you detain me, I will not eat any of your food. But if you prepare a burnt offering, offer it to the LORD." (Manoah did not realise that it was the angel of the LORD.)

17Then Manoah enquired of the angel of the LORD, "What is your name, so that we may honour you when your word comes true?"

18He replied, "Why do you ask my name? It is beyond understanding." 19Then Manoah took a young goat, together with the grain offering, and sacrificed it on a rock to the LORD. And the LORD did an amazing thing while Manoah and his wife watched: 20As the flame blazed up from the altar towards heaven, the angel of the LORD ascended in the flame. Seeing this, Manoah and his wife fell with their faces to the ground. 21When the angel of the LORD

did not show himself again to Manoah
and his wife, Manoah realised that it
was the angel of the LORD.
22"We are doomed to die!" he said to
his wife. "We have seen God!"
23But his wife answered, "If the LORD
had meant to kill us, he would not have
accepted a burnt offering and grain
offering from our hands, nor shown us
all these things or now told us this."
24The woman gave birth to a boy and
named him Samson. He grew and the
LORD blessed him, 25and the Spirit of
the LORD began to stir him while he was
in Mahaneh Dan, between Zorah and
Eshtaol.

NEW TESTAMENT READING
John 6:60–7:13

Many Disciples Desert Jesus

60On hearing it, many of his disciples
said, "This is a hard teaching. Who can
accept it?"
61Aware that his disciples were
grumbling about this, Jesus said to
them, "Does this offend you? 62What if
you see the Son of Man ascend to where
he was before! 63The Spirit gives life;
the flesh counts for nothing. The words
I have spoken to you are spirit and they
are life. 64Yet there are some of you
who do not believe." For Jesus had
known from the beginning which of
them did not believe and who would
betray him. 65He went on to say, "This
is why I told you that no-one can come
to me unless the Father has enabled
him."
66From this time many of his disciples
turned back and no longer followed
him.
67"You do not want to leave too, do
you?" Jesus asked the Twelve.
68Simon Peter answered him, "Lord,
to whom shall we go? You have the
words of eternal life. 69We believe and
know that you are the Holy One of
God."
70Then Jesus replied, "Have I not
chosen you, the Twelve? Yet one of you
is a devil!" 71(He meant Judas, the son
of Simon Iscariot, who, though one of
the Twelve, was later to betray him.)

Jesus Goes to the Feast of Tabernacles

7 After this, Jesus went around in
Galilee, purposely staying away
from Judea because the Jews there were
waiting to take his life. 2But when the
Jewish Feast of Tabernacles was near,
3Jesus' brothers said to him, "You
ought to leave here and go to Judea, so
that your disciples may see the miracles
you do. 4No-one who wants to become a
public figure acts in secret. Since you
are doing these things, show yourself to
the world." 5For even his own brothers
did not believe in him.
6Therefore Jesus told them, "The
right time for me has not yet come; for
you any time is right. 7The world cannot
hate you, but it hates me because I
testify that what it does is evil. 8You go
to the Feast. I am not yet going up to this
Feast, because for me the right time has
not yet come." 9Having said this, he
stayed in Galilee.
10However, after his brothers had left
for the Feast, he went also, not publicly,
but in secret. 11Now at the Feast the
Jews were watching for him and asking,
"Where is that man?"
12Among the crowds there was widespread whispering about him. Some
said, "He is a good man."
Others replied, "No, he deceives the
people." 13But no-one would say anything publicly about him for fear of the
Jews.

READING FROM PSALMS
Psalm 59:9–17

9O my Strength, I watch for you;
you, O God, are my fortress, 10my
loving God.

God will go before me
and will let me gloat over those
who slander me.

[11]But do not kill them, O Lord our
shield,
or my people will forget.
In your might make them wander
about,
and bring them down.
[12]For the sins of their mouths,
for the words of their lips,
let them be caught in their pride.
For the curses and lies they utter,
[13] consume them in wrath,
consume them till they are no more.
Then it will be known to the ends of
the earth
that God rules over Jacob. *Selah*

[14]They return at evening,
snarling like dogs,
and prowl about the city.
[15]They wander about for food
and howl if not satisfied.
[16]But I will sing of your strength,
in the morning I will sing of your
love;
for you are my fortress,
my refuge in times of trouble.

[17]O my Strength, I sing praise to
you;
you, O God, are my fortress, my
loving God.

DAY 132

MAY 12

OLD TESTAMENT READING
Judges 14:1–15:20

Samson's Marriage

14 Samson went down to Timnah
and saw there a young Philistine
woman. [2]When he returned, he said to
his father and mother, "I have seen a
Philistine woman in Timnah; now get
her for me as my wife."
[3]His father and mother replied, "Isn't
there an acceptable woman among your
relatives or among all our people? Must
you go to the uncircumcised Philistines
to get a wife?"
But Samson said to his father, "Get
her for me. She's the right one for me."
[4](His parents did not know that this was
from the LORD, who was seeking an
occasion to confront the Philistines; for
at that time they were ruling over
Israel.) [5]Samson went down to Timnah
together with his father and mother. As
they approached the vineyards of Timnah, suddenly a young lion came roaring towards him. [6]The Spirit of the
LORD came upon him in power so that
he tore the lion apart with his bare
hands as he might have torn a young
goat. But he told neither his father nor
his mother what he had done. [7]Then he
went down and talked with the woman,
and he liked her.
[8]Some time later, when he went back
to marry her, he turned aside to look at
the lion's carcass. In it was a swarm of
bees and some honey, [9]which he
scooped out with his hands and ate as he
went along. When he rejoined his
parents, he gave them some, and they
too ate it. But he did not tell them that
he had taken the honey from the lion's
carcass.
[10]Now his father went down to see the
woman. And Samson made a feast
there, as was customary for bride-
grooms. [11]When he appeared, he was
given thirty companions.
[12]"Let me tell you a riddle," Samson
said to them. "If you can give me the
answer within the seven days of the
feast, I will give you thirty linen garments and thirty sets of clothes. [13]If you
can't tell me the answer, you must give
me thirty linen garments and thirty sets
of clothes."
"Tell us your riddle," they said.
"Let's hear it."
[14]He replied,

"Out of the eater, something to eat;
out of the strong, something
sweet."

For three days they could not give the
answer.
15On the fourth day, they said to Samson's wife, "Coax your husband into
explaining the riddle for us, or we will
burn you and your father's household to
death. Did you invite us here to rob
us?"
16Then Samson's wife threw herself
on him, sobbing, "You hate me! You
don't really love me. You've given my
people a riddle, but you haven't told me
the answer."
"I haven't even explained it to my
father or mother," he replied, "so why
should I explain it to you?" 17She cried
the whole seven days of the feast. So on
the seventh day he finally told her, because she continued to press him. She in
turn explained the riddle to her people.
18Before sunset on the seventh day
the men of the town said to him,

"What is sweeter than honey?
What is stronger than a lion?"

Samson said to them,

"If you had not ploughed with my
heifer,
you would not have solved my
riddle."

19Then the Spirit of the LORD came
upon him in power. He went down to
Ashkelon, struck down thirty of their
men, stripped them of their belongings
and gave their clothes to those who had
explained the riddle. Burning with
anger, he went up to his father's house.
20And Samson's wife was given to the
friend who had attended him at his
wedding.

Samson's Vengeance on the Philistines

15 Later on, at the time of wheat
harvest, Samson took a young
goat and went to visit his wife. He said,
"I'm going to my wife's room." But her
father would not let him go in.
2"I was so sure you thoroughly hated
her," he said, "that I gave her to your
friend. Isn't her younger sister more
attractive? Take her instead."
3Samson said to them, "This time I
have a right to get even with the Philistines; I will really harm them." 4So he
went out and caught three hundred
foxes and tied them tail to tail in pairs.
He then fastened a torch to every pair of
tails, 5lit the torches and let the foxes
loose in the standing corn of the Philistines. He burned up the shocks and
standing corn, together with the
vineyards and olive groves.
6When the Philistines asked, "Who
did this?" they were told, "Samson, the
Timnite's son-in-law, because his wife
was given to his friend."
So the Philistines went up and burned
her and her father to death. 7Samson
said to them, "Since you've acted like
this, I won't stop until I get my revenge
on you." 8He attacked them viciously
and slaughtered many of them. Then he
went down and stayed in a cave in the
rock of Etam.
9The Philistines went up and camped
in Judah, spreading out near Lehi.
10The men of Judah asked, "Why have
you come to fight us?"
"We have come to take Samson prisoner," they answered, "to do to him as
he did to us."
11Then three thousand men from
Judah went down to the cave in the rock
of Etam and said to Samson, "Don't
you realise that the Philistines are rulers
over us? What have you done to us?"
He answered, "I merely did to them
what they did to me."
12They said to him, "We've come to
tie you up and hand you over to the
Philistines."
Samson said, "Swear to me that you
won't kill me yourselves."
13"Agreed," they answered. "We
will only tie you up and hand you over to
them. We will not kill you." So they
bound him with two new ropes and led

him up from the rock. [14]As he approached Lehi, the Philistines came towards him shouting. The Spirit of the LORD came upon him in power. The ropes on his arms became like charred flax, and the bindings dropped from his hands. [15]Finding a fresh jaw-bone of a donkey, he grabbed it and struck down a thousand men.

[16]Then Samson said,

"With a donkey's jaw-bone
  I have made donkeys of them.
With a donkey's jaw-bone
  I have killed a thousand men."

[17]When he finished speaking, he threw away the jaw-bone; and the place was called Ramath Lehi.

[18]Because he was very thirsty, he cried out to the LORD, "You have given your servant this great victory. Must I now die of thirst and fall into the hands of the uncircumcised?" [19]Then God opened up the hollow place in Lehi, and water came out of it. When Samson drank, his strength returned and he revived. So the spring was called En Hakkore, and it is still there in Lehi.

[20]Samson led Israel for twenty years in the days of the Philistines.

NEW TESTAMENT READING
John 7:14–44

Jesus Teaches at the Feast

[14]Not until halfway through the Feast did Jesus go up to the temple courts and begin to teach. [15]The Jews were amazed and asked, "How did this man get such learning without having studied?"

[16]Jesus answered, "My teaching is not my own. It comes from him who sent me. [17]If anyone chooses to do God's will, he will find out whether my teaching comes from God or whether I speak on my own. [18]He who speaks on his own does so to gain honour for himself, but he who works for the honour of the one who sent him is a man of truth; there is nothing false about him. [19]Has not Moses given you the law? Yet not one of you keeps the law. Why are you trying to kill me?"

[20]"You are demon-possessed," the crowd answered. "Who is trying to kill you?"

[21]Jesus said to them, "I did one miracle, and you are all astonished. [22]Yet, because Moses gave you circumcision (though actually it did not come from Moses, but from the patriarchs), you circumcise a child on the Sabbath. [23]Now if a child can be circumcised on the Sabbath so that the law of Moses may not be broken, why are you angry with me for healing the whole man on the Sabbath? [24]Stop judging by mere appearances, and make a right judgment."

Is Jesus the Christ?

[25]At that point some of the people of Jerusalem began to ask, "Isn't this the man they are trying to kill? [26]Here he is, speaking publicly, and they are not saying a word to him. Have the authorities really concluded that he is the Christ? [27]But we know where this man is from; when the Christ comes, no-one will know where he is from."

[28]Then Jesus, still teaching in the temple courts, cried out, "Yes, you know me, and you know where I am from. I am not here on my own, but he who sent me is true. You do not know him, [29]but I know him because I am from him and he sent me."

[30]At this they tried to seize him, but no-one laid a hand on him, because his time had not yet come. [31]Still, many in the crowd put their faith in him. They said, "When the Christ comes, will he do more miraculous signs than this man?"

[32]The Pharisees heard the crowd whispering such things about him. Then the chief priests and the Pharisees sent temple guards to arrest him.

[33]Jesus said, "I am with you for only a short time, and then I go to the one who sent me. [34]You will look for me, but you

will not find me; and where I am, you
cannot come."
35The Jews said to one another,
"Where does this man intend to go that
we cannot find him? Will he go where
our people live scattered among the
Greeks, and teach the Greeks? 36What
did he mean when he said, 'You will
look for me, but you will not find me,'
and 'Where I am, you cannot come'?"
37On the last and greatest day of the
Feast, Jesus stood and said in a loud
voice, "If anyone is thirsty, let him
come to me and drink. 38Whoever believes in me, as the Scripture has said,
streams of living water will flow from
within him." 39By this he meant the
Spirit, whom those who believed in him
were later to receive. Up to that time
the Spirit had not been given, since
Jesus had not yet been glorified.
40On hearing his words, some of the
people said, "Surely this man is the
Prophet."
41Others said, "He is the Christ."
Still others asked, "How can the
Christ come from Galilee? 42Does not
the Scripture say that the Christ will
come from David's family and from
Bethlehem, the town where David
lived?" 43Thus the people were divided
because of Jesus. 44Some wanted to
seize him, but no-one laid a hand on
him.

READING FROM PROVERBS
Proverbs 11:29–12:7

29He who brings trouble on his family
will inherit only wind,
and the fool will be servant to the
wise.

30The fruit of the righteous is a tree of
life,
and he who wins souls is wise.

31If the righteous receive their due on
earth,
how much more the ungodly and
the sinner!

12 Whoever loves discipline loves
knowledge,
but he who hates correction is
stupid.

2A good man obtains favour from the
LORD,
but the LORD condemns a crafty
man.

3A man cannot be established through
wickedness,
but the righteous cannot be
uprooted.

4A wife of noble character is her
husband's crown,
but a disgraceful wife is like decay
in his bones.

5The plans of the righteous are just,
but the advice of the wicked is
deceitful.

6The words of the wicked lie in wait
for blood,
but the speech of the upright
rescues them.

7Wicked men are overthrown and are
no more,
but the house of the righteous
stands firm.

DAY 133

MAY 13

OLD TESTAMENT READING
Judges 16:1–17:13

Samson and Delilah

16 One day Samson went to Gaza,
where he saw a prostitute. He
went in to spend the night with her.
2The people of Gaza were told, "Samson is here!" So they surrounded the
place and lay in wait for him all night at
the city gate. They made no move during the night, saying, "At dawn we'll kill
him."
3But Samson lay there only until the
middle of the night. Then he got up and
took hold of the doors of the city gate,
together with the two posts, and tore
them loose, bar and all. He lifted them
to his shoulders and carried them to the
top of the hill that faces Hebron.
4Some time later, he fell in love with a
woman in the Valley of Sorek whose
name was Delilah. 5The rulers of the
Philistines went to her and said, "See if
you can lure him into showing you the
secret of his great strength and how we
can overpower him so that we may tie
him up and subdue him. Each one of us
will give you eleven hundred shekels of
silver."
6So Delilah said to Samson, "Tell me
the secret of your great strength and
how you can be tied up and subdued."
7Samson answered her, "If anyone
ties me with seven fresh thongs that
have not been dried, I'll become as
weak as any other man."
8Then the rulers of the Philistines
brought her seven fresh thongs that had
not been dried, and she tied him with
them. 9With men hidden in the room,
she called to him, "Samson, the Philistines are upon you!" But he snapped
the thongs as easily as a piece of string
snaps when it comes close to a flame.
So the secret of his strength was not
discovered.
10Then Delilah said to Samson, "You
have made a fool of me; you lied to me.
Come now, tell me how you can be
tied."
11He said, "If anyone ties me securely
with new ropes that have never been
used, I'll become as weak as any other
man."
12So Delilah took new ropes and tied
him with them. Then, with men hidden
in the room, she called to him, "Samson, the Philistines are upon you!" But
he snapped the ropes off his arms as if
they were threads.
13Delilah then said to Samson, "Until
now, you have been making a fool of me
and lying to me. Tell me how you can be
tied."
He replied, "If you weave the seven
braids of my head into the fabric ⌊on the
loom⌋ and tighten it with the pin, I'll
become as weak as any other man." So
while he was sleeping, Delilah took the
seven braids of his head, wove them
into the fabric 14and tightened it with
the pin.
Again she called to him, "Samson,
the Philistines are upon you!" He
awoke from his sleep and pulled up the
pin and the loom, with the fabric.
15Then she said to him, "How can you
say, 'I love you,' when you won't con-
fide in me? This is the third time you
have made a fool of me and haven't told
me the secret of your great strength."
16With such nagging she prodded him
day after day until he was tired to death.
17So he told her everything. "No
razor has ever been used on my head,"
he said, "because I have been a Nazirite
set apart to God since birth. If my head
were shaved, my strength would leave
me, and I would become as weak as any
other man."
18When Delilah saw that he had told
her everything, she sent word to the
rulers of the Philistines, "Come back
once more; he has told me everything."

So the rulers of the Philistines returned
with the silver in their hands. 19Having
put him to sleep on her lap, she called a
man to shave off the seven braids of his
hair, and so began to subdue him. And
his strength left him.
20Then she called, "Samson, the Philistines are upon you!"
He awoke from his sleep and
thought, "I'll go out as before and shake
myself free." But he did not know that
the LORD had left him.
21Then the Philistines seized him,
gouged out his eyes and took him down
to Gaza. Binding him with bronze
shackles, they set him to grinding in the
prison. 22But the hair on his head began
to grow again after it had been shaved.

The Death of Samson

23Now the rulers of the Philistines
assembled to offer a great sacrifice to
Dagon their god and to celebrate,
saying, "Our god has delivered Samson, our enemy, into our hands."
24When the people saw him, they
praised their god, saying,

"Our god has delivered our enemy
into our hands,
the one who laid waste our land
and multiplied our slain."

25While they were in high spirits, they
shouted, "Bring out Samson to entertain us." So they called Samson out of
the prison, and he performed for them.
When they stood him among the pillars, 26Samson said to the servant who
held his hand, "Put me where I can feel
the pillars that support the temple, so
that I may lean against them." 27Now
the temple was crowded with men and
women; all the rulers of the Philistines
were there, and on the roof were about
three thousand men and women watching Samson perform. 28Then Samson
prayed to the LORD, "O Sovereign
LORD, remember me. O God, please
strengthen me just once more, and let
me with one blow get revenge on the
Philistines for my two eyes." 29Then
Samson reached towards the two central pillars on which the temple stood.
Bracing himself against them, his right
hand on the one and his left hand on the
other, 30Samson said, "Let me die with
the Philistines!" Then he pushed with
all his might, and down came the temple
on the rulers and all the people in it.
Thus he killed many more when he died
than while he lived.
31Then his brothers and his father's
whole family went down to get him.
They brought him back and buried him
between Zorah and Eshtaol in the tomb
of Manoah his father. He had led Israel
twenty years.

Micah's Idols

17 Now a man named Micah from
the hill country of Ephraim 2said
to his mother, "The eleven hundred
shekels of silver that were taken from
you and about which I heard you utter a
curse—I have that silver with me; I
took it."
Then his mother said, "The LORD
bless you, my son!"
3When he returned the eleven hundred shekels of silver to his mother, she
said, "I solemnly consecrate my silver
to the LORD for my son to make a carved
image and a cast idol. I will give it back
to you."
4So he returned the silver to his
mother, and she took two hundred
shekels of silver and gave them to a
silversmith, who made them into the
image and the idol. And they were put
in Micah's house.
5Now this man Micah had a shrine,
and he made an ephod and some idols
and installed one of his sons as his
priest. 6In those days Israel had no king;
everyone did as he saw fit.
7A young Levite from Bethlehem in
Judah, who had been living within the
clan of Judah, 8left that town in search
of some other place to stay. On his way
he came to Micah's house in the hill
country of Ephraim.

9Micah asked him, "Where are you
from?"
"I'm a Levite from Bethlehem in
Judah," he said, "and I'm looking for a
place to stay."
10Then Micah said to him, "Live with
me and be my father and priest, and I'll
give you ten shekels of silver a year,
your clothes and your food." 11So the
Levite agreed to live with him, and the
young man was to him like one of his
sons. 12Then Micah installed the Levite,
and the young man became his priest
and lived in his house. 13And Micah
said, "Now I know that the LORD will be
good to me, since this Levite has become my priest."

NEW TESTAMENT READING

John 7:45–8:11

Unbelief of the Jewish Leaders

45Finally the temple guards went back
to the chief priests and Pharisees, who
asked them, "Why didn't you bring him
in?"
46"No-one ever spoke the way this
man does," the guards declared.
47"You mean he has deceived you
also?" the Pharisees retorted. 48"Has
any of the rulers or of the Pharisees
believed in him? 49No! But this mob
that knows nothing of the law—there is
a curse on them."
50Nicodemus, who had gone to Jesus
earlier and who was one of their own
number, asked, 51"Does our law condemn a man without first hearing him to
find out what he is doing?"
52They replied, "Are you from
Galilee, too? Look into it, and you will
find that a prophet does not come out of
Galilee."

[The earliest and most reliable manuscripts and other ancient witnesses do not have John 7:53–8:11]

53Then each went to his own home.
8 But Jesus went to the Mount of
Olives. 2At dawn he appeared
again in the temple courts, where all the
people gathered round him, and he sat
down to teach them. 3The teachers of
the law and the Pharisees brought in a
woman caught in adultery. They made
her stand before the group 4and said to
Jesus, "Teacher, this woman was
caught in the act of adultery. 5In the
Law Moses commanded us to stone
such women. Now what do you say?"
6They were using this question as a trap,
in order to have a basis for accusing
him.
But Jesus bent down and started to
write on the ground with his finger.
7When they kept on questioning him,
he straightened up and said to them, "If
any one of you is without sin, let him be
the first to throw a stone at her." 8Again
he stooped down and wrote on the
ground.
9At this, those who heard began to go
away one at a time, the older ones first,
until only Jesus was left, with the
woman still standing there. 10Jesus
straightened up and asked her,
"Woman, where are they? Has no-one
condemned you?"
11"No-one, sir," she said.
"Then neither do I condemn you,"
Jesus declared. "Go now and leave your
life of sin."

READING FROM PSALMS

Psalm 60:1–4

For the director of music. To ˪the tune of˩ "The Lily of the Covenant". A *miktam* of David. For teaching. When he fought Aram Naharaim and Aram Zobah, and when Joab returned and struck down twelve thousand Edomites in the Valley of Salt.

1You have rejected us, O God, and
burst forth upon us;
you have been angry—now restore
us!
2You have shaken the land and torn it
open;
mend its fractures, for it is
quaking.

[3]You have shown your people
desperate times;
you have given us wine that makes
us stagger.

[4]But for those who fear you, you have
raised a banner
to be unfurled against the bow.
Selah

MAY 14

DAY 134

OLD TESTAMENT READING

Judges 18:1–19:30

Danites Settle in Laish

18 In those days Israel had no king.
And in those days the tribe of
the Danites was seeking a place of their
own where they might settle, because
they had not yet come into an inheritance among the tribes of Israel. [2]So the
Danites sent five warriors from Zorah
and Eshtaol to spy out the land and
explore it. These men represented all
their clans. They told them, "Go,
explore the land."

The men entered the hill country of
Ephraim and came to the house of
Micah, where they spent the night.
[3]When they were near Micah's house,
they recognised the voice of the young
Levite; so they turned in there and
asked him, "Who brought you here?
What are you doing in this place? Why
are you here?"

[4]He told them what Micah had done
for him, and said, "He has hired me and
I am his priest."

[5]Then they said to him, "Please
enquire of God to learn whether our
journey will be successful."

[6]The priest answered them, "Go in
peace. Your journey has the LORD's
approval."

[7]So the five men left and came to
Laish, where they saw that the people
were living in safety, like the Sidonians,
unsuspecting and secure. And since
their land lacked nothing, they were
prosperous. Also, they lived a long way
from the Sidonians and had no relationship with anyone else.

[8]When they returned to Zorah and
Eshtaol, their brothers asked them,
"How did you find things?"

[9]They answered, "Come on, let's
attack them! We have seen that the land
is very good. Aren't you going to do
something? Don't hesitate to go there
and take it over. [10]When you get there,
you will find an unsuspecting people
and a spacious land that God has put
into your hands, a land that lacks
nothing whatever."

[11]Then six hundred men from the clan
of the Danites, armed for battle, set out
from Zorah and Eshtaol. [12]On their way
they set up camp near Kiriath Jearim in
Judah. This is why the place west of
Kiriath Jearim is called Mahaneh Dan
to this day. [13]From there they went on
to the hill country of Ephraim and
came to Micah's house.

[14]Then the five men who had spied
out the land of Laish said to their
brothers, "Do you know that one of
these houses has an ephod, other household gods, a carved image and a cast
idol? Now you know what to do." [15]So
they turned in there and went to the
house of the young Levite at Micah's
place and greeted him. [16]The six hundred Danites, armed for battle, stood at
the entrance to the gate. [17]The five men
who had spied out the land went inside
and took the carved image, the ephod,
the other household gods and the cast
idol while the priest and the six hundred
armed men stood at the entrance to the
gate.

18When these men went into Micah's
house and took the carved image, the
ephod, the other household gods and
the cast idol, the priest said to them,
"What are you doing?"
19They answered him, "Be quiet!
Don't say a word. Come with us, and be
our father and priest. Isn't it better that
you serve a tribe and clan in Israel as
priest rather than just one man's household?" 20Then the priest was glad. He
took the ephod, the other household
gods and the carved image and went
along with the people. 21Putting their
little children, their livestock and their
possessions in front of them, they
turned away and left.
22When they had gone some distance
from Micah's house, the men who lived
near Micah were called together and
overtook the Danites. 23As they
shouted after them, the Danites turned
and said to Micah, "What's the matter
with you that you called out your men to
fight?"
24He replied, "You took the gods I
made, and my priest, and went away.
What else do I have? How can you ask,
'What's the matter with you?'"
25The Danites answered, "Don't
argue with us, or some hot-tempered
men will attack you, and you and your
family will lose your lives." 26So the
Danites went their way, and Micah,
seeing that they were too strong for
him, turned round and went back
home.
27Then they took what Micah had
made, and his priest, and went on to
Laish, against a peaceful and unsuspecting people. They attacked them
with the sword and burned down their
city. 28There was no-one to rescue them
because they lived a long way from
Sidon and had no relationship with anyone else. The city was in a valley near
Beth Rehob.
The Danites rebuilt the city and settled there. 29They named it Dan after
their forefather Dan, who was born to
Israel—though the city used to be called Laish. 30There the Danites set up for
themselves the idols, and Jonathan son
of Gershom, the son of Moses, and his
sons were priests for the tribe of Dan
until the time of the captivity of the
land. 31They continued to use the idols
Micah had made, all the time the house
of God was in Shiloh.

A Levite and His Concubine

19 In those days Israel had no king.
Now a Levite who lived in a
remote area in the hill country of
Ephraim took a concubine from Bethlehem in Judah. 2But she was unfaithful
to him. She left him and went back to
her father's house in Bethlehem, Judah.
After she had been there for four
months, 3her husband went to her to
persuade her to return. He had with him
his servant and two donkeys. She took
him into her father's house, and when
her father saw him, he gladly welcomed
him. 4His father-in-law, the girl's
father, prevailed upon him to stay; so he
remained with him three days, eating
and drinking, and sleeping there.
5On the fourth day they got up early
and he prepared to leave, but the girl's
father said to his son-in-law, "Refresh
yourself with something to eat; then you
can go." 6So the two of them sat down
to eat and drink together. Afterwards
the girl's father said, "Please stay
tonight and enjoy yourself." 7And
when the man got up to go, his father-
in-law persuaded him, so he stayed
there that night. 8On the morning of the
fifth day, when he rose to go, the girl's
father said, "Refresh yourself. Wait till
afternoon!" So the two of them ate
together.
9Then when the man, with his concubine and his servant, got up to leave,
his father-in-law, the girl's father, said,
"Now look, it's almost evening. Spend
the night here; the day is nearly over.
Stay and enjoy yourself. Early tomorrow morning you can get up and be on
your way home." 10But, unwilling to
stay another night, the man left and

went towards Jebus (that is, Jerusalem), with his two saddled donkeys
and his concubine.
11When they were near Jebus and the
day was almost gone, the servant said to
his master, "Come, let's stop at this city
of the Jebusites and spend the night."
12His master replied, "No. We won't
go into an alien city, whose people are
not Israelites. We will go on to
Gibeah." 13He added, "Come, let's try
to reach Gibeah or Ramah and spend
the night in one of those places." 14So
they went on, and the sun set as they
neared Gibeah in Benjamin. 15There
they stopped to spend the night. They
went and sat in the city square, but
no-one took them into his home for the
night.
16That evening an old man from the
hill country of Ephraim, who was living
in Gibeah (the men of the place were
Benjamites), came in from his work in
the fields. 17When he looked and saw
the traveller in the city square, the old
man asked, "Where are you going?
Where did you come from?"
18He answered, "We are on our way
from Bethlehem in Judah to a remote
area in the hill country of Ephraim
where I live. I have been to Bethlehem
in Judah and now I am going to the
house of the LORD. No-one has taken
me into his house. 19We have both straw
and fodder for our donkeys and bread
and wine for ourselves your servants
—me, your maidservant, and the young
man with us. We don't need anything."
20"You are welcome at my house,"
the old man said. "Let me supply whatever you need. Only don't spend the
night in the square." 21So he took him
into his house and fed his donkeys.
After they had washed their feet, they
had something to eat and drink.
22While they were enjoying themselves, some of the wicked men of the
city surrounded the house. Pounding on
the door, they shouted to the old man
who owned the house, "Bring out the
man who came to your house so we can
have sex with him."
23The owner of the house went outside and said to them, "No, my friends,
don't be so vile. Since this man is my
guest, don't do this disgraceful thing.
24Look, here is my virgin daughter, and
his concubine. I will bring them out to
you now, and you can use them and do
to them whatever you wish. But to this
man, don't do such a disgraceful thing."
25But the men would not listen to
him. So the man took his concubine and
sent her outside to them, and they raped
her and abused her throughout the
night, and at dawn they let her go. 26At
daybreak the woman went back to the
house where her master was staying, fell
down at the door and lay there until
daylight.
27When her master got up in the
morning and opened the door of the
house and stepped out to continue on
his way, there lay his concubine, fallen
in the doorway of the house, with her
hands on the threshold. 28He said to
her, "Get up; let's go." But there was
no answer. Then the man put her on his
donkey and set out for home.
29When he reached home, he took a
knife and cut up his concubine, limb by
limb, into twelve parts and sent them
into all the areas of Israel. 30Everyone
who saw it said, "Such a thing has never
been seen or done, not since the day the
Israelites came up out of Egypt. Think
about it! Consider it! Tell us what to
do!"

NEW TESTAMENT READING
John 8:12–30

The Validity of Jesus' Testimony

12When Jesus spoke again to the people, he said, "I am the light of the world.
Whoever follows me will never walk in
darkness, but will have the light of life."
13The Pharisees challenged him,
"Here you are, appearing as your own
witness; your testimony is not valid."
14Jesus answered, "Even if I testify

on my own behalf, my testimony is
valid, for I know where I came from and
where I am going. But you have no idea
where I come from or where I am going.
15You judge by human standards; I pass
judgment on no-one. 16But if I do
judge, my decisions are right, because I
am not alone. I stand with the Father,
who sent me. 17In your own Law it is
written that the testimony of two men is
valid. 18I am one who testifies for myself; my other witness is the Father, who
sent me."
19Then they asked him, "Where is
your father?"

"You do not know me or my Father,"
Jesus replied. "If you knew me, you
would know my Father also." 20He
spoke these words while teaching in the
temple area near the place where the
offerings were put. Yet no-one seized
him, because his time had not yet come.
21Once more Jesus said to them, "I
am going away, and you will look for
me, and you will die in your sin. Where I
go, you cannot come."
22This made the Jews ask, "Will he
kill himself? Is that why he says, 'Where
I go, you cannot come'?"
23But he continued, "You are from
below; I am from above. You are of this
world; I am not of this world. 24I told
you that you would die in your sins; if
you do not believe that I am ⌞the one I
claim to be⌟, you will indeed die in your
sins."
25"Who are you?" they asked.

"Just what I have been claiming all
along," Jesus replied. 26"I have much to
say in judgment of you. But he who sent
me is reliable, and what I have heard
from him I tell the world."
27They did not understand that he
was telling them about his Father. 28So
Jesus said, "When you have lifted up
the Son of Man, then you will know that
I am ⌞the one I claim to be⌟ and that I do
nothing on my own but speak just what
the Father has taught me. 29The one
who sent me is with me; he has not left
me alone, for I always do what pleases
him." 30Even as he spoke, many put
their faith in him.

READING FROM PSALMS

Psalm 60:5–12

5Save us and help us with your right
hand,
that those you love may be
delivered.
6God has spoken from his sanctuary:
"In triumph I will parcel out
Shechem
and measure off the Valley of
Succoth.
7Gilead is mine, and Manasseh is
mine;
Ephraim is my helmet,
Judah my sceptre.
8Moab is my washbasin,
upon Edom I toss my sandal;
over Philistia I shout in triumph."

9Who will bring me to the fortified
city?
Who will lead me to Edom?
10Is it not you, O God, you who have
rejected us
and no longer go out with our
armies?
11Give us aid against the enemy,
for the help of man is worthless.
12With God we shall gain the victory,
and he will trample down our
enemies.

MAY 15

DAY 135

OLD TESTAMENT READING

Judges 20:1–21:25

Israelites Fight the Benjamites

20 Then all the Israelites from Dan to Beersheba and from the land of Gilead came out as one man and assembled before the LORD in Mizpah. 2The leaders of all the people of the tribes of Israel took their places in the assembly of the people of God, four hundred thousand soldiers armed with swords. 3(The Benjamites heard that the Israelites had gone up to Mizpah.) Then the Israelites said, "Tell us how this awful thing happened."

4So the Levite, the husband of the murdered woman, said, "I and my concubine came to Gibeah in Benjamin to spend the night. 5During the night the men of Gibeah came after me and surrounded the house, intending to kill me. They raped my concubine, and she died. 6I took my concubine, cut her into pieces and sent one piece to each region of Israel's inheritance, because they committed this lewd and disgraceful act in Israel. 7Now, all you Israelites, speak up and give your verdict."

8All the people rose as one man, saying, "None of us will go home. No, not one of us will return to his house. 9But now this is what we'll do to Gibeah: We'll go up against it as the lot directs. 10We'll take ten men out of every hundred from all the tribes of Israel, and a hundred from a thousand, and a thousand from ten thousand, to get provisions for the army. Then, when the army arrives at Gibeahin Benjamin, it can give them what they deserve for all this vileness done in Israel." 11So all the men of Israel got together and united as one man against the city.

12The tribes of Israel sent men throughout the tribe of Benjamin, saying, "What about this awful crime that was committed among you? 13Now surrender those wicked men of Gibeah so that we may put them to death and purge the evil from Israel."

But the Benjamites would not listen to their fellow Israelites. 14From their towns they came together at Gibeah to fight against the Israelites. 15At once the Benjamites mobilised twenty-six thousand swordsmen from their towns, in addition to seven hundred chosen men from those living in Gibeah. 16Among all these soldiers there were seven hundred chosen men who were left-handed, each of whom could sling a stone at a hair and not miss.

17Israel, apart from Benjamin, mustered four hundred thousand swordsmen, all of them fighting men.

18The Israelites went up to Bethel and enquired of God. They said, "Who of us shall go first to fight against the Benjamites?"

The LORD replied, "Judah shall go first."

19The next morning the Israelites got up and pitched camp near Gibeah. 20The men of Israel went out to fight the Benjamites and took up battle positions against them at Gibeah. 21The Benjamites came out of Gibeah and cut down twenty-two thousand Israelites on the battlefield that day. 22But the men of Israel encouraged one another and again took up their positions where they had stationed themselves the first day. 23The Israelites went up and wept before the LORD until evening, and they enquired of the LORD. They said, "Shall we go up again to battle against the Benjamites, our brothers?"

The LORD answered, "Go up against them."

24Then the Israelites drew near to Benjamin the second day. 25This time, when the Benjamites came out from Gibeah to oppose them, they cut down another eighteen thousand Israelites, all of them armed with swords.

26Then the Israelites, all the people, went up to Bethel, and there they sat weeping before the LORD. They fasted that day until evening and presented burnt offerings and fellowship offerings to the LORD. 27And the Israelites enquired of the LORD. (In those days the ark of the covenant of God was there, 28with Phinehas son of Eleazar, the son of Aaron, ministering before it.) They asked, "Shall we go up again to battle with Benjamin our brother, or not?"

The LORD responded, "Go, for tomorrow I will give them into your hands."

29Then Israel set an ambush around Gibeah. 30They went up against the Benjamites on the third day and took up positions against Gibeah as they had done before. 31The Benjamites came out to meet them and were drawn away from the city. They began to inflict casualties on the Israelites as before, so that about thirty men fell in the open field and on the roads—the one leading to Bethel and the other to Gibeah.

32While the Benjamites were saying, "We are defeating them as before," the Israelites were saying, "Let's retreat and draw them away from the city to the roads."

33All the men of Israel moved from their places and took up positions at Baal Tamar, and the Israelite ambush charged out of its place on the west of Gibeah. 34Then ten thousand of Israel's finest men made a frontal attack on Gibeah. The fighting was so heavy that the Benjamites did not realise how near disaster was. 35The LORD defeated Benjamin before Israel, and on that day the Israelites struck down 25,100 Benjamites, all armed with swords. 36Then the Benjamites saw that they were beaten.

Now the men of Israel had given way before Benjamin, because they relied on the ambush they had set near Gibeah. 37The men who had been in ambush made a sudden dash into Gibeah, spread out and put the whole city to the sword. 38The men of Israel had arranged with the ambush that they should send up a great cloud of smoke from the city, 39and then the men of Israel would turn in the battle.

The Benjamites had begun to inflict casualties on the men of Israel (about thirty), and they said, "We are defeating them as in the first battle." 40But when the column of smoke began to rise from the city, the Benjamites turned and saw the smoke of the whole city going up into the sky. 41Then the men of Israel turned on them, and the men of Benjamin were terrified, because they realised that disaster had come upon them. 42So they fled before the Israelites in the direction of the desert, but they could not escape the battle. And the men of Israel who came out of the towns cut them down there. 43They surrounded the Benjamites, chased them and easily overran them in the vicinity of Gibeah on the east. 44Eighteen thousand Benjamites fell, all of them valiant fighters. 45As they turned and fled towards the desert to the rock of Rimmon, the Israelites cut down five thousand men along the roads. They kept pressing after the Benjamites as far as Gidom and struck down two thousand more.

46On that day twenty-five thousand Benjamite swordsmen fell, all of them valiant fighters. 47But six hundred men turned and fled into the desert to the rock of Rimmon, where they stayed for four months. 48The men of Israel went back to Benjamin and put all the towns to the sword, including the animals and everything else they found. All the towns they came across they set on fire.

Wives for the Benjamites

21 The men of Israel had taken an oath at Mizpah: "Not one of us will give his daughter in marriage to a Benjamite."

2The people went to Bethel, where they sat before God until evening, raising their voices and weeping bitterly.

3“O LORD, the God of Israel,” they
cried, “why has this happened to Israel?
Why should one tribe be missing from
Israel today?”

4Early the next day the people built
an altar and presented burnt offerings
and fellowship offerings.

5Then the Israelites asked, “Who
from all the tribes of Israel has failed to
assemble before the LORD?” For they
had taken a solemn oath that anyone
who failed to assemble before the LORD
at Mizpah should certainly be put to
death.

6Now the Israelites grieved for their
brothers, the Benjamites. “Today one
tribe is cut off from Israel,” they said.
7“How can we provide wives for those
who are left, since we have taken an
oath by the LORD not to give them any
of our daughters in marriage?” 8Then
they asked, “Which one of the tribes of
Israel failed to assemble before the
LORD at Mizpah?” They discovered
that no-one from Jabesh Gilead had
come to the camp for the assembly. 9For
when they counted the people, they
found that none of the people of Jabesh
Gilead were there.

10So the assembly sent twelve
thousand fighting men with instructions
to go to Jabesh Gilead and put to the
sword those living there, including the
women and children. 11“This is what
you are to do,” they said. “Kill every
male and every woman who is not a
virgin.” 12They found among the people
living in Jabesh Gilead four hundred
young women who had never slept with
a man, and they took them to the camp
at Shiloh in Canaan.

13Then the whole assembly sent an
offer of peace to the Benjamites at the
rock of Rimmon. 14So the Benjamites
returned at that time and were given the
women of Jabesh Gilead who had been
spared. But there were not enough for
all of them.

15The people grieved for Benjamin,
because the LORD had made a gap in the
tribes of Israel. 16And the elders of the
assembly said, “With the women of
Benjamin destroyed, how shall we provide wives for the men who are left?
17The Benjamite survivors must have
heirs,” they said, “so that a tribe of
Israel will not be wiped out. 18We can’t
give them our daughters as wives, since
we Israelites have taken this oath:
‘Cursed be anyone who gives a wife to a
Benjamite.’ 19But look, there is the
annual festival of the LORD in Shiloh, to
the north of Bethel, and east of the road
that goes from Bethel to Shechem, and
to the south of Lebonah.”

20So they instructed the Benjamites,
saying, “Go and hide in the vineyards
21and watch. When the girls of Shiloh
come out to join in the dancing, then
rush from the vineyards and each of you
seize a wife from the girls of Shiloh and
go to the land of Benjamin. 22When
their fathers or brothers complain to us,
we will say to them, ‘Do us a kindness
by helping them, because we did not get
wives for them during the war, and you
are innocent, since you did not give
your daughters to them.’”

23So that is what the Benjamites did.
While the girls were dancing, each man
caught one and carried her off to be his
wife. Then they returned to their inheritance and rebuilt the towns and settled
in them.

24At that time the Israelites left that
place and went home to their tribes and
clans, each to his own inheritance.

25In those days Israel had no king;
everyone did as he saw fit.

NEW TESTAMENT READING

John 8:31–59

The Children of Abraham

31To the Jews who had believed him,
Jesus said, “If you hold to my teaching,
you are really my disciples. 32Then you
will know the truth, and the truth will
set you free.”

33They answered him, “We are Abraham’s descendants and have never been

slaves of anyone. How can you say that
we shall be set free?"
34Jesus replied, "I tell you the truth,
everyone who sins is a slave to sin.
35Now a slave has no permanent place in
the family, but a son belongs to it for
ever. 36So if the Son sets you free, you
will be free indeed. 37I know you are
Abraham's descendants. Yet you are
ready to kill me, because you have no
room for my word. 38I am telling you
what I have seen in the Father's presence, and you do what you have heard
from your father."
39"Abraham is our father," they
answered.
"If you were Abraham's children,"
said Jesus, "then you would do the
things Abraham did. 40As it is, you are
determined to kill me, a man who has
told you the truth that I heard from
God. Abraham did not do such things.
41You are doing the things your own
father does."
"We are not illegitimate children,"
they protested. "The only Father we
have is God himself."

The Children of the Devil

42Jesus said to them, "If God were
your Father, you would love me, for I
came from God and now am here. I
have not come on my own; but he sent
me. 43Why is my language not clear to
you? Because you are unable to hear
what I say. 44You belong to your father,
the devil, and you want to carry out
your father's desire. He was a murderer
from the beginning, not holding to the
truth, for there is no truth in him. When
he lies, he speaks his native language,
for he is a liar and the father of lies.
45Yet because I tell the truth, you do
not believe me! 46Can any of you
prove me guilty of sin? If I am telling
the truth, why don't you believe me?
47He who belongs to God hears
what God says. The reason you do
not hear is that you do not belong to
God."

The Claims of Jesus About Himself

48The Jews answered him, "Aren't
we right in saying that you are a Samaritan and demon-possessed?"
49"I am not possessed by a demon,"
said Jesus, "but I honour my Father and
you dishonour me. 50I am not seeking
glory for myself; but there is one who
seeks it, and he is the judge. 51I tell you
the truth, if anyone keeps my word, he
will never see death."
52At this the Jews exclaimed, "Now
we know that you are demon-
possessed! Abraham died and so did the
prophets, yet you say that if anyone
keeps your word, he will never taste
death. 53Are you greater than our father
Abraham? He died, and so did the
prophets. Who do you think you are?"
54Jesus replied, "If I glorify myself,
my glory means nothing. My Father,
whom you claim as your God, is the one
who glorifies me. 55Though you do not
know him, I know him. If I said I did
not, I would be a liar like you, but I do
know him and keep his word. 56Your
father Abraham rejoiced at the thought
of seeing my day; he saw it and was
glad."
57"You are not yet fifty years old,"
the Jews said to him, "and you have
seen Abraham!"
58"I tell you the truth," Jesus
answered, "before Abraham was born,
I am!" 59At this, they picked up stones
to stone him, but Jesus hid himself,
slipping away from the temple grounds.

READING FROM PSALMS

Psalm 61:1–8

For the director of music. With stringed instruments. Of David.

1Hear my cry, O God;
listen to my prayer.

2From the ends of the earth I call to
you,
I call as my heart grows faint;

lead me to the rock that is higher
than I.
[3]For you have been my refuge,
a strong tower against the foe.

[4]I long to dwell in your tent for ever
and take refuge in the shelter of
your wings. *Selah*
[5]For you have heard my vows, O God;
you have given me the heritage of
those who fear your name.

[6]Increase the days of the king's life,
his years for many generations.
[7]May he be enthroned in God's
presence for ever;
appoint your love and faithfulness
to protect him.

[8]Then will I ever sing praise to your
name
and fulfil my vows day after day.

MAY 16

DAY 136

OLD TESTAMENT READING
Ruth 1:1–2:23

Naomi and Ruth

1 In the days when the judges ruled,
there was a famine in the land, and
a man from Bethlehem in Judah,
together with his wife and two sons,
went to live for a while in the country of
Moab. [2]The man's name was
Elimelech, his wife's name Naomi, and
the names of his two sons were Mahlon
and Kilion. They were Ephrathites
from Bethlehem, Judah. And they went
to Moab and lived there.
[3]Now Elimelech, Naomi's husband,
died, and she was left with her two sons.
[4]They married Moabite women, one
named Orpah and the other Ruth.
After they had lived there about ten
years, [5]both Mahlon and Kilion also
died, and Naomi was left without her
two sons and her husband.
[6]When she heard in Moab that the
LORD had come to the aid of his people
by providing food for them, Naomi and
her daughters-in-law prepared to return
home from there. [7]With her two daughters-in-law she left the place where she
had been living and set out on the road
that would take them back to the land of
Judah.
[8]Then Naomi said to her two daughters-in-law, "Go back, each of you, to
your mother's home. May the LORD
show kindness to you, as you have
shown to your dead and to me. [9]May the
LORD grant that each of you will find
rest in the home of another husband."
Then she kissed them and they wept
aloud [10]and said to her, "We will go
back with you to your people."
[11]But Naomi said, "Return home, my
daughters. Why would you come with
me? Am I going to have any more sons,
who could become your husbands?
[12]Return home, my daughters; I am too
old to have another husband. Even if I
thought there was still hope for me—
even if I had a husband tonight and then
gave birth to sons—[13]would you wait
until they grew up? Would you remain
unmarried for them? No, my daughters.
It is more bitter for me than for you,
because the LORD's hand has gone out
against me!"
[14]At this they wept again. Then
Orpah kissed her mother-in-law good-
bye, but Ruth clung to her.
[15]"Look," said Naomi, "your sister-
in-law is going back to her people and
her gods. Go back with her."
[16]But Ruth replied, "Don't urge me
to leave you or to turn back from you.
Where you go I will go, and where you

stay I will stay. Your people will be my
people and your God my God. 17Where
you die I will die, and there I will be
buried. May the LORD deal with me, be
it ever so severely, if anything but death
separates you and me." 18When Naomi
realised that Ruth was determined to go
with her, she stopped urging her.

19So the two women went on until
they came to Bethlehem. When they
arrived in Bethlehem, the whole town
was stirred because of them, and the
women exclaimed, "Can this be
Naomi?"

20"Don't call me Naomi," she told
them. "Call me Mara, because the
Almighty has made my life very bitter.
21I went away full, but the LORD has
brought me back empty. Why call me
Naomi? The LORD has afflicted me; the
Almighty has brought misfortune upon
me."

22So Naomi returned from Moab
accompanied by Ruth the Moabitess,
her daughter-in-law, arriving in
Bethlehem as the barley harvest was
beginning.

Ruth Meets Boaz

2 Now Naomi had a relative on her
husband's side from the clan of
Elimelech, a man of standing, whose
name was Boaz.

2And Ruth the Moabitess said to
Naomi, "Let me go to the fields and
pick up the leftover grain behind anyone in whose eyes I find favour."

Naomi said to her, "Go ahead, my
daughter." 3So she went out and began
to glean in the fields behind the harvesters. As it turned out, she found
herself working in a field belonging to
Boaz, who was from the clan of
Elimelech.

4Just then Boaz arrived from Bethlehem and greeted the harvesters, "The
LORD be with you!"

"The LORD bless you!" they called
back.

5Boaz asked the foreman of his harvesters, "Whose young woman is that?"

6The foreman replied, "She is the
Moabitess who came back from Moab
with Naomi. 7She said, 'Please let me
glean and gather among the sheaves
behind the harvesters.' She went into
the field and has worked steadily from
morning till now, except for a short rest
in the shelter."

8So Boaz said to Ruth, "My daughter, listen to me. Don't go and glean in
another field and don't go away from
here. Stay here with my servant girls.
9Watch the field where the men are
harvesting, and follow along after the
girls. I have told the men not to touch
you. And whenever you are thirsty, go
and get a drink from the water jars the
men have filled."

10At this, she bowed down with her
face to the ground. She exclaimed,
"Why have I found such favour in your
eyes that you notice me—a foreigner?"

11Boaz replied, "I've been told all
about what you have done for your
mother-in-law since the death of your
husband—how you left your father and
mother and your homeland and came to
live with a people you did not know
before. 12May the LORD repay you for
what you have done. May you be richly
rewarded by the LORD, the God of
Israel, under whose wings you have
come to take refuge."

13"May I continue to find favour in
your eyes, my lord," she said. "You
have given me comfort and have spoken
kindly to your servant—though I do not
have the standing of one of your servant
girls."

14At mealtime Boaz said to her,
"Come over here. Have some bread
and dip it in the wine vinegar."

When she sat down with the harvesters, he offered her some roasted
grain. She ate all she wanted and had
some left over. 15As she got up to glean,
Boaz gave orders to his men, "Even if
she gathers among the sheaves, don't
embarrass her. 16Rather, pull out some
stalks for her from the bundles and
leave them for her to pick up, and don't
rebuke her."

17So Ruth gleaned in the field until evening. Then she threshed the barley she had gathered, and it amounted to about an ephah. 18She carried it back to town, and her mother-in-law saw how much she had gathered. Ruth also brought out and gave her what she had left over after she had eaten enough.

19Her mother-in-law asked her, "Where did you glean today? Where did you work? Blessed be the man who took notice of you!"

Then Ruth told her mother-in-law about the one at whose place she had been working. "The name of the man I worked with today is Boaz," she said.

20"The LORD bless him!" Naomi said to her daughter-in-law. "He has not stopped showing his kindness to the living and the dead." She added, "That man is our close relative; he is one of our kinsman-redeemers."

21Then Ruth the Moabitess said, "He even said to me, 'Stay with my workers until they finish harvesting all my grain.'"

22Naomi said to Ruth her daughter-in-law, "It will be good for you, my daughter, to go with his girls, because in someone else's field you might be harmed."

23So Ruth stayed close to the servant girls of Boaz to glean until the barley and wheat harvests were finished. And she lived with her mother-in-law.

NEW TESTAMENT READING
John 9:1–34

Jesus Heals a Man Born Blind

9 As he went along, he saw a man blind from birth. 2His disciples asked him, "Rabbi, who sinned, this man or his parents, that he was born blind?"

3"Neither this man nor his parents sinned," said Jesus, "but this happened so that the work of God might be displayed in his life. 4As long as it is day, we must do the work of him who sent me. Night is coming, when no-one can work. 5While I am in the world, I am the light of the world."

6Having said this, he spat on the ground, made some mud with the saliva, and put it on the man's eyes. 7"Go," he told him, "wash in the Pool of Siloam" (this word means Sent). So the man went and washed, and came home seeing.

8His neighbours and those who had formerly seen him begging asked, "Isn't this the same man who used to sit and beg?" 9Some claimed that he was.

Others said, "No, he only looks like him."

But he himself insisted, "I am the man."

10"How then were your eyes opened?" they demanded.

11He replied, "The man they call Jesus made some mud and put it on my eyes. He told me to go to Siloam and wash. So I went and washed, and then I could see."

12"Where is this man?" they asked him.

"I don't know," he said.

The Pharisees Investigate the Healing

13They brought to the Pharisees the man who had been blind. 14Now the day on which Jesus had made the mud and opened the man's eyes was a Sabbath. 15Therefore the Pharisees also asked him how he had received his sight. "He put mud on my eyes," the man replied, "and I washed, and now I see."

16Some of the Pharisees said, "This man is not from God, for he does not keep the Sabbath."

But others asked, "How can a sinner do such miraculous signs?" So they were divided.

17Finally they turned again to the blind man, "What have you to say about him? It was your eyes he opened."

The man replied, "He is a prophet."

18The Jews still did not believe that he had been blind and had received his

sight until they sent for the man's
parents. 19"Is this your son?" they
asked. "Is this the one you say was born
blind? How is it that now he can see?"
20"We know he is our son," the
parents answered, "and we know he
was born blind. 21But how he can see
now, or who opened his eyes, we don't
know. Ask him. He is of age; he will
speak for himself." 22His parents said
this because they were afraid of the
Jews, for already the Jews had decided
that anyone who acknowledged that
Jesus was the Christ would be put out of
the synagogue. 23That was why his
parents said, "He is of age; ask him."
24A second time they summoned the
man who had been blind. "Give glory to
God," they said. "We know this man is
a sinner."
25He replied, "Whether he is a sinner
or not, I don't know. One thing I do
know. I was blind but now I see!"
26Then they asked him, "What did he
do to you? How did he open your
eyes?"
27He answered, "I have told you
already and you did not listen. Why do
you want to hear it again? Do you want
to become his disciples, too?"
28Then they hurled insults at him and
said, "You are this fellow's disciple! We
are disciples of Moses! 29We know that
God spoke to Moses, but as for this
fellow, we don't even know where he
comes from."
30The man answered, "Now that is
remarkable! You don't know where he
comes from, yet he opened my eyes.
31We know that God does not listen to
sinners. He listens to the godly man who
does his will. 32Nobody has ever heard
of opening the eyes of a man born blind.
33If this man were not from God, he
could do nothing."
34To this they replied, "You were
steeped in sin at birth; how dare you
lecture us!" And they threw him out.

READING FROM PROVERBS

Proverbs 12:8–17

8A man is praised according to his
wisdom,
but men with warped minds are
despised.

9Better to be a nobody and yet have a
servant
than pretend to be somebody and
have no food.

10A righteous man cares for the needs
of his animal,
but the kindest acts of the wicked
are cruel.

11He who works his land will have
abundant food,
but he who chases fantasies lacks
judgment.

12The wicked desire the plunder of evil
men,
but the root of the righteous
flourishes.

13An evil man is trapped by his sinful
talk,
but a righteous man escapes
trouble.

14From the fruit of his lips a man is
filled with good things
as surely as the work of his hands
rewards him.

15The way of a fool seems right to him,
but a wise man listens to advice.

16A fool shows his annoyance at once,
but a prudent man overlooks an
insult.

17A truthful witness gives honest
testimony,
but a false witness tells lies.

MAY 17

OLD TESTAMENT READING
Ruth 3:1–4:22

Ruth and Boaz at the Threshing-Floor

3 One day Naomi her mother-in-law
said to her, "My daughter, should I
not try to find a home for you, where
you will be well provided for? 2Is not
Boaz, with whose servant girls you have
been, a kinsman of ours? Tonight he
will be winnowing barley on the
threshing-floor. 3Wash and perfume
yourself, and put on your best clothes.
Then go down to the threshing-floor,
but don't let him know you are there
until he has finished eating and drinking. 4When he lies down, note the place
where he is lying. Then go and uncover
his feet and lie down. He will tell you
what to do."

5"I will do whatever you say," Ruth
answered. 6So she went down to the
threshing-floor and did everything her
mother-in-law told her to do.

7When Boaz had finished eating and
drinking and was in good spirits, he
went over to lie down at the far end
of the grain pile. Ruth approached
quietly, uncovered his feet and lay
down. 8In the middle of the night something startled the man, and he turned
and discovered a woman lying at his
feet.

9"Who are you?" he asked.

"I am your servant Ruth," she said.
"Spread the corner of your garment
over me, since you are a kinsman-
redeemer."

10"The LORD bless you, my daughter," he replied. "This kindness is
greater than that which you showed
earlier: You have not run after the
younger men, whether rich or poor.
11And now, my daughter, don't be
afraid. I will do for you all you ask. All
my fellow townsmen know that you
are a woman of noble character.
12Although it is true that I am near of
kin, there is a kinsman-redeemer nearer
than I. 13Stay here for the night, and in
the morning if he wants to redeem,
good; let him redeem. But if he is not
willing, as surely as the LORD lives I will
do it. Lie here until morning."

14So she lay at his feet until morning,
but got up before anyone could be recognised; and he said, "Don't let it be
known that a woman came to the
threshing-floor."

15He also said, "Bring me the shawl
you are wearing and hold it out." When
she did so, he poured into it six measures of barley and put it on her. Then
he went back to town.

16When Ruth came to her mother-in-
law, Naomi asked, "How did it go, my
daughter?"

Then she told her everything Boaz
had done for her 17and added, "He gave
me these six measures of barley, saying,
'Don't go back to your mother-in-law
empty-handed.'"

18Then Naomi said, "Wait, my
daughter, until you find out what happens. For the man will not rest until the
matter is settled today."

Boaz Marries Ruth

4 Meanwhile Boaz went up to the
town gate and sat there. When the
kinsman-redeemer he had mentioned
came along, Boaz said, "Come over
here, my friend, and sit down." So he
went over and sat down.

2Boaz took ten of the elders of the
town and said, "Sit here," and they did
so. 3Then he said to the kinsman-
redeemer, "Naomi, who has come back
from Moab, is selling the piece of land
that belonged to our brother Elimelech.
4I thought I should bring the matter to
your attention and suggest that you buy
it in the presence of these seated here
and in the presence of the elders of my

people. If you will redeem it, do so. But
if you will not, tell me, so that I will
know. For no-one has the right to do it
except you, and I am next in line."
"I will redeem it," he said.
5Then Boaz said, "On the day you
buy the land from Naomi and from
Ruth the Moabitess, you acquire the
dead man's widow, in order to maintain
the name of the dead with his
property."
6At this, the kinsman-redeemer said,
"Then I cannot redeem it because I
might endanger my own estate. You
redeem it yourself. I cannot do it."
7(Now in earlier times in Israel, for
the redemption and transfer of property
to become final, one party took off his
sandal and gave it to the other. This was
the method of legalising transactions in
Israel.)
8So the kinsman-redeemer said to
Boaz, "Buy it yourself." And he removed his sandal.
9Then Boaz announced to the elders
and all the people, "Today you are witnesses that I have bought from Naomi
all the property of Elimelech, Kilion
and Mahlon. 10I have also acquired
Ruth the Moabitess, Mahlon's widow,
as my wife, in order to maintain the
name of the dead with his property, so
that his name will not disappear from
among his family or from the town records. Today you are witnesses!"
11Then the elders and all those at the
gate said, "We are witnesses. May the
LORD make the woman who is coming
into your home like Rachel and Leah,
who together built up the house of
Israel. May you have standing in
Ephrathah and be famous in Bethlehem. 12Through the offspring the
LORD gives you by this young woman,
may your family be like that of Perez,
whom Tamar bore to Judah."

The Genealogy of David

13So Boaz took Ruth and she became
his wife. Then he went to her, and the
LORD enabled her to conceive, and she
gave birth to a son. 14The women said to
Naomi: "Praise be to the LORD, who
this day has not left you without a kinsman-redeemer. May he become famous
throughout Israel! 15He will renew your
life and sustain you in your old age. For
your daughter-in-law, who loves you
and who is better to you than seven
sons, has given him birth."
16Then Naomi took the child, laid
him in her lap and cared for him. 17The
women living there said, "Naomi has a
son." And they named him Obed. He
was the father of Jesse, the father of
David.
18This, then, is the family line of
Perez:

Perez was the father of Hezron,
19Hezron the father of Ram,
Ram the father of Amminadab,
20Amminadab the father of Nahshon,
Nahshon the father of Salmon,
21Salmon the father of Boaz,
Boaz the father of Obed,
22Obed the father of Jesse,
and Jesse the father of David.

NEW TESTAMENT READING
John 9:35–10:21

Spiritual Blindness

35Jesus heard that they had thrown
him out, and when he found him, he
said, "Do you believe in the Son of
Man?"
36"Who is he, sir?" the man asked.
"Tell me so that I may believe in him."
37Jesus said, "You have now seen
him; in fact, he is the one speaking with
you."
38Then the man said, "Lord, I believe," and he worshipped him.
39Jesus said, "For judgment I have
come into this world, so that the blind
will see and those who see will become
blind."
40Some Pharisees who were with him
heard him say this and asked, "What?
Are we blind too?"

41Jesus said, "If you were blind, you
would not be guilty of sin; but now that
you claim you can see, your guilt
remains.

The Shepherd and His Flock

10 "I tell you the truth, the man
who does not enter the sheep
pen by the gate, but climbs in by some
other way, is a thief and a robber. 2The
man who enters by the gate is the
shepherd of his sheep. 3The watchman
opens the gate for him, and the sheep
listen to his voice. He calls his own
sheep by name and leads them out.
4When he has brought out all his own,
he goes on ahead of them, and his sheep
follow him because they know his voice.
5But they will never follow a stranger; in
fact, they will run away from him because they do not recognise a stranger's
voice." 6Jesus used this figure of
speech, but they did not understand
what he was telling them.

7Therefore Jesus said again, "I tell
you the truth, I am the gate for the
sheep. 8All who ever came before me
were thieves and robbers, but the sheep
did not listen to them. 9I am the gate;
whoever enters through me will be
saved. He will come in and go out, and
find pasture. 10The thief comes only to
steal and kill and destroy; I have come
that they may have life, and have it to
the full.

11"I am the good shepherd. The good
shepherd lays down his life for the
sheep. 12The hired hand is not the
shepherd who owns the sheep. So when
he sees the wolf coming, he abandons
the sheep and runs away. Then the wolf
attacks the flock and scatters it. 13The
man runs away because he is a hired
hand and cares nothing for the sheep.

14"I am the good shepherd; I know
my sheep and my sheep know me—
15just as the Father knows me and I
know the Father—and I lay down my
life for the sheep. 16I have other sheep
that are not of this sheep pen. I must
bring them also. They too will listen to
my voice, and there shall be one flock
and one shepherd. 17The reason my
Father loves me is that I lay down my
life—only to take it up again. 18No-one
takes it from me, but I lay it down of my
own accord. I have authority to lay it
down and authority to take it up again.
This command I received from my
Father."

19At these words the Jews were again
divided. 20Many of them said, "He is
demon-possessed and raving mad. Why
listen to him?"

21But others said, "These are not the
sayings of a man possessed by a demon.
Can a demon open the eyes of the
blind?"

READING FROM PSALMS
Psalm 62:1–12

For the director of music. For Jeduthun. A psalm of David.

1My soul finds rest in God alone;
  my salvation comes from him.
2He alone is my rock and my
    salvation;
  he is my fortress, I shall never be
    shaken.

3How long will you assault a man?
  Would all of you throw him
    down—
  this leaning wall, this tottering
    fence?
4They fully intend to topple him
  from his lofty place;
  they take delight in lies.
 With their mouths they bless,
  but in their hearts they curse.
Selah

5Find rest, O my soul, in God alone;
  my hope comes from him.
6He alone is my rock and my
    salvation;
  he is my fortress, I shall not be
    shaken.

7My salvation and my honour depend
on God;
he is my mighty rock, my refuge.
8Trust in him at all times, O people;
pour out your hearts to him,
for God is our refuge. *Selah*

9Lowborn men are but a breath,
the highborn are but a lie;
if weighed on a balance, they are
nothing;
together they are only a breath.

10Do not trust in extortion
or take pride in stolen goods;
though your riches increase,
do not set your heart on them.

11One thing God has spoken,
two things have I heard:
that you, O God, are strong,
12 and that you, O Lord, are loving.
Surely you will reward each person
according to what he has done.

DAY 138

MAY 18

OLD TESTAMENT READING
1 Samuel 1:1–2:26

The Birth of Samuel

1 There was a certain man from Ramathaim, a Zuphite from the hill country of Ephraim, whose name was Elkanah son of Jeroham, the son of Elihu, the son of Tohu, the son of Zuph, an Ephraimite. 2He had two wives; one was called Hannah and the other Peninnah. Peninnah had children, but Hannah had none.

3Year after year this man went up from his town to worship and sacrifice to the LORD Almighty at Shiloh, where Hophni and Phinehas, the two sons of Eli, were priests of the LORD. 4Whenever the day came for Elkanah to sacrifice, he would give portions of the meat to his wife Peninnah and to all her sons and daughters. 5But to Hannah he gave a double portion because he loved her, and the LORD had closed her womb. 6And because the LORD had closed her womb, her rival kept provoking her in order to irritate her. 7This went on year after year. Whenever Hannah went up to the house of the LORD, her rival provoked her till she wept and would not eat. 8Elkanah her husband would say to her, "Hannah, why are you weeping? Why don't you eat? Why are you downhearted? Don't I mean more to you than ten sons?"

9Once when they had finished eating and drinking in Shiloh, Hannah stood up. Now Eli the priest was sitting on a chair by the doorpost of the LORD's temple. 10In bitterness of soul Hannah wept much and prayed to the LORD. 11And she made a vow, saying, "O LORD Almighty, if you will only look upon your servant's misery and remember me, and not forget your servant but give her a son, then I will give him to the LORD for all the days of his life, and no razor will ever be used on his head."

12As she kept on praying to the LORD, Eli observed her mouth. 13Hannah was praying in her heart, and her lips were moving but her voice was not heard. Eli thought she was drunk 14and said to her, "How long will you keep on getting drunk? Get rid of your wine."

15"Not so, my lord," Hannah replied, "I am a woman who is deeply troubled. I have not been drinking wine or beer; I was pouring out my soul to the LORD. 16Do not take your servant for a wicked woman; I have been praying here out of my great anguish and grief."

17Eli answered, "Go in peace, and may the God of Israel grant you what you have asked of him."

18She said, "May your servant find
favour in your eyes." Then she went her
way and ate something, and her face
was no longer downcast.
19Early the next morning they arose
and worshipped before the LORD and
then went back to their home at Ramah.
Elkanah lay with Hannah his wife, and
the LORD remembered her. 20So in the
course of time Hannah conceived and
gave birth to a son. She named him
Samuel, saying, "Because I asked the
LORD for him."

Hannah Dedicates Samuel

21When the man Elkanah went up
with all his family to offer the annual
sacrifice to the LORD and to fulfil his
vow, 22Hannah did not go. She said to
her husband, "After the boy is weaned,
I will take him and present him before
the LORD, and he will live there
always."
23"Do what seems best to you," Elkanah her husband told her. "Stay here
until you have weaned him; only may
the LORD make good his word." So the
woman stayed at home and nursed her
son until she had weaned him.
24After he was weaned, she took the
boy with her, young as he was, along
with a three-year-old bull, an ephah of
flour and a skin of wine, and brought
him to the house of the LORD at Shiloh.
25When they had slaughtered the bull,
they brought the boy to Eli, 26and she
said to him, "As surely as you live, my
lord, I am the woman who stood here
beside you praying to the LORD. 27I
prayed for this child, and the LORD has
granted me what I asked of him. 28So
now I give him to the LORD. For his
whole life he shall be given over to the
LORD." And he worshipped the LORD
there.

Hannah's Prayer

2 Then Hannah prayed and said:

"My heart rejoices in the LORD;
in the LORD my horn is lifted high.
My mouth boasts over my enemies,
for I delight in your deliverance.

2"There is no-one holy like the LORD;
there is no-one besides you;
there is no Rock like our God.

3"Do not keep talking so proudly
or let your mouth speak such
arrogance,
for the LORD is a God who knows,
and by him deeds are weighed.

4"The bows of the warriors are
broken,
but those who stumbled are armed
with strength.
5Those who were full hire themselves
out for food,
but those who were hungry hunger
no more.
She who was barren has borne seven
children,
but she who has had many sons
pines away.

6"The LORD brings death and makes
alive;
he brings down to the grave and
raises up.
7The LORD sends poverty and wealth;
he humbles and he exalts.
8He raises the poor from the dust
and lifts the needy from the ash
heap;
he seats them with princes
and has them inherit a throne of
honour.

"For the foundations of the earth are
the LORD's;
upon them he has set the world.
9He will guard the feet of his saints,
but the wicked will be silenced in
darkness.

"It is not by strength that one
prevails;
10 those who oppose the LORD will be
shattered.
He will thunder against them from
heaven;
the LORD will judge the ends of the
earth.

"He will give strength to his king
and exalt the horn of his
anointed."

11Then Elkanah went home to
Ramah, but the boy ministered before
the LORD under Eli the priest.

Eli's Wicked Sons

12Eli's sons were wicked men; they
had no regard for the LORD. 13Now it
was the practice of the priests with the
people that whenever anyone offered a
sacrifice and while the meat was being
boiled, the servant of the priest would
come with a three-pronged fork in his
hand. 14He would plunge it into the pan
or kettle or cauldron or pot, and the
priest would take for himself whatever
the fork brought up. This is how they
treated all the Israelites who came to
Shiloh. 15But even before the fat was
burned, the servant of the priest would
come and say to the man who was sacrificing, "Give the priest some meat to
roast; he won't accept boiled meat from
you, but only raw."

16If the man said to him, "Let the fat
be burned up first, and then take whatever you want," the servant would then
answer, "No, hand it over now; if you
don't, I'll take it by force."

17This sin of the young men was very
great in the LORD's sight, for they
were treating the LORD's offering with
contempt.

18But Samuel was ministering before
the LORD—a boy wearing a linen
ephod. 19Each year his mother made
him a little robe and took it to him when
she went up with her husband to offer
the annual sacrifice. 20Eli would bless
Elkanah and his wife, saying, "May the
LORD give you children by this woman
to take the place of the one she prayed
for and gave to the LORD." Then they
would go home. 21And the LORD was
gracious to Hannah; she conceived and
gave birth to three sons and two daughters. Meanwhile, the boy Samuel grew
up in the presence of the LORD.

22Now Eli, who was very old, heard
about everything his sons were doing to
all Israel and how they slept with the
women who served at the entrance to
the Tent of Meeting. 23So he said to
them, "Why do you do such things? I
hear from all the people about these
wicked deeds of yours. 24No, my sons; it
is not a good report that I hear spreading among the LORD's people. 25If a
man sins against another man, God may
mediate for him; but if a man sins
against the LORD, who will intercede for
him?" His sons, however, did not listen
to their father's rebuke, for it was the
LORD's will to put them to death.

26And the boy Samuel continued to
grow in stature and in favour with the
LORD and with men.

NEW TESTAMENT READING

John 10:22–42

The Unbelief of the Jews

22Then came the Feast of Dedication
at Jerusalem. It was winter, 23and Jesus
was in the temple area walking in
Solomon's Colonnade. 24The Jews
gathered round him, saying, "How long
will you keep us in suspense? If you are
the Christ, tell us plainly."

25Jesus answered, "I did tell you, but
you do not believe. The miracles I do in
my Father's name speak for me, 26but
you do not believe because you are not
my sheep. 27My sheep listen to my
voice; I know them, and they follow me.
28I give them eternal life, and they shall
never perish; no-one can snatch them
out of my hand. 29My Father, who has
given them to me, is greater than all;
no-one can snatch them out of my
Father's hand. 30I and the Father are
one."

31Again the Jews picked up stones to
stone him, 32but Jesus said to them, "I
have shown you many great miracles
from the Father. For which of these do
you stone me?"

33"We are not stoning you for any
of these," replied the Jews, "but for

blasphemy, because you, a mere man, claim to be God."
34Jesus answered them, "Is it not written in your Law, 'I have said you are gods'? 35If he called them 'gods', to whom the word of God came—and the Scripture cannot be broken—36what about the one whom the Father set apart as his very own and sent into the world? Why then do you accuse me of blasphemy because I said, 'I am God's Son'? 37Do not believe me unless I do what my Father does. 38But if I do it, even though you do not believe me, believe the miracles, that you may know and understand that the Father is in me, and I in the Father." 39Again they tried to seize him, but he escaped their grasp.
40Then Jesus went back across the Jordan to the place where John had been baptising in the early days. Here he stayed 41and many people came to him. They said, "Though John never performed a miraculous sign, all that John said about this man was true."
42And in that place many believed in Jesus.

READING FROM PSALMS
Psalm 63:1–11

A psalm of David. When he was in the Desert of Judah.

1O God, you are my God,
earnestly I seek you;
my soul thirsts for you,
my body longs for you,
in a dry and weary land
where there is no water.

2I have seen you in the sanctuary
and beheld your power and your glory.
3Because your love is better than life,
my lips will glorify you.
4I will praise you as long as I live,
and in your name I will lift up my hands.
5My soul will be satisfied as with the richest of foods;
with singing lips my mouth will praise you.

6On my bed I remember you;
I think of you through the watches of the night.
7Because you are my help,
I sing in the shadow of your wings.
8My soul clings to you;
your right hand upholds me.

9They who seek my life will be destroyed;
they will go down to the depths of the earth.
10They will be given over to the sword
and become food for jackals.

11But the king will rejoice in God;
all who swear by God's name will praise him,
while the mouths of liars will be silenced.

MAY 19

OLD TESTAMENT READING
1 Samuel 2:27–4:22

Prophecy Against the House of Eli

27Now a man of God came to Eli and said to him, "This is what the LORD says: 'Did I not clearly reveal myself to your father's house when they were in Egypt under Pharaoh? 28I chose your father out of all the tribes of Israel to be my priest, to go up to my altar, to burn incense, and to wear an ephod in my presence. I also gave your father's house all the offerings made with fire by the Israelites. 29Why do you scorn my sacrifice and offering that I prescribed for my dwelling? Why do you honour your sons more than me by fattening yourselves on the choice parts of every offering made by my people Israel?'

30"Therefore the LORD, the God of Israel, declares: 'I promised that your house and your father's house would minister before me for ever.' But now the LORD declares: 'Far be it from me! Those who honour me I will honour, but those who despise me will be disdained. 31The time is coming when I will cut short your strength and the strength of your father's house, so that there will not be an old man in your family line
32and you will see distress in my dwelling. Although good will be done to Israel, in your family line there will never be an old man. 33Every one of you that I do not cut off from my altar will be spared only to blind your eyes with tears and to grieve your heart, and all your descendants will die in the prime of life.

34" 'And what happens to your two sons, Hophni and Phinehas, will be a sign to you—they will both die on the same day. 35I will raise up for myself a faithful priest, who will do according to what is in my heart and mind. I will firmly establish his house, and he will minister before my anointed one always. 36Then everyone left in your family line will come and bow down before him for a piece of silver and a crust of bread and plead, "Appoint me to some priestly office so that I can have food to eat." ' "

The LORD Calls Samuel

3 The boy Samuel ministered before the LORD under Eli. In those days the word of the LORD was rare; there were not many visions.

2One night Eli, whose eyes were becoming so weak that he could barely see, was lying down in his usual place. 3The lamp of God had not yet gone out, and Samuel was lying down in the temple of the LORD, where the ark of God was. 4Then the LORD called Samuel.

Samuel answered, "Here I am."
5And he ran to Eli and said, "Here I am; you called me."

But Eli said, "I did not call; go back and lie down." So he went and lay down.

6Again the LORD called, "Samuel!" And Samuel got up and went to Eli and said, "Here I am; you called me."

"My son," Eli said, "I did not call; go back and lie down."

7Now Samuel did not yet know the LORD: The word of the LORD had not yet been revealed to him.

8The LORD called Samuel a third time, and Samuel got up and went to Eli and said, "Here I am; you called me."

Then Eli realised that the LORD was calling the boy. 9So Eli told Samuel, "Go and lie down, and if he calls you, say, 'Speak, LORD, for your servant is listening.' " So Samuel went and lay down in his place.

10The LORD came and stood there, calling as at the other times, "Samuel! Samuel!"

Then Samuel said, "Speak, for your servant is listening."

11And the LORD said to Samuel: "See, I am about to do something in Israel that will make the ears of everyone who hears of it tingle. 12At that time I will carry out against Eli everything I spoke against his family—from beginning to end. 13For I told him that I would judge his family for ever because of the sin he knew about; his sons made themselves contemptible, and he failed to restrain them. 14Therefore, I swore to the house of Eli, 'The guilt of Eli's house will never be atoned for by sacrifice or offering.' "

15Samuel lay down until morning and then opened the doors of the house of the LORD. He was afraid to tell Eli the vision, 16but Eli called him and said, "Samuel, my son."

Samuel answered, "Here I am."

17"What was it he said to you?" Eli asked. "Do not hide it from me. May God deal with you, be it ever so severely, if you hide from me anything he told you." 18So Samuel told him everything, hiding nothing from him. Then Eli said, "He is the LORD; let him do what is good in his eyes."

19The LORD was with Samuel as he grew up, and he let none of his words fall to the ground. 20And all Israel from Dan to Beersheba recognised that Samuel was attested as a prophet of the LORD. 21The LORD continued to appear at Shiloh, and there he revealed himself to Samuel through his word.

4 And Samuel's word came to all Israel.

The Philistines Capture the Ark

Now the Israelites went out to fight against the Philistines. The Israelites camped at Ebenezer, and the Philistines at Aphek. 2The Philistines deployed their forces to meet Israel, and as the battle spread, Israel was defeated by the Philistines, who killed about four thousand of them on the battlefield. 3When the soldiers returned to camp, the elders of Israel asked, "Why did the LORD bring defeat upon us today before the Philistines? Let us bring the ark of the LORD's covenant from Shiloh, so that it may go with us and save us from the hand of our enemies."

4So the people sent men to Shiloh, and they brought back the ark of the covenant of the LORD Almighty, who is enthroned between the cherubim. And Eli's two sons, Hophni and Phinehas, were there with the ark of the covenant of God.

5When the ark of the LORD's covenant came into the camp, all Israel raised such a great shout that the ground shook. 6Hearing the uproar, the Philistines asked, "What's all this shouting in the Hebrew camp?"

When they learned that the ark of the LORD had come into the camp, 7the Philistines were afraid. "A god has come into the camp," they said. "We're in trouble! Nothing like this has happened before. 8Woe to us! Who will deliver us from the hand of these mighty gods? They are the gods who struck the Egyptians with all kinds of plagues in the desert. 9Be strong, Philistines! Be men, or you will be subject to the Hebrews, as they have been to you. Be men, and fight!"

10So the Philistines fought, and the Israelites were defeated and every man fled to his tent. The slaughter was very great; Israel lost thirty thousand foot soldiers. 11The ark of God was captured, and Eli's two sons, Hophni and Phinehas, died.

Death of Eli

12That same day a Benjamite ran from the battle line and went to Shiloh, his clothes torn and dust on his head. 13When he arrived, there was Eli sitting on his chair by the side of the road, watching, because his heart feared for the ark of God. When the man entered the town and told what had happened, the whole town sent up a cry.

14Eli heard the outcry and asked,

"What is the meaning of this uproar?"
The man hurried over to Eli, [15]who was ninety-eight years old and whose eyes were set so that he could not see. [16]He told Eli, "I have just come from the battle line; I fled from it this very day."

Eli asked, "What happened, my son?"

[17]The man who brought the news replied, "Israel fled before the Philistines, and the army has suffered heavy losses. Also your two sons, Hophni and Phinehas, are dead, and the ark of God has been captured."

[18]When he mentioned the ark of God, Eli fell backwards off his chair by the side of the gate. His neck was broken and he died, for he was an old man and heavy. He had led Israel for forty years.

[19]His daughter-in-law, the wife of Phinehas, was pregnant and near the time of delivery. When she heard the news that the ark of God had been captured and that her father-in-law and her husband were dead, she went into labour and gave birth, but was overcome by her labour pains. [20]As she was dying, the women attending her said, "Don't despair; you have given birth to a son." But she did not respond or pay any attention.

[21]She named the boy Ichabod, saying, "The glory has departed from Israel" —because of the capture of the ark of God and the deaths of her father-in-law and her husband. [22]She said, "The glory has departed from Israel, for the ark of God has been captured."

NEW TESTAMENT READING
John 11:1–44

The Death of Lazarus

11 Now a man named Lazarus was sick. He was from Bethany, the village of Mary and her sister Martha. [2]This Mary, whose brother Lazarus now lay sick, was the same one who poured perfume on the Lord and wiped his feet with her hair. [3]So the sisters sent word to Jesus, "Lord, the one you love is sick."

[4]When he heard this, Jesus said, "This sickness will not end in death. No, it is for God's glory so that God's Son may be glorified through it." [5]Jesus loved Martha and her sister and Lazarus. [6]Yet when he heard that Lazarus was sick, he stayed where he was two more days.

[7]Then he said to his disciples, "Let us go back to Judea."

[8]"But Rabbi," they said, "a short while ago the Jews tried to stone you, and yet you are going back there?"

[9]Jesus answered, "Are there not twelve hours of daylight? A man who walks by day will not stumble, for he sees by this world's light. [10]It is when he walks by night that he stumbles, for he has no light."

[11]After he had said this, he went on to tell them, "Our friend Lazarus has fallen asleep; but I am going there to wake him up."

[12]His disciples replied, "Lord, if he sleeps, he will get better." [13]Jesus had been speaking of his death, but his disciples thought he meant natural sleep.

[14]So then he told them plainly, "Lazarus is dead, [15]and for your sake I am glad I was not there, so that you may believe. But let us go to him."

[16]Then Thomas (called Didymus) said to the rest of the disciples, "Let us also go, that we may die with him."

Jesus Comforts the Sisters

[17]On his arrival, Jesus found that Lazarus had already been in the tomb for four days. [18]Bethany was less than two miles from Jerusalem, [19]and many Jews had come to Martha and Mary to comfort them in the loss of their brother. [20]When Martha heard that Jesus was coming, she went out to meet him, but Mary stayed at home.

[21]"Lord," Martha said to Jesus, "if you had been here, my brother would

not have died. 22But I know that even
now God will give you whatever you
ask."
23Jesus said to her, "Your brother
will rise again."
24Martha answered, "I know he will
rise again in the resurrection at the last
day."
25Jesus said to her, "I am the resurrection and the life. He who believes in
me will live, even though he dies; 26and
whoever lives and believes in me will
never die. Do you believe this?"
27"Yes, Lord," she told him, "I believe that you are the Christ, the Son of
God, who was to come into the world."
28And after she had said this, she
went back and called her sister Mary
aside. "The Teacher is here," she said,
"and is asking for you." 29When Mary
heard this, she got up quickly and went
to him. 30Now Jesus had not yet entered
the village, but was still at the place
where Martha had met him. 31When the
Jews who had been with Mary in the
house, comforting her, noticed how
quickly she got up and went out, they
followed her, supposing she was going
to the tomb to mourn there.
32When Mary reached the place
where Jesus was and saw him, she fell at
his feet and said, "Lord, if you had been
here, my brother would not have died."
33When Jesus saw her weeping, and
the Jews who had come along with her
also weeping, he was deeply moved in
spirit and troubled. 34"Where have you
laid him?" he asked.
"Come and see, Lord," they replied.
35Jesus wept.
36Then the Jews said, "See how he
loved him!"
37But some of them said, "Could not
he who opened the eyes of the blind
man have kept this man from dying?"

Jesus Raises Lazarus From the Dead

38Jesus, once more deeply moved,
came to the tomb. It was a cave with a
stone laid across the entrance. 39"Take
away the stone," he said.
"But, Lord," said Martha, the sister
of the dead man, "by this time there is a
bad odour, for he has been there four
days."
40Then Jesus said, "Did I not tell you
that if you believed, you would see the
glory of God?"
41So they took away the stone. Then
Jesus looked up and said, "Father, I
thank you that you have heard me.
42I knew that you always hear me,
but I said this for the benefit of the
people standing here, that they may
believe that you sent me."
43When he had said this, Jesus called
in a loud voice, "Lazarus, come out!"
44The dead man came out, his hands
and feet wrapped with strips of linen,
and a cloth around his face.
Jesus said to them, "Take off the
grave clothes and let him go."

READING FROM PSALMS
Psalm 64:1–10

For the director of music. A psalm of David.

1Hear me, O God, as I voice my complaint;
protect my life from the threat of the enemy.
2Hide me from the conspiracy of the wicked,
from that noisy crowd of evildoers.

3They sharpen their tongues like swords
and aim their words like deadly arrows.
4They shoot from ambush at the innocent man;
they shoot at him suddenly, without fear.

5They encourage each other in evil plans,
they talk about hiding their snares;
they say, "Who will see them?"

[6]They plot injustice and say,
"We have devised a perfect plan!"
Surely the mind and heart of man
are cunning.

[7]But God will shoot them with arrows;
suddenly they will be struck down.
[8]He will turn their own tongues
against them
and bring them to ruin;
all who see them will shake their
heads in scorn.

[9]All mankind will fear;
they will proclaim the works of God
and ponder what he has done.
[10]Let the righteous rejoice in the LORD
and take refuge in him;
let all the upright in heart praise
him!

DAY 140

MAY 20

OLD TESTAMENT READING
1 Samuel 5:1–7:17

The Ark in Ashdod and Ekron

5 After the Philistines had captured
the ark of God, they took it from
Ebenezer to Ashdod. [2]Then they carried the ark into Dagon's temple and set
it beside Dagon. [3]When the people of
Ashdod rose early the next day, there
was Dagon, fallen on his face on the
ground before the ark of the LORD!
They took Dagon and put him back in
his place. [4]But the following morning
when they rose, there was Dagon, fallen
on his face on the ground before the ark
of the LORD! His head and hands had
been broken off and were lying on the
threshold; only his body remained.
[5]That is why to this day neither the
priests of Dagon nor any others who
enter Dagon's temple at Ashdod step
on the threshold.

[6]The LORD's hand was heavy upon
the people of Ashdod and its vicinity; he
brought devastation upon them and
afflicted them with tumours. [7]When the
men of Ashdod saw what was happening, they said, "The ark of the god of
Israel must not stay here with us, because his hand is heavy upon us and
upon Dagon our god." [8]So they called
together all the rulers of the Philistines
and asked them, "What shall we do with
the ark of the god of Israel?"

They answered, "Have the ark of the
god of Israel moved to Gath." So they
moved the ark of the God of Israel.

[9]But after they had moved it, the
LORD's hand was against that city,
throwing it into a great panic. He
afflicted the people of the city, both
young and old, with an outbreak of
tumours. [10]So they sent the ark of God
to Ekron.

As the ark of God was entering
Ekron, the people of Ekron cried out,
"They have brought the ark of the god
of Israel round to us to kill us and our
people." [11]So they called together all
the rulers of the Philistines and said,
"Send the ark of the god of Israel away;
let it go back to its own place, or it will
kill us and our people." For death had
filled the city with panic; God's hand
was very heavy upon it. [12]Those who did
not die were afflicted with tumours, and
the outcry of the city went up to heaven.

The Ark Returned to Israel

6 When the ark of the LORD had
been in Philistine territory for
seven months, [2]the Philistines called for
the priests and the diviners and said,
"What shall we do with the ark of the
LORD? Tell us how we should send it
back to its place."

[3]They answered, "If you return the
ark of the god of Israel, do not send it

away empty, but by all means send a
guilt offering to him. Then you will be
healed, and you will know why his hand
has not been lifted from you."
[4]The Philistines asked, "What guilt
offering should we send to him?"

They replied, "Five gold tumours and
five gold rats, according to the number
of the Philistine rulers, because the
same plague has struck both you and
your rulers. [5]Make models of the
tumours and of the rats that are destroying the country, and pay honour to
Israel's god. Perhaps he will lift his hand
from you and your gods and your land.
[6]Why do you harden your hearts as the
Egyptians and Pharaoh did? When he
treated them harshly, did they not send
the Israelites out so that they could go
on their way?
[7]"Now then, get a new cart ready,
with two cows that have calved and have
never been yoked. Hitch the cows to the
cart, but take their calves away and pen
them up. [8]Take the ark of the LORD and
put it on the cart, and in a chest beside it
put the gold objects you are sending
back to him as a guilt offering. Send it
on its way, [9]but keep watching it. If it
goes up to its own territory, towards
Beth Shemesh, then the LORD has
brought this great disaster on us. But if
it does not, then we shall know that it
was not his hand that struck us and that
it happened to us by chance."
[10]So they did this. They took two such
cows and hitched them to the cart and
penned up their calves. [11]They placed
the ark of the LORD on the cart and
along with it the chest containing the
gold rats and the models of the tumours.
[12]Then the cows went straight up towards Beth Shemesh, keeping on the
road and lowing all the way; they did
not turn to the right or to the left. The
rulers of the Philistines followed them
as far as the border of Beth Shemesh.
[13]Now the people of Beth Shemesh
were harvesting their wheat in the valley, and when they looked up and saw
the ark, they rejoiced at the sight. [14]The
cart came to the field of Joshua of Beth
Shemesh, and there it stopped beside a
large rock. The people chopped up the
wood of the cart and sacrificed the cows
as a burnt offering to the LORD. [15]The
Levites took down the ark of the LORD,
together with the chest containing the
gold objects, and placed them on the
large rock. On that day the people of
Beth Shemesh offered burnt offerings
and made sacrifices to the LORD. [16]The
five rulers of the Philistines saw all this
and then returned that same day to
Ekron.
[17]These are the gold tumours the
Philistines sent as a guilt offering to the
LORD—one each for Ashdod, Gaza,
Ashkelon, Gath and Ekron. [18]And the
number of the gold rats was according
to the number of Philistine towns belonging to the five rulers—the fortified
towns with their country villages. The
large rock, on which they set the ark of
the LORD, is a witness to this day in the
field of Joshua of Beth Shemesh.
[19]But God struck down some of the
men of Beth Shemesh, putting seventy
of them to death because they had
looked into the ark of the LORD. The
people mourned because of the heavy
blow the LORD had dealt them, [20]and
the men of Beth Shemesh asked, "Who
can stand in the presence of the LORD,
this holy God? To whom will the ark go
up from here?"
[21]Then they sent messengers to the
people of Kiriath Jearim, saying, "The
Philistines have returned the ark of
the LORD. Come down and take it up to
7 your place." [1]So the men of Kiriath
Jearim came and took up the ark
of the LORD. They took it to Abinadab's house on the hill and consecrated
Eleazar his son to guard the ark of the
LORD.

Samuel Subdues the Philistines at Mizpah

[2]It was a long time, twenty years in
all, that the ark remained at Kiriath
Jearim, and all the people of Israel
mourned and sought after the LORD.

[3]And Samuel said to the whole house of
Israel, "If you are returning to the LORD
with all your hearts, then rid yourselves
of the foreign gods and the Ashtoreths
and commit yourselves to the LORD and
serve him only, and he will deliver you
out of the hand of the Philistines." [4]So
the Israelites put away their Baals and
Ashtoreths, and served the LORD only.
[5]Then Samuel said, "Assemble all
Israel at Mizpah and I will intercede
with the LORD for you." [6]When they
had assembled at Mizpah, they drew
water and poured it out before the
LORD. On that day they fasted and there
they confessed, "We have sinned
against the LORD." And Samuel was
leader of Israel at Mizpah.
[7]When the Philistines heard that
Israel had assembled at Mizpah, the
rulers of the Philistines came up to
attack them. And when the Israelites
heard of it, they were afraid because of
the Philistines. [8]They said to Samuel,
"Do not stop crying out to the LORD our
God for us, that he may rescue us from
the hand of the Philistines." [9]Then
Samuel took a suckling lamb and
offered it up as a whole burnt offering to
the LORD. He cried out to the LORD on
Israel's behalf, and the LORD answered
him.
[10]While Samuel was sacrificing the
burnt offering, the Philistines drew near
to engage Israel in battle. But that day
the LORD thundered with loud thunder
against the Philistines and threw them
into such a panic that they were routed
before the Israelites. [11]The men of
Israel rushed out of Mizpah and pursued the Philistines, slaughtering them
along the way to a point below Beth
Car.
[12]Then Samuel took a stone and set it
up between Mizpah and Shen. He
named it Ebenezer, saying, "Thus far
has the LORD helped us." [13]So the
Philistines were subdued and did not
invade Israelite territory again.

Throughout Samuel's lifetime, the
hand of the LORD was against the Philistines. [14]The towns from Ekron to Gath
that the Philistines had captured from
Israel were restored to her, and Israel
delivered the neighbouring territory
from the power of the Philistines. And
there was peace between Israel and the
Amorites.
[15]Samuel continued as judge over
Israel all the days of his life. [16]From year
to year he went on a circuit from Bethel
to Gilgal to Mizpah, judging Israel in all
those places. [17]But he always went back
to Ramah, where his home was, and
there he also judged Israel. And he built
an altar there to the LORD.

NEW TESTAMENT READING

John 11:45–12:11

The Plot to Kill Jesus

[45]Therefore many of the Jews who
had come to visit Mary, and had seen
what Jesus did, put their faith in him.
[46]But some of them went to the Pharisees and told them what Jesus had
done. [47]Then the chief priests and the
Pharisees called a meeting of the
Sanhedrin.

"What are we accomplishing?" they
asked. "Here is this man performing
many miraculous signs. [48]If we let him
go on like this, everyone will believe in
him, and then the Romans will come
and take away both our place and our
nation."
[49]Then one of them, named
Caiaphas, who was high priest that
year, spoke up, "You know nothing at
all! [50]You do not realise that it is better
for you that one man die for the people
than that the whole nation perish."
[51]He did not say this on his own, but
as high priest that year he prophesied
that Jesus would die for the Jewish nation, [52]and not only for that nation but
also for the scattered children of God,
to bring them together and make them
one. [53]So from that day on they plotted
to take his life.
[54]Therefore Jesus no longer moved
about publicly among the Jews. Instead

he withdrew to a region near the desert, to a village called Ephraim, where he stayed with his disciples.

55When it was almost time for the Jewish Passover, many went up from the country to Jerusalem for their ceremonial cleansing before the Passover.
56They kept looking for Jesus, and as they stood in the temple area they asked one another, "What do you think? Isn't he coming to the Feast at all?" 57But the chief priests and Pharisees had given orders that if anyone found out where Jesus was, he should report it so that they might arrest him.

Jesus Anointed at Bethany

12 Six days before the Passover, Jesus arrived at Bethany, where Lazarus lived, whom Jesus had raised
from the dead. 2Here a dinner was given in Jesus' honour. Martha served, while Lazarus was among those reclining at
the table with him. 3Then Mary took about a pint of pure nard, an expensive perfume; she poured it on Jesus' feet and wiped his feet with her hair. And the house was filled with the fragrance of the perfume.

4But one of his disciples, Judas Iscariot, who was later to betray him, objected, 5"Why wasn't this perfume sold and the money given to the poor? It was
worth a year's wages." 6He did not say this because he cared about the poor but because he was a thief; as keeper of the money bag, he used to help himself to what was put into it.

7"Leave her alone," Jesus replied. "⌊It was intended⌋ that she should save this perfume for the day of my burial.
8You will always have the poor among you, but you will not always have me."

9Meanwhile a large crowd of Jews found out that Jesus was there and came, not only because of him but also to see Lazarus, whom he had raised
from the dead. 10So the chief priests
made plans to kill Lazarus as well, 11for
on account of him many of the Jews were going over to Jesus and putting their faith in him.

READING FROM PROVERBS

Proverbs 12:18–27

18Reckless words pierce like a sword,
but the tongue of the wise brings healing.

19Truthful lips endure for ever,
but a lying tongue lasts only a moment.

20There is deceit in the hearts of those who plot evil,
but joy for those who promote peace.

21No harm befalls the righteous,
but the wicked have their fill of trouble.

22The LORD detests lying lips,
but he delights in men who are truthful.

23A prudent man keeps his knowledge to himself,
but the heart of fools blurts out folly.

24Diligent hands will rule,
but laziness ends in slave labour.

25An anxious heart weighs a man down,
but a kind word cheers him up.

26A righteous man is cautious in friendship,
but the way of the wicked leads them astray.

27The lazy man does not roast his game,
but the diligent man prizes his possessions.

DAY 141

MAY 21

OLD TESTAMENT READING
1 Samuel 8:1–10:8

Israel Asks for a King

8 When Samuel grew old, he
appointed his sons as judges for
Israel. [2]The name of his firstborn was
Joel and the name of his second was
Abijah, and they served at Beersheba.
[3]But his sons did not walk in his ways.
They turned aside after dishonest gain
and accepted bribes and perverted
justice.
[4]So all the elders of Israel gathered
together and came to Samuel at Ramah.
[5]They said to him, "You are old, and
your sons do not walk in your ways; now
appoint a king to lead us, such as all the
other nations have."
[6]But when they said, "Give us a king
to lead us," this displeased Samuel; so
he prayed to the LORD. [7]And the LORD
told him: "Listen to all that the people
are saying to you; it is not you they have
rejected, but they have rejected me as
their king. [8]As they have done from the
day I brought them up out of Egypt until
this day, forsaking me and serving other
gods, so they are doing to you. [9]Now
listen to them; but warn them solemnly
and let them know what the king who
will reign over them will do."
[10]Samuel told all the words of the
LORD to the people who were asking
him for a king. [11]He said, "This is what
the king who will reign over you will do:
He will take your sons and make them
serve with his chariots and horses, and
they will run in front of his chariots.
[12]Some he will assign to be commanders
of thousands and commanders of fifties,
and others to plough his ground and
reap his harvest, and still others to make
weapons of war and equipment for his
chariots. [13]He will take your daughters
to be perfumers and cooks and bakers.
[14]He will take the best of your fields and
vineyards and olive groves and give
them to his attendants. [15]He will take a
tenth of your grain and of your vintage
and give it to his officials and attendants. [16]Your menservants and maidservants and the best of your cattle and
donkeys he will take for his own use.
[17]He will take a tenth of your flocks, and
you yourselves will become his slaves.
[18]When that day comes, you will cry out
for relief from the king you have
chosen, and the LORD will not answer
you in that day."
[19]But the people refused to listen to
Samuel. "No!" they said. "We want a
king over us. [20]Then we shall be like all
the other nations, with a king to lead us
and to go out before us and fight our
battles."
[21]When Samuel heard all that the
people said, he repeated it before the
LORD. [22]The LORD answered, "Listen
to them and give them a king."
Then Samuel said to the men of
Israel, "Everyone is to go back to his
town."

Samuel Anoints Saul

9 There was a Benjamite, a man of
standing, whose name was Kish
son of Abiel, the son of Zeror, the son
of Becorath, the son of Aphiah of Benjamin. [2]He had a son named Saul, an
impressive young man without equal
among the Israelites—a head taller
than any of the others.
[3]Now the donkeys belonging to Saul's
father Kish were lost, and Kish said to
his son Saul, "Take one of the servants
with you and go and look for the donkeys." [4]So he passed through the hill
country of Ephraim and through the
area around Shalisha, but they did not
find them. They went on into the district
of Shaalim, but the donkeys were not
there. Then he passed through the territory of Benjamin, but they did not find
them.
[5]When they reached the district of

Zuph, Saul said to the servant who was with him, "Come, let's go back, or my father will stop thinking about the donkeys and start worrying about us."

6But the servant replied, "Look, in this town there is a man of God; he is highly respected, and everything he says comes true. Let's go there now. Perhaps he will tell us what way to take."

7Saul said to his servant, "If we go, what can we give the man? The food in our sacks is gone. We have no gift to take to the man of God. What do we have?"

8The servant answered him again. "Look," he said, "I have a quarter of a shekel of silver. I will give it to the man of God so that he will tell us what way to
take." 9(Formerly in Israel, if a man went to enquire of God, he would say, "Come, let us go to the seer," because the prophet of today used to be called a seer.)

10"Good," Saul said to his servant. "Come, let's go." So they set out for the town where the man of God was.

11As they were going up the hill to the town, they met some girls coming out to draw water, and they asked them, "Is the seer here?"

12"He is," they answered. "He's ahead of you. Hurry now; he has just come to our town today, for the people have a sacrifice at the high place. 13As
soon as you enter the town, you will find him before he goes up to the high place to eat. The people will not begin eating until he comes, because he must bless the sacrifice; afterwards, those who are invited will eat. Go up now; you should find him about this time."

14They went up to the town, and as they were entering it, there was Samuel, coming towards them on his way up to the high place.

15Now the day before Saul came, the LORD had revealed this to Samuel:
16"About this time tomorrow I will send you a man from the land of Benjamin. Anoint him leader over my people Israel; he will deliver my people from the hand of the Philistines. I have looked upon my people, for their cry has reached me."

17When Samuel caught sight of Saul, the LORD said to him, "This is the man I spoke to you about; he will govern my people."

18Saul approached Samuel in the gateway and asked, "Would you please tell me where the seer's house is?"

19"I am the seer," Samuel replied. "Go up ahead of me to the high place, for today you are to eat with me, and in the morning I will let you go and will tell
you all that is in your heart. 20As for the donkeys you lost three days ago, do not worry about them; they have been found. And to whom is all the desire of Israel turned, if not to you and all your father's family?"

21Saul answered, "But am I not a Benjamite, from the smallest tribe of Israel, and is not my clan the least of all the clans of the tribe of Benjamin? Why do you say such a thing to me?"

22Then Samuel brought Saul and his servant into the hall and seated them at the head of those who were invited
—about thirty in number. 23Samuel said to the cook, "Bring the piece of meat I gave you, the one I told you to lay aside."

24So the cook took up the leg with what was on it and set it in front of Saul. Samuel said, "Here is what has been kept for you. Eat, because it was set aside for you for this occasion, from the time I said, 'I have invited guests.'" And Saul dined with Samuel that day.

25After they came down from the high place to the town, Samuel talked with Saul on the roof of his house.
26They rose about daybreak and Samuel called to Saul on the roof, "Get ready, and I will send you on your way." When Saul got ready, he and Samuel went
outside together. 27As they were going down to the edge of the town, Samuel said to Saul, "Tell the servant to go on ahead of us"—and the servant did so —"but you stay here awhile, so that I may give you a message from God."

10 Then Samuel took a flask of oil
and poured it on Saul's head
and kissed him, saying, "Has not the
LORD anointed you leader over his
inheritance? 2When you leave me today, you will meet two men near
Rachel's tomb, at Zelzah on the border
of Benjamin. They will say to you, 'The
donkeys you set out to look for have
been found. And now your father has
stopped thinking about them and is
worried about you. He is asking, "What
shall I do about my son?"'
3"Then you will go on from there
until you reach the great tree of Tabor.
Three men going up to God at Bethel
will meet you there. One will be carrying three young goats, another three
loaves of bread, and another a skin of
wine. 4They will greet you and offer you
two loaves of bread, which you will
accept from them.
5"After that you will go to Gibeah of
God, where there is a Philistine outpost. As you approach the town, you
will meet a procession of prophets coming down from the high place with lyres,
tambourines, flutes and harps being
played before them, and they will be
prophesying. 6The Spirit of the LORD
will come upon you in power, and you
will prophesy with them; and you will be
changed into a different person. 7Once
these signs are fulfilled, do whatever
your hand finds to do, for God is with
you.
8"Go down ahead of me to Gilgal. I
will surely come down to you to sacrifice
burnt offerings and fellowship offerings,
but you must wait seven days until I
come to you and tell you what you are to
do."

NEW TESTAMENT READING
John 12:12–36

The Triumphal Entry

12The next day the great crowd that
had come for the Feast heard that Jesus
was on his way to Jerusalem. 13They
took palm branches and went out to
meet him, shouting,

"Hosanna!"

"Blessed is he who comes in the
name of the Lord!"

"Blessed is the King of Israel!"

14Jesus found a young donkey and sat
upon it, as it is written,

15"Do not be afraid, O Daughter of
Zion;
see, your king is coming,
seated on a donkey's colt."

16At first his disciples did not understand all this. Only after Jesus was glorified did they realise that these things
had been written about him and that
they had done these things to him.
17Now the crowd that was with him
when he called Lazarus from the tomb
and raised him from the dead continued
to spread the word. 18Many people, because they had heard that he had given
this miraculous sign, went out to meet
him. 19So the Pharisees said to one
another, "See, this is getting us nowhere. Look how the whole world has
gone after him!"

Jesus Predicts His Death

20Now there were some Greeks
among those who went up to worship at
the Feast. 21They came to Philip, who
was from Bethsaida in Galilee, with a
request. "Sir," they said, "we would
like to see Jesus." 22Philip went to tell
Andrew; Andrew and Philip in turn told
Jesus.
23Jesus replied, "The hour has come
for the Son of Man to be glorified. 24I
tell you the truth, unless a grain of
wheat falls to the ground and dies, it
remains only a single seed. But if it dies,
it produces many seeds. 25The man who
loves his life will lose it, while the man
who hates his life in this world will keep

it for eternal life. 26Whoever serves me
must follow me; and where I am, my
servant also will be. My Father will
honour the one who serves me.
27"Now my heart is troubled, and
what shall I say? 'Father, save me from
this hour'? No, it was for this very
reason I came to this hour. 28Father,
glorify your name!"

Then a voice came from heaven, "I have glorified it, and will glorify it
again." 29The crowd that was there and
heard it said it had thundered; others said an angel had spoken to him.

30Jesus said, "This voice was for your
benefit, not mine. 31Now is the time for
judgment on this world; now the prince
of this world will be driven out. 32But I,
when I am lifted up from the earth, will
draw all men to myself." 33He said this
to show the kind of death he was going to die.

34The crowd spoke up, "We have heard from the Law that the Christ will remain for ever, so how can you say, 'The Son of Man must be lifted up'? Who is this 'Son of Man'?"

35Then Jesus told them, "You are going to have the light just a little while longer. Walk while you have the light, before darkness overtakes you. The man who walks in the dark does not know where he is going. 36Put your trust
in the light while you have it, so that you may become sons of light." When he had finished speaking, Jesus left and hid himself from them.

READING FROM PSALMS

Psalm 65:1–13

For the director of music. A psalm of David. A song.

1Praise awaits you, O God, in Zion;
to you our vows will be fulfilled.
2O you who hear prayer,
to you all men will come.
3When we were overwhelmed by sins,
you forgave our transgressions.
4Blessed are those you choose
and bring near to live in your courts!
We are filled with the good things of your house,
of your holy temple.

5You answer us with awesome deeds of righteousness,
O God our Saviour,
the hope of all the ends of the earth
and of the farthest seas,
6who formed the mountains by your power,
having armed yourself with strength,
7who stilled the roaring of the seas,
the roaring of their waves,
and the turmoil of the nations.
8Those living far away fear your wonders;
where morning dawns and evening fades
you call forth songs of joy.

9You care for the land and water it;
you enrich it abundantly.
The streams of God are filled with water
to provide the people with corn,
for so you have ordained it.
10You drench its furrows
and level its ridges;
you soften it with showers
and bless its crops.
11You crown the year with your bounty,
and your carts overflow with abundance.
12The grasslands of the desert overflow;
the hills are clothed with gladness.
13The meadows are covered with flocks
and the valleys are mantled with corn;
they shout for joy and sing.

DAY 142

MAY 22

OLD TESTAMENT READING
1 Samuel 10:9–12:25

Saul Made King

9As Saul turned to leave Samuel,
God changed Saul's heart, and all these
signs were fulfilled that day. 10When
they arrived at Gibeah, a procession of
prophets met him; the Spirit of God
came upon him in power, and he joined
in their prophesying. 11When all those
who had formerly known him saw him
prophesying with the prophets, they
asked each other, "What is this that has
happened to the son of Kish? Is Saul
also among the prophets?"
12A man who lived there answered,
"And who is their father?" So it became
a saying: "Is Saul also among the
prophets?" 13After Saul stopped
prophesying, he went to the high place.
14Now Saul's uncle asked him and his
servant, "Where have you been?"
"Looking for the donkeys," he said.
"But when we saw they were not to be
found, we went to Samuel."
15Saul's uncle said, "Tell me what
Samuel said to you."
16Saul replied, "He assured us that
the donkeys had been found." But he
did not tell his uncle what Samuel had
said about the kingship.
17Samuel summoned the people of
Israel to the LORD at Mizpah 18and said
to them, "This is what the LORD, the
God of Israel, says: 'I brought Israel up
out of Egypt, and I delivered you from
the power of Egypt and all the kingdoms that oppressed you.' 19But you
have now rejected your God, who saves
you out of all your calamities and distresses. And you have said, 'No, set a
king over us.' So now present yourselves before the LORD by your tribes
and clans."
20When Samuel brought all the tribes
of Israel near, the tribe of Benjamin was
chosen. 21Then he brought forward the
tribe of Benjamin, clan by clan, and
Matri's clan was chosen. Finally Saul
son of Kish was chosen. But when they
looked for him, he was not to be found.
22So they enquired further of the LORD,
"Has the man come here yet?"
And the LORD said, "Yes, he has
hidden himself among the baggage."
23They ran and brought him out, and
as he stood among the people he was a
head taller than any of the others.
24Samuel said to all the people, "Do you
see the man the LORD has chosen?
There is no-one like him among all the
people."
Then the people shouted, "Long live
the king!"
25Samuel explained to the people the
regulations of the kingship. He wrote
them down on a scroll and deposited it
before the LORD. Then Samuel dismissed the people, each to his own home.
26Saul also went to his home in
Gibeah, accompanied by valiant men
whose hearts God had touched. 27But
some troublemakers said, "How can
this fellow save us?" They despised him
and brought him no gifts. But Saul kept
silent.

Saul Rescues the City of Jabesh

11 Nahash the Ammonite went up and besieged Jabesh Gilead.
And all the men of Jabesh said to him,
"Make a treaty with us, and we will be
subject to you."
2But Nahash the Ammonite replied,
"I will make a treaty with you only on
the condition that I gouge out the right
eye of every one of you and so bring
disgrace on all Israel."
3The elders of Jabesh said to him,
"Give us seven days so that we can send
messengers throughout Israel; if no-one
comes to rescue us, we will surrender to
you."

4When the messengers came to
Gibeah of Saul and reported these
terms to the people, they all wept aloud.
5Just then Saul was returning from the
fields, behind his oxen, and he asked,
"What is wrong with the people? Why
are they weeping?" Then they repeated
to him what the men of Jabesh had said.
6When Saul heard their words, the
Spirit of God came upon him in power,
and he burned with anger. 7He took a
pair of oxen, cut them into pieces, and
sent the pieces by messengers throughout Israel, proclaiming, "This is what
will be done to the oxen of anyone who
does not follow Saul and Samuel."
Then the terror of the LORD fell on the
people, and they turned out as one man.
8When Saul mustered them at Bezek,
the men of Israel numbered three hundred thousand and the men of Judah
thirty thousand.
9They told the messengers who had
come, "Say to the men of Jabesh
Gilead, 'By the time the sun is hot
tomorrow, you will be delivered.'"
When the messengers went and reported this to the men of Jabesh, they
were elated. 10They said to the Ammonites, "Tomorrow we will surrender to
you, and you can do to us whatever
seems good to you."
11The next day Saul separated his
men into three divisions; during the last
watch of the night they broke into the
camp of the Ammonites and slaughtered them until the heat of the day.
Those who survived were scattered, so
that no two of them were left together.

Saul Confirmed as King

12The people then said to Samuel,
"Who was it that asked, 'Shall Saul
reign over us?' Bring these men to us
and we will put them to death."
13But Saul said, "No-one shall be put
to death today, for this day the LORD
has rescued Israel."
14Then Samuel said to the people,
"Come, let us go to Gilgal and there
reaffirm the kingship." 15So all the people went to Gilgal and confirmed Saul as
king in the presence of the LORD. There
they sacrificed fellowship offerings before the LORD, and Saul and all the
Israelites held a great celebration.

Samuel's Farewell Speech

12 Samuel said to all Israel, "I have
listened to everything you said
to me and have set a king over you.
2Now you have a king as your leader. As
for me, I am old and grey, and my sons
are here with you. I have been your
leader from my youth until this day.
3Here I stand. Testify against me in the
presence of the LORD and his anointed.
Whose ox have I taken? Whose donkey
have I taken? Whom have I cheated?
Whom have I oppressed? From whose
hand have I accepted a bribe to make
me shut my eyes? If I have done any of
these, I will make it right."
4"You have not cheated or oppressed
us," they replied. "You have not taken
anything from anyone's hand."
5Samuel said to them, "The LORD is
witness against you, and also his
anointed is witness this day, that you
have not found anything in my hand."
"He is witness," they said.
6Then Samuel said to the people, "It
is the LORD who appointed Moses and
Aaron and brought your forefathers up
out of Egypt. 7Now then, stand here,
because I am going to confront you with
evidence before the LORD as to all the
righteous acts performed by the LORD
for you and your fathers.
8"After Jacob entered Egypt, they
cried to the LORD for help, and the
LORD sent Moses and Aaron, who
brought your forefathers out of Egypt
and settled them in this place.
9"But they forgot the LORD their
God; so he sold them into the hands of
Sisera, the commander of the army of
Hazor, and into the hands of the Philistines and the king of Moab, who fought
against them. 10They cried out to the
LORD and said, 'We have sinned; we

have forsaken the LORD and served the Baals and the Ashtoreths. But now deliver us from the hands of our enemies, and we will serve you.' 11Then the LORD sent Jerub-Baal, Barak, Jephthah and Samuel, and he delivered you from the hands of your enemies on every side, so that you lived securely.

12"But when you saw that Nahash king of the Ammonites was moving against you, you said to me, 'No, we want a king to rule over us'—even though the LORD your God was your king. 13Now here is the king you have chosen, the one you asked for; see, the LORD has set a king over you. 14If you fear the LORD and serve and obey him and do not rebel against his commands, and if both you and the king who reigns over you follow the LORD your God—good! 15But if you do not obey the LORD, and if you rebel against his commands, his hand will be against you, as it was against your fathers.

16"Now then, stand still and see this great thing the LORD is about to do before your eyes! 17Is it not wheat harvest now? I will call upon the LORD to send thunder and rain. And you will realise what an evil thing you did in the eyes of the LORD when you asked for a king."

18Then Samuel called upon the LORD, and that same day the LORD sent thunder and rain. So all the people stood in awe of the LORD and of Samuel.

19The people all said to Samuel, "Pray to the LORD your God for your servants so that we will not die, for we have added to all our other sins the evil of asking for a king."

20"Do not be afraid," Samuel replied. "You have done all this evil; yet do not turn away from the LORD, but serve the LORD with all your heart. 21Do not turn away after useless idols. They can do you no good, nor can they rescue you, because they are useless. 22For the sake of his great name the LORD will not reject his people, because the LORD was pleased to make you his own. 23As for me, far be it from me that I should sin against the LORD by failing to pray for you. And I will teach you the way that is good and right. 24But be sure to fear the LORD and serve him faithfully with all your heart; consider what great things he has done for you. 25Yet if you persist in doing evil, both you and your king will be swept away."

NEW TESTAMENT READING

John 12:37–13:17

The Jews Continue in Their Unbelief

37Even after Jesus had done all these miraculous signs in their presence, they still would not believe in him. 38This was to fulfil the word of Isaiah the prophet:

"Lord, who has believed our message
and to whom has the arm of the
Lord been revealed?"

39For this reason they could not believe, because, as Isaiah says elsewhere:

40"He has blinded their eyes
and deadened their hearts,
so they can neither see with their
eyes,
nor understand with their hearts,
nor turn—and I would heal them."

41Isaiah said this because he saw Jesus' glory and spoke about him.

42Yet at the same time many even among the leaders believed in him. But because of the Pharisees they would not confess their faith for fear they would be put out of the synagogue; 43for they loved praise from men more than praise from God.

44Then Jesus cried out, "When a man believes in me, he does not believe in me only, but in the one who sent me. 45When he looks at me, he sees the one who sent me. 46I have come into the world as a light, so that no-one who believes in me should stay in darkness.

47"As for the person who hears my

words but does not keep them, I do not judge him. For I did not come to judge the world, but to save it. 48There is a judge for the one who rejects me and does not accept my words; that very word which I spoke will condemn him at the last day. 49For I did not speak of my own accord, but the Father who sent me commanded me what to say and how to say it. 50I know that his command leads to eternal life. So whatever I say is just what the Father has told me to say."

Jesus Washes His Disciples' Feet

13 It was just before the Passover Feast. Jesus knew that the time had come for him to leave this world and go to the Father. Having loved his own who were in the world, he now showed them the full extent of his love.

2The evening meal was being served, and the devil had already prompted Judas Iscariot, son of Simon, to betray Jesus. 3Jesus knew that the Father had put all things under his power, and that he had come from God and was returning to God; 4so he got up from the meal, took off his outer clothing, and wrapped a towel round his waist. 5After that, he poured water into a basin and began to wash his disciples' feet, drying them with the towel that was wrapped round him.

6He came to Simon Peter, who said to him, "Lord, are you going to wash my feet?"

7Jesus replied, "You do not realise now what I am doing, but later you will understand."

8"No," said Peter, "you shall never wash my feet."

Jesus answered, "Unless I wash you, you have no part with me."

9"Then, Lord," Simon Peter replied, "not just my feet but my hands and my head as well!"

10Jesus answered, "A person who has had a bath needs only to wash his feet; his whole body is clean. And you are clean, though not every one of you." 11For he knew who was going to betray him, and that was why he said not every one was clean.

12When he had finished washing their feet, he put on his clothes and returned to his place. "Do you understand what I have done for you?" he asked them. 13"You call me 'Teacher' and 'Lord', and rightly so, for that is what I am. 14Now that I, your Lord and Teacher, have washed your feet, you also should wash one another's feet. 15I have set you an example that you should do as I have done for you. 16I tell you the truth, no servant is greater than his master, nor is a messenger greater than the one who sent him. 17Now that you know these things, you will be blessed if you do them.

READING FROM PSALMS
Psalm 66:1–12

For the director of music. A song. A psalm.

1Shout with joy to God, all the earth!
2 Sing the glory of his name;
make his praise glorious!
3Say to God, "How awesome are your
deeds!
So great is your power
that your enemies cringe before
you.
4All the earth bows down to you;
they sing praise to you,
they sing praise to your name."
Selah

5Come and see what God has done,
how awesome his works on man's
behalf!
6He turned the sea into dry land,
they passed through the waters on
foot—
come, let us rejoice in him.
7He rules for ever by his power,
his eyes watch the nations—
let not the rebellious rise up
against him. *Selah*

[8]Praise our God, O peoples,
let the sound of his praise be heard;
[9]he has preserved our lives
and kept our feet from slipping.
[10]For you, O God, tested us;
you refined us like silver.
[11]You brought us into prison
and laid burdens on our backs.
[12]You let men ride over our heads;
we went through fire and water,
but you brought us to a place of abundance.

DAY 143

MAY 23

OLD TESTAMENT READING
1 Samuel 13:1–14:23

Samuel Rebukes Saul

13 Saul was ⌞thirty⌟ years old when he became king, and he reigned over Israel for ⌞forty-⌟two years.

[2]Saul chose three thousand men from Israel; two thousand were with him at Michmash and in the hill country of Bethel, and a thousand were with Jonathan at Gibeah in Benjamin. The rest of the men he sent back to their homes.

[3]Jonathan attacked the Philistine outpost at Geba, and the Philistines heard about it. Then Saul had the trumpet blown throughout the land and said, "Let the Hebrews hear!" [4]So all Israel heard the news: "Saul has attacked the Philistine outpost, and now Israel has become an offence to the Philistines." And the people were summoned to join Saul at Gilgal.

[5]The Philistines assembled to fight Israel, with three thousand chariots, six thousand charioteers, and soldiers as numerous as the sand on the seashore. They went up and camped at Michmash, east of Beth Aven. [6]When the men of Israel saw that their situation was critical and that their army was hard pressed, they hid in caves and thickets, among the rocks, and in pits and cisterns. [7]Some Hebrews even crossed the Jordan to the land of Gad and Gilead.

Saul remained at Gilgal, and all the troops with him were quaking with fear. [8]He waited for seven days, the time set by Samuel; but Samuel did not come to Gilgal, and Saul's men began to scatter. [9]So he said, "Bring me the burnt offering and the fellowship offerings." And Saul offered up the burnt offering. [10]Just as he finished making the offering, Samuel arrived, and Saul went out to greet him.

[11]"What have you done?" asked Samuel.

Saul replied, "When I saw that the men were scattering, and that you did not come at the set time, and that the Philistines were assembling at Michmash, [12]I thought, 'Now the Philistines will come down against me at Gilgal, and I have not sought the LORD's favour.' So I felt compelled to offer the burnt offering."

[13]"You acted foolishly," Samuel said. "You have not kept the command the LORD your God gave you; if you had, he would have established your kingdom over Israel for all time. [14]But now your kingdom will not endure; the LORD has sought out a man after his own heart and appointed him leader of his people, because you have not kept the LORD's command."

[15]Then Samuel left Gilgal and went up to Gibeah in Benjamin, and Saul counted the men who were with him. They numbered about six hundred.

Israel Without Weapons

16Saul and his son Jonathan and the
men with them were staying in Gibeah
of Benjamin, while the Philistines
camped at Michmash. 17Raiding parties
went out from the Philistine camp in
three detachments. One turned towards
Ophrah in the vicinity of Shual,
18another towards Beth Horon, and the
third towards the borderland overlooking the Valley of Zeboim facing the
desert.

19Not a blacksmith could be found in
the whole land of Israel, because the
Philistines had said, "Otherwise the
Hebrews will make swords or spears!"
20So all Israel went down to the Philistines to have their ploughshares, mattocks, axes and sickles sharpened. 21The
price was two thirds of a shekel for
sharpening ploughshares and mattocks,
and a third of a shekel for sharpening
forks and axes and for repointing goads.

22So on the day of the battle not a
soldier with Saul and Jonathan had a
sword or spear in his hand; only Saul
and his son Jonathan had them.

Jonathan Attacks the Philistines

23Now a detachment of Philistines
had gone out to the pass at Michmash.

14 1One day Jonathan son of Saul
said to the young man bearing
his armour, "Come, let's go over to the
Philistine outpost on the other side."
But he did not tell his father.

2Saul was staying on the outskirts of
Gibeah under a pomegranate tree in
Migron. With him were about six hundred men, 3among whom was Ahijah,
who was wearing an ephod. He was a
son of Ichabod's brother Ahitub son of
Phinehas, the son of Eli, the LORD's
priest in Shiloh. No-one was aware that
Jonathan had left.

4On each side of the pass that Jonathan intended to cross to reach the
Philistine outpost was a cliff; one was
called Bozez, and the other Seneh.
5One cliff stood to the north towards
Michmash, the other to the south towards Geba.

6Jonathan said to his young armour-
bearer, "Come, let's go over to the
outpost of those uncircumcised fellows.
Perhaps the LORD will act on our behalf.
Nothing can hinder the LORD from
saving, whether by many or by few."

7"Do all that you have in mind," his
armour-bearer said. "Go ahead; I am
with you heart and soul."

8Jonathan said, "Come, then; we will
cross over towards the men and let them
see us. 9If they say to us, 'Wait there
until we come to you,' we will stay
where we are and not go up to them.
10But if they say, 'Come up to us,' we
will climb up, because that will be our
sign that the LORD has given them into
our hands."

11So both of them showed themselves
to the Philistine outpost. "Look!" said
the Philistines. "The Hebrews are
crawling out of the holes they were
hiding in." 12The men of the outpost
shouted to Jonathan and his armour-
bearer, "Come up to us and we'll teach
you a lesson."

So Jonathan said to his armour-
bearer, "Climb up after me; the LORD
has given them into the hand of Israel."

13Jonathan climbed up, using his
hands and feet, with his armour-bearer
right behind him. The Philistines fell
before Jonathan, and his armour-
bearer followed and killed behind him.
14In that first attack Jonathan and his
armour-bearer killed some twenty men
in an area of about half an acre.

Israel Routs the Philistines

15Then panic struck the whole army
—those in the camp and field, and those
in the outposts and raiding parties—
and the ground shook. It was a panic
sent by God.

16Saul's lookouts at Gibeah in Benjamin saw the army melting away in all
directions. 17Then Saul said to the men
who were with him, "Muster the forces

and see who has left us." When they
did, it was Jonathan and his armour-
bearer who were not there.
18Saul said to Ahijah, "Bring the ark
of God." (At that time it was with the
Israelites.) 19While Saul was talking to
the priest, the tumult in the Philistine
camp increased more and more. So Saul
said to the priest, "Withdraw your
hand."
20Then Saul and all his men assembled and went to the battle. They found
the Philistines in total confusion, striking each other with their swords.
21Those Hebrews who had previously
been with the Philistines and had gone
up with them to their camp went over to
the Israelites who were with Saul and
Jonathan. 22When all the Israelites who
had hidden in the hill country of
Ephraim heard that the Philistines were
on the run, they joined the battle in hot
pursuit. 23So the LORD rescued Israel
that day, and the battle moved on
beyond Beth Aven.

NEW TESTAMENT READING
John 13:18–38

Jesus Predicts His Betrayal

18"I am not referring to all of you; I
know those I have chosen. But this is to
fulfil the scripture: 'He who shares my
bread has lifted up his heel against me.'
19"I am telling you now before it happens, so that when it does happen you
will believe that I am He. 20I tell you the
truth, whoever accepts anyone I send
accepts me; and whoever accepts me
accepts the one who sent me."
21After he had said this, Jesus was
troubled in spirit and testified, "I tell
you the truth, one of you is going to
betray me."
22His disciples stared at one another,
at a loss to know which of them he
meant. 23One of them, the disciple
whom Jesus loved, was reclining next to
him. 24Simon Peter motioned to this
disciple and said, "Ask him which one
he means."
25Leaning back against Jesus, he
asked him, "Lord, who is it?"
26Jesus answered, "It is the one to
whom I will give this piece of bread
when I have dipped it in the dish."
Then, dipping the piece of bread, he
gave it to Judas Iscariot, son of Simon.
27As soon as Judas took the bread,
Satan entered into him.
"What you are about to do, do
quickly," Jesus told him, 28but no-one
at the meal understood why Jesus said
this to him. 29Since Judas had charge of
the money, some thought Jesus was
telling him to buy what was needed
for the Feast, or to give something to
the poor. 30As soon as Judas had
taken the bread, he went out. And it
was night.

Jesus Predicts Peter's Denial

31When he was gone, Jesus said,
"Now is the Son of Man glorified and
God is glorified in him. 32If God is
glorified in him, God will glorify the Son
in himself, and will glorify him at once.
33"My children, I will be with you
only a little longer. You will look for
me, and just as I told the Jews, so I tell
you now: Where I am going, you cannot
come.
34"A new command I give you: Love
one another. As I have loved you, so
you must love one another. 35By this all
men will know that you are my disciples, if you love one another."
36Simon Peter asked him, "Lord,
where are you going?"
Jesus replied, "Where I am going,
you cannot follow now, but you will
follow later."
37Peter asked, "Lord, why can't I
follow you now? I will lay down my
life for you."
38Then Jesus answered, "Will you
really lay down your life for me? I tell
you the truth, before the cock crows,
you will disown me three times!

READING FROM PSALMS
Psalm 66:13–20

13I will come to your temple with burnt
offerings
and fulfil my vows to you—
14vows my lips promised and my mouth
spoke
when I was in trouble.
15I will sacrifice fat animals to you
and an offering of rams;
I will offer bulls and goats. *Selah*
16Come and listen, all you who fear
God;
let me tell you what he has done for
me.
17I cried out to him with my mouth;
his praise was on my tongue.
18If I had cherished sin in my heart,
the Lord would not have listened;
19but God has surely listened
and heard my voice in prayer.
20Praise be to God,
who has not rejected my prayer
or withheld his love from me!

MAY 24

DAY 144

OLD TESTAMENT READING
1 Samuel 14:24–15:35

Jonathan Eats Honey

24Now the men of Israel were in distress that day, because Saul had bound
the people under an oath, saying,
"Cursed be any man who eats food
before evening comes, before I have
avenged myself on my enemies!" So
none of the troops tasted food.
25The entire army entered the woods,
and there was honey on the ground.
26When they went into the woods, they
saw the honey oozing out, yet no-one
put his hand to his mouth, because they
feared the oath. 27But Jonathan had not
heard that his father had bound the
people with the oath, so he reached out
the end of the staff that was in his hand
and dipped it into the honeycomb. He
raised his hand to his mouth, and his
eyes brightened. 28Then one of the soldiers told him, "Your father bound the
army under a strict oath, saying,
'Cursed be any man who eats food today!' That is why the men are faint."
29Jonathan said, "My father has
made trouble for the country. See how
my eyes brightened when I tasted a little
of this honey. 30How much better it
would have been if the men had eaten
today some of the plunder they took
from their enemies. Would not the
slaughter of the Philistines have been
even greater?"
31That day, after the Israelites had
struck down the Philistines from Michmash to Aijalon, they were exhausted.
32They pounced on the plunder and,
taking sheep, cattle and calves, they
butchered them on the ground and ate
them, together with the blood. 33Then
someone said to Saul, "Look, the men
are sinning against the LORD by eating
meat that has blood in it."

"You have broken faith," he said.
"Roll a large stone over here at once."
34Then he said, "Go out among the men
and tell them, 'Each of you bring me
your cattle and sheep, and slaughter
them here and eat them. Do not sin
against the LORD by eating meat with
blood still in it.'"

So everyone brought his ox that night
and slaughtered it there. 35Then Saul
built an altar to the LORD; it was the first
time he had done this.
36Saul said, "Let us go down after the
Philistines by night and plunder them
till dawn, and let us not leave one of
them alive."

"Do whatever seems best to you,"
they replied.
But the priest said, "Let us enquire of
God here."
37So Saul asked God, "Shall I go
down after the Philistines? Will you give
them into Israel's hand?" But God did
not answer him that day.
38Saul therefore said, "Come here,
all you who are leaders of the army, and
let us find out what sin has been committed today. 39As surely as the LORD who
rescues Israel lives, even if it lies with
my son Jonathan, he must die." But not
one of the men said a word.
40Saul then said to all the Israelites,
"You stand over there; I and Jonathan
my son will stand over here."
"Do what seems best to you," the
men replied.
41Then Saul prayed to the LORD, the
God of Israel, "Give me the right
answer." And Jonathan and Saul were
taken by lot, and the men were cleared.
42Saul said, "Cast the lot between me
and Jonathan my son." And Jonathan
was taken.
43Then Saul said to Jonathan, "Tell
me what you have done."
So Jonathan told him, "I merely
tasted a little honey with the end of my
staff. And now must I die?"
44Saul said, "May God deal with me,
be it ever so severely, if you do not die,
Jonathan."
45But the men said to Saul, "Should
Jonathan die—he who has brought
about this great deliverance in Israel?
Never! As surely as the LORD lives, not
a hair of his head shall fall to the
ground, for he did this today with God's
help." So the men rescued Jonathan,
and he was not put to death.
46Then Saul stopped pursuing the
Philistines, and they withdrew to their
own land.
47After Saul had assumed rule over
Israel, he fought against their enemies
on every side: Moab, the Ammonites,
Edom, the kings of Zobah, and the
Philistines. Wherever he turned, he inflicted punishment on them. 48He
fought valiantly and defeated the
Amalekites, delivering Israel from the
hands of those who had plundered
them.

Saul's Family

49Saul's sons were Jonathan, Ishvi
and Malki-Shua. The name of his older
daughter was Merab, and that of the
younger was Michal. 50His wife's name
was Ahinoam daughter of Ahimaaz.
The name of the commander of Saul's
army was Abner son of Ner, and Ner
was Saul's uncle. 51Saul's father Kish
and Abner's father Ner were sons of
Abiel.
52All the days of Saul there was bitter
war with the Philistines, and whenever
Saul saw a mighty or brave man, he took
him into his service.

The LORD Rejects Saul as King

15 Samuel said to Saul, "I am the
one the LORD sent to anoint you
king over his people Israel; so listen
now to the message from the LORD.
2This is what the LORD Almighty says: 'I
will punish the Amalekites for what
they did to Israel when they waylaid
them as they came up from Egypt.
3Now go, attack the Amalekites and
totally destroy everything that belongs
to them. Do not spare them; put to
death men and women, children and
infants, cattle and sheep, camels and
donkeys.'"
4So Saul summoned the men and
mustered them at Telaim—two hundred thousand foot soldiers and ten
thousand men from Judah. 5Saul went
to the city of Amalek and set an ambush
in the ravine. 6Then he said to the Kenites, "Go away, leave the Amalekites
so that I do not destroy you along with
them; for you showed kindness to all the
Israelites when they came up out of
Egypt." So the Kenites moved away
from the Amalekites.
7Then Saul attacked the Amalekites

all the way from Havilah to Shur, to the
east of Egypt. 8He took Agag king of
the Amalekites alive, and all his people
he totally destroyed with the sword.
9But Saul and the army spared Agag
and the best of the sheep and cattle, the
fat calves and lambs—everything that
was good. These they were unwilling to
destroy completely, but everything that
was despised and weak they totally
destroyed.

10Then the word of the LORD came to
Samuel: 11"I am grieved that I have
made Saul king, because he has turned
away from me and has not carried out
my instructions." Samuel was troubled,
and he cried out to the LORD all that
night.

12Early in the morning Samuel got up
and went to meet Saul, but he was told,
"Saul has gone to Carmel. There he has
set up a monument in his own honour
and has turned and gone on down to
Gilgal."

13When Samuel reached him, Saul
said, "The LORD bless you! I have carried out the LORD's instructions."

14But Samuel said, "What then is this
bleating of sheep in my ears? What is
this lowing of cattle that I hear?"

15Saul answered, "The soldiers
brought them from the Amalekites;
they spared the best of the sheep and
cattle to sacrifice to the LORD your God,
but we totally destroyed the rest."

16"Stop!" Samuel said to Saul. "Let
me tell you what the LORD said to me
last night."

"Tell me," Saul replied.

17Samuel said, "Although you were
once small in your own eyes, did you not
become the head of the tribes of Israel?
The LORD anointed you king over
Israel. 18And he sent you on a mission,
saying, 'Go and completely destroy
those wicked people, the Amalekites;
make war on them until you have wiped
them out.' 19Why did you not obey the
LORD? Why did you pounce on the
plunder and do evil in the eyes of
the LORD?"

20"But I did obey the LORD," Saul
said. "I went on the mission the LORD
assigned me. I completely destroyed the
Amalekites and brought back Agag
their king. 21The soldiers took sheep
and cattle from the plunder, the best of
what was devoted to God, in order to
sacrifice them to the LORD your God at
Gilgal."

22But Samuel replied:

"Does the LORD delight in burnt
offerings and sacrifices
as much as in obeying the voice of
the LORD?
To obey is better than sacrifice,
and to heed is better than the fat of
rams.
23For rebellion is like the sin of
divination,
and arrogance like the evil of
idolatry.
Because you have rejected the word
of the LORD,
he has rejected you as king."

24Then Saul said to Samuel, "I have
sinned. I violated the LORD's command
and your instructions. I was afraid of the
people and so I gave in to them. 25Now I
beg you, forgive my sin and come back
with me, so that I may worship the
LORD."

26But Samuel said to him, "I will not
go back with you. You have rejected the
word of the LORD, and the LORD has
rejected you as king over Israel!"

27As Samuel turned to leave, Saul
caught hold of the hem of his robe, and
it tore. 28Samuel said to him, "The
LORD has torn the kingdom of Israel
from you today and has given it to one
of your neighbours—to one better than
you. 29He who is the Glory of Israel
does not lie or change his mind; for he is
not a man, that he should change his
mind."

30Saul replied, "I have sinned. But
please honour me before the elders of
my people and before Israel; come back
with me, so that I may worship the
LORD your God." 31So Samuel went

back with Saul, and Saul worshipped
the LORD.
32Then Samuel said, "Bring me Agag
king of the Amalekites."
Agag came to him confidently, thinking, "Surely the bitterness of death is
past."
33But Samuel said,

"As your sword has made women
childless,
so will your mother be childless
among women."

And Samuel put Agag to death before
the LORD at Gilgal.
34Then Samuel left for Ramah, but
Saul went up to his home in Gibeah of
Saul. 35Until the day Samuel died, he
did not go to see Saul again, though
Samuel mourned for him. And the
LORD was grieved that he had made
Saul king over Israel.

NEW TESTAMENT READING

John 14:1–31

Jesus Comforts His Disciples

14 "Do not let your hearts be troubled. Trust in God; trust also in
me. 2In my Father's house are many
rooms; if it were not so, I would have
told you. I am going there to prepare a
place for you. 3And if I go and prepare a
place for you, I will come back and take
you to be with me that you also may be
where I am. 4You know the way to the
place where I am going."

Jesus the Way to the Father

5Thomas said to him, "Lord, we
don't know where you are going, so how
can we know the way?"
6Jesus answered, "I am the way and
the truth and the life. No-one comes to
the Father except through me. 7If you
really knew me, you would know my
Father as well. From now on, you do
know him and have seen him."
8Philip said, "Lord, show us the
Father and that will be enough for us."
9Jesus answered: "Don't you know
me, Philip, even after I have been
among you such a long time? Anyone
who has seen me has seen the Father.
How can you say, 'Show us the Father'?
10Don't you believe that I am in the
Father, and that the Father is in me?
The words I say to you are not just my
own. Rather, it is the Father, living in
me, who is doing his work. 11Believe me
when I say that I am in the Father and
the Father is in me; or at least believe on
the evidence of the miracles themselves. 12I tell you the truth, anyone
who has faith in me will do what I have
been doing. He will do even greater
things than these, because I am going to
the Father. 13And I will do whatever
you ask in my name, so that the Son may
bring glory to the Father. 14You may
ask me for anything in my name, and I
will do it.

Jesus Promises the Holy Spirit

15"If you love me, you will obey what
I command. 16And I will ask the Father,
and he will give you another Counsellor
to be with you for ever—17the Spirit of
truth. The world cannot accept him,
because it neither sees him nor knows
him. But you know him, for he lives
with you and will be in you. 18I will not
leave you as orphans; I will come to
you. 19Before long, the world will not
see me any more, but you will see me.
Because I live, you also will live. 20On
that day you will realise that I am in my
Father, and you are in me, and I am in
you. 21Whoever has my commands and
obeys them, he is the one who loves me.
He who loves me will be loved by my
Father, and I too will love him and show
myself to him."
22Then Judas (not Judas Iscariot)
said, "But, Lord, why do you intend to
show yourself to us and not to the
world?"

[23]Jesus replied, "If anyone loves me, he will obey my teaching. My Father will love him, and we will come to him and make our home with him. [24]He who does not love me will not obey my teaching. These words you hear are not my own; they belong to the Father who sent me.

[25]"All this I have spoken while still with you. [26]But the Counsellor, the Holy Spirit, whom the Father will send in my name, will teach you all things and will remind you of everything I have said to you. [27]Peace I leave with you; my peace I give you. I do not give to you as the world gives. Do not let your hearts be troubled and do not be afraid.

[28]"You heard me say, 'I am going away and I am coming back to you.' If you loved me, you would be glad that I am going to the Father, for the Father is greater than I. [29]I have told you now before it happens, so that when it does happen you will believe. [30]I will not speak with you much longer, for the prince of this world is coming. He has no hold on me, [31]but the world must learn that I love the Father and that I do exactly what my Father has commanded me.

"Come now; let us leave.

READING FROM PROVERBS

Proverbs 12:28–13:9

[28]In the way of righteousness there is
life;
along that path is immortality.

13 A wise son heeds his father's
instruction,
but a mocker does not listen to
rebuke.

[2]From the fruit of his lips a man
enjoys good things,
but the unfaithful have a craving
for violence.

[3]He who guards his lips guards his life,
but he who speaks rashly will come
to ruin.

[4]The sluggard craves and gets nothing,
but the desires of the diligent are
fully satisfied.

[5]The righteous hate what is false,
but the wicked bring shame and
disgrace.

[6]Righteousness guards the man of
integrity,
but wickedness overthrows the
sinner.

[7]One man pretends to be rich, yet has
nothing;
another pretends to be poor, yet
has great wealth.

[8]A man's riches may ransom his life,
but a poor man hears no threat.

[9]The light of the righteous shines
brightly,
but the lamp of the wicked is
snuffed out.

DAY 145

MAY 25

OLD TESTAMENT READING
1 Samuel 16:1–17:37

Samuel Anoints David

16 The LORD said to Samuel, "How
long will you mourn for Saul,
since I have rejected him as king over
Israel? Fill your horn with oil and be on
your way; I am sending you to Jesse of
Bethlehem. I have chosen one of his
sons to be king."
[2]But Samuel said, "How can I go?
Saul will hear about it and kill me."
The LORD said, "Take a heifer with
you and say, 'I have come to sacrifice to
the LORD.' [3]Invite Jesse to the sacrifice,
and I will show you what to do. You are
to anoint for me the one I indicate."
[4]Samuel did what the LORD said.
When he arrived at Bethlehem, the
elders of the town trembled when they
met him. They asked, "Do you come in
peace?"
[5]Samuel replied, "Yes, in peace; I
have come to sacrifice to the LORD.
Consecrate yourselves and come to the
sacrifice with me." Then he consecrated
Jesse and his sons and invited them to
the sacrifice.
[6]When they arrived, Samuel saw
Eliab and thought, "Surely the LORD's
anointed stands here before the LORD."
[7]But the LORD said to Samuel, 'Do
not consider his appearance or his
height, for I have rejected him. The
LORD does not look at the things man
looks at. Man looks at the outward
appearance, but the LORD looks at the
heart."
[8]Then Jesse called Abinadab and
made him pass in front of Samuel. But
Samuel said, "The LORD has not chosen
this one either." [9]Jesse then made
Shammah pass by, but Samuel said,
"Nor has the LORD chosen this one."
[10]Jesse made seven of his sons pass before Samuel, but Samuel said to him,
"The LORD has not chosen these." [11]So
he asked Jesse, "Are these all the sons
you have?"
"There is still the youngest," Jesse
answered, "but he is tending the
sheep."
Samuel said, "Send for him; we will
not sit down until he arrives."
[12]So he sent and had him brought in.
He was ruddy, with a fine appearance
and handsome features.
Then the LORD said, "Rise and
anoint him; he is the one."
[13]So Samuel took the horn of oil and
anointed him in the presence of his
brothers, and from that day on the
Spirit of the LORD came upon David
in power. Samuel then went to Ramah.

David in Saul's Service

[14]Now the Spirit of the LORD had
departed from Saul, and an evil spirit
from the LORD tormented him.
[15]Saul's attendants said to him, "See,
an evil spirit from God is tormenting
you. [16]Let our lord command his servants here to search for someone who
can play the harp. He will play when the
evil spirit from God comes upon you,
and you will feel better."
[17]So Saul said to his attendants, "Find
someone who plays well and bring him
to me."
[18]One of the servants answered, "I
have seen a son of Jesse of Bethlehem
who knows how to play the harp. He is a
brave man and a warrior. He speaks
well and is a fine-looking man. And the
LORD is with him."
[19]Then Saul sent messengers to Jesse
and said, "Send me your son David,
who is with the sheep." [20]So Jesse took
a donkey loaded with bread, a skin of
wine and a young goat and sent them
with his son David to Saul.
[21]David came to Saul and entered his
service. Saul liked him very much, and

David became one of his armour-
bearers. [22]Then Saul sent word to Jesse,
saying, "Allow David to remain in my
service, for I am pleased with him."
[23]Whenever the spirit from God came
upon Saul, David would take his harp
and play. Then relief would come to
Saul; he would feel better, and the evil
spirit would leave him.

David and Goliath

17 Now the Philistines gathered
their forces for war and assembled at Socoh in Judah. They pitched
camp at Ephes Dammim, between
Socoh and Azekah. [2]Saul and the
Israelites assembled and camped in the
Valley of Elah and drew up their battle
line to meet the Philistines. [3]The Philistines occupied one hill and the Israelites
another, with the valley between them.
[4]A champion named Goliath, who
was from Gath, came out of the Philistine camp. He was over nine feet tall.
[5]He had a bronze helmet on his head
and wore a coat of scale armour of
bronze weighing five thousand shekels;
[6]on his legs he wore bronze greaves, and
a bronze javelin was slung on his back.
[7]His spear shaft was like a weaver's rod,
and its iron point weighed six hundred
shekels. His shield-bearer went ahead
of him.
[8]Goliath stood and shouted to the
ranks of Israel, "Why do you come out
and line up for battle? Am I not a
Philistine, and are you not the servants
of Saul? Choose a man and have him
come down to me. [9]If he is able to fight
and kill me, we will become your subjects; but if I overcome him and kill
him, you will become our subjects and
serve us." [10]Then the Philistine said,
"This day I defy the ranks of Israel!
Give me a man and let us fight each
other." [11]On hearing the Philistine's
words, Saul and all the Israelites were
dismayed and terrified.
[12]Now David was the son of an
Ephrathite named Jesse, who was from
Bethlehem in Judah. Jesse had eight
sons, and in Saul's time he was old and
well advanced in years. [13]Jesse's three
oldest sons had followed Saul to the
war: The firstborn was Eliab; the
second, Abinadab; and the third,
Shammah. [14]David was the youngest.
The three oldest followed Saul, [15]but
David went back and forth from Saul to
tend his father's sheep at Bethlehem.
[16]For forty days the Philistine came
forward every morning and evening and
took his stand.
[17]Now Jesse said to his son David,
"Take this ephah of roasted grain and
these ten loaves of bread for your
brothers and hurry to their camp.
[18]Take along these ten cheeses to the
commander of their unit. See how your
brothers are and bring back some assurance from them. [19]They are with Saul
and all the men of Israel in the Valley of
Elah, fighting against the Philistines."
[20]Early in the morning David left the
flock with a shepherd, loaded up and set
out, as Jesse had directed. He reached
the camp as the army was going out to
its battle positions, shouting the war
cry. [21]Israel and the Philistines were
drawing up their lines facing each other.
[22]David left his things with the keeper of
supplies, ran to the battle lines and
greeted his brothers. [23]As he was talking with them, Goliath, the Philistine
champion from Gath, stepped out from
his lines and shouted his usual defiance,
and David heard it. [24]When the
Israelites saw the man, they all ran from
him in great fear.
[25]Now the Israelites had been saying,
"Do you see how this man keeps coming out? He comes out to defy Israel.
The king will give great wealth to the
man who kills him. He will also give him
his daughter in marriage and will exempt his father's family from taxes in
Israel."
[26]David asked the men standing near
him, "What will be done for the man
who kills this Philistine and removes
this disgrace from Israel? Who is this
uncircumcised Philistine that he should
defy the armies of the living God?"

27They repeated to him what they had
been saying and told him, “This is what
will be done for the man who kills him.”
28When Eliab, David’s oldest
brother, heard him speaking with the
men, he burned with anger at him and
asked, “Why have you come down
here? And with whom did you leave
those few sheep in the desert? I know
how conceited you are and how wicked
your heart is; you came down only to
watch the battle.”
29“Now what have I done?” said
David. “Can’t I even speak?” 30He then
turned away to someone else and
brought up the same matter, and the
men answered him as before. 31What
David said was overheard and reported
to Saul, and Saul sent for him.
32David said to Saul, “Let no-one
lose heart on account of this Philistine;
your servant will go and fight him.”
33Saul replied, “You are not able to
go out against this Philistine and fight
him; you are only a boy, and he has
been a fighting man from his youth.”
34But David said to Saul, “Your servant has been keeping his father’s
sheep. When a lion or a bear came and
carried off a sheep from the flock, 35I
went after it, struck it and rescued the
sheep from its mouth. When it turned
on me, I seized it by its hair, struck it
and killed it. 36Your servant has killed
both the lion and the bear; this uncircumcised Philistine will be like one of
them, because he has defied the armies
of the living God. 37The LORD who delivered me from the paw of the lion and
the paw of the bear will deliver me from
the hand of this Philistine.”
Saul said to David, “Go, and the
LORD be with you.”

NEW TESTAMENT READING

John 15:1–16:4

The Vine and the Branches

15 “I am the true vine, and my
Father is the gardener. 2He cuts
off every branch in me that bears no
fruit, while every branch that does bear
fruit he prunes so that it will be even
more fruitful. 3You are already clean
because of the word I have spoken to
you. 4Remain in me, and I will remain
in you. No branch can bear fruit by
itself; it must remain in the vine.
Neither can you bear fruit unless you
remain in me.
5“I am the vine; you are the branches.
If a man remains in me and I in him, he
will bear much fruit; apart from me you
can do nothing. 6If anyone does not
remain in me, he is like a branch that
is thrown away and withers; such
branches are picked up, thrown into the
fire and burned. 7If you remain in me
and my words remain in you, ask whatever you wish, and it will be given you.
8This is to my Father’s glory, that you
bear much fruit, showing yourselves to
be my disciples.
9“As the Father has loved me, so
have I loved you. Now remain in my
love. 10If you obey my commands, you
will remain in my love, just as I have
obeyed my Father’s commands and remain in his love. 11I have told you this so
that my joy may be in you and that your
joy may be complete. 12My command is
this: Love each other as I have loved
you. 13Greater love has no-one than
this, that he lay down his life for his
friends. 14You are my friends if you do
what I command. 15I no longer call you
servants, because a servant does not
know his master’s business. Instead, I
have called you friends, for everything
that I learned from my Father I have
made known to you. 16You did not
choose me, but I chose you and
appointed you to go and bear fruit—
fruit that will last. Then the Father will
give you whatever you ask in my name.
17This is my command: Love each
other.

The World Hates the Disciples

18“If the world hates you, keep in
mind that it hated me first. 19If you
belonged to the world, it would love you

as its own. As it is, you do not belong to
the world, but I have chosen you out of
the world. That is why the world hates
you. 20Remember the words I spoke to
you: 'No servant is greater than his
master. If they persecuted me, they will
persecute you also. If they obeyed my
teaching, they will obey yours also.
21They will treat you this way because of
my name, for they do not know the One
who sent me. 22If I had not come and
spoken to them, they would not be
guilty of sin. Now, however, they have
no excuse for their sin. 23He who hates
me hates my Father as well. 24If I had
not done among them what no-one else
did, they would not be guilty of sin. But
now they have seen these miracles, and
yet they have hated both me and my
Father. 25But this is to fulfil what is
written in their Law: 'They hated me
without reason.'

26"When the Counsellor comes,
whom I will send to you from the
Father, the Spirit of truth who goes out
from the Father, he will testify about
me. 27And you also must testify, for you
have been with me from the beginning.

16 "All this I have told you so that
you will not go astray. 2They will
put you out of the synagogue; in fact, a
time is coming when anyone who kills
you will think he is offering a service to
God. 3They will do such things because
they have not known the Father or me.
4I have told you this, so that when the
time comes you will remember that I
warned you. I did not tell you this at first
because I was with you.

READING FROM PSALMS

Psalm 67:1–7

For the director of music. With stringed instruments. A psalm. A song.

1May God be gracious to us and bless
us
and make his face shine upon us,
Selah
2that your ways may be known on
earth,
your salvation among all nations.

3May the peoples praise you, O God;
may all the peoples praise you.
4May the nations be glad and sing for
joy,
for you rule the peoples justly
and guide the nations of the earth.
Selah
5May the peoples praise you, O God;
may all the peoples praise you.

6Then the land will yield its harvest,
and God, our God, will bless us.
7God will bless us,
and all the ends of the earth will
fear him.

MAY 26

DAY 146

OLD TESTAMENT READING

1 Samuel 17:38–18:30

38Then Saul dressed David in his own
tunic. He put a coat of armour on him
and a bronze helmet on his head.
39David fastened on his sword over the
tunic and tried walking around, because
he was not used to them.

"I cannot go in these," he said to
Saul, "because I am not used to them."
So he took them off. 40Then he took his
staff in his hand, chose five smooth
stones from the stream, put them in the
pouch of his shepherd's bag and, with
his sling in his hand, approacned the
Philistine.

41Meanwhile, the Philistine, with his
shield-bearer in front of him, kept coming closer to David. 42He looked David

over and saw that he was only a boy, ruddy and handsome, and he despised him. 43He said to David, "Am I a dog, that you come at me with sticks?" And the Philistine cursed David by his gods. 44"Come here," he said, "and I'll give your flesh to the birds of the air and the beasts of the field!"

45David said to the Philistine, "You come against me with sword and spear and javelin, but I come against you in the name of the LORD Almighty, the God of the armies of Israel, whom you have defied. 46This day the LORD will hand you over to me, and I'll strike you down and cut off your head. Today I will give the carcasses of the Philistine army to the birds of the air and the beasts of the earth, and the whole world will know that there is a God in Israel. 47All those gathered here will know that it is not by sword or spear that the LORD saves; for the battle is the LORD's, and he will give all of you into our hands."

48As the Philistine moved closer to attack him, David ran quickly towards the battle line to meet him. 49Reaching into his bag and taking out a stone, he slung it and struck the Philistine on the forehead. The stone sank into his forehead, and he fell face down on the ground.

50So David triumphed over the Philistine with a sling and a stone; without a sword in his hand he struck down the Philistine and killed him.

51David ran and stood over him. He took hold of the Philistine's sword and drew it from the scabbard. After he killed him, he cut off his head with the sword.

When the Philistines saw that their hero was dead, they turned and ran. 52Then the men of Israel and Judah surged forward with a shout and pursued the Philistines to the entrance of Gath and to the gates of Ekron. Their dead were strewn along the Shaaraim road to Gath and Ekron. 53When the Israelites returned from chasing the Philistines, they plundered their camp. 54David took the Philistine's head and brought it to Jerusalem, and he put the Philistine's weapons in his own tent.

55As Saul watched David going out to meet the Philistine, he said to Abner, commander of the army, "Abner, whose son is that young man?"

Abner replied, "As surely as you live, O king, I don't know."

56The king said, "Find out whose son this young man is."

57As soon as David returned from killing the Philistine, Abner took him and brought him before Saul, with David still holding the Philistine's head.

58"Whose son are you, young man?" Saul asked him.

David said, "I am the son of your servant Jesse of Bethlehem."

Saul's Jealousy of David

18 After David had finished talking with Saul, Jonathan became one in spirit with David, and he loved him as himself. 2From that day Saul kept David with him and did not let him return to his father's house. 3And Jonathan made a covenant with David because he loved him as himself. 4Jonathan took off the robe he was wearing and gave it to David, along with his tunic, and even his sword, his bow and his belt.

5Whatever Saul sent him to do, David did it so successfully that Saul gave him a high rank in the army. This pleased all the people, and Saul's officers as well.

6When the men were returning home after David had killed the Philistine, the women came out from all the towns of Israel to meet King Saul with singing and dancing, with joyful songs and with tambourines and lutes. 7As they danced, they sang:

"Saul has slain his thousands,
  and David his tens of thousands."

8Saul was very angry; this refrain galled him. "They have credited David with tens of thousands," he thought, "but me with only thousands. What

more can he get but the kingdom?”
9And from that time on Saul kept a
jealous eye on David.

10The next day an evil spirit from God
came forcefully upon Saul. He was
prophesying in his house, while David
was playing the harp, as he usually did.
Saul had a spear in his hand 11and he
hurled it, saying to himself, “I'll pin
David to the wall.” But David eluded
him twice.

12Saul was afraid of David, because
the LORD was with David but had left
Saul. 13So he sent David away from him
and gave him command over a thousand
men, and David led the troops in their
campaigns. 14In everything he did he
had great success, because the LORD
was with him. 15When Saul saw how
successful he was, he was afraid of him.
16But all Israel and Judah loved David,
because he led them in their campaigns.

17Saul said to David, “Here is my
elder daughter Merab. I will give her to
you in marriage; only serve me bravely
and fight the battles of the LORD.” For
Saul said to himself, “I will not raise a
hand against him. Let the Philistines do
that!”

18But David said to Saul, “Who am I,
and what is my family or my father's
clan in Israel, that I should become the
king's son-in-law?” 19So when the time
came for Merab, Saul's daughter, to be
given to David, she was given in marriage to Adriel of Meholah.

20Now Saul's daughter Michal was in
love with David, and when they told
Saul about it, he was pleased. 21“I will
give her to him,” he thought, “so that
she may be a snare to him and so that
the hand of the Philistines may be
against him.” So Saul said to David,
“Now you have a second opportunity to
become my son-in-law.”

22Then Saul ordered his attendants:
“Speak to David privately and say,
‘Look, the king is pleased with you, and
his attendants all like you; now become
his son-in-law.’”

23They repeated these words to
David. But David said, “Do you think it
is a small matter to become the king's
son-in-law? I'm only a poor man and
little known.”

24When Saul's servants told him what
David had said, 25Saul replied, “Say to
David, ‘The king wants no other price
for the bride than a hundred Philistine
foreskins, to take revenge on his enemies.’” Saul's plan was to have David
fall by the hands of the Philistines.

26When the attendants told David
these things, he was pleased to become
the king's son-in-law. So before the
allotted time elapsed, 27David and his
men went out and killed two hundred
Philistines. He brought their foreskins
and presented the full number to the
king so that he might become the king's
son-in-law. Then Saul gave him his
daughter Michal in marriage.

28When Saul realised that the LORD
was with David and that his daughter
Michal loved David, 29Saul became still
more afraid of him, and he remained his
enemy for the rest of his days.

30The Philistine commanders continued to go out to battle, and as often
as they did, David met with more success than the rest of Saul's officers, and
his name became well known.

NEW TESTAMENT READING
John 16:5–17:5

The Work of the Holy Spirit

5“Now I am going to him who sent
me, yet none of you asks me, ‘Where
are you going?’ 6Because I have said
these things, you are filled with grief.
7But I tell you the truth: It is for your
good that I am going away. Unless I go
away, the Counsellor will not come to
you; but if I go, I will send him to you.
8When he comes, he will convict the
world of guilt in regard to sin and righteousness and judgment: 9in regard to
sin, because men do not believe in me;
10in regard to righteousness, because I
am going to the Father, where you can
see me no longer; 11and in regard to

judgment, because the prince of this
world now stands condemned.
12"I have much more to say to you,
more than you can now bear. 13But
when he, the Spirit of truth, comes, he
will guide you into all truth. He will not
speak on his own; he will speak only
what he hears, and he will tell you what
is yet to come. 14He will bring glory to
me by taking from what is mine and
making it known to you. 15All that belongs to the Father is mine. That is why I
said the Spirit will take from what is
mine and make it known to you.
16"In a little while you will see me no
more, and then after a little while you
will see me."

The Disciples' Grief Will Turn to Joy

17Some of his disciples said to one
another, "What does he mean by
saying, 'In a little while you will see me
no more, and then after a little while
you will see me,' and 'Because I am
going to the Father'?" 18They kept
asking, "What does he mean by 'a little
while'? We don't understand what he is
saying."
19Jesus saw that they wanted to ask
him about this, so he said to them, "Are
you asking one another what I meant
when I said, 'In a little while you will see
me no more, and then after a little while
you will see me'? 20I tell you the truth,
you will weep and mourn while the
world rejoices. You will grieve, but
your grief will turn to joy. 21A woman
giving birth to a child has pain because
her time has come; but when her baby is
born she forgets the anguish because of
her joy that a child is born into the
world. 22So with you: Now is your time
of grief, but I will see you again and you
will rejoice, and no-one will take away
your joy. 23In that day you will no
longer ask me anything. I tell you the
truth, my Father will give you whatever
you ask in my name. 24Until now you
have not asked for anything in my
name. Ask and you will receive, and
your joy will be complete.
25"Though I have been speaking
figuratively, a time is coming when I will
no longer use this kind of language but
will tell you plainly about my Father.
26In that day you will ask in my name. I
am not saying that I will ask the Father
on your behalf. 27No, the Father himself
loves you because you have loved me
and have believed that I came from
God. 28I came from the Father and
entered the world; now I am leaving the
world and going back to the Father."
29Then Jesus' disciples said, "Now
you are speaking clearly and without
figures of speech. 30Now we can see that
you know all things and that you do not
even need to have anyone ask you questions. This makes us believe that you
came from God."
31"You believe at last!" Jesus
answered. 32"But a time is coming, and
has come, when you will be scattered,
each to his own home. You will leave
me all alone. Yet I am not alone, for my
Father is with me.
33"I have told you these things, so
that in me you may have peace. In this
world you will have trouble. But take
heart! I have overcome the world."

Jesus Prays for Himself

17 After Jesus said this, he looked
towards heaven and prayed:

"Father, the time has come.
Glorify your Son, that your Son
may glorify you. 2For you granted
him authority over all people that
he might give eternal life to all
those you have given him. 3Now
this is eternal life: that they may
know you, the only true God, and
Jesus Christ, whom you have sent.
4I have brought you glory on earth
by completing the work you gave
me to do. 5And now, Father,
glorify me in your presence with
the glory I had with you before the
world began.

READING FROM PSALMS

Psalm 68:1–6

For the director of music. Of David. A psalm. A song.

1May God arise, may his enemies be
scattered;
may his foes flee before him.
2As smoke is blown away by the wind,
may you blow them away;
as wax melts before the fire,
may the wicked perish before God.
3But may the righteous be glad
and rejoice before God;
may they be happy and joyful.

4Sing to God, sing praise to his name,
extol him who rides on the
clouds—
his name is the LORD—
and rejoice before him.
5A father to the fatherless, a defender
of widows,
is God in his holy dwelling.
6God sets the lonely in families,
he leads forth the prisoners with
singing;
but the rebellious live in a
sun-scorched land.

MAY 27

DAY 147

OLD TESTAMENT READING

1 Samuel 19:1–20:42

Saul Tries to Kill David

19 Saul told his son Jonathan and
all the attendants to kill David.
But Jonathan was very fond of David
2and warned him, "My father Saul is
looking for a chance to kill you. Be on
your guard tomorrow morning; go into
hiding and stay there. 3I will go out and
stand with my father in the field where
you are. I'll speak to him about you and
will tell you what I find out."

4Jonathan spoke well of David to
Saul his father and said to him, "Let not
the king do wrong to his servant David;
he has not wronged you, and what he
has done has benefited you greatly. 5He
took his life in his hands when he killed
the Philistine. The LORD won a great
victory for all Israel, and you saw it and
were glad. Why then would you do
wrong to an innocent man like David by
killing him for no reason?"

6Saul listened to Jonathan and took
this oath: "As surely as the LORD lives,
David will not be put to death."

7So Jonathan called David and told
him the whole conversation. He
brought him to Saul, and David was
with Saul as before.

8Once more war broke out, and
David went out and fought the Philistines. He struck them with such force
that they fled before him.

9But an evil spirit from the LORD
came upon Saul as he was sitting in his
house with his spear in his hand. While
David was playing the harp, 10Saul tried
to pin him to the wall with his spear, but
David eluded him as Saul drove the
spear into the wall. That night David
made good his escape.

11Saul sent men to David's house to
watch it and to kill him in the morning.
But Michal, David's wife, warned him,
"If you don't run for your life tonight,
tomorrow you'll be killed." 12So Michal
let David down through a window, and
he fled and escaped. 13Then Michal
took an idol and laid it on the bed,
covering it with a garment and putting
some goats' hair at the head.

14When Saul sent the men to capture
David, Michal said, "He is ill."

15Then Saul sent the men back to see
David and told them, "Bring him up to
me in his bed so that I may kill him."
16But when the men entered, there was
the idol in the bed, and at the head was
some goats' hair.

17Saul said to Michal, "Why did you
deceive me like this and send my enemy
away so that he escaped?"

Michal told him, "He said to me, 'Let
me get away. Why should I kill you?'"

18When David had fled and made his
escape, he went to Samuel at Ramah
and told him all that Saul had done to
him. Then he and Samuel went to
Naioth and stayed there. 19Word came
to Saul: "David is in Naioth at Ramah";
20so he sent men to capture him. But
when they saw a group of prophets
prophesying, with Samuel standing
there as their leader, the Spirit of God
came upon Saul's men and they also
prophesied. 21Saul was told about it,
and he sent more men, and they
prophesied too. Saul sent men a third
time, and they also prophesied.
22Finally, he himself left for Ramah and
went to the great cistern at Secu. And
he asked, "Where are Samuel and
David?"

"Over in Naioth at Ramah," they
said.

23So Saul went to Naioth at Ramah.
But the Spirit of God came even upon
him, and he walked along prophesying
until he came to Naioth. 24He stripped
off his robes and also prophesied in
Samuel's presence. He lay that way all
that day and night. This is why people
say, "Is Saul also among the prophets?"

David and Jonathan

20 Then David fled from Naioth at
Ramah and went to Jonathan
and asked, "What have I done? What is
my crime? How have I wronged your
father, that he is trying to take my life?"

2"Never!" Jonathan replied. "You
are not going to die! Look, my father
doesn't do anything, great or small,
without confiding in me. Why should he
hide this from me? It's not so!"

3But David took an oath and said,
"Your father knows very well that I
have found favour in your eyes, and he
has said to himself, 'Jonathan must not
know this or he will be grieved.' Yet as
surely as the LORD lives and as you live,
there is only a step between me and
death."

4Jonathan said to David, "Whatever
you want me to do, I'll do for you."

5So David said, "Look, tomorrow is
the New Moon festival, and I am supposed to dine with the king; but let me
go and hide in the field until the evening
of the day after tomorrow. 6If your
father misses me at all, tell him, 'David
earnestly asked my permission to hurry
to Bethlehem, his home town, because
an annual sacrifice is being made there
for his whole clan.' 7If he says, 'Very
well,' then your servant is safe. But if he
loses his temper, you can be sure that he
is determined to harm me. 8As for you,
show kindness to your servant, for you
have brought him into a covenant with
you before the LORD. If I am guilty,
then kill me yourself! Why hand me
over to your father?"

9"Never!" Jonathan said. "If I had
the least inkling that my father was determined to harm you, wouldn't I tell
you?"

10David asked, "Who will tell me if
your father answers you harshly?"

11"Come," Jonathan said, "let's go
out into the field." So they went there
together.

12Then Jonathan said to David: "By
the LORD, the God of Israel, I will
surely sound out my father by this time
the day after tomorrow! If he is favourably disposed towards you, will I not
send you word and let you know? 13But
if my father is inclined to harm you, may
the LORD deal with me, be it ever so
severely, if I do not let you know and
send you away safely. May the LORD be
with you as he has been with my father.
14But show me unfailing kindness like
that of the LORD as long as I live, so that

I may not be killed, 15and do not ever
cut off your kindness from my family
—not even when the LORD has cut off
every one of David's enemies from the
face of the earth."
16So Jonathan made a covenant with
the house of David, saying, "May the
LORD call David's enemies to account."
17And Jonathan made David reaffirm
his oath out of love for him, because he
loved him as he loved himself.
18Then Jonathan said to David:
"Tomorrow is the New Moon festival.
You will be missed, because your seat
will be empty. 19The day after tomorrow, towards evening, go to the place
where you hid when this trouble began,
and wait by the stone Ezel. 20I will shoot
three arrows to the side of it, as though I
were shooting at a target. 21Then I will
send a boy and say, 'Go, find the
arrows.' If I say to him, 'Look, the
arrows are on this side of you; bring
them here,' then come, because, as
surely as the LORD lives, you are safe;
there is no danger. 22But if I say to the
boy, 'Look, the arrows are beyond
you,' then you must go, because the
LORD has sent you away. 23And about
the matter you and I discussed—
remember, the LORD is witness between
you and me for ever."
24So David hid in the field, and when
the New Moon festival came, the king
sat down to eat. 25He sat in his customary place by the wall, opposite
Jonathan, and Abner sat next to Saul,
but David's place was empty. 26Saul
said nothing that day, for he thought,
"Something must have happened to
David to make him ceremonially unclean—surely he is unclean." 27But the
next day, the second day of the month,
David's place was empty again. Then
Saul said to his son Jonathan, "Why
hasn't the son of Jesse come to the meal,
either yesterday or today?"
28Jonathan answered, "David
earnestly asked me for permission to go
to Bethlehem. 29He said, 'Let me go,
because our family is observing a sacrifice in the town and my brother has
ordered me to be there. If I have found
favour in your eyes, let me go to see my
brothers.' That is why he has not come
to the king's table."
30Saul's anger flared up at Jonathan
and he said to him, "You son of a
perverse and rebellious woman! Don't I
know that you have sided with the son
of Jesse to your own shame and to the
shame of the mother who bore you?
31As long as the son of Jesse lives on this
earth, neither you nor your kingdom
will be established. Now send and bring
him to me, for he must die!"
32"Why should he be put to death?
What has he done?" Jonathan asked his
father. 33But Saul hurled his spear at
him to kill him. Then Jonathan knew
that his father intended to kill David.
34Jonathan got up from the table in
fierce anger; on that second day of the
month he did not eat, because he was
grieved at his father's shameful treatment of David.
35In the morning Jonathan went out
to the field for his meeting with David.
He had a small boy with him, 36and he
said to the boy, "Run and find the
arrows I shoot." As the boy ran, he shot
an arrow beyond him. 37When the boy
came to the place where Jonathan's
arrow had fallen, Jonathan called out
after him, "Isn't the arrow beyond
you?" 38Then he shouted, "Hurry! Go
quickly! Don't stop!" The boy picked
up the arrow and returned to his master.
39(The boy knew nothing of all this; only
Jonathan and David knew.) 40Then
Jonathan gave his weapons to the boy
and said, "Go, carry them back to
town."
41After the boy had gone, David got
up from the south side ⌞of the stone⌟ and
bowed down before Jonathan three
times, with his face to the ground. Then
they kissed each other and wept
together—but David wept the most.
42Jonathan said to David, "Go in
peace, for we have sworn friendship
with each other in the name of the
LORD, saying, 'The LORD is witness between you and me, and between your

descendants and my descendants for
ever.'" Then David left, and Jonathan
went back to the town.

NEW TESTAMENT READING
John 17:6–26

Jesus Prays for His Disciples

6"I have revealed you to those
whom you gave me out of the
world. They were yours; you gave
them to me and they have obeyed
your word. 7Now they know that
everything you have given me
comes from you. 8For I gave them
the words you gave me and they
accepted them. They knew with
certainty that I came from you, and
they believed that you sent me. 9I
pray for them. I am not praying for
the world, but for those you have
given me, for they are yours. 10All I
have is yours, and all you have is
mine. And glory has come to me
through them. 11I will remain in the
world no longer, but they are still in
the world, and I am coming to you.
Holy Father, protect them by the
power of your name—the name
you gave me—so that they may be
one as we are one. 12While I was
with them, I protected them and
kept them safe by that name you
gave me. None has been lost except
the one doomed to destruction so
that Scripture would be fulfilled.

13"I am coming to you now, but I
say these things while I am still in
the world, so that they may have
the full measure of my joy within
them. 14I have given them your
word and the world has hated
them, for they are not of the world
any more than I am of the world.
15My prayer is not that you take
them out of the world but that you
protect them from the evil one.
16They are not of the world, even as
I am not of it. 17Sanctify them by
the truth; your word is truth. 18As
you sent me into the world, I have
sent them into the world. 19For
them I sanctify myself, that they
too may be truly sanctified.

Jesus Prays for All Believers

20"My prayer is not for them
alone. I pray also for those who will
believe in me through their message, 21that all of them may be one,
Father, just as you are in me and I
am in you. May they also be in us so
that the world may believe that you
have sent me. 22I have given them
the glory that you gave me, that
they may be one as we are one: 23I
in them and you in me. May they be
brought to complete unity to let the
world know that you sent me and
have loved them even as you have
loved me.

24"Father, I want those you have
given me to be with me where I am,
and to see my glory, the glory you
have given me because you loved
me before the creation of the
world.

25"Righteous Father, though the
world does not know you, I know
you, and they know that you have
sent me. 26I have made you known
to them, and will continue to make
you known in order that the love
you have for me may be in them
and that I myself may be in them."

READING FROM PSALMS
Psalm 68:7–14

7When you went out before your
people, O God,
when you marched through the
wasteland, *Selah*
8the earth shook,
the heavens poured down rain,
before God, the One of Sinai,
before God, the God of Israel.
9You gave abundant showers,
O God;

you refreshed your weary
inheritance.
10Your people settled in it,
and from your bounty, O God, you
provided for the poor.

11The Lord announced the word,
and great was the company of
those who proclaimed it:
12"Kings and armies flee in haste;
in the camps men divide the
plunder.
13Even while you sleep among the
campfires,
the wings of ⌊my⌋ dove are
sheathed with silver,
its feathers with shining gold."
14When the Almighty scattered the
kings in the land,
it was like snow fallen on Zalmon.

MAY 28

DAY 148

OLD TESTAMENT READING

1 Samuel 21:1–23:29

David at Nob

21 David went to Nob, to Ahimelech the priest. Ahimelech
trembled when he met him, and asked,
"Why are you alone? Why is no-one
with you?"
2David answered Ahimelech the
priest, "The king charged me with a
certain matter and said to me, 'No-one
is to know anything about your mission
and your instructions.' As for my men, I
have told them to meet me at a certain
place. 3Now then, what have you to
hand? Give me five loaves of bread, or
whatever you can find."
4But the priest answered David, "I
don't have any ordinary bread to hand;
however, there is some consecrated
bread here—provided the men have
kept themselves from women."
5David replied, "Indeed women have
been kept from us, as usual whenever I
set out. The men's things are holy even
on missions that are not holy. How
much more so today!" 6So the priest
gave him the consecrated bread, since
there was no bread there except the
bread of the Presence that had been
removed from before the LORD and replaced by hot bread on the day it was
taken away.
7Now one of Saul's servants was there
that day, detained before the LORD; he
was Doeg the Edomite, Saul's head
shepherd.
8David asked Ahimelech, "Don't
you have a spear or sword here? I
haven't brought my sword or any other
weapon, because the king's business
was urgent."
9The priest replied, "The sword of
Goliath the Philistine, whom you killed
in the Valley of Elah, is here; it is wrapped in a cloth behind the ephod. If you
want it, take it; there is no sword here
but that one."
David said, "There is none like it;
give it to me."

David at Gath

10That day David fled from Saul and
went to Achish king of Gath. 11But the
servants of Achish said to him, "Isn't
this David, the king of the land? Isn't he
the one they sing about in their dances:

"'Saul has slain his thousands,
and David his tens of thousands'?"

12David took these words to heart
and was very much afraid of Achish
king of Gath. 13So he feigned insanity in
their presence; and while he was in their
hands he acted like a madman, making

marks on the doors of the gate and
letting saliva run down his beard.
[14]Achish said to his servants, "Look
at the man! He is insane! Why bring him
to me? [15]Am I so short of madmen that
you have to bring this fellow here to
carry on like this in front of me? Must
this man come into my house?"

David at Adullam and Mizpah

22 David left Gath and escaped to
the cave of Adullam. When his
brothers and his father's household
heard about it, they went down to him
there. [2]All those who were in distress or
in debt or discontented gathered round
him, and he became their leader. About
four hundred men were with him.
[3]From there David went to Mizpah in
Moab and said to the king of Moab,
"Would you let my father and mother
come and stay with you until I learn
what God will do for me?" [4]So he left
them with the king of Moab, and they
stayed with him as long as David was in
the stronghold.
[5]But the prophet Gad said to David,
"Do not stay in the stronghold. Go into
the land of Judah." So David left and
went to the forest of Hereth.

Saul Kills the Priests of Nob

[6]Now Saul heard that David and his
men had been discovered. And Saul,
spear in hand, was seated under the
tamarisk tree on the hill at Gibeah, with
all his officials standing round him.
[7]Saul said to them, "Listen, men of
Benjamin! Will the son of Jesse give all
of you fields and vineyards? Will he
make all of you commanders of
thousands and commanders of hundreds? [8]Is that why you have all conspired against me? No-one tells me
when my son makes a covenant with the
son of Jesse. None of you is concerned
about me or tells me that my son has
incited my servant to lie in wait for me,
as he does today."
[9]But Doeg the Edomite, who was
standing with Saul's officials, said, "I
saw the son of Jesse come to Ahimelech
son of Ahitub at Nob. [10]Ahimelech enquired of the LORD for him; he also gave
him provisions and the sword of Goliath
the Philistine."
[11]Then the king sent for the priest
Ahimelech son of Ahitub and his
father's whole family, who were the
priests at Nob, and they all came to the
king. [12]Saul said, "Listen now, son of
Ahitub."
"Yes, my lord," he answered.
[13]Saul said to him, "Why have you
conspired against me, you and the son
of Jesse, giving him bread and a sword
and enquiring of God for him, so that he
has rebelled against me and lies in wait
for me, as he does today?"
[14]Ahimelech answered the king,
"Who of all your servants is as loyal as
David, the king's son-in-law, captain of
your bodyguard and highly respected in
your household? [15]Was that day the first
time I enquired of God for him? Of
course not! Let not the king accuse your
servant or any of his father's family, for
your servant knows nothing at all about
this whole affair."
[16]But the king said, "You shall surely
die, Ahimelech, you and your father's
whole family."
[17]Then the king ordered the guards at
his side: "Turn and kill the priests of the
LORD, because they too have sided with
David. They knew he was fleeing, yet
they did not tell me."
But the king's officials were not willing to raise a hand to strike the priests of
the LORD.
[18]The king then ordered Doeg, "You
turn and strike down the priests." So
Doeg the Edomite turned and struck
them down. That day he killed eighty-
five men who wore the linen ephod.
[19]He also put to the sword Nob, the
town of the priests, with its men and
women, its children and infants, and its
cattle, donkeys and sheep.
[20]But Abiathar, son of Ahimelech
son of Ahitub, escaped and fled to join
David. [21]He told David that Saul had

killed the priests of the LORD. 22Then
David said to Abiathar: "That day,
when Doeg the Edomite was there, I
knew he would be sure to tell Saul. I am
responsible for the death of your
father's whole family. 23Stay with me;
don't be afraid; the man who is seeking
your life is seeking mine also. You will
be safe with me."

David Saves Keilah

23 When David was told, "Look,
the Philistines are fighting
against Keilah and are looting the
threshing-floors," 2he enquired of the
LORD, saying, "Shall I go and attack
these Philistines?"

The LORD answered him, "Go,
attack the Philistines and save Keilah."

3But David's men said to him, "Here
in Judah we are afraid. How much
more, then, if we go to Keilah against
the Philistine forces!"

4Once again David enquired of the
LORD, and the LORD answered him,
"Go down to Keilah, for I am going to
give the Philistines into your hand." 5So
David and his men went to Keilah,
fought the Philistines and carried off
their livestock. He inflicted heavy losses
on the Philistines and saved the people
of Keilah. 6(Now Abiathar son of
Ahimelech had brought the ephod
down with him when he fled to David at
Keilah.)

Saul Pursues David

7Saul was told that David had gone to
Keilah, and he said, "God has handed
him over to me, for David has imprisoned himself by entering a town with
gates and bars." 8And Saul called up all
his forces for battle, to go down to
Keilah to besiege David and his men.

9When David learned that Saul was
plotting against him, he said to
Abiathar the priest, "Bring the ephod."
10David said, "O LORD, God of Israel,
your servant has heard definitely that
Saul plans to come to Keilah and
destroy the town on account of me.
11Will the citizens of Keilah surrender
me to him? Will Saul come down, as
your servant has heard? O LORD, God
of Israel, tell your servant."

And the LORD said, "He will."

12Again David asked, "Will the
citizens of Keilah surrender me and my
men to Saul?"

And the LORD said, "They will."

13So David and his men, about six
hundred in number, left Keilah and
kept moving from place to place. When
Saul was told that David had escaped
from Keilah, he did not go there.

14David stayed in the desert strongholds and in the hills of the Desert of
Ziph. Day after day Saul searched for
him, but God did not give David into his
hands.

15While David was at Horesh in the
Desert of Ziph, he learned that Saul had
come out to take his life. 16And Saul's
son Jonathan went to David at Horesh
and helped him to find strength in God.
17"Don't be afraid," he said. "My
father Saul will not lay a hand on you.
You shall be king over Israel, and I will
be second to you. Even my father Saul
knows this." 18The two of them made a
covenant before the LORD. Then
Jonathan went home, but David remained at Horesh.

19The Ziphites went up to Saul at
Gibeah and said, "Is not David hiding
among us in the strongholds at Horesh,
on the hill of Hakilah, south of Jeshimon? 20Now, O king, come down
whenever it pleases you to do so, and we
will be responsible for handing him over
to the king."

21Saul replied, "The LORD bless you
for your concern for me. 22Go and make
further preparation. Find out where
David usually goes and who has seen
him there. They tell me he is very crafty.
23Find out about all the hiding-places he
uses and come back to me with definite
information. Then I will go with you; if
he is in the area, I will track him down
among all the clans of Judah."

24So they set out and went to Ziph

ahead of Saul. Now David and his men
were in the Desert of Maon, in the
Arabah south of Jeshimon. 25Saul and
his men began the search, and when
David was told about it, he went down
to the rock and stayed in the Desert of
Maon. When Saul heard this, he went
into the Desert of Maon in pursuit of
David.

26Saul was going along one side of the
mountain, and David and his men were
on the other side, hurrying to get away
from Saul. As Saul and his forces were
closing in on David and his men to
capture them, 27a messenger came to
Saul, saying, "Come quickly! The Philistines are raiding the land." 28Then
Saul broke off his pursuit of David and
went to meet the Philistines. That is why
they call this place Sela Hammahlekoth.
29And David went up from there and
lived in the strongholds of En Gedi.

NEW TESTAMENT READING
John 18:1–24

Jesus Arrested

18 When he had finished praying,
Jesus left with his disciples and
crossed the Kidron Valley. On the other
side there was an olive grove, and he
and his disciples went into it.

2Now Judas, who betrayed him,
knew the place, because Jesus had often
met there with his disciples. 3So Judas
came to the grove, guiding a detachment of soldiers and some officials from
the chief priests and Pharisees. They
were carrying torches, lanterns and
weapons.

4Jesus, knowing all that was going to
happen to him, went out and asked
them, "Who is it you want?"

5"Jesus of Nazareth," they replied.

"I am he," Jesus said. (And Judas the
traitor was standing there with them.)
6When Jesus said, "I am he," they drew
back and fell to the ground.

7Again he asked them, "Who is it you
want?"

And they said, "Jesus of Nazareth."

8"I told you that I am he," Jesus
answered. "If you are looking for me,
then let these men go." 9This happened
so that the words he had spoken would
be fulfilled: "I have not lost one of those
you gave me."

10Then Simon Peter, who had a
sword, drew it and struck the high
priest's servant, cutting off his right ear.
(The servant's name was Malchus.)

11Jesus commanded Peter, "Put your
sword away! Shall I not drink the cup
the Father has given me?"

Jesus Taken to Annas

12Then the detachment of soldiers
with its commander and the Jewish officials arrested Jesus. They bound him
13and brought him first to Annas, who
was the father-in-law of Caiaphas, the
high priest that year. 14Caiaphas was the
one who had advised the Jews that it
would be good if one man died for the
people.

Peter's First Denial

15Simon Peter and another disciple
were following Jesus. Because this disciple was known to the high priest, he
went with Jesus into the high priest's
courtyard, 16but Peter had to wait outside at the door. The other disciple, who
was known to the high priest, came
back, spoke to the girl on duty there and
brought Peter in.

17"You are not one of his disciples,
are you?" the girl at the door asked
Peter.

He replied, "I am not."

18It was cold, and the servants and
officials stood round a fire they had
made to keep warm. Peter also was
standing with them, warming himself.

The High Priest Questions Jesus

19Meanwhile, the high priest questioned Jesus about his disciples and his
teaching.

[20]"I have spoken openly to the world," Jesus replied. "I always taught in synagogues or at the temple, where all the Jews come together. I said nothing in secret. [21]Why question me? Ask those who heard me. Surely they know what I said."

[22]When Jesus said this, one of the officials near by struck him in the face. "Is this the way you answer the high priest?" he demanded.

[23]"If I said something wrong," Jesus replied, "testify as to what is wrong. But if I spoke the truth, why did you strike me?" [24]Then Annas sent him, still bound, to Caiaphas the high priest.

READING FROM PROVERBS
Proverbs 13:10–19

[10]Pride only breeds quarrels,
but wisdom is found in those who take advice.

[11]Dishonest money dwindles away,
but he who gathers money little by little makes it grow.

[12]Hope deferred makes the heart sick,
but a longing fulfilled is a tree of life.

[13]He who scorns instruction will pay for it,
but he who respects a command is rewarded.

[14]The teaching of the wise is a fountain of life,
turning a man from the snares of death.

[15]Good understanding wins favour,
but the way of the unfaithful is hard.

[16]Every prudent man acts out of knowledge,
but a fool exposes his folly.

[17]A wicked messenger falls into trouble,
but a trustworthy envoy brings healing.

[18]He who ignores discipline comes to poverty and shame,
but whoever heeds correction is honoured.

[19]A longing fulfilled is sweet to the soul,
but fools detest turning from evil.

MAY 29

DAY 149

OLD TESTAMENT READING
1 Samuel 24:1–25:44

David Spares Saul's Life

24 After Saul returned from pursuing the Philistines, he was told, "David is in the Desert of En Gedi."
[2]So Saul took three thousand chosen men from all Israel and set out to look for David and his men near the Crags of the Wild Goats.

[3]He came to the sheep pens along the way; a cave was there, and Saul went in to relieve himself. David and his men were far back in the cave.
[4]The men said, "This is the day the LORD spoke of when he said to you, 'I will give your enemy into your hands for you to deal with as you wish.'" Then David crept up unnoticed and cut off a corner of Saul's robe.

[5]Afterwards, David was conscience-stricken for having cut off a corner of his robe.
[6]He said to his men, "The LORD forbid that I should do such a thing to

my master, the LORD's anointed, or lift
my hand against him; for he is the
anointed of the LORD." 7With these
words David rebuked his men and did
not allow them to attack Saul. And Saul
left the cave and went his way.

8Then David went out of the cave and
called out to Saul, "My lord the king!"
When Saul looked behind him, David
bowed down and prostrated himself
with his face to the ground. 9He said to
Saul, "Why do you listen when men say,
'David is bent on harming you'? 10This
day you have seen with your own eyes
how the LORD gave you into my hands
in the cave. Some urged me to kill you,
but I spared you; I said, 'I will not lift my
hand against my master, because he is
the LORD's anointed.' 11See, my father,
look at this piece of your robe in my
hand! I cut off the corner of your robe
but did not kill you. Now understand
and recognise that I am not guilty of
wrongdoing or rebellion. I have not
wronged you, but you are hunting me
down to take my life. 12May the LORD
judge between you and me. And may
the LORD avenge the wrongs you have
done to me, but my hand will not touch
you. 13As the old saying goes, 'From
evildoers come evil deeds,' so my hand
will not touch you.

14"Against whom has the king of
Israel come out? Whom are you pursuing? A dead dog? A flea? 15May the
LORD be our judge and decide between
us. May he consider my cause and uphold it; may he vindicate me by delivering me from your hand."

16When David finished saying this,
Saul asked, "Is that your voice, David
my son?" And he wept aloud. 17"You
are more righteous than I," he said.
"You have treated me well, but I have
treated you badly. 18You have just now
told me of the good you did to me; the
LORD gave me into your hands, but you
did not kill me. 19When a man finds his
enemy, does he let him get away unharmed? May the LORD reward you
well for the way you treated me today.
20I know that you will surely be king and
that the kingdom of Israel will be established in your hands. 21Now swear to me
by the LORD that you will not cut off my
descendants or wipe out my name from
my father's family."

22So David gave his oath to Saul.
Then Saul returned home, but David
and his men went up to the stronghold.

David, Nabal and Abigail

25 Now Samuel died, and all Israel
assembled and mourned for
him; and they buried him at his home in
Ramah.

Then David moved down into the
Desert of Maon. 2A certain man in
Maon, who had property there at Carmel, was very wealthy. He had a
thousand goats and three thousand
sheep, which he was shearing in Carmel. 3His name was Nabal and his wife's
name was Abigail. She was an intelligent and beautiful woman, but her husband, a Calebite, was surly and mean in
his dealings.

4While David was in the desert, he
heard that Nabal was shearing sheep.
5So he sent ten young men and said to
them, "Go up to Nabal at Carmel and
greet him in my name. 6Say to him:
'Long life to you! Good health to you
and your household! And good health
to all that is yours!

7" 'Now I hear that it is sheep-
shearing time. When your shepherds
were with us, we did not ill-treat them,
and the whole time they were at Carmel
nothing of theirs was missing. 8Ask your
own servants and they will tell you.
Therefore be favourable towards my
young men, since we come at a festive
time. Please give your servants and your
son David whatever you can find for
them.' "

9When David's men arrived, they
gave Nabal this message in David's
name. Then they waited.

10Nabal answered David's servants,
"Who is this David? Who is this son of
Jesse? Many servants are breaking
away from their masters these days.

11Why should I take my bread and
water, and the meat I have slaughtered
for my shearers, and give it to men
coming from who knows where?"
12David's men turned round and went
back. When they arrived, they reported
every word. 13David said to his men,
"Put on your swords!" So they put on
their swords, and David put on his.
About four hundred men went up with
David, while two hundred stayed with
the supplies.
14One of the servants told Nabal's
wife Abigail: "David sent messengers
from the desert to give our master his
greetings, but he hurled insults at them.
15Yet these men were very good to us.
They did not ill-treat us, and the whole
time we were out in the fields near them
nothing was missing. 16Night and day
they were a wall around us all the time
we were herding our sheep near them.
17Now think it over and see what you
can do, because disaster is hanging over
our master and his whole household.
He is such a wicked man that no-one can
talk to him."
18Abigail lost no time. She took two
hundred loaves of bread, two skins of
wine, five dressed sheep, five seahs of
roasted grain, a hundred cakes of raisins
and two hundred cakes of pressed figs,
and loaded them on donkeys. 19Then
she told her servants, "Go on ahead; I'll
follow you." But she did not tell her
husband Nabal.
20As she came riding her donkey into
a mountain ravine, there were David
and his men descending towards her,
and she met them. 21David had just
said, "It's been useless—all my watching over this fellow's property in the
desert so that nothing of his was missing. He has paid me back evil for good.
22May God deal with David, be it ever
so severely, if by morning I leave alive
one male of all who belong to him!"
23When Abigail saw David, she
quickly got off her donkey and bowed
down before David with her face to the
ground. 24She fell at his feet and said:
"My lord, let the blame be on me alone.
Please let your servant speak to you;
hear what your servant has to say.
25May my lord pay no attention to that
wicked man Nabal. He is just like his
name—his name is Fool, and folly goes
with him. But as for me, your servant, I
did not see the men my master sent.
26"Now since the LORD has kept you,
my master, from bloodshed and from
avenging yourself with your own hands,
as surely as the LORD lives and as you
live, may your enemies and all who
intend to harm my master be like Nabal.
27And let this gift, which your servant
has brought to my master, be given to
the men who follow you. 28Please forgive your servant's offence, for the
LORD will certainly make a lasting
dynasty for my master, because he
fights the LORD's battles. Let no wrongdoing be found in you as long as you
live. 29Even though someone is pursuing you to take your life, the life of my
master will be bound securely in the
bundle of the living by the LORD your
God. But the lives of your enemies he
will hurl away as from the pocket of a
sling. 30When the LORD has done for my
master every good thing he promised
concerning him and has appointed him
leader over Israel, 31my master will not
have on his conscience the staggering
burden of needless bloodshed or of having avenged himself. And when the
LORD has brought my master success,
remember your servant."
32David said to Abigail, "Praise be to
the LORD, the God of Israel, who has
sent you today to meet me. 33May you
be blessed for your good judgment and
for keeping me from bloodshed this day
and from avenging myself with my own
hands. 34Otherwise, as surely as the
LORD, the God of Israel, lives, who has
kept me from harming you, if you had
not come quickly to meet me, not one
male belonging to Nabal would have
been left alive by daybreak."
35Then David accepted from her
hand what she had brought to him and
said, "Go home in peace. I have heard
your words and granted your request."

36When Abigail went to Nabal, he
was in the house holding a banquet like
that of a king. He was in high spirits and
very drunk. So she told him nothing
until daybreak. 37Then in the morning,
when Nabal was sober, his wife told him
all these things, and his heart failed him
and he became like a stone. 38About ten
days later, the LORD struck Nabal and
he died.
39When David heard that Nabal was
dead, he said, "Praise be to the LORD,
who has upheld my cause against Nabal
for treating me with contempt. He has
kept his servant from doing wrong and
has brought Nabal's wrongdoing down
on his own head."

Then David sent word to Abigail,
asking her to become his wife. 40His
servants went to Carmel and said to
Abigail, "David has sent us to you to
take you to become his wife."
41She bowed down with her face to
the ground and said, "Here is your
maidservant, ready to serve you and
wash the feet of my master's servants."
42Abigail quickly got on a donkey and,
attended by her five maids, went with
David's messengers and became his
wife. 43David had also married Ahinoam of Jezreel, and they both were his
wives. 44But Saul had given his daughter
Michal, David's wife, to Paltiel son of
Laish, who was from Gallim.

NEW TESTAMENT READING
John 18:25–40

Peter's Second and Third Denials

25As Simon Peter stood warming
himself, he was asked, "You are not
one of his disciples, are you?"

He denied it, saying, "I am not."
26One of the high priest's servants, a
relative of the man whose ear Peter had
cut off, challenged him, "Didn't I see
you with him in the olive grove?"
27Again Peter denied it, and at that
moment a cock began to crow.

Jesus Before Pilate

28Then the Jews led Jesus from
Caiaphas to the palace of the Roman
governor. By now it was early morning,
and to avoid ceremonial uncleanness
the Jews did not enter the palace; they
wanted to be able to eat the Passover.
29So Pilate came out to them and asked,
"What charges are you bringing against
this man?"
30"If he were not a criminal," they
replied, "we would not have handed
him over to you."
31Pilate said, "Take him yourselves
and judge him by your own law."

"But we have no right to execute
anyone," the Jews objected. 32This happened so that the words Jesus had
spoken indicating the kind of death he
was going to die would be fulfilled.
33Pilate then went back inside the
palace, summoned Jesus and asked
him, "Are you the king of the Jews?"
34"Is that your own idea," Jesus
asked, "or did others talk to you about
me?"
35"Am I a Jew?" Pilate replied. "It
was your people and your chief priests
who handed you over to me. What is it
you have done?"
36Jesus said, "My kingdom is not of
this world. If it were, my servants would
fight to prevent my arrest by the Jews.
But now my kingdom is from another
place."
37"You are a king, then!" said Pilate.

Jesus answered, "You are right in
saying I am a king. In fact, for this
reason I was born, and for this I came
into the world, to testify to the truth.
Everyone on the side of truth listens to
me."
38"What is truth?" Pilate asked. With
this he went out again to the Jews and
said, "I find no basis for a charge against
him. 39But it is your custom for me to
release to you one prisoner at the time
of the Passover. Do you want me to
release 'the king of the Jews'?"
40They shouted back, "No, not him!
Give us Barabbas!" Now Barabbas had
taken part in a rebellion.

READING FROM PSALMS
Psalm 68:15–20

15The mountains of Bashan are
majestic mountains;
rugged are the mountains of
Bashan.
16Why gaze in envy, O rugged
mountains,
at the mountain where God
chooses to reign,
where the LORD himself will dwell
for ever?
17The chariots of God are tens of
thousands
and thousands of thousands;
the Lord ⌊has come⌋ from Sinai
into his sanctuary.
18When you ascended on high,
you led captives in your train;
you received gifts from men,
even from the rebellious—
that you, O LORD God, might
dwell there.

19Praise be to the Lord, to God our
Saviour,
who daily bears our burdens.
Selah
20Our God is a God who saves;
from the Sovereign LORD comes
escape from death.

MAY 30

DAY 150

OLD TESTAMENT READING
1 Samuel 26:1–28:25

David Again Spares Saul's Life

26 The Ziphites went to Saul at
Gibeah and said, "Is not David
hiding on the hill of Hakilah, which
faces Jeshimon?"
2So Saul went down to the Desert of
Ziph, with his three thousand chosen
men of Israel, to search there for David.
3Saul made his camp beside the road on
the hill of Hakilah facing Jeshimon, but
David stayed in the desert. When he
saw that Saul had followed him there,
4he sent out scouts and learned that Saul
had definitely arrived.
5Then David set out and went to the
place where Saul had camped. He saw
where Saul and Abner son of Ner, the
commander of the army, had lain down.
Saul was lying inside the camp, with the
army encamped around him.
6David then asked Ahimelech the
Hittite and Abishai son of Zeruiah,
Joab's brother, "Who will go down into
the camp with me to Saul?"
"I'll go with you," said Abishai.
7So David and Abishai went to the
army by night, and there was Saul, lying
asleep inside the camp with his spear
stuck in the ground near his head.
Abner and the soldiers were lying round
him.
8Abishai said to David, "Today God
has given your enemy into your hands.
Now let me pin him to the ground with
one thrust of my spear; I won't strike
him twice."
9But David said to Abishai, "Don't
destroy him! Who can lay a hand on the
LORD's anointed and be guiltless? 10As
surely as the LORD lives," he said, "the
LORD himself will strike him; either his
time will come and he will die, or he will
go into battle and perish. 11But the
LORD forbid that I should lay a hand on
the LORD's anointed. Now get the spear
and water jug that are near his head,
and let's go."
12So David took the spear and water
jug near Saul's head, and they left. No-
one saw or knew about it, nor did anyone wake up. They were all sleeping,
because the LORD had put them into a
deep sleep.

13 Then David crossed over to the other side and stood on top of the hill some distance away; there was a wide space between them. 14 He called out to the army and to Abner son of Ner, "Aren't you going to answer me, Abner?"

Abner replied, "Who are you who calls to the king?"

15 David said, "You're a man, aren't you? And who is like you in Israel? Why didn't you guard your lord the king? Someone came to destroy your lord the king. 16 What you have done is not good. As surely as the LORD lives, you and your men deserve to die, because you did not guard your master, the LORD's anointed. Look around you. Where are the king's spear and water jug that were near his head?"

17 Saul recognised David's voice and said, "Is that your voice, David my son?"

David replied, "Yes it is, my lord the king." 18 And he added, "Why is my lord pursuing his servant? What have I done, and what wrong am I guilty of? 19 Now let my lord the king listen to his servant's words. If the LORD has incited you against me, then may he accept an offering. If, however, men have done it, may they be cursed before the LORD! They have now driven me from my share in the LORD's inheritance and have said, 'Go, serve other gods.' 20 Now do not let my blood fall to the ground far from the presence of the LORD. The king of Israel has come out to look for a flea—as one hunts a partridge in the mountains."

21 Then Saul said, "I have sinned. Come back, David my son. Because you considered my life precious today, I will not try to harm you again. Surely I have acted like a fool and have erred greatly."

22 "Here is the king's spear," David answered. "Let one of your young men come over and get it. 23 The LORD rewards every man for his righteousness and faithfulness. The LORD gave you into my hands today, but I would not lay a hand on the LORD's anointed. 24 As surely as I valued your life today, so may the LORD value my life and deliver me from all trouble."

25 Then Saul said to David, "May you be blessed, my son David; you will do great things and surely triumph."

So David went on his way, and Saul returned home.

David Among the Philistines

27 But David thought to himself, "One of these days I shall be destroyed by the hand of Saul. The best thing I can do is to escape to the land of the Philistines. Then Saul will give up searching for me anywhere in Israel, and I will slip out of his hand."

2 So David and the six hundred men with him left and went over to Achish son of Maoch king of Gath. 3 David and his men settled in Gath with Achish. Each man had his family with him, and David had his two wives: Ahinoam of Jezreel and Abigail of Carmel, the widow of Nabal. 4 When Saul was told that David had fled to Gath, he no longer searched for him.

5 Then David said to Achish, "If I have found favour in your eyes, let a place be assigned to me in one of the country towns, that I may live there. Why should your servant live in the royal city with you?"

6 So on that day Achish gave him Ziklag, and it has belonged to the kings of Judah ever since. 7 David lived in Philistine territory for a year and four months.

8 Now David and his men went up and raided the Geshurites, the Girzites and the Amalekites. (From ancient times these peoples had lived in the land extending to Shur and Egypt.) 9 Whenever David attacked an area, he did not leave a man or woman alive, but took sheep and cattle, donkeys and camels, and clothes. Then he returned to Achish.

10 When Achish asked, "Where did you go raiding today?" David would say, "Against the Negev of Judah" or

"Against the Negev of Jerahmeel" or
"Against the Negev of the Kenites."
11He did not leave a man or woman
alive to be brought to Gath, for he
thought, "They might inform on us and
say, 'This is what David did.'" And
such was his practice as long as he lived
in Philistine territory. 12Achish trusted
David and said to himself, "He has
become so odious to his people, the
Israelites, that he will be my servant for
ever."

Saul and the Witch of Endor

28 In those days the Philistines
gathered their forces to fight
against Israel. Achish said to David,
"You must understand that you and
your men will accompany me in the
army."

2David said, "Then you will see for
yourself what your servant can do."

Achish replied, "Very well, I will
make you my bodyguard for life."

3Now Samuel was dead, and all Israel
had mourned for him and buried him in
his own town of Ramah. Saul had expelled the mediums and spiritists from the
land.

4The Philistines assembled and came
and set up camp at Shunem, while Saul
gathered all the Israelites and set up
camp at Gilboa. 5When Saul saw the
Philistine army, he was afraid; terror
filled his heart. 6He enquired of the
LORD, but the LORD did not answer him
by dreams or Urim or prophets. 7Saul
then said to his attendants, "Find me a
woman who is a medium, so that I may
go and enquire of her."

"There is one in Endor," they said.

8So Saul disguised himself, putting on
other clothes, and at night he and two
men went to the woman. "Consult a
spirit for me," he said, "and bring up for
me the one I name."

9But the woman said to him, "Surely
you know what Saul has done. He has
cut off the mediums and spiritists from
the land. Why have you set a trap for my
life to bring about my death?"

10Saul swore to her by the LORD, "As
surely as the LORD lives, you will not be
punished for this."

11Then the woman asked, "Whom
shall I bring up for you?"

"Bring up Samuel," he said.

12When the woman saw Samuel, she
cried out at the top of her voice and said
to Saul, "Why have you deceived me?
You are Saul!"

13The king said to her, "Don't be
afraid. What do you see?"

The woman said, "I see a spirit coming up out of the ground."

14"What does he look like?" he
asked.

"An old man wearing a robe is coming up," she said.

Then Saul knew it was Samuel, and
he bowed down and prostrated himself
with his face to the ground.

15Samuel said to Saul, "Why have
you disturbed me by bringing me up?"

"I am in great distress," Saul said.
"The Philistines are fighting against me,
and God has turned away from me. He
no longer answers me, either by
prophets or by dreams. So I have called
on you to tell me what to do."

16Samuel said, "Why do you consult
me, now that the LORD has turned away
from you and become your enemy?
17The LORD has done what he predicted
through me. The LORD has torn the
kingdom out of your hands and given it
to one of your neighbours—to David.
18Because you did not obey the LORD or
carry out his fierce wrath against the
Amalekites, the LORD has done this to
you today. 19The LORD will hand over
both Israel and you to the Philistines,
and tomorrow you and your sons will be
with me. The LORD will also hand over
the army of Israel to the Philistines."

20Immediately Saul fell full length on
the ground, filled with fear because of
Samuel's words. His strength was gone,
for he had eaten nothing all that day and
night.

21When the woman came to Saul and
saw that he was greatly shaken, she
said, "Look, your maidservant has

obeyed you. I took my life in my hands and did what you told me to do. 22Now please listen to your servant and let me give you some food so that you may eat and have the strength to go on your way."

23He refused and said, "I will not eat."

But his men joined the woman in urging him, and he listened to them. He got up from the ground and sat on the couch.

24The woman had a fattened calf at the house, which she slaughtered at once. She took some flour, kneaded it and baked bread without yeast. 25Then she set it before Saul and his men, and they ate. That same night they got up and left.

NEW TESTAMENT READING
John 19:1–27

Jesus Sentenced to be Crucified

19 Then Pilate took Jesus and had him flogged. 2The soldiers twisted together a crown of thorns and put it on his head. They clothed him in a purple robe 3and went up to him again and again, saying, "Hail, king of the Jews!" And they struck him in the face.

4Once more Pilate came out and said to the Jews, "Look, I am bringing him out to you to let you know that I find no basis for a charge against him." 5When Jesus came out wearing the crown of thorns and the purple robe, Pilate said to them, "Here is the man!"

6As soon as the chief priests and their officials saw him, they shouted, "Crucify! Crucify!"

But Pilate answered, "You take him and crucify him. As for me, I find no basis for a charge against him."

7The Jews insisted, "We have a law, and according to that law he must die, because he claimed to be the Son of God."

8When Pilate heard this, he was even more afraid, 9and he went back inside the palace. "Where do you come from?" he asked Jesus, but Jesus gave him no answer. 10"Do you refuse to speak to me?" Pilate said. "Don't you realise I have power either to free you or to crucify you?"

11Jesus answered, "You would have no power over me if it were not given to you from above. Therefore the one who handed me over to you is guilty of a greater sin."

12From then on, Pilate tried to set Jesus free, but the Jews kept shouting, "If you let this man go, you are no friend of Caesar. Anyone who claims to be a king opposes Caesar."

13When Pilate heard this, he brought Jesus out and sat down on the judge's seat at a place known as the Stone Pavement (which in Aramaic is Gabbatha). 14It was the day of Preparation of Passover Week, about the sixth hour.

"Here is your king," Pilate said to the Jews.

15But they shouted, "Take him away! Take him away! Crucify him!"

"Shall I crucify your king?" Pilate asked.

"We have no king but Caesar," the chief priests answered.

16Finally Pilate handed him over to them to be crucified.

The Crucifixion

So the soldiers took charge of Jesus. 17Carrying his own cross, he went out to the place of the Skull (which in Aramaic is called Golgotha). 18Here they crucified him, and with him two others—one on each side and Jesus in the middle.

19Pilate had a notice prepared and fastened to the cross. It read: JESUS OF NAZARETH, THE KING OF THE JEWS. 20Many of the Jews read this sign, for the place where Jesus was crucified was near the city, and the sign was written in Aramaic, Latin and Greek. 21The chief priests of the Jews protested to Pilate, "Do not write 'The King of the Jews', but that this man claimed to be king of the Jews."

22Pilate answered, "What I have written, I have written."

23When the soldiers crucified Jesus, they took his clothes, dividing them into four shares, one for each of them, with the undergarment remaining. This garment was seamless, woven in one piece from top to bottom.

24"Let's not tear it," they said to one another. "Let's decide by lot who will get it."

This happened that the scripture might be fulfilled which said,

"They divided my garments among
them
and cast lots for my clothing."

So this is what the soldiers did.

25Near the cross of Jesus stood his
mother, his mother's sister, Mary the
wife of Clopas, and Mary Magdalene.
26When Jesus saw his mother there, and
the disciple whom he loved standing
near by, he said to his mother, "Dear
woman, here is your son," 27and to the
disciple, "Here is your mother." From
that time on, this disciple took her into
his home.

READING FROM PSALMS

Psalm 68:21–27

21Surely God will crush the heads of his
enemies,
the hairy crowns of those who go
on in their sins.
22The Lord says, "I will bring them
from Bashan;
I will bring them from the depths of
the sea,
23that you may plunge your feet in the
blood of your foes,
while the tongues of your dogs
have their share."

24Your procession has come into view,
O God,
the procession of my God and King
into the sanctuary.
25In front are the singers, after them
the musicians;
with them are the maidens playing
tambourines.
26Praise God in the great congregation;
praise the LORD in the assembly of
Israel.
27There is the little tribe of Benjamin,
leading them,
there the great throng of Judah's
princes,
and there the princes of Zebulun
and of Naphtali.

MAY 31

DAY 151

OLD TESTAMENT READING

1 Samuel 29:1–31:13

Achish Sends David Back to Ziklag

29 The Philistines gathered all their
forces at Aphek, and Israel
camped by the spring in Jezreel. 2As the
Philistine rulers marched with their
units of hundreds and thousands, David
and his men were marching at the rear
with Achish. 3The commanders of the
Philistines asked, "What about these
Hebrews?"

Achish replied, "Is this not David, who was an officer of Saul king of Israel? He has already been with me for over a year, and from the day he left Saul until now, I have found no fault in him."

4But the Philistine commanders were
angry with him and said, "Send the man
back, that he may return to the place
you assigned him. He must not go with

us into battle, or he will turn against us
during the fighting. How better could he
regain his master's favour than by
taking the heads of our own men? 5Isn't
this the David they sang about in their
dances:

"'Saul has slain his thousands,
and David his tens of thousands'?"

6So Achish called David and said to
him, "As surely as the LORD lives, you
have been reliable, and I would be
pleased to have you serve with me in the
army. From the day you came to me
until now, I have found no fault in you,
but the rulers don't approve of you.
7Turn back and go in peace; do nothing
to displease the Philistine rulers."
8"But what have I done?" asked
David. "What have you found against
your servant from the day I came to you
until now? Why can't I go and fight
against the enemies of my lord the
king?"
9Achish answered, "I know that you
have been as pleasing in my eyes as an
angel of God; nevertheless, the Philistine commanders have said, 'He must
not go up with us into battle.' 10Now get
up early, along with your master's servants who have come with you, and
leave in the morning as soon as it is
light."
11So David and his men got up early
in the morning to go back to the land of
the Philistines, and the Philistines went
up to Jezreel.

David Destroys the Amalekites

30 David and his men reached Ziklag on the third day. Now the
Amalekites had raided the Negev and
Ziklag. They had attacked Ziklag and
burned it, 2and had taken captive the
women and all who were in it, both
young and old. They killed none of
them, but carried them off as they went
on their way.
3When David and his men came to
Ziklag, they found it destroyed by fire
and their wives and sons and daughters
taken captive. 4So David and his men
wept aloud until they had no strength
left to weep. 5David's two wives had
been captured—Ahinoam of Jezreel
and Abigail, the widow of Nabal of
Carmel. 6David was greatly distressed
because the men were talking of stoning
him; each one was bitter in spirit because of his sons and daughters. But
David found strength in the LORD his
God.
7Then David said to Abiathar the
priest, the son of Ahimelech, "Bring me
the ephod." Abiathar brought it to him,
8and David enquired of the LORD,
"Shall I pursue this raiding party? Will I
overtake them?"
"Pursue them," he answered. "You
will certainly overtake them and succeed in the rescue."
9David and the six hundred men with
him came to the Besor Ravine, where
some stayed behind, 10for two hundred
men were too exhausted to cross the
ravine. But David and four hundred
men continued the pursuit.
11They found an Egyptian in a field
and brought him to David. They gave
him water to drink and food to eat
—12part of a cake of pressed figs and
two cakes of raisins. He ate and was
revived, for he had not eaten any food
or drunk any water for three days and
three nights.
13David asked him, "To whom do
you belong, and where do you come
from?"
He said, "I am an Egyptian, the slave
of an Amalekite. My master abandoned
me when I became ill three days ago.
14We raided the Negev of the Kerethites
and the territory belonging to Judah
and the Negev of Caleb. And we burned
Ziklag."
15David asked him, "Can you lead me
down to this raiding party?"
He answered, "Swear to me before
God that you will not kill me or hand me
over to my master, and I will take you
down to them."
16He led David down, and there they

were, scattered over the countryside,
eating, drinking and revelling because
of the great amount of plunder they had
taken from the land of the Philistines
and from Judah. 17David fought them
from dusk until the evening of the next
day, and none of them got away, except
four hundred young men who rode off
on camels and fled. 18David recovered
everything the Amalekites had taken,
including his two wives. 19Nothing was
missing: young or old, boy or girl, plunder or anything else they had taken.
David brought everything back. 20He
took all the flocks and herds, and his
men drove them ahead of the other
livestock, saying, "This is David's
plunder."

21Then David came to the two hundred men who had been too exhausted
to follow him and who were left behind
at the Besor Ravine. They came out to
meet David and the people with him.
As David and his men approached, he
greeted them. 22But all the evil men and
troublemakers among David's followers said, "Because they did not go out
with us, we will not share with them the
plunder we recovered. However, each
man may take his wife and children and
go."

23David replied, "No, my brothers,
you must not do that with what the
LORD has given us. He has protected us
and handed over to us the forces that
came against us. 24Who will listen to
what you say? The share of the man who
stayed with the supplies is to be the
same as that of him who went down to
the battle. All shall share alike."
25David made this a statute and ordinance for Israel from that day to this.

26When David arrived in Ziklag, he
sent some of the plunder to the elders of
Judah, who were his friends, saying,
"Here is a present for you from the
plunder of the LORD's enemies."

27He sent it to those who were in
Bethel, Ramoth Negev and Jattir; 28to
those in Aroer, Siphmoth, Eshtemoa
29and Racal; to those in the towns of the
Jerahmeelites and the Kenites; 30to
those in Hormah, Bor Ashan, Athach
31and Hebron; and to those in all the
other places where David and his men
had roamed.

Saul Takes His Life

31 Now the Philistines fought
against Israel; the Israelites fled
before them, and many fell slain on
Mount Gilboa. 2The Philistines pressed
hard after Saul and his sons, and they
killed his sons Jonathan, Abinadab and
Malki-Shua. 3The fighting grew fierce
around Saul, and when the archers
overtook him, they wounded him
critically.

4Saul said to his armour-bearer,
"Draw your sword and run me through,
or these uncircumcised fellows will
come and run me through and abuse
me."

But the armour-bearer was terrified
and would not do it; so Saul took his
own sword and fell on it. 5When the
armour-bearer saw that Saul was dead,
he too fell on his sword and died with
him. 6So Saul and his three sons and his
armour-bearer and all his men died
together that same day.

7When the Israelites along the valley
and those across the Jordan saw that the
Israelite army had fled and that Saul and
his sons had died, they abandoned their
towns and fled. And the Philistines
came and occupied them.

8The next day, when the Philistines
came to strip the dead, they found Saul
and his three sons fallen on Mount Gilboa. 9They cut off his head and stripped
off his armour, and they sent messengers throughout the land of the Philistines to proclaim the news in the temple
of their idols and among their people.
10They put his armour in the temple of
the Ashtoreths and fastened his body to
the wall of Beth Shan.

11When the people of Jabesh Gilead
heard of what the Philistines had done
to Saul, 12all their valiant men journeyed through the night to Beth Shan.
They took down the bodies of Saul and

his sons from the wall of Beth Shan and
went to Jabesh, where they burned
them. 13Then they took their bones and
buried them under a tamarisk tree at
Jabesh, and they fasted seven days.

NEW TESTAMENT READING

John 19:28–20:9

The Death of Jesus

28Later, knowing that all was now
completed, and so that the Scripture
would be fulfilled, Jesus said, "I am
thirsty." 29A jar of wine vinegar was
there, so they soaked a sponge in it, put
the sponge on a stalk of the hyssop
plant, and lifted it to Jesus' lips. 30When
he had received the drink, Jesus said,
"It is finished." With that, he bowed his
head and gave up his spirit.

31Now it was the day of Preparation,
and the next day was to be a special
Sabbath. Because the Jews did not want
the bodies left on the crosses during the
Sabbath, they asked Pilate to have the
legs broken and the bodies taken down.
32The soldiers therefore came and
broke the legs of the first man who had
been crucified with Jesus, and then
those of the other. 33But when they
came to Jesus and found that he was
already dead, they did not break his
legs. 34Instead, one of the soldiers
pierced Jesus' side with a spear, bringing a sudden flow of blood and water.
35The man who saw it has given testimony, and his testimony is true. He
knows that he tells the truth, and he
testifies so that you also may believe.
36These things happened so that the
scripture would be fulfilled: "Not one of
his bones will be broken," 37and, as
another scripture says, "They will look
on the one they have pierced."

The Burial of Jesus

38Later, Joseph of Arimathea asked
Pilate for the body of Jesus. Now
Joseph was a disciple of Jesus, but
secretly because he feared the Jews.
With Pilate's permission, he came and
took the body away. 39He was accompanied by Nicodemus, the man who
earlier had visited Jesus at night.
Nicodemus brought a mixture of myrrh
and aloes, about seventy-five pounds.
40Taking Jesus' body, the two of them
wrapped it, with the spices, in strips of
linen. This was in accordance with Jewish burial customs. 41At the place where
Jesus was crucified, there was a garden,
and in the garden a new tomb, in which
no-one had ever been laid. 42Because it
was the Jewish day of Preparation and
since the tomb was near by, they laid
Jesus there.

The Empty Tomb

20 Early on the first day of the
week, while it was still dark,
Mary Magdalene went to the tomb and
saw that the stone had been removed
from the entrance. 2So she came running to Simon Peter and the other disciple, the one Jesus loved, and said,
"They have taken the Lord out of the
tomb, and we don't know where they
have put him!"

3So Peter and the other disciple
started for the tomb. 4Both were running, but the other disciple outran Peter
and reached the tomb first. 5He bent
over and looked in at the strips of linen
lying there but did not go in. 6Then
Simon Peter, who was behind him,
arrived and went into the tomb. He saw
the strips of linen lying there, 7as well as
the burial cloth that had been around
Jesus' head. The cloth was folded up by
itself, separate from the linen. 8Finally
the other disciple, who had reached the
tomb first, also went inside. He saw and
believed. 9(They still did not understand from Scripture that Jesus had to
rise from the dead.)

READING FROM PSALMS

Psalm 68:28–35

28Summon your power, O God;
show us your strength, O God, as
you have done before.

29Because of your temple at Jerusalem
kings will bring you gifts.
30Rebuke the beast among the reeds,
the herd of bulls among the calves
of the nations.
Humbled, may it bring bars of silver.
Scatter the nations who delight in
war.
31Envoys will come from Egypt;
Cush will submit herself to God.

32Sing to God, O kingdoms of the
earth,
sing praise to the Lord, *Selah*
33to him who rides the ancient skies
above,
who thunders with mighty voice.
34Proclaim the power of God,
whose majesty is over Israel,
whose power is in the skies.
35You are awesome, O God, in your
sanctuary;
the God of Israel gives power and
strength to his people.

Praise be to God!

JUNE 1

DAY 152

OLD TESTAMENT READING
2 Samuel 1:1–2:7

David Hears of Saul's Death

1 After the death of Saul, David returned from defeating the Amalekites and stayed in Ziklag two days.
2On the third day a man arrived from Saul's camp, with his clothes torn and with dust on his head. When he came to David, he fell to the ground to pay him honour.

3"Where have you come from?" David asked him.

He answered, "I have escaped from the Israelite camp."

4"What happened?" David asked. "Tell me."

He said, "The men fled from the battle. Many of them fell and died. And Saul and his son Jonathan are dead."

5Then David said to the young man who brought him the report, "How do you know that Saul and his son Jonathan are dead?"

6"I happened to be on Mount Gilboa," the young man said, "and there was Saul, leaning on his spear, with the chariots and riders almost upon him.
7When he turned round and saw me, he called out to me, and I said, 'What can I do?'

8"He asked me, 'Who are you?'

" 'An Amalekite,' I answered.

9"Then he said to me, 'Stand over me and kill me! I am in the throes of death, but I'm still alive.'

10"So I stood over him and killed him, because I knew that after he had fallen he could not survive. And I took the crown that was on his head and the band on his arm and have brought them here to my lord."

11Then David and all the men with him took hold of their clothes and tore them.
12They mourned and wept and fasted till evening for Saul and his son Jonathan, and for the army of the LORD and the house of Israel, because they had fallen by the sword.

13David said to the young man who brought him the report, "Where are you from?"

"I am the son of an alien, an Amalekite," he answered.

14David asked him, "Why were you not afraid to lift your hand to destroy the LORD's anointed?"

15Then David called one of his men and said, "Go, strike him down!" So he struck him down, and he died.
16For

David had said to him, "Your blood be on your own head. Your own mouth testified against you when you said, 'I killed the LORD's anointed.'"

David's Lament for Saul and Jonathan

17David took up this lament concerning Saul and his son Jonathan, 18and ordered that the men of Judah be taught this lament of the bow (it is written in the Book of Jashar):

19"Your glory, O Israel, lies slain on
your heights.
How the mighty have fallen!

20"Tell it not in Gath,
proclaim it not in the streets of
Ashkelon,
lest the daughters of the Philistines
be glad,
lest the daughters of the
uncircumcised rejoice.

21"O mountains of Gilboa,
may you have neither dew nor
rain,
nor fields that yield offerings ⌞of
grain⌟.
For there the shield of the mighty
was defiled,
the shield of Saul—no longer
rubbed with oil.
22From the blood of the slain,
from the flesh of the mighty,
the bow of Jonathan did not turn
back,
the sword of Saul did not return
unsatisfied.

23"Saul and Jonathan—
in life they were loved and
gracious,
and in death they were not
parted.
They were swifter than eagles,
they were stronger than lions.

24"O daughters of Israel,
weep for Saul,
who clothed you in scarlet and
finery,
who adorned your garments with
ornaments of gold.

25"How the mighty have fallen in
battle!
Jonathan lies slain on your
heights.
26I grieve for you, Jonathan my
brother;
you were very dear to me.
Your love for me was wonderful,
more wonderful than that of
women.

27"How the mighty have fallen!
The weapons of war have
perished!"

David Anointed King Over Judah

2 In the course of time, David enquired of the LORD. "Shall I go up to one of the towns of Judah?" he asked.

The LORD said, "Go up."

David asked, "Where shall I go?"

"To Hebron," the LORD answered.

2So David went up there with his two wives, Ahinoam of Jezreel and Abigail, the widow of Nabal of Carmel. 3David
also took the men who were with him, each with his family, and they settled in Hebron and its towns. 4Then the men of
Judah came to Hebron and there they anointed David king over the house of Judah.

When David was told that it was the men of Jabesh Gilead who had buried Saul, 5he sent messengers to the men of
Jabesh Gilead to say to them, "The LORD bless you for showing this kindness to Saul your master by burying
him. 6May the LORD now show you kindness and faithfulness, and I too will show you the same favour because you
have done this. 7Now then, be strong and brave, for Saul your master is dead, and the house of Judah has anointed me king over them."

NEW TESTAMENT READING
John 20:10–31

Jesus Appears to Mary Magdalene

10Then the disciples went back to
their homes, 11but Mary stood outside
the tomb crying. As she wept, she bent
over to look into the tomb 12and saw
two angels in white, seated where Jesus'
body had been, one at the head and the
other at the foot.
13They asked her, "Woman, why are
you crying?"
"They have taken my Lord away,"
she said, "and I don't know where they
have put him." 14At this, she turned
round and saw Jesus standing there, but
she did not realise that it was Jesus.
15"Woman," he said, "why are you
crying? Who is it you are looking for?"
Thinking he was the gardener, she
said, "Sir, if you have carried him away,
tell me where you have put him, and I
will get him."
16Jesus said to her, "Mary."
She turned towards him and cried out
in Aramaic, "Rabboni!" (which means
Teacher).
17Jesus said, "Do not hold on to me,
for I have not yet returned to the
Father. Go instead to my brothers and
tell them, 'I am returning to my Father
and your Father, to my God and your
God.'"
18Mary Magdalene went to the disciples with the news: "I have seen the
Lord!" And she told them that he had
said these things to her.

Jesus Appears to His Disciples

19On the evening of that first day of
the week, when the disciples were
together, with the doors locked for fear
of the Jews, Jesus came and stood
among them and said, "Peace be with
you!" 20After he said this, he showed
them his hands and side. The disciples
were overjoyed when they saw the
Lord.
21Again Jesus said, "Peace be with
you! As the Father has sent me, I am
sending you." 22And with that he
breathed on them and said, "Receive
the Holy Spirit. 23If you forgive anyone
his sins, they are forgiven; if you do not
forgive them, they are not forgiven."

Jesus Appears to Thomas

24Now Thomas (called Didymus),
one of the Twelve, was not with the
disciples when Jesus came. 25So the
other disciples told him, "We have seen
the Lord!"
But he said to them, "Unless I see the
nail marks in his hands and put my
finger where the nails were, and put my
hand into his side, I will not believe it."
26A week later his disciples were in
the house again, and Thomas was with
them. Though the doors were locked,
Jesus came and stood among them and
said, "Peace be with you!" 27Then he
said to Thomas, "Put your finger here;
see my hands. Reach out your hand and
put it into my side. Stop doubting and
believe."
28Thomas said to him, "My Lord and
my God!"
29Then Jesus told him, "Because you
have seen me, you have believed;
blessed are those who have not seen and
yet have believed."
30Jesus did many other miraculous
signs in the presence of his disciples,
which are not recorded in this book.
31But these are written that you may
believe that Jesus is the Christ, the Son
of God, and that by believing you may
have life in his name.

READING FROM PROVERBS
Proverbs 13:20–14:4

20He who walks with the wise grows
wise,
but a companion of fools suffers
harm.

21Misfortune pursues the sinner,
but prosperity is the reward of the
righteous.

22A good man leaves an inheritance for
his children's children,
but a sinner's wealth is stored up
for the righteous.

23A poor man's field may produce
abundant food,
but injustice sweeps it away.

24He who spares the rod hates his son,
but he who loves him is careful to
discipline him.

25The righteous eat to their hearts'
content,
but the stomach of the wicked goes
hungry.

14 The wise woman builds her
house,
but with her own hands the foolish
one tears hers down.

2He whose walk is upright fears the
LORD,
but he whose ways are devious
despises him.

3A fool's talk brings a rod to his back,
but the lips of the wise protect
them.

4Where there are no oxen, the manger
is empty,
but from the strength of an ox
comes an abundant harvest.

DAY 153

JUNE 2

OLD TESTAMENT READING
2 Samuel 2:8–3:21

War Between the Houses of David and Saul

8Meanwhile, Abner son of Ner, the
commander of Saul's army, had taken
Ish-Bosheth son of Saul and brought
him over to Mahanaim. 9He made him
king over Gilead, Ashuri and Jezreel,
and also over Ephraim, Benjamin and
all Israel.
10Ish-Bosheth son of Saul was forty
years old when he became king over
Israel, and he reigned two years. The
house of Judah, however, followed
David. 11The length of time David was
king in Hebron over the house of Judah
was seven years and six months.
12Abner son of Ner, together with the
men of Ish-Bosheth son of Saul, left
Mahanaim and went to Gibeon. 13Joab
son of Zeruiah and David's men went
out and met them at the pool of Gibeon.
One group sat down on one side of the
pool and one group on the other side.
14Then Abner said to Joab, "Let's
have some of the young men get up and
fight hand to hand in front of us."
"All right, let them do it," Joab said.
15So they stood up and were counted
off—twelve men for Benjamin and Ish-
Bosheth son of Saul, and twelve for
David. 16Then each man grabbed his
opponent by the head and thrust his
dagger into his opponent's side, and
they fell down together. So that place in
Gibeon was called Helkath Hazzurim.
17The battle that day was very fierce,
and Abner and the men of Israel were
defeated by David's men.
18The three sons of Zeruiah were
there: Joab, Abishai and Asahel. Now
Asahel was as fleet-footed as a wild
gazelle. 19He chased Abner, turning
neither to the right nor to the left as
he pursued him. 20Abner looked
behind him and asked, "Is that you,
Asahel?"
"It is," he answered.
21Then Abner said to him, "Turn
aside to the right or to the left; take on
one of the young men and strip him of

his weapons." But Asahel would not
stop chasing him.
22Again Abner warned Asahel, "Stop chasing me! Why should I strike you down? How could I look your brother Joab in the face?"
23But Asahel refused to give up the pursuit; so Abner thrust the butt of his spear into Asahel's stomach, and the spear came out through his back. He fell there and died on the spot. And every man stopped when he came to the place where Asahel had fallen and died.
24But Joab and Abishai pursued Abner, and as the sun was setting, they came to the hill of Ammah, near Giah on the way to the wasteland of Gibeon.
25Then the men of Benjamin rallied behind Abner. They formed themselves into a group and took their stand on top of a hill.
26Abner called out to Joab, "Must the sword devour for ever? Don't you realise that this will end in bitterness? How long before you order your men to stop pursuing their brothers?"
27Joab answered, "As surely as God lives, if you had not spoken, the men would have continued the pursuit of their brothers until morning."
28So Joab blew the trumpet, and all the men came to a halt; they no longer pursued Israel, nor did they fight any more.
29All that night Abner and his men marched through the Arabah. They crossed the Jordan, continued through the whole Bithron and came to Mahanaim.
30Then Joab returned from pursuing Abner and assembled all his men. Besides Asahel, nineteen of David's men
were found missing. 31But David's men had killed 360 Benjamites who were
with Abner. 32They took Asahel and buried him in his father's tomb at Bethlehem. Then Joab and his men marched all night and arrived at Hebron by daybreak.

3 The war between the house of Saul and the house of David lasted a long time. David grew stronger and stronger, while the house of Saul grew weaker and weaker.
2Sons were born to David in Hebron:
His firstborn was Amnon the son of Ahinoam of Jezreel;
3his second, Kileab the son of Abigail the widow of Nabal of Carmel;
the third, Absalom the son of Maacah daughter of Talmai king of Geshur;
4the fourth, Adonijah the son of Haggith;
the fifth, Shephatiah the son of Abital;
5and the sixth, Ithream the son of David's wife Eglah.
These were born to David in Hebron.

Abner Goes Over to David

6During the war between the house of Saul and the house of David, Abner had been strengthening his own position in
the house of Saul. 7Now Saul had had a concubine named Rizpah daughter of Aiah. And Ish-Bosheth said to Abner, "Why did you sleep with my father's concubine?"
8Abner was very angry because of what Ish-Bosheth said and he answered, "Am I a dog's head—on Judah's side? This very day I am loyal to the house of your father Saul and to his family and friends. I haven't handed you over to David. Yet now you accuse me of an offence involving this woman!
9May God deal with Abner, be it ever so severely, if I do not do for David what the LORD promised him on oath 10and
transfer the kingdom from the house of Saul and establish David's throne over Israel and Judah from Dan to Beersheba." 11Ish-Bosheth did not dare to
say another word to Abner, because he was afraid of him.
12Then Abner sent messengers on his behalf to say to David, "Whose land is it? Make an agreement with me, and I

will help you bring all Israel over to
you."
13"Good," said David. "I will make
an agreement with you. But I demand
one thing of you: Do not come into my
presence unless you bring Michal
daughter of Saul when you come to see
me." 14Then David sent messengers to
Ish-Bosheth son of Saul, demanding,
"Give me my wife Michal, whom I betrothed to myself for the price of a
hundred Philistine foreskins."
15So Ish-Bosheth gave orders and had
her taken away from her husband Paltiel son of Laish. 16Her husband,
however, went with her, weeping behind her all the way to Bahurim. Then
Abner said to him, "Go back home!"
So he went back.
17Abner conferred with the elders of
Israel and said, "For some time you
have wanted to make David your king.
18Now do it! For the LORD promised
David, 'By my servant David I will rescue my people Israel from the hand of
the Philistines and from the hand of all
their enemies.' "
19Abner also spoke to the Benjamites
in person. Then he went to Hebron to
tell David everything that Israel and the
whole house of Benjamin wanted to do.
20When Abner, who had twenty men
with him, came to David at Hebron,
David prepared a feast for him and his
men. 21Then Abner said to David, "Let
me go at once and assemble all Israel for
my lord the king, so that they may make
a compact with you, and that you may
rule over all that your heart desires." So
David sent Abner away, and he went in
peace.

NEW TESTAMENT READING
John 21:1–25

Jesus and the Miraculous Catch of Fish

21 Afterwards Jesus appeared
again to his disciples, by the Sea
of Tiberias. It happened this way:
2Simon Peter, Thomas (called Didymus), Nathanael from Cana in Galilee,
the sons of Zebedee, and two other
disciples were together. 3"I'm going out
to fish," Simon Peter told them, and
they said, "We'll go with you." So they
went out and got into the boat, but that
night they caught nothing.
4Early in the morning, Jesus stood on
the shore, but the disciples did not
realise that it was Jesus.
5He called out to them, "Friends,
haven't you any fish?"
"No," they answered.
6He said, "Throw your net on the
right side of the boat and you will find
some." When they did, they were unable to haul the net in because of the
large number of fish.
7Then the disciple whom Jesus loved
said to Peter, "It is the Lord!" As soon
as Simon Peter heard him say, "It is the
Lord," he wrapped his outer garment
around him (for he had taken it off) and
jumped into the water. 8The other disciples followed in the boat, towing the
net full of fish, for they were not far
from shore, about a hundred yards.
9When they landed, they saw a fire of
burning coals there with fish on it, and
some bread.
10Jesus said to them, "Bring some of
the fish you have just caught."
11Simon Peter climbed aboard and
dragged the net ashore. It was full of
large fish, 153, but even with so many
the net was not torn. 12Jesus said to
them, "Come and have breakfast."
None of the disciples dared ask him,
"Who are you?" They knew it was the
Lord. 13Jesus came, took the bread and
gave it to them, and did the same with
the fish. 14This was now the third time
Jesus appeared to his disciples after he
was raised from the dead.

Jesus Reinstates Peter

15When they had finished eating,
Jesus said to Simon Peter, "Simon son
of John, do you truly love me more than
these?"
"Yes, Lord," he said, "you know that
I love you."
Jesus said, "Feed my lambs."

16 Again Jesus said, "Simon son of
John, do you truly love me?"
He answered, "Yes, Lord, you know
that I love you."
Jesus said, "Take care of my sheep."
17 The third time he said to him,
"Simon son of John, do you love me?"
Peter was hurt because Jesus asked
him the third time, "Do you love me?"
He said, "Lord, you know all things;
you know that I love you."
Jesus said, "Feed my sheep.
18 I
tell you the truth, when you were
younger you dressed yourself and went
where you wanted; but when you are
old you will stretch out your hands,
and someone else will dress you and
lead you where you do not want to
go."
19 Jesus said this to indicate the
kind of death by which Peter would
glorify God. Then he said to him,
"Follow me!"
20 Peter turned and saw that the disciple whom Jesus loved was following
them. (This was the one who had leaned
back against Jesus at the supper and had
said, "Lord, who is going to betray
you?")
21 When Peter saw him, he
asked, "Lord, what about him?"
22 Jesus answered, "If I want him to
remain alive until I return, what is that
to you? You must follow me."
23 Because of this, the rumour spread
among the brothers that this disciple
would not die. But Jesus did not say that
he would not die; he only said, "If I
want him to remain alive until I return,
what is that to you?"
24 This is the disciple who testifies to
these things and who wrote them down.
We know that his testimony is true.
25 Jesus did many other things as well.
If every one of them were written down,
I suppose that even the whole world
would not have room for the books that
would be written.

READING FROM PSALMS

Psalm 69:1–12

For the director of music. To ⌞the tune of⌟ "Lilies". Of David.

1 Save me, O God,
for the waters have come up to my neck.
2 I sink in the miry depths,
where there is no foothold.
I have come into the deep waters;
the floods engulf me.
3 I am worn out calling for help;
my throat is parched.
My eyes fail,
looking for my God.
4 Those who hate me without reason
outnumber the hairs of my head;
many are my enemies without cause,
those who seek to destroy me.
I am forced to restore
what I did not steal.

5 You know my folly, O God;
my guilt is not hidden from you.

6 May those who hope in you
not be disgraced because of me,
O Lord, the LORD Almighty;
may those who seek you
not be put to shame because of me,
O God of Israel.
7 For I endure scorn for your sake,
and shame covers my face.
8 I am a stranger to my brothers,
an alien to my own mother's sons;
9 for zeal for your house consumes me,
and the insults of those who insult you fall on me.
10 When I weep and fast,
I must endure scorn;
11 when I put on sackcloth,
people make sport of me.
12 Those who sit at the gate mock me,
and I am the song of the drunkards.

JUNE 3

OLD TESTAMENT READING
2 Samuel 3:22–5:5

Joab Murders Abner

22Just then David's men and Joab returned from a raid and brought with them a great deal of plunder. But Abner was no longer with David in Hebron, because David had sent him away, and he had gone in peace.
23When Joab and all the soldiers with him arrived, he was told that Abner son of Ner had come to the king and that the king had sent him away and that he had gone in peace.
24So Joab went to the king and said, "What have you done? Look, Abner came to you. Why did you let him go? Now he is gone!
25You know Abner son of Ner; he came to deceive you and observe your movements and find out everything you are doing."
26Joab then left David and sent messengers after Abner, and they brought him back from the well of Sirah. But David did not know it.
27Now when Abner returned to Hebron, Joab took him aside into the gateway, as though to speak with him privately. And there, to avenge the blood of his brother Asahel, Joab stabbed him in the stomach, and he died.
28Later, when David heard about this, he said, "I and my kingdom are for ever innocent before the LORD concerning the blood of Abner son of Ner.
29May his blood fall upon the head of Joab and upon all his father's house! May Joab's house never be without someone who has a running sore or leprosy or who leans on a crutch or who falls by the sword or who lacks food."
30(Joab and his brother Abishai murdered Abner because he had killed their brother Asahel in the battle of Gibeon.)
31Then David said to Joab and all the people with him, "Tear your clothes and put on sackcloth and walk in mourning in front of Abner." King David himself walked behind the bier.
32They buried Abner in Hebron, and the king wept aloud at Abner's tomb. All the people wept also.
33The king sang this lament for Abner:

"Should Abner have died as the
lawless die?
34 Your hands were not bound,
your feet were not fettered.
You fell as one falls before wicked
men."

And all the people wept over him again.
35Then they all came and urged David to eat something while it was still day; but David took an oath, saying, "May God deal with me, be it ever so severely, if I taste bread or anything else before the sun sets!"
36All the people took note and were pleased; indeed, everything the king did pleased them.
37So on that day all the people and all Israel knew that the king had no part in the murder of Abner son of Ner.
38Then the king said to his men, "Do you not realise that a prince and a great man has fallen in Israel this day?
39And today, though I am the anointed king, I am weak, and these sons of Zeruiah are too strong for me. May the LORD repay the evildoer according to his evil deeds!"

Ish-Bosheth Murdered

4 When Ish-Bosheth son of Saul heard that Abner had died in Hebron, he lost courage, and all Israel became alarmed.
2Now Saul's son had two men who were leaders of raiding bands. One was named Baanah and the other Recab; they were sons of Rimmon the Beerothite from the tribe of Benjamin

—Beeroth is considered part of Benjamin, 3because the people of Beeroth fled to Gittaim and have lived there as aliens to this day.

4(Jonathan son of Saul had a son who was lame in both feet. He was five years old when the news about Saul and Jonathan came from Jezreel. His nurse picked him up and fled, but as she hurried to leave, he fell and became crippled. His name was Mephibosheth.)

5Now Recab and Baanah, the sons of Rimmon the Beerothite, set out for the house of Ish-Bosheth, and they arrived there in the heat of the day while he was taking his noonday rest. 6They went into the inner part of the house as if to get some wheat, and they stabbed him in the stomach. Then Recab and his brother Baanah slipped away.

7They had gone into the house while he was lying on the bed in his bedroom. After they stabbed and killed him, they cut off his head. Taking it with them, they travelled all night by way of the Arabah. 8They brought the head of Ish-Bosheth to David at Hebron and said to the king, "Here is the head of Ish-Bosheth son of Saul, your enemy, who tried to take your life. This day the LORD has avenged my lord the king against Saul and his offspring."

9David answered Recab and his brother Baanah, the sons of Rimmon the Beerothite, "As surely as the LORD lives, who has delivered me out of all trouble, 10when a man told me, 'Saul is dead,' and thought he was bringing good news, I seized him and put him to death in Ziklag. That was the reward I gave him for his news! 11How much more—when wicked men have killed an innocent man in his own house and on his own bed—should I not now demand his blood from your hand and rid the earth of you!"

12So David gave an order to his men, and they killed them. They cut off their hands and feet and hung the bodies by the pool in Hebron. But they took the head of Ish-Bosheth and buried it in Abner's tomb at Hebron.

David Becomes King Over Israel

5 All the tribes of Israel came to David at Hebron and said, "We are your own flesh and blood. 2In the past, while Saul was king over us, you were the one who led Israel on their military campaigns. And the LORD said to you, 'You shall shepherd my people Israel, and you shall become their ruler.'"

3When all the elders of Israel had come to King David at Hebron, the king made a compact with them at Hebron before the LORD, and they anointed David king over Israel.

4David was thirty years old when he became king, and he reigned for forty years. 5In Hebron he reigned over Judah for seven years and six months, and in Jerusalem he reigned over all Israel and Judah for thirty-three years.

NEW TESTAMENT READING
Acts 1:1–22

Jesus Taken Up Into Heaven

1 In my former book, Theophilus, I wrote about all that Jesus began to do and to teach 2until the day he was taken up to heaven, after giving instructions through the Holy Spirit to the apostles he had chosen. 3After his suffering, he showed himself to these men and gave many convincing proofs that he was alive. He appeared to them over a period of forty days and spoke about the kingdom of God. 4On one occasion, while he was eating with them, he gave them this command: "Do not leave Jerusalem, but wait for the gift my Father promised, which you have heard me speak about. 5For John baptised with water, but in a few days you will be baptised with the Holy Spirit."

6So when they met together, they asked him, "Lord, are you at this time going to restore the kingdom to Israel?"

7He said to them: "It is not for you to know the times or dates the Father has set by his own authority. 8But you will receive power when the Holy Spirit comes on you; and you will be my witnesses in Jerusalem, and in all Judea and Samaria, and to the ends of the earth."

9After he said this, he was taken up
before their very eyes, and a cloud hid
him from their sight.

10They were looking intently up into
the sky as he was going, when suddenly
two men dressed in white stood beside
them. 11"Men of Galilee," they said,
"why do you stand here looking into the sky? This same Jesus, who has been taken from you into heaven, will come back in the same way you have seen him go into heaven."

Matthias Chosen to Replace Judas

12Then they returned to Jerusalem
from the hill called the Mount of Olives,
a Sabbath day's walk from the city.
13When they arrived, they went upstairs
to the room where they were staying. Those present were Peter, John, James and Andrew; Philip and Thomas, Bartholomew and Matthew; James son of Alphaeus and Simon the Zealot, and
Judas son of James. 14They all joined
together constantly in prayer, along with the women and Mary the mother of Jesus, and with his brothers.

15In those days Peter stood up among
the believers (a group numbering about
a hundred and twenty) 16and said,
"Brothers, the Scripture had to be fulfilled which the Holy Spirit spoke long ago through the mouth of David concerning Judas, who served as guide for
those who arrested Jesus—17he was
one of our number and shared in this ministry."

18(With the reward he got for his
wickedness, Judas bought a field; there he fell headlong, his body burst open and all his intestines spilled out.
19Everyone in Jerusalem heard about
this, so they called that field in their language Akeldama, that is, Field of Blood.)

20"For," said Peter, "it is written in
the Book of Psalms,

"'May his place be deserted;
let there be no-one to dwell in it,'

and,

"'May another take his place of
leadership.'

21Therefore it is necessary to choose
one of the men who have been with us the whole time the Lord Jesus went in
and out among us, 22beginning from
John's baptism to the time when Jesus was taken up from us. For one of these must become a witness with us of his resurrection."

READING FROM PSALMS

Psalm 69:13–28

13But I pray to you, O LORD,
in the time of your favour;
in your great love, O God,
answer me with your sure
salvation.
14Rescue me from the mire,
do not let me sink;
deliver me from those who hate me,
from the deep waters.
15Do not let the floodwaters engulf me
or the depths swallow me up
or the pit close its mouth over me.
16Answer me, O LORD, out of the
goodness of your love;
in your great mercy turn to me.
17Do not hide your face from your
servant;
answer me quickly, for I am in
trouble.
18Come near and rescue me;
redeem me because of my foes.

19You know how I am scorned,
disgraced and shamed;
all my enemies are before you.
20Scorn has broken my heart
and has left me helpless;
I looked for sympathy, but there was
none,
for comforters, but I found none.

21They put gall in my food
and gave me vinegar for my thirst.

22May the table set before them
become a snare;
may it become retribution and a
trap.
23May their eyes be darkened so that
they cannot see,
and their backs be bent for ever.
24Pour out your wrath on them;
let your fierce anger overtake
them.
25May their place be deserted;
let there be no-one to dwell in their
tents.
26For they persecute those you wound
and talk about the pain of those
you hurt.
27Charge them with crime upon crime;
do not let them share in your
salvation.
28May they be blotted out of the book
of life
and not be listed with the
righteous.

JUNE 4

DAY 155

OLD TESTAMENT READING
2 Samuel 5:6–6:23

David Conquers Jerusalem

6The king and his men marched to
Jerusalem to attack the Jebusites, who
lived there. The Jebusites said to David,
"You will not get in here; even the blind
and the lame can ward you off." They
thought, "David cannot get in here."
7Nevertheless, David captured the fortress of Zion, the City of David.
8On that day, David said, "Anyone
who conquers the Jebusites will have to
use the water shaft to reach those 'lame
and blind' who are David's enemies."
That is why they say, "The 'blind and
lame' will not enter the palace."
9David then took up residence in the
fortress and called it the City of David.
He built up the area around it, from the
supporting terraces inward. 10And he
became more and more powerful, because the LORD God Almighty was with
him.
11Now Hiram king of Tyre sent messengers to David, along with cedar logs
and carpenters and stonemasons, and
they built a palace for David. 12And
David knew that the LORD had established him as king over Israel and had
exalted his kingdom for the sake of his
people Israel.
13After he left Hebron, David took
more concubines and wives in Jerusalem, and more sons and daughters
were born to him. 14These are the
names of the children born to him there:
Shammua, Shobab, Nathan, Solomon,
15Ibhar, Elishua, Nepheg, Japhia,
16Elishama, Eliada and Eliphelet.

David Defeats the Philistines

17When the Philistines heard that
David had been anointed king over
Israel, they went up in full force to
search for him, but David heard about it
and went down to the stronghold.
18Now the Philistines had come and
spread out in the Valley of Rephaim;
19so David enquired of the LORD, "Shall
I go and attack the Philistines? Will you
hand them over to me?"
The LORD answered him, "Go, for I
will surely hand the Philistines over to
you."
20So David went to Baal Perazim, and
there he defeated them. He said, "As
waters break out, the LORD has broken
out against my enemies before me." So
that place was called Baal Perazim.
21The Philistines abandoned their idols

there, and David and his men carried them off.

22 Once more the Philistines came up and spread out in the Valley of Rephaim; 23 so David enquired of the LORD, and he answered, "Do not go straight up, but circle round behind them and attack them in front of the balsam trees. 24 As soon as you hear the sound of marching in the tops of the balsam trees, move quickly, because that will mean the LORD has gone out in front of you to strike the Philistine army." 25 So David did as the LORD commanded him, and he struck down the Philistines all the way from Gibeon to Gezer.

The Ark Brought to Jerusalem

6 David again brought together out of Israel chosen men, thirty thousand in all. 2 He and all his men set out from Baalah of Judah to bring up from there the ark of God, which is called by the Name, the name of the LORD Almighty, who is enthroned between the cherubim that are on the ark. 3 They set the ark of God on a new cart and brought it from the house of Abinadab, which was on the hill. Uzzah and Ahio, sons of Abinadab, were guiding the new cart 4 with the ark of God on it, and Ahio was walking in front of it. 5 David and the whole house of Israel were celebrating with all their might before the LORD, with songs and with harps, lyres, tambourines, sistrums and cymbals.

6 When they came to the threshing-floor of Nacon, Uzzah reached out and took hold of the ark of God, because the oxen stumbled. 7 The LORD's anger burned against Uzzah because of his irreverent act; therefore God struck him down and he died there beside the ark of God.

8 Then David was angry because the LORD's wrath had broken out against Uzzah, and to this day that place is called Perez Uzzah.

9 David was afraid of the LORD that day and said, "How can the ark of the LORD ever come to me?" 10 He was not willing to take the ark of the LORD to be with him in the City of David. Instead, he took it aside to the house of Obed-Edom the Gittite. 11 The ark of the LORD remained in the house of Obed-Edom the Gittite for three months, and the LORD blessed him and his entire household.

12 Now King David was told, "The LORD has blessed the household of Obed-Edom and everything he has, because of the ark of God." So David went down and brought up the ark of God from the house of Obed-Edom to the City of David with rejoicing. 13 When those who were carrying the ark of the LORD had taken six steps, he sacrificed a bull and a fattened calf. 14 David, wearing a linen ephod, danced before the LORD with all his might, 15 while he and the entire house of Israel brought up the ark of the LORD with shouts and the sound of trumpets.

16 As the ark of the LORD was entering the City of David, Michal daughter of Saul watched from a window. And when she saw King David leaping and dancing before the LORD, she despised him in her heart.

17 They brought the ark of the LORD and set it in its place inside the tent that David had pitched for it, and David sacrificed burnt offerings and fellowship offerings before the LORD. 18 After he had finished sacrificing the burnt offerings and fellowship offerings, he blessed the people in the name of the LORD Almighty. 19 Then he gave a loaf of bread, a cake of dates and a cake of raisins to each person in the whole crowd of Israelites, both men and women. And all the people went to their homes.

20 When David returned home to bless his household, Michal daughter of Saul came out to meet him and said, "How the king of Israel has distinguished himself today, disrobing in the sight of the slave girls of his servants as any vulgar fellow would."

21David said to Michal, "It was before the LORD, who chose me rather
than your father or anyone from his
house when he appointed me ruler over
the LORD's people Israel—I will celebrate before the LORD. 22I will become
even more undignified than this, and I
will be humiliated in my own eyes. But
by these slave girls you spoke of, I will
be held in honour."
23And Michal daughter of Saul had
no children to the day of her death.

NEW TESTAMENT READING

Acts 1:23–2:21

23So they proposed two men: Joseph
called Barsabbas (also known as Justus)
and Matthias. 24Then they prayed,
"Lord, you know everyone's heart.
Show us which of these two you have
chosen 25to take over this apostolic
ministry, which Judas left to go where
he belongs." 26Then they cast lots, and
the lot fell to Matthias; so he was added
to the eleven apostles.

The Holy Spirit Comes at Pentecost

2 When the day of Pentecost came,
they were all together in one place.
2Suddenly a sound like the blowing of a
violent wind came from heaven and
filled the whole house where they were
sitting. 3They saw what seemed to be
tongues of fire that separated and came
to rest on each of them. 4All of them
were filled with the Holy Spirit and
began to speak in other tongues as the
Spirit enabled them.
5Now there were staying in Jerusalem
God-fearing Jews from every nation
under heaven. 6When they heard this
sound, a crowd came together in be-
wilderment, because each one heard
them speaking in his own language.
7Utterly amazed, they asked: "Are not
all these men who are speaking Galileans? 8Then how is it that each of us
hears them in his own native language?
9Parthians, Medes and Elamites; residents of Mesopotamia, Judea and Cappadocia, Pontus and Asia, 10Phrygia
and Pamphylia, Egypt and the parts of
Libya near Cyrene; visitors from Rome
11(both Jews and converts to Judaism);
Cretans and Arabs—we hear them declaring the wonders of God in our own
tongues!" 12Amazed and perplexed,
they asked one another, "What does
this mean?"
13Some, however, made fun of them
and said, "They have had too much
wine."

Peter Addresses the Crowd

14Then Peter stood up with the
Eleven, raised his voice and addressed
the crowd: "Fellow Jews and all of you
who live in Jerusalem, let me explain
this to you; listen carefully to what I say.
15These men are not drunk, as you suppose. It's only nine in the morning!
16No, this is what was spoken by the
prophet Joel:

17" 'In the last days, God says,
I will pour out my Spirit on all
people.
Your sons and daughters will
prophesy,
your young men will see visions,
your old men will dream dreams.
18Even on my servants, both men and
women,
I will pour out my Spirit in those
days,
and they will prophesy.
19I will show wonders in the heaven
above
and signs on the earth below,
blood and fire and billows of
smoke.
20The sun will be turned to darkness
and the moon to blood
before the coming of the great and
glorious day of the Lord.
21And everyone who calls
on the name of the Lord will be
saved.'

READING FROM PSALMS
Psalm 69:29–36

29I am in pain and distress;
may your salvation, O God,
protect me.

30I will praise God's name in song
and glorify him with thanksgiving.
31This will please the LORD more than
an ox,
more than a bull with its horns and
hoofs.
32The poor will see and be glad—
you who seek God, may your
hearts live!
33The LORD hears the needy
and does not despise his captive
people.

34Let heaven and earth praise him,
the seas and all that move in
them,
35for God will save Zion
and rebuild the cities of Judah.
Then people will settle there and
possess it;
36 the children of his servants will
inherit it,
and those who love his name will
dwell there.

DAY 156

JUNE 5

OLD TESTAMENT READING
2 Samuel 7:1–8:18

God's Promise to David

7 After the king was settled in his
palace and the LORD had given him
rest from all his enemies around him,
2he said to Nathan the prophet, "Here I
am, living in a palace of cedar, while the
ark of God remains in a tent."
3Nathan replied to the king, "Whatever you have in mind, go ahead and do
it, for the LORD is with you."
4That night the word of the LORD
came to Nathan, saying:

5"Go and tell my servant David,
'This is what the LORD says: Are
you the one to build me a house to
dwell in? 6I have not dwelt in a
house from the day I brought the
Israelites up out of Egypt to this
day. I have been moving from
place to place with a tent as my
dwelling. 7Wherever I have moved
with all the Israelites, did I ever say
to any of their rulers whom I commanded to shepherd my people
Israel, "Why have you not built me
a house of cedar?"'
8"Now then, tell my servant
David, 'This is what the LORD
Almighty says: I took you from the
pasture and from following the
flock to be ruler over my people
Israel. 9I have been with you
wherever you have gone, and I
have cut off all your enemies from
before you. Now I will make your
name great, like the names of the
greatest men of the earth. 10And I
will provide a place for my people
Israel and will plant them so that
they can have a home of their
own and no longer be disturbed.
Wicked people shall not oppress
them any more, as they did at the
beginning 11and have done ever
since the time I appointed leaders
over my people Israel. I will
also give you rest from all your
enemies.
"'The LORD declares to you that
the LORD himself will establish a
house for you: 12When your days
are over and you rest with your

fathers, I will raise up your
offspring to succeed you, who will
come from your own body, and I
will establish his kingdom. 13He is
the one who will build a house for
my Name, and I will establish the
throne of his kingdom for ever. 14I
will be his father, and he shall be
my son. When he does wrong, I will
punish him with the rod of men,
with floggings inflicted by men.
15But my love will never be taken
away from him, as I took it away
from Saul, whom I removed from
before you. 16Your house and your
kingdom shall endure for ever
before me; your throne shall be
established for ever.' "

17Nathan reported to David all the
words of this entire revelation.

David's Prayer

18Then King David went in and sat
before the LORD, and he said:

"Who am I, O Sovereign LORD,
and what is my family, that you
have brought me this far? 19And as
if this were not enough in your
sight, O Sovereign LORD, you have
also spoken about the future of the
house of your servant. Is this your
usual way of dealing with man, O
Sovereign LORD?

20"What more can David say to
you? For you know your servant, O
Sovereign LORD. 21For the sake of
your word and according to your
will, you have done this great thing
and made it known to your servant.

22"How great you are, O
Sovereign LORD! There is no-one
like you, and there is no God but
you, as we have heard with our own
ears. 23And who is like your people
Israel—the one nation on earth
that God went out to redeem as a
people for himself, and to make a
name for himself, and to perform
great and awesome wonders by
driving out nations and their gods
from before your people, whom
you redeemed from Egypt? 24You
have established your people Israel
as your very own for ever, and you,
O LORD, have become their God.

25"And now, LORD God, keep
for ever the promise you have
made concerning your servant and
his house. Do as you promised,
26so that your name will be great
for ever. Then men will say, 'The
LORD Almighty is God over Israel!'
And the house of your servant
David will be established before
you.

27"O LORD Almighty, God of
Israel, you have revealed this to
your servant, saying, 'I will build a
house for you.' So your servant has
found courage to offer you this
prayer. 28O Sovereign LORD, you
are God! Your words are trustworthy, and you have promised
these good things to your servant.
29Now be pleased to bless the
house of your servant, that it may
continue for ever in your sight; for
you, O Sovereign LORD, have
spoken, and with your blessing the
house of your servant will be blessed for ever."

David's Victories

8 In the course of time, David defeated the Philistines and subdued
them, and he took Metheg Ammah
from the control of the Philistines.

2David also defeated the Moabites.
He made them lie down on the ground
and measured them off with a length of
cord. Every two lengths of them were
put to death, and the third length was
allowed to live. So the Moabites became subject to David and brought
tribute.

3Moreover, David fought Hadadezer
son of Rehob, king of Zobah, when
he went to restore his control along
the Euphrates River. 4David captured
a thousand of his chariots, seven
thousand charioteers and twenty

thousand foot soldiers. He hamstrung
all but a hundred of the chariot horses.
5When the Arameans of Damascus
came to help Hadadezer king of Zobah,
David struck down twenty-two
thousand of them. 6He put garrisons in
the Aramean kingdom of Damascus,
and the Arameans became subject to
him and brought tribute. The LORD
gave David victory wherever he went.
7David took the gold shields that belonged to the officers of Hadadezer and
brought them to Jerusalem. 8From Tebah and Berothai, towns that belonged
to Hadadezer, King David took a great
quantity of bronze.
9When Tou king of Hamath heard
that David had defeated the entire army
of Hadadezer, 10he sent his son Joram to
King David to greet him and congratulate him on his victory in battle over
Hadadezer, who had been at war with
Tou. Joram brought with him articles of
silver and gold and bronze.
11King David dedicated these articles
to the LORD, as he had done with the
silver and gold from all the nations he
had subdued: 12Edom and Moab, the
Ammonites and the Philistines, and
Amalek. He also dedicated the plunder
taken from Hadadezer son of Rehob,
king of Zobah.
13And David became famous after he
returned from striking down eighteen
thousand Edomites in the Valley of
Salt.
14He put garrisons throughout Edom,
and all the Edomites became subject to
David. The LORD gave David victory
wherever he went.

David's Officials

15David reigned over all Israel, doing
what was just and right for all his people. 16Joab son of Zeruiah was over the
army; Jehoshaphat son of Ahilud was
recorder; 17Zadok son of Ahitub and
Ahimelech son of Abiathar were
priests; Seraiah was secretary;
18Benaiah son of Jehoiada was over the
Kerethites and Pelethites; and David's
sons were royal advisers.

NEW TESTAMENT READING
Acts 2:22–47

22"Men of Israel, listen to this: Jesus
of Nazareth was a man accredited by
God to you by miracles, wonders and
signs, which God did among you
through him, as you yourselves know.
23This man was handed over to you by
God's set purpose and foreknowledge;
and you, with the help of wicked men,
put him to death by nailing him to the
cross. 24But God raised him from the
dead, freeing him from the agony of
death, because it was impossible for
death to keep its hold on him. 25David
said about him:

" 'I saw the Lord always before me.
Because he is at my right hand,
I will not be shaken.
26Therefore my heart is glad and my
tongue rejoices;
my body also will live in hope,
27because you will not abandon me to
the grave,
nor will you let your Holy One see
decay.
28You have made known to me the
paths of life;
you will fill me with joy in your
presence.'

29"Brothers, I can tell you confidently
that the patriarch David died and was
buried, and his tomb is here to this day.
30But he was a prophet and knew that
God had promised him on oath that he
would place one of his descendants on
his throne. 31Seeing what was ahead, he
spoke of the resurrection of the Christ,
that he was not abandoned to the grave,
nor did his body see decay. 32God has
raised this Jesus to life, and we are all
witnesses of the fact. 33Exalted to the
right hand of God, he has received from
the Father the promised Holy Spirit and
has poured out what you now see and
hear. 34For David did not ascend to
heaven, and yet he said,

" 'The Lord said to my Lord:
"Sit at my right hand

35until I make your enemies
a footstool for your feet." '

36"Therefore let all Israel be assured of this: God has made this Jesus, whom you crucified, both Lord and Christ."

37When the people heard this, they were cut to the heart and said to Peter and the other apostles, "Brothers, what shall we do?"

38Peter replied, "Repent and be baptised, every one of you, in the name of Jesus Christ for the forgiveness of your sins. And you will receive the gift of the Holy Spirit.
39The promise is for you and your children and for all who are far off—for all whom the Lord our God will call."

40With many other words he warned them; and he pleaded with them, "Save yourselves from this corrupt generation."
41Those who accepted his message were baptised, and about three thousand were added to their number that day.

The Fellowship of the Believers

42They devoted themselves to the apostles' teaching and to the fellowship, to the breaking of bread and to prayer.
43Everyone was filled with awe, and many wonders and miraculous signs were done by the apostles.
44All the believers were together and had everything in common.
45Selling their possessions and goods, they gave to anyone as he had need.
46Every day they continued to meet together in the temple courts. They broke bread in their homes and ate together with glad and sincere hearts,
47praising God and enjoying the favour of all the people. And the Lord added to their number daily those who were being saved.

READING FROM PROVERBS

Proverbs 14:5–14

5A truthful witness does not deceive,
but a false witness pours out lies.

6The mocker seeks wisdom and finds none,
but knowledge comes easily to the discerning.

7Stay away from a foolish man,
for you will not find knowledge on his lips.

8The wisdom of the prudent is to give thought to their ways,
but the folly of fools is deception.

9Fools mock at making amends for sin,
but goodwill is found among the upright.

10Each heart knows its own bitterness,
and no-one else can share its joy.

11The house of the wicked will be destroyed,
but the tent of the upright will flourish.

12There is a way that seems right to a man,
but in the end it leads to death.

13Even in laughter the heart may ache,
and joy may end in grief.

14The faithless will be fully repaid for their ways,
and the good man rewarded for his.

OLD TESTAMENT READING
2 Samuel 9:1–10:19

David and Mephibosheth

9 David asked, "Is there anyone still left of the house of Saul to whom I can show kindness for Jonathan's sake?"
2Now there was a servant of Saul's household named Ziba. They called him to appear before David, and the king said to him, "Are you Ziba?"
"Your servant," he replied.
3The king asked, "Is there no-one still left of the house of Saul to whom I can show God's kindness?"
Ziba answered the king, "There is still a son of Jonathan; he is crippled in both feet."
4"Where is he?" the king asked.
Ziba answered, "He is at the house of Makir son of Ammiel in Lo Debar."
5So King David had him brought from Lo Debar, from the house of Makir son of Ammiel.
6When Mephibosheth son of Jonathan, the son of Saul, came to David, he bowed down to pay him honour.
David said, "Mephibosheth!"
"Your servant," he replied.
7"Don't be afraid," David said to him, "for I will surely show you kindness for the sake of your father Jonathan. I will restore to you all the land that belonged to your grandfather Saul, and you will always eat at my table."
8Mephibosheth bowed down and said, "What is your servant, that you should notice a dead dog like me?"
9Then the king summoned Ziba, Saul's servant, and said to him, "I have given your master's grandson everything that belonged to Saul and his
family. 10You and your sons and your servants are to farm the land for him and bring in the crops, so that your master's grandson may be provided for. And Mephibosheth, grandson of your master, will always eat at my table." (Now Ziba had fifteen sons and twenty servants.)
11Then Ziba said to the king, "Your servant will do whatever my lord the king commands his servant to do." So Mephibosheth ate at David's table like one of the king's sons.
12Mephibosheth had a young son named Mica, and all the members of Ziba's household were servants of
Mephibosheth. 13And Mephibosheth lived in Jerusalem, because he always ate at the king's table, and he was crippled in both feet.

David Defeats the Ammonites

10 In the course of time, the king of the Ammonites died, and his son Hanun succeeded him as king.
2David thought, "I will show kindness to Hanun son of Nahash, just as his father showed kindness to me." So David sent a delegation to express his sympathy to Hanun concerning his father.
When David's men came to the land
of the Ammonites, 3the Ammonite nobles said to Hanun their lord, "Do you think David is honouring your father by sending men to you to express sympathy? Hasn't David sent them to you to explore the city and spy it out and
overthrow it?" 4So Hanun seized David's men, shaved off half of each man's beard, cut off their garments in the middle at the buttocks, and sent them away.
5When David was told about this, he sent messengers to meet the men, for they were greatly humiliated. The king said, "Stay at Jericho till your beards have grown, and then come back."
6When the Ammonites realised that

they had become an offence to David's nostrils, they hired twenty thousand Aramean foot soldiers from Beth Rehob and Zobah, as well as the king of Maacah with a thousand men, and also twelve thousand men from Tob.

7On hearing this, David sent Joab out with the entire army of fighting men. 8The Ammonites came out and drew up in battle formation at the entrance to their city gate, while the Arameans of Zobah and Rehob and the men of Tob and Maacah were by themselves in the open country.

9Joab saw that there were battle lines in front of him and behind him; so he selected some of the best troops in Israel and deployed them against the Arameans. 10He put the rest of the men under the command of Abishai his brother and deployed them against the Ammonites. 11Joab said, "If the Arameans are too strong for me, then you are to come to my rescue; but if the Ammonites are too strong for you, then I will come to rescue you. 12Be strong and let us fight bravely for our people and the cities of our God. The LORD will do what is good in his sight."

13Then Joab and the troops with him advanced to fight the Arameans, and they fled before him. 14When the Ammonites saw that the Arameans were fleeing, they fled before Abishai and went inside the city. So Joab returned from fighting the Ammonites and came to Jerusalem.

15After the Arameans saw that they had been routed by Israel, they regrouped. 16Hadadezer had Arameans brought from beyond the River; they went to Helam, with Shobach the commander of Hadadezer's army leading them.

17When David was told of this, he gathered all Israel, crossed the Jordan and went to Helam. The Arameans formed their battle lines to meet David and fought against him. 18But they fled before Israel, and David killed seven hundred of their charioteers and forty thousand of their foot soldiers. He also struck down Shobach the commander of their army, and he died there. 19When all the kings who were vassals of Hadadezer saw that they had been defeated by Israel, they made peace with the Israelites and became subject to them.

So the Arameans were afraid to help the Ammonites any more.

NEW TESTAMENT READING

Acts 3:1–26

Peter Heals the Crippled Beggar

3 One day Peter and John were going up to the temple at the time of prayer—at three in the afternoon. 2Now a man crippled from birth was being carried to the temple gate called Beautiful, where he was put every day to beg from those going into the temple courts. 3When he saw Peter and John about to enter, he asked them for money. 4Peter looked straight at him, as did John. Then Peter said, "Look at us!" 5So the man gave them his attention, expecting to get something from them.

6Then Peter said, "Silver or gold I do not have, but what I have I give you. In the name of Jesus Christ of Nazareth, walk." 7Taking him by the right hand, he helped him up, and instantly the man's feet and ankles became strong. 8He jumped to his feet and began to walk. Then he went with them into the temple courts, walking and jumping, and praising God. 9When all the people saw him walking and praising God, 10they recognised him as the same man who used to sit begging at the temple gate called Beautiful, and they were filled with wonder and amazement at what had happened to him.

Peter Speaks to the Onlookers

11While the beggar held on to Peter and John, all the people were astonished and came running to them in the

place called Solomon's Colonnade.
12When Peter saw this, he said to them:
"Men of Israel, why does this surprise
you? Why do you stare at us as if by our
own power or godliness we had made
this man walk? 13The God of Abraham,
Isaac and Jacob, the God of our fathers,
has glorified his servant Jesus. You
handed him over to be killed, and you
disowned him before Pilate, though he
had decided to let him go. 14You disowned the Holy and Righteous One and
asked that a murderer be released to
you. 15You killed the author of life, but
God raised him from the dead. We are
witnesses of this. 16By faith in the name
of Jesus, this man whom you see and
know was made strong. It is Jesus' name
and the faith that comes through him
that has given this complete healing to
him, as you can all see.

17"Now, brothers, I know that you
acted in ignorance, as did your leaders.
18But this is how God fulfilled what he
had foretold through all the prophets,
saying that his Christ would suffer.
19Repent, then, and turn to God, so that
your sins may be wiped out, that times
of refreshing may come from the Lord,
20and that he may send the Christ, who
has been appointed for you—even
Jesus. 21He must remain in heaven
until the time comes for God to restore
everything, as he promised long ago
through his holy prophets. 22For Moses
said, 'The Lord your God will raise up
for you a prophet like me from among
your own people; you must listen to
everything he tells you. 23Anyone who
does not listen to him will be completely
cut off from among his people.'

24"Indeed, all the prophets from
Samuel on, as many as have spoken,
have foretold these days. 25And you are
heirs of the prophets and of the covenant God made with your fathers. He
said to Abraham, 'Through your
offspring all peoples on earth will be
blessed.' 26When God raised up his
servant, he sent him first to you to bless
you by turning each of you from your
wicked ways."

READING FROM PSALMS
Psalm 70:1–5

For the director of music. Of David.
A petition.

1Hasten, O God, to save me;
O LORD, come quickly to help me.
2May those who seek my life
be put to shame and confusion;
may all who desire my ruin
be turned back in disgrace.
3May those who say to me, "Aha!
Aha!"
turn back because of their shame.
4But may all who seek you
rejoice and be glad in you;
may those who love your salvation
always say,
"Let God be exalted!"

5Yet I am poor and needy;
come quickly to me, O God.
You are my help and my deliverer;
O LORD, do not delay.

JUNE 7

DAY 158

OLD TESTAMENT READING
2 Samuel 11:1–12:31

David and Bathsheba

11 In the spring, at the time when kings go off to war, David sent Joab out with the king's men and the whole Israelite army. They destroyed the Ammonites and besieged Rabbah. But David remained in Jerusalem.

[2]One evening David got up from his bed and walked around on the roof of the palace. From the roof he saw a woman bathing. The woman was very beautiful, [3]and David sent someone to find out about her. The man said, "Isn't this Bathsheba, the daughter of Eliam and the wife of Uriah the Hittite?" [4]Then David sent messengers to get her. She came to him, and he slept with her. (She had purified herself from her uncleanness.) Then she went back home. [5]The woman conceived and sent word to David, saying, "I am pregnant."

[6]So David sent this word to Joab: "Send me Uriah the Hittite." And Joab sent him to David. [7]When Uriah came to him, David asked him how Joab was, how the soldiers were and how the war was going. [8]Then David said to Uriah, "Go down to your house and wash your feet." So Uriah left the palace, and a gift from the king was sent after him. [9]But Uriah slept at the entrance to the palace with all his master's servants and did not go down to his house.

[10]When David was told, "Uriah did not go home," he asked him, "Haven't you just come from a distance? Why didn't you go home?"

[11]Uriah said to David, "The ark and Israel and Judah are staying in tents, and my master Joab and my lord's men are camped in the open fields. How could I go to my house to eat and drink and lie with my wife? As surely as you live, I will not do such a thing!"

[12]Then David said to him, "Stay here one more day, and tomorrow I will send you back." So Uriah remained in Jerusalem that day and the next. [13]At David's invitation, he ate and drank with him, and David made him drunk. But in the evening Uriah went out to sleep on his mat among his master's servants; he did not go home.

[14]In the morning David wrote a letter to Joab and sent it with Uriah. [15]In it he wrote, "Put Uriah in the front line where the fighting is fiercest. Then withdraw from him so that he will be struck down and die."

[16]So while Joab had the city under siege, he put Uriah at a place where he knew the strongest defenders were. [17]When the men of the city came out and fought against Joab, some of the men in David's army fell; moreover, Uriah the Hittite died.

[18]Joab sent David a full account of the battle. [19]He instructed the messenger: "When you have finished giving the king this account of the battle, [20]the king's anger may flare up, and he may ask you, 'Why did you get so close to the city to fight? Didn't you know they would shoot arrows from the wall? [21]Who killed Abimelech son of Jerub-Besheth? Didn't a woman throw an upper millstone on him from the wall, so that he died in Thebez? Why did you get so close to the wall?' If he asks you this, then say to him, 'Also, your servant Uriah the Hittite is dead.' "

[22]The messenger set out, and when he arrived he told David everything Joab had sent him to say. [23]The messenger said to David, "The men overpowered us and came out against us in the open, but we drove them back to the entrance to the city gate. [24]Then the archers shot arrows at your servants from the wall,

and some of the king's men died.
Moreover, your servant Uriah the Hittite is dead."
25David told the messenger, "Say this
to Joab: 'Don't let this upset you; the
sword devours one as well as another.
Press the attack against the city and
destroy it.' Say this to encourage Joab."
26When Uriah's wife heard that her
husband was dead, she mourned for
him. 27After the time of mourning was
over, David had her brought to his
house, and she became his wife and
bore him a son. But the thing David had
done displeased the LORD.

Nathan Rebukes David

12 The LORD sent Nathan to
David. When he came to him,
he said, "There were two men in a
certain town, one rich and the other
poor. 2The rich man had a very large
number of sheep and cattle, 3but the
poor man had nothing except one little
ewe lamb that he had bought. He raised
it, and it grew up with him and his
children. It shared his food, drank from
his cup and even slept in his arms. It was
like a daughter to him.
4"Now a traveller came to the rich
man, but the rich man refrained from
taking one of his own sheep or cattle to
prepare a meal for the traveller who had
come to him. Instead, he took the ewe
lamb that belonged to the poor man and
prepared it for the one who had come to
him."
5David burned with anger against the
man and said to Nathan, "As surely as
the LORD lives, the man who did this
deserves to die! 6He must pay for that
lamb four times over, because he did
such a thing and had no pity."
7Then Nathan said to David, "You
are the man! This is what the LORD, the
God of Israel, says: 'I anointed you king
over Israel, and I delivered you from
the hand of Saul. 8I gave your master's
house to you, and your master's wives
into your arms. I gave you the house of
Israel and Judah. And if all this had
been too little, I would have given you
even more. 9Why did you despise the
word of the LORD by doing what is evil
in his eyes? You struck down Uriah the
Hittite with the sword and took his wife
to be your own. You killed him with the
sword of the Ammonites. 10Now, therefore, the sword shall never depart from
your house, because you despised me
and took the wife of Uriah the Hittite to
be your own.'
11"This is what the LORD says: 'Out of
your own household I am going to bring
calamity upon you. Before your very
eyes I will take your wives and give
them to one who is close to you, and he
will lie with your wives in broad daylight. 12You did it in secret, but I will do
this thing in broad daylight before all
Israel.'"
13Then David said to Nathan, "I have
sinned against the LORD."
Nathan replied, "The LORD has
taken away your sin. You are not going
to die. 14But because by doing this you
have made the enemies of the LORD
show utter contempt, the son born to
you will die."
15After Nathan had gone home, the
LORD struck the child that Uriah's wife
had borne to David, and he became ill.
16David pleaded with God for the child.
He fasted and went into his house and
spent the nights lying on the ground.
17The elders of his household stood beside him to get him up from the ground,
but he refused, and he would not eat
any food with them.
18On the seventh day the child died.
David's servants were afraid to tell him
that the child was dead, for they
thought, "While the child was still living, we spoke to David but he would not
listen to us. How can we tell him the
child is dead? He may do something
desperate."
19David noticed that his servants
were whispering among themselves and
he realised that the child was dead. "Is
the child dead?" he asked.
"Yes," they replied, "he is dead."

[20]Then David got up from the
ground. After he had washed, put on
lotions and changed his clothes, he went
into the house of the LORD and worshipped. Then he went to his own house,
and at his request they served him food,
and he ate.
[21]His servants asked him, "Why are
you acting in this way? While the child
was alive, you fasted and wept, but now
that the child is dead, you get up and
eat!"
[22]He answered, "While the child was
still alive, I fasted and wept. I thought,
'Who knows? The LORD may be
gracious to me and let the child live.'
[23]But now that he is dead, why should
I fast? Can I bring him back again? I
will go to him, but he will not return to
me."
[24]Then David comforted his wife
Bathsheba, and he went to her and lay
with her. She gave birth to a son, and
they named him Solomon. The LORD
loved him; [25]and because the LORD
loved him, he sent word through
Nathan the prophet to name him
Jedidiah.
[26]Meanwhile Joab fought against
Rabbah of the Ammonites and captured the royal citadel. [27]Joab then sent
messengers to David, saying, "I have
fought against Rabbah and taken its
water supply. [28]Now muster the rest of
the troops and besiege the city and capture it. Otherwise I shall take the city,
and it will be named after me."
[29]So David mustered the entire army
and went to Rabbah, and attacked and
captured it. [30]He took the crown from
the head of their king—its weight was
a talent of gold, and it was set with
precious stones—and it was placed on
David's head. He took a great quantity
of plunder from the city [31]and brought
out the people who were there, consigning them to labour with saws and
with iron picks and axes, and he made
them work at brickmaking. He did
this to all the Ammonite towns. Then
David and his entire army returned to
Jerusalem.

NEW TESTAMENT READING
Acts 4:1–22

Peter and John Before the Sanhedrin

4 The priests and the captain of the
temple guard and the Sadducees
came up to Peter and John while they
were speaking to the people. [2]They
were greatly disturbed because the
apostles were teaching the people and
proclaiming in Jesus the resurrection of
the dead. [3]They seized Peter and John,
and because it was evening, they put
them in jail until the next day. [4]But
many who heard the message believed,
and the number of men grew to about
five thousand.
[5]The next day the rulers, elders and
teachers of the law met in Jerusalem.
[6]Annas the high priest was there, and so
were Caiaphas, John, Alexander and
the other men of the high priest's family. [7]They had Peter and John brought
before them and began to question
them: "By what power or what name
did you do this?"
[8]Then Peter, filled with the Holy
Spirit, said to them: "Rulers and elders
of the people! [9]If we are being called to
account today for an act of kindness
shown to a cripple and are asked how he
was healed, [10]then know this, you and
all the people of Israel: It is by the name
of Jesus Christ of Nazareth, whom you
crucified but whom God raised from the
dead, that this man stands before you
healed. [11]He is

" 'the stone you builders rejected,
which has become the capstone.'

[12]Salvation is found in no-one else, for
there is no other name under heaven
given to men by which we must be
saved."
[13]When they saw the courage of Peter
and John and realised that they were
unschooled, ordinary men, they were
astonished and they took note that

these men had been with Jesus. 14But
since they could see the man who had
been healed standing there with them,
there was nothing they could say. 15So
they ordered them to withdraw from the
Sanhedrin and then conferred together.
16"What are we going to do with these
men?" they asked. "Everybody living
in Jerusalem knows they have done an
outstanding miracle, and we cannot
deny it. 17But to stop this thing from
spreading any further among the people, we must warn these men to speak
no longer to anyone in this name."
18Then they called them in again and
commanded them not to speak or teach
at all in the name of Jesus. 19But Peter
and John replied, "Judge for yourselves
whether it is right in God's sight to obey
you rather than God. 20For we cannot
help speaking about what we have seen
and heard."
21After further threats they let them
go. They could not decide how to punish them, because all the people were
praising God for what had happened.
22For the man who was miraculously
healed was over forty years old.

READING FROM PSALMS
Psalm 71:1–8

1In you, O LORD, I have taken refuge;
let me never be put to shame.
2Rescue me and deliver me in your
righteousness;
turn your ear to me and save me.
3Be my rock of refuge,
to which I can always go;
give the command to save me,
for you are my rock and my fortress.
4Deliver me, O my God, from the
hand of the wicked,
from the grasp of evil and cruel men.

5For you have been my hope, O
Sovereign LORD,
my confidence since my youth.
6From my birth I have relied on you;
you brought me forth from my
mother's womb.
I will ever praise you.
7I have become like a portent to many,
but you are my strong refuge.
8My mouth is filled with your praise,
declaring your splendour all day
long.

DAY 159

JUNE 8

OLD TESTAMENT READING
2 Samuel 13:1–39

Amnon and Tamar

13 In the course of time, Amnon
son of David fell in love with
Tamar, the beautiful sister of Absalom
son of David.
2Amnon became frustrated to the
point of illness on account of his sister
Tamar, for she was a virgin, and it
seemed impossible for him to do anything to her.
3Now Amnon had a friend named
Jonadab son of Shimeah, David's
brother. Jonadab was a very shrewd
man. 4He asked Amnon, "Why do you,
the king's son, look so haggard morning
after morning? Won't you tell me?"
Amnon said to him, "I'm in love with
Tamar, my brother Absalom's sister."
5"Go to bed and pretend to be ill,"
Jonadab said. "When your father
comes to see you, say to him, 'I would
like my sister Tamar to come and give
me something to eat. Let her prepare
the food in my sight so that I may watch
her and then eat it from her hand.'"

[6]So Amnon lay down and pretended to be ill. When the king came to see him, Amnon said to him, "I would like my sister Tamar to come and make some special bread in my sight, so that I may eat from her hand."

[7]David sent word to Tamar at the palace: "Go to the house of your brother Amnon and prepare some food for him." [8]So Tamar went to the house of her brother Amnon, who was lying down. She took some dough, kneaded it, made the bread in his sight and baked it. [9]Then she took the pan and served him the bread, but he refused to eat.

"Send everyone out of here," Amnon said. So everyone left him. [10]Then Amnon said to Tamar, "Bring the food here into my bedroom so that I may eat from your hand." And Tamar took the bread she had prepared and brought it to her brother Amnon in his bedroom. [11]But when she took it to him to eat, he grabbed her and said, "Come to bed with me, my sister."

[12]"Don't, my brother!" she said to him. "Don't force me. Such a thing should not be done in Israel! Don't do this wicked thing. [13]What about me? Where could I get rid of my disgrace? And what about you? You would be like one of the wicked fools in Israel. Please speak to the king; he will not keep me from being married to you." [14]But he refused to listen to her, and since he was stronger than she, he raped her.

[15]Then Amnon hated her with intense hatred. In fact, he hated her more than he had loved her. Amnon said to her, "Get up and get out!"

[16]"No!" she said to him. "Sending me away would be a greater wrong than what you have already done to me."

But he refused to listen to her. [17]He called his personal servant and said, "Get this woman out of here and bolt the door after her." [18]So his servant put her out and bolted the door after her. She was wearing a richly ornamented robe, for this was the kind of garment the virgin daughters of the king wore. [19]Tamar put ashes on her head and tore the ornamented robe she was wearing. She put her hand on her head and went away, weeping aloud as she went.

[20]Her brother Absalom said to her, "Has that Amnon, your brother, been with you? Be quiet now, my sister; he is your brother. Don't take this thing to heart." And Tamar lived in her brother Absalom's house, a desolate woman.

[21]When King David heard all this, he was furious. [22]Absalom never said a word to Amnon, either good or bad; he hated Amnon because he had disgraced his sister Tamar.

Absalom Kills Amnon

[23]Two years later, when Absalom's sheep-shearers were at Baal Hazor near the border of Ephraim, he invited all the king's sons to come there. [24]Absalom went to the king and said, "Your servant has had shearers come. Will the king and his officials please join me?"

[25]"No, my son," the king replied. "All of us should not go; we would only be a burden to you." Although Absalom urged him, he still refused to go, but gave him his blessing.

[26]Then Absalom said, "If not, please let my brother Amnon come with us."

The king asked him, "Why should he go with you?" [27]But Absalom urged him, so he sent with him Amnon and the rest of the king's sons.

[28]Absalom ordered his men, "Listen! When Amnon is in high spirits from drinking wine and I say to you, 'Strike Amnon down,' then kill him. Don't be afraid. Have not I given you this order? Be strong and brave." [29]So Absalom's men did to Amnon what Absalom had ordered. Then all the king's sons got up, mounted their mules and fled.

[30]While they were on their way, the report came to David: "Absalom has struck down all the king's sons; not one of them is left." [31]The king stood up, tore his clothes and lay down on the

ground; and all his servants stood by
with their clothes torn.
32But Jonadab son of Shimeah,
David's brother, said, "My lord should
not think that they killed all the princes;
only Amnon is dead. This has been
Absalom's expressed intention ever
since the day that Amnon raped his
sister Tamar. 33My lord the king should
not be concerned about the report that
all the king's sons are dead. Only
Amnon is dead."
34Meanwhile, Absalom had fled.
Now the man standing watch looked
up and saw many people on the road
west of him, coming down the side of
the hill. The watchman went and told
the king, "I see men in the direction of
Horonaim, on the side of the hill."
35Jonadab said to the king, "See, the
king's sons are here; it has happened
just as your servant said."
36As he finished speaking, the king's
sons came in, wailing loudly. The king,
too, and all his servants wept very
bitterly.
37Absalom fled and went to Talmai
son of Ammihud, the king of Geshur.
But King David mourned for his son
every day.
38After Absalom fled and went to
Geshur, he stayed there for three years.
39And the spirit of the king longed to go
to Absalom, for he was consoled concerning Amnon's death.

NEW TESTAMENT READING
Acts 4:23–5:11

The Believers' Prayer

23On their release, Peter and John
went back to their own people and reported all that the chief priests and
elders had said to them. 24When they
heard this, they raised their voices
together in prayer to God. "Sovereign
Lord," they said, "you made the
heaven and the earth and the sea, and
everything in them. 25You spoke by the
Holy Spirit through the mouth of your
servant, our father David:

" 'Why do the nations rage
and the peoples plot in vain?
26The kings of the earth take their
stand
and the rulers gather together
against the Lord
and against his Anointed One.'

27Indeed Herod and Pontius Pilate met
together with the Gentiles and the people of Israel in this city to conspire
against your holy servant Jesus, whom
you anointed. 28They did what your
power and will had decided beforehand
should happen. 29Now, Lord, consider
their threats and enable your servants to
speak your word with great boldness.
30Stretch out your hand to heal and
perform miraculous signs and wonders
through the name of your holy servant
Jesus."
31After they prayed, the place where
they were meeting was shaken. And
they were all filled with the Holy Spirit
and spoke the word of God boldly.

The Believers Share Their Possessions

32All the believers were one in heart
and mind. No-one claimed that any of
his possessions was his own, but they
shared everything they had. 33With
great power the apostles continued to
testify to the resurrection of the Lord
Jesus, and much grace was upon them
all. 34There were no needy persons
among them. For from time to time
those who owned lands or houses sold
them, brought the money from the sales
35and put it at the apostles' feet, and it
was distributed to anyone as he had
need.
36Joseph, a Levite from Cyprus,
whom the apostles called Barnabas
(which means Son of Encouragement),
37sold a field he owned and brought the
money and put it at the apostles' feet.

Ananias and Sapphira

5 Now a man named Ananias,
together with his wife Sapphira,
also sold a piece of property. 2With his
wife's full knowledge he kept back part
of the money for himself, but brought
the rest and put it at the apostles' feet.
3Then Peter said, "Ananias, how is it
that Satan has so filled your heart that
you have lied to the Holy Spirit and
have kept for yourself some of the
money you received for the land?
4Didn't it belong to you before it was
sold? And after it was sold, wasn't the
money at your disposal? What made
you think of doing such a thing? You
have not lied to men but to God."
5When Ananias heard this, he fell
down and died. And great fear seized all
who heard what had happened. 6Then
the young men came forward, wrapped
up his body, and carried him out and
buried him.
7About three hours later his wife
came in, not knowing what had happened. 8Peter asked her, "Tell me, is
this the price you and Ananias got for
the land?"

"Yes," she said, "that is the price."
9Peter said to her, "How could you
agree to test the Spirit of the Lord?
Look! The feet of the men who buried
your husband are at the door, and they
will carry you out also."
10At that moment she fell down at his
feet and died. Then the young men
came in and, finding her dead, carried
her out and buried her beside her husband. 11Great fear seized the whole
church and all who heard about these
events.

READING FROM PSALMS

Psalm 71:9–18

9Do not cast me away when I am old;
do not forsake me when my
strength is gone.
10For my enemies speak against me;
those who wait to kill me conspire
together.
11They say, "God has forsaken him;
pursue him and seize him,
for no-one will rescue him."
12Be not far from me, O God;
come quickly, O my God, to help
me.
13May my accusers perish in shame;
may those who want to harm me
be covered with scorn and
disgrace.

14But as for me, I shall always have
hope;
I will praise you more and more.
15My mouth will tell of your
righteousness,
of your salvation all day long,
though I know not its measure.
16I will come and proclaim your mighty
acts, O Sovereign LORD;
I will proclaim your righteousness,
yours alone.
17Since my youth, O God, you have
taught me,
and to this day I declare your
marvellous deeds.
18Even when I am old and grey,
do not forsake me, O God,
till I declare your power to the next
generation,
your might to all who are to come.

DAY 160

JUNE 9

OLD TESTAMENT READING
2 Samuel 14:1–15:12

Absalom Returns to Jerusalem

14 Joab son of Zeruiah knew that
the king's heart longed for
Absalom. 2So Joab sent someone to
Tekoa and had a wise woman brought
from there. He said to her, "Pretend
you are in mourning. Dress in mourning
clothes, and don't use any cosmetic lotions. Act like a woman who has spent
many days grieving for the dead. 3Then
go to the king and speak these words to
him." And Joab put the words in her
mouth.
4When the woman from Tekoa went
to the king, she fell with her face to the
ground to pay him honour, and she said,
"Help me, O king!"
5The king asked her, "What is troubling you?"
She said, "I am indeed a widow; my
husband is dead. 6I your servant had
two sons. They got into a fight with each
other in the field, and no-one was there
to separate them. One struck the other
and killed him. 7Now the whole clan has
risen up against your servant; they say,
'Hand over the one who struck his
brother down, so that we may put him
to death for the life of his brother whom
he killed; then we will get rid of the heir
as well.' They would put out the only
burning coal I have left, leaving my
husband neither name nor descendant
on the face of the earth."
8The king said to the woman, "Go
home, and I will issue an order on your
behalf."
9But the woman from Tekoa said to
him, "My lord the king, let the blame
rest on me and on my father's family,
and let the king and his throne be without guilt."
10The king replied, "If anyone says
anything to you, bring him to me, and
he will not bother you again."
11She said, "Then let the king invoke
the LORD his God to prevent the avenger of blood from adding to the destruction, so that my son shall not be
destroyed."
"As surely as the LORD lives," he
said, "not one hair of your son's head
will fall to the ground."
12Then the woman said, "Let your
servant speak a word to my lord the
king."
"Speak," he replied.
13The woman said, "Why then have
you devised a thing like this against the
people of God? When the king says this,
does he not convict himself, for the king
has not brought back his banished son?
14Like water spilled on the ground,
which cannot be recovered, so we must
die. But God does not take away life;
instead, he devises ways so that a
banished person may not remain
estranged from him.
15"And now I have come to say this to
my lord the king because the people
have made me afraid. Your servant
thought, 'I will speak to the king;
perhaps he will do what his servant asks.
16Perhaps the king will agree to deliver
his servant from the hand of the man
who is trying to cut off both me and my
son from the inheritance God gave
us.'
17"And now your servant says, 'May
the word of my lord the king bring me
rest, for my lord the king is like an angel
of God in discerning good and evil. May
the LORD your God be with you.'"
18Then the king said to the woman,
"Do not keep from me the answer to
what I am going to ask you."
"Let my lord the king speak," the
woman said.
19The king asked, "Isn't the hand of
Joab with you in all this?"

The woman answered, "As surely as
you live, my lord the king, no-one can
turn to the right or to the left from
anything my lord the king says. Yes, it
was your servant Joab who instructed
me to do this and who put all these
words into the mouth of your servant.
20 Your servant Joab did this to change
the present situation. My lord has wisdom like that of an angel of God—he
knows everything that happens in the
land."

21 The king said to Joab, "Very well, I
will do it. Go, bring back the young man
Absalom."

22 Joab fell with his face to the ground
to pay him honour, and he blessed the
king. Joab said, "Today your servant
knows that he has found favour in your
eyes, my lord the king, because the king
has granted his servant's request."

23 Then Joab went to Geshur and
brought Absalom back to Jerusalem.
24 But the king said, "He must go to his
own house; he must not see my face."
So Absalom went to his own house and
did not see the face of the king.

25 In all Israel there was not a man so
highly praised for his handsome appearance as Absalom. From the top of his
head to the sole of his foot there was no
blemish in him. 26 Whenever he cut the
hair of his head—he used to cut his hair
from time to time when it became too
heavy for him—he would weigh it, and
its weight was two hundred shekels by
the royal standard.

27 Three sons and a daughter were
born to Absalom. The daughter's name
was Tamar, and she became a beautiful
woman.

28 Absalom lived for two years in Jerusalem without seeing the king's face.
29 Then Absalom sent for Joab in order
to send him to the king, but Joab refused to come to him. So he sent a
second time, but he refused to come.
30 Then he said to his servants, "Look,
Joab's field is next to mine, and he has
barley there. Go and set it on fire." So
Absalom's servants set the field on fire.

31 Then Joab did go to Absalom's
house and he said to him, "Why have
your servants set my field on fire?"

32 Absalom said to Joab, "Look, I
sent word to you and said, 'Come here
so that I can send you to the king to ask,
"Why have I come from Geshur? It
would be better for me if I were still
there!"' Now then, I want to see the
king's face, and if I am guilty of anything, let him put me to death."

33 So Joab went to the king and told
him this. Then the king summoned
Absalom, and he came in and bowed
down with his face to the ground before
the king. And the king kissed Absalom.

Absalom's Conspiracy

15 In the course of time, Absalom
provided himself with a chariot
and horses and with fifty men to run
ahead of him. 2 He would get up early
and stand by the side of the road leading
to the city gate. Whenever anyone came
with a complaint to be placed before the
king for a decision, Absalom would call
out to him, "What town are you from?"
He would answer, "Your servant is
from one of the tribes of Israel." 3 Then
Absalom would say to him, "Look,
your claims are valid and proper, but
there is no representative of the king to
hear you." 4 And Absalom would add,
"If only I were appointed judge in the
land! Then everyone who has a complaint or case could come to me and I
would see that he receives justice."

5 Also, whenever anyone approached
him to bow down before him, Absalom
would reach out his hand, take hold of
him and kiss him. 6 Absalom behaved in
this way towards all the Israelites who
came to the king asking for justice, and
so he stole the hearts of the men of
Israel.

7 At the end of four years, Absalom
said to the king, "Let me go to Hebron
and fulfil a vow I made to the LORD.
8 While your servant was living at
Geshur in Aram, I made this vow: 'If
the LORD takes me back to Jerusalem, I
will worship the LORD in Hebron.'"

9The king said to him, "Go in peace." So he went to Hebron.

10Then Absalom sent secret messengers throughout the tribes of Israel to say, "As soon as you hear the sound of the trumpets, then say, 'Absalom is king in Hebron.' " 11Two hundred men from Jerusalem had accompanied Absalom. They had been invited as guests and went quite innocently, knowing nothing about the matter. 12While Absalom was offering sacrifices, he also sent for Ahithophel the Gilonite, David's counsellor, to come from Giloh, his home town. And so the conspiracy gained strength, and Absalom's following kept on increasing.

NEW TESTAMENT READING

Acts 5:12–42

The Apostles Heal Many

12The apostles performed many miraculous signs and wonders among the people. And all the believers used to meet together in Solomon's Colonnade. 13No-one else dared join them, even though they were highly regarded by the people. 14Nevertheless, more and more men and women believed in the Lord and were added to their number. 15As a result, people brought the sick into the streets and laid them on beds and mats so that at least Peter's shadow might fall on some of them as he passed by. 16Crowds gathered also from the towns around Jerusalem, bringing their sick and those tormented by evil spirits, and all of them were healed.

The Apostles Persecuted

17Then the high priest and all his associates, who were members of the party of the Sadducees, were filled with jealousy. 18They arrested the apostles and put them in the public jail. 19But during the night an angel of the Lord opened the doors of the jail and brought them out. 20"Go, stand in the temple courts," he said, "and tell the people the full message of this new life."

21At daybreak they entered the temple courts, as they had been told, and began to teach the people.

When the high priest and his associates arrived, they called together the Sanhedrin—the full assembly of the elders of Israel—and sent to the jail for the apostles. 22But on arriving at the jail, the officers did not find them there. So they went back and reported, 23"We found the jail securely locked, with the guards standing at the doors; but when we opened them, we found no-one inside." 24On hearing this report, the captain of the temple guard and the chief priests were puzzled, wondering what would come of this.

25Then someone came and said, "Look! The men you put in jail are standing in the temple courts teaching the people." 26At that, the captain went with his officers and brought the apostles. They did not use force, because they feared that the people would stone them.

27Having brought the apostles, they made them appear before the Sanhedrin to be questioned by the high priest. 28"We gave you strict orders not to teach in this name," he said. "Yet you have filled Jerusalem with your teaching and are determined to make us guilty of this man's blood."

29Peter and the other apostles replied: "We must obey God rather than men! 30The God of our fathers raised Jesus from the dead—whom you had killed by hanging him on a tree. 31God exalted him to his own right hand as Prince and Saviour that he might give repentance and forgiveness of sins to Israel. 32We are witnesses of these things, and so is the Holy Spirit, whom God has given to those who obey him."

33When they heard this, they were furious and wanted to put them to death. 34But a Pharisee named Gamaliel, a teacher of the law, who was honoured by all the people, stood up in the Sanhedrin and ordered that the men be put outside for a little while. 35Then he

addressed them: "Men of Israel, consider carefully what you intend to do to
these men. 36Some time ago Theudas
appeared, claiming to be somebody,
and about four hundred men rallied to
him. He was killed, all his followers
were dispersed, and it all came to nothing. 37After him, Judas the Galilean
appeared in the days of the census and
led a band of people in revolt. He too
was killed, and all his followers were
scattered. 38Therefore, in the present
case I advise you: Leave these men
alone! Let them go! For if their purpose
or activity is of human origin, it will fail.
39But if it is from God, you will not be
able to stop these men; you will only
find yourselves fighting against God."

40His speech persuaded them. They called the apostles in and had them flogged. Then they ordered them not to speak in the name of Jesus, and let them go.

41The apostles left the Sanhedrin, rejoicing because they had been counted
worthy of suffering disgrace for the
Name. 42Day after day, in the temple
courts and from house to house, they
never stopped teaching and proclaiming
the good news that Jesus is the Christ.

READING FROM PROVERBS

Proverbs 14:15–24

15A simple man believes anything,
but a prudent man gives thought to his steps.

16A wise man fears the LORD and shuns evil,
but a fool is hotheaded and reckless.

17A quick-tempered man does foolish things,
and a crafty man is hated.

18The simple inherit folly,
but the prudent are crowned with knowledge.

19Evil men will bow down in the presence of the good,
and the wicked at the gates of the righteous.

20The poor are shunned even by their neighbours,
but the rich have many friends.

21He who despises his neighbour sins,
but blessed is he who is kind to the needy.

22Do not those who plot evil go astray?
But those who plan what is good find love and faithfulness.

23All hard work brings a profit,
but mere talk leads only to poverty.

24The wealth of the wise is their crown,
but the folly of fools yields folly.

JUNE 10

OLD TESTAMENT READING

2 Samuel 15:13–16:14

David Flees

13A messenger came and told David, "The hearts of the men of Israel are with Absalom."
14Then David said to all his officials who were with him in Jerusalem, "Come! We must flee, or none of us will escape from Absalom. We must leave immediately, or he will move quickly to overtake us and bring ruin upon us and put the city to the sword."
15The king's officials answered him, "Your servants are ready to do whatever our lord the king chooses."
16The king set out, with his entire household following him; but he left ten concubines to take care of the palace.
17So the king set out, with all the people following him, and they halted at a
place some distance away. 18All his men
marched past him, along with all the Kerethites and Pelethites; and all the six hundred Gittites who had accompanied him from Gath marched before the king.
19The king said to Ittai the Gittite, "Why should you come along with us? Go back and stay with King Absalom. You are a foreigner, an exile from your
homeland. 20You came only yesterday.
And today shall I make you wander about with us, when I do not know where I am going? Go back, and take your countrymen. May kindness and faithfulness be with you."
21But Ittai replied to the king, "As surely as the LORD lives, and as my lord the king lives, wherever my lord the king may be, whether it means life or death, there will your servant be."
22David said to Ittai, "Go ahead, march on." So Ittai the Gittite marched on with all his men and the families that were with him.
23The whole countryside wept aloud as all the people passed by. The king also crossed the Kidron Valley, and all the people moved on towards the desert.
24Zadok was there, too, and all the Levites who were with him were carrying the ark of the covenant of God. They set down the ark of God, and Abiathar offered sacrifices until all the people had finished leaving the city.
25Then the king said to Zadok, "Take the ark of God back into the city. If I find favour in the LORD's eyes, he will bring me back and let me see it and his
dwelling-place again. 26But if he says, 'I
am not pleased with you,' then I am ready; let him do to me whatever seems good to him."
27The king also said to Zadok the priest, "Aren't you a seer? Go back to the city in peace, with your son Ahimaaz and Jonathan son of Abiathar. You and Abiathar take your two sons
with you. 28I will wait at the fords in the
desert until word comes from you to
inform me." 29So Zadok and Abiathar
took the ark of God back to Jerusalem and stayed there.
30But David continued up the Mount of Olives, weeping as he went; his head was covered and he was barefoot. All the people with him covered their heads too and were weeping as they went
up. 31Now David had been told,
"Ahithophel is among the conspirators with Absalom." So David prayed, "O LORD, turn Ahithophel's counsel into foolishness."
32When David arrived at the summit, where people used to worship God, Hushai the Arkite was there to meet him, his robe torn and dust on his head.
33David said to him, "If you go with me,
you will be a burden to me. 34But if you
return to the city and say to Absalom, 'I will be your servant, O king; I was your father's servant in the past, but now I will be your servant,' then you can help

me by frustrating Ahithophel's advice.
35Won't the priests Zadok and Abiathar
be there with you? Tell them anything
you hear in the king's palace. 36Their
two sons, Ahimaaz son of Zadok and
Jonathan son of Abiathar, are there
with them. Send them to me with anything you hear."
37So David's friend Hushai arrived at
Jerusalem as Absalom was entering the
city.

David and Ziba

16 When David had gone a short distance beyond the summit, there was Ziba, the steward of Mephibosheth, waiting to meet him. He had a string of donkeys saddled and loaded with two hundred loaves of bread, a hundred cakes of raisins, a hundred cakes of figs and a skin of wine.
2The king asked Ziba, "Why have
you brought these?"

Ziba answered, "The donkeys are for the king's household to ride on, the bread and fruit are for the men to eat, and the wine is to refresh those who become exhausted in the desert."
3The king then asked, "Where is your
master's grandson?"

Ziba said to him, "He is staying in Jerusalem, because he thinks, 'Today the house of Israel will give me back my grandfather's kingdom.'"
4Then the king said to Ziba, "All that
belonged to Mephibosheth is now
yours."

"I humbly bow," Ziba said. "May I find favour in your eyes, my lord the king."

Shimei Curses David

5As King David approached Bahurim, a man from the same clan as
Saul's family came out from there. His
name was Shimei son of Gera, and he
cursed as he came out. 6He pelted
David and all the king's officials with
stones, though all the troops and the
special guard were on David's right and
left. 7As he cursed, Shimei said, "Get
out, get out, you man of blood, you
scoundrel! 8The LORD has repaid you
for all the blood you shed in the household of Saul, in whose place you have reigned. The LORD has handed the kingdom over to your son Absalom. You have come to ruin because you are a man of blood!"
9Then Abishai son of Zeruiah said to
the king, "Why should this dead dog curse my lord the king? Let me go over and cut off his head."
10But the king said, "What do you
and I have in common, you sons of Zeruiah? If he is cursing because the LORD said to him, 'Curse David,' who can ask, 'Why do you do this?'"
11David then said to Abishai and all
his officials, "My son, who is of my own flesh, is trying to take my life. How much more, then, this Benjamite! Leave him alone; let him curse, for the
LORD has told him to. 12It may be that
the LORD will see my distress and repay me with good for the cursing I am receiving today."
13So David and his men continued
along the road while Shimei was going
along the hillside opposite him, cursing
as he went and throwing stones at him
and showering him with dirt. 14The king
and all the people with him arrived at
their destination exhausted. And there
he refreshed himself.

NEW TESTAMENT READING
Acts 6:1–7:19

The Choosing of the Seven

6 In those days when the number of disciples was increasing, the Grecian Jews among them complained against the Hebraic Jews because their widows were being overlooked in the
daily distribution of food. 2So the
Twelve gathered all the disciples
together and said, "It would not be right
for us to neglect the ministry of the word
of God in order to wait on tables.
3Brothers, choose seven men from
among you who are known to be full of
the Spirit and wisdom. We will turn this

responsibility over to them [4]and will
give our attention to prayer and the
ministry of the word."
[5]This proposal pleased the whole
group. They chose Stephen, a man full
of faith and of the Holy Spirit; also
Philip, Procorus, Nicanor, Timon, Par-
menas, and Nicolas from Antioch, a
convert to Judaism. [6]They presented
these men to the apostles, who prayed
and laid their hands on them.
[7]So the word of God spread. The
number of disciples in Jerusalem increased rapidly, and a large number of
priests became obedient to the faith.

Stephen Seized

[8]Now Stephen, a man full of God's
grace and power, did great wonders and
miraculous signs among the people.
[9]Opposition arose, however, from
members of the Synagogue of the
Freedmen (as it was called)—Jews of
Cyrene and Alexandria as well as the
provinces of Cilicia and Asia. These
men began to argue with Stephen, [10]but
they could not stand up against his wisdom or the Spirit by whom he spoke.
[11]Then they secretly persuaded some
men to say, "We have heard Stephen
speak words of blasphemy against
Moses and against God."
[12]So they stirred up the people and
the elders and the teachers of the law.
They seized Stephen and brought him
before the Sanhedrin. [13]They produced
false witnesses, who testified, "This fellow never stops speaking against this
holy place and against the law. [14]For we
have heard him say that this Jesus of
Nazareth will destroy this place and
change the customs Moses handed
down to us."
[15]All who were sitting in the Sanhedrin looked intently at Stephen, and they
saw that his face was like the face of an
angel.

Stephen's Speech to the Sanhedrin

7 Then the high priest asked him,
"Are these charges true?"
[2]To this he replied: "Brothers and
fathers, listen to me! The God of glory
appeared to our father Abraham while
he was still in Mesopotamia, before he
lived in Haran. [3]'Leave your country
and your people,' God said, 'and go to
the land I will show you.'
[4]"So he left the land of the Chaldeans
and settled in Haran. After the death of
his father, God sent him to this land
where you are now living. [5]He gave him
no inheritance here, not even a foot of
ground. But God promised him that he
and his descendants after him would
possess the land, even though at that
time Abraham had no child. [6]God
spoke to him in this way: 'Your descendants will be strangers in a country not
their own, and they will be enslaved and
ill-treated for four hundred years. [7]But
I will punish the nation they serve as
slaves,' God said, 'and afterwards they
will come out of that country and
worship me in this place.' [8]Then he gave
Abraham the covenant of circumcision.
And Abraham became the father of
Isaac and circumcised him eight days
after his birth. Later Isaac became the
father of Jacob, and Jacob became the
father of the twelve patriarchs.
[9]"Because the patriarchs were
jealous of Joseph, they sold him as a
slave into Egypt. But God was with him
[10]and rescued him from all his troubles.
He gave Joseph wisdom and enabled
him to gain the goodwill of Pharaoh
king of Egypt; so he made him ruler
over Egypt and all his palace.
[11]"Then a famine struck all Egypt and
Canaan, bringing great suffering, and
our fathers could not find food. [12]When
Jacob heard that there was grain in
Egypt, he sent our fathers on their first
visit. [13]On their second visit, Joseph
told his brothers who he was, and Pharaoh learned about Joseph's family.
[14]After this, Joseph sent for his father
Jacob and his whole family, seventy-five
in all. [15]Then Jacob went down to
Egypt, where he and our fathers died.
[16]Their bodies were brought back to
Shechem and placed in the tomb that
Abraham had bought from the sons of

Hamor at Shechem for a certain sum of money.

[17]"As the time drew near for God to fulfil his promise to Abraham, the number of our people in Egypt greatly increased. [18]Then another king, who knew nothing about Joseph, became ruler of Egypt. [19]He dealt treacherously with our people and oppressed our forefathers by forcing them to throw out their newborn babies so that they would die.

READING FROM PSALMS
Psalm 71:19–24

[19]Your righteousness reaches to the
skies, O God,
you who have done great things.
Who, O God, is like you?
[20]Though you have made me see
troubles, many and bitter,
you will restore my life again;
from the depths of the earth
you will again bring me up.
[21]You will increase my honour
and comfort me once again.

[22]I will praise you with the harp
for your faithfulness, O my God;
I will sing praise to you with the lyre,
O Holy One of Israel.
[23]My lips will shout for joy
when I sing praise to you—
I, whom you have redeemed.
[24]My tongue will tell of your righteous
acts
all day long,
for those who wanted to harm me
have been put to shame and
confusion.

JUNE 11

DAY 162

OLD TESTAMENT READING
2 Samuel 16:15–18:18

The Advice of Hushai and Ahithophel

[15]Meanwhile, Absalom and all the men of Israel came to Jerusalem, and Ahithophel was with him. [16]Then Hushai the Arkite, David's friend, went to Absalom and said to him, "Long live the king! Long live the king!"

[17]Absalom asked Hushai, "Is this the love you show your friend? Why didn't you go with your friend?"

[18]Hushai said to Absalom, "No, the one chosen by the LORD, by these people and by all the men of Israel—his I will be, and I will remain with him. [19]Furthermore, whom should I serve? Should I not serve the son? Just as I served your father, so I will serve you."

[20]Absalom said to Ahithophel, "Give us your advice. What should we do?"

[21]Ahithophel answered, "Lie with your father's concubines whom he left to take care of the palace. Then all Israel will hear that you have made yourself an offence to your father's nostrils, and the hands of everyone with you will be strengthened." [22]So they pitched a tent for Absalom on the roof, and he lay with his father's concubines in the sight of all Israel.

[23]Now in those days the advice Ahithophel gave was like that of one who enquires of God. That was how both David and Absalom regarded all of Ahithophel's advice.

17 Ahithophel said to Absalom, "I would choose twelve thousand men and set out tonight in pursuit of David. [2]I would attack him while he is weary and weak. I would strike him with terror, and then all the people with him will flee. I would strike down only the king [3]and bring all the people back to you. The death of the man you seek will

mean the return of all; all the people
will be unharmed." 4This plan seemed
good to Absalom and to all the elders of
Israel.
5But Absalom said, "Summon also
Hushai the Arkite, so that we can hear
what he has to say." 6When Hushai
came to him, Absalom said,
"Ahithophel has given this advice.
Should we do what he says? If not, give
us your opinion."
7Hushai replied to Absalom, "The
advice Ahithophel has given is not good
this time. 8You know your father and
his men; they are fighters, and as fierce
as a wild bear robbed of her cubs. Besides, your father is an experienced
fighter; he will not spend the night with
the troops. 9Even now, he is hidden in a
cave or some other place. If he should
attack your troops first, whoever hears
about it will say, 'There has been a
slaughter among the troops who follow
Absalom.' 10Then even the bravest soldier, whose heart is like the heart of a
lion, will melt with fear, for all Israel
knows that your father is a fighter and
that those with him are brave.
11"So I advise you: Let all Israel,
from Dan to Beersheba—as numerous
as the sand on the seashore—be
gathered to you, with you yourself leading them into battle. 12Then we will
attack him wherever he may be found,
and we will fall on him as dew settles on
the ground. Neither he nor any of his
men will be left alive. 13If he withdraws
into a city, then all Israel will bring
ropes to that city, and we will drag it
down to the valley until not even a piece
of it can be found."
14Absalom and all the men of Israel
said, "The advice of Hushai the Arkite
is better than that of Ahithophel." For
the LORD had determined to frustrate
the good advice of Ahithophel in order
to bring disaster on Absalom.
15Hushai told Zadok and Abiathar,
the priests, "Ahithophel has advised
Absalom and the elders of Israel to do
such and such, but I have advised them
to do so and so. 16Now send a message
immediately and tell David, 'Do not
spend the night at the fords in the desert; cross over without fail, or the king
and all the people with him will be
swallowed up.'"
17Jonathan and Ahimaaz were
staying at En Rogel. A servant girl was
to go and inform them, and they were to
go and tell King David, for they could
not risk being seen entering the city.
18But a young man saw them and told
Absalom. So the two of them left
quickly and went to the house of a
man in Bahurim. He had a well in his
courtyard, and they climbed down
into it. 19His wife took a covering and
spread it out over the opening of the
well and scattered grain over it. No-one
knew anything about it.
20When Absalom's men came to the
woman at the house, they asked,
"Where are Ahimaaz and Jonathan?"

The woman answered them, "They
crossed over the brook." The men
searched but found no-one, so they
returned to Jerusalem.
21After the men had gone, the two
climbed out of the well and went to
inform King David. They said to him,
"Set out and cross the river at once;
Ahithophel has advised such and such
against you." 22So David and all the
people with him set out and crossed the
Jordan. By daybreak, no-one was left
who had not crossed the Jordan.
23When Ahithophel saw that his
advice had not been followed, he saddled his donkey and set out for his house
in his home town. He put his house in
order and then hanged himself. So he
died and was buried in his father's
tomb.
24David went to Mahanaim, and
Absalom crossed the Jordan with all
the men of Israel. 25Absalom had
appointed Amasa over the army in
place of Joab. Amasa was the son of a
man named Jether, an Israelite who had
married Abigail, the daughter of Nahash and sister of Zeruiah the mother of
Joab. 26The Israelites and Absalom
camped in the land of Gilead.

27When David came to Mahanaim,
Shobi son of Nahash from Rabbah of
the Ammonites, and Makir son of
Ammiel from Lo Debar, and Barzillai
the Gileadite from Rogelim 28brought
bedding and bowls and articles of pottery. They also brought wheat and barley, flour and roasted grain, beans and
lentils, 29honey and curds, sheep, and
cheese from cows' milk for David
and his people to eat. For they said,
"The people have become hungry and
tired and thirsty in the desert."

Absalom's Death

18 David mustered the men who
were with him and appointed
over them commanders of thousands
and commanders of hundreds. 2David
sent the troops out—a third under the
command of Joab, a third under Joab's
brother Abishai son of Zeruiah, and a
third under Ittai the Gittite. The king
told the troops, "I myself will surely
march out with you."
3But the men said, "You must not go
out; if we are forced to flee, they won't
care about us. Even if half of us die,
they won't care; but you are worth ten
thousand of us. It would be better now
for you to give us support from the
city."
4The king answered, "I will do whatever seems best to you."
So the king stood beside the gate
while all the men marched out in units
of hundreds and of thousands. 5The
king commanded Joab, Abishai and
Ittai, "Be gentle with the young man
Absalom for my sake." And all the
troops heard the king giving orders
concerning Absalom to each of the
commanders.
6The army marched into the field to
fight Israel, and the battle took place in
the forest of Ephraim. 7There the army
of Israel was defeated by David's men,
and the casualties that day were great
—twenty thousand men. 8The battle
spread out over the whole countryside,
and the forest claimed more lives that
day than the sword.
9Now Absalom happened to meet
David's men. He was riding his mule,
and as the mule went under the thick
branches of a large oak, Absalom's
head got caught in the tree. He was left
hanging in mid-air, while the mule he
was riding kept on going.
10When one of the men saw this, he
told Joab, "I have just seen Absalom
hanging in an oak tree."
11Joab said to the man who had told
him this, "What! You saw him? Why
didn't you strike him to the ground right
there? Then I would have had to give
you ten shekels of silver and a warrior's
belt."
12But the man replied, "Even if a
thousand shekels were weighed out
into my hands, I would not lift my
hand against the king's son. In our
hearing the king commanded you and
Abishai and Ittai, 'Protect the young
man Absalom for my sake.' 13And if
I had put my life in jeopardy—and
nothing is hidden from the king—you
would have kept your distance from
me."
14Joab said, "I am not going to wait
like this for you." So he took three
javelins in his hand and plunged them
into Absalom's heart while Absalom
was still alive in the oak tree. 15And
ten of Joab's armour-bearers surrounded Absalom, struck him and
killed him.
16Then Joab sounded the trumpet,
and the troops stopped pursuing Israel,
for Joab halted them. 17They took
Absalom, threw him into a big pit in the
forest and piled up a large heap of rocks
over him. Meanwhile, all the Israelites
fled to their homes.
18During his life-time Absalom had
taken a pillar and erected it in the King's
Valley as a monument to himself, for
he thought, "I have no son to carry
on the memory of my name." He
named the pillar after himself, and it
is called Absalom's Monument to this
day.

NEW TESTAMENT READING
Acts 7:20–43

20“At that time Moses was born, and
he was no ordinary child. For three
months he was cared for in his father’s
house. 21When he was placed outside,
Pharaoh’s daughter took him and
brought him up as her own son. 22Moses
was educated in all the wisdom of the
Egyptians and was powerful in speech
and action.

23“When Moses was forty years old,
he decided to visit his fellow Israelites.
24He saw one of them being ill-treated
by an Egyptian, so he went to his defence and avenged him by killing the
Egyptian. 25Moses thought that his own
people would realise that God was using
him to rescue them, but they did not.
26The next day Moses came upon two
Israelites who were fighting. He tried to
reconcile them by saying, ‘Men, you are
brothers; why do you want to hurt each
other?’

27“But the man who was ill-treating
the other pushed Moses aside and said,
‘Who made you ruler and judge over
us? 28Do you want to kill me as you
killed the Egyptian yesterday?’ 29When
Moses heard this, he fled to Midian,
where he settled as a foreigner and had
two sons.

30“After forty years had passed, an
angel appeared to Moses in the flames
of a burning bush in the desert near
Mount Sinai. 31When he saw this, he
was amazed at the sight. As he went
over to look more closely, he heard the
Lord’s voice: 32‘I am the God of your
fathers, the God of Abraham, Isaac and
Jacob.’ Moses trembled with fear and
did not dare to look.

33“Then the Lord said to him, ‘Take
off your sandals; the place where you
are standing is holy ground. 34I have
indeed seen the oppression of my
people in Egypt. I have heard their
groaning and have come down to set
them free. Now come, I will send you
back to Egypt.’

35“This is the same Moses whom they
had rejected with the words, ‘Who
made you ruler and judge?’ He was sent
to be their ruler and deliverer by God
himself, through the angel who
appeared to him in the bush. 36He led
them out of Egypt and did wonders and
miraculous signs in Egypt, at the Red
Sea and for forty years in the desert.

37“This is that Moses who told the
Israelites, ‘God will send you a prophet
like me from your own people.’ 38He
was in the assembly in the desert, with
the angel who spoke to him on Mount
Sinai, and with our fathers; and he received living words to pass on to us.

39“But our fathers refused to obey
him. Instead, they rejected him and in
their hearts turned back to Egypt.
40They told Aaron, ‘Make us gods who
will go before us. As for this fellow
Moses who led us out of Egypt—we
don’t know what has happened to him!’
41That was the time they made an idol in
the form of a calf. They brought sacrifices to it and held a celebration in
honour of what their hands had made.
42But God turned away and gave them
over to the worship of the heavenly
bodies. This agrees with what is written
in the book of the prophets:

“ ‘Did you bring me sacrifices and
  offerings
for forty years in the desert, O
  house of Israel?
43You have lifted up the shrine of
  Molech
and the star of your god Rephan,
the idols you made to worship.
Therefore I will send you into exile’
  beyond Babylon.

READING FROM PSALMS
Psalm 72:1–20

Of Solomon.

1Endow the king with your justice, O
  God,
the royal son with your
  righteousness.

2He will judge your people in
righteousness,
your afflicted ones with justice.
3The mountains will bring prosperity
to the people,
the hills the fruit of righteousness.
4He will defend the afflicted among
the people
and save the children of the needy;
he will crush the oppressor.

5He will endure as long as the sun,
as long as the moon, through all
generations.
6He will be like rain falling on a mown
field,
like showers watering the earth.
7In his days the righteous will flourish;
prosperity will abound till the
moon is no more.

8He will rule from sea to sea
and from the River to the ends of
the earth.
9The desert tribes will bow before him
and his enemies will lick the dust.
10The kings of Tarshish and of distant
shores
will bring tribute to him;
the kings of Sheba and Seba
will present him gifts.
11All kings will bow down to him
and all nations will serve him.

12For he will deliver the needy who cry
out,
the afflicted who have no-one to
help.
13He will take pity on the weak and the
needy
and save the needy from death.
14He will rescue them from oppression
and violence,
for precious is their blood in his
sight.

15Long may he live!
May gold from Sheba be given to
him.
May people ever pray for him
and bless him all day long.
16Let corn abound throughout the
land;
on the tops of the hills may it sway.
Let its fruit flourish like Lebanon;
let it thrive like the grass of the
field.
17May his name endure for ever;
may it continue as long as the sun.

All nations will be blessed through
him,
and they will call him blessed.

18Praise be to the LORD God, the God
of Israel,
who alone does marvellous deeds.
19Praise be to his glorious name for
ever;
may the whole earth be filled with
his glory.
Amen and Amen.

20This concludes the prayers of David
son of Jesse.

JUNE 12

OLD TESTAMENT READING
2 Samuel 18:19–19:43

David Mourns

19Now Ahimaaz son of Zadok said,
"Let me run and take the news to the
king that the LORD has delivered him
from the hand of his enemies."
20"You are not the one to take the
news today," Joab told him. "You may
take the news another time, but you
must not do so today, because the king's
son is dead."
21Then Joab said to a Cushite, "Go,
tell the king what you have seen." The
Cushite bowed down before Joab and
ran off.
22Ahimaaz son of Zadok again said to
Joab, "Come what may, please let me
run behind the Cushite."
But Joab replied, "My son, why do
you want to go? You don't have any
news that will bring you a reward."
23He said, "Come what may, I want
to run."
So Joab said, "Run!" Then Ahimaaz
ran by way of the plain and outran the
Cushite.
24While David was sitting between
the inner and outer gates, the watchman
went up to the roof of the gateway by
the wall. As he looked out, he saw a
man running alone. 25The watchman
called out to the king and reported it.
The king said, "If he is alone, he must
have good news." And the man came
closer and closer.
26Then the watchman saw another
man running, and he called down to the
gatekeeper, "Look, another man running alone!"
The king said, "He must be bringing
good news, too."
27The watchman said, "It seems to
me that the first one runs like Ahimaaz
son of Zadok."
"He's a good man," the king said.
"He comes with good news."
28Then Ahimaaz called out to the
king, "All is well!" He bowed down
before the king with his face to the
ground and said, "Praise be to the LORD
your God! He has delivered up the men
who lifted their hands against my lord
the king."
29The king asked, "Is the young man
Absalom safe?"
Ahimaaz answered, "I saw great confusion just as Joab was about to send the
king's servant and me, your servant, but
I don't know what it was."
30The king said, "Stand aside and
wait here." So he stepped aside and
stood there.
31Then the Cushite arrived and said,
"My lord the king, hear the good news!
The LORD has delivered you today from
all who rose up against you."
32The king asked the Cushite, "Is the
young man Absalom safe?"
The Cushite replied, "May the enemies of my lord the king and all who
rise up to harm you be like that young
man."
33The king was shaken. He went up to
the room over the gateway and wept.
As he went, he said: "O my son Absalom! My son, my son Absalom! If only I
had died instead of you—O Absalom,
my son, my son!"
19 Joab was told, "The king is
weeping and mourning for
Absalom." 2And for the whole army
the victory that day was turned into
mourning, because on that day the
troops heard it said, "The king is grieving for his son." 3The men stole into the
city that day as men steal in who are
ashamed when they flee from battle.
4The king covered his face and cried
aloud, "O my son Absalom! O Absalom, my son, my son!"
5Then Joab went into the house to the

king and said, "Today you have humiliated all your men, who have just saved
your life and the lives of your sons and
daughters and the lives of your wives
and concubines. 6You love those who
hate you and hate those who love you.
You have made it clear today that the
commanders and their men mean nothing to you. I see that you would be
pleased if Absalom were alive today
and all of us were dead. 7Now go out
and encourage your men. I swear by the
LORD that if you don't go out, not a man
will be left with you by nightfall. This
will be worse for you than all the calamities that have come upon you from your
youth till now."
8So the king got up and took his seat
in the gateway. When the men were
told, "The king is sitting in the gateway," they all came before him.

David Returns to Jerusalem

Meanwhile, the Israelites had fled to
their homes. 9Throughout the tribes of
Israel, the people were all arguing with
each other, saying, "The king delivered
us from the hand of our enemies; he is
the one who rescued us from the hand of
the Philistines. But now he has fled the
country because of Absalom; 10and
Absalom, whom we anointed to rule
over us, has died in battle. So why do
you say nothing about bringing the king
back?"
11King David sent this message to
Zadok and Abiathar, the priests: "Ask
the elders of Judah, 'Why should you be
the last to bring the king back to his
palace, since what is being said throughout Israel has reached the king at his
quarters? 12You are my brothers, my
own flesh and blood. So why should you
be the last to bring back the king?'
13And say to Amasa, 'Are you not my
own flesh and blood? May God deal
with me, be it ever so severely, if from
now on you are not the commander of
my army in place of Joab.'"
14He won over the hearts of all the
men of Judah as though they were one
man. They sent word to the king, "Return, you and all your men." 15Then the
king returned and went as far as the
Jordan.

Now the men of Judah had come to
Gilgal to go out and meet the king and
bring him across the Jordan. 16Shimei
son of Gera, the Benjamite from
Bahurim, hurried down with the men of
Judah to meet King David. 17With him
were a thousand Benjamites, along with
Ziba, the steward of Saul's household,
and his fifteen sons and twenty servants.
They rushed to the Jordan, where the
king was. 18They crossed at the ford to
take the king's household over and to
do whatever he wished.

When Shimei son of Gera crossed the
Jordan, he fell prostrate before the king
19and said to him, "May my lord not
hold me guilty. Do not remember how
your servant did wrong on the day my
lord the king left Jerusalem. May the
king put it out of his mind. 20For I your
servant know that I have sinned, but
today I have come here as the first of the
whole house of Joseph to come down
and meet my lord the king."
21Then Abishai son of Zeruiah said,
"Shouldn't Shimei be put to death for
this? He cursed the LORD's anointed."
22David replied, "What do you and I
have in common, you sons of Zeruiah?
This day you have become my adversaries! Should anyone be put to death in
Israel today? Do I not know that today I
am king over Israel?" 23So the king said
to Shimei, "You shall not die." And the
king promised him on oath.
24Mephibosheth, Saul's grandson,
also went down to meet the king. He
had not taken care of his feet or trimmed his moustache or washed his
clothes from the day the king left until
the day he returned safely. 25When he
came from Jerusalem to meet the king,
the king asked him, "Why didn't you go
with me, Mephibosheth?"
26He said, "My lord the king, since I
your servant am lame, I said, 'I will have
my donkey saddled and will ride on it,
so that I can go with the king.' But Ziba

my servant betrayed me. 27And he has
slandered your servant to my lord the
king. My lord the king is like an angel of
God; so do whatever pleases you. 28All
my grandfather's descendants deserved
nothing but death from my lord the
king, but you gave your servant a place
among those who sat at your table. So
what right do I have to make any more
appeals to the king?"
29The king said to him, "Why say
more? I order you and Ziba to divide
the fields."
30Mephibosheth said to the king,
"Let him take everything, now that my
lord the king has arrived home safely."
31Barzillai the Gileadite also came
down from Rogelim to cross the Jordan
with the king and to send him on his way
from there. 32Now Barzillai was a very
old man, eighty years of age. He had
provided for the king during his stay in
Mahanaim, for he was a very wealthy
man. 33The king said to Barzillai,
"Cross over with me and stay with me in
Jerusalem, and I will provide for you."
34But Barzillai answered the king,
"How many more years shall I live, that
I should go up to Jerusalem with the
king? 35I am now eighty years old. Can I
tell the difference between what is good
and what is not? Can your servant taste
what he eats and drinks? Can I still hear
the voices of men and women singers?
Why should your servant be an added
burden to my lord the king? 36Your
servant will cross over the Jordan with
the king for a short distance, but why
should the king reward me in this way?
37Let your servant return, that I may die
in my own town near the tomb of my
father and mother. But here is your
servant Kimham. Let him cross over
with my lord the king. Do for him whatever pleases you."
38The king said, "Kimham shall cross
over with me, and I will do for him
whatever pleases you. And anything
you desire from me I will do for you."
39So all the people crossed the Jordan, and then the king crossed over.
The king kissed Barzillai and gave him
his blessing, and Barzillai returned to
his home.
40When the king crossed over to Gilgal, Kimham crossed with him. All the
troops of Judah and half the troops of
Israel had taken the king over.
41Soon all the men of Israel were
coming to the king and saying to him,
"Why did our brothers, the men of
Judah, steal the king away and bring
him and his household across the Jordan, together with all his men?"
42All the men of Judah answered the
men of Israel, "We did this because the
king is closely related to us. Why are
you angry about it? Have we eaten any
of the king's provisions? Have we taken
anything for ourselves?"
43Then the men of Israel answered
the men of Judah, "We have ten shares
in the king; and besides, we have a
greater claim on David than you have.
So why do you treat us with contempt?
Were we not the first to speak of bringing back our king?"

But the men of Judah responded even more harshly than the men of Israel.

NEW TESTAMENT READING

Acts 7:44–8:3

44"Our forefathers had the tabernacle of the Testimony with them in
the desert. It had been made as God
directed Moses, according to the pattern he had seen. 45Having received the
tabernacle, our fathers under Joshua
brought it with them when they took the
land from the nations God drove out
before them. It remained in the land
until the time of David, 46who enjoyed
God's favour and asked that he might
provide a dwelling-place for the God of
Jacob. 47But it was Solomon who built
the house for him.
48"However, the Most High does not live in houses made by men. As the prophet says:

49" 'Heaven is my throne,
and the earth is my footstool.

What kind of house will you build for
me?
says the Lord.
Or where will my resting place be?
50Has not my hand made all these
things?'

51"You stiff-necked people, with uncircumcised hearts and ears! You are just like your fathers: You always resist the Holy Spirit!
52Was there ever a prophet your fathers did not persecute? They even killed those who predicted the coming of the Righteous One. And now you have betrayed and murdered him—
53you who have received the law that was put into effect through angels but have not obeyed it."

The Stoning of Stephen

54When they heard this, they were furious and gnashed their teeth at him.
55But Stephen, full of the Holy Spirit, looked up to heaven and saw the glory of God, and Jesus standing at the right hand of God.
56"Look," he said, "I see heaven open and the Son of Man standing at the right hand of God."
57At this they covered their ears and, yelling at the top of their voices, they all rushed at him,
58dragged him out of the city and began to stone him. Meanwhile, the witnesses laid their clothes at the feet of a young man named Saul.
59While they were stoning him, Stephen prayed, "Lord Jesus, receive my spirit."
60Then he fell on his knees and cried out, "Lord, do not hold this sin against them." When he had said this, he fell asleep.

8 And Saul was there, giving approval to his death.

The Church Persecuted and Scattered

On that day a great persecution broke out against the church at Jerusalem, and all except the apostles were scattered throughout Judea and Samaria.
2Godly men buried Stephen and mourned deeply for him.
3But Saul began to destroy the church. Going from house to house, he dragged off men and women and put them in prison.

READING FROM PSALMS
Psalm 73:1–14

A psalm of Asaph.

1Surely God is good to Israel,
to those who are pure in heart.

2But as for me, my feet had almost
slipped;
I had nearly lost my foothold.
3For I envied the arrogant
when I saw the prosperity of the
wicked.

4They have no struggles;
their bodies are healthy and strong.
5They are free from the burdens
common to man;
they are not plagued by human ills.
6Therefore pride is their necklace;
they clothe themselves with
violence.
7From their callous hearts comes
iniquity;
the evil conceits of their minds
know no limits.
8They scoff, and speak with malice;
in their arrogance they threaten
oppression.
9Their mouths lay claim to heaven,
and their tongues take possession
of the earth.
10Therefore their people turn to them
and drink up waters in abundance.
11They say, "How can God know?
Does the Most High have
knowledge?"

12This is what the wicked are like—
always carefree, they increase in
wealth.

13Surely in vain have I kept my heart
pure;
in vain have I washed my hands in
innocence.
14All day long I have been plagued;
I have been punished every
morning.

DAY 164

JUNE 13

OLD TESTAMENT READING

2 Samuel 20:1–21:22

Sheba Rebels Against David

20 Now a troublemaker named
Sheba son of Bicri, a Benjamite,
happened to be there. He sounded the
trumpet and shouted,

"We have no share in David,
no part in Jesse's son!
Every man to his tent, O Israel!"

2 So all the men of Israel deserted
David to follow Sheba son of Bicri. But
the men of Judah stayed by their king all
the way from the Jordan to Jerusalem.
3 When David returned to his palace
in Jerusalem, he took the ten concubines he had left to take care of the
palace and put them in a house under
guard. He provided for them, but did
not lie with them. They were kept in
confinement till the day of their death,
living as widows.
4 Then the king said to Amasa, "Summon the men of Judah to come to me
within three days, and be here yourself." 5 But when Amasa went to summon Judah, he took longer than the
time the king had set for him.
6 David said to Abishai, "Now Sheba
son of Bicri will do us more harm than
Absalom did. Take your master's men
and pursue him, or he will find fortified
cities and escape from us." 7 So Joab's
men and the Kerethites and Pelethites
and all the mighty warriors went out
under the command of Abishai. They
marched out from Jerusalem to pursue
Sheba son of Bicri.
8 While they were at the great rock in
Gibeon, Amasa came to meet them.
Joab was wearing his military tunic, and
strapped over it at his waist was a belt
with a dagger in its sheath. As he stepped forward, it dropped out of its
sheath.
9 Joab said to Amasa, "How are you,
my brother?" Then Joab took Amasa
by the beard with his right hand to kiss
him. 10 Amasa was not on his guard
against the dagger in Joab's hand, and
Joab plunged it into his belly, and his
intestines spilled out on the ground.
Without being stabbed again, Amasa
died. Then Joab and his brother
Abishai pursued Sheba son of Bicri.
11 One of Joab's men stood beside
Amasa and said, "Whoever favours
Joab, and whoever is for David, let him
follow Joab!" 12 Amasa lay wallowing in
his blood in the middle of the road, and
the man saw that all the troops came to a
halt there. When he realised that everyone who came up to Amasa stopped, he
dragged him from the road into a field
and threw a garment over him. 13 After
Amasa had been removed from the
road, all the men went on with Joab to
pursue Sheba son of Bicri.
14 Sheba passed through all the tribes
of Israel to Abel Beth Maacah and
through the entire region of the Berites,
who gathered together and followed
him. 15 All the troops with Joab came
and besieged Sheba in Abel Beth
Maacah. They built a siege ramp up to
the city, and it stood against the outer
fortifications. While they were battering the wall to bring it down, 16 a wise
woman called from the city, "Listen!
Listen! Tell Joab to come here so that I
can speak to him." 17 He went towards
her, and she asked, "Are you Joab?"
"I am," he answered.
She said, "Listen to what your servant has to say."
"I'm listening," he said.
18 She continued, "Long ago they
used to say, 'Get your answer at Abel,'
and that settled it. 19 We are the peaceful
and faithful in Israel. You are trying to
destroy a city that is a mother in Israel.
Why do you want to swallow up the
LORD's inheritance?"

20"Far be it from me!" Joab replied, "Far be it from me to swallow up or destroy! 21That is not the case. A man named Sheba son of Bicri, from the hill country of Ephraim, has lifted up his hand against the king, against David. Hand over this one man, and I'll withdraw from the city."

The woman said to Joab, "His head will be thrown to you from the wall."

22Then the woman went to all the people with her wise advice, and they cut off the head of Sheba son of Bicri and threw it to Joab. So he sounded the trumpet, and his men dispersed from the city, each returning to his home. And Joab went back to the king in Jerusalem.

23Joab was over Israel's entire army; Benaiah son of Jehoiada was over the Kerethites and Pelethites; 24Adoniram was in charge of forced labour; Jehoshaphat son of Ahilud was recorder; 25Sheva was secretary; Zadok and Abiathar were priests; 26and Ira the Jairite was David's priest.

The Gibeonites Avenged

21 During the reign of David, there was a famine for three successive years; so David sought the face of the LORD. The LORD said, "It is on account of Saul and his blood-stained house; it is because he put the Gibeonites to death."

2The king summoned the Gibeonites and spoke to them. (Now the Gibeonites were not a part of Israel but were survivors of the Amorites; the Israelites had sworn to ⌞spare⌟ them, but Saul in his zeal for Israel and Judah had tried to annihilate them.) 3David asked the Gibeonites, "What shall I do for you? How shall I make amends so that you will bless the LORD's inheritance?"

4The Gibeonites answered him, "We have no right to demand silver or gold from Saul or his family, nor do we have the right to put anyone in Israel to death."

"What do you want me to do for you?" David asked.

5They answered the king, "As for the man who destroyed us and plotted against us so that we have been decimated and have no place anywhere in Israel, 6let seven of his male descendants be given to us to be killed and exposed before the LORD at Gibeah of Saul—the LORD's chosen one."

So the king said, "I will give them to you."

7The king spared Mephibosheth son of Jonathan, the son of Saul, because of the oath before the LORD between David and Jonathan son of Saul. 8But the king took Armoni and Mephibosheth, the two sons of Aiah's daughter Rizpah, whom she had borne to Saul, together with the five sons of Saul's daughter Merab, whom she had borne to Adriel son of Barzillai the Meholathite. 9He handed them over to the Gibeonites, who killed and exposed them on a hill before the LORD. All seven of them fell together; they were put to death during the first days of harvest, just as the barley harvest was beginning.

10Rizpah daughter of Aiah took sackcloth and spread it out for herself on a rock. From the beginning of the harvest till the rain poured down from the heavens on the bodies, she did not let the birds of the air touch them by day or the wild animals by night. 11When David was told what Aiah's daughter Rizpah, Saul's concubine, had done, 12he went and took the bones of Saul and his son Jonathan from the citizens of Jabesh Gilead. (They had taken them secretly from the public square at Beth Shan, where the Philistines had hung them after they struck Saul down on Gilboa.) 13David brought the bones of Saul and his son Jonathan from there, and the bones of those who had been killed and exposed were gathered up.

14They buried the bones of Saul and his son Jonathan in the tomb of Saul's father Kish, at Zela in Benjamin, and did everything the king commanded.

After that, God answered prayer on behalf of the land.

Wars Against the Philistines

[15]Once again there was a battle between the Philistines and Israel. David went down with his men to fight against the Philistines, and he became exhausted. [16]And Ishbi-Benob, one of the descendants of Rapha, whose bronze spearhead weighed three hundred shekels and who was armed with a new ⌞sword⌟, said he would kill David. [17]But Abishai son of Zeruiah came to David's rescue; he struck the Philistine down and killed him. Then David's men swore to him, saying, "Never again will you go out with us to battle, so that the lamp of Israel will not be extinguished."

[18]In the course of time, there was another battle with the Philistines, at Gob. At that time Sibbecai the Hushathite killed Saph, one of the descendants of Rapha.

[19]In another battle with the Philistines at Gob, Elhanan son of Jaare-Oregim the Bethlehemite killed Goliath the Gittite, who had a spear with a shaft like a weaver's rod.

[20]In still another battle, which took place at Gath, there was a huge man with six fingers on each hand and six toes on each foot—twenty-four in all. He also was descended from Rapha. [21]When he taunted Israel, Jonathan son of Shimeah, David's brother, killed him.

[22]These four were descendants of Rapha in Gath, and they fell at the hands of David and his men.

NEW TESTAMENT READING

Acts 8:4–40

Philip in Samaria

[4]Those who had been scattered preached the word wherever they went. [5]Philip went down to a city in Samaria and proclaimed the Christ there. [6]When the crowds heard Philip and saw the miraculous signs he did, they all paid close attention to what he said. [7]With shrieks, evil spirits came out of many, and many paralytics and cripples were healed. [8]So there was great joy in that city.

Simon the Sorcerer

[9]Now for some time a man named Simon had practised sorcery in the city and amazed all the people of Samaria. He boasted that he was someone great, [10]and all the people, both high and low, gave him their attention and exclaimed, "This man is the divine power known as the Great Power." [11]They followed him because he had amazed them for a long time with his magic. [12]But when they believed Philip as he preached the good news of the kingdom of God and the name of Jesus Christ, they were baptised, both men and women. [13]Simon himself believed and was baptised. And he followed Philip everywhere, astonished by the great signs and miracles he saw.

[14]When the apostles in Jerusalem heard that Samaria had accepted the word of God, they sent Peter and John to them. [15]When they arrived, they prayed for them that they might receive the Holy Spirit, [16]because the Holy Spirit had not yet come upon any of them; they had simply been baptised into the name of the Lord Jesus. [17]Then Peter and John placed their hands on them, and they received the Holy Spirit.

[18]When Simon saw that the Spirit was given at the laying on of the apostles' hands, he offered them money [19]and said, "Give me also this ability so that everyone on whom I lay my hands may receive the Holy Spirit."

[20]Peter answered: "May your money perish with you, because you thought you could buy the gift of God with money! [21]You have no part or share in this ministry, because your heart is not right before God. [22]Repent of this

wickedness and pray to the Lord. Perhaps he will forgive you for having such
a thought in your heart. 23For I see that
you are full of bitterness and captive to
sin."
24Then Simon answered, "Pray to the Lord for me so that nothing you have said may happen to me."
25When they had testified and proclaimed the word of the Lord, Peter and John returned to Jerusalem, preaching the gospel in many Samaritan villages.

Philip and the Ethiopian

26Now an angel of the Lord said to Philip, "Go south to the road—the desert road—that goes down from
Jerusalem to Gaza." 27So he started
out, and on his way he met an Ethiopian eunuch, an important official in charge of all the treasury of Candace, queen of the Ethiopians. This man had gone to
Jerusalem to worship, 28and on his way
home was sitting in his chariot reading
the book of Isaiah the prophet. 29The
Spirit told Philip, "Go to that chariot and stay near it."
30Then Philip ran up to the chariot and heard the man reading Isaiah the prophet. "Do you understand what you are reading?" Philip asked.
31"How can I," he said, "unless someone explains it to me?" So he invited Philip to come up and sit with him.
32The eunuch was reading this passage of Scripture:

"He was led like a sheep to the slaughter,
and as a lamb before the shearer is silent,
so he did not open his mouth.
33In his humiliation he was deprived of justice.
Who can speak of his descendants?
For his life was taken from the earth."

34The eunuch asked Philip, "Tell me, please, who is the prophet talking about, himself or someone else?"
35Then Philip began with that very passage of Scripture and told him the good news about Jesus.
36As they travelled along the road, they came to some water and the eunuch said, "Look, here is water. Why
shouldn't I be baptised?" 38And he gave
orders to stop the chariot. Then both Philip and the eunuch went down into the water and Philip baptised him.
39When they came up out of the water, the Spirit of the Lord suddenly took Philip away, and the eunuch did not see him again, but went on his way rejoicing.
40Philip, however, appeared at
Azotus and travelled about, preaching the gospel in all the towns until he reached Caesarea.

READING FROM PROVERBS
Proverbs 14:25–35

25A truthful witness saves lives,
but a false witness is deceitful.

26He who fears the LORD has a secure fortress,
and for his children it will be a refuge.

27The fear of the LORD is a fountain of life,
turning a man from the snares of death.

28A large population is a king's glory,
but without subjects a prince is ruined.

29A patient man has great understanding,
but a quick-tempered man displays folly.

30A heart at peace gives life to the body,
but envy rots the bones.

31He who oppresses the poor shows contempt for their Maker,

but whoever is kind to the needy
honours God.

32When calamity comes, the wicked are
brought down,
but even in death the righteous
have a refuge.

33Wisdom reposes in the heart of the
discerning
and even among fools she lets
herself be known.

34Righteousness exalts a nation,
but sin is a disgrace to any people.

35A king delights in a wise servant,
but a shameful servant incurs his
wrath.

DAY 165

JUNE 14

OLD TESTAMENT READING
2 Samuel 22:1–23:7

David's Song of Praise

22 David sang to the LORD the
words of this song when the
LORD delivered him from the hand of all
his enemies and from the hand of Saul.
2He said:

"The LORD is my rock, my fortress
and my deliverer;
3 my God is my rock, in whom I take
refuge,
my shield and the horn of my
salvation.
He is my stronghold, my refuge and
my saviour—
from violent men you save me.
4I call to the LORD, who is worthy of
praise,
and I am saved from my enemies.

5"The waves of death swirled about
me;
the torrents of destruction
overwhelmed me.
6The cords of the grave coiled around
me;
the snares of death confronted me.
7In my distress I called to the LORD;
I called out to my God.
From his temple he heard my voice;
my cry came to his ears.

8"The earth trembled and quaked,
the foundations of the heavens
shook;
they trembled because he was
angry.
9Smoke rose from his nostrils;
consuming fire came from his
mouth,
burning coals blazed out of it.
10He parted the heavens and came
down;
dark clouds were under his feet.
11He mounted the cherubim and flew;
he soared on the wings of the wind.
12He made darkness his canopy around
him—
the dark rain clouds of the sky.
13Out of the brightness of his presence
bolts of lightning blazed forth.
14The LORD thundered from heaven;
the voice of the Most High
resounded.
15He shot arrows and scattered ⌊the
enemies⌋,
bolts of lightning and routed them.
16The valleys of the sea were exposed
and the foundations of the earth
laid bare
at the rebuke of the LORD,
at the blast of breath from his
nostrils.

17"He reached down from on high and
took hold of me;
he drew me out of deep waters.

18He rescued me from my powerful
enemy,
from my foes, who were too strong
for me.
19They confronted me in the day of my
disaster,
but the LORD was my support.
20He brought me out into a spacious
place;
he rescued me because he
delighted in me.

21"The LORD has dealt with me
according to my righteousness;
according to the cleanness of my
hands he has rewarded me.
22For I have kept the ways of the LORD;
I have not done evil by turning
from my God.
23All his laws are before me;
I have not turned away from his
decrees.
24I have been blameless before him
and have kept myself from sin.
25The LORD has rewarded me
according to my righteousness,
according to my cleanness in his
sight.

26"To the faithful you show yourself
faithful,
to the blameless you show yourself
blameless,
27to the pure you show yourself pure,
but to the crooked you show
yourself shrewd.
28You save the humble,
but your eyes are on the haughty to
bring them low.
29You are my lamp, O LORD;
the LORD turns my darkness into
light.
30With your help I can advance against
a troop;
with my God I can scale a wall.

31"As for God, his way is perfect;
the word of the LORD is flawless.
He is a shield
for all who take refuge in him.
32For who is God besides the LORD?
And who is the Rock except our
God?
33It is God who arms me with strength
and makes my way perfect.
34He makes my feet like the feet of a
deer;
he enables me to stand on the
heights.
35He trains my hands for battle;
my arms can bend a bow of bronze.
36You give me your shield of victory;
you stoop down to make me great.
37You broaden the path beneath me,
so that my ankles do not turn over.

38"I pursued my enemies and crushed
them;
I did not turn back till they were
destroyed.
39I crushed them completely, and they
could not rise;
they fell beneath my feet.
40You armed me with strength for
battle;
you made my adversaries bow at
my feet.
41You made my enemies turn their
backs in flight,
and I destroyed my foes.
42They cried for help, but there was
no-one to save them—
to the LORD, but he did not
answer.
43I beat them as fine as the dust of the
earth;
I pounded and trampled them like
mud in the streets.

44"You have delivered me from the
attacks of my people;
you have preserved me as the head
of nations.
People I did not know are subject to
me,
45 and foreigners come cringing to
me;
as soon as they hear me, they obey
me.
46They all lose heart;
they come trembling from their
strongholds.

47"The LORD lives! Praise be to my
Rock!

Exalted be God, the Rock, my
Saviour!
48He is the God who avenges me,
who puts the nations under me,
49 who sets me free from my enemies.
You exalted me above my foes;
from violent men you rescued me.
50Therefore I will praise you, O LORD,
among the nations;
I will sing praises to your name.
51He gives his king great victories;
he shows unfailing kindness to his
anointed,
to David and his descendants for
ever."

The Last Words of David

23 These are the last words of
David:

"The oracle of David son of Jesse,
the oracle of the man exalted by
the Most High,
the man anointed by the God of
Jacob,
Israel's singer of songs:

2"The Spirit of the LORD spoke
through me;
his word was on my tongue.
3The God of Israel spoke,
the Rock of Israel said to me:
'When one rules over men in
righteousness,
when he rules in the fear of God,
4he is like the light of morning at
sunrise
on a cloudless morning,
like the brightness after rain
that brings the grass from the
earth.'

5"Is not my house right with God?
Has he not made with me an
everlasting covenant,
arranged and secured in every
part?
Will he not bring to fruition my
salvation
and grant me my every desire?
6But evil men are all to be cast aside
like thorns,
which are not gathered with the
hand.
7Whoever touches thorns
uses a tool of iron or the shaft of a
spear;
they are burned up where they
lie."

NEW TESTAMENT READING
Acts 9:1–31

Saul's Conversion

9 Meanwhile, Saul was still breathing out murderous threats against
the Lord's disciples. He went to the
high priest 2and asked him for letters
to the synagogues in Damascus, so that
if he found any there who belonged to
the Way, whether men or women, he
might take them as prisoners to Jerusalem. 3As he neared Damascus on his
journey, suddenly a light from heaven
flashed around him. 4He fell to the
ground and heard a voice say to him,
"Saul, Saul, why do you persecute
me?"
5"Who are you, Lord?" Saul asked.
"I am Jesus, whom you are persecuting," he replied. 6"Now get up and
go into the city, and you will be told
what you must do."
7The men travelling with Saul stood
there speechless; they heard the sound
but did not see anyone. 8Saul got up
from the ground, but when he opened
his eyes he could see nothing. So they
led him by the hand into Damascus.
9For three days he was blind, and did
not eat or drink anything.
10In Damascus there was a disciple
named Ananias. The Lord called to him
in a vision, "Ananias!"
"Yes, Lord," he answered.
11The Lord told him, "Go to the
house of Judas on Straight Street and
ask for a man from Tarsus named Saul,
for he is praying. 12In a vision he has
seen a man named Ananias come and

place his hands on him to restore his
sight."
13"Lord," Ananias answered, "I
have heard many reports about this man
and all the harm he has done to your
saints in Jerusalem. 14And he has come
here with authority from the chief
priests to arrest all who call on your
name."
15But the Lord said to Ananias, "Go!
This man is my chosen instrument to
carry my name before the Gentiles and
their kings and before the people of
Israel. 16I will show him how much he
must suffer for my name."
17Then Ananias went to the house
and entered it. Placing his hands on
Saul, he said, "Brother Saul, the Lord
—Jesus, who appeared to you on the
road as you were coming here—has
sent me so that you may see again and
be filled with the Holy Spirit."
18Immediately, something like scales
fell from Saul's eyes, and he could see
again. He got up and was baptised,
19and after taking some food, he re-
gained his strength.

Saul in Damascus and Jerusalem

Saul spent several days with the disciples in Damascus. 20At once he began
to preach in the synagogues that Jesus is
the Son of God. 21All those who heard
him were astonished and asked, "Isn't
he the man who caused havoc in Jerusalem among those who call on this
name? And hasn't he come here to take
them as prisoners to the chief priests?"
22Yet Saul grew more and more powerful and baffled the Jews living in Damascus by proving that Jesus is the Christ.
23After many days had gone by, the
Jews conspired to kill him, 24but Saul
learned of their plan. Day and night
they kept close watch on the city gates in
order to kill him. 25But his followers
took him by night and lowered him in a
basket through an opening in the wall.
26When he came to Jerusalem, he
tried to join the disciples, but they were
all afraid of him, not believing that he
really was a disciple. 27But Barnabas
took him and brought him to the apostles. He told them how Saul on his
journey had seen the Lord and that the
Lord had spoken to him, and how in
Damascus he had preached fearlessly in
the name of Jesus. 28So Saul stayed with
them and moved about freely in Jerusalem, speaking boldly in the name of
the Lord. 29He talked and debated with
the Grecian Jews, but they tried to kill
him. 30When the brothers learned of
this, they took him down to Caesarea
and sent him off to Tarsus.
31Then the church throughout Judea,
Galilee and Samaria enjoyed a time of
peace. It was strengthened; and encouraged by the Holy Spirit, it grew in numbers, living in the fear of the Lord.

READING FROM PSALMS
Psalm 73:15–28

15If I had said, "I will speak thus,"
I would have betrayed your
children.
16When I tried to understand all this,
it was oppressive to me
17till I entered the sanctuary of God;
then I understood their final
destiny.

18Surely you place them on slippery
ground;
you cast them down to ruin.
19How suddenly are they destroyed,
completely swept away by terrors!
20As a dream when one awakes,
so when you arise, O Lord,
you will despise them as fantasies.

21When my heart was grieved
and my spirit embittered,
22I was senseless and ignorant;
I was a brute beast before you.

23Yet I am always with you;
you hold me by my right hand.

[24]You guide me with your counsel,
and afterwards you will take me
into glory.
[25]Whom have I in heaven but you?
And earth has nothing I desire
besides you.
[26]My flesh and my heart may fail,
but God is the strength of my heart
and my portion for ever.
[27]Those who are far from you will
perish;
you destroy all who are unfaithful
to you.
[28]But as for me, it is good to be near
God.
I have made the Sovereign LORD
my refuge;
I will tell of all your deeds.

DAY 166

JUNE 15

OLD TESTAMENT READING
2 Samuel 23:8–24:25

David's Mighty Men

[8]These are the names of David's mighty men:

Josheb-Basshebeth, a Tahkemonite, was chief of the Three; he raised his spear against eight hundred men, whom he killed in one encounter.

[9]Next to him was Eleazar son of Dodai the Ahohite. As one of the three mighty men, he was with David when they taunted the Philistines gathered ⌞at Pas Dammim⌟ for battle. Then the men of Israel retreated, [10]but he stood his ground and struck down the Philistines till his hand grew tired and froze to the sword. The LORD brought about a great victory that day. The troops returned to Eleazar, but only to strip the dead.

[11]Next to him was Shammah son of Agee the Hararite. When the Philistines banded together at a place where there was a field full of lentils, Israel's troops fled from them. [12]But Shammah took his stand in the middle of the field. He defended it and struck the Philistines down, and the LORD brought about a great victory.

[13]During harvest time, three of the thirty chief men came down to David at the cave of Adullam, while a band of Philistines was encamped in the Valley of Rephaim. [14]At that time David was in the stronghold, and the Philistine garrison was at Bethlehem. [15]David longed for water and said, "Oh, that someone would get me a drink of water from the well near the gate of Bethlehem!" [16]So the three mighty men broke through the Philistine lines, drew water from the well near the gate of Bethlehem and carried it back to David. But he refused to drink it; instead, he poured it out before the LORD. [17]"Far be it from me, O LORD, to do this!" he said. "Is it not the blood of men who went at the risk of their lives?" And David would not drink it.

Such were the exploits of the three mighty men.

[18]Abishai the brother of Joab son of Zeruiah was chief of the Three. He raised his spear against three hundred men, whom he killed, and so he became as famous as the Three. [19]Was he not held in greater honour than the Three? He became their commander, even though he was not included among them.

[20]Benaiah son of Jehoiada was a valiant fighter from Kabzeel, who performed great exploits. He struck down two of Moab's best men. He also went down into a pit on a snowy day and killed a lion. [21]And he struck down a huge Egyptian. Although the Egyptian had a spear in his hand, Benaiah went

against him with a club. He snatched the
spear from the Egyptian's hand and killed him with his own spear. 22Such were
the exploits of Benaiah son of Jehoiada;
he too was as famous as the three
mighty men. 23He was held in greater
honour than any of the Thirty, but he
was not included among the Three. And
David put him in charge of his bodyguard.

24Among the Thirty were:
Asahel the brother of Joab,
Elhanan son of Dodo from Beth-lehem,
25Shammah the Harodite,
Elika the Harodite,
26Helez the Paltite,
Ira son of Ikkesh from Tekoa,
27Abiezer from Anathoth,
Mebunnai the Hushathite,
28Zalmon the Ahohite,
Maharai the Netophathite,
29Heled son of Baanah the Netophathite,
Ithai son of Ribai from Gibeah in Benjamin,
30Benaiah the Pirathonite,
Hiddai from the ravines of Gaash,
31Abi-Albon the Arbathite,
Azmaveth the Barhumite,
32Eliahba the Shaalbonite,
the sons of Jashen,
Jonathan 33son of Shammah the Hararite,
Ahiam son of Sharar the Hararite,
34Eliphelet son of Ahasbai the Maacathite,
Eliam son of Ahithophel the Gilonite,
35Hezro the Carmelite,
Paarai the Arbite,
36Igal son of Nathan from Zobah,
the son of Hagri,
37Zelek the Ammonite,
Naharai the Beerothite, the armour-bearer of Joab son of Zeruiah,
38Ira the Ithrite,
Gareb the Ithrite
39and Uriah the Hittite.
There were thirty-seven in all.

David Counts the Fighting Men

24 Again the anger of the LORD
burned against Israel, and he incited David against them, saying, "Go
and take a census of Israel and Judah."
2So the king said to Joab and the army
commanders with him, "Go throughout
the tribes of Israel from Dan to Beersheba and enrol the fighting men, so
that I may know how many there are."
3But Joab replied to the king, "May
the LORD your God multiply the troops
a hundred times over, and may the eyes
of my lord the king see it. But why does
my lord the king want to do such a
thing?"
4The king's word, however, over-
ruled Joab and the army commanders;
so they left the presence of the king to
enrol the fighting men of Israel.
5After crossing the Jordan, they
camped near Aroer, south of the town
in the gorge, and then went through
Gad and on to Jazer. 6They went to
Gilead and the region of Tahtim Hod-
shi, and on to Dan Jaan and around
towards Sidon. 7Then they went towards the fortress of Tyre and all the
towns of the Hivites and Canaanites.
Finally, they went on to Beersheba in
the Negev of Judah.
8After they had gone through the entire land, they came back to Jerusalem
at the end of nine months and twenty
days.
9Joab reported the number of the
fighting men to the king: In Israel there
were eight hundred thousand able-
bodied men who could handle a sword,
and in Judah five hundred thousand.
10David was conscience-stricken after
he had counted the fighting men, and he
said to the LORD, "I have sinned greatly
in what I have done. Now, O LORD, I
beg you, take away the guilt of your
servant. I have done a very foolish
thing."

11Before David got up the next morning, the word of the LORD had come to
Gad the prophet, David's seer: 12"Go
and tell David, 'This is what the LORD
says: I am giving you three options.
Choose one of them for me to carry out
against you.'"
13So Gad went to David and said to
him, "Shall there come upon you three
years of famine in your land? Or three
months of fleeing from your enemies
while they pursue you? Or three days of
plague in your land? Now then, think it
over and decide how I should answer
the one who sent me."
14David said to Gad, "I am in deep
distress. Let us fall into the hands of the
LORD, for his mercy is great; but do not
let me fall into the hands of men."
15So the LORD sent a plague on Israel
from that morning until the end of the
time designated, and seventy thousand
of the people from Dan to Beersheba
died. 16When the angel stretched out his
hand to destroy Jerusalem, the LORD
was grieved because of the calamity and
said to the angel who was afflicting the
people, "Enough! Withdraw your
hand." The angel of the LORD was then
at the threshing-floor of Araunah the
Jebusite.
17When David saw the angel who was
striking down the people, he said to the
LORD, "I am the one who has sinned
and done wrong. These are but sheep.
What have they done? Let your hand
fall upon me and my family."

David Builds an Altar

18On that day Gad went to David and
said to him, "Go up and build an altar to
the LORD on the threshing-floor of
Araunah the Jebusite." 19So David
went up, as the LORD had commanded
through Gad. 20When Araunah looked
and saw the king and his men coming
towards him, he went out and bowed
down before the king with his face to the
ground.
21Araunah said, "Why has my lord
the king come to his servant?"
"To buy your threshing-floor,"
David answered, "so that I can build an
altar to the LORD, that the plague on the
people may be stopped."
22Araunah said to David, "Let my
lord the king take whatever pleases him
and offer it up. Here are oxen for the
burnt offering, and here are threshing-
sledges and ox yokes for the wood. 23O
king, Araunah gives all this to the
king." Araunah also said to him, "May
the LORD your God accept you."
24But the king replied to Araunah,
"No, I insist on paying you for it. I will
not sacrifice to the LORD my God burnt
offerings that cost me nothing."
So David bought the threshing-floor
and the oxen and paid fifty shekels of
silver for them. 25David built an altar to
the LORD there and sacrificed burnt
offerings and fellowship offerings. Then
the LORD answered prayer on behalf of
the land, and the plague on Israel was
stopped.

NEW TESTAMENT READING
Acts 9:32–10:23a

Aeneas and Dorcas

32As Peter travelled about the country, he went to visit the saints in Lydda.
33There he found a man named Aeneas,
a paralytic who had been bedridden for
eight years. 34"Aeneas," Peter said to
him, "Jesus Christ heals you. Get up
and tidy up your mat." Immediately
Aeneas got up. 35All those who lived in
Lydda and Sharon saw him and turned
to the Lord.
36In Joppa there was a disciple named
Tabitha (which, when translated, is
Dorcas), who was always doing good
and helping the poor. 37About that time
she became sick and died, and her body
was washed and placed in an upstairs
room. 38Lydda was near Joppa; so when
the disciples heard that Peter was in
Lydda, they sent two men to him and
urged him, "Please come at once!"
39Peter went with them, and when he
arrived he was taken upstairs to the

room. All the widows stood around
him, crying and showing him the robes
and other clothing that Dorcas had
made while she was still with them.
40Peter sent them all out of the room;
then he got down on his knees and
prayed. Turning towards the dead
woman, he said, "Tabitha, get up." She
opened her eyes, and seeing Peter she
sat up. 41He took her by the hand and
helped her to her feet. Then he called
the believers and the widows and presented her to them alive. 42This became
known all over Joppa, and many people
believed in the Lord. 43Peter stayed in
Joppa for some time with a tanner
named Simon.

Cornelius Calls for Peter

10 At Caesarea there was a man
named Cornelius, a centurion in
what was known as the Italian Regiment. 2He and all his family were
devout and God-fearing; he gave generously to those in need and prayed to
God regularly. 3One day at about three
in the afternoon he had a vision. He
distinctly saw an angel of God, who
came to him and said, "Cornelius!"
4Cornelius stared at him in fear.
"What is it, Lord?" he asked.
The angel answered, "Your prayers
and gifts to the poor have come up as a
memorial offering before God. 5Now
send men to Joppa to bring back a man
named Simon who is called Peter. 6He is
staying with Simon the tanner, whose
house is by the sea."
7When the angel who spoke to him
had gone, Cornelius called two of his
servants and a devout soldier who was
one of his attendants. 8He told them
everything that had happened and sent
them to Joppa.

Peter's Vision

9About noon the following day as
they were on their journey and
approaching the city, Peter went up on
the roof to pray. 10He became hungry
and wanted something to eat, and while
the meal was being prepared, he fell
into a trance. 11He saw heaven opened
and something like a large sheet being
let down to earth by its four corners. 12It
contained all kinds of four-footed animals, as well as reptiles of the earth and
birds of the air. 13Then a voice told him,
"Get up, Peter. Kill and eat."
14"Surely not, Lord!" Peter replied.
"I have never eaten anything impure or
unclean."
15The voice spoke to him a second
time, "Do not call anything impure that
God has made clean."
16This happened three times, and immediately the sheet was taken back to
heaven.
17While Peter was wondering about
the meaning of the vision, the men sent
by Cornelius found out where Simon's
house was and stopped at the gate.
18They called out, asking if Simon who
was known as Peter was staying there.
19While Peter was still thinking about
the vision, the Spirit said to him,
"Simon, three men are looking for you.
20So get up and go downstairs. Do not
hesitate to go with them, for I have sent
them."
21Peter went down and said to the
men, "I'm the one you're looking for.
Why have you come?"
22The men replied, "We have come
from Cornelius the centurion. He is a
righteous and God-fearing man, who is
respected by all the Jewish people. A
holy angel told him to have you come to
his house so that he could hear what you
have to say." 23Then Peter invited the
men into the house to be his guests.

READING FROM PSALMS
Psalm 74:1–9

A *maskil* of Asaph.

1Why have you rejected us for ever, O
God?
Why does your anger smoulder
against the sheep of your
pasture?

[2]Remember the people you purchased
of old,
the tribe of your inheritance,
whom you redeemed—
Mount Zion, where you dwelt.
[3]Turn your steps towards these
everlasting ruins,
all this destruction the enemy has
brought on the sanctuary.

[4]Your foes roared in the place where
you met with us;
they set up their standards as signs.
[5]They behaved like men wielding axes
to cut through a thicket of trees.
[6]They smashed all the carved
panelling
with their axes and hatchets.
[7]They burned your sanctuary to the
ground;
they defiled the dwelling-place of
your Name.
[8]They said in their hearts, "We will
crush them completely!"
They burned every place where
God was worshipped in the
land.
[9]We are given no miraculous signs;
no prophets are left,
and none of us knows how long this
will be.

DAY 167

JUNE 16

OLD TESTAMENT READING

1 Kings 1:1–2:12

Adonijah Sets Himself Up as King

1 When King David was old and well
advanced in years, he could not
keep warm even when they put covers
over him. [2]So his servants said to him,
"Let us look for a young virgin to attend
the king and take care of him. She can
lie beside him so that our lord the king
may keep warm."
[3]Then they searched throughout
Israel for a beautiful girl and found
Abishag, a Shunammite, and brought
her to the king. [4]The girl was very
beautiful; she took care of the king and
waited on him, but the king had no
intimate relations with her.
[5]Now Adonijah, whose mother was
Haggith, put himself forward and said,
"I will be king." So he got chariots and
horses ready, with fifty men to run
ahead of him. [6](His father had never
interfered with him by asking, "Why do
you behave as you do?" He was also
very handsome and was born next after
Absalom.)
[7]Adonijah conferred with Joab son of
Zeruiah and with Abiathar the priest,
and they gave him their support. [8]But
Zadok the priest, Benaiah son of
Jehoiada, Nathan the prophet, Shimei
and Rei and David's special guard did
not join Adonijah.
[9]Adonijah then sacrificed sheep, cattle and fattened calves at the Stone of
Zoheleth near En Rogel. He invited all
his brothers, the king's sons, and all the
men of Judah who were royal officials,
[10]but he did not invite Nathan the
prophet or Benaiah or the special guard
or his brother Solomon.
[11]Then Nathan asked Bathsheba,
Solomon's mother, "Have you not
heard that Adonijah, the son of Haggith, has become king without our lord
David's knowing it? [12]Now then, let me
advise you how you can save your own
life and the life of your son Solomon.
[13]Go in to King David and say to him,
'My lord the king, did you not swear to
me your servant: "Surely Solomon your
son shall be king after me, and he will sit
on my throne"? Why then has Adonijah
become king?' [14]While you are still

there talking to the king, I will come in
and confirm what you have said."
15So Bathsheba went to see the aged
king in his room, where Abishag the
Shunammite was attending him.
16Bathsheba bowed low and knelt before the king.
"What is it you want?" the king
asked.
17She said to him, "My lord, you
yourself swore to me your servant by
the LORD your God: 'Solomon your son
shall become king after me, and he will
sit on my throne.' 18But now Adonijah
has become king, and you, my lord the
king, do not know about it. 19He has
sacrificed great numbers of cattle, fattened calves, and sheep, and has invited
all the king's sons, Abiathar the priest
and Joab the commander of the army,
but he has not invited Solomon your
servant. 20My lord the king, the eyes of
all Israel are on you, to learn from you
who will sit on the throne of my lord the
king after him. 21Otherwise, as soon as
my lord the king is laid to rest with his
fathers, I and my son Solomon will be
treated as criminals."
22While she was still speaking with
the king, Nathan the prophet arrived.
23And they told the king, "Nathan the
prophet is here." So he went before
the king and bowed with his face to
the ground.
24Nathan said, "Have you, my lord
the king, declared that Adonijah shall
be king after you, and that he will sit on
your throne? 25Today he has gone down
and sacrificed great numbers of cattle,
fattened calves, and sheep. He has invited all the king's sons, the commanders of the army and Abiathar the
priest. Right now they are eating and
drinking with him and saying, 'Long live
King Adonijah!' 26But me your servant,
and Zadok the priest, and Benaiah son
of Jehoiada, and your servant Solomon
he did not invite. 27Is this something my
lord the king has done without letting
his servants know who should sit on
the throne of my lord the king after
him?"

David Makes Solomon King

28Then King David said, "Call in
Bathsheba." So she came into the king's
presence and stood before him.
29The king then took an oath: "As
surely as the LORD lives, who has delivered me out of every trouble, 30I will
surely carry out today what I swore to
you by the LORD, the God of Israel:
Solomon your son shall be king after
me, and he will sit on my throne in my
place."
31Then Bathsheba bowed low with
her face to the ground and, kneeling
before the king, said, "May my lord
King David live for ever!"
32King David said, "Call in Zadok the
priest, Nathan the prophet and Benaiah
son of Jehoiada." When they came before the king, 33he said to them: "Take
your lord's servants with you and set
Solomon my son on my own mule and
take him down to Gihon. 34There shall
Zadok the priest and Nathan the
prophet anoint him king over Israel.
Blow the trumpet and shout, 'Long live
King Solomon!' 35Then you are to go up
with him, and he is to come and sit on
my throne and reign in my place. I have
appointed him ruler over Israel and
Judah."
36Benaiah son of Jehoiada answered
the king, "Amen! May the LORD, the
God of my lord the king, so declare it.
37As the LORD was with my lord the
king, so may he be with Solomon to
make his throne even greater than the
throne of my lord King David!"
38So Zadok the priest, Nathan the
prophet, Benaiah son of Jehoiada, the
Kerethites and the Pelethites went
down and put Solomon on King David's
mule and escorted him to Gihon.
39Zadok the priest took the horn of oil
from the sacred tent and anointed Solomon. Then they sounded the trumpet
and all the people shouted, "Long live
King Solomon!" 40And all the people
went up after him, playing flutes and
rejoicing greatly, so that the ground
shook with the sound.

41 Adonijah and all the guests who
were with him heard it as they were
finishing their feast. On hearing the
sound of the trumpet, Joab asked,
"What's the meaning of all the noise in
the city?"
42 Even as he was speaking, Jonathan
son of Abiathar the priest arrived.
Adonijah said, "Come in. A worthy
man like you must be bringing good
news."
43 "Not at all!" Jonathan answered.
"Our lord King David has made Solomon king. 44 The king has sent with him
Zadok the priest, Nathan the prophet,
Benaiah son of Jehoiada, the Kerethites
and the Pelethites, and they have put
him on the king's mule, 45 and Zadok the
priest and Nathan the prophet have
anointed him king at Gihon. From there
they have gone up cheering, and the city
resounds with it. That's the noise you
hear. 46 Moreover, Solomon has taken
his seat on the royal throne. 47 Also, the
royal officials have come to congratulate our lord King David, saying, 'May
your God make Solomon's name more
famous than yours and his throne
greater than yours!' And the king
bowed in worship on his bed 48 and said,
'Praise be to the LORD, the God of
Israel, who has allowed my eyes to see a
successor on my throne today.'"
49 At this, all Adonijah's guests rose in
alarm and dispersed. 50 But Adonijah,
in fear of Solomon, went and took hold
of the horns of the altar. 51 Then Solomon was told, "Adonijah is afraid of
King Solomon and is clinging to the
horns of the altar. He says, 'Let King
Solomon swear to me today that he will
not put his servant to death with the
sword.'"
52 Solomon replied, "If he shows himself to be a worthy man, not a hair of his
head will fall to the ground; but if evil is
found in him, he will die." 53 Then King
Solomon sent men, and they brought
him down from the altar. And Adonijah
came and bowed down to King Solomon, and Solomon said, "Go to your
home."

David's Charge to Solomon

2 When the time drew near for David
to die, he gave a charge to Solomon
his son.
2 "I am about to go the way of all the
earth," he said. "So be strong, show
yourself a man, 3 and observe what the
LORD your God requires: Walk in his
ways, and keep his decrees and commands, his laws and requirements, as
written in the Law of Moses, so that
you may prosper in all you do and wherever you go, 4 and that the LORD may
keep his promise to me: 'If your descendants watch how they live, and if
they walk faithfully before me with all
their heart and soul, you will never
fail to have a man on the throne of
Israel.'
5 "Now you yourself know what Joab
son of Zeruiah did to me—what he did
to the two commanders of Israel's
armies, Abner son of Ner and Amasa
son of Jether. He killed them, shedding
their blood in peacetime as if in battle,
and with that blood stained the belt
round his waist and the sandals on his
feet. 6 Deal with him according to your
wisdom, but do not let his grey head go
down to the grave in peace.
7 "But show kindness to the sons of
Barzillai of Gilead and let them be
among those who eat at your table.
They stood by me when I fled from your
brother Absalom.
8 "And remember, you have with you
Shimei son of Gera, the Benjamite from
Bahurim, who called down bitter curses
on me the day I went to Mahanaim.
When he came down to meet me at the
Jordan, I swore to him by the LORD: 'I
will not put you to death by the sword.'
9 But now, do not consider him innocent. You are a man of wisdom; you
will know what to do to him. Bring
his grey head down to the grave in
blood."
10 Then David rested with his fathers
and was buried in the City of David.
11 He had reigned for forty years over
Israel—seven years in Hebron and

thirty-three in Jerusalem. 12So Solomon sat on the throne of his father David, and his rule was firmly established.

NEW TESTAMENT READING
Acts 10:23b–11:18

Peter at Cornelius' House

The next day Peter started out with them, and some of the brothers from Joppa went along. 24The following day he arrived in Caesarea. Cornelius was expecting them and had called together his relatives and close friends. 25As Peter entered the house, Cornelius met him and fell at his feet in reverence. 26But Peter made him get up. "Stand up," he said, "I am only a man myself."

27Talking with him, Peter went inside and found a large gathering of people. 28He said to them: "You are well aware that it is against our law for a Jew to associate with a Gentile or visit him. But God has shown me that I should not call any man impure or unclean. 29So when I was sent for, I came without raising any objection. May I ask why you sent for me?"

30Cornelius answered: "Four days ago I was in my house praying at this hour, at three in the afternoon. Suddenly a man in shining clothes stood before me 31and said, 'Cornelius, God has heard your prayer and remembered your gifts to the poor. 32Send to Joppa for Simon who is called Peter. He is a guest in the home of Simon the tanner, who lives by the sea.' 33So I sent for you immediately, and it was good of you to come. Now we are all here in the presence of God to listen to everything the Lord has commanded you to tell us."

34Then Peter began to speak: "I now realise how true it is that God does not show favouritism 35but accepts men from every nation who fear him and do what is right. 36You know the message God sent to the people of Israel, telling the good news of peace through Jesus Christ, who is Lord of all. 37You know what has happened throughout Judea, beginning in Galilee after the baptism that John preached—38how God anointed Jesus of Nazareth with the Holy Spirit and power, and how he went around doing good and healing all who were under the power of the devil, because God was with him.

39"We are witnesses of everything he did in the country of the Jews and in Jerusalem. They killed him by hanging him on a tree, 40but God raised him from the dead on the third day and caused him to be seen. 41He was not seen by all the people, but by witnesses whom God had already chosen—by us who ate and drank with him after he rose from the dead. 42He commanded us to preach to the people and to testify that he is the one whom God appointed as judge of the living and the dead. 43All the prophets testify about him that everyone who believes in him receives forgiveness of sins through his name."

44While Peter was still speaking these words, the Holy Spirit came on all who heard the message. 45The circumcised believers who had come with Peter were astonished that the gift of the Holy Spirit had been poured out even on the Gentiles. 46For they heard them speaking in tongues and praising God.

Then Peter said, 47"Can anyone keep these people from being baptised with water? They have received the Holy Spirit just as we have." 48So he ordered that they be baptised in the name of Jesus Christ. Then they asked Peter to stay with them for a few days.

Peter Explains His Actions

11 The apostles and the brothers throughout Judea heard that the Gentiles also had received the word of God. 2So when Peter went up to Jerusalem, the circumcised believers criticised him 3and said, "You went into the house of uncircumcised men and ate with them."

4Peter began and explained everything to them precisely as it had happened: 5"I was in the city of Joppa

praying, and in a trance I saw a vision. I
saw something like a large sheet being
let down from heaven by its four corners, and it came down to where I was.
6I looked into it and saw four-footed
animals of the earth, wild beasts, reptiles, and birds of the air. 7Then I heard
a voice telling me, 'Get up, Peter. Kill
and eat.'
8"I replied, 'Surely not, Lord!
Nothing impure or unclean has ever
entered my mouth.'
9"The voice spoke from heaven a
second time, 'Do not call anything impure that God has made clean.' 10This
happened three times, and then it was
pulled up to heaven again.
11"Right then three men who had
been sent to me from Caesarea stopped
at the house where I was staying. 12The
Spirit told me to have no hesitation
about going with them. These six
brothers also went with me, and we
entered the man's house. 13He told us
how he had seen an angel appear in his
house and say, 'Send to Joppa for
Simon who is called Peter. 14He will
bring you a message through which you
and all your household will be saved.'
15"As I began to speak, the Holy
Spirit came on them as he had come on
us at the beginning. 16Then I remembered what the Lord had said: 'John
baptised with water, but you will be
baptised with the Holy Spirit.' 17So if
God gave them the same gift as he gave
us, who believed in the Lord Jesus
Christ, who was I to think that I could
oppose God?"
18When they heard this, they had no
further objections and praised God,
saying, "So then, God has granted even
the Gentiles repentance unto life."

READING FROM PSALMS
Psalm 74:10–17

10How long will the enemy mock you,
O God?
Will the foe revile your name for
ever?
11Why do you hold back your hand,
your right hand?
Take it from the folds of your
garment and destroy them!

12But you, O God, are my king from of
old;
you bring salvation upon the earth.
13It was you who split open the sea by
your power;
you broke the heads of the monster
in the waters.
14It was you who crushed the heads of
Leviathan
and gave him as food to the
creatures of the desert.
15It was you who opened up springs
and streams;
you dried up the ever-flowing
rivers.
16The day is yours, and yours also the
night;
you established the sun and moon.
17It was you who set all the boundaries
of the earth;
you made both summer and
winter.

JUNE 17

OLD TESTAMENT READING
1 Kings 2:13–3:15

Solomon's Throne Established

13Now Adonijah, the son of Haggith,
went to Bathsheba, Solomon's mother.
Bathsheba asked him, "Do you come
peacefully?"
He answered, "Yes, peacefully."
14Then he added, "I have something to
say to you."
"You may say it," she replied.
15"As you know," he said, "the kingdom was mine. All Israel looked to me
as their king. But things changed, and
the kingdom has gone to my brother;
for it has come to him from the LORD.
16Now I have one request to make of
you. Do not refuse me."
"You may make it," she said.
17So he continued, "Please ask King
Solomon—he will not refuse you—to
give me Abishag the Shunammite as my
wife."
18"Very well," Bathsheba replied, "I
will speak to the king for you."
19When Bathsheba went to King
Solomon to speak to him for Adonijah,
the king stood up to meet her, bowed
down to her and sat down on his throne.
He had a throne brought for the king's
mother, and she sat down at his right
hand.
20"I have one small request to make
of you," she said. "Do not refuse me."
The king replied, "Make it, my
mother; I will not refuse you."
21So she said, "Let Abishag the Shunammite be given in marriage to your
brother Adonijah."
22King Solomon answered his
mother, "Why do you request Abishag
the Shunammite for Adonijah? You
might as well request the kingdom for
him—after all, he is my older brother
—yes, for him and for Abiathar the
priest and Joab son of Zeruiah!"
23Then King Solomon swore by the
LORD: "May God deal with me, be it
ever so severely, if Adonijah does not
pay with his life for this request! 24And
now, as surely as the LORD lives—he
who has established me securely on the
throne of my father David and has
founded a dynasty for me as he promised—Adonijah shall be put to death
today!" 25So King Solomon gave orders
to Benaiah son of Jehoiada, and he
struck down Adonijah and he died.
26To Abiathar the priest the king
said, "Go back to your fields in
Anathoth. You deserve to die, but I will
not put you to death now, because you
carried the ark of the Sovereign LORD
before my father David and shared all
my father's hardships." 27So Solomon
removed Abiathar from the priesthood
of the LORD, fulfilling the word the
LORD had spoken at Shiloh about the
house of Eli.
28When the news reached Joab, who
had conspired with Adonijah though
not with Absalom, he fled to the tent of
the LORD and took hold of the horns of
the altar. 29King Solomon was told that
Joab had fled to the tent of the LORD
and was beside the altar. Then Solomon
ordered Benaiah son of Jehoiada, "Go,
strike him down!"
30So Benaiah entered the tent of the
LORD and said to Joab, "The king says,
'Come out!'"
But he answered, "No, I will die
here."
Benaiah reported to the king, "This is
how Joab answered me."
31Then the king commanded Benaiah, "Do as he says. Strike him down
and bury him, and so clear me and my
father's house of the guilt of the innocent blood that Joab shed. 32The LORD
will repay him for the blood he shed,
because without the knowledge of my
father David he attacked two men and
killed them with the sword. Both of

them—Abner son of Ner, commander
of Israel's army, and Amasa son of
Jether, commander of Judah's army—
were better men and more upright than
he. 33May the guilt of their blood rest on
the head of Joab and his descendants for
ever. But on David and his descendants, his house and his throne, may
there be the LORD's peace for ever."
34So Benaiah son of Jehoiada went up
and struck down Joab and killed him,
and he was buried on his own landin the
desert. 35The king put Benaiah son of
Jehoiada over the army in Joab's position and replaced Abiathar with Zadok
the priest.
36Then the king sent for Shimei and
said to him, "Build yourself a house in
Jerusalem and live there, but do not go
anywhere else. 37The day you leave and
cross the Kidron Valley, you can be sure
you will die; your blood will be on your
own head."
38Shimei answered the king, "What
you say is good. Your servant will do as
my lord the king has said." And Shimei
stayed in Jerusalem for a long time.
39But three years later, two of
Shimei's slaves ran off to Achish son of
Maacah, king of Gath, and Shimei was
told, "Your slaves are in Gath." 40At
this, he saddled his donkey and went to
Achish at Gath in search of his slaves.
So Shimei went away and brought the
slaves back from Gath.
41When Solomon was told that
Shimei had gone from Jerusalem to
Gath and had returned, 42the king summoned Shimei and said to him, "Did I
not make you swear by the LORD and
warn you, 'On the day you leave to go
anywhere else, you can be sure you will
die'? At that time you said to me, 'What
you say is good. I will obey.' 43Why
then did you not keep your oath to the
LORD and obey the command I gave
you?"
44The king also said to Shimei, "You
know in your heart all the wrong you did
to my father David. Now the LORD will
repay you for your wrongdoing. 45But
King Solomon will be blessed, and
David's throne will remain secure before the LORD for ever."
46Then the king gave the order to
Benaiah son of Jehoiada, and he went
out and struck Shimei down and killed
him.
The kingdom was now firmly established in Solomon's hands.

Solomon Asks for Wisdom

3 Solomon made an alliance with
Pharaoh king of Egypt and married
his daughter. He brought her to the City
of David until he finished building his
palace and the temple of the LORD, and
the wall around Jerusalem. 2The people, however, were still sacrificing at the
high places, because a temple had not
yet been built for the Name of the
LORD. 3Solomon showed his love for
the LORD by walking according to the
statutes of his father David, except that
he offered sacrifices and burned incense
on the high places.
4The king went to Gibeon to offer
sacrifices, for that was the most important high place, and Solomon offered a
thousand burnt offerings on that altar.
5At Gibeon the LORD appeared to Solomon during the night in a dream, and
God said, "Ask for whatever you want
me to give you."
6Solomon answered, "You have
shown great kindness to your servant,
my father David, because he was faithful to you and righteous and upright in
heart. You have continued this great
kindness to him and have given him a
son to sit on his throne this very day.
7"Now, O LORD my God, you have
made your servant king in place of my
father David. But I am only a little child
and do not know how to carry out my
duties. 8Your servant is here among the
people you have chosen, a great people,
too numerous to count or number. 9So
give your servant a discerning heart to
govern your people and to distinguish
between right and wrong. For who is
able to govern this great people of
yours?"

10The Lord was pleased that Solomon
had asked for this. 11So God said to him,
"Since you have asked for this and not
for long life or wealth for yourself, nor
have asked for the death of your enemies but for discernment in administering justice, 12I will do what you have
asked. I will give you a wise and discerning heart, so that there will never have
been anyone like you, nor will there
ever be. 13Moreover, I will give you
what you have not asked for—both
riches and honour—so that in your lifetime you will have no equal among
kings. 14And if you walk in my ways and
obey my statutes and commands as
David your father did, I will give you a
long life." 15Then Solomon awoke—
and he realised it had been a dream.

He returned to Jerusalem, stood before the ark of the Lord's covenant and
sacrificed burnt offerings and fellowship
offerings. Then he gave a feast for all his
court.

NEW TESTAMENT READING
Acts 11:19–12:19a

The Church in Antioch

19Now those who had been scattered
by the persecution in connection with
Stephen travelled as far as Phoenicia,
Cyprus and Antioch, telling the message only to Jews. 20Some of them, however, men from Cyprus and Cyrene,
went to Antioch and began to speak to
Greeks also, telling them the good news
about the Lord Jesus. 21The Lord's
hand was with them, and a great number of people believed and turned to the
Lord.

22News of this reached the ears of the
church at Jerusalem, and they sent Barnabas to Antioch. 23When he arrived
and saw the evidence of the grace of
God, he was glad and encouraged them
all to remain true to the Lord with all
their hearts. 24He was a good man, full
of the Holy Spirit and faith, and a great
number of people were brought to the
Lord.

25Then Barnabas went to Tarsus to
look for Saul, 26and when he found him,
he brought him to Antioch. So for a
whole year Barnabas and Saul met with
the church and taught great numbers of
people. The disciples were called
Christians first at Antioch.

27During this time some prophets
came down from Jerusalem to Antioch.
28One of them, named Agabus, stood
up and through the Spirit predicted that
a severe famine would spread over the
entire Roman world. (This happened
during the reign of Claudius.) 29The
disciples, each according to his ability,
decided to provide help for the brothers
living in Judea. 30This they did, sending
their gift to the elders by Barnabas and
Saul.

Peter's Miraculous Escape From Prison

12 It was about this time that King
Herod arrested some who belonged to the church, intending to
persecute them. 2He had James, the
brother of John, put to death with the
sword. 3When he saw that this pleased
the Jews, he proceeded to seize Peter
also. This happened during the Feast of
Unleavened Bread. 4After arresting
him, he put him in prison, handing him
over to be guarded by four squads of
four soldiers each. Herod intended to
bring him out for public trial after the
Passover.

5So Peter was kept in prison, but the
church was earnestly praying to God for
him.

6The night before Herod was to bring
him to trial, Peter was sleeping between
two soldiers, bound with two chains,
and sentries stood guard at the entrance. 7Suddenly an angel of the Lord
appeared and a light shone in the cell.
He struck Peter on the side and woke
him up. "Quick, get up!" he said, and
the chains fell off Peter's wrists.

8Then the angel said to him, "Put on
your clothes and sandals." And Peter

did so. "Wrap your cloak around you
and follow me," the angel told him.
9Peter followed him out of the prison,
but he had no idea that what the angel
was doing was really happening; he
thought he was seeing a vision. 10They
passed the first and second guards and
came to the iron gate leading to the city.
It opened for them by itself, and they
went through it. When they had walked
the length of one street, suddenly the
angel left him.
11Then Peter came to himself and
said, "Now I know without a doubt that
the Lord sent his angel and rescued
me from Herod's clutches and from
everything the Jewish people were
anticipating."
12When this had dawned on him, he
went to the house of Mary the mother of
John, also called Mark, where many
people had gathered and were praying.
13Peter knocked at the outer entrance,
and a servant girl named Rhoda came to
answer the door. 14When she recognised Peter's voice, she was so overjoyed she ran back without opening it
and exclaimed, "Peter is at the door!"
15"You're out of your mind," they
told her. When she kept insisting that it
was so, they said, "It must be his
angel."
16But Peter kept on knocking, and
when they opened the door and saw
him, they were astonished. 17Peter
motioned with his hand for them to be
quiet and described how the Lord had
brought him out of prison. "Tell James
and the brothers about this," he said,
and then he left for another place.
18In the morning, there was no small
commotion among the soldiers as to
what had become of Peter. 19After
Herod had a thorough search made for
him and did not find him, he cross-
examined the guards and ordered that
they be executed.

READING FROM PROVERBS

Proverbs 15:1–10

15 A gentle answer turns away wrath,
but a harsh word stirs up anger.

2The tongue of the wise commends knowledge,
but the mouth of the fool gushes folly.

3The eyes of the LORD are everywhere,
keeping watch on the wicked and the good.

4The tongue that brings healing is a tree of life,
but a deceitful tongue crushes the spirit.

5A fool spurns his father's discipline,
but whoever heeds correction shows prudence.

6The house of the righteous contains great treasure,
but the income of the wicked brings them trouble.

7The lips of the wise spread knowledge;
not so the hearts of fools.

8The LORD detests the sacrifice of the wicked,
but the prayer of the upright pleases him.

9The LORD detests the way of the wicked
but he loves those who pursue righteousness.

10Stern discipline awaits him who leaves the path;
he who hates correction will die.

JUNE 18

OLD TESTAMENT READING
1 Kings 3:16–5:18

A Wise Ruling

16Now two prostitutes came to the
king and stood before him. 17One of
them said, "My lord, this woman and I
live in the same house. I had a baby
while she was there with me. 18The third
day after my child was born, this woman
also had a baby. We were alone; there
was no-one in the house but the two of
us.

19"During the night this woman's son
died because she lay on him. 20So she
got up in the middle of the night and
took my son from my side while I your
servant was asleep. She put him by her
breast and put her dead son by my
breast. 21The next morning, I got up to
nurse my son—and he was dead! But
when I looked at him closely in the
morning light, I saw that it wasn't the
son I had borne."

22The other woman said, "No! The
living one is my son; the dead one is
yours."

But the first one insisted, "No! The dead one is yours; the living one is mine." And so they argued before the king.

23The king said, "This one says, 'My
son is alive and your son is dead,' while
that one says, 'No! Your son is dead and
mine is alive.' "

24Then the king said, "Bring me a
sword." So they brought a sword for the
king. 25He then gave an order: "Cut the
living child in two and give half to one
and half to the other."

26The woman whose son was alive
was filled with compassion for her son
and said to the king, "Please, my lord,
give her the living baby! Don't kill
him!"

But the other said, "Neither I nor you shall have him. Cut him in two!"

27Then the king gave his ruling:
"Give the living baby to the first
woman. Do not kill him; she is his
mother."

28When all Israel heard the verdict
the king had given, they held the king in
awe, because they saw that he had wisdom from God to administer justice.

Solomon's Officials and Governors

4 So King Solomon ruled over all
Israel. 2And these were his chief
officials:

Azariah son of Zadok—the priest;
3Elihoreph and Ahijah, sons of Shisha—secretaries;
Jehoshaphat son of Ahilud—recorder;
4Benaiah son of Jehoiada—commander-in-chief;
Zadok and Abiathar—priests;
5Azariah son of Nathan—in charge of the district officers;
Zabud son of Nathan—a priest and personal adviser to the king;
6Ahishar—in charge of the palace;
Adoniram son of Abda—in charge of forced labour.

7Solomon also had twelve district
governors over all Israel, who supplied
provisions for the king and the royal
household. Each one had to provide
supplies for one month in the year.
8These are their names:

Ben-Hur—in the hill country of Ephraim;
9Ben-Deker—in Makaz, Shaalbim, Beth Shemesh and Elon Bethhanan;
10Ben-Hesed—in Arubboth (Socoh and all the land of Hepher were his);
11Ben-Abinadab—in Naphoth Dor

(he was married to Taphath
daughter of Solomon);
12Baana son of Ahilud—in Taanach
and Megiddo, and in all of Beth
Shan next to Zarethan below
Jezreel, from Beth Shan to Abel
Meholah across to Jokmeam;
13Ben-Geber—in Ramoth Gilead
(the settlements of Jair son of
Manasseh in Gilead were his, as
well as the district of Argob in
Bashan and its sixty large walled
cities with bronze gate bars);
14Ahinadab son of Iddo—in Mahanaim;
15Ahimaaz—in Naphtali (he had
married Basemath daughter of
Solomon);
16Baana son of Hushai—in Asher
and in Aloth;
17Jehoshaphat son of Paruah—in
Issachar;
18Shimei son of Ela—in Benjamin;
19Geber son of Uri—in Gilead (the
country of Sihon king of the
Amorites and the country of Og
king of Bashan). He was the only
governor over the district.

Solomon's Daily Provisions

20The people of Judah and Israel
were as numerous as the sand on the
seashore; they ate, they drank and they
were happy. 21And Solomon ruled over
all the kingdoms from the River to the
land of the Philistines, as far as the
border of Egypt. These countries
brought tribute and were Solomon's
subjects all his life.
22Solomon's daily provisions were
thirty cors of fine flour and sixty cors of
meal, 23ten head of stall-fed cattle,
twenty of pasture-fed cattle and a hundred sheep and goats, as well as deer,
gazelles, roebucks and choice fowl.
24For he ruled over all the kingdoms
west of the River, from Tiphsah to
Gaza, and had peace on all sides.
25During Solomon's lifetime Judah and
Israel, from Dan to Beersheba, lived in
safety, each man under his own vine and
fig-tree.
26Solomon had four thousand stalls
for chariot horses, and twelve thousand
horses.
27The district officers, each in his
month, supplied provisions for King
Solomon and all who came to the king's
table. They saw to it that nothing was
lacking. 28They also brought to the
proper place their quotas of barley and
straw for the chariot horses and the
other horses.

Solomon's Wisdom

29God gave Solomon wisdom and
very great insight, and a breadth of
understanding as measureless as the
sand on the seashore. 30Solomon's wisdom was greater than the wisdom of all
the men of the East, and greater than all
the wisdom of Egypt. 31He was wiser
than any other man, including Ethan
the Ezrahite—wiser than Heman, Calcol and Darda, the sons of Mahol. And
his fame spread to all the surrounding
nations. 32He spoke three thousand
proverbs and his songs numbered a
thousand and five. 33He described plant
life, from the cedar of Lebanon to the
hyssop that grows out of walls. He also
taught about animals and birds, reptiles
and fish. 34Men of all nations came to
listen to Solomon's wisdom, sent by all
the kings of the world, who had heard of
his wisdom.

Preparations for Building the Temple

5 When Hiram king of Tyre heard
that Solomon had been anointed
king to succeed his father David, he sent
his envoys to Solomon, because he had
always been on friendly terms with
David. 2Solomon sent back this message to Hiram:

3"You know that because of the
wars waged against my father

David from all sides, he could not
build a temple for the Name of the
LORD his God until the LORD put
his enemies under his feet. 4But
now the LORD my God has given
me rest on every side, and there is
no adversary or disaster. 5I intend,
therefore, to build a temple for the
Name of the LORD my God, as the
LORD told my father David, when
he said, 'Your son whom I will put
on the throne in your place will
build the temple for my Name.'

6"So give orders that cedars of
Lebanon be cut for me. My men
will work with yours, and I will pay
you for your men whatever wages
you set. You know that we have
no-one so skilled in felling timber
as the Sidonians."

7When Hiram heard Solomon's message, he was greatly pleased and said,
"Praise be to the LORD today, for he has
given David a wise son to rule over this
great nation."

8So Hiram sent word to Solomon:

"I have received the message
you sent me and will do all you
want in providing the cedar and
pine logs. 9My men will haul them
down from Lebanon to the sea, and
I will float them in rafts by sea to
the place you specify. There I will
separate them and you can take
them away. And you are to grant
my wish by providing food for my
royal household."

10In this way Hiram kept Solomon
supplied with all the cedar and pine logs
he wanted, 11and Solomon gave Hiram
twenty thousand cors of wheat as food
for his household, in addition to twenty
thousand baths of pressed olive oil.
Solomon continued to do this for Hiram
year after year. 12The LORD gave Solomon wisdom, just as he had promised
him. There were peaceful relations between Hiram and Solomon, and the two
of them made a treaty.

13King Solomon conscripted labourers from all Israel—thirty thousand
men. 14He sent them off to Lebanon in
shifts of ten thousand a month, so that
they spent one month in Lebanon and
two months at home. Adoniram was in
charge of the forced labour. 15Solomon
had seventy thousand carriers and
eighty thousand stonecutters in the
hills, 16as well as thirty-three hundred
foremen who supervised the project
and directed the workmen. 17At the
king's command they removed from the
quarry large blocks of quality stone to
provide a foundation of dressed stone
for the temple. 18The craftsmen of
Solomon and Hiram and the men of
Gebal cut and prepared the timber and
stone for the building of the temple.

NEW TESTAMENT READING

Acts 12:19b–13:12

Herod's Death

Then Herod went from Judea to
Caesarea and stayed there a while. 20He
had been quarrelling with the people of
Tyre and Sidon; they now joined
together and sought an audience with
him. Having secured the support of
Blastus, a trusted personal servant of
the king, they asked for peace, because
they depended on the king's country for
their food supply.

21On the appointed day Herod, wearing his royal robes, sat on his throne and
delivered a public address to the people. 22They shouted, "This is the voice
of a god, not of a man." 23Immediately,
because Herod did not give praise to
God, an angel of the Lord struck him
down, and he was eaten by worms and
died.

24But the word of God continued to
increase and spread.

25When Barnabas and Saul had
finished their mission, they returned
from Jerusalem, taking with them John,
also called Mark.

Barnabas and Saul Sent Off

13 In the church at Antioch there
were prophets and teachers:
Barnabas, Simeon called Niger, Lucius
of Cyrene, Manaen (who had been
brought up with Herod the tetrarch)
and Saul. 2While they were worshipping
the Lord and fasting, the Holy Spirit
said, "Set apart for me Barnabas and
Saul for the work to which I have called
them." 3So after they had fasted and
prayed, they placed their hands on them
and sent them off.

On Cyprus

4The two of them, sent on their way
by the Holy Spirit, went down to
Seleucia and sailed from there to Cyprus. 5When they arrived at Salamis,
they proclaimed the word of God in the
Jewish synagogues. John was with them
as their helper.
6They travelled through the whole
island until they came to Paphos. There
they met a Jewish sorcerer and false
prophet named Bar-Jesus, 7who was an
attendant of the proconsul, Sergius
Paulus. The proconsul, an intelligent
man, sent for Barnabas and Saul because he wanted to hear the word of
God. 8But Elymas the sorcerer (for that
is what his name means) opposed them
and tried to turn the proconsul from the
faith. 9Then Saul, who was also called
Paul, filled with the Holy Spirit, looked
straight at Elymas and said, 10"You are
a child of the devil and an enemy of
everything that is right! You are full of
all kinds of deceit and trickery. Will you
never stop perverting the right ways of
the Lord? 11Now the hand of the Lord is
against you. You are going to be blind,
and for a time you will be unable to see
the light of the sun."
Immediately mist and darkness came
over him, and he groped about, seeking
someone to lead him by the hand.
12When the proconsul saw what had
happened, he believed, for he was
amazed at the teaching about the Lord.

READING FROM PSALMS

Psalm 74:18–23

18Remember how the enemy has
mocked you, O LORD,
how foolish people have reviled
your name.
19Do not hand over the life of your
dove to wild beasts;
do not forget the lives of your
afflicted people for ever.
20Have regard for your covenant,
because haunts of violence fill the
dark places of the land.
21Do not let the oppressed retreat in
disgrace;
may the poor and needy praise
your name.
22Rise up, O God, and defend your
cause;
remember how fools mock you all
day long.
23Do not ignore the clamour of your
adversaries,
the uproar of your enemies, which
rises continually.

JUNE 19

DAY 170

OLD TESTAMENT READING
1 Kings 6:1–7:22

Solomon Builds the Temple

6 In the four hundred and eightieth year after the Israelites had come out of Egypt, in the fourth year of Solomon's reign over Israel, in the month of Ziv, the second month, he began to build the temple of the LORD.

[2]The temple that King Solomon built for the LORD was sixty cubits long, twenty wide and thirty high. [3]The portico at the front of the main hall of the temple extended the width of the temple, that is twenty cubits, and projected ten cubits from the front of the temple. [4]He made narrow clerestory windows in the temple. [5]Against the walls of the main hall and inner sanctuary he built a structure around the building, in which there were side rooms. [6]The lowest floor was five cubits wide, the middle floor six cubits and the third floor seven. He made offset ledges around the outside of the temple so that nothing would be inserted into the temple walls.

[7]In building the temple, only blocks dressed at the quarry were used, and no hammer, chisel or any other iron tool was heard at the temple site while it was being built.

[8]The entrance to the lowest floor was on the south side of the temple; a stairway led up to the middle level and from there to the third. [9]So he built the temple and completed it, roofing it with beams and cedar planks. [10]And he built the side rooms all along the temple. The height of each was five cubits, and they were attached to the temple by beams of cedar.

[11]The word of the LORD came to Solomon: [12]"As for this temple you are building, if you follow my decrees, carry out my regulations and keep all my commands and obey them, I will fulfil through you the promise I gave to David your father. [13]And I will live among the Israelites and will not abandon my people Israel."

[14]So Solomon built the temple and completed it. [15]He lined its interior walls with cedar boards, panelling them from the floor of the temple to the ceiling, and covered the floor of the temple with planks of pine. [16]He partitioned off twenty cubits at the rear of the temple with cedar boards from floor to ceiling to form within the temple an inner sanctuary, the Most Holy Place. [17]The main hall in front of this room was forty cubits long. [18]The inside of the temple was cedar, carved with gourds and open flowers. Everything was cedar; no stone was to be seen.

[19]He prepared the inner sanctuary within the temple to set the ark of the covenant of the LORD there. [20]The inner sanctuary was twenty cubits long, twenty wide and twenty high. He overlaid the inside with pure gold, and he also overlaid the altar of cedar. [21]Solomon covered the inside of the temple with pure gold, and he extended gold chains across the front of the inner sanctuary, which was overlaid with gold. [22]So he overlaid the whole interior with gold. He also overlaid with gold the altar that belonged to the inner sanctuary.

[23]In the inner sanctuary he made a pair of cherubim of olive wood, each ten cubits high. [24]One wing of the first cherub was five cubits long, and the other wing five cubits—ten cubits from wing tip to wing tip. [25]The second cherub also measured ten cubits, for the two cherubim were identical in size and shape. [26]The height of each cherub was ten cubits. [27]He placed the cherubim inside the innermost room of the temple, with their wings spread out. The wing of one cherub touched one wall, while the wing of

the other touched the other wall, and
their wings touched each other in the
middle of the room. 28He overlaid the
cherubim with gold.

29On the walls all round the temple,
in both the inner and outer rooms, he
carved cherubim, palm trees and open
flowers. 30He also covered the floors of
both the inner and outer rooms of the
temple with gold.

31For the entrance of the inner sanctuary he made doors of olive wood with
five-sided jambs. 32And on the two olive
wood doors he carved cherubim, palm
trees and open flowers, and overlaid the
cherubim and palm trees with beaten
gold. 33In the same way he made four-
sided jambs of olive wood for the entrance to the main hall. 34He also made
two pine doors, each having two leaves
that turned in sockets. 35He carved
cherubim, palm trees and open flowers
on them and overlaid them with gold
hammered evenly over the carvings.

36And he built the inner courtyard of
three courses of dressed stone and one
course of trimmed cedar beams.

37The foundation of the temple of the
LORD was laid in the fourth year, in the
month of Ziv. 38In the eleventh year in
the month of Bul, the eighth month, the
temple was finished in all its details
according to its specifications. He had
spent seven years building it.

Solomon Builds His Palace

7 It took Solomon thirteen years,
however, to complete the construction of his palace. 2He built the Palace
of the Forest of Lebanon a hundred
cubits long, fifty wide and thirty high,
with four rows of cedar columns supporting trimmed cedar beams. 3It was
roofed with cedar above the beams that
rested on the columns—forty-five
beams, fifteen to a row. 4Its windows
were placed high in sets of three, facing
each other. 5All the doorways had rectangular frames; they were in the front
part in sets of three, facing each other.

6He made a colonnade fifty cubits
long and thirty wide. In front of it was a
portico, and in front of that were pillars
and an overhanging roof.

7He built the throne hall, the Hall of
Justice, where he was to judge, and he
covered it with cedar from floor to ceiling. 8And the palace in which he was to
live, set farther back, was similar in
design. Solomon also made a palace like
this hall for Pharaoh's daughter, whom
he had married.

9All these structures, from the outside to the great courtyard and from
foundation to eaves, were made of
blocks of high-grade stone cut to size
and trimmed with a saw on their inner
and outer faces. 10The foundations were
laid with large stones of good quality,
some measuring ten cubits and some
eight. 11Above were high-grade stones,
cut to size, and cedar beams. 12The
great courtyard was surrounded by a
wall of three courses of dressed stone
and one course of trimmed cedar
beams, as was the inner courtyard of the
temple of the LORD with its portico.

The Temple's Furnishings

13King Solomon sent to Tyre and
brought Huram, 14whose mother was a
widow from the tribe of Naphtali and
whose father was a man of Tyre and a
craftsman in bronze. Huram was highly
skilled and experienced in all kinds of
bronze work. He came to King Solomon and did all the work assigned to
him.

15He cast two bronze pillars, each
eighteen cubits high and twelve cubits
round, by line. 16He also made two
capitals of cast bronze to set on the tops
of the pillars; each capital was five cubits
high. 17A network of interwoven chains
festooned the capitals on top of the
pillars, seven for each capital. 18He
made pomegranates in two rows encircling each network to decorate the
capitals on top of the pillars. He did the
same for each capital. 19The capitals on
top of the pillars in the portico were in
the shape of lilies, four cubits high. 20On

the capitals of both pillars, above the
bowl-shaped part next to the network,
were the two hundred pomegranates in
rows all around. 21He erected the pillars
at the portico of the temple. The pillar to
the south he named Jakin and the one
to the north Boaz. 22The capitals on top
were in the shape of lilies. And so the
work on the pillars was completed.

NEW TESTAMENT READING

Acts 13:13–41

In Pisidian Antioch

13From Paphos, Paul and his companions sailed to Perga in Pamphylia,
where John left them to return to Jerusalem. 14From Perga they went on to
Pisidian Antioch. On the Sabbath they
entered the synagogue and sat down.
15After the reading from the Law and
the Prophets, the synagogue rulers sent
word to them, saying, "Brothers, if you
have a message of encouragement for
the people, please speak."

16Standing up, Paul motioned with
his hand and said: "Men of Israel and
you Gentiles who worship God, listen
to me! 17The God of the people of Israel
chose our fathers; he made the people
prosper during their stay in Egypt, with
mighty power he led them out of that
country, 18he endured their conduct for
about forty years in the desert, 19he
overthrew seven nations in Canaan and
gave their land to his people as their
inheritance. 20All this took about 450
years.

"After this, God gave them judges
until the time of Samuel the prophet.
21Then the people asked for a king, and
he gave them Saul son of Kish, of the
tribe of Benjamin, who ruled for forty
years. 22After removing Saul, he made
David their king. He testified concerning him: 'I have found David son of
Jesse a man after my own heart; he will
do everything I want him to do.'

23"From this man's descendants God
has brought to Israel the Saviour Jesus,
as he promised. 24Before the coming of
Jesus, John preached repentance and
baptism to all the people of Israel. 25As
John was completing his work, he said:
'Who do you think I am? I am not that
one. No, but he is coming after me,
whose sandals I am not worthy to untie.'

26"Brothers, children of Abraham,
and you God-fearing Gentiles, it is to us
that this message of salvation has been
sent. 27The people of Jerusalem and
their rulers did not recognise Jesus, yet
in condemning him they fulfilled the
words of the prophets that are read
every Sabbath. 28Though they found no
proper ground for a death sentence,
they asked Pilate to have him executed.
29When they had carried out all that was
written about him, they took him down
from the tree and laid him in a tomb.
30But God raised him from the dead,
31and for many days he was seen by
those who had travelled with him from
Galilee to Jerusalem. They are now his
witnesses to our people.

32"We tell you the good news: What
God promised our fathers 33he has ful-
filled for us, their children, by raising up
Jesus. As it is written in the second
Psalm:

> " 'You are my Son;
> today I have become your Father.'

34The fact that God raised him from the
dead, never to decay, is stated in these
words:

> " 'I will give you the holy and sure
> blessings promised to David.'

35So it is stated elsewhere:

> " 'You will not let your Holy One see
> decay.'

36"For when David had served God's
purpose in his own generation, he fell
asleep; he was buried with his fathers
and his body decayed. 37But the one
whom God raised from the dead did not
see decay.

38"Therefore, my brothers, I want
you to know that through Jesus the
forgiveness of sins is proclaimed to you.
39Through him everyone who believes is
justified from everything you could not
be justified from by the law of Moses.
40Take care that what the prophets have
said does not happen to you:

41" 'Look, you scoffers,
wonder and perish,
for I am going to do something in
your days
that you would never believe,
even if someone told you.' "

READING FROM PSALMS
Psalm 75:1–10

For the director of music. ⌞To the tune of⌟ "Do Not Destroy". A psalm of Asaph. A song.

1We give thanks to you, O God,
we give thanks, for your Name is
near;
men tell of your wonderful deeds.

2You say, "I choose the appointed
time;
it is I who judge uprightly.
3When the earth and all its people
quake,
it is I who hold its pillars firm.
Selah
4To the arrogant I say, 'Boast no
more,'
and to the wicked, 'Do not lift up
your horns.
5Do not lift your horns against
heaven;
do not speak with outstretched
neck.' "

6No-one from the east or the west
or from the desert can exalt a man.
7But it is God who judges:
He brings one down, he exalts
another.
8In the hand of the LORD is a cup
full of foaming wine mixed with
spices;
he pours it out, and all the wicked of
the earth
drink it down to its very dregs.

9As for me, I will declare this for ever;
I will sing praise to the God of
Jacob.
10I will cut off the horns of all the
wicked,
but the horns of the righteous shall
be lifted up.

DAY 171

JUNE 20

OLD TESTAMENT READING
1 Kings 7:23–8:21

23He made the Sea of cast metal,
circular in shape, measuring ten cubits
from rim to rim and five cubits high. It
took a line of thirty cubits to measure
round it. 24Below the rim, gourds encircled it—ten to a cubit. The gourds were
cast in two rows in one piece with the
Sea.
25The Sea stood on twelve bulls, three
facing north, three facing west, three
facing south and three facing east. The
Sea rested on top of them, and their
hindquarters were towards the centre.
26It was a handbreadth in thickness, and
its rim was like the rim of a cup, like
a lily blossom. It held two thousand
baths.
27He also made ten movable stands of
bronze; each was four cubits long, four
wide and three high. 28This is how the
stands were made: They had side panels

attached to uprights. 29On the panels
between the uprights were lions, bulls
and cherubim—and on the uprights as
well. Above and below the lions and
bulls were wreaths of hammered work.
30Each stand had four bronze wheels
with bronze axles, and each had a basin
resting on four supports, cast with
wreaths on each side. 31On the inside of
the stand there was an opening that had
a circular frame one cubit deep. This
opening was round, and with its base-
work it measured a cubit and a half.
Around its opening there was engraving. The panels of the stands were
square, not round. 32The four wheels
were under the panels, and the axles of
the wheels were attached to the stand.
The diameter of each wheel was a cubit
and a half. 33The wheels were made like
chariot wheels; the axles, rims, spokes
and hubs were all of cast metal.
34Each stand had four handles, one
on each corner, projecting from the
stand. 35At the top of the stand there
was a circular band half a cubit deep.
The supports and panels were attached
to the top of the stand. 36He engraved
cherubim, lions and palm trees on the
surfaces of the supports and on the
panels, in every available space, with
wreaths all around. 37This is the way he
made the ten stands. They were all cast
in the same moulds and were identical
in size and shape.
38He then made ten bronze basins,
each holding forty baths and measuring
four cubits across, one basin to go on
each of the ten stands. 39He placed five
of the stands on the south side of the
temple and five on the north. He placed
the Sea on the south side, at the south-
east corner of the temple. 40He also
made the basins and shovels and sprinkling bowls.

So Huram finished all the work he had undertaken for King Solomon in the temple of the LORD:

41the two pillars;
the two bowl-shaped capitals on top of the pillars;
the two sets of network decorating the two bowl-shaped capitals on top of the pillars;
42the four hundred pomegranates for the two sets of network (two rows of pomegranates for each network, decorating the bowl-shaped capitals on top of the pillars);
43the ten stands with their ten basins;
44the Sea and the twelve bulls under it;
45the pots, shovels and sprinkling bowls.

All these objects that Huram made
for King Solomon for the temple of the
LORD were of burnished bronze. 46The
king had them cast in clay moulds in
the plain of the Jordan between Succoth and Zarethan. 47Solomon left all
these things unweighed, because there
were so many; the weight of the bronze
was not determined.

48Solomon also made all the furnishings that were in the LORD's temple:

the golden altar;
the golden table on which was the bread of the Presence;
49the lampstands of pure gold (five on the right and five on the left, in front of the inner sanctuary);
the gold floral work and lamps and tongs;
50the pure gold dishes, wick trimmers, sprinkling bowls, dishes and censers;
and the gold sockets for the doors of the innermost room, the Most Holy Place, and also for the doors of the main hall of the temple.

51When all the work King Solomon had done for the temple of the LORD was finished, he brought in the things his father David had dedicated—the silver and gold and the furnishings—and he placed them in the treasuries of the LORD's temple.

The Ark Brought to the Temple

8 Then King Solomon summoned
into his presence at Jerusalem the
elders of Israel, all the heads of the
tribes and the chiefs of the Israelite
families, to bring up the ark of the
LORD's covenant from Zion, the City of
David. [2]All the men of Israel came
together to King Solomon at the time of
the festival in the month of Ethanim,
the seventh month.
[3]When all the elders of Israel had
arrived, the priests took up the ark,
[4]and they brought up the ark of the
LORD and the Tent of Meeting and all
the sacred furnishings in it. The priests
and Levites carried them up, [5]and King
Solomon and the entire assembly of
Israel that had gathered about him were
before the ark, sacrificing so many
sheep and cattle that they could not be
recorded or counted.
[6]The priests then brought the ark of
the LORD's covenant to its place in the
inner sanctuary of the temple, the Most
Holy Place, and put it beneath the wings
of the cherubim. [7]The cherubim spread
their wings over the place of the ark and
overshadowed the ark and its carrying
poles. [8]These poles were so long that
their ends could be seen from the Holy
Place in front of the inner sanctuary, but
not from outside the Holy Place; and
they are still there today. [9]There was
nothing in the ark except the two stone
tablets that Moses had placed in it at
Horeb, where the LORD made a covenant with the Israelites after they
came out of Egypt.
[10]When the priests withdrew from the
Holy Place, the cloud filled the temple
of the LORD. [11]And the priests could not
perform their service because of the
cloud, for the glory of the LORD filled
his temple.
[12]Then Solomon said, "The LORD has
said that he would dwell in a dark cloud;
[13]I have indeed built a magnificent temple for you, a place for you to dwell for
ever."
[14]While the whole assembly of Israel
was standing there, the king turned
round and blessed them. [15]Then he
said:

"Praise be to the LORD, the God
of Israel, who with his own hand
has fulfilled what he promised with
his own mouth to my father David.
For he said, [16]'Since the day I
brought my people Israel out of
Egypt, I have not chosen a city in
any tribe of Israel to have a temple
built for my Name to be there, but
I have chosen David to rule my
people Israel.'
[17]"My father David had it in his
heart to build a temple for the
Name of the LORD, the God of
Israel. [18]But the LORD said to my
father David, 'Because it was in
your heart to build a temple for my
Name, you did well to have this in
your heart. [19]Nevertheless, you are
not the one to build the temple, but
your son, who is your own flesh and
blood—he is the one who will build
the temple for my Name.'
[20]"The LORD has kept the promise he made: I have succeeded
David my father and now I sit on
the throne of Israel, just as the
LORD promised, and I have built
the temple for the Name of the
LORD, the God of Israel. [21]I have
provided a place there for the ark,
in which is the covenant of the
LORD that he made with our fathers
when he brought them out of
Egypt."

NEW TESTAMENT READING
Acts 13:42–14:7

[42]As Paul and Barnabas were leaving
the synagogue, the people invited them
to speak further about these things on
the next Sabbath. [43]When the congregation was dismissed, many of the Jews
and devout converts to Judaism followed Paul and Barnabas, who talked
with them and urged them to continue
in the grace of God.

44On the next Sabbath almost the
whole city gathered to hear the word of
the Lord. 45When the Jews saw the
crowds, they were filled with jealousy
and talked abusively against what Paul
was saying.
46Then Paul and Barnabas answered
them boldly: "We had to speak the
word of God to you first. Since you
reject it and do not consider yourselves
worthy of eternal life, we now turn to
the Gentiles. 47For this is what the Lord
has commanded us:

"'I have made you a light for the
Gentiles,
that you may bring salvation to the
ends of the earth.'"

48When the Gentiles heard this, they
were glad and honoured the word of the
Lord; and all who were appointed for
eternal life believed.
49The word of the Lord spread
through the whole region. 50But the
Jews incited the God-fearing women of
high standing and the leading men of
the city. They stirred up persecution
against Paul and Barnabas, and expelled them from their region. 51So they
shook the dust from their feet in protest
against them and went to Iconium.
52And the disciples were filled with joy
and with the Holy Spirit.

In Iconium

14 At Iconium Paul and Barnabas
went as usual into the Jewish
synagogue. There they spoke so effec-
tively that a great number of Jews and
Gentiles believed. 2But the Jews who
refused to believe stirred up the Gentiles and poisoned their minds against
the brothers. 3So Paul and Barnabas
spent considerable time there, speaking
boldly for the Lord, who confirmed the
message of his grace by enabling them
to do miraculous signs and wonders.
4The people of the city were divided;
some sided with the Jews, others with
the apostles. 5There was a plot afoot
among the Gentiles and Jews, together
with their leaders, to ill-treat them and
stone them. 6But they found out about
it and fled to the Lycaonian cities of
Lystra and Derbe and to the surrounding country, 7where they continued to
preach the good news.

READING FROM PSALMS
Psalm 76:1–12

For the director of music. With stringed instruments. A psalm of Asaph. A song.

1In Judah God is known;
his name is great in Israel.
2His tent is in Salem,
his dwelling-place in Zion.
3There he broke the flashing arrows,
the shields and the swords, the
weapons of war. *Selah*

4You are resplendent with light,
more majestic than mountains rich
with game.
5Valiant men lie plundered,
they sleep their last sleep;
not one of the warriors
can lift his hands.
6At your rebuke, O God of Jacob,
both horse and chariot lie still.
7You alone are to be feared.
Who can stand before you when
you are angry?
8From heaven you pronounced
judgment,
and the land feared and was
quiet—
9when you, O God, rose up to judge,
to save all the afflicted of the land.
Selah
10Surely your wrath against men brings
you praise,
and the survivors of your wrath are
restrained.

11Make vows to the LORD your God
and fulfil them;
let all the neighbouring lands
bring gifts to the One to be feared.
12He breaks the spirit of rulers;
he is feared by the kings of the
earth.

DAY 172

JUNE 21

OLD TESTAMENT READING
1 Kings 8:22–9:9

Solomon's Prayer of Dedication

[22]Then Solomon stood before the
altar of the LORD in front of the whole
assembly of Israel, spread out his hands
towards heaven [23]and said:

"O LORD, God of Israel, there is
no God like you in heaven above or
on earth below—you who keep
your covenant of love with your
servants who continue wholeheartedly in your way. [24]You have
kept your promise to your servant
David my father; with your mouth
you have promised and with your
hand you have fulfilled it—as it is
today.

[25]"Now LORD, God of Israel,
keep for your servant David my
father the promises you made to
him when you said, 'You shall
never fail to have a man to sit
before me on the throne of Israel, if
only your sons are careful in all
they do to walk before me as you
have done.' [26]And now, O God of
Israel, let your word that you
promised your servant David my
father come true.

[27]"But will God really dwell on
earth? The heavens, even the highest heaven, cannot contain you.
How much less this temple I have
built! [28]Yet give attention to your
servant's prayer and his plea for
mercy, O LORD my God. Hear the
cry and the prayer that your servant is praying in your presence
this day. [29]May your eyes be open
towards this temple night and day,
this place of which you said, 'My
Name shall be there,' so that you
will hear the prayer your servant
prays towards this place. [30]Hear
the supplication of your servant
and of your people Israel when
they pray towards this place. Hear
from heaven, your dwelling-place,
and when you hear, forgive.

[31]"When a man wrongs his
neighbour and is required to take
an oath and he comes and swears
the oath before your altar in this
temple, [32]then hear from heaven
and act. Judge between your servants, condemning the guilty and
bringing down on his own head
what he has done. Declare the innocent not guilty, and so establish
his innocence.

[33]"When your people Israel have
been defeated by an enemy because they have sinned against you,
and when they turn back to you and
confess your name, praying and
making supplication to you in this
temple, [34]then hear from heaven
and forgive the sin of your people
Israel and bring them back to the
land you gave to their fathers.

[35]"When the heavens are shut up
and there is no rain because your
people have sinned against you,
and when they pray towards this
place and confess your name and
turn from their sin because you
have afflicted them, [36]then hear
from heaven and forgive the sin of
your servants, your people Israel.
Teach them the right way to live,
and send rain on the land you gave
your people for an inheritance.

[37]"When famine or plague
comes to the land, or blight or mildew, locusts or grasshoppers, or
when an enemy besieges them in
any of their cities, whatever disaster or disease may come, [38]and
when a prayer or plea is made by
any of your people Israel—each
one aware of the afflictions of his
own heart, and spreading out his

hands towards this temple—39then
hear from heaven, your dwelling-
place. Forgive and act; deal with
each man according to all he does,
since you know his heart (for you
alone know the hearts of all men),
40so that they will fear you all the
time they live in the land you gave
our fathers.

41"As for the foreigner who does
not belong to your people Israel
but has come from a distant land
because of your name—42for men
will hear of your great name and
your mighty hand and your outstretched arm—when he comes
and prays towards this temple,
43then hear from heaven, your
dwelling-place, and do whatever
the foreigner asks of you, so that all
the peoples of the earth may know
your name and fear you, as do your
own people Israel, and may know
that this house I have built bears
your Name.

44"When your people go to war
against their enemies, wherever
you send them, and when they pray
to the LORD towards the city you
have chosen and the temple I have
built for your Name, 45then hear
from heaven their prayer and their
plea, and uphold their cause.

46"When they sin against you—
for there is no-one who does not
sin—and you become angry with
them and give them over to the
enemy, who takes them captive to
his own land, far away or near;
47and if they have a change of heart
in the land where they are held
captive, and repent and plead with
you in the land of their conquerors
and say, 'We have sinned, we have
done wrong, we have acted wickedly'; 48and if they turn back to you
with all their heart and soul in the
land of their enemies who took
them captive, and pray to you towards the land you gave their
fathers, towards the city you have
chosen and the temple I have built
for your Name; 49then from
heaven, your dwelling-place, hear
their prayer and their plea, and
uphold their cause. 50And forgive
your people, who have sinned
against you; forgive all the offences
they have committed against you,
and cause their conquerors to show
them mercy; 51for they are your
people and your inheritance,
whom you brought out of Egypt,
out of that iron-smelting furnace.

52"May your eyes be open to
your servant's plea and to the plea
of your people Israel, and may you
listen to them whenever they cry
out to you. 53For you singled them
out from all the nations of the
world to be your own inheritance,
just as you declared through your
servant Moses when you, O
Sovereign LORD, brought our
fathers out of Egypt."

54When Solomon had finished all
these prayers and supplications to the
LORD, he rose from before the altar of
the LORD, where he had been kneeling
with his hands spread out towards
heaven. 55He stood and blessed the
whole assembly of Israel in a loud voice,
saying:

56"Praise be to the LORD, who
has given rest to his people Israel
just as he promised. Not one word
has failed of all the good promises
he gave through his servant Moses.
57May the LORD our God be with us
as he was with our fathers; may he
never leave us nor forsake us.
58May he turn our hearts to him, to
walk in all his ways and to keep the
commands, decrees and regulations he gave our fathers. 59And
may these words of mine, which I
have prayed before the LORD, be
near to the LORD our God day and
night, that he may uphold the cause
of his servant and the cause of his
people Israel according to each
day's need, 60so that all the peoples

of the earth may know that the
LORD is God and that there is no
other. 61But your hearts must be
fully committed to the LORD our
God, to live by his decrees and
obey his commands, as at this
time."

The Dedication of the Temple

62Then the king and all Israel with
him offered sacrifices before the LORD.
63Solomon offered a sacrifice of fellowship offerings to the LORD: twenty-two
thousand cattle and a hundred and
twenty thousand sheep and goats. So
the king and all the Israelites dedicated
the temple of the LORD.

64On that same day the king consecrated the middle part of the courtyard
in front of the temple of the LORD, and
there he offered burnt offerings, grain
offerings and the fat of the fellowship
offerings, because the bronze altar before the LORD was too small to hold the
burnt offerings, the grain offerings and
the fat of the fellowship offerings.

65So Solomon observed the festival at
that time, and all Israel with him—a
vast assembly, people from Lebo
Hamath to the Wadi of Egypt. They
celebrated it before the LORD our God
for seven days and seven days more,
fourteen days in all. 66On the following
day he sent the people away. They
blessed the king and then went home,
joyful and glad in heart for all the good
things the LORD had done for his
servant David and his people Israel.

The LORD Appears to Solomon

9 When Solomon had finished building the temple of the LORD and the
royal palace, and had achieved all he
had desired to do, 2the LORD appeared
to him a second time, as he had
appeared to him at Gibeon. 3The LORD
said to him:

"I have heard the prayer and
plea you have made before me; I
have consecrated this temple,
which you have built, by putting
my Name there for ever. My eyes
and my heart will always be there.

4"As for you, if you walk before
me in integrity of heart and uprightness, as David your father did,
and do all I command and observe
my decrees and laws, 5I will establish your royal throne over Israel
for ever, as I promised David your
father when I said, 'You shall never
fail to have a man on the throne of
Israel.'

6"But if you or your sons turn
away from me and do not observe
the commands and decrees I have
given you and go off to serve other
gods and worship them, 7then I will
cut off Israel from the land I have
given them and will reject this
temple I have consecrated for my
Name. Israel will then become a
byword and an object of ridicule
among all peoples. 8And though
this temple is now imposing, all
who pass by will be appalled and
will scoff and say, 'Why has the
LORD done such a thing to this land
and to this temple?' 9People will
answer, 'Because they have forsaken the LORD their God, who
brought their fathers out of Egypt,
and have embraced other gods,
worshipping and serving them—
that is why the LORD brought all
this disaster on them.'"

NEW TESTAMENT READING

Acts 14:8–28

In Lystra and Derbe

8In Lystra there sat a man crippled in
his feet, who was lame from birth and
had never walked. 9He listened to Paul
as he was speaking. Paul looked directly
at him, saw that he had faith to be
healed 10and called out, "Stand up on
your feet!" At that, the man jumped up
and began to walk.

11When the crowd saw what Paul had
done, they shouted in the Lycaonian
language, "The gods have come down
to us in human form!" 12Barnabas they
called Zeus, and Paul they called
Hermes because he was the chief
speaker. 13The priest of Zeus, whose
temple was just outside the city,
brought bulls and wreaths to the city
gates because he and the crowd wanted
to offer sacrifices to them.

14But when the apostles Barnabas
and Paul heard of this, they tore their
clothes and rushed out into the crowd,
shouting: 15"Men, why are you doing
this? We too are only men, human like
you. We are bringing you good news,
telling you to turn from these worthless
things to the living God, who made
heaven and earth and sea and everything in them. 16In the past, he let all
nations go their own way. 17Yet he has
not left himself without testimony: He
has shown kindness by giving you rain
from heaven and crops in their seasons;
he provides you with plenty of food and
fills your hearts with joy." 18Even with
these words, they had difficulty keeping
the crowd from sacrificing to them.

19Then some Jews came from Antioch and Iconium and won the crowd
over. They stoned Paul and dragged
him outside the city, thinking he was
dead. 20But after the disciples had
gathered round him, he got up and went
back into the city. The next day he and
Barnabas left for Derbe.

The Return to Antioch in Syria

21They preached the good news in
that city and won a large number of
disciples. Then they returned to Lystra,
Iconium and Antioch, 22strengthening
the disciples and encouraging them to
remain true to the faith. "We must go
through many hardships to enter the
kingdom of God," they said. 23Paul and
Barnabas appointed elders for them in
each church and, with prayer and fasting, committed them to the Lord, in
whom they had put their trust. 24After
going through Pisidia, they came into
Pamphylia, 25and when they had
preached the word in Perga, they went
down to Attalia.

26From Attalia they sailed back to
Antioch, where they had been committed to the grace of God for the work
they had now completed. 27On arriving
there, they gathered the church
together and reported all that God had
done through them and how he had
opened the door of faith to the Gentiles.
28And they stayed there a long time with
the disciples.

READING FROM PROVERBS

Proverbs 15:11–20

11Death and Destruction lie open
before the LORD—
how much more the hearts of men!

12A mocker resents correction;
he will not consult the wise.

13A happy heart makes the face
cheerful,
but heartache crushes the spirit.

14The discerning heart seeks
knowledge,
but the mouth of a fool feeds on
folly.

15All the days of the oppressed are
wretched,
but the cheerful heart has a
continual feast.

16Better a little with the fear of the
LORD
than great wealth with turmoil.

17Better a meal of vegetables where
there is love
than a fattened calf with hatred.

18A hot-tempered man stirs up
dissension,
but a patient man calms a quarrel.

[19]The way of the sluggard is blocked
with thorns,
but the path of the upright is a
highway.

[20]A wise son brings joy to his
father,
but a foolish man despises his
mother.

DAY 173

JUNE 22

OLD TESTAMENT READING
1 Kings 9:10–11:13

Solomon's Other Activities

[10]At the end of twenty years, during
which Solomon built these two buildings—the temple of the LORD and the
royal palace—[11]King Solomon gave
twenty towns in Galilee to Hiram king
of Tyre, because Hiram had supplied
him with all the cedar and pine and gold
he wanted. [12]But when Hiram went
from Tyre to see the towns that Solomon had given him, he was not pleased
with them. [13]"What kind of towns are
these you have given me, my brother?"
he asked. And he called them the Land
of Cabul, a name they have to this day.
[14]Now Hiram had sent to the king 120
talents of gold.

[15]Here is the account of the forced
labour King Solomon conscripted to
build the LORD's temple, his own
palace, the supporting terraces, the wall
of Jerusalem, and Hazor, Megiddo and
Gezer. [16](Pharaoh king of Egypt had
attacked and captured Gezer. He had
set it on fire. He killed its Canaanite
inhabitants, and then gave it as a wedding gift to his daughter, Solomon's
wife. [17]And Solomon rebuilt Gezer.)
He built up Lower Beth Horon,
[18]Baalath, and Tadmor in the desert,
within his land, [19]as well as all his store
cities and the towns for his chariots and
for his horses—whatever he desired to
build in Jerusalem, in Lebanon and
throughout all the territory he ruled.

[20]All the people left from the Amorites, Hittites, Perizzites, Hivites and
Jebusites (these peoples were not
Israelites), [21]that is, their descendants
remaining in the land, whom the
Israelites could not exterminate—these
Solomon conscripted for his slave
labour force, as it is to this day. [22]But
Solomon did not make slaves of any of
the Israelites; they were his fighting
men, his government officials, his
officers, his captains, and the commanders of his chariots and charioteers.
[23]They were also the chief officials in
charge of Solomon's projects—550 officials supervising the men who did the
work.

[24]After Pharaoh's daughter had come
up from the City of David to the palace
Solomon had built for her, he constructed the supporting terraces.

[25]Three times a year Solomon sacrificed burnt offerings and fellowship
offerings on the altar he had built for the
LORD, burning incense before the LORD
along with them, and so fulfilled the
temple obligations.

[26]King Solomon also built ships at
Ezion Geber, which is near Elath in
Edom, on the shore of the Red Sea.
[27]And Hiram sent his men—sailors who
knew the sea—to serve in the fleet with
Solomon's men. [28]They sailed to Ophir
and brought back 420 talents of gold,
which they delivered to King Solomon.

The Queen of Sheba Visits Solomon

10 When the queen of Sheba heard
about the fame of Solomon and
his relation to the name of the LORD,
she came to test him with hard questions. [2]Arriving at Jerusalem with a

very great caravan—with camels carrying spices, large quantities of gold,
and precious stones—she came to Solomon and talked with him about all that
she had on her mind. 3Solomon
answered all her questions; nothing was
too hard for the king to explain to her.
4When the queen of Sheba saw all the
wisdom of Solomon and the palace he
had built, 5the food on his table, the
seating of his officials, the attending
servants in their robes, his cupbearers,
and the burnt offerings he made at the
temple of the LORD, she was overwhelmed.

6She said to the king, "The report I
heard in my own country about your
achievements and your wisdom is true.
7But I did not believe these things until I
came and saw with my own eyes. Indeed, not even half was told me; in
wisdom and wealth you have far exceeded the report I heard. 8How happy
your men must be! How happy your
officials, who continually stand before
you and hear your wisdom! 9Praise be to
the LORD your God, who has delighted
in you and placed you on the throne of
Israel. Because of the LORD's eternal
love for Israel, he has made you king, to
maintain justice and righteousness."

10And she gave the king 120 talents of
gold, large quantities of spices, and precious stones. Never again were so many
spices brought in as those the queen of
Sheba gave to King Solomon.

11(Hiram's ships brought gold from
Ophir; and from there they brought
great cargoes of almug-wood and precious stones. 12The king used the almug-
wood to make supports for the temple
of the LORD and for the royal palace,
and to make harps and lyres for the
musicians. So much almug-wood has
never been imported or seen since that
day.)

13King Solomon gave the queen of
Sheba all she desired and asked for,
besides what he had given her out of his
royal bounty. Then she left and returned with her retinue to her own
country.

Solomon's Splendour

14The weight of the gold that Solomon received yearly was 666 talents,
15not including the revenues from merchants and traders and from all the Ara-
bian kings and the governors of the
land.

16King Solomon made two hundred
large shields of hammered gold; six
hundred bekas of gold went into each
shield. 17He also made three hundred
small shields of hammered gold, with
three minas of gold in each shield. The
king put them in the Palace of the Forest
of Lebanon.

18Then the king made a great throne
inlaid with ivory and overlaid with fine
gold. 19The throne had six steps, and its
back had a rounded top. On both sides
of the seat were armrests, with a lion
standing beside each of them. 20Twelve
lions stood on the six steps, one at either
end of each step. Nothing like it had
ever been made for any other kingdom.
21All King Solomon's goblets were
gold, and all the household articles in
the Palace of the Forest of Lebanon
were pure gold. Nothing was made of
silver, because silver was considered of
little value in Solomon's days. 22The
king had a fleet of trading ships at sea
along with the ships of Hiram. Once
every three years it returned carrying
gold, silver and ivory, and apes and
baboons.

23King Solomon was greater in riches
and wisdom than all the other kings of
the earth. 24The whole world sought
audience with Solomon to hear the wisdom God had put in his heart. 25Year
after year, everyone who came brought
a gift—articles of silver and gold, robes,
weapons and spices, and horses and
mules.

26Solomon accumulated chariots and
horses; he had fourteen hundred chariots and twelve thousand horses, which
he kept in the chariot cities and also
with him in Jerusalem. 27The king made
silver as common in Jerusalem as
stones, and cedar as plentiful as

sycamore-fig trees in the foothills.
28Solomon's horses were imported from
Egypt and from Kue—the royal merchants purchased them from Kue.
29They imported a chariot from Egypt
for six hundred shekels of silver, and a
horse for a hundred and fifty. They also
exported them to all the kings of the
Hittites and of the Arameans.

Solomon's Wives

11 King Solomon, however, loved
many foreign women besides
Pharaoh's daughter—Moabites, Ammonites, Edomites, Sidonians and Hittites. 2They were from nations about
which the LORD had told the Israelites,
"You must not intermarry with them,
because they will surely turn your hearts
after their gods." Nevertheless, Solomon held fast to them in love. 3He had
seven hundred wives of royal birth and
three hundred concubines, and his
wives led him astray. 4As Solomon grew
old, his wives turned his heart after
other gods, and his heart was not fully
devoted to the LORD his God, as the
heart of David his father had been. 5He
followed Ashtoreth the goddess of the
Sidonians, and Molech the detestable
god of the Ammonites. 6So Solomon
did evil in the eyes of the LORD; he did
not follow the LORD completely, as
David his father had done.

7On a hill east of Jerusalem, Solomon
built a high place for Chemosh the detestable god of Moab, and for Molech
the detestable god of the Ammonites.
8He did the same for all his foreign
wives, who burned incense and offered
sacrifices to their gods.

9The LORD became angry with Solomon because his heart had turned away
from the LORD, the God of Israel, who
had appeared to him twice. 10Although
he had forbidden Solomon to follow
other gods, Solomon did not keep the
LORD's command. 11So the LORD said to
Solomon, "Since this is your attitude
and you have not kept my covenant and
my decrees, which I commanded you, I
will most certainly tear the kingdom
away from you and give it to one of your
subordinates. 12Nevertheless, for the
sake of David your father, I will not do
it during your lifetime. I will tear it out
of the hand of your son. 13Yet I will not
tear the whole kingdom from him, but
will give him one tribe for the sake of
David my servant and for the sake of
Jerusalem, which I have chosen."

NEW TESTAMENT READING
Acts 15:1–21

The Council at Jerusalem

15 Some men came down from
Judea to Antioch and were
teaching the brothers: "Unless you are
circumcised, according to the custom
taught by Moses, you cannot be saved."
2This brought Paul and Barnabas into
sharp dispute and debate with them. So
Paul and Barnabas were appointed,
along with some other believers, to go
up to Jerusalem to see the apostles and
elders about this question. 3The church
sent them on their way, and as they
travelled through Phoenicia and Samaria, they told how the Gentiles had
been converted. This news made all the
brothers very glad. 4When they came to
Jerusalem, they were welcomed by the
church and the apostles and elders, to
whom they reported everything God
had done through them.

5Then some of the believers who belonged to the party of the Pharisees
stood up and said, "The Gentiles must
be circumcised and required to obey the
law of Moses."

6The apostles and elders met to consider this question. 7After much discussion, Peter got up and addressed them:
"Brothers, you know that some time
ago God made a choice among you that
the Gentiles might hear from my lips the
message of the gospel and believe.
8God, who knows the heart, showed
that he accepted them by giving the
Holy Spirit to them, just as he did to us.
9He made no distinction between us and

them, for he purified their hearts by
faith. 10Now then, why do you try to test
God by putting on the necks of the
disciples a yoke that neither we nor our
fathers have been able to bear? 11No!
We believe it is through the grace of our
Lord Jesus that we are saved, just as
they are."

12The whole assembly became silent
as they listened to Barnabas and Paul
telling about the miraculous signs and
wonders God had done among the Gentiles through them. 13When they
finished, James spoke up: "Brothers,
listen to me. 14Simon has described to us
how God at first showed his concern by
taking from the Gentiles a people for
himself. 15The words of the prophets
are in agreement with this, as it is
written:

16" 'After this I will return
and rebuild David's fallen tent.
Its ruins I will rebuild,
and I will restore it,
17that the remnant of men may seek the Lord,
and all the Gentiles who bear my name,
says the Lord, who does these things'
18 that have been known for ages.

19"It is my judgment, therefore, that
we should not make it difficult for the
Gentiles who are turning to God.
20Instead we should write to them, telling them to abstain from food polluted
by idols, from sexual immorality, from
the meat of strangled animals and from
blood. 21For Moses has been preached
in every city from the earliest times
and is read in the synagogues on every
Sabbath."

READING FROM PSALMS

Psalm 77:1–9

For the director of music. For Jeduthun. Of Asaph. A psalm.

1I cried out to God for help;
I cried out to God to hear me.
2When I was in distress, I sought the Lord;
at night I stretched out untiring hands
and my soul refused to be comforted.

3I remembered you, O God, and I groaned;
I mused, and my spirit grew faint. *Selah*
4You kept my eyes from closing;
I was too troubled to speak.
5I thought about the former days,
the years of long ago;
6I remembered my songs in the night.
My heart mused and my spirit enquired:

7"Will the Lord reject for ever?
Will he never show his favour again?
8Has his unfailing love vanished for ever?
Has his promise failed for all time?
9Has God forgotten to be merciful?
Has he in anger withheld his compassion?" *Selah*

DAY 174

JUNE 23

OLD TESTAMENT READING
1 Kings 11:14–12:24

Solomon's Adversaries

14 Then the LORD raised up against Solomon an adversary, Hadad the Edomite, from the royal line of Edom. 15 Earlier when David was fighting with Edom, Joab the commander of the army, who had gone up to bury the dead, had struck down all the men in Edom. 16 Joab and all the Israelites stayed there for six months, until they had destroyed all the men in Edom. 17 But Hadad, still only a boy, fled to Egypt with some Edomite officials who had served his father. 18 They set out from Midian and went to Paran. Then taking men from Paran with them, they went to Egypt, to Pharaoh king of Egypt, who gave Hadad a house and land and provided him with food.

19 Pharaoh was so pleased with Hadad that he gave him a sister of his own wife, Queen Tahpenes, in marriage. 20 The sister of Tahpenes bore him a son named Genubath, whom Tahpenes brought up in the royal palace. There Genubath lived with Pharaoh's own children.

21 While he was in Egypt, Hadad heard that David rested with his fathers and that Joab the commander of the army was also dead. Then Hadad said to Pharaoh, "Let me go, so that I may return to my own country."

22 "What have you lacked here that you want to go back to your own country?" Pharaoh asked.

"Nothing," Hadad replied, "but do let me go!"

23 And God raised up against Solomon another adversary, Rezon son of Eliada, who had fled from his master, Hadadezer king of Zobah. 24 He gathered men around him and became the leader of a band of rebels when David destroyed the forces ⌞of Zobah⌟; the rebels went to Damascus, where they settled and took control. 25 Rezon was Israel's adversary as long as Solomon lived, adding to the trouble caused by Hadad. So Rezon ruled in Aram and was hostile towards Israel.

Jeroboam Rebels Against Solomon

26 Also, Jeroboam son of Nebat rebelled against the king. He was one of Solomon's officials, an Ephraimite from Zeredah, and his mother was a widow named Zeruah.

27 Here is the account of how he rebelled against the king: Solomon had built the supporting terraces and had filled in the gap in the wall of the city of David his father. 28 Now Jeroboam was a man of standing, and when Solomon saw how well the young man did his work, he put him in charge of the whole labour force of the house of Joseph.

29 About that time Jeroboam was going out of Jerusalem, and Ahijah the prophet of Shiloh met him on the way, wearing a new cloak. The two of them were alone out in the country, 30 and Ahijah took hold of the new cloak he was wearing and tore it into twelve pieces. 31 Then he said to Jeroboam, "Take ten pieces for yourself, for this is what the LORD, the God of Israel, says: 'See, I am going to tear the kingdom out of Solomon's hand and give you ten tribes. 32 But for the sake of my servant David and the city of Jerusalem, which I have chosen out of all the tribes of Israel, he will have one tribe. 33 I will do this because they have forsaken me and worshipped Ashtoreth the goddess of the Sidonians, Chemosh the god of the Moabites, and Molech the god of the Ammonites, and have not walked in my ways, nor done what is right in my eyes, nor kept my statutes and laws as David, Solomon's father, did.

34“ ‘But I will not take the whole kingdom out of Solomon’s hand; I have
made him ruler all the days of his life for
the sake of David my servant, whom I
chose and who observed my commands
and statutes. 35I will take the kingdom
from his son’s hands and give you ten
tribes. 36I will give one tribe to his son so
that David my servant may always have
a lamp before me in Jerusalem, the city
where I chose to put my Name.
37However, as for you, I will take you,
and you will rule over all that your heart
desires; you will be king over Israel. 38If
you do whatever I command you and
walk in my ways and do what is right in
my eyes by keeping my statutes and
commands, as David my servant did, I
will be with you. I will build you a
dynasty as enduring as the one I built for
David and will give Israel to you. 39I will
humble David’s descendants because of
this, but not for ever.’ ”

40Solomon tried to kill Jeroboam, but
Jeroboam fled to Egypt, to Shishak the
king, and stayed there until Solomon’s
death.

Solomon’s Death

41As for the other events of Solomon’s reign—all he did and the wisdom
he displayed—are they not written in
the book of the annals of Solomon?
42Solomon reigned in Jerusalem over all
Israel for forty years. 43Then he rested
with his fathers and was buried in the
city of David his father. And Rehoboam his son succeeded him as king.

Israel Rebels Against Rehoboam

12 Rehoboam went to Shechem,
for all the Israelites had gone
there to make him king. 2When Jeroboam son of Nebat heard this (he was
still in Egypt, where he had fled from
King Solomon), he returned from
Egypt. 3So they sent for Jeroboam, and
he and the whole assembly of Israel
went to Rehoboam and said to him:
4“Your father put a heavy yoke on us,
but now lighten the harsh labour and
the heavy yoke he put on us, and we will
serve you.”

5Rehoboam answered, “Go away for
three days and then come back to me.”
So the people went away.

6Then King Rehoboam consulted the
elders who had served his father Solomon during his lifetime. “How would
you advise me to answer these people?”
he asked.

7They replied, “If today you will be a
servant to these people and serve them
and give them a favourable answer,
they will always be your servants.”

8But Rehoboam rejected the advice
the elders gave him and consulted the
young men who had grown up with him
and were serving him. 9He asked them,
“What is your advice? How should we
answer these people who say to me,
‘Lighten the yoke your father put on
us’?”

10The young men who had grown up
with him replied, “Tell these people
who have said to you, ‘Your father put a
heavy yoke on us, but make our yoke
lighter’—tell them, ‘My little finger is
thicker than my father’s waist. 11My
father laid on you a heavy yoke; I will
make it even heavier. My father
scourged you with whips; I will scourge
you with scorpions.’ ”

12Three days later Jeroboam and all
the people returned to Rehoboam, as
the king had said, “Come back to me in
three days.” 13The king answered the
people harshly. Rejecting the advice
given him by the elders, 14he followed
the advice of the young men and said,
“My father made your yoke heavy; I
will make it even heavier. My father
scourged you with whips; I will scourge
you with scorpions.” 15So the king did
not listen to the people, for this turn
of events was from the LORD, to fulfil
the word the LORD had spoken to Jeroboam son of Nebat through Ahijah the
Shilonite.

16When all Israel saw that the king
refused to listen to them, they answered
the king:

"What share do we have in David,
what part in Jesse's son?
To your tents, O Israel!
Look after your own house, O
David!"

So the Israelites went home. [17]But as for
the Israelites who were living in the
towns of Judah, Rehoboam still ruled
over them.
[18]King Rehoboam sent out Adoniram, who was in charge of forced
labour, but all Israel stoned him to
death. King Rehoboam, however, man-
aged to get into his chariot and escape to
Jerusalem. [19]So Israel has been in rebellion against the house of David to this
day.
[20]When all the Israelites heard that
Jeroboam had returned, they sent and
called him to the assembly and made
him king over all Israel. Only the tribe
of Judah remained loyal to the house of
David.
[21]When Rehoboam arrived in Jerusalem, he mustered the whole house of
Judah and the tribe of Benjamin—a
hundred and eighty thousand fighting
men—to make war against the house of
Israel and to regain the kingdom for
Rehoboam son of Solomon.
[22]But this word of God came to Shemaiah the man of God: [23]"Say to Rehoboam son of Solomon king of Judah,
to the whole house of Judah and Benjamin, and to the rest of the people,
[24]'This is what the LORD says: Do not go
up to fight against your brothers, the
Israelites. Go home, every one of you,
for this is my doing.'" So they obeyed
the word of the LORD and went home
again, as the LORD had ordered.

NEW TESTAMENT READING

Acts 15:22–41

The Council's Letter to Gentile Believers

[22]Then the apostles and elders, with
the whole church, decided to choose
some of their own men and send them to
Antioch with Paul and Barnabas. They
chose Judas (called Barsabbas) and
Silas, two men who were leaders among
the brothers. [23]With them they sent the
following letter:

The apostles and elders, your brothers,

To the Gentile believers in Antioch, Syria and Cilicia:

Greetings.

[24]We have heard that some went
out from us without our authoris-
ation and disturbed you, troubling
your minds by what they said. [25]So
we all agreed to choose some men
and send them to you with our dear
friends Barnabas and Paul—[26]men
who have risked their lives for the
name of our Lord Jesus Christ.
[27]Therefore we are sending Judas
and Silas to confirm by word of
mouth what we are writing. [28]It
seemed good to the Holy Spirit and
to us not to burden you with anything beyond the following requirements: [29]You are to abstain
from food sacrificed to idols, from
blood, from the meat of strangled
animals and from sexual immorality. You will do well to avoid these
things.

Farewell.

[30]The men were sent off and went
down to Antioch, where they gathered
the church together and delivered the
letter. [31]The people read it and were
glad for its encouraging message.
[32]Judas and Silas, who themselves were
prophets, said much to encourage and
strengthen the brothers. [33]After spending some time there, they were sent off
by the brothers with the blessing of
peace to return to those who had sent
them. [35]But Paul and Barnabas remained in Antioch, where they and
many others taught and preached the
word of the Lord.

Disagreement Between Paul and Barnabas

[36]Some time later Paul said to Barnabas, "Let us go back and visit the
brothers in all the towns where we
preached the word of the Lord and see
how they are doing." [37]Barnabas
wanted to take John, also called Mark,
with them, [38]but Paul did not think it
wise to take him, because he had deserted them in Pamphylia and had not
continued with them in the work.
[39]They had such a sharp disagreement
that they parted company. Barnabas
took Mark and sailed for Cyprus, [40]but
Paul chose Silas and left, commended
by the brothers to the grace of the Lord.
[41]He went through Syria and Cilicia,
strengthening the churches.

READING FROM PSALMS
Psalm 77:10–20

[10]Then I thought, "To this I will
appeal:
the years of the right hand of the
Most High."
[11]I will remember the deeds of the
LORD;
yes, I will remember your miracles
of long ago.
[12]I will meditate on all your works
and consider all your mighty deeds.

[13]Your ways, O God, are holy.
What god is so great as our God?
[14]You are the God who performs
miracles;
you display your power among the
peoples.
[15]With your mighty arm you redeemed
your people,
the descendants of Jacob and
Joseph. *Selah*

[16]The waters saw you, O God,
the waters saw you and writhed;
the very depths were convulsed.
[17]The clouds poured down water,
the skies resounded with thunder;
your arrows flashed back and forth.
[18]Your thunder was heard in the
whirlwind,
your lightning lit up the world;
the earth trembled and quaked.
[19]Your path led through the sea,
your way through the mighty
waters,
though your footprints were not
seen.

[20]You led your people like a flock
by the hand of Moses and Aaron.

JUNE 24

DAY 175

OLD TESTAMENT READING
1 Kings 12:25–14:20

Golden Calves at Bethel and Dan

[25]Then Jeroboam fortified Shechem
in the hill country of Ephraim and lived
there. From there he went out and built
up Peniel.
[26]Jeroboam thought to himself, "The
kingdom is now likely to revert to the
house of David. [27]If these people go up
to offer sacrifices at the temple of the
LORD in Jerusalem, they will again give
their allegiance to their lord, Rehoboam king of Judah. They will kill me
and return to King Rehoboam."
[28]After seeking advice, the king made
two golden calves. He said to the people, "It is too much for you to go up to
Jerusalem. Here are your gods, O
Israel, who brought you up out of
Egypt." [29]One he set up in Bethel, and
the other in Dan. [30]And this thing became a sin; the people went even as far
as Dan to worship the one there.

31Jeroboam built shrines on high
places and appointed priests from all
sorts of people, even though they were
not Levites. 32He instituted a festival on
the fifteenth day of the eighth month,
like the festival held in Judah, and
offered sacrifices on the altar. This he
did in Bethel, sacrificing to the calves he
had made. And at Bethel he also installed priests at the high places he had
made. 33On the fifteenth day of the
eighth month, a month of his own
choosing, he offered sacrifices on the
altar he had built at Bethel. So he instituted the festival for the Israelites and
went up to the altar to make offerings.

The Man of God From Judah

13 By the word of the LORD a man
of God came from Judah to
Bethel, as Jeroboam was standing by
the altar to make an offering. 2He cried
out against the altar by the word of the
LORD: "O altar, altar! This is what the
LORD says: 'A son named Josiah will be
born to the house of David. On you he
will sacrifice the priests of the high
places who now make offerings here,
and human bones will be burned on
you.'" 3That same day the man of God
gave a sign: "This is the sign the LORD
has declared: The altar will be split
apart and the ashes on it will be poured
out."

4When King Jeroboam heard what
the man of God cried out against the
altar at Bethel, he stretched out his
hand from the altar and said, "Seize
him!" But the hand he stretched out
towards the man shrivelled up, so that
he could not pull it back. 5Also, the
altar was split apart and its ashes poured
out according to the sign given by the
man of God by the word of the LORD.

6Then the king said to the man of
God, "Intercede with the LORD your
God and pray for me that my hand may
be restored." So the man of God inter-
ceded with the LORD, and the king's
hand was restored and became as it was
before.

7The king said to the man of God,
"Come home with me and have something to eat, and I will give you a gift."

8But the man of God answered the
king, "Even if you were to give me half
your possessions, I would not go with
you, nor would I eat bread or drink
water here. 9For I was commanded by
the word of the LORD: 'You must not
eat bread or drink water or return by the
way you came.'" 10So he took another
road and did not return by the way he
had come to Bethel.

11Now there was a certain old prophet
living in Bethel, whose sons came and
told him all that the man of God had
done there that day. They also told their
father what he had said to the king.
12Their father asked them, "Which way
did he go?" And his sons showed him
which road the man of God from Judah
had taken. 13So he said to his sons,
"Saddle the donkey for me." And when
they had saddled the donkey for him, he
mounted it 14and rode after the man of
God. He found him sitting under an oak
tree and asked, "Are you the man of
God who came from Judah?"

"I am," he replied.

15So the prophet said to him, "Come
home with me and eat."

16The man of God said, "I cannot
turn back and go with you, nor can I eat
bread or drink water with you in this
place. 17I have been told by the word of
the LORD: 'You must not eat bread or
drink water there or return by the way
you came.'"

18The old prophet answered, "I too
am a prophet, as you are. And an angel
said to me by the word of the LORD:
'Bring him back with you to your house
so that he may eat bread and drink
water.'" (But he was lying to him.) 19So
the man of God returned with him and
ate and drank in his house.

20While they were sitting at the table,
the word of the LORD came to the old
prophet who had brought him back.
21He cried out to the man of God who
had come from Judah, "This is what the
LORD says: 'You have defied the word

of the LORD and have not kept the
command the LORD your God gave you.
22You came back and ate bread and
drank water in the place where he told
you not to eat or drink. Therefore your
body will not be buried in the tomb of
your fathers.'"

23When the man of God had finished
eating and drinking, the prophet who
had brought him back saddled his donkey for him. 24As he went on his way, a
lion met him on the road and killed him,
and his body was thrown down on the
road, with both the donkey and the lion
standing beside it. 25Some people who
passed by saw the body thrown down
there, with the lion standing beside the
body, and they went and reported it in
the city where the old prophet lived.

26When the prophet who had brought
him back from his journey heard of it,
he said, "It is the man of God who
defied the word of the LORD. The LORD
has given him over to the lion, which has
mauled him and killed him, as the word
of the LORD had warned him."

27The prophet said to his sons,
"Saddle the donkey for me," and they
did so. 28Then he went out and found
the body thrown down on the road, with
the donkey and the lion standing beside
it. The lion had neither eaten the body
nor mauled the donkey. 29So the
prophet picked up the body of the man
of God, laid it on the donkey, and
brought it back to his own city to mourn
for him and bury him. 30Then he laid the
body in his own tomb, and they
mourned over him and said, "Oh, my
brother!"

31After burying him, he said to his
sons, "When I die, bury me in the grave
where the man of God is buried; lay my
bones beside his bones. 32For the message he declared by the word of the
LORD against the altar in Bethel and
against all the shrines on the high places
in the towns of Samaria will certainly
come true."

33Even after this, Jeroboam did not
change his evil ways, but once more
appointed priests for the high places
from all sorts of people. Anyone who
wanted to become a priest he consecrated for the high places. 34This was
the sin of the house of Jeroboam that
led to its downfall and to its destruction
from the face of the earth.

Ahijah's Prophecy Against Jeroboam

14 At that time Abijah son of Jeroboam became ill, 2and Jeroboam said to his wife, "Go, disguise
yourself, so that you won't be recognised as the wife of Jeroboam. Then go
to Shiloh. Ahijah the prophet is there
—the one who told me I would be king
over this people. 3Take ten loaves of
bread with you, some cakes and a jar of
honey, and go to him. He will tell you
what will happen to the boy." 4So Jeroboam's wife did what he said and went
to Ahijah's house in Shiloh.

Now Ahijah could not see; his sight
was gone because of his age. 5But the
LORD had told Ahijah, "Jeroboam's
wife is coming to ask you about her son,
for he is ill, and you are to give her such
and such an answer. When she arrives,
she will pretend to be someone else."

6So when Ahijah heard the sound of
her footsteps at the door, he said,
"Come in, wife of Jeroboam. Why this
pretence? I have been sent to you with
bad news. 7Go, tell Jeroboam that this
is what the LORD, the God of Israel,
says: 'I raised you up from among the
people and made you a leader over my
people Israel. 8I tore the kingdom away
from the house of David and gave it to
you, but you have not been like my
servant David, who kept my commands
and followed me with all his heart,
doing only what was right in my eyes.
9You have done more evil than all who
lived before you. You have made for
yourself other gods, idols made of
metal; you have provoked me to anger
and thrust me behind your back.

10" 'Because of this, I am going to
bring disaster on the house of Jeroboam. I will cut off from Jeroboam
every last male in Israel—slave or free.

I will burn up the house of Jeroboam as
one burns dung, until it is all gone.
11Dogs will eat those belonging to Jeroboam who die in the city, and the birds
of the air will feed on those who die in
the country. The LORD has spoken!'
12"As for you, go back home. When
you set foot in your city, the boy will
die. 13All Israel will mourn for him and
bury him. He is the only one belonging
to Jeroboam who will be buried, because he is the only one in the house of
Jeroboam in whom the LORD, the God
of Israel, has found anything good.
14"The LORD will raise up for himself
a king over Israel who will cut off the
family of Jeroboam. This is the day!
What? Yes, even now. 15And the LORD
will strike Israel, so that it will be like a
reed swaying in the water. He will uproot Israel from this good land that he
gave to their forefathers and scatter
them beyond the River, because they
provoked the LORD to anger by making
Asherah poles. 16And he will give Israel
up because of the sins Jeroboam has
committed and has caused Israel to
commit."
17Then Jeroboam's wife got up and
left and went to Tirzah. As soon as she
stepped over the threshold of the house,
the boy died. 18They buried him, and all
Israel mourned for him, as the LORD
had said through his servant the prophet
Ahijah.
19The other events of Jeroboam's
reign, his wars and how he ruled, are
written in the book of the annals of the
kings of Israel. 20He reigned for twenty-
two years and then rested with his
fathers. And Nadab his son succeeded
him as king.

NEW TESTAMENT READING

Acts 16:1–15

Timothy Joins Paul and Silas

16 He came to Derbe and then to
Lystra, where a disciple named
Timothy lived, whose mother was a
Jewess and a believer, but whose father
was a Greek. 2The brothers at Lystra
and Iconium spoke well of him. 3Paul
wanted to take him along on the journey, so he circumcised him because of
the Jews who lived in that area, for they
all knew that his father was a Greek.
4As they travelled from town to town,
they delivered the decisions reached by
the apostles and elders in Jerusalem for
the people to obey. 5So the churches
were strengthened in the faith and grew
daily in numbers.

Paul's Vision of the Man of Macedonia

6Paul and his companions travelled
throughout the region of Phrygia and
Galatia, having been kept by the Holy
Spirit from preaching the word in the
province of Asia. 7When they came to
the border of Mysia, they tried to enter
Bithynia, but the Spirit of Jesus would
not allow them to. 8So they passed by
Mysia and went down to Troas. 9During
the night Paul had a vision of a man of
Macedonia standing and begging him,
"Come over to Macedonia and help
us." 10After Paul had seen the vision,
we got ready at once to leave for Macedonia, concluding that God had called
us to preach the gospel to them.

Lydia's Conversion in Philippi

11From Troas we put out to sea and
sailed straight for Samothrace, and the
next day on to Neapolis. 12From there
we travelled to Philippi, a Roman col-
ony and the leading city of that district
of Macedonia. And we stayed there
several days.
13On the Sabbath we went outside the
city gate to the river, where we expected
to find a place of prayer. We sat down
and began to speak to the women who
had gathered there. 14One of those
listening was a woman named Lydia, a
dealer in purple cloth from the city of
Thyatira, who was a worshipper of
God. The Lord opened her heart to
respond to Paul's message. 15When she

and the members of her household were baptised, she invited us to her home. "If you consider me a believer in the Lord," she said, "come and stay at my house." And she persuaded us.

READING FROM PSALMS
Psalm 78:1–8

A *maskil* of Asaph.

1O my people, hear my teaching;
listen to the words of my mouth.
2I will open my mouth in parables,
I will utter hidden things, things
from of old—
3what we have heard and known,
what our fathers have told us.
4We will not hide them from their
children;
we will tell the next generation
the praiseworthy deeds of the LORD,
his power, and the wonders he has
done.
5He decreed statutes for Jacob
and established the law in Israel,
which he commanded our forefathers
to teach their children,
6so that the next generation would
know them,
even the children yet to be born,
and they in turn would tell their
children.
7Then they would put their trust in
God
and would not forget his deeds
but would keep his commands.
8They would not be like their
forefathers—
a stubborn and rebellious
generation,
whose hearts were not loyal to God,
whose spirits were not faithful to
him.

JUNE 25

DAY 176

OLD TESTAMENT READING
1 Kings 14:21–16:7

Rehoboam King of Judah

21Rehoboam son of Solomon was king in Judah. He was forty-one years old when he became king, and he reigned for seventeen years in Jerusalem, the city the LORD had chosen out of all the tribes of Israel in which to put his Name. His mother's name was Naamah; she was an Ammonite.

22Judah did evil in the eyes of the
LORD. By the sins they committed they stirred up his jealous anger more than
their fathers had done. 23They also
set up for themselves high places, sacred stones and Asherah poles on every high hill and under every spread-
ing tree. 24There were even male shrine-prostitutes in the land; the people engaged in all the detestable practices of the nations the LORD had driven out before the Israelites.

25In the fifth year of King Rehoboam,
Shishak king of Egypt attacked Jerusalem. 26He carried off the treasures of the temple of the LORD and the treasures of the royal palace. He took everything, including all the gold
shields Solomon had made. 27So King
Rehoboam made bronze shields to replace them and assigned these to the commanders of the guard on duty at the
entrance to the royal palace. 28Whenever the king went to the LORD's temple, the guards bore the shields, and afterwards they returned them to the guardroom.

29As for the other events of Rehoboam's reign, and all he did, are they

not written in the book of the annals of
the kings of Judah? [30]There was continual warfare between Rehoboam and
Jeroboam. [31]And Rehoboam rested
with his fathers and was buried with
them in the City of David. His mother's
name was Naamah; she was an Ammonite. And Abijah his son succeeded him
as king.

Abijah King of Judah

15 In the eighteenth year of the
reign of Jeroboam son of Nebat,
Abijah became king of Judah, [2]and he
reigned in Jerusalem for three years.
His mother's name was Maacah daughter of Abishalom.

[3]He committed all the sins his father
had done before him; his heart was not
fully devoted to the LORD his God, as
the heart of David his forefather had
been. [4]Nevertheless, for David's sake
the LORD his God gave him a lamp in
Jerusalem by raising up a son to succeed
him and by making Jerusalem strong.
[5]For David had done what was right in
the eyes of the LORD and had not failed
to keep any of the LORD's commands all
the days of his life—except in the case
of Uriah the Hittite.

[6]There was war between Rehoboam
and Jeroboam throughout ⌞Abijah's⌟
lifetime. [7]As for the other events of
Abijah's reign, and all he did, are they
not written in the book of the annals of
the kings of Judah? There was war between Abijah and Jeroboam. [8]And
Abijah rested with his fathers and was
buried in the City of David. And Asa his
son succeeded him as king.

Asa King of Judah

[9]In the twentieth year of Jeroboam
king of Israel, Asa became king of
Judah, [10]and he reigned in Jerusalem
for forty-one years. His grandmother's
name was Maacah daughter of
Abishalom.

[11]Asa did what was right in the eyes of
the LORD, as his father David had done.
[12]He expelled the male shrine-
prostitutes from the land and got rid of
all the idols his fathers had made. [13]He
even deposed his grandmother Maacah
from her position as queen mother, because she had made a repulsive Asherah
pole. Asa cut the pole down and burned
it in the Kidron Valley. [14]Although he
did not remove the high places, Asa's
heart was fully committed to the LORD
all his life. [15]He brought into the temple
of the LORD the silver and gold and
the articles that he and his father had
dedicated.

[16]There was war between Asa and
Baasha king of Israel throughout their
reigns. [17]Baasha king of Israel went up
against Judah and fortified Ramah to
prevent anyone from leaving or entering the territory of Asa king of Judah.

[18]Asa then took all the silver and gold
that was left in the treasuries of the
LORD's temple and of his own palace.
He entrusted it to his officials and sent
them to Ben-Hadad son of Tabrimmon,
the son of Hezion, the king of Aram,
who was ruling in Damascus. [19]"Let
there be a treaty between me and you,"
he said, "as there was between my
father and your father. See, I am sending you a gift of silver and gold. Now
break your treaty with Baasha king of
Israel so that he will withdraw from
me."

[20]Ben-Hadad agreed with King Asa
and sent the commanders of his forces
against the towns of Israel. He conquered Ijon, Dan, Abel Beth Maacah
and all Kinnereth in addition to Naphtali. [21]When Baasha heard this, he stopped building Ramah and withdrew to
Tirzah. [22]Then King Asa issued an
order to all Judah—no-one was exempt
—and they carried away from Ramah
the stones and timber Baasha had been
using there. With them King Asa built
up Geba in Benjamin, and also Mizpah.

[23]As for all the other events of Asa's
reign, all his achievements, all he did
and the cities he built, are they not
written in the book of the annals of the
kings of Judah? In his old age, however,

his feet became diseased. 24Then Asa
rested with his fathers and was buried
with them in the city of his father David.
And Jehoshaphat his son succeeded
him as king.

Nadab King of Israel

25Nadab son of Jeroboam became
king of Israel in the second year of Asa
king of Judah, and he reigned over
Israel for two years. 26He did evil in the
eyes of the LORD, walking in the ways of
his father and in his sin, which he had
caused Israel to commit.

27Baasha son of Ahijah of the house
of Issachar plotted against him, and he
struck him down at Gibbethon, a Philistine town, while Nadab and all Israel
were besieging it. 28Baasha killed
Nadab in the third year of Asa king of
Judah and succeeded him as king.

29As soon as he began to reign, he
killed Jeroboam's whole family. He did
not leave Jeroboam anyone that
breathed, but destroyed them all,
according to the word of the LORD given
through his servant Ahijah the Shilonite—30because of the sins Jeroboam
had committed and had caused Israel to
commit, and because he provoked the
LORD, the God of Israel, to anger.

31As for the other events of Nadab's
reign, and all he did, are they not written in the book of the annals of the kings
of Israel? 32There was war between Asa
and Baasha king of Israel throughout
their reigns.

Baasha King of Israel

33In the third year of Asa king of
Judah, Baasha son of Ahijah became
king of all Israel in Tirzah, and he
reigned for twenty-four years. 34He did
evil in the eyes of the LORD, walking in
the ways of Jeroboam and in his sin,
which he had caused Israel to commit.

16 Then the word of the LORD
came to Jehu son of Hanani
against Baasha: 2"I lifted you up from
the dust and made you leader of my
people Israel, but you walked in the
ways of Jeroboam and caused my people Israel to sin and to provoke me to
anger by their sins. 3So I am about to
consume Baasha and his house, and I
will make your house like that of Jeroboam son of Nebat. 4Dogs will eat those
belonging to Baasha who die in the city,
and the birds of the air will feed on those
who die in the country."

5As for the other events of Baasha's
reign, what he did and his achievements, are they not written in the book
of the annals of the kings of Israel?
6Baasha rested with his fathers and was
buried in Tirzah. And Elah his son succeeded him as king.

7Moreover, the word of the LORD
came through the prophet Jehu son of
Hanani to Baasha and his house, because of all the evil he had done in the
eyes of the LORD, provoking him to
anger by the things he did, and becoming like the house of Jeroboam—and
also because he destroyed it.

NEW TESTAMENT READING
Acts 16:16–40

Paul and Silas in Prison

16Once when we were going to the
place of prayer, we were met by a slave
girl who had a spirit by which she predicted the future. She earned a great
deal of money for her owners by for-
tune-telling. 17This girl followed Paul
and the rest of us, shouting, "These
men are servants of the Most High God,
who are telling you the way to be
saved." 18She kept this up for many
days. Finally Paul became so troubled
that he turned round and said to the
spirit, "In the name of Jesus Christ I
command you to come out of her!" At
that moment the spirit left her.

19When the owners of the slave girl
realised that their hope of making
money was gone, they seized Paul and
Silas and dragged them into the market-
place to face the authorities. 20They

brought them before the magistrates
and said, "These men are Jews, and are
throwing our city into an uproar 21by
advocating customs unlawful for us
Romans to accept or practise."
22The crowd joined in the attack
against Paul and Silas, and the magistrates ordered them to be stripped and
beaten. 23After they had been severely
flogged, they were thrown into prison,
and the jailer was commanded to guard
them carefully. 24Upon receiving such
orders, he put them in the inner cell and
fastened their feet in the stocks.
25About midnight Paul and Silas were
praying and singing hymns to God, and
the other prisoners were listening to
them. 26Suddenly there was such a violent earthquake that the foundations of
the prison were shaken. At once all the
prison doors flew open, and everybody's chains came loose. 27The jailer
woke up, and when he saw the prison
doors open, he drew his sword and was
about to kill himself because he thought
the prisoners had escaped. 28But Paul
shouted, "Don't harm yourself! We are
all here!"
29The jailer called for lights, rushed in
and fell trembling before Paul and Silas.
30He then brought them out and asked,
"Sirs, what must I do to be saved?"
31They replied, "Believe in the Lord
Jesus, and you will be saved—you and
your household." 32Then they spoke
the word of the Lord to him and to all
the others in his house. 33At that hour
of the night the jailer took them and
washed their wounds; then immediately
he and all his family were baptised.
34The jailer brought them into his house
and set a meal before them; he was filled
with joy because he had come to believe
in God—he and his whole family.
35When it was daylight, the magistrates sent their officers to the jailer
with the order: "Release those men."
36The jailer told Paul, "The magistrates
have ordered that you and Silas be released. Now you can leave. Go in
peace."
37But Paul said to the officers: "They
beat us publicly without a trial, even
though we are Roman citizens, and
threw us into prison. And now do they
want to get rid of us quietly? No! Let
them come themselves and escort us
out."
38The officers reported this to the
magistrates, and when they heard that
Paul and Silas were Roman citizens,
they were alarmed. 39They came to
appease them and escorted them from
the prison, requesting them to leave the
city. 40After Paul and Silas came out of
the prison, they went to Lydia's house,
where they met with the brothers and
encouraged them. Then they left.

READING FROM PROVERBS
Proverbs 15:21–30

21Folly delights a man who lacks
judgment,
but a man of understanding keeps a
straight course.

22Plans fail for lack of counsel,
but with many advisers they
succeed.

23A man finds joy in giving an apt
reply—
and how good is a timely word!

24The path of life leads upward for the
wise
to keep him from going down to
the grave.

25The LORD tears down the proud
man's house
but he keeps the widow's
boundaries intact.

26The LORD detests the thoughts of the
wicked,
but those of the pure are pleasing
to him.

27A greedy man brings trouble to his
family,
but he who hates bribes will live.

[28]The heart of the righteous weighs its answers,
but the mouth of the wicked gushes evil.

[29]The LORD is far from the wicked
but he hears the prayer of the righteous.

[30]A cheerful look brings joy to the heart,
and good news gives health to the bones.

JUNE 26

DAY 177

OLD TESTAMENT READING
1 Kings 16:8–18:15

Elah King of Israel

[8]In the twenty-sixth year of Asa king
of Judah, Elah son of Baasha became
king of Israel, and he reigned in Tirzah
for two years.
[9]Zimri, one of his officials, who had
command of half his chariots, plotted
against him. Elah was in Tirzah at the
time, getting drunk in the home of
Arza, the man in charge of the palace at
Tirzah. [10]Zimri came in, struck him
down and killed him in the twenty-
seventh year of Asa king of Judah. Then
he succeeded him as king.
[11]As soon as he began to reign and
was seated on the throne, he killed off
Baasha's whole family. He did not spare
a single male, whether relative or
friend. [12]So Zimri destroyed the whole
family of Baasha, in accordance with
the word of the LORD spoken against
Baasha through the prophet Jehu—
[13]because of all the sins Baasha and his
son Elah had committed and had caused
Israel to commit, so that they provoked
the LORD, the God of Israel, to anger by
their worthless idols.
[14]As for the other events of Elah's
reign, and all he did, are they not written in the book of the annals of the kings
of Israel?

Zimri King of Israel

[15]In the twenty-seventh year of Asa
king of Judah, Zimri reigned in Tirzah
for seven days. The army was encamped
near Gibbethon, a Philistine town.
[16]When the Israelites in the camp heard
that Zimri had plotted against the king
and murdered him, they proclaimed
Omri, the commander of the army, king
over Israel that very day there in the
camp. [17]Then Omri and all the Israelites
with him withdrew from Gibbethon and
laid siege to Tirzah. [18]When Zimri saw
that the city was taken, he went into the
citadel of the royal palace and set the
palace on fire around him. So he died,
[19]because of the sins he had committed,
doing evil in the eyes of the LORD and
walking in the ways of Jeroboam and in
the sin he had committed and had
caused Israel to commit.
[20]As for the other events of Zimri's
reign, and the rebellion he carried out,
are they not written in the book of the
annals of the kings of Israel?

Omri King of Israel

[21]Then the people of Israel were split
into two factions; half supported Tibni
son of Ginath for king, and the other
half supported Omri. [22]But Omri's followers proved stronger than those of
Tibni son of Ginath. So Tibni died and
Omri became king.
[23]In the thirty-first year of Asa king of
Judah, Omri became king of Israel, and
he reigned for twelve years, six of them
in Tirzah. [24]He bought the hill of
Samaria from Shemer for two talents of
silver and built a city on the hill, calling

it Samaria, after Shemer, the name of the former owner of the hill.

25But Omri did evil in the eyes of the LORD and sinned more than all those before him. 26He walked in all the ways of Jeroboam son of Nebat and in his sin, which he had caused Israel to commit, so that they provoked the LORD, the God of Israel, to anger by their worthless idols.

27As for the other events of Omri's reign, what he did and the things he achieved, are they not written in the book of the annals of the kings of Israel? 28Omri rested with his fathers and was buried in Samaria. And Ahab his son succeeded him as king.

Ahab Becomes King of Israel

29In the thirty-eighth year of Asa king of Judah, Ahab son of Omri became king of Israel, and he reigned in Samaria over Israel for twenty-two years. 30Ahab son of Omri did more evil in the eyes of the LORD than any of those before him. 31He not only considered it trivial to commit the sins of Jeroboam son of Nebat, but he also married Jezebel daughter of Ethbaal king of the Sidonians, and began to serve Baal and worship him. 32He set up an altar for Baal in the temple of Baal that he built in Samaria. 33Ahab also made an Asherah pole and did more to provoke the LORD, the God of Israel, to anger than did all the kings of Israel before him.

34In Ahab's time, Hiel of Bethel rebuilt Jericho. He laid its foundations at the cost of his firstborn son Abiram, and he set up its gates at the cost of his youngest son Segub, in accordance with the word of the LORD spoken by Joshua son of Nun.

Elijah Fed by Ravens

17 Now Elijah the Tishbite, from Tishbe in Gilead, said to Ahab, "As the LORD, the God of Israel, lives, whom I serve, there will be neither dew nor rain in the next few years except at my word."

2Then the word of the LORD came to Elijah: 3"Leave here, turn eastward and hide in the Kerith Ravine, east of the Jordan. 4You will drink from the brook, and I have ordered the ravens to feed you there."

5So he did what the LORD had told him. He went to the Kerith Ravine, east of the Jordan, and stayed there. 6The ravens brought him bread and meat in the morning and bread and meat in the evening, and he drank from the brook.

The Widow at Zarephath

7Some time later the brook dried up because there had been no rain in the land. 8Then the word of the LORD came to him: 9"Go at once to Zarephath of Sidon and stay there. I have commanded a widow in that place to supply you with food." 10So he went to Zarephath. When he came to the town gate, a widow was there gathering sticks. He called to her and asked, "Would you bring me a little water in a jar so I may have a drink?" 11As she was going to get it, he called, "And bring me, please, a piece of bread."

12"As surely as the LORD your God lives," she replied, "I don't have any bread—only a handful of flour in a jar and a little oil in a jug. I am gathering a few sticks to take home and make a meal for myself and my son, that we may eat it—and die."

13Elijah said to her, "Don't be afraid. Go home and do as you have said. But first make a small cake of bread for me from what you have and bring it to me, and then make something for yourself and your son. 14For this is what the LORD, the God of Israel, says: 'The jar of flour will not be used up and the jug of oil will not run dry until the day the LORD gives rain on the land.'"

15She went away and did as Elijah had told her. So there was food every day for Elijah and for the woman and her

family. 16For the jar of flour was not
used up and the jug of oil did not run
dry, in keeping with the word of the
LORD spoken by Elijah.

17Some time later the son of the
woman who owned the house became
ill. He grew worse and worse, and
finally stopped breathing. 18She said to
Elijah, "What do you have against
me, man of God? Did you come to
remind me of my sin and kill my son?"

19"Give me your son," Elijah replied.
He took him from her arms, carried him
to the upper room where he was
staying, and laid him on his bed. 20Then
he cried out to the LORD, "O LORD my
God, have you brought tragedy also
upon this widow I am staying with, by
causing her son to die?" 21Then he
stretched himself out on the boy three
times and cried to the LORD, "O LORD
my God, let this boy's life return to
him!"

22The LORD heard Elijah's cry, and
the boy's life returned to him, and he
lived. 23Elijah picked up the child and
carried him down from the room into
the house. He gave him to his mother
and said, "Look, your son is alive!"

24Then the woman said to Elijah,
"Now I know that you are a man of God
and that the word of the LORD from
your mouth is the truth."

Elijah and Obadiah

18 After a long time, in the third
year, the word of the LORD came
to Elijah: "Go and present yourself to
Ahab, and I will send rain on the land."
2So Elijah went to present himself to
Ahab.

Now the famine was severe in Samaria, 3and Ahab had summoned Obadiah, who was in charge of his palace.
(Obadiah was a devout believer in the
LORD. 4While Jezebel was killing off the
LORD's prophets, Obadiah had taken a
hundred prophets and hidden them in
two caves, fifty in each, and had supplied them with food and water.) 5Ahab
had said to Obadiah, "Go through the
land to all the springs and valleys.
Maybe we can find some grass to keep
the horses and mules alive so we will not
have to kill any of our animals." 6So
they divided the land they were to
cover, Ahab going in one direction
and Obadiah in another.

7As Obadiah was walking along, Elijah met him. Obadiah recognised him,
bowed down to the ground, and said,
"Is it really you, my lord Elijah?"

8"Yes," he replied. "Go tell your
master, 'Elijah is here.'"

9"What have I done wrong," asked
Obadiah, "that you are handing your
servant over to Ahab to be put to death?
10As surely as the LORD your God lives,
there is not a nation or kingdom where
my master has not sent someone to look
for you. And whenever a nation or kingdom claimed you were not there, he
made them swear they could not find
you. 11But now you tell me to go to my
master and say, 'Elijah is here.' 12I don't
know where the Spirit of the LORD may
carry you when I leave you. If I go and
tell Ahab and he doesn't find you, he
will kill me. Yet I your servant have
worshipped the LORD since my youth.
13Haven't you heard, my lord, what I
did while Jezebel was killing the
prophets of the LORD? I hid a hundred
of the LORD's prophets in two caves,
fifty in each, and supplied them with
food and water. 14And now you tell me
to go to my master and say, 'Elijah is
here.' He will kill me!"

15Elijah said, "As the LORD Almighty
lives, whom I serve, I will surely present
myself to Ahab today."

NEW TESTAMENT READING
Acts 17:1–21

In Thessalonica

17 When they had passed through
Amphipolis and Apollonia, they
came to Thessalonica, where there was

a Jewish synagogue. 2As his custom
was, Paul went into the synagogue, and
on three Sabbath days he reasoned with
them from the Scriptures, 3explaining
and proving that the Christ had to suffer
and rise from the dead. "This Jesus I am
proclaiming to you is the Christ," he
said. 4Some of the Jews were persuaded
and joined Paul and Silas, as did a large
number of God-fearing Greeks and not
a few prominent women.

5But the Jews were jealous; so they
rounded up some bad characters from
the market-place, formed a mob and
started a riot in the city. They rushed to
Jason's house in search of Paul and Silas
in order to bring them out to the crowd.
6But when they did not find them, they
dragged Jason and some other brothers
before the city officials, shouting:
"These men who have caused trouble
all over the world have now come here,
7and Jason has welcomed them into his
house. They are all defying Caesar's
decrees, saying that there is another
king, one called Jesus." 8When they
heard this, the crowd and the city officials were thrown into turmoil. 9Then
they put Jason and the others on bail
and let them go.

In Berea

10As soon as it was night, the brothers
sent Paul and Silas away to Berea. On
arriving there, they went to the Jewish
synagogue. 11Now the Bereans were of
more noble character than the Thessalonians, for they received the message
with great eagerness and examined the
Scriptures every day to see if what Paul
said was true. 12Many of the Jews believed, as did also a number of prominent Greek women and many Greek
men.

13When the Jews in Thessalonica
learned that Paul was preaching the
word of God at Berea, they went there
too, agitating the crowds and stirring
them up. 14The brothers immediately
sent Paul to the coast, but Silas and
Timothy stayed at Berea. 15The men
who escorted Paul brought him to
Athens and then left with instructions
for Silas and Timothy to join him as
soon as possible.

In Athens

16While Paul was waiting for them in
Athens, he was greatly distressed to see
that the city was full of idols. 17So he
reasoned in the synagogue with the
Jews and the God-fearing Greeks, as
well as in the market-place day by day
with those who happened to be there.
18A group of Epicurean and Stoic philo-
sophers began to dispute with him.
Some of them asked, "What is this bab-
bler trying to say?" Others remarked,
"He seems to be advocating foreign
gods." They said this because Paul was
preaching the good news about Jesus
and the resurrection. 19Then they took
him and brought him to a meeting of the
Areopagus, where they said to him,
"May we know what this new teaching
is that you are presenting? 20You are
bringing some strange ideas to our ears,
and we want to know what they mean."
21(All the Athenians and the foreigners
who lived there spent their time doing
nothing but talking about and listening
to the latest ideas.)

READING FROM PSALMS
Psalm 78:9–16

9The men of Ephraim, though armed
with bows,
turned back on the day of battle;
10they did not keep God's covenant
and refused to live by his law.
11They forgot what he had done,
the wonders he had shown them.
12He did miracles in the sight of their
fathers
in the land of Egypt, in the region
of Zoan.
13He divided the sea and led them
through;
he made the water stand firm like a
wall.

[14]He guided them with the cloud by
day
and with light from the fire all
night.
[15]He split the rocks in the desert
and gave them water as abundant
as the seas;
[16]he brought streams out of a rocky crag
and made water flow down like
rivers.

JUNE 27

DAY 178

OLD TESTAMENT READING
1 Kings 18:16–19:21

Elijah on Mount Carmel

[16]So Obadiah went to meet Ahab and
told him, and Ahab went to meet Elijah. [17]When he saw Elijah, he said to
him, "Is that you, you troubler of
Israel?"

[18]"I have not made trouble for
Israel," Elijah replied. "But you and
your father's family have. You have
abandoned the LORD's commands and
have followed the Baals. [19]Now summon the people from all over Israel to
meet me on Mount Carmel. And bring
the four hundred and fifty prophets of
Baal and the four hundred prophets of
Asherah, who eat at Jezebel's table."

[20]So Ahab sent word throughout all
Israel and assembled the prophets on
Mount Carmel. [21]Elijah went before
the people and said, "How long will you
waver between two opinions? If the
LORD is God, follow him; but if Baal is
God, follow him."

But the people said nothing.

[22]Then Elijah said to them, "I am the
only one of the LORD's prophets left,
but Baal has four hundred and fifty
prophets. [23]Get two bulls for us. Let
them choose one for themselves, and let
them cut it into pieces and put it on the
wood but not set fire to it. I will prepare
the other bull and put it on the wood but
not set fire to it. [24]Then you call on the
name of your god, and I will call on the
name of the LORD. The god who
answers by fire—he is God."

Then all the people said, "What you
say is good."

[25]Elijah said to the prophets of Baal,
"Choose one of the bulls and prepare it
first, since there are so many of you.
Call on the name of your god, but do not
light the fire." [26]So they took the bull
given them and prepared it.

Then they called on the name of Baal
from morning till noon. "O Baal,
answer us!" they shouted. But there
was no response; no-one answered.
And they danced around the altar they
had made.

[27]At noon Elijah began to taunt
them. "Shout louder!" he said. "Surely
he is a god! Perhaps he is deep in
thought, or busy, or travelling. Maybe
he is sleeping and must be awakened."
[28]So they shouted louder and slashed
themselves with swords and spears, as
was their custom, until their blood
flowed. [29]Midday passed, and they continued their frantic prophesying until
the time for the evening sacrifice. But
there was no response, no-one
answered, no-one paid attention.

[30]Then Elijah said to all the people,
"Come here to me." They came to him,
and he repaired the altar of the LORD,
which was in ruins. [31]Elijah took twelve
stones, one for each of the tribes descended from Jacob, to whom the word
of the LORD had come, saying, "Your
name shall be Israel." [32]With the stones
he built an altar in the name of the
LORD, and he dug a trench round it
large enough to hold two seahs of seed.
[33]He arranged the wood, cut the bull

into pieces and laid it on the wood. Then he said to them, "Fill four large jars with water and pour it on the offering and on the wood."

34"Do it again," he said, and they did it again.

"Do it a third time," he ordered, and they did it the third time. 35The water ran down around the altar and even filled the trench.

36At the time of sacrifice, the prophet Elijah stepped forward and prayed: "O LORD, God of Abraham, Isaac and Israel, let it be known today that you are God in Israel and that I am your servant and have done all these things at your command. 37Answer me, O LORD, answer me, so these people will know that you, O LORD, are God, and that you are turning their hearts back again."

38Then the fire of the LORD fell and burned up the sacrifice, the wood, the stones and the soil, and also licked up the water in the trench.

39When all the people saw this, they fell prostrate and cried, "The LORD—he is God! The LORD—he is God!"

40Then Elijah commanded them, "Seize the prophets of Baal. Don't let anyone get away!" They seized them, and Elijah had them brought down to the Kishon Valley and slaughtered there.

41And Elijah said to Ahab, "Go, eat and drink, for there is the sound of a heavy rain." 42So Ahab went off to eat and drink, but Elijah climbed to the top of Carmel, bent down to the ground and put his face between his knees.

43"Go and look towards the sea," he told his servant. And he went up and looked.

"There is nothing there," he said.

Seven times Elijah said, "Go back."

44The seventh time the servant reported, "A cloud as small as a man's hand is rising from the sea."

So Elijah said, "Go and tell Ahab, 'Hitch up your chariot and go down before the rain stops you.'"

45Meanwhile, the sky grew black with clouds, the wind rose, a heavy rain came on and Ahab rode off to Jezreel. 46The power of the LORD came upon Elijah and, tucking his cloak into his belt, he ran ahead of Ahab all the way to Jezreel.

Elijah Flees to Horeb

19 Now Ahab told Jezebel everything Elijah had done and how he had killed all the prophets with the sword. 2So Jezebel sent a messenger to Elijah to say, "May the gods deal with me, be it ever so severely, if by this time tomorrow I do not make your life like that of one of them."

3Elijah was afraid and ran for his life. When he came to Beersheba in Judah, he left his servant there, 4while he himself went a day's journey into the desert. He came to a broom tree, sat down under it and prayed that he might die. "I have had enough, LORD," he said. "Take my life; I am no better than my ancestors." 5Then he lay down under the tree and fell asleep.

All at once an angel touched him and said, "Get up and eat." 6He looked around, and there by his head was a cake of bread baked over hot coals, and a jar of water. He ate and drank and then lay down again.

7The angel of the LORD came back a second time and touched him and said, "Get up and eat, for the journey is too much for you." 8So he got up and ate and drank. Strengthened by that food, he travelled for forty days and forty nights until he reached Horeb, the mountain of God. 9There he went into a cave and spent the night.

The LORD Appears to Elijah

And the word of the LORD came to him: "What are you doing here, Elijah?"

10He replied, "I have been very zealous for the LORD God Almighty. The Israelites have rejected your covenant, broken down your altars, and put your prophets to death with the sword. I am the only one left, and now they are trying to kill me too."

11The LORD said, "Go out and stand on the mountain in the presence of the LORD, for the LORD is about to pass by."

Then a great and powerful wind tore the mountains apart and shattered the rocks before the LORD, but the LORD was not in the wind. After the wind there was an earthquake, but the LORD was not in the earthquake. 12After the earthquake came a fire, but the LORD was not in the fire. And after the fire came a gentle whisper. 13When Elijah heard it, he pulled his cloak over his face and went out and stood at the mouth of the cave.

Then a voice said to him, "What are you doing here, Elijah?"

14He replied, "I have been very zealous for the LORD God Almighty. The Israelites have rejected your covenant, broken down your altars, and put your prophets to death with the sword. I am the only one left, and now they are trying to kill me too."

15The LORD said to him, "Go back the way you came, and go to the Desert of Damascus. When you get there, anoint Hazael king over Aram. 16Also, anoint Jehu son of Nimshi king over Israel, and anoint Elisha son of Shaphat from Abel Meholah to succeed you as prophet. 17Jehu will put to death any who escape the sword of Hazael, and Elisha will put to death any who escape the sword of Jehu. 18Yet I reserve seven thousand in Israel—all whose knees have not bowed down to Baal and all whose mouths have not kissed him."

The Call of Elisha

19So Elijah went from there and found Elisha son of Shaphat. He was ploughing with twelve yoke of oxen, and he himself was driving the twelfth pair. Elijah went up to him and threw his cloak around him. 20Elisha then left his oxen and ran after Elijah. "Let me kiss my father and mother good-bye," he said, "and then I will come with you."

"Go back," Elijah replied. "What have I done to you?"

21So Elisha left him and went back. He took his yoke of oxen and slaughtered them. He burned the ploughing equipment to cook the meat and gave it to the people, and they ate. Then he set out to follow Elijah and became his attendant.

NEW TESTAMENT READING
Acts 17:22–18:8

22Paul then stood up in the meeting of the Areopagus and said: "Men of Athens! I see that in every way you are very religious. 23For as I walked around and looked carefully at your objects of worship, I even found an altar with this inscription: TO AN UNKNOWN GOD. Now what you worship as something unknown I am going to proclaim to you.

24"The God who made the world and everything in it is the Lord of heaven and earth and does not live in temples built by hands. 25And he is not served by human hands, as if he needed anything, because he himself gives all men life and breath and everything else. 26From one man he made every nation of men, that they should inhabit the whole earth; and he determined the times set for them and the exact places where they should live. 27God did this so that men would seek him and perhaps reach out for him and find him, though he is not far from each one of us. 28'For in him we live and move and have our being.' As some of your own poets have said, 'We are his offspring.'

29"Therefore since we are God's offspring, we should not think that the divine being is like gold or silver or stone—an image made by man's design and skill. 30In the past God overlooked such ignorance, but now he commands all people everywhere to repent. 31For he has set a day when he will judge the world with justice by the man he has appointed. He has given proof of this to all men by raising him from the dead."

32When they heard about the resurrection of the dead, some of them sneered, but others said, "We want to hear you again on this subject." 33At that, Paul left the Council. 34A few men became followers of Paul and believed. Among them was Dionysius, a member of the Areopagus, also a woman named Damaris, and a number of others.

In Corinth

18 After this, Paul left Athens and went to Corinth. 2There he met
a Jew named Aquila, a native of Pontus,
who had recently come from Italy with
his wife Priscilla, because Claudius had
ordered all the Jews to leave Rome.
Paul went to see them, 3and because he
was a tentmaker as they were, he stayed
and worked with them. 4Every Sabbath
he reasoned in the synagogue, trying to
persuade Jews and Greeks.

5When Silas and Timothy came from
Macedonia, Paul devoted himself exclusively to preaching, testifying to the
Jews that Jesus was the Christ. 6But
when the Jews opposed Paul and became abusive, he shook out his clothes
in protest and said to them, "Your
blood be on your own heads! I am clear
of my responsibility. From now on I will
go to the Gentiles."

7Then Paul left the synagogue and
went next door to the house of Titius
Justus, a worshipper of God. 8Crispus,
the synagogue ruler, and his entire
household believed in the Lord; and
many of the Corinthians who heard him
believed and were baptised.

READING FROM PSALMS
Psalm 78:17–31

17But they continued to sin against him,
rebelling in the desert against the Most High.
18They wilfully put God to the test
by demanding the food they craved.
19They spoke against God, saying,
"Can God spread a table in the desert?
20When he struck the rock, water gushed out,
and streams flowed abundantly.
But can he also give us food?
Can he supply meat for his people?"
21When the LORD heard them, he was very angry;
his fire broke out against Jacob,
and his wrath rose against Israel,
22for they did not believe in God
or trust in his deliverance.
23Yet he gave a command to the skies above
and opened the doors of the heavens;
24he rained down manna for the people to eat,
he gave them the grain of heaven.
25Men ate the bread of angels;
he sent them all the food they could eat.
26He let loose the east wind from the heavens
and led forth the south wind by his power.
27He rained meat down on them like dust,
flying birds like sand on the seashore.
28He made them come down inside their camp,
all around their tents.
29They ate till they had more than enough,
for he had given them what they craved.
30But before they turned from the food they craved,
even while it was still in their mouths,
31God's anger rose against them;
he put to death the sturdiest among them,
cutting down the young men of Israel.

JUNE 28

OLD TESTAMENT READING
1 Kings 20:1–21:29

Ben-Hadad Attacks Samaria

20 Now Ben-Hadad king of Aram mustered his entire army. Accompanied by thirty-two kings with their horses and chariots, he went up and besieged Samaria and attacked it. [2]He sent messengers into the city to Ahab king of Israel, saying, "This is what Ben-Hadad says: [3]'Your silver and gold are mine, and the best of your wives and children are mine.' "

[4]The king of Israel answered, "Just as you say, my lord the king. I and all I have are yours."

[5]The messengers came again and said, "This is what Ben-Hadad says: 'I sent to demand your silver and gold, your wives and your children. [6]But about this time tomorrow I am going to send my officials to search your palace and the houses of your officials. They will seize everything you value and carry it away.' "

[7]The king of Israel summoned all the elders of the land and said to them, "See how this man is looking for trouble! When he sent for my wives and my children, my silver and my gold, I did not refuse him."

[8]The elders and the people all answered, "Don't listen to him or agree to his demands."

[9]So he replied to Ben-Hadad's messengers, "Tell my lord the king, 'Your servant will do all you demanded the first time, but this demand I cannot meet.' " They left and took the answer back to Ben-Hadad.

[10]Then Ben-Hadad sent another message to Ahab: "May the gods deal with me, be it ever so severely, if enough dust remains in Samaria to give each of my men a handful."

[11]The king of Israel answered, "Tell him: 'One who puts on his armour should not boast like one who takes it off.' "

[12]Ben-Hadad heard this message while he and the kings were drinking in their tents, and he ordered his men: "Prepare to attack." So they prepared to attack the city.

Ahab Defeats Ben-Hadad

[13]Meanwhile a prophet came to Ahab king of Israel and announced, "This is what the LORD says: 'Do you see this vast army? I will give it into your hand today, and then you will know that I am the LORD.' "

[14]"But who will do this?" asked Ahab.

The prophet replied, "This is what the LORD says: 'The young officers of the provincial commanders will do it.' "

"And who will start the battle?" he asked.

The prophet answered, "You will."

[15]So Ahab summoned the young officers of the provincial commanders, 232 men. Then he assembled the rest of the Israelites, 7,000 in all. [16]They set out at noon while Ben-Hadad and the 32 kings allied with him were in their tents getting drunk. [17]The young officers of the provincial commanders went out first.

Now Ben-Hadad had dispatched scouts, who reported, "Men are advancing from Samaria."

[18]He said, "If they have come out for peace, take them alive; if they have come out for war, take them alive."

[19]The young officers of the provincial commanders marched out of the city with the army behind them [20]and each one struck down his opponent. At that, the Arameans fled, with the Israelites in pursuit. But Ben-Hadad king of Aram escaped on horseback with some of his

horsemen. 21The king of Israel advanced and overpowered the horses and
chariots and inflicted heavy losses on
the Arameans.
22Afterwards, the prophet came to
the king of Israel and said, "Strengthen
your position and see what must be
done, because next spring the king of
Aram will attack you again."
23Meanwhile, the officials of the king
of Aram advised him, "Their gods are
gods of the hills. That is why they were
too strong for us. But if we fight them on
the plains, surely we will be stronger
than they. 24Do this: Remove all the
kings from their commands and replace
them with other officers. 25You must
also raise an army like the one you
lost—horse for horse and chariot for
chariot—so we can fight Israel on the
plains. Then surely we will be stronger
than they." He agreed with them and
acted accordingly.
26The next spring Ben-Hadad mustered the Arameans and went up to
Aphek to fight against Israel. 27When
the Israelites were also mustered and
given provisions, they marched out to
meet them. The Israelites camped
opposite them like two small flocks of
goats, while the Arameans covered the
countryside.
28The man of God came up and told
the king of Israel, "This is what the
LORD says: 'Because the Arameans
think the LORD is a god of the hills and
not a god of the valleys, I will deliver
this vast army into your hands, and you
will know that I am the LORD.' "
29For seven days they camped opposite each other, and on the seventh day
the battle was joined. The Israelites
inflicted a hundred thousand casualties
on the Aramean foot soldiers in one
day. 30The rest of them escaped to the
city of Aphek, where the wall collapsed
on twenty-seven thousand of them.
And Ben-Hadad fled to the city and hid
in an inner room.
31His officials said to him, "Look, we
have heard that the kings of the house of
Israel are merciful. Let us go to the king
of Israel with sackcloth round our waists
and ropes round our heads. Perhaps he
will spare your life."
32Wearing sackcloth round their
waists and ropes round their heads, they
went to the king of Israel and said,
"Your servant Ben-Hadad says: 'Please
let me live.' "
The king answered, "Is he still alive?
He is my brother."
33The men took this as a good sign
and were quick to pick up his word.
"Yes, your brother Ben-Hadad!" they
said.
"Go and get him," the king said.
When Ben-Hadad came out, Ahab had
him come up into his chariot.
34"I will return the cities my father
took from your father," Ben-Hadad
offered. "You may set up your own
market areas in Damascus, as my father
did in Samaria."
⌊Ahab said,⌋ "On the basis of a treaty
I will set you free." So he made a treaty
with him, and let him go.

A Prophet Condemns Ahab

35By the word of the LORD one of the
sons of the prophets said to his companion, "Strike me with your weapon,"
but the man refused.
36So the prophet said, "Because you
have not obeyed the LORD, as soon as
you leave me a lion will kill you." And
after the man went away, a lion found
him and killed him.
37The prophet found another man
and said, "Strike me, please." So the
man struck him and wounded him.
38Then the prophet went and stood by
the road waiting for the king. He disguised himself with his headband down
over his eyes. 39As the king passed by,
the prophet called out to him, "Your
servant went into the thick of the battle,
and someone came to me with a captive
and said, 'Guard this man. If he is missing, it will be your life for his life, or
you must pay a talent of silver.' 40While
your servant was busy here and there,
the man disappeared."

"That is your sentence," the king of
Israel said. "You have pronounced it
yourself."
41Then the prophet quickly removed
the headband from his eyes, and the
king of Israel recognised him as one of
the prophets. 42He said to the king,
"This is what the LORD says: 'You have
set free a man I had determined should
die. Therefore it is your life for his life,
your people for his people.'" 43Sullen
and angry, the king of Israel went to his
palace in Samaria.

Naboth's Vineyard

21 Some time later there was an
incident involving a vineyard belonging to Naboth the Jezreelite. The
vineyard was in Jezreel, close to the
palace of Ahab king of Samaria. 2Ahab
said to Naboth, "Let me have your
vineyard to use for a vegetable garden,
since it is close to my palace. In exchange I will give you a better vineyard
or, if you prefer, I will pay you whatever
it is worth."
3But Naboth replied, "The LORD forbid that I should give you the inheritance of my fathers."
4So Ahab went home, sullen and
angry because Naboth the Jezreelite
had said, "I will not give you the inheritance of my fathers." He lay on his bed
sulking and refused to eat.
5His wife Jezebel came in and asked
him, "Why are you so sullen? Why
won't you eat?"
6He answered her, "Because I said to
Naboth the Jezreelite, 'Sell me your
vineyard; or if you prefer, I will give you
another vineyard in its place.' But he
said, 'I will not give you my vineyard.'"
7Jezebel his wife said, "Is this how
you act as king over Israel? Get up and
eat! Cheer up. I'll get you the vineyard
of Naboth the Jezreelite."
8So she wrote letters in Ahab's name,
placed his seal on them, and sent them
to the elders and nobles who lived in
Naboth's city with him. 9In those letters
she wrote:

"Proclaim a day of fasting and
seat Naboth in a prominent place
among the people. 10But seat two
scoundrels opposite him and have
them testify that he has cursed both
God and the king. Then take him
out and stone him to death."

11So the elders and nobles who lived
in Naboth's city did as Jezebel directed
in the letters she had written to them.
12They proclaimed a fast and seated
Naboth in a prominent place among the
people. 13Then two scoundrels came
and sat opposite him and brought
charges against Naboth before the people, saying, "Naboth has cursed both
God and the king." So they took him
outside the city and stoned him to
death. 14Then they sent word to
Jezebel: "Naboth has been stoned and
is dead."
15As soon as Jezebel heard that
Naboth had been stoned to death, she
said to Ahab, "Get up and take possession of the vineyard of Naboth the Jezreelite that he refused to sell you. He is
no longer alive, but dead." 16When
Ahab heard that Naboth was dead, he
got up and went down to take possession of Naboth's vineyard.
17Then the word of the LORD came to
Elijah the Tishbite: 18"Go down to
meet Ahab king of Israel, who rules in
Samaria. He is now in Naboth's
vineyard, where he has gone to take
possession of it. 19Say to him, 'This is
what the LORD says: Have you not murdered a man and seized his property?'
Then say to him, 'This is what the LORD
says: In the place where dogs licked up
Naboth's blood, dogs will lick up your
blood—yes, yours!'"
20Ahab said to Elijah, "So you have
found me, my enemy!"
"I have found you," he answered,
"because you have sold yourself to do
evil in the eyes of the LORD. 21'I am
going to bring disaster on you. I will
consume your descendants and cut off
from Ahab every last male in Israel
—slave or free. 22I will make your house

like that of Jeroboam son of Nebat and
that of Baasha son of Ahijah, because
you have provoked me to anger and
have caused Israel to sin.'

23"And also concerning Jezebel the
LORD says: 'Dogs will devour Jezebel by
the wall of Jezreel.'

24"Dogs will eat those belonging to
Ahab who die in the city, and the birds
of the air will feed on those who die in
the country."

25(There was never a man like Ahab,
who sold himself to do evil in the eyes of
the LORD, urged on by Jezebel his wife.
26He behaved in the vilest manner by
going after idols, like the Amorites the
LORD drove out before Israel.)

27When Ahab heard these words, he
tore his clothes, put on sackcloth and
fasted. He lay in sackcloth and went
around meekly.

28Then the word of the LORD came
to Elijah the Tishbite: 29"Have you
noticed how Ahab has humbled himself
before me? Because he has humbled
himself, I will not bring this disaster in
his day, but I will bring it on his house in
the days of his son."

NEW TESTAMENT READING
Acts 18:9–19:13

9One night the Lord spoke to Paul in
a vision: "Do not be afraid; keep on
speaking, do not be silent. 10For I am
with you, and no-one is going to attack
and harm you, because I have many
people in this city." 11So Paul stayed for
a year and a half, teaching them the
word of God.

12While Gallio was proconsul of
Achaia, the Jews made a united attack
on Paul and brought him into court.
13"This man," they charged, "is per-
suading the people to worship God in
ways contrary to the law."

14Just as Paul was about to speak,
Gallio said to the Jews, "If you Jews
were making a complaint about some
misdemeanour or serious crime, it
would be reasonable for me to listen to
you. 15But since it involves questions
about words and names and your own
law—settle the matter yourselves. I will
not be a judge of such things." 16So he
had them ejected from the court.
17Then they all turned on Sosthenes the
synagogue ruler and beat him in front of
the court. But Gallio showed no concern whatever.

Priscilla, Aquila and Apollos

18Paul stayed on in Corinth for some
time. Then he left the brothers and
sailed for Syria, accompanied by Priscilla and Aquila. Before he sailed, he
had his hair cut off at Cenchrea because
of a vow he had taken. 19They arrived at
Ephesus, where Paul left Priscilla and
Aquila. He himself went into the synagogue and reasoned with the Jews.
20When they asked him to spend more
time with them, he declined. 21But as he
left, he promised, "I will come back if it
is God's will." Then he set sail from
Ephesus. 22When he landed at
Caesarea, he went up and greeted the
church and then went down to Antioch.

23After spending some time in Antioch, Paul set out from there and
travelled from place to place throughout the region of Galatia and Phrygia,
strengthening all the disciples.

24Meanwhile a Jew named Apollos, a
native of Alexandria, came to Ephesus.
He was a learned man, with a thorough
knowledge of the Scriptures. 25He had
been instructed in the way of the Lord,
and he spoke with great fervour and
taught about Jesus accurately, though
he knew only the baptism of John. 26He
began to speak boldly in the synagogue.
When Priscilla and Aquila heard him,
they invited him to their home and explained to him the way of God more
adequately.

27When Apollos wanted to go to
Achaia, the brothers encouraged him
and wrote to the disciples there to welcome him. On arriving, he was a great
help to those who by grace had believed. 28For he vigorously refuted the

Jews in public debate, proving from the
Scriptures that Jesus was the Christ.

Paul in Ephesus

19 While Apollos was at Corinth,
Paul took the road through the
interior and arrived at Ephesus. There
he found some disciples 2and asked
them, "Did you receive the Holy Spirit
when you believed?"

They answered, "No, we have not
even heard that there is a Holy Spirit."

3So Paul asked, "Then what baptism
did you receive?"

"John's baptism," they replied.

4Paul said, "John's baptism was a
baptism of repentance. He told the people to believe in the one coming after
him, that is, in Jesus." 5On hearing this,
they were baptised into the name of the
Lord Jesus. 6When Paul placed his
hands on them, the Holy Spirit came on
them, and they spoke in tongues and
prophesied. 7There were about twelve
men in all.

8Paul entered the synagogue and
spoke boldly there for three months,
arguing persuasively about the kingdom
of God. 9But some of them became
obstinate; they refused to believe and
publicly maligned the Way. So Paul left
them. He took the disciples with him
and had discussions daily in the lecture
hall of Tyrannus. 10This went on for two
years, so that all the Jews and Greeks
who lived in the province of Asia heard
the word of the Lord.

11God did extraordinary miracles
through Paul, 12so that even handker-
chiefs and aprons that had touched him
were taken to the sick, and their illnesses were cured and the evil spirits
left them.

13Some Jews who went around driving out evil spirits tried to invoke the
name of the Lord Jesus over those who
were demon-possessed. They would
say, "In the name of Jesus, whom Paul
preaches, I command you to come out."

READING FROM PSALMS

Psalm 78:32–39

32In spite of all this, they kept on
sinning;
in spite of his wonders, they did not
believe.
33So he ended their days in futility
and their years in terror.
34Whenever God slew them, they
would seek him;
they eagerly turned to him again.
35They remembered that God was their
Rock,
that God Most High was their
Redeemer.
36But then they would flatter him with
their mouths,
lying to him with their tongues;
37their hearts were not loyal to him,
they were not faithful to his
covenant.
38Yet he was merciful;
he forgave their iniquities
and did not destroy them.
Time after time he restrained his
anger
and did not stir up his full wrath.
39He remembered that they were but
flesh,
a passing breeze that does not
return.

DAY 180 JUNE 29

OLD TESTAMENT READING
1 Kings 22:1–53

Micaiah Prophesies Against Ahab

22 For three years there was no war
between Aram and Israel. 2But
in the third year Jehoshaphat king of
Judah went down to see the king of
Israel. 3The king of Israel had said to his
officials, "Don't you know that Ramoth
Gilead belongs to us and yet we are
doing nothing to retake it from the king
of Aram?"
4So he asked Jehoshaphat, "Will you
go with me to fight against Ramoth
Gilead?"
Jehoshaphat replied to the king of
Israel, "I am as you are, my people as
your people, my horses as your horses."
5But Jehoshaphat also said to the king
of Israel, "First seek the counsel of the
LORD."
6So the king of Israel brought
together the prophets—about four
hundred men—and asked them, "Shall
I go to war against Ramoth Gilead, or
shall I refrain?"
"Go," they answered, "for the Lord
will give it into the king's hand."
7But Jehoshaphat asked, "Is there
not a prophet of the LORD here whom
we can enquire of?"
8The king of Israel answered
Jehoshaphat, "There is still one man
through whom we can enquire of the
LORD, but I hate him because he never
prophesies anything good about me,
but always bad. He is Micaiah son of
Imlah."
"The king should not say that,"
Jehoshaphat replied.
9So the king of Israel called one of his
officials and said, "Bring Micaiah son of
Imlah at once."
10Dressed in their royal robes, the
king of Israel and Jehoshaphat king of
Judah were sitting on their thrones at
the threshing-floor by the entrance of
the gate of Samaria, with all the
prophets prophesying before them.
11Now Zedekiah son of Kenaanah had
made iron horns and he declared, "This
is what the LORD says: 'With these you
will gore the Arameans until they are
destroyed.'"
12All the other prophets were
prophesying the same thing. "Attack
Ramoth Gilead and be victorious,"
they said, "for the LORD will give it into
the king's hand."
13The messenger who had gone to
summon Micaiah said to him, "Look,
as one man the other prophets are pre-
dicting success for the king. Let your
word agree with theirs, and speak
favourably."
14But Micaiah said, "As surely as the
LORD lives, I can tell him only what the
LORD tells me."
15When he arrived, the king asked
him, "Micaiah, shall we go to war
against Ramoth Gilead, or shall I
refrain?"
"Attack and be victorious," he
answered, "for the LORD will give it into
the king's hand."
16The king said to him, "How many
times must I make you swear to tell me
nothing but the truth in the name of the
LORD?"
17Then Micaiah answered, "I saw all
Israel scattered on the hills like sheep
without a shepherd, and the LORD said,
'These people have no master. Let each
one go home in peace.'"
18The king of Israel said to
Jehoshaphat, "Didn't I tell you that he
never prophesies anything good about
me, but only bad?"
19Micaiah continued, "Therefore
hear the word of the LORD: I saw the
LORD sitting on his throne with all the
host of heaven standing round him on
his right and on his left. 20And the
LORD said, 'Who will entice Ahab into

attacking Ramoth Gilead and going
to his death there?'
"One suggested this, and another
that. 21Finally, a spirit came forward,
stood before the LORD and said, 'I will
entice him.'
22"'By what means?' the LORD
asked.
"'I will go out and be a lying spirit in
the mouths of all his prophets,' he said.
"'You will succeed in enticing him,'
said the LORD. 'Go and do it.'
23"So now the LORD has put a lying
spirit in the mouths of all these prophets
of yours. The LORD has decreed disaster
for you."
24Then Zedekiah son of Kenaanah
went up and slapped Micaiah in the
face. "Which way did the spirit from the
LORD go when he went from me to
speak to you?" he asked.
25Micaiah replied, "You will find out
on the day you go to hide in an inner
room."
26The king of Israel then ordered,
"Take Micaiah and send him back to
Amon the ruler of the city and to Joash
the king's son 27and say, 'This is what
the king says: Put this fellow in prison
and give him nothing but bread and
water until I return safely.'"
28Micaiah declared, "If you ever return safely, the LORD has not spoken
through me." Then he added, "Mark
my words, all you people!"

Ahab Killed at Ramoth Gilead

29So the king of Israel and
Jehoshaphat king of Judah went up to
Ramoth Gilead. 30The king of Israel
said to Jehoshaphat, "I will enter the
battle in disguise, but you wear your
royal robes." So the king of Israel disguised himself and went into battle.
31Now the king of Aram had ordered
his thirty-two chariot commanders,
"Do not fight with anyone, small or
great, except the king of Israel."
32When the chariot commanders saw
Jehoshaphat, they thought, "Surely this
is the king of Israel." So they turned to
attack him, but when Jehoshaphat cried
out, 33the chariot commanders saw that
he was not the king of Israel and stopped pursuing him.
34But someone drew his bow at random and hit the king of Israel between
the sections of his armour. The king told
his chariot driver, "Wheel round and
get me out of the fighting. I've been
wounded." 35All day long the battle
raged, and the king was propped up in
his chariot facing the Arameans. The
blood from his wound ran onto the floor
of the chariot, and that evening he died.
36As the sun was setting, a cry spread
through the army: "Every man to his
town; everyone to his land!"
37So the king died and was brought to
Samaria, and they buried him there.
38They washed the chariot at a pool in
Samaria (where the prostitutes bathed),
and the dogs licked up his blood, as the
word of the LORD had declared.
39As for the other events of Ahab's
reign, including all he did, the palace he
built and inlaid with ivory, and the cities
he fortified, are they not written in the
book of the annals of the kings of Israel?
40Ahab rested with his fathers. And
Ahaziah his son succeeded him as king.

Jehoshaphat King of Judah

41Jehoshaphat son of Asa became
king of Judah in the fourth year of Ahab
king of Israel. 42Jehoshaphat was thirty-
five years old when he became king, and
he reigned in Jerusalem for twenty-five
years. His mother's name was Azubah
daughter of Shilhi. 43In everything he
walked in the ways of his father Asa and
did not stray from them; he did what
was right in the eyes of the LORD. The
high places, however, were not removed, and the people continued to
offer sacrifices and burn incense there.
44Jehoshaphat was also at peace with
the king of Israel.
45As for the other events of Jehoshaphat's reign, the things he achieved and
his military exploits, are they not written in the book of the annals of the kings

of Judah? 46He rid the land of the rest of the male shrine-prostitutes who remained there even after the reign of his father Asa. 47There was then no king in Edom; a deputy ruled.

48Now Jehoshaphat built a fleet of trading ships to go to Ophir for gold, but they never set sail—they were wrecked at Ezion Geber. 49At that time Ahaziah son of Ahab said to Jehoshaphat, "Let my men sail with your men," but Jehoshaphat refused.

50Then Jehoshaphat rested with his fathers and was buried with them in the city of David his father. And Jehoram his son succeeded him.

Ahaziah King of Israel

51Ahaziah son of Ahab became king of Israel in Samaria in the seventeenth year of Jehoshaphat king of Judah, and he reigned over Israel for two years. 52He did evil in the eyes of the LORD, because he walked in the ways of his father and mother and in the ways of Jeroboam son of Nebat, who caused Israel to sin. 53He served and worshipped Baal and provoked the LORD, the God of Israel, to anger, just as his father had done.

NEW TESTAMENT READING
Acts 19:14–41

14Seven sons of Sceva, a Jewish chief priest, were doing this. 15⌞One day⌟ the evil spirit answered them, "Jesus I know, and I know about Paul, but who are you?" 16Then the man who had the evil spirit jumped on them and overpowered them all. He gave them such a beating that they ran out of the house naked and bleeding.

17When this became known to the Jews and Greeks living in Ephesus, they were all seized with fear, and the name of the Lord Jesus was held in high honour. 18Many of those who believed now came and openly confessed their evil deeds. 19A number who had practised sorcery brought their scrolls together and burned them publicly. When they calculated the value of the scrolls, the total came to fifty thousand drachmas. 20In this way the word of the Lord spread widely and grew in power.

21After all this had happened, Paul decided to go to Jerusalem, passing through Macedonia and Achaia. "After I have been there," he said, "I must visit Rome also." 22He sent two of his helpers, Timothy and Erastus, to Macedonia, while he stayed in the province of Asia a little longer.

The Riot in Ephesus

23About that time there arose a great disturbance about the Way. 24A silversmith named Demetrius, who made silver shrines of Artemis, brought in no little business for the craftsmen. 25He called them together, along with the workmen in related trades, and said: "Men, you know we receive a good income from this business. 26And you see and hear how this fellow Paul has convinced and led astray large numbers of people here in Ephesus and in practically the whole province of Asia. He says that man-made gods are no gods at all. 27There is danger not only that our trade will lose its good name, but also that the temple of the great goddess Artemis will be discredited, and the goddess herself, who is worshipped throughout the province of Asia and the world, will be robbed of her divine majesty."

28When they heard this, they were furious and began shouting: "Great is Artemis of the Ephesians!" 29Soon the whole city was in an uproar. The people seized Gaius and Aristarchus, Paul's travelling companions from Macedonia, and rushed as one man into the theatre. 30Paul wanted to appear before the crowd, but the disciples would not let him. 31Even some of the officials of the province, friends of Paul, sent him a message begging him not to venture into the theatre.

32The assembly was in confusion:
Some were shouting one thing, some
another. Most of the people did not
even know why they were there. 33The
Jews pushed Alexander to the front,
and some of the crowd shouted instructions to him. He motioned for silence in
order to make a defence before the
people. 34But when they realised he was
a Jew, they all shouted in unison for
about two hours: "Great is Artemis of
the Ephesians!"
35The city clerk quietened the crowd
and said: "Men of Ephesus, doesn't all
the world know that the city of Ephesus
is the guardian of the temple of the great
Artemis and of her image, which fell
from heaven? 36Therefore, since these
facts are undeniable, you ought to be
quiet and not do anything rash. 37You
have brought these men here, though
they have neither robbed temples nor
blasphemed our goddess. 38If, then,
Demetrius and his fellow craftsmen
have a grievance against anybody, the
courts are open and there are procon-
suls. They can press charges. 39If there
is anything further you want to bring up,
it must be settled in a legal assembly.
40As it is, we are in danger of being
charged with rioting because of today's
events. In that case we would not be
able to account for this commotion,
since there is no reason for it." 41After
he had said this, he dismissed the
assembly.

READING FROM PROVERBS
Proverbs 15:31–16:7

31He who listens to a life-giving rebuke
will be at home among the wise.

32He who ignores discipline despises
himself,
but whoever heeds correction gains
understanding.

33The fear of the LORD teaches a man
wisdom,
and humility comes before honour.

16 To man belong the plans of the
heart,
but from the LORD comes the reply
of the tongue.

2All a man's ways seem innocent to
him,
but motives are weighed by the
LORD.

3Commit to the LORD whatever you
do,
and your plans will succeed.

4The LORD works out everything for
his own ends—
even the wicked for a day of
disaster.

5The LORD detests all the proud of
heart.
Be sure of this: They will not go
unpunished.

6Through love and faithfulness sin is
atoned for;
through the fear of the LORD a man
avoids evil.

7When a man's ways are pleasing to
the LORD,
he makes even his enemies live at
peace with him.

JUNE 30

OLD TESTAMENT READING
2 Kings 1:1–2:25

The LORD's Judgment on Ahaziah

1 After Ahab's death, Moab rebelled against Israel. 2Now Ahaziah had fallen through the lattice of his upper room in Samaria and injured himself. So he sent messengers, saying to them, "Go and consult Baal-Zebub, the god of Ekron, to see if I will recover from this injury."

3But the angel of the LORD said to Elijah the Tishbite, "Go up and meet the messengers of the king of Samaria and ask them, 'Is it because there is no God in Israel that you are going off to consult Baal-Zebub, the god of Ekron?' 4Therefore this is what the LORD says: 'You will not leave the bed you are lying on. You will certainly die!' " So Elijah went.

5When the messengers returned to the king, he asked them, "Why have you come back?"

6"A man came to meet us," they replied. "And he said to us, 'Go back to the king who sent you and tell him, "This is what the LORD says: Is it because there is no God in Israel that you are sending men to consult Baal-Zebub, the god of Ekron? Therefore you will not leave the bed you are lying on. You will certainly die!" ' "

7The king asked them, "What kind of man was it who came to meet you and told you this?"

8They replied, "He was a man with a garment of hair and with a leather belt round his waist."

The king said, "That was Elijah the Tishbite."

9Then he sent to Elijah a captain with his company of fifty men. The captain went up to Elijah, who was sitting on the top of a hill, and said to him, "Man of God, the king says, 'Come down!' "

10Elijah answered the captain, "If I am a man of God, may fire come down from heaven and consume you and your fifty men!" Then the fire fell from heaven and consumed the captain and his men.

11At this the king sent to Elijah another captain with his fifty men. The captain said to him, "Man of God, this is what the king says, 'Come down at once!' "

12"If I am a man of God," Elijah replied, "may fire come down from heaven and consume you and your fifty men!" Then the fire of God fell from heaven and consumed him and his fifty men.

13So the king sent a third captain with his fifty men. This third captain went up and fell on his knees before Elijah. "Man of God," he begged, "please have respect for my life and the lives of these fifty men, your servants! 14See, fire has fallen from heaven and consumed the first two captains and all their men. But now have respect for my life!"

15The angel of the LORD said to Elijah, "Go down with him; do not be afraid of him." So Elijah got up and went down with him to the king.

16He told the king, "This is what the LORD says: Is it because there is no God in Israel for you to consult that you have sent messengers to consult Baal-Zebub, the god of Ekron? Because you have done this, you will never leave the bed you are lying on. You will certainly die!" 17So he died, according to the word of the LORD that Elijah had spoken.

Because Ahaziah had no son, Joram succeeded him as king in the second year of Jehoram son of Jehoshaphat king of Judah. 18As for all the other events of Ahaziah's reign, and what he did, are they not written in the book of the annals of the kings of Israel?

Elijah Taken Up to Heaven

2 When the LORD was about to take
Elijah up to heaven in a whirlwind,
Elijah and Elisha were on their way
from Gilgal. 2Elijah said to Elisha,
"Stay here; the LORD has sent me to
Bethel."
But Elisha said, "As surely as the
LORD lives and as you live, I will not
leave you." So they went down to
Bethel.
3The company of the prophets at
Bethel came out to Elisha and asked,
"Do you know that the LORD is going to
take your master from you today?"
"Yes, I know," Elisha replied, "but
do not speak of it."
4Then Elijah said to him, "Stay here,
Elisha; the LORD has sent me to
Jericho."
And he replied, "As surely as the
LORD lives and as you live, I will not
leave you." So they went to Jericho.
5The company of the prophets at
Jericho went up to Elisha and asked
him, "Do you know that the LORD is
going to take your master from you
today?"
"Yes, I know," he replied, "but do
not speak of it."
6Then Elijah said to him, "Stay here;
the LORD has sent me to the Jordan."
And he replied, "As surely as the
LORD lives and as you live, I will not
leave you." So the two of them walked
on.
7Fifty men of the company of the
prophets went and stood at a distance,
facing the place where Elijah and Elisha
had stopped at the Jordan. 8Elijah took
his cloak, rolled it up and struck the
water with it. The water divided to the
right and to the left, and the two of them
crossed over on dry ground.
9When they had crossed, Elijah said
to Elisha, "Tell me, what can I do for
you before I am taken from you?"
"Let me inherit a double portion of
your spirit," Elisha replied.
10"You have asked a difficult thing,"
Elijah said, "yet if you see me when I
am taken from you, it will be yours
—otherwise not."
11As they were walking along and
talking together, suddenly a chariot of
fire and horses of fire appeared and
separated the two of them, and Elijah
went up to heaven in a whirlwind.
12Elisha saw this and cried out, "My
father! My father! The chariots and
horsemen of Israel!" And Elisha saw
him no more. Then he took hold of his
own clothes and tore them apart.
13He picked up the cloak that had
fallen from Elijah and went back and
stood on the bank of the Jordan. 14Then
he took the cloak that had fallen from
him and struck the water with it.
"Where now is the LORD, the God of
Elijah?" he asked. When he struck the
water, it divided to the right and to the
left, and he crossed over.
15The company of the prophets from
Jericho, who were watching, said, "The
spirit of Elijah is resting on Elisha."
And they went to meet him and bowed
to the ground before him. 16"Look,"
they said, "we your servants have fifty
able men. Let them go and look for your
master. Perhaps the Spirit of the LORD
has picked him up and set him down on
some mountain or in some valley."
"No," Elisha replied, "do not send
them."
17But they persisted until he was too
ashamed to refuse. So he said, "Send
them." And they sent fifty men, who
searched for three days but did not find
him. 18When they returned to Elisha,
who was staying in Jericho, he said to
them, "Didn't I tell you not to go?"

Healing of the Water

19The men of the city said to Elisha,
"Look, our lord, this town is well situated, as you can see, but the water is bad
and the land is unproductive."
20"Bring me a new bowl," he said,
"and put salt in it." So they brought it to
him.
21Then he went out to the spring and

threw the salt into it, saying, "This is
what the LORD says: 'I have healed this
water. Never again will it cause death or
make the land unproductive.'" 22And
the water has remained wholesome to
this day, according to the word Elisha
had spoken.

Elisha Is Jeered

23From there Elisha went up to
Bethel. As he was walking along the
road, some youths came out of the town
and jeered at him. "Go on up, you
baldhead!" they said. "Go on up, you
baldhead!" 24He turned round, looked
at them and called down a curse on
them in the name of the LORD. Then
two bears came out of the woods and
mauled forty-two of the youths. 25And
he went on to Mount Carmel and from
there returned to Samaria.

NEW TESTAMENT READING
Acts 20:1–38

Through Macedonia and Greece

20 When the uproar had ended,
Paul sent for the disciples and,
after encouraging them, said good-bye
and set out for Macedonia. 2He
travelled through that area, speaking
many words of encouragement to the
people, and finally arrived in Greece,
3where he stayed three months. Because the Jews made a plot against him
just as he was about to sail for Syria, he
decided to go back through Macedonia.
4He was accompanied by Sopater son of
Pyrrhus from Berea, Aristarchus and
Secundus from Thessalonica, Gaius
from Derbe, Timothy also, and Tychicus and Trophimus from the province of
Asia. 5These men went on ahead and
waited for us at Troas. 6But we sailed
from Philippi after the Feast of Unleavened Bread, and five days later
joined the others at Troas, where we
stayed seven days.

Eutychus Raised From the Dead at Troas

7On the first day of the week we came
together to break bread. Paul spoke to
the people and, because he intended to
leave the next day, kept on talking until
midnight. 8There were many lamps in
the upstairs room where we were meeting. 9Seated in a window was a young
man named Eutychus, who was sinking
into a deep sleep as Paul talked on and
on. When he was sound asleep, he fell
to the ground from the third storey and
was picked up dead. 10Paul went down,
threw himself on the young man and put
his arms around him. "Don't be
alarmed," he said. "He's alive!" 11Then
he went upstairs again and broke bread
and ate. After talking until daylight, he
left. 12The people took the young man
home alive and were greatly comforted.

Paul's Farewell to the Ephesian Elders

13We went on ahead to the ship and
sailed for Assos, where we were going
to take Paul aboard. He had made this
arrangement because he was going
there on foot. 14When he met us at
Assos, we took him aboard and went on
to Mitylene. 15The next day we set sail
from there and arrived off Kios. The
day after that we crossed over to Samos,
and on the following day arrived at
Miletus. 16Paul had decided to sail past
Ephesus to avoid spending time in the
province of Asia, for he was in a hurry
to reach Jerusalem, if possible, by the
day of Pentecost.

17From Miletus, Paul sent to Ephesus
for the elders of the church. 18When
they arrived, he said to them: "You
know how I lived the whole time I was
with you, from the first day I came into
the province of Asia. 19I served the
Lord with great humility and with tears,
although I was severely tested by the
plots of the Jews. 20You know that I
have not hesitated to preach anything
that would be helpful to you but have

taught you publicly and from house to
house. 21I have declared to both Jews
and Greeks that they must turn to God
in repentance and have faith in our Lord
Jesus.
22"And now, compelled by the Spirit,
I am going to Jerusalem, not knowing
what will happen to me there. 23I only
know that in every city the Holy Spirit
warns me that prison and hardships are
facing me. 24However, I consider my
life worth nothing to me, if only I may
finish the race and complete the task the
Lord Jesus has given me—the task of
testifying to the gospel of God's grace.
25"Now I know that none of you
among whom I have gone about
preaching the kingdom will ever see me
again. 26Therefore, I declare to you today that I am innocent of the blood of all
men. 27For I have not hesitated to proclaim to you the whole will of God.
28Keep watch over yourselves and all
the flock of which the Holy Spirit has
made you overseers. Be shepherds of
the church of God, which he bought
with his own blood. 29I know that after I
leave, savage wolves will come in
among you and will not spare the flock.
30Even from your own number men will
arise and distort the truth in order to
draw away disciples after them. 31So be
on your guard! Remember that for
three years I never stopped warning
each of you night and day with tears.
32"Now I commit you to God and to
the word of his grace, which can build
you up and give you an inheritance
among all those who are sanctified. 33I
have not coveted anyone's silver or gold
or clothing. 34You yourselves know that
these hands of mine have supplied my
own needs and the needs of my companions. 35In everything I did, I showed you
that by this kind of hard work we must
help the weak, remembering the words
the Lord Jesus himself said: 'It is more
blessed to give than to receive.'"
36When he had said this, he knelt
down with all of them and prayed.
37They all wept as they embraced him
and kissed him. 38What grieved them
most was his statement that they would
never see his face again. Then they
accompanied him to the ship.

READING FROM PSALMS

Psalm 78:40–55

40How often they rebelled against him
in the desert
and grieved him in the wasteland!
41Again and again they put God to the
test;
they vexed the Holy One of Israel.
42They did not remember his power—
the day he redeemed them from
the oppressor,
43the day he displayed his miraculous
signs in Egypt,
his wonders in the region of Zoan.
44He turned their rivers to blood;
they could not drink from their
streams.
45He sent swarms of flies that devoured
them,
and frogs that devastated them.
46He gave their crops to the
grasshopper,
their produce to the locust.
47He destroyed their vines with hail
and their sycamore-figs with sleet.
48He gave over their cattle to the hail,
their livestock to bolts of lightning.
49He unleashed against them his hot
anger,
his wrath, indignation and
hostility—
a band of destroying angels.
50He prepared a path for his anger;
he did not spare them from death
but gave them over to the plague.
51He struck down all the firstborn of
Egypt,
the firstfruits of manhood in the
tents of Ham.
52But he brought his people out like a
flock;
he led them like sheep through the
desert.
53He guided them safely, so they were
unafraid;

but the sea engulfed their enemies.
54Thus he brought them to the border
of his holy land,
to the hill country his right hand
had taken.
55He drove out nations before them
and allotted their lands to them as
an inheritance;
he settled the tribes of Israel in
their homes.

DAY 182

JULY 1

OLD TESTAMENT READING
2 Kings 3:1–4:37

Moab Revolts

3 Joram son of Ahab became king of
Israel in Samaria in the eighteenth
year of Jehoshaphat king of Judah, and
he reigned for twelve years. 2He did evil
in the eyes of the LORD, but not as his
father and mother had done. He got rid
of the sacred stone of Baal that his
father had made. 3Nevertheless he
clung to the sins of Jeroboam son of
Nebat, which he had caused Israel to
commit; he did not turn away from
them.
4Now Mesha king of Moab raised
sheep, and he had to supply the king of
Israel with a hundred thousand lambs
and with the wool of a hundred
thousand rams. 5But after Ahab died,
the king of Moab rebelled against the
king of Israel. 6So at that time King
Joram set out from Samaria and mobilised all Israel. 7He also sent this message to Jehoshaphat king of Judah:
"The king of Moab has rebelled against
me. Will you go with me to fight against
Moab?"
"I will go with you," he replied. "I am
as you are, my people as your people,
my horses as your horses."
8"By what route shall we attack?" he
asked.
"Through the Desert of Edom," he
answered.
9So the king of Israel set out with the
king of Judah and the king of Edom.
After a roundabout march of seven
days, the army had no more water for
themselves or for the animals with
them.
10"What!" exclaimed the king of
Israel. "Has the LORD called us three
kings together only to hand us over to
Moab?"
11But Jehoshaphat asked, "Is there
no prophet of the LORD here, that we
may enquire of the LORD through
him?"
An officer of the king of Israel
answered, "Elisha son of Shaphat is
here. He used to pour water on the
hands of Elijah."
12Jehoshaphat said, "The word of the
LORD is with him." So the king of Israel
and Jehoshaphat and the king of Edom
went down to him.
13Elisha said to the king of Israel,
"What do we have to do with each
other? Go to the prophets of your father
and the prophets of your mother."
"No," the king of Israel answered,
"because it was the LORD who called us
three kings together to hand us over to
Moab."
14Elisha said, "As surely as the LORD
Almighty lives, whom I serve, if I did
not have respect for the presence of
Jehoshaphat king of Judah, I would not
look at you or even notice you. 15But
now bring me a harpist."
While the harpist was playing, the
hand of the LORD came upon Elisha
16and he said, "This is what the LORD
says: Make this valley full of ditches.
17For this is what the LORD says: You
will see neither wind nor rain, yet this
valley will be filled with water, and you,

your cattle and your other animals will
drink. 18This is an easy thing in the eyes
of the LORD; he will also hand Moab
over to you. 19You will overthrow every
fortified city and every major town.
You will cut down every good tree, stop
up all the springs, and ruin every good
field with stones."

20The next morning, about the time
for offering the sacrifice, there it was
—water flowing from the direction of
Edom! And the land was filled with
water.

21Now all the Moabites had heard
that the kings had come to fight against
them; so every man, young and old,
who could bear arms was called up and
stationed on the border. 22When they
got up early in the morning, the sun was
shining on the water. To the Moabites
across the way, the water looked red
—like blood. 23"That's blood!" they
said. "Those kings must have fought
and slaughtered each other. Now to the
plunder, Moab!"

24But when the Moabites came to the
camp of Israel, the Israelites rose up
and fought them until they fled. And the
Israelites invaded the land and slaughtered the Moabites. 25They destroyed
the towns, and each man threw a stone
on every good field until it was covered.
They stopped up all the springs and cut
down every good tree. Only Kir
Hareseth was left with its stones in
place, but men armed with slings surrounded it and attacked it as well.

26When the king of Moab saw that the
battle had gone against him, he took
with him seven hundred swordsmen to
break through to the king of Edom, but
they failed. 27Then he took his firstborn
son, who was to succeed him as king,
and offered him as a sacrifice on the city
wall. The fury against Israel was great;
they withdrew and returned to their
own land.

The Widow's Oil

4 The wife of a man from the company of the prophets cried out to
Elisha, "Your servant my husband is
dead, and you know that he revered the
LORD. But now his creditor is coming to
take my two boys as his slaves."

2Elisha replied to her, "How can I
help you? Tell me, what do you have in
your house?"

"Your servant has nothing there at
all," she said, "except a little oil."

3Elisha said, "Go round and ask all
your neighbours for empty jars. Don't
ask for just a few. 4Then go inside and
shut the door behind you and your sons.
Pour oil into all the jars, and as each is
filled, put it to one side."

5She left him and afterwards shut the
door behind her and her sons. They
brought the jars to her and she kept
pouring. 6When all the jars were full,
she said to her son, "Bring me another
one."

But he replied, "There is not a jar
left." Then the oil stopped flowing.

7She went and told the man of God,
and he said, "Go, sell the oil and pay
your debts. You and your sons can live
on what is left."

The Shunammite's Son Restored to Life

8One day Elisha went to Shunem.
And a well-to-do woman was there,
who urged him to stay for a meal. So
whenever he came by, he stopped there
to eat. 9She said to her husband, "I
know that this man who often comes
our way is a holy man of God. 10Let's
make a small room on the roof and put
in it a bed and a table, a chair and a lamp
for him. Then he can stay there whenever he comes to us."

11One day when Elisha came, he went
up to his room and lay down there. 12He
said to his servant Gehazi, "Call the
Shunammite." So he called her, and she
stood before him. 13Elisha said to him,
"Tell her, 'You have gone to all this
trouble for us. Now what can be done
for you? Can we speak on your behalf to
the king or the commander of the
army?' "

She replied, "I have a home among
my own people."

14“What can be done for her?” Elisha asked.

Gehazi said, “Well, she has no son and her husband is old.”

15Then Elisha said, “Call her.” So he called her, and she stood in the doorway. 16“About this time next year,” Elisha said, “you will hold a son in your arms.”

“No, my lord,” she objected. “Don’t mislead your servant, O man of God!”

17But the woman became pregnant, and the next year about that same time she gave birth to a son, just as Elisha had told her.

18The child grew, and one day he went out to his father, who was with the reapers. 19“My head! My head!” he said to his father.

His father told a servant, “Carry him to his mother.” 20After the servant had lifted him up and carried him to his mother, the boy sat on her lap until noon, and then he died. 21She went up and laid him on the bed of the man of God, then shut the door and went out.

22She called her husband and said, “Please send me one of the servants and a donkey so I can go to the man of God quickly and return.”

23“Why go to him today?” he asked. “It’s not the New Moon or the Sabbath.”

“It’s all right,” she said.

24She saddled the donkey and said to her servant, “Lead on; don’t slow down for me unless I tell you.” 25So she set out and came to the man of God at Mount Carmel.

When he saw her in the distance, the man of God said to his servant Gehazi, “Look! There’s the Shunammite! 26Run to meet her and ask her, ‘Are you all right? Is your husband all right? Is your child all right?’ ”

“Everything is all right,” she said.

27When she reached the man of God at the mountain, she took hold of his feet. Gehazi came over to push her away, but the man of God said, “Leave her alone! She is in bitter distress, but the LORD has hidden it from me and has not told me why.”

28“Did I ask you for a son, my lord?” she said. “Didn’t I tell you, ‘Don’t raise my hopes’?”

29Elisha said to Gehazi, “Tuck your cloak into your belt, take my staff in your hand and run. If you meet anyone, do not greet him, and if anyone greets you, do not answer. Lay my staff on the boy’s face.”

30But the child’s mother said, “As surely as the LORD lives and as you live, I will not leave you.” So he got up and followed her.

31Gehazi went on ahead and laid the staff on the boy’s face, but there was no sound or response. So Gehazi went back to meet Elisha and told him, “The boy has not awakened.”

32When Elisha reached the house, there was the boy lying dead on his couch. 33He went in, shut the door on the two of them and prayed to the LORD. 34Then he got on the bed and lay upon the boy, mouth to mouth, eyes to eyes, hands to hands. As he stretched himself out upon him, the boy’s body grew warm. 35Elisha turned away and walked back and forth in the room and then got onto the bed and stretched out upon him once more. The boy sneezed seven times and opened his eyes.

36Elisha summoned Gehazi and said, “Call the Shunammite.” And he did. When she came, he said, “Take your son.” 37She came in, fell at his feet and bowed to the ground. Then she took her son and went out.

NEW TESTAMENT READING

Acts 21:1–26

On to Jerusalem

21 After we had torn ourselves away from them, we put out to sea and sailed straight to Cos. The next day we went to Rhodes and from there to Patara. 2We found a ship crossing over to Phoenicia, went on board and set sail. 3After sighting Cyprus and

passing to the south of it, we sailed on to
Syria. We landed at Tyre, where our
ship was to unload its cargo. 4Finding
the disciples there, we stayed with them
seven days. Through the Spirit they
urged Paul not to go on to Jerusalem.
5But when our time was up, we left and
continued on our way. All the disciples
and their wives and children accompanied us out of the city, and there on the
beach we knelt to pray. 6After saying
good-bye to each other, we went aboard
the ship, and they returned home.

7We continued our voyage from Tyre
and landed at Ptolemais, where we
greeted the brothers and stayed with
them for a day. 8Leaving the next day,
we reached Caesarea and stayed at the
house of Philip the evangelist, one of
the Seven. 9He had four unmarried
daughters who prophesied.

10After we had been there a number
of days, a prophet named Agabus came
down from Judea. 11Coming over to us,
he took Paul's belt, tied his own hands
and feet with it and said, "The Holy
Spirit says, 'In this way the Jews
of Jerusalem will bind the owner of
this belt and will hand him over to the
Gentiles.'"

12When we heard this, we and the
people there pleaded with Paul not to
go up to Jerusalem. 13Then Paul
answered, "Why are you weeping and
breaking my heart? I am ready not only
to be bound, but also to die in Jerusalem
for the name of the Lord Jesus."
14When he would not be dissuaded, we
gave up and said, "The Lord's will be
done."

15After this, we got ready and went
up to Jerusalem. 16Some of the disciples
from Caesarea accompanied us and
brought us to the home of Mnason,
where we were to stay. He was a man
from Cyprus and one of the early
disciples.

Paul's Arrival at Jerusalem

17When we arrived at Jerusalem, the
brothers received us warmly. 18The next
day Paul and the rest of us went to see
James, and all the elders were present.
19Paul greeted them and reported in
detail what God had done among the
Gentiles through his ministry.

20When they heard this, they praised
God. Then they said to Paul: "You see,
brother, how many thousands of Jews
have believed, and all of them are
zealous for the law. 21They have been
informed that you teach all the Jews
who live among the Gentiles to turn
away from Moses, telling them not to
circumcise their children or live according to our customs. 22What shall we do?
They will certainly hear that you have
come, 23so do what we tell you. There
are four men with us who have made a
vow. 24Take these men, join in their
purification rites and pay their expenses, so that they can have their
heads shaved. Then everybody will
know there is no truth in these reports
about you, but that you yourself are
living in obedience to the law. 25As for
the Gentile believers, we have written
to them our decision that they should
abstain from food sacrificed to idols,
from blood, from the meat of strangled
animals and from sexual immorality."

26The next day Paul took the men and
purified himself along with them. Then
he went to the temple to give notice of
the date when the days of purification
would end and the offering would be
made for each of them.

READING FROM PSALMS

Psalm 78:56–72

56But they put God to the test
and rebelled against the Most
High;
they did not keep his statutes.
57Like their fathers they were disloyal
and faithless,
as unreliable as a faulty bow.
58They angered him with their high
places;

they aroused his jealousy with their
idols.
59When God heard them, he was very
angry;
he rejected Israel completely.
60He abandoned the tabernacle of
Shiloh,
the tent he had set up among men.
61He sent ⌞the ark of⌟ his might into
captivity,
his splendour into the hands of the
enemy.
62He gave his people over to the sword;
he was very angry with his
inheritance.
63Fire consumed their young men,
and their maidens had no wedding
songs;
64their priests were put to the sword,
and their widows could not weep.

65Then the Lord awoke as from
sleep,
as a man wakes from the stupor of
wine.
66He beat back his enemies;
he put them to everlasting shame.
67Then he rejected the tents of Joseph,
he did not choose the tribe of
Ephraim;
68but he chose the tribe of Judah,
Mount Zion, which he loved.
69He built his sanctuary like the
heights,
like the earth that he established
for ever.
70He chose David his servant
and took him from the sheep pens;
71from tending the sheep he brought
him
to be the shepherd of his people
Jacob,
of Israel his inheritance.
72And David shepherded them with
integrity of heart;
with skilful hands he led them.

DAY 183

JULY 2

OLD TESTAMENT READING
2 Kings 4:38–6:23

Death in the Pot

38Elisha returned to Gilgal and there
was a famine in that region. While the
company of the prophets was meeting
with him, he said to his servant, "Put on
the large pot and cook some stew for
these men."
39One of them went out into the fields
to gather herbs and found a wild vine.
He gathered some of its gourds and
filled the fold of his cloak. When he
returned, he cut them up into the pot of
stew, though no-one knew what they
were. 40The stew was poured out for the
men, but as they began to eat it, they
cried out, "O man of God, there is
death in the pot!" And they could not
eat it.
41Elisha said, "Get some flour." He
put it into the pot and said, "Serve it to
the people to eat." And there was nothing harmful in the pot.

Feeding of a Hundred

42A man came from Baal Shalishah,
bringing the man of God twenty loaves
of barley bread baked from the first ripe
corn, along with some ears of new corn.
"Give it to the people to eat," Elisha
said.
43"How can I set this before a hundred men?" his servant asked.
But Elisha answered, "Give it to the
people to eat. For this is what the LORD
says: 'They will eat and have some left
over.'" 44Then he set it before them,
and they ate and had some left over,
according to the word of the LORD.

Naaman Healed of Leprosy

5 Now Naaman was commander of
the army of the king of Aram. He
was a great man in the sight of his
master and highly regarded, because
through him the LORD had given victory
to Aram. He was a valiant soldier, but
he had leprosy.
2Now bands from Aram had gone out
and had taken captive a young girl from
Israel, and she served Naaman's wife.
3She said to her mistress, "If only my
master would see the prophet who is
in Samaria! He would cure him of his
leprosy."
4Naaman went to his master and told
him what the girl from Israel had said.
5"By all means, go," the king of Aram
replied. "I will send a letter to the king
of Israel." So Naaman left, taking with
him ten talents of silver, six thousand
shekels of gold and ten sets of clothing.
6The letter that he took to the king of
Israel read: "With this letter I am sending my servant Naaman to you so that
you may cure him of his leprosy."
7As soon as the king of Israel read the
letter, he tore his robes and said, "Am I
God? Can I kill and bring back to life?
Why does this fellow send someone to
me to be cured of his leprosy? See how
he is trying to pick a quarrel with me!"
8When Elisha the man of God heard
that the king of Israel had torn his
robes, he sent him this message: "Why
have you torn your robes? Make the
man come to me and he will know that
there is a prophet in Israel." 9So Naaman went with his horses and chariots
and stopped at the door of Elisha's
house. 10Elisha sent a messenger to say
to him, "Go, wash yourself seven times
in the Jordan, and your flesh will be
restored and you will be cleansed."
11But Naaman went away angry and
said, "I thought that he would surely
come out to me and stand and call on
the name of the LORD his God, wave his
hand over the spot and cure me of my
leprosy. 12Are not Abana and Pharpar,
the rivers of Damascus, better than any
of the waters of Israel? Couldn't I wash
in them and be cleansed?" So he turned
and went off in a rage.
13Naaman's servants went to him and
said, "My father, if the prophet had told
you to do some great thing, would you
not have done it? How much more,
then, when he tells you, 'Wash and be
cleansed'?" 14So he went down and
dipped himself in the Jordan seven
times, as the man of God had told him,
and his flesh was restored and became
clean like that of a young boy.
15Then Naaman and all his attendants
went back to the man of God. He stood
before him and said, "Now I know that
there is no God in all the world except in
Israel. Please accept now a gift from
your servant."
16The prophet answered, "As surely
as the LORD lives, whom I serve, I will
not accept a thing." And even though
Naaman urged him, he refused.
17"If you will not," said Naaman,
"please let me, your servant, be given as
much earth as a pair of mules can carry,
for your servant will never again make
burnt offerings and sacrifices to any
other god but the LORD. 18But may the
LORD forgive your servant for this one
thing: When my master enters the temple of Rimmon to bow down and he is
leaning on my arm and I bow there
also—when I bow down in the temple
of Rimmon, may the LORD forgive your
servant for this."
19"Go in peace," Elisha said.
After Naaman had travelled some
distance, 20Gehazi, the servant of
Elisha the man of God, said to himself,
"My master was too easy on Naaman,
this Aramean, by not accepting from
him what he brought. As surely as the
LORD lives, I will run after him and get
something from him."
21So Gehazi hurried after Naaman.
When Naaman saw him running
towards him, he got down from the
chariot to meet him. "Is everything
all right?" he asked.
22"Everything is all right," Gehazi
answered. "My master sent me to say,

‘Two young men from the company of the prophets have just come to me from the hill country of Ephraim. Please give them a talent of silver and two sets of clothing.’ ”

23“By all means, take two talents,” said Naaman. He urged Gehazi to accept them, and then tied up the two talents of silver in two bags, with two sets of clothing. He gave them to two of his servants, and they carried them ahead of Gehazi. 24When Gehazi came to the hill, he took the things from the servants and put them away in the house. He sent the men away and they left. 25Then he went in and stood before his master Elisha.

“Where have you been, Gehazi?” Elisha asked.

“Your servant didn’t go anywhere,” Gehazi answered.

26But Elisha said to him, “Was not my spirit with you when the man got down from his chariot to meet you? Is this the time to take money, or to accept clothes, olive groves, vineyards, flocks, herds, or menservants and maidservants? 27Naaman’s leprosy will cling to you and to your descendants for ever.” Then Gehazi went from Elisha’s presence and he was leprous, as white as snow.

An Axe-Head Floats

6 The company of the prophets said to Elisha, “Look, the place where we meet with you is too small for us. 2Let us go to the Jordan, where each of us can get a pole; and let us build a place there for us to live.”

And he said, “Go.”

3Then one of them said, “Won’t you please come with your servants?”

“I will,” Elisha replied. 4And he went with them.

They went to the Jordan and began to cut down trees. 5As one of them was cutting down a tree, the iron axe-head fell into the water. “Oh, my lord,” he cried out, “it was borrowed!”

6The man of God asked, “Where did it fall?” When he showed him the place, Elisha cut a stick and threw it there, and made the iron float. 7“Lift it out,” he said. Then the man reached out his hand and took it.

Elisha Traps Blinded Arameans

8Now the king of Aram was at war with Israel. After conferring with his officers, he said, “I will set up my camp in such and such a place.”

9The man of God sent word to the king of Israel: “Beware of passing that place, because the Arameans are going down there.” 10So the king of Israel checked on the place indicated by the man of God. Time and again Elisha warned the king, so that he was on his guard in such places.

11This enraged the king of Aram. He summoned his officers and demanded of them, “Will you not tell me which of us is on the side of the king of Israel?”

12“None of us, my lord the king,” said one of his officers, “but Elisha, the prophet who is in Israel, tells the king of Israel the very words you speak in your bedroom.”

13“Go, find out where he is,” the king ordered, “so that I can send men and capture him.” The report came back: “He is in Dothan.” 14Then he sent horses and chariots and a strong force there. They went by night and surrounded the city.

15When the servant of the man of God got up and went out early the next morning, an army with horses and chariots had surrounded the city. “Oh, my lord, what shall we do?” the servant asked.

16“Don’t be afraid,” the prophet answered. “Those who are with us are more than those who are with them.”

17And Elisha prayed, “O LORD, open his eyes so that he may see.” Then the LORD opened the servant’s eyes, and he looked and saw the hills full of horses and chariots of fire all round Elisha.

18As the enemy came down towards him, Elisha prayed to the LORD, “Strike these people with blindness." So he struck them with blindness, as Elisha had asked.

19Elisha told them, "This is not the road and this is not the city. Follow me, and I will lead you to the man you are looking for." And he led them to Samaria.

20After they entered the city, Elisha said, "LORD, open the eyes of these men so that they can see." Then the LORD opened their eyes and they looked, and there they were, inside Samaria.

21When the king of Israel saw them, he asked Elisha, "Shall I kill them, my father? Shall I kill them?"

22"Do not kill them," he answered. "Would you kill men you have captured with your own sword or bow? Set food and water before them so that they may eat and drink and then go back to their master." 23So he prepared a great feast for them, and after they had finished eating and drinking, he sent them away, and they returned to their master. So the bands from Aram stopped raiding Israel's territory.

NEW TESTAMENT READING

Acts 21:27–22:21

Paul Arrested

27When the seven days were nearly over, some Jews from the province of Asia saw Paul at the temple. They stirred up the whole crowd and seized him, 28shouting, "Men of Israel, help us! This is the man who teaches all men everywhere against our people and our law and this place. And besides, he has brought Greeks into the temple area and defiled this holy place." 29(They had previously seen Trophimus the Ephesian in the city with Paul and assumed that Paul had brought him into the temple area.)

30The whole city was aroused, and the people came running from all directions. Seizing Paul, they dragged him from the temple, and immediately the gates were shut. 31While they were trying to kill him, news reached the commander of the Roman troops that the whole city of Jerusalem was in an uproar. 32He at once took some officers and soldiers and ran down to the crowd. When the rioters saw the commander and his soldiers, they stopped beating Paul.

33The commander came up and arrested him and ordered him to be bound with two chains. Then he asked who he was and what he had done. 34Some in the crowd shouted one thing and some another, and since the commander could not get at the truth because of the uproar, he ordered that Paul be taken into the barracks. 35When Paul reached the steps, the violence of the mob was so great he had to be carried by the soldiers. 36The crowd that followed kept shouting, "Away with him!"

Paul Speaks to the Crowd

37As the soldiers were about to take Paul into the barracks, he asked the commander, "May I say something to you?"

"Do you speak Greek?" he replied. 38"Aren't you the Egyptian who started a revolt and led four thousand terrorists out into the desert some time ago?"

39Paul answered, "I am a Jew, from Tarsus in Cilicia, a citizen of no ordinary city. Please let me speak to the people."

40Having received the commander's permission, Paul stood on the steps and motioned to the crowd. When they were all silent, he said to them

22

in Aramaic: 1"Brothers and fathers, listen now to my defence."

2When they heard him speak to them in Aramaic, they became very quiet.

Then Paul said: 3"I am a Jew, born in Tarsus of Cilicia, but brought up in this city. Under Gamaliel I was thoroughly trained in the law of our fathers and was

just as zealous for God as any of you are
today. 4I persecuted the followers of
this Way to their death, arresting both
men and women and throwing them
into prison, 5as also the high priest and
all the Council can testify. I even
obtained letters from them to their
brothers in Damascus, and went there
to bring these people as prisoners to
Jerusalem to be punished.

6"About noon as I came near Damascus, suddenly a bright light from heaven
flashed around me. 7I fell to the ground
and heard a voice say to me, 'Saul! Saul!
Why do you persecute me?'

8" 'Who are you, Lord?' I asked.

" 'I am Jesus of Nazareth, whom you
are persecuting,' he replied. 9My companions saw the light, but they did not
understand the voice of him who was
speaking to me.

10" 'What shall I do, Lord?' I asked.

" 'Get up,' the Lord said, 'and go into
Damascus. There you will be told all
that you have been assigned to do.'
11My companions led me by the hand
into Damascus, because the brilliance
of the light had blinded me.

12"A man named Ananias came to
see me. He was a devout observer of the
law and highly respected by all the Jews
living there. 13He stood beside me and
said, 'Brother Saul, receive your sight!'
And at that very moment I was able to
see him.

14"Then he said: 'The God of our
fathers has chosen you to know his will
and to see the Righteous One and to
hear words from his mouth. 15You will
be his witness to all men of what you
have seen and heard. 16And now what
are you waiting for? Get up, be baptised
and wash your sins away, calling on his
name.'

17"When I returned to Jerusalem and
was praying at the temple, I fell into a
trance 18and saw the Lord speaking.
'Quick!' he said to me. 'Leave Jerusalem immediately, because they will
not accept your testimony about me.'

19" 'Lord,' I replied, 'these men know
that I went from one synagogue to
another to imprison and beat those who
believe in you. 20And when the blood of
your martyr Stephen was shed, I stood
there giving my approval and guarding
the clothes of those who were killing
him.'

21"Then the Lord said to me, 'Go;
I will send you far away to the
Gentiles.' "

READING FROM PSALMS
Psalm 79:1–13

A psalm of Asaph.

1O God, the nations have invaded
  your inheritance;
 they have defiled your holy temple,
 they have reduced Jerusalem to
  rubble.
2They have given the dead bodies of
  your servants
 as food to the birds of the air,
 the flesh of your saints to the beasts
  of the earth.
3They have poured out blood like
  water
 all around Jerusalem,
 and there is no-one to bury the
  dead.
4We are objects of reproach to our
  neighbours,
 of scorn and derision to those
  around us.

5How long, O LORD? Will you be
  angry for ever?
 How long will your jealousy burn
  like fire?
6Pour out your wrath on the nations
 that do not acknowledge you,
on the kingdoms
 that do not call on your name;
7for they have devoured Jacob
 and destroyed his homeland.
8Do not hold against us the sins of the
  fathers;
 may your mercy come quickly to
  meet us,
 for we are in desperate need.

[9]Help us, O God our Saviour,
for the glory of your name;
deliver us and forgive our sins
for your name's sake.
[10]Why should the nations say,
"Where is their God?"
Before our eyes, make known among
the nations
that you avenge the outpoured
blood of your servants.
[11]May the groans of the prisoners come
before you;
by the strength of your arm
preserve those condemned to die.

[12]Pay back into the laps of our
neighbours seven times
the reproach they have hurled at
you, O Lord.
[13]Then we your people, the sheep of
your pasture,
will praise you for ever;
from generation to generation
we will recount your praise.

JULY 3

DAY 184

OLD TESTAMENT READING
2 Kings 6:24–8:15

Famine in Besieged Samaria

[24]Some time later, Ben-Hadad king of Aram mobilised his entire army and marched up and laid siege to Samaria.
[25]There was a great famine in the city; the siege lasted so long that a donkey's head sold for eighty shekels of silver, and a fourth of a cab of seed pods for five shekels.
[26]As the king of Israel was passing by on the wall, a woman cried to him, "Help me, my lord the king!"
[27]The king replied, "If the LORD does not help you, where can I get help for you? From the threshing-floor? From
the winepress?" [28]Then he asked her, "What's the matter?"
She answered, "This woman said to me, 'Give up your son so that we may eat him today, and tomorrow we'll eat
my son.' [29]So we cooked my son and ate him. The next day I said to her, 'Give up your son so that we may eat him,' but she had hidden him."
[30]When the king heard the woman's words, he tore his robes. As he went along the wall, the people looked, and there, underneath, he had sackcloth on
his body. [31]He said, "May God deal with me, be it ever so severely, if the head of Elisha son of Shaphat remains on his shoulders today!"
[32]Now Elisha was sitting in his house, and the elders were sitting with him. The king sent a messenger ahead, but before he arrived, Elisha said to the elders, "Don't you see how this murderer is sending someone to cut off my head? Look, when the messenger comes, shut the door and hold it shut against him. Is not the sound of his master's footsteps behind him?"
[33]While he was still talking to them, the messenger came down to him. And ⌞the king⌟ said, "This disaster is from the LORD. Why should I wait for the LORD any longer?"
7 Elisha said, "Hear the word of the LORD. This is what the LORD says: About this time tomorrow, a seah of flour will sell for a shekel and two seahs of barley for a shekel at the gate of Samaria."
[2]The officer on whose arm the king was leaning said to the man of God, "Look, even if the LORD should open the floodgates of the heavens, could this happen?"
"You will see it with your own eyes," answered Elisha, "but you will not eat any of it!"

The Siege Lifted

3Now there were four men with leprosy at the entrance of the city gate.
They said to each other, "Why stay here
until we die? 4If we say, 'We'll go into
the city'—the famine is there, and we
will die. And if we stay here, we will die.
So let's go over to the camp of the
Arameans and surrender. If they spare
us, we live; if they kill us, then we die."
5At dusk they got up and went to the
camp of the Arameans. When they
reached the edge of the camp, not a man
was there, 6for the Lord had caused the
Arameans to hear the sound of chariots
and horses and a great army, so that
they said to one another, "Look, the
king of Israel has hired the Hittite and
Egyptian kings to attack us!" 7So they
got up and fled in the dusk and abandoned their tents and their horses and
donkeys. They left the camp as it was
and ran for their lives.
8The men who had leprosy reached
the edge of the camp and entered one of
the tents. They ate and drank, and carried away silver, gold and clothes, and
went off and hid them. They returned
and entered another tent and took some
things from it and hid them also.
9Then they said to each other,
"We're not doing right. This is a day of
good news and we are keeping it to
ourselves. If we wait until daylight,
punishment will overtake us. Let's go at
once and report this to the royal
palace."
10So they went and called out to the
city gatekeepers and told them, "We
went into the Aramean camp and not a
man was there—not a sound of anyone
—only tethered horses and donkeys,
and the tents left just as they were."
11The gatekeepers shouted the news,
and it was reported within the palace.
12The king got up in the night and said
to his officers, "I will tell you what the
Arameans have done to us. They know
we are starving; so they have left the
camp to hide in the countryside, thinking, 'They will surely come out, and
then we will take them alive and get into
the city.'"
13One of his officers answered,
"Make some men take five of the horses
that are left in the city. Their plight will
be like that of all the Israelites left here
—yes, they will only be like all these
Israelites who are doomed. So let us
send them to find out what happened."
14So they selected two chariots with
their horses, and the king sent them
after the Aramean army. He commanded the drivers, "Go and find out what
has happened." 15They followed them
as far as the Jordan, and they found the
whole road strewn with the clothing and
equipment the Arameans had thrown
away in their headlong flight. So the
messengers returned and reported to
the king. 16Then the people went out
and plundered the camp of the Arameans. So a seah of flour sold for a
shekel, and two seahs of barley sold for
a shekel, as the LORD had said.
17Now the king had put the officer on
whose arm he leaned in charge of the
gate, and the people trampled him in
the gateway, and he died, just as the
man of God had foretold when the king
came down to his house. 18It happened
as the man of God had said to the king:
"About this time tomorrow, a seah of
flour will sell for a shekel and two seahs
of barley for a shekel at the gate of
Samaria."
19The officer had said to the man of
God, "Look, even if the LORD should
open the floodgates of the heavens,
could this happen?" The man of God
had replied, "You will see it with your
own eyes, but you will not eat any of it!"
20And that is exactly what happened to
him, for the people trampled him in the
gateway, and he died.

The Shunammite's Land Restored

8 Now Elisha had said to the woman
whose son he had restored to life,
"Go away with your family and stay for
a while wherever you can, because the
LORD has decreed a famine in the land

that will last seven years." 2The woman
proceeded to do as the man of God said.
She and her family went away and
stayed in the land of the Philistines for
seven years.
3At the end of the seven years she
came back from the land of the Philistines and went to the king to beg for her
house and land. 4The king was talking
to Gehazi, the servant of the man of
God, and had said, "Tell me about all
the great things Elisha has done." 5Just
as Gehazi was telling the king how
Elisha had restored the dead to life, the
woman whose son Elisha had brought
back to life came to beg the king for her
house and land.

Gehazi said, "This is the woman, my
lord the king, and this is her son whom
Elisha restored to life." 6The king asked
the woman about it, and she told him.

Then he assigned an official to her case and said to him, "Give back everything that belonged to her, including all the income from her land from the day she left the country until now."

Hazael Murders Ben-Hadad

7Elisha went to Damascus, and Ben-
Hadad king of Aram was ill. When the
king was told, "The man of God has
come all the way up here," 8he said to
Hazael, "Take a gift with you and go to
meet the man of God. Consult the LORD
through him; ask him, 'Will I recover
from this illness?'"
9Hazael went to meet Elisha, taking
with him as a gift forty camel-loads of all the finest wares of Damascus. He went in and stood before him, and said, "Your son Ben-Hadad king of Aram has sent me to ask, 'Will I recover from this illness?'"
10Elisha answered, "Go and say to
him, 'You will certainly recover'; but
the LORD has revealed to me that he will
in fact die." 11He stared at him with a
fixed gaze until Hazael felt ashamed.
Then the man of God began to weep.
12"Why is my lord weeping?" asked
Hazael.

"Because I know the harm you will do to the Israelites," he answered. "You will set fire to their fortified places, kill their young men with the sword, dash their little children to the ground, and rip open their pregnant women."
13Hazael said, "How could your servant, a mere dog, accomplish such a feat?"

"The LORD has shown me that you will become king of Aram," answered Elisha.
14Then Hazael left Elisha and re-
turned to his master. When Ben-Hadad
asked, "What did Elisha say to you?"
Hazael replied, "He told me that you
would certainly recover." 15But the
next day he took a thick cloth, soaked it
in water and spread it over the king's
face, so that he died. Then Hazael succeeded him as king.

NEW TESTAMENT READING
Acts 22:22–23:11

Paul the Roman Citizen

22The crowd listened to Paul until he said this. Then they raised their voices and shouted, "Rid the earth of him! He's not fit to live!"
23As they were shouting and throwing
off their cloaks and flinging dust into the
air, 24the commander ordered Paul to
be taken into the barracks. He directed
that he be flogged and questioned in
order to find out why the people were
shouting at him like this. 25As they
stretched him out to flog him, Paul said
to the centurion standing there, "Is it
legal for you to flog a Roman citizen
who hasn't even been found guilty?"
26When the centurion heard this, he
went to the commander and reported it.
"What are you going to do?" he asked.
"This man is a Roman citizen."
27The commander went to Paul and
asked, "Tell me, are you a Roman
citizen?"

"Yes, I am," he answered.

28Then the commander said, "I had
to pay a big price for my citizenship."
"But I was born a citizen," Paul
replied.
29Those who were about to question
him withdrew immediately. The commander himself was alarmed when he
realised that he had put Paul, a Roman
citizen, in chains.

Before the Sanhedrin

30The next day, since the commander
wanted to find out exactly why Paul was
being accused by the Jews, he released
him and ordered the chief priests and all
the Sanhedrin to assemble. Then he
brought Paul and had him stand before
them.
23 Paul looked straight at the Sanhedrin and said, "My brothers, I
have fulfilled my duty to God in all good
conscience to this day." 2At this the
high priest Ananias ordered those
standing near Paul to strike him on the
mouth. 3Then Paul said to him, "God
will strike you, you whitewashed wall!
You sit there to judge me according to
the law, yet you yourself violate the law
by commanding that I be struck!"
4Those who were standing near Paul
said, "You dare to insult God's high
priest?"
5Paul replied, "Brothers, I did not
realise that he was the high priest; for it
is written: 'Do not speak evil about the
ruler of your people.'"
6Then Paul, knowing that some of
them were Sadducees and the others
Pharisees, called out in the Sanhedrin,
"My brothers, I am a Pharisee, the son
of a Pharisee. I stand on trial because of
my hope in the resurrection of the
dead." 7When he said this, a dispute
broke out between the Pharisees and
the Sadducees, and the assembly was
divided. 8(The Sadducees say that there
is no resurrection, and that there are
neither angels nor spirits, but the
Pharisees acknowledge them all.)
9There was a great uproar, and some
of the teachers of the law who were
Pharisees stood up and argued vigorously. "We find nothing wrong with this
man," they said. "What if a spirit or an
angel has spoken to him?" 10The dispute became so violent that the commander was afraid Paul would be torn
to pieces by them. He ordered the
troops to go down and take him away
from them by force and bring him into
the barracks.
11The following night the Lord stood
near Paul and said, "Take courage! As
you have testified about me in Jerusalem, so you must also testify in
Rome."

READING FROM PROVERBS

Proverbs 16:8–17

8Better a little with righteousness
than much gain with injustice.

9In his heart a man plans his course,
but the LORD determines his steps.

10The lips of a king speak as an oracle,
and his mouth should not betray
justice.

11Honest scales and balances are from
the LORD;
all the weights in the bag are of his
making.

12Kings detest wrongdoing,
for a throne is established through
righteousness.

13Kings take pleasure in honest lips;
they value a man who speaks the
truth.

14A king's wrath is a messenger of
death,
but a wise man will appease it.

15When a king's face brightens, it
means life;
his favour is like a rain cloud in
spring.

[16]How much better to get wisdom than
gold,
to choose understanding rather
than silver!

[17]The highway of the upright avoids
evil;
he who guards his way guards his
life.

JULY 4

DAY 185

OLD TESTAMENT READING
2 Kings 8:16–9:37

Jehoram King of Judah

[16]In the fifth year of Joram son of
Ahab king of Israel, when Jehoshaphat
was king of Judah, Jehoram son of
Jehoshaphat began his reign as king of
Judah. [17]He was thirty-two years old
when he became king, and he reigned in
Jerusalem for eight years. [18]He walked
in the ways of the kings of Israel, as the
house of Ahab had done, for he married
a daughter of Ahab. He did evil in the
eyes of the LORD. [19]Nevertheless, for
the sake of his servant David, the LORD
was not willing to destroy Judah. He
had promised to maintain a lamp for
David and his descendants for ever.

[20]In the time of Jehoram, Edom rebelled against Judah and set up its own
king. [21]So Jehoram went to Zair with all
his chariots. The Edomites surrounded
him and his chariot commanders, but he
rose up and broke through by night; his
army, however, fled back home. [22]To
this day Edom has been in rebellion
against Judah. Libnah revolted at the
same time.

[23]As for the other events of Jehoram's reign, and all he did, are they
not written in the book of the annals of
the kings of Judah? [24]Jehoram rested
with his fathers and was buried with
them in the City of David. And Ahaziah
his son succeeded him as king.

Ahaziah King of Judah

[25]In the twelfth year of Joram son of
Ahab king of Israel, Ahaziah son of
Jehoram king of Judah began to reign.
[26]Ahaziah was twenty-two years old
when he became king, and he reigned in
Jerusalem for one year. His mother's
name was Athaliah, a granddaughter of
Omri king of Israel. [27]He walked in the
ways of the house of Ahab and did evil
in the eyes of the LORD, as the house of
Ahab had done, for he was related by
marriage to Ahab's family.

[28]Ahaziah went with Joram son of
Ahab to war against Hazael king of
Aram at Ramoth Gilead. The Arameans wounded Joram; [29]so King
Joram returned to Jezreel to recover
from the wounds the Arameans had
inflicted on him at Ramoth in his battle
with Hazael king of Aram.

Then Ahaziah son of Jehoram king of
Judah went down to Jezreel to see
Joram son of Ahab, because he had
been wounded.

Jehu Anointed King of Israel

9 The prophet Elisha summoned a
man from the company of the
prophets and said to him, "Tuck your
cloak into your belt, take this flask of oil
with you and go to Ramoth Gilead.
[2]When you get there, look for Jehu son
of Jehoshaphat, the son of Nimshi. Go
to him, get him away from his companions and take him into an inner room.
[3]Then take the flask and pour the oil on
his head and declare, 'This is what the
LORD says: I anoint you king over
Israel.' Then open the door and run;
don't delay!"

[4]So the young man, the prophet,

went to Ramoth Gilead. 5When he arrived, he found the army officers sitting together. "I have a message for you, commander," he said.

"For which of us?" asked Jehu.

"For you, commander," he replied.

6Jehu got up and went into the house. Then the prophet poured the oil on Jehu's head and declared, "This is what the LORD, the God of Israel, says: 'I anoint you king over the LORD's people Israel. 7You are to destroy the house of Ahab your master, and I will avenge the blood of my servants the prophets and the blood of all the LORD's servants shed by Jezebel. 8The whole house of Ahab will perish. I will cut off from Ahab every last male in Israel—slave or free. 9I will make the house of Ahab like the house of Jeroboam son of Nebat and like the house of Baasha son of Ahijah. 10As for Jezebel, dogs will devour her on the plot of ground at Jezreel, and no-one will bury her.' " Then he opened the door and ran.

11When Jehu went out to his fellow officers, one of them asked him, "Is everything all right? Why did this madman come to you?"

"You know the man and the sort of things he says," Jehu replied.

12"That's not true!" they said. "Tell us."

Jehu said, "Here is what he told me: 'This is what the LORD says: I anoint you king over Israel.' "

13They hurried and took their cloaks and spread them under him on the bare steps. Then they blew the trumpet and shouted, "Jehu is king!"

Jehu Kills Joram and Ahaziah

14So Jehu son of Jehoshaphat, the son of Nimshi, conspired against Joram. (Now Joram and all Israel had been defending Ramoth Gilead against Hazael king of Aram, 15but King Joram had returned to Jezreel to recover from the wounds the Arameans had inflicted on him in the battle with Hazael king of Aram.) Jehu said, "If this is the way you feel, don't let anyone slip out of the city to go and tell the news in Jezreel." 16Then he got into his chariot and rode to Jezreel, because Joram was resting there and Ahaziah king of Judah had gone down to see him.

17When the lookout standing on the tower in Jezreel saw Jehu's troops approaching, he called out, "I see some troops coming."

"Get a horseman," Joram ordered. "Send him to meet them and ask, 'Do you come in peace?' "

18The horseman rode off to meet Jehu and said, "This is what the king says: 'Do you come in peace?' "

"What do you have to do with peace?" Jehu replied. "Fall in behind me."

The lookout reported, "The messenger has reached them, but he isn't coming back."

19So the king sent out a second horseman. When he came to them he said, "This is what the king says: 'Do you come in peace?' "

Jehu replied, "What do you have to do with peace? Fall in behind me."

20The lookout reported, "He has reached them, but he isn't coming back either. The driving is like that of Jehu son of Nimshi—he drives like a madman."

21"Hitch up my chariot," Joram ordered. And when it was hitched up, Joram king of Israel and Ahaziah king of Judah rode out, each in his own chariot, to meet Jehu. They met him at the plot of ground that had belonged to Naboth the Jezreelite. 22When Joram saw Jehu he asked, "Have you come in peace, Jehu?"

"How can there be peace," Jehu replied, "as long as all the idolatry and witchcraft of your mother Jezebel abound?"

23Joram turned about and fled, calling out to Ahaziah, "Treachery, Ahaziah!"

24Then Jehu drew his bow and shot Joram between the shoulders. The arrow pierced his heart and he slumped

down in his chariot. 25Jehu said to Bid-
kar, his chariot officer, "Pick him up
and throw him on the field that belonged to Naboth the Jezreelite. Remember how you and I were riding
together in chariots behind Ahab his
father when the LORD made this
prophecy about him: 26'Yesterday I saw
the blood of Naboth and the blood of his
sons, declares the LORD, and I will
surely make you pay for it on this
plot of ground, declares the LORD.'
Now then, pick him up and throw him
on that plot, in accordance with the
word of the LORD."
27When Ahaziah king of Judah saw
what had happened, he fled up the road
to Beth Haggan. Jehu chased him,
shouting, "Kill him too!" They
wounded him in his chariot on the way
up to Gur near Ibleam, but he escaped
to Megiddo and died there. 28His servants took him by chariot to Jerusalem
and buried him with his fathers in his
tomb in the City of David. 29(In the
eleventh year of Joram son of Ahab,
Ahaziah had become king of Judah.)

Jezebel Killed

30Then Jehu went to Jezreel. When
Jezebel heard about it, she painted her
eyes, arranged her hair and looked out
of a window. 31As Jehu entered the
gate, she asked, "Have you come in
peace, Zimri, you murderer of your
master?"
32He looked up at the window and
called out, "Who is on my side? Who?"
Two or three eunuchs looked down at
him. 33"Throw her down!" Jehu said.
So they threw her down, and some of
her blood spattered the wall and the
horses as they trampled her underfoot.
34Jehu went in and ate and drank.
"Take care of that cursed woman," he
said, "and bury her, for she was a king's
daughter." 35But when they went out to
bury her, they found nothing except her
skull, her feet and her hands. 36They
went back and told Jehu, who said,
"This is the word of the LORD that he
spoke through his servant Elijah the
Tishbite: On the plot of ground at Jezreel dogs will devour Jezebel's flesh.
37Jezebel's body will be like refuse on
the ground in the plot at Jezreel, so that
no-one will be able to say, 'This is
Jezebel.'"

NEW TESTAMENT READING
Acts 23:12–35

The Plot to Kill Paul

12The next morning the Jews formed
a conspiracy and bound themselves with
an oath not to eat or drink until they had
killed Paul. 13More than forty men were
involved in this plot. 14They went to the
chief priests and elders and said, "We
have taken a solemn oath not to eat
anything until we have killed Paul.
15Now then, you and the Sanhedrin
petition the commander to bring him
before you on the pretext of wanting
more accurate information about his
case. We are ready to kill him before he
gets here."
16But when the son of Paul's sister
heard of this plot, he went into the
barracks and told Paul.
17Then Paul called one of the centurions and said, "Take this young man
to the commander; he has something
to tell him." 18So he took him to the
commander.
The centurion said, "Paul, the prisoner, sent for me and asked me to bring
this young man to you because he has
something to tell you."
19The commander took the young
man by the hand, drew him aside and
asked, "What is it you want to tell me?"
20He said: "The Jews have agreed to
ask you to bring Paul before the
Sanhedrin tomorrow on the pretext of
wanting more accurate information
about him. 21Don't give in to them,
because more than forty of them are
waiting in ambush for him. They have
taken an oath not to eat or drink until
they have killed him. They are ready

now, waiting for your consent to their
request."
[22]The commander dismissed the
young man and cautioned him, "Don't
tell anyone that you have reported this
to me."

Paul Transferred to Caesarea

[23]Then he called two of his centurions
and ordered them, "Get ready a detachment of two hundred soldiers, seventy
horsemen and two hundred spearmen
to go to Caesarea at nine tonight.
[24]Provide mounts for Paul so that he
may be taken safely to Governor
Felix."
[25]He wrote a letter as follows:

[26]Claudius Lysias,

To His Excellency, Governor Felix:

Greetings.

[27]This man was seized by the
Jews and they were about to kill
him, but I came with my troops and
rescued him, for I had learned that
he is a Roman citizen. [28]I wanted to
know why they were accusing him,
so I brought him to their Sanhedrin. [29]I found that the accusation
had to do with questions about
their law, but there was no charge
against him that deserved death or
imprisonment. [30]When I was informed of a plot to be carried out
against the man, I sent him to you
at once. I also ordered his accusers
to present to you their case against
him.

[31]So the soldiers, carrying out their
orders, took Paul with them during the
night and brought him as far as Antipat-
ris. [32]The next day they let the cavalry
go on with him, while they returned to
the barracks. [33]When the cavalry arrived in Caesarea, they delivered the
letter to the governor and handed Paul
over to him. [34]The governor read the
letter and asked what province he was
from. Learning that he was from Cilicia,
[35]he said, "I will hear your case when
your accusers get here." Then he
ordered that Paul be kept under guard
in Herod's palace.

READING FROM PSALMS
Psalm 80:1–7

For the director of music. To ⌊the tune of⌋ "The Lilies of the Covenant". Of Asaph. A psalm.

[1]Hear us, O Shepherd of Israel,
you who lead Joseph like a flock;
you who sit enthroned between the cherubim, shine forth
[2] before Ephraim, Benjamin and Manasseh.
Awaken your might;
come and save us.

[3]Restore us, O God;
make your face shine upon us,
that we may be saved.

[4]O LORD God Almighty,
how long will your anger smoulder
against the prayers of your people?
[5]You have fed them with the bread of tears;
you have made them drink tears by the bowlful.
[6]You have made us a source of contention to our neighbours,
and our enemies mock us.

[7]Restore us, O God Almighty;
make your face shine upon us,
that we may be saved.

OLD TESTAMENT READING
2 Kings 10:1–11:21

Ahab's Family Killed

10 Now there were in Samaria seventy sons of the house of Ahab. So Jehu wrote letters and sent them to Samaria: to the officials of Jezreel, to the elders and to the guardians of Ahab's children. He said, [2]"As soon as this letter reaches you, since your master's sons are with you and you have chariots and horses, a fortified city and weapons, [3]choose the best and most worthy of your master's sons and set him on his father's throne. Then fight for your master's house."

[4]But they were terrified and said, "If two kings could not resist him, how can we?"

[5]So the palace administrator, the city governor, the elders and the guardians sent this message to Jehu: "We are your servants and we will do anything you say. We will not appoint anyone as king; you do whatever you think best."

[6]Then Jehu wrote them a second letter, saying, "If you are on my side and will obey me, take the heads of your master's sons and come to me in Jezreel by this time tomorrow."

Now the royal princes, seventy of them, were with the leading men of the city, who were bringing them up. [7]When the letter arrived, these men took the princes and slaughtered all seventy of them. They put their heads in baskets and sent them to Jehu in Jezreel. [8]When the messenger arrived, he told Jehu, "They have brought the heads of the princes."

Then Jehu ordered, "Put them in two piles at the entrance of the city gate until morning."

[9]The next morning Jehu went out. He stood before all the people and said, "You are innocent. It was I who conspired against my master and killed him, but who killed all these? [10]Know then, that not a word the LORD has spoken against the house of Ahab will fail. The LORD has done what he promised through his servant Elijah." [11]So Jehu killed everyone in Jezreel who remained of the house of Ahab, as well as all his chief men, his close friends and his priests, leaving him no survivor.

[12]Jehu then set out and went towards Samaria. At Beth Eked of the Shepherds, [13]he met some relatives of Ahaziah king of Judah and asked, "Who are you?"

They said, "We are relatives of Ahaziah, and we have come down to greet the families of the king and of the queen mother."

[14]"Take them alive!" he ordered. So they took them alive and slaughtered them by the well of Beth Eked—forty-two men. He left no survivor.

[15]After he left there, he came upon Jehonadab son of Recab, who was on his way to meet him. Jehu greeted him and said, "Are you in accord with me, as I am with you?"

"I am," Jehonadab answered.

"If so," said Jehu, "give me your hand." So he did, and Jehu helped him up into the chariot. [16]Jehu said, "Come with me and see my zeal for the LORD." Then he had him ride along in his chariot.

[17]When Jehu came to Samaria, he killed all who were left there of Ahab's family; he destroyed them, according to the word of the LORD spoken to Elijah.

Ministers of Baal Killed

[18]Then Jehu brought all the people together and said to them, "Ahab served Baal a little; Jehu will serve him much. [19]Now summon all the prophets of Baal, all his ministers and all his

priests. See that no-one is missing, because I am going to hold a great sacrifice
for Baal. Anyone who fails to come will
no longer live." But Jehu was acting
deceptively in order to destroy the
ministers of Baal.
20 Jehu said, "Call an assembly in honour of Baal." So they proclaimed it.
21 Then he sent word throughout Israel,
and all the ministers of Baal came; not
one stayed away. They crowded into the
temple of Baal until it was full from one
end to the other. 22 And Jehu said to the
keeper of the wardrobe, "Bring robes
for all the ministers of Baal." So he
brought out robes for them.
23 Then Jehu and Jehonadab son of
Recab went into the temple of Baal.
Jehu said to the ministers of Baal,
"Look around and see that no servants
of the LORD are here with you—only
ministers of Baal." 24 So they went in to
make sacrifices and burnt offerings.
Now Jehu had posted eighty men outside with this warning: "If one of you
lets any of the men I am placing in your
hands escape, it will be your life for his
life."
25 As soon as Jehu had finished making the burnt offering, he ordered the
guards and officers: "Go in and kill
them; let no-one escape." So they cut
them down with the sword. The guards
and officers threw the bodies out and
then entered the inner shrine of the
temple of Baal. 26 They brought the
sacred stone out of the temple of Baal
and burned it. 27 They demolished the
sacred stone of Baal and tore down the
temple of Baal, and people have used it
for a latrine to this day.
28 So Jehu destroyed Baal worship in
Israel. 29 However, he did not turn away
from the sins of Jeroboam son of Nebat,
which he had caused Israel to commit
—the worship of the golden calves at
Bethel and Dan.
30 The LORD said to Jehu, "Because
you have done well in accomplishing
what is right in my eyes and have done
to the house of Ahab all I had in mind to
do, your descendants will sit on the
throne of Israel to the fourth generation." 31 Yet Jehu was not careful to
keep the law of the LORD, the God of
Israel, with all his heart. He did not turn
away from the sins of Jeroboam, which
he had caused Israel to commit.
32 In those days the LORD began to
reduce the size of Israel. Hazael overpowered the Israelites throughout their
territory 33 east of the Jordan in all the
land of Gilead (the region of Gad,
Reuben and Manasseh), from Aroer by
the Arnon Gorge through Gilead to
Bashan.
34 As for the other events of Jehu's
reign, all he did, and all his achievements, are they not written in the book
of the annals of the kings of Israel?
35 Jehu rested with his fathers and was
buried in Samaria. And Jehoahaz his
son succeeded him as king. 36 The time
that Jehu reigned over Israel in Samaria
was twenty-eight years.

Athaliah and Joash

11 When Athaliah the mother of
Ahaziah saw that her son was
dead, she proceeded to destroy the
whole royal family. 2 But Jehosheba, the
daughter of King Jehoram and sister of
Ahaziah, took Joash son of Ahaziah
and stole him away from among the
royal princes, who were about to be
murdered. She put him and his nurse in
a bedroom to hide him from Athaliah;
so he was not killed. 3 He remained hidden with his nurse at the temple of the
LORD for six years while Athaliah ruled
the land.
4 In the seventh year Jehoiada sent for
the commanders of units of a hundred,
the Carites and the guards and had them
brought to him at the temple of the
LORD. He made a covenant with them
and put them under oath at the temple
of the LORD. Then he showed them the
king's son. 5 He commanded them,
saying, "This is what you are to do: You
who are in the three companies that are
going on duty on the Sabbath—a third

of you guarding the royal palace, 6a third at the Sur Gate, and a third at the gate behind the guard, who take turns guarding the temple—7and you who are in the other two companies that normally go off Sabbath duty are all to guard the temple for the king. 8Station yourselves round the king, each man with his weapon in his hand. Anyone who approaches your ranks must be put to death. Stay close to the king wherever he goes."

9The commanders of units of a hundred did just as Jehoiada the priest ordered. Each one took his men—those who were going on duty on the Sabbath and those who were going off duty—and came to Jehoiada the priest. 10Then he gave the commanders the spears and shields that had belonged to King David and that were in the temple of the LORD. 11The guards, each with his weapon in his hand, stationed themselves round the king—near the altar and the temple, from the south side to the north side of the temple.

12Jehoiada brought out the king's son and put the crown on him; he presented him with a copy of the covenant and proclaimed him king. They anointed him, and the people clapped their hands and shouted, "Long live the king!"

13When Athaliah heard the noise made by the guards and the people, she went to the people at the temple of the LORD. 14She looked and there was the king, standing by the pillar, as the custom was. The officers and the trumpeters were beside the king, and all the people of the land were rejoicing and blowing trumpets. Then Athaliah tore her robes and called out, "Treason! Treason!"

15Jehoiada the priest ordered the commanders of units of a hundred, who were in charge of the troops: "Bring her out between the ranks and put to the sword anyone who follows her." For the priest had said, "She must not be put to death in the temple of the LORD." 16So they seized her as she reached the place where the horses enter the palace grounds, and there she was put to death.

17Jehoiada then made a covenant between the LORD and the king and people that they would be the LORD's people. He also made a covenant between the king and the people. 18All the people of the land went to the temple of Baal and tore it down. They smashed the altars and idols to pieces and killed Mattan the priest of Baal in front of the altars.

Then Jehoiada the priest posted guards at the temple of the LORD. 19He took with him the commanders of hundreds, the Carites, the guards and all the people of the land, and together they brought the king down from the temple of the LORD and went into the palace, entering by way of the gate of the guards. The king then took his place on the royal throne, 20and all the people of the land rejoiced. And the city was quiet, because Athaliah had been slain with the sword at the palace.

21Joash was seven years old when he began his reign.

NEW TESTAMENT READING
Acts 24:1–27

The Trial Before Felix

24 Five days later the high priest Ananias went down to Caesarea with some of the elders and a lawyer named Tertullus, and they brought their charges against Paul before the governor. 2When Paul was called in, Tertullus presented his case before Felix: "We have enjoyed a long period of peace under you, and your foresight has brought about reforms in this nation. 3Everywhere and in every way, most excellent Felix, we acknowledge this with profound gratitude. 4But in order not to weary you further, I would request that you be kind enough to hear us briefly.

5"We have found this man to be a troublemaker, stirring up riots among

the Jews all over the world. He is a
ringleader of the Nazarene sect 6and
even tried to desecrate the temple; so
we seized him. 8By examining him yourself you will be able to learn the truth
about all these charges we are bringing
against him."
9The Jews joined in the accusation,
asserting that these things were true.
10When the governor motioned for
him to speak, Paul replied: "I know that
for a number of years you have been a
judge over this nation; so I gladly make
my defence. 11You can easily verify that
no more than twelve days ago I went up
to Jerusalem to worship. 12My accusers
did not find me arguing with anyone at
the temple, or stirring up a crowd in the
synagogues or anywhere else in the city.
13And they cannot prove to you the
charges they are now making against
me. 14However, I admit that I worship
the God of our fathers as a follower of
the Way, which they call a sect. I believe
everything that agrees with the Law
and that is written in the Prophets,
15and I have the same hope in God
as these men, that there will be a resurrection of both the righteous and the
wicked. 16So I strive always to keep
my conscience clear before God and
man.
17"After an absence of several years,
I came to Jerusalem to bring my people
gifts for the poor and to present offerings. 18I was ceremonially clean when
they found me in the temple courts
doing this. There was no crowd with
me, nor was I involved in any disturbance. 19But there are some Jews from
the province of Asia, who ought to be
here before you and bring charges if
they have anything against me. 20Or
these who are here should state what
crime they found in me when I stood
before the Sanhedrin—21unless it was
this one thing I shouted as I stood in
their presence: 'It is concerning the
resurrection of the dead that I am on
trial before you today.'"
22Then Felix, who was well acquainted with the Way, adjourned the
proceedings. "When Lysias the commander comes," he said, "I will decide
your case." 23He ordered the centurion
to keep Paul under guard but to give
him some freedom and permit his
friends to take care of his needs.
24Several days later Felix came with
his wife Drusilla, who was a Jewess. He
sent for Paul and listened to him as he
spoke about faith in Christ Jesus. 25As
Paul discoursed on righteousness, self-
control and the judgment to come, Felix
was afraid and said, "That's enough for
now! You may leave. When I find it
convenient, I will send for you." 26At
the same time he was hoping that Paul
would offer him a bribe, so he sent for
him frequently and talked with him.
27When two years had passed, Felix
was succeeded by Porcius Festus, but
because Felix wanted to grant a favour
to the Jews, he left Paul in prison.

READING FROM PSALMS
Psalm 80:8–19

8You brought a vine out of Egypt;
you drove out the nations and
planted it.
9You cleared the ground for it,
and it took root and filled the land.
10The mountains were covered with its
shade,
the mighty cedars with its
branches.
11It sent out its boughs to the Sea,
its shoots as far as the River.

12Why have you broken down its walls
so that all who pass by pick its
grapes?
13Boars from the forest ravage it
and the creatures of the field feed
on it.
14Return to us, O God Almighty!
Look down from heaven and see!
Watch over this vine,
15 the root your right hand has
planted,
the son you have raised up for
yourself.

16Your vine is cut down, it is burned
with fire;
at your rebuke your people perish.
17Let your hand rest on the man at your
right hand,
the son of man you have raised up
for yourself.
18Then we will not turn away from you;
revive us, and we will call on your
name.

19Restore us, O LORD God Almighty;
make your face shine upon us,
that we may be saved.

JULY 6

DAY 187

OLD TESTAMENT READING
2 Kings 12:1–14:22

Joash Repairs the Temple

12 In the seventh year of Jehu, Joash became king, and he reigned in Jerusalem for forty years. His mother's name was Zibiah; she was from Beersheba.
2Joash did what was right in the eyes of the LORD all the years Jehoiada the priest instructed him.
3The high places, however, were not removed; the people continued to offer sacrifices and burn incense there.
4Joash said to the priests, "Collect all the money that is brought as sacred offerings to the temple of the LORD—the money collected in the census, the money received from personal vows and the money brought voluntarily to the temple.
5Let every priest receive the money from one of the treasurers, and let it be used to repair whatever damage is found in the temple."
6But by the twenty-third year of King Joash the priests still had not repaired the temple.
7Therefore King Joash summoned Jehoiada the priest and the other priests and asked them, "Why aren't you repairing the damage done to the temple? Take no more money from your treasurers, but hand it over for repairing the temple."
8The priests agreed that they would not collect any more money from the people and that they would not repair the temple themselves.
9Jehoiada the priest took a chest and bored a hole in its lid. He placed it beside the altar, on the right side as one enters the temple of the LORD. The priests who guarded the entrance put into the chest all the money that was brought to the temple of the LORD.
10Whenever they saw that there was a large amount of money in the chest, the royal secretary and the high priest came, counted the money that had been brought into the temple of the LORD and put it into bags.
11When the amount had been determined, they gave the money to the men appointed to supervise the work on the temple. With it they paid those who worked on the temple of the LORD—the carpenters and builders,
12the masons and stonecutters. They purchased timber and dressed stone for the repair of the temple of the LORD, and met all the other expenses of restoring the temple.
13The money brought into the temple was not spent for making silver basins, wick trimmers, sprinkling bowls, trumpets or any other articles of gold or silver for the temple of the LORD;
14it was paid to the workmen, who used it to repair the temple.
15They did not require an accounting from those to whom they gave the money to pay the workers, because they acted with complete honesty.
16The money from the guilt offerings and sin offerings was not

brought into the temple of the LORD; it
belonged to the priests.
17About this time Hazael king of
Aram went up and attacked Gath and
captured it. Then he turned to attack
Jerusalem. 18But Joash king of Judah
took all the sacred objects dedicated by
his fathers—Jehoshaphat, Jehoram
and Ahaziah, the kings of Judah—and
the gifts he himself had dedicated and
all the gold found in the treasuries of the
temple of the LORD and of the royal
palace, and he sent them to Hazael king
of Aram, who then withdrew from
Jerusalem.
19As for the other events of the reign
of Joash, and all he did, are they not
written in the book of the annals of the
kings of Judah? 20His officials conspired
against him and assassinated him at
Beth Millo, on the road down to Silla.
21The officials who murdered him were
Jozabad son of Shimeath and Jehozabad son of Shomer. He died and was
buried with his fathers in the City of
David. And Amaziah his son succeeded
him as king.

Jehoahaz King of Israel

13 In the twenty-third year of Joash
son of Ahaziah king of Judah,
Jehoahaz son of Jehu became king of
Israel in Samaria, and he reigned for
seventeen years. 2He did evil in the eyes
of the LORD by following the sins of
Jeroboam son of Nebat, which he had
caused Israel to commit, and he did not
turn away from them. 3So the LORD's
anger burned against Israel, and for a
long time he kept them under the power
of Hazael king of Aram and Ben-Hadad
his son.
4Then Jehoahaz sought the LORD's
favour, and the LORD listened to him,
for he saw how severely the king of
Aram was oppressing Israel. 5The LORD
provided a deliverer for Israel, and they
escaped from the power of Aram. So
the Israelites lived in their own homes
as they had before. 6But they did not
turn away from the sins of the house of
Jeroboam, which he had caused Israel
to commit; they continued in them.
Also, the Asherah pole remained standing in Samaria.
7Nothing had been left of the army of
Jehoahaz except fifty horsemen, ten
chariots and ten thousand foot soldiers,
for the king of Aram had destroyed the
rest and made them like the dust at
threshing time.
8As for the other events of the reign
of Jehoahaz, all he did and his achievements, are they not written in the book
of the annals of the kings of Israel?
9Jehoahaz rested with his fathers and
was buried in Samaria. And Jehoash his
son succeeded him as king.

Jehoash King of Israel

10In the thirty-seventh year of Joash
king of Judah, Jehoash son of Jehoahaz
became king of Israel in Samaria, and
he reigned for sixteen years. 11He did
evil in the eyes of the LORD and did not
turn away from any of the sins of Jeroboam son of Nebat, which he had
caused Israel to commit; he continued
in them.
12As for the other events of the reign
of Jehoash, all he did and his achievements, including his war against Amaziah king of Judah, are they not written
in the book of the annals of the kings of
Israel? 13Jehoash rested with his
fathers, and Jeroboam succeeded him
on the throne. Jehoash was buried in
Samaria with the kings of Israel.
14Now Elisha was suffering from the
illness from which he died. Jehoash king
of Israel went down to see him and wept
over him. "My father! My father!" he
cried. "The chariots and horsemen of
Israel!"
15Elisha said, "Get a bow and some
arrows," and he did so. 16"Take the
bow in your hands," he said to the king
of Israel. When he had taken it, Elisha
put his hands on the king's hands.
17"Open the east window," he said,
and he opened it. "Shoot!" Elisha said,

and he shot. "The LORD's arrow of victory, the arrow of victory over Aram!"
Elisha declared. "You will completely
destroy the Arameans at Aphek."
18Then he said, "Take the arrows,"
and the king took them. Elisha told
him, "Strike the ground." He struck it
three times and stopped. 19The man of
God was angry with him and said, "You
should have struck the ground five or six
times; then you would have defeated
Aram and completely destroyed it. But
now you will defeat it only three times."
20Elisha died and was buried.

Now Moabite raiders used to enter
the country every spring. 21Once while
some Israelites were burying a man,
suddenly they saw a band of raiders; so
they threw the man's body into Elisha's
tomb. When the body touched Elisha's
bones, the man came to life and stood
up on his feet.
22Hazael king of Aram oppressed
Israel throughout the reign of
Jehoahaz. 23But the LORD was gracious
to them and had compassion and
showed concern for them because of his
covenant with Abraham, Isaac and
Jacob. To this day he has been unwilling
to destroy them or banish them from his
presence.
24Hazael king of Aram died, and
Ben-Hadad his son succeeded him as
king. 25Then Jehoash son of Jehoahaz
recaptured from Ben-Hadad son of
Hazael the towns he had taken in battle
from his father Jehoahaz. Three times
Jehoash defeated him, and so he recovered the Israelite towns.

Amaziah King of Judah

14 In the second year of Jehoash
son of Jehoahaz king of Israel,
Amaziah son of Joash king of Judah
began to reign. 2He was twenty-five
years old when he became king, and he
reigned in Jerusalem for twenty-nine
years. His mother's name was Jehoaddin; she was from Jerusalem. 3He did
what was right in the eyes of the LORD,
but not as his father David had done. In
everything he followed the example of
his father Joash. 4The high places,
however, were not removed; the people
continued to offer sacrifices and burn
incense there.
5After the kingdom was firmly in his
grasp, he executed the officials who had
murdered his father the king. 6Yet he
did not put the sons of the assassins to
death, in accordance with what is written in the Book of the Law of Moses
where the LORD commanded: "Fathers
shall not be put to death for their children, nor children put to death for their
fathers; each is to die for his own sins."
7He was the one who defeated ten
thousand Edomites in the Valley of Salt
and captured Sela in battle, calling it
Joktheel, the name it has to this day.
8Then Amaziah sent messengers to
Jehoash son of Jehoahaz, the son of
Jehu, king of Israel, with the challenge:
"Come, meet me face to face."
9But Jehoash king of Israel replied to
Amaziah king of Judah: "A thistle in
Lebanon sent a message to a cedar in
Lebanon, 'Give your daughter to my
son in marriage.' Then a wild beast in
Lebanon came along and trampled the
thistle underfoot. 10You have indeed
defeated Edom and now you are arrogant. Glory in your victory, but stay at
home! Why ask for trouble and cause
your own downfall and that of Judah
also?"
11Amaziah, however, would not listen, so Jehoash king of Israel attacked.
He and Amaziah king of Judah faced
each other at Beth Shemesh in Judah.
12Judah was routed by Israel, and every
man fled to his home. 13Jehoash king of
Israel captured Amaziah king of Judah,
the son of Joash, the son of Ahaziah, at
Beth Shemesh. Then Jehoash went to
Jerusalem and broke down the wall of
Jerusalem from the Ephraim Gate to
the Corner Gate—a section about six
hundred feet long. 14He took all the
gold and silver and all the articles found
in the temple of the LORD and in the
treasuries of the royal palace. He also
took hostages and returned to Samaria.

15As for the other events of the reign of Jehoash, what he did and his achievements, including his war against Amaziah king of Judah, are they not written in the book of the annals of the kings of Israel? 16Jehoash rested with his fathers and was buried in Samaria with the kings of Israel. And Jeroboam his son succeeded him as king.

17Amaziah son of Joash king of Judah lived for fifteen years after the death of Jehoash son of Jehoahaz king of Israel. 18As for the other events of Amaziah's reign, are they not written in the book of the annals of the kings of Judah?

19They conspired against him in Jerusalem, and he fled to Lachish, but they sent men after him to Lachish and killed him there. 20He was brought back by horse and was buried in Jerusalem with his fathers, in the City of David.

21Then all the people of Judah took Azariah, who was sixteen years old, and made him king in place of his father Amaziah. 22He was the one who rebuilt Elath and restored it to Judah after Amaziah rested with his fathers.

NEW TESTAMENT READING

Acts 25:1–22

The Trial Before Festus

25 Three days after arriving in the province, Festus went up from Caesarea to Jerusalem, 2where the chief priests and Jewish leaders appeared before him and presented the charges against Paul. 3They urgently requested Festus, as a favour to them, to have Paul transferred to Jerusalem, for they were preparing an ambush to kill him along the way. 4Festus answered, "Paul is being held at Caesarea, and I myself am going there soon. 5Let some of your leaders come with me and press charges against the man there, if he has done anything wrong."

6After spending eight or ten days with them, he went down to Caesarea, and the next day he convened the court and ordered that Paul be brought before him. 7When Paul appeared, the Jews who had come down from Jerusalem stood around him, bringing many serious charges against him, which they could not prove.

8Then Paul made his defence: "I have done nothing wrong against the law of the Jews or against the temple or against Caesar."

9Festus, wishing to do the Jews a favour, said to Paul, "Are you willing to go up to Jerusalem and stand trial before me there on these charges?"

10Paul answered: "I am now standing before Caesar's court, where I ought to be tried. I have not done any wrong to the Jews, as you yourself know very well. 11If, however, I am guilty of doing anything deserving death, I do not refuse to die. But if the charges brought against me by these Jews are not true, no-one has the right to hand me over to them. I appeal to Caesar!"

12After Festus had conferred with his council, he declared: "You have appealed to Caesar. To Caesar you will go!"

Festus Consults King Agrippa

13A few days later King Agrippa and Bernice arrived at Caesarea to pay their respects to Festus. 14Since they were spending many days there, Festus discussed Paul's case with the king. He said: "There is a man here whom Felix left as a prisoner. 15When I went to Jerusalem, the chief priests and elders of the Jews brought charges against him and asked that he be condemned.

16"I told them that it is not the Roman custom to hand over any man before he has faced his accusers and has had an opportunity to defend himself against their charges. 17When they came here with me, I did not delay the case, but convened the court the next day and ordered the man to be brought in. 18When his accusers got up to speak, they did not charge him with any of the

crimes I had expected. 19Instead, they had some points of dispute with him about their own religion and about a dead man named Jesus whom Paul claimed was alive. 20I was at a loss how to investigate such matters; so I asked if he would be willing to go to Jerusalem and stand trial there on these charges.
21When Paul made his appeal to be held over for the Emperor's decision, I ordered him to be held until I could send him to Caesar."

22Then Agrippa said to Festus, "I would like to hear this man myself."

He replied, "Tomorrow you will hear him."

READING FROM PSALMS
Psalm 81:1–7

For the director of music. According to *gittith*. Of Asaph.

1Sing for joy to God our strength;
shout aloud to the God of Jacob!
2Begin the music, strike the tambourine,
play the melodious harp and lyre.

3Sound the ram's horn at the New Moon,
and when the moon is full, on the day of our Feast;
4this is a decree for Israel,
an ordinance of the God of Jacob.
5He established it as a statute for Joseph
when he went out against Egypt,
where we heard a language we did not understand.

6He says, "I removed the burden from their shoulders;
their hands were set free from the basket.
7In your distress you called and I rescued you,
I answered you out of a thundercloud;
I tested you at the waters of Meribah. *Selah*

JULY 7

DAY 188

OLD TESTAMENT READING
2 Kings 14:23–15:38

Jeroboam II King of Israel

23In the fifteenth year of Amaziah son of Joash king of Judah, Jeroboam son of Jehoash king of Israel became king in Samaria, and he reigned for forty-one years. 24He did evil in the eyes of the LORD and did not turn away from any of the sins of Jeroboam son of Nebat, which he had caused Israel to commit.
25He was the one who restored the boundaries of Israel from Lebo Hamath to the Sea of the Arabah, in accordance with the word of the LORD, the God of Israel, spoken through his servant Jonah son of Amittai, the prophet from Gath Hepher.

26The LORD had seen how bitterly everyone in Israel, whether slave or free, was suffering; there was no-one to help them. 27And since the LORD had not said he would blot out the name of Israel from under heaven, he saved them by the hand of Jeroboam son of Jehoash.

28As for the other events of Jeroboam's reign, all he did, and his military achievements, including how he recovered for Israel both Damascus and Hamath, which had belonged to Yaudi, are they not written in the book of the annals of the kings of Israel?
29Jeroboam rested with his fathers, the

kings of Israel. And Zechariah his son
succeeded him as king.

Azariah King of Judah

15 In the twenty-seventh year of
Jeroboam king of Israel, Azariah son of Amaziah king of Judah began
to reign. 2He was sixteen years old when
he became king, and he reigned in Jerusalem for fifty-two years. His mother's
name was Jecoliah; she was from Jerusalem. 3He did what was right in the
eyes of the LORD, just as his father
Amaziah had done. 4The high places,
however, were not removed; the people
continued to offer sacrifices and burn
incense there.
5The LORD afflicted the king with leprosy until the day he died, and he lived
in a separate house. Jotham the king's
son had charge of the palace and governed the people of the land.
6As for the other events of Azariah's
reign, and all he did, are they not written in the book of the annals of the kings
of Judah? 7Azariah rested with his
fathers and was buried near them in the
City of David. And Jotham his son succeeded him as king.

Zechariah King of Israel

8In the thirty-eighth year of Azariah
king of Judah, Zechariah son of Jeroboam became king of Israel in Samaria,
and he reigned for six months. 9He did
evil in the eyes of the LORD, as his
fathers had done. He did not turn away
from the sins of Jeroboam son of Nebat,
which he had caused Israel to commit.
10Shallum son of Jabesh conspired
against Zechariah. He attacked him in
front of the people, assassinated him
and succeeded him as king. 11The other
events of Zechariah's reign are written
in the book of the annals of the kings of
Israel. 12So the word of the LORD
spoken to Jehu was fulfilled: "Your descendants will sit on the throne of Israel
to the fourth generation."

Shallum King of Israel

13Shallum son of Jabesh became king
in the thirty-ninth year of Uzziah king of
Judah, and he reigned in Samaria for
one month. 14Then Menahem son of
Gadi went from Tirzah up to Samaria.
He attacked Shallum son of Jabesh in
Samaria, assassinated him and succeeded him as king.
15The other events of Shallum's
reign, and the conspiracy he led, are
written in the book of the annals of the
kings of Israel.
16At that time Menahem, starting out
from Tirzah, attacked Tiphsah and
everyone in the city and its vicinity,
because they refused to open their
gates. He sacked Tiphsah and ripped
open all the pregnant women.

Menahem King of Israel

17In the thirty-ninth year of Azariah
king of Judah, Menahem son of Gadi
became king of Israel, and he reigned in
Samaria for ten years. 18He did evil in
the eyes of the LORD. During his entire
reign he did not turn away from the sins
of Jeroboam son of Nebat, which he had
caused Israel to commit.
19Then Pul king of Assyria invaded
the land, and Menahem gave him a
thousand talents of silver to gain his
support and strengthen his own hold on
the kingdom. 20Menahem exacted this
money from Israel. Every wealthy man
had to contribute fifty shekels of silver
to be given to the king of Assyria. So the
king of Assyria withdrew and stayed in
the land no longer.
21As for the other events of
Menahem's reign, and all he did, are
they not written in the book of the
annals of the kings of Israel?
22Menahem rested with his fathers. And
Pekahiah his son succeeded him as king.

Pekahiah King of Israel

23In the fiftieth year of Azariah king
of Judah, Pekahiah son of Menahem

became king of Israel in Samaria, and
he reigned for two years. 24Pekahiah did
evil in the eyes of the LORD. He did not
turn away from the sins of Jeroboam
son of Nebat, which he had caused
Israel to commit. 25One of his chief
officers, Pekah son of Remaliah, conspired against him. Taking fifty men of
Gilead with him, he assassinated Pekahiah, along with Argob and Arieh, in
the citadel of the royal palace at Samaria. So Pekah killed Pekahiah and succeeded him as king.
26The other events of Pekahiah's
reign, and all he did, are written in the
book of the annals of the kings of Israel.

Pekah King of Israel

27In the fifty-second year of Azariah
king of Judah, Pekah son of Remaliah
became king of Israel in Samaria, and
he reigned for twenty years. 28He did
evil in the eyes of the LORD. He did not
turn away from the sins of Jeroboam
son of Nebat, which he had caused
Israel to commit.
29In the time of Pekah king of Israel,
Tiglath-Pileser king of Assyria came
and took Ijon, Abel Beth Maacah,
Janoah, Kedesh and Hazor. He took
Gilead and Galilee, including all the
land of Naphtali, and deported the people to Assyria. 30Then Hoshea son of
Elah conspired against Pekah son of
Remaliah. He attacked and assassinated him, and then succeeded him as
king in the twentieth year of Jotham son
of Uzziah.
31As for the other events of Pekah's
reign, and all he did, are they not written in the book of the annals of the kings
of Israel?

Jotham King of Judah

32In the second year of Pekah son of
Remaliah king of Israel, Jotham son of
Uzziah king of Judah began to reign.
33He was twenty-five years old when he
became king, and he reigned in Jerusalem for sixteen years. His mother's
name was Jerusha daughter of Zadok.
34He did what was right in the eyes of
the LORD, just as his father Uzziah had
done. 35The high places, however, were
not removed; the people continued to
offer sacrifices and burn incense there.
Jotham rebuilt the Upper Gate of the
temple of the LORD.
36As for the other events of Jotham's
reign, and what he did, are they not
written in the book of the annals of the
kings of Judah? 37(In those days the
LORD began to send Rezin king of Aram
and Pekah son of Remaliah against
Judah.) 38Jotham rested with his fathers
and was buried with them in the City of
David, the city of his father. And Ahaz
his son succeeded him as king.

NEW TESTAMENT READING
Acts 25:23–26:23

Paul Before Agrippa

23The next day Agrippa and Bernice
came with great pomp and entered the
audience room with the high ranking
officers and the leading men of the
city. At the command of Festus, Paul
was brought in. 24Festus said: "King
Agrippa, and all who are present with
us, you see this man! The whole Jewish
community has petitioned me about
him in Jerusalem and here in Caesarea,
shouting that he ought not to live any
longer. 25I found he had done nothing
deserving of death, but because he
made his appeal to the Emperor I decided to send him to Rome. 26But I have
nothing definite to write to His Majesty
about him. Therefore I have brought
him before all of you, and especially
before you, King Agrippa, so that as a
result of this investigation I may have
something to write. 27For I think it is
unreasonable to send on a prisoner
without specifying the charges against
him."
26 Then Agrippa said to Paul,
"You have permission to speak
for yourself."

So Paul motioned with his hand and
began his defence: 2"King Agrippa, I
consider myself fortunate to stand before you today as I make my defence
against all the accusations of the Jews,
3and especially so because you are well
acquainted with all the Jewish customs
and controversies. Therefore, I beg you
to listen to me patiently.

4"The Jews all know the way I have
lived ever since I was a child, from the
beginning of my life in my own country,
and also in Jerusalem. 5They have
known me for a long time and can testify, if they are willing, that according to
the strictest sect of our religion, I lived
as a Pharisee. 6And now it is because of
my hope in what God has promised our
fathers that I am on trial today. 7This
is the promise our twelve tribes are
hoping to see fulfilled as they earnestly
serve God day and night. O King, it is
because of this hope that the Jews are
accusing me. 8Why should any of you
consider it incredible that God raises
the dead?

9"I too was convinced that I ought to
do all that was possible to oppose the
name of Jesus of Nazareth. 10And that is
just what I did in Jerusalem. On the
authority of the chief priests I put many
of the saints in prison, and when they
were put to death, I cast my vote against
them. 11Many a time I went from one
synagogue to another to have them
punished, and I tried to force them to
blaspheme. In my obsession against
them, I even went to foreign cities to
persecute them.

12"On one of these journeys I was
going to Damascus with the authority
and commission of the chief priests.
13About noon, O King, as I was on the
road, I saw a light from heaven, brighter
than the sun, blazing around me and my
companions. 14We all fell to the ground,
and I heard a voice saying to me in
Aramaic, 'Saul, Saul, why do you persecute me? It is hard for you to kick
against the goads.'

15"Then I asked, 'Who are you,
Lord?'

" 'I am Jesus, whom you are persecuting,' the Lord replied. 16'Now get up
and stand on your feet. I have appeared
to you to appoint you as a servant and as
a witness of what you have seen of me
and what I will show you. 17I will rescue
you from your own people and from the
Gentiles. I am sending you to them 18to
open their eyes and turn them from
darkness to light, and from the power of
Satan to God, so that they may receive
forgiveness of sins and a place among
those who are sanctified by faith in me.'

19"So then, King Agrippa, I was not
disobedient to the vision from heaven.
20First to those in Damascus, then to
those in Jerusalem and in all Judea, and
to the Gentiles also, I preached that
they should repent and turn to God and
prove their repentance by their deeds.
21That is why the Jews seized me in the
temple courts and tried to kill me. 22But
I have had God's help to this very day,
and so I stand here and testify to small
and great alike. I am saying nothing
beyond what the prophets and Moses
said would happen—23that the Christ
would suffer and, as the first to rise from
the dead, would proclaim light to his
own people and to the Gentiles."

READING FROM PROVERBS
Proverbs 16:18–27

18Pride goes before destruction,
  a haughty spirit before a fall.

19Better to be lowly in spirit and among
    the oppressed
  than to share plunder with the
    proud.

20Whoever gives heed to instruction
    prospers,
  and blessed is he who trusts in the
    LORD.

21The wise in heart are called
    discerning,
  and pleasant words promote
    instruction.

22Understanding is a fountain of life to
those who have it,
but folly brings punishment to
fools.

23A wise man's heart guides his mouth,
and his lips promote instruction.

24Pleasant words are a honeycomb,
sweet to the soul and healing to the
bones.

25There is a way that seems right to a
man,
but in the end it leads to death.

26The labourer's appetite works for
him;
his hunger drives him on.

27A scoundrel plots evil,
and his speech is like a scorching
fire.

JULY 8

DAY 189

OLD TESTAMENT READING

2 Kings 16:1–17:41

Ahaz King of Judah

16 In the seventeenth year of
Pekah son of Remaliah, Ahaz
son of Jotham king of Judah began to
reign. 2Ahaz was twenty years old when
he became king, and he reigned in Jerusalem for sixteen years. Unlike David
his father, he did not do what was right
in the eyes of the LORD his God. 3He
walked in the ways of the kings of Israel
and even sacrificed his son in the fire,
following the detestable ways of the
nations the LORD had driven out before
the Israelites. 4He offered sacrifices and
burned incense at the high places, on
the hilltops and under every spreading
tree.

5Then Rezin king of Aram and Pekah
son of Remaliah king of Israel marched
up to fight against Jerusalem and besieged Ahaz, but they could not overpower him. 6At that time, Rezin king of
Aram recovered Elath for Aram by
driving out the men of Judah. Edomites
then moved into Elath and have lived
there to this day.

7Ahaz sent messengers to say to Tiglath-Pileser king of Assyria, "I am your
servant and vassal. Come up and save
me out of the hand of the king of Aram
and of the king of Israel who are attacking me." 8And Ahaz took the silver and
gold found in the temple of the LORD
and in the treasuries of the royal palace
and sent it as a gift to the king of Assyria. 9The king of Assyria complied by
attacking Damascus and capturing it.
He deported its inhabitants to Kir and
put Rezin to death.

10Then King Ahaz went to Damascus
to meet Tiglath-Pileser king of Assyria.
He saw an altar in Damascus and sent to
Uriah the priest a sketch of the altar,
with detailed plans for its construction.
11So Uriah the priest built an altar in
accordance with all the plans that King
Ahaz had sent from Damascus and
finished it before King Ahaz returned.
12When the king came back from
Damascus and saw the altar, he
approached it and presented offerings
on it. 13He offered up his burnt offering
and grain offering, poured out his drink
offering, and sprinkled the blood of his
fellowship offerings on the altar. 14The
bronze altar that stood before the LORD
he brought from the front of the temple
—from between the new altar and the
temple of the LORD—and put it on the
north side of the new altar.

15King Ahaz then gave these orders
to Uriah the priest: "On the large new
altar, offer the morning burnt offering

and the evening grain offering, the
king's burnt offering and his grain offering, and the burnt offering of all the
people of the land, and their grain offering and their drink offering. Sprinkle on
the altar all the blood of the burnt offerings and sacrifices. But I will use the
bronze altar for seeking guidance."
16And Uriah the priest did just as King
Ahaz had ordered.
17King Ahaz took away the side
panels and removed the basins from the
movable stands. He removed the Sea
from the bronze bulls that supported it
and set it on a stone base. 18He took
away the Sabbath canopy that had been
built at the temple and removed the
royal entrance outside the temple of
the LORD, in deference to the king of
Assyria.
19As for the other events of the reign
of Ahaz, and what he did, are they not
written in the book of the annals of the
kings of Judah? 20Ahaz rested with his
fathers and was buried with them in the
City of David. And Hezekiah his son
succeeded him as king.

Hoshea Last King of Israel

17 In the twelfth year of Ahaz king
of Judah, Hoshea son of Elah
became king of Israel in Samaria, and
he reigned for nine years. 2He did evil in
the eyes of the LORD, but not like the
kings of Israel who preceded him.
3Shalmaneser king of Assyria came
up to attack Hoshea, who had been
Shalmaneser's vassal and had paid him
tribute. 4But the king of Assyria discovered that Hoshea was a traitor, for
he had sent envoys to So king of Egypt,
and he no longer paid tribute to the king
of Assyria, as he had done year by year.
Therefore Shalmaneser seized him and
put him in prison. 5The king of Assyria
invaded the entire land, marched
against Samaria and laid siege to it for
three years. 6In the ninth year of
Hoshea, the king of Assyria captured
Samaria and deported the Israelites to
Assyria. He settled them in Halah, in
Gozan on the Habor River and in the
towns of the Medes.

Israel Exiled Because of Sin

7All this took place because the
Israelites had sinned against the LORD
their God, who had brought them out of
Egypt from under the power of Pharaoh
king of Egypt. They worshipped other
gods 8and followed the practices of the
nations the LORD had driven out before
them, as well as the practices that the
kings of Israel had introduced. 9The
Israelites secretly did things against the
LORD their God that were not right.
From watchtower to fortified city they
built themselves high places in all their
towns. 10They set up sacred stones and
Asherah poles on every high hill and
under every spreading tree. 11At every
high place they burned incense, as the
nations whom the LORD had driven out
before them had done. They did wicked
things that provoked the LORD to anger.
12They worshipped idols, though the
LORD had said, "You shall not do this."
13The LORD warned Israel and Judah
through all his prophets and seers:
"Turn from your evil ways. Observe my
commands and decrees, in accordance
with the entire Law that I commanded
your fathers to obey and that I delivered
to you through my servants the
prophets."
14But they would not listen and were
as stiff-necked as their fathers, who did
not trust in the LORD their God. 15They
rejected his decrees and the covenant
he had made with their fathers and the
warnings he had given them. They followed worthless idols and themselves
became worthless. They imitated the
nations around them although the LORD
had ordered them, "Do not do as they
do," and they did the things the LORD
had forbidden them to do.
16They forsook all the commands of
the LORD their God and made for themselves two idols cast in the shape of
calves, and an Asherah pole. They
bowed down to all the starry hosts, and

they worshipped Baal. 17They sacrificed
their sons and daughters in the fire.
They practised divination and sorcery
and sold themselves to do evil in the
eyes of the LORD, provoking him to
anger.

18So the LORD was very angry with
Israel and removed them from his presence. Only the tribe of Judah was left,
19and even Judah did not keep the commands of the LORD their God. They
followed the practices Israel had introduced. 20Therefore the LORD rejected
all the people of Israel; he afflicted them
and gave them into the hands of
plunderers, until he thrust them from
his presence.

21When he tore Israel away from the
house of David, they made Jeroboam
son of Nebat their king. Jeroboam enticed Israel away from following the
LORD and caused them to commit a
great sin. 22The Israelites persisted in all
the sins of Jeroboam and did not turn
away from them 23until the LORD removed them from his presence, as he
had warned through all his servants the
prophets. So the people of Israel were
taken from their homeland into exile in
Assyria, and they are still there.

Samaria Resettled

24The king of Assyria brought people
from Babylon, Cuthah, Avva, Hamath
and Sepharvaim and settled them in the
towns of Samaria to replace the
Israelites. They took over Samaria and
lived in its towns. 25When they first lived
there, they did not worship the LORD;
so he sent lions among them and they
killed some of the people. 26It was reported to the king of Assyria: "The
people you deported and resettled in
the towns of Samaria do not know what
the god of that country requires. He has
sent lions among them, which are killing
them off, because the people do not
know what he requires."

27Then the king of Assyria gave this
order: "Make one of the priests you
took captive from Samaria go back to
live there and teach the people what the
god of the land requires." 28So one of
the priests who had been exiled from
Samaria came to live in Bethel and
taught them how to worship the LORD.

29Nevertheless, each national group
made its own gods in the several towns
where they settled, and set them up in
the shrines the people of Samaria had
made at the high places. 30The men
from Babylon made Succoth Benoth,
the men from Cuthah made Nergal, and
the men from Hamath made Ashima;
31the Avvites made Nibhaz and Tartak,
and the Sepharvites burned their children in the fire as sacrifices to Adrammelech and Anammelech, the gods of
Sepharvaim. 32They worshipped the
LORD, but they also appointed all sorts
of their own people to officiate for them
as priests in the shrines at the high
places. 33They worshipped the LORD,
but they also served their own gods in
accordance with the customs of the
nations from which they had been
brought.

34To this day they persist in their former practices. They neither worship the
LORD nor adhere to the decrees and
ordinances, the laws and commands
that the LORD gave the descendants of
Jacob, whom he named Israel. 35When
the LORD made a covenant with the
Israelites, he commanded them: "Do
not worship any other gods or bow
down to them, serve them or sacrifice to
them. 36But the LORD, who brought you
up out of Egypt with mighty power and
outstretched arm, is the one you must
worship. To him you shall bow down
and to him offer sacrifices. 37You must
always be careful to keep the decrees
and ordinances, the laws and commands he wrote for you. Do not
worship other gods. 38Do not forget the
covenant I have made with you, and do
not worship other gods. 39Rather,
worship the LORD your God; it is he
who will deliver you from the hand of all
your enemies."

40They would not listen, however,
but persisted in their former practices.

41Even while these people were worshipping the LORD, they were serving
their idols. To this day their children
and grandchildren continue to do as
their fathers did.

NEW TESTAMENT READING
Acts 26:24–27:12

24At this point Festus interrupted
Paul's defence. "You are out of your
mind, Paul!" he shouted. "Your great
learning is driving you insane."
25"I am not insane, most excellent
Festus," Paul replied. "What I am
saying is true and reasonable. 26The
king is familiar with these things, and I
can speak freely to him. I am convinced
that none of this has escaped his notice,
because it was not done in a corner.
27King Agrippa, do you believe the
prophets? I know you do."
28Then Agrippa said to Paul, "Do
you think that in such a short time you
can persuade me to be a Christian?"
29Paul replied, "Short time or long
—I pray God that not only you but all
who are listening to me today may become what I am, except for these
chains."
30The king rose, and with him the
governor and Bernice and those sitting
with them. 31They left the room, and
while talking with one another, they
said, "This man is not doing anything
that deserves death or imprisonment."
32Agrippa said to Festus, "This man
could have been set free if he had not
appealed to Caesar."

Paul Sails for Rome

27 When it was decided that we
would sail for Italy, Paul and
some other prisoners were handed over
to a centurion named Julius, who belonged to the Imperial Regiment. 2We
boarded a ship from Adramyttium
about to sail for ports along the coast of
the province of Asia, and we put out to
sea. Aristarchus, a Macedonian from
Thessalonica, was with us.
3The next day we landed at Sidon;
and Julius, in kindness to Paul, allowed
him to go to his friends so they might
provide for his needs. 4From there we
put out to sea again and passed to the
lee of Cyprus because the winds were
against us. 5When we had sailed across
the open sea off the coast of Cilicia and
Pamphylia, we landed at Myra in Lycia.
6There the centurion found an Alexandrian ship sailing for Italy and put us on
board. 7We made slow headway for
many days and had difficulty arriving off
Cnidus. When the wind did not allow us
to hold our course, we sailed to the lee
of Crete, opposite Salmone. 8We
moved along the coast with difficulty
and came to a place called Fair Havens,
near the town of Lasea.
9Much time had been lost, and sailing
had already become dangerous because
by now it was after the Fast. So Paul
warned them, 10"Men, I can see that
our voyage is going to be disastrous and
bring great loss to ship and cargo, and
to our own lives also." 11But the centurion, instead of listening to what Paul
said, followed the advice of the pilot
and of the owner of the ship. 12Since the
harbour was unsuitable to winter in, the
majority decided that we should sail on,
hoping to reach Phoenix and winter
there. This was a harbour in Crete,
facing both south-west and north-west.

READING FROM PSALMS
Psalm 81:8–16

8"Hear, O my people, and I will warn
you—
if you would but listen to me, O
Israel!
9You shall have no foreign god among
you;
you shall not bow down to an alien
god.
10I am the LORD your God,
who brought you up out of Egypt.

Open wide your mouth and I will
fill it.

11"But my people would not listen to
me;
Israel would not submit to me.
12So I gave them over to their stubborn
hearts
to follow their own devices.

13"If my people would but listen to me,
if Israel would follow my ways,
14how quickly would I subdue their
enemies
and turn my hand against their
foes!
15Those who hate the LORD would
cringe before him,
and their punishment would last
for ever.
16But you would be fed with the finest
of wheat;
with honey from the rock I would
satisfy you."

JULY 9

DAY 190

OLD TESTAMENT READING

2 Kings 18:1–19:13

Hezekiah King of Judah

18 In the third year of Hoshea son
of Elah king of Israel, Hezekiah
son of Ahaz king of Judah began to
reign. 2He was twenty-five years old
when he became king, and he reigned in
Jerusalem for twenty-nine years. His
mother's name was Abijah daughter of
Zechariah. 3He did what was right in
the eyes of the LORD, just as his father
David had done. 4He removed the high
places, smashed the sacred stones and
cut down the Asherah poles. He broke
into pieces the bronze snake Moses had
made, for up to that time the Israelites
had been burning incense to it. (It was
called Nehushtan.)
5Hezekiah trusted in the LORD, the
God of Israel. There was no-one like
him among all the kings of Judah, either
before him or after him. 6He held fast to
the LORD and did not cease to follow
him; he kept the commands the LORD
had given Moses. 7And the LORD was
with him; he was successful in whatever
he undertook. He rebelled against the
king of Assyria and did not serve him.
8From watchtower to fortified city, he
defeated the Philistines, as far as Gaza
and its territory.
9In King Hezekiah's fourth year,
which was the seventh year of Hoshea
son of Elah king of Israel, Shalmaneser
king of Assyria marched against Samaria and laid siege to it. 10At the end of
three years the Assyrians took it. So
Samaria was captured in Hezekiah's
sixth year, which was the ninth year of
Hoshea king of Israel. 11The king of
Assyria deported Israel to Assyria and
settled them in Halah, in Gozan on the
Habor River, and in towns of the
Medes. 12This happened because they
had not obeyed the LORD their God, but
had violated his covenant—all that
Moses the servant of the LORD commanded. They neither listened to the
commands nor carried them out.
13In the fourteenth year of King
Hezekiah's reign, Sennacherib king of
Assyria attacked all the fortified cities
of Judah and captured them. 14So Hezekiah king of Judah sent this message to
the king of Assyria at Lachish: "I have
done wrong. Withdraw from me, and I
will pay whatever you demand of me."
The king of Assyria exacted from Hezekiah king of Judah three hundred talents
of silver and thirty talents of gold. 15So
Hezekiah gave him all the silver that

was found in the temple of the LORD
and in the treasuries of the royal palace.
16At this time Hezekiah king of Judah
stripped off the gold with which he had
covered the doors and doorposts of the
temple of the LORD, and gave it to the
king of Assyria.

Sennacherib Threatens Jerusalem

17The king of Assyria sent his supreme commander, his chief officer and his field commander with a large army, from Lachish to King Hezekiah at Jerusalem. They came up to Jerusalem and stopped at the aqueduct of the Upper Pool, on the road to the Washerman's
Field. 18They called for the king; and Eliakim son of Hilkiah the palace administrator, Shebna the secretary, and Joah son of Asaph the recorder went out to them.
19The field commander said to them, "Tell Hezekiah:

"'This is what the great king, the king of Assyria, says: On what are you basing this confidence of
yours? 20You say you have strategy and military strength—but you speak only empty words. On whom are you depending, that you rebel
against me? 21Look now, you are depending on Egypt, that splintered reed of a staff, which pierces a man's hand and wounds him if he leans on it! Such is Pharaoh king of Egypt to all who depend on him.
22And if you say to me, "We are depending on the LORD our God" —isn't he the one whose high places and altars Hezekiah removed, saying to Judah and Jerusalem, "You must worship before this altar in Jerusalem"?
23"'Come now, make a bargain with my master, the king of Assyria: I will give you two thousand horses—if you can put riders on
them! 24How can you repulse one officer of the least of my master's officials, even though you are depending on Egypt for chariots and
horsemen? 25Furthermore, have I come to attack and destroy this place without word from the LORD? The LORD himself told me to march against this country and destroy it.'"

26Then Eliakim son of Hilkiah, and Shebna and Joah said to the field commander, "Please speak to your servants in Aramaic, since we understand it. Don't speak to us in Hebrew in the hearing of the people on the wall."
27But the commander replied, "Was it only to your master and you that my master sent me to say these things, and not to the men sitting on the wall—who, like you, will have to eat their own filth and drink their own urine?"
28Then the commander stood and called out in Hebrew: "Hear the word of the great king, the king of Assyria!
29This is what the king says: Do not let Hezekiah deceive you. He cannot de-
liver you from my hand. 30Do not let
Hezekiah persuade you to trust in the LORD when he says, 'The LORD will surely deliver us; this city will not be given into the hand of the king of Assyria.'
31"Do not listen to Hezekiah. This is what the king of Assyria says: Make peace with me and come out to me. Then every one of you will eat from his own vine and fig-tree and drink water
from his own cistern, 32until I come and
take you to a land like your own, a land of grain and new wine, a land of bread and vineyards, a land of olive trees and honey. Choose life and not death!
"Do not listen to Hezekiah, for he is misleading you when he says, 'The
LORD will deliver us.' 33Has the god of
any nation ever delivered his land from the hand of the king of Assyria?
34Where are the gods of Hamath and Arpad? Where are the gods of Sepharvaim, Hena and Ivvah? Have they rescued Samaria from my hand? 35Who of
all the gods of these countries has been

able to save his land from me? How
then can the LORD deliver Jerusalem
from my hand?"
36 But the people remained silent and
said nothing in reply, because the king
had commanded, "Do not answer
him."
37 Then Eliakim son of Hilkiah the
palace administrator, Shebna the secretary and Joah son of Asaph the recorder
went to Hezekiah, with their clothes
torn, and told him what the field commander had said.

Jerusalem's Deliverance Foretold

19 When King Hezekiah heard
this, he tore his clothes and put
on sackcloth and went into the temple
of the LORD. 2 He sent Eliakim the
palace administrator, Shebna the
secretary and the leading priests, all
wearing sackcloth, to the prophet Isaiah
son of Amoz. 3 They told him, "This is
what Hezekiah says: This day is a day of
distress and rebuke and disgrace, as
when children come to the point of birth
and there is no strength to deliver them.
4 It may be that the LORD your God will
hear all the words of the field commander, whom his master, the king of
Assyria, has sent to ridicule the living
God, and that he will rebuke him for the
words the LORD your God has heard.
Therefore pray for the remnant that still
survives."
5 When King Hezekiah's officials
came to Isaiah, 6 Isaiah said to them,
"Tell your master, 'This is what the
LORD says: Do not be afraid of what you
have heard—those words with which
the underlings of the king of Assyria
have blasphemed me. 7 Listen! I am
going to put such a spirit in him that
when he hears a certain report, he will
return to his own country, and there
I will have him cut down with the
sword.'"
8 When the field commander heard
that the king of Assyria had left Lachish, he withdrew and found the king
fighting against Libnah.
9 Now Sennacherib received a report
that Tirhakah, the Cushite king ⌞of
Egypt⌟, was marching out to fight
against him. So he again sent messengers to Hezekiah with this word: 10 "Say
to Hezekiah king of Judah: Do not let
the god you depend on deceive you
when he says, 'Jerusalem will not be
handed over to the king of Assyria.'
11 Surely you have heard what the kings
of Assyria have done to all the countries, destroying them completely. And
will you be delivered? 12 Did the gods of
the nations that were destroyed by my
forefathers deliver them: the gods of
Gozan, Haran, Rezeph and the people
of Eden who were in Tel Assar?
13 Where is the king of Hamath, the king
of Arpad, the king of the city of Sepharvaim, or of Hena or Ivvah?"

NEW TESTAMENT READING
Acts 27:13–44

The Storm

13 When a gentle south wind began to
blow, they thought they had obtained
what they wanted; so they weighed
anchor and sailed along the shore of
Crete. 14 Before very long, a wind of
hurricane force, called the "north-
easter", swept down from the island.
15 The ship was caught by the storm and
could not head into the wind; so we gave
way to it and were driven along. 16 As we
passed to the lee of a small island called
Cauda, we were hardly able to make the
lifeboat secure. 17 When the men had
hoisted it aboard, they passed ropes
under the ship itself to hold it together.
Fearing that they would run aground on
the sand-bars of Syrtis, they lowered the
sea anchor and let the ship be driven
along. 18 We took such a violent battering from the storm that the next day
they began to throw the cargo overboard. 19 On the third day, they threw
the ship's tackle overboard with their
own hands. 20 When neither sun nor
stars appeared for many days and the

storm continued raging, we finally gave
up all hope of being saved.
21After the men had gone a long time
without food, Paul stood up before
them and said: "Men, you should have
taken my advice not to sail from Crete;
then you would have spared yourselves
this damage and loss. 22But now I urge
you to keep up your courage, because
not one of you will be lost; only the ship
will be destroyed. 23Last night an angel
of the God whose I am and whom I
serve stood beside me 24and said, 'Do
not be afraid, Paul. You must stand trial
before Caesar; and God has graciously
given you the lives of all who sail with
you.' 25So keep up your courage, men,
for I have faith in God that it will happen just as he told me. 26Nevertheless,
we must run aground on some island."

The Shipwreck

27On the fourteenth night we were
still being driven across the Adriatic
Sea, when about midnight the sailors
sensed they were approaching land.
28They took soundings and found that
the water was one hundred and twenty
feet deep. A short time later they took
soundings again and found it was ninety
feet deep. 29Fearing that we would be
dashed against the rocks, they dropped
four anchors from the stern and prayed
for daylight. 30In an attempt to escape
from the ship, the sailors let the lifeboat
down into the sea, pretending they were
going to lower some anchors from the
bow. 31Then Paul said to the centurion
and the soldiers, "Unless these men
stay with the ship, you cannot be
saved." 32So the soldiers cut the ropes
that held the lifeboat and let it fall away.
33Just before dawn Paul urged them
all to eat. "For the last fourteen days,"
he said, "you have been in constant
suspense and have gone without food
—you haven't eaten anything. 34Now I
urge you to take some food. You need it
to survive. Not one of you will lose a
single hair from his head." 35After he
said this, he took some bread and gave
thanks to God in front of them all. Then
he broke it and began to eat. 36They
were all encouraged and ate some food
themselves. 37Altogether there were
276 of us on board. 38When they had
eaten as much as they wanted, they
lightened the ship by throwing the grain
into the sea.
39When daylight came, they did not
recognise the land, but they saw a bay
with a sandy beach, where they decided
to run the ship aground if they could.
40Cutting loose the anchors, they left
them in the sea and at the same time
untied the ropes that held the rudders.
Then they hoisted the foresail to the
wind and made for the beach. 41But the
ship struck a sand-bar and ran aground.
The bow stuck fast and would not move,
and the stern was broken to pieces by
the pounding of the surf.
42The soldiers planned to kill the prisoners to prevent any of them from
swimming away and escaping. 43But the
centurion wanted to spare Paul's life
and kept them from carrying out their
plan. He ordered those who could swim
to jump overboard first and get to land.
44The rest were to get there on planks or
on pieces of the ship. In this way everyone reached land in safety.

READING FROM PSALMS
Psalm 82:1–8

A psalm of Asaph.

1God presides in the great assembly;
he gives judgment among the
"gods":

2"How long will you defend the unjust
and show partiality to the wicked?
Selah
3Defend the cause of the weak and
fatherless;
maintain the rights of the poor and
oppressed.
4Rescue the weak and needy;
deliver them from the hand of the
wicked.

5"They know nothing, they
understand nothing.
They walk about in darkness;
all the foundations of the earth are
shaken.

6"I said, 'You are "gods";
you are all sons of the Most High.'

7But you will die like mere men;
you will fall like every other
ruler."

8Rise up, O God, judge the earth,
for all the nations are your
inheritance.

JULY 10

DAY 191

OLD TESTAMENT READING
2 Kings 19:14–20:21

Hezekiah's Prayer

14Hezekiah received the letter from
the messengers and read it. Then he
went up to the temple of the LORD and
spread it out before the LORD.
15And
Hezekiah prayed to the LORD: "O
LORD, God of Israel, enthroned between the cherubim, you alone are God over all the kingdoms of the earth. You
have made heaven and earth.
16Give
ear, O LORD, and hear; open your eyes,
O LORD, and see; listen to the words
Sennacherib has sent to insult the living
God.

17"It is true, O LORD, that the Assyrian kings have laid waste these
nations and their lands.
18They have
thrown their gods into the fire and destroyed them, for they were not gods
but only wood and stone, fashioned by
men's hands.
19Now, O LORD our God,
deliver us from his hand, so that all
kingdoms on earth may know that you
alone, O LORD, are God."

Isaiah Prophesies Sennacherib's Fall

20Then Isaiah son of Amoz sent a
message to Hezekiah: "This is what the
LORD, the God of Israel, says: I have
heard your prayer concerning Sennacherib king of Assyria.
21This is the
word that the LORD has spoken against
him:

" 'The Virgin Daughter of Zion
despises you and mocks you.
The Daughter of Jerusalem
tosses her head as you flee.
22Who is it you have insulted and
blasphemed?
Against whom have you raised
your voice
and lifted your eyes in pride?
Against the Holy One of Israel!
23By your messengers
you have heaped insults on the
Lord.
And you have said,
"With my many chariots
I have ascended the heights of the
mountains,
the utmost heights of Lebanon.
I have cut down its tallest cedars,
the choicest of its pines.
I have reached its remotest parts,
the finest of its forests.
24I have dug wells in foreign lands
and drunk the water there.
With the soles of my feet
I have dried up all the streams of
Egypt."

25" 'Have you not heard?
Long ago I ordained it.
In days of old I planned it;
now I have brought it to pass,
that you have turned fortified cities
into piles of stone.

26 Their people, drained of power,
are dismayed and put to shame.
They are like plants in the field,
like tender green shoots,
like grass sprouting on the roof,
scorched before it grows up.

27 " 'But I know where you stay
and when you come and go
and how you rage against me.
28 Because you rage against me
and your insolence has reached my
ears,
I will put my hook in your nose
and my bit in your mouth,
and I will make you return
by the way you came.'

29 "This will be the sign for you, O
Hezekiah:

This year you will eat what grows by
itself,
and the second year what springs
from that.
But in the third year sow and reap,
plant vineyards and eat their fruit.
30 Once more a remnant of the house of
Judah
will take root below and bear fruit
above.
31 For out of Jerusalem will come a
remnant,
and out of Mount Zion a band of
survivors.

The zeal of the LORD Almighty will
accomplish this.

32 "Therefore this is what the LORD
says concerning the king of Assyria:

"He will not enter this city
or shoot an arrow here.
He will not come before it with shield
or build a siege ramp against it.
33 By the way that he came he will
return;
he will not enter this city,
declares the LORD.
34 I will defend this city and save it,
for my sake and for the sake of
David my servant."

35 That night the angel of the LORD
went out and put to death a hundred
and eighty-five thousand men in the
Assyrian camp. When the people got up
the next morning—there were all the
dead bodies! 36 So Sennacherib king of
Assyria broke camp and withdrew. He
returned to Nineveh and stayed there.
37 One day, while he was worshipping
in the temple of his god Nisroch, his
sons Adrammelech and Sharezer cut
him down with the sword, and they
escaped to the land of Ararat. And
Esarhaddon his son succeeded him as
king.

Hezekiah's Illness

20 In those days Hezekiah became
ill and was at the point of death.
The prophet Isaiah son of Amoz went to
him and said, "This is what the LORD
says: Put your house in order, because
you are going to die; you will not
recover."
2 Hezekiah turned his face to the wall
and prayed to the LORD, 3 "Remember,
O LORD, how I have walked before you
faithfully and with wholehearted devotion and have done what is good in your
eyes." And Hezekiah wept bitterly.
4 Before Isaiah had left the middle
court, the word of the LORD came to
him: 5 "Go back and tell Hezekiah, the
leader of my people, 'This is what the
LORD, the God of your father David,
says: I have heard your prayer and seen
your tears; I will heal you. On the third
day from now you will go up to the
temple of the LORD. 6 I will add fifteen
years to your life. And I will deliver you
and this city from the hand of the king of
Assyria. I will defend this city for my
sake and for the sake of my servant
David.' "
7 Then Isaiah said, "Prepare a poultice of figs." They did so and applied it
to the boil, and he recovered.
8 Hezekiah had asked Isaiah, "What
will be the sign that the LORD will heal
me and that I will go up to the temple of
the LORD on the third day from now?"

9 Isaiah answered, "This is the LORD's
sign to you that the LORD will do what
he has promised: Shall the shadow go
forward ten steps, or shall it go back ten
steps?"
10 "It is a simple matter for the shadow
to go forward ten steps," said Hezekiah. "Rather, have it go back ten
steps."
11 Then the prophet Isaiah called
upon the LORD, and the LORD made the
shadow go back the ten steps it had gone
down on the stairway of Ahaz.

Envoys From Babylon

12 At that time Merodach-Baladan
son of Baladan king of Babylon sent
Hezekiah letters and a gift, because he
had heard of Hezekiah's illness.
13 Hezekiah received the messengers
and showed them all that was in his
storehouses—the silver, the gold, the
spices and the fine oil—his armoury and
everything found among his treasures.
There was nothing in his palace or in all
his kingdom that Hezekiah did not show
them.
14 Then Isaiah the prophet went to
King Hezekiah and asked, "What did
those men say, and where did they come
from?"
"From a distant land," Hezekiah replied. "They came from Babylon."
15 The prophet asked, "What did they
see in your palace?"
"They saw everything in my palace,"
Hezekiah said. "There is nothing
among my treasures that I did not show
them."
16 Then Isaiah said to Hezekiah,
"Hear the word of the LORD: 17 The time
will surely come when everything in
your palace, and all that your fathers
have stored up until this day, will be
carried off to Babylon. Nothing will be
left, says the LORD. 18 And some of your
descendants, your own flesh and blood,
that will be born to you, will be taken
away, and they will become eunuchs in
the palace of the king of Babylon."
19 "The word of the LORD you have
spoken is good," Hezekiah replied. For
he thought, "Will there not be peace
and security in my lifetime?"
20 As for the other events of Hezekiah's reign, all his achievements and
how he made the pool and the tunnel by
which he brought water into the city,
are they not written in the book of
the annals of the kings of Judah?
21 Hezekiah rested with his fathers. And
Manasseh his son succeeded him as
king.

NEW TESTAMENT READING

Acts 28:1–16

Ashore on Malta

28 Once safely on shore, we found
out that the island was called
Malta. 2 The islanders showed us unusual kindness. They built a fire and
welcomed us all because it was raining
and cold. 3 Paul gathered a pile of brush-
wood and, as he put it on the fire, a
viper, driven out by the heat, fastened
itself on his hand. 4 When the islanders
saw the snake hanging from his hand,
they said to each other, "This man must
be a murderer; for though he escaped
from the sea, Justice has not allowed
him to live." 5 But Paul shook the snake
off into the fire and suffered no ill
effects. 6 The people expected him to
swell up or suddenly fall dead, but after
waiting a long time and seeing nothing
unusual happen to him, they changed
their minds and said he was a god.
7 There was an estate near by that
belonged to Publius, the chief official of
the island. He welcomed us to his home
and for three days entertained us hos-
pitably. 8 His father was sick in bed,
suffering from fever and dysentery.
Paul went in to see him and, after
prayer, placed his hands on him and
healed him. 9 When this had happened,
the rest of the sick on the island came
and were cured. 10 They honoured us in
many ways and when we were ready to
sail, they furnished us with the supplies
we needed.

Arrival at Rome

11After three months we put out to
sea in a ship that had wintered in the
island. It was an Alexandrian ship with
the figurehead of the twin gods Castor
and Pollux. 12We put in at Syracuse and
stayed there three days. 13From there
we set sail and arrived at Rhegium. The
next day the south wind came up, and
on the following day we reached
Puteoli. 14There we found some
brothers who invited us to spend a week
with them. And so we came to Rome.
15The brothers there had heard that we
were coming, and they travelled as far
as the Forum of Appius and the Three
Taverns to meet us. At the sight of these
men Paul thanked God and was encouraged. 16When we got to Rome, Paul was
allowed to live by himself, with a soldier
to guard him.

READING FROM PSALMS

Psalm 83:1–18

A song. A psalm of Asaph.

1O God, do not keep silent;
be not quiet, O God, be not still.
2See how your enemies are astir,
how your foes rear their heads.
3With cunning they conspire against
your people;
they plot against those you cherish.
4"Come," they say, "let us destroy
them as a nation,
that the name of Israel be
remembered no more."
5With one mind they plot together;
they form an alliance against you—
6the tents of Edom and the
Ishmaelites,
of Moab and the Hagrites,
7Gebal, Ammon and Amalek,
Philistia, with the people of Tyre.
8Even Assyria has joined them
to lend strength to the descendants
of Lot. *Selah*

9Do to them as you did to Midian,
as you did to Sisera and Jabin at
the river Kishon,
10who perished at Endor
and became like refuse on the
ground.
11Make their nobles like Oreb and
Zeeb,
all their princes like Zebah and
Zalmunna,
12who said, "Let us take possession
of the pasture-lands of God."

13Make them like tumble-weed, O my
God,
like chaff before the wind.
14As fire consumes the forest
or a flame sets the mountains
ablaze,
15so pursue them with your tempest
and terrify them with your storm.
16Cover their faces with shame
so that men will seek your name, O
LORD.

17May they ever be ashamed and
dismayed;
may they perish in disgrace.
18Let them know that you, whose name
is the LORD—
that you alone are the Most High
over all the earth.

JULY 11

DAY 192

OLD TESTAMENT READING
2 Kings 21:1–22:20

Manasseh King of Judah

21 Manasseh was twelve years old
when he became king, and he
reigned in Jerusalem for fifty-five years.
His mother's name was Hephzibah. 2He
did evil in the eyes of the LORD, following the detestable practices of the nations the LORD had driven out before
the Israelites. 3He rebuilt the high
places his father Hezekiah had destroyed; he also erected altars to Baal
and made an Asherah pole, as Ahab
king of Israel had done. He bowed
down to all the starry hosts and worshipped them. 4He built altars in the temple
of the LORD, of which the LORD had
said, "In Jerusalem I will put my
Name." 5In both courts of the temple of
the LORD, he built altars to all the starry
hosts. 6He sacrificed his own son in the
fire, practised sorcery and divination,
and consulted mediums and spiritists.
He did much evil in the eyes of the
LORD, provoking him to anger.

7He took the carved Asherah pole he
had made and put it in the temple, of
which the LORD had said to David and
to his son Solomon, "In this temple and
in Jerusalem, which I have chosen out
of all the tribes of Israel, I will put my
Name for ever. 8I will not again make
the feet of the Israelites wander from
the land I gave their forefathers, if only
they will be careful to do everything I
commanded them and will keep the
whole Law that my servant Moses gave
them." 9But the people did not listen.
Manasseh led them astray, so that they
did more evil than the nations the LORD
had destroyed before the Israelites.

10The LORD said through his servants
the prophets: 11"Manasseh king of
Judah has committed these detestable
sins. He has done more evil than the
Amorites who preceded him and has
led Judah into sin with his idols.
12Therefore this is what the LORD, the
God of Israel, says: I am going to bring
such disaster on Jerusalem and Judah
that the ears of everyone who hears of it
will tingle. 13I will stretch out over Jerusalem the measuring line used against
Samaria and the plumb-line used
against the house of Ahab. I will wipe
out Jerusalem as one wipes out a dish,
wiping it and turning it upside-down. 14I
will forsake the remnant of my inheritance and hand them over to their
enemies. They will be looted and plundered by all their foes, 15because they
have done evil in my eyes and have
provoked me to anger from the day
their forefathers came out of Egypt until this day."

16Moreover, Manasseh also shed so
much innocent blood that he filled Jerusalem from end to end—besides the sin
that he had caused Judah to commit, so
that they did evil in the eyes of the
LORD.

17As for the other events of Manasseh's reign, and all he did, including
the sin he committed, are they not written in the book of the annals of the kings
of Judah? 18Manasseh rested with his
fathers and was buried in his palace
garden, the garden of Uzza. And Amon
his son succeeded him as king.

Amon King of Judah

19Amon was twenty-two years old
when he became king, and he reigned in
Jerusalem for two years. His mother's
name was Meshullemeth daughter of
Haruz; she was from Jotbah. 20He did
evil in the eyes of the LORD, as his father
Manasseh had done. 21He walked in all
the ways of his father; he worshipped
the idols his father had worshipped, and
bowed down to them. 22He forsook the

LORD, the God of his fathers, and did not walk in the way of the LORD.

23Amon's officials conspired against him and assassinated the king in his palace. 24Then the people of the land killed all who had plotted against King Amon, and they made Josiah his son king in his place.

25As for the other events of Amon's reign, and what he did, are they not written in the book of the annals of the kings of Judah? 26He was buried in his grave in the garden of Uzza. And Josiah his son succeeded him as king.

The Book of the Law Found

22 Josiah was eight years old when he became king, and he reigned in Jerusalem for thirty-one years. His mother's name was Jedidah daughter of Adaiah; she was from Bozkath. 2He did what was right in the eyes of the LORD and walked in all the ways of his father David, not turning aside to the right or to the left.

3In the eighteenth year of his reign, King Josiah sent the secretary, Shaphan son of Azaliah, the son of Meshullam, to the temple of the LORD. He said: 4"Go up to Hilkiah the high priest and make him get ready the money that has been brought into the temple of the LORD, which the doorkeepers have collected from the people. 5Make them entrust it to the men appointed to supervise the work on the temple. And make these men pay the workers who repair the temple of the LORD—6the carpenters, the builders and the masons. Also make them purchase timber and dressed stone to repair the temple. 7But they need not account for the money entrusted to them, because they are acting faithfully."

8Hilkiah the high priest said to Shaphan the secretary, "I have found the Book of the Law in the temple of the LORD." He gave it to Shaphan, who read it. 9Then Shaphan the secretary went to the king and reported to him: "Your officials have paid out the money that was in the temple of the LORD and have entrusted it to the workers and supervisors at the temple." 10Then Shaphan the secretary informed the king, "Hilkiah the priest has given me a book." And Shaphan read from it in the presence of the king.

11When the king heard the words of the Book of the Law, he tore his robes. 12He gave these orders to Hilkiah the priest, Ahikam son of Shaphan, Acbor son of Micaiah, Shaphan the secretary and Asaiah the king's attendant: 13"Go and enquire of the LORD for me and for the people and for all Judah about what is written in this book that has been found. Great is the LORD's anger that burns against us because our fathers have not obeyed the words of this book; they have not acted in accordance with all that is written there concerning us."

14Hilkiah the priest, Ahikam, Acbor, Shaphan and Asaiah went to speak to the prophetess Huldah, who was the wife of Shallum son of Tikvah, the son of Harhas, keeper of the wardrobe. She lived in Jerusalem, in the Second District.

15She said to them, "This is what the LORD, the God of Israel, says: Tell the man who sent you to me, 16'This is what the LORD says: I am going to bring disaster on this place and its people, according to everything written in the book the king of Judah has read. 17Because they have forsaken me and burned incense to other gods and provoked me to anger by all the idols their hands have made, my anger will burn against this place and will not be quenched.' 18Tell the king of Judah, who sent you to enquire of the LORD, 'This is what the LORD, the God of Israel, says concerning the words you heard: 19Because your heart was responsive and you humbled yourself before the LORD when you heard what I have spoken against this place and its people, that they would become accursed and laid waste, and because you tore your robes and wept in my presence, I have heard you, declares the LORD.

20Therefore I will gather you to your
fathers, and you will be buried in peace.
Your eyes will not see all the disaster I
am going to bring on this place.'"

So they took her answer back to the king.

NEW TESTAMENT READING
Acts 28:17–31

Paul Preaches at Rome Under Guard

17Three days later he called together
the leaders of the Jews. When they had
assembled, Paul said to them: "My
brothers, although I have done nothing
against our people or against the customs of our ancestors, I was arrested in
Jerusalem and handed over to the Romans.
18They examined me and wanted
to release me, because I was not guilty
of any crime deserving death.
19But
when the Jews objected, I was compelled to appeal to Caesar—not that I had
any charge to bring against my own
people.
20For this reason I have asked to
see you and talk with you. It is because
of the hope of Israel that I am bound
with this chain."

21They replied, "We have not received any letters from Judea concerning you, and none of the brothers who
have come from there has reported or
said anything bad about you.
22But we
want to hear what your views are, for we
know that people everywhere are talking against this sect."

23They arranged to meet Paul on a
certain day, and came in even larger
numbers to the place where he was
staying. From morning till evening he
explained and declared to them the
kingdom of God and tried to convince
them about Jesus from the Law of
Moses and from the Prophets.
24Some
were convinced by what he said, but
others would not believe.
25They disagreed among themselves and began to
leave after Paul had made this final
statement: "The Holy Spirit spoke the
truth to your forefathers when he said
through Isaiah the prophet:

26" 'Go to this people and say,
"You will be ever hearing but never
understanding;
you will be ever seeing but never
perceiving."
27For this people's heart has become
calloused;
they hardly hear with their ears,
and they have closed their eyes.
Otherwise they might see with their
eyes,
hear with their ears,
understand with their hearts
and turn, and I would heal them.'

28"Therefore I want you to know that
God's salvation has been sent to the
Gentiles, and they will listen!"

30For two whole years Paul stayed
there in his own rented house and welcomed all who came to see him.
31Boldly and without hindrance he
preached the kingdom of God and
taught about the Lord Jesus Christ.

READING FROM PROVERBS
Proverbs 16:28–17:4

28A perverse man stirs up dissension,
and a gossip separates close
friends.

29A violent man entices his neighbour
and leads him down a path that is
not good.

30He who winks with his eye is plotting
perversity;
he who purses his lips is bent on
evil.

31Grey hair is a crown of splendour;
it is attained by a righteous life.

32Better a patient man than a warrior,
a man who controls his temper
than one who takes a city.

[33]The lot is cast into the lap,
but its every decision is from the
LORD.

17 Better a dry crust with peace
and quiet
than a house full of feasting, with
strife.

[2]A wise servant will rule over a
disgraceful son,
and will share the inheritance as
one of the brothers.

[3]The crucible for silver and the
furnace for gold,
but the LORD tests the heart.

[4]A wicked man listens to evil lips;
a liar pays attention to a malicious
tongue.

DAY 193

JULY 12

OLD TESTAMENT READING
2 Kings 23:1–24:7

Josiah Renews the Covenant

23 Then the king called together all
the elders of Judah and Jerusalem. [2]He went up to the temple of the
LORD with the men of Judah, the people
of Jerusalem, the priests and the
prophets—all the people from the least
to the greatest. He read in their hearing
all the words of the Book of the Covenant, which had been found in the
temple of the LORD. [3]The king stood by
the pillar and renewed the covenant in
the presence of the LORD—to follow the
LORD and keep his commands, regulations and decrees with all his heart and
all his soul, thus confirming the words of
the covenant written in this book. Then
all the people pledged themselves to the
covenant.
[4]The king ordered Hilkiah the high
priest, the priests next in rank and the
doorkeepers to remove from the temple
of the LORD all the articles made for
Baal and Asherah and all the starry
hosts. He burned them outside Jerusalem in the fields of the Kidron Valley
and took the ashes to Bethel. [5]He did
away with the pagan priests appointed
by the kings of Judah to burn incense on
the high places of the towns of Judah
and on those around Jerusalem—those
who burned incense to Baal, to the sun
and moon, to the constellations and to
all the starry hosts. [6]He took the Asherah pole from the temple of the LORD
to the Kidron Valley outside Jerusalem
and burned it there. He ground it to
powder and scattered the dust over the
graves of the common people. [7]He also
tore down the quarters of the male
shrine-prostitutes, which were in the
temple of the LORD and where women
did weaving for Asherah.
[8]Josiah brought all the priests from
the towns of Judah and desecrated the
high places, from Geba to Beersheba,
where the priests had burned incense.
He broke down the shrines at the gates
—at the entrance to the Gate of Joshua,
the city governor, which is on the left of
the city gate. [9]Although the priests
of the high places did not serve at the
altar of the LORD in Jerusalem, they ate
unleavened bread with their fellow
priests.
[10]He desecrated Topheth, which was
in the Valley of Ben Hinnom, so no-one
could use it to sacrifice his son or daughter in the fire to Molech. [11]He removed
from the entrance to the temple of the
LORD the horses that the kings of Judah
had dedicated to the sun. They were in

the court near the room of an official
named Nathan-Melech. Josiah then
burned the chariots dedicated to the
sun.
[12]He pulled down the altars the kings
of Judah had erected on the roof near
the upper room of Ahaz, and the altars
Manasseh had built in the two courts of
the temple of the LORD. He removed
them from there, smashed them to
pieces and threw the rubble into the
Kidron Valley. [13]The king also desecrated the high places that were east of
Jerusalem on the south of the Hill of
Corruption—the ones Solomon king
of Israel had built for Ashtoreth the vile
goddess of the Sidonians, for Chemosh
the vile god of Moab, and for Molech
the detestable god of the people of
Ammon. [14]Josiah smashed the sacred
stones and cut down the Asherah poles
and covered the sites with human
bones.
[15]Even the altar at Bethel, the high
place made by Jeroboam son of Nebat,
who had caused Israel to sin—even that
altar and high place he demolished. He
burned the high place and ground it to
powder, and burned the Asherah pole
also. [16]Then Josiah looked around, and
when he saw the tombs that were there
on the hillside, he had the bones removed from them and burned on the
altar to defile it, in accordance with
the word of the LORD proclaimed by the
man of God who foretold these things.
[17]The king asked, "What is that
tombstone I see?"
The men of the city said, "It marks
the tomb of the man of God who came
from Judah and pronounced against the
altar of Bethel the very things you have
done to it."
[18]"Leave it alone," he said. "Don't
let anyone disturb his bones." So they
spared his bones and those of the
prophet who had come from Samaria.
[19]Just as he had done at Bethel,
Josiah removed and defiled all the
shrines at the high places that the kings
of Israel had built in the towns of
Samaria that had provoked the LORD to
anger. [20]Josiah slaughtered all the
priests of those high places on the altars
and burned human bones on them.
Then he went back to Jerusalem.
[21]The king gave this order to all the
people: "Celebrate the Passover to the
LORD your God, as it is written in this
Book of the Covenant." [22]Not since the
days of the judges who led Israel, nor
throughout the days of the kings of
Israel and the kings of Judah, had any
such Passover been observed. [23]But in
the eighteenth year of King Josiah, this
Passover was celebrated to the LORD in
Jerusalem.
[24]Furthermore, Josiah got rid of the
mediums and spiritists, the household
gods, the idols and all the other detestable things seen in Judah and
Jerusalem. This he did to fulfil the requirements of the law written in the
book that Hilkiah the priest had discovered in the temple of the LORD.
[25]Neither before nor after Josiah was
there a king like him who turned to the
LORD as he did—with all his heart and
with all his soul and with all his strength,
in accordance with all the Law of
Moses.
[26]Nevertheless, the LORD did not turn
away from the heat of his fierce anger,
which burned against Judah because of
all that Manasseh had done to provoke
him to anger. [27]So the LORD said, "I will
remove Judah also from my presence as
I removed Israel, and I will reject Jerusalem, the city I chose, and this temple,
about which I said, 'There shall my
Name be.'"
[28]As for the other events of Josiah's
reign, and all he did, are they not written in the book of the annals of the kings
of Judah?
[29]While Josiah was king, Pharaoh
Neco king of Egypt went up to the
Euphrates River to help the king of
Assyria. King Josiah marched out to
meet him in battle, but Neco faced him
and killed him at Megiddo. [30]Josiah's
servants brought his body in a chariot
from Megiddo to Jerusalem and buried
him in his own tomb. And the people of

the land took Jehoahaz son of Josiah
and anointed him and made him king in
place of his father.

Jehoahaz King of Judah

31Jehoahaz was twenty-three years
old when he became king, and he
reigned in Jerusalem for three months.
His mother's name was Hamutal daughter of Jeremiah; she was from Libnah.
32He did evil in the eyes of the LORD,
just as his fathers had done. 33Pharaoh
Neco put him in chains at Riblah in the
land of Hamath so that he might not
reign in Jerusalem, and he imposed on
Judah a levy of a hundred talents of
silver and a talent of gold. 34Pharaoh
Neco made Eliakim son of Josiah king
in place of his father Josiah and changed
Eliakim's name to Jehoiakim. But he
took Jehoahaz and carried him off to
Egypt, and there he died. 35Jehoiakim
paid Pharaoh Neco the silver and gold
he demanded. In order to do so, he
taxed the land and exacted the silver
and gold from the people of the land
according to their assessments.

Jehoiakim King of Judah

36Jehoiakim was twenty-five years old
when he became king, and he reigned
in Jerusalem for eleven years. His
mother's name was Zebidah daughter
of Pedaiah; she was from Rumah.
37And he did evil in the eyes of the
LORD, just as his fathers had done.
24 During Jehoiakim's reign,
Nebuchadnezzar king of Babylon invaded the land, and Jehoiakim
became his vassal for three years. But
then he changed his mind and rebelled
against Nebuchadnezzar. 2The LORD
sent Babylonian, Aramean, Moabite
and Ammonite raiders against him. He
sent them to destroy Judah, in accordance with the word of the LORD proclaimed by his servants the prophets.
3Surely these things happened to Judah
according to the LORD's command, in
order to remove them from his presence because of the sins of Manasseh
and all he had done, 4including the
shedding of innocent blood. For he
had filled Jerusalem with innocent
blood, and the LORD was not willing
to forgive.
5As for the other events of
Jehoiakim's reign, and all he did, are
they not written in the book of the
annals of the kings of Judah?
6Jehoiakim rested with his fathers. And
Jehoiachin his son succeeded him as
king.
7The king of Egypt did not march out
from his own country again, because the
king of Babylon had taken all his territory, from the Wadi of Egypt to the
Euphrates River.

NEW TESTAMENT READING
Romans 1:1–17

1 Paul, a servant of Christ Jesus,
called to be an apostle and set
apart for the gospel of God—2the
gospel he promised beforehand
through his prophets in the Holy
Scriptures 3regarding his Son, who as
to his human nature was a descendant
of David, 4and who through the Spirit
of holiness was declared with power to
be the Son of God, by his resurrection
from the dead: Jesus Christ our Lord.
5Through him and for his name's sake,
we received grace and apostleship
to call people from among all the
Gentiles to the obedience that comes
from faith. 6And you also are among
those who are called to belong to Jesus
Christ.

7To all in Rome who are loved by
God and called to be saints:

Grace and peace to you from God
our Father and from the Lord Jesus
Christ.

Paul's Longing to Visit Rome

8First, I thank my God through Jesus
Christ for all of you, because your faith
is being reported all over the world.
9God, whom I serve with my whole
heart in preaching the gospel of his Son,
is my witness how constantly I remember you 10in my prayers at all times; and
I pray that now at last by God's will the
way may be opened for me to come to
you.

11I long to see you so that I may
impart to you some spiritual gift to
make you strong—12that is, that you
and I may be mutually encouraged by
each other's faith. 13I do not want you to
be unaware, brothers, that I planned
many times to come to you (but have
been prevented from doing so until
now) in order that I might have a harvest among you, just as I have had
among the other Gentiles.

14I am bound both to Greeks and
non-Greeks, both to the wise and the
foolish. 15That is why I am so eager to
preach the gospel also to you who are at
Rome.

16I am not ashamed of the gospel,
because it is the power of God for the
salvation of everyone who believes: first
for the Jew, then for the Gentile. 17For
in the gospel a righteousness from God
is revealed, a righteousness that is by
faith from first to last, just as it is written: "The righteous will live by faith."

READING FROM PSALMS
Psalm 84:1–7

For the director of music. According to *gittith*. Of the Sons of Korah. A psalm.

1How lovely is your dwelling-place,
O LORD Almighty!
2My soul yearns, even faints,
for the courts of the LORD;
my heart and my flesh cry out
for the living God.

3Even the sparrow has found a home,
and the swallow a nest for herself,
where she may have her young—
a place near your altar,
O LORD Almighty, my King and my God.
4Blessed are those who dwell in your house;
they are ever praising you. *Selah*

5Blessed are those whose strength is in you,
who have set their hearts on pilgrimage.
6As they pass through the Valley of Baca,
they make it a place of springs;
the autumn rains also cover it with pools.
7They go from strength to strength,
till each appears before God in Zion.

JULY 13

DAY 194

OLD TESTAMENT READING
2 Kings 24:8–25:30

Jehoiachin King of Judah

8Jehoiachin was eighteen years old
when he became king, and he reigned in
Jerusalem for three months. His
mother's name was Nehushta daughter
of Elnathan; she was from Jerusalem.
9He did evil in the eyes of the LORD, just
as his father had done.

10At that time the officers of
Nebuchadnezzar king of Babylon advanced on Jerusalem and laid siege to it,
11and Nebuchadnezzar himself came up
to the city while his officers were besieging it. 12Jehoiachin king of Judah, his

mother, his attendants, his nobles and
his officials all surrendered to him.
In the eighth year of the reign of the
king of Babylon, he took Jehoiachin
prisoner. 13As the LORD had declared,
Nebuchadnezzar removed all the treasures from the temple of the LORD and
from the royal palace, and took away all
the gold articles that Solomon king of
Israel had made for the temple of the
LORD. 14He carried into exile all Jerusalem: all the officers and fighting men,
and all the craftsmen and artisans—a
total of ten thousand. Only the poorest
people of the land were left.
15Nebuchadnezzar took Jehoiachin
captive to Babylon. He also took from
Jerusalem to Babylon the king's
mother, his wives, his officials and the
leading men of the land. 16The king of
Babylon also deported to Babylon the
entire force of seven thousand fighting
men, strong and fit for war, and a
thousand craftsmen and artisans. 17He
made Mattaniah, Jehoiachin's uncle,
king in his place and changed his name
to Zedekiah.

Zedekiah King of Judah

18Zedekiah was twenty-one years old
when he became king, and he reigned
in Jerusalem for eleven years. His
mother's name was Hamutal daughter
of Jeremiah; she was from Libnah. 19He
did evil in the eyes of the LORD, just as
Jehoiakim had done. 20It was because of
the LORD's anger that all this happened
to Jerusalem and Judah, and in the end
he thrust them from his presence.

The Fall of Jerusalem

Now Zedekiah rebelled against the
king of Babylon.

25 So in the ninth year of Zedekiah's reign, on the tenth day of
the tenth month, Nebuchadnezzar king
of Babylon marched against Jerusalem
with his whole army. He encamped outside the city and built siege works all
around it. 2The city was kept under
siege until the eleventh year of King
Zedekiah. 3By the ninth day of the
⌞fourth⌟ month the famine in the city
had become so severe that there was
no food for the people to eat. 4Then
the city wall was broken through, and
the whole army fled at night through the
gate between the two walls near the
king's garden, though the Babylonians
were surrounding the city. They fled
towards the Arabah, 5but the Babylonian army pursued the king and overtook him in the plains of Jericho. All his
soldiers were separated from him and
scattered, 6and he was captured. He
was taken to the king of Babylon at
Riblah, where sentence was pronounced on him. 7They killed the sons
of Zedekiah before his eyes. Then they
put out his eyes, bound him with bronze
shackles and took him to Babylon.
8On the seventh day of the fifth
month, in the nineteenth year of
Nebuchadnezzar king of Babylon,
Nebuzaradan commander of the imperial guard, an official of the king of
Babylon, came to Jerusalem. 9He set
fire to the temple of the LORD, the royal
palace and all the houses of Jerusalem.
Every important building he burned
down. 10The whole Babylonian army,
under the commander of the imperial
guard, broke down the walls around
Jerusalem. 11Nebuzaradan the commander of the guard carried into exile
the people who remained in the city,
along with the rest of the populace and
those who had gone over to the king of
Babylon. 12But the commander left behind some of the poorest people of the
land to work the vineyards and fields.
13The Babylonians broke up the
bronze pillars, the movable stands and
the bronze Sea that were at the temple
of the LORD and they carried the bronze
to Babylon. 14They also took away the
pots, shovels, wick trimmers, dishes
and all the bronze articles used in the
temple service. 15The commander of
the imperial guard took away the censers and sprinkling bowls—all that were
made of pure gold or silver.

[16]The bronze from the two pillars, the
Sea and the movable stands, which
Solomon had made for the temple of the
LORD, was more than could be weighed.
[17]Each pillar was twenty-seven feet
high. The bronze capital on top of one
pillar was four and a half feet high and
was decorated with a network and
pomegranates of bronze all around.
The other pillar, with its network, was
similar.
[18]The commander of the guard took
as prisoners Seraiah the chief priest,
Zephaniah the priest next in rank and
the three doorkeepers. [19]Of those still
in the city, he took the officer in charge
of the fighting men and five royal advisers. He also took the secretary who was
chief officer in charge of conscripting
the people of the land and sixty of his
men who were found in the city.
[20]Nebuzaradan the commander took
them all and brought them to the king of
Babylon at Riblah. [21]There at Riblah,
in the land of Hamath, the king had
them executed.
So Judah went into captivity, away
from her land.
[22]Nebuchadnezzar king of Babylon
appointed Gedaliah son of Ahikam, the
son of Shaphan, to be over the people
he had left behind in Judah. [23]When all
the army officers and their men heard
that the king of Babylon had appointed
Gedaliah as governor, they came to
Gedaliah at Mizpah—Ishmael son of
Nethaniah, Johanan son of Kareah,
Seraiah son of Tanhumeth the
Netophathite, Jaazaniah the son of the
Maacathite, and their men. [24]Gedaliah
took an oath to reassure them and their
men. "Do not be afraid of the Babylonian officials," he said. "Settle down in
the land and serve the king of Babylon,
and it will go well with you."
[25]In the seventh month, however,
Ishmael son of Nethaniah, the son of
Elishama, who was of royal blood,
came with ten men and assassinated
Gedaliah and also the men of Judah and
the Babylonians who were with him at
Mizpah. [26]At this, all the people from
the least to the greatest, together with
the army officers, fled to Egypt for fear
of the Babylonians.

Jehoiachin Released

[27]In the thirty-seventh year of the
exile of Jehoiachin king of Judah, in the
year Evil-Merodach became king of
Babylon, he released Jehoiachin from
prison on the twenty-seventh day of the
twelfth month. [28]He spoke kindly to
him and gave him a seat of honour
higher than those of the other kings
who were with him in Babylon. [29]So
Jehoiachin put aside his prison clothes
and for the rest of his life ate regularly at
the king's table. [30]Day by day the king
gave Jehoiachin a regular allowance as
long as he lived.

NEW TESTAMENT READING
Romans 1:18–32

God's Wrath Against Mankind

[18]The wrath of God is being revealed
from heaven against all the godlessness
and wickedness of men who suppress
the truth by their wickedness, [19]since
what may be known about God is plain
to them, because God has made it plain
to them. [20]For since the creation of the
world God's invisible qualities—his
eternal power and divine nature—have
been clearly seen, being understood
from what has been made, so that men
are without excuse.
[21]For although they knew God, they
neither glorified him as God nor gave
thanks to him, but their thinking became futile and their foolish hearts were
darkened. [22]Although they claimed to
be wise, they became fools [23]and exchanged the glory of the immortal God
for images made to look like mortal
man and birds and animals and reptiles.
[24]Therefore God gave them over in

the sinful desires of their hearts to sexual impurity for the degrading of their
bodies with one another. 25They exchanged the truth of God for a lie, and
worshipped and served created things
rather than the Creator—who is for
ever praised. Amen.
26Because of this, God gave them
over to shameful lusts. Even their
women exchanged natural relations for
unnatural ones. 27In the same way the
men also abandoned natural relations
with women and were inflamed with lust
for one another. Men committed indecent acts with other men, and received
in themselves the due penalty for their
perversion.
28Furthermore, since they did not
think it worth while to retain the knowledge of God, he gave them over to a
depraved mind, to do what ought not to
be done. 29They have become filled with
every kind of wickedness, evil, greed
and depravity. They are full of envy,
murder, strife, deceit and malice. They
are gossips, 30slanderers, God-haters,
insolent, arrogant and boastful; they
invent ways of doing evil; they disobey
their parents; 31they are senseless, faithless, heartless, ruthless. 32Although
they know God's righteous decree that
those who do such things deserve death,
they not only continue to do these very things but also approve of those who practise them.

READING FROM PSALMS

Psalm 84:8–12

8Hear my prayer, O LORD God
Almighty;
listen to me, O God of Jacob.
Selah
9Look upon our shield, O God;
look with favour on your anointed
one.

10Better is one day in your courts
than a thousand elsewhere;
I would rather be a doorkeeper in the
house of my God
than dwell in the tents of the
wicked.
11For the LORD God is a sun and shield;
the LORD bestows favour and
honour;
no good thing does he withhold
from those whose walk is
blameless.

12O LORD Almighty,
blessed is the man who trusts in
you.

DAY 195

JULY 14

OLD TESTAMENT READING

Jonah 1:1–4:11

Jonah Flees From the LORD

1 The word of the LORD came to
Jonah son of Amittai: 2"Go to the
great city of Nineveh and preach against
it, because its wickedness has come up
before me."
3But Jonah ran away from the LORD
and headed for Tarshish. He went down
to Joppa, where he found a ship bound
for that port. After paying the fare, he
went aboard and sailed for Tarshish to
flee from the LORD.
4Then the LORD sent a great wind on
the sea, and such a violent storm arose
that the ship threatened to break up.
5All the sailors were afraid and each
cried out to his own god. And they
threw the cargo into the sea to lighten
the ship.
But Jonah had gone below deck,

where he lay down and fell into a deep
sleep. 6The captain went to him and
said, "How can you sleep? Get up and
call on your god! Maybe he will take
notice of us, and we will not perish."
7Then the sailors said to each other,
"Come, let us cast lots to find out who is
responsible for this calamity." They
cast lots and the lot fell on Jonah.
8So they asked him, "Tell us, who is
responsible for making all this trouble
for us? What do you do? Where do you
come from? What is your country?
From what people are you?"
9He answered, "I am a Hebrew and I
worship the LORD, the God of heaven,
who made the sea and the land."
10This terrified them and they asked,
"What have you done?" (They knew he
was running away from the LORD, because he had already told them so.)
11The sea was getting rougher and
rougher. So they asked him, "What
should we do to you to make the sea
calm down for us?"
12"Pick me up and throw me into the
sea," he replied, "and it will become
calm. I know that it is my fault that this
great storm has come upon you."
13Instead, the men did their best to
row back to land. But they could not,
for the sea grew even wilder than before. 14Then they cried to the LORD, "O
LORD, please do not let us die for taking
this man's life. Do not hold us accountable for killing an innocent man, for
you, O LORD, have done as you
pleased." 15Then they took Jonah and
threw him overboard, and the raging
sea grew calm. 16At this the men greatly
feared the LORD, and they offered a
sacrifice to the LORD and made vows to
him.
17But the LORD provided a great fish
to swallow Jonah, and Jonah was inside
the fish three days and three nights.

Jonah's Prayer

2 From inside the fish Jonah prayed
to the LORD his God. 2He said:

"In my distress I called to the LORD,
and he answered me.
From the depths of the grave I called
for help,
and you listened to my cry.
3You hurled me into the deep,
into the very heart of the seas,
and the currents swirled about me;
all your waves and breakers
swept over me.
4I said, 'I have been banished
from your sight;
yet I will look again
towards your holy temple.'
5The engulfing waters threatened me,
the deep surrounded me;
seaweed was wrapped around my
head.
6To the roots of the mountains I sank
down;
the earth beneath barred me in for
ever.
But you brought my life up from the
pit,
O LORD my God.

7"When my life was ebbing away,
I remembered you, LORD,
and my prayer rose to you,
to your holy temple.

8"Those who cling to worthless idols
forfeit the grace that could be
theirs.
9But I, with a song of thanksgiving,
will sacrifice to you.
What I have vowed I will make good.
Salvation comes from the LORD."

10And the LORD commanded the fish,
and it vomited Jonah onto dry land.

Jonah Goes to Nineveh

3 Then the word of the LORD came to
Jonah a second time: 2"Go to the
great city of Nineveh and proclaim to it
the message I give you."
3Jonah obeyed the word of the LORD
and went to Nineveh. Now Nineveh was
a very important city—a visit required
three days. 4On the first day, Jonah

started into the city. He proclaimed: "Forty more days and Nineveh will be overturned." 5The Ninevites believed God. They declared a fast, and all of them, from the greatest to the least, put on sackcloth.

6When the news reached the king of Nineveh, he rose from his throne, took off his royal robes, covered himself with sackcloth and sat down in the dust. 7Then he issued a proclamation in Nineveh:

"By the decree of the king and his nobles:

Do not let any man or beast, herd or flock, taste anything; do not let them eat or drink. 8But let man and beast be covered with sackcloth. Let everyone call urgently on God. Let them give up their evil ways and their violence. 9Who knows? God may yet relent and with compassion turn from his fierce anger so that we will not perish."

10When God saw what they did and how they turned from their evil ways, he had compassion and did not bring upon them the destruction he had threatened.

Jonah's Anger at the L*ORD's Compassion*

4 But Jonah was greatly displeased and became angry. 2He prayed to the LORD, "O LORD, is this not what I said when I was still at home? That is why I was so quick to flee to Tarshish. I knew that you are a gracious and compassionate God, slow to anger and abounding in love, a God who relents from sending calamity. 3Now, O LORD, take away my life, for it is better for me to die than to live."

4But the LORD replied, "Have you any right to be angry?"

5Jonah went out and sat down at a place east of the city. There he made himself a shelter, sat in its shade and waited to see what would happen to the city. 6Then the LORD God provided a vine and made it grow up over Jonah to give shade for his head to ease his discomfort, and Jonah was very happy about the vine. 7But at dawn the next day God provided a worm, which chewed the vine so that it withered. 8When the sun rose, God provided a scorching east wind, and the sun blazed on Jonah's head so that he grew faint. He wanted to die, and said, "It would be better for me to die than to live."

9But God said to Jonah, "Do you have a right to be angry about the vine?"

"I do," he said. "I am angry enough to die."

10But the LORD said, "You have been concerned about this vine, though you did not tend it or make it grow. It sprang up overnight and died overnight. 11But Nineveh has more than a hundred and twenty thousand people who cannot tell their right hand from their left, and many cattle as well. Should I not be concerned about that great city?"

NEW TESTAMENT READING

Romans 2:1–16

God's Righteous Judgment

2 You, therefore, have no excuse, you who pass judgment on someone else, for at whatever point you judge the other, you are condemning yourself, because you who pass judgment do the same things. 2Now we know that God's judgment against those who do such things is based on truth. 3So when you, a mere man, pass judgment on them and yet do the same things, do you think you will escape God's judgment? 4Or do you show contempt for the riches of his kindness, tolerance and patience, not realising that God's kindness leads you towards repentance?

5But because of your stubbornness

and your unrepentant heart, you are
storing up wrath against yourself for the
day of God's wrath, when his righteous
judgment will be revealed. 6God "will
give to each person according to what
he has done". 7To those who by persist-
ence in doing good seek glory, honour
and immortality, he will give eternal
life. 8But for those who are self-seeking
and who reject the truth and follow evil,
there will be wrath and anger. 9There
will be trouble and distress for every
human being who does evil: first for the
Jew, then for the Gentile; 10but glory,
honour and peace for everyone who
does good: first for the Jew, then for the
Gentile. 11For God does not show
favouritism.

12All who sin apart from the law will
also perish apart from the law, and all
who sin under the law will be judged by
the law. 13For it is not those who hear
the law who are righteous in God's
sight, but it is those who obey the law
who will be declared righteous.
14(Indeed, when Gentiles, who do not
have the law, do by nature things required by the law, they are a law for
themselves, even though they do not
have the law, 15since they show that the
requirements of the law are written on
their hearts, their consciences also bearing witness, and their thoughts now
accusing, now even defending them.)
16This will take place on the day when
God will judge men's secrets through
Jesus Christ, as my gospel declares.

READING FROM PSALMS

Psalm 85:1–7

For the director of music. Of the Sons of Korah. A psalm.

1You showed favour to your land, O LORD;
you restored the fortunes of Jacob.
2You forgave the iniquity of your people
and covered all their sins. *Selah*
3You set aside all your wrath
and turned from your fierce anger.

4Restore us again, O God our Saviour,
and put away your displeasure towards us.
5Will you be angry with us for ever?
Will you prolong your anger through all generations?
6Will you not revive us again,
that your people may rejoice in you?
7Show us your unfailing love, O LORD,
and grant us your salvation.

JULY 15

DAY 196

OLD TESTAMENT READING

Amos 1:1–2:16

1 The words of Amos, one of the shepherds of Tekoa—what he saw concerning Israel two years before the earthquake, when Uzziah was king of Judah and Jeroboam son of Jehoash was king of Israel.

2He said:

"The LORD roars from Zion
and thunders from Jerusalem;
the pastures of the shepherds dry up,
and the top of Carmel withers."

Judgment on Israel's Neighbours

3This is what the LORD says:

"For three sins of Damascus,
even for four, I will not turn back ⌊my wrath⌋.

Because she threshed Gilead
with sledges having iron teeth,
4I will send fire upon the house of
Hazael
that will consume the fortresses of
Ben-Hadad.
5I will break down the gate of
Damascus;
I will destroy the king who is in the
Valley of Aven
and the one who holds the sceptre in
Beth Eden.
The people of Aram will go into
exile to Kir,"
says the LORD.

6This is what the LORD says:

"For three sins of Gaza,
even for four, I will not turn back
⌊my wrath⌋.
Because she took captive whole
communities
and sold them to Edom,
7I will send fire upon the walls of Gaza
that will consume her fortresses.
8I will destroy the king of Ashdod
and the one who holds the sceptre
in Ashkelon.
I will turn my hand against Ekron,
till the last of the Philistines is
dead,"
says the Sovereign LORD.

9This is what the LORD says:

"For three sins of Tyre,
even for four, I will not turn back
⌊my wrath⌋.
Because she sold whole communities
of captives to Edom,
disregarding a treaty of
brotherhood,
10I will send fire upon the walls of Tyre
that will consume her fortresses."

11This is what the LORD says:

"For three sins of Edom,
even for four, I will not turn back
⌊my wrath⌋.
Because he pursued his brother with
a sword,
stifling all compassion,
because his anger raged continually
and his fury flamed unchecked,
12I will send fire upon Teman
that will consume the fortresses of
Bozrah."

13This is what the LORD says:

"For three sins of Ammon,
even for four, I will not turn back
⌊my wrath⌋.
Because he ripped open the pregnant
women of Gilead
in order to extend his borders,
14I will set fire to the walls of Rabbah
that will consume her fortresses
amid war cries on the day of battle,
amid violent winds on a stormy
day.
15Her king will go into exile,
he and his officials together,"
says the LORD.

2 This is what the LORD says:

"For three sins of Moab,
even for four, I will not turn back
⌊my wrath⌋.
Because he burned, as if to lime,
the bones of Edom's king,
2I will send fire upon Moab
that will consume the fortresses of
Kerioth.
Moab will go down in great tumult
amid war cries and the blast of the
trumpet.
3I will destroy her ruler
and kill all her officials with him,"
says the LORD.

4This is what the LORD says:

"For three sins of Judah,
even for four, I will not turn back
⌊my wrath⌋.
Because they have rejected the law of
the LORD
and have not kept his decrees,

because they have been led astray by
false gods,
the gods their ancestors followed,
5I will send fire upon Judah
that will consume the fortresses of
Jerusalem."

Judgment on Israel

6This is what the LORD says:

"For three sins of Israel,
even for four, I will not turn back
⌞my wrath⌟.
They sell the righteous for silver,
and the needy for a pair of sandals.
7They trample on the heads of the
poor
as upon the dust of the ground
and deny justice to the oppressed.
Father and son use the same girl
and so profane my holy name.
8They lie down beside every altar
on garments taken in pledge.
In the house of their god
they drink wine taken as fines.

9"I destroyed the Amorite before
them,
though he was tall as the cedars
and strong as the oaks.
I destroyed his fruit above
and his roots below.

10"I brought you up out of Egypt,
and I led you for forty years in the
desert
to give you the land of the
Amorites.
11I also raised up prophets from among
your sons
and Nazirites from among your
young men.
Is this not true, people of Israel?"
declares the LORD.
12"But you made the Nazirites drink
wine
and commanded the prophets not
to prophesy.

13"Now then, I will crush you
as a cart crushes when loaded with
grain.
14The swift will not escape,
the strong will not muster their
strength,
and the warrior will not save his
life.
15The archer will not stand his ground,
the fleet-footed soldier will not get
away,
and the horseman will not save his
life.
16Even the bravest warriors
will flee naked on that day,"
declares the LORD.

NEW TESTAMENT READING
Romans 2:17–3:8

The Jews and the Law

17Now you, if you call yourself a Jew;
if you rely on the law and brag about
your relationship to God; 18if you know
his will and approve of what is superior
because you are instructed by the law;
19if you are convinced that you are a
guide for the blind, a light for those who
are in the dark, 20an instructor of the
foolish, a teacher of infants, because
you have in the law the embodiment of
knowledge and truth—21you, then,
who teach others, do you not teach
yourself? You who preach against
stealing, do you steal? 22You who say
that people should not commit adultery, do you commit adultery? You who
abhor idols, do you rob temples? 23You
who brag about the law, do you dishonour God by breaking the law? 24As
it is written: "God's name is blasphemed among the Gentiles because of
you."
25Circumcision has value if you
observe the law, but if you break the
law, you have become as though you
had not been circumcised. 26If those
who are not circumcised keep the law's
requirements, will they not be regarded
as though they were circumcised? 27The
one who is not circumcised physically
and yet obeys the law will condemn you

who, even though you have the written code and circumcision, are a lawbreaker.

[28]A man is not a Jew if he is only one outwardly, nor is circumcision merely outward and physical. [29]No, a man is a Jew if he is one inwardly; and circumcision is circumcision of the heart, by the Spirit, not by the written code. Such a man's praise is not from men, but from God.

God's Faithfulness

3 What advantage, then, is there in being a Jew, or what value is there in circumcision? [2]Much in every way! First of all, they have been entrusted with the very words of God.

[3]What if some did not have faith? Will their lack of faith nullify God's faithfulness? [4]Not at all! Let God be true, and every man a liar. As it is written:

"So that you may be proved right
when you speak
and prevail when you judge."

[5]But if our unrighteousness brings out God's righteousness more clearly, what shall we say? That God is unjust in bringing his wrath on us? (I am using a human argument.) [6]Certainly not! If that were so, how could God judge the world? [7]Someone might argue, "If my falsehood enhances God's truthfulness and so increases his glory, why am I still condemned as a sinner?" [8]Why not say—as we are being slanderously reported as saying and as some claim that we say—"Let us do evil that good may result"? Their condemnation is deserved.

READING FROM PROVERBS

Proverbs 17:5–14

[5]He who mocks the poor shows
contempt for their Maker;
whoever gloats over disaster will
not go unpunished.

[6]Children's children are a crown to the
aged,
and parents are the pride of their
children.

[7]Arrogant lips are unsuited to a fool—
how much worse lying lips to a
ruler!

[8]A bribe is a charm to the one who
gives it;
wherever he turns, he succeeds.

[9]He who covers over an offence
promotes love,
but whoever repeats the matter
separates close friends.

[10]A rebuke impresses a man of
discernment
more than a hundred lashes a fool.

[11]An evil man is bent only on rebellion;
a merciless official will be sent
against him.

[12]Better to meet a bear robbed of her
cubs
than a fool in his folly.

[13]If a man pays back evil for good,
evil will never leave his house.

[14]Starting a quarrel is like breaching a
dam;
so drop the matter before a dispute
breaks out.

OLD TESTAMENT READING
Amos 3:1–4:13

Witnesses Summoned Against Israel

3 Hear this word the LORD has spoken against you, O people of Israel—against the whole family I brought up out of Egypt:

2"You only have I chosen
of all the families of the earth;
therefore I will punish you
for all your sins."

3Do two walk together
unless they have agreed to do so?
4Does a lion roar in the thicket
when he has no prey?
Does he growl in his den
when he has caught nothing?
5Does a bird fall into a trap on the ground
where no snare has been set?
Does a trap spring up from the earth
when there is nothing to catch?
6When a trumpet sounds in a city,
do not the people tremble?
When disaster comes to a city,
has not the LORD caused it?

7Surely the Sovereign LORD does nothing
without revealing his plan
to his servants the prophets.

8The lion has roared—
who will not fear?
The Sovereign LORD has spoken—
who can but prophesy?

9Proclaim to the fortresses of Ashdod
and to the fortresses of Egypt:
"Assemble yourselves on the mountains of Samaria;
see the great unrest within her
and the oppression among her people."

10"They do not know how to do right,"
declares the LORD,
"who hoard plunder and loot in their fortresses."

11Therefore this is what the Sovereign LORD says:

"An enemy will overrun the land;
he will pull down your strongholds
and plunder your fortresses."

12This is what the LORD says:

"As a shepherd saves from the lion's mouth
only two leg bones or a piece of an ear,
so will the Israelites be saved,
those who sit in Samaria
on the edge of their beds
and in Damascus on their couches."

13"Hear this and testify against the house of Jacob," declares the Lord, the LORD God Almighty.

14"On the day I punish Israel for her sins,
I will destroy the altars of Bethel;
the horns of the altar will be cut off
and fall to the ground.
15I will tear down the winter house
along with the summer house;
the houses adorned with ivory will be destroyed
and the mansions will be demolished,"
declares the LORD.

Israel Has Not Returned to God

4 Hear this word, you cows of Bashan on Mount Samaria,
you women who oppress the poor
and crush the needy

and say to your husbands, "Bring
us some drinks!"
2The Sovereign LORD has sworn by his
holiness:
"The time will surely come
when you will be taken away with
hooks,
the last of you with fish-hooks.
3You will each go straight out
through breaks in the wall,
and you will be cast out towards
Harmon,"
declares the LORD.
4"Go to Bethel and sin;
go to Gilgal and sin yet more.
Bring your sacrifices every morning,
your tithes every three years.
5Burn leavened bread as a
thank-offering
and brag about your freewill
offerings—
boast about them, you Israelites,
for this is what you love to do,"
declares the Sovereign LORD.

6"I gave you empty stomachs in every
city
and lack of bread in every town,
yet you have not returned to me,"
declares the LORD.

7"I also withheld rain from you
when the harvest was still three
months away.
I sent rain on one town,
but withheld it from another.
One field had rain;
another had none and dried up.
8People staggered from town to town
for water
but did not get enough to drink,
yet you have not returned to me,"
declares the LORD.

9"Many times I struck your gardens
and vineyards,
I struck them with blight and
mildew.
Locusts devoured your fig and olive
trees,
yet you have not returned to me,"
declares the LORD.

10"I sent plagues among you
as I did to Egypt.
I killed your young men with the
sword,
along with your captured horses.
I filled your nostrils with the stench of
your camps,
yet you have not returned to me,"
declares the LORD.

11"I overthrew some of you
as I overthrew Sodom and
Gomorrah.
You were like a burning stick
snatched from the fire,
yet you have not returned to me,"
declares the LORD.

12"Therefore this is what I will do to
you, Israel,
and because I will do this to you,
prepare to meet your God, O
Israel."

13He who forms the mountains,
creates the wind,
and reveals his thoughts to man,
he who turns dawn to darkness,
and treads the high places of the
earth—
the LORD God Almighty is his
name.

NEW TESTAMENT READING
Romans 3:9–31

No-one Is Righteous

9What shall we conclude then? Are
we any better? Not at all! We have
already made the charge that Jews and
Gentiles alike are all under sin. 10As it is
written:

"There is no-one righteous, not even
one;
11 there is no-one who understands,
no-one who seeks God.
12All have turned away,
they have together become
worthless;

there is no-one who does good,
not even one."
13"Their throats are open graves;
their tongues practise deceit."
"The poison of vipers is on their
lips."
14 "Their mouths are full of cursing
and bitterness."
15"Their feet are swift to shed blood;
16 ruin and misery mark their ways,
17and the way of peace they do not
know."
18 "There is no fear of God before
their eyes."

19Now we know that whatever the law
says, it says to those who are under
the law, so that every mouth may be
silenced and the whole world held
accountable to God. 20Therefore no-
one will be declared righteous in his
sight by observing the law; rather,
through the law we become conscious of
sin.

Righteousness Through Faith

21But now a righteousness from God,
apart from law, has been made known,
to which the Law and the Prophets testify. 22This righteousness from God
comes through faith in Jesus Christ to
all who believe. There is no difference,
23for all have sinned and fall short of the
glory of God, 24and are justified freely
by his grace through the redemption
that came by Christ Jesus. 25God presented him as a sacrifice of atonement,
through faith in his blood. He did this to
demonstrate his justice, because in his
forbearance he had left the sins committed beforehand unpunished26—he did
it to demonstrate his justice at the
present time, so as to be just and the one
who justifies those who have faith in
Jesus.

27Where, then, is boasting? It is excluded. On what principle? On that of
observing the law? No, but on that of
faith. 28For we maintain that a man is
justified by faith apart from observing
the law. 29Is God the God of Jews only?
Is he not the God of Gentiles too? Yes,
of Gentiles too, 30since there is only one
God, who will justify the circumcised by
faith and the uncircumcised through
that same faith. 31Do we, then, nullify
the law by this faith? Not at all! Rather,
we uphold the law.

READING FROM PSALMS

Psalm 85:8–13

8I will listen to what God the LORD
will say;
he promises peace to his people,
his saints—
but let them not return to folly.
9Surely his salvation is near those who
fear him,
that his glory may dwell in our
land.

10Love and faithfulness meet together;
righteousness and peace kiss each
other.
11Faithfulness springs forth from the
earth,
and righteousness looks down from
heaven.
12The LORD will indeed give what is
good,
and our land will yield its harvest.
13Righteousness goes before him
and prepares the way for his steps.

OLD TESTAMENT READING
Amos 5:1–27

A Lament and Call to Repentance

5 Hear this word, O house of Israel, this lament I take up concerning you:

2"Fallen is Virgin Israel,
never to rise again,
deserted in her own land,
with no-one to lift her up."

3This is what the Sovereign LORD says:

"The city that marches out a thousand strong for Israel
will have only a hundred left;
the town that marches out a hundred strong
will have only ten left."

4This is what the LORD says to the house of Israel:

"Seek me and live;
5 do not seek Bethel,
do not go to Gilgal,
do not journey to Beersheba.
For Gilgal will surely go into exile,
and Bethel will be reduced to nothing."
6Seek the LORD and live,
or he will sweep through the house of Joseph like a fire;
it will devour,
and Bethel will have no-one to quench it.

7You who turn justice into bitterness
and cast righteousness to the ground
8(he who made the Pleiades and Orion,
who turns blackness into dawn
and darkens day into night,
who calls for the waters of the sea
and pours them out over the face of the land—
the LORD is his name—
9he flashes destruction on the stronghold
and brings the fortified city to ruin),
10you hate the one who reproves in court
and despise him who tells the truth.

11You trample on the poor
and force him to give you grain.
Therefore, though you have built stone mansions,
you will not live in them;
though you have planted lush vineyards,
you will not drink their wine.
12For I know how many are your offences
and how great your sins.

You oppress the righteous and take bribes
and you deprive the poor of justice in the courts.
13Therefore the prudent man keeps quiet in such times,
for the times are evil.

14Seek good, not evil,
that you may live.
Then the LORD God Almighty will be with you,
just as you say he is.
15Hate evil, love good;
maintain justice in the courts.
Perhaps the LORD God Almighty will have mercy
on the remnant of Joseph.

16Therefore this is what the Lord, the LORD God Almighty, says:

"There will be wailing in all the streets

and cries of anguish in every public
square.
The farmers will be summoned to
weep
and the mourners to wail.
17There will be wailing in all the
vineyards,
for I will pass through your midst,"
says the LORD.

The Day of the LORD

18Woe to you who long
for the day of the LORD!
Why do you long for the day of the
LORD?
That day will be darkness, not
light.
19It will be as though a man fled from a
lion
only to meet a bear,
as though he entered his house
and rested his hand on the wall
only to have a snake bite him.
20Will not the day of the LORD be
darkness, not light—
pitch-dark, without a ray of
brightness?

21"I hate, I despise your religious
feasts;
I cannot stand your assemblies.
22Even though you bring me burnt
offerings and grain offerings,
I will not accept them.
Though you bring choice fellowship
offerings,
I will have no regard for them.
23Away with the noise of your songs!
I will not listen to the music of your
harps.
24But let justice roll on like a river,
righteousness like a never-failing
stream!

25"Did you bring me sacrifices and
offerings
for forty years in the desert, O
house of Israel?
26You have lifted up the shrine of your
king,
the pedestal of your idols,
the star of your god—
which you made for yourselves.
27Therefore I will send you into exile
beyond Damascus,"
says the LORD, whose name is God
Almighty.

NEW TESTAMENT READING
Romans 4:1–15

Abraham Justified by Faith

4 What then shall we say that Abraham, our forefather, discovered in
this matter? 2If, in fact, Abraham was
justified by works, he had something to
boast about—but not before God.
3What does the Scripture say? "Abraham believed God, and it was credited
to him as righteousness."

4Now when a man works, his wages
are not credited to him as a gift, but as
an obligation. 5However, to the man
who does not work but trusts God who
justifies the wicked, his faith is credited
as righteousness. 6David says the same
thing when he speaks of the blessedness
of the man to whom God credits righteousness apart from works:

7"Blessed are they
whose transgressions are forgiven,
whose sins are covered.
8Blessed is the man
whose sin the Lord will never
count against him."

9Is this blessedness only for the circumcised, or also for the uncircumcised? We have been saying that
Abraham's faith was credited to him as
righteousness. 10Under what circumstances was it credited? Was it after he
was circumcised, or before? It was not
after, but before! 11And he received the
sign of circumcision, a seal of the righteousness that he had by faith while he
was still uncircumcised. So then, he is
the father of all who believe but have
not been circumcised, in order that

righteousness might be credited to them. 12And he is also the father of the circumcised who not only are circumcised but who also walk in the footsteps of the faith that our father Abraham had before he was circumcised.

13It was not through law that Abraham and his offspring received the promise that he would be heir of the world, but through the righteousness that comes by faith. 14For if those who live by law are heirs, faith has no value and the promise is worthless, 15because law brings wrath. And where there is no law there is no transgression.

READING FROM PSALMS
Psalm 86:1–10

A prayer of David.

1Hear, O LORD, and answer me,
for I am poor and needy.
2Guard my life, for I am devoted to you.
You are my God; save your servant
who trusts in you.
3Have mercy on me, O Lord,
for I call to you all day long.
4Bring joy to your servant,
for to you, O Lord,
I lift up my soul.

5You are forgiving and good, O Lord,
abounding in love to all who call to you.
6Hear my prayer, O LORD;
listen to my cry for mercy.
7In the day of my trouble I will call to you,
for you will answer me.

8Among the gods there is none like you, O Lord;
no deeds can compare with yours.
9All the nations you have made
will come and worship before you, O Lord;
they will bring glory to your name.
10For you are great and do marvellous deeds;
you alone are God.

DAY 199

JULY 18

OLD TESTAMENT READING
Amos 6:1–7:17

Woe to the Complacent

6 Woe to you who are complacent in Zion,
and to you who feel secure on Mount Samaria,
you notable men of the foremost nation,
to whom the people of Israel come!
2Go to Calneh and look at it;
go from there to great Hamath,
and then go down to Gath in Philistia.
Are they better off than your two kingdoms?
Is their land larger than yours?
3You put off the evil day
and bring near a reign of terror.
4You lie on beds inlaid with ivory
and lounge on your couches.
You dine on choice lambs
and fattened calves.
5You strum away on your harps like David
and improvise on musical instruments.
6You drink wine by the bowlful
and use the finest lotions,
but you do not grieve over the ruin of Joseph.

7Therefore you will be among the first
to go into exile;
your feasting and lounging will
end.

The LORD Abhors the Pride of Israel

8The Sovereign LORD has sworn by himself—the LORD God Almighty declares:

"I abhor the pride of Jacob
and detest his fortresses;
I will deliver up the city
and everything in it."

9If ten men are left in one house, they
too will die. 10And if a relative who is to burn the bodies comes to carry them out of the house and asks anyone still hiding there, "Is anyone with you?" and he says, "No," then he will say, "Hush! We must not mention the name of the LORD."

11For the LORD has given the
command,
and he will smash the great house
into pieces
and the small house into bits.

12Do horses run on the rocky crags?
Does one plough there with oxen?
But you have turned justice into
poison
and the fruit of righteousness into
bitterness—
13you who rejoice in the conquest of Lo
Debar
and say, "Did we not take Karnaim
by our own strength?"

14For the LORD God Almighty
declares,
"I will stir up a nation against you,
O house of Israel,
that will oppress you all the way
from Lebo Hamath to the valley of
the Arabah."

Locusts, Fire and a Plumb-Line

7 This is what the Sovereign LORD showed me: He was preparing swarms of locusts after the king's share had been harvested and just as the
second crop was coming up. 2When
they had stripped the land clean, I cried out, "Sovereign LORD, forgive! How can Jacob survive? He is so small!"
3So the LORD relented.
"This will not happen," the LORD said.
4This is what the Sovereign LORD showed me: The Sovereign LORD was calling for judgment by fire; it dried up the great deep and devoured the land.
5Then I cried out, "Sovereign LORD, I beg you, stop! How can Jacob survive? He is so small!"
6So the LORD relented.
"This will not happen either," the Sovereign LORD said.

7This is what he showed me: The Lord was standing by a wall that had been built true to plumb, with a plumb-
line in his hand. 8And the LORD asked
me, "What do you see, Amos?"
"A plumb-line," I replied.
Then the Lord said, "Look, I am setting a plumb-line among my people Israel; I will spare them no longer.

9"The high places of Isaac will be
destroyed
and the sanctuaries of Israel will be
ruined;
with my sword I will rise against
the house of Jeroboam."

Amos and Amaziah

10Then Amaziah the priest of Bethel sent a message to Jeroboam king of Israel: "Amos is raising a conspiracy against you in the very heart of Israel. The land cannot bear all his words.
11For this is what Amos is saying:

"'Jeroboam will die by the sword,
and Israel will surely go into exile,
away from their native land.'"

[12]Then Amaziah said to Amos, "Get out, you seer! Go back to the land of Judah. Earn your bread there and do your prophesying there. [13]Don't prophesy any more at Bethel, because this is the king's sanctuary and the temple of the kingdom."

[14]Amos answered Amaziah, "I was neither a prophet nor a prophet's son, but I was a shepherd, and I also took care of sycamore-fig trees. [15]But the LORD took me from tending the flock and said to me, 'Go, prophesy to my people Israel.' [16]Now then, hear the word of the LORD. You say,

" 'Do not prophesy against Israel,
and stop preaching against the
house of Isaac.'

[17]"Therefore this is what the LORD says:

" 'Your wife will become a prostitute
in the city,
and your sons and daughters will
fall by the sword.
Your land will be measured and
divided up,
and you yourself will die in a pagan
country.
And Israel will certainly go into exile,
away from their native land.' "

NEW TESTAMENT READING

Romans 4:16–5:11

[16]Therefore, the promise comes by faith, so that it may be by grace and may be guaranteed to all Abraham's offspring—not only to those who are of the law but also to those who are of the faith of Abraham. He is the father of us all. [17]As it is written: "I have made you a father of many nations." He is our father in the sight of God, in whom he believed—the God who gives life to the dead and calls things that are not as though they were.

[18]Against all hope, Abraham in hope believed and so became the father of many nations, just as it had been said to him, "So shall your offspring be." [19]Without weakening in his faith, he faced the fact that his body was as good as dead—since he was about a hundred years old—and that Sarah's womb was also dead. [20]Yet he did not waver through unbelief regarding the promise of God, but was strengthened in his faith and gave glory to God, [21]being fully persuaded that God had power to do what he had promised. [22]This is why "it was credited to him as righteousness." [23]The words "it was credited to him" were written not for him alone, [24]but also for us, to whom God will credit righteousness—for us who believe in him who raised Jesus our Lord from the dead. [25]He was delivered over to death for our sins and was raised to life for our justification.

Peace and Joy

5 Therefore, since we have been justified through faith, we have peace with God through our Lord Jesus Christ, [2]through whom we have gained access by faith into this grace in which we now stand. And we rejoice in the hope of the glory of God. [3]Not only so, but we also rejoice in our sufferings, because we know that suffering produces perseverance; [4]perseverance, character; and character, hope. [5]And hope does not disappoint us, because God has poured out his love into our hearts by the Holy Spirit, whom he has given us.

[6]You see, at just the right time, when we were still powerless, Christ died for the ungodly. [7]Very rarely will anyone die for a righteous man, though for a good man someone might possibly dare to die. [8]But God demonstrates his own love for us in this: While we were still sinners, Christ died for us.

[9]Since we have now been justified by his blood, how much more shall we be saved from God's wrath through him! [10]For if, when we were God's enemies, we were reconciled to him through the

death of his Son, how much more, having been reconciled, shall we be saved through his life! [11]Not only is this so, but we also rejoice in God through our Lord Jesus Christ, through whom we have now received reconciliation.

READING FROM PSALMS
Psalm 86:11–17

11Teach me your way, O LORD,
and I will walk in your truth;
give me an undivided heart,
that I may fear your name.
12I will praise you, O Lord my God,
with all my heart;
I will glorify your name for ever.
13For great is your love towards me;
you have delivered me from the
depths of the grave.

14The arrogant are attacking me, O
God;
a band of ruthless men seeks my
life—
men without regard for you.
15But you, O Lord, are a
compassionate and gracious
God,
slow to anger, abounding in love
and faithfulness.
16Turn to me and have mercy on me;
grant your strength to your servant
and save the son of your
maidservant.
17Give me a sign of your goodness,
that my enemies may see it and be
put to shame,
for you, O LORD, have helped me
and comforted me.

JULY 19

DAY 200

OLD TESTAMENT READING
Amos 8:1–9:15

A Basket of Ripe Fruit

8 This is what the Sovereign LORD showed me: a basket of ripe fruit.
2"What do you see, Amos?" he asked.
"A basket of ripe fruit," I answered.
Then the LORD said to me, "The time is ripe for my people Israel; I will spare them no longer.
3"In that day," declares the Sovereign LORD, "the songs in the temple will turn to wailing. Many, many bodies—flung everywhere! Silence!"

4Hear this, you who trample the
needy
and do away with the poor of the
land,
5saying,

"When will the New Moon be over
that we may sell grain,
and the Sabbath be ended
that we may market wheat?"—
skimping the measure,
boosting the price
and cheating with dishonest scales,
6buying the poor with silver
and the needy for a pair of sandals,
selling even the sweepings with the
wheat.

7The LORD has sworn by the Pride of Jacob: "I will never forget anything they have done.

8"Will not the land tremble for this,
and all who live in it mourn?
The whole land will rise like the Nile;
it will be stirred up and then sink
like the river of Egypt.

9"In that day," declares the Sovereign LORD,

"I will make the sun go down at noon
and darken the earth in broad daylight.
10I will turn your religious feasts into mourning
and all your singing into weeping.
I will make all of you wear sackcloth
and shave your heads.
I will make that time like mourning for an only son
and the end of it like a bitter day.

11"The days are coming," declares the Sovereign LORD,
"when I will send a famine through the land—
not a famine of food or a thirst for water,
but a famine of hearing the words of the LORD.
12Men will stagger from sea to sea
and wander from north to east,
searching for the word of the LORD,
but they will not find it.

13"In that day

"the lovely young women and strong young men
will faint because of thirst.
14They who swear by the shame of Samaria,
or say, 'As surely as your god lives, O Dan',
or, 'As surely as the god of Beersheba lives'—
they will fall,
never to rise again."

Israel to Be Destroyed

9 I saw the Lord standing by the altar, and he said:

"Strike the tops of the pillars
so that the thresholds shake.
Bring them down on the heads of all the people;
those who are left I will kill with the sword.
Not one will get away,
none will escape.
2Though they dig down to the depths of the grave,
from there my hand will take them.
Though they climb up to the heavens,
from there I will bring them down.
3Though they hide themselves on the top of Carmel,
there I will hunt them down and seize them.
Though they hide from me at the bottom of the sea,
there I will command the serpent to bite them.
4Though they are driven into exile by their enemies,
there I will command the sword to slay them.
I will fix my eyes upon them
for evil and not for good."

5The Lord, the LORD Almighty,
he who touches the earth and it melts,
and all who live in it mourn—
the whole land rises like the Nile,
then sinks like the river of Egypt—
6he who builds his lofty palace in the heavens
and sets its foundation on the earth,
who calls for the waters of the sea
and pours them out over the face of the land—
the LORD is his name.

7"Are not you Israelites
the same to me as the Cushites?"
declares the LORD.
"Did I not bring Israel up from Egypt,
the Philistines from Caphtor
and the Arameans from Kir?

8"Surely the eyes of the Sovereign LORD
are on the sinful kingdom.
I will destroy it
from the face of the earth—

yet I will not totally destroy
the house of Jacob,"
declares the LORD.
9"For I will give the command,
and I will shake the house of Israel
among all the nations
as grain is shaken in a sieve,
and not a pebble will reach the
ground.
10All the sinners among my people
will die by the sword,
all those who say,
'Disaster will not overtake or
meet us.'

Israel's Restoration

11"In that day I will restore
David's fallen tent.
I will repair its broken places,
restore its ruins,
and build it as it used to be,
12so that they may possess the remnant
of Edom
and all the nations that bear my
name,"
declares the LORD,
who will do these things.

13"The days are coming," declares
the LORD,

"when the reaper will be overtaken
by the ploughman
and the planter by the one treading
grapes.
New wine will drip from the
mountains
and flow from all the hills.
14I will bring back my exiled people
Israel;
they will rebuild the ruined cities
and live in them.
They will plant vineyards and drink
their wine;
they will make gardens and eat
their fruit.
15I will plant Israel in their own land,
never again to be uprooted
from the land I have given them,"
says the LORD your God.

NEW TESTAMENT READING
Romans 5:12–21

Death Through Adam, Life Through Christ

12Therefore, just as sin entered the
world through one man, and death
through sin, and in this way death came
to all men, because all sinned—13for
before the law was given, sin was in the
world. But sin is not taken into account
when there is no law. 14Nevertheless,
death reigned from the time of Adam to
the time of Moses, even over those who
did not sin by breaking a command, as
did Adam, who was a pattern of the one
to come.
15But the gift is not like the trespass.
For if the many died by the trespass of
the one man, how much more did God's
grace and the gift that came by the grace
of the one man, Jesus Christ, overflow
to the many! 16Again, the gift of God is
not like the result of the one man's sin:
The judgment followed one sin and
brought condemnation, but the gift
followed many trespasses and brought
justification. 17For if, by the trespass of
the one man, death reigned through
that one man, how much more will
those who receive God's abundant
provision of grace and of the gift of
righteousness reign in life through the
one man, Jesus Christ.
18Consequently, just as the result of
one trespass was condemnation for all
men, so also the result of one act of
righteousness was justification that
brings life for all men. 19For just as
through the disobedience of the one
man the many were made sinners, so
also through the obedience of the one
man the many will be made righteous.
20The law was added so that the trespass might increase. But where sin increased, grace increased all the more,
21so that, just as sin reigned in death, so
also grace might reign through righteousness to bring eternal life through
Jesus Christ our Lord.

READING FROM PROVERBS
Proverbs 17:15–24

15Acquitting the guilty and
condemning the innocent—
the LORD detests them both.

16Of what use is money in the hand of a
fool,
since he has no desire to get
wisdom?

17A friend loves at all times,
and a brother is born for adversity.

18A man lacking in judgment strikes
hands in pledge
and puts up security for his
neighbour.

19He who loves a quarrel loves sin;
he who builds a high gate invites
destruction.

20A man of perverse heart does not
prosper;
he whose tongue is deceitful falls
into trouble.

21To have a fool for a son brings grief;
there is no joy for the father of a
fool.

22A cheerful heart is good medicine,
but a crushed spirit dries up the
bones.

23A wicked man accepts a bribe in
secret
to pervert the course of justice.

24A discerning man keeps wisdom in
view,
but a fool's eyes wander to the ends
of the earth.

DAY 201

JULY 20

OLD TESTAMENT READING
Hosea 1:1–2:23

1 The word of the LORD that came to
Hosea son of Beeri during the
reigns of Uzziah, Jotham, Ahaz and
Hezekiah, kings of Judah, and during
the reign of Jeroboam son of Joash king
of Israel:

Hosea's Wife and Children

2When the LORD began to speak
through Hosea, the LORD said to him,
"Go, take to yourself an adulterous
wife and children of unfaithfulness, because the land is guilty of the vilest
adultery in departing from the LORD."
3So he married Gomer daughter of Dib-
laim, and she conceived and bore him a
son.

4Then the LORD said to Hosea, "Call
him Jezreel, because I will soon punish
the house of Jehu for the massacre at
Jezreel, and I will put an end to the
kingdom of Israel. 5In that day I will
break Israel's bow in the Valley of
Jezreel."

6Gomer conceived again and gave
birth to a daughter. Then the LORD said
to Hosea, "Call her Lo-Ruhamah, for I
will no longer show love to the house of
Israel, that I should at all forgive them.
7Yet I will show love to the house of
Judah; and I will save them—not by
bow, sword or battle, or by horses and
horsemen, but by the LORD their God."

8After she had weaned Lo-Ruhamah,
Gomer had another son. 9Then the
LORD said, "Call him Lo-Ammi, for you
are not my people, and I am not your
God.

[10]"Yet the Israelites will be like the sand on the seashore, which cannot be measured or counted. In the place where it was said to them, 'You are not my people', they will be called 'sons of the living God'. [11]The people of Judah and the people of Israel will be reunited, and they will appoint one leader and will come up out of the land, for great will be the day of Jezreel.

2 "Say of your brothers, 'My people', and of your sisters, 'My loved one'.

Israel Punished and Restored

[2]"Rebuke your mother, rebuke her,
for she is not my wife,
and I am not her husband.
Let her remove the adulterous look
from her face
and the unfaithfulness from
between her breasts.
[3]Otherwise I will strip her naked
and make her as bare as on the day
she was born;
I will make her like a desert,
turn her into a parched land,
and slay her with thirst.
[4]I will not show my love to her
children,
because they are the children of
adultery.
[5]Their mother has been unfaithful
and has conceived them in
disgrace.
She said, 'I will go after my lovers,
who give me my food and my
water,
my wool and my linen, my oil and
my drink.'
[6]Therefore I will block her path with
thornbushes;
I will wall her in so that she cannot
find her way.
[7]She will chase after her lovers but not
catch them;
she will look for them but not find
them.
Then she will say,
'I will go back to my husband as at
first,
for then I was better off than now.'
[8]She has not acknowledged that I was
the one
who gave her the grain, the new
wine and oil,
who lavished on her the silver and
gold—
which they used for Baal.

[9]"Therefore I will take away my grain
when it ripens,
and my new wine when it is ready.
I will take back my wool and my
linen,
intended to cover her nakedness.
[10]So now I will expose her lewdness
before the eyes of her lovers;
no-one will take her out of my
hands.
[11]I will stop all her celebrations:
her yearly festivals, her New
Moons,
her Sabbath days—all her
appointed feasts.
[12]I will ruin her vines and her fig-trees,
which she said were her pay from
her lovers;
I will make them a thicket,
and wild animals will devour them.
[13]I will punish her for the days
she burned incense to the Baals;
she decked herself with rings and
jewellery,
and went after her lovers,
but me she forgot,"
declares the LORD.

[14]"Therefore I am now going to allure
her;
I will lead her into the desert
and speak tenderly to her.
[15]There I will give her back her
vineyards,
and will make the Valley of Achor
a door of hope.
There she will sing as in the days of
her youth,
as in the day she came up out of
Egypt.

[16]"In that day," declares the LORD,
"you will call me 'my husband';
you will no longer call me 'my
master'.

[17]I will remove the names of the Baals
from her lips;
no longer will their names be
invoked.
[18]In that day I will make a covenant for
them
with the beasts of the field and the
birds of the air
and the creatures that move along
the ground.
Bow and sword and battle
I will abolish from the land,
so that all may lie down in safety.
[19]I will betroth you to me for ever;
I will betroth you in righteousness
and justice,
in love and compassion.
[20]I will betroth you in faithfulness,
and you will acknowledge the
LORD.

[21]"In that day I will respond,"
declares the LORD—
"I will respond to the skies,
and they will respond to the earth;
[22]and the earth will respond to the
grain,
the new wine and oil,
and they will respond to Jezreel.
[23]I will plant her for myself in the land;
I will show my love to the one I
called 'Not my loved one'.
I will say to those called 'Not my
people', 'You are my people';
and they will say, 'You are my
God.'"

NEW TESTAMENT READING
Romans 6:1–14

Dead to Sin, Alive in Christ

6 What shall we say, then? Shall we
go on sinning, so that grace may
increase? [2]By no means! We died to sin;
how can we live in it any longer? [3]Or
don't you know that all of us who were
baptised into Christ Jesus were baptised
into his death? [4]We were therefore
buried with him through baptism into
death in order that, just as Christ was
raised from the dead through the glory
of the Father, we too may live a new
life.
[5]If we have been united with him like
this in his death, we will certainly also
be united with him in his resurrection.
[6]For we know that our old self was
crucified with him so that the body of sin
might be done away with, that we
should no longer be slaves to sin—
[7]because anyone who has died has been
freed from sin.
[8]Now if we died with Christ, we believe that we will also live with him. [9]For
we know that since Christ was raised
from the dead, he cannot die again;
death no longer has mastery over him.
[10]The death he died, he died to sin once
for all; but the life he lives, he lives to
God.
[11]In the same way, count yourselves
dead to sin but alive to God in Christ
Jesus. [12]Therefore do not let sin reign in
your mortal body so that you obey its
evil desires. [13]Do not offer the parts of
your body to sin, as instruments of wickedness, but rather offer yourselves to
God, as those who have been brought
from death to life; and offer the parts of
your body to him as instruments of
righteousness. [14]For sin shall not be
your master, because you are not under
law, but under grace.

READING FROM PSALMS
Psalm 87:1–7

Of the Sons of Korah. A psalm. A song.

[1]He has set his foundation on the holy
mountain;
[2] the LORD loves the gates of Zion
more than all the dwellings of
Jacob.
[3]Glorious things are said of you,
O city of God: *Selah*
[4]"I will record Rahab and Babylon
among those who acknowledge
me—

Philistia too, and Tyre, along with
Cush—
and will say, 'This one was born in
Zion.'"

5Indeed, of Zion it will be said,
"This one and that one were born
in her,
and the Most High himself will
establish her."
6The LORD will write in the register of
the peoples:
"This one was born in Zion."
Selah
7As they make music they will sing,
"All my fountains are in you."

JULY 21

DAY 202

OLD TESTAMENT READING
Hosea 3:1–5:15

Hosea's Reconciliation With His Wife

3 The LORD said to me, "Go, show
your love to your wife again,
though she is loved by another and is an
adulteress. Love her as the LORD loves
the Israelites, though they turn to other
gods and love the sacred raisin cakes."
2So I bought her for fifteen shekels of
silver and about a homer and a lethek of
barley. 3Then I told her, "You are to
live with me for many days; you must
not be a prostitute or be intimate with
any man, and I will live with you."
4For the Israelites will live for many
days without king or prince, without
sacrifice or sacred stones, without
ephod or idol. 5Afterwards the Israelites will return and seek the LORD their
God and David their king. They will
come trembling to the LORD and to his
blessings in the last days.

The Charge Against Israel

4 Hear the word of the LORD,
you Israelites,
because the LORD has a charge to
bring
against you who live in the land:
"There is no faithfulness, no love,
no acknowledgment of God in the
land.
2There is only cursing, lying and
murder,
stealing and adultery;
they break all bounds,
and bloodshed follows bloodshed.
3Because of this the land mourns,
and all who live in it waste away;
the beasts of the field and the birds of
the air
and the fish of the sea are dying.

4"But let no man bring a charge,
let no man accuse another,
for your people are like those
who bring charges against a priest.
5You stumble day and night,
and the prophets stumble with you.
So I will destroy your mother—
6 my people are destroyed from lack
of knowledge.

"Because you have rejected
knowledge,
I also reject you as my priests;
because you have ignored the law of
your God,
I also will ignore your children.
7The more the priests increased,
the more they sinned against me;
they exchanged their Glory for
something disgraceful.
8They feed on the sins of my people
and relish their wickedness.
9And it will be: Like people, like
priests.

I will punish both of them for their
ways
and repay them for their deeds.

10"They will eat but not have enough;
they will engage in prostitution but
not increase,
because they have deserted the LORD
to give themselves 11to
prostitution,
to old wine and new,
which take away the understanding
12of my people.
They consult a wooden idol
and are answered by a stick of
wood.
A spirit of prostitution leads them
astray;
they are unfaithful to their God.
13They sacrifice on the mountaintops
and burn offerings on the hills,
under oak, poplar and terebinth,
where the shade is pleasant.
Therefore your daughters turn to
prostitution
and your daughters-in-law to
adultery.

14"I will not punish your daughters
when they turn to prostitution,
nor your daughters-in-law
when they commit adultery,
because the men themselves consort
with harlots
and sacrifice with
shrine-prostitutes—
a people without understanding
will come to ruin!

15"Though you commit adultery, O
Israel,
let not Judah become guilty.

"Do not go to Gilgal;
do not go up to Beth Aven.
And do not swear, 'As surely as the
LORD lives!'
16The Israelites are stubborn,
like a stubborn heifer.
How then can the LORD pasture them
like lambs in a meadow?
17Ephraim is joined to idols;
leave him alone!
18Even when their drinks are gone,
they continue their prostitution;
their rulers dearly love shameful
ways.
19A whirlwind will sweep them away,
and their sacrifices will bring them
shame.

Judgment Against Israel

5 "Hear this, you priests!
Pay attention, you Israelites!
Listen, O royal house!
This judgment is against you:
You have been a snare at Mizpah,
a net spread out on Tabor.
2The rebels are deep in slaughter.
I will discipline all of them.
3I know all about Ephraim;
Israel is not hidden from me.
Ephraim, you have now turned to
prostitution;
Israel is corrupt.

4"Their deeds do not permit them
to return to their God.
A spirit of prostitution is in their
heart;
they do not acknowledge the
LORD.
5Israel's arrogance testifies against
them;
the Israelites, even Ephraim,
stumble in their sin;
Judah also stumbles with them.
6When they go with their flocks and
herds
to seek the LORD,
they will not find him;
he has withdrawn himself from
them.
7They are unfaithful to the LORD;
they give birth to illegitimate
children.
Now their New Moon festivals
will devour them and their fields.

8"Sound the trumpet in Gibeah,
the horn in Ramah.

Raise the battle cry in Beth Aven;
lead on, O Benjamin.
9Ephraim will be laid waste
on the day of reckoning.
Among the tribes of Israel
I proclaim what is certain.
10Judah's leaders are like those
who move boundary stones.
I will pour out my wrath on them
like a flood of water.
11Ephraim is oppressed,
trampled in judgment,
intent on pursuing idols.
12I am like a moth to Ephraim,
like rot to the people of Judah.

13"When Ephraim saw his sickness,
and Judah his sores,
then Ephraim turned to Assyria,
and sent to the great king for help.
But he is not able to cure you,
not able to heal your sores.
14For I will be like a lion to Ephraim,
like a great lion to Judah.
I will tear them to pieces and go
away;
I will carry them off, with no-one
to rescue them.
15Then I will go back to my place
until they admit their guilt.
And they will seek my face;
in their misery they will earnestly
seek me."

NEW TESTAMENT READING
Romans 6:15–7:6

Slaves to Righteousness

15What then? Shall we sin because we are not under law but under grace? By no means!
16Don't you know that when you offer yourselves to someone to obey him as slaves, you are slaves to the one whom you obey—whether you are slaves to sin, which leads to death, or to obedience, which leads to righteousness?
17But thanks be to God that, though you used to be slaves to sin, you wholeheartedly obeyed the form of teaching to which you were entrusted.
18You have been set free from sin and have become slaves to righteousness.

19I put this in human terms because you are weak in your natural selves. Just as you used to offer the parts of your body in slavery to impurity and to ever-increasing wickedness, so now offer them in slavery to righteousness leading to holiness.
20When you were slaves to sin, you were free from the control of righteousness.
21What benefit did you reap at that time from the things you are now ashamed of? Those things result in death!
22But now that you have been set free from sin and have become slaves to God, the benefit you reap leads to holiness, and the result is eternal life.
23For the wages of sin is death, but the gift of God is eternal life in Christ Jesus our Lord.

An Illustration From Marriage

7 Do you not know, brothers—for I am speaking to men who know the law—that the law has authority over a man only as long as he lives?
2For example, by law a married woman is bound to her husband as long as he is alive, but if her husband dies, she is released from the law of marriage.
3So then, if she marries another man while her husband is still alive, she is called an adulteress. But if her husband dies, she is released from that law and is not an adulteress, even though she marries another man.

4So, my brothers, you also died to the law through the body of Christ, that you might belong to another, to him who was raised from the dead, in order that we might bear fruit to God.
5For when we were controlled by the sinful nature, the sinful passions aroused by the law were at work in our bodies, so that we bore fruit for death.
6But now, by dying to what once bound us, we have been released from the law so that we serve in the new way of the Spirit, and not in the old way of the written code.

READING FROM PSALMS
Psalm 88:1–9a

A song. A psalm of the Sons of Korah. For the director of music. According to *mahalath leannoth*. A *maskil* of Heman the Ezrahite.

1O LORD, the God who saves me,
day and night I cry out before you.
2May my prayer come before you;
turn your ear to my cry.

3For my soul is full of trouble
and my life draws near the grave.
4I am counted among those who go
down to the pit;
I am like a man without strength.
5I am set apart with the dead,
like the slain who lie in the grave,
whom you remember no more,
who are cut off from your care.

6You have put me in the lowest pit,
in the darkest depths.
7Your wrath lies heavily upon me;
you have overwhelmed me with all
your waves. *Selah*
8You have taken from me my closest
friends
and have made me repulsive to
them.
I am confined and cannot escape;
9 my eyes are dim with grief.

DAY 203

JULY 22

OLD TESTAMENT READING
Hosea 6:1–7:16

Israel Unrepentant

6 "Come, let us return to the LORD.
He has torn us to pieces
but he will heal us;
he has injured us
but he will bind up our wounds.
2After two days he will revive us;
on the third day he will restore us,
that we may live in his presence.
3Let us acknowledge the LORD;
let us press on to acknowledge
him.
As surely as the sun rises,
he will appear;
he will come to us like the winter
rains,
like the spring rains that water the
earth."

4"What can I do with you, Ephraim?
What can I do with you, Judah?
Your love is like the morning mist,
like the early dew that disappears.
5Therefore I cut you in pieces with my
prophets,
I killed you with the words of my
mouth;
my judgments flashed like
lightning upon you.
6For I desire mercy, not sacrifice,
and acknowledgment of God
rather than burnt offerings.
7Like Adam, they have broken the
covenant—
they were unfaithful to me there.
8Gilead is a city of wicked men,
stained with footprints of blood.
9As marauders lie in ambush for a
man,
so do bands of priests;
they murder on the road to Shechem,
committing shameful crimes.
10I have seen a horrible thing
in the house of Israel.
There Ephraim is given to
prostitution
and Israel is defiled.

11"Also for you, Judah,
a harvest is appointed.

"Whenever I would restore the
fortunes of my people,
7 1whenever I would heal Israel,
the sins of Ephraim are exposed
and the crimes of Samaria
revealed.
They practise deceit,
thieves break into houses,
bandits rob in the streets;
2but they do not realise
that I remember all their evil
deeds.
Their sins engulf them;
they are always before me.

3"They delight the king with their
wickedness,
the princes with their lies.
4They are all adulterers,
burning like an oven
whose fire the baker need not stir
from the kneading of the dough till
it rises.
5On the day of the festival of our king
the princes become inflamed with
wine,
and he joins hands with the
mockers.
6Their hearts are like an oven;
they approach him with intrigue.
Their passion smoulders all night;
in the morning it blazes like a
flaming fire.
7All of them are hot as an oven;
they devour their rulers.
All their kings fall,
and none of them calls on me.

8"Ephraim mixes with the nations;
Ephraim is a flat cake not turned
over.
9Foreigners sap his strength,
but he does not realise it.
His hair is sprinkled with grey,
but he does not notice.
10Israel's arrogance testifies against
him,
but despite all this
he does not return to the LORD his
God
or search for him.

11"Ephraim is like a dove,
easily deceived and senseless—
now calling to Egypt,
now turning to Assyria.
12When they go, I will throw my net
over them;
I will pull them down like birds of
the air.
When I hear them flocking together,
I will catch them.
13Woe to them,
because they have strayed from
me!
Destruction to them,
because they have rebelled against
me!
I long to redeem them
but they speak lies against me.
14They do not cry out to me from their
hearts
but wail upon their beds.
They gather together for grain and
new wine
but turn away from me.
15I trained them and strengthened
them,
but they plot evil against me.
16They do not turn to the Most High;
they are like a faulty bow.
Their leaders will fall by the sword
because of their insolent words.
For this they will be ridiculed
in the land of Egypt.

NEW TESTAMENT READING
Romans 7:7–25

Struggling With Sin

7What shall we say, then? Is the law
sin? Certainly not! Indeed I would not
have known what sin was except
through the law. For I would not have
known what coveting really was if the
law had not said, "Do not covet." 8But
sin, seizing the opportunity afforded by
the commandment, produced in me
every kind of covetous desire. For apart
from law, sin is dead. 9Once I was alive
apart from law; but when the commandment came, sin sprang to life and I died.

10I found that the very commandment
that was intended to bring life actually
brought death. 11For sin, seizing the
opportunity afforded by the commandment, deceived me, and through the
commandment put me to death. 12So
then, the law is holy, and the commandment is holy, righteous and good.
13Did that which is good, then, become death to me? By no means! But in
order that sin might be recognised as
sin, it produced death in me through
what was good, so that through the
commandment sin might become
utterly sinful.
14We know that the law is spiritual;
but I am unspiritual, sold as a slave to
sin. 15I do not understand what I do. For
what I want to do I do not do, but what I
hate I do. 16And if I do what I do not
want to do, I agree that the law is good.
17As it is, it is no longer I myself who do
it, but it is sin living in me. 18I know that
nothing good lives in me, that is, in my
sinful nature. For I have the desire to do
what is good, but I cannot carry it out.
19For what I do is not the good I want to
do; no, the evil I do not want to do
—this I keep on doing. 20Now if I do
what I do not want to do, it is no longer I
who do it, but it is sin living in me that
does it.
21So I find this law at work: When I
want to do good, evil is right there with
me. 22For in my inner being I delight in
God's law; 23but I see another law at
work in the members of my body,
waging war against the law of my mind
and making me a prisoner of the law of
sin at work within my members. 24What
a wretched man I am! Who will rescue
me from this body of death? 25Thanks
be to God—through Jesus Christ our
Lord!

So then, I myself in my mind am a slave to God's law, but in the sinful nature a slave to the law of sin.

READING FROM PSALMS

Psalm 88:9b–18

I call to you, O LORD, every day;
I spread out my hands to you.
10Do you show your wonders to the dead?
Do those who are dead rise up and praise you? *Selah*
11Is your love declared in the grave,
your faithfulness in Destruction?
12Are your wonders known in the place of darkness,
or your righteous deeds in the land of oblivion?

13But I cry to you for help, O LORD;
in the morning my prayer comes before you.
14Why, O LORD, do you reject me
and hide your face from me?

15From my youth I have been afflicted and close to death;
I have suffered your terrors and am in despair.
16Your wrath has swept over me;
your terrors have destroyed me.
17All day long they surround me like a flood;
they have completely engulfed me.
18You have taken my companions and loved ones from me;
the darkness is my closest friend.

OLD TESTAMENT READING

Hosea 8:1–9:17

Israel to Reap the Whirlwind

8 "Put the trumpet to your lips!
An eagle is over the house of the
LORD
because the people have broken my
covenant
and rebelled against my law.
2Israel cries out to me,
'O our God, we acknowledge you!'
3But Israel has rejected what is good;
an enemy will pursue him.
4They set up kings without my
consent;
they choose princes without my
approval.
With their silver and gold
they make idols for themselves
to their own destruction.
5Throw out your calf-idol, O Samaria!
My anger burns against them.
How long will they be incapable of
purity?
6 They are from Israel!
This calf—a craftsman has made it;
it is not God.
It will be broken in pieces,
that calf of Samaria.

7"They sow the wind
and reap the whirlwind.
The stalk has no head;
it will produce no flour.
Were it to yield grain,
foreigners would swallow it up.
8Israel is swallowed up;
now she is among the nations
like a worthless thing.
9For they have gone up to Assyria
like a wild donkey wandering
alone.
Ephraim has sold herself to lovers.
10Although they have sold themselves
among the nations,
I will now gather them together.
They will begin to waste away
under the oppression of the mighty
king.

11"Though Ephraim built many altars
for sin offerings,
these have become altars for
sinning.
12I wrote for them the many things of
my law,
but they regarded them as
something alien.
13They offer sacrifices given to me
and they eat the meat,
but the LORD is not pleased with
them.
Now he will remember their
wickedness
and punish their sins:
They will return to Egypt.
14Israel has forgotten his Maker
and built palaces;
Judah has fortified many towns.
But I will send fire upon their cities
that will consume their fortresses."

Punishment for Israel

9 Do not rejoice, O Israel;
do not be jubilant like the other
nations.
For you have been unfaithful to your
God;
you love the wages of a prostitute
at every threshing-floor.
2Threshing-floors and winepresses will
not feed the people;
the new wine will fail them.
3They will not remain in the LORD's
land;
Ephraim will return to Egypt
and eat unclean food in Assyria.
4They will not pour out wine offerings
to the LORD,
nor will their sacrifices please him.
Such sacrifices will be to them like
the bread of mourners;
all who eat them will be unclean.

This food will be for themselves;
it will not come into the temple of the LORD.

5What will you do on the day of your appointed feasts,
on the festival days of the LORD?
6Even if they escape from destruction,
Egypt will gather them,
and Memphis will bury them.
Their treasures of silver will be taken over by briers,
and thorns will overrun their tents.
7The days of punishment are coming,
the days of reckoning are at hand.
Let Israel know this.
Because your sins are so many
and your hostility so great,
the prophet is considered a fool,
the inspired man a maniac.
8The prophet, along with my God,
is the watchman over Ephraim,
yet snares await him on all his paths,
and hostility in the house of his God.
9They have sunk deep into corruption,
as in the days of Gibeah.
God will remember their wickedness
and punish them for their sins.

10"When I found Israel,
it was like finding grapes in the desert;
when I saw your fathers,
it was like seeing the early fruit on the fig-tree.
But when they came to Baal Peor,
they consecrated themselves to that shameful idol
and became as vile as the thing they loved.
11Ephraim's glory will fly away like a bird—
no birth, no pregnancy, no conception.
12Even if they bring up children,
I will bereave them of every one.
Woe to them
when I turn away from them!
13I have seen Ephraim, like Tyre,
planted in a pleasant place.
But Ephraim will bring out
their children to the slayer."
14Give them, O LORD—
what will you give them?
Give them wombs that miscarry
and breasts that are dry.

15"Because of all their wickedness in Gilgal,
I hated them there.
Because of their sinful deeds,
I will drive them out of my house.
I will no longer love them;
all their leaders are rebellious.
16Ephraim is blighted,
their root is withered,
they yield no fruit.
Even if they bear children,
I will slay their cherished offspring."
17My God will reject them
because they have not obeyed him;
they will be wanderers among the nations.

NEW TESTAMENT READING
Romans 8:1–17

Life Through the Spirit

8 Therefore, there is now no condemnation for those who are in
Christ Jesus, 2because through Christ
Jesus the law of the Spirit of life set me
free from the law of sin and death. 3For
what the law was powerless to do in that
it was weakened by the sinful nature,
God did by sending his own Son in the
likeness of sinful man to be a sin offering. And so he condemned sin in sinful
man, 4in order that the righteous requirements of the law might be fully met
in us, who do not live according to the
sinful nature but according to the Spirit.
5Those who live according to the sinful nature have their minds set on what
that nature desires; but those who live
in accordance with the Spirit have their
minds set on what the Spirit desires.
6The mind of sinful man is death, but
the mind controlled by the Spirit is life
and peace; 7the sinful mind is hostile to
God. It does not submit to God's law,

nor can it do so. [8]Those controlled by
the sinful nature cannot please God.
[9]You, however, are controlled not by
the sinful nature but by the Spirit, if the
Spirit of God lives in you. And if anyone
does not have the Spirit of Christ, he
does not belong to Christ. [10]But if
Christ is in you, your body is dead because of sin, yet your spirit is alive because of righteousness. [11]And if the
Spirit of him who raised Jesus from the
dead is living in you, he who raised
Christ from the dead will also give life to
your mortal bodies through his Spirit,
who lives in you.
[12]Therefore, brothers, we have an
obligation—but it is not to the sinful
nature, to live according to it. [13]For if
you live according to the sinful nature,
you will die; but if by the Spirit you put
to death the misdeeds of the body, you
will live, [14]because those who are led by
the Spirit of God are sons of God. [15]For
you did not receive a spirit that makes
you a slave again to fear, but you received the Spirit of sonship. And by him
we cry, "*Abba*, Father." [16]The Spirit
himself testifies with our spirit that we
are God's children. [17]Now if we are
children, then we are heirs—heirs of
God and co-heirs with Christ, if indeed
we share in his sufferings in order that
we may also share in his glory.

READING FROM PROVERBS
Proverbs 17:25–18:6

[25]A foolish son brings grief to his father
and bitterness to the one who bore
him.

[26]It is not good to punish an innocent
man,
or to flog officials for their
integrity.

[27]A man of knowledge uses words with
restraint,
and a man of understanding is
even-tempered.

[28]Even a fool is thought wise if he
keeps silent,
and discerning if he holds his
tongue.

18 An unfriendly man pursues
selfish ends;
he defies all sound judgment.

[2]A fool finds no pleasure in
understanding
but delights in airing his own
opinions.

[3]When wickedness comes, so does
contempt,
and with shame comes disgrace.

[4]The words of a man's mouth are deep
waters,
but the fountain of wisdom is a
bubbling brook.

[5]It is not good to be partial to the
wicked
or to deprive the innocent of
justice.

[6]A fool's lips bring him strife,
and his mouth invites a beating.

OLD TESTAMENT READING
Hosea 10:1–11:11

10 Israel was a spreading vine;
he brought forth fruit for
himself.
As his fruit increased,
he built more altars;
as his land prospered,
he adorned his sacred stones.
2Their heart is deceitful,
and now they must bear their guilt.
The LORD will demolish their altars
and destroy their sacred stones.

3Then they will say, "We have no king
because we did not revere the
LORD.
But even if we had a king,
what could he do for us?"
4They make many promises,
take false oaths
and make agreements;
therefore lawsuits spring up
like poisonous weeds in a ploughed
field.
5The people who live in Samaria fear
for the calf-idol of Beth Aven.
Its people will mourn over it,
and so will its idolatrous priests,
those who had rejoiced over its
splendour,
because it is taken from them into
exile.
6It will be carried to Assyria
as tribute for the great king.
Ephraim will be disgraced;
Israel will be ashamed of its
wooden idols.
7Samaria and its king will float away
like a twig on the surface of the
waters.
8The high places of wickedness will be
destroyed—
it is the sin of Israel.
Thorns and thistles will grow up
and cover their altars.
Then they will say to the mountains,
"Cover us!"
and to the hills, "Fall on us!"

9"Since the days of Gibeah, you have
sinned, O Israel,
and there you have remained.
Did not war overtake
the evildoers in Gibeah?
10When I please, I will punish them;
nations will be gathered against
them
to put them in bonds for their
double sin.
11Ephraim is a trained heifer
that loves to thresh;
so I will put a yoke
on her fair neck.
I will drive Ephraim,
Judah must plough,
and Jacob must break up the
ground.
12Sow for yourselves righteousness,
reap the fruit of unfailing love,
and break up your unploughed
ground;
for it is time to seek the LORD,
until he comes
and showers righteousness on
you.
13But you have planted wickedness,
you have reaped evil,
you have eaten the fruit of
deception.
Because you have depended on your
own strength
and on your many warriors,
14the roar of battle will rise against
your people,
so that all your fortresses will be
devastated—
as Shalman devastated Beth Arbel on
the day of battle,
when mothers were dashed to the
ground with their children.
15Thus will it happen to you, O Bethel,
because your wickedness is great.

When that day dawns,
the king of Israel will be
completely destroyed.

God's Love for Israel

11 "When Israel was a child, I loved him,
and out of Egypt I called my son.
2But the more I called Israel,
the further they went from me.
They sacrificed to the Baals
and they burned incense to images.
3It was I who taught Ephraim to walk,
taking them by the arms;
but they did not realise
it was I who healed them.
4I led them with cords of human kindness,
with ties of love;
I lifted the yoke from their neck
and bent down to feed them.

5"Will they not return to Egypt
and will not Assyria rule over them
because they refuse to repent?
6Swords will flash in their cities,
will destroy the bars of their gates
and put an end to their plans.
7My people are determined to turn from me.
Even if they call to the Most High,
he will by no means exalt them.

8"How can I give you up, Ephraim?
How can I hand you over, Israel?
How can I treat you like Admah?
How can I make you like Zeboiim?
My heart is changed within me;
all my compassion is aroused.
9I will not carry out my fierce anger,
nor will I turn and devastate Ephraim.
For I am God, and not man—
the Holy One among you.
I will not come in wrath.
10They will follow the LORD;
he will roar like a lion.
When he roars,
his children will come trembling
from the west.
11They will come trembling
like birds from Egypt,
like doves from Assyria.
I will settle them in their homes,"
declares the LORD.

NEW TESTAMENT READING
Romans 8:18–39

Future Glory

18I consider that our present sufferings are not worth comparing with the
glory that will be revealed in us. 19The
creation waits in eager expectation for
the sons of God to be revealed. 20For
the creation was subjected to frustration, not by its own choice, but by the
will of the one who subjected it, in hope
21that the creation itself will be liberated
from its bondage to decay and brought
into the glorious freedom of the children of God.

22We know that the whole creation
has been groaning as in the pains of
childbirth right up to the present time.
23Not only so, but we ourselves, who
have the firstfruits of the Spirit, groan
inwardly as we wait eagerly for our
adoption as sons, the redemption of our
bodies. 24For in this hope we were
saved. But hope that is seen is no hope
at all. Who hopes for what he already
has? 25But if we hope for what we do not
yet have, we wait for it patiently.

26In the same way, the Spirit helps us
in our weakness. We do not know what
we ought to pray for, but the Spirit
himself intercedes for us with groans
that words cannot express. 27And he
who searches our hearts knows the
mind of the Spirit, because the Spirit
intercedes for the saints in accordance
with God's will.

More Than Conquerors

28And we know that in all things God
works for the good of those who love
him, who have been called according to
his purpose. 29For those God foreknew

he also predestined to be conformed to
the likeness of his Son, that he might be
the firstborn among many brothers.
30And those he predestined, he also
called; those he called, he also justified;
those he justified, he also glorified.
31What, then, shall we say in response
to this? If God is for us, who can be
against us? 32He who did not spare his
own Son, but gave him up for us all
—how will he not also, along with him,
graciously give us all things? 33Who will
bring any charge against those whom
God has chosen? It is God who justifies.
34Who is he that condemns? Christ
Jesus, who died—more than that, who
was raised to life—is at the right hand of
God and is also interceding for us.
35Who shall separate us from the love of
Christ? Shall trouble or hardship or
persecution or famine or nakedness or
danger or sword? 36As it is written:

> "For your sake we face death all day long;
> we are considered as sheep to be slaughtered."

37No, in all these things we are more
than conquerors through him who loved
us. 38For I am convinced that neither
death nor life, neither angels nor demons, neither the present nor the future, nor any powers, 39neither height
nor depth, nor anything else in all creation, will be able to separate us from the
love of God that is in Christ Jesus our
Lord.

READING FROM PSALMS
Psalm 89:1–8

A *maskil* of Ethan the Ezrahite.

1I will sing of the LORD's great love for ever;
with my mouth I will make your faithfulness known through all generations.
2I will declare that your love stands firm for ever,
that you established your faithfulness in heaven itself.

3You said, "I have made a covenant with my chosen one,
I have sworn to David my servant,
4'I will establish your line for ever
and make your throne firm through all generations.' " *Selah*

5The heavens praise your wonders, O LORD,
your faithfulness too, in the assembly of the holy ones.
6For who in the skies above can compare with the LORD?
Who is like the LORD among the heavenly beings?
7In the council of the holy ones God is greatly feared;
he is more awesome than all who surround him.
8O LORD God Almighty, who is like you?
You are mighty, O LORD, and your faithfulness surrounds you.

OLD TESTAMENT READING

Hosea 11:12–14:9

Israel's Sin

12Ephraim has surrounded me with lies,
the house of Israel with deceit.
And Judah is unruly against God,
even against the faithful Holy One.

12 1Ephraim feeds on the wind;
he pursues the east wind all day
and multiplies lies and violence.
He makes a treaty with Assyria
and sends olive oil to Egypt.
2The LORD has a charge to bring against Judah;
he will punish Jacob according to his ways
and repay him according to his deeds.
3In the womb he grasped his brother's heel;
as a man he struggled with God.
4He struggled with the angel and overcame him;
he wept and begged for his favour.
He found him at Bethel
and talked with him there—
5the LORD God Almighty,
the LORD is his name of renown!
6But you must return to your God;
maintain love and justice,
and wait for your God always.

7The merchant uses dishonest scales;
he loves to defraud.
8Ephraim boasts,
"I am very rich; I have become wealthy.
With all my wealth they will not find in me
any iniquity or sin."

9"I am the LORD your God,
⌊who brought you⌋ out of Egypt;
I will make you live in tents again,
as in the days of your appointed feasts.

10I spoke to the prophets,
gave them many visions
and told parables through them."

11Is Gilead wicked?
Its people are worthless!
Do they sacrifice bulls in Gilgal?
Their altars will be like piles of stones
on a ploughed field.
12Jacob fled to the country of Aram;
Israel served to get a wife,
and to pay for her he tended sheep.
13The LORD used a prophet to bring Israel up from Egypt,
by a prophet he cared for him.
14But Ephraim has bitterly provoked him to anger;
his Lord will leave upon him the guilt of his bloodshed
and will repay him for his contempt.

The LORD's Anger Against Israel

13 When Ephraim spoke, men trembled;
he was exalted in Israel.
But he became guilty of Baal worship and died.
2Now they sin more and more;
they make idols for themselves from their silver,
cleverly fashioned images,
all of them the work of craftsmen.
It is said of these people,
"They offer human sacrifice
and kiss the calf-idols."
3Therefore they will be like the morning mist,
like the early dew that disappears,
like chaff swirling from a threshing-floor,
like smoke escaping through a window.

4"But I am the LORD your God,
⌊who brought you⌋ out of Egypt.

You shall acknowledge no God but me,
no Saviour except me.
5I cared for you in the desert,
in the land of burning heat.
6When I fed them, they were satisfied;
when they were satisfied, they became proud;
then they forgot me.
7So I will come upon them like a lion,
like a leopard I will lurk by the path.
8Like a bear robbed of her cubs,
I will attack them and rip them open.
Like a lion I will devour them;
a wild animal will tear them apart.

9"You are destroyed, O Israel,
because you are against me,
against your helper.
10Where is your king, that he may save you?
Where are your rulers in all your towns,
of whom you said,
'Give me a king and princes'?
11So in my anger I gave you a king,
and in my wrath I took him away.
12The guilt of Ephraim is stored up,
his sins are kept on record.
13Pains as of a woman in childbirth come to him,
but he is a child without wisdom;
when the time arrives,
he does not come to the opening of the womb.

14"I will ransom them from the power of the grave;
I will redeem them from death.
Where, O death, are your plagues?
Where, O grave, is your destruction?

"I will have no compassion,
15 even though he thrives among his brothers.
An east wind from the LORD will come,
blowing in from the desert;
his spring will fail
and his well dry up.
His storehouse will be plundered
of all its treasures.
16The people of Samaria must bear their guilt,
because they have rebelled against their God.
They will fall by the sword;
their little ones will be dashed to the ground,
their pregnant women ripped open."

Repentance to Bring Blessing

14 Return, O Israel, to the LORD your God.
Your sins have been your downfall!
2Take words with you
and return to the LORD.
Say to him:
"Forgive all our sins
and receive us graciously,
that we may offer the fruit of our lips.
3Assyria cannot save us;
we will not mount war-horses.
We will never again say 'Our gods'
to what our own hands have made,
for in you the fatherless find compassion."

4"I will heal their waywardness
and love them freely,
for my anger has turned away from them.
5I will be like the dew to Israel;
he will blossom like a lily.
Like a cedar of Lebanon
he will send down his roots;
6 his young shoots will grow.
His splendour will be like an olive tree,
his fragrance like a cedar of Lebanon.
7Men will dwell again in his shade.
He will flourish like the corn.
He will blossom like a vine,
and his fame will be like the wine from Lebanon.

8O Ephraim, what more have I to do
with idols?
I will answer him and care for him.
I am like a green pine tree;
your fruitfulness comes from me."

9Who is wise? He will realise these
things.
Who is discerning? He will
understand them.
The ways of the LORD are right;
the righteous walk in them,
but the rebellious stumble in them.

NEW TESTAMENT READING
Romans 9:1–21

God's Sovereign Choice

9 I speak the truth in Christ—I am
not lying, my conscience confirms
it in the Holy Spirit—2I have great sorrow and unceasing anguish in my heart.
3For I could wish that I myself were
cursed and cut off from Christ for the
sake of my brothers, those of my own
race, 4the people of Israel. Theirs is the
adoption as sons; theirs the divine
glory, the covenants, the receiving of
the law, the temple worship and the
promises. 5Theirs are the patriarchs,
and from them is traced the human
ancestry of Christ, who is God over all,
for ever praised! Amen.

6It is not as though God's word had
failed. For not all who are descended
from Israel are Israel. 7Nor because
they are his descendants are they all
Abraham's children. On the contrary,
"It is through Isaac that your offspring
will be reckoned." 8In other words, it is
not the natural children who are God's
children, but it is the children of the
promise who are regarded as Abraham's offspring. 9For this was how the
promise was stated: "At the appointed
time I will return, and Sarah will have a
son."

10Not only that, but Rebekah's children had one and the same father, our
father Isaac. 11Yet, before the twins
were born or had done anything good or
bad—in order that God's purpose in
election might stand: 12not by works but
by him who calls—she was told, "The
older will serve the younger." 13Just as it
is written: "Jacob I loved, but Esau I
hated."

14What then shall we say? Is God
unjust? Not at all! 15For he says to
Moses,

"I will have mercy on whom I have
mercy,
and I will have compassion on
whom I have compassion."

16It does not, therefore, depend on
man's desire or effort, but on God's
mercy. 17For the Scripture says to Pharaoh: "I raised you up for this very purpose, that I might display my power in
you and that my name might be proclaimed in all the earth." 18Therefore
God has mercy on whom he wants to
have mercy, and he hardens whom he
wants to harden.

19One of you will say to me: "Then
why does God still blame us? For who
resists his will?" 20But who are you, O
man, to talk back to God? "Shall what is
formed say to him who formed it, 'Why
did you make me like this?'" 21Does not
the potter have the right to make out of
the same lump of clay some pottery for
noble purposes and some for common
use?

READING FROM PSALMS
Psalm 89:9–13

9You rule over the surging sea;
when its waves mount up, you still
them.
10You crushed Rahab like one of the
slain;
with your strong arm you scattered
your enemies.
11The heavens are yours, and yours
also the earth;
you founded the world and all that
is in it.

12You created the north and the south;
Tabor and Hermon sing for joy at your name.

13Your arm is endued with power;
your hand is strong, your right hand exalted.

DAY 207

JULY 26

OLD TESTAMENT READING
1 Chronicles 1:1–2:17

Historical Records From Adam to Abraham

To Noah's Sons

1 Adam, Seth, Enosh, 2Kenan, Mahalalel, Jared, 3Enoch, Methuselah, Lamech, Noah.

4The sons of Noah:
Shem, Ham and Japheth.

The Japhethites

5The sons of Japheth:
Gomer, Magog, Madai, Javan, Tubal, Meshech and Tiras.
6The sons of Gomer:
Ashkenaz, Riphath and Togarmah.
7The sons of Javan:
Elishah, Tarshish, the Kittim and the Rodanim.

The Hamites

8The sons of Ham:
Cush, Mizraim, Put and Canaan.
9The sons of Cush:
Seba, Havilah, Sabta, Raamah and Sabteca.
The sons of Raamah:
Sheba and Dedan.
10Cush was the father of
Nimrod, who grew to be a mighty warrior on earth.
11Mizraim was the father of
the Ludites, Anamites, Lehabites, Naphtuhites, 12Pathrusites, Casluhites (from whom the Philistines came) and Caphtorites.
13Canaan was the father of
Sidon his firstborn, and of the Hittites, 14Jebusites, Amorites, Girgashites, 15Hivites, Arkites, Sinites, 16Arvadites, Zemarites and Hamathites.

The Semites

17The sons of Shem:
Elam, Asshur, Arphaxad, Lud and Aram.
The sons of Aram:
Uz, Hul, Gether and Meshech.
18Arphaxad was the father of Shelah, and Shelah the father of Eber.
19Two sons were born to Eber:
One was named Peleg, because in his time the earth was divided; his brother was named Joktan.
20Joktan was the father of
Almodad, Sheleph, Hazarmaveth, Jerah, 21Hadoram, Uzal, Diklah, 22Obal, Abimael, Sheba, 23Ophir, Havilah and Jobab. All these were sons of Joktan.

24Shem, Arphaxad, Shelah,
25Eber, Peleg, Reu,
26Serug, Nahor, Terah
27and Abram (that is, Abraham).

The Family of Abraham

28The sons of Abraham:
Isaac and Ishmael.

Descendants of Hagar

29These were their descendants:
Nebaioth the firstborn of

Ishmael, Kedar, Adbeel, Mibsam, 30Mishma, Dumah, Massa,
Hadad, Tema, 31Jetur, Naphish
and Kedemah. These were the
sons of Ishmael.

Descendants of Keturah

32The sons born to Keturah,
Abraham's concubine:
Zimran, Jokshan, Medan, Mid-
ian, Ishbak and Shuah.
The sons of Jokshan:
Sheba and Dedan.
33The sons of Midian:
Ephah, Epher, Hanoch, Abida
and Eldaah.
All these were descendants of
Keturah.

Descendants of Sarah

34Abraham was the father of Isaac.
The sons of Isaac:
Esau and Israel.

Esau's Sons

35The sons of Esau:
Eliphaz, Reuel, Jeush, Jalam
and Korah.
36The sons of Eliphaz:
Teman, Omar, Zepho, Gatam
and Kenaz;
by Timna: Amalek.
37The sons of Reuel:
Nahath, Zerah, Shammah and
Mizzah.

The People of Seir in Edom

38The sons of Seir:
Lotan, Shobal, Zibeon, Anah,
Dishon, Ezer and Dishan.
39The sons of Lotan:
Hori and Homam. Timna was
Lotan's sister.
40The sons of Shobal:
Alvan, Manahath, Ebal, Shepho
and Onam.
The sons of Zibeon:
Aiah and Anah.
41The son of Anah:
Dishon.
The sons of Dishon:
Hemdan, Eshban, Ithran and
Keran.
42The sons of Ezer:
Bilhan, Zaavan and Akan.
The sons of Dishan:
Uz and Aran.

The Rulers of Edom

43These were the kings who reigned
in Edom before any Israelite king
reigned:
Bela son of Beor, whose city was
named Dinhabah.
44When Bela died, Jobab son of
Zerah from Bozrah succeeded
him as king.
45When Jobab died, Husham from
the land of the Temanites succeeded him as king.
46When Husham died, Hadad son of
Bedad, who defeated Midian in
the country of Moab, succeeded
him as king. His city was named
Avith.
47When Hadad died, Samlah from
Masrekah succeeded him as
king.
48When Samlah died, Shaul from
Rehoboth on the river succeeded
him as king.
49When Shaul died, Baal-Hanan son
of Acbor succeeded him as king.
50When Baal-Hanan died, Hadad
succeeded him as king. His city
was named Pau, and his wife's
name was Mehetabel daughter
of Matred, the daughter of Me-
Zahab. 51Hadad also died.

The chiefs of Edom were:
Timna, Alvah, Jetheth, 52Oholi-
bamah, Elah, Pinon, 53Kenaz,
Teman, Mibzar, 54Magdiel and
Iram. These were the chiefs of
Edom.

Israel's Sons

2 These were the sons of Israel:
Reuben, Simeon, Levi, Judah,
Issachar, Zebulun, 2Dan,

Joseph, Benjamin, Naphtali, Gad and Asher.

Judah

To Hezron's Sons

3The sons of Judah:
Er, Onan and Shelah. These three were born to him by a Canaanite woman, the daughter of Shua. Er, Judah's firstborn, was wicked in the LORD's sight; so the LORD put him to death.
4Tamar, Judah's daughter-in-law, bore him Perez and Zerah. Judah had five sons in all.

5The sons of Perez:
Hezron and Hamul.
6The sons of Zerah:
Zimri, Ethan, Heman, Calcol and Darda—five in all.
7The son of Carmi:
Achar, who brought trouble on Israel by violating the ban on taking devoted things.
8The son of Ethan:
Azariah.
9The sons born to Hezron were:
Jerahmeel, Ram and Caleb.

From Ram Son of Hezron

10Ram was the father of
Amminadab, and Amminadab the father of Nahshon, the leader of the people of Judah.
11Nahshon was the father of Salmon, Salmon the father of Boaz,
12Boaz the father of Obed and Obed the father of Jesse.
13Jesse was the father of
Eliab his firstborn; the second son was Abinadab, the third Shimea, 14the fourth Nethanel,
the fifth Raddai, 15the sixth Ozem and the seventh David.
16Their sisters were Zeruiah and Abigail. Zeruiah's three sons were Abishai, Joab and Asahel.
17Abigail was the mother of Amasa, whose father was Jether the Ishmaelite.

NEW TESTAMENT READING
Romans 9:22–10:4

22What if God, choosing to show his
wrath and make his power known, bore
with great patience the objects of his
wrath—prepared for destruction?
23What if he did this to make the riches
of his glory known to the objects of his
mercy, whom he prepared in advance
for glory—24even us, whom he also
called, not only from the Jews but also
from the Gentiles? 25As he says in
Hosea:

"I will call them 'my people' who are
not my people;
and I will call her 'my loved one'
who is not my loved one,"

26and,

"It will happen that in the very place
where it was said to them,
'You are not my people,'
they will be called 'sons of the living
God'."

27Isaiah cries out concerning Israel:

"Though the number of the Israelites
be like the sand by the sea,
only the remnant will be saved.
28For the Lord will carry out
his sentence on earth with speed
and finality."

29It is just as Isaiah said previously:

"Unless the Lord Almighty
had left us descendants,
we would have become like Sodom,
we would have been like
Gomorrah."

Israel's Unbelief

30What then shall we say? That the
Gentiles, who did not pursue righteousness, have obtained it, a righteousness
that is by faith; 31but Israel, who pursued a law of righteousness, has not
attained it. 32Why not? Because they

pursued it not by faith but as if it were by works. They stumbled over the "stumbling-stone".
33As it is written:

"See, I lay in Zion a stone that causes
men to stumble
and a rock that makes them fall,
and the one who trusts in him will
never be put to shame."

10 Brothers, my heart's desire and prayer to God for the Israelites is that they may be saved.
2For I can testify about them that they are zealous for God, but their zeal is not based on knowledge.
3Since they did not know the righteousness that comes from God and sought to establish their own, they did not submit to God's righteousness.
4Christ is the end of the law so that there may be righteousness for everyone who believes.

READING FROM PSALMS
Psalm 89:14–18

14Righteousness and justice are the
foundation of your throne;
love and faithfulness go before
you.
15Blessed are those who have learned
to acclaim you,
who walk in the light of your
presence, O LORD.
16They rejoice in your name all day
long;
they exult in your righteousness.
17For you are their glory and
strength,
and by your favour you exalt our
horn.
18Indeed, our shield belongs to the
LORD,
our king to the Holy One of Israel.

JULY 27

DAY 208

OLD TESTAMENT READING
1 Chronicles 2:18–4:8

Caleb Son of Hezron

18Caleb son of Hezron had children by his wife Azubah (and by Jerioth). These were her sons: Jesher, Shobab and Ardon.
19When Azubah died, Caleb married Ephrath, who bore him Hur.
20Hur was the father of Uri, and Uri the father of Bezalel.
21Later, Hezron lay with the daughter of Makir the father of Gilead (he had married her when he was sixty years old), and she bore him Segub.
22Segub was the father of Jair, who controlled twenty-three towns in Gilead.
23(But Geshur and Aram captured Havvoth Jair, as well as Kenath with its surrounding settlements—sixty towns.) All these were descendants of Makir the father of Gilead.

24After Hezron died in Caleb Ephrathah, Abijah the wife of Hezron bore him Ashhur the father of Tekoa.

Jerahmeel Son of Hezron

25The sons of Jerahmeel the firstborn of Hezron:
Ram his firstborn, Bunah, Oren, Ozem and Ahijah.
26Jerahmeel had another wife, whose name was Atarah; she was the mother of Onam.
27The sons of Ram the firstborn of Jerahmeel:
Maaz, Jamin and Eker.
28The sons of Onam:
Shammai and Jada.

The sons of Shammai:
Nadab and Abishur.
29Abishur's wife was named Abihail, who bore him Ahban and Molid.
30The sons of Nadab:
Seled and Appaim. Seled died without children.
31The son of Appaim:
Ishi, who was the father of Sheshan.
Sheshan was the father of Ahlai.
32The sons of Jada, Shammai's brother:
Jether and Jonathan. Jether died without children.
33The sons of Jonathan:
Peleth and Zaza.
These were the descendants of Jerahmeel.
34Sheshan had no sons—only daughters.
He had an Egyptian servant named Jarha.
35Sheshan gave his daughter in marriage to his servant Jarha, and she bore him Attai.
36Attai was the father of Nathan,
Nathan the father of Zabad,
37Zabad the father of Ephlal,
Ephlal the father of Obed,
38Obed the father of Jehu,
Jehu the father of Azariah,
39Azariah the father of Helez,
Helez the father of Eleasah,
40Eleasah the father of Sismai,
Sismai the father of Shallum,
41Shallum the father of Jekamiah, and Jekamiah the father of Elishama.

The Clans of Caleb

42The sons of Caleb the brother of Jerahmeel:
Mesha his firstborn, who was the father of Ziph, and his son Mareshah, who was the father of Hebron.
43The sons of Hebron:
Korah, Tappuah, Rekem and
Shema. 44Shema was the father of Raham, and Raham the father of Jorkeam. Rekem was the father of Shammai.
45The son of Shammai was Maon, and Maon was the father of Beth Zur.
46Caleb's concubine Ephah was the mother of Haran, Moza and Gazez. Haran was the father of Gazez.
47The sons of Jahdai:
Regem, Jotham, Geshan, Pelet, Ephah and Shaaph.
48Caleb's concubine Maacah was the mother of Sheber and Tirhanah.
49She also gave birth to Shaaph the father of Madmannah and to Sheva the father of Macbenah and Gibea. Caleb's daughter was
Acsah. 50These were the descendants of Caleb.
The sons of Hur the firstborn of Ephrathah:
Shobal the father of Kiriath
Jearim, 51Salma the father of Bethlehem, and Hareph the father of Beth Gader.
52The descendants of Shobal the father of Kiriath Jearim were:
Haroeh, half the Manahathites,
53and the clans of Kiriath Jearim: the Ithrites, Puthites, Shumathites and Mishraites. From these descended the Zorathites and Eshtaolites.
54The descendants of Salma:
Bethlehem, the Netophathites, Atroth Beth Joab, half the
Manahathites, the Zorites, 55and the clans of scribes who lived at Jabez: the Tirathites, Shimeathites and Sucathites. These are the Kenites who came from Hammath, the father of the house of Recab.

The Sons of David

3 These were the sons of David born to him in Hebron:
The firstborn was Amnon the son of Ahinoam of Jezreel;
the second, Daniel the son of Abigail of Carmel;
2the third, Absalom the son of

Maacah daughter of Talmai king of Geshur;
the fourth, Adonijah the son of Haggith;
3the fifth, Shephatiah the son of Abital;
and the sixth, Ithream, by his wife Eglah.
4These six were born to David in Hebron, where he reigned for seven years and six months.
David reigned in Jerusalem for thirty-three years, 5and these were the children born to him there:
Shammua, Shobab, Nathan and Solomon. These four were by Bathsheba daughter of Ammiel.
6There were also Ibhar, Elishua, Eliphelet, 7Nogah, Nepheg, Japhia, 8Elishama, Eliada and Eliphelet—nine in all. 9All these were the sons of David, besides his sons by his concubines. And Tamar was their sister.

The Kings of Judah

10Solomon's son was Rehoboam,
Abijah his son,
Asa his son,
Jehoshaphat his son,
11Jehoram his son,
Ahaziah his son,
Joash his son,
12Amaziah his son,
Azariah his son,
Jotham his son,
13Ahaz his son,
Hezekiah his son,
Manasseh his son,
14Amon his son,
Josiah his son.
15The sons of Josiah:
Johanan the firstborn,
Jehoiakim the second son,
Zedekiah the third,
Shallum the fourth.
16The successors of Jehoiakim:
Jehoiachin his son,
and Zedekiah.

The Royal Line After the Exile

17The descendants of Jehoiachin the captive:
Shealtiel his son, 18Malkiram, Pedaiah, Shenazzar, Jekamiah, Hoshama and Nedabiah.
19The sons of Pedaiah:
Zerubbabel and Shimei.
The sons of Zerubbabel:
Meshullam and Hananiah.
Shelomith was their sister.
20There were also five others:
Hashubah, Ohel, Berekiah, Hasadiah and Jushab-Hesed.
21The descendants of Hananiah:
Pelatiah and Jeshaiah, and the sons of Rephaiah, of Arnan, of Obadiah and of Shecaniah.
22The descendants of Shecaniah:
Shemaiah and his sons:
Hattush, Igal, Bariah, Neariah and Shaphat—six in all.
23The sons of Neariah:
Elioenai, Hizkiah and Azrikam—three in all.
24The sons of Elioenai:
Hodaviah, Eliashib, Pelaiah, Akkub, Johanan, Delaiah and Anani—seven in all.

Other Clans of Judah

4 The descendants of Judah:
Perez, Hezron, Carmi, Hur and Shobal.
2Reaiah son of Shobal was the father of Jahath, and Jahath the father of Ahumai and Lahad. These were the clans of the Zorathites.
3These were the sons of Etam:
Jezreel, Ishma and Idbash. Their sister was named Hazzelelponi.
4Penuel was the father of Gedor, and Ezer the father of Hushah.
These were the descendants of Hur, the firstborn of Ephrathah and father of Bethlehem.
5Ashhur the father of Tekoa had two wives, Helah and Naarah.
6Naarah bore him Ahuzzam, Hepher, Temeni and Haahashtari. These were the descendants of Naarah.
7The sons of Helah:
Zereth, Zohar, Ethnan, 8and

Koz, who was the father of Anub
and Hazzobebah and of the clans
of Aharhel son of Harum.

NEW TESTAMENT READING
Romans 10:5–11:10

5Moses describes in this way the
righteousness that is by the law: "The
man who does these things will live by
them." 6But the righteousness that is by
faith says: "Do not say in your heart,
'Who will ascend into heaven?'" (that
is, to bring Christ down) 7"or 'Who will
descend into the deep?'" (that is, to
bring Christ up from the dead). 8But
what does it say? "The word is near you;
it is in your mouth and in your heart,"
that is, the word of faith we are proclaiming: 9That if you confess with your
mouth, "Jesus is Lord," and believe in
your heart that God raised him from the
dead, you will be saved. 10For it is with
your heart that you believe and are
justified, and it is with your mouth that
you confess and are saved. 11As the
Scripture says, "Anyone who trusts in
him will never be put to shame." 12For
there is no difference between Jew and
Gentile—the same Lord is Lord of all
and richly blesses all who call on him,
13for, "Everyone who calls on the name
of the Lord will be saved."

14How, then, can they call on the one
they have not believed in? And how can
they believe in the one of whom they
have not heard? And how can they hear
without someone preaching to them?
15And how can they preach unless they
are sent? As it is written, "How beautiful are the feet of those who bring good
news!"

16But not all the Israelites accepted
the good news. For Isaiah says, "Lord,
who has believed our message?"
17Consequently, faith comes from hearing the message, and the message is
heard through the word of Christ. 18But
I ask: Did they not hear? Of course they
did:

"Their voice has gone out into all the
earth,
their words to the ends of the
world."

19Again I ask: Did Israel not understand? First, Moses says,

"I will make you envious by those
who are not a nation;
I will make you angry by a nation
that has no understanding."

20And Isaiah boldly says,

"I was found by those who did not
seek me;
I revealed myself to those who did
not ask for me."

21But concerning Israel he says,

"All day long I have held out my
hands
to a disobedient and obstinate
people."

The Remnant of Israel

11 I ask then: Did God reject his
people? By no means! I am an
Israelite myself, a descendant of Abraham, from the tribe of Benjamin. 2God
did not reject his people, whom he foreknew. Don't you know what the Scripture says in the passage about Elijah
—how he appealed to God against
Israel: 3"Lord, they have killed your
prophets and torn down your altars; I
am the only one left, and they are trying
to kill me"? 4And what was God's
answer to him? "I have reserved for
myself seven thousand who have not
bowed the knee to Baal." 5So too, at the
present time there is a remnant chosen
by grace. 6And if by grace, then it is no
longer by works; if it were, grace would
no longer be grace.

7What then? What Israel sought so
earnestly it did not obtain, but the elect
did. The others were hardened, 8as it is
written:

"God gave them a spirit of stupor,
eyes so that they could not see
and ears so that they could not hear,
to this very day."

9And David says:

"May their table become a snare and a trap,
a stumbling-block and a retribution for them.
10May their eyes be darkened so they cannot see,
and their backs be bent for ever."

READING FROM PROVERBS
Proverbs 18:7–16

7A fool's mouth is his undoing,
and his lips are a snare to his soul.

8The words of a gossip are like choice morsels;
they go down to a man's inmost parts.

9One who is slack in his work
is brother to one who destroys.

10The name of the LORD is a strong tower;
the righteous run to it and are safe.

11The wealth of the rich is their fortified city;
they imagine it an unscalable wall.

12Before his downfall a man's heart is proud,
but humility comes before honour.

13He who answers before listening—
that is his folly and his shame.

14A man's spirit sustains him in sickness,
but a crushed spirit who can bear?

15The heart of the discerning acquires knowledge;
the ears of the wise seek it out.

16A gift opens the way for the giver
and ushers him into the presence of the great.

JULY 28

DAY 209

OLD TESTAMENT READING
1 Chronicles 4:9–5:26

9Jabez was more honourable than his
brothers. His mother had named him
Jabez, saying, "I gave birth to him in
pain." 10Jabez cried out to the God of
Israel, "Oh, that you would bless me
and enlarge my territory! Let your hand
be with me, and keep me from harm so
that I will be free from pain." And God
granted his request.

11Kelub, Shuhah's brother, was the
father of Mehir, who was the
father of Eshton. 12Eshton was
the father of Beth Rapha,
Paseah and Tehinnah the father
of Ir Nahash. These were the
men of Recah.

13The sons of Kenaz:
Othniel and Seraiah.
The sons of Othniel:
Hathath and Meonothai.
14Meonothai was the father of
Ophrah.
Seraiah was the father of Joab,
the father of Ge Harashim. It
was called this because its people
were craftsmen.

15The sons of Caleb son of Jephunneh:
Iru, Elah and Naam.
The son of Elah:
Kenaz.
16The sons of Jehallelel:
Ziph, Ziphah, Tiria and Asarel.
17The sons of Ezrah:
Jether, Mered, Epher and Jalon.
One of Mered's wives gave birth
to Miriam, Shammai and Ishbah
the father of Eshtemoa. 18(His
Judean wife gave birth to Jered
the father of Gedor, Heber the
father of Soco, and Jekuthiel the
father of Zanoah.) These were
the children of Pharaoh's daughter Bithiah, whom Mered had
married.
19The sons of Hodiah's wife, the sister of Naham:
the father of Keilah the Garmite,
and Eshtemoa the Maacathite.
20The sons of Shimon:
Amnon, Rinnah, Ben-Hanan
and Tilon.
The descendants of Ishi:
Zoheth and Ben-Zoheth.
21The sons of Shelah son of Judah:
Er the father of Lecah, Laadah
the father of Mareshah and the
clans of the linen workers at
Beth Ashbea, 22Jokim, the men
of Cozeba, and Joash and
Saraph, who ruled in Moab and
Jashubi Lehem. (These records
are from ancient times.) 23They
were the potters who lived at
Netaim and Gederah; they
stayed there and worked for the
king.

Simeon

24The descendants of Simeon:
Nemuel, Jamin, Jarib, Zerah
and Shaul;
25Shallum was Shaul's son, Mibsam
his son and Mishma his son.
26The descendants of Mishma:
Hammuel his son, Zaccur his son
and Shimei his son.

27Shimei had sixteen sons and six
daughters, but his brothers did not have
many children; so their entire clan did
not become as numerous as the people
of Judah. 28They lived in Beersheba,
Moladah, Hazar Shual, 29Bilhah,
Ezem, Tolad, 30Bethuel, Hormah, Ziklag, 31Beth Marcaboth, Hazar Susim,
Beth Biri and Shaaraim. These were
their towns until the reign of David.
32Their surrounding villages were
Etam, Ain, Rimmon, Token and
Ashan—five towns—33and all the villages around these towns as far as
Baalath. These were their settlements.
And they kept a genealogical record.

34Meshobab, Jamlech, Joshah son
of Amaziah, 35Joel, Jehu son of
Joshibiah, the son of Seraiah, the
son of Asiel, 36also Elioenai,
Jaakobah, Jeshohaiah, Asaiah,
Adiel, Jesimiel, Benaiah, 37and
Ziza son of Shiphi, the son of
Allon, the son of Jedaiah, the son
of Shimri, the son of Shemaiah.

38The men listed above by name were
leaders of their clans. Their families
increased greatly, 39and they went to
the outskirts of Gedor to the east of the
valley in search of pasture for their
flocks. 40They found rich, good pasture,
and the land was spacious, peaceful and
quiet. Some Hamites had lived there
formerly.

41The men whose names were listed
came in the days of Hezekiah king of
Judah. They attacked the Hamites in
their dwellings and also the Meunites
who were there and completely destroyed them, as is evident to this day.
Then they settled in their place, because
there was pasture for their flocks. 42And
five hundred of these Simeonites, led
by Pelatiah, Neariah, Rephaiah and
Uzziel, the sons of Ishi, invaded the
hill country of Seir. 43They killed the
remaining Amalekites who had escaped, and they have lived there to this
day.

Reuben

5 The sons of Reuben the firstborn of Israel (he was the firstborn, but when he defiled his father's marriage bed, his rights as firstborn were given to the sons of Joseph son of Israel; so he could not be listed in the genealogical record in accordance with his birthright,
2and though Judah was the strongest of his brothers and a ruler came from him, the rights of the firstborn belonged to
Joseph)—3the sons of Reuben the firstborn of Israel:

Hanoch, Pallu, Hezron and Carmi.

4The descendants of Joel:

Shemaiah his son, Gog his son,
Shimei his son, 5Micah his son,
Reaiah his son, Baal his son,
6and Beerah his son, whom Tiglath-Pileser king of Assyria took into exile. Beerah was a leader of the Reubenites.

7Their relatives by clans, listed according to their genealogical records:

Jeiel the chief, Zechariah, 8and
Bela son of Azaz, the son of Shema, the son of Joel. They settled in the area from Aroer to
Nebo and Baal Meon. 9To the
east they occupied the land up to the edge of the desert that extends to the Euphrates River, because their livestock had increased in Gilead.

10During Saul's reign they waged war against the Hagrites, who were defeated at their hands; they occupied the dwellings of the Hagrites throughout the entire region east of Gilead.

Gad

11The Gadites lived next to them in Bashan, as far as Salecah:

12Joel was the chief, Shapham the second, then Janai and Shaphat, in Bashan.

13Their relatives, by families, were:

Michael, Meshullam, Sheba, Jorai, Jacan, Zia and Eber—seven in all.
14These were the sons of Abihail son of Huri, the son of Jaroah, the son of Gilead, the son of Michael, the son of Jeshishai, the son of Jahdo, the son of Buz.

15Ahi son of Abdiel, the son of Guni, was head of their family.

16The Gadites lived in Gilead, in Bashan and its outlying villages, and on all the pasture-lands of Sharon as far as they extended.

17All these were entered in the genealogical records during the reigns of Jotham king of Judah and Jeroboam king of Israel.

18The Reubenites, the Gadites and the half-tribe of Manasseh had 44,760 men ready for military service—able-bodied men who could handle shield and sword, who could use a bow, and
who were trained for battle. 19They
waged war against the Hagrites, Jetur,
Naphish and Nodab. 20They were
helped in fighting them, and God handed the Hagrites and all their allies over to them, because they cried out to him during the battle. He answered their prayers, because they trusted in
him. 21They seized the livestock of the
Hagrites—fifty thousand camels, two hundred and fifty thousand sheep and two thousand donkeys. They also took one hundred thousand people captive,
22and many others fell slain, because the battle was God's. And they occupied the land until the exile.

The Half-Tribe of Manasseh

23The people of the half-tribe of Manasseh were numerous; they settled in the land from Bashan to Baal Hermon, that is, to Senir (Mount Hermon).

24These were the heads of their families: Epher, Ishi, Eliel, Azriel, Jeremiah, Hodaviah and Jahdiel. They were brave warriors, famous men, and heads
of their families. 25But they were unfaithful to the God of their fathers and prostituted themselves to the gods of

the peoples of the land, whom God had destroyed before them. 26So the God of Israel stirred up the spirit of Pul king of Assyria (that is, Tiglath-Pileser king of Assyria), who took the Reubenites, the Gadites and the half-tribe of Manasseh into exile. He took them to Halah, Habor, Hara and the river of Gozan, where they are to this day.

NEW TESTAMENT READING
Romans 11:11–32

Ingrafted Branches

11Again I ask: Did they stumble so as to fall beyond recovery? Not at all! Rather, because of their transgression, salvation has come to the Gentiles to make Israel envious. 12But if their transgression means riches for the world, and their loss means riches for the Gentiles, how much greater riches will their fulness bring!

13I am talking to you Gentiles. Inasmuch as I am the apostle to the Gentiles, I make much of my ministry 14in the hope that I may somehow arouse my own people to envy and save some of them. 15For if their rejection is the reconciliation of the world, what will their acceptance be but life from the dead? 16If the part of the dough offered as firstfruits is holy, then the whole batch is holy; if the root is holy, so are the branches.

17If some of the branches have been broken off, and you, though a wild olive shoot, have been grafted in among the others and now share in the nourishing sap from the olive root, 18do not boast over those branches. If you do, consider this: You do not support the root, but the root supports you. 19You will say then, "Branches were broken off so that I could be grafted in." 20Granted. But they were broken off because of unbelief, and you stand by faith. Do not be arrogant, but be afraid. 21For if God did not spare the natural branches, he will not spare you either.

22Consider therefore the kindness and sternness of God: sternness to those who fell, but kindness to you, provided that you continue in his kindness. Otherwise, you also will be cut off. 23And if they do not persist in unbelief, they will be grafted in, for God is able to graft them in again. 24After all, if you were cut out of an olive tree that is wild by nature, and contrary to nature were grafted into a cultivated olive tree, how much more readily will these, the natural branches, be grafted into their own olive tree!

All Israel Will Be Saved

25I do not want you to be ignorant of this mystery, brothers, so that you may not be conceited: Israel has experienced a hardening in part until the full number of the Gentiles has come in. 26And so all Israel will be saved, as it is written:

"The deliverer will come from Zion;
he will turn godlessness away from Jacob.
27And this is my covenant with them
when I take away their sins."

28As far as the gospel is concerned, they are enemies on your account; but as far as election is concerned, they are loved on account of the patriarchs, 29for God's gifts and his call are irrevocable. 30Just as you who were at one time disobedient to God have now received mercy as a result of their disobedience, 31so they too have now become disobedient in order that they too may now receive mercy as a result of God's mercy to you. 32For God has bound all men over to disobedience so that he may have mercy on them all.

READING FROM PSALMS
Psalm 89:19–29

19Once you spoke in a vision,
to your faithful people you said:
"I have bestowed strength on a warrior;

I have exalted a young man from
among the people.
20I have found David my servant;
with my sacred oil I have anointed
him.
21My hand will sustain him;
surely my arm will strengthen him.
22No enemy will subject him to
tribute;
no wicked man will oppress him.
23I will crush his foes before him
and strike down his adversaries.
24My faithful love will be with him,
and through my name his horn will
be exalted.
25I will set his hand over the sea,
his right hand over the rivers.
26He will call out to me, 'You are my
Father,
my God, the Rock my Saviour.'
27I will also appoint him my firstborn,
the most exalted of the kings of the
earth.
28I will maintain my love to him for
ever,
and my covenant with him will
never fail.
29I will establish his line for ever,
his throne as long as the heavens
endure.

JULY 29

DAY 210

OLD TESTAMENT READING
1 Chronicles 6:1–81

Levi

6 The sons of Levi:
Gershon, Kohath and Merari.
2The sons of Kohath:
Amram, Izhar, Hebron and Uzziel.
3The children of Amram:
Aaron, Moses and Miriam.
The sons of Aaron:
Nadab, Abihu, Eleazar and Ithamar.
4Eleazar was the father of Phinehas,
Phinehas the father of Abishua,
5Abishua the father of Bukki,
Bukki the father of Uzzi,
6Uzzi the father of Zerahiah,
Zerahiah the father of Meraioth,
7Meraioth the father of Amariah,
Amariah the father of Ahitub,
8Ahitub the father of Zadok,
Zadok the father of Ahimaaz,
9Ahimaaz the father of Azariah,
Azariah the father of Johanan,
10Johanan the father of Azariah (it
was he who served as priest in
the temple Solomon built in
Jerusalem),
11Azariah the father of Amariah,
Amariah the father of Ahitub,
12Ahitub the father of Zadok,
Zadok the father of Shallum,
13Shallum the father of Hilkiah,
Hilkiah the father of Azariah,
14Azariah the father of Seraiah,
and Seraiah the father of Jehozadak.
15Jehozadak was deported when the
LORD sent Judah and Jerusalem
into exile by the hand of
Nebuchadnezzar.

16The sons of Levi:
Gershon, Kohath and Merari.
17These are the names of the sons of
Gershon:
Libni and Shimei.
18The sons of Kohath:
Amram, Izhar, Hebron and Uzziel.
19The sons of Merari:
Mahli and Mushi.
These are the clans of the Levites
listed according to their fathers:

20Of Gershon:
Libni his son, Jehath his son,
Zimmah his son, 21Joah his son,
Iddo his son, Zerah his son
and Jeatherai his son.
22The descendants of Kohath:
Amminadab his son, Korah his son,
Assir his son, 23Elkanah his son,
Ebiasaph his son, Assir his son,
24Tahath his son, Uriel his son,
Uzziah his son and Shaul his son.
25The descendants of Elkanah:
Amasai, Ahimoth,
26Elkanah his son, Zophai his son,
Nahath his son, 27Eliab his son,
Jeroham his son, Elkanah his son
and Samuel his son.
28The sons of Samuel:
Joel the firstborn
and Abijah the second son.
29The descendants of Merari:
Mahli, Libni his son,
Shimei his son, Uzzah his son,
30Shimea his son, Haggiah his son
and Asaiah his son.

The Temple Musicians

31These are the men David put in charge of the music in the house of the LORD after the ark came to rest there.
32They ministered with music before the tabernacle, the Tent of Meeting, until Solomon built the temple of the LORD in Jerusalem. They performed their duties according to the regulations laid down for them.
33Here are the men who served, together with their sons:
From the Kohathites:
Heman, the musician,
the son of Joel, the son of Samuel,
34the son of Elkanah, the son of Jeroham,
the son of Eliel, the son of Toah,
35the son of Zuph, the son of Elkanah,
the son of Mahath, the son of Amasai,
36the son of Elkanah, the son of Joel,
the son of Azariah, the son of Zephaniah,
37the son of Tahath, the son of Assir,
the son of Ebiasaph, the son of Korah,
38the son of Izhar, the son of Kohath,
the son of Levi, the son of Israel;
39and Heman's associate Asaph, who served at his right hand:
Asaph son of Berekiah, the son of Shimea,
40the son of Michael, the son of Baaseiah,
the son of Malkijah, 41the son of Ethni,
the son of Zerah, the son of Adaiah,
42the son of Ethan, the son of Zimmah,
the son of Shimei, 43the son of Jahath,
the son of Gershon, the son of Levi;
44and from their associates, the Merarites, at his left hand:
Ethan son of Kishi, the son of Abdi,
the son of Malluch, 45the son of Hashabiah,
the son of Amaziah, the son of Hilkiah,
46the son of Amzi, the son of Bani,
the son of Shemer, 47the son of Mahli,
the son of Mushi, the son of Merari,
the son of Levi.

48Their fellow Levites were assigned to all the other duties of the tabernacle, the house of God.
49But Aaron and his descendants were the ones who presented offerings on the altar of burnt offering and on the altar of incense in connection with all that was done in the Most Holy Place, making atonement for Israel, in accordance with

all that Moses the servant of God had commanded.

[50]These were the descendants of Aaron:
Eleazar his son, Phinehas his son,
Abishua his son, [51]Bukki his son,
Uzzi his son, Zerahiah his son,
[52]Meraioth his son, Amariah his son,
Ahitub his son, [53]Zadok his son and Ahimaaz his son.

[54]These were the locations of their settlements allotted as their territory (they were assigned to the descendants of Aaron who were from the Kohathite clan, because the first lot was for them):
[55]They were given Hebron in Judah with its surrounding pasture-lands.
[56]But the fields and villages around the city were given to Caleb son of Jephunneh.
[57]So the descendants of Aaron were given Hebron (a city of refuge), and Libnah, Jattir, Eshtemoa,
[58]Hilen, Debir,
[59]Ashan, Juttah and Beth Shemesh, together with their pasture-lands.
[60]And from the tribe of Benjamin they were given Gibeon, Geba, Alemeth and Anathoth, together with their pasture-lands.

These towns, which were distributed among the Kohathite clans, were thirteen in all.

[61]The rest of Kohath's descendants were allotted ten towns from the clans of half the tribe of Manasseh.

[62]The descendants of Gershon, clan by clan, were allotted thirteen towns from the tribes of Issachar, Asher and Naphtali, and from the part of the tribe of Manasseh that is in Bashan.

[63]The descendants of Merari, clan by clan, were allotted twelve towns from the tribes of Reuben, Gad and Zebulun.

[64]So the Israelites gave the Levites these towns and their pasture-lands.
[65]From the tribes of Judah, Simeon and Benjamin they allotted the previously named towns.

[66]Some of the Kohathite clans were given as their territory towns from the tribe of Ephraim.

[67]In the hill country of Ephraim they were given Shechem (a city of refuge), and Gezer,
[68]Jokmeam, Beth Horon,
[69]Aijalon and Gath Rimmon, together with their pasture-lands.

[70]And from half the tribe of Manasseh the Israelites gave Aner and Bileam, together with their pasture-lands, to the rest of the Kohathite clans.

[71]The Gershonites received the following:
From the clan of the half-tribe of Manasseh
they received Golan in Bashan and also Ashtaroth, together with their pasture-lands;
[72]from the tribe of Issachar
they received Kedesh, Daberath,
[73]Ramoth and Anem, together with their pasture-lands;
[74]from the tribe of Asher
they received Mashal, Abdon,
[75]Hukok and Rehob, together with their pasture-lands;
[76]and from the tribe of Naphtali
they received Kedesh in Galilee, Hammon and Kiriathaim, together with their pasture-lands.

[77]The Merarites (the rest of the Levites) received the following:
From the tribe of Zebulun
they received Jokneam, Kartah, Rimmono and Tabor, together with their pasture-lands;
[78]from the tribe of Reuben across the Jordan east of Jericho
they received Bezer in the desert, Jahzah,
[79]Kedemoth and Mephaath, together with their pasture-lands;

80and from the tribe of Gad
they received Ramoth in Gilead, Mahanaim, 81Heshbon and Jazer, together with their pasture-lands.

NEW TESTAMENT READING
Romans 11:33–12:21

Doxology

33Oh, the depth of the riches of the
wisdom and knowledge of God!
How unsearchable his judgments,
and his paths beyond tracing out!
34"Who has known the mind of the
Lord?
Or who has been his counsellor?"
35"Who has ever given to God,
that God should repay him?"
36For from him and through him and to
him are all things.
To him be the glory for ever!
Amen.

Living Sacrifices

12 Therefore, I urge you, brothers,
in view of God's mercy, to offer
your bodies as living sacrifices, holy and
pleasing to God—this is your spiritual
act of worship. 2Do not conform any
longer to the pattern of this world, but
be transformed by the renewing of your
mind. Then you will be able to test and
approve what God's will is—his good,
pleasing and perfect will.
3For by the grace given me I say to
every one of you: Do not think of yourself more highly than you ought, but
rather think of yourself with sober judgment, in accordance with the measure
of faith God has given you. 4Just as each
of us has one body with many members,
and these members do not all have the
same function, 5so in Christ we who are
many form one body, and each member
belongs to all the others. 6We have
different gifts, according to the grace
given us. If a man's gift is prophesying,
let him use it in proportion to his faith.
7If it is serving, let him serve; if it is
teaching, let him teach; 8if it is encouraging, let him encourage; if it is
contributing to the needs of others, let him give generously; if it is leadership, let him govern diligently; if it is showing mercy, let him do it cheerfully.

Love

9Love must be sincere. Hate what is
evil; cling to what is good. 10Be devoted
to one another in brotherly love.
Honour one another above yourselves.
11Never be lacking in zeal, but keep
your spiritual fervour, serving the Lord.
12Be joyful in hope, patient in affliction,
faithful in prayer. 13Share with God's
people who are in need. Practise
hospitality.
14Bless those who persecute you;
bless and do not curse. 15Rejoice with
those who rejoice; mourn with those
who mourn. 16Live in harmony with
one another. Do not be proud, but be
willing to associate with people of low
position. Do not be conceited.
17Do not repay anyone evil for evil.
Be careful to do what is right in the eyes
of everybody. 18If it is possible, as far as
it depends on you, live at peace with
everyone. 19Do not take revenge, my
friends, but leave room for God's
wrath, for it is written: "It is mine to
avenge; I will repay," says the Lord.
20On the contrary:

"If your enemy is hungry, feed him;
if he is thirsty, give him something
to drink.
In doing this, you will heap burning
coals on his head."

21Do not be overcome by evil, but overcome evil with good.

READING FROM PSALMS
Psalm 89:30–37

30"If his sons forsake my law
and do not follow my statutes,
31if they violate my decrees
and fail to keep my commands,
32I will punish their sin with the rod,
their iniquity with flogging;

33but I will not take my love from him,
nor will I ever betray my
faithfulness.
34I will not violate my covenant
or alter what my lips have
uttered.
35Once for all, I have sworn by my
holiness—
and I will not lie to David—
36that his line will continue for ever
and his throne endure before me
like the sun;
37it will be established for ever like the
moon,
the faithful witness in the sky."
Selah

JULY 30

DAY 211

OLD TESTAMENT READING

1 Chronicles 7:1–9:1a

Issachar

7 The sons of Issachar:
Tola, Puah, Jashub and Shimron
—four in all.
2The sons of Tola:
Uzzi, Rephaiah, Jeriel, Jahmai,
Ibsam and Samuel—heads of
their families. During the reign
of David, the descendants of
Tola listed as fighting men in
their genealogy numbered
22,600.
3The son of Uzzi:
Izrahiah.
The sons of Izrahiah:
Michael, Obadiah, Joel and
Isshiah. All five of them were
chiefs. 4According to their family genealogy, they had 36,000
men ready for battle, for they
had many wives and children.
5The relatives who were fighting
men belonging to all the clans of
Issachar, as listed in their genealogy, were 87,000 in all.

Benjamin

6Three sons of Benjamin:
Bela, Beker and Jediael.
7The sons of Bela:
Ezbon, Uzzi, Uzziel, Jerimoth
and Iri, heads of families—five
in all. Their genealogical record
listed 22,034 fighting men.
8The sons of Beker:
Zemirah, Joash, Eliezer,
Elioenai, Omri, Jeremoth, Abijah, Anathoth and Alemeth. All
these were the sons of Beker.
9Their genealogical record listed
the heads of families and 20,200
fighting men.
10The son of Jediael:
Bilhan.
The sons of Bilhan:
Jeush, Benjamin, Ehud,
Kenaanah, Zethan, Tarshish
and Ahishahar. 11All these sons
of Jediael were heads of families.
There were 17,200 fighting men
ready to go out to war.
12The Shuppites and Huppites were
the descendants of Ir, and the
Hushites the descendants of
Aher.

Naphtali

13The sons of Naphtali:
Jahziel, Guni, Jezer and Shillem—the descendants of Bilhah.

Manasseh

14The descendants of Manasseh:
Asriel was his descendant
through his Aramean concubine.
She gave birth to Makir the father
of Gilead. 15Makir took a wife from

among the Huppites and Shuppites. His sister's name was Maacah.

Another descendant was named Zelophehad, who had only daughters.

16 Makir's wife Maacah gave birth to a son and named him Peresh. His brother was named Sheresh, and his sons were Ulam and Rakem.

17 The son of Ulam:
Bedan.

These were the sons of Gilead son of Makir, the son of Manasseh.
18 His sister Hammoleketh gave birth to Ishhod, Abiezer and Mahlah.

19 The sons of Shemida were:
Ahian, Shechem, Likhi and Aniam.

Ephraim

20 The descendants of Ephraim:
Shuthelah, Bered his son,
Tahath his son, Eleadah his son,
Tahath his son, 21 Zabad his son
and Shuthelah his son.

Ezer and Elead were killed by the native-born men of Gath, when they went down to seize their livestock.
22 Their father Ephraim mourned for them many days, and his relatives came to comfort him.
23 Then he lay with his wife again, and she became pregnant and gave birth to a son. He named him Beriah, because there had been misfortune in his family.
24 His daughter was Sheerah, who built Lower and Upper Beth Horon as well as Uzzen Sheerah.

25 Rephah was his son, Resheph his son,
Telah his son, Tahan his son,
26 Ladan his son, Ammihud his son,
Elishama his son, 27 Nun his son
and Joshua his son.

28 Their lands and settlements included Bethel and its surrounding villages, Naaran to the east, Gezer and its villages to the west, and Shechem and its villages all the way to Ayyah and its villages.
29 Along the borders of Manasseh were Beth Shan, Taanach, Megiddo and Dor, together with their villages. The descendants of Joseph son of Israel lived in these towns.

Asher

30 The sons of Asher:
Imnah, Ishvah, Ishvi and Beriah. Their sister was Serah.

31 The sons of Beriah:
Heber and Malkiel, who was the father of Birzaith.

32 Heber was the father of Japhlet, Shomer and Hotham and of their sister Shua.

33 The sons of Japhlet:
Pasach, Bimhal and Ashvath.
These were Japhlet's sons.

34 The sons of Shomer:
Ahi, Rohgah, Hubbah and Aram.

35 The sons of his brother Helem:
Zophah, Imna, Shelesh and Amal.

36 The sons of Zophah:
Suah, Harnepher, Shual, Beri,
Imrah, 37 Bezer, Hod, Shamma,
Shilshah, Ithran and Beera.

38 The sons of Jether:
Jephunneh, Pispah and Ara.

39 The sons of Ulla:
Arah, Hanniel and Rizia.

40 All these were descendants of Asher—heads of families, choice men, brave warriors and outstanding leaders. The number of men ready for battle, as listed in their genealogy, was 26,000.

The Genealogy of Saul the Benjamite

8 Benjamin was the father of Bela his firstborn,
Ashbel the second son, Aharah the third,
2 Nohah the fourth and Rapha the fifth.

3 The sons of Bela were:
Addar, Gera, Abihud,

[4]Abishua, Naaman, Ahoah, [5]Gera, Shephuphan and Huram.

[6]These were the descendants of Ehud, who were heads of families of those living in Geba and were deported to Manahath:

[7]Naaman, Ahijah and Gera, who deported them and who was the father of Uzza and Ahihud.

[8]Sons were born to Shaharaim in Moab after he had divorced his wives Hushim and Baara. [9]By his wife Hodesh he had Jobab, Zibia, Mesha, Malcam, [10]Jeuz, Sakia and Mirmah. These were his sons, heads of families. [11]By Hushim he had Abitub and Elpaal.

[12]The sons of Elpaal:

Eber, Misham, Shemed (who built Ono and Lod with its surrounding villages), [13]and Beriah and Shema, who were heads of families of those living in Aijalon and who drove out the inhabitants of Gath.

[14]Ahio, Shashak, Jeremoth, [15]Zebadiah, Arad, Eder, [16]Michael, Ishpah and Joha were the sons of Beriah.

[17]Zebadiah, Meshullam, Hizki, Heber, [18]Ishmerai, Izliah and Jobab were the sons of Elpaal.

[19]Jakim, Zicri, Zabdi, [20]Elienai, Zillethai, Eliel, [21]Adaiah, Beraiah and Shimrath were the sons of Shimei.

[22]Ishpan, Eber, Eliel, [23]Abdon, Zicri, Hanan, [24]Hananiah, Elam, Anthothijah, [25]Iphdeiah and Penuel were the sons of Shashak.

[26]Shamsherai, Shehariah, Athaliah, [27]Jaareshiah, Elijah and Zicri were the sons of Jeroham.

[28]All these were heads of families, chiefs as listed in their genealogy, and they lived in Jerusalem.

[29]Jeiel the father of Gibeon lived in Gibeon.

His wife's name was Maacah, [30]and his firstborn son was Abdon, followed by Zur, Kish, Baal, Ner, Nadab, [31]Gedor, Ahio, Zeker [32]and Mikloth, who was the father of Shimeah. They too lived near their relatives in Jerusalem.

[33]Ner was the father of Kish, Kish the father of Saul, and Saul the father of Jonathan, Malki-Shua, Abinadab and Esh-Baal.

[34]The son of Jonathan:

Merib-Baal, who was the father of Micah.

[35]The sons of Micah:

Pithon, Melech, Tarea and Ahaz.

[36]Ahaz was the father of Jehoaddah, Jehoaddah was the father of Alemeth, Azmeveth and Zimri, and Zimri was the father of Moza. [37]Moza was the father of Binea; Raphah was his son, Eleasah his son and Azel his son.

[38]Azel had six sons, and these were their names:

Azrikam, Bokeru, Ishmael, Sheariah, Obadiah and Hanan. All these were the sons of Azel.

[39]The sons of his brother Eshek:

Ulam his firstborn, Jeush the second son and Eliphelet the third. [40]The sons of Ulam were brave warriors who could handle the bow. They had many sons and grandsons—150 in all.

All these were descendants of Benjamin.

9 All Israel was listed in the genealogies in the book of the kings of Israel.

NEW TESTAMENT READING
Romans 13:1–14

Submission to the Authorities

13 Everyone must submit himself to the governing authorities, for there is no authority except that which

God has established. The authorities
that exist have been established by
God. 2Consequently, he who rebels
against the authority is rebelling against
what God has instituted, and those who
do so will bring judgment on themselves. 3For rulers hold no terror for
those who do right, but for those who do
wrong. Do you want to be free from fear
of the one in authority? Then do what is
right and he will commend you. 4For he
is God's servant to do you good. But if
you do wrong, be afraid, for he does
not bear the sword for nothing. He is
God's servant, an agent of wrath to
bring punishment on the wrongdoer.
5Therefore, it is necessary to submit to
the authorities, not only because of
possible punishment but also because of
conscience.

6This is also why you pay taxes, for
the authorities are God's servants, who
give their full time to governing. 7Give
everyone what you owe him: If you
owe taxes, pay taxes; if revenue, then
revenue; if respect, then respect; if
honour, then honour.

Love, for the Day Is Near

8Let no debt remain outstanding,
except the continuing debt to love
one another, for he who loves his
fellow-man has fulfilled the law. 9The
commandments, "Do not commit
adultery," "Do not murder," "Do not
steal," "Do not covet," and whatever
other commandment there may be, are
summed up in this one rule: "Love your
neighbour as yourself." 10Love does no
harm to its neighbour. Therefore love is
the fulfilment of the law.

11And do this, understanding the
present time. The hour has come for
you to wake up from your slumber,
because our salvation is nearer now
than when we first believed. 12The night
is nearly over; the day is almost here. So
let us put aside the deeds of darkness
and put on the armour of light. 13Let us
behave decently, as in the daytime, not
in orgies and drunkenness, not in sexual
immorality and debauchery, not in dissension and jealousy. 14Rather, clothe
yourselves with the Lord Jesus Christ,
and do not think about how to gratify
the desires of the sinful nature.

READING FROM PSALMS

Psalm 89:38–45

38But you have rejected, you have
spurned,
you have been very angry with
your anointed one.
39You have renounced the covenant
with your servant
and have defiled his crown in the
dust.
40You have broken through all his walls
and reduced his strongholds to
ruins.
41All who pass by have plundered him;
he has become the scorn of his
neighbours.
42You have exalted the right hand of
his foes;
you have made all his enemies
rejoice.
43You have turned back the edge of his
sword
and have not supported him in
battle.
44You have put an end to his splendour
and cast his throne to the ground.
45You have cut short the days of his
youth;
you have covered him with a
mantle of shame. *Selah*

OLD TESTAMENT READING
1 Chronicles 9:1b–10:14

The People in Jerusalem

The people of Judah were taken captive to Babylon because of their unfaithfulness. 2Now the first to resettle on
their own property in their own towns
were some Israelites, priests, Levites
and temple servants.
3Those from Judah, from Benjamin,
and from Ephraim and Manasseh who
lived in Jerusalem were:
4Uthai son of Ammihud, the son of
Omri, the son of Imri, the son of
Bani, a descendant of Perez son
of Judah.
5Of the Shilonites:
Asaiah the firstborn and his
sons.
6Of the Zerahites:
Jeuel.
The people from Judah numbered 690.
7Of the Benjamites:
Sallu son of Meshullam, the son
of Hodaviah, the son of Hassenuah;
8Ibneiah son of Jeroham; Elah
son of Uzzi, the son of Micri; and
Meshullam son of Shephatiah,
the son of Reuel, the son of
Ibnijah.
9The people from Benjamin, as
listed in their genealogy, numbered 956. All these men were
heads of their families.
10Of the priests:
Jedaiah; Jehoiarib; Jakin;
11Azariah son of Hilkiah, the son
of Meshullam, the son of Zadok,
the son of Meraioth, the son of
Ahitub, the official in charge of
the house of God;
12Adaiah son of Jeroham, the son
of Pashhur, the son of Malkijah;
and Maasai son of Adiel, the son
of Jahzerah, the son of Meshullam, the son of Meshillemith, the
son of Immer.
13The priests, who were heads of
families, numbered 1,760. They
were able men, responsible for
ministering in the house of God.
14Of the Levites:
Shemaiah son of Hasshub, the
son of Azrikam, the son of
Hashabiah, a Merarite; 15Bak-
bakkar, Heresh, Galal and
Mattaniah son of Mica, the son
of Zicri, the son of Asaph;
16Obadiah son of Shemaiah, the
son of Galal, the son of
Jeduthun; and Berekiah son of
Asa, the son of Elkanah, who
lived in the villages of the
Netophathites.
17The gatekeepers:
Shallum, Akkub, Talmon, Ahiman and their brothers, Shallum
their chief 18being stationed at
the King's Gate on the east, up
to the present time. These were
the gatekeepers belonging to the
camp of the Levites. 19Shallum
son of Kore, the son of
Ebiasaph, the son of Korah, and
his fellow gatekeepers from his
family (the Korahites) were responsible for guarding the
thresholds of the Tent just as
their fathers had been responsible for guarding the entrance to
the dwelling of the LORD. 20In
earlier times Phinehas son of
Eleazar was in charge of the
gatekeepers, and the LORD was
with him.
21Zechariah son of Meshelemiah
was the gatekeeper at the entrance to the Tent of Meeting.
22Altogether, those chosen to be
gatekeepers at the thresholds numbered 212. They were registered by
genealogy in their villages. The

gatekeepers had been assigned to their
positions of trust by David and Samuel
the seer. 23They and their descendants
were in charge of guarding the gates of
the house of the LORD—the house
called the Tent. 24The gatekeepers were
on the four sides: east, west, north and
south. 25Their brothers in their villages
had to come from time to time and share
their duties for seven-day periods. 26But
the four principal gatekeepers, who
were Levites, were entrusted with the
responsibility for the rooms and
treasuries in the house of God. 27They
would spend the night stationed round
the house of God, because they had to
guard it; and they had charge of the key
for opening it each morning.

28Some of them were in charge of the
articles used in the temple service; they
counted them when they were brought
in and when they were taken out.
29Others were assigned to take care of
the furnishings and all the other articles
of the sanctuary, as well as the flour and
wine, and the oil, incense and spices.
30But some of the priests took care of
mixing the spices. 31A Levite named
Mattithiah, the firstborn son of Shallum
the Korahite, was entrusted with the
responsibility for baking the offering
bread. 32Some of their Kohathite
brothers were in charge of preparing for
every Sabbath the bread set out on the
table.

33Those who were musicians, heads
of Levite families, stayed in the rooms
of the temple and were exempt from
other duties because they were responsible for the work day and night.

34All these were heads of Levite families, chiefs as listed in their genealogy,
and they lived in Jerusalem.

The Genealogy of Saul

35Jeiel the father of Gibeon lived in
Gibeon.
His wife's name was Maacah,
36and his firstborn son was
Abdon, followed by Zur, Kish,
Baal, Ner, Nadab, 37Gedor,
Ahio, Zechariah and Mikloth.
38Mikloth was the father of
Shimeam. They too lived near
their relatives in Jerusalem.

39Ner was the father of Kish, Kish
the father of Saul, and Saul the
father of Jonathan, Malki-Shua,
Abinadab and Esh-Baal.

40The son of Jonathan:
Merib-Baal, who was the father
of Micah.

41The sons of Micah:
Pithon, Melech, Tahrea and
Ahaz.
42Ahaz was the father of Jadah,
Jadah was the father of Alemeth,
Azmaveth and Zimri, and Zimri
was the father of Moza. 43Moza
was the father of Binea;
Rephaiah was his son, Eleasah
his son and Azel his son.

44Azel had six sons, and these were
their names:
Azrikam, Bokeru, Ishmael,
Sheariah, Obadiah and Hanan.
These were the sons of Azel.

Saul Takes His Life

10 Now the Philistines fought
against Israel; the Israelites fled
before them, and many fell slain on
Mount Gilboa. 2The Philistines pressed
hard after Saul and his sons, and they
killed his sons Jonathan, Abinadab and
Malki-Shua. 3The fighting grew fierce
around Saul, and when the archers
overtook him, they wounded him.

4Saul said to his armour-bearer,
"Draw your sword and run me through,
or these uncircumcised fellows will
come and abuse me."

But his armour-bearer was terrified
and would not do it; so Saul took his
own sword and fell on it. 5When the
armour-bearer saw that Saul was dead,
he too fell on his sword and died. 6So
Saul and his three sons died, and all his
house died together.

7When all the Israelites in the valley
saw that the army had fled and that Saul
and his sons had died, they abandoned

their towns and fled. And the Philistines
came and occupied them.
8The next day, when the Philistines
came to strip the dead, they found Saul
and his sons fallen on Mount Gilboa.
9They stripped him and took his head
and his armour, and sent messengers
throughout the land of the Philistines to
proclaim the news among their idols
and their people. 10They put his armour
in the temple of their gods and hung up
his head in the temple of Dagon.
11When all the inhabitants of Jabesh
Gilead heard of everything the Philistines had done to Saul, 12all their valiant
men went and took the bodies of Saul
and his sons and brought them to
Jabesh. Then they buried their bones
under the great tree in Jabesh, and they
fasted seven days.
13Saul died because he was unfaithful
to the LORD; he did not keep the word
of the LORD, and even consulted a
medium for guidance, 14and did not enquire of the LORD. So the LORD put him
to death and turned the kingdom over
to David son of Jesse.

NEW TESTAMENT READING
Romans 14:1–18

The Weak and the Strong

14 Accept him whose faith is weak,
without passing judgment on
disputable matters. 2One man's faith
allows him to eat everything, but
another man, whose faith is weak, eats
only vegetables. 3The man who eats
everything must not look down on him
who does not, and the man who does
not eat everything must not condemn
the man who does, for God has
accepted him. 4Who are you to judge
someone else's servant? To his own
master he stands or falls. And he will
stand, for the Lord is able to make him
stand.
5One man considers one day more
sacred than another; another man considers every day alike. Each one should
be fully convinced in his own mind. 6He
who regards one day as special, does so
to the Lord. He who eats meat, eats to
the Lord, for he gives thanks to God;
and he who abstains, does so to the
Lord and gives thanks to God. 7For
none of us lives to himself alone and
none of us dies to himself alone. 8If we
live, we live to the Lord; and if we die,
we die to the Lord. So, whether we live
or die, we belong to the Lord.
9For this very reason, Christ died and
returned to life so that he might be the
Lord of both the dead and the living.
10You, then, why do you judge your
brother? Or why do you look down on
your brother? For we will all stand
before God's judgment seat. 11It is
written:

"'As surely as I live,' says the Lord,
'Every knee will bow before me;
every tongue will confess to
God.'"

12So then, each of us will give an
account of himself to God.
13Therefore let us stop passing judgment on one another. Instead, make up
your mind not to put any stumbling-
block or obstacle in your brother's way.
14As one who is in the Lord Jesus, I am
fully convinced that no food is unclean
in itself. But if anyone regards something as unclean, then for him it is unclean. 15If your brother is distressed
because of what you eat, you are no
longer acting in love. Do not by your
eating destroy your brother for whom
Christ died. 16Do not allow what you
consider good to be spoken of as evil.
17For the kingdom of God is not a matter of eating and drinking, but of righteousness, peace and joy in the Holy
Spirit, 18because anyone who serves
Christ in this way is pleasing to God and
approved by men.

READING FROM PROVERBS
Proverbs 18:17–19:2

17The first to present his case seems
right,
till another comes forward and
questions him.

18Casting the lot settles disputes
and keeps strong opponents apart.

19An offended brother is more
unyielding than a fortified city,
and disputes are like the barred
gates of a citadel.

20From the fruit of his mouth a man's
stomach is filled;
with the harvest from his lips he is
satisfied.

21The tongue has the power of life and
death,
and those who love it will eat its
fruit.

22He who finds a wife finds what is
good
and receives favour from the
LORD.

23A poor man pleads for mercy,
but a rich man answers harshly.

24A man of many companions may
come to ruin,
but there is a friend who sticks
closer than a brother.

19 Better a poor man whose walk
is blameless
than a fool whose lips are perverse.

2It is not good to have zeal without
knowledge,
nor to be hasty and miss the way.

DAY 213

AUGUST 1

OLD TESTAMENT READING
1 Chronicles 11:1–12:22

David Becomes King Over Israel

11 All Israel came together to
David at Hebron and said, "We
are your own flesh and blood. 2In the
past, even while Saul was king, you
were the one who led Israel on their
military campaigns. And the LORD your
God said to you, 'You will shepherd my
people Israel, and you will become their
ruler.'"
3When all the elders of Israel had
come to King David at Hebron, he
made a compact with them at Hebron
before the LORD, and they anointed
David king over Israel, as the LORD had
promised through Samuel.

David Conquers Jerusalem

4David and all the Israelites marched
to Jerusalem (that is, Jebus). The Jebusites who lived there 5said to David,
"You will not get in here." Nevertheless, David captured the fortress of
Zion, the City of David.
6David had said, "Whoever leads the
attack on the Jebusites will become
commander-in-chief." Joab son of
Zeruiah went up first, and so he received the command.
7David then took up residence in the
fortress, and so it was called the City of
David. 8He built up the city around it,
from the supporting terraces to the surrounding wall, while Joab restored the
rest of the city. 9And David became
more and more powerful, because the
LORD Almighty was with him.

David's Mighty Men

[10]These were the chiefs of David's
mighty men—they, together with all
Israel, gave his kingship strong support
to extend it over the whole land, as the
LORD had promised—[11]this is the list of
David's mighty men:

Jashobeam, a Hacmonite, was chief
of the officers; he raised his spear
against three hundred men, whom he
killed in one encounter.

[12]Next to him was Eleazar son of
Dodai the Ahohite, one of the three
mighty men. [13]He was with David at Pas
Dammim when the Philistines gathered
there for battle. At a place where there
was a field full of barley, the troops fled
from the Philistines. [14]But they took
their stand in the middle of the field.
They defended it and struck the Philistines down, and the LORD brought
about a great victory.

[15]Three of the thirty chiefs came
down to David to the rock at the cave of
Adullam, while a band of Philistines
was encamped in the Valley of
Rephaim. [16]At that time David was in
the stronghold, and the Philistine garrison was at Bethlehem. [17]David longed
for water and said, "Oh, that someone
would get me a drink of water from the
well near the gate of Bethlehem!" [18]So
the Three broke through the Philistine
lines, drew water from the well near the
gate of Bethlehem and carried it back to
David. But he refused to drink it; instead, he poured it out before the LORD.
[19]"God forbid that I should do this!"
he said. "Should I drink the blood of
these men who went at the risk of their
lives?" Because they risked their lives
to bring it back, David would not drink
it.

Such were the exploits of the three
mighty men.

[20]Abishai the brother of Joab was
chief of the Three. He raised his spear
against three hundred men, whom he
killed, and so he became as famous as
the Three. [21]He was doubly honoured
above the Three and became their
commander, even though he was not
included among them.

[22]Benaiah son of Jehoiada was a
valiant fighter from Kabzeel, who performed great exploits. He struck down
two of Moab's best men. He also went
down into a pit on a snowy day and
killed a lion. [23]And he struck down an
Egyptian who was seven and a half
feet tall. Although the Egyptian had a
spear like a weaver's rod in his hand,
Benaiah went against him with a club.
He snatched the spear from the Egyptian's hand and killed him with his
own spear. [24]Such were the exploits of
Benaiah son of Jehoiada; he too was as
famous as the three mighty men. [25]He
was held in greater honour than any
of the Thirty, but he was not included
among the Three. And David put him
in charge of his bodyguard.

[26]The mighty men were:
Asahel the brother of Joab,
Elhanan son of Dodo from Beth-
lehem,
[27]Shammoth the Harorite,
Helez the Pelonite,
[28]Ira son of Ikkesh from Tekoa,
Abiezer from Anathoth,
[29]Sibbecai the Hushathite,
Ilai the Ahohite,
[30]Maharai the Netophathite,
Heled son of Baanah the
Netophathite,
[31]Ithai son of Ribai from Gibeah
in Benjamin,
Benaiah the Pirathonite,
[32]Hurai from the ravines of
Gaash,
Abiel the Arbathite,
[33]Azmaveth the Baharumite,
Eliahba the Shaalbonite,
[34]the sons of Hashem the Gizo-
nite,
Jonathan son of Shagee the
Hararite,
[35]Ahiam son of Sacar the Hara-
rite,
Eliphal son of Ur,
[36]Hepher the Mekerathite,
Ahijah the Pelonite,

37Hezro the Carmelite,
Naarai son of Ezbai,
38Joel the brother of Nathan,
Mibhar son of Hagri,
39Zelek the Ammonite,
Naharai the Berothite, the armour-bearer of Joab son of Zeruiah,
40Ira the Ithrite,
Gareb the Ithrite,
41Uriah the Hittite,
Zabad son of Ahlai,
42Adina son of Shiza the Reubenite, who was chief of the Reubenites, and the thirty with him,
43Hanan son of Maacah,
Joshaphat the Mithnite,
44Uzzia the Ashterathite,
Shama and Jeiel the sons of Hotham the Aroerite,
45Jediael son of Shimri,
his brother Joha the Tizite,
46Eliel the Mahavite,
Jeribai and Joshaviah the sons of Elnaam,
Ithmah the Moabite,
47Eliel, Obed and Jaasiel the Mezobaite.

Warriors Join David

12 These were the men who came
to David at Ziklag, while he was
banished from the presence of Saul son
of Kish (they were among the warriors
who helped him in battle; 2they were
armed with bows and were able to shoot arrows or to sling stones right-handed or left-handed; they were kinsmen of Saul from the tribe of Benjamin):

3Ahiezer their chief and Joash the sons of Shemaah the Gibeathite; Jeziel and Pelet the sons of Azmaveth; Beracah, Jehu the
Anathothite, 4and Ishmaiah the
Gibeonite, a mighty man among the Thirty, who was a leader of the Thirty; Jeremiah, Jahaziel, Johanan, Jozabad the Gederathite,
5Eluzai, Jerimoth, Bealiah, Shemariah and Shephatiah the Haruphite; 6Elkanah, Isshiah, Azarel, Joezer and Jashobeam the Korahites; 7and Joelah and Zebadiah the sons of Jeroham from Gedor.

8Some Gadites defected to David at his stronghold in the desert. They were brave warriors, ready for battle and able to handle the shield and spear. Their faces were the faces of lions, and they were as swift as gazelles in the mountains.

9Ezer was the chief,
Obadiah the second in command,
Eliab the third,
10Mishmannah the fourth, Jeremiah the fifth,
11Attai the sixth, Eliel the seventh,
12Johanan the eighth, Elzabad the ninth,
13Jeremiah the tenth and Macbannai the eleventh.

14These Gadites were army commanders; the least was a match for a hundred, and the greatest for a thousand.
15It was they who crossed the Jordan in the first month when it was overflowing all its banks, and they put to flight everyone living in the valleys, to the east and to the west.

16Other Benjamites and some men from Judah also came to David in his
stronghold. 17David went out to meet them and said to them, "If you have come to me in peace, to help me, I am ready to have you unite with me. But if you have come to betray me to my enemies when my hands are free from violence, may the God of our fathers see it and judge you."

18Then the Spirit came upon Amasai, chief of the Thirty, and he said:

"We are yours, O David!
We are with you, O son of Jesse!
Success, success to you,
and success to those who help you,
for your God will help you."

So David received them and made them leaders of his raiding bands.

19Some of the men of Manasseh defected to David when he went with the
Philistines to fight against Saul. (He and
his men did not help the Philistines because, after consultation, their rulers
sent him away. They said, "It will cost
us our heads if he deserts to his master
Saul.") 20When David went to Ziklag,
these were the men of Manasseh who
defected to him: Adnah, Jozabad,
Jediael, Michael, Jozabad, Elihu and
Zillethai, leaders of units of a thousand
in Manasseh. 21They helped David
against raiding bands, for all of them
were brave warriors, and they were
commanders in his army. 22Day after
day men came to help David, until he
had a great army, like the army of God.

NEW TESTAMENT READING
Romans 14:19–15:13

19Let us therefore make every effort
to do what leads to peace and to mutual
edification. 20Do not destroy the work
of God for the sake of food. All food is
clean, but it is wrong for a man to eat
anything that causes someone else to
stumble. 21It is better not to eat meat or
drink wine or to do anything else that
will cause your brother to fall.

22So whatever you believe about
these things keep between yourself and
God. Blessed is the man who does not
condemn himself by what he approves.
23But the man who has doubts is condemned if he eats, because his eating is
not from faith; and everything that does
not come from faith is sin.

15 We who are strong ought to bear
with the failings of the weak and
not to please ourselves. 2Each of us
should please his neighbour for his
good, to build him up. 3For even Christ
did not please himself but, as it is written: "The insults of those who insult you
have fallen on me." 4For everything that
was written in the past was written to
teach us, so that through endurance and
the encouragement of the Scriptures we
might have hope.

5May the God who gives endurance
and encouragement give you a spirit of
unity among yourselves as you follow
Christ Jesus, 6so that with one heart and
mouth you may glorify the God and
Father of our Lord Jesus Christ.

7Accept one another, then, just as
Christ accepted you, in order to bring
praise to God. 8For I tell you that Christ
has become a servant of the Jews on
behalf of God's truth, to confirm the
promises made to the patriarchs 9so that
the Gentiles may glorify God for his
mercy, as it is written:

"Therefore I will praise you among
the Gentiles;
I will sing hymns to your name."

10Again, it says,

"Rejoice, O Gentiles, with his
people."

11And again,

"Praise the Lord, all you Gentiles,
and sing praises to him, all you
peoples."

12And again, Isaiah says,

"The Root of Jesse will spring up,
one who will arise to rule over the
nations;
the Gentiles will hope in him."

13May the God of hope fill you with
all joy and peace as you trust in him, so
that you may overflow with hope by the
power of the Holy Spirit.

READING FROM PSALMS
Psalm 89:46–52

46How long, O LORD? Will you hide
yourself for ever?
How long will your wrath burn like
fire?
47Remember how fleeting is my life.

For what futility you have created
all men!
48What man can live and not see death,
or save himself from the power of
the grave? *Selah*
49O Lord, where is your former great
love,
which in your faithfulness you
swore to David?
50Remember, Lord, how your servant
has been mocked,
how I bear in my heart the taunts
of all the nations,
51the taunts with which your enemies
have mocked, O LORD,
with which they have mocked
every step of your anointed
one.

52Praise be to the LORD for ever!
Amen and Amen.

DAY 214

AUGUST 2

OLD TESTAMENT READING
1 Chronicles 12:23–14:17

Others Join David at Hebron

23These are the numbers of the men
armed for battle who came to David at
Hebron to turn Saul's kingdom over to
him, as the LORD had said:
24men of Judah, carrying shield and
spear—6,800 armed for battle;
25men of Simeon, warriors ready for
battle—7,100;
26men of Levi—4,600, 27including
Jehoiada, leader of the family of
Aaron with 3,700 men, 28and
Zadok, a brave young warrior,
with 22 officers from his family;
29men of Benjamin, Saul's kinsmen
—3,000, most of whom had
remained loyal to Saul's house
until then;
30men of Ephraim, brave warriors,
famous in their own clans—
20,800;
31men of half the tribe of Manasseh,
designated by name to come and
make David king—18,000;
32men of Issachar, who understood
the times and knew what Israel
should do—200 chiefs, with
all their relatives under their
command;
33men of Zebulun, experienced
soldiers prepared for battle with
every type of weapon, to help
David with undivided loyalty—
50,000;
34men of Naphtali—1,000 officers,
together with 37,000 men carrying
shields and spears;
35men of Dan, ready for battle—
28,600;
36men of Asher, experienced soldiers
prepared for battle—
40,000;
37and from east of the Jordan, men
of Reuben, Gad, and the half-tribe
of Manasseh, armed with
every type of weapon—120,000.
38All these were fighting men who
volunteered to serve in the ranks. They
came to Hebron fully determined to
make David king over all Israel. All the
rest of the Israelites were also of one
mind to make David king.
39The men
spent three days there with David, eating
and drinking, for their families had
supplied provisions for them.
40Also,
their neighbours from as far away as
Issachar, Zebulun and Naphtali came
bringing food on donkeys, camels,
mules and oxen. There were plentiful
supplies of flour, fig cakes, raisin cakes,
wine, oil, cattle and sheep, for there was
joy in Israel.

Bringing Back the Ark

13 David conferred with each of his officers, the commanders of thousands and commanders of hundreds. 2He then said to the whole assembly of Israel, "If it seems good to you and if it is the will of the LORD our God, let us send word far and wide to the rest of our brothers throughout the territories of Israel, and also to the priests and Levites who are with them in their towns and pasture-lands, to come and join us. 3Let us bring the ark of our God back to us, for we did not enquire of it during the reign of Saul." 4The whole assembly agreed to do this, because it seemed right to all the people.

5So David assembled all the Israelites, from the Shihor River in Egypt to Lebo Hamath, to bring the ark of God from Kiriath Jearim. 6David and all the Israelites with him went to Baalah of Judah (Kiriath Jearim) to bring up from there the ark of God the LORD, who is enthroned between the cherubim—the ark that is called by the Name.

7They moved the ark of God from Abinadab's house on a new cart, with Uzzah and Ahio guiding it. 8David and all the Israelites were celebrating with all their might before God, with songs and with harps, lyres, tambourines, cymbals and trumpets.

9When they came to the threshing-floor of Kidon, Uzzah reached out his hand to steady the ark, because the oxen stumbled. 10The LORD's anger burned against Uzzah, and he struck him down because he had put his hand on the ark. So he died there before God.

11Then David was angry because the LORD's wrath had broken out against Uzzah, and to this day that place is called Perez Uzzah.

12David was afraid of God that day and asked, "How can I ever bring the ark of God to me?" 13He did not take the ark to be with him in the City of David. Instead, he took it aside to the house of Obed-Edom the Gittite. 14The ark of God remained with the family of Obed-Edom in his house for three months, and the LORD blessed his household and everything he had.

David's House and Family

14 Now Hiram king of Tyre sent messengers to David, along with cedar logs, stonemasons and carpenters to build a palace for him. 2And David knew that the LORD had established him as king over Israel and that his kingdom had been highly exalted for the sake of his people Israel.

3In Jerusalem David took more wives and became the father of more sons and daughters. 4These are the names of the children born to him there: Shammua, Shobab, Nathan, Solomon, 5Ibhar, Elishua, Elpelet, 6Nogah, Nepheg, Japhia, 7Elishama, Beeliada and Eliphelet.

David Defeats the Philistines

8When the Philistines heard that David had been anointed king over all Israel, they went up in full force to search for him, but David heard about it and went out to meet them. 9Now the Philistines had come and raided the Valley of Rephaim; 10so David enquired of God: "Shall I go and attack the Philistines? Will you hand them over to me?"

The LORD answered him, "Go, I will hand them over to you."

11So David and his men went up to Baal Perazim, and there he defeated them. He said, "As waters break out, God has broken out against my enemies by my hand." So that place was called Baal Perazim. 12The Philistines had abandoned their gods there, and David gave orders to burn them in the fire.

13Once more the Philistines raided the valley; 14so David enquired of God again, and God answered him, "Do not go straight up, but circle round them and attack them in front of the balsam

trees. 15As soon as you hear the sound
of marching in the tops of the balsam
trees, move out to battle, because that
will mean God has gone out in front of
you to strike the Philistine army." 16So
David did as God commanded him, and
they struck down the Philistine army, all
the way from Gibeon to Gezer.
17So David's fame spread throughout
every land, and the LORD made all the
nations fear him.

NEW TESTAMENT READING
Romans 15:14–33

Paul the Minister to the Gentiles

14I myself am convinced, my
brothers, that you yourselves are full of
goodness, complete in knowledge and
competent to instruct one another. 15I
have written to you quite boldly on
some points, as if to remind you of them
again, because of the grace God gave
me 16to be a minister of Christ Jesus to
the Gentiles with the priestly duty of
proclaiming the gospel of God, so that
the Gentiles might become an offering
acceptable to God, sanctified by the
Holy Spirit.
17Therefore I glory in Christ Jesus in
my service to God. 18I will not venture
to speak of anything except what Christ
has accomplished through me in leading
the Gentiles to obey God by what I have
said and done—19by the power of signs
and miracles, through the power of the
Spirit. So from Jerusalem all the way
around to Illyricum, I have fully proclaimed the gospel of Christ. 20It has
always been my ambition to preach the
gospel where Christ was not known, so
that I would not be building on someone else's foundation. 21Rather, as it is
written:

"Those who were not told about him
will see,
and those who have not heard will
understand."

22This is why I have often been hindered
from coming to you.

Paul's Plan to Visit Rome

23But now that there is no more place
for me to work in these regions, and
since I have been longing for many
years to see you, 24I plan to do so when I
go to Spain. I hope to visit you while
passing through and to have you assist
me on my journey there, after I have
enjoyed your company for a while.
25Now, however, I am on my way to
Jerusalem in the service of the saints
there. 26For Macedonia and Achaia
were pleased to make a contribution for
the poor among the saints in Jerusalem.
27They were pleased to do it, and indeed
they owe it to them. For if the Gentiles
have shared in the Jews' spiritual blessings, they owe it to the Jews to share
with them their material blessings. 28So
after I have completed this task and
have made sure that they have received
this fruit, I will go to Spain and visit you
on the way. 29I know that when I come
to you, I will come in the full measure of
the blessing of Christ.
30I urge you, brothers, by our Lord
Jesus Christ and by the love of the
Spirit, to join me in my struggle by
praying to God for me. 31Pray that I
may be rescued from the unbelievers in
Judea and that my service in Jerusalem
may be acceptable to the saints there,
32so that by God's will I may come to
you with joy and together with you be
refreshed. 33The God of peace be with
you all. Amen.

READING FROM PSALMS
Psalm 90:1–10

A prayer of Moses the man of God.

1Lord, you have been our
dwelling-place
throughout all generations.

[2]Before the mountains were born
or you brought forth the earth and
the world,
from everlasting to everlasting you
are God.

[3]You turn men back to dust,
saying, "Return to dust, O sons of
men."
[4]For a thousand years in your sight
are like a day that has just gone
by,
or like a watch in the night.
[5]You sweep men away in the sleep of
death;
they are like the new grass of the
morning—
[6]though in the morning it springs up
new,
by evening it is dry and
withered.
[7]We are consumed by your anger
and terrified by your indignation.
[8]You have set our iniquities before
you,
our secret sins in the light of your
presence.
[9]All our days pass away under your
wrath;
we finish our years with a moan.
[10]The length of our days is seventy
years—
or eighty, if we have the strength;
yet their span is but trouble and
sorrow,
for they quickly pass, and we fly
away.

AUGUST 3

DAY 215

OLD TESTAMENT READING
1 Chronicles 15:1–16:36

The Ark Brought to Jerusalem

15 After David had constructed
buildings for himself in the City
of David, he prepared a place for the
ark of God and pitched a tent for it.
[2]Then David said, "No-one but the Levites may carry the ark of God, because
the LORD chose them to carry the ark of
the LORD and to minister before him for
ever."
[3]David assembled all Israel in Jerusalem to bring up the ark of the LORD to
the place he had prepared for it. [4]He
called together the descendants of
Aaron and the Levites:
[5]From the descendants of Kohath,
Uriel the leader and 120 relatives;
[6]from the descendants of Merari,
Asaiah the leader and 220 relatives;
[7]from the descendants of Gershon,
Joel the leader and 130 relatives;
[8]from the descendants of Elizaphan,
Shemaiah the leader and 200
relatives;
[9]from the descendants of Hebron,
Eliel the leader and 80 relatives;
[10]from the descendants of Uzziel,
Amminadab the leader and 112
relatives.
[11]Then David summoned Zadok and
Abiathar the priests, and Uriel, Asaiah,
Joel, Shemaiah, Eliel and Amminadab
the Levites. [12]He said to them, "You
are the heads of the Levitical families;
you and your fellow Levites are to consecrate yourselves and bring up the ark
of the LORD, the God of Israel, to the
place I have prepared for it. [13]It was
because you, the Levites, did not bring
it up the first time that the LORD our
God broke out in anger against us. We
did not enquire of him about how to do
it in the prescribed way." [14]So the

priests and Levites consecrated themselves in order to bring up the ark of the
LORD, the God of Israel. 15And the
Levites carried the ark of God with
the poles on their shoulders, as Moses
had commanded in accordance with
the word of the LORD.

16David told the leaders of the Levites to appoint their brothers as singers
to sing joyful songs, accompanied by
musical instruments: lyres, harps and
cymbals.

17So the Levites appointed Heman
son of Joel; from his brothers, Asaph
son of Berekiah; and from their
brothers the Merarites, Ethan son of
Kushaiah; 18and with them their
brothers next in rank: Zechariah,
Jaaziel, Shemiramoth, Jehiel, Unni,
Eliab, Benaiah, Maaseiah, Mattithiah,
Eliphelehu, Mikneiah, Obed-Edom
and Jeiel, the gatekeepers.

19The musicians Heman, Asaph and
Ethan were to sound the bronze cymbals; 20Zechariah, Aziel, Shemiramoth,
Jehiel, Unni, Eliab, Maaseiah and Benaiah were to play the lyres according to
alamoth, 21and Mattithiah, Eliphelehu,
Mikneiah, Obed-Edom, Jeiel and Azaziah were to play the harps, directing
according to *sheminith*. 22Kenaniah the
head Levite was in charge of the singing; that was his responsibility because
he was skilful at it.

23Berekiah and Elkanah were to be
doorkeepers for the ark. 24Shebaniah,
Joshaphat, Nethanel, Amasai, Zechariah, Benaiah and Eliezer the priests
were to blow trumpets before the ark of
God. Obed-Edom and Jehiah were also
to be doorkeepers for the ark.

25So David and the elders of Israel
and the commanders of units of a
thousand went to bring up the ark of the
covenant of the LORD from the house of
Obed-Edom, with rejoicing. 26Because
God had helped the Levites who were
carrying the ark of the covenant of the
LORD, seven bulls and seven rams were
sacrificed. 27Now David was clothed in a
robe of fine linen, as were all the Levites
who were carrying the ark, and as were
the singers, and Kenaniah, who was in
charge of the singing of the choirs.
David also wore a linen ephod. 28So all
Israel brought up the ark of the covenant of the LORD with shouts, with the
sounding of rams' horns and trumpets,
and of cymbals, and the playing of lyres
and harps.

29As the ark of the covenant of the
LORD was entering the City of David,
Michal daughter of Saul watched from a
window. And when she saw King David
dancing and celebrating, she despised
him in her heart.

16 They brought the ark of God
and set it inside the tent that
David had pitched for it, and they presented burnt offerings and fellowship
offerings before God. 2After David had
finished sacrificing the burnt offerings
and fellowship offerings, he blessed the
people in the name of the LORD. 3Then
he gave a loaf of bread, a cake of dates
and a cake of raisins to each Israelite
man and woman.

4He appointed some of the Levites to
minister before the ark of the LORD,
to make petition, to give thanks, and
to praise the LORD, the God of Israel: 5Asaph was the chief, Zechariah
second, then Jeiel, Shemiramoth,
Jehiel, Mattithiah, Eliab, Benaiah,
Obed-Edom and Jeiel. They were to
play the lyres and harps, Asaph was to
sound the cymbals, 6and Benaiah and
Jahaziel the priests were to blow the
trumpets regularly before the ark of the
covenant of God.

David's Psalm of Thanks

7That day David first committed to
Asaph and his associates this psalm of
thanks to the LORD:

8Give thanks to the LORD, call on his
name;
make known among the nations
what he has done.
9Sing to him, sing praise to him;
tell of all his wonderful acts.
10Glory in his holy name;

let the hearts of those who seek the
LORD rejoice.
11Look to the LORD and his strength;
seek his face always.
12Remember the wonders he has done,
his miracles, and the judgments he
pronounced,
13O descendants of Israel his servant,
O sons of Jacob, his chosen ones.

14He is the LORD our God;
his judgments are in all the earth.
15He remembers his covenant for ever,
the word he commanded, for a
thousand generations,
16the covenant he made with Abraham,
the oath he swore to Isaac.
17He confirmed it to Jacob as a decree,
to Israel as an everlasting
covenant:
18"To you I will give the land of
Canaan
as the portion you will inherit."

19When they were but few in number,
few indeed, and strangers in it,
20they wandered from nation to nation,
from one kingdom to another.
21He allowed no man to oppress them;
for their sake he rebuked kings:
22"Do not touch my anointed ones;
do my prophets no harm."

23Sing to the LORD, all the earth;
proclaim his salvation day after
day.
24Declare his glory among the nations,
his marvellous deeds among all
peoples.
25For great is the LORD and most
worthy of praise;
he is to be feared above all gods.
26For all the gods of the nations are
idols,
but the LORD made the heavens.
27Splendour and majesty are before
him;
strength and joy in his
dwelling-place.
28Ascribe to the LORD, O families of
nations,
ascribe to the LORD glory and
strength,
29 ascribe to the LORD the glory due
to his name.
Bring an offering and come before
him;
worship the LORD in the splendour
of his holiness.
30Tremble before him, all the earth!
The world is firmly established; it
cannot be moved.
31Let the heavens rejoice, let the earth
be glad;
let them say among the nations,
"The LORD reigns!"
32Let the sea resound, and all that is in
it;
let the fields be jubilant, and
everything in them!
33Then the trees of the forest will sing,
they will sing for joy before the
LORD,
for he comes to judge the earth.

34Give thanks to the LORD, for he is
good;
his love endures for ever.
35Cry out, "Save us, O God our
Saviour;
gather us and deliver us from the
nations,
that we may give thanks to your holy
name,
that we may glory in your praise."
36Praise be to the LORD, the God of
Israel,
from everlasting to everlasting.

Then all the people said "Amen" and "Praise the LORD."

NEW TESTAMENT READING
Romans 16:1–27

Personal Greetings

16 I commend to you our sister
Phoebe, a servant of the church
in Cenchrea. 2I ask you to receive her in
the Lord in a way worthy of the saints
and to give her any help she may need
from you, for she has been a great help
to many people, including me.

[3]Greet Priscilla and Aquila, my fellow-workers in Christ Jesus. [4]They risked their lives for me. Not only I but all the churches of the Gentiles are grateful to them.
[5]Greet also the church that meets at their house.
Greet my dear friend Epenetus, who was the first convert to Christ in the province of Asia.
[6]Greet Mary, who worked very hard for you.
[7]Greet Andronicus and Junias, my relatives who have been in prison with me. They are outstanding among the apostles, and they were in Christ before I was.
[8]Greet Ampliatus, whom I love in the Lord.
[9]Greet Urbanus, our fellow-worker in Christ, and my dear friend Stachys.
[10]Greet Apelles, tested and approved in Christ.
Greet those who belong to the household of Aristobulus.
[11]Greet Herodion, my relative.
Greet those in the household of Narcissus who are in the Lord.
[12]Greet Tryphena and Tryphosa, those women who work hard in the Lord.
Greet my dear friend Persis, another woman who has worked very hard in the Lord.
[13]Greet Rufus, chosen in the Lord, and his mother, who has been a mother to me, too.
[14]Greet Asyncritus, Phlegon, Hermes, Patrobas, Hermas and the brothers with them.
[15]Greet Philologus, Julia, Nereus and his sister, and Olympas and all the saints with them.
[16]Greet one another with a holy kiss.
All the churches of Christ send greetings.

[17]I urge you, brothers, to watch out for those who cause divisions and put obstacles in your way that are contrary to the teaching you have learned. Keep away from them. [18]For such people are not serving our Lord Christ, but their own appetites. By smooth talk and flattery they deceive the minds of naïve people. [19]Everyone has heard about your obedience, so I am full of joy over you; but I want you to be wise about what is good, and innocent about what is evil.

[20]The God of peace will soon crush Satan under your feet.

The grace of our Lord Jesus be with you.

[21]Timothy, my fellow-worker, sends his greetings to you, as do Lucius, Jason and Sosipater, my relatives.

[22]I, Tertius, who wrote down this letter, greet you in the Lord.

[23]Gaius, whose hospitality I and the whole church here enjoy, sends you his greetings.

Erastus, who is the city's director of public works, and our brother Quartus send you their greetings.

[25]Now to him who is able to establish you by my gospel and the proclamation of Jesus Christ, according to the revelation of the mystery hidden for long ages past, [26]but now revealed and made known through the prophetic writings by the command of the eternal God, so that all nations might believe and obey him—[27]to the only wise God be glory for ever through Jesus Christ! Amen.

READING FROM PSALMS
Psalm 90:11–17

[11]Who knows the power of your anger?
For your wrath is as great as the fear that is due to you.
[12]Teach us to number our days aright,
that we may gain a heart of wisdom.

[13]Relent, O LORD! How long will it be?
Have compassion on your servants.
[14]Satisfy us in the morning with your unfailing love,
that we may sing for joy and be glad all our days.
[15]Make us glad for as many days as you have afflicted us,

for as many years as we have seen
trouble.
16May your deeds be shown to your
servants,
your splendour to their
children.

17May the favour of the Lord our God
rest upon us;
establish the work of our hands for
us—
yes, establish the work of our
hands.

AUGUST 4

DAY 216

OLD TESTAMENT READING

1 Chronicles 16:37–18:17

37David left Asaph and his associates
before the ark of the covenant of the
LORD to minister there regularly,
according to each day's requirements.
38He also left Obed-Edom and his sixty-
eight associates to minister with them.
Obed-Edom son of Jeduthun, and also
Hosah, were gatekeepers.

39David left Zadok the priest and his
fellow priests before the tabernacle of
the LORD at the high place in Gibeon
40to present burnt offerings to the LORD
on the altar of burnt offering regularly,
morning and evening, in accordance
with everything written in the Law of
the LORD, which he had given Israel.
41With them were Heman and Jeduthun
and the rest of those chosen and designated by name to give thanks to the
LORD, "for his love endures for ever."
42Heman and Jeduthun were responsible for the sounding of the trumpets and
cymbals and for the playing of the other
instruments for sacred song. The sons of
Jeduthun were stationed at the gate.

43Then all the people left, each for his
own home, and David returned home to
bless his family.

God's Promise to David

17 After David was settled in his
palace, he said to Nathan the
prophet, "Here I am, living in a palace
of cedar, while the ark of the covenant
of the LORD is under a tent."

2Nathan replied to David, "Whatever you have in mind, do it, for God is
with you."

3That night the word of God came to
Nathan, saying:

4"Go and tell my servant David,
'This is what the LORD says: You
are not the one to build me a house
to dwell in. 5I have not dwelt in a
house from the day I brought Israel
up out of Egypt to this day. I have
moved from one tent site to
another, from one dwelling-place
to another. 6Wherever I have
moved with all the Israelites, did I
ever say to any of their leaders
whom I commanded to shepherd
my people, "Why have you not
built me a house of cedar?"'

7"Now then, tell my servant
David, 'This is what the LORD
Almighty says: I took you from the
pasture and from following the
flock, to be ruler over my people
Israel. 8I have been with you
wherever you have gone, and I
have cut off all your enemies from
before you. Now I will make your
name like the names of the greatest
men of the earth. 9And I will provide a place for my people Israel
and will plant them so that they can
have a home of their own and no
longer be disturbed. Wicked people will not oppress them any

more, as they did at the beginning
10and have done ever since the time
I appointed leaders over my people
Israel. I will also subdue all your
enemies.

" 'I declare to you that the LORD
will build a house for you: 11When
your days are over and you go to be
with your fathers, I will raise up
your offspring to succeed you, one
of your own sons, and I will establish his kingdom. 12He is the one
who will build a house for me, and I
will establish his throne for ever.
13I will be his father, and he will be
my son. I will never take my love
away from him, as I took it away
from your predecessor. 14I will set
him over my house and my kingdom for ever; his throne will be
established for ever.' "

15Nathan reported to David all the
words of this entire revelation.

David's Prayer

16Then King David went in and sat
before the LORD, and he said:

"Who am I, O LORD God, and
what is my family, that you have
brought me this far? 17And as if this
were not enough in your sight, O
God, you have spoken about the
future of the house of your servant.
You have looked on me as though I
were the most exalted of men, O
LORD God.

18"What more can David say to
you for honouring your servant?
For you know your servant, 19O
LORD. For the sake of your servant
and according to your will, you
have done this great thing and
made known all these great
promises.

20"There is no-one like you, O
LORD, and there is no God but you,
as we have heard with our own
ears. 21And who is like your people
Israel—the one nation on earth
whose God went out to redeem a
people for himself, and to make a
name for yourself, and to perform
great and awesome wonders by
driving out nations from before
your people, whom you redeemed
from Egypt? 22You made your people Israel your very own for ever,
and you, O LORD, have become
their God.

23"And now, LORD, let the
promise you have made concerning
your servant and his house be
established for ever. Do as you
promised, 24so that it will be established and that your name will be
great for ever. Then men will say,
'The LORD Almighty, the God over
Israel, is Israel's God!' And the
house of your servant David will be
established before you.

25"You, my God, have revealed
to your servant that you will build a
house for him. So your servant has
found courage to pray to you. 26O
LORD, you are God! You have
promised these good things to your
servant. 27Now you have been
pleased to bless the house of your
servant, that it may continue for
ever in your sight; for you, O
LORD, have blessed it, and it will be
blessed for ever."

David's Victories

18 In the course of time, David defeated the Philistines and subdued them, and he took Gath and its
surrounding villages from the control of
the Philistines.

2David also defeated the Moabites,
and they became subject to him and
brought tribute.

3Moreover, David fought Hadadezer
king of Zobah, as far as Hamath, when
he went to establish his control along
the Euphrates River. 4David captured
a thousand of his chariots, seven
thousand charioteers and twenty
thousand foot soldiers. He hamstrung
all but a hundred of the chariot horses.

5When the Arameans of Damascus
came to help Hadadezer king of Zobah,
David struck down twenty-two
thousand of them. 6He put garrisons in
the Aramean kingdom of Damascus,
and the Arameans became subject to
him and brought tribute. The LORD
gave David victory everywhere he
went.
7David took the gold shields carried
by the officers of Hadadezer and
brought them to Jerusalem. 8From
Tebah and Cun, towns that belonged to
Hadadezer, David took a great quantity
of bronze, which Solomon used to make
the bronze Sea, the pillars and various
bronze articles.
9When Tou king of Hamath heard
that David had defeated the entire army
of Hadadezer king of Zobah, 10he sent
his son Hadoram to King David to greet
him and congratulate him on his victory
in battle over Hadadezer, who had been
at war with Tou. Hadoram brought all
kinds of articles of gold and silver and
bronze.
11King David dedicated these articles
to the LORD, as he had done with the
silver and gold he had taken from all
these nations: Edom and Moab, the
Ammonites and the Philistines, and
Amalek.
12Abishai son of Zeruiah struck down
eighteen thousand Edomites in the Valley of Salt. 13He put garrisons in Edom,
and all the Edomites became subject to
David. The LORD gave David victory
everywhere he went.

David's Officials

14David reigned over all Israel, doing
what was just and right for all his people. 15Joab son of Zeruiah was over the
army; Jehoshaphat son of Ahilud was
recorder; 16Zadok son of Ahitub and
Ahimelech son of Abiathar were
priests; Shavsha was secretary;
17Benaiah son of Jehoiada was over the
Kerethites and Pelethites; and David's
sons were chief officials at the king's
side.

NEW TESTAMENT READING
1 Corinthians 1:1–17

1 Paul, called to be an apostle of
Christ Jesus by the will of God, and
our brother Sosthenes,

2To the church of God in Corinth, to
those sanctified in Christ Jesus and
called to be holy, together with all those
everywhere who call on the name of our
Lord Jesus Christ—their Lord and
ours:

3Grace and peace to you from God
our Father and the Lord Jesus Christ.

Thanksgiving

4I always thank God for you because
of his grace given you in Christ Jesus.
5For in him you have been enriched in
every way—in all your speaking and in
all your knowledge—6because our
testimony about Christ was confirmed
in you. 7Therefore you do not lack any
spiritual gift as you eagerly wait for our
Lord Jesus Christ to be revealed. 8He
will keep you strong to the end, so that
you will be blameless on the day of our
Lord Jesus Christ. 9God, who has called
you into fellowship with his Son Jesus
Christ our Lord, is faithful.

Divisions in the Church

10I appeal to you, brothers, in the
name of our Lord Jesus Christ, that all
of you agree with one another so that
there may be no divisions among you
and that you may be perfectly united in
mind and thought. 11My brothers, some
from Chloe's household have informed
me that there are quarrels among you.
12What I mean is this: One of you says,
"I follow Paul"; another, "I follow
Apollos"; another, "I follow Cephas";
still another, "I follow Christ."
13Is Christ divided? Was Paul crucified for you? Were you baptised into
the name of Paul? 14I am thankful that I

did not baptise any of you except Cris-
pus and Gaius, 15so no-one can say that
you were baptised into my name.
(16Yes, I also baptised the household of
Stephanas; beyond that, I don't remember if I baptised anyone else.) 17For
Christ did not send me to baptise, but to
preach the gospel—not with words of
human wisdom, lest the cross of Christ
be emptied of its power.

READING FROM PROVERBS

Proverbs 19:3–12

3A man's own folly ruins his life,
yet his heart rages against the LORD.

4Wealth brings many friends,
but a poor man's friend deserts him.

5A false witness will not go unpunished,
and he who pours out lies will not go free.

6Many curry favour with a ruler,
and everyone is the friend of a man who gives gifts.

7A poor man is shunned by all his relatives—
how much more do his friends avoid him!
Though he pursues them with pleading,
they are nowhere to be found.

8He who gets wisdom loves his own soul;
he who cherishes understanding prospers.

9A false witness will not go unpunished,
and he who pours out lies will perish.

10It is not fitting for a fool to live in luxury—
how much worse for a slave to rule over princes!

11A man's wisdom gives him patience;
it is to his glory to overlook an offence.

12A king's rage is like the roar of a lion,
but his favour is like dew on the grass.

DAY 217

AUGUST 5

OLD TESTAMENT READING

1 Chronicles 19:1–22:1

The Battle Against the Ammonites

19 In the course of time, Nahash
king of the Ammonites died,
and his son succeeded him as king.
2David thought, "I will show kindness
to Hanun son of Nahash, because his
father showed kindness to me." So
David sent a delegation to express his
sympathy to Hanun concerning his
father.
When David's men came to Hanun in
the land of the Ammonites to express
sympathy to him, 3the Ammonite
nobles said to Hanun, "Do you think
David is honouring your father by sending men to you to express sympathy?
Haven't his men come to you to explore
and spy out the country and overthrow
it?" 4So Hanun seized David's men,
shaved them, cut off their garments in
the middle at the buttocks, and sent
them away.
5When someone came and told David
about the men, he sent messengers to
meet them, for they were greatly

humiliated. The king said, "Stay at
Jericho till your beards have grown, and
then come back."

6When the Ammonites realised that
they had become an offence to David's
nostrils, Hanun and the Ammonites
sent a thousand talents of silver to hire
chariots and charioteers from Aram
Naharaim, Aram Maacah and Zobah.
7They hired thirty-two thousand chariots and charioteers, as well as the king
of Maacah with his troops, who came
and camped near Medeba, while the
Ammonites were mustered from their
towns and moved out for battle.

8On hearing this, David sent Joab out
with the entire army of fighting men.
9The Ammonites came out and drew up
in battle formation at the entrance to
their city, while the kings who had come
were by themselves in the open country.

10Joab saw that there were battle lines
in front of him and behind him; so he
selected some of the best troops in
Israel and deployed them against the
Arameans. 11He put the rest of the men
under the command of Abishai his
brother, and they were deployed
against the Ammonites. 12Joab said, "If
the Arameans are too strong for me,
then you are to rescue me; but if the
Ammonites are too strong for you, then
I will rescue you. 13Be strong and let us
fight bravely for our people and the
cities of our God. The LORD will do
what is good in his sight."

14Then Joab and the troops with him
advanced to fight the Arameans, and
they fled before him. 15When the
Ammonites saw that the Arameans
were fleeing, they too fled before his
brother Abishai and went inside the
city. So Joab went back to Jerusalem.

16After the Arameans saw that they
had been routed by Israel, they sent
messengers and had Arameans brought
from beyond the River, with Shophach
the commander of Hadadezer's army
leading them.

17When David was told of this, he
gathered all Israel and crossed the Jordan; he advanced against them and
formed his battle lines opposite them.
David formed his lines to meet the Arameans in battle, and they fought against
him. 18But they fled before Israel, and
David killed seven thousand of their
charioteers and forty thousand of their
foot soldiers. He also killed Shophach
the commander of their army.

19When the vassals of Hadadezer saw
that they had been defeated by Israel,
they made peace with David and became subject to him.

So the Arameans were not willing to
help the Ammonites any more.

The Capture of Rabbah

20 In the spring, at the time when
kings go off to war, Joab led out
the armed forces. He laid waste the land
of the Ammonites and went to Rabbah
and besieged it, but David remained in
Jerusalem. Joab attacked Rabbah and
left it in ruins. 2David took the crown
from the head of their king—its weight
was found to be a talent of gold, and
it was set with precious stones—and it
was placed on David's head. He took a
great quantity of plunder from the city
3and brought out the people who were
there, consigning them to labour with
saws and with iron picks and axes.
David did this to all the Ammonite
towns. Then David and his entire army
returned to Jerusalem.

War With the Philistines

4In the course of time, war broke out
with the Philistines, at Gezer. At that
time Sibbecai the Hushathite killed
Sippai, one of the descendants of the
Rephaites, and the Philistines were
subjugated.

5In another battle with the Philistines, Elhanan son of Jair killed Lahmi
the brother of Goliath the Gittite, who
had a spear with a shaft like a weaver's
rod.

6In still another battle, which took
place at Gath, there was a huge man
with six fingers on each hand and six
toes on each foot—twenty-four in all.
He also was descended from Rapha.

7When he taunted Israel, Jonathan son
of Shimea, David's brother, killed him.
8These were descendants of Rapha in
Gath, and they fell at the hands of
David and his men.

David Numbers the Fighting Men

21 Satan rose up against Israel and
incited David to take a census of
Israel. 2So David said to Joab and the
commanders of the troops, "Go and
count the Israelites from Beersheba to
Dan. Then report back to me so that I
may know how many there are."
3But Joab replied, "May the LORD
multiply his troops a hundred times
over. My lord the king, are they not all
my lord's subjects? Why does my lord
want to do this? Why should he bring
guilt on Israel?"
4The king's word, however, over-
ruled Joab; so Joab left and went
throughout Israel and then came back
to Jerusalem. 5Joab reported the number of the fighting men to David: In all
Israel there were one million one hundred thousand men who could handle a
sword, including four hundred and
seventy thousand in Judah.
6But Joab did not include Levi and
Benjamin in the numbering, because
the king's command was repulsive to
him. 7This command was also evil in the
sight of God; so he punished Israel.
8Then David said to God, "I have
sinned greatly by doing this. Now, I beg
you, take away the guilt of your servant.
I have done a very foolish thing."
9The LORD said to Gad, David's seer,
10"Go and tell David, 'This is what the
LORD says: I am giving you three
options. Choose one of them for me
to carry out against you.'"
11So Gad went to David and said to
him, "This is what the LORD says: 'Take
your choice: 12three years of famine,
three months of being swept away before your enemies, with their swords
overtaking you, or three days of the
sword of the LORD—days of plague in
the land with the angel of the LORD
ravaging every part of Israel.' Now
then, decide how I should answer the
one who sent me."
13David said to Gad, "I am in deep
distress. Let me fall into the hands of
the LORD, for his mercy is very great;
but do not let me fall into the hands of
men."
14So the LORD sent a plague on Israel,
and seventy thousand men of Israel fell
dead. 15And God sent an angel to destroy Jerusalem. But as the angel was
doing so, the LORD saw it and was
grieved because of the calamity and said
to the angel who was destroying the
people, "Enough! Withdraw your
hand." The angel of the LORD was then
standing at the threshing-floor of
Araunah the Jebusite.
16David looked up and saw the angel
of the LORD standing between heaven
and earth, with a drawn sword in his
hand extended over Jerusalem. Then
David and the elders, clothed in sackcloth, fell face down.
17David said to God, "Was it not I
who ordered the fighting men to be
counted? I am the one who has sinned
and done wrong. These are but sheep.
What have they done? O LORD my
God, let your hand fall upon me and my
family, but do not let this plague remain
on your people."
18Then the angel of the LORD ordered
Gad to tell David to go up and build an
altar to the LORD on the threshing-floor
of Araunah the Jebusite. 19So David
went up in obedience to the word that
Gad had spoken in the name of the
LORD.
20While Araunah was threshing
wheat, he turned and saw the angel; his
four sons who were with him hid themselves. 21Then David approached, and
when Araunah looked and saw him, he
left the threshing-floor and bowed down
before David with his face to the
ground.
22David said to him, "Let me have the
site of your threshing-floor so that I can
build an altar to the LORD, that the
plague on the people may be stopped.
Sell it to me at the full price."

[23]Araunah said to David, "Take it!
Let my lord the king do whatever
pleases him. Look, I will give the oxen
for the burnt offerings, the threshing-
sledges for the wood, and the wheat for
the grain offering. I will give all this."
[24]But King David replied to
Araunah, "No, I insist on paying the
full price. I will not take for the LORD
what is yours, or sacrifice a burnt offering that costs me nothing."
[25]So David paid Araunah six hundred
shekels of gold for the site. [26]David built
an altar to the LORD there and sacrificed
burnt offerings and fellowship offerings.
He called on the LORD, and the LORD
answered him with fire from heaven on
the altar of burnt offering.
[27]Then the LORD spoke to the angel,
and he put his sword back into its
sheath. [28]At that time, when David saw
that the LORD had answered him on the
threshing-floor of Araunah the Jebusite, he offered sacrifices there. [29]The
tabernacle of the LORD, which Moses
had made in the desert, and the altar of
burnt offering were at that time on the
high place at Gibeon. [30]But David could
not go before it to enquire of God,
because he was afraid of the sword of
the angel of the LORD.
22 Then David said, "The house of
the LORD God is to be here, and
also the altar of burnt offering for
Israel."

NEW TESTAMENT READING
1 Corinthians 1:18–2:5

Christ the Wisdom and Power of God

[18]For the message of the cross is
foolishness to those who are perishing,
but to us who are being saved it is the
power of God. [19]For it is written:

"I will destroy the wisdom of the
wise;
the intelligence of the intelligent I
will frustrate."

[20]Where is the wise man? Where is
the scholar? Where is the philosopher
of this age? Has not God made foolish
the wisdom of the world? [21]For since in
the wisdom of God the world through
its wisdom did not know him, God was
pleased through the foolishness of what
was preached to save those who believe.
[22]Jews demand miraculous signs and
Greeks look for wisdom, [23]but we
preach Christ crucified: a stumbling-
block to Jews and foolishness to Gentiles, [24]but to those whom God has
called, both Jews and Greeks, Christ
the power of God and the wisdom of
God. [25]For the foolishness of God is
wiser than man's wisdom, and the
weakness of God is stronger than man's
strength.
[26]Brothers, think of what you were
when you were called. Not many of you
were wise by human standards; not
many were influential; not many were
of noble birth. [27]But God chose the
foolish things of the world to shame the
wise; God chose the weak things of
the world to shame the strong. [28]He
chose the lowly things of this world and
the despised things—and the things
that are not—to nullify the things
that are, [29]so that no-one may boast
before him. [30]It is because of him that
you are in Christ Jesus, who has become for us wisdom from God—that
is, our righteousness, holiness and
redemption. [31]Therefore, as it is
written: "Let him who boasts boast
in the Lord."
2 When I came to you, brothers, I
did not come with eloquence or
superior wisdom as I proclaimed to you
the testimony about God. [2]For I resolved to know nothing while I was with
you except Jesus Christ and him crucified. [3]I came to you in weakness and
fear, and with much trembling. [4]My
message and my preaching were not
with wise and persuasive words, but
with a demonstration of the Spirit's
power, [5]so that your faith might not
rest on men's wisdom, but on God's
power.

READING FROM PSALMS
Psalm 91:1–8

1He who dwells in the shelter of the
Most High
will rest in the shadow of the
Almighty.
2I will say of the LORD, "He is my
refuge and my fortress,
my God, in whom I trust."

3Surely he will save you from the
fowler's snare
and from the deadly pestilence.
4He will cover you with his feathers,
and under his wings you will find
refuge;
his faithfulness will be your shield
and rampart.
5You will not fear the terror of night,
nor the arrow that flies by day,
6nor the pestilence that stalks in the
darkness,
nor the plague that destroys at
midday.
7A thousand may fall at your side,
ten thousand at your right hand,
but it will not come near you.
8You will only observe with your eyes
and see the punishment of the
wicked.

DAY 218

AUGUST 6

OLD TESTAMENT READING
1 Chronicles 22:2–23:32

Preparations for the Temple

2So David gave orders to assemble
the aliens living in Israel, and from
among them he appointed stonecutters
to prepare dressed stone for building
the house of God. 3He provided a large
amount of iron to make nails for the
doors of the gateways and for the
fittings, and more bronze than could be
weighed. 4He also provided more cedar
logs than could be counted, for the
Sidonians and Tyrians had brought
large numbers of them to David.

5David said, "My son Solomon is
young and inexperienced, and the
house to be built for the LORD should be
of great magnificence and fame and
splendour in the sight of all the nations.
Therefore I will make preparations for
it." So David made extensive preparations before his death.

6Then he called for his son Solomon
and charged him to build a house for the
LORD, the God of Israel. 7David said to
Solomon: "My son, I had it in my heart
to build a house for the Name of the
LORD my God. 8But this word of the
LORD came to me: 'You have shed
much blood and have fought many
wars. You are not to build a house for
my Name, because you have shed much
blood on the earth in my sight. 9But you
will have a son who will be a man of
peace and rest, and I will give him rest
from all his enemies on every side. His
name will be Solomon, and I will grant
Israel peace and quiet during his reign.
10He is the one who will build a house
for my Name. He will be my son, and I
will be his father. And I will establish
the throne of his kingdom over Israel
for ever.'

11"Now, my son, the LORD be with
you, and may you have success and
build the house of the LORD your God,
as he said you would. 12May the LORD
give you discretion and understanding
when he puts you in command over
Israel, so that you may keep the law of
the LORD your God. 13Then you will
have success if you are careful to
observe the decrees and laws that the
LORD gave to Moses for Israel. Be

strong and courageous. Do not be
afraid or discouraged.
14"I have taken great pains to provide
for the temple of the LORD a hundred
thousand talents of gold, a million talents of silver, quantities of bronze and
iron too great to be weighed, and wood
and stone. And you may add to them.
15You have many workmen: stonecutters, masons and carpenters, as well as
men skilled in every kind of work 16in
gold and silver, bronze and iron—
craftsmen beyond number. Now begin
the work, and the LORD be with you."
17Then David ordered all the leaders
of Israel to help his son Solomon. 18He
said to them, "Is not the LORD your
God with you? And has he not granted
you rest on every side? For he has
handed the inhabitants of the land over
to me, and the land is subject to the
LORD and to his people. 19Now devote
your heart and soul to seeking the LORD
your God. Begin to build the sanctuary
of the LORD God, so that you may bring
the ark of the covenant of the LORD and
the sacred articles belonging to God
into the temple that will be built for the
Name of the LORD."

The Levites

23 When David was old and full of
years, he made his son Solomon
king over Israel.
2He also gathered together all the
leaders of Israel, as well as the priests
and Levites. 3The Levites thirty years
old or more were counted, and the
total number of men was thirty-eight
thousand. 4David said, "Of these,
twenty-four thousand are to supervise
the work of the temple of the LORD and
six thousand are to be officials and
judges. 5Four thousand are to be
gatekeepers and four thousand are
to praise the LORD with the musical
instruments I have provided for that
purpose."
6David divided the Levites into
groups corresponding to the sons of
Levi: Gershon, Kohath and Merari.

Gershonites

7Belonging to the Gershonites:
Ladan and Shimei.
8The sons of Ladan:
Jehiel the first, Zetham and Joel
—three in all.
9The sons of Shimei:
Shelomoth, Haziel and Haran—
three in all.
These were the heads of the
families of Ladan.
10And the sons of Shimei:
Jahath, Ziza, Jeush and Beriah.
These were the sons of Shimei
—four in all.
11Jahath was the first and Ziza the
second, but Jeush and Beriah did
not have many sons; so they
were counted as one family with
one assignment.

Kohathites

12The sons of Kohath:
Amram, Izhar, Hebron and
Uzziel—four in all.
13The sons of Amram:
Aaron and Moses.
Aaron was set apart, he and his
descendants for ever, to consecrate the most holy things, to
offer sacrifices before the LORD,
to minister before him and to
pronounce blessings in his name
for ever. 14The sons of Moses the
man of God were counted as part
of the tribe of Levi.
15The sons of Moses:
Gershom and Eliezer.
16The descendants of Gershom:
Shubael was the first.
17The descendants of Eliezer:
Rehabiah was the first.
Eliezer had no other sons, but
the sons of Rehabiah were very
numerous.
18The sons of Izhar:
Shelomith was the first.
19The sons of Hebron:
Jeriah the first, Amariah the
second, Jahaziel the third and
Jekameam the fourth.

20 The sons of Uzziel:
Micah the first and Isshiah the second.

Merarites

21 The sons of Merari:
Mahli and Mushi.
The sons of Mahli:
Eleazar and Kish.
22 Eleazar died without having sons: he had only daughters.
Their cousins, the sons of Kish, married them.
23 The sons of Mushi:
Mahli, Eder and Jerimoth—three in all.

24 These were the descendants of Levi
by their families—the heads of families
as they were registered under their
names and counted individually, that is,
the workers twenty years old or more
who served in the temple of the LORD.
25 For David had said, "Since the LORD,
the God of Israel, has granted rest to his
people and has come to dwell in Jerusalem for ever, 26 the Levites no longer
need to carry the tabernacle or any of
the articles used in its service."
27 According to the last instructions of
David, the Levites were counted from
those twenty years old or more.
28 The duty of the Levites was to help
Aaron's descendants in the service of
the temple of the LORD: to be in charge
of the courtyards, the side rooms, the
purification of all sacred things and
the performance of other duties at the
house of God. 29 They were in charge of
the bread set out on the table, the flour
for the grain offerings, the unleavened
wafers, the baking and the mixing, and
all measurements of quantity and size.
30 They were also to stand every morning to thank and praise the LORD. They
were to do the same in the evening 31 and
whenever burnt offerings were presented to the LORD on Sabbaths and at
New Moon festivals and at appointed
feasts. They were to serve before the
LORD regularly in the proper number
and in the way prescribed for them.
32 And so the Levites carried out their
responsibilities for the Tent of Meeting,
for the Holy Place and, under their
brothers the descendants of Aaron, for
the service of the temple of the LORD.

NEW TESTAMENT READING
1 Corinthians 2:6–16

Wisdom From the Spirit

6 We do, however, speak a message of
wisdom among the mature, but not the
wisdom of this age or of the rulers of this
age, who are coming to nothing. 7 No,
we speak of God's secret wisdom, a
wisdom that has been hidden and that
God destined for our glory before time
began. 8 None of the rulers of this age
understood it, for if they had, they
would not have crucified the Lord of
glory. 9 However, as it is written:

"No eye has seen,
no ear has heard,
no mind has conceived
what God has prepared for those
who love him"—

10 but God has revealed it to us by his
Spirit.
The Spirit searches all things, even
the deep things of God. 11 For who
among men knows the thoughts of a
man except the man's spirit within him?
In the same way no-one knows the
thoughts of God except the Spirit of
God. 12 We have not received the spirit
of the world but the Spirit who is from
God, that we may understand what God
has freely given us. 13 This is what we
speak, not in words taught us by human
wisdom but in words taught by the
Spirit, expressing spiritual truths in
spiritual words. 14 The man without the
Spirit does not accept the things that
come from the Spirit of God, for they
are foolishness to him, and he cannot
understand them, because they are
spiritually discerned. 15 The spiritual
man makes judgments about all things,

but he himself is not subject to any man's judgment:

16"For who has known the mind of the
Lord
that he may instruct him?"

But we have the mind of Christ.

READING FROM PSALMS
Psalm 91:9–16

9If you make the Most High your
dwelling—
even the LORD, who is my refuge—
10then no harm will befall you,
no disaster will come near your
tent.
11For he will command his angels
concerning you
to guard you in all your ways;
12they will lift you up in their hands,
so that you will not strike your foot
against a stone.
13You will tread upon the lion and the
cobra;
you will trample the great lion and
the serpent.

14"Because he loves me," says the
LORD, "I will rescue him;
I will protect him, for he
acknowledges my name.
15He will call upon me, and I will
answer him;
I will be with him in trouble,
I will deliver him and honour him.
16With long life will I satisfy him
and show him my salvation."

AUGUST 7

DAY 219

OLD TESTAMENT READING
1 Chronicles 24:1–26:19

The Divisions of Priests

24 These were the divisions of the sons of Aaron:
The sons of Aaron were Nadab,
Abihu, Eleazar and Ithamar. 2But
Nadab and Abihu died before their father did, and they had no sons; so Eleazar and Ithamar served as the
priests. 3With the help of Zadok a descendant of Eleazar and Ahimelech a descendant of Ithamar, David separated them into divisions for their appointed order of ministering. 4A larger number of leaders were found among Eleazar's descendants than among Ithamar's, and they were divided accordingly: sixteen heads of families from Eleazar's descendants and eight heads of families from Ithamar's descendants. 5They divided them
impartially by drawing lots, for there were officials of the sanctuary and officials of God among the descendants of both Eleazar and Ithamar.
6The scribe Shemaiah son of Nethanel, a Levite, recorded their names in the presence of the king and of the officials: Zadok the priest, Ahimelech son of Abiathar and the heads of families of the priests and of the Levites—one family being taken from Eleazar and then one from Ithamar.

7The first lot fell to Jehoiarib,
the second to Jedaiah,
8the third to Harim,
the fourth to Seorim,
9the fifth to Malkijah,
the sixth to Mijamin,
10the seventh to Hakkoz,
the eighth to Abijah,
11the ninth to Jeshua,
the tenth to Shecaniah,

12the eleventh to Eliashib,
the twelfth to Jakim,
13the thirteenth to Huppah,
the fourteenth to Jeshebeab,
14the fifteenth to Bilgah,
the sixteenth to Immer,
15the seventeenth to Hezir,
the eighteenth to Happizzez,
16the nineteenth to Pethahiah,
the twentieth to Jehezkel,
17the twenty-first to Jakin,
the twenty-second to Gamul,
18the twenty-third to Delaiah
and the twenty-fourth to Maaziah.

19This was their appointed order of ministering when they entered the temple of the LORD, according to the regulations prescribed for them by their forefather Aaron, as the LORD, the God of Israel, had commanded him.

The Rest of the Levites

20As for the rest of the descendants of Levi:
from the sons of Amram: Shubael;
from the sons of Shubael: Jehdeiah.
21As for Rehabiah, from his sons: Isshiah was the first.
22From the Izharites: Shelomoth;
from the sons of Shelomoth: Jahath.
23The sons of Hebron: Jeriah the first, Amariah the second, Jahaziel the third and Jekameam the fourth.
24The son of Uzziel: Micah;
from the sons of Micah: Shamir.
25The brother of Micah: Isshiah;
from the sons of Isshiah: Zechariah.
26The sons of Merari: Mahli and Mushi.
The son of Jaaziah: Beno.
27The sons of Merari:
from Jaaziah: Beno, Shoham, Zaccur and Ibri.
28From Mahli: Eleazar, who had no sons.
29From Kish: the son of Kish: Jerahmeel.
30And the sons of Mushi: Mahli, Eder and Jerimoth.

These were the Levites, according to
their families. 31They also cast lots, just as their brothers the descendants of Aaron did, in the presence of King David and of Zadok, Ahimelech, and the heads of families of the priests and of the Levites. The families of the eldest brother were treated the same as those of the youngest.

The Singers

25 David, together with the commanders of the army, set apart some of the sons of Asaph, Heman and Jeduthun for the ministry of prophesying, accompanied by harps, lyres and cymbals. Here is the list of the men who performed this service:

2From the sons of Asaph:
Zaccur, Joseph, Nethaniah and Asarelah. The sons of Asaph were under the supervision of Asaph, who prophesied under the king's supervision.
3As for Jeduthun, from his sons:
Gedaliah, Zeri, Jeshaiah, Shimei, Hashabiah and Mattithiah, six in all, under the supervision of their father Jeduthun, who prophesied, using the harp in thanking and praising the LORD.
4As for Heman, from his sons:
Bukkiah, Mattaniah, Uzziel, Shubael and Jerimoth; Hananiah, Hanani, Eliathah, Giddalti and Romamti-Ezer; Joshbekashah, Mallothi, Hothir and Mahazioth.
5All these were sons of Heman the king's seer. They were given to him through the promises of God to exalt him. God gave Heman fourteen sons and three daughters.

6All these men were under the supervision of their fathers for the music of

the temple of the LORD, with cymbals,
lyres and harps, for the ministry at the
house of God. Asaph, Jeduthun and
Heman were under the supervision of
the king. 7Along with their relatives
—all of them trained and skilled in
music for the LORD—they numbered
288. 8Young and old alike, teacher as
well as student, cast lots for their duties.

9The first lot, which was for
Asaph, fell to Joseph,
his sons and relatives, 12
the second to Gedaliah,
he and his relatives
and sons, 12
10the third to Zaccur,
his sons and relatives, 12
11the fourth to Izri,
his sons and relatives, 12
12the fifth to Nethaniah,
his sons and relatives, 12
13the sixth to Bukkiah,
his sons and relatives, 12
14the seventh to Jesarelah,
his sons and relatives, 12
15the eighth to Jeshaiah,
his sons and relatives, 12
16the ninth to Mattaniah,
his sons and relatives, 12
17the tenth to Shimei,
his sons and relatives, 12
18the eleventh to Azarel,
his sons and relatives, 12
19the twelfth to Hashabiah,
his sons and relatives, 12
20the thirteenth to Shubael,
his sons and relatives, 12
21the fourteenth to
Mattithiah,
his sons and relatives, 12
22the fifteenth to Jerimoth,
his sons and relatives, 12
23the sixteenth to Hananiah,
his sons and relatives, 12
24the seventeenth to
Joshbakashah,
his sons and relatives, 12
25the eighteenth to Hanani,
his sons and relatives, 12
26the nineteenth to Mallothi,
his sons and relatives, 12
27the twentieth to Eliathah,
his sons and relatives, 12
28the twenty-first to Hothir,
his sons and relatives, 12
29the twenty-second to
Giddalti,
his sons and relatives, 12
30the twenty-third to
Mahazioth,
his sons and relatives, 12
31the twenty-fourth to
Romamti-Ezer,
his sons and relatives, 12

The Gatekeepers

26 The divisions of the gatekeepers:

From the Korahites: Meshelemiah
son of Kore, one of the sons of
Asaph.
2Meshelemiah had sons:
Zechariah the firstborn,
Jediael the second,
Zebadiah the third,
Jathniel the fourth,
3Elam the fifth,
Jehohanan the sixth
and Eliehoenai the seventh.
4Obed-Edom also had sons:
Shemaiah the firstborn,
Jehozabad the second,
Joah the third,
Sacar the fourth,
Nethanel the fifth,
5Ammiel the sixth,
Issachar the seventh
and Peullethai the eighth.
(For God had blessed Obed-
Edom.)

6His son Shemaiah also had sons,
who were leaders in their
father's family because they
were very capable men. 7The
sons of Shemaiah: Othni,
Rephael, Obed and Elzabad; his
relatives Elihu and Semakiah
were also able men. 8All these
were descendants of Obed-
Edom; they and their sons and

their relatives were capable men
with the strength to do the work
—descendants of Obed-Edom,
62 in all.
[9]Meshelemiah had sons and relatives, who were able men—18 in
all.

[10]Hosah the Merarite had sons:
Shimri the first (although he was
not the firstborn, his father had
appointed him the first),
[11]Hilkiah the second, Tabaliah
the third and Zechariah the
fourth. The sons and relatives of
Hosah were 13 in all.

[12]These divisions of the gatekeepers,
through their chief men, had duties for
ministering in the temple of the LORD,
just as their relatives had. [13]Lots were
cast for each gate, according to their
families, young and old alike.

[14]The lot for the East Gate fell to
Shelemiah. Then lots were cast for his
son Zechariah, a wise counsellor, and
the lot for the North Gate fell to him.
[15]The lot for the South Gate fell to
Obed-Edom, and the lot for the storehouse fell to his sons. [16]The lots for the
West Gate and the Shalleketh Gate on
the upper road fell to Shuppim and
Hosah.

Guard was alongside guard: [17]There
were six Levites a day on the east, four a
day on the north, four a day on the
south and two at a time at the storehouse. [18]As for the court to the west,
there were four at the road and two at
the court itself.

[19]These were the divisions of the
gatekeepers who were descendants of
Korah and Merari.

NEW TESTAMENT READING
1 Corinthians 3:1–23

On Divisions in the Church

3 Brothers, I could not address you
as spiritual but as worldly—mere
infants in Christ. [2]I gave you milk, not
solid food, for you were not yet ready
for it. Indeed, you are still not ready.
[3]You are still worldly. For since there is
jealousy and quarrelling among you,
are you not worldly? Are you not acting
like mere men? [4]For when one says, "I
follow Paul," and another, "I follow
Apollos," are you not mere men?

[5]What, after all, is Apollos? And
what is Paul? Only servants, through
whom you came to believe—as the
Lord has assigned to each his task. [6]I
planted the seed, Apollos watered it,
but God made it grow. [7]So neither he
who plants nor he who waters is anything, but only God, who makes things
grow. [8]The man who plants and the man
who waters have one purpose, and each
will be rewarded according to his own
labour. [9]For we are God's fellow-
workers; you are God's field, God's
building.

[10]By the grace God has given me, I
laid a foundation as an expert builder,
and someone else is building on it. But
each one should be careful how he
builds. [11]For no-one can lay any foundation other than the one already laid,
which is Jesus Christ. [12]If any man
builds on this foundation using gold,
silver, costly stones, wood, hay or
straw, [13]his work will be shown for what
it is, because the Day will bring it to
light. It will be revealed with fire, and
the fire will test the quality of each
man's work. [14]If what he has built survives, he will receive his reward. [15]If it is
burned up, he will suffer loss; he himself
will be saved, but only as one escaping
through the flames.

[16]Don't you know that you yourselves
are God's temple and that God's Spirit
lives in you? [17]If anyone destroys God's
temple, God will destroy him; for
God's temple is sacred, and you are
that temple.

[18]Do not deceive yourselves. If any
one of you thinks he is wise by the
standards of this age, he should become
a "fool" so that he may become wise.
[19]For the wisdom of this world is
foolishness in God's sight. As it is

written: "He catches the wise in their craftiness"; [20]and again, "The Lord knows that the thoughts of the wise are futile." [21]So then, no more boasting about men! All things are yours, [22]whether Paul or Apollos or Cephas or the world or life or death or the present or the future—all are yours, [23]and you are of Christ, and Christ is of God.

READING FROM PSALMS
Psalm 92:1–15

A psalm. A song. For the Sabbath day.

[1]It is good to praise the LORD
and make music to your name, O Most High,
[2]to proclaim your love in the morning
and your faithfulness at night,
[3]to the music of the ten-stringed lyre
and the melody of the harp.

[4]For you make me glad by your deeds, O LORD;
I sing for joy at the work of your hands.
[5]How great are your works, O LORD,
how profound your thoughts!
[6]The senseless man does not know,
fools do not understand,
[7]that though the wicked spring up like grass
and all evildoers flourish,
they will be for ever destroyed.

[8]But you, O LORD, are exalted for ever.

[9]For surely your enemies, O LORD,
surely your enemies will perish;
all evildoers will be scattered.
[10]You have exalted my horn like that of a wild ox;
fine oils have been poured upon me.
[11]My eyes have seen the defeat of my adversaries;
my ears have heard the rout of my wicked foes.

[12]The righteous will flourish like a palm tree,
they will grow like a cedar of Lebanon;
[13]planted in the house of the LORD,
they will flourish in the courts of our God.
[14]They will still bear fruit in old age,
they will stay fresh and green,
[15]proclaiming, "The LORD is upright;
he is my Rock, and there is no wickedness in him."

AUGUST 8

DAY 220

OLD TESTAMENT READING
1 Chronicles 26:20–27:34

The Treasurers and Other Officials

[20]Their fellow Levites were in charge of the treasuries of the house of God and the treasuries for the dedicated things.

[21]The descendants of Ladan, who were Gershonites through Ladan and who were heads of families belonging to Ladan the Gershonite, were Jehieli,
[22]the sons of Jehieli, Zetham and his brother Joel. They were in charge of the treasuries of the temple of the LORD.

[23]From the Amramites, the Izharites, the Hebronites and the Uzzielites:

[24]Shubael, a descendant of Gershom son of Moses, was the officer in charge of the treasuries. [25]His relatives through Eliezer: Rehabiah his son, Jeshaiah his son, Joram his son, Zicri his son and Shelomith his son. [26]Shelomith

and his relatives were in charge
of all the treasuries for the things
dedicated by King David, by the
heads of families who were the
commanders of thousands and
commanders of hundreds, and
by the other army commanders.
27Some of the plunder taken in
battle they dedicated for the repair of the temple of the LORD.
28And everything dedicated by
Samuel the seer and by Saul son
of Kish, Abner son of Ner and
Joab son of Zeruiah, and all the
other dedicated things were in
the care of Shelomith and his
relatives.
29From the Izharites: Kenaniah and
his sons were assigned duties
away from the temple, as officials and judges over Israel.
30From the Hebronites: Hashabiah
and his relatives—seventeen
hundred able men—were re-
sponsible in Israel west of the
Jordan for all the work of the
LORD and for the king's service.
31As for the Hebronites, Jeriah
was their chief according to the
genealogical records of their
families. In the fortieth year of
David's reign a search was made
in the records, and capable men
among the Hebronites were
found at Jazer in Gilead. 32Jeriah
had two thousand seven hundred
relatives, who were able men
and heads of families, and King
David put them in charge of the
Reubenites, the Gadites and the
half-tribe of Manasseh for every
matter pertaining to God and for
the affairs of the king.

Army Divisions

27 This is the list of the Israelites —heads of families, commanders of thousands and commanders of hundreds, and their officers, who served the king in all that concerned the army divisions that were on duty month by month throughout the year. Each division consisted of 24,000 men.

2In charge of the first division, for the
first month, was Jashobeam son of
Zabdiel. There were 24,000 men in
his division. 3He was a descendant
of Perez and chief of all the army
officers for the first month.
4In charge of the division for the
second month was Dodai the Ahohite; Mikloth was the leader of his
division. There were 24,000 men in
his division.
5The third army commander, for the
third month, was Benaiah son of
Jehoiada the priest. He was chief
and there were 24,000 men in his
division. 6This was the Benaiah
who was a mighty man among the
Thirty and was over the Thirty. His
son Ammizabad was in charge of
his division.
7The fourth, for the fourth month, was
Asahel the brother of Joab; his son
Zebadiah was his successor. There
were 24,000 men in his division.
8The fifth, for the fifth month, was the
commander Shamhuth the Izra-
hite. There were 24,000 men in his
division.
9The sixth, for the sixth month, was Ira
the son of Ikkesh the Tekoite.
There were 24,000 men in his
division.
10The seventh, for the seventh month,
was Helez the Pelonite, an
Ephraimite. There were 24,000
men in his division.
11The eighth, for the eighth month, was
Sibbecai the Hushathite, a Zerahite. There were 24,000 men in his
division.
12The ninth, for the ninth month, was
Abiezer the Anathothite, a Benjamite. There were 24,000 men in his
division.
13The tenth, for the tenth month, was
Maharai the Netophathite, a Zerahite. There were 24,000 men in his
division.
14The eleventh, for the eleventh month,

was Benaiah the Pirathonite, an Ephraimite. There were 24,000 men in his division.
15The twelfth, for the twelfth month, was Heldai the Netophathite, from the family of Othniel. There were 24,000 men in his division.

Officers of the Tribes

16The officers over the tribes of Israel:

over the Reubenites: Eliezer son of Zicri;
over the Simeonites: Shephatiah son of Maacah;
17over Levi: Hashabiah son of Kemuel;
over Aaron: Zadok;
18over Judah: Elihu, a brother of David;
over Issachar: Omri son of Michael;
19over Zebulun: Ishmaiah son of Obadiah;
over Naphtali: Jerimoth son of Azriel;
20over the Ephraimites: Hoshea son of Azaziah;
over half the tribe of Manasseh: Joel son of Pedaiah;
21over the half-tribe of Manasseh in Gilead: Iddo son of Zechariah;
over Benjamin: Jaasiel son of Abner;
22over Dan: Azarel son of Jeroham.
These were the officers over the tribes of Israel.

23David did not take the number of the men twenty years old or less, because the LORD had promised to make Israel as numerous as the stars in the sky.
24Joab son of Zeruiah began to count the men but did not finish. Wrath came on Israel on account of this numbering, and the number was not entered in the book of the annals of King David.

The King's Overseers

25Azmaveth son of Adiel was in charge of the royal storehouses.

Jonathan son of Uzziah was in charge of the storehouses in the outlying districts, in the towns, the villages and the watchtowers.

26Ezri son of Kelub was in charge of the field workers who farmed the land.

27Shimei the Ramathite was in charge of the vineyards.

Zabdi the Shiphmite was in charge of the produce of the vineyards for the wine vats.

28Baal-Hanan the Gederite was in charge of the olive and sycamore-fig trees in the western foothills.

Joash was in charge of the supplies of olive oil.

29Shitrai the Sharonite was in charge of the herds grazing in Sharon.

Shaphat son of Adlai was in charge of the herds in the valleys.

30Obil the Ishmaelite was in charge of the camels.

Jehdeiah the Meronothite was in charge of the donkeys.

31Jaziz the Hagrite was in charge of the flocks.

All these were the officials in charge of King David's property.

32Jonathan, David's uncle, was a counsellor, a man of insight and a scribe. Jehiel son of Hacmoni took care of the king's sons.

33Ahithophel was the king's counsellor.

Hushai the Arkite was the king's friend.
34Ahithophel was succeeded by Jehoiada son of Benaiah and by Abiathar.

Joab was the commander of the royal army.

NEW TESTAMENT READING
1 Corinthians 4:1–21

Apostles of Christ

4 So then, men ought to regard us as servants of Christ and as those entrusted with the secret things of God.
2Now it is required that those who have

been given a trust must prove faithful. [3]I
care very little if I am judged by you or
by any human court; indeed, I do not
even judge myself. [4]My conscience is
clear, but that does not make me innocent. It is the Lord who judges me.
[5]Therefore judge nothing before the appointed time; wait till the Lord comes.
He will bring to light what is hidden
in darkness and will expose the motives
of men's hearts. At that time each will
receive his praise from God.

[6]Now, brothers, I have applied these
things to myself and Apollos for your
benefit, so that you may learn from us
the meaning of the saying, "Do not go
beyond what is written." Then you will
not take pride in one man over against
another. [7]For who makes you different
from anyone else? What do you have
that you did not receive? And if you did
receive it, why do you boast as though
you did not?

[8]Already you have all you want!
Already you have become rich! You
have become kings—and that without
us! How I wish that you really had become kings so that we might be kings
with you! [9]For it seems to me that God
has put us apostles on display at the end
of the procession, like men condemned
to die in the arena. We have been made
a spectacle to the whole universe, to
angels as well as to men. [10]We are fools
for Christ, but you are so wise in Christ!
We are weak, but you are strong! You
are honoured, we are dishonoured!
[11]To this very hour we go hungry and
thirsty, we are in rags, we are brutally
treated, we are homeless. [12]We work
hard with our own hands. When we are
cursed, we bless; when we are persecuted, we endure it; [13]when we are
slandered, we answer kindly. Up to this
moment we have become the scum of
the earth, the refuse of the world.

[14]I am not writing this to shame you,
but to warn you, as my dear children.
[15]Even though you have ten thousand
guardians in Christ, you do not have
many fathers, for in Christ Jesus I became your father through the gospel.
[16]Therefore I urge you to imitate me.
[17]For this reason I am sending to you
Timothy, my son whom I love, who is
faithful in the Lord. He will remind you
of my way of life in Christ Jesus, which
agrees with what I teach everywhere in
every church.

[18]Some of you have become arrogant,
as if I were not coming to you. [19]But I
will come to you very soon, if the Lord is
willing, and then I will find out not only
how these arrogant people are talking,
but what power they have. [20]For the
kingdom of God is not a matter of talk
but of power. [21]What do you prefer?
Shall I come to you with a whip, or in
love and with a gentle spirit?

READING FROM PROVERBS
Proverbs 19:13–22

[13]A foolish son is his father's ruin,
and a quarrelsome wife is like a
constant dripping.

[14]Houses and wealth are inherited from
parents,
but a prudent wife is from the
LORD.

[15]Laziness brings on deep sleep,
and the shiftless man goes hungry.

[16]He who obeys instructions guards his
life,
but he who is contemptuous of his
ways will die.

[17]He who is kind to the poor lends to
the LORD,
and he will reward him for what he
has done.

[18]Discipline your son, for in that there
is hope;
do not be a willing party to his
death.

[19]A hot-tempered man must pay the
penalty;

if you rescue him, you will have to
do it again.

[20]Listen to advice and accept
instruction,
and in the end you will be wise.

[21]Many are the plans in a man's heart,
but it is the LORD's purpose that
prevails.

[22]What a man desires is unfailing love;
better to be poor than a liar.

AUGUST 9

DAY 221

OLD TESTAMENT READING
1 Chronicles 28:1–29:30

David's Plans for the Temple

28 David summoned all the officials of Israel to assemble at
Jerusalem: the officers over the tribes,
the commanders of the divisions in the
service of the king, the commanders of
thousands and commanders of hundreds, and the officials in charge of all
the property and livestock belonging to
the king and his sons, together with the
palace officials, the mighty men and all
the brave warriors.

[2]King David rose to his feet and said:
"Listen to me, my brothers and my
people. I had it in my heart to build a
house as a place of rest for the ark of the
covenant of the LORD, for the footstool
of our God, and I made plans to build it.
[3]But God said to me, 'You are not to
build a house for my Name, because
you are a warrior and have shed blood.'

[4]"Yet the LORD, the God of Israel,
chose me from my whole family to be
king over Israel for ever. He chose
Judah as leader, and from the house of
Judah he chose my family, and from my
father's sons he was pleased to make me
king over all Israel. [5]Of all my sons
—and the LORD has given me many
—he has chosen my son Solomon to sit
on the throne of the kingdom of the
LORD over Israel. [6]He said to me, 'Solomon your son is the one who will build
my house and my courts, for I have
chosen him to be my son, and I will be
his father. [7]I will establish his kingdom
for ever if he is unswerving in carrying
out my commands and laws, as is being
done at this time.'

[8]"So now I charge you in the sight of
all Israel and of the assembly of the
LORD, and in the hearing of our God:
Be careful to follow all the commands of
the LORD your God, that you may possess this good land and pass it on as an
inheritance to your descendants for
ever.

[9]"And you, my son Solomon, acknowledge the God of your father, and
serve him with wholehearted devotion
and with a willing mind, for the LORD
searches every heart and understands
every motive behind the thoughts. If
you seek him, he will be found by you;
but if you forsake him, he will reject you
for ever. [10]Consider now, for the LORD
has chosen you to build a temple as a
sanctuary. Be strong and do the work."

[11]Then David gave his son Solomon
the plans for the portico of the temple,
its buildings, its storerooms, its upper
parts, its inner rooms and the place of
atonement. [12]He gave him the plans of
all that the Spirit had put in his mind for
the courts of the temple of the LORD and
all the surrounding rooms, for the
treasuries of the temple of God and for
the treasuries for the dedicated things.
[13]He gave him instructions for the divisions of the priests and Levites, and for
all the work of serving in the temple of
the LORD, as well as for all the articles to

be used in its service. 14He designated
the weight of gold for all the gold articles to be used in various kinds of service, and the weight of silver for all the
silver articles to be used in various kinds
of service: 15the weight of gold for the
gold lampstands and their lamps, with
the weight for each lampstand and its
lamps; and the weight of silver for each
silver lampstand and its lamps, according to the use of each lampstand; 16the
weight of gold for each table for consecrated bread; the weight of silver for the
silver tables; 17the weight of pure gold
for the forks, sprinkling bowls and
pitchers; the weight of gold for each
gold dish; the weight of silver for each
silver dish; 18and the weight of the refined gold for the altar of incense. He
also gave him the plan for the chariot,
that is, the cherubim of gold that spread
their wings and shelter the ark of the
covenant of the LORD.
19"All this," David said, "I have in
writing from the hand of the LORD upon
me, and he gave me understanding in all
the details of the plan."
20David also said to Solomon his son,
"Be strong and courageous, and do the
work. Do not be afraid or discouraged,
for the LORD God, my God, is with you.
He will not fail you or forsake you until
all the work for the service of the temple
of the LORD is finished. 21The divisions
of the priests and Levites are ready for
all the work on the temple of God, and
every willing man skilled in any craft
will help you in all the work. The officials and all the people will obey your
every command."

Gifts for Building the Temple

29 Then King David said to the
whole assembly: "My son Solomon, the one whom God has chosen, is
young and inexperienced. The task is
great, because this palatial structure
is not for man but for the LORD God.
2With all my resources I have provided
for the temple of my God—gold for the
gold work, silver for the silver, bronze
for the bronze, iron for the iron and
wood for the wood, as well as onyx for
the settings, turquoise, stones of various
colours, and all kinds of fine stone and
marble—all of these in large quantities.
3Besides, in my devotion to the temple
of my God I now give my personal
treasures of gold and silver for the temple of my God, over and above everything I have provided for this holy
temple: 4three thousand talents of gold
(gold of Ophir) and seven thousand
talents of refined silver, for the over-
laying of the walls of the buildings, 5for
the gold work and the silver work, and
for all the work to be done by the craftsmen. Now, who is willing to consecrate
himself today to the LORD?"
6Then the leaders of families, the
officers of the tribes of Israel, the commanders of thousands and commanders
of hundreds, and the officials in charge
of the king's work gave willingly. 7They
gave towards the work on the temple of
God five thousand talents and ten
thousand darics of gold, ten thousand
talents of silver, eighteen thousand talents of bronze and a hundred thousand
talents of iron. 8Any who had precious
stones gave them to the treasury of the
temple of the LORD in the custody of
Jehiel the Gershonite. 9The people rejoiced at the willing response of their
leaders, for they had given freely and
wholeheartedly to the LORD. David the
king also rejoiced greatly.

David's Prayer

10David praised the LORD in the presence of the whole assembly, saying,

"Praise be to you, O LORD,
God of our father Israel,
from everlasting to everlasting.
11Yours, O LORD, is the greatness and
the power
and the glory and the majesty and
the splendour,
for everything in heaven and earth
is yours.

Yours, O LORD, is the kingdom;
you are exalted as head over all.
12Wealth and honour come from you;
you are the ruler of all things.
In your hands are strength and power
to exalt and give strength to all.
13Now, our God, we give you thanks,
and praise your glorious name.

14"But who am I, and who are my
people, that we should be able to give as
generously as this? Everything comes
from you, and we have given you only
what comes from your hand. 15We are
aliens and strangers in your sight, as
were all our forefathers. Our days on
earth are like a shadow, without hope.
16O LORD our God, as for all this abundance that we have provided for building you a temple for your Holy Name, it
comes from your hand, and all of it
belongs to you. 17I know, my God, that
you test the heart and are pleased with
integrity. All these things have I given
willingly and with honest intent. And
now I have seen with joy how willingly
your people who are here have given to
you. 18O LORD, God of our fathers
Abraham, Isaac and Israel, keep this
desire in the hearts of your people for
ever, and keep their hearts loyal to you.
19And give my son Solomon the
wholehearted devotion to keep your
commands, requirements and decrees
and to do everything to build the
palatial structure for which I have
provided."

20Then David said to the whole
assembly, "Praise the LORD your God."
So they all praised the LORD, the God of
their fathers; they bowed low and fell
prostrate before the LORD and the king.

Solomon Acknowledged as King

21The next day they made sacrifices to
the LORD and presented burnt offerings
to him: a thousand bulls, a thousand
rams and a thousand male lambs,
together with their drink offerings, and
other sacrifices in abundance for all
Israel. 22They ate and drank with great
joy in the presence of the LORD that
day.

Then they acknowledged Solomon
son of David as king a second time,
anointing him before the LORD to be
ruler and Zadok to be priest. 23So Solomon sat on the throne of the LORD as
king in place of his father David. He
prospered and all Israel obeyed him.
24All the officers and mighty men, as
well as all of King David's sons, pledged
their submission to King Solomon.

25The LORD highly exalted Solomon
in the sight of all Israel and bestowed on
him royal splendour such as no king
over Israel ever had before.

The Death of David

26David son of Jesse was king over all
Israel. 27He ruled over Israel for forty
years—seven in Hebron and thirty-
three in Jerusalem. 28He died at a good
old age, having enjoyed long life,
wealth and honour. His son Solomon
succeeded him as king.

29As for the events of King David's
reign, from beginning to end, they are
written in the records of Samuel the
seer, the records of Nathan the prophet
and the records of Gad the seer,
30together with the details of his reign
and power, and the circumstances that
surrounded him and Israel and the kingdoms of all the other lands.

NEW TESTAMENT READING

1 Corinthians 5:1–13

Expel the Immoral Brother!

5 It is actually reported that there is
sexual immorality among you, and
of a kind that does not occur even
among pagans: A man has his father's
wife. 2And you are proud! Shouldn't
you rather have been filled with grief
and have put out of your fellowship the
man who did this? 3Even though I am
not physically present, I am with you in

spirit. And I have already passed judgment on the one who did this, just as if I
were present. 4When you are assembled
in the name of our Lord Jesus and I am
with you in spirit, and the power of our
Lord Jesus is present, 5hand this man
over to Satan, so that the sinful nature
may be destroyed and his spirit saved on
the day of the Lord.
6Your boasting is not good. Don't
you know that a little yeast works
through the whole batch of dough? 7Get
rid of the old yeast that you may be a
new batch without yeast—as you really
are. For Christ, our Passover lamb, has
been sacrificed. 8Therefore let us keep
the Festival, not with the old yeast, the
yeast of malice and wickedness, but
with bread without yeast, the bread of
sincerity and truth.
9I have written to you in my letter not
to associate with sexually immoral people—10not at all meaning the people of
this world who are immoral, or the
greedy and swindlers, or idolaters. In
that case you would have to leave this
world. 11But now I am writing to you
that you must not associate with anyone
who calls himself a brother but is
sexually immoral or greedy, an idolater
or a slanderer, a drunkard or a swindler.
With such a man do not even eat.
12What business is it of mine to judge
those outside the church? Are you not
to judge those inside? 13God will judge
those outside. "Expel the wicked man
from among you."

READING FROM PSALMS
Psalm 93:1–5

1The LORD reigns, he is robed in majesty;
the LORD is robed in majesty
and is armed with strength.
The world is firmly established;
it cannot be moved.
2Your throne was established long ago;
you are from all eternity.

3The seas have lifted up, O LORD,
the seas have lifted up their voice;
the seas have lifted up their pounding waves.
4Mightier than the thunder of the great waters,
mightier than the breakers of the sea—
the LORD on high is mighty.

5Your statutes stand firm;
holiness adorns your house
for endless days, O LORD.

DAY 222

AUGUST 10

OLD TESTAMENT READING
2 Chronicles 1:1–17

Solomon Asks for Wisdom

1 Solomon son of David established
himself firmly over his kingdom,
for the LORD his God was with him and
made him exceedingly great.
2Then Solomon spoke to all Israel
—to the commanders of thousands and
commanders of hundreds, to the judges
and to all the leaders in Israel, the heads
of families—3and Solomon and the
whole assembly went to the high place
at Gibeon, for God's Tent of Meeting
was there, which Moses the LORD's servant had made in the desert. 4Now
David had brought up the ark of God
from Kiriath Jearim to the place he had
prepared for it, because he had pitched
a tent for it in Jerusalem. 5But the
bronze altar that Bezalel son of Uri, the
son of Hur, had made was in Gibeon in

front of the tabernacle of the LORD; so
Solomon and the assembly enquired of
him there. 6Solomon went up to the
bronze altar before the LORD in the
Tent of Meeting and offered a thousand
burnt offerings on it.
7That night God appeared to Solomon and said to him, "Ask for whatever
you want me to give you."
8Solomon answered God, "You have
shown great kindness to David my
father and have made me king in his
place. 9Now, LORD God, let your promise to my father David be confirmed, for
you have made me king over a people
who are as numerous as the dust of the
earth. 10Give me wisdom and knowledge, that I may lead this people, for
who is able to govern this great people
of yours?"
11God said to Solomon, "Since this is
your heart's desire and you have not
asked for wealth, riches or honour, nor
for the death of your enemies, and since
you have not asked for a long life but for
wisdom and knowledge to govern my
people over whom I have made you
king, 12therefore wisdom and knowledge will be given you. And I will also
give you wealth, riches and honour,
such as no king who was before you ever
had and none after you will have."
13Then Solomon went to Jerusalem
from the high place at Gibeon, from
before the Tent of Meeting. And he
reigned over Israel.
14Solomon accumulated chariots and
horses; he had fourteen hundred chariots and twelve thousand horses, which
he kept in the chariot cities and also
with him in Jerusalem. 15The king made
silver and gold as common in Jerusalem
as stones, and cedar as plentiful as
sycamore-fig trees in the foothills.
16Solomon's horses were imported from
Egypt and from Kue—the royal merchants purchased them from Kue.
17They imported a chariot from Egypt
for six hundred shekels of silver, and a
horse for a hundred and fifty. They also
exported them to all the kings of the
Hittites and of the Arameans.

NEW TESTAMENT READING
1 Corinthians 6:1–20

Lawsuits Among Believers

6 If any of you has a dispute with
another, dare he take it before the
ungodly for judgment instead of before
the saints? 2Do you not know that the
saints will judge the world? And if you
are to judge the world, are you not
competent to judge trivial cases? 3Do
you not know that we will judge angels?
How much more the things of this life!
4Therefore, if you have disputes about
such matters, appoint as judges even
men of little account in the church! 5I
say this to shame you. Is it possible that
there is nobody among you wise enough
to judge a dispute between believers?
6But instead, one brother goes to law
against another—and this in front of
unbelievers!
7The very fact that you have lawsuits
among you means you have been completely defeated already. Why not
rather be wronged? Why not rather be
cheated? 8Instead, you yourselves cheat
and do wrong, and you do this to your
brothers.
9Do you not know that the wicked
will not inherit the kingdom of God? Do
not be deceived: Neither the sexually
immoral nor idolaters nor adulterers
nor male prostitutes nor homosexual
offenders 10nor thieves nor the greedy
nor drunkards nor slanderers nor
swindlers will inherit the kingdom of
God. 11And that is what some of you
were. But you were washed, you were
sanctified, you were justified in the
name of the Lord Jesus Christ and by
the Spirit of our God.

Sexual Immorality

12"Everything is permissible for me"
—but not everything is beneficial.
"Everything is permissible for me"—
but I will not be mastered by anything.
13"Food for the stomach and the
stomach for food"—but God will

destroy them both. The body is not meant for sexual immorality, but for the Lord, and the Lord for the body.
14By his power God raised the Lord from the dead, and he will raise us also.
15Do you not know that your bodies are members of Christ himself? Shall I then take the members of Christ and unite them with a prostitute? Never!
16Do you not know that he who unites himself with a prostitute is one with her in body? For it is said, "The two will become one flesh." 17But he who unites himself with the Lord is one with him in spirit.

18Flee from sexual immorality. All other sins a man commits are outside his body, but he who sins sexually sins against his own body. 19Do you not know that your body is a temple of the Holy Spirit, who is in you, whom you have received from God? You are not your own; 20you were bought at a price. Therefore honour God with your body.

READING FROM PSALMS

Psalm 94:1–11

1O Lord, the God who avenges,
O God who avenges, shine forth.
2Rise up, O Judge of the earth;
pay back to the proud what they deserve.
3How long will the wicked, O Lord,
how long will the wicked be jubilant?

4They pour out arrogant words;
all the evildoers are full of boasting.
5They crush your people, O Lord;
they oppress your inheritance.
6They slay the widow and the alien;
they murder the fatherless.
7They say, "The Lord does not see;
the God of Jacob pays no heed."

8Take heed, you senseless ones among the people;
you fools, when will you become wise?
9Does he who implanted the ear not hear?
Does he who formed the eye not see?
10Does he who disciplines nations not punish?
Does he who teaches man lack knowledge?
11The Lord knows the thoughts of man;
he knows that they are futile.

DAY 223

AUGUST 11

OLD TESTAMENT READING

Ecclesiastes 1:1–3:22

Everything Is Meaningless

1 The words of the Teacher, son of David, king of Jerusalem:

2"Meaningless! Meaningless!"
says the Teacher.
"Utterly meaningless!
Everything is meaningless."
3What does man gain from all his labour
at which he toils under the sun?
4Generations come and generations go,
but the earth remains for ever.
5The sun rises and the sun sets,
and hurries back to where it rises.
6The wind blows to the south
and turns to the north;
round and round it goes,
ever returning on its course.

[7]All streams flow into the sea,
yet the sea is never full.
To the place the streams come from,
there they return again.
[8]All things are wearisome,
more than one can say.
The eye never has enough of seeing,
nor the ear its fill of hearing.
[9]What has been will be again,
what has been done will be done again;
there is nothing new under the sun.
[10]Is there anything of which one can say,
"Look! This is something new"?
It was here already, long ago;
it was here before our time.
[11]There is no remembrance of men of old,
and even those who are yet to come
will not be remembered
by those who follow.

Wisdom Is Meaningless

[12]I, the Teacher, was king over Israel in Jerusalem. [13]I devoted myself to study and to explore by wisdom all that is done under heaven. What a heavy burden God has laid on men! [14]I have seen all the things that are done under the sun; all of them are meaningless, a chasing after the wind.

[15]What is twisted cannot be straightened;
what is lacking cannot be counted.

[16]I thought to myself, "Look, I have grown and increased in wisdom more than anyone who has ruled over Jerusalem before me; I have experienced much of wisdom and knowledge."
[17]Then I applied myself to the understanding of wisdom, and also of madness and folly, but I learned that this, too, is a chasing after the wind.

[18]For with much wisdom comes much sorrow;
the more knowledge, the more grief.

Pleasures Are Meaningless

2 I thought in my heart, "Come now, I will test you with pleasure to find out what is good." But that also proved
to be meaningless. [2]"Laughter," I said, "is foolish. And what does pleasure
accomplish?" [3]I tried cheering myself with wine, and embracing folly—my mind still guiding me with wisdom. I wanted to see what was worth while for men to do under heaven during the few days of their lives.
[4]I undertook great projects: I built houses for myself and planted
vineyards. [5]I made gardens and parks and planted all kinds of fruit trees in
them. [6]I made reservoirs to water
groves of flourishing trees. [7]I bought male and female slaves and had other slaves who were born in my house. I also owned more herds and flocks than
anyone in Jerusalem before me. [8]I amassed silver and gold for myself, and the treasure of kings and provinces. I acquired men and women singers, and a harem as well—the delights of the heart
of man. [9]I became greater by far than anyone in Jerusalem before me. In all this my wisdom stayed with me.

[10]I denied myself nothing my eyes desired;
I refused my heart no pleasure.
My heart took delight in all my work,
and this was the reward for all my labour.
[11]Yet when I surveyed all that my hands had done
and what I had toiled to achieve,
everything was meaningless, a chasing after the wind;
nothing was gained under the sun.

Wisdom and Folly Are Meaningless

[12]Then I turned my thoughts to consider wisdom,
and also madness and folly.
What more can the king's successor do
than what has already been done?

13I saw that wisdom is better than folly,
just as light is better than darkness.
14The wise man has eyes in his head,
while the fool walks in the
darkness;
but I came to realise
that the same fate overtakes them
both.

15Then I thought in my heart,

"The fate of the fool will overtake me
also.
What then do I gain by being
wise?"
I said in my heart,
"This too is meaningless."
16For the wise man, like the fool, will
not be long remembered;
in days to come both will be
forgotten.
Like the fool, the wise man too must
die!

Toil Is Meaningless

17So I hated life, because the work
that is done under the sun was grievous
to me. All of it is meaningless, a chasing
after the wind. 18I hated all the things I
had toiled for under the sun, because I
must leave them to the one who comes
after me. 19And who knows whether he
will be a wise man or a fool? Yet he will
have control over all the work into
which I have poured my effort and skill
under the sun. This too is meaningless.
20So my heart began to despair over all
my toilsome labour under the sun. 21For
a man may do his work with wisdom,
knowledge and skill, and then he must
leave all he owns to someone who has
not worked for it. This too is meaningless and a great misfortune. 22What
does a man get for all the toil and
anxious striving with which he labours
under the sun? 23All his days his work is
pain and grief; even at night his mind
does not rest. This too is meaningless.
24A man can do nothing better than to
eat and drink and find satisfaction in his
work. This too, I see, is from the hand
of God, 25for without him, who can eat
or find enjoyment? 26To the man who
pleases him, God gives wisdom, knowledge and happiness, but to the sinner he
gives the task of gathering and storing
up wealth to hand it over to the one who
pleases God. This too is meaningless, a
chasing after the wind.

A Time for Everything

3 There is a time for everything,
and a season for every activity
under heaven:

2 a time to be born and a time to die,
a time to plant and a time to
uproot,
3 a time to kill and a time to heal,
a time to tear down and a time to
build,
4 a time to weep and a time to laugh,
a time to mourn and a time to
dance,
5 a time to scatter stones and a time
to gather them,
a time to embrace and a time to
refrain,
6 a time to search and a time to give
up,
a time to keep and a time to throw
away,
7 a time to tear and a time to mend,
a time to be silent and a time to
speak,
8 a time to love and a time to hate,
a time for war and a time for
peace.

9What does the worker gain from his
toil? 10I have seen the burden God has
laid on men. 11He has made everything
beautiful in its time. He has also set
eternity in the hearts of men; yet they
cannot fathom what God has done from
beginning to end. 12I know that there is
nothing better for men than to be happy
and do good while they live. 13That
everyone may eat and drink, and find
satisfaction in all his toil—this is the gift
of God. 14I know that everything God
does will endure for ever; nothing can

be added to it and nothing taken from it.
God does it so that men will revere him.

15Whatever is has already been,
and what will be has been before;
and God will call the past to
account.

16And I saw something else under the
sun:

In the place of judgment—
wickedness was there,
in the place of justice—wickedness
was there.

17I thought in my heart,

"God will bring to judgment
both the righteous and the wicked,
for there will be a time for every
activity,
a time for every deed."

18I also thought, "As for men, God
tests them so that they may see that they
are like the animals. 19Man's fate is like
that of the animals; the same fate awaits
them both: As one dies, so dies the
other. All have the same breath; man
has no advantage over the animal.
Everything is meaningless. 20All go to
the same place; all come from dust, and
to dust all return. 21Who knows if the
spirit of man rises upward and if the
spirit of the animal goes down into
the earth?"
22So I saw that there is nothing better
for a man than to enjoy his work, because that is his lot. For who can bring
him to see what will happen after him?

NEW TESTAMENT READING

1 Corinthians 7:1–16

Marriage

7 Now for the matters you wrote
about: It is good for a man not to
marry. 2But since there is so much immorality, each man should have his own
wife, and each woman her own husband. 3The husband should fulfil his
marital duty to his wife, and likewise the
wife to her husband. 4The wife's body
does not belong to her alone but also to
her husband. In the same way, the husband's body does not belong to him
alone but also to his wife. 5Do not deprive each other except by mutual consent and for a time, so that you may
devote yourselves to prayer. Then come
together again so that Satan will not
tempt you because of your lack of self-
control. 6I say this as a concession, not
as a command. 7I wish that all men were
as I am. But each man has his own gift
from God; one has this gift, another has
that.
8Now to the unmarried and the
widows I say: It is good for them to stay
unmarried, as I am. 9But if they cannot
control themselves, they should marry,
for it is better to marry than to burn with
passion.
10To the married I give this command
(not I, but the Lord): A wife must not
separate from her husband. 11But if
she does, she must remain unmarried
or else be reconciled to her husband.
And a husband must not divorce his
wife.
12To the rest I say this (I, not the
Lord): If any brother has a wife who is
not a believer and she is willing to live
with him, he must not divorce her.
13And if a woman has a husband who is
not a believer and he is willing to live
with her, she must not divorce him.
14For the unbelieving husband has been
sanctified through his wife, and the unbelieving wife has been sanctified
through her believing husband. Otherwise your children would be unclean,
but as it is, they are holy.
15But if the unbeliever leaves, let him
do so. A believing man or woman is not
bound in such circumstances; God has
called us to live in peace. 16How do you
know, wife, whether you will save your
husband? Or, how do you know,
husband, whether you will save your
wife?

READING FROM PSALMS
Psalm 94:12–23

12Blessed is the man you discipline, O
LORD,
the man you teach from your law;
13you grant him relief from days of
trouble,
till a pit is dug for the wicked.
14For the LORD will not reject his
people;
he will never forsake his
inheritance.
15Judgment will again be founded on
righteousness,
and all the upright in heart will
follow it.

16Who will rise up for me against the
wicked?
Who will take a stand for me
against evildoers?
17Unless the LORD had given me help,
I would soon have dwelt in the
silence of death.
18When I said, "My foot is slipping,"
your love, O LORD, supported
me.
19When anxiety was great within me,
your consolation brought joy to my
soul.

20Can a corrupt throne be allied with
you—
one that brings on misery by its
decrees?
21They band together against the
righteous
and condemn the innocent to
death.
22But the LORD has become my
fortress,
and my God the rock in whom I
take refuge.
23He will repay them for their sins
and destroy them for their
wickedness;
the LORD our God will destroy
them.

DAY 224

AUGUST 12

OLD TESTAMENT READING
Ecclesiastes 4:1–6:12

Oppression, Toil, Friendlessness

4 Again I looked and saw all the oppression that was taking place under the sun:

I saw the tears of the oppressed—
and they have no comforter;
power was on the side of their
oppressors—
and they have no comforter.
2And I declared that the dead,
who had already died,
are happier than the living,
who are still alive.
3But better than both
is he who has not yet been,
who has not seen the evil
that is done under the sun.

4And I saw that all labour and all achievement spring from man's envy of his neighbour. This too is meaningless, a chasing after the wind.

5The fool folds his hands
and ruins himself.
6Better one handful with tranquillity
than two handfuls with toil
and chasing after the wind.

7Again I saw something meaningless under the sun:

8There was a man all alone;
he had neither son nor brother.

There was no end to his toil,
yet his eyes were not content with his wealth.
"For whom am I toiling," he asked,
"and why am I depriving myself of enjoyment?"
This too is meaningless—
a miserable business!

9Two are better than one,
because they have a good return for their work:
10If one falls down,
his friend can help him up.
But pity the man who falls
and has no-one to help him up!
11Also, if two lie down together, they will keep warm.
But how can one keep warm alone?
12Though one may be overpowered,
two can defend themselves.
A cord of three strands is not quickly broken.

Advancement Is Meaningless

13Better a poor but wise youth than an old but foolish king who no longer knows how to take warning. 14The youth may have come from prison to the kingship, or he may have been born in poverty within his kingdom. 15I saw that all who lived and walked under the sun followed the youth, the king's successor. 16There was no end to all the people who were before them. But those who came later were not pleased with the successor. This too is meaningless, a chasing after the wind.

Stand in Awe of God

5 Guard your steps when you go to the house of God. Go near to listen rather than to offer the sacrifice of fools, who do not know that they do wrong.

2Do not be quick with your mouth,
do not be hasty in your heart
to utter anything before God.
God is in heaven
and you are on earth,
so let your words be few.
3As a dream comes when there are many cares,
so the speech of a fool when there are many words.

4When you make a vow to God, do not delay in fulfilling it. He has no pleasure in fools; fulfil your vow. 5It is better not to vow than to make a vow and not fulfil it. 6Do not let your mouth lead you into sin. And do not protest to the ⌊temple⌋ messenger, "My vow was a mistake." Why should God be angry at what you say and destroy the work of your hands? 7Much dreaming and many words are meaningless. Therefore stand in awe of God.

Riches Are Meaningless

8If you see the poor oppressed in a district, and justice and rights denied, do not be surprised at such things; for one official is eyed by a higher one, and over them both are others higher still. 9The increase from the land is taken by all; the king himself profits from the fields.

10Whoever loves money never has money enough;
whoever loves wealth is never satisfied with his income.
This too is meaningless.

11As goods increase,
so do those who consume them.
And what benefit are they to the owner
except to feast his eyes on them?

12The sleep of a labourer is sweet,
whether he eats little or much,
but the abundance of a rich man
permits him no sleep.

13I have seen a grievous evil under the sun:

wealth hoarded to the harm of its
owner,
14 or wealth lost through some
misfortune,
so that when he has a son
there is nothing left for him.
15Naked a man comes from his
mother's womb,
and as he comes, so he departs.
He takes nothing from his labour
that he can carry in his hand.

16This too is a grievous evil:

As a man comes, so he departs,
and what does he gain,
since he toils for the wind?
17All his days he eats in darkness,
with great frustration, affliction
and anger.

18Then I realised that it is good and
proper for a man to eat and drink, and
to find satisfaction in his toilsome
labour under the sun during the few
days of life God has given him—for this
is his lot. 19Moreover, when God gives
any man wealth and possessions, and
enables him to enjoy them, to accept his
lot and be happy in his work—this is a
gift of God. 20He seldom reflects on the
days of his life, because God keeps him
occupied with gladness of heart.

6 I have seen another evil under the
sun, and it weighs heavily on men:
2God gives a man wealth, possessions
and honour, so that he lacks nothing his
heart desires, but God does not enable
him to enjoy them, and a stranger enjoys them instead. This is meaningless,
a grievous evil.

3A man may have a hundred children
and live many years; yet no matter how
long he lives, if he cannot enjoy his
prosperity and does not receive proper
burial, I say that a stillborn child is
better off than he. 4It comes without
meaning, it departs in darkness, and in
darkness its name is shrouded. 5Though
it never saw the sun or knew anything, it
has more rest than does that man—
6even if he lives a thousand years twice
over but fails to enjoy his prosperity.
Do not all go to the same place?

7All man's efforts are for his mouth,
yet his appetite is never satisfied.
8What advantage has a wise man
over a fool?
What does a poor man gain
by knowing how to conduct himself
before others?
9Better what the eye sees
than the roving of the appetite.
This too is meaningless,
a chasing after the wind.

10Whatever exists has already been
named,
and what man is has been known;
no man can contend
with one who is stronger than he.
11The more the words,
the less the meaning,
and how does that profit anyone?

12For who knows what is good for a
man in life, during the few and
meaningless days he passes through like
a shadow? Who can tell him what will
happen under the sun after he is gone?

NEW TESTAMENT READING
1 Corinthians 7:17–35

17Nevertheless, each one should retain the place in life that the Lord
assigned to him and to which God has
called him. This is the rule I lay down in
all the churches. 18Was a man already
circumcised when he was called? He
should not become uncircumcised. Was
a man uncircumcised when he was
called? He should not be circumcised.
19Circumcision is nothing and uncircumcision is nothing. Keeping God's
commands is what counts. 20Each one
should remain in the situation which he
was in when God called him. 21Were
you a slave when you were called?
Don't let it trouble you—although if

you can gain your freedom, do so. 22For
he who was a slave when he was called
by the Lord is the Lord's freedman;
similarly, he who was a free man when
he was called is Christ's slave. 23You
were bought at a price; do not become
slaves of men. 24Brothers, each man, as
responsible to God, should remain in
the situation God called him to.

25Now about virgins: I have no command from the Lord, but I give a judgment as one who by the Lord's mercy is
trustworthy. 26Because of the present
crisis, I think that it is good for you to
remain as you are. 27Are you married?
Do not seek a divorce. Are you unmarried? Do not look for a wife. 28But if you
do marry, you have not sinned; and if a
virgin marries, she has not sinned.
But those who marry will face many
troubles in this life, and I want to spare
you this.

29What I mean, brothers, is that the
time is short. From now on those who
have wives should live as if they had
none; 30those who mourn, as if they did
not; those who are happy, as if they
were not; those who buy something, as
if it were not theirs to keep; 31those who
use the things of the world, as if not
engrossed in them. For this world in its
present form is passing away.

32I would like you to be free from
concern. An unmarried man is concerned about the Lord's affairs—how
he can please the Lord. 33But a married
man is concerned about the affairs of
this world—how he can please his wife
—34and his interests are divided. An
unmarried woman or virgin is concerned about the Lord's affairs: Her
aim is to be devoted to the Lord in both
body and spirit. But a married woman is
concerned about the affairs of this
world—how she can please her husband. 35I am saying this for your own
good, not to restrict you, but that you
may live in a right way in undivided
devotion to the Lord.

READING FROM PROVERBS

Proverbs 19:23–20:4

23The fear of the LORD leads to life:
Then one rests content, untouched by trouble.

24The sluggard buries his hand in the dish;
he will not even bring it back to his mouth!

25Flog a mocker, and the simple will learn prudence;
rebuke a discerning man, and he will gain knowledge.

26He who robs his father and drives out his mother
is a son who brings shame and disgrace.

27Stop listening to instruction, my son,
and you will stray from the words of knowledge.

28A corrupt witness mocks at justice,
and the mouth of the wicked gulps down evil.

29Penalties are prepared for mockers,
and beatings for the backs of fools.

20 Wine is a mocker and beer a brawler;
whoever is led astray by them is not wise.

2A king's wrath is like the roar of a lion;
he who angers him forfeits his life.

3It is to a man's honour to avoid strife,
but every fool is quick to quarrel.

4A sluggard does not plough in season;
so at harvest time he looks but finds nothing.

AUGUST 13

OLD TESTAMENT READING
Ecclesiastes 7:1–9:12

Wisdom

7 A good name is better than fine
perfume,
and the day of death better than
the day of birth.
2It is better to go to a house of
mourning
than to go to a house of feasting,
for death is the destiny of every man;
the living should take this to heart.
3Sorrow is better than laughter,
because a sad face is good for the
heart.
4The heart of the wise is in the house
of mourning,
but the heart of fools is in the
house of pleasure.
5It is better to heed a wise man's
rebuke
than to listen to the song of fools.
6Like the crackling of thorns under
the pot,
so is the laughter of fools.
This too is meaningless.

7Extortion turns a wise man into a
fool,
and a bribe corrupts the heart.

8The end of a matter is better than its
beginning,
and patience is better than pride.
9Do not be quickly provoked in your
spirit,
for anger resides in the lap of fools.

10Do not say, "Why were the old days
better than these?"
For it is not wise to ask such
questions.

11Wisdom, like an inheritance, is a
good thing
and benefits those who see the sun.
12Wisdom is a shelter
as money is a shelter,
but the advantage of knowledge is
this:
that wisdom preserves the life of its
possessor.

13Consider what God has done:

Who can straighten
what he has made crooked?
14When times are good, be happy;
but when times are bad, consider:
God has made the one
as well as the other.
Therefore, a man cannot discover
anything about his future.

15In this meaningless life of mine I
have seen both of these:

a righteous man perishing in his
righteousness,
and a wicked man living long in his
wickedness.
16Do not be over-righteous,
neither be overwise—
why destroy yourself?
17Do not be overwicked,
and do not be a fool—
why die before your time?
18It is good to grasp the one
and not let go of the other.
The man who fears God will avoid
all ⌞extremes⌟.

19Wisdom makes one wise man more
powerful
than ten rulers in a city.

20There is not a righteous man on earth
who does what is right and never
sins.

21Do not pay attention to every word
people say,
or you may hear your servant
cursing you—

[22]for you know in your heart
that many times you yourself have cursed others.

[23]All this I tested by wisdom and I said,

"I am determined to be wise"—
but this was beyond me.
[24]Whatever wisdom may be,
it is far off and most profound—
who can discover it?
[25]So I turned my mind to understand,
to investigate and to search out
wisdom and the scheme of things
and to understand the stupidity of wickedness
and the madness of folly.

[26]I find more bitter than death
the woman who is a snare,
whose heart is a trap
and whose hands are chains.
The man who pleases God will escape her,
but the sinner she will ensnare.

[27]"Look," says the Teacher, "this is what I have discovered:

"Adding one thing to another to discover the scheme of things—
[28] while I was still searching
but not finding—
I found one ⌊upright⌋ man among a thousand,
but not one ⌊upright⌋ woman among them all.
[29]This only have I found:
God made mankind upright,
but men have gone in search of many schemes."

8 Who is like the wise man?
Who knows the explanation of things?
Wisdom brightens a man's face
and changes its hard appearance.

Obey the King

[2]Obey the king's command, I say,
because you took an oath before God.
[3]Do not be in a hurry to leave the king's
presence. Do not stand up for a bad
cause, for he will do whatever he
pleases. [4]Since a king's word is
supreme, who can say to him, "What
are you doing?"

[5]Whoever obeys his command will come to no harm,
and the wise heart will know the proper time and procedure.
[6]For there is a proper time and procedure for every matter,
though a man's misery weighs heavily upon him.

[7]Since no man knows the future,
who can tell him what is to come?
[8]No man has power over the wind to contain it;
so no-one has power over the day of his death.
As no-one is discharged in time of war,
so wickedness will not release those who practise it.

[9]All this I saw, as I applied my mind
to everything done under the sun.
There is a time when a man lords it over
others to his own hurt. [10]Then too, I saw
the wicked buried—those who used to
come and go from the holy place and
receive praise in the city where they did
this. This too is meaningless.
[11]When the sentence for a crime is not
quickly carried out, the hearts of the
people are filled with schemes to do
wrong. [12]Although a wicked man commits a hundred crimes and still lives a
long time, I know that it will go better
with God-fearing men, who are reverent before God. [13]Yet because the
wicked do not fear God, it will not go
well with them, and their days will not
lengthen like a shadow.
[14]There is something else meaningless that occurs on earth: righteous men
who get what the wicked deserve, and
wicked men who get what the righteous
deserve. This too, I say, is meaningless.
[15]So I commend the enjoyment of life,

because nothing is better for a man under the sun than to eat and drink and be glad. Then joy will accompany him in his work all the days of the life God has given him under the sun.

16When I applied my mind to know wisdom and to observe man's labour on earth—his eyes not seeing sleep day or night—17then I saw all that God has done. No-one can comprehend what goes on under the sun. Despite all his efforts to search it out, man cannot discover its meaning. Even if a wise man claims he knows, he cannot really comprehend it.

A Common Destiny for All

9 So I reflected on all this and concluded that the righteous and the wise and what they do are in God's hands, but no man knows whether love or hate awaits him. 2All share a common destiny—the righteous and the wicked, the good and the bad, the clean and the unclean, those who offer sacrifices and those who do not.

As it is with the good man,
so with the sinner;
as it is with those who take oaths,
so with those who are afraid to
take them.

3This is the evil in everything that happens under the sun: The same destiny overtakes all. The hearts of men, moreover, are full of evil and there is madness in their hearts while they live, and afterwards they join the dead. 4Anyone who is among the living has hope—even a live dog is better off than a dead lion!

5For the living know that they will die,
but the dead know nothing;
they have no further reward,
and even the memory of them is
forgotten.
6Their love, their hate
and their jealousy have long since
vanished;
never again will they have a part
in anything that happens under the
sun.

7Go, eat your food with gladness, and drink your wine with a joyful heart, for it is now that God favours what you do. 8Always be clothed in white, and always anoint your head with oil. 9Enjoy life with your wife, whom you love, all the days of this meaningless life that God has given you under the sun—all your meaningless days. For this is your lot in life and in your toilsome labour under the sun. 10Whatever your hand finds to do, do it with all your might, for in the grave, where you are going, there is neither working nor planning nor knowledge nor wisdom.

11I have seen something else under the sun:

The race is not to the swift
or the battle to the strong,
nor does food come to the wise
or wealth to the brilliant
or favour to the learned;
but time and chance happen to them
all.

12Moreover, no man knows when his hour will come:

As fish are caught in a cruel net,
or birds are taken in a snare,
so men are trapped by evil times
that fall unexpectedly upon them.

NEW TESTAMENT READING
1 Corinthians 7:36–8:13

36If anyone thinks he is acting improperly towards the virgin he is engaged to, and if she is getting on in years and he feels he ought to marry, he should do as he wants. He is not sinning. They should get married. 37But the man who has settled the matter in his own mind, who is under no compulsion but

has control over his own will, and who
has made up his mind not to marry the
virgin—this man also does the right
thing. 38So then, he who marries the
virgin does right, but he who does not
marry her does even better.
39A woman is bound to her husband
as long as he lives. But if her husband
dies, she is free to marry anyone she
wishes, but he must belong to the Lord.
40In my judgment, she is happier if she
stays as she is—and I think that I too
have the Spirit of God.

Food Sacrificed to Idols

8 Now about food sacrificed to idols:
We know that we all possess
knowledge. Knowledge puffs up, but
love builds up. 2The man who thinks he
knows something does not yet know as
he ought to know. 3But the man who
loves God is known by God.
4So then, about eating food sacrificed
to idols: We know that an idol is nothing
at all in the world and that there is no
God but one. 5For even if there are
so-called gods, whether in heaven or on
earth (as indeed there are many "gods"
and many "lords"), 6yet for us there is
but one God, the Father, from whom all
things came and for whom we live; and
there is but one Lord, Jesus Christ,
through whom all things came and
through whom we live.
7But not everyone knows this. Some
people are still so accustomed to idols
that when they eat such food they think
of it as having been sacrificed to an idol,
and since their conscience is weak, it is
defiled. 8But food does not bring us
near to God; we are no worse if we do
not eat, and no better if we do.
9Be careful, however, that the exercise of your freedom does not become a
stumbling-block to the weak. 10For if
anyone with a weak conscience sees you
who have this knowledge eating in an
idol's temple, won't he be emboldened
to eat what has been sacrificed to idols?
11So this weak brother, for whom Christ
died, is destroyed by your knowledge.
12When you sin against your brothers in
this way and wound their weak conscience, you sin against Christ. 13There-
fore, if what I eat causes my brother to
fall into sin, I will never eat meat again,
so that I will not cause him to fall.

READING FROM PSALMS
Psalm 95:1–11

1Come, let us sing for joy to the LORD;
  let us shout aloud to the Rock of
    our salvation.
2Let us come before him with
    thanksgiving
  and extol him with music and song.

3For the LORD is the great God,
  the great King above all gods.
4In his hand are the depths of the
    earth,
  and the mountain peaks belong to
    him.
5The sea is his, for he made it,
  and his hands formed the dry land.

6Come, let us bow down in worship,
  let us kneel before the LORD our
    Maker;
7for he is our God
  and we are the people of his
    pasture,
  the flock under his care.

Today, if you hear his voice,
8 do not harden your hearts as you
    did at Meribah,
  as you did that day at Massah in the
    desert,
9where your fathers tested and tried
    me,
  though they had seen what I did.
10For forty years I was angry with that
    generation;
  I said, "They are a people whose
    hearts go astray,
  and they have not known my
    ways."
11So I declared on oath in my anger,
  "They shall never enter my rest."

OLD TESTAMENT READING
Ecclesiastes 9:13–12:14

Wisdom Better Than Folly

13I also saw under the sun this example of wisdom that greatly impressed
me: 14There was once a small city with
only a few people in it. And a powerful
king came against it, surrounded it and
built huge siegeworks against it. 15Now
there lived in that city a man poor but
wise, and he saved the city by his wisdom. But nobody remembered that
poor man. 16So I said, "Wisdom is better than strength." But the poor man's
wisdom is despised, and his words are
no longer heeded.

17The quiet words of the wise are more
to be heeded
than the shouts of a ruler of fools.
18Wisdom is better than weapons of
war,
but one sinner destroys much
good.

10 As dead flies give perfume a
bad smell,
so a little folly outweighs wisdom
and honour.
2The heart of the wise inclines to the
right,
but the heart of the fool to the left.
3Even as he walks along the road,
the fool lacks sense
and shows everyone how stupid
he is.
4If a ruler's anger rises against you,
do not leave your post;
calmness can lay great errors to
rest.

5There is an evil I have seen under the
sun,
the sort of error that arises from a
ruler:
6Fools are put in many high positions,
while the rich occupy the low ones.
7I have seen slaves on horseback,
while princes go on foot like slaves.

8Whoever digs a pit may fall into it;
whoever breaks through a wall
may be bitten by a snake.
9Whoever quarries stones may be
injured by them;
whoever splits logs may be
endangered by them.

10If the axe is dull
and its edge unsharpened,
more strength is needed
but skill will bring success.

11If a snake bites before it is charmed,
there is no profit for the charmer.

12Words from a wise man's mouth are
gracious,
but a fool is consumed by his own
lips.
13At the beginning his words are folly;
at the end they are wicked
madness—
14 and the fool multiplies words.

No-one knows what is coming—
who can tell him what will happen
after him?

15A fool's work wearies him;
he does not know the way to town.

16Woe to you, O land whose king was a
servant
and whose princes feast in the
morning.
17Blessed are you, O land whose king is
of noble birth
and whose princes eat at a proper
time—
for strength and not for
drunkenness.

18If a man is lazy, the rafters sag;
if his hands are idle, the house
leaks.

19A feast is made for laughter,
and wine makes life merry,
but money is the answer for everything.

20Do not revile the king even in your thoughts,
or curse the rich in your bedroom,
because a bird of the air may carry your words,
and a bird on the wing may report what you say.

Bread Upon the Waters

11 Cast your bread upon the waters,
for after many days you will find it again.
2Give portions to seven, yes to eight,
for you do not know what disaster may come upon the land.

3If clouds are full of water,
they pour rain upon the earth.
Whether a tree falls to the south or to the north,
in the place where it falls, there will it lie.
4Whoever watches the wind will not plant;
whoever looks at the clouds will not reap.

5As you do not know the path of the wind,
or how the body is formed in a mother's womb,
so you cannot understand the work of God,
the Maker of all things.

6Sow your seed in the morning,
and at evening let not your hands be idle,
for you do not know which will succeed,
whether this or that,
or whether both will do equally well.

Remember Your Creator While Young

7Light is sweet,
and it pleases the eyes to see the sun.
8However many years a man may live,
let him enjoy them all.
But let him remember the days of darkness,
for they will be many.
Everything to come is meaningless.

9Be happy, young man, while you are young,
and let your heart give you joy in the days of your youth.
Follow the ways of your heart
and whatever your eyes see,
but know that for all these things
God will bring you to judgment.
10So then, banish anxiety from your heart
and cast off the troubles of your body,
for youth and vigour are meaningless.

12 Remember your Creator
in the days of your youth,
before the days of trouble come
and the years approach when you will say,
"I find no pleasure in them"—
2before the sun and the light
and the moon and the stars grow dark,
and the clouds return after the rain;
3when the keepers of the house tremble,
and the strong men stoop,
when the grinders cease because they are few,
and those looking through the windows grow dim;
4when the doors to the street are closed
and the sound of grinding fades;
when men rise up at the sound of birds,
but all their songs grow faint;

5when men are afraid of heights
and of dangers in the streets;
when the almond tree blossoms
and the grasshopper drags himself along
and desire no longer is stirred.
Then man goes to his eternal home
and mourners go about the streets.

6Remember him—before the silver cord is severed,
or the golden bowl is broken;
before the pitcher is shattered at the spring,
or the wheel broken at the well,
7and the dust returns to the ground it came from,
and the spirit returns to God who gave it.

8"Meaningless! Meaningless!" says the Teacher.
"Everything is meaningless!"

The Conclusion of the Matter

9Not only was the Teacher wise, but also he imparted knowledge to the people. He pondered and searched out and set in order many proverbs.
10The Teacher searched to find just the right words, and what he wrote was upright and true.

11The words of the wise are like goads, their collected sayings like firmly embedded nails—given by one Shepherd.
12Be warned, my son, of anything in addition to them.

Of making many books there is no end, and much study wearies the body.

13Now all has been heard;
here is the conclusion of the matter:
Fear God and keep his commandments,
for this is the whole ⌊duty⌋ of man.
14For God will bring every deed into judgment,
including every hidden thing,
whether it is good or evil.

NEW TESTAMENT READING
1 Corinthians 9:1–18

The Rights of an Apostle

9 Am I not free? Am I not an apostle? Have I not seen Jesus our Lord? Are you not the result of my work in the Lord?
2Even though I may not be an apostle to others, surely I am to you! For you are the seal of my apostleship in the Lord.

3This is my defence to those who sit in judgment on me.
4Don't we have the right to food and drink?
5Don't we have the right to take a believing wife along with us, as do the other apostles and the Lord's brothers and Cephas?
6Or is it only I and Barnabas who must work for a living?

7Who serves as a soldier at his own expense? Who plants a vineyard and does not eat of its grapes? Who tends a flock and does not drink of the milk?
8Do I say this merely from a human point of view? Doesn't the Law say the same thing?
9For it is written in the Law of Moses: "Do not muzzle an ox while it is treading out the grain." Is it about oxen that God is concerned?
10Surely he says this for us, doesn't he? Yes, this was written for us, because when the ploughman ploughs and the thresher threshes, they ought to do so in the hope of sharing in the harvest.
11If we have sown spiritual seed among you, is it too much if we reap a material harvest from you?
12If others have this right of support from you, shouldn't we have it all the more?

But we did not use this right. On the contrary, we put up with anything rather than hinder the gospel of Christ.
13Don't you know that those who work in the temple get their food from the temple, and those who serve at the altar share in what is offered on the altar?
14In the same way, the Lord has commanded that those who preach the gospel should receive their living from the gospel.

15But I have not used any of these

rights. And I am not writing this in the hope that you will do such things for me. I would rather die than have anyone deprive me of this boast. [16]Yet when I
preach the gospel, I cannot boast, for I am compelled to preach. Woe to me if I do not preach the gospel! [17]If I preach
voluntarily, I have a reward; if not voluntarily, I am simply discharging the trust committed to me. [18]What then is
my reward? Just this: that in preaching the gospel I may offer it free of charge, and so not make use of my rights in preaching it.

READING FROM PSALMS
Psalm 96:1–13

[1]Sing to the LORD a new song;
sing to the LORD, all the earth.
[2]Sing to the LORD, praise his name;
proclaim his salvation day after day.
[3]Declare his glory among the nations,
his marvellous deeds among all peoples.

[4]For great is the LORD and most worthy of praise;
he is to be feared above all gods.
[5]For all the gods of the nations are idols,
but the LORD made the heavens.
[6]Splendour and majesty are before him;
strength and glory are in his sanctuary.

[7]Ascribe to the LORD, O families of nations,
ascribe to the LORD glory and strength.
[8]Ascribe to the LORD the glory due to his name;
bring an offering and come into his courts.
[9]Worship the LORD in the splendour of his holiness;
tremble before him, all the earth.

[10]Say among the nations, "The LORD reigns."
The world is firmly established, it cannot be moved;
he will judge the peoples with equity.
[11]Let the heavens rejoice, let the earth be glad;
let the sea resound, and all that is in it;
[12] let the fields be jubilant, and everything in them.
Then all the trees of the forest will sing for joy;
[13] they will sing before the LORD, for he comes,
he comes to judge the earth.
He will judge the world in righteousness
and the peoples in his truth.

AUGUST 15

DAY 227

OLD TESTAMENT READING
2 Chronicles 2:1–5:1

Preparations for Building the Temple

2 Solomon gave orders to build a temple for the Name of the LORD and a royal palace for himself. [2]He conscripted seventy thousand men as carriers and eighty thousand as stone-cutters in the hills and thirty-six hundred as foremen over them.

[3]Solomon sent this message to Hiram king of Tyre:

"Send me cedar logs as you did for my father David when you sent him cedar to build a palace to live

in. 4Now I am about to build a
temple for the Name of the LORD
my God and to dedicate it to him
for burning fragrant incense before
him, for setting out the consecrated
bread regularly, and for making
burnt offerings every morning and
evening and on Sabbaths and New
Moons and at the appointed feasts
of the LORD our God. This is a
lasting ordinance for Israel.
5"The temple I am going to build
will be great, because our God is
greater than all other gods. 6But
who is able to build a temple for
him, since the heavens, even the
highest heavens, cannot contain
him? Who then am I to build a
temple for him, except as a place to
burn sacrifices before him?
7"Send me, therefore, a man
skilled to work in gold and silver,
bronze and iron, and in purple,
crimson and blue yarn, and experienced in the art of engraving, to
work in Judah and Jerusalem with
my skilled craftsmen, whom my
father David provided.
8"Send me also cedar, pine and
algum logs from Lebanon, for I
know that your men are skilled in
cutting timber there. My men shall
work with yours 9to provide me
with plenty of timber, because the
temple I build must be large and
magnificent. 10I will give your servants, the woodsmen who cut the
timber, twenty thousand cors of
ground wheat, twenty thousand
cors of barley, twenty thousand
baths of wine and twenty thousand baths of olive oil."

11Hiram king of Tyre replied by letter
to Solomon:

"Because the LORD loves his
people, he has made you their
king."

12And Hiram added:

"Praise be to the LORD, the God
of Israel, who made heaven and
earth! He has given King David a
wise son, endowed with intelligence and discernment, who will
build a temple for the LORD and a
palace for himself.
13"I am sending you Huram-
Abi, a man of great skill, 14whose
mother was from Dan and whose
father was from Tyre. He is trained
to work in gold and silver, bronze
and iron, stone and wood, and with
purple and blue and crimson yarn
and fine linen. He is experienced in
all kinds of engraving and can execute any design given to him. He
will work with your craftsmen and
with those of my lord, David your
father.
15"Now let my lord send his servants the wheat and barley and the
olive oil and wine he promised,
16and we will cut all the logs from
Lebanon that you need and will
float them in rafts by sea down to
Joppa. You can then take them up
to Jerusalem."

17Solomon took a census of all the
aliens who were in Israel, after the census his father David had taken; and they
were found to be 153,600. 18He assigned
70,000 of them to be carriers and 80,000
to be stonecutters in the hills, with 3,600
foremen over them to keep the people
working.

Solomon Builds the Temple

3 Then Solomon began to build the
temple of the LORD in Jerusalem
on Mount Moriah, where the LORD had
appeared to his father David. It was on
the threshing-floor of Araunah the
Jebusite, the place provided by David.
2He began building on the second day of
the second month in the fourth year of
his reign.
3The foundation Solomon laid for
building the temple of God was sixty
cubits long and twenty cubits wide

(using the cubit of the old standard).
4The portico at the front of the temple
was twenty cubits long across the width
of the building and twenty cubits high.

He overlaid the inside with pure gold.
5He panelled the main hall with pine
and covered it with fine gold and decorated it with palm tree and chain
designs. 6He adorned the temple with
precious stones. And the gold he used
was gold of Parvaim. 7He overlaid the
ceiling beams, door-frames, walls and
doors of the temple with gold, and he
carved cherubim on the walls.

8He built the Most Holy Place, its
length corresponding to the width of the
temple—twenty cubits long and twenty
cubits wide. He overlaid the inside with
six hundred talents of fine gold. 9The
gold nails weighed fifty shekels. He also
overlaid the upper parts with gold.

10In the Most Holy Place he made a
pair of sculptured cherubim and overlaid them with gold. 11The total wing-
span of the cherubim was twenty cubits.
One wing of the first cherub was five
cubits long and touched the temple
wall, while its other wing, also five
cubits long, touched the wing of the
other cherub. 12Similarly one wing of
the second cherub was five cubits long
and touched the other temple wall, and
its other wing, also five cubits long,
touched the wing of the first cherub.
13The wings of these cherubim extended
twenty cubits. They stood on their feet,
facing the main hall.

14He made the curtain of blue, purple
and crimson yarn and fine linen, with
cherubim worked into it.

15In the front of the temple he made
two pillars, which ⌊together⌋ were
thirty-five cubits long, each with a capital on top measuring five cubits. 16He
made interwoven chains and put them
on top of the pillars. He also made a
hundred pomegranates and attached
them to the chains. 17He erected the
pillars in the front of the temple, one to
the south and one to the north. The one
to the south he named Jakin and the one
to the north Boaz.

The Temple's Furnishings

4 He made a bronze altar twenty
cubits long, twenty cubits wide and
ten cubits high. 2He made the Sea of cast
metal, circular in shape, measuring
ten cubits from rim to rim and five
cubits high. It took a line of thirty
cubits to measure round it. 3Below
the rim, figures of bulls encircled
it—ten to a cubit. The bulls were
cast in two rows in one piece with the
Sea.

4The Sea stood on twelve bulls, three
facing north, three facing west, three
facing south and three facing east. The
Sea rested on top of them, and their
hindquarters were towards the centre.
5It was a handbreadth in thickness, and
its rim was like the rim of a cup, like a
lily blossom. It held three thousand
baths.

6He then made ten basins for washing
and placed five on the south side and
five on the north. In them the things to
be used for the burnt offerings were
rinsed, but the Sea was to be used by the
priests for washing.

7He made ten gold lampstands
according to the specifications for them
and placed them in the temple, five on
the south side and five on the north.

8He made ten tables and placed them
in the temple, five on the south side and
five on the north. He also made a hundred gold sprinkling bowls.

9He made the courtyard of the
priests, and the large court and the
doors for the court, and overlaid
the doors with bronze. 10He placed the
Sea on the south side, at the south-east
corner.

11He also made the pots and shovels
and sprinkling bowls.

So Huram finished the work he had
undertaken for King Solomon in the
temple of God:

12the two pillars;
the two bowl-shaped capitals on
top of the pillars;
the two sets of network decorating

the two bowl-shaped capitals on top of the pillars;
13the four hundred pomegranates for the two sets of network (two rows of pomegranates for each network, decorating the bowl-shaped capitals on top of the pillars);
14the stands with their basins;
15the Sea and the twelve bulls under it;
16the pots, shovels, meat forks and all related articles.

All the objects that Huram-Abi made
for King Solomon for the temple of the
LORD were of polished bronze. 17The
king had them cast in clay moulds in
the plain of the Jordan between Succoth
and Zarethan. 18All these things that
Solomon made amounted to so much
that the weight of the bronze was not
determined.
19Solomon also made all the furnishings that were in God's temple:

the golden altar;
the tables on which was the bread of the Presence;
20the lampstands of pure gold with their lamps, to burn in front of the inner sanctuary as prescribed;
21the gold floral work and lamps and tongs (they were solid gold);
22the pure gold wick trimmers, sprinkling bowls, dishes and censers; and the gold doors of the temple: the inner doors to the Most Holy Place and the doors of the main hall.

5 When all the work Solomon had done for the temple of the LORD was finished, he brought in the things his father David had dedicated—the silver and gold and all the furnishings—and he placed them in the treasuries of God's temple.

NEW TESTAMENT READING

1 Corinthians 9:19–10:13

19Though I am free and belong to no
man, I make myself a slave to everyone,
to win as many as possible. 20To the
Jews I became like a Jew, to win the
Jews. To those under the law I became
like one under the law (though I myself
am not under the law), so as to win
those under the law. 21To those not
having the law I became like one not
having the law (though I am not free
from God's law but am under Christ's
law), so as to win those not having the
law. 22To the weak I became weak, to
win the weak. I have become all things
to all men so that by all possible means I
might save some. 23I do all this for the
sake of the gospel, that I may share in its
blessings.
24Do you not know that in a race all
the runners run, but only one gets the
prize? Run in such a way as to get the
prize. 25Everyone who competes in
the games goes into strict training. They
do it to get a crown that will not last; but
we do it to get a crown that will last for
ever. 26Therefore I do not run like a
man running aimlessly; I do not fight
like a man beating the air. 27No, I beat
my body and make it my slave so that
after I have preached to others, I myself
will not be disqualified for the prize.

Warnings From Israel's History

10 For I do not want you to be
ignorant of the fact, brothers,
that our forefathers were all under the
cloud and that they all passed through
the sea. 2They were all baptised into
Moses in the cloud and in the sea. 3They
all ate the same spiritual food 4and
drank the same spiritual drink; for they
drank from the spiritual rock that
accompanied them, and that rock was
Christ. 5Nevertheless, God was not
pleased with most of them; their bodies
were scattered over the desert.
6Now these things occurred as examples to keep us from setting our hearts

on evil things as they did. [7]Do not be
idolaters, as some of them were; as it is
written: "The people sat down to eat
and drink and got up to indulge in pagan
revelry." [8]We should not commit sexual
immorality, as some of them did—and
in one day twenty-three thousand of
them died. [9]We should not test the
Lord, as some of them did—and were
killed by snakes. [10]And do not grumble,
as some of them did—and were killed
by the destroying angel.

[11]These things happened to them as
examples and were written down as
warnings for us, on whom the fulfilment
of the ages has come. [12]So, if you think
you are standing firm, be careful that
you don't fall! [13]No temptation has
seized you except what is common to
man. And God is faithful; he will not let
you be tempted beyond what you can
bear. But when you are tempted, he will
also provide a way out so that you can
stand up under it.

READING FROM PSALMS
Psalm 97:1–12

[1]The LORD reigns, let the earth be
glad;
let the distant shores rejoice.

[2]Clouds and thick darkness surround
him;
righteousness and justice are the
foundation of his throne.
[3]Fire goes before him
and consumes his foes on every
side.
[4]His lightning lights up the world;
the earth sees and trembles.
[5]The mountains melt like wax before
the LORD,
before the Lord of all the earth.
[6]The heavens proclaim his
righteousness,
and all the peoples see his glory.

[7]All who worship images are put to
shame,
those who boast in idols—
worship him, all you gods!

[8]Zion hears and rejoices
and the villages of Judah are glad
because of your judgments, O
LORD.
[9]For you, O LORD, are the Most High
over all the earth;
you are exalted far above all gods.

[10]Let those who love the LORD hate
evil,
for he guards the lives of his
faithful ones
and delivers them from the hand of
the wicked.
[11]Light is shed upon the righteous
and joy on the upright in heart.
[12]Rejoice in the LORD, you who are
righteous,
and praise his holy name.

DAY 228

AUGUST 16

OLD TESTAMENT READING
2 Chronicles 5:2–7:10

The Ark Brought to the Temple

2Then Solomon summoned to Jerusalem the elders of Israel, all the heads of the tribes and the chiefs of the Israelite families, to bring up the ark of the LORD's covenant from Zion, the City of David. 3And all the men of Israel came together to the king at the time of the festival in the seventh month.

4When all the elders of Israel had arrived, the Levites took up the ark, 5and they brought up the ark and the Tent of Meeting and all the sacred furnishings in it. The priests, who were Levites, carried them up; 6and King Solomon and the entire assembly of Israel that had gathered about him were before the ark, sacrificing so many sheep and cattle that they could not be recorded or counted.

7The priests then brought the ark of the LORD's covenant to its place in the inner sanctuary of the temple, the Most Holy Place, and put it beneath the wings of the cherubim. 8The cherubim spread their wings over the place of the ark and covered the ark and its carrying poles. 9These poles were so long that their ends, extending from the ark, could be seen from in front of the inner sanctuary, but not from outside the Holy Place; and they are still there today. 10There was nothing in the ark except the two tablets that Moses had placed in it at Horeb, where the LORD made a covenant with the Israelites after they came out of Egypt.

11The priests then withdrew from the Holy Place. All the priests who were there had consecrated themselves, regardless of their divisions. 12All the Levites who were musicians—Asaph, Heman, Jeduthun and their sons and relatives—stood on the east side of the altar, dressed in fine linen and playing cymbals, harps and lyres. They were accompanied by 120 priests sounding trumpets. 13The trumpeters and singers joined in unison, as with one voice, to give praise and thanks to the LORD. Accompanied by trumpets, cymbals and other instruments, they raised their voices in praise to the LORD and sang:

"He is good;
his love endures for ever."

Then the temple of the LORD was filled with a cloud, 14and the priests could not perform their service because of the cloud, for the glory of the LORD filled the temple of God.

6 Then Solomon said, "The LORD has said that he would dwell in a dark cloud; 2I have built a magnificent temple for you, a place for you to dwell for ever."

3While the whole assembly of Israel was standing there, the king turned round and blessed them. 4Then he said:

"Praise be to the LORD, the God of Israel, who with his hands has fulfilled what he promised with his mouth to my father David. For he said, 5'Since the day I brought my people out of Egypt, I have not chosen a city in any tribe of Israel to have a temple built for my Name to be there, nor have I chosen anyone to be the leader over my people Israel. 6But now I have chosen Jerusalem for my Name to be there, and I have chosen David to rule my people Israel.'

7"My father David had it in his heart to build a temple for the Name of the LORD, the God of Israel. 8But the LORD said to my father David, 'Because it was in your heart to build a temple for my

Name, you did well to have this in
your heart. 9Nevertheless, you are
not the one to build the temple, but
your son, who is your own flesh and
blood—he is the one who will build
the temple for my Name.'
10"The LORD has kept the promise he made. I have succeeded
David my father and now I sit on
the throne of Israel, just as the
LORD promised, and I have built
the temple for the Name of the
LORD, the God of Israel. 11There I
have placed the ark, in which is the
covenant of the LORD that he made
with the people of Israel."

Solomon's Prayer of Dedication

12Then Solomon stood before the
altar of the LORD in front of the whole
assembly of Israel and spread out his
hands. 13Now he had made a bronze
platform, five cubits long, five cubits
wide and three cubits high, and had
placed it in the centre of the outer court.
He stood on the platform and then knelt
down before the whole assembly of
Israel and spread out his hands towards
heaven. 14He said:

"O LORD, God of Israel, there is
no God like you in heaven or on
earth—you who keep your covenant of love with your servants
who continue wholeheartedly in
your way. 15You have kept your
promise to your servant David my
father; with your mouth you have
promised and with your hand you
have fulfilled it—as it is today.
16"Now LORD, God of Israel,
keep for your servant David my
father the promises you made to
him when you said, 'You shall
never fail to have a man to sit before me on the throne of Israel, if
only your sons are careful in all
they do to walk before me according to my law, as you have done.'
17And now, O LORD, God of
Israel, let your word that you
promised your servant David come
true.
18"But will God really dwell on
earth with men? The heavens, even
the highest heavens, cannot contain you. How much less this temple that I have built! 19Yet give
attention to your servant's prayer
and his plea for mercy, O LORD my
God. Hear the cry and the prayer
that your servant is praying in your
presence. 20May your eyes be open
towards this temple day and night,
this place of which you said you
would put your Name there. May
you hear the prayer your servant
prays towards this place. 21Hear
the supplications of your servant
and of your people Israel when
they pray towards this place. Hear
from heaven, your dwelling-place;
and when you hear, forgive.
22"When a man wrongs his
neighbour and is required to take
an oath and he comes and swears
the oath before your altar in this
temple, 23then hear from heaven
and act. Judge between your servants, repaying the guilty by bringing down on his own head what he
has done. Declare the innocent
not guilty and so establish his
innocence.
24"When your people Israel have
been defeated by an enemy because they have sinned against you
and when they turn back and confess your name, praying and making supplication before you in this
temple, 25then hear from heaven
and forgive the sin of your people
Israel and bring them back to the
land you gave to them and their
fathers.
26"When the heavens are shut up
and there is no rain because your
people have sinned against you,
and when they pray towards this
place and confess your name and
turn from their sin because you
have afflicted them, 27then hear
from heaven and forgive the sin of

your servants, your people Israel.
Teach them the right way to live,
and send rain on the land that
you gave your people for an
inheritance.
[28]"When famine or plague
comes to the land, or blight or mildew, locusts or grasshoppers, or
when enemies besiege them in any
of their cities, whatever disaster or
disease may come, [29]and when a
prayer or plea is made by any of
your people Israel—each one
aware of his afflictions and pains,
and spreading out his hands towards this temple—[30]then hear
from heaven, your dwelling-place.
Forgive, and deal with each man
according to all he does, since you
know his heart (for you alone know
the hearts of men), [31]so that they
will fear you and walk in your ways
all the time they live in the land that
you gave our fathers.
[32]"As for the foreigner who does
not belong to your people Israel
but has come from a distant land
because of your great name and
your mighty hand and your outstretched arm—when he comes
and prays towards this temple,
[33]then hear from heaven, your
dwelling-place, and do whatever
the foreigner asks of you, so that all
the peoples of the earth may know
your name and fear you, as do your
own people Israel, and may know
that this house that I have built
bears your Name.
[34]"When your people go to war
against their enemies, wherever
you send them, and when they pray
to you towards this city you have
chosen and the temple I have built
for your Name, [35]then hear from
heaven their prayer and their plea,
and uphold their cause.
[36]"When they sin against you—
for there is no-one who does not
sin—and you become angry with
them and give them over to the
enemy, who takes them captive to
a land far away or near; [37]and if
they have a change of heart in the
land where they are held captive,
and repent and plead with you in
the land of their captivity and say,
'We have sinned, we have done
wrong and acted wickedly'; [38]and if
they turn back to you with all their
heart and soul in the land of their
captivity where they were taken,
and pray towards the land that you
gave their fathers, towards the city
you have chosen and towards the
temple that I have built for your
Name; [39]then from heaven, your
dwelling-place, hear their prayer
and their pleas, and uphold their
cause. And forgive your people,
who have sinned against you.
[40]"Now, my God, may your eyes
be open and your ears attentive to
the prayers offered in this place.

[41]"Now arise, O LORD God, and
come to your resting place,
you and the ark of your might.
May your priests, O LORD God,
be clothed with salvation,
may your saints rejoice in your
goodness.
[42]O LORD God, do not reject your
anointed one.
Remember the great love
promised to David your
servant."

The Dedication of the Temple

7 When Solomon finished praying,
fire came down from heaven and
consumed the burnt offering and the
sacrifices, and the glory of the LORD
filled the temple. [2]The priests could not
enter the temple of the LORD because
the glory of the LORD filled it. [3]When all
the Israelites saw the fire coming down
and the glory of the LORD above the
temple, they knelt on the pavement
with their faces to the ground, and they
worshipped and gave thanks to the
LORD, saying,

"He is good;
his love endures for ever."

4Then the king and all the people
offered sacrifices before the LORD.
5And King Solomon offered a sacrifice
of twenty-two thousand head of cattle
and a hundred and twenty thousand
sheep and goats. So the king and all the
people dedicated the temple of God.
6The priests took their positions, as did
the Levites with the LORD's musical instruments, which King David had made
for praising the LORD and which were
used when he gave thanks, saying, "His
love endures for ever." Opposite the
Levites, the priests blew their trumpets,
and all the Israelites were standing.
7Solomon consecrated the middle
part of the courtyard in front of the
temple of the LORD, and there he
offered burnt offerings and the fat of
the fellowship offerings, because the
bronze altar he had made could not hold
the burnt offerings, the grain offerings
and the fat portions.
8So Solomon observed the festival at
that time for seven days, and all Israel
with him—a vast assembly, people
from Lebo Hamath to the Wadi of
Egypt. 9On the eighth day they held an
assembly, for they had celebrated the
dedication of the altar for seven days
and the festival for seven days more.
10On the twenty-third day of the
seventh month he sent the people to
their homes, joyful and glad in heart for
the good things the LORD had done for
David and Solomon and for his people
Israel.

NEW TESTAMENT READING
1 Corinthians 10:14–11:1

Idol Feasts and the Lord's Supper

14Therefore, my dear friends, flee
from idolatry. 15I speak to sensible
people; judge for yourselves what I say.
16Is not the cup of thanksgiving for
which we give thanks a participation in
the blood of Christ? And is not the
bread that we break a participation in
the body of Christ? 17Because there is
one loaf, we, who are many, are one
body, for we all partake of the one loaf.
18Consider the people of Israel: Do
not those who eat the sacrifices participate in the altar? 19Do I mean then that
a sacrifice offered to an idol is anything,
or that an idol is anything? 20No, but the
sacrifices of pagans are offered to demons, not to God, and I do not want
you to be participants with demons.
21You cannot drink the cup of the Lord
and the cup of demons too; you cannot
have a part in both the Lord's table and
the table of demons. 22Are we trying to
arouse the Lord's jealousy? Are we
stronger than he?

The Believer's Freedom

23"Everything is permissible"—but
not everything is beneficial. "Everything is permissible"—but not everything is constructive. 24Nobody should
seek his own good, but the good of
others.
25Eat anything sold in the meat market without raising questions of conscience, 26for, "The earth is the Lord's,
and everything in it."
27If some unbeliever invites you to a
meal and you want to go, eat whatever
is put before you without raising questions of conscience. 28But if anyone says
to you, "This has been offered in sacrifice," then do not eat it, both for the
sake of the man who told you and for
conscience' sake—29the other man's
conscience, I mean, not yours. For why
should my freedom be judged by
another's conscience? 30If I take part in
the meal with thankfulness, why am I
denounced because of something I
thank God for?
31So whether you eat or drink or
whatever you do, do it all for the glory
of God. 32Do not cause anyone to stumble, whether Jews, Greeks or the
church of God—33even as I try to
please everybody in every way. For I am

not seeking my own good but the good
of many, so that they may be saved.
11 [1]Follow my example, as I follow
the example of Christ.

READING FROM PROVERBS
Proverbs 20:5–14

5The purposes of a man's heart are
deep waters,
but a man of understanding draws
them out.

6Many a man claims to have unfailing
love,
but a faithful man who can find?

7The righteous man leads a blameless
life;
blessed are his children after him.

8When a king sits on his throne to
judge,
he winnows out all evil with his
eyes.

9Who can say, "I have kept my heart
pure;
I am clean and without sin"?

10Differing weights and differing
measures—
the LORD detests them both.

11Even a child is known by his actions,
by whether his conduct is pure and
right.

12Ears that hear and eyes that see—
the LORD has made them both.

13Do not love sleep or you will grow
poor;
stay awake and you will have food
to spare.

14"It's no good, it's no good!" says the
buyer;
then off he goes and boasts about
his purchase.

DAY 229

AUGUST 17

OLD TESTAMENT READING
2 Chronicles 7:11–9:31

The LORD Appears to Solomon

11When Solomon had finished the
temple of the LORD and the royal
palace, and had succeeded in carrying
out all he had in mind to do in the
temple of the LORD and in his own
palace, 12the LORD appeared to him at
night and said:

"I have heard your prayer and
have chosen this place for myself as
a temple for sacrifices.
13"When I shut up the heavens
so that there is no rain, or command locusts to devour the land or
send a plague among my people,
14if my people, who are called by
my name, will humble themselves
and pray and seek my face and turn
from their wicked ways, then will I
hear from heaven and will forgive
their sin and will heal their land.
15Now my eyes will be open and
my ears attentive to the prayers
offered in this place. 16I have
chosen and consecrated this temple
so that my Name may be there for
ever. My eyes and my heart will
always be there.
17"As for you, if you walk before
me as David your father did, and
do all I command, and observe my
decrees and laws, 18I will establish
your royal throne, as I covenanted
with David your father when I said,
'You shall never fail to have a man
to rule over Israel.'

[19]"But if you turn away and forsake the decrees and commands I
have given you and go off to serve
other gods and worship them,
[20]then I will uproot Israel from my
land, which I have given them, and
will reject this temple which I have
consecrated for my Name. I will
make it a byword and an object of
ridicule among all peoples. [21]And
though this temple is now so imposing, all who pass by will be appalled and say, 'Why has the LORD
done such a thing to this land and to
this temple?' [22]People will answer,
'Because they have forsaken the
LORD, the God of their fathers,
who brought them out of Egypt,
and have embraced other gods,
worshipping and serving them—
that is why he brought all this
disaster on them.'"

Solomon's Other Activities

8 At the end of twenty years, during
which Solomon built the temple of
the LORD and his own palace, [2]Solomon
rebuilt the villages that Hiram had given
him, and settled Israelites in them.
[3]Solomon then went to Hamath Zobah
and captured it. [4]He also built up Tadmor in the desert and all the store cities
he had built in Hamath. [5]He rebuilt
Upper Beth Horon and Lower Beth
Horon as fortified cities, with walls and
with gates and bars, [6]as well as Baalath
and all his store cities, and all the cities
for his chariots and for his horses—
whatever he desired to build in Jerusalem, in Lebanon and throughout all
the territory that he ruled.
[7]All the people left from the Hittites,
Amorites, Perizzites, Hivites and Jebusites (these peoples were not Israelites),
[8]that is, their descendants remaining in
the land, whom the Israelites had not
destroyed—these Solomon conscripted
for his slave labour force, as it is to this
day. [9]But Solomon did not make slaves
of the Israelites for his work; they were
his fighting men, commanders of his
captains, and commanders of his chariots and charioteers. [10]They were also
King Solomon's chief officials—two
hundred and fifty officials supervising
the men.
[11]Solomon brought Pharaoh's daughter up from the City of David to the
palace he had built for her, for he said,
"My wife must not live in the palace of
David king of Israel, because the places
the ark of the LORD has entered are
holy."
[12]On the altar of the LORD that he had
built in front of the portico, Solomon
sacrificed burnt offerings to the LORD,
[13]according to the daily requirement for
offerings commanded by Moses for
Sabbaths, New Moons and the three
annual feasts—the Feast of Unleavened Bread, the Feast of Weeks
and the Feast of Tabernacles. [14]In keeping with the ordinance of his father
David, he appointed the divisions of the
priests for their duties and the Levites to
lead the praise and to assist the priests
according to each day's requirement.
He also appointed the gatekeepers by
divisions for the various gates, because
this was what David the man of God had
ordered. [15]They did not deviate from
the king's commands to the priests or to
the Levites in any matter, including that
of the treasuries.
[16]All Solomon's work was carried
out, from the day the foundation of the
temple of the LORD was laid until its
completion. So the temple of the LORD
was finished.
[17]Then Solomon went to Ezion Geber and Elath on the coast of Edom.
[18]And Hiram sent him ships commanded by his own officers, men who knew
the sea. These with Solomon's men,
sailed to Ophir and brought back four
hundred and fifty talents of gold, which
they delivered to King Solomon.

The Queen of Sheba Visits Solomon

9 When the queen of Sheba heard of
Solomon's fame, she came to Jeru-
salem to test him with hard questions.
Arriving with a very great caravan—

with camels carrying spices, large quantities of gold, and precious stones—she came to Solomon and talked with him about all she had on her mind. 2Solomon answered all her questions; nothing was too hard for him to explain to her. 3When the queen of Sheba saw the wisdom of Solomon, as well as the palace he had built, 4the food on his table, the seating of his officials, the attending servants in their robes, the cupbearers in their robes and the burnt offerings he made at the temple of the LORD, she was overwhelmed.

5She said to the king, "The report I heard in my own country about your achievements and your wisdom is true. 6But I did not believe what they said until I came and saw with my own eyes. Indeed, not even half the greatness of your wisdom was told me; you have far exceeded the report I heard. 7How happy your men must be! How happy your officials, who continually stand before you and hear your wisdom! 8Praise be to the LORD your God, who has delighted in you and placed you on his throne as king to rule for the LORD your God. Because of the love of your God for Israel and his desire to uphold them for ever, he has made you king over them, to maintain justice and righteousness."

9Then she gave the king 120 talents of gold, large quantities of spices, and precious stones. There had never been such spices as those the queen of Sheba gave to King Solomon.

10(The men of Hiram and the men of Solomon brought gold from Ophir; they also brought algum-wood and precious stones. 11The king used the algum-wood to make steps for the temple of the LORD and for the royal palace, and to make harps and lyres for the musicians. Nothing like them had ever been seen in Judah.)

12King Solomon gave the queen of Sheba all she desired and asked for; he gave her more than she had brought to him. Then she left and returned with her retinue to her own country.

Solomon's Splendour

13The weight of the gold that Solomon received yearly was 666 talents, 14not including the revenues brought in by merchants and traders. Also all the kings of Arabia and the governors of the land brought gold and silver to Solomon.

15King Solomon made two hundred large shields of hammered gold; six hundred bekas of hammered gold went into each shield. 16He also made three hundred small shields of hammered gold, with three hundred bekas of gold in each shield. The king put them in the Palace of the Forest of Lebanon.

17Then the king made a great throne inlaid with ivory and overlaid with pure gold. 18The throne had six steps, and a footstool of gold was attached to it. On both sides of the seat were armrests, with a lion standing beside each of them. 19Twelve lions stood on the six steps, one at either end of each step. Nothing like it had ever been made for any other kingdom. 20All King Solomon's goblets were gold, and all the household articles in the Palace of the Forest of Lebanon were pure gold. Nothing was made of silver, because silver was considered of little value in Solomon's day. 21The king had a fleet of trading ships manned by Hiram's men. Once every three years it returned, carrying gold, silver and ivory, and apes and baboons.

22King Solomon was greater in riches and wisdom than all the other kings of the earth. 23All the kings of the earth sought audience with Solomon to hear the wisdom God had put in his heart. 24Year after year, everyone who came brought a gift—articles of silver and gold, and robes, weapons and spices, and horses and mules.

25Solomon had four thousand stalls for horses and chariots, and twelve thousand horses, which he kept in the chariot cities and also with him in Jerusalem. 26He ruled over all the kings from the River to the land of the Philistines, as far as the border of Egypt. 27The king made silver as common in Jerusalem as stones, and cedar as plentiful as sycamore-fig trees in the foothills. 28Solomon's horses were imported from Egypt and from all other countries.

Solomon's Death

29As for the other events of Solomon's reign, from beginning to end, are they not written in the records of Nathan the prophet, in the prophecy of Ahijah the Shilonite and in the visions of Iddo the seer concerning Jeroboam son of Nebat? 30Solomon reigned in Jerusalem over all Israel for forty years. 31Then he rested with his fathers and was buried in the city of David his father. And Rehoboam his son succeeded him as king.

NEW TESTAMENT READING
1 Corinthians 11:2–34

Propriety in Worship

2I praise you for remembering me in everything and for holding to the teachings, just as I passed them on to you.

3Now I want you to realise that the head of every man is Christ, and the head of the woman is man, and the head of Christ is God. 4Every man who prays or prophesies with his head covered dishonours his head. 5And every woman who prays or prophesies with her head uncovered dishonours her head—it is just as though her head were shaved. 6If a woman does not cover her head, she should have her hair cut off; and if it is a disgrace for a woman to have her hair cut or shaved off, she should cover her head. 7A man ought not to cover his head, since he is the image and glory of God; but the woman is the glory of man. 8For man did not come from woman, but woman from man; 9neither was man created for woman, but woman for man. 10For this reason, and because of the angels, the woman ought to have a sign of authority on her head.

11In the Lord, however, woman is not independent of man, nor is man independent of woman. 12For as woman came from man, so also man is born of woman. But everything comes from God. 13Judge for yourselves: Is it proper for a woman to pray to God with her head uncovered? 14Does not the very nature of things teach you that if a man has long hair, it is a disgrace to him, 15but that if a woman has long hair, it is her glory? For long hair is given to her as a covering. 16If anyone wants to be contentious about this, we have no other practice—nor do the churches of God.

The Lord's Supper

17In the following directives I have no praise for you, for your meetings do more harm than good. 18In the first place, I hear that when you come together as a church, there are divisions among you, and to some extent I believe it. 19No doubt there have to be differences among you to show which of you have God's approval. 20When you come together, it is not the Lord's Supper you eat, 21for as you eat, each of you goes ahead without waiting for anybody else. One remains hungry, another gets drunk. 22Don't you have homes to eat and drink in? Or do you despise the church of God and humiliate those who have nothing? What shall I say to you? Shall I praise you for this? Certainly not!

23For I received from the Lord what I also passed on to you: The Lord Jesus, on the night he was betrayed, took bread, 24and when he had given thanks, he broke it and said, "This is my body, which is for you; do this in remembrance of me." 25In the same way, after supper he took the cup, saying, "This cup is the new covenant in my blood; do this, whenever you drink it,

in remembrance of me." 26For whenever you eat this bread and drink this
cup, you proclaim the Lord's death
until he comes.
27Therefore, whoever eats the bread
or drinks the cup of the Lord in an
unworthy manner will be guilty of sinning against the body and blood of the
Lord. 28A man ought to examine himself before he eats of the bread and
drinks of the cup. 29For anyone who
eats and drinks without recognising the
body of the Lord eats and drinks judgment on himself. 30That is why many
among you are weak and sick, and a
number of you have fallen asleep. 31But
if we judged ourselves, we would not
come under judgment. 32When we are
judged by the Lord, we are being disciplined so that we will not be condemned
with the world.
33So then, my brothers, when you
come together to eat, wait for each
other. 34If anyone is hungry, he should
eat at home, so that when you meet
together it may not result in judgment.

And when I come I will give further directions.

READING FROM PSALMS
Psalm 98:1–9

A psalm.

1Sing to the LORD a new song,
for he has done marvellous things;
his right hand and his holy arm
have worked salvation for him.
2The LORD has made his salvation known
and revealed his righteousness to the nations.
3He has remembered his love
and his faithfulness to the house of Israel;
all the ends of the earth have seen
the salvation of our God.

4Shout for joy to the LORD, all the earth,
burst into jubilant song with music;
5make music to the LORD with the harp,
with the harp and the sound of singing,
6with trumpets and the blast of the ram's horn—
shout for joy before the LORD, the King.

7Let the sea resound, and everything in it,
the world, and all who live in it.
8Let the rivers clap their hands,
let the mountains sing together for joy;
9let them sing before the LORD,
for he comes to judge the earth.
He will judge the world in righteousness
and the peoples with equity.

AUGUST 18

OLD TESTAMENT READING
Song of Songs 1:1–4:16

1 Solomon's Song of Songs.

Beloved

2Let him kiss me with the kisses of his mouth—
for your love is more delightful than wine.
3Pleasing is the fragrance of your perfumes;
your name is like perfume poured out.
No wonder the maidens love you!
4Take me away with you—let us hurry!
Let the king bring me into his chambers.

Friends

We rejoice and delight in you;
we will praise your love more than wine.

Beloved

How right they are to adore you!

5Dark am I, yet lovely,
O daughters of Jerusalem,
dark like the tents of Kedar,
like the tent curtains of Solomon.
6Do not stare at me because I am dark,
because I am darkened by the sun.
My mother's sons were angry with me
and made me take care of the vineyards;
my own vineyard I have neglected.
7Tell me, you whom I love, where you graze your flock
and where you rest your sheep at midday.
Why should I be like a veiled woman
beside the flocks of your friends?

Friends

8If you do not know, most beautiful of women,
follow the tracks of the sheep
and graze your young goats
by the tents of the shepherds.

Lover

9I liken you, my darling, to a mare
harnessed to one of the chariots of Pharaoh.
10Your cheeks are beautiful with ear-rings,
your neck with strings of jewels.
11We will make you ear-rings of gold,
studded with silver.

Beloved

12While the king was at his table,
my perfume spread its fragrance.
13My lover is to me a sachet of myrrh
resting between my breasts.
14My lover is to me a cluster of henna blossoms
from the vineyards of En Gedi.

Lover

15How beautiful you are, my darling!
Oh, how beautiful!
Your eyes are doves.

Beloved

16How handsome you are, my lover!
Oh, how charming!
And our bed is verdant.

Lover

17The beams of our house are cedars;
our rafters are firs.

Beloved

2 I am a rose of Sharon,
a lily of the valleys.

Lover

2Like a lily among thorns
is my darling among the maidens.

Beloved

3Like an apple tree among the trees of the forest
is my lover among the young men.
I delight to sit in his shade,
and his fruit is sweet to my taste.
4He has taken me to the banquet hall,
and his banner over me is love.
5Strengthen me with raisins,
refresh me with apples,
for I am faint with love.
6His left arm is under my head,
and his right arm embraces me.
7Daughters of Jerusalem, I charge you
by the gazelles and by the does of the field:
Do not arouse or awaken love
until it so desires.

8Listen! My lover!
Look! Here he comes,
leaping across the mountains,
bounding over the hills.
9My lover is like a gazelle or a young stag.
Look! There he stands behind our wall,
gazing through the windows,
peering through the lattice.
10My lover spoke and said to me,
"Arise, my darling,
my beautiful one, and come with me.
11See! The winter is past;
the rains are over and gone.
12Flowers appear on the earth;
the season of singing has come,
the cooing of doves
is heard in our land.
13The fig-tree forms its early fruit;
the blossoming vines spread their fragrance.
Arise, come, my darling;
my beautiful one, come with me."

Lover

14My dove in the clefts of the rock,
in the hiding-places on the mountainside,
show me your face,
let me hear your voice;
for your voice is sweet,
and your face is lovely.
15Catch for us the foxes,
the little foxes
that ruin the vineyards,
our vineyards that are in bloom.

Beloved

16My lover is mine and I am his;
he browses among the lilies.
17Until the day breaks
and the shadows flee,
turn, my lover,
and be like a gazelle
or like a young stag
on the rugged hills.

3 All night long on my bed
I looked for the one my heart loves;
I looked for him but did not find him.
2I will get up now and go about the city,
through its streets and squares;
I will search for the one my heart loves.
So I looked for him but did not find him.
3The watchmen found me
as they made their rounds in the city.
"Have you seen the one my heart loves?"
4Scarcely had I passed them
when I found the one my heart loves.
I held him and would not let him go
till I had brought him to my mother's house,
to the room of the one who conceived me.

5Daughters of Jerusalem, I charge you
by the gazelles and by the does of
the field:
Do not arouse or awaken love
until it so desires.

6Who is this coming up from the
desert
like a column of smoke,
perfumed with myrrh and incense
made from all the spices of the
merchant?
7Look! It is Solomon's carriage,
escorted by sixty warriors,
the noblest of Israel,
8all of them wearing the sword,
all experienced in battle,
each with his sword at his side,
prepared for the terrors of the
night.
9King Solomon made for himself the
carriage;
he made it of wood from Lebanon.
10Its posts he made of silver,
its base of gold.
Its seat was upholstered with purple,
its interior lovingly inlaid
by the daughters of Jerusalem.
11Come out, you daughters of Zion,
and look at King Solomon wearing
the crown,
the crown with which his mother
crowned him
on the day of his wedding,
the day his heart rejoiced.

Lover

4 How beautiful you are, my
darling!
Oh, how beautiful!
Your eyes behind your veil are
doves.
Your hair is like a flock of goats
descending from Mount Gilead.
2Your teeth are like a flock of sheep
just shorn,
coming up from the washing.
Each has its twin;
not one of them is alone.
3Your lips are like a scarlet ribbon;
your mouth is lovely.
Your temples behind your veil
are like the halves of a
pomegranate.
4Your neck is like the tower of David,
built with elegance;
on it hang a thousand shields,
all of them shields of warriors.
5Your two breasts are like two fawns,
like twin fawns of a gazelle
that browse among the lilies.
6Until the day breaks
and the shadows flee,
I will go to the mountain of myrrh
and to the hill of incense.
7All beautiful you are, my darling;
there is no flaw in you.

8Come with me from Lebanon, my
bride,
come with me from Lebanon.
Descend from the crest of Amana,
from the top of Senir, the summit
of Hermon,
from the lions' dens
and the mountain haunts of the
leopards.
9You have stolen my heart, my sister,
my bride;
you have stolen my heart
with one glance of your eyes,
with one jewel of your necklace.
10How delightful is your love, my
sister, my bride!
How much more pleasing is your
love than wine,
and the fragrance of your perfume
than any spice!
11Your lips drop sweetness as the
honeycomb, my bride;
milk and honey are under your
tongue.
The fragrance of your garments is
like that of Lebanon.
12You are a garden locked up, my
sister, my bride;
you are a spring enclosed, a sealed
fountain.
13Your plants are an orchard of
pomegranates
with choice fruits,
with henna and nard,

14 nard and saffron,
calamus and cinnamon,
with every kind of incense tree,
with myrrh and aloes
and all the finest spices.
15You are a garden fountain,
a well of flowing water
streaming down from Lebanon.

Beloved

16Awake, north wind,
and come, south wind!
Blow on my garden,
that its fragrance may spread
abroad.
Let my lover come into his garden
and taste its choice fruits.

NEW TESTAMENT READING

1 Corinthians 12:1–26

Spiritual Gifts

12 Now about spiritual gifts,
brothers, I do not want you to be
ignorant. 2You know that when you
were pagans, somehow or other you
were influenced and led astray to mute
idols. 3Therefore I tell you that no-one
who is speaking by the Spirit of God
says, "Jesus be cursed," and no-one can
say, "Jesus is Lord," except by the Holy
Spirit.
4There are different kinds of gifts, but
the same Spirit. 5There are different
kinds of service, but the same Lord.
6There are different kinds of working,
but the same God works all of them in
all men.
7Now to each one the manifestation
of the Spirit is given for the common
good. 8To one there is given through the
Spirit the message of wisdom, to
another the message of knowledge by
means of the same Spirit, 9to another
faith by the same Spirit, to another gifts
of healing by that one Spirit, 10to
another miraculous powers, to another
prophecy, to another distinguishing between spirits, to another speaking in
different kinds of tongues, and to still
another the interpretation of tongues.
11All these are the work of one and the
same Spirit, and he gives them to each
one, just as he determines.

One Body, Many Parts

12The body is a unit, though it is made
up of many parts; and though all its
parts are many, they form one body. So
it is with Christ. 13For we were all baptised by one Spirit into one body—
whether Jews or Greeks, slave or free
—and we were all given the one Spirit to
drink.
14Now the body is not made up of one
part but of many. 15If the foot should
say, "Because I am not a hand, I do not
belong to the body," it would not for
that reason cease to be part of the body.
16And if the ear should say, "Because I
am not an eye, I do not belong to the
body," it would not for that reason
cease to be part of the body. 17If the
whole body were an eye, where would
the sense of hearing be? If the whole
body were an ear, where would the
sense of smell be? 18But in fact God has
arranged the parts in the body, every
one of them, just as he wanted them to
be. 19If they were all one part, where
would the body be? 20As it is, there are
many parts, but one body.
21The eye cannot say to the hand, "I
don't need you!" And the head cannot
say to the feet, "I don't need you!" 22On
the contrary, those parts of the body
that seem to be weaker are indispens-
able, 23and the parts that we think are
less honourable we treat with special
honour. And the parts that are unpre-
sentable are treated with special mod-
esty, 24while our presentable parts need
no special treatment. But God has combined the members of the body and has
given greater honour to the parts that
lacked it, 25so that there should be no
division in the body, but that its parts
should have equal concern for each
other. 26If one part suffers, every part
suffers with it; if one part is honoured,
every part rejoices with it.

READING FROM PSALMS
Psalm 99:1–9

1The LORD reigns,
let the nations tremble;
he sits enthroned between the cherubim,
let the earth shake.
2Great is the LORD in Zion;
he is exalted over all the nations.
3Let them praise your great and awesome name—
he is holy.

4The King is mighty, he loves justice—
you have established equity;
in Jacob you have done
what is just and right.
5Exalt the LORD our God
and worship at his footstool;
he is holy.

6Moses and Aaron were among his priests,
Samuel was among those who called on his name;
they called on the LORD
and he answered them.
7He spoke to them from the pillar of cloud;
they kept his statutes and the decrees he gave them.

8O LORD our God,
you answered them;
you were to Israel a forgiving God,
though you punished their misdeeds.
9Exalt the LORD our God
and worship at his holy mountain,
for the LORD our God is holy.

AUGUST 19

DAY 231

OLD TESTAMENT READING
Song of Songs 5:1–8:14

Lover

5 I have come into my garden, my sister, my bride;
I have gathered my myrrh with my spice.
I have eaten my honeycomb and my honey;
I have drunk my wine and my milk.

Friends

Eat, O friends, and drink;
drink your fill, O lovers.

Beloved

2I slept but my heart was awake.
Listen! My lover is knocking:
"Open to me, my sister, my darling,
my dove, my flawless one.
My head is drenched with dew,
my hair with the dampness of the night."
3I have taken off my robe—
must I put it on again?
I have washed my feet—
must I soil them again?
4My lover thrust his hand through the latch-opening;
my heart began to pound for him.
5I arose to open for my lover,
and my hands dripped with myrrh,
my fingers with flowing myrrh,
on the handles of the lock.
6I opened for my lover,
but my lover had left; he was gone.
My heart sank at his departure.
I looked for him but did not find him.
I called him but he did not answer.

7The watchmen found me
as they made their rounds in the city.
They beat me, they bruised me;
they took away my cloak,
those watchmen of the walls!
8O daughters of Jerusalem, I charge you—
if you find my lover,
what will you tell him?
Tell him I am faint with love.

Friends

9How is your beloved better than others,
most beautiful of women?
How is your beloved better than others,
that you charge us so?

Beloved

10My lover is radiant and ruddy,
outstanding among ten thousand.
11His head is purest gold;
his hair is wavy
and black as a raven.
12His eyes are like doves
by the water streams,
washed in milk,
mounted like jewels.
13His cheeks are like beds of spice
yielding perfume.
His lips are like lilies
dripping with myrrh.
14His arms are rods of gold
set with chrysolite.
His body is like polished ivory
decorated with sapphires.
15His legs are pillars of marble
set on bases of pure gold.
His appearance is like Lebanon,
choice as its cedars.
16His mouth is sweetness itself;
he is altogether lovely.
This is my lover, this my friend,
O daughters of Jerusalem.

Friends

6 Where has your lover gone,
most beautiful of women?
Which way did your lover turn,
that we may look for him with you?

Beloved

2My lover has gone down to his garden,
to the beds of spices,
to browse in the gardens
and to gather lilies.
3I am my lover's and my lover is mine;
he browses among the lilies.

Lover

4You are beautiful, my darling, as Tirzah,
lovely as Jerusalem,
majestic as troops with banners.
5Turn your eyes from me;
they overwhelm me.
Your hair is like a flock of goats
descending from Gilead.
6Your teeth are like a flock of sheep
coming up from the washing.
Each has its twin,
not one of them is alone.
7Your temples behind your veil
are like the halves of a pomegranate.
8Sixty queens there may be,
and eighty concubines,
and virgins beyond number;
9but my dove, my perfect one, is unique,
the only daughter of her mother,
the favourite of the one who bore her.
The maidens saw her and called her blessed;
the queens and concubines praised her.

Friends

10Who is this that appears like the dawn,
fair as the moon, bright as the sun,
majestic as the stars in procession?

Lover

11I went down to the grove of nut trees
to look at the new growth in the valley,
to see if the vines had budded
or the pomegranates were in bloom.
12Before I realised it,
my desire set me among the royal chariots of my people.

Friends

13Come back, come back, O Shulammite;
come back, come back, that we may gaze on you!

Lover

Why would you gaze on the Shulammite
as on the dance of Mahanaim?

7 How beautiful your sandalled feet,
O prince's daughter!
Your graceful legs are like jewels,
the work of a craftsman's hands.
2Your navel is a rounded goblet
that never lacks blended wine.
Your waist is a mound of wheat
encircled by lilies.
3Your breasts are like two fawns,
twins of a gazelle.
4Your neck is like an ivory tower.
Your eyes are the pools of Heshbon
by the gate of Bath Rabbim.
Your nose is like the tower of Lebanon
looking towards Damascus.
5Your head crowns you like Mount Carmel.
Your hair is like royal tapestry;
the king is held captive by its tresses.
6How beautiful you are and how pleasing,
O love, with your delights!
7Your stature is like that of the palm,
and your breasts like clusters of fruit.
8I said, "I will climb the palm tree;
I will take hold of its fruit."
May your breasts be like the clusters of the vine,
the fragrance of your breath like apples,
9 and your mouth like the best wine.

Beloved

May the wine go straight to my lover,
flowing gently over lips and teeth.
10I belong to my lover,
and his desire is for me.
11Come, my lover, let us go to the countryside,
let us spend the night in the villages.
12Let us go early to the vineyards
to see if the vines have budded,
if their blossoms have opened,
and if the pomegranates are in bloom—
there I will give you my love.
13The mandrakes send out their fragrance,
and at our door is every delicacy,
both new and old,
that I have stored up for you, my lover.

8 If only you were to me like a brother,
who was nursed at my mother's breasts!
Then, if I found you outside,
I would kiss you,
and no-one would despise me.
2I would lead you
and bring you to my mother's house—
she who has taught me.
I would give you spiced wine to drink,
the nectar of my pomegranates.
3His left arm is under my head
and his right arm embraces me.
4Daughters of Jerusalem, I charge you:
Do not arouse or awaken love
until it so desires.

Friends

5Who is this coming up from the
desert
leaning on her lover?

Beloved

Under the apple tree I roused you;
there your mother conceived you,
there she who was in labour gave
you birth.
6Place me like a seal over your heart,
like a seal on your arm;
for love is as strong as death,
its jealousy unyielding as the grave.
It burns like blazing fire,
like a mighty flame.
7Many waters cannot quench love;
rivers cannot wash it away.
If one were to give
all the wealth of his house for love,
it would be utterly scorned.

Friends

8We have a young sister,
and her breasts are not yet grown.
What shall we do for our sister
for the day she is spoken for?
9If she is a wall,
we will build towers of silver on
her.
If she is a door,
we will enclose her with panels of
cedar.

Beloved

10I am a wall,
and my breasts are like towers.
Thus I have become in his eyes
like one bringing contentment.
11Solomon had a vineyard in Baal
Hamon;
he let out his vineyard to tenants.
Each was to bring for its fruit
a thousand shekels of silver.
12But my own vineyard is mine to give;
the thousand shekels are for you,
O Solomon,
and two hundred are for those who
tend its fruit.

Lover

13You who dwell in the gardens
with friends in attendance,
let me hear your voice!

Beloved

14Come away, my lover,
and be like a gazelle
or like a young stag
on the spice-laden mountains.

NEW TESTAMENT READING
1 Corinthians 12:27–13:13

27Now you are the body of Christ, and
each one of you is a part of it. 28And in
the church God has appointed first of
all apostles, second prophets, third
teachers, then workers of miracles, also
those having gifts of healing, those able
to help others, those with gifts of
administration, and those speaking in
different kinds of tongues. 29Are all
apostles? Are all prophets? Are all
teachers? Do all work miracles? 30Do
all have gifts of healing? Do all speak in
tongues? Do all interpret? 31But eagerly
desire the greater gifts.

Love

And now I will show you the most excellent way.
13 If I speak in the tongues of men
and of angels, but have not love,
I am only a resounding gong or a clang-
ing cymbal. 2If I have the gift of prophecy and can fathom all mysteries and
all knowledge, and if I have a faith that
can move mountains, but have not love,
I am nothing. 3If I give all I possess to
the poor and surrender my body to
the flames, but have not love, I gain
nothing.
4Love is patient, love is kind. It does
not envy, it does not boast, it is not
proud. 5It is not rude, it is not self-
seeking, it is not easily angered, it keeps

no record of wrongs. 6Love does not
delight in evil but rejoices with the
truth. 7It always protects, always trusts,
always hopes, always perseveres.
8Love never fails. But where there
are prophecies, they will cease; where
there are tongues, they will be stilled;
where there is knowledge, it will pass
away. 9For we know in part and we
prophesy in part, 10but when perfection
comes, the imperfect disappears.
11When I was a child, I talked like a
child, I thought like a child, I reasoned
like a child. When I became a man, I put
childish ways behind me. 12Now we see
but a poor reflection as in a mirror; then
we shall see face to face. Now I know in
part; then I shall know fully, even as I
am fully known.
13And now these three remain: faith,
hope and love. But the greatest of these
is love.

READING FROM PSALMS
Psalm 100:1–5

A psalm. For giving thanks.

1Shout for joy to the LORD, all the
earth.
2 Worship the LORD with gladness;
come before him with joyful songs.
3Know that the LORD is God.
It is he who made us, and we are
his;
we are his people, the sheep of his
pasture.

4Enter his gates with thanksgiving
and his courts with praise;
give thanks to him and praise his
name.
5For the LORD is good and his love
endures for ever;
his faithfulness continues through
all generations.

AUGUST 20

DAY 232

OLD TESTAMENT READING
2 Chronicles 10:1–12:16

Israel Rebels Against Rehoboam

10 Rehoboam went to Shechem,
for all the Israelites had gone
there to make him king. 2When Jeroboam son of Nebat heard this (he was in
Egypt, where he had fled from King
Solomon), he returned from Egypt. 3So
they sent for Jeroboam, and he and all
Israel went to Rehoboam and said to
him: 4"Your father put a heavy yoke on
us, but now lighten the harsh labour and
the heavy yoke he put on us, and we will
serve you."
5Rehoboam answered, "Come back
to me in three days." So the people
went away.
6Then King Rehoboam consulted the
elders who had served his father Solomon during his lifetime. "How would
you advise me to answer these people?"
he asked.
7They replied, "If you will be kind to
these people and please them and give
them a favourable answer, they will
always be your servants."
8But Rehoboam rejected the advice
the elders gave him and consulted the
young men who had grown up with him
and were serving him. 9He asked them,
"What is your advice? How should we
answer these people who say to me,
'Lighten the yoke your father put on
us'?"
10The young men who had grown up
with him replied, "Tell the people who
have said to you, 'Your father put a
heavy yoke on us, but make our yoke
lighter'—tell them, 'My little finger is
thicker than my father's waist. 11My
father laid on you a heavy yoke; I will
make it even heavier. My father

scourged you with whips; I will scourge
you with scorpions.' "
12Three days later Jeroboam and all
the people returned to Rehoboam, as
the king had said, "Come back to me in
three days." 13The king answered them
harshly. Rejecting the advice of the
elders, 14he followed the advice of the
young men and said, "My father made
your yoke heavy; I will make it even
heavier. My father scourged you with
whips; I will scourge you with scorpions." 15So the king did not listen to
the people, for this turn of events was
from God, to fulfil the word that the
LORD had spoken to Jeroboam son of
Nebat through Ahijah the Shilonite.
16When all Israel saw that the king
refused to listen to them, they answered
the king:

"What share do we have in David,
what part in Jesse's son?
To your tents, O Israel!
Look after your own house, O
David!"

So all the Israelites went home. 17But as
for the Israelites who were living in the
towns of Judah, Rehoboam still ruled
over them.
18King Rehoboam sent out Adoniram, who was in charge of forced
labour, but the Israelites stoned him to
death. King Rehoboam, however, man-
aged to get into his chariot and escape to
Jerusalem. 19So Israel has been in rebellion against the house of David to
this day.
11 When Rehoboam arrived in
Jerusalem, he mustered the
house of Judah and Benjamin—a hundred and eighty thousand fighting men
—to make war against Israel and to
regain the kingdom for Rehoboam.
2But this word of the LORD came to
Shemaiah the man of God: 3"Say to
Rehoboam son of Solomon king of
Judah and to all the Israelites in Judah
and Benjamin, 4'This is what the LORD
says: Do not go up to fight against your
brothers. Go home, every one of you,
for this is my doing.' " So they obeyed
the words of the LORD and turned back
from marching against Jeroboam.

Rehoboam Fortifies Judah

5Rehoboam lived in Jerusalem and
built up towns for defence in Judah:
6Bethlehem, Etam, Tekoa, 7Beth Zur,
Soco, Adullam, 8Gath, Mareshah,
Ziph, 9Adoraim, Lachish, Azekah,
10Zorah, Aijalon and Hebron. These
were fortified cities in Judah and Benjamin. 11He strengthened their defences and put commanders in them,
with supplies of food, olive oil and wine.
12He put shields and spears in all the
cities, and made them very strong. So
Judah and Benjamin were his.
13The priests and Levites from all
their districts throughout Israel sided
with him. 14The Levites even abandoned their pasture-lands and property,
and came to Judah and Jerusalem because Jeroboam and his sons had rejected them as priests of the LORD.
15And he appointed his own priests for
the high places and for the goat and calf
idols he had made. 16Those from every
tribe of Israel who set their hearts on
seeking the LORD, the God of Israel,
followed the Levites to Jerusalem to
offer sacrifices to the LORD, the God of
their fathers. 17They strengthened the
kingdom of Judah and supported Rehoboam son of Solomon for three years,
walking in the ways of David and Solomon during this time.

Rehoboam's Family

18Rehoboam married Mahalath, who
was the daughter of David's son Jerimoth and of Abihail, the daughter of
Jesse's son Eliab. 19She bore him sons:
Jeush, Shemariah and Zaham. 20Then
he married Maacah daughter of Absalom, who bore him Abijah, Attai, Ziza
and Shelomith. 21Rehoboam loved
Maacah daughter of Absalom more
than any of his other wives and concubines. In all he had eighteen wives

and sixty concubines, twenty-eight sons
and sixty daughters.
22Rehoboam appointed Abijah son
of Maacah to be the chief prince among
his brothers, in order to make him king.
23He acted wisely, dispersing some of
his sons throughout the districts of
Judah and Benjamin, and to all the
fortified cities. He gave them abundant
provisions and took many wives for
them.

Shishak Attacks Jerusalem

12 After Rehoboam's position as
king was established and he had
become strong, he and all Israel with
him abandoned the law of the LORD.
2Because they had been unfaithful to
the LORD, Shishak king of Egypt attacked Jerusalem in the fifth year of
King Rehoboam. 3With twelve hundred
chariots and sixty thousand horsemen
and the innumerable troops of Libyans,
Sukkites and Cushites that came with
him from Egypt, 4he captured the fortified cities of Judah and came as far as
Jerusalem.
5Then the prophet Shemaiah came to
Rehoboam and to the leaders of Judah
who had assembled in Jerusalem for
fear of Shishak, and he said to them,
"This is what the LORD says: 'You have
abandoned me; therefore I now abandon you to Shishak.'"
6The leaders of Israel and the king
humbled themselves and said, "The
LORD is just."
7When the LORD saw that they humbled themselves, this word of the LORD
came to Shemaiah: "Since they have
humbled themselves, I will not destroy
them but will soon give them deliverance. My wrath will not be poured out
on Jerusalem through Shishak. 8They
will, however, become subject to him,
so that they may learn the difference
between serving me and serving the
kings of other lands."
9When Shishak king of Egypt attacked Jerusalem, he carried off the
treasures of the temple of the LORD and
the treasures of the royal palace. He
took everything, including the gold
shields that Solomon had made. 10So
King Rehoboam made bronze shields to
replace them and assigned these to the
commanders of the guard on duty at the
entrance to the royal palace. 11When-
ever the king went to the LORD's temple, the guards went with him, bearing
the shields, and afterwards they returned them to the guardroom.
12Because Rehoboam humbled himself, the LORD's anger turned from him,
and he was not totally destroyed. Indeed, there was some good in Judah.
13King Rehoboam established himself firmly in Jerusalem and continued
as king. He was forty-one years old
when he became king, and he reigned
for seventeen years in Jerusalem, the
city the LORD had chosen out of all the
tribes of Israel in which to put his Name.
His mother's name was Naamah; she
was an Ammonite. 14He did evil because he had not set his heart on seeking
the LORD.
15As for the events of Rehoboam's
reign, from beginning to end, are they
not written in the records of Shemaiah
the prophet and of Iddo the seer that
deal with genealogies? There was continual warfare between Rehoboam and
Jeroboam. 16Rehoboam rested with his
fathers and was buried in the City of
David. And Abijah his son succeeded
him as king.

NEW TESTAMENT READING
1 Corinthians 14:1–19

Gifts of Prophecy and Tongues

14 Follow the way of love and
eagerly desire spiritual gifts,
especially the gift of prophecy. 2For
anyone who speaks in a tongue does not
speak to men but to God. Indeed, no-
one understands him; he utters mysteries with his spirit. 3But everyone who
prophesies speaks to men for their
strengthening, encouragement and

comfort. 4He who speaks in a tongue
edifies himself, but he who prophesies
edifies the church. 5I would like every
one of you to speak in tongues, but I
would rather have you prophesy. He
who prophesies is greater than one who
speaks in tongues, unless he interprets,
so that the church may be edified.
6Now, brothers, if I come to you and
speak in tongues, what good will I be to
you, unless I bring you some revelation
or knowledge or prophecy or word of
instruction? 7Even in the case of lifeless
things that make sounds, such as the
flute or harp, how will anyone know
what tune is being played unless there is
a distinction in the notes? 8Again, if the
trumpet does not sound a clear call, who
will get ready for battle? 9So it is with
you. Unless you speak intelligible
words with your tongue, how will anyone know what you are saying? You
will just be speaking into the air.
10Undoubtedly there are all sorts of languages in the world, yet none of them is
without meaning. 11If then I do not
grasp the meaning of what someone is
saying, I am a foreigner to the speaker,
and he is a foreigner to me. 12So it is
with you. Since you are eager to have
spiritual gifts, try to excel in gifts that
build up the church.
13For this reason anyone who speaks
in a tongue should pray that he may
interpret what he says. 14For if I pray in
a tongue, my spirit prays, but my mind
is unfruitful. 15So what shall I do? I will
pray with my spirit, but I will also pray
with my mind; I will sing with my spirit,
but I will also sing with my mind. 16If
you are praising God with your spirit,
how can one who finds himself among
those who do not understand say
"Amen" to your thanksgiving, since he
does not know what you are saying?
17You may be giving thanks well
enough, but the other man is not
edified.
18I thank God that I speak in tongues
more than all of you. 19But in the church
I would rather speak five intelligible
words to instruct others than ten
thousand words in a tongue.

READING FROM PROVERBS

Proverbs 20:15–24

15Gold there is, and rubies in
abundance,
but lips that speak knowledge are a
rare jewel.

16Take the garment of one who puts up
security for a stranger;
hold it in pledge if he does it for a
wayward woman.

17Food gained by fraud tastes sweet to
a man,
but he ends up with a mouth full of
gravel.

18Make plans by seeking advice;
if you wage war, obtain guidance.

19A gossip betrays a confidence;
so avoid a man who talks too
much.

20If a man curses his father or mother,
his lamp will be snuffed out in pitch
darkness.

21An inheritance quickly gained at the
beginning
will not be blessed at the end.

22Do not say, "I'll pay you back for this
wrong!"
Wait for the LORD, and he will
deliver you.

23The LORD detests differing weights,
and dishonest scales do not please
him.

24A man's steps are directed by the
LORD.
How then can anyone understand
his own way?

AUGUST 21

DAY 233

OLD TESTAMENT READING

2 Chronicles 13:1–15:19

Abijah King of Judah

13 In the eighteenth year of the reign of Jeroboam, Abijah became king of Judah, 2and he reigned in Jerusalem for three years. His mother's name was Maacah, a daughter of Uriel of Gibeah.

There was war between Abijah and Jeroboam. 3Abijah went into battle with a force of four hundred thousand able fighting men, and Jeroboam drew up a battle line against him with eight hundred thousand able troops.

4Abijah stood on Mount Zemaraim, in the hill country of Ephraim, and said, "Jeroboam and all Israel, listen to me! 5Don't you know that the LORD, the God of Israel, has given the kingship of Israel to David and his descendants for ever by a covenant of salt? 6Yet Jeroboam son of Nebat, an official of Solomon son of David, rebelled against his master. 7Some worthless scoundrels gathered around him and opposed Rehoboam son of Solomon when he was young and indecisive and not strong enough to resist them.

8"And now you plan to resist the kingdom of the LORD, which is in the hands of David's descendants. You are indeed a vast army and have with you the golden calves that Jeroboam made to be your gods. 9But didn't you drive out the priests of the LORD, the sons of Aaron, and the Levites, and make priests of your own as the peoples of other lands do? Whoever comes to consecrate himself with a young bull and seven rams may become a priest of what are not gods.

10"As for us, the LORD is our God, and we have not forsaken him. The priests who serve the LORD are sons of Aaron, and the Levites assist them. 11Every morning and evening they present burnt offerings and fragrant incense to the LORD. They set out the bread on the ceremonially clean table and light the lamps on the gold lampstand every evening. We are observing the requirements of the LORD our God. But you have forsaken him. 12God is with us; he is our leader. His priests with their trumpets will sound the battle cry against you. Men of Israel, do not fight against the LORD, the God of your fathers, for you will not succeed."

13Now Jeroboam had sent troops round to the rear, so that while he was in front of Judah the ambush was behind them. 14Judah turned and saw that they were being attacked at both front and rear. Then they cried out to the LORD. The priests blew their trumpets 15and the men of Judah raised the battle cry. At the sound of their battle cry, God routed Jeroboam and all Israel before Abijah and Judah. 16The Israelites fled before Judah, and God delivered them into their hands. 17Abijah and his men inflicted heavy losses on them, so that there were five hundred thousand casualties among Israel's able men. 18The men of Israel were subdued on that occasion, and the men of Judah were victorious because they relied on the LORD, the God of their fathers.

19Abijah pursued Jeroboam and took from him the towns of Bethel, Jeshanah and Ephron, with their surrounding villages. 20Jeroboam did not regain power during the time of Abijah. And the LORD struck him down and he died.

21But Abijah grew in strength. He married fourteen wives and had twenty-two sons and sixteen daughters.

22The other events of Abijah's reign, what he did and what he said, are written in the annotations of the prophet Iddo.

14 And Abijah rested with his fathers and was buried in the City of David. Asa his son succeeded

him as king, and in his days the country
was at peace for ten years.

Asa King of Judah

2Asa did what was good and right in
the eyes of the LORD his God. 3He
removed the foreign altars and the high
places, smashed the sacred stones and
cut down the Asherah poles. 4He commanded Judah to seek the LORD, the
God of their fathers, and to obey his
laws and commands. 5He removed the
high places and incense altars in every
town in Judah, and the kingdom was at
peace under him. 6He built up the fortified cities of Judah, since the land was
at peace. No-one was at war with him
during those years, for the LORD gave
him rest.

7"Let us build up these towns," he
said to Judah, "and put walls round
them, with towers, gates and bars. The
land is still ours, because we have
sought the LORD our God; we sought
him and he has given us rest on every
side." So they built and prospered.

8Asa had an army of three hundred
thousand men from Judah, equipped
with large shields and with spears, and
two hundred and eighty thousand from
Benjamin, armed with small shields and
with bows. All these were brave fighting
men.

9Zerah the Cushite marched out
against them with a vast army and three
hundred chariots, and came as far as
Mareshah. 10Asa went out to meet him,
and they took up battle positions in the
Valley of Zephathah near Mareshah.

11Then Asa called to the LORD his
God and said, "LORD, there is no-one
like you to help the powerless against
the mighty. Help us, O LORD our God,
for we rely on you, and in your name we
have come against this vast army. O
LORD, you are our God; do not let man
prevail against you."

12The LORD struck down the Cushites
before Asa and Judah. The Cushites
fled, 13and Asa and his army pursued
them as far as Gerar. Such a great number of Cushites fell that they could not
recover; they were crushed before the
LORD and his forces. The men of Judah
carried off a large amount of plunder.
14They destroyed all the villages around
Gerar, for the terror of the LORD had
fallen upon them. They plundered all
these villages, since there was much
booty there. 15They also attacked the
camps of the herdsmen and carried off
droves of sheep and goats and camels.
Then they returned to Jerusalem.

Asa's Reform

15 The Spirit of God came upon
Azariah son of Oded. 2He went
out to meet Asa and said to him, "Listen to me, Asa and all Judah and Benjamin. The LORD is with you when you
are with him. If you seek him, he will be
found by you, but if you forsake him, he
will forsake you. 3For a long time Israel
was without the true God, without a
priest to teach and without the law. 4But
in their distress they turned to the
LORD, the God of Israel, and sought
him, and he was found by them. 5In
those days it was not safe to travel
about, for all the inhabitants of the
lands were in great turmoil. 6One nation was being crushed by another and
one city by another, because God was
troubling them with every kind of distress. 7But as for you, be strong and
do not give up, for your work will be
rewarded."

8When Asa heard these words and
the prophecy of Azariah son of Oded
the prophet, he took courage. He removed the detestable idols from the
whole land of Judah and Benjamin and
from the towns he had captured in the
hills of Ephraim. He repaired the altar
of the LORD that was in front of the
portico of the LORD's temple.

9Then he assembled all Judah and
Benjamin and the people from
Ephraim, Manasseh and Simeon who
had settled among them, for large numbers had come over to him from Israel
when they saw that the LORD his God
was with him.

10They assembled at Jerusalem in the
third month of the fifteenth year of
Asa's reign. 11At that time they sacrificed to the LORD seven hundred head
of cattle and seven thousand sheep and
goats from the plunder they had
brought back. 12They entered into a
covenant to seek the LORD, the God of
their fathers, with all their heart and
soul. 13All who would not seek the
LORD, the God of Israel, were to be put
to death, whether small or great, man or
woman. 14They took an oath to the
LORD with loud acclamation, with
shouting and with trumpets and horns.
15All Judah rejoiced about the oath because they had sworn it wholeheartedly.
They sought God eagerly, and he was
found by them. So the LORD gave them
rest on every side.
16King Asa also deposed his grandmother Maacah from her position as
queen mother, because she had made a
repulsive Asherah pole. Asa cut the
pole down, broke it up and burned it in
the Kidron Valley. 17Although he did
not remove the high places from Israel,
Asa's heart was fully committed ⌊to the
LORD⌋ all his life. 18He brought into the
temple of God the silver and gold and
the articles that he and his father had
dedicated.
19There was no more war until the
thirty-fifth year of Asa's reign.

NEW TESTAMENT READING
1 Corinthians 14:20–40

20Brothers, stop thinking like children. In regard to evil be infants, but in
your thinking be adults. 21In the Law it
is written:

"Through men of strange tongues
and through the lips of foreigners
I will speak to this people,
but even then they will not listen to
me,"
says the Lord.

22Tongues, then, are a sign, not for
believers but for unbelievers; prophecy,
however, is for believers, not for unbelievers. 23So if the whole church
comes together and everyone speaks in
tongues, and some who do not understand or some unbelievers come in, will
they not say that you are out of your
mind? 24But if an unbeliever or someone who does not understand comes in
while everybody is prophesying, he will
be convinced by all that he is a sinner
and will be judged by all, 25and the
secrets of his heart will be laid bare. So
he will fall down and worship God,
exclaiming, "God is really among you!"

Orderly Worship

26What then shall we say, brothers?
When you come together, everyone has
a hymn, or a word of instruction, a
revelation, a tongue or an interpretation. All of these must be done for the
strengthening of the church. 27If anyone
speaks in a tongue, two—or at the most
three—should speak, one at a time, and
someone must interpret. 28If there is no
interpreter, the speaker should keep
quiet in the church and speak to himself
and God.
29Two or three prophets should
speak, and the others should weigh
carefully what is said. 30And if a revelation comes to someone who is sitting
down, the first speaker should stop.
31For you can all prophesy in turn so
that everyone may be instructed and
encouraged. 32The spirits of prophets
are subject to the control of prophets.
33For God is not a God of disorder but
of peace.
As in all the congregations of the
saints, 34women should remain silent in
the churches. They are not allowed to
speak, but must be in submission, as the
Law says. 35If they want to enquire
about something, they should ask their
own husbands at home; for it is disgraceful for a woman to speak in the
church.
36Did the word of God originate with
you? Or are you the only people it has
reached? 37If anybody thinks he is a

prophet or spiritually gifted, let him acknowledge that what I am writing to
you is the Lord's command. 38If he
ignores this, he himself will be ignored.
39Therefore, my brothers, be eager to prophesy, and do not forbid speaking in
tongues. 40But everything should be
done in a fitting and orderly way.

READING FROM PSALMS
Psalm 101:1–8

Of David. A psalm.

1I will sing of your love and justice;
to you, O LORD, I will sing praise.
2I will be careful to lead a blameless life—
when will you come to me?

I will walk in my house
with blameless heart.
3I will set before my eyes
no vile thing.

The deeds of faithless men I hate;
they shall not cling to me.
4Men of perverse heart shall be far from me;
I will have nothing to do with evil.

5Whoever slanders his neighbour in secret,
him will I put to silence;
whoever has haughty eyes and a proud heart,
him will I not endure.

6My eyes will be on the faithful in the land,
that they may dwell with me;
he whose walk is blameless
will minister to me.

7No-one who practises deceit
will dwell in my house;
no-one who speaks falsely
will stand in my presence.

8Every morning I will put to silence
all the wicked in the land;
I will cut off every evildoer
from the city of the LORD.

DAY 234

AUGUST 22

OLD TESTAMENT READING
2 Chronicles 16:1–18:27

Asa's Last Years

16 In the thirty-sixth year of Asa's reign Baasha king of Israel went up against Judah and fortified Ramah to prevent anyone from leaving or entering the territory of Asa king of Judah.
2Asa then took the silver and gold out of the treasuries of the LORD's temple and of his own palace and sent it to Ben-Hadad king of Aram, who was ruling in Damascus.
3"Let there be a treaty between me and you," he said, "as there was between my father and your father. See, I am sending you silver and gold. Now break your treaty with Baasha king of Israel so that he will withdraw from me."
4Ben-Hadad agreed with King Asa and sent the commanders of his forces against the towns of Israel. They conquered Ijon, Dan, Abel Maim and all the store cities of Naphtali.
5When Baasha heard this, he stopped building Ramah and abandoned his work.
6Then King Asa brought all the men of Judah, and they carried away from Ramah the stones and timber Baasha had been using. With them he built up Geba and Mizpah.

7At that time Hanani the seer came to
Asa king of Judah and said to him:
"Because you relied on the king of
Aram and not on the LORD your God,
the army of the king of Aram has
escaped from your hand. 8Were not the
Cushites and Libyans a mighty army
with great numbers of chariots and
horsemen? Yet when you relied on the
LORD, he delivered them into your
hand. 9For the eyes of the LORD range
throughout the earth to strengthen
those whose hearts are fully committed
to him. You have done a foolish thing,
and from now on you will be at war."

10Asa was angry with the seer because
of this; he was so enraged that he put
him in prison. At the same time Asa
brutally oppressed some of the people.

11The events of Asa's reign, from beginning to end, are written in the book
of the kings of Judah and Israel. 12In the
thirty-ninth year of his reign Asa was
afflicted with a disease in his feet.
Though his disease was severe, even in
his illness he did not seek help from the
LORD, but only from the physicians.
13Then in the forty-first year of his reign
Asa died and rested with his fathers.
14They buried him in the tomb that he
had cut out for himself in the City of
David. They laid him on a bier covered
with spices and various blended perfumes, and they made a huge fire in his
honour.

Jehoshaphat King of Judah

17 Jehoshaphat his son succeeded
him as king and strengthened
himself against Israel. 2He stationed
troops in all the fortified cities of Judah
and put garrisons in Judah and in the
towns of Ephraim that his father Asa
had captured.

3The LORD was with Jehoshaphat because in his early years he walked in the
ways that his father David had followed. He did not consult the Baals 4but
sought the God of his father and followed his commands rather than the
practices of Israel. 5The LORD established the kingdom under his control;
and all Judah brought gifts to
Jehoshaphat, so that he had great
wealth and honour. 6His heart was devoted to the ways of the LORD; furthermore, he removed the high places and
the Asherah poles from Judah.

7In the third year of his reign he sent
his officials Ben-Hail, Obadiah,
Zechariah, Nethanel and Micaiah to
teach in the towns of Judah. 8With them
were certain Levites—Shemaiah,
Nethaniah, Zebadiah, Asahel, Shemiramoth, Jehonathan, Adonijah, Tobijah
and Tob-Adonijah—and the priests
Elishama and Jehoram. 9They taught
throughout Judah, taking with them the
Book of the Law of the LORD; they went
round to all the towns of Judah and
taught the people.

10The fear of the LORD fell on all the
kingdoms of the lands surrounding
Judah, so that they did not make war
with Jehoshaphat. 11Some Philistines
brought Jehoshaphat gifts and silver as
tribute, and the Arabs brought him
flocks: seven thousand seven hundred
rams and seven thousand seven hundred goats.

12Jehoshaphat became more and
more powerful; he built forts and store
cities in Judah 13and had large supplies
in the towns of Judah. He also kept
experienced fighting men in Jerusalem.
14Their enrolment by families was as
follows:

From Judah, commanders of units of 1,000:
Adnah the commander, with 300,000 fighting men;
15next, Jehohanan the commander, with 280,000;
16next, Amasiah son of Zicri, who volunteered himself for the service of the LORD, with 200,000.
17From Benjamin:
Eliada, a valiant soldier, with 200,000 men armed with bows and shields;

18next, Jehozabad, with 180,000
men armed for battle.

19These were the men who served the
king, besides those he stationed in the
fortified cities throughout Judah.

Micaiah Prophesies Against Ahab

18 Now Jehoshaphat had great
wealth and honour, and he
allied himself with Ahab by marriage.
2Some years later he went down to visit
Ahab in Samaria. Ahab slaughtered
many sheep and cattle for him and the
people with him and urged him to attack
Ramoth Gilead. 3Ahab king of Israel
asked Jehoshaphat king of Judah, "Will
you go with me against Ramoth
Gilead?"
Jehoshaphat replied, "I am as you
are, and my people as your people;
we will join you in the war." 4But
Jehoshaphat also said to the king of
Israel, "First seek the counsel of the
LORD."
5So the king of Israel brought
together the prophets—four hundred
men—and asked them, "Shall we go to
war against Ramoth Gilead, or shall I
refrain?"
"Go," they answered, "for God will
give it into the king's hand."
6But Jehoshaphat asked, "Is there
not a prophet of the LORD here whom
we can enquire of?"
7The king of Israel answered
Jehoshaphat, "There is still one man
through whom we can enquire of the
LORD, but I hate him because he never
prophesies anything good about me,
but always bad. He is Micaiah son of
Imlah."
"The king should not say that,"
Jehoshaphat replied.
8So the king of Israel called one of his
officials and said, "Bring Micaiah son of
Imlah at once."
9Dressed in their royal robes, the
king of Israel and Jehoshaphat king of
Judah were sitting on their thrones at
the threshing-floor by the entrance to
the gate of Samaria, with all the
prophets prophesying before them.
10Now Zedekiah son of Kenaanah had
made iron horns, and he declared,
"This is what the LORD says: 'With
these you will gore the Arameans until
they are destroyed.'"
11All the other prophets were
prophesying the same thing. "Attack
Ramoth Gilead and be victorious,"
they said, "for the LORD will give it into
the king's hand."
12The messenger who had gone to
summon Micaiah said to him, "Look, as
one man the other prophets are pre-
dicting success for the king. Let your
word agree with theirs, and speak
favourably."
13But Micaiah said, "As surely as the
LORD lives, I can tell him only what my
God says."
14When he arrived, the king asked
him, "Micaiah, shall we go to war
against Ramoth Gilead, or shall I
refrain?"
"Attack and be victorious," he
answered, "for they will be given into
your hand."
15The king said to him, "How many
times must I make you swear to tell me
nothing but the truth in the name of the
LORD?"
16Then Micaiah answered, "I saw all
Israel scattered on the hills like sheep
without a shepherd, and the LORD said,
'These people have no master. Let each
one go home in peace.'"
17The king of Israel said to
Jehoshaphat, "Didn't I tell you that he
never prophesies anything good about
me, but only bad?"
18Micaiah continued, "Therefore
hear the word of the LORD: I saw the
LORD sitting on his throne with all the
host of heaven standing on his right and
on his left. 19And the LORD said, 'Who
will entice Ahab king of Israel into
attacking Ramoth Gilead and going to
his death there?'
"One suggested this, and another
that. 20Finally, a spirit came forward,

stood before the LORD and said, 'I will
entice him.'
"'By what means?' the LORD asked.
21"'I will go and be a lying spirit in the
mouths of all his prophets,' he said.
"'You will succeed in enticing him,'
said the LORD. 'Go and do it.'
22"So now the LORD has put a lying
spirit in the mouths of these prophets of
yours. The LORD has decreed disaster
for you."
23Then Zedekiah son of Kenaanah
went up and slapped Micaiah in the
face. "Which way did the spirit from the
LORD go when he went from me to
speak to you?" he asked.
24Micaiah replied, "You will find out
on the day you go to hide in an inner
room."
25The king of Israel then ordered,
"Take Micaiah and send him back to
Amon the ruler of the city and to Joash
the king's son, 26and say, 'This is what
the king says: Put this fellow in prison
and give him nothing but bread and
water until I return safely.'"
27Micaiah declared, "If you ever return safely, the LORD has not spoken
through me." Then he added, "Mark
my words, all you people!"

NEW TESTAMENT READING
1 Corinthians 15:1–34

The Resurrection of Christ

15 Now, brothers, I want to remind
you of the gospel I preached to
you, which you received and on which
you have taken your stand. 2By this
gospel you are saved, if you hold firmly
to the word I preached to you. Otherwise, you have believed in vain.
3For what I received I passed on to
you as of first importance: that Christ
died for our sins according to the Scriptures, 4that he was buried, that he was
raised on the third day according to the
Scriptures, 5and that he appeared to
Peter, and then to the Twelve. 6After
that, he appeared to more than five
hundred of the brothers at the same
time, most of whom are still living,
though some have fallen asleep. 7Then
he appeared to James, then to all the
apostles, 8and last of all he appeared to
me also, as to one abnormally born.
9For I am the least of the apostles and
do not even deserve to be called an
apostle, because I persecuted the
church of God. 10But by the grace of
God I am what I am, and his grace to me
was not without effect. No, I worked
harder than all of them—yet not I, but
the grace of God that was with me.
11Whether, then, it was I or they, this is
what we preach, and this is what you
believed.

The Resurrection of the Dead

12But if it is preached that Christ has
been raised from the dead, how can
some of you say that there is no resurrection of the dead? 13If there is no
resurrection of the dead, then not even
Christ has been raised. 14And if Christ
has not been raised, our preaching is
useless and so is your faith. 15More than
that, we are then found to be false witnesses about God, for we have testified
about God that he raised Christ from
the dead. But he did not raise him if in
fact the dead are not raised. 16For if the
dead are not raised, then Christ has not
been raised either. 17And if Christ has
not been raised, your faith is futile; you
are still in your sins. 18Then those also
who have fallen asleep in Christ are lost.
19If only for this life we have hope in
Christ, we are to be pitied more than all
men.
20But Christ has indeed been raised
from the dead, the firstfruits of those
who have fallen asleep. 21For since
death came through a man, the resurrection of the dead comes also through a
man. 22For as in Adam all die, so in
Christ all will be made alive. 23But each
in his own turn: Christ, the firstfruits;
then, when he comes, those who belong
to him. 24Then the end will come, when
he hands over the kingdom to God the

Father after he has destroyed all dominion, authority and power. 25For he must
reign until he has put all his enemies
under his feet. 26The last enemy to be
destroyed is death. 27For he "has put
everything under his feet". Now when it
says that "everything" has been put
under him, it is clear that this does not
include God himself, who put everything under Christ. 28When he has done
this, then the Son himself will be made
subject to him who put everything
under him, so that God may be all in all.
29Now if there is no resurrection,
what will those do who are baptised for
the dead? If the dead are not raised at
all, why are people baptised for them?
30And as for us, why do we endanger
ourselves every hour? 31I die every day
—I mean that, brothers—just as surely
as I glory over you in Christ Jesus our
Lord. 32If I fought wild beasts in Ephesus for merely human reasons, what
have I gained? If the dead are not
raised,

"Let us eat and drink,
for tomorrow we die."

33Do not be misled: "Bad company corrupts good character." 34Come back to
your senses as you ought, and stop sinning; for there are some who are ignorant of God—I say this to your shame.

READING FROM PSALMS

Psalm 102:1–11

A prayer of an afflicted man. When he is faint and pours out his lament before the LORD.

1Hear my prayer, O LORD;
let my cry for help come to you.
2Do not hide your face from me
when I am in distress.
Turn your ear to me;
when I call, answer me quickly.

3For my days vanish like smoke;
my bones burn like glowing embers.
4My heart is blighted and withered like grass;
I forget to eat my food.
5Because of my loud groaning
I am reduced to skin and bones.
6I am like a desert owl,
like an owl among the ruins.
7I lie awake; I have become
like a bird alone on a roof.
8All day long my enemies taunt me;
those who rail against me use my name as a curse.
9For I eat ashes as my food
and mingle my drink with tears
10because of your great wrath,
for you have taken me up and thrown me aside.
11My days are like the evening shadow;
I wither away like grass.

DAY 235

AUGUST 23

OLD TESTAMENT READING

2 Chronicles 18:28–21:3

Ahab Killed at Ramoth Gilead

28So the king of Israel and
Jehoshaphat king of Judah went up to
Ramoth Gilead. 29The king of Israel
said to Jehoshaphat, "I will enter the
battle in disguise, but you wear your
royal robes." So the king of Israel disguised himself and went into battle.
30Now the king of Aram had ordered
his chariot commanders, "Do not fight
with anyone, small or great, except the
king of Israel." 31When the chariot
commanders saw Jehoshaphat, they
thought, "This is the king of Israel." So
they turned to attack him, but
Jehoshaphat cried out, and the LORD

helped him. God drew them away from him, 32for when the chariot commanders saw that he was not the king of Israel, they stopped pursuing him.

33But someone drew his bow at random and hit the king of Israel between the sections of his armour. The king told the chariot driver, "Wheel around and get me out of the fighting. I've been wounded." 34All day long the battle raged, and the king of Israel propped himself up in his chariot facing the Arameans until evening. Then at sunset he died.

19 When Jehoshaphat king of Judah returned safely to his palace in Jerusalem, 2Jehu the seer, the son of Hanani, went out to meet him and said to the king, "Should you help the wicked and love those who hate the LORD? Because of this, the wrath of the LORD is upon you. 3There is, however, some good in you, for you have rid the land of the Asherah poles and have set your heart on seeking God."

Jehoshaphat Appoints Judges

4Jehoshaphat lived in Jerusalem, and he went out again among the people from Beersheba to the hill country of Ephraim and turned them back to the LORD, the God of their fathers. 5He appointed judges in the land, in each of the fortified cities of Judah. 6He told them, "Consider carefully what you do, because you are not judging for man but for the LORD, who is with you whenever you give a verdict. 7Now let the fear of the LORD be upon you. Judge carefully, for with the LORD our God there is no injustice or partiality or bribery."

8In Jerusalem also, Jehoshaphat appointed some of the Levites, priests and heads of Israelite families to administer the law of the LORD and to settle disputes. And they lived in Jerusalem. 9He gave them these orders: "You must serve faithfully and wholeheartedly in the fear of the LORD. 10In every case that comes before you from your fellow countrymen who live in the cities—whether bloodshed or other concerns of the law, commands, decrees or ordinances—you are to warn them not to sin against the LORD; otherwise his wrath will come on you and your brothers. Do this, and you will not sin.

11"Amariah the chief priest will be over you in any matter concerning the LORD, and Zebadiah son of Ishmael, the leader of the tribe of Judah, will be over you in any matter concerning the king, and the Levites will serve as officials before you. Act with courage, and may the LORD be with those who do well."

Jehoshaphat Defeats Moab and Ammon

20 After this, the Moabites and Ammonites with some of the Meunites came to make war on Jehoshaphat.

2Some men came and told Jehoshaphat, "A vast army is coming against you from Edom, from the other side of the Sea. It is already in Hazazon Tamar" (that is, En Gedi). 3Alarmed, Jehoshaphat resolved to enquire of the LORD, and he proclaimed a fast for all Judah. 4The people of Judah came together to seek help from the LORD; indeed, they came from every town in Judah to seek him.

5Then Jehoshaphat stood up in the assembly of Judah and Jerusalem at the temple of the LORD in the front of the new courtyard 6and said:

> "O LORD, God of our fathers, are you not the God who is in heaven? You rule over all the kingdoms of the nations. Power and might are in your hand, and no-one can withstand you. 7O our God, did you not drive out the inhabitants of this land before your people Israel and give it for ever to the descendants of Abraham your friend? 8They have lived in it and have built in it a sanctuary for your Name, saying, 9'If calamity comes

upon us, whether the sword of
judgment, or plague or famine, we
will stand in your presence before
this temple that bears your Name
and will cry out to you in our distress, and you will hear us and save
us.’
10“But now here are men from
Ammon, Moab and Mount Seir,
whose territory you would not
allow Israel to invade when they
came from Egypt; so they turned
away from them and did not destroy them. 11See how they are repaying us by coming to drive us out
of the possession you gave us as an
inheritance. 12O our God, will you
not judge them? For we have no
power to face this vast army that is
attacking us. We do not know what
to do, but our eyes are upon you.”

13All the men of Judah, with their
wives and children and little ones, stood
there before the LORD.
14Then the Spirit of the LORD came
upon Jahaziel son of Zechariah, the son
of Benaiah, the son of Jeiel, the son of
Mattaniah, a Levite and descendant of
Asaph, as he stood in the assembly.
15He said, “Listen, King Jehoshaphat
and all who live in Judah and Jerusalem!
This is what the LORD says to you: ‘Do
not be afraid or discouraged because of
this vast army. For the battle is not
yours, but God’s. 16Tomorrow march
down against them. They will be climb-
ing up by the Pass of Ziz, and you will
find them at the end of the gorge in the
Desert of Jeruel. 17You will not have to
fight this battle. Take up your positions;
stand firm and see the deliverance the
LORD will give you, O Judah and Jerusalem. Do not be afraid; do not be
discouraged. Go out to face them
tomorrow, and the LORD will be with
you.’ ”
18Jehoshaphat bowed with his face to
the ground, and all the people of Judah
and Jerusalem fell down in worship before the LORD. 19Then some Levites
from the Kohathites and Korahites
stood up and praised the LORD, the God
of Israel, with a very loud voice.
20Early in the morning they left for
the Desert of Tekoa. As they set out,
Jehoshaphat stood and said, “Listen to
me, Judah and people of Jerusalem!
Have faith in the LORD your God and
you will be upheld; have faith in his
prophets and you will be successful.”
21After consulting the people,
Jehoshaphat appointed men to sing to
the LORD and to praise him for the
splendour of his holiness as they went
out at the head of the army, saying:

“Give thanks to the LORD,
for his love endures for ever.”

22As they began to sing and praise,
the LORD set ambushes against the men
of Ammon and Moab and Mount Seir
who were invading Judah, and they
were defeated. 23The men of Ammon
and Moab rose up against the men from
Mount Seir to destroy and annihilate
them. After they finished slaughtering
the men from Seir, they helped to destroy one another.
24When the men of Judah came to the
place that overlooks the desert and
looked towards the vast army, they saw
only dead bodies lying on the ground;
no-one had escaped. 25So Jehoshaphat
and his men went to carry off their
plunder, and they found among them a
great amount of equipment and clothing and also articles of value—more
than they could take away. There was so
much plunder that it took three days to
collect it. 26On the fourth day they
assembled in the Valley of Beracah,
where they praised the LORD. This is
why it is called the Valley of Beracah to
this day.
27Then, led by Jehoshaphat, all the
men of Judah and Jerusalem returned
joyfully to Jerusalem, for the LORD had
given them cause to rejoice over their
enemies. 28They entered Jerusalem and

went to the temple of the LORD with
harps and lutes and trumpets.
29The fear of God came upon all the
kingdoms of the countries when they
heard how the LORD had fought against
the enemies of Israel. 30And the kingdom of Jehoshaphat was at peace, for
his God had given him rest on every
side.

The End of Jehoshaphat's Reign

31So Jehoshaphat reigned over
Judah. He was thirty-five years old
when he became king of Judah, and he
reigned in Jerusalem for twenty-five
years. His mother's name was Azubah
daughter of Shilhi. 32He walked in the
ways of his father Asa and did not stray
from them; he did what was right in the
eyes of the LORD. 33The high places,
however, were not removed, and the
people still had not set their hearts on
the God of their fathers.
34The other events of Jehoshaphat's
reign, from beginning to end, are written in the annals of Jehu son of Hanani,
which are recorded in the book of the
kings of Israel.
35Later, Jehoshaphat king of Judah
made an alliance with Ahaziah king of
Israel, who was guilty of wickedness.
36He agreed with him to construct a fleet
of trading ships. After these were built
at Ezion Geber, 37Eliezer son of Doda-
vahu of Mareshah prophesied against
Jehoshaphat, saying, "Because you
have made an alliance with Ahaziah,
the LORD will destroy what you have
made." The ships were wrecked and
were not able to set sail to trade.
21 Then Jehoshaphat rested with
his fathers and was buried with
them in the City of David. And Jehoram his son succeeded him as king.
2Jehoram's brothers, the sons of
Jehoshaphat, were Azariah, Jehiel,
Zechariah, Azariahu, Michael and
Shephatiah. All these were sons of
Jehoshaphat king of Israel. 3Their
father had given them many gifts of
silver and gold and articles of value, as
well as fortified cities in Judah, but he
had given the kingdom to Jehoram because he was his firstborn son.

NEW TESTAMENT READING
1 Corinthians 15:35–49

The Resurrection Body

35But someone may ask, "How are
the dead raised? With what kind of
body will they come?" 36How foolish!
What you sow does not come to life
unless it dies. 37When you sow, you do
not plant the body that will be, but just a
seed, perhaps of wheat or of something
else. 38But God gives it a body as he has
determined, and to each kind of seed he
gives its own body. 39All flesh is not the
same: Men have one kind of flesh,
animals have another, birds another
and fish another. 40There are also
heavenly bodies and there are earthly
bodies; but the splendour of the
heavenly bodies is one kind, and the
splendour of the earthly bodies is
another. 41The sun has one kind of
splendour, the moon another and the
stars another; and star differs from star
in splendour.
42So will it be with the resurrection of
the dead. The body that is sown is
perishable, it is raised imperishable; 43it
is sown in dishonour, it is raised in
glory; it is sown in weakness, it is raised
in power; 44it is sown a natural body, it is
raised a spiritual body.
If there is a natural body, there is also
a spiritual body. 45So it is written: "The
first man Adam became a living being";
the last Adam, a life-giving spirit. 46The
spiritual did not come first, but the natural, and after that the spiritual. 47The
first man was of the dust of the earth,
the second man from heaven. 48As was
the earthly man, so are those who are
of the earth; and as is the man from
heaven, so also are those who are of
heaven. 49And just as we have borne the
likeness of the earthly man, so shall we
bear the likeness of the man from
heaven.

READING FROM PSALMS
Psalm 102:12–17

12But you, O LORD, sit enthroned for ever;
your renown endures through all generations.
13You will arise and have compassion on Zion,
for it is time to show favour to her;
the appointed time has come.
14For her stones are dear to your servants;
her very dust moves them to pity.
15The nations will fear the name of the LORD,
all the kings of the earth will revere your glory.
16For the LORD will rebuild Zion
and appear in his glory.
17He will respond to the prayer of the destitute;
he will not despise their plea.

DAY 236

AUGUST 24

OLD TESTAMENT READING
2 Chronicles 21:4–23:21

Jehoram King of Judah

4When Jehoram established himself
firmly over his father's kingdom, he put
all his brothers to the sword along with
some of the princes of Israel. 5Jehoram
was thirty-two years old when he became king, and he reigned in Jerusalem
for eight years. 6He walked in the ways
of the kings of Israel, as the house of
Ahab had done, for he married a daughter of Ahab. He did evil in the eyes of
the LORD. 7Nevertheless, because of
the covenant the LORD had made with
David, the LORD was not willing to destroy the house of David. He had promised to maintain a lamp for him and his
descendants for ever.

8In the time of Jehoram, Edom rebelled against Judah and set up its own
king. 9So Jehoram went there with his
officers and all his chariots. The Edomites surrounded him and his chariot
commanders, but he rose up and broke
through by night. 10To this day Edom
has been in rebellion against Judah.

Libnah revolted at the same time,
because Jehoram had forsaken the
LORD, the God of his fathers. 11He had
also built high places on the hills of
Judah and had caused the people of
Jerusalem to prostitute themselves and
had led Judah astray.

12Jehoram received a letter from Elijah the prophet, which said:

"This is what the LORD, the God of
your father David, says: 'You have
not walked in the ways of your
father Jehoshaphat or of Asa king
of Judah. 13But you have walked in
the ways of the kings of Israel, and
you have led Judah and the people
of Jerusalem to prostitute themselves, just as the house of Ahab
did. You have also murdered your
own brothers, members of your
father's house, men who were better than you. 14So now the LORD is
about to strike your people, your
sons, your wives and everything
that is yours, with a heavy blow.
15You yourself will be very ill with a
lingering disease of the bowels, until the disease causes your bowels
to come out.'"

16The LORD aroused against Jehoram
the hostility of the Philistines and of the
Arabs who lived near the Cushites.
17They attacked Judah, invaded it and
carried off all the goods found in the
king's palace, together with his sons and

wives. Not a son was left to him except
Ahaziah, the youngest.
18After all this, the LORD afflicted
Jehoram with an incurable disease of
the bowels. 19In the course of time, at
the end of the second year, his bowels
came out because of the disease, and he
died in great pain. His people made no
fire in his honour, as they had for his
fathers.
20Jehoram was thirty-two years old
when he became king, and he reigned in
Jerusalem for eight years. He passed
away, to no-one's regret, and was
buried in the City of David, but not in
the tombs of the kings.

Ahaziah King of Judah

22 The people of Jerusalem made
Ahaziah, Jehoram's youngest
son, king in his place, since the raiders,
who came with the Arabs into the camp,
had killed all the older sons. So Ahaziah
son of Jehoram king of Judah began to
reign.
2Ahaziah was twenty-two years old
when he became king, and he reigned in
Jerusalem for one year. His mother's
name was Athaliah, a granddaughter of
Omri.
3He too walked in the ways of the
house of Ahab, for his mother encouraged him in doing wrong. 4He did evil in
the eyes of the LORD, as the house of
Ahab had done, for after his father's
death they became his advisers, to his
undoing. 5He also followed their counsel when he went with Joram son of
Ahab king of Israel to war against
Hazael king of Aram at Ramoth
Gilead. The Arameans wounded
Joram; 6so he returned to Jezreel to
recover from the wounds they had inflicted on him at Ramoth in his battle
with Hazael king of Aram.

Then Ahaziah son of Jehoram king of
Judah went down to Jezreel to see
Joram son of Ahab because he had been
wounded.
7Through Ahaziah's visit to Joram,
God brought about Ahaziah's downfall.
When Ahaziah arrived, he went out
with Joram to meet Jehu son of Nimshi,
whom the LORD had anointed to destroy the house of Ahab. 8While Jehu
was executing judgment on the house of
Ahab, he found the princes of Judah
and the sons of Ahaziah's relatives, who
had been attending Ahaziah, and he
killed them. 9He then went in search of
Ahaziah, and his men captured him
while he was hiding in Samaria. He was
brought to Jehu and put to death. They
buried him, for they said, "He was a son
of Jehoshaphat, who sought the LORD
with all his heart." So there was no-one
in the house of Ahaziah powerful
enough to retain the kingdom.

Athaliah and Joash

10When Athaliah the mother of Ahaziah saw that her son was dead, she
proceeded to destroy the whole royal
family of the house of Judah. 11But
Jehosheba, the daughter of King Jehoram, took Joash son of Ahaziah and
stole him away from among the royal
princes who were about to be murdered
and put him and his nurse in a bedroom. Because Jehosheba, the daughter
of King Jehoram and wife of the priest
Jehoiada, was Ahaziah's sister, she hid
the child from Athaliah so that she
could not kill him. 12He remained hidden with them at the temple of God for
six years while Athaliah ruled the land.

23 In the seventh year Jehoiada
showed his strength. He made a
covenant with the commanders of units
of a hundred: Azariah son of Jeroham,
Ishmael son of Jehohanan, Azariah son
of Obed, Maaseiah son of Adaiah, and
Elishaphat son of Zicri. 2They went
throughout Judah and gathered the Levites and the heads of Israelite families
from all the towns. When they came to
Jerusalem, 3the whole assembly made a
covenant with the king at the temple of
God.

Jehoiada said to them, "The king's
son shall reign, as the LORD promised
concerning the descendants of David.

4Now this is what you are to do: A third
of you priests and Levites who are going
on duty on the Sabbath are to keep
watch at the doors, 5a third of you at the
royal palace and a third at the Foundation Gate, and all the other men are to
be in the courtyards of the temple of the
LORD. 6No-one is to enter the temple of
the LORD except the priests and Levites
on duty; they may enter because they
are consecrated, but all the other men
are to guard what the LORD has assigned
to them. 7The Levites are to station
themselves round the king, each man
with his weapons in his hand. Anyone
who enters the temple must be put to
death. Stay close to the king wherever
he goes."

8The Levites and all the men of Judah
did just as Jehoiada the priest ordered.
Each one took his men—those who
were going on duty on the Sabbath and
those who were going off duty—for
Jehoiada the priest had not released any
of the divisions. 9Then he gave the commanders of units of a hundred the
spears and the large and small shields
that had belonged to King David and
that were in the temple of God. 10He
stationed all the men, each with his
weapon in his hand, round the king
—near the altar and the temple, from
the south side to the north side of the
temple.

11Jehoiada and his sons brought out
the king's son and put the crown on him;
they presented him with a copy of the
covenant and proclaimed him king.
They anointed him and shouted, "Long
live the king!"

12When Athaliah heard the noise of
the people running and cheering the
king, she went to them at the temple of
the LORD. 13She looked, and there was
the king, standing by his pillar at the
entrance. The officers and the trumpeters were beside the king, and all the
people of the land were rejoicing and
blowing trumpets, and singers with
musical instruments were leading the
praises. Then Athaliah tore her robes
and shouted, "Treason! Treason!"

14Jehoiada the priest sent out the
commanders of units of a hundred, who
were in charge of the troops, and said to
them: "Bring her out between the ranks
and put to the sword anyone who follows her." For the priest had said, "Do
not put her to death at the temple of the
LORD." 15So they seized her as she
reached the entrance of the Horse Gate
on the palace grounds, and there they
put her to death.

16Jehoiada then made a covenant that
he and the people and the king would be
the LORD's people. 17All the people
went to the temple of Baal and tore it
down. They smashed the altars and
idols and killed Mattan the priest of
Baal in front of the altars.

18Then Jehoiada placed the oversight
of the temple of the LORD in the hands
of the priests, who were Levites, to
whom David had made assignments in
the temple, to present the burnt offerings of the LORD as written in the Law of
Moses, with rejoicing and singing, as
David had ordered. 19He also stationed
doorkeepers at the gates of the LORD's
temple so that no-one who was in any
way unclean might enter.

20He took with him the commanders
of hundreds, the nobles, the rulers of
the people and all the people of the land
and brought the king down from the
temple of the LORD. They went into the
palace through the Upper Gate and
seated the king on the royal throne,
21and all the people of the land rejoiced.
And the city was quiet, because Athaliah had been slain with the sword.

NEW TESTAMENT READING
1 Corinthians 15:50–16:4

50I declare to you, brothers, that flesh
and blood cannot inherit the kingdom
of God, nor does the perishable inherit
the imperishable. 51Listen, I tell you a
mystery: We will not all sleep, but we
will all be changed—52in a flash, in the
twinkling of an eye, at the last trumpet.

For the trumpet will sound, the dead will be raised imperishable, and we will be changed. 53For the perishable must clothe itself with the imperishable, and the mortal with immortality. 54When the perishable has been clothed with the imperishable, and the mortal with immortality, then the saying that is written will come true: "Death has been swallowed up in victory."

55"Where, O death, is your victory?
Where, O death, is your sting?"

56The sting of death is sin, and the power of sin is the law. 57But thanks be to God! He gives us the victory through our Lord Jesus Christ.

58Therefore, my dear brothers, stand firm. Let nothing move you. Always give yourselves fully to the work of the Lord, because you know that your labour in the Lord is not in vain.

The Collection for God's People

16 Now about the collection for God's people: Do what I told the Galatian churches to do. 2On the first day of every week, each one of you should set aside a sum of money in keeping with his income, saving it up, so that when I come no collections will have to be made. 3Then, when I arrive, I will give letters of introduction to the men you approve and send them with your gift to Jerusalem. 4If it seems advisable for me to go also, they will accompany me.

READING FROM PROVERBS

Proverbs 20:25–21:4

25It is a trap for a man to dedicate
something rashly
and only later to consider his vows.

26A wise king winnows out the wicked;
he drives the threshing wheel over
them.

27The lamp of the LORD searches the
spirit of a man;
it searches out his inmost being.

28Love and faithfulness keep a king
safe;
through love his throne is made
secure.

29The glory of young men is their
strength,
grey hair the splendour of the old.

30Blows and wounds cleanse away evil,
and beatings purge the inmost
being.

21 The king's heart is in the hand
of the LORD;
he directs it like a watercourse
wherever he pleases.

2All a man's ways seem right to him,
but the LORD weighs the heart.

3To do what is right and just
is more acceptable to the LORD
than sacrifice.

4Haughty eyes and a proud heart,
the lamp of the wicked, are sin!

DAY 237

AUGUST 25

OLD TESTAMENT READING
2 Chronicles 24:1–25:28

Joash Repairs the Temple

24 Joash was seven years old when
he became king, and he reigned
in Jerusalem for forty years. His
mother's name was Zibiah; she was
from Beersheba. 2Joash did what was
right in the eyes of the LORD all the
years of Jehoiada the priest. 3Jehoiada
chose two wives for him, and he had
sons and daughters.

4Some time later Joash decided to
restore the temple of the LORD. 5He
called together the priests and Levites
and said to them, "Go to the towns of
Judah and collect the money due
annually from all Israel, to repair the
temple of your God. Do it now." But
the Levites did not act at once.

6Therefore the king summoned
Jehoiada the chief priest and said to
him, "Why haven't you required the
Levites to bring in from Judah and Jerusalem the tax imposed by Moses the
servant of the LORD and by the assembly of Israel for the Tent of the
Testimony?"

7Now the sons of that wicked woman
Athaliah had broken into the temple of
God and had used even its sacred ob-
jects for the Baals.

8At the king's command, a chest was
made and placed outside, at the gate of
the temple of the LORD. 9A proclamation was then issued in Judah and Jerusalem that they should bring to the
LORD the tax that Moses the servant of
God had required of Israel in the desert.
10All the officials and all the people
brought their contributions gladly,
dropping them into the chest until it was
full. 11Whenever the chest was brought
in by the Levites to the king's officials
and they saw that there was a large
amount of money, the royal secretary
and the officer of the chief priest would
come and empty the chest and carry it
back to its place. They did this regularly
and collected a great amount of money.
12The king and Jehoiada gave it to the
men who carried out the work required
for the temple of the LORD. They hired
masons and carpenters to restore the
LORD's temple, and also workers in iron
and bronze to repair the temple.

13The men in charge of the work were
diligent, and the repairs progressed
under them. They rebuilt the temple of
God according to its original design and
reinforced it. 14When they had finished,
they brought the rest of the money to
the king and Jehoiada, and with it were
made articles for the LORD's temple:
articles for the service and for the burnt
offerings, and also dishes and other objects of gold and silver. As long as
Jehoiada lived, burnt offerings were
presented continually in the temple of
the LORD.

15Now Jehoiada was old and full of
years, and he died at the age of a hundred and thirty. 16He was buried with
the kings in the City of David, because
of the good he had done in Israel for
God and his temple.

The Wickedness of Joash

17After the death of Jehoiada, the
officials of Judah came and paid homage to the king, and he listened to them.
18They abandoned the temple of the
LORD, the God of their fathers, and
worshipped Asherah poles and idols.
Because of their guilt, God's anger
came upon Judah and Jerusalem.
19Although the LORD sent prophets to
the people to bring them back to him,
and though they testified against them,
they would not listen.

20Then the Spirit of God came upon
Zechariah son of Jehoiada the priest.
He stood before the people and said,
"This is what God says: 'Why do you
disobey the LORD's commands? You

will not prosper. Because you have forsaken the LORD, he has forsaken you.' "

21But they plotted against him, and by order of the king they stoned him to death in the courtyard of the LORD's temple. 22King Joash did not remember the kindness Zechariah's father Jehoiada had shown him but killed his son, who said as he lay dying, "May the LORD see this and call you to account."

23At the turn of the year, the army of Aram marched against Joash; it invaded Judah and Jerusalem and killed all the leaders of the people. They sent all the plunder to their king in Damascus. 24Although the Aramean army had come with only a few men, the LORD delivered into their hands a much larger army. Because Judah had forsaken the LORD, the God of their fathers, judgment was executed on Joash. 25When the Arameans withdrew, they left Joash severely wounded. His officials conspired against him for murdering the son of Jehoiada the priest, and they killed him in his bed. So he died and was buried in the City of David, but not in the tombs of the kings.

26Those who conspired against him were Zabad, son of Shimeath an Ammonite woman, and Jehozabad, son of Shimrith a Moabite woman. 27The account of his sons, the many prophecies about him, and the record of the restoration of the temple of God are written in the annotations on the book of the kings. And Amaziah his son succeeded him as king.

Amaziah King of Judah

25 Amaziah was twenty-five years old when he became king, and he reigned in Jerusalem for twenty-nine years. His mother's name was Jehoaddin; she was from Jerusalem. 2He did what was right in the eyes of the LORD, but not wholeheartedly. 3After the kingdom was firmly in his control, he executed the officials who had murdered his father the king. 4Yet he did not put their sons to death, but acted in accordance with what is written in the Law, in the Book of Moses, where the LORD commanded: "Fathers shall not be put to death for their children, nor children put to death for their fathers; each is to die for his own sins."

5Amaziah called the people of Judah together and assigned them according to their families to commanders of thousands and commanders of hundreds for all Judah and Benjamin. He then mustered those twenty years old or more and found that there were three hundred thousand men ready for military service, able to handle the spear and shield. 6He also hired a hundred thousand fighting men from Israel for a hundred talents of silver.

7But a man of God came to him and said, "O king, these troops from Israel must not march with you, for the LORD is not with Israel—not with any of the people of Ephraim. 8Even if you go and fight courageously in battle, God will overthrow you before the enemy, for God has the power to help or to overthrow."

9Amaziah asked the man of God, "But what about the hundred talents I paid for these Israelite troops?"

The man of God replied, "The LORD can give you much more than that."

10So Amaziah dismissed the troops who had come to him from Ephraim and sent them home. They were furious with Judah and left for home in a great rage.

11Amaziah then marshalled his strength and led his army to the Valley of Salt, where he killed ten thousand men of Seir. 12The army of Judah also captured ten thousand men alive, took them to the top of a cliff and threw them down so that all were dashed to pieces.

13Meanwhile the troops that Amaziah had sent back and had not allowed to take part in the war raided Judean towns from Samaria to Beth Horon. They killed three thousand people and carried off great quantities of plunder.

14When Amaziah returned from slaughtering the Edomites, he brought back the gods of the people of Seir. He set them up as his own gods, bowed down to them and burned sacrifices to them. 15The anger of the LORD burned against Amaziah, and he sent a prophet to him, who said, "Why do you consult this people's gods, which could not save their own people from your hand?"

16While he was still speaking, the king said to him, "Have we appointed you an adviser to the king? Stop! Why be struck down?"

So the prophet stopped but said, "I know that God has determined to destroy you, because you have done this and have not listened to my counsel."

17After Amaziah king of Judah consulted his advisers, he sent this challenge to Jehoash son of Jehoahaz, the son of Jehu, king of Israel: "Come, meet me face to face."

18But Jehoash king of Israel replied to Amaziah king of Judah, "A thistle in Lebanon sent a message to a cedar in Lebanon, 'Give your daughter to my son in marriage.' Then a wild beast in Lebanon came along and trampled the thistle underfoot. 19You say to yourself that you have defeated Edom, and now you are arrogant and proud. But stay at home! Why ask for trouble and cause your own downfall and that of Judah also?"

20Amaziah, however, would not listen, for God so worked that he might hand them over to ⌊Jehoash⌋, because they sought the gods of Edom. 21So Jehoash king of Israel attacked. He and Amaziah king of Judah faced each other at Beth Shemesh in Judah. 22Judah was routed by Israel, and every man fled to his home. 23Jehoash king of Israel captured Amaziah king of Judah, the son of Joash, the son of Ahaziah, at Beth Shemesh. Then Jehoash brought him to Jerusalem and broke down the wall of Jerusalem from the Ephraim Gate to the Corner Gate—a section about six hundred feet long. 24He took all the gold and silver and all the articles found in the temple of God that had been in the care of Obed-Edom, together with the palace treasures and the hostages, and returned to Samaria.

25Amaziah son of Joash king of Judah lived for fifteen years after the death of Jehoash son of Jehoahaz king of Israel. 26As for the other events of Amaziah's reign, from beginning to end, are they not written in the book of the kings of Judah and Israel? 27From the time that Amaziah turned away from following the LORD, they conspired against him in Jerusalem and he fled to Lachish, but they sent men after him to Lachish and killed him there. 28He was brought back by horse and was buried with his fathers in the City of Judah.

NEW TESTAMENT READING

1 Corinthians 16:5–24

Personal Requests

5After I go through Macedonia, I will come to you—for I will be going through Macedonia. 6Perhaps I will stay with you awhile, or even spend the winter, so that you can help me on my journey, wherever I go. 7I do not want to see you now and make only a passing visit; I hope to spend some time with you, if the Lord permits. 8But I will stay on at Ephesus until Pentecost, 9because a great door for effective work has opened to me, and there are many who oppose me.

10If Timothy comes, see to it that he has nothing to fear while he is with you, for he is carrying on the work of the Lord, just as I am. 11No-one, then, should refuse to accept him. Send him on his way in peace so that he may return to me. I am expecting him along with the brothers.

12Now about our brother Apollos: I strongly urged him to go to you with the brothers. He was quite unwilling to go now, but he will go when he has the opportunity.

13Be on your guard; stand firm in the faith; be men of courage; be strong. 14Do everything in love.

15You know that the household of

Stephanas were the first converts in Achaia, and they have devoted themselves to the service of the saints. I urge you, brothers, 16to submit to such as these and to everyone who joins in the work, and labours at it. 17I was glad when Stephanas, Fortunatus and Achaicus arrived, because they have supplied what was lacking from you. 18For they refreshed my spirit and yours also. Such men deserve recognition.

Final Greetings

19The churches in the province of Asia send you greetings. Aquila and Priscilla greet you warmly in the Lord, and so does the church that meets at their house. 20All the brothers here send you greetings. Greet one another with a holy kiss.

21I, Paul, write this greeting in my own hand.

22If anyone does not love the Lord —a curse be on him. Come, O Lord!

23The grace of the Lord Jesus be with you.

24My love to all of you in Christ Jesus. Amen.

READING FROM PSALMS

Psalm 102:18–28

18Let this be written for a future
generation,
that a people not yet created may
praise the LORD:
19"The LORD looked down from his
sanctuary on high,
from heaven he viewed the
earth,
20to hear the groans of the prisoners
and release those condemned to
death."
21So the name of the LORD will be
declared in Zion
and his praise in Jerusalem
22when the peoples and the kingdoms
assemble to worship the LORD.

23In the course of my life he broke my
strength;
he cut short my days.
24So I said:
"Do not take me away, O my God,
in the midst of my days;
your years go on through all
generations.
25In the beginning you laid the
foundations of the earth,
and the heavens are the work of
your hands.
26They will perish, but you remain;
they will all wear out like a
garment.
Like clothing you will change them
and they will be discarded.
27But you remain the same,
and your years will never end.
28The children of your servants will live
in your presence;
their descendants will be
established before you."

DAY 238

AUGUST 26

OLD TESTAMENT READING
2 Chronicles 26:1–28:27

Uzziah King of Judah

26 Then all the people of Judah
took Uzziah, who was sixteen
years old, and made him king in place of
his father Amaziah. 2He was the one
who rebuilt Elath and restored it to
Judah after Amaziah rested with his
fathers.
3Uzziah was sixteen years old when
he became king, and he reigned in Jerusalem for fifty-two years. His mother's
name was Jecoliah; she was from Jerusalem. 4He did what was right in the
eyes of the LORD, just as his father
Amaziah had done. 5He sought God
during the days of Zechariah, who instructed him in the fear of God. As long
as he sought the LORD, God gave him
success.
6He went to war against the Philistines and broke down the walls of Gath,
Jabneh and Ashdod. He then rebuilt
towns near Ashdod and elsewhere
among the Philistines. 7God helped him
against the Philistines and against the
Arabs who lived in Gur Baal and
against the Meunites. 8The Ammonites
brought tribute to Uzziah, and his fame
spread as far as the border of Egypt,
because he had become very powerful.
9Uzziah built towers in Jerusalem at
the Corner Gate, at the Valley Gate and
at the angle of the wall, and he fortified
them. 10He also built towers in the desert and dug many cisterns, because he
had much livestock in the foothills and
in the plain. He had people working his
fields and vineyards in the hills and in
the fertile lands, for he loved the soil.
11Uzziah had a well-trained army,
ready to go out by divisions according to
their numbers as mustered by Jeiel the
secretary and Maaseiah the officer
under the direction of Hananiah, one of
the royal officials. 12The total number of
family leaders over the fighting men was
2,600. 13Under their command was an
army of 307,500 men trained for war, a
powerful force to support the king
against his enemies. 14Uzziah provided
shields, spears, helmets, coats of
armour, bows and slingstones for the
entire army. 15In Jerusalem he made
machines designed by skilful men for
use on the towers and on the corner
defences to shoot arrows and hurl large
stones. His fame spread far and wide,
for he was greatly helped until he became powerful.
16But after Uzziah became powerful,
his pride led to his downfall. He was
unfaithful to the LORD his God, and
entered the temple of the LORD to burn
incense on the altar of incense.
17Azariah the priest with eighty other
courageous priests of the LORD followed him in. 18They confronted him
and said, "It is not right for you,
Uzziah, to burn incense to the LORD.
That is for the priests, the descendants
of Aaron, who have been consecrated
to burn incense. Leave the sanctuary,
for you have been unfaithful; and you
will not be honoured by the LORD
God."
19Uzziah, who had a censer in his
hand ready to burn incense, became
angry. While he was raging at the priests
in their presence before the incense
altar in the LORD's temple, leprosy
broke out on his forehead. 20When
Azariah the chief priest and all the other
priests looked at him, they saw that he
had leprosy on his forehead, so they
hurried him out. Indeed, he himself was
eager to leave, because the LORD had
afflicted him.
21King Uzziah had leprosy until the
day he died. He lived in a separate
house—leprous, and excluded from the
temple of the LORD. Jotham his son had
charge of the palace and governed the
people of the land.

22The other events of Uzziah's reign,
from beginning to end, are recorded by
the prophet Isaiah son of Amoz.
23Uzziah rested with his fathers and was
buried near them in a field for burial
that belonged to the kings, for people
said, "He had leprosy." And Jotham his
son succeeded him as king.

Jotham King of Judah

27 Jotham was twenty-five years
old when he became king, and
he reigned in Jerusalem for sixteen
years. His mother's name was Jerusha
daughter of Zadok. 2He did what was
right in the eyes of the LORD, just as his
father Uzziah had done, but unlike him
he did not enter the temple of the LORD.
The people, however, continued their
corrupt practices. 3Jotham rebuilt the
Upper Gate of the temple of the LORD
and did extensive work on the wall at
the hill of Ophel. 4He built towns in the
Judean hills and forts and towers in the
wooded areas.
5Jotham made war on the king of the
Ammonites and conquered them. That
year the Ammonites paid him a hundred talents of silver, ten thousand cors
of wheat and ten thousand cors of barley. The Ammonites brought him the
same amount also in the second and
third years.
6Jotham grew powerful because he
walked steadfastly before the LORD his
God.
7The other events in Jotham's reign,
including all his wars and the other
things he did, are written in the book of
the kings of Israel and Judah. 8He was
twenty-five years old when he became
king, and he reigned in Jerusalem for
sixteen years. 9Jotham rested with his
fathers and was buried in the City of
David. And Ahaz his son succeeded
him as king.

Ahaz King of Judah

28 Ahaz was twenty years old when
he became king, and he reigned
in Jerusalem for sixteen years. Unlike
David his father, he did not do what was
right in the eyes of the LORD. 2He
walked in the ways of the kings of Israel
and also made cast idols for worshipping the Baals. 3He burned sacrifices in
the Valley of Ben Hinnom and sacrificed his sons in the fire, following
the detestable ways of the nations that
the LORD had driven out before the
Israelites. 4He offered sacrifices and
burned incense at the high places, on
the hilltops and under every spreading
tree.
5Therefore the LORD his God handed
him over to the king of Aram. The
Arameans defeated him and took many
of his people as prisoners and brought
them to Damascus.
He was also given into the hands of
the king of Israel, who inflicted heavy
casualties on him. 6In one day Pekah
son of Remaliah killed a hundred and
twenty thousand soldiers in Judah—
because Judah had forsaken the LORD,
the God of their fathers. 7Zicri, an
Ephraimite warrior, killed Maaseiah
the king's son, Azrikam the officer in
charge of the palace, and Elkanah,
second to the king. 8The Israelites took
captive from their kinsmen two hundred thousand wives, sons and daughters. They also took a great deal of
plunder, which they carried back to
Samaria.
9But a prophet of the LORD named
Oded was there, and he went out to
meet the army when it returned to
Samaria. He said to them, "Because the
LORD, the God of your fathers, was
angry with Judah, he gave them into
your hand. But you have slaughtered
them in a rage that reaches to heaven.
10And now you intend to make the men
and women of Judah and Jerusalem
your slaves. But aren't you also guilty of
sins against the LORD your God? 11Now
listen to me! Send back your fellow
countrymen that you have taken as prisoners, for the LORD's fierce anger rests
on you."
12Then some of the leaders in
Ephraim—Azariah son of Jehohanan,

Berekiah son of Meshillemoth, Jehiz-
kiah son of Shallum, and Amasa son of
Hadlai—confronted those who were
arriving from the war. 13"You must
not bring those prisoners here," they
said, "or we will be guilty before the
LORD. Do you intend to add to our
sin and guilt? For our guilt is already
great, and his fierce anger rests on
Israel."

14So the soldiers gave up the prisoners and plunder in the presence of the
officials and all the assembly. 15The men
designated by name took the prisoners,
and from the plunder they clothed all
who were naked. They provided them
with clothes and sandals, food and
drink, and healing balm. All those who
were weak they put on donkeys. So they
took them back to their fellow countrymen at Jericho, the City of Palms, and
returned to Samaria.

16At that time King Ahaz sent to the
king of Assyria for help. 17The Edomites had again come and attacked Judah
and carried away prisoners, 18while the
Philistines had raided towns in the
foothills and in the Negev of Judah.
They captured and occupied Beth
Shemesh, Aijalon and Gederoth, as
well as Soco, Timnah and Gimzo, with
their surrounding villages. 19The LORD
had humbled Judah because of Ahaz
king of Israel, for he had promoted
wickedness in Judah and had been most
unfaithful to the LORD. 20Tiglath-
Pileser king of Assyria came to him,
but gave him trouble instead of help.
21Ahaz took some of the things from
the temple of the LORD and from the
royal palace and from the princes and
presented them to the king of Assyria,
but that did not help him.

22In his time of trouble King Ahaz
became even more unfaithful to the
LORD. 23He offered sacrifices to the
gods of Damascus, who had defeated
him; for he thought, "Since the gods of
the kings of Aram have helped them, I
will sacrifice to them so that they will
help me." But they were his downfall
and the downfall of all Israel.

24Ahaz gathered together the furnishings from the temple of God and
took them away. He shut the doors of
the LORD's temple and set up altars at
every street corner in Jerusalem. 25In
every town in Judah he built high places
to burn sacrifices to other gods and provoked the LORD, the God of his fathers,
to anger.

26The other events of his reign and all
his ways, from beginning to end, are
written in the book of the kings of Judah
and Israel. 27Ahaz rested with his
fathers and was buried in the city of
Jerusalem, but he was not placed in the
tombs of the kings of Israel. And Hezekiah his son succeeded him as king.

NEW TESTAMENT READING
2 Corinthians 1:1–11

1 Paul, an apostle of Christ Jesus by
the will of God, and Timothy our
brother,

To the church of God in Corinth,
together with all the saints throughout
Achaia:

2Grace and peace to you from God
our Father and the Lord Jesus Christ.

The God of All Comfort

3Praise be to the God and Father of
our Lord Jesus Christ, the Father of
compassion and the God of all comfort,
4who comforts us in all our troubles, so
that we can comfort those in any trouble
with the comfort we ourselves have received from God. 5For just as the sufferings of Christ flow over into our lives, so
also through Christ our comfort overflows. 6If we are distressed, it is for your
comfort and salvation; if we are comforted, it is for your comfort, which
produces in you patient endurance of
the same sufferings we suffer. 7And our
hope for you is firm, because we know

that just as you share in our sufferings, so also you share in our comfort.

8We do not want you to be uninformed, brothers, about the hardships we suffered in the province of Asia. We were under great pressure, far beyond our ability to endure, so that we despaired even of life. 9Indeed, in our
hearts we felt the sentence of death. But this happened that we might not rely on ourselves but on God, who raises the
dead. 10He has delivered us from such a deadly peril, and he will deliver us. On him we have set our hope that he will
continue to deliver us, 11as you help us by your prayers. Then many will give thanks on our behalf for the gracious favour granted us in answer to the prayers of many.

READING FROM PSALMS

Psalm 103:1–12

Of David.

1Praise the LORD, O my soul;
all my inmost being, praise his holy name.
2Praise the LORD, O my soul,
and forget not all his benefits—
3who forgives all your sins
and heals all your diseases,
4who redeems your life from the pit
and crowns you with love and compassion,
5who satisfies your desires with good things
so that your youth is renewed like the eagle's.

6The LORD works righteousness
and justice for all the oppressed.

7He made known his ways to Moses,
his deeds to the people of Israel:
8The LORD is compassionate and gracious,
slow to anger, abounding in love.
9He will not always accuse,
nor will he harbour his anger for ever;
10he does not treat us as our sins deserve
or repay us according to our iniquities.
11For as high as the heavens are above the earth,
so great is his love for those who fear him;
12as far as the east is from the west,
so far has he removed our transgressions from us.

AUGUST 27

DAY 239

OLD TESTAMENT READING

2 Chronicles 29:1–31:1

Hezekiah Purifies the Temple

29 Hezekiah was twenty-five years old when he became king, and he reigned in Jerusalem for twenty-nine years. His mother's name was Abijah daughter of Zechariah. 2He did what
was right in the eyes of the LORD, just as his father David had done.
3In the first month of the first year of his reign, he opened the doors of the temple of the LORD and repaired them.
4He brought in the priests and the Levites, assembled them in the square on the east side 5and said, "Listen to me, Levites! Consecrate yourselves now and consecrate the temple of the LORD, the God of your fathers. Remove all defilement from the sanctuary. 6Our
fathers were unfaithful; they did evil in the eyes of the LORD our God and forsook him. They turned their faces away from the LORD's dwelling-place and turned their backs on him. 7They also

shut the doors of the portico and put out
the lamps. They did not burn incense or
present any burnt offerings at the sanctuary to the God of Israel. 8Therefore,
the anger of the LORD has fallen on
Judah and Jerusalem; he has made
them an object of dread and horror and
scorn, as you can see with your own
eyes. 9This is why our fathers have fallen by the sword and why our sons and
daughters and our wives are in captivity. 10Now I intend to make a covenant
with the LORD, the God of Israel, so
that his fierce anger will turn away from
us. 11My sons, do not be negligent now,
for the LORD has chosen you to stand
before him and serve him, to minister
before him and to burn incense."

12Then these Levites set to work:
from the Kohathites,
Mahath son of Amasai and Joel
son of Azariah;
from the Merarites,
Kish son of Abdi and Azariah son
of Jehallelel;
from the Gershonites,
Joah son of Zimmah and Eden
son of Joah;
13from the descendants of Elizaphan,
Shimri and Jeiel;
from the descendants of Asaph,
Zechariah and Mattaniah;
14from the descendants of Heman,
Jehiel and Shimei;
from the descendants of Jeduthun,
Shemaiah and Uzziel.

15When they had assembled their
brothers and consecrated themselves,
they went in to purify the temple of the
LORD, as the king had ordered, following the word of the LORD. 16The priests
went into the sanctuary of the LORD to
purify it. They brought out to the courtyard of the LORD's temple everything
unclean that they found in the temple of
the LORD. The Levites took it and carried it out to the Kidron Valley. 17They
began the consecration on the first day
of the first month, and by the eighth day
of the month they reached the portico of
the LORD. For eight more days they
consecrated the temple of the LORD
itself, finishing in the sixteenth day of
the first month.

18Then they went in to King Hezekiah
and reported: "We have purified the
entire temple of the LORD, the altar of
burnt offering with all its utensils, and
the table for setting out the consecrated
bread, with all its articles. 19We have
prepared and consecrated all the articles that King Ahaz removed in his unfaithfulness while he was king. They are
now in front of the LORD's altar."

20Early the next morning King Hezekiah gathered the city officials together
and went up to the temple of the LORD.
21They brought seven bulls, seven rams,
seven male lambs and seven male goats
as a sin offering for the kingdom, for the
sanctuary and for Judah. The king commanded the priests, the descendants of
Aaron, to offer these on the altar of the
LORD. 22So they slaughtered the bulls,
and the priests took the blood and
sprinkled it on the altar; next they
slaughtered the rams and sprinkled
their blood on the altar; then they
slaughtered the lambs and sprinkled
their blood on the altar. 23The goats for
the sin offering were brought before the
king and the assembly, and they laid
their hands on them. 24The priests then
slaughtered the goats and presented
their blood on the altar for a sin offering
to atone for all Israel, because the king
had ordered the burnt offering and the
sin offering for all Israel.

25He stationed the Levites in the temple of the LORD with cymbals, harps and
lyres in the way prescribed by David
and Gad the king's seer and Nathan
the prophet; this was commanded by
the LORD through his prophets. 26So the
Levites stood ready with David's instruments, and the priests with their
trumpets.

27Hezekiah gave the order to sacrifice
the burnt offering on the altar. As the
offering began, singing to the LORD began also, accompanied by trumpets and
the instruments of David king of Israel.
28The whole assembly bowed in
worship, while the singers sang and the

trumpeters played. All this continued
until the sacrifice of the burnt offering
was completed.
29When the offerings were finished,
the king and everyone present with him
knelt down and worshipped. 30King
Hezekiah and his officials ordered the
Levites to praise the LORD with the
words of David and of Asaph the seer.
So they sang praises with gladness and
bowed their heads and worshipped.
31Then Hezekiah said, "You have
now dedicated yourselves to the LORD.
Come and bring sacrifices and thank-
offerings to the temple of the LORD." So
the assembly brought sacrifices and
thank-offerings, and all whose hearts
were willing brought burnt offerings.
32The number of burnt offerings the
assembly brought was seventy bulls, a
hundred rams and two hundred male
lambs—all of them for burnt offerings
to the LORD. 33The animals consecrated
as sacrifices amounted to six hundred
bulls and three thousand sheep and
goats. 34The priests, however, were too
few to skin all the burnt offerings; so
their kinsmen the Levites helped them
until the task was finished and until
other priests had been consecrated, for
the Levites had been more conscien-
tious in consecrating themselves than
the priests had been. 35There were
burnt offerings in abundance, together
with the fat of the fellowship offerings
and the drink offerings that accompanied the burnt offerings.

So the service of the temple of the
LORD was re-established. 36Hezekiah
and all the people rejoiced at what God
had brought about for his people, because it was done so quickly.

Hezekiah Celebrates the Passover

30 Hezekiah sent word to all Israel
and Judah and also wrote letters
to Ephraim and Manasseh, inviting
them to come to the temple of the LORD
in Jerusalem and celebrate the Passover
to the LORD, the God of Israel. 2The
king and his officials and the whole
assembly in Jerusalem decided to celebrate the Passover in the second month.
3They had not been able to celebrate it
at the regular time because not enough
priests had consecrated themselves and
the people had not assembled in Jerusalem. 4The plan seemed right both to
the king and to the whole assembly.
5They decided to send a proclamation
throughout Israel, from Beersheba to
Dan, calling the people to come to Jerusalem and celebrate the Passover to the
LORD, the God of Israel. It had not been
celebrated in large numbers according
to what was written.
6At the king's command, couriers
went throughout Israel and Judah with
letters from the king and from his
officials, which read:

> "People of Israel, return to the
> LORD, the God of Abraham, Isaac
> and Israel, that he may return to
> you who are left, who have escaped
> from the hand of the kings of
> Assyria. 7Do not be like your
> fathers and brothers, who were un-
> faithful to the LORD, the God of
> their fathers, so that he made them
> an object of horror, as you see. 8Do
> not be stiff-necked, as your fathers
> were; submit to the LORD. Come to
> the sanctuary, which he has conse-
> crated for ever. Serve the LORD
> your God, so that his fierce anger
> will turn away from you. 9If you
> return to the LORD, then your
> brothers and your children will be
> shown compassion by their captors
> and will come back to this land, for
> the LORD your God is gracious and
> compassionate. He will not turn his
> face from you if you return to
> him."

10The couriers went from town to
town in Ephraim and Manasseh, as far
as Zebulun, but the people scorned and
ridiculed them. 11Nevertheless, some
men of Asher, Manasseh and Zebulun
humbled themselves and went to Jerusalem. 12Also in Judah the hand of God
was on the people to give them unity of

mind to carry out what the king and his
officials had ordered, following the
word of the LORD.
13A very large crowd of people
assembled in Jerusalem to celebrate
the Feast of Unleavened Bread in the
second month. 14They removed the
altars in Jerusalem and cleared away
the incense altars and threw them into
the Kidron Valley.
15They slaughtered the Passover
lamb on the fourteenth day of the
second month. The priests and the Levites were ashamed and consecrated
themselves and brought burnt offerings
to the temple of the LORD. 16Then they
took up their regular positions as prescribed in the Law of Moses the man of
God. The priests sprinkled the blood
handed to them by the Levites. 17Since
many in the crowd had not consecrated
themselves, the Levites had to kill the
Passover lambs for all those who were
not ceremonially clean and could not
consecrate ⌞their lambs⌟ to the LORD.
18Although most of the many people
who came from Ephraim, Manasseh,
Issachar and Zebulun had not purified
themselves, yet they ate the Passover,
contrary to what was written. But Hezekiah prayed for them, saying, "May the
LORD, who is good, pardon everyone
19who sets his heart on seeking God
—the LORD, the God of his fathers
—even if he is not clean according to the
rules of the sanctuary." 20And the LORD
heard Hezekiah and healed the people.
21The Israelites who were present in
Jerusalem celebrated the Feast of Unleavened Bread for seven days with
great rejoicing, while the Levites and
priests sang to the LORD every day,
accompanied by the LORD's instruments of praise.
22Hezekiah spoke encouragingly to
all the Levites, who showed good
understanding of the service of the
LORD. For the seven days they ate their
assigned portion and offered fellowship
offerings and praised the LORD, the God
of their fathers.
23The whole assembly then agreed to
celebrate the festival seven more days;
so for another seven days they celebrated joyfully. 24Hezekiah king of
Judah provided a thousand bulls and
seven thousand sheep and goats for the
assembly, and the officials provided
them with a thousand bulls and ten
thousand sheep and goats. A great
number of priests consecrated themselves. 25The entire assembly of Judah
rejoiced, along with the priests and Levites and all who had assembled from
Israel, including the aliens who had
come from Israel and those who lived in
Judah. 26There was great joy in Jerusalem, for since the days of Solomon
son of David king of Israel there had
been nothing like this in Jerusalem.
27The priests and the Levites stood to
bless the people, and God heard them,
for their prayer reached heaven, his
holy dwelling-place.

31 When all this had ended, the
Israelites who were there went
out to the towns of Judah, smashed the
sacred stones and cut down the Asherah
poles. They destroyed the high places
and the altars throughout Judah and
Benjamin and in Ephraim and Manasseh. After they had destroyed all of
them, the Israelites returned to their
own towns and to their own property.

NEW TESTAMENT READING

2 Corinthians 1:12–22

Paul's Change of Plans

12Now this is our boast: Our conscience testifies that we have conducted
ourselves in the world, and especially in
our relations with you, in the holiness
and sincerity that are from God. We
have done so not according to worldly
wisdom but according to God's grace.
13For we do not write to you anything
you cannot read or understand. And I
hope that, 14as you have understood us
in part, you will come to understand
fully that you can boast of us just as we
will boast of you in the day of the Lord
Jesus.

15Because I was confident of this, I
planned to visit you first so that you
might benefit twice. 16I planned to visit
you on my way to Macedonia and to
come back to you from Macedonia, and
then to have you send me on my way to
Judea. 17When I planned this, did I do it
lightly? Or do I make my plans in a
worldly manner so that in the same
breath I say, "Yes, yes" and "No, no"?
18But as surely as God is faithful, our
message to you is not "Yes" and "No".
19For the Son of God, Jesus Christ, who
was preached among you by me and
Silas and Timothy, was not "Yes" and
"No", but in him it has always been
"Yes". 20For no matter how many
promises God has made, they are
"Yes" in Christ. And so through him
the "Amen" is spoken by us to the glory
of God. 21Now it is God who makes
both us and you stand firm in Christ. He
anointed us, 22set his seal of ownership
on us, and put his Spirit in our hearts as
a deposit, guaranteeing what is to come.

READING FROM PSALMS
Psalm 103:13–22

13As a father has compassion on his
children,
so the LORD has compassion on
those who fear him;
14for he knows how we are formed,
he remembers that we are dust.
15As for man, his days are like grass,
he flourishes like a flower of the
field;
16the wind blows over it and it is gone,
and its place remembers it no
more.
17But from everlasting to everlasting
the LORD's love is with those who
fear him,
and his righteousness with their
children's children—
18with those who keep his covenant
and remember to obey his
precepts.

19The LORD has established his throne
in heaven,
and his kingdom rules over all.

20Praise the LORD, you his angels,
you mighty ones who do his
bidding,
who obey his word.
21Praise the LORD, all his heavenly
hosts,
you his servants who do his will.
22Praise the LORD, all his works
everywhere in his dominion.

Praise the LORD, O my soul.

AUGUST 28

DAY 240

OLD TESTAMENT READING
2 Chronicles 31:2–33:20

Contributions for Worship

2Hezekiah assigned the priests and
Levites to divisions—each of them
according to their duties as priests or
Levites—to offer burnt offerings and
fellowship offerings, to minister, to give
thanks and to sing praises at the gates of
the LORD's dwelling. 3The king contributed from his own possessions for the
morning and evening burnt offerings
and for the burnt offerings on the Sabbaths, New Moons and appointed feasts
as written in the Law of the LORD. 4He
ordered the people living in Jerusalem
to give the portion due to the priests and
Levites so that they could devote themselves to the Law of the LORD. 5As soon
as the order went out, the Israelites

generously gave the firstfruits of their
grain, new wine, oil and honey and all
that the fields produced. They brought a
great amount, a tithe of everything.
6The men of Israel and Judah who lived
in the towns of Judah also brought a
tithe of their herds and flocks and a tithe
of the holy things dedicated to the LORD
their God, and they piled them in
heaps. 7They began doing this in the
third month and finished in the seventh
month. 8When Hezekiah and his officials came and saw the heaps, they
praised the LORD and blessed his people
Israel.

9Hezekiah asked the priests and Levites about the heaps; 10and Azariah the
chief priest, from the family of Zadok,
answered, "Since the people began to
bring their contributions to the temple
of the LORD, we have had enough to eat
and plenty to spare, because the LORD
has blessed his people, and this great
amount is left over."

11Hezekiah gave orders to prepare
storerooms in the temple of the LORD,
and this was done. 12Then they faithfully brought in the contributions, tithes
and dedicated gifts. Conaniah, a Levite,
was in charge of these things, and his
brother Shimei was next in rank.
13Jehiel, Azaziah, Nahath, Asahel,
Jerimoth, Jozabad, Eliel, Ismakiah,
Mahath and Benaiah were supervisors
under Conaniah and Shimei his
brother, by appointment of King Hezekiah and Azariah the official in charge
of the temple of God.

14Kore son of Imnah the Levite,
keeper of the East Gate, was in charge
of the freewill offerings given to God,
distributing the contributions made to
the LORD and also the consecrated gifts.
15Eden, Miniamin, Jeshua, Shemaiah,
Amariah and Shecaniah assisted him
faithfully in the towns of the priests,
distributing to their fellow priests
according to their divisions, old and
young alike.

16In addition, they distributed to the
males three years old or more whose
names were in the genealogical records
—all who would enter the temple of the
LORD to perform the daily duties of
their various tasks, according to their
responsibilities and their divisions.
17And they distributed to the priests
enrolled by their families in the
genealogical records and likewise to the
Levites twenty years old or more,
according to their responsibilities and
their divisions. 18They included all the
little ones, the wives, and the sons and
daughters of the whole community
listed in these genealogical records.
For they were faithful in consecrating
themselves.

19As for the priests, the descendants
of Aaron, who lived on the farm lands
around their towns or in any other
towns, men were designated by name to
distribute portions to every male among
them and to all who were recorded in
the genealogies of the Levites.

20This is what Hezekiah did throughout Judah, doing what was good and
right and faithful before the LORD his
God. 21In everything that he undertook
in the service of God's temple and in
obedience to the law and the commands, he sought his God and worked
wholeheartedly. And so he prospered.

Sennacherib Threatens Jerusalem

32 After all that Hezekiah had so
faithfully done, Sennacherib
king of Assyria came and invaded
Judah. He laid siege to the fortified
cities, thinking to conquer them for
himself. 2When Hezekiah saw that Sennacherib had come and that he intended
to make war on Jerusalem, 3he consulted with his officials and military staff
about blocking off the water from the
springs outside the city, and they helped
him. 4A large force of men assembled,
and they blocked all the springs and the
stream that flowed through the land.
"Why should the kings of Assyria come
and find plenty of water?" they said.
5Then he worked hard repairing all the
broken sections of the wall and building

towers on it. He built another wall outside that one and reinforced the supporting terraces of the City of David. He
also made large numbers of weapons
and shields.
6He appointed military officers over
the people and assembled them before
him in the square at the city gate and
encouraged them with these words:
7"Be strong and courageous. Do not be
afraid or discouraged because of the
king of Assyria and the vast army with
him, for there is a greater power with us
than with him. 8With him is only the
arm of flesh, but with us is the LORD our
God to help us and to fight our battles."
And the people gained confidence from
what Hezekiah the king of Judah said.
9Later, when Sennacherib king of
Assyria and all his forces were laying
siege to Lachish, he sent his officers to
Jerusalem with this message for Hezekiah king of Judah and for all the people
of Judah who were there:

10"This is what Sennacherib king
of Assyria says: On what are you
basing your confidence, that you
remain in Jerusalem under siege?
11When Hezekiah says, 'The LORD
our God will save us from the hand
of the king of Assyria,' he is misleading you, to let you die of hunger and thirst. 12Did not Hezekiah
himself remove this god's high
places and altars, saying to Judah
and Jerusalem, 'You must worship
before one altar and burn sacrifices
on it'?
13"Do you not know what I and
my fathers have done to all the
peoples of the other lands? Were
the gods of those nations ever able
to deliver their land from my hand?
14Who of all the gods of these nations that my fathers destroyed has
been able to save his people from
me? How then can your god deliver
you from my hand? 15Now do not
let Hezekiah deceive you and mislead you like this. Do not believe
him, for no god of any nation or
kingdom has been able to deliver
his people from my hand or the
hand of my fathers. How much less
will your god deliver you from my
hand!"

16Sennacherib's officers spoke further against the LORD God and against
his servant Hezekiah. 17The king also
wrote letters insulting the LORD, the
God of Israel, and saying this against
him: "Just as the gods of the peoples of
the other lands did not rescue their people from my hand, so the god of Hezekiah will not rescue his people from my
hand." 18Then they called out in Hebrew to the people of Jerusalem who
were on the wall, to terrify them and
make them afraid in order to capture
the city. 19They spoke about the God of
Jerusalem as they did about the gods of
the other peoples of the world—the
work of men's hands.
20King Hezekiah and the prophet
Isaiah son of Amoz cried out in prayer
to heaven about this. 21And the LORD
sent an angel, who annihilated all the
fighting men and the leaders and
officers in the camp of the Assyrian
king. So he withdrew to his own land in
disgrace. And when he went into the
temple of his god, some of his sons cut
him down with the sword.
22So the LORD saved Hezekiah and
the people of Jerusalem from the hand
of Sennacherib king of Assyria and
from the hand of all others. He took
care of them on every side. 23Many
brought offerings to Jerusalem for the
LORD and valuable gifts for Hezekiah
king of Judah. From then on he was
highly regarded by all the nations.

Hezekiah's Pride, Success and Death

24In those days Hezekiah became ill
and was at the point of death. He
prayed to the LORD, who answered him
and gave him a miraculous sign. 25But
Hezekiah's heart was proud and he did
not respond to the kindness shown him;
therefore the LORD's wrath was on him

and on Judah and Jerusalem. 26Then
Hezekiah repented of the pride of his
heart, as did the people of Jerusalem;
therefore the LORD's wrath did not
come upon them during the days of
Hezekiah.

27Hezekiah had very great riches and
honour, and he made treasuries for his
silver and gold and for his precious
stones, spices, shields and all kinds of
valuables. 28He also made buildings to
store the harvest of grain, new wine and
oil; and he made stalls for various kinds
of cattle, and pens for the flocks. 29He
built villages and acquired great numbers of flocks and herds, for God had
given him very great riches.

30It was Hezekiah who blocked the
upper outlet of the Gihon spring and
channelled the water down to the west
side of the City of David. He succeeded
in everything he undertook. 31But when
envoys were sent by the rulers of Babylon to ask him about the miraculous
sign that had occurred in the land, God
left him to test him and to know everything that was in his heart.

32The other events of Hezekiah's
reign and his acts of devotion are written in the vision of the prophet Isaiah
son of Amoz in the book of the kings of
Judah and Israel. 33Hezekiah rested
with his fathers and was buried on the
hill where the tombs of David's descendants are. All Judah and the people of
Jerusalem honoured him when he died.
And Manasseh his son succeeded him as
king.

Manasseh King of Judah

33 Manasseh was twelve years old
when he became king, and he
reigned in Jerusalem for fifty-five years.
2He did evil in the eyes of the LORD,
following the detestable practices of the
nations the LORD had driven out before
the Israelites. 3He rebuilt the high
places his father Hezekiah had demolished; he also erected altars to the
Baals and made Asherah poles. He
bowed down to all the starry hosts and
worshipped them. 4He built altars in the
temple of the LORD, of which the LORD
had said, "My Name will remain in
Jerusalem for ever." 5In both courts of
the temple of the LORD, he built altars
to all the starry hosts. 6He sacrificed his
sons in the fire in the Valley of Ben
Hinnom, practised sorcery, divination
and witchcraft, and consulted mediums
and spiritists. He did much evil in the
eyes of the LORD, provoking him to
anger.

7He took the carved image he had
made and put it in God's temple, of
which God had said to David and to his
son Solomon, "In this temple and in
Jerusalem, which I have chosen out of
all the tribes of Israel, I will put my
Name for ever. 8I will not again make
the feet of the Israelites leave the land I
assigned to your forefathers, if only
they will be careful to do everything that
I commanded them concerning all the
laws, decrees and ordinances given
through Moses." 9But Manasseh led
Judah and the people of Jerusalem
astray, so that they did more evil than
the nations the LORD had destroyed
before the Israelites.

10The LORD spoke to Manasseh and
his people, but they paid no attention.
11So the LORD brought against them the
army commanders of the king of Assyria, who took Manasseh prisoner,
put a hook in his nose, bound him
with bronze shackles and took him to
Babylon. 12In his distress he sought
the favour of the LORD his God and
humbled himself greatly before the
God of his fathers. 13And when he
prayed to him, the LORD was moved by
his entreaty and listened to his plea; so
he brought him back to Jerusalem and
to his kingdom. Then Manasseh knew
that the LORD is God.

14Afterwards he rebuilt the outer wall
of the City of David, west of the Gihon
spring in the valley, as far as the entrance of the Fish Gate and encircling
the hill of Ophel; he also made it much
higher. He stationed military commanders in all the fortified cities in Judah.

15He got rid of the foreign gods and
removed the image from the temple of
the LORD, as well as all the altars he had
built on the temple hill and in Jerusalem; and he threw them out of the
city. 16Then he restored the altar of the
LORD and sacrificed fellowship offerings
and thank-offerings on it, and told
Judah to serve the LORD, the God of
Israel. 17The people, however, continued to sacrifice at the high places, but
only to the LORD their God.
18The other events of Manasseh's
reign, including his prayer to his God
and the words the seers spoke to him in
the name of the LORD, the God of
Israel, are written in the annals of the
kings of Israel. 19His prayer and how
God was moved by his entreaty, as well
as all his sins and unfaithfulness, and the
sites where he built high places and set
up Asherah poles and idols before he
humbled himself—all are written in the
records of the seers. 20Manasseh rested
with his fathers and was buried in his
palace. And Amon his son succeeded
him as king.

NEW TESTAMENT READING
2 Corinthians 1:23–2:11

23I call God as my witness that it was
in order to spare you that I did not
return to Corinth. 24Not that we lord it
over your faith, but we work with you
for your joy, because it is by faith you
2 stand firm. 1So I made up my mind
that I would not make another
painful visit to you. 2For if I grieve you,
who is left to make me glad but you
whom I have grieved? 3I wrote as I did
so that when I came I should not be
distressed by those who ought to make
me rejoice. I had confidence in all of
you, that you would all share my joy.
4For I wrote to you out of great distress
and anguish of heart and with many
tears, not to grieve you but to let you
know the depth of my love for you.

Forgiveness for the Sinner

5If anyone has caused grief, he has
not so much grieved me as he has
grieved all of you, to some extent—not
to put it too severely. 6The punishment
inflicted on him by the majority is sufficient for him. 7Now instead, you ought
to forgive and comfort him, so that he
will not be overwhelmed by excessive
sorrow. 8I urge you, therefore, to
reaffirm your love for him. 9The reason
I wrote to you was to see if you would
stand the test and be obedient in everything. 10If you forgive anyone, I also
forgive him. And what I have forgiven
—if there was anything to forgive—I
have forgiven in the sight of Christ for
your sake, 11in order that Satan might
not outwit us. For we are not unaware
of his schemes.

READING FROM PROVERBS
Proverbs 21:5–16

5The plans of the diligent lead to profit
as surely as haste leads to poverty.

6A fortune made by a lying tongue
is a fleeting vapour and a deadly
snare.

7The violence of the wicked will drag
them away,
for they refuse to do what is right.

8The way of the guilty is devious,
but the conduct of the innocent is
upright.

9Better to live on a corner of the roof
than share a house with a
quarrelsome wife.

10The wicked man craves evil;
his neighbour gets no mercy from
him.

11When a mocker is punished, the
simple gain wisdom;

when a wise man is instructed, he
gets knowledge.

12The Righteous One takes note of the
house of the wicked
and brings the wicked to ruin.

13If a man shuts his ears to the cry of
the poor,
he too will cry out and not be
answered.

14A gift given in secret soothes anger,
and a bribe concealed in the cloak
pacifies great wrath.

15When justice is done, it brings joy to
the righteous
but terror to evildoers.

16A man who strays from the path of
understanding
comes to rest in the company of the
dead.

DAY 241

AUGUST 29

OLD TESTAMENT READING

2 Chronicles 33:21–35:19

Amon King of Judah

21Amon was twenty-two years old
when he became king, and he reigned in
Jerusalem for two years. 22He did evil in
the eyes of the LORD, as his father Manasseh had done. Amon worshipped
and offered sacrifices to all the idols
Manasseh had made. 23But unlike his
father Manasseh, he did not humble
himself before the LORD; Amon increased his guilt.
24Amon's officials conspired against
him and assassinated him in his palace.
25Then the people of the land killed all
who had plotted against King Amon,
and they made Josiah his son king in his
place.

Josiah's Reforms

34 Josiah was eight years old when
he became king, and he reigned
in Jerusalem for thirty-one years. 2He
did what was right in the eyes of the
LORD and walked in the ways of his
father David, not turning aside to the
right or to the left.
3In the eighth year of his reign, while
he was still young, he began to seek the
God of his father David. In his twelfth
year he began to purge Judah and Jerusalem of high places, Asherah poles,
carved idols and cast images. 4Under his
direction the altars of the Baals were
torn down; he cut to pieces the incense
altars that were above them, and
smashed the Asherah poles, the idols
and the images. These he broke to
pieces and scattered over the graves of
those who had sacrificed to them. 5He
burned the bones of the priests on their
altars, and so he purged Judah and Jerusalem. 6In the towns of Manasseh,
Ephraim and Simeon, as far as Naphtali, and in the ruins around them, 7he
tore down the altars and the Asherah
poles and crushed the idols to powder
and cut to pieces all the incense altars
throughout Israel. Then he went back
to Jerusalem.
8In the eighteenth year of Josiah's
reign, to purify the land and the temple,
he sent Shaphan son of Azaliah and
Maaseiah the ruler of the city, with Joah
son of Joahaz, the recorder, to repair
the temple of the LORD his God.
9They went to Hilkiah the high
priest and gave him the money that had
been brought into the temple of God,
which the Levites who were the doorkeepers had collected from the people

of Manasseh, Ephraim and the entire
remnant of Israel and from all the
people of Judah and Benjamin and the
inhabitants of Jerusalem. [10]Then they
entrusted it to the men appointed to
supervise the work on the LORD's
temple. These men paid the workers
who repaired and restored the temple.
[11]They also gave money to the carpenters and builders to purchase dressed
stone, and timber for joists and beams
for the buildings that the kings of
Judah had allowed to fall into ruin.
[12]The men did the work faithfully.
Over them to direct them were Jahath
and Obadiah, Levites descended from
Merari, and Zechariah and Meshullam,
descended from Kohath. The Levites
—all who were skilled in playing musical instruments—[13]had charge of the
labourers and supervised all the workers from job to job. Some of the Levites
were secretaries, scribes and doorkeepers.

The Book of the Law Found

[14]While they were bringing out the
money that had been taken into the
temple of the LORD, Hilkiah the priest
found the Book of the Law of the LORD
that had been given through Moses.
[15]Hilkiah said to Shaphan the secretary,
"I have found the Book of the Law in
the temple of the LORD." He gave it to
Shaphan.
[16]Then Shaphan took the book to the
king and reported to him: "Your officials are doing everything that has
been committed to them. [17]They have
paid out the money that was in the
temple of the LORD and have entrusted
it to the supervisors and workers."
[18]Then Shaphan the secretary informed
the king, "Hilkiah the priest has given
me a book." And Shaphan read from it
in the presence of the king.
[19]When the king heard the words of
the Law, he tore his robes. [20]He gave
these orders to Hilkiah, Ahikam son of
Shaphan, Abdon son of Micah,
Shaphan the secretary and Asaiah the
king's attendant: [21]"Go and enquire of
the LORD for me and for the remnant in
Israel and Judah about what is written
in this book that has been found. Great
is the LORD's anger that is poured out on
us because our fathers have not kept the
word of the LORD; they have not acted
in accordance with all that is written in
this book."
[22]Hilkiah and those the king had sent
with him went to speak to the
prophetess Huldah, who was the wife of
Shallum son of Tokhath, the son of
Hasrah, keeper of the wardrobe. She
lived in Jerusalem, in the Second
District.
[23]She said to them, "This is what the
LORD, the God of Israel, says: Tell the
man who sent you to me, [24]'This is what
the LORD says: I am going to bring
disaster on this place and its people
—all the curses written in the book that
has been read in the presence of the
king of Judah. [25]Because they have forsaken me and burned incense to other
gods and provoked me to anger by all
that their hands have made, my anger
will be poured out on this place and will
not be quenched.' [26]Tell the king of
Judah, who sent you to enquire of the
LORD, 'This is what the LORD, the God
of Israel, says concerning the words you
heard: [27]Because your heart was responsive and you humbled yourself
before God when you heard what he
spoke against this place and its people,
and because you humbled yourself before me and tore your robes and wept in
my presence, I have heard you, declares
the LORD. [28]Now I will gather you to
your fathers, and you will be buried in
peace. Your eyes will not see all the
disaster I am going to bring on this place
and on those who live here.'"
So they took her answer back to the
king.
[29]Then the king called together all the
elders of Judah and Jerusalem. [30]He
went up to the temple of the LORD with
the men of Judah, the people of Jerusalem, the priests and the Levites—all
the people from the least to the

greatest. He read in their hearing all the words of the Book of the Covenant, which had been found in the temple of the LORD. 31The king stood by his pillar and renewed the covenant in the presence of the LORD—to follow the LORD and keep his commands, regulations and decrees with all his heart and all his soul, and to obey the words of the covenant written in this book.

32Then he made everyone in Jerusalem and Benjamin pledge themselves to it; the people of Jerusalem did this in accordance with the covenant of God, the God of their fathers.

33Josiah removed all the detestable idols from all the territory belonging to the Israelites, and he made all who were present in Israel serve the LORD their God. As long as he lived, they did not fail to follow the LORD, the God of their fathers.

Josiah Celebrates the Passover

35 Josiah celebrated the Passover to the LORD in Jerusalem, and the Passover lamb was slaughtered on the fourteenth day of the first month. 2He appointed the priests to their duties and encouraged them in the service of the LORD's temple. 3He said to the Levites, who instructed all Israel and who had been consecrated to the LORD: "Put the sacred ark in the temple that Solomon son of David king of Israel built. It is not to be carried about on your shoulders. Now serve the LORD your God and his people Israel. 4Prepare yourselves by families in your divisions, according to the directions written by David king of Israel and by his son Solomon.

5"Stand in the holy place with a group of Levites for each sub-division of the families of your fellow countrymen, the lay people. 6Slaughter the Passover lambs, consecrate yourselves and prepare ⌞the lambs⌟ for your fellow countrymen, doing what the LORD commanded through Moses."

7Josiah provided for all the lay people who were there a total of thirty thousand sheep and goats for the Passover offerings, and also three thousand cattle—all from the king's own possessions.

8His officials also contributed voluntarily to the people and the priests and Levites. Hilkiah, Zechariah and Jehiel, the administrators of God's temple, gave the priests two thousand six hundred Passover offerings and three hundred cattle. 9Also Conaniah along with Shemaiah and Nethanel, his brothers, and Hashabiah, Jeiel and Jozabad, the leaders of the Levites, provided five thousand Passover offerings and five hundred head of cattle for the Levites.

10The service was arranged and the priests stood in their places with the Levites in their divisions as the king had ordered. 11The Passover lambs were slaughtered, and the priests sprinkled the blood handed to them, while the Levites skinned the animals. 12They set aside the burnt offerings to give them to the sub-divisions of the families of the people to offer to the LORD, as is written in the Book of Moses. They did the same with the cattle. 13They roasted the Passover animals over the fire as prescribed, and boiled the holy offerings in pots, cauldrons and pans and served them quickly to all the people. 14After this, they made preparations for themselves and for the priests, because the priests, the descendants of Aaron, were sacrificing the burnt offerings and the fat portions until nightfall. So the Levites made preparations for themselves and for the Aaronic priests.

15The musicians, the descendants of Asaph, were in the places prescribed by David, Asaph, Heman and Jeduthun the king's seer. The gatekeepers at each gate did not need to leave their posts, because their fellow Levites made the preparations for them.

16So at that time the entire service of the LORD was carried out for the celebration of the Passover and the offering of burnt offerings on the altar of the LORD, as King Josiah had

ordered. [17]The Israelites who were
present celebrated the Passover at that
time and observed the Feast of Unleavened Bread for seven days. [18]The
Passover had not been observed like
this in Israel since the days of the
prophet Samuel; and none of the kings
of Israel had ever celebrated such a
Passover as did Josiah, with the priests,
the Levites and all Judah and Israel who
were there with the people of Jerusalem. [19]This Passover was celebrated
in the eighteenth year of Josiah's reign.

NEW TESTAMENT READING
2 Corinthians 2:12–3:6

Ministers of the New Covenant

[12]Now when I went to Troas to preach
the gospel of Christ and found that the
Lord had opened a door for me, [13]I still
had no peace of mind, because I did not
find my brother Titus there. So I said
good-bye to them and went on to
Macedonia.

[14]But thanks be to God, who always
leads us in triumphal procession in
Christ and through us spreads everywhere the fragrance of the knowledge
of him. [15]For we are to God the aroma
of Christ among those who are being
saved and those who are perishing. [16]To
the one we are the smell of death; to the
other, the fragrance of life. And who is
equal to such a task? [17]Unlike so many,
we do not peddle the word of God for
profit. On the contrary, in Christ we
speak before God with sincerity, like
men sent from God.

3 Are we beginning to commend
ourselves again? Or do we need,
like some people, letters of recom-
mendation to you or from you? [2]You
yourselves are our letter, written on our
hearts, known and read by everybody.
[3]You show that you are a letter from
Christ, the result of our ministry, written not with ink but with the Spirit of the
living God, not on tablets of stone but
on tablets of human hearts.

[4]Such confidence as this is ours
through Christ before God. [5]Not that
we are competent in ourselves to claim
anything for ourselves, but our compe-
tence comes from God. [6]He has made
us competent as ministers of a new
covenant—not of the letter but of the
Spirit; for the letter kills, but the Spirit
gives life.

READING FROM PSALMS
Psalm 104:1–18

[1]Praise the LORD, O my soul.

O LORD my God, you are very great;
you are clothed with splendour and
majesty.
[2]He wraps himself in light as with a
garment;
he stretches out the heavens like a
tent
[3] and lays the beams of his upper
chambers on their waters.
He makes the clouds his chariot
and rides on the wings of the wind.
[4]He makes winds his messengers,
flames of fire his servants.

[5]He set the earth on its foundations;
it can never be moved.
[6]You covered it with the deep as with
a garment;
the waters stood above the
mountains.
[7]But at your rebuke the waters fled,
at the sound of your thunder they
took to flight;
[8]they flowed over the mountains,
they went down into the valleys,
to the place you assigned for them.
[9]You set a boundary they cannot
cross;
never again will they cover the
earth.

[10]He makes springs pour water into the
ravines;
it flows between the mountains.

[11]They give water to all the beasts of
the field;
the wild donkeys quench their
thirst.
[12]The birds of the air nest by the
waters;
they sing among the branches.
[13]He waters the mountains from his
upper chambers;
the earth is satisfied by the fruit of
his work.
[14]He makes grass grow for the cattle,
and plants for man to cultivate—
bringing forth food from the earth:
[15]wine that gladdens the heart of man,
oil to make his face shine,
and bread that sustains his heart.
[16]The trees of the LORD are well
watered,
the cedars of Lebanon that he
planted.
[17]There the birds make their nests;
the stork has its home in the pine
trees.
[18]The high mountains belong to the
wild goats;
the crags are a refuge for the
conies.

DAY 242

AUGUST 30

OLD TESTAMENT READING

2 Chronicles 35:20–36:23

The Death of Josiah

[20]After all this, when Josiah had set
the temple in order, Neco king of Egypt
went up to fight at Carchemish on the
Euphrates, and Josiah marched out to
meet him in battle. [21]But Neco sent
messengers to him saying, "What quarrel is there between you and me, O king
of Judah? It is not you I am attacking at
this time, but the house with which I am
at war. God has told me to hurry; so
stop opposing God, who is with me, or
he will destroy you."

[22]Josiah, however, would not turn
away from him, but disguised himself to
engage him in battle. He would not
listen to what Neco had said at God's
command but went to fight him on the
plain of Megiddo.

[23]Archers shot King Josiah, and he
told his officers, "Take me away; I am
badly wounded." [24]So they took him
out of his chariot, put him in the other
chariot he had and brought him to Jerusalem, where he died. He was buried in
the tombs of his fathers, and all Judah
and Jerusalem mourned for him.

[25]Jeremiah composed laments for
Josiah, and to this day all the men and
women singers commemorate Josiah in
the laments. These became a tradition
in Israel and are written in the Laments.

[26]The other events of Josiah's reign
and his acts of devotion, according to
what is written in the Law of the LORD
—[27]all the events, from beginning to
end, are written in the book of the kings
36 of Israel and Judah. [1]And the
people of the land took
Jehoahaz son of Josiah and made him
king in Jerusalem in place of his father.

Jehoahaz King of Judah

[2]Jehoahaz was twenty-three years old
when he became king, and he reigned in
Jerusalem for three months. [3]The king
of Egypt dethroned him in Jerusalem
and imposed on Judah a levy of a hundred talents of silver and a talent of gold.
[4]The king of Egypt made Eliakim, a
brother of Jehoahaz, king over Judah
and Jerusalem and changed Eliakim's
name to Jehoiakim. But Neco took
Eliakim's brother Jehoahaz and carried
him off to Egypt.

Jehoiakim King of Judah

5Jehoiakim was twenty-five years old
when he became king, and he reigned in
Jerusalem for eleven years. He did evil
in the eyes of the LORD his God.
6Nebuchadnezzar king of Babylon
attacked him and bound him with
bronze shackles to take him to Babylon.
7Nebuchadnezzar also took to Babylon
articles from the temple of the LORD
and put them in his temple there.
8The other events of Jehoiakim's
reign, the detestable things he did and
all that was found against him, are written in the book of the kings of Israel and
Judah. And Jehoiachin his son succeeded him as king.

Jehoiachin King of Judah

9Jehoiachin was eighteen years old
when he became king, and he reigned in
Jerusalem for three months and ten
days. He did evil in the eyes of the
LORD. 10In the spring, King Nebuchadnezzar sent for him and brought him to
Babylon, together with articles of value
from the temple of the LORD, and he
made Jehoiachin's uncle, Zedekiah,
king over Judah and Jerusalem.

Zedekiah King of Judah

11Zedekiah was twenty-one years old
when he became king, and he reigned in
Jerusalem for eleven years. 12He did
evil in the eyes of the LORD his God and
did not humble himself before Jeremiah
the prophet, who spoke the word of the
LORD. 13He also rebelled against King
Nebuchadnezzar, who had made him
take an oath in God's name. He became
stiff-necked and hardened his heart and
would not turn to the LORD, the God of
Israel. 14Furthermore, all the leaders of
the priests and the people became more
and more unfaithful, following all the
detestable practices of the nations and
defiling the temple of the LORD, which
he had consecrated in Jerusalem.

The Fall of Jerusalem

15The LORD, the God of their fathers,
sent word to them through his messengers again and again, because he had
pity on his people and on his dwelling-
place. 16But they mocked God's messengers, despised his words and scoffed
at his prophets until the wrath of the
LORD was aroused against his people
and there was no remedy. 17He brought
up against them the king of the Babylonians, who killed their young men with
the sword in the sanctuary, and spared
neither young man nor young woman,
old man or aged. God handed all of
them over to Nebuchadnezzar. 18He
carried to Babylon all the articles from
the temple of God, both large and
small, and the treasures of the LORD's
temple and the treasures of the king and
his officials. 19They set fire to God's
temple and broke down the wall of Jerusalem; they burned all the palaces and
destroyed everything of value there.
20He carried into exile to Babylon the
remnant who escaped from the sword,
and they became servants to him and his
sons until the kingdom of Persia came to
power. 21The land enjoyed its sabbath
rests; all the time of its desolation it
rested, until the seventy years were
completed in fulfilment of the word of
the LORD spoken by Jeremiah.
22In the first year of Cyrus king of
Persia, in order to fulfil the word of the
LORD spoken by Jeremiah, the LORD
moved the heart of Cyrus king of Persia
to make a proclamation throughout his
realm and to put it in writing:

23"This is what Cyrus king of Persia
says:

"'The LORD, the God of heaven,
has given me all the kingdoms of
the earth and he has appointed me
to build a temple for him at Jerusalem in Judah. Anyone of his people among you—may the LORD his
God be with him, and let him go
up.'"

NEW TESTAMENT READING
2 Corinthians 3:7–18

The Glory of the New Covenant

7Now if the ministry that brought
death, which was engraved in letters on
stone, came with glory, so that the
Israelites could not look steadily at the
face of Moses because of its glory,
fading though it was, 8will not the
ministry of the Spirit be even more
glorious? 9If the ministry that condemns men is glorious, how much more
glorious is the ministry that brings
righteousness! 10For what was glorious
has no glory now in comparison with the
surpassing glory. 11And if what was
fading away came with glory, how
much greater is the glory of that which
lasts!

12Therefore, since we have such a
hope, we are very bold. 13We are not
like Moses, who would put a veil over
his face to keep the Israelites from
gazing at it while the radiance was
fading away. 14But their minds were
made dull, for to this day the same veil
remains when the old covenant is read.
It has not been removed, because only
in Christ is it taken away. 15Even to
this day when Moses is read, a veil
covers their hearts. 16But whenever anyone turns to the Lord, the veil is taken
away. 17Now the Lord is the Spirit, and
where the Spirit of the Lord is, there
is freedom. 18And we, who with
unveiled faces all reflect the Lord's
glory, are being transformed into his
likeness with ever-increasing glory,
which comes from the Lord, who is
the Spirit.

READING FROM PSALMS
Psalm 104:19–30

19The moon marks off the seasons,
and the sun knows when to go down.
20You bring darkness, it becomes night,
and all the beasts of the forest prowl.
21The lions roar for their prey
and seek their food from God.
22The sun rises, and they steal away;
they return and lie down in their dens.
23Then man goes out to his work,
to his labour until evening.

24How many are your works, O LORD!
In wisdom you made them all;
the earth is full of your creatures.
25There is the sea, vast and spacious,
teeming with creatures beyond number—
living things both large and small.
26There the ships go to and fro,
and the leviathan, which you formed to frolic there.

27These all look to you
to give them their food at the proper time.
28When you give it to them,
they gather it up;
when you open your hand,
they are satisfied with good things.
29When you hide your face,
they are terrified;
when you take away their breath,
they die and return to the dust.
30When you send your Spirit,
they are created,
and you renew the face of the earth.

OLD TESTAMENT READING

Micah 1:1–4:13

1 The word of the LORD that came to
Micah of Moresheth during the
reigns of Jotham, Ahaz and Hezekiah,
kings of Judah—the vision he saw concerning Samaria and Jerusalem.

2Hear, O peoples, all of you,
listen, O earth and all who are in it,
that the Sovereign LORD may witness against you,
the Lord from his holy temple.

Judgment Against Samaria and Jerusalem

3Look! The LORD is coming from his dwelling-place;
he comes down and treads the high places of the earth.
4The mountains melt beneath him
and the valleys split apart,
like wax before the fire,
like water rushing down a slope.
5All this is because of Jacob's transgression,
because of the sins of the house of Israel.
What is Jacob's transgression?
Is it not Samaria?
What is Judah's high place?
Is it not Jerusalem?

6"Therefore I will make Samaria a heap of rubble,
a place for planting vineyards.
I will pour her stones into the valley
and lay bare her foundations.
7All her idols will be broken to pieces;
all her temple gifts will be burned with fire;
I will destroy all her images.
Since she gathered her gifts from the wages of prostitutes,
as the wages of prostitutes they will again be used."

Weeping and Mourning

8Because of this I will weep and wail;
I will go about barefoot and naked.
I will howl like a jackal
and moan like an owl.
9For her wound is incurable;
it has come to Judah.
It has reached the very gate of my people,
even to Jerusalem itself.
10Tell it not in Gath;
weep not at all.
In Beth Ophrah
roll in the dust.
11Pass on in nakedness and shame,
you who live in Shaphir.
Those who live in Zaanan
will not come out.
Beth Ezel is in mourning;
its protection is taken from you.
12Those who live in Maroth writhe in pain,
waiting for relief,
because disaster has come from the LORD,
even to the gate of Jerusalem.
13You who live in Lachish,
harness the team to the chariot.
You were the beginning of sin
to the Daughter of Zion,
for the transgressions of Israel
were found in you.
14Therefore you will give parting gifts
to Moresheth Gath.
The town of Aczib will prove deceptive
to the kings of Israel.
15I will bring a conqueror against you
who live in Mareshah.
He who is the glory of Israel
will come to Adullam.
16Shave your heads in mourning
for the children in whom you delight;
make yourselves as bald as the vulture,
for they will go from you into exile.

Man's Plans and God's

2 Woe to those who plan iniquity,
to those who plot evil on their beds!
At morning's light they carry it out
because it is in their power to do it.
2They covet fields and seize them,
and houses, and take them.
They defraud a man of his home,
a fellow-man of his inheritance.

3Therefore, the LORD says:

"I am planning disaster against this people,
from which you cannot save yourselves.
You will no longer walk proudly,
for it will be a time of calamity.
4In that day men will ridicule you;
they will taunt you with this mournful song:
'We are utterly ruined;
my people's possession is divided up.
He takes it from me!
He assigns our fields to traitors.' "

5Therefore you will have no-one in the assembly of the LORD
to divide the land by lot.

False Prophets

6"Do not prophesy," their prophets say.
"Do not prophesy about these things;
disgrace will not overtake us."
7Should it be said, O house of Jacob:
"Is the Spirit of the LORD angry?
Does he do such things?"

"Do not my words do good
to him whose ways are upright?
8Lately my people have risen up
like an enemy.
You strip off the rich robe
from those who pass by without a care,
like men returning from battle.
9You drive the women of my people
from their pleasant homes.
You take away my blessing
from their children for ever.
10Get up, go away!
For this is not your resting place,
because it is defiled,
it is ruined, beyond all remedy.
11If a liar and deceiver comes and says,
'I will prophesy for you plenty of wine and beer,'
he would be just the prophet for this people!

Deliverance Promised

12"I will surely gather all of you, O Jacob;
I will surely bring together the remnant of Israel.
I will bring them together like sheep in a pen,
like a flock in its pasture;
the place will throng with people.
13One who breaks open the way will go up before them;
they will break through the gate and go out.
Their king will pass through before them,
the LORD at their head."

Leaders and Prophets Rebuked

3 Then I said,

"Listen, you leaders of Jacob,
you rulers of the house of Israel.
Should you not know justice,
2 you who hate good and love evil;
who tear the skin from my people
and the flesh from their bones;
3who eat my people's flesh,
strip off their skin
and break their bones in pieces;
who chop them up like meat for the pan,
like flesh for the pot."

4Then they will cry out to the LORD,
but he will not answer them.
At that time he will hide his face from them
because of the evil they have done.

5This is what the LORD says:

"As for the prophets
who lead my people astray,
if one feeds them,
they proclaim 'peace';
if he does not,
they prepare to wage war against
him.
6Therefore night will come over you,
without visions,
and darkness, without divination.
The sun will set for the prophets,
and the day will go dark for them.
7The seers will be ashamed
and the diviners disgraced.
They will all cover their faces
because there is no answer from
God."

8But as for me, I am filled with power,
with the Spirit of the LORD,
and with justice and might,
to declare to Jacob his transgression,
to Israel his sin.
9Hear this, you leaders of the house of
Jacob,
you rulers of the house of Israel,
who despise justice
and distort all that is right;
10who build Zion with bloodshed,
and Jerusalem with wickedness.
11Her leaders judge for a bribe,
her priests teach for a price,
and her prophets tell fortunes for
money.
Yet they lean upon the LORD and say,
"Is not the LORD among us?
No disaster will come upon us."
12Therefore because of you,
Zion will be ploughed like a field,
Jerusalem will become a heap of
rubble,
the temple hill a mound overgrown
with thickets.

The Mountain of the LORD

4 In the last days

the mountain of the LORD's temple
will be established
as chief among the mountains;
it will be raised above the hills,
and peoples will stream to it.

2Many nations will come and say,

"Come, let us go up to the mountain
of the LORD,
to the house of the God of Jacob.
He will teach us his ways,
so that we may walk in his paths."
The law will go out from Zion,
the word of the LORD from
Jerusalem.
3He will judge between many peoples
and will settle disputes for strong
nations far and wide.
They will beat their swords into
ploughshares
and their spears into pruning
hooks.
Nation will not take up sword against
nation,
nor will they train for war any
more.
4Every man will sit under his own vine
and under his own fig-tree,
and no-one will make them afraid,
for the LORD Almighty has spoken.
5All the nations may walk
in the name of their gods;
we will walk in the name of the LORD
our God for ever and ever.

The LORD's Plan

6"In that day," declares the LORD,

"I will gather the lame;
I will assemble the exiles
and those I have brought to grief.
7I will make the lame a remnant,
those driven away a strong nation.
The LORD will rule over them in
Mount Zion
from that day and for ever.
8As for you, O watchtower of the
flock,
O stronghold of the Daughter of
Zion,
the former dominion will be restored
to you;

kingship will come to the Daughter
of Jerusalem."

9 Why do you now cry aloud—
have you no king?
Has your counsellor perished,
that pain seizes you like that of a
woman in labour?
10 Writhe in agony, O Daughter of
Zion,
like a woman in labour,
for now you must leave the city
to camp in the open field.
You will go to Babylon;
there you will be rescued.
There the LORD will redeem you
out of the hand of your enemies.

11 But now many nations
are gathered against you.
They say, "Let her be defiled,
let our eyes gloat over Zion!"
12 But they do not know
the thoughts of the LORD;
they do not understand his plan,
he who gathers them like sheaves
to the threshing-floor.

13 "Rise and thresh, O Daughter of
Zion,
for I will give you horns of iron;
I will give you hoofs of bronze
and you will break to pieces many
nations."

You will devote their ill-gotten gains
to the LORD,
their wealth to the Lord of all the
earth.

NEW TESTAMENT READING
2 Corinthians 4:1–18

Treasures in Jars of Clay

4 Therefore, since through God's mercy we have this ministry, we do
not lose heart.
2 Rather, we have renounced secret and shameful ways; we do not use deception, nor do we distort the word of God. On the contrary, by setting forth the truth plainly we commend ourselves to every man's conscience in the sight of God.
3 And even if our gospel is veiled, it is veiled to those who are perishing.
4 The god of this age has blinded the minds of unbelievers, so that they cannot see the light of the gospel of the glory of Christ, who is the image of God.
5 For we do not preach ourselves, but Jesus Christ as Lord, and ourselves as your servants for Jesus' sake.
6 For God, who said, "Let light shine out of darkness," made his light shine in our hearts to give us the light of the knowledge of the glory of God in the face of Christ.

7 But we have this treasure in jars of clay to show that this all-surpassing power is from God and not from us.
8 We are hard pressed on every side, but not crushed; perplexed, but not in despair;
9 persecuted, but not abandoned; struck down, but not destroyed.
10 We always carry around in our body the death of Jesus, so that the life of Jesus may also be revealed in our body.
11 For we who are alive are always being given over to death for Jesus' sake, so that his life may be revealed in our mortal body.
12 So then, death is at work in us, but life is at work in you.

13 It is written: "I believed; therefore I have spoken." With that same spirit of faith we also believe and therefore speak,
14 because we know that the one who raised the Lord Jesus from the dead will also raise us with Jesus and present us with you in his presence.
15 All this is for your benefit, so that the grace that is reaching more and more people may cause thanksgiving to overflow to the glory of God.

16 Therefore we do not lose heart. Though outwardly we are wasting away, yet inwardly we are being renewed day by day.
17 For our light and momentary troubles are achieving for us an eternal glory that far outweighs them all.
18 So we fix our eyes not on what is seen, but on what is unseen. For what is seen is temporary, but what is unseen is eternal.

READING FROM PSALMS
Psalm 104:31–35

31May the glory of the LORD endure for ever;
may the LORD rejoice in his works—
32he who looks at the earth, and it trembles,
who touches the mountains, and they smoke.

33I will sing to the LORD all my life;
I will sing praise to my God as long as I live.
34May my meditation be pleasing to him,
as I rejoice in the LORD.
35But may sinners vanish from the earth
and the wicked be no more.

Praise the LORD, O my soul.

Praise the LORD.

SEPTEMBER 1

DAY 244

OLD TESTAMENT READING
Micah 5:1–7:20

A Promised Ruler From Bethlehem

5 Marshal your troops, O city of troops,
for a siege is laid against us.
They will strike Israel's ruler
on the cheek with a rod.

2"But you, Bethlehem Ephrathah,
though you are small among the clans of Judah,
out of you will come for me
one who will be ruler over Israel,
whose origins are from of old,
from ancient times."

3Therefore Israel will be abandoned
until the time when she who is in labour gives birth
and the rest of his brothers return
to join the Israelites.

4He will stand and shepherd his flock
in the strength of the LORD,
in the majesty of the name of the LORD his God.
And they will live securely, for then his greatness
will reach to the ends of the earth.
5 And he will be their peace.

Deliverance and Destruction

When the Assyrian invades our land
and marches through our fortresses,
we will raise against him seven shepherds,
even eight leaders of men.
6They will rule the land of Assyria
with the sword,
the land of Nimrod with drawn sword.
He will deliver us from the Assyrian
when he invades our land
and marches into our borders.

7The remnant of Jacob will be
in the midst of many peoples
like dew from the LORD,
like showers on the grass,
which do not wait for man
or linger for mankind.
8The remnant of Jacob will be among the nations,
in the midst of many peoples,
like a lion among the beasts of the forest,
like a young lion among flocks of sheep,
which mauls and mangles as it goes,
and no-one can rescue.

[9]Your hand will be lifted up in
triumph over your enemies,
and all your foes will be destroyed.

[10]"In that day," declares the LORD,

"I will destroy your horses from
among you
and demolish your chariots.
[11]I will destroy the cities of your land
and tear down all your strongholds.
[12]I will destroy your witchcraft
and you will no longer cast spells.
[13]I will destroy your carved images
and your sacred stones from among
you;
you will no longer bow down
to the work of your hands.
[14]I will uproot from among you your
Asherah poles
and demolish your cities.
[15]I will take vengeance in anger and
wrath
upon the nations that have not
obeyed me."

The LORD's Case Against Israel

6 Listen to what the LORD says:

"Stand up, plead your case before
the mountains;
let the hills hear what you have to
say.
[2]Hear, O mountains, the LORD's
accusation;
listen, you everlasting foundations
of the earth.
For the LORD has a case against his
people;
he is lodging a charge against
Israel.

[3]"My people, what have I done to
you?
How have I burdened you?
Answer me.
[4]I brought you up out of Egypt
and redeemed you from the land of
slavery.
I sent Moses to lead you,
also Aaron and Miriam.
[5]My people, remember
what Balak king of Moab
counselled
and what Balaam son of Beor
answered.
Remember ⌞your journey⌟ from
Shittim to Gilgal,
that you may know the righteous
acts of the LORD."

[6]With what shall I come before the
LORD
and bow down before the exalted
God?
Shall I come before him with burnt
offerings,
with calves a year old?
[7]Will the LORD be pleased with
thousands of rams,
with ten thousand rivers of oil?
Shall I offer my firstborn for my
transgression,
the fruit of my body for the sin of
my soul?
[8]He has showed you, O man, what is
good.
And what does the LORD require
of you?
To act justly and to love mercy
and to walk humbly with your
God.

Israel's Guilt and Punishment

[9]Listen! The LORD is calling to the
city—
and to fear your name is wisdom—
"Heed the rod and the One who
appointed it.
[10]Am I still to forget, O wicked house,
your ill-gotten treasures
and the short ephah, which is
accursed?
[11]Shall I acquit a man with dishonest
scales,
with a bag of false weights?
[12]Her rich men are violent;
her people are liars
and their tongues speak
deceitfully.
[13]Therefore, I have begun to destroy
you,
to ruin you because of your sins.

14You will eat but not be satisfied;
your stomach will still be empty.
You will store up but save nothing,
because what you save I will give to the sword.
15You will plant but not harvest;
you will press olives but not use the oil on yourselves,
you will crush grapes but not drink the wine.
16You have observed the statutes of Omri
and all the practices of Ahab's house,
and you have followed their traditions.
Therefore I will give you over to ruin
and your people to derision;
you will bear the scorn of the nations."

Israel's Misery

7 What misery is mine!
I am like one who gathers summer fruit
at the gleaning of the vineyard;
there is no cluster of grapes to eat,
none of the early figs that I crave.
2The godly have been swept from the land;
not one upright man remains.
All men lie in wait to shed blood;
each hunts his brother with a net.
3Both hands are skilled in doing evil;
the ruler demands gifts,
the judge accepts bribes,
the powerful dictate what they desire—
they all conspire together.
4The best of them is like a brier,
the most upright worse than a thorn hedge.
The day of your watchmen has come,
the day God visits you.
Now is the time of their confusion.
5Do not trust a neighbour;
put no confidence in a friend.
Even with her who lies in your embrace
be careful of your words.
6For a son dishonours his father,
a daughter rises up against her mother,
a daughter-in-law against her mother-in-law—
a man's enemies are the members of his own household.

7But as for me, I watch in hope for the LORD,
I wait for God my Saviour;
my God will hear me.

Israel Will Rise

8Do not gloat over me, my enemy!
Though I have fallen, I will rise.
Though I sit in darkness,
the LORD will be my light.
9Because I have sinned against him,
I will bear the LORD's wrath,
until he pleads my case
and establishes my right.
He will bring me out into the light;
I will see his righteousness.
10Then my enemy will see it
and will be covered with shame,
she who said to me,
"Where is the LORD your God?"
My eyes will see her downfall;
even now she will be trampled underfoot
like mire in the streets.

11The day for building your walls will come,
the day for extending your boundaries.
12In that day people will come to you
from Assyria and the cities of Egypt,
even from Egypt to the Euphrates
and from sea to sea
and from mountain to mountain.
13The earth will become desolate
because of its inhabitants,
as the result of their deeds.

Prayer and Praise

14Shepherd your people with your staff,
the flock of your inheritance,

which lives by itself in a forest,
in fertile pasture-lands.
Let them feed in Bashan and Gilead
as in days long ago.

15"As in the days when you came out of
Egypt,
I will show them my wonders."

16Nations will see and be ashamed,
deprived of all their power.
They will lay their hands on their
mouths
and their ears will become deaf.
17They will lick dust like a snake,
like creatures that crawl on the
ground.
They will come trembling out of their
dens;
they will turn in fear to the LORD
our God
and will be afraid of you.
18Who is a God like you,
who pardons sin and forgives the
transgression
of the remnant of his inheritance?
You do not stay angry for ever
but delight to show mercy.
19You will again have compassion on
us;
you will tread our sins underfoot
and hurl all our iniquities into the
depths of the sea.
20You will be true to Jacob,
and show mercy to Abraham,
as you pledged on oath to our fathers
in days long ago.

NEW TESTAMENT READING
2 Corinthians 5:1–10

Our Heavenly Dwelling

5 Now we know that if the earthly
tent we live in is destroyed, we
have a building from God, an eternal
house in heaven, not built by human
hands. 2Meanwhile we groan, longing
to be clothed with our heavenly dwelling, 3because when we are clothed, we
will not be found naked. 4For while we
are in this tent, we groan and are burdened, because we do not wish to be
unclothed but to be clothed with our
heavenly dwelling, so that what is mortal may be swallowed up by life. 5Now it
is God who has made us for this very
purpose and has given us the Spirit as a
deposit, guaranteeing what is to come.
6Therefore we are always confident
and know that as long as we are at home
in the body we are away from the Lord.
7We live by faith, not by sight. 8We are
confident, I say, and would prefer to be
away from the body and at home with
the Lord. 9So we make it our goal to
please him, whether we are at home in
the body or away from it. 10For we must
all appear before the judgment seat of
Christ, that each one may receive what
is due to him for the things done while in
the body, whether good or bad.

READING FROM PROVERBS
Proverbs 21:17–26

17He who loves pleasure will become
poor;
whoever loves wine and oil will
never be rich.

18The wicked become a ransom for the
righteous,
and the unfaithful for the upright.

19Better to live in a desert
than with a quarrelsome and
ill-tempered wife.

20In the house of the wise are stores of
choice food and oil,
but a foolish man devours all he
has.

21He who pursues righteousness and
love
finds life, prosperity and honour.

22A wise man attacks the city of the
mighty

and pulls down the stronghold in
which they trust.

23He who guards his mouth and his
tongue
keeps himself from calamity.

24The proud and arrogant man—
"Mocker" is his name;
he behaves with overweening
pride.

25The sluggard's craving will be the
death of him,
because his hands refuse to work.
26All day long he craves for more,
but the righteous give without
sparing.

SEPTEMBER 2

DAY 245

OLD TESTAMENT READING
Isaiah 1:1–2:22

1 The vision concerning Judah and
Jerusalem that Isaiah son of Amoz
saw during the reigns of Uzziah,
Jotham, Ahaz and Hezekiah, kings of
Judah.

A Rebellious Nation

2Hear, O heavens! Listen, O earth!
For the LORD has spoken:
"I reared children and brought them
up,
but they have rebelled against me.
3The ox knows his master,
the donkey his owner's manger,
but Israel does not know,
my people do not understand."

4Ah, sinful nation,
a people loaded with guilt,
a brood of evildoers,
children given to corruption!
They have forsaken the LORD;
they have spurned the Holy One of
Israel
and turned their backs on him.

5Why should you be beaten any more?
Why do you persist in rebellion?
Your whole head is injured,
your whole heart afflicted.
6From the sole of your foot to the top
of your head
there is no soundness—
only wounds and bruises
and open sores,
not cleansed or bandaged
or soothed with oil.

7Your country is desolate,
your cities burned with fire;
your fields are being stripped by
foreigners
right before you,
laid waste as when overthrown by
strangers.
8The Daughter of Zion is left
like a shelter in a vineyard,
like a hut in a field of melons,
like a city under siege.
9Unless the LORD Almighty
had left us some survivors,
we would have become like Sodom,
we would have been like
Gomorrah.

10Hear the word of the LORD,
you rulers of Sodom;
listen to the law of our God,
you people of Gomorrah!
11"The multitude of your sacrifices—
what are they to me?" says the
LORD.
"I have more than enough of burnt
offerings,
of rams and the fat of fattened
animals;
I have no pleasure
in the blood of bulls and lambs and
goats.

12When you come to appear before me,
who has asked this of you,
this trampling of my courts?
13Stop bringing meaningless offerings!
Your incense is detestable to me.
New Moons, Sabbaths and
convocations—
I cannot bear your evil assemblies.
14Your New Moon festivals and your
appointed feasts
my soul hates.
They have become a burden to me;
I am weary of bearing them.
15When you spread out your hands in
prayer,
I will hide my eyes from you;
even if you offer many prayers,
I will not listen.
Your hands are full of blood;
16 wash and make yourselves clean.
Take your evil deeds
out of my sight!
Stop doing wrong,
17 learn to do right!
Seek justice,
encourage the oppressed.
Defend the cause of the fatherless,
plead the case of the widow.

18"Come now, let us reason together,"
says the LORD.
"Though your sins are like scarlet,
they shall be as white as snow;
though they are red as crimson,
they shall be like wool.
19If you are willing and obedient,
you will eat the best from the land;
20but if you resist and rebel,
you will be devoured by the
sword."
For the mouth of the LORD has
spoken.

21See how the faithful city
has become a harlot!
She once was full of justice;
righteousness used to dwell in
her—
but now murderers!
22Your silver has become dross,
your choice wine is diluted with
water.
23Your rulers are rebels,
companions of thieves;
they all love bribes
and chase after gifts.
They do not defend the cause of the
fatherless;
the widow's case does not come
before them.
24Therefore the Lord, the LORD
Almighty,
the Mighty One of Israel, declares:
"Ah, I will get relief from my foes
and avenge myself on my enemies.
25I will turn my hand against you;
I will thoroughly purge away your
dross
and remove all your impurities.
26I will restore your judges as in days of
old,
your counsellors as at the
beginning.
Afterwards you will be called
the City of Righteousness,
the Faithful City."

27Zion will be redeemed with justice,
her penitent ones with
righteousness.
28But rebels and sinners will both be
broken,
and those who forsake the LORD
will perish.
29"You will be ashamed because of the
sacred oaks
in which you have delighted;
you will be disgraced because of the
gardens
that you have chosen.
30You will be like an oak with fading
leaves,
like a garden without water.
31The mighty man will become tinder
and his work a spark;
both will burn together,
with no-one to quench the fire."

The Mountain of the LORD

2 This is what Isaiah son of Amoz saw concerning Judah and Jerusalem:

2In the last days

the mountain of the LORD's temple
will be established
as chief among the mountains;
it will be raised above the hills,
and all nations will stream to it.

3Many peoples will come and say,

"Come, let us go up to the mountain
of the LORD,
to the house of the God of Jacob.
He will teach us his ways,
so that we may walk in his paths."
The law will go out from Zion,
the word of the LORD from
Jerusalem.
4He will judge between the nations
and will settle disputes for many
peoples.
They will beat their swords into
ploughshares
and their spears into pruning
hooks.
Nation will not take up sword against
nation,
nor will they train for war any
more.

5Come, O house of Jacob,
let us walk in the light of the LORD.

The Day of the LORD

6You have abandoned your people,
the house of Jacob.
They are full of superstitions from
the East;
they practise divination like the
Philistines
and clasp hands with pagans.
7Their land is full of silver and gold;
there is no end to their treasures.
Their land is full of horses;
there is no end to the chariots.
8Their land is full of idols;
they bow down to the work of their
hands,
to what their fingers have made.
9So man will be brought low
and mankind humbled—
do not forgive them.

10Go into the rocks,
hide in the ground
from dread of the LORD
and the splendour of his majesty!
11The eyes of the arrogant man will be
humbled
and the pride of men brought low;
the LORD alone will be exalted in that
day.

12The LORD Almighty has a day in
store
for all the proud and lofty,
for all that is exalted
(and they will be humbled),
13for all the cedars of Lebanon, tall and
lofty,
and all the oaks of Bashan,
14for all the towering mountains
and all the high hills,
15for every lofty tower
and every fortified wall,
16for every trading ship
and every stately vessel.
17The arrogance of man will be brought
low
and the pride of men humbled;
the LORD alone will be exalted in that
day,
18 and the idols will totally disappear.

19Men will flee to caves in the rocks
and to holes in the ground
from the dread of the LORD
and the splendour of his majesty,
when he rises to shake the earth.
20In that day men will throw away
to the rodents and bats
their idols of silver and idols of gold,
which they made to worship.
21They will flee to caverns in the rocks
and to the overhanging crags
from dread of the LORD
and the splendour of his majesty,
when he rises to shake the earth.

22Stop trusting in man,
who has but a breath in his nostrils.
Of what account is he?

NEW TESTAMENT READING
2 Corinthians 5:11–6:2

The Ministry of Reconciliation

11Since, then, we know what it is to
fear the Lord, we try to persuade men.
What we are is plain to God, and I hope
it is also plain to your conscience. 12We
are not trying to commend ourselves to
you again, but are giving you an opportunity to take pride in us, so that you can
answer those who take pride in what is
seen rather than in what is in the heart.
13If we are out of our mind, it is for the
sake of God; if we are in our right mind,
it is for you. 14For Christ's love compels
us, because we are convinced that one
died for all, and therefore all died.
15And he died for all, that those who
live should no longer live for themselves
but for him who died for them and was
raised again.

16So from now on we regard no-one
from a worldly point of view. Though
we once regarded Christ in this way, we
do so no longer. 17Therefore, if anyone
is in Christ, he is a new creation; the old
has gone, the new has come! 18All this is
from God, who reconciled us to himself
through Christ and gave us the ministry
of reconciliation: 19that God was recon-
ciling the world to himself in Christ, not
counting men's sins against them. And
he has committed to us the message of
reconciliation. 20We are therefore
Christ's ambassadors, as though God
were making his appeal through us.
We implore you on Christ's behalf: Be
reconciled to God. 21God made him
who had no sin to be sin for us, so that in
him we might become the righteousness
of God.

6 As God's fellow-workers we urge you not to receive God's grace in vain. 2For he says,

"In the time of my favour I heard
you,
and in the day of salvation I helped
you."

I tell you, now is the time of God's favour, now is the day of salvation.

READING FROM PSALMS
Psalm 105:1–11

1Give thanks to the LORD, call on his
name;
make known among the nations
what he has done.
2Sing to him, sing praise to him;
tell of all his wonderful acts.
3Glory in his holy name;
let the hearts of those who seek the
LORD rejoice.
4Look to the LORD and his strength;
seek his face always.

5Remember the wonders he has done,
his miracles, and the judgments he
pronounced,
6O descendants of Abraham his
servant,
O sons of Jacob, his chosen ones.
7He is the LORD our God;
his judgments are in all the earth.

8He remembers his covenant for ever,
the word he commanded, for a
thousand generations,
9the covenant he made with
Abraham,
the oath he swore to Isaac.
10He confirmed it to Jacob as a decree,
to Israel as an everlasting
covenant:
11"To you I will give the land of
Canaan
as the portion you will inherit."

OLD TESTAMENT READING
Isaiah 3:1–5:7

Judgment on Jerusalem and Judah

3 See now, the Lord,
the LORD Almighty,
is about to take from Jerusalem and Judah
both supply and support:
all supplies of food and all supplies of water,
2 the hero and warrior,
the judge and prophet,
the soothsayer and elder,
3 the captain of fifty and man of rank,
the counsellor, skilled craftsman
and clever enchanter.

4 I will make boys their officials;
mere children will govern them.
5 People will oppress each other—
man against man, neighbour against neighbour.
The young will rise up against the old,
the base against the honourable.

6 A man will seize one of his brothers
at his father's home, and say,
"You have a cloak, you be our leader;
take charge of this heap of ruins!"
7 But in that day he will cry out,
"I have no remedy.
I have no food or clothing in my house;
do not make me the leader of the people."

8 Jerusalem staggers,
Judah is falling;
their words and deeds are against the LORD,
defying his glorious presence.
9 The look on their faces testifies against them;
they parade their sin like Sodom;
they do not hide it.
Woe to them!
They have brought disaster upon themselves.

10 Tell the righteous it will be well with them,
for they will enjoy the fruit of their deeds.
11 Woe to the wicked! Disaster is upon them!
They will be paid back for what their hands have done.

12 Youths oppress my people,
women rule over them.
O my people, your guides lead you astray;
they turn you from the path.

13 The LORD takes his place in court;
he rises to judge the people.
14 The LORD enters into judgment
against the elders and leaders of his people:
"It is you who have ruined my vineyard;
the plunder from the poor is in your houses.
15 What do you mean by crushing my people
and grinding the faces of the poor?"
declares the Lord, the LORD Almighty.

16 The LORD says,
"The women of Zion are haughty,
walking along with outstretched necks,
flirting with their eyes,
tripping along with mincing steps,
with ornaments jingling on their ankles.
17 Therefore the Lord will bring sores
on the heads of the women of Zion;

the LORD will make their scalps
bald."

18In that day the Lord will snatch
away their finery: the bangles and headbands and crescent necklaces, 19the
ear-rings and bracelets and veils, 20the
head-dresses and ankle chains and
sashes, the perfume bottles and charms,
21the signet rings and nose rings, 22the
fine robes and the capes and cloaks, the
purses 23and mirrors, and the linen garments and tiaras and shawls.

24Instead of fragrance there will be a
stench;
instead of a sash, a rope;
instead of well-dressed hair,
baldness;
instead of fine clothing, sackcloth;
instead of beauty, branding.
25Your men will fall by the sword,
your warriors in battle.
26The gates of Zion will lament and
mourn;
destitute, she will sit on the
ground.

4 In that day seven women
will take hold of one man
and say, "We will eat our own food
and provide our own clothes;
only let us be called by your name.
Take away our disgrace!"

The Branch of the LORD

2In that day the Branch of the LORD
will be beautiful and glorious, and the
fruit of the land will be the pride and
glory of the survivors in Israel. 3Those
who are left in Zion, who remain in
Jerusalem, will be called holy, all who
are recorded among the living in Jerusalem. 4The Lord will wash away the
filth of the women of Zion; he will
cleanse the bloodstains from Jerusalem
by a spirit of judgment and a spirit of
fire. 5Then the LORD will create over all
of Mount Zion and over those who
assemble there a cloud of smoke by day
and a glow of flaming fire by night; over
all the glory will be a canopy. 6It will be
a shelter and shade from the heat of the
day, and a refuge and hiding-place from
the storm and rain.

The Song of the Vineyard

5 I will sing for the one I love
a song about his vineyard:
My loved one had a vineyard
on a fertile hillside.
2He dug it up and cleared it of stones
and planted it with the choicest
vines.
He built a watchtower in it
and cut out a winepress as well.
Then he looked for a crop of good
grapes,
but it yielded only bad fruit.

3"Now you dwellers in Jerusalem and
men of Judah,
judge between me and my
vineyard.
4What more could have been done for
my vineyard
than I have done for it?
When I looked for good grapes,
why did it yield only bad?
5Now I will tell you
what I am going to do to my
vineyard:
I will take away its hedge,
and it will be destroyed;
I will break down its wall,
and it will be trampled.
6I will make it a wasteland,
neither pruned nor cultivated,
and briers and thorns will grow
there.
I will command the clouds
not to rain on it."

7The vineyard of the LORD Almighty
is the house of Israel,
and the men of Judah
are the garden of his delight.
And he looked for justice, but saw
bloodshed;
for righteousness, but heard cries
of distress.

NEW TESTAMENT READING
2 Corinthians 6:3–7:1

Paul's Hardships

3We put no stumbling-block in anyone's path, so that our ministry will not
be discredited. 4Rather, as servants of
God we commend ourselves in every
way: in great endurance; in troubles,
hardships and distresses; 5in beatings,
imprisonments and riots; in hard work,
sleepless nights and hunger; 6in purity,
understanding, patience and kindness;
in the Holy Spirit and in sincere love; 7in
truthful speech and in the power of
God; with weapons of righteousness in
the right hand and in the left; 8through
glory and dishonour, bad report and
good report; genuine, yet regarded as
impostors; 9known, yet regarded as unknown; dying, and yet we live on;
beaten, and yet not killed; 10sorrowful,
yet always rejoicing; poor, yet making
many rich; having nothing, and yet
possessing everything.

11We have spoken freely to you,
Corinthians, and opened wide our
hearts to you. 12We are not withholding
our affection from you, but you are
withholding yours from us. 13As a fair
exchange—I speak as to my children
—open wide your hearts also.

Do Not Be Yoked With Unbelievers

14Do not be yoked together with unbelievers. For what do righteousness
and wickedness have in common? Or
what fellowship can light have with
darkness? 15What harmony is there between Christ and Belial? What does a
believer have in common with an unbeliever? 16What agreement is there between the temple of God and idols? For
we are the temple of the living God. As
God has said: "I will live with them and
walk among them, and I will be their
God, and they will be my people."

17"Therefore come out from them
and be separate,
says the Lord.
Touch no unclean thing,
and I will receive you."
18"I will be a Father to you,
and you will be my sons and
daughters,
says the Lord Almighty."

7 Since we have these promises, dear
friends, let us purify ourselves from
everything that contaminates body and
spirit, perfecting holiness out of reverence for God.

READING FROM PSALMS
Psalm 105:12–22

12When they were but few in number,
few indeed, and strangers in it,
13they wandered from nation to nation,
from one kingdom to another.
14He allowed no-one to oppress them;
for their sake he rebuked kings:
15"Do not touch my anointed ones;
do my prophets no harm."

16He called down famine on the land
and destroyed all their supplies of
food;
17and he sent a man before them—
Joseph, sold as a slave.
18They bruised his feet with shackles,
his neck was put in irons,
19till what he foretold came to pass,
till the word of the LORD proved
him true.
20The king sent and released him,
the ruler of peoples set him free.
21He made him master of his
household,
ruler over all he possessed,
22to instruct his princes as he pleased
and teach his elders wisdom.

SEPTEMBER 4

OLD TESTAMENT READING
Isaiah 5:8–8:10

Woes and Judgments

8Woe to you who add house to house
and join field to field
till no space is left
and you live alone in the land.

9The LORD Almighty has declared in my hearing:

"Surely the great houses will become desolate,
the fine mansions left without occupants.
10A ten-acre vineyard will produce only a bath of wine,
a homer of seed only an ephah of grain."

11Woe to those who rise early in the morning
to run after their drinks,
who stay up late at night
till they are inflamed with wine.
12They have harps and lyres at their banquets,
tambourines and flutes and wine,
but they have no regard for the deeds of the LORD,
no respect for the work of his hands.
13Therefore my people will go into exile
for lack of understanding;
their men of rank will die of hunger
and their masses will be parched with thirst.
14Therefore the grave enlarges its appetite
and opens its mouth without limit;
into it will descend their nobles and masses
with all their brawlers and revellers.
15So man will be brought low
and mankind humbled,
the eyes of the arrogant humbled.
16But the LORD Almighty will be exalted by his justice,
and the holy God will show himself holy by his righteousness.
17Then sheep will graze as in their own pasture;
lambs will feed among the ruins of the rich.

18Woe to those who draw sin along with cords of deceit,
and wickedness as with cart ropes,
19to those who say, "Let God hurry,
let him hasten his work
so that we may see it.
Let it approach,
let the plan of the Holy One of Israel come,
so that we may know it."

20Woe to those who call evil good
and good evil,
who put darkness for light
and light for darkness,
who put bitter for sweet
and sweet for bitter.

21Woe to those who are wise in their own eyes
and clever in their own sight.

22Woe to those who are heroes at drinking wine
and champions at mixing drinks,
23who acquit the guilty for a bribe,
but deny justice to the innocent.

24Therefore, as tongues of fire lick up straw
and as dry grass sinks down in the flames,
so their roots will decay
and their flowers blow away like dust;

for they have rejected the law of the
LORD Almighty
and spurned the word of the Holy
One of Israel.
25Therefore the LORD's anger burns
against his people;
his hand is raised and he strikes
them down.
The mountains shake,
and the dead bodies are like refuse
in the streets.

Yet for all this, his anger is not turned
away,
his hand is still upraised.

26He lifts up a banner for the distant
nations,
he whistles for those at the ends of
the earth.
Here they come,
swiftly and speedily!
27Not one of them grows tired or
stumbles,
not one slumbers or sleeps;
not a belt is loosened at the waist,
not a sandal thong is broken.
28Their arrows are sharp,
all their bows are strung;
their horses' hoofs seem like flint,
their chariot wheels like a
whirlwind.
29Their roar is like that of the lion,
they roar like young lions;
they growl as they seize their prey
and carry it off with no-one to
rescue.
30In that day they will roar over it
like the roaring of the sea.
And if one looks at the land,
he will see darkness and distress;
even the light will be darkened by
the clouds.

Isaiah's Commission

6 In the year that King Uzziah died, I
saw the Lord seated on a throne,
high and exalted, and the train of his
robe filled the temple. 2Above him were
seraphs, each with six wings: With two
wings they covered their faces, with
two they covered their feet, and with
two they were flying. 3And they were
calling to one another:

"Holy, holy, holy is the LORD
Almighty;
the whole earth is full of his glory."

4At the sound of their voices the doorposts and thresholds shook and the
temple was filled with smoke.
5"Woe to me!" I cried. "I am ruined!
For I am a man of unclean lips, and I live
among a people of unclean lips, and my
eyes have seen the King, the LORD
Almighty."
6Then one of the seraphs flew to me
with a live coal in his hand, which he had
taken with tongs from the altar. 7With it
he touched my mouth and said, "See,
this has touched your lips; your guilt is
taken away and your sin atoned for."
8Then I heard the voice of the Lord
saying, "Whom shall I send? And who
will go for us?"
And I said, "Here am I. Send me!"
9He said, "Go and tell this people:

"'Be ever hearing, but never
understanding;
be ever seeing, but never
perceiving.'
10Make the heart of this people
calloused;
make their ears dull
and close their eyes.
Otherwise they might see with their
eyes,
hear with their ears,
understand with their hearts,
and turn and be healed."

11Then I said, "For how long, O
Lord?"
And he answered:

"Until the cities lie ruined
and without inhabitant,
until the houses are left deserted
and the fields ruined and ravaged,
12until the LORD has sent everyone far
away
and the land is utterly forsaken.

13And though a tenth remains in the
land,
it will again be laid waste.
But as the terebinth and oak
leave stumps when they are cut
down,
so the holy seed will be the stump
in the land."

The Sign of Immanuel

7 When Ahaz son of Jotham, the son
of Uzziah, was king of Judah, King
Rezin of Aram and Pekah son of Remaliah king of Israel marched up to
fight against Jerusalem, but they could
not overpower it.
2Now the house of David was told,
"Aram has allied itself with Ephraim";
so the hearts of Ahaz and his people
were shaken, as the trees of the forest
are shaken by the wind.
3Then the LORD said to Isaiah, "Go
out, you and your son Shear-Jashub, to
meet Ahaz at the end of the aqueduct of
the Upper Pool, on the road to the
Washerman's Field. 4Say to him, 'Be
careful, keep calm and don't be afraid.
Do not lose heart because of these two
smouldering stubs of firewood—
because of the fierce anger of Rezin and
Aram and of the son of Remaliah.
5Aram, Ephraim and Remaliah's son
have plotted your ruin, saying, 6"Let us
invade Judah; let us tear it apart and
divide it among ourselves, and make the
son of Tabeel king over it." 7Yet this is
what the Sovereign LORD says:

" 'It will not take place,
it will not happen,
8for the head of Aram is Damascus,
and the head of Damascus is only
Rezin.
Within sixty-five years
Ephraim will be too shattered to be
a people.
9The head of Ephraim is Samaria,
and the head of Samaria is only
Remaliah's son.
If you do not stand firm in your faith,
you will not stand at all.' "

10Again the LORD spoke to Ahaz,
11"Ask the LORD your God for a sign,
whether in the deepest depths or in the
highest heights."
12But Ahaz said, "I will not ask; I will
not put the LORD to the test."
13Then Isaiah said, "Hear now, you
house of David! Is it not enough to try
the patience of men? Will you try the
patience of my God also? 14Therefore
the Lord himself will give you a sign:
The virgin will be with child and will
give birth to a son, and will call him
Immanuel. 15He will eat curds and
honey when he knows enough to reject
the wrong and choose the right. 16But
before the boy knows enough to reject
the wrong and choose the right, the
land of the two kings you dread will
be laid waste. 17The LORD will bring
on you and on your people and on
the house of your father a time unlike
any since Ephraim broke away from
Judah—he will bring the king of
Assyria."
18In that day the LORD will whistle for
flies from the distant streams of Egypt
and for bees from the land of Assyria.
19They will all come and settle in the
steep ravines and in the crevices in the
rocks, on all the thornbushes and at all
the water holes. 20In that day the Lord
will use a razor hired from beyond the
River—the king of Assyria—to shave
your head and the hair of your legs, and
to take off your beards also. 21In that
day, a man will keep alive a young cow
and two goats. 22And because of the
abundance of the milk they give, he will
have curds to eat. All who remain in the
land will eat curds and honey. 23In that
day, in every place where there were a
thousand vines worth a thousand silver
shekels, there will be only briers and
thorns. 24Men will go there with bow
and arrow, for the land will be covered
with briers and thorns. 25As for all the
hills once cultivated by the hoe, you will
no longer go there for fear of the briers
and thorns; they will become places
where cattle are turned loose and where
sheep run.

Assyria, the LORD's Instrument

8 The LORD said to me, "Take a
large scroll and write on it with an
ordinary pen: Maher-Shalal-Hash-Baz.
2And I will call in Uriah the priest and
Zechariah son of Jeberekiah as reliable
witnesses for me."

3Then I went to the prophetess, and
she conceived and gave birth to a son.
And the LORD said to me, "Name him
Maher-Shalal-Hash-Baz. 4Before the
boy knows how to say 'My father' or
'My mother', the wealth of Damascus
and the plunder of Samaria will be
carried off by the king of Assyria."

5The LORD spoke to me again:

6"Because this people has rejected
the gently flowing waters of
Shiloah
and rejoices over Rezin
and the son of Remaliah,
7therefore the Lord is about to bring
against them
the mighty floodwaters of the
River—
the king of Assyria with all his
pomp.
It will overflow all its channels,
run over all its banks
8and sweep on into Judah, swirling
over it,
passing through it and reaching up
to the neck.
Its outspread wings will cover the
breadth of your land,
O Immanuel!"

9Raise the war cry, you nations, and
be shattered!
Listen, all you distant lands.
Prepare for battle, and be shattered!
Prepare for battle, and be
shattered!
10Devise your strategy, but it will be
thwarted;
propose your plan, but it will not
stand,
for God is with us.

NEW TESTAMENT READING
2 Corinthians 7:2–16

Paul's Joy

2Make room for us in your hearts. We
have wronged no-one, we have corrupted no-one, we have exploited no-
one. 3I do not say this to condemn you; I
have said before that you have such a
place in our hearts that we would live or
die with you. 4I have great confidence in
you; I take great pride in you. I am
greatly encouraged; in all our troubles
my joy knows no bounds.

5For when we came into Macedonia,
this body of ours had no rest, but we
were harassed at every turn—conflicts
on the outside, fears within. 6But God,
who comforts the downcast, comforted
us by the coming of Titus, 7and not only
by his coming but also by the comfort
you had given him. He told us about
your longing for me, your deep sorrow,
your ardent concern for me, so that my
joy was greater than ever.

8Even if I caused you sorrow by my
letter, I do not regret it. Though I did
regret it—I see that my letter hurt you,
but only for a little while—9yet now I
am happy, not because you were made
sorry, but because your sorrow led you
to repentance. For you became sorrowful as God intended and so were not
harmed in any way by us. 10Godly sorrow brings repentance that leads to
salvation and leaves no regret, but
worldly sorrow brings death. 11See what
this godly sorrow has produced in you:
what earnestness, what eagerness to
clear yourselves, what indignation,
what alarm, what longing, what concern, what readiness to see justice done.
At every point you have proved
yourselves to be innocent in this matter.
12So even though I wrote to you, it was
not on account of the one who did the
wrong or of the injured party, but rather
that before God you could see for
yourselves how devoted to us you are.
13By all this we are encouraged.

In addition to our own encouragement, we were especially delighted to

see how happy Titus was, because his
spirit has been refreshed by all of you.
14I had boasted to him about you, and
you have not embarrassed me. But just
as everything we said to you was true, so
our boasting about you to Titus has
proved to be true as well. 15And his
affection for you is all the greater
when he remembers that you were all
obedient, receiving him with fear
and trembling. 16I am glad I can have
complete confidence in you.

READING FROM PSALMS
Psalm 105:23–36

23Then Israel entered Egypt;
Jacob lived as an alien in the land of Ham.
24The LORD made his people very fruitful;
he made them too numerous for their foes,
25whose hearts he turned to hate his people,
to conspire against his servants.
26He sent Moses his servant,
and Aaron, whom he had chosen.
27They performed his miraculous signs among them,
his wonders in the land of Ham.
28He sent darkness and made the land dark—
for had they not rebelled against his words?
29He turned their waters into blood,
causing their fish to die.
30Their land teemed with frogs,
which went up into the bedrooms of their rulers.
31He spoke, and there came swarms of flies,
and gnats throughout their country.
32He turned their rain into hail,
with lightning throughout their land;
33he struck down their vines and fig-trees
and shattered the trees of their country.
34He spoke, and the locusts came,
grasshoppers without number;
35they ate up every green thing in their land,
ate up the produce of their soil.
36Then he struck down all the firstborn in their land,
the firstfruits of all their manhood.

DAY 248

SEPTEMBER 5

OLD TESTAMENT READING
Isaiah 8:11–10:19

Fear God

11The LORD spoke to me with his
strong hand upon me, warning me not
to follow the way of this people. He
said:

12"Do not call conspiracy
everything that these people call conspiracy;
do not fear what they fear,
and do not dread it.
13The LORD Almighty is the one you are to regard as holy,
he is the one you are to fear,
he is the one you are to dread,
14and he will be a sanctuary;
but for both houses of Israel he will be
a stone that causes men to stumble
and a rock that makes them fall.
And for the people of Jerusalem he will be
a trap and a snare.

15Many of them will stumble;
they will fall and be broken,
they will be snared and captured."

16Bind up the testimony
and seal up the law among my
disciples.
17I will wait for the LORD,
who is hiding his face from the
house of Jacob.
I will put my trust in him.

18Here am I, and the children the
LORD has given me. We are signs and
symbols in Israel from the LORD
Almighty, who dwells on Mount Zion.
19When men tell you to consult
mediums and spiritists, who whisper
and mutter, should not a people enquire
of their God? Why consult the dead on
behalf of the living? 20To the law and to
the testimony! If they do not speak
according to this word, they have no
light of dawn. 21Distressed and hungry,
they will roam through the land; when
they are famished, they will become
enraged and, looking upward, will curse
their king and their God. 22Then they
will look towards the earth and see only
distress and darkness and fearful
gloom, and they will be thrust into utter
darkness.

To Us a Child Is Born

9 Nevertheless, there will be no more gloom for those who were in distress. In the past he humbled the land of Zebulun and the land of Naphtali, but in the future he will honour Galilee of the Gentiles, by the way of the sea, along the Jordan—

2The people walking in darkness
have seen a great light;
on those living in the land of the
shadow of death
a light has dawned.
3You have enlarged the nation
and increased their joy;
they rejoice before you
as people rejoice at the harvest,
as men rejoice
when dividing the plunder.
4For as in the day of Midian's defeat,
you have shattered
the yoke that burdens them,
the bar across their shoulders,
the rod of their oppressor.
5Every warrior's boot used in battle
and every garment rolled in blood
will be destined for burning,
will be fuel for the fire.
6For to us a child is born,
to us a son is given,
and the government will be on his
shoulders.
And he will be called
Wonderful Counsellor, Mighty
God,
Everlasting Father, Prince of
Peace.
7Of the increase of his government
and peace
there will be no end.
He will reign on David's throne
and over his kingdom,
establishing and upholding it
with justice and righteousness
from that time on and for ever.
The zeal of the LORD Almighty
will accomplish this.

The LORD's Anger Against Israel

8The Lord has sent a message against
Jacob;
it will fall on Israel.
9All the people will know it—
Ephraim and the inhabitants of
Samaria—
who say with pride
and arrogance of heart,
10"The bricks have fallen down,
but we will rebuild with dressed
stone;
the fig-trees have been felled,
but we will replace them with
cedars."
11But the LORD has strengthened
Rezin's foes against them
and has spurred their enemies on.
12Arameans from the east and
Philistines from the west

have devoured Israel with open
mouth.

Yet for all this, his anger is not turned
away,
his hand is still upraised.

13But the people have not returned to
him who struck them,
nor have they sought the LORD
Almighty.
14So the LORD will cut off from Israel
both head and tail,
both palm branch and reed in a
single day;
15the elders and prominent men are the
head,
the prophets who teach lies are the
tail.
16Those who guide this people mislead
them,
and those who are guided are led
astray.
17Therefore the Lord will take no
pleasure in the young men,
nor will he pity the fatherless and
widows,
for everyone is ungodly and wicked,
every mouth speaks vileness.

Yet for all this, his anger is not turned
away,
his hand is still upraised.

18Surely wickedness burns like a fire;
it consumes briers and thorns,
it sets the forest thickets ablaze,
so that it rolls upward in a column
of smoke.
19By the wrath of the LORD Almighty
the land will be scorched
and the people will be fuel for the
fire;
no-one will spare his brother.
20On the right they will devour,
but still be hungry;
on the left they will eat,
but not be satisfied.
Each will feed on the flesh of his own
offspring:
21 Manasseh will feed on Ephraim,
and Ephraim on Manasseh;
together they will turn against
Judah.

Yet for all this, his anger is not turned
away,
his hand is still upraised.

10 Woe to those who make unjust
laws,
to those who issue oppressive
decrees,
2to deprive the poor of their rights
and withhold justice from the
oppressed of my people,
making widows their prey
and robbing the fatherless.
3What will you do on the day of
reckoning,
when disaster comes from afar?
To whom will you run for help?
Where will you leave your riches?
4Nothing will remain but to cringe
among the captives
or fall among the slain.

Yet for all this, his anger is not
turned away,
his hand is still upraised.

God's Judgment on Assyria

5"Woe to the Assyrian, the rod of my
anger,
in whose hand is the club of my
wrath!
6I send him against a godless nation,
I dispatch him against a people
who anger me,
to seize loot and snatch plunder,
and to trample them down like
mud in the streets.
7But this is not what he intends,
this is not what he has in mind;
his purpose is to destroy,
to put an end to many nations.
8'Are not my commanders all kings?'
he says.
9 'Has not Calno fared like
Carchemish?
Is not Hamath like Arpad,
and Samaria like Damascus?
10As my hand seized the kingdoms of
the idols,

kingdoms whose images excelled
those of Jerusalem and
Samaria—
11shall I not deal with Jerusalem and
her images
as I dealt with Samaria and her
idols?'"

12When the Lord has finished all his work against Mount Zion and Jerusalem, he will say, "I will punish the king of Assyria for the wilful pride of his heart and the haughty look in his eyes.
13For he says:

"'By the strength of my hand I have
done this,
and by my wisdom, because I have
understanding.
I removed the boundaries of nations,
I plundered their treasures;
like a mighty one I subdued their
kings.
14As one reaches into a nest,
so my hand reached for the wealth
of the nations;
as men gather abandoned eggs,
so I gathered all the countries;
not one flapped a wing,
or opened its mouth to chirp.'"

15Does the axe raise itself above him
who swings it,
or the saw boast against him who
uses it?
As if a rod were to wield him who lifts
it up,
or a club brandish him who is not
wood!
16Therefore, the Lord, the LORD
Almighty,
will send a wasting disease upon his
sturdy warriors;
under his pomp a fire will be kindled
like a blazing flame.
17The Light of Israel will become a fire,
their Holy One a flame;
in a single day it will burn and
consume
his thorns and his briers.
18The splendour of his forests and
fertile fields
it will completely destroy,
as when a sick man wastes away.
19And the remaining trees of his forests
will be so few
that a child could write them down.

NEW TESTAMENT READING
2 Corinthians 8:1–15

Generosity Encouraged

8 And now, brothers, we want you to
know about the grace that God has
given the Macedonian churches. 2Out
of the most severe trial, their overflowing joy and their extreme poverty welled up in rich generosity. 3For I
testify that they gave as much as they were able, and even beyond their ability. Entirely on their own, 4they
urgently pleaded with us for the privilege of sharing in this service to the saints. 5And they did not do as we expected, but they gave themselves first to the Lord and then to us in keeping with God's will. 6So we urged Titus, since he had earlier made a beginning, to bring also to completion this act of grace on your part. 7But just as you excel in everything—in faith, in speech, in knowledge, in complete earnestness and in your love for us—see that you also excel in this grace of giving.

8I am not commanding you, but I want to test the sincerity of your love by comparing it with the earnestness of others. 9For you know the grace of our Lord Jesus Christ, that though he was rich, yet for your sakes he became poor, so that you through his poverty might become rich.

10And here is my advice about what is best for you in this matter: Last year you were the first not only to give but also to have the desire to do so. 11Now finish
the work, so that your eager willingness to do it may be matched by your completion of it, according to your means.
12For if the willingness is there, the gift is acceptable according to what one has, not according to what he does not have.

[13]Our desire is not that others might
be relieved while you are hard pressed,
but that there might be equality. [14]At
the present time your plenty will supply
what they need, so that in turn their
plenty will supply what you need. Then
there will be equality, [15]as it is written:
"He who gathered much did not have
too much, and he who gathered little
did not have too little."

READING FROM PROVERBS
Proverbs 21:27–22:6

[27]The sacrifice of the wicked is
detestable—
how much more so when brought
with evil intent!

[28]A false witness will perish,
and whoever listens to him will be
destroyed for ever.

[29]A wicked man puts up a bold front,
but an upright man gives thought
to his ways.

[30]There is no wisdom, no insight, no
plan
that can succeed against the
LORD.

[31]The horse is made ready for the day
of battle,
but victory rests with the LORD.

22 A good name is more desirable
than great riches;
to be esteemed is better than silver
or gold.

[2]Rich and poor have this in common:
The LORD is the Maker of them all.

[3]A prudent man sees danger and takes
refuge,
but the simple keep going and
suffer for it.

[4]Humility and the fear of the LORD
bring wealth and honour and life.

[5]In the paths of the wicked lie thorns
and snares,
but he who guards his soul stays far
from them.

[6]Train a child in the way he should go,
and when he is old he will not turn
from it.

DAY 249 SEPTEMBER 6

OLD TESTAMENT READING
Isaiah 10:20–13:22

The Remnant of Israel

[20]In that day the remnant of Israel,
the survivors of the house of Jacob,
will no longer rely on him
who struck them down
but will truly rely on the LORD,
the Holy One of Israel.
[21]A remnant will return, a remnant of
Jacob
will return to the Mighty God.
[22]Though your people, O Israel, be like
the sand by the sea,
only a remnant will return.
Destruction has been decreed,
overwhelming and righteous.
[23]The Lord, the LORD Almighty, will
carry out
the destruction decreed upon the
whole land.

[24]Therefore, this is what the Lord,
the LORD Almighty, says:

"O my people who live in Zion,
do not be afraid of the Assyrians,
who beat you with a rod
and lift up a club against you, as Egypt did.
25Very soon my anger against you will end
and my wrath will be directed to their destruction."

26The LORD Almighty will lash them with a whip,
as when he struck down Midian at the rock of Oreb;
and he will raise his staff over the waters,
as he did in Egypt.
27In that day their burden will be lifted from your shoulders,
their yoke from your neck;
the yoke will be broken
because you have grown so fat.

28They enter Aiath;
they pass through Migron;
they store supplies at Michmash.
29They go over the pass, and say,
"We will camp overnight at Geba."
Ramah trembles;
Gibeah of Saul flees.
30Cry out, O Daughter of Gallim!
Listen, O Laishah!
Poor Anathoth!
31Madmenah is in flight;
the people of Gebim take cover.
32This day they will halt at Nob;
they will shake their fist
at the mount of the Daughter of Zion,
at the hill of Jerusalem.

33See, the Lord, the LORD Almighty,
will lop off the boughs with great power.
The lofty trees will be felled,
the tall ones will be brought low.
34He will cut down the forest thickets with an axe;
Lebanon will fall before the Mighty One.

The Branch From Jesse

11 A shoot will come up from the stump of Jesse;
from his roots a Branch will bear fruit.
2The Spirit of the LORD will rest on him—
the Spirit of wisdom and of understanding,
the Spirit of counsel and of power,
the Spirit of knowledge and of the fear of the LORD—
3and he will delight in the fear of the LORD.

He will not judge by what he sees with his eyes,
or decide by what he hears with his ears;
4but with righteousness he will judge the needy,
with justice he will give decisions for the poor of the earth.
He will strike the earth with the rod of his mouth;
with the breath of his lips he will slay the wicked.
5Righteousness will be his belt
and faithfulness the sash round his waist.

6The wolf will live with the lamb,
the leopard will lie down with the goat,
the calf and the lion and the yearling together;
and a little child will lead them.
7The cow will feed with the bear,
their young will lie down together,
and the lion will eat straw like the ox.
8The infant will play near the hole of the cobra,
and the young child put his hand into the viper's nest.
9They will neither harm nor destroy
on all my holy mountain,
for the earth will be full of the knowledge of the LORD
as the waters cover the sea.

10In that day the Root of Jesse will
stand as a banner for the peoples; the
nations will rally to him, and his place of
rest will be glorious. 11In that day the
Lord will reach out his hand a second
time to reclaim the remnant that is left
of his people from Assyria, from Lower
Egypt, from Upper Egypt, from Cush,
from Elam, from Babylonia, from
Hamath and from the islands of the sea.

12He will raise a banner for the nations
and gather the exiles of Israel;
he will assemble the scattered people
of Judah
from the four quarters of the earth.
13Ephraim's jealousy will vanish,
and Judah's enemies will be cut off;
Ephraim will not be jealous of Judah,
nor Judah hostile towards
Ephraim.
14They will swoop down on the slopes
of Philistia to the west;
together they will plunder the
people to the east.
They will lay hands on Edom and
Moab,
and the Ammonites will be subject
to them.
15The LORD will dry up
the gulf of the Egyptian sea;
with a scorching wind he will sweep
his hand
over the Euphrates River.
He will break it up into seven streams
so that men can cross over in
sandals.
16There will be a highway for the
remnant of his people
that is left from Assyria,
as there was for Israel
when they came up from Egypt.

Songs of Praise

12 In that day you will say:

"I will praise you, O LORD.
Although you were angry with me,
your anger has turned away
and you have comforted me.
2Surely God is my salvation;
I will trust and not be afraid.
The LORD, the LORD, is my strength
and my song;
he has become my salvation."
3With joy you will draw water
from the wells of salvation.

4In that day you will say:

"Give thanks to the LORD, call on his
name;
make known among the nations
what he has done,
and proclaim that his name is
exalted.
5Sing to the LORD, for he has done
glorious things;
let this be known to all the world.
6Shout aloud and sing for joy, people
of Zion,
for great is the Holy One of Israel
among you."

A Prophecy Against Babylon

13 An oracle concerning Babylon
that Isaiah son of Amoz saw:

2Raise a banner on a bare hilltop,
shout to them;
beckon to them
to enter the gates of the nobles.
3I have commanded my holy ones;
I have summoned my warriors to
carry out my wrath—
those who rejoice in my triumph.

4Listen, a noise on the mountains,
like that of a great multitude!
Listen, an uproar among the
kingdoms,
like nations massing together!
The LORD Almighty is mustering
an army for war.
5They come from faraway lands,
from the ends of the heavens—
the LORD and the weapons of his
wrath—
to destroy the whole country.

6Wail, for the day of the LORD is near;
it will come like destruction from
the Almighty.

7Because of this, all hands will go limp,
every man's heart will melt.
8Terror will seize them,
pain and anguish will grip them;
they will writhe like a woman in labour.
They will look aghast at each other,
their faces aflame.

9See, the day of the LORD is coming
—a cruel day, with wrath and fierce anger—
to make the land desolate
and destroy the sinners within it.
10The stars of heaven and their constellations
will not show their light.
The rising sun will be darkened
and the moon will not give its light.
11I will punish the world for its evil,
the wicked for their sins.
I will put an end to the arrogance of the haughty
and will humble the pride of the ruthless.
12I will make man scarcer than pure gold,
more rare than the gold of Ophir.
13Therefore I will make the heavens tremble;
and the earth will shake from its place
at the wrath of the LORD Almighty,
in the day of his burning anger.

14Like a hunted gazelle,
like sheep without a shepherd,
each will return to his own people,
each will flee to his native land.
15Whoever is captured will be thrust through;
all who are caught will fall by the sword.
16Their infants will be dashed to pieces before their eyes;
their houses will be looted and their wives ravished.
17See, I will stir up against them the Medes,
who do not care for silver
and have no delight in gold.
18Their bows will strike down the young men;
they will have no mercy on infants
nor will they look with compassion on children.
19Babylon, the jewel of kingdoms,
the glory of the Babylonians' pride,
will be overthrown by God
like Sodom and Gomorrah.
20She will never be inhabited
or lived in through all generations;
no Arab will pitch his tent there,
no shepherd will rest his flocks there.
21But desert creatures will lie there,
jackals will fill her houses;
there the owls will dwell,
and there the wild goats will leap about.
22Hyenas will howl in her strongholds,
jackals in her luxurious palaces.
Her time is at hand,
and her days will not be prolonged.

NEW TESTAMENT READING
2 Corinthians 8:16–9:5

Titus Sent to Corinth

16I thank God, who put into the heart of Titus the same concern I have for you. 17For Titus not only welcomed our appeal, but he is coming to you with much enthusiasm and on his own initiative. 18And we are sending along with him the brother who is praised by all the churches for his service to the gospel.
19What is more, he was chosen by the churches to accompany us as we carry the offering, which we administer in order to honour the Lord himself and to show our eagerness to help. 20We want to avoid any criticism of the way we administer this liberal gift. 21For we are taking pains to do what is right, not only in the eyes of the Lord but also in the eyes of men.

22In addition, we are sending with them our brother who has often proved

to us in many ways that he is zealous,
and now even more so because of his
great confidence in you. 23As for Titus,
he is my partner and fellow-worker
among you; as for our brothers, they are
representatives of the churches and an
honour to Christ. 24Therefore show
these men the proof of your love and the
reason for our pride in you, so that the
churches can see it.

9 There is no need for me to write to
you about this service to the saints.
2For I know your eagerness to help, and
I have been boasting about it to the
Macedonians, telling them that since
last year you in Achaia were ready to
give; and your enthusiasm has stirred
most of them to action. 3But I am sending the brothers in order that our boasting about you in this matter should not
prove hollow, but that you may be
ready, as I said you would be. 4For if
any Macedonians come with me and
find you unprepared, we—not to say
anything about you—would be
ashamed of having been so confident.
5So I thought it necessary to urge the
brothers to visit you in advance and
finish the arrangements for the generous gift you had promised. Then it will
be ready as a generous gift, not as one
grudgingly given.

READING FROM PSALMS
Psalm 105:37–45

37He brought out Israel, laden with
silver and gold,
and from among their tribes
no-one faltered.
38Egypt was glad when they left,
because dread of Israel had fallen
on them.
39He spread out a cloud as a covering,
and a fire to give light at night.
40They asked, and he brought them
quail
and satisfied them with the bread
of heaven.
41He opened the rock, and water
gushed out;
like a river it flowed in the desert.
42For he remembered his holy promise
given to his servant Abraham.
43He brought out his people with
rejoicing,
his chosen ones with shouts of joy;
44he gave them the lands of the nations,
and they fell heir to what others
had toiled for—
45that they might keep his precepts
and observe his laws.

Praise the LORD.

DAY 250

SEPTEMBER 7

OLD TESTAMENT READING
Isaiah 14:1–16:14

14 The LORD will have compassion
on Jacob;
once again he will choose Israel
and will settle them in their own
land.
Aliens will join them
and unite with the house of Jacob.
2Nations will take them
and bring them to their own place.
And the house of Israel will possess
the nations
as menservants and maidservants
in the LORD's land.
They will make captives of their
captors
and rule over their oppressors.

3On the day the LORD gives you relief
from suffering and turmoil and cruel
bondage, 4you will take up this taunt
against the king of Babylon:

How the oppressor has come to an
end!
How his fury has ended!
5The LORD has broken the rod of the
wicked,
the sceptre of the rulers,
6which in anger struck down peoples
with unceasing blows,
and in fury subdued nations
with relentless aggression.
7All the lands are at rest and at peace;
they break into singing.
8Even the pine trees and the cedars of
Lebanon
exult over you and say,
"Now that you have been laid low,
no woodsman comes to cut us
down."

9The grave below is all astir
to meet you at your coming;
it rouses the spirits of the departed to
greet you—
all those who were leaders in the
world;
it makes them rise from their
thrones—
all those who were kings over the
nations.
10They will all respond,
they will say to you,
"You also have become weak, as we
are;
you have become like us."
11All your pomp has been brought
down to the grave,
along with the noise of your harps;
maggots are spread out beneath you
and worms cover you.

12How you have fallen from heaven,
O morning star, son of the dawn!
You have been cast down to the earth,
you who once laid low the nations!
13You said in your heart,
"I will ascend to heaven;
I will raise my throne
above the stars of God;
I will sit enthroned on the mount of
assembly,
on the utmost heights of the sacred
mountain.
14I will ascend above the tops of the
clouds;
I will make myself like the Most
High."
15But you are brought down to the
grave,
to the depths of the pit.

16Those who see you stare at you,
they ponder your fate:
"Is this the man who shook the earth
and made kingdoms tremble,
17the man who made the world a
desert,
who overthrew its cities
and would not let his captives go
home?"

18All the kings of the nations lie in
state,
each in his own tomb.
19But you are cast out of your tomb
like a rejected branch;
you are covered with the slain,
with those pierced by the sword,
those who descend to the stones of
the pit.
Like a corpse trampled underfoot,
20 you will not join them in burial,
for you have destroyed your land
and killed your people.

The offspring of the wicked
will never be mentioned again.
21Prepare a place to slaughter his sons
for the sins of their forefathers;
they are not to rise to inherit the land
and cover the earth with their
cities.

22"I will rise up against them,"
declares the LORD Almighty.
"I will cut off from Babylon her name
and survivors,
her offspring and descendants,"
declares the LORD.
23"I will turn her into a place for owls
and into swampland;
I will sweep her with the broom of
destruction,"
declares the LORD Almighty.

A Prophecy Against Assyria

24The LORD Almighty has sworn,

"Surely, as I have planned, so it will
be,
and as I have purposed, so it will
stand.
25I will crush the Assyrian in my land;
on my mountains I will trample
him down.
His yoke will be taken from my
people,
and his burden removed from their
shoulders."

26This is the plan determined for the
whole world;
this is the hand stretched out over
all nations.
27For the LORD Almighty has
purposed, and who can thwart
him?
His hand is stretched out, and who
can turn it back?

A Prophecy Against the Philistines

28This oracle came in the year King Ahaz died:

29Do not rejoice, all you Philistines,
that the rod that struck you is
broken;
from the root of that snake will spring
up a viper,
its fruit will be a darting, venomous
serpent.
30The poorest of the poor will find
pasture,
and the needy will lie down in
safety.
But your root I will destroy by
famine;
it will slay your survivors.

31Wail, O gate! Howl, O city!
Melt away, all you Philistines!
A cloud of smoke comes from the
north,
and there is not a straggler in its
ranks.
32What answer shall be given
to the envoys of that nation?
"The LORD has established Zion,
and in her his afflicted people will
find refuge."

A Prophecy Against Moab

15 An oracle concerning Moab:

Ar in Moab is ruined,
destroyed in a night!
Kir in Moab is ruined,
destroyed in a night!
2Dibon goes up to its temple,
to its high places to weep;
Moab wails over Nebo and
Medeba.
Every head is shaved
and every beard cut off.
3In the streets they wear sackcloth;
on the roofs and in the public
squares
they all wail,
prostrate with weeping.
4Heshbon and Elealeh cry out,
their voices are heard all the way to
Jahaz.
Therefore the armed men of Moab
cry out,
and their hearts are faint.

5My heart cries out over Moab;
her fugitives flee as far as Zoar,
as far as Eglath Shelishiyah.
They go up the way to Luhith,
weeping as they go;
on the road to Horonaim
they lament their destruction.
6The waters of Nimrim are dried up
and the grass is withered;
the vegetation is gone
and nothing green is left.
7So the wealth they have acquired and
stored up
they carry away over the Ravine of
the Poplars.
8Their outcry echoes along the border
of Moab;
their wailing reaches as far as
Eglaim,
their lamentation as far as Beer
Elim.

9Dimon's waters are full of blood,
but I will bring still more upon
Dimon—
a lion upon the fugitives of Moab
and upon those who remain in the
land.

16 Send lambs as tribute to the
ruler of the land,
from Sela, across the desert,
to the mount of the Daughter of
Zion.
2Like fluttering birds
pushed from the nest,
so are the women of Moab
at the fords of the Arnon.

3"Give us counsel,
render a decision.
Make your shadow like night—
at high noon.
Hide the fugitives,
do not betray the refugees.
4Let the Moabite fugitives stay with
you;
be their shelter from the
destroyer."

The oppressor will come to an end,
and destruction will cease;
the aggressor will vanish from the
land.
5In love a throne will be established;
in faithfulness a man will sit on it—
one from the house of David—
one who in judging seeks justice
and speeds the cause of
righteousness.

6We have heard of Moab's pride—
her overweening pride and conceit,
her pride and her insolence—
but her boasts are empty.
7Therefore the Moabites wail,
they wail together for Moab.
Lament and grieve
for the men of Kir Hareseth.
8The fields of Heshbon wither,
the vines of Sibmah also.
The rulers of the nations
have trampled down the choicest
vines,
which once reached Jazer
and spread towards the desert.
Their shoots spread out
and went as far as the sea.
9So I weep, as Jazer weeps,
for the vines of Sibmah.
O Heshbon, O Elealeh,
I drench you with tears!
The shouts of joy over your ripened
fruit
and over your harvests have been
stilled.
10Joy and gladness are taken away from
the orchards;
no-one sings or shouts in the
vineyards;
no-one treads out wine at the presses,
for I have put an end to the
shouting.
11My heart laments for Moab like a
harp,
my inmost being for Kir Hareseth.
12When Moab appears at her high
place,
she only wears herself out;
when she goes to her shrine to pray,
it is to no avail.

13This is the word the LORD has
already spoken concerning Moab. 14But
now the LORD says: "Within three
years, as a servant bound by contract
would count them, Moab's splendour
and all her many people will be despised, and her survivors will be very
few and feeble."

NEW TESTAMENT READING
2 Corinthians 9:6–15

Sowing Generously

6Remember this: Whoever sows
sparingly will also reap sparingly, and
whoever sows generously will also reap
generously. 7Each man should give
what he has decided in his heart to give,
not reluctantly or under compulsion,
for God loves a cheerful giver. 8And
God is able to make all grace abound to
you, so that in all things at all times,

having all that you need, you will abound in every good work. [9]As it is written:

"He has scattered abroad his gifts to the poor;
his righteousness endures for ever."

[10]Now he who supplies seed to the sower and bread for food will also supply and increase your store of seed and will enlarge the harvest of your righteousness. [11]You will be made rich in every way so that you can be generous on every occasion, and through us your generosity will result in thanksgiving to God.

[12]This service that you perform is not only supplying the needs of God's people but is also overflowing in many expressions of thanks to God. [13]Because of the service by which you have proved yourselves, men will praise God for the obedience that accompanies your confession of the gospel of Christ, and for your generosity in sharing with them and with everyone else. [14]And in their prayers for you their hearts will go out to you, because of the surpassing grace God has given you. [15]Thanks be to God for his indescribable gift!

READING FROM PSALMS
Psalm 106:1–15

[1]Praise the LORD.

Give thanks to the LORD, for he is good;
his love endures for ever.
[2]Who can proclaim the mighty acts of the LORD
or fully declare his praise?
[3]Blessed are they who maintain justice,
who constantly do what is right.
[4]Remember me, O LORD, when you show favour to your people,
come to my aid when you save them,
[5]that I may enjoy the prosperity of your chosen ones,
that I may share in the joy of your nation
and join your inheritance in giving praise.

[6]We have sinned, even as our fathers did;
we have done wrong and acted wickedly.
[7]When our fathers were in Egypt,
they gave no thought to your miracles;
they did not remember your many kindnesses,
and they rebelled by the sea, the Red Sea.
[8]Yet he saved them for his name's sake,
to make his mighty power known.
[9]He rebuked the Red Sea, and it dried up;
he led them through the depths as through a desert.
[10]He saved them from the hand of the foe;
from the hand of the enemy he redeemed them.
[11]The waters covered their adversaries;
not one of them survived.
[12]Then they believed his promises
and sang his praise.

[13]But they soon forgot what he had done
and did not wait for his counsel.
[14]In the desert they gave in to their craving;
in the wasteland they put God to the test.
[15]So he gave them what they asked for,
but sent a wasting disease upon them.

OLD TESTAMENT READING
Isaiah 17:1–19:25

An Oracle Against Damascus

17 An oracle concerning Damascus:

"See, Damascus will no longer be a city
but will become a heap of ruins.
2The cities of Aroer will be deserted
and left to flocks, which will lie down,
with no-one to make them afraid.
3The fortified city will disappear from Ephraim,
and royal power from Damascus;
the remnant of Aram will be
like the glory of the Israelites,"
declares the LORD Almighty.

4"In that day the glory of Jacob will fade;
the fat of his body will waste away.
5It will be as when a reaper gathers the standing corn
and harvests the corn with his arm—
as when a man gleans ears of corn
in the Valley of Rephaim.
6Yet some gleanings will remain,
as when an olive tree is beaten,
leaving two or three olives on the topmost branches,
four or five on the fruitful boughs,"
declares the LORD,
the God of Israel.

7In that day men will look to their Maker
and turn their eyes to the Holy One of Israel.
8They will not look to the altars,
the work of their hands,
and they will have no regard for the Asherah poles
and the incense altars their fingers have made.

9In that day their strong cities, which
they left because of the Israelites, will
be like places abandoned to thickets
and undergrowth. And all will be
desolation.

10You have forgotten God your Saviour;
you have not remembered the Rock, your fortress.
Therefore, though you set out the finest plants
and plant imported vines,
11though on the day you set them out,
you make them grow,
and on the morning when you plant them, you bring them to bud,
yet the harvest will be as nothing
in the day of disease and incurable pain.

12Oh, the raging of many nations—
they rage like the raging sea!
Oh, the uproar of the peoples—
they roar like the roaring of great waters!
13Although the peoples roar like the roar of surging waters,
when he rebukes them they flee far away,
driven before the wind like chaff on the hills,
like tumble-weed before a gale.
14In the evening, sudden terror!
Before the morning, they are gone!
This is the portion of those who loot us,
the lot of those who plunder us.

A Prophecy Against Cush

18 Woe to the land of whirring wings
along the rivers of Cush,
2which sends envoys by sea
in papyrus boats over the water.

Go, swift messengers,
to a people tall and smooth-skinned,
to a people feared far and wide,
an aggressive nation of strange speech,
whose land is divided by rivers.
3All you people of the world,
you who live on the earth,
when a banner is raised on the mountains,
you will see it,
and when a trumpet sounds,
you will hear it.
4This is what the LORD says to me:
"I will remain quiet and will look on from my dwelling-place,
like shimmering heat in the sunshine,
like a cloud of dew in the heat of harvest."
5For, before the harvest, when the blossom is gone
and the flower becomes a ripening grape,
he will cut off the shoots with pruning knives,
and cut down and take away the spreading branches.
6They will all be left to the mountain birds of prey
and to the wild animals;
the birds will feed on them all summer,
the wild animals all winter.

7At that time gifts will be brought to the LORD Almighty

from a people tall and smooth-skinned,
from a people feared far and wide,
an aggressive nation of strange speech,
whose land is divided by rivers—

the gifts will be brought to Mount Zion, the place of the Name of the LORD Almighty.

A Prophecy About Egypt

19 An oracle concerning Egypt:

See, the LORD rides on a swift cloud
and is coming to Egypt.
The idols of Egypt tremble before him,
and the hearts of the Egyptians melt within them.

2"I will stir up Egyptian against Egyptian—
brother will fight against brother,
neighbour against neighbour,
city against city,
kingdom against kingdom.
3The Egyptians will lose heart,
and I will bring their plans to nothing;
they will consult the idols and the spirits of the dead,
the mediums and the spiritists.
4I will hand the Egyptians over
to the power of a cruel master,
and a fierce king will rule over them,"
declares the Lord, the LORD Almighty.

5The waters of the river will dry up,
and the river bed will be parched and dry.
6The canals will stink;
the streams of Egypt will dwindle and dry up.
The reeds and rushes will wither,
7 also the plants along the Nile,
at the mouth of the river.
Every sown field along the Nile
will become parched, will blow away and be no more.
8The fishermen will groan and lament,
all who cast hooks into the Nile;
those who throw nets on the water
will pine away.
9Those who work with combed flax
will despair,
the weavers of fine linen will lose hope.
10The workers in cloth will be dejected,
and all the wage earners will be sick at heart.

11The officials of Zoan are nothing but fools;
the wise counsellors of Pharaoh
give senseless advice.

How can you say to Pharaoh,
"I am one of the wise men,
a disciple of the ancient kings"?

12 Where are your wise men now?
Let them show you and make known
what the LORD Almighty
has planned against Egypt.
13 The officials of Zoan have become fools,
the leaders of Memphis are deceived;
the cornerstones of her peoples
have led Egypt astray.
14 The LORD has poured into them
a spirit of dizziness;
they make Egypt stagger in all that she does,
as a drunkard staggers around in his vomit.
15 There is nothing Egypt can do—
head or tail, palm branch or reed.

16 In that day the Egyptians will be
like women. They will shudder with fear
at the uplifted hand that the LORD
Almighty raises against them. 17 And
the land of Judah will bring terror to the
Egyptians; everyone to whom Judah is
mentioned will be terrified, because of
what the LORD Almighty is planning
against them.
18 In that day five cities in Egypt will
speak the language of Canaan and
swear allegiance to the LORD Almighty.
One of them will be called the City of
Destruction.
19 In that day there will be an altar to
the LORD in the heart of Egypt, and a
monument to the LORD at its border.
20 It will be a sign and witness to the
LORD Almighty in the land of Egypt.
When they cry out to the LORD because
of their oppressors, he will send them a
saviour and defender, and he will rescue
them. 21 So the LORD will make himself
known to the Egyptians, and in that day
they will acknowledge the LORD. They
will worship with sacrifices and grain
offerings; they will make vows to the
LORD and keep them. 22 The LORD will
strike Egypt with a plague; he will strike
them and heal them. They will turn to
the LORD, and he will respond to their
pleas and heal them.
23 In that day there will be a highway
from Egypt to Assyria. The Assyrians
will go to Egypt and the Egyptians to
Assyria. The Egyptians and Assyrians
will worship together. 24 In that day
Israel will be the third, along with Egypt
and Assyria, a blessing on the earth.
25 The LORD Almighty will bless them,
saying, "Blessed be Egypt my people,
Assyria my handiwork, and Israel my
inheritance."

NEW TESTAMENT READING

2 Corinthians 10:1–18

Paul's Defence of His Ministry

10 By the meekness and gentleness
of Christ, I appeal to you—I,
Paul, who am "timid" when face to face
with you, but "bold" when away! 2 I beg
you that when I come I may not have to
be as bold as I expect to be towards
some people who think that we live by
the standards of this world. 3 For though
we live in the world, we do not wage war
as the world does. 4 The weapons we
fight with are not the weapons of the
world. On the contrary, they have divine power to demolish strongholds. 5 We
demolish arguments and every pretension that sets itself up against the
knowledge of God, and we take captive
every thought to make it obedient to
Christ. 6 And we will be ready to punish
every act of disobedience, once your
obedience is complete.
7 You are looking only on the surface
of things. If anyone is confident that he
belongs to Christ, he should consider
again that we belong to Christ just as
much as he. 8 For even if I boast somewhat freely about the authority the
Lord gave us for building you up rather
than pulling you down, I will not be
ashamed of it. 9 I do not want to seem to
be trying to frighten you with my letters.

[10]For some say, "His letters are weighty
and forceful, but in person he is unim-
pressive and his speaking amounts to
nothing." [11]Such people should realise
that what we are in our letters when we
are absent, we will be in our actions
when we are present.

[12]We do not dare to classify or compare ourselves with some who commend themselves. When they measure
themselves by themselves and compare
themselves with themselves, they are
not wise. [13]We, however, will not boast
beyond proper limits, but will confine
our boasting to the field God has
assigned to us, a field that reaches even
to you. [14]We are not going too far in our
boasting, as would be the case if we had
not come to you, for we did get as far as
you with the gospel of Christ. [15]Neither
do we go beyond our limits by boasting
of work done by others. Our hope is
that, as your faith continues to grow,
our area of activity among you will
greatly expand, [16]so that we can preach
the gospel in the regions beyond you.
For we do not want to boast about work
already done in another man's territory.
[17]But, "Let him who boasts boast in the
Lord." [18]For it is not the one who commends himself who is approved, but the
one whom the Lord commends.

READING FROM PSALMS

Psalm 106:16–31

[16]In the camp they grew envious of
Moses
and of Aaron, who was
consecrated to the LORD.
[17]The earth opened up and swallowed
Dathan;
it buried the company of Abiram.
[18]Fire blazed among their followers;
a flame consumed the wicked.
[19]At Horeb they made a calf
and worshipped an idol cast from
metal.
[20]They exchanged their Glory
for an image of a bull, which eats
grass.
[21]They forgot the God who saved
them,
who had done great things in
Egypt,
[22]miracles in the land of Ham
and awesome deeds by the Red
Sea.
[23]So he said he would destroy them—
had not Moses, his chosen one,
stood in the breach before him
to keep his wrath from destroying
them.

[24]Then they despised the pleasant land;
they did not believe his promise.
[25]They grumbled in their tents
and did not obey the LORD.
[26]So he swore to them with uplifted
hand
that he would make them fall in the
desert,
[27]make their descendants fall among
the nations
and scatter them throughout the
lands.

[28]They yoked themselves to the Baal of
Peor
and ate sacrifices offered to lifeless
gods;
[29]they provoked the LORD to anger by
their wicked deeds;
and a plague broke out among
them.
[30]But Phinehas stood up and
intervened,
and the plague was checked.
[31]This was credited to him as
righteousness
for endless generations to come.

SEPTEMBER 9

OLD TESTAMENT READING
Isaiah 20:1–23:18

A Prophecy Against Egypt and Cush

20 In the year that the supreme
commander, sent by Sargon
king of Assyria, came to Ashdod and
attacked and captured it—2at that time
the LORD spoke through Isaiah son of
Amoz. He said to him, "Take off the
sackcloth from your body and the sandals from your feet." And he did so,
going around stripped and barefoot.
3Then the LORD said, "Just as my
servant Isaiah has gone stripped and
barefoot for three years, as a sign and
portent against Egypt and Cush, 4so the
king of Assyria will lead away stripped
and barefoot the Egyptian captives and
Cushite exiles, young and old, with buttocks bared—to Egypt's shame. 5Those
who trusted in Cush and boasted in
Egypt will be afraid and put to shame.
6In that day the people who live on this
coast will say, 'See what has happened
to those we relied on, those we fled to
for help and deliverance from the king
of Assyria! How then can we escape?' "

A Prophecy Against Babylon

21 An oracle concerning the Desert by the Sea:

Like whirlwinds sweeping through
the southland,
an invader comes from the desert,
from a land of terror.

2A dire vision has been shown to me:
The traitor betrays, the looter
takes loot.
Elam, attack! Media, lay siege!
I will bring to an end all the
groaning she caused.

3At this my body is racked with pain,
pangs seize me, like those of a
woman in labour;
I am staggered by what I hear,
I am bewildered by what I see.
4My heart falters,
fear makes me tremble;
the twilight I longed for
has become a horror to me.

5They set the tables,
they spread the rugs,
they eat, they drink!
Get up, you officers,
oil the shields!

6This is what the Lord says to me:

"Go, post a lookout
and have him report what he sees.
7When he sees chariots
with teams of horses,
riders on donkeys
or riders on camels,
let him be alert,
fully alert."

8And the lookout shouted,

"Day after day, my lord, I stand on
the watchtower;
every night I stay at my post.
9Look, here comes a man in a chariot
with a team of horses.
And he gives back the answer:
'Babylon has fallen, has fallen!
All the images of its gods
lie shattered on the ground!' "

10O my people, crushed on the
threshing-floor,
I tell you what I have heard
from the LORD Almighty,
from the God of Israel.

A Prophecy Against Edom

11An oracle concerning Dumah:

Someone calls to me from Seir,
"Watchman, what is left of the
night?

Watchman, what is left of the night?"
12 The watchman replies,
"Morning is coming, but also the night.
If you would ask, then ask;
and come back yet again."

A Prophecy Against Arabia

13 An oracle concerning Arabia:

You caravans of Dedanites,
who camp in the thickets of Arabia,
14 bring water for the thirsty;
you who live in Tema,
bring food for the fugitives.
15 They flee from the sword,
from the drawn sword,
from the bent bow
and from the heat of battle.

16 This is what the Lord says to me:
"Within one year, as a servant bound by
contract would count it, all the pomp of
Kedar will come to an end. 17 The sur-
vivors of the bowmen, the warriors of
Kedar, will be few." The LORD, the
God of Israel, has spoken.

A Prophecy About Jerusalem

22 An oracle concerning the Valley of Vision:

What troubles you now,
that you have all gone up on the roofs,
2 O town full of commotion,
O city of tumult and revelry?
Your slain were not killed by the sword,
nor did they die in battle.
3 All your leaders have fled together;
they have been captured without using the bow.
All you who were caught were taken prisoner together,
having fled while the enemy was still far away.
4 Therefore I said, "Turn away from me;
let me weep bitterly.
Do not try to console me
over the destruction of my people."

5 The Lord, the LORD Almighty, has a day
of tumult and trampling and terror
in the Valley of Vision,
a day of battering down walls
and of crying out to the mountains.
6 Elam takes up the quiver,
with her charioteers and horses;
Kir uncovers the shield.
7 Your choicest valleys are full of chariots,
and horsemen are posted at the city gates;
8 the defences of Judah are stripped away.

And you looked in that day
to the weapons in the Palace of the Forest;
9 you saw that the City of David
had many breaches in its defences;
you stored up water
in the Lower Pool.
10 You counted the buildings in Jerusalem
and tore down houses to strengthen the wall.
11 You built a reservoir between the two walls
for the water of the Old Pool,
but you did not look to the One who made it,
or have regard for the One who planned it long ago.

12 The Lord, the LORD Almighty,
called you on that day
to weep and to wail,
to tear out your hair and put on sackcloth.
13 But see, there is joy and revelry,
slaughtering of cattle and killing of sheep,
eating of meat and drinking of wine!

"Let us eat and drink," you say,
"for tomorrow we die!"

14The LORD Almighty has revealed this in my hearing: "Till your dying day this sin will not be atoned for," says the Lord, the LORD Almighty.

15This is what the Lord, the LORD Almighty, says:

"Go, say to this steward,
to Shebna, who is in charge of the palace:
16What are you doing here and who gave you permission
to cut out a grave for yourself here,
hewing your grave on the height
and chiselling your resting place in the rock?
17"Beware, the LORD is about to take firm hold of you
and hurl you away, O you mighty man.
18He will roll you up tightly like a ball
and throw you into a large country.
There you will die
and there your splendid chariots will remain—
you disgrace to your master's house!
19I will depose you from your office,
and you will be ousted from your position.

20"In that day I will summon my servant, Eliakim son of Hilkiah. 21I will
clothe him with your robe and fasten
your sash around him and hand your
authority over to him. He will be a
father to those who live in Jerusalem
and to the house of Judah. 22I will place
on his shoulder the key to the house of
David; what he opens no-one can shut,
and what he shuts no-one can open. 23I
will drive him like a peg into a firm
place; he will be a seat of honour for the
house of his father. 24All the glory of his
family will hang on him: its offspring
and offshoots—all its lesser vessels,
from the bowls to all the jars.

25"In that day," declares the LORD
Almighty, "the peg driven into the firm
place will give way; it will be sheared off
and will fall, and the load hanging on it
will be cut down." The LORD has
spoken.

A Prophecy About Tyre

23 An oracle concerning Tyre:

Wail, O ships of Tarshish!
For Tyre is destroyed
and left without house or harbour.
From the land of Cyprus
word has come to them.

2Be silent, you people of the island
and you merchants of Sidon,
whom the seafarers have enriched.
3On the great waters
came the grain of the Shihor;
the harvest of the Nile was the revenue of Tyre,
and she became the market-place of the nations.

4Be ashamed, O Sidon, and you, O fortress of the sea,
for the sea has spoken:
"I have neither been in labour nor given birth;
I have neither reared sons nor brought up daughters."
5When word comes to Egypt,
they will be in anguish at the report from Tyre.

6Cross over to Tarshish;
wail, you people of the island.
7Is this your city of revelry,
the old, old city,
whose feet have taken her
to settle in far-off lands?
8Who planned this against Tyre,
the bestower of crowns,
whose merchants are princes,
whose traders are renowned in the earth?
9The LORD Almighty planned it,
to bring low the pride of all glory

and to humble all who are
renowned on the earth.

10Till your land as along the Nile,
O Daughter of Tarshish,
for you no longer have a harbour.
11The LORD has stretched out his hand
over the sea
and made its kingdoms tremble.
He has given an order concerning
Phoenicia
that her fortresses be destroyed.
12He said, "No more of your revelling,
O Virgin Daughter of Sidon, now
crushed!

"Up, cross over to Cyprus;
even there you will find no rest."
13Look at the land of the Babylonians,
this people that is now of no
account!
The Assyrians have made it
a place for desert creatures;
they raised up their siege towers,
they stripped its fortresses bare
and turned it into a ruin.

14Wail, you ships of Tarshish;
your fortress is destroyed!

15At that time Tyre will be forgotten
for seventy years, the span of a king's
life. But at the end of these seventy
years, it will happen to Tyre as in the
song of the prostitute:

16"Take up a harp, walk through the
city,
O prostitute forgotten;
play the harp well, sing many a song,
so that you will be remembered."

17At the end of seventy years, the
LORD will deal with Tyre. She will return to her hire as a prostitute and will
ply her trade with all the kingdoms on
the face of the earth. 18Yet her profit
and her earnings will be set apart for the
LORD; they will not be stored up or
hoarded. Her profits will go to those
who live before the LORD, for abundant
food and fine clothes.

NEW TESTAMENT READING

2 Corinthians 11:1–15

Paul and the False Apostles

11 I hope you will put up with a
little of my foolishness; but you
are already doing that. 2I am jealous for
you with a godly jealousy. I promised
you to one husband, to Christ, so that I
might present you as a pure virgin to
him. 3But I am afraid that just as Eve
was deceived by the serpent's cunning,
your minds may somehow be led astray
from your sincere and pure devotion to
Christ. 4For if someone comes to you
and preaches a Jesus other than the
Jesus we preached, or if you receive a
different spirit from the one you received, or a different gospel from the
one you accepted, you put up with it
easily enough. 5But I do not think I am
in the least inferior to those "super-
apostles". 6I may not be a trained
speaker, but I do have knowledge. We
have made this perfectly clear to you in
every way.

7Was it a sin for me to lower myself in
order to elevate you by preaching the
gospel of God to you free of charge? 8I
robbed other churches by receiving support from them so as to serve you. 9And
when I was with you and needed something, I was not a burden to anyone, for
the brothers who came from Macedonia
supplied what I needed. I have kept
myself from being a burden to you in
any way, and will continue to do so.
10As surely as the truth of Christ is in
me, nobody in the regions of Achaia
will stop this boasting of mine. 11Why?
Because I do not love you? God knows I
do! 12And I will keep on doing what I
am doing in order to cut the ground
from under those who want an opportunity to be considered equal with us in
the things they boast about.

13For such men are false apostles,
deceitful workmen, masquerading as
apostles of Christ. 14And no wonder,
for Satan himself masquerades as an
angel of light. 15It is not surprising,

then, if his servants masquerade as servants of righteousness. Their end will be what their actions deserve.

READING FROM PROVERBS
Proverbs 22:7–16

7The rich rule over the poor,
and the borrower is servant to the lender.

8He who sows wickedness reaps trouble,
and the rod of his fury will be destroyed.

9A generous man will himself be blessed,
for he shares his food with the poor.

10Drive out the mocker, and out goes strife;
quarrels and insults are ended.

11He who loves a pure heart and whose speech is gracious
will have the king for his friend.

12The eyes of the LORD keep watch over knowledge,
but he frustrates the words of the unfaithful.

13The sluggard says, "There is a lion outside!"
or, "I will be murdered in the streets!"

14The mouth of an adulteress is a deep pit;
he who is under the LORD's wrath will fall into it.

15Folly is bound up in the heart of a child,
but the rod of discipline will drive it far from him.

16He who oppresses the poor to increase his wealth
and he who gives gifts to the rich—both come to poverty.

SEPTEMBER 10

DAY 253

OLD TESTAMENT READING
Isaiah 24:1–26:21

The LORD's Devastation of the Earth

24 See, the LORD is going to lay waste the earth
and devastate it;
he will ruin its face
and scatter its inhabitants—
2it will be the same
for priests as for people,
for master as for servant,
for mistress as for maid,
for seller as for buyer,
for borrower as for lender,
for debtor as for creditor.
3The earth will be completely laid waste
and totally plundered.
The LORD has spoken this word.

4The earth dries up and withers,
the world languishes and withers,
the exalted of the earth languish.
5The earth is defiled by its people;
they have disobeyed the laws,
violated the statutes
and broken the everlasting covenant.
6Therefore a curse consumes the earth;

its people must bear their
guilt.
Therefore earth's inhabitants are
burned up,
and very few are left.
7The new wine dries up and the vine
withers;
all the merrymakers groan.
8The gaiety of the tambourines is
stilled,
the noise of the revellers has
stopped,
the joyful harp is silent.
9No longer do they drink wine with a
song;
the beer is bitter to its drinkers.
10The ruined city lies desolate;
the entrance to every house is
barred.
11In the streets they cry out for wine;
all joy turns to gloom,
all gaiety is banished from the
earth.
12The city is left in ruins,
its gate is battered to pieces.
13So will it be on the earth
and among the nations,
as when an olive tree is beaten,
or as when gleanings are left after
the grape harvest.

14They raise their voices, they shout for
joy;
from the west they acclaim the
LORD's majesty.
15Therefore in the east give glory to the
LORD;
exalt the name of the LORD, the
God of Israel,
in the islands of the sea.
16From the ends of the earth we hear
singing:
"Glory to the Righteous One."

But I said, "I waste away, I waste
away!
Woe to me!
The treacherous betray!
With treachery the treacherous
betray!"
17Terror and pit and snare await you,
O people of the earth.
18Whoever flees at the sound of terror
will fall into a pit;
whoever climbs out of the pit
will be caught in a snare.

The floodgates of the heavens are
opened,
the foundations of the earth shake.
19The earth is broken up,
the earth is split asunder,
the earth is thoroughly shaken.
20The earth reels like a drunkard,
it sways like a hut in the wind;
so heavy upon it is the guilt of its
rebellion
that it falls—never to rise again.

21In that day the LORD will punish
the powers in the heavens above
and the kings on the earth below.
22They will be herded together
like prisoners bound in a dungeon;
they will be shut up in prison
and be punished after many days.
23The moon will be abashed, the sun
ashamed;
for the LORD Almighty will reign
on Mount Zion and in Jerusalem,
and before its elders, gloriously.

Praise to the LORD

25 O LORD, you are my God;
I will exalt you and praise your
name,
for in perfect faithfulness
you have done marvellous things,
things planned long ago.
2You have made the city a heap of
rubble,
the fortified town a ruin,
the foreigners' stronghold a city no
more;
it will never be rebuilt.
3Therefore strong peoples will honour
you;
cities of ruthless nations will revere
you.
4You have been a refuge for the poor,
a refuge for the needy in his
distress,
a shelter from the storm
and a shade from the heat.

For the breath of the ruthless
is like a storm driving against a wall
5 and like the heat of the desert.
You silence the uproar of foreigners;
as heat is reduced by the shadow of a cloud,
so the song of the ruthless is stilled.

6On this mountain the LORD Almighty will prepare
a feast of rich food for all peoples,
a banquet of aged wine—
the best of meats and the finest of wines.
7On this mountain he will destroy
the shroud that enfolds all peoples,
the sheet that covers all nations;
8 he will swallow up death for ever.
The Sovereign LORD will wipe away the tears
from all faces;
he will remove the disgrace of his people
from all the earth.
The LORD has spoken.

9In that day they will say,

"Surely this is our God;
we trusted in him, and he saved us.
This is the LORD, we trusted in him;
let us rejoice and be glad in his salvation."

10The hand of the LORD will rest on this mountain;
but Moab will be trampled under him
as straw is trampled down in the manure.
11They will spread out their hands in it,
as a swimmer spreads out his hands to swim.
God will bring down their pride
despite the cleverness of their hands.
12He will bring down your high fortified walls
and lay them low;
he will bring them down to the ground,
to the very dust.

A Song of Praise

26 In that day this song will be sung in the land of Judah:

We have a strong city;
God makes salvation
its walls and ramparts.
2Open the gates
that the righteous nation may enter,
the nation that keeps faith.
3You will keep in perfect peace
him whose mind is steadfast,
because he trusts in you.
4Trust in the LORD for ever,
for the LORD, the LORD, is the Rock eternal.
5He humbles those who dwell on high,
he lays the lofty city low;
he levels it to the ground
and casts it down to the dust.
6Feet trample it down—
the feet of the oppressed,
the footsteps of the poor.

7The path of the righteous is level;
O upright One, you make the way of the righteous smooth.
8Yes, LORD, walking in the way of your laws,
we wait for you;
your name and renown
are the desire of our hearts.
9My soul yearns for you in the night;
in the morning my spirit longs for you.
When your judgments come upon the earth,
the people of the world learn righteousness.
10Though grace is shown to the wicked,
they do not learn righteousness;
even in a land of uprightness they go on doing evil
and regard not the majesty of the LORD.
11O LORD, your hand is lifted high,
but they do not see it.
Let them see your zeal for your people and be put to shame;
let the fire reserved for your enemies consume them.

12LORD, you establish peace for us;
all that we have accomplished you
have done for us.
13O LORD, our God, other lords
besides you have ruled over us,
but your name alone do we
honour.
14They are now dead, they live no
more;
those departed spirits do not rise.
You punished them and brought
them to ruin;
you wiped out all memory of them.
15You have enlarged the nation, O
LORD;
you have enlarged the nation.
You have gained glory for yourself;
you have extended all the borders
of the land.

16LORD, they came to you in their
distress;
when you disciplined them,
they could barely whisper a prayer.
17As a woman with child and about to
give birth
writhes and cries out in her pain,
so were we in your presence, O
LORD.
18We were with child, we writhed in
pain,
but we gave birth to wind.
We have not brought salvation to the
earth;
we have not given birth to people
of the world.

19But your dead will live;
their bodies will rise.
You who dwell in the dust,
wake up and shout for joy.
Your dew is like the dew of the
morning;
the earth will give birth to her
dead.

20Go, my people, enter your rooms
and shut the doors behind you;
hide yourselves for a little while
until his wrath has passed by.
21See, the LORD is coming out of his
dwelling
to punish the people of the earth
for their sins.
The earth will disclose the blood shed
upon her;
she will conceal her slain no longer.

NEW TESTAMENT READING
2 Corinthians 11:16–33

Paul Boasts About His Sufferings

16I repeat: Let no-one take me for a
fool. But if you do, then receive me just
as you would a fool, so that I may do a
little boasting. 17In this self-confident
boasting I am not talking as the Lord
would, but as a fool. 18Since many are
boasting in the way the world does, I too
will boast. 19You gladly put up with
fools since you are so wise! 20In fact, you
even put up with anyone who enslaves
you or exploits you or takes advantage
of you or pushes himself forward or
slaps you in the face. 21To my shame I
admit that we were too weak for that!

What anyone else dares to boast
about—I am speaking as a fool—I
also dare to boast about. 22Are they
Hebrews? So am I. Are they Israelites?
So am I. Are they Abraham's descendants? So am I. 23Are they servants of
Christ? (I am out of my mind to talk like
this.) I am more. I have worked much
harder, been in prison more frequently,
been flogged more severely, and been
exposed to death again and again.
24Five times I received from the Jews
the forty lashes minus one. 25Three
times I was beaten with rods, once I was
stoned, three times I was shipwrecked, I
spent a night and a day in the open sea,
26I have been constantly on the move. I
have been in danger from rivers, in
danger from bandits, in danger from my
own countrymen, in danger from Gentiles; in danger in the city, in danger in
the country, in danger at sea; and in
danger from false brothers. 27I have
laboured and toiled and have often
gone without sleep; I have known

hunger and thirst and have often gone
without food; I have been cold and
naked. 28Besides everything else, I face
daily the pressure of my concern for all
the churches. 29Who is weak, and I do
not feel weak? Who is led into sin, and
I do not inwardly burn?
30If I must boast, I will boast of the
things that show my weakness. 31The
God and Father of the Lord Jesus, who
is to be praised for ever, knows that I am
not lying. 32In Damascus the governor
under King Aretas had the city of the
Damascenes guarded in order to arrest
me. 33But I was lowered in a basket
from a window in the wall and slipped
through his hands.

READING FROM PSALMS

Psalm 106:32–39

32By the waters of Meribah they
angered the LORD,
and trouble came to Moses because
of them;
33for they rebelled against the Spirit of
God,
and rash words came from Moses'
lips.

34They did not destroy the peoples
as the LORD had commanded
them,
35but they mingled with the nations
and adopted their customs.
36They worshipped their idols,
which became a snare to them.
37They sacrificed their sons
and their daughters to demons.
38They shed innocent blood,
the blood of their sons and
daughters,
whom they sacrificed to the idols of
Canaan,
and the land was desecrated by
their blood.
39They defiled themselves by what they
did;
by their deeds they prostituted
themselves.

SEPTEMBER 11

DAY 254

OLD TESTAMENT READING

Isaiah 27:1–28:29

Deliverance of Israel

27 In that day,
the LORD will punish with his
sword,
his fierce, great and powerful
sword,
Leviathan the gliding serpent,
Leviathan the coiling serpent;
he will slay the monster of the sea.

2In that day—

"Sing about a fruitful vineyard:
3 I, the LORD, watch over it;
I water it continually.
I guard it day and night
so that no-one may harm it.
4 I am not angry.
If only there were briers and thorns
confronting me!
I would march against them in
battle;
I would set them all on fire.
5Or else let them come to me for
refuge;
let them make peace with me,
yes, let them make peace with me."

6In days to come Jacob will take root,
Israel will bud and blossom
and fill all the world with fruit.

7Has ⌞the LORD⌟ struck her
as he struck down those who struck
her?

Has she been killed
as those were killed who killed her?
8By warfare and exile you contend with her—
with his fierce blast he drives her out,
as on a day the east wind blows.
9By this, then, will Jacob's guilt be atoned for,
and this will be the full fruitage of the removal of his sin:
When he makes all the altar stones
to be like chalk stones crushed to pieces,
no Asherah poles or incense altars
will be left standing.
10The fortified city stands desolate,
an abandoned settlement, forsaken like the desert;
there the calves graze,
there they lie down;
they strip its branches bare.
11When its twigs are dry, they are broken off
and women come and make fires with them.
For this is a people without understanding;
so their Maker has no compassion on them,
and their Creator shows them no favour.

12In that day the LORD will thresh
from the flowing Euphrates to the Wadi
of Egypt, and you, O Israelites, will be
gathered up one by one. 13And in that
day a great trumpet will sound. Those
who were perishing in Assyria and those
who were exiled in Egypt will come and
worship the LORD on the holy mountain
in Jerusalem.

Woe to Ephraim

28 Woe to that wreath, the pride of Ephraim's drunkards,
to the fading flower, his glorious beauty,
set on the head of a fertile valley—
to that city, the pride of those laid low by wine!
2See, the Lord has one who is powerful and strong.
Like a hailstorm and a destructive wind,
like a driving rain and a flooding downpour,
he will throw it forcefully to the ground.
3That wreath, the pride of Ephraim's drunkards,
will be trampled underfoot.
4That fading flower, his glorious beauty,
set on the head of a fertile valley,
will be like a fig ripe before harvest—
as soon as someone sees it and takes it in his hand,
he swallows it.

5In that day the LORD Almighty
will be a glorious crown,
a beautiful wreath
for the remnant of his people.
6He will be a spirit of justice
to him who sits in judgment,
a source of strength
to those who turn back the battle at the gate.

7And these also stagger from wine
and reel from beer:
Priests and prophets stagger from beer
and are befuddled with wine;
they reel from beer,
they stagger when seeing visions,
they stumble when rendering decisions.
8All the tables are covered with vomit
and there is not a spot without filth.

9"Who is it he is trying to teach?
To whom is he explaining his message?
To children weaned from their milk,
to those just taken from the breast?
10For it is:
Do and do, do and do,
rule on rule, rule on rule;
a little here, a little there."

11 Very well then, with foreign lips and
strange tongues
God will speak to this people,
12 to whom he said,
"This is the resting-place, let the
weary rest";
and, "This is the place of repose"—
but they would not listen.
13 So then, the word of the LORD to
them will become:
Do and do, do and do,
rule on rule, rule on rule;
a little here, a little there—
so that they will go and fall
backwards,
be injured and snared and
captured.

14 Therefore hear the word of the
LORD, you scoffers
who rule this people in Jerusalem.
15 You boast, "We have entered into a
covenant with death,
with the grave we have made an
agreement.
When an overwhelming scourge
sweeps by,
it cannot touch us,
for we have made a lie our refuge
and falsehood our hiding-place."

16 So this is what the Sovereign LORD says:

"See, I lay a stone in Zion,
a tested stone,
a precious cornerstone for a sure
foundation;
the one who trusts will never be
dismayed.
17 I will make justice the measuring line
and righteousness the plumb-line;
hail will sweep away your refuge, the
lie,
and water will overflow your
hiding-place.
18 Your covenant with death will be
annulled;
your agreement with the grave will
not stand.
When the overwhelming scourge
sweeps by,
you will be beaten down by it.
19 As often as it comes it will carry you
away;
morning after morning, by day and
by night,
it will sweep through."

The understanding of this message
will bring sheer terror.
20 The bed is too short to stretch out on,
the blanket too narrow to wrap
around you.
21 The LORD will rise up as he did at
Mount Perazim,
he will rouse himself as in the
Valley of Gibeon—
to do his work, his strange work,
and perform his task, his alien
task.
22 Now stop your mocking,
or your chains will become heavier;
the Lord, the LORD Almighty, has
told me
of the destruction decreed against
the whole land.

23 Listen and hear my voice;
pay attention and hear what I say.
24 When a farmer ploughs for planting,
does he plough continually?
Does he keep on breaking up and
harrowing the soil?
25 When he has levelled the surface,
does he not sow caraway and
scatter cummin?
Does he not plant wheat in its place,
barley in its plot,
and spelt in its field?
26 His God instructs him
and teaches him the right way.

27 Caraway is not threshed with a
sledge,
nor is a cartwheel rolled over
cummin;
caraway is beaten out with a rod,
and cummin with a stick.
28 Grain must be ground to make bread;
so one does not go on threshing it
for ever.
Though he drives the wheels of his
threshing-cart over it,
his horses do not grind it.

29All this also comes from the LORD
Almighty,
wonderful in counsel and
magnificent in wisdom.

NEW TESTAMENT READING
2 Corinthians 12:1–10

Paul's Vision and His Thorn

12 I must go on boasting. Although
there is nothing to be gained, I
will go on to visions and revelations
from the Lord. 2I know a man in Christ
who fourteen years ago was caught up
to the third heaven. Whether it was in
the body or out of the body I do not
know—God knows. 3And I know that
this man—whether in the body or apart
from the body I do not know, but God
knows—4was caught up to paradise. He
heard inexpressible things, things that
man is not permitted to tell. 5I will boast
about a man like that, but I will not
boast about myself, except about my
weaknesses. 6Even if I should choose to
boast, I would not be a fool, because I
would be speaking the truth. But I refrain, so no-one will think more of me
than is warranted by what I do or say.
7To keep me from becoming conceited because of these surpassingly
great revelations, there was given me a
thorn in my flesh, a messenger of Satan,
to torment me. 8Three times I pleaded
with the Lord to take it away from me.
9But he said to me, "My grace is sufficient for you, for my power is made
perfect in weakness." Therefore I will
boast all the more gladly about my
weaknesses, so that Christ's power may
rest on me. 10That is why, for Christ's
sake, I delight in weaknesses, in insults, in hardships, in persecutions, in difficulties. For when I am weak, then I am strong.

READING FROM PSALMS
Psalm 106:40–48

40Therefore the LORD was angry with
his people
and abhorred his inheritance.
41He handed them over to the nations,
and their foes ruled over them.
42Their enemies oppressed them
and subjected them to their power.
43Many times he delivered them,
but they were bent on rebellion
and they wasted away in their sin.

44But he took note of their distress
when he heard their cry;
45for their sake he remembered his
covenant
and out of his great love he
relented.
46He caused them to be pitied
by all who held them captive.

47Save us, O LORD our God,
and gather us from the nations,
that we may give thanks to your holy
name
and glory in your praise.

48Praise be to the LORD, the God of
Israel,
from everlasting to everlasting.
Let all the people say, "Amen!"

Praise the LORD.

SEPTEMBER 12

OLD TESTAMENT READING
Isaiah 29:1–30:18

Woe to David's City

29 Woe to you, Ariel, Ariel,
the city where David settled!
Add year to year
and let your cycle of festivals go on.
2Yet I will besiege Ariel;
she will mourn and lament,
she will be to me like an altar hearth.
3I will encamp against you all around;
I will encircle you with towers
and set up my siege works against you.
4Brought low, you will speak from the ground;
your speech will mumble out of the dust.
Your voice will come ghostlike from the earth;
out of the dust your speech will whisper.

5But your many enemies will become like fine dust,
the ruthless hordes like blown chaff.
Suddenly, in an instant,
6 the LORD Almighty will come
with thunder and earthquake and great noise,
with windstorm and tempest and flames of a devouring fire.
7Then the hordes of all the nations that fight against Ariel,
that attack her and her fortress and besiege her,
will be as it is with a dream,
with a vision in the night—
8as when a hungry man dreams that he is eating,
but he awakens, and his hunger remains;
as when a thirsty man dreams that he is drinking,
but he awakens faint, with his thirst unquenched.
So will it be with the hordes of all the nations
that fight against Mount Zion.

9Be stunned and amazed,
blind yourselves and be sightless;
be drunk, but not from wine,
stagger, but not from beer.
10The LORD has brought over you a deep sleep:
He has sealed your eyes (the prophets);
he has covered your heads (the seers).

11For you this whole vision is nothing
but words sealed in a scroll. And if you
give the scroll to someone who can
read, and say to him, "Read this,
please," he will answer, "I can't; it is
sealed." 12Or if you give the scroll to
someone who cannot read, and say,
"Read this, please," he will answer, "I
don't know how to read."

13The Lord says:

"These people come near to me with their mouth
and honour me with their lips,
but their hearts are far from me.
Their worship of me
is made up only of rules taught by men.
14Therefore once more I will astound these people
with wonder upon wonder;
the wisdom of the wise will perish,
the intelligence of the intelligent will vanish."
15Woe to those who go to great depths
to hide their plans from the LORD,

who do their work in darkness and
think,
"Who sees us? Who will know?"
16You turn things upside down,
as if the potter were thought to be
like the clay!
Shall what is formed say to him who
formed it,
"He did not make me"?
Can the pot say of the potter,
"He knows nothing"?
17In a very short time, will not Lebanon
be turned into a fertile field
and the fertile field seem like a
forest?
18In that day the deaf will hear the
words of the scroll,
and out of gloom and darkness
the eyes of the blind will see.
19Once more the humble will rejoice in
the LORD;
the needy will rejoice in the Holy
One of Israel.
20The ruthless will vanish,
the mockers will disappear,
and all who have an eye for evil will
be cut down—
21those who with a word make a man
out to be guilty,
who ensnare the defender in court
and with false testimony deprive
the innocent of justice.

22Therefore this is what the LORD,
who redeemed Abraham, says to the
house of Jacob:

"No longer will Jacob be ashamed;
no longer will their faces grow
pale.
23When they see among them their
children,
the work of my hands,
they will keep my name holy;
they will acknowledge the holiness
of the Holy One of Jacob,
and will stand in awe of the God of
Israel.
24Those who are wayward in spirit will
gain understanding;
those who complain will accept
instruction."

Woe to the Obstinate Nation

30 "Woe to the obstinate
children,"
declares the LORD,
"to those who carry out plans that are
not mine,
forming an alliance, but not by my
Spirit,
heaping sin upon sin;
2who go down to Egypt
without consulting me;
who look for help to Pharaoh's
protection,
to Egypt's shade for refuge.
3But Pharaoh's protection will be to
your shame,
Egypt's shade will bring you
disgrace.
4Though they have officials in Zoan
and their envoys have arrived in
Hanes,
5everyone will be put to shame
because of a people useless to
them,
who bring neither help nor
advantage,
but only shame and disgrace."

6An oracle concerning the animals of
the Negev:

Through a land of hardship and
distress,
of lions and lionesses,
of adders and darting snakes,
the envoys carry their riches on
donkeys' backs,
their treasures on the humps of
camels,
to that unprofitable nation,
7 to Egypt, whose help is utterly
useless.
Therefore I call her
Rahab the Do-Nothing.

8Go now, write it on a tablet for them,
inscribe it on a scroll,
that for the days to come
it may be an everlasting witness.
9These are rebellious people, deceitful
children,

children unwilling to listen to the
LORD's instruction.
10They say to the seers,
"See no more visions!"
and to the prophets,
"Give us no more visions of what is right!
Tell us pleasant things,
prophesy illusions.
11Leave this way,
get off this path,
and stop confronting us
with the Holy One of Israel!"

12Therefore, this is what the Holy One of Israel says:

"Because you have rejected this message,
relied on oppression
and depended on deceit,
13this sin will become for you
like a high wall, cracked and bulging,
that collapses suddenly, in an instant.
14It will break in pieces like pottery,
shattered so mercilessly
that among its pieces not a fragment will be found
for taking coals from a hearth
or scooping water out of a cistern."

15This is what the Sovereign LORD, the Holy One of Israel, says:

"In repentance and rest is your salvation,
in quietness and trust is your strength,
but you would have none of it.
16You said, 'No, we will flee on horses.'
Therefore you will flee!
You said, 'We will ride off on swift horses.'
Therefore your pursuers will be swift!
17A thousand will flee
at the threat of one;
at the threat of five
you will all flee away,
till you are left
like a flagstaff on a mountaintop,
like a banner on a hill."

18Yet the LORD longs to be gracious to you;
he rises to show you compassion.
For the LORD is a God of justice.
Blessed are all who wait for him!

NEW TESTAMENT READING

2 Corinthians 12:11–21

Paul's Concern for the Corinthians

11I have made a fool of myself, but
you drove me to it. I ought to have been
commended by you, for I am not in the
least inferior to the "super-apostles",
even though I am nothing. 12The things
that mark an apostle—signs, wonders
and miracles—were done among you
with great perseverance. 13How were
you inferior to the other churches, except that I was never a burden to you?
Forgive me this wrong!

14Now I am ready to visit you for the
third time, and I will not be a burden to
you, because what I want is not your
possessions but you. After all, children
should not have to save up for their
parents, but parents for their children.
15So I will very gladly spend for you
everything I have and expend myself as
well. If I love you more, will you love
me less? 16Be that as it may, I have not
been a burden to you. Yet, crafty fellow
that I am, I caught you by trickery!
17Did I exploit you through any of the
men I sent you? 18I urged Titus to go to
you and I sent our brother with him.
Titus did not exploit you, did he? Did
we not act in the same spirit and follow
the same course?

19Have you been thinking all along
that we have been defending ourselves
to you? We have been speaking in the
sight of God as those in Christ; and
everything we do, dear friends, is for
your strengthening. 20For I am afraid
that when I come I may not find you as I

want you to be, and you may not find me as you want me to be. I fear that there may be quarrelling, jealousy, outbursts of anger, factions, slander, gossip, arrogance and disorder. 21I am afraid that when I come again my God will humble me before you, and I will be grieved over many who have sinned earlier and have not repented of the impurity, sexual sin and debauchery in which they have indulged.

READING FROM PSALMS

Psalm 107:1–9

1Give thanks to the LORD, for he is good;
his love endures for ever.
2Let the redeemed of the LORD say this—
those he redeemed from the hand of the foe,
3those he gathered from the lands,
from east and west, from north and south.

4Some wandered in desert wastelands,
finding no way to a city where they could settle.
5They were hungry and thirsty,
and their lives ebbed away.
6Then they cried out to the LORD in their trouble,
and he delivered them from their distress.
7He led them by a straight way
to a city where they could settle.
8Let them give thanks to the LORD for his unfailing love
and his wonderful deeds for men,
9for he satisfies the thirsty
and fills the hungry with good things.

DAY 256

SEPTEMBER 13

OLD TESTAMENT READING

Isaiah 30:19–32:20

19O people of Zion, who live in Jerusalem, you will weep no more. How
gracious he will be when you cry for
help! As soon as he hears, he will
answer you. 20Although the Lord gives
you the bread of adversity and the water
of affliction, your teachers will be hidden no more; with your own eyes you
will see them. 21Whether you turn to the
right or to the left, your ears will hear a
voice behind you, saying, "This is the
way; walk in it." 22Then you will defile
your idols overlaid with silver and your
images covered with gold; you will
throw them away like a menstrual cloth
and say to them, "Away with you!"

23He will also send you rain for the
seed you sow in the ground, and the
food that comes from the land will be
rich and plentiful. In that day your
cattle will graze in broad meadows.
24The oxen and donkeys that work the
soil will eat fodder and mash, spread out
with fork and shovel. 25In the day of
great slaughter, when the towers fall,
streams of water will flow on every high
mountain and every lofty hill. 26The
moon will shine like the sun, and the
sunlight will be seven times brighter,
like the light of seven full days, when
the LORD binds up the bruises of
his people and heals the wounds he
inflicted.

27See, the Name of the LORD comes from afar,
with burning anger and dense clouds of smoke;
his lips are full of wrath,
and his tongue is a consuming fire.

28His breath is like a rushing torrent,
rising up to the neck.
He shakes the nations in the sieve of destruction;
he places in the jaws of the peoples
a bit that leads them astray.
29And you will sing
as on the night you celebrate a holy festival;
your hearts will rejoice
as when people go up with flutes
to the mountain of the LORD,
to the Rock of Israel.
30The LORD will cause men to hear his majestic voice
and will make them see his arm coming down
with raging anger and consuming fire,
with cloudburst, thunderstorm and hail.
31The voice of the LORD will shatter Assyria;
with his sceptre he will strike them down.
32Every stroke the LORD lays on them
with his punishing rod
will be to the music of tambourines and harps,
as he fights them in battle with the blows of his arm.
33Topheth has long been prepared;
it has been made ready for the king.
Its fire pit has been made deep and wide,
with an abundance of fire and wood;
the breath of the LORD,
like a stream of burning sulphur,
sets it ablaze.

Woe to Those Who Rely on Egypt

31 Woe to those who go down to Egypt for help,
who rely on horses,
who trust in the multitude of their chariots
and in the great strength of their horsemen,
but do not look to the Holy One of Israel,
or seek help from the LORD.
2Yet he too is wise and can bring disaster;
he does not take back his words.
He will rise up against the house of the wicked,
against those who help evildoers.
3But the Egyptians are men and not God;
their horses are flesh and not spirit.
When the LORD stretches out his hand,
he who helps will stumble,
he who is helped will fall;
both will perish together.

4This is what the LORD says to me:

"As a lion growls,
a great lion over his prey—
and though a whole band of shepherds
is called together against him,
he is not frightened by their shouts
or disturbed by their clamour—
so the LORD Almighty will come down
to do battle on Mount Zion and on its heights.
5Like birds hovering overhead,
the LORD Almighty will shield Jerusalem;
he will shield it and deliver it,
he will 'pass over' it and will rescue it."

6Return to him you have so greatly
revolted against, O Israelites. 7For in
that day every one of you will reject the
idols of silver and gold your sinful hands
have made.

8"Assyria will fall by a sword that is not of man;
a sword, not of mortals, will devour them.
They will flee before the sword
and their young men will be put to forced labour.
9Their stronghold will fall because of terror;

at sight of the battle standard their
commanders will panic,"
declares the LORD,
whose fire is in Zion,
whose furnace is in Jerusalem.

The Kingdom of Righteousness

32 See, a king will reign in righteousness
and rulers will rule with justice.
2Each man will be like a shelter from the wind
and a refuge from the storm,
like streams of water in the desert
and the shadow of a great rock in a thirsty land.

3Then the eyes of those who see will no longer be closed,
and the ears of those who hear will listen.
4The mind of the rash will know and understand,
and the stammering tongue will be fluent and clear.
5No longer will the fool be called noble
nor the scoundrel be highly respected.
6For the fool speaks folly,
his mind is busy with evil:
He practises ungodliness
and spreads error concerning the LORD;
the hungry he leaves empty
and from the thirsty he withholds water.
7The scoundrel's methods are wicked,
he makes up evil schemes
to destroy the poor with lies,
even when the plea of the needy is just.
8But the noble man makes noble plans,
and by noble deeds he stands.

The Women of Jerusalem

9You women who are so complacent,
rise up and listen to me;
you daughters who feel secure,
hear what I have to say!
10In little more than a year
you who feel secure will tremble;
the grape harvest will fail,
and the harvest of fruit will not come.
11Tremble, you complacent women;
shudder, you daughters who feel secure!
Strip off your clothes,
put sackcloth round your waists.
12Beat your breasts for the pleasant fields,
for the fruitful vines
13and for the land of my people,
a land overgrown with thorns and briers—
yes, mourn for all houses of merriment
and for this city of revelry.
14The fortress will be abandoned,
the noisy city deserted;
citadel and watchtower will become a wasteland for ever,
the delight of donkeys, a pasture for flocks,
15till the Spirit is poured upon us from on high,
and the desert becomes a fertile field,
and the fertile field seems like a forest.
16Justice will dwell in the desert
and righteousness live in the fertile field.
17The fruit of righteousness will be peace;
the effect of righteousness will be quietness and confidence for ever.
18My people will live in peaceful dwelling-places,
in secure homes,
in undisturbed places of rest.
19Though hail flattens the forest
and the city is levelled completely,
20how blessed you will be,
sowing your seed by every stream,
and letting your cattle and donkeys range free.

NEW TESTAMENT READING
2 Corinthians 13:1–14

Final Warnings

13 This will be my third visit to you.
"Every matter must be established by the testimony of two or three
witnesses." 2I already gave you a warning when I was with you the second
time. I now repeat it while absent: On
my return I will not spare those who
sinned earlier or any of the others,
3since you are demanding proof that
Christ is speaking through me. He is not
weak in dealing with you, but is powerful among you. 4For to be sure, he was
crucified in weakness, yet he lives by
God's power. Likewise, we are weak in
him, yet by God's power we will live
with him to serve you.
5Examine yourselves to see whether
you are in the faith; test yourselves. Do
you not realise that Christ Jesus is
in you—unless, of course, you fail the
test? 6And I trust that you will discover
that we have not failed the test. 7Now
we pray to God that you will not do
anything wrong. Not that people will
see that we have stood the test but that
you will do what is right even though we
may seem to have failed. 8For we cannot do anything against the truth, but
only for the truth. 9We are glad whenever we are weak but you are strong;
and our prayer is for your perfection.
10This is why I write these things when I
am absent, that when I come I may not
have to be harsh in my use of authority
—the authority the Lord gave me for
building you up, not for tearing you
down.

Final Greetings

11Finally, brothers, good-bye. Aim
for perfection, listen to my appeal, be of
one mind, live in peace. And the God of
love and peace will be with you.
12Greet one another with a holy kiss.
13All the saints send their greetings.
14May the grace of the Lord Jesus
Christ, and the love of God, and the
fellowship of the Holy Spirit be with you
all.

READING FROM PROVERBS
Proverbs 22:17–27

Sayings of the Wise

17Pay attention and listen to the sayings
of the wise;
apply your heart to what I teach,
18for it is pleasing when you keep them
in your heart
and have all of them ready on your
lips.
19So that your trust may be in the
LORD,
I teach you today, even you.
20Have I not written thirty sayings for
you,
sayings of counsel and knowledge,
21teaching you true and reliable words,
so that you can give sound answers
to him who sent you?

22Do not exploit the poor because they
are poor
and do not crush the needy in
court,
23for the LORD will take up their case
and will plunder those who plunder
them.

24Do not make friends with a
hot-tempered man,
do not associate with one easily
angered,
25or you may learn his ways
and get yourself ensnared.

26Do not be a man who strikes hands in
pledge
or puts up security for debts;
27if you lack the means to pay,
your very bed will be snatched
from under you.

OLD TESTAMENT READING

Isaiah 33:1–35:10

Distress and Help

33 Woe to you, O destroyer,
you who have not been destroyed!
Woe to you, O traitor,
you who have not been betrayed!
When you stop destroying,
you will be destroyed;
when you stop betraying,
you will be betrayed.

2O LORD, be gracious to us;
we long for you.
Be our strength every morning,
our salvation in time of distress.
3At the thunder of your voice, the peoples flee;
when you rise up, the nations scatter.
4Your plunder, O nations, is harvested as by young locusts;
like a swarm of locusts men pounce on it.

5The LORD is exalted, for he dwells on high;
he will fill Zion with justice and righteousness.
6He will be the sure foundation for your times,
a rich store of salvation and wisdom and knowledge;
the fear of the LORD is the key to this treasure.

7Look, their brave men cry aloud in the streets;
the envoys of peace weep bitterly.
8The highways are deserted,
no travellers are on the roads.
The treaty is broken,
its witnesses are despised,
no-one is respected.
9The land mourns and wastes away,
Lebanon is ashamed and withers;
Sharon is like the Arabah,
and Bashan and Carmel drop their leaves.

10"Now will I arise," says the LORD.
"Now will I be exalted;
now will I be lifted up.
11You conceive chaff,
you give birth to straw;
your breath is a fire that consumes you.
12The peoples will be burned as if to lime;
like cut thornbushes they will be set ablaze."

13You who are far away, hear what I have done;
you who are near, acknowledge my power!
14The sinners in Zion are terrified;
trembling grips the godless:
"Who of us can dwell with the consuming fire?
Who of us can dwell with everlasting burning?"
15He who walks righteously
and speaks what is right,
who rejects gain from extortion
and keeps his hand from accepting bribes,
who stops his ears against plots of murder
and shuts his eyes against contemplating evil—
16this is the man who will dwell on the heights,
whose refuge will be the mountain fortress.
His bread will be supplied,
and water will not fail him.

17Your eyes will see the king in his beauty
and view a land that stretches afar.
18In your thoughts you will ponder the former terror:
"Where is that chief officer?

Where is the one who took the
revenue?
Where is the officer in charge of
the towers?"
19You will see those arrogant people no
more,
those people of an obscure speech,
with their strange,
incomprehensible tongue.

20Look upon Zion, the city of our
festivals;
your eyes will see Jerusalem,
a peaceful abode, a tent that will
not be moved;
its stakes will never be pulled up,
nor any of its ropes broken.
21There the LORD will be our Mighty
One.
It will be like a place of broad
rivers and streams.
No galley with oars will ride them,
no mighty ship will sail them.
22For the LORD is our judge,
the LORD is our lawgiver,
the LORD is our king;
it is he who will save us.

23Your rigging hangs loose:
The mast is not held secure,
the sail is not spread.
Then an abundance of spoils will be
divided
and even the lame will carry off
plunder.
24No-one living in Zion will say, "I am
ill";
and the sins of those who dwell
there will be forgiven.

Judgment Against the Nations

34 Come near, you nations, and
listen;
pay attention, you peoples!
Let the earth hear, and all that is
in it,
the world, and all that comes out
of it!
2The LORD is angry with all nations;
his wrath is upon all their armies.
He will totally destroy them,
he will give them over to slaughter.
3Their slain will be thrown out,
their dead bodies will send up a
stench;
the mountains will be soaked with
their blood.
4All the stars of the heavens will be
dissolved
and the sky rolled up like a scroll;
all the starry host will fall
like withered leaves from the vine,
like shrivelled figs from the
fig-tree.

5My sword has drunk its fill in the
heavens;
see, it descends in judgment on
Edom,
the people I have totally
destroyed.
6The sword of the LORD is bathed in
blood,
it is covered with fat—
the blood of lambs and goats,
fat from the kidneys of rams.
For the LORD has a sacrifice in
Bozrah
and a great slaughter in Edom.
7And the wild oxen will fall with them,
the bull calves and the great bulls.
Their land will be drenched with
blood,
and the dust will be soaked with
fat.

8For the LORD has a day of vengeance,
a year of retribution, to uphold
Zion's cause.
9Edom's streams will be turned into
pitch,
her dust into burning sulphur;
her land will become blazing pitch!
10It will not be quenched night and day;
its smoke will rise for ever.
From generation to generation it will
lie desolate;
no-one will ever pass through it
again.
11The desert owl and screech owl will
possess it;
the great owl and the raven will
nest there.

God will stretch out over Edom
the measuring line of chaos
and the plumb-line of desolation.
12Her nobles will have nothing there to
be called a kingdom,
all her princes will vanish away.
13Thorns will overrun her citadels,
nettles and brambles her
strongholds.
She will become a haunt for jackals,
a home for owls.
14Desert creatures will meet with
hyenas,
and wild goats will bleat to each
other;
there the night creatures will also
repose
and find for themselves places of
rest.
15The owl will nest there and lay eggs,
she will hatch them, and care for
her young under the shadow of
her wings;
there also the falcons will gather,
each with its mate.

16Look in the scroll of the LORD and read:

None of these will be missing,
not one will lack her mate.
For it is his mouth that has given the
order,
and his Spirit will gather them
together.
17He allots their portions;
his hand distributes them by
measure.
They will possess it for ever
and dwell there from generation to
generation.

Joy of the Redeemed

35 The desert and the parched
land will be glad;
the wilderness will rejoice and
blossom.
Like the crocus, 2it will burst into
bloom;
it will rejoice greatly and shout for
joy.
The glory of Lebanon will be given to
it,
the splendour of Carmel and
Sharon;
they will see the glory of the LORD,
the splendour of our God.

3Strengthen the feeble hands,
steady the knees that give way;
4say to those with fearful hearts,
"Be strong, do not fear;
your God will come,
he will come with vengeance;
with divine retribution
he will come to save you."

5Then will the eyes of the blind be
opened
and the ears of the deaf unstopped.
6Then will the lame leap like a deer,
and the mute tongue shout for joy.
Water will gush forth in the
wilderness
and streams in the desert.
7The burning sand will become a pool,
the thirsty ground bubbling
springs.
In the haunts where jackals once lay,
grass and reeds and papyrus will
grow.

8And a highway will be there;
it will be called the Way of
Holiness.
The unclean will not journey on it;
it will be for those who walk in that
Way;
wicked fools will not go about on it.
9No lion will be there,
nor will any ferocious beast get up
on it;
they will not be found there.
But only the redeemed will walk
there,
10 and the ransomed of the LORD will
return.
They will enter Zion with singing;
everlasting joy will crown their
heads.
Gladness and joy will overtake them,
and sorrow and sighing will flee
away.

NEW TESTAMENT READING
Galatians 1:1–24

1 Paul, an apostle—sent not from
men nor by man, but by Jesus
Christ and God the Father, who raised
him from the dead—[2]and all the
brothers with me,

To the churches in Galatia:

[3]Grace and peace to you from God
our Father and the Lord Jesus Christ,
[4]who gave himself for our sins to rescue
us from the present evil age, according
to the will of our God and Father, [5]to
whom be glory for ever and ever.
Amen.

No Other Gospel

[6]I am astonished that you are so
quickly deserting the one who called
you by the grace of Christ and are turning to a different gospel—[7]which is
really no gospel at all. Evidently some
people are throwing you into confusion
and are trying to pervert the gospel of
Christ. [8]But even if we or an angel from
heaven should preach a gospel other
than the one we preached to you, let
him be eternally condemned! [9]As we
have already said, so now I say again: If
anybody is preaching to you a gospel
other than what you accepted, let him
be eternally condemned!

[10]Am I now trying to win the approval
of men, or of God? Or am I trying to
please men? If I were still trying to
please men, I would not be a servant of
Christ.

Paul Called by God

[11]I want you to know, brothers, that
the gospel I preached is not something
that man made up. [12]I did not receive it
from any man, nor was I taught it;
rather, I received it by revelation from
Jesus Christ.

[13]For you have heard of my previous
way of life in Judaism, how intensely I
persecuted the church of God and tried
to destroy it. [14]I was advancing in Judaism beyond many Jews of my own age
and was extremely zealous for the traditions of my fathers. [15]But when God,
who set me apart from birth and called
me by his grace, was pleased [16]to reveal
his Son in me so that I might preach him
among the Gentiles, I did not consult
any man, [17]nor did I go up to Jerusalem
to see those who were apostles before
I was, but I went immediately into
Arabia and later returned to Damascus.

[18]Then after three years, I went up to
Jerusalem to get acquainted with Peter
and stayed with him fifteen days. [19]I saw
none of the other apostles—only
James, the Lord's brother. [20]I assure
you before God that what I am writing
to you is no lie. [21]Later I went to Syria
and Cilicia. [22]I was personally unknown
to the churches of Judea that are in
Christ. [23]They only heard the report:
"The man who formerly persecuted us
is now preaching the faith he once tried
to destroy." [24]And they praised God
because of me.

READING FROM PSALMS
Psalm 107:10–22

[10]Some sat in darkness and the deepest
gloom,
prisoners suffering in iron chains,
[11]for they had rebelled against the
words of God
and despised the counsel of the
Most High.
[12]So he subjected them to bitter
labour;
they stumbled, and there was
no-one to help.
[13]Then they cried to the LORD in their
trouble,
and he saved them from their
distress.
[14]He brought them out of darkness and
the deepest gloom
and broke away their chains.

[15]Let them give thanks to the LORD for
his unfailing love
and his wonderful deeds for men,
[16]for he breaks down gates of bronze
and cuts through bars of iron.

[17]Some became fools through their
rebellious ways
and suffered affliction because of
their iniquities.
[18]They loathed all food
and drew near the gates of death.
[19]Then they cried to the LORD in their
trouble,
and he saved them from their
distress.
[20]He sent forth his word and healed
them;
he rescued them from the grave.
[21]Let them give thanks to the LORD for
his unfailing love
and his wonderful deeds for men.
[22]Let them sacrifice thank-offerings
and tell of his works with songs of
joy.

DAY 258

SEPTEMBER 15

OLD TESTAMENT READING
Isaiah 36:1–37:38

Sennacherib Threatens Jerusalem

36 In the fourteenth year of King
Hezekiah's reign, Sennacherib
king of Assyria attacked all the fortified
cities of Judah and captured them.
[2]Then the king of Assyria sent his field
commander with a large army from
Lachish to King Hezekiah at Jerusalem.
When the commander stopped at the
aqueduct of the Upper Pool, on the
road to the Washerman's Field,
[3]Eliakim son of Hilkiah the palace
administrator, Shebna the secretary,
and Joah son of Asaph the recorder
went out to him.

[4]The field commander said to them,
"Tell Hezekiah,

" 'This is what the great king, the
king of Assyria, says: On what are
you basing this confidence of
yours? [5]You say you have strategy
and military strength—but you
speak only empty words. On whom
are you depending, that you rebel
against me? [6]Look now, you are
depending on Egypt, that splintered reed of a staff, which pierces
a man's hand and wounds him if he
leans on it! Such is Pharaoh king of
Egypt to all who depend on him.
[7]And if you say to me, "We are
depending on the LORD our God"
—isn't he the one whose high
places and altars Hezekiah removed, saying to Judah and Jerusalem, "You must worship before
this altar"?

[8]" 'Come now, make a bargain
with my master, the king of Assyria: I will give you two thousand
horses—if you can put riders on
them! [9]How then can you repulse
one officer of the least of my master's officials, even though you are
depending on Egypt for chariots
and horsemen? [10]Furthermore,
have I come to attack and destroy
this land without the LORD? The
LORD himself told me to march
against this country and destroy
it.' "

[11]Then Eliakim, Shebna and Joah
said to the field commander, "Please
speak to your servants in Aramaic,
since we understand it. Don't speak to
us in Hebrew in the hearing of the
people on the wall."

[12]But the commander replied, "Was

it only to your master and you that my
master sent me to say these things, and
not to the men sitting on the wall—
who, like you, will have to eat their own
filth and drink their own urine?"
13Then the commander stood and
called out in Hebrew, "Hear the words
of the great king, the king of Assyria!
14This is what the king says: Do not
let Hezekiah deceive you. He cannot
deliver you! 15Do not let Hezekiah
persuade you to trust in the LORD when
he says, 'The LORD will surely deliver
us; this city will not be given into the
hand of the king of Assyria.'
16"Do not listen to Hezekiah. This is
what the king of Assyria says: Make
peace with me and come out to me.
Then every one of you will eat from his
own vine and fig-tree and drink water
from his own cistern, 17until I come and
take you to a land like your own—a
land of corn and new wine, a land of
bread and vineyards.
18"Do not let Hezekiah mislead you
when he says, 'The LORD will deliver
us.' Has the god of any nation ever
delivered his land from the hand of the
king of Assyria? 19Where are the gods
of Hamath and Arpad? Where are the
gods of Sepharvaim? Have they rescued
Samaria from my hand? 20Who of all the
gods of these countries has been able to
save his land from me? How then can
the LORD deliver Jerusalem from my
hand?"
21But the people remained silent and
said nothing in reply, because the king
had commanded, "Do not answer
him."
22Then Eliakim son of Hilkiah the
palace administrator, Shebna the secretary, and Joah son of Asaph the recorder went to Hezekiah, with their
clothes torn, and told him what the field
commander had said.

Jerusalem's Deliverance Foretold

37 When King Hezekiah heard
this, he tore his clothes and put
on sackcloth and went into the temple
of the LORD. 2He sent Eliakim the
palace administrator, Shebna the
secretary, and the leading priests, all
wearing sackcloth, to the prophet Isaiah
son of Amoz. 3They told him, "This is
what Hezekiah says: This day is a day of
distress and rebuke and disgrace, as
when children come to the point of birth
and there is no strength to deliver them.
4It may be that the LORD your God will
hear the words of the field commander,
whom his master, the king of Assyria,
has sent to ridicule the living God, and
that he will rebuke him for the words
the LORD your God has heard. Therefore pray for the remnant that still
survives."
5When King Hezekiah's officials
came to Isaiah, 6Isaiah said to them,
"Tell your master, 'This is what the
LORD says: Do not be afraid of what you
have heard—those words with which
the underlings of the king of Assyria
have blasphemed me. 7Listen! I am
going to put a spirit in him so that when
he hears a certain report, he will return
to his own country, and there I will have
him cut down with the sword.'"
8When the field commander heard
that the king of Assyria had left Lachish, he withdrew and found the king
fighting against Libnah.
9Now Sennacherib received a report
that Tirhakah, the Cushite king ⌞of
Egypt⌟, was marching out to fight
against him. When he heard it, he sent
messengers to Hezekiah with this word:
10"Say to Hezekiah king of Judah: Do
not let the god you depend on deceive
you when he says, 'Jerusalem will not be
handed over to the king of Assyria.'
11Surely you have heard what the kings
of Assyria have done to all the countries, destroying them completely. And
will you be delivered? 12Did the gods of
the nations that were destroyed by my
forefathers deliver them—the gods of
Gozan, Haran, Rezeph and the people
of Eden who were in Tel Assar?
13Where is the king of Hamath, the king
of Arpad, the king of the city of Sepharvaim, or of Hena or Ivvah?"

Hezekiah's Prayer

14Hezekiah received the letter from
the messengers and read it. Then he
went up to the temple of the LORD and
spread it out before the LORD. 15And
Hezekiah prayed to the LORD: 16"O
LORD Almighty, God of Israel, enthroned between the cherubim, you
alone are God over all the kingdoms of
the earth. You have made heaven and
earth. 17Give ear, O LORD, and hear;
open your eyes, O LORD, and see; listen
to all the words Sennacherib has sent to
insult the living God.

18"It is true, O LORD, that the Assyrian kings have laid waste all these
peoples and their lands. 19They have
thrown their gods into the fire and destroyed them, for they were not gods
but only wood and stone, fashioned by
human hands. 20Now, O LORD our
God, deliver us from his hand, so that
all kingdoms on earth may know that
you alone, O LORD, are God."

Sennacherib's Fall

21Then Isaiah son of Amoz sent a
message to Hezekiah: "This is what the
LORD, the God of Israel, says: Because
you have prayed to me concerning Sennacherib king of Assyria, 22this is the
word the LORD has spoken against him:

"The Virgin Daughter of Zion
despises and mocks you.
The Daughter of Jerusalem
tosses her head as you flee.
23Who is it you have insulted and blasphemed?
Against whom have you raised your voice
and lifted your eyes in pride?
Against the Holy One of Israel!
24By your messengers
you have heaped insults on the Lord.
And you have said,
'With my many chariots
I have ascended the heights of the mountains,
the utmost heights of Lebanon.
I have cut down its tallest cedars,
the choicest of its pines.
I have reached its remotest heights,
the finest of its forests.
25I have dug wells in foreign lands
and drunk the water there.
With the soles of my feet
I have dried up all the streams of Egypt.'

26"Have you not heard?
Long ago I ordained it.
In days of old I planned it;
now I have brought it to pass,
that you have turned fortified cities
into piles of stone.
27Their people, drained of power,
are dismayed and put to shame.
They are like plants in the field,
like tender green shoots,
like grass sprouting on the roof,
scorched before it grows up.

28"But I know where you stay
and when you come and go
and how you rage against me.
29Because you rage against me
and because your insolence has reached my ears,
I will put my hook in your nose
and my bit in your mouth,
and I will make you return
by the way you came.

30"This will be the sign for you, O Hezekiah:

"This year you will eat what grows by itself,
and the second year what springs from that.
But in the third year sow and reap,
plant vineyards and eat their fruit.
31Once more a remnant of the house of Judah
will take root below and bear fruit above.
32For out of Jerusalem will come a remnant,
and out of Mount Zion a band of survivors.

The zeal of the LORD Almighty
will accomplish this.

33“Therefore this is what the LORD
says concerning the king of Assyria:

“He will not enter this city
or shoot an arrow here.
He will not come before it with shield
or build a siege ramp against it.
34By the way that he came he will
return;
he will not enter this city,”
declares the LORD.
35“I will defend this city and save it,
for my sake and for the sake of
David my servant!”

36Then the angel of the LORD went
out and put to death a hundred and
eighty-five thousand men in the Assyrian camp. When the people got up
the next morning—there were all the
dead bodies! 37So Sennacherib king of
Assyria broke camp and withdrew. He
returned to Nineveh and stayed there.
38One day, while he was worshipping
in the temple of his god Nisroch, his
sons Adrammelech and Sharezer cut
him down with the sword, and they
escaped to the land of Ararat. And
Esarhaddon his son succeeded him as
king.

NEW TESTAMENT READING
Galatians 2:1–10

Paul Accepted by the Apostles

2 Fourteen years later I went up
again to Jerusalem, this time with
Barnabas. I took Titus along also. 2I
went in response to a revelation and set
before them the gospel that I preach
among the Gentiles. But I did this
privately to those who seemed to be
leaders, for fear that I was running or
had run my race in vain. 3Yet not even
Titus, who was with me, was compelled
to be circumcised, even though he was a
Greek. 4⌊This matter arose⌋ because
some false brothers had infiltrated our
ranks to spy on the freedom we have in
Christ Jesus and to make us slaves. 5We
did not give in to them for a moment, so
that the truth of the gospel might remain with you.
6As for those who seemed to be important—whatever they were makes no
difference to me; God does not judge
by external appearance—those men
added nothing to my message. 7On the
contrary, they saw that I had been entrusted with the task of preaching the
gospel to the Gentiles, just as Peter had
been to the Jews. 8For God, who was at
work in the ministry of Peter as an
apostle to the Jews, was also at work in
my ministry as an apostle to the Gentiles. 9James, Peter and John, those
reputed to be pillars, gave me and Barnabas the right hand of fellowship when
they recognised the grace given to me.
They agreed that we should go to the
Gentiles, and they to the Jews. 10All
they asked was that we should continue
to remember the poor, the very thing I
was eager to do.

READING FROM PSALMS
Psalm 107:23–32

23Others went out on the sea in ships;
they were merchants on the mighty
waters.
24They saw the works of the LORD,
his wonderful deeds in the deep.
25For he spoke and stirred up a tempest
that lifted high the waves.
26They mounted up to the heavens and
went down to the depths;
in their peril their courage melted
away.
27They reeled and staggered like
drunken men;
they were at their wits’ end.
28Then they cried out to the LORD in
their trouble,

and he brought them out of their
distress.
29He stilled the storm to a whisper;
the waves of the sea were hushed.
30They were glad when it grew calm,
and he guided them to their desired
haven.
31Let them give thanks to the LORD for
his unfailing love
and his wonderful deeds for men.
32Let them exalt him in the assembly of
the people
and praise him in the council of the
elders.

DAY 259

SEPTEMBER 16

OLD TESTAMENT READING
Isaiah 38:1–40:31

Hezekiah's Illness

38 In those days Hezekiah became
ill and was at the point of death.
The prophet Isaiah son of Amoz went to
him and said, "This is what the LORD
says: Put your house in order, because
you are going to die; you will not
recover."
2Hezekiah turned his face to the wall
and prayed to the LORD, 3"Remember,
O LORD, how I have walked before you
faithfully and with wholehearted devotion and have done what is good in
your eyes." And Hezekiah wept
bitterly.
4Then the word of the LORD came to
Isaiah: 5"Go and tell Hezekiah, 'This is
what the LORD, the God of your father
David, says: I have heard your prayer
and seen your tears; I will add fifteen
years to your life. 6And I will deliver
you and this city from the hand of the
king of Assyria. I will defend this city.
7" 'This is the LORD's sign to you that
the LORD will do what he has promised:
8I will make the shadow cast by the sun
go back the ten steps it has gone down
on the stairway of Ahaz.' " So the sunlight went back the ten steps it had gone
down.

9A writing of Hezekiah king of Judah
after his illness and recovery:

10I said, "In the prime of my life
must I go through the gates of
death
and be robbed of the rest of my
years?"
11I said, "I will not again see the LORD,
the LORD, in the land of the living;
no longer will I look on mankind,
or be with those who now dwell in
this world.
12Like a shepherd's tent my house
has been pulled down and taken
from me.
Like a weaver I have rolled up my
life,
and he has cut me off from the
loom;
day and night you made an end of
me.
13I waited patiently till dawn,
but like a lion he broke all my
bones;
day and night you made an end of
me.
14I cried like a swift or thrush,
I moaned like a mourning dove.
My eyes grew weak as I looked to the
heavens.
I am troubled; O Lord, come to my
aid!"

15But what can I say?
He has spoken to me, and he
himself has done this.
I will walk humbly all my years
because of this anguish of my soul.
16Lord, by such things men live;
and my spirit finds life in them too.

You restored me to health
and let me live.
17Surely it was for my benefit
that I suffered such anguish.
In your love you kept me
from the pit of destruction;
you have put all my sins
behind your back.
18For the grave cannot praise you,
death cannot sing your praise;
those who go down to the pit
cannot hope for your faithfulness.
19The living, the living—they praise
you,
as I am doing today;
fathers tell their children
about your faithfulness.

20The LORD will save me,
and we will sing with stringed
instruments
all the days of our lives
in the temple of the LORD.

21Isaiah had said, "Prepare a poultice of figs and apply it to the boil, and he will recover."
22Hezekiah had asked, "What will be the sign that I will go up to the temple of the LORD?"

Envoys From Babylon

39 At that time Merodach-Baladan son of Baladan king of Babylon sent Hezekiah letters and a gift, because he had heard of his illness and recovery.
2Hezekiah received the envoys gladly and showed them what was in his storehouses—the silver, the gold, the spices, the fine oil, his entire armoury and everything found among his treasures. There was nothing in his palace or in all his kingdom that Hezekiah did not show them.
3Then Isaiah the prophet went to King Hezekiah and asked, "What did those men say, and where did they come from?"
"From a distant land," Hezekiah replied. "They came to me from Babylon."
4The prophet asked, "What did they see in your palace?"
"They saw everything in my palace," Hezekiah said. "There is nothing among my treasures that I did not show them."
5Then Isaiah said to Hezekiah, "Hear
the word of the LORD Almighty: 6The
time will surely come when everything in your palace, and all that your fathers have stored up until this day, will be carried off to Babylon. Nothing will be
left, says the LORD. 7And some of your
descendants, your own flesh and blood who will be born to you, will be taken away, and they will become eunuchs in the palace of the king of Babylon."
8"The word of the LORD you have spoken is good," Hezekiah replied. For he thought, "There will be peace and security in my lifetime."

Comfort for God's People

40 Comfort, comfort my people,
says your God.
2Speak tenderly to Jerusalem,
and proclaim to her
that her hard service has been
completed,
that her sin has been paid for,
that she has received from the LORD's
hand
double for all her sins.

3A voice of one calling:
"In the desert prepare
the way for the LORD;
make straight in the wilderness
a highway for our God.
4Every valley shall be raised up,
every mountain and hill made low;
the rough ground shall become level,
the rugged places a plain.
5And the glory of the LORD will be
revealed,
and all mankind together will
see it.
For the mouth of the
LORD has spoken."

6A voice says, "Cry out."
And I said, "What shall I cry?"

"All men are like grass,
and all their glory is like the flowers of the field.
7The grass withers and the flowers fall,
because the breath of the LORD blows on them.
Surely the people are grass.
8The grass withers and the flowers fall,
but the word of our God stands for ever."

9You who bring good tidings to Zion,
go up on a high mountain.
You who bring good tidings to Jerusalem,
lift up your voice with a shout,
lift it up, do not be afraid;
say to the towns of Judah,
"Here is your God!"
10See, the Sovereign LORD comes with power,
and his arm rules for him.
See, his reward is with him,
and his recompense accompanies him.
11He tends his flock like a shepherd:
He gathers the lambs in his arms
and carries them close to his heart;
he gently leads those that have young.

12Who has measured the waters in the hollow of his hand,
or with the breadth of his hand marked off the heavens?
Who has held the dust of the earth in a basket,
or weighed the mountains on the scales
and the hills in a balance?
13Who has understood the mind of the LORD,
or instructed him as his counsellor?
14Whom did the LORD consult to enlighten him,
and who taught him the right way?
Who was it that taught him knowledge
or showed him the path of understanding?

15Surely the nations are like a drop in a bucket;
they are regarded as dust on the scales;
he weighs the islands as though they were fine dust.
16Lebanon is not sufficient for altar fires,
nor its animals enough for burnt offerings.
17Before him all the nations are as nothing;
they are regarded by him as worthless
and less than nothing.

18To whom, then, will you compare God?
What image will you compare him to?
19As for an idol, a craftsman casts it,
and a goldsmith overlays it with gold
and fashions silver chains for it.
20A man too poor to present such an offering
selects wood that will not rot.
He looks for a skilled craftsman
to set up an idol that will not topple.

21Do you not know?
Have you not heard?
Has it not been told you from the beginning?
Have you not understood since the earth was founded?
22He sits enthroned above the circle of the earth,
and its people are like grasshoppers.
He stretches out the heavens like a canopy,
and spreads them out like a tent to live in.
23He brings princes to naught
and reduces the rulers of this world to nothing.
24No sooner are they planted,
no sooner are they sown,
no sooner do they take root in the ground,
than he blows on them and they wither,

and a whirlwind sweeps them away
like chaff.

25"To whom will you compare me?
Or who is my equal?" says the
Holy One.
26Lift your eyes and look to the
heavens:
Who created all these?
He who brings out the starry host one
by one,
and calls them each by name.
Because of his great power and
mighty strength,
not one of them is missing.

27Why do you say, O Jacob,
and complain, O Israel,
"My way is hidden from the LORD;
my cause is disregarded by my
God"?
28Do you not know?
Have you not heard?
The LORD is the everlasting God,
the Creator of the ends of the
earth.
He will not grow tired or weary,
and his understanding no-one can
fathom.
29He gives strength to the weary
and increases the power of the
weak.
30Even youths grow tired and weary,
and young men stumble and fall;
31but those who hope in the LORD
will renew their strength.
They will soar on wings like eagles;
they will run and not grow weary,
they will walk and not be faint.

NEW TESTAMENT READING
Galatians 2:11–3:9

Paul Opposes Peter

11When Peter came to Antioch, I
opposed him to his face, because he was
clearly in the wrong. 12Before certain
men came from James, he used to eat
with the Gentiles. But when they arrived, he began to draw back and separate himself from the Gentiles because
he was afraid of those who belonged to
the circumcision group. 13The other
Jews joined him in his hypocrisy, so that
by their hypocrisy even Barnabas was
led astray.
14When I saw that they were not
acting in line with the truth of the gospel, I said to Peter in front of them all,
"You are a Jew, yet you live like a
Gentile and not like a Jew. How is it,
then, that you force Gentiles to follow
Jewish customs?
15"We who are Jews by birth and not
'Gentile sinners' 16know that a man is
not justified by observing the law, but
by faith in Jesus Christ. So we, too, have
put our faith in Christ Jesus that we may
be justified by faith in Christ and not by
observing the law, because by observing
the law no-one will be justified.
17"If, while we seek to be justified in
Christ, it becomes evident that we
ourselves are sinners, does that mean
that Christ promotes sin? Absolutely
not! 18If I rebuild what I destroyed, I
prove that I am a law-breaker. 19For
through the law I died to the law so that
I might live for God. 20I have been
crucified with Christ and I no longer
live, but Christ lives in me. The life I live
in the body, I live by faith in the Son of
God, who loved me and gave himself
for me. 21I do not set aside the grace of
God, for if righteousness could be
gained through the law, Christ died for
nothing!"

Faith or Observance of the Law

3 You foolish Galatians! Who has
bewitched you? Before your very
eyes Jesus Christ was clearly portrayed
as crucified. 2I would like to learn just
one thing from you: Did you receive the
Spirit by observing the law, or by believing what you heard? 3Are you so foolish? After beginning with the Spirit, are
you now trying to attain your goal by
human effort? 4Have you suffered so

much for nothing—if it really was for nothing? 5Does God give you his Spirit and work miracles among you because you observe the law, or because you believe what you heard?

6Consider Abraham: "He believed God, and it was credited to him as righteousness." 7Understand, then, that those who believe are children of Abraham. 8The Scripture foresaw that God would justify the Gentiles by faith, and announced the gospel in advance to Abraham: "All nations will be blessed through you." 9So those who have faith are blessed along with Abraham, the man of faith.

READING FROM PSALMS
Psalm 107:33–43

33He turned rivers into a desert,
flowing springs into thirsty ground,
34and fruitful land into a salt waste,
because of the wickedness of those who lived there.
35He turned the desert into pools of water
and the parched ground into flowing springs;
36there he brought the hungry to live,
and they founded a city where they could settle.
37They sowed fields and planted vineyards
that yielded a fruitful harvest;
38he blessed them, and their numbers greatly increased,
and he did not let their herds diminish.

39Then their numbers decreased, and they were humbled
by oppression, calamity and sorrow;
40he who pours contempt on nobles
made them wander in a trackless waste.
41But he lifted the needy out of their affliction
and increased their families like flocks.
42The upright see and rejoice,
but all the wicked shut their mouths.

43Whoever is wise, let him heed these things
and consider the great love of the LORD.

DAY 260

SEPTEMBER 17

OLD TESTAMENT READING
Isaiah 41:1–42:25

The Helper of Israel

41 "Be silent before me, you islands!
Let the nations renew their strength!
Let them come forward and speak;
let us meet together at the place of judgment.

2"Who has stirred up one from the east,
calling him in righteousness to his service?
He hands nations over to him
and subdues kings before him.
He turns them to dust with his sword,
to wind-blown chaff with his bow.
3He pursues them and moves on unscathed,
by a path his feet have not travelled before.
4Who has done this and carried it through,
calling forth the generations from the beginning?

I, the LORD—with the first of them
and with the last—I am he."
5The islands have seen it and fear;
the ends of the earth tremble.
They approach and come forward;
6 each helps the other
and says to his brother, "Be
strong!"
7The craftsman encourages the
goldsmith,
and he who smooths with the
hammer
spurs on him who strikes the anvil.
He says of the welding, "It is good."
He nails down the idol so that it
will not topple.

8"But you, O Israel, my servant,
Jacob, whom I have chosen,
you descendants of Abraham my
friend,
9I took you from the ends of the earth,
from its farthest corners I called
you.
I said, 'You are my servant';
I have chosen you and have not
rejected you.
10So do not fear, for I am with you;
do not be dismayed, for I am your
God.
I will strengthen you and help you;
I will uphold you with my righteous
right hand.

11"All who rage against you
will surely be ashamed and
disgraced;
those who oppose you
will be as nothing and perish.
12Though you search for your enemies,
you will not find them.
Those who wage war against you
will be as nothing at all.
13For I am the LORD, your God,
who takes hold of your right hand
and says to you, Do not fear;
I will help you.
14Do not be afraid, O worm Jacob,
O little Israel,
for I myself will help you," declares
the LORD,
your Redeemer, the Holy One of
Israel.
15"See, I will make you into a
threshing-sledge,
new and sharp, with many teeth.
You will thresh the mountains and
crush them,
and reduce the hills to chaff.
16You will winnow them, the wind will
pick them up,
and a gale will blow them away.
But you will rejoice in the LORD
and glory in the Holy One of
Israel.

17"The poor and needy search for
water,
but there is none;
their tongues are parched with
thirst.
But I the LORD will answer them;
I, the God of Israel, will not
forsake them.
18I will make rivers flow on barren
heights,
and springs within the valleys.
I will turn the desert into pools of
water,
and the parched ground into
springs.
19I will put in the desert
the cedar and the acacia, the
myrtle and the olive.
I will set pines in the wasteland,
the fir and the cypress together,
20so that people may see and know,
may consider and understand,
that the hand of the LORD has done
this,
that the Holy One of Israel has
created it.

21"Present your case," says the LORD.
"Set forth your arguments," says
Jacob's King.
22"Bring in ⌞your idols⌟ to tell us
what is going to happen.
Tell us what the former things were,
so that we may consider them
and know their final outcome.
Or declare to us the things to come,

23 tell us what the future holds,
so that we may know you are gods.
Do something, whether good or bad,
so that we will be dismayed and filled with fear.
24 But you are less than nothing
and your works are utterly worthless;
he who chooses you is detestable.

25 "I have stirred up one from the north, and he comes—
one from the rising sun who calls on my name.
He treads on rulers as if they were mortar,
as if he were a potter treading the clay.
26 Who told of this from the beginning,
so that we could know,
or beforehand, so that we could say, 'He was right'?
No-one told of this,
no-one foretold it,
no-one heard any words from you.
27 I was the first to tell Zion, 'Look, here they are!'
I gave to Jerusalem a messenger of good tidings.
28 I look but there is no-one—
no-one among them to give counsel,
no-one to give answer when I ask them.
29 See, they are all false!
Their deeds amount to nothing;
their images are but wind and confusion.

The Servant of the Lord

42 "Here is my servant, whom I uphold,
my chosen one in whom I delight;
I will put my Spirit on him
and he will bring justice to the nations.
2 He will not shout or cry out,
or raise his voice in the streets.
3 A bruised reed he will not break,
and a smouldering wick he will not snuff out.
In faithfulness he will bring forth justice;
4 he will not falter or be discouraged
till he establishes justice on earth.
In his law the islands will put their hope."

5 This is what God the Lord says—
he who created the heavens and stretched them out,
who spread out the earth and all that comes out of it,
who gives breath to its people,
and life to those who walk on it:
6 "I, the Lord, have called you in righteousness;
I will take hold of your hand.
I will keep you and will make you
to be a covenant for the people
and a light for the Gentiles,
7 to open eyes that are blind,
to free captives from prison
and to release from the dungeon
those who sit in darkness.

8 "I am the Lord; that is my name!
I will not give my glory to another
or my praise to idols.
9 See, the former things have taken place,
and new things I declare;
before they spring into being
I announce them to you."

Song of Praise to the Lord

10 Sing to the Lord a new song,
his praise from the ends of the earth,
you who go down to the sea, and all that is in it,
you islands, and all who live in them.
11 Let the desert and its towns raise their voices;
let the settlements where Kedar lives rejoice.
Let the people of Sela sing for joy;
let them shout from the mountaintops.
12 Let them give glory to the Lord
and proclaim his praise in the islands.

13The LORD will march out like a
mighty man,
like a warrior he will stir up his
zeal;
with a shout he will raise the battle
cry
and will triumph over his enemies.

14"For a long time I have kept silent,
I have been quiet and held myself
back.
But now, like a woman in childbirth,
I cry out, I gasp and pant.
15I will lay waste the mountains and
hills
and dry up all their vegetation;
I will turn rivers into islands
and dry up the pools.
16I will lead the blind by ways they have
not known,
along unfamiliar paths I will guide
them;
I will turn the darkness into light
before them
and make the rough places smooth.
These are the things I will do;
I will not forsake them.
17But those who trust in idols,
who say to images, 'You are our
gods,'
will be turned back in utter shame.

Israel Blind and Deaf

18"Hear, you deaf;
look, you blind, and see!
19Who is blind but my servant,
and deaf like the messenger I send?
Who is blind like the one committed
to me,
blind like the servant of the LORD?
20You have seen many things, but have
paid no attention;
your ears are open, but you hear
nothing."
21It pleased the LORD
for the sake of his righteousness
to make his law great and glorious.
22But this is a people plundered and
looted,
all of them trapped in pits
or hidden away in prisons.
They have become plunder,
with no-one to rescue them;
they have been made loot,
with no-one to say, "Send them
back."

23Which of you will listen to this
or pay close attention in time to
come?
24Who handed Jacob over to become
loot,
and Israel to the plunderers?
Was it not the LORD,
against whom we have sinned?
For they would not follow his ways;
they did not obey his law.
25So he poured out on them his burning
anger,
the violence of war.
It enveloped them in flames, yet they
did not understand;
it consumed them, but they did not
take it to heart.

NEW TESTAMENT READING

Galatians 3:10–25

10All who rely on observing the law
are under a curse, for it is written:
"Cursed is everyone who does not continue to do everything written in the
Book of the Law." 11Clearly no-one is
justified before God by the law, because, "The righteous will live by faith."
12The law is not based on faith; on the
contrary, "The man who does these
things will live by them." 13Christ redeemed us from the curse of the law by
becoming a curse for us, for it is written:
"Cursed is everyone who is hung on a
tree." 14He redeemed us in order that
the blessing given to Abraham might
come to the Gentiles through Christ
Jesus, so that by faith we might receive
the promise of the Spirit.

The Law and the Promise

15Brothers, let me take an example
from everyday life. Just as no-one can

set aside or add to a human covenant
that has been duly established, so it is in
this case.
16The promises were spoken
to Abraham and to his seed. The Scripture does not say "and to seeds", meaning many people, but "and to your seed", meaning one person, who is
Christ.
17What I mean is this: The law, introduced 430 years later, does not set aside the covenant previously established by God and thus do away with the
promise.
18For if the inheritance depends on the law, then it no longer depends on a promise; but God in his grace gave it to Abraham through a promise.

19What, then, was the purpose of the law? It was added because of transgressions until the Seed to whom the promise referred had come. The law was put into effect through angels by a
mediator.
20A mediator, however, does not represent just one party; but God is one.

21Is the law, therefore, opposed to the promises of God? Absolutely not! For if a law had been given that could impart life, then righteousness would certainly have come by the law.
22But the Scripture declares that the whole world is a prisoner of sin, so that what was promised, being given through faith in Jesus Christ, might be given to those who believe.

23Before this faith came, we were held prisoners by the law, locked up until faith should be revealed.
24So the law was put in charge to lead us to Christ that we might be justified by faith.
25Now that faith has come, we are no longer under the supervision of the law.

READING FROM PROVERBS

Proverbs 22:28–23:9

28Do not move an ancient boundary
stone
set up by your forefathers.

29Do you see a man skilled in his work?
He will serve before kings;
he will not serve before obscure
men.

23 When you sit to dine with a
ruler,
note well what is before you,
2and put a knife to your throat
if you are given to gluttony.
3Do not crave his delicacies,
for that food is deceptive.

4Do not wear yourself out to get rich;
have the wisdom to show restraint.
5Cast but a glance at riches, and they
are gone,
for they will surely sprout wings
and fly off to the sky like an eagle.

6Do not eat the food of a stingy man,
do not crave his delicacies;
7for he is the kind of man
who is always thinking about the
cost.
"Eat and drink," he says to you,
but his heart is not with you.
8You will vomit up the little you have
eaten
and will have wasted your
compliments.

9Do not speak to a fool,
for he will scorn the wisdom of
your words.

OLD TESTAMENT READING
Isaiah 43:1–44:23

Israel's Only Saviour

43 But now, this is what the LORD says—
he who created you, O Jacob,
he who formed you, O Israel:
"Fear not, for I have redeemed you;
I have summoned you by name;
you are mine.
2When you pass through the waters,
I will be with you;
and when you pass through the rivers,
they will not sweep over you.
When you walk through the fire,
you will not be burned;
the flames will not set you ablaze.
3For I am the LORD, your God,
the Holy One of Israel, your Saviour;
I give Egypt for your ransom,
Cush and Seba in your stead.
4Since you are precious and honoured in my sight,
and because I love you,
I will give men in exchange for you,
and people in exchange for your life.
5Do not be afraid, for I am with you;
I will bring your children from the east
and gather you from the west.
6I will say to the north, 'Give them up!'
and to the south, 'Do not hold them back.'
Bring my sons from afar
and my daughters from the ends of the earth—
7everyone who is called by my name,
whom I created for my glory,
whom I formed and made."
8Lead out those who have eyes but are blind,
who have ears but are deaf.
9All the nations gather together
and the peoples assemble.
Which of them foretold this
and proclaimed to us the former things?
Let them bring in their witnesses to prove they were right,
so that others may hear and say,
"It is true."
10"You are my witnesses," declares the LORD,
"and my servant whom I have chosen,
so that you may know and believe me
and understand that I am he.
Before me no god was formed,
nor will there be one after me.
11I, even I, am the LORD,
and apart from me there is no saviour.
12I have revealed and saved and proclaimed—
I, and not some foreign god among you.
You are my witnesses," declares the LORD, "that I am God.
13 Yes, and from ancient days I am he.
No-one can deliver out of my hand.
When I act, who can reverse it?"

God's Mercy and Israel's Unfaithfulness

14This is what the LORD says—
your Redeemer, the Holy One of Israel:
"For your sake I will send to Babylon
and bring down as fugitives all the Babylonians,
in the ships in which they took pride.
15I am the LORD, your Holy One,
Israel's Creator, your King."

16This is what the LORD says—
he who made a way through the sea,
a path through the mighty waters,

17who drew out the chariots and horses,
the army and reinforcements together,
and they lay there, never to rise again,
extinguished, snuffed out like a wick:
18"Forget the former things;
do not dwell on the past.
19See, I am doing a new thing!
Now it springs up; do you not perceive it?
I am making a way in the desert
and streams in the wasteland.
20The wild animals honour me,
the jackals and the owls,
because I provide water in the desert
and streams in the wasteland,
to give drink to my people, my chosen,
21 the people I formed for myself
that they may proclaim my praise.

22"Yet you have not called upon me, O Jacob,
you have not wearied yourselves for me, O Israel.
23You have not brought me sheep for burnt offerings,
nor honoured me with your sacrifices.
I have not burdened you with grain offerings
nor wearied you with demands for incense.
24You have not bought any fragrant calamus for me,
or lavished on me the fat of your sacrifices.
But you have burdened me with your sins
and wearied me with your offences.

25"I, even I, am he who blots out
your transgressions, for my own sake,
and remembers your sins no more.
26Review the past for me,
let us argue the matter together;
state the case for your innocence.
27Your first father sinned;
your spokesmen rebelled against me.
28So I will disgrace the dignitaries of your temple,
and I will consign Jacob to destruction
and Israel to scorn.

Israel the Chosen

44 "But now listen, O Jacob, my servant,
Israel, whom I have chosen.
2This is what the LORD says—
he who made you, who formed you in the womb,
and who will help you:
Do not be afraid, O Jacob, my servant,
Jeshurun, whom I have chosen.
3For I will pour water on the thirsty land,
and streams on the dry ground;
I will pour out my Spirit on your offspring,
and my blessing on your descendants.
4They will spring up like grass in a meadow,
like poplar trees by flowing streams.
5One will say, 'I belong to the LORD';
another will call himself by the name of Jacob;
still another will write on his hand,
'The LORD's',
and will take the name Israel.

The LORD, Not Idols

6"This is what the LORD says—
Israel's King and Redeemer, the LORD Almighty:
I am the first and I am the last;
apart from me there is no God.
7Who then is like me? Let him proclaim it.
Let him declare and lay out before me
what has happened since I
established my ancient people,

and what is yet to come—
yes, let him foretell what will come.
8 Do not tremble, do not be afraid.
Did I not proclaim this and foretell it long ago?
You are my witnesses. Is there any God besides me?
No, there is no other Rock; I know not one."

9 All who make idols are nothing,
and the things they treasure are worthless.
Those who would speak up for them are blind;
they are ignorant, to their own shame.
10 Who shapes a god and casts an idol,
which can profit him nothing?
11 He and his kind will be put to shame;
craftsmen are nothing but men.
Let them all come together and take their stand;
they will be brought down to terror and infamy.

12 The blacksmith takes a tool
and works with it in the coals;
he shapes an idol with hammers,
he forges it with the might of his arm.
He gets hungry and loses his strength;
he drinks no water and grows faint.
13 The carpenter measures with a line
and makes an outline with a marker;
he roughs it out with chisels
and marks it with compasses.
He shapes it in the form of man,
of man in all his glory,
that it may dwell in a shrine.
14 He cut down cedars,
or perhaps took a cypress or oak.
He let it grow among the trees of the forest,
or planted a pine, and the rain made it grow.
15 It is man's fuel for burning;
some of it he takes and warms himself,
he kindles a fire and bakes bread.
But he also fashions a god and worships it;
he makes an idol and bows down to it.
16 Half of the wood he burns in the fire;
over it he prepares his meal,
he roasts his meat and eats his fill.
He also warms himself and says,
"Ah! I am warm; I see the fire."
17 From the rest he makes a god, his idol;
he bows down to it and worships.
He prays to it and says,
"Save me; you are my god."
18 They know nothing, they understand nothing;
their eyes are plastered over so that they cannot see,
and their minds closed so that they cannot understand.
19 No-one stops to think,
no-one has the knowledge or understanding to say,
"Half of it I used for fuel;
I even baked bread over its coals,
I roasted meat and I ate.
Shall I make a detestable thing from what is left?
Shall I bow down to a block of wood?"
20 He feeds on ashes, a deluded heart misleads him;
he cannot save himself, or say,
"Is not this thing in my right hand a lie?"

21 "Remember these things, O Jacob,
for you are my servant, O Israel.
I have made you, you are my servant;
O Israel, I will not forget you.
22 I have swept away your offences like a cloud,
your sins like the morning mist.
Return to me,
for I have redeemed you."

23 Sing for joy, O heavens, for the LORD has done this;
shout aloud, O earth beneath.
Burst into song, you mountains,
you forests and all your trees,
for the LORD has redeemed Jacob,
he displays his glory in Israel.

NEW TESTAMENT READING
Galatians 3:26–4:20

Sons of God

26You are all sons of God through
faith in Christ Jesus, 27for all of you who
were baptised into Christ have clothed
yourselves with Christ. 28There is
neither Jew nor Greek, slave nor free,
male nor female, for you are all one in
Christ Jesus. 29If you belong to Christ,
then you are Abraham's seed, and heirs
according to the promise.

4 What I am saying is that as long as
the heir is a child, he is no different
from a slave, although he owns the
whole estate. 2He is subject to guardians and trustees until the time set by his
father. 3So also, when we were children, we were in slavery under the basic
principles of the world. 4But when the
time had fully come, God sent his Son,
born of a woman, born under law, 5to
redeem those under law, that we might
receive the full rights of sons. 6Because
you are sons, God sent the Spirit of his
Son into our hearts, the Spirit who calls
out, "*Abba*, Father." 7So you are no
longer a slave, but a son; and since you
are a son, God has made you also an
heir.

Paul's Concern for the Galatians

8Formerly, when you did not know
God, you were slaves to those who by
nature are not gods. 9But now that you
know God—or rather are known by
God—how is it that you are turning
back to those weak and miserable principles? Do you wish to be enslaved by
them all over again? 10You are observing special days and months and seasons
and years! 11I fear for you, that somehow I have wasted my efforts on you.

12I plead with you, brothers, become
like me, for I became like you. You
have done me no wrong. 13As you
know, it was because of an illness that I
first preached the gospel to you. 14Even
though my illness was a trial to you, you
did not treat me with contempt or scorn.
Instead, you welcomed me as if I were
an angel of God, as if I were Christ Jesus
himself. 15What has happened to all
your joy? I can testify that, if you could
have done so, you would have torn out
your eyes and given them to me. 16Have
I now become your enemy by telling
you the truth?

17Those people are zealous to win you
over, but for no good. What they want is
to alienate you ⌊from us⌋, so that you
may be zealous for them. 18It is fine to
be zealous, provided the purpose is
good, and to be so always and not just
when I am with you. 19My dear children, for whom I am again in the pains
of childbirth until Christ is formed in
you, 20how I wish I could be with you
now and change my tone, because I am
perplexed about you!

READING FROM PSALMS
Psalm 108:1–5

A song. A psalm of David.

1My heart is steadfast, O God;
  I will sing and make music with all
    my soul.
2Awake, harp and lyre!
  I will awaken the dawn.
3I will praise you, O LORD, among the
    nations;
  I will sing of you among the
    peoples.
4For great is your love, higher than
    the heavens;
  your faithfulness reaches to the
    skies.
5Be exalted, O God, above the
    heavens,
  and let your glory be over all the
    earth.

OLD TESTAMENT READING
Isaiah 44:24–46:13

Jerusalem to Be Inhabited

24"This is what the LORD says—
your Redeemer, who formed you in the womb:

I am the LORD,
who has made all things,
who alone stretched out the heavens,
who spread out the earth by myself,

25who foils the signs of false prophets
and makes fools of diviners,
who overthrows the learning of the wise
and turns it into nonsense,
26who carries out the words of his servants
and fulfils the predictions of his messengers,

who says of Jerusalem, 'It shall be inhabited,'
of the towns of Judah, 'They shall be built,'
and of their ruins, 'I will restore them,'
27who says to the watery deep, 'Be dry,
and I will dry up your streams,'
28who says of Cyrus, 'He is my shepherd
and will accomplish all that I please;
he will say of Jerusalem, "Let it be rebuilt,"
and of the temple, "Let its foundations be laid."'

45 "This is what the LORD says to his anointed,
to Cyrus, whose right hand I take hold of
to subdue nations before him
and to strip kings of their armour,
to open doors before him
so that gates will not be shut:

2I will go before you
and will level the mountains;
I will break down gates of bronze
and cut through bars of iron.
3I will give you the treasures of darkness,
riches stored in secret places,
so that you may know that I am the LORD,
the God of Israel, who summons you by name.
4For the sake of Jacob my servant,
of Israel my chosen,
I summon you by name
and bestow on you a title of honour,
though you do not acknowledge me.
5I am the LORD, and there is no other;
apart from me there is no God.
I will strengthen you,
though you have not acknowledged me,
6so that from the rising of the sun
to the place of its setting
men may know there is none besides me.
I am the LORD, and there is no other.
7I form the light and create darkness,
I bring prosperity and create disaster;
I, the LORD, do all these things.

8"You heavens above, rain down righteousness;
let the clouds shower it down.
Let the earth open wide,
let salvation spring up,
let righteousness grow with it;
I, the LORD, have created it.

9"Woe to him who quarrels with his Maker,
to him who is but a potsherd
among the potsherds on the ground.

Does the clay say to the potter,
'What are you making?'
Does your work say,
'He has no hands'?
10Woe to him who says to his father,
'What have you begotten?'
or to his mother,
'What have you brought to birth?'

11"This is what the LORD says—
the Holy One of Israel, and its Maker:
Concerning things to come,
do you question me about my children,
or give me orders about the work of my hands?
12It is I who made the earth
and created mankind upon it.
My own hands stretched out the heavens;
I marshalled their starry hosts.
13I will raise up Cyrus in my righteousness:
I will make all his ways straight.
He will rebuild my city
and set my exiles free,
but not for a price or reward,
says the LORD Almighty."

14This is what the LORD says:

"The products of Egypt and the merchandise of Cush,
and those tall Sabeans—
they will come over to you
and will be yours;
they will trudge behind you,
coming over to you in chains.
They will bow down before you
and plead with you, saying,
'Surely God is with you, and there is no other;
there is no other god.'"

15Truly you are a God who hides himself,
O God and Saviour of Israel.
16All the makers of idols will be put to shame and disgraced;
they will go off into disgrace together.
17But Israel will be saved by the LORD
with an everlasting salvation;
you will never be put to shame or disgraced,
to ages everlasting.

18For this is what the LORD says—
he who created the heavens,
he is God;
he who fashioned and made the earth,
he founded it;
he did not create it to be empty,
but formed it to be inhabited—
he says:
"I am the LORD,
and there is no other.
19I have not spoken in secret,
from somewhere in a land of darkness;
I have not said to Jacob's descendants,
'Seek me in vain.'
I, the LORD, speak the truth;
I declare what is right.

20"Gather together and come;
assemble, you fugitives from the nations.
Ignorant are those who carry about idols of wood,
who pray to gods that cannot save.
21Declare what is to be, present it—
let them take counsel together.
Who foretold this long ago,
who declared it from the distant past?
Was it not I, the LORD?
And there is no God apart from me,
a righteous God and a Saviour;
there is none but me.

22"Turn to me and be saved,
all you ends of the earth;
for I am God, and there is no other.
23By myself I have sworn,
my mouth has uttered in all integrity
a word that will not be revoked:
Before me every knee will bow;
by me every tongue will swear.

[24]They will say of me, 'In the LORD
alone
are righteousness and strength.'"
All who have raged against him
will come to him and be put to
shame.
[25]But in the LORD all the descendants
of Israel
will be found righteous and will
exult.

Gods of Babylon

46 Bel bows down, Nebo stoops
low;
their idols are borne by beasts of
burden.
The images that are carried about are
burdensome,
a burden for the weary.
[2]They stoop and bow down together;
unable to rescue the burden,
they themselves go off into
captivity.

[3]"Listen to me, O house of Jacob,
all you who remain of the house of
Israel,
you whom I have upheld since you
were conceived,
and have carried since your birth.
[4]Even to your old age and grey hairs
I am he, I am he who will sustain
you.
I have made you and I will carry you;
I will sustain you and I will rescue
you.

[5]"To whom will you compare me or
count me equal?
To whom will you liken me that we
may be compared?
[6]Some pour out gold from their bags
and weigh out silver on the scales;
they hire a goldsmith to make it into
a god,
and they bow down and worship it.
[7]They lift it to their shoulders and
carry it;
they set it up in its place, and there
it stands.
From that spot it cannot move.
Though one cries out to it, it does not
answer;
it cannot save him from his
troubles.

[8]"Remember this, fix it in mind,
take it to heart, you rebels.
[9]Remember the former things, those
of long ago;
I am God, and there is no other;
I am God, and there is none like
me.
[10]I make known the end from the
beginning,
from ancient times, what is still to
come.
I say: My purpose will stand,
and I will do all that I please.
[11]From the east I summon a bird of
prey;
from a far-off land, a man to fulfil
my purpose.
What I have said, that will I bring
about;
what I have planned, that will I do.
[12]Listen to me, you stubborn-hearted,
you who are far from
righteousness.
[13]I am bringing my righteousness near,
it is not far away;
and my salvation will not be
delayed.
I will grant salvation to Zion,
my splendour to Israel.

NEW TESTAMENT READING
Galatians 4:21–5:6

Hagar and Sarah

[21]Tell me, you who want to be under
the law, are you not aware of what the
law says? [22]For it is written that Abraham had two sons, one by the slave
woman and the other by the free
woman. [23]His son by the slave woman
was born in the ordinary way; but his
son by the free woman was born as the
result of a promise.
[24]These things may be taken figuratively, for the women represent two

covenants. One covenant is from
Mount Sinai and bears children who are
to be slaves: This is Hagar. 25Now
Hagar stands for Mount Sinai in Arabia
and corresponds to the present city of
Jerusalem, because she is in slavery
with her children. 26But the Jerusalem
that is above is free, and she is our
mother. 27For it is written:

"Be glad, O barren woman,
who bears no children;
break forth and cry aloud,
you who have no labour pains;
because more are the children of the
desolate woman
than of her who has a husband."

28Now you, brothers, like Isaac, are
children of promise. 29At that time the
son born in the ordinary way persecuted
the son born by the power of the Spirit.
It is the same now. 30But what does the
Scripture say? "Get rid of the slave
woman and her son, for the slave
woman's son will never share in the
inheritance with the free woman's son."
31Therefore, brothers, we are not children of the slave woman, but of the free
woman.

Freedom in Christ

5 It is for freedom that Christ has set
us free. Stand firm, then, and do
not let yourselves be burdened again by
a yoke of slavery.

2Mark my words! I, Paul, tell you that
if you let yourselves be circumcised,
Christ will be of no value to you at all.
3Again I declare to every man who lets
himself be circumcised that he is required to obey the whole law. 4You who
are trying to be justified by law have
been alienated from Christ; you have
fallen away from grace. 5But by faith we
eagerly await through the Spirit the
righteousness for which we hope. 6For
in Christ Jesus neither circumcision nor
uncircumcision has any value. The only
thing that counts is faith expressing itself through love.

READING FROM PSALMS
Psalm 108:6–13

6Save us and help us with your right
hand,
that those you love may be
delivered.
7God has spoken from his sanctuary:
"In triumph I will parcel out
Shechem
and measure off the Valley of
Succoth.
8Gilead is mine, Manasseh is mine;
Ephraim is my helmet,
Judah my sceptre.
9Moab is my washbasin,
upon Edom I toss my sandal;
over Philistia I shout in triumph."

10Who will bring me to the fortified
city?
Who will lead me to Edom?
11Is it not you, O God, you who have
rejected us
and no longer go out with our
armies?
12Give us aid against the enemy,
for the help of man is worthless.
13With God we shall gain the victory,
and he will trample down our
enemies.

SEPTEMBER 20

OLD TESTAMENT READING
Isaiah 47:1–49:7

The Fall of Babylon

47 "Go down, sit in the dust,
Virgin Daughter of Babylon;
sit on the ground without a throne,
Daughter of the Babylonians.
No more will you be called
tender or delicate.
2Take millstones and grind flour;
take off your veil.
Lift up your skirts, bare your legs,
and wade through the streams.
3Your nakedness will be exposed
and your shame uncovered.
I will take vengeance;
I will spare no-one."

4Our Redeemer—the LORD Almighty
is his name—
is the Holy One of Israel.

5"Sit in silence, go into darkness,
Daughter of the Babylonians;
no more will you be called
queen of kingdoms.
6I was angry with my people
and desecrated my inheritance;
I gave them into your hand,
and you showed them no mercy.
Even on the aged
you laid a very heavy yoke.
7You said, 'I will continue for ever—
the eternal queen!'
But you did not consider these things
or reflect on what might happen.

8"Now then, listen, you wanton
creature,
lounging in your security
and saying to yourself,
'I am, and there is none besides
me.
I will never be a widow
or suffer the loss of children.'
9Both of these will overtake you
in a moment, on a single day:
loss of children and widowhood.
They will come upon you in full
measure,
in spite of your many sorceries
and all your potent spells.
10You have trusted in your wickedness
and have said, 'No-one sees me.'
Your wisdom and knowledge mislead
you
when you say to yourself,
'I am, and there is none besides
me.'
11Disaster will come upon you,
and you will not know how to
conjure it away.
A calamity will fall upon you
that you cannot ward off with a
ransom;
a catastrophe you cannot foresee
will suddenly come upon you.

12"Keep on, then, with your magic
spells
and with your many sorceries,
which you have laboured at since
childhood.
Perhaps you will succeed,
perhaps you will cause terror.
13All the counsel you have received has
only worn you out!
Let your astrologers come forward,
those stargazers who make
predictions month by month,
let them save you from what is
coming upon you.
14Surely they are like stubble;
the fire will burn them up.
They cannot even save themselves
from the power of the flame.
Here are no coals to warm anyone;
here is no fire to sit by.
15That is all they can do for you—
these you have laboured with
and trafficked with since
childhood.
Each of them goes on in his error;
there is not one that can save you.

Stubborn Israel

48 "Listen to this, O house of
Jacob,
you who are called by the name of
Israel
and come from the line of Judah,
you who take oaths in the name of
the LORD
and invoke the God of Israel—
but not in truth or righteousness—
2you who call yourselves citizens of
the holy city
and rely on the God of Israel—
the LORD Almighty is his name:
3I foretold the former things long ago,
my mouth announced them and I
made them known;
then suddenly I acted, and they
came to pass.
4For I knew how stubborn you were;
the sinews of your neck were iron,
your forehead was bronze.
5Therefore I told you these things long
ago;
before they happened I announced
them to you
so that you could not say,
'My idols did them;
my wooden image and metal god
ordained them.'
6You have heard these things; look at
them all.
Will you not admit them?
"From now on I will tell you of new
things,
of hidden things unknown to you.
7They are created now, and not long
ago;
you have not heard of them before
today.
So you cannot say,
'Yes, I knew of them.'
8You have neither heard nor
understood;
from of old your ear has not been
open.
Well do I know how treacherous you
are;
you were called a rebel from birth.
9For my own name's sake I delay my
wrath;
for the sake of my praise I hold it
back from you,
so as not to cut you off.
10See, I have refined you, though not as
silver;
I have tested you in the furnace of
affliction.
11For my own sake, for my own sake, I
do this.
How can I let myself be defamed?
I will not yield my glory to another.

Israel Freed

12"Listen to me, O Jacob,
Israel, whom I have called:
I am he;
I am the first and I am the last.
13My own hand laid the foundations of
the earth,
and my right hand spread out the
heavens;
when I summon them,
they all stand up together.

14"Come together, all of you, and
listen:
Which of ⌊the idols⌋ has foretold
these things?
The LORD's chosen ally
will carry out his purpose against
Babylon;
his arm will be against the
Babylonians.
15I, even I, have spoken;
yes, I have called him.
I will bring him,
and he will succeed in his mission.

16"Come near me and listen to this:

"From the first announcement I have
not spoken in secret;
at the time it happens, I am there."

And now the Sovereign LORD has
sent me,
with his Spirit.

17This is what the LORD says—
your Redeemer, the Holy One of
Israel:

"I am the LORD your God,
who teaches you what is best for you,
who directs you in the way you should go.
18If only you had paid attention to my commands,
your peace would have been like a river,
your righteousness like the waves of the sea.
19Your descendants would have been like the sand,
your children like its numberless grains;
their name would never be cut off
nor destroyed from before me."

20Leave Babylon,
flee from the Babylonians!
Announce this with shouts of joy
and proclaim it.
Send it out to the ends of the earth;
say, "The LORD has redeemed his servant Jacob."
21They did not thirst when he led them through the deserts;
he made water flow for them from the rock;
he split the rock
and water gushed out.

22"There is no peace," says the LORD,
"for the wicked."

The Servant of the LORD

49 Listen to me, you islands;
hear this, you distant nations:
Before I was born the LORD called me;
from my birth he has made mention of my name.
2He made my mouth like a sharpened sword,
in the shadow of his hand he hid me;
he made me into a polished arrow
and concealed me in his quiver.
3He said to me, "You are my servant,
Israel, in whom I will display my splendour."
4But I said, "I have laboured to no purpose;
I have spent my strength in vain
and for nothing.
Yet what is due to me is in the LORD's hand,
and my reward is with my God."

5And now the LORD says—
he who formed me in the womb to be his servant
to bring Jacob back to him
and gather Israel to himself,
for I am honoured in the eyes of the LORD
and my God has been my strength—
6he says:
"It is too small a thing for you to be my servant
to restore the tribes of Jacob
and bring back those of Israel I have kept.
I will also make you a light for the Gentiles,
that you may bring my salvation to the ends of the earth."

7This is what the LORD says—
the Redeemer and Holy One of Israel—
to him who was despised and abhorred by the nation,
to the servant of rulers:
"Kings will see you and rise up,
princes will see and bow down,
because of the LORD, who is faithful,
the Holy One of Israel, who has chosen you."

NEW TESTAMENT READING

Galatians 5:7–26

7You were running a good race. Who
cut in on you and kept you from obeying
the truth? 8That kind of persuasion does
not come from the one who calls you.
9"A little yeast works through the

whole batch of dough." 10I am confident
in the Lord that you will take no other
view. The one who is throwing you into
confusion will pay the penalty, whoever
he may be. 11Brothers, if I am still
preaching circumcision, why am I still
being persecuted? In that case the offence of the cross has been abolished.
12As for those agitators, I wish they
would go the whole way and emasculate
themselves!
13You, my brothers, were called to be
free. But do not use your freedom to
indulge the sinful nature; rather, serve
one another in love. 14The entire law is
summed up in a single command: "Love
your neighbour as yourself." 15If you
keep on biting and devouring each
other, watch out or you will be destroyed by each other.

Life by the Spirit

16So I say, live by the Spirit, and you
will not gratify the desires of the sinful
nature. 17For the sinful nature desires
what is contrary to the Spirit, and the
Spirit what is contrary to the sinful nature. They are in conflict with each
other, so that you do not do what you
want. 18But if you are led by the Spirit,
you are not under law.
19The acts of the sinful nature are
obvious: sexual immorality, impurity
and debauchery; 20idolatry and witchcraft; hatred, discord, jealousy, fits of
rage, selfish ambition, dissensions, factions 21and envy; drunkenness, orgies,
and the like. I warn you, as I did before,
that those who live like this will not
inherit the kingdom of God.
22But the fruit of the Spirit is love,
joy, peace, patience, kindness, goodness, faithfulness, 23gentleness and self-control. Against such things there is no
law. 24Those who belong to Christ Jesus
have crucified the sinful nature with its
passions and desires. 25Since we live by
the Spirit, let us keep in step with the
Spirit. 26Let us not become conceited,
provoking and envying each other.

READING FROM PSALMS
Psalm 109:1–20

For the director of music. Of David. A psalm.

1O God, whom I praise,
do not remain silent,
2for wicked and deceitful men
have opened their mouths against me;
they have spoken against me with lying tongues.
3With words of hatred they surround me;
they attack me without cause.
4In return for my friendship they accuse me,
but I am a man of prayer.
5They repay me evil for good,
and hatred for my friendship.

6Appoint an evil man to oppose him;
let an accuser stand at his right hand.
7When he is tried, let him be found guilty,
and may his prayers condemn him.
8May his days be few;
may another take his place of leadership.
9May his children be fatherless
and his wife a widow.
10May his children be wandering beggars;
may they be driven from their ruined homes.
11May a creditor seize all he has;
may strangers plunder the fruits of his labour.
12May no-one extend kindness to him
or take pity on his fatherless children.
13May his descendants be cut off,
their names blotted out from the next generation.
14May the iniquity of his fathers be remembered before the LORD;
may the sin of his mother never be blotted out.
15May their sins always remain before the LORD,

that he may cut off the memory of
them from the earth.

16For he never thought of doing a
kindness,
but hounded to death the poor
and the needy and the
broken-hearted.
17He loved to pronounce a curse—
may it come on him;
he found no pleasure in blessing—
may it be far from him.
18He wore cursing as his garment;
it entered into his body like water,
into his bones like oil.
19May it be like a cloak wrapped about
him,
like a belt tied for ever round him.
20May this be the LORD's payment to
my accusers,
to those who speak evil of me.

SEPTEMBER 21

DAY 264

OLD TESTAMENT READING
Isaiah 49:8–51:16

Restoration of Israel

8This is what the LORD says:

"In the time of my favour I will
answer you,
and in the day of salvation I will
help you;
I will keep you and will make you
to be a covenant for the people,
to restore the land
and to reassign its desolate
inheritances,
9to say to the captives, 'Come out,'
and to those in darkness,
'Be free!'

"They will feed beside the roads
and find pasture on every barren
hill.
10They will neither hunger nor thirst,
nor will the desert heat or the sun
beat upon them.
He who has compassion on them will
guide them
and lead them beside springs of
water.
11I will turn all my mountains into
roads,
and my highways will be raised up.
12See, they will come from afar—
some from the north, some from
the west,
some from the region of Aswan."

13Shout for joy, O heavens;
rejoice, O earth;
burst into song, O mountains!
For the LORD comforts his people
and will have compassion on his
afflicted ones.

14But Zion said, "The LORD has
forsaken me,
the Lord has forgotten me."

15"Can a mother forget the baby at her
breast
and have no compassion on the
child she has borne?
Though she may forget,
I will not forget you!
16See, I have engraved you on the
palms of my hands;
your walls are ever before me.
17Your sons hasten back,
and those who laid you waste
depart from you.
18Lift up your eyes and look around;
all your sons gather and come to
you.
As surely as I live," declares the
LORD,

"you will wear them all as
ornaments;
you will put them on, like a bride.

19"Though you were ruined and made
desolate
and your land laid waste,
now you will be too small for your
people,
and those who devoured you will
be far away.
20The children born during your
bereavement
will yet say in your hearing,
'This place is too small for us;
give us more space to live in.'
21Then you will say in your heart,
'Who bore me these?
I was bereaved and barren;
I was exiled and rejected.
Who brought these up?
I was left all alone,
but these—where have they come
from?'"

22This is what the Sovereign LORD says:

"See, I will beckon to the Gentiles,
I will lift up my banner to the
peoples;
they will bring your sons in their arms
and carry your daughters on their
shoulders.
23Kings will be your foster fathers,
and their queens your nursing
mothers.
They will bow down before you with
their faces to the ground;
they will lick the dust at your feet.
Then you will know that I am the
LORD;
those who hope in me will not be
disappointed."

24Can plunder be taken from warriors,
or captives rescued from the fierce?

25But this is what the LORD says:

"Yes, captives will be taken from
warriors,
and plunder retrieved from the
fierce;
I will contend with those who
contend with you,
and your children I will save.
26I will make your oppressors eat their
own flesh;
they will be drunk on their own
blood, as with wine.
Then all mankind will know
that I, the LORD, am your Saviour,
your Redeemer, the Mighty One of
Jacob."

Israel's Sin and the Servant's Obedience

50 This is what the LORD says:

"Where is your mother's certificate
of divorce
with which I sent her away?
Or to which of my creditors
did I sell you?
Because of your sins you were sold;
because of your transgressions
your mother was sent away.
2When I came, why was there no-one?
When I called, why was there
no-one to answer?
Was my arm too short to ransom
you?
Do I lack the strength to rescue
you?
By a mere rebuke I dry up the sea,
I turn rivers into a desert;
their fish rot for lack of water
and die of thirst.
3I clothe the sky with darkness
and make sackcloth its covering."

4The Sovereign LORD has given me an
instructed tongue,
to know the word that sustains the
weary.
He wakens me morning by morning,
wakens my ear to listen like one
being taught.
5The Sovereign LORD has opened my
ears,
and I have not been rebellious;
I have not drawn back.

6I offered my back to those who beat
me,
my cheeks to those who pulled out
my beard;
I did not hide my face
from mocking and spitting.
7Because the Sovereign LORD helps
me,
I will not be disgraced.
Therefore have I set my face like
flint,
and I know I will not be put to
shame.
8He who vindicates me is near.
Who then will bring charges
against me?
Let us face each other!
Who is my accuser?
Let him confront me!
9It is the Sovereign LORD who helps
me.
Who is he who will condemn me?
They will all wear out like a garment;
the moths will eat them up.

10Who among you fears the LORD
and obeys the word of his servant?
Let him who walks in the dark,
who has no light,
trust in the name of the LORD
and rely on his God.
11But now, all you who light fires
and provide yourselves with
flaming torches,
go, walk in the light of your fires
and of the torches you have set
ablaze.
This is what you shall receive from
my hand:
You will lie down in torment.

Everlasting Salvation for Zion

51 "Listen to me, you who pursue
righteousness
and who seek the LORD:
Look to the rock from which you
were cut
and to the quarry from which you
were hewn;
2look to Abraham, your father,
and to Sarah, who gave you birth.
When I called him he was but one,
and I blessed him and made him
many.
3The LORD will surely comfort Zion
and will look with compassion on
all her ruins;
he will make her deserts like Eden,
her wastelands like the garden of
the LORD.
Joy and gladness will be found in her,
thanksgiving and the sound of
singing.

4"Listen to me, my people;
hear me, my nation:
The law will go out from me;
my justice will become a light to
the nations.
5My righteousness draws near
speedily,
my salvation is on the way,
and my arm will bring justice to the
nations.
The islands will look to me
and wait in hope for my arm.
6Lift up your eyes to the heavens,
look at the earth beneath;
the heavens will vanish like smoke,
the earth will wear out like a
garment
and its inhabitants die like flies.
But my salvation will last for ever,
my righteousness will never fail.

7"Hear me, you who know what is
right,
you people who have my law in
your hearts:
Do not fear the reproach of men
or be terrified by their insults.
8For the moth will eat them up like a
garment;
the worm will devour them like
wool.
But my righteousness will last for
ever,
my salvation through all
generations."

9Awake, awake! Clothe yourself with
strength,
O arm of the LORD;

awake, as in days gone by,
as in generations of old.
Was it not you who cut Rahab to pieces,
who pierced that monster through?
10 Was it not you who dried up the sea,
the waters of the great deep,
who made a road in the depths of the sea
so that the redeemed might cross over?
11 The ransomed of the LORD will return.
They will enter Zion with singing;
everlasting joy will crown their heads.
Gladness and joy will overtake them,
and sorrow and sighing will flee away.

12 "I, even I, am he who comforts you.
Who are you that you fear mortal men,
the sons of men, who are but grass,
13 that you forget the LORD your Maker,
who stretched out the heavens
and laid the foundations of the earth,
that you live in constant terror every day
because of the wrath of the oppressor,
who is bent on destruction?
For where is the wrath of the oppressor?
14 The cowering prisoners will soon be set free;
they will not die in their dungeon,
nor will they lack bread.
15 For I am the LORD your God,
who churns up the sea so that its waves roar—
the LORD Almighty is his name.
16 I have put my words in your mouth
and covered you with the shadow of my hand—
I who set the heavens in place,
who laid the foundations of the earth,
and who say to Zion, 'You are my people.'"

NEW TESTAMENT READING
Galatians 6:1–18

Doing Good to All

6 Brothers, if someone is caught in a
sin, you who are spiritual should
restore him gently. But watch yourself,
or you also may be tempted. 2 Carry
each other's burdens, and in this way
you will fulfil the law of Christ. 3 If anyone thinks he is something when he is
nothing, he deceives himself. 4 Each one
should test his own actions. Then he can
take pride in himself, without comparing himself to somebody else, 5 for each
one should carry his own load.

6 Anyone who receives instruction in
the word must share all good things with
his instructor.

7 Do not be deceived: God cannot be
mocked. A man reaps what he sows.
8 The one who sows to please his sinful
nature, from that nature will reap
destruction; the one who sows to please
the Spirit, from the Spirit will reap eternal life. 9 Let us not become weary in
doing good, for at the proper time we
will reap a harvest if we do not give up.
10 Therefore, as we have opportunity,
let us do good to all people, especially
to those who belong to the family of
believers.

Not Circumcision but a New Creation

11 See what large letters I use as I write
to you with my own hand!

12 Those who want to make a good
impression outwardly are trying to com-
pel you to be circumcised. The only
reason they do this is to avoid being
persecuted for the cross of Christ. 13 Not
even those who are circumcised obey
the law, yet they want you to be circumcised that they may boast about your
flesh. 14 May I never boast except in the
cross of our Lord Jesus Christ, through
which the world has been crucified to
me, and I to the world. 15 Neither circumcision nor uncircumcision means
anything; what counts is a new creation.

16Peace and mercy to all who follow this
rule, even to the Israel of God.
17Finally, let no-one cause me
trouble, for I bear on my body the
marks of Jesus.
18The grace of our Lord Jesus Christ
be with your spirit, brothers. Amen.

READING FROM PROVERBS
Proverbs 23:10–18

10Do not move an ancient boundary
stone
or encroach on the fields of the
fatherless,
11for their Defender is strong;
he will take up their case against
you.
12Apply your heart to instruction
and your ears to words of
knowledge.

13Do not withhold discipline from a
child;
if you punish him with the rod, he
will not die.
14Punish him with the rod
and save his soul from death.

15My son, if your heart is wise,
then my heart will be glad;
16my inmost being will rejoice
when your lips speak what is right.

17Do not let your heart envy sinners,
but always be zealous for the fear
of the LORD.
18There is surely a future hope for you,
and your hope will not be cut off.

SEPTEMBER 22

DAY 265

OLD TESTAMENT READING
Isaiah 51:17–54:17

The Cup of the LORD's Wrath

17Awake, awake!
Rise up, O Jerusalem,
you who have drunk from the hand of
the LORD
the cup of his wrath,
you who have drained to its dregs
the goblet that makes men stagger.
18Of all the sons she bore
there was none to guide her;
of all the sons she brought up
there was none to take her by the
hand.
19These double calamities have come
upon you—
who can comfort you?—
ruin and destruction, famine and
sword—
who can console you?
20Your sons have fainted;
they lie at the head of every street,
like antelope caught in a net.
They are filled with the wrath of the
LORD
and the rebuke of your God.

21Therefore hear this, you afflicted
one,
made drunk, but not with wine.
22This is what your Sovereign LORD
says,
your God, who defends his people:
"See, I have taken out of your hand
the cup that made you stagger;
from that cup, the goblet of my
wrath,
you will never drink again.
23I will put it into the hands of your
tormentors,
who said to you,
'Fall prostrate that we may walk
over you.'

And you made your back like the
ground,
like a street to be walked over."

52 Awake, awake, O Zion,
clothe yourself with strength.
Put on your garments of splendour,
O Jerusalem, the holy city.
The uncircumcised and defiled
will not enter you again.
2Shake off your dust;
rise up, sit enthroned, O
Jerusalem.
Free yourself from the chains on your
neck,
O captive Daughter of Zion.

3For this is what the LORD says:

"You were sold for nothing,
and without money you will be
redeemed."

4For this is what the Sovereign LORD
says:

"At first my people went down to
Egypt to live;
lately, Assyria has oppressed
them.

5"And now what do I have here?"
declares the LORD.

"For my people have been taken
away for nothing,
and those who rule them mock,"
declares the LORD.
"And all day long
my name is constantly
blasphemed.
6Therefore my people will know my
name;
therefore in that day they will
know
that it is I who foretold it.
Yes, it is I."

7How beautiful on the mountains
are the feet of those who bring
good news,
who proclaim peace,
who bring good tidings,
who proclaim salvation,
who say to Zion,
"Your God reigns!"
8Listen! Your watchmen lift up their
voices;
together they shout for joy.
When the LORD returns to Zion,
they will see it with their own eyes.
9Burst into songs of joy together,
you ruins of Jerusalem,
for the LORD has comforted his
people,
he has redeemed Jerusalem.
10The LORD will lay bare his holy arm
in the sight of all the nations,
and all the ends of the earth will see
the salvation of our God.

11Depart, depart, go out from there!
Touch no unclean thing!
Come out from it and be pure,
you who carry the vessels of the
LORD.
12But you will not leave in haste
or go in flight;
for the LORD will go before you,
the God of Israel will be your rear
guard.

The Suffering and Glory of the Servant

13See, my servant will act wisely;
he will be raised and lifted up and
highly exalted.
14Just as there were many who were
appalled at him—
his appearance was so disfigured
beyond that of any man
and his form marred beyond
human likeness—
15so will he sprinkle many nations,
and kings will shut their mouths
because of him.
For what they were not told, they will
see,
and what they have not heard, they
will understand.

53 Who has believed our message
and to whom has the arm of the
LORD been revealed?

[2]He grew up before him like a tender shoot,
and like a root out of dry ground.
He had no beauty or majesty to attract us to him,
nothing in his appearance that we should desire him.
[3]He was despised and rejected by men,
a man of sorrows, and familiar with suffering.
Like one from whom men hide their faces
he was despised, and we esteemed him not.

[4]Surely he took up our infirmities
and carried our sorrows,
yet we considered him stricken by God,
smitten by him, and afflicted.
[5]But he was pierced for our transgressions,
he was crushed for our iniquities;
the punishment that brought us peace was upon him,
and by his wounds we are healed.
[6]We all, like sheep, have gone astray,
each of us has turned to his own way;
and the LORD has laid on him
the iniquity of us all.

[7]He was oppressed and afflicted,
yet he did not open his mouth;
he was led like a lamb to the slaughter,
and as a sheep before her shearers is silent,
so he did not open his mouth.
[8]By oppression and judgment he was taken away.
And who can speak of his descendants?
For he was cut off from the land of the living;
for the transgression of my people he was stricken.
[9]He was assigned a grave with the wicked,
and with the rich in his death,
though he had done no violence,
nor was any deceit in his mouth.

[10]Yet it was the LORD's will to crush him and cause him to suffer,
and though the LORD makes his life a guilt offering,
he will see his offspring and prolong his days,
and the will of the LORD will prosper in his hand.
[11]After the suffering of his soul,
he will see the light ⌊of life⌋ and be satisfied;
by his knowledge my righteous servant will justify many,
and he will bear their iniquities.
[12]Therefore I will give him a portion among the great,
and he will divide the spoils with the strong,
because he poured out his life unto death,
and was numbered with the transgressors.
For he bore the sin of many,
and made intercession for the transgressors.

The Future Glory of Zion

54 "Sing, O barren woman,
you who never bore a child;
burst into song, shout for joy,
you who were never in labour;
because more are the children of the desolate woman
than of her who has a husband,"
says the LORD.
[2]"Enlarge the place of your tent,
stretch your tent curtains wide,
do not hold back;
lengthen your cords,
strengthen your stakes.
[3]For you will spread out to the right and to the left;
your descendants will dispossess nations
and settle in their desolate cities.

[4]"Do not be afraid; you will not suffer shame.
Do not fear disgrace; you will not be humiliated.
You will forget the shame of your youth

and remember no more the
reproach of your widowhood.
5For your Maker is your husband—
the LORD Almighty is his name—
the Holy One of Israel is your
Redeemer;
he is called the God of all the
earth.
6The LORD will call you back
as if you were a wife deserted and
distressed in spirit—
a wife who married young,
only to be rejected," says your
God.
7"For a brief moment I abandoned
you,
but with deep compassion I will
bring you back.
8In a surge of anger
I hid my face from you for a
moment,
but with everlasting kindness
I will have compassion on you,"
says the LORD your Redeemer.

9"To me this is like the days of Noah,
when I swore that the waters of
Noah would never again cover
the earth.
So now I have sworn not to be angry
with you,
never to rebuke you again.
10Though the mountains be shaken
and the hills be removed,
yet my unfailing love for you will not
be shaken
nor my covenant of peace be
removed,"
says the LORD, who has
compassion on you.

11"O afflicted city, lashed by storms
and not comforted,
I will build you with stones of
turquoise,
your foundations with sapphires.
12I will make your battlements of
rubies,
your gates of sparkling jewels,
and all your walls of precious
stones.
13All your sons will be taught by the
LORD,
and great will be your children's
peace.
14In righteousness you will be
established:
Tyranny will be far from you;
you will have nothing to fear.
Terror will be far removed;
it will not come near you.
15If anyone does attack you, it will not
be my doing;
whoever attacks you will surrender
to you.

16"See, it is I who created the
blacksmith
who fans the coals into flame
and forges a weapon fit for its
work.
And it is I who have created the
destroyer to work havoc;
17 no weapon forged against you will
prevail,
and you will refute every tongue
that accuses you.
This is the heritage of the servants of
the LORD,
and this is their vindication from
me,"
declares the LORD.

NEW TESTAMENT READING
Ephesians 1:1–23

1 Paul, an apostle of Christ Jesus by the will of God,

To the saints in Ephesus, the faithful in Christ Jesus:

2Grace and peace to you from God our Father and the Lord Jesus Christ.

Spiritual Blessings in Christ

3Praise be to the God and Father of our Lord Jesus Christ, who has blessed

us in the heavenly realms with every
spiritual blessing in Christ. 4For he
chose us in him before the creation of
the world to be holy and blameless in his
sight. In love 5he predestined us to be
adopted as his sons through Jesus
Christ, in accordance with his pleasure
and will—6to the praise of his glorious
grace, which he has freely given us in
the One he loves. 7In him we have
redemption through his blood, the forgiveness of sins, in accordance with the
riches of God's grace 8that he lavished
on us with all wisdom and understanding. 9And he made known to us the
mystery of his will according to his good
pleasure, which he purposed in Christ,
10to be put into effect when the times
will have reached their fulfilment—to
bring all things in heaven and on earth
together under one head, even Christ.

11In him we were also chosen, having
been predestined according to the plan
of him who works out everything in
conformity with the purpose of his will,
12in order that we, who were the first to
hope in Christ, might be for the praise
of his glory. 13And you also were included in Christ when you heard the
word of truth, the gospel of your salvation. Having believed, you were
marked in him with a seal, the promised
Holy Spirit, 14who is a deposit guaranteeing our inheritance until the redemption of those who are God's possession
—to the praise of his glory.

Thanksgiving and Prayer

15For this reason, ever since I heard
about your faith in the Lord Jesus and
your love for all the saints, 16I have not
stopped giving thanks for you, remembering you in my prayers. 17I keep
asking that the God of our Lord Jesus
Christ, the glorious Father, may give
you the Spirit of wisdom and revelation,
so that you may know him better. 18I
pray also that the eyes of your heart may
be enlightened in order that you may
know the hope to which he has called
you, the riches of his glorious inheritance in the saints, 19and his incompar-
ably great power for us who believe.
That power is like the working of his
mighty strength, 20which he exerted in
Christ when he raised him from the
dead and seated him at his right hand in
the heavenly realms, 21far above all rule
and authority, power and dominion,
and every title that can be given, not
only in the present age but also in the
one to come. 22And God placed all
things under his feet and appointed him
to be head over everything for the
church, 23which is his body, the fulness
of him who fills everything in every way.

READING FROM PSALMS

Psalm 109:21–31

21But you, O Sovereign LORD,
deal well with me for your name's sake;
out of the goodness of your love,
deliver me.
22For I am poor and needy,
and my heart is wounded within me.
23I fade away like an evening shadow;
I am shaken off like a locust.
24My knees give way from fasting;
my body is thin and gaunt.
25I am an object of scorn to my accusers;
when they see me, they shake their heads.

26Help me, O LORD my God;
save me in accordance with your love.
27Let them know that it is your hand,
that you, O LORD, have done it.
28They may curse, but you will bless;
when they attack they will be put to shame,
but your servant will rejoice.
29My accusers will be clothed with disgrace
and wrapped in shame as in a cloak.

30With my mouth I will greatly extol
the LORD;
in the great throng I will praise
him.
31For he stands at the right hand of the
needy one,
to save his life from those who
condemn him.

DAY 266

SEPTEMBER 23

OLD TESTAMENT READING

Isaiah 55:1–57:13

Invitation to the Thirsty

55 "Come, all you who are thirsty,
come to the waters;
and you who have no money,
come, buy and eat!
Come, buy wine and milk
without money and without cost.
2Why spend money on what is not
bread,
and your labour on what does not
satisfy?
Listen, listen to me, and eat what is
good,
and your soul will delight in the
richest of fare.
3Give ear and come to me;
hear me, that your soul may live.
I will make an everlasting covenant
with you,
my faithful love promised to
David.
4See, I have made him a witness to the
peoples,
a leader and commander of the
peoples.
5Surely you will summon nations you
know not,
and nations that do not know you
will hasten to you,
because of the LORD your God,
the Holy One of Israel,
for he has endowed you with
splendour."

6Seek the LORD while he may be
found;
call on him while he is near.
7Let the wicked forsake his way
and the evil man his thoughts.
Let him turn to the LORD, and he will
have mercy on him,
and to our God, for he will freely
pardon.

8"For my thoughts are not your
thoughts,
neither are your ways my ways,"
declares the LORD.
9"As the heavens are higher than the
earth,
so are my ways higher than your
ways
and my thoughts than your
thoughts.
10As the rain and the snow
come down from heaven,
and do not return to it
without watering the earth
and making it bud and flourish,
so that it yields seed for the sower
and bread for the eater,
11so is my word that goes out from my
mouth:
It will not return to me empty,
but will accomplish what I desire
and achieve the purpose for which
I sent it.
12You will go out in joy
and be led forth in peace;
the mountains and hills
will burst into song before you,
and all the trees of the field
will clap their hands.
13Instead of the thornbush will grow
the pine tree,
and instead of briers the myrtle will
grow.

This will be for the LORD's renown,
for an everlasting sign,
which will not be destroyed."

Salvation for Others

56 This is what the LORD says:

"Maintain justice
and do what is right,
for my salvation is close at hand
and my righteousness will soon be revealed.
2Blessed is the man who does this,
the man who holds it fast,
who keeps the Sabbath without desecrating it,
and keeps his hand from doing any evil."
3Let no foreigner who has bound himself to the LORD say,
"The LORD will surely exclude me from his people."
And let not any eunuch complain,
"I am only a dry tree."

4For this is what the LORD says:

"To the eunuchs who keep my Sabbaths,
who choose what pleases me
and hold fast to my covenant—
5to them I will give within my temple
and its walls
a memorial and a name
better than sons and daughters;
I will give them an everlasting name
that will not be cut off.
6And foreigners who bind themselves to the LORD
to serve him,
to love the name of the LORD,
and to worship him,
all who keep the Sabbath without desecrating it
and who hold fast to my covenant—
7these I will bring to my holy mountain
and give them joy in my house of prayer.
Their burnt offerings and sacrifices
will be accepted on my altar;
for my house will be called
a house of prayer for all nations."
8The Sovereign LORD declares—
he who gathers the exiles of Israel:
"I will gather still others to them
besides those already gathered."

God's Accusation Against the Wicked

9Come, all you beasts of the field,
come and devour, all you beasts of the forest!
10Israel's watchmen are blind,
they all lack knowledge;
they are all mute dogs,
they cannot bark;
they lie around and dream,
they love to sleep.
11They are dogs with mighty appetites;
they never have enough.
They are shepherds who lack understanding;
they all turn to their own way,
each seeks his own gain.
12"Come," each one cries, "let me get wine!
Let us drink our fill of beer!
And tomorrow will be like today,
or even far better."

57 The righteous perish,
and no-one ponders it in his heart;
devout men are taken away,
and no-one understands
that the righteous are taken away
to be spared from evil.
2Those who walk uprightly
enter into peace;
they find rest as they lie in death.

3"But you—come here, you sons of a sorceress,
you offspring of adulterers and prostitutes!
4Whom are you mocking?
At whom do you sneer
and stick out your tongue?
Are you not a brood of rebels,
the offspring of liars?

[5]You burn with lust among the oaks
and under every spreading tree;
you sacrifice your children in the ravines
and under the overhanging crags.

[6]⌊The idols⌋ among the smooth stones of the ravines are your portion;
they, they are your lot.
Yes, to them you have poured out drink offerings
and offered grain offerings.
In the light of these things, should I relent?
[7]You have made your bed on a high and lofty hill;
there you went up to offer your sacrifices.
[8]Behind your doors and your doorposts
you have put your pagan symbols.
Forsaking me, you uncovered your bed,
you climbed into it and opened it wide;
you made a pact with those whose beds you love,
and you looked on their nakedness.
[9]You went to Molech with olive oil
and increased your perfumes.
You sent your ambassadors far away;
you descended to the grave itself!
[10]You were wearied by all your ways,
but you would not say, 'It is hopeless.'
You found renewal of your strength,
and so you did not faint.

[11]"Whom have you so dreaded and feared
that you have been false to me,
and have neither remembered me
nor pondered this in your hearts?
Is it not because I have long been silent
that you do not fear me?
[12]I will expose your righteousness and your works,
and they will not benefit you.
[13]When you cry out for help,
let your collection ⌊of idols⌋ save you!
The wind will carry all of them off,
a mere breath will blow them away.
But the man who makes me his refuge
will inherit the land
and possess my holy mountain."

NEW TESTAMENT READING
Ephesians 2:1–22

Made Alive in Christ

2 As for you, you were dead in your
transgressions and sins, [2]in which
you used to live when you followed the
ways of this world and of the ruler of the
kingdom of the air, the spirit who is now
at work in those who are disobedient.
[3]All of us also lived among them at one
time, gratifying the cravings of our sinful nature and following its desires and
thoughts. Like the rest, we were by
nature objects of wrath. [4]But because of
his great love for us, God, who is rich in
mercy, [5]made us alive with Christ even
when we were dead in transgressions
—it is by grace you have been saved.
[6]And God raised us up with Christ and
seated us with him in the heavenly
realms in Christ Jesus, [7]in order that in
the coming ages he might show the
incomparable riches of his grace, expressed in his kindness to us in Christ
Jesus. [8]For it is by grace you have been
saved, through faith—and this not from
yourselves, it is the gift of God—[9]not by
works, so that no-one can boast. [10]For
we are God's workmanship, created in
Christ Jesus to do good works, which
God prepared in advance for us to do.

One in Christ

[11]Therefore, remember that formerly
you who are Gentiles by birth and called
"uncircumcised" by those who call
themselves "the circumcision" (that

done in the body by the hands of men)
—12 remember that at that time you
were separate from Christ, excluded
from citizenship in Israel and foreigners
to the covenants of the promise, without hope and without God in the world.
13 But now in Christ Jesus you who once
were far away have been brought near
through the blood of Christ.
14 For he himself is our peace, who has
made the two one and has destroyed the
barrier, the dividing wall of hostility,
15 by abolishing in his flesh the law with
its commandments and regulations. His
purpose was to create in himself one
new man out of the two, thus making
peace, 16 and in this one body to reconcile both of them to God through the
cross, by which he put to death their
hostility. 17 He came and preached
peace to you who were far away and
peace to those who were near. 18 For
through him we both have access to the
Father by one Spirit.
19 Consequently, you are no longer
foreigners and aliens, but fellow-
citizens with God's people and members of God's household, 20 built on
the foundation of the apostles and
prophets, with Christ Jesus himself as
the chief cornerstone. 21 In him the
whole building is joined together and
rises to become a holy temple in the
Lord. 22 And in him you too are being
built together to become a dwelling in
which God lives by his Spirit.

READING FROM PSALMS
Psalm 110:1–7

Of David. A psalm.

1 The LORD says to my Lord:
  "Sit at my right hand
until I make your enemies
  a footstool for your feet."

2 The LORD will extend your mighty
    sceptre from Zion;
  you will rule in the midst of your
    enemies.
3 Your troops will be willing
  on your day of battle.
Arrayed in holy majesty,
  from the womb of the dawn
  you will receive the dew of your
    youth.

4 The LORD has sworn
  and will not change his mind:
"You are a priest for ever,
  in the order of Melchizedek."

5 The Lord is at your right hand;
  he will crush kings on the day of his
    wrath.
6 He will judge nations, heaping up the
    dead
  and crushing the rulers of the
    whole earth.
7 He will drink from a brook beside the
    way;
  therefore he will lift up his head.

SEPTEMBER 24

OLD TESTAMENT READING
Isaiah 57:14–59:21

Comfort for the Contrite

14And it will be said:

"Build up, build up, prepare the
road!
Remove the obstacles out of the
way of my people."
15For this is what the high and lofty
One says—
he who lives for ever, whose name
is holy:
"I live in a high and holy place,
but also with him who is contrite
and lowly in spirit,
to revive the spirit of the lowly
and to revive the heart of the
contrite.
16I will not accuse for ever,
nor will I always be angry,
for then the spirit of man would grow
faint before me—
the breath of man that I have
created.
17I was enraged by his sinful greed;
I punished him, and hid my face in
anger,
yet he kept on in his wilful ways.
18I have seen his ways, but I will heal
him;
I will guide him and restore
comfort to him,
19 creating praise on the lips of the
mourners in Israel.
Peace, peace, to those far and near,"
says the LORD. "And I will heal
them."
20But the wicked are like the tossing
sea,
which cannot rest,
whose waves cast up mire and
mud.
21"There is no peace," says my God,
"for the wicked."

True Fasting

58 "Shout it aloud, do not hold
back.
Raise your voice like a trumpet.
Declare to my people their rebellion
and to the house of Jacob their
sins.
2For day after day they seek me out;
they seem eager to know my ways,
as if they were a nation that does
what is right
and has not forsaken the
commands of its God.
They ask me for just decisions
and seem eager for God to come
near them.
3'Why have we fasted,' they say,
'and you have not seen it?
Why have we humbled ourselves,
and you have not noticed?'

"Yet on the day of your fasting, you
do as you please
and exploit all your workers.
4Your fasting ends in quarrelling and
strife,
and in striking each other with
wicked fists.
You cannot fast as you do today
and expect your voice to be heard
on high.
5Is this the kind of fast I have chosen,
only a day for a man to humble
himself?
Is it only for bowing one's head like a
reed
and for lying on sackcloth and
ashes?
Is that what you call a fast,
a day acceptable to the LORD?

6"Is not this the kind of fasting I have
chosen:
to loose the chains of injustice
and untie the cords of the yoke,
to set the oppressed free
and break every yoke?

7Is it not to share your food with the
hungry
and to provide the poor wanderer
with shelter—
when you see the naked, to clothe
him,
and not to turn away from your
own flesh and blood?
8Then your light will break forth like
the dawn,
and your healing will quickly
appear;
then your righteousness will go
before you,
and the glory of the LORD will be
your rear guard.
9Then you will call, and the LORD will
answer;
you will cry for help, and he will
say: Here am I.

"If you do away with the yoke of
oppression,
with the pointing finger and
malicious talk,
10and if you spend yourselves on behalf
of the hungry
and satisfy the needs of the
oppressed,
then your light will rise in the
darkness,
and your night will become like the
noonday.
11The LORD will guide you always;
he will satisfy your needs in a
sun-scorched land
and will strengthen your frame.
You will be like a well-watered
garden,
like a spring whose waters never
fail.
12Your people will rebuild the ancient
ruins
and will raise up the age-old
foundations;
you will be called Repairer of Broken
Walls,
Restorer of Streets with Dwellings.

13"If you keep your feet from breaking
the Sabbath
and from doing as you please on
my holy day,
if you call the Sabbath a delight
and the LORD's holy day
honourable,
and if you honour it by not going your
own way
and not doing as you please or
speaking idle words,
14then you will find your joy in the
LORD,
and I will cause you to ride on the
heights of the land
and to feast on the inheritance of
your father Jacob."
The mouth of the LORD
has spoken.

Sin, Confession and Redemption

59 Surely the arm of the LORD is
not too short to save,
nor his ear too dull to hear.
2But your iniquities have separated
you from your God;
your sins have hidden his face from
you,
so that he will not hear.
3For your hands are stained with
blood,
your fingers with guilt.
Your lips have spoken lies,
and your tongue mutters wicked
things.
4No-one calls for justice;
no-one pleads his case with
integrity.
They rely on empty arguments and
speak lies;
they conceive trouble and give
birth to evil.
5They hatch the eggs of vipers
and spin a spider's web.
Whoever eats their eggs will die,
and when one is broken, an adder
is hatched.
6Their cobwebs are useless for
clothing;
they cannot cover themselves with
what they make.
Their deeds are evil deeds,
and acts of violence are in their
hands.
7Their feet rush into sin;

they are swift to shed innocent
blood.
Their thoughts are evil thoughts;
ruin and destruction mark their
ways.
8The way of peace they do not know;
there is no justice in their paths.
They have turned them into crooked
roads;
no-one who walks in them will
know peace.

9So justice is far from us,
and righteousness does not reach
us.
We look for light, but all is darkness;
for brightness, but we walk in deep
shadows.
10Like the blind we grope along the
wall,
feeling our way like men without
eyes.
At midday we stumble as if it were
twilight;
among the strong, we are like the
dead.
11We all growl like bears;
we moan mournfully like doves.
We look for justice, but find none;
for deliverance, but it is far away.

12For our offences are many in your
sight,
and our sins testify against us.
Our offences are ever with us,
and we acknowledge our iniquities:
13rebellion and treachery against the
LORD,
turning our backs on our God,
fomenting oppression and revolt,
uttering lies our hearts have
conceived.
14So justice is driven back,
and righteousness stands at a
distance;
truth has stumbled in the streets,
honesty cannot enter.
15Truth is nowhere to be found,
and whoever shuns evil becomes a
prey.

The LORD looked and was displeased
that there was no justice.
16He saw that there was no-one,
he was appalled that there was
no-one to intervene;
so his own arm worked salvation for
him,
and his own righteousness
sustained him.
17He put on righteousness as his
breastplate,
and the helmet of salvation on his
head;
he put on the garments of vengeance
and wrapped himself in zeal as in a
cloak.
18According to what they have done,
so will he repay
wrath to his enemies
and retribution to his foes;
he will repay the islands their due.
19From the west, men will fear the
name of the LORD,
and from the rising of the sun, they
will revere his glory.
For he will come like a pent-up flood
that the breath of the LORD drives
along.

20"The Redeemer will come to Zion,
to those in Jacob who repent of
their sins,"
declares the LORD.

21"As for me, this is my covenant with
them," says the LORD. "My Spirit, who
is on you, and my words that I have put
in your mouth will not depart from your
mouth, or from the mouths of your
children, or from the mouths of their
descendants from this time on and for
ever," says the LORD.

NEW TESTAMENT READING
Ephesians 3:1–21

Paul the Preacher to the Gentiles

3 For this reason I, Paul, the prisoner
of Christ Jesus for the sake of you
Gentiles—
2Surely you have heard about the administration of God's grace that was

given to me for you, [3]that is, the mystery made known to me by revelation,
as I have already written briefly. [4]In
reading this, then, you will be able to
understand my insight into the mystery
of Christ, [5]which was not made known
to men in other generations as it has
now been revealed by the Spirit to
God's holy apostles and prophets. [6]This
mystery is that through the gospel the
Gentiles are heirs together with Israel,
members together of one body, and
sharers together in the promise in Christ
Jesus.
[7]I became a servant of this gospel by
the gift of God's grace given me through
the working of his power. [8]Although I
am less than the least of all God's people, this grace was given me: to preach
to the Gentiles the unsearchable riches
of Christ, [9]and to make plain to everyone the administration of this mystery,
which for ages past was kept hidden in
God, who created all things. [10]His intent was that now, through the church,
the manifold wisdom of God should be
made known to the rulers and authorities in the heavenly realms, [11]ac-
cording to his eternal purpose which he
accomplished in Christ Jesus our Lord.
[12]In him and through faith in him we
may approach God with freedom and
confidence. [13]I ask you, therefore, not
to be discouraged because of my sufferings for you, which are your glory.

A Prayer for the Ephesians

[14]For this reason I kneel before the
Father, [15]from whom his whole family
in heaven and on earth derives its name.
[16]I pray that out of his glorious riches he
may strengthen you with power through
his Spirit in your inner being, [17]so that
Christ may dwell in your hearts through
faith. And I pray that you, being rooted
and established in love, [18]may have
power, together with all the saints, to
grasp how wide and long and high and
deep is the love of Christ, [19]and to know
this love that surpasses knowledge—
that you may be filled to the measure of
all the fulness of God.

[20]Now to him who is able to do im-
measurably more than all we ask or
imagine, according to his power that is
at work within us, [21]to him be glory in
the church and in Christ Jesus throughout all generations, for ever and ever!
Amen.

READING FROM PSALMS

Psalm 111:1–10

[1]Praise the LORD.

I will extol the LORD with all my heart
in the council of the upright and in the assembly.

[2]Great are the works of the LORD;
they are pondered by all who delight in them.
[3]Glorious and majestic are his deeds,
and his righteousness endures for ever.
[4]He has caused his wonders to be remembered;
the LORD is gracious and compassionate.
[5]He provides food for those who fear him;
he remembers his covenant for ever.
[6]He has shown his people the power of his works,
giving them the lands of other nations.
[7]The works of his hands are faithful and just;
all his precepts are trustworthy.
[8]They are steadfast for ever and ever,
done in faithfulness and uprightness.
[9]He provided redemption for his people;
he ordained his covenant for ever—
holy and awesome is his name.

[10]The fear of the LORD is the beginning of wisdom;
all who follow his precepts have good understanding.
To him belongs eternal praise.

DAY 268 **SEPTEMBER 25**

OLD TESTAMENT READING
Isaiah 60:1–62:12

The Glory of Zion

60 "Arise, shine, for your light has come,
and the glory of the LORD rises upon you.
2See, darkness covers the earth
and thick darkness is over the peoples,
but the LORD rises upon you
and his glory appears over you.
3Nations will come to your light,
and kings to the brightness of your dawn.

4"Lift up your eyes and look about you:
All assemble and come to you;
your sons come from afar,
and your daughters are carried on the arm.
5Then you will look and be radiant,
your heart will throb and swell with joy;
the wealth on the seas will be brought to you,
to you the riches of the nations will come.
6Herds of camels will cover your land,
young camels of Midian and Ephah.
And all from Sheba will come,
bearing gold and incense
and proclaiming the praise of the LORD.
7All Kedar's flocks will be gathered to you,
the rams of Nebaioth will serve you;
they will be accepted as offerings on my altar,
and I will adorn my glorious temple.

8"Who are these that fly along like clouds,
like doves to their nests?
9Surely the islands look to me;
in the lead are the ships of Tarshish,
bringing your sons from afar,
with their silver and gold,
to the honour of the LORD your God,
the Holy One of Israel,
for he has endowed you with splendour.

10"Foreigners will rebuild your walls,
and their kings will serve you.
Though in anger I struck you,
in favour I will show you compassion.
11Your gates will always stand open,
they will never be shut, day or night,
so that men may bring you the wealth of the nations—
their kings led in triumphal procession.
12For the nation or kingdom that will not serve you will perish;
it will be utterly ruined.

13"The glory of Lebanon will come to you,
the pine, the fir and the cypress together,
to adorn the place of my sanctuary;
and I will glorify the place of my feet.
14The sons of your oppressors will come bowing before you;
all who despise you will bow down at your feet
and will call you the City of the LORD,
Zion of the Holy One of Israel.

15"Although you have been forsaken and hated,
with no-one travelling through,

I will make you the everlasting pride
and the joy of all generations.
16You will drink the milk of nations
and be nursed at royal breasts.
Then you will know that I, the LORD,
am your Saviour,
your Redeemer, the Mighty One of
Jacob.
17Instead of bronze I will bring you
gold,
and silver in place of iron.
Instead of wood I will bring you
bronze,
and iron in place of stones.
I will make peace your governor
and righteousness your ruler.
18No longer will violence be heard in
your land,
nor ruin or destruction within your
borders,
but you will call your walls Salvation
and your gates Praise.
19The sun will no more be your light by
day,
nor will the brightness of the moon
shine on you,
for the LORD will be your everlasting
light,
and your God will be your glory.
20Your sun will never set again,
and your moon will wane no more;
the LORD will be your everlasting
light,
and your days of sorrow will end.
21Then will all your people be righteous
and they will possess the land for
ever.
They are the shoot I have planted,
the work of my hands,
for the display of my splendour.
22The least of you will become a
thousand,
the smallest a mighty nation.
I am the LORD;
in its time I will do this swiftly."

The Year of the LORD's Favour

61 The Spirit of the Sovereign
LORD is on me,
because the LORD has anointed me
to preach good news to the poor.
He has sent me to bind up the
broken-hearted,
to proclaim freedom for the
captives
and release from darkness for the
prisoners,
2to proclaim the year of the LORD's
favour
and the day of vengeance of our
God,
to comfort all who mourn,
3 and provide for those who grieve in
Zion—
to bestow on them a crown of beauty
instead of ashes,
the oil of gladness
instead of mourning,
and a garment of praise
instead of a spirit of despair.
They will be called oaks of
righteousness,
a planting of the LORD
for the display of his splendour.

4They will rebuild the ancient ruins
and restore the places long
devastated;
they will renew the ruined cities
that have been devastated for
generations.
5Aliens will shepherd your flocks;
foreigners will work your fields and
vineyards.
6And you will be called priests of the
LORD,
you will be named ministers of our
God.
You will feed on the wealth of
nations,
and in their riches you will boast.

7Instead of their shame
my people will receive a double
portion,
and instead of disgrace
they will rejoice in their
inheritance;
and so they will inherit a double
portion in their land,
and everlasting joy will be theirs.

8"For I, the LORD, love justice;
I hate robbery and iniquity.
In my faithfulness I will reward them
and make an everlasting covenant with them.
9Their descendants will be known among the nations
and their offspring among the peoples.
All who see them will acknowledge
that they are a people the LORD has blessed."

10I delight greatly in the LORD;
my soul rejoices in my God.
For he has clothed me with garments of salvation
and arrayed me in a robe of righteousness,
as a bridegroom adorns his head like a priest,
and as a bride adorns herself with her jewels.
11For as the soil makes the young plant come up
and a garden causes seeds to grow,
so the Sovereign LORD will make righteousness and praise
spring up before all nations.

Zion's New Name

62 For Zion's sake I will not keep silent,
for Jerusalem's sake I will not remain quiet,
till her righteousness shines out like the dawn,
her salvation like a blazing torch.
2The nations will see your righteousness,
and all kings your glory;
you will be called by a new name
that the mouth of the LORD will bestow.
3You will be a crown of splendour in the LORD's hand,
a royal diadem in the hand of your God.
4No longer will they call you Deserted,
or name your land Desolate.
But you will be called Hephzibah,
and your land Beulah;
for the LORD will take delight in you,
and your land will be married.
5As a young man marries a maiden,
so will your sons marry you;
as a bridegroom rejoices over his bride,
so will your God rejoice over you.

6I have posted watchmen on your walls, O Jerusalem;
they will never be silent day or night.
You who call on the LORD,
give yourselves no rest,
7and give him no rest till he establishes Jerusalem
and makes her the praise of the earth.

8The LORD has sworn by his right hand
and by his mighty arm:
"Never again will I give your grain
as food for your enemies,
and never again will foreigners drink the new wine
for which you have toiled;
9but those who harvest it will eat it
and praise the LORD,
and those who gather the grapes will drink it
in the courts of my sanctuary."

10Pass through, pass through the gates!
Prepare the way for the people.
Build up, build up the highway!
Remove the stones.
Raise a banner for the nations.

11The LORD has made proclamation
to the ends of the earth:
"Say to the Daughter of Zion,
'See, your Saviour comes!
See, his reward is with him,
and his recompense accompanies him.'"
12They will be called the Holy People,
the Redeemed of the LORD;
and you will be called Sought After,
the City No Longer Deserted.

NEW TESTAMENT READING
Ephesians 4:1–16

Unity in the Body of Christ

4 As a prisoner for the Lord, then, I urge you to live a life worthy of the calling you have received. 2Be completely humble and gentle; be patient, bearing with one another in love. 3Make every effort to keep the unity of the Spirit through the bond of peace. 4There is one body and one Spirit—just as you were called to one hope when you were called—5one Lord, one faith, one baptism; 6one God and Father of all, who is over all and through all and in all.

7But to each one of us grace has been given as Christ apportioned it. 8This is why it says:

"When he ascended on high,
he led captives in his train
and gave gifts to men."

9(What does "he ascended" mean except that he also descended to the lower, earthly regions? 10He who descended is the very one who ascended higher than all the heavens, in order to fill the whole universe.) 11It was he who gave some to be apostles, some to be prophets, some to be evangelists, and some to be pastors and teachers, 12to prepare God's people for works of service, so that the body of Christ may be built up 13until we all reach unity in the faith and in the knowledge of the Son of God and become mature, attaining to the whole measure of the fulness of Christ.

14Then we will no longer be infants, tossed back and forth by the waves, and blown here and there by every wind of teaching and by the cunning and craftiness of men in their deceitful scheming. 15Instead, speaking the truth in love, we will in all things grow up into him who is the Head, that is, Christ. 16From him the whole body, joined and held together by every supporting ligament, grows and builds itself up in love, as each part does its work.

READING FROM PROVERBS
Proverbs 23:19–28

19Listen, my son, and be wise,
and keep your heart on the right path.
20Do not join those who drink too much wine
or gorge themselves on meat,
21for drunkards and gluttons become poor,
and drowsiness clothes them in rags.

22Listen to your father, who gave you life,
and do not despise your mother when she is old.
23Buy the truth and do not sell it;
get wisdom, discipline and understanding.
24The father of a righteous man has great joy;
he who has a wise son delights in him.
25May your father and mother be glad;
may she who gave you birth rejoice!

26My son, give me your heart
and let your eyes keep to my ways,
27for a prostitute is a deep pit
and a wayward wife is a narrow well.
28Like a bandit she lies in wait,
and multiplies the unfaithful among men.

DAY 269

SEPTEMBER 26

OLD TESTAMENT READING
Isaiah 63:1–65:16

God's Day of Vengeance and Redemption

63 Who is this coming from Edom,
from Bozrah, with his garments
stained crimson?
Who is this, robed in splendour,
striding forward in the greatness of
his strength?

"It is I, speaking in righteousness,
mighty to save."

2Why are your garments red,
like those of one treading the
winepress?

3"I have trodden the winepress alone;
from the nations no-one was with
me.
I trampled them in my anger
and trod them down in my wrath;
their blood spattered my garments,
and I stained all my clothing.
4For the day of vengeance was in my
heart,
and the year of my redemption has
come.
5I looked, but there was no-one to
help,
I was appalled that no-one gave
support;
so my own arm worked salvation for
me,
and my own wrath sustained me.
6I trampled the nations in my anger;
in my wrath I made them drunk
and poured their blood on the
ground."

Praise and Prayer

7I will tell of the kindnesses of the
LORD,
the deeds for which he is to be
praised,
according to all the LORD has done
for us—
yes, the many good things he has
done
for the house of Israel,
according to his compassion and
many kindnesses.
8He said, "Surely they are my people,
sons who will not be false to me";
and so he became their Saviour.
9In all their distress he too was
distressed,
and the angel of his presence saved
them.
In his love and mercy he redeemed
them;
he lifted them up and carried them
all the days of old.
10Yet they rebelled
and grieved his Holy Spirit.
So he turned and became their enemy
and he himself fought against
them.

11Then his people recalled the days of
old,
the days of Moses and his people—
where is he who brought them
through the sea,
with the shepherd of his flock?
Where is he who set
his Holy Spirit among them,
12who sent his glorious arm of power
to be at Moses' right hand,
who divided the waters before them,
to gain for himself everlasting
renown,
13who led them through the depths?
Like a horse in open country,
they did not stumble;
14like cattle that go down to the plain,
they were given rest by the Spirit of
the LORD.
This is how you guided your people
to make for yourself a glorious
name.

15Look down from heaven and see
from your lofty throne, holy and glorious.
Where are your zeal and your might?
Your tenderness and compassion
are withheld from us.
16But you are our Father,
though Abraham does not know us
or Israel acknowledge us;
you, O LORD, are our Father,
our Redeemer from of old is your name.
17Why, O LORD, do you make us
wander from your ways
and harden our hearts so that we
do not revere you?
Return for the sake of your servants,
the tribes that are your inheritance.
18For a little while your people
possessed your holy place,
but now our enemies have
trampled down your sanctuary.
19We are yours from of old;
but you have not ruled over them,
they have not been called by your name.

64 Oh, that you would rend the heavens and come down,
that the mountains would tremble before you!
2As when fire sets twigs ablaze
and causes water to boil,
come down to make your name
known to your enemies
and cause the nations to quake
before you!
3For when you did awesome things
that we did not expect,
you came down, and the
mountains trembled before you.
4Since ancient times no-one has heard,
no ear has perceived,
no eye has seen any God besides you,
who acts on behalf of those who
wait for him.
5You come to the help of those who
gladly do right,
who remember your ways.
But when we continued to sin against them,
you were angry.
How then can we be saved?
6All of us have become like one who is unclean,
and all our righteous acts are like filthy rags;
we all shrivel up like a leaf,
and like the wind our sins sweep us away.
7No-one calls on your name
or strives to lay hold of you;
for you have hidden your face from us
and made us waste away because
of our sins.

8Yet, O LORD, you are our Father.
We are the clay, you are the potter;
we are all the work of your hand.
9Do not be angry beyond measure, O LORD;
do not remember our sins for ever.
Oh, look upon us we pray,
for we are all your people.
10Your sacred cities have become a desert;
even Zion is a desert, Jerusalem a desolation.
11Our holy and glorious temple, where
our fathers praised you,
has been burned with fire,
and all that we treasured lies in ruins.
12After all this, O LORD, will you hold
yourself back?
Will you keep silent and punish us
beyond measure?

Judgment and Salvation

65 "I revealed myself to those who did not ask for me;
I was found by those who did not seek me.
To a nation that did not call on my name,
I said, 'Here am I, here am I.'
2All day long I have held out my hands
to an obstinate people,

who walk in ways not good,
pursuing their own imaginations—
3a people who continually provoke me
to my very face,
offering sacrifices in gardens
and burning incense on altars of
brick;
4who sit among the graves
and spend their nights keeping
secret vigil;
who eat the flesh of pigs,
and whose pots hold broth of
unclean meat;
5who say, 'Keep away; don't come
near me,
for I am too sacred for you!'
Such people are smoke in my
nostrils,
a fire that keeps burning all day.

6"See, it stands written before me;
I will not keep silent but will pay
back in full;
I will pay it back into their laps—
7both your sins and the sins of your
fathers,"
says the LORD.
"Because they burned sacrifices on
the mountains
and defied me on the hills,
I will measure into their laps
the full payment for their former
deeds."

8This is what the LORD says:

"As when juice is still found in a
cluster of grapes
and men say, 'Don't destroy it,
there is yet some good in it,'
so will I do on behalf of my servants;
I will not destroy them all.
9I will bring forth descendants from
Jacob,
and from Judah those who will
possess my mountains;
my chosen people will inherit them,
and there will my servants live.
10Sharon will become a pasture for
flocks,
and the Valley of Achor a resting
place for herds,
for my people who seek me.

11"But as for you who forsake the
LORD
and forget my holy mountain,
who spread a table for Fortune
and fill bowls of mixed wine for
Destiny,
12I will destine you for the sword,
and you will all bend down for the
slaughter;
for I called but you did not answer,
I spoke but you did not listen.
You did evil in my sight
and chose what displeases me."

13Therefore this is what the Sovereign
LORD says:

"My servants will eat,
but you will go hungry;
my servants will drink,
but you will go thirsty;
my servants will rejoice,
but you will be put to shame.
14My servants will sing
out of the joy of their hearts,
but you will cry out
from anguish of heart
and wail in brokenness of spirit.
15You will leave your name
to my chosen ones as a curse;
the Sovereign LORD will put you to
death,
but to his servants he will give
another name.
16Whoever invokes a blessing in the
land
will do so by the God of truth;
he who takes an oath in the land
will swear by the God of truth.
For the past troubles will be forgotten
and hidden from my eyes.

NEW TESTAMENT READING
Ephesians 4:17–5:7

Living as Children of Light

17So I tell you this, and insist on it in the Lord, that you must no longer live as the Gentiles do, in the futility of their

thinking. 18They are darkened in their
understanding and separated from the
life of God because of the ignorance
that is in them due to the hardening of
their hearts. 19Having lost all sensi-
tivity, they have given themselves over
to sensuality so as to indulge in every
kind of impurity, with a continual lust
for more.

20You, however, did not come to
know Christ that way. 21Surely you
heard of him and were taught in him in
accordance with the truth that is in
Jesus. 22You were taught, with regard
to your former way of life, to put off
your old self, which is being corrupted
by its deceitful desires; 23to be made
new in the attitude of your minds; 24and
to put on the new self, created to be like
God in true righteousness and holiness.

25Therefore each of you must put off
falsehood and speak truthfully to his
neighbour, for we are all members of
one body. 26"In your anger do not sin":
Do not let the sun go down while you
are still angry, 27and do not give the
devil a foothold. 28He who has been
stealing must steal no longer, but must
work, doing something useful with his
own hands, that he may have something
to share with those in need.

29Do not let any unwholesome talk
come out of your mouths, but only what
is helpful for building others up according to their needs, that it may benefit
those who listen. 30And do not grieve
the Holy Spirit of God, with whom you
were sealed for the day of redemption.
31Get rid of all bitterness, rage and
anger, brawling and slander, along with
every form of malice. 32Be kind and
compassionate to one another, forgiving each other, just as in Christ God
forgave you.

5 Be imitators of God, therefore, as
dearly loved children 2and live a
life of love, just as Christ loved us and
gave himself up for us as a fragrant
offering and sacrifice to God.

3But among you there must not be
even a hint of sexual immorality, or of
any kind of impurity, or of greed,
because these are improper for God's
holy people. 4Nor should there be ob-
scenity, foolish talk or coarse joking,
which are out of place, but rather
thanksgiving. 5For of this you can be
sure: No immoral, impure or greedy
person—such a man is an idolater—
has any inheritance in the kingdom of
Christ and of God. 6Let no-one deceive
you with empty words, for because of
such things God's wrath comes on
those who are disobedient. 7Therefore
do not be partners with them.

READING FROM PSALMS
Psalm 112:1–10

1Praise the LORD.

Blessed is the man who fears the
LORD,
who finds great delight in his
commands.

2His children will be mighty in the
land;
the generation of the upright will
be blessed.
3Wealth and riches are in his house,
and his righteousness endures for
ever.
4Even in darkness light dawns for the
upright,
for the gracious and compassionate
and righteous man.
5Good will come to him who is
generous and lends freely,
who conducts his affairs with
justice.
6Surely he will never be shaken;
a righteous man will be
remembered for ever.
7He will have no fear of bad news;
his heart is steadfast, trusting in the
LORD.
8His heart is secure, he will have no
fear;
in the end he will look in triumph
on his foes.

[9]He has scattered abroad his gifts to
the poor,
his righteousness endures for
ever;
his horn will be lifted high in
honour.
[10]The wicked man will see and be
vexed,
he will gnash his teeth and waste
away;
the longings of the wicked will
come to nothing.

DAY 270

SEPTEMBER 27

OLD TESTAMENT READING
Isaiah 65:17–66:24

New Heavens and a New Earth

[17]"Behold, I will create
new heavens and a new earth.
The former things will not be
remembered,
nor will they come to mind.
[18]But be glad and rejoice for ever
in what I will create,
for I will create Jerusalem to be a
delight
and its people a joy.
[19]I will rejoice over Jerusalem
and take delight in my people;
the sound of weeping and of crying
will be heard in it no more.

[20]"Never again will there be in it
an infant who lives but a few days,
or an old man who does not live
out his years;
he who dies at a hundred
will be thought a mere youth;
he who fails to reach a hundred
will be considered accursed.
[21]They will build houses and dwell in
them;
they will plant vineyards and eat
their fruit.
[22]No longer will they build houses and
others live in them,
or plant and others eat.
For as the days of a tree,
so will be the days of my people;
my chosen ones will long enjoy
the works of their hands.
[23]They will not toil in vain
or bear children doomed to
misfortune;
for they will be a people blessed by
the LORD,
they and their descendants with
them.
[24]Before they call I will answer;
while they are still speaking I will
hear.
[25]The wolf and the lamb will feed
together,
and the lion will eat straw like the
ox,
but dust will be the serpent's food.
They will neither harm nor destroy
on all my holy mountain,"
says the LORD.

Judgment and Hope

66 This is what the LORD says:

"Heaven is my throne,
and the earth is my footstool.
Where is the house you will build for
me?
Where will my resting place be?
[2]Has not my hand made all these
things,
and so they came into being?"
declares the LORD.

"This is the one I esteem:
he who is humble and contrite in
spirit,
and trembles at my word.
[3]But whoever sacrifices a bull
is like one who kills a man,

and whoever offers a lamb,
like one who breaks a dog's neck;
whoever makes a grain offering
is like one who presents pig's
blood,
and whoever burns memorial
incense,
like one who worships an idol.
They have chosen their own ways,
and their souls delight in their
abominations;
4so I also will choose harsh treatment
for them
and will bring upon them what they
dread.
For when I called, no-one answered,
when I spoke, no-one listened.
They did evil in my sight
and chose what displeases me."

5Hear the word of the LORD,
you who tremble at his word;
"Your brothers who hate you,
and exclude you because of my
name, have said,
'Let the LORD be glorified,
that we may see your joy!'
Yet they will be put to shame.
6Hear that uproar from the city,
hear that noise from the temple!
It is the sound of the LORD
repaying his enemies all they
deserve.

7"Before she goes into labour,
she gives birth;
before the pains come upon her,
she delivers a son.
8Who has ever heard of such a thing?
Who has ever seen such things?
Can a country be born in a day
or a nation be brought forth in a
moment?
Yet no sooner is Zion in labour
than she gives birth to her children.
9Do I bring to the moment of birth
and not give delivery?" says the
LORD.
"Do I close up the womb
when I bring to delivery?" says
your God.

10"Rejoice with Jerusalem and be glad
for her,
all you who love her;
rejoice greatly with her,
all you who mourn over her.
11For you will nurse and be satisfied
at her comforting breasts;
you will drink deeply
and delight in her overflowing
abundance."

12For this is what the LORD says:

"I will extend peace to her like a
river,
and the wealth of nations like a
flooding stream;
you will nurse and be carried on her
arm
and dandled on her knees.
13As a mother comforts her child,
so will I comfort you;
and you will be comforted over
Jerusalem."

14When you see this, your heart will
rejoice
and you will flourish like grass;
the hand of the LORD will be made
known to his servants,
but his fury will be shown to his
foes.
15See, the LORD is coming with fire,
and his chariots are like a
whirlwind;
he will bring down his anger with
fury,
and his rebuke with flames of fire.
16For with fire and with his sword
the LORD will execute judgment
upon all men,
and many will be those slain by the
LORD.

17"Those who consecrate and purify
themselves to go into the gardens, following the one in the midst of those who
eat the flesh of pigs and rats and other
abominable things—they will meet
their end together," declares the LORD.
18"And I, because of their actions and
their imaginations, am about to come

and gather all nations and tongues, and they will come and see my glory.

19"I will set a sign among them, and I will send some of those who survive to the nations—to Tarshish, to the Libyans and Lydians (famous as archers), to Tubal and Greece, and to the distant islands that have not heard of my fame or seen my glory. They will proclaim my glory among the nations. 20And they will bring all your brothers, from all the nations, to my holy mountain in Jerusalem as an offering to the LORD—on horses, in chariots and wagons, and on mules and camels," says the LORD. "They will bring them, as the Israelites bring their grain offerings, to the temple of the LORD in ceremonially clean vessels. 21And I will select some of them also to be priests and Levites," says the LORD.

22"As the new heavens and the new earth that I make will endure before me," declares the LORD, "so will your name and descendants endure. 23From one New Moon to another and from one Sabbath to another, all mankind will come and bow down before me," says the LORD. 24"And they will go out and look upon the dead bodies of those who rebelled against me; their worm will not die, nor will their fire be quenched, and they will be loathsome to all mankind."

NEW TESTAMENT READING
Ephesians 5:8–33

8For you were once darkness, but now you are light in the Lord. Live as children of light 9(for the fruit of the light consists in all goodness, righteousness and truth) 10and find out what pleases the Lord. 11Have nothing to do with the fruitless deeds of darkness, but rather expose them. 12For it is shameful even to mention what the disobedient do in secret. 13But everything exposed by the light becomes visible, 14for it is light that makes everything visible. This is why it is said:

"Wake up, O sleeper,
  rise from the dead,
and Christ will shine on you."

15Be very careful, then, how you live—not as unwise but as wise, 16making the most of every opportunity, because the days are evil. 17Therefore do not be foolish, but understand what the Lord's will is. 18Do not get drunk on wine, which leads to debauchery. Instead, be filled with the Spirit. 19Speak to one another with psalms, hymns and spiritual songs. Sing and make music in your heart to the Lord, 20always giving thanks to God the Father for everything, in the name of our Lord Jesus Christ.

21Submit to one another out of reverence for Christ.

Wives and Husbands

22Wives, submit to your husbands as to the Lord. 23For the husband is the head of the wife as Christ is the head of the church, his body, of which he is the Saviour. 24Now as the church submits to Christ, so also wives should submit to their husbands in everything.

25Husbands, love your wives, just as Christ loved the church and gave himself up for her 26to make her holy, cleansing her by the washing with water through the word, 27and to present her to himself as a radiant church, without stain or wrinkle or any other blemish, but holy and blameless. 28In this same way, husbands ought to love their wives as their own bodies. He who loves his wife loves himself. 29After all, no-one ever hated his own body, but he feeds and cares for it, just as Christ does the church—30for we are members of his body. 31"For this reason a man will leave his father and mother and be united to his wife, and the two will become one flesh." 32This is a profound mystery—but I am talking about Christ and the church. 33However, each one of you also must love his wife as he loves himself, and the wife must respect her husband.

READING FROM PSALMS
Psalm 113:1–9

1Praise the LORD.

Praise, O servants of the LORD,
praise the name of the LORD.
2Let the name of the LORD be praised,
both now and for evermore.
3From the rising of the sun to the
place where it sets,
the name of the LORD is to be
praised.

4The LORD is exalted over all the
nations,
his glory above the heavens.
5Who is like the LORD our God,
the One who sits enthroned on
high,
6who stoops down to look
on the heavens and the earth?

7He raises the poor from the dust
and lifts the needy from the ash
heap;
8he seats them with princes,
with the princes of their people.
9He settles the barren woman in her
home
as a happy mother of children.

Praise the LORD.

SEPTEMBER 28

DAY 271

OLD TESTAMENT READING
Nahum 1:1–3:19

1 An oracle concerning Nineveh. The book of the vision of Nahum the Elkoshite.

The LORD's Anger Against Nineveh

2The LORD is a jealous and avenging
God;
the LORD takes vengeance and is
filled with wrath.
The LORD takes vengeance on his
foes
and maintains his wrath against his
enemies.
3The LORD is slow to anger and great
in power;
the LORD will not leave the guilty
unpunished.
His way is in the whirlwind and the
storm,
and clouds are the dust of his feet.
4He rebukes the sea and dries it up;
he makes all the rivers run dry.
Bashan and Carmel wither
and the blossoms of Lebanon fade.
5The mountains quake before him
and the hills melt away.
The earth trembles at his presence,
the world and all who live in it.
6Who can withstand his indignation?
Who can endure his fierce anger?
His wrath is poured out like fire;
the rocks are shattered before him.

7The LORD is good,
a refuge in times of trouble.
He cares for those who trust in him,
8 but with an overwhelming flood
he will make an end of ⌞Nineveh⌟;
he will pursue his foes into
darkness.

9Whatever they plot against the LORD
he will bring to an end;
trouble will not come a second
time.
10They will be entangled among thorns
and drunk from their wine;
they will be consumed like dry
stubble.
11From you, ⌞O Nineveh,⌟ has one
come forth
who plots evil against the LORD
and counsels wickedness.

[12]This is what the LORD says:

"Although they have allies and are numerous,
they will be cut off and pass away.
Although I have afflicted you, ⌞O Judah,⌟
I will afflict you no more.
[13]Now I will break their yoke from your neck
and tear your shackles away."

[14]The LORD has given a command concerning you, ⌞Nineveh⌟:
"You will have no descendants to bear your name.
I will destroy the carved images and cast idols
that are in the temple of your gods.
I will prepare your grave,
for you are vile."

[15]Look, there on the mountains,
the feet of one who brings good news,
who proclaims peace!
Celebrate your festivals, O Judah,
and fulfil your vows.
No more will the wicked invade you;
they will be completely destroyed.

Nineveh to Fall

2 An attacker advances against you, ⌞Nineveh⌟.
Guard the fortress,
watch the road,
brace yourselves,
marshal all your strength!

[2]The LORD will restore the splendour of Jacob
like the splendour of Israel,
though destroyers have laid them waste
and have ruined their vines.

[3]The shields of his soldiers are red;
the warriors are clad in scarlet.
The metal on the chariots flashes
on the day they are made ready;
the spears of pine are brandished.
[4]The chariots storm through the streets,
rushing back and forth through the squares.
They look like flaming torches;
they dart about like lightning.

[5]He summons his picked troops,
yet they stumble on their way.
They dash to the city wall;
the protective shield is put in place.
[6]The river gates are thrown open
and the palace collapses.
[7]It is decreed that ⌞the city⌟
be exiled and carried away.
Its slave girls moan like doves
and beat upon their breasts.
[8]Nineveh is like a pool,
and its water is draining away.
"Stop! Stop!" they cry,
but no-one turns back.
[9]Plunder the silver!
Plunder the gold!
The supply is endless,
the wealth from all its treasures!
[10]She is pillaged, plundered, stripped!
Hearts melt, knees give way,
bodies tremble, every face grows pale.

[11]Where now is the lions' den,
the place where they fed their young,
where the lion and lioness went,
and the cubs, with nothing to fear?
[12]The lion killed enough for his cubs
and strangled the prey for his mate,
filling his lairs with the kill
and his dens with the prey.

[13]"I am against you,"
declares the LORD Almighty.
"I will burn up your chariots in smoke,
and the sword will devour your young lions.
I will leave you no prey on the earth.
The voices of your messengers
will no longer be heard."

Woe to Nineveh

3 Woe to the city of blood,
full of lies,
full of plunder,
never without victims!
2 The crack of whips,
the clatter of wheels,
galloping horses
and jolting chariots!
3 Charging cavalry,
flashing swords
and glittering spears!
Many casualties,
piles of dead,
bodies without number,
people stumbling over the corpses—
4 all because of the wanton lust of a harlot,
alluring, the mistress of sorceries,
who enslaved nations by her prostitution
and peoples by her witchcraft.

5 "I am against you," declares the LORD Almighty.
"I will lift your skirts over your face.
I will show the nations your nakedness
and the kingdoms your shame.
6 I will pelt you with filth,
I will treat you with contempt
and make you a spectacle.
7 All who see you will flee from you and say,
'Nineveh is in ruins—who will mourn for her?'
Where can I find anyone to comfort you?"

8 Are you better than Thebes,
situated on the Nile,
with water around her?
The river was her defence,
the waters her wall.
9 Cush and Egypt were her boundless strength;
Put and Libya were among her allies.
10 Yet she was taken captive
and went into exile.
Her infants were dashed to pieces
at the head of every street.
Lots were cast for her nobles,
and all her great men were put in chains.
11 You too will become drunk;
you will go into hiding
and seek refuge from the enemy.

12 All your fortresses are like fig-trees
with their first ripe fruit;
when they are shaken,
the figs fall into the mouth of the eater.
13 Look at your troops—
they are all women!
The gates of your land
are wide open to your enemies;
fire has consumed their bars.

14 Draw water for the siege,
strengthen your defences!
Work the clay,
tread the mortar,
repair the brickwork!
15 There the fire will devour you;
the sword will cut you down
and, like grasshoppers, consume you.
Multiply like grasshoppers,
multiply like locusts!
16 You have increased the number of your merchants
till they are more than the stars of the sky,
but like locusts they strip the land
and then fly away.
17 Your guards are like locusts,
your officials like swarms of locusts
that settle in the walls on a cold day—
but when the sun appears they fly away,
and no-one knows where.

18 O king of Assyria, your shepherds slumber;
your nobles lie down to rest.
Your people are scattered on the mountains
with no-one to gather them.

[19]Nothing can heal your wound;
your injury is fatal.
Everyone who hears the news about
you
claps his hands at your fall,
for who has not felt
your endless cruelty?

NEW TESTAMENT READING
Ephesians 6:1–24

Children and Parents

6 Children, obey your parents in the
Lord, for this is right. [2]"Honour
your father and mother"—which is the
first commandment with a promise—
[3]"that it may go well with you and that
you may enjoy long life on the earth."
[4]Fathers, do not exasperate your children; instead, bring them up in the
training and instruction of the Lord.

Slaves and Masters

[5]Slaves, obey your earthly masters
with respect and fear, and with sincerity
of heart, just as you would obey Christ.
[6]Obey them not only to win their favour
when their eye is on you, but like slaves
of Christ, doing the will of God from
your heart. [7]Serve wholeheartedly, as if
you were serving the Lord, not men,
[8]because you know that the Lord will
reward everyone for whatever good he
does, whether he is slave or free.
[9]And masters, treat your slaves in the
same way. Do not threaten them, since
you know that he who is both their
Master and yours is in heaven, and
there is no favouritism with him.

The Armour of God

[10]Finally, be strong in the Lord and in
his mighty power. [11]Put on the full
armour of God so that you can take
your stand against the devil's schemes.
[12]For our struggle is not against flesh
and blood, but against the rulers,
against the authorities, against the
powers of this dark world and against
the spiritual forces of evil in the
heavenly realms. [13]Therefore put on
the full armour of God, so that when the
day of evil comes, you may be able to
stand your ground, and after you have
done everything, to stand. [14]Stand firm
then, with the belt of truth buckled
round your waist, with the breastplate
of righteousness in place, [15]and with
your feet fitted with the readiness that
comes from the gospel of peace. [16]In
addition to all this, take up the shield of
faith, with which you can extinguish all
the flaming arrows of the evil one.
[17]Take the helmet of salvation and the
sword of the Spirit, which is the word of
God. [18]And pray in the Spirit on all
occasions with all kinds of prayers and
requests. With this in mind, be alert and
always keep on praying for all the
saints.
[19]Pray also for me, that whenever I
open my mouth, words may be given me
so that I will fearlessly make known the
mystery of the gospel, [20]for which I am
an ambassador in chains. Pray that I
may declare it fearlessly, as I should.

Final Greetings

[21]Tychicus, the dear brother and
faithful servant in the Lord, will tell you
everything, so that you also may know
how I am and what I am doing. [22]I am
sending him to you for this very purpose, that you may know how we are,
and that he may encourage you.
[23]Peace to the brothers, and love with
faith from God the Father and the Lord
Jesus Christ. [24]Grace to all who love our
Lord Jesus Christ with an undying love.

READING FROM PSALMS
Psalm 114:1–8

[1]When Israel came out of Egypt,
the house of Jacob from a people
of foreign tongue,

2Judah became God's sanctuary,
Israel his dominion.

3The sea looked and fled,
the Jordan turned back;
4the mountains skipped like rams,
the hills like lambs.

5Why was it, O sea, that you fled,
O Jordan, that you turned back,
6you mountains, that you skipped like rams,
you hills, like lambs?

7Tremble, O earth, at the presence of the Lord,
at the presence of the God of Jacob,
8who turned the rock into a pool,
the hard rock into springs of water.

SEPTEMBER 29

DAY 272

OLD TESTAMENT READING
Zephaniah 1:1–3:20

1 The word of the LORD that came to Zephaniah son of Cushi, the son of Gedaliah, the son of Amariah, the son of Hezekiah, during the reign of Josiah son of Amon king of Judah:

Warning of Coming Destruction

2"I will sweep away everything
from the face of the earth,"
declares the LORD.
3"I will sweep away both men and animals;
I will sweep away the birds of the air
and the fish of the sea.
The wicked will have only heaps of rubble
when I cut off man from the face of the earth,"
declares the LORD.

Against Judah

4"I will stretch out my hand against Judah
and against all who live in Jerusalem.
I will cut off from this place every remnant of Baal,
the names of the pagan and the idolatrous priests—
5those who bow down on the roofs
to worship the starry host,
those who bow down and swear by the LORD
and who also swear by Molech,
6those who turn back from following the LORD
and neither seek the LORD nor enquire of him.
7Be silent before the Sovereign LORD,
for the day of the LORD is near.
The LORD has prepared a sacrifice;
he has consecrated those he has invited.
8On the day of the LORD's sacrifice
I will punish the princes
and the king's sons
and all those clad
in foreign clothes.
9On that day I will punish
all who avoid stepping on the threshold,
who fill the temple of their gods
with violence and deceit.

10"On that day," declares the LORD,
"a cry will go up from the Fish Gate,
wailing from the New Quarter,
and a loud crash from the hills.
11Wail, you who live in the market district;
all your merchants will be wiped out,

all who trade with silver will be
ruined.
12At that time I will search Jerusalem
with lamps
and punish those who are
complacent,
who are like wine left on its dregs,
who think, 'The LORD will do
nothing,
either good or bad.'
13Their wealth will be plundered,
their houses demolished.
They will build houses
but not live in them;
they will plant vineyards
but not drink the wine.

The Great Day of the LORD

14"The great day of the LORD is near—
near and coming quickly.
Listen! The cry on the day of the
LORD will be bitter,
the shouting of the warrior there.
15That day will be a day of wrath,
a day of distress and anguish,
a day of trouble and ruin,
a day of darkness and gloom,
a day of clouds and blackness,
16a day of trumpet and battle cry
against the fortified cities
and against the corner towers.
17I will bring distress on the people
and they will walk like blind men,
because they have sinned against
the LORD.
Their blood will be poured out like
dust
and their entrails like filth.
18Neither their silver nor their gold
will be able to save them
on the day of the LORD's wrath.
In the fire of his jealousy
the whole world will be consumed,
for he will make a sudden end
of all who live in the earth."

2 Gather together, gather together,
O shameful nation,
2before the appointed time arrives
and that day sweeps on like chaff,
before the fierce anger of the LORD
comes upon you,
before the day of the LORD's wrath
comes upon you.
3Seek the LORD, all you humble of the
land,
you who do what he commands.
Seek righteousness, seek humility;
perhaps you will be sheltered
on the day of the LORD's anger.

Against Philistia

4Gaza will be abandoned
and Ashkelon left in ruins.
At midday Ashdod will be emptied
and Ekron uprooted.
5Woe to you who live by the sea,
O Kerethite people;
the word of the LORD is against you,
O Canaan, land of the Philistines.

"I will destroy you,
and none will be left."

6The land by the sea, where the
Kerethites dwell,
will be a place for shepherds and
sheep pens.
7It will belong to the remnant of the
house of Judah;
there they will find pasture.
In the evening they will lie down
in the houses of Ashkelon.
The LORD their God will care for
them;
he will restore their fortunes.

Against Moab and Ammon

8"I have heard the insults of Moab
and the taunts of the Ammonites,
who insulted my people
and made threats against their
land.
9Therefore, as surely as I live,"
declares the LORD Almighty, the
God of Israel,
"surely Moab will become like
Sodom,
the Ammonites like Gomorrah—
a place of weeds and salt pits,
a wasteland for ever.

The remnant of my people will
plunder them;
the survivors of my nation will
inherit their land."

10This is what they will get in return for
their pride,
for insulting and mocking the
people of the LORD Almighty.
11The LORD will be awesome to them
when he destroys all the gods of the
land.
The nations on every shore will
worship him,
every one in its own land.

Against Cush

12"You too, O Cushites,
will be slain by my sword."

Against Assyria

13He will stretch out his hand against
the north
and destroy Assyria,
leaving Nineveh utterly desolate
and dry as the desert.
14Flocks and herds will lie down there,
creatures of every kind.
The desert owl and the screech owl
will roost on her columns.
Their calls will echo through the
windows,
rubble will be in the doorways,
the beams of cedar will be exposed.
15This is the carefree city
that lived in safety.
She said to herself,
"I am, and there is none besides
me."
What a ruin she has become,
a lair for wild beasts!
All who pass by her scoff
and shake their fists.

The Future of Jerusalem

3 Woe to the city of oppressors,
rebellious and defiled!
2She obeys no-one,
she accepts no correction.
She does not trust in the LORD,
she does not draw near to her God.
3Her officials are roaring lions,
her rulers are evening wolves,
who leave nothing for the morning.
4Her prophets are arrogant;
they are treacherous men.
Her priests profane the sanctuary
and do violence to the law.
5The LORD within her is righteous;
he does no wrong.
Morning by morning he dispenses his
justice,
and every new day he does not fail,
yet the unrighteous know no
shame.

6"I have cut off nations;
their strongholds are demolished.
I have left their streets deserted,
with no-one passing through.
Their cities are destroyed;
no-one will be left—no-one
at all.
7I said to the city,
'Surely you will fear me
and accept correction!'
Then her dwelling would not be cut
off,
nor all my punishments come upon
her.
But they were still eager
to act corruptly in all they did.
8Therefore wait for me," declares the
LORD,
"for the day I will stand up to
testify.
I have decided to assemble the
nations,
to gather the kingdoms
and to pour out my wrath on them—
all my fierce anger.
The whole world will be consumed
by the fire of my jealous anger.

9"Then will I purify the lips of the
peoples,
that all of them may call on the
name of the LORD
and serve him shoulder to
shoulder.

10From beyond the rivers of Cush
my worshippers, my scattered people,
will bring me offerings.
11On that day you will not be put to shame
for all the wrongs you have done to me,
because I will remove from this city
those who rejoice in their pride.
Never again will you be haughty
on my holy hill.
12But I will leave within you
the meek and humble,
who trust in the name of the LORD.
13The remnant of Israel will do no wrong;
they will speak no lies,
nor will deceit be found in their mouths.
They will eat and lie down
and no-one will make them afraid."

14Sing, O Daughter of Zion;
shout aloud, O Israel!
Be glad and rejoice with all your heart,
O Daughter of Jerusalem!
15The LORD has taken away your punishment,
he has turned back your enemy.
The LORD, the King of Israel, is with you;
never again will you fear any harm.
16On that day they will say to Jerusalem,
"Do not fear, O Zion;
do not let your hands hang limp.
17The LORD your God is with you,
he is mighty to save.
He will take great delight in you,
he will quiet you with his love,
he will rejoice over you with singing."

18"The sorrows for the appointed feasts
I will remove from you;
they are a burden and a reproach to you.
19At that time I will deal
with all who oppressed you;
I will rescue the lame
and gather those who have been scattered.
I will give them praise and honour
in every land where they were put to shame.
20At that time I will gather you;
at that time I will bring you home.
I will give you honour and praise
among all the peoples of the earth
when I restore your fortunes
before your very eyes,"
says the LORD.

NEW TESTAMENT READING

Philippians 1:1–26

1 Paul and Timothy, servants of Christ Jesus,

To all the saints in Christ Jesus at Philippi, together with the overseers and deacons:

2Grace and peace to you from God our Father and the Lord Jesus Christ.

Thanksgiving and Prayer

3I thank my God every time I remember you. 4In all my prayers for all of you,
I always pray with joy 5because of your
partnership in the gospel from the first
day until now, 6being confident of this,
that he who began a good work in you will carry it on to completion until the day of Christ Jesus.

7It is right for me to feel this way about all of you, since I have you in my heart; for whether I am in chains or defending and confirming the gospel, all of you share in God's grace with me.
8God can testify how I long for all of you with the affection of Christ Jesus.

9And this is my prayer: that your love may abound more and more in knowl-
edge and depth of insight, 10so that you may be able to discern what is best and may be pure and blameless until the day
of Christ, 11filled with the fruit of right-
eousness that comes through Jesus Christ—to the glory and praise of God.

Paul's Chains Advance the Gospel

12Now I want you to know, brothers,
that what has happened to me has really
served to advance the gospel. 13As a
result, it has become clear throughout
the whole palace guard and to everyone else that I am in chains for Christ.
14Because of my chains, most of the
brothers in the Lord have been encouraged to speak the word of God more
courageously and fearlessly.
15It is true that some preach Christ
out of envy and rivalry, but others out of
goodwill. 16The latter do so in love,
knowing that I am put here for the
defence of the gospel. 17The former
preach Christ out of selfish ambition,
not sincerely, supposing that they can
stir up trouble for me while I am in
chains. 18But what does it matter? The
important thing is that in every way,
whether from false motives or true,
Christ is preached. And because of this
I rejoice.
Yes, and I will continue to rejoice,
19for I know that through your prayers
and the help given by the Spirit of Jesus
Christ, what has happened to me will
turn out for my deliverance. 20I eagerly
expect and hope that I will in no way be
ashamed, but will have sufficient courage so that now as always Christ will be
exalted in my body, whether by life or
by death. 21For to me, to live is Christ
and to die is gain. 22If I am to go on
living in the body, this will mean fruitful
labour for me. Yet what shall I choose?
I do not know! 23I am torn between the
two: I desire to depart and be with
Christ, which is better by far; 24but it is
more necessary for you that I remain in
the body. 25Convinced of this, I know
that I will remain, and I will continue
with all of you for your progress and joy
in the faith, 26so that through my being
with you again your joy in Christ Jesus
will overflow on account of me.

READING FROM PROVERBS

Proverbs 23:29–24:4

29Who has woe? Who has sorrow?
Who has strife? Who has complaints?
Who has needless bruises? Who has bloodshot eyes?
30Those who linger over wine,
who go to sample bowls of mixed wine.
31Do not gaze at wine when it is red,
when it sparkles in the cup,
when it goes down smoothly!
32In the end it bites like a snake
and poisons like a viper.
33Your eyes will see strange sights
and your mind imagine confusing things.
34You will be like one sleeping on the high seas,
lying on top of the rigging.
35"They hit me," you will say, "but I'm not hurt!
They beat me, but I don't feel it!
When will I wake up
so I can find another drink?"

24 Do not envy wicked men,
do not desire their company;
2for their hearts plot violence,
and their lips talk about making trouble.

3By wisdom a house is built,
and through understanding it is established;
4through knowledge its rooms are filled
with rare and beautiful treasures.

DAY 273

SEPTEMBER 30

OLD TESTAMENT READING
Jeremiah 1:1–2:30

1 The words of Jeremiah son of Hilkiah, one of the priests at Anathoth
in the territory of Benjamin. 2The word
of the LORD came to him in the thirteenth year of the reign of Josiah son of
Amon king of Judah, 3and through the
reign of Jehoiakim son of Josiah king of
Judah, down to the fifth month of the
eleventh year of Zedekiah son of Josiah
king of Judah, when the people of Jerusalem went into exile.

The Call of Jeremiah

4The word of the LORD came to me,
saying,

5"Before I formed you in the womb I
knew you,
before you were born I set you
apart;
I appointed you as a prophet to the
nations."

6"Ah, Sovereign LORD," I said, "I do
not know how to speak; I am only a
child."
7But the LORD said to me, "Do not
say, 'I am only a child.' You must go to
everyone I send you to and say whatever I command you. 8Do not be afraid
of them, for I am with you and will
rescue you," declares the LORD.
9Then the LORD reached out his hand
and touched my mouth and said to me,
"Now, I have put my words in your
mouth. 10See, today I appoint you over
nations and kingdoms to uproot and
tear down, to destroy and overthrow, to
build and to plant."
11The word of the LORD came to me:
"What do you see, Jeremiah?"
"I see the branch of an almond tree,"
I replied.
12The LORD said to me, "You have
seen correctly, for I am watching to see
that my word is fulfilled."
13The word of the LORD came to me
again: "What do you see?"
"I see a boiling pot, tilting away from
the north," I answered.
14The LORD said to me, "From the
north disaster will be poured out on all
who live in the land. 15I am about to
summon all the peoples of the northern
kingdoms," declares the LORD.

"Their kings will come and set up
their thrones
in the entrance of the gates of
Jerusalem;
they will come against all her
surrounding walls
and against all the towns of Judah.
16I will pronounce my judgments on my
people
because of their wickedness in
forsaking me,
in burning incense to other gods
and in worshipping what their
hands have made.

17"Get yourself ready! Stand up and
say to them whatever I command you.
Do not be terrified by them, or I will
terrify you before them. 18Today I have
made you a fortified city, an iron pillar
and a bronze wall to stand against the
whole land—against the kings of
Judah, its officials, its priests and the
people of the land. 19They will fight
against you but will not overcome you,
for I am with you and will rescue you,"
declares the LORD.

Israel Forsakes God

2 The word of the LORD came to me:
2"Go and proclaim in the hearing
of Jerusalem:

"'I remember the devotion of your
youth,
how as a bride you loved me

and followed me through the desert,
through a land not sown.
3Israel was holy to the LORD,
the firstfruits of his harvest;
all who devoured her were held
guilty,
and disaster overtook them,'"
declares the LORD.

4Hear the word of the LORD, O house
of Jacob,
all you clans of the house of Israel.

5This is what the LORD says:

"What fault did your fathers find in
me,
that they strayed so far from me?
They followed worthless idols
and became worthless themselves.
6They did not ask, 'Where is the
LORD,
who brought us up out of Egypt
and led us through the barren
wilderness,
through a land of deserts and rifts,
a land of drought and darkness,
a land where no-one travels and
no-one lives?'
7I brought you into a fertile land
to eat its fruit and rich produce.
But you came and defiled my land
and made my inheritance
detestable.
8The priests did not ask,
'Where is the LORD?'
Those who deal with the law did not
know me;
the leaders rebelled against me.
The prophets prophesied by Baal,
following worthless idols.

9"Therefore I bring charges against
you again,"
declares the LORD.
"And I will bring charges against
your children's children.
10Cross over to the coasts of Kittim and
look,
send to Kedar and observe closely;
see if there has ever been anything
like this:
11Has a nation ever changed its gods?
(Yet they are not gods at all.)
But my people have exchanged their
Glory
for worthless idols.
12Be appalled at this, O heavens,
and shudder with great horror,"
declares the LORD.
13"My people have committed two
sins:
They have forsaken me,
the spring of living water,
and have dug their own cisterns,
broken cisterns that cannot hold
water.
14Is Israel a servant, a slave by birth?
Why then has he become plunder?
15Lions have roared;
they have growled at him.
They have laid waste his land;
his towns are burned and deserted.
16Also, the men of Memphis and
Tahpanhes
have shaved the crown of your
head.
17Have you not brought this on
yourselves
by forsaking the LORD your God
when he led you in the way?
18Now why go to Egypt
to drink water from the Shihor?
And why go to Assyria
to drink water from the River?
19Your wickedness will punish you;
your backsliding will rebuke you.
Consider then and realise
how evil and bitter it is for you
when you forsake the LORD your God
and have no awe of me,"
declares the Lord,
the LORD Almighty.

20"Long ago you broke off your yoke
and tore off your bonds;
you said, 'I will not serve you!'
Indeed, on every high hill
and under every spreading tree
you lay down as a prostitute.
21I had planted you like a choice vine
of sound and reliable stock.
How then did you turn against me
into a corrupt, wild vine?

22Although you wash yourself with
soda
and use an abundance of soap,
the stain of your guilt is still before
me,"
declares the Sovereign LORD.
23"How can you say, 'I am not defiled;
I have not run after the Baals'?
See how you behaved in the valley;
consider what you have done.
You are a swift she-camel
running here and there,
24a wild donkey accustomed to the
desert,
sniffing the wind in her craving—
in her heat who can restrain her?
Any males that pursue her need not
tire themselves;
at mating time they will find her.
25Do not run until your feet are bare
and your throat is dry.
But you said, 'It's no use!
I love foreign gods,
and I must go after them.'

26"As a thief is disgraced when he is
caught,
so the house of Israel is
disgraced—
they, their kings and their officials,
their priests and their prophets.
27They say to wood, 'You are my
father,'
and to stone, 'You gave me birth.'
They have turned their backs to me
and not their faces;
yet when they are in trouble, they
say,
'Come and save us!'
28Where then are the gods you made
for yourselves?
Let them come if they can save you
when you are in trouble!
For you have as many gods
as you have towns, O Judah.

29"Why do you bring charges against
me?
You have all rebelled against me,"
declares the LORD.
30"In vain I punished your people;
they did not respond to correction.
Your sword has devoured your
prophets
like a ravening lion.

NEW TESTAMENT READING
Philippians 1:27–2:11

27Whatever happens, conduct yourselves in a manner worthy of the gospel
of Christ. Then, whether I come and see
you or only hear about you in my absence, I will know that you stand firm in
one spirit, contending as one man for
the faith of the gospel 28without being
frightened in any way by those who
oppose you. This is a sign to them that
they will be destroyed, but that you will
be saved—and that by God. 29For it has
been granted to you on behalf of Christ
not only to believe on him, but also to
suffer for him, 30since you are going
through the same struggle you saw I
had, and now hear that I still have.

Imitating Christ's Humility

2 If you have any encouragement
from being united with Christ, if
any comfort from his love, if any fellowship with the Spirit, if any tenderness and compassion, 2then make my
joy complete by being like-minded,
having the same love, being one in spirit
and purpose. 3Do nothing out of selfish
ambition or vain conceit, but in humility
consider others better than yourselves.
4Each of you should look not only to
your own interests, but also to the interests of others.
5Your attitude should be the same as
that of Christ Jesus:

6Who, being in very nature God,
did not consider equality with God
something to be grasped,
7but made himself nothing,
taking the very nature of a servant,
being made in human likeness.
8And being found in appearance as a
man,

he humbled himself
and became obedient to
death—even death on a cross!
9Therefore God exalted him to the
highest place
and gave him the name that is
above every name,
10that at the name of Jesus every knee
should bow,
in heaven and on earth and under
the earth,
11and every tongue confess that Jesus
Christ is Lord,
to the glory of God the Father.

READING FROM PSALMS
Psalm 115:1–11

1Not to us, O LORD, not to us
but to your name be the glory,
because of your love and
faithfulness.

2Why do the nations say,
"Where is their God?"

3Our God is in heaven;
he does whatever pleases him.
4But their idols are silver and gold,
made by the hands of men.
5They have mouths, but cannot speak,
eyes, but they cannot see;
6they have ears, but cannot hear,
noses, but they cannot smell;
7they have hands, but cannot feel,
feet, but they cannot walk;
nor can they utter a sound with
their throats.
8Those who make them will be like
them,
and so will all who trust in them.

9O house of Israel, trust in the
LORD—
he is their help and shield.
10O house of Aaron, trust in the
LORD—
he is their help and shield.
11You who fear him, trust in the
LORD—
he is their help and shield.

OCTOBER 1

DAY 274

OLD TESTAMENT READING
Jeremiah 2:31–4:9

31"You of this generation, consider the word of the LORD:

"Have I been a desert to Israel
or a land of great darkness?
Why do my people say, 'We are free
to roam;
we will come to you no more'?
32Does a maiden forget her jewellery,
a bride her wedding ornaments?
Yet my people have forgotten me,
days without number.
33How skilled you are at pursuing love!
Even the worst of women can learn
from your ways.
34On your clothes men find
the lifeblood of the innocent poor,
though you did not catch them
breaking in.
Yet in spite of all this
35 you say, 'I am innocent;
he is not angry with me.'
But I will pass judgment on you
because you say, 'I have not
sinned.'
36Why do you go about so much,
changing your ways?
You will be disappointed by Egypt
as you were by Assyria.
37You will also leave that place
with your hands on your head,
for the LORD has rejected those you
trust;
you will not be helped by them.

3 "If a man divorces his wife
and she leaves him and marries
another man,
should he return to her again?
Would not the land be completely
defiled?
But you have lived as a prostitute
with many lovers—
would you now return to me?"
declares the LORD.
2"Look up to the barren heights and
see.
Is there any place where you have
not been ravished?
By the roadside you sat waiting for
lovers,
sat like a nomad in the desert.
You have defiled the land
with your prostitution and
wickedness.
3Therefore the showers have been
withheld,
and no spring rains have fallen.
Yet you have the brazen look of a
prostitute;
you refuse to blush with shame.
4Have you not just called to me:
'My Father, my friend from my
youth,
5will you always be angry?
Will your wrath continue for ever?'
This is how you talk,
but you do all the evil you can."

Unfaithful Israel

6During the reign of King Josiah, the
LORD said to me, "Have you seen what
faithless Israel has done? She has gone
up on every high hill and under every
spreading tree and has committed adultery there. 7I thought that after she had
done all this she would return to me but
she did not, and her unfaithful sister
Judah saw it. 8I gave faithless Israel her
certificate of divorce and sent her away
because of all her adulteries. Yet I saw
that her unfaithful sister Judah had no
fear; she also went out and committed
adultery. 9Because Israel's immorality
mattered so little to her, she defiled the
land and committed adultery with stone
and wood. 10In spite of all this, her
unfaithful sister Judah did not return to
me with all her heart, but only in pretence," declares the LORD.
11The LORD said to me, "Faithless
Israel is more righteous than unfaithful
Judah. 12Go, proclaim this message
towards the north:

" 'Return, faithless Israel,' declares
the LORD,
'I will frown on you no longer,
for I am merciful,' declares the
LORD,
'I will not be angry for ever.
13Only acknowledge your guilt—
you have rebelled against the LORD
your God,
you have scattered your favours to
foreign gods
under every spreading tree,
and have not obeyed me,' "
declares the LORD.

14"Return, faithless people," declares the LORD, "for I am your husband. I will choose you—one from a
town and two from a clan—and bring
you to Zion. 15Then I will give you
shepherds after my own heart, who will
lead you with knowledge and understanding. 16In those days, when your
numbers have increased greatly in the
land," declares the LORD, "men will no
longer say, 'The ark of the covenant of
the LORD.' It will never enter their
minds or be remembered; it will not be
missed, nor will another one be made.
17At that time they will call Jerusalem
The Throne of the LORD, and all nations
will gather in Jerusalem to honour the
name of the LORD. No longer will they
follow the stubbornness of their evil
hearts. 18In those days the house of
Judah will join the house of Israel, and
together they will come from a northern
land to the land I gave your forefathers
as an inheritance.
19"I myself said,

" 'How gladly would I treat you like
sons

and give you a desirable land,
the most beautiful inheritance of
any nation.'
I thought you would call me 'Father'
and not turn away from following
me.
20But like a woman unfaithful to her
husband,
so you have been unfaithful to me,
O house of Israel,"
declares the LORD.

21A cry is heard on the barren heights,
the weeping and pleading of the
people of Israel,
because they have perverted their
ways
and have forgotten the LORD their
God.

22"Return, faithless people;
I will cure you of backsliding."

"Yes, we will come to you,
for you are the LORD our God.
23Surely the ⌞idolatrous⌟ commotion on
the hills
and mountains is a deception;
surely in the LORD our God
is the salvation of Israel.
24From our youth shameful gods have
consumed
the fruits of our fathers' labour—
their flocks and herds,
their sons and daughters.
25Let us lie down in our shame,
and let our disgrace cover us.
We have sinned against the LORD our
God,
both we and our fathers;
from our youth till this day
we have not obeyed the LORD our
God."

4 "If you will return, O Israel,
return to me,"
declares the LORD.
"If you put your detestable idols out
of my sight
and no longer go astray,
2and if in a truthful, just and righteous
way
you swear, 'As surely as the LORD
lives,'
then the nations will be blessed by
him
and in him they will glory."

3This is what the LORD says to the
men of Judah and to Jerusalem:

"Break up your unploughed ground
and do not sow among thorns.
4Circumcise yourselves to the LORD,
circumcise your hearts,
you men of Judah and people of
Jerusalem,
or my wrath will break out and burn
like fire
because of the evil you have
done—
burn with no-one to quench it.

Disaster From the North

5"Announce in Judah and proclaim in
Jerusalem and say:
'Sound the trumpet throughout the
land!'
Cry aloud and say:
'Gather together!
Let us flee to the fortified cities!'
6Raise the signal to go to Zion!
Flee for safety without delay!
For I am bringing disaster from the
north,
even terrible destruction."

7A lion has come out of his lair;
a destroyer of nations has set out.
He has left his place
to lay waste your land.
Your towns will lie in ruins
without inhabitant.
8So put on sackcloth,
lament and wail,
for the fierce anger of the LORD
has not turned away from us.

9"In that day," declares the LORD,
"the king and the officials will lose
heart,
the priests will be horrified,
and the prophets will be appalled."

NEW TESTAMENT READING
Philippians 2:12–30

Shining as Stars

12Therefore, my dear friends, as you
have always obeyed—not only in my
presence, but now much more in my
absence—continue to work out your
salvation with fear and trembling, 13for
it is God who works in you to will and to
act according to his good purpose.
14Do everything without complaining
or arguing, 15so that you may become
blameless and pure, children of God
without fault in a crooked and depraved
generation, in which you shine like stars
in the universe 16as you hold out the
word of life—in order that I may boast
on the day of Christ that I did not run or
labour for nothing. 17But even if I am
being poured out like a drink offering
on the sacrifice and service coming from
your faith, I am glad and rejoice with all
of you. 18So you too should be glad and
rejoice with me.

Timothy and Epaphroditus

19I hope in the Lord Jesus to send
Timothy to you soon, that I also may be
cheered when I receive news about you.
20I have no-one else like him, who takes
a genuine interest in your welfare. 21For
everyone looks out for his own interests, not those of Jesus Christ. 22But
you know that Timothy has proved himself, because as a son with his father he
has served with me in the work of the
gospel. 23I hope, therefore, to send him
as soon as I see how things go with me.
24And I am confident in the Lord that I
myself will come soon.
25But I think it is necessary to send
back to you Epaphroditus, my brother,
fellow-worker and fellow-soldier, who
is also your messenger, whom you sent
to take care of my needs. 26For he longs
for all of you and is distressed because
you heard he was ill. 27Indeed he was ill,
and almost died. But God had mercy on
him, and not on him only but also on
me, to spare me sorrow upon sorrow.
28Therefore I am all the more eager to
send him, so that when you see him
again you may be glad and I may have
less anxiety. 29Welcome him in the Lord
with great joy, and honour men like
him, 30because he almost died for the
work of Christ, risking his life to make
up for the help you could not give me.

READING FROM PSALMS
Psalm 115:12–18

12The LORD remembers us and will
bless us:
He will bless the house of Israel,
he will bless the house of Aaron,
13he will bless those who fear the
LORD—
small and great alike.

14May the LORD make you increase,
both you and your children.
15May you be blessed by the LORD,
the Maker of heaven and earth.

16The highest heavens belong to the
LORD,
but the earth he has given to man.
17It is not the dead who praise the
LORD,
those who go down to silence;
18it is we who extol the LORD,
both now and for evermore.

Praise the LORD.

OLD TESTAMENT READING
Jeremiah 4:10–5:31

10Then I said, "Ah, Sovereign LORD,
how completely you have deceived this
people and Jerusalem by saying, 'You
will have peace,' when the sword is at
our throats."
11At that time this people and Jerusalem will be told, "A scorching wind
from the barren heights in the desert
blows towards my people, but not to
winnow or cleanse; 12a wind too strong
for that comes from me. Now I pronounce my judgments against them."

13Look! He advances like the clouds,
his chariots come like a whirlwind,
his horses are swifter than eagles.
Woe to us! We are ruined!
14O Jerusalem, wash the evil from your heart and be saved.
How long will you harbour wicked thoughts?
15A voice is announcing from Dan,
proclaiming disaster from the hills of Ephraim.
16"Tell this to the nations,
proclaim it to Jerusalem:
'A besieging army is coming from a distant land,
raising a war cry against the cities of Judah.
17They surround her like men guarding a field,
because she has rebelled against me,'"
declares the LORD.
18"Your own conduct and actions
have brought this upon you.
This is your punishment.
How bitter it is!
How it pierces to the heart!"

19Oh, my anguish, my anguish!
I writhe in pain.
Oh, the agony of my heart!
My heart pounds within me,
I cannot keep silent.
For I have heard the sound of the trumpet;
I have heard the battle cry.
20Disaster follows disaster;
the whole land lies in ruins.
In an instant my tents are destroyed,
my shelter in a moment.
21How long must I see the battle standard
and hear the sound of the trumpet?

22"My people are fools;
they do not know me.
They are senseless children;
they have no understanding.
They are skilled in doing evil;
they know not how to do good."

23I looked at the earth,
and it was formless and empty;
and at the heavens,
and their light was gone.
24I looked at the mountains,
and they were quaking;
all the hills were swaying.
25I looked, and there were no people;
every bird in the sky had flown away.
26I looked, and the fruitful land was a desert;
all its towns lay in ruins
before the LORD, before his fierce anger.

27This is what the LORD says:

"The whole land will be ruined,
though I will not destroy it completely.
28Therefore the earth will mourn
and the heavens above grow dark,
because I have spoken and will not relent,
I have decided and will not turn back."

29At the sound of horsemen and archers
every town takes to flight.

Some go into the thickets;
some climb up among the rocks.
All the towns are deserted;
no-one lives in them.

30What are you doing, O devastated one?
Why dress yourself in scarlet
and put on jewels of gold?
Why shade your eyes with paint?
You adorn yourself in vain.
Your lovers despise you;
they seek your life.

31I hear a cry as of a woman in labour,
a groan as of one bearing her first child—
the cry of the Daughter of Zion
gasping for breath,
stretching out her hands and saying,
"Alas! I am fainting;
my life is given over to murderers."

Not One Is Upright

5 "Go up and down the streets of Jerusalem,
look around and consider,
search through her squares.
If you can find but one person
who deals honestly and seeks the truth,
I will forgive this city.
2Although they say, 'As surely as the LORD lives,'
still they are swearing falsely."

3O LORD, do not your eyes look for truth?
You struck them, but they felt no pain;
you crushed them but they refused correction.
They made their faces harder than stone
and refused to repent.
4I thought, "These are only the poor;
they are foolish,
for they do not know the way of the LORD,
the requirements of their God.
5So I will go to the leaders
and speak to them;
surely they know the way of the LORD,
the requirements of their God."
But with one accord they too had broken off the yoke
and torn off the bonds.
6Therefore a lion from the forest will attack them,
a wolf from the desert will ravage them,
a leopard will lie in wait near their towns
to tear to pieces any who venture out,
for their rebellion is great
and their backslidings many.

7"Why should I forgive you?
Your children have forsaken me
and sworn by gods that are not gods.
I supplied all their needs,
yet they committed adultery
and thronged to the houses of prostitutes.
8They are well-fed, lusty stallions,
each neighing for another man's wife.
9Should I not punish them for this?"
declares the LORD.
"Should I not avenge myself
on such a nation as this?

10"Go through her vineyards and ravage them,
but do not destroy them completely.
Strip off her branches,
for these people do not belong to the LORD.
11The house of Israel and the house of Judah
have been utterly unfaithful to me,"
declares the LORD.

12They have lied about the LORD;
they said, "He will do nothing!
No harm will come to us;
we will never see sword or famine.

13The prophets are but wind
and the word is not in them;
so let what they say be done to
them."

14Therefore this is what the LORD God Almighty says:

"Because the people have spoken
these words,
I will make my words in your
mouth a fire
and these people the wood it
consumes.
15O house of Israel," declares the
LORD,
"I am bringing a distant nation
against you—
an ancient and enduring nation,
a people whose language you do
not know,
whose speech you do not
understand.
16Their quivers are like an open grave;
all of them are mighty warriors.
17They will devour your harvests and
food,
devour your sons and daughters;
they will devour your flocks and
herds,
devour your vines and fig-trees.
With the sword they will destroy
the fortified cities in which you
trust.

18"Yet even in those days," declares
the LORD, "I will not destroy you completely. 19And when the people ask,
'Why has the LORD our God done all
this to us?' you will tell them, 'As you
have forsaken me and served foreign
gods in your own land, so now you will
serve foreigners in a land not your own.'

20"Announce this to the house of Jacob
and proclaim it in Judah:
21Hear this, you foolish and senseless
people,
who have eyes but do not see,
who have ears but do not hear:
22Should you not fear me?" declares
the LORD.
"Should you not tremble in my
presence?
I made the sand a boundary for the
sea,
an everlasting barrier it cannot
cross.
The waves may roll, but they cannot
prevail;
they may roar, but they cannot
cross it.
23But these people have stubborn and
rebellious hearts;
they have turned aside and gone
away.
24They do not say to themselves,
'Let us fear the LORD our God,
who gives autumn and spring rains in
season,
who assures us of the regular weeks
of harvest.'
25Your wrongdoings have kept these
away;
your sins have deprived you of
good.

26"Among my people are wicked men
who lie in wait like men who snare
birds
and like those who set traps to
catch men.
27Like cages full of birds,
their houses are full of deceit;
they have become rich and powerful
28 and have grown fat and sleek.
Their evil deeds have no limit;
they do not plead the case of the
fatherless to win it,
they do not defend the rights of the
poor.
29Should I not punish them for this?"
declares the LORD.
"Should I not avenge myself
on such a nation as this?

30"A horrible and shocking thing
has happened in the land:
31The prophets prophesy lies,
the priests rule by their own
authority,
and my people love it this way.
But what will you do in the end?

NEW TESTAMENT READING
Philippians 3:1–4:1

No Confidence in the Flesh

3 Finally, my brothers, rejoice in the
Lord! It is no trouble for me to
write the same things to you again, and
it is a safeguard for you.
[2]Watch out for those dogs, those men
who do evil, those mutilators of the
flesh. [3]For it is we who are the circumcision, we who worship by the Spirit of
God, who glory in Christ Jesus, and
who put no confidence in the flesh—
[4]though I myself have reasons for such
confidence.
If anyone else thinks he has reasons
to put confidence in the flesh, I have
more: [5]circumcised on the eighth day,
of the people of Israel, of the tribe of
Benjamin, a Hebrew of Hebrews; in
regard to the law, a Pharisee; [6]as for
zeal, persecuting the church; as for
legalistic righteousness, faultless.
[7]But whatever was to my profit I now
consider loss for the sake of Christ.
[8]What is more, I consider everything a
loss compared to the surpassing greatness of knowing Christ Jesus my Lord,
for whose sake I have lost all things. I
consider them rubbish, that I may gain
Christ [9]and be found in him, not having
a righteousness of my own that comes
from the law, but that which is through
faith in Christ—the righteousness that
comes from God and is by faith. [10]I want
to know Christ and the power of his
resurrection and the fellowship of
sharing in his sufferings, becoming like
him in his death, [11]and so, somehow, to
attain to the resurrection from the dead.

Pressing on Towards the Goal

[12]Not that I have already obtained all
this, or have already been made perfect,
but I press on to take hold of that for
which Christ Jesus took hold of me.
[13]Brothers, I do not consider myself yet
to have taken hold of it. But one thing I
do: Forgetting what is behind and
straining towards what is ahead, [14]I
press on towards the goal to win the
prize for which God has called me
heavenwards in Christ Jesus.
[15]All of us who are mature should
take such a view of things. And if on
some point you think differently, that
too God will make clear to you. [16]Only
let us live up to what we have already
attained.
[17]Join with others in following my
example, brothers, and take note of
those who live according to the pattern
we gave you. [18]For, as I have often told
you before and now say again even with
tears, many live as enemies of the cross
of Christ. [19]Their destiny is destruction,
their god is their stomach, and their
glory is in their shame. Their mind is on
earthly things. [20]But our citizenship is in
heaven. And we eagerly await a Saviour
from there, the Lord Jesus Christ,
[21]who, by the power that enables him to
bring everything under his control, will
transform our lowly bodies so that they
will be like his glorious body.

4 Therefore, my brothers, you whom
I love and long for, my joy and
crown, that is how you should stand firm
in the Lord, dear friends!

READING FROM PSALMS
Psalm 116:1–11

[1]I love the LORD, for he heard my
voice;
he heard my cry for mercy.
[2]Because he turned his ear to me,
I will call on him as long as I live.

[3]The cords of death entangled me,
the anguish of the grave came upon
me;
I was overcome by trouble and
sorrow.
[4]Then I called on the name of the
LORD:
"O LORD, save me!"

5The LORD is gracious and righteous;
our God is full of compassion.
6The LORD protects the
simple-hearted;
when I was in great need, he saved
me.

7Be at rest once more, O my soul,
for the LORD has been good to you.

8For you, O LORD, have delivered my
soul from death,
my eyes from tears,
my feet from stumbling,
9that I may walk before the LORD
in the land of the living.
10I believed; therefore I said,
"I am greatly afflicted."
11And in my dismay I said,
"All men are liars."

OCTOBER 3

DAY 276

OLD TESTAMENT READING

Jeremiah 6:1–7:29

Jerusalem Under Siege

6 "Flee for safety, people of
Benjamin!
Flee from Jerusalem!
Sound the trumpet in Tekoa!
Raise the signal over Beth
Hakkerem!
For disaster looms out of the north,
even terrible destruction.
2I will destroy the Daughter of Zion,
so beautiful and delicate.
3Shepherds with their flocks will come
against her;
they will pitch their tents round
her,
each tending his own portion."

4"Prepare for battle against her!
Arise, let us attack at noon!
But, alas, the daylight is fading,
and the shadows of evening grow
long.
5So arise, let us attack at night
and destroy her fortresses!"

6This is what the LORD Almighty
says:

"Cut down the trees
and build siege ramps against
Jerusalem.
This city must be punished;
it is filled with oppression.
7As a well pours out its water,
so she pours out her wickedness.
Violence and destruction resound in
her;
her sickness and wounds are ever
before me.
8Take warning, O Jerusalem,
or I will turn away from you
and make your land desolate
so that no-one can live in it."

9This is what the LORD Almighty
says:

"Let them glean the remnant of
Israel
as thoroughly as a vine;
pass your hand over the branches
again,
like one gathering grapes."

10To whom can I speak and give
warning?
Who will listen to me?
Their ears are closed
so that they cannot hear.
The word of the LORD is offensive to
them;
they find no pleasure in it.
11But I am full of the wrath of the
LORD,
and I cannot hold it in.

"Pour it out on the children in the street
and on the young men gathered together;
both husband and wife will be caught in it,
and the old, those weighed down with years.
12Their houses will be turned over to others,
together with their fields and their wives,
when I stretch out my hand
against those who live in the land,"
declares the LORD.
13"From the least to the greatest,
all are greedy for gain;
prophets and priests alike,
all practise deceit.
14They dress the wound of my people
as though it were not serious.
'Peace, peace,' they say,
when there is no peace.
15Are they ashamed of their loathsome conduct?
No, they have no shame at all;
they do not even know how to blush.
So they will fall among the fallen;
they will be brought down when I punish them,"
says the LORD.

16This is what the LORD says:

"Stand at the crossroads and look;
ask for the ancient paths,
ask where the good way is, and walk in it,
and you will find rest for your souls.
But you said, 'We will not walk in it.'
17I appointed watchmen over you and said,
'Listen to the sound of the trumpet!'
But you said, 'We will not listen.'
18Therefore hear, O nations;
observe, O witnesses,
what will happen to them.
19Hear, O earth:
I am bringing disaster on this people,
the fruit of their schemes,
because they have not listened to my words
and have rejected my law.
20What do I care about incense from Sheba
or sweet calamus from a distant land?
Your burnt offerings are not acceptable;
your sacrifices do not please me."

21Therefore this is what the LORD says:

"I will put obstacles before this people.
Fathers and sons alike will stumble over them;
neighbours and friends will perish."

22This is what the LORD says:

"Look, an army is coming
from the land of the north;
a great nation is being stirred up
from the ends of the earth.
23They are armed with bow and spear;
they are cruel and show no mercy.
They sound like the roaring sea
as they ride on their horses;
they come like men in battle formation
to attack you, O Daughter of Zion."

24We have heard reports about them,
and our hands hang limp.
Anguish has gripped us,
pain like that of a woman in labour.
25Do not go out to the fields
or walk on the roads,
for the enemy has a sword,
and there is terror on every side.
26O my people, put on sackcloth
and roll in ashes;
mourn with bitter wailing
as for an only son,
for suddenly the destroyer
will come upon us.

27“I have made you a tester of metals
and my people the ore,
that you may observe
and test their ways.
28They are all hardened rebels,
going about to slander.
They are bronze and iron;
they all act corruptly.
29The bellows blow fiercely
to burn away the lead with fire,
but the refining goes on in vain;
the wicked are not purged out.
30They are called rejected silver,
because the LORD has rejected
them.”

False Religion Worthless

7 This is the word that came to Jeremiah from the LORD: 2“Stand at
the gate of the LORD’s house and there
proclaim this message:
“ ‘Hear the word of the LORD, all you
people of Judah who come through
these gates to worship the LORD. 3This
is what the LORD Almighty, the God of
Israel, says: Reform your ways and your
actions, and I will let you live in this
place. 4Do not trust in deceptive words
and say, “This is the temple of the
LORD, the temple of the LORD, the
temple of the LORD!” 5If you really
change your ways and your actions and
deal with each other justly, 6if you do
not oppress the alien, the fatherless or
the widow and do not shed innocent
blood in this place, and if you do not
follow other gods to your own harm,
7then I will let you live in this place, in
the land I gave to your forefathers for
ever and ever. 8But look, you are
trusting in deceptive words that are
worthless.
9“ ‘Will you steal and murder, commit adultery and perjury, burn incense
to Baal and follow other gods you have
not known, 10and then come and stand
before me in this house, which bears my
Name, and say, “We are safe”—safe to
do all these detestable things? 11Has this
house, which bears my Name, become a
den of robbers to you? But I have been
watching! declares the LORD.
12“ ‘Go now to the place in Shiloh
where I first made a dwelling for my
Name, and see what I did to it because
of the wickedness of my people Israel.
13While you were doing all these things,
declares the LORD, I spoke to you again
and again, but you did not listen; I
called you, but you did not answer.
14Therefore, what I did to Shiloh I will
now do to the house that bears my
Name, the temple you trust in, the place
I gave to you and your fathers. 15I will
thrust you from my presence, just as I
did all your brothers, the people of
Ephraim.’
16“So do not pray for this people nor
offer any plea or petition for them; do
not plead with me, for I will not listen to
you. 17Do you not see what they are
doing in the towns of Judah and in the
streets of Jerusalem? 18The children
gather wood, the fathers light the fire,
and the women knead the dough and
make cakes of bread for the Queen of
Heaven. They pour out drink offerings
to other gods to provoke me to anger.
19But am I the one they are provoking?
declares the LORD. Are they not rather
harming themselves, to their own
shame?
20“ ‘Therefore this is what the
Sovereign LORD says: My anger and my
wrath will be poured out on this place,
on man and beast, on the trees of the
field and on the fruit of the ground, and
it will burn and not be quenched.
21“ ‘This is what the LORD Almighty,
the God of Israel, says: Go ahead, add
your burnt offerings to your other sacrifices and eat the meat yourselves!
22For when I brought your forefathers
out of Egypt and spoke to them, I did
not just give them commands about
burnt offerings and sacrifices, 23but I
gave them this command: Obey me,
and I will be your God and you will be
my people. Walk in all the ways I command you, that it may go well with you.
24But they did not listen or pay attention; instead, they followed the stubborn inclinations of their evil hearts.
They went backward and not forward.

[25]From the time your forefathers left Egypt until now, day after day, again and again I sent you my servants the prophets. [26]But they did not listen to me or pay attention. They were stiff-necked and did more evil than their forefathers.'

[27]"When you tell them all this, they will not listen to you; when you call to them, they will not answer. [28]Therefore say to them, 'This is the nation that has not obeyed the LORD its God or responded to correction. Truth has perished; it has vanished from their lips. [29]Cut off your hair and throw it away; take up a lament on the barren heights, for the LORD has rejected and abandoned this generation that is under his wrath.

NEW TESTAMENT READING
Philippians 4:2–23

Exhortations

[2]I plead with Euodia and I plead with Syntyche to agree with each other in the Lord. [3]Yes, and I ask you, loyal yokefellow, help these women who have contended at my side in the cause of the gospel, along with Clement and the rest of my fellow-workers, whose names are in the book of life.

[4]Rejoice in the Lord always. I will say it again: Rejoice! [5]Let your gentleness be evident to all. The Lord is near. [6]Do not be anxious about anything, but in everything, by prayer and petition, with thanksgiving, present your requests to God. [7]And the peace of God, which transcends all understanding, will guard your hearts and your minds in Christ Jesus.

[8]Finally, brothers, whatever is true, whatever is noble, whatever is right, whatever is pure, whatever is lovely, whatever is admirable—if anything is excellent or praiseworthy—think about such things. [9]Whatever you have learned or received or heard from me, or seen in me—put it into practice. And the God of peace will be with you.

Thanks for Their Gifts

[10]I rejoice greatly in the Lord that at last you have renewed your concern for me. Indeed, you have been concerned, but you had no opportunity to show it. [11]I am not saying this because I am in need, for I have learned to be content whatever the circumstances. [12]I know what it is to be in need, and I know what it is to have plenty. I have learned the secret of being content in any and every situation, whether well fed or hungry, whether living in plenty or in want. [13]I can do everything through him who gives me strength.

[14]Yet it was good of you to share in my troubles. [15]Moreover, as you Philippians know, in the early days of your acquaintance with the gospel, when I set out from Macedonia, not one church shared with me in the matter of giving and receiving, except you only; [16]for even when I was in Thessalonica, you sent me aid again and again when I was in need. [17]Not that I am looking for a gift, but I am looking for what may be credited to your account. [18]I have received full payment and even more; I am amply supplied, now that I have received from Epaphroditus the gifts you sent. They are a fragrant offering, an acceptable sacrifice, pleasing to God. [19]And my God will meet all your needs according to his glorious riches in Christ Jesus.

[20]To our God and Father be glory for ever and ever. Amen.

Final Greetings

[21]Greet all the saints in Christ Jesus. The brothers who are with me send greetings. [22]All the saints send you greetings, especially those who belong to Caesar's household.

[23]The grace of the Lord Jesus Christ be with your spirit. Amen.

READING FROM PROVERBS
Proverbs 24:5–14

5A wise man has great power,
and a man of knowledge increases strength;
6for waging war you need guidance,
and for victory many advisers.

7Wisdom is too high for a fool;
in the assembly at the gate he has nothing to say.

8He who plots evil
will be known as a schemer.
9The schemes of folly are sin,
and men detest a mocker.

10If you falter in times of trouble,
how small is your strength!
11Rescue those being led away to death;
hold back those staggering towards slaughter.
12If you say, "But we knew nothing about this,"
does not he who weighs the heart perceive it?
Does not he who guards your life know it?
Will he not repay each person according to what he has done?

13Eat honey, my son, for it is good;
honey from the comb is sweet to your taste.
14Know also that wisdom is sweet to your soul;
if you find it, there is a future hope for you,
and your hope will not be cut off.

OCTOBER 4

DAY 277

OLD TESTAMENT READING
Jeremiah 7:30–9:16

The Valley of Slaughter

30"'The people of Judah have done
evil in my eyes, declares the LORD.
They have set up their detestable idols
in the house that bears my Name and
have defiled it. 31They have built the
high places of Topheth in the Valley of
Ben Hinnom to burn their sons and
daughters in the fire—something I did
not command, nor did it enter my mind.
32So beware, the days are coming, declares the LORD, when people will no
longer call it Topheth or the Valley of
Ben Hinnom, but the Valley of Slaughter, for they will bury the dead in
Topheth until there is no more room.
33Then the carcasses of this people will
become food for the birds of the air and
the beasts of the earth, and there will be
no-one to frighten them away. 34I will
bring an end to the sounds of joy and
gladness and to the voices of bride
and bridegroom in the towns of Judah
and the streets of Jerusalem, for the
land will become desolate.

8 "'At that time, declares the LORD,
the bones of the kings and officials
of Judah, the bones of the priests and
prophets, and the bones of the people of
Jerusalem will be removed from their
graves. 2They will be exposed to the sun
and the moon and all the stars of the
heavens, which they have loved and
served and which they have followed
and consulted and worshipped. They
will not be gathered up or buried, but
will be like refuse lying on the ground.
3Wherever I banish them, all the survivors of this evil nation will prefer
death to life, declares the LORD
Almighty.'

Sin and Punishment

4"Say to them, 'This is what the LORD says:

" 'When men fall down, do they not get up?
When a man turns away, does he not return?
5Why then have these people turned away?
Why does Jerusalem always turn away?
They cling to deceit;
they refuse to return.
6I have listened attentively,
but they do not say what is right.
No-one repents of his wickedness,
saying, "What have I done?"
Each pursues his own course
like a horse charging into battle.
7Even the stork in the sky
knows her appointed seasons,
and the dove, the swift and the thrush
observe the time of their migration.
But my people do not know
the requirements of the LORD.

8" 'How can you say, "We are wise,
for we have the law of the LORD,"
when actually the lying pen of the scribes
has handled it falsely?
9The wise will be put to shame;
they will be dismayed and trapped.
Since they have rejected the word of the LORD,
what kind of wisdom do they have?
10Therefore I will give their wives to other men
and their fields to new owners.
From the least to the greatest,
all are greedy for gain;
prophets and priests alike,
all practise deceit.
11They dress the wound of my people
as though it were not serious.
"Peace, peace," they say,
when there is no peace.
12Are they ashamed of their loathsome conduct?
No, they have no shame at all;
they do not even know how to blush.
So they will fall among the fallen;
they will be brought down when they are punished,
says the LORD.

13" 'I will take away their harvest,
declares the LORD.
There will be no grapes on the vine.
There will be no figs on the tree,
and their leaves will wither.
What I have given them
will be taken from them.' "

14"Why are we sitting here?
Gather together!
Let us flee to the fortified cities
and perish there!
For the LORD our God has doomed us to perish
and given us poisoned water to drink,
because we have sinned against him.
15We hoped for peace
but no good has come,
for a time of healing
but there was only terror.
16The snorting of the enemy's horses
is heard from Dan;
at the neighing of their stallions
the whole land trembles.
They have come to devour
the land and everything in it,
the city and all who live there."

17"See, I will send venomous snakes among you,
vipers that cannot be charmed,
and they will bite you,"
declares the LORD.

18O my Comforter in sorrow,
my heart is faint within me.
19Listen to the cry of my people
from a land far away:
"Is the LORD not in Zion?
Is her King no longer there?"

"Why have they provoked me to
anger with their images,
with their worthless foreign idols?"

20"The harvest is past,
the summer has ended,
and we are not saved."

21Since my people are crushed, I am
crushed;
I mourn, and horror grips me.
22Is there no balm in Gilead?
Is there no physician there?
Why then is there no healing
for the wound of my people?

9 1Oh, that my head were a spring
of water
and my eyes a fountain of tears!
I would weep day and night
for the slain of my people.
2Oh, that I had in the desert
a lodging place for travellers,
so that I might leave my people
and go away from them;
for they are all adulterers,
a crowd of unfaithful people.

3"They make ready their tongue
like a bow, to shoot lies;
it is not by truth
that they triumph in the land.
They go from one sin to another;
they do not acknowledge me,"
declares the LORD.
4"Beware of your friends;
do not trust your brothers.
For every brother is a deceiver,
and every friend a slanderer.
5Friend deceives friend,
and no-one speaks the truth.
They have taught their tongues to lie;
they weary themselves with
sinning.
6You live in the midst of deception;
in their deceit they refuse to
acknowledge me,"
declares the LORD.

7Therefore this is what the LORD
Almighty says:

"See, I will refine and test them,
for what else can I do
because of the sin of my people?
8Their tongue is a deadly arrow;
it speaks with deceit.
With his mouth each speaks cordially
to his neighbour,
but in his heart he sets a trap for
him.
9Should I not punish them for this?"
declares the LORD.
"Should I not avenge myself
on such a nation as this?"

10I will weep and wail for the
mountains
and take up a lament concerning
the desert pastures.
They are desolate and untravelled,
and the lowing of cattle is not
heard.
The birds of the air have fled
and the animals are gone.

11"I will make Jerusalem a heap of
ruins,
a haunt of jackals;
and I will lay waste the towns of
Judah
so that no-one can live there."

12What man is wise enough to understand this? Who has been instructed by
the LORD and can explain it? Why has
the land been ruined and laid waste like
a desert that no-one can cross?
13The LORD said, "It is because they
have forsaken my law, which I set before them; they have not obeyed me or
followed my law. 14Instead, they have
followed the stubbornness of their
hearts; they have followed the Baals,
as their fathers taught them."
15Therefore, this is what the LORD
Almighty, the God of Israel, says: "See,
I will make this people eat bitter food
and drink poisoned water. 16I will scatter them among nations that neither
they nor their fathers have known, and I
will pursue them with the sword until I
have destroyed them."

NEW TESTAMENT READING
Colossians 1:1–23

1 Paul, an apostle of Christ Jesus by the will of God, and Timothy our brother,

2To the holy and faithful brothers in Christ at Colosse:

Grace and peace to you from God our Father.

Thanksgiving and Prayer

3We always thank God, the Father of our Lord Jesus Christ, when we pray for you, 4because we have heard of your faith in Christ Jesus and of the love you have for all the saints—5the faith and love that spring from the hope that is stored up for you in heaven and that you have already heard about in the word of truth, the gospel 6that has come to you. All over the world this gospel is bearing fruit and growing, just as it has been doing among you since the day you heard it and understood God's grace in all its truth. 7You learned it from Epaphras, our dear fellow-servant, who is a faithful minister of Christ on our behalf, 8and who also told us of your love in the Spirit.

9For this reason, since the day we heard about you, we have not stopped praying for you and asking God to fill you with the knowledge of his will through all spiritual wisdom and understanding. 10And we pray this in order that you may live a life worthy of the Lord and may please him in every way: bearing fruit in every good work, growing in the knowledge of God, 11being strengthened with all power according to his glorious might so that you may have great endurance and patience, and joyfully 12giving thanks to the Father, who has qualified you to share in the inheritance of the saints in the kingdom of light. 13For he has rescued us from the dominion of darkness and brought us into the kingdom of the Son he loves, 14in whom we have redemption, the forgiveness of sins.

The Supremacy of Christ

15He is the image of the invisible God, the firstborn over all creation. 16For by him all things were created: things in heaven and on earth, visible and invisible, whether thrones or powers or rulers or authorities; all things were created by him and for him. 17He is before all things, and in him all things hold together. 18And he is the head of the body, the church; he is the beginning and the firstborn from among the dead, so that in everything he might have the supremacy. 19For God was pleased to have all his fulness dwell in him, 20and through him to reconcile to himself all things, whether things on earth or things in heaven, by making peace through his blood, shed on the cross.

21Once you were alienated from God and were enemies in your minds because of your evil behaviour. 22But now he has reconciled you by Christ's physical body through death to present you holy in his sight, without blemish and free from accusation—23if you continue in your faith, established and firm, not moved from the hope held out in the gospel. This is the gospel that you heard and that has been proclaimed to every creature under heaven, and of which I, Paul, have become a servant.

READING FROM PSALMS
Psalm 116:12–19

12How can I repay the LORD
for all his goodness to me?
13I will lift up the cup of salvation
and call on the name of the LORD.
14I will fulfil my vows to the LORD
in the presence of all his people.

15Precious in the sight of the LORD
is the death of his saints.

16O LORD, truly I am your servant;
I am your servant, the son of your maidservant;
you have freed me from my chains.

17I will sacrifice a thank-offering to you
and call on the name of the LORD.

18I will fulfil my vows to the LORD
in the presence of all his people,
19in the courts of the house of the LORD—
in your midst, O Jerusalem.

Praise the LORD.

OCTOBER 5

DAY 278

OLD TESTAMENT READING

Jeremiah 9:17–11:17

17This is what the LORD Almighty says:

"Consider now! Call for the wailing women to come;
send for the most skilful of them.
18Let them come quickly
and wail over us
till our eyes overflow with tears
and water streams from our eyelids.
19The sound of wailing is heard from Zion:
'How ruined we are!
How great is our shame!
We must leave our land
because our houses are in ruins.'"

20Now, O women, hear the word of the LORD;
open your ears to the words of his mouth.
Teach your daughters how to wail;
teach one another a lament.
21Death has climbed in through our windows
and has entered our fortresses;
it has cut off the children from the streets
and the young men from the public squares.

22Say, "This is what the LORD declares:

"'The dead bodies of men will lie
like refuse on the open field,
like cut corn behind the reaper,
with no-one to gather them.'"

23This is what the LORD says:

"Let not the wise man boast of his wisdom
or the strong man boast of his strength
or the rich man boast of his riches,
24but let him who boasts boast about this:
that he understands and knows me,
that I am the LORD, who exercises kindness,
justice and righteousness on earth,
for in these I delight,"
declares the LORD.

25"The days are coming," declares
the LORD, "when I will punish all who
are circumcised only in the flesh—
26Egypt, Judah, Edom, Ammon, Moab
and all who live in the desert in distant
places. For all these nations are really
uncircumcised, and even the whole
house of Israel is uncircumcised in
heart."

God and Idols

10 Hear what the LORD says to you,
O house of Israel. 2This is what
the LORD says:

"Do not learn the ways of the nations
or be terrified by signs in the sky,
though the nations are terrified by them.
3For the customs of the peoples are worthless;
they cut a tree out of the forest,
and a craftsman shapes it with his chisel.
4They adorn it with silver and gold;
they fasten it with hammer and nails
so that it will not totter.
5Like a scarecrow in a melon patch,
their idols cannot speak;
they must be carried
because they cannot walk.
Do not fear them;
they can do no harm
nor can they do any good."

6No-one is like you, O LORD;
you are great,
and your name is mighty in power.
7Who should not revere you,
O King of the nations?
This is your due.
Among all the wise men of the nations
and in all their kingdoms,
there is no-one like you.
8They are all senseless and foolish;
they are taught by worthless wooden idols.
9Hammered silver is brought from Tarshish
and gold from Uphaz.
What the craftsman and goldsmith have made
is then dressed in blue and purple—
all made by skilled workers.
10But the LORD is the true God;
he is the living God, the eternal King.
When he is angry, the earth trembles;
the nations cannot endure his wrath.

11"Tell them this: 'These gods, who
did not make the heavens and the earth,
will perish from the earth and from
under the heavens.'"

12But God made the earth by his power;
he founded the world by his wisdom
and stretched out the heavens by his understanding.
13When he thunders, the waters in the heavens roar;
he makes clouds rise from the ends of the earth.
He sends lightning with the rain
and brings out the wind from his storehouses.

14Everyone is senseless and without knowledge;
every goldsmith is shamed by his idols.
His images are a fraud;
they have no breath in them.
15They are worthless, the objects of mockery;
when their judgment comes, they will perish.
16He who is the Portion of Jacob is not like these,
for he is the Maker of all things,
including Israel, the tribe of his inheritance—
the LORD Almighty is his name.

Coming Destruction

17Gather up your belongings to leave the land,
you who live under siege.
18For this is what the LORD says:
"At this time I will hurl out
those who live in this land;
I will bring distress on them
so that they may be captured."

19Woe to me because of my injury!
My wound is incurable!
Yet I said to myself,
"This is my sickness, and I must endure it."
20My tent is destroyed;
all its ropes are snapped.

My sons are gone from me and are no
more;
no-one is left now to pitch my tent
or to set up my shelter.
21The shepherds are senseless
and do not enquire of the LORD;
so they do not prosper
and all their flock is scattered.
22Listen! The report is coming—
a great commotion from the land of
the north!
It will make the towns of Judah
desolate,
a haunt of jackals.

Jeremiah's Prayer

23I know, O LORD, that a man's life is
not his own;
it is not for man to direct his steps.
24Correct me, LORD, but only with
justice—
not in your anger,
lest you reduce me to nothing.
25Pour out your wrath on the nations
that do not acknowledge you,
on the peoples who do not call on
your name.
For they have devoured Jacob;
they have devoured him
completely
and destroyed his homeland.

The Covenant Is Broken

11 This is the word that came to
Jeremiah from the LORD:
2"Listen to the terms of this covenant
and tell them to the people of Judah and
to those who live in Jerusalem. 3Tell
them that this is what the LORD, the
God of Israel, says: 'Cursed is the man
who does not obey the terms of this
covenant—4the terms I commanded
your forefathers when I brought them
out of Egypt, out of the iron-smelting
furnace.' I said, 'Obey me and do everything I command you, and you will be
my people, and I will be your God.
5Then I will fulfil the oath I swore to
your forefathers, to give them a land
flowing with milk and honey'—the land
you possess today."

I answered, "Amen, LORD."

6The LORD said to me, "Proclaim all
these words in the towns of Judah and in
the streets of Jerusalem: 'Listen to the
terms of this covenant and follow them.
7From the time I brought your forefathers up from Egypt until today, I
warned them again and again, saying,
"Obey me." 8But they did not listen or
pay attention; instead, they followed
the stubbornness of their evil hearts. So
I brought on them all the curses of the
covenant I had commanded them to
follow but that they did not keep.'"

9Then the LORD said to me, "There is
a conspiracy among the people of Judah
and those who live in Jerusalem. 10They
have returned to the sins of their forefathers, who refused to listen to my
words. They have followed other gods
to serve them. Both the house of Israel
and the house of Judah have broken the
covenant I made with their forefathers.
11Therefore this is what the LORD says:
'I will bring on them a disaster they
cannot escape. Although they cry out to
me, I will not listen to them. 12The
towns of Judah and the people of Jerusalem will go and cry out to the gods to
whom they burn incense, but they will
not help them at all when disaster
strikes. 13You have as many gods as you
have towns, O Judah; and the altars you
have set up to burn incense to that
shameful god Baal are as many as the
streets of Jerusalem.'

14"Do not pray for this people nor
offer any plea or petition for them, because I will not listen when they call to
me in the time of their distress.

15"What is my beloved doing in my
temple
as she works out her evil schemes
with many?
Can consecrated meat avert ⌞your
punishment⌟?
When you engage in your
wickedness,
then you rejoice."

[16]The LORD called you a thriving olive
tree
with fruit beautiful in form.
But with the roar of a mighty storm
he will set it on fire,
and its branches will be broken.

[17]The LORD Almighty, who planted you, has decreed disaster for you, because the house of Israel and the house of Judah have done evil and provoked me to anger by burning incense to Baal.

NEW TESTAMENT READING
Colossians 1:24–2:5

Paul's Labour for the Church

[24]Now I rejoice in what was suffered
for you, and I fill up in my flesh what is
still lacking in regard to Christ's afflictions, for the sake of his body, which is
the church. [25]I have become its servant
by the commission God gave me to
present to you the word of God in its
fulness—[26]the mystery that has been
kept hidden for ages and generations,
but is now disclosed to the saints. [27]To
them God has chosen to make known
among the Gentiles the glorious riches
of this mystery, which is Christ in you,
the hope of glory.
[28]We proclaim him, admonishing and
teaching everyone with all wisdom, so
that we may present everyone perfect in
Christ. [29]To this end I labour, struggling
with all his energy, which so powerfully
works in me.

2 I want you to know how much I am
struggling for you and for those at
Laodicea, and for all who have not met
me personally. [2]My purpose is that they
may be encouraged in heart and united
in love, so that they may have the full
riches of complete understanding, in
order that they may know the mystery
of God, namely, Christ, [3]in whom are
hidden all the treasures of wisdom and
knowledge. [4]I tell you this so that no-
one may deceive you by fine-sounding
arguments. [5]For though I am absent
from you in body, I am present with you
in spirit and delight to see how orderly
you are and how firm your faith in
Christ is.

READING FROM PSALMS
Psalm 117:1–2

[1]Praise the LORD, all you nations;
extol him, all you peoples.
[2]For great is his love towards us,
and the faithfulness of the LORD
endures for ever.

Praise the LORD.

DAY 279

OCTOBER 6

OLD TESTAMENT READING
Jeremiah 11:18–13:27

Plot Against Jeremiah

[18]Because the LORD revealed their
plot to me, I knew it, for at that time he
showed me what they were doing. [19]I
had been like a gentle lamb led to the
slaughter; I did not realise that they had
plotted against me, saying,

"Let us destroy the tree and its fruit;
let us cut him off from the land of
the living,
that his name be remembered no
more."
[20]But, O LORD Almighty, you who
judge righteously
and test the heart and mind,
let me see your vengeance upon them,
for to you I have committed my
cause.

[21]"Therefore this is what the LORD says about the men of Anathoth who are seeking your life and saying, 'Do not prophesy in the name of the LORD or you will die by our hands'—[22]therefore this is what the LORD Almighty says: 'I will punish them. Their young men will die by the sword, their sons and daughters by famine. [23]Not even a remnant will be left to them, because I will bring disaster on the men of Anathoth in the year of their punishment.'"

Jeremiah's Complaint

12 You are always righteous, O LORD,
when I bring a case before you.
Yet I would speak with you about your justice:
Why does the way of the wicked prosper?
Why do all the faithless live at ease?
[2]You have planted them, and they have taken root;
they grow and bear fruit.
You are always on their lips
but far from their hearts.
[3]Yet you know me, O LORD;
you see me and test my thoughts about you.
Drag them off like sheep to be butchered!
Set them apart for the day of slaughter!
[4]How long will the land lie parched
and the grass in every field be withered?
Because those who live in it are wicked,
the animals and birds have perished.
Moreover, the people are saying,
"He will not see what happens to us."

God's Answer

[5]"If you have raced with men on foot
and they have worn you out,
how can you compete with horses?
If you stumble in safe country,
how will you manage in the thickets by the Jordan?
[6]Your brothers, your own family—
even they have betrayed you;
they have raised a loud cry against you.
Do not trust them,
though they speak well of you.

[7]"I will forsake my house,
abandon my inheritance;
I will give the one I love
into the hands of her enemies.
[8]My inheritance has become to me
like a lion in the forest.
She roars at me;
therefore I hate her.
[9]Has not my inheritance become to me
like a speckled bird of prey
that other birds of prey surround and attack?
Go and gather all the wild beasts;
bring them to devour.
[10]Many shepherds will ruin my vineyard
and trample down my field;
they will turn my pleasant field
into a desolate wasteland.
[11]It will be made a wasteland,
parched and desolate before me;
the whole land will be laid waste
because there is no-one who cares.
[12]Over all the barren heights in the desert
destroyers will swarm,
for the sword of the LORD will devour
from one end of the land to the other;
no-one will be safe.
[13]They will sow wheat but reap thorns;
they will wear themselves out but gain nothing.
So bear the shame of your harvest
because of the LORD's fierce anger."

[14]This is what the LORD says: "As for
all my wicked neighbours who seize the
inheritance I gave to my people Israel, I
will uproot them from their lands and I

will uproot the house of Judah from
among them. 15But after I uproot them,
I will again have compassion and will
bring each of them back to his own
inheritance and his own country. 16And
if they learn well the ways of my people
and swear by my name, saying, 'As
surely as the LORD lives'—even as they
once taught my people to swear by Baal
—then they will be established among
my people. 17But if any nation does
not listen, I will completely uproot and
destroy it," declares the LORD.

A Linen Belt

13 This is what the LORD said to
me: "Go and buy a linen belt
and put it round your waist, but do not
let it touch water." 2So I bought a belt,
as the LORD directed, and put it round
my waist.

3Then the word of the LORD came to
me a second time: 4"Take the belt you
bought and are wearing round your
waist, and go now to Perath and hide it
there in a crevice in the rocks." 5So I
went and hid it at Perath, as the LORD
told me.

6Many days later the LORD said to
me, "Go now to Perath and get the belt
I told you to hide there." 7So I went to
Perath and dug up the belt and took it
from the place where I had hidden it,
but now it was ruined and completely
useless.

8Then the word of the LORD came to
me: 9"This is what the LORD says: 'In
the same way I will ruin the pride of
Judah and the great pride of Jerusalem.
10These wicked people, who refuse to
listen to my words, who follow the stubbornness of their hearts and go after
other gods to serve and worship them,
will be like this belt—completely useless! 11For as a belt is bound round a
man's waist, so I bound the whole house
of Israel and the whole house of Judah
to me,' declares the LORD, 'to be my
people for my renown and praise and
honour. But they have not listened.'

Wineskins

12"Say to them: 'This is what the
LORD, the God of Israel, says: Every
wineskin should be filled with wine.'
And if they say to you, 'Don't we know
that every wineskin should be filled with
wine?' 13then tell them, 'This is what the
LORD says: I am going to fill with drunkenness all who live in this land, including the kings who sit on David's throne,
the priests, the prophets and all those
living in Jerusalem. 14I will smash them
one against the other, fathers and sons
alike, declares the LORD. I will allow no
pity or mercy or compassion to keep me
from destroying them.'"

Threat of Captivity

15Hear and pay attention,
do not be arrogant,
for the LORD has spoken.
16Give glory to the LORD your God
before he brings the darkness,
before your feet stumble
on the darkening hills.
You hope for light,
but he will turn it to thick darkness
and change it to deep gloom.
17But if you do not listen,
I will weep in secret
because of your pride;
my eyes will weep bitterly,
overflowing with tears,
because the LORD's flock will be
taken captive.

18Say to the king and to the queen
mother,
"Come down from your thrones,
for your glorious crowns
will fall from your heads."
19The cities in the Negev will be shut
up,
and there will be no-one to open
them.
All Judah will be carried into exile,
carried completely away.

20Lift up your eyes and see
those who are coming from the
north.

Where is the flock that was entrusted
to you,
the sheep of which you boasted?
21 What will you say when ⌞the LORD⌟
sets over you
those you cultivated as your special
allies?
Will not pain grip you
like that of a woman in labour?
22 And if you ask yourself,
"Why has this happened to
me?"—
it is because of your many sins
that your skirts have been torn off
and your body ill-treated.
23 Can the Ethiopian change his skin
or the leopard its spots?
Neither can you do good
who are accustomed to doing evil.

24 "I will scatter you like chaff
driven by the desert wind.
25 This is your lot,
the portion I have decreed for
you,"
declares the LORD,
"because you have forgotten me
and trusted in false gods.
26 I will pull up your skirts over your
face
that your shame may be seen—
27 your adulteries and lustful neighings,
your shameless prostitution!
I have seen your detestable acts
on the hills and in the fields.
Woe to you, O Jerusalem!
How long will you be unclean?"

NEW TESTAMENT READING

Colossians 2:6–23

Freedom From Human Regulations Through Life With Christ

6 So then, just as you received Christ
Jesus as Lord, continue to live in him,
7 rooted and built up in him, strengthened in the faith as you were taught,
and overflowing with thankfulness.
8 See to it that no-one takes you captive through hollow and deceptive
philosophy, which depends on human
tradition and the basic principles of this
world rather than on Christ.
9 For in Christ all the fulness of the
Deity lives in bodily form, 10 and you
have been given fulness in Christ, who is
the Head over every power and authority. 11 In him you were also circumcised,
in the putting off of the sinful nature,
not with a circumcision done by the
hands of men but with the circumcision
done by Christ, 12 having been buried
with him in baptism and raised with him
through your faith in the power of God,
who raised him from the dead.
13 When you were dead in your sins
and in the uncircumcision of your sinful
nature, God made you alive with Christ.
He forgave us all our sins, 14 having cancelled the written code, with its regulations, that was against us and that
stood opposed to us; he took it away,
nailing it to the cross. 15 And having
disarmed the powers and authorities, he
made a public spectacle of them, tri-
umphing over them by the cross.
16 Therefore do not let anyone judge
you by what you eat or drink, or with
regard to a religious festival, a New
Moon celebration or a Sabbath day.
17 These are a shadow of the things that
were to come; the reality, however, is
found in Christ. 18 Do not let anyone
who delights in false humility and the
worship of angels disqualify you for the
prize. Such a person goes into great
detail about what he has seen, and his
unspiritual mind puffs him up with idle
notions. 19 He has lost connection with
the Head, from whom the whole body,
supported and held together by its liga-
ments and sinews, grows as God causes
it to grow.
20 Since you died with Christ to the
basic principles of this world, why, as
though you still belonged to it, do you
submit to its rules: 21 "Do not handle!
Do not taste! Do not touch!"? 22 These
are all destined to perish with use,
because they are based on human
commands and teachings. 23 Such regulations indeed have an appearance of

wisdom, with their self-imposed worship, their false humility and their harsh treatment of the body, but they lack any value in restraining sensual indulgence.

READING FROM PSALMS
Psalm 118:1–16

1Give thanks to the LORD, for he is
good;
his love endures for ever.

2Let Israel say:
"His love endures for ever."
3Let the house of Aaron say:
"His love endures for ever."
4Let those who fear the LORD say:
"His love endures for ever."

5In my anguish I cried to the LORD,
and he answered by setting me
free.
6The LORD is with me; I will not be
afraid.
What can man do to me?
7The LORD is with me; he is my
helper.
I will look in triumph on my
enemies.

8It is better to take refuge in the LORD
than to trust in man.
9It is better to take refuge in the LORD
than to trust in princes.

10All the nations surrounded me,
but in the name of the LORD I cut
them off.
11They surrounded me on every side,
but in the name of the LORD I cut
them off.
12They swarmed around me like bees,
but they died out as quickly as
burning thorns;
in the name of the LORD I cut them
off.

13I was pushed back and about to fall,
but the LORD helped me.
14The LORD is my strength and my
song;
he has become my salvation.

15Shouts of joy and victory
resound in the tents of the
righteous:
"The LORD's right hand has done
mighty things!
16 The LORD's right hand is lifted
high;
the LORD's right hand has done
mighty things!"

DAY 280

OCTOBER 7

OLD TESTAMENT READING
Jeremiah 14:1–15:21

Drought, Famine, Sword

14 This is the word of the LORD to Jeremiah concerning the drought:

2"Judah mourns,
her cities languish;
they wail for the land,
and a cry goes up from Jerusalem.
3The nobles send their servants for
water;
they go to the cisterns
but find no water.
They return with their jars unfilled;
dismayed and despairing,
they cover their heads.
4The ground is cracked
because there is no rain in the land;
the farmers are dismayed
and cover their heads.
5Even the doe in the field

deserts her newborn fawn
because there is no grass.
6Wild donkeys stand on the barren heights
and pant like jackals;
their eyesight fails
for lack of pasture."

7Although our sins testify against us,
O LORD, do something for the sake of your name.
For our backsliding is great;
we have sinned against you.
8O Hope of Israel,
its Saviour in times of distress,
why are you like a stranger in the land,
like a traveller who stays only a night?
9Why are you like a man taken by surprise,
like a warrior powerless to save?
You are among us, O LORD,
and we bear your name;
do not forsake us!

10This is what the LORD says about
this people:

"They greatly love to wander;
they do not restrain their feet.
So the LORD does not accept them;
he will now remember their wickedness
and punish them for their sins."

11Then the LORD said to me, "Do not
pray for the well-being of this people.
12Although they fast, I will not listen to
their cry; though they offer burnt offerings and grain offerings, I will not
accept them. Instead, I will destroy
them with the sword, famine and
plague."
13But I said, "Ah, Sovereign LORD,
the prophets keep telling them, 'You
will not see the sword or suffer famine.
Indeed, I will give you lasting peace in
this place.'"
14Then the LORD said to me, "The
prophets are prophesying lies in my
name. I have not sent them or
appointed them or spoken to them.
They are prophesying to you false
visions, divinations, idolatries and the
delusions of their own minds. 15There-
fore, this is what the LORD says about
the prophets who are prophesying in my
name: I did not send them, yet they are
saying, 'No sword or famine will touch
this land.' Those same prophets will
perish by sword and famine. 16And the
people they are prophesying to will be
thrown out into the streets of Jerusalem
because of the famine and sword. There
will be no-one to bury them or their
wives, their sons or their daughters. I
will pour out on them the calamity they
deserve.

17"Speak this word to them:

"'Let my eyes overflow with tears
night and day without ceasing;
for my virgin daughter—my people—
has suffered a grievous wound,
a crushing blow.
18If I go into the country,
I see those slain by the sword;
if I go into the city,
I see the ravages of famine.
Both prophet and priest
have gone to a land they know not.'"

19Have you rejected Judah completely?
Do you despise Zion?
Why have you afflicted us
so that we cannot be healed?
We hoped for peace
but no good has come,
for a time of healing
but there is only terror.
20O LORD, we acknowledge our wickedness
and the guilt of our fathers;
we have indeed sinned against you.
21For the sake of your name do not despise us;
do not dishonour your glorious throne.
Remember your covenant with us
and do not break it.

22Do any of the worthless idols of the nations bring rain?
Do the skies themselves send down showers?
No, it is you, O LORD our God.
Therefore our hope is in you,
for you are the one who does all this.

15 Then the LORD said to me:
"Even if Moses and Samuel
were to stand before me, my heart
would not go out to this people. Send
them away from my presence! Let them
go! 2And if they ask you, 'Where shall
we go?' tell them, 'This is what the
LORD says:

" 'Those destined for death, to death;
those for the sword, to the sword;
those for starvation, to starvation;
those for captivity, to captivity.'

3"I will send four kinds of destroyers
against them," declares the LORD, "the
sword to kill and the dogs to drag away
and the birds of the air and the beasts of
the earth to devour and destroy. 4I will
make them abhorrent to all the kingdoms of the earth because of what Manasseh son of Hezekiah king of Judah
did in Jerusalem.

5"Who will have pity on you, O Jerusalem?
Who will mourn for you?
Who will stop to ask how you are?
6You have rejected me," declares the LORD.
"You keep on backsliding.
So I will lay hands on you and destroy you;
I can no longer show compassion.
7I will winnow them with a winnowing fork
at the city gates of the land.
I will bring bereavement and destruction on my people,
for they have not changed their ways.
8I will make their widows more numerous
than the sand of the sea.
At midday I will bring a destroyer
against the mothers of their young men;
suddenly I will bring down on them
anguish and terror.
9The mother of seven will grow faint
and breathe her last.
Her sun will set while it is still day;
she will be disgraced and humiliated.
I will put the survivors to the sword
before their enemies,"
declares the LORD.

10Alas, my mother, that you gave me birth,
a man with whom the whole land strives and contends!
I have neither lent nor borrowed,
yet everyone curses me.

11The LORD said,

"Surely I will deliver you for a good purpose;
surely I will make your enemies plead with you
in times of disaster and times of distress.

12"Can a man break iron—
iron from the north—or bronze?
13Your wealth and your treasures
I will give as plunder, without charge,
because of all your sins
throughout your country.
14I will enslave you to your enemies
in a land you do not know,
for my anger will kindle a fire
that will burn against you."

15You understand, O LORD;
remember me and care for me.
Avenge me on my persecutors.
You are long-suffering—do not take me away;
think of how I suffer reproach for your sake.
16When your words came, I ate them;
they were my joy and my heart's delight,

for I bear your name,
O LORD God Almighty.
17 I never sat in the company of
revellers,
never made merry with them;
I sat alone because your hand was on
me
and you had filled me with
indignation.
18 Why is my pain unending
and my wound grievous and
incurable?
Will you be to me like a deceptive
brook,
like a spring that fails?

19 Therefore this is what the LORD
says:

"If you repent, I will restore you
that you may serve me;
if you utter worthy, not worthless,
words,
you will be my spokesman.
Let this people turn to you,
but you must not turn to them.
20 I will make you a wall to this people,
a fortified wall of bronze;
they will fight against you
but will not overcome you,
for I am with you
to rescue and save you,"
declares the LORD.
21 "I will save you from the hands of the
wicked
and redeem you from the grasp of
the cruel."

NEW TESTAMENT READING
Colossians 3:1–4:1

Rules for Holy Living

3 Since, then, you have been raised
with Christ, set your hearts on
things above, where Christ is seated at
the right hand of God. 2 Set your minds
on things above, not on earthly things.
3 For you died, and your life is now
hidden with Christ in God. 4 When
Christ, who is your life, appears, then
you also will appear with him in glory.
5 Put to death, therefore, whatever
belongs to your earthly nature: sexual
immorality, impurity, lust, evil desires
and greed, which is idolatry. 6 Because
of these, the wrath of God is coming.
7 You used to walk in these ways, in the
life you once lived. 8 But now you must
rid yourselves of all such things as these:
anger, rage, malice, slander and filthy
language from your lips. 9 Do not lie to
each other, since you have taken off
your old self with its practices 10 and
have put on the new self, which is being
renewed in knowledge in the image of
its Creator. 11 Here there is no Greek or
Jew, circumcised or uncircumcised,
barbarian, Scythian, slave or free, but
Christ is all, and is in all.
12 Therefore, as God's chosen people,
holy and dearly loved, clothe yourselves
with compassion, kindness, humility,
gentleness and patience. 13 Bear with
each other and forgive whatever griev-
ances you may have against one
another. Forgive as the Lord forgave
you. 14 And over all these virtues put on
love, which binds them all together in
perfect unity.
15 Let the peace of Christ rule in your
hearts, since as members of one body
you were called to peace. And be thankful. 16 Let the word of Christ dwell in you
richly as you teach and admonish one
another with all wisdom, and as you sing
psalms, hymns and spiritual songs with
gratitude in your hearts to God. 17 And
whatever you do, whether in word or
deed, do it all in the name of the Lord
Jesus, giving thanks to God the Father
through him.

Rules for Christian Households

18 Wives, submit to your husbands, as
is fitting in the Lord.
19 Husbands, love your wives and do
not be harsh with them.
20 Children, obey your parents in
everything, for this pleases the Lord.
21 Fathers, do not embitter your children, or they will become discouraged.

[22]Slaves, obey your earthly masters in everything; and do it, not only when their eye is on you and to win their favour, but with sincerity of heart and reverence for the Lord. [23]Whatever you do, work at it with all your heart, as working for the Lord, not for men, [24]since you know that you will receive an inheritance from the Lord as a reward. It is the Lord Christ you are serving. [25]Anyone who does wrong will be repaid for his wrong, and there is no favouritism.

4 Masters, provide your slaves with what is right and fair, because you know that you also have a Master in heaven.

READING FROM PROVERBS
Proverbs 24:15–22

[15]Do not lie in wait like an outlaw
against a righteous man's house,
do not raid his dwelling-place;
[16]for though a righteous man falls seven times, he rises again,
but the wicked are brought down by calamity.

[17]Do not gloat when your enemy falls;
when he stumbles, do not let your heart rejoice,
[18]or the LORD will see and disapprove
and turn his wrath away from him.

[19]Do not fret because of evil men
or be envious of the wicked,
[20]for the evil man has no future hope,
and the lamp of the wicked will be snuffed out.

[21]Fear the LORD and the king, my son,
and do not join with the rebellious,
[22]for those two will send sudden destruction upon them,
and who knows what calamities they can bring?

DAY 281

OCTOBER 8

OLD TESTAMENT READING
Jeremiah 16:1–17:27

Day of Disaster

16 Then the word of the LORD came to me: [2]"You must not marry and have sons or daughters in this place." [3]For this is what the LORD says about the sons and daughters born in this land and about the women who are their mothers and the men who are their fathers: [4]"They will die of deadly diseases. They will not be mourned or buried but will be like refuse lying on the ground. They will perish by sword and famine, and their dead bodies will become food for the birds of the air and the beasts of the earth."

[5]For this is what the LORD says: "Do not enter a house where there is a funeral meal; do not go to mourn or show sympathy, because I have withdrawn my blessing, my love and my pity from this people," declares the LORD. [6]"Both high and low will die in this land. They will not be buried or mourned, and no-one will cut himself or shave his head for them. [7]No-one will offer food to comfort those who mourn for the dead—not even for a father or a mother —nor will anyone give them a drink to console them.

[8]"And do not enter a house where there is feasting and sit down to eat and drink. [9]For this is what the LORD Almighty, the God of Israel, says: Before your eyes and in your days I will bring an end to the sounds of joy and gladness and to the voices of bride and bridegroom in this place.

10"When you tell these people all this
and they ask you, 'Why has the LORD
decreed such a great disaster against us?
What wrong have we done? What sin
have we committed against the LORD
our God?' 11then say to them, 'It is
because your fathers forsook me,' declares the LORD, 'and followed other
gods and served and worshipped them.
They forsook me and did not keep my
law. 12But you have behaved more
wickedly than your fathers. See how
each of you is following the stubbornness of his evil heart instead of obeying
me. 13So I will throw you out of this land
into a land neither you nor your fathers
have known, and there you will serve
other gods day and night, for I will show
you no favour.'

14"However, the days are coming,"
declares the LORD, "when men will no
longer say, 'As surely as the LORD lives,
who brought the Israelites up out of
Egypt,' 15but they will say, 'As surely as
the LORD lives, who brought the
Israelites up out of the land of the north
and out of all the countries where he
had banished them.' For I will restore
them to the land I gave to their forefathers.

16"But now I will send for many
fishermen," declares the LORD, "and
they will catch them. After that I will
send for many hunters, and they will
hunt them down on every mountain and
hill and from the crevices of the rocks.
17My eyes are on all their ways; they are
not hidden from me, nor is their sin
concealed from my eyes. 18I will repay
them double for their wickedness and
their sin, because they have defiled my
land with the lifeless forms of their vile
images and have filled my inheritance
with their detestable idols."

19O LORD, my strength and my
fortress,
my refuge in time of distress,
to you the nations will come
from the ends of the earth and say,
"Our fathers possessed nothing but
false gods,
worthless idols that did them no
good.
20Do men make their own gods?
Yes, but they are not gods!"

21"Therefore I will teach them—
this time I will teach them
my power and might.
Then they will know
that my name is the LORD.

17 "Judah's sin is engraved with an
iron tool,
inscribed with a flint point,
on the tablets of their hearts
and on the horns of their altars.
2Even their children remember
their altars and Asherah poles
beside the spreading trees
and on the high hills.
3My mountain in the land
and your wealth and all your
treasures
I will give away as plunder,
together with your high places,
because of sin throughout your
country.
4Through your own fault you will lose
the inheritance I gave you.
I will enslave you to your enemies
in a land you do not know,
for you have kindled my anger,
and it will burn for ever."

5This is what the LORD says:

"Cursed is the one who trusts in man,
who depends on flesh for his
strength
and whose heart turns away from
the LORD.
6He will be like a bush in the
wastelands;
he will not see prosperity when it
comes.
He will dwell in the parched places of
the desert,
in a salt land where no-one lives.

7"But blessed is the man who trusts in
the LORD,
whose confidence is in him.

8 He will be like a tree planted by the water
that sends out its roots by the stream.
It does not fear when heat comes;
its leaves are always green.
It has no worries in a year of drought
and never fails to bear fruit."

9 The heart is deceitful above all things
and beyond cure.
Who can understand it?

10 "I the LORD search the heart
and examine the mind,
to reward a man according to his conduct,
according to what his deeds deserve."

11 Like a partridge that hatches eggs it did not lay
is the man who gains riches by unjust means.
When his life is half gone, they will desert him,
and in the end he will prove to be a fool.

12 A glorious throne, exalted from the beginning,
is the place of our sanctuary.
13 O LORD, the hope of Israel,
all who forsake you will be put to shame.
Those who turn away from you will be written in the dust
because they have forsaken the LORD,
the spring of living water.

14 Heal me, O LORD, and I shall be healed;
save me and I shall be saved,
for you are the one I praise.
15 They keep saying to me,
"Where is the word of the LORD?
Let it now be fulfilled!"
16 I have not run away from being your shepherd;
you know I have not desired the day of despair.
What passes my lips is open before you.
17 Do not be a terror to me;
you are my refuge in the day of disaster.
18 Let my persecutors be put to shame,
but keep me from shame;
let them be terrified,
but keep me from terror.
Bring on them the day of disaster;
destroy them with double destruction.

Keeping the Sabbath Holy

19 This is what the LORD said to me:
"Go and stand at the gate of the people,
through which the kings of Judah go in
and out; stand also at all the other gates
of Jerusalem. 20 Say to them, 'Hear the
word of the LORD, O kings of Judah and
all people of Judah and everyone living
in Jerusalem who come through these
gates. 21 This is what the LORD says: Be
careful not to carry a load on the Sabbath day or bring it through the gates of
Jerusalem. 22 Do not bring a load out of
your houses or do any work on the
Sabbath, but keep the Sabbath day
holy, as I commanded your forefathers.
23 Yet they did not listen or pay attention; they were stiff-necked and would
not listen or respond to discipline. 24 But
if you are careful to obey me, declares
the LORD, and bring no load through
the gates of this city on the Sabbath, but
keep the Sabbath day holy by not doing
any work on it, 25 then kings who sit on
David's throne will come through the
gates of this city with their officials.
They and their officials will come riding
in chariots and on horses, accompanied
by the men of Judah and those living in
Jerusalem, and this city will be inhabited for ever. 26 People will come from
the towns of Judah and the villages
around Jerusalem, from the territory of
Benjamin and the western foothills,
from the hill country and the Negev,
bringing burnt offerings and sacrifices,
grain offerings, incense and thank-
offerings to the house of the LORD.

27But if you do not obey me to keep the
Sabbath day holy by not carrying any
load as you come through the gates of
Jerusalem on the Sabbath day, then I
will kindle an unquenchable fire in the
gates of Jerusalem that will consume
her fortresses.'"

NEW TESTAMENT READING
Colossians 4:2–18

Further Instructions

2Devote yourselves to prayer, being
watchful and thankful. 3And pray for
us, too, that God may open a door for
our message, so that we may proclaim
the mystery of Christ, for which I am in
chains. 4Pray that I may proclaim it
clearly, as I should. 5Be wise in the way
you act towards outsiders; make the
most of every opportunity. 6Let your
conversation be always full of grace,
seasoned with salt, so that you may
know how to answer everyone.

Final Greetings

7Tychicus will tell you all the news
about me. He is a dear brother, a faithful minister and fellow-servant in the
Lord. 8I am sending him to you for the
express purpose that you may know
about our circumstances and that he
may encourage your hearts. 9He is
coming with Onesimus, our faithful
and dear brother, who is one of you.
They will tell you everything that is
happening here.

10My fellow-prisoner Aristarchus
sends you his greetings, as does Mark,
the cousin of Barnabas. (You have received instructions about him; if he
comes to you, welcome him.) 11Jesus,
who is called Justus, also sends greetings. These are the only Jews among my
fellow-workers for the kingdom of God,
and they have proved a comfort to me.
12Epaphras, who is one of you and a
servant of Christ Jesus, sends greetings.
He is always wrestling in prayer for you,
that you may stand firm in all the will of
God, mature and fully assured. 13I
vouch for him that he is working hard
for you and for those at Laodicea and
Hierapolis. 14Our dear friend Luke, the
doctor, and Demas send greetings.
15Give my greetings to the brothers at
Laodicea, and to Nympha and the
church in her house.

16After this letter has been read to
you, see that it is also read in the church
of the Laodiceans and that you in turn
read the letter from Laodicea.

17Tell Archippus: "See to it that you
complete the work you have received in
the Lord."

18I, Paul, write this greeting in my
own hand. Remember my chains.
Grace be with you.

READING FROM PSALMS
Psalm 118:17–29

17I will not die but live,
and will proclaim what the LORD
has done.
18The LORD has chastened me severely,
but he has not given me over to
death.

19Open for me the gates of
righteousness;
I will enter and give thanks to the
LORD.
20This is the gate of the LORD
through which the righteous may
enter.
21I will give you thanks, for you
answered me;
you have become my salvation.

22The stone the builders rejected
has become the capstone;
23the LORD has done this,
and it is marvellous in our eyes.
24This is the day the LORD has made;
let us rejoice and be glad in it.

25O LORD, save us;
O LORD, grant us success.
26Blessed is he who comes in the name
of the LORD.

From the house of the LORD we
bless you.
27The LORD is God,
and he has made his light shine
upon us.
With boughs in hand, join in the
festal procession
up to the horns of the altar.
28You are my God, and I will give
thanks;
you are my God, and I will exalt
you.
29Give thanks to the LORD, for he is
good;
his love endures for ever.

DAY 282

OCTOBER 9

OLD TESTAMENT READING

Jeremiah 18:1–20:18

At the Potter's House

18 This is the word that came to
Jeremiah from the LORD: 2"Go
down to the potter's house, and there I
will give you my message." 3So I went
down to the potter's house, and I saw
him working at the wheel. 4But the
pot he was shaping from the clay was
marred in his hands; so the potter
formed it into another pot, shaping it as
seemed best to him.
5Then the word of the LORD came to
me: 6"O house of Israel, can I not do
with you as this potter does?" declares
the LORD. "Like clay in the hand of the
potter, so are you in my hand, O house
of Israel. 7If at any time I announce that
a nation or kingdom is to be uprooted,
torn down and destroyed, 8and if that
nation I warned repents of its evil, then
I will relent and not inflict on it the
disaster I had planned. 9And if at
another time I announce that a nation
or kingdom is to be built up and
planted, 10and if it does evil in my sight
and does not obey me, then I will reconsider the good I had intended to do
for it.
11"Now therefore say to the people of
Judah and those living in Jerusalem,
'This is what the LORD says: Look! I am
preparing a disaster for you and de-
vising a plan against you. So turn from
your evil ways, each one of you, and
reform your ways and your actions.'
12But they will reply, 'It's no use. We
will continue with our own plans; each
of us will follow the stubbornness of his
evil heart.'"

13Therefore this is what the LORD
says:

"Enquire among the nations:
Who has ever heard anything like
this?
A most horrible thing has been done
by Virgin Israel.
14Does the snow of Lebanon
ever vanish from its rocky slopes?
Do its cool waters from distant
sources
ever cease to flow?
15Yet my people have forgotten me;
they burn incense to worthless
idols,
which made them stumble in their
ways
and in the ancient paths.
They made them walk in bypaths
and on roads not built up.
16Their land will be laid waste,
an object of lasting scorn;
all who pass by will be appalled
and will shake their heads.
17Like a wind from the east,
I will scatter them before their
enemies;
I will show them my back and not my
face
in the day of their disaster."

18They said, "Come, let's make plans
against Jeremiah; for the teaching of the
law by the priest will not be lost, nor will
counsel from the wise, nor the word
from the prophets. So come, let's attack
him with our tongues and pay no attention to anything he says."

19Listen to me, O LORD;
  hear what my accusers are saying!
20Should good be repaid with evil?
  Yet they have dug a pit for me.
Remember that I stood before you
  and spoke on their behalf
  to turn your wrath away from
    them.
21So give their children over to famine;
  hand them over to the power of the
    sword.
Let their wives be made childless and
    widows;
  let their men be put to death,
  their young men slain by the sword
    in battle.
22Let a cry be heard from their houses
  when you suddenly bring invaders
    against them,
for they have dug a pit to capture me
  and have hidden snares for my
    feet.
23But you know, O LORD,
  all their plots to kill me.
Do not forgive their crimes
  or blot out their sins from your
    sight.
Let them be overthrown before you;
  deal with them in the time of your
    anger.

19 This is what the LORD says: "Go
and buy a clay jar from a potter.
Take along some of the elders of the
people and of the priests 2and go out to
the Valley of Ben Hinnom, near the
entrance of the Potsherd Gate. There
proclaim the words I tell you, 3and say,
'Hear the word of the LORD, O kings of
Judah and people of Jerusalem. This is
what the LORD Almighty, the God of
Israel, says: Listen! I am going to bring
a disaster on this place that will make
the ears of everyone who hears of it
tingle. 4For they have forsaken me and
made this a place of foreign gods; they
have burned sacrifices in it to gods that
neither they nor their fathers nor the
kings of Judah ever knew, and they
have filled this place with the blood of
the innocent. 5They have built the high
places of Baal to burn their sons in the
fire as offerings to Baal—something I
did not command or mention, nor did it
enter my mind. 6So beware, the days
are coming, declares the LORD, when
people will no longer call this place
Topheth or the Valley of Ben Hinnom,
but the Valley of Slaughter.

7" 'In this place I will ruin the plans of
Judah and Jerusalem. I will make them
fall by the sword before their enemies,
at the hands of those who seek their
lives, and I will give their carcasses as
food to the birds of the air and the
beasts of the earth. 8I will devastate this
city and make it an object of scorn; all
who pass by will be appalled and will
scoff because of all its wounds. 9I will
make them eat the flesh of their sons
and daughters, and they will eat one
another's flesh during the stress of the
siege imposed on them by the enemies
who seek their lives.'

10"Then break the jar while those
who go with you are watching, 11and say
to them, 'This is what the LORD Almighty says: I will smash this nation and
this city just as this potter's jar is
smashed and cannot be repaired. They
will bury the dead in Topheth until
there is no more room. 12This is what I
will do to this place and to those who
live here, declares the LORD. I will
make this city like Topheth. 13The
houses in Jerusalem and those of the
kings of Judah will be defiled like this
place, Topheth—all the houses where
they burned incense on the roofs to all
the starry hosts and poured out drink
offerings to other gods.' "

14Jeremiah then returned from
Topheth, where the LORD had sent him
to prophesy, and stood in the court of
the LORD's temple and said to all the
people, 15"This is what the LORD

Almighty, the God of Israel, says: 'Listen! I am going to bring on this city and
the villages around it every disaster I
pronounced against them, because they
were stiff-necked and would not listen
to my words.'"

Jeremiah and Pashhur

20 When the priest Pashhur son of
Immer, the chief officer in the
temple of the LORD, heard Jeremiah
prophesying these things, 2he had Jeremiah the prophet beaten and put in the
stocks at the Upper Gate of Benjamin
at the LORD's temple. 3The next day,
when Pashhur released him from the
stocks, Jeremiah said to him, "The
LORD's name for you is not Pashhur, but
Magor-Missabib. 4For this is what the
LORD says: 'I will make you a terror to
yourself and to all your friends; with
your own eyes you will see them fall by
the sword of their enemies. I will hand
all Judah over to the king of Babylon,
who will carry them away to Babylon or
put them to the sword. 5I will hand over
to their enemies all the wealth of this
city—all its products, all its valuables
and all the treasures of the kings of
Judah. They will take it away as plunder
and carry it off to Babylon. 6And you,
Pashhur, and all who live in your house
will go into exile to Babylon. There you
will die and be buried, you and all your
friends to whom you have prophesied
lies.'"

Jeremiah's Complaint

7O LORD, you deceived me, and I was deceived;
you overpowered me and prevailed.
I am ridiculed all day long;
everyone mocks me.
8Whenever I speak, I cry out
proclaiming violence and destruction.
So the word of the LORD has brought me
insult and reproach all day long.
9But if I say, "I will not mention him
or speak any more in his name,"
his word is in my heart like a fire,
a fire shut up in my bones.
I am weary of holding it in;
indeed, I cannot.
10I hear many whispering,
"Terror on every side!
Report him! Let's report him!"
All my friends
are waiting for me to slip, saying,
"Perhaps he will be deceived;
then we will prevail over him
and take our revenge on him."

11But the LORD is with me like a mighty warrior;
so my persecutors will stumble and not prevail.
They will fail and be thoroughly disgraced;
their dishonour will never be forgotten.
12O LORD Almighty, you who examine the righteous
and probe the heart and mind,
let me see your vengeance upon them,
for to you I have committed my cause.

13Sing to the LORD!
Give praise to the LORD!
He rescues the life of the needy
from the hands of the wicked.

14Cursed be the day I was born!
May the day my mother bore me
not be blessed!
15Cursed be the man who brought my father the news,
who made him very glad, saying,
"A child is born to you—a son!"
16May that man be like the towns
the LORD overthrew without pity.
May he hear wailing in the morning,
a battle cry at noon.
17For he did not kill me in the womb,
with my mother as my grave,
her womb enlarged for ever.
18Why did I ever come out of the womb
to see trouble and sorrow
and to end my days in shame?

NEW TESTAMENT READING
1 Thessalonians 1:1–2:16

1 Paul, Silas and Timothy,

To the church of the Thessalonians in
God the Father and the Lord Jesus
Christ:

Grace and peace to you.

Thanksgiving for the Thessalonians' Faith

2We always thank God for all of you,
mentioning you in our prayers. 3We
continually remember before our God
and Father your work produced by
faith, your labour prompted by love,
and your endurance inspired by hope in
our Lord Jesus Christ.
4For we know, brothers loved by
God, that he has chosen you, 5because
our gospel came to you not simply with
words, but also with power, with the
Holy Spirit and with deep conviction.
You know how we lived among you for
your sake. 6You became imitators of us
and of the Lord; in spite of severe suffering, you welcomed the message with
the joy given by the Holy Spirit. 7And
so you became a model to all the believers in Macedonia and Achaia. 8The
Lord's message rang out from you not
only in Macedonia and Achaia—your
faith in God has become known everywhere. Therefore we do not need to say
anything about it, 9for they themselves
report what kind of reception you gave
us. They tell how you turned to God
from idols to serve the living and true
God, 10and to wait for his Son from
heaven, whom he raised from the dead
—Jesus, who rescues us from the
coming wrath.

Paul's Ministry in Thessalonica

2 You know, brothers, that our visit
to you was not a failure. 2We had
previously suffered and been insulted in
Philippi, as you know, but with the help
of our God we dared to tell you his
gospel in spite of strong opposition.
3For the appeal we make does not
spring from error or impure motives,
nor are we trying to trick you. 4On the
contrary, we speak as men approved by
God to be entrusted with the gospel.
We are not trying to please men but
God, who tests our hearts. 5You know
we never used flattery, nor did we put
on a mask to cover up greed—God is
our witness. 6We were not looking for
praise from men, not from you or anyone else.
As apostles of Christ we could have
been a burden to you, 7but we were
gentle among you, like a mother caring
for her little children. 8We loved you so
much that we were delighted to share
with you not only the gospel of God but
our lives as well, because you had become so dear to us. 9Surely you remember, brothers, our toil and hardship; we
worked night and day in order not to be
a burden to anyone while we preached
the gospel of God to you.
10You are witnesses, and so is God, of
how holy, righteous and blameless we
were among you who believed. 11For
you know that we dealt with each of
you as a father deals with his own
children, 12encouraging, comforting and
urging you to live lives worthy of God,
who calls you into his kingdom and
glory.
13And we also thank God continually
because, when you received the word of
God, which you heard from us, you
accepted it not as the word of men, but
as it actually is, the word of God, which
is at work in you who believe. 14For you,
brothers, became imitators of God's
churches in Judea, which are in Christ
Jesus: You suffered from your own
countrymen the same things those
churches suffered from the Jews, 15who
killed the Lord Jesus and the prophets
and also drove us out. They displease
God and are hostile to all men 16in their
effort to keep us from speaking to the
Gentiles so that they may be saved. In

this way they always heap up their sins
to the limit. The wrath of God has come
upon them at last.

READING FROM PSALMS
Psalm 119:1–8

א Aleph

1Blessed are they whose ways are
blameless,
who walk according to the law of
the LORD.
2Blessed are they who keep his
statutes
and seek him with all their heart.
3They do nothing wrong;
they walk in his ways.
4You have laid down precepts
that are to be fully obeyed.
5Oh, that my ways were steadfast
in obeying your decrees!
6Then I would not be put to shame
when I consider all your
commands.
7I will praise you with an upright heart
as I learn your righteous laws.
8I will obey your decrees;
do not utterly forsake me.

DAY 283

OCTOBER 10

OLD TESTAMENT READING
Jeremiah 21:1–23:8

God Rejects Zedekiah's Request

21 The word came to Jeremiah
from the LORD when King Zedekiah sent to him Pashhur son of Malkijah and the priest Zephaniah son of
Maaseiah. They said: 2"Enquire now of
the LORD for us because Nebuchadnezzar king of Babylon is attacking us.
Perhaps the LORD will perform wonders
for us as in times past so that he will
withdraw from us."
3But Jeremiah answered them, "Tell
Zedekiah, 4'This is what the LORD, the
God of Israel, says: I am about to turn
against you the weapons of war that are
in your hands, which you are using to
fight the king of Babylon and the
Babylonians who are outside the wall
besieging you. And I will gather them
inside this city. 5I myself will fight
against you with an outstretched hand
and a mighty arm in anger and fury and
great wrath. 6I will strike down those
who live in this city—both men and
animals—and they will die of a terrible
plague. 7After that, declares the LORD,
I will hand over Zedekiah king of
Judah, his officials and the people in this
city who survive the plague, sword and
famine, to Nebuchadnezzar king of
Babylon and to their enemies who seek
their lives. He will put them to the
sword; he will show them no mercy or
pity or compassion.'
8"Furthermore, tell the people, 'This
is what the LORD says: See, I am setting
before you the way of life and the way of
death. 9Whoever stays in this city will
die by the sword, famine or plague. But
whoever goes out and surrenders to the
Babylonians who are besieging you will
live; he will escape with his life. 10I have
determined to do this city harm and not
good, declares the LORD. It will be
given into the hands of the king of Babylon, and he will destroy it with fire.'
11"Moreover, say to the royal house
of Judah, 'Hear the word of the LORD;
12O house of David, this is what the
LORD says:

"'Administer justice every morning;
rescue from the hand of his
oppressor
the one who has been robbed,

or my wrath will break out and burn
like fire
because of the evil you have
done—
burn with no-one to quench it.
13I am against you, ⌞Jerusalem,⌟
you who live above this valley
on the rocky plateau,
declares the LORD—
you who say, "Who can come against
us?
Who can enter our refuge?"
14I will punish you as your deeds
deserve,
declares the LORD.
I will kindle a fire in your forests
that will consume everything
around you.'"

Judgment Against Evil Kings

22 This is what the LORD says: "Go
down to the palace of the king of
Judah and proclaim this message there:
2'Hear the word of the LORD, O king of
Judah, you who sit on David's throne
—you, your officials and your people
who come through these gates. 3This is
what the LORD says: Do what is just
and right. Rescue from the hand of
his oppressor the one who has been
robbed. Do no wrong or violence to the
alien, the fatherless or the widow, and
do not shed innocent blood in this place.
4For if you are careful to carry out these
commands, then kings who sit on
David's throne will come through the
gates of this palace, riding in chariots
and on horses, accompanied by their
officials and their people. 5But if you do
not obey these commands, declares the
LORD, I swear by myself that this palace
will become a ruin.'"
6For this is what the LORD says about
the palace of the king of Judah:

"Though you are like Gilead to me,
like the summit of Lebanon,
I will surely make you like a desert,
like towns not inhabited.
7I will send destroyers against you,
each man with his weapons,
and they will cut up your fine cedar
beams
and throw them into the fire.

8"People from many nations will pass
by this city and will ask one another,
'Why has the LORD done such a thing to
this great city?' 9And the answer will be:
'Because they have forsaken the covenant of the LORD their God and have
worshipped and served other gods.'"

10Do not weep for the dead ⌞king⌟ or
mourn his loss;
rather, weep bitterly for him who is
exiled,
because he will never return
nor see his native land again.

11For this is what the LORD says about
Shallum son of Josiah, who succeeded
his father as king of Judah but has gone
from this place: "He will never return.
12He will die in the place where they
have led him captive; he will not see this
land again."

13"Woe to him who builds his palace by
unrighteousness,
his upper rooms by injustice,
making his countrymen work for
nothing,
not paying them for their labour.
14He says, 'I will build myself a great
palace
with spacious upper rooms.'
So he makes large windows in it,
panels it with cedar
and decorates it in red.

15Does it make you a king
to have more and more cedar?
Did not your father have food and
drink?
He did what was right and just,
so all went well with him.
16He defended the cause of the poor
and needy,
and so all went well.
Is that not what it means to know
me?"
declares the LORD.

17"But your eyes and your heart
are set only on dishonest gain,
on shedding innocent blood
and on oppression and extortion."

18Therefore this is what the LORD says
about Jehoiakim son of Josiah king of
Judah:

"They will not mourn for him:
'Alas, my brother! Alas, my sister!'
They will not mourn for him:
'Alas, my master! Alas, his
splendour!'
19He will have the burial of a donkey—
dragged away and thrown
outside the gates of Jerusalem."

20"Go up to Lebanon and cry out,
let your voice be heard in Bashan,
cry out from Abarim,
for all your allies are crushed.
21I warned you when you felt secure,
but you said, 'I will not listen!'
This has been your way from your
youth;
you have not obeyed me.
22The wind will drive all your
shepherds away,
and your allies will go into exile.
Then you will be ashamed and
disgraced
because of all your wickedness.
23You who live in 'Lebanon',
who are nestled in cedar buildings,
how you will groan when pangs come
upon you,
pain like that of a woman in
labour!

24"As surely as I live," declares the
LORD, "even if you, Jehoiachin son of
Jehoiakim king of Judah, were a signet
ring on my right hand, I would still pull
you off. 25I will hand you over to those
who seek your life, those you fear—to
Nebuchadnezzar king of Babylon and
to the Babylonians. 26I will hurl you and
the mother who gave you birth into
another country, where neither of you
was born, and there you both will die.
27You will never come back to the land
you long to return to."

28Is this man Jehoiachin a despised,
broken pot,
an object no-one wants?
Why will he and his children be
hurled out,
cast into a land they do not know?
29O land, land, land,
hear the word of the LORD!
30This is what the LORD says:
"Record this man as if childless,
a man who will not prosper in his
lifetime,
for none of his offspring will prosper,
none will sit on the throne of David
or rule any more in Judah."

The Righteous Branch

23 "Woe to the shepherds who are
destroying and scattering the
sheep of my pasture!" declares the
LORD. 2Therefore this is what the LORD,
the God of Israel, says to the shepherds
who tend my people: "Because you
have scattered my flock and driven
them away and have not bestowed care
on them, I will bestow punishment on
you for the evil you have done," declares the LORD. 3"I myself will gather
the remnant of my flock out of all the
countries where I have driven them and
will bring them back to their pasture,
where they will be fruitful and increase
in number. 4I will place shepherds over
them who will tend them, and they will
no longer be afraid or terrified, nor will
any be missing," declares the LORD.

5"The days are coming," declares the
LORD,
"when I will raise up to David a
righteous Branch,
a King who will reign wisely
and do what is just and right in the
land.
6In his days Judah will be saved
and Israel will live in safety.
This is the name by which he will be
called:
The LORD Our Righteousness.

7"So then, the days are coming," declares the LORD, "when people will no

longer say, 'As surely as the LORD lives,
who brought the Israelites up out of
Egypt,' 8but they will say, 'As surely as
the LORD lives, who brought the descendants of Israel up out of the land of
the north and out of all the countries
where he had banished them.' Then
they will live in their own land."

NEW TESTAMENT READING
1 Thessalonians 2:17–3:13

Paul's Longing to See the Thessalonians

17But, brothers, when we were torn
away from you for a short time (in person, not in thought), out of our intense
longing we made every effort to see
you. 18For we wanted to come to you
—certainly I, Paul, did, again and again
—but Satan stopped us. 19For what is
our hope, our joy, or the crown in which
we will glory in the presence of our Lord
Jesus Christ when he comes? Is it not
you? 20Indeed, you are our glory and
joy.

3 So when we could stand it no
longer, we thought it best to be left
by ourselves in Athens. 2We sent
Timothy, who is our brother and God's
fellow-worker in spreading the gospel of
Christ, to strengthen and encourage
you in your faith, 3so that no-one would
be unsettled by these trials. You know
quite well that we were destined for
them. 4In fact, when we were with you,
we kept telling you that we would be
persecuted. And it turned out that way,
as you well know. 5For this reason,
when I could stand it no longer, I sent to
find out about your faith. I was afraid
that in some way the tempter might
have tempted you and our efforts might
have been useless.

Timothy's Encouraging Report

6But Timothy has just now come to us
from you and has brought good news
about your faith and love. He has told
us that you always have pleasant
memories of us and that you long to see
us, just as we also long to see you.
7Therefore, brothers, in all our distress
and persecution we were encouraged
about you because of your faith. 8For
now we really live, since you are standing firm in the Lord. 9How can we thank
God enough for you in return for all the
joy we have in the presence of our God
because of you? 10Night and day we
pray most earnestly that we may see you
again and supply what is lacking in your
faith.

11Now may our God and Father himself and our Lord Jesus clear the way for
us to come to you. 12May the Lord make
your love increase and overflow for
each other and for everyone else, just as
ours does for you. 13May he strengthen
your hearts so that you will be blameless
and holy in the presence of our God and
Father when our Lord Jesus comes with
all his holy ones.

READING FROM PSALMS
Psalm 119:9–16

ב Beth

9How can a young man keep his way
pure?
By living according to your word.
10I seek you with all my heart;
do not let me stray from your
commands.
11I have hidden your word in my heart
that I might not sin against you.
12Praise be to you, O LORD;
teach me your decrees.
13With my lips I recount
all the laws that come from your
mouth.
14I rejoice in following your statutes
as one rejoices in great riches.
15I meditate on your precepts
and consider your ways.
16I delight in your decrees;
I will not neglect your word.

OCTOBER 11

OLD TESTAMENT READING
Jeremiah 23:9–25:14

Lying Prophets

9Concerning the prophets:

My heart is broken within me;
all my bones tremble.
I am like a drunken man,
like a man overcome by wine,
because of the LORD
and his holy words.
10The land is full of adulterers;
because of the curse the land lies parched
and the pastures in the desert are withered.
The ⌞prophets⌟ follow an evil course
and use their power unjustly.

11"Both prophet and priest are godless;
even in my temple I find their wickedness,"
declares the LORD.
12"Therefore their path will become slippery;
they will be banished to darkness
and there they will fall.
I will bring disaster on them
in the year they are punished,"
declares the LORD.

13"Among the prophets of Samaria
I saw this repulsive thing:
They prophesied by Baal
and led my people Israel astray.
14And among the prophets of Jerusalem
I have seen something horrible:
They commit adultery and live a lie.
They strengthen the hands of evildoers,
so that no-one turns from his wickedness.
They are all like Sodom to me;
the people of Jerusalem are like Gomorrah."

15Therefore, this is what the LORD Almighty says concerning the prophets:

"I will make them eat bitter food
and drink poisoned water,
because from the prophets of Jerusalem
ungodliness has spread throughout the land."

16This is what the LORD Almighty says:

"Do not listen to what the prophets are prophesying to you;
they fill you with false hopes.
They speak visions from their own minds,
not from the mouth of the LORD.
17They keep saying to those who despise me,
'The LORD says: You will have peace.'
And to all who follow the stubbornness of their hearts
they say, 'No harm will come to you.'
18But which of them has stood in the council of the LORD
to see or to hear his word?
Who has listened and heard his word?
19See, the storm of the LORD
will burst out in wrath,
a whirlwind swirling down
on the heads of the wicked.
20The anger of the LORD will not turn back
until he fully accomplishes
the purposes of his heart.
In days to come
you will understand it clearly.
21I did not send these prophets,
yet they have run with their message;
I did not speak to them,
yet they have prophesied.
22But if they had stood in my council,

they would have proclaimed my
words to my people
and would have turned them from
their evil ways
and from their evil deeds.

23"Am I only a God nearby,"
declares the LORD,
"and not a God far away?
24Can anyone hide in secret places
so that I cannot see him?"
declares the LORD.
"Do not I fill heaven and earth?"
declares the LORD.

25"I have heard what the prophets say
who prophesy lies in my name. They
say, 'I had a dream! I had a dream!'
26How long will this continue in the
hearts of these lying prophets, who
prophesy the delusions of their own
minds? 27They think the dreams they
tell one another will make my people
forget my name, just as their fathers
forgot my name through Baal worship.
28Let the prophet who has a dream tell
his dream, but let the one who has my
word speak it faithfully. For what has
straw to do with grain?" declares the
LORD. 29"Is not my word like fire,"
declares the LORD, "and like a hammer
that breaks a rock in pieces?
30"Therefore," declares the LORD, "I
am against the prophets who steal from
one another words supposedly from
me. 31Yes," declares the LORD, "I am
against the prophets who wag their own
tongues and yet declare, 'The LORD
declares.' 32Indeed, I am against those
who prophesy false dreams," declares
the LORD. "They tell them and lead my
people astray with their reckless lies,
yet I did not send or appoint them. They
do not benefit these people in the
least," declares the LORD.

False Oracles and False Prophets

33"When these people, or a prophet
or a priest, ask you, 'What is the oracle
of the LORD?' say to them, 'What
oracle? I will forsake you, declares the
LORD.' 34If a prophet or a priest or
anyone else claims, 'This is the oracle of
the LORD,' I will punish that man and
his household. 35This is what each of
you keeps on saying to his friend or
relative: 'What is the LORD's answer?'
or 'What has the LORD spoken?' 36But
you must not mention 'the oracle of the
LORD' again, because every man's own
word becomes his oracle and so you
distort the words of the living God, the
LORD Almighty, our God. 37This is
what you keep saying to a prophet:
'What is the LORD's answer to you?'
or 'What has the LORD spoken?'
38Although you claim, 'This is the
oracle of the LORD,' this is what the
LORD says: You used the words, 'This
is the oracle of the LORD,' even though
I told you that you must not claim, 'This
is the oracle of the LORD.' 39Therefore,
I will surely forget you and cast you
out of my presence along with the city
I gave to you and your fathers. 40I will
bring upon you everlasting disgrace
—everlasting shame that will not be
forgotten."

Two Baskets of Figs

24 After Jehoiachin son of
Jehoiakim king of Judah and the
officials, the craftsmen and the artisans
of Judah were carried into exile from
Jerusalem to Babylon by Nebuchadnezzar king of Babylon, the LORD showed
me two baskets of figs placed in front of
the temple of the LORD. 2One basket
had very good figs, like those that ripen
early; the other basket had very poor
figs, so bad that they could not be eaten.
3Then the LORD asked me, "What do
you see, Jeremiah?"

"Figs," I answered. "The good ones
are very good, but the poor ones are so
bad that they cannot be eaten."

4Then the word of the LORD came to
me: 5"This is what the LORD, the God of
Israel, says: 'Like these good figs, I
regard as good the exiles from Judah,
whom I sent away from this place to the
land of the Babylonians. 6My eyes will

watch over them for their good, and I
will bring them back to this land. I will
build them up and not tear them down; I
will plant them and not uproot them.
7I will give them a heart to know me,
that I am the LORD. They will be my
people, and I will be their God, for they
will return to me with all their heart.
8" 'But like the poor figs, which are so
bad that they cannot be eaten,' says the
LORD, 'so will I deal with Zedekiah king
of Judah, his officials and the survivors
from Jerusalem, whether they remain in
this land or live in Egypt. 9I will make
them abhorrent and an offence to all the
kingdoms of the earth, a reproach and
a byword, an object of ridicule and
cursing, wherever I banish them. 10I will
send the sword, famine and plague
against them until they are destroyed
from the land I gave to them and their
fathers.' "

Seventy Years of Captivity

25 The word came to Jeremiah concerning all the people of Judah
in the fourth year of Jehoiakim son of
Josiah king of Judah, which was the first
year of Nebuchadnezzar king of Babylon. 2So Jeremiah the prophet said to
all the people of Judah and to all those
living in Jerusalem: 3For twenty-three
years—from the thirteenth year of
Josiah son of Amon king of Judah until
this very day—the word of the LORD
has come to me and I have spoken to
you again and again, but you have not
listened.
4And though the LORD has sent all his
servants the prophets to you again and
again, you have not listened or paid any
attention. 5They said, "Turn now, each
of you, from your evil ways and your
evil practices, and you can stay in the
land the LORD gave to you and your
fathers for ever and ever. 6Do not follow other gods to serve and worship
them; do not provoke me to anger with
what your hands have made. Then I will
not harm you."
7"But you did not listen to me," declares the LORD, "and you have provoked me with what your hands have
made, and you have brought harm to
yourselves."
8Therefore the LORD Almighty says
this: "Because you have not listened
to my words, 9I will summon all the
peoples of the north and my servant
Nebuchadnezzar king of Babylon," declares the LORD, "and I will bring them
against this land and its inhabitants and
against all the surrounding nations. I
will completely destroy them and make
them an object of horror and scorn, and
an everlasting ruin. 10I will banish from
them the sounds of joy and gladness,
the voices of bride and bridegroom, the
sound of millstones and the light of the
lamp. 11This whole country will become
a desolate wasteland, and these nations
will serve the king of Babylon for
seventy years.
12"But when the seventy years are
fulfilled, I will punish the king of Babylon and his nation, the land of the
Babylonians, for their guilt," declares
the LORD, "and will make it desolate for
ever. 13I will bring upon that land all the
things I have spoken against it, all that
are written in this book and prophesied
by Jeremiah against all the nations.
14They themselves will be enslaved by
many nations and great kings; I will
repay them according to their deeds and
the work of their hands."

NEW TESTAMENT READING
1 Thessalonians 4:1–18

Living to Please God

4 Finally, brothers, we instructed
you how to live in order to please
God, as in fact you are living. Now we
ask you and urge you in the Lord Jesus
to do this more and more. 2For you
know what instructions we gave you by
the authority of the Lord Jesus.
3It is God's will that you should be
sanctified: that you should avoid sexual
immorality; 4that each of you should

learn to control his own body in a way
that is holy and honourable, 5not in
passionate lust like the heathen, who do
not know God; 6and that in this matter
no-one should wrong his brother or take
advantage of him. The Lord will punish
men for all such sins, as we have already
told you and warned you. 7For God did
not call us to be impure, but to live a
holy life. 8Therefore, he who rejects
this instruction does not reject man but
God, who gives you his Holy Spirit.

9Now about brotherly love we do not
need to write to you, for you yourselves
have been taught by God to love each
other. 10And in fact, you do love all the
brothers throughout Macedonia. Yet
we urge you, brothers, to do so more
and more.

11Make it your ambition to lead a
quiet life, to mind your own business
and to work with your hands, just as we
told you, 12so that your daily life may
win the respect of outsiders and so that
you will not be dependent on anybody.

The Coming of the Lord

13Brothers, we do not want you to be
ignorant about those who fall asleep, or
to grieve like the rest of men, who have
no hope. 14We believe that Jesus died
and rose again and so we believe that
God will bring with Jesus those who
have fallen asleep in him. 15According
to the Lord's own word, we tell you that
we who are still alive, who are left till
the coming of the Lord, will certainly
not precede those who have fallen
asleep. 16For the Lord himself will come
down from heaven, with a loud command, with the voice of the archangel
and with the trumpet call of God, and
the dead in Christ will rise first. 17After
that, we who are still alive and are left
will be caught up together with them in
the clouds to meet the Lord in the air.
And so we will be with the Lord for
ever. 18Therefore encourage each other
with these words.

READING FROM PROVERBS

Proverbs 24:23–34

Further Sayings of the Wise

23These also are sayings of the wise:

To show partiality in judging is not
good:
24Whoever says to the guilty, "You are
innocent"—
peoples will curse him and nations
denounce him.
25But it will go well with those who
convict the guilty,
and rich blessing will come upon
them.

26An honest answer
is like a kiss on the lips.

27Finish your outdoor work
and get your fields ready;
after that, build your house.

28Do not testify against your neighbour
without cause,
or use your lips to deceive.
29Do not say, "I'll do to him as he has
done to me;
I'll pay that man back for what he
did."

30I went past the field of the sluggard,
past the vineyard of the man who
lacks judgment;
31thorns had come up everywhere,
the ground was covered with
weeds,
and the stone wall was in ruins.
32I applied my heart to what I observed
and learned a lesson from what I
saw:
33A little sleep, a little slumber,
a little folding of the hands to
rest—
34and poverty will come on you like a
bandit
and scarcity like an armed man.

DAY 285

OCTOBER 12

OLD TESTAMENT READING
Jeremiah 25:15–26:24

The Cup of God's Wrath

15This is what the LORD, the God of
Israel, said to me: "Take from my hand
this cup filled with the wine of my wrath
and make all the nations to whom I send
you drink it. 16When they drink it, they
will stagger and go mad because of the
sword I will send among them."
17So I took the cup from the LORD's
hand and made all the nations to whom
he sent me drink it: 18Jerusalem and the
towns of Judah, its kings and officials, to
make them a ruin and an object of
horror and scorn and cursing, as they
are today; 19Pharaoh king of Egypt, his
attendants, his officials and all his people, 20and all the foreign people there;
all the kings of Uz; all the kings of the
Philistines (those of Ashkelon, Gaza,
Ekron, and the people left at Ashdod);
21Edom, Moab and Ammon; 22all the
kings of Tyre and Sidon; the kings of the
coastlands across the sea; 23Dedan,
Tema, Buz and all who are in distant
places; 24all the kings of Arabia and all
the kings of the foreign people who live
in the desert; 25all the kings of Zimri,
Elam and Media; 26and all the kings of
the north, near and far, one after the
other—all the kingdoms on the face of
the earth. And after all of them, the
king of Sheshach will drink it too.
27"Then tell them, 'This is what the
LORD Almighty, the God of Israel, says:
Drink, get drunk and vomit, and fall to
rise no more because of the sword I will
send among you.' 28But if they refuse to
take the cup from your hand and drink,
tell them, 'This is what the LORD
Almighty says: You must drink it!
29See, I am beginning to bring disaster
on the city that bears my Name, and will
you indeed go unpunished? You will
not go unpunished, for I am calling
down a sword upon all who live on the
earth, declares the LORD Almighty.'
30"Now prophesy all these words
against them and say to them:

"'The LORD will roar from on high;
he will thunder from his holy
dwelling
and roar mightily against his land.
He will shout like those who tread
the grapes,
shout against all who live on the
earth.
31The tumult will resound to the ends
of the earth,
for the LORD will bring charges
against the nations;
he will bring judgment on all
mankind
and put the wicked to the sword,'"
declares the LORD.

32This is what the LORD Almighty
says:

"Look! Disaster is spreading
from nation to nation;
a mighty storm is rising
from the ends of the earth."

33At that time those slain by the LORD
will be everywhere—from one end of
the earth to the other. They will not be
mourned or gathered up or buried, but
will be like refuse lying on the ground.

34Weep and wail, you shepherds;
roll in the dust, you leaders of the
flock.
For your time to be slaughtered has
come;
you will fall and be shattered like
fine pottery.
35The shepherds will have nowhere to
flee,
the leaders of the flock no place to
escape.
36Hear the cry of the shepherds,

the wailing of the leaders of the
flock,
for the LORD is destroying their
pasture.
37The peaceful meadows will be laid
waste
because of the fierce anger of the
LORD.
38Like a lion he will leave his lair,
and their land will become desolate
because of the sword of the oppressor
and because of the LORD's fierce
anger.

Jeremiah Threatened With Death

26 Early in the reign of Jehoiakim
son of Josiah king of Judah, this
word came from the LORD: 2"This is
what the LORD says: Stand in the courtyard of the LORD's house and speak to
all the people of the towns of Judah who
come to worship in the house of the
LORD. Tell them everything I command
you; do not omit a word. 3Perhaps they
will listen and each will turn from his
evil way. Then I will relent and not
bring on them the disaster I was planning because of the evil they have done.
4Say to them, 'This is what the LORD
says: If you do not listen to me and
follow my law, which I have set before
you, 5and if you do not listen to the
words of my servants the prophets,
whom I have sent to you again and again
(though you have not listened), 6then I
will make this house like Shiloh and this
city an object of cursing among all the
nations of the earth.' "
7The priests, the prophets and all the
people heard Jeremiah speak these
words in the house of the LORD. 8But as
soon as Jeremiah finished telling all the
people everything the LORD had commanded him to say, the priests, the
prophets and all the people seized him
and said, "You must die! 9Why do you
prophesy in the LORD's name that this
house will be like Shiloh and this city
will be desolate and deserted?" And all
the people crowded around Jeremiah in
the house of the LORD.
10When the officials of Judah heard
about these things, they went up from
the royal palace to the house of the
LORD and took their places at the entrance of the New Gate of the LORD's
house. 11Then the priests and the
prophets said to the officials and all the
people, "This man should be sentenced
to death because he has prophesied
against this city. You have heard it with
your own ears!"
12Then Jeremiah said to all the officials and all the people: "The LORD
sent me to prophesy against this house
and this city all the things you have
heard. 13Now reform your ways and
your actions and obey the LORD your
God. Then the LORD will relent and not
bring the disaster he has pronounced
against you. 14As for me, I am in your
hands; do with me whatever you think is
good and right. 15Be assured, however,
that if you put me to death, you will
bring the guilt of innocent blood on
yourselves and on this city and on those
who live in it, for in truth the LORD has
sent me to you to speak all these words
in your hearing."
16Then the officials and all the people
said to the priests and the prophets,
"This man should not be sentenced to
death! He has spoken to us in the name
of the LORD our God."
17Some of the elders of the land
stepped forward and said to the entire
assembly of people, 18"Micah of
Moresheth prophesied in the days of
Hezekiah king of Judah. He told all the
people of Judah, 'This is what the LORD
Almighty says:

" 'Zion will be ploughed like a field,
Jerusalem will become a heap of
rubble,
the temple hill a mound overgrown
with thickets.'

19"Did Hezekiah king of Judah or anyone else in Judah put him to death? Did
not Hezekiah fear the LORD and seek
his favour? And did not the LORD relent, so that he did not bring the disaster
he pronounced against them? We are

about to bring a terrible disaster on
ourselves!"
20(Now Uriah son of Shemaiah from
Kiriath Jearim was another man who
prophesied in the name of the LORD; he
prophesied the same things against this
city and this land as Jeremiah did.
21When King Jehoiakim and all his
officers and officials heard his words,
the king sought to put him to death. But
Uriah heard of it and fled in fear to
Egypt. 22King Jehoiakim, however,
sent Elnathan son of Acbor to Egypt,
along with some other men. 23They
brought Uriah out of Egypt and took
him to King Jehoiakim, who had him
struck down with a sword and his body
thrown into the burial place of the
common people.)
24Furthermore, Ahikam son of
Shaphan supported Jeremiah, and so he
was not handed over to the people to be
put to death.

NEW TESTAMENT READING
1 Thessalonians 5:1–28

5 Now, brothers, about times and
dates we do not need to write to
you, 2for you know very well that the
day of the Lord will come like a thief in
the night. 3While people are saying,
"Peace and safety", destruction will
come on them suddenly, as labour pains
on a pregnant woman, and they will not
escape.
4But you, brothers, are not in darkness so that this day should surprise you
like a thief. 5You are all sons of the light
and sons of the day. We do not belong
to the night or to the darkness. 6So then,
let us not be like others, who are asleep,
but let us be alert and self-controlled.
7For those who sleep, sleep at night,
and those who get drunk, get drunk at
night. 8But since we belong to the day,
let us be self-controlled, putting on faith
and love as a breastplate, and the hope
of salvation as a helmet. 9For God did
not appoint us to suffer wrath but to
receive salvation through our Lord
Jesus Christ. 10He died for us so that,
whether we are awake or asleep, we
may live together with him. 11Therefore
encourage one another and build each
other up, just as in fact you are doing.

Final Instructions

12Now we ask you, brothers, to respect those who work hard among you,
who are over you in the Lord and who
admonish you. 13Hold them in the highest regard in love because of their work.
Live in peace with each other. 14And we
urge you, brothers, warn those who are
idle, encourage the timid, help the
weak, be patient with everyone. 15Make
sure that nobody pays back wrong for
wrong, but always try to be kind to each
other and to everyone else.
16Be joyful always; 17pray continually; 18give thanks in all circumstances,
for this is God's will for you in Christ
Jesus.
19Do not put out the Spirit's fire; 20do
not treat prophecies with contempt.
21Test everything. Hold on to the good.
22Avoid every kind of evil.
23May God himself, the God of
peace, sanctify you through and
through. May your whole spirit, soul
and body be kept blameless at the
coming of our Lord Jesus Christ. 24The
one who calls you is faithful and he will
do it.

25Brothers, pray for us. 26Greet all
the brothers with a holy kiss. 27I charge
you before the Lord to have this letter
read to all the brothers.
28The grace of our Lord Jesus Christ
be with you.

READING FROM PSALMS
Psalm 119:17–24

ג Gimel

17Do good to your servant, and I will
live;
I will obey your word.
18Open my eyes that I may see
wonderful things in your law.

[19]I am a stranger on earth;
do not hide your commands from
me.
[20]My soul is consumed with longing
for your laws at all times.
[21]You rebuke the arrogant, who are
cursed
and who stray from your
commands.
[22]Remove from me scorn and
contempt,
for I keep your statutes.
[23]Though rulers sit together and
slander me,
your servant will meditate on your
decrees.
[24]Your statutes are my delight;
they are my counsellors.

OCTOBER 13

DAY 286

OLD TESTAMENT READING

Jeremiah 27:1–29:23

Judah to Serve Nebuchadnezzar

27 Early in the reign of Zedekiah
son of Josiah king of Judah, this
word came to Jeremiah from the LORD:
[2]This is what the LORD said to me:
"Make a yoke out of straps and crossbars and put it on your neck. [3]Then send
word to the kings of Edom, Moab,
Ammon, Tyre and Sidon through the
envoys who have come to Jerusalem to
Zedekiah king of Judah. [4]Give them a
message for their masters and say, 'This
is what the LORD Almighty, the God of
Israel, says: "Tell this to your masters:
[5]With my great power and outstretched
arm I made the earth and its people and
the animals that are on it, and I give it to
anyone I please. [6]Now I will hand all
your countries over to my servant
Nebuchadnezzar king of Babylon; I will
make even the wild animals subject to
him. [7]All nations will serve him and his
son and his grandson until the time for
his land comes; then many nations and
great kings will subjugate him.

[8]" ' "If, however, any nation or kingdom will not serve Nebuchadnezzar
king of Babylon or bow its neck under
his yoke, I will punish that nation with
the sword, famine and plague, declares
the LORD, until I destroy it by his hand.
[9]So do not listen to your prophets, your
diviners, your interpreters of dreams,
your mediums or your sorcerers who
tell you, 'You will not serve the king of
Babylon.' [10]They prophesy lies to you
that will only serve to remove you far
from your lands; I will banish you and
you will perish. [11]But if any nation will
bow its neck under the yoke of the king
of Babylon and serve him, I will let
that nation remain in its own land to
till it and to live there, declares the
LORD." ' "

[12]I gave the same message to Zedekiah king of Judah. I said, "Bow your
neck under the yoke of the king of
Babylon; serve him and his people, and
you will live. [13]Why will you and your
people die by the sword, famine and
plague with which the LORD has
threatened any nation that will not
serve the king of Babylon? [14]Do not
listen to the words of the prophets who
say to you, 'You will not serve the king
of Babylon,' for they are prophesying
lies to you. [15]'I have not sent them,'
declares the LORD. 'They are prophesying lies in my name. Therefore, I will
banish you and you will perish, both
you and the prophets who prophesy to
you.' "

[16]Then I said to the priests and all
these people, "This is what the LORD
says: Do not listen to the prophets who
say, 'Very soon now the articles from
the LORD's house will be brought back

from Babylon.' They are prophesying
lies to you. 17Do not listen to them.
Serve the king of Babylon, and you will
live. Why should this city become a
ruin? 18If they are prophets and have
the word of the LORD, let them plead
with the LORD Almighty that the furnishings remaining in the house of the
LORD and in the palace of the king of
Judah and in Jerusalem not be taken to
Babylon. 19For this is what the LORD
Almighty says about the pillars, the
Sea, the movable stands and the other
furnishings that are left in this city,
20which Nebuchadnezzar king of Babylon did not take away when he carried
Jehoiachin son of Jehoiakim king of
Judah into exile from Jerusalem to
Babylon, along with all the nobles of
Judah and Jerusalem—21yes, this is
what the LORD Almighty, the God of
Israel, says about the things that are left
in the house of the LORD and in the
palace of the king of Judah and in Jerusalem: 22'They will be taken to Babylon
and there they will remain until the day
I come for them,' declares the LORD.
'Then I will bring them back and restore
them to this place.'"

The False Prophet Hananiah

28 In the fifth month of that same
year, the fourth year, early in
the reign of Zedekiah king of Judah, the
prophet Hananiah son of Azzur, who
was from Gibeon, said to me in the
house of the LORD in the presence of the
priests and all the people: 2"This is what
the LORD Almighty, the God of Israel,
says: 'I will break the yoke of the king of
Babylon. 3Within two years I will bring
back to this place all the articles of the
LORD's house that Nebuchadnezzar
king of Babylon removed from here and
took to Babylon. 4I will also bring back
to this place Jehoiachin son of
Jehoiakim king of Judah and all the
other exiles from Judah who went to
Babylon,' declares the LORD, 'for
I will break the yoke of the king of
Babylon.'"

5Then the prophet Jeremiah replied
to the prophet Hananiah before the
priests and all the people who were
standing in the house of the LORD. 6He
said, "Amen! May the LORD do so! May
the LORD fulfil the words you have
prophesied by bringing the articles of
the LORD's house and all the exiles
back to this place from Babylon.
7Nevertheless, listen to what I have to
say in your hearing and in the hearing of
all the people: 8From early times the
prophets who preceded you and me
have prophesied war, disaster and
plague against many countries and great
kingdoms. 9But the prophet who
prophesies peace will be recognised as
one truly sent by the LORD only if his
prediction comes true."

10Then the prophet Hananiah took
the yoke off the neck of the prophet
Jeremiah and broke it, 11and he said
before all the people, "This is what the
LORD says: 'In the same way will I break
the yoke of Nebuchadnezzar king of
Babylon off the neck of all the nations
within two years.'" At this, the prophet
Jeremiah went on his way.

12Shortly after the prophet Hananiah
had broken the yoke off the neck of the
prophet Jeremiah, the word of the
LORD came to Jeremiah: 13"Go and tell
Hananiah, 'This is what the LORD says:
You have broken a wooden yoke, but in
its place you will get a yoke of iron.
14This is what the LORD Almighty, the
God of Israel, says: I will put an iron
yoke on the necks of all these nations to
make them serve Nebuchadnezzar king
of Babylon, and they will serve him. I
will even give him control over the wild
animals.'"

15Then the prophet Jeremiah said to
Hananiah the prophet, "Listen, Hananiah! The LORD has not sent you, yet
you have persuaded this nation to trust
in lies. 16Therefore, this is what the
LORD says: 'I am about to remove you
from the face of the earth. This very
year you are going to die, because you
have preached rebellion against the
LORD.'"

17In the seventh month of that same
year, Hananiah the prophet died.

A Letter to the Exiles

29 This is the text of the letter that
the prophet Jeremiah sent from
Jerusalem to the surviving elders among
the exiles and to the priests, the
prophets and all the other people
Nebuchadnezzar had carried into exile
from Jerusalem to Babylon. 2(This was
after King Jehoiachin and the queen
mother, the court officials and the leaders of Judah and Jerusalem, the craftsmen and the artisans had gone into exile
from Jerusalem.) 3He entrusted the
letter to Elasah son of Shaphan and to
Gemariah son of Hilkiah, whom Zedekiah king of Judah sent to King
Nebuchadnezzar in Babylon. It said:

4This is what the LORD Almighty, the God of Israel, says to
all those I carried into exile from
Jerusalem to Babylon: 5"Build
houses and settle down; plant gardens and eat what they produce.
6Marry and have sons and daughters; find wives for your sons and
give your daughters in marriage, so
that they too may have sons and
daughters. Increase in number
there; do not decrease. 7Also, seek
the peace and prosperity of the city
to which I have carried you into
exile. Pray to the LORD for it, because if it prospers, you too will
prosper." 8Yes, this is what the
LORD Almighty, the God of Israel,
says: "Do not let the prophets and
diviners among you deceive you.
Do not listen to the dreams you
encourage them to have. 9They are
prophesying lies to you in my
name. I have not sent them," declares the LORD.

10This is what the LORD says:
"When seventy years are completed for Babylon, I will come to
you and fulfil my gracious promise
to bring you back to this place.
11For I know the plans I have for
you," declares the LORD, "plans to
prosper you and not to harm you,
plans to give you hope and a future.
12Then you will call upon me and
come and pray to me, and I will
listen to you. 13You will seek me
and find me when you seek me with
all your heart. 14I will be found by
you," declares the LORD, "and will
bring you back from captivity. I will
gather you from all the nations and
places where I have banished you,"
declares the LORD, "and will bring
you back to the place from which I
carried you into exile."

15You may say, "The LORD has
raised up prophets for us in Babylon," 16but this is what the LORD
says about the king who sits on
David's throne and all the people
who remain in this city, your countrymen who did not go with you
into exile—17yes, this is what the
LORD Almighty says: "I will send
the sword, famine and plague
against them and I will make them
like poor figs that are so bad they
cannot be eaten. 18I will pursue
them with the sword, famine and
plague and will make them abhorrent to all the kingdoms of the
earth and an object of cursing and
horror, of scorn and reproach,
among all the nations where I drive
them. 19For they have not listened
to my words," declares the LORD,
"words that I sent to them again
and again by my servants the
prophets. And you exiles have not
listened either," declares the
LORD.

20Therefore, hear the word of
the LORD, all you exiles whom I
have sent away from Jerusalem to
Babylon. 21This is what the LORD
Almighty, the God of Israel, says
about Ahab son of Kolaiah and
Zedekiah son of Maaseiah, who
are prophesying lies to you in my
name: "I will hand them over to
Nebuchadnezzar king of Babylon,

and he will put them to death before your very eyes. [22]Because of
them, all the exiles from Judah who
are in Babylon will use this curse:
'The LORD treat you like Zedekiah
and Ahab, whom the king of Babylon burned in the fire.' [23]For they
have done outrageous things in
Israel; they have committed adultery with their neighbours' wives
and in my name have spoken lies,
which I did not tell them to do. I
know it and am a witness to it,"
declares the LORD.

NEW TESTAMENT READING
2 Thessalonians 1:1–12

1 Paul, Silas and Timothy,

To the church of the Thessalonians in God our Father and the Lord Jesus Christ:

[2]Grace and peace to you from God the Father and the Lord Jesus Christ.

Thanksgiving and Prayer

[3]We ought always to thank God for
you, brothers, and rightly so, because
your faith is growing more and more,
and the love every one of you has for
each other is increasing. [4]There-
fore among God's churches we boast
about your perseverance and faith in
all the persecutions and trials you are
enduring.
[5]All this is evidence that God's judgment is right, and as a result you will be
counted worthy of the kingdom of God,
for which you are suffering. [6]God is
just: He will pay back trouble to those
who trouble you [7]and give relief to you
who are troubled, and to us as well. This
will happen when the Lord Jesus is revealed from heaven in blazing fire with
his powerful angels. [8]He will punish
those who do not know God and do not
obey the gospel of our Lord Jesus.
[9]They will be punished with everlasting
destruction and shut out from the presence of the Lord and from the majesty
of his power [10]on the day he comes to be
glorified in his holy people and to be
marvelled at among all those who have
believed. This includes you, because
you believed our testimony to you.
[11]With this in mind, we constantly
pray for you, that our God may count
you worthy of his calling, and that by his
power he may fulfil every good purpose
of yours and every act prompted by
your faith. [12]We pray this so that the
name of our Lord Jesus may be glorified
in you, and you in him, according to the
grace of our God and the Lord Jesus
Christ.

READING FROM PSALMS
Psalm 119:25–32

ד Daleth

[25]I am laid low in the dust;
preserve my life according to your word.
[26]I recounted my ways and you answered me;
teach me your decrees.
[27]Let me understand the teaching of your precepts;
then I will meditate on your wonders.
[28]My soul is weary with sorrow;
strengthen me according to your word.
[29]Keep me from deceitful ways;
be gracious to me through your law.
[30]I have chosen the way of truth;
I have set my heart on your laws.
[31]I hold fast to your statutes, O LORD;
do not let me be put to shame.
[32]I run in the path of your commands,
for you have set my heart free.

OCTOBER 14

DAY 287

OLD TESTAMENT READING
Jeremiah 29:24–31:14

Message to Shemaiah

24Tell Shemaiah the Nehelamite,
25"This is what the LORD Almighty, the
God of Israel, says: You sent letters in
your own name to all the people in
Jerusalem, to Zephaniah son of
Maaseiah the priest, and to all the other
priests. You said to Zephaniah, 26'The
LORD has appointed you priest in place
of Jehoiada to be in charge of the house
of the LORD; you should put any madman who acts like a prophet into the
stocks and neck-irons. 27So why have
you not reprimanded Jeremiah from
Anathoth, who poses as a prophet
among you? 28He has sent this message
to us in Babylon: It will be a long time.
Therefore build houses and settle
down; plant gardens and eat what they
produce.' "
29Zephaniah the priest, however,
read the letter to Jeremiah the prophet.
30Then the word of the LORD came to
Jeremiah: 31"Send this message to all
the exiles: 'This is what the LORD says
about Shemaiah the Nehelamite: Because Shemaiah has prophesied to you,
even though I did not send him, and has
led you to believe a lie, 32this is what the
LORD says: I will surely punish Shemaiah the Nehelamite and his descendants. He will have no-one left among
his people, nor will he see the good
things I will do for my people, declares
the LORD, because he has preached rebellion against me.' "

Restoration of Israel

30 This is the word that came to
Jeremiah from the LORD: 2"This
is what the LORD, the God of Israel,
says: 'Write in a book all the words I
have spoken to you. 3The days are
coming,' declares the LORD, 'when I
will bring my people Israel and Judah
back from captivity and restore them to
the land I gave to their forefathers to
possess,' says the LORD."
4These are the words the LORD spoke
concerning Israel and Judah: 5"This is
what the LORD says:

" 'Cries of fear are heard—
terror, not peace.
6Ask and see:
Can a man bear children?
Then why do I see every strong man
with his hands on his stomach like
a woman in labour,
every face turned deathly pale?
7How awful that day will be!
None will be like it.
It will be a time of trouble for Jacob,
but he will be saved out of it.

8" 'In that day,' declares the LORD
Almighty,
'I will break the yoke off their
necks
and will tear off their bonds;
no longer will foreigners enslave
them.
9Instead, they will serve the LORD
their God
and David their king,
whom I will raise up for them.

10" 'So do not fear, O Jacob my
servant;
do not be dismayed, O Israel,'
declares the LORD.
'I will surely save you out of a distant
place,
your descendants from the land of
their exile.
Jacob will again have peace and
security,
and no-one will make him afraid.
11I am with you and will save you,'
declares the LORD.

'Though I completely destroy all the
nations
among which I scatter you,
I will not completely destroy you.
I will discipline you but only with
justice;
I will not let you go entirely
unpunished.'

12"This is what the LORD says:

" 'Your wound is incurable,
your injury beyond healing.
13There is no-one to plead your cause,
no remedy for your sore,
no healing for you.
14All your allies have forgotten you;
they care nothing for you.
I have struck you as an enemy would
and punished you as would the
cruel,
because your guilt is so great
and your sins so many.
15Why do you cry out over your
wound,
your pain that has no cure?
Because of your great guilt and many
sins
I have done these things to you.

16" 'But all who devour you will be
devoured;
all your enemies will go into exile.
Those who plunder you will be
plundered;
all who make spoil of you I will
despoil.
17But I will restore you to health
and heal your wounds,'
declares the LORD,
'because you are called an outcast,
Zion for whom no-one cares.'

18"This is what the LORD says:

" 'I will restore the fortunes of
Jacob's tents
and have compassion on his
dwellings;
the city will be rebuilt on her ruins,
and the palace will stand in its
proper place.
19From them will come songs of
thanksgiving
and the sound of rejoicing.
I will add to their numbers,
and they will not be decreased;
I will bring them honour,
and they will not be disdained.
20Their children will be as in days of
old,
and their community will be
established before me;
I will punish all who oppress them.
21Their leader will be one of their own;
their ruler will arise from among
them.
I will bring him near and he will come
close to me,
for who is he who will devote
himself
to be close to me?'
declares the LORD.
22" 'So you will be my people,
and I will be your God.' "

23See, the storm of the LORD
will burst out in wrath,
a driving wind swirling down
on the heads of the wicked.
24The fierce anger of the LORD will not
turn back
until he fully accomplishes
the purposes of his heart.
In days to come
you will understand this.

31 "At that time," declares the
LORD, "I will be the God of all
the clans of Israel, and they will be my
people."
2This is what the LORD says:

"The people who survive the sword
will find favour in the desert;
I will come to give rest to Israel."

3The LORD appeared to us in the past,
saying:

"I have loved you with an everlasting
love;
I have drawn you with
loving-kindness.

4I will build you up again
and you will be rebuilt, O Virgin Israel.
Again you will take up your tambourines
and go out to dance with the joyful.
5Again you will plant vineyards
on the hills of Samaria;
the farmers will plant them
and enjoy their fruit.
6There will be a day when watchmen cry out
on the hills of Ephraim,
'Come, let us go up to Zion,
to the LORD our God.'"

7This is what the LORD says:

"Sing with joy for Jacob;
shout for the foremost of the nations.
Make your praises heard, and say,
'O LORD, save your people,
the remnant of Israel.'
8See, I will bring them from the land of the north
and gather them from the ends of the earth.
Among them will be the blind and the lame,
expectant mothers and women in labour;
a great throng will return.
9They will come with weeping;
they will pray as I bring them back.
I will lead them beside streams of water
on a level path where they will not stumble,
because I am Israel's father,
and Ephraim is my firstborn son.

10"Hear the word of the LORD, O nations;
proclaim it in distant coastlands:
'He who scattered Israel will gather them
and will watch over his flock like a shepherd.'
11For the LORD will ransom Jacob
and redeem them from the hand of those stronger than they.
12They will come and shout for joy on the heights of Zion;
they will rejoice in the bounty of the LORD—
the grain, the new wine and the oil,
the young of the flocks and herds.
They will be like a well-watered garden,
and they will sorrow no more.
13Then maidens will dance and be glad,
young men and old as well.
I will turn their mourning into gladness;
I will give them comfort and joy instead of sorrow.
14I will satisfy the priests with abundance,
and my people will be filled with my bounty,"
declares the LORD.

NEW TESTAMENT READING
2 Thessalonians 2:1–17

The Man of Lawlessness

2 Concerning the coming of our Lord
Jesus Christ and our being
gathered to him, we ask you, brothers,
2not to become easily unsettled or
alarmed by some prophecy, report or
letter supposed to have come from us,
saying that the day of the Lord has
already come. 3Don't let anyone deceive you in any way, for ⌞that day will
not come⌟ until the rebellion occurs and
the man of lawlessness is revealed, the
man doomed to destruction. 4He will
oppose and will exalt himself over
everything that is called God or is
worshipped, so that he sets himself
up in God's temple, proclaiming himself to be God.

5Don't you remember that when I
was with you I used to tell you these
things? 6And now you know what is
holding him back, so that he may be
revealed at the proper time. 7For the
secret power of lawlessness is already at
work; but the one who now holds it back
will continue to do so till he is taken out

of the way. [8]And then the lawless one
will be revealed, whom the Lord Jesus
will overthrow with the breath of his
mouth and destroy by the splendour of
his coming. [9]The coming of the lawless
one will be in accordance with the
work of Satan displayed in all kinds of
counterfeit miracles, signs and wonders, [10]and in every sort of evil that
deceives those who are perishing. They
perish because they refused to love the
truth and so be saved. [11]For this reason
God sends them a powerful delusion so
that they will believe the lie [12]and so
that all will be condemned who have not
believed the truth but have delighted in
wickedness.

Stand Firm

[13]But we ought always to thank God
for you, brothers loved by the Lord,
because from the beginning God chose
you to be saved through the sanctifying
work of the Spirit and through belief in
the truth. [14]He called you to this
through our gospel, that you might
share in the glory of our Lord Jesus
Christ. [15]So then, brothers, stand firm
and hold to the teachings we passed on
to you, whether by word of mouth or by
letter.
[16]May our Lord Jesus Christ himself
and God our Father, who loved us and
by his grace gave us eternal encouragement and good hope, [17]encourage your
hearts and strengthen you in every good
deed and word.

READING FROM PSALMS
Psalm 119:33–40

ה He

[33]Teach me, O LORD, to follow your
decrees;
then I will keep them to the end.
[34]Give me understanding, and I will
keep your law
and obey it with all my heart.
[35]Direct me in the path of your
commands,
for there I find delight.
[36]Turn my heart towards your statutes
and not towards selfish gain.
[37]Turn my eyes away from worthless
things;
preserve my life according to your
word.
[38]Fulfil your promise to your servant,
so that you may be feared.
[39]Take away the disgrace I dread,
for your laws are good.
[40]How I long for your precepts!
Preserve my life in your
righteousness.

DAY 288

OCTOBER 15

OLD TESTAMENT READING
Jeremiah 31:15–32:25

[15]This is what the LORD says:

"A voice is heard in Ramah,
mourning and great weeping,
Rachel weeping for her children
and refusing to be comforted,
because her children are no more."

[16]This is what the LORD says:

"Restrain your voice from weeping
and your eyes from tears,
for your work will be rewarded,"
declares the LORD.
"They will return from the land of
the enemy.
[17]So there is hope for your future,"
declares the LORD.

"Your children will return to their
own land.

18"I have surely heard Ephraim's
moaning:
'You disciplined me like an unruly
calf,
and I have been disciplined.
Restore me, and I will return,
because you are the LORD my God.
19After I strayed,
I repented;
after I came to understand,
I beat my breast.
I was ashamed and humiliated
because I bore the disgrace of my
youth.'
20Is not Ephraim my dear son,
the child in whom I delight?
Though I often speak against him,
I still remember him.
Therefore my heart yearns for him;
I have great compassion for him,"
declares the LORD.

21"Set up road signs;
put up guideposts.
Take note of the highway,
the road that you take.
Return, O Virgin Israel,
return to your towns.
22How long will you wander,
O unfaithful daughter?
The LORD will create a new thing on
earth—
a woman will surround a man."

23This is what the LORD Almighty,
the God of Israel, says: "When I bring
them back from captivity, the people in
the land of Judah and in its towns will
once again use these words: 'The LORD
bless you, O righteous dwelling, O
sacred mountain.' 24People will live
together in Judah and all its towns—
farmers and those who move about with
their flocks. 25I will refresh the weary
and satisfy the faint."
26At this I awoke and looked around.
My sleep had been pleasant to me.
27"The days are coming," declares
the LORD, "when I will plant the house
of Israel and the house of Judah with the
offspring of men and of animals. 28Just
as I watched over them to uproot and
tear down, and to overthrow, destroy
and bring disaster, so I will watch over
them to build and to plant," declares
the LORD. 29"In those days people will
no longer say,

'The fathers have eaten sour grapes,
and the children's teeth are set on
edge.'

30Instead, everyone will die for his own
sin; whoever eats sour grapes—his own
teeth will be set on edge.

31"The time is coming," declares the
LORD,
"when I will make a new covenant
with the house of Israel
and with the house of Judah.
32It will not be like the covenant
I made with their forefathers
when I took them by the hand
to lead them out of Egypt,
because they broke my covenant,
though I was a husband to them,"
declares the LORD.
33"This is the covenant that I will make
with the house of Israel
after that time," declares the
LORD.
"I will put my law in their minds
and write it on their hearts.
I will be their God,
and they will be my people.
34No longer will a man teach his
neighbour,
or a man his brother, saying,
'Know the LORD,'
because they will all know me,
from the least of them to the
greatest,"
declares the LORD.
"For I will forgive their wickedness
and will remember their sins no
more."

35This is what the LORD says,

he who appoints the sun
to shine by day,
who decrees the moon and stars
to shine by night,

who stirs up the sea
so that its waves roar—
the LORD Almighty is his name:
36"Only if these decrees vanish from
my sight,"
declares the LORD,
"will the descendants of Israel ever
cease
to be a nation before me."

37This is what the LORD says:

"Only if the heavens above can be
measured
and the foundations of the earth
below be searched out
will I reject all the descendants of
Israel
because of all they have done,"
declares the LORD.

38"The days are coming," declares
the LORD, "when this city will be rebuilt
for me from the Tower of Hananel to
the Corner Gate. 39The measuring line
will stretch from there straight to the hill
of Gareb and then turn to Goah. 40The
whole valley where dead bodies and
ashes are thrown, and all the terraces
out to the Kidron Valley on the east as
far as the corner of the Horse Gate, will
be holy to the LORD. The city will never
again be uprooted or demolished."

Jeremiah Buys a Field

32 This is the word that came to
Jeremiah from the LORD in the
tenth year of Zedekiah king of Judah,
which was the eighteenth year of
Nebuchadnezzar. 2The army of the king
of Babylon was then besieging Jerusalem, and Jeremiah the prophet was
confined in the courtyard of the guard in
the royal palace of Judah.
3Now Zedekiah king of Judah had
imprisoned him there, saying, "Why do
you prophesy as you do? You say, 'This
is what the LORD says: I am about to
hand this city over to the king of Babylon, and he will capture it. 4Zedekiah
king of Judah will not escape out of the
hands of the Babylonians but will certainly be handed over to the king of
Babylon, and will speak with him face
to face and see him with his own eyes.
5He will take Zedekiah to Babylon,
where he will remain until I deal with
him, declares the LORD. If you fight
against the Babylonians, you will not
succeed.'"
6Jeremiah said, "The word of the
LORD came to me: 7Hanamel son of
Shallum your uncle is going to come to
you and say, 'Buy my field at Anathoth,
because as nearest relative it is your
right and duty to buy it.'
8"Then, just as the LORD had said, my
cousin Hanamel came to me in the
courtyard of the guard and said, 'Buy
my field at Anathoth in the territory
of Benjamin. Since it is your right to
redeem it and possess it, buy it for
yourself.'
"I knew that this was the word of the
LORD; 9so I bought the field at Anathoth
from my cousin Hanamel and weighed
out for him seventeen shekels of silver.
10I signed and sealed the deed, had it
witnessed, and weighed out the silver
on the scales. 11I took the deed of purchase—the sealed copy containing the
terms and conditions, as well as the
unsealed copy—12and I gave this deed
to Baruch son of Neriah, the son of
Mahseiah, in the presence of my cousin
Hanamel and of the witnesses who had
signed the deed and of all the Jews
sitting in the courtyard of the guard.
13"In their presence I gave Baruch
these instructions: 14'This is what the
LORD Almighty, the God of Israel, says:
Take these documents, both the sealed
and unsealed copies of the deed of
purchase, and put them in a clay jar so
that they will last a long time. 15For this
is what the LORD Almighty, the God of
Israel, says: Houses, fields and
vineyards will again be bought in this
land.'
16"After I had given the deed of purchase to Baruch son of Neriah, I prayed
to the LORD:

17"Ah, Sovereign LORD, you have
made the heavens and the earth by

your great power and outstretched
arm. Nothing is too hard for you.
18You show love to thousands but
bring the punishment for the
fathers' sins into the laps of their
children after them. O great and
powerful God, whose name is the
LORD Almighty, 19great are your
purposes and mighty are your
deeds. Your eyes are open to all
the ways of men; you reward everyone according to his conduct and as
his deeds deserve. 20You performed miraculous signs and wonders in Egypt and have continued
them to this day, both in Israel and
among all mankind, and have
gained the renown that is still
yours. 21You brought your people
Israel out of Egypt with signs and
wonders, by a mighty hand and an
outstretched arm and with great
terror. 22You gave them this land
you had sworn to give to their forefathers, a land flowing with milk
and honey. 23They came in and
took possession of it, but they did
not obey you or follow your law;
they did not do what you commanded them to do. So you brought all
this disaster upon them.

24"See how the siege ramps are
built up to take the city. Because of
the sword, famine and plague, the
city will be handed over to the
Babylonians who are attacking it.
What you said has happened, as
you now see. 25And though the city
will be handed over to the Babylonians, you, O Sovereign LORD, say
to me, 'Buy the field with silver and
have the transaction witnessed.'"

NEW TESTAMENT READING
2 Thessalonians 3:1–18

Request for Prayer

3 Finally, brothers, pray for us that
the message of the Lord may
spread rapidly and be honoured, just as
it was with you. 2And pray that we may
be delivered from wicked and evil men,
for not everyone has faith. 3But the
Lord is faithful, and he will strengthen
and protect you from the evil one. 4We
have confidence in the Lord that you are
doing and will continue to do the things
we command. 5May the Lord direct
your hearts into God's love and Christ's
perseverance.

Warning Against Idleness

6In the name of the Lord Jesus Christ,
we command you, brothers, to keep
away from every brother who is idle and
does not live according to the teaching
you received from us. 7For you
yourselves know how you ought to follow our example. We were not idle
when we were with you, 8nor did we eat
anyone's food without paying for it. On
the contrary, we worked night and day,
labouring and toiling so that we would
not be a burden to any of you. 9We did
this, not because we do not have the
right to such help, but in order to make
ourselves a model for you to follow.
10For even when we were with you, we
gave you this rule: "If a man will not
work, he shall not eat."

11We hear that some among you are
idle. They are not busy; they are busybodies. 12Such people we command and
urge in the Lord Jesus Christ to settle
down and earn the bread they eat.
13And as for you, brothers, never tire of
doing what is right.

14If anyone does not obey our instruction in this letter, take special note of
him. Do not associate with him, in order
that he may feel ashamed. 15Yet do not
regard him as an enemy, but warn him
as a brother.

Final Greetings

16Now may the Lord of peace himself
give you peace at all times and in every
way. The Lord be with all of you.

17I, Paul, write this greeting in my
own hand, which is the distinguishing

mark in all my letters. This is how I write.

18The grace of our Lord Jesus Christ be with you all.

READING FROM PROVERBS
Proverbs 25:1–10

More Proverbs of Solomon

25 These are more proverbs of Solomon, copied by the men of Hezekiah king of Judah:

2It is the glory of God to conceal a matter;
to search out a matter is the glory of kings.

3As the heavens are high and the earth is deep,
so the hearts of kings are unsearchable.

4Remove the dross from the silver,
and out comes material for the silversmith;
5remove the wicked from the king's presence,
and his throne will be established through righteousness.

6Do not exalt yourself in the king's presence,
and do not claim a place among great men;
7it is better for him to say to you,
"Come up here,"
than for him to humiliate you before a nobleman.

What you have seen with your eyes
8 do not bring hastily to court,
for what will you do in the end
if your neighbour puts you to shame?

9If you argue your case with a neighbour,
do not betray another man's confidence,
10or he who hears it may shame you
and you will never lose your bad reputation.

DAY 289

OCTOBER 16

OLD TESTAMENT READING
Jeremiah 32:26–34:22

26Then the word of the LORD came to
Jeremiah: 27"I am the LORD, the God of
all mankind. Is anything too hard for
me? 28Therefore, this is what the LORD
says: I am about to hand this city over to
the Babylonians and to Nebuchadnezzar king of Babylon, who will capture it.
29The Babylonians who are attacking
this city will come in and set it on fire; they will burn it down, along with the houses where the people provoked me to anger by burning incense on the roofs to Baal and by pouring out drink offerings to other gods.
30"The people of Israel and Judah have done nothing but evil in my sight from their youth; indeed, the people of Israel have done nothing but provoke me with what their hands have made,
declares the LORD. 31From the day it
was built until now, this city has so aroused my anger and wrath that I must
remove it from my sight. 32The people
of Israel and Judah have provoked me by all the evil they have done—they, their kings and officials, their priests and prophets, the men of Judah and the
people of Jerusalem. 33They turned
their backs to me and not their faces; though I taught them again and again, they would not listen or respond to discipline. 34They set up their abominable
idols in the house that bears my Name

and defiled it. 35They built high places
for Baal in the Valley of Ben Hinnom to
sacrifice their sons and daughters to
Molech, though I never commanded,
nor did it enter my mind, that they
should do such a detestable thing and so
make Judah sin.

36"You are saying about this city, 'By
the sword, famine and plague it will be
handed over to the king of Babylon';
but this is what the LORD, the God of
Israel, says: 37I will surely gather them
from all the lands where I banish them
in my furious anger and great wrath; I
will bring them back to this place and let
them live in safety. 38They will be my
people, and I will be their God. 39I will
give them singleness of heart and action, so that they will always fear me for
their own good and the good of their
children after them. 40I will make an
everlasting covenant with them: I will
never stop doing good to them, and I
will inspire them to fear me, so that they
will never turn away from me. 41I will
rejoice in doing them good and will
assuredly plant them in this land with all
my heart and soul.

42"This is what the LORD says: As I
have brought all this great calamity on
this people, so I will give them all the
prosperity I have promised them.
43Once more fields will be bought in this
land of which you say, 'It is a desolate
waste, without men or animals, for it
has been handed over to the Babylonians.' 44Fields will be bought for silver,
and deeds will be signed, sealed and
witnessed in the territory of Benjamin,
in the villages around Jerusalem, in the
towns of Judah and in the towns of the
hill country, of the western foothills and
of the Negev, because I will restore
their fortunes, declares the LORD."

Promise of Restoration

33 While Jeremiah was still confined in the courtyard of the
guard, the word of the LORD came to
him a second time: 2"This is what the
LORD says, he who made the earth, the
LORD who formed it and established
it—the LORD is his name: 3'Call to me
and I will answer you and tell you great
and unsearchable things you do not
know.' 4For this is what the LORD, the
God of Israel, says about the houses in
this city and the royal palaces of Judah
that have been torn down to be used
against the siege ramps and the sword
5in the fight with the Babylonians: 'They
will be filled with the dead bodies of the
men I will slay in my anger and wrath. I
will hide my face from this city because
of all its wickedness.

6" 'Nevertheless, I will bring health
and healing to it; I will heal my people
and will let them enjoy abundant
peace and security. 7I will bring Judah
and Israel back from captivity and will
rebuild them as they were before. 8I will
cleanse them from all the sin they have
committed against me and will forgive
all their sins of rebellion against me.
9Then this city will bring me renown,
joy, praise and honour before all nations on earth that hear of all the good
things I do for it; and they will be in awe
and will tremble at the abundant
prosperity and peace I provide for it.'

10"This is what the LORD says: 'You
say about this place, "It is a desolate
waste, without men or animals." Yet in
the towns of Judah and the streets of
Jerusalem that are deserted, inhabited
by neither men nor animals, there will
be heard once more 11the sounds of joy
and gladness, the voices of bride and
bridegroom, and the voices of those
who bring thank-offerings to the house
of the LORD, saying,

"Give thanks to the LORD Almighty,
  for the LORD is good;
  his love endures for ever."

For I will restore the fortunes of the
land as they were before,' says the
LORD.

12"This is what the LORD Almighty
says: 'In this place, desolate and without men or animals—in all its towns

there will again be pastures for
shepherds to rest their flocks. [13]In the
towns of the hill country, of the western
foothills and of the Negev, in the territory of Benjamin, in the villages around
Jerusalem and in the towns of Judah,
flocks will again pass under the hand of
the one who counts them,' says the
LORD.
[14]" 'The days are coming,' declares
the LORD, 'when I will fulfil the gracious
promise I made to the house of Israel
and to the house of Judah.

[15]" 'In those days and at that time
I will make a righteous Branch
sprout from David's line;
he will do what is just and right in
the land.
[16]In those days Judah will be saved
and Jerusalem will live in safety.
This is the name by which it will be
called:
The LORD Our Righteousness.'

[17]For this is what the LORD says: 'David
will never fail to have a man to sit on the
throne of the house of Israel, [18]nor
will the priests, who are Levites, ever
fail to have a man to stand before me
continually to offer burnt offerings, to
burn grain offerings and to present
sacrifices.' "
[19]The word of the LORD came to Jeremiah: [20]"This is what the LORD says: 'If
you can break my covenant with the day
and my covenant with the night, so that
day and night no longer come at their
appointed time, [21]then my covenant
with David my servant—and my covenant with the Levites who are priests
ministering before me—can be broken
and David will no longer have a descendant to reign on his throne. [22]I will make
the descendants of David my servant
and the Levites who minister before me
as countless as the stars of the sky and as
measureless as the sand on the
seashore.' "
[23]The word of the LORD came to Jeremiah: [24]"Have you not noticed that
these people are saying, 'The LORD has
rejected the two kingdoms he chose'?
So they despise my people and no longer regard them as a nation. [25]This is
what the LORD says: 'If I have not established my covenant with day and night
and the fixed laws of heaven and earth,
[26]then I will reject the descendants of
Jacob and David my servant and will
not choose one of his sons to rule over
the descendants of Abraham, Isaac and
Jacob. For I will restore their fortunes
and have compassion on them.' "

Warning to Zedekiah

34 While Nebuchadnezzar king of
Babylon and all his army and all
the kingdoms and peoples in the empire
he ruled were fighting against Jerusalem
and all its surrounding towns, this word
came to Jeremiah from the LORD:
[2]"This is what the LORD, the God of
Israel, says: Go to Zedekiah king of
Judah and tell him, 'This is what the
LORD says: I am about to hand this city
over to the king of Babylon, and he will
burn it down. [3]You will not escape from
his grasp but will surely be captured and
handed over to him. You will see the
king of Babylon with your own eyes,
and he will speak with you face to face.
And you will go to Babylon.
[4]" 'Yet hear the promise of the LORD,
O Zedekiah king of Judah. This is what
the LORD says concerning you: You will
not die by the sword; [5]you will die
peacefully. As people made a funeral
fire in honour of your fathers, the
former kings who preceded you, so
they will make a fire in your honour and
lament, "Alas, O master!" I myself
make this promise, declares the
LORD.' "
[6]Then Jeremiah the prophet told all
this to Zedekiah king of Judah, in Jerusalem, [7]while the army of the king of
Babylon was fighting against Jerusalem
and the other cities of Judah that were
still holding out—Lachish and Azekah.
These were the only fortified cities left
in Judah.

Freedom for Slaves

8The word came to Jeremiah from the
LORD after King Zedekiah had made a
covenant with all the people in Jerusalem to proclaim freedom for the
slaves. 9Everyone was to free his Hebrew slaves, both male and female;
no-one was to hold a fellow Jew in
bondage. 10So all the officials and people who entered into this covenant
agreed that they would free their male
and female slaves and no longer hold
them in bondage. They agreed, and set
them free. 11But afterwards they
changed their minds and took back the
slaves they had freed and enslaved them
again.

12Then the word of the LORD came to
Jeremiah: 13"This is what the LORD, the
God of Israel, says: I made a covenant
with your forefathers when I brought
them out of Egypt, out of the land of
slavery. I said, 14'Every seventh year
each of you must free any fellow Hebrew who has sold himself to you. After
he has served you for six years, you
must let him go free.' Your fathers,
however, did not listen to me or pay
attention to me. 15Recently you repented and did what is right in my sight:
Each of you proclaimed freedom to his
countrymen. You even made a covenant before me in the house that bears
my Name. 16But now you have turned
round and profaned my name; each of
you has taken back the male and female
slaves you had set free to go where they
wished. You have forced them to become your slaves again.

17"Therefore, this is what the LORD
says: You have not obeyed me; you
have not proclaimed freedom for your
fellow countrymen. So I now proclaim
'freedom' for you, declares the LORD
—'freedom' to fall by the sword, plague
and famine. I will make you abhorrent
to all the kingdoms of the earth. 18The
men who have violated my covenant
and have not fulfilled the terms of the
covenant they made before me, I will
treat like the calf they cut in two and
then walked between its pieces. 19The
leaders of Judah and Jerusalem, the
court officials, the priests and all
the people of the land who walked between the pieces of the calf, 20I will hand
over to their enemies who seek their
lives. Their dead bodies will become
food for the birds of the air and the
beasts of the earth.

21"I will hand Zedekiah king of Judah
and his officials over to their enemies
who seek their lives, to the army of the
king of Babylon, which has withdrawn
from you. 22I am going to give the order,
declares the LORD, and I will bring them
back to this city. They will fight against
it, take it and burn it down. And I will
lay waste the towns of Judah so that
no-one can live there."

NEW TESTAMENT READING
1 Timothy 1:1–20

1 Paul, an apostle of Christ Jesus by
the command of God our Saviour
and of Christ Jesus our hope,

2To Timothy my true son in the faith:

Grace, mercy and peace from God
the Father and Christ Jesus our Lord.

Warning Against False Teachers of the Law

3As I urged you when I went into
Macedonia, stay there in Ephesus so
that you may command certain men not
to teach false doctrines any longer 4nor
to devote themselves to myths and
endless genealogies. These promote
controversies rather than God's work
—which is by faith. 5The goal of this
command is love, which comes from a
pure heart and a good conscience and a
sincere faith. 6Some have wandered
away from these and turned to
meaningless talk. 7They want to be
teachers of the law, but they do not
know what they are talking about or
what they so confidently affirm.

8We know that the law is good if one
uses it properly. 9We also know that law
is made not for the righteous but for
lawbreakers and rebels, the ungodly
and sinful, the unholy and irreligious;
for those who kill their fathers or
mothers, for murderers, 10for adulterers and perverts, for slave traders and
liars and perjurers—and for whatever
else is contrary to the sound doctrine
11that conforms to the glorious gospel of
the blessed God, which he entrusted to
me.

The Lord's Grace to Paul

12I thank Christ Jesus our Lord, who
has given me strength, that he considered me faithful, appointing me to
his service. 13Even though I was once a
blasphemer and a persecutor and a
violent man, I was shown mercy because I acted in ignorance and unbelief.
14The grace of our Lord was poured out
on me abundantly, along with the faith
and love that are in Christ Jesus.

15Here is a trustworthy saying that
deserves full acceptance: Christ Jesus
came into the world to save sinners—of
whom I am the worst. 16But for that
very reason I was shown mercy so that
in me, the worst of sinners, Christ Jesus
might display his unlimited patience as
an example for those who would believe
on him and receive eternal life. 17Now
to the King eternal, immortal, invisible,
the only God, be honour and glory for
ever and ever. Amen.

18Timothy, my son, I give you this
instruction in keeping with the prophecies once made about you, so that by
following them you may fight the good
fight, 19holding on to faith and a good
conscience. Some have rejected these
and so have shipwrecked their faith.
20Among them are Hymenaeus and
Alexander, whom I have handed over
to Satan to be taught not to blaspheme.

READING FROM PSALMS

Psalm 119:41–48

ו Waw

41May your unfailing love come to me,
O LORD,
your salvation according to your
promise;
42then I will answer the one who taunts
me,
for I trust in your word.
43Do not snatch the word of truth from
my mouth,
for I have put my hope in your
laws.
44I will always obey your law,
for ever and ever.
45I will walk about in freedom,
for I have sought out your
precepts.
46I will speak of your statutes before
kings
and will not be put to shame,
47for I delight in your commands
because I love them.
48I lift up my hands to your commands,
which I love,
and I meditate on your decrees.

OCTOBER 17

DAY 290

OLD TESTAMENT READING

Jeremiah 35:1–37:21

The Recabites

35 This is the word that came to Jeremiah from the LORD during the reign of Jehoiakim son of Josiah king of Judah: 2"Go to the Recabite family and invite them to come to one of the side rooms of the house of the LORD and give them wine to drink."

3So I went to get Jaazaniah son of Jeremiah, the son of Habazziniah, and his brothers and all his sons—the whole family of the Recabites. 4I brought them into the house of the LORD, into the room of the sons of Hanan son of Igdaliah the man of God. It was next to the room of the officials, which was over that of Maaseiah son of Shallum the door-keeper. 5Then I set bowls full of wine and some cups before the men of the Recabite family and said to them, "Drink some wine."

6But they replied, "We do not drink wine, because our forefather Jonadab son of Recab gave us this command: 'Neither you nor your descendants must ever drink wine. 7Also you must never build houses, sow seed or plant vineyards; you must never have any of these things, but must always live in tents. Then you will live a long time in the land where you are nomads.' 8We have obeyed everything our forefather Jonadab son of Recab commanded us. Neither we nor our wives nor our sons and daughters have ever drunk wine 9or built houses to live in or had vineyards, fields or crops. 10We have lived in tents and have fully obeyed everything our forefather Jonadab commanded us. 11But when Nebuchadnezzar king of Babylon invaded this land, we said, 'Come, we must go to Jerusalem to escape the Babylonian and Aramean armies.' So we have remained in Jerusalem."

12Then the word of the LORD came to Jeremiah, saying: 13"This is what the LORD Almighty, the God of Israel, says: Go and tell the men of Judah and the people of Jerusalem, 'Will you not learn a lesson and obey my words?' declares the LORD. 14'Jonadab son of Recab ordered his sons not to drink wine and this command has been kept. To this day they do not drink wine, because they obey their forefather's command. But I have spoken to you again and again, yet you have not obeyed me. 15Again and again I sent all my servants the prophets to you. They said, "Each of you must turn from your wicked ways and reform your actions; do not follow other gods to serve them. Then you shall live in the land I have given to you and your fathers." But you have not paid attention or listened to me. 16The descendants of Jonadab son of Recab have carried out the command their forefather gave them, but these people have not obeyed me.'

17"Therefore, this is what the LORD God Almighty, the God of Israel, says: 'Listen! I am going to bring on Judah and on everyone living in Jerusalem every disaster I pronounced against them. I spoke to them, but they did not listen; I called to them, but they did not answer.'"

18Then Jeremiah said to the family of the Recabites, "This is what the LORD Almighty, the God of Israel, says: 'You have obeyed the command of your forefather Jonadab and have followed all his instructions and have done everything he ordered.' 19Therefore, this is what the LORD Almighty, the God of Israel, says: 'Jonadab son of Recab shall never fail to have a man to serve me.'"

Jehoiakim Burns Jeremiah's Scroll

36 In the fourth year of Jehoiakim son of Josiah king of Judah, this word came to Jeremiah from the LORD:

2"Take a scroll and write on it all the
words I have spoken to you concerning
Israel, Judah and all the other nations
from the time I began speaking to you in
the reign of Josiah till now. 3Perhaps
when the people of Judah hear about
every disaster I plan to inflict on them,
each of them will turn from his wicked
way; then I will forgive their wickedness
and their sin."

4So Jeremiah called Baruch son of
Neriah, and while Jeremiah dictated all
the words the LORD had spoken to him,
Baruch wrote them on the scroll. 5Then
Jeremiah told Baruch, "I am restricted;
I cannot go to the LORD's temple. 6So
you go to the house of the LORD on a
day of fasting and read to the people
from the scroll the words of the LORD
that you wrote as I dictated. Read them
to all the people of Judah who come in
from their towns. 7Perhaps they will
bring their petition before the LORD,
and each will turn from his wicked ways,
for the anger and wrath pronounced
against this people by the LORD are
great."

8Baruch son of Neriah did everything
Jeremiah the prophet told him to do; at
the LORD's temple he read the words of
the LORD from the scroll. 9In the ninth
month of the fifth year of Jehoiakim son
of Josiah king of Judah, a time of fasting
before the LORD was proclaimed for all
the people in Jerusalem and those who
had come from the towns of Judah.
10From the room of Gemariah son of
Shaphan the secretary, which was in the
upper courtyard at the entrance of the
New Gate of the temple, Baruch read to
all the people at the LORD's temple the
words of Jeremiah from the scroll.

11When Micaiah son of Gemariah,
the son of Shaphan, heard all the words
of the LORD from the scroll, 12he went
down to the secretary's room in the
royal palace, where all the officials were
sitting: Elishama the secretary, Delaiah
son of Shemaiah, Elnathan son of
Acbor, Gemariah son of Shaphan,
Zedekiah son of Hananiah, and all the
other officials. 13After Micaiah told
them everything he had heard Baruch
read to the people from the scroll, 14all
the officials sent Jehudi son of Nethaniah, the son of Shelemiah, the son of
Cushi, to say to Baruch, "Bring the
scroll from which you have read to the
people and come." So Baruch son of
Neriah went to them with the scroll in
his hand. 15They said to him, "Sit down,
please, and read it to us."

So Baruch read it to them. 16When
they heard all these words, they looked
at each other in fear and said to Baruch,
"We must report all these words to the
king." 17Then they asked Baruch, "Tell
us, how did you come to write all this?
Did Jeremiah dictate it?"

18"Yes," Baruch replied, "he dictated all these words to me, and I wrote
them in ink on the scroll."

19Then the officials said to Baruch,
"You and Jeremiah, go and hide. Don't
let anyone know where you are."

20After they put the scroll in the room
of Elishama the secretary, they went to
the king in the courtyard and reported
everything to him. 21The king sent Jehudi to get the scroll, and Jehudi
brought it from the room of Elishama
the secretary and read it to the king and
all the officials standing beside him. 22It
was the ninth month and the king was
sitting in the winter apartment, with a
fire burning in the brazier in front of
him. 23Whenever Jehudi had read three
or four columns of the scroll, the king
cut them off with a scribe's knife and
threw them into the brazier, until the
entire scroll was burned in the fire.
24The king and all his attendants who
heard all these words showed no fear,
nor did they tear their clothes. 25Even
though Elnathan, Delaiah and Gemariah urged the king not to burn the scroll,
he would not listen to them. 26Instead,
the king commanded Jerahmeel, a son
of the king, Seraiah son of Azriel and
Shelemiah son of Abdeel to arrest
Baruch the scribe and Jeremiah the
prophet. But the LORD had hidden
them.

27After the king burned the scroll

containing the words that Baruch had
written at Jeremiah's dictation, the
word of the LORD came to Jeremiah:
28"Take another scroll and write on it all
the words that were on the first scroll,
which Jehoiakim king of Judah burned
up. 29Also tell Jehoiakim king of Judah,
'This is what the LORD says: You
burned that scroll and said, "Why did
you write on it that the king of Babylon
would certainly come and destroy this
land and cut off both men and animals
from it?" 30Therefore, this is what the
LORD says about Jehoiakim king of
Judah: He will have no-one to sit on the
throne of David; his body will be
thrown out and exposed to the heat by
day and the frost by night. 31I will punish him and his children and his attendants for their wickedness; I will bring
on them and those living in Jerusalem
and the people of Judah every disaster I
pronounced against them, because they
have not listened.'"

32So Jeremiah took another scroll and
gave it to the scribe Baruch son of
Neriah, and as Jeremiah dictated,
Baruch wrote on it all the words of the
scroll that Jehoiakim king of Judah had
burned in the fire. And many similar
words were added to them.

Jeremiah in Prison

37 Zedekiah son of Josiah was
made king of Judah by
Nebuchadnezzar king of Babylon; he
reigned in place of Jehoiachin son of
Jehoiakim. 2Neither he nor his attendants nor the people of the land paid
any attention to the words the LORD had
spoken through Jeremiah the prophet.

3King Zedekiah, however, sent
Jehucal son of Shelemiah with the priest
Zephaniah son of Maaseiah to Jeremiah
the prophet with this message: "Please
pray to the LORD our God for us."

4Now Jeremiah was free to come and
go among the people, for he had not yet
been put in prison. 5Pharaoh's army had
marched out of Egypt, and when the
Babylonians who were besieging Jerusalem heard the report about them,
they withdrew from Jerusalem.

6Then the word of the LORD came to
Jeremiah the prophet: 7"This is what
the LORD, the God of Israel, says: Tell
the king of Judah, who sent you to
enquire of me, 'Pharaoh's army, which
has marched out to support you, will go
back to its own land, to Egypt. 8Then
the Babylonians will return and attack
this city; they will capture it and burn it
down.'

9"This is what the LORD says: Do not
deceive yourselves, thinking, 'The
Babylonians will surely leave us.' They
will not! 10Even if you were to defeat the
entire Babylonian army that is attacking
you and only wounded men were left in
their tents, they would come out and
burn this city down."

11After the Babylonian army had
withdrawn from Jerusalem because of
Pharaoh's army, 12Jeremiah started to
leave the city to go to the territory of
Benjamin to get his share of the property among the people there. 13But
when he reached the Benjamin Gate,
the captain of the guard, whose name
was Irijah son of Shelemiah, the son of
Hananiah, arrested him and said, "You
are deserting to the Babylonians!"

14"That's not true!" Jeremiah said. "I
am not deserting to the Babylonians."
But Irijah would not listen to him;
instead, he arrested Jeremiah and
brought him to the officials. 15They
were angry with Jeremiah and had him
beaten and imprisoned in the house of
Jonathan the secretary, which they had
made into a prison.

16Jeremiah was put into a vaulted cell
in a dungeon, where he remained a long
time. 17Then King Zedekiah sent for
him and had him brought to the palace,
where he asked him privately, "Is there
any word from the LORD?"

"Yes," Jeremiah replied, "you will
be handed over to the king of Babylon."

18Then Jeremiah said to King Zedekiah, "What crime have I committed
against you or your officials or this

people, that you have put me in
prison? 19Where are your prophets who
prophesied to you, 'The king of
Babylon will not attack you or this
land'? 20But now, my lord the king,
please listen. Let me bring my petition
before you: Do not send me back to
the house of Jonathan the secretary,
or I shall die there."

21King Zedekiah then gave orders for
Jeremiah to be placed in the courtyard
of the guard and given bread from the
street of the bakers each day until all the
bread in the city was gone. So Jeremiah
remained in the courtyard of the guard.

NEW TESTAMENT READING
1 Timothy 2:1–15

Instructions on Worship

2 I urge, then, first of all, that requests, prayers, intercession and
thanksgiving be made for everyone—
2for kings and all those in authority, that
we may live peaceful and quiet lives in
all godliness and holiness. 3This is good,
and pleases God our Saviour, 4who
wants all men to be saved and to come
to a knowledge of the truth. 5For there
is one God and one mediator between
God and men, the man Christ Jesus,
6who gave himself as a ransom for all
men—the testimony given in its proper
time. 7And for this purpose I was
appointed a herald and an apostle—I
am telling the truth, I am not lying
—and a teacher of the true faith to the
Gentiles.

8I want men everywhere to lift up
holy hands in prayer, without anger or
disputing.

9I also want women to dress mod-
estly, with decency and propriety, not
with braided hair or gold or pearls or
expensive clothes, 10but with good
deeds, appropriate for women who profess to worship God.

11A woman should learn in quietness
and full submission. 12I do not permit a
woman to teach or to have authority
over a man; she must be silent. 13For
Adam was formed first, then Eve.
14And Adam was not the one deceived;
it was the woman who was deceived and
became a sinner. 15But women will be
saved through childbearing—if they
continue in faith, love and holiness with
propriety.

READING FROM PSALMS
Psalm 119:49–56

ז Zayin

49Remember your word to your
servant,
for you have given me hope.
50My comfort in my suffering is this:
Your promise preserves my life.
51The arrogant mock me without
restraint,
but I do not turn from your law.
52I remember your ancient laws, O
Lord,
and I find comfort in them.
53Indignation grips me because of the
wicked,
who have forsaken your law.
54Your decrees are the theme of my
song
wherever I lodge.
55In the night I remember your name,
O Lord,
and I will keep your law.
56This has been my practice:
I obey your precepts.

OCTOBER 18

DAY 291

OLD TESTAMENT READING

Jeremiah 38:1–40:6

Jeremiah Thrown Into a Cistern

38 Shephatiah son of Mattan, Gedaliah son of Pashhur, Jehucal son of Shelemiah, and Pashhur son of Malkijah heard what Jeremiah was telling all the people when he said, 2"This is what the LORD says: 'Whoever stays in this city will die by the sword, famine or plague, but whoever goes over to the Babylonians will live. He will escape with his life; he will live.' 3And this is what the LORD says: 'This city will certainly be handed over to the army of the king of Babylon, who will capture it.'"

4Then the officials said to the king, "This man should be put to death. He is discouraging the soldiers who are left in this city, as well as all the people, by the things he is saying to them. This man is not seeking the good of these people but their ruin."

5"He is in your hands," King Zedekiah answered. "The king can do nothing to oppose you."

6So they took Jeremiah and put him into the cistern of Malkijah, the king's son, which was in the courtyard of the guard. They lowered Jeremiah by ropes into the cistern; it had no water in it, only mud, and Jeremiah sank down into the mud.

7But Ebed-Melech, a Cushite, an official in the royal palace, heard that they had put Jeremiah into the cistern. While the king was sitting in the Benjamin Gate, 8Ebed-Melech went out of the palace and said to him, 9"My lord the king, these men have acted wickedly in all they have done to Jeremiah the prophet. They have thrown him into a cistern, where he will starve to death when there is no longer any bread in the city."

10Then the king commanded Ebed-Melech the Cushite, "Take thirty men from here with you and lift Jeremiah the prophet out of the cistern before he dies."

11So Ebed-Melech took the men with him and went to a room under the treasury in the palace. He took some old rags and worn-out clothes from there and let them down with ropes to Jeremiah in the cistern. 12Ebed-Melech the Cushite said to Jeremiah, "Put these old rags and worn-out clothes under your arms to pad the ropes." Jeremiah did so, 13and they pulled him up with the ropes and lifted him out of the cistern. And Jeremiah remained in the courtyard of the guard.

Zedekiah Questions Jeremiah Again

14Then King Zedekiah sent for Jeremiah the prophet and had him brought to the third entrance to the temple of the LORD. "I am going to ask you something," the king said to Jeremiah. "Do not hide anything from me."

15Jeremiah said to Zedekiah, "If I give you an answer, will you not kill me? Even if I did give you counsel, you would not listen to me."

16But King Zedekiah swore this oath secretly to Jeremiah: "As surely as the LORD lives, who has given us breath, I will neither kill you nor hand you over to those who are seeking your life."

17Then Jeremiah said to Zedekiah, "This is what the LORD God Almighty, the God of Israel, says: 'If you surrender to the officers of the king of Babylon, your life will be spared and this city will not be burned down; you and your family will live. 18But if you will not surrender to the officers of the king of Babylon, this city will be handed over to the Babylonians and they will burn it

down; you yourself will not escape from
their hands.' "
19King Zedekiah said to Jeremiah, "I
am afraid of the Jews who have gone
over to the Babylonians, for the
Babylonians may hand me over to them
and they will ill-treat me."
20"They will not hand you over,"
Jeremiah replied. "Obey the LORD by
doing what I tell you. Then it will go
well with you, and your life will be
spared. 21But if you refuse to surrender,
this is what the LORD has revealed to
me: 22All the women left in the palace
of the king of Judah will be brought
out to the officials of the king of
Babylon. Those women will say to
you:

"'They misled you and overcame
    you—
  those trusted friends of yours.
Your feet are sunk in the mud;
  your friends have deserted you.'

23"All your wives and children will be
brought out to the Babylonians. You
yourself will not escape from their
hands but will be captured by the king of
Babylon; and this city will be burned
down."
24Then Zedekiah said to Jeremiah,
"Do not let anyone know about this
conversation, or you may die. 25If the
officials hear that I talked with you, and
they come to you and say, 'Tell us what
you said to the king and what the king
said to you; do not hide it from us or we
will kill you,' 26then tell them, 'I was
pleading with the king not to send
me back to Jonathan's house to die
there.'"
27All the officials did come to Jeremiah and question him, and he told
them everything the king had ordered
him to say. So they said no more to him,
for no-one had heard his conversation
with the king.
28And Jeremiah remained in the
courtyard of the guard until the day
Jerusalem was captured.

The Fall of Jerusalem

39 This is how Jerusalem was
taken: 1In the ninth year of
Zedekiah king of Judah, in the tenth
month, Nebuchadnezzar king of Babylon marched against Jerusalem with
his whole army and laid siege to it. 2And
on the ninth day of the fourth month of
Zedekiah's eleventh year, the city wall
was broken through. 3Then all the officials of the king of Babylon came and
took seats in the Middle Gate: Nergal-
Sharezer of Samgar, Nebo-Sarsekim a
chief officer, Nergal-Sharezer a high official and all the other officials of the
king of Babylon. 4When Zedekiah king
of Judah and all the soldiers saw them,
they fled; they left the city at night by
way of the king's garden, through the
gate between the two walls, and headed
towards the Arabah.
5But the Babylonian army pursued
them and overtook Zedekiah in the
plains of Jericho. They captured him
and took him to Nebuchadnezzar king
of Babylon at Riblah in the land of
Hamath, where he pronounced sentence on him. 6There at Riblah the king
of Babylon slaughtered the sons of
Zedekiah before his eyes and also killed
all the nobles of Judah. 7Then he put
out Zedekiah's eyes and bound him
with bronze shackles to take him to
Babylon.
8The Babylonians set fire to the royal
palace and the houses of the people and
broke down the walls of Jerusalem.
9Nebuzaradan commander of the imperial guard carried into exile to Babylon the people who remained in the
city, along with those who had gone
over to him, and the rest of the people.
10But Nebuzaradan the commander of
the guard left behind in the land of
Judah some of the poor people, who
owned nothing; and at that time he gave
them vineyards and fields.
11Now Nebuchadnezzar king of
Babylon had given these orders about
Jeremiah through Nebuzaradan commander of the imperial guard: 12"Take

him and look after him; don't harm him but do for him whatever he asks." [13]So Nebuzaradan the commander of the guard, Nebushazban a chief officer, Nergal-Sharezer a high official and all the other officers of the king of Babylon [14]sent and had Jeremiah taken out of the courtyard of the guard. They handed him over to Gedaliah son of Ahikam, the son of Shaphan, to take him back to his home. So he remained among his own people.

[15]While Jeremiah had been confined in the courtyard of the guard, the word of the LORD came to him: [16]"Go and tell Ebed-Melech the Cushite, 'This is what the LORD Almighty, the God of Israel, says: I am about to fulfil my words against this city through disaster, not prosperity. At that time they will be fulfilled before your eyes. [17]But I will rescue you on that day, declares the LORD; you will not be handed over to those you fear. [18]I will save you; you will not fall by the sword but will escape with your life, because you trust in me, declares the LORD.'"

Jeremiah Freed

40 The word came to Jeremiah from the LORD after Nebuzaradan commander of the imperial guard had released him at Ramah. He had found Jeremiah bound in chains among all the captives from Jerusalem and Judah who were being carried into exile to Babylon. [2]When the commander of the guard found Jeremiah, he said to him, "The LORD your God decreed this disaster for this place. [3]And now the LORD has brought it about; he has done just as he said he would. All this happened because you people sinned against the LORD and did not obey him. [4]But today I am freeing you from the chains on your wrists. Come with me to Babylon, if you like, and I will look after you; but if you do not want to, then don't come. Look, the whole country lies before you; go wherever you please." [5]However, before Jeremiah turned to go, Nebuzaradan added, "Go back to Gedaliah son of Ahikam, the son of Shaphan, whom the king of Babylon has appointed over the towns of Judah, and live with him among the people, or go anywhere else you please."

Then the commander gave him provisions and a present and let him go. [6]So Jeremiah went to Gedaliah son of Ahikam at Mizpah and stayed with him among the people who were left behind in the land.

NEW TESTAMENT READING
1 Timothy 3:1–16

Overseers and Deacons

3 Here is a trustworthy saying: If anyone sets his heart on being an overseer, he desires a noble task. [2]Now the overseer must be above reproach, the husband of but one wife, temperate, self-controlled, respectable, hospitable, able to teach, [3]not given to drunkenness, not violent but gentle, not quarrelsome, not a lover of money. [4]He must manage his own family well and see that his children obey him with proper respect. [5](If anyone does not know how to manage his own family, how can he take care of God's church?) [6]He must not be a recent convert, or he may become conceited and fall under the same judgment as the devil. [7]He must also have a good reputation with outsiders, so that he will not fall into disgrace and into the devil's trap.

[8]Deacons, likewise, are to be men worthy of respect, sincere, not indulging in much wine, and not pursuing dishonest gain. [9]They must keep hold of the deep truths of the faith with a clear conscience. [10]They must first be tested;

and then if there is nothing against
them, let them serve as deacons.
11In the same way, their wives are to
be women worthy of respect, not malicious talkers but temperate and trustworthy in everything.
12A deacon must be the husband of
but one wife and must manage his children and his household well. 13Those
who have served well gain an excellent
standing and great assurance in their
faith in Christ Jesus.
14Although I hope to come to you
soon, I am writing you these instructions so that, 15if I am delayed, you will
know how people ought to conduct
themselves in God's household, which
is the church of the living God, the pillar
and foundation of the truth. 16Beyond
all question, the mystery of godliness is
great:

He appeared in a body,
was vindicated by the Spirit,
was seen by angels,
was preached among the nations,
was believed on in the world,
was taken up in glory.

READING FROM PSALMS
Psalm 119:57–64

ח Heth

57You are my portion, O LORD;
I have promised to obey your words.
58I have sought your face with all my heart;
be gracious to me according to your promise.
59I have considered my ways
and have turned my steps to your statutes.
60I will hasten and not delay
to obey your commands.
61Though the wicked bind me with ropes,
I will not forget your law.
62At midnight I rise to give you thanks
for your righteous laws.
63I am a friend to all who fear you,
to all who follow your precepts.
64The earth is filled with your love, O LORD;
teach me your decrees.

DAY 292

OCTOBER 19

OLD TESTAMENT READING
Jeremiah 40:7–42:22

Gedaliah Assassinated

7When all the army officers and their
men who were still in the open country
heard that the king of Babylon had
appointed Gedaliah son of Ahikam as
governor over the land and had put him
in charge of the men, women and children who were the poorest in the land
and who had not been carried into exile
to Babylon, 8they came to Gedaliah at
Mizpah—Ishmael son of Nethaniah,
Johanan and Jonathan the sons of
Kareah, Seraiah son of Tanhumeth, the
sons of Ephai the Netophathite, and
Jaazaniah the son of the Maacathite,
and their men. 9Gedaliah son of Ahikam, the son of Shaphan, took an oath
to reassure them and their men. "Do
not be afraid to serve the Babylonians,"
he said. "Settle down in the land and
serve the king of Babylon, and it will go
well with you. 10I myself will stay in
Mizpah to represent you before the
Babylonians who come to us, but you
are to harvest the wine, summer fruit
and oil, and put them in your storage
jars, and live in the towns you have
taken over."

11When all the Jews in Moab,
Ammon, Edom and all the other countries heard that the king of Babylon had
left a remnant in Judah and had
appointed Gedaliah son of Ahikam, the
son of Shaphan, as governor over them,
12they all came back to the land of
Judah, to Gedaliah at Mizpah, from all
the countries where they had been scattered. And they harvested an abundance of wine and summer fruit.
13Johanan son of Kareah and all the
army officers still in the open country
came to Gedaliah at Mizpah 14and said
to him, "Don't you know that Baalis
king of the Ammonites has sent Ishmael
son of Nethaniah to take your life?" But
Gedaliah son of Ahikam did not believe
them.
15Then Johanan son of Kareah said
privately to Gedaliah in Mizpah, "Let
me go and kill Ishmael son of Nethaniah, and no-one will know it. Why
should he take your life and cause all the
Jews who are gathered around you to be
scattered and the remnant of Judah to
perish?"
16But Gedaliah son of Ahikam said to
Johanan son of Kareah, "Don't do such
a thing! What you are saying about
Ishmael is not true."

41 In the seventh month Ishmael
son of Nethaniah, the son of
Elishama, who was of royal blood and
had been one of the king's officers,
came with ten men to Gedaliah son of
Ahikam at Mizpah. While they were
eating together there, 2Ishmael son of
Nethaniah and the ten men who were
with him got up and struck down Gedaliah son of Ahikam, the son of Shaphan,
with the sword, killing the one whom
the king of Babylon had appointed as
governor over the land. 3Ishmael also
killed all the Jews who were with Gedaliah at Mizpah, as well as the Babylonian soldiers who were there.
4The day after Gedaliah's assassin-
ation, before anyone knew about it,
5eighty men who had shaved off their
beards, torn their clothes and cut themselves came from Shechem, Shiloh and
Samaria, bringing grain offerings and
incense with them to the house of the
LORD. 6Ishmael son of Nethaniah went
out from Mizpah to meet them, weeping as he went. When he met them, he
said, "Come to Gedaliah son of Ahikam." 7When they went into the city,
Ishmael son of Nethaniah and the men
who were with him slaughtered them
and threw them into a cistern. 8But ten
of them said to Ishmael, "Don't kill us!
We have wheat and barley, oil and
honey, hidden in a field." So he let them
alone and did not kill them with the
others. 9Now the cistern where he threw
all the bodies of the men he had killed
along with Gedaliah was the one King
Asa had made as part of his defence
against Baasha king of Israel. Ishmael
son of Nethaniah filled it with the dead.
10Ishmael made captives of all the rest
of the people who were in Mizpah—the
king's daughters along with all the
others who were left there, over whom
Nebuzaradan commander of the imperial guard had appointed Gedaliah
son of Ahikam. Ishmael son of Nethaniah took them captive and set out to
cross over to the Ammonites.
11When Johanan son of Kareah and
all the army officers who were with him
heard about all the crimes Ishmael son
of Nethaniah had committed, 12they
took all their men and went to fight
Ishmael son of Nethaniah. They caught
up with him near the great pool in
Gibeon. 13When all the people Ishmael
had with him saw Johanan son of
Kareah and the army officers who were
with him, they were glad. 14All the
people Ishmael had taken captive at
Mizpah turned and went over to Johanan son of Kareah. 15But Ishmael son
of Nethaniah and eight of his men
escaped from Johanan and fled to the
Ammonites.

Flight to Egypt

16Then Johanan son of Kareah and all
the army officers who were with him led

away all the survivors from Mizpah
whom he had recovered from Ishmael
son of Nethaniah after he had assassinated Gedaliah son of Ahikam: the
soldiers, women, children and court
officials he had brought from Gibeon.
17And they went on, stopping at Geruth
Kimham near Bethlehem on their way
to Egypt 18to escape the Babylonians.
They were afraid of them because
Ishmael son of Nethaniah had killed
Gedaliah son of Ahikam, whom the
king of Babylon had appointed as governor over the land.

42 Then all the army officers, including Johanan son of Kareah
and Jezaniah son of Hoshaiah, and
all the people from the least to the
greatest approached 2Jeremiah the
prophet and said to him, "Please hear
our petition and pray to the LORD
your God for this entire remnant. For
as you now see, though we were once
many, now only a few are left. 3Pray
that the LORD your God will tell us
where we should go and what we should
do."

4"I have heard you," replied Jeremiah the prophet. "I will certainly pray
to the LORD your God as you have
requested; I will tell you everything the
LORD says and will keep nothing back
from you."

5Then they said to Jeremiah, "May
the LORD be a true and faithful witness
against us if we do not act in accordance
with everything the LORD your God
sends you to tell us. 6Whether it is
favourable or unfavourable, we will
obey the LORD our God, to whom we
are sending you, so that it will go well
with us, for we will obey the LORD our
God."

7Ten days later the word of the LORD
came to Jeremiah. 8So he called
together Johanan son of Kareah and all
the army officers who were with him
and all the people from the least to the
greatest. 9He said to them, "This is
what the LORD, the God of Israel, to
whom you sent me to present your
petition, says: 10'If you stay in this
land, I will build you up and not tear
you down; I will plant you and not uproot you, for I am grieved over the
disaster I have inflicted on you. 11Do
not be afraid of the king of Babylon,
whom you now fear. Do not be afraid
of him, declares the LORD, for I am
with you and will save you and deliver
you from his hands. 12I will show you
compassion so that he will have compassion on you and restore you to
your land.'

13"However, if you say, 'We will not
stay in this land,' and so disobey the
LORD your God, 14and if you say, 'No,
we will go and live in Egypt, where we
will not see war or hear the trumpet or
be hungry for bread,' 15then hear the
word of the LORD, O remnant of Judah.
This is what the LORD Almighty, the
God of Israel, says: 'If you are determined to go to Egypt and you do go to
settle there, 16then the sword you fear
will overtake you there, and the famine
you dread will follow you into Egypt,
and there you will die. 17Indeed, all who
are determined to go to Egypt to settle
there will die by the sword, famine and
plague; not one of them will survive or
escape the disaster I will bring on them.'
18This is what the LORD Almighty, the
God of Israel, says: 'As my anger and
wrath have been poured out on those
who lived in Jerusalem, so will my wrath
be poured out on you when you go to
Egypt. You will be an object of cursing
and horror, of condemnation and reproach; you will never see this place
again.'

19"O remnant of Judah, the LORD has
told you, 'Do not go to Egypt.' Be sure
of this: I warn you today 20that you
made a fatal mistake when you sent me
to the LORD your God and said, 'Pray to
the LORD our God for us; tell us everything he says and we will do it.' 21I have
told you today, but you still have not
obeyed the LORD your God in all he sent
me to tell you. 22So now, be sure of this:
You will die by the sword, famine and
plague in the place where you want to
go to settle."

NEW TESTAMENT READING
1 Timothy 4:1–16

Instructions to Timothy

4 The Spirit clearly says that in later times some will abandon the faith and follow deceiving spirits and things taught by demons. [2]Such teachings come through hypocritical liars, whose consciences have been seared as with a hot iron. [3]They forbid people to marry and order them to abstain from certain foods, which God created to be received with thanksgiving by those who believe and who know the truth. [4]For everything God created is good, and nothing is to be rejected if it is received with thanksgiving, [5]because it is consecrated by the word of God and prayer.

[6]If you point these things out to the brothers, you will be a good minister of Christ Jesus, brought up in the truths of the faith and of the good teaching that you have followed. [7]Have nothing to do with godless myths and old wives' tales; rather, train yourself to be godly. [8]For physical training is of some value, but godliness has value for all things, holding promise for both the present life and the life to come.

[9]This is a trustworthy saying that deserves full acceptance [10](and for this we labour and strive), that we have put our hope in the living God, who is the Saviour of all men, and especially of those who believe.

[11]Command and teach these things. [12]Don't let anyone look down on you because you are young, but set an example for the believers in speech, in life, in love, in faith and in purity. [13]Until I come, devote yourself to the public reading of Scripture, to preaching and to teaching. [14]Do not neglect your gift, which was given you through a prophetic message when the body of elders laid their hands on you.

[15]Be diligent in these matters; give yourself wholly to them, so that everyone may see your progress. [16]Watch your life and doctrine closely. Persevere in them, because if you do, you will save both yourself and your hearers.

READING FROM PROVERBS
Proverbs 25:11–20

[11]A word aptly spoken
is like apples of gold in settings of silver.

[12]Like an ear-ring of gold or an ornament of fine gold
is a wise man's rebuke to a listening ear.

[13]Like the coolness of snow at harvest time
is a trustworthy messenger to those who send him;
he refreshes the spirit of his masters.

[14]Like clouds and wind without rain
is a man who boasts of gifts he does not give.

[15]Through patience a ruler can be persuaded,
and a gentle tongue can break a bone.

[16]If you find honey, eat just enough—
too much of it, and you will vomit.

[17]Seldom set foot in your neighbour's house—
too much of you, and he will hate you.

[18]Like a club or a sword or a sharp arrow
is the man who gives false testimony against his neighbour.

[19]Like a bad tooth or a lame foot
is reliance on the unfaithful in times of trouble.

[20]Like one who takes away a garment on a cold day,
or like vinegar poured on soda,
is one who sings songs to a heavy heart.

OCTOBER 20

OLD TESTAMENT READING
Jeremiah 43:1–45:5

43 When Jeremiah finished telling
the people all the words of the
LORD their God—everything the LORD
had sent him to tell them—2Azariah
son of Hoshaiah and Johanan son of
Kareah and all the arrogant men said to
Jeremiah, "You are lying! The LORD
our God has not sent you to say, 'You
must not go to Egypt to settle there.'
3But Baruch son of Neriah is inciting
you against us to hand us over to the
Babylonians, so that they may kill us or
carry us into exile to Babylon."
4So Johanan son of Kareah and all the
army officers and all the people disobeyed the LORD's command to stay in
the land of Judah. 5Instead, Johanan
son of Kareah and all the army officers
led away all the remnant of Judah who
had come back to live in the land of
Judah from all the nations where they
had been scattered. 6They also led away
all the men, women and children and
the king's daughters whom Nebuzaradan commander of the imperial guard
had left with Gedaliah son of Ahikam,
the son of Shaphan, and Jeremiah the
prophet and Baruch son of Neriah. 7So
they entered Egypt in disobedience to
the LORD and went as far as Tahpanhes.
8In Tahpanhes the word of the LORD
came to Jeremiah: 9"While the Jews are
watching, take some large stones with
you and bury them in clay in the brick
pavement at the entrance to Pharaoh's
palace in Tahpanhes. 10Then say to
them, 'This is what the LORD Almighty,
the God of Israel, says: I will send for
my servant Nebuchadnezzar king of
Babylon, and I will set his throne over
these stones I have buried here; he will
spread his royal canopy above them.
11He will come and attack Egypt, bringing death to those destined for death,
captivity to those destined for captivity,
and the sword to those destined for the
sword. 12He will set fire to the temples of
the gods of Egypt; he will burn their
temples and take their gods captive. As
a shepherd wraps his garment round
him, so will he wrap Egypt round himself and depart from there unscathed.
13There in the temple of the sun in
Egypt he will demolish the sacred pillars
and will burn down the temples of the
gods of Egypt.'"

Disaster Because of Idolatry

44 This word came to Jeremiah
concerning all the Jews living in
Lower Egypt—in Migdol, Tahpanhes
and Memphis—and in Upper Egypt:
2"This is what the LORD Almighty, the
God of Israel, says: You saw the great
disaster I brought on Jerusalem and on
all the towns of Judah. Today they lie
deserted and in ruins 3because of the
evil they have done. They provoked me
to anger by burning incense and by worshipping other gods that neither they
nor you nor your fathers ever knew.
4Again and again I sent my servants the
prophets, who said, 'Do not do this
detestable thing that I hate!' 5But they
did not listen or pay attention; they did
not turn from their wickedness or stop
burning incense to other gods. 6There-
fore, my fierce anger was poured out; it
raged against the towns of Judah and
the streets of Jerusalem and made them
the desolate ruins they are today.
7"Now this is what the LORD God
Almighty, the God of Israel, says: Why
bring such great disaster on yourselves
by cutting off from Judah the men and
women, the children and infants, and so
leave yourselves without a remnant?
8Why provoke me to anger with what
your hands have made, burning incense
to other gods in Egypt, where you have
come to live? You will destroy yourselves and make yourselves an object of

cursing and reproach among all the
nations on earth. [9]Have you forgotten
the wickedness committed by your
fathers and by the kings and queens of
Judah and the wickedness committed
by you and your wives in the land of
Judah and the streets of Jerusalem?
[10]To this day they have not humbled
themselves or shown reverence, nor
have they followed my law and the decrees I set before you and your fathers.

[11]"Therefore, this is what the LORD
Almighty, the God of Israel, says: I am
determined to bring disaster on you and
to destroy all Judah. [12]I will take away
the remnant of Judah who were determined to go to Egypt to settle there.
They will all perish in Egypt; they will
fall by the sword or die from famine.
From the least to the greatest, they will
die by sword or famine. They will become an object of cursing and horror, of
condemnation and reproach. [13]I will
punish those who live in Egypt with the
sword, famine and plague, as I punished
Jerusalem. [14]None of the remnant of
Judah who have gone to live in Egypt
will escape or survive to return to the
land of Judah, to which they long to
return and live; none will return except
a few fugitives."

[15]Then all the men who knew that
their wives were burning incense to
other gods, along with all the women
who were present—a large assembly
—and all the people living in Lower and
Upper Egypt, said to Jeremiah, [16]"We
will not listen to the message you have
spoken to us in the name of the LORD!
[17]We will certainly do everything we
said we would: We will burn incense to
the Queen of Heaven and will pour out
drink offerings to her just as we and our
fathers, our kings and our officials did in
the towns of Judah and in the streets of
Jerusalem. At that time we had plenty
of food and were well off and suffered
no harm. [18]But ever since we stopped
burning incense to the Queen of
Heaven and pouring out drink offerings
to her, we have had nothing and have
been perishing by sword and famine."

[19]The women added, "When we
burned incense to the Queen of Heaven
and poured out drink offerings to her,
did not our husbands know that we were
making cakes like her image and pouring out drink offerings to her?"

[20]Then Jeremiah said to all the people, both men and women, who were
answering him, [21]"Did not the LORD
remember and think about the incense
burned in the towns of Judah and the
streets of Jerusalem by you and your
fathers, your kings and your officials
and the people of the land? [22]When the
LORD could no longer endure your
wicked actions and the detestable things
you did, your land became an object of
cursing and a desolate waste without
inhabitants, as it is today. [23]Because
you have burned incense and have sinned against the LORD and have not
obeyed him or followed his law or his
decrees or his stipulations, this disaster
has come upon you, as you now see."

[24]Then Jeremiah said to all the people, including the women, "Hear the
word of the LORD, all you people of
Judah in Egypt. [25]This is what the LORD
Almighty, the God of Israel, says: You
and your wives have shown by your
actions what you promised when you
said, 'We will certainly carry out the
vows we made to burn incense and pour
out drink offerings to the Queen of
Heaven.'

"Go ahead then, do what you promised! Keep your vows! [26]But hear the
word of the LORD, all Jews living in
Egypt: 'I swear by my great name,' says
the LORD, 'that no-one from Judah living anywhere in Egypt shall ever again
invoke my name or swear, "As surely as
the Sovereign LORD lives." [27]For I am
watching over them for harm, not for
good; the Jews in Egypt will perish by
sword and famine until they are all destroyed. [28]Those who escape the sword
and return to the land of Judah from
Egypt will be very few. Then the whole
remnant of Judah who came to live in
Egypt will know whose word will stand
—mine or theirs.

29“ ‘This will be the sign to you that I
will punish you in this place,’ declares
the LORD, ‘so that you will know that
my threats of harm against you will
surely stand.’ 30This is what the LORD
says: ‘I am going to hand Pharaoh
Hophra king of Egypt over to his enemies who seek his life, just as I
handed Zedekiah king of Judah over
to Nebuchadnezzar king of Babylon,
the enemy who was seeking his life.’ ”

A Message to Baruch

45 This is what Jeremiah the
prophet told Baruch son of
Neriah in the fourth year of Jehoiakim
son of Josiah king of Judah, after
Baruch had written on a scroll the words
Jeremiah was then dictating: 2“This is
what the LORD, the God of Israel, says
to you, Baruch: 3You said, ‘Woe to me!
The LORD has added sorrow to my pain;
I am worn out with groaning and find no
rest.’ ”

4⌊The LORD said,⌋ “Say this to him:
‘This is what the LORD says: I will overthrow what I have built and uproot what
I have planted, throughout the land.
5Should you then seek great things for
yourself? Seek them not. For I will
bring disaster on all people, declares the
LORD, but wherever you go I will let you
escape with your life.’ ”

NEW TESTAMENT READING
1 Timothy 5:1–6:2

Advice About Widows, Elders and Slaves

5 Do not rebuke an older man
harshly, but exhort him as if he
were your father. Treat younger men as
brothers, 2older women as mothers,
and younger women as sisters, with
absolute purity.

3Give proper recognition to those
widows who are really in need. 4But if a
widow has children or grandchildren,
these should learn first of all to put their
religion into practice by caring for
their own family and so repaying
their parents and grandparents, for this
is pleasing to God. 5The widow who is
really in need and left all alone puts her
hope in God and continues night and
day to pray and to ask God for help.
6But the widow who lives for pleasure is
dead even while she lives. 7Give the
people these instructions, too, so that
no-one may be open to blame. 8If anyone does not provide for his relatives,
and especially for his immediate family,
he has denied the faith and is worse than
an unbeliever.

9No widow may be put on the list of
widows unless she is over sixty, has been
faithful to her husband, 10and is well
known for her good deeds, such as
bringing up children, showing hospitality, washing the feet of the saints,
helping those in trouble and devoting
herself to all kinds of good deeds.

11As for younger widows, do not put
them on such a list. For when their
sensual desires overcome their dedication to Christ, they want to marry.
12Thus they bring judgment on themselves, because they have broken their
first pledge. 13Besides, they get into the
habit of being idle and going about from
house to house. And not only do they
become idlers, but also gossips and
busybodies, saying things they ought
not to. 14So I counsel younger widows to
marry, to have children, to manage
their homes and to give the enemy no
opportunity for slander. 15Some have in
fact already turned away to follow
Satan.

16If any woman who is a believer has
widows in her family, she should help
them and not let the church be burdened with them, so that the church can
help those widows who are really in
need.

17The elders who direct the affairs of
the church well are worthy of double
honour, especially those whose work is
preaching and teaching. 18For the Scripture says, “Do not muzzle the ox while

it is treading out the grain," and "The
worker deserves his wages." 19Do not
entertain an accusation against an elder
unless it is brought by two or three
witnesses. 20Those who sin are to be
rebuked publicly, so that the others may
take warning.

21I charge you, in the sight of God
and Christ Jesus and the elect angels,
to keep these instructions without
partiality, and to do nothing out of
favouritism.

22Do not be hasty in the laying on of
hands, and do not share in the sins of
others. Keep yourself pure.

23Stop drinking only water, and use a
little wine because of your stomach and
your frequent illnesses.

24The sins of some men are obvious,
reaching the place of judgment ahead of
them; the sins of others trail behind
them. 25In the same way, good deeds
are obvious, and even those that are not
cannot be hidden.

6 All who are under the yoke of slavery should consider their masters
worthy of full respect, so that God's
name and our teaching may not be
slandered. 2Those who have believing
masters are not to show less respect for
them because they are brothers. Instead, they are to serve them even better, because those who benefit from
their service are believers, and dear to
them. These are the things you are to
teach and urge on them.

READING FROM PSALMS
Psalm 119:65–72

ט Teth

65Do good to your servant
according to your word, O LORD.
66Teach me knowledge and good
judgment,
for I believe in your commands.
67Before I was afflicted I went astray,
but now I obey your word.
68You are good, and what you do is
good;
teach me your decrees.
69Though the arrogant have smeared
me with lies,
I keep your precepts with all my
heart.
70Their hearts are callous and
unfeeling,
but I delight in your law.
71It was good for me to be afflicted
so that I might learn your decrees.
72The law from your mouth is more
precious to me
than thousands of pieces of silver
and gold.

OCTOBER 21

DAY 294

OLD TESTAMENT READING
Jeremiah 46:1–47:7

A Message About Egypt

46 This is the word of the LORD that
came to Jeremiah the prophet
concerning the nations:

2Concerning Egypt:

This is the message against the army
of Pharaoh Neco king of Egypt, which
was defeated at Carchemish on the
Euphrates River by Nebuchadnezzar
king of Babylon in the fourth year of
Jehoiakim son of Josiah king of Judah:

3"Prepare your shields, both large and
small,
and march out for battle!
4Harness the horses,
mount the steeds!
Take your positions
with helmets on!

Polish your spears,
put on your armour!
5What do I see?
They are terrified,
they are retreating,
their warriors are defeated.
They flee in haste
without looking back,
and there is terror on every side,"
declares the LORD.

6"The swift cannot flee
nor the strong escape.
In the north by the River Euphrates
they stumble and fall.

7"Who is this that rises like the Nile,
like rivers of surging waters?
8Egypt rises like the Nile,
like rivers of surging waters.
She says, 'I will rise and cover the earth;
I will destroy cities and their people.'
9Charge, O horses!
Drive furiously, O charioteers!
March on, O warriors—
men of Cush and Put who carry shields,
men of Lydia who draw the bow.
10But that day belongs to the Lord, the LORD Almighty—
a day of vengeance, for vengeance on his foes.
The sword will devour till it is satisfied,
till it has quenched its thirst with blood.
For the Lord, the LORD Almighty, will offer sacrifice
in the land of the north by the River Euphrates.

11"Go up to Gilead and get balm,
O Virgin Daughter of Egypt.
But you multiply remedies in vain;
there is no healing for you.
12The nations will hear of your shame;
your cries will fill the earth.
One warrior will stumble over another;
both will fall down together."

13This is the message the LORD spoke to Jeremiah the prophet about the coming of Nebuchadnezzar king of Babylon to attack Egypt:

14"Announce this in Egypt, and proclaim it in Migdol;
proclaim it also in Memphis and Tahpanhes:
'Take your positions and get ready,
for the sword devours those around you.'
15Why will your warriors be laid low?
They cannot stand, for the LORD will push them down.
16They will stumble repeatedly;
they will fall over each other.
They will say, 'Get up, let us go back
to our own people and our native lands,
away from the sword of the oppressor.'
17There they will exclaim,
'Pharaoh king of Egypt is only a loud noise;
he has missed his opportunity.'

18"As surely as I live," declares the King,
whose name is the LORD Almighty,
"one will come who is like Tabor among the mountains,
like Carmel by the sea.
19Pack your belongings for exile,
you who live in Egypt,
for Memphis will be laid waste
and lie in ruins without inhabitant.

20"Egypt is a beautiful heifer,
but a gadfly is coming
against her from the north.
21The mercenaries in her ranks
are like fattened calves.
They too will turn and flee together,
they will not stand their ground,
for the day of disaster is coming upon them,
the time for them to be punished.
22Egypt will hiss like a fleeing serpent
as the enemy advances in force;
they will come against her with axes,
like men who cut down trees.

23They will chop down her forest,"
declares the LORD,
"dense though it be.
They are more numerous than
locusts,
they cannot be counted.
24The Daughter of Egypt will be put to
shame,
handed over to the people of the
north."

25The LORD Almighty, the God of
Israel, says: "I am about to bring
punishment on Amon god of Thebes,
on Pharaoh, on Egypt and her gods and
her kings, and on those who rely on
Pharaoh. 26I will hand them over to
those who seek their lives, to
Nebuchadnezzar king of Babylon and
his officers. Later, however, Egypt will
be inhabited as in times past," declares
the LORD.

27"Do not fear, O Jacob my servant;
do not be dismayed, O Israel.
I will surely save you out of a distant
place,
and your descendants from the
land of their exile.
Jacob will again have peace and
security,
and no-one will make him afraid.
28Do not fear, O Jacob my servant,
for I am with you," declares the
LORD.
"Though I completely destroy all the
nations
among which I scatter you,
I will not completely destroy you.
I will discipline you but only with
justice;
I will not let you go entirely
unpunished."

A Message About the Philistines

47 This is the word of the LORD that came to Jeremiah the prophet concerning the Philistines before Pharaoh attacked Gaza:

2This is what the LORD says:

"See how the waters are rising in the
north;
they will become an overflowing
torrent.
They will overflow the land and
everything in it,
the towns and those who live in
them.
The people will cry out;
all who dwell in the land will wail
3at the sound of the hoofs of galloping
steeds,
at the noise of enemy chariots
and the rumble of their wheels.
Fathers will not turn to help their
children;
their hands will hang limp.
4For the day has come
to destroy all the Philistines
and to cut off all survivors
who could help Tyre and Sidon.
The LORD is about to destroy the
Philistines,
the remnant from the coasts of
Caphtor.
5Gaza will shave her head in
mourning;
Ashkelon will be silenced.
O remnant on the plain,
how long will you cut yourselves?

6" 'Ah, sword of the LORD,' ⌞you cry,⌟
'how long till you rest?
Return to your scabbard;
cease and be still.'
7But how can it rest
when the LORD has commanded it,
when he has ordered it
to attack Ashkelon and the coast?"

NEW TESTAMENT READING
1 Timothy 6:3–21

Love of Money

3If anyone teaches false doctrines and
does not agree to the sound instruction
of our Lord Jesus Christ and to godly
teaching, 4he is conceited and understands nothing. He has an unhealthy

interest in controversies and quarrels
about words that result in envy, strife,
malicious talk, evil suspicions 5and constant friction between men of corrupt
mind, who have been robbed of the
truth and who think that godliness is a
means to financial gain.

6But godliness with contentment is
great gain. 7For we brought nothing
into the world, and we can take nothing
out of it. 8But if we have food and
clothing, we will be content with that.
9People who want to get rich fall into
temptation and a trap and into many
foolish and harmful desires that plunge
men into ruin and destruction. 10For the
love of money is a root of all kinds of
evil. Some people, eager for money,
have wandered from the faith and
pierced themselves with many griefs.

Paul's Charge to Timothy

11But you, man of God, flee from all
this, and pursue righteousness, godliness, faith, love, endurance and gentleness. 12Fight the good fight of the faith.
Take hold of the eternal life to which
you were called when you made your
good confession in the presence of
many witnesses. 13In the sight of God,
who gives life to everything, and of
Christ Jesus, who while testifying before Pontius Pilate made the good confession, I charge you 14to keep this
command without spot or blame until
the appearing of our Lord Jesus Christ,
15which God will bring about in his own
time—God, the blessed and only
Ruler, the King of kings and Lord of
lords, 16who alone is immortal and who
lives in unapproachable light, whom no-
one has seen or can see. To him be
honour and might for ever. Amen.

17Command those who are rich in this
present world not to be arrogant nor to
put their hope in wealth, which is so
uncertain, but to put their hope in God,
who richly provides us with everything
for our enjoyment. 18Command them to
do good, to be rich in good deeds, and
to be generous and willing to share. 19In
this way they will lay up treasure for
themselves as a firm foundation for the
coming age, so that they may take hold
of the life that is truly life.

20Timothy, guard what has been entrusted to your care. Turn away from
godless chatter and the opposing ideas
of what is falsely called knowledge,
21which some have professed and in so
doing have wandered from the faith.

Grace be with you.

READING FROM PSALMS
Psalm 119:73–80

ʾ Yodh

73Your hands made me and formed me;
give me understanding to learn your commands.
74May those who fear you rejoice when they see me,
for I have put my hope in your word.
75I know, O LORD, that your laws are righteous,
and in faithfulness you have afflicted me.
76May your unfailing love be my comfort,
according to your promise to your servant.
77Let your compassion come to me that I may live,
for your law is my delight.
78May the arrogant be put to shame for wronging me without cause;
but I will meditate on your precepts.
79May those who fear you turn to me,
those who understand your statutes.
80May my heart be blameless towards your decrees,
that I may not be put to shame.

OLD TESTAMENT READING

Jeremiah 48:1–49:6

A Message About Moab

48 Concerning Moab:

This is what the LORD Almighty, the God of Israel, says:

"Woe to Nebo, for it will be ruined.
Kiriathaim will be disgraced and captured;
the stronghold will be disgraced and shattered.
2Moab will be praised no more;
in Heshbon men will plot her downfall:
'Come, let us put an end to that nation.'
You too, O Madmen, will be silenced;
the sword will pursue you.
3Listen to the cries from Horonaim,
cries of great havoc and destruction.
4Moab will be broken;
her little ones will cry out.
5They go up the way to Luhith,
weeping bitterly as they go;
on the road down to Horonaim
anguished cries over the destruction are heard.
6Flee! Run for your lives;
become like a bush in the desert.
7Since you trust in your deeds and riches,
you too will be taken captive,
and Chemosh will go into exile,
together with his priests and officials.
8The destroyer will come against every town,
and not a town will escape.
The valley will be ruined
and the plateau destroyed,
because the LORD has spoken.
9Put salt on Moab,
for she will be laid waste;
her towns will become desolate,
with no-one to live in them.

10"A curse on him who is lax in doing the LORD's work!
A curse on him who keeps his sword from bloodshed!

11"Moab has been at rest from youth,
like wine left on its dregs,
not poured from one jar to another—
she has not gone into exile.
So she tastes as she did,
and her aroma is unchanged.
12But days are coming,"
declares the LORD,
"when I will send men who pour from jars,
and they will pour her out;
they will empty her jars
and smash her jugs.
13Then Moab will be ashamed of Chemosh,
as the house of Israel was ashamed
when they trusted in Bethel.

14"How can you say, 'We are warriors,
men valiant in battle'?
15Moab will be destroyed and her towns invaded;
her finest young men will go down in the slaughter,"
declares the King, whose name is the LORD Almighty.
16"The fall of Moab is at hand;
her calamity will come quickly.
17Mourn for her, all who live around her,
all who know her fame;
say, 'How broken is the mighty sceptre,
how broken the glorious staff!'

18"Come down from your glory
and sit on the parched ground,

O inhabitants of the Daughter of
Dibon,
for he who destroys Moab
will come up against you
and ruin your fortified cities.
19Stand by the road and watch,
you who live in Aroer.
Ask the man fleeing and the woman
escaping,
ask them, 'What has happened?'
20Moab is disgraced, for she is
shattered.
Wail and cry out!
Announce by the Arnon
that Moab is destroyed.
21Judgment has come to the plateau—
to Holon, Jahzah and Mephaath,
22 to Dibon, Nebo and Beth
Diblathaim,
23 to Kiriathaim, Beth Gamul and
Beth Meon,
24 to Kerioth and Bozrah—
to all the towns of Moab, far and
near.
25Moab's horn is cut off;
her arm is broken,"
declares the LORD.

26"Make her drunk,
for she has defied the LORD.
Let Moab wallow in her vomit;
let her be an object of ridicule.
27Was not Israel the object of your
ridicule?
Was she caught among thieves,
that you shake your head in scorn
whenever you speak of her?
28Abandon your towns and dwell
among the rocks,
you who live in Moab.
Be like a dove that makes its nest
at the mouth of a cave.

29"We have heard of Moab's pride—
her overweening pride and conceit,
her pride and arrogance
and the haughtiness of her heart.
30I know her insolence but it is futile,"
declares the LORD,
"and her boasts accomplish
nothing.
31Therefore I wail over Moab,
for all Moab I cry out,
I moan for the men of Kir
Hareseth.
32I weep for you, as Jazer weeps,
O vines of Sibmah.
Your branches spread as far as the
sea;
they reached as far as the sea of
Jazer.
The destroyer has fallen
on your ripened fruit and grapes.
33Joy and gladness are gone
from the orchards and fields of
Moab.
I have stopped the flow of wine from
the presses;
no-one treads them with shouts of
joy.
Although there are shouts,
they are not shouts of joy.

34"The sound of their cry rises
from Heshbon to Elealeh and
Jahaz,
from Zoar as far as Horonaim and
Eglath Shelishiyah,
for even the waters of Nimrim are
dried up.
35In Moab I will put an end
to those who make offerings on the
high places
and burn incense to their gods,"
declares the LORD.
36"So my heart laments for Moab like a
flute;
it laments like a flute for the men of
Kir Hareseth.
The wealth they acquired is gone.
37Every head is shaved
and every beard cut off;
every hand is slashed
and every waist is covered with
sackcloth.
38On all the roofs in Moab
and in the public squares
there is nothing but mourning,
for I have broken Moab
like a jar that no-one wants,"
declares the LORD.
39"How shattered she is! How they
wail!
How Moab turns her back in
shame!

Moab has become an object of
 ridicule,
 an object of horror to all those
 around her."

40This is what the LORD says:

"Look! An eagle is swooping down,
 spreading its wings over Moab.
41Kerioth will be captured
 and the strongholds taken.
In that day the hearts of Moab's
 warriors
 will be like the heart of a woman in
 labour.
42Moab will be destroyed as a nation
 because she defied the LORD.
43Terror and pit and snare await you,
 O people of Moab,"
 declares the LORD.
44"Whoever flees from the terror
 will fall into a pit,
whoever climbs out of the pit
 will be caught in a snare;
for I will bring upon Moab
 the year of her punishment,"
 declares the LORD.

45"In the shadow of Heshbon
 the fugitives stand helpless,
for a fire has gone out from Heshbon,
 a blaze from the midst of Sihon;
it burns the foreheads of Moab,
 the skulls of the noisy boasters.
46Woe to you, O Moab!
 The people of Chemosh are
 destroyed;
your sons are taken into exile
 and your daughters into captivity.

47"Yet I will restore the fortunes of
 Moab
 in days to come,"
 declares the LORD.

Here ends the judgment on Moab.

A Message About Ammon

49 Concerning the Ammonites:

This is what the LORD says:

"Has Israel no sons?
 Has she no heirs?
Why then has Molech taken
 possession of Gad?
 Why do his people live in its
 towns?
2But the days are coming,"
 declares the LORD,
"when I will sound the battle cry
 against Rabbah of the Ammonites;
it will become a mound of ruins,
 and its surrounding villages will be
 set on fire.
Then Israel will drive out
 those who drove her out,"
 says the LORD.
3"Wail, O Heshbon, for Ai is
 destroyed!
 Cry out, O inhabitants of Rabbah!
Put on sackcloth and mourn;
 rush here and there inside the
 walls,
for Molech will go into exile,
 together with his priests and
 officials.
4Why do you boast of your valleys,
 boast of your valleys so fruitful?
O unfaithful daughter,
 you trust in your riches and say,
 'Who will attack me?'
5I will bring terror on you
 from all those around you,"
 declares the Lord,
 the LORD Almighty.
"Every one of you will be driven
 away,
 and no-one will gather the
 fugitives.

6"Yet afterwards, I will restore the
 fortunes of the Ammonites,"
 declares the LORD.

NEW TESTAMENT READING

2 Timothy 1:1–18

1 Paul, an apostle of Christ Jesus by the will of God, according to the promise of life that is in Christ Jesus,

2To Timothy, my dear son:

Grace, mercy and peace from God the Father and Christ Jesus our Lord.

Encouragement to Be Faithful

3I thank God, whom I serve, as my
forefathers did, with a clear conscience,
as night and day I constantly remember
you in my prayers. 4Recalling your
tears, I long to see you, so that I may be
filled with joy. 5I have been reminded of
your sincere faith, which first lived in
your grandmother Lois and in your
mother Eunice and, I am persuaded,
now lives in you also. 6For this reason I
remind you to fan into flame the gift of
God, which is in you through the laying
on of my hands. 7For God did not give
us a spirit of timidity, but a spirit of
power, of love and of self-discipline.
8So do not be ashamed to testify
about our Lord, or ashamed of me his
prisoner. But join with me in suffering
for the gospel, by the power of God,
9who has saved us and called us to a holy
life—not because of anything we have
done but because of his own purpose
and grace. This grace was given us in
Christ Jesus before the beginning of
time, 10but it has now been revealed
through the appearing of our Saviour,
Christ Jesus, who has destroyed death
and has brought life and immortality to
light through the gospel. 11And of this
gospel I was appointed a herald and an
apostle and a teacher. 12That is why I
am suffering as I am. Yet I am not
ashamed, because I know whom I have
believed, and am convinced that he is
able to guard what I have entrusted to
him for that day.
13What you heard from me, keep as
the pattern of sound teaching, with faith
and love in Christ Jesus. 14Guard the
good deposit that was entrusted to you
—guard it with the help of the Holy
Spirit who lives in us.
15You know that everyone in the
province of Asia has deserted me, including Phygelus and Hermogenes.
16May the Lord show mercy to the
household of Onesiphorus, because he
often refreshed me and was not
ashamed of my chains. 17On the contrary, when he was in Rome, he
searched hard for me until he found
me. 18May the Lord grant that he will
find mercy from the Lord on that day!
You know very well in how many ways
he helped me in Ephesus.

READING FROM PSALMS
Psalm 119:81–88

כ Kaph

81My soul faints with longing for your salvation,
but I have put my hope in your word.
82My eyes fail, looking for your promise;
I say, "When will you comfort me?"
83Though I am like a wineskin in the smoke,
I do not forget your decrees.
84How long must your servant wait?
When will you punish my persecutors?
85The arrogant dig pitfalls for me,
contrary to your law.
86All your commands are trustworthy;
help me, for men persecute me without cause.
87They almost wiped me from the earth,
but I have not forsaken your precepts.
88Preserve my life according to your love,
and I will obey the statutes of your mouth.

OCTOBER 23

OLD TESTAMENT READING
Jeremiah 49:7–50:10

A Message About Edom

7Concerning Edom:

This is what the LORD Almighty says:

"Is there no longer wisdom in
Teman?
Has counsel perished from the
prudent?
Has their wisdom decayed?
8Turn and flee, hide in deep caves,
you who live in Dedan,
for I will bring disaster on Esau
at the time I punish him.
9If grape-pickers came to you,
would they not leave a few grapes?
If thieves came during the night,
would they not steal only as much
as they wanted?
10But I will strip Esau bare;
I will uncover his hiding-places,
so that he cannot conceal himself.
His children, relatives and
neighbours will perish,
and he will be no more.
11Leave your orphans; I will protect
their lives.
Your widows too can trust in me."

12This is what the LORD says: "If
those who do not deserve to drink the
cup must drink it, why should you go
unpunished? You will not go unpunished, but must drink it. 13I swear by
myself," declares the LORD, "that Bozrah will become a ruin and an object of
horror, of reproach and of cursing; and
all its towns will be in ruins for ever."

14I have heard a message from the
LORD:
An envoy was sent to the nations to
say,
"Assemble yourselves to attack it!
Rise up for battle!"

15"Now I will make you small among
the nations,
despised among men.
16The terror you inspire
and the pride of your heart have
deceived you,
you who live in the clefts of the rocks,
who occupy the heights of the hill.
Though you build your nest as high as
the eagle's,
from there I will bring you down,"
declares the LORD.
17"Edom will become an object of
horror;
all who pass by will be appalled and
will scoff
because of all its wounds.
18As Sodom and Gomorrah were
overthrown,
along with their neighbouring
towns,"
says the LORD,
"so no-one will live there;
no man will dwell in it.

19"Like a lion coming up from Jordan's
thickets
to a rich pasture-land,
I will chase Edom from its land in an
instant.
Who is the chosen one I will
appoint for this?
Who is like me and who can
challenge me?
And what shepherd can stand
against me?"
20Therefore, hear what the LORD has
planned against Edom,
what he has purposed against those
who live in Teman:
The young of the flock will be
dragged away;
he will completely destroy their
pasture because of them.
21At the sound of their fall the earth
will tremble;
their cry will resound to the Red
Sea.

22Look! An eagle will soar and swoop
down,
spreading its wings over Bozrah.
In that day the hearts of Edom's
warriors
will be like the heart of a woman in
labour.

A Message About Damascus

23Concerning Damascus:

"Hamath and Arpad are dismayed,
for they have heard bad news.
They are disheartened,
troubled like the restless sea.
24Damascus has become feeble,
she has turned to flee
and panic has gripped her;
anguish and pain have seized her,
pain like that of a woman in labour.
25Why has the city of renown not been
abandoned,
the town in which I delight?
26Surely, her young men will fall in the
streets;
all her soldiers will be silenced in
that day,"
declares the LORD Almighty.
27"I will set fire to the walls of
Damascus;
it will consume the fortresses of
Ben-Hadad."

A Message About Kedar and Hazor

28Concerning Kedar and the kingdoms of Hazor, which Nebuchadnezzar king of Babylon attacked:

This is what the LORD says:

"Arise, and attack Kedar
and destroy the people of the East.
29Their tents and their flocks will be
taken;
their shelters will be carried off
with all their goods and camels.
Men will shout to them,
'Terror on every side!'
30"Flee quickly away!
Stay in deep caves, you who live in
Hazor,"
declares the LORD.
"Nebuchadnezzar king of Babylon
has plotted against you;
he has devised a plan against you.

31"Arise and attack a nation at ease,
which lives in confidence,"
declares the LORD,
"a nation that has neither gates nor
bars;
its people live alone.
32Their camels will become plunder,
and their large herds will be booty.
I will scatter to the winds those who
are in distant places
and will bring disaster on them
from every side,"
declares the LORD.
33"Hazor will become a haunt of
jackals,
a desolate place for ever.
No-one will live there;
no man will dwell in it."

A Message About Elam

34This is the word of the LORD that came to Jeremiah the prophet concerning Elam, early in the reign of Zedekiah king of Judah:

35This is what the LORD Almighty says:

"See, I will break the bow of Elam,
the mainstay of their might.
36I will bring against Elam the four
winds
from the four quarters of the
heavens;
I will scatter them to the four winds,
and there will not be a nation
where Elam's exiles do not go.
37I will shatter Elam before their foes,
before those who seek their lives;
I will bring disaster upon them,
even my fierce anger,"
declares the LORD.
"I will pursue them with the sword
until I have made an end of them.
38I will set my throne in Elam
and destroy her king and officials,"
declares the LORD.

39"Yet I will restore the fortunes of
Elam
in days to come,"
declares the LORD.

A Message About Babylon

50 This is the word the LORD spoke through Jeremiah the prophet concerning Babylon and the land of the Babylonians:

2"Announce and proclaim among the
nations,
lift up a banner and proclaim it;
keep nothing back, but say,
'Babylon will be captured;
Bel will be put to shame,
Marduk filled with terror.
Her images will be put to shame
and her idols filled with terror.'
3A nation from the north will attack
her
and lay waste her land.
No-one will live in it;
both men and animals will flee
away.

4"In those days, at that time,"
declares the LORD,
"the people of Israel and the people
of Judah together
will go in tears to seek the LORD
their God.
5They will ask the way to Zion
and turn their faces towards it.
They will come and bind themselves
to the LORD
in an everlasting covenant
that will not be forgotten.

6"My people have been lost sheep;
their shepherds have led them
astray
and caused them to roam on the
mountains.
They wandered over mountain and
hill
and forgot their own resting place.
7Whoever found them devoured
them;
their enemies said, 'We are not
guilty,
for they sinned against the LORD,
their true pasture,
the LORD, the hope of their
fathers.'

8"Flee out of Babylon;
leave the land of the Babylonians,
and be like the goats that lead the
flock.
9For I will stir up and bring against
Babylon
an alliance of great nations from
the land of the north.
They will take up their positions
against her,
and from the north she will be
captured.
Their arrows will be like skilled
warriors
who do not return empty-handed.
10So Babylonia will be plundered;
all who plunder her will have their
fill,"
declares the LORD.

NEW TESTAMENT READING
2 Timothy 2:1–26

2 You then, my son, be strong in the
grace that is in Christ Jesus. 2And
the things you have heard me say in the
presence of many witnesses entrust to
reliable men who will also be qualified
to teach others. 3Endure hardship with
us like a good soldier of Christ Jesus.
4No-one serving as a soldier gets involved in civilian affairs—he wants to
please his commanding officer.
5Similarly, if anyone competes as an
athlete, he does not receive the victor's
crown unless he competes according to
the rules. 6The hardworking farmer
should be the first to receive a share of
the crops. 7Reflect on what I am saying,
for the Lord will give you insight into all
this.

8Remember Jesus Christ, raised from
the dead, descended from David. This
is my gospel, 9for which I am suffering
even to the point of being chained
like a criminal. But God's word is
not chained. 10Therefore I endure

everything for the sake of the elect, that
they too may obtain the salvation that
is in Christ Jesus, with eternal glory.
11Here is a trustworthy saying:

If we died with him,
we will also live with him;
12if we endure,
we will also reign with him.
If we disown him,
he will also disown us;
13if we are faithless,
he will remain faithful,
for he cannot disown himself.

A Workman Approved by God

14Keep reminding them of these
things. Warn them before God against
quarrelling about words; it is of no
value, and only ruins those who listen.
15Do your best to present yourself to
God as one approved, a workman who
does not need to be ashamed and who
correctly handles the word of truth.
16Avoid godless chatter, because those
who indulge in it will become more and
more ungodly. 17Their teaching will
spread like gangrene. Among them are
Hymenaeus and Philetus, 18who have
wandered away from the truth. They
say that the resurrection has already
taken place, and they destroy the faith
of some. 19Nevertheless, God's solid
foundation stands firm, sealed with this
inscription: "The Lord knows those
who are his," and, "Everyone who confesses the name of the Lord must turn
away from wickedness."
20In a large house there are articles
not only of gold and silver, but also of
wood and clay; some are for noble purposes and some for ignoble. 21If a man
cleanses himself from the latter, he will
be an instrument for noble purposes,
made holy, useful to the Master and
prepared to do any good work.
22Flee the evil desires of youth, and
pursue righteousness, faith, love and
peace, along with those who call on the
Lord out of a pure heart. 23Don't have
anything to do with foolish and stupid
arguments, because you know they
produce quarrels. 24And the Lord's servant must not quarrel; instead, he must
be kind to everyone, able to teach, not
resentful. 25Those who oppose him he
must gently instruct, in the hope that
God will grant them repentance leading
them to a knowledge of the truth, 26and
that they will come to their senses and
escape from the trap of the devil, who
has taken them captive to do his will.

READING FROM PROVERBS

Proverbs 25:21–26:2

21If your enemy is hungry, give him
food to eat;
if he is thirsty, give him water to
drink.
22In doing this, you will heap burning
coals on his head,
and the LORD will reward you.

23As a north wind brings rain,
so a sly tongue brings angry looks.

24Better to live on a corner of the roof
than share a house with a
quarrelsome wife.

25Like cold water to a weary soul
is good news from a distant land.

26Like a muddied spring or a polluted
well
is a righteous man who gives way to
the wicked.

27It is not good to eat too much honey,
nor is it honourable to seek one's
own honour.

28Like a city whose walls are broken
down
is a man who lacks self-control.

26 Like snow in summer or rain in
harvest,
honour is not fitting for a fool.
2Like a fluttering sparrow or a darting
swallow,
an undeserved curse does not come
to rest.

OCTOBER 24

DAY 297

OLD TESTAMENT READING
Jeremiah 50:11–51:14

11"Because you rejoice and are glad,
you who pillage my inheritance,
because you frolic like a heifer
threshing corn
and neigh like stallions,
12your mother will be greatly ashamed;
she who gave you birth will be
disgraced.
She will be the least of the nations—
a wilderness, a dry land, a desert.
13Because of the LORD's anger she will
not be inhabited
but will be completely desolate.
All who pass Babylon will be
horrified and scoff
because of all her wounds.

14"Take up your positions round
Babylon,
all you who draw the bow.
Shoot at her! Spare no arrows,
for she has sinned against the
LORD.
15Shout against her on every side!
She surrenders, her towers fall,
her walls are torn down.
Since this is the vengeance of the
LORD,
take vengeance on her;
do to her as she has done to others.
16Cut off from Babylon the sower,
and the reaper with his sickle at
harvest.
Because of the sword of the
oppressor
let everyone return to his own
people,
let everyone flee to his own land.

17"Israel is a scattered flock
that lions have chased away.
The first to devour him
was the king of Assyria;
the last to crush his bones
was Nebuchadnezzar king of
Babylon."

18Therefore this is what the LORD
Almighty, the God of Israel, says:

"I will punish the king of Babylon
and his land
as I punished the king of Assyria.
19But I will bring Israel back to his own
pasture
and he will graze on Carmel and
Bashan;
his appetite will be satisfied
on the hills of Ephraim and Gilead.
20In those days, at that time,"
declares the LORD,
"search will be made for Israel's
guilt,
but there will be none,
and for the sins of Judah,
but none will be found,
for I will forgive the remnant I
spare.

21"Attack the land of Merathaim
and those who live in Pekod.
Pursue, kill and completely destroy
them,"
declares the LORD.
"Do everything I have commanded
you.
22The noise of battle is in the land,
the noise of great destruction!
23How broken and shattered
is the hammer of the whole earth!
How desolate is Babylon
among the nations!
24I set a trap for you, O Babylon,
and you were caught before you
knew it;
you were found and captured
because you opposed the LORD.
25The LORD has opened his arsenal
and brought out the weapons of his
wrath,
for the Sovereign LORD Almighty has
work to do
in the land of the Babylonians.
26Come against her from afar.
Break open her granaries;
pile her up like heaps of grain.

Completely destroy her
and leave her no remnant.
27Kill all her young bulls;
let them go down to the slaughter!
Woe to them! For their day has
come,
the time for them to be punished.
28Listen to the fugitives and refugees
from Babylon
declaring in Zion
how the LORD our God has taken
vengeance,
vengeance for his temple.

29"Summon archers against Babylon,
all those who draw the bow.
Encamp all round her;
let no-one escape.
Repay her for her deeds;
do to her as she has done.
For she defied the LORD,
the Holy One of Israel.
30Therefore, her young men will fall in
the streets;
all her soldiers will be silenced in
that day,"
declares the LORD.
31"See, I am against you, O arrogant
one,"
declares the Lord, the LORD
Almighty,
"for your day has come,
the time for you to be punished.
32The arrogant one will stumble and
fall
and no-one will help her up;
I will kindle a fire in her towns
that will consume all who are
around her."

33This is what the LORD Almighty says:

"The people of Israel are oppressed,
and the people of Judah as well.
All their captors hold them fast,
refusing to let them go.
34Yet their Redeemer is strong;
the LORD Almighty is his name.
He will vigorously defend their cause
so that he may bring rest to their
land,
but unrest to those who live in
Babylon.

35"A sword against the Babylonians!"
declares the LORD—
"against those who live in Babylon
and against her officials and wise
men!
36A sword against her false prophets!
They will become fools.
A sword against her warriors!
They will be filled with terror.
37A sword against her horses and
chariots
and all the foreigners in her ranks!
They will become women.
A sword against her treasures!
They will be plundered.
38A drought on her waters!
They will dry up.
For it is a land of idols,
idols that will go mad with terror.

39"So desert creatures and hyenas will
live there,
and there the owl will dwell.
It will never again be inhabited
or lived in from generation to
generation.
40As God overthrew Sodom and
Gomorrah
along with their neighbouring
towns,"
declares the LORD,
"so no-one will live there;
no man will dwell in it.

41"Look! An army is coming from the
north;
a great nation and many kings
are being stirred up from the ends
of the earth.
42They are armed with bows and
spears;
they are cruel and without mercy.
They sound like the roaring sea
as they ride on their horses;
they come like men in battle
formation
to attack you, O Daughter of
Babylon.

43The king of Babylon has heard
reports about them,
and his hands hang limp.
Anguish has gripped him,
pain like that of a woman in
labour.
44Like a lion coming up from Jordan's
thickets
to a rich pasture-land,
I will chase Babylon from its land in
an instant.
Who is the chosen one I will
appoint for this?
Who is like me and who can
challenge me?
And what shepherd can stand
against me?"
45Therefore, hear what the LORD has
planned against Babylon,
what he has purposed against the
land of the Babylonians:
The young of the flock will be
dragged away;
he will completely destroy their
pasture because of them.
46At the sound of Babylon's capture
the earth will tremble;
its cry will resound among the
nations.

51 This is what the LORD says:

"See, I will stir up the spirit of a
destroyer
against Babylon and the people of
Leb Kamai.
2I will send foreigners to Babylon
to winnow her and to devastate her
land;
they will oppose her on every side
in the day of her disaster.
3Let not the archer string his bow,
nor let him put on his armour.
Do not spare her young men;
completely destroy her army.
4They will fall down slain in Babylon,
fatally wounded in her streets.
5For Israel and Judah have not been
forsaken
by their God, the LORD Almighty,
though their land is full of guilt
before the Holy One of Israel.

6"Flee from Babylon!
Run for your lives!
Do not be destroyed because of
her sins.
It is time for the LORD's vengeance;
he will pay her what she deserves.
7Babylon was a gold cup in the LORD's
hand;
she made the whole earth drunk.
The nations drank her wine;
therefore they have now gone
mad.
8Babylon will suddenly fall and be
broken.
Wail over her!
Get balm for her pain;
perhaps she can be healed.

9" 'We would have healed Babylon,
but she cannot be healed;
let us leave her and each go to his
own land,
for her judgment reaches to the
skies,
it rises as high as the clouds.'

10" 'The LORD has vindicated us;
come, let us tell in Zion
what the LORD our God has done.'

11"Sharpen the arrows,
take up the shields!
The LORD has stirred up the kings of
the Medes,
because his purpose is to destroy
Babylon.
The LORD will take vengeance,
vengeance for his temple.
12Lift up a banner against the walls of
Babylon!
Reinforce the guard,
station the watchmen,
prepare an ambush!
The LORD will carry out his purpose,
his decree against the people of
Babylon.
13You who live by many waters
and are rich in treasures,
your end has come,
the time for you to be cut off.
14The LORD Almighty has sworn by
himself:

I will surely fill you with men, as
with a swarm of locusts,
and they will shout in triumph over
you.

NEW TESTAMENT READING
2 Timothy 3:1–17

Godlessness in the Last Days

3 But mark this: There will be terrible times in the last days. 2People
will be lovers of themselves, lovers of
money, boastful, proud, abusive, disobedient to their parents, ungrateful,
unholy, 3without love, unforgiving,
slanderous, without self-control, brutal,
not lovers of the good, 4treacherous,
rash, conceited, lovers of pleasure
rather than lovers of God—5having a
form of godliness but denying its power.
Have nothing to do with them.

6They are the kind who worm their
way into homes and gain control over
weak-willed women, who are loaded
down with sins and are swayed by all
kinds of evil desires, 7always learning
but never able to acknowledge the
truth. 8Just as Jannes and Jambres
opposed Moses, so also these men
oppose the truth—men of depraved
minds, who, as far as the faith is concerned, are rejected. 9But they will not
get very far because, as in the case of
those men, their folly will be clear to
everyone.

Paul's Charge to Timothy

10You, however, know all about my
teaching, my way of life, my purpose,
faith, patience, love, endurance, 11per-
secutions, sufferings—what kinds of
things happened to me in Antioch, Iconium and Lystra, the persecutions I endured. Yet the Lord rescued me from
all of them. 12In fact, everyone who
wants to live a godly life in Christ Jesus
will be persecuted, 13while evil men and
impostors will go from bad to worse,
deceiving and being deceived. 14But as
for you, continue in what you have
learned and have become convinced of,
because you know those from whom
you learned it, 15and how from infancy
you have known the holy Scriptures,
which are able to make you wise for
salvation through faith in Christ Jesus.
16All Scripture is God-breathed and is
useful for teaching, rebuking, correct-
ing and training in righteousness, 17so
that the man of God may be thoroughly
equipped for every good work.

READING FROM PSALMS
Psalm 119:89–96

ל Lamedh

89Your word, O LORD, is eternal;
it stands firm in the heavens.
90Your faithfulness continues through
all generations;
you established the earth, and it
endures.
91Your laws endure to this day,
for all things serve you.
92If your law had not been my delight,
I would have perished in my
affliction.
93I will never forget your precepts,
for by them you have preserved my
life.
94Save me, for I am yours;
I have sought out your precepts.
95The wicked are waiting to destroy
me,
but I will ponder your statutes.
96To all perfection I see a limit;
but your commands are boundless.

OLD TESTAMENT READING
Jeremiah 51:15–64

15"He made the earth by his power;
he founded the world by his wisdom
and stretched out the heavens by his understanding.
16When he thunders, the waters in the heavens roar;
he makes clouds rise from the ends of the earth.
He sends lightning with the rain
and brings out the wind from his storehouses.

17"Every man is senseless and without knowledge;
every goldsmith is shamed by his idols.
His images are a fraud;
they have no breath in them.
18They are worthless, the objects of mockery;
when their judgment comes, they will perish.
19He who is the Portion of Jacob is not like these,
for he is the Maker of all things,
including the tribe of his inheritance—
the LORD Almighty is his name.

20"You are my war club,
my weapon for battle—
with you I shatter nations,
with you I destroy kingdoms,
21with you I shatter horse and rider,
with you I shatter chariot and driver,
22with you I shatter man and woman,
with you I shatter old man and youth,
with you I shatter young man and maiden,
23with you I shatter shepherd and flock,
with you I shatter farmer and oxen,
with you I shatter governors and officials.

24"Before your eyes I will repay Babylon and all who live in Babylonia for all the wrong they have done in Zion," declares the LORD.

25"I am against you, O destroying mountain,
you who destroy the whole earth,"
declares the LORD.
"I will stretch out my hand against you,
roll you off the cliffs,
and make you a burnt-out mountain.
26No rock will be taken from you for a cornerstone,
nor any stone for a foundation,
for you will be desolate for ever,"
declares the LORD.

27"Lift up a banner in the land!
Blow the trumpet among the nations!
Prepare the nations for battle against her;
summon against her these kingdoms:
Ararat, Minni and Ashkenaz.
Appoint a commander against her;
send up horses like a swarm of locusts.
28Prepare the nations for battle against her—
the kings of the Medes,
their governors and all their officials,
and all the countries they rule.
29The land trembles and writhes,
for the LORD's purposes against Babylon stand—
to lay waste the land of Babylon
so that no-one will live there.
30Babylon's warriors have stopped fighting;
they remain in their strongholds.

Their strength is exhausted;
they have become like women.
Her dwellings are set on fire;
the bars of her gates are broken.
31One courier follows another
and messenger follows messenger
to announce to the king of Babylon
that his entire city is captured,
32the river crossings seized,
the marshes set on fire,
and the soldiers terrified."

33This is what the LORD Almighty, the God of Israel, says:

"The Daughter of Babylon is like a threshing-floor
at the time it is trampled;
the time to harvest her will soon come."

34"Nebuchadnezzar king of Babylon has devoured us,
he has thrown us into confusion,
he has made us an empty jar.
Like a serpent he has swallowed us
and filled his stomach with our delicacies,
and then has spewed us out.
35May the violence done to our flesh be upon Babylon,"
say the inhabitants of Zion.
"May our blood be on those who live in Babylonia,"
says Jerusalem.

36Therefore, this is what the LORD says:

"See, I will defend your cause
and avenge you;
I will dry up her sea
and make her springs dry.
37Babylon will be a heap of ruins,
a haunt of jackals,
an object of horror and scorn,
a place where no-one lives.
38Her people all roar like young lions,
they growl like lion cubs.
39But while they are aroused,
I will set out a feast for them
and make them drunk,
so that they shout with laughter—
then sleep for ever and not awake,"
declares the LORD.
40"I will bring them down
like lambs to the slaughter,
like rams and goats.

41"How Sheshach will be captured,
the boast of the whole earth seized!
What a horror Babylon will be
among the nations!
42The sea will rise over Babylon;
its roaring waves will cover her.
43Her towns will be desolate,
a dry and desert land,
a land where no-one lives,
through which no man travels.
44I will punish Bel in Babylon
and make him spew out what he has swallowed.
The nations will no longer stream to him.
And the wall of Babylon will fall.

45"Come out of her, my people!
Run for your lives!
Run from the fierce anger of the LORD.
46Do not lose heart or be afraid
when rumours are heard in the land;
one rumour comes this year, another the next,
rumours of violence in the land
and of ruler against ruler.
47For the time will surely come
when I will punish the idols of Babylon;
her whole land will be disgraced
and her slain will all lie fallen within her.
48Then heaven and earth and all that is in them
will shout for joy over Babylon,
for out of the north
destroyers will attack her,"
declares the LORD.

49"Babylon must fall because of Israel's slain,
just as the slain in all the earth
have fallen because of Babylon.

50You who have escaped the sword,
leave and do not linger!
Remember the LORD in a distant land,
and think on Jerusalem."

51"We are disgraced,
for we have been insulted
and shame covers our faces,
because foreigners have entered
the holy places of the LORD's house."

52"But days are coming," declares the LORD,
"when I will punish her idols,
and throughout her land
the wounded will groan.
53Even if Babylon reaches the sky
and fortifies her lofty stronghold,
I will send destroyers against her,"
declares the LORD.

54"The sound of a cry comes from Babylon,
the sound of great destruction
from the land of the Babylonians.
55The LORD will destroy Babylon;
he will silence her noisy din.
Waves ⌞of enemies⌟ will rage like great waters;
the roar of their voices will resound.
56A destroyer will come against Babylon;
her warriors will be captured,
and their bows will be broken.
For the LORD is a God of retribution;
he will repay in full.
57I will make her officials and wise men drunk,
her governors, officers and warriors as well;
they will sleep for ever and not awake,"
declares the King, whose name is the LORD Almighty.

58This is what the LORD Almighty says:

"Babylon's thick wall will be levelled
and her high gates set on fire;
the peoples exhaust themselves for nothing,
the nations' labour is only fuel for the flames."

59This is the message Jeremiah gave to the staff officer Seraiah son of Neriah, the son of Mahseiah, when he went to Babylon with Zedekiah king of Judah in the fourth year of his reign.
60Jeremiah had written on a scroll about all the disasters that would come upon Babylon—all that had been recorded concerning Babylon. 61He said to Seraiah, "When you get to Babylon, see that you read all these words aloud.
62Then say, 'O LORD, you have said you will destroy this place, so that neither man nor animal will live in it; it will be desolate for ever.' 63When you finish reading this scroll, tie a stone to it and throw it into the Euphrates. 64Then say, 'So will Babylon sink to rise no more because of the disaster I will bring upon her. And her people will fall.' "

The words of Jeremiah end here.

NEW TESTAMENT READING
2 Timothy 4:1–22

4 In the presence of God and of Christ Jesus, who will judge the living and the dead, and in view of his appearing and his kingdom, I give you this charge: 2Preach the Word; be prepared in season and out of season; correct, rebuke and encourage—with great patience and careful instruction.
3For the time will come when men will not put up with sound doctrine. Instead, to suit their own desires, they will gather around them a great number of teachers to say what their itching ears want to hear. 4They will turn their ears away from the truth and turn aside to myths. 5But you, keep your head in all situations, endure hardship, do the work of an evangelist, discharge all the duties of your ministry.

6For I am already being poured out
like a drink offering, and the time has
come for my departure. 7I have fought
the good fight, I have finished the race, I
have kept the faith. 8Now there is in
store for me the crown of righteousness,
which the Lord, the righteous Judge,
will award to me on that day—and not
only to me, but also to all who have
longed for his appearing.

Personal Remarks

9Do your best to come to me quickly,
10for Demas, because he loved this
world, has deserted me and has gone to
Thessalonica. Crescens has gone to
Galatia, and Titus to Dalmatia. 11Only
Luke is with me. Get Mark and bring
him with you, because he is helpful to
me in my ministry. 12I sent Tychicus
to Ephesus. 13When you come, bring
the cloak that I left with Carpus at
Troas, and my scrolls, especially the
parchments.
14Alexander the metalworker did me
a great deal of harm. The Lord will
repay him for what he has done. 15You
too should be on your guard against
him, because he strongly opposed our
message.
16At my first defence, no-one came to
my support, but everyone deserted me.
May it not be held against them. 17But
the Lord stood at my side and gave me
strength, so that through me the message might be fully proclaimed and all
the Gentiles might hear it. And I was
delivered from the lion's mouth. 18The
Lord will rescue me from every evil
attack and will bring me safely to his
heavenly kingdom. To him be glory for
ever and ever. Amen.

Final Greetings

19Greet Priscilla and Aquila and the
household of Onesiphorus. 20Erastus
stayed in Corinth, and I left Trophimus
sick in Miletus. 21Do your best to get
here before winter. Eubulus greets you,
and so do Pudens, Linus, Claudia and
all the brothers.
22The Lord be with your spirit. Grace
be with you.

READING FROM PSALMS
Psalm 119:97–104

מ Mem

97Oh, how I love your law!
  I meditate on it all day long.
98Your commands make me wiser than my enemies,
  for they are ever with me.
99I have more insight than all my teachers,
  for I meditate on your statutes.
100I have more understanding than the elders,
  for I obey your precepts.
101I have kept my feet from every evil path
  so that I might obey your word.
102I have not departed from your laws,
  for you yourself have taught me.
103How sweet are your words to my taste,
  sweeter than honey to my mouth!
104I gain understanding from your precepts;
  therefore I hate every wrong path.

OCTOBER 26

DAY 299

OLD TESTAMENT READING
Jeremiah 52:1–34

The Fall of Jerusalem

52 Zedekiah was twenty-one years
old when he became king, and
he reigned in Jerusalem for eleven
years. His mother's name was Hamutal
daughter of Jeremiah; she was from
Libnah. 2He did evil in the eyes of the
LORD, just as Jehoiakim had done. 3It
was because of the LORD's anger that all
this happened to Jerusalem and Judah,
and in the end he thrust them from his
presence.

Now Zedekiah rebelled against the
king of Babylon.

4So in the ninth year of Zedekiah's
reign, on the tenth day of the tenth
month, Nebuchadnezzar king of Babylon marched against Jerusalem with
his whole army. They camped outside
the city and built siege works all around
it. 5The city was kept under siege until
the eleventh year of King Zedekiah.

6By the ninth day of the fourth month
the famine in the city had become so
severe that there was no food for the
people to eat. 7Then the city wall was
broken through, and the whole army
fled. They left the city at night through
the gate between the two walls near the
king's garden, though the Babylonians
were surrounding the city. They fled
towards the Arabah, 8but the Babylonian army pursued King Zedekiah and
overtook him in the plains of Jericho.
All his soldiers were separated from
him and scattered, 9and he was
captured.

He was taken to the king of Babylon
at Riblah in the land of Hamath, where
he pronounced sentence on him.
10There at Riblah the king of Babylon
slaughtered the sons of Zedekiah before his eyes; he also killed all the officials of Judah. 11Then he put out
Zedekiah's eyes, bound him with
bronze shackles and took him to Babylon, where he put him in prison till the
day of his death.

12On the tenth day of the fifth month,
in the nineteenth year of Nebuchadnezzar king of Babylon, Nebuzaradan commander of the imperial guard, who
served the king of Babylon, came to
Jerusalem. 13He set fire to the temple of
the LORD, the royal palace and all the
houses of Jerusalem. Every important building he burned down. 14The
whole Babylonian army under the commander of the imperial guard broke
down all the walls around Jerusalem.
15Nebuzaradan the commander of the
guard carried into exile some of the
poorest people and those who remained
in the city, along with the rest of the
craftsmen and those who had gone over
to the king of Babylon. 16But Nebuzaradan left behind the rest of the poorest
people of the land to work the vineyards
and fields.

17The Babylonians broke up the
bronze pillars, the movable stands and
the bronze Sea that were at the temple
of the LORD and they carried all the
bronze to Babylon. 18They also took
away the pots, shovels, wick trimmers,
sprinkling bowls, dishes and all the
bronze articles used in the temple service. 19The commander of the imperial
guard took away the basins, censers,
sprinkling bowls, pots, lampstands,
dishes and bowls used for drink offerings—all that were made of pure gold
or silver.

20The bronze from the two pillars, the
Sea and the twelve bronze bulls under
it, and the movable stands, which King
Solomon had made for the temple of the
LORD, was more than could be weighed.
21Each of the pillars was eighteen cubits
high and twelve cubits in circumfer-
ence; each was four fingers thick, and
hollow. 22The bronze capital on the top

of the one pillar was five cubits high and
was decorated with a network and
pomegranates of bronze all around.
The other pillar, with its pomegranates,
was similar. 23There were ninety-six
pomegranates on the sides; the total
number of pomegranates above the surrounding network was a hundred.

24The commander of the guard took
as prisoners Seraiah the chief priest,
Zephaniah the priest next in rank and
the three doorkeepers. 25Of those still
in the city, he took the officer in charge
of the fighting men, and seven royal
advisers. He also took the secretary
who was chief officer in charge of conscripting the people of the land and sixty
of his men who were found in the city.
26Nebuzaradan the commander took
them all and brought them to the king of
Babylon at Riblah. 27There at Riblah,
in the land of Hamath, the king had
them executed.

So Judah went into captivity, away
from her land. 28This is the number of
the people Nebuchadnezzar carried
into exile:

in the seventh year, 3,023 Jews;
29in Nebuchadnezzar's eighteenth year,
832 people from Jerusalem;
30in his twenty-third year,
745 Jews taken into exile by
Nebuzaradan
the commander of the imperial
guard.
There were 4,600 people in all.

Jehoiachin Released

31In the thirty-seventh year of the
exile of Jehoiachin king of Judah, in the
year Evil-Merodach became king of
Babylon, he released Jehoiachin king of
Judah and freed him from prison on the
twenty-fifth day of the twelfth month.
32He spoke kindly to him and gave him a
seat of honour higher than those of the
other kings who were with him in Babylon. 33So Jehoiachin put aside his
prison clothes and for the rest of his life
ate regularly at the king's table. 34Day
by day the king of Babylon gave
Jehoiachin a regular allowance as long
as he lived, till the day of his death.

NEW TESTAMENT READING

Titus 1:1–16

1 Paul, a servant of God and an apostle of Jesus Christ for the faith of
God's elect and the knowledge of the
truth that leads to godliness—2a faith
and knowledge resting on the hope of
eternal life, which God, who does not
lie, promised before the beginning of
time, 3and at his appointed season he
brought his word to light through the
preaching entrusted to me by the command of God our Saviour,

4To Titus, my true son in our common faith:

Grace and peace from God the
Father and Christ Jesus our Saviour.

Titus' Task on Crete

5The reason I left you in Crete was
that you might straighten out what was
left unfinished and appoint elders in
every town, as I directed you. 6An elder
must be blameless, the husband of but
one wife, a man whose children believe
and are not open to the charge of being
wild and disobedient. 7Since an overseer is entrusted with God's work, he
must be blameless—not overbearing,
not quick-tempered, not given to
drunkenness, not violent, not pursuing
dishonest gain. 8Rather he must be hospitable, one who loves what is good,
who is self-controlled, upright, holy and
disciplined. 9He must hold firmly to the
trustworthy message as it has been
taught, so that he can encourage others
by sound doctrine and refute those who
oppose it.

10For there are many rebellious people, mere talkers and deceivers, especially those of the circumcision group.
11They must be silenced, because they
are ruining whole households by
teaching things they ought not to teach
—and that for the sake of dishonest
gain. 12Even one of their own prophets

has said, "Cretans are always liars, evil brutes, lazy gluttons." 13This testimony is true. Therefore, rebuke them sharply, so that they will be sound in the faith 14and will pay no attention to Jewish myths or to the commands of those who reject the truth. 15To the pure, all things are pure, but to those who are corrupted and do not believe, nothing is pure. In fact, both their minds and consciences are corrupted. 16They claim to know God, but by their actions they deny him. They are detestable, disobedient and unfit for doing anything good.

READING FROM PSALMS
Psalm 119:105–112

נ Nun

105Your word is a lamp to my feet
and a light for my path.
106I have taken an oath and confirmed it,
that I will follow your righteous laws.
107I have suffered much;
preserve my life, O LORD,
according to your word.
108Accept, O LORD, the willing praise of my mouth,
and teach me your laws.
109Though I constantly take my life in my hands,
I will not forget your law.
110The wicked have set a snare for me,
but I have not strayed from your precepts.
111Your statutes are my heritage for ever;
they are the joy of my heart.
112My heart is set on keeping your decrees
to the very end.

OCTOBER 27

DAY 300

OLD TESTAMENT READING
Habakkuk 1:1–3:19

1 The oracle that Habakkuk the prophet received.

Habakkuk's Complaint

2How long, O LORD, must I call for help,
but you do not listen?
Or cry out to you, "Violence!"
but you do not save?
3Why do you make me look at injustice?
Why do you tolerate wrong?
Destruction and violence are before me;
there is strife, and conflict abounds.
4Therefore the law is paralysed,
and justice never prevails.
The wicked hem in the righteous,
so that justice is perverted.

The LORD's Answer

5"Look at the nations and watch—
and be utterly amazed.
For I am going to do something in your days
that you would not believe,
even if you were told.
6I am raising up the Babylonians,
that ruthless and impetuous people,
who sweep across the whole earth
to seize dwelling-places not their own.
7They are a feared and dreaded people;
they are a law to themselves
and promote their own honour.

8Their horses are swifter than
leopards,
fiercer than wolves at dusk.
Their cavalry gallops headlong;
their horsemen come from afar.
They fly like a vulture swooping to
devour;
9 they all come bent on violence.
Their hordes advance like a desert
wind
and gather prisoners like sand.
10They deride kings
and scoff at rulers.
They laugh at all fortified cities;
they build earthen ramps and
capture them.
11Then they sweep past like the wind
and go on—
guilty men, whose own strength is
their god."

Habakkuk's Second Complaint

12O LORD, are you not from
everlasting?
My God, my Holy One, we will not
die.
O LORD, you have appointed them to
execute judgment;
O Rock, you have ordained them
to punish.
13Your eyes are too pure to look on
evil;
you cannot tolerate wrong.
Why then do you tolerate the
treacherous?
Why are you silent while the
wicked
swallow up those more righteous
than themselves?
14You have made men like fish in the
sea,
like sea creatures that have no
ruler.
15The wicked foe pulls all of them up
with hooks,
he catches them in his net,
he gathers them up in his drag-net;
and so he rejoices and is glad.
16Therefore he sacrifices to his net
and burns incense to his drag-net,
for by his net he lives in luxury
and enjoys the choicest food.
17Is he to keep on emptying his net,
destroying nations without mercy?

2 I will stand at my watch
and station myself on the ramparts;
I will look to see what he will say to
me,
and what answer I am to give to
this complaint.

The LORD's Answer

2Then the LORD replied:

"Write down the revelation
and make it plain on tablets
so that a herald may run with it.
3For the revelation awaits an
appointed time;
it speaks of the end
and will not prove false.
Though it linger, wait for it;
it will certainly come and will not
delay.

4"See, he is puffed up;
his desires are not upright—
but the righteous will live by his
faith—
5indeed, wine betrays him;
he is arrogant and never at rest.
Because he is as greedy as the grave
and like death is never satisfied,
he gathers to himself all the nations
and takes captive all the peoples.

6"Will not all of them taunt him with
ridicule and scorn, saying,

"'Woe to him who piles up stolen
goods
and makes himself wealthy by
extortion!
How long must this go on?'
7Will not your debtors suddenly arise?
Will they not wake up and make
you tremble?
Then you will become their victim.
8Because you have plundered many
nations,

the peoples who are left will
plunder you.
For you have shed man's blood;
you have destroyed lands and cities
and everyone in them.

9"Woe to him who builds his realm by
unjust gain
to set his nest on high,
to escape the clutches of ruin!
10You have plotted the ruin of many
peoples,
shaming your own house and
forfeiting your life.
11The stones of the wall will cry out,
and the beams of the woodwork
will echo it.

12"Woe to him who builds a city with
bloodshed
and establishes a town by crime!
13Has not the LORD Almighty
determined
that the people's labour is only fuel
for the fire,
that nations exhaust themselves for
nothing?
14For the earth will be filled with the
knowledge of the glory of the
LORD,
as the waters cover the sea.

15"Woe to him who gives drink to his
neighbours,
pouring it from the wineskin till
they are drunk,
so that he can gaze on their naked
bodies.
16You will be filled with shame instead
of glory.
Now it is your turn! Drink and be
exposed!
The cup from the LORD's right hand
is coming round to you,
and disgrace will cover your glory.
17The violence you have done to
Lebanon will overwhelm you,
and your destruction of animals
will terrify you.
For you have shed man's blood;
you have destroyed lands and cities
and everyone in them.

18"Of what value is an idol, since a man
has carved it?
Or an image that teaches lies?
For he who makes it trusts in his own
creation;
he makes idols that cannot speak.
19Woe to him who says to wood, 'Come
to life!'
Or to lifeless stone, 'Wake up!'
Can it give guidance?
It is covered with gold and silver;
there is no breath in it.
20But the LORD is in his holy temple;
let all the earth be silent before
him."

Habakkuk's Prayer

3 A prayer of Habakkuk the prophet. On *shigionoth*.

2LORD, I have heard of your fame;
I stand in awe of your deeds, O
LORD.
Renew them in our day,
in our time make them known;
in wrath remember mercy.

3God came from Teman,
the Holy One from Mount Paran.
Selah
His glory covered the heavens
and his praise filled the earth.
4His splendour was like the sunrise;
rays flashed from his hand,
where his power was hidden.
5Plague went before him;
pestilence followed his steps.
6He stood, and shook the earth;
he looked, and made the nations
tremble.
The ancient mountains crumbled
and the age-old hills collapsed.
His ways are eternal.
7I saw the tents of Cushan in distress,
the dwellings of Midian in anguish.

8Were you angry with the rivers, O
LORD?
Was your wrath against the
streams?

Did you rage against the sea
when you rode with your horses
and your victorious chariots?
9You uncovered your bow,
you called for many arrows. *Selah*
You split the earth with rivers;
10 the mountains saw you and
writhed.
Torrents of water swept by;
the deep roared
and lifted its waves on high.

11Sun and moon stood still in the
heavens
at the glint of your flying arrows,
at the lightning of your flashing
spear.
12In wrath you strode through the earth
and in anger you threshed the
nations.
13You came out to deliver your people,
to save your anointed one.
You crushed the leader of the land of
wickedness,
you stripped him from head to
foot. *Selah*
14With his own spear you pierced his
head
when his warriors stormed out to
scatter us,
gloating as though about to devour
the wretched who were in hiding.
15You trampled the sea with your
horses,
churning the great waters.

16I heard and my heart pounded,
my lips quivered at the sound;
decay crept into my bones,
and my legs trembled.
Yet I will wait patiently for the day of
calamity
to come on the nation invading us.
17Though the fig-tree does not bud
and there are no grapes on the
vines,
though the olive crop fails
and the fields produce no food,
though there are no sheep in the pen
and no cattle in the stalls,
18yet I will rejoice in the LORD,
I will be joyful in God my Saviour.
19The Sovereign LORD is my strength;
he makes my feet like the feet of a
deer,
he enables me to go on the heights.

For the director of music. On my
stringed instruments.

NEW TESTAMENT READING
Titus 2:1–15

What Must Be Taught to Various Groups

2 You must teach what is in accord
with sound doctrine. 2Teach the
older men to be temperate, worthy of
respect, self-controlled, and sound in
faith, in love and in endurance.
3Likewise, teach the older women to
be reverent in the way they live, not to
be slanderers or addicted to much wine,
but to teach what is good. 4Then they
can train the younger women to love
their husbands and children, 5to be self-
controlled and pure, to be busy at
home, to be kind, and to be subject to
their husbands, so that no-one will
malign the word of God.
6Similarly, encourage the young men
to be self-controlled. 7In everything set
them an example by doing what is
good. In your teaching show integrity,
seriousness 8and soundness of speech
that cannot be condemned, so that
those who oppose you may be ashamed
because they have nothing bad to say
about us.
9Teach slaves to be subject to their
masters in everything, to try to please
them, not to talk back to them, 10and
not to steal from them, but to show that
they can be fully trusted, so that in every
way they will make the teaching about
God our Saviour attractive.
11For the grace of God that brings
salvation has appeared to all men. 12It
teaches us to say "No" to ungodliness
and worldly passions, and to live self-
controlled, upright and godly lives in
this present age, 13while we wait for the

blessed hope—the glorious appearing of our great God and Saviour, Jesus Christ, [14]who gave himself for us to redeem us from all wickedness and to purify for himself a people that are his very own, eager to do what is good.
[15]These, then, are the things you should teach. Encourage and rebuke with all authority. Do not let anyone despise you.

READING FROM PROVERBS
Proverbs 26:3–12

[3]A whip for the horse, a halter for the donkey,
and a rod for the backs of fools!

[4]Do not answer a fool according to his folly,
or you will be like him yourself.

[5]Answer a fool according to his folly,
or he will be wise in his own eyes.

[6]Like cutting off one's feet or drinking violence
is the sending of a message by the hand of a fool.

[7]Like a lame man's legs that hang limp
is a proverb in the mouth of a fool.

[8]Like tying a stone in a sling
is the giving of honour to a fool.

[9]Like a thornbush in a drunkard's hand
is a proverb in the mouth of a fool.

[10]Like an archer who wounds at random
is he who hires a fool or any passer-by.

[11]As a dog returns to its vomit,
so a fool repeats his folly.

[12]Do you see a man wise in his own eyes?
There is more hope for a fool than for him.

OCTOBER 28

DAY 301

OLD TESTAMENT READING
Lamentations 1:1–2:6

1 How deserted lies the city,
once so full of people!
How like a widow is she,
who once was great among the nations!
She who was queen among the provinces
has now become a slave.

[2]Bitterly she weeps at night,
tears are upon her cheeks.
Among all her lovers
there is none to comfort her.
All her friends have betrayed her;
they have become her enemies.

[3]After affliction and harsh labour,
Judah has gone into exile.
She dwells among the nations;
she finds no resting place.
All who pursue her have overtaken her
in the midst of her distress.

[4]The roads to Zion mourn,
for no-one comes to her appointed feasts.
All her gateways are desolate,
her priests groan,
her maidens grieve,
and she is in bitter anguish.

[5]Her foes have become her masters;
her enemies are at ease.

The LORD has brought her grief
because of her many sins.
Her children have gone into exile,
captive before the foe.

6All the splendour has departed
from the Daughter of Zion.
Her princes are like deer
that find no pasture;
in weakness they have fled
before the pursuer.

7In the days of her affliction and wandering
Jerusalem remembers all the treasures
that were hers in days of old.
When her people fell into enemy hands,
there was no-one to help her.
Her enemies looked at her
and laughed at her destruction.

8Jerusalem has sinned greatly
and so has become unclean.
All who honoured her despise her,
for they have seen her nakedness;
she herself groans
and turns away.

9Her filthiness clung to her skirts;
she did not consider her future.
Her fall was astounding;
there was none to comfort her.
"Look, O LORD, on my affliction,
for the enemy has triumphed."

10The enemy laid hands
on all her treasures;
she saw pagan nations
enter her sanctuary—
those you had forbidden
to enter your assembly.

11All her people groan
as they search for bread;
they barter their treasures for food
to keep themselves alive.
"Look, O LORD, and consider,
for I am despised."

12"Is it nothing to you, all you who pass by?
Look around and see.
Is any suffering like my suffering
that was inflicted on me,
that the LORD brought on me
in the day of his fierce anger?

13"From on high he sent fire,
sent it down into my bones.
He spread a net for my feet
and turned me back.
He made me desolate,
faint all the day long.

14"My sins have been bound into a yoke;
by his hands they were woven together.
They have come upon my neck
and the Lord has sapped my strength.
He has handed me over
to those I cannot withstand.

15"The Lord has rejected
all the warriors in my midst;
he has summoned an army against me
to crush my young men.
In his winepress the Lord has trampled
the Virgin Daughter of Judah.

16"This is why I weep
and my eyes overflow with tears.
No-one is near to comfort me,
no-one to restore my spirit.
My children are destitute
because the enemy has prevailed."

17Zion stretches out her hands,
but there is no-one to comfort her.
The LORD has decreed for Jacob
that his neighbours become his foes;
Jerusalem has become
an unclean thing among them.

18"The LORD is righteous,
yet I rebelled against his command.
Listen, all you peoples;
look upon my suffering.
My young men and maidens
have gone into exile.

19"I called to my allies
but they betrayed me.
My priests and my elders
perished in the city
while they searched for food
to keep themselves alive.

20"See, O LORD, how distressed I am!
I am in torment within,
and in my heart I am disturbed,
for I have been most rebellious.
Outside, the sword bereaves;
inside, there is only death.

21"People have heard my groaning,
but there is no-one to comfort me.
All my enemies have heard of my
distress;
they rejoice at what you have
done.
May you bring the day you have
announced
so that they may become like me.

22"Let all their wickedness come
before you;
deal with them
as you have dealt with me
because of all my sins.
My groans are many
and my heart is faint."

2 How the Lord has covered the
Daughter of Zion
with the cloud of his anger!
He has hurled down the splendour of
Israel
from heaven to earth;
he has not remembered his footstool
in the day of his anger.

2Without pity the Lord has swallowed
up
all the dwellings of Jacob;
in his wrath he has torn down
the strongholds of the Daughter of
Judah.
He has brought her kingdom and its
princes
down to the ground in dishonour.

3In fierce anger he has cut off
every horn of Israel.
He has withdrawn his right hand
at the approach of the enemy.
He has burned in Jacob like a flaming
fire
that consumes everything around
it.

4Like an enemy he has strung his bow;
his right hand is ready.
Like a foe he has slain
all who were pleasing to the eye;
he has poured out his wrath like fire
on the tent of the Daughter of
Zion.

5The Lord is like an enemy;
he has swallowed up Israel.
He has swallowed up all her palaces
and destroyed her strongholds.
He has multiplied mourning and
lamentation
for the Daughter of Judah.

6He has laid waste his dwelling like a
garden;
he has destroyed his place of
meeting.
The LORD has made Zion forget
her appointed feasts and her
Sabbaths;
in his fierce anger he has spurned
both king and priest.

NEW TESTAMENT READING
Titus 3:1–15

Doing What is Good

3 Remind the people to be subject to rulers and authorities, to be obedient, to be ready to do whatever is good,
2to slander no-one, to be peaceable and considerate, and to show true humility towards all men.

3At one time we too were foolish, disobedient, deceived and enslaved by all kinds of passions and pleasures. We lived in malice and envy, being hated and hating one another.
4But when the kindness and love of God our Saviour appeared,
5he saved us, not because of

righteous things we had done, but because of his mercy. He saved us through
the washing of rebirth and renewal by
the Holy Spirit, 6whom he poured out
on us generously through Jesus Christ
our Saviour, 7so that, having been justified by his grace, we might become
heirs having the hope of eternal life.
8This is a trustworthy saying. And I
want you to stress these things, so that
those who have trusted in God may be
careful to devote themselves to doing
what is good. These things are excellent
and profitable for everyone.
9But avoid foolish controversies and
genealogies and arguments and quarrels about the law, because these are
unprofitable and useless. 10Warn a divi-
sive person once, and then warn him a
second time. After that, have nothing to
do with him. 11You may be sure that
such a man is warped and sinful; he is
self-condemned.

Final Remarks

12As soon as I send Artemas or Tychicus to you, do your best to come to me
at Nicopolis, because I have decided to
winter there. 13Do everything you can
to help Zenas the lawyer and Apollos
on their way and see that they have
everything they need. 14Our people
must learn to devote themselves to
doing what is good, in order that they
may provide for daily necessities and
not live unproductive lives.
15Everyone with me sends you greetings. Greet those who love us in the
faith.

Grace be with you all.

READING FROM PSALMS
Psalm 119:113–120

ס Samekh

113I hate double-minded men,
but I love your law.
114You are my refuge and my shield;
I have put my hope in your word.
115Away from me, you evildoers,
that I may keep the commands of my God!
116Sustain me according to your promise, and I shall live;
do not let my hopes be dashed.
117Uphold me, and I shall be delivered;
I shall always have regard for your decrees.
118You reject all who stray from your decrees,
for their deceitfulness is in vain.
119All the wicked of the earth you discard like dross;
therefore I love your statutes.
120My flesh trembles in fear of you;
I stand in awe of your laws.

DAY 302

OCTOBER 29

OLD TESTAMENT READING
Lamentations 2:7–3:39

7The Lord has rejected his altar
and abandoned his sanctuary.
He has handed over to the enemy
the walls of her palaces;
they have raised a shout in the house of the LORD
as on the day of an appointed feast.
8The LORD determined to tear down
the wall around the Daughter of Zion.
He stretched out a measuring line
and did not withhold his hand from destroying.
He made ramparts and walls lament;
together they wasted away.

9Her gates have sunk into the ground;
their bars he has broken and destroyed.
Her king and her princes are exiled among the nations,
the law is no more,
and her prophets no longer find visions from the LORD.

10The elders of the Daughter of Zion
sit on the ground in silence;
they have sprinkled dust on their heads
and put on sackcloth.
The young women of Jerusalem
have bowed their heads to the ground.

11My eyes fail from weeping,
I am in torment within,
my heart is poured out on the ground
because my people are destroyed,
because children and infants faint
in the streets of the city.

12They say to their mothers,
"Where is bread and wine?"
as they faint like wounded men
in the streets of the city,
as their lives ebb away
in their mothers' arms.

13What can I say for you?
With what can I compare you,
O Daughter of Jerusalem?
To what can I liken you,
that I may comfort you,
O Virgin Daughter of Zion?
Your wound is as deep as the sea.
Who can heal you?

14The visions of your prophets
were false and worthless;
they did not expose your sin
to ward off your captivity.
The oracles they gave you
were false and misleading.

15All who pass your way
clap their hands at you;
they scoff and shake their heads
at the Daughter of Jerusalem:
"Is this the city that was called
the perfection of beauty,
the joy of the whole earth?"

16All your enemies open their mouths
wide against you;
they scoff and gnash their teeth
and say, "We have swallowed her up.
This is the day we have waited for;
we have lived to see it."

17The LORD has done what he planned;
he has fulfilled his word,
which he decreed long ago.
He has overthrown you without pity,
he has let the enemy gloat over you,
he has exalted the horn of your foes.

18The hearts of the people
cry out to the Lord.
O wall of the Daughter of Zion,
let your tears flow like a river
day and night;
give yourself no relief,
your eyes no rest.

19Arise, cry out in the night,
as the watches of the night begin;
pour out your heart like water
in the presence of the Lord.
Lift up your hands to him
for the lives of your children,
who faint from hunger
at the head of every street.

20"Look, O LORD, and consider:
Whom have you ever treated like this?
Should women eat their offspring,
the children they have cared for?
Should priest and prophet be killed
in the sanctuary of the Lord?

21"Young and old lie together
in the dust of the streets;
my young men and maidens
have fallen by the sword.
You have slain them in the day of your anger;
you have slaughtered them without pity.

22"As you summon to a feast day,
so you summoned against me
terrors on every side.
In the day of the LORD's anger
no-one escaped or survived;
those I cared for and reared,
my enemy has destroyed."

3 I am the man who has seen affliction
by the rod of his wrath.
2He has driven me away and made me walk
in darkness rather than light;
3indeed, he has turned his hand against me
again and again, all day long.

4He has made my skin and my flesh grow old
and has broken my bones.
5He has besieged me and surrounded me
with bitterness and hardship.
6He has made me dwell in darkness
like those long dead.

7He has walled me in so that I cannot escape;
he has weighed me down with chains.
8Even when I call out or cry for help,
he shuts out my prayer.
9He has barred my way with blocks of stone;
he has made my paths crooked.

10Like a bear lying in wait,
like a lion in hiding,
11he dragged me from the path and mangled me
and left me without help.
12He drew his bow
and made me the target for his arrows.

13He pierced my heart
with arrows from his quiver.
14I became the laughing-stock of all my people;
they mock me in song all day long.
15He has filled me with bitter herbs
and sated me with gall.

16He has broken my teeth with gravel;
he has trampled me in the dust.
17I have been deprived of peace;
I have forgotten what prosperity is.
18So I say, "My splendour is gone
and all that I had hoped from the LORD."

19I remember my affliction and my wandering,
the bitterness and the gall.
20I well remember them,
and my soul is downcast within me.
21Yet this I call to mind
and therefore I have hope:

22Because of the LORD's great love we are not consumed,
for his compassions never fail.
23They are new every morning;
great is your faithfulness.
24I say to myself, "The LORD is my portion;
therefore I will wait for him."

25The LORD is good to those whose hope is in him,
to the one who seeks him;
26it is good to wait quietly
for the salvation of the LORD.
27It is good for a man to bear the yoke
while he is young.

28Let him sit alone in silence,
for the LORD has laid it on him.
29Let him bury his face in the dust—
there may yet be hope.
30Let him offer his cheek to one who would strike him,
and let him be filled with disgrace.

31For men are not cast off
by the Lord for ever.
32Though he brings grief, he will show compassion,
so great is his unfailing love.
33For he does not willingly bring affliction
or grief to the children of men.

34To crush underfoot
all prisoners in the land,

35to deny a man his rights
before the Most High,
36to deprive a man of justice—
would not the Lord see such
things?

37Who can speak and have it happen
if the Lord has not decreed it?
38Is it not from the mouth of the Most
High
that both calamities and good
things come?
39Why should any living man complain
when punished for his sins?

NEW TESTAMENT READING
Philemon 1–25

1Paul, a prisoner of Christ Jesus, and
Timothy our brother,

To Philemon our dear friend and
fellow-worker, 2to Apphia our sister,
to Archippus our fellow-soldier and to
the church that meets in your home:

3Grace to you and peace from God
our Father and the Lord Jesus Christ.

Thanksgiving and Prayer

4I always thank my God as I remember you in my prayers, 5because I hear
about your faith in the Lord Jesus and
your love for all the saints. 6I pray that
you may be active in sharing your faith,
so that you will have a full understanding of every good thing we have in
Christ. 7Your love has given me great
joy and encouragement, because you,
brother, have refreshed the hearts of
the saints.

Paul's Plea for Onesimus

8Therefore, although in Christ I
could be bold and order you to do what
you ought to do, 9yet I appeal to you on
the basis of love. I then, as Paul—an old
man and now also a prisoner of Christ
Jesus—10I appeal to you for my son
Onesimus, who became my son while I
was in chains. 11Formerly he was useless
to you, but now he has become useful
both to you and to me.

12I am sending him—who is my very
heart—back to you. 13I would have
liked to keep him with me so that he
could take your place in helping me
while I am in chains for the gospel.
14But I did not want to do anything
without your consent, so that any
favour you do will be spontaneous and
not forced. 15Perhaps the reason he was
separated from you for a little while was
that you might have him back for good
—16no longer as a slave, but better than
a slave, as a dear brother. He is very
dear to me but even dearer to you, both
as a man and as a brother in the Lord.

17So if you consider me a partner,
welcome him as you would welcome
me. 18If he has done you any wrong or
owes you anything, charge it to me. 19I,
Paul, am writing this with my own hand.
I will pay it back—not to mention that
you owe me your very self. 20I do wish,
brother, that I may have some benefit
from you in the Lord; refresh my heart
in Christ. 21Confident of your obedience, I write to you, knowing that you
will do even more than I ask.

22And one thing more: Prepare a
guest room for me, because I hope to be
restored to you in answer to your
prayers.

23Epaphras, my fellow-prisoner in
Christ Jesus, sends you greetings.
24And so do Mark, Aristarchus, Demas
and Luke, my fellow-workers.

25The grace of the Lord Jesus Christ
be with your spirit.

READING FROM PSALMS
Psalm 119:121–128

ע Ayin

121I have done what is righteous and
just;
do not leave me to my oppressors.

122Ensure your servant's well-being;
let not the arrogant oppress me.
123My eyes fail, looking for your salvation,
looking for your righteous promise.
124Deal with your servant according to your love
and teach me your decrees.
125I am your servant; give me discernment
that I may understand your statutes.
126It is time for you to act, O LORD;
your law is being broken.
127Because I love your commands
more than gold, more than pure gold,
128and because I consider all your precepts right,
I hate every wrong path.

DAY 303

OCTOBER 30

OLD TESTAMENT READING

Lamentations 3:40–5:22

40Let us examine our ways and test them,
and let us return to the LORD.
41Let us lift up our hearts and our hands
to God in heaven, and say:
42"We have sinned and rebelled
and you have not forgiven.

43"You have covered yourself with anger and pursued us;
you have slain without pity.
44You have covered yourself with a cloud
so that no prayer can get through.
45You have made us scum and refuse
among the nations.

46"All our enemies have opened their mouths
wide against us.
47We have suffered terror and pitfalls,
ruin and destruction."
48Streams of tears flow from my eyes
because my people are destroyed.

49My eyes will flow unceasingly,
without relief,
50until the LORD looks down
from heaven and sees.
51What I see brings grief to my soul
because of all the women of my city.

52Those who were my enemies without cause
hunted me like a bird.
53They tried to end my life in a pit
and threw stones at me;
54the waters closed over my head,
and I thought I was about to be cut off.

55I called on your name, O LORD,
from the depths of the pit.
56You heard my plea: "Do not close your ears
to my cry for relief."
57You came near when I called you,
and you said, "Do not fear."

58O Lord, you took up my case;
you redeemed my life.
59You have seen, O LORD, the wrong done to me.
Uphold my cause!
60You have seen the depth of their vengeance,
all their plots against me.

61O LORD, you have heard their insults,
all their plots against me—
62what my enemies whisper and mutter
against me all day long.
63Look at them! Sitting or standing,
they mock me in their songs.

64Pay them back what they deserve, O
LORD,
for what their hands have done.
65Put a veil over their hearts,
and may your curse be on them!
66Pursue them in anger and destroy
them
from under the heavens of the
LORD.

4 How the gold has lost its lustre,
the fine gold become dull!
The sacred gems are scattered
at the head of every street.

2How the precious sons of Zion,
once worth their weight in gold,
are now considered as pots of clay,
the work of a potter's hands!

3Even jackals offer their breasts
to nurse their young,
but my people have become heartless
like ostriches in the desert.

4Because of thirst the infant's tongue
sticks to the roof of its mouth;
the children beg for bread,
but no-one gives it to them.

5Those who once ate delicacies
are destitute in the streets.
Those nurtured in purple
now lie on ash heaps.

6The punishment of my people
is greater than that of Sodom,
which was overthrown in a moment
without a hand turned to help her.

7Their princes were brighter than
snow
and whiter than milk,
their bodies more ruddy than rubies,
their appearance like sapphires.

8But now they are blacker than soot;
they are not recognised in the
streets.
Their skin has shrivelled on their
bones;
it has become as dry as a stick.

9Those killed by the sword are better
off
than those who die of famine;
racked with hunger, they waste away
for lack of food from the field.

10With their own hands compassionate
women
have cooked their own children,
who became their food
when my people were destroyed.

11The LORD has given full vent to his
wrath;
he has poured out his fierce anger.
He kindled a fire in Zion
that consumed her foundations.

12The kings of the earth did not
believe,
nor did any of the world's people,
that enemies and foes could enter
the gates of Jerusalem.

13But it happened because of the sins of
her prophets
and the iniquities of her priests,
who shed within her
the blood of the righteous.

14Now they grope through the streets
like men who are blind.
They are so defiled with blood
that no-one dares to touch their
garments.

15"Go away! You are unclean!" men
cry to them.
"Away! Away! Don't touch us!"
When they flee and wander about,
people among the nations say,
"They can stay here no longer."

16The LORD himself has scattered
them;
he no longer watches over them.
The priests are shown no honour,
the elders no favour.

17Moreover, our eyes failed,
looking in vain for help;
from our towers we watched
for a nation that could not save us.

18Men stalked us at every step,
so we could not walk in our streets.
Our end was near, our days were numbered,
for our end had come.

19Our pursuers were swifter
than eagles in the sky;
they chased us over the mountains
and lay in wait for us in the desert.

20The LORD's anointed, our very life breath,
was caught in their traps.
We thought that under his shadow
we would live among the nations.

21Rejoice and be glad, O Daughter of Edom,
you who live in the land of Uz.
But to you also the cup will be passed;
you will be drunk and stripped naked.

22O Daughter of Zion, your punishment will end;
he will not prolong your exile.
But, O Daughter of Edom, he will punish your sin
and expose your wickedness.

5 Remember, O LORD, what has happened to us;
look, and see our disgrace.
2Our inheritance has been turned over to aliens,
our homes to foreigners.
3We have become orphans and fatherless,
our mothers like widows.
4We must buy the water we drink;
our wood can be had only at a price.
5Those who pursue us are at our heels;
we are weary and find no rest.
6We submitted to Egypt and Assyria
to get enough bread.
7Our fathers sinned and are no more,
and we bear their punishment.
8Slaves rule over us,
and there is none to free us from their hands.
9We get our bread at the risk of our lives
because of the sword in the desert.
10Our skin is hot as an oven,
feverish from hunger.
11Women have been ravished in Zion,
and virgins in the towns of Judah.
12Princes have been hung up by their hands;
elders are shown no respect.
13Young men toil at the millstones;
boys stagger under loads of wood.
14The elders are gone from the city gate;
the young men have stopped their music.
15Joy is gone from our hearts;
our dancing has turned to mourning.
16The crown has fallen from our head.
Woe to us, for we have sinned!
17Because of this our hearts are faint;
because of these things our eyes grow dim
18for Mount Zion, which lies desolate,
with jackals prowling over it.

19You, O LORD, reign for ever;
your throne endures from generation to generation.
20Why do you always forget us?
Why do you forsake us so long?
21Restore us to yourself, O LORD, that we may return;
renew our days as of old
22unless you have utterly rejected us
and are angry with us beyond measure.

NEW TESTAMENT READING
Hebrews 1:1–14

The Son Superior to Angels

1 In the past God spoke to our forefathers through the prophets at
many times and in various ways, 2but in
these last days he has spoken to us by his
Son, whom he appointed heir of all
things, and through whom he made the
universe. 3The Son is the radiance of

God's glory and the exact representation of his being, sustaining all things by his powerful word. After he had provided purification for sins, he sat down at the right hand of the Majesty in
heaven. 4So he became as much superior to the angels as the name he has inherited is superior to theirs.
5For to which of the angels did God ever say,

"You are my Son;
today I have become your Father"?

Or again,

"I will be his Father,
and he will be my Son"?

6And again, when God brings his firstborn into the world, he says,

"Let all God's angels worship him."

7In speaking of the angels he says,

"He makes his angels winds,
his servants flames of fire."

8But about the Son he says,

"Your throne, O God, will last for ever and ever,
and righteousness will be the sceptre of your kingdom.
9You have loved righteousness and hated wickedness;
therefore God, your God, has set you above your companions
by anointing you with the oil of joy."

10He also says,

"In the beginning, O Lord, you laid the foundations of the earth,
and the heavens are the work of your hands.
11They will perish, but you remain;
they will all wear out like a garment.
12You will roll them up like a robe;
like a garment they will be changed.
But you remain the same,
and your years will never end."

13To which of the angels did God ever say,

"Sit at my right hand
until I make your enemies
a footstool for your feet"?

14Are not all angels ministering spirits sent to serve those who will inherit salvation?

READING FROM PSALMS
Psalm 119:129–136

פ Pe

129Your statutes are wonderful;
therefore I obey them.
130The unfolding of your words gives light;
it gives understanding to the simple.
131I open my mouth and pant,
longing for your commands.
132Turn to me and have mercy on me,
as you always do to those who love your name.
133Direct my footsteps according to your word;
let no sin rule over me.
134Redeem me from the oppression of men,
that I may obey your precepts.
135Make your face shine upon your servant
and teach me your decrees.
136Streams of tears flow from my eyes,
for your law is not obeyed.

OCTOBER 31

OLD TESTAMENT READING
Obadiah 1–21

1The vision of Obadiah.

This is what the Sovereign LORD says about Edom—

We have heard a message from the LORD:
An envoy was sent to the nations to say,
"Rise, and let us go against her for battle"—

2"See, I will make you small among the nations;
you will be utterly despised.
3The pride of your heart has deceived you,
you who live in the clefts of the rocks
and make your home on the heights,
you who say to yourself,
'Who can bring me down to the ground?'
4Though you soar like the eagle
and make your nest among the stars,
from there I will bring you down,"
declares the LORD.
5"If thieves came to you,
if robbers in the night—
Oh, what a disaster awaits you—
would they not steal only as much as they wanted?
If grape pickers came to you,
would they not leave a few grapes?
6But how Esau will be ransacked,
his hidden treasures pillaged!
7All your allies will force you to the border;
your friends will deceive and overpower you;
those who eat your bread will set a trap for you,
but you will not detect it.

8"In that day," declares the LORD,
"will I not destroy the wise men of Edom,
men of understanding in the mountains of Esau?
9Your warriors, O Teman, will be terrified,
and everyone in Esau's mountains
will be cut down in the slaughter.
10Because of the violence against your brother Jacob,
you will be covered with shame;
you will be destroyed for ever.
11On the day you stood aloof
while strangers carried off his wealth
and foreigners entered his gates
and cast lots for Jerusalem,
you were like one of them.
12You should not look down on your brother
in the day of his misfortune,
nor rejoice over the people of Judah
in the day of their destruction,
nor boast so much
in the day of their trouble.
13You should not march through the gates of my people
in the day of their disaster,
nor look down on them in their calamity
in the day of their disaster,
nor seize their wealth
in the day of their disaster.
14You should not wait at the crossroads
to cut down their fugitives,
nor hand over their survivors
in the day of their trouble.

15"The day of the LORD is near
for all nations.
As you have done, it will be done to you;
your deeds will return upon your own head.
16Just as you drank on my holy hill,
so all the nations will drink continually;

they will drink and drink
and be as if they had never been.
17But on Mount Zion will be
deliverance;
it will be holy,
and the house of Jacob
will possess its inheritance.
18The house of Jacob will be a fire
and the house of Joseph a flame;
the house of Esau will be stubble,
and they will set it on fire and
consume it.
There will be no survivors
from the house of Esau."
The LORD has spoken.

19People from the Negev will occupy
the mountains of Esau,
and people from the foothills will
possess
the land of the Philistines.
They will occupy the fields of
Ephraim and Samaria,
and Benjamin will possess Gilead.
20This company of Israelite exiles who
are in Canaan
will possess ⌞the land⌟ as far as
Zarephath;
the exiles from Jerusalem who are in
Sepharad
will possess the towns of the
Negev.
21Deliverers will go up on Mount Zion
to govern the mountains of Esau.
And the kingdom will be the
LORD's.

NEW TESTAMENT READING

Hebrews 2:1–18

Warning to Pay Attention

2 We must pay more careful attention, therefore, to what we have
heard, so that we do not drift away. 2For
if the message spoken by angels was
binding, and every violation and disobedience received its just punishment,
3how shall we escape if we ignore such a
great salvation? This salvation, which
was first announced by the Lord, was
confirmed to us by those who heard
him. 4God also testified to it by signs,
wonders and various miracles, and gifts
of the Holy Spirit distributed according
to his will.

Jesus Made Like His Brothers

5It is not to angels that he has subjected the world to come, about which
we are speaking. 6But there is a place
where someone has testified:

"What is man that you are mindful of
him,
the son of man that you care for
him?
7You made him a little lower than the
angels;
you crowned him with glory and
honour
8 and put everything under his feet."

In putting everything under him, God
left nothing that is not subject to him.
Yet at present we do not see everything
subject to him. 9But we see Jesus, who
was made a little lower than the angels,
now crowned with glory and honour
because he suffered death, so that by
the grace of God he might taste death
for everyone.
10In bringing many sons to glory, it
was fitting that God, for whom and
through whom everything exists, should
make the author of their salvation perfect through suffering. 11Both the one
who makes men holy and those who are
made holy are of the same family. So
Jesus is not ashamed to call them
brothers. 12He says,

"I will declare your name to my
brothers;
in the presence of the congregation
I will sing your praises."

13And again,

"I will put my trust in him."

And again he says,

"Here am I, and the children God
has given me."

14Since the children have flesh and
blood, he too shared in their humanity
so that by his death he might destroy
him who holds the power of death—
that is, the devil—15and free those who
all their lives were held in slavery by
their fear of death. 16For surely it is not
angels he helps, but Abraham's descendants. 17For this reason he had to
be made like his brothers in every way,
in order that he might become a merciful and faithful high priest in service to
God, and that he might make atonement for the sins of the people.
18Because he himself suffered when he
was tempted, he is able to help those
who are being tempted.

READING FROM PROVERBS
Proverbs 26:13–22

13The sluggard says, "There is a lion in
the road,
a fierce lion roaming the streets!"
14As a door turns on its hinges,
so a sluggard turns on his bed.

15The sluggard buries his hand in the
dish;
he is too lazy to bring it back to his
mouth.

16The sluggard is wiser in his own eyes
than seven men who answer
discreetly.
17Like one who seizes a dog by the ears
is a passer-by who meddles in a
quarrel not his own.

18Like a madman shooting
firebrands or deadly arrows
19is a man who deceives his neighbour
and says, "I was only joking!"

20Without wood a fire goes out;
without gossip a quarrel dies down.

21As charcoal to embers and as wood to
fire,
so is a quarrelsome man for
kindling strife.

22The words of a gossip are like choice
morsels;
they go down to a man's inmost
parts.

DAY 305

NOVEMBER 1

OLD TESTAMENT READING
Joel 1:1–2:17

1 The word of the LORD that came to
Joel son of Pethuel.

An Invasion of Locusts

2Hear this, you elders;
listen, all who live in the land.
Has anything like this ever happened
in your days
or in the days of your forefathers?
3Tell it to your children,
and let your children tell it to their
children,
and their children to the next
generation.
4What the locust swarm has left
the great locusts have eaten;
what the great locusts have left
the young locusts have eaten;
what the young locusts have left
other locusts have eaten.
5Wake up, you drunkards, and weep!
Wail, all you drinkers of wine;

wail because of the new wine,
for it has been snatched from your lips.
6A nation has invaded my land,
powerful and without number;
it has the teeth of a lion,
the fangs of a lioness.
7It has laid waste my vines
and ruined my fig-trees.
It has stripped off their bark
and thrown it away,
leaving their branches white.

8Mourn like a virgin in sackcloth
grieving for the husband of her youth.
9Grain offerings and drink offerings
are cut off from the house of the LORD.
The priests are in mourning,
those who minister before the LORD.
10The fields are ruined,
the ground is dried up;
the grain is destroyed,
the new wine is dried up,
the oil fails.
11Despair, you farmers,
wail, you vine growers;
grieve for the wheat and the barley,
because the harvest of the field is destroyed.
12The vine is dried up
and the fig-tree is withered;
the pomegranate, the palm and the apple tree—
all the trees of the field—are dried up.
Surely the joy of mankind
is withered away.

A Call to Repentance

13Put on sackcloth, O priests, and mourn;
wail, you who minister before the altar.
Come, spend the night in sackcloth,
you who minister before my God;
for the grain offerings and drink offerings
are withheld from the house of your God.
14Declare a holy fast;
call a sacred assembly.
Summon the elders
and all who live in the land
to the house of the LORD your God,
and cry out to the LORD.

15Alas for that day!
For the day of the LORD is near;
it will come like destruction from the Almighty.

16Has not the food been cut off
before our very eyes—
joy and gladness
from the house of our God?
17The seeds are shrivelled
beneath the clods.
The storehouses are in ruins,
the granaries have been broken down,
for the grain has dried up.
18How the cattle moan!
The herds mill about
because they have no pasture;
even the flocks of sheep are suffering.

19To you, O LORD, I call,
for fire has devoured the open pastures
and flames have burned up all the trees of the field.
20Even the wild animals pant for you;
the streams of water have dried up
and fire has devoured the open pastures.

An Army of Locusts

2 Blow the trumpet in Zion;
sound the alarm on my holy hill.
Let all who live in the land tremble,
for the day of the LORD is coming.
It is close at hand—
2 a day of darkness and gloom,
a day of clouds and blackness.
Like dawn spreading across the mountains
a large and mighty army comes,
such as never was of old
nor ever will be in ages to come.

[3]Before them fire devours,
behind them a flame blazes.
Before them the land is like the garden of Eden,
behind them, a desert waste—
nothing escapes them.
[4]They have the appearance of horses;
they gallop along like cavalry.
[5]With a noise like that of chariots
they leap over the mountaintops,
like a crackling fire consuming stubble,
like a mighty army drawn up for battle.

[6]At the sight of them, nations are in anguish;
every face turns pale.
[7]They charge like warriors;
they scale walls like soldiers.
They all march in line,
not swerving from their course.
[8]They do not jostle each other;
each marches straight ahead.
They plunge through defences
without breaking ranks.
[9]They rush upon the city;
they run along the wall.
They climb into the houses;
like thieves they enter through the windows.

[10]Before them the earth shakes,
the sky trembles,
the sun and moon are darkened,
and the stars no longer shine.
[11]The LORD thunders
at the head of his army;
his forces are beyond number,
and mighty are those who obey his command.
The day of the LORD is great;
it is dreadful.
Who can endure it?

Rend Your Heart

[12]"Even now," declares the LORD,
"return to me with all your heart,
with fasting and weeping and mourning."
[13]Rend your heart
and not your garments.
Return to the LORD your God,
for he is gracious and compassionate,
slow to anger and abounding in love,
and he relents from sending calamity.
[14]Who knows? He may turn and have pity
and leave behind a blessing—
grain offerings and drink offerings
for the LORD your God.

[15]Blow the trumpet in Zion,
declare a holy fast,
call a sacred assembly.
[16]Gather the people,
consecrate the assembly;
bring together the elders,
gather the children,
those nursing at the breast.
Let the bridegroom leave his room
and the bride her chamber.
[17]Let the priests, who minister before the LORD,
weep between the temple porch and the altar.
Let them say, "Spare your people, O LORD.
Do not make your inheritance an object of scorn,
a byword among the nations.
Why should they say among the peoples,
'Where is their God?'"

NEW TESTAMENT READING
Hebrews 3:1–19

Jesus Greater Than Moses

3 Therefore, holy brothers, who share in the heavenly calling, fix your thoughts on Jesus, the apostle and high priest whom we confess. [2]He was faithful to the one who appointed him, just as Moses was faithful in all God's house. [3]Jesus has been found worthy of greater honour than Moses, just as the

builder of a house has greater honour
than the house itself. 4For every house
is built by someone, but God is the
builder of everything. 5Moses was faithful as a servant in all God's house, testifying to what would be said in the
future. 6But Christ is faithful as a son
over God's house. And we are his
house, if we hold on to our courage and
the hope of which we boast.

Warning Against Unbelief

7So, as the Holy Spirit says:

"Today, if you hear his voice,
8 do not harden your hearts
as you did in the rebellion,
during the time of testing in the desert,
9where your fathers tested and tried me
and for forty years saw what I did.
10That is why I was angry with that generation,
and I said, 'Their hearts are always going astray,
and they have not known my ways.'
11So I declared on oath in my anger,
'They shall never enter my rest.' "

12See to it, brothers, that none of you
has a sinful, unbelieving heart that turns
away from the living God. 13But encourage one another daily, as long as it
is called Today, so that none of you may
be hardened by sin's deceitfulness.
14We have come to share in Christ if we
hold firmly till the end the confidence
we had at first. 15As has just been said:

"Today, if you hear his voice,
do not harden your hearts
as you did in the rebellion."

16Who were they who heard and rebelled? Were they not all those Moses
led out of Egypt? 17And with whom was
he angry for forty years? Was it not with
those who sinned, whose bodies fell in
the desert? 18And to whom did God
swear that they would never enter his
rest if not to those who disobeyed? 19So
we see that they were not able to enter,
because of their unbelief.

READING FROM PSALMS

Psalm 119:137–144

צ Tsadhe

137Righteous are you, O LORD,
and your laws are right.
138The statutes you have laid down are righteous;
they are fully trustworthy.
139My zeal wears me out,
for my enemies ignore your words.
140Your promises have been thoroughly tested,
and your servant loves them.
141Though I am lowly and despised,
I do not forget your precepts.
142Your righteousness is everlasting
and your law is true.
143Trouble and distress have come upon me,
but your commands are my delight.
144Your statutes are for ever right;
give me understanding that I may live.

DAY 306

NOVEMBER 2

OLD TESTAMENT READING
Joel 2:18–3:21

The LORD's Answer

18 Then the LORD will be jealous for his land
and take pity on his people.

19 The LORD will reply to them:

"I am sending you grain, new wine and oil,
enough to satisfy you fully;
never again will I make you
an object of scorn to the nations.

20 "I will drive the northern army far from you,
pushing it into a parched and barren land,
with its front columns going into the eastern sea
and those in the rear into the western sea.
And its stench will go up;
its smell will rise."

Surely he has done great things.
21 Be not afraid, O land;
be glad and rejoice.
Surely the LORD has done great things.
22 Be not afraid, O wild animals,
for the open pastures are becoming green.
The trees are bearing their fruit;
the fig-tree and the vine yield their riches.
23 Be glad, O people of Zion,
rejoice in the LORD your God,
for he has given you
the autumn rains in righteousness.
He sends you abundant showers,
both autumn and spring rains, as before.
24 The threshing-floors will be filled with grain;
the vats will overflow with new wine and oil.

25 "I will repay you for the years the locusts have eaten—
the great locust and the young locust,
the other locusts and the locust swarm—
my great army that I sent among you.
26 You will have plenty to eat, until you are full,
and you will praise the name of the LORD your God,
who has worked wonders for you;
never again will my people be shamed.
27 Then you will know that I am in Israel,
that I am the LORD your God,
and that there is no other;
never again will my people be shamed.

The Day of the LORD

28 "And afterwards,
I will pour out my Spirit on all people.
Your sons and daughters will prophesy,
your old men will dream dreams,
your young men will see visions.
29 Even on my servants, both men and women,
I will pour out my Spirit in those days.
30 I will show wonders in the heavens
and on the earth,
blood and fire and billows of smoke.
31 The sun will be turned to darkness
and the moon to blood
before the coming of the great and dreadful day of the LORD.
32 And everyone who calls
on the name of the LORD will be saved;
for on Mount Zion and in Jerusalem
there will be deliverance,
as the LORD has said,

among the survivors
whom the LORD calls.

The Nations Judged

3 "In those days and at that time,
when I restore the fortunes of
Judah and Jerusalem,
2I will gather all nations
and bring them down to the Valley
of Jehoshaphat.
There I will enter into judgment
against them
concerning my inheritance, my
people Israel,
for they scattered my people among
the nations
and divided up my land.
3They cast lots for my people
and traded boys for prostitutes;
they sold girls for wine
that they might drink.

4"Now what have you against me, O
Tyre and Sidon and all you regions of
Philistia? Are you repaying me for
something I have done? If you are
paying me back, I will swiftly and
speedily return on your own heads what
you have done. 5For you took my silver
and my gold and carried off my finest
treasures to your temples. 6You sold the
people of Judah and Jerusalem to the
Greeks, that you might send them far
from their homeland.

7"See, I am going to rouse them out
of the places to which you sold them,
and I will return on your own heads
what you have done. 8I will sell your
sons and daughters to the people of
Judah, and they will sell them to the
Sabeans, a nation far away." The LORD
has spoken.

9Proclaim this among the nations:
Prepare for war!
Rouse the warriors!
Let all the fighting men draw near
and attack.
10Beat your ploughshares into swords
and your pruning hooks into
spears.
Let the weakling say,
"I am strong!"
11Come quickly, all you nations from
every side,
and assemble there.

Bring down your warriors, O LORD!

12"Let the nations be roused;
let them advance into the Valley of
Jehoshaphat,
for there I will sit
to judge all the nations on every
side.
13Swing the sickle,
for the harvest is ripe.
Come, trample the grapes,
for the winepress is full
and the vats overflow—
so great is their wickedness!"

14Multitudes, multitudes
in the valley of decision!
For the day of the LORD is near
in the valley of decision.
15The sun and moon will be darkened,
and the stars no longer shine.
16The LORD will roar from Zion
and thunder from Jerusalem;
the earth and the sky will tremble.
But the LORD will be a refuge for his
people,
a stronghold for the people of
Israel.

Blessings for God's People

17"Then you will know that I, the LORD
your God,
dwell in Zion, my holy hill.
Jerusalem will be holy;
never again will foreigners invade
her.

18"In that day the mountains will drip
new wine,
and the hills will flow with milk;
all the ravines of Judah will run
with water.
A fountain will flow out of the LORD's
house
and will water the valley of acacias.
19But Egypt will be desolate,
Edom a desert waste,

because of violence done to the
people of Judah,
in whose land they shed innocent
blood.
20Judah will be inhabited for ever
and Jerusalem through all
generations.
21Their bloodguilt, which I have not
pardoned,
I will pardon."

The LORD dwells in Zion!

NEW TESTAMENT READING
Hebrews 4:1–13

A Sabbath-rest for the People of God

4 Therefore, since the promise of entering his rest still stands, let us be careful that none of you be found to have fallen short of it.
2For we also have
had the gospel preached to us, just as they did; but the message they heard was of no value to them, because those who heard did not combine it with faith.
3Now we who have believed enter that rest, just as God has said,

"So I declared on oath in my anger,
'They shall never enter my rest.'"

And yet his work has been finished since the creation of the world.
4For somewhere he has spoken about the seventh day in these words: "And on the seventh day God rested from all his work."
5And again in the passage above he says, "They shall never enter my rest."

6It still remains that some will enter that rest, and those who formerly had the gospel preached to them did not go in, because of their disobedience.
7Therefore God again set a certain day, calling it Today, when a long time later he spoke through David, as was said before:

"Today, if you hear his voice,
do not harden your hearts."

8For if Joshua had given them rest, God would not have spoken later about another day.
9There remains, then, a Sabbath-rest for the people of God;
10for anyone who enters God's rest also rests from his own work, just as God did from his.
11Let us, therefore, make every effort to enter that rest, so that no-one will fall by following their example of disobedience.

12For the word of God is living and active. Sharper than any double-edged sword, it penetrates even to dividing soul and spirit, joints and marrow; it judges the thoughts and attitudes of the heart.
13Nothing in all creation is hidden from God's sight. Everything is uncovered and laid bare before the eyes of him to whom we must give account.

READING FROM PSALMS
Psalm 119:145–152

ק Qoph

145I call with all my heart; answer me,
O LORD,
and I will obey your decrees.
146I call out to you; save me
and I will keep your statutes.
147I rise before dawn and cry for help;
I have put my hope in your word.
148My eyes stay open through the
watches of the night,
that I may meditate on your
promises.
149Hear my voice in accordance with
your love;
preserve my life, O LORD,
according to your laws.
150Those who devise wicked schemes
are near,
but they are far from your law.
151Yet you are near, O LORD,
and all your commands are true.
152Long ago I learned from your
statutes
that you established them to last
for ever.

NOVEMBER 3

DAY 307

OLD TESTAMENT READING

Ezekiel 1:1–3:27

The Living Creatures and the Glory of the LORD

1 In the thirtieth year, in the fourth
month on the fifth day, while I was
among the exiles by the Kebar River,
the heavens were opened and I saw
visions of God.
2On the fifth of the month—it was the
fifth year of the exile of King Jehoiachin
—3the word of the LORD came to Ezekiel the priest, the son of Buzi, by the
Kebar River in the land of the Babylonians. There the hand of the LORD was
upon him.
4I looked, and I saw a windstorm
coming out of the north—an immense
cloud with flashing lightning and surrounded by brilliant light. The centre of
the fire looked like glowing metal, 5and
in the fire was what looked like four
living creatures. In appearance their
form was that of a man, 6but each of
them had four faces and four wings.
7Their legs were straight; their feet were
like those of a calf and gleamed like
burnished bronze. 8Under their wings
on their four sides they had the hands of
a man. All four of them had faces and
wings, 9and their wings touched one
another. Each one went straight ahead;
they did not turn as they moved.
10Their faces looked like this: Each of
the four had the face of a man, and on
the right side each had the face of a lion,
and on the left the face of an ox; each
also had the face of an eagle. 11Such
were their faces. Their wings were
spread out upwards; each had two
wings, one touching the wing of another
creature on either side, and two wings
covering its body. 12Each one went
straight ahead. Wherever the spirit
would go, they would go, without turning as they went. 13The appearance of
the living creatures was like burning
coals of fire or like torches. Fire moved
back and forth among the creatures; it
was bright, and lightning flashed out of
it. 14The creatures sped back and forth
like flashes of lightning.
15As I looked at the living creatures, I
saw a wheel on the ground beside each
creature with its four faces. 16This was
the appearance and structure of the
wheels: They sparkled like chrysolite,
and all four looked alike. Each
appeared to be made like a wheel intersecting a wheel. 17As they moved,
they would go in any one of the four
directions the creatures faced; the
wheels did not turn about as the creatures went. 18Their rims were high and
awesome, and all four rims were full of
eyes all around.
19When the living creatures moved,
the wheels beside them moved; and
when the living creatures rose from
the ground, the wheels also rose.
20Wherever the spirit would go, they
would go, and the wheels would rise
along with them, because the spirit of
the living creatures was in the wheels.
21When the creatures moved, they also
moved; when the creatures stood still,
they also stood still; and when the creatures rose from the ground, the wheels
rose along with them, because the spirit
of the living creatures was in the wheels.
22Spread out above the heads of the
living creatures was what looked like an
expanse, sparkling like ice, and awesome. 23Under the expanse their wings
were stretched out one towards the
other, and each had two wings covering
its body. 24When the creatures moved, I
heard the sound of their wings, like the
roar of rushing waters, like the voice
of the Almighty, like the tumult of
an army. When they stood still, they
lowered their wings.
25Then there came a voice from
above the expanse over their heads as
they stood with lowered wings. 26Above

the expanse over their heads was what looked like a throne of sapphire, and high above on the throne was a figure like that of a man. [27]I saw that from what appeared to be his waist up he looked like glowing metal, as if full of fire, and that from there down he looked like fire; and brilliant light surrounded him. [28]Like the appearance of a rainbow in the clouds on a rainy day, so was the radiance around him.

This was the appearance of the likeness of the glory of the LORD. When I saw it, I fell face down, and I heard the voice of one speaking.

Ezekiel's Call

2 He said to me, "Son of man, stand up on your feet and I will speak to you." [2]As he spoke, the Spirit came into me and raised me to my feet, and I heard him speaking to me.

[3]He said: "Son of man, I am sending you to the Israelites, to a rebellious nation that has rebelled against me; they and their fathers have been in revolt against me to this very day. [4]The people to whom I am sending you are obstinate and stubborn. Say to them, 'This is what the Sovereign LORD says.' [5]And whether they listen or fail to listen —for they are a rebellious house—they will know that a prophet has been among them. [6]And you, son of man, do not be afraid of them or their words. Do not be afraid, though briers and thorns are all around you and you live among scorpions. Do not be afraid of what they say or terrified by them, though they are a rebellious house. [7]You must speak my words to them, whether they listen or fail to listen, for they are rebellious. [8]But you, son of man, listen to what I say to you. Do not rebel like that rebellious house; open your mouth and eat what I give you."

[9]Then I looked, and I saw a hand stretched out to me. In it was a scroll, [10]which he unrolled before me. On both sides of it were written words of lament and mourning and woe.

3 And he said to me, "Son of man, eat what is before you, eat this scroll; then go and speak to the house of Israel." [2]So I opened my mouth, and he gave me the scroll to eat.

[3]Then he said to me, "Son of man, eat this scroll I am giving you and fill your stomach with it." So I ate it, and it tasted as sweet as honey in my mouth.

[4]He then said to me: "Son of man, go now to the house of Israel and speak my words to them. [5]You are not being sent to a people of obscure speech and difficult language, but to the house of Israel—[6]not to many peoples of obscure speech and difficult language, whose words you cannot understand. Surely if I had sent you to them, they would have listened to you. [7]But the house of Israel is not willing to listen to you because they are not willing to listen to me, for the whole house of Israel is hardened and obstinate. [8]But I will make you as unyielding and hardened as they are. [9]I will make your forehead like the hardest stone, harder than flint. Do not be afraid of them or terrified by them, though they are a rebellious house."

[10]And he said to me, "Son of man, listen carefully and take to heart all the words I speak to you. [11]Go now to your countrymen in exile and speak to them. Say to them, 'This is what the Sovereign LORD says,' whether they listen or fail to listen."

[12]Then the Spirit lifted me up, and I heard behind me a loud rumbling sound —May the glory of the LORD be praised in his dwelling-place!—[13]the sound of the wings of the living creatures brushing against each other and the sound of the wheels beside them, a loud rumbling sound. [14]The Spirit then lifted me up and took me away, and I went in bitterness and in the anger of my spirit, with the strong hand of the LORD upon me. [15]I came to the exiles who lived at Tel Abib near the Kebar River. And there, where they were living, I sat among them for seven days— overwhelmed.

Warning to Israel

16At the end of seven days the word of
the LORD came to me. 17"Son of man, I
have made you a watchman for the
house of Israel; so hear the word I speak
and give them warning from me.
18When I say to a wicked man, 'You will
surely die,' and you do not warn him or
speak out to dissuade him from his evil
ways in order to save his life, that
wicked man will die for his sin, and I will
hold you accountable for his blood.
19But if you do warn the wicked man
and he does not turn from his wickedness or from his evil ways, he will die for
his sin; but you will have saved yourself.

20"Again, when a righteous man
turns from his righteousness and does
evil, and I put a stumbling-block before
him, he will die. Since you did not warn
him, he will die for his sin. The righteous things he did will not be remembered, and I will hold you accountable
for his blood. 21But if you do warn the
righteous man not to sin and he does not
sin, he will surely live because he took
warning, and you will have saved
yourself."

22The hand of the LORD was upon me
there, and he said to me, "Get up and
go out to the plain, and there I will
speak to you." 23So I got up and went
out to the plain. And the glory of the
LORD was standing there, like the glory
I had seen by the Kebar River, and I fell
face down.

24Then the Spirit came into me and
raised me to my feet. He spoke to me
and said: "Go, shut yourself inside your
house. 25And you, son of man, they will
tie with ropes; you will be bound so that
you cannot go out among the people. 26I
will make your tongue stick to the roof
of your mouth so that you will be silent
and unable to rebuke them, though they
are a rebellious house. 27But when I
speak to you, I will open your mouth
and you shall say to them, 'This is what
the Sovereign LORD says.' Whoever will
listen let him listen, and whoever will
refuse let him refuse; for they are a
rebellious house.

NEW TESTAMENT READING

Hebrews 4:14–5:10

Jesus the Great High Priest

14Therefore, since we have a great
high priest who has gone through the
heavens, Jesus the Son of God, let us
hold firmly to the faith we profess. 15For
we do not have a high priest who is
unable to sympathise with our weaknesses, but we have one who has been
tempted in every way, just as we are
—yet was without sin. 16Let us then
approach the throne of grace with confidence, so that we may receive mercy
and find grace to help us in our time of
need.

5 Every high priest is selected from
among men and is appointed to
represent them in matters related to
God, to offer gifts and sacrifices for sins.
2He is able to deal gently with those who
are ignorant and are going astray, since
he himself is subject to weakness. 3This
is why he has to offer sacrifices for his
own sins, as well as for the sins of the
people.

4No-one takes this honour upon himself; he must be called by God, just as
Aaron was. 5So Christ also did not take
upon himself the glory of becoming a
high priest. But God said to him,

"You are my Son;
today I have become your Father."

6And he says in another place,

"You are a priest for ever,
in the order of Melchizedek."

7During the days of Jesus' life on
earth, he offered up prayers and petitions with loud cries and tears to the one
who could save him from death, and he
was heard because of his reverent submission. 8Although he was a son, he
learned obedience from what he suffered 9and, once made perfect, he became the source of eternal salvation for
all who obey him 10and was designated
by God to be high priest in the order of
Melchizedek.

READING FROM PSALMS
Psalm 119:153–160

ר Resh

153 Look upon my suffering and deliver
me,
for I have not forgotten your law.
154 Defend my cause and redeem me;
preserve my life according to your
promise.
155 Salvation is far from the wicked,
for they do not seek out your
decrees.
156 Your compassion is great, O LORD;
preserve my life according to your
laws.
157 Many are the foes who persecute
me,
but I have not turned from your
statutes.
158 I look on the faithless with loathing,
for they do not obey your word.
159 See how I love your precepts;
preserve my life, O LORD,
according to your love.
160 All your words are true;
all your righteous laws are eternal.

DAY 308

NOVEMBER 4

OLD TESTAMENT READING
Ezekiel 4:1–6:14

Siege of Jerusalem Symbolised

4 "Now, son of man, take a clay tablet, put it in front of you and draw
the city of Jerusalem on it. 2 Then lay
siege to it: Erect siege works against it,
build a ramp up to it, set up camps
against it and put battering-rams
around it. 3 Then take an iron pan, place
it as an iron wall between you and the
city and turn your face towards it. It will
be under siege, and you shall besiege it.
This will be a sign to the house of Israel.
4 "Then lie on your left side and put
the sin of the house of Israel upon yourself. You are to bear their sin for the
number of days you lie on your side. 5 I
have assigned you the same number of
days as the years of their sin. So for 390
days you will bear the sin of the house of
Israel.
6 "After you have finished this, lie
down again, this time on your right side,
and bear the sin of the house of Judah. I
have assigned you 40 days, a day for
each year. 7 Turn your face towards the
siege of Jerusalem and with bared arm
prophesy against her. 8 I will tie you up
with ropes so that you cannot turn from
one side to the other until you have
finished the days of your siege.
9 "Take wheat and barley, beans and
lentils, millet and spelt; put them in a
storage jar and use them to make bread
for yourself. You are to eat it during the
390 days you lie on your side. 10 Weigh
out twenty shekels of food to eat each
day and eat it at set times. 11 Also measure out a sixth of a hin of water and
drink it at set times. 12 Eat the food as
you would a barley cake; bake it in the
sight of the people, using human excrement for fuel." 13 The LORD said, "In
this way the people of Israel will eat
defiled food among the nations where I
will drive them."
14 Then I said, "Not so, Sovereign
LORD! I have never defiled myself.
From my youth until now I have never
eaten anything found dead or torn by
wild animals. No unclean meat has ever
entered my mouth."
15 "Very well," he said, "I will let you
bake your bread over cow manure instead of human excrement."
16 He then said to me: "Son of man, I
will cut off the supply of food in Jerusalem. The people will eat rationed
food in anxiety and drink rationed

water in despair, 17for food and water
will be scarce. They will be appalled at
the sight of each other and will waste
away because of their sin.

5 "Now, son of man, take a sharp
sword and use it as a barber's razor
to shave your head and your beard.
Then take a set of scales and divide up
the hair. 2When the days of your siege
come to an end, burn a third of the hair
with fire inside the city. Take a third and
strike it with the sword all around the
city. And scatter a third to the wind. For
I will pursue them with drawn sword.
3But take a few strands of hair and tuck
them away in the folds of your garment.
4Again, take a few of these and throw
them into the fire and burn them up. A
fire will spread from there to the whole
house of Israel.

5"This is what the Sovereign LORD
says: This is Jerusalem, which I have set
in the centre of the nations, with countries all around her. 6Yet in her wickedness she has rebelled against my laws
and decrees more than the nations and
countries around her. She has rejected
my laws and has not followed my
decrees.

7"Therefore this is what the
Sovereign LORD says: You have been
more unruly than the nations around
you and have not followed my decrees
or kept my laws. You have not even
conformed to the standards of the nations around you.

8"Therefore this is what the
Sovereign LORD says: I myself am
against you, Jerusalem, and I will inflict
punishment on you in the sight of the
nations. 9Because of all your detestable
idols, I will do to you what I have never
done before and will never do again.
10Therefore in your midst fathers will
eat their children, and children will eat
their fathers. I will inflict punishment on
you and will scatter all your survivors to
the winds. 11Therefore as surely as I
live, declares the Sovereign LORD, because you have defiled my sanctuary
with all your vile images and detestable
practices, I myself will withdraw my
favour; I will not look on you with pity
or spare you. 12A third of your people
will die of the plague or perish by
famine inside you; a third will fall by the
sword outside your walls; and a third I
will scatter to the winds and pursue with
drawn sword.

13"Then my anger will cease and my
wrath against them will subside, and I
will be avenged. And when I have spent
my wrath upon them, they will know
that I the LORD have spoken in my zeal.

14"I will make you a ruin and a reproach among the nations around you,
in the sight of all who pass by. 15You will
be a reproach and a taunt, a warning
and an object of horror to the nations
around you when I inflict punishment
on you in anger and in wrath and with
stinging rebuke. I the LORD have
spoken. 16When I shoot at you with my
deadly and destructive arrows of
famine, I will shoot to destroy you. I will
bring more and more famine upon you
and cut off your supply of food. 17I will
send famine and wild beasts against
you, and they will leave you childless.
Plague and bloodshed will sweep
through you, and I will bring the sword
against you. I the LORD have spoken."

A Prophecy Against the Mountains of Israel

6 The word of the LORD came to me:
2"Son of man, set your face against
the mountains of Israel; prophesy
against them 3and say: 'O mountains of
Israel, hear the word of the Sovereign
LORD. This is what the Sovereign LORD
says to the mountains and hills, to the
ravines and valleys: I am about to bring
a sword against you, and I will destroy
your high places. 4Your altars will be
demolished and your incense altars will
be smashed; and I will slay your people
in front of your idols. 5I will lay the dead
bodies of the Israelites in front of their
idols, and I will scatter your bones
around your altars. 6Wherever you live,
the towns will be laid waste and the high
places demolished, so that your altars
will be laid waste and devastated, your

idols smashed and ruined, your incense
altars broken down, and what you have
made wiped out. 7Your people will fall
slain among you, and you will know that
I am the LORD.
8" 'But I will spare some, for some of
you will escape the sword when you are
scattered among the lands and nations.
9Then in the nations where they have
been carried captive, those who escape
will remember me—how I have been
grieved by their adulterous hearts,
which have turned away from me, and
by their eyes, which have lusted after
their idols. They will loathe themselves
for the evil they have done and for all
their detestable practices. 10And they
will know that I am the LORD; I did not
threaten in vain to bring this calamity on
them.
11" 'This is what the Sovereign LORD
says: Strike your hands together and
stamp your feet and cry out "Alas!"
because of all the wicked and detestable
practices of the house of Israel, for they
will fall by the sword, famine and plague. 12He that is far away will die of the
plague, and he that is near will fall by
the sword, and he that survives and is
spared will die of famine. So will I spend
my wrath upon them. 13And they will
know that I am the LORD, when their
people lie slain among their idols
around their altars, on every high hill
and on all the mountaintops, under
every spreading tree and every leafy
oak—places where they offered fragrant incense to all their idols. 14And I
will stretch out my hand against them
and make the land a desolate waste
from the desert to Diblah—wherever
they live. Then they will know that I am
the LORD.' "

NEW TESTAMENT READING
Hebrews 5:11–6:12

Warning Against Falling Away

11We have much to say about this, but
it is hard to explain because you are
slow to learn. 12In fact, though by this
time you ought to be teachers, you need
someone to teach you the elementary
truths of God's word all over again. You
need milk, not solid food! 13Anyone
who lives on milk, being still an infant,
is not acquainted with the teaching
about righteousness. 14But solid food is
for the mature, who by constant use
have trained themselves to distinguish
good from evil.
6 Therefore let us leave the
elementary teachings about Christ
and go on to maturity, not laying again
the foundation of repentance from acts
that lead to death, and of faith in God,
2instruction about baptisms, the laying
on of hands, the resurrection of the
dead, and eternal judgment. 3And God
permitting, we will do so.
4It is impossible for those who have
once been enlightened, who have tasted
the heavenly gift, who have shared in
the Holy Spirit, 5who have tasted the
goodness of the word of God and the
powers of the coming age, 6if they fall
away, to be brought back to repentance, because to their loss they are
crucifying the Son of God all over
again and subjecting him to public
disgrace.
7Land that drinks in the rain often
falling on it and that produces a
crop useful to those for whom it is
farmed receives the blessing of God.
8But land that produces thorns and
thistles is worthless and is in danger
of being cursed. In the end it will be
burned.
9Even though we speak like this, dear
friends, we are confident of better
things in your case—things that accompany salvation. 10God is not unjust; he
will not forget your work and the love
you have shown him as you have helped
his people and continue to help them.
11We want each of you to show this
same diligence to the very end, in order
to make your hope sure. 12We do not
want you to become lazy, but to imitate
those who through faith and patience
inherit what has been promised.

READING FROM PROVERBS
Proverbs 26:23–27:4

23Like a coating of glaze over
earthenware
are fervent lips with an evil heart.

24A malicious man disguises himself
with his lips,
but in his heart he harbours
deceit.
25Though his speech is charming, do
not believe him,
for seven abominations fill his
heart.
26His malice may be concealed by
deception,
but his wickedness will be exposed
in the assembly.

27If a man digs a pit, he will fall
into it;
if a man rolls a stone, it will roll
back on him.

28A lying tongue hates those it hurts,
and a flattering mouth works ruin.

27 Do not boast about tomorrow,
for you do not know what a day
may bring forth.

2Let another praise you, and not your
own mouth;
someone else, and not your own
lips.

3Stone is heavy and sand a burden,
but provocation by a fool is heavier
than both.

4Anger is cruel and fury
overwhelming,
but who can stand before jealousy?

NOVEMBER 5

DAY 309

OLD TESTAMENT READING
Ezekiel 7:1–9:11

The End Has Come

7 The word of the LORD came to me:
2"Son of man, this is what the
Sovereign LORD says to the land of
Israel: The end! The end has come upon
the four corners of the land. 3The end is
now upon you and I will unleash my
anger against you. I will judge you
according to your conduct and repay
you for all your detestable practices. 4I
will not look on you with pity or spare
you; I will surely repay you for your
conduct and the detestable practices
among you. Then you will know that I
am the LORD.

5"This is what the Sovereign LORD
says: Disaster! An unheard-of disaster
is coming. 6The end has come! The end
has come! It has roused itself against
you. It has come! 7Doom has come
upon you—you who dwell in the land.
The time has come, the day is near;
there is panic, not joy, upon the mountains. 8I am about to pour out my wrath
on you and spend my anger against you;
I will judge you according to your conduct and repay you for all your detestable practices. 9I will not look on you
with pity or spare you; I will repay you
in accordance with your conduct and
the detestable practices among you.
Then you will know that it is I the LORD
who strikes the blow.

10"The day is here! It has come!
Doom has burst forth, the rod has
budded, arrogance has blossomed!
11Violence has grown into a rod to punish wickedness; none of the people will
be left, none of that crowd—no wealth,
nothing of value. 12The time has come,
the day has arrived. Let not the buyer
rejoice nor the seller grieve, for wrath is
upon the whole crowd. 13The seller will

not recover the land he has sold as long
as both of them live, for the vision concerning the whole crowd will not be
reversed. Because of their sins, not one
of them will preserve his life. 14Though
they blow the trumpet and get everything ready, no-one will go into battle,
for my wrath is upon the whole crowd.
15"Outside is the sword, inside are
plague and famine; those in the country
will die by the sword, and those in the
city will be devoured by famine and
plague. 16All who survive and escape
will be in the mountains, moaning like
doves of the valleys, each because of his
sins. 17Every hand will go limp, and
every knee will become as weak as
water. 18They will put on sackcloth and
be clothed with terror. Their faces will
be covered with shame and their heads
will be shaved. 19They will throw their
silver into the streets, and their gold will
be an unclean thing. Their silver and
gold will not be able to save them in the
day of the LORD's wrath. They will not
satisfy their hunger or fill their stomachs
with it, for it has made them stumble
into sin. 20They were proud of their
beautiful jewellery and used it to make
their detestable idols and vile images.
Therefore I will turn these into an unclean thing for them. 21I will hand it all
over as plunder to foreigners and as loot
to the wicked of the earth, and they will
defile it. 22I will turn my face away from
them, and they will desecrate my treasured place; robbers will enter it and
desecrate it.
23"Prepare chains, because the land is
full of bloodshed and the city is full of
violence. 24I will bring the most wicked
of the nations to take possession of their
houses; I will put an end to the pride of
the mighty, and their sanctuaries will be
desecrated. 25When terror comes, they
will seek peace, but there will be none.
26Calamity upon calamity will come,
and rumour upon rumour. They will try
to get a vision from the prophet; the
teaching of the law by the priest will be
lost, as will the counsel of the elders.
27The king will mourn, the prince will be
clothed with despair, and the hands of
the people of the land will tremble. I
will deal with them according to their
conduct, and by their own standards I
will judge them. Then they will know
that I am the LORD."

Idolatry in the Temple

8 In the sixth year, in the sixth month
on the fifth day, while I was sitting
in my house and the elders of Judah
were sitting before me, the hand of the
Sovereign LORD came upon me there. 2I
looked, and I saw a figure like that of a
man. From what appeared to be his
waist down he was like fire, and from
there up his appearance was as bright as
glowing metal. 3He stretched out what
looked like a hand and took me by the
hair of my head. The Spirit lifted me
up between earth and heaven and in
visions of God he took me to Jerusalem,
to the entrance to the north gate of the
inner court, where the idol that pro-
vokes to jealousy stood. 4And there
before me was the glory of the God of
Israel, as in the vision I had seen in the
plain.
5Then he said to me, "Son of man,
look towards the north." So I looked,
and in the entrance north of the gate of
the altar I saw this idol of jealousy.
6And he said to me, "Son of man, do
you see what they are doing—the
utterly detestable things the house of
Israel is doing here, things that will
drive me far from my sanctuary? But
you will see things that are even more
detestable."
7Then he brought me to the entrance
to the court. I looked, and I saw a hole
in the wall. 8He said to me, "Son of
man, now dig into the wall." So I dug
into the wall and saw a doorway there.
9And he said to me, "Go in and see
the wicked and detestable things they
are doing here." 10So I went in and
looked, and I saw portrayed all over the
walls all kinds of crawling things and
detestable animals and all the idols of
the house of Israel. 11In front of them

stood seventy elders of the house of
Israel, and Jaazaniah son of Shaphan
was standing among them. Each had a
censer in his hand, and a fragrant cloud
of incense was rising.
12He said to me, "Son of man, have
you seen what the elders of the house of
Israel are doing in the darkness, each at
the shrine of his own idol? They say,
'The LORD does not see us; the LORD
has forsaken the land.'" 13Again, he
said, "You will see them doing things
that are even more detestable."
14Then he brought me to the entrance
to the north gate of the house of the
LORD, and I saw women sitting there,
mourning for Tammuz. 15He said to me,
"Do you see this, son of man? You will
see things that are even more detestable
than this."
16He then brought me into the inner
court of the house of the LORD, and
there at the entrance to the temple,
between the portico and the altar, were
about twenty-five men. With their
backs towards the temple of the LORD
and their faces towards the east, they
were bowing down to the sun in the
east.
17He said to me, "Have you seen this,
son of man? Is it a trivial matter for the
house of Judah to do the detestable
things they are doing here? Must they
also fill the land with violence and continually provoke me to anger? Look at
them putting the branch to their nose!
18Therefore I will deal with them in
anger; I will not look on them with pity
or spare them. Although they shout in
my ears, I will not listen to them."

Idolaters Killed

9 Then I heard him call out in a loud
voice, "Bring the guards of the city
here, each with a weapon in his hand."
2And I saw six men coming from the
direction of the upper gate, which faces
north, each with a deadly weapon in his
hand. With them was a man clothed in
linen who had a writing kit at his side.
They came in and stood beside the
bronze altar.
3Now the glory of the God of Israel
went up from above the cherubim,
where it had been, and moved to the
threshold of the temple. Then the LORD
called to the man clothed in linen who
had the writing kit at his side 4and said
to him, "Go throughout the city of Jerusalem and put a mark on the foreheads
of those who grieve and lament over all
the detestable things that are done in
it."
5As I listened, he said to the others,
"Follow him through the city and kill,
without showing pity or compassion.
6Slaughter old men, young men and
maidens, women and children, but do
not touch anyone who has the mark.
Begin at my sanctuary." So they began
with the elders who were in front of the
temple.
7Then he said to them, "Defile the
temple and fill the courts with the slain.
Go!" So they went out and began killing
throughout the city. 8While they were
killing and I was left alone, I fell face
down, crying out, "Ah, Sovereign
LORD! Are you going to destroy the
entire remnant of Israel in this outpouring of your wrath on Jerusalem?"
9He answered me, "The sin of the
house of Israel and Judah is exceedingly
great; the land is full of bloodshed and
the city is full of injustice. They say,
'The LORD has forsaken the land; the
LORD does not see.' 10So I will not look
on them with pity or spare them, but I
will bring down on their own heads what
they have done."
11Then the man in linen with the
writing kit at his side brought back
word, saying, "I have done as you
commanded."

NEW TESTAMENT READING
Hebrews 6:13–7:10

The Certainty of God's Promise

13When God made his promise to
Abraham, since there was no-one
greater for him to swear by, he swore by

himself, [14]saying, "I will surely bless you and give you many descendants." [15]And so after waiting patiently, Abraham received what was promised.

[16]Men swear by someone greater than themselves, and the oath confirms what is said and puts an end to all argument. [17]Because God wanted to make the unchanging nature of his purpose very clear to the heirs of what was promised, he confirmed it with an oath. [18]God did this so that, by two unchangeable things in which it is impossible for God to lie, we who have fled to take hold of the hope offered to us may be greatly encouraged. [19]We have this hope as an anchor for the soul, firm and secure. It enters the inner sanctuary behind the curtain, [20]where Jesus, who went before us, has entered on our behalf. He has become a high priest for ever, in the order of Melchizedek.

Melchizedek the Priest

7 This Melchizedek was king of Salem and priest of God Most High. He met Abraham returning from the defeat of the kings and blessed him, [2]and Abraham gave him a tenth of everything. First, his name means "king of righteousness"; then also, "king of Salem" means "king of peace". [3]Without father or mother, without genealogy, without beginning of days or end of life, like the Son of God he remains a priest for ever.

[4]Just think how great he was: Even the patriarch Abraham gave him a tenth of the plunder! [5]Now the law requires the descendants of Levi who become priests to collect a tenth from the people—that is, their brothers—even though their brothers are descended from Abraham. [6]This man, however, did not trace his descent from Levi, yet he collected a tenth from Abraham and blessed him who had the promises. [7]And without doubt the lesser person is blessed by the greater. [8]In the one case, the tenth is collected by men who die; but in the other case, by him who is declared to be living. [9]One might even say that Levi, who collects the tenth, paid the tenth through Abraham, [10]because when Melchizedek met Abraham, Levi was still in the body of his ancestor.

READING FROM PSALMS
Psalm 119:161–168

שׁ Sin and Shin

161 Rulers persecute me without cause,
but my heart trembles at your word.
162 I rejoice in your promise
like one who finds great spoil.
163 I hate and abhor falsehood
but I love your law.
164 Seven times a day I praise you
for your righteous laws.
165 Great peace have they who love your law,
and nothing can make them stumble.
166 I wait for your salvation, O LORD,
and I follow your commands.
167 I obey your statutes,
for I love them greatly.
168 I obey your precepts and your statutes,
for all my ways are known to you.

NOVEMBER 6

DAY 310

OLD TESTAMENT READING
Ezekiel 10:1–12:28

The Glory Departs From the Temple

10 I looked, and I saw the likeness of a throne of sapphire above the expanse that was over the heads of the cherubim. 2The LORD said to the man clothed in linen, "Go in among the wheels beneath the cherubim. Fill your hands with burning coals from among the cherubim and scatter them over the city." And as I watched, he went in.

3Now the cherubim were standing on the south side of the temple when the man went in, and a cloud filled the inner court. 4Then the glory of the LORD rose from above the cherubim and moved to the threshold of the temple. The cloud filled the temple, and the court was full of the radiance of the glory of the LORD. 5The sound of the wings of the cherubim could be heard as far away as the outer court, like the voice of God Almighty when he speaks.

6When the LORD commanded the man in linen, "Take fire from among the wheels, from among the cherubim," the man went in and stood beside a wheel. 7Then one of the cherubim reached out his hand to the fire that was among them. He took up some of it and put it into the hands of the man in linen, who took it and went out. 8(Under the wings of the cherubim could be seen what looked like the hands of a man.)

9I looked, and I saw beside the cherubim four wheels, one beside each of the cherubim; the wheels sparkled like chrysolite. 10As for their appearance, the four of them looked alike; each was like a wheel intersecting a wheel. 11As they moved, they would go in any one of the four directions the cherubim faced; the wheels did not turn about as the cherubim went. The cherubim went in whatever direction the head faced, without turning as they went. 12Their entire bodies, including their backs, their hands and their wings, were completely full of eyes, as were their four wheels. 13I heard the wheels being called "the whirling wheels". 14Each of the cherubim had four faces: One face was that of a cherub, the second the face of a man, the third the face of a lion, and the fourth the face of an eagle.

15Then the cherubim rose upwards. These were the living creatures I had seen by the Kebar River. 16When the cherubim moved, the wheels beside them moved; and when the cherubim spread their wings to rise from the ground, the wheels did not leave their side. 17When the cherubim stood still, they also stood still; and when the cherubim rose, they rose with them, because the spirit of the living creatures was in them.

18Then the glory of the LORD departed from over the threshold of the temple and stopped above the cherubim. 19While I watched, the cherubim spread their wings and rose from the ground, and as they went, the wheels went with them. They stopped at the entrance to the east gate of the LORD's house, and the glory of the God of Israel was above them.

20These were the living creatures I had seen beneath the God of Israel by the Kebar River, and I realised that they were cherubim. 21Each had four faces and four wings, and under their wings were what looked like the hands of a man. 22Their faces had the same appearance as those I had seen by the Kebar River. Each one went straight ahead.

Judgment on Israel's Leaders

11 Then the Spirit lifted me up and brought me to the gate of the house of the LORD that faces east. There

at the entrance to the gate were twenty-
five men, and I saw among them Jaazaniah son of Azzur and Pelatiah son of
Benaiah, leaders of the people. 2The
LORD said to me, "Son of man, these
are the men who are plotting evil and
giving wicked advice in this city. 3They
say, 'Will it not soon be time to build
houses? This city is a cooking pot, and
we are the meat.' 4Therefore prophesy
against them; prophesy, son of man."
5Then the Spirit of the LORD came
upon me, and he told me to say: "This is
what the LORD says: That is what you
are saying, O house of Israel, but I
know what is going through your mind.
6You have killed many people in this
city and filled its streets with the dead.
7"Therefore this is what the
Sovereign LORD says: The bodies you
have thrown there are the meat and this
city is the pot, but I will drive you out of
it. 8You fear the sword, and the sword is
what I will bring against you, declares
the Sovereign LORD. 9I will drive you
out of the city and hand you over to
foreigners and inflict punishment on
you. 10You will fall by the sword, and I
will execute judgment on you at the
borders of Israel. Then you will know
that I am the LORD. 11This city will not
be a pot for you, nor will you be the
meat in it; I will execute judgment on
you at the borders of Israel. 12And you
will know that I am the LORD, for
you have not followed my decrees or
kept my laws but have conformed to
the standards of the nations around
you."
13Now as I was prophesying, Pelatiah
son of Benaiah died. Then I fell face
down and cried out in a loud voice,
"Ah, Sovereign LORD! Will you completely destroy the remnant of Israel?"
14The word of the LORD came to me:
15"Son of man, your brothers—your
brothers who are your blood-relatives
and the whole house of Israel—are
those of whom the people of Jerusalem
have said, 'They are far away from the
LORD; this land was given to us as our
possession.'

Promised Return of Israel

16"Therefore say: 'This is what the
Sovereign LORD says: Although I sent
them far away among the nations and
scattered them among the countries, yet
for a little while I have been a sanctuary
for them in the countries where they
have gone.'
17"Therefore say: 'This is what the
Sovereign LORD says: I will gather you
from the nations and bring you back
from the countries where you have been
scattered, and I will give you back the
land of Israel again.'
18"They will return to it and remove
all its vile images and detestable idols.
19I will give them an undivided heart
and put a new spirit in them; I will
remove from them their heart of stone
and give them a heart of flesh. 20Then
they will follow my decrees and be careful to keep my laws. They will be my
people, and I will be their God. 21But as
for those whose hearts are devoted to
their vile images and detestable idols, I
will bring down on their own heads what
they have done, declares the Sovereign
LORD."
22Then the cherubim, with the wheels
beside them, spread their wings, and
the glory of the God of Israel was above
them. 23The glory of the LORD went up
from within the city and stopped above
the mountain east of it. 24The Spirit
lifted me up and brought me to the
exiles in Babylonia in the vision given by
the Spirit of God.
Then the vision I had seen went up
from me, 25and I told the exiles everything the LORD had shown me.

The Exile Symbolised

12 The word of the LORD came to
me: 2"Son of man, you are living
among a rebellious people. They have
eyes to see but do not see and ears to
hear but do not hear, for they are a
rebellious people.
3"Therefore, son of man, pack your
belongings for exile and in the daytime,
as they watch, set out and go from

where you are to another place.
Perhaps they will understand, though
they are a rebellious house. 4During the
daytime, while they watch, bring out
your belongings packed for exile. Then
in the evening, while they are watching,
go out like those who go into exile.
5While they watch, dig through the wall
and take your belongings out through it.
6Put them on your shoulder as they are
watching and carry them out at dusk.
Cover your face so that you cannot see
the land, for I have made you a sign to
the house of Israel."

7So I did as I was commanded. During the day I brought out my things
packed for exile. Then in the evening
I dug through the wall with my hands.
I took my belongings out at dusk, carrying them on my shoulders while they
watched.

8In the morning the word of the LORD
came to me: 9"Son of man, did not that
rebellious house of Israel ask you,
'What are you doing?'

10"Say to them, 'This is what the
Sovereign LORD says: This oracle concerns the prince in Jerusalem and the
whole house of Israel who are there.'
11Say to them, 'I am a sign to you.'

"As I have done, so it will be done to
them. They will go into exile as captives.

12"The prince among them will put
his things on his shoulder at dusk and
leave, and a hole will be dug in the wall
for him to go through. He will cover his
face so that he cannot see the land. 13I
will spread my net for him, and he will
be caught in my snare; I will bring him
to Babylonia, the land of the Chaldeans, but he will not see it, and there
he will die. 14I will scatter to the winds
all those around him—his staff and all
his troops—and I will pursue them with
drawn sword.

15"They will know that I am the
LORD, when I disperse them among
the nations and scatter them through
the countries. 16But I will spare a few
of them from the sword, famine and
plague, so that in the nations where
they go they may acknowledge all their
detestable practices. Then they will
know that I am the LORD."

17The word of the LORD came to me:
18"Son of man, tremble as you eat your
food, and shudder in fear as you drink
your water. 19Say to the people of the
land: 'This is what the Sovereign LORD
says about those living in Jerusalem and
in the land of Israel: They will eat their
food in anxiety and drink their water in
despair, for their land will be stripped of
everything in it because of the violence
of all who live there. 20The inhabited
towns will be laid waste and the land will
be desolate. Then you will know that I
am the LORD.' "

21The word of the LORD came to me:
22"Son of man, what is this proverb you
have in the land of Israel: 'The days go
by and every vision comes to nothing'?
23Say to them, 'This is what the
Sovereign LORD says: I am going to put
an end to this proverb, and they will no
longer quote it in Israel.' Say to them,
'The days are near when every vision
will be fulfilled. 24For there will be no
more false visions or flattering divinations among the people of Israel. 25But I
the LORD will speak what I will, and it
shall be fulfilled without delay. For in
your days, you rebellious house, I will
fulfil whatever I say, declares the
Sovereign LORD.' "

26The word of the LORD came to me:
27"Son of man, the house of Israel is
saying, 'The vision he sees is for many
years from now, and he prophesies
about the distant future.'

28"Therefore say to them, 'This is
what the Sovereign LORD says: None of
my words will be delayed any longer;
whatever I say will be fulfilled, declares
the Sovereign LORD.' "

NEW TESTAMENT READING
Hebrews 7:11–28

Jesus Like Melchizedek

11If perfection could have been
attained through the Levitical priesthood (for on the basis of it the law was

given to the people), why was there still
need for another priest to come—one
in the order of Melchizedek, not in the
order of Aaron? [12]For when there is a
change of the priesthood, there must
also be a change of the law. [13]He of
whom these things are said belonged to
a different tribe, and no-one from that
tribe has ever served at the altar. [14]For it
is clear that our Lord descended from
Judah, and in regard to that tribe Moses
said nothing about priests. [15]And what
we have said is even more clear if
another priest like Melchizedek
appears, [16]one who has become a priest
not on the basis of a regulation as to his
ancestry but on the basis of the power
of an indestructible life. [17]For it is
declared:

"You are a priest for ever,
in the order of Melchizedek."

[18]The former regulation is set aside
because it was weak and useless [19](for
the law made nothing perfect), and a
better hope is introduced, by which we
draw near to God.
[20]And it was not without an oath!
Others became priests without any
oath, [21]but he became a priest with an
oath when God said to him:

"The Lord has sworn
and will not change his mind:
'You are a priest for ever.'"

[22]Because of this oath, Jesus has
become the guarantee of a better
covenant.
[23]Now there have been many of those
priests, since death prevented them
from continuing in office; [24]but because
Jesus lives for ever, he has a permanent
priesthood. [25]Therefore he is able to
save completely those who come to God
through him, because he always lives to
intercede for them.
[26]Such a high priest meets our need
—one who is holy, blameless, pure, set
apart from sinners, exalted above the
heavens. [27]Unlike the other high
priests, he does not need to offer sacrifices day after day, first for his own
sins, and then for the sins of the people.
He sacrificed for their sins once for all
when he offered himself. [28]For the law
appoints as high priests men who are
weak; but the oath, which came after
the law, appointed the Son, who has
been made perfect for ever.

READING FROM PSALMS

Psalm 119:169–176

ת Taw

[169]May my cry come before you, O
LORD;
give me understanding according
to your word.
[170]May my supplication come before
you;
deliver me according to your
promise.
[171]May my lips overflow with praise,
for you teach me your decrees.
[172]May my tongue sing of your word,
for all your commands are
righteous.
[173]May your hand be ready to help me,
for I have chosen your precepts.
[174]I long for your salvation, O LORD,
and your law is my delight.
[175]Let me live that I may praise you,
and may your laws sustain me.
[176]I have strayed like a lost sheep.
Seek your servant,
for I have not forgotten your
commands.

NOVEMBER 7

DAY 311

OLD TESTAMENT READING

Ezekiel 13:1–15:8

False Prophets Condemned

13 The word of the LORD came to
me: 2“Son of man, prophesy
against the prophets of Israel who are
now prophesying. Say to those who
prophesy out of their own imagination:
‘Hear the word of the LORD! 3This is
what the Sovereign LORD says: Woe to
the foolish prophets who follow their
own spirit and have seen nothing! 4Your
prophets, O Israel, are like jackals
among ruins. 5You have not gone up to
the breaks in the wall to repair it for the
house of Israel so that it will stand firm
in the battle on the day of the LORD.
6Their visions are false and their divinations a lie. They say, “The LORD declares”, when the LORD has not sent
them; yet they expect their words to
be fulfilled. 7Have you not seen false
visions and uttered lying divinations
when you say, “The LORD declares”,
though I have not spoken?

8“ ‘Therefore this is what the
Sovereign LORD says: Because of your
false words and lying visions, I am
against you, declares the Sovereign
LORD. 9My hand will be against the
prophets who see false visions and utter
lying divinations. They will not belong
to the council of my people or be listed
in the records of the house of Israel, nor
will they enter the land of Israel. Then
you will know that I am the Sovereign
LORD.

10“ ‘Because they lead my people
astray, saying, “Peace”, when there is
no peace, and because, when a flimsy
wall is built, they cover it with
whitewash, 11therefore tell those who
cover it with whitewash that it is going
to fall. Rain will come in torrents, and I
will send hailstones hurtling down, and
violent winds will burst forth. 12When
the wall collapses, will people not ask
you, “Where is the whitewash you
covered it with?”

13“ ‘Therefore this is what the
Sovereign LORD says: In my wrath I will
unleash a violent wind, and in my anger
hailstones and torrents of rain will fall
with destructive fury. 14I will tear down
the wall you have covered with
whitewash and will level it to the ground
so that its foundation will be laid bare.
When it falls, you will be destroyed in it;
and you will know that I am the LORD.
15So I will spend my wrath against the
wall and against those who covered it
with whitewash. I will say to you, “The
wall is gone and so are those who
whitewashed it, 16those prophets of
Israel who prophesied to Jerusalem and
saw visions of peace for her when there
was no peace, declares the Sovereign
LORD.” ’

17“Now, son of man, set your face
against the daughters of your people
who prophesy out of their own imagination. Prophesy against them 18and say,
‘This is what the Sovereign LORD says:
Woe to the women who sew magic
charms on all their wrists and make veils
of various lengths for their heads in
order to ensnare people. Will you ensnare the lives of my people but preserve your own? 19You have profaned
me among my people for a few handfuls
of barley and scraps of bread. By lying
to my people, who listen to lies, you
have killed those who should not have
died and have spared those who should
not live.

20“ ‘Therefore this is what the
Sovereign LORD says: I am against your
magic charms with which you ensnare
people like birds and I will tear them
from your arms; I will set free the people that you ensnare like birds. 21I will
tear off your veils and save my people
from your hands, and they will no longer fall prey to your power. Then you
will know that I am the LORD.

22Because you disheartened the righteous with your lies, when I had brought
them no grief, and because you encouraged the wicked not to turn from their
evil ways and so save their lives,
23therefore you will no longer see false
visions or practise divination. I will save
my people from your hands. And then
you will know that I am the LORD.' "

Idolaters Condemned

14 Some of the elders of Israel
came to me and sat down in
front of me. 2Then the word of the LORD
came to me: 3"Son of man, these men
have set up idols in their hearts and put
wicked stumbling-blocks before their
faces. Should I let them enquire of me at
all? 4Therefore speak to them and tell
them, 'This is what the Sovereign LORD
says: When any Israelite sets up idols in
his heart and puts a wicked stumbling-
block before his face and then goes to a
prophet, I the LORD will answer him
myself in keeping with his great idolatry. 5I will do this to recapture the
hearts of the people of Israel, who have
all deserted me for their idols.'

6"Therefore say to the house of
Israel, 'This is what the Sovereign LORD
says: Repent! Turn from your idols and
renounce all your detestable practices!

7" 'When any Israelite or any alien
living in Israel separates himself from
me and sets up idols in his heart and puts
a wicked stumbling-block before his
face and then goes to a prophet to enquire of me, I the LORD will answer him
myself. 8I will set my face against that
man and make him an example and a
byword. I will cut him off from my
people. Then you will know that I am
the LORD.

9" 'And if the prophet is enticed to
utter a prophecy, I the LORD have enticed that prophet, and I will stretch out
my hand against him and destroy him
from among my people Israel. 10They
will bear their guilt—the prophet will
be as guilty as the one who consults him.
11Then the people of Israel will no longer stray from me, nor will they defile
themselves any more with all their sins.
They will be my people, and I will be
their God, declares the Sovereign
LORD.' "

Judgment Inescapable

12The word of the LORD came to me:
13"Son of man, if a country sins against
me by being unfaithful and I stretch out
my hand against it to cut off its food
supply and send famine upon it and kill
its men and their animals, 14even if
these three men—Noah, Daniel and
Job—were in it, they could save only
themselves by their righteousness, declares the Sovereign LORD.

15"Or if I send wild beasts through
that country and they leave it childless
and it becomes desolate so that no-one
can pass through it because of the
beasts, 16as surely as I live, declares the
Sovereign LORD, even if these three
men were in it, they could not save their
own sons or daughters. They alone
would be saved, but the land would be
desolate.

17"Or if I bring a sword against that
country and say, 'Let the sword pass
throughout the land,' and I kill its men
and their animals, 18as surely as I live,
declares the Sovereign LORD, even if
these three men were in it, they could
not save their own sons or daughters.
They alone would be saved.

19"Or if I send a plague into that land
and pour out my wrath upon it through
bloodshed, killing its men and their
animals, 20as surely as I live, declares
the Sovereign LORD, even if Noah,
Daniel and Job were in it, they could
save neither son nor daughter. They
would save only themselves by their
righteousness.

21"For this is what the Sovereign
LORD says: How much worse will it
be when I send against Jerusalem my
four dreadful judgments—sword and
famine and wild beasts and plague—to
kill its men and their animals! 22Yet

there will be some survivors—sons and
daughters who will be brought out of it.
They will come to you, and when you
see their conduct and their actions, you
will be consoled regarding the disaster I
have brought upon Jerusalem—every
disaster I have brought upon it. 23You
will be consoled when you see their
conduct and their actions, for you will
know that I have done nothing in it
without cause, declares the Sovereign
LORD."

Jerusalem, a Useless Vine

15 The word of the LORD came to
me: 2"Son of man, how is the
wood of a vine better than that of a
branch on any of the trees in the forest?
3Is wood ever taken from it to make
anything useful? Do they make pegs
from it to hang things on? 4And after it
is thrown on the fire as fuel and the fire
burns both ends and chars the middle, is
it then useful for anything? 5If it was not
useful for anything when it was whole,
how much less can it be made into something useful when the fire has burned it
and it is charred?

6"Therefore this is what the
Sovereign LORD says: As I have given
the wood of the vine among the trees of
the forest as fuel for the fire, so will I
treat the people living in Jerusalem. 7I
will set my face against them. Although
they have come out of the fire, the fire
will yet consume them. And when I set
my face against them, you will know
that I am the LORD. 8I will make the
land desolate because they have been
unfaithful, declares the Sovereign
LORD."

NEW TESTAMENT READING
Hebrews 8:1–13

The High Priest of a New Covenant

8 The point of what we are saying is
this: We do have such a high priest,
who sat down at the right hand of the
throne of the Majesty in heaven, 2and
who serves in the sanctuary, the true
tabernacle set up by the Lord, not by
man.

3Every high priest is appointed to
offer both gifts and sacrifices, and so it
was necessary for this one also to have
something to offer. 4If he were on earth,
he would not be a priest, for there are
already men who offer the gifts prescribed by the law. 5They serve at a
sanctuary that is a copy and shadow of
what is in heaven. This is why Moses
was warned when he was about to build
the tabernacle: "See to it that you make
everything according to the pattern
shown you on the mountain." 6But
the ministry Jesus has received is as
superior to theirs as the covenant of
which he is mediator is superior to the
old one, and it is founded on better
promises.

7For if there had been nothing wrong
with that first covenant, no place would
have been sought for another. 8But God
found fault with the people and said:

"The time is coming, declares the
Lord,
when I will make a new covenant
with the house of Israel
and with the house of Judah.
9It will not be like the covenant
I made with their forefathers
when I took them by the hand
to lead them out of Egypt,
because they did not remain faithful
to my covenant,
and I turned away from them,
declares the Lord.
10This is the covenant I will make with
the house of Israel
after that time, declares the Lord.
I will put my laws in their minds
and write them on their hearts.
I will be their God,
and they will be my people.
11No longer will a man teach his
neighbour,
or a man his brother, saying,
'Know the Lord,'
because they will all know me,

from the least of them to the
greatest.
12For I will forgive their wickedness
and will remember their sins no
more."

13By calling this covenant "new", he has made the first one obsolete; and what is obsolete and ageing will soon disappear.

READING FROM PSALMS
Psalm 120:1–7

A song of ascents.

1I call on the LORD in my distress,
and he answers me.
2Save me, O LORD, from lying lips
and from deceitful tongues.

3What will he do to you,
and what more besides, O deceitful
tongue?
4He will punish you with a warrior's
sharp arrows,
with burning coals of the broom
tree.

5Woe to me that I dwell in Meshech,
that I live among the tents of
Kedar!
6Too long have I lived
among those who hate peace.
7I am a man of peace;
but when I speak, they are for war.

DAY 312

NOVEMBER 8

OLD TESTAMENT READING
Ezekiel 16:1–63

An Allegory of Unfaithful Jerusalem

16 The word of the LORD came to
me: 2"Son of man, confront
Jerusalem with her detestable practices
3and say, 'This is what the Sovereign
LORD says to Jerusalem: Your ancestry
and birth were in the land of the
Canaanites; your father was an Amorite
and your mother a Hittite. 4On the day
you were born your cord was not cut,
nor were you washed with water to
make you clean, nor were you rubbed
with salt or wrapped in cloths. 5No-one
looked on you with pity or had compassion enough to do any of these things for
you. Rather, you were thrown out into
the open field, for on the day you were
born you were despised.
6" 'Then I passed by and saw you
kicking about in your blood, and as you
lay there in your blood I said to you,
"Live!" 7I made you grow like a plant of
the field. You grew up and developed
and became the most beautiful of
jewels. Your breasts were formed and
your hair grew, you who were naked
and bare.
8" 'Later I passed by, and when I
looked at you and saw that you were old
enough for love, I spread the corner of
my garment over you and covered your
nakedness. I gave you my solemn oath
and entered into a covenant with you,
declares the Sovereign LORD, and you
became mine.
9" 'I bathed you with water and
washed the blood from you and put
ointments on you. 10I clothed you with
an embroidered dress and put leather
sandals on you. I dressed you in fine
linen and covered you with costly garments. 11I adorned you with jewellery: I
put bracelets on your arms and a necklace around your neck, 12and I put a ring
on your nose, ear-rings on your ears and
a beautiful crown on your head. 13So
you were adorned with gold and silver;

your clothes were of fine linen and
costly fabric and embroidered cloth.
Your food was fine flour, honey and
olive oil. You became very beautiful
and rose to be a queen. 14And your
fame spread among the nations on
account of your beauty, because the
splendour I had given you made your
beauty perfect, declares the Sovereign
LORD.

15" 'But you trusted in your beauty
and used your fame to become a prostitute. You lavished your favours on anyone who passed by and your beauty
became his. 16You took some of your
garments to make gaudy high places,
where you carried on your prostitution.
Such things should not happen, nor
should they ever occur. 17You also took
the fine jewellery I gave you, the jewellery made of my gold and silver, and you
made for yourself male idols and engaged in prostitution with them. 18And
you took your embroidered clothes to
put on them, and you offered my oil and
incense before them. 19Also the food I
provided for you—the fine flour, olive
oil and honey I gave you to eat—you
offered as fragrant incense before them.
That is what happened, declares the
Sovereign LORD.

20" 'And you took your sons and
daughters whom you bore to me and
sacrificed them as food to the idols. Was
your prostitution not enough? 21You
slaughtered my children and sacrificed
them to the idols. 22In all your detestable practices and your prostitution you
did not remember the days of your
youth, when you were naked and bare,
kicking about in your blood.

23" 'Woe! Woe to you, declares the
Sovereign LORD. In addition to all your
other wickedness, 24you built a mound
for yourself and made a lofty shrine in
every public square. 25At the head of
every street you built your lofty shrines
and degraded your beauty, offering
your body with increasing promiscuity
to anyone who passed by. 26You engaged in prostitution with the Egyptians, your lustful neighbours, and
provoked me to anger with your increasing promiscuity. 27So I stretched
out my hand against you and reduced
your territory; I gave you over to the
greed of your enemies, the daughters of
the Philistines, who were shocked by
your lewd conduct. 28You engaged in
prostitution with the Assyrians too, because you were insatiable; and even
after that, you still were not satisfied.
29Then you increased your promiscuity
to include Babylonia, a land of merchants, but even with this you were not
satisfied.

30" 'How weak-willed you are, declares the Sovereign LORD, when you
do all these things, acting like a brazen
prostitute! 31When you built your
mounds at the head of every street and
made your lofty shrines in every public
square, you were unlike a prostitute,
because you scorned payment.

32" 'You adulterous wife! You prefer
strangers to your own husband! 33Every
prostitute receives a fee, but you give
gifts to all your lovers, bribing them to
come to you from everywhere for your
illicit favours. 34So in your prostitution
you are the opposite of others; no-one
runs after you for your favours. You are
the very opposite, for you give payment
and none is given to you.

35" 'Therefore, you prostitute, hear
the word of the LORD! 36This is what the
Sovereign LORD says: Because you
poured out your wealth and exposed
your nakedness in your promiscuity
with your lovers, and because of all your
detestable idols, and because you gave
them your children's blood, 37therefore
I am going to gather all your lovers, with
whom you found pleasure, those you
loved as well as those you hated. I will
gather them against you from all around
and will strip you in front of them, and
they will see all your nakedness. 38I will
sentence you to the punishment of
women who commit adultery and who
shed blood; I will bring upon you the
blood vengeance of my wrath and
jealous anger. 39Then I will hand you
over to your lovers, and they will tear

down your mounds and destroy your
lofty shrines. They will strip you of your
clothes and take your fine jewellery and
leave you naked and bare. 40They will
bring a mob against you, who will stone
you and hack you to pieces with their
swords. 41They will burn down your
houses and inflict punishment on you in
the sight of many women. I will put a
stop to your prostitution, and you will
no longer pay your lovers. 42Then my
wrath against you will subside and my
jealous anger will turn away from you; I
will be calm and no longer angry.

43" 'Because you did not remember
the days of your youth but enraged me
with all these things, I will surely bring
down on your head what you have
done, declares the Sovereign LORD.
Did you not add lewdness to all your
other detestable practices?

44" 'Everyone who quotes proverbs
will quote this proverb about you:
"Like mother, like daughter." 45You
are a true daughter of your mother, who
despised her husband and her children;
and you are a true sister of your sisters,
who despised their husbands and their
children. Your mother was a Hittite and
your father an Amorite. 46Your older
sister was Samaria, who lived to the
north of you with her daughters; and
your younger sister, who lived to the
south of you with her daughters, was
Sodom. 47You not only walked in their
ways and copied their detestable practices, but in all your ways you soon
became more depraved than they. 48As
surely as I live, declares the Sovereign
LORD, your sister Sodom and her
daughters never did what you and your
daughters have done.

49" 'Now this was the sin of your sister
Sodom: She and her daughters were
arrogant, overfed and unconcerned;
they did not help the poor and needy.
50They were haughty and did detestable
things before me. Therefore I did away
with them as you have seen. 51Samaria
did not commit half the sins you did.
You have done more detestable things
than they, and have made your sisters
seem righteous by all these things you
have done. 52Bear your disgrace, for
you have furnished some justification
for your sisters. Because your sins were
more vile than theirs, they appear more
righteous than you. So then, be
ashamed and bear your disgrace, for
you have made your sisters appear
righteous.

53" 'However, I will restore the fortunes of Sodom and her daughters and
of Samaria and her daughters, and your
fortunes along with them, 54so that you
may bear your disgrace and be ashamed
of all you have done in giving them
comfort. 55And your sisters, Sodom
with her daughters and Samaria with
her daughters, will return to what they
were before; and you and your daughters will return to what you were before.
56You would not even mention your
sister Sodom in the day of your pride,
57before your wickedness was uncovered. Even so, you are now scorned
by the daughters of Edom and all her
neighbours and the daughters of the
Philistines—all those around you who
despise you. 58You will bear the consequences of your lewdness and your
detestable practices, declares the
LORD.

59" 'This is what the Sovereign LORD
says: I will deal with you as you deserve,
because you have despised my oath by
breaking the covenant. 60Yet I will remember the covenant I made with you
in the days of your youth, and I will
establish an everlasting covenant with
you. 61Then you will remember your
ways and be ashamed when you receive
your sisters, both those who are older
than you and those who are younger. I
will give them to you as daughters, but
not on the basis of my covenant with
you. 62So I will establish my covenant
with you, and you will know that I am
the LORD. 63Then, when I make atonement for you for all you have done, you
will remember and be ashamed and
never again open your mouth because
of your humiliation, declares the
Sovereign LORD.' "

NEW TESTAMENT READING
Hebrews 9:1–15

Worship in the Earthly Tabernacle

9 Now the first covenant had regulations for worship and also an
earthly sanctuary. 2A tabernacle was set
up. In its first room were the lampstand,
the table and the consecrated bread;
this was called the Holy Place. 3Behind
the second curtain was a room called the
Most Holy Place, 4which had the golden
altar of incense and the gold-covered
ark of the covenant. This ark contained
the gold jar of manna, Aaron's staff that
had budded, and the stone tablets of the
covenant. 5Above the ark were the
cherubim of the Glory, overshadowing
the atonement cover. But we cannot
discuss these things in detail now.
6When everything had been arranged
like this, the priests entered regularly
into the outer room to carry on their
ministry. 7But only the high priest entered the inner room, and that only
once a year, and never without blood,
which he offered for himself and for the
sins the people had committed in ignorance. 8The Holy Spirit was showing by
this that the way into the Most Holy
Place had not yet been disclosed as long
as the first tabernacle was still standing.
9This is an illustration for the present
time, indicating that the gifts and sacrifices being offered were not able to
clear the conscience of the worshipper.
10They are only a matter of food and
drink and various ceremonial washings
—external regulations applying until
the time of the new order.

The Blood of Christ

11When Christ came as high priest of
the good things that are already here, he
went through the greater and more perfect tabernacle that is not man-made,
that is to say, not a part of this creation.
12He did not enter by means of the
blood of goats and calves; but he entered the Most Holy Place once for all
by his own blood, having obtained eternal redemption. 13The blood of goats
and bulls and the ashes of a heifer
sprinkled on those who are ceremonially unclean sanctify them so that
they are outwardly clean. 14How much
more, then, will the blood of Christ,
who through the eternal Spirit offered
himself unblemished to God, cleanse
our consciences from acts that lead to
death, so that we may serve the living
God!
15For this reason Christ is the
mediator of a new covenant, that those
who are called may receive the promised eternal inheritance—now that he
has died as a ransom to set them free
from the sins committed under the first
covenant.

READING FROM PROVERBS
Proverbs 27:5–14

5Better is open rebuke
than hidden love.

6Wounds from a friend can be trusted,
but an enemy multiplies kisses.

7He who is full loathes honey,
but to the hungry even what is
bitter tastes sweet.

8Like a bird that strays from its nest
is a man who strays from his home.

9Perfume and incense bring joy to the
heart,
and the pleasantness of one's
friend springs from his earnest
counsel.

10Do not forsake your friend and the
friend of your father,
and do not go to your brother's
house when disaster strikes
you—
better a neighbour nearby than a
brother far away.

11Be wise, my son, and bring joy to my
heart;
then I can answer anyone who
treats me with contempt.

12The prudent see danger and take
refuge,
but the simple keep going and
suffer for it.

13Take the garment of one who puts up
security for a stranger;
hold it in pledge if he does it for a
wayward woman.

14If a man loudly blesses his neighbour
early in the morning,
it will be taken as a curse.

DAY 313

NOVEMBER 9

OLD TESTAMENT READING
Ezekiel 17:1–18:32

Two Eagles and a Vine

17 The word of the LORD came to me: 2"Son of man, set forth an allegory and tell the house of Israel a parable. 3Say to them, 'This is what the Sovereign LORD says: A great eagle with powerful wings, long feathers and full plumage of varied colours came to Lebanon. Taking hold of the top of a cedar, 4he broke off its topmost shoot and carried it away to a land of merchants, where he planted it in a city of traders.

5" 'He took some of the seed of your land and put it in fertile soil. He planted it like a willow by abundant water, 6and it sprouted and became a low, spreading vine. Its branches turned towards him, but its roots remained under it. So it became a vine and produced branches and put out leafy boughs.

7" 'But there was another great eagle with powerful wings and full plumage. The vine now sent out its roots towards him from the plot where it was planted and stretched out its branches to him for water. 8It had been planted in good soil by abundant water so that it would produce branches, bear fruit and become a splendid vine.'

9"Say to them, 'This is what the Sovereign LORD says: Will it thrive? Will it not be uprooted and stripped of its fruit so that it withers? All its new growth will wither. It will not take a strong arm or many people to pull it up by the roots. 10Even if it is transplanted, will it thrive? Will it not wither completely when the east wind strikes it—wither away in the plot where it grew?' "

11Then the word of the LORD came to me: 12"Say to this rebellious house, 'Do you not know what these things mean?' Say to them: 'The king of Babylon went to Jerusalem and carried off her king and her nobles, bringing them back with him to Babylon. 13Then he took a member of the royal family and made a treaty with him, putting him under oath. He also carried away the leading men of the land, 14so that the kingdom would be brought low, unable to rise again, surviving only by keeping his treaty. 15But the king rebelled against him by sending his envoys to Egypt to get horses and a large army. Will he succeed? Will he who does such things escape? Will he break the treaty and yet escape?

16" 'As surely as I live, declares the Sovereign LORD, he shall die in Babylon, in the land of the king who put him on the throne, whose oath he despised and whose treaty he broke. 17Pharaoh with his mighty army and great horde will be of no help to him in war, when

ramps are built and siege works erected
to destroy many lives. 18He despised the
oath by breaking the covenant. Because
he had given his hand in pledge and yet
did all these things, he shall not escape.
19" 'Therefore this is what the
Sovereign LORD says: As surely as I
live, I will bring down on his head my
oath that he despised and my covenant
that he broke. 20I will spread my net for
him, and he will be caught in my snare. I
will bring him to Babylon and execute
judgment upon him there because he
was unfaithful to me. 21All his fleeing
troops will fall by the sword, and the
survivors will be scattered to the winds.
Then you will know that I the LORD
have spoken.
22" 'This is what the Sovereign LORD
says: I myself will take a shoot from the
very top of a cedar and plant it; I will
break off a tender sprig from its topmost
shoots and plant it on a high and lofty
mountain. 23On the mountain heights of
Israel I will plant it; it will produce
branches and bear fruit and become a
splendid cedar. Birds of every kind will
nest in it; they will find shelter in the
shade of its branches. 24All the trees of
the field will know that I the LORD bring
down the tall tree and make the low tree
grow tall. I dry up the green tree and
make the dry tree flourish.
" 'I the LORD have spoken, and I will
do it.' "

The Soul Who Sins Will Die

18 The word of the LORD came to
me: 2"What do you people mean
by quoting this proverb about the land
of Israel:

" 'The fathers eat sour grapes,
and the children's teeth are set on
edge'?

3"As surely as I live, declares the
Sovereign LORD, you will no longer
quote this proverb in Israel. 4For every
living soul belongs to me, the father as
well as the son—both alike belong to
me. The soul who sins is the one who
will die.

5"Suppose there is a righteous man
who does what is just and right.
6He does not eat at the mountain
shrines
or look to the idols of the house of
Israel.
He does not defile his neighbour's
wife
or lie with a woman during her
period.
7He does not oppress anyone,
but returns what he took in pledge
for a loan.
He does not commit robbery,
but gives his food to the hungry
and provides clothing for the
naked.
8He does not lend at usury
or take excessive interest.
He withholds his hand from doing
wrong
and judges fairly between man and
man.
9He follows my decrees
and faithfully keeps my laws.
That man is righteous;
he will surely live,
declares the Sovereign LORD.

10"Suppose he has a violent son, who
sheds blood or does any of these other
things 11(though the father has done
none of them):

"He eats at the mountain shrines.
He defiles his neighbour's wife.
12He oppresses the poor and needy.
He commits robbery.
He does not return what he took in
pledge.
He looks to the idols.
He does detestable things.
13He lends at usury and takes excessive
interest.

Will such a man live? He will not! Because he has done all these detestable
things, he will surely be put to death and
his blood will be on his own head.

14"But suppose this son has a son who
sees all the sins his father commits, and
though he sees them, he does not do
such things:

15"He does not eat at the mountain
shrines
or look to the idols of the house of
Israel.
He does not defile his neighbour's
wife.
16He does not oppress anyone
or require a pledge for a loan.
He does not commit robbery,
but gives his food to the hungry
and provides clothing for the
naked.
17He withholds his hand from sin
and takes no usury or excessive
interest.
He keeps my laws and follows my
decrees.

He will not die for his father's sin; he
will surely live. 18But his father will die
for his own sin, because he practised
extortion, robbed his brother and did
what was wrong among his people.
19"Yet you ask, 'Why does the son
not share the guilt of his father?' Since
the son has done what is just and right
and has been careful to keep all my
decrees, he will surely live. 20The soul
who sins is the one who will die. The son
will not share the guilt of the father, nor
will the father share the guilt of the son.
The righteousness of the righteous man
will be credited to him, and the wickedness of the wicked will be charged
against him.
21"But if a wicked man turns away
from all the sins he has committed and
keeps all my decrees and does what is
just and right, he will surely live; he will
not die. 22None of the offences he has
committed will be remembered against
him. Because of the righteous things he
has done, he will live. 23Do I take any
pleasure in the death of the wicked?
declares the Sovereign LORD. Rather,
am I not pleased when they turn from
their ways and live?
24"But if a righteous man turns from
his righteousness and commits sin and
does the same detestable things the
wicked man does, will he live? None of
the righteous things he has done will be
remembered. Because of the unfaithfulness he is guilty of and because of the
sins he has committed, he will die.
25"Yet you say, 'The way of the Lord
is not just.' Hear, O house of Israel: Is
my way unjust? Is it not your ways that
are unjust? 26If a righteous man turns
from his righteousness and commits sin,
he will die for it; because of the sin he
has committed he will die. 27But if a
wicked man turns away from the wickedness he has committed and does what
is just and right, he will save his life.
28Because he considers all the offences
he has committed and turns away from
them, he will surely live; he will not die.
29Yet the house of Israel says, 'The way
of the Lord is not just.' Are my ways
unjust, O house of Israel? Is it not your
ways that are unjust?
30"Therefore, O house of Israel, I will
judge you, each one according to his
ways, declares the Sovereign LORD. Repent! Turn away from all your offences;
then sin will not be your downfall. 31Rid
yourselves of all the offences you have
committed, and get a new heart and a
new spirit. Why will you die, O house of
Israel? 32For I take no pleasure in the
death of anyone, declares the Sovereign
LORD. Repent and live!

NEW TESTAMENT READING
Hebrews 9:16–28

16In the case of a will, it is necessary to
prove the death of the one who made it,
17because a will is in force only when
somebody has died; it never takes effect
while the one who made it is living.
18This is why even the first covenant was
not put into effect without blood.
19When Moses had proclaimed every
commandment of the law to all the
people, he took the blood of calves,
together with water, scarlet wool and

branches of hyssop, and sprinkled the
scroll and all the people. [20]He said,
"This is the blood of the covenant,
which God has commanded you to
keep." [21]In the same way, he sprinkled
with the blood both the tabernacle and
everything used in its ceremonies. [22]In
fact, the law requires that nearly everything be cleansed with blood, and without the shedding of blood there is no
forgiveness.
[23]It was necessary, then, for the
copies of the heavenly things to be
purified with these sacrifices, but the
heavenly things themselves with better
sacrifices than these. [24]For Christ did
not enter a man-made sanctuary that
was only a copy of the true one; he
entered heaven itself, now to appear for
us in God's presence. [25]Nor did he enter
heaven to offer himself again and again,
the way the high priest enters the Most
Holy Place every year with blood that is
not his own. [26]Then Christ would have
had to suffer many times since the creation of the world. But now he has
appeared once for all at the end of the
ages to do away with sin by the sacrifice
of himself. [27]Just as man is destined to
die once, and after that to face judgment, [28]so Christ was sacrificed once to
take away the sins of many people; and
he will appear a second time, not to bear
sin, but to bring salvation to those who
are waiting for him.

READING FROM PSALMS
Psalm 121:1–8

A song of ascents.

[1]I lift up my eyes to the hills—
where does my help come from?
[2]My help comes from the LORD,
the Maker of heaven and earth.

[3]He will not let your foot slip—
he who watches over you will not
slumber;
[4]indeed, he who watches over Israel
will neither slumber nor sleep.

[5]The LORD watches over you—
the LORD is your shade at your
right hand;
[6]the sun will not harm you by day,
nor the moon by night.

[7]The LORD will keep you from all
harm—
he will watch over your life;
[8]the LORD will watch over your
coming and going
both now and for evermore.

NOVEMBER 10

DAY 314

OLD TESTAMENT READING
Ezekiel 19:1–20:44

A Lament for Israel's Princes

19 "Take up a lament concerning
the princes of Israel [2]and say:

" 'What a lioness was your mother
among the lions!
She lay down among the young lions
and reared her cubs.
[3]She brought up one of her cubs,
and he became a strong lion.
He learned to tear the prey
and he devoured men.
[4]The nations heard about him,
and he was trapped in their pit.
They led him with hooks
to the land of Egypt.

[5]" 'When she saw her hope unfulfilled,
her expectation gone,
she took another of her cubs
and made him a strong lion.
[6]He prowled among the lions,
for he was now a strong lion.

He learned to tear the prey
and he devoured men.
7 He broke down their strongholds
and devastated their towns.
The land and all who were in it
were terrified by his roaring.
8 Then the nations came against him,
those from regions round about.
They spread their net for him,
and he was trapped in their pit.
9 With hooks they pulled him into a cage
and brought him to the king of Babylon.
They put him in prison,
so his roar was heard no longer
on the mountains of Israel.

10 " 'Your mother was like a vine in your vineyard
planted by the water;
it was fruitful and full of branches
because of abundant water.
11 Its branches were strong,
fit for a ruler's sceptre.
It towered high
above the thick foliage,
conspicuous for its height
and for its many branches.
12 But it was uprooted in fury
and thrown to the ground.
The east wind made it shrivel,
it was stripped of its fruit;
its strong branches withered
and fire consumed them.
13 Now it is planted in the desert,
in a dry and thirsty land.
14 Fire spread from one of its main branches
and consumed its fruit.
No strong branch is left on it
fit for a ruler's sceptre.'

This is a lament and is to be used as a lament."

Rebellious Israel

20 In the seventh year, in the fifth month on the tenth day, some of the elders of Israel came to enquire of the LORD, and they sat down in front of me.

2 Then the word of the LORD came to
me: 3 "Son of man, speak to the elders of
Israel and say to them, 'This is what the
Sovereign LORD says: Have you come
to enquire of me? As surely as I live, I
will not let you enquire of me, declares
the Sovereign LORD.'
4 "Will you judge them? Will you
judge them, son of man? Then confront
them with the detestable practices of
their fathers 5 and say to them: 'This is
what the Sovereign LORD says: On the
day I chose Israel, I swore with uplifted
hand to the descendants of the house of
Jacob and revealed myself to them in
Egypt. With uplifted hand I said to
them, "I am the LORD your God." 6 On
that day I swore to them that I would
bring them out of Egypt into a land I
had searched out for them, a land flowing
with milk and honey, the most
beautiful of all lands. 7 And I said to
them, "Each of you, get rid of the vile
images you have set your eyes on, and
do not defile yourselves with the idols of
Egypt. I am the LORD your God."
8 " 'But they rebelled against me and
would not listen to me; they did not get
rid of the vile images they had set their
eyes on, nor did they forsake the idols of
Egypt. So I said I would pour out my
wrath on them and spend my anger
against them in Egypt. 9 But for the sake
of my name I did what would keep it
from being profaned in the eyes of the
nations they lived among and in whose
sight I had revealed myself to the
Israelites by bringing them out of
Egypt. 10 Therefore I led them out of
Egypt and brought them into the desert.
11 I gave them my decrees and made
known to them my laws, for the man
who obeys them will live by them.
12 Also I gave them my Sabbaths as a
sign between us, so they would know
that I the LORD made them holy.
13 " 'Yet the people of Israel rebelled
against me in the desert. They did not
follow my decrees but rejected my laws
—although the man who obeys them
will live by them—and they utterly
desecrated my Sabbaths. So I said I

would pour out my wrath on them and
destroy them in the desert. 14But for the
sake of my name I did what would keep
it from being profaned in the eyes of the
nations in whose sight I had brought
them out. 15Also with uplifted hand I
swore to them in the desert that I would
not bring them into the land I had given
them—a land flowing with milk and
honey, most beautiful of all lands—
16because they rejected my laws and did
not follow my decrees and desecrated
my Sabbaths. For their hearts were devoted to their idols. 17Yet I looked on
them with pity and did not destroy them
or put an end to them in the desert. 18I
said to their children in the desert, "Do
not follow the statutes of your fathers or
keep their laws or defile yourselves with
their idols. 19I am the LORD your God;
follow my decrees and be careful to
keep my laws. 20Keep my Sabbaths
holy, that they may be a sign between
us. Then you will know that I am the
LORD your God."
21" 'But the children rebelled against
me: They did not follow my decrees,
they were not careful to keep my laws
—although the man who obeys them
will live by them—and they desecrated
my Sabbaths. So I said I would pour out
my wrath on them and spend my anger
against them in the desert. 22But I withheld my hand, and for the sake of my
name I did what would keep it from
being profaned in the eyes of the nations in whose sight I had brought them
out. 23Also with uplifted hand I swore
to them in the desert that I would disperse them among the nations and
scatter them through the countries,
24because they had not obeyed my laws
but had rejected my decrees and desecrated my Sabbaths, and their eyes
⌞lusted⌟ after their fathers' idols. 25I also
gave them over to statutes that were not
good and laws they could not live by; 26I
let them become defiled through their
gifts—the sacrifice of every firstborn
—that I might fill them with horror so
that they would know that I am the
LORD.'

27"Therefore, son of man, speak to
the people of Israel and say to them,
'This is what the Sovereign LORD says:
In this also your fathers blasphemed me
by forsaking me: 28When I brought
them into the land I had sworn to give
them and they saw any high hill or any
leafy tree, there they offered their sacrifices, made offerings that provoked
me to anger, presented their fragrant
incense and poured out their drink
offerings. 29Then I said to them: What is
this high place you go to?' " (It is called
Bamah to this day.)

Judgment and Restoration

30"Therefore say to the house of
Israel: 'This is what the Sovereign LORD
says: Will you defile yourselves the way
your fathers did and lust after their vile
images? 31When you offer your gifts
—the sacrifice of your sons in the fire
—you continue to defile yourselves with
all your idols to this day. Am I to let you
enquire of me, O house of Israel? As
surely as I live, declares the Sovereign
LORD, I will not let you enquire of me.
32" 'You say, "We want to be like the
nations, like the peoples of the world,
who serve wood and stone." But what
you have in mind will never happen.
33As surely as I live, declares the
Sovereign LORD, I will rule over you
with a mighty hand and an outstretched
arm and with outpoured wrath. 34I will
bring you from the nations and gather
you from the countries where you have
been scattered—with a mighty hand
and an outstretched arm and with outpoured wrath. 35I will bring you into the
desert of the nations and there, face to
face, I will execute judgment upon you.
36As I judged your fathers in the desert
of the land of Egypt, so I will judge you,
declares the Sovereign LORD. 37I will
take note of you as you pass under my
rod, and I will bring you into the bond of
the covenant. 38I will purge you of those
who revolt and rebel against me.
Although I will bring them out of the
land where they are living, yet they will

not enter the land of Israel. Then you
will know that I am the LORD.
39“ ‘As for you, O house of Israel, this
is what the Sovereign LORD says: Go
and serve your idols, every one of you!
But afterwards you will surely listen to
me and no longer profane my holy name
with your gifts and idols. 40For on my
holy mountain, the high mountain of
Israel, declares the Sovereign LORD,
there in the land the entire house of
Israel will serve me, and there I will
accept them. There I will require your
offerings and your choice gifts, along
with all your holy sacrifices. 41I will
accept you as fragrant incense when I
bring you out from the nations and
gather you from the countries where
you have been scattered, and I will show
myself holy among you in the sight of
the nations. 42Then you will know that I
am the LORD, when I bring you into the
land of Israel, the land I had sworn with
uplifted hand to give to your fathers.
43There you will remember your conduct and all the actions by which you
have defiled yourselves, and you will
loathe yourselves for all the evil you
have done. 44You will know that I am
the LORD, when I deal with you for my
name's sake and not according to your
evil ways and your corrupt practices, O
house of Israel, declares the Sovereign
LORD.’ ”

NEW TESTAMENT READING
Hebrews 10:1–18

Christ's Sacrifice Once for All

10 The law is only a shadow of the
good things that are coming—
not the realities themselves. For this
reason it can never, by the same sacrifices repeated endlessly year after
year, make perfect those who draw near
to worship. 2If it could, would they not
have stopped being offered? For the
worshippers would have been cleansed
once for all, and would no longer have
felt guilty for their sins. 3But those sacrifices are an annual reminder of sins,
4because it is impossible for the blood of
bulls and goats to take away sins.
5Therefore, when Christ came into
the world, he said:

“Sacrifice and offering you did not
desire,
but a body you prepared for me;
6with burnt offerings and sin offerings
you were not pleased.
7Then I said, ‘Here I am—it is written
about me in the scroll—
I have come to do your will, O
God.’ ”

8First he said, “Sacrifices and offerings,
burnt offerings and sin offerings you did
not desire, nor were you pleased with
them” (although the law required them
to be made). 9Then he said, “Here I am,
I have come to do your will.” He sets
aside the first to establish the second.
10And by that will, we have been made
holy through the sacrifice of the body of
Jesus Christ once for all.
11Day after day every priest stands
and performs his religious duties; again
and again he offers the same sacrifices,
which can never take away sins. 12But
when this priest had offered for all time
one sacrifice for sins, he sat down at the
right hand of God. 13Since that time he
waits for his enemies to be made his
footstool, 14because by one sacrifice he
has made perfect for ever those who are
being made holy.
15The Holy Spirit also testifies to us
about this. First he says:

16“This is the covenant I will make with
them
after that time, says the Lord.
I will put my laws in their hearts,
and I will write them on their
minds.”

17Then he adds:

“Their sins and lawless acts
I will remember no more.”

18And where these have been forgiven,
there is no longer any sacrifice for sin.

READING FROM PSALMS
Psalm 122:1–9

A song of ascents. Of David.

1I rejoiced with those who said to me,
"Let us go to the house of the LORD."
2Our feet are standing
in your gates, O Jerusalem.

3Jerusalem is built like a city
that is closely compacted together.
4That is where the tribes go up,
the tribes of the LORD,
to praise the name of the LORD
according to the statute given to Israel.

5There the thrones for judgment stand,
the thrones of the house of David.

6Pray for the peace of Jerusalem:
"May those who love you be secure.
7May there be peace within your walls
and security within your citadels."
8For the sake of my brothers and friends,
I will say, "Peace be within you."
9For the sake of the house of the LORD our God,
I will seek your prosperity.

NOVEMBER 11

DAY 315

OLD TESTAMENT READING
Ezekiel 20:45–22:22

Prophecy Against the South

45The word of the LORD came to me:
46"Son of man, set your face towards
the south; preach against the south and
prophesy against the forest of the southland. 47Say to the southern forest: 'Hear
the word of the LORD. This is what the
Sovereign LORD says: I am about to set
fire to you, and it will consume all your
trees, both green and dry. The blazing
flame will not be quenched, and every
face from south to north will be scorched by it. 48Everyone will see that I the
LORD have kindled it; it will not be
quenched.' "
49Then I said, "Ah, Sovereign LORD!
They are saying of me, 'Isn't he just
telling parables?' "

Babylon, God's Sword of Judgment

21 The word of the LORD came to
me: 2"Son of man, set your face
against Jerusalem and preach against
the sanctuary. Prophesy against the
land of Israel 3and say to her: 'This is
what the LORD says: I am against you. I
will draw my sword from its scabbard
and cut off from you both the righteous
and the wicked. 4Because I am going to
cut off the righteous and the wicked, my
sword will be unsheathed against everyone from south to north. 5Then all people will know that I the LORD have
drawn my sword from its scabbard; it
will not return again.'
6"Therefore groan, son of man!
Groan before them with broken heart
and bitter grief. 7And when they ask
you, 'Why are you groaning?' you shall
say, 'Because of the news that is coming. Every heart will melt and every
hand go limp; every spirit will become
faint and every knee become as weak as
water.' It is coming! It will surely take
place, declares the Sovereign LORD."
8The word of the LORD came to me:
9"Son of man, prophesy and say, 'This
is what the Lord says:

" 'A sword, a sword,
sharpened and polished—

10sharpened for the slaughter,
polished to flash like lightning!

" 'Shall we rejoice in the sceptre of my son ⌞Judah⌟? The sword despises every such stick.

11" 'The sword is appointed to be polished,
to be grasped with the hand;
it is sharpened and polished,
made ready for the hand of the slayer.
12Cry out and wail, son of man,
for it is against my people;
it is against all the princes of Israel.
They are thrown to the sword
along with my people.
Therefore beat your breast.

13" 'Testing will surely come. And what if the sceptre ⌞of Judah⌟, which the sword despises, does not continue? declares the Sovereign LORD.'

14"So then, son of man, prophesy
and strike your hands together.
Let the sword strike twice,
even three times.
It is a sword for slaughter—
a sword for great slaughter,
closing in on them from every side.
15So that hearts may melt
and the fallen be many,
I have stationed the sword for slaughter
at all their gates.
Oh! It is made to flash like lightning,
it is grasped for slaughter.
16O sword, slash to the right,
then to the left,
wherever your blade is turned.
17I too will strike my hands together,
and my wrath will subside.
I the LORD have spoken."

18The word of the LORD came to me:
19"Son of man, mark out two roads for
the sword of the king of Babylon to
take, both starting from the same country.
Make a signpost where the road
branches off to the city. 20Mark out one
road for the sword to come against Rabbah of the Ammonites and another against Judah and fortified Jerusalem.
21For the king of Babylon will stop at
the fork in the road, at the junction of
the two roads, to seek an omen: He will
cast lots with arrows, he will consult his
idols, he will examine the liver. 22Into
his right hand will come the lot for Jerusalem, where he is to set up battering-rams, to give the command to slaughter, to sound the battle cry, to set battering-rams against the gates, to build a ramp and to erect siege works.
23It will seem like a false omen to those
who have sworn allegiance to him, but he will remind them of their guilt and take them captive.
24"Therefore this is what the Sovereign LORD says: 'Because you people have brought to mind your guilt by your open rebellion, revealing your sins in all that you do—because you have done this, you will be taken captive.
25" 'O profane and wicked prince of Israel, whose day has come, whose time of punishment has reached its climax,
26this is what the Sovereign LORD says:
Take off the turban, remove the crown. It will not be as it was: The lowly will be exalted and the exalted will be brought
low. 27A ruin! A ruin! I will make it a
ruin! It will not be restored until he comes to whom it rightfully belongs; to him I will give it.'
28"And you, son of man, prophesy and say, 'This is what the Sovereign LORD says about the Ammonites and their insults:

" 'A sword, a sword,
drawn for the slaughter,
polished to consume
and to flash like lightning!
29Despite false visions concerning you
and lying divinations about you,
it will be laid on the necks
of the wicked who are to be slain,
whose day has come,
whose time of punishment has reached its climax.

[30]Return the sword to its scabbard.
In the place where you were created,
in the land of your ancestry,
I will judge you.
[31]I will pour out my wrath upon you
and breathe out my fiery anger against you;
I will hand you over to brutal men,
men skilled in destruction.
[32]You will be fuel for the fire,
your blood will be shed in your land,
you will be remembered no more;
for I the LORD have spoken.' "

Jerusalem's Sins

22 The word of the LORD came to
me: [2]"Son of man, will you
judge her? Will you judge this city of
bloodshed? Then confront her with all
her detestable practices [3]and say: 'This
is what the Sovereign LORD says: O city
that brings on herself doom by shedding
blood in her midst and defiles herself by
making idols, [4]you have become guilty
because of the blood you have shed and
have become defiled by the idols you
have made. You have brought your
days to a close, and the end of your
years has come. Therefore I will make
you an object of scorn to the nations and
a laughing-stock to all the countries.
[5]Those who are near and those who are
far away will mock you, O infamous
city, full of turmoil.
[6]" 'See how each of the princes of
Israel who are in you uses his power to
shed blood. [7]In you they have treated
father and mother with contempt; in
you they have oppressed the alien and
ill-treated the fatherless and the widow.
[8]You have despised my holy things and
desecrated my Sabbaths. [9]In you are
slanderous men bent on shedding
blood; in you are those who eat at the
mountain shrines and commit lewd acts.
[10]In you are those who dishonour their
fathers' bed; in you are those who
violate women during their period,
when they are ceremonially unclean.
[11]In you one man commits a detestable
offence with his neighbour's wife,
another shamefully defiles his daughter-
in-law, and another violates his sister,
his own father's daughter. [12]In you men
accept bribes to shed blood; you take
usury and excessive interest and make
unjust gain from your neighbours by
extortion. And you have forgotten me,
declares the Sovereign LORD.
[13]" 'I will surely strike my hands
together at the unjust gain you have
made and at the blood you have shed in
your midst. [14]Will your courage endure
or your hands be strong in the day I deal
with you? I the LORD have spoken, and
I will do it. [15]I will disperse you among
the nations and scatter you through the
countries; and I will put an end to your
uncleanness. [16]When you have been defiled in the eyes of the nations, you will
know that I am the LORD.' "
[17]Then the word of the LORD came to
me: [18]"Son of man, the house of Israel
has become dross to me; all of them are
the copper, tin, iron and lead left inside
a furnace. They are but the dross of
silver. [19]Therefore this is what the
Sovereign LORD says: 'Because you
have all become dross, I will gather you
into Jerusalem. [20]As men gather silver,
copper, iron, lead and tin into a furnace
to melt it with a fiery blast, so will I
gather you in my anger and my wrath
and put you inside the city and melt you.
[21]I will gather you and I will blow on you
with my fiery wrath, and you will be
melted inside her. [22]As silver is melted
in a furnace, so you will be melted inside
her, and you will know that I the LORD
have poured out my wrath upon you.' "

NEW TESTAMENT READING
Hebrews 10:19–39

A Call to Persevere

[19]Therefore, brothers, since we have
confidence to enter the Most Holy Place
by the blood of Jesus, [20]by a new and

living way opened for us through the
curtain, that is, his body, 21and since we
have a great priest over the house of
God, 22let us draw near to God with a
sincere heart in full assurance of faith,
having our hearts sprinkled to cleanse
us from a guilty conscience and having
our bodies washed with pure water.
23Let us hold unswervingly to the hope
we profess, for he who promised is
faithful. 24And let us consider how we
may spur one another on towards love
and good deeds. 25Let us not give up
meeting together, as some are in the
habit of doing, but let us encourage one
another—and all the more as you see
the Day approaching.

26If we deliberately keep on sinning
after we have received the knowledge of
the truth, no sacrifice for sins is left,
27but only a fearful expectation of judgment and of raging fire that will consume the enemies of God. 28Anyone
who rejected the law of Moses died
without mercy on the testimony of two
or three witnesses. 29How much more
severely do you think a man deserves to
be punished who has trampled the Son
of God under foot, who has treated as
an unholy thing the blood of the covenant that sanctified him, and who has
insulted the Spirit of grace? 30For we
know him who said, "It is mine to
avenge; I will repay," and again, "The
Lord will judge his people." 31It is a
dreadful thing to fall into the hands of
the living God.

32Remember those earlier days after
you had received the light, when you
stood your ground in a great contest in
the face of suffering. 33Sometimes you
were publicly exposed to insult and
persecution; at other times you stood
side by side with those who were so
treated. 34You sympathised with those
in prison and joyfully accepted the confiscation of your property, because you
knew that you yourselves had better
and lasting possessions.

35So do not throw away your confidence; it will be richly rewarded. 36You
need to persevere so that when you
have done the will of God, you will
receive what he has promised. 37For in
just a very little while,

"He who is coming will come and will
not delay.
38 But my righteous one will live by
faith.
And if he shrinks back,
I will not be pleased with him."

39But we are not of those who shrink
back and are destroyed, but of those
who believe and are saved.

READING FROM PSALMS

Psalm 123:1–4

A song of ascents.

1I lift up my eyes to you,
to you whose throne is in heaven.
2As the eyes of slaves look to the hand
of their master,
as the eyes of a maid look to the
hand of her mistress,
so our eyes look to the LORD our
God,
till he shows us his mercy.

3Have mercy on us, O LORD, have
mercy on us,
for we have endured much
contempt.
4We have endured much ridicule from
the proud,
much contempt from the arrogant.

NOVEMBER 12

OLD TESTAMENT READING

Ezekiel 22:23–23:49

[23]Again the word of the LORD came to me: [24]"Son of man, say to the land, 'You are a land that has had no rain or showers in the day of wrath.' [25]There is a conspiracy of her princes within her like a roaring lion tearing its prey; they devour people, take treasures and precious things and make many widows within her. [26]Her priests do violence to my law and profane my holy things; they do not distinguish between the holy and the common; they teach that there is no difference between the unclean and the clean; and they shut their eyes to the keeping of my Sabbaths, so that I am profaned among them. [27]Her officials within her are like wolves tearing their prey; they shed blood and kill people to make unjust gain. [28]Her prophets whitewash these deeds for them by false visions and lying divinations. They say, 'This is what the Sovereign LORD says'—when the LORD has not spoken. [29]The people of the land practise extortion and commit robbery; they oppress the poor and needy and ill-treat the alien, denying them justice.

[30]"I looked for a man among them who would build up the wall and stand before me in the gap on behalf of the land so that I would not have to destroy it, but I found none. [31]So I will pour out my wrath on them and consume them with my fiery anger, bringing down on their own heads all they have done, declares the Sovereign LORD."

Two Adulterous Sisters

23 The word of the LORD came to me: [2]"Son of man, there were two women, daughters of the same mother. [3]They became prostitutes in Egypt, engaging in prostitution from their youth. In that land their breasts were fondled and their virgin bosoms caressed. [4]The older was named Oholah, and her sister was Oholibah. They were mine and gave birth to sons and daughters. Oholah is Samaria, and Oholibah is Jerusalem.

[5]"Oholah engaged in prostitution while she was still mine; and she lusted after her lovers, the Assyrians—warriors [6]clothed in blue, governors and commanders, all of them handsome young men, and mounted horsemen. [7]She gave herself as a prostitute to all the elite of the Assyrians and defiled herself with all the idols of everyone she lusted after. [8]She did not give up the prostitution she began in Egypt, when during her youth men slept with her, caressed her virgin bosom and poured out their lust upon her.

[9]"Therefore I handed her over to her lovers, the Assyrians, for whom she lusted. [10]They stripped her naked, took away her sons and daughters and killed her with the sword. She became a byword among women, and punishment was inflicted on her.

[11]"Her sister Oholibah saw this, yet in her lust and prostitution she was more depraved than her sister. [12]She too lusted after the Assyrians—governors and commanders, warriors in full dress, mounted horsemen, all handsome young men. [13]I saw that she too defiled herself; both of them went the same way.

[14]"But she carried her prostitution still further. She saw men portrayed on a wall, figures of Chaldeansportrayed in red, [15]with belts round their waists and flowing turbans on their heads; all of them looked like Babylonian chariot officers, natives of Chaldea. [16]As soon as she saw them, she lusted after them and sent messengers to them in Chaldea. [17]Then the Babylonians came to her, to the bed of love, and in their lust

they defiled her. After she had been defiled by them, she turned away from them in disgust. 18When she carried on her prostitution openly and exposed her nakedness, I turned away from her in disgust, just as I had turned away from her sister. 19Yet she became more and more promiscuous as she recalled the days of her youth, when she was a prostitute in Egypt. 20There she lusted after her lovers, whose genitals were like those of donkeys and whose emission was like that of horses. 21So you longed for the lewdness of your youth, when in Egypt your bosom was caressed and your young breasts fondled.

22"Therefore, Oholibah, this is what the Sovereign LORD says: I will stir up your lovers against you, those you turned away from in disgust, and I will bring them against you from every side —23the Babylonians and all the Chaldeans, the men of Pekod and Shoa and Koa, and all the Assyrians with them, handsome young men, all of them governors and commanders, chariot officers and men of high rank, all mounted on horses. 24They will come against you with weapons, chariots and wagons and with a throng of people; they will take up positions against you on every side with large and small shields and with helmets. I will turn you over to them for punishment, and they will punish you according to their standards. 25I will direct my jealous anger against you, and they will deal with you in fury. They will cut off your noses and your ears, and those of you who are left will fall by the sword. They will take away your sons and daughters, and those of you who are left will be consumed by fire. 26They will also strip you of your clothes and take your fine jewellery. 27So I will put a stop to the lewdness and prostitution you began in Egypt. You will not look on these things with longing or remember Egypt any more.

28"For this is what the Sovereign LORD says: I am about to hand you over to those you hate, to those you turned away from in disgust. 29They will deal with you in hatred and take away everything you have worked for. They will leave you naked and bare, and the shame of your prostitution will be exposed. Your lewdness and promiscuity 30have brought this upon you, because you lusted after the nations and defiled yourself with their idols. 31You have gone the way of your sister; so I will put her cup into your hand.

32"This is what the Sovereign LORD says:

"You will drink your sister's cup,
  a cup large and deep;
it will bring scorn and derision,
  for it holds so much.
33You will be filled with drunkenness
    and sorrow,
  the cup of ruin and desolation,
  the cup of your sister Samaria.
34You will drink it and drain it dry;
  you will dash it to pieces
  and tear your breasts.

I have spoken, declares the Sovereign LORD.

35"Therefore this is what the Sovereign LORD says: Since you have forgotten me and thrust me behind your back, you must bear the consequences of your lewdness and prostitution."

36The LORD said to me: "Son of man, will you judge Oholah and Oholibah? Then confront them with their detestable practices, 37for they have committed adultery and blood is on their hands. They committed adultery with their idols; they even sacrificed their children, whom they bore to me, as food for them. 38They have also done this to me: At that same time they defiled my sanctuary and desecrated my Sabbaths. 39On the very day they sacrificed their children to their idols, they entered my sanctuary and desecrated it. That is what they did in my house.

40"They even sent messengers for men who came from far away, and when they arrived you bathed yourself for them, painted your eyes and put on your jewellery. 41You sat on an elegant couch, with a table spread before it on which you had placed the incense and oil that belonged to me.

42"The noise of a carefree crowd was around her; Sabeans were brought from the desert along with men from the rabble, and they put bracelets on the arms of the woman and her sister and beautiful crowns on their heads. 43Then I said about the one worn out by adultery, 'Now let them use her as a prostitute, for that is all she is.' 44And they slept with her. As men sleep with a prostitute, so they slept with those lewd women, Oholah and Oholibah. 45But righteous men will sentence them to the punishment of women who commit adultery and shed blood, because they are adulterous and blood is on their hands.

46"This is what the Sovereign LORD says: Bring a mob against them and give them over to terror and plunder. 47The mob will stone them and cut them down with their swords; they will kill their sons and daughters and burn down their houses.

48"So I will put an end to lewdness in the land, that all women may take warning and not imitate you. 49You will suffer the penalty for your lewdness and bear the consequences of your sins of idolatry. Then you will know that I am the Sovereign LORD."

NEW TESTAMENT READING
Hebrews 11:1–16

By Faith

11 Now faith is being sure of what we hope for and certain of what we do not see. 2This is what the ancients were commended for.

3By faith we understand that the universe was formed at God's command, so that what is seen was not made out of what was visible.

4By faith Abel offered God a better sacrifice than Cain did. By faith he was commended as a righteous man, when God spoke well of his offerings. And by faith he still speaks, even though he is dead.

5By faith Enoch was taken from this life, so that he did not experience death; he could not be found, because God had taken him away. For before he was taken, he was commended as one who pleased God. 6And without faith it is impossible to please God, because anyone who comes to him must believe that he exists and that he rewards those who earnestly seek him.

7By faith Noah, when warned about things not yet seen, in holy fear built an ark to save his family. By his faith he condemned the world and became heir of the righteousness that comes by faith.

8By faith Abraham, when called to go to a place he would later receive as his inheritance, obeyed and went, even though he did not know where he was going. 9By faith he made his home in the promised land like a stranger in a foreign country; he lived in tents, as did Isaac and Jacob, who were heirs with him of the same promise. 10For he was looking forward to the city with foundations, whose architect and builder is God.

11By faith Abraham, even though he was past age—and Sarah herself was barren—was enabled to become a father because he considered him faithful who had made the promise. 12And so from this one man, and he as good as dead, came descendants as numerous as the stars in the sky and as countless as the sand on the seashore.

13All these people were still living by faith when they died. They did not receive the things promised; they only saw them and welcomed them from a distance. And they admitted that they were aliens and strangers on earth. 14People who say such things show that they are looking for a country of their own. 15If they had been thinking of the country they had left, they would have had opportunity to return. 16Instead, they were longing for a better country—a heavenly one. Therefore God is not ashamed to be called their God, for he has prepared a city for them.

READING FROM PROVERBS

Proverbs 27:15–22

15A quarrelsome wife is like
a constant dripping on a rainy day;
16restraining her is like restraining the wind
or grasping oil with the hand.

17As iron sharpens iron,
so one man sharpens another.

18He who tends a fig-tree will eat its fruit,
and he who looks after his master will be honoured.

19As water reflects a face,
so a man's heart reflects the man.

20Death and Destruction are never satisfied,
and neither are the eyes of man.

21The crucible for silver and the furnace for gold,
but man is tested by the praise he receives.

22Though you grind a fool in a mortar,
grinding him like grain with a pestle,
you will not remove his folly from him.

DAY 317

NOVEMBER 13

OLD TESTAMENT READING

Ezekiel 24:1–25:17

The Cooking Pot

24 In the ninth year, in the tenth month on the tenth day, the word of the LORD came to me: 2"Son of man, record this date, this very date, because the king of Babylon has laid siege to Jerusalem this very day. 3Tell this rebellious house a parable and say to them: 'This is what the Sovereign LORD says:

" 'Put on the cooking pot; put it on
and pour water into it.
4Put into it the pieces of meat,
all the choice pieces—the leg and the shoulder.
Fill it with the best of these bones;
5 take the pick of the flock.
Pile wood beneath it for the bones;
bring it to the boil
and cook the bones in it.

6" 'For this is what the Sovereign LORD says:

" 'Woe to the city of bloodshed,
to the pot now encrusted,
whose deposit will not go away!
Empty it piece by piece
without casting lots for them.

7" 'For the blood she shed is in her midst:
She poured it on the bare rock;
she did not pour it on the ground,
where the dust would cover it.
8To stir up wrath and take revenge
I put her blood on the bare rock,
so that it would not be covered.

9" 'Therefore this is what the Sovereign LORD says:

" 'Woe to the city of bloodshed!
I, too, will pile the wood high.
10So heap on the wood
and kindle the fire.

Cook the meat well,
mixing in the spices;
and let the bones be charred.
11Then set the empty pot on the coals
till it becomes hot and its copper
glows
so its impurities may be melted
and its deposit burned away.
12It has frustrated all efforts;
its heavy deposit has not been
removed,
not even by fire.

13" 'Now your impurity is lewdness.
Because I tried to cleanse you but you
would not be cleansed from your impurity, you will not be clean again until my
wrath against you has subsided.

14" 'I the LORD have spoken. The
time has come for me to act. I will not
hold back; I will not have pity, nor will I
relent. You will be judged according to
your conduct and your actions, declares
the Sovereign LORD.' "

Ezekiel's Wife Dies

15The word of the LORD came to me:
16"Son of man, with one blow I am
about to take away from you the delight
of your eyes. Yet do not lament or weep
or shed any tears. 17Groan quietly; do
not mourn for the dead. Keep your
turban fastened and your sandals on
your feet; do not cover the lower part of
your face or eat the customary food ⌊of
mourners⌋."
18So I spoke to the people in the
morning, and in the evening my wife
died. The next morning I did as I had
been commanded.
19Then the people asked me, "Won't
you tell us what these things have to do
with us?"
20So I said to them, "The word of the
LORD came to me: 21Say to the house of
Israel, 'This is what the Sovereign LORD
says: I am about to desecrate my sanctuary—the stronghold in which you take
pride, the delight of your eyes, the object of your affection. The sons and
daughters you left behind will fall by the
sword. 22And you will do as I have
done. You will not cover the lower part
of your face or eat the customary food
⌊of mourners⌋. 23You will keep your
turbans on your heads and your sandals
on your feet. You will not mourn or
weep but will waste away because of
your sins and groan among yourselves.
24Ezekiel will be a sign to you; you will
do just as he has done. When this happens, you will know that I am the
Sovereign LORD.'
25"And you, son of man, on the day I
take away their stronghold, their joy
and glory, the delight of their eyes, their
heart's desire, and their sons and
daughters as well—26on that day a fugitive will come to tell you the news. 27At
that time your mouth will be opened;
you will speak with him and will no
longer be silent. So you will be a sign to
them, and they will know that I am the
LORD."

A Prophecy Against Ammon

25 The word of the LORD came to
me: 2"Son of man, set your face
against the Ammonites and prophesy
against them. 3Say to them, 'Hear the
word of the Sovereign LORD. This is
what the Sovereign LORD says: Because
you said "Aha!" over my sanctuary
when it was desecrated and over the
land of Israel when it was laid waste and
over the people of Judah when they
went into exile, 4therefore I am going to
give you to the people of the East as a
possession. They will set up their camps
and pitch their tents among you; they
will eat your fruit and drink your milk.
5I will turn Rabbah into a pasture for
camels and Ammon into a resting place
for sheep. Then you will know that I am
the LORD. 6For this is what the
Sovereign LORD says: Because you have
clapped your hands and stamped your
feet, rejoicing with all the malice of
your heart against the land of Israel,
7therefore I will stretch out my hand
against you and give you as plunder to

the nations. I will cut you off from the nations and exterminate you from the countries. I will destroy you, and you will know that I am the LORD.'"

A Prophecy Against Moab

8"This is what the Sovereign LORD says: 'Because Moab and Seir said, "Look, the house of Judah has become like all the other nations," 9therefore I will expose the flank of Moab, beginning at its frontier towns—Beth Jeshimoth, Baal Meon and Kiriathaim—the glory of that land. 10I will give Moab along with the Ammonites to the people of the East as a possession, so that the Ammonites will not be remembered among the nations; 11and I will inflict punishment on Moab. Then they will know that I am the LORD.'"

A Prophecy Against Edom

12"This is what the Sovereign LORD says: 'Because Edom took revenge on the house of Judah and became very guilty by doing so, 13therefore this is what the Sovereign LORD says: I will stretch out my hand against Edom and kill its men and their animals. I will lay it waste, and from Teman to Dedan they will fall by the sword. 14I will take vengeance on Edom by the hand of my people Israel, and they will deal with Edom in accordance with my anger and my wrath; they will know my vengeance, declares the Sovereign LORD.'"

A Prophecy Against Philistia

15"This is what the Sovereign LORD says: 'Because the Philistines acted in vengeance and took revenge with malice in their hearts, and with ancient hostility sought to destroy Judah, 16therefore this is what the Sovereign LORD says: I am about to stretch out my hand against the Philistines, and I will cut off the Kerethites and destroy those remaining along the coast. 17I will carry out great vengeance on them and punish them in my wrath. Then they will know that I am the LORD, when I take vengeance on them.'"

NEW TESTAMENT READING

Hebrews 11:17–40

17By faith Abraham, when God tested him, offered Isaac as a sacrifice. He who had received the promises was about to sacrifice his one and only son, 18even though God had said to him, "It is through Isaac that your offspring will be reckoned." 19Abraham reasoned that God could raise the dead, and figuratively speaking, he did receive Isaac back from death.

20By faith Isaac blessed Jacob and Esau in regard to their future.

21By faith Jacob, when he was dying, blessed each of Joseph's sons, and worshipped as he leaned on the top of his staff.

22By faith Joseph, when his end was near, spoke about the exodus of the Israelites from Egypt and gave instructions about his bones.

23By faith Moses' parents hid him for three months after he was born, because they saw he was no ordinary child, and they were not afraid of the king's edict.

24By faith Moses, when he had grown up, refused to be known as the son of Pharaoh's daughter. 25He chose to be ill-treated along with the people of God rather than to enjoy the pleasures of sin for a short time. 26He regarded disgrace for the sake of Christ as of greater value than the treasures of Egypt, because he was looking ahead to his reward. 27By faith he left Egypt, not fearing the king's anger; he persevered because he saw him who is invisible. 28By faith he kept the Passover and the sprinkling of blood, so that the destroyer of the firstborn would not touch the firstborn of Israel.

29By faith the people passed through the Red Sea as on dry land; but when

the Egyptians tried to do so, they were
drowned.
30By faith the walls of Jericho fell,
after the people had marched around
them for seven days.
31By faith the prostitute Rahab, because she welcomed the spies, was not
killed with those who were disobedient.
32And what more shall I say? I do not
have time to tell about Gideon, Barak,
Samson, Jephthah, David, Samuel and
the prophets, 33who through faith conquered kingdoms, administered justice,
and gained what was promised; who
shut the mouths of lions, 34quenched
the fury of the flames, and escaped the
edge of the sword; whose weakness was
turned to strength; and who became
powerful in battle and routed foreign
armies. 35Women received back their
dead, raised to life again. Others were
tortured and refused to be released, so
that they might gain a better resurrection. 36Some faced jeers and flogging,
while still others were chained and put
in prison. 37They were stoned; they
were sawn in two; they were put to
death by the sword. They went about in
sheepskins and goatskins, destitute,
persecuted and ill-treated—38the world
was not worthy of them. They wandered in deserts and mountains, and in
caves and holes in the ground.
39These were all commended for their
faith, yet none of them received what
had been promised. 40God had planned
something better for us so that only
together with us would they be made
perfect.

READING FROM PSALMS
Psalm 124:1–8

A song of ascents. Of David.

1If the LORD had not been on our
side—
let Israel say—
2if the LORD had not been on our side
when men attacked us,
3when their anger flared against us,
they would have swallowed us
alive;
4the flood would have engulfed us,
the torrent would have swept
over us,
5the raging waters
would have swept us away.

6Praise be to the LORD,
who has not let us be torn by their
teeth.
7We have escaped like a bird
out of the fowler's snare;
the snare has been broken,
and we have escaped.
8Our help is in the name of the LORD,
the Maker of heaven and earth.

NOVEMBER 14

DAY 318

OLD TESTAMENT READING
Ezekiel 26:1–27:36

A Prophecy Against Tyre

26 In the eleventh year, on the first
day of the month, the word of
the LORD came to me: 2"Son of man,
because Tyre has said of Jerusalem,
'Aha! The gate to the nations is broken,
and its doors have swung open to me;
now that she lies in ruins I will prosper,'
3therefore this is what the Sovereign
LORD says: I am against you, O Tyre,
and I will bring many nations against
you, like the sea casting up its waves.
4They will destroy the walls of Tyre and
pull down her towers; I will scrape away
her rubble and make her a bare rock.
5Out in the sea she will become a place

to spread fishing nets, for I have
spoken, declares the Sovereign LORD.
She will become plunder for the nations, [6]and her settlements on the mainland will be ravaged by the sword. Then
they will know that I am the LORD.
[7]"For this is what the Sovereign LORD
says: From the north I am going to bring
against Tyre Nebuchadnezzar king of
Babylon, king of kings, with horses and
chariots, with horsemen and a great
army. [8]He will ravage your settlements
on the mainland with the sword; he will
set up siege works against you, build a
ramp up to your walls and raise his
shields against you. [9]He will direct the
blows of his battering-rams against your
walls and demolish your towers with his
weapons. [10]His horses will be so many
that they will cover you with dust. Your
walls will tremble at the noise of the war
horses, wagons and chariots when he
enters your gates as men enter a city
whose walls have been broken through.
[11]The hoofs of his horses will trample all
your streets; he will kill your people
with the sword, and your strong pillars
will fall to the ground. [12]They will plunder your wealth and loot your merchandise; they will break down your walls
and demolish your fine houses and
throw your stones, timber and rubble
into the sea. [13]I will put an end to your
noisy songs, and the music of your harps
will be heard no more. [14]I will make you
a bare rock, and you will become a place
to spread fishing nets. You will never be
rebuilt, for I the LORD have spoken,
declares the Sovereign LORD.
[15]"This is what the Sovereign LORD
says to Tyre: Will not the coastlands
tremble at the sound of your fall, when
the wounded groan and the slaughter
takes place in you? [16]Then all the
princes of the coast will step down from
their thrones and lay aside their robes
and take off their embroidered garments. Clothed with terror, they will
sit on the ground, trembling every
moment, appalled at you. [17]Then they
will take up a lament concerning you
and say to you:

" 'How you are destroyed, O city of
renown,
peopled by men of the sea!
You were a power on the seas,
you and your citizens;
you put your terror
on all who lived there.
[18]Now the coastlands tremble
on the day of your fall;
the islands in the sea
are terrified at your collapse.'

[19]"This is what the Sovereign LORD
says: When I make you a desolate city,
like cities no longer inhabited, and
when I bring the ocean depths over you
and its vast waters cover you, [20]then I
will bring you down with those who go
down to the pit, to the people of long
ago. I will make you dwell in the earth
below, as in ancient ruins, with those
who go down to the pit, and you will not
return or take your place in the land of
the living. [21]I will bring you to a horrible
end and you will be no more. You will
be sought, but you will never again be
found, declares the Sovereign LORD."

A Lament for Tyre

27 The word of the LORD came to
me: [2]"Son of man, take up a
lament concerning Tyre. [3]Say to Tyre,
situated at the gateway to the sea, merchant of peoples on many coasts, 'This
is what the Sovereign LORD says:

" 'You say, O Tyre,
"I am perfect in beauty."
[4]Your domain was on the high seas;
your builders brought your beauty
to perfection.
[5]They made all your timbers
of pine trees from Senir;
they took a cedar from Lebanon
to make a mast for you.
[6]Of oaks from Bashan
they made your oars;
of cypress wood from the coasts of
Cyprus
they made your deck, inlaid with
ivory.

7Fine embroidered linen from Egypt
was your sail
and served as your banner;
your awnings were of blue and purple
from the coasts of Elishah.
8Men of Sidon and Arvad were your
oarsmen;
your skilled men, O Tyre, were
aboard as your seamen.
9Veteran craftsmen of Gebal were on
board
as shipwrights to caulk your seams.
All the ships of the sea and their
sailors
came alongside to trade for your
wares.

10" 'Men of Persia, Lydia and Put
served as soldiers in your army.
They hung their shields and helmets
on your walls,
bringing you splendour.
11Men of Arvad and Helech
manned your walls on every side;
men of Gammad
were in your towers.
They hung their shields around your
walls;
they brought your beauty to
perfection.

12" 'Tarshish did business with you
because of your great wealth of goods;
they exchanged silver, iron, tin and lead
for your merchandise.
13" 'Greece, Tubal and Meshech
traded with you; they exchanged slaves
and articles of bronze for your wares.
14" 'Men of Beth Togarmah exchanged work horses, war horses and
mules for your merchandise.
15" 'The men of Rhodes traded with
you, and many coastlands were your
customers; they paid you with ivory
tusks and ebony.
16" 'Aram did business with you because of your many products; they
exchanged turquoise, purple fabric,
embroidered work, fine linen, coral
and rubies for your merchandise.
17" 'Judah and Israel traded with you;
they exchanged wheat from Minnith
and confections, honey, oil and balm for
your wares.
18" 'Damascus, because of your many
products and great wealth of goods, did
business with you in wine from Helbon
and wool from Zahar.
19" 'Danites and Greeks from Uzal
bought your merchandise; they exchanged wrought iron, cassia and calamus for your wares.
20" 'Dedan traded in saddle blankets
with you.
21" 'Arabia and all the princes of
Kedar were your customers; they did
business with you in lambs, rams and
goats.
22" 'The merchants of Sheba and
Raamah traded with you; for your merchandise they exchanged the finest of all
kinds of spices and precious stones, and
gold.
23" 'Haran, Canneh and Eden and
merchants of Sheba, Asshur and Kil-
mad traded with you. 24In your market-
place they traded with you beautiful
garments, blue fabric, embroidered
work and multicoloured rugs with cords
twisted and tightly knotted.

25" 'The ships of Tarshish serve
as carriers for your wares.
You are filled with heavy cargo
in the heart of the sea.
26Your oarsmen take you
out to the high seas.
But the east wind will break you to
pieces
in the heart of the sea.
27Your wealth, merchandise and
wares,
your mariners, seamen and
shipwrights,
your merchants and all your soldiers,
and everyone else on board
will sink into the heart of the sea
on the day of your shipwreck.
28The shorelands will quake
when your seamen cry out.
29All who handle the oars
will abandon their ships;
the mariners and all the seamen
will stand on the shore.

[30]They will raise their voice
and cry bitterly over you;
they will sprinkle dust on their heads
and roll in ashes.
[31]They will shave their heads because
of you
and will put on sackcloth.
They will weep over you with anguish
of soul
and with bitter mourning.
[32]As they wail and mourn over you,
they will take up a lament
concerning you:
"Who was ever silenced like Tyre,
surrounded by the sea?"
[33]When your merchandise went out on
the seas,
you satisfied many nations;
with your great wealth and your
wares
you enriched the kings of the earth.
[34]Now you are shattered by the sea
in the depths of the waters;
your wares and all your company
have gone down with you.
[35]All who live in the coastlands
are appalled at you;
their kings shudder with horror
and their faces are distorted with
fear.
[36]The merchants among the nations
hiss at you;
you have come to a horrible end
and will be no more.'"

NEW TESTAMENT READING
Hebrews 12:1–13

God Disciplines His Sons

12 Therefore, since we are surrounded by such a great cloud of
witnesses, let us throw off everything
that hinders and the sin that so easily
entangles, and let us run with perseverance the race marked out for us. [2]Let us
fix our eyes on Jesus, the author and
perfecter of our faith, who for the joy
set before him endured the cross, scorn-
ing its shame, and sat down at the right
hand of the throne of God. [3]Consider
him who endured such opposition from
sinful men, so that you will not grow
weary and lose heart.
[4]In your struggle against sin, you
have not yet resisted to the point of
shedding your blood. [5]And you have
forgotten that word of encouragement
that addresses you as sons:

"My son, do not make light of the
Lord's discipline,
and do not lose heart when he
rebukes you,
[6]because the Lord disciplines those he
loves,
and he punishes everyone he
accepts as a son."

[7]Endure hardship as discipline; God
is treating you as sons. For what son is
not disciplined by his father? [8]If you are
not disciplined (and everyone under-
goes discipline), then you are illegitimate children and not true sons.
[9]Moreover, we have all had human
fathers who disciplined us and we respected them for it. How much more
should we submit to the Father of our
spirits and live! [10]Our fathers disciplined us for a little while as they
thought best; but God disciplines us for
our good, that we may share in his
holiness. [11]No discipline seems pleasant
at the time, but painful. Later on,
however, it produces a harvest of righteousness and peace for those who have
been trained by it.
[12]Therefore, strengthen your feeble
arms and weak knees! [13]"Make level
paths for your feet," so that the lame
may not be disabled, but rather healed.

READING FROM PSALMS
Psalm 125:1–5

A song of ascents.

[1]Those who trust in the LORD are like
Mount Zion,
which cannot be shaken but
endures for ever.

[2]As the mountains surround
Jerusalem,
so the LORD surrounds his
people
both now and for evermore.

[3]The sceptre of the wicked will not
remain
over the land allotted to the
righteous,
for then the righteous might use
their hands to do evil.
[4]Do good, O LORD, to those who are
good,
to those who are upright in heart.
[5]But those who turn to crooked ways
the LORD will banish with the
evildoers.

Peace be upon Israel.

NOVEMBER 15

DAY 319

OLD TESTAMENT READING
Ezekiel 28:1–29:21

A Prophecy Against the King of Tyre

28 The word of the LORD came to
me: [2]"Son of man, say to the
ruler of Tyre, 'This is what the
Sovereign LORD says:

" 'In the pride of your heart
you say, "I am a god;
I sit on the throne of a god
in the heart of the seas."
But you are a man and not a god,
though you think you are as wise as
a god.
[3]Are you wiser than Daniel?
Is no secret hidden from you?
[4]By your wisdom and understanding
you have gained wealth for
yourself
and amassed gold and silver
in your treasuries.
[5]By your great skill in trading
you have increased your wealth,
and because of your wealth
your heart has grown proud.

[6]" 'Therefore this is what the
Sovereign LORD says:

" 'Because you think you are wise,
as wise as a god,
[7]I am going to bring foreigners against
you,
the most ruthless of nations;
they will draw their swords against
your beauty and wisdom
and pierce your shining splendour.
[8]They will bring you down to the pit,
and you will die a violent death
in the heart of the seas.
[9]Will you then say, "I am a god,"
in the presence of those who kill
you?
You will be but a man, not a god,
in the hands of those who slay you.
[10]You will die the death of the
uncircumcised
at the hands of foreigners.

I have spoken, declares the Sovereign
LORD.' "

[11]The word of the LORD came to me:
[12]"Son of man, take up a lament concerning the king of Tyre and say to him:
'This is what the Sovereign LORD says:

" 'You were the model of perfection,
full of wisdom and perfect in
beauty.
[13]You were in Eden,
the garden of God;
every precious stone adorned you:
ruby, topaz and emerald,
chrysolite, onyx and jasper,
sapphire, turquoise and beryl.

Your settings and mountings were
made of gold;
on the day you were created they
were prepared.
14You were anointed as a guardian
cherub,
for so I ordained you.
You were on the holy mount of God;
you walked among the fiery stones.
15You were blameless in your ways
from the day you were created
till wickedness was found in you.
16Through your widespread trade
you were filled with violence,
and you sinned.
So I drove you in disgrace from the
mount of God,
and I expelled you, O guardian
cherub,
from among the fiery stones.
17Your heart became proud
on account of your beauty,
and you corrupted your wisdom
because of your splendour.
So I threw you to the earth;
I made a spectacle of you before
kings.
18By your many sins and dishonest
trade
you have desecrated your
sanctuaries.
So I made a fire come out from you,
and it consumed you,
and I reduced you to ashes on the
ground
in the sight of all who were
watching.
19All the nations who knew you
are appalled at you;
you have come to a horrible end
and will be no more.'"

A Prophecy Against Sidon

20The word of the LORD came to me:
21"Son of man, set your face against
Sidon; prophesy against her 22and say:
'This is what the Sovereign LORD says:

"'I am against you, O Sidon,
and I will gain glory within you.
They will know that I am the LORD,
when I inflict punishment on her
and show myself holy within her.
23I will send a plague upon her
and make blood flow in her streets.
The slain will fall within her,
with the sword against her on every
side.
Then they will know that I am the
LORD.

24"'No longer will the people of
Israel have malicious neighbours who
are painful briers and sharp thorns.
Then they will know that I am the
Sovereign LORD.
25"'This is what the Sovereign LORD
says: When I gather the people of Israel
from the nations where they have been
scattered, I will show myself holy
among them in the sight of the nations.
Then they will live in their own land,
which I gave to my servant Jacob.
26They will live there in safety and will
build houses and plant vineyards; they
will live in safety when I inflict punishment on all their neighbours who
maligned them. Then they will know
that I am the LORD their God.'"

A Prophecy Against Egypt

29 In the tenth year, in the tenth
month on the twelfth day, the
word of the LORD came to me: 2"Son of
man, set your face against Pharaoh king
of Egypt and prophesy against him and
against all Egypt. 3Speak to him and
say: 'This is what the Sovereign LORD
says:

"'I am against you, Pharaoh king of
Egypt,
you great monster lying among
your streams.
You say, "The Nile is mine;
I made it for myself."
4But I will put hooks in your jaws
and make the fish of your streams
stick to your scales.
I will pull you out from among your
streams,
with all the fish sticking to your
scales.

[5]I will leave you in the desert,
you and all the fish of your
streams.
You will fall on the open field
and not be gathered or picked up.
I will give you as food
to the beasts of the earth and the
birds of the air.

[6]Then all who live in Egypt will know
that I am the LORD.

"'You have been a staff of reed for
the house of Israel. [7]When they grasped
you with their hands, you splintered and
you tore open their shoulders; when
they leaned on you, you broke and their
backs were wrenched.
[8]"'Therefore this is what the
Sovereign LORD says: I will bring a
sword against you and kill your men
and their animals. [9]Egypt will become
a desolate wasteland. Then they will
know that I am the LORD.
"'Because you said, "The Nile is
mine; I made it," [10]therefore I am
against you and against your streams,
and I will make the land of Egypt a ruin
and a desolate waste from Migdol to
Aswan, as far as the border of Cush.
[11]No foot of man or animal will pass
through it; no-one will live there for
forty years. [12]I will make the land of
Egypt desolate among devastated
lands, and her cities will lie desolate for
forty years among ruined cities. And I
will disperse the Egyptians among the
nations and scatter them through the
countries.
[13]"'Yet this is what the Sovereign
LORD says: At the end of forty years I
will gather the Egyptians from the nations where they were scattered. [14]I will
bring them back from captivity and return them to Upper Egypt, the land of
their ancestry. There they will be a
lowly kingdom. [15]It will be the lowliest
of kingdoms and will never again exalt
itself above the other nations. I will
make it so weak that it will never again
rule over the nations. [16]Egypt will no
longer be a source of confidence for the
people of Israel but will be a reminder
of their sin in turning to her for help.
Then they will know that I am the
Sovereign LORD.'"

[17]In the twenty-seventh year, in the
first month on the first day, the word of
the LORD came to me. [18]"Son of man,
Nebuchadnezzar king of Babylon drove
his army in a hard campaign against
Tyre; every head was rubbed bare and
every shoulder made raw. Yet he and
his army got no reward from the campaign he led against Tyre. [19]Therefore
this is what the Sovereign LORD says: I
am going to give Egypt to Nebuchadnezzar king of Babylon, and he will
carry off its wealth. He will loot and
plunder the land as pay for his army. [20]I
have given him Egypt as a reward for his
efforts because he and his army did it for
me, declares the Sovereign LORD.
[21]"On that day I will make a horn
grow for the house of Israel, and I will
open your mouth among them. Then
they will know that I am the LORD."

NEW TESTAMENT READING
Hebrews 12:14–29

Warning Against Refusing God

[14]Make every effort to live in peace
with all men and to be holy; without
holiness no-one will see the Lord. [15]See
to it that no-one misses the grace of God
and that no bitter root grows up to cause
trouble and defile many. [16]See that no-
one is sexually immoral, or is godless
like Esau, who for a single meal sold his
inheritance rights as the oldest son.
[17]Afterwards, as you know, when he
wanted to inherit this blessing, he was
rejected. He could bring about no
change of mind, though he sought the
blessing with tears.
[18]You have not come to a mountain
that can be touched and that is burning
with fire; to darkness, gloom and storm;
[19]to a trumpet blast or to such a voice
speaking words that those who heard it

begged that no further word be spoken
to them, [20]because they could not bear
what was commanded: "If even an
animal touches the mountain, it must be
stoned." [21]The sight was so terrifying
that Moses said, "I am trembling with
fear."

[22]But you have come to Mount Zion,
to the heavenly Jerusalem, the city of
the living God. You have come to
thousands upon thousands of angels in
joyful assembly, [23]to the church of the
firstborn, whose names are written in
heaven. You have come to God, the
judge of all men, to the spirits of righteous men made perfect, [24]to Jesus the
mediator of a new covenant, and to the
sprinkled blood that speaks a better
word than the blood of Abel.

[25]See to it that you do not refuse him
who speaks. If they did not escape when
they refused him who warned them on
earth, how much less will we, if we turn
away from him who warns us from
heaven? [26]At that time his voice shook
the earth, but now he has promised,
"Once more I will shake not only the
earth but also the heavens." [27]The
words "once more" indicate the removing of what can be shaken—that is,
created things—so that what cannot be
shaken may remain.

[28]Therefore, since we are receiving a
kingdom that cannot be shaken, let us
be thankful, and so worship God
acceptably with reverence and awe,
[29]for our "God is a consuming fire."

READING FROM PSALMS
Psalm 126:1–6

A song of ascents.

[1]When the LORD brought back the
captives to Zion,
we were like men who dreamed.
[2]Our mouths were filled with laughter,
our tongues with songs of joy.
Then it was said among the nations,
"The LORD has done great things
for them."
[3]The LORD has done great things for
us,
and we are filled with joy.

[4]Restore our fortunes, O LORD,
like streams in the Negev.
[5]Those who sow in tears
will reap with songs of joy.
[6]He who goes out weeping,
carrying seed to sow,
will return with songs of joy,
carrying sheaves with him.

DAY 320

NOVEMBER 16

OLD TESTAMENT READING
Ezekiel 30:1–31:18

A Lament for Egypt

30 The word of the LORD came to
me: [2]"Son of man, prophesy and
say: 'This is what the Sovereign LORD
says:

" 'Wail and say,
"Alas for that day!"
[3]For the day is near,
the day of the LORD is near—
a day of clouds,
a time of doom for the nations.
[4]A sword will come against Egypt,
and anguish will come upon Cush.
When the slain fall in Egypt,
her wealth will be carried away
and her foundations torn down.

[5]Cush and Put, Lydia and all Arabia,
Libya and the people of the covenant

land will fall by the sword along with Egypt.

[6]" 'This is what the LORD says:

" 'The allies of Egypt will fall
and her proud strength will fail.
From Migdol to Aswan
they will fall by the sword within her,
declares the Sovereign LORD.
[7]" 'They will be desolate
among desolate lands,
and their cities will lie
among ruined cities.
[8]Then they will know that I am the LORD,
when I set fire to Egypt
and all her helpers are crushed.

[9]" 'On that day messengers will go out from me in ships to frighten Cush out of her complacency. Anguish will take hold of them on the day of Egypt's doom, for it is sure to come.

[10]" 'This is what the Sovereign LORD says:

" 'I will put an end to the hordes of Egypt
by the hand of Nebuchadnezzar king of Babylon.
[11]He and his army—the most ruthless of nations—
will be brought in to destroy the land.
They will draw their swords against Egypt
and fill the land with the slain.
[12]I will dry up the streams of the Nile
and sell the land to evil men;
by the hand of foreigners
I will lay waste the land and everything in it.

I the LORD have spoken.

[13]" 'This is what the Sovereign LORD says:

" 'I will destroy the idols
and put an end to the images in Memphis.
No longer will there be a prince in Egypt,
and I will spread fear throughout the land.
[14]I will lay waste Upper Egypt,
set fire to Zoan
and inflict punishment on Thebes.
[15]I will pour out my wrath on Pelusium,
the stronghold of Egypt,
and cut off the hordes of Thebes.
[16]I will set fire to Egypt;
Pelusium will writhe in agony.
Thebes will be taken by storm;
Memphis will be in constant distress.
[17]The young men of Heliopolis and Bubastis
will fall by the sword,
and the cities themselves will go into captivity.
[18]Dark will be the day at Tahpanhes
when I break the yoke of Egypt;
there her proud strength will come to an end.
She will be covered with clouds,
and her villages will go into captivity.
[19]So I will inflict punishment on Egypt,
and they will know that I am the LORD.' "

[20]In the eleventh year, in the first
month on the seventh day, the word of
the LORD came to me: [21]"Son of man, I
have broken the arm of Pharaoh king of
Egypt. It has not been bound up for
healing or put in a splint so as to become
strong enough to hold a sword.
[22]Therefore this is what the Sovereign
LORD says: I am against Pharaoh king of
Egypt. I will break both his arms, the
good arm as well as the broken one, and
make the sword fall from his hand. [23]I
will disperse the Egyptians among the
nations and scatter them through the
countries. [24]I will strengthen the arms of
the king of Babylon and put my sword in
his hand, but I will break the arms of
Pharaoh, and he will groan before him
like a mortally wounded man. [25]I will
strengthen the arms of the king of Babylon, but the arms of Pharaoh will fall

limp. Then they will know that I am the LORD, when I put my sword into the hand of the king of Babylon and he brandishes it against Egypt. 26I will disperse the Egyptians among the nations and scatter them through the countries. Then they will know that I am the LORD."

A Cedar in Lebanon

31 In the eleventh year, in the third month on the first day, the word of the LORD came to me: 2"Son of man, say to Pharaoh king of Egypt and to his hordes:

"'Who can be compared with you in
majesty?
3Consider Assyria, once a cedar in
Lebanon,
with beautiful branches
overshadowing the forest;
it towered on high,
its top above the thick foliage.
4The waters nourished it,
deep springs made it grow tall;
their streams flowed
all around its base
and sent their channels
to all the trees of the field.
5So it towered higher
than all the trees of the field;
its boughs increased
and its branches grew long,
spreading because of abundant
waters.
6All the birds of the air
nested in its boughs,
all the beasts of the field
gave birth under its branches;
all the great nations
lived in its shade.
7It was majestic in beauty,
with its spreading boughs,
for its roots went down
to abundant waters.
8The cedars in the garden of God
could not rival it,
nor could the pine trees
equal its boughs,
nor could the plane trees
compare with its branches—
no tree in the garden of God
could match its beauty.
9I made it beautiful
with abundant branches,
the envy of all the trees of Eden
in the garden of God.

10"'Therefore this is what the Sovereign LORD says: Because it towered on high, lifting its top above the thick foliage, and because it was proud of its
height, 11I handed it over to the ruler of the nations, for him to deal with according to its wickedness. I cast it aside,
12and the most ruthless of foreign nations cut it down and left it. Its boughs fell on the mountains and in all the valleys; its branches lay broken in all the ravines of the land. All the nations of the earth came out from under its shade
and left it. 13All the birds of the air settled on the fallen tree, and all the beasts of the field were among its bran-
ches. 14Therefore no other trees by the waters are ever to tower proudly on high, lifting their tops above the thick foliage. No other trees so well-watered are ever to reach such a height; they are all destined for death, for the earth below, among mortal men, with those who go down to the pit.
15"'This is what the Sovereign LORD says: On the day it was brought down to the grave I covered the deep springs with mourning for it; I held back its streams, and its abundant waters were restrained. Because of it I clothed Lebanon with gloom, and all the trees of the
field withered away. 16I made the nations tremble at the sound of its fall when I brought it down to the grave with those who go down to the pit. Then all the trees of Eden, the choicest and best of Lebanon, all the trees that were well-watered, were consoled in the
earth below. 17Those who lived in its shade, its allies among the nations, had also gone down to the grave with it, joining those killed by the sword.
18"'Which of the trees of Eden can be compared with you in splendour and majesty? Yet you, too, will be brought

down with the trees of Eden to the earth
below; you will lie among the uncircumcised, with those killed by the sword.
"'This is Pharaoh and all his hordes,
declares the Sovereign LORD.'"

NEW TESTAMENT READING
Hebrews 13:1–25

Concluding Exhortations

13 Keep on loving each other as
brothers. 2Do not forget to entertain strangers, for by so doing some
people have entertained angels without
knowing it. 3Remember those in prison
as if you were their fellow-prisoners,
and those who are ill-treated as if you
yourselves were suffering.
4Marriage should be honoured by all,
and the marriage bed kept pure, for
God will judge the adulterer and all the
sexually immoral. 5Keep your lives free
from the love of money and be content
with what you have, because God has
said,

"Never will I leave you;
never will I forsake you."

6So we say with confidence,

"The Lord is my helper; I will not be
afraid.
What can man do to me?"

7Remember your leaders, who spoke
the word of God to you. Consider the
outcome of their way of life and imitate
their faith. 8Jesus Christ is the same
yesterday and today and for ever.
9Do not be carried away by all kinds
of strange teachings. It is good for our
hearts to be strengthened by grace, not
by ceremonial foods, which are of no
value to those who eat them. 10We have
an altar from which those who minister
at the tabernacle have no right to eat.
11The high priest carries the blood of
animals into the Most Holy Place as a
sin offering, but the bodies are burned
outside the camp. 12And so Jesus also
suffered outside the city gate to make
the people holy through his own blood.
13Let us, then, go to him outside the
camp, bearing the disgrace he bore.
14For here we do not have an enduring
city, but we are looking for the city that
is to come.
15Through Jesus, therefore, let us
continually offer to God a sacrifice of
praise—the fruit of lips that confess his
name. 16And do not forget to do good
and to share with others, for with such
sacrifices God is pleased.
17Obey your leaders and submit to
their authority. They keep watch over
you as men who must give an account.
Obey them so that their work will be a
joy, not a burden, for that would be of
no advantage to you.
18Pray for us. We are sure that we
have a clear conscience and desire to
live honourably in every way. 19I particularly urge you to pray so that I may be
restored to you soon.
20May the God of peace, who through
the blood of the eternal covenant
brought back from the dead our Lord
Jesus, that great Shepherd of the sheep,
21equip you with everything good for
doing his will, and may he work in us
what is pleasing to him, through Jesus
Christ, to whom be glory for ever and
ever. Amen.

22Brothers, I urge you to bear with
my word of exhortation, for I have written you only a short letter.
23I want you to know that our brother
Timothy has been released. If he arrives
soon, I will come with him to see you.
24Greet all your leaders and all God's
people. Those from Italy send you their
greetings.
25Grace be with you all.

READING FROM PROVERBS
Proverbs 27:23–28:6

23Be sure you know the condition of
your flocks,
give careful attention to your
herds;

24for riches do not endure for ever,
and a crown is not secure for all generations.
25When the hay is removed and new growth appears
and the grass from the hills is gathered in,
26the lambs will provide you with clothing,
and the goats with the price of a field.
27You will have plenty of goats' milk
to feed you and your family
and to nourish your servant girls.

28 The wicked man flees
though no-one pursues,
but the righteous are as bold as a lion.

2When a country is rebellious, it has many rulers,
but a man of understanding and knowledge maintains order.

3A ruler who oppresses the poor
is like a driving rain that leaves no crops.

4Those who forsake the law praise the wicked,
but those who keep the law resist them.

5Evil men do not understand justice,
but those who seek the LORD understand it fully.

6Better a poor man whose walk is blameless
than a rich man whose ways are perverse.

DAY 321

NOVEMBER 17

OLD TESTAMENT READING
Ezekiel 32:1–33:20

A Lament for Pharaoh

32 In the twelfth year, in the
twelfth month on the first day,
the word of the LORD came to me:
2"Son of man, take up a lament concerning Pharaoh king of Egypt and say
to him:

" 'You are like a lion among the nations;
you are like a monster in the seas
thrashing about in your streams,
churning the water with your feet
and muddying the streams.

3" 'This is what the Sovereign LORD says:

" 'With a great throng of people
I will cast my net over you,
and they will haul you up in my net.
4I will throw you on the land
and hurl you on the open field.
I will let all the birds of the air settle on you
and all the beasts of the earth
gorge themselves on you.
5I will spread your flesh on the mountains
and fill the valleys with your remains.
6I will drench the land with your flowing blood
all the way to the mountains,
and the ravines will be filled with your flesh.
7When I snuff you out, I will cover the heavens
and darken their stars;
I will cover the sun with a cloud,
and the moon will not give its light.

8All the shining lights in the heavens
I will darken over you;
I will bring darkness over your land,
declares the Sovereign LORD.
9I will trouble the hearts of many peoples
when I bring about your destruction among the nations,
among lands you have not known.
10I will cause many peoples to be appalled at you,
and their kings will shudder with horror because of you
when I brandish my sword before them.
On the day of your downfall
each of them will tremble
every moment for his life.

11" 'For this is what the Sovereign LORD says:

" 'The sword of the king of Babylon
will come against you.
12I will cause your hordes to fall
by the swords of mighty men—
the most ruthless of all nations.
They will shatter the pride of Egypt,
and all her hordes will be overthrown.
13I will destroy all her cattle
from beside abundant waters
no longer to be stirred by the foot of man
or muddied by the hoofs of cattle.
14Then I will let her waters settle
and make her streams flow like oil,
declares the Sovereign LORD.
15When I make Egypt desolate
and strip the land of everything in it,
when I strike down all who live there,
then they will know that I am the LORD.'

16"This is the lament they will chant for her. The daughters of the nations will chant it; for Egypt and all her hordes they will chant it, declares the Sovereign LORD."

17In the twelfth year, on the fifteenth day of the month, the word of the LORD
came to me: 18"Son of man, wail for the hordes of Egypt and consign to the earth below both her and the daughters of mighty nations, with those who go down to the pit. 19Say to them, 'Are you more favoured than others? Go down and be laid among the uncircumcised.'
20They will fall among those killed by the sword. The sword is drawn; let her be dragged off with all her hordes.
21From within the grave the mighty leaders will say of Egypt and her allies, 'They have come down and they lie with the uncircumcised, with those killed by the sword.'

22"Assyria is there with her whole army; she is surrounded by the graves of all her slain, all who have fallen by the sword. 23Their graves are in the depths of the pit and her army lies around her grave. All who had spread terror in the land of the living are slain, fallen by the sword.

24"Elam is there, with all her hordes around her grave. All of them are slain, fallen by the sword. All who had spread terror in the land of the living went down uncircumcised to the earth below. They bear their shame with those who go down to the pit. 25A bed is made for her among the slain, with all her hordes around her grave. All of them are uncircumcised, killed by the sword. Because their terror had spread in the land of the living, they bear their shame with those who go down to the pit; they are laid among the slain.

26"Meshech and Tubal are there, with all their hordes around their graves. All of them are uncircumcised, killed by the sword because they spread their terror in the land of the living.
27Do they not lie with the other uncircumcised warriors who have fallen, who went down to the grave with their weapons of war, whose swords were placed under their heads? The punishment for their sins rested on their bones, though the terror of these warriors had stalked through the land of the living.

28"You too, O Pharaoh, will be

broken and will lie among the uncircumcised, with those killed by the
sword.
29"Edom is there, her kings and all
her princes; despite their power, they
are laid with those killed by the sword.
They lie with the uncircumcised, with
those who go down to the pit.
30"All the princes of the north and all
the Sidonians are there; they went down
with the slain in disgrace despite the
terror caused by their power. They lie
uncircumcised with those killed by the
sword and bear their shame with those
who go down to the pit.
31"Pharaoh—he and all his army—
will see them and he will be consoled for
all his hordes that were killed by the
sword, declares the Sovereign LORD.
32Although I had him spread terror in
the land of the living, Pharaoh and all
his hordes will be laid among the uncircumcised, with those killed by the
sword, declares the Sovereign LORD."

Ezekiel a Watchman

33 The word of the LORD came to
me: 2"Son of man, speak to your
countrymen and say to them: 'When I
bring the sword against a land, and the
people of the land choose one of their
men and make him their watchman,
3and he sees the sword coming against
the land and blows the trumpet to warn
the people, 4then if anyone hears the
trumpet but does not take warning and
the sword comes and takes his life, his
blood will be on his own head. 5Since he
heard the sound of the trumpet but did
not take warning, his blood will be on
his own head. If he had taken warning,
he would have saved himself. 6But if the
watchman sees the sword coming and
does not blow the trumpet to warn the
people and the sword comes and takes
the life of one of them, that man will be
taken away because of his sin, but I will
hold the watchman accountable for his
blood.'
7"Son of man, I have made you a
watchman for the house of Israel; so
hear the word I speak and give them
warning from me. 8When I say to the
wicked, 'O wicked man, you will surely
die,' and you do not speak out to dissuade him from his ways, that wicked
man will die for his sin, and I will hold
you accountable for his blood. 9But if
you do warn the wicked man to turn
from his ways and he does not do so, he
will die for his sin, but you will be saved
yourself.
10"Son of man, say to the house of
Israel, 'This is what you are saying:
"Our offences and sins weigh us down,
and we are wasting away because of
them. How then can we live?"' 11Say to
them, 'As surely as I live, declares the
Sovereign LORD, I take no pleasure in
the death of the wicked, but rather that
they turn from their ways and live.
Turn! Turn from your evil ways! Why
will you die, O house of Israel?'
12"Therefore, son of man, say to your
countrymen, 'The righteousness of the
righteous man will not save him when
he disobeys, and the wickedness of the
wicked man will not cause him to fall
when he turns from it. The righteous
man, if he sins, will not be allowed to
live because of his former righteousness.' 13If I tell the righteous man that
he will surely live, but then he trusts in
his righteousness and does evil, none of
the righteous things he has done will be
remembered; he will die for the evil he
has done. 14And if I say to the wicked
man, 'You will surely die,' but he then
turns away from his sin and does what is
just and right—15if he gives back what
he took in pledge for a loan, returns
what he has stolen, follows the decrees
that give life, and does no evil, he will
surely live; he will not die. 16None of the
sins he has committed will be remembered against him. He has done what is
just and right; he will surely live.
17"Yet your countrymen say, 'The
way of the Lord is not just.' But it is
their way that is not just. 18If a righteous
man turns from his righteousness and
does evil, he will die for it. 19And if a

wicked man turns away from his wickedness and does what is just and right,
he will live by doing so. [20]Yet, O house
of Israel, you say, 'The way of the Lord
is not just.' But I will judge each of you
according to his own ways."

NEW TESTAMENT READING
James 1:1–27

1 James, a servant of God and of the
Lord Jesus Christ,

To the twelve tribes scattered among
the nations:

Greetings.

Trials and Temptations

[2]Consider it pure joy, my brothers,
whenever you face trials of many kinds,
[3]because you know that the testing of
your faith develops perseverance.
[4]Perseverance must finish its work so
that you may be mature and complete,
not lacking anything. [5]If any of you
lacks wisdom, he should ask God, who
gives generously to all without finding
fault, and it will be given to him. [6]But
when he asks, he must believe and not
doubt, because he who doubts is like a
wave of the sea, blown and tossed by the
wind. [7]That man should not think he
will receive anything from the Lord; [8]he
is a double-minded man, unstable in all
he does.

[9]The brother in humble circumstances ought to take pride in his high
position. [10]But the one who is rich
should take pride in his low position,
because he will pass away like a wild
flower. [11]For the sun rises with scorching heat and withers the plant; its
blossom falls and its beauty is destroyed. In the same way, the rich man
will fade away even while he goes about
his business.

[12]Blessed is the man who perseveres
under trial, because when he has stood
the test, he will receive the crown of life
that God has promised to those who
love him.

[13]When tempted, no-one should say,
"God is tempting me." For God cannot
be tempted by evil, nor does he tempt
anyone; [14]but each one is tempted
when, by his own evil desire, he is dragged away and enticed. [15]Then, after
desire has conceived, it gives birth to
sin; and sin, when it is full-grown, gives
birth to death.

[16]Don't be deceived, my dear
brothers. [17]Every good and perfect gift
is from above, coming down from the
Father of the heavenly lights, who does
not change like shifting shadows. [18]He
chose to give us birth through the word
of truth, that we might be a kind of
firstfruits of all he created.

Listening and Doing

[19]My dear brothers, take note of this:
Everyone should be quick to listen,
slow to speak and slow to become
angry, [20]for man's anger does not bring
about the righteous life that God desires. [21]Therefore, get rid of all moral
filth and the evil that is so prevalent, and
humbly accept the word planted in you,
which can save you.

[22]Do not merely listen to the word,
and so deceive yourselves. Do what it
says. [23]Anyone who listens to the word
but does not do what it says is like a man
who looks at his face in a mirror [24]and,
after looking at himself, goes away and
immediately forgets what he looks like.
[25]But the man who looks intently into
the perfect law that gives freedom, and
continues to do this, not forgetting what
he has heard, but doing it—he will be
blessed in what he does.

[26]If anyone considers himself religious and yet does not keep a tight rein
on his tongue, he deceives himself and
his religion is worthless. [27]Religion that
God our Father accepts as pure and
faultless is this: to look after orphans
and widows in their distress and to keep
oneself from being polluted by the
world.

READING FROM PSALMS

Psalm 127:1–5

A song of ascents. Of Solomon.

1Unless the LORD builds the house,
its builders labour in vain.
Unless the LORD watches over the
city,
the watchmen stand guard in vain.
2In vain you rise early
and stay up late,
toiling for food to eat—
for he grants sleep to those he
loves.

3Sons are a heritage from the LORD,
children a reward from him.
4Like arrows in the hands of a warrior
are sons born in one's youth.
5Blessed is the man
whose quiver is full of them.
They will not be put to shame
when they contend with their
enemies in the gate.

DAY 322

NOVEMBER 18

OLD TESTAMENT READING

Ezekiel 33:21–35:15

Jerusalem's Fall Explained

21In the twelfth year of our exile, in
the tenth month on the fifth day, a man
who had escaped from Jerusalem came
to me and said, "The city has fallen!"
22Now the evening before the man arrived, the hand of the LORD was upon
me, and he opened my mouth before
the man came to me in the morning. So
my mouth was opened and I was no
longer silent.
23Then the word of the LORD came to
me: 24"Son of man, the people living in
those ruins in the land of Israel are
saying, 'Abraham was only one man,
yet he possessed the land. But we are
many; surely the land has been given to
us as our possession.' 25Therefore say to
them, 'This is what the Sovereign LORD
says: Since you eat meat with the blood
still in it and look to your idols and shed
blood, should you then possess the
land? 26You rely on your sword, you do
detestable things, and each of you defiles his neighbour's wife. Should you
then possess the land?'
27"Say this to them: 'This is what the
Sovereign LORD says: As surely as I
live, those who are left in the ruins will
fall by the sword, those out in the country I will give to the wild animals to be
devoured, and those in strongholds and
caves will die of a plague. 28I will make
the land a desolate waste, and her proud
strength will come to an end, and the
mountains of Israel will become desolate so that no-one will cross them.
29Then they will know that I am the
LORD, when I have made the land a
desolate waste because of all the detestable things they have done.'
30"As for you, son of man, your countrymen are talking together about you
by the walls and at the doors of the
houses, saying to each other, 'Come
and hear the message that has come
from the LORD.' 31My people come to
you, as they usually do, and sit before
you to listen to your words, but they do
not put them into practice. With their
mouths they express devotion, but their
hearts are greedy for unjust gain.
32Indeed, to them you are nothing more
than one who sings love songs with a
beautiful voice and plays an instrument
well, for they hear your words but do
not put them into practice.
33"When all this comes true—and it
surely will—then they will know that a
prophet has been among them."

Shepherds and Sheep

34 The word of the LORD came to
me: 2“Son of man, prophesy
against the shepherds of Israel; prophesy and say to them: ‘This is what the
Sovereign LORD says: Woe to the
shepherds of Israel who only take care
of themselves! Should not shepherds
take care of the flock? 3You eat the
curds, clothe yourselves with the wool
and slaughter the choice animals, but
you do not take care of the flock. 4You
have not strengthened the weak or
healed the sick or bound up the injured.
You have not brought back the strays or
searched for the lost. You have ruled
them harshly and brutally. 5So they
were scattered because there was no
shepherd, and when they were scattered they became food for all the wild
animals. 6My sheep wandered over all
the mountains and on every high hill.
They were scattered over the whole
earth, and no-one searched or looked
for them.

7“ ‘Therefore, you shepherds, hear
the word of the LORD: 8As surely as I
live, declares the Sovereign LORD, because my flock lacks a shepherd and so
has been plundered and has become
food for all the wild animals, and because my shepherds did not search for
my flock but cared for themselves rather
than for my flock, 9therefore, O
shepherds, hear the word of the LORD:
10This is what the Sovereign LORD says:
I am against the shepherds and will hold
them accountable for my flock. I will
remove them from tending the flock so
that the shepherds can no longer feed
themselves. I will rescue my flock from
their mouths, and it will no longer be
food for them.

11“ ‘For this is what the Sovereign
LORD says: I myself will search for my
sheep and look after them. 12As a
shepherd looks after his scattered flock
when he is with them, so will I look after
my sheep. I will rescue them from all the
places where they were scattered on a
day of clouds and darkness. 13I will
bring them out from the nations and
gather them from the countries, and I
will bring them into their own land. I
will pasture them on the mountains of
Israel, in the ravines and in all the settlements in the land. 14I will tend them in a
good pasture, and the mountain heights
of Israel will be their grazing land.
There they will lie down in good grazing
land, and there they will feed in a rich
pasture on the mountains of Israel. 15I
myself will tend my sheep and make
them lie down, declares the Sovereign
LORD. 16I will search for the lost and
bring back the strays. I will bind up the
injured and strengthen the weak, but
the sleek and the strong I will destroy. I
will shepherd the flock with justice.

17“ ‘As for you, my flock, this is what
the Sovereign LORD says: I will judge
between one sheep and another, and
between rams and goats. 18Is it not
enough for you to feed on the good
pasture? Must you also trample the rest
of your pasture with your feet? Is it not
enough for you to drink clear water?
Must you also muddy the rest with your
feet? 19Must my flock feed on what you
have trampled and drink what you have
muddied with your feet?

20“ ‘Therefore this is what the
Sovereign LORD says to them: See, I
myself will judge between the fat sheep
and the lean sheep. 21Because you
shove with flank and shoulder, butting
all the weak sheep with your horns until
you have driven them away, 22I will save
my flock, and they will no longer be
plundered. I will judge between one
sheep and another. 23I will place over
them one shepherd, my servant David,
and he will tend them; he will tend them
and be their shepherd. 24I the LORD will
be their God, and my servant David will
be prince among them. I the LORD have
spoken.

25“ ‘I will make a covenant of peace
with them and rid the land of wild beasts
so that they may live in the desert and
sleep in the forests in safety. 26I will
bless them and the places surrounding
my hill. I will send down showers in

season; there will be showers of blessing. 27The trees of the field will yield
their fruit and the ground will yield its
crops; the people will be secure in their
land. They will know that I am the
LORD, when I break the bars of their
yoke and rescue them from the hands of
those who enslaved them. 28They will
no longer be plundered by the nations,
nor will wild animals devour them.
They will live in safety, and no-one will
make them afraid. 29I will provide for
them a land renowned for its crops, and
they will no longer be victims of famine
in the land or bear the scorn of the
nations. 30Then they will know that I,
the LORD their God, am with them and
that they, the house of Israel, are my
people, declares the Sovereign LORD.
31You my sheep, the sheep of my pasture, are people, and I am your God,
declares the Sovereign LORD.' "

A Prophecy Against Edom

35 The word of the LORD came to
me: 2"Son of man, set your face
against Mount Seir; prophesy against it
3and say: 'This is what the Sovereign
LORD says: I am against you, Mount
Seir, and I will stretch out my hand
against you and make you a desolate
waste. 4I will turn your towns into ruins
and you will be desolate. Then you will
know that I am the LORD.

5" 'Because you harboured an ancient
hostility and delivered the Israelites
over to the sword at the time of their
calamity, the time their punishment
reached its climax, 6therefore as surely
as I live, declares the Sovereign LORD, I
will give you over to bloodshed and it
will pursue you. Since you did not hate
bloodshed, bloodshed will pursue you.
7I will make Mount Seir a desolate
waste and cut off from it all who come
and go. 8I will fill your mountains with
the slain; those killed by the sword will
fall on your hills and in your valleys and
in all your ravines. 9I will make you
desolate for ever; your towns will not be
inhabited. Then you will know that I am
the LORD.

10" 'Because you have said, "These
two nations and countries will be ours
and we will take possession of them,"
even though I the LORD was there,
11therefore as surely as I live, declares
the Sovereign LORD, I will treat you in
accordance with the anger and jealousy
you showed in your hatred of them and I
will make myself known among them
when I judge you. 12Then you will know
that I the LORD have heard all the contemptible things you have said against
the mountains of Israel. You said,
"They have been laid waste and have
been given over to us to devour." 13You
boasted against me and spoke against
me without restraint, and I heard it.
14This is what the Sovereign LORD says:
While the whole earth rejoices, I will
make you desolate. 15Because you rejoiced when the inheritance of the
house of Israel became desolate, that is
how I will treat you. You will be desolate, O Mount Seir, you and all of
Edom. Then they will know that I am
the LORD.' "

NEW TESTAMENT READING
James 2:1–26

Favouritism Forbidden

2 My brothers, as believers in our
glorious Lord Jesus Christ, don't
show favouritism. 2Suppose a man
comes into your meeting wearing a gold
ring and fine clothes, and a poor man in
shabby clothes also comes in. 3If you
show special attention to the man wearing fine clothes and say, "Here's a good
seat for you," but say to the poor man,
"You stand there" or "Sit on the floor
by my feet," 4have you not discrimin-
ated among yourselves and become
judges with evil thoughts?

5Listen, my dear brothers: Has not
God chosen those who are poor in the
eyes of the world to be rich in faith and
to inherit the kingdom he promised

those who love him? 6But you have insulted the poor. Is it not the rich who are exploiting you? Are they not the ones who are dragging you into court? 7Are they not the ones who are slandering the noble name of him to whom you belong?

8If you really keep the royal law found in Scripture, "Love your neighbour as yourself," you are doing right. 9But if you show favouritism, you sin and are convicted by the law as lawbreakers. 10For whoever keeps the whole law and yet stumbles at just one point is guilty of breaking all of it. 11For he who said, "Do not commit adultery," also said, "Do not murder." If you do not commit adultery but do commit murder, you have become a lawbreaker.

12Speak and act as those who are going to be judged by the law that gives freedom, 13because judgment without mercy will be shown to anyone who has not been merciful. Mercy triumphs over judgment!

Faith and Deeds

14What good is it, my brothers, if a man claims to have faith but has no deeds? Can such faith save him? 15Suppose a brother or sister is without clothes and daily food. 16If one of you says to him, "Go, I wish you well; keep warm and well fed," but does nothing about his physical needs, what good is it? 17In the same way, faith by itself, if it is not accompanied by action, is dead.

18But someone will say, "You have faith; I have deeds."

Show me your faith without deeds, and I will show you my faith by what I do. 19You believe that there is one God. Good! Even the demons believe that —and shudder.

20You foolish man, do you want evidence that faith without deeds is useless? 21Was not our ancestor Abraham considered righteous for what he did when he offered his son Isaac on the altar? 22You see that his faith and his actions were working together, and his faith was made complete by what he did. 23And the scripture was fulfilled that says, "Abraham believed God, and it was credited to him as righteousness," and he was called God's friend. 24You see that a person is justified by what he does and not by faith alone.

25In the same way, was not even Rahab the prostitute considered righteous for what she did when she gave lodging to the spies and sent them off in a different direction? 26As the body without the spirit is dead, so faith without deeds is dead.

READING FROM PSALMS

Psalm 128:1–6

A song of ascents.

1Blessed are all who fear the LORD,
who walk in his ways.
2You will eat the fruit of your labour;
blessings and prosperity will be
yours.
3Your wife will be like a fruitful vine
within your house;
your sons will be like olive shoots
round your table.
4Thus is the man blessed
who fears the LORD.

5May the LORD bless you from Zion
all the days of your life;
may you see the prosperity of
Jerusalem,
6 and may you live to see your
children's children.

Peace be upon Israel.

DAY 323

NOVEMBER 19

OLD TESTAMENT READING
Ezekiel 36:1–37:28

A Prophecy to the Mountains of Israel

36 “Son of man, prophesy to the
mountains of Israel and say, ‘O
mountains of Israel, hear the word of
the LORD. 2This is what the Sovereign
LORD says: The enemy said of you,
“Aha! The ancient heights have become our possession.”’ 3Therefore
prophesy and say, ‘This is what the
Sovereign LORD says: Because they ravaged and hounded you from every side
so that you became the possession of the
rest of the nations and the object of
people’s malicious talk and slander,
4therefore, O mountains of Israel, hear
the word of the Sovereign LORD: This is
what the Sovereign LORD says to the
mountains and hills, to the ravines and
valleys, to the desolate ruins and the
deserted towns that have been plundered and ridiculed by the rest of the
nations around you—5this is what the
Sovereign LORD says: In my burning
zeal I have spoken against the rest of the
nations, and against Edom, for with
glee and with malice in their hearts they
made my land their own possession so
that they might plunder its pasture-
land.’ 6Therefore prophesy concerning
the land of Israel and say to the mountains and hills, to the ravines and valleys: ‘This is what the Sovereign LORD
says: I speak in my jealous wrath because you have suffered the scorn of the
nations. 7Therefore this is what the
Sovereign LORD says: I swear with uplifted hand that the nations around you
will also suffer scorn.

8“ ‘But you, O mountains of Israel,
will produce branches and fruit for my
people Israel, for they will soon come
home. 9I am concerned for you and will
look on you with favour; you will be
ploughed and sown, 10and I will multiply the number of people upon you,
even the whole house of Israel. The
towns will be inhabited and the ruins
rebuilt. 11I will increase the number of
men and animals upon you, and they
will be fruitful and become numerous. I
will settle people on you as in the past
and will make you prosper more than
before. Then you will know that I am
the LORD. 12I will cause people, my
people Israel, to walk upon you. They
will possess you, and you will be
their inheritance; you will never again
deprive them of their children.

13“ ‘This is what the Sovereign LORD
says: Because people say to you, “You
devour men and deprive your nation of
its children,” 14therefore you will no
longer devour men or make your nation
childless, declares the Sovereign LORD.
15No longer will I make you hear the
taunts of the nations, and no longer will
you suffer the scorn of the peoples or
cause your nation to fall, declares the
Sovereign LORD.’ ”

16Again the word of the LORD came
to me: 17“Son of man, when the people
of Israel were living in their own land,
they defiled it by their conduct and their
actions. Their conduct was like a
woman’s monthly uncleanness in my
sight. 18So I poured out my wrath on
them because they had shed blood in
the land and because they had defiled it
with their idols. 19I dispersed them
among the nations, and they were scattered through the countries; I judged
them according to their conduct and
their actions. 20And wherever they went
among the nations they profaned my
holy name, for it was said of them,
‘These are the LORD’s people, and yet
they had to leave his land.’ 21I had concern for my holy name, which the house
of Israel profaned among the nations
where they had gone.

22“Therefore say to the house of

Israel, 'This is what the Sovereign LORD says: It is not for your sake, O house of Israel, that I am going to do these things, but for the sake of my holy name, which you have profaned among the nations where you have gone. 23 I will show the holiness of my great name, which has been profaned among the nations, the name you have profaned among them. Then the nations will know that I am the LORD, declares the Sovereign LORD, when I show myself holy through you before their eyes.

24 " 'For I will take you out of the nations; I will gather you from all the countries and bring you back into your own land. 25 I will sprinkle clean water on you, and you will be clean; I will cleanse you from all your impurities and from all your idols. 26 I will give you a new heart and put a new spirit in you; I will remove from you your heart of stone and give you a heart of flesh. 27 And I will put my Spirit in you and move you to follow my decrees and be careful to keep my laws. 28 You will live in the land I gave your forefathers; you will be my people, and I will be your God. 29 I will save you from all your uncleanness. I will call for the corn and make it plentiful and will not bring famine upon you. 30 I will increase the fruit of the trees and the crops of the field, so that you will no longer suffer disgrace among the nations because of famine. 31 Then you will remember your evil ways and wicked deeds, and you will loathe yourselves for your sins and detestable practices. 32 I want you to know that I am not doing this for your sake, declares the Sovereign LORD. Be ashamed and disgraced for your conduct, O house of Israel!

33 " 'This is what the Sovereign LORD says: On the day I cleanse you from all your sins, I will resettle your towns, and the ruins will be rebuilt. 34 The desolate land will be cultivated instead of lying desolate in the sight of all who pass through it. 35 They will say, "This land that was laid waste has become like the garden of Eden; the cities that were lying in ruins, desolate and destroyed, are now fortified and inhabited." 36 Then the nations around you that remain will know that I the LORD have rebuilt what was destroyed and have replanted what was desolate. I the LORD have spoken, and I will do it.'

37 "This is what the Sovereign LORD says: Once again I will yield to the plea of the house of Israel and do this for them: I will make their people as numerous as sheep, 38 as numerous as the flocks for offerings at Jerusalem during her appointed feasts. So will the ruined cities be filled with flocks of people. Then they will know that I am the LORD."

The Valley of Dry Bones

37 The hand of the LORD was upon me, and he brought me out by the Spirit of the LORD and set me in the middle of a valley; it was full of bones. 2 He led me to and fro among them, and I saw a great many bones on the floor of the valley, bones that were very dry. 3 He asked me, "Son of man, can these bones live?"

I said, "O Sovereign LORD, you alone know."

4 Then he said to me, "Prophesy to these bones and say to them, 'Dry bones, hear the word of the LORD! 5 This is what the Sovereign LORD says to these bones: I will make breath enter you, and you will come to life. 6 I will attach tendons to you and make flesh come upon you and cover you with skin; I will put breath in you, and you will come to life. Then you will know that I am the LORD.' "

7 So I prophesied as I was commanded. And as I was prophesying, there was a noise, a rattling sound, and the bones came together, bone to bone. 8 I looked, and tendons and flesh appeared on them and skin covered them, but there was no breath in them.

9 Then he said to me, "Prophesy to the breath; prophesy, son of man, and say to it, 'This is what the Sovereign

LORD says: Come from the four winds,
O breath, and breathe into these slain,
that they may live.'" 10So I prophesied
as he commanded me, and breath entered them; they came to life and stood
up on their feet—a vast army.
11Then he said to me: "Son of man,
these bones are the whole house of
Israel. They say, 'Our bones are dried
up and our hope is gone; we are cut off.'
12Therefore prophesy and say to them:
'This is what the Sovereign LORD says:
O my people, I am going to open your
graves and bring you up from them; I
will bring you back to the land of Israel.
13Then you, my people, will know that I
am the LORD, when I open your graves
and bring you up from them. 14I will put
my Spirit in you and you will live, and I
will settle you in your own land. Then
you will know that I the LORD have
spoken, and I have done it, declares the
LORD.'"

One Nation Under One King

15The word of the LORD came to me:
16"Son of man, take a stick of wood and
write on it, 'Belonging to Judah and the
Israelites associated with him.' Then
take another stick of wood, and write
on it, 'Ephraim's stick, belonging to
Joseph and all the house of Israel associated with him.' 17Join them together
into one stick so that they will become
one in your hand.
18"When your countrymen ask you,
'Won't you tell us what you mean by
this?' 19say to them, 'This is what the
Sovereign LORD says: I am going to take
the stick of Joseph—which is in
Ephraim's hand—and of the Israelite
tribes associated with him, and join it to
Judah's stick, making them a single
stick of wood, and they will become one
in my hand.' 20Hold before their eyes
the sticks you have written on 21and say
to them, 'This is what the Sovereign
LORD says: I will take the Israelites out
of the nations where they have gone. I
will gather them from all around and
bring them back into their own land. 22I
will make them one nation in the land,
on the mountains of Israel. There will
be one king over all of them and they
will never again be two nations or be
divided into two kingdoms. 23They will
no longer defile themselves with their
idols and vile images or with any of their
offences, for I will save them from all
their sinful backsliding, and I will
cleanse them. They will be my people,
and I will be their God.
24"'My servant David will be king
over them, and they will all have one
shepherd. They will follow my laws and
be careful to keep my decrees. 25They
will live in the land I gave to my servant
Jacob, the land where your fathers
lived. They and their children and their
children's children will live there for
ever, and David my servant will be their
prince for ever. 26I will make a covenant
of peace with them; it will be an everlasting covenant. I will establish them
and increase their numbers, and I will
put my sanctuary among them for ever.
27My dwelling-place will be with them; I
will be their God, and they will be my
people. 28Then the nations will know
that I the LORD make Israel holy, when
my sanctuary is among them for ever.'"

NEW TESTAMENT READING
James 3:1–18

Taming the Tongue

3 Not many of you should presume
to be teachers, my brothers, because you know that we who teach will
be judged more strictly. 2We all stumble
in many ways. If anyone is never at fault
in what he says, he is a perfect man, able
to keep his whole body in check.
3When we put bits into the mouths of
horses to make them obey us, we can
turn the whole animal. 4Or take ships as
an example. Although they are so large
and are driven by strong winds, they are
steered by a very small rudder wherever
the pilot wants to go. 5Likewise the

tongue is a small part of the body, but it
makes great boasts. Consider what a
great forest is set on fire by a small
spark. 6The tongue also is a fire, a world
of evil among the parts of the body. It
corrupts the whole person, sets the
whole course of his life on fire, and is
itself set on fire by hell.
7All kinds of animals, birds, reptiles
and creatures of the sea are being tamed
and have been tamed by man, 8but no
man can tame the tongue. It is a restless
evil, full of deadly poison.
9With the tongue we praise our Lord
and Father, and with it we curse men,
who have been made in God's likeness.
10Out of the same mouth come praise
and cursing. My brothers, this should
not be. 11Can both fresh water and salt
water flow from the same spring? 12My
brothers, can a fig-tree bear olives, or a
grapevine bear figs? Neither can a salt
spring produce fresh water.

Two Kinds of Wisdom

13Who is wise and understanding
among you? Let him show it by his good
life, by deeds done in the humility that
comes from wisdom. 14But if you harbour bitter envy and selfish ambition in
your hearts, do not boast about it or
deny the truth. 15Such "wisdom" does
not come down from heaven but is
earthly, unspiritual, of the devil. 16For
where you have envy and selfish ambition, there you find disorder and
every evil practice.
17But the wisdom that comes from
heaven is first of all pure; then peace-
loving, considerate, submissive, full of
mercy and good fruit, impartial and sincere. 18Peacemakers who sow in peace
raise a harvest of righteousness.

READING FROM PSALMS
Psalm 129:1–8

A song of ascents.

1They have greatly oppressed me from
my youth—
let Israel say—
2they have greatly oppressed me from
my youth,
but they have not gained the
victory over me.
3Ploughmen have ploughed my back
and made their furrows long.
4But the LORD is righteous;
he has cut me free from the cords
of the wicked.

5May all who hate Zion
be turned back in shame.
6May they be like grass on the roof,
which withers before it can grow;
7with it the reaper cannot fill his
hands,
nor the one who gathers fill his
arms.
8May those who pass by not say,
"The blessing of the LORD be upon
you;
we bless you in the name of the
LORD."

DAY 324

NOVEMBER 20

OLD TESTAMENT READING
Ezekiel 38:1–39:29

A Prophecy Against Gog

38 The word of the LORD came to
me: 2"Son of man, set your face
against Gog, of the land of Magog, the
chief prince of Meshech and Tubal;
prophesy against him 3and say: 'This is
what the Sovereign LORD says: I am
against you, O Gog, chief prince of
Meshech and Tubal. 4I will turn you
around, put hooks in your jaws and
bring you out with your whole army
—your horses, your horsemen fully
armed, and a great horde with large and
small shields, all of them brandishing
their swords. 5Persia, Cush and Put will
be with them, all with shields and helmets, 6also Gomer with all its troops,
and Beth Togarmah from the far north
with all its troops—the many nations
with you.
7" 'Get ready; be prepared, you and
all the hordes gathered about you, and
take command of them. 8After many
days you will be called to arms. In future
years you will invade a land that has
recovered from war, whose people were
gathered from many nations to the
mountains of Israel, which had long
been desolate. They had been brought
out from the nations, and now all of
them live in safety. 9You and all your
troops and the many nations with you
will go up, advancing like a storm; you
will be like a cloud covering the land.
10" 'This is what the Sovereign LORD
says: On that day thoughts will come
into your mind and you will devise an
evil scheme. 11You will say, "I will invade a land of unwalled villages; I will
attack a peaceful and unsuspecting people—all of them living without walls
and without gates and bars. 12I will
plunder and loot and turn my hand
against the resettled ruins and the people gathered from the nations, rich in
livestock and goods, living at the centre
of the land." 13Sheba and Dedan and
the merchants of Tarshish and all her
villages will say to you, "Have you come
to plunder? Have you gathered your
hordes to loot, to carry off silver and
gold, to take away livestock and goods
and to seize much plunder?" '
14"Therefore, son of man, prophesy
and say to Gog: 'This is what the
Sovereign LORD says: In that day, when
my people Israel are living in safety, will
you not take notice of it? 15You will
come from your place in the far north,
you and many nations with you, all of
them riding on horses, a great horde, a
mighty army. 16You will advance
against my people Israel like a cloud
that covers the land. In days to come, O
Gog, I will bring you against my land, so
that the nations may know me when I
show myself holy through you before
their eyes.
17" 'This is what the Sovereign LORD
says: Are you not the one I spoke of
in former days by my servants the
prophets of Israel? At that time they
prophesied for years that I would bring
you against them. 18This is what will
happen in that day: When Gog attacks
the land of Israel, my hot anger will be
aroused, declares the Sovereign LORD.
19In my zeal and fiery wrath I declare
that at that time there shall be a great
earthquake in the land of Israel. 20The
fish of the sea, the birds of the air, the
beasts of the field, every creature that
moves along the ground, and all the
people on the face of the earth will
tremble at my presence. The mountains
will be overturned, the cliffs will crum-
ble and every wall will fall to the
ground. 21I will summon a sword against
Gog on all my mountains, declares the
Sovereign LORD. Every man's sword

will be against his brother. 22I will execute judgment upon him with plague
and bloodshed; I will pour down torrents of rain, hailstones and burning
sulphur on him and on his troops and on
the many nations with him. 23And so I
will show my greatness and my holiness,
and I will make myself known in the
sight of many nations. Then they will
know that I am the LORD.'

39 "Son of man, prophesy against
Gog and say: 'This is what the
Sovereign LORD says: I am against you,
O Gog, chief prince of Meshech and
Tubal. 2I will turn you around and drag
you along. I will bring you from the far
north and send you against the mountains of Israel. 3Then I will strike your
bow from your left hand and make your
arrows drop from your right hand. 4On
the mountains of Israel you will fall, you
and all your troops and the nations with
you. I will give you as food to all kinds of
carrion birds and to the wild animals.
5You will fall in the open field, for I
have spoken, declares the Sovereign
LORD. 6I will send fire on Magog and on
those who live in safety in the coastlands, and they will know that I am the
LORD.

7" 'I will make known my holy name
among my people Israel. I will no longer
let my holy name be profaned, and the
nations will know that I the LORD am
the Holy One in Israel. 8It is coming! It
will surely take place, declares the
Sovereign LORD. This is the day I have
spoken of.

9" 'Then those who live in the towns
of Israel will go out and use the weapons
for fuel and burn them up—the small
and large shields, the bows and arrows,
the war clubs and spears. For seven
years they will use them for fuel. 10They
will not need to gather wood from the
fields or cut it from the forests, because
they will use the weapons for fuel. And
they will plunder those who plundered
them and loot those who looted them,
declares the Sovereign LORD.

11" 'On that day I will give Gog a
burial place in Israel, in the valley of
those who travel east towards the Sea. It
will block the way of travellers, because
Gog and all his hordes will be buried
there. So it will be called the Valley of
Hamon Gog.

12" 'For seven months the house of
Israel will be burying them in order to
cleanse the land. 13All the people of the
land will bury them, and the day I am
glorified will be a memorable day for
them, declares the Sovereign LORD.

14" 'Men will be regularly employed
to cleanse the land. Some will go
throughout the land and, in addition to
them, others will bury those that remain
on the ground. At the end of the seven
months they will begin their search.
15As they go through the land and one
of them sees a human bone, he will set
up a marker beside it until the grave-
diggers have buried it in the Valley of
Hamon Gog. 16(Also a town called
Hamonah will be there.) And so they
will cleanse the land.'

17"Son of man, this is what the
Sovereign LORD says: Call out to every
kind of bird and all the wild animals:
'Assemble and come together from all
around to the sacrifice I am preparing
for you, the great sacrifice on the mountains of Israel. There you will eat flesh
and drink blood. 18You will eat the flesh
of mighty men and drink the blood of
the princes of the earth as if they were
rams and lambs, goats and bulls—all of
them fattened animals from Bashan.
19At the sacrifice I am preparing for
you, you will eat fat till you are glutted
and drink blood till you are drunk. 20At
my table you will eat your fill of horses
and riders, mighty men and soldiers of
every kind,' declares the Sovereign
LORD.

21"I will display my glory among the
nations, and all the nations will see the
punishment I inflict and the hand I lay
upon them. 22From that day forward the
house of Israel will know that I am the
LORD their God. 23And the nations will
know that the people of Israel went into
exile for their sin, because they were
unfaithful to me. So I hid my face from

them and handed them over to their
enemies, and they all fell by the sword.
24I dealt with them according to their
uncleanness and their offences, and I
hid my face from them.
25"Therefore this is what the
Sovereign LORD says: I will now bring
Jacob back from captivity and will have
compassion on all the people of Israel,
and I will be zealous for my holy name.
26They will forget their shame and all
the unfaithfulness they showed towards
me when they lived in safety in their
land with no-one to make them afraid.
27When I have brought them back from
the nations and have gathered them
from the countries of their enemies, I
will show myself holy through them in
the sight of many nations. 28Then they
will know that I am the LORD their God,
for though I sent them into exile among
the nations, I will gather them to their
own land, not leaving any behind. 29I
will no longer hide my face from them,
for I will pour out my Spirit on the house
of Israel, declares the Sovereign
LORD."

NEW TESTAMENT READING
James 4:1–17

Submit Yourselves to God

4 What causes fights and quarrels
among you? Don't they come from
your desires that battle within you?
2You want something but don't get it.
You kill and covet, but you cannot have
what you want. You quarrel and fight.
You do not have, because you do not
ask God. 3When you ask, you do not
receive, because you ask with wrong
motives, that you may spend what you
get on your pleasures.
4You adulterous people, don't you
know that friendship with the world is
hatred towards God? Anyone who
chooses to be a friend of the world
becomes an enemy of God. 5Or do you
think Scripture says without reason that
the spirit he caused to live in us envies
intensely? 6But he gives us more grace.
That is why Scripture says:

"God opposes the proud
but gives grace to the humble."

7Submit yourselves, then, to God.
Resist the devil, and he will flee from
you. 8Come near to God and he will
come near to you. Wash your hands,
you sinners, and purify your hearts, you
double-minded. 9Grieve, mourn and
wail. Change your laughter to mourning
and your joy to gloom. 10Humble
yourselves before the Lord, and he will
lift you up.
11Brothers, do not slander one
another. Anyone who speaks against
his brother or judges him speaks against
the law and judges it. When you judge
the law, you are not keeping it, but
sitting in judgment on it. 12There is only
one Lawgiver and Judge, the one who is
able to save and destroy. But you—who
are you to judge your neighbour?

Boasting About Tomorrow

13Now listen, you who say, "Today or
tomorrow we will go to this or that city,
spend a year there, carry on business
and make money." 14Why, you do not
even know what will happen tomorrow.
What is your life? You are a mist that
appears for a little while and then
vanishes. 15Instead, you ought to say,
"If it is the Lord's will, we will live and
do this or that." 16As it is, you boast and
brag. All such boasting is evil. 17Any-
one, then, who knows the good he
ought to do and doesn't do it, sins.

READING FROM PROVERBS
Proverbs 28:7–17

7He who keeps the law is a discerning
son,
but a companion of gluttons
disgraces his father.

[8]He who increases his wealth by
exorbitant interest
amasses it for another, who will be
kind to the poor.

[9]If anyone turns a deaf ear to the law,
even his prayers are detestable.

[10]He who leads the upright along an
evil path
will fall into his own trap,
but the blameless will receive a
good inheritance.

[11]A rich man may be wise in his own
eyes,
but a poor man who has
discernment sees through him.

[12]When the righteous triumph, there is
great elation;
but when the wicked rise to power,
men go into hiding.

[13]He who conceals his sins does not
prosper,
but whoever confesses and
renounces them finds mercy.

[14]Blessed is the man who always fears
the LORD,
but he who hardens his heart falls
into trouble.

[15]Like a roaring lion or a charging bear
is a wicked man ruling over a
helpless people.

[16]A tyrannical ruler lacks judgment,
but he who hates ill-gotten gain will
enjoy a long life.

[17]A man tormented by the guilt of
murder
will be a fugitive till death;
let no-one support him.

NOVEMBER 21

DAY 325

OLD TESTAMENT READING
Ezekiel 40:1–49

The New Temple Area

40 In the twenty-fifth year of our
exile, at the beginning of the
year, on the tenth of the month, in the
fourteenth year after the fall of the city
—on that very day the hand of the LORD
was upon me and he took me there. [2]In
visions of God he took me to the land of
Israel and set me on a very high mountain, on whose south side were some
buildings that looked like a city. [3]He
took me there, and I saw a man whose
appearance was like bronze; he was
standing in the gateway with a linen
cord and a measuring rod in his hand.
[4]The man said to me, "Son of man, look
with your eyes and hear with your ears
and pay attention to everything I am
going to show you, for that is why you
have been brought here. Tell the house
of Israel everything you see."

The East Gate to the Outer Court

[5]I saw a wall completely surrounding
the temple area. The length of the
measuring rod in the man's hand was six
long cubits, each of which was a cubit
and a handbreadth. He measured the
wall; it was one measuring rod thick and
one rod high.

[6]Then he went to the gate facing east.
He climbed its steps and measured the
threshold of the gate; it was one rod
deep. [7]The alcoves for the guards were
one rod long and one rod wide, and the
projecting walls between the alcoves
were five cubits thick. And the
threshold of the gate next to the portico
facing the temple was one rod deep.

8Then he measured the portico of the gateway; 9it was eight cubits deep and its jambs were two cubits thick. The portico of the gateway faced the temple.

10Inside the east gate were three alcoves on each side; the three had the same measurements, and the faces of the projecting walls on each side had the same measurements. 11Then he measured the width of the entrance to the gateway; it was ten cubits and its length was thirteen cubits. 12In front of each alcove was a wall one cubit high, and the alcoves were six cubits square. 13Then he measured the gateway from the top of the rear wall of one alcove to the top of the opposite one; the distance was twenty-five cubits from one parapet opening to the opposite one. 14He measured along the faces of the projecting walls all around the inside of the gateway—sixty cubits. The measurement was up to the portico facing the courtyard. 15The distance from the entrance of the gateway to the far end of its portico was fifty cubits. 16The alcoves and the projecting walls inside the gateway were surmounted by narrow parapet openings all round, as was the portico; the openings all round faced inward. The faces of the projecting walls were decorated with palm trees.

The Outer Court

17Then he brought me into the outer court. There I saw some rooms and a pavement that had been constructed all round the court; there were thirty rooms along the pavement. 18It abutted the sides of the gateways and was as wide as they were long; this was the lower pavement. 19Then he measured the distance from the inside of the lower gateway to the outside of the inner court; it was a hundred cubits on the east side as well as on the north.

The North Gate

20Then he measured the length and width of the gate facing north, leading into the outer court. 21Its alcoves—three on each side—its projecting walls and its portico had the same measurements as those of the first gateway. It was fifty cubits long and twenty-five cubits wide. 22Its openings, its portico and its palm tree decorations had the same measurements as those of the gate facing east. Seven steps led up to it, with its portico opposite them. 23There was a gate to the inner court facing the north gate, just as there was on the east. He measured from one gate to the opposite one; it was a hundred cubits.

The South Gate

24Then he led me to the south side and I saw a gate facing south. He measured its jambs and its portico, and they had the same measurements as the others. 25The gateway and its portico had narrow openings all round, like the openings of the others. It was fifty cubits long and twenty-five cubits wide. 26Seven steps led up to it, with its portico opposite them; it had palm tree decorations on the faces of the projecting walls on each side. 27The inner court also had a gate facing south, and he measured from this gate to the outer gate on the south side; it was a hundred cubits.

Gates to the Inner Court

28Then he brought me into the inner court through the south gate, and he measured the south gate; it had the same measurements as the others. 29Its alcoves, its projecting walls and its portico had the same measurements as the others. The gateway and its portico had openings all round. It was fifty cubits long and twenty-five cubits wide. 30(The porticoes of the gateways around the inner court were twenty-five cubits wide and five cubits deep.) 31Its portico faced the outer court; palm trees decorated its jambs, and eight steps led up to it.

32Then he brought me to the inner court on the east side, and he measured

the gateway; it had the same measurements as the others. 33Its alcoves, its
projecting walls and its portico had the
same measurements as the others. The
gateway and its portico had openings
all round. It was fifty cubits long and
twenty-five cubits wide. 34Its portico
faced the outer court; palm trees
decorated the jambs on either side, and
eight steps led up to it.
35Then he brought me to the north
gate and measured it. It had the same
measurements as the others, 36as did its
alcoves, its projecting walls and its portico, and it had openings all round. It
was fifty cubits long and twenty-five
cubits wide. 37Its portico faced the outer
court; palm trees decorated the jambs
on either side, and eight steps led up to
it.

The Rooms for Preparing Sacrifices

38A room with a doorway was by the
portico in each of the inner gateways,
where the burnt offerings were washed.
39In the portico of the gateway were two
tables on each side, on which the burnt
offerings, sin offerings and guilt offerings were slaughtered. 40By the outside
wall of the portico of the gateway, near
the steps at the entrance to the north
gateway were two tables, and on the
other side of the steps were two tables.
41So there were four tables on one side
of the gateway and four on the other
—eight tables in all—on which the sacrifices were slaughtered. 42There were
also four tables of dressed stone for the
burnt offerings, each a cubit and a half
long, a cubit and a half wide and a cubit
high. On them were placed the utensils
for slaughtering the burnt offerings and
the other sacrifices. 43And double-
pronged hooks, each a handbreadth
long, were attached to the wall all
around. The tables were for the flesh of
the offerings.

Rooms for the Priests

44Outside the inner gate, within the
inner court, were two rooms, one at the
side of the north gate and facing south,
and another at the side of the south gate
and facing north. 45He said to me, "The
room facing south is for the priests who
have charge of the temple, 46and the
room facing north is for the priests who
have charge of the altar. These are the
sons of Zadok, who are the only Levites
who may draw near to the LORD to
minister before him."
47Then he measured the court: It was
square—a hundred cubits long and a
hundred cubits wide. And the altar was
in front of the temple.

The Temple

48He brought me to the portico of the
temple and measured the jambs of the
portico; they were five cubits wide on
either side. The width of the entrance
was fourteen cubits and its projecting
walls were three cubits wide on either
side. 49The portico was twenty cubits
wide, and twelve cubits from front to
back. It was reached by a flight of stairs,
and there were pillars on each side of
the jambs.

NEW TESTAMENT READING
James 5:1–20

Warning to Rich Oppressors

5 Now listen, you rich people, weep
and wail because of the misery that
is coming upon you. 2Your wealth has
rotted, and moths have eaten your
clothes. 3Your gold and silver are cor-
roded. Their corrosion will testify
against you and eat your flesh like fire.
You have hoarded wealth in the last
days. 4Look! The wages you failed to
pay the workmen who mowed your
fields are crying out against you. The
cries of the harvesters have reached the
ears of the Lord Almighty. 5You have
lived on earth in luxury and self-
indulgence. You have fattened yourselves in the day of slaughter. 6You

have condemned and murdered innocent men, who were not opposing you.

Patience in Suffering

7Be patient, then, brothers, until the
Lord's coming. See how the farmer
waits for the land to yield its valuable
crop and how patient he is for the
autumn and spring rains. 8You too, be
patient and stand firm, because the
Lord's coming is near. 9Don't grumble
against each other, brothers, or you will
be judged. The Judge is standing at the
door!

10Brothers, as an example of patience
in the face of suffering, take the
prophets who spoke in the name of the
Lord. 11As you know, we consider
blessed those who have persevered.
You have heard of Job's perseverance
and have seen what the Lord finally
brought about. The Lord is full of compassion and mercy.

12Above all, my brothers, do not
swear—not by heaven or by earth or
by anything else. Let your "Yes" be
yes, and your "No", no, or you will be
condemned.

The Prayer of Faith

13Is any one of you in trouble? He
should pray. Is anyone happy? Let him
sing songs of praise. 14Is any one of you
sick? He should call the elders of the
church to pray over him and anoint him
with oil in the name of the Lord. 15And
the prayer offered in faith will make the
sick person well; the Lord will raise him
up. If he has sinned, he will be forgiven.
16Therefore confess your sins to each
other and pray for each other so that
you may be healed. The prayer of a
righteous man is powerful and effective.

17Elijah was a man just like us. He
prayed earnestly that it would not rain,
and it did not rain on the land for three
and a half years. 18Again he prayed, and
the heavens gave rain, and the earth
produced its crops.

19My brothers, if one of you should
wander from the truth and someone
should bring him back, 20remember
this: Whoever turns a sinner from the
error of his way will save him from
death and cover over a multitude of
sins.

READING FROM PSALMS

Psalm 130:1–8

A song of ascents.

1Out of the depths I cry to you, O
LORD;
2 O Lord, hear my voice.
Let your ears be attentive
to my cry for mercy.

3If you, O LORD, kept a record of sins,
O Lord, who could stand?
4But with you there is forgiveness;
therefore you are feared.

5I wait for the LORD, my soul waits,
and in his word I put my hope.
6My soul waits for the Lord
more than watchmen wait for the
morning,
more than watchmen wait for the
morning.

7O Israel, put your hope in the LORD,
for with the LORD is unfailing love
and with him is full redemption.
8He himself will redeem Israel
from all their sins.

NOVEMBER 22

DAY 326

OLD TESTAMENT READING

Ezekiel 41:1–42:20

41 Then the man brought me to the outer sanctuary and measured the jambs; the width of the jambs was six cubits on each side. 2The entrance was ten cubits wide, and the projecting walls on each side of it were five cubits wide. He also measured the outer sanctuary; it was forty cubits long and twenty cubits wide.

3Then he went into the inner sanctuary and measured the jambs of the entrance; each was two cubits wide. The entrance was six cubits wide, and the projecting walls on each side of it were seven cubits wide. 4And he measured the length of the inner sanctuary; it was twenty cubits, and its width was twenty cubits across the end of the outer sanctuary. He said to me, "This is the Most Holy Place."

5Then he measured the wall of the temple; it was six cubits thick, and each side room round the temple was four cubits wide. 6The side rooms were on three levels, one above another, thirty on each level. There were ledges all round the wall of the temple to serve as supports for the side rooms, so that the supports were not inserted into the wall of the temple. 7The side rooms all round the temple were wider at each successive level. The structure surrounding the temple was built in ascending stages, so that the rooms widened as one went upward. A stairway went up from the lowest floor to the top floor through the middle floor.

8I saw that the temple had a raised base all round it, forming the foundation of the side rooms. It was the length of the rod, six long cubits. 9The outer wall of the side rooms was five cubits thick. The open area between the side rooms of the temple 10and the ⌞priests'⌟ rooms was twenty cubits wide all round the temple. 11There were entrances to the side rooms from the open area, one on the north and another on the south; and the base adjoining the open area was five cubits wide all round.

12The building facing the temple courtyard on the west side was seventy cubits wide. The wall of the building was five cubits thick all round, and its length was ninety cubits.

13Then he measured the temple; it was a hundred cubits long, and the temple courtyard and the building with its walls were also a hundred cubits long. 14The width of the temple courtyard on the east, including the front of the temple, was a hundred cubits.

15Then he measured the length of the building facing the courtyard at the rear of the temple, including its galleries on each side; it was a hundred cubits.

The outer sanctuary, the inner sanctuary and the portico facing the court, 16as well as the thresholds and the narrow windows and galleries round the three of them—everything beyond and including the threshold was covered with wood. The floor, the wall up to the windows, and the windows were covered. 17In the space above the outside of the entrance to the inner sanctuary and on the walls at regular intervals all round the inner and outer sanctuary 18were carved cherubim and palm trees. Palm trees alternated with cherubim. Each cherub had two faces: 19the face of a man towards the palm tree on one side and the face of a lion towards the palm tree on the other. They were carved all round the whole temple. 20From the floor to the area above the entrance, cherubim and palm trees were carved on the wall of the outer sanctuary.

21The outer sanctuary had a rectangular door-frame, and the one at the front of the Most Holy Place was similar. 22There was a wooden altar three cubits high and two cubits square; its corners, its base and its sides were of wood. The man said to me, "This is the table that is before the LORD." 23Both the outer sanctuary and the Most Holy Place had double doors. 24Each door had two leaves—two hinged leaves for each door. 25And on the doors of the outer sanctuary were carved cherubim and palm trees like those carved on the walls, and there was a wooden overhang on the front of the portico. 26On the side walls of the portico were narrow windows with palm trees carved on each side. The side rooms of the temple also had overhangs.

Rooms for the Priests

42 Then the man led me northward into the outer court and brought me to the rooms opposite the temple courtyard and opposite the outer wall on the north side. 2The building whose door faced north was a hundred cubits long and fifty cubits wide. 3Both in the section twenty cubits from the inner court and in the section opposite the pavement of the outer court, gallery faced gallery at the three levels. 4In front of the rooms was an inner passageway ten cubits wide and a hundred cubits long. Their doors were on the north. 5Now the upper rooms were narrower, for the galleries took more space from them than from the rooms on the lower and middle floors of the building. 6The rooms on the third floor had no pillars, as the courts had; so they were smaller in floor space than those on the lower and middle floors. 7There was an outer wall parallel to the rooms and the outer court; it extended in front of the rooms for fifty cubits. 8While the row of rooms on the side next to the outer court was fifty cubits long, the row on the side nearest the sanctuary was a hundred cubits long. 9The lower rooms had an entrance on the east side as one enters them from the outer court.

10On the south side along the length of the wall of the outer court, adjoining the temple courtyard and opposite the outer wall, were rooms 11with a passageway in front of them. These were like the rooms on the north; they had the same length and width, with similar exits and dimensions. Similar to the doorways on the north 12were the doorways of the rooms on the south. There was a doorway at the beginning of the passageway that was parallel to the corresponding wall extending eastward, by which one enters the rooms.

13Then he said to me, "The north and south rooms facing the temple courtyard are the priests' rooms, where the priests who approach the LORD will eat the most holy offerings. There they will put the most holy offerings—the grain offerings, the sin offerings and the guilt offerings—for the place is holy. 14Once the priests enter the holy precincts, they are not to go into the outer court until they leave behind the garments in which they minister, for these are holy. They are to put on other clothes before they go near the places that are for the people."

15When he had finished measuring what was inside the temple area, he led me out by the east gate and measured the area all around: 16He measured the east side with the measuring rod; it was five hundred cubits. 17He measured the north side; it was five hundred cubits by the measuring rod. 18He measured the south side; it was five hundred cubits by the measuring rod. 19Then he turned to the west side and measured; it was five hundred cubits by the measuring rod. 20So he measured the area on all four sides. It had a wall round it, five hundred cubits long and five hundred cubits wide, to separate the holy from the common.

NEW TESTAMENT READING

1 Peter 1:1–2:3

1 Peter, an apostle of Jesus Christ,

To God's elect, strangers in the world, scattered throughout Pontus,

Galatia, Cappadocia, Asia and Bithynia, 2who have been chosen according to the foreknowledge of God the
Father, through the sanctifying work of
the Spirit, for obedience to Jesus Christ
and sprinkling by his blood:

Grace and peace be yours in abundance.

Praise to God for a Living Hope

3Praise be to the God and Father of
our Lord Jesus Christ! In his great
mercy he has given us new birth into a
living hope through the resurrection of
Jesus Christ from the dead, 4and into an
inheritance that can never perish, spoil
or fade—kept in heaven for you, 5who
through faith are shielded by God's
power until the coming of the salvation
that is ready to be revealed in the last
time. 6In this you greatly rejoice,
though now for a little while you may
have had to suffer grief in all kinds of
trials. 7These have come so that your
faith—of greater worth than gold,
which perishes even though refined by
fire—may be proved genuine and may
result in praise, glory and honour when
Jesus Christ is revealed. 8Though you
have not seen him, you love him; and
even though you do not see him now,
you believe in him and are filled with an
inexpressible and glorious joy, 9for you
are receiving the goal of your faith, the
salvation of your souls.

10Concerning this salvation, the
prophets, who spoke of the grace that
was to come to you, searched intently
and with the greatest care, 11trying to
find out the time and circumstances to
which the Spirit of Christ in them was
pointing when he predicted the sufferings of Christ and the glories that would
follow. 12It was revealed to them that
they were not serving themselves but
you, when they spoke of the things that
have now been told you by those who
have preached the gospel to you by the
Holy Spirit sent from heaven. Even
angels long to look into these things.

Be Holy

13Therefore, prepare your minds for
action; be self-controlled; set your hope
fully on the grace to be given you when
Jesus Christ is revealed. 14As obedient
children, do not conform to the evil
desires you had when you lived in ignorance. 15But just as he who called you is
holy, so be holy in all you do; 16for it is
written: "Be holy, because I am holy."

17Since you call on a Father who
judges each man's work impartially,
live your lives as strangers here in reverent fear. 18For you know that it was
not with perishable things such as silver
or gold that you were redeemed from
the empty way of life handed down to
you from your forefathers, 19but with
the precious blood of Christ, a lamb
without blemish or defect. 20He was
chosen before the creation of the world,
but was revealed in these last times for
your sake. 21Through him you believe in
God, who raised him from the dead and
glorified him, and so your faith and
hope are in God.

22Now that you have purified
yourselves by obeying the truth so that
you have sincere love for your brothers,
love one another deeply, from the
heart. 23For you have been born again,
not of perishable seed, but of imperishable, through the living and enduring
word of God. 24For,

"All men are like grass,
  and all their glory is like the
    flowers of the field;
the grass withers and the flowers fall,
25 but the word of the Lord stands for
    ever."

And this is the word that was preached
to you.

2 Therefore, rid yourselves of all
malice and all deceit, hypocrisy,
envy, and slander of every kind. 2Like
newborn babies, crave pure spiritual
milk, so that by it you may grow up in
your salvation, 3now that you have
tasted that the Lord is good.

READING FROM PSALMS
Psalm 131:1–3

A song of ascents. Of David.

1My heart is not proud, O LORD,
my eyes are not haughty;
I do not concern myself with great matters
or things too wonderful for me.
2But I have stilled and quietened my soul;
like a weaned child with its mother,
like a weaned child is my soul within me.

3O Israel, put your hope in the LORD
both now and for evermore.

DAY 327

NOVEMBER 23

OLD TESTAMENT READING
Ezekiel 43:1–44:31

The Glory Returns to the Temple

43 Then the man brought me to the
gate facing east, 2and I saw the
glory of the God of Israel coming from
the east. His voice was like the roar of
rushing waters, and the land was radiant
with his glory. 3The vision I saw was like
the vision I had seen when he came to
destroy the city and like the visions I
had seen by the Kebar River, and I fell
face down. 4The glory of the LORD entered the temple through the gate facing
east. 5Then the Spirit lifted me up and
brought me into the inner court, and the
glory of the LORD filled the temple.
6While the man was standing beside
me, I heard someone speaking to me
from inside the temple. 7He said: "Son
of man, this is the place of my throne
and the place for the soles of my feet.
This is where I will live among the
Israelites for ever. The house of Israel
will never again defile my holy name
—neither they nor their kings—by their
prostitution and the lifeless idols of
their kings at their high places. 8When
they placed their threshold next to
my threshold and their doorposts beside
my doorposts, with only a wall between
me and them, they defiled my holy
name by their detestable practices. So I
destroyed them in my anger. 9Now let
them put away from me their prostitution and the lifeless idols of their kings,
and I will live among them for ever.
10"Son of man, describe the temple to
the people of Israel, that they may be
ashamed of their sins. Let them consider the plan, 11and if they are ashamed
of all they have done, make known to
them the design of the temple—its
arrangement, its exits and entrances—
its whole design and all its regulations
and laws. Write these down before
them so that they may be faithful to its
design and follow all its regulations.
12"This is the law of the temple: All
the surrounding area on top of the
mountain will be most holy. Such is the
law of the temple.

The Altar

13"These are the measurements of
the altar in long cubits, that cubit being
a cubit and a handbreadth: Its gutter is a
cubit deep and a cubit wide, with a rim
of one span around the edge. And this is
the height of the altar: 14From the gutter
on the ground up to the lower edge it is
two cubits high and a cubit wide, and
from the smaller ledge up to the larger
ledge it is four cubits high and a cubit
wide. 15The altar hearth is four cubits
high, and four horns project upward
from the hearth. 16The altar hearth is
square, twelve cubits long and twelve

cubits wide. 17The upper ledge also is
square, fourteen cubits long and fourteen cubits wide, with a rim of half a
cubit and a gutter of a cubit all round.
The steps of the altar face east."

18Then he said to me, "Son of man,
this is what the Sovereign LORD says:
These will be the regulations for sacrificing burnt offerings and sprinkling
blood upon the altar when it is built:
19You are to give a young bull as a sin
offering to the priests, who are Levites,
of the family of Zadok, who come near
to minister before me, declares the
Sovereign LORD. 20You are to take
some of its blood and put it on the four
horns of the altar and on the four corners of the upper ledge and all round the
rim, and so purify the altar and make
atonement for it. 21You are to take the
bull for the sin offering and burn it in the
designated part of the temple area outside the sanctuary.

22"On the second day you are to offer
a male goat without defect for a sin
offering, and the altar is to be purified as
it was purified with the bull. 23When you
have finished purifying it, you are to
offer a young bull and a ram from the
flock, both without defect. 24You are to
offer them before the LORD, and the
priests are to sprinkle salt on them and
sacrifice them as a burnt offering to the
LORD.

25"For seven days you are to provide
a male goat daily for a sin offering; you
are also to provide a young bull and a
ram from the flock, both without defect.
26For seven days they are to make
atonement for the altar and cleanse it;
thus they will dedicate it. 27At the end of
these days, from the eighth day on, the
priests are to present your burnt offerings and fellowship offerings on the
altar. Then I will accept you, declares
the Sovereign LORD."

The Prince, the Levites, the Priests

44 Then the man brought me back
to the outer gate of the sanctuary, the one facing east, and it was shut.
2The LORD said to me, "This gate is to
remain shut. It must not be opened;
no-one may enter through it. It is to
remain shut because the LORD, the God
of Israel, has entered through it. 3The
prince himself is the only one who may
sit inside the gateway to eat in the presence of the LORD. He is to enter by way
of the portico of the gateway and go out
the same way."

4Then the man brought me by way of
the north gate to the front of the temple.
I looked and saw the glory of the LORD
filling the temple of the LORD, and I fell
face down.

5The LORD said to me, "Son of man,
look carefully, listen closely and give
attention to everything I tell you concerning all the regulations regarding the
temple of the LORD. Give attention to
the entrance of the temple and all the
exits of the sanctuary. 6Say to the rebellious house of Israel, 'This is what the
Sovereign LORD says: Enough of your
detestable practices, O house of Israel!
7In addition to all your other detestable
practices, you brought foreigners uncircumcised in heart and flesh into my
sanctuary, desecrating my temple while
you offered me food, fat and blood, and
you broke my covenant. 8Instead of
carrying out your duty in regard to my
holy things, you put others in charge of
my sanctuary. 9This is what the
Sovereign LORD says: No foreigner uncircumcised in heart and flesh is to enter
my sanctuary, not even the foreigners
who live among the Israelites.

10" 'The Levites who went far from
me when Israel went astray and who
wandered from me after their idols must
bear the consequences of their sin.
11They may serve in my sanctuary, having charge of the gates of the temple and
serving in it; they may slaughter the
burnt offerings and sacrifices for the
people and stand before the people and
serve them. 12But because they served
them in the presence of their idols
and made the house of Israel fall into
sin, therefore I have sworn with uplifted hand that they must bear the

consequences of their sin, declares
the Sovereign LORD. 13They are not to
come near to serve me as priests or
come near any of my holy things or my
most holy offerings; they must bear the
shame of their detestable practices.
14Yet I will put them in charge of the
duties of the temple and all the work
that is to be done in it.
15" 'But the priests, who are Levites
and descendants of Zadok and who
faithfully carried out the duties of my
sanctuary when the Israelites went
astray from me, are to come near to
minister before me; they are to stand
before me to offer sacrifices of fat and
blood, declares the Sovereign LORD.
16They alone are to enter my sanctuary;
they alone are to come near my table
to minister before me and perform my
service.
17" 'When they enter the gates of the
inner court, they are to wear linen
clothes; they must not wear any woollen
garment while ministering at the gates
of the inner court or inside the temple.
18They are to wear linen turbans on
their heads and linen undergarments
round their waists. They must not wear
anything that makes them perspire.
19When they go out into the outer court
where the people are, they are to take
off the clothes they have been ministering in and leave them in the sacred
rooms, and put on other clothes, so that
they do not consecrate the people by
means of their garments.
20" 'They must not shave their heads
or let their hair grow long, but they are
to keep the hair of their heads trimmed.
21No priest is to drink wine when he
enters the inner court. 22They must not
marry widows or divorced women; they
may marry only virgins of Israelite descent or widows of priests. 23They are to
teach my people the difference between
the holy and the common and show
them how to distinguish between the
unclean and the clean.
24" 'In any dispute, the priests are to
serve as judges and decide it according
to my ordinances. They are to keep my
laws and my decrees for all my
appointed feasts, and they are to keep
my Sabbaths holy.
25" 'A priest must not defile himself
by going near a dead person; however,
if the dead person was his father or
mother, son or daughter, brother or
unmarried sister, then he may defile
himself. 26After he is cleansed, he must
wait seven days. 27On the day he goes
into the inner court of the sanctuary to
minister in the sanctuary, he is to offer a
sin offering for himself, declares the
Sovereign LORD.
28" 'I am to be the only inheritance
the priests have. You are to give them
no possession in Israel; I will be their
possession. 29They will eat the grain
offerings, the sin offerings and the guilt
offerings; and everything in Israel devoted to the LORD will belong to them.
30The best of all the firstfruits and of all
your special gifts will belong to the
priests. You are to give them the first
portion of your ground meal so that a
blessing may rest on your household.
31The priests must not eat anything,
bird or animal, found dead or torn by
wild animals.

NEW TESTAMENT READING
1 Peter 2:4–25

The Living Stone and a Chosen People

4As you come to him, the living Stone
—rejected by men but chosen by God
and precious to him—5you also, like
living stones, are being built into a spiritual house to be a holy priesthood,
offering spiritual sacrifices acceptable
to God through Jesus Christ. 6For in
Scripture it says:

"See, I lay a stone in Zion,
  a chosen and precious cornerstone,
and the one who trusts in him
  will never be put to shame."

7Now to you who believe, this stone
is precious. But to those who do not
believe,

"The stone the builders rejected
has become the capstone,"

8and,

"A stone that causes men to stumble
and a rock that makes them fall."

They stumble because they disobey the message—which is also what they were destined for.

9But you are a chosen people, a royal priesthood, a holy nation, a people belonging to God, that you may declare the praises of him who called you out of darkness into his wonderful light. 10Once you were not a people, but now you are the people of God; once you had not received mercy, but now you have received mercy.

11Dear friends, I urge you, as aliens and strangers in the world, to abstain from sinful desires, which war against your soul. 12Live such good lives among the pagans that, though they accuse you of doing wrong, they may see your good deeds and glorify God on the day he visits us.

Submission to Rulers and Masters

13Submit yourselves for the Lord's sake to every authority instituted among men: whether to the king, as the supreme authority, 14or to governors, who are sent by him to punish those who do wrong and to commend those who do right. 15For it is God's will that by doing good you should silence the ignorant talk of foolish men. 16Live as free men, but do not use your freedom as a cover-up for evil; live as servants of God. 17Show proper respect to everyone: Love the brotherhood of believers, fear God, honour the king.

18Slaves, submit yourselves to your masters with all respect, not only to those who are good and considerate, but also to those who are harsh. 19For it is commendable if a man bears up under the pain of unjust suffering because he is conscious of God. 20But how is it to your credit if you receive a beating for doing wrong and endure it? But if you suffer for doing good and you endure it, this is commendable before God. 21To this you were called, because Christ suffered for you, leaving you an example, that you should follow in his steps.

22"He committed no sin,
and no deceit was found in his
mouth."

23When they hurled their insults at him, he did not retaliate; when he suffered, he made no threats. Instead, he entrusted himself to him who judges justly. 24He himself bore our sins in his body on the tree, so that we might die to sins and live for righteousness; by his wounds you have been healed. 25For you were like sheep going astray, but now you have returned to the Shepherd and Overseer of your souls.

READING FROM PSALMS

Psalm 132:1–18

A song of ascents.

1O LORD, remember David
and all the hardships he endured.

2He swore an oath to the LORD
and made a vow to the Mighty One
of Jacob:
3"I will not enter my house
or go to my bed—
4I will allow no sleep to my eyes,
no slumber to my eyelids,
5till I find a place for the LORD,
a dwelling for the Mighty One of
Jacob."

6We heard it in Ephrathah,
we came upon it in the fields of
Jaar:
7"Let us go to his dwelling-place;
let us worship at his footstool—
8arise, O LORD, and come to your
resting place,

you and the ark of your might.
9May your priests be clothed with
righteousness;
may your saints sing for joy."

10For the sake of David your servant,
do not reject your anointed one.

11The LORD swore an oath to David,
a sure oath that he will not revoke:
"One of your own descendants
I will place on your throne—
12if your sons keep my covenant
and the statutes I teach them,
then their sons shall sit
on your throne for ever and ever."

13For the LORD has chosen Zion,
he has desired it for his dwelling:
14"This is my resting place for ever and
ever;
here I will sit enthroned, for I have
desired it—
15I will bless her with abundant
provisions;
her poor will I satisfy with food.
16I will clothe her priests with
salvation,
and her saints shall ever sing for
joy.

17"Here I will make a horn grow for
David
and set up a lamp for my anointed
one.
18I will clothe his enemies with shame,
but the crown on his head shall be
resplendent."

DAY 328

NOVEMBER 24

OLD TESTAMENT READING
Ezekiel 45:1–46:24

Division of the Land

45 " 'When you allot the land as an
inheritance, you are to present
to the LORD a portion of the land as a
sacred district, 25,000 cubits long and
20,000 cubits wide; the entire area will
be holy. 2Of this, a section 500 cubits
square is to be for the sanctuary, with 50
cubits around it for open land. 3In the
sacred district, measure off a section
25,000 cubits long and 10,000 cubits
wide. In it will be the sanctuary, the
Most Holy Place. 4It will be the sacred
portion of the land for the priests, who
minister in the sanctuary and who draw
near to minister before the LORD. It will
be a place for their houses as well as a
holy place for the sanctuary. 5An area
25,000 cubits long and 10,000 cubits
wide will belong to the Levites, who
serve in the temple, as their possession
for towns to live in.

6" 'You are to give the city as its property an area 5,000 cubits wide and
25,000 cubits long, adjoining the sacred
portion; it will belong to the whole
house of Israel.
7" 'The prince will have the land
bordering each side of the area formed
by the sacred district and the property
of the city. It will extend westward from
the west side and eastward from the east
side, running lengthwise from the western to the eastern border parallel to one
of the tribal portions. 8This land will be
his possession in Israel. And my princes
will no longer oppress my people but
will allow the house of Israel to possess
the land according to their tribes.
9" 'This is what the Sovereign LORD
says: You have gone far enough, O
princes of Israel! Give up your violence
and oppression and do what is just and
right. Stop dispossessing my people, declares the Sovereign LORD. 10You are to
use accurate scales, an accurate ephah
and an accurate bath. 11The ephah and

the bath are to be the same size, the
bath containing a tenth of a homer and
the ephah a tenth of a homer; the homer
is to be the standard measure for both.
12 The shekel is to consist of twenty
gerahs. Twenty shekels plus twenty-five
shekels plus fifteen shekels equal one
mina.

Offerings and Holy Days

13 " 'This is the special gift you are to
offer: a sixth of an ephah from each
homer of wheat and a sixth of an ephah
from each homer of barley. 14 The prescribed portion of oil, measured by the
bath, is a tenth of a bath from each cor
(which consists of ten baths or one
homer, for ten baths are equivalent to a
homer). 15 Also one sheep is to be taken
from every flock of two hundred from
the well-watered pastures of Israel.
These will be used for the grain offerings, burnt offerings and fellowship
offerings to make atonement for the
people, declares the Sovereign LORD.
16 All the people of the land will participate in this special gift for the use of the
prince in Israel. 17 It will be the duty of
the prince to provide the burnt offerings, grain offerings and drink offerings
at the festivals, the New Moons and the
Sabbaths—at all the appointed feasts of
the house of Israel. He will provide the
sin offerings, grain offerings, burnt
offerings and fellowship offerings to
make atonement for the house of Israel.

18 " 'This is what the Sovereign LORD
says: In the first month on the first day
you are to take a young bull without
defect and purify the sanctuary. 19 The
priest is to take some of the blood of the
sin offering and put it on the doorposts
of the temple, on the four corners of the
upper ledge of the altar and on the
gateposts of the inner court. 20 You are
to do the same on the seventh day of the
month for anyone who sins unintentionally or through ignorance; so you
are to make atonement for the temple.

21 " 'In the first month on the fourteenth day you are to observe the Passover, a feast lasting seven days, during
which you shall eat bread made without
yeast. 22 On that day the prince is to
provide a bull as a sin offering for himself and for all the people of the land.
23 Every day during the seven days of the
Feast he is to provide seven bulls and
seven rams without defect as a burnt
offering to the LORD, and a male goat
for a sin offering. 24 He is to provide as a
grain offering an ephah for each bull
and an ephah for each ram, along with a
hin of oil for each ephah.

25 " 'During the seven days of the
Feast, which begins in the seventh
month on the fifteenth day, he is to
make the same provision for sin offerings, burnt offerings, grain offerings
and oil.

46 " 'This is what the Sovereign
LORD says: The gate of the inner
court facing east is to be shut on the six
working days, but on the Sabbath day
and on the day of the New Moon it is to
be opened. 2 The prince is to enter from
the outside through the portico of the
gateway and stand by the gatepost. The
priests are to sacrifice his burnt offering
and his fellowship offerings. He is to
worship at the threshold of the gateway
and then go out, but the gate will not be
shut until evening. 3 On the Sabbaths
and New Moons the people of the land
are to worship in the presence of the
LORD at the entrance to that gateway.
4 The burnt offering the prince brings to
the LORD on the Sabbath day is to be six
male lambs and a ram, all without defect. 5 The grain offering given with the
ram is to be an ephah, and the grain
offering with the lambs is to be as much
as he pleases, along with a hin of oil for
each ephah. 6 On the day of the New
Moon he is to offer a young bull, six
lambs and a ram, all without defect. 7 He
is to provide as a grain offering one
ephah with the bull, one ephah with the
ram, and with the lambs as much as he
wants to give, along with a hin of oil
with each ephah. 8 When the prince
enters, he is to go in through the portico
of the gateway, and he is to come out
the same way.

9" 'When the people of the land come
before the LORD at the appointed
feasts, whoever enters by the north gate
to worship is to go out by the south gate;
and whoever enters by the south gate is
to go out by the north gate. No-one is to
return through the gate by which he
entered, but each is to go out by the
opposite gate. 10The prince is to be
among them, going in when they go in
and going out when they go out.

11" 'At the festivals and the appointed
feasts, the grain offering is to be an
ephah with a bull, an ephah with a ram,
and with the lambs as much as one
pleases, along with a hin of oil for each
ephah. 12When the prince provides a
freewill offering to the LORD—whether
a burnt offering or fellowship offerings
—the gate facing east is to be opened
for him. He shall offer his burnt offering
or his fellowship offerings as he does on
the Sabbath day. Then he shall go out,
and after he has gone out, the gate will
be shut.

13" 'Every day you are to provide a
year-old lamb without defect for a burnt
offering to the LORD; morning by morning you shall provide it. 14You are also
to provide with it morning by morning a
grain offering, consisting of a sixth of an
ephah with a third of a hin of oil to
moisten the flour. The presenting of this
grain offering to the LORD is a lasting
ordinance. 15So the lamb and the grain
offering and the oil shall be provided
morning by morning for a regular burnt
offering.

16" 'This is what the Sovereign LORD
says: If the prince makes a gift from his
inheritance to one of his sons, it will also
belong to his descendants; it is to be
their property by inheritance. 17If,
however, he makes a gift from his inheritance to one of his servants, the
servant may keep it until the year of
freedom; then it will revert to the
prince. His inheritance belongs to his
sons only; it is theirs. 18The prince must
not take any of the inheritance of the
people, driving them off their property.
He is to give his sons their inheritance
out of his own property, so that none of
my people will be separated from his
property.' "

19Then the man brought me through
the entrance at the side of the gate to the
sacred rooms facing north, which belonged to the priests, and showed me a
place at the western end. 20He said to
me, "This is the place where the priests
will cook the guilt offering and the sin
offering and bake the grain offering, to
avoid bringing them into the outer court
and consecrating the people."

21He then brought me to the outer
court and led me round to its four corners, and I saw in each corner another
court. 22In the four corners of the outer
court were enclosed courts, forty cubits
long and thirty cubits wide; each of the
courts in the four corners was the same
size. 23Around the inside of each of the
four courts was a ledge of stone, with
places for fire built all round under the
ledge. 24He said to me, "These are the
kitchens where those who minister at
the temple will cook the sacrifices of the
people."

NEW TESTAMENT READING
1 Peter 3:1–22

Wives and Husbands

3 Wives, in the same way be submissive to your husbands so that, if any
of them do not believe the word, they
may be won over without words by the
behaviour of their wives, 2when they
see the purity and reverence of your
lives. 3Your beauty should not come
from outward adornment, such as
braided hair and the wearing of gold
jewellery and fine clothes. 4Instead, it
should be that of your inner self, the
unfading beauty of a gentle and quiet
spirit, which is of great worth in God's
sight. 5For this is the way the holy
women of the past who put their hope in
God used to make themselves beautiful. They were submissive to their own

husbands, 6like Sarah, who obeyed
Abraham and called him her master.
You are her daughters if you do what is
right and do not give way to fear.
7Husbands, in the same way be considerate as you live with your wives, and
treat them with respect as the weaker
partner and as heirs with you of the
gracious gift of life, so that nothing will
hinder your prayers.

Suffering for Doing Good

8Finally, all of you, live in harmony
with one another; be sympathetic, love
as brothers, be compassionate and
humble. 9Do not repay evil with evil or
insult with insult, but with blessing, because to this you were called so that you
may inherit a blessing. 10For,

"Whoever would love life
and see good days
must keep his tongue from evil
and his lips from deceitful speech.
11He must turn from evil and do good;
he must seek peace and pursue it.
12For the eyes of the Lord are on the
righteous
and his ears are attentive to their
prayer,
but the face of the Lord is against
those who do evil."

13Who is going to harm you if you are
eager to do good? 14But even if you
should suffer for what is right, you are
blessed. "Do not fear what they fear; do
not be frightened." 15But in your hearts
set apart Christ as Lord. Always be
prepared to give an answer to everyone
who asks you to give the reason for the
hope that you have. But do this with
gentleness and respect, 16keeping a
clear conscience, so that those who
speak maliciously against your good behaviour in Christ may be ashamed of
their slander. 17It is better, if it is God's
will, to suffer for doing good than for
doing evil. 18For Christ died for sins
once for all, the righteous for the unrighteous, to bring you to God. He was
put to death in the body but made alive
by the Spirit, 19through whom also he
went and preached to the spirits in
prison 20who disobeyed long ago when
God waited patiently in the days of
Noah while the ark was being built. In it
only a few people, eight in all, were
saved through water, 21and this water
symbolises baptism that now saves you
also—not the removal of dirt from the
body but the pledge of a good conscience towards God. It saves you by
the resurrection of Jesus Christ, 22who
has gone into heaven and is at God's
right hand—with angels, authorities
and powers in submission to him.

READING FROM PROVERBS
Proverbs 28:18–28

18He whose walk is blameless is kept
safe,
but he whose ways are perverse
will suddenly fall.

19He who works his land will have
abundant food,
but the one who chases fantasies
will have his fill of poverty.

20A faithful man will be richly blessed,
but one eager to get rich will not go
unpunished.

21To show partiality is not good—
yet a man will do wrong for a piece
of bread.

22A stingy man is eager to get rich
and is unaware that poverty awaits
him.

23He who rebukes a man will in the end
gain more favour
than he who has a flattering
tongue.

24He who robs his father or mother
and says, "It's not wrong"—

he is partner to him who
destroys.
25A greedy man stirs up dissension,
but he who trusts in the LORD will
prosper.
26He who trusts in himself is a fool,
but he who walks in wisdom is kept
safe.
27He who gives to the poor will lack
nothing,
but he who closes his eyes to them
receives many curses.
28When the wicked rise to power,
people go into hiding;
but when the wicked perish, the
righteous thrive.

DAY 329

NOVEMBER 25

OLD TESTAMENT READING
Ezekiel 47:1–48:35

The River From the Temple

47 The man brought me back to the
entrance of the temple, and I
saw water coming out from under the
threshold of the temple towards the east
(for the temple faced east). The water
was coming down from under the south
side of the temple, south of the altar.
2He then brought me out through the
north gate and led me round the outside
to the outer gate facing east, and the
water was flowing from the south side.
3As the man went eastward with a
measuring line in his hand, he measured
off a thousand cubits and then led me
through water that was ankle-deep. 4He
measured off another thousand cubits
and led me through water that was
knee-deep. He measured off another
thousand and led me through water that
was up to the waist. 5He measured off
another thousand, but now it was a river
that I could not cross, because the water
had risen and was deep enough to swim
in—a river that no-one could cross. 6He
asked me, "Son of man, do you see
this?"

Then he led me back to the bank of
the river. 7When I arrived there, I saw a
great number of trees on each side of
the river. 8He said to me, "This water
flows towards the eastern region and
goes down into the Arabah, where it
enters the Sea. When it empties into the
Sea, the water there becomes fresh.
9Swarms of living creatures will live
wherever the river flows. There will be
large numbers of fish, because this
water flows there and makes the salt
water fresh; so where the river flows
everything will live. 10Fishermen will
stand along the shore; from En Gedi to
En Eglaim there will be places for
spreading nets. The fish will be of many
kinds—like the fish of the Great Sea.
11But the swamps and marshes will not
become fresh; they will be left for salt.
12Fruit trees of all kinds will grow on
both banks of the river. Their leaves will
not wither, nor will their fruit fail.
Every month they will bear, because the
water from the sanctuary flows to them.
Their fruit will serve for food and their
leaves for healing."

The Boundaries of the Land

13This is what the Sovereign LORD
says: "These are the boundaries by
which you are to divide the land for an
inheritance among the twelve tribes of
Israel, with two portions for Joseph.
14You are to divide it equally among
them. Because I swore with uplifted
hand to give it to your forefathers, this
land will become your inheritance.

15"This is to be the boundary of the land:

"On the north side it will run from the Great Sea by the Hethlon road past Lebo Hamath to Zedad, 16Berothah and Sibraim (which lies on the border between Damascus and Hamath), as far as Hazer Hatticon, which is on the border of Hauran. 17The boundary will extend from the sea to Hazar Enan, along the northern border of Damascus, with the border of Hamath to the north. This will be the north boundary.
18"On the east side the boundary will run between Hauran and Damascus, along the Jordan between Gilead and the land of Israel, to the eastern sea and as far as Tamar. This will be the east boundary.
19"On the south side it will run from Tamar as far as the waters of Meribah Kadesh, then along the Wadi ⌊of Egypt⌋ to the Great Sea. This will be the south boundary.
20"On the west side, the Great Sea will be the boundary to a point opposite Lebo Hamath. This will be the west boundary.

21"You are to distribute this land among yourselves according to the tribes of Israel. 22You are to allot it as an inheritance for yourselves and for the aliens who have settled among you and who have children. You are to consider them as native-born Israelites; along with you they are to be allotted an inheritance among the tribes of Israel. 23In whatever tribe the alien settles, there you are to give him his inheritance," declares the Sovereign LORD.

The Division of the Land

48 "These are the tribes, listed by name: At the northern frontier, Dan will have one portion; it will follow the Hethlon road to Lebo Hamath; Hazar Enan and the northern border of Damascus next to Hamath will be part of its border from the east side to the west side.

2"Asher will have one portion; it will border the territory of Dan from east to west.

3"Naphtali will have one portion; it will border the territory of Asher from east to west.

4"Manasseh will have one portion; it will border the territory of Naphtali from east to west.

5"Ephraim will have one portion; it will border the territory of Manasseh from east to west.

6"Reuben will have one portion; it will border the territory of Ephraim from east to west.

7"Judah will have one portion; it will border the territory of Reuben from east to west.

8"Bordering the territory of Judah from east to west will be the portion you are to present as a special gift. It will be 25,000 cubits wide, and its length from east to west will equal one of the tribal portions; the sanctuary will be in the centre of it.

9"The special portion you are to offer to the LORD will be 25,000 cubits long and 10,000 cubits wide. 10This will be the sacred portion for the priests. It will be 25,000 cubits long on the north side, 10,000 cubits wide on the west side, 10,000 cubits wide on the east side and 25,000 cubits long on the south side. In the centre of it will be the sanctuary of the LORD. 11This will be for the consecrated priests, the Zadokites, who were faithful in serving me and did not go astray as the Levites did when the Israelites went astray. 12It will be a special gift to them from the sacred portion of the land, a most holy portion, bordering the territory of the Levites.

13"Alongside the territory of the priests, the Levites will have an allotment 25,000 cubits long and 10,000 cubits wide. Its total length will be 25,000 cubits and its width 10,000 cubits. 14They must not sell or exchange any of it. This is the best of the land, and

must not pass into other hands, because
it is holy to the LORD.
15 "The remaining area, 5,000 cubits
wide and 25,000 cubits long, will be for
the common use of the city, for houses
and for pasture-land. The city will be in
the centre of it 16 and will have these
measurements: the north side 4,500
cubits, the south side 4,500 cubits, the
east side 4,500 cubits, and the west side
4,500 cubits. 17 The pasture-land for the
city will be 250 cubits on the north, 250
cubits on the south, 250 cubits on the
east, and 250 cubits on the west. 18 What
remains of the area, bordering on the
sacred portion and running the length of
it, will be 10,000 cubits on the east side
and 10,000 cubits on the west side. Its
produce will supply food for the workers of the city. 19 The workers from the
city who farm it will come from all the
tribes of Israel. 20 The entire portion will
be a square, 25,000 cubits on each side.
As a special gift you will set aside the
sacred portion, along with the property
of the city.
21 "What remains on both sides of the
area formed by the sacred portion and
the city property will belong to the
prince. It will extend eastward from the
25,000 cubits of the sacred portion to
the eastern border, and westward from
the 25,000 cubits to the western border.
Both these areas running the length of
the tribal portions will belong to the
prince, and the sacred portion with the
temple sanctuary will be in the centre of
them. 22 So the property of the Levites
and the property of the city will lie in the
centre of the area that belongs to the
prince. The area belonging to the prince
will lie between the border of Judah and
the border of Benjamin.
23 "As for the rest of the tribes: Benjamin will have one portion; it will extend from the east side to the west side.
24 "Simeon will have one portion; it
will border the territory of Benjamin
from east to west.
25 "Issachar will have one portion; it
will border the territory of Simeon from
east to west.
26 "Zebulun will have one portion; it
will border the territory of Issachar
from east to west.
27 "Gad will have one portion; it will
border the territory of Zebulun from
east to west.
28 "The southern boundary of Gad
will run south from Tamar to the waters
of Meribah Kadesh, then along the
Wadi ⌞of Egypt⌟ to the Great Sea.
29 "This is the land you are to allot as
an inheritance to the tribes of Israel,
and these will be their portions," declares the Sovereign LORD.

The Gates of the City

30 "These will be the exits of the city:
Beginning on the north side, which is
4,500 cubits long, 31 the gates of the city
will be named after the tribes of Israel.
The three gates on the north side will be
the gate of Reuben, the gate of Judah
and the gate of Levi.
32 "On the east side, which is 4,500
cubits long, will be three gates: the gate
of Joseph, the gate of Benjamin and the
gate of Dan.
33 "On the south side, which measures
4,500 cubits, will be three gates: the
gate of Simeon, the gate of Issachar and
the gate of Zebulun.
34 "On the west side, which is 4,500
cubits long, will be three gates: the gate
of Gad, the gate of Asher and the gate
of Naphtali.
35 "The distance all around will be
18,000 cubits.
"And the name of the city from that
time on will be:

THE LORD IS THERE."

NEW TESTAMENT READING
1 Peter 4:1–19

Living for God

4 Therefore, since Christ suffered in
his body, arm yourselves also with
the same attitude, because he who has

suffered in his body is done with sin. 2As
a result, he does not live the rest of his
earthly life for evil human desires, but
rather for the will of God. 3For you have
spent enough time in the past doing
what pagans choose to do—living in
debauchery, lust, drunkenness, orgies,
carousing and detestable idolatry.
4They think it strange that you do not
plunge with them into the same flood of
dissipation, and they heap abuse on
you. 5But they will have to give account
to him who is ready to judge the living
and the dead. 6For this is the reason the
gospel was preached even to those who
are now dead, so that they might be
judged according to men in regard to
the body, but live according to God in
regard to the spirit.

7The end of all things is near. Therefore be clear minded and self-controlled
so that you can pray. 8Above all, love
each other deeply, because love covers
over a multitude of sins. 9Offer hospitality to one another without grumbling. 10Each one should use whatever
gift he has received to serve others,
faithfully administering God's grace in
its various forms. 11If anyone speaks, he
should do it as one speaking the very
words of God. If anyone serves, he
should do it with the strength God provides, so that in all things God may be
praised through Jesus Christ. To him be
the glory and the power for ever and
ever. Amen.

Suffering for Being a Christian

12Dear friends, do not be surprised at
the painful trial you are suffering, as
though something strange were happening to you. 13But rejoice that you
participate in the sufferings of Christ, so
that you may be overjoyed when his
glory is revealed. 14If you are insulted
because of the name of Christ, you are
blessed, for the Spirit of glory and of
God rests on you. 15If you suffer, it
should not be as a murderer or thief or
any other kind of criminal, or even as a
meddler. 16However, if you suffer as a
Christian, do not be ashamed, but
praise God that you bear that name.
17For it is time for judgment to begin
with the family of God; and if it begins
with us, what will the outcome be for
those who do not obey the gospel of
God? 18And,

"If it is hard for the righteous to be
saved,
what will become of the ungodly
and the sinner?"

19So then, those who suffer according
to God's will should commit themselves
to their faithful Creator and continue to
do good.

READING FROM PSALMS

Psalm 133:1–3

A song of ascents. Of David.

1How good and pleasant it is
when brothers live together in
unity!
2It is like precious oil poured on the
head,
running down on the beard,
running down on Aaron's beard,
down upon the collar of his robes.
3It is as if the dew of Hermon
were falling on Mount Zion.
For there the LORD bestows his
blessing,
even life for evermore.

DAY 330

NOVEMBER 26

OLD TESTAMENT READING
Daniel 1:1–2:23

Daniel's Training in Babylon

1 In the third year of the reign of
Jehoiakim king of Judah, Nebuchadnezzar king of Babylon came to
Jerusalem and besieged it. 2And the
Lord delivered Jehoiakim king of Judah
into his hand, along with some of the
articles from the temple of God. These
he carried off to the temple of his god in
Babylonia and put in the treasure-house
of his god.
3Then the king ordered Ashpenaz,
chief of his court officials, to bring in
some of the Israelites from the royal
family and the nobility—4young men
without any physical defect, handsome,
showing aptitude for every kind of
learning, well informed, quick to understand, and qualified to serve in the
king's palace. He was to teach them the
language and literature of the Babylonians. 5The king assigned them a daily
amount of food and wine from the
king's table. They were to be trained for
three years, and after that they were to
enter the king's service.
6Among these were some from
Judah: Daniel, Hananiah, Mishael and
Azariah. 7The chief official gave them
new names: to Daniel, the name Belteshazzar; to Hananiah, Shadrach; to
Mishael, Meshach; and to Azariah,
Abednego.
8But Daniel resolved not to defile
himself with the royal food and wine,
and he asked the chief official for permission not to defile himself in this way.
9Now God had caused the official to
show favour and sympathy to Daniel,
10but the official told Daniel, "I am
afraid of my lord the king, who has
assigned your food and drink. Why
should he see you looking worse than
the other young men of your age? The
king would then have my head because
of you."
11Daniel then said to the guard whom
the chief official had appointed over
Daniel, Hananiah, Mishael and Azariah, 12"Please test your servants for ten
days: Give us nothing but vegetables to
eat and water to drink. 13Then compare
our appearance with that of the young
men who eat the royal food, and treat
your servants in accordance with what
you see." 14So he agreed to this and
tested them for ten days.
15At the end of the ten days they
looked healthier and better nourished
than any of the young men who ate the
royal food. 16So the guard took away
their choice food and the wine they
were to drink and gave them vegetables
instead.
17To these four young men God gave
knowledge and understanding of all
kinds of literature and learning. And
Daniel could understand visions and
dreams of all kinds.
18At the end of the time set by the
king to bring them in, the chief official
presented them to Nebuchadnezzar.
19The king talked with them, and he
found none equal to Daniel, Hananiah,
Mishael and Azariah; so they entered
the king's service. 20In every matter of
wisdom and understanding about which
the king questioned them, he found
them ten times better than all the
magicians and enchanters in his whole
kingdom.
21And Daniel remained there until
the first year of King Cyrus.

Nebuchadnezzar's Dream

2 In the second year of his reign,
Nebuchadnezzar had dreams; his
mind was troubled and he could not
sleep. 2So the king summoned the
magicians, enchanters, sorcerers and
astrologers to tell him what he had

dreamed. When they came in and stood
before the king, 3he said to them, "I
have had a dream that troubles me and I
want to know what it means."
4Then the astrologers answered the
king in Aramaic, "O king, live for ever!
Tell your servants the dream, and we
will interpret it."
5The king replied to the astrologers,
"This is what I have firmly decided: If
you do not tell me what my dream was
and interpret it, I will have you cut into
pieces and your houses turned into piles
of rubble. 6But if you tell me the dream
and explain it, you will receive from me
gifts and rewards and great honour. So
tell me the dream and interpret it for
me."
7Once more they replied, "Let the
king tell his servants the dream, and we
will interpret it."
8Then the king answered, "I am certain that you are trying to gain time,
because you realise that this is what I
have firmly decided: 9If you do not tell
me the dream, there is just one penalty
for you. You have conspired to tell me
misleading and wicked things, hoping
the situation will change. So then, tell
me the dream, and I will know that you
can interpret it for me."
10The astrologers answered the king,
"There is not a man on earth who can do
what the king asks! No king, however
great and mighty, has ever asked such a
thing of any magician or enchanter or
astrologer. 11What the king asks is too
difficult. No-one can reveal it to the
king except the gods, and they do not
live among men."
12This made the king so angry and
furious that he ordered the execution of
all the wise men of Babylon. 13So the
decree was issued to put the wise men to
death, and men were sent to look for
Daniel and his friends to put them to
death.
14When Arioch, the commander of
the king's guard, had gone out to put to
death the wise men of Babylon, Daniel
spoke to him with wisdom and tact.
15He asked the king's officer, "Why did
the king issue such a harsh decree?"
Arioch then explained the matter to
Daniel. 16At this, Daniel went in to the
king and asked for time, so that he
might interpret the dream for him.
17Then Daniel returned to his house
and explained the matter to his friends
Hananiah, Mishael and Azariah. 18He
urged them to plead for mercy from the
God of heaven concerning this mystery,
so that he and his friends might not be
executed with the rest of the wise men
of Babylon. 19During the night the mystery was revealed to Daniel in a vision.
Then Daniel praised the God of heaven
20and said:

"Praise be to the name of God for
ever and ever;
wisdom and power are his.
21He changes times and seasons;
he sets up kings and deposes them.
He gives wisdom to the wise
and knowledge to the discerning.
22He reveals deep and hidden things;
he knows what lies in darkness,
and light dwells with him.
23I thank and praise you, O God of my
fathers:
You have given me wisdom and
power,
you have made known to me what we
asked of you,
you have made known to us the
dream of the king."

NEW TESTAMENT READING
1 Peter 5:1–14

To Elders and Young Men

5 To the elders among you, I appeal
as a fellow-elder, a witness of
Christ's sufferings and one who also will
share in the glory to be revealed: 2Be
shepherds of God's flock that is under
your care, serving as overseers—not
because you must, but because you are
willing, as God wants you to be; not
greedy for money, but eager to serve;
3not lording it over those entrusted to

you, but being examples to the flock.
4And when the Chief Shepherd
appears, you will receive the crown of
glory that will never fade away.
5Young men, in the same way be
submissive to those who are older. All
of you, clothe yourselves with humility
towards one another, because,

"God opposes the proud
but gives grace to the humble."

6Humble yourselves, therefore, under
God's mighty hand, that he may lift you
up in due time. 7Cast all your anxiety on
him because he cares for you.
8Be self-controlled and alert. Your
enemy the devil prowls around like a
roaring lion looking for someone to devour. 9Resist him, standing firm in the
faith, because you know that your
brothers throughout the world are
undergoing the same kind of sufferings.
10And the God of all grace, who
called you to his eternal glory in
Christ, after you have suffered a little
while, will himself restore you and
make you strong, firm and steadfast.
11To him be the power for ever and
ever. Amen.

Final Greetings

12With the help of Silas, whom I regard as a faithful brother, I have written
to you briefly, encouraging you and testifying that this is the true grace of God.
Stand fast in it.
13She who is in Babylon, chosen
together with you, sends you her greetings, and so does my son Mark. 14Greet
one another with a kiss of love.
Peace to all of you who are in Christ.

READING FROM PSALMS
Psalm 134:1–3

A song of ascents.

1Praise the LORD, all you servants of
the LORD
who minister by night in the house
of the LORD.
2Lift up your hands in the sanctuary
and praise the LORD.

3May the LORD, the Maker of heaven
and earth,
bless you from Zion.

DAY 331

NOVEMBER 27

OLD TESTAMENT READING
Daniel 2:24–3:12

Daniel Interprets the Dream

24Then Daniel went to Arioch, whom
the king had appointed to execute the
wise men of Babylon, and said to him,
"Do not execute the wise men of Babylon. Take me to the king, and I will
interpret his dream for him."
25Arioch took Daniel to the king at
once and said, "I have found a man
among the exiles from Judah who can
tell the king what his dream means."
26The king asked Daniel (also called
Belteshazzar), "Are you able to tell me
what I saw in my dream and interpret
it?"
27Daniel replied, "No wise man, enchanter, magician or diviner can explain
to the king the mystery he has asked
about, 28but there is a God in heaven
who reveals mysteries. He has shown
King Nebuchadnezzar what will happen
in days to come. Your dream and the
visions that passed through your mind
as you lay on your bed are these:
29"As you were lying there, O king,
your mind turned to things to come, and

the revealer of mysteries showed you
what is going to happen. 30As for me,
this mystery has been revealed to me,
not because I have greater wisdom than
other living men, but so that you, O
king, may know the interpretation and
that you may understand what went
through your mind.

31"You looked, O king, and there
before you stood a large statue—an
enormous, dazzling statue, awesome in
appearance. 32The head of the statue
was made of pure gold, its chest and
arms of silver, its belly and thighs of
bronze, 33its legs of iron, its feet partly
of iron and partly of baked clay. 34While
you were watching, a rock was cut out,
but not by human hands. It struck the
statue on its feet of iron and clay and
smashed them. 35Then the iron, the
clay, the bronze, the silver and the gold
were broken to pieces at the same time
and became like chaff on a threshing-
floor in the summer. The wind swept
them away without leaving a trace. But
the rock that struck the statue became a
huge mountain and filled the whole
earth.

36"This was the dream, and now we
will interpret it to the king. 37You, O
king, are the king of kings. The God of
heaven has given you dominion and
power and might and glory; 38in your
hands he has placed mankind and the
beasts of the field and the birds of the
air. Wherever they live, he has made
you ruler over them all. You are that
head of gold.

39"After you, another kingdom will
rise, inferior to yours. Next, a third
kingdom, one of bronze, will rule over
the whole earth. 40Finally, there will be
a fourth kingdom, strong as iron—for
iron breaks and smashes everything—
and as iron breaks things to pieces, so it
will crush and break all the others.
41Just as you saw that the feet and toes
were partly of baked clay and partly of
iron, so this will be a divided kingdom;
yet it will have some of the strength of
iron in it, even as you saw iron mixed
with clay. 42As the toes were partly iron
and partly clay, so this kingdom will be
partly strong and partly brittle. 43And
just as you saw the iron mixed with
baked clay, so the people will be a mixture and will not remain united, any
more than iron mixes with clay.

44"In the time of those kings, the God
of heaven will set up a kingdom that will
never be destroyed, nor will it be left to
another people. It will crush all those
kingdoms and bring them to an end, but
it will itself endure for ever. 45This is the
meaning of the vision of the rock cut out
of a mountain, but not by human hands
—a rock that broke the iron, the
bronze, the clay, the silver and the gold
to pieces.

"The great God has shown the king
what will take place in the future. The
dream is true and the interpretation is
trustworthy."

46Then King Nebuchadnezzar fell
prostrate before Daniel and paid him
honour and ordered that an offering
and incense be presented to him. 47The
king said to Daniel, "Surely your God is
the God of gods and the Lord of kings
and a revealer of mysteries, for you
were able to reveal this mystery."

48Then the king placed Daniel in a
high position and lavished many gifts on
him. He made him ruler over the entire
province of Babylon and placed him in
charge of all its wise men. 49Moreover,
at Daniel's request the king appointed
Shadrach, Meshach and Abednego
administrators over the province of
Babylon, while Daniel himself remained at the royal court.

The Image of Gold and the Fiery Furnace

3 King Nebuchadnezzar made an image of gold, ninety feet high and
nine feet wide, and set it up on the plain
of Dura in the province of Babylon. 2He
then summoned the satraps, prefects,
governors, advisers, treasurers, judges,
magistrates and all the other provincial
officials to come to the dedication of the
image he had set up. 3So the satraps,

prefects, governors, advisers, treasurers, judges, magistrates and all the other provincial officials assembled for the dedication of the image that King Nebuchadnezzar had set up, and they stood before it.

4Then the herald loudly proclaimed, "This is what you are commanded to do, O peoples, nations and men of every language: 5As soon as you hear the sound of the horn, flute, zither, lyre, harp, pipes and all kinds of music, you must fall down and worship the image of gold that King Nebuchadnezzar has set up. 6Whoever does not fall down and worship will immediately be thrown into a blazing furnace."

7Therefore, as soon as they heard the sound of the horn, flute, zither, lyre, harp and all kinds of music, all the peoples, nations and men of every language fell down and worshipped the image of gold that King Nebuchadnezzar had set up.

8At this time some astrologers came forward and denounced the Jews. 9They said to King Nebuchadnezzar, "O king, live for ever! 10You have issued a decree, O king, that everyone who hears the sound of the horn, flute, zither, lyre, harp, pipes and all kinds of music must fall down and worship the image of gold, 11and that whoever does not fall down and worship will be thrown into a blazing furnace. 12But there are some Jews whom you have set over the affairs of the province of Babylon—Shadrach, Meshach and Abednego—who pay no attention to you, O king. They neither serve your gods nor worship the image of gold you have set up."

NEW TESTAMENT READING
2 Peter 1:1–21

1 Simon Peter, a servant and apostle of Jesus Christ,

To those who through the righteousness of our God and Saviour Jesus Christ have received a faith as precious as ours:

2Grace and peace be yours in abundance through the knowledge of God and of Jesus our Lord.

Making One's Calling and Election Sure

3His divine power has given us everything we need for life and godliness through our knowledge of him who called us by his own glory and goodness. 4Through these he has given us his very great and precious promises, so that through them you may participate in the divine nature and escape the corruption in the world caused by evil desires.

5For this very reason, make every effort to add to your faith goodness; and to goodness, knowledge; 6and to knowledge, self-control; and to self-control, perseverance; and to perseverance, godliness; 7and to godliness, brotherly kindness; and to brotherly kindness, love. 8For if you possess these qualities in increasing measure, they will keep you from being ineffective and unproductive in your knowledge of our Lord Jesus Christ. 9But if anyone does not have them, he is short-sighted and blind, and has forgotten that he has been cleansed from his past sins.

10Therefore, my brothers, be all the more eager to make your calling and election sure. For if you do these things, you will never fall, 11and you will receive a rich welcome into the eternal kingdom of our Lord and Saviour Jesus Christ.

Prophecy of Scripture

12So I will always remind you of these things, even though you know them and are firmly established in the truth you now have. 13I think it is right to refresh your memory as long as I live in the tent of this body, 14because I know that I will soon put it aside, as our Lord Jesus Christ has made clear to me. 15And I

will make every effort to see that after
my departure you will always be able to
remember these things.
16 We did not follow cleverly invented
stories when we told you about the
power and coming of our Lord Jesus
Christ, but we were eye-witnesses of his
majesty. 17 For he received honour and
glory from God the Father when the
voice came to him from the Majestic
Glory, saying, "This is my Son, whom I
love; with him I am well pleased." 18 We
ourselves heard this voice that came
from heaven when we were with him on
the sacred mountain.
19 And we have the word of the
prophets made more certain, and you
will do well to pay attention to it, as to a
light shining in a dark place, until the
day dawns and the morning star rises in
your hearts. 20 Above all, you must
understand that no prophecy of Scripture came about by the prophet's own
interpretation. 21 For prophecy never
had its origin in the will of man, but men
spoke from God as they were carried
along by the Holy Spirit.

READING FROM PSALMS
Psalm 135:1–12

1 Praise the LORD.

Praise the name of the LORD;
praise him, you servants of the LORD,
2 you who minister in the house of the LORD,
in the courts of the house of our God.

3 Praise the LORD, for the LORD is good;
sing praise to his name, for that is pleasant.
4 For the LORD has chosen Jacob to be his own,
Israel to be his treasured possession.

5 I know that the LORD is great,
that our Lord is greater than all gods.
6 The LORD does whatever pleases him,
in the heavens and on the earth,
in the seas and all their depths.
7 He makes clouds rise from the ends of the earth;
he sends lightning with the rain
and brings out the wind from his storehouses.

8 He struck down the firstborn of Egypt,
the firstborn of men and animals.
9 He sent his signs and wonders into your midst, O Egypt,
against Pharaoh and all his servants.
10 He struck down many nations
and killed mighty kings—
11 Sihon king of the Amorites,
Og king of Bashan
and all the kings of Canaan—
12 and he gave their land as an inheritance,
an inheritance to his people Israel.

DAY 332

NOVEMBER 28

OLD TESTAMENT READING
Daniel 3:13–4:18

13Furious with rage, Nebuchadnezzar
summoned Shadrach, Meshach and
Abednego. So these men were brought
before the king, 14and Nebuchadnezzar
said to them, "Is it true, Shadrach,
Meshach and Abednego, that you do
not serve my gods or worship the image
of gold I have set up? 15Now when you
hear the sound of the horn, flute, zither,
lyre, harp, pipes and all kinds of music,
if you are ready to fall down and
worship the image I made, very good.
But if you do not worship it, you will be
thrown immediately into a blazing furnace. Then what god will be able to
rescue you from my hand?"
16Shadrach, Meshach and Abednego
replied to the king, "O Nebuchadnezzar, we do not need to defend ourselves
before you in this matter. 17If we are
thrown into the blazing furnace, the
God we serve is able to save us from it,
and he will rescue us from your hand, O
king. 18But even if he does not, we want
you to know, O king, that we will not
serve your gods or worship the image of
gold you have set up."
19Then Nebuchadnezzar was furious
with Shadrach, Meshach and Abednego, and his attitude towards them
changed. He ordered the furnace to be
heated seven times hotter than usual
20and commanded some of the strongest
soldiers in his army to tie up Shadrach,
Meshach and Abednego and throw
them into the blazing furnace. 21So
these men, wearing their robes, trous-
ers, turbans and other clothes, were
bound and thrown into the blazing furnace. 22The king's command was so
urgent and the furnace so hot that the
flames of the fire killed the soldiers who
took up Shadrach, Meshach and Abednego, 23and these three men, firmly
tied, fell into the blazing furnace.
24Then King Nebuchadnezzar leaped
to his feet in amazement and asked his
advisers, "Weren't there three men that
we tied up and threw into the fire?"
They replied, "Certainly, O king."
25He said, "Look! I see four men
walking around in the fire, unbound and
unharmed, and the fourth looks like a
son of the gods."
26Nebuchadnezzar then approached
the opening of the blazing furnace and
shouted, "Shadrach, Meshach and
Abednego, servants of the Most High
God, come out! Come here!"
So Shadrach, Meshach and Abednego came out of the fire, 27and the
satraps, prefects, governors and royal
advisers crowded around them. They
saw that the fire had not harmed their
bodies, nor was a hair of their heads
singed; their robes were not scorched,
and there was no smell of fire on them.
28Then Nebuchadnezzar said,
"Praise be to the God of Shadrach,
Meshach and Abednego, who has sent
his angel and rescued his servants! They
trusted in him and defied the king's
command and were willing to give up
their lives rather than serve or worship
any god except their own God.
29Therefore I decree that the people of
any nation or language who say anything against the God of Shadrach,
Meshach and Abednego be cut into
pieces and their houses be turned into
piles of rubble, for no other god can
save in this way."
30Then the king promoted Shadrach,
Meshach and Abednego in the province
of Babylon.

Nebuchadnezzar's Dream of a Tree

4 King Nebuchadnezzar,

To the peoples, nations and men
of every language, who live in all
the world:

May you prosper greatly!

[2]It is my pleasure to tell you about the miraculous signs and wonders that the Most High God has performed for me.

3 How great are his signs,
how mighty his wonders!
His kingdom is an eternal
kingdom;
his dominion endures from
generation to generation.

[4]I, Nebuchadnezzar, was at home in my palace, contented and
prosperous. [5]I had a dream that
made me afraid. As I was lying in my bed, the images and visions that passed through my mind terrified
me. [6]So I commanded that all the
wise men of Babylon be brought before me to interpret the dream
for me. [7]When the magicians, en-
chanters, astrologers and diviners came, I told them the dream, but they could not interpret it for me.
[8]Finally, Daniel came into my
presence and I told him the dream. (He is called Belteshazzar, after the name of my god, and the spirit of the holy gods is in him.)
[9]I said, "Belteshazzar, chief of the magicians, I know that the spirit of the holy gods is in you, and no mystery is too difficult for you. Here is my dream; interpret it for
me. [10]These are the visions I saw
while lying in my bed: I looked, and there before me stood a tree in the middle of the land. Its height
was enormous. [11]The tree grew
large and strong and its top touched the sky; it was visible to
the ends of the earth. [12]Its leaves
were beautiful, its fruit abundant, and on it was food for all. Under it the beasts of the field found shelter, and the birds of the air lived in its branches; from it every creature was fed.
[13]"In the visions I saw while lying
in my bed, I looked, and there before me was a messenger, a holy one, coming down from heaven.
[14]He called in a loud voice: 'Cut
down the tree and trim off its branches; strip off its leaves and scatter its fruit. Let the animals flee from under it and the birds from its branches. [15]But let the stump and its
roots, bound with iron and bronze, remain in the ground, in the grass of the field.
" 'Let him be drenched with the dew of heaven, and let him live with the animals among the plants
of the earth. [16]Let his mind be
changed from that of a man and let him be given the mind of an animal, till seven times pass by for him.
[17]" 'The decision is announced
by messengers, the holy ones declare the verdict, so that the living may know that the Most High is sovereign over the kingdoms of men and gives them to anyone he wishes and sets over them the lowliest of men.'
[18]"This is the dream that I, King
Nebuchadnezzar, had. Now, Belteshazzar, tell me what it means, for none of the wise men in my kingdom can interpret it for me. But you can, because the spirit of the holy gods is in you."

NEW TESTAMENT READING
2 Peter 2:1–22

False Teachers and Their Destruction

2 But there were also false prophets among the people, just as there will be false teachers among you. They will secretly introduce destructive heresies, even denying the sovereign Lord who bought them—bringing swift destruction on themselves. [2]Many will follow
their shameful ways and will bring the
way of truth into disrepute. [3]In their

greed these teachers will exploit you with stories they have made up. Their condemnation has long been hanging over them, and their destruction has not been sleeping.

4For if God did not spare angels when they sinned, but sent them to hell, putting them into gloomy dungeons to be held for judgment; 5if he did not spare the ancient world when he brought the flood on its ungodly people, but protected Noah, a preacher of righteousness, and seven others; 6if he condemned the cities of Sodom and Gomorrah by burning them to ashes, and made them an example of what is going to happen to the ungodly; 7and if he rescued Lot, a righteous man, who was distressed by the filthy lives of lawless men 8(for that righteous man, living among them day after day, was tormented in his righteous soul by the lawless deeds he saw and heard)—9if this is so, then the Lord knows how to rescue godly men from trials and to hold the unrighteous for the day of judgment, while continuing their punishment. 10This is especially true of those who follow the corrupt desire of the sinful nature and despise authority.

Bold and arrogant, these men are not afraid to slander celestial beings; 11yet even angels, although they are stronger and more powerful, do not bring slanderous accusations against such beings in the presence of the Lord. 12But these men blaspheme in matters they do not understand. They are like brute beasts, creatures of instinct, born only to be caught and destroyed, and like beasts they too will perish.

13They will be paid back with harm for the harm they have done. Their idea of pleasure is to carouse in broad daylight. They are blots and blemishes, revelling in their pleasures while they feast with you. 14With eyes full of adultery, they never stop sinning; they seduce the unstable; they are experts in greed—an accursed brood! 15They have left the straight way and wandered off to follow the way of Balaam son of Beor, who loved the wages of wickedness. 16But he was rebuked for his wrongdoing by a donkey—a beast without speech—who spoke with a man's voice and restrained the prophet's madness.

17These men are springs without water and mists driven by a storm. Blackest darkness is reserved for them. 18For they mouth empty, boastful words and, by appealing to the lustful desires of sinful human nature, they entice people who are just escaping from those who live in error. 19They promise them freedom, while they themselves are slaves of depravity—for a man is a slave to whatever has mastered him. 20If they have escaped the corruption of the world by knowing our Lord and Saviour Jesus Christ and are again entangled in it and overcome, they are worse off at the end than they were at the beginning. 21It would have been better for them not to have known the way of righteousness, than to have known it and then to turn their backs on the sacred command that was passed on to them. 22Of them the proverbs are true: "A dog returns to its vomit," and, "A sow that is washed goes back to her wallowing in the mud."

READING FROM PROVERBS
Proverbs 29:1–9

29 A man who remains
stiff-necked after many rebukes
will suddenly be destroyed—
without remedy.

2When the righteous thrive, the
people rejoice;
when the wicked rule, the people
groan.

3A man who loves wisdom brings joy
to his father,
but a companion of prostitutes
squanders his wealth.

[4]By justice a king gives a country
stability,
but one who is greedy for bribes
tears it down.

[5]Whoever flatters his neighbour
is spreading a net for his feet.

[6]An evil man is snared by his own sin,
but a righteous one can sing and be
glad.

[7]The righteous care about justice for
the poor,
but the wicked have no such
concern.

[8]Mockers stir up a city,
but wise men turn away anger.

[9]If a wise man goes to court with a
fool,
the fool rages and scoffs, and there
is no peace.

NOVEMBER 29

DAY 333

OLD TESTAMENT READING

Daniel 4:19–5:16

Daniel Interprets the Dream

[19]Then Daniel (also called Belteshazzar) was greatly perplexed
for a time, and his thoughts terrified him. So the king said, "Belteshazzar, do not let the dream or
its meaning alarm you."

Belteshazzar answered, "My
lord, if only the dream applied to
your enemies and its meaning to
your adversaries! [20]The tree you
saw, which grew large and strong,
with its top touching the sky, visible to the whole earth, [21]with
beautiful leaves and abundant
fruit, providing food for all, giving
shelter to the beasts of the field,
and having nesting places in its
branches for the birds of the air
—[22]you, O king, are that tree! You
have become great and strong;
your greatness has grown until it
reaches the sky, and your dominion extends to distant parts of the
earth.

[23]"You, O king, saw a messenger, a holy one, coming down from
heaven and saying, 'Cut down the
tree and destroy it, but leave the
stump, bound with iron and
bronze, in the grass of the field,
while its roots remain in the
ground. Let him be drenched with
the dew of heaven; let him live like
the wild animals, until seven times
pass by for him.'

[24]"This is the interpretation, O
king, and this is the decree the
Most High has issued against my
lord the king: [25]You will be driven
away from people and will live with
the wild animals; you will eat grass
like cattle and be drenched with the
dew of heaven. Seven times will
pass by for you until you acknowledge that the Most High is
sovereign over the kingdoms of
men and gives them to anyone he
wishes. [26]The command to leave
the stump of the tree with its roots
means that your kingdom will be
restored to you when you acknowledge that Heaven rules. [27]There-
fore, O king, be pleased to accept
my advice: Renounce your sins by
doing what is right, and your wickedness by being kind to the oppressed. It may be that then your
prosperity will continue."

The Dream Is Fulfilled

[28]All this happened to King Nebuchadnezzar. [29]Twelve months

later, as the king was walking on
the roof of the royal palace of Babylon, [30]he said, "Is not this the
great Babylon I have built as the
royal residence, by my mighty
power and for the glory of my
majesty?"
[31]The words were still on his lips
when a voice came from heaven,
"This is what is decreed for you,
King Nebuchadnezzar: Your royal
authority has been taken from you.
[32]You will be driven away from
people and will live with the wild
animals; you will eat grass like cattle. Seven times will pass by for you
until you acknowledge that the
Most High is sovereign over the
kingdoms of men and gives them to
anyone he wishes."
[33]Immediately what had been
said about Nebuchadnezzar was
fulfilled. He was driven away from
people and ate grass like cattle. His
body was drenched with the dew of
heaven until his hair grew like the
feathers of an eagle and his nails
like the claws of a bird.

[34]At the end of that time, I,
Nebuchadnezzar, raised my eyes
towards heaven, and my sanity was
restored. Then I praised the Most
High; I honoured and glorified him
who lives for ever.

His dominion is an eternal
    dominion;
  his kingdom endures from
    generation to generation.
35 All the peoples of the earth
  are regarded as nothing.
He does as he pleases
  with the powers of heaven
  and the peoples of the earth.
No-one can hold back his hand
  or say to him: "What have you
    done?"

[36]At the same time that my sanity was restored, my honour and
splendour were returned to me for
the glory of my kingdom. My advisers and nobles sought me out, and I
was restored to my throne and became even greater than before.
[37]Now I, Nebuchadnezzar, praise
and exalt and glorify the King of
heaven, because everything he
does is right and all his ways are
just. And those who walk in pride
he is able to humble.

The Writing on the Wall

5 King Belshazzar gave a great banquet for a thousand of his nobles
and drank wine with them. [2]While Belshazzar was drinking his wine, he gave
orders to bring in the gold and silver
goblets that Nebuchadnezzar his father
had taken from the temple in Jerusalem, so that the king and his nobles,
his wives and his concubines might
drink from them. [3]So they brought in
the gold goblets that had been taken
from the temple of God in Jerusalem,
and the king and his nobles, his wives
and his concubines drank from them.
[4]As they drank the wine, they praised
the gods of gold and silver, of bronze,
iron, wood and stone.
[5]Suddenly the fingers of a human
hand appeared and wrote on the plaster
of the wall, near the lampstand in the
royal palace. The king watched the
hand as it wrote. [6]His face turned pale
and he was so frightened that his knees
knocked together and his legs gave way.
[7]The king called out for the enchanters, astrologers and diviners to be
brought and said to these wise men of
Babylon, "Whoever reads this writing
and tells me what it means will be
clothed in purple and have a gold chain
placed around his neck, and he will
be made the third highest ruler in the
kingdom."
[8]Then all the king's wise men came
in, but they could not read the writing or
tell the king what it meant. [9]So King
Belshazzar became even more terrified
and his face grew more pale. His nobles
were baffled.

10The queen, hearing the voices of the
king and his nobles, came into the banquet hall. "O king, live for ever!" she
said. "Don't be alarmed! Don't look so
pale! 11There is a man in your kingdom
who has the spirit of the holy gods in
him. In the time of your father he was
found to have insight and intelligence
and wisdom like that of the gods. King
Nebuchadnezzar your father—your
father the king, I say—appointed him
chief of the magicians, enchanters,
astrologers and diviners. 12This man
Daniel, whom the king called Belteshazzar, was found to have a keen mind
and knowledge and understanding, and
also the ability to interpret dreams, explain riddles and solve difficult problems. Call for Daniel, and he will tell
you what the writing means."

13So Daniel was brought before the
king, and the king said to him, "Are you
Daniel, one of the exiles my father the
king brought from Judah? 14I have
heard that the spirit of the gods is in you
and that you have insight, intelligence
and outstanding wisdom. 15The wise
men and enchanters were brought before me to read this writing and tell me
what it means, but they could not explain it. 16Now I have heard that you are
able to give interpretations and to solve
difficult problems. If you can read this
writing and tell me what it means, you
will be clothed in purple and have a gold
chain placed around your neck, and you
will be made the third highest ruler in
the kingdom."

NEW TESTAMENT READING
2 Peter 3:1–18

The Day of the Lord

3 Dear friends, this is now my second
letter to you. I have written both of
them as reminders to stimulate you to
wholesome thinking. 2I want you to recall the words spoken in the past by the
holy prophets and the command given
by our Lord and Saviour through your
apostles.

3First of all, you must understand that
in the last days scoffers will come,
scoffing and following their own evil
desires. 4They will say, "Where is this
'coming' he promised? Ever since our
fathers died, everything goes on as it has
since the beginning of creation." 5But
they deliberately forget that long ago by
God's word the heavens existed and the
earth was formed out of water and by
water. 6By these waters also the world
of that time was deluged and destroyed.
7By the same word the present heavens
and earth are reserved for fire, being
kept for the day of judgment and destruction of ungodly men.

8But do not forget this one thing, dear
friends: With the Lord a day is like a
thousand years, and a thousand years
are like a day. 9The Lord is not slow in
keeping his promise, as some understand slowness. He is patient with you,
not wanting anyone to perish, but
everyone to come to repentance.

10But the day of the Lord will come
like a thief. The heavens will disappear
with a roar; the elements will be destroyed by fire, and the earth and
everything in it will be laid bare.

11Since everything will be destroyed
in this way, what kind of people ought
you to be? You ought to live holy and
godly lives 12as you look forward to the
day of God and speed its coming. That
day will bring about the destruction of
the heavens by fire, and the elements
will melt in the heat. 13But in keeping
with his promise we are looking forward
to a new heaven and a new earth, the
home of righteousness.

14So then, dear friends, since you are
looking forward to this, make every
effort to be found spotless, blameless
and at peace with him. 15Bear in mind
that our Lord's patience means salvation, just as our dear brother Paul
also wrote to you with the wisdom that
God gave him. 16He writes the same
way in all his letters, speaking in them of
these matters. His letters contain some
things that are hard to understand,
which ignorant and unstable people

distort, as they do the other Scriptures, to their own destruction.

17Therefore, dear friends, since you already know this, be on your guard so that you may not be carried away by the error of lawless men and fall from your secure position. 18But grow in the grace and knowledge of our Lord and Saviour Jesus Christ. To him be glory both now and for ever! Amen.

READING FROM PSALMS
Psalm 135:13–21

13Your name, O LORD, endures for
ever,
your renown, O LORD, through all
generations.
14For the LORD will vindicate his
people
and have compassion on his
servants.

15The idols of the nations are silver and
gold,
made by the hands of men.
16They have mouths, but cannot speak,
eyes, but they cannot see;
17they have ears, but cannot hear,
nor is there breath in their mouths.
18Those who make them will be like
them,
and so will all who trust in them.

19O house of Israel, praise the LORD;
O house of Aaron, praise the
LORD;
20O house of Levi, praise the LORD;
you who fear him, praise the LORD.
21Praise be to the LORD from Zion,
to him who dwells in Jerusalem.

Praise the LORD.

DAY 334

NOVEMBER 30

OLD TESTAMENT READING
Daniel 5:17–6:28

17Then Daniel answered the king, "You may keep your gifts for yourself and give your rewards to someone else. Nevertheless, I will read the writing for the king and tell him what it means.

18"O king, the Most High God gave your father Nebuchadnezzar sovereignty and greatness and glory and splendour.
19Because of the high position he gave him, all the peoples and nations and men of every language dreaded and feared him. Those the king wanted to put to death, he put to death; those he wanted to spare, he spared; those he wanted to promote, he promoted; and those he wanted to humble, he humbled.
20But when his heart became arrogant and hardened with pride, he was deposed from his royal throne and stripped of his glory.
21He was driven away from people and given the mind of an animal; he lived with the wild donkeys and ate grass like cattle; and his body was drenched with the dew of heaven, until he acknowledged that the Most High God is sovereign over the kingdoms of men and sets over them anyone he wishes.

22"But you his son, O Belshazzar, have not humbled yourself, though you knew all this.
23Instead, you have set yourself up against the Lord of heaven. You had the goblets from his temple brought to you, and you and your nobles, your wives and your concubines drank wine from them. You praised the gods of silver and gold, of bronze, iron, wood and stone, which cannot see or hear or understand. But you did not honour the God who holds in his hand your life and all your ways.
24Therefore

he sent the hand that wrote the
inscription.
25"This is the inscription that was
written:

MENE, MENE, TEKEL, PARSIN

26"This is what these words mean:

Mene: God has numbered the
days of your reign and
brought it to an end.
27*Tekel*: You have been weighed
on the scales and found
wanting.
28*Peres*: Your kingdom is divided and given to the
Medes and Persians."

29Then at Belshazzar's command,
Daniel was clothed in purple, a gold
chain was placed around his neck, and
he was proclaimed the third highest
ruler in the kingdom.
30That very night Belshazzar, king of
the Babylonians, was slain, 31and
Darius the Mede took over the kingdom, at the age of sixty-two.

Daniel in the Den of Lions

6 It pleased Darius to appoint 120
satraps to rule throughout the kingdom, 2with three administrators over
them, one of whom was Daniel. The
satraps were made accountable to them
so that the king might not suffer loss.
3Now Daniel so distinguished himself
among the administrators and the satraps by his exceptional qualities that the
king planned to set him over the whole
kingdom. 4At this, the administrators
and the satraps tried to find grounds for
charges against Daniel in his conduct of
government affairs, but they were
unable to do so. They could find no
corruption in him, because he was
trustworthy and neither corrupt nor
negligent. 5Finally these men said, "We
will never find any basis for charges
against this man Daniel unless it has
something to do with the law of his
God."
6So the administrators and the satraps went as a group to the king and
said: "O King Darius, live for ever!
7The royal administrators, prefects, satraps, advisers and governors have all
agreed that the king should issue an
edict and enforce the decree that anyone who prays to any god or man during
the next thirty days, except to you, O
king, shall be thrown into the lions' den.
8Now, O king, issue the decree and put
it in writing so that it cannot be altered
—in accordance with the laws of the
Medes and Persians, which cannot be
repealed." 9So King Darius put the
decree in writing.
10Now when Daniel learned that the
decree had been published, he went
home to his upstairs room where the
windows opened towards Jerusalem.
Three times a day he got down on his
knees and prayed, giving thanks to his
God, just as he had done before. 11Then
these men went as a group and found
Daniel praying and asking God for
help. 12So they went to the king and
spoke to him about his royal decree:
"Did you not publish a decree that during the next thirty days anyone who
prays to any god or man except to you,
O king, would be thrown into the lions'
den?"
The king answered, "The decree
stands—in accordance with the laws of
the Medes and Persians, which cannot
be repealed."
13Then they said to the king, "Daniel,
who is one of the exiles from Judah,
pays no attention to you, O king, or to
the decree you put in writing. He still
prays three times a day." 14When the
king heard this, he was greatly distressed; he was determined to rescue
Daniel and made every effort until sun-
down to save him.
15Then the men went as a group to the
king and said to him, "Remember, O
king, that according to the law of the
Medes and Persians no decree or edict
that the king issues can be changed."
16So the king gave the order, and they
brought Daniel and threw him into the

lions' den. The king said to Daniel, "May your God, whom you serve continually, rescue you!"

[17]A stone was brought and placed over the mouth of the den, and the king sealed it with his own signet ring and with the rings of his nobles, so that Daniel's situation might not be changed. [18]Then the king returned to his palace and spent the night without eating and without any entertainment being brought to him. And he could not sleep.

[19]At the first light of dawn, the king got up and hurried to the lions' den. [20]When he came near the den, he called to Daniel in an anguished voice, "Daniel, servant of the living God, has your God, whom you serve continually, been able to rescue you from the lions?"

[21]Daniel answered, "O king, live for ever! [22]My God sent his angel, and he shut the mouths of the lions. They have not hurt me, because I was found innocent in his sight. Nor have I ever done any wrong before you, O king."

[23]The king was overjoyed and gave orders to lift Daniel out of the den. And when Daniel was lifted from the den, no wound was found on him, because he had trusted in his God.

[24]At the king's command, the men who had falsely accused Daniel were brought in and thrown into the lions' den, along with their wives and children. And before they reached the floor of the den, the lions overpowered them and crushed all their bones.

[25]Then King Darius wrote to all the peoples, nations and men of every language throughout the land:

"May you prosper greatly!

[26]"I issue a decree that in every part of my kingdom people must fear and reverence the God of Daniel.

"For he is the living God
and he endures for ever;
his kingdom will not be destroyed,
his dominion will never end.
[27] He rescues and he saves;
he performs signs and wonders
in the heavens and on the earth.
He has rescued Daniel
from the power of the lions."

[28]So Daniel prospered during the reign of Darius and the reign of Cyrus the Persian.

NEW TESTAMENT READING

1 John 1:1–2:11

The Word of Life

1 That which was from the beginning, which we have heard, which we have seen with our eyes, which we have looked at and our hands have touched—this we proclaim concerning the Word of life. [2]The life appeared; we have seen it and testify to it, and we proclaim to you the eternal life, which was with the Father and has appeared to us. [3]We proclaim to you what we have seen and heard, so that you also may have fellowship with us. And our fellowship is with the Father and with his Son, Jesus Christ. [4]We write this to make our joy complete.

Walking in the Light

[5]This is the message we have heard from him and declare to you: God is light; in him there is no darkness at all. [6]If we claim to have fellowship with him yet walk in the darkness, we lie and do not live by the truth. [7]But if we walk in the light, as he is in the light, we have fellowship with one another, and the blood of Jesus, his Son, purifies us from all sin.

[8]If we claim to be without sin, we deceive ourselves and the truth is not in us. [9]If we confess our sins, he is faithful and just and will forgive us our sins and purify us from all unrighteousness. [10]If we claim we have not sinned, we make

him out to be a liar and his word has no
place in our lives.
2 My dear children, I write this to
you so that you will not sin. But if
anybody does sin, we have one who
speaks to the Father in our defence
—Jesus Christ, the Righteous One. 2He
is the atoning sacrifice for our sins, and
not only for ours but also for the sins of
the whole world.
3We know that we have come to
know him if we obey his commands.
4The man who says, "I know him," but
does not do what he commands is a liar,
and the truth is not in him. 5But if
anyone obeys his word, God's love is
truly made complete in him. This is how
we know we are in him: 6Whoever
claims to live in him must walk as Jesus
did.
7Dear friends, I am not writing you a
new command but an old one, which
you have had since the beginning. This
old command is the message you have
heard. 8Yet I am writing you a new
command; its truth is seen in him and
you, because the darkness is passing
and the true light is already shining.
9Anyone who claims to be in the light
but hates his brother is still in the darkness. 10Whoever loves his brother lives
in the light, and there is nothing in him
to make him stumble. 11But whoever
hates his brother is in the darkness and
walks around in the darkness; he does
not know where he is going, because the
darkness has blinded him.

READING FROM PSALMS

Psalm 136:1–12

1Give thanks to the LORD, for he is
good.
His love endures for ever.
2Give thanks to the God of gods.
His love endures for ever.
3Give thanks to the Lord of lords:
His love endures for ever.

4to him who alone does great
wonders,
His love endures for ever.
5who by his understanding made the
heavens,
His love endures for ever.
6who spread out the earth upon the
waters,
His love endures for ever.
7who made the great lights—
His love endures for ever.
8the sun to govern the day,
His love endures for ever.
9the moon and stars to govern the
night;
His love endures for ever.

10to him who struck down the firstborn
of Egypt
His love endures for ever.
11and brought Israel out from among
them
His love endures for ever.
12with a mighty hand and outstretched
arm;
His love endures for ever.

DECEMBER 1

OLD TESTAMENT READING
Daniel 7:1–8:14

Daniel's Dream of Four Beasts

7 In the first year of Belshazzar king of Babylon, Daniel had a dream, and visions passed through his mind as he was lying on his bed. He wrote down the substance of his dream.

2Daniel said: "In my vision at night I looked, and there before me were the four winds of heaven churning up the great sea. 3Four great beasts, each different from the others, came up out of the sea.

4"The first was like a lion, and it had the wings of an eagle. I watched until its wings were torn off and it was lifted from the ground so that it stood on two feet like a man, and the heart of a man was given to it.

5"And there before me was a second beast, which looked like a bear. It was raised up on one of its sides, and it had three ribs in its mouth between its teeth. It was told, 'Get up and eat your fill of flesh!'

6"After that, I looked, and there before me was another beast, one that looked like a leopard. And on its back it had four wings like those of a bird. This beast had four heads, and it was given authority to rule.

7"After that, in my vision at night I looked, and there before me was a fourth beast—terrifying and frightening and very powerful. It had large iron teeth; it crushed and devoured its victims and trampled underfoot whatever was left. It was different from all the former beasts, and it had ten horns.

8"While I was thinking about the horns, there before me was another horn, a little one, which came up among them; and three of the first horns were uprooted before it. This horn had eyes like the eyes of a man and a mouth that spoke boastfully.

9"As I looked,

"thrones were set in place,
  and the Ancient of Days took his seat.
His clothing was as white as snow;
  the hair of his head was white like wool.
His throne was flaming with fire,
  and its wheels were all ablaze.
10A river of fire was flowing,
  coming out from before him.
Thousands upon thousands attended him;
  ten thousand times ten thousand stood before him.
The court was seated,
  and the books were opened.

11"Then I continued to watch because of the boastful words the horn was speaking. I kept looking until the beast was slain and its body destroyed and thrown into the blazing fire. 12(The other beasts had been stripped of their authority, but were allowed to live for a period of time.)

13"In my vision at night I looked, and there before me was one like a son of man, coming with the clouds of heaven. He approached the Ancient of Days and was led into his presence. 14He was given authority, glory and sovereign power; all peoples, nations and men of every language worshipped him. His dominion is an everlasting dominion that will not pass away, and his kingdom is one that will never be destroyed.

The Interpretation of the Dream

15"I, Daniel, was troubled in spirit, and the visions that passed through my mind disturbed me. 16I approached one of those standing there and asked him the true meaning of all this.

"So he told me and gave me the interpretation of these things: 17'The four
great beasts are four kingdoms that will
rise from the earth. 18But the saints of
the Most High will receive the kingdom
and will possess it for ever—yes, for
ever and ever.'
19"Then I wanted to know the true
meaning of the fourth beast, which was
different from all the others and most
terrifying, with its iron teeth and bronze
claws—the beast that crushed and devoured its victims and trampled underfoot whatever was left. 20I also wanted
to know about the ten horns on its head
and about the other horn that came up,
before which three of them fell—the
horn that looked more imposing than
the others and that had eyes and a
mouth that spoke boastfully. 21As I
watched, this horn was waging war
against the saints and defeating them,
22until the Ancient of Days came and
pronounced judgment in favour of
the saints of the Most High, and the
time came when they possessed the
kingdom.
23"He gave me this explanation: 'The
fourth beast is a fourth kingdom that
will appear on earth. It will be different
from all the other kingdoms and will
devour the whole earth, trampling it
down and crushing it. 24The ten horns
are ten kings who will come from this
kingdom. After them another king will
arise, different from the earlier ones; he
will subdue three kings. 25He will speak
against the Most High and oppress his
saints and try to change the set times
and the laws. The saints will be handed
over to him for a time, times and half a
time.
26" 'But the court will sit, and his
power will be taken away and completely destroyed for ever. 27Then the
sovereignty, power and greatness of the
kingdoms under the whole heaven will
be handed over to the saints, the people
of the Most High. His kingdom will be
an everlasting kingdom, and all rulers
will worship and obey him.'
28"This is the end of the matter. I,
Daniel, was deeply troubled by my
thoughts, and my face turned pale, but I
kept the matter to myself."

Daniel's Vision of a Ram and a Goat

8 In the third year of King Belshazzar's reign, I, Daniel, had a vision,
after the one that had already appeared
to me. 2In my vision I saw myself in the
citadel of Susa in the province of Elam;
in the vision I was beside the Ulai
Canal. 3I looked up, and there before
me was a ram with two horns, standing
beside the canal, and the horns were
long. One of the horns was longer than
the other but grew up later. 4I watched
the ram as he charged towards the west
and the north and the south. No animal
could stand against him, and none could
rescue from his power. He did as he
pleased and became great.
5As I was thinking about this, suddenly a goat with a prominent horn
between his eyes came from the west,
crossing the whole earth without
touching the ground. 6He came towards
the two-horned ram I had seen standing
beside the canal and charged at him in
great rage. 7I saw him attack the ram
furiously, striking the ram and shatter-
ing his two horns. The ram was powerless to stand against him; the goat
knocked him to the ground and trampled on him, and none could rescue the
ram from his power. 8The goat became
very great, but at the height of his power
his large horn was broken off, and in its
place four prominent horns grew up
towards the four winds of heaven.
9Out of one of them came another
horn, which started small but grew in
power to the south and to the east and
towards the Beautiful Land. 10It grew
until it reached the host of the heavens,
and it threw some of the starry host
down to the earth and trampled on
them. 11It set itself up to be as great as
the Prince of the host; it took away the
daily sacrifice from him, and the place
of his sanctuary was brought low.
12Because of rebellion, the host ⌞of the

saints⌋ and the daily sacrifice were given
over to it. It prospered in everything it
did, and truth was thrown to the
ground.
13 Then I heard a holy one speaking,
and another holy one said to him, "How
long will it take for the vision to be
fulfilled—the vision concerning the
daily sacrifice, the rebellion that causes
desolation, and the surrender of the
sanctuary and of the host that will be
trampled underfoot?"
14 He said to me, "It will take 2,300
evenings and mornings; then the sanctuary will be reconsecrated."

NEW TESTAMENT READING
1 John 2:12–27

12 I write to you, dear children,
because your sins have been
forgiven on account of his
name.
13 I write to you, fathers,
because you have known him who
is from the beginning.
I write to you, young men,
because you have overcome the
evil one.
I write to you, dear children,
because you have known the
Father.
14 I write to you, fathers,
because you have known him who
is from the beginning.
I write to you, young men,
because you are strong,
and the word of God lives in you,
and you have overcome the evil
one.

Do Not Love the World

15 Do not love the world or anything in
the world. If anyone loves the world,
the love of the Father is not in him.
16 For everything in the world—the
cravings of sinful man, the lust of his
eyes and the boasting of what he has and
does—comes not from the Father but
from the world. 17 The world and its
desires pass away, but the man who
does the will of God lives for ever.

Warning Against Antichrists

18 Dear children, this is the last hour;
and as you have heard that the antichrist
is coming, even now many antichrists
have come. This is how we know it is the
last hour. 19 They went out from us, but
they did not really belong to us. For if
they had belonged to us, they would
have remained with us; but their going
showed that none of them belonged to
us.
20 But you have an anointing from the
Holy One, and all of you know the
truth. 21 I do not write to you because
you do not know the truth, but because
you do know it and because no lie comes
from the truth. 22 Who is the liar? It is
the man who denies that Jesus is the
Christ. Such a man is the antichrist—he
denies the Father and the Son. 23 No-
one who denies the Son has the Father;
whoever acknowledges the Son has the
Father also.
24 See that what you have heard from
the beginning remains in you. If it does,
you also will remain in the Son and in
the Father. 25 And this is what he promised us—even eternal life.
26 I am writing these things to you
about those who are trying to lead you
astray. 27 As for you, the anointing
you received from him remains in you,
and you do not need anyone to teach
you. But as his anointing teaches you
about all things and as that anointing is
real, not counterfeit—just as it has
taught you, remain in him.

READING FROM PSALMS
Psalm 136:13–26

13 to him who divided the Red Sea
asunder
His love endures for ever.
14 and brought Israel through the midst
of it,
His love endures for ever.

[15]but swept Pharaoh and his army into the Red Sea;
His love endures for ever.

[16]to him who led his people through the desert,
His love endures for ever.
[17]who struck down great kings,
His love endures for ever.
[18]and killed mighty kings—
His love endures for ever.
[19]Sihon king of the Amorites
His love endures for ever.
[20]and Og king of Bashan—
His love endures for ever.
[21]and gave their land as an inheritance,
His love endures for ever.
[22]an inheritance to his servant Israel;
His love endures for ever.

[23]to the One who remembered us in our low estate
His love endures for ever.
[24]and freed us from our enemies,
His love endures for ever.
[25]and who gives food to every creature.
His love endures for ever.

[26]Give thanks to the God of heaven.
His love endures for ever.

DECEMBER 2

DAY 336

OLD TESTAMENT READING
Daniel 8:15–9:19

The Interpretation of the Vision

[15]While I, Daniel, was watching the
vision and trying to understand it, there
before me stood one who looked like a
man. [16]And I heard a man's voice from
the Ulai calling, "Gabriel, tell this man
the meaning of the vision."
[17]As he came near the place where I
was standing, I was terrified and fell
prostrate. "Son of man," he said to me,
"understand that the vision concerns
the time of the end."
[18]While he was speaking to me, I was
in a deep sleep, with my face to the
ground. Then he touched me and raised
me to my feet.
[19]He said: "I am going to tell you
what will happen later in the time of
wrath, because the vision concerns the
appointed time of the end. [20]The two-
horned ram that you saw represents the
kings of Media and Persia. [21]The shaggy
goat is the king of Greece, and the large
horn between his eyes is the first king.
[22]The four horns that replaced the
one that was broken off represent four
kingdoms that will emerge from his
nation but will not have the same power.
[23]"In the latter part of their reign,
when rebels have become completely
wicked, a stern-faced king, a master of
intrigue, will arise. [24]He will become
very strong, but not by his own power.
He will cause astounding devastation
and will succeed in whatever he does.
He will destroy the mighty men and the
holy people. [25]He will cause deceit to
prosper, and he will consider himself
superior. When they feel secure, he will
destroy many and take his stand against
the Prince of princes. Yet he will be
destroyed, but not by human power.
[26]"The vision of the evenings and
mornings that has been given you is
true, but seal up the vision, for it concerns the distant future."
[27]I, Daniel, was exhausted and lay ill
for several days. Then I got up and
went about the king's business. I was
appalled by the vision; it was beyond
understanding.

Daniel's Prayer

9 In the first year of Darius son of
Xerxes (a Mede by descent), who
was made ruler over the Babylonian

kingdom—[2]in the first year of his reign,
I, Daniel, understood from the Scriptures, according to the word of the
LORD given to Jeremiah the prophet,
that the desolation of Jerusalem would
last seventy years. [3]So I turned to the
Lord God and pleaded with him in
prayer and petition, in fasting, and in
sackcloth and ashes.
[4]I prayed to the LORD my God and
confessed:

"O Lord, the great and awesome
God, who keeps his covenant of
love with all who love him and obey
his commands, [5]we have sinned
and done wrong. We have been
wicked and have rebelled; we have
turned away from your commands
and laws. [6]We have not listened to
your servants the prophets, who
spoke in your name to our kings,
our princes and our fathers, and to
all the people of the land.
[7]"Lord, you are righteous, but
this day we are covered with shame
—the men of Judah and people of
Jerusalem and all Israel, both near
and far, in all the countries where
you have scattered us because of
our unfaithfulness to you. [8]O
LORD, we and our kings, our
princes and our fathers are covered
with shame because we have sinned against you. [9]The Lord our
God is merciful and forgiving, even
though we have rebelled against
him; [10]we have not obeyed the
LORD our God or kept the laws he
gave us through his servants the
prophets. [11]All Israel has trans-
gressed your law and turned away,
refusing to obey you.
"Therefore the curses and sworn
judgments written in the Law of
Moses, the servant of God, have
been poured out on us, because we
have sinned against you. [12]You
have fulfilled the words spoken
against us and against our rulers by
bringing upon us great disaster.
Under the whole heaven nothing
has ever been done like what has
been done to Jerusalem. [13]Just as it
is written in the Law of Moses, all
this disaster has come upon us, yet
we have not sought the favour of
the LORD our God by turning from
our sins and giving attention to
your truth. [14]The LORD did not
hesitate to bring the disaster upon
us, for the LORD our God is righteous in everything he does; yet we
have not obeyed him.
[15]"Now, O Lord our God, who
brought your people out of Egypt
with a mighty hand and who made
for yourself a name that endures to
this day, we have sinned, we have
done wrong. [16]O Lord, in keeping
with all your righteous acts, turn
away your anger and your wrath
from Jerusalem, your city, your
holy hill. Our sins and the iniquities
of our fathers have made Jerusalem and your people an object of
scorn to all those around us.
[17]"Now, our God, hear the
prayers and petitions of your servant. For your sake, O Lord, look
with favour on your desolate sanctuary. [18]Give ear, O God, and
hear; open your eyes and see the
desolation of the city that bears
your Name. We do not make requests of you because we are righteous, but because of your great
mercy. [19]O Lord, listen! O Lord,
forgive! O Lord, hear and act! For
your sake, O my God, do not delay, because your city and your
people bear your Name."

NEW TESTAMENT READING
1 John 2:28–3:10

Children of God

[28]And now, dear children, continue
in him, so that when he appears we may
be confident and unashamed before him
at his coming.
[29]If you know that he is righteous,

you know that everyone who does what
is right has been born of him.

3 How great is the love the Father
has lavished on us, that we should
be called children of God! And that is
what we are! The reason the world does
not know us is that it did not know him.
2Dear friends, now we are children of
God, and what we will be has not yet
been made known. But we know that
when he appears, we shall be like him,
for we shall see him as he is. 3Everyone
who has this hope in him purifies himself, just as he is pure.
4Everyone who sins breaks the law; in
fact, sin is lawlessness. 5But you know
that he appeared so that he might take
away our sins. And in him is no sin.
6No-one who lives in him keeps on sinning. No-one who continues to sin has
either seen him or known him.
7Dear children, do not let anyone
lead you astray. He who does what is
right is righteous, just as he is righteous.
8He who does what is sinful is of the
devil, because the devil has been sinning from the beginning. The reason the
Son of God appeared was to destroy the
devil's work. 9No-one who is born of
God will continue to sin, because God's
seed remains in him; he cannot go on
sinning, because he has been born of
God. 10This is how we know who the
children of God are and who the children of the devil are: Anyone who does
not do what is right is not a child of God;
nor is anyone who does not love his
brother.

READING FROM PROVERBS
Proverbs 29:10–18

10Bloodthirsty men hate a man of
integrity
and seek to kill the upright.

11A fool gives full vent to his anger,
but a wise man keeps himself under
control.

12If a ruler listens to lies,
all his officials become wicked.

13The poor man and the oppressor
have this in common:
The LORD gives sight to the eyes of
both.

14If a king judges the poor with
fairness,
his throne will always be secure.

15The rod of correction imparts
wisdom,
but a child left to himself disgraces
his mother.

16When the wicked thrive, so does sin,
but the righteous will see their
downfall.

17Discipline your son, and he will give
you peace;
he will bring delight to your soul.

18Where there is no revelation, the
people cast off restraint;
but blessed is he who keeps the
law.

DAY 337

DECEMBER 3

OLD TESTAMENT READING
Daniel 9:20–11:1

The Seventy "Sevens"

20While I was speaking and praying,
confessing my sin and the sin of my
people Israel and making my request to
the LORD my God for his holy hill—
21while I was still in prayer, Gabriel, the
man I had seen in the earlier vision,
came to me in swift flight about the time
of the evening sacrifice. 22He instructed
me and said to me, "Daniel, I have now
come to give you insight and understanding. 23As soon as you began to
pray, an answer was given, which I have
come to tell you, for you are highly
esteemed. Therefore, consider the message and understand the vision:
24"Seventy 'sevens' are decreed for
your people and your holy city to finish
transgression, to put an end to sin, to
atone for wickedness, to bring in everlasting righteousness, to seal up vision
and prophecy and to anoint the most
holy.
25"Know and understand this: From
the issuing of the decree to restore and
rebuild Jerusalem until the Anointed
One, the ruler, comes, there will be
seven 'sevens', and sixty-two 'sevens'. It
will be rebuilt with streets and a trench,
but in times of trouble. 26After the sixty-
two 'sevens', the Anointed One will be
cut off and will have nothing. The people of the ruler who will come will destroy the city and the sanctuary. The end
will come like a flood: War will continue
until the end, and desolations have been
decreed. 27He will confirm a covenant
with many for one 'seven'. In the middle
of the 'seven' he will put an end to
sacrifice and offering. And on a wing ⌞of
the temple⌟ he will set up an abomination that causes desolation, until the
end that is decreed is poured out on
him."

Daniel's Vision of a Man

10 In the third year of Cyrus king of
Persia, a revelation was given to
Daniel (who was called Belteshazzar).
Its message was true and it concerned a
great war. The understanding of the
message came to him in a vision.
2At that time I, Daniel, mourned for
three weeks. 3I ate no choice food; no
meat or wine touched my lips; and I
used no lotions at all until the three
weeks were over.
4On the twenty-fourth day of the first
month, as I was standing on the bank of
the great river, the Tigris, 5I looked up
and there before me was a man dressed
in linen, with a belt of the finest gold
round his waist. 6His body was like
chrysolite, his face like lightning, his
eyes like flaming torches, his arms and
legs like the gleam of burnished bronze,
and his voice like the sound of a
multitude.
7I, Daniel, was the only one who saw
the vision; the men with me did not see
it, but such terror overwhelmed them
that they fled and hid themselves. 8So
I was left alone, gazing at this great
vision; I had no strength left, my
face turned deathly pale and I was helpless. 9Then I heard him speaking, and as
I listened to him, I fell into a deep sleep,
my face to the ground.
10A hand touched me and set me
trembling on my hands and knees. 11He
said, "Daniel, you who are highly
esteemed, consider carefully the words
I am about to speak to you, and stand
up, for I have now been sent to you."
And when he said this to me, I stood up
trembling.
12Then he continued, "Do not be
afraid, Daniel. Since the first day that
you set your mind to gain understanding
and to humble yourself before your
God, your words were heard, and I
have come in response to them. 13But

the prince of the Persian kingdom resisted me twenty-one days. Then
Michael, one of the chief princes, came
to help me, because I was detained
there with the king of Persia. 14Now I
have come to explain to you what will
happen to your people in the future, for
the vision concerns a time yet to come."
15While he was saying this to me, I
bowed with my face towards the ground
and was speechless. 16Then one who
looked like a man touched my lips, and I
opened my mouth and began to speak.
I said to the one standing before me,
"I am overcome with anguish because
of the vision, my lord, and I am helpless. 17How can I, your servant, talk
with you, my lord? My strength is gone
and I can hardly breathe."
18Again the one who looked like a
man touched me and gave me strength.
19"Do not be afraid, O man highly
esteemed," he said. "Peace! Be strong
now; be strong."

When he spoke to me, I was strengthened and said, "Speak, my lord, since
you have given me strength."
20So he said, "Do you know why I
have come to you? Soon I will return to
fight against the prince of Persia, and
when I go, the prince of Greece will
come; 21but first I will tell you what is
written in the Book of Truth. (No-one
supports me against them except
11 Michael, your prince. 1And in
the first year of Darius the
Mede, I took my stand to support and
protect him.)

NEW TESTAMENT READING
1 John 3:11–4:6

Love One Another

11This is the message you heard from
the beginning: We should love one
another. 12Do not be like Cain, who
belonged to the evil one and murdered
his brother. And why did he murder
him? Because his own actions were evil
and his brother's were righteous. 13Do
not be surprised, my brothers, if the
world hates you. 14We know that we
have passed from death to life, because
we love our brothers. Anyone who does
not love remains in death. 15Anyone
who hates his brother is a murderer, and
you know that no murderer has eternal
life in him.
16This is how we know what love is:
Jesus Christ laid down his life for us.
And we ought to lay down our lives for
our brothers. 17If anyone has material
possessions and sees his brother in need
but has no pity on him, how can the love
of God be in him? 18Dear children, let
us not love with words or tongue but
with actions and in truth. 19This then is
how we know that we belong to the
truth, and how we set our hearts at rest
in his presence 20whenever our hearts
condemn us. For God is greater than
our hearts, and he knows everything.
21Dear friends, if our hearts do not
condemn us, we have confidence before
God 22and receive from him anything
we ask, because we obey his commands
and do what pleases him. 23And this is
his command: to believe in the name of
his Son, Jesus Christ, and to love one
another as he commanded us. 24Those
who obey his commands live in him, and
he in them. And this is how we know
that he lives in us: We know it by the
Spirit he gave us.

Test the Spirits

4 Dear friends, do not believe every
spirit, but test the spirits to see
whether they are from God, because
many false prophets have gone out into
the world. 2This is how you can recognise the Spirit of God: Every spirit that
acknowledges that Jesus Christ has
come in the flesh is from God, 3but
every spirit that does not acknowledge
Jesus is not from God. This is the spirit
of the antichrist, which you have heard
is coming and even now is already in the
world.

[4]You, dear children, are from God and have overcome them, because the one who is in you is greater than the one who is in the world. [5]They are from the world and therefore speak from the viewpoint of the world, and the world listens to them. [6]We are from God, and whoever knows God listens to us; but whoever is not from God does not listen to us. This is how we recognise the Spirit of truth and the spirit of falsehood.

READING FROM PSALMS
Psalm 137:1–9

[1]By the rivers of Babylon we sat and wept
when we remembered Zion.
[2]There on the poplars
we hung our harps,
[3]for there our captors asked us for songs,
our tormentors demanded songs of joy;
they said, "Sing us one of the songs of Zion!"

[4]How can we sing the songs of the LORD
while in a foreign land?
[5]If I forget you, O Jerusalem,
may my right hand forget ⌞its skill⌟.
[6]May my tongue cling to the roof of my mouth
if I do not remember you,
if I do not consider Jerusalem
my highest joy.

[7]Remember, O LORD, what the Edomites did
on the day Jerusalem fell.
"Tear it down," they cried,
"tear it down to its foundations!"

[8]O Daughter of Babylon, doomed to destruction,
happy is he who repays you
for what you have done to us—
[9]he who seizes your infants
and dashes them against the rocks.

DAY 338

DECEMBER 4

OLD TESTAMENT READING
Daniel 11:2–35

The Kings of the South and the North

[2]"Now then, I tell you the truth: Three more kings will appear in Persia, and then a fourth, who will be far richer than all the others. When he has gained power by his wealth, he will stir up everyone against the kingdom of Greece. [3]Then a mighty king will appear, who will rule with great power and do as he pleases. [4]After he has appeared, his empire will be broken up and parcelled out towards the four winds of heaven. It will not go to his descendants, nor will it have the power he exercised, because his empire will be uprooted and given to others.

[5]"The king of the South will become strong, but one of his commanders will become even stronger than he and will rule his own kingdom with great power. [6]After some years, they will become allies. The daughter of the king of the South will go to the king of the North to make an alliance, but she will not retain her power, and he and his power will not last. In those days she will be handed over, together with her royal escort and her father and the one who supported her.

[7]"One from her family line will arise to take her place. He will attack the forces of the king of the North and enter his fortress; he will fight against them and be victorious. [8]He will also seize their gods, their metal images and their

valuable articles of silver and gold and
carry them off to Egypt. For some years
he will leave the king of the North
alone. [9]Then the king of the North will
invade the realm of the king of the
South but will retreat to his own country. [10]His sons will prepare for war and
assemble a great army, which will sweep
on like an irresistible flood and carry the
battle as far as his fortress.

[11]"Then the king of the South will
march out in rage and fight against the
king of the North, who will raise a large
army, but it will be defeated. [12]When
the army is carried off, the king of the
South will be filled with pride and will
slaughter many thousands, yet he will
not remain triumphant. [13]For the king
of the North will muster another army,
larger than the first; and after several
years, he will advance with a huge army
fully equipped.

[14]"In those times many will rise
against the king of the South. The violent men among your own people will
rebel in fulfilment of the vision, but
without success. [15]Then the king of the
North will come and build up siege
ramps and will capture a fortified city.
The forces of the South will be powerless to resist; even their best troops will
not have the strength to stand. [16]The
invader will do as he pleases; no-one
will be able to stand against him. He will
establish himself in the Beautiful Land
and will have the power to destroy it.
[17]He will determine to come with the
might of his entire kingdom and will
make an alliance with the king of the
South. And he will give him a daughter
in marriage in order to overthrow the
kingdom, but his plans will not succeed
or help him. [18]Then he will turn his
attention to the coastlands and will take
many of them, but a commander will
put an end to his insolence and will
turn his insolence back upon him.
[19]After this, he will turn back towards
the fortresses of his own country but
will stumble and fall, to be seen no
more.

[20]"His successor will send out a tax
collector to maintain the royal splendour. In a few years, however, he will
be destroyed, yet not in anger or in
battle.

[21]"He will be succeeded by a
contemptible person who has not been
given the honour of royalty. He will
invade the kingdom when its people feel
secure, and he will seize it through intrigue. [22]Then an overwhelming army will
be swept away before him; both it and
a prince of the covenant will be destroyed. [23]After coming to an agreement with him, he will act deceitfully,
and with only a few people he will rise
to power. [24]When the richest provinces
feel secure, he will invade them and will
achieve what neither his fathers nor his
forefathers did. He will distribute plunder, loot and wealth among his followers. He will plot the overthrow of
fortresses—but only for a time.

[25]"With a large army he will stir up his
strength and courage against the king of
the South. The king of the South will
wage war with a large and very powerful
army, but he will not be able to stand
because of the plots devised against
him. [26]Those who eat from the king's
provisions will try to destroy him; his
army will be swept away, and many will
fall in battle. [27]The two kings, with their
hearts bent on evil, will sit at the same
table and lie to each other, but to no
avail, because an end will still come at
the appointed time. [28]The king of the
North will return to his own country
with great wealth, but his heart will be
set against the holy covenant. He will
take action against it and then return to
his own country.

[29]"At the appointed time he will invade the South again, but this time the
outcome will be different from what it
was before. [30]Ships of the western
coastlands will oppose him, and he will
lose heart. Then he will turn back and
vent his fury against the holy covenant.
He will return and show favour to those
who forsake the holy covenant.

[31]"His armed forces will rise up to
desecrate the temple fortress and will

abolish the daily sacrifice. Then they
will set up the abomination that causes
desolation. 32With flattery he will corrupt those who have violated the covenant, but the people who know their
God will firmly resist him.

33"Those who are wise will instruct
many, though for a time they will fall by
the sword or be burned or captured or
plundered. 34When they fall, they will
receive a little help, and many who are
not sincere will join them. 35Some of the
wise will stumble, so that they may be
refined, purified and made spotless until
the time of the end, for it will still come
at the appointed time.

NEW TESTAMENT READING
1 John 4:7–21

God's Love and Ours

7Dear friends, let us love one
another, for love comes from God.
Everyone who loves has been born of
God and knows God. 8Whoever does
not love does not know God, because
God is love. 9This is how God showed
his love among us: He sent his one and
only Son into the world that we might
live through him. 10This is love: not that
we loved God, but that he loved us and
sent his Son as an atoning sacrifice for
our sins. 11Dear friends, since God so
loved us, we also ought to love one
another. 12No-one has ever seen God;
but if we love one another, God lives in
us and his love is made complete in us.

13We know that we live in him and he
in us, because he has given us of his
Spirit. 14And we have seen and testify
that the Father has sent his Son to be the
Saviour of the world. 15If anyone acknowledges that Jesus is the Son of
God, God lives in him and he in God.
16And so we know and rely on the love
God has for us.

God is love. Whoever lives in love
lives in God, and God in him. 17In this
way, love is made complete among us so
that we will have confidence on the day
of judgment, because in this world we
are like him. 18There is no fear in love.
But perfect love drives out fear, because fear has to do with punishment.
The one who fears is not made perfect in
love.

19We love because he first loved us.
20If anyone says, "I love God," yet
hates his brother, he is a liar. For anyone who does not love his brother,
whom he has seen, cannot love God,
whom he has not seen. 21And he has
given us this command: Whoever loves
God must also love his brother.

READING FROM PSALMS
Psalm 138:1–8

Of David.

1I will praise you, O LORD, with all my
heart;
before the "gods" I will sing your
praise.
2I will bow down towards your holy
temple
and will praise your name
for your love and your faithfulness,
for you have exalted above all things
your name and your word.
3When I called, you answered me;
you made me bold and
stout-hearted.

4May all the kings of the earth praise
you, O LORD,
when they hear the words of your
mouth.
5May they sing of the ways of the
LORD,
for the glory of the LORD is great.

6Though the LORD is on high, he looks
upon the lowly,
but the proud he knows from afar.
7Though I walk in the midst of
trouble,
you preserve my life;
you stretch out your hand against the
anger of my foes,

with your right hand you save
me.
8The LORD will fulfil ⌞his purpose⌟ for
me;
your love, O LORD, endures for
ever—
do not abandon the works of your
hands.

DECEMBER 5

DAY 339

OLD TESTAMENT READING
Daniel 11:36–12:13

The King Who Exalts Himself

36"The king will do as he pleases. He will exalt and magnify himself above every god and will say unheard-of things against the God of gods. He will be successful until the time of wrath is completed, for what has been determined must take place.
37He will show no regard for the gods of his fathers or for the one desired by women, nor will he regard any god, but will exalt himself above them all.
38Instead of them, he will honour a god of fortresses; a god unknown to his fathers he will honour with gold and silver, with precious stones and costly gifts.
39He will attack the mightiest fortresses with the help of a foreign god and will greatly honour those who acknowledge him. He will make them rulers over many people and will distribute the land at a price.

40"At the time of the end the king of the South will engage him in battle, and the king of the North will storm out against him with chariots and cavalry and a great fleet of ships. He will invade many countries and sweep through them like a flood.
41He will also invade the Beautiful Land. Many countries will fall, but Edom, Moab and the leaders of Ammon will be delivered from his hand.
42He will extend his power over many countries; Egypt will not escape.
43He will gain control of the treasures of gold and silver and all the riches of Egypt, with the Libyans and Nubians in submission.
44But reports from the east and the north will alarm him, and he will set out in a great rage to destroy and annihilate many.
45He will pitch his royal tents between the seas at the beautiful holy mountain. Yet he will come to his end, and no-one will help him.

The End Times

12 "At that time Michael, the great prince who protects your people, will arise. There will be a time of distress such as has not happened from the beginning of nations until then. But at that time your people—everyone whose name is found written in the book—will be delivered.
2Multitudes who sleep in the dust of the earth will awake: some to everlasting life, others to shame and everlasting contempt.
3Those who are wise will shine like the brightness of the heavens, and those who lead many to righteousness, like the stars for ever and ever.
4But you, Daniel, close up and seal the words of the scroll until the time of the end. Many will go here and there to increase knowledge."

5Then I, Daniel, looked, and there before me stood two others, one on this bank of the river and one on the opposite bank.
6One of them said to the man clothed in linen, who was above the waters of the river, "How long will it be before these astonishing things are fulfilled?"

7The man clothed in linen, who was

above the waters of the river, lifted his
right hand and his left hand towards
heaven, and I heard him swear by him
who lives for ever, saying, "It will be for
a time, times and half a time. When
the power of the holy people has been
finally broken, all these things will be
completed."
8I heard, but I did not understand. So
I asked, "My lord, what will the outcome of all this be?"
9He replied, "Go your way, Daniel,
because the words are closed up and
sealed until the time of the end. 10Many
will be purified, made spotless and refined, but the wicked will continue to be
wicked. None of the wicked will understand, but those who are wise will
understand.
11"From the time that the daily sacrifice is abolished and the abomination
that causes desolation is set up, there
will be 1,290 days. 12Blessed is the one
who waits for and reaches the end of the
1,335 days.
13"As for you, go your way till the
end. You will rest, and then at the end
of the days you will rise to receive your
allotted inheritance."

NEW TESTAMENT READING
1 John 5:1–21

Faith in the Son of God

5
Everyone who believes that Jesus
is the Christ is born of God, and
everyone who loves the father loves his
child as well. 2This is how we know that
we love the children of God: by loving
God and carrying out his commands.
3This is love for God: to obey his commands. And his commands are not
burdensome, 4for everyone born of
God overcomes the world. This is the
victory that has overcome the world,
even our faith. 5Who is it that overcomes the world? Only he who believes
that Jesus is the Son of God.
6This is the one who came by water
and blood—Jesus Christ. He did not
come by water only, but by water and
blood. And it is the Spirit who testifies,
because the Spirit is the truth. 7For
there are three that testify: 8the Spirit,
the water and the blood; and the three
are in agreement. 9We accept man's
testimony, but God's testimony is
greater because it is the testimony of
God, which he has given about his Son.
10Anyone who believes in the Son of
God has this testimony in his heart.
Anyone who does not believe God has
made him out to be a liar, because he
has not believed the testimony God has
given about his Son. 11And this is the
testimony: God has given us eternal
life, and this life is in his Son. 12He who
has the Son has life; he who does not
have the Son of God does not have life.

Concluding Remarks

13I write these things to you who believe in the name of the Son of God so
that you may know that you have eternal life. 14This is the confidence we have
in approaching God: that if we ask anything according to his will, he hears us.
15And if we know that he hears us—
whatever we ask—we know that we
have what we asked of him.
16If anyone sees his brother commit a
sin that does not lead to death, he
should pray and God will give him life. I
refer to those whose sin does not lead to
death. There is a sin that leads to death.
I am not saying that he should pray
about that. 17All wrongdoing is sin, and
there is sin that does not lead to death.
18We know that anyone born of God
does not continue to sin; the one who
was born of God keeps him safe, and
the evil one cannot harm him. 19We
know that we are children of God, and
that the whole world is under the control of the evil one. 20We know also that
the Son of God has come and has given
us understanding, so that we may know
him who is true. And we are in him who
is true—even in his Son Jesus Christ.
He is the true God and eternal life.
21Dear children, keep yourselves
from idols.

READING FROM PSALMS

Psalm 139:1–10

For the director of music. Of David.
A psalm.

1O LORD, you have searched me
and you know me.
2You know when I sit and when I
rise;
you perceive my thoughts from
afar.
3You discern my going out and my
lying down;
you are familiar with all my ways.
4Before a word is on my tongue
you know it completely, O LORD.
5You hem me in—behind and before;
you have laid your hand upon me.
6Such knowledge is too wonderful for
me,
too lofty for me to attain.

7Where can I go from your Spirit?
Where can I flee from your
presence?
8If I go up to the heavens, you are
there;
if I make my bed in the depths, you
are there.
9If I rise on the wings of the dawn,
if I settle on the far side of the sea,
10even there your hand will guide me,
your right hand will hold me fast.

DECEMBER 6

DAY 340

OLD TESTAMENT READING

Haggai 1:1–2:23

A Call to Build the House of the LORD

1 In the second year of King Darius,
on the first day of the sixth month,
the word of the LORD came through the
prophet Haggai to Zerubbabel son of
Shealtiel, governor of Judah, and to
Joshua son of Jehozadak, the high
priest:

2This is what the LORD Almighty
says: "These people say, 'The time has
not yet come for the LORD's house to be
built.'"

3Then the word of the LORD came
through the prophet Haggai: 4"Is it a
time for you yourselves to be living in
your panelled houses, while this house
remains a ruin?"

5Now this is what the LORD Almighty
says: "Give careful thought to your
ways. 6You have planted much, but
have harvested little. You eat, but
never have enough. You drink,
but never have your fill. You put on
clothes, but are not warm. You earn
wages, only to put them in a purse with
holes in it."

7This is what the LORD Almighty
says: "Give careful thought to your
ways. 8Go up into the mountains and
bring down timber and build the house,
so that I may take pleasure in it and be
honoured," says the LORD. 9"You
expected much, but see, it turned out to
be little. What you brought home, I
blew away. Why?" declares the LORD
Almighty. "Because of my house,
which remains a ruin, while each of you
is busy with his own house. 10Therefore,
because of you the heavens have withheld their dew and the earth its crops.
11I called for a drought on the fields and
the mountains, on the grain, the new
wine, the oil and whatever the ground
produces, on men and cattle, and on the
labour of your hands."

12Then Zerubbabel son of Shealtiel,
Joshua son of Jehozadak, the high
priest, and the whole remnant of the
people obeyed the voice of the LORD
their God and the message of the
prophet Haggai, because the LORD

their God had sent him. And the people
feared the LORD.
13Then Haggai, the LORD's messenger, gave this message of the LORD to
the people: "I am with you," declares
the LORD. 14So the LORD stirred up the
spirit of Zerubbabel son of Shealtiel,
governor of Judah, and the spirit of
Joshua son of Jehozadak, the high
priest, and the spirit of the whole remnant of the people. They came and began work on the house of the LORD
Almighty, their God, 15on the twenty-
fourth day of the sixth month in the
second year of King Darius.

The Promised Glory of the New House

2 On the twenty-first day of the
seventh month, the word of the
LORD came through the prophet Haggai: 2"Speak to Zerubbabel son of
Shealtiel, governor of Judah, to Joshua
son of Jehozadak, the high priest, and
to the remnant of the people. Ask them,
3'Who of you is left who saw this house
in its former glory? How does it look to
you now? Does it not seem to you like
nothing? 4But now be strong, O Zerubbabel,' declares the LORD. 'Be strong,
O Joshua son of Jehozadak, the high
priest. Be strong, all you people of the
land,' declares the LORD, 'and work.
For I am with you,' declares the LORD
Almighty. 5'This is what I covenanted
with you when you came out of Egypt.
And my Spirit remains among you. Do
not fear.'
6"This is what the LORD Almighty
says: 'In a little while I will once more
shake the heavens and the earth, the sea
and the dry land. 7I will shake all
nations, and the desired of all nations
will come, and I will fill this house
with glory,' says the LORD Almighty.
8'The silver is mine and the gold is
mine,' declares the LORD Almighty.
9'The glory of this present house will be
greater than the glory of the former
house,' says the LORD Almighty. 'And
in this place I will grant peace,' declares
the LORD Almighty."

Blessings for a Defiled People

10On the twenty-fourth day of the
ninth month, in the second year of
Darius, the word of the LORD came to
the prophet Haggai: 11"This is what the
LORD Almighty says: 'Ask the priests
what the law says: 12If a person carries
consecrated meat in the fold of his garment, and that fold touches some bread
or stew, some wine, oil or other food,
does it become consecrated?'"
The priests answered, "No."
13Then Haggai said, "If a person defiled by contact with a dead body
touches one of these things, does it become defiled?"
"Yes," the priests replied, "it becomes defiled."
14Then Haggai said, "'So it is with
this people and this nation in my sight,'
declares the LORD. 'Whatever they do
and whatever they offer there is defiled.
15"'Now give careful thought to this
from this day on—consider how things
were before one stone was laid on
another in the LORD's temple. 16When
anyone came to a heap of twenty measures, there were only ten. When anyone went to a wine vat to draw fifty
measures, there were only twenty. 17I
struck all the work of your hands with
blight, mildew and hail, yet you did not
turn to me,' declares the LORD. 18'From
this day on, from this twenty-fourth day
of the ninth month, give careful thought
to the day when the foundation of the
LORD's temple was laid. Give careful
thought: 19Is there yet any seed left in
the barn? Until now, the vine and the
fig-tree, the pomegranate and the olive
tree have not borne fruit.
"'From this day on I will bless you.'"

Zerubbabel the LORD's Signet Ring

20The word of the LORD came to Haggai a second time on the twenty-fourth
day of the month: 21"Tell Zerubbabel
governor of Judah that I will shake the
heavens and the earth. 22I will overturn
royal thrones and shatter the power of

the foreign kingdoms. I will overthrow chariots and their drivers; horses and their riders will fall, each by the sword of his brother.

23"'On that day,' declares the LORD Almighty, 'I will take you, my servant Zerubbabel son of Shealtiel,' declares the LORD, 'and I will make you like my signet ring, for I have chosen you,' declares the LORD Almighty."

NEW TESTAMENT READING
2 John 1–13

1The elder,

To the chosen lady and her children, whom I love in the truth—and not I only, but also all who know the truth
—2because of the truth, which lives in us and will be with us for ever:

3Grace, mercy and peace from God the Father and from Jesus Christ, the Father's Son, will be with us in truth and love.

4It has given me great joy to find some of your children walking in the truth,
just as the Father commanded us. 5And
now, dear lady, I am not writing you a new command but one we have had from the beginning. I ask that we love
one another. 6And this is love: that we
walk in obedience to his commands. As you have heard from the beginning, his command is that you walk in love.
7Many deceivers, who do not acknowledge Jesus Christ as coming in the flesh, have gone out into the world. Any such person is the deceiver and the
antichrist. 8Watch out that you do not
lose what you have worked for, but that
you may be rewarded fully. 9Anyone
who runs ahead and does not continue in the teaching of Christ does not have God; whoever continues in the teaching
has both the Father and the Son. 10If
anyone comes to you and does not bring this teaching, do not take him into your
house or welcome him. 11Anyone who
welcomes him shares in his wicked work.
12I have much to write to you, but I do not want to use paper and ink. Instead, I hope to visit you and talk with you face to face, so that our joy may be complete.

13The children of your chosen sister send their greetings.

READING FROM PROVERBS
Proverbs 29:19–27

19A servant cannot be corrected by
mere words;
though he understands, he will not
respond.

20Do you see a man who speaks in
haste?
There is more hope for a fool than
for him.

21If a man pampers his servant from
youth,
he will bring grief in the end.

22An angry man stirs up dissension,
and a hot-tempered one commits
many sins.

23A man's pride brings him low,
but a man of lowly spirit gains
honour.

24The accomplice of a thief is his own
enemy;
he is put under oath and dare not
testify.

25Fear of man will prove to be a snare,
but whoever trusts in the LORD is
kept safe.

26Many seek an audience with a ruler,
but it is from the LORD that man
gets justice.

27The righteous detest the dishonest;
the wicked detest the upright.

DAY 341

DECEMBER 7

OLD TESTAMENT READING
Zechariah 1:1–4:14

A Call to Return to the LORD

1 In the eighth month of the second
year of Darius, the word of the
LORD came to the prophet Zechariah
son of Berekiah, the son of Iddo:
[2]"The LORD was very angry with your
forefathers. [3]Therefore tell the people:
This is what the LORD Almighty says:
'Return to me,' declares the LORD
Almighty, 'and I will return to you,'
says the LORD Almighty. [4]Do not be
like your forefathers, to whom the
earlier prophets proclaimed: This is
what the LORD Almighty says: 'Turn
from your evil ways and your evil practices.' But they would not listen or pay
attention to me, declares the LORD.
[5]Where are your forefathers now? And
the prophets, do they live for ever? [6]But
did not my words and my decrees,
which I commanded my servants the
prophets, overtake your forefathers?
"Then they repented and said, 'The
LORD Almighty has done to us what our
ways and practices deserve, just as he
determined to do.' "

The Man Among the Myrtle Trees

[7]On the twenty-fourth day of the
eleventh month, the month of Shebat,
in the second year of Darius, the word
of the LORD came to the prophet
Zechariah son of Berekiah, the son of
Iddo.
[8]During the night I had a vision—and
there before me was a man riding a red
horse! He was standing among the
myrtle trees in a ravine. Behind him
were red, brown and white horses.
[9]I asked, "What are these, my lord?"
The angel who was talking with me
answered, "I will show you what they
are."
[10]Then the man standing among the
myrtle trees explained, "They are the
ones the LORD has sent to go throughout the earth."
[11]And they reported to the angel of
the LORD, who was standing among the
myrtle trees, "We have gone throughout the earth and found the whole world
at rest and in peace."
[12]Then the angel of the LORD said,
"LORD Almighty, how long will you
withhold mercy from Jerusalem and
from the towns of Judah, which you
have been angry with these seventy
years?" [13]So the LORD spoke kind and
comforting words to the angel who
talked with me.
[14]Then the angel who was speaking to
me said, "Proclaim this word: This is
what the LORD Almighty says: 'I am
very jealous for Jerusalem and Zion,
[15]but I am very angry with the nations
that feel secure. I was only a little angry,
but they added to the calamity.'
[16]"Therefore, this is what the LORD
says: 'I will return to Jerusalem with
mercy, and there my house will be rebuilt. And the measuring line will be
stretched out over Jerusalem,' declares
the LORD Almighty.
[17]"Proclaim further: This is what the
LORD Almighty says: 'My towns will
again overflow with prosperity, and the
LORD will again comfort Zion and
choose Jerusalem.' "

Four Horns and Four Craftsmen

[18]Then I looked up—and there before me were four horns! [19]I asked the
angel who was speaking to me, "What
are these?"
He answered me, "These are the
horns that scattered Judah, Israel and
Jerusalem."
[20]Then the LORD showed me four
craftsmen. [21]I asked, "What are these
coming to do?"
He answered, "These are the horns
that scattered Judah so that no-one

could raise his head, but the craftsmen
have come to terrify them and throw
down these horns of the nations who
lifted up their horns against the land of
Judah to scatter its people."

A Man With a Measuring Line

2 Then I looked up—and there before me was a man with a measuring line in his hand! 2I asked, "Where
are you going?"

He answered me, "To measure Jerusalem, to find out how wide and how
long it is."

3Then the angel who was speaking to
me left, and another angel came to meet
him 4and said to him: "Run, tell that
young man, 'Jerusalem will be a city
without walls because of the great number of men and livestock in it. 5And I
myself will be a wall of fire around it,'
declares the LORD, 'and I will be its
glory within.'

6"Come! Come! Flee from the land of
the north," declares the LORD, "for I
have scattered you to the four winds of
heaven," declares the LORD.

7"Come, O Zion! Escape, you who
live in the Daughter of Babylon!" 8For
this is what the LORD Almighty says:
"After he has honoured me and has sent
me against the nations that have plundered you—for whoever touches you
touches the apple of his eye—9I will
surely raise my hand against them so
that their slaves will plunder them.
Then you will know that the LORD
Almighty has sent me.

10"Shout and be glad, O Daughter of
Zion. For I am coming, and I will live
among you," declares the LORD.
11"Many nations will be joined with the
LORD in that day and will become my
people. I will live among you and you
will know that the LORD Almighty has
sent me to you. 12The LORD will inherit
Judah as his portion in the holy land and
will again choose Jerusalem. 13Be still
before the LORD, all mankind, because
he has roused himself from his holy
dwelling."

Clean Garments for the High Priest

3 Then he showed me Joshua the
high priest standing before the
angel of the LORD, and Satan standing
at his right side to accuse him. 2The
LORD said to Satan, "The LORD rebuke
you, Satan! The LORD, who has chosen
Jerusalem, rebuke you! Is not this man
a burning stick snatched from the fire?"

3Now Joshua was dressed in filthy
clothes as he stood before the angel.
4The angel said to those who were
standing before him, "Take off his filthy
clothes."

Then he said to Joshua, "See, I have
taken away your sin, and I will put rich
garments on you."

5Then I said, "Put a clean turban on
his head." So they put a clean turban on
his head and clothed him, while the
angel of the LORD stood by.

6The angel of the LORD gave this
charge to Joshua: 7"This is what the
LORD Almighty says: 'If you will walk in
my ways and keep my requirements,
then you will govern my house and have
charge of my courts, and I will give you
a place among these standing here.

8" 'Listen, O high priest Joshua and
your associates seated before you, who
are men symbolic of things to come: I
am going to bring my servant, the
Branch. 9See, the stone I have set in
front of Joshua! There are seven eyes on
that one stone, and I will engrave an
inscription on it,' says the LORD
Almighty, 'and I will remove the sin of
this land in a single day.

10" 'In that day each of you will invite
his neighbour to sit under his vine and
fig-tree,' declares the LORD Almighty."

The Gold Lampstand and the Two Olive Trees

4 Then the angel who talked with me
returned and wakened me, as a
man is wakened from his sleep. 2He
asked me, "What do you see?"

I answered, "I see a solid gold lampstand with a bowl at the top and seven
lights on it, with seven channels to the

lights. 3Also there are two olive trees by
it, one on the right of the bowl and the
other on its left."
4I asked the angel who talked with
me, "What are these, my lord?"
5He answered, "Do you not know
what these are?"
"No, my lord," I replied.
6So he said to me, "This is the word of
the LORD to Zerubbabel: 'Not by might
nor by power, but by my Spirit,' says the
LORD Almighty.
7"What are you, O mighty mountain?
Before Zerubbabel you will become
level ground. Then he will bring out the
capstone to shouts of 'God bless it! God
bless it!'"
8Then the word of the LORD came to
me: 9"The hands of Zerubbabel have
laid the foundation of this temple; his
hands will also complete it. Then you
will know that the LORD Almighty has
sent me to you.
10"Who despises the day of small
things? Men will rejoice when they see
the plumb-line in the hand of Zerubbabel.
"(These seven are the eyes of the
LORD, which range throughout the
earth.)"
11Then I asked the angel, "What are
these two olive trees on the right and the
left of the lampstand?"
12Again I asked him, "What are these
two olive branches beside the two gold
pipes that pour out golden oil?"
13He replied, "Do you not know what
these are?"
"No, my lord," I said.
14So he said, "These are the two who
are anointed to serve the Lord of all the
earth."

NEW TESTAMENT READING

3 John 1–14

1The elder,

To my dear friend Gaius, whom I
love in the truth.

2Dear friend, I pray that you may
enjoy good health and that all may go
well with you, even as your soul is getting along well. 3It gave me great joy to
have some brothers come and tell about
your faithfulness to the truth and how
you continue to walk in the truth. 4I
have no greater joy than to hear that my
children are walking in the truth.
5Dear friend, you are faithful in what
you are doing for the brothers, even
though they are strangers to you. 6They
have told the church about your love.
You will do well to send them on their
way in a manner worthy of God. 7It was
for the sake of the Name that they went
out, receiving no help from the pagans.
8We ought therefore to show hospitality
to such men so that we may work
together for the truth.
9I wrote to the church, but Diotrephes, who loves to be first, will have
nothing to do with us. 10So if I come, I
will call attention to what he is doing,
gossiping maliciously about us. Not
satisfied with that, he refuses to welcome the brothers. He also stops those
who want to do so and puts them out of
the church.
11Dear friend, do not imitate what is
evil but what is good. Anyone who does
what is good is from God. Anyone who
does what is evil has not seen God.
12Demetrius is well spoken of by everyone—and even by the truth itself. We
also speak well of him, and you know
that our testimony is true.
13I have much to write to you, but I do
not want to do so with pen and ink. 14I
hope to see you soon, and we will talk
face to face.

Peace to you. The friends here send their greetings. Greet the friends there by name.

READING FROM PSALMS

Psalm 139:11–16

11If I say, "Surely the darkness will
hide me
and the light become night around
me,"

[12]even the darkness will not be dark to
you;
the night will shine like the day,
for darkness is as light to you.

[13]For you created my inmost being;
you knit me together in my
mother's womb.
[14]I praise you because I am fearfully
and wonderfully made;
your works are wonderful,
I know that full well.
[15]My frame was not hidden from you
when I was made in the secret
place.
When I was woven together in the
depths of the earth,
16 your eyes saw my unformed body.
All the days ordained for me
were written in your book
before one of them came to be.

DECEMBER 8

DAY 342

OLD TESTAMENT READING
Zechariah 5:1–8:23

The Flying Scroll

5 I looked again—and there before
me was a flying scroll!
[2]He asked me, "What do you see?"
I answered, "I see a flying scroll,
thirty feet long and fifteen feet wide."
[3]And he said to me, "This is the curse
that is going out over the whole land; for
according to what it says on one side,
every thief will be banished, and
according to what it says on the other,
everyone who swears falsely will be
banished. [4]The LORD Almighty declares, 'I will send it out, and it will enter
the house of the thief and the house of
him who swears falsely by my name. It
will remain in his house and destroy it,
both its timbers and its stones.'"

The Woman in a Basket

[5]Then the angel who was speaking
to me came forward and said to me,
"Look up and see what this is that is
appearing."
[6]I asked, "What is it?"
He replied, "It is a measuring basket." And he added, "This is the iniquity of the people throughout the
land."
[7]Then the cover of lead was raised,
and there in the basket sat a woman!
[8]He said, "This is wickedness," and he
pushed her back into the basket and
pushed the lead cover down over its
mouth.
[9]Then I looked up—and there before
me were two women, with the wind in
their wings! They had wings like those
of a stork, and they lifted up the basket
between heaven and earth.
[10]"Where are they taking the basket?" I asked the angel who was speaking to me.
[11]He replied, "To the country of
Babylonia to build a house for it. When
it is ready, the basket will be set there in
its place."

Four Chariots

6 I looked up again—and there before me were four chariots coming
out from between two mountains—
mountains of bronze! [2]The first chariot
had red horses, the second black, [3]the
third white, and the fourth dappled—
all of them powerful. [4]I asked the angel
who was speaking to me, "What are
these, my lord?"
[5]The angel answered me, "These are
the four spirits of heaven, going out
from standing in the presence of the
Lord of the whole world. [6]The one with

the black horses is going towards the
north country, the one with the white
horses towards the west, and the one
with the dappled horses towards the
south."
7When the powerful horses went out,
they were straining to go throughout the
earth. And he said, "Go throughout
the earth!" So they went throughout the
earth.
8Then he called to me, "Look, those
going towards the north country have
given my Spirit rest in the land of the
north."

A Crown for Joshua

9The word of the LORD came to me:
10"Take ⌞silver and gold⌟ from the
exiles Heldai, Tobijah and Jedaiah,
who have arrived from Babylon. Go the
same day to the house of Josiah son of
Zephaniah. 11Take the silver and gold
and make a crown, and set it on the
head of the high priest, Joshua son of
Jehozadak. 12Tell him this is what the
LORD Almighty says: 'Here is the man
whose name is the Branch, and he will
branch out from his place and build the
temple of the LORD. 13It is he who will
build the temple of the LORD, and he
will be clothed with majesty and will sit
and rule on his throne. And he will be a
priest on his throne. And there will be
harmony between the two.' 14The
crown will be given to Heldai, Tobijah,
Jedaiah and Hen son of Zephaniah as a
memorial in the temple of the LORD.
15Those who are far away will come and
help to build the temple of the LORD,
and you will know that the LORD
Almighty has sent me to you. This will
happen if you diligently obey the LORD
your God."

Justice and Mercy, Not Fasting

7 In the fourth year of King Darius,
the word of the LORD came to
Zechariah on the fourth day of the ninth
month, the month of Kislev. 2The people of Bethel had sent Sharezer and
Regem-Melech, together with their
men, to entreat the LORD 3by asking the
priests of the house of the LORD
Almighty and the prophets, "Should I
mourn and fast in the fifth month, as I
have done for so many years?"
4Then the word of the LORD Almighty came to me: 5"Ask all the
people of the land and the priests,
'When you fasted and mourned in the
fifth and seventh months for the past
seventy years, was it really for me that
you fasted? 6And when you were eating
and drinking, were you not just feasting
for yourselves? 7Are these not the
words the LORD proclaimed through the
earlier prophets when Jerusalem and its
surrounding towns were at rest and
prosperous, and the Negev and the
western foothills were settled?'"
8And the word of the LORD came
again to Zechariah: 9"This is what the
LORD Almighty says: 'Administer true
justice; show mercy and compassion to
one another. 10Do not oppress the
widow or the fatherless, the alien or the
poor. In your hearts do not think evil of
each other.'
11"But they refused to pay attention;
stubbornly they turned their backs and
stopped up their ears. 12They made
their hearts as hard as flint and would
not listen to the law or to the words that
the LORD Almighty had sent by his
Spirit through the earlier prophets. So
the LORD Almighty was very angry.
13"'When I called, they did not listen;
so when they called, I would not listen,'
says the LORD Almighty. 14'I scattered
them with a whirlwind among all the
nations, where they were strangers. The
land was left so desolate behind them
that no-one could come or go. This
is how they made the pleasant land
desolate.'"

The LORD Promises to Bless Jerusalem

8 Again the word of the LORD
Almighty came to me. 2This is what
the LORD Almighty says: "I am very
jealous for Zion; I am burning with
jealousy for her."

3This is what the LORD says: "I will
return to Zion and dwell in Jerusalem.
Then Jerusalem will be called the City
of Truth, and the mountain of the
LORD Almighty will be called the Holy
Mountain."
4This is what the LORD Almighty
says: "Once again men and women of
ripe old age will sit in the streets of
Jerusalem, each with cane in hand because of his age. 5The city streets will be
filled with boys and girls playing there."
6This is what the LORD Almighty
says: "It may seem marvellous to the
remnant of this people at that time, but
will it seem marvellous to me?" declares
the LORD Almighty.
7This is what the LORD Almighty
says: "I will save my people from the
countries of the east and the west. 8I will
bring them back to live in Jerusalem;
they will be my people, and I will be
faithful and righteous to them as their
God."
9This is what the LORD Almighty
says: "You who now hear these words
spoken by the prophets who were there
when the foundation was laid for the
house of the LORD Almighty, let your
hands be strong so that the temple may
be built. 10Before that time there were
no wages for man or beast. No-one
could go about his business safely because of his enemy, for I had turned
every man against his neighbour. 11But
now I will not deal with the remnant of
this people as I did in the past," declares
the LORD Almighty.
12"The seed will grow well, the vine
will yield its fruit, the ground will produce its crops, and the heavens will drop
their dew. I will give all these things as
an inheritance to the remnant of this
people. 13As you have been an object of
cursing among the nations, O Judah and
Israel, so will I save you, and you will be
a blessing. Do not be afraid, but let your
hands be strong."
14This is what the LORD Almighty
says: "Just as I had determined to bring
disaster upon you and showed no pity
when your fathers angered me," says
the LORD Almighty, 15"so now I have
determined to do good again to Jerusalem and Judah. Do not be afraid.
16These are the things you are to do:
Speak the truth to each other, and render true and sound judgment in your
courts; 17do not plot evil against your
neighbour, and do not love to swear
falsely. I hate all this," declares the
LORD.
18Again the word of the LORD
Almighty came to me. 19This is what the
LORD Almighty says: "The fasts of the
fourth, fifth, seventh and tenth months
will become joyful and glad occasions
and happy festivals for Judah. Therefore love truth and peace."
20This is what the LORD Almighty
says: "Many peoples and the inhabitants of many cities will yet come, 21and
the inhabitants of one city will go to
another and say, 'Let us go at once to
entreat the LORD and seek the LORD
Almighty. I myself am going.' 22And
many peoples and powerful nations will
come to Jerusalem to seek the LORD
Almighty and to entreat him."
23This is what the LORD Almighty
says: "In those days ten men from all
languages and nations will take firm
hold of one Jew by the hem of his robe
and say, 'Let us go with you, because we
have heard that God is with you.'"

NEW TESTAMENT READING

Jude 1–25

1Jude, a servant of Jesus Christ and a
brother of James,

To those who have been called, who
are loved by God the Father and kept by
Jesus Christ:

2Mercy, peace and love be yours in
abundance.

The Sin and Doom of Godless Men

3Dear friends, although I was very
eager to write to you about the salvation
we share, I felt I had to write and urge
you to contend for the faith that was

once for all entrusted to the saints. 4For
certain men whose condemnation was
written about long ago have secretly
slipped in among you. They are godless
men, who change the grace of our God
into a licence for immorality and deny
Jesus Christ our only Sovereign and
Lord.
5Though you already know all this, I
want to remind you that the Lord delivered his people out of Egypt, but
later destroyed those who did not believe. 6And the angels who did not keep
their positions of authority but abandoned their own home—these he has
kept in darkness, bound with everlasting chains for judgment on the great
Day. 7In a similar way, Sodom and
Gomorrah and the surrounding towns
gave themselves up to sexual immorality and perversion. They serve as an
example of those who suffer the punishment of eternal fire.
8In the very same way, these dream-
ers pollute their own bodies, reject authority and slander celestial beings.
9But even the archangel Michael, when
he was disputing with the devil about
the body of Moses, did not dare to bring
a slanderous accusation against him,
but said, "The Lord rebuke you!" 10Yet
these men speak abusively against
whatever they do not understand; and
what things they do understand by instinct, like unreasoning animals—these
are the very things that destroy them.
11Woe to them! They have taken the
way of Cain; they have rushed for profit
into Balaam's error; they have been
destroyed in Korah's rebellion.
12These men are blemishes at your
love feasts, eating with you without the
slightest qualm—shepherds who feed
only themselves. They are clouds without rain, blown along by the wind;
autumn trees, without fruit and uprooted—twice dead. 13They are wild
waves of the sea, foaming up their
shame; wandering stars, for whom
blackest darkness has been reserved for
ever.
14Enoch, the seventh from Adam,
prophesied about these men: "See, the
Lord is coming with thousands upon
thousands of his holy ones 15to judge
everyone, and to convict all the ungodly
of all the ungodly acts they have done in
the ungodly way, and of all the harsh
words ungodly sinners have spoken
against him." 16These men are grumb-
lers and fault-finders; they follow their
own evil desires; they boast about themselves and flatter others for their own
advantage.

A Call to Persevere

17But, dear friends, remember what
the apostles of our Lord Jesus Christ
foretold. 18They said to you, "In the last
times there will be scoffers who will
follow their own ungodly desires."
19These are the men who divide you,
who follow mere natural instincts and
do not have the Spirit.
20But you, dear friends, build yourselves up in your most holy faith and
pray in the Holy Spirit. 21Keep
yourselves in God's love as you wait for
the mercy of our Lord Jesus Christ to
bring you to eternal life.
22Be merciful to those who doubt;
23snatch others from the fire and save
them; to others show mercy, mixed with
fear—hating even the clothing stained
by corrupted flesh.

Doxology

24To him who is able to keep you from
falling and to present you before his
glorious presence without fault and with
great joy—25to the only God our
Saviour be glory, majesty, power and
authority, through Jesus Christ our
Lord, before all ages, now and for evermore! Amen.

READING FROM PSALMS

Psalm 139:17–24

17How precious to me are your
thoughts, O God!
How vast is the sum of them!

[18]Were I to count them,
they would outnumber the grains of sand.
When I awake,
I am still with you.

[19]If only you would slay the wicked, O God!
Away from me, you bloodthirsty men!
[20]They speak of you with evil intent;
your adversaries misuse your name.
[21]Do I not hate those who hate you, O LORD,
and abhor those who rise up against you?
[22]I have nothing but hatred for them;
I count them my enemies.

[23]Search me, O God, and know my heart;
test me and know my anxious thoughts.
[24]See if there is any offensive way in me,
and lead me in the way everlasting.

DECEMBER 9

DAY 343

OLD TESTAMENT READING

Zechariah 9:1–11:17

Judgment on Israel's Enemies

An Oracle

9 The word of the LORD is against the land of Hadrach
and will rest upon Damascus—
for the eyes of men and all the tribes of Israel
are on the LORD—
[2]and upon Hamath too, which borders on it,
and upon Tyre and Sidon, though they are very skilful.
[3]Tyre has built herself a stronghold;
she has heaped up silver like dust,
and gold like the dirt of the streets.
[4]But the Lord will take away her possessions
and destroy her power on the sea,
and she will be consumed by fire.
[5]Ashkelon will see it and fear;
Gaza will writhe in agony,
and Ekron too, for her hope will wither.
Gaza will lose her king
and Ashkelon will be deserted.
[6]Foreigners will occupy Ashdod,
and I will cut off the pride of the Philistines.
[7]I will take the blood from their mouths,
the forbidden food from between their teeth.
Those who are left will belong to our God
and become leaders in Judah,
and Ekron will be like the Jebusites.
[8]But I will defend my house
against marauding forces.
Never again will an oppressor overrun my people,
for now I am keeping watch.

The Coming of Zion's King

[9]Rejoice greatly, O Daughter of Zion!
Shout, Daughter of Jerusalem!
See, your king comes to you,
righteous and having salvation,
gentle and riding on a donkey,
on a colt, the foal of a donkey.
[10]I will take away the chariots from Ephraim
and the war-horses from Jerusalem,
and the battle-bow will be broken.
He will proclaim peace to the nations.

His rule will extend from sea to sea
and from the River to the ends of
the earth.
11 As for you, because of the blood of
my covenant with you,
I will free your prisoners from the
waterless pit.
12 Return to your fortress, O prisoners
of hope;
even now I announce that I will
restore twice as much to you.
13 I will bend Judah as I bend my bow
and fill it with Ephraim.
I will rouse your sons, O Zion,
against your sons, O Greece,
and make you like a warrior's
sword.

The LORD Will Appear

14 Then the LORD will appear over
them;
his arrow will flash like lightning.
The Sovereign LORD will sound the
trumpet;
he will march in the storms of the
south,
15 and the LORD Almighty will shield
them.
They will destroy
and overcome with slingstones.
They will drink and roar as with wine;
they will be full like a bowl
used for sprinkling the corners of
the altar.
16 The LORD their God will save them
on that day
as the flock of his people.
They will sparkle in his land
like jewels in a crown.
17 How attractive and beautiful they will
be!
Grain will make the young men
thrive,
and new wine the young women.

The LORD Will Care for Judah

10 Ask the LORD for rain in the
springtime;
it is the LORD who makes the storm
clouds.
He gives showers of rain to men,
and plants of the field to everyone.
2 The idols speak deceit,
diviners see visions that lie;
they tell dreams that are false,
they give comfort in vain.
Therefore the people wander like
sheep
oppressed for lack of a shepherd.

3 "My anger burns against the
shepherds,
and I will punish the leaders;
for the LORD Almighty will care
for his flock, the house of Judah,
and make them like a proud horse
in battle.
4 From Judah will come the
cornerstone,
from him the tent peg,
from him the battle-bow,
from him every ruler.
5 Together they will be like mighty men
trampling the muddy streets in
battle.
Because the LORD is with them,
they will fight and overthrow the
horsemen.

6 "I will strengthen the house of Judah
and save the house of Joseph.
I will restore them
because I have compassion on
them.
They will be as though
I had not rejected them,
for I am the LORD their God
and I will answer them.
7 The Ephraimites will become like
mighty men,
and their hearts will be glad as with
wine.
Their children will see it and be
joyful;
their hearts will rejoice in the
LORD.
8 I will signal for them
and gather them in.
Surely I will redeem them;
they will be as numerous as before.
9 Though I scatter them among the
peoples,

yet in distant lands they will
remember me.
They and their children will survive,
and they will return.
10I will bring them back from Egypt
and gather them from Assyria.
I will bring them to Gilead and
Lebanon,
and there will not be room enough
for them.
11They will pass through the sea of
trouble;
the surging sea will be subdued
and all the depths of the Nile will
dry up.
Assyria's pride will be brought down
and Egypt's sceptre will pass away.
12I will strengthen them in the LORD
and in his name they will walk,"
declares the LORD.

11 Open your doors, O Lebanon,
so that fire may devour your
cedars!
2Wail, O pine tree, for the cedar has
fallen;
the stately trees are ruined!
Wail, oaks of Bashan;
the dense forest has been cut
down!
3Listen to the wail of the shepherds:
their rich pastures are destroyed!
Listen to the roar of the lions;
the lush thicket of the Jordan is
ruined!

Two Shepherds

4This is what the LORD my God says:
"Pasture the flock marked for slaughter.
5Their buyers slaughter them and
go unpunished. Those who sell them
say, 'Praise the LORD, I am rich!' Their
own shepherds do not spare them. 6For
I will no longer have pity on the people
of the land," declares the LORD. "I will
hand everyone over to his neighbour
and his king. They will oppress the land,
and I will not rescue them from their
hands."
7So I pastured the flock marked for
slaughter, particularly the oppressed of
the flock. Then I took two staffs and
called one Favour and the other Union,
and I pastured the flock. 8In one month
I got rid of the three shepherds.
The flock detested me, and I grew
weary of them 9and said, "I will not be
your shepherd. Let the dying die, and
the perishing perish. Let those who are
left eat one another's flesh."
10Then I took my staff called Favour
and broke it, revoking the covenant I
had made with all the nations. 11It was
revoked on that day, and so the afflicted
of the flock who were watching me
knew it was the word of the LORD.
12I told them, "If you think it best,
give me my pay; but if not, keep it." So
they paid me thirty pieces of silver.
13And the LORD said to me, "Throw it
to the potter"—the handsome price at
which they priced me! So I took the
thirty pieces of silver and threw them
into the house of the LORD to the potter.
14Then I broke my second staff called
Union, breaking the brotherhood between Judah and Israel.
15Then the LORD said to me, "Take
again the equipment of a foolish shepherd.
16For I am going to raise up a
shepherd over the land who will not
care for the lost, or seek the young, or
heal the injured, or feed the healthy,
but will eat the meat of the choice
sheep, tearing off their hoofs.

17"Woe to the worthless shepherd,
who deserts the flock!
May the sword strike his arm and his
right eye!
May his arm be completely
withered,
his right eye totally blinded!"

NEW TESTAMENT READING
Revelation 1:1–20

Prologue

1 The revelation of Jesus Christ,
which God gave him to show his
servants what must soon take place. He

made it known by sending his angel to
his servant John, 2who testifies to everything he saw—that is, the word of God
and the testimony of Jesus Christ.
3Blessed is the one who reads the words
of this prophecy, and blessed are those
who hear it and take to heart what is
written in it, because the time is near.

Greetings and Doxology

4John,

To the seven churches in the province of Asia:

Grace and peace to you from him
who is, and who was, and who is to
come, and from the seven spirits before
his throne, 5and from Jesus Christ, who
is the faithful witness, the firstborn from
the dead, and the ruler of the kings of
the earth.

To him who loves us and has freed us
from our sins by his blood, 6and has
made us to be a kingdom and priests to
serve his God and Father—to him be
glory and power for ever and ever!
Amen.

7Look, he is coming with the clouds,
and every eye will see him,
even those who pierced him;
and all the peoples of the earth will
mourn because of him.
So shall it be! Amen.

8"I am the Alpha and the Omega,"
says the Lord God, "who is, and
who was, and who is to come, the
Almighty."

One Like a Son of Man

9I, John, your brother and companion in the suffering and kingdom
and patient endurance that are ours in
Jesus, was on the island of Patmos because of the word of God and the testimony of Jesus. 10On the Lord's Day I
was in the Spirit, and I heard behind me
a loud voice like a trumpet, 11which
said: "Write on a scroll what you see
and send it to the seven churches:
to Ephesus, Smyrna, Pergamum,
Thyatira, Sardis, Philadelphia and
Laodicea."
12I turned round to see the voice that
was speaking to me. And when I turned
I saw seven golden lampstands, 13and
among the lampstands was someone
"like a son of man", dressed in a robe
reaching down to his feet and with a
golden sash round his chest. 14His head
and hair were white like wool, as white
as snow, and his eyes were like blazing
fire. 15His feet were like bronze glowing
in a furnace, and his voice was like the
sound of rushing waters. 16In his right
hand he held seven stars, and out of his
mouth came a sharp double-edged
sword. His face was like the sun shining
in all its brilliance.
17When I saw him, I fell at his feet as
though dead. Then he placed his right
hand on me and said: "Do not be afraid.
I am the First and the Last. 18I am the
Living One; I was dead, and behold I
am alive for ever and ever! And I hold
the keys of death and Hades.
19"Write, therefore, what you have
seen, what is now and what will take
place later. 20The mystery of the seven
stars that you saw in my right hand and
of the seven golden lampstands is this:
The seven stars are the angels of the
seven churches, and the seven lampstands are the seven churches.

READING FROM PSALMS

Psalm 140:1–5

For the director of music. A psalm of David.

1Rescue me, O LORD, from evil men;
protect me from men of violence,
2who devise evil plans in their hearts
and stir up war every day.

[3]They make their tongues as sharp as
a serpent's;
the poison of vipers is on their lips.
Selah

[4]Keep me, O LORD, from the hands of
the wicked;
protect me from men of violence
who plan to trip my feet.
[5]Proud men have hidden a snare for
me;
they have spread out the cords of
their net
and have set traps for me along my
path.
Selah

DECEMBER 10

DAY 344

OLD TESTAMENT READING
Zechariah 12:1–14:21

Jerusalem's Enemies to Be Destroyed

An Oracle

12 This is the word of the LORD
concerning Israel. The LORD,
who stretches out the heavens, who lays
the foundation of the earth, and who
forms the spirit of man within him, declares: [2]"I am going to make Jerusalem
a cup that sends all the surrounding
peoples reeling. Judah will be besieged
as well as Jerusalem. [3]On that day,
when all the nations of the earth are
gathered against her, I will make Jerusalem an immovable rock for all the
nations. All who try to move it will
injure themselves. [4]On that day I will
strike every horse with panic and its
rider with madness," declares the
LORD. "I will keep a watchful eye over
the house of Judah, but I will blind all
the horses of the nations. [5]Then the
leaders of Judah will say in their hearts,
'The people of Jerusalem are strong,
because the LORD Almighty is their
God.'
[6]"On that day I will make the leaders
of Judah like a brazier in a woodpile,
like a flaming torch among sheaves.
They will consume right and left all the
surrounding peoples, but Jerusalem will
remain intact in her place.
[7]"The LORD will save the dwellings of
Judah first, so that the honour of the
house of David and of Jerusalem's inhabitants may not be greater than that
of Judah. [8]On that day the LORD will
shield those who live in Jerusalem, so
that the feeblest among them will be
like David, and the house of David will
be like God, like the Angel of the LORD
going before them. [9]On that day I will
set out to destroy all the nations that
attack Jerusalem.

Mourning for the One They Pierced

[10]"And I will pour out on the house of
David and the inhabitants of Jerusalem
a spirit of grace and supplication. They
will look on me, the one they have
pierced, and they will mourn for him as
one mourns for an only child, and grieve
bitterly for him as one grieves for a
firstborn son. [11]On that day the weeping
in Jerusalem will be great, like the
weeping of Hadad Rimmon in the plain
of Megiddo. [12]The land will mourn,
each clan by itself, with their wives by
themselves: the clan of the house of
David and their wives, the clan of the
house of Nathan and their wives, [13]the
clan of the house of Levi and their
wives, the clan of Shimei and their
wives, [14]and all the rest of the clans and
their wives.

Cleansing From Sin

13 "On that day a fountain will be
opened to the house of David
and the inhabitants of Jerusalem, to
cleanse them from sin and impurity.

2"On that day, I will banish the
names of the idols from the land, and
they will be remembered no more,"
declares the LORD Almighty. "I will
remove both the prophets and the spirit
of impurity from the land. 3And if anyone still prophesies, his father and
mother, to whom he was born, will say
to him, 'You must die, because you
have told lies in the LORD's name.'
When he prophesies, his own parents
will stab him.

4"On that day every prophet will be
ashamed of his prophetic vision. He will
not put on a prophet's garment of hair in
order to deceive. 5He will say, 'I am not
a prophet. I am a farmer; the land has
been my livelihood since my youth.' 6If
someone asks him, 'What are these
wounds on your body?' he will answer,
'The wounds I was given at the house of
my friends.'

The Shepherd Struck, the Sheep Scattered

7"Awake, O sword, against my
shepherd,
against the man who is close to
me!"
declares the LORD Almighty.
"Strike the shepherd,
and the sheep will be scattered,
and I will turn my hand against the
little ones.
8In the whole land," declares the
LORD,
"two-thirds will be struck down
and perish;
yet one-third will be left in it.
9This third I will bring into the fire;
I will refine them like silver
and test them like gold.
They will call on my name
and I will answer them;
I will say, 'They are my people,'
and they will say, 'The LORD is our
God.'"

The LORD Comes and Reigns

14 A day of the LORD is coming
when your plunder will be
divided among you.

2I will gather all the nations to Jerusalem to fight against it; the city will be
captured, the houses ransacked, and
the women raped. Half of the city will
go into exile, but the rest of the people
will not be taken from the city.

3Then the LORD will go out and fight
against those nations, as he fights in the
day of battle. 4On that day his feet will
stand on the Mount of Olives, east of
Jerusalem, and the Mount of Olives will
be split in two from east to west, forming a great valley, with half of the mountain moving north and half moving
south. 5You will flee by my mountain
valley, for it will extend to Azel. You
will flee as you fled from the earthquake
in the days of Uzziah king of Judah.
Then the LORD my God will come, and
all the holy ones with him.

6On that day there will be no light, no
cold or frost. 7It will be a unique day,
without daytime or night-time—a day
known to the LORD. When evening
comes, there will be light.

8On that day living water will flow out
from Jerusalem, half to the eastern sea
and half to the western sea, in summer
and in winter.

9The LORD will be king over the
whole earth. On that day there will be
one LORD, and his name the only name.

10The whole land, from Geba to Rimmon, south of Jerusalem, will become
like the Arabah. But Jerusalem will be
raised up and remain in its place, from
the Benjamin Gate to the site of the
First Gate, to the Corner Gate, and
from the Tower of Hananel to the royal
winepresses. 11It will be inhabited;
never again will it be destroyed. Jerusalem will be secure.

12This is the plague with which the
LORD will strike all the nations that
fought against Jerusalem: Their flesh
will rot while they are still standing on
their feet, their eyes will rot in their
sockets, and their tongues will rot in
their mouths. 13On that day men will be
stricken by the LORD with great panic.
Each man will seize the hand of
another, and they will attack each

other. [14]Judah too will fight at Jerusalem. The wealth of all the surrounding nations will be collected—great quantities of gold and silver and clothing. [15]A similar plague will strike the horses and mules, the camels and donkeys, and all the animals in those camps.

[16]Then the survivors from all the nations that have attacked Jerusalem will go up year after year to worship the King, the LORD Almighty, and to celebrate the Feast of Tabernacles. [17]If any of the peoples of the earth do not go up to Jerusalem to worship the King, the LORD Almighty, they will have no rain. [18]If the Egyptian people do not go up and take part, they will have no rain. The LORD will bring on them the plague he inflicts on the nations that do not go up to celebrate the Feast of Tabernacles. [19]This will be the punishment of Egypt and the punishment of all the nations that do not go up to celebrate the Feast of Tabernacles.

[20]On that day HOLY TO THE LORD will be inscribed on the bells of the horses, and the cooking pots in the LORD's house will be like the sacred bowls in front of the altar. [21]Every pot in Jerusalem and Judah will be holy to the LORD Almighty, and all who come to sacrifice will take some of the pots and cook in them. And on that day there will no longer be a Canaanite in the house of the LORD Almighty.

NEW TESTAMENT READING
Revelation 2:1–17

To the Church in Ephesus

2 "To the angel of the church in Ephesus write:

These are the words of him who holds the seven stars in his right hand and walks among the seven golden lampstands: [2]I know your deeds, your hard work and your perseverance. I know that you cannot tolerate wicked men, that you have tested those who claim to be apostles but are not, and have found them false. [3]You have persevered and have endured hardships for my name, and have not grown weary.

[4]Yet I hold this against you: You have forsaken your first love. [5]Remember the height from which you have fallen! Repent and do the things you did at first. If you do not repent, I will come to you and remove your lampstand from its place. [6]But you have this in your favour: You hate the practices of Nicolaitans, which I also hate.

[7]He who has an ear, let him hear what the Spirit says to the churches. To him who overcomes, I will give the right to eat from the tree of life, which is in the paradise of God.

To the Church in Smyrna

[8]"To the angel of the church in Smyrna write:

These are the words of him who is the First and the Last, who died and came to life again. [9]I know your afflictions and your poverty—yet you are rich! I know the slander of those who say they are Jews and are not, but are a synagogue of Satan. [10]Do not be afraid of what you are about to suffer. I tell you, the devil will put some of you in prison to test you, and you will suffer persecution for ten days. Be faithful, even to the point of death, and I will give you the crown of life.

[11]He who has an ear, let him hear what the Spirit says to the churches. He who overcomes will not be hurt at all by the second death.

To the Church in Pergamum

[12]"To the angel of the church in Pergamum write:

These are the words of him who
has the sharp, double-edged
sword. 13I know where you live
—where Satan has his throne. Yet
you remain true to my name. You
did not renounce your faith in me,
even in the days of Antipas, my
faithful witness, who was put to
death in your city—where Satan
lives.
14Nevertheless, I have a few
things against you: You have people there who hold to the teaching
of Balaam, who taught Balak to
entice the Israelites to sin by eating
food sacrificed to idols and by
committing sexual immorality.
15Likewise you also have those who
hold to the teaching of the Nicolaitans. 16Repent therefore! Otherwise, I will soon come to you and
will fight against them with the
sword of my mouth.
17He who has an ear, let him hear
what the Spirit says to the churches. To him who overcomes, I will
give some of the hidden manna. I
will also give him a white stone with
a new name written on it, known
only to him who receives it.

READING FROM PROVERBS
Proverbs 30:1–10

Sayings of Agur

30 The sayings of Agur son of Jakeh—an oracle:

This man declared to Ithiel,
to Ithiel and to Ucal:

2"I am the most ignorant of men;
I do not have a man's
understanding.
3I have not learned wisdom,
nor have I knowledge of the Holy
One.
4Who has gone up to heaven and
come down?
Who has gathered up the wind in
the hollow of his hands?
Who has wrapped up the waters in
his cloak?
Who has established all the ends of
the earth?
What is his name, and the name of
his son?
Tell me if you know!

5"Every word of God is flawless;
he is a shield to those who take
refuge in him.
6Do not add to his words,
or he will rebuke you and prove
you a liar.

7"Two things I ask of you, O LORD;
do not refuse me before I die:
8Keep falsehood and lies far from me;
give me neither poverty nor riches,
but give me only my daily bread.
9Otherwise, I may have too much and
disown you
and say, 'Who is the LORD?'
Or I may become poor and steal,
and so dishonour the name of my
God.

10"Do not slander a servant to his
master,
or he will curse you, and you will
pay for it.

DECEMBER 11 DAY 345

OLD TESTAMENT READING
Esther 1:1–2:18

Queen Vashti Deposed

1 This is what happened during the
time of Xerxes, the Xerxes who
ruled over 127 provinces stretching
from India to Cush: 2At that time King
Xerxes reigned from his royal throne in
the citadel of Susa, 3and in the third
year of his reign he gave a banquet for
all his nobles and officials. The military
leaders of Persia and Media, the
princes, and the nobles of the provinces
were present.
4For a full 180 days he displayed the
vast wealth of his kingdom and the
splendour and glory of his majesty.
5When these days were over, the king
gave a banquet, lasting seven days, in
the enclosed garden of the king's
palace, for all the people from the least
to the greatest, who were in the citadel
of Susa. 6The garden had hangings of
white and blue linen, fastened with
cords of white linen and purple material
to silver rings on marble pillars. There
were couches of gold and silver on a
mosaic pavement of porphyry, marble,
mother-of-pearl and other costly
stones. 7Wine was served in goblets of
gold, each one different from the other,
and the royal wine was abundant, in
keeping with the king's liberality. 8By
the king's command each guest was
allowed to drink in his own way, for the
king instructed all the wine stewards to
serve each man what he wished.
9Queen Vashti also gave a banquet
for the women in the royal palace of
King Xerxes.
10On the seventh day, when King
Xerxes was in high spirits from wine, he
commanded the seven eunuchs who
served him—Mehuman, Biztha, Harbona, Bigtha, Abagtha, Zethar and
Carcas—11to bring before him Queen
Vashti, wearing her royal crown, in
order to display her beauty to the
people and nobles, for she was lovely to
look at. 12But when the attendants delivered the king's command, Queen
Vashti refused to come. Then the king
became furious and burned with anger.
13Since it was customary for the king
to consult experts in matters of law
and justice, he spoke with the wise
men who understood the times 14and
were closest to the king—Carshena,
Shethar, Admatha, Tarshish, Meres,
Marsena and Memucan, the seven
nobles of Persia and Media who had
special access to the king and were
highest in the kingdom.
15"According to law, what must be
done to Queen Vashti?" he asked. "She
has not obeyed the command of King
Xerxes that the eunuchs have taken to
her."
16Then Memucan replied in the presence of the king and the nobles, "Queen
Vashti has done wrong, not only against
the king but also against all the nobles
and the peoples of all the provinces of
King Xerxes. 17For the queen's conduct
will become known to all the women,
and so they will despise their husbands
and say, 'King Xerxes commanded
Queen Vashti to be brought before him,
but she would not come.' 18This very
day the Persian and Median women of
the nobility who have heard about the
queen's conduct will respond to all the
king's nobles in the same way. There
will be no end of disrespect and discord.
19"Therefore, if it pleases the king,
let him issue a royal decree and let it be
written in the laws of Persia and Media,
which cannot be repealed, that Vashti is
never again to enter the presence of
King Xerxes. Also let the king give her
royal position to someone else who is
better than she. 20Then when the king's
edict is proclaimed throughout all his
vast realm, all the women will respect

their husbands, from the least to the
greatest."
21 The king and his nobles were
pleased with this advice, so the king did
as Memucan proposed. 22 He sent dispatches to all parts of the kingdom, to
each province in its own script and to
each people in its own language, proclaiming in each people's tongue that
every man should be ruler over his own
household.

Esther Made Queen

2 Later when the anger of King
Xerxes had subsided, he remembered Vashti and what she had done
and what he had decreed about her.
2 Then the king's personal attendants
proposed, "Let a search be made for
beautiful young virgins for the king.
3 Let the king appoint commissioners in
every province of his realm to bring all
these beautiful girls into the harem at
the citadel of Susa. Let them be placed
under the care of Hegai, the king's
eunuch, who is in charge of the women;
and let beauty treatments be given to
them. 4 Then let the girl who pleases the
king be queen instead of Vashti." This
advice appealed to the king, and he
followed it.
5 Now there was in the citadel of Susa
a Jew of the tribe of Benjamin, named
Mordecai son of Jair, the son of Shimei,
the son of Kish, 6 who had been carried
into exile from Jerusalem by Nebuchadnezzar king of Babylon, among those
taken captive with Jehoiachin king of
Judah. 7 Mordecai had a cousin named
Hadassah, whom he had brought up
because she had neither father nor
mother. This girl, who was also known
as Esther, was lovely in form and features, and Mordecai had taken her as
his own daughter when her father and
mother died.
8 When the king's order and edict had
been proclaimed, many girls were
brought to the citadel of Susa and put
under the care of Hegai. Esther also was
taken to the king's palace and entrusted
to Hegai, who had charge of the harem.
9 The girl pleased him and won his
favour. Immediately he provided her
with her beauty treatments and special
food. He assigned to her seven maids
selected from the king's palace and
moved her and her maids into the best
place in the harem.
10 Esther had not revealed her
nationality and family background, because Mordecai had forbidden her to do
so. 11 Every day he walked to and fro
near the courtyard of the harem to find
out how Esther was and what was happening to her.
12 Before a girl's turn came to go in to
King Xerxes, she had to complete
twelve months of beauty treatments
prescribed for the women, six months
with oil of myrrh and six with perfumes
and cosmetics. 13 And this is how she
would go to the king: Anything she
wanted was given to her to take with her
from the harem to the king's palace.
14 In the evening she would go there and
in the morning return to another part of
the harem to the care of Shaashgaz, the
king's eunuch who was in charge of the
concubines. She would not return to
the king unless he was pleased with her
and summoned her by name.
15 When the turn came for Esther (the
girl Mordecai had adopted, the daughter of his uncle Abihail) to go to the
king, she asked for nothing other than
what Hegai, the king's eunuch who was
in charge of the harem, suggested. And
Esther won the favour of everyone who
saw her. 16 She was taken to King Xerxes
in the royal residence in the tenth
month, the month of Tebeth, in the
seventh year of his reign.
17 Now the king was attracted to
Esther more than to any of the other
women, and she won his favour and
approval more than any of the other
virgins. So he set a royal crown on her
head and made her queen instead of
Vashti. 18 And the king gave a great
banquet, Esther's banquet, for all his
nobles and officials. He proclaimed a
holiday throughout the provinces and
distributed gifts with royal liberality.

NEW TESTAMENT READING
Revelation 2:18–3:6

To the Church in Thyatira

18“To the angel of the church in
Thyatira write:

These are the words of the Son of
God, whose eyes are like blazing
fire and whose feet are like burnished bronze. 19I know your
deeds, your love and faith, your
service and perseverance, and that
you are now doing more than you
did at first.
20Nevertheless, I have this
against you: You tolerate that
woman Jezebel, who calls herself a
prophetess. By her teaching she
misleads my servants into sexual
immorality and the eating of food
sacrificed to idols. 21I have given
her time to repent of her immorality, but she is unwilling. 22So I will
cast her on a bed of suffering, and I
will make those who commit adultery with her suffer intensely, unless they repent of her ways. 23I will
strike her children dead. Then all
the churches will know that I am he
who searches hearts and minds,
and I will repay each of you according to your deeds. 24Now I say to
the rest of you in Thyatira, to you
who do not hold to her teaching
and have not learned Satan's so-
called deep secrets (I will not impose any other burden on you):
25Only hold on to what you have
until I come.
26To him who overcomes and
does my will to the end, I will give
authority over the nations—

27‘He will rule them with an iron
sceptre;
he will dash them to pieces
like pottery’—

just as I have received authority
from my Father. 28I will also give
him the morning star. 29He who has
an ear, let him hear what the Spirit
says to the churches.

To the Church in Sardis

3 “To the angel of the church in
Sardis write:

These are the words of him who
holds the seven spirits of God and
the seven stars. I know your deeds;
you have a reputation of being
alive, but you are dead. 2Wake up!
Strengthen what remains and is
about to die, for I have not found
your deeds complete in the sight of
my God. 3Remember, therefore,
what you have received and heard;
obey it, and repent. But if you do
not wake up, I will come like a
thief, and you will not know at
what time I will come to you.
4Yet you have a few people in
Sardis who have not soiled their
clothes. They will walk with me,
dressed in white, for they are
worthy. 5He who overcomes will,
like them, be dressed in white. I
will never blot out his name from
the book of life, but will acknowledge his name before my Father
and his angels. 6He who has an ear,
let him hear what the Spirit says to
the churches.

READING FROM PSALMS
Psalm 140:6–13

6O LORD, I say to you, “You are my
God.”
Hear, O LORD, my cry for mercy.
7O Sovereign LORD, my strong
deliverer,
who shields my head in the day of
battle—
8do not grant the wicked their desires,
O LORD;
do not let their plans succeed,
or they will become proud. *Selah*

[9]Let the heads of those who surround
me
be covered with the trouble their
lips have caused.
[10]Let burning coals fall upon them;
may they be thrown into the fire,
into miry pits, never to rise.
[11]Let slanderers not be established in
the land;
may disaster hunt down men of
violence.

[12]I know that the LORD secures justice
for the poor
and upholds the cause of the needy.
[13]Surely the righteous will praise your
name
and the upright will live before you.

DAY 346 DECEMBER 12

OLD TESTAMENT READING
Esther 2:19–5:14

Mordecai Uncovers a Conspiracy

[19]When the virgins were assembled a
second time, Mordecai was sitting at
the king's gate. [20]But Esther had kept
secret her family background and
nationality just as Mordecai had told
her to do, for she continued to follow
Mordecai's instructions as she had done
when he was bringing her up.

[21]During the time Mordecai was sitting at the king's gate, Bigthana and
Teresh, two of the king's officers who
guarded the doorway, became angry
and conspired to assassinate King
Xerxes. [22]But Mordecai found out
about the plot and told Queen Esther,
who in turn reported it to the king,
giving credit to Mordecai. [23]And when
the report was investigated and found to
be true, the two officials were hanged
on a gallows. All this was recorded in
the book of the annals in the presence of
the king.

Haman's Plot to Destroy the Jews

3 After these events, King Xerxes
honoured Haman son of Hammedatha, the Agagite, elevating him and
giving him a seat of honour higher than
that of all the other nobles. [2]All the
royal officials at the king's gate knelt
down and paid honour to Haman, for
the king had commanded this concerning him. But Mordecai would not kneel
down or pay him honour.

[3]Then the royal officials at the king's
gate asked Mordecai, "Why do you disobey the king's command?" [4]Day after
day they spoke to him but he refused to
comply. Therefore they told Haman
about it to see whether Mordecai's
behaviour would be tolerated, for he
had told them he was a Jew.

[5]When Haman saw that Mordecai
would not kneel down or pay him honour, he was enraged. [6]Yet having
learned who Mordecai's people were,
he scorned the idea of killing only Mordecai. Instead Haman looked for a way
to destroy all Mordecai's people, the
Jews, throughout the whole kingdom of
Xerxes.

[7]In the twelfth year of King Xerxes,
in the first month, the month of Nisan,
they cast the *pur* (that is, the lot) in the
presence of Haman to select a day and
month. And the lot fell on the twelfth
month, the month of Adar.

[8]Then Haman said to King Xerxes,
"There is a certain people dispersed and
scattered among the peoples in all the
provinces of your kingdom whose customs are different from those of all
other people and who do not obey the
king's laws; it is not in the king's best

interest to tolerate them. 9If it pleases
the king, let a decree be issued to destroy them, and I will put ten thousand talents of silver into the royal
treasury for the men who carry out
this business."
10So the king took his signet ring from
his finger and gave it to Haman son of
Hammedatha, the Agagite, the enemy
of the Jews. 11"Keep the money," the
king said to Haman, "and do with the
people as you please."
12Then on the thirteenth day of the
first month the royal secretaries were
summoned. They wrote out in the script
of each province and in the language of
each people all Haman's orders to the
king's satraps, the governors of the various provinces and the nobles of the
various peoples. These were written in
the name of King Xerxes himself and
sealed with his own ring. 13Dispatches
were sent by couriers to all the king's
provinces with the order to destroy, kill
and annihilate all the Jews—young and
old, women and little children—on a
single day, the thirteenth day of the
twelfth month, the month of Adar, and
to plunder their goods. 14A copy of the
text of the edict was to be issued as law
in every province and made known to
the people of every nationality so that
they would be ready for that day.
15Spurred on by the king's command,
the couriers went out, and the edict was
issued in the citadel of Susa. The king
and Haman sat down to drink, but the
city of Susa was bewildered.

Mordecai Persuades Esther to Help

4 When Mordecai learned of all that
had been done, he tore his clothes,
put on sackcloth and ashes, and went
out into the city, wailing loudly and
bitterly. 2But he went only as far as the
king's gate, because no-one clothed in
sackcloth was allowed to enter it. 3In
every province to which the edict and
order of the king came, there was great
mourning among the Jews, with fasting,
weeping and wailing. Many lay in sackcloth and ashes.
4When Esther's maids and eunuchs
came and told her about Mordecai, she
was in great distress. She sent clothes
for him to put on instead of his sackcloth, but he would not accept them.
5Then Esther summoned Hathach, one
of the king's eunuchs assigned to attend
her, and ordered him to find out what
was troubling Mordecai and why.
6So Hathach went out to Mordecai in
the open square of the city in front of
the king's gate. 7Mordecai told him
everything that had happened to him,
including the exact amount of money
Haman had promised to pay into the
royal treasury for the destruction of the
Jews. 8He also gave him a copy of
the text of the edict for their annihil-
ation, which had been published in Susa,
to show to Esther and explain it to her,
and he told him to urge her to go into
the king's presence to beg for mercy
and plead with him for her people.
9Hathach went back and reported to
Esther what Mordecai had said. 10Then
she instructed him to say to Mordecai,
11"All the king's officials and the people
of the royal provinces know that for any
man or woman who approaches the
king in the inner court without being
summoned the king has but one law:
that he be put to death. The only excep-
tion to this is for the king to extend the
gold sceptre to him and spare his life.
But thirty days have passed since I was
called to go to the king."
12When Esther's words were reported to Mordecai, 13he sent back this
answer: "Do not think that because you
are in the king's house you alone of all
the Jews will escape. 14For if you remain
silent at this time, relief and deliverance
for the Jews will arise from another
place, but you and your father's family
will perish. And who knows but that
you have come to royal position for such
a time as this?"
15Then Esther sent this reply to Mordecai: 16"Go, gather together all the
Jews who are in Susa, and fast for me.
Do not eat or drink for three days, night
or day. I and my maids will fast as you

do. When this is done, I will go to the king, even though it is against the law. And if I perish, I perish."

17So Mordecai went away and carried out all of Esther's instructions.

Esther's Request to the King

5 On the third day Esther put on her royal robes and stood in the inner court of the palace, in front of the king's hall. The king was sitting on his royal throne in the hall, facing the entrance.
2When he saw Queen Esther standing in the court, he was pleased with her and held out to her the gold sceptre that was in his hand. So Esther approached and touched the tip of the sceptre.

3Then the king asked, "What is it, Queen Esther? What is your request? Even up to half the kingdom, it will be given you."

4"If it pleases the king," replied Esther, "let the king, together with Haman, come today to a banquet I have prepared for him."

5"Bring Haman at once," the king said, "so that we may do what Esther asks."

So the king and Haman went to the banquet Esther had prepared. 6As they were drinking wine, the king again asked Esther, "Now what is your petition? It will be given you. And what is your request? Even up to half the kingdom, it will be granted."

7Esther replied, "My petition and my request is this: 8If the king regards me with favour and if it pleases the king to grant my petition and fulfil my request, let the king and Haman come tomorrow to the banquet I will prepare for them. Then I will answer the king's question."

Haman's Rage Against Mordecai

9Haman went out that day happy and in high spirits. But when he saw Mordecai at the king's gate and observed that he neither rose nor showed fear in his presence, he was filled with rage against Mordecai. 10Nevertheless, Haman restrained himself and went home.

Calling together his friends and Zeresh, his wife, 11Haman boasted to them about his vast wealth, his many sons, and all the ways the king had honoured him and how he had elevated him above the other nobles and officials. 12"And that's not all," Haman added. "I'm the only person Queen Esther invited to accompany the king to the banquet she gave. And she has invited me along with the king tomorrow.
13But all this gives me no satisfaction as long as I see that Jew Mordecai sitting at the king's gate."

14His wife Zeresh and all his friends said to him, "Have a gallows built, seventy-five feet high, and ask the king in the morning to have Mordecai hanged on it. Then go with the king to the dinner and be happy." This suggestion delighted Haman, and he had the gallows built.

NEW TESTAMENT READING

Revelation 3:7–22

To the Church in Philadelphia

7"To the angel of the church in Philadelphia write:

> These are the words of him who is holy and true, who holds the key of David. What he opens no-one can shut, and what he shuts no-one can open. 8I know your deeds. See, I have placed before you an open door that no-one can shut. I know that you have little strength, yet you have kept my word and have not denied my name. 9I will make those who are of the synagogue of Satan, who claim to be Jews though they are not, but are liars—I will make them come and fall down at your feet and acknowledge that I have loved you. 10Since you have kept my command to endure patiently, I will also keep you from the hour of trial that is going to come upon the whole world to test those who live on the earth.

11I am coming soon. Hold on to
what you have, so that no-one will
take your crown. 12Him who overcomes I will make a pillar in the
temple of my God. Never again
will he leave it. I will write on him
the name of my God and the name
of the city of my God, the new
Jerusalem, which is coming down
out of heaven from my God; and I
will also write on him my new
name. 13He who has an ear, let him
hear what the Spirit says to the
churches.

To the Church in Laodicea

14"To the angel of the church in
Laodicea write:

These are the words of the
Amen, the faithful and true witness, the ruler of God's creation.
15I know your deeds, that you are
neither cold nor hot. I wish you
were either one or the other! 16So,
because you are lukewarm—
neither hot nor cold—I am about
to spit you out of my mouth. 17You
say, 'I am rich; I have acquired
wealth and do not need a thing.'
But you do not realise that you are
wretched, pitiful, poor, blind and
naked. 18I counsel you to buy from
me gold refined in the fire, so that
you can become rich; and white
clothes to wear, so that you can
cover your shameful nakedness;
and salve to put on your eyes, so
that you can see.

19Those whom I love I rebuke
and discipline. So be earnest, and
repent. 20Here I am! I stand at the
door and knock. If anyone hears
my voice and opens the door, I will
come in and eat with him, and he
with me.

21To him who overcomes, I will
give the right to sit with me on my
throne, just as I overcame and sat
down with my Father on his
throne. 22He who has an ear, let
him hear what the Spirit says to the
churches."

READING FROM PSALMS

Psalm 141:1–10

A psalm of David.

1O LORD, I call to you; come quickly
to me.
Hear my voice when I call to you.
2May my prayer be set before you like
incense;
may the lifting up of my hands be
like the evening sacrifice.

3Set a guard over my mouth, O LORD;
keep watch over the door of my
lips.
4Let not my heart be drawn to what is
evil,
to take part in wicked deeds
with men who are evildoers;
let me not eat of their delicacies.

5Let a righteous man strike me—it is a
kindness;
let him rebuke me—it is oil on my
head.
My head will not refuse it.

Yet my prayer is ever against the
deeds of evildoers;
6 their rulers will be thrown down
from the cliffs,
and the wicked will learn that my
words were well spoken.
7⌊They will say,⌋ "As one ploughs and
breaks up the earth,
so our bones have been scattered
at the mouth of the grave."

8But my eyes are fixed on you, O
Sovereign LORD;
in you I take refuge—do not give
me over to death.
9Keep me from the snares they have
laid for me,
from the traps set by evildoers.
10Let the wicked fall into their own
nets,
while I pass by in safety.

DAY 347

DECEMBER 13

OLD TESTAMENT READING
Esther 6:1–8:17

Mordecai Honoured

6 That night the king could not sleep;
so he ordered the book of the
chronicles, the record of his reign, to be
brought in and read to him. 2It was
found recorded there that Mordecai
had exposed Bigthana and Teresh, two
of the king's officers who guarded the
doorway, who had conspired to assassinate King Xerxes.
3"What honour and recognition has
Mordecai received for this?" the king
asked.
"Nothing has been done for him," his
attendants answered.
4The king said, "Who is in the
court?" Now Haman had just entered
the outer court of the palace to speak to
the king about hanging Mordecai on the
gallows he had erected for him.
5His attendants answered, "Haman is
standing in the court."
"Bring him in," the king ordered.
6When Haman entered, the king
asked him, "What should be done for
the man the king delights to honour?"
Now Haman thought to himself,
"Who is there that the king would
rather honour than me?" 7So he
answered the king, "For the man the
king delights to honour, 8have them
bring a royal robe the king has worn and
a horse the king has ridden, one with a
royal crest placed on its head. 9Then let
the robe and horse be entrusted to one
of the king's most noble princes. Let
them robe the man the king delights to
honour, and lead him on the horse
through the city streets, proclaiming before him, 'This is what is done for the
man the king delights to honour!' "
10"Go at once," the king commanded
Haman. "Get the robe and the horse
and do just as you have suggested for
Mordecai the Jew, who sits at the king's
gate. Do not neglect anything you have
recommended."
11So Haman got the robe and the
horse. He robed Mordecai, and led him
on horseback through the city streets,
proclaiming before him, "This is what is
done for the man the king delights to
honour!"
12Afterwards Mordecai returned to
the king's gate. But Haman rushed
home, with his head covered, in grief,
13and told Zeresh his wife and all his
friends everything that had happened to
him.
His advisers and his wife Zeresh said
to him, "Since Mordecai, before whom
your downfall has started, is of Jewish
origin, you cannot stand against him
—you will surely come to ruin!"
14While they were still talking with him,
the king's eunuchs arrived and hurried
Haman away to the banquet Esther had
prepared.

Haman Hanged

7 So the king and Haman went to
dine with Queen Esther, 2and as
they were drinking wine on that second
day, the king again asked, "Queen
Esther, what is your petition? It will be
given you. What is your request? Even
up to half the kingdom, it will be
granted."
3Then Queen Esther answered, "If I
have found favour with you, O king,
and if it pleases your majesty, grant me
my life—this is my petition. And spare
my people—this is my request. 4For I
and my people have been sold for destruction and slaughter and annihila-
tion. If we had merely been sold as male
and female slaves, I would have kept
quiet, because no such distress would
justify disturbing the king."
5King Xerxes asked Queen Esther,
"Who is he? Where is the man who has
dared to do such a thing?"

6Esther said, "The adversary and enemy is this vile Haman."

Then Haman was terrified before the king and queen. 7The king got up in a rage, left his wine and went out into the palace garden. But Haman, realising that the king had already decided his fate, stayed behind to beg Queen Esther for his life.

8Just as the king returned from the palace garden to the banquet hall, Haman was falling on the couch where Esther was reclining.

The king exclaimed, "Will he even molest the queen while she is with me in the house?"

As soon as the word left the king's mouth, they covered Haman's face. 9Then Harbona, one of the eunuchs attending the king, said, "A gallows seventy-five feet high stands by Haman's house. He had it made for Mordecai, who spoke up to help the king."

The king said, "Hang him on it!" 10So they hanged Haman on the gallows he had prepared for Mordecai. Then the king's fury subsided.

The King's Edict on Behalf of the Jews

8 That same day King Xerxes gave Queen Esther the estate of Haman, the enemy of the Jews. And Mordecai came into the presence of the king, for Esther had told how he was related to her. 2The king took off his signet ring, which he had reclaimed from Haman, and presented it to Mordecai. And Esther appointed him over Haman's estate.

3Esther again pleaded with the king, falling at his feet and weeping. She begged him to put an end to the evil plan of Haman the Agagite, which he had devised against the Jews. 4Then the king extended the gold sceptre to Esther and she arose and stood before him.

5"If it pleases the king," she said, "and if he regards me with favour and thinks it the right thing to do, and if he is pleased with me, let an order be written overruling the dispatches that Haman son of Hammedatha, the Agagite, devised and wrote to destroy the Jews in all the king's provinces. 6For how can I bear to see disaster fall on my people? How can I bear to see the destruction of my family?"

7King Xerxes replied to Queen Esther and to Mordecai the Jew, "Because Haman attacked the Jews, I have given his estate to Esther, and they have hanged him on the gallows. 8Now write another decree in the king's name on behalf of the Jews as seems best to you, and seal it with the king's signet ring —for no document written in the king's name and sealed with his ring can be revoked."

9At once the royal secretaries were summoned—on the twenty-third day of the third month, the month of Sivan. They wrote out all Mordecai's orders to the Jews, and to the satraps, governors and nobles of the 127 provinces stretching from India to Cush. These orders were written in the script of each province and the language of each people and also to the Jews in their own script and language. 10Mordecai wrote in the name of King Xerxes, sealed the dispatches with the king's signet ring, and sent them by mounted couriers, who rode fast horses especially bred for the king.

11The king's edict granted the Jews in every city the right to assemble and protect themselves; to destroy, kill and annihilate any armed force of any nationality or province that might attack them and their women and children; and to plunder the property of their enemies. 12The day appointed for the Jews to do this in all the provinces of King Xerxes was the thirteenth day of the twelfth month, the month of Adar. 13A copy of the text of the edict was to be issued as law in every province and made known to the people of every nationality so that the Jews would be ready on that day to avenge themselves on their enemies.

14The couriers, riding the royal horses, raced out, spurred on by the

king's command. And the edict was also
issued in the citadel of Susa.
15Mordecai left the king's presence
wearing royal garments of blue and
white, a large crown of gold and a purple robe of fine linen. And the city of
Susa held a joyous celebration. 16For
the Jews it was a time of happiness and
joy, gladness and honour. 17In every
province and in every city, wherever the
edict of the king went, there was joy and
gladness among the Jews, with feasting
and celebrating. And many people of
other nationalities became Jews because fear of the Jews had seized them.

NEW TESTAMENT READING

Revelation 4:1–11

The Throne in Heaven

4 After this I looked, and there before me was a door standing open
in heaven. And the voice I had first
heard speaking to me like a trumpet
said, "Come up here, and I will show
you what must take place after this."
2At once I was in the Spirit, and there
before me was a throne in heaven with
someone sitting on it. 3And the one who
sat there had the appearance of jasper
and carnelian. A rainbow, resembling
an emerald, encircled the throne.
4Surrounding the throne were twenty-
four other thrones, and seated on them
were twenty-four elders. They were
dressed in white and had crowns of gold
on their heads. 5From the throne came
flashes of lightning, rumblings and peals
of thunder. Before the throne, seven
lamps were blazing. These are the seven
spirits of God. 6Also before the throne
there was what looked like a sea of
glass, clear as crystal.
In the centre, around the throne,
were four living creatures, and they
were covered with eyes, in front and
behind. 7The first living creature was
like a lion, the second was like an ox,
the third had a face like a man, the
fourth was like a flying eagle. 8Each of
the four living creatures had six wings
and was covered with eyes all around,
even under his wings. Day and night
they never stop saying:

"Holy, holy, holy
is the Lord God Almighty,
who was, and is, and is to come."

9Whenever the living creatures give
glory, honour and thanks to him who
sits on the throne and who lives for ever
and ever, 10the twenty-four elders fall
down before him who sits on the throne,
and worship him who lives for ever and
ever. They lay their crowns before the
throne and say:

11"You are worthy, our Lord and God,
to receive glory and honour and
power,
for you created all things,
and by your will they were created
and have their being."

READING FROM PSALMS

Psalm 142:1–7

A *maskil* of David. When he was in the
cave. A prayer.

1I cry aloud to the LORD;
I lift up my voice to the LORD for
mercy.
2I pour out my complaint before him;
before him I tell my trouble.

3When my spirit grows faint within
me,
it is you who know my way.
In the path where I walk
men have hidden a snare for me.
4Look to my right and see;
no-one is concerned for me.
I have no refuge;
no-one cares for my life.

5I cry to you, O LORD;
I say, "You are my refuge,
my portion in the land of the
living."

[6]Listen to my cry,
for I am in desperate need;
rescue me from those who pursue
me,
for they are too strong
for me.
[7]Set me free from my prison,
that I may praise your name.

Then the righteous will gather about
me
because of your goodness to me.

DECEMBER 14

DAY 348

OLD TESTAMENT READING

Esther 9:1–10:3

Triumph of the Jews

9 On the thirteenth day of the twelfth
month, the month of Adar, the
edict commanded by the king was to be
carried out. On this day the enemies of
the Jews had hoped to overpower them,
but now the tables were turned and the
Jews got the upper hand over those who
hated them. [2]The Jews assembled in
their cities in all the provinces of King
Xerxes to attack those seeking their
destruction. No-one could stand against
them, because the people of all the
other nationalities were afraid of them.
[3]And all the nobles of the provinces, the
satraps, the governors and the king's
administrators helped the Jews, because fear of Mordecai had seized them.
[4]Mordecai was prominent in the palace;
his reputation spread throughout the
provinces, and he became more and
more powerful.

[5]The Jews struck down all their
enemies with the sword, killing and
destroying them, and they did what
they pleased to those who hated them.
[6]In the citadel of Susa, the Jews killed
and destroyed five hundred men. [7]They
also killed Parshandatha, Dalphon,
Aspatha, [8]Poratha, Adalia, Aridatha,
[9]Parmashta, Arisai, Aridai and
Vaizatha, [10]the ten sons of Haman son
of Hammedatha, the enemy of the
Jews. But they did not lay their hands
on the plunder.

[11]The number of those slain in the
citadel of Susa was reported to the king
that same day. [12]The king said to Queen
Esther, "The Jews have killed and destroyed five hundred men and the ten
sons of Haman in the citadel of Susa.
What have they done in the rest of the
king's provinces? Now what is your
petition? It will be given you. What is
your request? It will also be granted."

[13]"If it pleases the king," Esther
answered, "give the Jews in Susa permission to carry out this day's edict
tomorrow also, and let Haman's ten
sons be hanged on gallows."

[14]So the king commanded that this be
done. An edict was issued in Susa, and
they hanged the ten sons of Haman.
[15]The Jews in Susa came together on the
fourteenth day of the month of Adar,
and they put to death in Susa three
hundred men, but they did not lay their
hands on the plunder.

[16]Meanwhile, the remainder of the
Jews who were in the king's provinces
also assembled to protect themselves
and get relief from their enemies. They
killed seventy-five thousand of them but
did not lay their hands on the plunder.
[17]This happened on the thirteenth day
of the month of Adar, and on the fourteenth they rested and made it a day of
feasting and joy.

Purim Celebrated

[18]The Jews in Susa, however, had
assembled on the thirteenth and fourteenth, and then on the fifteenth they

rested and made it a day of feasting and joy.

19That is why rural Jews—those living in villages—observe the fourteenth of the month of Adar as a day of joy and feasting, a day for giving presents to each other.

20Mordecai recorded these events, and he sent letters to all the Jews throughout the provinces of King Xerxes, near and far, 21to have them celebrate annually the fourteenth and fifteenth days of the month of Adar 22as the time when the Jews got relief from their enemies, and as the month when their sorrow was turned into joy and their mourning into a day of celebration. He wrote to them to observe the days as days of feasting and joy and giving presents of food to one another and gifts to the poor.

23So the Jews agreed to continue the celebration they had begun, doing what Mordecai had written to them. 24For Haman son of Hammedatha, the Agagite, the enemy of all the Jews, had plotted against the Jews to destroy them and had cast the *pur* (that is, the lot) for their ruin and destruction. 25But when the plot came to the king's attention, he issued written orders that the evil scheme Haman had devised against the Jews should come back on to his own head, and that he and his sons should be hanged on the gallows. 26(Therefore these days were called Purim, from the word *pur*.) Because of everything written in this letter and because of what they had seen and what had happened to them, 27the Jews took it upon themselves to establish the custom that they and their descendants and all who join them should without fail observe these two days every year, in the way prescribed and at the time appointed. 28These days should be remembered and observed in every generation by every family, and in every province and in every city. And these days of Purim should never cease to be celebrated by the Jews, nor should the memory of them die out among their descendants.

29So Queen Esther, daughter of Abihail, along with Mordecai the Jew, wrote with full authority to confirm this second letter concerning Purim. 30And Mordecai sent letters to all the Jews in the 127 provinces of the kingdom of Xerxes—words of goodwill and assurance—31to establish these days of Purim at their designated times, as Mordecai the Jew and Queen Esther had decreed for them, and as they had established for themselves and their descendants in regard to their times of fasting and lamentation. 32Esther's decree confirmed these regulations about Purim, and it was written down in the records.

The Greatness of Mordecai

10 King Xerxes imposed tribute throughout the empire, to its distant shores. 2And all his acts of power and might, together with a full account of the greatness of Mordecai to which the king had raised him, are they not written in the book of the annals of the kings of Media and Persia? 3Mordecai the Jew was second in rank to King Xerxes, pre-eminent among the Jews, and held in high esteem by his many fellow Jews, because he worked for the good of his people and spoke up for the welfare of all the Jews.

NEW TESTAMENT READING
Revelation 5:1–14

The Scroll and the Lamb

5 Then I saw in the right hand of him who sat on the throne a scroll with writing on both sides and sealed with seven seals. 2And I saw a mighty angel proclaiming in a loud voice, "Who is worthy to break the seals and open the scroll?" 3But no-one in heaven or on earth or under the earth could open the scroll or even look inside it. 4I wept and wept because no-one was found who was worthy to open the scroll or look inside. 5Then one of the elders said to

me, "Do not weep! See, the Lion of the
tribe of Judah, the Root of David, has
triumphed. He is able to open the scroll
and its seven seals."
6Then I saw a Lamb, looking as if it
had been slain, standing in the centre of
the throne, encircled by the four living
creatures and the elders. He had seven
horns and seven eyes, which are the
seven spirits of God sent out into all the
earth. 7He came and took the scroll
from the right hand of him who sat on
the throne. 8And when he had taken it,
the four living creatures and the twenty-
four elders fell down before the Lamb.
Each one had a harp and they were
holding golden bowls full of incense,
which are the prayers of the saints.
9And they sang a new song:

"You are worthy to take the scroll
and to open its seals,
because you were slain,
and with your blood you purchased
men for God
from every tribe and language and
people and nation.
10You have made them to be a
kingdom and priests to serve
our God,
and they will reign on the earth."

11Then I looked and heard the voice
of many angels, numbering thousands
upon thousands, and ten thousand
times ten thousand. They encircled the
throne and the living creatures and the
elders. 12In a loud voice they sang:

"Worthy is the Lamb, who was slain,
to receive power and wealth and
wisdom and strength
and honour and glory and praise!"

13Then I heard every creature in
heaven and on earth and under the
earth and on the sea, and all that is in
them, singing:

"To him who sits on the throne and
to the Lamb
be praise and honour and glory and
power,
for ever and ever!"

14The four living creatures said,
"Amen", and the elders fell down and
worshipped.

READING FROM PROVERBS
Proverbs 30:11–23

11"There are those who curse their
fathers
and do not bless their mothers;
12those who are pure in their own eyes
and yet are not cleansed of their
filth;
13those whose eyes are ever so
haughty,
whose glances are so disdainful;
14those whose teeth are swords
and whose jaws are set with knives
to devour the poor from the earth,
the needy from among mankind.

15"The leech has two daughters.
'Give! Give!' they cry.

"There are three things that are
never satisfied,
four that never say, 'Enough!':
16the grave, the barren womb,
land, which is never satisfied with
water,
and fire, which never says,
'Enough!'

17"The eye that mocks a father,
that scorns obedience to a mother,
will be pecked out by the ravens of
the valley,
will be eaten by the vultures.

18"There are three things that are too
amazing for me,
four that I do not understand:

19the way of an eagle in the sky,
the way of a snake on a rock,
the way of a ship on the high seas,
and the way of a man with a maiden.

20"This is the way of an adulteress:
She eats and wipes her mouth
and says, 'I've done nothing
wrong.'

21"Under three things the earth
trembles,
under four it cannot bear up:
22a servant who becomes king,
a fool who is full of food,
23an unloved woman who is
married,
and a maidservant who displaces
her mistress.

DAY 349

DECEMBER 15

OLD TESTAMENT READING

Malachi 1:1–2:16

1 An oracle: The word of the LORD to Israel through Malachi.

Jacob Loved, Esau Hated

2"I have loved you," says the LORD.
"But you ask, 'How have you loved us?'
"Was not Esau Jacob's brother?" the LORD says. "Yet I have loved Jacob,
3but Esau I have hated, and I have turned his mountains into a wasteland and left his inheritance to the desert jackals."
4Edom may say, "Though we have been crushed, we will rebuild the ruins."
But this is what the LORD Almighty says: "They may build, but I will demolish. They will be called the Wicked Land, a people always under the wrath of the LORD.
5You will see it with your own eyes and say, 'Great is the LORD—even beyond the borders of Israel!'

Blemished Sacrifices

6"A son honours his father, and a servant his master. If I am a father, where is the honour due to me? If I am a master, where is the respect due to me?" says the LORD Almighty. "It is you, O priests, who show contempt for my name.
"But you ask, 'How have we shown contempt for your name?'
7"You place defiled food on my altar.
"But you ask, 'How have we defiled you?'
"By saying that the LORD's table is contemptible.
8When you bring blind animals for sacrifice, is that not wrong? When you sacrifice crippled or diseased animals, is that not wrong? Try offering them to your governor! Would he be pleased with you? Would he accept you?" says the LORD Almighty.
9"Now implore God to be gracious to us. With such offerings from your hands, will he accept you?"—says the LORD Almighty.
10"Oh, that one of you would shut the temple doors, so that you would not light useless fires on my altar! I am not pleased with you," says the LORD Almighty, "and I will accept no offering from your hands.
11My name will be great among the nations, from the rising to the setting of the sun. In every place incense and pure offerings will be brought to my name, because my name will be great among the nations," says the LORD Almighty.
12"But you profane it by saying of the Lord's table, 'It is defiled', and of its

food, ‘It is contemptible.’ 13And you say, ‘What a burden!’ and you sniff at it contemptuously,” says the LORD Almighty.

“When you bring injured, crippled or diseased animals and offer them as sacrifices, should I accept them from your hands?” says the LORD. 14“Cursed is the cheat who has an acceptable male in his flock and vows to give it, but then sacrifices a blemished animal to the Lord. For I am a great king,” says the LORD Almighty, “and my name is to be feared among the nations.

Admonition for the Priests

2 “And now this admonition is for you, O priests. 2If you do not listen, and if you do not set your heart to honour my name,” says the LORD Almighty, “I will send a curse upon you, and I will curse your blessings. Yes, I have already cursed them, because you have not set your heart to honour me.

3“Because of you I will rebuke your descendants; I will spread on your faces the offal from your festival sacrifices, and you will be carried off with it. 4And you will know that I have sent you this admonition so that my covenant with Levi may continue,” says the LORD Almighty. 5“My covenant was with him, a covenant of life and peace, and I gave them to him; this called for reverence and he revered me and stood in awe of my name. 6True instruction was in his mouth and nothing false was found on his lips. He walked with me in peace and uprightness, and turned many from sin.

7“For the lips of a priest ought to preserve knowledge, and from his mouth men should seek instruction—because he is the messenger of the LORD Almighty. 8But you have turned from the way and by your teaching have caused many to stumble; you have violated the covenant with Levi,” says the LORD Almighty. 9“So I have caused you to be despised and humiliated before all the people, because you have not followed my ways but have shown partiality in matters of the law.”

Judah Unfaithful

10Have we not all one Father? Did not one God create us? Why do we profane the covenant of our fathers by breaking faith with one another?

11Judah has broken faith. A detestable thing has been committed in Israel and in Jerusalem: Judah has desecrated the sanctuary the LORD loves, by marrying the daughter of a foreign god. 12As for the man who does this, whoever he may be, may the LORD cut him off from the tents of Jacob—even though he brings offerings to the LORD Almighty.

13Another thing you do: You flood the LORD’s altar with tears. You weep and wail because he no longer pays attention to your offerings or accepts them with pleasure from your hands. 14You ask, “Why?” It is because the LORD is acting as the witness between you and the wife of your youth, because you have broken faith with her, though she is your partner, the wife of your marriage covenant.

15Has not ⌞the LORD⌟ made them one? In flesh and spirit they are his. And why one? Because he was seeking godly offspring. So guard yourself in your spirit, and do not break faith with the wife of your youth.

16“I hate divorce,” says the LORD God of Israel, “and I hate a man’s covering himself with violence as well as with his garment,” says the LORD Almighty.

So guard yourself in your spirit, and do not break faith.

NEW TESTAMENT READING

Revelation 6:1–17

The Seals

6 I watched as the Lamb opened the first of the seven seals. Then I heard one of the four living creatures

say in a voice like thunder, "Come!" 2I
looked, and there before me was a
white horse! Its rider held a bow, and he
was given a crown, and he rode out as a
conqueror bent on conquest.
3When the Lamb opened the second
seal, I heard the second living creature
say, "Come!" 4Then another horse
came out, a fiery red one. Its rider was
given power to take peace from the
earth and to make men slay each other.
To him was given a large sword.
5When the Lamb opened the third
seal, I heard the third living creature
say, "Come!" I looked, and there before me was a black horse! Its rider was
holding a pair of scales in his hand.
6Then I heard what sounded like a voice
among the four living creatures, saying,
"A quart of wheat for a day's wages, and
three quarts of barley for a day's wages,
and do not damage the oil and the
wine!"
7When the Lamb opened the fourth
seal, I heard the voice of the fourth
living creature say, "Come!" 8I looked,
and there before me was a pale horse!
Its rider was named Death, and Hades
was following close behind him. They
were given power over a fourth of the
earth to kill by sword, famine and plague, and by the wild beasts of the earth.
9When he opened the fifth seal, I saw
under the altar the souls of those who
had been slain because of the word of
God and the testimony they had main-
tained. 10They called out in a loud
voice, "How long, Sovereign Lord,
holy and true, until you judge the inhabitants of the earth and avenge our
blood?" 11Then each of them was given
a white robe, and they were told to wait
a little longer, until the number of their
fellow-servants and brothers who were
to be killed as they had been was
completed.
12I watched as he opened the sixth
seal. There was a great earthquake. The
sun turned black like sackcloth made of
goat hair, the whole moon turned blood
red, 13and the stars in the sky fell to
earth, as late figs drop from a fig-tree
when shaken by a strong wind. 14The
sky receded like a scroll, rolling up, and
every mountain and island was removed
from its place.
15Then the kings of the earth, the
princes, the generals, the rich, the
mighty, and every slave and every free
man hid in caves and among the rocks of
the mountains. 16They called to the
mountains and the rocks, "Fall on us
and hide us from the face of him who sits
on the throne and from the wrath of the
Lamb! 17For the great day of their wrath
has come, and who can stand?"

READING FROM PSALMS
Psalm 143:1–12

A psalm of David.

1O LORD, hear my prayer,
listen to my cry for mercy;
in your faithfulness and righteousness
come to my relief.
2Do not bring your servant into
judgment,
for no-one living is righteous
before you.

3The enemy pursues me,
he crushes me to the ground;
he makes me dwell in darkness
like those long dead.
4So my spirit grows faint within me;
my heart within me is dismayed.

5I remember the days of long ago;
I meditate on all your works
and consider what your hands have
done.
6I spread out my hands to you;
my soul thirsts for you like a
parched land. *Selah*

7Answer me quickly, O LORD;
my spirit fails.
Do not hide your face from me
or I will be like those who go down
to the pit.

8Let the morning bring me word of
your unfailing love,
for I have put my trust in
you.
Show me the way I should go,
for to you I lift up my soul.
9Rescue me from my enemies, O
LORD,
for I hide myself in you.
10Teach me to do your will,
for you are my God;
may your good Spirit
lead me on level ground.

11For your name's sake, O LORD,
preserve my life;
in your righteousness, bring me out
of trouble.
12In your unfailing love, silence my
enemies;
destroy all my foes,
for I am your servant.

DECEMBER 16

DAY 350

OLD TESTAMENT READING
Malachi 2:17–4:6

The Day of Judgment

17You have wearied the LORD with your words.

"How have we wearied him?" you ask.

By saying, "All who do evil are good in the eyes of the LORD, and he is pleased with them" or "Where is the God of justice?"

3 "See, I will send my messenger, who will prepare the way before me. Then suddenly the Lord you are seeking will come to his temple; the messenger of the covenant, whom you desire, will come," says the Lord Almighty.

2But who can endure the day of his coming? Who can stand when he appears? For he will be like a refiner's fire or a launderer's soap. 3He will sit as
a refiner and purifier of silver; he will purify the Levites and refine them like gold and silver. Then the LORD will have men who will bring offerings in righteousness, 4and the offerings of
Judah and Jerusalem will be acceptable to the LORD, as in days gone by, as in former years.

5"So I will come near to you for judgment. I will be quick to testify against sorcerers, adulterers and perjurers, against those who defraud labourers of their wages, who oppress the widows and the fatherless, and deprive aliens of justice, but do not fear me," says the LORD Almighty.

Robbing God

6"I the LORD do not change. So you, O descendants of Jacob, are not destroyed. 7Ever since the time of your
forefathers you have turned away from my decrees and have not kept them. Return to me, and I will return to you," says the LORD Almighty.

"But you ask, 'How are we to return?'

8"Will a man rob God? Yet you rob me.

"But you ask, 'How do we rob you?'

"In tithes and offerings. 9You are
under a curse—the whole nation of you —because you are robbing me. 10Bring
the whole tithe into the storehouse, that there may be food in my house. Test me in this," says the LORD Almighty, "and see if I will not throw open the floodgates of heaven and pour out so much blessing that you will not have room

enough for it. 11I will prevent pests from
devouring your crops, and the vines in
your fields will not cast their fruit," says
the LORD Almighty. 12"Then all the
nations will call you blessed, for yours
will be a delightful land," says the LORD
Almighty.
13"You have said harsh things against
me," says the LORD.
"Yet you ask, 'What have we said
against you?'
14"You have said, 'It is futile to serve
God. What did we gain by carrying out
his requirements and going about like
mourners before the LORD Almighty?
15But now we call the arrogant blessed.
Certainly the evildoers prosper, and
even those who challenge God
escape.' "
16Then those who feared the LORD
talked with each other, and the LORD
listened and heard. A scroll of remembrance was written in his presence
concerning those who feared the LORD
and honoured his name.
17"They will be mine," says the LORD
Almighty, "in the day when I make up
my treasured possession. I will spare
them, just as in compassion a man
spares his son who serves him. 18And
you will again see the distinction between the righteous and the wicked,
between those who serve God and those
who do not.

The Day of the LORD

4 "Surely the day is coming; it will
burn like a furnace. All the arrogant and every evildoer will be stubble,
and that day that is coming will set them
on fire," says the LORD Almighty. "Not
a root or a branch will be left to them.
2But for you who revere my name, the
sun of righteousness will rise with healing in its wings. And you will go out
and leap like calves released from the
stall. 3Then you will trample down the
wicked; they will be ashes under the
soles of your feet on the day when I do
these things," says the LORD Almighty.
4"Remember the law of my servant
Moses, the decrees and laws I gave him
at Horeb for all Israel.
5"See, I will send you the prophet
Elijah before that great and dreadful
day of the LORD comes. 6He will turn
the hearts of the fathers to their children, and the hearts of the children to
their fathers; or else I will come and
strike the land with a curse."

NEW TESTAMENT READING
Revelation 7:1–17

144,000 Sealed

7 After this I saw four angels standing at the four corners of the earth,
holding back the four winds of the earth
to prevent any wind from blowing on
the land or on the sea or on any tree.
2Then I saw another angel coming up
from the east, having the seal of the
living God. He called out in a loud voice
to the four angels who had been given
power to harm the land and the sea:
3"Do not harm the land or the sea or the
trees until we put a seal on the foreheads of the servants of our God."
4Then I heard the number of those who
were sealed: 144,000 from all the tribes
of Israel.

5From the tribe of Judah 12,000 were
sealed,
from the tribe of Reuben 12,000,
from the tribe of Gad 12,000,
6from the tribe of Asher 12,000,
from the tribe of Naphtali 12,000,
from the tribe of Manasseh 12,000,
7from the tribe of Simeon 12,000,
from the tribe of Levi 12,000,
from the tribe of Issachar 12,000,
8from the tribe of Zebulun 12,000,
from the tribe of Joseph 12,000,
from the tribe of Benjamin 12,000.

The Great Multitude in White Robes

9After this I looked and there before
me was a great multitude that no-one

could count, from every nation, tribe,
people and language, standing before
the throne and in front of the Lamb.
They were wearing white robes and
were holding palm branches in their
hands. [10]And they cried out in a loud
voice:

"Salvation belongs to our God,
who sits on the throne,
and to the Lamb."

[11]All the angels were standing round the
throne and around the elders and the
four living creatures. They fell down on
their faces before the throne and worshipped God, [12]saying:

"Amen!
Praise and glory
and wisdom and thanks and honour
and power and strength
be to our God for ever and ever.
Amen!"

[13]Then one of the elders asked me,
"These in white robes—who are they,
and where did they come from?"
[14]I answered, "Sir, you know."
And he said, "These are they who
have come out of the great tribulation;
they have washed their robes and made
them white in the blood of the Lamb.
[15]Therefore,

"they are before the throne of God
and serve him day and night in his temple;
and he who sits on the throne will
spread his tent over them.
[16]Never again will they hunger;
never again will they thirst.
The sun will not beat upon them,
nor any scorching heat.
[17]For the Lamb at the centre of the
throne will be their shepherd;
he will lead them to springs of
living water.
And God will wipe away every tear
from their eyes."

READING FROM PSALMS
Psalm 144:1–8

Of David.

[1]Praise be to the LORD my Rock,
who trains my hands for war,
my fingers for battle.
[2]He is my loving God and my fortress,
my stronghold and my deliverer,
my shield, in whom I take refuge,
who subdues peoples under me.

[3]O LORD, what is man that you care
for him,
the son of man that you think of
him?
[4]Man is like a breath;
his days are like a fleeting shadow.

[5]Part your heavens, O LORD, and
come down;
touch the mountains, so that they
smoke.
[6]Send forth lightning and scatter ⌊the
enemies⌋;
shoot your arrows and rout them.
[7]Reach down your hand from on high;
deliver me and rescue me
from the mighty waters,
from the hands of foreigners
[8]whose mouths are full of lies,
whose right hands are deceitful.

DAY 351

DECEMBER 17

OLD TESTAMENT READING
Ezra 1:1–2:67

Cyrus Helps the Exiles to Return

1 In the first year of Cyrus king of
Persia, in order to fulfil the word
of the LORD spoken by Jeremiah, the
LORD moved the heart of Cyrus king of
Persia to make a proclamation through-
out his realm and to put it in writing:

2"This is what Cyrus king of Persia
says:
" 'The LORD, the God of heaven,
has given me all the kingdoms of
the earth and he has appointed me
to build a temple for him at Jerusalem in Judah. 3Anyone of his
people among you—may his God
be with him, and let him go up to
Jerusalem in Judah and build the
temple of the LORD, the God of
Israel, the God who is in Jerusalem. 4And the people of any
place where survivors may now be
living are to provide him with silver
and gold, with goods and livestock,
and with freewill offerings for the
temple of God in Jerusalem.' "

5Then the family heads of Judah and
Benjamin, and the priests and Levites
—everyone whose heart God had
moved—prepared to go up and build
the house of the LORD in Jerusalem.
6All their neighbours assisted them with
articles of silver and gold, with goods
and livestock, and with valuable gifts, in
addition to all the freewill offerings.
7Moreover, King Cyrus brought out the
articles belonging to the temple of the
LORD, which Nebuchadnezzar had carried away from Jerusalem and had
placed in the temple of his god. 8Cyrus
king of Persia had them brought by
Mithredath the treasurer, who counted
them out to Sheshbazzar the prince of
Judah.

9This was the inventory:

gold dishes	30
silver dishes	1,000
silver pans	29
10gold bowls	30
matching silver bowls	410
other articles	1,000

11In all, there were 5,400 articles of
gold and of silver. Sheshbazzar brought
all these along when the exiles came up
from Babylon to Jerusalem.

The List of the Exiles Who Returned

2 Now these are the people of the
province who came up from the
captivity of the exiles, whom Nebuchadnezzar king of Babylon had taken
captive to Babylon (they returned to
Jerusalem and Judah, each to his own
town, 2in company with Zerubbabel,
Jeshua, Nehemiah, Seraiah, Reelaiah,
Mordecai, Bilshan, Mispar, Bigvai,
Rehum and Baanah):

The list of the men of the people of
Israel:

3the descendants of Parosh	2,172
4of Shephatiah	372
5of Arah	775
6of Pahath-Moab (through the line of Jeshua and Joab)	2,812
7of Elam	1,254
8of Zattu	945
9of Zaccai	760
10of Bani	642
11of Bebai	623
12of Azgad	1,222
13of Adonikam	666
14of Bigvai	2,056
15of Adin	454
16of Ater (through Hezekiah)	98
17of Bezai	323
18of Jorah	112
19of Hashum	223
20of Gibbar	95

21the men of Bethlehem	123
22of Netophah	56
23of Anathoth	128
24of Azmaveth	42
25of Kiriath Jearim, Kephirah and Beeroth	743
26of Ramah and Geba	621
27of Michmash	122
28of Bethel and Ai	223
29of Nebo	52
30of Magbish	156
31of the other Elam	1,254
32of Harim	320
33of Lod, Hadid and Ono	725
34of Jericho	345
35of Senaah	3,630

36The priests:

the descendants of Jedaiah (through the family of Jeshua)	973
37of Immer	1,052
38of Pashhur	1,247
39of Harim	1,017

40The Levites:

the descendants of Jeshua and Kadmiel (through the line of Hodaviah)	74

41The singers:

the descendants of Asaph	128

42The gatekeepers of the temple:

the descendants of Shallum, Ater, Talmon, Akkub, Hatita and Shobai	139

43The temple servants:

the descendants of
Ziha, Hasupha, Tabbaoth,
44Keros, Siaha, Padon,
45Lebanah, Hagabah, Akkub,
46Hagab, Shalmai, Hanan,
47Giddel, Gahar, Reaiah,
48Rezin, Nekoda, Gazzam,
49Uzza, Paseah, Besai,
50Asnah, Meunim, Nephussim,
51Bakbuk, Hakupha, Harhur,
52Bazluth, Mehida, Harsha,
53Barkos, Sisera, Temah,
54Neziah and Hatipha

55The descendants of the servants of Solomon:

the descendants of
Sotai, Hassophereth, Peruda,
56Jaala, Darkon, Giddel,
57Shephatiah, Hattil,
Pokereth-Hazzebaim and Ami

58The temple servants and the descendants of the servants of Solomon	392

59The following came up from
the towns of Tel Melah, Tel Harsha, Kerub, Addon and Immer,
but they could not show that their
families were descended from
Israel:

60The descendants of Delaiah, Tobiah and Nekoda	652

61And from among the priests:

The descendants of
Hobaiah, Hakkoz and Barzillai
(a man who had married a
daughter of Barzillai the
Gileadite and was called by that
name).
62These searched for their family
records, but they could not find
them and so were excluded from
the priesthood as unclean. 63The
governor ordered them not to eat
any of the most sacred food until
there was a priest ministering with
the Urim and Thummim.

64The whole company numbered
42,360, 65besides their 7,337 menservants and maidservants; and
they also had 200 men and women

singers. 66They had 736 horses, 245
mules, 67435 camels and 6,720
donkeys.

NEW TESTAMENT READING
Revelation 8:1–9:12

The Seventh Seal and the Golden Censer

8 When he opened the seventh seal,
there was silence in heaven for
about half an hour.
2And I saw the seven angels who
stand before God, and to them were
given seven trumpets.
3Another angel, who had a golden
censer, came and stood at the altar.
He was given much incense to offer,
with the prayers of all the saints, on
the golden altar before the throne.
4The smoke of the incense, together
with the prayers of the saints, went up
before God from the angel's hand.
5Then the angel took the censer, filled it
with fire from the altar, and hurled it on
the earth; and there came peals of thunder, rumblings, flashes of lightning and
an earthquake.

The Trumpets

6Then the seven angels who had the
seven trumpets prepared to sound
them.
7The first angel sounded his trumpet,
and there came hail and fire mixed with
blood, and it was hurled down upon the
earth. A third of the earth was burned
up, a third of the trees were burned up,
and all the green grass was burned up.
8The second angel sounded his trumpet, and something like a huge mountain, all ablaze, was thrown into the sea.
A third of the sea turned into blood,
9a third of the living creatures in the
sea died, and a third of the ships were
destroyed.
10The third angel sounded his trumpet, and a great star, blazing like a
torch, fell from the sky on a third of the
rivers and on the springs of water—
11the name of the star is Wormwood. A
third of the waters turned bitter, and
many people died from the waters that
had become bitter.
12The fourth angel sounded his trumpet, and a third of the sun was struck, a
third of the moon, and a third of the
stars, so that a third of them turned
dark. A third of the day was without
light, and also a third of the night.
13As I watched, I heard an eagle that
was flying in mid-air call out in a loud
voice: "Woe! Woe! Woe to the inhabitants of the earth, because of the trumpet blasts about to be sounded by the
other three angels!"
9 The fifth angel sounded his trumpet, and I saw a star that had fallen
from the sky to the earth. The star was
given the key to the shaft of the Abyss.
2When he opened the Abyss, smoke
rose from it like the smoke from a gigan-
tic furnace. The sun and sky were
darkened by the smoke from the Abyss.
3And out of the smoke locusts came
down upon the earth and were given
power like that of scorpions of the
earth. 4They were told not to harm the
grass of the earth or any plant or tree,
but only those people who did not have
the seal of God on their foreheads.
5They were not given power to kill
them, but only to torture them for five
months. And the agony they suffered
was like that of the sting of a scorpion
when it strikes a man. 6During those
days men will seek death, but will not
find it; they will long to die, but death
will elude them.
7The locusts looked like horses prepared for battle. On their heads they
wore something like crowns of gold,
and their faces resembled human faces.
8Their hair was like women's hair, and
their teeth were like lions' teeth. 9They
had breastplates like breastplates of
iron, and the sound of their wings was
like the thundering of many horses and
chariots rushing into battle. 10They had
tails and stings like scorpions, and in
their tails they had power to torment

people for five months. 11They had as
king over them the angel of the Abyss,
whose name in Hebrew is Abaddon,
and in Greek, Apollyon.
12The first woe is past; two other woes
are yet to come.

READING FROM PSALMS

Psalm 144:9–15

9I will sing a new song to you, O God;
on the ten-stringed lyre I will make
music to you,
10to the One who gives victory to kings,
who delivers his servant David
from the deadly sword.

11Deliver me and rescue me
from the hands of foreigners
whose mouths are full of lies,
whose right hands are deceitful.

12Then our sons in their youth
will be like well-nurtured plants,
and our daughters will be like pillars
carved to adorn a palace.
13Our barns will be filled
with every kind of provision.
Our sheep will increase by thousands,
by tens of thousands in our fields;
14 our oxen will draw heavy loads.
There will be no breaching of walls,
no going into captivity,
no cry of distress in our streets.

15Blessed are the people of whom this
is true;
blessed are the people whose God
is the LORD.

DECEMBER 18

DAY 352

OLD TESTAMENT READING

Ezra 2:68–4:5

68When they arrived at the house of
the LORD in Jerusalem, some of the
heads of the families gave freewill offerings towards the rebuilding of the house
of God on its site. 69According to their
ability they gave to the treasury for
this work 61,000 drachmas of gold,
5,000 minas of silver and 100 priestly
garments.
70The priests, the Levites, the singers, the gatekeepers and the temple servants settled in their own towns, along
with some of the other people, and the
rest of the Israelites settled in their
towns.

Rebuilding the Altar

3 When the seventh month came and
the Israelites had settled in their
towns, the people assembled as one
man in Jerusalem. 2Then Jeshua son of
Jozadak and his fellow priests and
Zerubbabel son of Shealtiel and his
associates began to build the altar of the
God of Israel to sacrifice burnt offerings
on it, in accordance with what is written
in the Law of Moses the man of God.
3Despite their fear of the peoples
around them, they built the altar on its
foundation and sacrificed burnt offerings on it to the LORD, both the morning
and evening sacrifices. 4Then in accordance with what is written, they celebrated the Feast of Tabernacles with the
required number of burnt offerings prescribed for each day. 5After that, they
presented the regular burnt offerings,
the New Moon sacrifices and the sacrifices for all the appointed sacred feasts
of the LORD, as well as those brought as
freewill offerings to the LORD. 6On the
first day of the seventh month they began to offer burnt offerings to the LORD,

though the foundation of the LORD's
temple had not yet been laid.

Rebuilding the Temple

7Then they gave money to the masons
and carpenters, and gave food and
drink and oil to the people of Sidon and
Tyre, so that they would bring cedar
logs by sea from Lebanon to Joppa, as
authorised by Cyrus king of Persia.
8In the second month of the second
year after their arrival at the house of
God in Jerusalem, Zerubbabel son of
Shealtiel, Jeshua son of Jozadak and the
rest of their brothers (the priests and the
Levites and all who had returned from
the captivity to Jerusalem) began the
work, appointing Levites twenty years
of age and older to supervise the
building of the house of the LORD.
9Jeshua and his sons and brothers and
Kadmiel and his sons (descendants of
Hodaviah) and the sons of Henadad
and their sons and brothers—all Levites—joined together in supervising
those working on the house of God.
10When the builders laid the foundation of the temple of the LORD, the
priests in their vestments and with trumpets, and the Levites (the sons of
Asaph) with cymbals, took their places
to praise the LORD, as prescribed by
David king of Israel. 11With praise and
thanksgiving they sang to the LORD:

"He is good;
his love to Israel endures for
ever."

And all the people gave a great shout of
praise to the LORD, because the foundation of the house of the LORD was laid.
12But many of the older priests and
Levites and family heads, who had seen
the former temple, wept aloud when
they saw the foundation of this temple
being laid, while many others shouted
for joy. 13No-one could distinguish the
sound of the shouts of joy from the
sound of weeping, because the people
made so much noise. And the sound
was heard far away.

Opposition to the Rebuilding

4
When the enemies of Judah and
Benjamin heard that the exiles
were building a temple for the LORD,
the God of Israel, 2they came to Zerubbabel and to the heads of the families
and said, "Let us help you build because, like you, we seek your God and
have been sacrificing to him since the
time of Esarhaddon king of Assyria,
who brought us here."
3But Zerubbabel, Jeshua and the rest
of the heads of the families of Israel
answered, "You have no part with us in
building a temple to our God. We alone
will build it for the LORD, the God of
Israel, as King Cyrus, the king of Persia,
commanded us."
4Then the peoples around them set
out to discourage the people of Judah
and make them afraid to go on building.
5They hired counsellors to work against
them and frustrate their plans during
the entire reign of Cyrus king of Persia
and down to the reign of Darius king of
Persia.

NEW TESTAMENT READING

Revelation 9:13–10:11

13The sixth angel sounded his trumpet, and I heard a voice coming from the
horns of the golden altar that is before
God. 14It said to the sixth angel who had
the trumpet, "Release the four angels
who are bound at the great river Euphrates." 15And the four angels who had
been kept ready for this very hour and
day and month and year were released
to kill a third of mankind. 16The number
of the mounted troops was two hundred
million. I heard their number.
17The horses and riders I saw in my
vision looked like this: Their breastplates were fiery red, dark blue, and
yellow as sulphur. The heads of the

horses resembled the heads of lions,
and out of their mouths came fire,
smoke and sulphur. 18A third of mankind was killed by the three plagues of
fire, smoke and sulphur that came out of
their mouths. 19The power of the horses
was in their mouths and in their tails; for
their tails were like snakes, having
heads with which they inflict injury.
20The rest of mankind that were not
killed by these plagues still did not repent of the work of their hands; they did
not stop worshipping demons, and idols
of gold, silver, bronze, stone and wood
—idols that cannot see or hear or walk.
21Nor did they repent of their murders,
their magic arts, their sexual immorality
or their thefts.

The Angel and the Little Scroll

10 Then I saw another mighty angel
coming down from heaven. He
was robed in a cloud, with a rainbow
above his head; his face was like the
sun, and his legs were like fiery pillars.
2He was holding a little scroll, which lay
open in his hand. He planted his right
foot on the sea and his left foot on the
land, 3and he gave a loud shout like
the roar of a lion. When he shouted, the
voices of the seven thunders spoke.
4And when the seven thunders spoke, I
was about to write; but I heard a voice
from heaven say, "Seal up what the
seven thunders have said and do not
write it down."
5Then the angel I had seen standing
on the sea and on the land raised his
right hand to heaven. 6And he swore by
him who lives for ever and ever, who
created the heavens and all that is in
them, the earth and all that is in it, and
the sea and all that is in it, and said,
"There will be no more delay! 7But in
the days when the seventh angel is
about to sound his trumpet, the mystery
of God will be accomplished, just as
he announced to his servants the
prophets."
8Then the voice that I had heard from
heaven spoke to me once more: "Go,
take the scroll that lies open in the hand
of the angel who is standing on the sea
and on the land."
9So I went to the angel and asked him
to give me the little scroll. He said to
me, "Take it and eat it. It will turn your
stomach sour, but in your mouth it will
be as sweet as honey." 10I took the little
scroll from the angel's hand and ate it. It
tasted as sweet as honey in my mouth,
but when I had eaten it, my stomach
turned sour. 11Then I was told, "You
must prophesy again about many peoples, nations, languages and kings."

READING FROM PROVERBS
Proverbs 30:24–33

24"Four things on earth are small,
yet they are extremely wise:
25Ants are creatures of little strength,
yet they store up their food in the
summer;
26conies are creatures of little power,
yet they make their home in the
crags;
27locusts have no king,
yet they advance together in ranks;
28a lizard can be caught with the hand,
yet it is found in kings' palaces.

29"There are three things that are
stately in their stride,
four that move with stately
bearing:
30a lion, mighty among beasts,
who retreats before nothing;
31a strutting cock, a he-goat,
and a king with his army around
him.

32"If you have played the fool and
exalted yourself,
or if you have planned evil,
clap your hand over your mouth!
33For as churning the milk produces
butter,
and as twisting the nose produces
blood,
so stirring up anger produces
strife."

DAY 353

DECEMBER 19

OLD TESTAMENT READING
Ezra 4:6–5:17

Later Opposition Under Xerxes and Artaxerxes

6At the beginning of the reign of
Xerxes, they lodged an accusation
against the people of Judah and
Jerusalem.
7And in the days of Artaxerxes king
of Persia, Bishlam, Mithredath, Tabeel
and the rest of his associates wrote a
letter to Artaxerxes. The letter was
written in Aramaic script and in the
Aramaic language.
8Rehum the commanding officer and
Shimshai the secretary wrote a letter
against Jerusalem to Artaxerxes the
king as follows:

9Rehum the commanding officer
and Shimshai the secretary,
together with the rest of their
associates—the judges and officials over the men from Tripolis,
Persia, Erech and Babylon, the
Elamites of Susa, 10and the other
people whom the great and honourable Ashurbanipal deported
and settled in the city of Samaria
and elsewhere in Trans-Euphrates.

11(This is a copy of the letter they sent
him.)

To King Artaxerxes,

From your servants, the men of
Trans-Euphrates:

12The king should know that the
Jews who came up to us from you
have gone to Jerusalem and are rebuilding that rebellious and wicked
city. They are restoring the walls
and repairing the foundations.
13Furthermore, the king should
know that if this city is built and its
walls are restored, no more taxes,
tribute or duty will be paid, and the
royal revenues will suffer. 14Now
since we are under obligation to the
palace and it is not proper for us to
see the king dishonoured, we are
sending this message to inform the
king, 15so that a search may be
made in the archives of your prede-
cessors. In these records you will
find that this city is a rebellious city,
troublesome to kings and provinces, a place of rebellion from
ancient times. That is why this city
was destroyed. 16We inform the
king that if this city is built and its
walls are restored, you will be left
with nothing in Trans-Euphrates.

17The king sent this reply:

To Rehum the commanding
officer, Shimshai the secretary and
the rest of their associates living in
Samaria and elsewhere in Trans-
Euphrates:

Greetings.

18The letter you sent us has been
read and translated in my presence. 19I issued an order and a
search was made, and it was found
that this city has a long history of
revolt against kings and has been a
place of rebellion and sedition.
20Jerusalem has had powerful kings
ruling over the whole of Trans-
Euphrates, and taxes, tribute and
duty were paid to them. 21Now
issue an order to these men to stop
work, so that this city will not be
rebuilt until I so order. 22Be careful
not to neglect this matter. Why let
this threat grow, to the detriment
of the royal interests?

[23]As soon as the copy of the letter of King Artaxerxes was read to Rehum and Shimshai the secretary and their associates, they went immediately to the Jews in Jerusalem and compelled them by force to stop.

[24]Thus the work on the house of God in Jerusalem came to a standstill until the second year of the reign of Darius king of Persia.

Tattenai's Letter to Darius

5 Now Haggai the prophet and
Zechariah the prophet, a descendant of Iddo, prophesied to the Jews in
Judah and Jerusalem in the name of the
God of Israel, who was over them.
[2]Then Zerubbabel son of Shealtiel and
Jeshua son of Jozadak set to work to
rebuild the house of God in Jerusalem.
And the prophets of God were with
them, helping them.
[3]At that time Tattenai, governor of
Trans-Euphrates, and Shethar-Bozenai
and their associates went to them and
asked, "Who authorised you to rebuild
this temple and restore this structure?"
[4]They also asked, "What are the names
of the men constructing this building?"
[5]But the eye of their God was watching
over the elders of the Jews, and they
were not stopped until a report could
go to Darius and his written reply be
received.
[6]This is a copy of the letter that Tattenai, governor of Trans-Euphrates, and
Shethar-Bozenai and their associates,
the officials of Trans-Euphrates, sent to
King Darius. [7]The report they sent him
read as follows:

To King Darius:

Cordial greetings.

[8]The king should know that we
went to the district of Judah, to the
temple of the great God. The people are building it with large stones
and placing the timbers in the
walls. The work is being carried on
with diligence and is making rapid
progress under their direction.
[9]We questioned the elders and
asked them, "Who authorised you
to rebuild this temple and restore
this structure?" [10]We also asked
them their names, so that we could
write down the names of their leaders for your information.
[11]This is the answer they gave us:

"We are the servants of the God
of heaven and earth, and we are
rebuilding the temple that was built
many years ago, one that a great
king of Israel built and finished.
[12]But because our fathers angered
the God of heaven, he handed
them over to Nebuchadnezzar the
Chaldean, king of Babylon, who
destroyed this temple and deported the people to Babylon.
[13]"However, in the first year of
Cyrus king of Babylon, King Cyrus
issued a decree to rebuild this
house of God. [14]He even removed
from the temple of Babylon the
gold and silver articles of the house
of God, which Nebuchadnezzar
had taken from the temple in Jerusalem and brought to the temple in
Babylon.
"Then King Cyrus gave them to
a man named Sheshbazzar, whom
he had appointed governor, [15]and
he told him, 'Take these articles
and go and deposit them in the
temple in Jerusalem. And rebuild
the house of God on its site.' [16]So
this Sheshbazzar came and laid the
foundations of the house of God in
Jerusalem. From that day to the
present it has been under construction but is not yet finished."

[17]Now if it pleases the king, let a
search be made in the royal archives of Babylon to see if King
Cyrus did in fact issue a decree to
rebuild this house of God in Jerusalem. Then let the king send us his
decision in this matter.

NEW TESTAMENT READING
Revelation 11:1–19

The Two Witnesses

11 I was given a reed like a measuring rod and was told, "Go and
measure the temple of God and the
altar, and count the worshippers there.
2But exclude the outer court; do not
measure it, because it has been given to
the Gentiles. They will trample on the
holy city for 42 months. 3And I will give
power to my two witnesses, and they
will prophesy for 1,260 days, clothed in
sackcloth." 4These are the two olive
trees and the two lampstands that stand
before the Lord of the earth. 5If anyone
tries to harm them, fire comes from
their mouths and devours their enemies. This is how anyone who wants to
harm them must die. 6These men have
power to shut up the sky so that it will
not rain during the time they are
prophesying; and they have power to
turn the waters into blood and to strike
the earth with every kind of plague as
often as they want.
7Now when they have finished their
testimony, the beast that comes up from
the Abyss will attack them, and overpower and kill them. 8Their bodies will
lie in the street of the great city, which is
figuratively called Sodom and Egypt,
where also their Lord was crucified.
9For three and a half days men from
every people, tribe, language and nation will gaze on their bodies and refuse
them burial. 10The inhabitants of the
earth will gloat over them and will
celebrate by sending each other gifts,
because these two prophets had
tormented those who live on earth.
11But after the three and a half days a
breath of life from God entered them,
and they stood on their feet, and terror
struck those who saw them. 12Then they
heard a loud voice from heaven saying
to them, "Come up here." And they
went up to heaven in a cloud, while their
enemies looked on.
13At that very hour there was a severe
earthquake and a tenth of the city collapsed. Seven thousand people were
killed in the earthquake, and the survivors were terrified and gave glory to the
God of heaven.
14The second woe has passed; the
third woe is coming soon.

The Seventh Trumpet

15The seventh angel sounded his
trumpet, and there were loud voices in
heaven, which said:

"The kingdom of the world has
become the kingdom of our
Lord and of his Christ,
and he will reign for ever and
ever."

16And the twenty-four elders, who were
seated on their thrones before God, fell
on their faces and worshipped God,
17saying:

"We give thanks to you, Lord God
Almighty,
the One who is and who was,
because you have taken your great
power
and have begun to reign.
18The nations were angry;
and your wrath has come.
The time has come for judging the
dead,
and for rewarding your servants
the prophets
and your saints and those who
reverence your name,
both small and great—
and for destroying those who destroy
the earth."

19Then God's temple in heaven was
opened, and within his temple was seen
the ark of his covenant. And there came
flashes of lightning, rumblings, peals of
thunder, an earthquake and a great
hailstorm.

READING FROM PSALMS
Psalm 145:1–7

A psalm of praise. Of David.

1I will exalt you, my God the King;
I will praise your name for ever and ever.
2Every day I will praise you
and extol your name for ever and ever.

3Great is the LORD and most worthy of praise;
his greatness no-one can fathom.
4One generation will commend your works to another;
they will tell of your mighty acts.
5They will speak of the glorious splendour of your majesty,
and I will meditate on your wonderful works.
6They will tell of the power of your awesome works,
and I will proclaim your great deeds.
7They will celebrate your abundant goodness
and joyfully sing of your righteousness.

DECEMBER 20

DAY 354

OLD TESTAMENT READING
Ezra 6:1–7:10

The Decree of Darius

6 King Darius then issued an order, and they searched in the archives stored in the treasury at Babylon.
2A scroll was found in the citadel of Ecbatana in the province of Media, and this was written on it:

Memorandum:

3In the first year of King Cyrus, the king issued a decree concerning the temple of God in Jerusalem:

Let the temple be rebuilt as a place to present sacrifices, and let its foundations be laid. It is to be ninety feet high and ninety feet wide,
4with three courses of large stones and one of timbers. The costs are to be paid by the royal treasury.
5Also, the gold and silver articles of the house of God, which Nebuchadnezzar took from the temple in Jerusalem and brought to Babylon, are to be returned to their places in the temple in Jerusalem; they are to be deposited in the house of God.

6Now then, Tattenai, governor of Trans-Euphrates, and Shethar-Bozenai and you, their fellow officials of that province, stay away from there.
7Do not interfere with the work on this temple of God. Let the governor of the Jews and the Jewish elders rebuild this house of God on its site.

8Moreover, I hereby decree what you are to do for these elders of the Jews in the construction of this house of God:

The expenses of these men are to be fully paid out of the royal treasury, from the revenues of Trans-Euphrates, so that the work will not stop.
9Whatever is needed—young bulls, rams, male lambs for burnt offerings to the God of heaven, and wheat, salt, wine and oil, as requested by the priests in Jerusalem—must be given them daily without fail,
10so that they may offer sacrifices pleasing to the God of heaven and pray for the

well-being of the king and his sons.
11Furthermore, I decree that if
anyone changes this edict, a beam
is to be pulled from his house and
he is to be lifted up and impaled on
it. And for this crime his house is to
be made a pile of rubble. 12May
God, who has caused his Name to
dwell there, overthrow any king or
people who lifts a hand to change
this decree or to destroy this temple in Jerusalem.
I Darius have decreed it. Let it
be carried out with diligence.

Completion and Dedication of the Temple

13Then, because of the decree King
Darius had sent, Tattenai, governor of
Trans-Euphrates, and Shethar-Bozenai
and their associates carried it out with
diligence. 14So the elders of the Jews
continued to build and prosper under
the preaching of Haggai the prophet
and Zechariah, a descendant of Iddo.
They finished building the temple
according to the command of the God
of Israel and the decrees of Cyrus,
Darius and Artaxerxes, kings of Persia.
15The temple was completed on the
third day of the month Adar, in the sixth
year of the reign of King Darius.
16Then the people of Israel—the
priests, the Levites and the rest of the
exiles—celebrated the dedication of
the house of God with joy. 17For the
dedication of this house of God they
offered a hundred bulls, two hundred
rams, four hundred male lambs and, as
a sin offering for all Israel, twelve male
goats, one for each of the tribes of
Israel. 18And they installed the priests
in their divisions and the Levites in their
groups for the service of God at Jerusalem, according to what is written in
the Book of Moses.

The Passover

19On the fourteenth day of the first
month, the exiles celebrated the Passover. 20The priests and Levites had
purified themselves and were all ceremonially clean. The Levites slaughtered
the Passover lamb for all the exiles, for
their brothers the priests and for themselves. 21So the Israelites who had returned from the exile ate it, together
with all who had separated themselves
from the unclean practices of their Gentile neighbours in order to seek the
LORD, the God of Israel. 22For seven
days they celebrated with joy the Feast
of Unleavened Bread, because the
LORD had filled them with joy by changing the attitude of the king of Assyria,
so that he assisted them in the work on
the house of God, the God of Israel.

Ezra Comes to Jerusalem

7 After these things, during the reign
of Artaxerxes king of Persia, Ezra
son of Seraiah, the son of Azariah, the
son of Hilkiah, 2the son of Shallum,
the son of Zadok, the son of Ahitub,
3the son of Amariah, the son of Azariah, the son of Meraioth, 4the son of
Zerahiah, the son of Uzzi, the son of
Bukki, 5the son of Abishua, the son
of Phinehas, the son of Eleazar, the
son of Aaron the chief priest—6this
Ezra came up from Babylon. He was
a teacher well versed in the Law of
Moses, which the LORD, the God of
Israel, had given. The king had granted
him everything he asked, for the hand
of the LORD his God was on him.
7Some of the Israelites, including
priests, Levites, singers, gate-keepers
and temple servants, also came up to
Jerusalem in the seventh year of King
Artaxerxes.
8Ezra arrived in Jerusalem in the fifth
month of the seventh year of the king.
9He had begun his journey from Babylon on the first day of the first month,
and he arrived in Jerusalem on the first
day of the fifth month, for the gracious
hand of his God was on him. 10For Ezra
had devoted himself to the study and
observance of the Law of the LORD, and
to teaching its decrees and laws in
Israel.

NEW TESTAMENT READING
Revelation 12:1–13:1a

The Woman and the Dragon

12 A great and wondrous sign
appeared in heaven: a woman
clothed with the sun, with the moon
under her feet and a crown of twelve
stars on her head. 2She was pregnant
and cried out in pain as she was about to
give birth. 3Then another sign appeared
in heaven: an enormous red dragon
with seven heads and ten horns and
seven crowns on his heads. 4His tail
swept a third of the stars out of the sky
and flung them to the earth. The dragon
stood in front of the woman who was
about to give birth, so that he might
devour her child the moment it was
born. 5She gave birth to a son, a male
child, who will rule all the nations with
an iron sceptre. And her child was
snatched up to God and to his throne.
6The woman fled into the desert to a
place prepared for her by God, where
she might be taken care of for 1,260
days.

7And there was war in heaven.
Michael and his angels fought against
the dragon, and the dragon and his
angels fought back. 8But he was not
strong enough, and they lost their place
in heaven. 9The great dragon was
hurled down—that ancient serpent
called the devil, or Satan, who leads
the whole world astray. He was hurled
to the earth, and his angels with him.

10Then I heard a loud voice in heaven
say:

"Now have come the salvation and
the power and the kingdom of
our God,
and the authority of his Christ.
For the accuser of our brothers,
who accuses them before our God
day and night,
has been hurled down.
11They overcame him
by the blood of the Lamb
and by the word of their testimony;
they did not love their lives so much
as to shrink from death.
12Therefore rejoice, you heavens
and you who dwell in them!
But woe to the earth and the sea,
because the devil has gone down to
you!
He is filled with fury,
because he knows that his time is
short."

13When the dragon saw that he had
been hurled to the earth, he pursued the
woman who had given birth to the male
child. 14The woman was given the two
wings of a great eagle, so that she might
fly to the place prepared for her in the
desert, where she would be taken care
of for a time, times and half a time, out
of the serpent's reach. 15Then from his
mouth the serpent spewed water like a
river, to overtake the woman and sweep
her away with the torrent. 16But the
earth helped the woman by opening its
mouth and swallowing the river that the
dragon had spewed out of his mouth.
17Then the dragon was enraged at the
woman and went off to make war
against the rest of her offspring—those
who obey God's commandments and
hold to the testimony of Jesus.
13 1And the dragon stood on the
shore of the sea.

READING FROM PSALMS
Psalm 145:8–13a

8The LORD is gracious and
compassionate,
slow to anger and rich in love.
9The LORD is good to all;
he has compassion on all he has
made.
10All you have made will praise you, O
LORD;
your saints will extol you.
11They will tell of the glory of your
kingdom
and speak of your might,

[12]so that all men may know of your
mighty acts
and the glorious splendour of your
kingdom.

[13]Your kingdom is an everlasting
kingdom,
and your dominion endures
through all generations.

DAY 355

DECEMBER 21

OLD TESTAMENT READING

Ezra 7:11–8:14

King Artaxerxes' Letter to Ezra

[11]This is a copy of the letter King Artaxerxes had given to Ezra the priest and teacher, a man learned in matters concerning the commands and decrees of the LORD for Israel:

[12]Artaxerxes, king of kings,

To Ezra the priest, a teacher of the Law of the God of heaven:

Greetings.

[13]Now I decree that any of the
Israelites in my kingdom, including
priests and Levites, who wish to go
to Jerusalem with you, may go.
[14]You are sent by the king and his
seven advisers to enquire about
Judah and Jerusalem with regard
to the Law of your God, which is in
your hand. [15]Moreover, you are to
take with you the silver and gold
that the king and his advisers have
freely given to the God of Israel,
whose dwelling is in Jerusalem,
[16]together with all the silver and
gold you may obtain from the province of Babylon, as well as the
freewill offerings of the people and
priests for the temple of their God
in Jerusalem. [17]With this money be
sure to buy bulls, rams and male
lambs, together with their grain
offerings and drink offerings, and
sacrifice them on the altar of the
temple of your God in Jerusalem.

[18]You and your brother Jews
may then do whatever seems best
with the rest of the silver and gold,
in accordance with the will of your
God. [19]Deliver to the God of Jerusalem all the articles entrusted to
you for worship in the temple of
your God. [20]And anything else
needed for the temple of your God
that you may have occasion to
supply, you may provide from the
royal treasury.

[21]Now I, King Artaxerxes, order
all the treasurers of Trans-Euphrates to provide with diligence whatever Ezra the priest, a
teacher of the Law of the God of
heaven, may ask of you—[22]up to a
hundred talents of silver, a hundred
cors of wheat, a hundred baths of
wine, a hundred baths of olive oil,
and salt without limit. [23]Whatever
the God of heaven has prescribed,
let it be done with diligence for the
temple of the God of heaven. Why
should there be wrath against the
realm of the king and of his sons?
[24]You are also to know that you
have no authority to impose taxes,
tribute or duty on any of the
priests, Levites, singers, gatekeepers, temple servants or other
workers at this house of God.

[25]And you, Ezra, in accordance
with the wisdom of your God,
which you possess, appoint magistrates and judges to administer
justice to all the people of Trans-Euphrates—all who know the laws
of your God. And you are to teach
any who do not know them.

26Whoever does not obey the law of your God and the law of the king must surely be punished by death, banishment, confiscation of property, or imprisonment.

27Praise be to the LORD, the God of our fathers, who has put it into the king's heart to bring honour to the house of the LORD in Jerusalem in this way 28and who has extended his good favour to me before the king and his advisers and all the king's powerful officials. Because the hand of the LORD my God was on me, I took courage and gathered leading men from Israel to go up with me.

List of the Family Heads Returning With Ezra

8 These are the family heads and those registered with them who came up with me from Babylon during the reign of King Artaxerxes:

2of the descendants of Phinehas, Gershom;
of the descendants of Ithamar, Daniel;
of the descendants of David, Hattush 3of the descendants of Shecaniah;

of the descendants of Parosh, Zechariah, and with him were registered 150 men;
4of the descendants of Pahath-Moab, Eliehoenai son of Zerahiah, and with him 200 men;
5of the descendants of Zattu, Shecaniah son of Jahaziel, and with him 300 men;
6of the descendants of Adin, Ebed son of Jonathan, and with him 50 men;
7of the descendants of Elam, Jeshaiah son of Athaliah, and with him 70 men;
8of the descendants of Shephatiah, Zebadiah son of Michael, and with him 80 men;
9of the descendants of Joab, Obadiah son of Jehiel, and with him 218 men;
10of the descendants of Bani, Shelomith son of Josiphiah, and with him 160 men;
11of the descendants of Bebai, Zechariah son of Bebai, and with him 28 men;
12of the descendants of Azgad, Johanan son of Hakkatan, and with him 110 men;
13of the descendants of Adonikam, the last ones, whose names were Eliphelet, Jeuel and Shemaiah, and with them 60 men;
14of the descendants of Bigvai, Uthai and Zaccur, and with them 70 men.

NEW TESTAMENT READING
Revelation 13:1b–18

The Beast out of the Sea

And I saw a beast coming out of the
sea. He had ten horns and seven heads,
with ten crowns on his horns, and on
each head a blasphemous name. 2The
beast I saw resembled a leopard, but
had feet like those of a bear and a mouth
like that of a lion. The dragon gave the
beast his power and his throne and great
authority. 3One of the heads of the
beast seemed to have had a fatal wound,
but the fatal wound had been healed.
The whole world was astonished and
followed the beast. 4Men worshipped
the dragon because he had given
authority to the beast, and they also
worshipped the beast and asked, "Who
is like the beast? Who can make war
against him?"

5The beast was given a mouth to utter
proud words and blasphemies and to
exercise his authority for forty-two
months. 6He opened his mouth to blaspheme God, and to slander his name
and his dwelling-place and those who
live in heaven. 7He was given power to

make war against the saints and to conquer them. And he was given authority
over every tribe, people, language and
nation. 8All inhabitants of the earth will
worship the beast—all whose names
have not been written in the book of life
belonging to the Lamb that was slain
from the creation of the world.
9He who has an ear, let him hear.

10If anyone is to go into captivity,
into captivity he will go.
If anyone is to be killed with the
sword,
with the sword he will be killed.

This calls for patient endurance and faithfulness on the part of the saints.

The Beast out of the Earth

11Then I saw another beast, coming
out of the earth. He had two horns like a
lamb, but he spoke like a dragon. 12He
exercised all the authority of the first
beast on his behalf, and made the earth
and its inhabitants worship the first
beast, whose fatal wound had been
healed. 13And he performed great and
miraculous signs, even causing fire to
come down from heaven to earth in full
view of men. 14Because of the signs he
was given power to do on behalf of the
first beast, he deceived the inhabitants
of the earth. He ordered them to set up
an image in honour of the beast who was
wounded by the sword and yet lived.
15He was given power to give breath to
the image of the first beast, so that it
could speak and cause all who refused
to worship the image to be killed. 16He
also forced everyone, small and great,
rich and poor, free and slave, to receive
a mark on his right hand or on his
forehead, 17so that no-one could buy or
sell unless he had the mark, which is the
name of the beast or the number of his
name.
18This calls for wisdom. If anyone has
insight, let him calculate the number of
the beast, for it is man's number. His
number is 666.

READING FROM PSALMS

Psalm 145:13b–21

The LORD is faithful to all his
promises
and loving towards all he has made.
14The LORD upholds all those who fall
and lifts up all who are bowed
down.
15The eyes of all look to you,
and you give them their food at the
proper time.
16You open your hand
and satisfy the desires of every
living thing.

17The LORD is righteous in all his ways
and loving towards all he has
made.
18The LORD is near to all who call on
him,
to all who call on him in truth.
19He fulfils the desires of those who
fear him;
he hears their cry and saves them.
20The LORD watches over all who love
him,
but all the wicked he will destroy.

21My mouth will speak in praise of the
LORD.
Let every creature praise his holy
name
for ever and ever.

DECEMBER 22

OLD TESTAMENT READING

Ezra 8:15–9:15

The Return to Jerusalem

[15]I assembled them at the canal that flows towards Ahava, and we camped there three days. When I checked among the people and the priests, I found no Levites there. [16]So I summoned Eliezer, Ariel, Shemaiah, Elnathan, Jarib, Elnathan, Nathan, Zechariah and Meshullam, who were leaders, and Joiarib and Elnathan, who were men of learning, [17]and I sent them to Iddo, the leader in Casiphia. I told them what to say to Iddo and his kinsmen, the temple servants in Casiphia, so that they might bring attendants to us for the house of our God. [18]Because the gracious hand of our God was on us, they brought us Sherebiah, a capable man, from the descendants of Mahli son of Levi, the son of Israel, and Sherebiah's sons and brothers, 18 men; [19]and Hashabiah, together with Jeshaiah from the descendants of Merari, and his brothers and nephews, 20 men. [20]They also brought 220 of the temple servants —a body that David and the officials had established to assist the Levites. All were registered by name.

[21]There, by the Ahava Canal, I proclaimed a fast, so that we might humble ourselves before our God and ask him for a safe journey for us and our children, with all our possessions. [22]I was ashamed to ask the king for soldiers and horsemen to protect us from enemies on the road, because we had told the king, "The gracious hand of our God is on everyone who looks to him, but his great anger is against all who forsake him." [23]So we fasted and petitioned our God about this, and he answered our prayer.

[24]Then I set apart twelve of the leading priests, together with Sherebiah, Hashabiah and ten of their brothers, [25]and I weighed out to them the offering of silver and gold and the articles that the king, his advisers, his officials and all Israel present there had donated for the house of our God. [26]I weighed out to them 650 talents of silver, silver articles weighing 100 talents, 100 talents of gold, [27]20 bowls of gold valued at 1,000 darics, and two fine articles of polished bronze, as precious as gold.

[28]I said to them, "You as well as these articles are consecrated to the LORD. The silver and gold are a freewill offering to the LORD, the God of your fathers. [29]Guard them carefully until you weigh them out in the chambers of the house of the LORD in Jerusalem before the leading priests and the Levites and the family heads of Israel." [30]Then the priests and Levites received the silver and gold and sacred articles that had been weighed out to be taken to the house of our God in Jerusalem.

[31]On the twelfth day of the first month we set out from the Ahava Canal to go to Jerusalem. The hand of our God was on us, and he protected us from enemies and bandits along the way. [32]So we arrived in Jerusalem, where we rested three days.

[33]On the fourth day, in the house of our God, we weighed out the silver and gold and the sacred articles into the hands of Meremoth son of Uriah, the priest. Eleazar son of Phinehas was with him, and so were the Levites Jozabad son of Jeshua and Noadiah son of Binnui. [34]Everything was accounted for by number and weight, and the entire weight was recorded at that time.

[35]Then the exiles who had returned from captivity sacrificed burnt offerings to the God of Israel: twelve bulls for all Israel, ninety-six rams, seventy-seven male lambs and, as a sin offering, twelve male goats. All this was a burnt offering

to the LORD. [36]They also delivered the king's orders to the royal satraps and to the governors of Trans-Euphrates who then gave assistance to the people and to the house of God.

Ezra's Prayer About Intermarriage

9 After these things had been done, the leaders came to me and said, "The people of Israel, including the priests and the Levites, have not kept themselves separate from the neighbouring peoples with their detestable practices, like those of the Canaanites, Hittites, Perizzites, Jebusites, Ammonites, Moabites, Egyptians and Amorites. [2]They have taken some of their daughters as wives for themselves and their sons, and have mingled the holy race with the peoples around them. And the leaders and officials have led the way in this unfaithfulness."

[3]When I heard this, I tore my tunic and cloak, pulled hair from my head and beard and sat down appalled. [4]Then everyone who trembled at the words of the God of Israel gathered round me because of this unfaithfulness of the exiles. And I sat there appalled until the evening sacrifice.

[5]Then, at the evening sacrifice, I rose from my self-abasement, with my tunic and cloak torn, and fell on my knees with my hands spread out to the LORD my God [6]and prayed:

"O my God, I am too ashamed and disgraced to lift up my face to you, my God, because our sins are higher than our heads and our guilt has reached to the heavens. [7]From the days of our forefathers until now, our guilt has been great. Because of our sins, we and our kings and our priests have been subjected to the sword and captivity, to pillage and humiliation at the hand of foreign kings, as it is today.

[8]"But now, for a brief moment, the LORD our God has been gracious in leaving us a remnant and giving us a firm place in his sanctuary, and so our God gives light to our eyes and a little relief in our bondage. [9]Though we are slaves, our God has not deserted us in our bondage. He has shown us kindness in the sight of the kings of Persia: He has granted us new life to rebuild the house of our God and repair its ruins, and he has given us a wall of protection in Judah and Jerusalem.

[10]"But now, O our God, what can we say after this? For we have disregarded the commands [11]you gave through your servants the prophets when you said: 'The land you are entering to possess is a land polluted by the corruption of its peoples. By their detestable practices they have filled it with their impurity from one end to the other. [12]Therefore, do not give your daughters in marriage to their sons or take their daughters for your sons. Do not seek a treaty of friendship with them at any time, that you may be strong and eat the good things of the land and leave it to your children as an everlasting inheritance.'

[13]"What has happened to us is a result of our evil deeds and our great guilt, and yet, our God, you have punished us less than our sins have deserved and have given us a remnant like this. [14]Shall we again break your commands and intermarry with the peoples who commit such detestable practices? Would you not be angry enough with us to destroy us, leaving us no remnant or survivor? [15]O LORD, God of Israel, you are righteous! We are left this day as a remnant. Here we are before you in our guilt, though because of it not one of us can stand in your presence."

NEW TESTAMENT READING
Revelation 14:1–13

The Lamb and the 144,000

14 Then I looked, and there before
me was the Lamb, standing on
Mount Zion, and with him 144,000 who
had his name and his Father's name
written on their foreheads. 2And I
heard a sound from heaven like the roar
of rushing waters and like a loud peal of
thunder. The sound I heard was like
that of harpists playing their harps.
3And they sang a new song before the
throne and before the four living creatures and the elders. No-one could learn
the song except the 144,000 who had
been redeemed from the earth. 4These
are those who did not defile themselves
with women, for they kept themselves
pure. They follow the Lamb wherever
he goes. They were purchased from
among men and offered as firstfruits to
God and the Lamb. 5No lie was found in
their mouths; they are blameless.

The Three Angels

6Then I saw another angel flying in
mid-air, and he had the eternal gospel
to proclaim to those who live on the
earth—to every nation, tribe, language
and people. 7He said in a loud voice,
"Fear God and give him glory, because
the hour of his judgment has come.
Worship him who made the heavens,
the earth, the sea and the springs of
water."

8A second angel followed and said,
"Fallen! Fallen is Babylon the Great,
which made all the nations drink the
maddening wine of her adulteries."

9A third angel followed them and said
in a loud voice: "If anyone worships the
beast and his image and receives his
mark on the forehead or on the hand,
10he, too, will drink of the wine of God's
fury, which has been poured full
strength into the cup of his wrath. He
will be tormented with burning sulphur
in the presence of the holy angels and of
the Lamb. 11And the smoke of their
torment rises for ever and ever. There is
no rest day or night for those who
worship the beast and his image, or for
anyone who receives the mark of his
name." 12This calls for patient endurance on the part of the saints who obey
God's commandments and remain
faithful to Jesus.

13Then I heard a voice from heaven
say, "Write: Blessed are the dead who
die in the Lord from now on."

"Yes," says the Spirit, "they will rest
from their labour, for their deeds will
follow them."

READING FROM PROVERBS
Proverbs 31:1–9

Sayings of King Lemuel

31 The sayings of King Lemuel—
an oracle his mother taught him:

2"O my son, O son of my womb,
O son of my vows,
3do not spend your strength on
women,
your vigour on those who ruin
kings.

4"It is not for kings, O Lemuel—
not for kings to drink wine,
not for rulers to crave beer,
5lest they drink and forget what the
law decrees,
and deprive all the oppressed of
their rights.
6Give beer to those who are perishing,
wine to those who are in anguish;
7let them drink and forget their
poverty
and remember their misery no
more.

8"Speak up for those who cannot
speak for themselves,
for the rights of all who are
destitute.
9Speak up and judge fairly;
defend the rights of the poor and
needy."

DAY 357 **DECEMBER 23**

OLD TESTAMENT READING
Ezra 10:1–44

The People's Confession of Sin

10 While Ezra was praying and
confessing, weeping and throwing himself down before the house of
God, a large crowd of Israelites—men,
women and children—gathered round
him. They too wept bitterly. 2Then Shecaniah son of Jehiel, one of the descendants of Elam, said to Ezra, "We have
been unfaithful to our God by marrying
foreign women from the peoples
around us. But in spite of this, there is
still hope for Israel. 3Now let us make a
covenant before our God to send away
all these women and their children, in
accordance with the counsel of my lord
and of those who fear the commands of
our God. Let it be done according to the
Law. 4Rise up; this matter is in your
hands. We will support you, so take
courage and do it."
5So Ezra rose up and put the leading
priests and Levites and all Israel under
oath to do what had been suggested.
And they took the oath. 6Then Ezra
withdrew from before the house of God
and went to the room of Jehohanan son
of Eliashib. While he was there, he ate
no food and drank no water, because he
continued to mourn over the unfaithfulness of the exiles.
7A proclamation was then issued
throughout Judah and Jerusalem for all
the exiles to assemble in Jerusalem.
8Anyone who failed to appear within
three days would forfeit all his property,
in accordance with the decision of the
officials and elders, and would himself
be expelled from the assembly of the
exiles.

9Within the three days, all the men of
Judah and Benjamin had gathered in
Jerusalem. And on the twentieth day of
the ninth month, all the people were
sitting in the square before the house of
God, greatly distressed by the occasion
and because of the rain. 10Then Ezra the
priest stood up and said to them, "You
have been unfaithful; you have married
foreign women, adding to Israel's guilt.
11Now make confession to the LORD,
the God of your fathers, and do his will.
Separate yourselves from the peoples
around you and from your foreign
wives."
12The whole assembly responded
with a loud voice: "You are right! We
must do as you say. 13But there are
many people here and it is the rainy
season; so we cannot stand outside. Besides, this matter cannot be taken care
of in a day or two, because we have
sinned greatly in this thing. 14Let our
officials act for the whole assembly.
Then let everyone in our towns who has
married a foreign woman come at a set
time, along with the elders and judges
of each town, until the fierce anger of
our God in this matter is turned away
from us." 15Only Jonathan son of
Asahel and Jahzeiah son of Tikvah,
supported by Meshullam and Shabbethai the Levite, opposed this.
16So the exiles did as was proposed.
Ezra the priest selected men who were
family heads, one from each family division, and all of them designated by
name. On the first day of the tenth
month they sat down to investigate the
cases, 17and by the first day of the first
month they finished dealing with all the
men who had married foreign women.

Those Guilty of Intermarriage

18Among the descendants of the
priests, the following had married foreign women:

From the descendants of Jeshua
son of Jozadak, and his brothers:

Maaseiah, Eliezer, Jarib and Gedaliah. 19(They all gave their hands in pledge to put away their wives, and for their guilt they each presented a ram from the flock as a guilt offering.)

20From the descendants of Immer:
Hanani and Zebadiah.

21From the descendants of Harim:
Maaseiah, Elijah, Shemaiah, Jehiel and Uzziah.

22From the descendants of Pashhur:
Elioenai, Maaseiah, Ishmael, Nethanel, Jozabad and Elasah.

23Among the Levites:

Jozabad, Shimei, Kelaiah (that is Kelita), Pethahiah, Judah and Eliezer.

24From the singers:
Eliashib.

From the gatekeepers:
Shallum, Telem and Uri.

25And among the other Israelites:

From the descendants of Parosh:
Ramiah, Izziah, Malkijah, Mijamin, Eleazar, Malkijah and Benaiah.

26From the descendants of Elam:
Mattaniah, Zechariah, Jehiel, Abdi, Jeremoth and Elijah.

27From the descendants of Zattu:
Elioenai, Eliashib, Mattaniah, Jeremoth, Zabad and Aziza.

28From the descendants of Bebai:
Jehohanan, Hananiah, Zabbai and Athlai.

29From the descendants of Bani:
Meshullam, Malluch, Adaiah, Jashub, Sheal and Jeremoth.

30From the descendants of Pahath-Moab:
Adna, Kelal, Benaiah, Maaseiah, Mattaniah, Bezalel, Binnui and Manasseh.

31From the descendants of Harim:
Eliezer, Ishijah, Malkijah, Shemaiah, Shimeon, 32Benjamin, Malluch and Shemariah.

33From the descendants of Hashum:
Mattenai, Mattattah, Zabad, Eliphelet, Jeremai, Manasseh and Shimei.

34From the descendants of Bani:
Maadai, Amram, Uel,
35Benaiah, Bedeiah, Keluhi,
36Vaniah, Meremoth, Eliashib,
37Mattaniah, Mattenai and Jaasu.

38From the descendants of Binnui:
Shimei, 39Shelemiah, Nathan,
Adaiah, 40Macnadebai, Shashai,
Sharai, 41Azarel, Shelemiah,
Shemariah, 42Shallum, Amariah and Joseph.

43From the descendants of Nebo:
Jeiel, Mattithiah, Zabad, Zebina, Jaddai, Joel and Benaiah.

44All these had married foreign women, and some of them had children by these wives.

NEW TESTAMENT READING
Revelation 14:14–15:8

The Harvest of the Earth

14I looked, and there before me was a
white cloud, and seated on the cloud
was one "like a son of man" with a
crown of gold on his head and a sharp
sickle in his hand. 15Then another angel
came out of the temple and called in a
loud voice to him who was sitting on the
cloud, "Take your sickle and reap, because the time to reap has come, for the
harvest of the earth is ripe." 16So he
who was seated on the cloud swung his
sickle over the earth, and the earth was
harvested.

17Another angel came out of the temple in heaven, and he too had a sharp
sickle. 18Still another angel, who had
charge of the fire, came from the altar
and called in a loud voice to him who
had the sharp sickle, "Take your sharp
sickle and gather the clusters of grapes
from the earth's vine, because its grapes
are ripe." 19The angel swung his sickle

on the earth, gathered its grapes and
threw them into the great winepress of
God's wrath. 20They were trampled in
the winepress outside the city, and
blood flowed out of the press, rising as
high as the horses' bridles for a distance
of 1,600 stadia.

Seven Angels With Seven Plagues

15 I saw in heaven another great
and marvellous sign: seven
angels with the seven last plagues—
last, because with them God's wrath is
completed. 2And I saw what looked like
a sea of glass mixed with fire and, standing beside the sea, those who had been
victorious over the beast and his image
and over the number of his name. They
held harps given them by God 3and sang
the song of Moses the servant of God
and the song of the Lamb:

"Great and marvellous are your
deeds,
Lord God Almighty.
Just and true are your ways,
King of the ages.
4Who will not fear you, O Lord,
and bring glory to your name?
For you alone are holy.
All nations will come
and worship before you,
for your righteous acts have been
revealed."

5After this I looked and in heaven
the temple, that is, the tabernacle of the
Testimony, was opened. 6Out of the
temple came the seven angels with
the seven plagues. They were dressed
in clean, shining linen and wore golden
sashes round their chests. 7Then one of
the four living creatures gave to the
seven angels seven golden bowls filled
with the wrath of God, who lives for
ever and ever. 8And the temple was
filled with smoke from the glory of God
and from his power, and no-one could
enter the temple until the seven plagues
of the seven angels were completed.

READING FROM PSALMS

Psalm 146:1–10

1Praise the LORD.

Praise the LORD, O my soul.
2 I will praise the LORD all my life;
I will sing praise to my God as long
as I live.

3Do not put your trust in princes,
in mortal men, who cannot save.
4When their spirit departs, they return
to the ground;
on that very day their plans come
to nothing.

5Blessed is he whose help is the God
of Jacob,
whose hope is in the LORD his
God,
6the Maker of heaven and earth,
the sea, and everything in them—
the LORD, who remains faithful for
ever.
7He upholds the cause of the
oppressed
and gives food to the hungry.
The LORD sets prisoners free,
8 the LORD gives sight to the blind,
the LORD lifts up those who are
bowed down,
the LORD loves the righteous.
9The LORD watches over the alien
and sustains the fatherless and the
widow,
but he frustrates the ways of the
wicked.

10The LORD reigns for ever,
your God, O Zion, for all
generations.

Praise the LORD.

DECEMBER 24

DAY 358

OLD TESTAMENT READING

Nehemiah 1:1–2:20

Nehemiah's Prayer

1 The words of Nehemiah son of Hacaliah:

In the month of Kislev in the twentieth year, while I was in the citadel of Susa, 2Hanani, one of my brothers, came from Judah with some other men, and I questioned them about the Jewish remnant that survived the exile, and also about Jerusalem.

3They said to me, "Those who survived the exile and are back in the province are in great trouble and disgrace. The wall of Jerusalem is broken down, and its gates have been burned with fire."

4When I heard these things, I sat down and wept. For some days I mourned and fasted and prayed before the God of heaven. 5Then I said:

"O LORD, God of heaven, the great and awesome God, who keeps his covenant of love with those who love him and obey his commands, 6let your ear be attentive and your eyes open to hear the prayer your servant is praying before you day and night for your servants, the people of Israel. I confess the sins we Israelites, including myself and my father's house, have committed against you. 7We have acted very wickedly towards you. We have not obeyed the commands, decrees and laws you gave your servant Moses.

8"Remember the instruction you gave your servant Moses, saying, 'If you are unfaithful, I will scatter you among the nations, 9but if you return to me and obey my commands, then even if your exiled people are at the farthest horizon, I will gather them from there and bring them to the place I have chosen as a dwelling for my Name.'

10"They are your servants and your people, whom you redeemed by your great strength and your mighty hand. 11O Lord, let your ear be attentive to the prayer of this your servant and to the prayer of your servants who delight in revering your name. Give your servant success today by granting him favour in the presence of this man."

I was cupbearer to the king.

Artaxerxes Sends Nehemiah to Jerusalem

2 In the month of Nisan in the twentieth year of King Artaxerxes, when wine was brought for him, I took the wine and gave it to the king. I had not been sad in his presence before; 2so the king asked me, "Why does your face look so sad when you are not ill? This can be nothing but sadness of heart."

I was very much afraid, 3but I said to the king, "May the king live for ever! Why should my face not look sad when the city where my fathers are buried lies in ruins, and its gates have been destroyed by fire?"

4The king said to me, "What is it you want?"

Then I prayed to the God of heaven, 5and I answered the king, "If it pleases the king and if your servant has found favour in his sight, let him send me to the city in Judah where my fathers are buried so that I can rebuild it."

6Then the king, with the queen sitting beside him, asked me, "How long will your journey take, and when will you get back?" It pleased the king to send me; so I set a time.

[7]I also said to him, "If it pleases the
king, may I have letters to the governors
of Trans-Euphrates, so that they will
provide me safe-conduct until I arrive in
Judah? [8]And may I have a letter to
Asaph, keeper of the king's forest, so he
will give me timber to make beams for
the gates of the citadel by the temple
and for the city wall and for the residence I will occupy?" And because the
gracious hand of my God was upon me,
the king granted my requests. [9]So I
went to the governors of Trans-
Euphrates and gave them the king's
letters. The king had also sent army
officers and cavalry with me.
[10]When Sanballat the Horonite and
Tobiah the Ammonite official heard
about this, they were very much disturbed that someone had come to promote the welfare of the Israelites.

Nehemiah Inspects Jerusalem's Walls

[11]I went to Jerusalem, and after
staying there three days [12]I set out during the night with a few men. I had not
told anyone what my God had put in my
heart to do for Jerusalem. There were
no mounts with me except the one I was
riding on.
[13]By night I went out through the
Valley Gate towards the Jackal Well
and the Dung Gate, examining the walls
of Jerusalem, which had been broken
down, and its gates, which had been
destroyed by fire. [14]Then I moved on
towards the Fountain Gate and the
King's Pool, but there was not enough
room for my mount to get through; [15]so
I went up the valley by night, examining
the wall. Finally, I turned back and
re-entered through the Valley Gate.
[16]The officials did not know where I had
gone or what I was doing, because as yet
I had said nothing to the Jews or the
priests or nobles or officials or any
others who would be doing the work.
[17]Then I said to them, "You see the
trouble we are in: Jerusalem lies in
ruins, and its gates have been burned
by fire. Come, let us rebuild the wall
of Jerusalem, and we will no longer be
in disgrace." [18]I also told them about
the gracious hand of my God upon me
and what the king had said to me.
They replied, "Let us start rebuilding." So they began this good work.
[19]But when Sanballat the Horonite,
Tobiah the Ammonite official and
Geshem the Arab heard about it, they
mocked and ridiculed us. "What is this
you are doing?" they asked. "Are you
rebelling against the king?"
[20]I answered them by saying, "The
God of heaven will give us success. We
his servants will start rebuilding, but as
for you, you have no share in Jerusalem
or any claim or historic right to it."

NEW TESTAMENT READING

Revelation 16:1–21

The Seven Bowls of God's Wrath

16 Then I heard a loud voice from
the temple saying to the seven
angels, "Go, pour out the seven bowls
of God's wrath on the earth."
[2]The first angel went and poured out
his bowl on the land, and ugly and painful sores broke out on the people who
had the mark of the beast and worshipped his image.
[3]The second angel poured out his
bowl on the sea, and it turned into blood
like that of a dead man, and every living
thing in the sea died.
[4]The third angel poured out his bowl
on the rivers and springs of water, and
they became blood. [5]Then I heard the
angel in charge of the waters say:

"You are just in these judgments,
you who are and who were, the
Holy One,
because you have so judged;
[6]for they have shed the blood of your
saints and prophets,
and you have given them blood to
drink as they deserve."

7And I heard the altar respond:

"Yes, Lord God Almighty,
true and just are your judgments."

8The fourth angel poured out his
bowl on the sun, and the sun was given
power to scorch people with fire. 9They
were seared by the intense heat and
they cursed the name of God, who had
control over these plagues, but they
refused to repent and glorify him.
10The fifth angel poured out his bowl
on the throne of the beast, and his kingdom was plunged into darkness. Men
gnawed their tongues in agony 11and
cursed the God of heaven because of
their pains and their sores, but they
refused to repent of what they had
done.
12The sixth angel poured out his bowl
on the great river Euphrates, and its
water was dried up to prepare the way
for the kings from the East. 13Then I
saw three evil spirits that looked like
frogs; they came out of the mouth of the
dragon, out of the mouth of the beast
and out of the mouth of the false
prophet. 14They are spirits of demons
performing miraculous signs, and they
go out to the kings of the whole world,
to gather them for the battle on the
great day of God Almighty.
15"Behold, I come like a thief! Blessed is he who stays awake and keeps his
clothes with him, so that he may not go
naked and be shamefully exposed."
16Then they gathered the kings
together to the place that in Hebrew is
called Armageddon.
17The seventh angel poured out his
bowl into the air, and out of the temple
came a loud voice from the throne,
saying, "It is done!" 18Then there came
flashes of lightning, rumblings, peals of
thunder and a severe earthquake. No
earthquake like it has ever occurred
since man has been on earth, so
tremendous was the quake. 19The great
city split into three parts, and the cities
of the nations collapsed. God remembered Babylon the Great and gave her
the cup filled with the wine of the fury of
his wrath. 20Every island fled away and
the mountains could not be found.
21From the sky huge hailstones of about
a hundred pounds each fell upon men.
And they cursed God on account of the
plague of hail, because the plague was
so terrible.

READING FROM PSALMS

Psalm 147:1–11

1Praise the LORD.

How good it is to sing praises to our God,
how pleasant and fitting to praise him!

2The LORD builds up Jerusalem;
he gathers the exiles of Israel.
3He heals the broken-hearted
and binds up their wounds.

4He determines the number of the stars
and calls them each by name.
5Great is our Lord and mighty in power;
his understanding has no limit.
6The LORD sustains the humble
but casts the wicked to the ground.

7Sing to the LORD with thanksgiving;
make music to our God on the harp.
8He covers the sky with clouds;
he supplies the earth with rain
and makes grass grow on the hills.
9He provides food for the cattle
and for the young ravens when they call.

10His pleasure is not in the strength of the horse,
nor his delight in the legs of a man;
11the LORD delights in those who fear him,
who put their hope in his unfailing love.

OLD TESTAMENT READING
Nehemiah 3:1–4:23

Builders of the Wall

3 Eliashib the high priest and his fellow priests went to work and rebuilt the Sheep Gate. They dedicated it
and set its doors in place, building as far
as the Tower of the Hundred, which
they dedicated, and as far as the Tower
of Hananel. 2The men of Jericho built
the adjoining section, and Zaccur son of
Imri built next to them.

3The Fish Gate was rebuilt by the
sons of Hassenaah. They laid its beams
and put its doors and bolts and bars in
place. 4Meremoth son of Uriah, the son
of Hakkoz, repaired the next section.
Next to him Meshullam son of Berekiah, the son of Meshezabel, made repairs, and next to him Zadok son of
Baana also made repairs. 5The next
section was repaired by the men of
Tekoa, but their nobles would not put
their shoulders to the work under their
supervisors.

6The Jeshanah Gate was repaired by
Joiada son of Paseah and Meshullam
son of Besodeiah. They laid its beams
and put its doors and bolts and bars in
place. 7Next to them, repairs were
made by men from Gibeon and Mizpah
—Melatiah of Gibeon and Jadon of
Meronoth—places under the authority
of the governor of Trans-Euphrates.
8Uzziel son of Harhaiah, one of the
goldsmiths, repaired the next section;
and Hananiah, one of the perfume-
makers, made repairs next to that. They
restored Jerusalem as far as the Broad
Wall. 9Rephaiah son of Hur, ruler of a
half-district of Jerusalem, repaired the
next section. 10Adjoining this, Jedaiah
son of Harumaph made repairs opposite his house, and Hattush son of
ashabneiah made repairs next to him.
lkijah son of Harim and Hasshub
son of Pahath-Moab repaired another
section and the Tower of the Ovens.
12Shallum son of Hallohesh, ruler of
a half-district of Jerusalem, repaired
the next section with the help of his
daughters.

13The Valley Gate was repaired by
Hanun and the residents of Zanoah.
They rebuilt it and put its doors and
bolts and bars in place. They also repaired five hundred yards of the wall as
far as the Dung Gate.

14The Dung Gate was repaired by
Malkijah son of Recab, ruler of the
district of Beth Hakkerem. He rebuilt it
and put its doors and bolts and bars in
place.

15The Fountain Gate was repaired by
Shallun son of Col-Hozeh, ruler of the
district of Mizpah. He rebuilt it, roofing
it over and putting its doors and bolts
and bars in place. He also repaired the
wall of the Pool of Siloam, by the King's
Garden, as far as the steps going down
from the City of David. 16Beyond him,
Nehemiah son of Azbuk, ruler of a half-
district of Beth Zur, made repairs up to
a point opposite the tombs of David, as
far as the artificial pool and the House
of the Heroes.

17Next to him, the repairs were made
by the Levites under Rehum son of
Bani. Beside him, Hashabiah, ruler of
half the district of Keilah, carried out
repairs for his district. 18Next to him,
the repairs were made by their countrymen under Binnui son of Henadad,
ruler of the other half-district of Keilah.
19Next to him, Ezer son of Jeshua, ruler
of Mizpah, repaired another section,
from a point facing the ascent to the
armoury as far as the angle. 20Next to
him, Baruch son of Zabbai zealously
repaired another section, from the
angle to the entrance of the house of

Eliashib the high priest. 21Next to him,
Meremoth son of Uriah, the son of
Hakkoz, repaired another section, from
the entrance of Eliashib's house to the
end of it.
22The repairs next to him were made
by the priests from the surrounding region. 23Beyond them, Benjamin and
Hasshub made repairs in front of their
house; and next to them, Azariah son of
Maaseiah, the son of Ananiah, made
repairs beside his house. 24Next to him,
Binnui son of Henadad repaired
another section, from Azariah's house
to the angle and the corner, 25and Palal
son of Uzai worked opposite the angle
and the tower projecting from the upper
palace near the court of the guard. Next
to him, Pedaiah son of Parosh 26and the
temple servants living on the hill of
Ophel made repairs up to a point opposite the Water Gate towards the east
and the projecting tower. 27Next to
them, the men of Tekoa repaired
another section, from the great projecting tower to the wall of Ophel.

28Above the Horse Gate, the priests
made repairs, each in front of his own
house. 29Next to them, Zadok son of
Immer made repairs opposite his house.
Next to him, Shemaiah son of Shecaniah, the guard at the East Gate, made
repairs. 30Next to him, Hananiah son of
Shelemiah, and Hanun, the sixth son of
Zalaph, repaired another section. Next
to them, Meshullam son of Berekiah
made repairs opposite his living quarters. 31Next to him, Malkijah, one of
the goldsmiths, made repairs as far
as the house of the temple servants
and the merchants, opposite the In-
spection Gate, and as far as the room
above the corner; 32and between the
room above the corner and the Sheep
Gate the goldsmiths and merchants
made repairs.

Opposition to the Rebuilding

4 When Sanballat heard that we
were rebuilding the wall, he became angry and was greatly incensed.
He ridiculed the Jews, 2and in the presence of his associates and the army of
Samaria, he said, "What are those
feeble Jews doing? Will they restore
their wall? Will they offer sacrifices?
Will they finish in a day? Can they bring
the stones back to life from those heaps
of rubble—burned as they are?"
3Tobiah the Ammonite, who was at
his side, said, "What they are building
—if even a fox climbed up on it, he
would break down their wall of stones!"

4Hear us, O our God, for we are
despised. Turn their insults back on
their own heads. Give them over as
plunder in a land of captivity. 5Do not
cover up their guilt or blot out their sins
from your sight, for they have thrown
insults in the face of the builders.

6So we rebuilt the wall till all of it
reached half its height, for the people
worked with all their heart.
7But when Sanballat, Tobiah, the
Arabs, the Ammonites and the men of
Ashdod heard that the repairs to Jerusalem's walls had gone ahead and that
the gaps were being closed, they were
very angry. 8They all plotted together to
come and fight against Jerusalem and
stir up trouble against it. 9But we
prayed to our God and posted a guard
day and night to meet this threat.
10Meanwhile, the people in Judah
said, "The strength of the labourers is
giving out, and there is so much rubble
that we cannot rebuild the wall."
11Also our enemies said, "Before
they know it or see us, we will be right
there among them and will kill them and
put an end to the work."
12Then the Jews who lived near them
came and told us ten times over,
"Wherever you turn, they will attack
us."
13Therefore I stationed some of the
people behind the lowest points of the
wall at the exposed places, posting them
by families, with their swords, spears
and bows. 14After I looked things over,
I stood up and said to the nobles, the
officials and the rest of the people,

"Don't be afraid of them. Remember
the Lord, who is great and awesome,
and fight for your brothers, your sons
and your daughters, your wives and
your homes."
15When our enemies heard that we
were aware of their plot and that God
had frustrated it, we all returned to the
wall, each to his own work.
16From that day on, half of my men
did the work, while the other half were
equipped with spears, shields, bows and
armour. The officers posted themselves
behind all the people of Judah 17who
were building the wall. Those who carried materials did their work with one
hand and held a weapon in the other,
18and each of the builders wore his
sword at his side as he worked. But the
man who sounded the trumpet stayed
with me.
19Then I said to the nobles, the officials and the rest of the people, "The
work is extensive and spread out, and
we are widely separated from each
other along the wall. 20Wherever you
hear the sound of the trumpet, join us
there. Our God will fight for us!"
21So we continued the work with half
the men holding spears, from the first
light of dawn till the stars came out. 22At
that time I also said to the people,
"Have every man and his helper stay
inside Jerusalem at night, so that they
can serve us as guards by night and
workmen by day." 23Neither I nor my
brothers nor my men nor the guards
with me took off our clothes; each had
his weapon, even when he went for
water.

NEW TESTAMENT READING
Revelation 17:1–18

The Woman on the Beast

17 One of the seven angels who had
the seven bowls came and said
me, "Come, I will show you the
punishment of the great prostitute,
who sits on many waters. 2With her the
kings of the earth committed adultery
and the inhabitants of the earth
were intoxicated with the wine of her
adulteries."
3Then the angel carried me away in
the Spirit into a desert. There I saw a
woman sitting on a scarlet beast that
was covered with blasphemous names
and had seven heads and ten horns.
4The woman was dressed in purple and
scarlet, and was glittering with gold,
precious stones and pearls. She held a
golden cup in her hand, filled with
abominable things and the filth of her
adulteries. 5This title was written on her
forehead:

MYSTERY
BABYLON THE GREAT
THE MOTHER OF PROSTITUTES
AND OF THE ABOMINATIONS
OF THE EARTH.

6I saw that the woman was drunk with
the blood of the saints, the blood of
those who bore testimony to Jesus.
When I saw her, I was greatly astonished. 7Then the angel said to me:
"Why are you astonished? I will explain
to you the mystery of the woman and of
the beast she rides, which has the seven
heads and ten horns. 8The beast, which
you saw, once was, now is not, and will
come up out of the Abyss and go to
his destruction. The inhabitants of
the earth whose names have not been
written in the book of life from the creation of the world will be astonished
when they see the beast, because he
once was, now is not, and yet will
come.
9"This calls for a mind with wisdom.
The seven heads are seven hills on
which the woman sits. 10They are also
seven kings. Five have fallen, one is, the
other has not yet come; but when he
does come, he must remain for a little
while. 11The beast who once was, and

now is not, is an eighth king. He belongs to the seven and is going to his
destruction.
12"The ten horns you saw are ten
kings who have not yet received a kingdom, but who for one hour will receive
authority as kings along with the beast.
13They have one purpose and will
give their power and authority to the
beast. 14They will make war against the
Lamb, but the Lamb will overcome
them because he is Lord of lords
and King of kings—and with him
will be his called, chosen and faithful
followers."
15Then the angel said to me, "The
waters you saw, where the prostitute
sits, are peoples, multitudes, nations
and languages. 16The beast and the ten
horns you saw will hate the prostitute.
They will bring her to ruin and leave her
naked; they will eat her flesh and burn
her with fire. 17For God has put it into
their hearts to accomplish his purpose
by agreeing to give the beast their
power to rule, until God's words are
fulfilled. 18The woman you saw is the
great city that rules over the kings of
the earth."

READING FROM PSALMS
Psalm 147:12–20

12Extol the LORD, O Jerusalem;
praise your God, O Zion,
13for he strengthens the bars of your
gates
and blesses your people within
you.
14He grants peace to your borders
and satisfies you with the finest of
wheat.

15He sends his command to the earth;
his word runs swiftly.
16He spreads the snow like wool
and scatters the frost like ashes.
17He hurls down hail like pebbles.
Who can withstand his icy blast?
18He sends his word and melts them;
he stirs up his breezes, and the
waters flow.

19He has revealed his word to Jacob,
his laws and decrees to Israel.
20He has done this for no other nation;
they do not know his laws.

Praise the LORD.

DECEMBER 26

DAY 360

OLD TESTAMENT READING
Nehemiah 5:1–7:3

Nehemiah Helps the Poor

5 Now the men and their wives raised
a great outcry against their Jewish
brothers. 2Some were saying, "We and
our sons and daughters are numerous;
in order for us to eat and stay alive, we
must get grain."
3Others were saying, "We are mort-
gaging our fields, our vineyards and our
homes to get grain during the famine."
4Still others were saying, "We have
had to borrow money to pay the king's
tax on our fields and vineyards.
5Although we are of the same flesh and
blood as our countrymen and though
our sons are as good as theirs, yet we
have to subject our sons and daughters
to slavery. Some of our daughters have
already been enslaved, but we are
powerless, because our fields and our
vineyards belong to others."
6When I heard their outcry and these
charges, I was very angry. 7I pondered
them in my mind and then accused the
nobles and officials. I told them, "You
are exacting usury from your own countrymen!" So I called together a large

meeting to deal with them 8and said:
"As far as possible, we have bought
back our Jewish brothers who were sold
to the Gentiles. Now you are selling
your brothers, only for them to be sold
back to us!" They kept quiet, because
they could find nothing to say.
9So I continued, "What you are doing
is not right. Shouldn't you walk in the
fear of our God to avoid the reproach of
our Gentile enemies? 10I and my
brothers and my men are also lending
the people money and grain. But let the
exacting of usury stop! 11Give back
to them immediately their fields,
vineyards, olive groves and houses, and
also the usury you are charging them
—the hundredth part of the money,
grain, new wine and oil."
12"We will give it back," they said.
"And we will not demand anything
more from them. We will do as you
say."
Then I summoned the priests and
made the nobles and officials take an
oath to do what they had promised. 13I
also shook out the folds of my robe and
said, "In this way may God shake out of
his house and possessions every man
who does not keep this promise. So may
such a man be shaken out and
emptied!"
At this the whole assembly said,
"Amen," and praised the LORD. And
the people did as they had promised.
14Moreover, from the twentieth year
of King Artaxerxes, when I was
appointed to be their governor in the
land of Judah, until his thirty-second
year—twelve years—neither I nor my
brothers ate the food allotted to the
governor. 15But the earlier governors
—those preceding me—placed a heavy
burden on the people and took forty
shekels of silver from them in addition
to food and wine. Their assistants also
lorded it over the people. But out of
reverence for God I did not act like that.
16Instead, I devoted myself to the work
on this wall. All my men were assem-
led there for the work; we did not
uire any land.
17Furthermore, a hundred and fifty
Jews and officials ate at my table, as well
as those who came to us from the surrounding nations. 18Each day one ox,
six choice sheep and some poultry were
prepared for me, and every ten days an
abundant supply of wine of all kinds. In
spite of all this, I never demanded the
food allotted to the governor, because
the demands were heavy on these
people.
19Remember me with favour, O my
God, for all I have done for these
people.

Further Opposition to the Rebuilding

6 When word came to Sanballat,
Tobiah, Geshem the Arab and the
rest of our enemies that I had rebuilt the
wall and not a gap was left in it—
though up to that time I had not set the
doors in the gates—2Sanballat and
Geshem sent me this message: "Come,
let us meet together in one of the villages on the plain of Ono."
But they were scheming to harm me;
3so I sent messengers to them with this
reply: "I am carrying on a great project
and cannot go down. Why should the
work stop while I leave it and go down
to you?" 4Four times they sent me the
same message, and each time I gave
them the same answer.
5Then, the fifth time, Sanballat sent
his assistant to me with the same message, and in his hand was an unsealed
letter 6in which was written:

> "It is reported among the na-
> tions—and Geshem says it is true
> —that you and the Jews are plot-
> ting to revolt, and therefore you
> are building the wall. Moreover,
> according to these reports you are
> about to become their king 7and
> have even appointed prophets to
> make this proclamation about you
> in Jerusalem: 'There is a king in
> Judah!' Now this report will get
> back to the king; so come, let us
> confer together."

[8]I sent him this reply: "Nothing like what you are saying is happening; you are just making it up out of your head."

[9]They were all trying to frighten us, thinking, "Their hands will get too weak for the work, and it will not be completed."

⌞But I prayed,⌟ "Now strengthen my hands."

[10]One day I went to the house of Shemaiah son of Delaiah, the son of Mehetabel, who was shut in at his home. He said, "Let us meet in the house of God, inside the temple, and let us close the temple doors, because men are coming to kill you—by night they are coming to kill you."

[11]But I said, "Should a man like me run away? Or should one like me go into the temple to save his life? I will not go!" [12]I realised that God had not sent him, but that he had prophesied against me because Tobiah and Sanballat had hired him. [13]He had been hired to intimidate me so that I would commit a sin by doing this, and then they would give me a bad name to discredit me.

[14]Remember Tobiah and Sanballat, O my God, because of what they have done; remember also the prophetess Noadiah and the rest of the prophets who have been trying to intimidate me.

The Completion of the Wall

[15]So the wall was completed on the twenty-fifth of Elul, in fifty-two days. [16]When all our enemies heard about this, all the surrounding nations were afraid and lost their self-confidence, because they realised that this work had been done with the help of our God.

[17]Also, in those days the nobles of Judah were sending many letters to Tobiah, and replies from Tobiah kept coming to them. [18]For many in Judah were under oath to him, since he was son-in-law to Shecaniah son of Arah, and his son Jehohanan had married the daughter of Meshullam son of Berekiah. [19]Moreover, they kept reporting to me his good deeds and then telling him what I said. And Tobiah sent letters to intimidate me.

7 After the wall had been rebuilt and I had set the doors in place, the gatekeepers and the singers and the Levites were appointed. [2]I put in charge of Jerusalem my brother Hanani, along with Hananiah the commander of the citadel, because he was a man of integrity and feared God more than most men do. [3]I said to them, "The gates of Jerusalem are not to be opened until the sun is hot. While the gatekeepers are still on duty, make them shut the doors and bar them. Also appoint residents of Jerusalem as guards, some at their posts and some near their own houses."

NEW TESTAMENT READING
Revelation 18:1–17a

The Fall of Babylon

18 After this I saw another angel coming down from heaven. He had great authority, and the earth was illuminated by his splendour. [2]With a mighty voice he shouted:

"Fallen! Fallen is Babylon the Great!
She has become a home for
demons
and a haunt for every evil spirit,
a haunt for every unclean and
detestable bird.
[3]For all the nations have drunk
the maddening wine of her
adulteries.
The kings of the earth committed
adultery with her,
and the merchants of the earth
grew rich from her excessive
luxuries."

[4]Then I heard another voice from heaven say:

"Come out of her, my people,
so that you will not share in her
sins,

so that you will not receive any of
her plagues;
[5]for her sins are piled up to heaven,
and God has remembered her
crimes.
[6]Give back to her as she has given;
pay her back double for what she
has done.
Mix her a double portion from her
own cup.
[7]Give her as much torture and grief
as the glory and luxury she gave
herself.
In her heart she boasts,
'I sit as queen; I am not a widow,
and I will never mourn.'
[8]Therefore in one day her plagues will
overtake her:
death, mourning and famine.
She will be consumed by fire,
for mighty is the Lord God who
judges her.

[9]"When the kings of the earth who
committed adultery with her and shared
her luxury see the smoke of her burning, they will weep and mourn over her.
[10]Terrified at her torment, they will
stand far off and cry:

"'Woe! Woe, O great city,
O Babylon, city of power!
In one hour your doom has come!'

[11]"The merchants of the earth will
weep and mourn over her because no-
one buys their cargoes any more—
[12]cargoes of gold, silver, precious stones
and pearls; fine linen, purple, silk and
scarlet cloth; every sort of citron wood,
and articles of every kind made of ivory,
costly wood, bronze, iron and marble;
[13]cargoes of cinnamon and spice, of incense, myrrh and frankincense, of wine
and olive oil, of fine flour and wheat;
cattle and sheep; horses and carriages;
and bodies and souls of men.
[14]"They will say, 'The fruit you
longed for is gone from you. All your
riches and splendour have vanished,
never to be recovered.' [15]The merchants who sold these things and gained
their wealth from her will stand far off,
terrified at her torment. They will weep
and mourn [16]and cry out:

"'Woe! Woe, O great city,
dressed in fine linen, purple and
scarlet,
and glittering with gold, precious
stones and pearls!
[17]In one hour such great wealth has
been brought to ruin!'

READING FROM PROVERBS
Proverbs 31:10–20

Epilogue: The Wife of Noble Character

[10]A wife of noble character who can
find?
She is worth far more than rubies.
[11]Her husband has full confidence in
her
and lacks nothing of value.
[12]She brings him good, not harm,
all the days of her life.
[13]She selects wool and flax
and works with eager hands.
[14]She is like the merchant ships,
bringing her food from afar.
[15]She gets up while it is still dark;
she provides food for her family
and portions for her servant girls.
[16]She considers a field and buys it;
out of her earnings she plants a
vineyard.
[17]She sets about her work vigorously;
her arms are strong for her tasks.
[18]She sees that her trading is profitable,
and her lamp does not go out at
night.
[19]In her hand she holds the distaff
and grasps the spindle with her
fingers.
[20]She opens her arms to the poor
and extends her hands to the
needy.

DECEMBER 27

DAY 361

OLD TESTAMENT READING

Nehemiah 7:4–8:18

The List of the Exiles Who Returned

4 Now the city was large and spacious,
but there were few people in it, and the
houses had not yet been rebuilt. 5 So my
God put it into my heart to assemble the
nobles, the officials and the common
people for registration by families. I
found the genealogical record of those
who had been the first to return. This is
what I found written there:

6 These are the people of the
province who came up from the
captivity of the exiles whom Nebuchadnezzar king of Babylon had
taken captive (they returned to
Jerusalem and Judah, each to his
own town, 7 in company with
Zerubbabel, Jeshua, Nehemiah,
Azariah, Raamiah, Nahamani,
Mordecai, Bilshan, Mispereth,
Bigvai, Nehum and Baanah):

The list of the men of Israel:

8 the descendants of Parosh	2,172
9 of Shephatiah	372
10 of Arah	652
11 of Pahath-Moab (through the line of Jeshua and Joab)	2,818
12 of Elam	1,254
13 of Zattu	845
14 of Zaccai	760
15 of Binnui	648
16 of Bebai	628
17 of Azgad	2,322
18 of Adonikam	667
19 of Bigvai	2,067
20 of Adin	655
21 of Ater (through Hezekiah)	98
22 of Hashum	328
23 of Bezai	324
24 of Hariph	112
25 of Gibeon	95
26 the men of Bethlehem and Netophah	188
27 of Anathoth	128
28 of Beth Azmaveth	42
29 of Kiriath Jearim, Kephirah and Beeroth	743
30 of Ramah and Geba	621
31 of Michmash	122
32 of Bethel and Ai	123
33 of the other Nebo	52
34 of the other Elam	1,254
35 of Harim	320
36 of Jericho	345
37 of Lod, Hadid and Ono	721
38 of Senaah	3,930

39 The priests:

the descendants of Jedaiah (through the family of Jeshua)	973
40 of Immer	1,052
41 of Pashhur	1,247
42 of Harim	1,017

43 The Levites:

the descendants of Jeshua (through Kadmiel through the line of Hodaviah)	74

44 The singers:

the descendants of Asaph	148

45 The gatekeepers:

the descendants of Shallum, Ater, Talmon, Akkub, Hatita and Shobai	138

46 The temple servants:

the descendants of
Ziha, Hasupha, Tabbaoth,
47 Keros, Sia, Padon,
48 Lebana, Hagaba, Shalmai,
49 Hanan, Giddel, Gahar,

[50]Reaiah, Rezin, Nekoda,
[51]Gazzam, Uzza, Paseah,
[52]Besai, Meunim, Nephussim,
[53]Bakbuk, Hakupha, Harhur,
[54]Bazluth, Mehida, Harsha,
[55]Barkos, Sisera, Temah,
[56]Neziah and Hatipha

[57]The descendants of the servants of Solomon:

the descendants of
Sotai, Sophereth, Perida,
[58]Jaala, Darkon, Giddel,
[59]Shephatiah, Hattil, Pokereth-Hazzebaim and Amon

[60]The temple servants and the descendants of the servants of Solomon 392

[61]The following came up from the towns of Tel Melah, Tel Harsha, Kerub, Addon and Immer, but they could not show that their families were descended from Israel:

[62]the descendants of
Delaiah, Tobiah and Nekoda 642

[63]And from among the priests:

the descendants of
Hobaiah, Hakkoz and Barzillai (a man who had married a daughter of Barzillai the Gileadite and was called by that name).

[64]These searched for their family records, but they could not find them and so were excluded from the priesthood as unclean. [65]The governor, therefore, ordered them not to eat any of the most sacred food until there should be a priest ministering with the Urim and Thummim.

[66]The whole company numbered 42,360, [67]besides their 7,337 menservants and maidservants; and they also had 245 men and women singers. [68]There were 736 horses, 245 mules, [69]435 camels and 6,720 donkeys.

[70]Some of the heads of the families contributed to the work. The governor gave to the treasury 1,000 drachmas of gold, 50 bowls and 530 garments for priests. [71]Some of the heads of the families gave to the treasury for the work 20,000 drachmas of gold and 2,200 minas of silver. [72]The total given by the rest of the people was 20,000 drachmas of gold, 2,000 minas of silver and 67 garments for priests.

[73]The priests, the Levites, the gatekeepers, the singers and the temple servants, along with certain of the people and the rest of the Israelites, settled in their own towns.

Ezra Reads the Law

When the seventh month came and the Israelites had settled in their towns,
8 [1]all the people assembled as one man in the square before the Water Gate. They told Ezra the scribe to bring out the Book of the Law of Moses, which the LORD had commanded for Israel.

[2]So on the first day of the seventh month, Ezra the priest brought the Law before the assembly, which was made up of men and women and all who were able to understand. [3]He read it aloud from daybreak till noon as he faced the square before the Water Gate in the presence of the men, women and others who could understand. And all the people listened attentively to the Book of the Law.

[4]Ezra the scribe stood on a high wooden platform built for the occasion. Beside him on his right stood Mattithiah, Shema, Anaiah, Uriah, Hilkiah and Maaseiah; and on his left were Pedaiah, Mishael, Malkijah, Hashum, Hashbaddanah, Zechariah and Meshullam.

5Ezra opened the book. All the people could see him because he was standing above them; and as he opened it, the
people all stood up. 6Ezra praised the
LORD, the great God; and all the people
lifted their hands and responded,
"Amen! Amen!" Then they bowed
down and worshipped the LORD with
their faces to the ground.
7The Levites—Jeshua, Bani, Sherebiah, Jamin, Akkub, Shabbethai,
Hodiah, Maaseiah, Kelita, Azariah,
Jozabad, Hanan and Pelaiah—
instructed the people in the Law while
the people were standing there. 8They
read from the Book of the Law of God,
making it clear and giving the meaning
so that the people could understand
what was being read.
9Then Nehemiah the governor, Ezra
the priest and scribe, and the Levites
who were instructing the people said to
them all, "This day is sacred to the
LORD your God. Do not mourn or
weep." For all the people had been
weeping as they listened to the words of
the Law.
10Nehemiah said, "Go and enjoy
choice food and sweet drinks, and send
some to those who have nothing prepared. This day is sacred to our Lord.
Do not grieve, for the joy of the LORD is
your strength."
11The Levites calmed all the people
saying, "Be still, for this is a sacred day.
Do not grieve."
12Then all the people went away to
eat and drink, to send portions of food
and to celebrate with great joy, because
they now understood the words that had
been made known to them.
13On the second day of the month,
the heads of all the families, along with
the priests and the Levites, gathered
round Ezra the scribe to give attention
to the words of the Law. 14They found
written in the Law, which the LORD had
commanded through Moses, that the
Israelites were to live in booths during
the feast of the seventh month 15and
that they should proclaim this word and
spread it throughout their towns and in
Jerusalem: "Go out into the hill country
and bring back branches from olive and
wild olive trees, and from myrtles,
palms and shade trees, to make booths"
—as it is written.
16So the people went out and brought
back branches and built themselves
booths on their own roofs, in their
courtyards, in the courts of the house of
God and in the square by the Water
Gate and the one by the Gate of
Ephraim. 17The whole company that
had returned from exile built booths
and lived in them. From the days of
Joshua son of Nun until that day, the
Israelites had not celebrated it like this.
And their joy was very great.
18Day after day, from the first day to
the last, Ezra read from the Book of the
Law of God. They celebrated the feast
for seven days, and on the eighth day, in
accordance with the regulation, there
was an assembly.

NEW TESTAMENT READING

Revelation 18:17b–19:10

"Every sea captain, and all who
travel by ship, the sailors, and all who
earn their living from the sea, will stand
far off. 18When they see the smoke of
her burning, they will exclaim, 'Was
there ever a city like this great city?'
19They will throw dust on their heads,
and with weeping and mourning cry
out:

"'Woe! Woe, O great city,
where all who had ships on the sea
became rich through her wealth!
In one hour she has been brought to
ruin!
20Rejoice over her, O heaven!
Rejoice, saints and apostles and
prophets!
God has judged her for the way she
treated you.'"

21Then a mighty angel picked up a
boulder the size of a large millstone and
threw it into the sea, and said:

"With such violence
the great city of Babylon will be
thrown down,
never to be found again.
22The music of harpists and musicians,
flute players and trumpeters,
will never be heard in you again.
No workman of any trade
will ever be found in you again.
The sound of a millstone
will never be heard in you again.
23The light of a lamp
will never shine in you again.
The voice of bridegroom and bride
will never be heard in you again.
Your merchants were the world's
great men.
By your magic spell all the nations
were led astray.
24In her was found the blood of
prophets and of the saints,
and of all who have been killed on
the earth."

Hallelujah!

19 After this I heard what sounded like the roar of a great multitude in heaven shouting:

"Hallelujah!
Salvation and glory and power
belong to our God,
2 for true and just are his judgments.
He has condemned the great
prostitute
who corrupted the earth by her
adulteries.
He has avenged on her the blood of
his servants."

3And again they shouted:

"Hallelujah!
The smoke from her goes up for ever
and ever."

4The twenty-four elders and the four living creatures fell down and worshipped God, who was seated on the throne. And they cried:

"...men, Hallelujah!"

5Then a voice came from the throne, saying:

"Praise our God,
all you his servants,
you who fear him,
both small and great!"

6Then I heard what sounded like a great multitude, like the roar of rushing waters and like loud peals of thunder, shouting:

"Hallelujah!
For our Lord God Almighty
reigns.
7Let us rejoice and be glad
and give him glory!
For the wedding of the Lamb has
come,
and his bride has made herself
ready.
8Fine linen, bright and clean,
was given her to wear."

(Fine linen stands for the righteous acts of the saints.)

9Then the angel said to me, "Write: 'Blessed are those who are invited to the wedding supper of the Lamb!'" And he added, "These are the true words of God."

10At this I fell at his feet to worship him. But he said to me, "Do not do it! I am a fellow-servant with you and with your brothers who hold to the testimony of Jesus. Worship God! For the testimony of Jesus is the spirit of prophecy."

READING FROM PSALMS

Psalm 148:1–6

1Praise the LORD.

Praise the LORD from the heavens,
praise him in the heights above.
2Praise him, all his angels,
praise him, all his heavenly hosts.

3Praise him, sun and moon,
praise him, all you shining stars.
4Praise him, you highest heavens
and you waters above the skies.
5Let them praise the name of the LORD,
for he commanded and they were created.
6He set them in place for ever and ever;
he gave a decree that will never pass away.

DECEMBER 28

DAY 362

OLD TESTAMENT READING

Nehemiah 9:1–37

The Israelites Confess Their Sins

9 On the twenty-fourth day of the same month, the Israelites gathered together, fasting and wearing sackcloth and having dust on their heads. 2Those of Israelite descent had separated themselves from all foreigners. They stood in their places and confessed their sins and the wickedness of their fathers. 3They stood where they were and read from the Book of the Law of the LORD their God for a quarter of the day, and spent another quarter in confession and in worshipping the LORD their God. 4Standing on the stairs were the Levites—Jeshua, Bani, Kadmiel, Shebaniah, Bunni, Sherebiah, Bani and Kenani—who called with loud voices to the LORD their God. 5And the Levites—Jeshua, Kadmiel, Bani, Hashabneiah, Sherebiah, Hodiah, Shebaniah and Pethahiah—said: "Stand up and praise the LORD your God, who is from everlasting to everlasting."

"Blessed be your glorious name, and may it be exalted above all blessing and praise. 6You alone are the LORD. You made the heavens, even the highest heavens, and all their starry host, the earth and all that is on it, the seas and all that is in them. You give life to everything, and the multitudes of heaven worship you.

7"You are the LORD God, who chose Abram and brought him out of Ur of the Chaldeans and named him Abraham. 8You found his heart faithful to you, and you made a covenant with him to give to his descendants the land of the Canaanites, Hittites, Amorites, Perizzites, Jebusites and Girgashites. You have kept your promise because you are righteous.

9"You saw the suffering of our forefathers in Egypt; you heard their cry at the Red Sea. 10You sent miraculous signs and wonders against Pharaoh, against all his officials and all the people of his land, for you knew how arrogantly the Egyptians treated them. You made a name for yourself, which remains to this day. 11You divided the sea before them, so that they passed through it on dry ground, but you hurled their pursuers into the depths, like a stone into mighty waters. 12By day you led them with a pillar of cloud, and by night with a pillar of fire to give them light on the way they were to take.

13"You came down on Mount Sinai; you spoke to them from heaven. You gave them regulations and laws that are just and right, and decrees and commands that are good. 14You made known to them your holy Sabbath and gave them commands, decrees and laws through your servant Moses.

15In their hunger you gave them
bread from heaven and in their
thirst you brought them water from
the rock; you told them to go in and
take possession of the land you had
sworn with uplifted hand to give
them.
16"But they, our forefathers, became arrogant and stiff-necked,
and did not obey your commands.
17They refused to listen and failed
to remember the miracles you performed among them. They became
stiff-necked and in their rebellion
appointed a leader in order to return to their slavery. But you are a
forgiving God, gracious and compassionate, slow to anger and
abounding in love. Therefore you
did not desert them, 18even when
they cast for themselves an image
of a calf and said, 'This is your god,
who brought you up out of Egypt,'
or when they committed awful
blasphemies.
19"Because of your great compassion you did not abandon them
in the desert. By day the pillar of
cloud did not cease to guide them
on their path, nor the pillar of fire
by night to shine on the way they
were to take. 20You gave your good
Spirit to instruct them. You did not
withhold your manna from their
mouths, and you gave them water
for their thirst. 21For forty years
you sustained them in the desert;
they lacked nothing, their clothes
did not wear out nor did their feet
become swollen.
22"You gave them kingdoms and
nations, allotting to them even the
remotest frontiers. They took over
the country of Sihon king of Heshbon and the country of Og king of
Bashan. 23You made their sons as
numerous as the stars in the sky,
and you brought them into the land
that you told their fathers to enter
and possess. 24Their sons went in
nd took possession of the land.
[illegible] subdued before them the
Canaanites, who lived in the land;
you handed the Canaanites over to
them, along with their kings and
the peoples of the land, to deal with
them as they pleased. 25They captured fortified cities and fertile
land; they took possession of
houses filled with all kinds of good
things, wells already dug, vineyards, olive groves and fruit trees
in abundance. They ate to the full
and were well-nourished; they
revelled in your great goodness.
26"But they were disobedient
and rebelled against you; they put
your law behind their backs. They
killed your prophets, who had
admonished them in order to turn
them back to you; they committed
awful blasphemies. 27So you
handed them over to their enemies, who oppressed them. But
when they were oppressed they
cried out to you. From heaven you
heard them, and in your great compassion you gave them deliverers,
who rescued them from the hand of
their enemies.
28"But as soon as they were at
rest, they again did what was evil in
your sight. Then you abandoned
them to the hand of their enemies
so that they ruled over them. And
when they cried out to you again,
you heard from heaven, and in
your compassion you delivered
them time after time.
29"You warned them to return to
your law, but they became arrogant and disobeyed your commands. They sinned against your
ordinances, by which a man will
live if he obeys them. Stubbornly
they turned their backs on you,
became stiff-necked and refused to
listen. 30For many years you were
patient with them. By your Spirit
you admonished them through
your prophets. Yet they paid no
attention, so you handed them
over to the neighbouring peoples.
31But in your great mercy you did

not put an end to them or abandon
them, for you are a gracious and
merciful God.
32"Now therefore, O our God,
the great, mighty and awesome
God, who keeps his covenant of
love, do not let all this hardship
seem trifling in your eyes—the
hardship that has come upon us,
upon our kings and leaders, upon
our priests and prophets, upon our
fathers and all your people, from
the days of the kings of Assyria
until today. 33In all that has happened to us, you have been just;
you have acted faithfully, while we
did wrong. 34Our kings, our leaders, our priests and our fathers did
not follow your law; they did not
pay attention to your commands or
the warnings you gave them.
35Even while they were in their
kingdom, enjoying your great
goodness to them in the spacious
and fertile land you gave them,
they did not serve you or turn from
their evil ways.
36"But see, we are slaves today,
slaves in the land you gave our
forefathers so that they could eat
its fruit and the other good things it
produces. 37Because of our sins, its
abundant harvest goes to the kings
you have placed over us. They rule
over our bodies and our cattle
as they please. We are in great
distress.

NEW TESTAMENT READING
Revelation 19:11–21

The Rider on the White Horse

11I saw heaven standing open and
there before me was a white horse,
whose rider is called Faithful and True.
With justice he judges and makes war.
12His eyes are like blazing fire, and on
his head are many crowns. He has a
name written on him that no-one knows
but he himself. 13He is dressed in a robe
dipped in blood, and his name is the
Word of God. 14The armies of heaven
were following him, riding on white
horses and dressed in fine linen, white
and clean. 15Out of his mouth comes a
sharp sword with which to strike down
the nations. "He will rule them with an
iron sceptre." He treads the winepress
of the fury of the wrath of God Almighty. 16On his robe and on his thigh
he has this name written:

KING OF KINGS AND LORD OF LORDS.

17And I saw an angel standing in the
sun, who cried in a loud voice to all the
birds flying in mid-air, "Come, gather
together for the great supper of God,
18so that you may eat the flesh of kings,
generals, and mighty men, of horses
and their riders, and the flesh of all
people, free and slave, small and
great."
19Then I saw the beast and the kings
of the earth and their armies gathered
together to make war against the rider
on the horse and his army. 20But the
beast was captured, and with him
the false prophet who had performed
the miraculous signs on his behalf. With
these signs he had deluded those who
had received the mark of the beast and
worshipped his image. The two of them
were thrown alive into the fiery lake of
burning sulphur. 21The rest of them
were killed with the sword that came
out of the mouth of the rider on the
horse, and all the birds gorged themselves on their flesh.

READING FROM PSALMS
Psalm 148:7–14

7Praise the LORD from the earth,
you great sea creatures and all
ocean depths,
8lightning and hail, snow and clouds,
stormy winds that do his bidding,
9you mountains and all hills,
fruit trees and all cedars,

[10]wild animals and all cattle,
small creatures and flying birds,
[11]kings of the earth and all nations,
you princes and all rulers on earth,
[12]young men and maidens,
old men and children.

[13]Let them praise the name of the LORD,
for his name alone is exalted;
his splendour is above the earth and the heavens.
[14]He has raised up for his people a horn,
the praise of all his saints,
of Israel, the people close to his heart.

Praise the LORD.

DAY 363

DECEMBER 29

OLD TESTAMENT READING
Nehemiah 9:38–11:21

The Agreement of the People

[38]"In view of all this, we are making a binding agreement, putting it in writing, and our leaders, our Levites and our priests are affixing their seals to it."

10 Those who sealed it were:

Nehemiah the governor, the son of Hacaliah.

Zedekiah, [2]Seraiah, Azariah, Jeremiah,
[3]Pashhur, Amariah, Malkijah,
[4]Hattush, Shebaniah, Malluch,
[5]Harim, Meremoth, Obadiah,
[6]Daniel, Ginnethon, Baruch,
[7]Meshullam, Abijah, Mijamin,
[8]Maaziah, Bilgai and Shemaiah.
These were the priests.

[9]The Levites:

Jeshua son of Azaniah,
Binnui of the sons of Henadad, Kadmiel,
[10]and their associates:
Shebaniah, Hodiah, Kelita,
Pelaiah, Hanan,
[11]Mica, Rehob, Hashabiah,
[12]Zaccur, Sherebiah, Shebaniah,
[13]Hodiah, Bani and Beninu.

[14]The leaders of the people:

Parosh, Pahath-Moab, Elam, Zattu, Bani,
[15]Bunni, Azgad, Bebai,
[16]Adonijah, Bigvai, Adin,
[17]Ater, Hezekiah, Azzur,
[18]Hodiah, Hashum, Bezai,
[19]Hariph, Anathoth, Nebai,
[20]Magpiash, Meshullam, Hezir,
[21]Meshezabel, Zadok, Jaddua,
[22]Pelatiah, Hanan, Anaiah,
[23]Hoshea, Hananiah, Hasshub,
[24]Hallohesh, Pilha, Shobek,
[25]Rehum, Hashabnah, Maaseiah,
[26]Ahiah, Hanan, Anan,
[27]Malluch, Harim and Baanah.

[28]"The rest of the people—priests, Levites, gatekeepers, singers, temple servants and all who separated themselves from the neighbouring peoples for the sake of the Law of God, together with their wives and all their sons and daughters who are able to understand—
[29]all these now join their brothers the nobles, and bind themselves with a curse and an oath to follow the Law of God given through Moses the servant of

God and to obey carefully all the
commands, regulations and decrees of the LORD our Lord.
30"We promise not to give our
daughters in marriage to the peoples around us or take their daughters for our sons.
31"When the neighbouring peoples bring merchandise or grain to
sell on the Sabbath, we will not buy
from them on the Sabbath or on
any holy day. Every seventh year
we will forgo working the land and
will cancel all debts.
32"We assume the responsibility
for carrying out the commands to
give a third of a shekel each year for
the service of the house of our
God: 33for the bread set out on the
table; for the regular grain offerings and burnt offerings; for the
offerings on the Sabbaths, New
Moon festivals and appointed
feasts; for the holy offerings; for sin
offerings to make atonement for
Israel; and for all the duties of the
house of our God.
34"We—the priests, the Levites
and the people—have cast lots to
determine when each of our families is to bring to the house of our
God at set times each year a contribution of wood to burn on the
altar of the LORD our God, as it is
written in the Law.
35"We also assume responsibility
for bringing to the house of the
LORD each year the firstfruits of
our crops and of every fruit tree.
36"As it is also written in the
Law, we will bring the firstborn of
our sons and of our cattle, of our
herds and of our flocks to the house
of our God, to the priests ministering there.
37"Moreover, we will bring to
the storerooms of the house of our
God, to the priests, the first of our
ground meal, of our ⌞grain⌟ offerings, of the fruit of all our trees and
of our new wine and oil. And we
will bring a tithe of our crops to the
Levites, for it is the Levites who
collect the tithes in all the towns
where we work. 38A priest descended from Aaron is to accompany the Levites when they receive
the tithes, and the Levites are to
bring a tenth of the tithes up to
the house of our God, to the
storerooms of the treasury. 39The
people of Israel, including the Levites, are to bring their contributions of grain, new wine and oil to
the storerooms where the articles
for the sanctuary are kept and
where the ministering priests, the
gatekeepers and the singers stay.
"We will not neglect the house of
our God."

The New Residents of Jerusalem

11 Now the leaders of the people
settled in Jerusalem, and the
rest of the people cast lots to bring one
out of every ten to live in Jerusalem, the
holy city, while the remaining nine were
to stay in their own towns. 2The people
commended all the men who volunteered to live in Jerusalem.
3These are the provincial leaders who
settled in Jerusalem (now some
Israelites, priests, Levites, temple servants and descendants of Solomon's
servants lived in the towns of Judah,
each on his own property in the various towns, 4while other people from
both Judah and Benjamin lived in
Jerusalem):

From the descendants of Judah:

Athaiah son of Uzziah, the son of
Zechariah, the son of Amariah, the
son of Shephatiah, the son of
Mahalalel, a descendant of Perez;
5and Maaseiah son of Baruch, the
son of Col-Hozeh, the son of
Hazaiah, the son of Adaiah, the
son of Joiarib, the son of Zechariah, a descendant of Shelah. 6The
descendants of Perez who lived in
Jerusalem totalled 468 able men.

7From the descendants of Benjamin:

Sallu son of Meshullam, the son of Joed, the son of Pedaiah, the son of Kolaiah, the son of Maaseiah, the son of Ithiel, the son of Jeshaiah, 8and his followers, Gabbai and Sallai—928 men. 9Joel son of Zicri was their chief officer, and Judah son of Hassenuah was over the Second District of the city.

10From the priests:

Jedaiah; the son of Joiarib; Jakin; 11Seraiah son of Hilkiah, the son of Meshullam, the son of Zadok, the son of Meraioth, the son of Ahitub, supervisor in the house of God, 12and their associates, who carried on work for the temple—822 men; Adaiah son of Jeroham, the son of Pelaliah, the son of Amzi, the son of Zechariah, the son of Pashhur, the son of Malkijah, 13and his associates, who were heads of families—242 men; Amashsai son of Azarel, the son of Ahzai, the son of Meshillemoth, the son of Immer, 14and his associates, who were able men—128 men. Their chief officer was Zabdiel son of Haggedolim.

15From the Levites:

Shemaiah son of Hasshub, the son of Azrikam, the son of Hashabiah, the son of Bunni; 16Shabbethai and Jozabad, two of the heads of the Levites, who had charge of the outside work of the house of God; 17Mattaniah son of Mica, the son of Zabdi, the son of Asaph, the director who led in thanksgiving and prayer; Bakbukiah, second among his associates; and Abda son of Shammua, the son of Galal, the son of Jeduthun. 18The Levites in the holy city totalled 284.

… gatekeepers:

Akkub, Talmon and their associates, who kept watch at the gates —172 men.

20The rest of the Israelites, with the priests and Levites, were in all the towns of Judah, each on his ancestral property.

21The temple servants lived on the hill of Ophel, and Ziha and Gishpa were in charge of them.

NEW TESTAMENT READING

Revelation 20:1–15

The Thousand Years

20 And I saw an angel coming down out of heaven, having the key to the Abyss and holding in his hand a great chain. 2He seized the dragon, that ancient serpent, who is the devil, or Satan, and bound him for a thousand years. 3He threw him into the Abyss, and locked and sealed it over him, to keep him from deceiving the nations any more until the thousand years were ended. After that, he must be set free for a short time.

4I saw thrones on which were seated those who had been given authority to judge. And I saw the souls of those who had been beheaded because of their testimony for Jesus and because of the word of God. They had not worshipped the beast or his image and had not received his mark on their foreheads or their hands. They came to life and reigned with Christ for a thousand years. 5(The rest of the dead did not come to life until the thousand years were ended.) This is the first resurrection. 6Blessed and holy are those who have part in the first resurrection. The second death has no power over them, but they will be priests of God and of Christ and will reign with him for a thousand years.

Satan's Doom

7When the thousand years are over, Satan will be released from his prison

[8]and will go out to deceive the nations in the four corners of the earth—Gog and Magog—to gather them for battle. In number they are like the sand on the seashore. [9]They marched across the breadth of the earth and surrounded the camp of God's people, the city he loves. But fire came down from heaven and devoured them. [10]And the devil, who deceived them, was thrown into the lake of burning sulphur, where the beast and the false prophet had been thrown. They will be tormented day and night for ever and ever.

The Dead Are Judged

[11]Then I saw a great white throne and him who was seated on it. Earth and sky fled from his presence, and there was no place for them. [12]And I saw the dead, great and small, standing before the throne, and books were opened. Another book was opened, which is the book of life. The dead were judged according to what they had done as recorded in the books. [13]The sea gave up the dead that were in it, and death and Hades gave up the dead that were in them, and each person was judged according to what he had done. [14]Then death and Hades were thrown into the lake of fire. The lake of fire is the second death. [15]If anyone's name was not found written in the book of life, he was thrown into the lake of fire.

READING FROM PSALMS
Psalm 149:1–9

[1]Praise the LORD.

Sing to the LORD a new song,
his praise in the assembly of the saints.

[2]Let Israel rejoice in their Maker;
let the people of Zion be glad in their King.
[3]Let them praise his name with dancing
and make music to him with tambourine and harp.
[4]For the LORD takes delight in his people;
he crowns the humble with salvation.
[5]Let the saints rejoice in this honour
and sing for joy on their beds.

[6]May the praise of God be in their mouths
and a double-edged sword in their hands,
[7]to inflict vengeance on the nations
and punishment on the peoples,
[8]to bind their kings with fetters,
their nobles with shackles of iron,
[9]to carry out the sentence written against them.
This is the glory of all his saints.

Praise the LORD.

DECEMBER 30

DAY 364

OLD TESTAMENT READING
Nehemiah 11:22–12:47

[22]The chief officer of the Levites in Jerusalem was Uzzi son of Bani, the son of Hashabiah, the son of Mattaniah, the son of Mica. Uzzi was one of Asaph's descendants, who were the singers responsible for the service of the house of God. [23]The singers were under the king's orders, which regulated their daily activity.

[24]Pethahiah son of Meshezabel, one of the descendants of Zerah son of Judah, was the king's agent in all affairs relating to the people.

[25]As for the villages with their fields, some of the people of Judah lived in

Kiriath Arba and its surrounding settlements, in Dibon and its settlements, in
Jekabzeel and its villages, 26in Jeshua,
in Moladah, in Beth Pelet, 27in Hazar
Shual, in Beersheba and its settlements,
28in Ziklag, in Meconah and its settlements, 29in En Rimmon, in Zorah, in
Jarmuth, 30Zanoah, Adullam and their
villages, in Lachish and its fields, and in
Azekah and its settlements. So they
were living all the way from Beersheba
to the Valley of Hinnom.
31The descendants of the Benjamites
from Geba lived in Michmash, Aija,
Bethel and its settlements, 32in
Anathoth, Nob and Ananiah, 33in
Hazor, Ramah and Gittaim, 34in Ha-
did, Zeboim and Neballat, 35in Lod
and Ono, and in the Valley of the
Craftsmen.
36Some of the divisions of the Levites
of Judah settled in Benjamin.

Priests and Levites

12 These were the priests and Levites who returned with Zerubbabel son of Shealtiel and with Jeshua:

Seraiah, Jeremiah, Ezra,
2Amariah, Malluch, Hattush,
3Shecaniah, Rehum, Meremoth,
4Iddo, Ginnethon, Abijah,
5Mijamin, Moadiah, Bilgah,
6Shemaiah, Joiarib, Jedaiah,
7Sallu, Amok, Hilkiah and Jedaiah.

These were the leaders of the priests
and their associates in the days of
Jeshua.
8The Levites were Jeshua, Binnui,
Kadmiel, Sherebiah, Judah, and also
Mattaniah, who, together with his
associates, was in charge of the songs of
thanksgiving. 9Bakbukiah and Unni,
their associates, stood opposite them in
the services.
10Jeshua was the father of Joiakim,
Joiakim the father of Eliashib, Eliashib
the father of Joiada, 11Joiada the father
of Jonathan, and Jonathan the father of
Jaddua.
12In the days of Joiakim, these were
the heads of the priestly families:

of Seraiah's family, Meraiah;
of Jeremiah's, Hananiah;
13of Ezra's, Meshullam;
of Amariah's, Jehohanan;
14of Malluch's, Jonathan;
of Shecaniah's, Joseph;
15of Harim's, Adna;
of Meremoth's, Helkai;
16of Iddo's, Zechariah;
of Ginnethon's, Meshullam;
17of Abijah's, Zicri;
of Miniamin's and of Moadiah's,
Piltai;
18of Bilgah's, Shammua;
of Shemaiah's, Jehonathan;
19of Joiarib's, Mattenai;
of Jedaiah's, Uzzi;
20of Sallu's, Kallai;
of Amok's, Eber;
21of Hilkiah's, Hashabiah;
of Jedaiah's, Nethanel.

22The family heads of the Levites in
the days of Eliashib, Joiada, Johanan
and Jaddua, as well as those of the
priests, were recorded in the reign of
Darius the Persian. 23The family heads
among the descendants of Levi up to the
time of Johanan son of Eliashib were
recorded in the book of the annals.
24And the leaders of the Levites were
Hashabiah, Sherebiah, Jeshua son of
Kadmiel, and their associates, who
stood opposite them to give praise and
thanksgiving, one section responding to
the other, as prescribed by David the
man of God.
25Mattaniah, Bakbukiah, Obadiah,
Meshullam, Talmon and Akkub were
gatekeepers who guarded the
storerooms at the gates. 26They served
in the days of Joiakim son of Jeshua, the
son of Jozadak, and in the days of Nehemiah the governor and of Ezra the
priest and scribe.

Dedication of the Wall of Jerusalem

27At the dedication of the wall of
Jerusalem, the Levites were sought out
from where they lived and were brought
to Jerusalem to celebrate joyfully the
dedication with songs of thanksgiving

and with the music of cymbals, harps
and lyres. 28The singers also were
brought together from the region
around Jerusalem—from the villages of
the Netophathites, 29from Beth Gilgal,
and from the area of Geba and
Azmaveth, for the singers had built villages for themselves around Jerusalem.
30When the priests and Levites had
purified themselves ceremonially, they
purified the people, the gates and the
wall.

31I had the leaders of Judah go up on
top of the wall. I also assigned two large
choirs to give thanks. One was to pro-
ceed on top of the wall to the right,
towards the Dung Gate. 32Hoshaiah
and half the leaders of Judah followed
them, 33along with Azariah, Ezra,
Meshullam, 34Judah, Benjamin, Shemaiah, Jeremiah, 35as well as some
priests with trumpets, and also Zechariah son of Jonathan, the son of Shemaiah, the son of Mattaniah, the son
of Micaiah, the son of Zaccur, the
son of Asaph, 36and his associates—
Shemaiah, Azarel, Milalai, Gilalai,
Maai, Nethanel, Judah and Hanani—
with musical instruments ⌞prescribed
by⌟ David the man of God. Ezra the
scribe led the procession. 37At the
Fountain Gate they continued directly
up the steps of the City of David on the
ascent to the wall and passed above the
house of David to the Water Gate on
the east.

38The second choir proceeded in the
opposite direction. I followed them on
top of the wall, together with half the
people—past the Tower of the Ovens
to the Broad Wall, 39over the Gate of
Ephraim, the Jeshanah Gate, the Fish
Gate, the Tower of Hananel and the
Tower of the Hundred, as far as the
Sheep Gate. At the Gate of the Guard
they stopped.

40The two choirs that gave thanks
then took their places in the house of
God; so did I, together with half the
officials, 41as well as the priests—
Eliakim, Maaseiah, Miniamin,
Micaiah, Elioenai, Zechariah and
Hananiah with their trumpets—42and
also Maaseiah, Shemaiah, Eleazar,
Uzzi, Jehohanan, Malkijah, Elam and
Ezer. The choirs sang under the direc-
tion of Jezrahiah. 43And on that day
they offered great sacrifices, rejoicing
because God had given them great joy.
The women and children also rejoiced.
The sound of rejoicing in Jerusalem
could be heard far away.

44At that time men were appointed to
be in charge of the storerooms for the
contributions, firstfruits and tithes.
From the fields around the towns they
were to bring into the storerooms the
portions required by the Law for the
priests and the Levites, for Judah was
pleased with the ministering priests and
Levites. 45They performed the service
of their God and the service of purification, as did also the singers and
gatekeepers, according to the commands of David and his son Solomon.
46For long ago, in the days of David and
Asaph, there had been directors for the
singers and for the songs of praise and
thanksgiving to God. 47So in the days of
Zerubbabel and of Nehemiah, all Israel
contributed the daily portions for the
singers and gatekeepers. They also set
aside the portion for the other Levites,
and the Levites set aside the portion for
the descendants of Aaron.

NEW TESTAMENT READING
Revelation 21:1–27

The New Jerusalem

21 Then I saw a new heaven and a
new earth, for the first heaven
and the first earth had passed away, and
there was no longer any sea. 2I saw the
Holy City, the new Jerusalem, coming
down out of heaven from God, prepared as a bride beautifully dressed for
her husband. 3And I heard a loud voice
from the throne saying, "Now the
dwelling of God is with men, and he will
live with them. They will be his people,

and God himself will be with them and
be their God. 4He will wipe every tear
from their eyes. There will be no more
death or mourning or crying or pain, for
the old order of things has passed
away."
5He who was seated on the throne
said, "I am making everything new!"
Then he said, "Write this down, for
these words are trustworthy and true."
6He said to me: "It is done. I am the
Alpha and the Omega, the Beginning
and the End. To him who is thirsty I will
give to drink without cost from the
spring of the water of life. 7He who
overcomes will inherit all this, and I will
be his God and he will be my son. 8But
the cowardly, the unbelieving, the vile,
the murderers, the sexually immoral,
those who practise magic arts, the idolaters and all liars—their place will be in
the fiery lake of burning sulphur. This is
the second death."
9One of the seven angels who had the
seven bowls full of the seven last plagues came and said to me, "Come, I will
show you the bride, the wife of the
Lamb." 10And he carried me away in
the Spirit to a mountain great and high,
and showed me the Holy City, Jerusalem, coming down out of heaven from
God. 11It shone with the glory of God,
and its brilliance was like that of a very
precious jewel, like a jasper, clear as
crystal. 12It had a great, high wall with
twelve gates, and with twelve angels at
the gates. On the gates were written the
names of the twelve tribes of Israel.
13There were three gates on the east,
three on the north, three on the south
and three on the west. 14The wall of the
city had twelve foundations, and on
them were the names of the twelve
apostles of the Lamb.
15The angel who talked with me had a
measuring rod of gold to measure the
city, its gates and its walls. 16The city
was laid out like a square, as long as it
was wide. He measured the city with the
od and found it to be 12,000 stadia in
th, and as wide and high as it is long.
neasured its wall and it was 144
cubits thick, by man's measurement,
which the angel was using. 18The wall
was made of jasper, and the city of pure
gold, as pure as glass. 19The foundations
of the city walls were decorated with
every kind of precious stone. The first
foundation was jasper, the second
sapphire, the third chalcedony, the
fourth emerald, 20the fifth sardonyx, the
sixth carnelian, the seventh chrysolite,
the eighth beryl, the ninth topaz, the
tenth chrysoprase, the eleventh jacinth,
and the twelfth amethyst. 21The twelve
gates were twelve pearls, each gate
made of a single pearl. The great street
of the city was of pure gold, like trans-
parent glass.
22I did not see a temple in the city,
because the Lord God Almighty and
the Lamb are its temple. 23The city does
not need the sun or the moon to shine
on it, for the glory of God gives it light,
and the Lamb is its lamp. 24The nations
will walk by its light, and the kings of the
earth will bring their splendour into it.
25On no day will its gates ever be shut,
for there will be no night there. 26The
glory and honour of the nations will be
brought into it. 27Nothing impure will
ever enter it, nor will anyone who does
what is shameful or deceitful, but only
those whose names are written in the
Lamb's book of life.

READING FROM PROVERBS

Proverbs 31:21–31

21When it snows, she has no fear for
her household;
for all of them are clothed in
scarlet.
22She makes coverings for her bed;
she is clothed in fine linen and
purple.
23Her husband is respected at the city
gate,
where he takes his seat among the
elders of the land.
24She makes linen garments and sells
them,

and supplies the merchants with
sashes.
25She is clothed with strength and
dignity;
she can laugh at the days to
come.
26She speaks with wisdom,
and faithful instruction is on her
tongue.
27She watches over the affairs of her
household
and does not eat the bread of
idleness.
28Her children arise and call her
blessed;
her husband also, and he praises
her:
29"Many women do noble things,
but you surpass them all."
30Charm is deceptive, and beauty is
fleeting;
but a woman who fears the LORD is
to be praised.
31Give her the reward she has earned,
and let her works bring her praise
at the city gate.

DECEMBER 31

DAY 365

OLD TESTAMENT READING
Nehemiah 13:1–31

Nehemiah's Final Reforms

13 On that day the Book of Moses
was read aloud in the hearing of
the people and there it was found written that no Ammonite or Moabite
should ever be admitted into the assembly of God, 2because they had not met
the Israelites with food and water but
had hired Balaam to call a curse down
on them. (Our God, however, turned
the curse into a blessing.) 3When the
people heard this law, they excluded
from Israel all who were of foreign
descent.

4Before this, Eliashib the priest had
been put in charge of the storerooms of
the house of our God. He was closely
associated with Tobiah, 5and he had
provided him with a large room formerly used to store the grain offerings
and incense and temple articles, and
also the tithes of grain, new wine and oil
prescribed for the Levites, singers and
gatekeepers, as well as the contributions for the priests.

6But while all this was going on, I was
not in Jerusalem, for in the thirty-
second year of Artaxerxes king of
Babylon I had returned to the king.
Some time later I asked his permission
7and came back to Jerusalem. Here I
learned about the evil thing Eliashib
had done in providing Tobiah a room
in the courts of the house of God. 8I
was greatly displeased and threw all
Tobiah's household goods out of the
room. 9I gave orders to purify the
rooms, and then I put back into them
the equipment of the house of God,
with the grain offerings and the incense.

10I also learned that the portions
assigned to the Levites had not been
given to them, and that all the Levites
and singers responsible for the service
had gone back to their own fields. 11So I
rebuked the officials and asked them,
"Why is the house of God neglected?"
Then I called them together and stationed them at their posts.

12All Judah brought the tithes of
grain, new wine and oil into the
storerooms. 13I put Shelemiah the
priest, Zadok the scribe, and a Levite
named Pedaiah in charge of the
storerooms and made Hanan son of
Zaccur, the son of Mattaniah, their
assistant, because these men were considered trustworthy. They were made
responsible for distributing the supplies
to their brothers.

[14]Remember me for this, O my God, and do not blot out what I have so faithfully done for the house of my God and its services.

[15]In those days I saw men in Judah treading winepresses on the Sabbath and bringing in grain and loading it on donkeys, together with wine, grapes, figs and all other kinds of loads. And they were bringing all this into Jerusalem on the Sabbath. Therefore I warned them against selling food on that day. [16]Men from Tyre who lived in Jerusalem were bringing in fish and all kinds of merchandise and selling them in Jerusalem on the Sabbath to the people of Judah. [17]I rebuked the nobles of Judah and said to them, "What is this wicked thing you are doing—desecrating the Sabbath day? [18]Didn't your forefathers do the same things, so that our God brought all this calamity upon us and upon this city? Now you are stirring up more wrath against Israel by desecrating the Sabbath."

[19]When evening shadows fell on the gates of Jerusalem before the Sabbath, I ordered the doors to be shut and not opened until the Sabbath was over. I stationed some of my own men at the gates so that no load could be brought in on the Sabbath day. [20]Once or twice the merchants and sellers of all kinds of goods spent the night outside Jerusalem. [21]But I warned them and said, "Why do you spend the night by the wall? If you do this again, I will lay hands on you." From that time on they no longer came on the Sabbath. [22]Then I commanded the Levites to purify themselves and go and guard the gates in order to keep the Sabbath day holy.

Remember me for this also, O my God, and show mercy to me according to your great love.

[23]Moreover, in those days I saw men of Judah who had married women from Ashdod, Ammon and Moab. [24]Half of their children spoke the language of Ashdod or the language of one of the other peoples, and did not know how to speak the language of Judah. [25]I rebuked them and called curses down on them. I beat some of the men and pulled out their hair. I made them take an oath in God's name and said: "You are not to give your daughters in marriage to their sons, nor are you to take their daughters in marriage for your sons or for yourselves. [26]Was it not because of marriages like these that Solomon king of Israel sinned? Among the many nations there was no king like him. He was loved by his God, and God made him king over all Israel, but even he was led into sin by foreign women. [27]Must we hear now that you too are doing all this terrible wickedness and are being unfaithful to our God by marrying foreign women?"

[28]One of the sons of Joiada son of Eliashib the high priest was son-in-law to Sanballat the Horonite. And I drove him away from me.

[29]Remember them, O my God, because they defiled the priestly office and the covenant of the priesthood and of the Levites.

[30]So I purified the priests and the Levites of everything foreign, and assigned them duties, each to his own task. [31]I also made provision for contributions of wood at designated times, and for the firstfruits.

Remember me with favour, O my God.

NEW TESTAMENT READING
Revelation 22:1–21

The River of Life

22 Then the angel showed me the river of the water of life, as clear as crystal, flowing from the throne of God and of the Lamb [2]down the middle of the great street of the city. On each side of the river stood the tree of life, bearing twelve crops of fruit, yielding its fruit every month. And the leaves of the

tree are for the healing of the nations.
3No longer will there be any curse. The
throne of God and of the Lamb will be
in the city, and his servants will serve
him. 4They will see his face, and his
name will be on their foreheads. 5There
will be no more night. They will not
need the light of a lamp or the light of
the sun, for the Lord God will give them
light. And they will reign for ever and
ever.
6The angel said to me, "These words
are trustworthy and true. The Lord, the
God of the spirits of the prophets, sent
his angel to show his servants the things
that must soon take place."

Jesus Is Coming

7"Behold, I am coming soon! Blessed
is he who keeps the words of the
prophecy in this book."

8I, John, am the one who heard and
saw these things. And when I had heard
and seen them, I fell down to worship at
the feet of the angel who had been
showing them to me. 9But he said to me,
"Do not do it! I am a fellow-servant
with you and with your brothers the
prophets and of all who keep the words
of this book. Worship God!"
10Then he told me, "Do not seal up
the words of the prophecy of this book,
because the time is near. 11Let him who
does wrong continue to do wrong; let
him who is vile continue to be vile; let
him who does right continue to do right;
and let him who is holy continue to be
holy."

12"Behold, I am coming soon! My
reward is with me, and I will give to
everyone according to what he has
done. 13I am the Alpha and the Omega,
the First and the Last, the Beginning
and the End.
14"Blessed are those who wash their
robes, that they may have the right to
the tree of life and may go through the
gates into the city. 15Outside are the
dogs, those who practise magic arts,
the sexually immoral, the murderers,
the idolaters and everyone who loves
and practises falsehood.
16"I, Jesus, have sent my angel to give
you this testimony for the churches. I
am the Root and the Offspring of
David, and the bright Morning Star."

17The Spirit and the bride say,
"Come!" And let him who hears say,
"Come!" Whoever is thirsty, let him
come; and whoever wishes, let him take
the free gift of the water of life.

18I warn everyone who hears the
words of the prophecy of this book: If
anyone adds anything to them, God will
add to him the plagues described in this
book. 19And if anyone takes words
away from this book of prophecy, God
will take away from him his share in the
tree of life and in the holy city, which
are described in this book.
20He who testifies to these things
says, "Yes, I am coming soon."
Amen. Come, Lord Jesus.
21The grace of the Lord Jesus be with
God's people. Amen.

READING FROM PSALMS
Psalm 150:1–6

1Praise the LORD.

Praise God in his sanctuary;
    praise him in his mighty heavens.
2Praise him for his acts of power;
    praise him for his surpassing
        greatness.
3Praise him with the sounding of the
        trumpet,
    praise him with the harp and lyre,
4praise him with tambourine and
        dancing,
    praise him with the strings and
        flute,
5praise him with the clash of cymbals,
    praise him with resounding
        cymbals.

6Let everything that has breath praise
        the LORD.

Praise the LORD.

NEW INTERNATIONAL VERSION

Notes and Maps

NEW INTERNATIONAL VERSION

Notes and Maps

TABLE OF CONTENTS

THE BIBLE AT A GLANCE

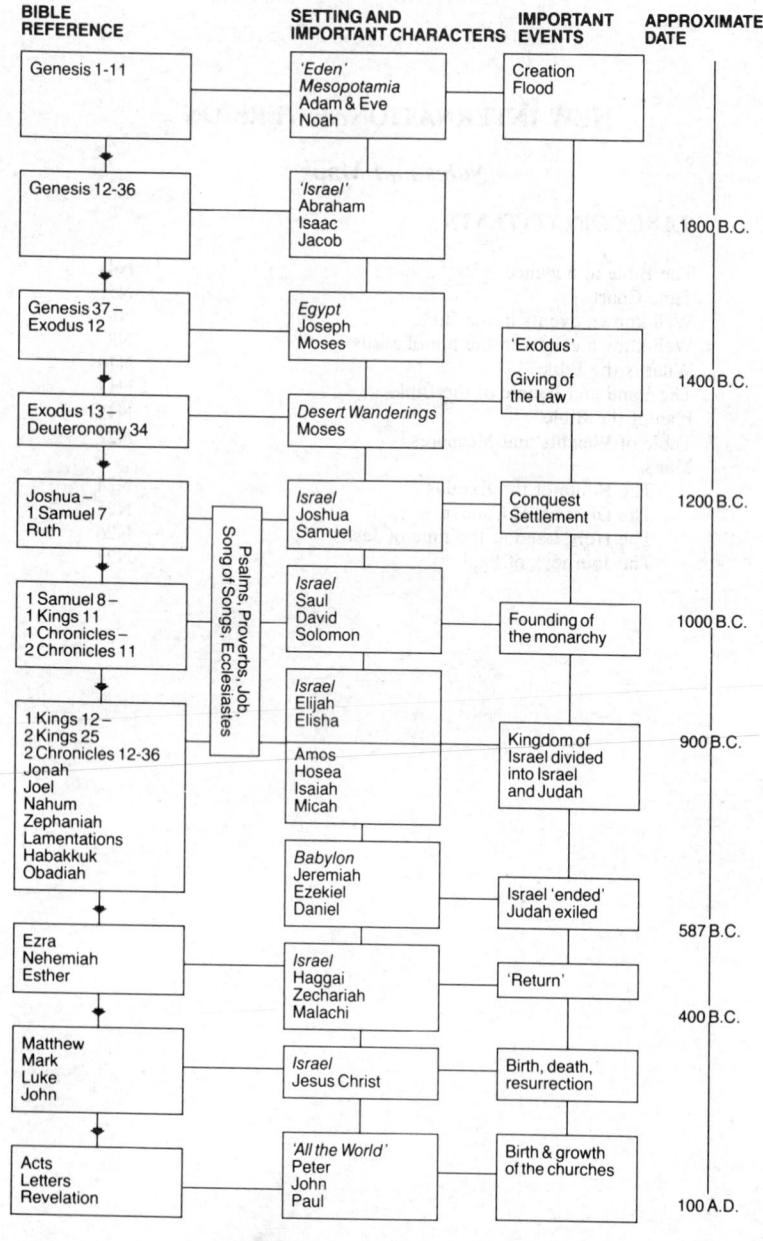

BIBLE REFERENCE		SETTING AND IMPORTANT CHARACTERS	IMPORTANT EVENTS	APPROXIMATE DATE
Genesis 1-11		*'Eden'* *Mesopotamia* Adam & Eve Noah	Creation Flood	
Genesis 12-36		*'Israel'* Abraham Isaac Jacob		1800 B.C.
Genesis 37 – Exodus 12		*Egypt* Joseph Moses	'Exodus' Giving of the Law	1400 B.C.
Exodus 13 – Deuteronomy 34		*Desert Wanderings* Moses		
Joshua – 1 Samuel 7 Ruth		*Israel* Joshua Samuel	Conquest Settlement	1200 B.C.
1 Samuel 8 – 1 Kings 11 1 Chronicles – 2 Chronicles 11	Psalms, Proverbs, Job, Song of Songs, Ecclesiastes	*Israel* Saul David Solomon	Founding of the monarchy	1000 B.C.
1 Kings 12 – 2 Kings 25 2 Chronicles 12-36 Jonah Joel Nahum Zephaniah Lamentations Habakkuk Obadiah		*Israel* Elijah Elisha Amos Hosea Isaiah Micah	Kingdom of Israel divided into Israel and Judah	900 B.C.
		Babylon Jeremiah Ezekiel Daniel	Israel 'ended' Judah exiled	587 B.C.
Ezra Nehemiah Esther		*Israel* Haggai Zechariah Malachi	'Return'	400 B.C.
Matthew Mark Luke John		*Israel* Jesus Christ	Birth, death, resurrection	
Acts Letters Revelation		*'All the World'* Peter John Paul	Birth & growth of the churches	100 A.D.

TIME CHART

INTRODUCTORY NOTES

Over the last hundred years or so we have gained a better understanding of the history of the Jewish nation as it relates to world history. This is partly a result of the work of archaeologists combined with scientific ways of dating their discoveries. Thus we can be more accurate in dating biblical events.

Nevertheless, the further back into history we go the less is it possible to pinpoint a precise date. After about 1000 B.C. we can be more definite about dates, but before this (2000–1000 B.C.) there may be differences of up to 100 years. The dates marked with * on the chart below are those which are particularly debated although generally accepted. The abbreviation *c.* means 'about' (Latin 'circa'). ** means 'somewhere within this period'.

Surprisingly, it is harder to pinpoint many New Testament dates! The New Testament itself gives us fewer clues than the Old Testament about historical details. It is especially difficult to say precisely when many of the books were written, so all the dates in the chart are not the only dates suggested.

Biblical Period and where it is recorded	World Events	
BEGINNINGS OF TIME Genesis 1–11		
Abraham c.2000–1825** Isaac c.1900–1725** Jacob c.1800–1700** Joseph c.1720–1550** Jacob and his eleven sons join Joseph in Egypt c.1700	Middle Bronze Age 1950–1550	2000 B.C.
↓		
EXODUS FROM EGYPT AND CONQUEST OF CANAAN Exodus–Joshua		
Moses Exodus 1280/1260* Desert Wanderings Joshua Fall of Jericho 1240/1220*	Pharaoh Rameses II 1290–1224	1300 B.C.
↓		
DEATH OF JOSHUA TO THE FIRST KING Judges–1 Samuel 12		1200 B.C.
Joshua 1300–1190* The Judges 1220/1200–1050/1045 Samuel 1075–1035 Saul 1050/1045–1010	PHILISTINES Iron Age	
↓		
ISRAEL'S GOLDEN AGE 1 Samuel 13–1 Kings 11 (1 Chronicles 10–2 Chronicles 9)		1000 B.C.
David 1010–970 Solomon 970–930	PHILISTINES	
↓		

THE TWO KINGDOMS 1 Kings 12–2 Kings 17 (2 Chronicles 10–28)

Israel: The Northern Kingdom	*Prophets*		
			930 B.C.
930–909 Jeroboam I			
909–908 Nabad			
908–885 Baasha			
885–884 Elah			
884 Zimri			
884 Tibni			
884–873 Omri			
873–853 Ahab	Elijah		
853–852 Ahaziah	"		
852–841 Joram	Elisha		
841–813 Jehu	"		
813–798 Jehoahaz			800 B.C.
798–781 Jehoash	?Jonah		
781–753 Jeroboam II	Amos c.760–750	Tiglath Pileser III	
753–752 Zechariah	Hosea c.750–725	of ASSYRIA 745–727	
752 Shallum	"		
752–741 Menahem	"		
741–739 Pekahiah	"		
739–731 Pekah	"		
731–722 Hoshea	"	Shalmanezer V of	
		ASSYRIA 727–722	
Fall of Samaria, capital of Israel 722			

TIME CHART (2)

Judah: The Southern Kingdom	*Prophets*		
930–913 Rehoboam			930 B.C.
913–910 Abijam			
910–869 Asa			
869–848 Jehoshaphat			
841–835 Athaliah			
835–796 Joash			800 B.C.
796–767 Amaziah		Tiglath Pileser III	
767–739 Azariah (Uzziah)		of ASSYRIA 745–727	
739–731 Jotham	Isaiah 740–701		
731–715 Ahaz	„	Shalmanezer V of	
	Micah 725–701	ASSYRIA 727–722	

LAST DAYS OF JUDAH 1 Kings 18–25 (2 Chronicles 29–36)

	Prophets		
715–686 Hezekiah	Isaiah/Micah	Sennacherib of	
710 Siege of Jerusalem		ASSYRIA	700 B.C.
686–641 Manasseh			
641–639 Amon			
639–609 Josiah	Jeremiah/?Zephaniah/?Jonah	Fall of Nineveh,	
	?Nahum/?Habakkuk/?Joel	capital of ASSYRIA	
	Lamentations	612	
609 Jehoahaz			
609–597 Jehoiakim		Nebuchadrezzar of	
605 Daniel deported to Babylon		BABYLON	600 B.C.
597 Jehoiachin 'First' deportation to Babylon	Ezekiel 593–571		
597–587 Zedekiah 'Second' deportation to Babylon	Obadiah		
562 Further deportation to Babylon			

EXILE AND RETURN Ezra, Nehemiah, Esther, Haggai, Zechariah, Malachi, Isaiah 40–66

	Prophets		
539 Fall of Babylon		Cyrus of PERSIA	
538 Cyrus' Decree First Return to Jerusalem			
	Haggai 520	Artaxerxes of PERSIA	
515 Dedication of second Jerusalem temple	Zechariah 520		
	Malachi c.500–450		
			500 B.C.
445 Nehemiah arrives in Jerusalem			
428** Ezra arrives in Jerusalem			

BETWEEN THE TESTAMENTS (1 & 2 Maccabees, in the APOCRYPHA)

336–323 Alexander the Great of GREECE	Fall of PERSIA 331	
323 Greek Empire divided into Ptolemaic (Egypt) and Seleucid (Syria and Mesopotamia)		300 B.C.
323–198 Israel a Ptolemaic state		
198–166 Israel a Seleucid state	Antiochus Epiphanes,	200 B.C.
167 Desecration of Jerusalem temple	SELEUCID king 175–163	
Maccabean Revolt		
165 Jerusalem temple rededicated		
142 Jewish Independence		
63 Pompey of Rome annexes Jerusalem		100 B.C.
40 B.C.–4 A.D. Herod the Great		

TIME CHART (3)

LIFE OF JESUS Matthew, Mark, Luke, John

?4 B.C.	Birth of John the Baptist	27B.C. – 14A.D. Caesar Augustus of ROME	
?4	Birth of Jesus		
?29 A.D.	Baptism of Jesus	26 – 30A.D. Pontius Pilate	
30/33 A.D.	Crucifixion		30 A.D.

↓

THE EARLY CHURCH Acts & Letters

		Literature			
35	Paul's conversion	49/50	Galatians	41 – 54 Claudius	
47	Paul's first missionary journey	50 – 51	1&2 Thessalonians		
		55 – 56	1&2 Corinthians		
49	Important Church Council	58	Romans		
50 – 52	Paul's second missionary journey	**50 – 62	James		50 A.D.
		61	Philemon, Colossians, Ephesians		
53 – 57	Paul's third missionary journey			54 – 68 Nero	
64	Death of Paul in Rome	62	Philippians		
70	Fall of Jerusalem to Rome	**62 – 64	1 Peter		
		**63/64	1&2 Timothy, Titus		
		64 – 68	Mark	81 – 96 Domitian	100 A.D.
		**65 – 68	2 Peter		
		70	Hebrews		
		80	Matthew		
		**65 – 80	Jude		
		**75 – 85	Luke, Acts		
		**70 – 100	John		
		**90 – 100	1,2,3, John		
		**90 – 95	Revelation		

WELL-KNOWN EVENTS IN THE BIBLE

Creation **Genesis** 1–2
The first sin **Genesis** 3
Cain kills Abel **Genesis** 4
Noah and the Ark **Genesis** 6–9
Sodom and Gomorrah **Genesis** 18–19
Abraham sacrifices Isaac **Genesis** 22
Jacob's Dream **Genesis** 28:10–22
Joseph's coat of many colours **Genesis** 37
Moses in the bullrushes **Exodus** 2
Moses and the burning bush **Exodus** 3
Plagues on Egypt **Exodus** 7–11
The first Passover **Exodus** 12
The Exodus **Exodus** 12–13
Crossing the Red Sea **Exodus** 13–14
Manna and quail **Exodus** 16
Water from the rock **Exodus** 17
The Ten Commandments **Exodus** 20
Balaam's donkey **Numbers** 22
Death of Moses **Deuteronomy** 34
Crossing the Jordan **Joshua** 3
The Battle of Jericho **Joshua** 6
Gideon and the fleece **Judges** 6–7
Samson and Delilah **Judges** 13–16
Samuel called by God **1 Samuel** 1–3
David and Goliath **1 Samuel** 17
David and Bathsheba **2 Samuel** 11
Solomon builds the Temple **1 Kings** 6–7, **2 Chronicles** 3–4
Elijah and the priests of Baal **1 Kings** 18
The miracles of Elisha **2 Kings** 4–5
'The Lord is my Shepherd' **Psalm** 23
Benefits of Wisdom **Proverbs** 3
Sayings of the wise **Proverbs** 22
The Wife of noble character **Proverbs** 31
'To us a child is born' **Isaiah** 9
Ezekiel and the dry bones **Ezekiel** 37
The fiery furnace **Daniel** 3
Writing on the wall **Daniel** 5
Daniel in the lions' den **Daniel** 6
Hosea and his adulterous wife **Hosea** 1–3
Jonah and the fish **Jonah** 1
Coming of the Holy Spirit at Pentecost **Acts** 2
Death of Stephen **Acts** 6–7
Conversion of Saul **Acts** 9:1–31
Paul's shipwreck **Acts** 27–28

WELL-KNOWN EVENTS IN THE LIFE OF JESUS

Birth **Matthew** 1–2; **Luke** 1–2
Baptism **Matthew** 3:13–17; **Mark** 1:9–11; **Luke** 3:21–22
Temptation **Matthew** 4:1–11; **Mark** 1:12–13; **Luke** 4:1–13
The transfiguration **Matthew** 17:1–13; **Mark** 9:2–13; **Luke** 9:28–36
The triumphal entry into Jerusalem **Matthew** 21:1–11; **Mark** 11:1–11; **Luke** 19:28–44; **John** 12:12–19
Jesus clears the temple **Matthew** 21:12–13; **Mark** 11:15–19; **Luke** 19:45–48; **John** 2:12–25
The widow's offering **Mark** 12:41–44; **Luke** 21:1–4
The last supper **Matthew** 26:17–30; **Mark** 14:12–26; **Luke** 22:7–38; **John** 13:21–30
Jesus washes his disciples' feet **John** 13:1–17
Jesus at Gethsemane **Matthew** 26:36–46; **Mark** 14:32–42; **Luke** 22:39–46
Judas betrays Jesus **Matthew** 26:47–56; **Mark** 14:43–50; **Luke** 22:1–6, 47–53; **John** 18:1–11
Peter denies Jesus **Matthew** 26:69–75; **Mark** 14:66–72; **Luke** 22:54–62; **John** 18:15–18, 25–27
The trial and crucifixion **Matthew** 26:57–27:66; **Mark** 15:1–47; **Luke** 22:66–23:56; **John** 18:28–19:42
Resurrection and ascension **Matthew** 28:1–20; **Mark** 16:1–20; **Luke** 24:1–53; **John** 20:1–21:25

SELECTED MIRACLES OF JESUS

Man with leprosy **Matthew** 8:2–4; **Mark** 1:40–42; **Luke** 5:12–13
Roman centurion's servant **Matthew** 8:5–13; **Luke** 7:1–10
Calming the storm **Matthew** 8:23–27; **Mark** 4:37–41; **Luke** 8:22–25
Two demon-possessed men **Matthew** 8:28–34; **Mark** 5:1–15; **Luke** 8:26–39
Paralysed man **Matthew** 9:2–7; **Mark** 2:3–12; **Luke** 5:18–25
Jairus's daughter **Matthew** 9:18–19, 23–25; **Mark** 5:22–24, 38–42; **Luke** 8:41–42, 49–56
Woman with bleeding **Matthew** 9:20–22; **Mark** 5:25–29; **Luke** 8:43–48
Walking on water **Matthew** 14:25; **Mark** 6:48–51; **John** 6:19–21
5000 people fed **Matthew** 14:15–21; **Mark** 6:35–44; **Luke** 9:12–17; **John** 6:5–13
Canaanite woman's daughter **Matthew** 15:21–28; **Mark** 7:24–30
4000 people fed **Matthew** 15:32–38; **Mark** 8:1–9
Boy with a demon **Matthew** 17:14–18; **Mark** 9:17–29; **Luke** 9:38–43
Fig-tree withered **Matthew** 21:18–22; **Mark** 11:12–14, 20–25
Man possessed (in synagogue) **Mark** 1:23–26; **Luke** 4:33–35
Catch of fish **Luke** 5:4–11
Widow's son at Nain **Luke** 7:11–15
Crippled woman **Luke** 13:11–13
Ten men with leprosy **Luke** 17:11–19
The high-priest's servant **Luke** 22:50–51
Water turned to wine **John** 2:1–11
Official's son at Capernaum **John** 4:46–54
Sick man at pool of Bethesda **John** 5:1–9
Man born blind **John** 9:1–7
Lazarus **John** 11:1–44
Another catch of fish **John** 21:1–11

SELECTED PARABLES OF JESUS

Lamp under a bowl **Matthew** 5:14–15; **Mark** 4:21–22; **Luke** 8:16; 11:33
House on the rock **Matthew** 7:24–27; **Luke** 6:47–49
New cloth **Matthew** 9:16; **Mark** 2:21; **Luke** 5:36
New wine in old wineskins **Matthew** 9:17; **Mark** 2:22; **Luke** 5:37–38
Sower **Matthew** 13:3–8, 18–23; **Mark** 4:3–8, 14–20; **Luke** 8:5–8, 11–15
Weeds **Matthew** 13:24–30, 36–43
Mustard seed **Matthew** 13:31–32; **Mark** 4:30–32; **Luke** 13:18–19
Yeast **Matthew** 13:33; **Luke** 13:20–21
Hidden treasure **Matthew** 13:44
Valuable pearl **Matthew** 13:45–46
Owner of a house **Matthew** 13:52
Lost sheep **Matthew** 18:12–14; **Luke** 15:4–7
Unforgiving servant **Matthew** 18:23–34
Workers in the vineyard **Matthew** 20:1–16
Wicked tenants **Matthew** 21:33–44; **Mark** 12:1–11; **Luke** 20:9–18
Wedding feast **Matthew** 22:2–14
Faithful and wise servant **Matthew** 24:45–51; **Luke** 12:42–48
Ten virgins **Matthew** 25:1–13
Talents **Matthew** 25:14–30; **Luke** 19:12–27
Sheep and goats **Matthew** 25:31–46
Watchful servants **Mark** 13:35–37; **Luke** 12:35–40
Good samaritan **Luke** 10:30–37
Friend at midnight **Luke** 11:5–8
Rich fool **Luke** 12:16–21
Wedding feast **Luke** 14:7–14
Great banquet **Luke** 14:16–24
Cost of discipleship **Luke** 14:28–33
Lost coin **Luke** 15:8–10
Lost (prodigal) son **Luke** 15:11–32
Rich man and Lazarus **Luke** 16:19–31
Pharisee and tax collector **Luke** 18:10–14

WHAT IS THE BIBLE?

Although one book, the Bible contains sixty-six individual books. Within each of these there is often a variety of writing such as poetry, prose, biography, letters, family trees, official records, songs and prayers. It is important to recognise the type of writing when we are reading so that we read the Bible on its own terms. To read poetry, for example, as if it was an excerpt from an official record, would make it very difficult to understand.

POETRY

The main division is between prose and poetry. Several of the Old Testament books are written completely in poetry: Psalms, the Song of Songs and Lamentations for instance. Most of the book of Job is written in poetic form, and other poems are found in prose passages, for example, Exodus 15; Judges 5 and 1 Samuel 2. Modern translations show quite clearly where poetry is used and it is easy to see that most of the prophetic books are written in poetic form. In the New Testament there is some poetry, for example, Mary's Song (Luke 1:46–55), Zechariah's Song (Luke 1:68–79) and Philippians 2:6–11.

There is an important difference between Hebrew/Jewish poetry and modern poetry. Hebrew poetry uses **rhythm** and not rhyme. It also uses **'parallelism'** which means that the idea or thought in one line is repeated in the next line in a different way and using different words. A glance at any poetic passage will illustrate this, for example:

Job 33:4 'The Spirit of God has made me;
the breath of the Almighty
gives me life.'

There are also many **different types of poetry**. The Song of Songs and the book of Job are each written as a play with various actors. In the Psalms there are poetic songs and prayers for many different occasions: songs of thanksgiving, songs for pilgrims, songs for the coronation of a king, prayers for the congregation and prayers for individuals. In the New Testament it is probable that Philippians 2:6–11, for example, was a hymn sung by the first Christians.

LAW

Israel's laws are found in the books of Exodus through to Deuteronomy. These formed the foundation of the life of the nation and of its relationship with God. Thus the law is regarded as an expression of God's character and will; the law shows how God wants his people to behave, to worship, and to live in society.

The best known list of laws is the Ten Commandments (Exodus 20). These are a summary of the essential points of the many laws contained in Exodus through to Deuteronomy. Three groups of laws have been drawn out: Covenant Law or the **Book of the Covenant** (Exodus 21–23), which contains moral, civil and religious laws. **The Holiness Code** (Leviticus 17–26) which, as its name suggests, arises from the frequent statements, 'I the LORD am holy—I who make you holy' (Leviticus 21:8). This law 'book' sets out rules for worship, especially about priests and sacrifices. **The Deuteronomic Code** (Deuteronomy 12–25) is set out like a sermon and includes warnings about the consequences of breaking the laws.

These laws touch on every area of life, not only religion. There are laws about family life (marriage etc.), human rights, theft, damage to property, personal and food hygiene and so on. Many of them are uncompromising, or absolute statements: 'You shall/shall not' (as in Exodus 20), but many are what we call 'case laws': 'if . . . then'—what to do in particular situations.

There are no new lists of commandments in the New Testament, though some regard the **Sermon on the Mount** (Matthew 5–7) as the new law for Christians. The standards set out there are even more difficult to achieve than in the Old Testament law. Some Christians therefore regard these as ideals to be aimed at, even if they can never fully attain them. Paul has much to say about the law (and uses the word in different ways), but basically he teaches that while it is good, it is limited. This is because people can never earn God's love—it is given freely.

A SPECIAL KIND OF HISTORY

There is much in the Bible which helps us to piece together the early history of the Jewish nation and later, the early church. The history books of the Old Testament are Joshua through to 2 Kings, and 1 and 2 Chronicles record some of the same events. There are historical passages in Isaiah and Jeremiah, and parts of Genesis, Exodus and Numbers could be described as 'history'. In the New Testament there are some historical references in the Gospels and Acts.

In the Hebrew Bible Joshua–2 Kings are grouped together and called 'The Former Prophets'. This will help us to understand that biblical history is not history told for its own sake, but history told from a particular point of view. It does not tell us everything that happened but only those events which show how God is at work in his world, developing his plan in the Jewish nation and later in the church. This does not mean that this history is unreliable, for archaeology and comparative studies of other nations show it to be trustworthy.

There are many references in the Old Testament books of history which show that the writers and editors used older writings and records. For example Joshua 10:13 and 2 Samuel 1:18 refer to 'The Book of Jashar'; 1 Kings 11:41 to the 'annals of Solomon' and 1 Chronicles 29:29 to 'the records of Nathan the prophet and the records of Gad the seer'. Reference is also made to particular people writing down God's words: Exodus 24:4 (Moses); 1 Samuel 10:25 (Samuel). The many family trees (genealogies) were other sources used by the writers. In the New Testament the writer of Luke and Acts indicates that he has investigated other accounts (Luke 1:3).

PROPHECY

There are many prophetic books in the Old Testament and they are grouped together from Isaiah through to Malachi. The popular idea of prophecy is that it is the prediction of future events, but biblical prophecy is much more than this. The prophets announced God's message not only, or necessarily, about the future, but very often about the present. Frequently they began with the words, 'This is what the Lord says'. They spoke God's word and that meant that they condemned social injustice and sham worship. They exposed mistaken, cosy ideas about God and his laws and warned the people that God must punish them if they did not mend their ways.

The prophets communicated what they had to say in many different ways: dialogue, narrative, poetry, picture language and drama. Many prophets have given us an account of how God called them to their work. Their conviction was that they said what God had told them to say, but how they received those words we do not know.

There are a few references to prophets writing down at least some of their message: Isaiah 30:8 (Isaiah), and Jeremiah 30:2 (Jeremiah). Jeremiah 36 also tells us that Jeremiah dictated some of his message to Baruch who must have been a follower of his.

Other prophecies have both an immediate and a long term meaning; they were fulfilled in the prophet's lifetime or soon after, but only partly so. The New Testament writers understood this and show how many of the Old Testament promises were finally fulfilled in the life, death and resurrection of Jesus.

APOCALYPTIC

This is a particular type of prophetic literature found notably in Daniel (chapters 6–12) and Revelation, but also in Isaiah 24–27, Ezekiel 38–39, Zechariah 9–14 (the first part of the book is apocalyptic in thought) and Mark 13, which is known as 'the little Apocalypse'. The word comes from Greek, and means 'unveiling' or 'revealing' and the book of Revelation is often called 'The Apocalypse' since it is the unveiling or revealing of the future. Apocalyptic writing is full of strange symbols and creatures, as well as angels. The interpretation of apocalyptic writing gives rise to a variety of points of view.

WISDOM

We know that many ancient nations had 'wisdom writings'. Job, Ecclesiastes and Proverbs are the main biblical Wisdom books, but many of the Psalms belong to this type of writing (for example, 1, 34, 37, 73 etc). Wisdom writing was interested in the problems of existence: why are we here? why are things the way they are? why do people suffer? In its simplest and earliest form wisdom was communicated in riddles (Judges 14:14; 1 Samuel 24:13 for example) and the proverbs found in the biblical book of that name. The book of Proverbs is full of statements and observations, often amusing, about life. Sometimes they are presented as if a father or teacher were talking to his son or student, teaching him how to behave in various situations.

GOSPEL

Although there are four Gospels the word actually applies to what they contain, for the announcement that a new age has begun with Jesus **is** the gospel, which means 'good news'. The Gospels are, nevertheless, a new and particular kind of biblical literature. It is important to understand that the Gospels are not biographies; they do not simply recount the life of Jesus. Rather, each Gospel presents the story of Jesus from a particular viewpoint, and each has a distinctive way of telling the story. Matthew has grouped Jesus' teaching together; Mark is a vivid, fast-moving story; Luke has beautiful pen sketches of many of the people who featured in the story of Jesus; John is a deeply religious, almost otherworldly study.

Scholars have discussed the writing of the Gospels a great deal. A very early record tells us that Mark wrote down Peter's memories of Jesus. Luke was probably written by the man who helped Paul in some of his missionary work.

LETTERS

The writers of the New Testament letters follow the 'rules' for letter writing of the first century A.D. This began with an opening sentence giving the name of the writer and the recipient. Then followed a general greeting and enquiry into the health of the recipient. The main section of the letter was concluded with a personal greeting. However, the New Testament letters are much longer than the average 150–200 words of the letters of that period. Even Philemon, the shortest, is 470 words. Paul's letters are usually characterised by a main section which deals first with teaching and then with the way Christians should put into practice what they have learned. Although most of the New Testament letters tell us the name of the author some do not.

There are some interesting letters in the Old Testament. The best example is in Jeremiah 29, but others are found in 1 Kings 21; 2 Chronicles 30; Ezra 4 and 5 and Nehemiah 6.

THE LAND AND PEOPLE OF THE BIBLE

GEOGRAPHY

NAME: The place in which the story of the Bible is set has been known by different names in its history:

Canaan is the earliest reference to the country (Genesis 10:19; 11:31). As Genesis 12:6 shows, the name is associated with the people who lived there: Canaanites.

Israel or 'the land of Israel', is the name used as the Old Testament progresses (e.g. 1 Samuel 13:19). When the nation was divided the northern part was called **'Israel'**, and the southern area **'Judah'**. In the New Testament period under the Romans, the land was divided into provinces such as 'Judea' and 'Galilee'.

Palestine has also been used, as for example, in the earlier part of this century. It is associated with the **'Philistines'** who once occupied the coastal area to the west of Israel—the 'land of the Philistines' or 'Philistia'.

Today, the whole area is so divided that the various titles only confuse!

PHYSICAL FEATURES: The land of Israel is small, roughly the size of Wales, 150–200 miles long and 100 miles at its widest point. It is a land of great contrasts. Travelling in an easterly direction from the Mediterranean Sea there is a coastal plain from which the land slopes gently at first, then more steeply to the central highlands of Judea. It then drops sharply to the Jordan rift valley and rises again to a mountainous plateau in the Trans-Jordan area. Travelling from north to south the land descends steadily from Mount Hermon (9000 feet) to the Dead Sea (1275 feet below sea level).

LANDSCAPE: The present landscape is very different from what it was in the early Old Testament period. Then the northern central area and Trans-Jordan were covered by lush forest, and the plains nearer the coast were sand dunes, lagoons, swamp and forest. In the north-west and central areas (where most of the Bible story is set) there were fertile plains. The southern area was desert scrub.

CLIMATE: There are great variations in the climate which falls roughly between temperate and tropical, with wet winters and hot, dry summers (May/June–September/October). Climate varies with the height above sea level, distance from the coast, etc. **Rainfall** is vital and while the rainy season is predictable there are great variations from year to year. In the Bible there are references to:

'the early rains'–mid-October: (Autumn) which make ploughing possible. This is followed by the rainy season proper, November–March, with most rain falling in December and January.

'the latter rains' or 'spring rains'—vital to mature the grain.

Rainfall averages lessen from north to south and from west to east. During the summer, dew and morning mist bring moisture to the coastal areas and the plains, and this is of vital importance. Drought and famine were constant factors which had to be reckoned with.

OCCUPATIONS:

Agriculture. The people of the Bible, and particularly of Old Testament times, were farmers. Almost everyone would have had their own smallholding, growing what was needed for food, and keeping sheep, goats and cattle. Goats provided milk, and their skins were used to make tents. Sheep provided milk and wool, and occasionally meat. By New Testament times it was fairly common to keep chickens.

Though a large part of the land was desert and rock, and therefore unsuitable for farming, the areas of lower Galilee were fertile. Barley was grown in the fertile valleys (such as the Jordan valley), and wheat in the Plain of Jezreel. Flax for making linen, and millet were also grown. Pomegranates, melons, dates, cucumbers, figs and nuts were important crops providing a supplement to water in the long hot season. On the lower hills there were vineyards—the vine is an important symbol in the Bible (e.g. Isaiah 5:7; John 15:1). Olives were eaten for food, and their oil was used for lighting, cooking, medicine, and soap for washing. **Harvesting** began in March (Flax) and proceeded with barley (April/May), wheat (May/June), grapes (July–October), figs (August/September) and olives (October/November).

Other Occupations

FISHING: Whole communities made their living from fishing, as the New Testament Gospels show. Lake Galilee was the focus for this.

MINING: The mining of iron and copper in the area of Ezion Geber began around 1000 B.C. Chemical salts and pitch were found in the Dead Sea area.

POTTERY: Although there are several references to potters and their craft in the Bible, there was nothing distinctive about Israelite pottery.

FROM TENTS TO TOWNS

THE TRIBE: The story of Israel begins with Abraham. He lived a 'semi-nomadic' life (i.e. travelling from place to place and living in tents) much as the modern Bedouin today. The tribe would include the entire family, from the head of the family/tribe, through the various generations to the youngest member. Servants and large numbers of animals would be included.

EARLY COMMUNITIES: After the settlement in Canaan under Joshua's leadership, the twelve tribes gradually settled into small farming communities or villages, which later became walled towns and cities. Towns were small with about 150–200 houses.

LATER DEVELOPMENTS: Under the kings, and especially Solomon, towns became larger and the gap between rich and poor widened as farms were taken over, and even tenant farmers were forced off their land.

NEW TESTAMENT TIMES: By New Testament times towns were planned more carefully, though life was still quite rural. Jerusalem probably had a quarter of a million inhabitants in the time of Jesus. The Romans, famed for their civil engineering, did much to improve conditions by building drainage schemes, aqueducts etc. They also created 'provinces', some of which were governed by a governor or proconsul, and others (where troops were stationed) by a procurator. Some cities were given special status as Roman colonies and were governed by magistrates. Philippi was one of these. Roman citizenship was another privilege and Paul was proud of his.

HOW PEOPLE LIVED

The Bible covers a period of some 2000 years so there were changes in some customs and in the way people lived. It is only possible to look at a few of these customs in this section.

FAMILY LIFE:

Circumcision. Eight days after birth a boy was circumcised. Other races practised circumcision but it had religious meaning for the Jews. It reminded them that God had chosen them and that they were different from other people.

Education. Learning was based on 'the Scriptures', particularly the Laws in the Pentateuch. The many festivals helped children to learn about the history of Israel. Children were taught at home, but by New Testament times boys would go to the synagogue school.

The eldest son succeeded his father. While both boys and girls would help on the farm, girls would also help in the home. Women did all the food preparation, water carrying, spinning, weaving, and the making of clothes.

Marriage. This was arranged by parents, and throughout biblical times there was an insistence that marriage should take place only between fellow Israelites, though many disregarded this, as the Old Testament shows. The **engagement** was binding and a 'bride price' (mohar) would be paid to the bride's father, and a dowry by the bride's father. These could be paid in servants, land, property or work, not only in money. **Divorce** was allowed, but the actual grounds for this were not clear and were still being debated in Jesus' time.

Death. There were clear mourning rites which lasted seven days. The body had to be buried within 24 hours, either in a cave, or for the rich, a specially prepared tomb. There was no clear understanding of a **life beyond death** in the Old Testament. It was believed that the dead went to a 'place of shadows' called 'Sheol'. By the New Testament period the Pharisees believed in a physical resurrection, and certainly many of the ordinary people did as well (see John 11).

JUSTICE AND ADMINISTRATION:

Early period. After the settlement, when towns began to be established, the entrance ('the gate') became the meeting place and a kind of law-court, where cases were heard and judgment given. Under Solomon an organised administration and government began to emerge, and community and military service was introduced.

Later period. Towards the end of the Old Testament period families of priests began to emerge with wide powers and influence. Together with 'elders' these priests formed a central governing body called **'the Sanhedrin'** or 'the Council'. It had wide civil and administrative powers and its own police force. It was this court that tried Jesus, and later, some of his followers.

ISRAEL AND HER NEIGHBOURS

Although Israel was a tiny country its position in relation to the nations which surround it gave it a strategic importance. This is because it formed a kind of land bridge between powerful nations: Egypt in the south and Mesopotamia in the north were constantly struggling with each other for possession, influence and control of vital trade routes. An understanding of this helps us to see why, in the Old Testament in particular, there was constant warfare and threat of invasion.

SUMERIA. This probably forms the background culture to Genesis 1–11. It is the oldest culture of which we know, and dates to at least 4500 B.C., so that Sumeria is often called 'the cradle of civilisation'. It lay near the Persian Gulf, between the Tigris and Euphrates rivers (modern S. Iraq). Its largest city was **Ur** from which Abraham's family came. Sumerians were scientists, mathematicians and astronomers, but their greatest contribution to civilisation was **writing**, which they seem to have invented. The earliest understandable writing dates from 3200 B.C., and many later languages developed from this. Sumeria had been finally absorbed by the Semites by 1750 B.C., but its legacy of writings lived on.

EGYPT. In Genesis and Exodus the founding fathers of Israel (Abraham, Isaac etc.) travelled constantly to and from Egypt. Egyptian civilisation is very old and reaches back at least to 3000 B.C. It was an advanced culture and Egyptians had special interest in dreams and their interpretation, as well as in poetry, proverbs and story-writing. Their king was called 'Pharaoh' (his Majesty) and was regarded as a god.

At the end of the Old Testament period Egypt's power had dwindled so that she often tried to form political alliances with other nations, including Israel, to keep herself going.

CANAANITES. These were the main racial group in Palestine at the time of the Conquest. They lived in small 'city-states' or 'fortress towns', built on hill summits. Other tribal groups lived alongside them, such as Amorites, Perizzites, etc. (see Exodus 33:2). The significance of the Canaanites for Israel's history is in their religion. This was a nature religion, its chief god being Baal, the storm god, and provider (or withholder) of rain.

PHILISTINES. They appear to have been part of a general movement of tribes known as 'Sea People', who came to the coastal areas of Palestine from Crete, Cyprus and the Aegean Islands. The territory was known as 'the land of the Philistines' or 'Philistia'. They had five settlements or 'city-states': Gaza, Ashkelon, Gath, Ashdod and Ekron which formed a closely knit and very efficient social and military unit. Their chief god was Dagon.

There was constant border warfare between Israel and the Philistines throughout the period of the Judges and until King David finally defeated them.

SYRIA. Also called Aram (after the Aramean tribes who settled here), Syria lay to the north of Israel. Its chief city was Damascus. Aramaic was probably the language of these early settlers. Relationships between Israel and Syria varied between border warfare, independent existence and alliance.

In the New Testament Antioch in Syria was an important centre of early Christianity, and it was there that the followers of Jesus were first called Christians.

ASSYRIA. This lay in north Mesopotamia (the northern part of modern Iraq). It was an ancient nation, settled at least by *c.* 2300 B.C., but its importance for the history of Israel spans a period of some 200 years (850–650 B.C.) during which Israel became part of the Assyrian empire. Their capital city was Asshur (their chief god had the same name), but later Nineveh became the capital city until Assyria fell to the Babylonians in 612 B.C. Assyria was a cruel, but very efficient, military nation who resettled conquered peoples away from their own land, thus breaking their national identity. This fate befell the Northern Kingdom of Israel in 722 B.C. Kings mentioned in the OT are **Tiglath-Pileser III** (744–727 B.C.—2 Ki 15:29), **Shalmaneser V** (726–722 B.C.—2 Ki 17:3), **Sargon II** (721–705 B.C.—Isa 20:1), **Sennacherib** (704–681 B.C.—2 Ki 18:13), **Esarhaddon** (681–669 B.C.—2 Ki 19:37) and **Ashurbanipal** (660–627 B.C.—Ezr 4:10).

BABYLON. Babylonian history reaches back to the Sumerian period from which it derives many of its cultural traditions. It lay in what is now Southern Iraq. The Assyrian Empire passed to Babylon under king Nebuchadnezzar. Both Ezekiel and Daniel were exiled to Babylon, and Ezra the scribe returned to Israel from Babylon, although by then Babylon had itself fallen to the Persian king, Cyrus, in 539 B.C.

PERSIA. Persians were originally travelling Indo-Europeans from Southern Russia, who settled in what is now modern Iran about 1000 B.C. Their capital was Susa, where Nehemiah was based, while the book of Esther gives an inside view of life in the royal palace there. We learn about Persian policy towards conquered peoples from 2 Chronicles and Ezra, both of which contain a decree of king Cyrus. It shows that Persia encouraged subject nations to continue their own religion and culture. Kings mentioned in the OT are **Cyrus II**, the Great (or Darius the Mede, 559–530 B.C.; 2 Ch 36:22–23; Ezr 1:1–4; Da 1:21); **Darius I**, the Great (522–486 B.C.; Ezr 4:5; Ne 12:22; Hag 1:1; Zec 1:1), **Artaxerxes** (465–424 B.C.; Ezr 7:1, 21–26; Ne 2:1–8), **Darius II** (424–404 B.C.; Ne 12:22).

Persian power was overthrown by Alexander the Great of Greece in 331 B.C.

GREECE. It was Alexander the Great who was responsible for the spread of Greek civilisation throughout the vast Greek empire. Greek cities were established all over the empire, and Greek philosophy, science, morality, customs and language spread everywhere (including Israel) even after Alexander's death when his empire was divided between his four generals.

ROME. In 63 B.C. much of Israel was incorporated into the Roman province of Syria when Pompey marched into Jerusalem. Over the next few decades there was a lot of rivalry among Roman leaders, but in 31 B.C. Octavian emerged as sole ruler of the Empire. In 27 B.C. he took the name Augustus and it was during his rule that Jesus was born (Luke 2:1). Rome brought many benefits to the world: for example, roads which made travelling and trade so much easier. Latin and Greek were the official language throughout the empire and this helped the early Christian missionaries as they went everywhere preaching.

Despite the fact that subject nations were allowed to follow their own customs and religion, the Jews hated Rome. In the time of Jesus Roman troops were stationed in Judea, and Jewish hopes that God would intervene and deliver them became very strong. Resistance to Roman rule increased during the period A.D. 60–70 and in A.D. 70. Rome retaliated by destroying the Temple in Jerusalem.

Persecution of Christians seems to have been unusual, but the book of Revelation may indicate a firmer line being taken against the Christian church.

PLAN OF THE BIBLE

GENESIS
As its name implies this book is about origins or beginnings—of the universe, of the different nations, of sin, and of the Jewish people. The first eleven chapters reach back to the beginning of time and deal with questions that we all ask: who made the world? where did we come from? why is there suffering and evil in the world?

In chapters 12–50 we move from the general (the human race) to the particular as we learn how God moved into the chaos and confusion and chose one man, Abraham. God directed him to settle in the land of Israel and he and his descendants, Isaac and Jacob, are known as the patriarchs (fathers) or founders of Israel. Jacob's twelve sons are the beginnings of the twelve tribes. Through Joseph, one of his sons, the whole family settle in Egypt.

EXODUS
The centre-piece of this book is God's deliverance of emergent Israel from Egypt and the book's name means 'going out'. Some four hundred years separate Genesis and Exodus, during which time Egyptian attitudes to the settlers changed from peaceful co-existence to hostility and oppression. Moses emerged to lead God's people out of Egypt, their destination being the land of Israel. At the mountain of Sinai God gave Moses the laws which were to form the basis of the newly-formed nation's life. These are summed up in the Ten Commandments.

LEVITICUS
This is a book of further laws or rules, mainly for Israel's worship, and in particular about sacrifice and the priesthood. A keyword is 'holiness', for the intention of the laws was to help the people relate to God and in so doing to reflect his character in daily life.

NUMBERS
The first ten chapters continue in the legal atmosphere of Leviticus. The name of the book arises from the various censuses or numberings taken prior to breaking camp and leaving Sinai. The remaining chapters are a sad record of almost forty years wandering in the desert and of complaints and rebellion against Moses and God.

DEUTERONOMY
The setting of the book is the border of the land of Israel. It is presented as three sermons of Moses in which he surveys the journey from Egypt, the people's rebellion and God's patient loyalty. He restates and underlines some of the laws of Exodus, Leviticus and Numbers (thus the book's title, which means 'second law-giving'), and stresses the need for obedience after they have settled in Israel. The book closes with some final words of Moses and his death.

JOSHUA
The first twelve chapters tell us about the initial occupation of Israel under its new leader, Joshua. The remaining chapters outline the planned territorial division among the twelve tribes. Many of the native people still had to be conquered.

JUDGES
This book continues the story of the conquest of the land of Israel which involved conflict with various tribes both in and around Israel. Interwoven in the account is the constant disobedience to God alternating with a turning back to him, and his patient loyalty which is demonstrated in various leaders (called 'judges') who emerged to rally the tribes to fight their enemies.

RUTH
This is a story of family loyalty and loyalty to God and to his laws. It is set in the same period as Judges. The central character, Ruth, was not an Israelite but came to believe in God and, through her marriage to an Israelite called Boaz, became the great-grandmother of David and an ancestor of Jesus.

1 SAMUEL
The first and second books of Samuel recount Israel's history in the crucial transition from intermittent leadership to monarchy. The books take their name from the prophet who appointed the first two kings, Saul and David.

1 Samuel picks up from the book of Judges and shows how the continued harassment from neighbouring tribes made the people ask for a king.

2 SAMUEL
This is about Israel's second, and best known king, David. The book opens against a background of civil war following the death of Saul in battle. Later in the book we read of intrigue among David's sons over the succession. It was David who established Jerusalem as Israel's capital.

1 KINGS
The two books of Kings cover the history of Israel over a period of almost four hundred years.

The first eleven chapters of 1 Kings concern David's son, Solomon, the third king of Israel. His importance centres on his building of the Jerusalem Temple, the focal point of Israel's worship. His son, Rehoboam, inherited a dissatisfied nation and due to his foolish attitude ten of the tribes formed themselves into a separate state under a former official of Solomon's called Jeroboam. Subsequently this state is known as Israel, or the Northern Kingdom, and the remaining two tribes as Judah, or the Southern Kingdom. The history of these two states is recounted in interwoven accounts in the remaining chapters of 1 and 2 Kings. Elijah, an important prophet, dominates the end of 1 Kings.

2 KINGS

The death of Elijah and the emergence of the prophet Elisha occupy the early chapters of 2 Kings. The remaining sweep of the history covers some three hundred years, and from a religious point of view is all downhill apart from one or two religious revivals promoted by the reigning monarch. The end of the Northern Kingdom comes a century and a half before that of Judah, but in both cases it is understood as the inevitable punishment for turning away from God.

1 CHRONICLES

The two books of Chronicles cover the same period as Samuel and Kings but from a particular point of view. The writer, known as 'The Chronicler', shows that David laid the foundations of Israel's worship even though he did not build the Temple. In the first nine chapters he uses family trees to trace the history of Israel from Adam to the return from Exile to show that Judah is the true people of God.

2 CHRONICLES

Solomon, the builder of the Temple, is the subject of chapters 1–9. It becomes obvious in the remaining chapters that interest lies only in the history of Judah, through whom God would continue his purpose. Special attention is also given to kings who promoted religious reform. The end of the book goes beyond 2 Kings as it hints that the period in exile in Babylon is about to end. Persia has taken over the Babylonian empire.

EZRA

This follows on in time immediately from 2 Chronicles. The Persian king has issued a decree which allows the Jews to return to Israel and to rebuild the Jerusalem Temple. In chapters 3–6 we learn that initially the altar was rebuilt and sacrifices resumed but opposition halted the temple rebuilding for many years. Finally, it was completed and dedicated. Some time later (chapters 7–10) Ezra, an expert on the Jewish law, was sent from Babylon to help and guide the newly-established community. The main problem was that the Jews were intermarrying with other nations, thereby threatening the survival of national identity.

NEHEMIAH

Another leader in establishing the new community, Nehemiah organised the rebuilding of the walls round Jerusalem, so vital to its security (chapters 1–7). Once this was done Ezra read the law (from the first five books of the Bible) to the people and led them in a confession of their disobedience to God and then to a promise to obey him in the future (chapters 8–10). Nehemiah also carried through several social reforms (chapters 11–13).

ESTHER

The setting of this story is the Persian king's palace in the same period as Ezra–Nehemiah. Esther, a Jew, became a Persian queen and was able to save the Jews in the Persian empire from a plot to exterminate them.

JOB

The story of Job is found in the first two and the last chapter of the book. Satan is allowed to bring several major tragedies into the life of this good and religious man. The main section of the book is a discussion between Job and three friends (a fourth makes a brief appearance) as to why Job has suffered so much trouble. The questions raised are not only about human suffering but about God: is he fair? is he even good? Traditional, trite answers are shown to be inadequate.

PSALMS

Here are sacred songs, poems and prayers which originated in Israel's worship and her experience of God. They are traditionally associated with David but reflect centuries of individual and corporate responses to God. Human emotions of anger, despair, sadness, guilt, doubt, joy, praise and adoration are expressed. Themes include the Law, Jerusalem and its Temple, Israel's history, the natural world, human suffering and God's justice.

PROVERBS

The first nine chapters are written as though a father, or perhaps a teacher, is giving advice to a son or student. After this each verse presents a proverb as we know proverbs today—concise, common sense and often witty statements about wise, successful living. Dominant themes include: poverty, justice, pride, self-control, drunkenness, anger, speaking wisely.

ECCLESIASTES

The name of this book means something like 'The Teacher' and the central word is 'meaningless'. The writer examines every aspect of life: wealth, social position, professional success and pleasure and concludes that they are futile because of the fact of death which comes to everyone. The only positive suggestion is that we should enjoy whatever God has given us, and in 12:13 the Teacher states his conclusion: 'Fear God and keep his Commandments'.

SONG OF SONGS

This is presented in poetic form as a 'song' about the wonder of sexual love. There are at least two individual speakers, a man and a woman, and a group called 'friends'. There are conversations between them, but also thoughts of each lover about the other. Many see the Song as a symbol of God's love for his people.

ISAIAH

This book relates to a period of some three hundred years. Chapters 1–39 are set in the closing years of the Northern Kingdom when Judah was still relatively safe. Isaiah worked in Jerusalem warning its people that God's judgment must fall on them because of social injustice and religious hypocrisy. To successive kings of Judah he advised dependence on God's guidance and protection rather than on political alliances with foreign nations. Jerusalem is spared the same fate as the Northern Kingdom for the time being.

Chapters 40–55 are concerned with the Jewish exiles in Babylon. The message is one of comfort: God is about to do something new and the punishment and pain of the past are over. The return to the land of Israel will recall the deliverance from Egypt.

In the final section of the book, which is set in the period after the temple had been rebuilt, there is evidence that the new community is in danger of slipping back into old patterns of behaviour. Alongside warnings is a vision of the greatness of God and his plans for the blessing of the Jews and through them, of all nations.

JEREMIAH

This prophet worked in the closing years of Judah. His message was one of warning: God's judgment must come if the people persist in rebelling against him. Indeed, judgment has become inevitable and they would be wise to recognise that God was using Babylon to punish them. When the ruling classes were exiled to Babylon Jeremiah told them that God would work out his plans through the exiles. At the same time he tried to encourage those who remained in Judah to accept their fate, but his words fell on deaf ears. Within the book we have several insights into what this unpopular prophet was thinking and feeling.

LAMENTATIONS

This is a funeral song about the devastated city of Jerusalem, possibly written by Jeremiah. Each chapter is a complete poem and in each the mood changes from anguish and despair in the recognition that punishment was deserved, to hope in God's love and mercy. Prayer is made that God will once again show these to his people.

EZEKIEL

This prophet was exiled to Babylon and his work was among the exiles there. He may have been a priest and a key theme of the book is God's holiness. The book is full of strange symbolism, visions and accounts of how the prophet often presented his message through drama. Roughly, the first thirty-three chapters convey a similar message to that of Jeremiah and at a similar period: Jerusalem will be captured by Babylon and the temple will be destroyed. Once this had taken place Ezekiel's message was one of comfort (chapters 33–39): God will bring back his people to their own country one day. Meanwhile, in Babylon they will learn that God can be worshipped even though there is no temple or they cannot offer sacrifice. Chapters 40–48 are a detailed vision of the future which centres on the Temple.

DANIEL

Daniel was also an exile in Babylon but was chosen to live in the Babylonian court and to train for the civil service. Despite this privilege we learn that Daniel, and later three of his friends, refused to give up their Jewish faith. God blessed their loyalty and Daniel was respected and consulted by the Babylonian, and later the Persian kings, particularly because of his ability to interpret dreams. The second part of the book (chapters 7–12) includes some detailed visions full of strange symbols and not always easy to interpret.

HOSEA

This prophet lived and worked in the Northern Kingdom in the closing years of its existence. Through his own experience of a broken marriage Hosea gained a deep insight into Israel's relationship to God. The covenant made at Sinai was like a marriage, but like Hosea's own wife Israel had left God to worship Canaanite gods. Hosea speaks movingly of the sadness God feels because of his love for Israel even though she deserves to be punished.

JOEL

We are not sure when Joel lived. In chapter 1 he speaks of the devastation caused by a plague of locusts. This may have been a real event or a vision but in either case it is a symbol of the invading army which God will use to punish his people (2:1–11). Joel calls the people to turn back to God while there is still time and speaks of a special outpouring of God's Spirit (2:12–32). Chapter 3 concerns a final and universal judgment.

AMOS

This prophet came from the Southern Kingdom but worked in the Northern Kingdom slightly earlier than Hosea. In chapters 1–2 he speaks of God's judgment on the surrounding nations but also on the complacent Northern Kingdom. In chapter 3 he announces that God has broken off the covenant agreement with his people in the Northern Kingdom and the next few chapters show why: oppression, social injustice, religious hypocrisy. Five visions (chapters 7–9) show that there is still time to turn back to God, but in the last two visions punishment is inevitable. A hope for something beyond God's judgment is expressed in the last few verses.

OBADIAH

This is the shortest Old Testament book and we know nothing about the prophet. The theme is the punishment of Edom, which lay to the south-east of the Dead Sea. The

Edomites were descendants of Esau and thus related to the Israelites, yet they were long-standing enemies. The reference in this book suggests that when Jerusalem fell to the Babylonian army in 587 B.C. the Edomites did nothing to help and maybe even took some advantage of Judah's fate. While Edom disappeared from history Obadiah foretells the return of Israel to her own land.

JONAH

God told the prophet Jonah to go and warn the people of Nineveh, capital of Assyria (a cruel enemy of Israel) that God was going to punish her. After attempts to evade God's orders Jonah reluctantly preached in the city and the Ninevites turned to God. Jonah was furious with God for showing mercy to such wicked people and God tries to demonstrate to the prophet that he feels compassion even for Israel's enemies.

MICAH

This prophet lived and worked a little later than Amos and Hosea and about the same time as Isaiah and what he has to say is very similar to them. He worked in the Southern Kingdom and condemned social injustice and inequality, and corruption among the political and religious leaders. God must punish his people but beyond that Micah speaks of a future which will centre on the Jerusalem temple when a descendant of David will emerge to lead God's people against her enemies (chapters 4–7). 6:6–8 seems to sum up the message, not only of Micah, but of all the prophets of this period.

NAHUM

This prophet announces the destruction of Nineveh, capital of Assyria. In the opening verses Nahum speaks of God as 'slow to anger' but also that he will 'not leave the guilty unpunished'. It is for this reason that God must now punish Nineveh for extreme cruelty. Chapters 2 and 3 are a poem about the siege of Nineveh. This took place in 612 B.C.

HABAKKUK

Because Habakkuk mentions Babylon (1:6) it is assumed that he worked at the end of the seventh century B.C. The prophet questions God about his justice: why does he turn a blind eye to cruelty and wickedness? how can he use wicked people to punish people who are better than them? God gives no direct answer (chapter 2) but promises that one day he will punish all oppression and injustice. Chapter 3 is a poem about God coming to punish all wickedness and concludes with a statement by the prophet of his trust in God, no matter what happens.

ZEPHANIAH

Zephaniah worked just before Jeremiah. The theme of the book is God's universal judgment. Chapter 1 deals with the judgment of Israel but 2:1–3 promises that this may be averted if they turn back to God. The remainder of chapter 2 foretells the punishment of some of Israel's neighbours. Beyond the judgment of Jerusalem the prophet sees hope (chapter 3).

HAGGAI

Haggai and Zechariah belong to the same period (520 B.C.). Many Jews had returned to Israel to rebuild their national life. Initially they worked with enthusiasm but opposition brought the work of rebuilding the Temple to a standstill. Haggai rallied the people, showing that the economic difficulties they were experiencing were because they had their priorities wrong. The important thing for their national life was God's 'house' and God had greater things in store if they would only learn to put him first.

ZECHARIAH

Like Haggai, this prophet encouraged the people to take up the work they had left off and complete the Temple building. His messages are given in a series of visions in chapters 1–8 and concern other issues as well as the rebuilding. Chapters 9–14 are in a different form, more typical of prophetic messages. Their theme is the future age: Israel's deliverance, God's triumph and the work of the Messiah.

MALACHI

This book indicates that after the time of Haggai and Zechariah things deteriorated again. The people felt disappointed with God (1:2–5), the religious leaders were corrupt and slipshod in their duties (1:6–2:9), and everybody disobedient to God's laws (2:10–16) while at the same time treating him with contempt (2:17–3:18). Chapter 4 looks forward to the time when injustice will be dealt with and those who are loyal to God will be restored.

MATTHEW

The first three Gospels follow a similar pattern and are often known as the 'Synoptic Gospels' because they 'see together' the life of Jesus. Yet each has its own particular emphasis.

Matthew begins by tracing Jesus' family history back to Abraham and recounts various incidents concerned with Jesus' birth (chapters 1–2). His is a carefully organised Gospel and he is especially interested in what Jesus said: the Sermon on the Mount (chapters 5–7), parables about the kingdom of heaven (chapter 13) and parables about the end of time (chapter 25). He also shows that Jesus is the Messiah spoken of in the Old Testament.

MARK

This Gospel concentrates mainly on what Jesus did, although the writer does include some of Jesus' teaching. Within the first few chapters several miracles are recorded. He does not speak about Jesus' birth but begins with John the Baptist's work and Jesus' baptism and temptations. Chapters 1–9 are about Jesus' work in Galilee, chapters 10–15 his journey to Jerusalem ending in his death, and chapter 16 about his resurrection. 16:9–20 was added later, probably by the early church.

LUKE

The first two chapters of this Gospel contain several unique incidents related to Jesus' birth and early life. Luke traces Jesus' family tree to Adam, which underlines the emphasis on Jesus as the Saviour of the whole world. He stresses that Jesus is concerned for minority groups, for the poor and the oppressed. Other prominent themes are prayer, joy and the Holy Spirit. He often cross-references events to dates in secular history. He is also the author of Acts.

JOHN

It is obvious from the first verse that this Gospel is very different in atmosphere to the other three. Jesus' miracles are called 'signs', Jesus does not speak of the 'kingdom' but of 'eternal life'. There are no parables but several long, rather complex sermons which are usually linked to one of the signs. Thus when Jesus heals a blind man he speaks of himself as 'the light of the world'. These 'I am' sayings are quite distinctive to this Gospel and the accounts of Jesus' appearances after his resurrection are also unique.

ACTS

This is the 'second instalment' of the story begun in Luke's Gospel and tells us what happened in the early church in the first thirty years or so. It begins with the ascension of Jesus (chapter 1) and the coming of the Holy Spirit at Pentecost (chapter 2). The next ten chapters show how the gospel spread beyond the locality of Jerusalem as far as Samaria. Peter, Stephen and James are the main characters. Chapters 13–28 centre on Paul and his three missionary tours taking the gospel to Greece and Europe. The whole book shows that the main source of opposition to the 'new religion' came from the Jews, not the Roman government.

ROMANS

This is the first of twenty-one letters found in the New Testament. They are very important because they give us an inside view of life in the earliest Christian churches and the teaching of their leaders. Paul had not been to Rome when he wrote this letter. It is the most detailed account of an important part of his teaching: that the only way to be accepted by God was to rely on what Jesus did through his death and resurrection (chapters 1–8). In chapters 9–11 Paul expresses the hope that although the Jews have largely refused this teaching they will one day accept it. Romans follows the pattern of most of Paul's letters: the first part is teaching and the second practical application in real life. Thus chapters 12–16 speak of how Christians should behave in the church and in the world.

1 CORINTHIANS

This and the following letter were written to a church in the Greek city of Corinth which Paul had visited (Acts 18:1–21). Paul had heard that there were various problems in the church: party politics (chapters 1–4), moral problems (chapter 5), Christians taking each other to court (chapter 6), marriage (chapter 7), special difficulties arising from living in a city full of temples to various gods (chapters 8–10), the organisation of worship (chapters 11–14) and intellectual problems with life after death (chapter 15).

2 CORINTHIANS

Between this and the previous letter Paul visited the church. There had been a lot of criticism and even hostility shown to him, and his authority as a leader had been called into question. Relationships had improved but Paul finds it necessary to stress the genuineness of his authority as an apostle (chapters 2–3, 10–13). The letter shows how deeply Paul felt (chapter 7). Chapter 5 contains further teaching on life after death, and chapters 8–9 give details about an appeal for financial help for a group of churches facing hardship.

GALATIANS

This is probably the first of Paul's letters and its theme is similar to that of Romans. It is apparent that many Jews felt that non-Jews becoming Christians should keep the Jewish law and in particular the food laws, and be circumcised. (Acts also tells us this.) The heart of Paul's teaching on this view is found in 2:14–21: a right relationship with God is possible only through Jesus, and nothing else is required. Chapters 5–6 show that this does not mean we can do as we like. Christians are called to 'serve one another in love' and the Holy Spirit is given to help them do this.

EPHESIANS

This letter may have been written to several churches in and around the important city of Ephesus. Paul founded this church on his third missionary tour (Acts 18:23–20:1). The clear theme of the letter is unity: God's plan is to bring to an end all that divides men and women, social classes, cultures, nations and religions. Jesus Christ is the unifying force, as the head 'unites' the human body. Chapters 4–6 show that this unity is very practical: it is worked out in good relationships in the family, the church and the work place.

PHILIPPIANS

Paul established this church on his second missionary tour (Acts 16:6–40), and this letter was written some ten or twelve years after that visit. It is a warm, personal letter to a church for which he felt a deep affection. He speaks of his imprisonment which has resulted in the gospel being preached to Roman personnel (chapter 1). Chapter 2 contains an important statement about Jesus as the servant who was willing to give up his rights for the good of others, and Paul encourages the church to follow that example.

COLOSSIANS

The church was founded by Epaphras, one of Paul's converts. The contents of the letter make it clear that wrong teaching was creeping into the church. In the face of this Paul stresses the true gospel: Jesus is absolutely central. He existed before time began and he is the one who brings God and the human race together again (chapter 1). Rituals, regulations, philosophical reasonings and self-denial are not what is required (chapter 2) but right relationships and attitudes in the church, the family, the work place and the world (chapters 3–4).

1 THESSALONIANS

Paul founded this church on his second missionary tour (Acts 17:1–9) amid a lot of opposition from Jews. This and 2 Thessalonians are among Paul's earliest letters. No doubt because the Jews had continued to undermine his reputation Paul begins by insisting that he is a true apostle (chapters 1–2). From chapter 3 we learn that Timothy had been sent to the church and had returned to Paul with an encouraging report. In chapters 4 and 5 Paul deals with two questions: what happens to Christians when they die? and when will Jesus return?

2 THESSALONIANS

The Thessalonian church did not fully understand what Paul had said in his first letter (1 Thessalonians) about Jesus' return. They had also been confused by other teachers who said that Jesus had already returned. Furthermore, some church members had even opted out of responsibilities on the basis that if Jesus was about to return there was not much point in going to work! Paul deals with all these difficulties.

1 TIMOTHY

Paul had met Timothy on his second missionary tour (Acts 16:1–3) and Timothy had worked with him. Now he was a leader in the church at Ephesus and Paul writes to encourage him and give him advice about organising the church there. He writes about public prayer, the appointment of leaders, help for widows and attitudes to slaves (chapters 2–5). He warns about those who teach differently to what has been taught by recognised leaders.

2 TIMOTHY

This is more personal than 1 Timothy and was written at the end of Paul's life. He warns Timothy that wrong teaching is on the increase and people will easily be deceived. In the face of this Timothy must stand by the truth, which will take courage.

TITUS

In a similar way to Timothy, Titus was a leader in the church on the island of Crete. Paul writes as he did in 1 Timothy, about the organisation and leadership of the church, correct teaching in the face of error and right attitudes in the church, the work place and the world.

PHILEMON

Philemon was probably a convert of Paul's and now a church worker. Onesimus, one of his slaves, had run away but had met Paul and become a Christian. Paul writes to Philemon to say that he is sending Onesimus back to his master and appeals to Philemon to do what would have been unusual in those days—to forgive and reinstate Onesimus.

HEBREWS

We do not know who wrote this letter, nor who the readers were. Since the writer's theme is that the Temple and its ceremonies were temporary pointers to Christianity it is probable that the original readers were Jews. The keyword for this letter is 'better'. Jesus has offered a better (and the last) sacrifice (chapters 4–7). He is 'better' than all that has gone before: greater than the angels (chapters 1–2), greater than Moses (chapter 3). The New Covenant has replaced the Old (chapters 8–10). In the closing chapters he writes to encourage his readers to keep going in the face of difficulties and hostility. The people of the Old Testament did wonderful things because they relied on God (chapter 11). Christians must follow their example and the example of Jesus (chapter 12).

JAMES

James may have been Jesus' brother who was also the first leader of the church in Jerusalem. It could be the first of the New Testament letters to be written, and it is very practical. The main themes are: if we say we are Christians we must also live like Christians; discrimination of any kind is wrong, as is oppression of the poor and the weak; Christians should be self-controlled, especially in what they say.

1 PETER

This letter was written to Christians in the Black Sea coastal area, probably in the early 60s A.D. The theme is suffering, and probably the readers were facing real persecution because they were Christians. Christians must not be surprised if they experience opposition and persecution; Jesus, their example, certainly did! Indeed, they may be full of hope and joy because they are sharing with Jesus in this way. Throughout the letter there are also practical guidelines on Christian behaviour.

2 PETER

The letter opens with the same emphasis as in 1 Peter on Christian behaviour. Chapters 2 and 3 are a strong onslaught against those who mislead by wrong teaching and the writer speaks in detail of their future punishment. This leads him to speak of the return of Jesus.

1 JOHN

It is probable that the writer of this letter and 2 and 3 John was also the writer of the Gospel of John and the book of Revelation. It is clear that the Christians to whom he wrote 1 John were worried by teachers of strange ideas. They were saying they had special understanding of spiritual matters. This meant that they were claiming to be perfect on the one hand, and that Jesus could not have been a real man on the other. In reply John stresses the certainty that Christians have: 'we know' is a favourite phrase. One of the clear proofs that people are Christians is that they love other Christians.

2 JOHN

This letter is written to 'the chosen lady' which probably refers to a church, not an individual. Some of the themes found in 1 John are taken up here: loving God means doing what he has told us to do and loving others. The writer warns about teachers of wrong ideas.

3 JOHN

This letter is addressed to someone called Gaius who is praised for the way he is standing by the truth. A man called Diotrephes is setting himself up as a leader and turning away representatives of the writer.

JUDE

Many believe that Jude was a brother of Jesus. His letter uses almost the same words as 2 Peter 2:1–3:3 to condemn all who mislead by their wrong teaching. He too writes of their future punishment and encourages his readers to keep to the teaching they were given originally.

REVELATION

This letter was written to seven churches in Asia Minor which are named in the course of messages to them from Jesus in chapters 2–3. John had a vision of Jesus which he describes in chapter 1. In chapters 4–5 he has another vision of Jesus and in the course of this Jesus takes a scroll from the hand 'of him who sat on the throne'. The rest of the book recounts what happens as Jesus opens this scroll. These chapters are full of difficult symbols which we do not fully understand and we cannot be certain of their meaning. But the basic message of the book is that God is in control and all evil will eventually be destroyed.

Table of Weights and Measures

BIBLICAL UNIT		APPROXIMATE IMPERIAL EQUIVALENT	APPROXIMATE METRIC EQUIVALENT
WEIGHTS			
talent	*(60 minas)*	75 pounds	34 kilograms
mina	*(50 shekels)*	1¼ pounds	0.6 kilogram
shekel	*(2 bekas)*	⅖ ounce	11.5 grams
pim	*(⅔ shekel)*	¼ ounce	7.7 grams
beka	*(10 gerahs)*	⅕ ounce	5.8 grams
gerah		1/50 ounce	0.6 gram
LENGTH			
cubit		18 inches	0.5 metre
span		9 inches	23 centimetres
handbreadth		3 inches	8 centimetres
CAPACITY			
Dry Measure			
cor [homer]	*(10 ephahs)*	6 bushels	220 litres
lethek	*(5 ephahs)*	3 bushels	110 litres
ephah	*(10 omers)*	⅗ bushel	22 litres
seah	*(⅓ ephah)*	13 pints	7.3 litres
omer	*(1/10 ephah)*	4 pints	2 litres
cab	*(1/18 ephah)*	2 pints	1 litre
Liquid Measure			
bath	*(1 ephah)*	5 gallons	22 litres
hin	*(⅙ bath)*	7 pints	4 litres
log	*(1/72 bath)*	½ pint	0.3 litre

The figures of the table are calculated on the basis of a shekel equalling 11.5 grams, a cubit equalling 18 inches and an ephah equalling 22 litres. It is based upon the best available information, but it is not intended to be mathematically precise; like the measurement equivalents in the footnotes, it merely gives approximate amounts and distances. Weights and measures differed somewhat at various times and places in the ancient world. There is uncertainty particularly about the ephah and the bath; further discoveries may give more light on these units of capacity.

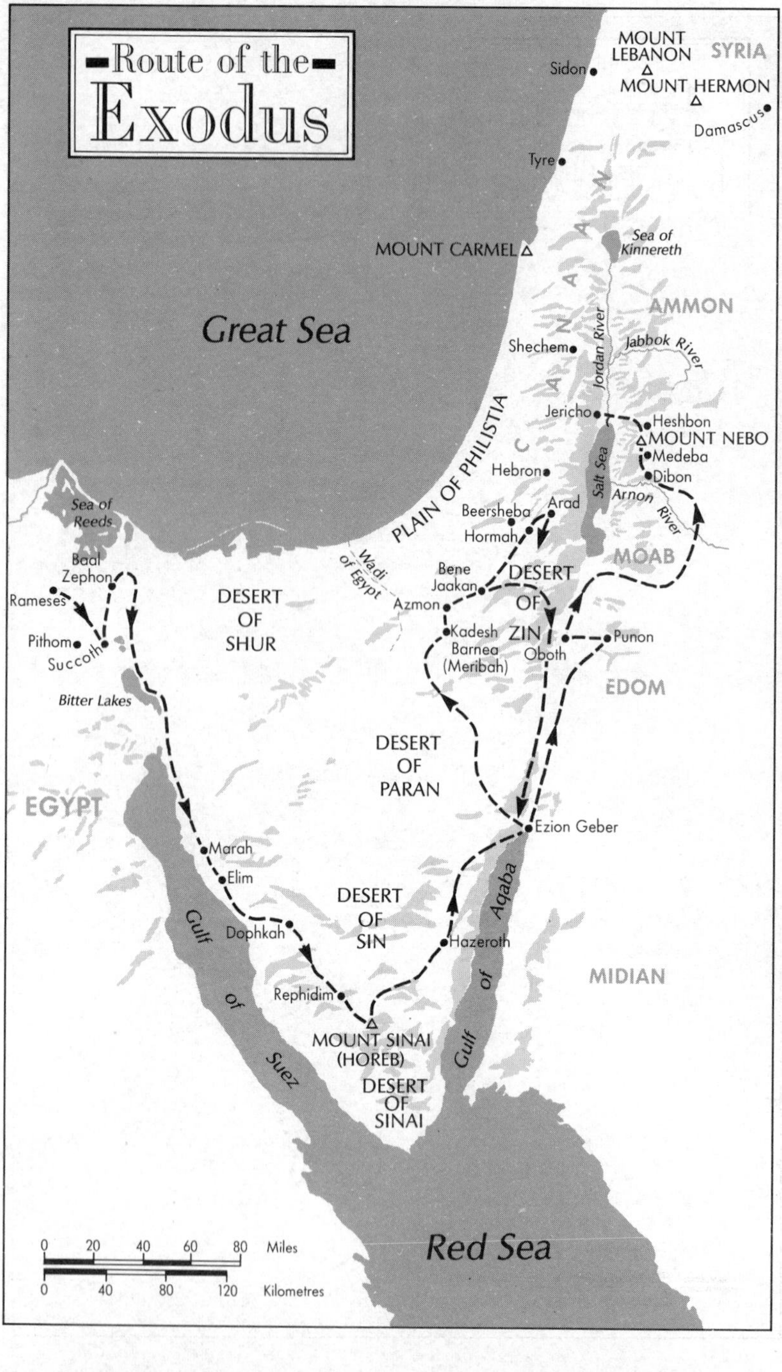
Route of the Exodus
MOUNT LEBANON
SYRIA
Sidon
MOUNT HERMON
Damascus
Tyre
CANAAN
Sea of Kinnereth
MOUNT CARMEL
AMMON
Great Sea
Shechem
Jordan River
Jabbok River
PLAIN OF PHILISTIA
Jericho
Heshbon
MOUNT NEBO
Medeba
Hebron
Salt Sea
Dibon
Sea of Reeds
Arad
Arnon River
Beersheba
Hormah
MOAB
Baal Zephon
Wadi of Egypt
Bene Jaakan
DESERT OF ZIN
Rameses
DESERT OF SHUR
Azmon
Pithom
Succoth
Kadesh Barnea (Meribah)
Oboth
Punon
Bitter Lakes
EDOM
DESERT OF PARAN
EGYPT
Ezion Geber
Marah
Elim
DESERT OF SIN
Gulf of Aqaba
Dophkah
Hazeroth
MIDIAN
Gulf of Suez
Rephidim
MOUNT SINAI (HOREB)
DESERT OF SINAI
Red Sea
0 20 40 60 80 Miles
0 40 80 120 Kilometres

The Division of Canaan

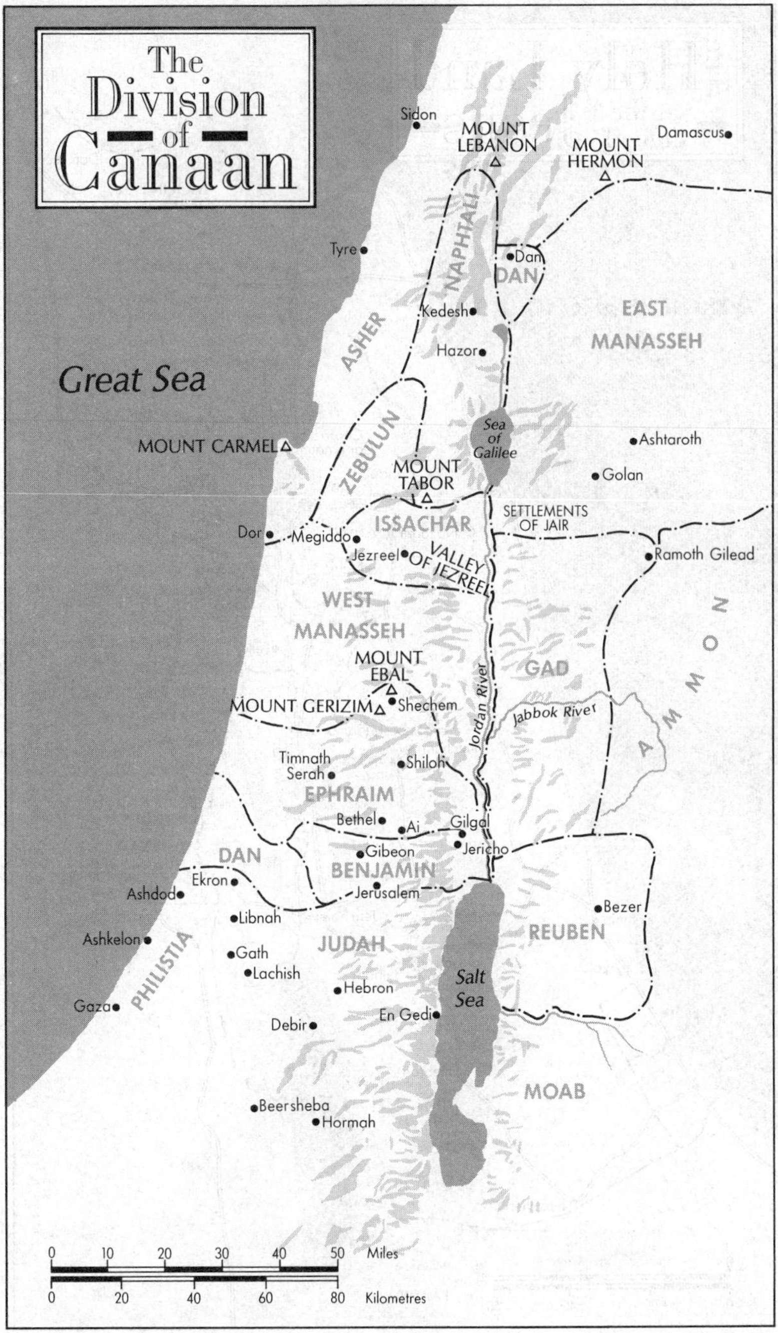

The Holy Land at the time of Jesus
Mediterranean Sea
PHOENICIA
SYRIA
Sidon
Damascus
MOUNT HERMON
Tyre
Caesarea Philippi
GALILEE
Chorazin
Capernaum
Bethsaida
Ptolemais
Cana
Sea of Galilee
Magadan
MOUNT CARMEL
Tiberias
Nazareth
Nain
Gadara
Caesarea
Pella
DECAPOLIS
Sebaste (Samaria)
Shechem
Sychar
SAMARIA
River Jordan
Joppa
Arimathea
Ephraim
PEREA
Philadelphia
Jericho
Jamnia
Emmaus
Jerusalem
Bethany
Azotus
Bethlehem
Ashkelon
JUDEA
Hebron
Gaza
Salt Sea (Dead Sea)
IDUMEA
Beersheba
NABATEA
0 10 20 30 40 Miles
0 20 40 60 Kilometres

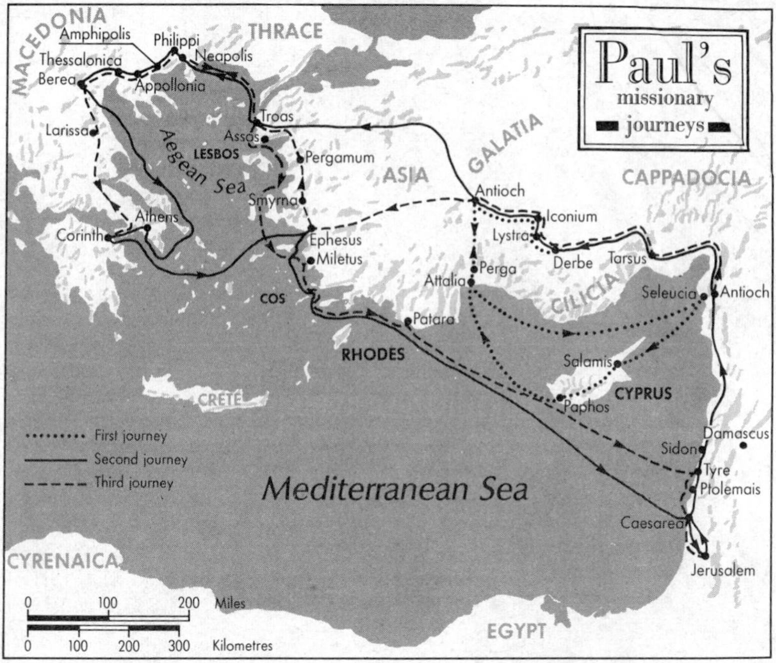
Paul's
missionary
journeys
MACEDONIA
THRACE
Amphipolis
Philippi
Neapolis
Thessalonica
Berea
Appollonia
Troas
Larissa
Assos
LESBOS
Aegean Sea
Pergamum
ASIA
GALATIA
CAPPADOCIA
Smyrna
Antioch
Iconium
Lystra
Athens
Corinth
Ephesus
Miletus
Derbe
Tarsus
Perga
Attalia
CILICIA
Seleucia
Antioch
COS
Patara
RHODES
Salamis
CYPRUS
CRETE
Paphos
First journey
Second journey
Third journey
Damascus
Sidon
Tyre
Ptolemais
Mediterranean Sea
Caesarea
Jerusalem
CYRENAICA
0 100 200 Miles
0 100 200 300 Kilometres
EGYPT

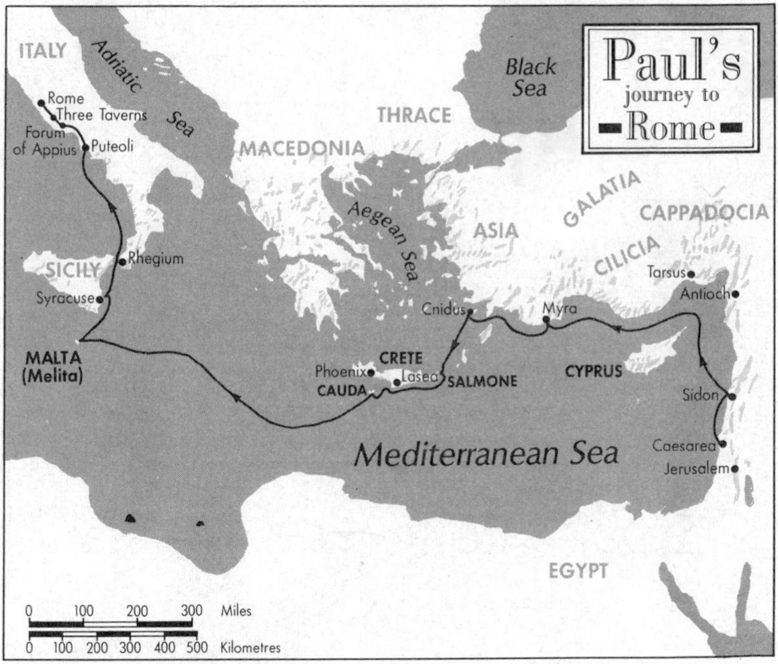
Paul's
journey to
Rome
ITALY
Adriatic Sea
Black Sea
Rome
Three Taverns
Forum of Appius
Puteoli
THRACE
MACEDONIA
Aegean Sea
GALATIA
CAPPADOCIA
ASIA
CILICIA
SICILY
Rhegium
Tarsus
Antioch
Syracuse
Cnidus
Myra
MALTA (Melita)
CRETE
Phoenix
Lasea
SALMONE
CAUDA
CYPRUS
Sidon
Mediterranean Sea
Caesarea
Jerusalem
EGYPT
0 100 200 300 Miles
0 100 200 300 400 500 Kilometres